D1711970

Separation of Powers Law

Separation of Powers Law

Cases and Materials

FOURTH EDITION

Peter M. Shane

JACOB E. DAVIS AND JACOB E. DAVIS II CHAIR IN LAW
THE OHIO STATE UNIVERSITY MORITZ COLLEGE OF LAW

Harold H. Bruff

ROSENBAUM PROFESSOR OF LAW EMERITUS AND DEAN EMERITUS
UNIVERSITY OF COLORADO LAW SCHOOL

Neil J. Kinkopf

PROFESSOR OF LAW
GEORGIA STATE UNIVERSITY COLLEGE OF LAW

CAROLINA ACADEMIC PRESS
Durham, North Carolina

ISBN 978-1-53100-259-6
eISBN 978-1-53100-260-2
LCCN 2017957040

Carolina Academic Press, LLC
700 Kent Street
Durham, North Carolina 27701
Telephone (919) 489-7486
Fax (919) 493-5668
www.cap-press.com

Printed in the United States of America

For Martha and Beth
p.m.s.

For all of my students over all of the years
h.h.b.

For my family
n.k.

Contents

Table of Cases

Preface

When two of us published our 1988 text, *The Law of Presidential Power: Cases and Materials*, which has since morphed into what are now four editions of *Separation of Powers Law: Cases and Materials*, it is safe to say we had no idea of what the next decades would witness in our particular research and teaching domain. "Far-fetched" does not begin to capture how we would have described the ideas that Congress might impeach a President for lying about a sexual affair, that the Supreme Court would intercede in a state vote recount in a way that would effectively decide a presidential election, or that the executive branch would claim inherent authority to hold U.S. citizens indefinitely, and without counsel or hearing, as "enemy combatants." We could not have imagined the horrific events of September 11, 2001, whose impact on the nation's constitutional thinking is still unfolding a decade and a half later.

Yet while each of these events has now become part of the separation of powers landscape, nothing really prepared us for the tone and conduct of the 2016 election or for the style of governance that has characterized the opening months of the Donald J. Trump Administration. The increasing willingness of each branch to test the limits of its authority beyond what had been conventional boundaries had long ago led us to rethink earlier assumptions and conclusions. But the current Administration's defiance of so many norms that prior Administrations considered standard operating procedure — norm-breaching behavior conspicuously in evidence from the President himself — has spawned significant and often intellectually challenging constitutional and administrative law disputes at a pace arguably without post-New Deal precedent. Indeed, it must be noted that the "locking down" of this volume's contents on November 8, 2017 may well mean that, even by the time of publication a few months hence, our supporting web site will already be featuring significant supplementary materials.

Readers of our 2011 volume will note that the Fourth Edition features some significant changes. Foremost among these is the addition of a third author, Neil Kinkopf, a prolific writer on separation of powers issues and, like his collaborators, an alumnus of the Justice Department's Office of Legal Counsel. Reflecting intense controversies of the last seven years, this volume also includes expanded treatment of the President's role in immigration law and an entirely reworked subchapter on the presidential obligation to take care that the laws be faithfully executed. We have for the first time included discussion of the Foreign Emoluments Clause. And we have broken our exploration of war powers into two separate chapters. Chapter Six continues to focus on what might be called, "Warmaking Classic," i.e., the allocation of authority between Congress and the President when it comes to repelling invasion (or an equivalent threat) or deploying military assets in a conflict between nation-states. Chapter Seven focuses on national security controversies related to what has variously been called the "war on terror," "the long war," and even "the forever war." As we go to press, the blurring of legal categories that have traditionally dominated war powers doctrine has been dramatically illustrated by a presidential suggestion (echoing two Senators) that a civilian Islamic State sympathizer who murdered eight people in Manhattan by driving his truck onto a bicycle path be transferred to military custody at the Guantánamo Bay Naval Base as an enemy combatant. That this suggestion is virtually certain not to be implemented does not belie how differently key government actors are now thinking about war powers.

To make room for new materials, we have sharply reduced the number of primary documents in our appendix, removing a lot of material that even we were rarely using in our classes.

We continue to regard our volume as innovative for law schools because its subject matter is not well covered by the mainstream curriculum. We regard it as innovative for undergraduate and graduate courses on the Presidency and Congress because of its emphasis on primary materials at the expense of discursive secondary text.

As law teachers, we have found the value of this project for our students to be at least twofold. First, despite the ever-increasing importance of all aspects of public law in our national life, legal curricula tend to focus predominantly on the operation of the courts and, with the exception of criminal law and, in some schools, a first-year offering on legislation and regulation, the menu of required law school courses still tilts heavily towards private law. These materials, we hope, afford readers a clearer picture of how the elected branches of government operate and of how complex are the processes of national policymaking and execution of the laws. Although bits and pieces of the overall picture may appear in courses on constitutional law, administrative law, international law, and legislation, we find that a systematic overview of the elected branches better highlights and puts into context such processes as law enforcement, program administration, budgeting and accounting, and the implementation of foreign and military policy.

Second, as the ever-increasing number of legal cases involving separation of powers attests, the subject of this work has become and is likely to remain a central national concern. The Nixon Presidency precipitated a major shift in legal attitude towards judicial oversight of the separation of powers. The decades since have by no means seen any contrary trend. The burden that the executive branch shoulders for solving domestic and foreign problems requires citizens to concern themselves ever more with the issues surrounding executive effectiveness and accountability. Persistent political and institutional competition between President and Congress—plus the public's increasingly strident distrust of government generally—likewise require citizens to focus on complex issues surrounding the scope and implementation of Congress's proper roles. These materials help to prepare students of law and political science to participate in these debates more knowledgeably.

Teachers who prefer in their courses a continued stress on presidential issues will find that this volume still permits that approach. Indeed, a thorough exploration of the applicability of law to either Congress's or the President's functions has an additional advantage. It highlights the crucial non-litigative role of legal counsel that, in all fields, legal curricula tend to underemphasize. Perhaps because most discussion materials in law school classes consist of reported cases, the impression is created that law is determined primarily in the courtroom and that arguing cases is what "real lawyers" do. Most hard legal questions facing Congress or the President must be decided, at least in the first instance, within each respective branch and on the basis of relatively little prior judicial guidance. In exploring each branch's view of things, the following materials rely substantially on sources other than judicial opinions to which the presidential or congressional lawyers would resort in order to solve a difficult problem. We have also tried to raise on a number of occasions what we take to be critical ethical questions that face public lawyers who engage in the counseling function. The most ambitious of these is a section on the "torture memos" that appears in Chapter Seven.

Three final notes on style: First, although we try to avoid using a masculine generic to describe all people, we continue to use "he" as an occasional pronoun for "the President" because of the historical circumstance that this country has not yet elected a woman to the presidency. Second, although we have marked textual deletions in the excerpted materials, we often omit, without any printed signal, footnote material and citations to cases or other authorities that may appear in the excerpts. Third, in citing relevant secondary literature, we use forms of citation that are conventional among legal academics, but which may be unusual for political scientists and their students.

This work has owed a great deal over the years to many research and production assistants. We remain especially indebted to the team that worked on the Third Eduition: to Ashley Carter '12, Yasmine Harik '12, and Benjamin Wilhelm '11, all of the Moritz College of Law at The Ohio State University. We are also grateful to a group of faithful "adopters," who have graciously shared with us their suggestions and reactions over a period of many years—Marshall Breger, at Catholic University; David Martin and Saikrishna Prakash, at the University of Virginia; and William Marshall, at the University of North Carolina–Chapel Hill. We are thankful for their friendship and insights.

Peter M. Shane
Columbus, Ohio

Harold H. Bruff
Boulder, Colorado

Neil Kinkopf
Atlanta, Georgia

November, 2017

Separation of Powers Law

Chapter 1

Introduction

The feature that distinguishes our national government from all those that had gone before is its structure. Our system of separated powers with checks and balances is accepted by Americans with more faith than understanding. Perhaps the system's record of survival with little formal change for more than two centuries is enough to justify it. (Such an approach, though, does beg the question: as compared to what?) Our hope in this book is to supplement faith with understanding. Although that may imperil the faith for some readers, we do not take that conclusion. We think that a critical exploration of the structure of our government will show that its survival is less a matter of accident than design, and that its successes outnumber its failures.

This is not to say that our system is perfect—we conclude our exploration with a chapter outlining some modifications and alternatives that astute observers have suggested. First, though, one needs to understand our complex government as it operates under the body of law and practice that has fleshed out the bare bones of the Constitution. We begin with a brief review of some constitutional history that should inform the reader's understanding of the succeeding chapters. For introductory treatments of separation of powers generally, see Harold H. Bruff, Balance of Forces: Separation of Powers Law in the Administrative State (2006); Louis Fisher, Constitutional Conflicts Between Congress and the President (2014); William B. Gwyn, The Meaning of the Separation of Powers (1965); M.J.C. Vile, Constitutionalism and the Separation of Powers (1967).

A. Constitutional History

Of good constitutional histories there are many, and all are longer than what follows here. So we provide only a sketch of matters most pertinent to this introductory book, and refer our readers to the following corpus of distinguished works as a way for them to begin their own explorations: The Founders' Constitution (Philip B. Kurland & Ralph Lerner eds., 1987); Akhil R. Amar, America's Constitution: A Biography (2006); Leonard W. Levy, Essays on the Making of the Constitution (1969); Forrest McDonald, Novus Ordo Seclorum (1985); Charles C. Thach, The Creation of the Presidency, 1775–1789 (1923); Melvin I. Urofsky & Paul Finkelman, A March of Liberty, A Constitutional History of the United States (2011); Garry Wills, Explaining America: The

FEDERALIST (1981); GORDON S. WOOD, THE CREATION OF THE AMERICAN REPUBLIC, 1776–1787 (1969).

1. Atlantic Legacy

Separation of powers theories first took shape during the English Civil War in the seventeenth century. Precursor ideas can be traced, though, to the ancient republics of Greece and Rome. By 1600, England had a rudimentary division of functions among Parliament, the Crown, and the common law courts. Parliament possessed most of the power of the purse; the Crown held various ill-defined prerogatives; the common law judges claimed the power to bind even the king by law.

During this eventful century, England experienced a Civil War leading to regicide, Cromwell's Commonwealth, restoration of the monarchy, and a final Glorious Revolution that deposed another king and confirmed the ascendancy of Parliament. It was during the Commonwealth that separation of powers ideas formed. Since at least the time of the ancient historian Polybius, theories of mixed government had dominated political discourse. These held that a combination of the elements of monarchy, aristocracy, and democracy could best assure a balanced and stable government. Now that the old system had broken down, some new formulation was needed. Separation of powers principles were articulated by John Lilburne and by James Harrington, who incorporated the new ideas in his OCEANA (1656), which helped to transmit them to Americans. With restoration of the monarchy these theories receded in England.

We lack the space to develop fully the rich history of seventeenth century England, even as it relates to the topic of this book. *See generally* MAURICE ASHLEY, ENGLAND IN THE SEVENTEENTH CENTURY (1952); CHRISTOPHER HILL, THE CENTURY OF REVOLUTION, 1603–1714 (1961); SIMON SCHAMA, 2 A HISTORY OF BRITAIN, THE WARS OF THE BRITISH 1603–1776 (2001); GEORGE M. TREVELYAN, 2 HISTORY OF ENGLAND, THE TUDORS AND THE STUART ERA (3D ED. 1953). For purposes of the American experience, however, we note several lessons that Americans could draw from an elementary knowledge of this history.

First, the adoption of two temporary written constitutions during the Commonwealth suggested that a document could provide a permanent charter of government. Second, the English experience proved the need to bolster legislative autonomy. To prevent executive dominance, the legislature had to control elections, membership, and meetings. Legislators also needed protection from arrest and from suspension of their laws by the executive. Third, the autonomy and role of the courts required definition, including protection from executive pressure and dismissal. Fourth, it was obvious that civilians must wield effective control of the military. Fifth, impeachment abuses showed that there should be more sensitive devices to control the executive.

Finally, the issue of joint legislative-executive officeholding would have to be addressed in any system of divided responsibilities. After the restoration, the Crown began a practice of "corrupting" the legislature by employing its members in an effort to sway their loyalties and retain power. The practice fundamentally threatened legislative independence. In America, forbidding joint officeholding would be a central means of maintaining separate branches of government.

Americans understood the English revolutionary experience largely through the work of Locke and Montesquieu. John Locke's Two Treatises of Government (Peter Laslett ed., 1967) was first published in 1690. Locke's model of government divided the legislative power between the Crown and a two-house legislature. In a separate branch from the legislature were executive functions (internal affairs), federative ones (external affairs), and the judiciary. Locke's categories of executive and federative power drew from old distinctions about the portions of a king's prerogative that could or could not be limited by the legislature. Locke also saw a need for residual executive power that would not rest on prior legislative authorization. He emphasized the need for an independent judiciary, and for legislators to make general laws to which they would be subjected. Maurice Cranston, John Locke (1985).

The Baron de Montesquieu's celebrated The Spirit of the Laws (Anne M. Cohler et al. eds., 1989), first published in 1748, became, along with Locke's Second Treatise, the political authority most widely cited by our founding generation. Montesquieu converted traditional mixture theory into a set of checks in a system of separated powers. He saw that although checks conflicted with a principle of pure separation of powers, they could stop encroachments and promote efficiency.

Montesquieu's principal contributions were to make a clearer separation of executive and legislative functions than had his predecessors, and to emphasize the importance of a separate and independent judiciary. He prescribed a bicameral legislature. A separate executive would possess veto power over legislation and would command the army. An independent judiciary would provide a vital bulwark against tyranny. Anne M. Cohler, Montesquieu's Comparative Politics and the Spirit of American Constitutionalism (1988).

2. Government in Colonial America

English colonies, unlike those of other nations, had a substantial degree of local self-government. Especially at the beginning, colonial governments featured a complex blending of functions rather than separated powers. The ruling bodies could legislate for their people, but not contrary to the laws of England. By 1765, colonial legislatures held control of finance, like the House of Commons. Legislatures also commonly exercised judicial functions, trying cases and granting appellate relief. The royal governors exercised veto powers over colonial assemblies, and could create courts and appoint and remove judges. The colonial councils, usually appointed by the Crown, advised the governor, acted as the upper house of the legislature, and sat as the supreme court.

Blended form of Government

3. Revolutionary State Governments

Americans adopted the separation of powers for their newly independent states. *See generally* WILLI P. ADAMS, THE FIRST AMERICAN CONSTITUTIONS: REPUBLICAN IDEOLOGY AND THE MAKING OF THE STATE CONSTITUTIONS IN THE REVOLUTIONARY ERA (1980); Robert F. Williams, *"Experience Must Be Our Only Guide": The State Constitutional Experience of the Framers of the Federal Constitution,* 15 HASTINGS CONST. L.Q. 403 (1988). The new state constitutions often contained ringing endorsements of separation of powers principles. To those who had resisted kingly tyranny, the purpose of separation was to prevent executive manipulation of the judiciary and especially the legislature. The resulting structures were prone to an unanticipated problem — legislative abuse of the other branches and of the people.

Understandably, Americans proceeded by revising existing colonial structures. In practice, the states vested power almost entirely in the legislatures, bringing them close to the people by providing a one-year term of office. Dominating the new state governments, the legislatures assumed not only their existing functions, such as controlling courts and issuing judgments, but also a number of previously executive functions, such as declaring war, conducting foreign policy, and issuing pardons. Ten states divided their legislatures into two houses. The senates, converted from the colonial councils, were meant to promote stability by means of their smaller size, longer tenure, and staggered terms. Most states had special property qualifications for senatorial candidates, but direct election by the people not by the lower house.

The new governments contained a core guarantee of separation of powers that sharply distinguished them from the British: prohibitions on holding office in more than one branch. For Americans had feared and resented the colonial governors' use of "corruption" to control legislators by appointing them to executive or judicial posts.

Nothing in experience or in traditional theories told Americans how to select an executive. It was obvious, though, that the mode of selection was crucial to the authority of the office. Except for New York, the state constitutions of 1776–78 subordinated the executive to the legislature. The states provided for election by the assembly (often annually and often with rotation in office). They also appended councils selected by the assembly or by the people. Most enumerated executive functions were subject to control by the council.

The state constitutions stripped the governor of the veto and all prerogatives. Most or all executive actions were subject to overruling by someone. Impeachment was included despite its desuetude in England. No state allowed the governor alone to appoint officers — the legislatures held that power, alone or concurrently with him. These weak governors were consistent with strict separation of powers theory, but not with effective government, as war pressures would soon demonstrate.

Most of the states excluded the judges from the upper houses of the legislature and stripped the governors and councils of the judicial role. No new state placed judicial tenure at the executive's pleasure; most chose legislative appointment. Judges were not to be independent of the people. Some had terms of years; others were subject to removal.

The new constitutions of Virginia and especially Pennsylvania created relatively radical schemes featuring legislative dominance. In 1777, New York provided the leading example of a conservative constitution, one that eventually influenced the Federal Constitution. This constitution contained an executive with significant authority, on which the presidency would be modeled. The governor received "the supreme executive power and authority of the State." He was commander-in-chief, could pardon criminals, could recommend legislation, and was charged "to take care that the laws are executed to the best of his ability." The governor was chosen by the electorate, not the legislature, for a three-year term with eligibility for reelection. He had both a qualified power of appointment and a qualified veto. In place of a general privy council, there were councils of appointment (with senators) and of revision (with judges).

In the new states, legislatures, as the people's representatives, thought they could alter constitutions, especially under the exigency of war. Executives and courts were defenseless. Legislatures dictated to them by laws they could not oppose. The courts were vulnerable because legislatures had traditionally performed adjudicative functions.

Eventually, a reaction to legislative dominance set in. James Madison objected to the great volume and changeability of laws in the new legislatures. He saw the problem as one of oppressive majorities, because that was where the real power lay. In 1787, Madison wrote VICES OF THE POLITICAL SYSTEM OF THE UNITED STATES. He listed the defects of state governments: noncompliance with congressional requisitions, encroachment on national authority, violation of treaties, trespasses on each other, and a lack of guarantees against internal violence.

Thomas Jefferson's NOTES ON THE STATE OF VIRGINIA complained that: "All the powers of government, legislative, executive, and judiciary, result to the legislative body." (WILLIAM PEDEN ED., 1954, AT 120). It now seemed that "173 despots would surely be as oppressive as one." The Virginia Constitution had forbidden any branch to exercise another's power, "[b]ut no barrier was provided between these several powers." Because the executive and judiciary were dependent on the legislature for subsistence, or even continuance, in office, they would not complain of its encroachments. Jefferson argued that power must be "so divided and balanced among several bodies . . . that no one could transcend their legal limits, without being effectually checked and restrained by the others." *Id.* Thus checks and balances reappeared as a primary element of a reformed system.

Most proposed reforms focused on maintaining separation of the three functions of government. Obviously, power had to be taken from the lower houses and given to the senates, the courts, and the governors. Popular election of governors would establish independence from the legislatures. Rotation in office now seemed to promote weakness and instability. An executive power to veto legislation would prevent encroachments. Legislative appointment of officers had led to faction and corruption; executive appointment would aid independence. Legislative exercise of judicial powers, a century-old practice, now seemed improper. Also, judges should be freed of dependence on the legislature by executive appointment and tenure during good behavior.

4. The Articles of Confederation

The nature of union, and not its desirability, was the major issue in 1776. John Adams observed that the colonies could choose between declaring themselves "a sovereign state, or a number of confederated sovereign states." MERRILL JENSEN, THE ARTICLES OF CONFEDERATION 167 (1940). Although formal parties did not exist during the Revolution, there were broad differences in outlook. Radical republicans generally trusted their state legislatures and distrusted all distant central government. Conservatives hoped to construct a strong central authority that could regulate trade, control western lands, settle interstate disputes, and protect property rights generally.

In 1777, Congress adopted the Articles of Confederation and sent them to the states for ratification, which had to be unanimous. Under the Articles, the powers of Congress included conducting war and foreign affairs, regulating coinage and post offices, appointing army and navy officers, and requisitioning troops. Congress had no power to tax or to regulate trade. To prevent any grant of undefined residual powers to Congress, Article 2 stipulated that each state retained every power not expressly delegated. Important decisions needed the consent of nine states, almost three-quarters. Most important, amending the Articles required unanimity. One recalcitrant state could — and would — block needed reforms.

The Articles forbade anyone to sit in Congress for more than three of any six years. An incompatibility clause in Article 5 provided: "nor shall any person, being a delegate, be capable of holding any office under the United States" for a salary. The delegates added a provision guaranteeing free speech and immunity from arrest for members of Congress, except for treason, felony, or breach of the peace.

The Articles omitted any permanent executive, and provided only for a committee of states to sit while Congress was in recess. The committee could exercise powers entrusted to it, not including such important matters as declaring war, entering treaties, or appropriating money. The committee could appoint a member "to preside," but not for more than one year in three. Also lacking any federal judiciary, the Articles made Congress the last resort in disputes between states, under a complex arbitral process.

Congress had created more of an alliance than a nation. The Articles certainly dispersed power effectively. Congress, having no power to make rules binding citizens, was less a legislative body than an executive or administrative one. Under the pressure of wartime necessity, Congress evolved substantially. Eventually Congress became less an active administrator and more a maker of policies for permanent subordinates. It created mixed boards composed of its own members and others, for admiralty, war, and the treasury. Washington pressed for further reform.

> The need for a separate executive was becoming clear. Hamilton complained about want of method and energy in the administration . . . and the want of a proper executive. Congress have kept the power too much in their own hands and have meddled too much with details of every sort. Congress is, properly, a deliberative corps, and it forgets itself when it attempts to play the executive. It is impossible such a body, numerous as it is, and constantly fluctuating, can ever act with sufficient decision or with system. (THACH, *supra*, at 64.)

Jefferson later echoed this argument:

> I think it very material to separate in the hands of Congress the Executive and Legislative powers, as the judiciary already are in some degree. . . . The want of it has been the source of more evil than we have experienced from any other cause. Nothing is so embarrassing as the details of execution. The smallest trifle of that kind occupies as long as the most important act of legislation, and takes the place of everything else. (*Id.* at 70.)

Finally, in 1781, executive departments of foreign affairs, war, marine, and treasury were formed. Peace followed, and Congress withered. In 1785–86, Congress went without a quorum of nine states for all but a few days. Shays' Rebellion frightened moderates everywhere as mobs blocked courts from convening. In February 1787, Congress finally voted to ask the states to send delegates to Philadelphia. Given the colonial experience with central power, the creation of an effective national government would be as great a political revolution as the one in 1776.

5. The Constitutional Convention

Statements that "the framers" intended something are treacherous. Today, it is difficult to identify decisive influences on a text that evolved from a series of compromises. The process, which called for majority votes of the states, was marked by internal divisions in the delegations, close votes, and fluctuating outcomes. Often it was difficult to identify the interests of particular states in proposed structural features of the new national government. *See generally* CATHERINE DRINKER BOWEN, MIRACLE AT PHILADELPHIA (1966); CLINTON ROSSITER, 1787, THE GRAND CONVENTION (1966); CARL VAN DOREN, THE GREAT REHEARSAL (1948).

On the eve of the Constitutional Convention, Madison drafted the Virginia plan, which effectively set the agenda. It separated legislative and executive personnel through an ineligibility clause. A chief executive (of undetermined number) would be elected by the legislature without possibility for reelection. A council of revision having executive and judicial members would hold a qualified veto of national laws and an absolute veto of state laws. Overall, separation of powers was less prominent in the plan than was concentration of power in Congress.

The delegates began by passing a resolution calling for replacement of the Articles with a national government composed of three branches. The delegates then debated the Virginia plan in committee of the whole. Madison also called for granting the executive powers to effectuate national laws, to appoint officers, and to "execute such other powers not Legislative nor Judiciary in their nature" as Congress delegated.

James Wilson responded that the executive should rest on the whole people, not the states, and should be independent of the legislature. He thought a unitary executive would provide "energy, dispatch, and responsibility." 1 Max Farrand, The Records of the Federal Convention of 1787, 65 (rev. ed. 1966). Wilson wanted an absolute veto in a council of revision, and election by the people with eligibility for reelection. His plan, which was obviously based on New York, would have put the executive on an equal plane with the legislature, instead of Madison's more subordinated model.

Delegates opposed to a strong executive, such as George Mason and Roger Sherman, now made their case for an administrative executive, who should be "nothing more than an institution for carrying the will of the legislature into effect." *Id.* They lost — Wilson's proposal for a single executive passed, 7–3. Since all states but New York had a general council to restrict the governor, this was a real move toward efficiency and responsibility. The Convention preliminarily chose legislative election to a single, seven-year term, impeachment for "malpractice or neglect of duty," and no council of revision but a veto. National power to coerce the states was gone; indeed, state legislatures were to elect senators. The executive's duties were to execute the laws and to make appointments, except for judges, who were to be appointed by the Senate.

Then the New Jersey counterproposal shifted the focus from the executive to representation. Although it was defeated, the plan had important effects. It had a plural executive, to be chosen by the legislature for a single term. Its powers were to execute the law, to control the military, and to appoint officers, including judges. Operating on the states not the citizens, this plan revealed its infeasibility by authorizing the executive to call out the troops to coerce a state. For the most part, its version of congressional powers was adopted, and it contained the germ of the supremacy clause. Wilson objected to its unicameral legislature, explaining that a legislature should be divided within itself into distinct and independent branches, to foster both liberty and stability.

Debate on the composition of Congress continued. In July the Convention adopted Franklin's suggestion for equal representation of states in the Senate, balanced by having money bills originate in the House. The compromise passed narrowly, and the delegates returned to the executive. The small states, having gained the Senate, wanted to empower it at the expense of the executive, which was seen as a large-state office. A complex discussion of election, eligibility for reelection, and length of term ensued. After considering seven distinct alternatives, the delegates reverted to the original plan.

The Convention recessed while a Committee of Detail drafted a document embodying the decisions to date. The committee, mostly lawyers, considered a plan for the executive that closely followed New York's. An enumeration of executive powers emerged that would remain unchanged by the Convention. It specified that the "executive power" would be in a single person. The President's powers would include being commander-in-chief, receiving ambassadors, making appointments, exercising a conditional veto, and issuing pardons.

The Committee of Detail also enumerated congressional powers. Congress received authority to regulate commerce, make war, raise armies, call up the militia, establish courts, and appoint a treasurer. The Senate was to have exclusive power to make treaties and to appoint ambassadors and justices.

Debate on the draft began. The Convention had not seriously addressed the President's relation to administration. In August, it considered proposals for a council to supply nonbinding advice to the President, and even for a cabinet council and a constitutional organization of the executive departments. The Convention eventually dropped these matters of detail, except for the "Opinions Clause."

The Convention made various other changes in the report of the Committee of Detail. Congress was given power to declare rather than to make war, in order to allow Presidents to repel sudden attacks and to avoid confusion with the conduct of war, an executive function. The Senate had evolved into a kind of executive council, which might sit constantly, managing foreign affairs.

At the end of August, the Committee of Eleven was formed to address unresolved issues. Matters referred included presidential election and reelection, the role of the Senate in conducting foreign affairs and selecting judges, the method of impeachment, ineligibility and incompatibility, and the right of the House to initiate revenue bills. The committee broke the deadlock over the executive by inventing the Electoral College. The state legislatures retained power to pick the electors or to let the people do so. The small states were guaranteed weighted minimum representation, while the large ones won proportionality otherwise. In the absence of a majority the people's branch would decide, voting by states.

Following the committee's recommendations, the Convention modified the relations between President and Senate. The executive received appointment and treaty powers with the Senate's concurrence. The President's term was to be four years, with reelection allowed. Impeachments were to be tried in the Senate on a two-thirds vote. The House gained the power to originate revenue bills, an important matter to the large states.

The major decisions having been made, the Committee of Style touched up the drafting. It included Hamilton and Madison; Gouverneur Morris, an accomplished stylist, "wrote" the Constitution. Freed by the Convention's poor internal recordkeeping (there was no complete, official draft) and by the general fatigue, the committee included some new features, such as the contracts clause. Its product was amended again and finally adopted. The Convention appended a resolution recommending that Congress forward the proposed Constitution to the states for submission to conventions of delegates chosen by the people. Congress and all the state legislatures subsequently agreed.

By 1787, both separation of powers and checks and balances were widely accepted as general principles. Madison provided the key link by arguing that checks maintain separation—they combine to guarantee a Constitution's paper provisions. There was spirited disagreement over the institutional arrangements that could satisfy separation of powers. The Constitution's major attribute of formal separation of powers is its separation of personnel. Equally important is its creation of an independent political base for the presidency. Combined with executive nomination of judges and guarantees of their tenure, this severing of the executive from dependence on Congress created three truly independent branches.

Executive power remained vague in the minds of men who wanted neither another king nor another Confederation. Even in England, the concept had always been difficult to define, partly because it included residuary powers not allocated elsewhere. The Convention's most important qualifications on executive power were the conditional nature of the veto and the senatorial checks on appointments and treaties.

The very delicate issue of "corruption" was compromised by forbidding the joint holding of legislative and executive office, but allowing the appointment of former legislators to executive offices, except for those created or for which salaries were increased during their tenure in Congress. The framers, with a new theory of executive responsibility to the people, saw no reason to adopt the responsibility to the legislature that England was still struggling to accomplish.

The judiciary received the least attention, because it was regarded as the least powerful branch. There was agreement that it should be independent, with tenure during good behavior. Congress was left free to create lower courts and to decide the size of the Supreme Court. Although there was no explicit debate over judicial review of legislation, at least eight delegates, including Madison and Wilson, did remark that the judicial function would include review of legislation, and no one argued the contrary. The power of judicial review, which had been asserted in the courts in three or four dicta and one or two decisions, remained an inchoate idea in America.

6. Expounding and Ratifying the Constitution

Both the Constitution and its supporting arguments displayed the Enlightenment's interest in social mechanics. The challenge was to use republican institutions to develop the best elements of human nature and dampen the worst. The FEDERALIST PAPERS appeared in an effort to obtain ratification in the critical state of New York. (The BENJAMIN F. WRIGHT EDITION, 1961, has a good introduction.) Publius took a balanced view of human nature, as part good and part evil. For example, in No. 76, Hamilton argued that "[t]he supposition of universal venality . . . is little less an error in political reasoning than the supposition of universal rectitude."

Factions had abused the state governments; controlling them lay at the heart of the federalists' program. The Constitution contained two main devices to harness our complex behavior: the nature of representation and the structure of the national government. Madison's famous argument in No. 10 explored the former; here we concentrate on the latter.

The contribution of the structure of government to public virtue depended on a complex analysis. Madison's task in Numbers 47–51 was to justify abandonment of strict separation of powers in favor of a system relying heavily on checks and balances. The opening discussion in No. 47 declared that separate branches were needed to prevent undue concentrations of power, and quickly shifted to the more controversial blending of powers to create checks and balances. In No. 48, Madison explained that "parchment barriers" such as those in the state constitutions would not ensure separation in practice without a constitutional control in each branch over the others. Each branch must have adequate defenses; none could have a superior right of setting the boundaries. Multiple representation plus separation of powers and checks and balances would prevent corruption of the overall balance by preventing any officer from acquiring power over the others. In No. 51, Madison added a layer of competing officeholders to that of the interest groups he had discussed in No. 10. Ambition should be made to countervail ambition. Having the officers check each other to remedy "the defect of better motives" would let private interest "be a sentinel over the public rights."

The courts provided the federalists with a possible stabilizer to keep the other two branches in balance. The prospect of judicial review created problems of limiting judicial supremacy, however. In No. 78, Hamilton tried to assuage such fears, by arguing that the courts would provide salutary checks on Congress. He noted that interpretation of statutes could serve as one check. Outright invalidation of legislation was justified by the supremacy of the constituent act over both court and legislature. Indeed, the absence of a court would violate the "celebrated maxim" of separation of powers, because lawmakers would be left to judge their own cause. In No. 81, he argued that impeachment threats would suffice to prevent courts from abusing their power.

The Federalist Papers met a vigorous response. The antifederalists feared that the President could become king for life because of the long term, reelection eligibility, absence of a council, and commander-in-chief and appointment powers. The Senate could become "a fixed and unchangeable body of men" allied to the President through shared powers over legislation, treaties, and appointments. For a concise introduction to their views, *see* Herbert J. Storing, What the Anti-Federalists Were For, the introductory essay to his seven-volume The Complete Anti-Federalist (1981).

Ratification was a close battle, full of political manipulation. Pennsylvania federalists forced an immediate vote, to prevent effective organization of the opposition. South Carolina came in by a single vote. Massachusetts was close but favorable. The spring of 1788, with eight of nine needed ratifications complete, saw an upsurge of antifederalist sentiment, rallying around the call for a bill of rights. Then New Hampshire's ratification created the new nation, which still needed Virginia and New York to be viable. Virginia joined after a promise that a bill of rights would follow ratification. New York, long leaning to the antis, weakened under the barrages of Hamilton and ratified narrowly. The new Constitution was a going concern.

B. Approaches to Separation of Powers Analysis

More than two centuries of practice and legal disputation under the government the framers made have created a substantial legacy of materials bearing on legal issues surrounding the structure of our national government, as the rest of this book will reveal. Today, lawyers inhabiting all three branches of the government and the private sector as well encounter these issues regularly. Indeed, because state governments usually incorporate separation of powers principles, state constitutional law often borrows concepts from federal doctrine (although it need not do so).

How should a lawyer—or law student—approach a separation of powers problem? Unfortunately, there is no simple answer to this question. For its part, the Supreme Court has displayed a number of different approaches. The Court often mixes them in a single case, and, in any event, the boundaries between them are often indistinct. Nevertheless, it should aid understanding and analysis to attempt a preliminary catalog here, so that you can apply it to the cases. We have identified at least the following categories of approaches, and principal questions that they raise, in the Court's opinions:

1. Textual

Because it is a written constitution we are expounding, it is natural for the Court to lay at least some stress on the meaning of the text. You may be familiar with the interpretive strategies that are usually thought appropriate for the open-textured constitutional guarantees of due process and equal protection—should the same strategies apply to separation of powers issues? For arguments that different kinds of constitutional provisions should evoke different interpretive approaches, *see* Peter M. Shane, *Conventionalism in Constitutional Interpretation and the Place of Administrative Agencies,* 36 Am. U. L. Rev. 573 (1987); Frederick Schauer, *Easy Cases,* 58 S. Cal. L. Rev. 399 (1985).

The cases place quite variant reliance on the text. Sometimes they purport to give it conclusive weight. Also, some of the cases employ canons of construction, with their notorious manipulability. If the text seems clear, to what extent should other techniques of analysis be employed? If the text seems ambiguous, how much should it confine decision, if at all? What kinds of implications should be drawn from the text? *See generally Symposium, Textualism and the Constitution,* 66 Geo. Wash. L. Rev. 1081 (1998).

The most prominent "textualist" on the recent Court was the late Justice Antonin Scalia, who argued that the words of the Constitution should be read as they would have been commonly understood at the time they were written. Antonin Scalia, A Matter of Interpretation: Federal Courts and the Law (1997). Even he, however, sometimes appeared to depart from obvious textual readings, perhaps most prominently in connection with the Eleventh Amendment, which explicitly bars only suits against states in federal court brought by citizens of other states or of a foreign state. Justice Scalia nonetheless joined in opinions interpreting the Amendment as barring all unconsented suits against states that are based on federal law, even if brought in state courts. See, e.g., *Alden v. Maine*, 527 U.S. 706 (1999).

2. Original Intent

We have enough constitutional history of the development of the text and of interpretations given it by the framers to tempt the Court to search for original intent. Indeed, one school of thought would confine the Court to analysis of the text and accompanying indicia of original intent. See Leonard W. Levy, Original Intent and the Framers' Constitution (1989); Edwin Meese, *Toward a Jurisprudence of Original Intention*, 2 Benchmark 1 (1986); Caleb Nelson, *Originalism and Interpretive Conventions*, 70 U. Chi. L. Rev. 519 (2003); H. Jefferson Powell, *Rules for Originalists*, 73 Va. L. Rev. 659 (1987); William H. Rehnquist, *The Notion of a Living Constitution*, 54 Tex. L. Rev. 693 (1976).

Advocates of an original intent approach face some obstacles. First, there are serious problems in imputing one intention to any product of group decisionmaking. Second, consider our outline of constitutional history. Many modern problems are simply not addressed there. Third, the records of the Constitutional Convention are far from a complete transcript of the proceedings, and serious doubt surrounds the accuracy of some of them. See James H. Hutson, *The Creation of the Constitution: The Integrity of the Documentary Record*, 65 Tex. L. Rev. 1 (1986). It now appears that James Madison substantially revised his influential notes of the Convention over the years before their publication. Mary S. Bilder, Madison's Hand: Revising the Constitutional Convention (2015). And fourth, a lively debate surrounds the question whether the framers themselves accepted or rejected a jurisprudence of original intent. See Jack N. Rakove, Original Meanings: Politics and Ideas in the Making of the Constitution (1996); Jack N. Rakove, ed., Interpreting the Constitution, The Debate Over Original Intent (1990).

Whose intent counts? The Court often credits the influential views of the authors of the Federalist Papers or records of the Constitutional Convention. Yet how do we discover and weigh the intent of the thirteen ratifying conventions in the states? The Court often gives special weight to the "contemporaneous construction" of the Constitution by the framers after ratification, especially in the First Congress. Yet perhaps these actions reflected perceived needs to depart from original intent in light of experience. For example, Madison himself eventually abandoned his initial opposition to the constitutionality of the Bank of the United States, citing "repeated recognitions . . . of [its] validity . . . in acts of the legislative, executive, and judicial branches of the Government." Drew R. McCoy, The Last of the Fathers 81 (1989). For a review of the varying and evolving views of the framers as our government established itself, see Joseph M. Lynch, Negotiating the Constitution: The Earliest Debates Over Original Intent (1999).

Other puzzling questions remain. If history suggests an original meaning that seems inconsistent with the text, which should govern? If the original meaning seems inappropriate to present conditions, may it be disregarded?

Moreover, the use of original intent raises an obvious normative question: Especially because the framers drafted a Constitution so difficult to amend, why should a contemporary Court be bound by their intentions when at odds with the views of a majority of modern Americans?

The Court often decides separation of powers cases by using a process of reasoning logically from the text of the Constitution and what is known about the framers' intent. The usual term for this approach is formalism; notice that it tends to obscure the presence of any other reasons for decision, such as value preferences.

3. Structural/Functional

Structural arguments make appeal to "inferences from the existence of constitutional structures and the relationships which the Constitution ordains among those structures." Phillip Bobbitt, Constitutional Fate: A Theory of the Constitution 74 (1984). It is a method first given modern scholarly prominence in the work of the late Charles Black. See Charles L. Black, Structure and Relationship in Constitutional Law (1969). Structural analysis seems especially apt for separation of powers issues. Yet it suffers serious problems of specificity and limits. For example, the Constitution creates separate branches for the three functions of legislation, execution, and judging. Does that imply rigid boundaries between them? Are government entities, such as independent agencies, that do not fit neatly in the tripartite scheme of legislative, executive, and judicial powers forbidden?

One mode of interpretation, which may be seen as a variety of structural interpretation, is functionalism. Functionalism accepts that the Constitution embodies a set of foundational premises about how the branches of government were supposed to work, but rejects a strict formalist reading that would confine each branch exclusively to functions fitting classical labels. Observing that the activities of government are very diverse, and often resist easy characterization, functionalists prefer to ask whether a particular institutional arrangement invades the "core functions" of one of the branches. If not, they—like the Court, when it is operating in the functionalist mode—would uphold such an arrangement when challenged. See M. Elizabeth Magill, *The Real Separation in Separation of Powers Law*, 86 Va. L. Rev. 1127 (2000); Thomas W. Merrill, *The Constitutional Principle of Separation of Powers*, 1991

Sup. Ct. Rev. 225; Peter L. Strauss, *The Place of Agencies in Government: Separation of Powers and the Fourth Branch*, 84 Colum. L. Rev. 573 (1984).

4. Institutional Competence

This is a style of interpretation closely related to structural analysis. The three constitutional branches differ in their institutional nature. What does that suggest for the particular tasks that should be allocated to each branch? For example, the judiciary, enjoying life tenure and salary protections, is well situated to play a countermajoritarian role in American life. How far does that go in justifying judicial review as it now exists? Similarly, the presidency enjoys the advantages in "energy, dispatch, and responsibility" that accrue to its unitary structure. What does that suggest for the allocation of foreign relations responsibilities between President and Congress?

5. Historical Practice

Through their historically developed practices, the three branches have provided possible answers for many of the Constitution's ambiguities and silences. In what circumstances should the Court honor these? What if they seem to conflict with the text or original intent? What requisites such as duration, consistency, and visibility should be expected of a practice before it attains prescriptive weight? *See* Michael J. Glennon, *The Use of Custom in Resolving Separation of Powers Disputes*, 64 B.U. L. Rev. 109 (1984). What if the other branches object or acquiesce? Of special interest here is the status of some legislation, such as the War Powers Resolution, that addresses the distribution of power that has developed incrementally, and tries to set enduring limits. These statutes, along with traditional practices, can achieve a kind of quasi-constitutional status even where a practice has not ripened into constitutional gloss.

6. Values

This term is meant to cover a host of effects on interpretation that stem from values that an interpreter holds, but that are not obviously related to conventional methods of constitutional interpretation. *See generally* Sanford Levinson, Constitutional Faith (1988); Philip Bobbitt, Constitutional Fate (1982); John H. Ely, Democracy and Distrust: A Theory of Judicial Review (1980). These values can, of course, have many sources, such as a sense of necessity in a particular situation or a person's own political philosophy. The operative values are sometimes more obscure in separation of powers cases than in the individual rights cases where their presence and effects are so often openly debated.

Not surprisingly, value judgments inhere in the Supreme Court's efforts to draw the line between law and politics. Thus, the Court often pursues prudential values, whether explicitly or not, in deciding whether to reach the merits of separation of powers disputes. The doctrines of standing and political questions embody these values. *See* Jesse H. Choper, Judicial Review and the National Political Process: A Functional Reconsideration of the Role of the Supreme Court (1980).

Individual Justices continue to engage in ancient debates, traceable to Hamilton and Jefferson, between strict and loose construction of the Constitution, and between interpretations that concentrate and those that disperse the powers of the national government. Similarly, in defining executive power, the Court weighs the comparative values of rules and discretion ("a government of laws, and not of men"). These tradeoffs can be quite complex and subtle. For example, even when recognizing discretion the Court can compensate by implying requirements for legal controls that assure accountability. And the Court can cloak any or all of these kinds of value judgments in neutral garb (such as textual analysis) or obfuscation (such as reference to undefined "inherent" powers). What are the appropriate sources of a lawyer's or judge's separation of powers values, and what role should they play in interpretation?

For an essay that connects the debate over interpretive method to debates about the legitimacy of judicial review more generally, see Peter Shane, "Analyzing Constitutions," in R.A.W. Rhodes, Sarah A. Binder, and Bert A. Rockman, The Oxford Handbook of Political Institutions (2006).

C. The Ambiguities of Executive Power: Competing Theories of the Presidency

Our brief constitutional history noted that the vagueness of Article II presents special problems for the interpreter. These problems are only magnified by the tendency of the great crises of our national history to pose questions of executive power. So we pause to introduce competing theories of presidential power. Academics have produced a vast literature on the Presidency. Some places to enter this realm include: Harold J. Krent, Presidential Powers (2005); Leonard W. Levy & Louis Fisher eds., Encyclopedia of the American Presidency (1994); Forrest McDonald, The American Presidency, An Intellectual History (1994); Peter M. Shane, Madison's Nightmare: How Executive Power Threatens American Democracy (2009).

As we shall see in this book, all three federal branches interpret the Constitution continuously as they perform their assigned functions. The executive is distinctive in that final interpretation lies in the hands of one person — the President. In Untrodden Ground: How Presidents Interpret the Constitution (2015), Harold H. Bruff explores the history and impact of presidential interpretation. *See also* Akhil R. Amar, America's Unwritten Constitution (2015); Ken Gormley, ed., The Presidents and the Constitution: A Living History (2016). Bruff summarizes his findings, *supra* at 3–4:

[F]ive main factors appear to drive presidential interpretation; they lie more in history and politics than in law as conventionally understood. First, each president sees the Constitution through the lens of his own character and experience. Presidents approach the document in ways that reflect their temperament (for example, Buchanan's cowardice, Lincoln's courage, Andrew Johnson's rigidity) . . . .

Second, a president's political values and priorities affect his view of the Constitution in fundamental ways. Each incoming president encounters the political opportunities and constraints of the day. Sometimes the scope of available political choice is wide, sometimes narrow. Some of our presidents have reconstructed the politics of their day by their behavior in office — Jefferson, Jackson, Lincoln, Franklin Roosevelt, Reagan. In doing so they find a wide scope for constitutional interpretation as well. Thus politics and law move together, guided with varying degrees of success by presidents. Whatever their capacities, all presidents have interpretive options. For example, . . . whether a president believes in a vigorous or restrained role for the federal government affects his constitutional interpretations comprehensively.

Third, the incentives that the presidency contains steer presidents once they assume the office, whatever their prior views may have been. For most presidents, a broad view of the powers of the office is essential to achieving political goals. Hence, the Whig presidents of the nineteenth century often found themselves abandoning party orthodoxy, which favored a quite restrained presidency, in favor of the vigorous views that other incumbents have adopted.

Fourth, the practical problems of the day drive interpretation. Of course, no president controls his own agenda more than partially. Fate intervenes. As Lincoln remarked, events control presidents to an important extent. Perceived necessity demands a solution that works today, whatever its implications for tomorrow or its basis in yesterday.

Fifth, presidents view themselves in historical perspective, and want to be compared with their most illustrious predecessors, not the least of them. Therefore they rummage among the available precedents that could be invoked to lend both legitimacy and luster to a new decision. They avoid precedents that invite comparison to the presidency's worst moments.

Now let us examine some influential presidential interpretations in the Presidents' own words.

1. Washington

As he took office, George Washington was already a national hero, universally known as the commander of the victorious army during the Revolution. He had been unanimously elected by the Electoral College, giving him freedom to act above partisan politics. *See generally* RICHARD N. SMITH, PATRIARCH, GEORGE WASHINGTON AND THE NEW AMERICAN NATION (1993); RALPH KETCHAM, PRESIDENTS ABOVE PARTY, THE FIRST AMERICAN PRESIDENCY, 1789–1829 (1984).

Washington's influence on the Presidency would be magnified because he had no precedents to follow; instead, he would be creating precedent. He was well aware of his unique position in history (NORMAN J. SMALL, SOME PRESIDENTIAL INTERPRETATIONS OF THE PRESIDENCY 14 (1932)):

> In our progress toward political happiness my station is new, and if I may use the expression, I walk on untrodden ground. There is scarcely an action, the motive of which may not be subject to a double interpretation. There is scarcely any part of my conduct which may not hereafter be drawn into precedent. Under such a view of the duties inherent in my arduous office, I could not but feel a diffidence in myself on the one hand, and an anxiety for the community.

Washington consciously avoided important substantive tests of presidential power. The nation had just emerged from twenty years of turmoil, and the new government was just beginning to gain popular acceptance—now was not the time for such tests:

> [I]n this very early stage of affairs, and at a period so little removed from an exhausting war, the public welfare and safety evidently enjoin a conduct of circumspection, moderation, and forbearance. (*Id.* at 14.)

Several important issues arose during Washington's terms of office. His 1793 "Proclamation of Neutrality" in the war between France and Britain raised serious questions regarding presidential power to make foreign policy. While Washington himself said little, debate erupted in the Cabinet between Treasury Secretary Hamilton and Secretary of State Jefferson. *See* JOHN P. ROCHE & LEONARD W. LEVY, THE PRESIDENCY 10–12 (1964). Hamilton argued that the Proclamation was authorized by a grant of power in Article II:

> The second article of the Constitution of the United States, section first, establishes this general proposition, "the EXECUTIVE POWER shall be vested in a president of the United States of America." The same article, in a succeeding section, proceeds to delineate particular cases of executive power. . . . It would not consist with the rules of sound construction, to consider this enumeration of particular authorities, as derogating from the more comprehensive grant in the general clause, further than as it may be coupled with express restrictions or limitations. . . . The difficulty of a complete enumeration of all the cases of executive authority, would naturally dictate the use of general terms, and would render it improbable, that a specification of certain particulars was designed as a substitute for those terms, when antecedently used. . . . The enumeration ought therefore to be considered, as intended merely to specify the principal articles implied in the definition of executive power; leaving the rest to flow from the general grant of that power.

James Madison, who fifteen years later was himself to become President, responded with the Jeffersonian position:

> If we consult, for a moment, the nature and operation of the two powers to declare war and to make treaties it will be impossible not to see that they can never fall within a proper definition of executive powers. The natural province of the executive magistrate is to execute laws, as that of the legislature is to make laws. All his acts, therefore, properly executive, must presuppose the existence of the laws to be executed. A treaty is not an execution of the laws; it does not pre-suppose the existence of laws. It is, on the contrary, to have itself the force of a *law*, and to be carried into *execution*, like all *other laws*, by the *executive magistrate*. To say then that the power of making treaties which are confessedly laws, belongs naturally to the department which is to execute laws, is to say, that the executive department naturally includes a legislative power. In theory this is an absurdity . . . in practice a tyranny. . . . Another important inference to be noted is, that the powers of making war and treaty being substantially of a legislative, not an executive nature, the rule of interpreting exceptions strictly, must narrow instead of enlarging executive pretensions on those subjects.

These arguments are classic statements of broad and narrow views of constitutional interpretation. They echo the famous clash between Hamilton and Jefferson in 1791 over the constitutionality of the Bank of the United States. *See* J. Willard Hurst, *Alexander Hamilton, Law Maker*, 78 Colum. L. Rev. 483 (1978). Hamilton's views persuaded Washington in both instances.

The historical prominence of the Hamilton/Jefferson debate over the nature of constitutional interpretation has obscured the presence of a third point of view, that of our first Attorney General, Edmund Randolph. Washington asked Randolph for his views on the constitutionality of the bank bill, and Randolph responded with a careful and cautious analysis that lacked the flash of his famous contemporaries. Randolph concluded that Congress lacked constitutional authority to charter a bank. For his opinion on The Constitutionality of the Bank Bill (1791) and an accompanying critique he generated of the arguments then circulating, see H. Jefferson Powell, The Constitution and the Attorneys General 3–10 (1999).

2. Jefferson

When Thomas Jefferson assumed the Presidency in 1801, it was widely assumed that, pursuant to his strict constructionist views, executive power would be severely restricted. Although Jefferson may have had an honest intention to reduce the President's role, his tenure expanded it. *See* Dumas Malone, Jefferson and His Time, vol. 4, Jefferson the President, First Term, 1801–1805 (1970); vol. 5, Jefferson the President, Second Term, 1805–1809 (1975).

The clearest example of this reversal is Jefferson's purchase of the Louisiana territory from France. He had, at first, felt that such a purchase exceeded the constitutional power of both the President and Congress: "To take a single step beyond the boundaries specifically drawn is to take possession of a boundless field of power, no longer susceptible of any definitions." 8 The Writings of Thomas Jefferson 244 (Paul L. Ford ed., 1899). But he also saw the territory as a great opportunity for the country, one which might be lost by waiting for congressional action or a constitutional amendment. Accordingly, he found a power in his office to act as a "guardian" for the people, even for an action technically outside the Constitution:

> The executive in seizing the fugitive occurrence, which so much advances the good of their country, has done an act beyond the Constitution. The Legislature in casting behind them metaphysical subtleties, and risking themselves like faithful servants, must ratify and pay for it, and throw themselves upon their country for doing for them unauthorized, what we know they would have done for themselves had they been in a situation to do it. It is the case of the guardian, investing the money of its ward in purchasing an important adjacent territory; and saying to him when of age, I did this for your good; I pretend to no right to bind you; you may disavow me and I must get out of the scrape as I can; I thought it my duty to risk myself for you. But we shall not be disavowed by the nation, and their act of indemnity will confirm and not weaken the Constitution by more strongly marking out its lines. *Id.*

Jefferson continued to advocate a strict construction of the Constitution. His actions, however, set a precedent for a strong Presidency, one which would be taken to heart by several later executives.

3. Jackson

The next major expansion in the powers of the Presidency took place in the 1830s, under the administration of Andrew Jackson. Jackson was the first "people's" President. *See* Arthur M. Schlesinger, Jr., The Age of Jackson (1950). By his time, all but a few states were selecting presidential electors by popular vote, thus clearly tying the President directly to the people. Also, more than any previous President, Jackson was one of the "common people." Far from an aristocrat, he came from the backwoods of the frontier, and achieved national fame as a hard-fighting general in wars against the British and the Indians.

Jackson became the first executive to appeal to the people over the heads of their legislative representatives. He claimed a role as the sole true representative of the people (Arthur B. Tourtellot, The Presidents on the Presidency 35 (1964)):

> We are *one people* in the choice of President and Vice-President. Here the States have no other agency than to direct the mode in which the votes shall be given. The candidates having the majority of all the votes are chosen . . . .
> The people, then, and not the States, are represented in the executive branch.

Jackson found many ways in which to exercise power. He fought the Bank of the United States, and succeeded in having it abolished. He battled Congress. Previous Presidents had wielded the veto power sparingly, usually on grounds that legislation was unconstitutional. Jackson vetoed any legislation with which he strongly disagreed. Also, he fought John Marshall and the Supreme Court. The story goes that, when the Court denied the states power to regulate Indian territory in 1832, Jackson mockingly declared, "Well, John Marshall has made his decision, now let him enforce it." ROCHE & LEVY, *supra*, at 13. Jackson consistently maintained that he could determine the constitutionality of legislation, regardless of what the Supreme Court ruled. He vetoed a bill to re-establish the Bank of the United States, although the constitutionality of its predecessor had been upheld in *McCulloch v. Maryland*, 17 U.S. (4 Wheat.) 316 (1819). He explained (TOURTELLOT, *supra*, at 268–69):

> The Congress, the Executive, and the Court must each for itself be guided by its own opinion of the Constitution. Each public officer who takes an oath to support the Constitution swears that he will support it as he understands it, and not as it is understood by others. It is as much the duty of the House of Representatives, of the Senate, and of the President to decide upon the constitutionality of any bill or resolution which may be presented to them for passage or approval as it is for the supreme judges when it may be brought before them for judicial decision. The opinion of the judges has no more authority over Congress than the opinion of Congress has over the judges, and on that point the President is independent of both. The authority of the Supreme Court must not, therefore, be permitted to control the Congress or the Executive when acting in their legislative capacities, but to have only such influence as the force of their reasoning may deserve.

4. Buchanan

After Jackson's retirement in 1836, the power of the Presidency receded dramatically. The period 1836–1861 saw mostly weak, short-lived Presidencies, as nine Presidents assumed office. At the same time, Congress was enjoying its Golden Age. Led by such men as Daniel Webster, Henry Clay, and John Calhoun, the legislature overshadowed the executive.

The administration of James Buchanan ended this period with the Presidency—and the nation—in shambles. In late 1860 and early 1861, as the southern states were announcing their secession from the Union, Buchanan maintained that there was little he could do to resolve the crisis. In his last State of the Union message he said of the Presidency (TOURTELLOT, *supra*, at 417):

> Wisely limited and restrained as is his power under our Constitution and laws, he alone can accomplish but little for good or for evil on such a momentous question. . . . From the very nature of his office, and its high responsibilities, he must necessarily be conservative. The stern duty of administering

the vast and complicated concerns of this government affords in itself a guarantee that he will not attempt any violation of a clear constitutional right. After all, he is no more than the chief executive officer of the government. His province is not to make but to execute the laws. . . . Apart from the execution of the laws, so far as this may be practicable, the Executive has no authority to decide what shall be the relations between the federal government and South Carolina.

5. Lincoln

Buchanan's successor, Abraham Lincoln, held an entirely different view of the President's power to respond to secession. *See* DANIEL FARBER, LINCOLN'S CONSTITUTION (2003); JAMES G. RANDALL, CONSTITUTIONAL PROBLEMS UNDER LINCOLN (REV. ED. 1951). Rejecting constitutional niceties concerning executive power, Lincoln maintained that his duty was to save the federal Union—and that he was justified in taking any action to achieve that end, even if it were otherwise unconstitutional. As he wrote to Samuel Chase: "These rebels are violating the Constitution to destroy the Union; I will violate the Constitution, if necessary, to save the Union; and I suspect, Chase, that our Constitution is going to have a rough time of it before we get done with this row." (WARD H. LAMON, RECOLLECTIONS OF ABRAHAM LINCOLN 221 (1911)).

The Constitution did, in fact, have "a rough time of it" before the war was over. During his four years in office, Lincoln took a series of dramatic and constitutionally questionable steps. Although no declaration of war had been made, he called for new troops, declared a blockade against southern ports, and commenced military action. Basic civil liberties, including habeas corpus, were suspended. *See* MARK E. NEELY, JR., THE FATE OF LIBERTY: ABRAHAM LINCOLN AND CIVIL LIBERTIES (1991). And in 1863 Lincoln unilaterally ordered the emancipation of all slaves within rebel territory, without congressional approval, as a war measure.

Lincoln justified these actions as necessary to save the Union. As he explained this "doctrine of necessity" (TOURTELLOT, *supra*, at 399):

[M]y oath to preserve the Constitution to the best of my ability imposed upon me the duty of preserving, by every indispensable means, that government. . . . Was it possible to lose the nation and yet preserve the Constitution? By general law, life and limb must be protected, yet often a limb must be amputated to save a life; but a life is never wisely given to save a limb. I felt that measures otherwise unconstitutional might become lawful by becoming indispensable to the preservation of the Constitution through the preservation of the nation. Right or wrong, I assumed this ground, and now avow it. I could not feel that, to the best of my ability, I had even tried to preserve the Constitution, if, to save slavery or any minor matter, I should permit the wreck of government, country, and Constitution all together.

6. Wilson on the Post-Civil War Presidency

The dramatic increase in executive power brought about by Lincoln was, however, not to continue beyond the Civil War. Although Andrew Johnson, Lincoln's successor, tried to exercise strong authority, he did not possess either the ability or popular support necessary to succeed. Congress reasserted its powers. Johnson eventually faced an impeachment trial in the Senate for defying Congress. He escaped conviction by one vote, but the Presidency was not soon to recover. Beginning with the election of General Ulysses Grant in 1868, weak and unassertive Presidents were to hold office for most of the rest of the century. The dominance of Congress, as in the antebellum years, had returned.

The sickly state of the Presidency during this era was noted in 1885 in CONGRESSIONAL GOVERNMENT: A STUDY IN AMERICAN POLITICS, by Woodrow Wilson, the future President who was then a doctoral candidate at Johns Hopkins University. Wilson believed that the "balance of powers" set up by the Constitution had been destroyed. Congress, in fact if not in theory, was the supreme branch of government (*Id.* at 28):

> The noble charter of fundamental law given us by the Convention of 1787 is still our Constitution; but it is now our *form of government* rather in name than in reality, the form of the Constitution being one of nicely adjusted, ideal balances, whilst the actual form of our present government is simply a scheme of congressional supremacy. . . .

Wilson urged solving the problem of legislative dominance by adoption of a system more like the British one, in which the President could act as a "Prime Minister." He rejected the idea, however, that the President could take extra-constitutional actions in times of crisis. Instead, the President should try to induce Congress to grant his requests.

By 1900, Wilson thought that his early views of government had become out of date, as the President was once again "at the front of affairs" (*Id.* at 22, Preface to the Fifteenth Printing). Like any good scholar, Wilson wrote a successor volume to present his new views. In CONSTITUTIONAL GOVERNMENT IN THE UNITED STATES 69 (1908), he said of the President:

> He may be both the leader of his party and the leader of the nation, or he may be one or the other. If he lead the nation, his party can hardly resist him. His office is anything he has the sagacity and force to make it.

When he reached the presidency, Wilson certainly tried to play this role, and sometimes succeeded. See AUGUST HECKSCHER, WOODROW WILSON (1991).

7. Theodore Roosevelt and Taft

Even before Wilson had the chance to implement his ideas in practice, the Presidency began to awake from its slumber. The revival began under William McKinley during the Spanish-American War. It crested when Theodore Roosevelt assumed office. Roosevelt was an enthusiastic disciple of Lincoln's broad theory of presidential power. While Lincoln had been careful to justify his actions on the basis of wartime emergency, however, Roosevelt faced no such crisis. The breadth of his views therefore exceeded those held by any of his predecessors.

Roosevelt explicitly rejected the idea that specific constitutional authorization was needed for a President to act. As he explained this "residuum of powers" theory (THEODORE ROOSEVELT, AN AUTOBIOGRAPHY 388 (1913)):

> [I insisted] upon the theory that the executive power was limited only by specific restrictions and prohibitions appearing in the Constitution or imposed by the Congress under its Constitutional powers. My view was that every executive officer . . . was a steward of the people bound actively and affirmatively to do all he could for the people, and not to content himself with the negative merit of keeping his talents undamaged in a napkin. I declined to adopt the view that what was imperatively necessary for the Nation could not be done by the President unless he could find some specific authorization to do it. My belief was that it was not only his right but his duty to do anything that the needs of the Nation demanded unless such action was forbidden by the Constitution or by the laws. . . . I did not usurp power, but I did greatly broaden the use of executive power.

Roosevelt did not hesitate to use the power he claimed. He took the initiative in foreign affairs by building the Panama Canal, intervening in Santo Domingo and Cuba, and — against the express wishes of Congress — by sending the U.S. fleet on a world-wide tour. Domestically, he became personally involved in everything from coal strikes to trust-busting. He was not deterred by those who criticized his use of power (TOURTELLOT, *supra*, at 116):

> While President I have *been* President, emphatically; I have used every ounce of power there was in the office and I have not cared a rap for the criticisms of those who spoke of my "usurpation of power"; for I knew that the talk was all nonsense and that there was no usurpation. I believe that the efficiency of this Government depends upon its possessing a strong central executive, and wherever I could establish a precedent for strength in the executive . . . I have felt not merely that my action was right in itself, but that . . . I was establishing a precedent of value.

When Roosevelt retired from the Presidency in 1908, he picked William Howard Taft to be his successor, apparently confident that Taft shared his views on the Presidency and would carry on his policies. Disappointment awaited, however. Taft, a future Chief Justice, not only did not share Roosevelt's broad view of the office — he held a nearly opposite view. He strongly opposed Roosevelt's theory. Directly addressing his predecessor, Taft wrote in 1916 (ROCHE & LEVY, *supra*, at 25):

> My judgment is that the view of . . . Mr. Roosevelt, ascribing an undefined residuum of power to the President is an unsafe doctrine and that it might

lead under emergencies to results of an arbitrary character, doing irremediable injustice to private right. The mainspring of such a view is that the Executive is charged with responsibility for the welfare of all the people in a general way, that he is to play the part of a Universal Providence and set all things right, and that anything that in his judgment will help the people he ought to do, unless he is expressly forbidden not to do it. The wide field of action that this would give to the Executive one can hardly limit.

Taft argued for a strict construction of Article II. The executive, he reasoned, should exercise only power that is expressly or impliedly granted by the Constitution (*Id.* at 23–24):

The true view of the Executive functions is, as I conceive it, that the President can exercise no power which cannot be fairly and reasonably traced to some specific grant of power or justly implied and included within such express grant as proper and necessary to its exercise. Such specific grant must be either in the Federal Constitution or in an act of Congress passed in pursuance thereof. There is no undefined residuum of power which he can exercise because it seems to him to be in the public interest. . . . The grants of Executive power are necessarily in general terms in order not to embarrass the Executive within a field of action plainly marked for him, but his jurisdiction must be justified and vindicated by affirmative constitutional or statutory provision, or it does not exist.

8. Franklin Roosevelt

In the decade following World War I, the Presidency again became less active. The country was enjoying a period of peace and prosperity, decreasing the need for a strong and active executive. Warren Harding and Calvin Coolidge asserted no broad views of executive power. Coolidge spent much time cleaning up the Teapot Dome scandal that he had inherited from Harding. *See* Laton McCartney, The Teapot Dome Scandal (2008). Herbert Hoover took a more activist view of the office, but exercised its powers cautiously, especially at the onset of the Great Depression.

The election of Franklin Roosevelt led to an enduring transformation in the power of the presidency. *See* James M. Burns, Roosevelt: The Lion and the Fox (1956); Richard E. Neustadt, Presidential Power and the Modern Presidents: The Politics of Leadership from Roosevelt to Reagan (1990). Although Roosevelt wrote very little on his theories of the presidency, it is clear that he was willing to exercise power whenever he felt it necessary. While Roosevelt apparently had no specific plan when he assumed office, he did feel that action of some sort was required. Within a year, Congress had approved his legislative proposals for programs and agencies, often controlled directly or indirectly by the President, that affected almost every aspect of economic life. Also, he frequently spoke directly to the nation through a series of press conferences and "fireside chats," thus altering the President's relationship with the people. His leadership role grew even more in 1941, with the outbreak of war.

In 1937, Roosevelt became the first President since Andrew Jackson to launch a major assault on the judicial branch, through his "court-packing" plan. In defending the plan, he described the government as a three-horse team (*Fireside Chat, March 9, 1937, in* THE PUBLIC PAPERS AND ADDRESSES OF FRANKLIN D. ROOSEVELT (SAMUEL I. ROSENMAN ED., 1950)):

> The three horses are, of course, the three branches of government — the Congress, the Executive and the Courts. Two of the horses are pulling in unison today; the third is not. Those who have intimated that the President of the United States is trying to drive that team, overlook the simple fact that the President, as Chief Executive, is himself one of the three horses.

Nevertheless, many observers did not see things the same way, and felt that Roosevelt was trying to drive the team himself. Herbert Hoover, for example, warned that F.D.R. was amassing a dangerous amount of power (ADDRESSES UPON THE AMERICAN ROAD 238 (1961)):

> There has been a gigantic and insidious building up of personal power of the President during these two terms [1933–1940]. The President himself admits these powers provide shackles upon liberty which may be dangerous.... In building up these powers the independence of the Supreme Court, the Congress and the local government has been degraded.

Whether or not Roosevelt assumed too much power, his administration permanently altered the role of the executive. At the end of his twelve years in office, the presidency had much greater importance than ever before. To a large extent, he can be credited with the creation of the "modern Presidency."

9. Truman through Carter

A generation after World War II, the growth in executive power that had been catalyzed by the New Deal and the Cold War was so marked that Arthur Schlesinger, Jr., chose THE IMPERIAL PRESIDENCY as the title of his influential study in 1974. (We will encounter specific claims of power by the postwar Presidents throughout this book, and will merely note some broad contours here.) President Truman, although not a theorist by nature, pushed the boundaries of executive power through his activist exercise of his office, especially during the Korean War. President Eisenhower, despite his cautious nature, reacted to the Cold War by stating broad claims of executive power through his subordinates. President Kennedy's successful resolution of the Cuban Missile Crisis showed that presidential leadership could stave off everyone's worst nightmare, nuclear war.

President Johnson, drawing on Truman's legacy and faced with increasing congressional restiveness over the Vietnam War, elaborated a broad theory of independent presidential authority in foreign and military affairs. President Nixon, beset by widespread public dissent from his Vietnam policy and by a Democratic Congress largely hostile to his domestic agenda, went even further in asserting unilateral presidential authority not only for foreign and military affairs, but also for the domestic protection of national security, budgeting, and the protection of confidential information.

The collapse of the Nixon presidency in the Watergate scandal, coupled with Congress's new assertiveness in foreign affairs because of Vietnam, produced a brief era of separation of powers accommodation between 1974 and 1980. This is not to say that Presidents Ford and Carter were unmindful of their presidential prerogatives. President Ford relied extensively on his veto powers and engaged in unilateral military actions in Southeast Asia. President Carter substantially increased the central role of the White House in overseeing government regulatory policy. Yet neither President strongly resisted Congress's legislative innovations regarding such matters as the control of presidential records and the authorization of special prosecutors. With one unsuccessful exception, President Carter pointedly refused to follow President Nixon's attempts to invoke executive privilege as a means of withholding information from Congress. Apparently, the Imperial Presidency was passé.

10. Reagan and George H.W. Bush

The return of the White House to Republican control in 1981 led to a resurgence of executive arguments for constitutionally based unilateral presidential power in both domestic and foreign affairs. Because President Reagan's political agenda was at odds with the prevailing sentiment of the Democratic House (and, during his final two years in office, with the Democratic Senate), constitutional debates were especially sharp concerning such matters as executive privilege and presidential nonenforcement of assertedly unconstitutional laws. The Reagan era saw the rise of a theory of the "unitary executive," which claimed strong supervisory powers for the President over the Executive Branch. *See generally* STEVEN G. CALABRESI AND CHRISTOPHER S. YOO, THE UNITARY EXECUTIVE: PRESIDENTIAL POWER FROM WASHINGTON TO BUSH (2008). Under the George H.W. Bush Administration, the Office of Legal Counsel took the unconventional step of crystallizing the Administration's separation of powers view into a general framework for assessing congressional-executive relations. *See Common Legislative Encroachments on Executive Branch Constitutional Authority*, 13 Op. O.L.C. 299 (1989) (the "Barr Memorandum").

Although the first President Bush usually followed a less confrontational relationship with Congress than his predecessor, he also expressed some frustrations that many modern Presidents have felt. For example, he chastised Congress for excessive oversight and for bundling unrelated matters into a single bill, which frustrated his veto power. For an argument that he evaded Congress rather than confront it, see CHARLES TIEFER, THE SEMI-SOVEREIGN PRESIDENCY: THE BUSH ADMINISTRATION'S STRATEGY OF GOVERNING WITHOUT CONGRESS (1994).

11. Clinton

Like most of his modern predecessors, President Clinton was too busy being President to spin theories about the office. His two terms, however, were certainly eventful. His first two years in office featured Democratic majorities in both houses of Congress. Perhaps because of this, his administration was marked by two characteristics that suggested a determined effort to promote a cordial relationship with Congress. First, Clinton avoided direct confrontation with Congress—he vetoed no bills at all during the 103d Congress, and never formally claimed executive privilege. Even Franklin Roosevelt found himself vetoing many bills generated by Democratic Congresses. Second, Clinton's program for regulatory management, which we review in Chapter Four, was much more attentive to congressional policymaking than the Reagan-Bush program had been. For an account of the complex and frenetic efforts of the Clinton administration to enact an economic program, see Bob Woodward, The Agenda: Inside the Clinton White House (1994).

The midterm elections of 1994 delivered both houses to the Republicans, and led to a more confrontational set of relationships between President and Congress that endured for the balance of Clinton's time in office. The nadir was the unsuccessful attempt to impeach and remove him, which we examine in Chapter Three. Intriguingly, however, the Clinton Justice Department sought to supersede the Barr Memorandum, *supra*, with its own comprehensive memorandum on the law of interbranch relations—a memo that eschewed reliance on the "unitary executive" theory of presidential power as a way of drawing proverbial lines in the sand against congressional initiatives. *See The Constitutional Separation of Powers Between the President and Congress, reprinted in* H. Jefferson Powell, The Constitution and the Attorneys General 617 (1999).

12. George W. Bush

The second President Bush reached office after one of the most spectacularly controversial elections in American history, featuring an extended crisis that culminated in a Supreme Court decision determining the final outcome. In Chapter Eight, we explore the issues surrounding the deepest intrusion of the courts into the electoral process in our history.

The George W. Bush Administration was notable also for asserting especially aggressive claims of inherent executive power that could not be supervised by Congress or the courts. Such claims accelerated after the terror attacks of September 11, 2001. See Harold H. Bruff, Bad Advice: Bush's Lawyers in the War on Terror (2009); Peter M. Shane, Madison's Nightmare: How Executive Power Threatens American Democracy (2009). The chapters that follow will explore many of these claims on issues including executive privilege, presidential signing statements, unitary presidency theory, the President's national security authorities, and war powers.

13. Obama

From his earliest official memoranda and executive orders, President Obama sought to distance himself philosophically from the most ambitious George W. Bush claims of executive power, and to demonstrate a greater willingness to frame assertions of presidential authority—even in the national security area—as based in statute and subject to oversight. This was typically done either by renouncing particular initiatives of the prior Administration (*e.g.*, harsh interrogation techniques for alleged enemy combatants) or establishing processes that would subject claims of inherent executive authority to more rigorous and higher-level legal review.

The new Administration's philosophical differences with George W. Bush, however, did not always produce operational differences between the Administrations. Thus, for example, while President Obama largely curtailed the use of presidential signing statements to claim executive prerogative to ignore particular statutes, he continued a fairly aggressive practice of asserting the state secrets privilege in national security litigation. Because President Obama eschewed the articulation of any systematic theory of executive power, his tenure seemed to many observers more pragmatic than ideologically driven. Though willing to assert unilateral presidential authority where he believed it necessary, he avoided the appearance of making such claims reflexively, but limited his more aggressive claims of authority to contexts where he deemed it unnecessary to fulfilling an important presidential objective. In a comment made before he became President, Obama prefigured the approach he would take to constitutional interpretation (BRUFF, *supra*, at 427):

> [In difficult cases,] adherence to precedent and rules of construction and interpretation will only get you through the 25th mile of the marathon. The last mile can only be determined on the basis of one's deepest values, one's core concerns, one's broader perspective on how the world works, and the depth and breadth of one's empathy . . . . In those difficult cases, the critical ingredient is supplied by what is in the [interpreter's] heart.

In many ways, this comment captures what all American Presidents have done as they interpreted the Constitution.

14. Trump

This volume went to press too early in the Trump Administration to permit any general assessment of the new President's approach to issues of executive authority. However, having achieved electoral victory through an aggressively personalist campaign based largely on claims about his decisiveness, business success and negotiating acumen, the new President took office amid significant public anxiety that he would bring a more authoritarian approach to the exercise of power than perhaps any president since Richard Nixon. Specific predictions seem hazardous, however, because— as the materials in this volume illustrate—expectations for presidential behavior vis-à-vis the other branches of government and more generally are largely based on a set of informal norms or conventions that are nowhere formally codified. Throughout both his campaign and during the transition period, Trump showed little patience for the observance of customary political and institutional norms. Prior to the 2016 campaign, for example, it would have been thought improper for Presidents (and by implication, presidential candidates) personally to choose named targets for criminal prosecution or to make public statements as to the criminal guilt or innocence of parties under government investigation. Such personal involvement would have conflicted sharply with a norm of avoiding the appearance of politicization in federal law enforcement. Yet at an October 2016 rally, Trump said with regard to his opponent, Hillary Clinton: "I will ask my attorney general to appoint a special prosecutor" to investigate Secretary Clinton's alleged corruption, adding, "She has to go to jail." Peter W. Stevenson, *A brief history of the 'Lock her up!' chant by Trump supporters against Clinton*, WASH. POST (Nov. 22, 2016), https://www.washingtonpost.com /news/the-fix/wp/2016/11/22/a-brief-history-of-the-lock-her-up-chant-as-it-looks -like-trump-might-not-even-try/?utm_term=.a551a13d8b16. Even when seeming to rescind that apparent promise following his victory, Trump articulated the decision as a personal one, saying, "It's just not something that I feel strongly about," and "I don't want to hurt the Clintons, I really don't." Julie Hirschfeld Davis and Michael D. Shearnov, *Donald Trump Drops Threat of New Hillary Clinton Investigation*, N.Y. TIMES (Nov. 22, 2016), https://www.nytimes.com/2016/11/22/us/politics/donald-trump -hillary-clinton-investigation.html?_r=0.

Thus, both President Trump's background and his early approaches to the presidential office raise three fundamental questions: whether he will abide or change longstanding conventions, how he will exercise his formal powers, and whether he will abide or challenge the rule of law in the United States. Consider, for example, that, with the unfolding of a Justice Department Special Counsel's criminal investigation into the activities of individuals (including family members) involved in his 2016 campaign, President Trump, unlike prior presidents, has publicly and repeatedly renewed calls for criminal investigation of his opponents. In a November 2, 2017 radio interview, he stated: "The saddest thing is that because I'm the President of the United States, I am not supposed to be involved with the Justice Department," and, "I am really not involved with the Justice Department. I'd like to let it run itself. But honestly, they should be looking at the Democrats." Eli Watkins, *Donald Trump laments he's 'not supposed' to influence DOJ, FBI*, CNN.COM (Nov. 3, 2017), http://www.cnn.com/2017/11/02/politics/donald-trump-justice-department -fbi/index.html.

D. An Institutional Overview

Applying a Constitution written over two hundred years ago for a small, rural nation to today's massive federal government is no easy task. In 1789, the practical operation of the government was rather like that of a small town today—the constitutional officers participated personally in all the important decisions made by their branches, and the interrelation between them was often a matter of simple conversation. Today, our government confronts problems of size and decentralization in all three branches.

Congress, having grown to 535 members, delegates much important decision-making to its committees and subcommittees, and to legions of unelected staff personnel. The President now sits atop a considerable personal bureaucracy whose core for administration, the Office of Management and Budget (OMB), attempts to control the vast executive establishment where most policy is made. The Supreme Court, at the apex of a constantly growing pyramid of lower federal courts that finally decide most federal questions, struggles to manage the articulation of national law.

What follows is an overview of the structure of each of the three branches of government. As you read it, you will see that each is far from monolithic—a characteristic that complicates many aspects of modern separation of powers analysis. By now, you are familiar with the concept that all three branches interpret the Constitution. Notice the institutional structures that the two "political" branches possess for this function, and consider whether these structures could be improved.

1. Congress

For an introduction to Congress, see Donald C. Bacon, Roger H. Davidson, & Morton Keller, eds., The Encyclopedia of the United States Congress (1995); Abner J. Mikva & Patti B. Saris, The American Congress, The First Branch (1983); Walter J. Oleszek, Mark J. Oleszek, Elizabeth Rybicki & Bill Heniff, Jr., Congressional Procedures and the Policy Process (2016); Charles Tiefer, Congressional Practice and Procedure: A Reference, Research, and Legislative Guide (1989).

If a legislature of 535 individuals tried to do all its business in "committee of the whole," with neither internal structure nor procedural rules, chaos would result. Priority-setting would be impossible. A policy decision made by today's majority could be undone by tomorrow's. Ever since the opening of the First Congress, there have been internal rules in both houses to provide structure and procedure. These rules promote expertise by funneling issues to groups of Members and staff who work on them regularly. And they promote policy stability by allowing leaders, committees, and even individual members (in the case of the filibuster) to prevent bills from passing. The fact that these devices are "extraconstitutional" has not reduced their importance to the operation of Congress.

In the early twenty-first century, Congress is in substantial disarray. *See generally* Thomas E. Mann & Norman J. Ornstein, The Broken Branch: How Congress Is Failing America and How to Get It Back on Track (2006) and It's Even Worse Than It Was: How the American Constitutional System Collided

WITH THE NEW POLITICS OF EXTREMISM (2016). To the extent that Congress lacks internal control of its legislative process, it is vulnerable to domination by the hierarchically organized executive. (For example, during most of the administration of the second President Bush, dominated it was.) There is a long-term structural problem at work here. The framers' expectation that there would be a natural tension between the political branches did not take account of the effects of political parties. When the same party holds both the presidency and Congress, as it did during most of Bush's tenure, party discipline fundamentally erodes Madison's plan that ambition would offset ambition. Daryl J. Levinson & Richard H. Pildes, *Separation of Parties, Not Powers*, 119 HARV. L. REV. 2311 (2006). Instead, the dominant party's political program can be formulated by the executive and forced through Congress, as long as party discipline holds.

Several modern developments within Congress have eroded cooperation. A traditional informal congressional norm has been that "politics stops at the water's edge," that is, policy concerning foreign affairs and wars should be made in a bipartisan manner. This tradition diminished party control. Since about the 1970s, however, Congress has undergone some structural changes that hamper policy coordination in general and bipartisanship in particular. *See generally* JULIAN E. ZELIZER, ON CAPITOL HILL: THE STRUGGLE TO REFORM CONGRESS AND ITS CONSEQUENCES, 1948–2000 (2004); E. SCOTT ADLER, WHY CONGRESSIONAL REFORMS FAIL: REELECTION AND THE HOUSE COMMITTEE SYSTEM (2002); ROBERT V. REMINI, THE HOUSE: THE HISTORY OF THE HOUSE OF REPRESENTATIVES (2006). A decentralization of power within Congress was partly responsible, as a reform movement after Watergate broke the power of a handful of committee "barons" who had held tight the reins of power and had dictated the legislative agenda. As power flowed to myriad subcommittee chairs, it became difficult to coordinate policymaking or to reach across the aisle. When the Republicans took control of Congress in 1994, they recentralized power by strengthening the party leadership. In the House, redistricting gerrymanders have produced many safe districts for Members of Congress from both parties. The effect of this change has been polarizing: relatively conservative Republicans and relatively liberal Democrats have little in common, and little incentive to cooperate with each other. Moreover, the balance of power in both houses has often been on the razor's edge. Both parties have focused more on seeking the electoral victory that would allow them to organize the houses than on compromising with the other party, which might only lead to defeat at the polls. In this superheated partisan atmosphere, traditional norms of cooperation within Congress had broken down by 2001, and have not recovered since.

Nowadays, many aspects of congressional procedure are undergoing internal and external criticism, as Congress struggles to perform its Herculean responsibilities. In 1992, Congress formed a special Joint Committee on the Organization of Congress, to examine issues of structure and process comprehensively. It recommended various reform steps, but Congress has done little to implement them. *See* Final Report of the Joint Committee on the Organization of Congress, S. Rep. No. 103–215 &

H.R. Rep. No. 413, 103d Cong., 1st Sess. (1993); *see generally* E. Scott Adler, Why Congressional Reforms Fail: Reelection and the House Committee System (2002); Julian E. Zelizer, On Capitol Hill: The Struggle to Reform Congress and Its Consequences, 1948–2000 (2004).

Congress has a substantial bureaucracy of its own. The Senate and House have about 17,500 employees, and there are numerous satellite entities: the Architect of the Capitol, the Congressional Budget Office, the Government Accountability Office, the Government Printing Office, and the Library of Congress. Altogether, the total number of congressional employees is almost 30,000.

Congress also has created an institutional capacity to represent itself in court. *See* Charles Tiefer, *The Senate and House Counsel Offices: Dilemmas of Representing in Court the Institutional Congressional Client*, 61 L. & Contemp. Probs 47 (Spring 1998). For many years, Congress relied on representation by the Justice Department or by occasional private counsel. As the number of separation of powers cases in which Congress and the executive were opposed rose in the 1970s, it became apparent that Congress needed its own counsel. The Ethics in Government Act of 1978, Pub. L. No. 95-521, created the Office of Senate Legal Counsel. *See* 2 U.S.C. § 288. The Counsel is authorized to defend official actions of the Senate, its committees, its Members, and its employees, to sue for the enforcement of subpoenas, and to appear as amicus curiae. An early version of the Ethics bill would have created an Office of Congressional Legal Counsel, but the House was not prepared to agree to a joint office. The Office of the Clerk of the House performs functions similar to those of the Senate Counsel.

2. The Executive

Today the Presidency includes a substantial bureaucracy within the Executive Office of the President (EOP). The EOP has about 1,700 employees, and the White House Office within it, which contains the President's immediate staff, has about 400 employees. This staff organization supervises the 2.6 million employees in the executive branch as a whole. Considering the size of the EOP alone, a modern President keeps quite busy supervising his *own* bureaucracy, to say nothing of controlling the scurrying millions throughout his branch of government.

According to Stephen Hess, Organizing The Presidency, 1–3 (1966), life at the apex of the executive branch was once simpler:

> Presidents had been given vast emergency powers before the New Deal, always in anticipation of war or during its conduct. But the concept of the powerful Chief Executive was otherwise alien to the American ethic. According to the White House Chief Usher, before World War I Woodrow Wilson "worked but three or four hours a day and spent much of his time happily and quietly, sitting around with his family." . . . The pace of the White House was reflected in the modest size of its staff when Franklin Roosevelt

took office. It soon became obvious, however, that the existing arrangements were inadequate to meet both the new responsibilities that Congress had given the President and the people's rising expectations of what they wished the federal government to do. . . . With Roosevelt's blessing, [Congress created] an Executive Office of the President and additional all-purpose White House aides. . . . World War II and its aftermath, the country's new role as a world leader, and national fears of economic dislocation, thrust additional burdens on the President and accelerated the trend toward White House centralization . . . . [T]he growth of the White House establishment reflects a conscious effort over four decades to impose a presidential presence on an executive conglomerate, which today is too vast for personal supervision. It also is a manifestation of the multiple roles that have been given to or assumed by Presidents: Commander in Chief, primary proposer of legislation and chief lobbyist, top executive in the executive branch, guardian of the economy, negotiator with other nations, head of state, party leader, and moral leader.

A President allots his time and organizes his administration along the lines of the diverse functions he must perform, hires different people to support him in his different duties, and organizes those around him to accommodate his perceptions of his task. Roosevelt constructed a circle with himself at the hub. Eisenhower designed a pyramid with himself at the apex. A President chooses the degree of tidiness or chaos that best supports his work habits. He chooses the amount of advice he wants to get from within government and how much he wants to receive from outside. He decides to give competing assignments and overlapping jurisdictions or to rely on aides with specific and tightly defined responsibilities. He selects between formal lines of command and informal arrangements. He chooses between the advice of specialists and generalists.

More detail about enduring problems in organizing the modern Presidency is provided from a congressional perspective in Presidential Staffing—A Brief Overview, Subcomm. on Employee Ethics and Utilization, House Comm. on Post Office and Civil Service, 95th Cong., 2d Sess., 55–61 (1978):

The President's principal source of assistants . . . continues to be the White House Office staff and the personnel of selected Executive Office agencies. These aides are . . . envisioned as having "no power to make decisions or issue instructions in their own right" and "possessed of high competence, great vigor, and a passion for anonymity."

In spite of these high hopes, White House assistants to succeeding presidents, since 1939, have become highly conspicuous, multiple in number, possessed of great power, and virtually unaccountable to anyone but the Chief Executive for their actions. The number of presidential advisers and policy aides within the White House Office and the larger Executive Office has exhibited generally steady growth, regardless of national or international events, changes of administration, or differing management styles of Chief Executives. . . . Managerial authority and program responsibility has been given over to presidential assistants because other coordinating and administrative guidance institutions, such as the Cabinet, have proven to be unsuitable for these functions. . . .

Thus, it is the White House Office and the Executive Office satellites which have come to better serve the President as coordinators of executive functions. And as managers of the Government, as well, they have come to play policy roles, refining policy suggestions and sometimes even the access of other policymakers to the Chief Executive. But, as Theodore Sorensen has noted, such a role carries with it certain dangers.

> A White House adviser may see a departmental problem in a wider context than a Secretary, but he also has less contact with actual operations and pressures, with Congress and interested groups. If his own staff grows too large, his office may become only another department, another level of clearances and concurrences instead of a personal instrument of the President. If his confidential relationship with the President causes either one to be too uncritical of the other's judgment, errors may go uncorrected. If he develops . . . a confidence in his own competence which outruns the fact, his contribution may be more mischievous than useful. If, on the other hand, he defers too readily to the authority of the renowned experts and Cabinet powers, then the President is denied the skeptical, critical service his staff should be providing. [DECISION-MAKING IN THE WHITE HOUSE 71–72 (1963).]

The most recent experiments with Cabinet government were those of the Reagan administration. His first term saw the formation of seven domestic policy Cabinet councils, in which the secretaries of departments having related subject matter responsibilities met in efforts to coordinate policy. This structure proved unwieldy, however, and was replaced in the second term with two streamlined Cabinet councils, one for economics and one for all other domestic policy. Notwithstanding these elaborate structures, observers found that important issues often bypassed the councils in favor of direct decision by powerful officials such as Office of Management and Budget Director David Stockman. *See* Ronald Brownstein & Dick Kirschten, *Cabinet Government*, 18 NAT'L J. 1582 (June 28, 1986).

The process of presidential decisionmaking is formalized enough to merit summary here. The following outline focuses on the President's implementation of his diverse statutory powers, but it applies to many decisions with constitutional overtones as well. Harold H. Bruff, *Judicial Review and the President's Statutory Powers*, 68 VA. L. REV. 1, 14–17 (1982):

Although the process that precedes a President's implementation of his statutory powers varies somewhat from administration to administration—indeed, from day to day—it follows an overall pattern. Few impending decisions reach the White House without previous, often extensive, analysis in one or more of the executive agencies. Thus, when the time comes for the President to exercise his discretion, an administrative record exists in the bureaucracy—a mass of raw data, analysis, and opinion from both within and without the government. This "record" is ordinarily far too massive and unwieldy for any actual transmittal to the White House; in any event, no one there would have either the time or the inclination to pore through it. Therefore, although statutes do not always require agencies to forward formal recommendations to the President prior to his decision, agencies normally do so, if only to summarize and evaluate the administrative record they have compiled. . . .

Accompanying the policy materials that reach the White House is legal analysis, again from several sources. The interested agencies are likely to provide opinions from their general counsels' offices. Legal analysis from the agencies may conflict regarding the extent of the President's discretion in the matter. Moreover, the White House staff is likely to suspect that the general counsels' work product reflects the orientation of their clients. Accordingly, they turn to lawyers whose client is the President—the Counsel to the President, and, for "outside counsel," the Office of Legal Counsel in the Department of Justice.

While the President's staff reviews and digests the policy and legal materials that were generated in the agencies, a somewhat separate process of policy and legal debate is likely to arise within the White House. Once it becomes known that a presidential decision is near, interested parties of all kinds—agency heads, Congressmen, private parties—may descend on those having an influence on the decision, including the President himself.

When the time arrives for a formal presidential decision, the mechanics are fairly simple, and essentially similar from administration to administration. The White House staff or an agency official prepares a decision memorandum for the President, in order to present concisely the major policy options or recommendations that have survived debate within the administration. It usually reflects, although it may not discuss, legal analysis of the extent of permissible discretion under the statute or statutes involved. Each option is likely to be accompanied by outlines of the arguments favoring and disfavoring its adoption. These arguments may be confined to a rather legalistic presentation of relevant policy concerns, or they may branch off into frank discussion of political considerations having little or no legal relevance to the decision. The President reads the memorandum, perhaps discusses it with his advisers, and then decides, usually initialing or marking the options memorandum to indicate his choice. His reasons for selecting a particular option may or may not be those presented by the memorandum, and they may or may not be revealed to his advisers.

Because this process is an informal one not governed by statutory procedures, it is subject to exceptions. Especially when there is pressure to reach a decision on short notice, the process often becomes an almost entirely oral one composed of hurried telephone conversations and meetings between the White House staff and their policy and legal advisers in the agencies. Whether from the press of events or otherwise, some presidential decisions occur without full consultation with the President's lawyers. Indeed, there is sometimes an effort by the White House staff to prevent an interested agency — or even anyone outside a select group of presidential advisers — from knowing that a statutory decision is imminent. The usual motivation for such secrecy is to prevent opposition to, or widespread disclosure of, a policy initiative coming from within the White House. Thus, presidential decisions are sometimes made without knowledge of whether they are legal.

Unlike his recent predecessors, President George W. Bush eschewed the use of decision memos in favor of a decision-making process that was usually oral — the President discussed an issue with advisers, considered it, and informed senior staff of his decision. *See Governing the Cabinet*, 35 NAT'L J. 236–37 (Jan. 25, 2003).

In the foregoing description, note the interplay — and the implied competition for influence — between the President's policy advisers and his legal advisers. The President has a number of kinds of legal advisers, not all working directly for him. *See generally Government Lawyering* (Neal Devins, special ed.), 61 LAW & CONTEMP. PROBS. Nos. 1 & 2 (Winter & Spring 1998). The Counsel to the President, with a staff of about thirty lawyers, is in the White House. *See* Jeremy Rabkin, *At the President's Side: The Role of the White House Counsel in Constitutional Policy*, 56 LAW & CONTEMP. PROBS. 63 (1993). Many of the lawyers in the Office of Management and Budget are also engaged in preparing advice or doing other legal work directly or indirectly for the President.

The Department of Justice, with its thousands of lawyers, is the major repository of "outside" legal advice for the White House. An Executive Order requires proposed Executive Orders to be submitted to the Attorney General "for his consideration as to both form and legality." 1 C.F.R. § 19.2(b) (1980). The Attorney General's disapproval will ordinarily halt processing of an Order. Within the Department, this review function has been delegated to the Office of Legal Counsel (OLC). With over twenty lawyers, OLC has the principal responsibility for advising the Attorney General, the White House, and other agencies on questions of presidential power. *See* Douglas W. Kmiec, *OLC's Opinion Writing Function: The Legal Adhesive for a Unitary Executive*, 15 CARDOZO L. REV. 337 (1993); John O. McGinnis, *Models of the Opinion Function of the Attorney General: A Normative, Descriptive, and Historical Prolegomenon*, *id.* at 375.

Lawyers in the various executive agencies also furnish advice to the White House. And, of course, the President can seek legal advice from personal advisers who hold no government office. For the memoirs of a highly influential informal adviser to several Presidents, see CLARK CLIFFORD, COUNSEL TO THE PRESIDENT (1991).

Consider the difference, if any, that the role of presidential adviser should make in a lawyer's normal behavior. Is the relationship like any other lawyer/client one? Should the role of the "in-house" counsel to the President differ from that of "outside" counsel in the Department of Justice and elsewhere in the executive branch? If it seems to you that the oath to defend the Constitution that the President and all government lawyers take should affect the answer to these questions, consider how many concrete questions it is likely to answer.

3. The Judiciary

A combination of docket overload and regional division of authority has largely decentralized the federal judiciary. At the apex of the judicial branch, the capacity of the Supreme Court as presently constituted is essentially fixed at about 150 decisions per year after full briefing and argument. *See* Peter L. Strauss, *One Hundred Fifty Cases per Year: Some Implications of the Supreme Court's Limited Resources for Judicial Review of Agency Action*, 87 COLUM. L. REV. 1093 (1987). In recent years the Court has decided about 75 cases per year. (2015 Year-end Report on the Federal Judiciary, *in* State of the Federal Judiciary: Annual Reports of the Chief Justice of the Supreme Court of the United States.) Hence the Court, in an effort to decide its most important cases carefully, is operating at about half of its theoretical maximum capacity.

The courts of appeals are divided into the eleven numbered regional circuits, the District of Columbia Circuit, and the Federal Circuit. *See generally* ERWIN C. SURRENCY, HISTORY OF THE FEDERAL COURTS (2d ed. 2002). It is the appellate court level that largely accounts for concerns surrounding the federal courts. *See* FEDERAL JUDICIAL CENTER, STRUCTURAL AND OTHER ALTERNATIVES FOR THE FEDERAL COURTS OF APPEALS (1993); RICHARD A. POSNER, THE FEDERAL COURTS, CHALLENGE AND REFORM (1996); Harold H. Bruff, *Coordinating Judicial Review in Administrative Law*, 39 UCLA L. REV. 1193 (1992). The 191 circuit judges now receive about 60,000 appeals per year. The caseload has risen much faster than the number of judges— from 1960 to 1987, the caseload per judge nearly tripled. To handle the flood, these courts now decide about a third of their cases without oral argument and rely upon growing numbers of law clerks and staff attorneys. Able judges complain about the increasingly bureaucratic routine, which leaves little time for reflection on the path of the law. As with the district courts, courts of appeal lack the discretion to turn away cases they do not wish to decide. But as with the Supreme Court, there are structural limitations to their size. Courts of appeal are collegial and cannot function well after they have reached a certain size. The D.C. Circuit, currently at twelve members, is of middling size; the Ninth Circuit, at twenty-eight, is the giant.

The Supreme Court's capacity to review and coordinate the activities of the courts of appeals is extremely limited. In 1924, the Court reviewed about one in ten decisions of the courts of appeals; nowadays, the proportion has shrunk to about one in 200. This means that the thirteen courts of appeals are now almost always the final deciders of federal law. Even if the third of the courts of appeals' caseload that receives summary adjudication is removed from the calculus, the Supreme Court reviews only a small fraction of the appellate decisions. (The success rate for certiorari petitions is about 1%.) This is a tenfold decrease from the 1924 figure, a decline that cannot be inconsequential.

Observers have debated whether the Court eventually resolves the most important conflicts among the circuits regarding federal law. *Compare* SAMUEL ESTREICHER & JOHN E. SEXTON, REDEFINING THE SUPREME COURT'S ROLE (1986) *with* Thomas E. Baker & Douglas D. McFarland, *The Need for a New National Court*, 100 HARV. L. REV. 1400 (1987). In any event, the Court's remoteness has at least two effects. First, much time can pass while cases that present issues that are ripe for decision jostle in the queue. Meanwhile, uncertainty breeds repeated litigation of the same issues in the lower courts and hampers confident planning of life's affairs. Second, the Court's receding presence as manager of its branch of government increases slack in the system, allowing litigants and judges to treat the prospect of Supreme Court review as too unlikely to affect their behavior in routine litigation. For the judicial branch as a whole, the capacity to articulate a coherent body of national law is vitiated.

In a decentralized system, the government as a litigant often finds itself subject to conflicting court orders either in different circuits, or within a circuit. Executive agencies have responded by refusing to "acquiesce" in court orders issued below the Supreme Court level. Of course, agencies honor court orders for the litigating parties; nonacquiescence is the refusal to accord them any broader effect on an intercircuit or intracircuit basis. We consider this issue in Chapter Four.

Although the judiciary is the least bureaucratized of the three federal branches, it cannot escape this phenomenon entirely. The main institutional aid to judicial administration is the Administrative Office of the United States Courts, created in 1939. The Federal Judicial Center exists to study the operation of the courts and to aid the Judicial Conference, which is the formal organization of the federal judges. The Conference, along with governing the operation of the federal judicial system, has sought ways to improve its relations with Congress. *See* ROBERT A. KATZMANN, COURTS AND CONGRESS (1997).

Chapter 2

Framework: The Separation and Confluence of Powers

Every political constitution in which different bodies share the supreme power is only enabled to exist by the forbearance of those among whom this power is distributed.

—Lord John Russell, quoted in WOODROW WILSON,
CONGRESSIONAL GOVERNMENT 163 (1885).

The Framers bequeathed us a complex and (they hoped) balanced scheme of government. They well knew that their system could fail in either of two fundamental ways. On one hand, perhaps the separations between the branches would turn out to be mere "parchment barriers" in practice, and undue amounts of power would flow to one branch (Congress, they thought). On the other, perhaps the barriers would prove too strong, the checks and balances too debilitating, and the government would collapse in a heap of ineffectiveness and mutual recrimination. At various points in our history, one or the other of these systemic failures has been widely diagnosed. For example, Lincoln's critics called him a dictator; the Progressives thought our government's structure paralyzed reform efforts. As you begin exploring this field with us, pause a moment to make your own evaluation of the State of the Union today—and then revisit that judgment at the end of the book to see if it has changed.

This chapter canvasses the most basic legal relationships among the branches. Throughout, we will see that the legal and practical powers held by each branch are a function of its interrelation with each of the others. These powers evolve over time, and not always in ways that contemporaries can easily detect.

A. Analytic Framework: The Rule of Law and the Realm of Politics

1. The Executive and the Judiciary

We begin with *Marbury v. Madison*, a foundational case in both constitutional and administrative law. Of course, *Marbury* is best known for its assertion of judicial power to review the constitutionality of federal statutes, a question requiring the Court to determine its proper relationship to Congress. We do not include those portions of the opinion here, because they receive lavish attention in basic Constitutional Law courses. We focus more closely on a less-noticed portion of the opinion, in which the Court considered its proper relationship to the executive.

Before you read *Marbury*, we have some preliminary matters for you to consider. As we noted in Chapter One, proposed executive actions are usually reviewed for their legality by the Department of Justice. This process raises issues of professional responsibility that pervade this book. The following excerpt both provides some background on *Marbury* and, through an extended and very realistic hypothetical, presents recurring ethical dilemmas of the executive adviser. As you read *Marbury*, then, consider your response to the following questions, put by Dean Norman Redlich in a symposium reported in Assn. of the Bar of the City of New York, Professional Responsibility of the Lawyer, The Murky Divide Between Right and Wrong 97–101 (1976):

> You may recall the facts that led up to *Marbury v. Madison*: Thomas Jefferson was elected President of the United States in November of 1800. . . . [O]n February 27th, 1801, just one week before the new administration was to take office, the old Congress passed a law creating some forty-two justices of the peace for the District of Columbia, with five-year terms. President Adams promptly appointed them all; they were promptly confirmed by the Senate, and the commissions were all signed by the then Secretary of State, John Marshall. . . . Now, imagine yourselves as the new Attorney General of the United States on the morning of March 5th, 1801. You, the new Attorney General, Levi Lincoln, are sitting in your office, . . . and suddenly there is a knock at the door and in walks James Madison, the new Secretary of State. . . . Madison says, "You know, the darnedest thing happened. You won't believe this, but I came into my office this morning and . . . I found . . . [f]our commissions for justice of the peace signed by John Marshall. In his hurry to get out of here to be Chief Justice, he just left them here. . . . And one of them belongs to this fellow, Marbury, and you know how the President feels about Marbury! He's . . . a political opponent, and I think you really ought not to send this commission to Marbury. I'd like your opinion as to what we ought to do."

> And so you go all out and research the question, and you legitimately reach the conclusion, based upon your best understanding of the law, that . . . he is entitled to this job. You are about to inform your client, the Secretary of State, about this, when the President of the United States walks in and he says, "I understand that you've been asked for an opinion by Madison. Madison won't act without one, and I want you to advise Madison that he should withhold this commission. These are 'midnight' jobs; . . . there is no reason why our opponents should get these lucrative jobs. I want this commission withheld and I want you to render an opinion which says that he has the

right to withhold them." What does the Attorney General do under these circumstances? . . .

Next scene: You have not rendered your opinion. . . . The President and the Secretary of State turn to you as Attorney General and say to you, "Mr. Lincoln, we understand you're having a problem. We don't want to ask you to say anything you don't believe in; we are just going to withhold the commission anyway." And you say, "Why do you want to do that? I've told you . . . Marbury has a clear right to this commission." "Well," says the President, "This is our chance to show that the courts can't control the executive branch of the Government. Suppose that Marshall *does* issue an order commanding us to give this commission to Marbury; how is he going to enforce it? This is our chance to show that the Federalist control of the judiciary can't push the people's representative—namely, the President—around." . . .

Next scene: The President and James Madison say, "Mr. Attorney General, we know you don't think we can win on the merits, but no one can be completely sure. Isn't that right? Besides, we think we should have a court decision on the question of whether someone is entitled to an appointment if all the steps in the process have not been completed. And the final step in this process, namely, delivery of the commission, has not been completed. We think this is an important issue. We think that the courts have no business interfering in the process of appointment. We are not going to *defy* the courts if we are wrong; we are going to obey the court order; but we are saying that *you*, Mr. Attorney General, should not decide this issue; it's an issue that should be decided by the courts; it's too important to be decided by default." . . .

My final scene in this drama comes up when you prepare the argument. The President and the Secretary of State call you in and say, "Mr. Attorney General, how are you preparing to handle this case?" Remember, you have refused to deliver the commission, Marbury has brought his lawsuit . . . in the Supreme Court of the United States, claiming that the Supreme Court has original jurisdiction pursuant to an Act of Congress which, in the view of Mr. Marbury, gives the Court original jurisdiction to issue a mandamus to the Secretary of State to compel the delivery of the commission. That's the posture of the lawsuit.

You say, "Well, Mr. President, I am going to make [several] arguments. I've got them neatly laid out in the papers. Here they are: *One*: the Supreme Court has no jurisdiction to hear this case because Congress never gave the Supreme Court the power to issue writs of mandamus in this type of case. The only thing Congress did was to give the Supreme Court power to issue writs of mandamus in cases where they otherwise had jurisdiction, but there is no grant of jurisdiction to hear this case. . . . *Point number two*: If I have read the statute wrong, and if Congress *did* give the Supreme Court the power to issue a writ of mandamus in this case, it is unconstitutional because Congress cannot enlarge the original jurisdiction of the Supreme Court. If it did so, it is contrary to the Constitution and it is the obligation of the Supreme Court to declare the Act unconstitutional. My *third* argument is that if there is jurisdiction and if it comes out that what Congress did was constitutional, the Court has no right to interfere with the political power of the President. Nothing is more discretionary than appointment. This appointment was never completed. And so the Court has no right to order an appointment. . . ."

The President and the Secretary of State listen to all this and they say, "Oh, no. It is perfectly all right to argue that the Congress never gave the Supreme Court jurisdiction—that is, the first argument—but we are not going to have you arguing that, if Congress *did* give them jurisdiction, the Court can declare it unconstitutional." You say, "Don't you want to win?" And they say, "Not on *that* ground. We'd much prefer that they decide against us, and let him try to enforce his order, than that we win because they say Congress didn't have the power to authorize the Supreme Court to push us around. Because Marshall is going to be in a position of being able to say that he not only has the power to tell the Congress what to do, but also has the power to tell *us* what to do, and we are not going to get into that situation."

The Attorney General says, "Look, Mr. President, what if the Court says, 'Mr. Attorney General, does the Congress have the power to enlarge the jurisdiction of the Supreme Court?' What do I say?" The President says, "You answer the question, 'Yes.' Because if you answer, 'No,' then you are going to give the Supreme Court the opportunity to declare this Act of Congress unconstitutional and I don't want that to happen." Suppose you really think that the better argument is that Congress does *not* have the power to enlarge the jurisdiction of the Supreme Court, and you think it is very important for the country that at the outset of our national experience, the concepts of a limiting Constitution and of judicial review be established, do you still go in and handle this case in the Court in the way in which the President says you should?

Marbury v. Madison

5 U.S. (1 Cranch) 137 (1803)

Chief Justice MARSHALL delivered the opinion of the Court.

At the last term, on the affidavits then read and filed with the clerk, a rule was granted in this case, requiring the secretary of state to show cause why a mandamus should not issue, directing him to deliver to William Marbury his commission as a justice of the peace for the county of Washington, in the district of Columbia. No cause has been shown, and the present motion is for a mandamus. . . . The first object of inquiry is, [h]as the applicant a right to the commission he demands?

His right originates in an act of Congress passed in February 1801, concerning the district of Columbia. . . . [T]his law enacts, "that there shall be appointed . . . such number of discreet persons to be justices of the peace as the president of the United States shall, from time to time, think expedient, to continue in office for five years." It appears from the affidavits, that in compliance with this law, a commission for William Marbury as a justice of peace . . . was signed by John Adams, then president of the United States; after which the seal of the United States was affixed to it; but the commission has never reached the person for whom it was made out.

In order to determine whether he is entitled to this commission, it becomes necessary to inquire whether he has been appointed to the office. For if he has been appointed, the law continues him in office for five years, and he is entitled to the possession of those evidences of office, which, being completed, became his property. . . . The last act to be done by the president, is the signature of the commission. He has then acted on the advice and consent of the senate to his own nomination. The time for deliberation has then passed. He has decided. His judgment, on the advice and consent of the senate concurring with his nomination, has been made, and the officer is appointed. . . .

The commission being signed, the subsequent duty of the secretary of state is prescribed by law, and not to be guided by the will of the president. He is to affix the seal of the United States to the commission, and is to record it. . . . It is the duty of the secretary of state to conform to the law, and in this he is an officer of the United States, bound to obey the laws. He acts, in this respect, . . . under the authority of law, and not by the instructions of the president. It is a ministerial act which the law enjoins on a particular officer for a particular purpose. . . .

It is therefore decidedly the opinion of the court, that when a commission has been signed by the president, the appointment is made; and that the commission is complete when the seal of the United States has been affixed to it by the secretary of state. . . . [W]hen the officer is not removable at the will of the executive, the appointment is not revocable and cannot be annulled. It has conferred legal rights which cannot be resumed. . . .

Mr. Marbury, then, since his commission was signed by the president and sealed by the secretary of state, was appointed; and as the law creating the office gave the officer a right to hold for five years independent of the executive, the appointment was not revocable; but vested in the officer legal rights which are protected by the laws of his country. To withhold the commission, therefore, is an act deemed by the court not warranted by law, but violative of a vested legal right.

This brings us to the second inquiry; which is, [i]f he has a right, and that right has been violated, do the laws of his country afford him a remedy? The very essence of civil liberty certainly consists in the right of every individual to claim the protection of the laws, whenever he receives an injury. One of the first duties of government is to afford that protection. In Great Britain the king himself is sued in the respectful form of a petition, and he never fails to comply with the judgment of his court. . . . The government of the United States has been emphatically termed a government of laws, and not of men. It will certainly cease to deserve this high appellation, if the laws furnish no remedy for the violation of a vested legal right. . . .

Is the act of delivering or withholding a commission to be considered as a mere political act belonging to the executive department alone, for the performance of which entire confidence is placed by our constitution in the supreme executive; and for any misconduct respecting which, the injured individual has no remedy? That there may be such cases is not to be questioned; but that every act of duty to be performed in any of the great departments of government constitutes such a case, is not to be admitted. . . . [W]hether the legality of an act of the head of a department be examinable in a court of justice or not, must always depend on the nature of that act. If some acts be examinable, and others not, there must be some rule of law to guide the court in the exercise of its jurisdiction. . . .

By the Constitution of the United States, the President is invested with certain important political powers, in the exercise of which he is to use his own discretion, and is accountable only to his country in his political character, and to his own conscience. To aid him in the performance of these duties, he is authorized to appoint certain officers, who act by his authority and in conformity with his orders. In such cases, their acts are his acts; and whatever opinion may be entertained of the manner in which executive discretion may be used, still there exists, and can exist, no power to control that discretion. The subjects are political. They respect the nation, not individual rights, and being entrusted to the executive, the decision of the executive is conclusive. The application of this remark will be perceived by adverting to the act of Congress for establishing the department of foreign affairs. This officer, as his duties were prescribed by that act, is to conform precisely to the will of the president. He is the mere organ by whom that will is communicated. The acts of such an officer, as an officer, can never be examinable by the courts.

But when the legislature proceeds to impose on that officer other duties; when he is directed peremptorily to perform certain acts; when the rights of individuals are dependent on the performance of those acts; he is so far the officer of the law; is amenable to the laws for his conduct; and cannot at his discretion sport away the vested rights of others. . . .

If this be the rule, let us inquire how it applies to the case under the consideration of the court. The power of nominating to the senate, and the power of appointing the person nominated, are political powers, to be exercised by the President according to his own discretion. When he has made an appointment, he has exercised his whole power, and his discretion has been completely applied to the case. . . .

The question whether a right has vested or not, is, in its nature, judicial, and must be tried by the judicial authority. . . . It is, then, the opinion of the Court, . . . [t]hat, having this legal title to the office, he has a consequent right to the commission; a refusal to deliver which is a plain violation of that right, for which the laws of his country afford him a remedy. It remains to be inquired whether, [h]e is entitled to the remedy for which he applies. This depends on . . . [t]he nature of the writ applied for [a]nd . . . [t]he power of this court.

1st. The nature of the writ. Blackstone, in the third volume of his Commentaries, page 110, defines a mandamus to be, "a command issuing in the king's name from the court of king's bench, and directed to any person, corporation, or inferior court of judicature within the king's dominions, requiring them to do some particular thing therein specified which appertains to their office and duty, and which the court of king's bench has previously determined, or at least supposes, to be consonant to right and justice." . . .

Still, to render the mandamus a proper remedy, the officer to whom it is to be directed, must be one to whom, on legal principles, such writ may be directed; and the person applying for it must be without any other specific and legal remedy. . . . The intimate political relation, subsisting between the President of the United States and the heads of departments, necessarily renders any legal investigation of the acts of one of those high officers peculiarly irksome, as well as delicate; and excites some hesitation with respect to the propriety of entering into such investigation. . . . The province of the court is, solely, to decide on the rights of individuals, not to inquire how the executive, or executive officers, perform duties in which they have a discretion. Questions, in their nature political, or which are, by the constitution and laws, submitted to the executive, can never be made in this court.

But, if this be not such a question; if so far from being an intrusion into the secrets of the cabinet, it respects a paper, which, according to law, is upon record, and to a copy of which the law gives a right, on the payment of ten cents; . . . what is there in the exalted station of the officer, which shall bar a citizen from asserting, in a court of justice, his legal rights, or shall forbid a court to listen to the claim; or to issue a mandamus, directing the performance of a duty, not depending on executive discretion, but on particular acts of Congress and the general principles of law? . . . It is not by the office of the person to whom the writ is directed, but the nature of the thing to be done, that the propriety or impropriety of issuing a mandamus is to be determined. . . . This, then, is a plain case of a mandamus, either to deliver the commission, or a copy of it from the record; and it only remains to be inquired, [w]hether it can issue from this court?

[Chief Justice MARSHALL concluded, in the remainder of the Court's unanimous opinion, that the writ of mandamus could not issue from the Supreme Court in this case because Congress could not constitutionally vest original jurisdiction in the Supreme Court to hear suits for mandamus against officers of the United States.]

———————

1. *Professional Responsibility.* First, let us return to the ethical questions with which we preceded *Marbury*. A response to some of Dean Redlich's questions comes from Bruce E. Fein, *Promoting the President's Policies Through Legal Advocacy: An*

[handwritten margin note: ∅ have Original Juris so ∅ Power to hear case for 1st time]

Ethical Imperative of the Government Attorney, 30 FED. BAR NEWS & J. 406, 408 (Sept./Oct. 1983):

> [T]he discovery by a government attorney of precedent that seemingly would condemn a Presidential policy does not ordain the conclusion that no responsible legal argument can be assembled to vindicate the policy. To the contrary, in most such situations, rational reasons can be adduced for modifying or reversing the adverse precedent, or distinguishing it, in order to effectuate the President's policy goal. The government attorney is ethically bound to develop when necessary plausible arguments for altering or overturning existing law. This duty is comparable to the ethical norm governing private attorneys that endorses advocacy of any non-frivolous constructions dependent on modification or reversal of existing law, without regard to the attorney's professional opinion as to the likelihood that the construction will ultimately prevail. If a government attorney cannot ungrudgingly adhere to the ethical imperative requiring promotion of the President's policies through legal advocacy, then he might seriously consider voluntary resignation from the Executive Branch.

This argument embodies the traditional rule that when appearing in court, a lawyer may advance claims that are "not frivolous, which includes a good faith argument" for altering existing law. AMERICAN BAR ASS'N, MODEL RULES OF PROFESSIONAL CONDUCT 3.1 (2003). Since a frivolous argument should have little chance of success in court and tends to attract negative publicity, not much constraint attends instructing trial lawyers to do better than that. Yet if the same stance is applied to the provision of confidential counseling to the executive, the incentive to craft responsible arguments that is created by the presence of a neutral arbiter disappears. The contexts are fundamentally different.

Therefore, the counseling function is governed by a different rule: that the lawyer is expected to "exercise independent professional judgment and render candid advice." ABA MODEL RULES 2.1. The rule continues: "In rendering advice, a lawyer may refer not only to law but to other considerations such as moral, economic, social and political factors, that may be relevant to the client's situation." An accompanying comment explains that although "a lawyer is not a moral advisor as such, moral and ethical considerations impinge upon most legal questions and may decisively influence how the law will be applied." Thus, the consequences of conduct that the law might allow should be considered and explained to the client. Another comment cautions that "[a] client is entitled to straightforward advice expressing the lawyer's honest assessment. Legal advice often involves unpleasant facts and alternatives that a client may be disinclined to confront."

Compare the views of PETER M. SHANE, in MADISON'S NIGHTMARE: HOW EXECUTIVE POWER THREATENS AMERICAN DEMOCRACY 83 (2009):

> [I]t is . . . essential that government lawyers understand their unique roles as both advisers and advocates. In adversarial proceedings before courts of

law, it may be fine for each of two contesting sides, including the government, to have a zealous, and not wholly impartial defense, while the judge acts as a neutral decision maker. But government lawyers, in their advisory function, must themselves play a more objective, even quasi-adjudicative role. They must give the law their most conscientious interpretation. If they do not, there will frequently be no one else effectively situated to do the job of assuring diligence in legal compliance. Government lawyers imbued with the ideology of presidentialism too easily abandon their professional obligations as advisers and too readily become ethically blinkered advocates for unchecked executive power. Especially in their advisory role, government lawyers must remember that their "client" is the American people, and not the ephemeral roster of incumbent federal officer holders.

In *Legal Disagreement and Negotiation in a Government of Laws: The Case of Executive Privilege Claims Against Congress*, 71 Minn. L. Rev. 461, 491–92 (1987) Shane elaborates:

A government of laws . . . is a government in which officials feel obligated to look to legal points of reference to describe and justify official behavior. This obligation is treated as important, even if not always performed well and even if, because law and political interest may coincide, it is sometimes superfluous. It is deemed important that government officials at least exercise the self-discipline of questioning the legal significance of their acts and, often, of providing explicit justification for those acts in legal terms. It is the habitual commitment to this interpretive regime that perhaps most pervasively differentiates a government of laws from a government of unadorned power.

A former Deputy Assistant Attorney General reports the views of a President (Letter from Larry A. Hammond to Peter M. Shane, Jan. 7, 1986):

In many instances, . . . Jimmy Carter was not interested in playing the "lawmaker as advocate" game. . . . Carter made it known, very clearly, that if there was a legal question in a policy paper, he wanted to know whether the options were lawful or not lawful. . . . He knew that lawyers could "advocate" any position, but he wanted his Attorney General to tell him what the correct legal answer was, and he was prepared to live by it.

The competing ethical stances suggested in this note are sometimes explored by posing the question, "Who is a government lawyer's client?" Does a Justice Department attorney advising the White House on a matter of presidential authority represent the United States, the President, the Presidency, the Department of Justice, the people? Robert P. Lawry, *Who Is the Client of the Federal Government Lawyer? An Analysis of the Wrong Question?* 47 Fed. Bar J. 61 (1978), argues that because a government lawyer's obligations depend on the context, it is misleading to ask this question. Instead, he argues that a government lawyer has three central ethical concerns: 1) identifying whose directions he or she should take, and on what subjects;

2) identifying whose confidences should be respected, and with whom they may be shared; and 3) determining what role his or her own judgment should play in deciding what to do. For a strong expression of the view that government attorneys solely represent the executive branch and the President, as its head, see Geoffrey P. Miller, *Government Lawyers' Ethics in a System of Checks and Balances*, 54 U. CHI. L. REV. 1293 (1987). Professor Miller argues that any attempt by federal attorneys to represent the public interest is incoherent. He believes that our system of separated and checked powers provides ample mechanisms to assert positions contrary to those of the executive, and that an executive branch attorney may support any initiative that is not contrary to law. Note that this problem of client identification exists in some form for all attorneys who advise large organizations. Indeed, throughout this book, you may find it profitable to compare the problems posed for government attorneys with those of corporate or other private institutional attorneys, and ask whether the different roles should imply different professional attitudes or obligations.

For interesting perspectives on the role and obligations of the Attorney General and of government attorneys, see *Government Lawyering* (Neal Devins, special ed.), 61 LAW & CONTEMP. PROBS. NOS. 1 & 2 (Winter & Spring 1998). Many of the most important constitutional opinions of the Attorneys General are collected in H. JEFFERSON POWELL, THE CONSTITUTION AND THE ATTORNEYS GENERAL (1999).

Regarding *judicial* ethics, was it proper for John Marshall, as the former Secretary of State who had received Marbury's commission, to have decided this case? He was probably the best witness about the disposition of the commissions. Marbury's lawyer was reduced to calling other witnesses (including Marshall's brother, who had delivered some of them), in an inconclusive effort to prove what happened to them. Also, does Chief Justice Marshall decide that Secretary Marshall failed to perform a ministerial duty to Marbury? If so, should a judge decide a case that may bring his or her own conduct into question?

2. Politics v. Law. Marbury distinguished the executive's political discretion, which the courts could not control, from its statutory duties to individuals, which the courts could determine. What was Marshall's apparent source for these categories? Was he merely translating the traditional mandamus law distinction between ministerial and discretionary acts into a constitutional context? See GEORGE L. HASKINS & HERBERT A. JOHNSON, FOUNDATIONS OF POWER: JOHN MARSHALL 1801–15 (2 HISTORY OF THE SUPREME COURT OF THE UNITED STATES) (1981), arguing that the law/politics distinction was crucial to Marshall's great achievement as Chief Justice: the establishment of the rule of law as the basis of Supreme Court jurisprudence. They point out that eighteenth-century courts were viewed as an arm of the administration, and engaged in political as well as strictly legal activities. In *Marbury*, Marshall rejected that political role, yet claimed a vital legal role. (As elsewhere in the opinion, Marshall used a retreat in one direction to cover an advance in another.) Haskins & Johnson conclude, at 406:

> In a sense the Court under Marshall had accepted a sharply diminished role in politics, but in so limiting its activities it had secured a better control

of law, the jurisdiction to which it had undoubted entitlement. Removing itself from partisan politics, it entrenched itself as the constitutional guardian of individual rights against the excesses and vagaries of popular government in a disturbingly new egalitarian age. In beating a strategic retreat before the armies of Jeffersonian legislators, the judges arrived at a delineation of judicial power such that even their detractors were forced to concede the validity of their pretensions, and Republican judges found incumbent Federalist judges to be of one mind with them. Upon this consensus was built the foundations of the Supreme Court of the United States as we know it today.

Marbury's line between law and politics is not self-defining. Instead, value questions inhere in deciding which issues of separation of powers or individual rights to remove from the sphere of democratic politics for resolution by the courts. Therefore, we need to qualify Marshall's assertion (made in support of the power of judicial review) that "[i]t is emphatically the province and duty of the judicial department to say what the law is."

What deference was the executive bound to give to Marshall's dicta about the Court's power over the executive? Recall the quotation in Chapter One from a later President, Andrew Jackson, arguing that each branch "must be guided by its own opinion of the Constitution." If the executive is prepared to obey the order of a court having jurisdiction of a controversy, has it any broader duty to honor judicial statements of "what the law is"? *See generally* Symposium, *Perspectives on the Authoritativeness of Supreme Court Decisions*, 61 TUL. L. REV. 977 (1987). We consider this issue in Chapter Four.

For the full story of the *Marbury* litigation, see CLIFF SLOAN & DAVID McKEAN, THE GREAT DECISION (2009).

3. *Judicial Deference?* Both of the other branches routinely take positions on statutory and constitutional issues—to what extent should the courts defer to their views? This question pervades modern constitutional law in general, and separation of powers in particular, as we shall see. And it has an analogue in administrative law that is also pertinent throughout these materials. Reviewing courts generally defer to administrative interpretations of statutes, within the limits of reason and ascertainable legislative intent. *See Chevron, U.S.A., Inc. v. Natural Resources Defense Council, Inc.*, 467 U.S. 837 (1984). Should Marshall have given some deference to the executive's presumed interpretation of the pertinent statutes as making appointments complete only upon delivery of the commissions? *See generally* Henry P. Monaghan, Marbury *and the Administrative State*, 83 COLUM. L. REV. 1 (1983).

Should Marshall have deferred *completely* to the executive's statutory interpretation, on grounds that it presented an unreviewable political question? That would have acknowledged the value content of the law/politics line, but it would have altered fundamentally the development of administrative law, according to Harold H. Bruff, *Judicial Review and the President's Statutory Powers*, 68 VA. L. REV. 1, 9–10 (1982):

Marbury laid the foundation of American administrative law by affirming both the power of Congress to limit the President's discretion and the power of the courts to interpret and enforce those limits. The Court decided the latter issue without an analytic demonstration of the need for judicial intervention. The alternative of deferring to the executive would have required reliance in part on the executive's own constitutional duty to execute the laws faithfully, and in part on the opportunity for Congress to enter the fray. In *Marbury*, the Court appeared to find sufficient justification for its intervention in the need for judicial protection of individual rights against executive infringement.

There are additional reasons why it would be unwise to treat the President's statutory duties as political questions. A government having two policy-making branches that are in constant competition needs an arbiter to identify the locus of responsibility in particular cases. The alternative would be to force Congress to work its will with the executive through means that would frequently be excessive or unrelated to the controversy at hand. This would introduce unnecessary inefficiencies into the operation of government. More seriously, it would accord Congress both too much and too little power to enforce its existing statutes. Congress would have insufficient power insofar as the President's role as head of his party would enable him to forestall effective legislative response. Congress would have excessive power in two ways. First, Congress could effectively alter existing statutes without following the constitutional process for amending them, simply by acceding to presidential decisions inconsistent with them. Second, the President would lose an important means of defending the legitimacy of his actions. A judicial determination that executive action is consistent with statutory authority enables a President to blunt charges that he has overstepped his role in defiance of the institutional interests of Congress.

4. *Accountability.* Marshall states that every right, in the American constitutional system, must have legal redress. In his article on executive privilege (*supra*, at 490–91), Shane relates this concept to accountability:

> The distribution of different powers among the branches, with the inevitability of some confrontation, makes unavoidable some occasions on which one branch can poignantly remind another of the importance of pursuing justification through legal reasoning. Justice Marshall's opinion in *Marbury v. Madison* can be read from just such a perspective. In statements that were technically dicta, Marshall constitutionalized the traditional distinction in the law of mandamus between judicially reviewable ministerial acts and unreviewable political acts for which a government officer is not accountable in court. He did so in the face of his undoubted awareness that presidential exercises of political discretion could result in constitutional violations which the courts, under *Marbury*, could not remedy. For example, it would presumably be unconstitutional for the President, with purely invidious

motives, to veto those congressional enactments, and only those enactments, that had the effect of improving the social position of American Blacks. Yet, following Marshall's reasoning, no judicial sanction could enjoin such behavior. Indeed, no judicial sanction could compel Congress to override the President's vetoes, or to impeach him for his behavior.

Despite the potential for unjust results created by situations such as this, Marshall, without apparent irony, describes our government as a "government of laws" in which the "laws" furnish a remedy for the violation of a "vested legal right." If "laws furnish[ing a] remedy," in Marshall's words, were interpreted simply to mean "courts furnishing mandatory relief," Marshall's characterization of our government as a government of laws would be wrong.

It is possible, however, to interpret *Marbury* in a different light. Each branch of the government has a role in maintaining the ideal of the government of laws. The judicial branch, as *Marbury* illustrates, is not solely responsible for providing remedies for unconstitutional behavior. Prospectively, the allegiance of the executive branch to legal norms affords a kind of preliminary injunction against such behavior. That same sense of obligation may lead Congress, in the face of necessity, to vest jurisdiction in an appropriate court to review the Executive's acts. Failing that, an obligation to impeach may arise. Such remedies may not be perfect. As in Marbury's case, they may fail. They do, however, exist, and *Marbury* may be read as an exhortation to their use.

Do you agree with Shane's view of the potential power of legal interpretation as a mechanism of accountability? How do you assess the significance of the extraordinary amount of interpretive activity that in fact goes on throughout the federal bureaucracy? As you read the various judicial opinions that follow, consider whether they lend credence to Shane's assertion that the branches often send messages to one another, reminding them of their obligations (even if unenforceable) under law. Is this an appropriate judicial function?

5. *Why Discuss Remedy?* Could Marshall have persuasively characterized Marbury as not having a legal right under the facts presented, thus avoiding the question of remedy? For example, note the Court's assumptions about Marbury's removability from office. Would the case have been decided differently had the Court assumed that Marbury was removable by the President at will?

6. *Theoretical v. Practical Remedies.* Had mandamus issued and had Madison failed to comply, could the Court have held him in contempt? What if he had been ordered to resist by President Jefferson? (In that case, it might have been Jefferson in 1803, not Jackson in 1832, making the famous challenge to Marshall to enforce his decision!) Should the Court's inability to execute such a sanction determine whether a legal right exists against the executive (or against Congress)?

7. *Chief of State, or Chief Clerk?* Can Congress vest ministerial duties directly in the President? What would be the extent of judicial authority over the President

should Congress vest a ministerial duty in him? We will return to these questions in Chapter Four, when we consider the applicability of administrative procedure statutes to the President.

Note on Obtaining Judicial Review of Executive Actions

Marbury raised as many questions as it answered regarding methods of obtaining judicial review of presidential actions. Madison did not appear by counsel or in person in response to the Court's order to show cause — the Jeffersonians regarded it as an outrageous intrusion on executive authority. *See* HASKINS & JOHNSON, *supra*, at 183–86. And, of course, Marshall's disposition of the constitutional question made it unnecessary for him to issue mandamus to an executive officer, although he asserted the power to do so. Therefore, questions lingered about the amenability of the President himself to judicial process, and about other limits to judicial power over the executive. It would be many years before definitive answers were provided to some of these questions.

First, notice the mode of review sought by Marbury — mandamus, one of the extraordinary writs in English law, brought into American law with the adoption of the common law. Marshall, to define the scope of the writ, invoked the traditional English doctrine that mandamus will issue to compel an officer to perform a "ministerial" duty, but not to exercise discretion in a particular way. Thus, Marshall adapted a writ that was designed to control the King's officers to control the President and his officers. This technique of adapting common law doctrines and remedies to American administrative law has continued to the present day. For example, the Court later elaborated on the ministerial/discretionary distinction for mandamus, in *Roberts v. United States*, 176 U.S. 219, 231 (1900):

> Every statute to some extent requires construction by the public officer whose duties may be defined therein. Such officer must read the law, . . . in order to form a judgment from its language what duty he is . . . to perform. But that does not necessarily . . . make the duty of the officer anything other than a purely ministerial one. If the law direct him to perform an act in regard to which no discretion is committed to him, and which, upon the facts existing, he is bound to perform, then that act is ministerial, although depending upon a statute which requires, in some degree, a construction of its language by the officer.

Today, 28 U.S.C. § 1361 codifies mandamus by granting federal jurisdiction "of any action in the nature of mandamus to compel an officer . . . to perform a duty owed to the plaintiff."

Testing the implications of *Marbury* required exercising, rather than merely asserting, judicial power. The Court, and Marshall, soon found opportunities. In *Little v. Barreme*, 6 U.S. (2 Cranch) 170 (1804), the Court unanimously upheld an award of damages against a ship captain who, on orders of the President, seized a ship coming to the United States from France. Marshall's opinion said that the President might have power to seize ships without special statutory authority, but that the Nonintercourse Act had "prescribed . . . the manner in which this law shall be carried into execution," and that a noncomplying seizure was illegal.

In *Little*, however, the Court issued no compulsory process to the President. A celebrated case soon gave Marshall that opportunity. Sitting on circuit in the treason trial of Aaron Burr, Marshall issued a subpoena to President Jefferson for evidence material to the case. *United States v. Burr*, 25 F. Cas. 30 (C.C. Va. 1807) (No. 14, 692-D). He rejected any absolute presidential immunity from judicial process (25 F. Cas. at 34):

> Of the many points of difference which exist between the first magistrate in England and the first magistrate of the United States, in respect to the personal dignity conferred on them by the constitutions of their respective nations, the court will only select and mention two. It is a principle of the English constitution that the king can do no wrong, that no blame can be imputed to him, that he cannot be named in debate. By the Constitution of the United States, the president, as well as any other officer of the government, may be impeached, and may be removed from office on high crimes and misdemeanors. By the constitution of Great Britain, the crown is hereditary, and the monarch can never be a subject. By that of the United States, the President is elected from the mass of the people, and, on the expiration of the time for which he is elected, returns to the mass of the people again. How essentially this difference of circumstances must vary the policy of the laws of the two countries, in reference to the personal dignity of the executive chief, will be perceived by every person.

Burr provided no definitive resolution, however. Jefferson "voluntarily" complied with the subpoena, protesting any obligation to do so. For the full story, see Paul A. Freund, *Foreword: On Presidential Privilege, The Supreme Court, 1973 Term*, 88 HARV. L. REV. 13, 23–30 (1974).

In the quoted passage from *Burr*, Marshall referred obliquely to the common law doctrine of sovereign immunity, that "the king can do no wrong." In *Cohens v. Virginia*, 19 U.S. (6 Wheat.) 264 (1821), he assumed that the doctrine applied to the United States. It was, he said, "the universally received opinion . . . that no suit can be commenced or prosecuted against the United States; that the judiciary act does not authorize such suits." (19 U.S. at 411). Despite this thin pedigree, sovereign immunity entered our law, and still forbids unconsented suits against the United States. *See* Antonin Scalia, *Historical Anomalies in Administrative Law*, YEARBOOK 1985, 103, 105.

In order to avoid having sovereign immunity bar review of the legality of ordinary administrative action, the courts had to evolve a fiction. Injunctive suits were brought against officers in their "personal" capacity so that relief did not formally run against the government, although the point of the lawsuit was to produce that effect. *Ex Parte Young*, 209 U.S. 123 (1908). Eventually, Congress waived sovereign immunity for injunctive relief against the United States. 5 U.S.C. § 702. (Damages actions still require a specific statutory waiver.) Today, the standard method for challenging administrative action (absent a special statutory grant of review authority) is a suit invoking federal question jurisdiction under 28 U.S.C. § 1331 and seeking an injunction, perhaps coupled with a request for declaratory relief under 28 U.S.C. §§ 2201–02. And the mandamus statute provides another avenue for relief.

None of these statutes, however, specifically authorizes review of presidential action. Partly for that reason, Marbury's strategy of suing a subordinate officer who is executing the President's policies remains dominant. The first case to issue mandamus against an officer was *Kendall v. United States ex rel. Stokes*, 37 U.S. (12 Pet.) 524 (1838). A dispute arose between the Postmaster General and some contractors over amounts owing for the carriage of mail. Eventually, Congress passed a statute calling for another official to settle the claims and for the Postmaster to pay the amount awarded. The Postmaster declined to pay the full amount of the award; the contractors sought mandamus. It was clear to the Court that under ordinary mandamus principles, the Postmaster's action was purely ministerial—to pay whatever amount had been awarded. The only complicating factor was the breadth of the Postmaster's defense. There had been, said the Court, "a very extended range of argument on the independence and duties" of the executive. Nevertheless, the President did not stand in the way—he had notified Congress of the Postmaster's actions, without endorsing them. In that posture of the case, the Court upheld issuance of the writ. In an opinion by Justice Thompson, the Court responded to the argument that it had heard with some broad views of its own (37 U.S. at 612–13):

> It was urged at the bar, that the postmaster-general was alone subject to the direction and control of the president, with respect to the execution of the duty imposed upon him by this law; and this right of the president is claimed, as growing out of the obligation imposed upon him by the Constitution, to take care that the laws be faithfully executed. This is a doctrine that cannot receive the sanction of this court. It would be vesting in the President a dispensing power, which has no countenance for its support, in any part of the Constitution; and is asserting a principle, which, . . . would be clothing the President with a power entirely to control the legislation of Congress, and paralyze the administration of justice. To contend, that the obligation imposed on the President to see the laws faithfully executed, implies a power to forbid their execution, is a novel construction of the Constitution, and entirely inadmissible.

A more serious challenge to presidential power followed the Civil War. Mississippi challenged the constitutionality of the Reconstruction Acts by seeking an injunction against presidential enforcement. Before the Supreme Court, Attorney General Stanbery argued that the courts could not issue an order to the President because the power to do so would entail the power to punish his disobedience by contempt, and that sanction would effectively remove him from office, usurping the impeachment power of Congress. In *Mississippi v. Johnson*, 71 U.S. (4 Wall.) 475 (1867), the

Court denied the injunction. Chief Justice Chase stressed that this facial attack on the Acts did not involve an effort to compel the President to perform a ministerial act. Characterizing the President's military duties under the Acts as "purely executive and political," the Court refused to intervene. Thus, the outcome in *Mississippi v. Johnson* probably turned on the presence of nonjusticiable political questions and on the unripeness of the challenge, rather than on the amenability of the President to suit. It is one of a series of cases in which the Court successfully avoided ruling on the constitutionality of Reconstruction.

The Court finally held that the President is subject to judicial process in *United States v. Nixon*, 418 U.S. 683 (1974), excerpted in Chapter Three. Surprisingly, the *Nixon* Court made no direct analysis of the President's amenability to compulsory process, instead subsuming the question under the issue of the extent of his executive privilege to resist disclosure of confidential communications. The amenability issue did receive direct scrutiny, however, in an earlier stage of the litigation. In *Nixon v. Sirica*, 487 F.2d 700 (D.C. Cir. 1973), the court would not find the President immune from process (487 F.2d at 710–12):

> Thus, to find the President immune from judicial process, we must read out of *Burr* and *Youngstown* [excerpted *infra*] the underlying principles that the eminent jurists in each case thought they were establishing. The Constitution makes no mention of special presidential immunities. Indeed, the Executive Branch generally is afforded none. This silence cannot be ascribed to oversight. James Madison raised the question of Executive privileges during the Constitutional Convention, and Senators and Representatives enjoy an express, if limited, immunity from arrest, and an express privilege from inquiry concerning "Speech and Debate" on the floors of Congress. Lacking textual support, counsel for the President nonetheless would have us infer immunity from the President's political mandate, or from his vulnerability to impeachment, or from his broad discretionary powers. These are invitations to refashion the Constitution, and we reject them. . . .

> Nor does the Impeachment Clause imply immunity from routine court process. . . . The legality of judicial orders should not be confused with the legal consequences of their breach; for the courts in this country always assume that their orders will be obeyed, especially when addressed to responsible government officials.

An issue left open after *United States v. Nixon*, the availability of contempt against Cabinet officers, was litigated in *In re The Attorney General of the United States*, 596 F.2d 58 (2d Cir.), *cert. denied*, 444 U.S. 903 (1979). In 1973, the Socialist Workers Party (SWP) and others sued the Federal Bureau of Investigation (FBI), alleging that the plaintiffs had been subjected to an unlawful investigation aimed at destroying their organizations. In the course of the litigation, the FBI refused to release 18 files under a discovery order by the District Court, on the ground of "informant privilege." The District Court consequently held the Attorney General in civil contempt. The Court of Appeals held that contempt was inappropriate because of the availability of sanctions that were more reasonable in light of the consequences of contempt and the plaintiff's case. The court said (596 F.2d at 65):

> [H]olding the Attorney General of the United States in contempt to ensure compliance with a court order should be a last resort, to be undertaken only after all other means to achieve the ends legitimately sought by the court have been exhausted. Judged by these standards, the action of the trial court unfortunately falls short, for in our view the court insufficiently considered issue-related sanctions. The Federal Rules of Civil Procedure permit many sanctions other than contempt alternatives that the court did not sufficiently explore except to reject the Government's proposals.

In the SWP litigation, the Attorney General "interposed" himself as the defendant decisionmaker, after issuance of a court order to the FBI. Could the President have done so? If the Attorney General had been held in contempt, what would have been the appropriate penalty? Incarceration? A fine? What do your answers to these questions suggest concerning the legitimacy or the utility of the contempt sanction?

Consider again whether, had mandamus issued against Secretary Madison, the Court could properly have held him in contempt. Could a court legitimately determine that the gravity of resistance to a court order in any one case outweighed the interference with the operation of the executive branch that incarcerating a Cabinet official—assuming a U.S. Marshal would do so—would entail?

Review the foregoing case law: what role should the prospect of litigation play in the process of legal interpretation by government lawyers? Do the courts have sufficient sanctions to earn the respect of those inclined to adhere to executive interpretations of law in the face of contrary judicial opinion?

Finally, consider in this context, as you will in many others, the extent to which this case law demonstrates the wisdom of the remark by Lord Russell with which we began this chapter.

2. The Executive and Congress (as Mediated by the Courts)

This section first considers the scope of the President's powers when Congress has not legislated. Does he possess "inherent" powers? To what extent is the faithful execution clause, with or without additional textual support in the Constitution, a sufficient legal basis for a presidential initiative in domestic affairs? Consider especially how, if the legal issues in the materials that follow were presented to you in your planning role as legal counsel, you would approach the analysis.

We then turn to two basic situations involving relevant legislation. First, we consider the possibility that executive administration of a statute, acquiesced in by Congress, can modify the apparent meaning of the statute. Second, we examine the "Steel Seizure" case, *Youngstown*, which represents the modern Supreme Court's most thorough discussion of congressional restraints on presidential power.

Two Supreme Court cases decided in the late nineteenth century, *In re Neagle*, 135 U.S. 1 (1890), and *In re Debs*, 158 U.S. 564 (1895), stated broad support for presidential actions taken without statutory authorization. In BALANCE OF FORCES, SEPARATION OF POWERS LAW IN THE ADMINISTRATIVE STATE 94–97 (2006), HAROLD H. BRUFF analyzes the two cases:

> *In re Neagle* arose from a true Wild West episode. A highly unstable California couple, the Terrys, had threatened the life of Supreme Court Justice Field. Without any specific statutory authority, the President assigned Deputy U.S. Marshal Neagle to protect Field on a circuit-riding trip to the west coast. The Terrys boarded a train on which Field was riding and assaulted him; Neagle shot David Terry dead. When the State of California charged Neagle with homicide, he invoked a federal habeas corpus statute that authorized release of a person being held "in custody for an act done . . . in pursuance of a law of the United States." California argued that the habeas statute was inapplicable, because no federal statute had authorized Neagle's protection of Justice Field. When the case reached the Supreme Court, Justice Miller's opinion concluded that "any obligation fairly and properly inferrible" from the Constitution or from the general scope of Neagle's statutory duties would protect him under the habeas statute. The Court focused on the President's constitutional duty faithfully to execute the laws, and asked rhetorically:
>
> > Is this duty limited to the enforcement of acts of Congress or of treaties of the United States according to their *express terms*, or does it include the rights, duties and obligations growing out of the Constitution itself, our international relations, and all the protection implied by the nature of the government under the Constitution? . . . We cannot doubt the power of the President to take measures for the protection of a judge of one of the courts of the United States, who, while in the discharge of the duties of his office, is threatened with a personal attack which may probably result in his death. . . . [I]f the prisoner is held in the state court to answer for an act which he was authorized to do by the law of the United States, . . . he *cannot* be guilty of a crime under the law of the State of California.
>
> No legal realist can be surprised that the Supreme Court would find sufficient constitutional authority in the executive to protect the Justices themselves from mayhem. Maybe *Neagle* stands for no more than that, but such a reading would be unnecessarily cramped. The decision does clearly proscribe any state criminal liability for the performance by a United States employee of a function derived from the general scope of the employee's duties, unless Congress consents. More broadly, the facts of *Neagle* reveal that the statutes empowering executive officers have gaps that sometimes leave the President without a statutory basis for responding to emergencies. The context can be as colorful and limited as *Neagle* itself, or as grim and momentous as the crisis Lincoln faced at his inauguration.

In *Neagle*, the Court visibly struggled to find a theory to support presidential action. To do so, it read the Faithful Execution Clause as more than a cross-reference to preexisting statutes: the clause justified enforcing rights "growing out of the Constitution itself," and out of "the nature of the government." These vague phrases, which were not needed to sustain the result in the case, might justify anything. Executive advisers have cited *Neagle* as support for almost any conceivable response to emergencies. At a minimum, the case does show the need for a presidential power to protect federal officials from danger. Its logic also suggests a power to protect other American citizens, who possess rights under the Constitution. It would certainly be surprising if the chief executive of any nation were powerless to shield the nation's officers and citizens from harm. Accordingly, *Neagle* is often cited for the proposition that the President may take such actions as using the armed forces to rescue Americans illegally detained abroad. A President who needs to take immediate protective steps, especially when there is little or no time to ask Congress for authority, can fairly rely on *Neagle*, but the case does not support major commitments of the nation's forces under the cloak of the Court's broadest phrases.

In re Debs grew out of the bitter Pullman strike of 1894, during which railroad workers refused to service Pullman cars until the Company agreed to arbitrate its differences with them. By shutting down the railroads, the strike threatened the primary method of interstate transport of persons, mail, and essential commodities. Without statutory authority, the government obtained a sweeping injunction against the socialist labor leader Eugene Debs, prohibiting him from communicating with railway employees concerning the strike. His arrest for violating the order succeeded in breaking the morale of the strikers. Debs's petition for habeas corpus challenged his conviction for contempt and brought the validity of the injunction before the Supreme Court.

A unanimous Court ruled against Debs. Justice Brewer, perceiving the strike as a dangerous conspiracy against interstate commerce, argued that the federal government should not be restricted to criminal prosecutions against those who had obstructed commerce. Instead, force could be used: "The entire strength of the nation may be used to enforce in any part of the land the full and free exercise of all national powers and the security of all rights entrusted by the Constitution to its care." Lesser measures were also appropriate, because "the right to use force does not exclude the right of appeal to the courts for a judicial determination and for the exercise of all their powers of prevention." Indeed, the Court thought it praiseworthy of the government to employ the courts rather than the sword. Therefore, the executive had "a right to apply to its own courts for any proper assistance" in performing its duties.

The *Debs* Court was in no mood for subtleties. Two main reservations to its broad statements are necessary. First, use of either the militia or federal troops to execute the laws involves compliance with various statutory limitations. Second, arguments that greater powers automatically include lesser ones encounter severe criticism in constitutional law, because they deflect attention away from the presence or absence of justification for actions actually taken, toward hypothetical alternatives that may not be realistic. Nevertheless, the *Debs* decision is valuable for its creation of an incentive for the executive to eschew the use of force in favor of a resort to judicial process. Even if the executive might be denied an injunction on the merits, as would occur many years later in the *Pentagon Papers* litigation, the *Debs* precedent is useful for its dampening of concerns that the courts will reject an application for their aid at the threshold. Since *Debs* empowered the courts as well as the executive, we can be confident that this portion of its reasoning will prove durable. An unauthorized appeal to the courts for their aid can still fail, however, due to generally applicable limits on federal court consideration of the merits of controversies.

In re Neagle is invariably cited in Department of Justice legal memoranda as legitimating a broad implied power to take all steps necessary and proper for the enforcement of federal law, even in the face of apparent conflict with state law obligations. *See generally* The Story of *In re Neagle*: Sex, Money, Politics, Perjury, Homicide, Federalism, and Executive Power, in Presidential Power Stories 133 (Christopher H. Schroeder & Curtis A. Bradley eds., 2008). Relying in part on *Neagle* and *Debs*, however, Professor Henry Monaghan, in *The Protective Power of the Presidency*, 93 Colum. L. Rev. 1, 11, 66 (1993), goes further:

> [T]he considerable debate on the issue of a presidential emergency power has obscured the existence of a narrower, inherent executive authority, namely, an executive "protective" power. I contend that the constitutional conception of a Chief Executive authorized to enforce the laws includes a general authority to protect and defend the personnel, property, and instrumentalities of the United States from harm. While the occasion for exercise of this presidential authority will often arise in emergencies, some relatively small, such as assigning a marshal to protect the life of a judge, the protective power is, strictly speaking, *not* a doctrine of emergency power. For example, acting without statutory authority, the Executive has standing to enforce the contract or property rights of the United States. . . .

> [I]nherent in the concept of the American Chief Executive is the power (and perhaps the duty) to use force as necessary to enforce federal law when a breakdown in the normal civil process has occurred, and not only to defend the United States against sudden attack, but also to "protect" the government's personnel, property, and instrumentalities. While this latter "protective" power finds its clearest illustrations in cases of immediate danger,

it is, in principle, not so limited. It includes the general right of the executive, without express statutory authority, to make contracts and, more importantly, to sue to protect the personnel and the property interests of the United States, and when necessary to use force and other resources to protect them.

Monaghan traces the roots of his theory as far back as the views of John Locke. Monaghan would limit the power to actions not contrary to law, including the common law rights of private persons. We will return to issues about the existence and nature of a presidential protective power in Chapter Four. For now, notice that it plays a role in the cases that follow.

Introductory Note on Executive Orders

When Presidents want to make commands to the executive bureaucracy or to the public more generally, they typically issue what can most generically be called "executive orders." As you will see in this book, these orders can take a bewildering variety of forms. These range from documents formally styled Executive Orders (which appear in numbered form in the Federal Register), to Proclamations (which are usually addressed to the public), to various national security directives (which are often secret), to simple memoranda or notes to subordinates (which are meant to be mandatory). The legality of all of these commands depends on whatever blend of constitutional and statutory support the President can find for them. We have just seen two examples — the simple assignment of a Marshal to accompany a Justice in *Neagle* and a directive to the Justice Department to file a lawsuit in *Debs*. Others are about to follow in *Midwest Oil* and *Youngstown, infra. See generally* GRAHAM G. DODDS, TAKE UP YOUR PEN: UNILATERAL PRESIDENTIAL DIRECTIVES IN AMERICAN POLITICS (2013); KENNETH R. MAYER, WITH THE STROKE OF A PEN, EXECUTIVE ORDERS AND PRESIDENTIAL POWER (2001); Hugh C. Keenan, *Executive Orders: A Brief History of Their Use and the President's Power to Issue Them, in* Sen. Special Comm. on Nat'l Emergencies and Delegated Emergency Powers, 93d Cong., 2d Sess., Executive Orders in Times of War and National Emergency 20 (Comm. Print 1974). To find executive orders, go to 3 C.F.R., or for orders from the Clinton administration or later, go to www.archives.gov/federal-register/index.html.

In modern times, presidential use of executive orders to form policy has become highly controversial. It should not be surprising that the aggressive figure of Theodore Roosevelt looms large over the development of modern practices — and the controversy that surrounds them. See HAROLD H. BRUFF, UNTRODDEN GROUND: HOW PRESIDENTS INTERPRET THE CONSTITUTION 200 (2015):

> TR's technique for expanding presidential power was to read existing statutory authority very broadly. He knew that Congress could rarely muster the votes necessary to override his actions. Roosevelt implemented his statutory interpretations by issuing various executive orders to the bureaucracy. Signing almost as many orders as all of his predecessors combined, he brought the executive order to its modern prominence as a means of managing

the executive. This practice had great consequences for twentieth century presidents as the nation entered an era of statutory empowerment of the federal government. As the corpus of statutes grew, so did the opportunities for presidential interpretive activity. Roosevelt's expanded use of executive orders created a "new norm" for his successors, who continued frequent use of the practice once TR had demonstrated its utility. After issuing orders, presidents would rely on their veto power to stop Congress from retracting or modifying delegations of power that they had treated expansively.

Most of President Roosevelt's conservation accomplishments depended on executive orders. An early decision epitomized his style. In response to a request to form a wildlife refuge on federal land in Florida, he responded: "Is there any law that will prevent me from declaring Pelican Island a Federal Bird Reservation? Very well, then I so declare it." During his presidency, TR formed federal conservation reserves of many kinds and even took steps to save the buffalo from extinction.

A freewheeling presidential style like TR's may succeed in escaping a congressional statutory override, but how will it fare against legal challenge in court? The following case involves a statute whose text seems to forbid the action taken by the executive. How does the Court find a way to uphold President Taft?

––––––––––

United States v. Midwest Oil Co.
236 U.S. 459 (1915)

Justice LAMAR delivered the opinion of the court.

All public lands containing petroleum or other mineral oils and chiefly valuable therefor, have been declared by Congress to be "free and open to occupation, exploration and purchase by citizens of the United States . . . under regulations prescribed by law." Act of February 11, 1897, c. 216, 29 Stat. 526.

As these regulations permitted exploration and location without the payment of any sum, and as title could be obtained for a merely nominal amount, many persons availed themselves of the provisions of the statute. Large areas of California were explored; and petroleum having been found, locations were made. . . . [O]il was so rapidly extracted that on September 7, 1909, the Director of the Geological Survey made a report to the Secretary of the Interior which . . . called attention to the fact that, while there was a limited supply of coal on the Pacific coast and the value of oil as a fuel had been fully demonstrated, yet at the rate at which oil lands in California were being patented by private parties it would "be impossible for the people of the United States to continue ownership of oil lands for more than a few months. After that the Government will be obliged to repurchase the very oil that it has practically given away. . . ." "In view of the increasing use of fuel by the American Navy there would appear to be an immediate necessity for assuring the conservation of a proper supply of petroleum for the Government's own use . . ." and "pending the enactment of adequate legislation on this subject, the filing of claims to oil lands in the State of California should be suspended."

This recommendation was approved by the Secretary of the Interior. Shortly afterwards he brought the matter to the attention of the President who, on September 27, 1909, issued the following Proclamation:

"Temporary Petroleum Withdrawal No. 5."

"In aid of proposed legislation affecting the use and disposition of the petroleum deposits on the public domain, all public lands in the accompanying lists are hereby temporarily withdrawn from all forms of location, settlement, selection, filing, entry, or disposal under the mineral or nonmineral public-land laws. All locations or claims existing and valid on this date may proceed to entry in the usual manner after field investigation and examination."

The list attached described an area aggregating 3,041,000 acres in California and Wyoming—though, of course, the order only applied to the public lands therein, the acreage of which is not shown. On March 27, 1910, six months after the publication of the Proclamation, William T. Henshaw and others entered upon a quarter section of this public land in Wyoming so withdrawn. They made explorations, bored a well, discovered oil and thereafter assigned their interest to the Appellees, who took possession and extracted large quantities of oil. On May 4, 1910, they filed a location certificate.

As the explorations by the original claimants, and the subsequent operation of the well, were both long after the date of the President's Proclamation, the Government filed, in the District Court . . . a Bill in Equity against the Midwest Oil Company and the other Appellees, seeking to recover the land and to obtain an accounting for 50,000 barrels of oil alleged to have been illegally extracted. The court sustained the defendant's demurrer and dismissed the bill. [Appeals followed.]

On the part of the Government it is urged that the President, as Commander-in-Chief of the Army and Navy, had power to make the order for the purpose of retaining and preserving a source of supply of fuel for the Navy, instead of allowing the oil land to be taken up for a nominal sum, the Government being then obliged to purchase at a great cost what it had previously owned. It is argued that the President, charged with the care of the public domain, could, by virtue of the executive power vested in him by the Constitution (Art. 2, § 1), and also in conformity with the tacit consent of Congress, withdraw, in the public interest, any public land from entry or location by private parties.

The Appellees, on the other hand, insist that there is no dispensing power in the Executive and that he could not suspend a statute or withdraw from entry or location any land which Congress had affirmatively declared should be free and open to acquisition by citizens of the United States. They further insist that the withdrawal order is absolutely void since it appears on its face to be a mere attempt to suspend a statute—supposed to be unwise—in order to allow Congress to pass another more in accordance with what the Executive thought to be in the public interest.

1. We need not consider whether, as an original question, the President could have withdrawn from private acquisition what Congress had made free and open to occupation and purchase. The case can be determined on other grounds and in the light of the legal consequences flowing from a long continued practice to make orders like the one here involved. For the President's proclamation of September 27, 1909, is by no means the first instance in which the Executive, by a special order, has withdrawn land which Congress, by general statute, had thrown open to acquisition by citizens. And while it is not known when the first of these orders was made, it is certain that "the practice dates from an early period in the history of the government." *Grisar v. McDowell*, 6 Wall. 381 [(1867)]. Scores and hundreds of these orders have been made; and treating them as they must be, as the act of the President, an examination of official publications will show that . . . he has during the past 80 years, without express statutory authority—but under the claim of power so to do—made a multitude of Executive Orders which operated to withdraw public land that would otherwise have been open to private acquisition. They affected every kind of land— mineral and nonmineral. The size of the tracts varied from a few square rods to many square miles and the amount withdrawn has aggregated millions of acres. The number of such instances cannot, of course, be accurately given, but the extent of the practice can best be appreciated by a consideration of what is believed to be a correct enumeration of such Executive Orders mentioned in public documents.

They show that prior to the year 1910 there had been issued:

99 Executive Orders establishing or enlarging Indian Reservations;

109 Executive Orders establishing or enlarging Military Reservations and setting apart land for water, timber, fuel, hay, signal stations, target ranges and rights of way for use in connection with Military Reservations;

44 Executive Orders establishing Bird Reserves.

In the sense that these lands may have been intended for public use, they were reserved for a public purpose. But they were not reserved in pursuance of law or by virtue of any general or special statutory authority. For, it is to be specially noted that there was no act of Congress providing for Bird Reserves or for these Indian Reservations. There was no law for the establishment of these Military Reservations or defining their size or location. There was no statute empowering the President to withdraw any of these lands from settlement or to reserve them for any of the purposes indicated.

But when it appeared that the public interest would be served by withdrawing or reserving parts of the public domain, nothing was more natural than to retain what the Government already owned. And in making such orders, which were thus useful to the public, no private interest was injured. For prior to the initiation of some right given by law the citizen had no enforceable interest in the public statute and no private right in land which was the property of the people. The President was in a

[handwritten margin note:] Pres has withdrawn land before, nothing new

[handwritten margin note:] it was in the public interest to retain land

position to know when the public interest required particular portions of the people's lands to be withdrawn from entry or location; his action inflicted no wrong upon any private citizen, and being subject to disaffirmance by Congress, could occasion no harm to the interest of the public at large. Congress did not repudiate the power claimed or the withdrawal orders made. On the contrary it uniformly and repeatedly acquiesced in the practice and, as shown by these records, there had been, prior to 1910, at least 252 Executive Orders making reservations for useful, though non-statutory purposes.

This right of the President to make reservations, and thus withdraw land from private acquisition, was expressly recognized in *Grisar v. McDowell*, 6 Wall. 364, 381 (1867), where it was said that "from an early period in the history of the Government it has been the practice of the President to order, from time to time, as the exigencies of the public service required, parcels of land belonging to the United States to be reserved from sale and set apart for public uses."

But notwithstanding this decision and the continuity of this practice, the absence of express statutory authority was the occasion of doubt being expressed as to the power of the President to make these orders. The matter was therefore several times referred to the law officers of the Government for an opinion on the subject. One of them stated (1889) (19 Op. 370) that the validity of such orders rested on "a long-established and long-recognized power in the President to withhold from sale or settlement, at discretion, portions of the public domain." [The Court cited two similar attorney general opinions from 1881.]

Similar views were expressed by officers in the Land Department. Indeed, one of the strongest assertions of the existence of the power is the frequently quoted statement of Secretary Teller made in 1881:

> "That the power resides in the Executive from an early period in the history
> of the country to make reservations has never been denied either legisla-
> tively or judicially, but on the contrary has been recognized. It constitutes
> in fact a part of the Land Office Law, exists *ex necessitati rei*, is indispens-
> able to the public weal and in that light, by different laws enacted as herein
> indicated, has been referred to as an existing undisputed power too well
> settled ever to be disputed." 1 L.D., 338 (1881–3).

2. It may be argued that while these facts and rulings prove a usage they do not establish its validity. But government is a practical affair intended for practical men. Both officers, law-makers and citizens naturally adjust themselves to any long-continued action of the Executive Department—on the presumption that unauthorized acts would not have been allowed to be so often repeated as to crystallize into a regular practice. That presumption is not reasoning in a circle but the basis of a wise and quieting rule that in determining the meaning of a statute or the existence of a power, weight shall be given to the usage itself—even when the validity of the practice is the subject of investigation. . . .

3 . . . [D]ecisions [supporting the Court's conclusion] do not, of course, mean . . . that the Executive can by his course of action create a power. But they do clearly indicate that the long-continued practice, known to and acquiesced in by Congress, would raise a presumption that the withdrawals had been made in pursuance of its consent or of a recognized administrative power of the Executive in the management of the public lands. This is particularly true in view of the fact that the land is property of the United States and that the land laws are not of a legislative character in the highest sense of the term (Art. 4, § 3) "but savor somewhat of mere rules prescribed by an owner of property for its disposal." *Butte City Water Co. v. Baker*, 196 U.S. 126 [(1905)].

These rules or laws for the disposal of public land are necessarily general in their nature. Emergencies may occur, or conditions may so change as to require that the agent in charge should, in the public interest, withhold the land from sale; and while no such express authority has been granted, there is nothing in the nature of the power exercised which prevents Congress from granting it by implication just as could be done by any other owner of property under similar conditions. The power of the Executive, as agent in charge, to retain that property from sale need not necessarily be expressed in writing . . . .

[margin, handwritten: Power ∅ need to be in writing]

The Executive, as agent, was in charge of the public domain; by a multitude of orders extending over a long period of time and affecting vast bodies of land, in many States and Territories, he withdrew large areas in the public interest. These orders were known to Congress, as principal, and in not a single instance was the act of the agent disapproved. Its acquiescence all the more readily operated as an implied grant of power in view of the fact that its exercise was not only useful to the public but did not interfere with any vested right of the citizen.

[margin, handwritten: Congress ∅ object before]

4. The appellees . . . make a distinction between a . . . Reservation for a purpose, not provided for by existing legislation, and a Withdrawal made in aid of future legislation. It would mean that a Permanent Reservation . . . would be valid, while a mere Temporary Withdrawal to enable Congress to legislate in the public interest would be invalid. . . . [A]s the greater includes the less, the power to make permanent reservations includes power to make temporary withdrawals. . . .

5. . . . [T]hat the existence of this power was recognized and its exercise by the Executive assented to by Congress, is emphasized by the fact that the above-mentioned withdrawals were issued after the Report which the Secretary of the Interior made in 1902, in response to a resolution of the Senate calling for information "as to what, if any, of the public lands have been withdrawn from disposition under the settlement or other laws by order of the Commissioner of the General Land Office and *what, if any, authority of law exists for such order of withdrawal.*"

The answer to this specific inquiry was . . . the elaborate and detailed report of the Commissioner of the Land Office. . . . This report refers to *Withdrawals* and not to *Reservations*. It is most important in connection with the present inquiry as to whether Congress knew of the practice to make temporary withdrawals and knowingly assented thereto. It will be noted that the Resolution called on the Department to state the extent of such withdrawals and the authority by which they were made. The officer of the Land Department in his answer shows that there have been a large number of withdrawals made for good but for non-statutory reasons. He shows that these 92 orders had been made by virtue of a long-continued practice and under claim of a right to take such action in the public interest "as exigencies might demand . . ." Congress with notice of this practice and of this claim of authority, received the Report. Neither at that session nor afterwards did it ever repudiate the action taken or the power claimed. Its silence was acquiescence. Its acquiescence was equivalent to consent to continue the practice until the power was revoked by some subsequent action by Congress.

Congresses silence was acquiescence

6. Nor is the position of the appellees strengthened by the act of June 25, 1910 (36 Stat. 847), [passed after the withdrawals contested in this case] to authorize the President to make withdrawals of public lands and requiring a list of the same to be filed with Congress. . . . The legislative history of the statute shows that there was no . . . intent and no purpose to make the Act retroactive or to disaffirm what the agent in charge had already done. . . .

The case is therefore remanded to the District Court with directions that the decree dismissing the Bill be *Reversed*.

Justice DAY, with whom concurred Justice McKENNA and Justice VAN DEVANTER, dissenting:

. . . It is . . . explicitly recognized, as was already apparent from the terms of the Constitution itself, that the sole authority to dispose of the public lands was vested in the Congress and in no other branch of the Federal Government. The right of the Executive to withdraw lands which Congress has declared shall be open and free to settlement upon terms which Congress has itself prescribed, is said to arise from the tacit consent of Congress in long acquiescence in such executive action resulting in an implied authority from Congress to make such withdrawals in the public interest as the Executive deems proper and necessary. There is nothing in the Constitution suggesting or authorizing such augmentation of executive authority or justifying him in thus acting in aid of a power which the Framers of the Constitution saw fit to vest exclusively in the legislative branch of the Government . . . .

The constitutional authority of the President of the United States (Art. II, §§ 1, 3), includes the executive power of the Nation and the duty to see that the laws are faithfully executed. . . . Under this clause his duty is not limited to the enforcement of acts of Congress according to their express terms. It includes "the rights and obligations growing out of the Constitution itself, our international relations, and all the protection implied by the nature of the government under the Constitution." *In re Neagle*, 135 U.S. 1. The Constitution does not confer upon him any power to enact laws or to suspend or repeal such as the Congress enacts. *Kendall v. United States*, 12 Pet. 524, 613 . . . . In other words, it may be fairly said that a given withdrawal must have been expressly authorized by Congress or there must be that clear implication of congressional authority which is equivalent to express authority; and when such authority is wanting there can be no executive withdrawal of lands from the operation of an act of Congress which would otherwise control. . . .

Justice McREYNOLDS took no part in the decision of this case.

———————

1. *"A Foolish Consistency . . ."* Was President Taft's basis for the withdrawal order consistent with his general views on executive power, which we outlined in Chapter One? Justice Jackson thought not: *see Youngstown Sheet & Tube Co. v. Sawyer*, 343 U.S. 579, 634 n.1 (1952), where in the context of discussing competing views of executive power he said: "It even seems that President Taft cancels out Professor Taft. Compare his Temporary Petroleum Withdrawal No. 5 of September 27, 1909, *United States v. Midwest Oil Co.*, with his appraisal of executive power in Our Chief Magistrate and His Powers 139–40" [quoted in Chapter One].

2. *"Inherent" Executive Powers.* In *Midwest Oil*, the executive argued that the President's power as Commander-in-Chief and the clause vesting executive power in him supported the order. Why, within twenty-five years after *Neagle* and *Debs*, did the majority not rest decision on that basis—or even cite the earlier cases? Wasn't the President's constitutional argument on the facts of *Midwest Oil* as strong as any argument based on the facts of those cases?

3. *The Public Lands Context.* To what extent does *Midwest Oil* appear to be a case confined to the public lands context? At least we can say that this is a hospitable context for its invocation. Harold H. Bruff, *Executive Power and the Public Lands,* 76 U. Colo. L. Rev. 503 (2005). Ever since the administration of Theodore Roosevelt, Presidents have created new national monuments under the authority of the Antiquities Act of 1906, 16 U.S.C. § 431 (1982).

The Antiquities Act authorizes the President:

> to declare by public proclamation historic landmarks, historic and pre-historic structures, and other objects of historic or scientific interest that are situated upon the lands owned or controlled by the Government of the United States to be national monuments, and may reserve as a part thereof parcels of land, the limits of which in all cases shall be confined to the smallest area compatible with the proper care and management of the objects to be protected.

Although the statutory language most readily calls to mind such phenomena as Indian burial mounds and surrounding lands the Act has been used for "objects" as large as the Grand Canyon and the 89.6 million-acre Papahānaumokuākea Marine National Monument near Hawaii! The courts have upheld these actions. *See generally* Harold H. Bruff, *Judicial Review and the President's Statutory Powers,* 68 Va. L. Rev. 1, 36–39 (1982). Because Presidents Nixon and Reagan have so far been the only Presidents since 1906 not to invoke Antiquities Act authority to create national monuments, it seems a safe bet that the precedent for broad interpretation of the Act that Theodore Roosevelt first set will continue indefinitely under future Presidents.

4. *The "Acquiescence Doctrine."* *Midwest Oil* is best known as the source of the Court's doctrine that Congress can impliedly authorize executive action by acquiescing in it. (Is this just a statutory doctrine, or can it work for the Constitution as well? Recall James Madison's conclusion, quoted in Chapter One, that the behavior of all three branches had removed his earlier doubts about the constitutionality of a bank.) In any event, do the facts of *Midwest Oil* present a strong case for acquiescence?

What is the basis for the doctrine? It is commonplace to say that courts will defer to reasonable executive interpretations of statutes. The interpreting agency, after all, may have helped to draft the statute, and its experience in administration is surely worth something. How far beyond this does *Midwest Oil* go in deferring to long-standing executive branch interpretations of statutes and the Constitution? Review the kinds of evidence proffered by the Court for its conclusion that Congress authorized temporary withdrawals in aid of legislation. Are all equally probative?

Professor Monaghan, *supra* at 44–47, says of the case:

> *United States v. Midwest Oil Co.* is occasionally cited as a decision — the *only* decision, I should add — in which the Supreme Court upheld presidential law-making contrary to the terms of an Act of Congress. That interpretation, however, is untenable. Nothing in the Court's opinion or in the dissent suggested that the Court had endorsed such far-reaching doctrine. Fairly read, however, *Midwest Oil* does recognize the existence of some presidential authority to "burden private rights" even absent direct statutory authority. . . .
>
> *Midwest Oil* can support several different propositions. Considerable language in the Court's opinion, for example, could justifiably limit the decision to no more than a fact-specific implied delegation case — with the President's construction of the access statute reasonable in light of a long-standing administrative practice. For me, that reading does not quite fit. No [broad] umbrella provision existed under which the executive order could, at least formally, be subsumed. . . . *Midwest Oil* could also be confined to that presidential regulatory power necessarily incident to the President's role as "chief administrator" in connection with government lands and perhaps other property. . . .
>
> In fact, *Midwest Oil* has not been confined as a precedent to the notion of President as chief administrator. . . . [T]he Court understands the decision to sanction presidential conduct invading private rights if this conduct is supported by congressional acquiescence or tacit consent, and the question then becomes what congressional conduct suffices for that purpose. Congressional inaction is not enough; *Midwest Oil* requires that, fairly read, "adjacent" congressional legislation must presume the validity of a prior presidential practice.

5. *Deja Vu All Over Again*. *Midwest Oil* will be an important precedent in several major cases in this book: *Dames & Moore v. Regan* and *Haig v. Agee*, reprinted in Chapter Five, and the *Steel Seizure* case, which follows. After you have read these cases, reevaluate the status of the acquiescence doctrine.

Youngstown Sheet & Tube Co. v. Sawyer

343 U.S. 579 (1952)

Justice BLACK delivered the opinion of the Court.

We are asked to decide whether the President was acting within his constitutional power when he issued an order directing the Secretary of Commerce to take possession of and operate most of the Nation's steel mills. The mill owners argue that the President's order amounts to lawmaking, a legislative function which the Constitution has expressly confided to the Congress and not to the President. The Government's position is that the order was made on findings of the President that his action was necessary to avert a national catastrophe which would inevitably result from a stoppage of steel production, and that in meeting this grave emergency the President was acting within the aggregate of his constitutional powers as the Nation's Chief Executive and the Commander in Chief of the Armed Forces of the United States. The issue emerges here from the following series of events:

In the latter part of 1951, a dispute arose between the steel companies and their employees over terms and conditions that should be included in new collective bargaining agreements. Long-continued conferences failed to resolve the dispute. On December 18, 1951, the employees' representative, United Steelworkers of America, C.I.O., gave notice of an intention to strike when the existing bargaining agreements expired on December 31. The Federal Mediation and Conciliation Service then intervened in an effort to get labor and management to agree. This failing, the President on December 22, 1951, referred the dispute to the Federal Wage Stabilization Board to investigate and make recommendations for fair and equitable terms of settlement. This Board's report resulted in no settlement. On April 4, 1952, the Union gave notice of a nation-wide strike called to begin at 12:01 a.m. April 9. The indispensability of steel as a component of substantially all weapons and other war materials led the President to believe that the proposed work stoppage would immediately jeopardize our national defense and that governmental seizure of the steel mills was necessary in order to assure the continued availability of steel. Reciting these considerations for his action, the President, a few hours before the strike was to begin, issued Executive Order 10340. . . . The order directed the Secretary of Commerce to take possession of most of the steel mills and keep them running. The Secretary immediately issued his own possessory orders, calling upon the presidents of the various seized companies to serve as operating managers for the United States. They were directed to carry on their activities in accordance with regulations and directions of the Secretary. The next morning the President sent a message to Congress

[handwritten margin notes: "Order = law making which Pres ¢ do"; "Strike"; "∅ steel = jeopardize national defense"]

reporting his action. Twelve days later he sent a second message. Congress has taken no action.

Obeying the Secretary's orders under protest, the companies brought proceedings against him in the District Court. Their complaints charged that the seizure was not authorized by an act of Congress or by any constitutional provisions. The District Court was asked to declare the orders of the President and the Secretary invalid and to issue preliminary and permanent injunctions restraining their enforcement. Opposing the motion for preliminary injunction, the United States asserted that a strike disrupting steel production for even a brief period would so endanger the well-being and safety of the Nation that the President had "inherent power" to do what he had done—power "supported by the Constitution, by historical precedent, and by court decisions." The Government also contended that in any event no preliminary injunction should be issued because the companies had made no showing that their available legal remedies were inadequate or that their injuries from seizure would be irreparable. Holding against the Government on all points, the District Court on April 30 issued a preliminary injunction restraining the Secretary from "continuing the seizure and possession of the plants . . . and from acting under the purported authority of Executive Order No. 10340." 103 F. Supp. 569. On the same day the Court of Appeals stayed the District Court's injunction. Deeming it best that the issues raised be promptly decided by this Court, we granted certiorari on May 3 and set the cause for argument on May 12. . . .

I.

[The Court first rejected the Government's argument that injunctive relief should be denied because damages were adequate to compensate for the harm suffered. The Court thought that difficulties in measuring and awarding damages justified a finding of irreparable injury.]

II.

The President's power, if any, to issue the order must stem either from an act of Congress or from the Constitution itself. There is no statute that expressly authorizes the President to take possession of property as he did here. Nor is there any act of Congress to which our attention has been directed from which such a power can fairly be implied. Indeed, we do not understand the Government to rely on statutory authorization for this seizure. There are two statutes which do authorize the President to take both personal and real property under certain conditions. However, the Government admits that these conditions were not met and that the President's order was not rooted in either of the statutes. The Government refers to the seizure provisions of one of these statutes (§ 201(b) of the Defense Production Act) as "much too cumbersome, involved, and time-consuming for the crisis which was at hand."

Moreover, the use of the seizure technique to solve labor disputes in order to prevent work stoppages was not only unauthorized by any congressional enactment; prior to this controversy, Congress had refused to adopt that method of settling labor disputes. When the Taft-Hartley Act was under consideration in 1947, Congress rejected an amendment which would have authorized such governmental seizures in cases of emergency. Apparently it was thought that the technique of seizure, like that of compulsory arbitration, would interfere with the process of collective bargaining. Consequently, the plan Congress adopted in that Act did not provide for seizure under any circumstances. Instead, the plan sought to bring about settlements by use of the customary devices of mediation, conciliation, investigation by boards of inquiry, and public reports. In some instances temporary injunctions were authorized to provide cooling-off periods. All this failing, unions were left free to strike after a secret vote by employees as to whether they wished to accept their employers' final settlement offer.

Mediation > Seizure for labor stuff

It is clear that if the President had authority to issue the order he did, it must be found in some provision of the Constitution. And it is not claimed that express constitutional language grants this power to the President. The contention is that presidential power should be implied from the aggregate of his powers under the Constitution. Particular reliance is placed on provisions in Article II which say that "The executive Power shall be vested in a President . . ."; that "he shall take Care that the Laws be faithfully executed"; and that he "shall be Commander in Chief of the Army and Navy of the United States."

The order cannot properly be sustained as an exercise of the President's military power as Commander in Chief of the Armed Forces. The Government attempts to do so by citing a number of cases upholding broad powers in military commanders engaged in day-to-day fighting in a theater of war. Such cases need not concern us here. Even though "theater of war" be an expanding concept, we cannot with faithfulness to our constitutional system hold that the Commander in Chief of the Armed Forces has the ultimate power as such to take possession of private property in order to keep labor disputes from stopping production. This is a job for the Nation's lawmakers, not for its military authorities.

Commander in Chief power ≠ go this far

Nor can the seizure order be sustained because of the several constitutional provisions that grant executive power to the President. In the framework of our Constitution, the President's power to see that the laws are faithfully executed refutes the idea that he is to be a lawmaker. The Constitution limits his functions in the lawmaking process to the recommending of laws he thinks wise and the vetoing of laws he thinks bad. And the Constitution is neither silent nor equivocal about who shall make laws which the President is to execute. The first section of the first article says that "All legislative Powers herein granted shall be vested in a Congress of the United States. . . ." After granting many powers to the Congress, Article I goes on to provide that Congress may "make all Laws which shall be necessary and proper for carrying into Execution the foregoing Powers and all other Powers vested by this Constitution in the Government of the United States, or in any Department or Officer thereof."

hes going around Congress

The President's order does not direct that a congressional policy be executed in a manner prescribed by Congress—it directs that a presidential policy be executed in a manner prescribed by the President. . . . The power of Congress to adopt such public policies as those proclaimed by the order is beyond question. It can authorize the taking of private property for public use. It can make laws regulating the relationships between employers and employees, prescribing rules designed to settle labor disputes, and fixing wages and working conditions in certain fields of our economy. The Constitution did not subject this law-making power of Congress to presidential or military supervision or control.

It is said that other Presidents without congressional authority have taken possession of private business enterprises in order to settle labor disputes. But even if this be true, Congress has not thereby lost its exclusive constitutional authority to make laws necessary and proper to carry out the powers vested by the Constitution "in the Government of the United States, or in any Department or Officer thereof." The Founders of this Nation entrusted the law making power to the Congress alone in both good and bad times. It would do no good to recall the historical events, the fears of power and the hopes for freedom that lay behind their choice. Such a review would but confirm our holding that this seizure order cannot stand.

The judgment of the District Court is affirmed.

Justice FRANKFURTER, concurring.

. . . Congress in 1947 was . . . called upon to consider whether governmental seizure should be used to avoid serious industrial shutdowns. Congress decided against conferring such power generally and in advance, without special congressional enactment to meet each particular need. Under the urgency of telephone and coal strikes in the winter of 1946, Congress addressed itself to the problems raised by "national emergency" strikes and lockouts. The termination of wartime seizure powers on December 31, 1946, brought these matters to the attention of Congress with vivid impact. A proposal that the President be given powers to seize plants to avert a shutdown where the "health or safety" of the nation was endangered was thoroughly canvassed by Congress and rejected. No room for doubt remains that the proponents as well as the opponents of the bill which became the Labor Management Relations Act of 1947 clearly understood that as a result of that legislation the only recourse for preventing a shutdown in any basic industry, after failure of mediation, was Congress. . . .

But it is now claimed that the President has seizure power by virtue of the Defense Production Act of 1950 and its Amendments. And the claim is based on the occurrence of new events—Korea and the need for stabilization, etc.—although it was well known that seizure power was withheld by the Act of 1947 and although the President, whose specific requests for other authority were in the main granted by Congress, never suggested that in view of the new events he needed the power of seizure which Congress in its judgment had decided to withhold from him. The utmost that the Korean conflict may imply is that it may have been desirable to have given the President further authority, a freer hand in these matters. Absence of authority in the President to deal with a crisis does not imply want of power in the Government. Conversely the fact that power exists in the Government does not vest it in the President. . . .

No authority that has since been given to the President can by any fair process of statutory construction be deemed to withdraw the restriction or change the will of Congress as expressed by a body of enactments, culminating in the Labor Management Relations Act of 1947. . . .

Apart from his vast share of responsibility for the conduct of our foreign relations, the embracing function of the President is that "he shall take Care that the Laws be faithfully executed. . . ." Art. II, § 3. The nature of that authority has for me been comprehensively indicated by Mr. Justice Holmes. "The duty of the President to see that the laws be executed is a duty that does not go beyond the laws or require him to achieve more than Congress sees fit to leave within his power." *Myers v. United States*, 272 U.S. 52, 177. . . .

To be sure, the content of the three authorities of government is not to be derived from an abstract analysis. The areas are partly interacting, not wholly disjointed. The Constitution is a framework for government. Therefore the way the framework has consistently operated fairly establishes that it has operated according to its true nature. Deeply embedded traditional ways of conducting government cannot supplant the Constitution or legislation, but they give meaning to the words of a text or supply them. It is an inadmissibly narrow conception of American constitutional law to confine it to the words of the Constitution and to disregard the gloss which life has written upon them. In short, a systematic, unbroken, executive practice, long pursued to the knowledge of the Congress and never before questioned, engaged in by Presidents who have also sworn to uphold the Constitution, making as it were such exercise of power part of the structure of our government, may be treated as a gloss on "executive Power" vested in the President by § 1 of Art. II.

Such was the case of *United States v. Midwest Oil Co.*, 236 U.S. 459. The contrast between the circumstances of that case and this one helps to draw a clear line between authority not explicitly conferred yet authorized to be exercised by the President and the denial of such authority. In both instances it was the concern of Congress under express constitutional grant to make rules and regulations for the problems with which the President dealt. In the one case he was dealing with the protection of property belonging to the United States; in the other with the enforcement of the Commerce Clause and with raising and supporting armies and maintaining the Navy. In the *Midwest Oil* case, lands which Congress had opened for entry were, over a period of 80 years and in 252 instances, and by Presidents learned and unlearned in the law, temporarily withdrawn from entry so as to enable Congress to deal with such withdrawals. No remotely comparable practice can be vouched for executive seizure of property at a time when this country was not at war, in the only constitutional way in which it can be at war. It would pursue the irrelevant to reopen the controversy over the constitutionality of some acts of Lincoln during the Civil War. *See* J.G. Randall, Constitutional Problems under Lincoln (Revised ed. 1951). Suffice it to say that he seized railroads in territory where armed hostilities had already interrupted the movement of troops to the beleaguered Capital, and his order was ratified by the Congress. . . .

Down to the World War II period, . . . the record is barren of instances comparable to the one before us. Of twelve seizures by President Roosevelt prior to the enactment of the War Labor Disputes Act in June 1943, three were sanctioned by existing law, and six others were effected after Congress, on December 8, 1941, had declared the existence of a state of war. In this case, reliance on the powers that flow from declared war has been commendably disclaimed by the Solicitor General. Thus the list of executive assertions of the power of seizure in circumstances comparable to the present reduces to three in the six-month period from June to December of 1941. We need not split hairs in comparing those actions to the one before us, though much might be said by way of differentiation. Without passing on their validity, as we are not called upon to do, it suffices to say that these three isolated instances do not add up, either in number, scope, duration or contemporaneous legal justification, to the kind of executive construction of the Constitution revealed in the *Midwest Oil* case. Nor do they come to us sanctioned by long-continued acquiescence of Congress giving decisive weight to a construction by the Executive of its powers. . . .

Justice JACKSON, concurring in the judgment and opinion of the Court.

That comprehensive and undefined presidential powers hold both practical advantages and grave dangers for the country will impress anyone who has served as legal adviser to a President in time of transition and public anxiety. While an interval of detached reflection may temper teachings of that experience, they probably are a more realistic influence on my views than the conventional materials of judicial decision which seem unduly to accentuate doctrine and legal fiction. But as we approach the question of presidential power, we half overcome mental hazards by recognizing them. The opinions of judges, no less than executives and publicists, often suffer the infirmity of confusing the issue of a power's validity with the cause it is invoked to promote, of confounding the permanent executive office with its temporary occupant. The tendency is strong to emphasize transient results upon policies—such as wages or stabilization—and lose sight of enduring consequences upon the balanced power structure of our Republic.

A judge, like an executive adviser, may be surprised at the poverty of really useful and unambiguous authority applicable to concrete problems of executive power as they actually present themselves. Just what our forefathers did envision, or would have envisioned had they foreseen modern conditions, must be divined from materials almost as enigmatic as the dreams Joseph was called upon to interpret for Pharaoh. A century and a half of partisan debate and scholarly speculation yields no net result but only supplies more or less apt quotations from respected sources on each side of any question. They largely cancel each other. And court decisions are indecisive because of the judicial practice of dealing with the largest questions in the most narrow way.

The actual art of governing under our Constitution does not and cannot conform to judicial definitions of the power of any of its branches based on isolated clauses or even single Articles torn from context. While the Constitution diffuses power the better to secure liberty, it also contemplates that practice will integrate the dispersed powers into a workable government. It enjoins upon its branches separateness but interdependence, autonomy but reciprocity. Presidential powers are not fixed but fluctuate, depending upon their disjunction or conjunction with those of Congress. We may well begin by a somewhat over-simplified grouping of practical situations in which a President may doubt, or others may challenge, his powers, and by distinguishing roughly the legal consequences of this factor of relativity.

1. When the President acts pursuant to an express or implied authorization of Congress, his authority is at its maximum, for it includes all that he possesses in his own right plus all that Congress can delegate. In these circumstances, and in these only, may he be said (for what it may be worth), to personify the federal sovereignty. If his act is held unconstitutional under these circumstances, it usually means that the Federal Government as an undivided whole lacks power. A seizure executed by the President pursuant to an Act of Congress would be supported by the strongest of presumptions and the widest latitude of judicial interpretation, and the burden of persuasion would rest heavily upon any who might attack it.

2. When the President acts in absence of either a congressional grant or denial of authority, he can only rely upon his own independent powers, but there is a zone of twilight in which he and Congress may have concurrent authority, or in which its distribution is uncertain. Therefore, congressional inertia, indifference or quiescence may sometimes, at least as a practical matter, enable, if not invite, measures on independent presidential responsibility. In this area, any actual test of power is likely to depend on the imperatives of events and contemporary imponderables rather than on abstract theories of law.

3. When the President takes measures incompatible with the expressed or implied will of Congress, his power is at its lowest ebb, for then he can rely only upon his own constitutional powers minus any constitutional powers of Congress over the matter. Courts can sustain exclusive presidential control in such a case only by disabling the Congress from acting upon the subject. Presidential claim to a power at once so conclusive and preclusive must be scrutinized with caution, for what is at stake is the equilibrium established by our constitutional system.

Into which of these classifications does this executive seizure of the steel industry fit? It is eliminated from the first by admission, for it is conceded that no congressional authorization exists for this seizure. That takes away also the support of the many precedents and declarations which were made in relation, and must be confined, to this category.

Can it then be defended under flexible tests available to the second category? It seems clearly eliminated from that class because Congress has not left seizure of private property an open field but has covered it by three statutory policies inconsistent with this seizure. In cases where the purpose is to supply needs of the Government itself, two courses are provided: one, seizure of a plant which fails to comply with obligatory orders placed by the Government, another, condemnation of facilities, including temporary use under the power of eminent domain. The third is applicable where it is the general economy of the country that is to be protected rather than exclusive governmental interests. None of these were invoked. In choosing a different and inconsistent way of his own, the President cannot claim that it is necessitated or invited by failure of Congress to legislate upon the occasions, grounds and methods for seizure of industrial properties.

This leaves the current seizure to be justified only by the severe tests under the third grouping, where it can be supported only by any remainder of executive power after subtraction of such powers as Congress may have over the subject. In short, we can sustain the President only by holding that seizure of such strike-bound industries is within his domain and beyond control by Congress. Thus, this Court's first review of such seizures occurs under circumstances which leave presidential power most vulnerable to attack and in the least favorable of possible constitutional postures. . . .

The Solicitor General seeks the power of seizure in three clauses of the Executive Article, the first reading, "The executive Power shall be vested in a President of the United States of America." Lest I be thought to exaggerate, I quote the interpretation which his brief puts upon it: "In our view, this clause constitutes a grant of all the executive powers of which the Government is capable." If that be true, it is difficult to see why the forefathers bothered to add several specific items, including some trifling ones.

The example of such unlimited executive power that must have most impressed the forefathers was the prerogative exercised by George III, and the description of its evils in the Declaration of Independence leads me to doubt that they were creating their new Executive in his image. Continental European examples were no more appealing. And if we seek instruction from our own times, we can match it only from the executive powers in those governments we disparagingly describe as totalitarian. I cannot accept the view that this clause is a grant in bulk of all conceivable executive power but regard it as an allocation to the presidential office of the generic powers thereafter stated.

The clause on which the Government next relies is that "The President shall be Commander in Chief of the Army and Navy of the United States. . . ." These cryptic words have given rise to some of the most persistent controversies in our constitutional history. Of course, they imply something more than an empty title. But just what authority goes with the name has plagued presidential advisers who would not waive or narrow it by nonassertion yet cannot say where it begins or ends. It undoubtedly puts the Nation's armed forces under presidential command. Hence, this loose appellation is sometimes advanced as support for any presidential action, internal or external, involving use of force, the idea being that it vests power to do anything, anywhere, that can be done with an army or navy.

That seems to be the logic of an argument tendered at our bar—that the President having, on his own responsibility, sent American troops abroad derives from that act "affirmative power" to seize the means of producing a supply of steel for them.

To quote, "Perhaps the most forceful illustrations of the scope of Presidential power in this connection is the fact that American troops in Korea, whose safety and effectiveness are so directly involved here, were sent to the field by an exercise of the President's constitutional powers." Thus, it is said he has invested himself with "war powers."

I cannot foresee all that it might entail if the Court should indorse this argument. Nothing in our Constitution is plainer than that declaration of a war is entrusted only to Congress. Of course, a state of war may in fact exist without a formal declaration. But no doctrine that the Court could promulgate would seem to me more sinister and alarming than that a President whose conduct of foreign affairs is so largely uncontrolled, and often even is unknown, can vastly enlarge his mastery over the internal affairs of the country by his own commitment of the Nation's armed forces to some foreign venture. I do not, however, find it necessary or appropriate to consider the legal status of the Korean enterprise to discountenance argument based on it.

Assuming that we are in a war *de facto*, whether it is or is not a war *de jure*, does that empower the Commander in Chief to seize industries he thinks necessary to supply our army? The Constitution expressly places in Congress power "to raise and *support* Armies" and "to *provide* and *maintain* a Navy." (Emphasis supplied.) This certainly lays upon Congress primary responsibility for supplying the armed forces. Congress alone controls the raising of revenues and their appropriation and may determine in what manner and by what means they shall be spent for military and naval procurement. I suppose no one would doubt that Congress can take over war supply as a Government enterprise. On the other hand, if Congress sees fit to rely on free private enterprise collectively bargaining with free labor for support and maintenance of our armed forces, can the Executive because of lawful disagreements incidental to that process, seize the facility for operation upon Government-imposed terms? . . .

We should not use this occasion to circumscribe, much less to contract, the lawful role of the President as Commander in Chief. I should indulge the widest latitude of interpretation to sustain his exclusive function to command the instruments of national force, at least when turned against the outside world for the security of our society. But, when it is turned inward, not because of rebellion but because of a lawful economic struggle between industry and labor, it should have no such indulgence. His command power is not such an absolute as might be implied from that office in a militaristic system but is subject to limitations consistent with a constitutional Republic whose law and policy-making branch is a representative Congress. The purpose of lodging dual titles in one man was to insure that the civilian would control the military, not to enable the military to subordinate the presidential office. . . .

The third clause in which the Solicitor General finds seizure powers is that "he shall take Care that the Laws be faithfully executed. . . ." That authority must be matched against words of the Fifth Amendment that "No person shall be . . . deprived of life, liberty, or property, without due process of law. . . ." One gives a governmental authority that reaches so far as there is law, the other gives a private right that authority shall go no farther. These signify about all there is of the principle that ours is a government of laws, not of men, and that we submit ourselves to rulers only if under rules.

The Solicitor General lastly grounds support of the seizure upon nebulous, inherent powers never expressly granted but said to have accrued to the office from the customs and claims of preceding administrations. The plea is for a resulting power to deal with a crisis or an emergency according to the necessities of the case, the unarticulated assumption being that necessity knows no law.

Loose and irresponsible use of adjectives colors all non-legal and much legal discussion of presidential powers. "Inherent" powers, "implied" powers, "incidental" powers, "plenary" powers, "war" powers and "emergency" powers are used, often interchangeably and without fixed or ascertainable meanings. The vagueness and generality of the clauses that set forth presidential powers afford a plausible basis for pressures within and without an administration for presidential action beyond that supported by those whose responsibility it is to defend his actions in court. The claim of inherent and unrestricted presidential powers has long been a persuasive dialectical weapon in political controversy. While it is not surprising that counsel should grasp support from such unadjudicated claims of power, a judge cannot accept self-serving press statements of the attorney for one of the interested parties as authority in answering a constitutional question, even if the advocate was himself. But prudence has counseled that actual reliance on such nebulous claims stop short of provoking a judicial test. . . .

The appeal, however, that we declare the existence of inherent powers *ex necessitate* to meet an emergency asks us to do what many think would be wise, although it is something the forefathers omitted. They knew what emergencies were, knew the pressures they engender for authoritative action, knew, too, how they afford a ready pretext for usurpation. We may also suspect that they suspected that emergency powers would tend to kindle emergencies. Aside from suspension of the privilege of the writ of habeas corpus in time of rebellion or invasion, when the public safety may require it, they made no express provision for exercise of extraordinary authority because of a crisis. I do not think we rightfully may so amend their work, and, if we could, I am not convinced it would be wise to do so, although many modern nations have forthrightly recognized that war and economic crises may upset the normal balance between liberty and authority. Their experience with emergency powers may not be irrelevant to the argument here that we should say that the Executive, of his own volition, can invest himself with undefined emergency powers.

Germany, after the First World War, framed the Weimar Constitution, designed to secure her liberties in the Western tradition. However, the President of the Republic, without concurrence of the Reichstag, was empowered temporarily to suspend any or all individual rights if public safety and order were seriously disturbed or endangered. This proved a temptation to every government, whatever its shade of opinion, and in 13 years suspension of rights was invoked on more than 250 occasions. Finally, Hitler persuaded President Von Hindenberg to suspend all such rights, and they were never restored. . . .

Great Britain also has fought both World Wars under a sort of temporary dictatorship created by legislation. As Parliament is not bound by written constitutional limitations, it established a crisis government simply by delegation to its Ministers of a larger measure than usual of its own unlimited power, which is exercised under its supervision by Ministers whom it may dismiss. This has been called the "high-water mark in the voluntary surrender of liberty," but, as Churchill put it, "Parliament stands custodian of these surrendered liberties, and its most sacred duty will be to restore them in their fullness when victory has crowned our exertions and our perseverance." Thus, parliamentary control made emergency powers compatible with freedom.

This contemporary foreign experience may be inconclusive as to the wisdom of lodging emergency powers somewhere in a modern government. But it suggests that emergency powers are consistent with free government only when their control is lodged elsewhere than in the Executive who exercises them. That is the safeguard that would be nullified by our adoption of the "inherent powers" formula. Nothing in my experience convinces me that such risks are warranted by any real necessity, although such powers would, of course, be an executive convenience.

In the practical working of our Government we already have evolved a technique within the framework of the Constitution by which normal executive powers may be considerably expanded to meet an emergency. Congress may and has granted extraordinary authorities which lie dormant in normal times but may be called into play by the Executive in war or upon proclamation of a national emergency. In 1939, upon congressional request, the Attorney General listed ninety-nine such separate statutory grants by Congress of emergency or war-time executive powers. They were invoked from time to time as need appeared. Under this procedure we retain Government by law — special, temporary law, perhaps, but law nonetheless. The public may know the extent and limitations of the powers that can be asserted, and persons affected may be informed from the statute of their rights and duties.

In view of the ease, expedition and safety with which Congress can grant and has granted large emergency powers, certainly ample to embrace this crisis, I am quite unimpressed with the argument that we should affirm possession of them without statute. Such power either has no beginning or it has no end. If it exists, it need submit to no legal restraint. I am not alarmed that it would plunge us straightway into dictatorship, but it is at least a step in that wrong direction.

As to whether there is imperative necessity for such powers, it is relevant to note the gap that exists between the President's paper powers and his real powers. The Constitution does not disclose the measure of the actual controls wielded by the modern presidential office. That instrument must be understood as an Eighteenth-Century sketch of a government hoped for, not as a blueprint of the Government that is. Vast accretions of federal power, eroded from that reserved by the States, have magnified the scope of presidential activity. Subtle shifts take place in the centers of real power that do not show on the face of the Constitution.

Executive power has the advantage of concentration in a single head in whose choice the whole Nation has a part, making him the focus of public hopes and expectations. In drama, magnitude and finality his decisions so far overshadow any others that almost alone he fills the public eye and ear. No other personality in public life can begin to compete with him in access to the public mind through modern methods of communications. By his prestige as head of state and his influence upon public opinion, he exerts a leverage upon those who are supposed to check and balance his power which often cancels their effectiveness.

Moreover, rise of the party system has made a significant extraconstitutional supplement to real executive power. No appraisal of his necessities is realistic which overlooks that he heads a political system as well as a legal system. Party loyalties and interests, sometimes more binding than law, extend his effective control into branches of government other than his own and he often may win, as a political leader, what he cannot command under the Constitution. Indeed, Woodrow Wilson, commenting on the President as leader both of his party and of the Nation, observed, "If he rightly interpret the national thought and boldly insist upon it, he is irresistible. . . . His office is anything he has the sagacity and force to make it." I cannot be brought to believe that this country will suffer if the Court refuses further to aggrandize the presidential office, already so potent and so relatively immune from judicial review, at the expense of Congress. . . .

[Justice DOUGLAS concurred, characterizing the presidential action as an unauthorized taking of property, which was legislative in nature and therefore invalid. Justices BURTON and CLARK also concurred, stating that Congress had specified methods for dealing with this kind of crisis, with which the President had not complied. Justice CLARK went on to say that in the absence of such legislation, "the President's independent power to act depends upon the gravity of the situation confronting the nation."]

Chief Justice VINSON, with whom Justice REED and Justice MINTON join, dissenting.

. . . In passing upon the question of presidential powers in this case, we must first consider the context in which those powers were exercised. Those who suggest that this is a case involving extraordinary powers should be mindful that these are extraordinary times. A world not yet recovered from the devastation of World War II has been forced to face the threat of another and more terrifying global conflict. . . .

In 1950, when the United Nations called upon member nations "to render every assistance" to repel aggression in Korea, the United States furnished its vigorous support. For almost two full years, our armed forces have been fighting in Korea, suffering casualties of over 108,000 men. Hostilities have not abated. . . . Congressional support of the action in Korea has been manifested by provisions for increased military manpower and equipment and for economic stabilization, as hereinafter described. . . . Congress also directed the President to build up our own defenses. Congress, recognizing the "grim fact . . . that the United States is now engaged in a struggle for survival" and that "it is imperative that we now take those necessary steps to make our strength equal to the peril of the hour," granted authority to draft men into the armed forces. As a result, we now have over 3,500,000 men in our armed forces.

Appropriations for the Department of Defense, which had averaged less than $13 billion per year for the three years before attack in Korea, were increased by Congress to $48 billion for fiscal year 1951 and to $60 billion for fiscal year 1952. . . . The bulk of the increase is for military equipment and supplies—guns, tanks, ships, planes and ammunition—all of which require steel. . . . Congress recognized the impact of these defense programs upon the economy. Following the attack in Korea, the President asked for authority to requisition property and to allocate and fix priorities for scarce goods. In the Defense Production Act of 1950, Congress granted the powers requested and, in *addition*, granted power to stabilize prices and wages and to provide for settlement of labor disputes arising in the defense program. . . .

The President has the duty to execute the foregoing legislative programs. Their successful execution depends upon continued production of steel and stabilized prices for steel. Accordingly, when the collective bargaining agreements between the Nation's steel producers and their employees, represented by the United Steel Workers, were due to expire on December 31, 1951, and a strike shutting down the entire basic steel industry was threatened, the President acted to avert a complete shutdown of steel production. . . .

[On] April 9, 1952, the President addressed the following Message to Congress:

"*To the Congress of the United States*:

"The Congress is undoubtedly aware of the recent events which have taken place in connection with the management-labor dispute in the steel industry. These events culminated in the action which was taken last night to provide for temporary operation of the steel mills by the Government. I took this action with the utmost reluctance. The idea of Government operation of the steel mills is thoroughly distasteful to me and I want to see it ended as soon as possible. However, in the situation which confronted me yesterday, I felt that I could make no other choice. The other alternatives appeared to be even worse—so much worse that I could not accept them.

"One alternative would have been to permit a shut-down in the steel industry. The effects of such a shut-down would have been so immediate and damaging with respect to our efforts to support our Armed Forces and to protect our national security that it made this alternative unthinkable. The only way that I know of, other than Government operation, by which a steel shut-down could have been avoided was to grant the demands of the steel industry for a large price increase. I believed and the officials in charge of our stabilization agencies believed that this would have wrecked our stabilization program. I was unwilling to accept the incalculable damage which might be done to our country by following such a course.

"Accordingly, it was my judgment that Government operation of the steel mills for a temporary period was the least undesirable of the courses of action which lay open. In the circumstances, I believed it to be, and now believe it to be, my duty and within my powers as President to follow that course of action. It may be that the Congress will deem some other course to be wiser. . . . I do not believe the Congress will favor any of these courses of action, but that is a matter for the Congress to determine. . . . On the basis of the facts that are known to me at this time, I do not believe that immediate congressional action is essential; but I would, of course, be glad to cooperate in developing any legislative proposals which the Congress may wish to consider. . . ."

Twelve days passed without action by Congress. On April 21, 1952, the President sent a letter to the President of the Senate in which he again described the purpose and need for his action and again stated his position that "The Congress can, if it wishes, reject the course of action I have followed in this matter." Congress has not so acted to this date.

Meanwhile, plaintiffs instituted this action in the District Court to compel defendant to return possession of the steel mills seized under Executive Order 10340. . . . We . . . assume without deciding that the courts may go behind a President's finding of fact that an emergency exists. But there is not the slightest basis for suggesting that the President's finding in this case can be undermined. Plaintiffs moved for a preliminary injunction before answer or hearing. Defendant opposed the motion, filing uncontroverted affidavits of Government officials describing the facts underlying the President's order. . . . Accordingly, if the President has any power under the Constitution to meet a critical situation in the absence of express statutory authorization, there is no basis whatever for criticizing the exercise of such power in this case. . . .

[I]n this case, we need only look to history and time-honored principles of constitutional law—principles that have been applied consistently by all branches of the Government throughout our history. . . . A review of executive action demonstrates that our Presidents have on many occasions exhibited the leadership contemplated by the Framers when they made the President Commander-in-Chief, and imposed upon him the trust to "take Care that the Laws be faithfully executed." With or without explicit statutory authorization, Presidents have at such times dealt with national emergencies by acting promptly and resolutely to enforce legislative programs, at least to save those programs until Congress could act. Congress and the courts have responded to such executive initiative with consistent approval.

Our first President displayed at once the leadership contemplated by the Framers. When the national revenue laws were openly flouted in some sections of Pennsylvania, President Washington, without waiting for a call from the state government, summoned the militia and took decisive steps to secure the faithful execution of the laws. When international disputes engendered by the French revolution threatened to involve this country in war, and while congressional policy remained uncertain, Washington issued his Proclamation of Neutrality. Hamilton, whose defense of the Proclamation has endured the test of time, invoked the argument that the Executive has the duty to do that which will preserve peace until Congress acts and, in addition, pointed to the need for keeping the Nation informed of the requirements of existing laws and treaties as part of the faithful execution of the laws. . . .

Jefferson's initiative in the Louisiana Purchase, the Monroe Doctrine, and Jackson's removal of Government deposits from the Bank of the United States further serve to demonstrate by deed what the Framers described by word when they vested the whole of the executive power in the President.

Without declaration of war, President Lincoln took energetic action with the outbreak of the War Between the States. He summoned troops and paid them out of the Treasury without appropriation therefor. He proclaimed a naval blockade of the Confederacy and seized ships violating that blockade. Congress, far from denying the validity of these acts, gave them express approval. The most striking action of President Lincoln was the Emancipation Proclamation, issued in aid of the successful prosecution of the War Between the States, but wholly without statutory authority. In an action furnishing a most apt precedent for this case, President Lincoln without statutory authority directed the seizure of rail and telegraph lines leading to Washington. Many months later, Congress recognized and confirmed the power of the President to seize railroads and telegraph lines and provided criminal penalties for interference with Government operation. . . .

In *In re Neagle*, 135 U.S. 1 (1890), this Court held that a federal officer had acted in line of duty when he was guarding a Justice of this Court riding circuit. It was conceded that there was no specific statute authorizing the President to assign such a guard. President Hayes authorized the wide-spread use of federal troops during the Railroad Strike of 1877. President Cleveland also used the troops in the Pullman Strike of 1895 and his action is of special significance. No statute authorized this action. . . . But the President's concern was that federal laws relating to the free flow of interstate commerce and the mails be continuously and faithfully executed without interruption. To further this aim his agents sought and obtained the injunction upheld by this Court in *In re Debs*, 158 U.S. 564 (1895) . . . .

In 1909, President Taft was informed that government-owned oil lands were being patented by private parties at such a rate that public oil lands would be depleted in a matter of months. Although Congress had explicitly provided that these lands were open to purchase by United States citizens, the President nevertheless ordered the lands withdrawn from sale "[i]n aid of proposed legislation." In *United States v. Midwest Oil Co.*, 236 U.S. 459 (1915), the President's action was sustained as consistent with executive practice throughout our history. . . .

During World War I, President Wilson established a War Labor Board without awaiting specific direction by Congress. . . . [T]he Board had as its purpose the prevention of strikes and lockouts interfering with the production of goods to meet the emergency. Effectiveness of the War Labor Board decision was accomplished by Presidential action, including seizure of industrial plants. Seizure of the Nation's railroads was also ordered by President Wilson.

Beginning with the Bank Holiday Proclamation and continuing through World War II, executive leadership and initiative were characteristic of President Franklin D. Roosevelt's administration. . . . In May of 1941, the danger from the Axis belligerents having become clear, the President proclaimed "an unlimited national emergency" calling for mobilization of the Nation's defenses to repel aggression. The President took the initiative in strengthening our defenses by acquiring rights from the British Government to establish air bases in exchange for overage destroyers. . . .

More recently, President Truman acted to repel aggression by employing our armed forces in Korea. Upon the intervention of the Chinese Communists, the President proclaimed the existence of an unlimited national emergency requiring the speedy build-up of our defense establishment. Congress responded by providing for increased manpower and weapons for our armed forces, by increasing military aid . . . and enacting economic stabilization measures. . . .

Focusing now on the situation confronting the President on the night of April 8, 1952, we cannot but conclude that the President was performing his duty under the Constitution to "take Care that the Laws be faithfully executed" — a duty described by President Benjamin Harrison as "the central idea of the office." The President reported to Congress the morning after the seizure that he acted because a work stoppage in steel production would immediately imperil the safety of the Nation by preventing execution of the legislative programs for procurement of military equipment. And, while a shutdown could be averted by granting the price concessions requested by plaintiffs, granting such concessions would disrupt the price stabilization program also enacted by Congress. Rather than fail to execute either legislative program, the President acted to execute both.

Much of the argument in this case has been directed at straw men. We do not now have before us the case of a President acting solely on the basis of his own notions of the public welfare. Nor is there any question of unlimited executive power in this case. The President himself closed the door to any such claim when he sent his Message to Congress stating his purpose to abide by any action of Congress, whether approving or disapproving his seizure action. Here, the President immediately made sure that Congress was fully informed of the temporary action he had taken only to preserve the legislative programs from destruction until Congress could act.

The absence of a specific statute authorizing seizure of the steel mills as a mode of executing the laws — both the military procurement program and the anti-inflation program — has not until today been thought to prevent the President from executing the laws. Unlike an administrative commission confined to the enforcement of the statute under which it was created, or the head of a department when administering a particular statute, the President is a constitutional officer charged with taking care that a "mass of legislation be executed." Flexibility as to mode of execution to meet critical situations is a matter of practical necessity. This practical construction of the "Take Care" clause, advocated by John Marshall, was adopted by this Court in *In re Neagle, In re Debs* and other cases. . . .

There is no statute prohibiting seizure as a method of enforcing legislative programs. Congress has in no wise indicated that its legislation is not to be executed by the taking of private property (subject of course to the payment of just compensation) if its legislation cannot otherwise be executed. Indeed, the Universal Military Training and Service Act authorizes the seizure of any plant that fails to fill a Government contract or the properties of any steel producer that fails to allocate steel as directed for defense production. And the Defense Production Act authorizes the President to requisition equipment and condemn real property needed without delay in the defense effort. Where Congress authorizes seizure in instances not necessarily crucial to the defense program, it can hardly be said to have disclosed an intention to prohibit seizures where essential to the execution of that legislative program. . . .

The President's action served the same purposes as a judicial stay entered to maintain the status quo in order to preserve the jurisdiction of a court. . . . In *United States v. Midwest Oil Co.*, 236 U.S. 459, this Court approved executive action where, as here, the President acted to preserve an important matter until Congress could act—even though his action in that case was contrary to an express statute. In this case, there is no statute prohibiting the action taken by the President in a matter not merely important but threatening the very safety of the Nation. Executive inaction in such a situation, courting national disaster, is foreign to the concept of energy and initiative in the Executive as created by the Founding Fathers. The Constitution was itself "adopted in a period of grave emergency. . . . While emergency does not create power, emergency may furnish the occasion for the exercise of power." The Framers knew, as we should know in these times of peril, that there is real danger in Executive weakness. There is no cause to fear Executive tyranny so long as the laws of Congress are being faithfully executed. Certainly there is no basis for fear of dictatorship when the Executive acts, as he did in this case, only to save the situation until Congress could act.

Plaintiffs place their primary emphasis on the . . . Taft-Hartley Act, but do not contend that that Act contains any provision prohibiting seizure. . . . Taft-Hartley preserves the right to strike in any emergency, however serious, subject only to an 80-day delay in cases of strikes imperiling the national health and safety. . . . Plaintiffs admit that the emergency procedures of Taft-Hartley are not mandatory. Nevertheless, plaintiffs apparently argue that, since Congress did provide the 80-day injunction method for dealing with emergency strikes, the President cannot claim that an emergency exists until the procedures of Taft-Hartley have been exhausted. This argument . . . loses all force when viewed in light of the statutory pattern confronting the President in this case.

In Title V of the Defense Production Act of 1950, Congress . . . authorized the President to initiate labor-management conferences and to take action appropriate to carrying out the recommendations of such conferences and the provisions of Title V. Due regard is to be given to collective bargaining practice and stabilization policies and no action taken is to be inconsistent with Taft-Hartley and other laws. . . . The President authorized the Wage Stabilization Board (WSB), which administers the wage stabilization functions of Title IV of the Defense Production Act, also to deal with labor disputes affecting the defense program. . . .

When the President acted on April 8, he had exhausted the procedures for settlement available to him. Taft-Hartley was a route parallel to, not connected with, the WSB procedure. The strike had been delayed 99 days as contrasted with the maximum delay of 80 days under Taft-Hartley. There had been a hearing on the issues in dispute and bargaining which promised settlement up to the very hour before seizure had broken down. Faced with immediate national peril through stoppage in steel production on the one hand and faced with destruction of the wage and price legislative programs on the other, the President took temporary possession of the steel mills as the only course open to him consistent with his duty to take care that the laws be faithfully executed . . . .

———

1. *An Unlimited Executive?* Like many of the separation of powers cases in this book, *Youngstown* was litigated under great time pressure, and in the glare of intense national publicity. For histories of the case, see MAEVA MARCUS, TRUMAN AND THE STEEL SEIZURE CASE (1977); ALAN F. WESTIN, THE ANATOMY OF A CONSTITUTIONAL LAW CASE (1958); Patricia L. Bellia, *The Story of the* Steel Seizure *Case*, in PRESIDENTIAL POWER STORIES 233 (CHRISTOPHER H. SCHROEDER & CURTIS A. BRADLEY EDS., 2008). Such trying circumstances can adversely affect the quality of the advocacy for both sides. A famous colloquy that haunted the government throughout occurred between Assistant Attorney General Baldridge and Judge Pine in the District Court (WESTIN, *supra*, at 64):

> *Mr. Baldridge*: Section 1, Article II, of the Constitution reposes all of the executive power in the Chief Executive. I think that the distinction that the Constitution itself makes between the powers of the Executive and the powers of the legislative branch of the Government are significant and important. In so far as the Executive is concerned, all executive power is vested in the President. In so far as legislative powers are concerned, the Congress has only those powers that are specifically delegated to it, plus the implied power to carry out the powers specifically enumerated.
>
> *The Court*: So, when the sovereign people adopted the Constitution, it . . . limited the powers of the Congress and limited the powers of the judiciary, but it did not limit the powers of the Executive. Is that what you say?
>
> *Mr. Baldridge*: That is the way we read Article II of the Constitution.
>
> *The Court*: I see. . . .

Baldridge's argument produced an immediate storm of criticism. (Indeed, public and press reaction to the seizure was negative throughout.) President Truman himself issued a disclaimer (WESTIN, *supra*, at 67): "The powers of the President are derived from the Constitution, and they are limited, of course, by the provisions of the Constitution, particularly those that protect the rights of individuals." The government issued another disclaimer in the form of a "Supplemental Memorandum" that it filed in District Court, but the damage was done. The steel companies never tired of repeating Baldridge's assertion in their briefs.

Baldridge's assertion of nearly unlimited executive powers in *Youngstown* was far from an isolated example of this kind of argument. In MADISON'S NIGHTMARE, *supra* at 27–29, Peter M. Shane introduces a distinction between presidentialism and pluralism to which we will recur repeatedly in these pages:

> On one side of the debate are *presidentialists,* advocates of what former Vice President Al Gore has perhaps most famously criticized as "the unilateral executive." They interpret the constitutional design as creating a largely autonomous executive branch, in which the President enjoys a robust range of inherent authorities, both foreign and domestic, which are beyond the power of Congress to regulate or the authority of the courts to review. If they are right, then we are legally required to have a unilateral presidency, unless the Constitution is to be amended.

> On the other side are those who might most accurately be called the constitutional *pluralists*. Pluralists interpret the checks and balances system to emphasize the roles that the Constitution assigns to the multiple institutions of our national government in holding each other to account. In the pluralist view, the scope of permissible presidential initiative depends very much on the actions of Congress and the courts.

> There is, however, a potential disconnect between the debates over constitutional theory and the realities of actual government practice. Assume that the Presidentialists are right, and the President is legally entitled to exercise unilateral authority over a wide range of domestic and national affairs. In theory, such a President would be entitled to decide unilaterally to create a form of governance that was actually highly consultative with Congress and open to significant debate within the executive. If the President has unilateral power, he could unilaterally decide he wants to behave in a politically pluralist fashion.

> The converse is also true. Even if the Constitution permits Congress and the courts to check the presidency, they are not legally compelled to do so. In exercising their own discretion, judges and legislators may choose to be so deferential or so acquiescent towards the President that the pluralist presidency in operation could look a lot like the unilateral presidency that the Presidentialists prefer. There is thus an important distinction to be drawn between a description of the presidency in terms of the powers that formally attach to the office — what might be called "the legal presidency" — and a description of the presidency in terms of how particular presidents

decide to deploy those formal powers—which we can call "the behavioral presidency."

It is just on this point, however, that the contest between presidentialism and pluralism is assymetrical. In general, presidents want more, not less unilateral power. Presidential performance is typically measured by accomplishment, and the pace and volume of accomplishment for which presidents can take full credit can be diminished to the extent presidents have to take the time to accommodate Congress and the courts in bringing their initiatives to fruition. Presidents' lives are easier, politically speaking, the more authority they can wield without accountability to the other two branches. Thus, if the Presidentialists are right about the nature of the *legal presidency*, they will almost certainly get their way in terms of the operation of the *behavioral presidency*. A President who is legally entitled to exercise power unilaterally will almost surely want to use that power to consolidate, not to diffuse presidential authority—and we will have a unilateral presidency in both theory and operation. Under a presidentialist regime, it is not clear how or why public pressure to conduct executive branch affairs in a more pluralist mode would have any effect.

On the other hand, even if the pluralists are right about the law, Americans still run a never-ending risk of an excessively unilateral executive. That is because both Congress and the courts have significant incentives to defer to presidents, even when they technically have authority to hold presidents in check. Congressional members from the President's party may be deferential to preserve what they perceive to be the overall strength of their party. Congress may prefer to keep public attention focused on the President with regard to hard policy decisions, so that members of either party do not pay a price at election time for unpopular outcomes. This is a common explanation, for example, why Congress tends to be so quiescent in presidential military adventures.

For their part, courts become involved in disputes over executive authority only episodically, and are anxious about decision making in areas where they might lack expertise or could be perceived as intruding in policy making, as opposed to legal interpretation. Judges, moreover, are well aware of the limits that exist to their remedial powers should they decide an Administration is violating the law. In extreme cases, they may defer to the President out of concern that judicial aggressiveness will simply be met by defiance.

2. *Emergency Powers.* What *were* the best arguments available to the government in *Youngstown*? For the arguments actually made in the Supreme Court, review Chief Justice Vinson's dissent, which tracks parts of the government's briefs closely. (Apparently, Vinson played another, less savory role in the litigation. ROBERT J. DONOVAN, TUMULTUOUS YEARS, THE PRESIDENCY OF HARRY S. TRUMAN 1949–53, 386–87 (1982), reports that Vinson, a close friend of Truman's, advised the President that it would be constitutional to seize the mills.) The government stressed the emergency nature

of the seizure, and placed it against the background of other emergency actions by past Presidents. Here the lawyers reflected the personal views of the President:

> From his reading of history, Truman was convinced his action fell within his powers as President and Commander in Chief. In a state of national emergency, Lincoln had suspended the right to *habeas corpus*, he would point out. Tom Clark, now on the Supreme Court, had once, as Attorney General, advised him that a President, faced with a calamitous strike, had the "inherent" power to prevent a paralysis of the national economy.

DAVID MCCULLOUGH, TRUMAN 896–97 (1992). In his concurrence, Justice Clark suggested that courts can and should assess degrees of emergency. Do you agree? How should the government have argued the respective institutional competence of the branches on this point? Justice Clark was explicitly willing to entertain the possibility of presidential emergency powers in situations where no statute forbids a particular action. Justice Jackson's concurrence at least implicitly agrees, doesn't it? Hence Justice Black's confident assertions about the need for positive statutory authority for presidential lawmaking did not command a majority of the Court.

3. *Judicial Precedent.* The government also stressed the series of cases we have just reviewed, *Neagle, Debs,* and *Midwest Oil.* As a litigant or a judge in *Youngstown,* how much weight would you have assigned these precedents? Where does *Youngstown* leave them? Do you agree with Chief Justice Vinson's characterization of *Midwest Oil* as involving an action "contrary to an express statute"?

4. *Limitation by Implication.* Justices Frankfurter and Jackson attached great significance to congressional rejection in 1947 of a proposal to confer seizure authority on the executive, which would have permitted actions such as President Truman's. Is this a legitimate approach? Should Congress, in rejecting a proposal, be deemed to legislate that the authority proposed is forbidden? Or, alternatively, is the fact that Congress knew of a proposal and rejected it simply part of a relevant "adjudicative context"? Should it be persuasive for the government to argue that Congress did not foresee the particular emergency that arose in 1952, so that its rejection of advance seizure authority should not be construed as a blanket denial?

5. *The Relevance of Alternatives.* President Truman could have invoked the Taft-Hartley Act to stop the strike for eighty days, but declined to do so. He argued that there would be a temporary shutdown for a week or two while the Act's mechanism was engaged, and that the strike could resume after the "cooling-off period" if no settlement had been reached. Donovan, *supra,* at 385. What weight should the courts give to the availability of a statutory alternative to a presidential action, and to the President's reasons for eschewing it? Similarly, what weight should the courts have given to Truman's messages to Congress, inviting ratification of his action, and to congressional silence in response? If Congress has provided a statutory avenue for presidential action, must it also affirmatively negate other courses he might prefer, either in advance or in the event?

Can a court go behind a President's stated justifications to his "real" reasons for refusing to invoke statutory authority? In *Youngstown*, the underlying stakes were whether the union would receive a wage increase, and whether the steel companies would receive a compensating price increase. President Truman was a friend of labor and an enemy of the Taft-Hartley Act. He thought the unions deserved a wage increase (which they could be granted if the government could operate the mills), and that the companies should absorb the cost with little or no price increase. Is that a good reason to forego available statutory remedies?

6. *Zones of Power.* Justice Jackson's three categories of congressional-executive interaction are famous, because despite their simplicity they are useful initial guides to analysis. Consider the following summary of Jackson's approach: there exist zones of exclusive executive power and of exclusive legislative power, which each branch may exercise without interference by the other, and:

> a twilight zone of concurrent power, [in which] either the President or Congress can act in the absence of initiative by the other. If both attempt to act in ways that bring their wills into conflict, the deadlock must be resolved in favor of congressional action through valid legislation, which includes legislation passed over a presidential veto.

Pollack, et al., *Indochina: The Constitutional Crisis*, Pt. II, 116 CONG. REC. 16,478 (1978). Is this accurate? In preparing legal advice to the President on a question of first impression, how do you think you would be influenced by this analysis?

7. *Injunction or Damages?* Should the Court have avoided the ultimate constitutional issues by accepting the government's claim that "just compensation" under the Fifth Amendment would be available as a fully adequate remedy?

8. *Justice Jackson v. General Jackson.* President Roosevelt's Attorney General throughout 1940 and during most of 1941 was Robert H. Jackson. In that role, he had supported controversial exercises of presidential power in the transfer of over-age destroyers to Great Britain in exchange for air bases, *see* 39 OP. A.G. 484, and the seizure of the North American Aviation Plant. *Id.* at 343 U.S. 649 & n.17, he distinguished that seizure from the one at bar, and remarked: "I do not regard it as a precedent for this, but, even if I did, I should not bind present judicial judgment by earlier partisan advocacy." Should a court disregard Attorney General opinions as merely an advocate's statements on behalf of a client? Do you think Attorneys General view their role that way?

9. *Applying* Youngstown. As a Department of Justice lawyer, what advice would you render in the following circumstances: during a recess of Congress, natural disaster hits the State of Washington: a week's continuous rain makes air travel extremely hazardous; flooding makes main roads impassable. To save hundreds of lives in the flooded areas, the government must transport food and medical supplies. Only rail transportation can accomplish the task, and the relevant railroad is on strike. The President asks the Attorney General if he has authority to seize the railroad for 12 hours. No statute expressly permits or forbids a seizure; a previous

administration had proposed the enactment of such authority and the proposal died in committee.

Would your advice differ if no proposal had been submitted? Would your advice differ if Congress had voted on the proposal and defeated it? Would it make a difference if the Secretary of Labor is arguing against a seizure on grounds that it will effectively end the strike and that weather reports indicate that air drops may be feasible sometime soon?

10. *Later Executive Orders Under the* Youngstown *Framework.* As we have seen in *Youngstown*, presidents use executive orders to implement many of their most important initiatives, basing them on any combination of constitutional and statutory authority that is thought to be available. Thus, these orders often dwell in Justice Jackson's zone of twilight, where authority is neither clearly present nor absent. Although interstitial, the programs involved may prove surprisingly durable. For a history of two prominent examples, orders promoting civil rights in government-related activities and orders seeking economic stabilization, see Joel Fleishman & Arthur Aufses, *Law and Orders: The Problem of Presidential Legislation*, 40 Law & Contemp. Probs. 1 (1976). Lower federal courts have often been friendly to presidential executive orders. A prominent example is *AFL-CIO v. Kahn*, 618 F. 2d 784 (D.C. Cir.) (en banc), *cert. denied*, 443 U.S. 915 (1979), which upheld an executive order denying Government contracts above $5 million to companies that refused to comply with "voluntary" wage and price standards. Later cases apparently extending a presumption of regularity to executive orders include American *Federation of Government Employees v. Reagan*, 870 F.2d 723 (D.C. Cir. 1989) (holding that the Federal Service Labor-Management Relations Act did not require the President to incorporate written findings into an executive order implementing his statutory authority to exempt certain agencies from coverage). *But see Chamber of Commerce v. Reich*, 57 F. 3d 1099 (D.C. Cir. 1995)(invalidating an executive order forbidding federal contractors from permanently replacing lawfully striking employees where the president had based the order on the same statutory authority upheld in *AFL-CIO v. Kahn*); *Reyes v. U.S. Department of Immigration and Naturalization*, 910 F.2d 611 (9th Cir. 1990) (invalidating executive order imposing restriction on geographical areas within which Philippine national who had served in U.S. military could serve and be eligible for naturalization pursuant to Immigration and Naturalization Act, which authorized no such restrictions).

11. *The Effects of 9/11.* Should the lessons of the terrorist attacks in 2001 include a need to reconsider *Youngstown*? *See* Youngstown *at Fifty, A Symposium*, 19 Const. Comm. 1 (2002); Christopher Bryant & Carl Tobias, Youngstown *Revisited*, 29 Hastings Const. L.Q. 263 (2002). We consider the war on terror after 9/11 extensively in later chapters.

Note on Private Enforcement of Executive Orders

In *In re Surface Mining Regulation Litigation*, 627 F.2d 1346 (D.C. Cir. 1980), the Court of Appeals reviewed a series of challenges to interim regulations issued by the

Secretary of the Interior under the Surface Mining Control and Reclamation Act of 1977, 30 U.S.C. § 1201 *et seq.* A number of coal mining companies and trade associations challenged the regulations because, among other things, the Secretary of the Interior assertedly failed to prepare a formal economic and inflationary impact analysis as required by Exec. Order No. 11,281. The court's response to this challenge provides a concise statement of the general rule concerning the private enforcement of obligations imposed on executive branch officials by executive orders (627 F.2d at 1357):

> Executive Order No. 11821 "require[s] that all major legislative proposals, regulations, and rules emanating from the executive branch of the Government include a statement certifying that the inflationary impact of such actions on the Nation has been carefully considered." OMB Circular No. A-107, which was issued to implement [it], directs agency heads to consider the effects of proposed regulations on inflation, employment, and energy supply and demand, and establishes criteria for identifying regulations that may have such an impact. In *Independent Meat Packers Ass'n v. Butz*, 526 F.2d 228, 236 (8th Cir. 1975), *cert. denied*, 424 U.S. 966 (1976), the . . . Eighth Circuit held that "Executive Order No. 11821 was intended primarily as a managerial tool for implementing the President's personal economic policies and not as a legal framework enforceable by private civil action" and, "therefore, that the district court erroneously set aside the revised [Department of Agriculture] regulations . . . because of alleged deficiencies in the impact statement." This court has also declared that executive orders without specific foundation in congressional action are not judicially enforceable in private civil suits. *See Manhattan-Bronx Postal Union v. Gronouski*, 350 F.2d 451, 456–57 (1965), *cert. denied*, 382 U.S. 978 (1966) (Executive Order No. 10988). Thus, Executive Order No. 11821 and OMB Circular No. A-107 provide no basis for overturning the interim regulations.

See also Louisiana ex rel. Guste v. Verity, 681 F. Supp. 1178, 1181–82 (E.D. La. 1988), *aff'd*, 853 F.2d 322 (5th Cir. 1988) (holding Exec. Order No. 12,291 not judicially enforceable).

What accounts for this judicial unwillingness to allow private parties to enforce presidential directives? Frequently, executive orders contain disclaimers of any intent to create private rights of action. Is that the answer, or is the President simply without power to confer jurisdiction on federal courts by any action of his own? Could one argue persuasively that executive orders that have direct private beneficiaries, such as those protecting civil rights, should be privately enforceable, but that orders lacking such beneficiaries, such as those requiring cost-benefit analysis, should not? For an argument that courts should explore the intent of any statutes that authorize executive orders to see whether private enforcement should be allowed, see John E. Noyes, *Executive Orders, Presidential Intent, and Private Rights of Action*, 59 Tex. L. Rev. 837 (1981).

3. Congress and the Judiciary: Statutory Control of Federal Jurisdiction

From the beginning, Congress has exercised substantial power over the federal courts. The Constitution grants Congress the power "To constitute Tribunals inferior to the Supreme Court," and confers appellate jurisdiction on the Supreme Court "with such exceptions, and under such Regulations as the Congress shall make." The Judiciary Act of 1789 did not give all of the potential judicial power to the federal courts (for example, there was no general grant of federal question jurisdiction until 1875). And Congress soon began rearranging the inferior courts.

Everyone knows that congressional power over federal court jurisdiction is broad; the problem is one of limits, which have never been clearly identified. Courses in Federal Jurisdiction plumb the depths of these mysteries (without reaching the bottom). Here we examine the major cases concerning congressional restriction of jurisdiction to help set the separation of powers framework; in a later section we outline congressional distribution of the judicial power to institutions other than the federal courts (principally the executive).

Congress can affect judicial behavior by formally altering federal court structure and jurisdiction, as we shall see. Less obviously, congressional *inaction* can also send signals to the courts. The courts, like the executive, are in constant need of legislative aid — substantive, procedural, and monetary. They may desire new jurisdiction or hope to lose existing responsibilities. In modern times of caseload crisis, they constantly need added judgeships and increased support personnel and facilities. And although the Constitution forbids the diminution of judicial salaries, Congress is under no obligation to *raise* salaries, even in times of inflation when a constant salary loses purchasing power. *United States v. Will*, 449 U.S. 200 (1980). So Congress can send signals to the courts just by denying their legislative needs. *See* Neal Devins, *Congress as Culprit: How Lawmakers Spurred on the Court's Anti-Congress Crusade*, 51 DUKE L.J. 435, 454–58 (2001); Todd D. Peterson, *Controlling the Federal Courts Through the Appropriations Process*, 1998 WISC. L. REV. 993.

Congressional power over federal jurisdiction may help legitimate the power of judicial review, because the courts are not wholly free of democratic control. The interplay between the reciprocal powers of judicial review and congressional control at the time of *Marbury* provides some grist for appraising this possibility. *See* JAMES F. SIMON, WHAT KIND OF NATION: THOMAS JEFFERSON, JOHN MARSHALL, AND THE EPIC STRUGGLE TO CREATE A UNITED STATES (2002); DONALD O. DEWEY, MARSHALL V. JEFFERSON: THE POLITICAL BACKGROUND OF *MARBURY V. MADISON*, chs. 4–5 (1970).

In 1801, in the last weeks of John Adams' presidency, the lame-duck Federalist Congress passed a statute to reform the judiciary. The new act relieved Supreme Court Justices of their circuit-riding duties and created new circuit judges to fill the gap. It also reduced the number of Justices from six to five at the next vacancy. Both of these provisions were justifiable. Circuit-riding on early nineteenth-century roads was the bane of the Justices' existence, and there is obvious merit to having an odd number of Justices to avoid tie votes. Yet the act sparked partisan outrage from the incoming Republicans, because Adams would be able to make many new Federalist "midnight judges" (and justices of the peace like Marbury as well), and because President Jefferson would lose his first opportunity to nominate a Justice.

In 1802, the newly Republican Congress repealed the act of 1801, and also altered the timing of Supreme Court terms in a way that kept the Court from sitting between December 1801, and February 1803. This had the effect (and probably the intention) of delaying both the pending *Marbury* litigation and any judicial response to the repealer. For there was substantial opinion that the repealer was unconstitutional, and would be invalidated by the courts. DEWEY, *supra*, at 70–74. The possible defects in the legislation were that it deprived the new circuit judges of their jobs, and that it made Justices part-time inferior court judges by restoring circuit-riding. A test case was ready: *Stuart v. Laird*, 5 U.S. (1 Cranch) 299 (1803), in which objection was made to transferring a litigation to the old-style circuit court, where a Justice sat. For the plaintiffs, Charles Lee (who also argued for Marbury) made both constitutional arguments, and explicitly called for invalidating the legislation. Opposing counsel argued only that the Court *should not* exercise judicial review, not that it *could not*. DEWEY, *supra*, at 182. Even in Congress, Republicans seemed to assume that the Court could void the legislation — if it dared!

Marbury was small potatoes next to *Stuart*. The latter raised broad issues about the shape of the federal judiciary, and the challenged legislation was obviously a major part of a partisan war over the courts. *See* DAVID P. CURRIE, THE CONSTITUTION IN THE SUPREME COURT: THE FIRST HUNDRED YEARS, 1789–1888, at 74–77 (1985). If the doctrine of judicial review had been announced — and enforced — in *Stuart*, the Court would have seemed to be taking a partisan role itself, contrary to the neutral stance Marshall wanted for it. Moreover, the Court would have invited serious retaliation by outraged Republicans in Congress. Instead, six days after *Marbury*, the Court upheld the legislation. Justice Paterson's opinion said that rearranging the circuits was constitutional because "Congress have constitutional authority to establish from time to time such inferior tribunals as they may think proper." Justices could sit in lower courts because "practice and acquiescence under [the Constitution] for a period of several years, commencing with the organization of the judicial system, affords an irresistible answer, and has indeed fixed the construction." Acquiescence, no less, after a period of twelve years!

Set in this larger context, *Marbury* is an even greater strategic victory for the Marshall Court than is commonly supposed. So from the very beginning of our Republic, Congress and the courts have possessed weapons to fight each other. What constitutional conclusions should we draw from the imbroglio of 1801–1803, concerning Congress's power over the courts?

The next major confrontation on the field of jurisdictional restriction occurred during a time of even more heated politics — Reconstruction. Since the Constitution contemplates neither secession nor reconstruction, much of Congress's postwar legislation was open to constitutional challenge. Moreover, military arrests and prosecutions, begun during the war, continued afterwards, in apparent violation of several provisions of the Bill of Rights. (*See* Mark E. Neely, Jr., The Fate of Liberty: Abraham Lincoln and Civil Liberties 177–79 (1991). On the constitutional merits of the prosecutions, see *Ex Parte Milligan*, excerpted in Chapter Six.) As you will recall from our summary of *Mississippi v. Johnson*, earlier in this chapter, the Court never did pass on the constitutionality of the main Reconstruction legislation. When a case involving a military arrest posed an apparent threat that it might do so, however, Congress intervened with a jurisdictional restriction.

A newspaper editor, McCardle, was arrested and held in custody by the Army for trial before a military commission, on charges that he had published incendiary and libelous articles. He sought *habeas corpus* under a federal statute passed on February 5th, 1867, which provided that the federal courts, in addition to their existing jurisdiction, would have power to grant writs of *habeas corpus* in all cases where any person was restrained of his or her liberty in violation of the Constitution, or of any treaty or law of the United States. The act also provided for appeals from the Circuit Courts to the Supreme Court.

McCardle, having lost below, appealed to the Supreme Court, where argument was held on the merits early in March 1868. By the end of the month, and before any decision from the Court, Congress had passed, over the President's veto, a statute providing:

> That so much of the act approved February 5, 1867 . . . as authorized an appeal from the judgment of the Circuit Court to the Supreme Court of the United States, or the exercise of any such jurisdiction by said Supreme Court, on appeals which have been, or may hereafter be taken, be, and the same is hereby repealed. (Act of March 27, 1868, 15 Stat. 44.)

The Court's attention was directed to the statute, and after the Chief Justice returned from presiding at President Johnson's impeachment trial, argument was heard on the effect of the repeal. Counsel for McCardle argued that the Constitution vested the judicial power in the courts directly, and that Congress lacked power to abridge it, else congressional inaction could vitiate the power of a co-ordinate branch. Suppose, he asked, Congress simply repealed the Judiciary Act of 1789 — would all federal jurisdiction fall with it? He then argued that Congress was exercising judicial power in this case, for if:

> Congress had specifically enacted "that the Supreme Court of the United States shall never publicly give judgment in the case of McCardle, already argued, and on which we anticipate that it will soon deliver judgment, contrary to the views of the majority in Congress, of what it ought to decide," its purpose to interfere specifically with and prevent the judgment in this very case would not have been more real or, as a fact, more universally known.

Thus the challenge to the Court's power was fundamental. Was its response adequate?

Ex Parte McCardle

74 U.S. (7 Wall.) 506 (1868)

Chief Justice CHASE delivered the opinion of the court.

The first question necessarily is that of jurisdiction; for, if the act of March 1868, takes away the jurisdiction defined by the act of February 1867, it is useless, if not improper, to enter into any discussion of other questions. It is quite true, as was argued by the counsel for the petitioner, that the appellate jurisdiction of this court is not derived from acts of Congress. It is, strictly speaking, conferred by the Constitution. But it is conferred "with such exceptions and under such regulations as Congress shall make."

It is unnecessary to consider whether, if Congress had made no exceptions and no regulations, this court might not have exercised general appellate jurisdiction under rules prescribed by itself. For among the earliest acts of the first Congress, at its first session, was the act of September 24th, 1789, to establish the judicial courts of the United States. That act provided for the organization of this court, and prescribed regulations for the exercise of its jurisdiction.

The source of that jurisdiction, and the limitations of it by the Constitution and by statute, have been on several occasions subjects of consideration here. In the case of *Durousseau v. The United States*, [10 U.S. (6 Cranch) 307, 312 (1810)] particularly, the whole matter was carefully examined, and the court held, that while "the appellate powers of this court are not given by the judicial act, but are given by the Constitution," they are, nevertheless, "limited and regulated by that act, and by such other acts as have been passed on the subject." The court said, further, that the judicial act was an exercise of the power given by the Constitution to Congress "of making exceptions to the appellate jurisdiction of the Supreme Court." "They have described affirmatively," said the court, "its jurisdiction, and this affirmative description has been understood to imply a negation of the exercise of such appellate power as is not comprehended within it."

The principle that the affirmation of appellate jurisdiction implies the negation of all such jurisdiction not affirmed having been thus established, it was an almost necessary consequence that acts of Congress, providing for the exercise of jurisdiction, should come to be spoken of as acts granting jurisdiction, and not as acts making exceptions to the constitutional grant of it. The exception to appellate jurisdiction in the case before us, however, is not an inference from the affirmation of other appellate jurisdiction. It is made in terms. The provision of the act of 1867, affirming the appellate jurisdiction of this court in cases of habeas corpus is expressly repealed. It is hardly possible to imagine a plainer instance of positive exception.

We are not at liberty to inquire into the motives of the legislature. We can only examine into its power under the Constitution; and the power to make exceptions to the appellate jurisdiction of this court is given by express words.

What, then, is the effect of the repealing act upon the case before us? We cannot doubt as to this. Without jurisdiction the court cannot proceed at all in any cause. Jurisdiction is power to declare the law, and when it ceases to exist, the only function remaining to the court is that of announcing the fact and dismissing the cause. And this is not less clear upon authority than upon principle. . . .

It is quite clear, therefore, that this Court cannot proceed to pronounce judgment in this case, for it has no longer jurisdiction of the appeal; and judicial duty is not less fitly performed by declining ungranted jurisdiction than in exercising firmly that which the Constitution and the laws confer. Counsel seem to have supposed, if effect be given to the repealing act in question, that the whole appellate power of the court, in cases of habeas corpus, is denied. But this is an error. The act of 1868 does not except from that jurisdiction any cases but appeals from Circuit Courts under the act of 1867. It does not affect the jurisdiction which was previously exercised.

The appeal of the petitioner in this case must be dismissed for want of jurisdiction.

————————

1. *Congressional Motivation.* One might suppose that Chief Justice Chase, fresh from presiding at the near removal of a President by the radical Congress, was in no mood for a confrontation of his own. For histories of the case, see CHARLES FAIRMAN, RECONSTRUCTION AND REUNION 1864–88, 4 HISTORY OF THE SUPREME COURT OF THE UNITED STATES 433–514 (1971); William W. Van Alstyne, *A Critical Guide to* Ex Parte McCardle, 15 ARIZ. L. REV. 229 (1973). Although the Court often says, as in *McCardle*, that it does not probe the motives of a legislature, in fact it does so occasionally and quite unpredictably. *See* John H. Ely, *Legislative and Administrative Motivation in Constitutional Law,* 79 YALE L.J. 1205 (1970). Consider whether it does so in the very next case in this book. *McCardle* shows the potential for jurisdictional legislation to be a pretext to obtain a result that Congress fears it cannot obtain directly. Should this kind of legislation then receive *more* rather than less judicial scrutiny, compared to others? Which way does it cut that the Court would be protecting itself?

2. *The Nature of Federal Jurisdiction.* As *McCardle* makes clear, fundamental doctrine holds that the Constitution confers judicial power directly, but statutes regulating jurisdiction are treated as if that were not the case. Does it make sense for one of the branches to concede what appears to be its main source of ultimate power to protect itself against the others?

3. *The Scope of* McCardle. Note the Court's remark, near the end of its brief opinion, that the challenged act was only a partial removal of appellate jurisdiction. Could you write a narrower opinion for the Court that would not confront Congress? In *Ex parte Yerger,* 75 U.S. (8 Wall.) 75 (1869), the Court considered another petition for *habeas corpus* from a prisoner being held for trial by military court. The Court

found that earlier statutes, including one enacted in 1789, gave sufficient authority to free an unlawfully held prisoner.

The apparent sweep of *McCardle* was soon qualified by the case that follows — but how much?

———————

United States v. Klein

80 U.S. (13 Wall.) 128 (1872)

Chief Justice CHASE delivered the opinion of the court.

The general question in this case is whether or not the proviso relating to suits for the proceeds of abandoned and captured property in the Court of Claims, contained in the appropriation act of July 12th, 1870, [16 Stat. 235] debars the defendant in error from recovering . . . the proceeds of certain cotton . . . which came into the possession of the agents of the Treasury Department as captured or abandoned property, and the proceeds of which were paid . . . into the Treasury. . . .

The [Abandoned and Captured Property Act of March 12th, 1863, 12 Stat. 820] directs the officers of the Treasury Department to take into their possession and make sale of all property abandoned by its owners or captured by the national forces, and to pay the proceeds into the national treasury. [The Act provides] that any person claiming to have been the owner of such property might prefer his claim to the proceeds thereof, and, on proof that he had never given aid or comfort to the rebellion, receive the amount after deducting expenses. . . .

If you ¢ help the Confederates, you can have it back

[O]n the 17th of July, 1862, Congress had already passed an act . . . which authorized the President, "at any time hereafter, by proclamation, to extend to persons who may have participated in the existing rebellion, in any State or part thereof, pardon and amnesty, with such exceptions and at such time and on such conditions as he may deem expedient for the public welfare." . . . [O]n the 8th of December, 1863, the President issued a proclamation, in which he referred to that act, and offered a full pardon, with restoration of all rights of property, except as to slaves . . . to [former rebels who] would take and keep inviolate a prescribed oath. By this oath the person . . . was required to promise that he would thenceforth support the Constitution of the United States and the union of the States . . . . [In the following years, Presidents Lincoln and Johnson issued a series of pardon proclamations that were similar to the initial one. Finally, a full pardon was granted] on the 25th of December 1868, without exception, unconditionally and without reservation, to all who had participated in the rebellion, with restoration of rights of property as before. No oath was required. . . .

Then full Pardon

[Meanwhile the Court had decided in *Ex parte Garland*, 71 U.S. 333 (1867)] that the President's power of pardon "is not subject to legislation;" that "Congress can neither limit the effect of his pardon, nor exclude from its exercise any class of offenders." . . . It was competent for the President to annex to his offer of pardon any conditions or qualifications he should see fit. . . . [Upon compliance, t]he restoration of the proceeds became the absolute right of the persons pardoned, on application within two years from the close of the war. . . .

[T]he owner of the cotton in this case . . . had done certain acts which this court has adjudged to be acts in aid of the rebellion; but he abandoned the cotton to the agent of the Treasury Department, . . . and he took, and has not violated, the amnesty oath under the President's proclamation. Upon this case the Court of Claims pronounced him entitled to a judgment for the net proceeds in the Treasury. This decree was rendered on the 26th of May, 1869; the appeal to this court . . . was filed here on the 11th of December, 1869. The judgment of the court in the case of [*United States v. Padelford*, 9 Wall. 531] which, in its essential features, was the same with this case, was rendered on the 30th of April, 1870. It affirmed the judgment of the Court of Claims in his favor.

Soon afterwards the provision in question was introduced as a proviso to the clause in the general appropriation bill, appropriating a sum of money for the payment of judgments of the Court of Claims, and became a part of the act, with perhaps little consideration in either House of Congress.

This proviso declares in substance that no pardon . . . [or] oath . . . shall be admissible in evidence in support of any claim against the United States in the Court of Claims, or to establish the right of any claimant to bring suit in that court; nor, if already put in evidence, shall be used or considered on behalf of the claimant, by said court, or by the appellate court on appeal. Proof of loyalty is required to be made according to the provisions of certain statutes, irrespective of the effect of any executive proclamation, pardon, or amnesty, . . . and when judgment has been already rendered on other proof of loyalty, the Supreme Court, on appeal, shall have no further jurisdiction of the cause, and shall dismiss the same for want of jurisdiction. It is further provided that whenever any pardon, granted to any suitor in the Court of Claims, for the proceeds of captured and abandoned property, shall recite in substance that the person pardoned took part in the late rebellion, or was guilty of any act of rebellion or disloyalty, and shall have been accepted in writing without express disclaimer and protestation against the fact so recited, such pardon or acceptance shall be taken as conclusive evidence in the Court of Claims, and on appeal, that the claimant did give aid to the rebellion; and on proof of such pardon, or acceptance, which proof may be made summarily on motion or otherwise, the jurisdiction of the court shall cease, and the suit shall be forthwith dismissed.

The substance of this enactment is that an acceptance of a pardon, without disclaimer, shall be conclusive evidence of the acts pardoned, but shall be null and void as evidence of the rights conferred by it, both in the Court of Claims and in this court on appeal. . . .

The Court of Claims is . . . constituted one of those inferior courts which Congress authorizes, and has jurisdiction of contracts between the government and the citizen, from which appeal regularly lies to this court. Undoubtedly the legislature

Pardon = conclusive evidence of aiding the rebellion ≠ evidence of rights

has complete control over the organization and existence of that court and may confer or withhold the right of appeal from its decisions. And if this act did nothing more, it would be our duty to give it effect. If it simply denied the right of appeal in a particular class of cases, there could be no doubt that it must be regarded as an exercise of the power of Congress to make "such exceptions from the appellate jurisdiction" as should seem to it expedient.

But the language of the proviso shows plainly that it does not intend to withhold appellate jurisdiction except as a means to an end. Its great and controlling purpose is to deny to pardons granted by the President the effect which this court had adjudged them to have. The proviso declares that pardons shall not be considered by this court on appeal. We had already decided that it was our duty to consider them and give them effect, in cases like the present, as equivalent to proof of loyalty. . . . [T]he denial of jurisdiction to this court, as well as to the Court of Claims, is founded solely on the application of a rule of decision, in causes pending, prescribed by Congress. The court has jurisdiction of the cause to a given point; but when it ascertains that a certain state of things exists, its jurisdiction is to cease and it is required to dismiss the cause for want of jurisdiction.

It seems to us that this is not an exercise of the acknowledged power of Congress to make exceptions and prescribe regulations to the appellate power. The court is required to ascertain the existence of certain facts and thereupon to declare that its jurisdiction on appeal has ceased, by dismissing the bill. What is this but to prescribe a rule for the decision of a cause in a particular way? In the case before us, the Court of Claims has rendered judgment for the claimant and an appeal has been taken to this court. We are directed to dismiss the appeal, if we find that the judgment must be affirmed, because of a pardon granted to the intestate of the claimants. Can we do so without allowing one party to the controversy to decide it in its own favor? Can we do so without allowing that the legislature may prescribe rules of decision to the Judicial Department of the government in cases pending before it?

We think not; and thus thinking, we do not at all question what was decided in the case of *Pennsylvania v. Wheeling Bridge Company* [59 U.S. (18 How.) 429 (1855)]. In that case, after a decree in this court that the bridge, in the then state of the law, was a nuisance and must be abated as such, Congress passed an act legalizing the structure and making it a post-road; and the court, on a motion for process to enforce the decree, held that the bridge had ceased to be a nuisance by the exercise of the constitutional powers of Congress, and denied the motion. No arbitrary rule of decision was prescribed in that case, but the court was left to apply its ordinary rules to the new circumstances created by the act. In the case before us no new circumstances have been created by legislation. But the court is forbidden to give the effect to evidence which, in its own judgment, such evidence should have, and is directed to give it an effect precisely contrary.

We must think that Congress has inadvertently passed the limit which separates the legislative from the judicial power. It is of vital importance that these powers be kept distinct. . . . Congress has already provided that the Supreme Court shall have jurisdiction of the judgments of the Court of Claims on appeal. Can it prescribe a rule in conformity with which the court must deny to itself the jurisdiction thus conferred, because and only because its decision, in accordance with settled law, must be adverse to the government and favorable to the suitor? This question seems to us to answer itself.

The rule prescribed is also liable to just exception as impairing the effect of a pardon, and thus infringing the constitutional power of the Executive. It is the intention of the Constitution that each of the great co-ordinate departments of the government— the Legislative, the Executive, and the Judicial—shall be, in its sphere, independent of the others. To the executive alone is intrusted the power of pardon; and it is granted without limit. . . . Now it is clear that the legislature cannot change the effect of such a pardon any more than the executive can change a law. Yet this is attempted by the provision under consideration. The court is required to receive special pardons as evidence of guilt and to treat them as null and void. It is required to disregard pardons granted by proclamation on condition, though the condition has been fulfilled, and to deny them their legal effect. This certainly impairs the executive authority and directs the court to be instrumental to that end. . . .

[The Court affirmed the Court of Claims.]

Justice MILLER (with whom concurred Justice BRADLEY), dissenting.

. . . I do agree to the proposition that the proviso to the act of July 12th, 1870, is unconstitutional, so far as it attempts to prescribe to the judiciary the effect to be given to an act of pardon or amnesty by the President. This power of pardon is confided to the President by the Constitution, and whatever may be its extent or its limits, the legislative branch of the government cannot impair its force of effect in a judicial proceeding in a constitutional court. But I have not been able to bring my mind to concur in the proposition that, under the act concerning captured and abandoned property, there remains in the former owner, who had given aid and comfort to the rebellion, any interest whatever in the property or its proceeds when it had been sold and paid into the treasury. . . .

————————

1. *Categorizing* Klein. Is *Klein* a pardon power case, or a jurisdiction limiting case? It seems hard to imagine a clearer invasion of the President's pardon power than this statute, and the Court is unanimous on the point. So *Klein* may just stand for the proposition that Congress may not use the technique of jurisdiction limitation to achieve a separate constitutional violation. *See* Gordon G. Young, *Congressional Regulation of Federal Courts' Jurisdiction and Processes:* United States v. Klein *Revisited*, 1981 WIS. L. REV. 1189. In that case, it appears that the Court has jurisdiction to detect and condemn such violations, notwithstanding contrary implications in *McCardle*.

2. *Invading the Judicial Power.* The Court also objects that Congress has intruded on judicial power. Apparently, it is constitutional to "den[y] the right of appeal in a particular class of cases," but not to "prescribe rules of decision" in pending cases. Is

this distinction tenable? Consider the Court's distinction of the *Wheeling Bridge* case—is it persuasive?

In *Robertson v. Seattle Audubon Soc'y*, 503 U.S. 429 (1992), the Court unanimously upheld legislation against a *Klein* challenge, although the statute mentioned pending cases by name and declared that government forest management according to certain specified criteria would meet requirements of prior statutes as interpreted in those cases. The Court thought this was an amendment of existing law under *Wheeling Bridge*, and not a direction of decision in pending cases without amending any law, as in *Klein*. The Court did not reach an argument that "even a change in law, prospectively applied, would be unconstitutional if the change swept no more broadly, or little more broadly, than the range of applications at issue in the pending cases." Would that be a good description of *Klein*—or a good modification of *Klein*?

In *Plaut v. Spendthrift Farm, Inc.*, 514 U.S. 211 (1995), the Court invalidated a provision of securities law that required federal courts to reinstate civil fraud actions that the Court had previously held to be time-barred. Justice Scalia's opinion emphasized that Article III authorizes the courts to decide cases conclusively, without legislative interference with their final judgments. He distinguished *Wheeling Bridge* as involving alteration of the prospective effect of an injunction.

Finally, in *Bank Markazi v. Peterson*, 136 S.Ct. 1310 (2016), the Court upheld a statute requiring courts to apply a new legal standard in a pending and specifically identified postjudgment enforcement proceeding involving damages actions against state sponsors of terrorism. Justice Ginsburg's opinion invoked *Robertson*, concluding that Congress had changed the applicable law even though the effect was to determine the outcome in a particular litigation.

The *Klein* Court also objected to allowing "one party to a controversy to decide it in its own favor." That does sound terrible, but isn't it clear that Congress could have simply reasserted sovereign immunity in all abandoned property cases that had not reached final judgment?

Certainly, *McCardle* and *Klein* leave us a murky legacy. Modern scholars have struggled, with more words than effect, to identify the limits to congressional control of federal jurisdiction. One enduring formulation is from Henry Hart's famous article, *The Power of Congress to Limit the Jurisdiction of Federal Courts: An Exercise in Dialectic*, 66 Harv. L. Rev. 1362, 1365 (1953): Congress cannot "destroy the essential role of the Supreme Court in the constitutional plan." Obviously, the Court's role in the constitutional plan is far from self-identifying, but Hart at least focuses our attention on the possibility of trying to protect some version of the Court's "core functions" from congressional interference. For views of scholars who believe congressional power to be especially broad, see Gerald Gunther, *Congressional Power to Curtail Federal Court Jurisdiction: An Opinionated Guide to the Ongoing Debate*, 36 Stan. L. Rev. 895 (1984); Herbert Wechsler, *The Courts and the Constitution*, 65 Colum. L. Rev. 1001 (1965). For the views of those who find limits to congressional power, especially when constitutional claims are involved, see Akhil R. Amar, *A*

Neo-Federalist View of Article III: Separating the Two Tiers of Federal Jurisdiction, 65 B.U. L. REV. 205 (1985); Lawrence Sager, *Foreword: Constitutional Limitations on Congress' Authority to Regulate the Jurisdiction of the Federal Courts,* 95 HARV. L. REV. 17 (1981); Laurence H. Tribe, *Jurisdictional Gerrymandering: Zoning Disfavored Rights Out of the Federal Courts,* 16 HARV. C.R.-C.L. L. REV. 129 (1981).

Considering that congressional power to remove federal jurisdiction is at least quite broad, and perhaps entirely unconstrained, its most surprising feature may be the infrequency with which it has actually occurred. *See* LAURENCE H. TRIBE, 1 AMERICAN CONSTITUTIONAL LAW § 3-5 (3d ed. 2000). During the 1980s, a series of bills were proposed in Congress to limit federal court jurisdiction over cases involving controversial subject matter such as school prayer and abortion. With the exception of some restrictions on busing to integrate schools, none of the bills passed. Even the busing bills were operationally inconsequential, however — they allowed judges to ignore the restrictions when necessary. What accounts for this gap between potential power and its actual exercise? Some answers might include: the value that Americans place on protection of constitutional rights, the expectation that a practice of responding to disliked court opinions with jurisdictional restrictions is one that more than one side could engage in, and the acceptance of Lord Russell's aphorism. Regarding the latter, see Barry Friedman, *A Different Dialogue: The Supreme Court, Congress and Federal Jurisdiction,* 85 Nw. U. L. REV. 1 (1990), arguing that legal uncertainty leads to a process of interaction between Congress and the courts over allocations of federal jurisdiction. For a frankly pessimistic perspective on congressional-judicial relations with regard to areas of procedural rulemaking that require mutual respect and accommodation, see Stephen B. Burbank, *Procedure, Politics and Power: The Role of Congress,* 79 NOTRE DAME L. REV. 101 (2004).

4. Judicial Self-Restraint

The traditional canon that judges should exercise restraint in deciding constitutional issues is alive and well, if not consistently followed. *Compare* Cass R. Sunstein, ONE CASE AT A TIME, JUDICIAL MINIMALISM ON THE SUPREME COURT (1999), *with* Larry D. Kramer, *The Supreme Court, 2000 Term, Foreword: We the Court,* 115 HARV. L. REV. 4 (2001). The culture of the federal courts contains competing values: recognition of the duty to decide legal issues, even difficult ones, alongside awareness of the need to defer appropriately to the political branches. Consider also the preceding section of this casebook. Federal judges, although possessed of a high degree of individual independence, inhabit a branch that they know is vulnerable to assault by the other branches. *See* John A. Ferejohn & Larry D. Kramer, *Independent Judges, Dependent Judiciary: Institutionalizing Judicial Restraint,* 77 N.Y.U. L. REV. 962 (2002). Hence for judges, as for people generally, self-restraint tends to waver in practice.

The Supreme Court has developed a number of doctrines that it can invoke to justify refusing to reach the merits of a separation of powers controversy. These doctrines are an amalgam of two basic elements that are often hard to distinguish in the opinions. First, the Court often says that limitations on its power are implicit in Article III's definition of federal judicial power as extending only to various categories of "Cases" and "Controversies." Second, the Court often cites "prudential" concerns related to preserving its institutional position in the nation when it declines to decide a thorny issue. *See generally* Lea Brilmayer, *The Jurisprudence of Article III: Perspectives on the "Case or Controversy" Requirement,* 93 HARV. L. REV. 297 (1979); Michael C. Dorf, *Dicta and Article III,* 142 U. PA. L. REV. 1997 (1994). We have already encountered one of the most prominent of these techniques of self-denial, the political question doctrine, which originated in *Marbury.* A number of cases in this book will consider invoking it. We introduce it here, along with another major avoidance doctrine, standing, and a brief summary of the other issues that are often lumped under the general term "justiciability."

In his concurring opinion in *Goldwater v. Carter,* 444 U.S. 996 (1979) (excerpted in Chapter Five) Justice Powell gave a useful, brief restatement of modern political question analysis:

> As set forth in the seminal case of *Baker v. Carr,* 369 U.S. 186, 217 (1962), the doctrine incorporates three inquiries: (i) Does the issue involve resolution of questions committed by the text of the Constitution to a coordinate branch of Government? (ii) Would resolution of the question demand that a court move beyond areas of judicial expertise? (iii) Do prudential considerations counsel against judicial intervention? . . . First, the existence of "a textually demonstrable constitutional commitment of the issue to a coordinate political department," ibid., turns on an examination of the constitutional provisions governing the exercise of the power in question. . . . Second, [a court asks if there is a] "lack of judicially discoverable and manageable standards for resolving" [a] case; [or whether] a decision [is] impossible "without an initial policy determination of a kind clearly for nonjudicial discretion." *Baker v. Carr,* 369 U.S. at 217. . . . Finally, the political-question doctrine rests in part on prudential concerns calling for mutual respect among the three branches of Government. Thus, the Judicial Branch should avoid "the potentiality of embarrassment [that would result] from multifarious pronouncements by various departments on one question." Similarly, the doctrine restrains judicial action where there is an "unusual need for unquestioning adherence to a political decision already made." *Baker v. Carr,* 369 U.S. at 217.

The first of these factors—the "textual commitment" one—has caused the greatest controversy. For example, in *Powell v. McCormack,* 395 U.S. 486 (1969) (excerpted in Chapter Three), the Court held that a congressional decision to exclude a member was justiciable. The Court said that, in order to determine whether a textual commitment to another branch exists, "we must interpret the Constitution," and proceeded to examine the clause in Article I, §5, that grants Congress the power to judge the qualifications of its members. Because the Court read the clause narrowly, there was no broad grant of power to Congress to exclude members without judicial review.

The Court's decision in *Powell* led observers to suggest that the "textual commit-ment" issue is the core of the political question doctrine, and that the doctrine itself is almost indistinguishable from the merits. *See generally* Symposium, *Comments on Powell v. McCormack,* 17 UCLA L. Rev. 1 (1969). Professor Terrence Sandalow con-cluded, *id.* at 172–73:

> Having begun by asking the right question, whether there was a "constitu-tional commitment of the issue" to the House, the Court proceeded to answer a quite different one, whether the "qualifications" which Article I, Section 5 authorized the House to "judge" were only those specified in [the Constitution]. The opinion reflects, in short, a classic instance of confusion between "jurisdiction"—the power to decide—and "the merits"—the cor-rectness of decisions. The source of this confusion, it seems fairly clear, is the Court's assumption that it bears "responsibility . . . to act as the ultimate interpreter of the Constitution." [quoting the Court, 395 U.S. at 549.] On that premise, it is but a short step to the conclusion that the Court is obli-gated to intervene when another branch of government acts in a manner prohibited by the Constitution.

Professor Louis Henkin, in *Is There a "Political Question" Doctrine?* 85 Yale L.J. 597 (1976), argues that the judiciary does not need to be blind to any part of the Consti-tution. He thinks that many of the political question cases could as easily have held that the action in question was within constitutional limits, and therefore was open only to political challenge. *See also* Mark Tushnet, *Law and Prudence in the Law of Justiciability: The Transformation of the Political Question Doctrine,* 80 N.C. L. Rev. 1203 (2002), arguing that the doctrine has declined along with the possibility that the Court's decisions will be overturned politically.

For the view that courts should regard all constitutional issues concerning the respective powers of Congress and the President as nonjusticiable, see Jesse Choper, Judicial Review and the National Political Process 260–379 (1980), *reviewed by* Carl McGowan, *Constitutional Adjudication: Deciding When to Decide,* 79 Mich. L. Rev. 616 (1980); Henry P. Monaghan, *Book Review,* 94 Harv. L. Rev. 296 (1980). *See also* J. Peter Mulhern, *In Defense of the Political Question Doctrine,* 137 U. Pa. L. Rev. 1 (1988).

Another prominent doctrinal consequence of the case or controversy requirement is the Court's refusal, since the earliest days, to issue "advisory opinions." In 1793, President Washington asked for an opinion from the Supreme Court on twenty-nine questions relating to treaties with France. Both colonial and English practices sup-ported such a request. The Constitutional Convention, however, had considered autho-rizing the advisory opinion practice, and had declined to do so. The Justices declined Washington's request, "considering themselves," John Marshall explained later, "merely as constituting a legal tribunal for the decision of controversies brought before them in legal form." James Bradley Thayer, Oliver Wendell Holmes, and Felix Frank-furter on John Marshall 57 (1967); *see also Muskrat v. United States,* 219 U.S. 346 (1911); Stewart Jay, Most Humble Servants: The Advisory Role of Early Judges (1997).

The Supreme Court also requires federal litigants to have "standing" to make their claims in court. *See generally* William A. Fletcher, *The Structure of Standing*, 98 Yale L.J. 221 (1988); Cass R. Sunstein, *Standing and the Privatization of Public Law*, 88 Colum. L. Rev. 1432 (1988). The Court's standing cases are notoriously confused and contradictory, perhaps because the prudential aspects of justiciability play an especially prominent role in them. Nevertheless, the Court also routinely states a case or controversy component to the standing inquiry. In *Allen v. Wright*, 468 U.S. 737 (1984), Justice O'Connor explained:

> Standing doctrine embraces several judicially self-imposed limits on the exercise of federal jurisdiction, such as the general prohibition on a litigant's raising another person's legal rights, the rule barring adjudication of generalized grievances more appropriately addressed in the representative branches, and the requirement that a plaintiff's complaint fall within the zone of interests protected by the law invoked. The requirement of standing, however, has a core component derived directly from the Constitution. A plaintiff must allege personal injury fairly traceable to the defendant's allegedly unlawful conduct and likely to be redressed by the requested relief. Like the prudential component, the constitutional component of standing doctrine incorporates concepts concededly not susceptible of precise definition. The injury alleged must be, for example, " 'distinct and palpable,' " and not "abstract" or "conjectural" or "hypothetical." The injury must be "fairly" traceable to the challenged action, and relief from the injury must be "likely" to follow from a favorable decision.

In separation of powers cases, nongovernmental plaintiffs have often had to rely on the broadest possible grounds for standing, because the connection between the government action complained of and any injury to the plaintiff has been quite indirect. The broadest traditional category has been taxpayer standing—since we are all, alas, taxpayers. But for many years the Court seemed to have erected an insurmountable barrier to this kind of standing. In *Frothingham v. Mellon*, 262 U.S. 447 (1923), it rejected a taxpayer's challenge to federal spending that promoted the health of mothers and infants. Yet in *Flast v. Cohen*, 392 U.S. 83 (1968), the Court opened the door to taxpayer standing in at least some circumstances by allowing a challenge to federal aid to religious schools. For federal spending programs such as those involved in these cases, if taxpayers lacked standing it was likely that no plaintiff was available to force the government to obey the Constitution.

Yet the modern Supreme Court continues to deny standing to particular plaintiffs in circumstances where it is unlikely anyone else can establish standing. In these cases, the practical effect of the court's decision equates to a ruling that an issue is a political question. Under either doctrine, important constitutional issues that the Court declines to review are left to the two political branches for resolution. The doctrinal difference is that a standing holding only says "not you," instead of "never," leaving the other branches to wonder whether the Court might someday find a suitable plaintiff if sufficiently tempted to do so. Perhaps using standing doctrine reduces pressure on the political branches to take responsibility for their actions. Two companion cases from the Vietnam War era illustrate this effect.

In *United States v. Richardson*, 418 U.S. 166 (1974), a taxpayer brought a challenge to a provision of the Central Intelligence Agency Act of 1949 (50 U.S.C. § 403a et seq.) that allows secret CIA spending, on grounds that it violated Art. I, § 9, cl. 7, of the Constitution which provides:

> "No Money shall be drawn from the Treasury, but in Consequence of Appropriations made by Law; and a regular Statement and Account of the Receipts and Expenditures of all public Money shall be published from time to time."

Chief Justice Burger's opinion for the Court rejected Richardson's standing to sue, citing *Frothingham* and distinguishing *Flast*: "Respondent is seeking 'to employ a federal court as a forum in which to air his generalized grievances about the conduct of government.'" Concluding, the Court noted that "It can be argued that if respondent is not permitted to litigate this issue, no one can do so. In a very real sense, the absence of any particular individual or class to litigate these claims gives support to the argument that the subject matter is committed to the surveillance of Congress, and ultimately to the political process."

The Chief Justice also wrote the opinion in the companion case, *Schlesinger v. Reservists Committee to Stop the War,* 418 U.S. 208 (1974). Opponents of the Vietnam War had challenged the eligibility of Members of Congress to hold commissions in the Armed Forces Reserve during their continuance in office. (At the time suit was filed, 130 Members of the 91st Congress were members of the Reserves.) The plaintiffs relied on the Incompatibility Clause of the Constitution, Article I, § 6, cl. 2, which provides that "no Person holding any Office under the United States, shall be a Member of either House during his Continuance in Office." As in *Richardson*, the Court concluded that the interests of the plaintiffs (here, in avoiding undue executive influence in Congress) were shared with all other citizens and hence were nonjusticiable. Congress took no action to end the practice of allowing its members to hold Reserve commissions.

"What's the Constitution between friends?" is the perhaps apocryphal response of a Tammany politician to President Cleveland's remark that he would not support a bill because it was unconstitutional. *See* LOUIS FISHER, THE CONSTITUTION BETWEEN FRIENDS, at v (1978). The problem it reveals is the possibility that the political branches may agree to support an unconstitutional practice that no private plaintiff may challenge. In its footnote 11, the *Richardson* Court, in the course of suggesting the outlines of a political question holding, discussed the available control on secret spending by the executive:

> Although we need not reach or decide precisely what is meant by "a regular Statement and Account," it is clear that Congress has plenary power to exact any reporting and accounting it considers appropriate in the public interest. It is therefore open to serious question whether the Framers of the

Constitution ever imagined that general directives to the Congress or the Executive would be subject to enforcement by an individual citizen. While the available evidence is neither qualitatively nor quantitatively conclusive, historical analysis of the genesis of cl. 7 suggests that it was intended to permit some degree of secrecy of governmental operations. The ultimate weapon of enforcement available to the Congress would, of course, be the "power of the purse." . . . Not controlling, but surely not unimportant, are nearly two centuries of acceptance of a reading of cl. 7 as vesting in Congress plenary power to spell out the details of precisely when and with what specificity Executive agencies must report the expenditure of appropriated funds and to exempt certain secret activities from comprehensive public reporting.

Is this fully responsive to Richardson's complaint? He wanted to know the CIA's budget, which is secret by statute. Wasn't his objection really to the conduct of *both* branches in building a largely secret national security apparatus? The framers—veterans of revolutionary war and intrigue—do seem to have assumed the need for some secret spending. Still, until about World War II, Congress complied with the Statement and Account clause except for relatively small amounts of money. It was development of the atomic bomb with secret funds that ushered in a new era. By the early twenty-first century, amounts of more than $40 billion were hidden in the appropriations for our national security agencies. The actual figures were available to each member of Congress. Eventually, efforts succeeded within Congress to have the aggregate amount of secret spending for all agencies published. Hence, the political process to which the Court remitted Richardson eventually provided a remedy, however incomplete.

The Court's most recent national security standing decision is consistent with the Vietnam era cases. In *Clapper v. Amnesty International USA*, 568 U.S. 398 (2013), the Court denied standing to persons who feared that their communications would be intercepted by the National Security Agency as part of its electronic eavesdropping to discover terror threats (which we cover in Chapters Five and Seven). Although the plaintiffs alleged that their work required them to engage in sensitive international communications that were particularly likely to be intercepted by the NSA and directly challenged the constitutionality of the NSA's activities, Justice Alito's opinion for the Court rejected their claim as unduly speculative. The plaintiffs' assertion that there was "an objectively reasonable likelihood" that their communications would be intercepted failed to satisfy the constitutional standing requirement for an injury in fact that is "certainly impending," said the Court. Justice Breyer's opinion for four dissenters would have found enough prospect of harm to avoid dismissing the case. Because the NSA refuses to reveal whom it has surveilled, the result in *Clapper* once again appears to remit a serious constitutional controversy to the political process.

Thus American courts have not adopted the concept of the "public action," a right in any citizen to hold the government accountable to law. *See* Louis Jaffe, Judicial Control of Administrative Action 459–500 (1965). Should they? In

Schlesinger, the majority revealed its concern that citizenship standing to contest constitutional violations would have "no boundaries." It has often been observed that the *Flast* criteria for taxpayer standing are invented ways to allow Establishment Clause challenges to federal spending without opening the gates to other taxpayer or citizen suits. Why not do something similar for separation of powers cases? The Court might look for situations where the political process will not correct itself, as it has in reapportionment cases. Are these two cases examples of that? Or the Court could have held that *Richardson* involved a direct constitutional duty to the citizens, and that *Schlesinger* involved plaintiffs with a grievance distinct from that of other citizens, as the dissents in the cases would have held. What would the implications for other cases have been?

Does standing doctrine reflect only Article III concerns about cases and controversies, or does it have an ultimate basis in the separation of powers? *See* Antonin Scalia, *The Doctrine of Standing as an Essential Element of the Separation of Powers*, 17 Suffolk U.L. Rev. 881 (1983). In *Lujan v. Defenders of Wildlife*, 504 U.S. 555 (1992), Justice Scalia obtained the Supreme Court's imprimatur for the view suggested by his article title. The case involved a challenge to a rule that limited the applicability of the Endangered Species Act to federal actions taken within the United States, by a plaintiff who could not show personal injury caused by the action. In an opinion refusing to allow invocation of a "citizen-suit" provision of the Act, 16 U.S.C. § 1540(g), Scalia wrote:

> We have consistently held that a plaintiff raising only a generally available grievance about government — claiming only harm to his and every citizen's interest in proper application of the Constitution and laws, and seeking relief that no more directly and tangibly benefits him than it does the public at large — does not state an Article III case or controversy.... To be sure, our generalized-grievance cases have typically involved Government violation of procedures assertedly ordained by the Constitution rather than the Congress. But there is absolutely no basis for making the Article III inquiry turn on the source of the asserted right. Whether the courts were to act on their own, or at the invitation of Congress, in ignoring the concrete injury requirement described in our cases, they would be discarding a principle fundamental to the separate and distinct constitutional role of the Third Branch — one of the essential elements that identifies those "Cases" and "Controversies" that are the business of the courts rather than of the political branches. "The province of the court," as Chief Justice Marshall said in *Marbury v. Madison*, 1 Cranch, 137, 170 (1803) "is, solely, to decide on the rights of individuals." Vindicating the public interest (including the public interest in government observance of the Constitution and laws) is the function of Congress and the Chief Executive. The question presented here is whether the public interest in proper administration of the laws (specifically, in agencies' observance of a particular, statutorily prescribed procedure) can be converted into an individual right by a statute that denominates

it as such, and that permits all citizens (or, for that matter, a subclass of citizens who suffer no distinctive concrete harm) to sue. If the concrete injury requirement has the separation-of-powers significance we have always said, the answer must be obvious: To permit Congress to convert the undifferentiated public interest in executive officers' compliance with the law into an "individual right" vindicable in the courts is to permit Congress to transfer from the President to the courts the Chief Executive's most important constitutional duty, to "take Care that the Laws be faithfully executed," Art. II, § 3. . . . We have always rejected that vision of our role. . . .

The Court has subsequently shown itself more hospitable to attending to citizen grievances than Justice Scalia's *Lujan* opinion might suggest. Over his dissent (joined by two others), in *FEC v. Akins*, 524 U.S. 11 (1998), the Court recognized an "informational injury" as sufficient for standing. A group of voters had challenged the FEC's refusal to subject a certain organization to the reporting and disclosure requirements of federal election law. *Akins* is quite difficult to distinguish from *Richardson* except that Congress expressly created a statutory cause of action against the FEC. Hence the Court may be deferring to Congress concerning whether to create citizen actions. If so, is such a policy justifiable in light of the congressional conflicts of interest entailed in a case like *Richardson*? And what does this make of the apparent premise of *Richardson* and *Schlesinger* that the adjudication in federal courts of "generalized grievances" would violate Article III?

Moreover, with Justice Scalia writing, the Court upheld Congress's authority to confer standing to pursue *qui tam* actions, in which a private party receives a monetary award for uncovering fraud against the government. *Vermont Agency of Natural Resources v. United States*, 529 U.S. 765 (2000), discussed in Chapter Four. Justice Scalia thought the routine acceptance of *qui tam* suits in the late 18th century made it historically implausible that such suits should be deemed incompatible with Article III. His opinion purported to reserve the question of compatibility with Article II, a somewhat puzzling suggestion since the identical history would presumably be determinative to an originalist like Scalia in an Article II challenge, as well.

Justice Scalia's opinion in *Lujan* has received substantial critical attention. *See* Cass R. Sunstein, *What's Standing After* Lujan? *Of Citizen Suits, "Injuries," and Article III*, 91 MICH. L. REV. 163 (1992). Professor Sunstein argues that the "injury in fact" requirement is a recent invention of federal judges, without support in the history or text of Article III. Canvassing the history of the law of standing, he concludes that citizen suits were accepted during our founding period in both England and America. Describing the injury in fact requirement as value-laden and misleading, he would replace it with an inquiry into whether the law (the Constitution, relevant statutes, or federal common law) has conferred a cause of action on the plaintiffs.

Professor Shane has criticized the Court's zigzagging standing jurisprudence as a misguided effort to make "standing" do the job of identifying substantively plausible plaintiffs in public law that "cause of action" does in private law. He deems recent torturous doctrinal efforts to justify standing limitations as driven by a misguided view (attributable largely to Justice Scalia) that the aim of standing doctrine is to protect executive branch discretion from judicial interference. He argues that standing barriers—most notably, the requirement for a concrete adversarial dispute susceptible to final determination by a court—are:

> better understood as an effort to protect judicial power. . . . [I]t would weaken the judiciary vis-a-vis the other branches for courts to render merely advisory opinions or judgments in suits that are factually underdeveloped, or in suits in which the judicial determination could be administratively altered. Giving a judicial imprimatur to collusive suits would represent an abandonment of the court's public dispute resolution function altogether. It is to protect only against these important, but limited concerns that standing rules ought to be fashioned and followed. The work of keeping the judiciary out of the business of the other branches is a separate matter, and handled amply through the political question doctrine and rules on justiciability.

Peter M. Shane, *Returning Separation of Powers Analysis to its Normative Roots: The Constitutionality of* Qui Tam *Actions and Other Private Suits to Enforce Civil Penalties*, 30 Environmental L. Reporter 11,081,11,103 (2000).

The standing of Members of Congress to sue presents special separation of powers problems. We outline them here and return to them in Chapter Four. In *Raines v. Byrd*, 521 U.S. 811 (1997), six Members of Congress who had voted against the Line Item Veto Act challenged its constitutionality. As we will see later in this chapter, the Court later invalidated the Act, which authorized the President to "cancel" items in appropriations statutes. In *Raines*, the Court denied standing to the legislators even though the Act explicitly attempted to grant standing to any Member of Congress to bring such a suit. The plaintiffs had claimed injury by impairment of the effectiveness of their votes on appropriations. The Court concluded that this alleged "institutional injury is wholly abstract and widely dispersed." It noted that the legislators could repeal the Act or exempt appropriations from it, and that other plaintiffs could challenge the Act (as, they later did, successfully). The Court distinguished situations in which a Member is singled out for unfavorable treatment (*Powell v. McCormack, supra*) and those in which legislators' votes are completely nullified by an action they challenge.

B. Combining Powers in the Executive

Separation of powers doctrine has long struggled with the problem of limits to Congress's discretion to structure and empower the other two branches. In this section we first consider the delegation doctrine, which states limits to the power of Congress to transfer broad authority to the executive. We then summarize doctrine concerning legislative transfer of adjudicative power to the executive. The result of these delegations of power is that the executive exercises functions typical of all three constitutional branches of government. This feature pervades American administrative law, and continues to raise basic questions about the legitimacy of our modern administrative state.

1. Delegation of Legislative Powers

Article I, Section One, of the Constitution provides that "[a]ll legislative powers herein granted shall be vested in . . . Congress;" Section Eight authorizes Congress to "make all Laws . . . necessary and proper for carrying into Execution the foregoing Powers, and all other Powers vested by this Constitution in the Government of the United States, or in any Department or Officer thereof." Read together, how much latitude do these clauses give Congress to empower the executive to form policy?

Early American republican theory held that the people's sovereignty was not transferred to the legislature. Instead, the legislature was a limited agent, entrusted with powers to be exercised as instructed by the people. John Locke had stressed the corollary idea that entrusted power could not be further delegated to others. This is a simple, appealing notion: if the legislature is a trustee, any large transfer of its power seems a plain evasion of responsibility. The problem is only worsened when the transfer of power is to a politically unresponsible bureaucracy, instead of the President himself. Yet executive power was surely intended to consist mainly of responsibility to implement powers that were conferred by statutes.

Both the assumption that Congress may grant the executive some measure of discretion and the concern that underlies the delegation doctrine surfaced at the Constitutional Convention. Madison moved that the President be authorized "to execute such other powers (not legislative nor judiciary in their nature) as may from time to time be delegated by the national Legislature." 1 MAX FARRAND, THE RECORDS OF THE FEDERAL CONVENTION OF 1787, 67 (REV. ED. 1966) (Madison's notes). The suggestion was defeated after an argument that the phrase was surplusage to the general power to execute the laws, although Madison demurred that it might "serve to prevent doubts and misconstructions." The parenthetical phrase, however, came not from Madison but from Pinckney, who proposed its addition to forestall any delegation of "improper powers."

Apparently, then, the framers thought that Congress would need to delegate discretion to the executive, but that somewhere there were limits. Both early congressional actions and the fragmentary case law of the framers' generation are consistent with such a general attitude. Between 1794 and 1810, Congress repeatedly authorized the President to lay or remove trade embargoes, amid some discussion whether the power to initiate or suspend a law was an exclusive legislative function that could not be delegated. Louis Fisher, *Delegating Power to the President*, 19 EMORY J. PUBLIC L. 251, 253–56 (1970). In *The Brig Aurora*, 11 U.S. (7 Cranch) 382 (1813), the Supreme Court gave the problem short shrift. The Court upheld a delegation to the President to lift embargoes when France and England "ceased to violate the neutral commerce of the United States." To an argument that Congress had unconstitutionally transferred its legislative power to the President, the Court (per Justice Johnson) responded that "we can see no sufficient reason, why the legislature should not exercise its discretion in reviving the [statute] either expressly or conditionally, as their judgment should direct."

Chief Justice Marshall's contribution to the subject occurred in *Wayman v. Southard*, 23 U.S. (10 Wheat.) 1 (1825), a case involving a delegation of power to the courts, not the executive. The Judiciary Act of 1789 had authorized the courts to make rules for the conduct of their business. Marshall rejected a challenge to the constitutionality of this provision (23 U.S. at 42–43, 46):

> It will not be contended that Congress can delegate to the Courts, or to any other tribunals, powers which are strictly and exclusively legislative. But Congress may certainly delegate to others, powers which the legislature may rightfully exercise itself. . . . The line has not been exactly drawn which separates these important subjects, which must be entirely regulated by the legislature itself, from those of less interest, in which a general provision may be made, and power given to those who are to act under such general provisions to fill up the details. . . . The difference between the departments undoubtedly is, that the legislature makes, the executive executes, and the judiciary construes the law; but the maker of the law may commit something to the discretion of the other departments, and the precise boundary of this power is a subject of delicate and difficult inquiry, into which a Court will not enter unnecessarily.

Marshall was right—the limits of permissible delegation raise a "delicate and difficult inquiry," as later cases have shown. Until well into this century, the major delegation cases (except for *Wayman*) all involved direct grants of power to the President (rather than to subordinate officers) in the field of foreign relations. The Court displayed a willingness to uphold the delegations, perhaps because the need for executive discretion in foreign affairs is readily apparent. Yet, as we see in Marshall's gropings in *Wayman*, the Court was never very comfortable in its articulation of underlying theory.

A leading case, *Field v. Clark*, 143 U.S. 649 (1892), illustrates the problems. A statute allowed the President to suspend free import of certain goods if he found that the exporting country was not according American goods reciprocal treatment. For the Court, the first Justice Harlan stated a strict rule: "That Congress cannot delegate legislative power to the President is a principle universally recognized as vital to the integrity and maintenance of the system of government ordained by the Constitution." He then upheld the statute, however, by characterizing the President's role as limited to fact-finding, and therefore execution: "He was the mere agent of the law-making department to ascertain and declare the event upon which its expressed will was to take effect."

In *Field*, the Court essayed a functional distinction between legislative and executive power, between policymaking and factfinding. Of course, there is no clear line between these functions. *Field* itself illustrates this—the operative terms of the statute called on the President to act when he deemed foreign duties "reciprocally unequal and unreasonable." Plainly, a new doctrinal formulation was needed, one that would allow Congress to grant substantial policymaking discretion to the growing federal bureaucracy. Early in the twentieth century, the Court shifted to a requirement that legislation contain "standards" to limit the scope of executive discretion. A prominent case is *J. W. Hampton, Jr. & Co. v. United States*, 276 U.S. 394 (1928), in which the Court upheld another statute allowing the President to equalize tariff rates. The Court concluded that "if Congress shall lay down . . . an intelligible principle to which the [executive] is directed to conform, [that] is not a forbidden delegation of legislative power."

The standards requirement appeared to be an ideal marriage of principle with necessity. Congress cannot legislate in advance for every eventuality, and wisdom may lie in deferring to the executive's greater capacity to respond to unfolding events. Yet if an "intelligible principle" exists to guide the executive, the rule of law can be preserved. Nevertheless, the Court quickly began honoring the standards doctrine mainly in the breach, as it approved a series of extremely broad delegations to administrative agencies. For example, the Court allowed railroad regulation under "just and reasonable rates," broadcast licensing in the "public interest, convenience, or necessity," and trade regulation of "unfair methods of competition." To many observers, the doctrine seemed to lack teeth. The onset of the Great Depression in the 1930s would alter that perception, if temporarily.

The primary delegation cases of the 1930s involved the National Industrial Recovery Act of 1933 (NIRA), at one time President Roosevelt's flagship legislation. Like all major cases, they must be understood in historical context, and the context for these was truly extraordinary. It included FDR's war with the Court, which we consider with materials on judicial appointments and the ill-fated Court-packing plan (Chapter Four *infra*). It also included the explosion of legislative and executive activity, beginning with the "Hundred Days," that transformed both the face of American government and the Presidency.

In the depths of the economic emergency at Roosevelt's inauguration, the analogy to wartime crisis was easy to make. Early New Deal legislation borrowed government structure and procedure from emergency responses to World War I. Indeed, FDR's first official action, declaration of a bank holiday, rested for authority on the Trading with the Enemy Act of 1917. *See* Belknap, *The New Deal and the Emergency Powers Doctrine*, 62 TEX. L. REV. 67, 73 (1983). It was hoped that judicial precedent accommodating the wartime actions could be relied on as well, but that was not to be.

An introduction to the times and to the NIRA is provided by JAMES MAC-GREGOR BURNS, in ROOSEVELT: THE LION AND THE FOX 166–93 (1956). As you read this history, consider what lessons it contains for Congress in delegating power in times of crisis, and for the executive in exercising it. Also, consider the effect of this background on the Supreme Court in its later consideration of the constitutional issues:

Summoned by the new President, Congress convened in special session on Thursday, March 9. . . . By unanimous consent Democratic leaders introduced an emergency banking act to confirm Roosevelt's proclamation and to grant him new powers over banking and currency. Completed by the President and his advisers at two o'clock that morning, the bill was still in rough form. But even during the meager forty minutes allotted to the debate, shouts of "Vote! Vote!" echoed from the floor. . . . The House promptly passed the bill without a record vote; the Senate approved it a few hours later; the President signed it by nine o'clock. . . . [A] host of presidential advisers were at work in a dozen agencies, in hotel rooms, anywhere they could find a desk, drawing up bills. The result was more of the fast and staccato action that would go down in history as the "Hundred Days." . . .

Roosevelt was following no master program—no "economic panaceas or fancy plans," as he later called them derisively. . . . The Chief Executive was Chief Legislator. It was only at the level of the presidential office that party interests, the crisscrossing legislative blocs, and the bustling bureaucrats were given some measure of integration in meeting national problems. . . . Nothing better exemplified this pragmatism—both in the manner it was drawn up and in its major provisions—than the National Industrial Recovery Act. . . . As the mainspring of the early New Deal, this measure for two years embodied its hopes and its liabilities. . . .

[T]he NRA had its immediate origin with a number of persons working separately in Washington during the interregnum . . . . Would Roosevelt's strategy of combining many disparate proposals, thereby gaining support from various elements in Congress, offset the voting strength of the opposition should the dissident groups combine against the bill? His strategy worked, but only because . . . ticklish political issues were left to the President to decide by delegation of power. . . . The final act was a compromise among many groups and theories. Industrial councils could draw up codes of fair competition, but these had to be approved by the President. These codes were exempted from antitrust laws, but monopolistic practices were still barred. . . . In an entirely different title of the bill, over three billion dollars were authorized for a huge spending effort through public works. . . .

If the New Deal had circus-like qualities during the first years, the center ring was occupied by the National Recovery Administration, and the ringmaster presented a fresh new visage on the American scene. General Hugh S. Johnson looked like the old cavalry man that he was. . . . Johnson's main task was to induce businessmen to draw up codes of fair competition, which on the President's approval had the full force of law. Administered under the general's supervision by a code authority in each industry, the codes were supposed to stop wasteful competition, to bring about more orderly pricing and selling policies, and to establish higher wages, shorter hours, and better working conditions for workers. . . .

Within weeks the NRA burst on the American people like a national call to arms. The NRA eagle was suddenly in every shop window. . . . Almost at the start the President had virtually lost control of the NRA. He told the cabinet one day how Johnson . . . had rushed into his office, and handed the President three codes to sign. As Roosevelt was signing the last one, Johnson looked at his watch, said he had five minutes to catch his plane, and dashed out, the codes in his pocket. "He hasn't been seen since," Roosevelt added brightly. The President was hardly more than a front man. . . . Johnson himself had to delegate huge policy-making powers to hastily summoned businessmen who might or might not be representative of the myriad interests in their industries. And in the first flush of enthusiasm the NRA coverage was extended so far that the machinery was nearly swamped. . . . Roosevelt trimmed NRA's powers, limited its jurisdiction, eased Johnson out, and put a more domesticated chief, Donald Richberg, in his place. But by the time the Supreme Court [considered the NRA's constitutionality], it was near administrative and political collapse.

Against this backdrop, the Supreme Court decided two challenges to the NIRA. The first involved the NIRA's attempt to protect the petroleum industry from a flood of newly discovered oil that was depressing the market. Section 9(c), 48 Stat. 200 (1933), authorized the President to prohibit the transportation in interstate commerce of petroleum produced in excess of the amount permitted by any state law. The President issued an executive order prohibiting such "hot oil." Oil producers and refiners sought an injunction against the program. In *Panama Refining Co. v. Ryan*, 293 U.S. 388 (1935), the Supreme Court held section 9(c) unconstitutional, in an opinion by Chief Justice Hughes:

Section 9(c) does not state whether, or in what circumstances or under what conditions, the President is to prohibit the transportation of the amount of petroleum . . . produced in excess of the state's permission. It establishes no criterion to govern the President's course. It does not require any finding by the President as a condition of his action. The Congress in § 9(c) thus declares no policy as to the transportation of the excess production. So far as this section is concerned, it gives to the President an unlimited authority to determine the policy and to lay down the prohibition, or not to lay it down, as he may see fit. And disobedience to his order is made a crime punishable by fine and imprisonment. . . .

The Congress manifestly is not permitted to abdicate, or to transfer to others, the essential legislative functions with which it is . . . vested. Undoubtedly legislation must often be adapted to complex conditions involving a host of details with which the national legislature cannot deal directly. The Constitution has never been regarded as denying to the Congress the necessary resources of flexibility and practicality which will enable it to perform its function in laying down policies and establishing standards, while leaving to select instrumentalities the making of subordinate rules within prescribed limits and the determination of facts to which the policy as declared by the legislature is to apply. Without capacity to give authorizations of that sort we should have the anomaly of a legislative power which in many circumstances calling for its exertion would be but a futility. But . . . in every case in which the question has been raised, the Court has recognized that there are limits on delegation which there is no constitutional authority to transcend. We think that §9(c) goes beyond those limits. As to the transportation of oil products in excess of state permission, the Congress has declared no policy, has established no standard, has laid down no rule. . . . If §9(c) were held valid, it would be idle to pretend that anything would be left of limitations upon the power of the Congress to delegate its law-making function. . . .

Justice Cardozo dissented, agreeing that a standard was needed, but concluding that one could be implied from the statute:

[The President] has choice, though within limits, as to the occasion, but none whatever as to the means. The means have been prescribed by Congress. There has been no grant to the Executive of any roving commission to inquire into evils and then, upon discovering them, do anything he pleases. . . . If we look to the whole structure of the statute, the test is plainly this, that the President is to forbid the transportation of the oil when he believes, in the light of the conditions of the industry as disclosed from time to time, that the prohibition will tend to effectuate the declared policies of the act. . . . He is to [choose] action or inaction according to its observed effect upon industrial recovery—the ultimate end . . . to which all the other ends are tributary and mediate.

A challenge to the heart of the NIRA reached the Court in *A.L.A. Schechter Poultry Corp. v. United States*, 295 U.S. 495 (1935). Section 3 provided that trade associations could promulgate codes of "fair competition," which, upon approval by the President, would have the force of law. The President was authorized to approve a code only if he found that the trade association was representative of the industry, that the code was not designed to promote monopolies, and that the code would carry out the general policies of the Act. A trade group proposed a "poultry code"; the President approved it; the Schechters were convicted for violating it. They appealed.

In another opinion by Chief Justice Hughes, the Supreme Court invalidated the statute, on two grounds. First, the Court held that Congress had exceeded its powers to regulate interstate commerce. (Other New Deal legislation also fell for this reason, until the Court's famous "switch in time" that led to wholesale approval of New Deal legislation.) Second, the Court held that the code-making authority conferred by section 3 was an unconstitutional delegation of legislative power. Again the Chief Justice found no adequate standard in the Act. He then distinguished the recent cases that had upheld broad delegations of authority to administrative agencies:

The Federal Trade Commission Act (§5) introduced the expression "unfair methods of competition," which were declared to be unlawful. That was an expression new in the law. . . . What are "unfair methods of competition" are thus to be determined in particular instances, upon evidence, in the light of particular competitive conditions and of what is found to be a specific and substantial public interest. To make this possible, Congress set up a special procedure. A Commission, a quasi-judicial body, was created. Provision was made for formal complaint, for notice and hearing, for appropriate findings of fact supported by adequate evidence, and for judicial review to give assurance that the action of the Commission is taken within its statutory authority.

In providing for codes, the [NIRA] dispenses with this administrative procedure and with any administrative procedure of an analogous character. But the difference between the code plan of the Recovery Act and the scheme of the Federal Trade Commission Act lies not only in procedure but in subject matter. . . . The "fair competition" of the codes has a much broader range [than the FTC's delegation] and a new significance. . . .

Such a sweeping delegation of legislative power finds no support in the decisions upon which the Government relies. By the Interstate Commerce Act, Congress has itself provided a code of laws regulating the activities of the common carriers subject to the Act, in order to assure the performance of their services upon just and reasonable terms, with adequate facilities and without unjust discrimination. Congress from time to time has elaborated its requirements, as needs have been disclosed. To facilitate the application of the standards prescribed by the Act, Congress has provided an expert body. That administrative agency, in dealing with particular cases, is required to act upon notice and hearings, and its orders must be supported by findings of fact which in turn are sustained by evidence. . . .

Similarly, we have held that the Radio Act of 1927 established standards to govern radio communications and, in view of the limited number of available broadcasting frequencies, Congress authorized allocation and licenses. The authority of the [Federal Radio] Commission to grant licenses "as public convenience, interest or necessity requires" was limited by the nature of radio communications, and by the scope, character, and quality of the services to be rendered and the relative advantages to be derived through distribution of facilities. These standards established by Congress were to be enforced upon hearing, and evidence, by an administrative body acting under statutory restrictions adapted to the particular activity.

This time Justice Cardozo concurred:

The delegated power of legislation which has found expression in this code is not canalized within banks that keep it from overflowing. It is unconfined and vagrant. . . . Here, in the case before us, is an attempted delegation not confined to any [actions] identified or described by reference to a standard. Here in effect is a roving commission to inquire into evils and upon discovery correct them.

If codes of fair competition are codes eliminating "unfair" methods of competition ascertained upon inquiry to prevail in one industry or another, there is no unlawful delegation of legislative functions when the President is directed to inquire into such practices and denounce them when discovered. For many years a like power has been committed to the Federal Trade Commission with the approval of this court in a long series of decisions. Delegation in such circumstances is born of the necessities of the occasion. The industries of the country are too many and diverse to make it possible for Congress, in respect of matters such as these, to legislate directly with adequate appreciation of varying conditions. . . . But there is another conception of codes of fair competition, [by which] a code is not to be restricted to the elimination of business practices that would be characterized by general acceptation as oppressive or unfair. It is to include whatever ordinances may be desirable or helpful for the well-being or prosperity of the industry affected. . . . What is fair, as thus conceived, is not something to be contrasted with what is unfair or fraudulent or tricky. The extension becomes as wide as the field of industrial regulation. If that conception shall prevail, anything that Congress may do within the limits of the Commerce Clause for the betterment of business may be done by the President upon the recommendation of a trade association by calling it a code. This is delegation running riot. No such plenitude of power is susceptible of transfer. The statute, however, aims at nothing less, as one can learn both from its terms and from the administrative practice under it. Nothing less is aimed at by the code now submitted to our scrutiny.

These two cases certainly did not bow to the governmental exigencies created by the Great Depression. The Court has often upheld broad delegations of power to the President in wartime (*see, e.g.,* BELKNAP, *supra*). Is there to be no way for Congress to grant peacetime emergency powers even when, in contrast to *Youngstown*, it wants to do so? This last question suggests the extent to which *Schechter Poultry* is inconsistent with the rest of the case law that you will see in this book. For example, compare a decision the next year — *United States v. Curtiss-Wright Export Corp.*, 299 U.S. 304 (1936) (excerpted in Chapter Five), in which the Court upheld a delegation of power to the President to prohibit arms sales to countries engaged in armed conflict in South America. The Court said that legislation in "the international field must often accord to the President a degree of discretion and freedom from statutory restriction which would not be admissible were domestic affairs alone involved." Might not the same be said for the difference between domestic emergencies and ordinary times?

In *Schechter Poultry*, notice the Court's emphasis on fair procedure to distinguish this delegation from other broad ones that it had approved. Is that a real distinction, or just a makeweight? Isn't the underlying concern of the delegation doctrine with congressional control of *substance*, and isn't fair procedure an independent requirement of due process or administrative law? In any event, the chaotic administration of the NRA certainly seemed to take its toll on the government's chances in *Schechter Poultry*. Congress later enacted a comprehensive code of federal administrative procedure, in the Administrative Procedure Act (APA) of 1946, 5 U.S.C. § 551 *et seq.* We will encounter the APA repeatedly in these materials.

Another major challenge to an economic control program involved World War II price controls, administered by the Office of Price Administration (OPA). This time the Supreme Court upheld the statute, in an opinion by Chief Justice Stone in *Yakus v. United States*, 321 U.S. 414 (1944):

> That Congress has constitutional authority to prescribe commodity prices as a war emergency measure, and that the Act was adopted by Congress in the exercise of that power, are not questioned here. . . .
>
> Congress enacted the Emergency Price Control Act in pursuance of a defined policy and required that the prices fixed by the Administrator should further that policy and conform to standards prescribed by the Act. The boundaries of the field of the Administrator's permissible action are marked by the statute. It directs that the prices fixed shall effectuate the declared policy of the Act to stabilize commodity prices so as to prevent wartime inflation and its enumerated disruptive causes and effects. In addition the prices established must be fair and equitable, and in fixing them the Administrator is directed to give due consideration, so far as practicable, to prevailing prices during the designated base period, with prescribed administrative adjustments to compensate for enumerated disturbing factors affecting prices. . . .
>
> The Act is unlike the National Industrial Recovery Act considered in *Schechter Poultry Corp. v. United States*, which proclaimed in the broadest terms its purpose "to rehabilitate industry and to conserve natural resources." It prescribed no method of attaining that end save by the establishment of codes of fair competition, the nature of whose permissible provisions was left undefined. It provided no standards to which those codes were to conform. The function of formulating the codes was delegated, not to a public official responsible to Congress or the Executive, but to private individuals engaged in the industries to be regulated. . . .
>
> Acting within its constitutional power to fix prices it is for Congress to say whether the data on the basis of which prices are to be fixed are to be confined within a narrow or a broad range. In either case the only concern of courts is to ascertain whether the will of Congress has been obeyed. This depends not upon the breadth of the definition of the facts or conditions which the administrative officer is to find but upon the determination whether the definition sufficiently marks the field within which the Administrator is to

act so that it may be known whether he has kept within it in compliance with the legislative will. . . . Only if we could say that there is an absence of standards for the guidance of the Administrator's action, so that it would be impossible in a proper proceeding to ascertain whether the will of Congress has been obeyed, would we be justified in overriding its choice of means for effecting its declared purpose of preventing inflation. The standards prescribed by the present Act, with the aid of the "statement of the considerations" required to be made by the Administrator, are sufficiently definite and precise to enable Congress, the courts and the public to ascertain whether the Administrator, in fixing the designated prices, has conformed to those standards. . . .

In *Yakus*, the Court mentioned congressional war powers as a basis for the statute. Yet did the Court's analysis and outcome seem to place any real reliance on the war powers? *Yakus* now counterbalances *Schechter Poultry*. Indeed, *Yakus* initiated a string of decisions rejecting delegation doctrine challenges to domestic legislation that has continued unbroken to the present.

Examining these decisions, Justice Antonin Scalia, himself a former professor of administrative law, offered an explanation of the weakness of the delegation doctrine in a dissenting opinion in *Mistretta v. United States*, 488 U.S. 361, 388 (1989):

> [W]hile the doctrine of unconstitutional delegation is unquestionably a fundamental element of our constitutional system, it is not an element readily enforceable by the courts. Once it is conceded, as it must be, that no statute can be entirely precise, and that some judgments, even some judgments involving policy considerations, must be left to the officers executing the law and to the judges applying it, the debate over unconstitutional delegation becomes a debate not over a point of principle but over a question of degree. As Chief Justice Taft expressed the point for the Court in the landmark case of *J. W. Hampton, Jr., & Co. v. United States*, the limits of delegation "must be fixed according to common sense and the inherent necessities of the governmental co-ordination." Since Congress is no less endowed with common sense than we are, and better equipped to inform itself of the "necessities" of government; and since the factors bearing upon those necessities are both multifarious and (in the nonpartisan sense) highly political — including, for example, whether the Nation is at war, or whether for other reasons "emergency is instinct in the situation," it is small wonder that we have almost never felt qualified to second-guess Congress regarding the permissible degree of policy judgment that can be left to those executing or applying the law. As the Court points out, we have invoked the doctrine of unconstitutional delegation to invalidate a law only twice in our history, over half a century ago. What legislated standard, one must wonder, can possibly be too vague to survive judicial scrutiny, when we have repeatedly upheld, in various contexts, a "public interest" standard?

Note: Finding an "Intelligible Principle" in Vague Statutory Text

Justice Scalia's analysis in *Mistretta* asks a critical question: should the Court ever find that statutory text lacks any intelligible principle and is therefore invalid? The extraordinary financial crisis of 2008 gave rise to an example of this problem. In September of 2008, with major financial firms failing and securities markets in crisis, President Bush's Treasury Secretary, Henry Paulson, submitted a short draft bill to Congress to address the crisis. After a quick congressional touchup, Congress enacted the Economic Emergency Stabilization Act of 2008, which provided, in part, that the Secretary of the Treasury was authorized "to establish the Troubled Asset Relief Program (or "TARP") to purchase, and to make and fund commitments to purchase, troubled assets from any financial institution, on such terms and conditions as are determined by the Secretary, and in accordance with this Act and the policies and procedures developed and published by the Secretary." Pub. L. 110-343, § 101, 110th Cong., 2d Sess. (2008). TARP authorized purchases of up to $700 billion in assets. Plainly this was a sweeping delegation of power to meet a rapidly evolving crisis. Paulson actually used much of the initial appropriation to buy stock in financial intermediaries rather than to buy their troubled assets, and the Bush Administration construed "financial institutions" broadly enough in December 2008, to include General Motors and Chrysler. If a plaintiff with standing (who would that be?) had challenged TARP in court, should the Supreme Court have found an "intelligible principle" in it? How should the Court have gone about making that determination?

Since the Court has not invalidated a Congressional delegation for over a half century, it should be obvious to you that some broad, and even careless, standards have survived. Why do you think the federal courts usually strain so hard to find a sufficient standard instead of following the lead of the New Deal cases and voiding broad delegations so that Congress must resolve fundamental policy issues? While considering the TARP problem, note a response once offered by the Supreme Court in the process of approving a broad delegation to the Secretary of the Interior to apportion the water of the Colorado River, in *Arizona v. California*, 373 U.S. 546 (1963). The Court remarked that if the Secretary abused his broad powers, Congress could alter them by amending the statute. Is that an adequate control on broadly delegated powers, considering the length of Congress's agenda and the usual difficulty of statutory revision? Does your answer change when the delegate is the President himself, in view of the likelihood that he will veto any restriction of previously granted powers? Consider this question in connection with the materials on presidential veto powers that appear later in this chapter.

Although the standards requirement is not vigorously enforced by the courts, a number of issues concerning it remain. In *Touby v. United States*, 500 U.S. 160 (1991), the Court upheld the power of the Attorney General temporarily to designate a drug as a controlled substance (possession of which is a crime), pending further administrative processes that would produce permanent designation. The Court conceded that some of its cases could be read to say that more specific standards are necessary for regulations carrying criminal sanctions than for other delegations of power. It was not necessary to resolve the issue, however, because the statute met any heightened specificity requirement. Do you think the Court *should* require more specific standards for such delegations? If so, how strict should courts be?

Perhaps some subject matter is entirely nondelegable, no matter what the specificity of accompanying standards. Could Congress create an Impeachment Commission and authorize it to exercise that power? See James Freedman, Crisis and Legitimacy: The Administrative Process and American Government 80–86 (1978).

Skinner v. Mid-America Pipeline Co., 490 U.S. 212 (1989), involved a statute authorizing the Secretary of Transportation to establish user fees to recover the costs of administering pipeline safety programs. The company challenged the statute as an unconstitutional delegation of the power to tax. (In *National Cable Television Ass'n v. United States*, 415 U.S. 336 (1974), the Court had suggested the viability of such an argument.) The company argued for a heightened standards requirement, urging that the Framers required taxes to originate in the House of Representatives in order to keep close political accountability over the decision to impose them. The Court noted that Congress often legislates taxes "with remarkable specificity," but refused to recognize a special constitutional duty to do so. The Court was aware of the difficulty of administering a special rule for "taxes," due to the problem of distinguishing them from fees or from the cost burdens of ordinary regulation.

Does the identity of a particular delegate matter to the constitutional analysis? In a very curious decision, the Court once suggested that how power is distributed *within* the executive branch might receive constitutional scrutiny. In *Hampton v. Mow Sun Wong*, 426 U.S. 88 (1976), the Court invalidated a Civil Service rule excluding aliens from federal employment. Although the Court relied on due process, not the delegation doctrine, Justice Stevens' rationale had delegation overtones. He argued that proffered justifications for the restriction, such as to encourage naturalization, were remote from Civil Service responsibilities. He admitted that both Congress and the President had apparently acquiesced in the rule. Nevertheless, he concluded that, if Congress or the President had imposed the restriction directly, such justifications might be credited, but not when the Government's personnel office formulated the rule. Do Congress and the President then have a duty to allocate decisions within the executive according to subject matter expertise?

In *Touby*, objection was made to allowing the Attorney General to designate illegal drugs:

> Petitioners concede that Congress may legitimately authorize someone in the Executive Branch to schedule drugs temporarily, but argue that it must be someone other than the Attorney General because he wields the power to prosecute crimes. They insist that allowing the Attorney General both to schedule a particular drug and to prosecute those who manufacture that drug violates the principle of separation of powers. . . . This argument has no

basis in our separation-of-powers jurisprudence. The principle of separation of powers focuses on the distribution of powers *among* the three coequal Branches; it does not speak to the manner in which authority is parceled out within a single Branch.

Is *Touby* a better candidate for extending separation of powers analysis than *Mow Sun Wong* was, because of the presence of conflict of interest problems? Is the earlier case still good law?

Although delegation disputes typically involve the allocation of authority between Congress and the executive, one scholar has argued that Congress undermines the executive when it relies on persons who are not federal officers to implement the laws—state officials, private experts, producer groups, and other private citizens. *See* Harold J. Krent, *Fragmenting the Unitary Executive: Congressional Delegations of Administrative Authority Outside the Federal Government*, 85 Nw. L. Rev. 62 (1990); *but see* Neil Kinkopf, *Of Devolution, Privatization, and Globalization: Separation of Powers Limits on Congressional Authority to Assign Power to Non-Federal Actors*, 50 Rut. L. Rev. 331 (1998). Given the expanding role of "cooperative federalism" and privatization as techniques for the implementation of federal government goals, this is a concern with potentially broad implications.

The Supreme Court's most recent major delegation case is *Whitman v. American Trucking Ass'ns, Inc.*, 531 U.S. 457 (2001). A court of appeals had invalidated § 109(b)(1) of the Clean Air Act, which requires the Environmental Protection Agency to set air quality standards which, "allowing an adequate margin of safety, are requisite to protect the public health." Writing for the Court, Justice Scalia agreed with the court of appeals that the statute forbade EPA to consider cost in setting the standards—the delegation was indeed a broad one. Nevertheless, the Court unanimously upheld it. As a preliminary matter, the Court rejected an argument that the EPA could cure an overbroad delegation by adopting a limiting construction of the statute: "Whether the statute delegates legislative power is a question for the courts, and an agency's voluntary self-denial has no bearing on the answer." After reviewing its precedents, the Court concluded that the challenged delegation "fits comfortably within the scope of discretion permitted" by them.

Scholars, inspecting *American Trucking* in the rear-view mirror, have come to various conclusions. Here is a sampling: 1) There is really no such thing as a constitutional nondelegation principle, Eric A. Posner & Adrian Vermeule, *Interring the Nondelegation Principle*, 69 U. Chi. L. Rev. 1721 (2002). 2) There is, but the courts are not going to enforce it, Gary Lawson, *Delegation and Original Meaning*, 88 Va. L. Rev. 327 (2002). 3) The doctrine has an indirect effect, causing courts to adopt narrowing constructions of statutes to avoid invalidating them, Cass R. Sunstein, *Nondelegation Canons*, 67 U. Chi. L. Rev. 315 (2000); John F. Manning, *The Nondelegation Doctrine as a Canon of Avoidance*, 2000 Sup. Ct. Rev. 223. 4) The courts don't really do that. David M. Driesen, *Loose Canons: Statutory Construction and the New Nondelegation Doctrine*, 64 U. Pitt. L. Rev. 1 (2002). 5) Courts should turn to the protections against arbitrariness that administrative law offers in order to control agencies. Lisa Schultz Bressman, *Disciplining Delegations After* Whitman v. American Trucking Ass'ns, 87 Corn. L. Rev. 452 (2002).

Another oblique use of the doctrine is illustrated by *Zemel v. Rusk*, 381 U.S. 1 (1965). In approving restrictions on travel to Cuba, the Court adopted standards that it found in administrative practice—it held that the Act authorized "only those ... restrictions which it could fairly be argued were adopted by Congress in light of prior administrative practice." In a subsequent case, *Haig v. Agee*, 453 U.S. 280 (1981), excerpted in Chapter Five, the *Zemel* technique appeared again, amid a spirited dispute on the Court over whether the administrative practice in question was "sufficiently substantial and consistent" to warrant the conclusion that Congress had approved it. Hence, even if *American Trucking* forbids agencies to cure overbroad statutes themselves, they can offer a limiting construction for judicial adoption.

Some scholars, undeterred by the Supreme Court's continuing unresponsiveness, have continued to urge enforcement of the delegation doctrine. David Schoenbrod, Power Without Responsibility: How Congress Abuses the People Through Delegation (1993); Peter Aranson, Ernest Gellhorn & Glen O. Robinson, *A Theory of Delegation*, 68 Cornell L. Rev. 1 (1982). A leading proponent of reviving the delegation doctrine is Theodore Lowi. A representative sample of his views is The End of Liberalism: Ideology, Policy, and the Crisis of Public Authority 298–99 (1969), in which he indicts what he characterizes as "interest group liberalism," that is the distribution of positive Government power among interest groups to the detriment of the general public interest and the "rule of law":

> Restoration of the *Schechter* rule would be dramatic because it would mean return to the practice of occasional Supreme Court invalidation of congressional acts. Nothing is more dramatic than the confrontation of these two jealous Branches, the more so due to its infrequent occurrence in recent years. But there is no reason to fear judicial usurpation. Under present conditions, when Congress delegates without a shred of guidance, the courts usually end up rewriting many of the statutes in the course of "construction." Since the Court's present procedure is always to try to find an acceptable meaning of a statute in order to avoid invalidating it, the Court is legislating constantly. A blanket invalidation under the *Schechter* rule is a Court order for Congress to do its own work. Therefore the rule of law is a restraint upon rather than an expansion of the judicial function.
>
> There is also no reason to fear reduction of government power as a result of serious application of the *Schechter* rule. ... Historically, rule of law, especially statute law, is the essence of positive government. A bureaucracy in the service of a strong and clear statute is more effective than ever. Granted, the rule-of-law requirement is likely to make more difficult the framing and passage of some policies. But why should any program be acceptable if the partisans cannot fairly clearly state purpose and means?

For critiques of the doctrine's utility, see Jerry L. Mashaw, *Prodelegation: Why Administrators Should Make Political Decisions*, 1 J.L. ECON. & ORG. 81 (1985); Harold H. Bruff, *Judicial Review and the President's Statutory Powers*, 68 VA. L. REV. 1, 25–29 (1982). Bruff argues:

> In general, . . . the delegation doctrine's present utility as a meaningful restraint on Congress is low. . . . Reviving the doctrine for statutes delegating power to the President would be unwise, however. Some of the reasons for this conclusion are relevant whether the delegation is to the President or to an agency. The courts are properly reluctant to employ the doctrine vigorously, in part because it involves a constitutional decision that overrides a congressional judgment regarding the amount of discretion that should be accorded the executive in a particular context. Moreover, the doctrine may foster judicial subjectivity, because no one has articulated neutral principles for deciding how specific a particular delegation should have to be. Finally, invocation of the doctrine to invalidate a statute invites a judicial confrontation with Congress, which may be unwilling or unable to articulate precise standards. In short, the delegation doctrine, which was designed to help maintain the separation of powers between Congress and the executive, fails because it requires courts to assume a role that they sense oversteps separation of powers limits on their own relationship with Congress.
>
> A revived delegation doctrine would create special problems were courts to apply it to statutes granting power to the President. First, broad delegations to the President are often entirely appropriate or even necessary—his emergency statutory powers are an obvious example. Indeed, where the President has independent constitutional powers, as in foreign affairs, Congress may doubt its authority to bind him closely. Moreover, the accountability concerns at the center of the delegation doctrine are partially met when a grant of power is to the President himself, with his direct political responsibility. Although the doctrine's purpose of keeping policymaking in *Congress* is not met, at least delegations to the President do not transfer responsibility to an appointed bureaucrat. Furthermore, the ultimate power to intervene to correct overenthusiastic presidential initiatives remains with Congress.
>
> It is possible to make too much of this point, however. The Constitution's checks on the legislative process are weakened if Congress may delegate power without restriction. The effect is to shift the burden of overcoming institutional inertia from the initial formation of policy through legislation to the generation of legislation to override a presidential initiative. Notwithstanding Congress's assent to it, this effect is deleterious to the policymaking process that the Constitution envisions. The Framers designed their checks on the legislative process not only to control Congress but also to minimize the amount of lawmaking to which the public would be subjected. By transferring broad authority to the executive, which has fewer

internal impediments to forming decisions, Congress increases the amount of lawmaking that is likely to occur.

Nevertheless, the courts can do no more than to hold the delegation doctrine in reserve in case of a particularly egregious congressional abdication of power to the President, and to [take] into account all available controls on executive discretion. Among these controls is statutory interpretation, a judicial function that is made both more important and more difficult to exercise by the delegation doctrine's failure to provide an effective means to force Congress to set policy standards for executive action.

2. Allocating Adjudicative Power Outside the Judiciary

Congressional allocations of adjudicative power, like those of other governmental powers, have spawned a separation of powers jurisprudence. The ultimate issues are profound and difficult; the case law is notoriously confused—and confusing. For comprehensive analyses of the issues treated briefly in this section, see Richard H. Fallon, *Of Legislative Courts, Administrative Agencies, and Article III*, 101 HARV. L. REV. 915 (1988); Gordon Young, *Public Rights and the Federal Judicial Power: From* Murray's Lessee *Through* Crowell *to* Schor, 35 BUFF. L. REV. 765 (1987); the classic exploration remains Henry M. Hart, Jr., *The Power of Congress to Limit the Jurisdiction of the Federal Courts: An Exercise in Dialectic*, 66 HARV. L. REV. 1362 (1953).

Article III creates the "judicial Power of the United States," but the federal courts have never been its sole repository. For example, state courts have always decided federal questions and cases within federal diversity jurisdiction. Even within the federal government, no obvious theory underlies the distribution of adjudicative business among the available fora. The catalogue includes article III courts, article III adjuncts (such as bankruptcy courts), "legislative" courts (such as the Tax Court), and administrative agencies.

Executive branch agencies in particular adjudicate vast numbers of controversies that could have been placed in the federal courts, for example Social Security disability determinations. If the federal courts had been assigned these cases, a greatly enlarged judiciary and an equally shrunken executive would have resulted. Moreover, some functionally adjudicative activities are "executive" in either of two constitutional senses—that they *may* be vested in the executive, or that they *may not* be transferred to the courts. Examples of the former category early appeared, when the first Congress enacted statutes vesting determinations of veterans' benefits and customs duties in executive officers. Examples of the latter category are the President's exercise of law-applying judgments pursuant to responsibilities conferred on him by the Constitution or by some statutes.

The underlying problem is that law-applying judgments can be described as either executive or judicial, since both branches perform them every day. Indeed, prior to the writings of Montesquieu, it had been common to regard judicial power as embraced within the executive "magisterial" power. Plainly, a simple formalist distinction will not suffice for separation of powers purposes. Chief Justice Marshall perceived this point:

> That [a Treasury officer's setting of the amount of a duty] may be, in an enlarged sense, a judicial act, must be admitted. . . . In this sense the act of the President in calling out the militia under [a statute] or of a commissioner who makes a certificate for the extradition of a criminal, under a treaty, is judicial. *Ex parte Randolph*, 20 F. Cas. 242, 254 (C.C.D. Va. 1833) (No. 11,558).

Marshall's awareness of the lack of a clear test for allocating adjudicative functions may explain his creation of a theory of legislative courts in *American Insurance Co. v. Canter*, 26 U.S. (1 Pet.) 511 (1828). The Court held that the establishment of Florida's territorial court, whose judges had four-year terms, was a valid exercise of the legislative powers of Congress. Notwithstanding strong criticism of Marshall's sweeping rationale, the idea that Congress can rely on its article I powers to create adjudicative bodies has endured. Indeed, if executive bodies having few or none of the traditional tenure and process safeguards of the courts may adjudicate, why not allow closer approximations? The problem, then, is one of limits.

The Supreme Court has struggled to identify adjudicative functions that *must* remain in federal courts, those that *may* be placed in the executive, and those that *must* be placed in the executive. *Crowell v. Benson*, 285 U.S. 22 (1932), initially established the constitutionality of delegating adjudicative power to administrative agencies. Congress had created a workers' compensation scheme for longshoremen and had authorized an agency to decide claims under procedures resembling those later codified in the Administrative Procedure Act (APA). The Court rejected a due process assault on administrative fact-finding, because judicial review could assure the presence of substantial evidence for the award. Article III did not require that the subject matter, which was within the federal judicial power, be allocated to the courts. It sufficed that reviewing courts retained power to decide issues of law.

The *Crowell* Court did hold, however, that courts must perform independent review of issues of "constitutional" or "jurisdictional" fact that determined the power of the agency over the dispute, such as whether an accident had occurred on navigable waters. Here the Court invoked earlier cases that have not been followed in recent years, but that have never been overruled. In *Ohio Valley Water Co. v. Ben Avon Borough*, 253 U.S. 287 (1920), the Court had held that *de novo* judicial review must be applied to the facts underlying a claim that rate regulation was "confiscatory" because it did not allow a reasonable rate of return and was therefore a taking of property without just compensation. *See also St. Joseph Stock Yards Co. v. United States,* 298 U.S. 38 (1936). In *Ng Fung Ho v. White*, 259 U.S. 276 (1922), individuals facing deportation argued that they were citizens and therefore not deportable. The Court held that deportation could not occur without a *de novo* determination of the "essential jurisdictional fact" of citizenship.

The requirement for *de novo* review of "constitutional facts" and "jurisdictional facts" met withering criticism, and the Court seems quietly to have dropped it. Both the misguided impulses that originally accounted for these requirements and the reasons for abandoning them seem easy enough to understand today. The cases arose from perceptions that only traditional judicial processes could be trusted with the resolution of constitutional issues, and that agencies should not be allowed to decide issues on which their very power to act depended. Now that agency adjudication is regularized under the APA, and now that courts have evolved ways of extending limited but still meaningful review to agency fact determinations, no strong reason remains for the courts to bear the burdens of *de novo* review. Moreover, there are powerful reasons *not* to engage in unrestrained review. Resolving fact issues is often at the heart of the policymaking discretion that Congress creates agencies to exercise.

Matters long thought settled by *Crowell* were cast into doubt by the Court's decision in *Northern Pipeline Construction Co. v. Marathon Pipe Line Co.*, 458 U.S. 50 (1982). A statute authorized bankruptcy judges to decide all issues pertinent to proceedings in their courts — including claims arising under state law — with review by article III judges. (The bankruptcy judges lacked life tenure or salary protection, but had powers closely resembling those of federal judges.) A badly divided Court held that the bankruptcy judges' authority to decide state-law claims violated article III. A plurality of four justices signed a formalist opinion that defined some matters as inherently judicial in the sense that federal courts must decide them in the first instance rather than supervise them through appellate review. Existing exceptions to mandatory article III jurisdiction failed to include bankruptcy matters. The exception that is pertinent here concerned "public rights." The plurality defined public rights narrowly, as claims against government but not controversies between private persons arising incident to a federal program. Thus, the dichotomy between public and private rights appeared to flow from the concept of sovereign immunity. Congress, free to deny all relief for claims against the government, could take the lesser step of allocating the claims to an alternative forum. By refusing to define public rights to include controversies between private persons that were regulated pursuant to the substantive powers of Congress, the plurality cast doubt on the holding of *Crowell*.

Two concurring justices took the more limited position that state-law claims removed from a state tribunal must go to an article III court. The three dissenters pointed out the inconsistency of the plurality's formulation with the ordinary pattern of administrative adjudication. They thought that the bankruptcy scheme satisfied a functional inquiry, which entailed examining the strength of congressional interests in placing decision-making authority in another forum. Moreover, they emphasized the statute's preservation of judicial review and found no danger of aggrandizement by the other branches at the expense of the courts as long as the subject matter was not especially significant to the political branches.

The use of the public rights doctrine, which the Court has never explained coherently, originated in a conclusory passage in *Murray's Lessee v. Hoboken Land & Improvement Co.*, 59 U.S. (18 How.) 272, 284 (1856), in which the Court upheld a summary procedure for the government to recoup funds from one of its customs collectors:

> [W]e do not consider Congress can either withdraw from judicial cognizance any matter which, from its nature, is the subject of a suit at the common law, or in equity, or admiralty; nor, on the other hand, can it bring under the judicial power a matter which, from its nature, is not a subject for judicial determination. At the same time there are matters, involving public rights, which may be presented in such form that the judicial power is capable of acting on them, and which are susceptible of judicial determination, but which Congress may or may not bring within the cognizance of the courts of the United States, as it may deem proper.

Northern Pipeline demonstrates that formalism's broad sweep is inappropriate for allocations of adjudicative power among the branches, especially when it is stated in terms of the unhelpful "public rights" doctrine. Agencies have often been created to obtain speedy and informal adjudication by a fact finder with expertise in the subject matter. By shunting fact-intensive adjudications to agencies, Congress frees the federal courts to carry out their central responsibilities of interpreting the Constitution and statutes.

Hence, some later cases have curtailed the implications of *Northern Pipeline*. *See Thomas v. Union Carbide Agricultural Products Co.*, 473 U.S. 568, 594 (1985), in which the Court upheld mandatory arbitration requirements in a federal pesticide regulation program. It concluded that Congress could authorize an agency to "allocate costs and benefits among voluntary participants" in a regulatory program without providing an article III adjudication. Justice O'Connor interpreted *Northern Pipeline* as holding only that Congress could not give a non-article III court power to decide state-law contract actions without the litigant's consent and subject only to ordinary appellate review. *See* Harold H. Bruff, *Public Programs, Private Deciders: The Constitutionality of Arbitration in Federal Programs*, 67 TEX. L. REV. 441 (1989); *Constitutional Limits on Federal Government Participation in Binding Arbitration*, 19 OP. O.L.C. 208 (1995).

Although some of the language in Justice O'Connor's opinion in *Thomas* suggests that article III courts must hear all common-law claims, the Court has since modified its stance. In *Commodity Futures Trading Commission v. Schor*, 478 U.S. 833 (1986), the Court upheld the authority of the Commodity Futures Trading Commission (CFTC) to entertain state-law counterclaims in reparation proceedings, in which disgruntled customers seek redress for brokers' violations of statutes or regulations. The Commodity Exchange Act authorized CFTC adjudicators to decide counterclaims arising out of transactions properly alleged in a complaint. Schor filed a claim for reparations, and the defendants counterclaimed for debt. Justice O'Connor's opinion for seven Justices relied in part on consent—Schor chose the CFTC's "prompt" and "inexpensive" procedure instead of a lawsuit. The Court also performed a more general analysis of the requisites of article III:

Schor claims that . . . [Congress may not authorize] the initial adjudication of common law counterclaims by the CFTC, an administrative agency whose adjudicatory officers do not enjoy the tenure and salary protections embodied in Article III. . . . [T]he constitutionality of a given congressional delegation of adjudicative functions to a non-Article III body must be assessed by reference to the purposes underlying the requirements of Article III. This inquiry, in turn, is guided by the principle that "practical attention to substance rather than doctrinaire reliance on formal categories should inform application of Article III." *Thomas.* Article III, § 1, serves both to protect "the role of the independent judiciary within the constitutional scheme of tripartite government," and to safeguard litigants' "right to have claims decided before judges who are free from potential domination by other branches of government." . . . [O]ur prior discussions of Article III, § 1's guarantee of an independent and impartial adjudication by the federal judiciary of matters within the judicial power of the United States intimated that this guarantee serves to protect primarily personal, rather than structural, interests. Our precedents also demonstrate, however, that Article III does not confer on litigants an absolute right to the plenary consideration of every nature of claim by an Article III court. Moreover, as a personal right, Article III's guarantee of an impartial and independent federal adjudication is subject to waiver, just as are other personal constitutional rights that dictate the procedures by which civil and criminal matters must be tried. . . .

[O]ur precedents establish that Article III, § 1, not only preserves to litigants their interest in an impartial and independent federal adjudication of claims within the judicial power of the United States, but also serves as "an inseparable element of the constitutional system of checks and balances." *Northern Pipeline.* Article III, § 1 safeguards the role of the Judicial Branch in our tripartite system by barring congressional attempts "to transfer jurisdiction [to non-Article III tribunals] for the purpose of emasculating" constitutional courts, *National Insurance Co. v. Tidewater Co.*, 337 U.S. 582, 644 (1949) (Vinson, C.J., dissenting), and thereby preventing "the encroachment or aggrandizement of one branch at the expense of the other." . . . [T]he parties cannot by consent cure the constitutional difficulty for the same reason that the parties by consent cannot confer on federal courts subject-matter jurisdiction beyond the limitations imposed by Article III, § 2. When these Article III limitations are at issue, notions of consent and waiver cannot be dispositive because the limitations serve institutional interests that the parties cannot be expected to protect.

In determining the extent to which a given congressional decision to authorize the adjudication of Article III business in a non-Article III tribunal impermissibly threatens the institutional integrity of the Judicial Branch, the Court has declined to adopt formalistic and unbending rules, [which might] . . . unduly constrict Congress' ability to take needed and innovative action pursuant to its Article I powers. . . . Among the factors upon which we have focused are the extent to which the "essential attributes of judicial power" are reserved to Article III courts, and, conversely, the extent to which the non-Article III forum exercises the range of jurisdiction and powers normally vested only in Article III courts, the origins and importance of the right to be adjudicated, and the concerns that drove Congress to depart from the requirements of Article III.

An examination of the relative allocation of powers between the CFTC and Article III courts . . . demonstrates that the congressional scheme does not impermissibly intrude on the province of the judiciary. The CFTC's adjudicatory powers depart from the traditional agency model in just one respect: the CFTC's jurisdiction over common law counterclaims. While wholesale importation of concepts of pendent or ancillary jurisdiction into the agency context may create greater constitutional difficulties, we decline to endorse an absolute prohibition on such jurisdiction out of fear of where some hypothetical "slippery slope" may deposit us. . . . In the instant cases, . . . the CEA leaves far more of the "essential attributes of judicial power" to Article III courts than did that portion of the Bankruptcy Act found unconstitutional in *Northern Pipeline*. The CEA scheme in fact hews closely to the agency model approved by the Court in *Crowell v. Benson*. The CFTC, like the agency in *Crowell*, deals only with a "particularized area of law," whereas the jurisdiction of the bankruptcy courts found unconstitutional in *Northern Pipeline* extended to broadly "all civil proceedings arising under title 11 or arising in or related to cases under title 11." CFTC orders, like those of the agency in *Crowell*, but unlike those of the bankruptcy courts under the 1978 Act, are enforceable only by order of the district court. . . . Finally, the CFTC, unlike the bankruptcy courts under the 1978 Act, does not exercise "all ordinary powers of district courts," and thus may not, for instance, preside over jury trials or issue writs of habeas corpus. . . .

We have explained that "the public rights doctrine reflects simply a pragmatic understanding that when Congress selects a quasi-judicial method of resolving matters that 'could be conclusively determined by the Executive and Legislative Branches,' the danger of encroaching on the judicial powers is less than when private rights, which are normally within the purview of the judiciary, are relegated as an initial matter to administrative adjudication." . . . Accordingly, where private, common law rights are at stake, our examination of the congressional attempt to control the manner in which those rights are adjudicated has been searching. In this litigation, however, . . . we are persuaded that the congressional authorization of limited CFTC jurisdiction over a narrow class of common law claims as an incident to the CFTC's primary, and unchallenged, adjudicative function does not create a substantial threat to the separation of powers. . . . Congress may make available a quasi-judicial mechanism through which willing parties may, at their option, elect to resolve their differences.

This is not to say, of course, that if Congress created a phalanx of non-Article III tribunals equipped to handle the entire business of the Article III courts without any Article III supervision or control and without evidence of valid and specific legislative necessities, the fact that the parties had the election to proceed in their forum of choice would necessarily save the scheme from constitutional attack. . . . [But w]hen Congress authorized the CFTC to adjudicate counterclaims, its primary focus was on making effective a specific and limited federal regulatory scheme, not on allocating jurisdiction among federal tribunals. . . . [T]his case raises no question of the aggrandizement of congressional power at the expense of a coordinate branch. Instead, the separation of powers question presented in this litigation is whether Congress impermissibly undermined, without appreciable expansion of its own power, the role of the Judicial Branch. . . . We conclude that the limited jurisdiction that the CFTC asserts over state law claims as a necessary incident to the adjudication of federal claims willingly submitted by the parties for initial agency adjudication does not contravene separation of powers principles or Article III.

Justices Brennan and Marshall, dissenting, argued that the majority was allowing the undue dilution of judicial authority in service of legislative convenience.

In both *Thomas* and *Schor,* the Court thought the challenged schemes were consistent with the original purpose of article III's protections: to guarantee the independence of adjudication from political pressure emanating from the executive or Congress. In *Thomas,* the Court remarked that shifting from agency adjudicators to private arbitrators "surely does not diminish the likelihood of impartial decision-making, free from political influence." Similarly, in *Schor* it noted that Congress had placed adjudication in an independent agency, which would be "relatively immune from the 'political winds that sweep Washington.'"

In *Granfinanciera, S.A. v. Nordberg,* 492 U.S. 33 (1989), the Court held that a person who had not submitted a claim against a bankruptcy trustee had a right to a jury trial when sued by the trustee to recover an allegedly fraudulent money transfer. Justice Brennan's majority opinion revisited the cases:

[O]ur decisions point to the conclusion that, if a statutory cause of action is legal in nature, the question whether the Seventh Amendment permits Congress to assign its adjudication to a tribunal that does not employ juries as factfinders requires the same answer as the question whether Article III allows Congress to assign adjudication of that cause of action to a non-Article III tribunal. . . . [I]f Congress may assign the adjudication of a statutory cause of action to a non-Article III tribunal, then the Seventh Amendment poses no independent bar to the adjudication of that action by a nonjury factfinder. . . .

[W]e therefore rely on our decisions exploring the restrictions Article III places on Congress' choice of adjudicative bodies to resolve disputes over statutory rights to determine whether petitioners are entitled to a jury trial.

In our most recent discussion of the "public rights" doctrine as it bears on Congress' power to commit adjudication of a statutory cause of action to a non-Article III tribunal, we rejected the view that "a matter of public rights must at a minimum arise 'between the government and others.'" We held, instead, that the Federal Government need not be a party for a case to revolve around "public rights." The crucial question, in cases not involving the Federal Government, is whether "Congress, acting for a valid legislative purpose pursuant to its constitutional powers under Article I, [has] create[d] a seemingly 'private' right that is so closely integrated into a public regulatory scheme as to be a matter appropriate for agency resolution with limited involvement by the Article III judiciary." *Thomas.* If a statutory right is not closely intertwined with a federal regulatory program Congress has power to enact, and if that right neither belongs to nor exists against the Federal Government, then it must be adjudicated by an Article III court. If the right is legal in nature, then it carries with it the Seventh Amendment's guarantee of a jury trial.

The majority went on to conclude that the trustee's claim was not intertwined with a regulatory program as were those in *Schor*; it was a "private right." Therefore, the right to a jury trial attached. Justice Scalia, concurring, questioned the majority's definition of public rights:

> The notion that the power to adjudicate a legal controversy between two private parties may be assigned to a non-Article III, yet federal, tribunal is entirely inconsistent with the origins of the public rights doctrine.... It is clear that what we meant by public rights were not rights important to the public, or rights created by the public, but rights of the public—that is, rights pertaining to claims brought by or against the United States. For central to our reasoning was the device of waiver of sovereign immunity.... I would return to the longstanding principle that the public rights doctrine requires, at a minimum, that the United States be a party to the adjudication.

Dissenting, Justices White, Blackmun, and O'Connor thought that juries were out of place in the integrated scheme of bankruptcy law.

Finally, in *Stern v. Marshall*, 564 U.S. 462 (2011), the Court invalidated a provision of federal bankruptcy law that allowed bankruptcy courts to enter final judgments in common law counterclaims asserted by a debtor in response to claims against an estate. The case involved highly complicated and even lurid facts, not all of which bear repetition here. One Vickie Lynn Marshall (popularly known as Anna Nicole Smith) had filed for bankruptcy protection to avoid liability in a case in which she had defaulted. Eventually she counterclaimed for damages against her own former stepson, on grounds of tortious interference with a large gift from her late husband. The Bankruptcy Court entered judgment in her favor for over $400 million. When the case reached the Supreme Court (for the second time), the Court held that Ms. Marshall's counterclaim did not satisfy the requirements for agency adjudication set forth in *CFTC v. Schor*. Chief Justice Roberts wrote a majority opinion summarizing the state of the law:

> Shortly after *Northern Pipeline*, the Court rejected the limitation of the public rights exception to actions involving the Government as a party. The Court has continued, however, to limit the exception to cases in which the claim at issue derives from a federal regulatory scheme, or in which resolution of the claim by an expert government agency is deemed essential to a limited regulatory objective within the agency's authority. In other words, it is still the case that what makes a right "public" rather than private is that the right is integrally related to particular federal government action.
>
> *Schor* concerned a statutory scheme that created a procedure for customers injured by a broker's violation of the federal commodities law to seek reparations from the broker before the Commodity Futures Trading Commission (CFTC). A customer filed such a claim to recover a debit balance in his account, while the broker filed a lawsuit in Federal District Court to recover the same amount as lawfully due from the customer. The broker later submitted its claim to the CFTC, but after that agency ruled against the customer, the customer argued that agency jurisdiction over the broker's counterclaim violated Article III. This Court disagreed, but only after observing that (1) the claim and the counterclaim concerned a "single dispute"—the same account balance; (2) the CFTC's assertion of authority involved only "a narrow class of common law claims" in a " 'particularized area of law' "; (3) the area of law in question was governed by "a specific and limited federal regulatory scheme" as to which the agency had "obvious expertise"; (4) the parties had freely elected to resolve their differences before the CFTC; and (5) CFTC orders were "enforceable only by order of the district court." Most significantly, given that the customer's reparations claim before the agency and the broker's counterclaim were competing claims to the same amount, the Court repeatedly emphasized that it was "necessary" to allow the agency to exercise jurisdiction over the broker's claim, or else "the reparations procedure would have been confounded."

Hence the jurisprudence of article III remains in flux. Do you see any way to provide it some certainty without either dismantling the administrative state or granting Congress a free hand?

C. Fundamental Checks and Balances

We conclude our introductory tour of the separation of powers landscape with a review of three of the most basic checks and balances in the system. All of these will hover in the background—or emerge into the foreground—in many of the controversies covered in this book. The first two, the President's veto and Congress's power of the purse, initially seem to be ways for each of the two branches to ignore the other's needs and desires, while asserting its fundamental power to veto legislation or to refuse funding. Yet we may find that more often, these checks and balances knit the two branches together in mutual dependency. (The veto brings Congress to the President; the power of the purse brings the President to Congress.)

The third topic is perhaps the most fundamental check of all—the ever-present opportunity for those dissatisfied with the behavior of one of the branches to seek amendment of the Constitution. We will look briefly at the amendment process and its many imponderables.

1. Veto Powers

In this section we consider veto powers of various sorts. First, we explore the President's conditional power to veto legislation, and pause to note related powers to initiate and press legislation within Congress. Then we introduce a special form of the presidential veto: the pocket veto, which occurs upon the adjournment of Congress. Next, we turn to "legislative vetoes," devices for Congress to disapprove executive action, and to their invalidation by the Supreme Court. (We review the Supreme Court's invalidation of an effort by Congress to grant the President an "item veto" later in this chapter, with the budgetary materials to which it relates.)

a. The President's Veto

The key presidential check on the legislative process is the constitutional requirement, under Art. I, §7, that all actions of Congress having public effect, whatever their form, must be presented to the President for approval or veto. A bill or resolution may be enacted over the President's veto only by a vote of two-thirds of each house of Congress (i.e., by at least two-thirds of a quorum of each house, *Missouri Pacific Ry. Co. v. Kansas*, 248 U.S. 276 (1919)). There is some evidence that both the veto and the override powers have grown in political importance in recent years, perhaps because of increasing difficulties that Presidents face in bargaining effectively with congressional leaders for their support of presidential goals. David McKay, *Presidential Strategy and the Veto Power: A Reappraisal*, 104 POL. SCI. Q. 447 (1989). Still, Presidents vary substantially in their veto practices. On one end of the scale is Franklin Roosevelt, who vetoed hundreds of bills. On the other are William Clinton, who vetoed no bills in the 103d Congress, the first time that had happened since 1853, George W. Bush, who vetoed only ten bills in his two terms of office, and Barack Obama, who vetoed twelve.[1] http://www.senate.gov/reference/Legislation/Vetoes/ObamaBH.htm

---

1. In 2009 and 2010, Obama withheld his signature from two bills, yet returned them to the originating House even though the period for signature expired during a congressional recess. The

For *Some Thoughts on the Veto*, we turn to Professor Charles Black, 40 Law & Contemp. Probs. 87, 93–98 (1976), who emphasizes the great power the veto accords the
President due to the difficulty of override:

> Let's take the House of Representatives. . . . The usual situation, where
> there is a general opposition between the President and the House, is where
> the President is of a different party from the House majority. Now the one
> simple factor that is steady is party loyalty, reenforced by patronage. Let us
> take a Congress much like the present one, with about 290 Democrats and
> about 145 Republicans — figures I pick for the exact two to one ratio — and
> with a Republican President. In our politics, this is about as high as the
> majority in the House is likely to get. We ought to assume, until some reason
> to the contrary appears, that equal percentages of Democrats and Republi-
> cans will, in the long run, defect, both as to Democrats supporting the Pres-
> ident and as to Republicans voting to override. But if (in our 290–145 House)
> ten per cent of the Republicans and ten per cent of the Democrats switch
> sides, the override loses by something like 275–160, a . . . failure of override
> by a wide margin.
>
> How big a Democratic majority would it take to get around this? The
> answer, of course, depends on the percentage of defection. Assuming, *pro
> forma*, the same 10 per cent defection across party fences both ways, you
> would need 308 Democrats and 127 Republicans to have a "veto-proof"
> Congress. . . . On a party vote, with defections in equal proportions, override
> loses heavily in any imaginable House of Representatives. Let us assume,
> since there is no reason not to, that the same situation exists in the Senate.
> And then (as reality requires, for a few overrides do occur) let us soften our
> assumptions a bit, . . . and say, . . . that override in either House has, say, one
> chance in four. It is important to note that this would mean that override in
> both Houses has one chance in 4 [squared] or 16, which is not far from what
> we find through history. . . . (Parenthetically, the situation is even worse
> where the majority party is the President's own, for in that case the party
> loyalty of the majority runs to the President, and against override. F. D.
> Roosevelt vetoed [372] bills; [9] were overridden.) . . . .
>
> What are the consequences for American politics? First and most obviously,
> the majorities, even quite large, in . . . the House and the Senate are power-
> less to fix American policy on anything, foreign or domestic, so long as Con-
> gress sticks to the forthright expression of policy judgment in a single bill,
> and attempts neither circumvention of the veto by "rider," nor reprisal. . . .
> The result is, inevitably, that actual veto can be rather rare even now — the
> tip of the iceberg, to coin a phrase. For the practical task of the leadership of

---

count of presidential vetoes maintained by the Clerk of the House did not count these as pocket
vetoes. http://history.house.gov/Institution/Presidential-Vetoes/Presidential-Vetoes/.

the House of Representatives and the Senate, in reality and as perceived by that leadership, is not to draft and pass a bill that seems good to strong working majorities in the House and Senate. It is to produce a bill, acceptable to those majorities, or reluctantly swallowed by those majorities, that may get by a veto. I say and stress "may" because there is no means of compelling the President to announce in advance what his action will be on a bill, or what amendments it will take to buy his signature. Very often, the general direction of his views is known. But exactly how much movement toward those views will be necessary is normally not known.

I suppose here one begins to enter the field of force of games theory. . . . One player must move toward placating his opponent, while only the opponent knows what it will take to placate him—or perhaps has not yet decided what it will take. . . . Very often—perhaps typically—the result has to be a compromise which rests on no clear policy, which may be worse than the following-out of either policy—and which may be vetoed anyway. That is the real situation in which the veto power puts Congress, and every citizen should be brought to understand it. There is one way out, as matters now stand. That is for Congress to accept, virtually verbatim, whatever "recommendations" the President makes. . . .

Let me move on to a third and quite crucial point about the veto. [T]here is an asymmetry here: The President may veto any independent action of Congress—indeed, no independent action of Congress, having the force of law, exists, except for the possibility . . . of override. But Congress may not veto any independent action of the President, for the peculiar reason that its action in this regard would itself be subject to Presidential veto. . . . If the President believes that an Act of Congress encroaches upon his office, he may, under the strictest and most ancient standards, veto it; so, also, if he believes an Act of Congress unconstitutional. If Congress, however, believes that an action of the President encroaches on its powers, or is unconstitutional on other grounds, it may not veto it, because the congressional veto, to have effect as law, must be by concurrence of both Houses, and so, under Article I, § 7, is subject to Presidential veto. . . .

It is against this background that one must consider the oft-repeated formula . . . that the President's powers, insofar as they derive from the general "executive power," are interstitial and tentative, since Congress may undo what the President has done. True, in a sense. But not very important, since the disaffirming congressional action is subject to veto. Not true at all, if what one means is that majorities of, say, 65 per cent in each House—an enormous preponderance—may effectively disapprove and annul the presidential action. The result of this asymmetry is that the President, with what might be thought meager textual powers, is institutionally almost untrammeled, since he may veto disapproving action by the very body to which he is supposedly subject, while that body, textually empowered to an enormous degree, is institutionally bound toe and neck by the veto. This institutional reason for the development of Presidential power must be added to . . . the structural suitability of the Presidency for the exercise of power, as contrasted with the built-in many headedness of Congress.

Certainly the overall statistics confirm Black's argument that the veto is a powerful presidential weapon. According to one count, by 2016, there had been 1506 regular vetoes, and 1066 pocket vetoes, for a total of 2572. Of the regular vetoes, 111, or 7.4%, were overridden (pocket vetoes, which are discussed below, are absolute). Compilations are kept at http://history.house.gov/Institution/Presidential-Vetoes /Presidential-Vetoes/. Still, might Black's case be somewhat overstated? He compares the veto to a game in which each side is uncertain of the other's strategy. In that situation, won't a President, wishing to avoid the considerable embarrassment of an override, have an incentive to make concessions to strongly held views in Congress? Presidents have even been known to swallow bills they detest rather than be punished with an override. Thus, it seems that President and Congress have reciprocal influence in the legislative process, and that raw statistics on overrides tell only part of a very rich story. *See* Richard A. Watson, Presidential Vetoes and Public Policy (1993); for an interesting game-theoretic approach to the President's veto, see William N. Eskridge, Jr. & John Ferejohn, *The Article I, Section 7 Game*, 80 Geo. L.J. 523 (1992).

There is a longstanding controversy over the appropriate uses of the veto. Although The Federalist argued that the President could exercise his veto on either constitutional or policy grounds (*see INS v. Chadha, infra*), the first Presidents rarely exercised a veto and most of the early ones were constitutionally based (including the first one, Washington's 1791 veto of a bill apportioning representatives). Characteristically, Jefferson thought that the veto was solely a shield against congressional encroachment on the executive; Hamilton found it apt for a bill objectionable on any ground. *See* Carl McGowan, *The President's Veto Power: An Important Instrument of Conflict in Our Constitutional System*, 23 San Diego L. Rev. 791, 798–806 (1986). Before Andrew Jackson's famous veto in 1832 of the rechartering of the Second Bank of the United States, there had been only 21 vetoes, 6 of which were based on other than constitutional grounds. Richard M. Pious, The American Presidency 60 (1979).

Our increased reliance on legislation in modern times, and the accompanying veto opportunities, renew the question of the appropriate scope of the veto. Judge McGowan, *supra* at 806–08, sides with Hamilton:

> There are . . . persuasive policy reasons for viewing the veto power as a broad tool of presidential review. At the Constitutional Convention, the Framers discussed and designed the veto as an integral component in our separation of powers scheme. But to be an effective check on the federal legislature, the veto need not and should not be limited to bills encroaching on the executive realm. The legislative branch can overreach without encroaching on the executive. Members of Congress often produce legislation that is the result

of pressure employed by special interest groups. Indeed, while the legislative process is a model of compromise, the final product may be nothing more than an aggregation of narrow, special-interest proposals. . . . Even the Framers recognized that laws could be enacted in the heat of factionalism. It is both appropriate and desirable that interest groups have access to our lawmakers.

The presidency can be characterized in a similar fashion. All elective officials must necessarily be responsive to interest groups in today's political environment. But the President represents a more national voter constituency, as compared to a single legislator. A presidential veto can moderate legislation for the national good or skew legislation toward the President's personal agenda. Each of these results is desirable. Since the veto clearly contemplates presidential participation in the difficult task of legislating, there is no good reason why the President should don blinders and ignore the full range of his policy, and even political interests. . . . [I]f the President is a representative of *all* the people, there is no reason to limit his powers to respond to his constituency, at least in the absence of a clear, constitutional mandate to do so. There is certainly no *express* limitation on the veto power. . . .

Of course, it is important to recognize that a broad veto power enables a recalcitrant President to interfere with positive congressional programs. We often view the legislative branch as responsible for designing comprehensive solutions to our nation's problems. Without the support of the President, however, Congress' task can be far more difficult. . . . The fact that the President is often supported on veto overrides by his own political party (thus explaining the low override rate) does not cast his veto in a dark light. Rather it validates the political, and possibly popular acceptance of his position. Moreover, when Congress is populated by a majority of members of the opposite party, it is not defenseless against a systematic use of the veto. At some point, the President's reliance on a negative power in the face of continued congressional initiatives will produce untoward political consequences for the executive. Additionally, the President must work with Congress if he is to achieve his own agenda. Thus, Congress can use its role in other lawmaking to force a President to moderate particular vetoes, just as a President uses his vetoes to moderate Congress.

The great disadvantage of the veto power from the President's perspective is its current availability only on an all-or-nothing basis. If objectionable features appear in a bill the President otherwise wants enacted, the President must choose whether to exercise the veto and risk not having a "clean bill" approved, or to swallow the Act, objectionable sections and all. Modern Presidents have tried to edge their way around this difficulty by drafting signing statements that accompany a bill that is becoming law, but specifying their constitutional objections.

Signing statements caused sharp controversy during the administration of President George W. Bush. Peter M. Shane provides a critique in MADISON'S NIGHTMARE, supra at 132–42:

> When the President vetoes a bill, the Constitution directs him to return Congress's bill to the first House that voted on it, along with his "objections." There is no constitutional requirement for the President to make any statement with regard to those bills he actually signs. Presidents, however, have taken various occasions to promulgate "signing statements" for legislation they are approving. These statements often tout the benefits that the legislation is projected to achieve, but may also state the President's policy reservations with respect to aspects of the new law. On occasions that were relatively rare — until the Bush Administration — Presidents had also used signing statements to indicate doubts about the constitutionality of particular provisions of the newly enacted statutes they were signing. In such cases, Presidents typically say that they will implement or interpret the statutory provision in question to minimize the perceived constitutional difficulty.
>
> The propriety of this practice is debatable. After all, each President swears to protect and defend the Constitution. If he thinks part of some bill is unconstitutional, should he not feel duty-bound to veto what Congress has enacted? There are good reasons, however, why Presidents may think differently. Most obviously, a great deal of legislation takes the form of a fairly complex package, some of which a President may think is urgently required for the good of the country. Requiring him to veto an entire bill because some narrow feature of the package is arguably unconstitutional may be exacting too high a price in terms of sacrificing the public interest as embodied in those parts of the new law that the President thinks are salutary. Moreover, a President might responsibly take the position that, in the ordinary case, the courts are available to address questions of law. Courts are perhaps better positioned to decide on questions of unconstitutionality. If a provision of an enacted bill is unconstitutional in a way that inflicts harm on particular members of the public, anyone harmed can sue to vindicate their rights. A court most often can effectively excise the offending provision from the law.
>
> On a number of occasions, however, Presidents have stated constitutional objections precisely because the law is arguably objectionable in a way that would be very difficult for a private party to challenge in court. In such cases, the President may object because there would not be an effective judicial alternative to test the constitutionality of the offending legal provision. Prior to the Bush Administration, a fairly common constitutional objection in signing statements involved a legislative practice called the "legislative veto." [These are considered later in this chapter.]

only need to explain veto ∅ endorsements

In objecting to legislative vetoes, Presidents were objecting to a practice that threatened to undermine their own central role in the scheme of checks and balances, and their objections were based on both strong constitutional argument and strong arguments of public policy. It is thus not surprising they would provide the occasion for a number of presidential signing statements asserting their unconstitutionality.

By one count, however, the total number of statutory provisions to which Presidents objected on constitutional grounds between the administration of James Monroe and the beginning of the first Reagan Administration was 101. The advent of the Reagan Administration, however, marked a significant increase in the frequency of the device, plus a dramatic departure in terms of its intended institutional significance. Attorney General Edwin Meese persuaded the company that publishes new laws also to publish the President's signing statements. The signing statements were intended to become, as one report explained, "a strategic weapon in a campaign to influence the way legislation was interpreted by the courts and Executive agencies." [REPORT OF THE AMERICAN BAR ASSOCIATION TASK FORCE ON PRESIDENTIAL SIGNING STATEMENTS AND THE SEPARATION OF POWERS DOCTRINE, at 10 (Aug. 2006), available at http://www.abanet.org/op/signingstatements/aba _final_signing_statements_recommendation-report_7-24-06.pdf.]

Over the course of two administrations, President Reagan, through his signing statements, objected to or unilaterally reinterpreted 71 statutory provisions. [T. J. HALSTEAD, PRESIDENTIAL SIGNING STATEMENTS: CONSTITUTIONAL AND INSTITUTIONAL IMPLICATIONS 3 (CRS Report for Congress Apr. 13, 2007).] In a single term, President George H.W. Bush objected to 146. Most of the objections involved the President's asserted foreign policy powers, although many reflected the Administration's full embrace of the unitary executive theory and some of the more expansive claims of presidentialist constitutionalism. President Clinton used the signing statement device also, his objections to 105 statutory provisions exceeding the record of President Reagan, although more modest than the record of President Bush 41. In terms of robust presidentialism, however, none of these three Presidents can compete with the record of the George W. Bush Administration. In his first six years in office, President George W. Bush raised nearly 1400 constitutional objections to roughly 1000 statutory provisions, over three times the total of his 42 predecessors combined. But it is not just the numbers that made the Bush signing statements distinctive. Unlike the long-standing presidential objections to legislative vetoes, the Bush objections were frequently based on no legal authority whatever and had nothing to do with any plausible version of the public interest.

So many examples exist of the bizarreness of this practice that I take, almost at random, the President's signing statement for the 2006 Postal Accountability and Enhancement Act. That Act amends the law describing an agency called the Postal Regulatory Commission. As amended, this rather undramatic law now reads as follows:

> The Postal Regulatory Commission is composed of 5 Commissioners, appointed by the President, by and with the advice and consent of the Senate. The Commissioners shall be chosen solely on the basis of their technical qualifications, professional standing, and demonstrated expertise in economics, accounting, law, or public administration, and may be removed by the President only for cause. Each individual appointed to the Commission shall have the qualifications and expertise necessary to carry out the enhanced responsibilities accorded Commissioners under the Postal Accountability and Enhancement Act. Not more than 3 of the Commissioners may be adherents of the same political party. [Pub. L. No. 109-435, 120 Stat. 3198 (2006).]

In signing the Act, the President objected to this provision as one of two in the Act that "purport to limit the qualifications of the pool of persons from whom the President may select appointees in a manner that rules out a large portion of those persons best qualified by experience and knowledge to fill the positions." [Statement on Signing the Postal Accountability and Enhancement Act, 42 Weekly Comp. Pres. Docs. 2196 (2006).] He then went on to state that the executive branch would construe these provisions "in a manner consistent with the Appointments Clause of the Constitution." In other words, President Bush wanted to go on record as objecting to this innocuous statute as a violation of his power to nominate and appoint officers of the United States, and said he would read the law in some unspecified manner that would be consistent with his authority.

Putting aside constitutional issues for a moment, what exactly could the President be thinking here? The statute invites the President to nominate new commission members "on the basis of their technical qualifications, professional standing, and demonstrated expertise in economics, accounting, law, or public administration." What "large portion of those persons best qualified by experience and knowledge" could possibly be excluded by this requirement? The statute does say the President may not appoint more than three of the five commission members from any one political party. He thus has to find at least two Democrats, two Republicans, two independents or some combination in addition to any three Commission members who belong to the same party. It boggles the mind to think of this as a substantial limit on the President's capacity to identify the best qualified person for any given opening . . . . The only tenable reason for objecting would be the formalist syllogism: Congress may not constitutionally demand that the President nominate John Smith or Jill Jones, in particular, for any particular office. To the presidential formalist, this implies that Congress may impose no constraints on the President at all regarding his choice of nominee . . . .

Many of President Bush's constitutional objections fall within areas about which Presidents are typically protective. Of the nearly 1400 objections lodged in signing statements between 2001 and 2006, 84 mention potential interference with commander-in-chief powers, 144 mention interference with his constitutional authorities regarding diplomacy and foreign affairs, and another 183 point to alleged violations of the President's constitutional authorities to withhold or control access to information to protect foreign relations or national security, sometimes mentioning also his power to protect executive branch deliberative processes or the performance of the executive's constitutional duties.

Even in these traditional contexts, however, the substance of the President's objections is often extreme and hypertechnical. For example, one provision alleged to raise issues regarding executive privilege was a legal requirement in the Intelligence Authorization Act for Fiscal Year 2002 that certain reports to congressional intelligence committees must be in writing and include an executive summary. [Pub. L. No. 107-108, § 305, 115 Stat. 1398 (2001), codified at 50 U.S.C. § 413a; Statement on Signing the Intelligence Authorization Act for Fiscal Year 2002, 37 Weekly Comp. Pres. Docs. 1835 (2001).] Similarly, the President found a violation of his foreign affairs powers in provisions of the so-called "Syria Accountability and Lebanese Sovereignty Restoration Act of 2003" that required him to take certain actions against Syria unless "the President either determines and certifies to the Congress that the Government of Syria has taken specific actions, or determines that it is in the national security interest of the United States to waive such requirements and reports the reasons for that determination to the Congress." [Pub. L. 108-175, § 5(a)(b), 117 Stat. 2482, 2487–88 (2003); Statement on Signing the Syria Accountability and Lebanese Sovereignty Restoration Act of 2003, 39 Weekly Comp. Pres. Docs. 1795 (2003).] In other words, Congress violates the Constitution — according to President Bush — when it requires him either to perform an act or not perform it, at his sole discretion . . . .

Going beyond these somewhat astonishing claims in areas of traditional presidential concern, there are hundreds in wholly novel areas. For example, the President objected to 214 legally imposed reporting requirements as interfering with his constitutional authority to recommend measures to Congress. Apparently, President Bush believes that the President's entitlement to speak his mind to Congress entails a prohibition on Congress demanding any other reports or recommendations from the executive branch. This is an historically baseless argument. As our original Secretary of the Treasury, Alexander Hamilton — the most presidentialist of the framers — clearly found himself as responsible for filing reports with Congress as to the President. [Gerhard Casper, *An Essay in Separation of Powers: Some Early Versions and Practices*, 30 Wm. & Mary L. Rev. 211, 240–242; Jerry L. Mashaw, *Recovering American Administrative Law: Federalist Foundations 1787–1801*,

115 YALE L. J. 1256, 1284–87 (2006).] Any constitutional infirmity in the requirement of executive reports to Congress is entirely a figment of the contemporary presidentialist imagination.

In his first six years in office, President George W. Bush lodged 346 objections based on Congress's alleged interference with the President's control over the "unitary executive." Many of these assertions seem to be merely "piling on" with regard to other, narrower objections. Thus, when the President objects to a congressional mandate that some executive branch official do something with regard to foreign affairs, the President may object on both the foreign affairs ground—i.e., Congress may not make foreign policy—and the unitary executive ground, i.e., Congress may not the President how to use his subordinates. Likewise, when the President objects to a congressional requirement that a subordinate member of the executive branch file a report with Congress, on the ground that this violates the President's "recommendations" power, he may also object on unitary executive grounds, again, that Congress is telling someone subordinate to the President what to do.

Beyond these merely cumulative "unitary executive" objections, some invocations of the unitary executive appear to be distinctively rooted in the Bush Administration's imagined authority to direct personally the discretionary activity of every member of the executive branch on any subject, regardless of what the law prescribes. For example, one statutory provision to which the President objected on "unitary executive grounds" is Section 115 of a 2002 "Act to Provide for Improvement of Federal Education Research, Statistics, Evaluation, Information, and Dissemination and for Other Purposes." [Pub. L. 107-279, § 115, 116 Stat 1940, 1948 (2002).] The act creates an Institute of Education Sciences within the Department of Education, to be run by a Director and a board. Section 115 requires the Director to propose Institute priorities for Board approval. The President of the United States, of course, has no inherent constitutional power over education. Yet, executive branch lawyers seem to imagine that it somehow violates the separation of powers either to allow the Director to recommend priorities or for the Board to decide on those priorities, without presidential intervention. [Statement on signing legislation to provide for improvement of federal education research, statistics, evaluation, information, dissemination and for other purposes 38 Weekly Comp. Pres. Docs. 1995 (2002).] . . . These examples all demonstrate the expansive interpretive tendency described above with regard to the President's appointment power. The strategy is to insist, in bright-line terms, for the most ambitious and rigid assertions of any conceded executive power. But why have these signing statements proliferated now? The views they embody, even if earlier GOP presidents pushed them less aggressively, were certainly held also by leading legal thinkers under both Presidents Reagan and George H.W. Bush. As legal formalists,

[handwritten margin note: Congress ∅ make foreign policy + congress ∅ tell Pres how to use his subordinates]

the lawyers in earlier Administrations would surely have appreciated, as much as George W. Bush Administration lawyers, the existence of some formal documents embodying their presidentialist claims that could be cited as a species of legal precedent for their arguments. Moreover, Bush's recent GOP predecessors, facing Congresses controlled by Democrats, actually had less political room to work their will than he had until 2007. One thus might have expected to find them even more strident than Bush 43 in asserting their prerogatives of unilateral action.

As it happens, however, what seems to have tempted George W. Bush to use signing statements so aggressively is not their political necessity, but rather the fact he could get away with them in the face of a largely quiescent Congress. From 2001–2006, and especially after Republicans took the Senate in 2002, Congress most often did not stand up to the President on his claims of unilateral power. The President set forth his objections so frequently because Congress was not pushing back. Had Congress been standing up for its own prerogatives with customary institutional vigor, one would have expected ambitious signing statements to be matched with equally robust rhetorical responses—or more—from the House and Senate. That simply did not happen . . . . What happened from 2001–06 was Bush Administration exploitation of congressional passivity to generate a series of documentary artifacts that can impersonate as legal authority for unilateral presidentialist legal interpretation.

It might well be asked how much all of this lawyerly complexity really matters. Even if we concede that the President is fabricating baseless constitutional objections to the statutory qualifications for Postal Rate Commissioners or the obligation of the Secretary of Agriculture to listen to an advisory board on specialty crops, this may not seem worthy of public agitation. But it does matter, in two important respects.

First, . . . the signing statements are intended to help legitimate a specific form of presidentialist initiative that is less known to the public than such matters as wiretapping and warmaking, but, in terms of day to day governance, arguably more significant. This is the recent revolution in the President's relationship to the policymaking bureaucracy—the agencies that regulate virtually every aspect of Americans' social and economic activity, including critical matters of public health and safety. Our recent Presidents have asserted unprecedented authority to determine how all such policy is made, and their signing statements could be used as something that looks like legal authority for executive usurpation. They are formal documents, officially anthologized and electronically searchable. They are connected to an assigned presidential role in the constitutional order. Legally speaking, their content is discretionary with the President. If they say something often enough, these presidential utterances, thus solemnized, may begin to look like law. They are duly executed and ceremonially delivered. They are citable. They are precedents of a sort. One is tempted, however, to say that they are *faux* law in just the way creation science is *faux* science. Left unchallenged, they may still have the power to cow Congress and shape the behavior of executive underlings.

But the second point is that the George W. Bush signing statements and the Administration's litigiousness over executive privilege are part of the more general presidentialist ethos of government . . . . Presidentialism is a form of institutional ambition that feeds on itself, and presidential signing statements are both a reflection of and encouragement to a psychology of constitutional entitlement. The future of specialty crops may be less newsworthy than Guantanamo or NSA wiretapping, but the sense of unilateral authority that fuels the President's stance on obscure matters helps to maintain the attitudes—the norms of governance—that lead to other, more consequential claims of unilateral executive authority. An important function of the George W. Bush signing statements is that they serve as reminders to Administration members, and especially to Administration lawyers, of how the President wants the Administration to behave: claim maximum power, concede minimum authority to the other branches. . . . [T]he signing statements embody both a disregard for the institutional authorities of the other branches—especially Congress—and a disregard for the necessity to ground legal claims in plausible law. Such is the legal face of contemporary presidentialism.

See also Symposium, *The Last Word? The Constitutional Implications of Presidential Signing Statements*, 16 Wm. & Mary Bill of Rights J. 231 (2007).

Soon after taking office, President Obama issued a Memorandum on Presidential Signing Statements, reprinted in Peter Augustine Lawler (Editor), Robert Martin Schaefer, eds., American Political Rhetoric: Essential Speeches and Writings On Founding Principles and Contemporary Controversies 92 (6th ed. 2010). Would this approach be well calculated to fix the problems Professor Shane identifies? (Obama wound up issuing a total of twenty-one statements containing constitutional objections or reservations with regard to statutes he was signing into law. They voiced 104 objections to roughly eighty-nine enumerated provisions of law; it is hard to be more precise because a number of statements lodge objections to "certain provisions" or "numerous provisions," without citing them more specifically.)

Memorandum for the Heads of Executive Departments and Agencies On Presidential Signing Statements

March 9, 2009

For nearly two centuries, Presidents have issued statements addressing constitutional or other legal questions upon signing bills into law (signing statements).

Particularly since omnibus bills have become prevalent, signing statements have often been used to ensure that concerns about the constitutionality of discrete statutory provisions do not require a veto of the entire bill.

In recent years, there has been considerable public discussion and criticism of the use of signing statements to raise constitutional objections to statutory provisions. There is no doubt that the practice of issuing such statements can be abused. Constitutional signing statements should not be used to suggest that the President will disregard statutory requirements on the basis of policy disagreements. At the same time, such signing statements serve a legitimate function in our system, at least when based on well-founded constitutional objections. In appropriately limited circumstances, they represent an exercise of the President's constitutional obligation to take care that the laws be faithfully executed, and they promote a healthy dialogue between the executive branch and the Congress.

With these considerations in mind and based upon advice of the Department of Justice, I will issue signing statements to address constitutional concerns only when it is appropriate to do so as a means of discharging my constitutional responsibilities. In issuing signing statements, I shall adhere to the following principles:

1. The executive branch will take appropriate and timely steps, whenever practicable, to inform the Congress of its constitutional concerns about pending legislation. Such communication should facilitate the efforts of the executive branch and the Congress to work together to address these concerns during the legislative process, thus minimizing the number of occasions on which I am presented with an enrolled bill that may require a signing statement.

2. Because legislation enacted by the Congress comes with a presumption of constitutionality, I will strive to avoid the conclusion that any part of an enrolled bill is unconstitutional. In exercising my responsibility to determine whether a provision of an enrolled bill is unconstitutional, I will act with caution and restraint, based only on interpretations of the Constitution that are well-founded.

3. To promote transparency and accountability, I will ensure that signing statements identify my constitutional concerns about a statutory provision with sufficient specificity to make clear the nature and basis of the constitutional objection.

4. I will announce in signing statements that I will construe a statutory provision in a manner that avoids a constitutional problem only if that construction is a legitimate one.

To ensure that all signing statements previously issued are followed only when consistent with these principles, executive branch departments and agencies are directed to seek the advice of the Attorney General before relying on signing statements issued prior to the date of this memorandum as the basis for disregarding, or otherwise refusing to comply with, any provision of a statute.

This memorandum is not intended to, and does not, create any right or benefit, substantive or procedural, enforceable at law or in equity by any party against the United States, its departments, agencies, or entities, its officers, employees, or agents, or any other person.

This memorandum shall be published in the Federal Register.

BARACK OBAMA

Presidential signing statements also sometimes give the President's interpretation of the meaning of a new statute. Should courts consider such a statement to be part of the legislative history of the statute, or, alternatively, as an executive interpretation of the statute to which some judicial deference is due under ordinary principles of administrative law? (Generally, they have not.) For a comprehensive review of the issues by Assistant Attorney General Walter Dellinger of the Clinton administration, see *The Legal Significance of Presidential Signing Statements*, 17 Op. O.L.C. No. 11 (1993), *reprinted in* H. JEFFERSON POWELL, THE CONSTITUTION AND THE ATTORNEYS GENERAL 563–72 (1999).

In addition to the veto power, the Constitution contemplates that the President will participate in the legislative process by "recommend[ing] to their Consideration such Measures as he shall judge necessary and expedient. . . ." Art. II, § 3. Judge McGowan's point that "the President must work with Congress if he is to achieve his own agenda" is one that some Presidents have grasped better than others. Critical as it is to his overall success, the President's role as legislative initiator and advocate lies mostly in the province of political science rather than law. It has been argued, however, that it may impinge on the President's power of legislative proposal for Congress to forbid the use of appropriations for the purpose of advocating or even studying particular policies. J. Gregory Sidak, *The Recommendation Clause*, 77 GEO. L.J. 2079 (1989).

b. Pocket Vetoes

In one circumstance the President has what amounts to an absolute veto. Under Art. I, § 7, the President must return vetoed legislation to the house from which it originated, with his objections, for possible override. If the President fails to return a bill within ten days, excepting Sundays, it becomes law, "unless Congress by their Adjournment prevent its Return, in which Case it shall not be a Law." When the President prevents a bill from becoming law in this last way, it is called a "pocket veto," and Congress must pass an entirely new piece of legislation in its next session, which the President again may disapprove.

The limits of the President's pocket veto power are explored by HAROLD H. BRUFF, in BALANCE OF FORCES, *supra* at 227–31:

> This seems a most obscure provision of the Constitution, but an unfortunate ambiguity has led to repeated litigation and enduring doubt about its meaning. The problem arises as follows. If the President neither signs nor vetoes a bill for ten days while Congress is in session, it becomes law. If he

[handwritten margin note: if [] sign or veto a bill in 10 days, it becomes law]

behaves the same way during a constitutional "adjournment" of Congress, there is a successful pocket veto. Therefore, the validity of legislation can depend on the definition of "adjournment," and about that there is much uncertainty.

The records of the Constitutional Convention do not mention the pocket veto. The framers did extensively debate whether the President should have a veto and whether Congress should be able to override it. The pocket veto clause came from the Committee of Detail's draft constitution. It appears to be a safeguard against evasions of the qualified veto by either branch. The President cannot prevent override by refusing to sign or return a bill; Congress cannot prevent a veto by adjourning so that the President cannot return a bill. No one doubts that the final adjournment of each Congress is a pocket veto opportunity. Because renewed legislation will be considered by a new and differently composed Congress, the President has been deprived of his opportunity to return the bill with his objections to the old Congress. The disputes concern "intersession" adjournments, which occur between the first and second sessions of each Congress, and "intrasession" adjournments, for example over holidays, which may last only a few days.

In *The Pocket Veto Case*, [279 U.S. 655 (1929).] the Supreme Court held that an intersession adjournment provided the President a pocket veto opportunity. Justice Sanford's opinion concluded that an "adjournment" includes any occasion on which a house of Congress is not in session, because the President is always prevented from returning a bill to that house. Rejecting an argument that the bill could be given to an agent of the originating house, he stressed the potential for uncertainty about the effectiveness of an attempted return, and for long delay before reconsideration by Congress could take place. The Court's support for a broad pocket veto power did not last long, however. In *Wright v. United States*, [302 U.S. 583 (1938),] the Court considered the effectiveness of the President's return of a bill on the tenth day, during a three-day adjournment of the originating house. Chief Justice Hughes wrote an opinion holding that return had not been prevented. Delivery of the veto message to the Secretary of the Senate was effective, and an override opportunity remained. Revisiting its broad statements in the *Pocket Veto Case*, the Court began by arguing that the Constitution provides that only an adjournment by "the Congress" can prevent a return; here, only the Senate had adjourned. Moreover, there was no "practical difficulty" in making a return: "The organization of the Senate continued and was intact. The Secretary of the Senate was functioning and was able to receive, and did receive, the bill." Thus, the Court no longer condemned the use of an agent — nothing in the Constitution forbade the practice. Neither uncertainty about the status of a bill nor indefinite delay seemed a problem when the organization of a house remained operative during a short intrasession adjournment.

The change in judicial attitudes toward pocket vetoes that *Wright* reveals probably responded to an intervening constitutional amendment. The Twentieth Amendment, ratified in 1933, made Congress a modern institution — just in time for the Hundred Days and the New Deal. Under the original Constitution, Members of Congress were elected in the fall for a term that began in March, but since the Constitution also required Congress to convene each December, over a year would pass between a Member's election and actual service. A new Congress would have its first session beginning the December after its election year, and would meet until the summer. The second session would be a lame-duck one that could last until terms expired the next March. The inefficiencies of this pattern were obvious, but were tolerable in a nation that expected little of its legislature. The Amendment altered terms to begin in January, and called for Congress to convene each year in that month. This change, together with the practical needs of the nation during the New Deal, converted Congress from a part-time body that would adjourn for many months at a time to the nearly full-time one we know today.

Two decisions of the D.C. Circuit Court of Appeals have tried to apply the teachings of the two Supreme Court decisions. *Kennedy v. Sampson,* [511 F.2d 430 (D.C. Cir. 1974),] involved President Nixon's attempted pocket veto of the Family Practice of Medicine Act during a five-day Christmas recess of the Senate. The court held that return was not prevented by such an intrasession adjournment by a house, as long as it had arranged for receipt of veto messages. The court thought that the concerns of the *Pocket Veto Case* about uncertainty or delay were outdated. Perhaps because the bill had passed initially by almost unanimous votes in both houses, the administration declined to appeal, and the bill was published as a law. In *Barnes v. Kline,* [759 F.2d 21 (D.C. Cir. 1985), *vacated sub. nom.* Burke v. Barnes, 497 U.S. 361 (1987),] some Representatives sued to nullify President Reagan's attempted intersession pocket veto of a bill that restricted military assistance to El Salvador. *Barnes* raised the question whether the holding of the *Pocket Veto Case* could be ignored by a lower court, on the authority of *Wright.* Judge McGowan's opinion held that intersession adjournments no longer provided a pocket veto opportunity. He read *Wright* to establish two propositions. First, only when the President was "truly deprived" of a return opportunity would a pocket veto be available; otherwise, Congress's override power would be sacrificed unnecessarily. Second, return would not be prevented if there was an agent to receive messages and if delay and uncertainty were not present. Applying these considerations, he concluded that intersession adjournments, which are now shorter than some intrasession ones, no longer prevent return messages. Still, historical practice clouded the issue somewhat. From Jefferson to Nixon, Presidents had treated intersession adjournments as pocket veto opportunities, and Congress had acquiesced in all 272 instances.

The court pointed out, though, that this understanding was based on the long adjournment patterns of the past. Thus, Presidents Ford and Carter had begun to send return messages to Congress between sessions. President Reagan had restored the more confrontational earlier practice.

If *Barnes* is correct, as I believe it is, only final adjournments of Congress provide a pocket veto opportunity. The nature of Congress has indeed changed in a way that affects the logic of the Pocket Veto Clause, as the Twentieth Amendment signifies. Moreover, the *Pocket Veto Case* rested on weak reasoning. The concern about uncertain status of legislation if agents are used is easy to meet. Every county courthouse can track filings; so can Congress. The concern about delay was more real when intersession adjournments were long, but even then, every bill not signed into law after the first session would languish extensively—nothing seems distinctive about override issues. If the result of this analysis is to reduce the pocket veto to minimum scope, we need not grieve. The evasions that the framers tried to forestall would be prevented—Presidents could not refuse to take action on bills, and Congress could not sneak out of town to prevent returns. The qualified veto, as we have seen, is so powerful that Presidents do not need capacious pockets. Use of the ordinary veto process subjects proposed legislation to the maximum winnowing process, compared to absolute pocket vetoes. The logjam of legislation that typically occurs at the end of each Congress will still provide the President an ample choice of bills to pocket. If *Barnes* is wrong, all intersession adjournments and perhaps some intrasession ones also present pocket veto opportunities. The Justice Department, moving not an inch beyond the facts of *Wright*, has taken the position that any intrasession adjournment of more than three days allows pocket vetoes. The Supreme Court needs to clarify the status of the *Pocket Veto Case*. A bill pocketed at intersession may or may not be law; no one knows. If it has been finally vetoed, an override vote will not restore it. If not, no vote is necessary.

Presidents have the greatest temptation to extend the pocket veto when bills have enough support to make override probable. When in doubt, Presidents have returned bills to the originating house with a message announcing a pocket veto, hoping that at least a regular veto has occurred. Congress has considered legislating to specify that only final adjournments are occasions for pocket vetoes. [Butler C. Derrick, Jr., *Stitching the Hole in the President's Pocket: A Legislative Solution to the Pocket-Veto Controversy*, 31 HARV. J. LEGIS. 321 (1994).] The effectiveness of such a statute is uncertain, however—even if the President does not pocket it! The Court might uphold such a statute for two reasons. First, it would be consistent with *Wright* and the court of appeals cases. Second, Congress can always restrict the President's pocket veto opportunities to final adjournments by timing presentment so that no adjournment occurs until after the return period expires.

c. "Legislative Vetoes"

Most recent scholarly analysis of the significance of the President's veto powers has occurred in discussions of the so-called "legislative veto." Legislative veto is a shorthand phrase referring to any mechanism through which Congress employs a resolution of one or both of its houses to approve or disapprove executive exercise of delegated authority. These resolutions purport to have mandatory effect, although they are not submitted to the President for approval or veto. For example, using a "one-house veto" Congress may delegate to an agency the authority to promulgate a rule, but provide that the rule shall not go into effect if it is "disapproved" by either house of Congress. Similarly, under a "committee approval" provision, Congress may delegate rulemaking authority to an agency, but provide that the rule shall not go into effect unless it is approved by the committees of the House and Senate having subject matter jurisdiction over the agency. A two-house veto takes the form of a *concurrent* resolution, which is a resolution of both houses not submitted to the President. (This should not be confused with a *joint* resolution, which is presented to the President and is essentially the same as ordinary legislation.) For a comprehensive history of the legislative veto, see H. Lee Watson, *Congress Steps Out: A Look at Congressional Control of the Executive*, 63 Calif. L. Rev. 983 (1975).

After decades of doubt and disagreement about the constitutionality of the legislative veto, the Supreme Court finally considered the issue in a landmark case, *INS v. Chadha*, which follows. Justice White's dissent in *Chadha* provides an introduction by recounting the variety of uses that Congress had found for the legislative veto, and the impetus that led to increasing reliance on it through the years:

> The prominence of the legislative veto mechanism in our contemporary political system and its importance to Congress can hardly be overstated. It has become a central means by which Congress secures the accountability of executive and independent agencies. Without the legislative veto, Congress is faced with a Hobson's choice: either to refrain from delegating the necessary authority, leaving itself with a hopeless task of writing laws with the requisite specificity to cover endless special circumstances across the entire policy landscape, or in the alternative, to abdicate its law-making function to the executive branch and independent agencies. To choose the former leaves major national problems unresolved; to opt for the latter risks unaccountable policymaking by those not elected to fill that role. Accordingly, over the past five decades, the legislative veto has been placed in nearly 200 statutes. The device is known in every field of governmental concern: reorganization, budgets, foreign affairs, war powers, and regulation of trade, safety, energy, the environment and the economy.
>
> The legislative veto developed initially in response to the problems of reorganizing the sprawling government structure created in response to the Depression. The Reorganization Acts established the chief model for the legislative veto. When President Hoover requested authority to reorganize the government in 1929, he ... proposed that the Executive "should act upon

approval of a joint committee of Congress or with the reservation of power of revision by Congress within some limited period adequate for its consideration." Pub. Papers 432 (1929). Congress followed President Hoover's suggestion and authorized reorganization subject to legislative review. Act of June 30, 1932, ch. 314, §407, 47 Stat. 382, 414. . . . Over the years, the provision was used extensively. Presidents submitted 115 reorganization plans to Congress of which 23 were disapproved by Congress pursuant to legislative veto provisions.

Shortly after adoption of the Reorganization Act of 1939, Congress and the President applied the legislative veto procedure to resolve the delegation problem for national security and foreign affairs. World War II occasioned the need to transfer greater authority to the President in these areas. The legislative veto offered the means by which Congress could confer additional authority while preserving its own constitutional role. During World War II, Congress enacted over thirty statutes conferring powers on the Executive with legislative veto provisions. President Roosevelt accepted the veto as the necessary price for obtaining exceptional authority.

Over the quarter century following World War II, Presidents continued to accept legislative vetoes by one or both Houses as constitutional, while regularly denouncing provisions by which Congressional committees reviewed Executive activity. The legislative veto balanced delegations of statutory authority in new areas of governmental involvement: the space program, international agreements on nuclear energy, tariff arrangements, and adjustment of federal pay rates.

During the 1970's the legislative veto was important in resolving a series of major constitutional disputes between the President and Congress over claims of the President to broad impoundment, war, and national emergency powers. The key provision of the War Powers Resolution authorizes the termination by concurrent resolution of the use of armed forces in hostilities. A similar measure resolved the problem posed by Presidential claims of inherent power to impound appropriations. Congressional Budget and Impoundment Control Act of 1974, 31 U.S.C. §1403. . . . This compromise provided the President with flexibility, while preserving ultimate Congressional control over the budget. . . . These statutes were followed by others resolving similar problems: the National Emergencies Act, 50 U.S.C. §1622 (1976), resolving the longstanding problems with unchecked Executive emergency power; the Arms Export Control Act, 22 U.S.C. §2776(b) (1976), resolving the problem of foreign arms sales; and the Nuclear Non-Proliferation Act of 1978, 42 U.S.C. §§2160(f), 2155(b), 2157(b), 2158, 2153(d) (Supp. IV. 1980), resolving the problem of exports of nuclear technology. . . .

Presidents from Franklin Roosevelt through Reagan resisted legislative veto provisions on both constitutional and policy grounds, often noting their reservations while signing bills containing veto provisions. There were several policy-based objections. First, veto provisions create uncertainty in the administration of government programs. Second, they afford opportunities for undisclosed political pressure to influence administration, at the expense of meaningful public participation. Third, they provide an incentive for agencies to make policy through cumbersome adjudication, which is not vulnerable to legislative veto. Finally, they increase the importance of responsible congressional oversight of the details of the myriad government programs. Ironically, the veto, which was designed to increase congressional control of the executive, may actually have decreased that control whenever Congress did not give active review to an executive action. The reason is that availability of the veto device seems to have encouraged Congress to make broader delegations than it otherwise would, in hopes of checking policy as it formed at the implementing stage. *See* Harold H. Bruff & Ernest Gellhorn, *Congressional Control of Administrative Regulation: A Study of Legislative Vetoes*, 90 Harv. L. Rev. 1369 (1977).

Immigration and Naturalization Service v. Chadha

462 U.S. 919 (1983)

Chief Justice BURGER delivered the opinion of the Court.

[This case] presents a challenge to the constitutionality of the provision in §244(c)(2) of the Immigration and Nationality Act, 8 U.S.C. §1254(c)(2), authorizing one House of Congress, by resolution, to invalidate the decision of the Executive Branch, pursuant to authority delegated by Congress to the Attorney General . . . to allow a particular deportable alien to remain in the United States.

I

Chadha is an East Indian who was born in Kenya and holds a British passport. He was lawfully admitted to the United States in 1966 on a nonimmigrant student visa. His visa expired on June 30, 1972. On October 11, 1973, the District Director of the Immigration and Naturalization Service ordered Chadha to show cause why he should not be deported for having "remained in the United States for a longer time than permitted." . . . [A] deportation hearing was held before an immigration judge [at which] Chadha conceded that he was deportable for overstaying his visa and the hearing was adjourned to enable him to file an application for suspension of deportation under §244(a)(1) of the Act, [which] provides:

> (a) . . . the Attorney General may, in his discretion, suspend deportation and adjust the status to that of an alien lawfully admitted for permanent residence, in the case of an alien who applies to the Attorney General for suspension of deportation and—

> (1) is deportable under any law of the United States . . . and proves that . . . he was and is a person of good moral character; and is a person whose deportation would, in the opinion of the Attorney General, result in extreme hardship. . . .

[Handwritten margin notes:]
President said he's gotta go but they ¢ want that

he admits he fucked up and over stayed + they said he could file a app for suspension of deportation

AG will suspend deport if you can show hardship+ have a good guy

After Chadha submitted his application . . . the deportation hearing was resumed. . . . On the basis of evidence adduced at the hearing, affidavits submitted with the application, and the results of a character investigation conducted by the INS, the immigration judge, on June 25, 1974, ordered that Chadha's deportation be suspended. The immigration judge found that Chadha met the requirements of § 244(a)(1) . . . .

Pursuant to § 244(c)(1) of the Act, the immigration judge suspended Chadha's deportation and a report of the suspension was transmitted to Congress. Once the Attorney General's recommendation for suspension of Chadha's deportation was conveyed to Congress, Congress had the power under § 244(c)(2) of the Act to veto the Attorney General's determination that Chadha should not be deported. Section 244(c)(2) provides:

> (2) In the case of an alien specified in paragraph (1) of subsection (a) of this subsection —

> if . . . either the Senate or the House of Representatives passes a resolution stating in substance that it does not favor the suspension of such deportation, the Attorney General shall thereupon deport such alien or authorize the alien's voluntary departure at his own expense under the order of deportation in the manner provided by law. If, within the time above specified, neither the Senate nor the House of Representatives shall pass such a resolution, the Attorney General shall cancel deportation proceedings. . . .

On December 12, 1975, Representative Eilberg, Chairman of the Judiciary Subcommittee on Immigration, Citizenship, and International Law, introduced a resolution opposing "the granting of permanent residence in the United States to [six] aliens," including Chadha. The resolution was referred to the House Committee on the Judiciary. On December 16, 1975, the resolution was discharged from further consideration by the House Committee . . . and submitted to the House of Representatives for a vote. The resolution had not been printed and was not made available to other Members of the House prior to or at the time it was voted on. So far as the record before us shows, the House consideration of the resolution was based on Representative Eilberg's statement from the floor that:

> [i]t was the feeling of the committee, after reviewing 340 cases, that the aliens contained in the resolution [Chadha and five others] did not meet these statutory requirements, particularly as it relates to hardship; and it is the opinion of the committee that their deportation should not be suspended.

The resolution was passed without debate or recorded vote. Since the House action was pursuant to § 244(c)(2), the resolution was not treated as an Article I legislative act; it was not submitted to the Senate or presented to the President for his action.

After the House veto of the Attorney General's decision to allow Chadha to remain in the United States, the immigration judge reopened the deportation proceedings to implement the House order deporting Chadha. Chadha moved to terminate the proceedings on the ground that § 244(c)(2) is unconstitutional. The immigration judge held that he had no authority to rule on the constitutional validity of § 244(c)(2). On November 8, 1976, Chadha was ordered deported pursuant to the House action. . . .

Chadha filed a petition for review of the deportation order in the United States Court of Appeals for the Ninth Circuit. The Immigration and Naturalization Service agreed with Chadha's position before the Court of Appeals and joined him in arguing that § 244(c)(2) is unconstitutional. In light of the importance of the question, the Court of Appeals invited both the Senate and the House of Representatives to file briefs *amici curiae*. . . . [T]he Court of Appeals held that the House was without constitutional authority to order Chadha's deportation. . . . The essence of its holding was that § 244(c)(2) violates the constitutional doctrine of separation of powers. We granted certiorari . . . and we now affirm.

appeals Ct say house ∅ have authority to order his deportation

II

Before we address the important question of the constitutionality of the one-House veto provision of § 244(c)(2), we first consider several challenges to the authority of this Court to resolve the issue raised. . . .

B

Severability

Congress . . . contends that the provision for the one-House veto in § 244(c)(2) cannot be severed from § 244. Congress argues that if the provision for the one-House veto is held unconstitutional, all of § 244 must fall. If § 244 in its entirety is violative of the Constitution, it follows that the Attorney General has no authority to suspend Chadha's deportation under § 244(a)(1) and Chadha would be deported. From this, Congress argues that Chadha lacks standing to challenge the constitutionality of the one-House veto provision because he could receive no relief even if his constitutional challenge proves successful.

Congress says if 244c2 is bad so is 244, so ∅ auth to suspend + They say ∅ standing blc ∅ relief

Only recently this Court reaffirmed that the invalid portions of a statute are to be severed "[u]nless it is evident that the Legislature would not have enacted those provisions which are within its power, independently of that which is not." *Buckley v. Valeo*, 424 U.S. 1, 108 (1976). Here, however, we need not embark on that elusive inquiry since Congress itself has provided the answer to the question of severability in § 406 of the Immigration and Nationality Act, which provides:

> If any particular provision of this Act, or the application thereof to any person or circumstance, is held invalid, *the remainder of the Act and the application of such provision to other persons or circumstances shall not be affected thereby*. (Emphasis added.)

"shall ∅ be affected"

This language is unambiguous and gives rise to a presumption that Congress did not intend the validity of the Act as a whole, or of any part of the Act, to depend upon whether the veto clause of § 244(c)(2) was invalid. . . . Congress could not have more plainly authorized the presumption that the provision for a one-House veto in § 244(c)(2) is severable from the remainder of § 244 and the Act of which it is a part.

The presumption as to the severability of the one-House veto provision in §244(c)(2) is supported by the legislative history of §244. That section and its precursors supplanted the long established pattern of dealing with deportations like Chadha's on a case-by-case basis through private bills. . . . [T]here is insufficient evidence that Congress would have continued to subject itself to the onerous burdens of private bills had it known that §244(c)(2) would be held unconstitutional.

A provision is further presumed severable if what remains after severance "is fully operative as a law." *Champlin Refining Co. v. Corporation Comm'n*, 286 U.S., at 234 [(1932)]. There can be no doubt that §244 is "fully operative" and workable administrative machinery without the veto provision in §244(c)(2) . . . .

III

A

We turn now to the question whether action of one House of Congress under §244(c)(2) violates strictures of the Constitution. We begin, of course, with the presumption that the challenged statute is valid. Its wisdom is not the concern of the courts; if a challenged action does not violate the Constitution, it must be sustained. . . . By the same token, the fact that a given law or procedure is efficient, convenient, and useful in facilitating functions of government, standing alone, will not save it if it is contrary to the Constitution. Convenience and efficiency are not the primary objectives—or the hallmarks—of democratic government and our inquiry is sharpened rather than blunted by the fact that Congressional veto provisions are appearing with increasing frequency in statutes which delegate authority to executive and independent agencies . . . .

Explicit and unambiguous provisions of the Constitution prescribe and define the respective functions of the Congress and of the Executive in the legislative process. Since the precise terms of those familiar provisions are critical to the resolution of this case, we set them out verbatim. Art. I provides:

> All legislative Powers herein granted shall be vested in a Congress of the United States, which shall consist of a Senate *and* a House of Representatives. Art. I, §1. (Emphasis added).

> Every Bill which shall have passed the House of Representatives *and* the Senate, *shall*, before it becomes a Law, be presented to the President of the United States; . . . Art. I, §7, cl. 2. (Emphasis added).

> *Every* Order, Resolution, or Vote to which the Concurrence of the Senate and House of Representatives may be necessary (except on a question of Adjournment) *shall* be presented to the President of the United States; and before the Same shall take Effect, *shall* be approved by him, or being disapproved by him, *shall* be repassed by two thirds of the Senate and House of Representatives, according to the Rules and Limitations prescribed in the Case of a Bill. Art. I, §7, cl. 3. (Emphasis added).

These provisions of Art. I are integral parts of the constitutional design for the separation of powers. We . . . find that the purposes underlying the Presentment Clauses, Art. I, § 7, cls. 2, 3, and the bicameral requirement of Art. I, § 1 and § 7, cl. 2, guide our resolution of the important question presented in this case. The very structure of the articles delegating and separating powers under Arts. I, II, and III exemplify the concept of separation of powers and we now turn to Art. I.

B

The Presentment Clauses

The records of the Constitutional Convention reveal that the requirement that all legislation be presented to the President before becoming law was uniformly accepted by the Framers. Presentment to the President and the Presidential veto were considered so imperative that the draftsmen took special pains to assure that these requirements could not be circumvented. During the final debate on Art. I, § 7, cl. 2, James Madison expressed concern that it might easily be evaded by the simple expedient of calling a proposed law a "resolution" or "vote" rather than a "bill." 2 M. Farrand, The Records of the Federal Convention of 1787, 301–02. As a consequence, Art. I, § 7, cl. 3, was added.

The decision to provide the President with a limited and qualified power to nullify proposed legislation by veto was based on the profound conviction of the Framers that the powers conferred on Congress were the powers to be most carefully circumscribed. It is beyond doubt that lawmaking was a power to be shared by both Houses and the President. In The Federalist No. 73, Hamilton focused on the President's role in making laws:

> If even no propensity had ever discovered itself in the legislative body to invade the rights of the Executive, the rules of just reasoning and theoretic propriety would of themselves teach us that the one ought not to be left to the mercy of the other, but ought to possess a constitutional and effectual power of self-defense.

See also The Federalist No. 51. In his Commentaries on the Constitution, Joseph Story makes the same point. 1 J. Story, Commentaries on the Constitution of the United States 614–615 (1858).

The President's role in the lawmaking process also reflects the Framers' careful efforts to check whatever propensity a particular Congress might have to enact oppressive, improvident, or ill-considered measures. The President's veto role in the legislative process was described later during public debate on ratification:

> It establishes a salutary check upon the legislative body, calculated to guard the community against the effects of faction, precipitancy, or of any impulse unfriendly to the public good which may happen to influence a majority of that body. . . . The primary inducement to conferring the power in question upon the Executive is to enable him to defend himself; the secondary one is to increase the chances in favor of the community against the passing

of bad laws through haste, inadvertence, or design. The Federalist No. 73 (A. Hamilton).

The Court also has observed that the Presentment Clauses serve the important purpose of assuring that a "national" perspective is grafted on the legislative process:

> The President is a representative of the people just as the members of the Senate and of the House are, and it may be, at some times, on some subjects, that the President elected by all the people is rather more representative of them all than are the members of either body of the Legislature whose constituencies are local and not countrywide.... *Myers v. United States*, 272 U.S., at 123.

C

Bicameralism

The bicameral requirement of Art. I, §§ 1, 7 was of scarcely less concern to the Framers than was the Presidential veto and indeed the two concepts are interdependent. By providing that no law could take effect without the concurrence of the prescribed majority of the Members of both Houses, the Framers reemphasized their belief, already remarked upon in connection with the Presentment Clauses, that legislation should not be enacted unless it has been carefully and fully considered by the Nation's elected officials.... These observations are consistent with what many of the Framers expressed, none more cogently than Hamilton in pointing up the need to divide and disperse power in order to protect liberty:

> In republican government, the legislative authority necessarily predominates. The remedy for this inconveniency is to divide the legislature into different branches; and to render them, by different modes of election and different principles of action, as little connected with each other as the nature of their common functions and their common dependence on the society will admit. The Federalist No. 51.

However familiar, it is useful to recall that apart from their fear that special interests could be favored at the expense of public needs, the Framers were also concerned, although not of one mind, over the apprehensions of the smaller states.... It need hardly be repeated here that the Great Compromise, under which one House was viewed as representing the people and the other the states, allayed the fears of both the large and small states.

We see therefore that the Framers were acutely conscious that the bicameral requirement and the Presentment Clauses would serve essential constitutional functions. The President's participation in the legislative process was to protect the Executive Branch from Congress and to protect the whole people from improvident laws. The division of the Congress into two distinctive bodies assures that the legislative power would be exercised only after opportunity for full study and debate in separate settings. The President's unilateral veto power, in turn, was limited by the power of two thirds of both Houses of Congress to overrule a veto thereby precluding final arbitrary action of one person. *See* 1 M. Farrand, at 99–104. It emerges clearly that the prescription for legislative action in Art. I, §§ 1, 7 represents the Framers' decision that the legislative power of the Federal government be exercised in accord with a single, finely wrought and exhaustively considered, procedure.

IV

The Constitution sought to divide the delegated powers of the new federal government into three defined categories, legislative, executive and judicial, to assure, as nearly as possible, that each Branch of government would confine itself to its assigned responsibility. The hydraulic pressure inherent within each of the separate Branches to exceed the outer limits of its power, even to accomplish desirable objectives, must be resisted. Although not "hermetically" sealed from one another, the powers delegated to the three Branches are functionally identifiable. . . . [W]e must nevertheless establish that the challenged action under § 244(c)(2) is of the kind to which the procedural requirements of Art. I, § 7 apply. Not every action taken by either House is subject to the bicameralism and presentment requirements of Art. I. Whether actions taken by either House are, in law and fact, an exercise of legislative power depends not on their form but upon "whether they contain matter which is properly to be regarded as legislative in its character and effect." S.Rep. No. 1335, 54th Cong., 2d Sess., 8 (1897).

Examination of the action taken here by one House pursuant to § 244(c)(2) reveals that it was essentially legislative in purpose and effect. In purporting to exercise power defined in Art. I, § 8, cl. 4 to "establish an uniform Rule of Naturalization," the House took action that had the purpose and effect of altering the legal rights, duties and relations of persons, including the Attorney General, Executive Branch officials and Chadha, all outside the legislative branch. Section 244(c)(2) purports to authorize one House of Congress to require the Attorney General to deport an individual alien whose deportation otherwise would be canceled under § 244. The one-House veto operated in this case to overrule the Attorney General and mandate Chadha's deportation; absent the House action, Chadha would remain in the United States. Congress has *acted* and its action has altered Chadha's status.

The legislative character of the one-House veto in this case is confirmed by the character of the Congressional action it supplants. Neither the House of Representatives nor the Senate contends that, absent the veto provision in § 244(c)(2), either of them, or both of them acting together, could effectively require the Attorney General to deport an alien once the Attorney General, in the exercise of legislatively delegated authority, had determined the alien should remain in the United States. Without the challenged provision in § 244(c)(2), this could have been achieved, if at all, only by legislation requiring deportation. Similarly, a veto by one House of Congress under § 244(c)(2) cannot be justified as an attempt at amending the standards set out in

§ 244(a)(1), or as a repeal of § 244 as applied to Chadha. Amendment and repeal of statutes, no less than enactment, must conform with Art. I.

The nature of the decision implemented by the one-House veto in this case further manifests its legislative character. After long experience with the clumsy, time consuming private bill procedure, Congress made a deliberate choice to delegate to the Executive Branch, and specifically to the Attorney General, the authority to allow deportable aliens to remain in this country in certain specified circumstances. It is not disputed that this choice to delegate authority is precisely the kind of decision that can be implemented only in accordance with the procedures set out in Art. I. Disagreement with the Attorney General's decision on Chadha's deportation — that is, Congress' decision to deport Chadha — no less than Congress' original choice to delegate to the Attorney General the authority to make that decision, involves determinations of policy that Congress can implement in only one way; bicameral passage followed by presentment to the President. Congress must abide by its delegation of authority until that delegation is legislatively altered or revoked.

Finally, we see that when the Framers intended to authorize either House of Congress to act alone and outside of its prescribed bicameral legislative role, they narrowly and precisely defined the procedure for such action. There are but four provisions in the Constitution, explicit and unambiguous, by which one House may act alone with the unreviewable force of law, not subject to the President's veto:

(a) The House of Representatives alone was given the power to initiate impeachments. Art. I, § 2, cl. 6;

(b) The Senate alone was given the power to conduct trials following impeachment on charges initiated by the House and to convict following trial. Art. I, § 3, cl. 5;

(c) The Senate alone was given final unreviewable power to approve or to disapprove presidential appointments. Art. II, § 2, cl. 2;

(d) The Senate alone was given unreviewable power to ratify treaties negotiated by the President. Art. II, § 2, cl. 2.

Clearly, when the Draftsmen sought to confer special powers on one House, independent of the other House, or of the President, they did so in explicit, unambiguous terms. These carefully defined exceptions from presentment and bicameralism underscore the difference between the legislative functions of Congress and other unilateral but important and binding one-House acts provided for in the Constitution. . . . [T]hey provide further support for the conclusion that Congressional authority is not to be implied and for the conclusion that the veto provided for in § 244(c)(2) is not authorized by the constitutional design of the powers of the Legislative Branch. . . .

V

We hold that the Congressional veto provision in § 244(c)(2) is severable from the Act and that it is unconstitutional. Accordingly, the judgment of the Court of Appeals is

Affirmed.

Justice POWELL, concurring in the judgment.

The Court's decision, based on the Presentment Clauses, Art. I, § 7, cls. 2 and 3, apparently will invalidate every use of the legislative veto. The breadth of this holding gives one pause. Congress has included the veto in literally hundreds of statutes, dating back to the 1930s. . . . [T]he respect due its judgment as a coordinate branch of Government cautions that our holding should be no more extensive than necessary to decide this case. In my view, the case may be decided on a narrower ground. When Congress finds that a particular person does not satisfy the statutory criteria for permanent residence in this country it has assumed a judicial function in violation of the principle of separation of powers. Accordingly, I concur only in the judgment.

I

A

The Framers perceived that "[t]he accumulation of all powers legislative, executive and judiciary in the same hands, whether of one, a few or many, and whether hereditary, self appointed, or elective, may justly be pronounced the very definition of tyranny." The Federalist No. 47 (J. Madison). . . . One abuse that was prevalent during the Confederation was the exercise of judicial power by the state legislatures. The Framers were well acquainted with the danger of subjecting the determination of the rights of one person to the "tyranny of shifting majorities." . . . It was to prevent the recurrence of such abuses that the Framers vested the executive, legislative, and judicial powers in separate branches. Their concern that a legislature should not be able unilaterally to impose a substantial deprivation on one person was expressed not only in this general allocation of power, but also in more specific provisions, such as the Bill of Attainder Clause, Art. I, § 9, cl. 3. . . . This Clause, and the separation of powers doctrine generally, reflect the Framers' concern that trial by a legislature lacks the safeguards necessary to prevent the abuse of power.

B

. . . Functionally, the doctrine may be violated in two ways. One branch may interfere impermissibly with the other's performance of its constitutionally assigned function. *See Nixon v. Administrator of General Services*, 433 U.S. 425, 433 (1977); *United States v. Nixon*, 418 U.S. 683 (1974). Alternatively, the doctrine may be violated when one branch assumes a function that more properly is entrusted to another. *See Youngstown Sheet & Tube Co. v. Sawyer, supra*, 343 U.S., at 587 (1952). This case presents the latter situation.

II

. . . On its face, the House's action appears clearly adjudicatory. The House did not enact a general rule; rather it made its own determination that six specific persons did not comply with certain statutory criteria. It thus undertook the type of decision that traditionally has been left to other branches. Even if the House did not make a *de novo* determination, but simply reviewed the Immigration and Naturalization

Service's findings, it still assumed a function ordinarily entrusted to the federal courts. . . .

The impropriety of the House's assumption of this function is confirmed by the fact that its action raises the very danger the Framers sought to avoid—the exercise of unchecked power. In deciding whether Chadha deserves to be deported, Congress is not subject to any internal constraints that prevent it from arbitrarily depriving him of the right to remain in this country. Unlike the judiciary or an administrative agency, Congress is not bound by established substantive rules. Nor is it subject to the procedural safeguards, such as the right to counsel and a hearing before an impartial tribunal, that are present when a court or an agency adjudicates individual rights. The only effective constraint on Congress' power is political, but Congress is most accountable politically when it prescribes rules of general applicability. When it decides rights of specific persons, those rights are subject to "the tyranny of a shifting majority." . . . In my view, when Congress undertook to apply its rules to Chadha, it exceeded the scope of its constitutionally prescribed authority . . . .

Justice WHITE, dissenting.

. . . The history of the legislative veto . . . makes clear that it has not been a sword with which Congress has struck out to aggrandize itself at the expense of the other branches—the concerns of Madison and Hamilton. Rather, the veto has been a means of defense, a reservation of ultimate authority necessary if Congress is to fulfill its designated role under Article I as the nation's lawmaker. While the President has often objected to particular legislative vetoes, generally those left in the hands of congressional committees, the Executive has more often agreed to legislative review as the price for a broad delegation of authority. To be sure, the President may have preferred unrestricted power, but that could be precisely why Congress thought it essential to retain a check on the exercise of delegated authority. . . .

III

. . . [T]he Third Part of the Court's opinion, is entirely unexceptionable. It does not, however, answer the constitutional question before us. The power to exercise a legislative veto is not the power to write new law without bicameral approval or presidential consideration. The veto must be authorized by statute and may only negative what an Executive department or independent agency has proposed. On its face, the legislative veto no more allows one House of Congress to make law than does the presidential veto confer such power upon the President. . . .

A

The terms of the Presentment Clauses suggest only that bills and their equivalent are subject to the requirements of bicameral passage and presentment to the President. . . . [T]he historical background of the Presentation Clause . . . reveals only that the Framers were concerned with limiting the methods for enacting new legislation. . . . There is no record that the Convention contemplated, let alone intended, that these Article I requirements would someday be invoked to restrain the scope of Congressional authority pursuant to duly-enacted law. When the Convention did turn its attention to the scope of Congress' lawmaking power, the Framers were expansive. The Necessary and Proper Clause . . . [means] that Congress may "exercise its best judgment in the selection of measures, to carry into execution the constitutional powers of the government," and "avail itself of experience, to exercise its reason, and to accommodate its legislation to circumstances." *McCulloch v. Maryland*, 4 Wheat. 316, 415–16, 420 (1819).

B

The Court heeded this counsel in approving the modern administrative state. The Court's holding today that all legislative-type action must be enacted through the lawmaking process ignores that legislative authority is routinely delegated to the Executive branch, to the independent regulatory agencies, and to private individuals and groups. . . . This Court's decisions sanctioning such delegations make clear that Article I does not require all action with the effect of legislation to be passed as a law. . . . For some time, the sheer amount of law — the substantive rules that regulate private conduct and direct the operation of government — made by the agencies has far outnumbered the lawmaking engaged in by Congress through the traditional process. There is no question but that agency rulemaking is lawmaking in any functional or realistic sense of the term. . . . When agencies are authorized to prescribe law through substantive rulemaking, the administrator's regulation is not only due deference, but is accorded "legislative effect." These regulations bind courts and officers of the federal government, may pre-empt state law, and grant rights to and impose obligations on the public. In sum, they have the force of law.

If Congress may delegate lawmaking power to independent and executive agencies, it is most difficult to understand Article I as forbidding Congress from also reserving a check on legislative power for itself. Absent the veto, the agencies receiving delegations of legislative or quasi-legislative power may issue regulations having the force of law without bicameral approval and without the President's signature. It is thus not apparent why the reservation of a veto over the exercise of that legislative power must be subject to a more exacting test. In both cases, it is enough that the initial statutory authorizations comply with the Article I requirements.

. . . While most authority to issue rules and regulations is given to the executive branch and the independent regulatory agencies, statutory delegations to private persons have also passed this Court's scrutiny. . . . Assuming [these cases] remain sound law, the Court's decision today suggests that Congress may place a "veto" power over suspensions of deportation in private hands or in the hands of an independent agency, but is forbidden from reserving such authority for itself. Perhaps this odd result could be justified on other constitutional grounds, such as the separation of powers, but certainly it cannot be defended as consistent with the Court's view of the Article I presentment and bicameralism commands. . . .

[T]he Court concedes that certain administrative agency action, such as rulemaking, "may resemble lawmaking". . . . Such rules and adjudications by the agencies meet the Court's own definition of legislative action for they "alter[ ] the legal rights, duties, and relations of persons . . . outside the legislative branch," and involve "determinations of policy." Under the Court's analysis, the Executive Branch and the independent agencies may make rules with the effect of law while Congress, in whom the Framers confided the legislative power, Art. I, § 1, may not exercise a veto which precludes such rules from having operative force. If the effective functioning of a complex modern government requires the delegation of vast authority which, by virtue of its breadth, is legislative or "quasi-legislative" in character, I cannot accept that Article I — which is, after all, the source of the non-delegation doctrine — should forbid Congress from qualifying that grant with a legislative veto.

C

The Court also takes no account of perhaps the most relevant consideration: However resolutions of disapproval under § 244(c)(2) are formally characterized, in reality, a departure from the status quo occurs only upon the concurrence of opinion among the House, Senate, and President. . . . The central concern of the presentation and bicameralism requirements of Article I is that when a departure from the legal status quo is undertaken, it is done with the approval of the President and both Houses of Congress. . . . This interest is fully satisfied by the operation of § 244(c)(2). The President's approval is found in the Attorney General's action in recommending to Congress that the deportation order for a given alien be suspended. The House and the Senate indicate their approval of the Executive's action by not passing a resolution of disapproval within the statutory period. Thus, a change in the legal status quo — the deportability of the alien — is consummated only with the approval of each of the three relevant actors. The disagreement of any one of the three maintains the alien's pre-existing status: the Executive may choose not to recommend suspension; the House and Senate may each veto the recommendation. The effect on the rights and obligations of the affected individuals and upon the legislative system is precisely the same as if a private bill were introduced but failed to receive the necessary approval. . . .

I now briefly consider possible objections to the analysis. First, it may be asserted that Chadha's status before legislative disapproval is one of nondeportation and that the exercise of the veto, unlike the failure of a private bill, works a change in the status quo. This position plainly ignores the statutory language. At no place in § 244 has Congress delegated to the Attorney General any final power to determine which aliens shall be allowed to remain in the United States. . . . Second, it may be said that this approach leads to the incongruity that the two-House veto is more suspect than its one-House brother. Although the idea may be initially counter-intuitive, . . . [i]f the Attorney General's action is a proposal for legislation, then the disapproval of but a single House is all that is required to prevent its passage. . . . The two-House version may present a different question. . . . Third, it may be objected that Congress cannot indicate its approval of legislative change by inaction. . . . Certainly the legislative veto is no more susceptible to this attack than the Court's increasingly common practice of according weight to the failure of Congress to disturb an Executive or independent agency's action. . . .

IV

. . . The legislative veto provision does not "prevent the Executive Branch from accomplishing its constitutionally assigned functions." First, it is clear that the Executive Branch has no "constitutionally assigned" function of suspending the deportation of aliens. . . . Nor can it be said that the inherent function of the Executive Branch in executing the law is involved. *The Steel Seizure Case* resolved that the Article II mandate for the President to execute the law is a directive to enforce the law which Congress has written. "The duty of the President to see that the laws be executed is a duty that does not go beyond the laws or require him to achieve more than Congress sees fit to leave within his power." *Myers v. United States*, 272 U.S., at 177 (Holmes, J., dissenting). Here, §244 grants the executive only a qualified suspension authority and it is only that authority which the President is constitutionally authorized to execute. . . . In comparison to private bills, which must be initiated in the Congress and which allow a Presidential veto to be overridden by a two-thirds majority in both Houses of Congress, §244 augments rather than reduces the executive branch's authority. . . .

Nor does §244 infringe on the judicial power, as Justice Powell would hold. . . . The Act provides for judicial review of the refusal of the Attorney General to suspend a deportation and to transmit a recommendation to Congress. But the courts have not been given the authority to review whether an alien should be given permanent status; review is limited to whether the Attorney General has properly applied the statutory standards for essentially denying the alien a recommendation that his deportable status be changed by the Congress. Moreover, there is no constitutional obligation to provide any judicial review whatever for a failure to suspend deportation. . . .

I do not suggest that all legislative vetoes are necessarily consistent with separation of powers principles. A legislative check on an inherently executive function, for example, that of initiating prosecutions, poses an entirely different question. But the legislative veto device here—and in many other settings—is far from an instance of legislative tyranny over the Executive. It is a necessary check on the unavoidably expanding power of the agencies, both executive and independent, as they engage in exercising authority delegated by Congress. . . .

Justice REHNQUIST, with whom Justice WHITE joins, dissenting.

. . . Because I believe that Congress did not intend the one-House veto provision of §244(c)(2) to be severable, I dissent. . . . Congress has never indicated that it would be willing to permit suspensions of deportation unless it could retain some sort of veto. . . .

----

1. *Critiquing the Majority.* Which method of separation of powers analysis does the Court use in *Chadha*? Its opinion is notoriously opaque. The Court's response to Justice White's detailed dissent was mostly confined to its footnote 16:

> Congress protests that affirming the Court of Appeals in this case will sanction "lawmaking by the Attorney General. . . . To be sure, some administrative

agency action—rule making, for example—may resemble "lawmaking." *See* 5 U.S.C. § 551(4), which defines an agency's "rule" as "the whole or part of an agency statement of general or particular applicability and future effect designed to implement, interpret, or prescribe *law* or policy. . . ." This Court has referred to agency activity as being "quasi-legislative" in character. . . . When the Attorney General performs his duties pursuant to § 244, he does not exercise "legislative" power. The bicameral process is not necessary as a check on the Executive's administration of the laws because his administrative activity cannot reach beyond the limits of the statute that created it—a statute duly enacted pursuant to Art. I, §§ 1, 7. . . . It is clear, therefore, that the Attorney General acts in his presumptively Art. II capacity when he administers the Immigration and Nationality Act. Executive action under legislatively delegated authority that might resemble "legislative" action in some respects is not subject to the approval of both Houses of Congress and the President for the reason that the Constitution does not so require. . . .

Is this a persuasive response to the dissent? E. Donald Elliott, *INS v. Chadha: The Administrative Constitution, the Constitution, and the Legislative Veto*, 1983 Sup. Ct. Rev. 125, at 134–35, 144–47, analyzes the Court's approach as follows:

> The core of the Court's reasoning is conceptual and formalistic: the legislative veto is "legislative" because it has the effect of "altering legal rights." The legislative veto "alters legal rights," however, only because the Court chooses to characterize its effect that way. The Court's manipulation of legal categories could just as easily be turned to support the opposite conclusion that the legislative veto does not alter legal rights. . . . Even if it could be said that Chadha had acquired "legal rights," how were those rights "altered" by the House resolution? After all, the statute authorizing the Attorney General to suspend deportation on grounds of hardship also provided that either house of Congress could veto the Attorney General's action. Why was the nature of Chadha's legal rights not defined by the statute creating them? . . . These questions imply, not that the Court's analysis is incorrect, but that it is arbitrary. . . .
>
> The underlying source of the problems is jurisprudential. The Court insists that the texts of the presentment clauses and the vesting of legislative power in a bicameral Congress dispose of the legislative veto ex proprio vigore. But constitutional texts do not apply themselves. Justice White is surely right that the Constitution is silent on the "precise question" of the legislative veto and neither "directly authorize[s]" nor "prohibit[s]" it. In order to treat the texts as dispositive, the Court must tacitly assume the postulate which should be under examination: whether the legislative veto is congressional action of the sort to which the requirements of bicameralism and presentment should apply. To answer this question necessarily requires a perspective from outside the system: "Syllogism" alone is incapable of resolving such questions. . . .

[To the Court, the] growth of the bureaucracy in the Executive branch and in agencies independent of presidential control is not of constitutional significance because it raises a nice point of classification that can be laid to rest once the Court decides whether the legal category "executive" or "legislative" is more appropriate. . . . [Yet t]he growth of lawmaking power in a vast administrative bureaucracy may be seen as a threat to the essence of the constitutional principle of separation of powers. Madison . . . summarized that fundamental constitutional principle in Federalist No. 51 as "contriving the interior structure of the government as that its several constituent parts may, by their mutual relations, be the means of keeping each other in their proper places." The "constant aim" of this strategy, Madison continues, "is to divide and arrange the several offices in such a manner as that each may be a check on the other." It is ironic that the Court in *Chadha*, in the name of the constitutional principles of checks and balances and separation of powers, ends up striking down one of the few existing checks on lawmaking by the bureaucracy.

Can you formulate a more complete rationale for the Court's decision? For one effort to do so, see Harold H. Bruff, *The Incompatibility Principle*, 59 ADMIN L. REV. 225, 246–48 (2007):

The *Chadha* Court never did connect its conclusions to the purposes of bicameralism and presentation. By making that connection, it is possible to articulate a more complete rationale for the Court's action. The structure of Article I serves three purposes. The Court identified two of them—preventing encroachments on the executive and dampening the effects of faction. [For the ways in which the legislative veto aided factions, see Harold H. Bruff, *Legislative Formality, Administrative Rationality*, 63 TEX. L. REV. 207, 220–22 (1984).] The third is to reduce the amount of legislation that would burden the people. The legislative veto interferes with the realization of all three. When Congress sent the President a bill containing a legislative veto provision, it simultaneously contravened two of the purposes of Article I. First, it proposed an encroachment on executive power. In both theory and practice, legislative veto provisions gave Congress a share in the execution of the law, in a way that infringed the [principle underlying the Incompatibility Clause of the Constitution]. When no legislative veto authority is present, the executive bears sole legal responsibility for statutory implementation. With a veto, one or both houses share that responsibility due to their power to choose whether to override executive action or leave it alone. In practice, programs containing veto provisions featured much more direct participation by congressional committees in formulating executive actions than is otherwise the case. The committees possessed this increased leverage because it was relatively easy to pass a veto resolution, compared to ordinary legislation. It was not just that the agreement of the other house and the President was not needed. A veto resolution did not call for an affirmative and perhaps controversial statement of policy by the house passing it. It simply rejected the particular executive policy in question, and could be justified by the institutional congressional need to keep the executive under control.

If legislative vetoes encroached on executive power, why did Presidents sign so many statutes containing them? The reason is that the executive wanted power that Congress would not delegate without a veto condition. Hence statutes containing vetoes expanded the power of the federal government, compared to ordinary legislation. Presidents yielded to the temptation to enter improper bargains with Congress, receiving increased executive power but sharing it with Congress. This pattern evaded the attempt of the framers to make the process of legislation cumbersome enough to minimize federal legislation, leaving the states and the people free to govern themselves.

The Court could also have pointed out that Congress, by virtue of the Incompatibility Clause, is forbidden to engage in execution. To the framing generation, the spectacle of Congress and the President bargaining to expand their joint power by evading the limits of the Presentation Clauses would have seemed "corruption" at its worst, by trading on mutual influence. Moreover, the Framers-in-Government debated the permissible limits of congressional delegation of power to the executive in quite modern terms, revealing their shared view that the legislative/executive boundary required enforcement. [*See* David P. Currie, The Constitution in Congress, The Federalist Period 1789–1801, at 147–49, 246–47 (1997)].

In contrast, Professor Shane has argued that the Court's justification was *more* elaborate than necessary. In *Conventionalism in Constitutional Interpretation and the Place of Administrative Agencies*, 36 Am. U. L. Rev. 573, 585–86 (1987), he argues that a textualist resolution of *Chadha* is sufficient:

> It is difficult to see how two-house vetoes, not presented to the President, can pass muster under [the Presentment Clauses] . . . . If that is true, then the question in *INS v. Chadha* was essentially, is there any reason to think that one-house vetoes are more permissible than two-house vetoes? . . . No matter what purpose is ascribed to article I, section 7, I cannot imagine an affirmative answer to that question.

See also Harold J. Krent, *Separating the Strands in Separation of Powers Controversies*, 74 Va. L. Rev. 1253 (1988) (arguing that the Constitution prescribes, in a way that is capable of relatively formal implementation, how and when each branch may act, but leaves open to a balancing analysis those cases when one branch acts within express constitutional constraints, although in a manner that intrudes on another branch's domain). In light of this argument, consider Justice White's admission that his view of the Constitution leads to the "counter-intuitive" conclusion that two-house vetoes are more vulnerable than the one-house form. Does that reveal a fundamental defect in his argument?

The "reverse legislation" theory is discussed further in Peter M. Shane, *The Separation of Powers and the Rule of Law: The Virtues of Seeing the Trees*, 30 Wm. & Mary L. Rev. 375, 380–81 n.27 (1989). In Shane's view, what *does* require fuller explanation is the normative basis for conventional textualism as a mode of constitutional interpretation. He argues that for provisions such as those in Articles I and II "which describe conventionally understood structures and processes," textualist interpretation is more accessible, more certain, and more likely to vindicate the Constitution's underlying functional premises than alternative approaches. *Id.* at 593–97. Additionally, *some* formalism in constitutional interpretation "gives voice to our aspirations for control and accountability as part of justice. It would be advantageous . . . if textualism in constitutional interpretation vis-a-vis administrative agencies passes the message to government officials that, sometimes, we just want them to do what they are told." *Id.* at 598. For a similar analysis, see Geoffrey P. Miller, *Independent Agencies*, 1986 Sup. Ct. Rev. 41, 52–58.

2. Chadha's *Scope.* How broad is the scope of the *Chadha* ruling? Do you agree that it has swept away all forms of the legislative veto? *See generally* Peter L. Strauss, *Was There a Baby in the Bathwater? A Comment on the Supreme Court's Legislative Veto Decision*, 1983 Duke L.J. 789, for an argument that the Court should have distinguished legislative vetoes that directly address difficult separation of powers controversies between the branches from those governing ordinary administration. In your view, which is more vulnerable? We will consider the issue of the appropriate scope of *Chadha* in direct interbranch controversies twice below, in connection with legislative vetoes in the Impoundment Control Act (later in this chapter) and the War Powers Resolution (Chapter Six).

3. *Severability.* Severability issues proliferated after *Chadha*. In *Alaska Airlines, Inc. v. Brock*, 480 U.S. 678 (1987), the Court decided its first post-*Chadha* severability case. In the course of holding that a legislative veto contained in the Airline Deregulation Act of 1978 was severable, the Court gave some general guidance. Regarding the part of the severability test that asks whether the statute is "fully operative" without the unconstitutional portion, the Court noted that "by its very nature" a legislative veto is separate from the substantive provisions, since it is contemplated that Congress will ordinarily refrain from employing it. From this the Court concluded that the statute's operability without the veto would "indicate little" about congressional intent regarding severability. The Court went on to say:

> The more relevant inquiry is whether the statute will function in a *manner consistent with the intent of Congress*. . . . [I]t is necessary to recognize that the absence of the veto necessarily alters the balance of powers between the Legislative and Executive Branches. . . . Thus, it is not only appropriate to evaluate the importance of the veto in the original legislative bargain, but also to consider the nature of the delegated authority that Congress made subject to a veto. Some delegations . . . may have been so controversial or so broad that Congress would have been unwilling to make the delegation

without a strong oversight mechanism. The final test . . . is the traditional one: the unconstitutional provision must be severed unless the statute created in its absence is legislation that Congress would not have enacted.

Note that, as in *Chadha*, some statutes have severability clauses even when the legislative veto may have been essential to the "legislative bargain." Should a court ever ignore such a clause and hold that a legislative veto in a statute having one is nonseverable?

4. *Independent Agencies.* Do you agree with the Court's implication that all executive activity is the same and that the independent agencies present no special considerations? After *Chadha*, the Court summarily affirmed decisions invalidating legislative vetoes applicable to rulemaking by independent agencies, *U.S. House of Representatives v. FTC*, 463 U.S. 1216 (1983); *Process Gas Consumers Group v. Consumer Energy Council of America*, 463 U.S. 1216 (1983).

5. *Concurrent Resolutions.* In the FTC case cited *supra*, the Court summarily affirmed a decision invalidating a two-House veto.

6. *Replacements.* What steps should Congress take to oversee the executive in the wake of *Chadha*? Some have proposed a constitutional amendment to restore the veto. *See* Dennis DeConcini & Robert Faucher, *The Legislative Veto: A Constitutional Amendment*, 21 Harv. J. Legis. 29 (1984). Of course, Congress retains its ordinary oversight devices, such as hearings with a view to altering legislation or appropriations.

Some new devices have been adopted, such as subjecting executive action to joint resolutions of approval or disapproval before it becomes effective. Of course, Congress may always alter delegated power by statute; these techniques add something new by changing the internal rules of Congress to ensure speedy floor consideration of the resolutions, without possibility of amendment. In that way, Congress can mimic the legislative veto without running afoul of *Chadha*. *See* Stephen Breyer, *The Legislative Veto After* Chadha, 72 Geo. L.J. 785 (1984). Congress has enacted a requirement that federal regulations lie before it for 60 legislative days, during which time Congress can employ expedited process to pass a joint resolution of disapproval. Congressional Review Act (CRA) of 1996, 5 U.S.C. §801 et seq. *See generally* Daniel Cohen & Peter L. Strauss, *Congressional Review of Agency Regulations*, 49 Admin. L. Rev. 95 (1997); Morton Rosenberg, *Whatever Happened to Congressional Review of Agency Rulemaking? A Brief Overview, Assessment, and Proposal for Reform*, 51 Admin. L. Rev. 1051 (1999).

The impact of the CRA has seen two distinct phases. Between 1995 and the end of the Obama Administration, Congress disapproved only one regulation, invalidating an eleventh-hour Clinton Administration ergonomics standard for workplaces. Congressional Research Serv., Congressional Review of Agency Rulemaking 5–6 (2002). Yet agencies had forwarded over 46,000 rules during this period to the Government Accountability Office and Congress for review, of which 700 were classified as "major." Statement of Gary Kepplinger, General Counsel, Government

Accountability Office, Before the Subcommittee on Commercial and Administrative Law, Committee on the Judiciary, House of Representatives re: Congressional Review Act 5 (GAO-08-268T) (Nov. 6, 2007). Perhaps even more remarkably, the Congressional Research Service reported in late 2009:

> GAO periodically compares the list of rules that are submitted to it with the rules that are published in the Federal Register to determine whether any covered rules have not been submitted. Between 1999 and 2009, GAO sent the Office of Information and Regulatory Affairs (OIRA) within the Office of Management and Budget at least five letters listing more than 1,000 substantive final rules that GAO said it had not received. In each of those letters, GAO encouraged OIRA to use the information to ensure that the agencies complied with the CRA. The most recent of these letters was sent to OIRA in May 2009, and listed 101 substantive rules that were published during FY2008 that GAO said had not been submitted. The missing rules were issued by different agencies, including the Departments of Agriculture, Commerce, Transportation, and Homeland Security. The topics covered by these rules varied, and included chemical facility anti-terrorism standards, designation of critical habitats for endangered species, the administration of direct farm loan programs, oil and gas lease operations, and changes to workplace drug and alcohol programs.

Curtis W. Copeland, *Congressional Review Act: Rules Not Submitted to GAO and Congress* (CRS Dec. 29, 2009).

Republican control of both Houses of Congress in 2017, however, together with the election of Donald J. Trump as president, saw the CRA spring into action. The CRA gives each new Congress an extra seventy-five legislative (for the House) or session (for the Senate) days to review rules reported to Congress within 60 legislative days of the adjournment of its prior session. This gave the GOP-controlled elected branches the opportunity to review Obama Administration rules going back to mid-June 2016, and Congress responded by voiding fourteen major rules. (A roster of the repealed rules appears at http://www.progressivereform.org/assaultscratargets.cfm.) Given the statute's fast-track procedures — no filibusters are allowed — these rules were revoked with relatively little debate despite their often significant content.

Its long period of dormancy led some observers to regard the CRA as a failed experiment. How would you assess the CRA in terms of its likely impacts on the administrative process? What amendments, if any, might you propose to the CRA to increase the executive branch's accountability for its rulemaking activity? Or would you eliminate the Act because you think it gives Congress too much leeway to abolish rules without its own accountability?

7. *So What?* Since *Chadha*, Congress has continued to include legislative veto provisions in new legislation. Although the executive claims that these have no legal effect, Congress clearly expects, and often obtains, informal compliance with them. *See* Louis Fisher, Congressional Abdication on War and Spending 180–81

(2000), reporting that Congress has often attached committee veto provisions to agency use of appropriated funds. The executive must then obey the committee if it wants the money. *See also* Michael J. Berry, The Modern Legislative Veto: Macropolitical Conflict and the Legacy of *Chadha* (2016); Louis Fisher, Constitutional Conflicts Between Congress and the President (2014). Should the courts respond to this situation in any way? Who would have standing to object?

8. Chadha's *Implications for the Use of Legislative History.* The ordinary sources of legislative history, such as committee reports, are not subject to the controls of bicameral consideration and presentment to the President, unlike the text of a bill. Does the logic of *Chadha* require that courts ignore these materials? See John Manning, *Textualism as a Nondelegation Doctrine*, 97 Colum. L. Rev. 673 (1997), making that argument, and a response by Peter L. Strauss, *The Courts and the Congress: Should Judges Disdain Political History?* 98 Colum. L. Rev. 242 (1998).

2. Congress's "Power of the Purse"

No picture of basic executive-legislative relations is complete without a rudimentary sketch of the way that the federal government spends money. Usually, there are three important stages (we mention exceptions below). First, the executive branch furnishes Congress a budget for the government. Second, Congress translates the budget into appropriations of funds. Third, actual expenditures occur in the daily operations of the agencies.

This section of the chapter begins with an overview of budget and spending processes. Next we examine congressional controls on executive expenditures, and constitutional limits to their exercise. We then explore executive management of spending, and the contentious question of impoundment of appropriated funds. Finally, we explore the rise and fall of the item veto.

a. Overview of Budget and Spending Processes

The Constitution gives Congress the authority to tax and spend "for the common Defence and general Welfare of the United States." (Art. I, §8, cl. 1) In *United States v. Butler*, 297 U.S. 1 (1936), the Supreme Court settled a longstanding controversy by holding that the power to tax and spend is not limited to implementation of other substantive powers of Congress, such as the Commerce Clause, but is a freestanding power to pursue the "general welfare." Madison had contended for the narrow view of the clause, stressing that ours is a government of limited and enumerated powers; the Court sided with Hamilton, who, later buttressed by Story, advanced the broad view. (Nevertheless, the *Butler* Court struck down the statute at bar for invading the rights of the states reserved by the Tenth Amendment.) In subsequent years, the Court has realized the promise of *Butler* by approving a vast range of federal expenditures.

In the absence of important substantive limits to the power to tax and spend, congressional process takes on special importance. *See generally* Allen Schick, The

Federal Budget: Politics, Policy, Process (3d ed. 2007); Louis Fisher, *Congressional Abdication on War and Spending* (2000); Elizabeth Garrett, *The Congressional Budget Process: Strengthening the Party-in-Government*, 100 Colum. L. Rev. 702 (2000).

Rules of both the House and the Senate require that legislation authorizing a substantive program be enacted before any appropriations are made. Assuming the existence of authorizing legislation, appropriations bills traditionally begin in the House Appropriations Committee. This very powerful committee is divided into twelve functional subcommittees, such as Agriculture and Defense, each of which submits its own appropriations bill. Formulated in a subcommittee and amended by the full committee, a bill then proceeds to the floor of the House. Once passed by the House, it goes to the Senate Appropriations Committee. Due to constraints of time and energy, the Senate committee traditionally acts as an appellate forum. Changes may also be made, of course, when the bills reach the Senate floor, or in conference with the House.

Today, the central procedural question is how these separate spending decisions should be aggregated into a national fiscal policy, a budget. Through the end of the nineteenth century, customs revenues were large enough, and federal expenditures small enough, that budgets were not a major problem. Prior to World War I, neither Congress nor the President had a comprehensive budgeting system. The Budget and Accounting Act of 1921, 42 Stat. 20, reformed the financial machinery of the executive branch by setting up the Bureau of the Budget and the General Accounting Office (now the Government Accountability Office). The Act grants the GAO broad powers to investigate all matters relating to the use of public funds, and requires it to report annually to Congress the results of its audits.

The creation of the Bureau of the Budget centralized executive branch fiscal management under the President. Previously, federal agencies had made direct requests to Congress for appropriations. The Act required all agencies to submit their appropriations proposals to the Bureau of the Budget. (Congress has sometimes granted ad hoc exceptions to this requirement, especially for the independent agencies.) Under the Nixon Administration, the Bureau was reorganized and renamed the Office of Management and Budget (OMB).

A *congressional* budget procedure was introduced by the Congressional Budget and Impoundment Control Act of 1974, Pub. L. No. 93-344, 88 Stat. 297. For the first time, the Act required Congress to review overall expenditures and revenues systematically, and to determine what actions its appropriations and revenue committees should take to meet broad fiscal goals. Previously, taxing and spending bills percolated up through the various subcommittees and committees, with no procedure to force Congress to decide between another dollar for butter and another dollar for guns.

Indeed, by 1974, only about 60 percent of federal spending was subject to annual appropriations procedure at all. The rest either did not require yearly appropriations or created promises that Congress felt obligated to meet. Such "backdoor spending" is accomplished through several devices, such as authorizing agencies to borrow or to enter contracts in advance of appropriations, through permanent or multi-year appropriations, or through entitlement programs in which Congress makes payments to individuals mandatory through fixed formulas.

In hopes of instilling fiscal discipline, the Act set a detailed timetable for passing a legislative budget. Unfortunately, budgeting has remained a last-minute, chaotic process in which only some of the 12 regular appropriations bills are passed on time — or at all. (We explore some of the consequences below.) Thus, although Congress can help itself to frame the issues involved in budgeting, making the hard underlying choices remains as painful as ever.

The 1974 Act established a two-stage budgeting process, by which Congress was to adopt a first resolution each spring, setting broad targets for the individual appropriations bills, and then a second resolution on the eve of the new fiscal year (which begins on October 1st), making final decisions in light of the bills as they had passed, and ordering reconciliation of the bills with the overall budget. This process, however, proved cumbersome and unrealistic.

Congress simplified the timetable with the Balanced Budget and Emergency Deficit Control Act of 1985 (the "Gramm-Rudman-Hollings Act"), Pub. L. No. 99-177, 99 Stat. 1038. The Act contained declining target figures for the overall deficit for the ensuing fiscal years, on a path that would reach zero in a few years. Congress also provided for a single budget resolution in the spring. The Act's complicated enforcement mechanism employed deficit estimates to be made in the summer by the Comptroller General, after considering estimates from the Congressional Budget Office and OMB. Implementation was to be by presidential sequestration orders as necessary to meet the Act's targets. The Comptroller's participation in this scheme was held to be unconstitutional in *Bowsher v. Synar* (excerpted in Chapter Four).

In 1987, responding to *Bowsher*, Congress restored the automatic deficit-reduction features of the 1985 legislation, with some modifications. The Comptroller General was replaced by the OMB Director, who was to estimate deficits after giving "due regard" to deficit estimates from the Congressional Budget Office. A constitutional issue remained, however: may Congress delegate such broad power over spending to *anyone*? Considering the 1985 Act, Congressman Jack Brooks argued not, in *Gramm-Rudman: Can Congress and the President Pass This Buck?* 64 Tex. L. Rev. 131 (1985).

After several years' experience, strong doubts persisted whether Gramm-Rudman-Hollings was working. Although significant deficit reduction occurred between 1985 and 1989, experts generally credited most of the change to economic expansion and growing reserves in the Social Security trust fund. Indeed, critics asserted that the Act's major force had been to promote accounting "gimmicks" by both Congress and the White House to meet the Act's targets.

In 1990, the White House and congressional leadership convened a "budget summit" to find yet another approach to controlling the burgeoning deficit. Their agreement ultimately spawned a comprehensive rewrite of Gramm-Rudman-Hollings:

The Budget Enforcement Act of 1990 (BEA), Pub. Law No. 101-508, 104 Stat. 1388. The BEA replaced fixed, multi-year targets for deficit or surplus amounts with adjustable yearly targeting, to allow current economic conditions to be reflected. It then created separate processes for the two basic kinds of federal spending. "Discretionary spending" included the third of the budget that is appropriated annually (defense, agency operations, and many grants such as foreign aid). Here specific caps were to be set for broad categories of spending, and any appropriations bill in excess was out of order.

For "direct spending," (mostly the entitlement programs, such as Medicaid or food stamps), spending from year to year is driven by eligibility of individual recipients under the governing statutes. Here, the BEA instituted the "PAYGO" rules, under which any statutory change that would either increase direct spending or reduce revenues had to be offset by other spending cuts or other new revenue, to preserve fiscal neutrality. If Congress violated either kind of restriction, OMB was granted sequester authority. (Social security receipts and expenditures are not counted in the budget calculations.)

Since 1990, the budget has had a roller-coaster ride. At first, the red ink flowed unabated. The deficits for fiscal 1991 ($269 billion) and 1992 ($290 billion) exceeded any previous deficits. But by the end of the decade, the boom of the '90s (and the BEA?) actually produced surpluses, which appeared to be longlasting. Thereafter a spate of terrorism, war, and tax cuts has restarted the parade of deficits.

The deficit story in the twenty-first century is not a happy one. President Bush cut taxes and then increased spending on defense and national security. He "signed every spending bill passed by Congress, even when the amounts greatly exceeded his budget requests." SCHICK, *supra* at 117. The BEA expired in 2002. Congress then tried to limit spending in its budget resolutions each year, with each house adopting its own approach. The absence of binding PAYGO rules (except as adopted by the House for 2007) made it more difficult to control spending. The financial crisis and recession of 2008 then made everything worse. The Bush and Obama administrations engaged in vigorous deficit spending to stop the economic slide. In 2010, the Obama administration obtained a statutory restoration of PAYGO as a means to address soaring deficits. As a result of all this, the Congressional Budget Office estimated the 2010 budget deficit at $1.6 trillion, the highest percentage of GDP since World War II. *See generally* ALAN J. AUERBACH & WILLIAM G. GALE, THE ECONOMIC CRISIS AND THE FISCAL CRISIS: 2009 AND BEYOND, AN UPDATE (2009).

The usual inability of the federal government to balance its budget has led to proposals for constitutional reform of the process. For a sampling of the diverse views on the wisdom of a constitutional amendment requiring a balanced budget, see THE CONSTITUTION AND THE BUDGET (W. S. MOORE & RUDOLPH G. PENNER EDS. 1980); Jeffery A. Needleman, *Deconstructing the Balanced Budget Amendment: Fiscal Folly, Monetary Madness*, 44 UCLA L. REV. 1289 (1997); Theodore P. Seto, *Drafting a Federal Balanced Budget Amendment That Does What it is Supposed To Do (And No More)*, 106 YALE L.J. 1449 (1997); E. Donald Elliott, *Constitutional Conventions and the*

Deficit, 1985 DUKE L.J. 1077. For an analysis of the role of supermajority rules as a cure for excess spending, see John O. McGinnis & Michael B. Rappaport, *Supermajority Rules as a Constitutional Solution*, 40 WM. & MARY L. REV. 365 (1999).

At the beginning of the 104th Congress, the House passed H.J. Res. 1, proposing the following constitutional amendment:

> SECTION 1. Total outlays for any fiscal year shall not exceed total receipts for that fiscal year, unless three-fifths of the whole number of each House of Congress shall provide by law for a specific excess of outlays over receipts by a roll call vote.

> SECTION 2. The limit on the debt of the United States held by the public shall not be increased, unless three-fifths of the whole number of each House shall provide by law for such an increase by a roll call vote.

> SECTION 3. Prior to each fiscal year, the President shall transmit to the Congress a proposed budget for the United States Government for that fiscal year in which total outlays do not exceed total receipts.

> SECTION 4. No bill to increase revenue shall become law unless approved by a majority of the whole number of each House by a roll call vote.

> SECTION 5. The Congress may waive the provisions of this article for any fiscal year in which a declaration of war is in effect. The provisions of this article may be waived for any fiscal year in which the United States is engaged in military conflict which causes an imminent and serious military threat to national security and is so declared by a joint resolution, adopted by a majority of the whole number of each House, which becomes law.

> SECTION 6. The Congress shall enforce and implement this article by appropriate legislation, which may rely on estimates of outlays and receipts.

> SECTION 7. Total receipts shall include all receipts of the United States Government except those derived from borrowing. Total outlays shall include all outlays of the United States Government except for those for repayment of debt principal.

> SECTION 8. This article shall take effect beginning with fiscal year 2002 or with the second fiscal year beginning after its ratification, whichever is later.

When this proposal reached the Senate, it added a sentence to § 6: "The judicial power of the United States shall not extend to any case or controversy arising under this Article except as may be specifically authorized by legislation adopted pursuant to this section." The Senate then narrowly failed to reach the two-thirds majority necessary to send the proposed amendment to the states for ratification. The short-term impetus behind the amendment evaporated as — surprise! — the budget came into balance in succeeding years. It should not surprise the reader that recent experience with surging deficits has renewed interest in an amendment. A new version, substantially similar to the one above, was proposed by Senators Graham and DeMint in 2007. Should the events of the following decade alter the prospects for passage of this amendment?

What would the effects of this amendment be? One of us opined that if a predecessor version of the amendment were to have operational force:

> . . . [I]t is . . . likely Congress would seek to render the amendment enforceable by vesting in the President powers either to adjust tax rates as may be necessary to secure predetermined levels of revenue or to sequester funds in order to reduce expenditures. Whether authority to vary tax rates could actually be constitutionally delegated to the executive is itself debatable. The Supreme Court might well consider the taxing power so significant that it may be exercised only by Congress.
>
> Whether the enforcement mechanism involves taxes, sequestration, or some combination, Congress would have to be aware that vesting such authorities in the executive would in large measure be abdicating to the executive much of Congress's authority to make policy through appropriations. To see this, it is necessary only to recall that any budget, on the first day of the new fiscal year, is dependent on expenditure and revenue predictions that must, in some measure, prove inaccurate. Imagine, then, that the executive is charged — when expenditures out pace revenues — to sequester funds sufficient to bring the budget into balance, unless Congress itself changes its intended allocation of appropriations. To the extent the executive has discretion to target its sequestration selectively, the relative strength and emphases to be assigned different programs will become a matter of presidential, rather than congressional determination. If the executive is limited to across-the-board sequestration, Congress, too, will be denied the ability to assert its revised budgetary priorities — unless it can come up with a revised appropriations measure that (a) the President likes better than an across-the-board sequestration, or (b) enjoys sufficient support in Congress to withstand a presidential veto. Again, the leverage Congress has lost over the budgetary process is enormous. Although Congress may continue to check the President to the extent initial appropriations set a ceiling on the fiscal year's expenditures, Congress will lose any meaningful way to check the President's policy priorities once evolving fiscal realities make adjustments in spending necessary. To reiterate Montesquieu: The executive power would "become legislative in the most important point of legislation."

Letter from Peter M. Shane to Rep. Dave Nagle, June 4, 1992, *reprinted at* 138 Cong. Rec. H4442, H4444 (daily ed. June 9, 1992). Experience with the various statutory reform efforts to date, and with the debate over balanced budget amendment proposals, poses two daunting questions. First, can any structural or procedural mechanism yield budgetary discipline absent an interbranch substantive agreement over spending levels and priorities? Second, can Congress and the President design any mechanism that effectuates budget control without unconstitutionally altering the distribution of power over spending and appropriations?

b. Congressional Control of Spending

In recent decades, Congress has rarely managed to enact all twelve appropriations bills before the start of the new fiscal year. As a result, Congress has had to rely on "continuing resolutions," i.e., joint resolutions containing budget authority for large numbers of agencies, which are designed to serve during the interim between the start of the fiscal year and the passage of a regular appropriations bill. In recent years, "budget summits" between Presidents and Congress over the details of omnibus spending resolutions have produced occasional interbranch consensus on priorities, as in 1990, but the process is ad hoc. Political pressures often become intense in connection with these emergency spending measures, leading to jeopardy that a lapse in appropriations will occur if Congress cannot agree on an extension in time, or if the President exercises a veto.

Among the most famous contretemps was the series of government shutdowns that occurred in 1995–96 during a political standoff between President Clinton and the 104th Congress. *See* Schick, *supra*, at 228–30. Republican leaders tried to use the appropriations process to make major policy changes, daring President Clinton to use his veto power. He surprised them by his willingness to do so. Thirteen continuing resolutions were enacted but parts of the government were shut down twice. Eventually a compromise emerged that left spending patterns mostly unchanged; politics crowned President Clinton the victor when the dust finally settled.

More of the same occurred in the Obama administration, as Professor Bruff recounts in Untrodden Ground, *supra*, at 453–54:

> After the Obama administration's first two years, which featured important legislation addressing the economic crisis and establishing a national medical plan, acrimonious deadlock stifled ordinary legislation. An initial low point occurred in 2011, when the House of Representatives used the need to raise the statutory ceiling on the national debt to accommodate the stimulus as a lever to try to force deep spending cuts. Delicate negotiations between the president and House Speaker John Boehner eventually broke down, with fingers pointing everywhere.
>
> With national default looming, suggestions arose that the president simply ignore the debt limit in favor of enforcing other statutory provisions that appropriated funds. In part, this step would rely on arguments dating from the *Youngstown* case, that the president has a duty to reconcile conflicts in the statutes. The argument also relied on a heretofore obscure provision in the Fourteenth Amendment stating that the validity of the public debt of the United States "shall not be questioned." President Obama rejected these proposals out of hand. The constitutional provision was arguably relevant and controlling — Congress inserted it into the amendment to foreclose challenges to its Civil War legislation creating greenback currency and funding pensions. Modern spending legislation is not fundamentally different. But

the president was surely aware that a practical problem foreclosed any attempt to breach the debt limit. Efforts by the government to borrow in violation of the limit would be unlikely to find buyers, given doubts about enforceability of the government's promises to pay. The president and congressional leaders soldiered on.

Congress eventually resolved the crisis for the time being by extending the debt limit in return for onerous and widespread "sequesters" of spending (that is, budget cuts) to take effect in the future. In an effort to discipline both branches, Congress was supposing that the approaching deadline for the unappealing cuts would force another, less draconian, compromise. Of course, no compromise followed, and the sequesters took effect.

Worse was in store. In the fall of 2013, continuing political deadlock produced a partial shutdown of the government that lasted for sixteen days and once again threatened default on the national debt. Apparently chastened by the negative public reaction to this wasteful and debilitating practice of governing from self-induced crisis to crisis, Congress then managed a small feat of bipartisanship at the end of the year, enacting a budget that will allow the government to operate more normally. Optimism would be premature. Until a sea change in American politics reduces the deep partisan conflict that is presently refracted through Congress, it is difficult to perceive a way out of this mess.

How should the executive respond to a lapse in appropriations for an agency, or for a large portion of the government? Here is an exploration of the problems from HAROLD H. BRUFF, BALANCE OF FORCES, *supra* at 253–56:

The problem is complicated by the existence of the Antideficiency Act, [31 U.S.C. §§ 1341–42,] a venerable statute that attempts (as its title suggests) to prevent executive officers from creating government obligations for which there are no appropriations ("deficiencies"), but which Congress will feel morally obligated to pay. The Act forbids obligations in advance of appropriations, unless they are "authorized by law," and permits the government to employ the personal service of its employees without appropriations only in "cases of emergency involving the safety of human life or the protection of property." During the Carter administration, two Attorney General Opinions grappled with these problems. Both opinions took a cautious view of executive power that conceded the textual and historic locus of the power of the purse in Congress. First, when the Federal Trade Commission suffered a lapse in appropriations, the Attorney General opined that the agency must shut down, even if there was every practical expectation of renewed funding. [4 Op. O.L.C. 16 (1980).] There was little choice—the FTC could make no contracts and obligate no further funds except as authorized by law. Also, the agency could no longer employ the services of its employees. The Attorney General did think, though, that the FTC could "fulfill certain legal obligations connected with the orderly termination of agency operations." Congress, having sent the FTC a rather blunt message of its displeasure over current policy, subsequently resuscitated the agency.

In October, 1980, Congress failed to enact eleven of the thirteen appropriations bills, and provided no continuing spending authority. The Attorney General revisited the issues in a greatly expanded context. [Authority for the Continuance of Governmental Functions During a Temporary Lapse in Appropriations, 43 Op. Att'y Gen. 293 (1981); *see* Alan L. Feld, *Shutting Down the Government*, 69 B.U. L. Rev. 971 (1989).] Following the opinions of his predecessors and of the Comptrollers General, he opined that expenditures would be "authorized by law" either if there were such express authority as multi-year appropriations, or if there were implied authority of a sufficiently clear kind. Here, the Attorney General thought that the Antideficiency Act merely codified the relevant legal inquiry that would exist in its absence, "a requirement of legal authority for the obligation of public funds." Implied authority could fairly be drawn, however, only from specific duties imposed on officers, and not from the broad terms of an agency's enabling act. The Attorney General explained:

> Thus, for example, when Congress specifically authorizes contracts to be entered into for the accomplishment of a particular purpose, the delegated officer may negotiate such contracts even before Congress appropriates all the funds necessary for their fulfillment. On the other hand, when authority for the performance of a specific function rests on a particular appropriation that proves inadequate to the fulfillment of its purpose, the responsible officer is not authorized to obligate further funds for that purpose in the absence of additional appropriations. This rule prevails even though the [action] may be a reasonable means for fulfilling general responsibilities that Congress has delegated to the official in broad terms, but without conferring specific authority to enter into contracts or otherwise obligate funds in advance of appropriations.

The Attorney General went on to say that a "nearly Government-wide" lapse of appropriations raised another, deeper question of executive authority, stemming from the President's constitutional powers. He was reluctant to read the Antideficiency Act as "precluding exercises of executive power through which the President, acting alone or through his subordinates, could have obligated funds in advance of appropriations had [it] not been enacted." Since such a reading could raise "grave" constitutional questions, it should be avoided. The Attorney General explained:

> The President, of course, cannot legislate his own obligational authorities; the legislative power rests with Congress. . . . [T]he Antideficiency Act is not the only source of law or the only exercise of congressional power that must be weighed in determining whether the President has authority for an initiative that obligates funds in advance of

appropriations. The President's obligational authority may be strengthened in connection with initiatives that are grounded in the peculiar institutional powers and competency of the President. His authority will be further buttressed in connection with any initiative that is consistent with statutes—and thus with the exercise of legislative power in an area of concurrent authority—that are more narrowly drawn than the Antideficiency Act and that would otherwise authorize the President to carry out his constitutionally assigned tasks in the manner he contemplates.

He would attempt no catalogue of protected presidential functions, but thought it pertinent whether they "would assist the President in fulfilling his peculiar constitutional role." Turning to the bar to paying employees except to protect life or property, the Attorney General called for a "reasonable connection" between a government function and safety of life or property. Examples might be FBI criminal investigations and Department of Agriculture meat inspections. Thus, the Attorney General was prepared to take an aggressive stance where presidential powers or emergency needs of government could be invoked.

Considering Congress' current budgeting difficulties, it should enact a permanent appropriations act, providing that upon any lapse in regular appropriations, funds are appropriated for an agency at the same level as under its most recent authority, until the passage of a subsequent appropriations bill. This statute would remove both existing uncertainty about which functions may continue during appropriations lapses and the inefficiency that has attended partial agency shutdowns in the past. In the absence of such a statute, Presidents should continue those functions that are most proximate to their independent constitutional powers over national security and foreign affairs. They should also continue to read the Antideficiency Act's authority to protect life and property in light of the constitutional power of faithful execution, which applies to substantive statutes that create various government duties as well as appropriations measures. A good faith interpretation of this combination of constitutional and statutory powers should certainly support the Attorney General's "reasonable connection" test for continuing government functions.

Do you agree with Professor Bruff's recommendation for a permanent appropriations act to deal with all future lapses in appropriations? The opinion of Attorney General Benjamin Civiletti, quoted by Professor Bruff, concludes: "As the law is now written, the nation must rely initially for the efficient operation of government on the timely and responsible functioning of the legislative process. . . . Any inconvenience that this system, in extreme circumstances, may bode is outweighed, in my estimation, by the salutary distribution of power that it embodies." How would the Bruff proposal change the distribution of power between the elected branches?

In 1990, Congress amended 31 U.S.C. § 1342 to include the following sentence:

> As used in this section, the term "emergencies involving the safety of human life or the protection of property" does not include ongoing, regular functions of government the suspension of which would not imminently threaten the safety of human life or the protection of property.

Is the Attorney General's discovery of "orderly shutdown" authority plausible under the revised wording?

Is Congress constitutionally required to provide any funds whatsoever for the operation of the executive branch, aside from the President's salary? Professor Charles Black, in *Some Thoughts on the Veto*, 40 LAW & CONTEMP. PROBS. 87, 89 (1976), presents a vision that:

> arose from my asking myself, "To what state could Congress, without violating the Constitution, reduce the President?" I arrived at a picture of a man living in a modest apartment, with perhaps one secretary to answer mail; that is where one appropriation bill could put him, at the beginning of a new term.

Do you share this vision of a President constitutionally shorn of all the trappings and implements of office? If not, what is the minimum Congress must provide, and who could force it to provide that? For a lengthy argument that "the President, without violating the Constitution or statutory law, may obligate the Treasury provided that Congress has failed to appropriate the minimum amount necessary for him to perform the duties and exercise the prerogatives given him by Article II of the Constitution," see J. Gregory Sidak, *The President's Power of the Purse*, 1989 DUKE L.J. 1163, 1163 (1989). For the contrary view, see Kate Stith, *Congress' Power of the Purse*, 97 YALE L.J. 1343 (1988).

A recurrent constitutional question surrounds congressional restrictions on executive use of appropriations. We know that after *Butler* and its progeny, Congress has wide discretion over spending. Does that mean that Congress has *more* power to control executive action through the technique of conditioning appropriations than it would have through a direct limitation on a substantive grant of power? The following case shows how these problems arise.

Brown v. Califano

627 F.2d 1221 (D.C. Cir. 1980)

BAZELON, Senior Circuit Judge:

Darryl and David Brown and sixteen other public school children, the appellants, challenge the constitutionality of amendments that restrict federal methods for assuring nondiscrimination in public schools receiving federal support. The amendments essentially prevent the Department of Health, Education, and Welfare (HEW) from requiring "the transportation of any student to a school other than the school

Can't term funds to induce busing

which is nearest the student's home." The district court found that the existence of an alternative federal avenue to effect transportation remedies saves these amendments from constitutional challenge on their face. The district court explicitly left open the possibility of future challenges to the amendments as applied. For the reasons described below, we affirm.

I. BACKGROUND

... Title VI of the [Civil Rights] Act prohibits discrimination on the ground of race, color, or national origin under any program receiving federal financial assistance. [42 U.S.C. §2000d] ... [T]he Act permits the Executive to avoid providing support to noncomplying public school districts, and to use the threat of fund-termination to persuade or induce recipients to dismantle vestiges of segregation.

Through agreement with other executive departments, HEW assumed responsibility for Title VI enforcement with respect to most federal financial assistance to elementary, secondary and higher education . . . HEW diligently followed rules it promulgated under Title VI and brought some six hundred administrative proceedings against noncomplying districts. Then, between March 1970 and February 1971, HEW brought no enforcement proceedings. At the same time, HEW continued to advance federal funds to schools HEW found in violation of Title VI.

Based on factual findings of this sort, Judge Pratt in *Adams v. Richardson* [356 F. Supp. 92 (D.D.C. 1973)] and Judge Sirica in . . . this case ordered declaratory and injunctive relief requiring HEW to resume enforcement under Title VI. Those decisions disapproved of HEW's conduct but left its regulations in place to guide future enforcement. Under these regulations, HEW requires elementary and secondary school applicants and recipients to provide assurances of their compliance with desegregation plans. . . . HEW can pursue enforcement through fund termination proceedings within the agency. . . . The regulations specify the primary alternative to fund-termination: referral to the Department of Justice with a recommendation of appropriate legal action. . . .

Enacted as floor amendments to appropriation bills, the amendments challenged here lack careful explanation or description of their intended effect on HEW's enforcement procedures under Title VI. Their general purpose, however, is clear. Congress wanted to ensure that no student would be transported beyond the school nearest his home because of an HEW requirement. Of course, as members of Congress were aware, HEW never had the authority to order any particular remedial plan. Its enforcement authority permits it only to . . . seek enforcement through fund-termination proceedings or referral to the Department of Justice. Nonetheless, as the legislative debates also acknowledge, the power to threaten fund-termination . . . can often work coercively. Thus, Congress explicitly intended that HEW could not use this power to require, "directly or indirectly," student transportation beyond the school closest to their home. . . .

[I]t is clear that the amendments leave intact HEW's entire administrative enforcement process, including fund-termination, for violations not calling for transportation remedies. But the legislative debates do not identify when and through what procedures HEW can avoid funding schools known to violate the Constitution and Title VI. Congress apparently intended HEW to retain the power to refer cases to the Department of Justice for appropriate legal action. Congress neglected, however, to specify the steps HEW may take before a referral. . . .

II. THE AMENDMENTS AND EFFECTIVE DESEGREGATION ENFORCEMENT

The amendments here at issue make no classification along impermissible lines, but that does not prevent an equal protection challenge. Interference with the remedies necessary to implement the promise of *Brown v. Board of Education*, 347 U.S. 483 (1954), could well rise to the level of impermissible discriminatory effect and purpose. . . . Appellants argue that, by restricting HEW's ability to require busing remedies, the amendments demonstrate discriminatory intent to interfere with desegregation. Presumably, this claim attaches to HEW's statutory obligation under Title VI to achieve equality in federally-funded schools and to the Executive's duty to "take care that the Laws [are] faithfully executed."

Thus, appellants assert that the amendments . . . violate the Fifth Amendment by eliminating "the single, proven, and most effective remedy for desegregating schools receiving federal aid." There are actually two prongs to this claim: the amendments will effectively inhibit desegregation and thereby dilute the guarantees of the Fifth Amendment; and the amendments reflect an impermissible legislative motivation to inhibit desegregation. Because the amendments on their face leave open many apparently effective avenues for desegregation, we are not persuaded by either argument.

A. *Construing the Amendments*

. . . The amendments can be interpreted here to advance a permissible purpose, with no general inhibition of desegregation. Although individual supporters broadly attacked busing as a desegregation remedy, we do not find these statements expressive of the entire legislature's intent. Were they representative, we would be confronted with grave constitutional difficulties. Instead, we recognize the primary focus of the congressional debates on the role of HEW as an enforcement agency. An explicit, major purpose of the amendments was to take "HEW out of the busing business." In other words, Congress wanted to ensure that mandatory busing orders derive either from local school officials or federal courts.

Accordingly, the amendments . . . do not in any way restrict HEW's authority to threaten or actually terminate funds with respect to any other desegregation remedy which would suffice. Thus, HEW can reject fund applications which fail to provide for magnet schools, faculty desegregation, school construction or school closings that enhance desegregation, or other nontransportation remedies it deems necessary for compliance with Title VI and the Constitution. For those noncomplying school districts which HEW believes require transportation remedies, the amendments clearly eliminate use of the fund-termination option to induce busing. At the same time, nothing in their language or legislative history . . . precludes HEW from referring such cases to the Department of Justice, with recommendations for appropriate legal action. . . . The government argues that the amendments do not prevent HEW from threatening referral to the Department of Justice in order to increase HEW's leverage in persuading offending districts to "voluntarily" reassign students. We agree, with this proviso: HEW cannot delay in taking necessary steps to bring about compliance. . . .

B. *Dilution of Equal Protection Guarantees*

The amendments would be constitutionally flawed if they diluted rather than enforced equal protection guarantees. . . . [Since they allow fund-termination except to induce busing and since] the amendments also leave in place the enforcement options at the Department of Justice, we cannot find that on their face they "restrict, abrogate, or dilute" the guarantee of equal protection. Where a choice of alternative enforcement routes is available, and the one preferred is not demonstrably less effective, Congress has the power to exercise its preference.

C. *Legislative Motivation*

Absent discriminatory effect, judicial inquiry into legislative motivation is unnecessary, as well as undesirable. Obviously, the foreseeable effect of these amendments is increased litigation for court-ordered desegregation, and settlements supervised by HEW and the courts — not unremedied segregation. Thus, statements by individual congressmen that reveal opposition to busing or to student assignment to achieve desegregation, do not by themselves establish constitutional flaws in the amendments.

III. PROHIBITION AGAINST GOVERNMENT SUPPORT FOR SEGREGATION

More problematic is appellants' charge that the amendments interfere with the government's obligation not to support segregated schools. . . . Distinct from its duty to enforce the law, the Executive must not itself participate in unlawful discrimination. . . . To avoid the cloud of constitutional doubt, we must assume that Congress did not intend the amendments to force federal financial support of illegal discrimination. Thus, the amendments cannot be read to prevent HEW from fulfilling its obligation to assure no federal moneys support segregated schools. . . . In particular instances, HEW may be required to 1) refer a case to the Department of Justice for appropriate action; 2) terminate funds through HEW's administrative procedures; or 3) alert the President that a case may require Executive impoundment of funds. Appellants and other private individuals certainly are not barred from challenging HEW's failure to take any such steps. . . .

Affirmed.

———————

1. *Does Technique Matter?* From either a political or constitutional point of view, was Congress better advised to limit busing through the appropriations process rather than through substantive or jurisdictional legislation?

2. *Managing Federal Litigation.* Is there any constitutional obstacle to appropriations limitations that allow the Department of Justice to bring certain lawsuits but attempt to control how such lawsuits shall be tried? Should any such congressional directives be viewed as posing ethical problems for government lawyers? At the time of the *Brown* litigation, how would you have advised the federal agencies involved on the nature of their legal obligations? As the Obama Administration deliberated over the possible criminal prosecution of alleged 9/11 "mastermind" Khalid Sheikh Mohammed, some Members of Congress threatened to sponsor legislation requiring federal criminal prosecutors to try Mohammed, if ever, only before a military commission, rather than an Article III court. Would such a restriction raise any constitutional or ethical issues? (On the role of military commissions after 9/11, see Chapter Seven.)

3. *Preventing Discrimination Via the Tax Code.* Would it be unconstitutional for Congress to permit tax exemptions for racially discriminatory private schools? (In *Bob Jones University v. United States*, 461 U.S. 574 (1983), the Court held that Congress had authorized the IRS to deny exemptions for such schools, and could constitutionally do so.) Assuming that Congress *must* deny such exemptions, may it nevertheless deny funds to the IRS to investigate the racially discriminatory practices of tax-exempt institutions?

4. *Mandatory Impoundment?* Notice one option the court identifies for preventing government funds from aiding discriminatory activity: presidential impoundment. In a footnote, the court said: "Impoundment takes on special importance where the Executive believes the expenditure would violate a constitutional provision." Does the existence of this option cast doubt on the constitutional necessity for authorizing Department of Justice lawsuits, or must the impoundment option be shown to be realistic? As you read the materials in the next section of this chapter, consider the soundness of the court's view of impoundment.

Note that, in order to avoid funding racially discriminatory schools, the President need not actually impound funds—the executive branch could simply shift funds from racially discriminatory school districts to nondiscriminatory districts, without actually spending any less money. If the President has the power to order such shifting, what administrative protections would need to be afforded the purportedly discriminatory school districts? Could Congress expressly deny the President power to alter the administrative allotment of federal grant funds in order to require busing? What if the Supreme Court squarely held that, in particular cases, busing is essential to the vindication of individual rights under the Constitution?

5. *Lord Russell Again.* The potential for governmental havoc posed by appropriations disputes illustrates again Lord Russell's point in the opening quotation for this chapter: the success of our government depends largely on each branch's willingness not to press what arguably are its powers to their logical extremes.

c. Executive Control of Spending

For appropriations, as for substantive statutory actions, Congress bounds executive discretion within varying limits. At one extreme is a lump sum for a broadly defined purpose; at the other is an appropriation broken down by "line items," each for a specific use. The nation's experience while governed by those who had framed the Constitution illustrates the scope of the possible variations. (The story is told in a good general introduction to the issues in this section, Louis Fisher, Presidential Spending Power 60–61 (1975).) The first appropriations act in 1789 simply provided lump sums for four general categories of expenditures, for example $137,000 for the War Department. A period of much greater itemization soon followed, however. By 1793, appropriations had descended to such minutiae as $450 for the Treasurer's office supplies. This trend was actually encouraged by the newly inaugurated Jefferson, who urged Congress to appropriate "specific sums to every specific purpose susceptible of definition." (Hamilton trenchantly termed this "preposterous.") Experience soon convinced Jefferson, however, that at least from the standpoint of the executive, "too minute a specification has its evil as well as a too general one." Congress, he had come to believe, should repose a temporary trust in the executive, which could be "put an end to if abused." Congress has subsequently displayed an appreciation for the principles that Jefferson eventually adopted. In applying them, Congress has varied the specificity of its appropriations greatly, according to the subject matter, the temper of the times, and the degree of trust reposed in the President.

It has long been accepted that Congress may direct expenditure in at least some circumstances. That is the principle established by *Kendall v. United States ex rel. Stokes*, 37 U.S. 524 (1838), discussed earlier in this chapter, in which the Court upheld issuance of mandamus to the Postmaster General to pay government contractors an award for their services as determined by an arbitrator. A statute had set up the arbitration procedure and had commanded payment of the award.

Notwithstanding implications that might be taken from *Kendall*, federal spending is not a purely mechanical function, but one invested with varying degrees of executive discretion. Despite the surface precision of appropriations, expressed as they are in numbers, they do not necessarily confer less executive discretion than do substantive delegations. There is often a respectable argument that a particular appropriation is a ceiling on expenditure, not a specific directive, as our discussion of impoundment will reveal. Also, the executive possesses a number of techniques for manipulating spending, which can convert appropriations from one purpose to another. Moreover, the delegation doctrine, which purports to restrain the breadth of substantive delegations of power, has only rarely been applied to appropriations. For a summary rejection of an argument that an appropriation violated the delegation doctrine, see *Cincinnati Soap Co. v. United States*, 301 U.S. 308, 321 (1937).

It may be useful to distinguish positive from negative executive spending decisions. Positive discretion results in expenditure. It includes shifting appropriations among budgeted accounts within one statutory category of appropriations (reprogramming), timing expenditures to affect the availability or amount of appropriations, and obligating funds that have yet to be appropriated. The extent of executive discretion concerning such matters has never been authoritatively determined, although the effect can be to alter substantially the expenditure patterns anticipated in both executive budgets and congressional appropriations. Negative discretion, which refers to decisions that result in withholding appropriated amounts from expenditure, also takes numerous forms, which tend to be lumped together under the general term "impoundment." Examples include the formation of reserves and the withholding of contract authority. A practical difference between positive and negative discretion may favor implying broader executive authority for the latter—impounded funds remain available for Congress to appropriate to the purpose of its choice.

Broad, lump sum appropriations are common in periods of war or economic crisis. (Smaller contingency funds of diverse sorts are scattered in appropriations in ordinary times.) At times, the consequence has been to grant a President virtually unfettered control over large sums. For example, at the end of Franklin Roosevelt's first term, it was estimated that Congress had given him discretionary authority over $15.4 billion, as compared to $1.6 billion for all previous Presidents.

The more common practice, however, has been for Congress to itemize sufficiently to produce executive branch grumbling through the years. Often the executive can draw support from public administration school theories of budgeting, which have traditionally favored executive responsibility for spending decisions. Whether in response to these pressures or from felt needs of its own, Congress has moved somewhat toward broader "program" budgeting in recent decades. In doing so, Congress has increased its needs to monitor spending as it occurs, instead of specifying acceptable uses of money in advance.

Not all congressional controls on spending appear in the appropriations statutes themselves. As we have seen, instructions appear in the committee reports, hearings, and floor debates. Notwithstanding the Supreme Court's decision in *Chadha, supra,* many of these instructions require committee approval for particular kinds of spending decisions—whether or not these instructions are constitutional! If congressional wishes are ignored, or if the promises implied by the executive's budget requests are not met, Congress can retaliate the next year with cutbacks, restrictive conditions, and line itemization. Still, budgets are prepared far enough in advance of actual expenditure that a perfect fit cannot be expected. Accordingly, the committees are prepared to tolerate a certain amount of reprogramming of funds within statutory accounts, and of executive impoundments. (There is also authority to transfer funds from one statutory account to another. It is conferred exclusively, and sometimes broadly, by statute.)

The following case explores both the effect of instructions in the legislative history of appropriations on executive discretion and the reviewability in court of executive spending decisions.

Lincoln v. Vigil

508 U.S. 182 (1993)

Justice SOUTER delivered the opinion of the [unanimous] Court:

For several years in the late 1970s and early 1980s, the Indian Health Service provided diagnostic and treatment services, referred to collectively as the Indian Children's Program, to handicapped Indian children in the Southwest. In 1985, the Service decided to reallocate the Program's resources to a nationwide effort to assist such children. We hold that the Service's decision to discontinue the Program was "committed to agency discretion by law" and therefore not subject to judicial review under the Administrative Procedure Act, 5 U.S.C. § 701(a)(2) . . . .

The Indian Health Service, an agency within the Public Health Service of the Department of Health and Human Services, provides health care for some 1.5 million American Indian and Alaska Native people. The Service receives yearly lump-sum appropriations from Congress and expends the funds under authority of the Snyder Act, 25 U.S.C. § 13, and the Indian Health Care Improvement Act, 25 U.S.C. § 1601 et seq. So far as it concerns us here, the Snyder Act authorizes the Service to "expend such moneys as Congress may from time to time appropriate, for the benefit, care, and assistance of the Indians," for the "relief of distress and conservation of health." The Improvement Act authorizes expenditures for, inter alia, Indian mental-health care, and specifically for "therapeutic and residential treatment centers." . . . This case concerns a collection of related services, commonly known as the Indian Children's Program, that the Service provided from 1978 to 1985. . . . Congress never expressly appropriated funds for these centers. In 1978, however, the Service allocated approximately $292,000 from its fiscal year 1978 appropriation to its office in Albuquerque, New Mexico, for the planning and development of a pilot project for handicapped Indian children, which became known as the Indian Children's Program. . . . Congress never authorized or appropriated monies expressly for the Program, and the Service continued to pay for its regional activities out of annual lump-sum appropriations from 1980 to 1985, during which period the Service repeatedly apprised Congress of the Program's continuing operation. . . .

In August 1985, the Service determined that Program staff hitherto assigned to provide direct clinical services should be reassigned as consultants to other nationwide Service programs, and discontinued the direct clinical services to Indian children in the Southwest. . . . Respondents, handicapped Indian children eligible to receive services through the Program, subsequently brought this action for declaratory and injunctive relief . . . [alleging] that the Service's decision to discontinue direct clinical services violated the . . . Snyder Act, the Improvement Act, [and] the Administrative Procedure Act. . . .

First is the question whether it was error for the Court of Appeals to hold the substance of the Service's decision to terminate the Program reviewable under the APA. The Act provides that "[a] person suffering legal wrong because of agency action, or adversely affected or aggrieved by agency action within the meaning of a relevant statute, is entitled to judicial review thereof," 5 U.S.C. § 702, and we have read the Act as embodying a "basic presumption of judicial review." This is "just" a presumption, however, and under § 701(a)(2) agency action is not subject to judicial review "to the extent that" such action "is committed to agency discretion by law." As we explained in *Heckler v. Chaney*, 470 U.S. 821, 830 (1985), § 701(a)(2) makes it clear that "review is not to be had" in those rare circumstances where the relevant statute "is drawn so that a court would have no meaningful standard against which to judge the agency's exercise of discretion." "In such a case, the statute ('law') can be taken to have 'committed' the decisionmaking to the agency's judgment absolutely." . . .

The allocation of funds from a lump-sum appropriation is another administrative decision traditionally regarded as committed to agency discretion. After all, the very point of a lump-sum appropriation is to give an agency the capacity to adapt to changing circumstances and meet its statutory responsibilities in what it sees as the most effective or desirable way. . . . For this reason, a fundamental principle of appropriations law is that where "Congress merely appropriates lump-sum amounts without statutorily restricting what can be done with those funds, a clear inference arises that it does not intend to impose legally binding restrictions, and indicia in committee reports and other legislative history as to how the funds should or are expected to be spent do not establish any legal requirements on" the agency. *LTV Aerospace Corp.*, 55 Comp. Gen. 307, 319 (1975); *cf. American Hospital Ass'n v. NLRB*, 499 U.S. 606 (1991) (statements in committee reports do not have the force of law); *Tennessee Valley Authority v. Hill*, 437 U.S. 153, 191 (1978) ("Expressions of committees dealing with requests for appropriations cannot be equated with statutes enacted by Congress"). Put another way, a lump-sum appropriation reflects a congressional recognition that an agency must be allowed "flexibility to shift . . . funds within a particular . . . appropriation account so that" the agency "can make necessary adjustments for 'unforeseen developments'" and "'changing requirements.'" *LTV Aerospace Corp., supra*, at 318.

Like the decision [in *Heckler v. Chaney*] against instituting enforcement proceedings, then, an agency's allocation of funds from a lump-sum appropriation requires "a complicated balancing of a number of factors which are peculiarly within its expertise": whether its "resources are best spent" on one program or another; whether it "is likely to succeed" in fulfilling its statutory mandate; whether a particular program "best fits the agency's overall policies"; and, "indeed, whether the agency has enough resources" to fund a program "at all." As in *Heckler*, so here, the "agency is far better equipped than the courts to deal with the many variables involved in the proper ordering of its priorities." Of course, an agency is not free simply to disregard statutory responsibilities: Congress may always circumscribe agency discretion to allocate resources by putting restrictions in the operative statutes (though not, as we have seen, just in the legislative history). And, of course, we hardly need to note that an agency's decision to ignore congressional expectations may expose it to grave political consequences. But as long as the agency allocates funds from a lump-sum appropriation to meet permissible statutory objectives, § 701(a)(2) gives the courts no leave to intrude. "To [that] extent," the decision to allocate funds "is committed to agency discretion by law." § 701(a)(2).

The Service's decision to discontinue the Program is accordingly unreviewable under § 701(a)(2). As the Court of Appeals recognized, the appropriations Acts for the relevant period do not so much as mention the Program, and both the Snyder Act and the Improvement Act likewise speak about Indian health only in general terms. It is true that the Service repeatedly apprised Congress of the Program's continued operation, but, as we have explained, these representations do not translate through the medium of legislative history into legally binding obligations. The reallocation of agency resources to assist handicapped Indian children nationwide clearly falls within the Service's statutory mandate to provide health care to Indian people. . . . The decision to terminate the Program was committed to the Service's discretion. . . .

App acts ∅ mention the program

————

1. *Promises, Promises.* Apparently, the *Lincoln* Court believes that the appropriations committees have enough political power to police executive compliance with promises made in the appropriations process, and do not need the aid of the courts, at the instance of private litigants, to do so. Or does the case embody a consequence of the logic of *Chadha* that we suggested above—that Congress may make law only by statute, and not through legislative history? The persistence of legislative veto provisions in this field may mean that Congress doesn't need law on its side—clear signals are enough when appropriations are involved.

2. *Reviewability.* As *Lincoln* explains, the Court has found executive action to be unreviewable when statutes are drawn so broadly that there is no meaningful standard for a court to apply. Is this doctrine a derivative of the political question doctrine, which also inquires about manageable judicial standards? Doesn't the Court's formulation of unreviewability admit that the delegation doctrine does not always require standards?

3. *Challenging Federal Spending.* Recall the *Richardson* case *supra,* denying taxpayer or citizen standing to enforce constitutional restrictions on secret spending. The combination of standing and reviewability doctrines creates a formidable barrier to private challenges to federal spending, doesn't it?

Note on Impoundment of Funds

Although Presidents have probably impounded funds since the first administration, few controversies arose in the early years. (The historical summary which follows relies substantially on FISHER, *supra*; *see also* Roy E. Brownell II, *The Constitutional Status of the President's Impoundment of National Security Funds*, 12 SETON HALL CONST. L.J. 1 (2001); Nile Stanton, *History and Practice of Executive Impoundment of Appropriated Funds*, 53 NEB. L. REV. 1 (1974).) It quickly became clear that the nature of the appropriations process required some kinds of executive impoundments.

First, since predictions of cost are always somewhat uncertain even if the goods or services are precisely identified, the executive can sometimes fulfill Congress's purpose for less than the amount appropriated. Second, in the interval between appropriation and expenditure, changing circumstances may remove the original reason for the appropriation. In a famous early example, Jefferson declined to spend an amount appropriated for gunboats because a "favorable and peaceable turn of affairs" on the Mississippi had rendered the expenditure unnecessary. (FISHER, *supra*, at 150.) Thus, perhaps every appropriation carries an implied authorization to impound the money if to spend it would not advance the original purpose. Third, the process of apportionment, by which the timing of spending a year's appropriation is scheduled to avoid deficiencies at the end, can produce a surplus as readily as a shortfall. This process can include the conscious sequestration of a reserve for unforeseen requirements.

The first controversial impoundment occurred when President Grant refused to spend river and harbor funds for "works of purely private interest," as opposed to national interests. The pork barrel aspects of public works legislation have led several Presidents to delete some projects authorized by Congress while executing others. Congress has not always reacted vigorously. For example, although Grant's action produced some incandescent rhetoric in the House of Representatives ("Upon what meat hath this our Caesar fed?"), the House later accepted the President's position that the appropriation was not mandatory.

A few court decisions in the late 19th century mentioned impoundments, but they offered no guidance as to the lawfulness of the practice. Four Attorney General opinions rendered during this period, however, all asserted that the President's impoundment power depended upon the intent of Congress. The Attorneys General did not rely entirely on Congress's appropriations language to determine legislative intent. For example, Attorney General Lamont, in 1896, opined that a sum that Congress indicated "shall be expended" for a specified project did not have to be expended if the project could be completed for less. He asserted that economizing would accord with Congress's intent.

In the modern era, extensive impoundments began when Franklin Roosevelt withheld public works and other funds in response to emergency conditions created by the depression and World War II. Notwithstanding some dissatisfaction with Roosevelt's actions, Congress amended the Antideficiency Act in 1950 to authorize the President to establish reserves "to provide for contingencies, or to effect savings whenever savings are made possible by or through changes in requirements, greater efficiency of operations, or other developments subsequent to" the appropriation.

After the war, Presidents continued to impound funds, sometimes in large amounts. Much of the controversy concerned defense appropriations for weapons systems. Here the President's power as Commander in Chief was offered as a constitutional justification for impoundment. Also, the executive's special informational advantages in national security and foreign affairs helped to thwart congressional opposition.

Not surprisingly, Presidents usually prevailed, although considerable maneuvering was sometimes required. President Johnson broadened the argument to include inherent authority to impound funds for domestic programs.

Although Congress has long been prepared to allow routine "programmatic" impoundments (such as to prevent waste), other impoundments have raised much more controversy because they appeared to negate the policy decisions made by appropriations. These "policy impoundments," which fall into several categories, are for the most part a phenomenon of the last fifty years. They have engendered arguments over whether such broad statutory language as the Antideficiency Act's "other developments" phrase should be read to authorize policy impoundments.

The impoundment issue finally became acute when President Nixon impounded unprecedented proportions of appropriations, as much as 20 percent of "controllable" federal expenditures. A number of programs were to be terminated outright. Again, however, Congress did not respond unambiguously. For example, in 1972 the Department of Agriculture announced a change that effectively terminated one class of rural development loans and replaced them with loans made available at somewhat higher interest rates and under more stringent qualification standards. Congress reacted by considering legislation completely restoring the loan program. Yet the compromise measure that eventually passed did not mandate the spending of any funds, and the administrator was given unprecedented statutory discretion in return for an informal promise to make the funds available under the program for at least three years.

Reasons advanced for the Nixon impoundments were usually general ones of fiscal integrity, such as the need to control inflation. Where particular projects were to be deleted, as in public works, there was usually no effort to justify the choices as the result of any criteria other than presence in the President's budget. Accompanying legal arguments consisted of a distortion of the historical record through claims that nothing new was occurring, and an oversimplification of previous constitutional arguments in support of a conclusion that the President could impound essentially without limitation. *See* Ralph S. Abascal & John R. Kramer, *Presidential Impoundment Part I: Historical Genesis and Constitutional Framework*, 62 Geo. L.J. 1549 (1974); *Part II: Judicial and Legislative Responses*, 63 Geo. L.J. 149 (1974).

The Nixon impoundments finally provoked both judicial and legislative response. Neither, however, produced a definitive resolution of the permissible extent of impoundment. A series of lower court cases challenging particular impoundments generally produced defeats for the executive. For example, in *Missouri Highway Commission v. Volpe*, 479 F.2d 1099 (8th Cir. 1973), the court held that the Secretary of Transportation could not lawfully refuse to obligate highway funds which had been allocated to the state of Missouri on the ground that such expenditures would aggravate inflationary pressures in the economy. The court held that even if the governing statute were not mandatory, the Secretary lacked power to impound funds for reasons not related to the program being administered.

The Supreme Court's only foray into the issues occurred in *Train v. City of New York*, 420 U.S. 35 (1975). In 1972, Congress amended the Federal Water Pollution Control Act to provide federal financing for municipal sewage treatment works, in the form of 75% grants. The amendments authorized the appropriation of amounts "not to exceed" $5 billion for the program's first year, with greater amounts thereafter. The bill provided that the authorized sums "shall be allotted" to the states by EPA according to a formula, whereupon grant applications for the amounts allotted, once approved, would become contractual obligations of the United States. President Nixon vetoed the bill as "budget-wrecking;" Congress promptly overrode the veto. The President then instructed EPA to allot no more than $2 billion in the first year of the program, with further large reductions in subsequent years. The City of New York sued for a declaration that EPA was required to allot the full amount of the authorization, and prevailed.

The case reached the Supreme Court in the wake of the Nixon resignation. The executive had abandoned broad claims of constitutional impoundment power; only statutory issues remained. The executive now claimed only discretion as to the timing of expenditure. Therefore, the Court was not deciding a contested issue when it read the legislative history to mandate "a firm commitment of substantial sums" to meet water pollution problems, one not subject to a "seemingly limitless" power to withhold funds. The Court considered the effect of two changes to the statutory language that had been added in conference in hopes of avoiding a veto. These eliminated a requirement that "all" sums be allotted, and added "not to exceed" to the sum authorized for expenditure. The changes had been explained in Congress as allowing some flexibility consistent with the basic commitment involved. (Similar ambiguity attended the veto override.) The Court decided that whatever discretion there was should be exercised at the later obligation stage, not for allotments.

Thus, the Court was able to sidestep the important issue of the amount of spending discretion conferred by the statute, because that issue would arise at a later stage of administration. Surely, the Court was correct to invalidate the President's impoundment at the allotment stage, because it amounted to an effort to ignore congressional authorization of the program. That was an issue on which the President had exercised his veto and had been overridden. To uphold that impoundment would have accorded the President an absolute veto, not a conditional one. Therefore, *Train* appears to delineate at least some role for the courts in reviewing impoundments — otherwise, Presidents could terminate congressionally mandated programs by withholding their funding. Still, the Court left the thorniest issues open: what the limits to policy impoundment might be, and how a court could draw the lines.

In *Train*, then, the President's action was not at the late stages of program implementation, involving project selection and funding. If he had impounded funds for particular projects on grounds of the inefficiency that is so typical of pork barrel appropriations, a different issue would have been presented. Similarly, if the impoundment had been at a program-wide level, for example 10% of all program funds, but had occurred after enough time had passed since the authorization to allow an

argument for changed circumstances (such as unanticipated budgetary developments or actual waste in the administration of the program), an issue distinguishable from *Train* would be presented. In either case, a court faced with a suit to compel
expenditure could stay its hand in favor of a "remand to Congress" to allow the
President to test support for his action. An advantage of this approach for the courts
would be that it would minimize their inquiry into issues of degree surrounding the
permissibility of policy impoundments. How do you think the courts should address
these problems?

Congress responded to the impoundment crisis of the Nixon administration with
the Congressional Budget and Impoundment Control Act of 1974, Pub. L. No. 93-344,
88 Stat. 297, which set up a procedure for impoundments. Proposals to rescind appropriations entirely were to be submitted to Congress, where they would be without
effect unless approved by a bill passed within a specified period. Proposals to defer
spending temporarily within the fiscal year were to be valid unless disapproved by a
one-house legislative veto. Congress attempted to avoid any constitutional confrontation over the Act, however, by including a disclaimer that it was not to be construed
as "asserting or conceding the constitutional powers or limitations of either the
Congress or the President." At the same time, Congress deleted the Antideficiency
Act's authorization to create reserves in response to "other developments," to forestall
its use in support of policy impoundments.

The Supreme Court's invalidation of legislative vetoes in *Chadha, supra,* raised
severability issues regarding the deferral provision in the Impoundment Control
Act. In *City of New Haven v. United States,* 809 F. 2d 900 (D.C. Cir. 1987), the court
held that the veto provision was not severable from the deferral authority, because
Congress was trying mightily to reduce executive discretion and would not have
tolerated an increase in that discretion by a grant of unreviewable deferrable authority. The court made a sharp distinction between programmatic and policy impoundments, finding the former a way to serve congressional intent and the latter a way to
negate it. The court gave the following example:

> "As a hypothetical example, one might consider a congressional appropria-
> tion of $10,000,000 to construct a new highway between Washington, D.C.
> and New York. If inclement weather threatened completion of the construc-
> tion project, the President might seek to defer the expenditure of the appro-
> priated funds for "programmatic" reasons. However, if the President believed
> that the project was inflationary, he might attempt to delay the expenditure
> of the funds for "policy" reasons."

Is the difference that clear? What if the President impounds the portion of the highway funds that would pay construction worker wage increases, on grounds that the
increases both render the project no longer cost-effective and contribute to general
inflation?

In its 1987 legislation restoring automatic deficit reduction procedures, Congress
included a provision designed to codify *New Haven*. The Act prohibited policy

deferrals (2 U.S.C. §684(b), see Statutory Appendix) and allowed programmatic deferrals only (1) for contingencies, (2) for efficiency, or (3) as specifically provided for by law. Did that solve the problems?

Rescissions now occur when the President proposes them and Congress enacts ratifying legislation. After a spate of successful rescission proposals at the outset of the Reagan presidency, the approval rate has dropped to about 20%. *See* SCHICK, *supra*, at 288.

Finally, what is the constitutional status of impoundment? Consider the history of interbranch conflict through 1974, and the disclaimer in the Act. Would it be constitutional for Congress to require particular amounts of money to be spent for foreign affairs or military purposes? Does the "take Care" clause give the President some residual constitutional authority even for domestic spending?

d. The Item Veto

For many years, Presidents sought authority to veto line items in appropriations bills, pointing to the fact that governors of most of the states possess this power. Eventually, Congress acquiesced—but the Supreme Court did not.

Clinton v. City of New York

524 U.S. 417 (1998)

Justice STEVENS delivered the opinion of the Court.

[Under t]he Line Item Veto Act (Act), 2 U.S.C. §691 et seq., . . . the President exercised his authority to cancel one provision in the Balanced Budget Act of 1997, and two provisions in the Taxpayer Relief Act of 1997. Appellees, claiming that they had been injured by two of those cancellations, filed these cases [and we hold] that the cancellation procedures set forth in the Act violate the Presentment Clause, Art. I, §7, cl. 2, of the Constitution.

I

We begin by reviewing the canceled items that are at issue in these cases. Title XIX of the Social Security Act authorizes the Federal Government to transfer huge sums of money to the States to help finance medical care for the indigent. *See* 42 U.S.C. §1396d(b). In 1991, Congress directed that those federal subsidies be reduced by the amount of certain taxes levied by the States on health care providers. [The Department of Health and Human Services (HHS) notified the State of New York that some of its taxes were covered by the 1991 Act. A prolonged squabble ensued, with amounts as high as $2.6 billion in controversy. Eventually,] New York turned to Congress for relief. On August 5, 1997, Congress enacted a law that resolved the issue in New York's favor. Section 4722(c) of the Balanced Budget Act of 1997 identifies the disputed taxes and provides that they "are deemed to be permissible health care related taxes and in compliance with the requirements" of the relevant provisions of the 1991 statute. On August 11, 1997, the President sent identical notices to the Senate and to the House of Representatives canceling "one item of new direct spending," specifying § 4722(c) as that item, and stating that he had determined that "this cancellation will reduce the Federal budget deficit." He explained that § 4722(c) would have permitted New York "to continue relying upon impermissible provider taxes to finance its Medicaid program" and that "[t]his preferential treatment would have increased Medicaid costs, would have treated New York differently from all other States, and would have established a costly precedent for other States to request comparable treatment."

Said #4722 allows NY to rely on TP's to fund medicare

A person who realizes a profit from the sale of securities is generally subject to a capital gains tax. Under existing law, however, an ordinary business corporation can acquire a . . . food processing or refining company, in a . . . transaction in which no gain is recognized to the seller, see 26 U.S.C. §§ 354(a), 368(a); the seller's tax payment, therefore, is deferred. If, however, the purchaser is a farmers' cooperative, the [seller] . . . cannot obtain the benefits of tax deferral. In § 968 of the Taxpayer Relief Act of 1997, Congress amended § 1042 of the Internal Revenue Code to permit owners of certain food refiners and processors to defer the recognition of gain if they sell their stock to eligible farmers' cooperatives. The purpose of the amendment, as repeatedly explained by its sponsors, was "to facilitate the transfer of refiners and processors to farmers' cooperatives." The amendment to § 1042 was one of the 79 "limited tax benefits" authorized by the Taxpayer Relief Act of 1997 and specifically identified in Title XVII of that Act as "subject to [the] line item veto."

On the same date that he canceled the "item of new direct spending" involving New York's health care programs, the President also canceled this limited tax benefit. In his explanation of that action, the President endorsed the objective of encouraging "value-added farming through the purchase by farmers' cooperatives of refiners or processors of agricultural goods," but concluded that the provision lacked safeguards and also "failed to target its benefits to small-and-medium-size cooperatives."

II

Appellees filed two separate actions against the President and other federal officials challenging these two cancellations. The plaintiffs in the first case are the City of New York, two hospital associations, one hospital, and two unions representing health care employees. The plaintiffs in the second are [the Snake River] farmers' cooperative consisting of about 30 potato growers in Idaho and an individual farmer who is a member and officer of the cooperative. The District Court consolidated the two cases and determined that at least one of the plaintiffs in each had standing under Article III of the Constitution. . . .

On the merits, the District Court held that the cancellations did not conform to the constitutionally mandated procedures for the enactment or repeal of laws in two respects. First, the laws that resulted after the cancellations "were different from those consented to by both Houses of Congress." Moreover, the President violated Article I "when he unilaterally canceled provisions of duly enacted statutes." As a separate basis for its decision, the District Court also held that the Act "impermissibly disrupts the balance of powers among the three branches of government."

III

As in the prior challenge to the Line Item Veto Act, we initially confront jurisdictional questions. . . . We are . . . unpersuaded by the Government's argument that appellees' challenge to the constitutionality of the Act is nonjusticiable. . . . [T]hese cases differ from *Raines,* not only because the President's exercise of his cancellation authority has removed any concern about the ripeness of the dispute, but more importantly because the parties have alleged a "personal stake" in having an actual injury redressed rather than an "institutional injury" that is "abstract and widely dispersed." . . .

IV

The Line Item Veto Act gives the President the power to "cancel in whole" three types of provisions that have been signed into law: "(1) any dollar amount of discretionary budget authority; (2) any item of new direct spending; or (3) any limited tax benefit." 2 U.S.C. § 691(a). It is undisputed that the New York case involves an "item of new direct spending" and that the Snake River case involves a "limited tax benefit" as those terms are defined in the Act. It is also undisputed that each of those provisions had been signed into law pursuant to Article I, § 7, of the Constitution before it was canceled.

The Act requires the President to adhere to precise procedures whenever he exercises his cancellation authority. In identifying items for cancellation he must consider the legislative history, the purposes, and other relevant information about the items. He must determine, with respect to each cancellation, that it will "(i) reduce the Federal budget deficit; (ii) not impair any essential Government functions; and (iii) not harm the national interest." Moreover, he must transmit a special message to Congress notifying it of each cancellation within five calendar days (excluding Sundays) after the enactment of the canceled provision. It is undisputed that the President meticulously followed these procedures in these cases.

A cancellation takes effect upon receipt by Congress of the special message from the President. If, however, a "disapproval bill" pertaining to a special message is enacted into law, the cancellations set forth in that message become "null and void." The Act sets forth a detailed expedited procedure for the consideration of a "disapproval bill," but no such bill was passed for either of the cancellations involved in these cases. A majority vote of both Houses is sufficient to enact a disapproval bill. The Act does not grant the President the authority to cancel a disapproval bill, but he does, of course, retain his constitutional authority to veto such a bill.

The effect of a cancellation is plainly stated in § 691e, which defines the principal terms used in the Act. With respect to both an item of new direct spending and a limited tax benefit, the cancellation prevents the item "from having legal force or effect." Thus, under the plain text of the statute, the two actions of the President that are challenged in these cases prevented one section of the Balanced Budget Act of 1997 and one section of the Taxpayer Relief Act of 1997 "from having legal force or effect." The remaining provisions of those statutes, with the exception of the second canceled item in the latter, continue to have the same force and effect as they had when signed into law.

In both legal and practical effect, the President has amended two Acts of Congress by repealing a portion of each. "[R]epeal of statutes, no less than enactment, must conform with Art. I." *INS v. Chadha.* There is no provision in the Constitution that authorizes the President to enact, to amend, or to repeal statutes . . . . [A]fter a bill has passed both Houses of Congress, but "before it become[s] a Law," it must be presented to the President. If he approves it, "he shall sign it, but if not he shall return it, with his Objections to that House in which it shall have originated, who shall enter the Objections at large on their Journal, and proceed to reconsider it." Art. I, § 7, cl. 2. His "return" of a bill, which is usually described as a "veto," is subject to being overridden by a two-thirds vote in each House.

There are important differences between the President's "return" of a bill pursuant to Article I, § 7, and the exercise of the President's cancellation authority pursuant to the Line Item Veto Act. The constitutional return takes place before the bill becomes law; the statutory cancellation occurs after the bill becomes law. The constitutional return is of the entire bill; the statutory cancellation is of only a part. Although the Constitution expressly authorizes the President to play a role in the process of enacting statutes, it is silent on the subject of unilateral Presidential action that either repeals or amends parts of duly enacted statutes.

There are powerful reasons for construing constitutional silence on this profoundly important issue as equivalent to an express prohibition . . . Our first President understood the text of the Presentment Clause as requiring that he either "approve all the parts of a Bill, or reject it in toto." What has emerged in these cases from the President's exercise of his statutory cancellation powers, however, are truncated versions of two bills that passed both Houses of Congress. They are not the product of the "finely wrought" procedure that the Framers designed . . . .

V

The Government advances two related arguments to support its position that despite the unambiguous provisions of the Act, cancellations do not amend or repeal properly enacted statutes in violation of the Presentment Clause. First, relying primarily on *Field v. Clark*, the Government contends that the cancellations were merely exercises of discretionary authority granted to the President by the Balanced Budget Act and the Taxpayer Relief Act read in light of the previously enacted Line Item Veto Act. Second, the Government submits that the substance of the authority to cancel tax and spending items "is, in practical effect, no more and no less than the power to 'decline to spend' specified sums of money, or to 'decline to implement' specified tax measures." Neither argument is persuasive.

In *Field v. Clark*, the Court upheld . . . [a statute] that directed the President to suspend [a tariff exemption] "whenever, and so often" as he should be satisfied that any country producing and exporting those products imposed duties on the agricultural products of the United States that he deemed to be reciprocally unequal and unreasonable. The section then specified the duties to be imposed on those products during any such suspension. . . . [There are] three critical differences between the power to suspend the exemption from import duties and the power to cancel portions of a duly enacted statute. First, the exercise of the suspension power was contingent upon a condition that did not exist when the Tariff Act was passed: the imposition of "reciprocally unequal and unreasonable" import duties by other countries. In contrast, the exercise of the cancellation power within five days after the enactment of the Balanced Budget and Tax Reform Acts necessarily was based on the same conditions that Congress evaluated when it passed those statutes. Second, under the Tariff Act, when the President determined that the contingency had arisen, he had a duty to suspend; in contrast, while it is true that the President was required by the Act to make three determinations before he canceled a provision, those determinations did not qualify his discretion to cancel or not to cancel. Finally, whenever the President suspended an exemption under the Tariff Act, he was executing the policy that Congress had embodied in the statute. In contrast, whenever the President cancels an item of new direct spending or a limited tax benefit he is rejecting the policy judgment made by Congress and relying on his own policy judgment.

Thus, the conclusion in *Field v. Clark* that the suspensions mandated by the Tariff Act were not exercises of legislative power does not undermine our opinion that cancellations pursuant to the Line Item Veto Act are the functional equivalent of partial repeals of Acts of Congress that fail to satisfy Article I, § 7. . . . [W]hen enacting the statutes discussed in *Field*, Congress itself made the decision to suspend or repeal the particular provisions at issue upon the occurrence of particular events subsequent to enactment, and it left only the determination of whether such events occurred up to the President. The Line Item Veto Act authorizes the President himself to effect the repeal of laws, for his own policy reasons, without observing the procedures set out in Article I, § 7. The fact that Congress intended such a result is of no moment. Although Congress presumably anticipated that the President might cancel some of the items in the Balanced Budget Act and in the Taxpayer Relief Act, Congress cannot alter the procedures set out in Article I, § 7, without amending the Constitution.

Neither are we persuaded by the Government's contention that the President's authority to cancel new direct spending and tax benefit items is no greater than his traditional authority to decline to spend appropriated funds. The Government has reviewed in some detail the series of statutes in which Congress has given the Executive broad discretion over the expenditure of appropriated funds. For example, the First Congress appropriated "sum[s] not exceeding" specified amounts to be spent on various Government operations. In those statutes, as in later years, the President was given wide discretion with respect to both the amounts to be spent and how the money would be allocated among different functions. It is argued that the Line Item Veto Act merely confers comparable discretionary authority over the expenditure of appropriated funds. The critical difference between this statute and all of its predecessors, however, is that unlike any of them, this Act gives the President the unilateral power to change the text of duly enacted statutes. None of the Act's predecessors could even arguably have been construed to authorize such a change.

VI

Although they are implicit in what we have already written, the profound importance of these cases makes it appropriate to emphasize three points. First, we express no opinion about the wisdom of the procedures authorized by the Line Item Veto Act. Many members of both major political parties who have served in the Legislative and the Executive Branches have long advocated the enactment of such procedures for the purpose of "ensur[ing] greater fiscal accountability in Washington." H.R. Conf. Rep. 104–491, p. 15 (1996). Second, ... because we conclude that the Act's cancellation provisions violate Article I, § 7, of the Constitution, we find it unnecessary to consider the District Court's alternative holding that the Act "impermissibly disrupts the balance of powers among the three branches of government." Third, our decision rests on the narrow ground that the procedures authorized by the Line Item Veto Act are not authorized by the Constitution. . . . If there is to be a new procedure in which the President will play a different role in determining the final text of what may "become a law," such change must come not by legislation but through the amendment procedures set forth in Article V of the Constitution. The judgment of the District Court is affirmed.

Justice KENNEDY, concurring.

. . . Liberty is always at stake when one or more of the branches seek to transgress the separation of powers. Separation of powers was designed to implement a fundamental insight: Concentration of power in the hands of a single branch is a threat to liberty. . . . [When] the people delegate some degree of control to a remote central authority, one branch of government ought not possess the power to shape their destiny without a sufficient check from the other two. In this vision, liberty demands limits on the ability of any one branch to influence basic political decisions. . . . It follows that if a citizen who is taxed has the measure of the tax or the decision to spend determined by the Executive alone, without adequate control by the citizen's Representatives in Congress, liberty is threatened . . . .

The principal object of the statute, it is true, was not to enhance the President's power to reward one group and punish another, to help one set of taxpayers and hurt another, to favor one State and ignore another. Yet these are its undeniable effects. The law establishes a new mechanism which gives the President the sole ability to hurt a group that is a visible target, in order to disfavor the group or to extract further concessions from Congress . . . . That a congressional cession of power is voluntary does not make it innocuous. . . . By increasing the power of the President beyond what the Framers envisioned, the statute compromises the political liberty of our citizens, liberty which the separation of powers seeks to secure. . . .

Justice SCALIA, with whom Justice O'CONNOR joins, and with whom Justice BREYER joins as to Part III, concurring in part and dissenting in part.

[U]nlike the Court I find the President's cancellation of spending items to be entirely in accord with the Constitution. . . .

III

Article I, § 7, of the Constitution obviously prevents the President from canceling a law that Congress has not authorized him to cancel. . . . It was certainly arguable, as an original matter, that Art. I, § 7, also prevents the President from canceling a law which itself authorizes the President to cancel it. But as the Court acknowledges, that argument has long since been made and rejected. In 1809, Congress passed a law authorizing the President to cancel trade restrictions against Great Britain and France if either revoked edicts directed at the United States. Joseph Story regarded the conferral of that authority as entirely unremarkable in *The Orono*, 18 F. Cas. 830, No. 10,585 (CCD Mass. 1812). The Tariff Act of 1890 authorized the President to "suspend, by proclamation to that effect" certain of its provisions if he determined that other countries were imposing "reciprocally unequal and unreasonable" duties. This Court upheld the constitutionality of that Act in *Field v. Clark*, reciting the history since 1798 of statutes conferring upon the President the power to, inter alia, "discontinue the prohibitions and restraints hereby enacted and declared," "suspend the operation of the aforesaid act," and "declare the provisions of this act to be inoperative."

As much as the Court goes on about Art. I, § 7, therefore, that provision does not demand the result the Court reaches. It no more categorically prohibits the Executive reduction of congressional dispositions in the course of implementing statutes that authorize such reduction, than it categorically prohibits the Executive augmentation of congressional dispositions in the course of implementing statutes that authorize such augmentation—generally known as substantive rulemaking. There are, to be sure, limits upon the former just as there are limits upon the latter—and I am prepared to acknowledge that the limits upon the former may be much more severe. Those limits are established, however, not by some categorical prohibition of Art. I, § 7, which our cases conclusively disprove, but by what has come to be known as the doctrine of unconstitutional delegation of legislative authority: When authorized Executive reduction or augmentation is allowed to go too far, it usurps the nondelegable function of Congress and violates the separation of powers.

It is this doctrine, and not the Presentment Clause, . . . that is the issue presented by the statute before us here. That is why the Court is correct to distinguish prior authorizations of Executive cancellation, such as the one involved in *Field*, on the ground that they were contingent upon an Executive finding of fact, and on the ground that they related to the field of foreign affairs, an area where the President has a special " 'degree of discretion and freedom.' " These distinctions have nothing to do with whether the details of Art. I, § 7, have been complied with, but everything to do with whether the authorizations went too far by transferring to the Executive a degree of political, lawmaking power that our traditions demand be retained by the Legislative Branch.

I turn, then, to the crux of the matter: whether Congress's authorizing the President to cancel an item of spending gives him a power that our history and traditions show must reside exclusively in the Legislative Branch. I may note, to begin with, that the Line Item Veto Act is not the first statute to authorize the President to "cancel" spending items. In *Bowsher v. Synar*, 478 U.S. 714 (1986), we addressed the constitutionality of the Balanced Budget and Emergency Deficit Control Act of 1985, which required the President, if the federal budget deficit exceeded a certain amount, to issue a "sequestration" order mandating spending reductions specified by the Comptroller General. The effect of sequestration was that "amounts sequestered . . . shall be permanently cancelled." We held that the Act was unconstitutional, not because it impermissibly gave the Executive legislative power, but because it gave the Comptroller General, an officer of the Legislative Branch over whom Congress retained removal power, "the ultimate authority to determine the budget cuts to be made, functions . . . plainly entailing execution of the law in constitutional terms." The President's discretion under the Line Item Veto Act is certainly broader than the Comptroller General's discretion was under the 1985 Act, but it is no broader than the discretion traditionally granted the President in his execution of spending laws.

Insofar as the degree of political, "lawmaking" power conferred upon the Executive is concerned, there is not a dime's worth of difference between Congress's authorizing the President to cancel a spending item, and Congress's authorizing money to be spent on a particular item at the President's discretion. And the latter has been done since the founding of the Nation. From 1789–1791, the First Congress made lump-sum appropriations for the entire Government — "sum[s] not exceeding" specified amounts for broad purposes. From a very early date Congress also made permissive individual appropriations, leaving the decision whether to spend the money to the President's unfettered discretion. In 1803, it appropriated $50,000 for the President to build "not exceeding fifteen gun boats, to be armed, manned and fitted out, and employed for such purposes as in his opinion the public service may require." President Jefferson reported that "[t]he sum of fifty thousand dollars appropriated by Congress for providing gun boats remains unexpended. The favorable and peaceable turn of affairs on the Mississippi rendered an immediate execution of that law unnecessary." Examples of appropriations committed to the discretion of the President abound in our history. During the Civil War, an Act appropriated over $76 million to be divided among various items "as the exigencies of the service may require." During the Great Depression, Congress appropriated $950 million "for such projects and/or purposes and under such rules and regulations as the President in his discretion may prescribe," and $4 billion for general classes of projects, the money to be spent "in the discretion and under the direction of the President." The constitutionality of such appropriations has never seriously been questioned. Rather, "[t]hat Congress has wide discretion in the matter of prescribing details of expenditures for which it appropriates must, of course, be plain." Appropriations and other acts of Congress are replete with instances of general appropriations of large amounts, to be allotted and expended as directed by designated government agencies." *Cincinnati Soap Co. v. United States*, 301 U.S. 308, 321–322 (1937).

Certain Presidents have claimed Executive authority to withhold appropriated funds even absent an express conferral of discretion to do so. In 1876, for example, President Grant reported to Congress that he would not spend money appropriated for certain harbor and river improvements, because "[u]nder no circumstances [would he] allow expenditures upon works not clearly national," and in his view, the appropriations were for "works of purely private or local interest, in no sense national." President Franklin D. Roosevelt impounded funds appropriated for a flood control reservoir and levee in Oklahoma. President Truman ordered the impoundment of hundreds of millions of dollars that had been appropriated for military aircraft. President Nixon, the Mahatma Gandhi of all impounders, asserted at a press conference in 1973 that his "constitutional right" to impound appropriated funds was "absolutely clear." Our decision two years later in *Train v. City of New York*, 420 U.S. 35 (1975), proved him wrong, but it implicitly confirmed that Congress may confer discretion upon the Executive to withhold appropriated funds, even funds appropriated for a specific purpose. The statute at issue in *Train* authorized spending "not to exceed" specified sums for certain projects, and directed that such "[s]ums authorized to be appropriated . . . shall be allotted" by the Administrator of the Environmental Protection Agency. Upon enactment of this statute, the President directed the Administrator to allot no more than a certain part of the amount authorized. This Court held, as a matter of statutory interpretation, that the statute did not grant the Executive discretion to withhold the funds, but required allotment of the full amount authorized.

The short of the matter is this: Had the Line Item Veto Act authorized the President to "decline to spend" any item of spending contained in the Balanced Budget Act of 1997, there is not the slightest doubt that authorization would have been constitutional. What the Line Item Veto Act does instead—authorizing the President to "cancel" an item of spending—is technically different. But the technical difference does not relate to the technicalities of the Presentment Clause, which have been fully complied with; and the doctrine of unconstitutional delegation, which is at issue here, is preeminently not a doctrine of technicalities. The title of the Line Item Veto Act, which was perhaps designed to simplify for public comprehension, or perhaps merely to comply with the terms of a campaign pledge, has succeeded in faking out the Supreme Court. The President's action it authorizes in fact is not a line-item veto and thus does not offend Art. I, §7; and insofar as the substance of that action is concerned, it is no different from what Congress has permitted the President to do since the formation of the Union. . . .

Justice BREYER, with whom Justice O'CONNOR and Justice SCALIA join as to Part III, dissenting.

I agree with the Court that the parties have standing, but I do not agree with its ultimate conclusion. In my view the Line Item Veto Act (Act) does not violate any specific textual constitutional command, nor does it violate any implicit separation-of-powers principle. Consequently, I believe that the Act is constitutional.

I approach the constitutional question before us with three general consider-ations in mind. First, the Act represents a legislative effort to provide the President with the power to give effect to some, but not to all, of the expenditure and revenue-diminishing provisions contained in a single massive appropriations bill. And this objective is constitutionally proper. When our Nation was founded, Congress could easily have provided the President with this kind of power. In that time period, our population was less than 4 million, federal employees numbered fewer than 5,000, annual federal budget outlays totaled approximately $4 million, and the entire oper-ative text of Congress' first general appropriations law read as follows:

> "Be it enacted . . . [t]hat there be appropriated for the service of the present year, to be paid out of the monies which arise, either from the requisitions heretofore made upon the several states, or from the duties on import and tonnage, the following sums, viz. A sum not exceeding two hundred and sixteen thousand dollars for defraying the expenses of the civil list, under the late and present government; a sum not exceeding one hundred and thirty-seven thousand dollars for defraying the expenses of the depart-ment of war; a sum not exceeding one hundred and ninety thousand dol-lars for discharging the warrants issued by the late board of treasury, and remaining unsatisfied; and a sum not exceeding ninety-six thousand dol-lars for paying the pensions to invalids." Act of Sept. 29, 1789, ch. 23, § 1, 1 Stat. 95.

At that time, a Congress, wishing to give a President the power to select among appropriations, could simply have embodied each appropriation in a separate bill, each bill subject to a separate Presidential veto.

Today, however, our population is about 250 million, the Federal Government employs more than 4 million people, the annual federal budget is $1.5 trillion, and a typical budget appropriations bill may have a dozen titles, hundreds of sections, and spread across more than 500 pages of the Statutes at Large. Congress cannot divide such a bill into thousands, or tens of thousands, of separate appropriations bills, each one of which the President would have to sign, or to veto, separately. Thus, the question is whether the Constitution permits Congress to choose a partic-ular novel means to achieve this same, constitutionally legitimate, end.

Second, the case in part requires us to focus upon the Constitution's generally phrased structural provisions, provisions that delegate all "legislative" power to Con-gress and vest all "executive" power in the President. The Court, when applying these provisions, has interpreted them generously in terms of the institutional arrange-ments that they permit. . . . Third, we need not here referee a dispute among the other two branches. These three background circumstances mean that, when one measures the literal words of the Act against the Constitution's literal commands, the fact that the Act may closely resemble a different, literally unconstitutional, arrangement is beside the point. . . . The background circumstances also mean that we are to inter-pret nonliteral separation-of-powers principles in light of the need for "workable government." *Youngstown Sheet and Tube Co.*, (Jackson, J., concurring). If we apply those principles in light of that objective, as this Court has applied them in the past, the Act is constitutional.

III

The Court believes that the Act violates the literal text of the Constitution. A simple syllogism captures its basic reasoning: Major Premise: The Constitution sets forth an exclusive method for enacting, repealing, or amending laws. Minor Premise: The Act authorizes the President to "repea[l] or amen[d]" laws in a different way, namely by announcing a cancellation of a portion of a previously enacted law. Conclusion: The Act is inconsistent with the Constitution. I find this syllogism unconvincing, however, because its Minor Premise is faulty. When the President "canceled" the two appropriation measures now before us, he did not repeal any law nor did he amend any law. He simply followed the law, leaving the statutes, as they are literally written, intact. . . . Literally speaking, the President has not "repealed" or "amended" anything. He has simply executed a power conferred upon him by Congress, which power is contained in laws that were enacted in compliance with the exclusive method set forth in the Constitution. . . . This is not the first time that Congress has delegated to the President or to others this kind of power—a contingent power to deny effect to certain statutory language. . . .

IV

Because I disagree with the Court's holding of literal violation, I must consider whether the Act nonetheless violates separation-of-powers principles. . . . There are three relevant separation-of-powers questions here: (1) Has Congress given the President the wrong kind of power, i.e., "non-Executive" power? (2) Has Congress given the President the power to "encroach" upon Congress' own constitutionally reserved territory? (3) Has Congress given the President too much power, violating the doctrine of "nondelegation?" . . . [T]he answer to all these questions is "no."

Viewed conceptually, the power the Act conveys is the right kind of power. It is "executive." As explained above, an exercise of that power "executes" the Act. Conceptually speaking, it closely resembles the kind of delegated authority—to spend or not to spend appropriations, to change or not to change tariff rates—that Congress has frequently granted the President, any differences being differences in degree, not kind . . . .

The Act does not undermine what this Court has often described as the principal function of the separation-of-powers, which is to maintain the tripartite structure of the Federal Government—and thereby protect individual liberty—by providing a "safeguard against the encroachment or aggrandizement of one branch at the expense of the other." *Buckley v. Valeo; Mistretta v. United States.* In contrast to these cases, one cannot say that the Act "encroaches" upon Congress' power, when Congress retained the power to insert, by simple majority, into any future appropriations bill, into any section of any such bill, or into any phrase of any section, a provision that says the Act will not apply. Congress also retained the power to "disapprov[e]," and thereby reinstate, any of the President's cancellations. And it is Congress that drafts and enacts the appropriations statutes that are subject to the Act in the first place—and thereby defines the outer limits of the President's cancellation authority. . . . Indeed, the President acts only in response to, and on the terms set by, the Congress.

Nor can one say that the Act's basic substantive objective is constitutionally improper, for the earliest Congresses could, and often did, confer on the President this sort of discretionary authority over spending. . . . Nor can one say the Act's grant of power "aggrandizes" the Presidential office. The grant is limited to the context of the budget. It is limited to the power to spend, or not to spend, particular appropriated items, and the power to permit, or not to permit, specific limited exemptions from generally applicable tax law from taking effect. These powers, . . . resemble those the President has exercised in the past on other occasions. The delegation of those powers to the President may strengthen the Presidency, but any such change in Executive Branch authority seems minute when compared with the changes worked by delegations of other kinds of authority that the Court in the past has upheld.

The "nondelegation" doctrine represents an added constitutional check upon Congress' authority to delegate power to the Executive Branch. . . . Congress has frequently delegated the President the authority to spend, or not to spend, particular sums of money . . . . The President, unlike most agency decisionmakers, is an elected official. He is responsible to the voters, who, in principle, will judge the manner in which he exercises his delegated authority. Whether the President's expenditure decisions, for example, are arbitrary is a matter that in the past has been left primarily to those voters to consider. And this Court has made clear that judicial review is less appropriate when the President's own discretion, rather than that of an agency, is at stake. *See Dalton v. Specter.* These matters reflect in part the Constitution's own delegation of "executive Power" to "a President," Art. II, § 1; and we must take this into account when applying the Constitution's nondelegation doctrine to questions of Presidential authority. Consequently I believe that the power the Act grants the President to prevent spending items from taking effect does not violate the "nondelegation" doctrine . . . .

In sum, I recognize that the Act before us is novel. . . . The means chosen do not amount literally to the enactment, repeal, or amendment of a law. Nor, for that matter, do they amount literally to the "line item veto" that the Act's title announces. Those means do not violate any basic separation-of-powers principle. They do not improperly shift the constitutionally foreseen balance of power from Congress to the President. Nor, since they comply with separation-of-powers principles, do they threaten the liberties of individual citizens. They represent an experiment that may, or may not, help representative government work better. The Constitution, in my view, authorizes Congress and the President to try novel methods in this way. Consequently, with respect, I dissent.

———————

1. *Chadha II* or *Field II*? For the Justices, characterization of the Line Item Veto was crucial. Which position persuades you: that it was making new law, and obviously

invalid under *Chadha*, or that it was an acceptable delegation by statute, as in *Field*? To put it another way, do you agree with Justice Scalia that the title of the statute "fak[ed] out the Supreme Court?" *See* Elizabeth Garrett, *Accountability and Restraint: The Federal Budget Process and the Line Item Veto Act,* 20 CARDOZO L. REV. 871 (1999), and Saikrishna B. Prakash, *Deviant Executive Lawmaking,* 67 GEO. WASH. L. REV. 1 (1998), for affirmative answers to that question. One of us has also chimed in with the dissents. Harold H. Bruff, *The Incompatibility Principle,* 59 ADMIN. L. REV. 225, 250–51 (2007):

> *Clinton* is a formalist opinion much in the style of *Chadha*. This time, though, the Court was wrong. The two former professors of administrative law on the Court, Justices Scalia and Breyer (joined by Justice O'Connor), furnished the correct analysis. They characterized the Act as making a delegation to the executive that was subject to the usual need for legislative standards, which were present . . . . In both *Chadha* and *Clinton*, the statutory authorizations for legislative or item vetoes had been enacted through the full constitutional process for legislation. The difference lay in the identity of the recipient of the delegated power. In *Chadha*, power flowed to one or both houses of Congress to control the implementation of executive power, in violation of the incompatibility principle [that underlies the Incompatibility Clause of the Constitution]. In *Clinton*, power flowed to the President to make policy choices within the range of discretion conferred by statute, in compliance with the incompatibility principle. This distinction also accords with traditional practice under the Constitution. Appropriating funds is clearly a function solely for Congress; spending those funds is an executive function that is controlled by the appropriations statutes but ordinarily contains substantial amounts of discretion.

2. *A Powerful Tool?* The Court's footnote 24 remarked: "Congress failed to act upon proposed legislation to disapprove these cancellations. Indeed, despite the fact that the President has canceled at least 82 items since the Act was passed, . . . Congress has enacted only one law, over a Presidential veto, disapproving any cancellation . . . [(involving] the cancellation of 38 military construction spending items)." Hence the early returns showed that item vetoes would rarely be overridden, a result that should not surprise us, considering the materials on the presidential veto earlier in this chapter. Should that affect the constitutional analysis? The White House estimated that the 82 exercises of the veto during the life of the statute saved $2 billion. Is that impressive in budgets that neared $2 trillion during these years?

3. *Impoundment Compared.* Impoundment has long offered Presidents a functional analogue to the item veto, as Justice Scalia emphasizes and as we have seen in this chapter. (Indeed, impoundment is more flexible than some variants of the item veto, because it allows reducing rather than wholly eliminating categories of spending.) Do our materials on impoundment affect your view of the desirability of an item veto?

4. *Does It Already Exist?* Some have suggested that the President has always had an item veto. The argument is based on the fact that the anti-evasion clause of Article I says that, in addition to "Bills," every "Order, Resolution, or Vote" for which the concurrence of the two houses is necessary must be presented to the President for his possible veto. That would include many internal portions of bills. In 1989, Professors Laurence Tribe and Philip Kurland provided their written opinion, on the request of Senator Edward Kennedy, that any presidential attempt to exercise a line-item veto would be unconstitutional. They cited "commonsense reading of the constitutional text," and historical evidence that the framers anticipated multi-subject appropriations bills that the President would have to veto or approve in their entirety. For the text of their letter and an attempt to show the constitutional argument to be less clear-cut than Tribe and Kurland suggest, see J. Gregory Sidak & Thomas A. Smith, *Four Faces of the Item Veto: A Reply to Tribe and Kurland,* 84 Nw. U. L. Rev. 437 (1990). For a comprehensive rebuttal of the argument for an existing line-item veto, see Michael B. Rappaport, *The President's Veto and the Constitution,* 87 Nw. U. L. Rev. 735 (1993).

5. *Evading* Clinton. Recall that the President's veto power applies to "bills." In an early version of what became the item veto statute, the Senate called for dividing each appropriations measure into as many bills as there are items. The President could then veto any item, subject of course to override. This technique would certainly be cumbersome. After *Clinton*, would it be constitutional?

3. Amending the Constitution

The ultimate check on any of the branches' abuse of its power is a constitutional amendment constraining it for the future. Amendments have affected our system of separated powers in important ways, although the design of the framers remains remarkably intact. The amendments that have altered the structure of the federal government have been: XII (1804), changing the ballot process for the presidency; XVII (1913), providing for popular election of Senators; XX (1933), altering the terms of the President and Members of Congress, and specifying presidential succession; XXII (1951), limiting Presidents to two terms; XXV (1967), providing procedures to replace Vice Presidents and for presidential disability; and XXVII (1992), forbidding congressional pay raises to take effect until after the next election.

Article V of the Constitution, which governs the amendment process, has its own set of processes that do not necessarily parallel those for more everyday functions like legislation. This point became clear early in our history, when litigants asserted that the Eleventh Amendment had not been properly adopted because it had not been presented to the President for his possible veto. In *Hollingsworth v. Virginia*, 3 Dall. 378 (1798), the Court held that presidential approval was unnecessary for a proposed constitutional amendment which had passed both Houses of Congress by the requisite two-thirds majority. Although the Court stated no rationale, it may have mattered that the Bill of Rights also lacked presidential presentation, and would have been jeopardized by a contrary holding in *Hollingsworth*.

The statute that governs the official adoption of amendments that have been ratified is 1 U.S.C. § 106b:

> Whenever official notice is received at the National Archives and Records Administration that any amendment proposed to the Constitution of the United States has been adopted, according to the provisions of the Constitution, the Archivist of the United States shall forthwith cause the amendment to be published, with his certificate, specifying the States by which the same may have been adopted, and that the same has become valid, to all intents and purposes, as a part of the Constitution of the United States.

This statute has been the same for many years, except that the Secretary of State (until 1951) and then the Administrator of General Services (until 1984) formerly performed the functions now assigned to the Archivist. Its source is the Act of April 20, 1818, 3 Stat. 439.

The most recent amendment, the Twenty-Seventh, has the most extended history of all. It was drafted by Madison as the second article of the original Bill of Rights, and proposed to the state legislatures by the First Congress. It contained no time limit. Only six of the states, however, ratified it by the time the Bill of Rights was adopted in 1791. About a century later, Ohio ratified it to protest a congressional "salary grab" — whereupon Congress repealed the pay raise. The amendment then lay dormant for almost another century, until a university student wrote a paper concluding that it might still be alive, and then proceeded to urge state legislatures to adopt it. After 1983, there occurred a spate of ratifications, many by states like Colorado that were not even gleams in the framers' eyes in 1791.

When the necessary three-fourths of the states had ratified Madison's amendment in 1992, the Archivist certified it as effective. No one knew for certain whether the action of the states alone was necessary, whether the Archivist's certification was conclusive, whether congressional acceptance would be conclusive — or whether the amendment was too stale to be adopted at all! Congress was, however, in no political position to resist a restriction on its own pay increases, and both houses proceeded to adopt a resolution confirming the Archivist's decision, by overwhelming margins. Thus, more than two centuries after its adoption, the Constitution continues to feel the hand of James Madison. (The full story is told in RICHARD B. BERNSTEIN WITH JEROME AGEL, AMENDING AMERICA 243–48 (1993).) In *Boehner v. Anderson*, 30 F.3d 156 (D.C. Cir. 1994), the court rejected a challenge based on the Amendment to the annual cost of living adjustment for Members of Congress. It held that the legislation creating the adjustment complied with the Amendment; therefore, automatic increases could take effect. What would Madison say?

Which branch should decide whether a proposed amendment has been properly ratified? Is the answer that is provided by the following case equally appropriate for every kind of amendment?

Coleman v. Miller

307 U.S. 433 (1939)

Opinion of the Court by Chief Justice HUGHES, announced by Justice STONE.

In June, 1924, the Congress proposed an amendment to the Constitution, known as the Child Labor Amendment [providing that "Congress shall have power to limit, regulate, and prohibit the labor of persons under eighteen years of age."]. In January, 1925, the Legislature of Kansas adopted a resolution rejecting the proposed amendment. . . . In January, 1937, a resolution . . . was introduced in the Senate of Kansas ratifying the proposed amendment. [It passed narrowly in the Senate.] The resolution was later adopted by the House of Representatives. . . . This original proceeding in mandamus was then brought in the Supreme Court of Kansas by . . . the twenty senators who had voted against the resolution, and three members of the House of Representatives, to . . . restrain the . . . Secretary of State of Kansas from authenticating it and delivering it to the Governor. The petition . . . set forth the prior rejection of the proposed amendment and alleged that in the period from June, 1924, to March, 1927, the amendment had been rejected by both houses of the legislatures of twenty-six States, and had been ratified in only five States, and that by reason of that rejection and the failure of ratification within a reasonable time the proposed amendment had lost its vitality. . . .

The Supreme Court . . . held that . . . the proposed amendment retained its original vitality, and that . . . "the act of ratification of the proposed amendment by the legislature of Kansas was final and complete." The writ of mandamus was accordingly denied. This Court granted certiorari. . . . [The majority held that the Kansas legislators had standing to litigate federal issues concerning the ratification before the Supreme Court. It then considered the] effect of the previous rejection of the amendment and of the lapse of time since its submission.

1. The state court adopted the view . . . that a state legislature which has rejected an amendment proposed by the Congress may later ratify. The argument in support of that view is that Article V says nothing of rejection but speaks only of ratification and provides that a proposed amendment shall be valid as part of the Constitution when ratified by three-fourths of the States; that the power to ratify . . . persists despite a previous rejection. The opposing view . . . [holds] that ratification if once given cannot afterwards be rescinded and the amendment rejected, and it is urged that the same effect in the exhaustion of the State's power to act should be ascribed to rejection; that a State can act "but once, either by convention or through its legislature."

Historic instances are cited. . . . The question did arise in connection with the adoption of the Fourteenth Amendment. The legislatures of Georgia, North Carolina and South Carolina had rejected the amendment in November and December, 1866. New governments were erected in those States (and in others) under the direction of Congress. The new legislatures ratified the amendment. . . . Ohio and New Jersey first ratified and then passed resolutions withdrawing their consent. As there were then thirty-seven States, twenty-eight were needed to constitute the requisite three-fourths. . . . On July 20th, [1868, Secretary of State] Seward issued a proclamation reciting the ratification by twenty-eight States, including North Carolina, South Carolina, Ohio and New Jersey, and stating that it appeared that Ohio and New Jersey had since passed resolutions withdrawing their consent and that "it is deemed a matter of doubt and uncertainty whether such resolutions are not irregular, invalid and therefore ineffectual." The Secretary certified that if the ratifying resolutions of Ohio and New Jersey were still in full force and effect, notwithstanding the attempted withdrawal, the amendment had become a part of the Constitution. On the following day the Congress adopted a concurrent resolution which, reciting that three-fourths of the States having ratified (the list including North Carolina, South Carolina, Ohio and New Jersey), declared the Fourteenth Amendment to be a part of the Constitution and that it should be duly promulgated as such by the Secretary of State. Accordingly, Secretary Seward, on July 28th, issued his proclamation embracing the States mentioned in the congressional resolution and adding Georgia [which had just ratified].

Thus the political departments of the Government dealt with the effect both of previous rejection and of attempted withdrawal and determined that both were ineffectual in the presence of an actual ratification. . . . This decision by the political departments of the Government as to the validity of the adoption of the Fourteenth Amendment has been accepted. We think that in accordance with this historic precedent the question of the efficacy of ratifications by state legislatures, in the light of previous rejection or attempted withdrawal, should be regarded as a political question pertaining to the political departments, with the ultimate authority in the Congress in the exercise of its control over the promulgation of the adoption of the amendment.

The precise question as now raised is whether, when the legislature of the State, as we have found, has actually ratified the proposed amendment, the Court should restrain the state officers from certifying the ratification to the Secretary of State, because of an earlier rejection, and thus prevent the question from coming before the political departments. We find no basis in either Constitution or statute for such judicial action. Article V, speaking solely of ratification, contains no provision as to rejection. Nor has the Congress enacted a statute relating to rejections. The statutory provision with respect to constitutional amendments . . . presupposes official notice to the Secretary of State when a state legislature has adopted a resolution of ratification. We see no warrant for judicial interference with the performance of that duty.

2. The more serious question is whether the proposal by the Congress of the amendment had lost its vitality through lapse of time and hence it could not be ratified by the Kansas legislature in 1937. The argument of petitioners stresses the fact that nearly thirteen years elapsed between the proposal in 1924 and the ratification in question. It is said that when the amendment was proposed there was a definitely adverse popular sentiment and that at the end of 1925 there had been rejection by both houses of the legislatures of sixteen States and ratification by only four States,

and that it was not until about 1933 that an aggressive campaign was started in favor of the amendment. In reply, it is urged that Congress did not fix a limit of time for ratification and that an unreasonably long time had not elapsed since the submission; that the conditions which gave rise to the amendment had not been eliminated; that the prevalence of child labor, the diversity of state laws and the disparity in their administration, with the resulting competitive inequalities, continued to exist. Reference is also made to the fact that a number of the States have treated the amendment as still pending and that in the proceedings of the national government there have been indications of the same view. It is said that there were fourteen ratifications in 1933, four in 1935, one in 1936, and three in 1937.

We have held that the Congress in proposing an amendment may fix a reasonable time for ratification. *Dillon v. Gloss*, 256 U.S. 368 (1921). There we sustained the action of the Congress in providing in the proposed Eighteenth Amendment that it should be inoperative unless ratified within seven years. No limitation of time for ratification is provided in the instant case either in the proposed amendment or in the resolution of submission. But petitioners contend that, in the absence of a limitation by the Congress, the Court can and should decide what is a reasonable period within which ratification may be had. . . . But it does not follow that, whenever Congress has not exercised that power, the Court should take upon itself the responsibility of deciding what constitutes a reasonable time and determine accordingly the validity of ratifications. . . .

Where are to be found the criteria for such a judicial determination? None are to be found in Constitution or statute. In their endeavor to answer this question petitioners' counsel have suggested that at least two years should be allowed; that six years would not seem to be unreasonably long; that seven years had been used by the Congress as a reasonable period; that one year, six months and thirteen days was the average time used in passing upon amendments which have been ratified since the first ten amendments; that three years, six months and twenty-five days has been the longest time used in ratifying. To this list of variables, counsel add that "the nature and extent of publicity and the activity of the public and of the legislatures of the several States in relation to any particular proposal should be taken into consideration." That statement is pertinent, but there are additional matters to be examined and weighed. When a proposed amendment springs from a conception of economic needs, it would be necessary, in determining whether a reasonable time had elapsed since its submission, to consider the economic conditions prevailing in the country, whether these had so far changed since the submission as to make the proposal no longer responsive to the conception which inspired it or whether conditions were such as to intensify the feeling of need and the appropriateness of the proposed remedial action. In short, the question of a reasonable time in many cases would involve, as in this case it does involve, an appraisal of a great variety of relevant conditions, political, social and economic, which can hardly be said to be within the appropriate range of evidence receivable in a court of justice and as to which it would be an extravagant extension of judicial authority to assert judicial notice as the basis of deciding a controversy with respect to the validity of an amendment actually ratified. On the other hand, these conditions are appropriate for the consideration of the political departments of the Government. The questions they involve are essentially political and not justiciable. They can be decided by the Congress with the full knowledge and appreciation ascribed to the national legislature of the political, social and economic conditions which have prevailed during the period since the submission of the amendment.

Our decision that the Congress has the power under Article V to fix a reasonable limit of time for ratification in proposing an amendment proceeds upon the assumption that the question, what is a reasonable time, lies within the congressional province. If it be deemed that such a question is an open one when the limit has not been fixed in advance, we think that it should also be regarded as an open one for the consideration of the Congress when, in the presence of certified ratifications by three-fourths of the States, the time arrives for the promulgation of the adoption of the amendment. The decision by the Congress, in its control of the action of the Secretary of State, of the question whether the amendment had been adopted within a reasonable time would not be subject to review by the courts.

It would unduly lengthen this opinion to attempt to review our decisions as to the class of questions deemed to be political and not justiciable. In determining whether a question falls within that category, the appropriateness under our system of government of attributing finality to the action of the political departments and also the lack of satisfactory criteria for a judicial determination are dominant considerations. . . .

For the reasons we have stated, . . . we think that the Congress in controlling the promulgation of the adoption of a constitutional amendment has the final determination of the question whether by lapse of time its proposal of the amendment had lost its vitality prior to the required ratifications. . . . As we find no reason for disturbing the decision of the Supreme Court of Kansas in denying the mandamus sought by petitioners, its judgment is affirmed. . . .

Concurring opinion by Justice BLACK, in which Justice ROBERTS, Justice FRANKFURTER and Justice DOUGLAS join.

. . . The Constitution grants Congress exclusive power to control submission of constitutional amendments. Final determination by Congress that ratification by three-fourths of the States has taken place "is conclusive upon the courts." . . . [A] proclaimed amendment must be accepted as a part of the Constitution, leaving to the judiciary its traditional authority of interpretation. To the extent that the Court's opinion in the present case even impliedly assumes a power to make judicial interpretation of the exclusive constitutional authority of Congress over submission and ratification of amendments, we are unable to agree. . . .

[I]t is apparent that judicial review of or pronouncements upon a supposed limitation of a "reasonable time" within which Congress may accept ratification; . . . or whether a State may reverse its action once taken upon a proposed amendment; and kindred questions, are all consistent only with an ultimate control over the amending process in the courts. . . .

No such division between the political and judicial branches of the government is made by Article V which grants power over the amending of the Constitution to Congress alone. Undivided control of that process has been given by the Article exclusively and completely to Congress. The process itself is "political" in its entirety, from submission until an amendment becomes part of the Constitution, and is not subject to judicial guidance, control or interference at any point.

Since Congress has sole and complete control over the amending process, subject to no judicial review, the views of any court upon this process cannot be binding upon Congress, and insofar as *Dillon v. Gloss* attempts judicially to impose a limitation upon the right of Congress to determine final adoption of an amendment, it should be disapproved. If Congressional determination that an amendment has been completed and become a part of the Constitution is final and removed from examination by the courts, as the Court's present opinion recognizes, surely the steps leading to that condition must be subject to the scrutiny, control and appraisal of none save the Congress, the body having exclusive power to make that final determination. . . .

Justice BUTLER, dissenting. . . .

In *Dillon v. Gloss*, 256 U.S. 368, one imprisoned for transportation of intoxicating liquor in violation of . . . the National Prohibition Act, instituted habeas corpus proceedings to obtain his release on the ground that the Eighteenth Amendment was invalid because the resolution proposing it declared that it should not be operative unless ratified within seven years. The Amendment was ratified in less than a year and a half. We definitely held that Article V impliedly requires amendments submitted to be ratified within a reasonable time after proposal; that Congress may fix a reasonable time for ratification, and that the period of seven years fixed by the Congress was reasonable.

We said:

> "It will be seen that this article says nothing about the time within which ratification may be had—neither that it shall be unlimited nor that it shall be fixed by Congress. . . . We do not find anything in the Article which suggests that an amendment once proposed is to be open to ratification for all time, or that ratification in some of the States may be separated from that in others by many years and yet be effective. We do find that which strongly suggests the contrary. First, proposal and ratification are not treated as unrelated acts, but as succeeding steps in a single endeavor, the natural inference being that they are not to be widely separated in time. Secondly, it is only when there is deemed to be a necessity therefor that amendments are to be proposed, the reasonable implication being that when proposed they are to be considered and disposed of presently. Thirdly, as ratification is but the expression of the approbation of the people and is to be effective when had

in three-fourths of the States, there is a fair implication that it must be sufficiently contemporaneous in that number of States to reflect the will of the people in all sections at relatively the same period, which of course ratification scattered through a long series of years would not do. . . . [The need for a time limit] becomes even more manifest when what is comprehended in the other view is considered; for, according to it, four amendments proposed long ago—two in 1789, one in 1810, and one in 1861—are still pending and in a situation where their ratification in some of the States many years since by representatives of generations now largely forgotten may be effectively supplemented in enough more States to make three-fourths by representatives of the present or some future generation. To that view few would be able to subscribe, and in our opinion it is quite untenable. . . ."

Upon the reasoning of our opinion in that case, I would hold that more than a reasonable time had elapsed. . . .

Justice McREYNOLDS joins in this opinion.

———

1. *Who Decides?* To most of the Justices in *Coleman*, issues concerning whether an amendment has been ratified lie solely within the province of Congress. Why should that be? Consider the usual foci of the political question doctrine. First, perhaps there is a textual commitment in Article V to Congress, as the majority and concurring Justices suggest, but is the fact that Congress has explicit power to decide between the legislative and convention modes of ratification enough to commit all other issues to them? Second, are there manageable judicial standards? The argument over the wisdom of the dicta in *Dillon* will give you both sides of that issue.

The third main type of political question consideration, whether there are institutional imperatives that force the Court to stay its hand, may explain *Coleman* best. First, note the Court's recital of the history of the Fourteenth Amendment. The legality of that ratification was bound up in such sensitive questions as whether Congress could compel a seceded state's ratification as a condition on full reentry into the Union. In 1868, the radical Congress that was about to impeach a President for defying it would not have taken judicial intervention kindly. So this history may have reminded the Court of the potential horrors of conflict over ratification. Perhaps some legal questions are best left unaddressed in court, in the interests of repose.

Second, the Child Labor Amendment was an effort to overturn Supreme Court precedent holding that the Commerce Clause did not grant Congress such power. The Court may not have wished to get into the business of reviewing attempts to override its own decisions. But are we happy leaving *all* these issues to Congress—especially if an amendment is to constrain *that* body's prerogatives? Consider the history of the Twenty-Seventh Amendment—what should the courts have done had Congress resolved that the amendment had *not* been duly ratified?

Professor Walter Dellinger has argued, in *The Legitimacy of Constitutional Change: Rethinking the Amendment Process*, 97 Harv. L. Rev. 386 (1983), that *Coleman*'s abandonment of a role for judicial review in the amendment process is wrong, because it allows debilitating uncertainty about the status of amendments. For a rejoinder, see Laurence H. Tribe, *A Constitution We Are Amending: In Defense of a Restrained Judicial Role*, 97 Harv. L.Rev. 433 (1983).

2. *Vitality and the Twenty-Seventh Amendment.* The *Dillon* Court thought that some judicial supervision of the vitality of old amendment proposals was needed, lest one of those first proposed in 1789 somehow be ratified. That fear may have seemed to be an imaginary horrible in 1921, but a future generation made it real with the Twenty-Seventh Amendment. Perhaps the history of that amendment lays the *Dillon* Court's position to rest, in favor of Justice Black's position in *Coleman*. If so, is that a good thing—do you think *Dillon* should be revived and applied to invalidate the Twenty-Seventh Amendment? *See* Stewart Dalzell & Eric J. Beste, *Is the Twenty-Seventh Amendment 200 Years Too Late?* 62 Geo. Wash. L. Rev. 501 (1994) ("yes"); Michael S. Paulsen, *A General Theory of Article V: The Constitutional Lessons of the Twenty-Seventh Amendment*, 103 Yale L.J. 677 (1993) ("no").

3. *The Convention Quandary.* The uncertainties that surround the amendment process multiply when constitutional conventions are considered. Article V clearly provides for the possibility of a convention, upon the call of two-thirds of the state legislatures. Could a convention called for a particular purpose be held to its instructions? The 1787 Convention clearly outran its own charter, so perhaps not. In any event, who decides? *See* Russell L. Caplan, Constitutional Brinksmanship, Amending the Constitution by National Convention (1988). For arguments in favor of a new constitutional convention, see Sanford Levinson, Our Undemocratic Constitution: Where the Constitution Goes Wrong (and How We the People Can Correct It) (2008); Larry J. Sabato, A More Perfect Constitution (2007).

Chapter 3

Autonomy and Mutual Accountability among the Branches

This chapter reviews the ways each branch protects its autonomy from the others, and the compensating ways that the branches hold one another to account — thereby limiting and defining their autonomy. We begin by examining the power of Congress to determine the membership of all three branches. Impeachment is Congress's ultimate weapon against personnel of the other two branches. Congress also exercises power over its own membership. We then consider the immunities from suit of the members of each branch. This section introduces a process of implying immunities that continues in the following section's examination of the branches' implied privileges from disclosing information. Finally, we review the powers of Congress to adjust the accountability of all three branches by legislation.

A. Congressional Power over the Membership of the Branches

1. Impeachment

a. "High Crimes and Misdemeanors"

Article II, § 4 of the Constitution provides: "The president, vice president, and all civil officers of the United States, shall be removed from office on impeachment for, and conviction of, treason, bribery, or other high crimes and misdemeanors." Under Article I, § 2, the House of Representatives "shall have the sole power of impeachment." Section 3 then grants the Senate "the sole power to try all impeachments." Conviction requires "the concurrence of two-thirds of the members present." Judgment "shall not extend further than to removal from office and disqualification" to hold future office, "but the party convicted shall nevertheless be ... subject to indictment, trial, judgment, and punishment, according to law."

This laconic text raises a number of major issues. First, what is the substantive meaning of high crimes and misdemeanors? The main possibilities are: 1) all crimes; 2) all felonies; 3) some or all crimes that relate to performance of the office; 4) some or all abuses of power, whether or not technically criminal in nature; 5) whatever the necessary majorities in the House and Senate believe is sufficient (as then-Representative

Gerald Ford once famously argued). Second, what processes are appropriate for the two Houses to follow? That is, should the House conduct its own factfinding, or may it accept a record compiled by a prosecutor or in a criminal trial? Is the House like a grand jury, needing only reason to believe an impeachable offense has been committed, or should it find that an offense has occurred, and if so, under what standard of proof? What does it mean for the Senate to "try" someone? Should it act on a record compiled by the House or by some other institution, or should it hear witnesses? Again, what is the standard of proof—the criminal reasonable doubt standard, or something less? Third, are sanctions other than removal and disqualification available, such as censure? And fourth, may criminal prosecution, especially of a President, occur before removal, as it explicitly may afterwards?

Until the 1970s, modern Americans could be forgiven for regarding impeachment as a quaint holdover from British precedents, a process that had been rendered ineffective by two ill-advised and failed impeachments earlier in our history. These, of course, were the trials of Justice Samuel Chase in 1805 and President Andrew Johnson in 1868. *See* WILLIAM H. REHNQUIST, GRAND INQUESTS: THE HISTORIC IMPEACHMENTS OF JUSTICE SAMUEL CHASE AND PRESIDENT ANDREW JOHNSON (1992); DAVID O. STEWART, IMPEACHED: THE TRIAL OF PRESIDENT ANDREW JOHNSON AND THE FIGHT FOR LINCOLN'S LEGACY (2009). Both disputes were highly politicized. Chase was impeached by Republicans in Congress at the instigation of Thomas Jefferson as part of his war on the Federalist judiciary. Johnson was impeached by radicals in Congress as part of the battle over control of Reconstruction. Both were acquitted. The Chief Justice's book argues that these trials threatened the Framers' "two original contributions to the art of government"—the independent, not parliamentary executive, and the independent judiciary empowered to invalidate legislation. He concludes (at 278): "The importance of these two acquittals in our constitutional history can hardly be overstated. . . . [T]hese two 'cases'—decided not by the courts but by the United States Senate—surely contributed as much to the maintenance of our tripartite federal system of government as any case decided by any court." For valuable analyses of impeachment and its problems, see MICHAEL J. GERHARDT, THE FEDERAL IMPEACHMENT PROCESS: A CONSTITUTIONAL AND HISTORICAL ANALYSIS (2d ed. 2000); CHARLES L. BLACK, IMPEACHMENT: A HANDBOOK (1974).

Within twenty-five years at the close of the twentieth century, two Presidents faced impeachment. Richard Nixon resigned as the House prepared to impeach him; Bill Clinton survived impeachment and trial. As these controversies begin to recede into history, Americans need to assess what they have done to the presidency, to Congress, and to the nation. We begin with an analysis that was prepared to guide the House as it considered the impeachment of Richard Nixon in the wake of the Watergate scandal. Despite the dispassionate tone of the House Judiciary Committee staff report, the House was under Democratic control, and it is worth considering to what degree the study should be read as an advocacy document. The executive branch likewise proffered scholarly studies on impeachment, with the prefatory disclaimers that they were not to be regarded as taking an official position, and, indeed, were not intended to reach "ultimate conclusions." Office of Legal Counsel, U.S. Department of Justice, Legal Aspects of Impeachment: An Overview (with 4 appendices) (1974). President Nixon argued that impeachment could be based only on criminal offenses. *See* James D. St. Clair, *et al.*, *Analysis of the Constitutional Standard for Presidential Impeachment, in* Presidential Impeachment: A Documentary Overview 40–73 (M. B. Schnapper ed., 1974). For another view generally concurring with the House study that follows, see Committee on Legislation, Association of the Bar of the City of New York, The Law of Presidential Impeachment (1974).

Constitutional Grounds for Presidential Impeachment

Report by the Staff of the Impeachment Inquiry of the House Committee on the Judiciary (Comm. Print), 93d Cong., 2d Sess. (1974)

I. Introduction

. . . This memorandum offers no fixed standards for determining whether grounds for [the] impeachment [of Richard Nixon] exist. The framers did not write a fixed standard. Instead they adopted from English history a standard sufficiently general and flexible to meet future circumstances and events, the nature and character of which they could not foresee.

II. The Historical Origins of Impeachment

The Constitution provides that the President ". . . shall be removed from Office on Impeachment for, and Conviction of, Treason, Bribery, or other high Crimes and Misdemeanors." The framers could have written simply "or other crimes" as indeed they did in the provision for extradition of criminal offenders from one state to another. They did not do that. If they had meant simply to denote seriousness, they could have done so directly. They did not do that either. They adopted instead a unique phrase used for centuries in English parliamentary impeachments, for the meaning of which one must look to history. . . .

A. THE ENGLISH PARLIAMENTARY PRACTICE

Alexander Hamilton wrote, in No. 65 of The Federalist, that Great Britain had served as "the model from which [impeachment] has been borrowed." . . . Parliament developed the impeachment process as a means to exercise some measure of control over the power of the King. An impeachment proceeding in England was a direct method of bringing to account the King's ministers and favorites — men who might otherwise have been beyond reach. Impeachment, at least in its early history, has been called "the most powerful weapon in the political armory, short of civil war." . . .

At the time of the Constitutional Convention the phrase "high Crimes and Misdemeanors" had been in use for over 400 years in impeachment proceedings in Parliament . . . .

Two points emerge from the 400 years of English parliamentary experience with the phrase "high Crimes and Misdemeanors." First, the particular allegations of misconduct alleged damage to the state in such forms as misapplication of funds, abuse of official power, neglect of duty, encroachment on Parliament's prerogatives, corruption, and betrayal of trust. Second, the phrase "high Crimes and Misdemeanors" was confined to parliamentary impeachments; it had no roots in the ordinary criminal law, and the particular allegations of misconduct under that heading were not necessarily limited to common law or statutory derelictions or crimes.

B. THE INTENTION OF THE FRAMERS

The debates on impeachment at the Constitutional Convention in Philadelphia focus principally on its applicability to the President. The framers sought to create a responsible though strong executive; they hoped, in the words of Elbridge Gerry of Massachusetts, that "the maxim would never be adopted here that the chief Magistrate could do [no] wrong." Impeachment was to be one of the central elements of executive responsibility in the framework of the new government as they conceived it.

The constitutional grounds for impeachment of the President received little direct attention in the Convention; the phrase "other high Crimes and Misdemeanors" was ultimately added to "Treason" and "Bribery" with virtually no debate. There is evidence, however, that the framers were aware of the technical meaning the phrase had acquired in English impeachments. . . .

1. THE PURPOSE OF THE IMPEACHMENT REMEDY

Among the weaknesses of the Articles of Confederation apparent to the delegates to the Constitutional Convention was that they provided for a purely legislative form of government whose ministers were subservient to Congress. One of the first decisions of the delegates was that their new plan should include a separate executive, judiciary, and legislature. However, the framers sought to avoid the creation of a too-powerful executive. The Revolution had been fought against the tyranny of a king and his council, and the framers sought to build in safeguards against executive abuse and usurpation of power . . . . [T]he impeachability of the President was considered to be an important element of his responsibility. Impeachment had been included in the proposals before the Constitutional Convention from its beginning. A specific provision, making the executive removable from office on impeachment and conviction for "malpractice or neglect of duty," was unanimously adopted even before it was decided that the executive would be a single person.

The only major debate on the desirability of impeachment occurred when it was moved that the provision for impeachment be dropped, a motion that was defeated by a vote of eight states to two. . . . The one argument made by the opponents of impeachment to which no direct response was made during the debate was that the executive would be too dependent on the legislature—that, as Charles Pinckney put it, the legislature would hold impeachment "as a rod over the Executive and by that means effectually destroy his independence." That issue, which involved the forum for trying impeachments and the mode of electing the executive, troubled the Convention until its closing days. Throughout its deliberations on ways to avoid executive subservience to the legislature, however, the Convention never reconsidered its early decision to make the executive removable through the process of impeachment.

2. ADOPTION OF "HIGH CRIMES AND MISDEMEANORS"

Briefly, and late in the Convention, the framers addressed the question how to describe the grounds for impeachment consistent with its intended function. They did so only after the mode of the President's election was settled in a way that did not make him (in the words of James Wilson) "the Minion of the Senate." The draft of the Constitution then before the Convention provided for his removal upon impeachment and conviction for "treason or bribery." George Mason objected that these grounds were too limited:

> Why is the provision restrained to Treason & bribery only? Treason as defined in the Constitution will not reach many great and dangerous offenses. Hastings is not guilty of Treason. Attempts to subvert the Constitution may not be Treason as above defined—As bills of attainder which have saved the British Constitution are forbidden, it is the more necessary to extend the power of impeachments.

Mason then moved to add the word "maladministration" to the other two grounds. Maladministration was a term in use in six of the thirteen state constitutions as a ground for impeachment, including Mason's home state of Virginia. When James Madison objected that "so vague a term will be equivalent to a tenure during pleasure of the Senate," Mason withdrew "maladministration" and substituted "high crimes and misdemeanors agst. the State," which was adopted eight states to three, apparently with no further debate.

That the framers were familiar with English parliamentary impeachment proceedings is clear. . . . Blackstone's *Commentaries on the Laws of England*—a work cited by delegates in other portions of the Convention's deliberations and which Madison later described (in the Virginia ratifying convention) as "a book which is in every man's hand"—included "high misdemeanors" as one term for positive offenses "against the king and government." The "first and principal" high misdemeanor, according to Blackstone, was "mal-administration of such high officers, as are in public trust and employment," usually punished by the method of parliamentary impeachment . . . .

3. GROUNDS FOR IMPEACHMENT

Mason's suggestion to add "maladministration," Madison's objection to it as "vague," and Mason's substitution of "high crimes and misdemeanors agst. the State" are the only comments in the Philadelphia convention specifically directed to the constitutional language describing the grounds for impeachment of the President. Mason's objection to limiting the grounds to treason and bribery was that treason would "not reach many great and dangerous offenses" including "[a]ttempts to subvert the Constitution." His willingness to substitute "high Crimes and Misdemeanors," . . . suggests that he believed "high Crimes and Misdemeanors" would cover the offenses about which he was concerned.

Contemporaneous comments on the scope of impeachment are persuasive as to the intention of the framers. In Federalist No. 65, Alexander Hamilton described the subject of impeachment as

> those offenses which proceed from the misconduct of public men, or, in other words, from the abuse or violation of some public trust. They are of a nature which may with peculiar propriety be denominated POLITICAL, as they relate chiefly to injuries done immediately to the society itself.

Comments in the state ratifying conventions also suggest that those who adopted the Constitution viewed impeachment as a remedy for usurpation or abuse of power or serious breach of trust. . . . [T]he framers who discussed impeachment in the state ratifying conventions, as well as other delegates who favored the Constitution, implied that it reached offenses against the government, and especially abuses of constitutional duties. The opponents did not argue that the grounds for impeachment had been limited to criminal offenses . . . .

C. THE AMERICAN IMPEACHMENT CASES

Thirteen officers have been impeached by the House since 1787; one President, one cabinet officer, one United States Senator, and ten Federal judges. In addition there have been numerous resolutions and investigations in the House not resulting in impeachment. However, the action of the House in declining to impeach an officer is not particularly illuminating. The reasons for failing to impeach are generally not stated, and may have rested upon a failure of proof, legal insufficiency of the grounds, political judgment, the press of legislative business, or the closeness of the expiration of the session of Congress. On the other hand, when the House has voted to impeach an officer, a majority of the Members necessarily have concluded that the conduct alleged constituted grounds for impeachment.

Does Article III, Section 1 of the Constitution, which states that judges "shall hold their Offices during good Behavior," limit the relevance of the ten impeachments of judges with respect to presidential impeachment standards as has been argued by some? It does not. The argument is that "good behavior" implies an additional ground for impeachment of judges not applicable to other civil officers. However, the only impeachment provision discussed in the Convention and included in the Constitution is Article II, Section 4, which by its express terms, applies to all civil officers, including judges, and defines impeachment offenses as "Treason, Bribery, and other high Crimes and Misdemeanors." . . .

Each of the thirteen American impeachments involved charges of misconduct incompatible with the official position of the officeholder. This conduct falls into three broad categories: (1) exceeding the constitutional bounds of the powers of the office in derogation of the powers of another branch of government; (2) behaving in a manner grossly incompatible with the proper function and purpose of the office; and (3) employing the power of the office for an improper purpose or for personal gain.

1. EXCEEDING THE POWERS OF THE OFFICE IN DEROGATION OF THOSE OF ANOTHER BRANCH OF GOVERNMENT

. . . . The impeachment of President Andrew Johnson in 1868 . . . rested on allegations that he had exceeded the power of his office and had failed to respect the prerogatives of Congress. The Johnson impeachment grew out of a bitter partisan struggle over the implementation of Reconstruction in the South following the Civil War. Johnson was charged with violation of the Tenure of Office Act, which purported to take away the President's authority to remove members of his own cabinet and specifically provided that violation would be a "high misdemeanor," as well as a crime. Believing the Act unconstitutional, Johnson removed Secretary of War Edwin M. Stanton and was impeached three days later. . . . The removal of Stanton[, however,] was more a catalyst for the impeachment than a fundamental cause. The issue between the President and Congress was which of them should have the constitutional — and ultimately even the military — power to make and enforce Reconstruction policy in the South. The Johnson impeachment, like the British impeachments of great ministers, involved issues of state going to the heart of the constitutional division of executive and legislative power.

2. BEHAVING IN A MANNER GROSSLY INCOMPATIBLE WITH THE PROPER FUNCTION AND PURPOSE OF THE OFFICE

Judge John Pickering was impeached in 1803, largely for intoxication on the bench. . . . Seventy-three years later another judge, Mark Delahay, was impeached for intoxication both on and off the bench but resigned before articles of impeachment were adopted. A similar concern with conduct incompatible with the proper exercise of judicial office appears in the decision of the House to impeach Associate Supreme Court Justice Samuel Chase in 1804. The [Democratic-Republican-controlled] House alleged that [federalist] Justice Chase had permitted his partisan views to influence his conduct of two trials held while he was conducting circuit court several years earlier. . . . Judge West H. Humphreys was impeached in 1862 on charges that he joined the Confederacy without resigning his federal judgeship. . . . Judicial favoritism and failure to give impartial consideration to cases before him were also among the allegations in the impeachment of Judge George W. English in 1926.

3. EMPLOYING THE POWER OF THE OFFICE FOR AN IMPROPER PURPOSE OR PERSONAL GAIN

Two types of official conduct for improper purposes have been alleged in past impeachments. The first type involves vindictive use of their office by federal judges; the second, the use of office for personal gain. Judge James H. Peck was impeached in 1826 for charging with contempt a lawyer who had publicly criticized one of his decisions, imprisoning him, and ordering his disbarment for 18 months. . . . Some of the articles in the impeachment of Judge Charles Swayne (1903) alleged that he maliciously and unlawfully imprisoned two lawyers and a litigant for contempt.

Six impeachments have alleged the use of office for personal gain or the appearance of financial impropriety while in office. Secretary of War William W. Belknap was impeached in 1876 of high crimes and misdemeanors for conduct that probably constituted bribery and certainly involved the use of his office for highly improper purposes: receiving substantial annual payments through an intermediary in return for his appointing a particular post trader at a frontier military post in Indian territory. The impeachments of Judges Charles Swayne (1903), Robert W. Archibald (1912), and George W. English (1926) each involved charges of the use of office for direct or indirect personal monetary gain. . . .

III. The Criminality Issue

The phrase "high Crimes and Misdemeanors" may connote "criminality" to some. This likely is the predicate for some of the contentions that only an indictable crime can constitute impeachable conduct. Other advocates of an indictable-offense requirement would establish a criminal standard of impeachable conduct because that standard is definite, can be known in advance and reflects a contemporary legal view of what conduct should be punished. A requirement of criminality would require resort to familiar criminal laws and concepts to serve as standards in the impeachment process. Furthermore, this would pose problems concerning the applicability of standards of proof and the like pertaining to the trial of crimes.

The central issue raised by these concerns is whether requiring an indictable offense as an essential element of impeachable conduct is consistent with the purposes and intent of the framers in establishing the impeachment power and in setting a constitutional standard for the exercise of that power . . . The impeachment of a President must occur only for reasons at least as pressing as those needs of government that give rise to the creation of criminal offenses. But this does not mean that the various elements of proof, defenses, and other substantive concepts surrounding an indictable offense control the impeachment process. Nor does it mean that state or federal criminal codes are necessarily the place to turn to provide a standard under the United States Constitution. Impeachment is a constitutional remedy. The framers intended that the impeachment language they employed should reflect the grave misconduct that so injures or abuses our constitutional institutions and form of government as to justify impeachment . . . .

Impeachment and the criminal law serve fundamentally different purposes. Impeachment is the first step in a remedial process—removal from office and possible disqualification from holding future office. The purpose of impeachment is not personal punishment; its function is primarily to maintain constitutional government. Furthermore, the Constitution itself provides that impeachment is no substitute for the ordinary process of criminal law since it specifies that impeachment does not immunize the officer from criminal liability for his wrongdoing.

The general applicability of the criminal law also makes it inappropriate as the standard for a process applicable to a highly specific situation such as removal of a President. The criminal law sets a general standard of conduct that all must follow. It does not address itself to the abuses of presidential power. In an impeachment proceeding a President is called to account for abusing powers that only a President possesses.

Other characteristics of the criminal law make criminality inappropriate as an essential element of impeachable conduct. While the failure to act may be a crime, the traditional focus of criminal law is prohibitory. Impeachable conduct, on the other hand, may include the serious failure to discharge the affirmative duties imposed on the President by the Constitution. Unlike a criminal case, the cause for the removal of a President may be based on his entire course of conduct in office. In particular situations, it may be a course of conduct more than individual acts that has a tendency to subvert constitutional government. To confine impeachable conduct to indictable offenses may well be to set a standard so restrictive as not to reach conduct that might adversely affect the system of government. Some of the most grievous offenses against our constitutional form of government may not entail violations of the criminal law. . . .

Impeachment of Richard M. Nixon, President of the United States

H. Rep. No. 1305, 93d Cong., 2d Sess. (1974)

The committee on the Judiciary . . . recommends that the House exercise its constitutional power to impeach Richard M. Nixon, President of the United States, and that articles of impeachment be exhibited to the Senate as follows: . . .

ARTICLE I

In his conduct of the office of President of the United States, Richard M. Nixon, in violation of his constitutional oath faithfully to execute the office of President of the United States and to the best of his ability, preserve, protect and defend the Constitution of the United States, and in violation of his constitutional duty to take care that the laws be faithfully executed, has prevented, obstructed, and impeded the administration of justice in that:

On June 17, 1972, and prior thereto, agents of the Committee for the Re-election of the President committed unlawful entry of the headquarters of the Democratic National Committee in Washington, District of Columbia, for the purpose of securing political intelligence. Subsequent thereto, Richard M. Nixon, using the powers of his high office, engaged personally and through his subordinates and agents, in a course of conduct or plan designed to delay, impede, and obstruct the investigation of such unlawful entry; to cover up, conceal and protect those responsible; and to conceal the existence and scope of other unlawful covert activities.

The means used to implement this course of conduct or plan included one or more of the following:

(1) making or causing to be made false or misleading statements to lawfully authorized investigative officers and employees of the United States;

(2) withholding relevant and material evidence or information from lawfully authorized investigative officers and employees of the United States;

(3) approving, condoning, acquiescing in, and counseling witnesses with respect to the giving of false or misleading statements to lawfully authorized investigative officers and employees of the United States and false or misleading testimony in duly instituted judicial and congressional proceedings;

(4) interfering or endeavoring to interfere with the conduct of investigations by the Department of Justice of the United States, the Federal Bureau of Investigation, the Office of Watergate Special Prosecution Force, and Congressional Committees;

(5) approving, condoning, and acquiescing in, the surreptitious payment of substantial sums of money for the purpose of obtaining the silence or influencing the testimony of witnesses, potential witnesses or individuals who participated in such unlawful entry and other illegal activities;

(6) endeavoring to misuse the Central Intelligence Agency, an agency of the United States; . . .

(9) endeavoring to cause prospective defendants, and individuals duly tried and convicted, to expect favored treatment and consideration in return for their silence or false testimony or rewarding individuals for their silence or false testimony. . . .

Wherefore Richard M. Nixon, by such conduct, warrants impeachment and trial, and removal from office.

ARTICLE II

Using the powers of the office of President of the United States, Richard M. Nixon, in violation of his constitutional oath faithfully to execute the office of President of the United States and, to the best of his ability, preserve, protect and defend the Constitution of the United States, and in disregard of his constitutional duty to take care that the laws be faithfully executed, has repeatedly engaged in conduct violating the constitutional rights of citizens, impairing the due and proper administration of justice and the conduct of lawful inquiries, or contravening the laws governing agencies of the executive branch and the purposes of these agencies.

This conduct has included one or more of the following:

(1) He has, acting personally and through his subordinates and agents, endeavored to obtain from the Internal Revenue Service, in violation of the constitutional rights of citizens, confidential information contained in income tax returns for purposes not authorized by law, and to cause, in violation of the constitutional rights of citizens, income tax audits or other income tax investigations to be initiated or conducted in a discriminatory manner.

(2) He misused the Federal Bureau of Investigation, the Secret Service, and other executive personnel, in violation or disregard of the constitutional rights of citizens, by directing or authorizing such agencies or personnel to conduct or continue electronic surveillance or other investigations for purposes unrelated to national security, the enforcement of laws, or any other lawful function of his office; . . . .

(3) He has, acting personally and through his subordinates and agents, in violation or disregard of the constitutional rights of citizens, authorized and permitted to be maintained a secret investigative unit within the office of the President, financed in part with money derived from campaign contributions, which unlawfully utilized the resources of the Central Intelligence Agency, engaged in covert and unlawful activities, and attempted to prejudice the constitutional right of an accused to a fair trial.

(4) He has failed to take care that the laws were faithfully executed by failing to act when he knew or had reason to know that his close subordinates endeavored to impede and frustrate lawful inquiries by duly constituted executive, judicial, and legislative entities concerning the unlawful entry into the headquarters of the Democratic National Committee, and the cover-up thereof, ...

(5) In disregard of the rule of law, he knowingly misused the executive power by interfering with agencies of the executive branch, including the Federal Bureau of Investigation, the Criminal Division, and the Office of Watergate Special Prosecution Force, of the Department of Justice, and the Central Intelligence Agency, in violation of his duty to take care that the laws be faithfully executed. . . .

Wherefore Richard M. Nixon, by such conduct, warrants impeachment and trial, and removal from office.

ARTICLE III

In his conduct of the office of President of the United States, Richard M. Nixon, contrary to his oath faithfully to execute the office of President of the United States and, to the best of his ability, preserve, protect, and defend the Constitution of the United States, and in violation of his constitutional duty to take care that the laws be faithfully executed, has failed without lawful cause or excuse to produce papers and things as directed by duly authorized subpoenas issued by the Committee on the Judiciary of the House of Representatives on April 11, 1974, May 15, 1974, May 30, 1974, and June 24, 1974, and willfully disobeyed such subpoenas. The subpoenaed papers and things were deemed necessary by the Committee in order to resolve by direct evidence fundamental, factual questions relating to Presidential direction, knowledge, or approval of actions demonstrated by other evidence to be substantial grounds for impeachment of the President. In refusing to produce these papers and things, Richard M. Nixon [assumed] to himself functions and judgments necessary to the exercise of the sole power of impeachment vested by the Constitution in the House of Representatives. . . .

Wherefore Richard M. Nixon, by such conduct, warrants impeachment and trial, and removal from office.

---

1. *Sufficiency of the Charges.* Do you believe that all of the counts contained in the first two articles of impeachment voted against Richard Nixon amounted to

impeachable offenses? (When you read material later in this chapter concerning executive privilege and Congress, consider the sufficiency of the proposed Article III, focusing on Nixon's resistance to congressional subpoenas. Would a President's refusal to obey Congress's subpoenas always amount to an impeachable offense, or would your conclusion depend on the nature of the congressional inquiry at issue?)

2. *Rejected Charges.* The House Committee also considered and rejected a series of other possible charges. We will discuss the most serious of these, allegations on the concealment of information about bombing operations in Cambodia, with materials on the Vietnam War in Chapter Six. The other charges concerned Nixon's personal enrichment through tax evasion and excess government expenditures to improve his private properties. We consider whether "private" derelictions should be impeachable offenses in connection with the Clinton impeachment, where the issue took center stage. For now, note that successful impeachments of federal judges often follow convictions for tax evasion. Do those cases provide good precedents for presidential impeachment, or should Presidents be held to some different standard?

3. *Wallowing in Watergate.* The story of the journalistic investigations that gave impetus to the Nixon impeachment efforts is told in Bob Woodward and Carl Bernstein, All the President's Men (1974). The same authors recount the President's resignation in the face of certain impeachment in The Final Days (1976). For a popular account of the work of the House Judiciary Committee in connection with Watergate, see Howard Fields, High Crimes and Misdemeanors (1978). An account of the scandal and Congress's response told by the Senate's most conspicuous leader during the Watergate period is Samuel J. Ervin, Jr., The Whole Truth: The Watergate Conspiracy (1980). And for a retrospective, see *Symposium, The Presidency: Twenty-five Years After Watergate*, 43 St. Louis U. L.J. 723 (1999).

President Nixon's resignation on the eve of impeachment left many issues tantalizingly unresolved. It is too much to say that the Clinton impeachment resolved them, but it certainly produced ample grist for analysis. As with the Nixon case, by the time Clinton faced impeachment and trial, the facts were widely known to the American public. What had happened was not as much in issue as whether impeachment was warranted.

The misconduct underlying President Clinton's impeachment was his illicit affair with White House intern Monica Lewinsky. By itself, this dalliance was the stuff of scandal not impeachment, but it acquired a legal overlay that eventually formed the basis for the charges against him. The unraveling began when the Supreme Court decided in *Clinton v. Jones* (excerpted later in this chapter) that a President has no constitutional immunity against civil litigation concerning conduct unrelated to his office, and occurring prior to its commencement. Discovery in Paula Jones's suit against Clinton for sexual harassment during his tenure as Governor of Arkansas then led to a deposition in which Clinton denied a sexual relationship with Monica Lewinsky.

Independent Counsel Kenneth Starr, whose charter to investigate the "White-water" matter had expanded to encompass issues related to the Jones case, brought Clinton before a grand jury to investigate whether he had perjured himself in the civil deposition. Starr also pursued allegations that Clinton had obstructed justice by offering to obtain employment for Ms. Lewinsky in order to buy her silence in response to Starr's investigation. As evidence of Clinton's affair with Lewinsky continued to emerge, his denials became more strained, and were eventually replaced with a confession of "inappropriate intimate contact." Starr then concluded his investigation and submitted a highly detailed report to the House of Representatives, with a recommendation that "there is substantial and credible information that President Clinton committed acts that may constitute grounds for impeachment." The House immediately made the report, with all its salacious material, public. The final version of the report, filed by Ken Starr's successor as Independent Counsel, Robert W. Ray, is: Final Report of the Independent Counsel In Re: Madison Guaranty Savings & Loan Association, Regarding Monica Lewinsky and Others, filed with the United States Court of Appeals for the District of Columbia Circuit, Division for the Purpose of Appointing Independent Counsels, Division No. 94-1 (2001), available at http://icreport.access.gpo.gov/lewinsky.html.

On December 19, 1998, the House, relying on the Starr report, voted to impeach Clinton for perjury before the grand jury and for obstruction of justice. Hence proposed articles I and III of the four recommended by the House Judiciary Committee (see below) became articles I and II before the Senate. Voting patterns on the impeachment proposals in the House of Representatives and the Senate are described in Peter M. Shane, *When Interbranch Norms Break Down: Of Arms-for-Hostages, "Orderly Shutdowns," Presidential Impeachments, and Judicial Coups*, 12 CORNELL J. L. & PUB. POL. 503, 523 (2003):

> Th[e] investigation ultimately resulted in the approval by the House Judiciary Committee of four Articles of Impeachment on December 16, 1998, all by straight party-lines vote, except for a single article—alleging perjury in the Paula Jones deposition—on which Republican Representative Lindsay Graham, a former criminal prosecutor, voted, "No." On December 19, the lame-duck House passed the article alleging grand jury perjury by a vote of 228–206, with five Democrats supporting the article and five Republicans opposing it. An obstruction of justice article passed 221 to 212, but would likely have been defeated if held upon the seating of the 106th Congress, in which the Democrats held five more House seats. The two other articles, alleging perjury in the Jones deposition and misstatements in Clinton's written responses to Judiciary Committee questions, were both rejected. On February 12, 1999, the Republican-controlled Senate voted to acquit Clinton by votes of 55–45 on the perjury count, and 50–50 on the obstruction of justice count. The Republicans, who would have needed 67 votes to prevail, could not achieve a clear majority on either article, even in a Senate in which they held 55 seats.

The Senate held proceedings lasting about a month, with one day resembling a trial in that videotaped depositions of three witnesses, including Monica Lewinsky, were presented. The rest was motions practice and arguments. After the Senate acquitted Clinton, a motion to censure the President lost on procedural grounds.

Materials surrounding the Clinton impeachment are voluminous. For selections see MERRILL MCLOUGHLIN ED., THE IMPEACHMENT AND TRIAL OF PRESIDENT CLINTON: THE OFFICIAL TRANSCRIPTS, FROM THE HOUSE JUDICIARY COMMITTEE HEARINGS TO THE SENATE TRIAL (1999); EMILY FIELD VAN TASSEL & PAUL FINKEL-MAN, IMPEACHABLE OFFENSES, A DOCUMENTARY HISTORY FROM 1787 TO THE PRESENT (1999). We include three items: the articles recommended by the House Judiciary Committee, the House Managers' presentation to the Senate urging conviction on the two articles that passed the House, and the President's defense brief in the Senate.

H. Res. 611

105th Congress, 2d Session, Report No. 105-830 (1998)

Resolved, That William Jefferson Clinton, President of the United States, is impeached for high crimes and misdemeanors, and that the following articles of impeachment be exhibited to the United States Senate: . . .

ARTICLE I

In his conduct while President of the United States, William Jefferson Clinton, in violation of his constitutional oath faithfully to execute the office of President of the United States and, to the best of his ability, preserve, protect, and defend the Constitution of the United States, and in violation of his constitutional duty to take care that the laws be faithfully executed, has willfully corrupted and manipulated the judicial process of the United States for his personal gain and exoneration, impeding the administration of justice, in that:

On August 17, 1998, William Jefferson Clinton swore to tell the truth, the whole truth, and nothing but the truth before a Federal grand jury of the United States. Contrary to that oath, William Jefferson Clinton willfully provided perjurious, false and misleading testimony to the grand jury concerning one or more of the following: (1) the nature and details of his relationship with a subordinate Government employee; (2) prior perjurious, false and misleading testimony he gave in a Federal civil rights action brought against him; (3) prior false and misleading statements he allowed his attorney to make to a Federal judge in that civil rights action; and (4) his corrupt efforts to influence the testimony of witnesses and to impede the discovery of evidence in that civil rights action. . . .

Wherefore, William Jefferson Clinton, by such conduct, warrants impeachment and trial, and removal from office and disqualification to hold and enjoy any office of honor, trust, or profit under the United States.

ARTICLE II

In his conduct while President of the United States, William Jefferson Clinton, in violation of his constitutional oath faithfully to execute the office of President of the United States and, to the best of his ability, preserve, protect, and defend the Constitution of the United States, and in violation of his constitutional duty to take care that the laws be faithfully executed, has willfully corrupted and manipulated the judicial process of the United States for his personal gain and exoneration, impeding the administration of justice, in that:

(1) On December 23, 1997, William Jefferson Clinton, in sworn answers to written questions asked as part of a Federal civil rights action brought against him, willfully provided perjurious, false and misleading testimony in response to questions deemed relevant by a Federal judge concerning conduct and proposed conduct with subordinate employees.

(2) On January 17, 1998, William Jefferson Clinton swore under oath to tell the truth, the whole truth, and nothing but the truth in a deposition given as part of a Federal civil rights action brought against him. Contrary to that oath, William Jefferson Clinton willfully provided perjurious, false and misleading testimony in response to questions deemed relevant by a Federal judge concerning the nature and details of his relationship with a subordinate Government employee, his knowledge of that employee's involvement and participation in the civil rights action brought against him, and his corrupt efforts to influence the testimony of that employee. . . .

Wherefore, William Jefferson Clinton, by such conduct, warrants impeachment and trial, and removal from office and disqualification to hold and enjoy any office of honor, trust, or profit under the United States.

ARTICLE III

In his conduct while President of the United States, William Jefferson Clinton, in violation of his constitutional oath faithfully to execute the office of President of the United States and, to the best of his ability, preserve, protect, and defend the Constitution of the United States, and in violation of his constitutional duty to take care that the laws be faithfully executed, has prevented, obstructed, and impeded the administration of justice, and has to that end engaged personally, and through his subordinates and agents, in a course of conduct or scheme designed to delay, impede, cover up, and conceal the existence of evidence and testimony related to a Federal civil rights action brought against him in a duly instituted judicial proceeding.

The means used to implement this course of conduct or scheme included one or more of the following acts:

(1) On or about December 17, 1997, William Jefferson Clinton corruptly encouraged a witness in a Federal civil rights action brought against him to execute a sworn affidavit in that proceeding that he knew to be perjurious, false and misleading.

(2) On or about December 17, 1997, William Jefferson Clinton corruptly encouraged a witness in a Federal civil rights action brought against him to give perjurious,

false and misleading testimony if and when called to testify personally in that proceeding.

(3) On or about December 28, 1997, William Jefferson Clinton corruptly engaged in, encouraged, or supported a scheme to conceal evidence that had been subpoenaed in a Federal civil rights action brought against him.

(4) Beginning on or about December 7, 1997, and continuing through and including January 14, 1998, William Jefferson Clinton intensified and succeeded in an effort to secure job assistance to a witness in a Federal civil rights action brought against him in order to corruptly prevent the truthful testimony of that witness in that proceeding at a time when the truthful testimony of that witness would have been harmful to him.

(5) On January 17, 1998, at his deposition in a Federal civil rights action brought against him, William Jefferson Clinton corruptly allowed his attorney to make false and misleading statements to a Federal judge characterizing an affidavit, in order to prevent questioning deemed relevant by the judge. Such false and misleading statements were subsequently acknowledged by his attorney in a communication to that judge.

(6) On or about January 18 and January 20–21, 1998, William Jefferson Clinton related a false and misleading account of events relevant to a Federal civil rights action brought against him to a potential witness in that proceeding, in order to corruptly influence the testimony of that witness.

(7) On or about January 21, 23 and 26, 1998, William Jefferson Clinton made false and misleading statements to potential witnesses in a Federal grand jury proceeding in order to corruptly influence the testimony of those witnesses. The false and misleading statements made by William Jefferson Clinton were repeated by the witnesses to the grand jury, causing the grand jury to receive false and misleading information. . . .

Wherefore, William Jefferson Clinton, by such conduct, warrants impeachment and trial, and removal from office and disqualification to hold and enjoy any office of honor, trust, or profit under the United States.

ARTICLE IV

Using the powers and influence of the office of President of the United States, William Jefferson Clinton, in violation of his constitutional oath faithfully to execute the office of President of the United States and, to the best of his ability, preserve, protect, and defend the Constitution of the United States, and in disregard of his constitutional duty to take care that the laws be faithfully executed, has engaged in conduct that resulted in misuse and abuse of his high office, impaired the due and proper administration of justice and the conduct of lawful inquiries, and contravened the authority of the legislative branch and the truth seeking purpose of a coordinate investigative proceeding, in that, as President, William Jefferson Clinton refused and failed to respond to certain written requests for admission and willfully made perjurious, false and misleading sworn statements in response to certain written requests for admission propounded to him as part of the impeachment inquiry authorized by the House of Representatives of the Congress of the United States. William Jefferson Clinton, in refusing and failing to respond and in making perjurious, false and misleading statements, assumed to himself functions and judgments necessary to the exercise of the sole power of impeachment vested by the Constitution in the House of Representatives and exhibited contempt for the inquiry. . . .

Wherefore, William Jefferson Clinton, by such conduct, warrants impeachment and trial, and removal from office and disqualification to hold and enjoy any office of honor, trust, or profit under the United States.

Trial Memorandum of the United States House of Representatives

In The Senate Of The United States, Sitting as a Court of Impeachment, In Re Impeachment of President William Jefferson Clinton. Now comes the United States House of Representatives, by and through its duly authorized Managers, and respectfully submits to the United States Senate its Brief in connection with the Impeachment Trial of William Jefferson Clinton, President of the United States.

The President is charged in two Articles with: 1) Perjury and false and misleading testimony and statements under oath before a federal grand jury (Article I), and 2) engaging in a course of conduct or scheme to delay and obstruct justice (Article II).

The evidence contained in the record, when viewed as a unified whole, overwhelmingly supports both charges.

Perjury and False Statements Under Oath. President Clinton deliberately and willfully testified falsely under oath when he appeared before a federal grand jury on August 17, 1998. Although what follows is not exhaustive, some of the more overt examples will serve to illustrate.

At the very outset, the President read a prepared statement, which itself contained totally false assertions and other clearly misleading information.

The President relied on his statement nineteen times in his testimony when questioned about his relationship with Ms. Lewinsky . . . .

He falsely claimed that his actions with Ms. Lewinsky did not fall within the definition of "sexual relations" that was given at his deposition.

He falsely testified that he answered questions truthfully at his deposition concerning, among other subjects, whether he had been alone with Ms. Lewinsky . . . .

Obstruction of Justice. The President engaged in an ongoing scheme to obstruct both the Jones civil case and the grand jury. Further, he undertook a continuing and concerted plan to tamper with witnesses and prospective witnesses for the purpose of causing those witnesses to provide false and misleading testimony. Examples abound:

The President and Ms. Lewinsky concocted a cover story to conceal their relationship, and the President suggested that she employ that story if subpoenaed in the Jones case.

The President suggested that Ms. Lewinsky provide an affidavit to avoid testifying in the Jones case, when he knew that the affidavit would need to be false to accomplish its purpose . . . .

The President attempted to influence the expected testimony of his secretary, Ms. Currie, by providing her with a false account of his meetings with Ms. Lewinsky.

The President provided several of his top aides with elaborate lies about his relationship with Ms. Lewinsky, so that those aides would convey the false information to the public and to the grand jury. When he did this, he knew that those aides would likely be called to testify, while he was declining several invitations to testify. By this action, he obstructed and delayed the operation of the grand jury . . . .

The President lied repeatedly under oath in his deposition in the Jones case, and thereby obstructed justice in that case . . . .

The President employed the power of his office to procure a job for Ms. Lewinsky after she signed the false affidavit by causing his friend to exert extraordinary efforts for that purpose.

The foregoing are merely accusations of an ongoing pattern of obstruction of justice, and witness tampering extending over a period of several months, and having the effect of seriously compromising the integrity of the entire judicial system.

The effect of the President's misconduct has been devastating in several respects. 1) He violated repeatedly his oath to "preserve, protect and defend the Constitution of the United States." 2) He ignored his constitutional duty as chief law enforcement officer to "take care that the laws be faithfully executed." 3) He deliberately and unlawfully obstructed Paula Jones's rights as a citizen to due process and the equal protection of the laws, though he had sworn to protect those rights. 4) By his pattern of lies under oath, misleading statements and deceit, he has seriously undermined the integrity and credibility of the Office of President and thereby the honor and integrity of the United States. 5) His pattern of perjuries, obstruction of justice, and witness tampering has affected the truth seeking process which is the foundation of our legal system. 6) By mounting an assault in the truth seeking process, he has attacked the entire Judicial Branch of government.

The Articles of Impeachment that the House has preferred state offenses that warrant, if proved, the conviction and removal from office of President William Jefferson Clinton. The Articles charge that the President has committed perjury before a federal grand jury and that he obstructed justice in a federal civil rights action. The Senate's own precedents establish beyond doubt that perjury warrants conviction and removal. During the 1980s, the Senate convicted and removed three federal judges for committing perjury. Obstruction of justice undermines the judicial system in the same fashion that perjury does, and it also warrants conviction and removal. Under our Constitution, judges are impeached under the same standard as

Presidents—treason, bribery, or other high crimes and misdemeanors. Thus, these judicial impeachments for perjury set the standard here. Finally, the Senate's own precedents further establish that the President's crimes need not arise directly out of his official duties. Two of the three judges removed in the 1980s were removed for perjury that had nothing to do with their official duties. . . .

This case is not about sex or private conduct. It is about multiple obstructions of justice, perjury, false and misleading statements, and witness tampering—all committed or orchestrated by the President of the United States. Before addressing the President's lies and obstruction, it is important to place the events in the proper context. If this were only about private sex we would not now be before the Senate . . . .

Some "experts" have questioned whether the President's deportment affects his office, the government of the United States or the dignity and honor of the country. . . . [T]he President is the spokesman for the government and the people of the United States concerning both domestic and foreign matters. His honesty and integrity, therefore, directly influence the credibility of this country. . . . Again: there is no such thing as non-serious lying under oath. Every time a witness lies, that witness chips a stone from the foundation of our entire legal system. Likewise, every act of obstruction of justice, of witness tampering or of perjury adversely affects the judicial branch of government. . . . Apart from all else, the President's illegal actions constitute an attack upon and utter disregard for the truth, and for the rule of law. Much worse, they manifest an arrogant disdain not only for the rights of his fellow citizens, but also for the functions and the integrity of the other two co-equal branches of our constitutional system. . . . The President mounted a direct assault upon the truth-seeking process which is the very essence and foundation of the Judicial Branch. Not content with that, though, Mr. Clinton renewed his lies, half-truths and obstruction to this Congress when he filed his answers to simple requests to admit or deny. In so doing, he also demonstrated his lack of respect for the constitutional functions of the Legislative Branch. . . .

The Articles state offenses that warrant the President's conviction and removal from office. The Senate's own precedents establish that perjury and obstruction warrant conviction and removal from office. Those same precedents establish that the perjury and obstruction need not have any direct connection to the officer's official duties. In the 1980s, the Senate convicted and removed from office three federal judges for making perjurious statements. . . .

To avoid the conclusive force of these recent precedents—and in particular the exact precedent supporting impeachment for, conviction, and removal for perjury—the only recourse for the President's defenders is to argue that a high crime or misdemeanor for a judge is not necessarily a high crime or misdemeanor for the President. The arguments advanced in support of this dubious proposition do not withstand serious scrutiny. The Constitution provides that Article III judges "shall hold their Offices during good Behavior," U.S. Const. Art. III, 1. Thus, these arguments suggest that judges are impeachable for "misbehavior" while other federal officials are only impeachable for treason, bribery, and other high crimes and misdemeanors.

The staff of the House Judiciary Committee in the 1970s and the National Commission on Judicial Discipline and Removal in the 1990s both issued reports rejecting these arguments. . . . Moreover, even assuming that presidential high crimes and misdemeanors could be different from judicial ones, surely the President ought not be held to a lower standard of impeachability than judges. In the course of the 1980s judicial impeachments, Congress emphasized unequivocally that the removal from office of federal judges guilty of crimes indistinguishable from those currently charged against the President was essential to the preservation of the rule of law. If the perjury of just one judge so undermines the rule of law as to make it intolerable that he remain in office, then how much more so does perjury committed by the President of the United States, who alone is charged with the duty "to take Care that the Laws be faithfully executed." . . . When a President, as chief law enforcement officer of the United States, commits perjury, he violates this constitutional oath unique to his office and casts doubt on the notion that we are a nation ruled by laws and not men . . . .

Although Congress has never adopted a fixed definition of "high crimes and misdemeanors," much of the background and history of the impeachment process contradicts the President's claim that these offenses are private and therefore do not warrant conviction and removal. Two reports prepared in 1974 on the background and history of impeachment are particularly helpful in evaluating the President's defense. Both reports support the conclusion that the facts in this case compel the conviction and removal of President Clinton . . . .

That the President's perjury and obstruction do not directly involve his official conduct does not diminish their significance. The record is clear that federal officials have been impeached for reasons other than official misconduct. . . . Nothing in the text, structure, or history of the Constitution suggests that officials are subject to impeachment only for official misconduct. Perjury and obstruction of justice— even regarding a private matter—are offenses that substantially affect the President's official duties because they are grossly incompatible with his preeminent duty to "take care that the laws be faithfully executed." Regardless of their genesis, perjury and obstruction of justice are acts of public misconduct—they cannot be dismissed as understandable or trivial. Perjury and obstruction of justice are not private matters; they are crimes against the system of justice, for which impeachment, conviction, and removal are appropriate. . . .

This is a defining moment for the Presidency as an institution, because if the President is not convicted as a consequence of the conduct that has been portrayed, then no House of Representatives will ever be able to impeach again and no Senate will ever convict. The bar will be so high that only a convicted felon or a traitor will need to be concerned. Experts pointed to the fact that the House refused to impeach President Nixon for lying on an income tax return. Can you imagine a future President, faced with possible impeachment, pointing to the perjuries, lies, obstructions, and tampering with witnesses by the current occupant of the office as not rising to the level of high crimes and misdemeanors? If this is not enough, what is? . . .

Answer of President William Jefferson Clinton to the Articles of Impeachment

January 11, 1999

. . . The charges in the two Articles of Impeachment do not permit the conviction and removal from office of a duly elected President. The President has acknowledged conduct with Ms. Lewinsky that was improper. But . . . [t]he charges in the articles do not rise to the level of "high Crimes and Misdemeanors" as contemplated by the Founding Fathers, and they do not satisfy the rigorous constitutional standard applied throughout our Nation's history. Accordingly, the Articles of Impeachment should be dismissed.

President Clinton denies that he made perjurious, false and misleading statements before the federal grand jury on August 17, 1998. . . . There is a myth about President Clinton's testimony before the grand jury. The myth is that the President failed to admit his improper intimate relationship with Ms. Monica Lewinsky. The myth is perpetuated by Article I, which accuses the President of lying about "the nature and details of his relationship" with Ms. Lewinsky.

The fact is that the President specifically acknowledged to the grand jury that he had an improper intimate relationship with Ms. Lewinsky. He said so, plainly and clearly: "When I was alone with Ms. Lewinsky on certain occasions in early 1996 and once in early 1997, I engaged in conduct that was wrong. These encounters . . . did involve inappropriate intimate contact." The President described to the grand jury how the relationship began and how it ended at his insistence early in 1997 — long before any public attention or scrutiny. . . . The President read a prepared statement to the grand jury acknowledging his relationship with Ms. Lewinsky. The statement was offered at the beginning of his testimony to focus the questioning in a manner that would allow the Office of Independent Counsel to obtain necessary information without unduly dwelling on the salacious details of the relationship. The President's statement was followed by almost four hours of questioning. If it is charged that his statement was in any respect perjurious, false and misleading, the President denies it. The President also denies that the statement was in any way an attempt to thwart the investigation. . . . The President was truthful when he testified before the grand jury that he did not engage in sexual relations with Ms. Lewinsky as he understood that term to be defined by the *Jones* lawyers during their questioning of him in that deposition. The President further denies that his other statements to the grand jury about the nature and details of his relationship with Ms. Lewinsky were perjurious, false, and misleading. . . .

––––––––––

1. *Criminal Prosecution and Impeachment.* Article I, § 3 of the Constitution provides explicitly that impeachment may be followed by criminal prosecution. But may prosecution *precede* impeachment? For lesser officials, such as district judges, it often has come first. The Watergate Special Prosecutor declined to seek the indictment of President Nixon; nor did Independent Counsel Starr seek to indict President

Clinton. Could a sitting President be subjected to criminal prosecution? Professor Philip B. Kurland, in WATERGATE AND THE CONSTITUTION 135 (1978), thought not, because the President "is the sole indispensable man in government." *Accord* Akhil Reed Amar, *On Prosecuting Presidents*, 27 HOFSTRA L. REV. 671 (1999). For the contrary view, see Eric M. Freedman, *On Protecting Accountability*, 27 HOFSTRA L. REV. 677 (1999), and by the same author, *The Law as King and the King as Law: Is a President Immune from Criminal Prosecution Before Impeachment?* 20 HASTINGS CONST. L.Q. 7 (1992).

2. *The Executive Branch's Position.* In 1973, the Office of Legal Counsel undertook a review of the amenability to criminal prosecution of all civil officers. OLC concluded that the president is immune from criminal prosecution while in office, but that every other civil officer is subject to criminal prosecution while in office. The reasoning of the opinion is in line with Professor Kurland's view: Because the president is the single head of the executive branch, a criminal prosecution of the president would debilitate that branch uniquely and prevent it from performing its constitutional functions. *See* Memorandum from Robert G. Dixon, Jr., Assistant Attorney General, Office of Legal Counsel, Re: Amenability of the President, Vice President and other Civil Officers to Federal Criminal Prosecution while in Office (Sept. 24, 1973). The issue arose later that year when grand jury proceedings commenced against sitting Vice President Spiro Agnew. When Agnew's lawyers moved to enjoin the proceedings, the Department of Justice filed a brief opposing Agnew and reiterating the view of the OLC memo that only the president is immune from criminal prosecution while in office. Agnew resigned his office and pleaded guilty to tax evasion. More recently, and for reasons that are not at all clear, OLC decided to reexamine the question. It opined that the 1973 memo's conclusions "remain sound and that subsequent developments in the law validate both the analytical framework applied and the conclusions reached at that time." *See A Sitting President's Amenability to Indictment and Criminal Prosecution*, 24 OP. O.L.C. 222, 223 (October 6, 2000).

3. *Low Crimes and Misdemeanors*? Many scholars weighed in on the issue of the constitutional sufficiency of the charges against President Clinton. *See Symposium, Background and History of Impeachment*, 67 GEO. WASH. L. REV. 601 (1999), reproducing testimony given by leading constitutional scholars before the House Judiciary Committee in November 1998; see also *Symposium, The Constitution Under Clinton: A Critical Assessment* (Neil Kinkopf, special ed.), 63 LAW & CONTEMP. PROBS. 1 (2000); *A Symposium on the Impeachment of William Jefferson Clinton: Reflections on the Process, the Results, and the Future*, 28 HOFSTRA L. REV. 291 (1999). Not surprisingly, a range of views has emerged. Professor Cass R. Sunstein, in *Impeaching the President*, 147 U. PA. L. REV. 279 (1998), argues that the focus of the impeachment clause is to pursue "a narrow category of egregious or large-scale abuses of authority that comes from the exercise of distinctly presidential powers." Other crimes, he argues, should usually be prosecuted after the President leaves office, and he regards the issue whether any ordinary crimes are impeachable as undecided to date. In agreement is Professor Michael J. Gerhardt, *The Lessons of Impeachment*

History, 67 GEO. WASH. L. REV. 603 (1999), referring to the constitutional text as "technical terms of art that refer to political crimes . . . serious abuses of official power or serious breaches of the public trust." From this premise it is an easy step to conclude, as does Professor Jack N. Rakove, in *Statement on the Background and History of Impeachment, id.* at 682, that Clinton's misconduct was "essentially private and non-official even if subsequent proceedings gave it a legal and public character." Rakove, emphasizing the framers' fear of congressional domination of the presidency, counsels against an expansive reading of the clause.

Taking the opposite tack, Professor Stephen B. Presser asks *Would George Washington Have Wanted Bill Clinton Impeached?, id.* at 666, and answers yes. He emphasizes that the allegations were of comprehensive "criminal interference with the legal process," resembling many of the English precedents, and overall "a pattern of conduct that involved injury to the state and a betrayal of his constitutional duties" for personal gain. For further development of the view that impeachment need not be limited to abuses of office, see two articles by Professor Jonathan Turley, *The Executive Function Theory, The Hamilton Affair, and other Constitutional Mythologies*, 77 N. C. L. REV. 1791 (1999), and *Reflections on Murder, Misdemeanors, and Madison*, 28 HOFSTRA L. REV. 439 (1999) (a public/private dichotomy is a "mere artificiality in a process designed to deal with the perceived legitimacy of a President to govern").

4. *Impeachment Process: Politics or Law?* Closely related to the issue of defining impeachable offenses is the issue of the appropriate conduct of the House and Senate in impeachment cases. For federal judges, the process has been lawyerly, typically asking whether a particular felony conviction should support impeachment. For Presidents, however, the sanitized air of a trial is probably impossible to achieve—and may be undesirable as well. Professor John O. McGinnis, in *Impeachment: The Structural Understanding*, 67 GEO. WASH. L. REV. 650 (1999), argues that the framers assigned impeachment to the deeply political institution of Congress because they sought the "prudential" judgment of that body, to address "any objective misconduct so serious that it poses an unacceptable risk to the public rather than . . . some fixed list of offenses or a set of offenses determined by some abstract rule." For similar views, see Jonathan Turley, *Congress as Grand Jury: The Role of the House of Representatives in the Impeachment of an American President, id.* at 735 ("Ultimately, an impeachment says more about the values and expectations of a society than it does about the conduct of a President."); and *Senate Trials and Factional Disputes: Impeachment as a Madisonian Device*, 49 DUKE L.J. 1 (1999). If presidential impeachments are at bottom political in the larger sense of the term, it is inevitable that Congress will receive public pressure concerning its own behavior—pressure that may determine the outcome. *See* Frank O. Bowman III & Stephen L. Sepinuck, *"High Crimes and Misdemeanors": Defining the Constitutional Limits on Presidential Impeachment*, 72 S. CAL. L. REV. 1517, 1563 (1999), arguing that the Clinton acquittal was "a vehicle to express disapproval of a method of politics more destructive of the public welfare than the continuance in office of one severely flawed individual."

For procedural reviews and analysis of the Clinton case, see Asa Hutchinson, *Did the Senate Trial Satisfy the Constitution and the Demands of Justice?* 28 HOFSTRA L. REV. 393 (1999) ("No," in the view of one of the House Managers); Charles Tiefer, *The Senate Impeachment Trial for President Clinton, id.* at 407 (1999). For an argument that Chief Justice Rehnquist's restrained role as presiding officer was *too* restrained to properly shape the trial, see Michael F. Williams, *Rehnquist's Renunciation? The Chief Justice's Constitutional Duty to "Preside" Over Impeachment Trials,* 104 W. VA. L. REV. 457 (2002).

5. *The Censure Alternative.* Professor Joseph Isenbergh, in IMPEACHMENT AND PRESIDENTIAL IMMUNITY FROM JUDICIAL PROCESS (1998), argued that removal and disqualification were not the only remedies available to Congress in a formal impeachment; conviction followed by censure was also permissible. For a debate over this issue, see Akhil Reed Amar, *On Impeaching Presidents, Appendix, A Constitutional Conversation,* 28 HOFSTRA L. REV. 291, 317–41 (1999). A perhaps blunter appraisal is Peter M. Shane, *A Detour into Constitutional Absurdity,* N.Y. TIMES, Jan. 27, 1999, at A27.

6. *Impeachment and the Future.* In the wake of the Clinton impeachment, MICHAEL J. GERHARDT, THE FEDERAL IMPEACHMENT PROCESS: A CONSTITUTIONAL AND HISTORICAL ANALYSIS 192–94 (2d ed. 2000), concludes that impeachment has not been abused in America. Its use has been rare, he notes, and he speculates that the Clinton acquittal may have strengthened the presidency by identifying "a zone of misconduct for which presidents . . . are not potentially impeachable." *See also* Susan Low Bloch, *A Report Card on the Impeachment: Judging the Institutions that Judged President Clinton,* 63 LAW & CONTEMP. PROBS. 143 (2000) ("The constitutional design worked reasonably well."). Do you concur? Does any presidential impeachment, even a failed one, make this a more "thinkable" option? If so, is that effect good or bad?

7. *The Bottom Line: A Plague on Both Their Houses?* Judge Richard Posner, in AN AFFAIR OF STATE: THE INVESTIGATION, IMPEACHMENT, AND TRIAL OF PRESIDENT CLINTON 91–92 (1999), observes that the Clinton imbroglio offers:

> two diametrically opposed narratives to choose between. In one, a reckless, lawless, immoral President commits a series of crimes in order to conceal a tawdry and shameful affair, crimes compounded by a campaign of public lying and slanders. A prosecutor could easily draw up a thirty-count indictment against the President. In the other narrative, the confluence of a stupid law (the independent counsel law), a marginal lawsuit begotten and nursed by political partisanship, a naïve and imprudent judicial decision by the Supreme Court in that suit, and the irresistible human impulse to conceal one's sexual improprieties, allows a trivial sexual escapade (what Clinton and Lewinsky called "fooling around" or "messing around") to balloon into a grotesque and gratuitous constitutional drama. The problem is that both narratives are correct.

So where do you come out on all this? For still more opinions, see LEONARD V. KAPLAN & BEVERLY I. MORAN, EDS., AFTERMATH: THE CLINTON IMPEACHMENT AND

THE PRESIDENCY IN THE AGE OF POLITICAL SPECTACLE (2001); JEFFREY TOOBIN, A VAST CONSPIRACY (1999).

8. *Apology or Apologia?* At the end of the day, Clinton admitted wrongdoing and accepted suspension from the Arkansas bar and a waiver of any right to legal fees in return for Independent Counsel Ray's agreement not to indict. He said, "I acknowledge having knowingly violated Judge Wright's discovery orders in my deposition in that case. I tried to walk a fine line between acting lawfully and testifying falsely, but I now recognize that I did not fully accomplish this goal and that certain of my responses to questions about Ms. Lewinsky were false." "I Hope My Actions Today Will Help Bring Closure," WASH. POST, Jan. 20, 2001, at A19, available at 2001 WL 2538067. In light of this admission, was his lawyers' trial statement in the Senate problematic in any respect?

9. The *"Russia Thing."* The Trump Administration has been embroiled in scandal from its inception over the influence of Russia in the 2016 election. About a month before the election, the Obama administration revealed that the U.S. government believed Russia was behind computer hacks directed at the Democratic National Committee and Hillary Clinton campaign Chairman John Podesta, and was trying to interfere with the election. An FBI counterintelligence investigation begun in July, 2016 brought to light that a number of individuals closely associated with the Trump campaign had had contacts with Russian officials, Eugene Kiely, *Timeline of Russia Investigation*, POLITICO (June 7, 2017, updated), http://www.factcheck.org/2017/06/timeline-russia-investigation/, a fact that the campaign had repeatedly denied. It has also since been revealed that "Russian agents intending to sow discord among American citizens" made extensive use of social media; for example, they "disseminated inflammatory posts that reached 126 million users on Facebook, published more than 131,000 messages on Twitter and uploaded over 1,000 videos to Google's YouTube service." Mike Isaac and Daisuke Wakabayashi, *Russian Influence Reached 126 Million Through Facebook Alone*, N.Y. TIMES (Oct. 30, 2017), https://www.nytimes.com/2017/10/30/technology/facebook-google-russia.html.

The story took a dramatic turn just as this volume was going to press. On October 30, 2017, the office of the Justice Department Special Counsel who was appointed to investigate the matter revealed that George Papadopoulos, a former foreign policy adviser to the Trump campaign, had pleaded guilty in July, 2017, to lying to the FBI about campaign outreach to the Russians. Specifically, court documents, available at https://www.justice.gov/file/1007346/download, detail Papadopolous's efforts to contact Russian officials, who claimed to possess thousands of Democratic emails and other "dirt" on Hillary Clinton. Mr. Papadopolous's conviction and the fact of his ongoing cooperation with the Justice Department were revealed on the same day that Paul Manafort, President Trump's former campaign manager, was indicted on charges of conspiracy to launder money, conspiracy against the United States, being an unregistered agent of a foreign principal, false and misleading statements under the Foreign Agents Registration Act, and other charges.

This is not likely to be end of what President Trump has dismissively called "the Russia thing." For example, although not indicted as of early November, 2017, another campaign adviser, General Michael Flynn, is known to have held meetings—in potential violation of the Logan Act—with Russian officials during the transition period to set up a back channel for U.S.-Russian communications once President-elect Trump was inaugurated. General Flynn, who had been named to be Trump's National Security Adviser, applied for renewal of his security clearance in February 2017, but failed to disclose these contacts or to report income he had received from Russian sources. When reports to this effect began to surface, Flynn misled Trump Administration officials, including Vice President Mike Pence, regarding his connections with the Russian government. On February 13, President Trump fired General Flynn for lying to the Vice President.

Other associates of the Trump campaign with significant ties to the Russian government include advisers Carter Page and Roger Stone, and son-in-law Jared Kushner. In addition, the first Senator to endorse Donald Trump for president was now-Attorney General Jeff Sessions. During the campaign Sen. Sessions twice met with Russian Ambassador Sergey Kislyak. After President Trump nominated Senator Sessions to be Attorney General, Sessions testified at his confirmation hearings that he "did not have communications with the Russians." After the fact of his meetings with Ambassador Kislyak became public, Mr. Sessions recused himself from the investigation into Russian involvement in the 2016 presidential campaign.

At the time President Trump took office, the official in charge of the federal investigation of Russian influence in the 2016 presidential election was FBI Director James Comey. Director Comey had already achieved broad public notoriety. After George W. Bush appointed him to serve as Deputy Attorney General, Comey (along with Attorney General John Ashcroft and Assistant Attorney General Jack Goldsmith) stood up to the White House in refusing to re-authorize an aspect of the Administration's Terrorist Surveillance Program. This episode helped Comey solidify a reputation for integrity and non-partisanship and largely explains why President Obama appointed this Republican to be FBI Director.

In July 2016, Director Comey announced that the FBI was recommending that the Justice Department not pursue charges against Hillary Clinton for conducting official business as Secretary of State over a private email server she maintained in the basement of her home, even though classified material appeared on the server. The announcement had two unusual elements. First, the FBI typically does not make its recommendations public, but rather leaves the final decision and the announcement to one of the FBI director's superiors—the Attorney General or the Deputy Attorney General—at Main Justice. Second, Comey went beyond announcing that there would be no charges and criticized Secretary Clinton's carelessness in handling classified information. Such commentary is highly unusual under any circumstances, but especially so when the subject of the comments is a candidate for president. Then on October 28, 2016, as the presidential campaign was drawing to a close, Comey announced that the FBI was re-opening the investigation of Secretary Clinton because of additional emails that were found in the course of an unrelated investigation into the husband of one of Secretary Clinton's advisers. On November 6, just days before the election, Comey announced that the reopened investigation was again being closed.

On May 9, 2017, President Trump fired James Comey as FBI Director. The initial White House announcement stated that the firing was because of a memorandum prepared by newly appointed Deputy Attorney General Rod Rosenstein. The memo recommended that Comey be terminated because of his mishandling of the Hillary Clinton email investigation. The memo specifically asserted that Comey had overstepped his authority making the July 2016 announcement recommending against prosecution and in commenting further on Clinton's carelessness. President Trump almost immediately undermined this narrative, however. In an interview, the President stated that he made his decision to fire Comey independently of the Deputy Attorney General's memorandum and that his reason for the firing had nothing to do with the Clinton email investigation. Rather, President Trump declared that he had fired Comey because of "this Russia thing."

On June 8, 2017, James Comey testified before the Senate Intelligence Committee, which had opened its own inquiry into possible Russian interference in the 2016 presidential election. Comey's dramatic testimony included a number of significant claims. First, at the conclusion of a national security briefing by top executive officials in the oval office, President Trump asked to speak to Director Comey alone. He specifically raised the FBI's reported investigation of General Flynn and said, "I hope you can see your way clear to letting this go, to letting Flynn go. He is a good guy. I hope you can let this go." Comey testified that, despite the "I hope" phrasing, he understood President Trump to be issuing an order to cease the investigation. For his part, President Trump denied making the statement or in any way indicating that Comey should stop the investigation. Second, in two subsequent telephone conversations with Director Comey, President Trump described the Russia investigation as "a cloud" that was impairing the President's ability to do his job. Previous to these discussions, President Trump had a private dinner with Comey in the White House at which time the President informed Comey that "I need loyalty, I expect loyalty." This pattern of conduct led Comey to conclude, "I was fired because of the Russia investigation. I was fired, in some way, to change, or the endeavor was to change, the way the Russia investigation was being conducted." President Trump has denied that he endeavored to affect the Russia investigation.

Further legal developments will no doubt continue to unfold even as this volume heads to publication, and it is far too early to predict specific outcomes. The investigations of the Department of Justice, which have been turned over to a Special Counsel, and the Senate and House Intelligence Committees remain in full force. Moreover, what evidence we have regarding the President's personal involvement—principally the Comey testimony—is contested. The matter nonetheless illuminates a number of important points and raises important questions about the impeachment power. Because of the incomplete and contested nature of the information we have, we regard the following discussion as hypothetical and do not mean to express a view on the "Russia thing."

a. *Does an offense have to be a formal crime to be impeachable?* Much of the commentary on events recounted by former FBI Director Comey has focused on the issue of whether the President's conduct fits the legal definition of obstruction of justice. 18 U.S.C. § 1503 (prohibiting conduct that "corruptly or by threats or force, or by any threatening letter or communication, influences, obstructs, or impedes, or endeavors to influence, obstruct, or impede, the due administration of justice.") Suppose President Trump endeavored to impede the investigation but did not do so in a manner that falls within the statutory definition of "corrupt" or "threatening." Should the President then be insulated from impeachment or should Congress be understood to have the authority to protect the nation from a President who obstructs the due administration of justice?

b. *Can unintentional conduct be impeachable?* Aside from the President's conduct relating to the Russia investigation, it is clear that quite a few of the President's close advisers have had some contacts with the Russian government or individuals and entities connected with the Kremlin. Assuming the worst case with respect to these advisers—that they are willful agents of the Russian government—but that the President was unaware of these advisers' true motives, would such circumstances provide legal grounds for the House to initiate impeachment proceedings? In such an instance, the President lacks ill-intent and therefore, in all likelihood, the *mens rea* requisite to commit a significant crime. It is conceivable that the House would regard the President as having jeopardized the nation by employing a coterie of disloyal advisers and so to be unfit to remain in office—not because the President is personally endeavoring to do harm, but because the President cannot be trusted to protect the nation against the machinations of foreign powers. Should this be sufficient grounds for impeachment?

c. *The political safeguards of separation of powers.* The two preceding notes raise questions that might incline one to take a relatively expansive view of what constitutes "high crimes and misdemeanors." The concern about doing so is that an open-ended impeachment power could render the President subservient to Congress. James Madison raised this objection to an early draft of the Constitution, which empowered Congress to impeach the president for "maladministration." Madison considered maladministration "so vague a term [that it] will be equivalent to tenure during [the] pleasure of the Senate." 2 MAX FARRAND, RECORDS OF THE FEDERAL CONVENTION OF 1787, 550 (1911). The most practically significant check against congressional abuse of the impeachment power is not the legal definition of "high crimes and misdemeanors" but the impeachment process itself. While the House of Representatives holds the power to impeach a civil officer by a simple majority, no consequence follows from an impeachment vote. In order for an impeachment to have a legal consequence, it must be presented to the Senate for a trial and vote of conviction, which vote requires a two-thirds supermajority. This process has operated to ensure that an officer may be removed from office through impeachment only where there is broad bipartisan agreement that the officer has actually engaged in conduct that justifies this sanction.

Consider what this means in the context of the Russia matter as set forth above. One of the more explosive charges leveled during Mr. Comey's testimony is that the President pressured him to drop the investigation of General Flynn (again, President Trump denies this). But note what Comey relates the President as having said: "I hope you can see your way to letting . . . Flynn go." Comey asserts that in context he understood this as conveying a clear order from the President. Be that as it may, the actual words the President used do not expressly issue an order, and getting to that conclusion requires construction that may or may not be justified. Faced with competing plausible constructions of the statements and events, is it not realistic to think members of the President's party in Congress will choose the innocent construction? Doesn't the constitutional process — especially the supermajority requirement — operate to establish a strong presumption of presidential innocence?

d. *Impeachment as a remedy for pre-presidential misconduct.* Imagine that a candidate for President colludes with a foreign power to hack into the United States's balloting system (which is not maintained by the federal government but rather is maintained by the states) in order to directly rig the outcome of the presidential election. This would seem to be clear grounds for impeachment. It is not clear, however, that the impeachment power extends to conduct undertaken by one who is not, at that time, a civil officer of the United States. Somewhat analogously, the Senate has twice refused to convict a former official who acted corruptly in office but who resigned before the Senate could conclude a trial of the matter. *See* MICHAEL J. GERHARDT, THE FEDERAL IMPEACHMENT PROCESS, *supra* at 79. It is noteworthy that conviction in this circumstance would not be a futile gesture because the punishment for conviction can, at the Senate's discretion, extend beyond removal from office to include a disability to hold office ever again. *See* U.S. CONST. art. I, § 3, cl. 7. These precedents indicate a reluctance to apply the impeachment power in a way that covers consequences falling outside the term of office. Moreover, as discussed in note 3 *supra*, some commentators have argued that the scope of impeachable offenses should be limited to those that involve the abuse of official power. *See* Cass Sunstein, *Impeaching the President*, 147 U. PA. L. REV. 279 (1998), *but see* Neil J. Kinkopf, *The Scope of "High Crimes and Misdemeanors" after the Impeachment of President Clinton*, 63 LAW & CONTEMP. PROBS. 201 (2000). The presidential candidate we have hypothesized does not hold office and so cannot have engaged in conduct that abuses the power of office in conspiring with a foreign power to fix an election.

e. *Is Election-Related Misconduct a Special Case?* It is standard to note that the impeachment and removal power co-exists in serious tension with our democratic commitments, at least when applied to a sitting president, because the removal of a president undoes the result of an election and, in this very direct sense, subverts the will of the people. Congress has frequently cited this as a reason for being hesitant to pursue presidential impeachments. Should this impulse to defer to democracy, so to speak, apply with equal force where the alleged misconduct goes to the legitimacy of the election itself?

b. A Judicial Role?

If a President contends that the "offenses" alleged against him are not "high crimes and misdemeanors" under the Constitution, should he be able to seek judicial review of that question? Before a Senate trial? After conviction? The following case, involving not President Nixon but a federal judge also named Nixon, clearly was decided with the former President's case in mind.

Nixon v. United States
506 U.S. 224 (1993)

Chief Justice REHNQUIST delivered the opinion of the Court.

Petitioner Walter L. Nixon, Jr., asks this court to decide whether Senate Rule XI, which allows a committee of Senators to hear evidence against an individual who has been impeached and to report that evidence to the full Senate, violates the Impeachment Trial Clause, Art. I, § 3, cl. 6. That Clause provides that the "Senate shall have the sole Power to try all Impeachments." But before we reach the merits of such a claim, we must decide whether it is "justiciable," that is, whether it is a claim that may be resolved by the courts. We conclude that it is not.

Nixon, a former Chief Judge of the United States District Court for the Southern District of Mississippi, was convicted by a jury of two counts of making false statements before a federal grand jury and sentenced to prison. The grand jury investigation stemmed from reports that Nixon had accepted a gratuity from a Mississippi businessman in exchange for asking a local district attorney to halt the prosecution of the businessman's son. . . .

On May 10, 1989, the House of Representatives adopted three articles of impeachment for high crimes and misdemeanors. The first two articles charged Nixon with giving false testimony before the grand jury and the third article charged him with bringing disrepute on the Federal Judiciary. After the House presented the articles to the Senate, the Senate voted to invoke its own Impeachment Rule XI, under which the presiding officer appoints a committee of Senators to "receive evidence and take testimony." The Senate committee held four days of hearings, during which 10 witnesses, including Nixon, testified. Pursuant to Rule XI, the committee presented the full Senate with a complete transcript of the proceeding and a report stating the uncontested facts and summarizing the evidence on the contested facts. Nixon and the House impeachment managers submitted extensive final briefs to the full Senate and delivered arguments from the Senate floor during the three hours set aside for oral argument in front of that body. Nixon himself gave a personal appeal, and several Senators posed questions directly to both parties. The Senate voted by more than the constitutionally required two-thirds majority to convict Nixon on the first two articles. The presiding officer then entered judgment removing Nixon from his office as United States District Judge.

Nixon thereafter commenced the present suit, arguing that Senate Rule XI violates the constitutional grant of authority to the Senate to "try" all impeachments because it prohibits the whole Senate from taking part in the evidentiary hearings.... The District Court held that his claim was nonjusticiable, and the Court of Appeals for the District of Columbia Circuit agreed.

A controversy is nonjusticiable—i.e., involves a political question—where there is "a textually demonstrable constitutional commitment of the issue to a coordinate political department; or a lack of judicially discoverable and manageable standards for resolving it. . . ." *Baker v. Carr*, 369 U.S. 186, 217, (1962). But the courts must, in the first instance, interpret the text in question and determine whether and to what extent the issue is textually committed. *Powell v. McCormack*, 395 U.S. 486, 519, (1969). As the discussion that follows makes clear, the concept of a textual commitment to a coordinate political department is not completely separate from the concept of a lack of judicially discoverable and manageable standards for resolving it; the lack of judicially manageable standards may strengthen the conclusion that there is a textually demonstrable commitment to a coordinate branch.

In this case, we must examine Art. I, § 3, cl. 6, to determine the scope of authority conferred upon the Senate by the Framers regarding impeachment.... The language and structure of this Clause are revealing. The first sentence is a grant of authority to the Senate, and the word "sole" indicates that this authority is reposed in the Senate and nowhere else. The next two sentences specify requirements to which the Senate proceedings shall conform.... Petitioner argues that the word "try" in the first sentence imposes by implication an additional requirement on the Senate in that the proceedings must be in the nature of a judicial trial . . . . The word "try," both in 1787 and later, has considerably broader meanings than those to which petitioner would limit it . . . . Based on the variety of definitions, . . . we cannot say that the Framers used the word "try" as an implied limitation on the method by which the Senate might proceed in trying impeachments. . . .

[T]he first sentence of Clause 6 . . . provides that "the Senate shall have the sole Power to try all Impeachments." We think that the word "sole" is of considerable significance. Indeed, the word "sole" appears only one other time in the Constitution—with respect to the House of Representatives' "*sole* Power of Impeachment." Art. I, § 2, cl. 5. The common sense meaning of the word "sole" is that the Senate alone shall have authority to determine whether an individual should be acquitted or convicted . . . .

The history and contemporary understanding of the impeachment provisions support our reading of the constitutional language. The parties do not offer evidence of a single word in the history of the Constitutional Convention or in contemporary commentary that even alludes to the possibility of judicial review in the context of the impeachment powers. This silence is quite meaningful in light of the several explicit references to the availability of judicial review as a check on the Legislature's power with respect to bills of attainder, ex post facto laws, and statutes.

The Framers labored over the question of where the impeachment power should lie. Significantly, in at least two considered scenarios the power was placed with the Federal Judiciary. *See* 1 Farrand 21–22 (Virginia Plan); *id.*, at 244 (New Jersey Plan). Indeed, Madison and the Committee of Detail proposed that the Supreme Court should have the power to determine impeachments. Despite these proposals, the Convention ultimately decided that the Senate would have [it]. According to Alexander Hamilton, the Senate was the "most fit depositary of this important trust" because its members are representatives of the people. *See* The Federalist No. 65, p. 440 (J. Cooke ed., 1961). The Supreme Court was not the proper body because the Framers "doubted whether the members of that tribunal would, at all times, be endowed with so eminent a portion of fortitude as would be called for in the execution of so difficult a task" or whether the Court "would possess the degree of credit and authority" to carry out its judgment if it conflicted with the accusation brought by the Legislature—the people's representative. *See id.*, at 441. . . .

There are two additional reasons why the Judiciary, and the Supreme Court in particular, were not chosen to have any role in impeachments. First, the Framers recognized that most likely there would be two sets of proceedings for individuals who commit impeachable offenses—the impeachment trial and a separate criminal trial. In fact, the Constitution explicitly provides for two separate proceedings. *See* Art. I, § 3, cl. 7. The Framers deliberately separated the two forums to avoid raising the specter of bias and to ensure independent judgments. . . . Certainly judicial review of the Senate's "trial" would introduce the same risk of bias as would participation in the trial itself. Second, judicial review would be inconsistent with the Framers' insistence that our system be one of checks and balances. In our constitutional system, impeachment was designed to be the only check on the Judicial Branch by the Legislature. On the topic of judicial accountability, Hamilton wrote:

"The precautions for their responsibility are comprised in the article respecting impeachments. They are liable to be impeached for mal-conduct by the house of representatives, and tried by the senate, and if convicted, may be dismissed from office and disqualified for holding any other. *This is the only provision on the point, which is consistent with the necessary independence of the judicial character, and is the only one which we find in our own constitution in respect to our own judges.*" *Id.*, No. 79, pp. 532–33 (emphasis added).

Judicial involvement in impeachment proceedings, even if only for purposes of judicial review, is counterintuitive because it would eviscerate the "important constitutional check" placed on the Judiciary by the Framers. Nixon's argument would place final reviewing authority with respect to impeachments in the hands of the same body that the impeachment process is meant to regulate.

Nevertheless, Nixon argues that judicial review is necessary in order to place a check on the Legislature. . . . The Framers anticipated this objection and created two constitutional safeguards to keep the Senate in check. The first safeguard is that the whole of the impeachment power is divided between the two legislative bodies, with the House given the right to accuse and the Senate given the right to judge.

This split of authority "avoids the inconvenience of making the same persons both accusers and judges; and guards against the danger of persecution from the prevalency of a factious spirit in either of those branches." The second safeguard is the two-thirds supermajority vote requirement. . . .

In addition to the textual commitment argument, we are persuaded that the lack of finality and the difficulty of fashioning relief counsel against justiciability. We agree with the Court of Appeals that opening the door of judicial review . . . would "expose the political life of the country to months, or perhaps years, of chaos." This lack of finality would manifest itself most dramatically if the President were impeached. The legitimacy of any successor, and hence his effectiveness, would be impaired severely, not merely while the judicial process was running its course, but during any retrial that a differently constituted Senate might conduct if its first judgment of conviction were invalidated. Equally uncertain is the question of what relief a court may give other than simply setting aside the judgment of conviction. Could it order the reinstatement of a convicted federal judge, or order Congress to create an additional judgeship if the seat had been filled in the interim? . . .

For the foregoing reasons, the judgment of the Court of Appeals is Affirmed.

Justice WHITE, with whom Justice BLACKMUN joins, concurring in the judgment.

. . . [I would] reach the merits of the claim. I concur in the judgment because the Senate fulfilled its constitutional obligation to "try" petitioner. It should be said at the outset that, as a practical matter, it will likely make little difference whether the Court's or my view controls this case. This is so because the Senate has very wide discretion in specifying impeachment trial procedures and because it is extremely unlikely that the Senate would abuse its discretion and insist on a procedure that could not be deemed a trial by reasonable judges. . . . When asked at oral argument whether [the Constitution] would be satisfied if, after a House vote to impeach, the Senate, without any procedure whatsoever, unanimously found the accused guilty of being "a bad guy," counsel for the United States answered that the Government's theory "leads me to answer that question yes." . . . I would not issue an invitation to the Senate to find an excuse, in the name of other pressing business, to be dismissive of its critical role in the impeachment process. . . .

[T]here can be little doubt that the Framers came to the view at the Convention that the trial of officials' public misdeeds should be conducted by representatives of the people; that the fledgling judiciary lacked the wherewithal to adjudicate political intrigues; that the judiciary ought not to try both impeachments and subsequent criminal cases emanating from them; and that the impeachment power must reside in the Legislative Branch to provide a check on the largely unaccountable judiciary.

The majority's review of the historical record . . . does not explain, however, the sweeping statement that the judiciary was "not chosen to have any role in impeachments." Not a single word in the historical materials . . . addresses judicial review of the Impeachment Trial Clause. . . . What the relevant history mainly reveals is deep ambivalence among many of the Framers over the very institution of impeachment, which, by its nature, is not easily reconciled with our system of checks and balances. As they clearly recognized, the branch of the Federal Government which is possessed of the authority to try impeachments, by having final say over the membership of each branch, holds a potentially unanswerable power over the others. In addition, that branch, insofar as it is called upon to try not only members of other branches, but also its own, will have the advantage of being the judge of its own members' causes . . . .

The historical evidence reveals above all else that the Framers were deeply concerned about placing in any branch the "awful discretion, which a court of impeachments must necessarily have." The Federalist No. 65, p. 441 (J. Cooke ed., 1961). Viewed against this history, the discord between the majority's position and the basic principles of checks and balances underlying the Constitution's separation of powers is clear. In essence, the majority suggests that the Framers conferred upon Congress a potential tool of legislative dominance yet at the same time rendered Congress' exercise of that power one of the very few areas of legislative authority immune from any judicial review. . . . [I]t is the Court's finding of nonjusticiability that truly upsets the Framers' careful design. In a truly balanced system, impeachments tried by the Senate would serve as a means of controlling the largely unaccountable judiciary, even as judicial review would ensure that the Senate adhered to a minimal set of procedural standards in conducting impeachment trials.

The majority also contends that the term "try" does not present a judicially manageable standard. . . . The majority's conclusion that "try" is incapable of meaningful judicial construction is not without irony. One might think that if any class of concepts would fall within the definitional abilities of the judiciary, it would be that class having to do with procedural justice. Examination of the remaining question — whether proceedings in accordance with Senate Rule XI are compatible with the Impeachment Trial Clause — confirms this intuition.

Petitioner bears the rather substantial burden of demonstrating that, simply by employing the word "try," the Constitution prohibits the Senate from relying on a fact-finding committee. It is clear that the Framers were familiar with English impeachment practice and with that of the States. . . . It is also noteworthy that the delegation of fact-finding by judicial and quasi-judicial bodies was hardly unknown to the Framers. Jefferson, at least, was aware that the House of Lords sometimes delegated fact-finding in impeachment trials to committees and recommended use of the same to the Senate. T. Jefferson, A Manual of Parliamentary Practice for the Use of the Senate of the United States §LIII (2d ed. 1812). The States also had on occasion employed legislative committees to investigate whether to draw up articles of impeachment. . . . Particularly in light of the Constitution's grant to each House of the power to "determine the Rules of its Proceedings," the existence of legislative and judicial delegation strongly suggests that the Impeachment Trial Clause was not designed to prevent employment of a factfinding committee. . . .

Justice SOUTER, concurring in the judgment.

I agree with the Court that this case presents a nonjusticiable political question . . . [T]he functional nature of the political question doctrine requires analysis of "the precise facts and posture of the particular case," and precludes "resolution by any semantic cataloguing." Whatever considerations feature most prominently in a particular case, the political question doctrine . . . [derives] in large part from prudential concerns about the respect we owe the political departments. . . . [A]pplication of the doctrine ultimately turns, as Learned Hand put it, on "how importunately the occasion demands an answer." *L. Hand, The Bill of Rights* 15 (1958).

This occasion does not demand an answer. . . . It seems fair to conclude that the Clause contemplates that the Senate may determine, within broad boundaries, such subsidiary issues as the procedures for receipt and consideration of evidence necessary to satisfy its duty to "try" impeachments. . . . One can, nevertheless, envision different and unusual circumstances that might justify a more searching review of impeachment proceedings. If the Senate were to act in a manner seriously threatening the integrity of its results, convicting, say, upon a coin-toss, or upon a summary determination that an officer of the United States was simply " 'a bad guy,' " judicial interference might well be appropriate. In such circumstances, the Senate's action might be so far beyond the scope of its constitutional authority, and the consequent impact on the Republic so great, as to merit a judicial response despite the prudential concerns that would ordinarily counsel silence. . . .

[The concurring opinion of Justice STEVENS is omitted]

––––––––––

1. *Political Question or Constitutional Discretion?* Justice White remarks that it probably makes "little difference" whether his approach or the majority's is taken, in view of the wide procedural discretion he would recognize in the Senate. Indeed, the Justices seem to be arguing not about Judge Nixon, who received plenty of fair process, but about other impeachment controversies that loom in recent history or in the imagination. Given the majority's concern about reviewing presidential impeachments, is the real basis of its opinion not the two strands of political question doctrine that it discusses most, but the residual institutional considerations that often seem to play so strong a role in these cases? In view of the extensive consideration given by the majority to the text and history of the Constitution, how far removed is their actual determination from Justice White's? (Recall the view of some observers that the doctrine is a poorly disguised judgment that a branch is within its constitutional discretion.)

2. *Reviewing Impeachments.* Considering our overall constitutional structure, how should we regard judicial review of impeachments—would it be adding an inappropriate and unwarranted check, or would it be preserving the overall balance of the system in the same way that judicial review does otherwise? Would judicial review have been a help or a hindrance if it had followed a conviction of Justice Chase, or of Presidents Johnson, Nixon, or Clinton? Consider the Justices' debate about the "bad guy" hypothetical—did the Solicitor General give the best answer?

Suppose, as was once proposed, that former Justice Douglas had been impeached for marrying too often and writing leftish books. Should the Court have reviewed whether those are impeachable offenses? That is, are both procedural and substantive issues about impeachments now political questions?

3. *Committee Process.* What do you think of the use of a committee to perform part of the impeachment process? Are there substantial arguments that this delegation is bad *per se*, or should one's view depend on how it operates? For a critique of the current procedures as unfair, see Note, *Committee Impeachment Trials: The Best Solution?* 80 Geo. L.J. 163 (1991).

4. *Disciplining Federal Judges.* The Judicial Councils Reform and Judicial Conduct and Disability Act of 1980, Pub. L. No. 96-458, 94 Stat. 2035, codified at 28 U.S. Code §§ 331–32, 372, 604, created a mechanism to consider and respond to complaints against federal judges. If a complaint about a judge's conduct is filed with the appropriate court of appeals, the judicial council of the circuit is empowered, after various preliminary investigative steps, to punish the judge by means such as a reprimand, a temporary suspension, or a transfer of the judge's cases. If the situation appears to warrant removal, the inquiry moves to the Judicial Conference of the United States for reporting to the House of Representatives. For analysis of the Act, see Michael J. Gerhardt, The Federal Impeachment Process: A Constitutional and Historical Analysis 100–102 (2d ed. 2000); Robert W. Kastenmeier & Michael Remington, *Judicial Discipline: A Legislative Perspective*, 76 Ky. L.J. 763 (1987–88).

After having impeached and removed three federal judges within just over two years, Congress decided broadly to address issues of judicial discipline. It created a National Commission on Judicial Discipline and Removal to study the problems and report recommendations (Pub. L. No. 101-650, 104 Stat. 5124). The Commission, a distinguished group chaired by former Congressman Robert W. Kastenmeier, issued its Report of the National Commission on Judicial Discipline and Removal (1993). The Commission did not recommend constitutional reform. It concluded that federal judges could constitutionally be prosecuted, convicted, and jailed by federal or state authorities, but that statutes attempting to provide for removal of federal judges by means other than impeachment would be unconstitutional. The Commission thought that the circuit councils could control the caseload of judges under inquiry, but that a statute suspending compensation in the event of a conviction would be unconstitutional. Regarding impeachment proceedings, the Commission urged better cooperation between executive and congressional authorities in potential removal situations and suggested some ways to streamline and to ensure the fairness of the process. It did not call for abandonment of the Senate's Rule XI process for delegating trial responsibilities to a committee. *See* Peter M. Shane, *Who May Discipline or Remove Federal Judges? A Constitutional Analysis*, 142 U. Pa. L. Rev. 209 (1993); Todd D. Peterson, *The Role of the Executive Branch in the Discipline and Removal of Federal Judges*, 1993 U. Ill. L. Rev. 809.

2. Membership in Congress

a. Exclusion and Expulsion

Powell v. McCormack

395 U.S. 486 (1969)

Chief Justice WARREN delivered the opinion of the Court.

In November 1966, petitioner Adam Clayton Powell, Jr., was duly elected from the 18th Congressional District of New York to serve in the United States House of Representatives for the 90th Congress. However, pursuant to a House resolution, he was not permitted to take his seat. Powell (and some of the voters of his district) then filed suit in Federal District Court, claiming that the House could exclude him only if it found he failed to meet the standing requirements of age, citizenship, and residence contained in Art. I, § 2, of the Constitution — requirements the House specifically found Powell met — and thus had excluded him unconstitutionally. . . . We have determined that . . . petitioner Powell is entitled to a declaratory judgment that he was unlawfully excluded from the 90th Congress.

I.

During the 89th Congress, a Special Subcommittee on Contracts . . . conducted an investigation into the expenditures of the Committee on Education and Labor, of which petitioner Adam Clayton Powell, Jr., was chairman. The Special Subcommittee issued a report concluding that Powell and certain staff employees had deceived the House authorities as to travel expenses. The report also indicated there was strong evidence that certain illegal salary payments had been made to Powell's wife at his direction. No formal action was taken during the 89th Congress. . . .

When the 90th Congress met to organize in January 1967, Powell was asked to step aside while the oath was administered to the other members-elect. . . . [The House created] a Select Committee to determine Powell's eligibility. The Select Committee . . . issued an invitation to Powell to testify . . . [concerning] Powell's qualifications as to age, citizenship, and residency; . . . and "matters of . . . alleged official misconduct since January 3, 1961." . . . After the Committee denied in part Powell's request that certain adversary-type procedures be followed, Powell testified. He would, however, give information relating only to his age, citizenship, and residency; upon the advice of counsel, he refused to answer other questions.

. . . [T]he Select Committee . . . informed Powell that its responsibility . . . [included] "inquir[ing] into the question of whether you should be punished or expelled." . . . Powell's attorneys . . . urged that punishment or expulsion was not possible until a member had been seated. Then, on February 23, 1967, the Committee issued its report, finding that Powell met the standing qualifications of Art. I, § 2. However, the Committee further reported that Powell had asserted an unwarranted privilege and immunity from the processes of the courts of New York; that he had wrongfully diverted House funds for the use of others and himself; and that he had made false reports on expenditures of foreign currency to the Committee on House Administration. The Committee recommended that Powell be sworn and seated as a member of the 90th Congress but that he be censured by the House, fined $40,000 and be deprived of his seniority.

The report was presented to the House. . . . An amendment to the resolution was . . . offered; it called for the exclusion of Powell and a declaration that his seat was vacant. The Speaker ruled that a majority vote of the House would be sufficient to pass the resolution if it were so amended. After further debate, the amendment was adopted by a vote of 248 to 176. Then the House adopted by a vote of 307 to 116 House Resolution No. 278 in its amended form, thereby excluding Powell. . . . Powell and 13 voters of the 18th Congressional District of New York subsequently instituted this suit . . . John W. McCormack was named in his official capacity as Speaker, and the Clerk of the House of Representatives, the Sergeant at Arms and the Doorkeeper were named individually and in their official capacities. . . . While the case was pending on our docket, the 90th Congress officially terminated and the 91st Congress was seated. In November 1968, Powell was again elected as the representative of the 18th Congressional District of New York and he was seated by the 91st Congress. The resolution seating Powell also fined him $25,000. . . .

[The Court held that the case was not moot, because Powell continued to claim back salary from the 90th Congress, and, in passages excerpted *infra*, that congressional immunity did not bar the suit.]

IV.

The resolution excluding petitioner Powell was adopted by a vote in excess of two-thirds of the 434 Members of Congress — 307 to 116. Article I, § 5, grants the House authority to expel a member "with the Concurrence of two thirds." Respondents assert that the House may expel a member for any reason whatsoever and that, since a two-thirds vote was obtained, the procedure by which Powell was denied his seat in the 90th Congress should be regarded as an expulsion, not an exclusion. . . . [T]heir attempt to equate exclusion with expulsion would require . . . speculation that the House would have voted to expel Powell had it been faced with that question. . . .

Nor is the distinction between exclusion and expulsion merely one of form. The misconduct for which Powell was charged occurred prior to the convening of the 90th Congress. On several occasions the House has debated whether a member can be expelled for actions taken during a prior Congress and the House's own manual of procedure applicable in the 90th Congress states that "both Houses have distrusted their power to punish in such cases." The House rules manual reflects positions taken by prior Congresses. . . .

Members of the House having expressed a belief that such strictures apply to its own power to expel, we will not assume that two-thirds of its members would have expelled Powell for his prior conduct had the Speaker announced that House

Resolution No. 278 was for expulsion rather than exclusion. Finally, the proceedings which culminated in Powell's exclusion cast considerable doubt upon respondents' assumption that the two-thirds vote necessary to expel would have been mustered. [*See* Robert Eckhardt, *The Adam Clayton Powell Case*, 45 Texas L. Rev. 1205 (1967).] ... We must reject respondents' suggestion that we overrule the Speaker and hold that, although the House manifested an intent to exclude Powell, its action should be tested by whatever standards may govern an expulsion.

VI.

... [W]e must determine whether ... this case presents a political question because under Art. I, § 5, there has been a "textually demonstrable constitutional commitment" to the House of the "adjudicatory power" to determine Powell's qualifications. Thus it is argued that the House, and the House alone, has power to determine who is qualified to be a member. In order to determine whether there has been a textual commitment to a co-ordinate department of the Government, we must interpret the Constitution. In other words, we must first determine what power the Constitution confers upon the House through Art. I, § 5, before we can determine to what extent, if any, the exercise of that power is subject to judicial review. ...

If examination of § 5 disclosed that the Constitution gives the House judicially unreviewable power to set qualifications for membership and to judge whether prospective members meet those qualifications, further review of the House determination might well be barred by the political question doctrine. On the other hand, if the Constitution gives the House power to judge only whether elected members possess the three standing qualifications set forth in the Constitution, further consideration would be necessary to determine whether any of the other formulations of the political question doctrine are "inextricable from the case at bar." ...

In order to determine the scope of any "textual commitment" under Art. I, § 5, we necessarily must determine the meaning of the phrase to "be the Judge of the Qualifications of its own Members." Our examination of the relevant historical materials leads us to the conclusion that ... the Constitution leaves the House without authority to exclude any person, duly elected by his constituents, who meets all the requirements for membership expressly prescribed in the Constitution.

a. The Pre-Convention Precedents

... By 1782, after a long struggle, the arbitrary exercise of the power to exclude was unequivocally repudiated by ... the most notorious English election dispute of the 18th century—the John Wilkes case. While serving as a member of Parliament in 1763, Wilkes published an attack on a recent peace treaty with France, calling it a product of bribery and condemning the Crown's ministers as "'the tools of despotism and corruption.'" *R. Postgate, That Devil Wilkes* 53 (1929). Wilkes and others who were involved ... were arrested. Prior to Wilkes' trial, the House of Commons expelled him for publishing "a false, scandalous, and seditious libel." ... He was elected to the next Parliament, ... [which] declared him ineligible for membership and ordered that he be "expelled this House." ...

Wilkes . . . unsuccessfully campaigned to have the resolutions expelling him and declaring him incapable of re-election expunged from the record. Finally, in 1782, the House of Commons voted to expunge them, resolving that the prior House actions were "subversive of the rights of the whole body of electors of this kingdom." With the successful resolution of Wilkes' long and bitter struggle for the right of the British electorate to be represented by men of their own choice, it is evident that . . . English practice did not support . . . the right to exclude members-elect for general misconduct not within standing qualifications. . . . Wilkes' struggle and his ultimate victory had a significant impact in the American colonies. His . . . pursuit of the right to be seated in Parliament became a cause celebre for the colonists. . . . It is within this historical context that we must examine the Convention debates in 1787, just five years after Wilkes' final victory.

b. Convention Debates

. . . [P]etitioners argue that the proceedings manifest the Framers' unequivocal intention to deny either branch of Congress the authority to add to or otherwise vary the membership qualifications expressly set forth in the Constitution. . . . We have concluded that the records of the debates, viewed in the . . . light of the distinction the Framers made between the power to expel and the power to exclude, indicate that petitioners' ultimate conclusion is correct.

. . . By the end of July, the delegates adopted, with a minimum of debate, age requirements for membership in both the Senate and the House. The Convention then appointed a Committee of Detail to draft a constitution incorporating these and other resolutions adopted during the preceding months. . . . The Committee reported in early August, proposing no change in the age requirement; however, it did recommend adding citizenship and residency requirements for membership. After first debating what the precise requirements should be, . . . the delegates unanimously adopted the three qualifications embodied in Art. I, § 2.

On August 10, the Convention considered the Committee of Detail's proposal that the "Legislature of the United States shall have authority to establish such uniform qualifications of the members of each House, with regard to property, as to the said Legislature shall seem expedient." The debate on this proposal discloses much about the views of the Framers on the issue of qualifications. For example, James Madison urged its rejection, stating that the proposal would vest "an improper & dangerous power in the Legislature. The qualifications of electors and elected were fundamental articles in a Republican Govt. and ought to be fixed by the Constitution. If the Legislature could regulate those of either, it can by degrees subvert the Constitution. . . . It was a power also, which might be made subservient to the views of one faction agst. another. Qualifications founded on artificial distinctions may be devised, by the stronger in order to keep out partisans of [a weaker] faction."

Significantly, Madison's argument was not aimed at the imposition of a property qualification as such, but rather at the delegation to the Congress of the discretionary power to establish any qualifications. The parallel between Madison's arguments and those made in Wilkes' behalf is striking. In view of what followed Madison's speech, it appears that on this critical day the Framers were facing and then reject-ing the possibility that the legislature would have power to usurp the "indisputable right [of the people] to return whom they thought proper" to the legislature. . . . Later the same day, the Convention adopted without debate the provision authorizing each House to be "the judge of the . . . qualifications of its own members."

One other decision made the same day is very important to determining the mean-ing of Art. I, § 5. When the delegates reached the Committee of Detail's proposal to empower each House to expel its members, Madison "observed that the right of expulsion . . . was too important to be exercised by a bare majority of a quorum: and in emergencies [one] faction might be dangerously abused." He therefore moved that "with the concurrence of two-thirds" be inserted. . . . [T]he motion was unani-mously approved without debate, although Gouverneur Morris noted his opposition. The importance of this decision cannot be over-emphasized. . . . [P]rior to 1787 the legislative powers to judge qualifications and to expel were exercised by a majority vote. . . . Thus, the Convention's decision to increase the vote required to expel, . . . while at the same time not similarly restricting the power to judge qualifications, is compelling evidence that they considered the latter already limited by the standing qualifications previously adopted. . . .

Petitioners also argue that the post-Convention debates over the Constitution's ratification support their interpretation of § 5. For example, they emphasize Hamil-ton's reply to the antifederalist charge that the new Constitution favored the wealthy and well-born:

> "The truth is that there is no method of securing to the rich the preference apprehended but by prescribing qualifications of property either for those who may elect or be elected. But this forms no part of the power to be con-ferred upon the national government. . . . *The qualifications of the persons who may choose or be chosen, . . . are defined and fixed in the Constitution, and are unalterable by the legislature.*" The Federalist Papers 371 (Mentor ed., 1961). (Emphasis in last sentence added.)

Madison had expressed similar views in an earlier essay, and his arguments at the Convention leave no doubt about his agreement with Hamilton on this issue. . . . The debates at the state conventions also demonstrate the Framers' under-standing that the qualifications for members of Congress had been fixed in the Constitution. . . .

c. Post-Ratification

. . . Unquestionably, both the House and the Senate have excluded members-elect for reasons other than their failure to meet the Constitution's standing quali-fications. For almost the first 100 years of its existence, however, Congress strictly limited its power to judge the qualifications of its members to those enumerated in the Constitution. . . . [This practice] came under heavy attack, however, "during the stress of civil war [but initially] the House of Representatives declined to exercise the power [to exclude], even under circumstances of great provocation." The abandonment of such restraint, however, was among the casualties of the general upheaval produced in war's wake. In 1868, the House voted for the first time in its history to exclude a member-elect. It refused to seat two duly elected representatives for giving aid and comfort to the Confederacy.... From that time until the present, congressional practice has been erratic; and on the few occasions when a member-elect was excluded although he met all the qualifications set forth in the Constitution, there were frequently vigorous dissents. Even the annotations to the official manual of procedure for the 90th Congress manifest doubt as to the House's power to exclude a member-elect who has met the constitutionally prescribed qualifications.

Had these congressional exclusion precedents been more consistent, their precedential value still would be quite limited. That an unconstitutional action has been taken before surely does not render that same action any less unconstitutional at a later date.... Obviously, ... the precedential value of these cases tends to increase in proportion to their proximity to the Convention in 1787. And, what evidence we have of Congress' early understanding confirms our conclusion that the House is without power to exclude any member-elect who meets the Constitution's requirements for membership.

d. Conclusion

Had the intent of the Framers emerged from these materials with less clarity, we would nevertheless have been compelled to resolve any ambiguity in favor of a narrow construction of the scope of Congress' power to exclude members-elect. A fundamental principle of our representative democracy is, in Hamilton's words, "that the people should choose whom they please to govern them." As Madison pointed out at the Convention, this principle is undermined as much by limiting whom the people can select as by limiting the franchise itself. In apparent agreement with this basic philosophy, the Convention adopted his suggestion limiting the power to expel. To allow essentially that same power to be exercised under the guise of judging qualifications, would be to ignore Madison's warning, borne out in the Wilkes case and some of Congress' own post-Civil War exclusion cases, against "vesting an improper & dangerous power in the Legislature." Moreover, it would effectively nullify the Convention's decision to require a two-thirds vote for expulsion. Unquestionably, Congress has an interest in preserving its institutional integrity, but in most cases that interest can be sufficiently safeguarded by the exercise of its power to punish its members for disorderly behavior and, in extreme cases, to expel a member with the concurrence of two-thirds....

For these reasons, we have concluded that Art. I, § 5, is at most a "textually demonstrable commitment" to Congress to judge only the qualifications expressly set forth in the Constitution. Therefore, the "textual commitment" formulation of the political question doctrine does not bar federal courts from adjudicating petitioners' claims.... [C]learly there are "judicially ... manageable standards." ... Thus, we conclude that petitioners' claim is not barred by the political question doctrine....

Therefore, we hold that, since Adam Clayton Powell, Jr., was duly elected by the voters of the 18th Congressional District of New York and was not ineligible to serve under any provision of the Constitution, the House was without power to exclude him from its membership . . .

[Justice STEWART dissented on grounds of mootness. His opinion and Justice DOUGLAS' concurring opinion are omitted.]

---

1. *Distinguishing* Nixon. Why can the Court review Congress's grounds for excluding a Member, but not its process for impeachments? The *Nixon* case, *supra*, distinguished *Powell* as follows:

> We held that, in light of the three requirements specified in the Constitution, the word "qualifications" — of which the House was to be the Judge — was of a precise, limited nature. Our conclusion in *Powell* was based on the fixed meaning of "qualifications" set forth in Art. I, § 2. The claim by the House that its power to "be the Judge of the Elections, Returns and Qualifications of its own Members" was a textual commitment of unreviewable authority was defeated by the existence of this separate provision specifying the only qualifications which might be imposed for House membership. The decision as to whether a member satisfied these qualifications was placed with the House, but the decision as to what these qualifications consisted of was not.

Persuasive? Note that the *Powell* opinion says only that "at most" the question whether a Member meets the standing qualifications is committed to Congress. What if the House of Representatives had solemnly announced that Powell, then obviously and provably middle-aged, did not meet the minimum age of 25 for a Representative? If you think the Court would find a way to review such a determination to prevent abuse of the exclusion power, what justifies holding aspects of the impeachment process wholly unreviewable? Note that the *Powell* Court's justification for constraining Congress is the people's right to "choose whom they please." Perhaps, then, it is congressional actions that do not determine who may be a Member of Congress which will be treated as political questions, for example impeachment process.

2. *Exclusion v. Expulsion.* What does the Court suggest about the reviewability of expulsions? It emphasizes historical problems with abuse of both exclusion and expulsion, in this country and England. Is the supermajority requirement enough of a safeguard that courts can stay their hands? If not, it seems to make little sense to review one and not the other.

b. Term Limits

Frustrated with the behavior of their Members of Congress, many states enacted limitations on the number of terms an individual could serve. For example, an amendment to the Arkansas Constitution prohibited candidates from running for Congress if they had served three terms in the House or two in the Senate. The purpose was to replace unresponsive professional legislators with citizen-legislators in the classic republican mold. *See generally* GEORGE F. WILL, RESTORATION: CONGRESS, TERM LIMITS AND THE RECOVERY OF DELIBERATIVE DEMOCRACY (1993). Of course, such limits necessarily forfeit vast amounts of expertise and dedication by removing the good legislators along with the bad. Both the wisdom and the constitutionality of term limits soon became matters of sharp controversy. A challenge to the Arkansas limitation reached the Supreme Court.

In *U.S. Term Limits v. Thornton*, 514 U.S. 779 (1995), the Court held, 5–4, that state-imposed term limits for Members of Congress are unconstitutional. Relying on *Powell*, the majority decided that term limits constitute forbidden additions to the list of qualifications for membership that Article I contains. Justice Stevens first reaffirmed *Powell*'s conclusion that *Congress* may not add to the Constitution's qualifications, lest it infringe the principle "that the people should choose whom they please to govern them." Turning to state-imposed limits, he concluded that the framers meant the Constitution to be the "exclusive source" of qualifications for Congress, so that the states were divested of all power to add others. Essentially, he reasoned that the characteristics of Congress were matters of federal power, and were not left with the states under the Tenth Amendment. As with restrictions on congressional power to add qualifications, democratic principles favoring free voter choice reinforced constitutional history. The majority also thought it important that the qualifications for Congress be uniform nationwide.

A spirited dissent by Justice Thomas argued that the Constitution is "simply silent" on the question of term limits. Therefore, he would have upheld them as a power reserved to the states under the Tenth Amendment. He also argued that the limits could be justified as within the acknowledged power of the states to regulate ballot access. To the dissent, there was no small irony in the majority's invocation of democratic principles to strike down term limits provisions that had been enacted by substantial majorities of voters in many states.

Do you agree with the majority in *U.S. Term Limits*, or would you, with the dissent, have resolved all doubts in favor of preserving a role for the states in imposing limits? *See* Kathleen M. Sullivan, *Dueling Sovereignties*: U.S. Term Limits, Inc. v. Thornton, 109 HARV. L. REV. 78 (1995).

B. Immunities of Government Officers

1. Congressional Immunity

In Powell v. McCormack, supra, the Court discussed the scope of the immunity from judicial process that the Constitution grants Members of Congress:

> Respondents assert that the Speech or Debate Clause . . . , Art. I, §6, is an absolute bar to petitioners' action. This Court has on four prior occasions— *Dombrowski v. Eastland*, 387 U.S. 82 (1967); *United States v. Johnson*, 383 U.S. 169 (1966); *Tenney v. Brandhove*, 341 U.S. 367 (1951); and *Kilbourn v.*

Thompson, 103 U.S. 168 (1881) — been called upon to determine if allegedly unconstitutional action taken by legislators or legislative employees is insulated from judicial review by the Speech or Debate Clause. . . .

The Speech or Debate Clause, adopted by the Constitutional Convention without debate or opposition, finds its roots in the conflict between Parliament and the Crown culminating in the Glorious Revolution of 1688 and the English Bill of Rights of 1689. [The Court noted that "The English Bill of Rights contained a provision substantially identical to Art. I, § 6: 'That the Freedom of Speech, and Debates or Proceedings in Parliament, ought not to be impeached or questioned in any Court or Place out of Parliament.'"] Drawing upon this history, we concluded in *United States v. Johnson, supra*, that the purpose of this clause was "to prevent intimidation [of legislators] by the executive and accountability before a possibly hostile judiciary." Although the clause sprang from a fear of seditious libel actions instituted by the Crown to punish unfavorable speeches made in Parliament, we have held that it would be a "narrow view" to confine the protection of the Speech or Debate Clause to words spoken in debate. Committee reports, resolutions, and the act of voting are equally covered, as are "things generally done in a session of the House by one of its members in relation to the business before it." *Kilbourn v. Thompson, supra.* Furthermore, the clause not only provides a defense on the merits but also protects a legislator from the burden of defending himself.

Our cases make it clear that the legislative immunity created by the Speech or Debate Clause performs an important function in representative government. It insures that legislators are free to represent the interests of their constituents without fear that they will be later called to task in the courts for that representation. Thus . . . the writings of James Wilson . . . [show] the reason for legislative immunity: "In order to enable and encourage a representative of the publick to discharge his publick trust with firmness and success, it is indispensably necessary, that he should enjoy the fullest liberty of speech, and that he should be protected from the resentment of every one, however powerful, to whom the exercise of that liberty may occasion offence." [1 The Works of James Wilson 421 (R. McCloskey ed., 1967).]

Legislative immunity does not, of course, bar all judicial review of legislative acts. That issue was settled by implication as early as 1803, see *Marbury v. Madison*, 1 Cranch 137, and expressly in *Kilbourn v. Thompson,* the first of this Court's cases interpreting the reach of the Speech or Debate Clause. Challenged in *Kilbourn* was the constitutionality of a House Resolution ordering the arrest and imprisonment of a recalcitrant witness who had refused to respond to a subpoena issued by a House investigating committee. While holding that the Speech or Debate Clause barred Kilbourn's action for false imprisonment brought against several members of the House, the Court nevertheless reached the merits of Kilbourn's attack and decided that, since the

House had no power to punish for contempt, Kilbourn's imprisonment pursuant to the resolution was unconstitutional. It therefore allowed Kilbourn to bring his false imprisonment action against Thompson, the House's Sergeant at Arms, who had executed the warrant for Kilbourn's arrest.

The Court first articulated in *Kilbourn* and followed in *Dombrowski v. Eastland* the doctrine that, although an action against a Congressman may be barred by the Speech or Debate Clause, legislative employees who participated in the unconstitutional activity are responsible for their acts. . . . The purpose of the protection afforded legislators is not to forestall judicial review of legislative action but to insure that legislators are not distracted from or hindered in the performance of their legislative tasks by being called into court to defend their actions. . . . [T]hough this action may be dismissed against the Congressmen petitioners are entitled to maintain their action against House employees and to judicial review of the propriety of the decision to exclude petitioner Powell. . . .

In reviewing the development of the case law on congressional immunity from suit, the *Powell* Court stressed the need to protect Members of Congress from intimidation and distraction in the performance of their duties. This protection from litigation, however, protects the Members personally, and not the institution, as the outcome in *Powell* attests. If the rule were otherwise, judicial review could hardly exist.

Powell affirmed that congressional aides are sometimes subject to process when the Members they serve are not. Still, the Court has recognized a derivative immunity for staff members, albeit of a limited nature. The leading case follows.

Gravel v. United States

408 U.S. 606 (1972)

[This litigation arose in the wake of public disclosure of the "Pentagon Papers," a classified government study of the conduct of the Vietnam War. (In Chapter Five we consider the litigation in which the executive sought to enjoin newspaper publication of the papers.) At the height of the controversy over whether the papers should become public, Senator Mike Gravel convened his obscure Subcommittee on Buildings and Grounds, read portions of the papers, and then placed them in the public record. A grand jury investigating possible violations of federal law issued a subpoena to one of his aides, a Dr. Rodberg, and the Senator intervened to quash it as violative of his Speech or Debate privilege. The Supreme Court considered the appropriate scope of protective orders governing questioning of the aide.]

Opinion of the Court by Justice WHITE.

I

Because the claim is that a Member's aide shares the Member's constitutional privilege, we consider first whether and to what extent Senator Gravel himself is exempt from process or inquiry by a grand jury investigating the commission of a crime. . . . The last sentence of [Art. I, § 6, cl. 1] provides Members of Congress with two distinct privileges. Except in cases of "Treason, Felony and Breach of the Peace," the Clause shields Members from arrest while attending or traveling to and from a session of their House. History reveals, and prior cases so hold, that this part of the Clause exempts Members from arrest in civil cases only. "When the Constitution was adopted, arrests in civil suits were still common in America. It is only to such arrests that the provision applies." *Long v. Ansell*, 293 U.S. 76, 83 (1934) . . . . Nor does freedom from arrest confer immunity on a Member from service of process as a defendant in civil matters, or as a witness in a criminal case. . . . It is, therefore, sufficiently plain that the constitutional freedom from arrest does not exempt Members of Congress from the operation of the ordinary criminal laws, even though imprisonment may prevent or interfere with the performance of their duties as Members. Indeed, implicit in the narrow scope of the privilege of freedom from arrest is, as Jefferson noted, the judgment that legislators ought not to stand above the law they create but ought generally to be bound by it as are ordinary persons. *T. Jefferson, Manual of Parliamentary Practice*, S. Doc. No. 92-1, p. 437 (1971).

. . . [T]he last portion of § 6 affords Members of Congress another vital privilege — they may not be questioned in any other place for any speech or debate in either House. The claim is . . . [of protection] from criminal or civil liability and from questioning elsewhere than in the Senate, with respect to the events occurring at the subcommittee hearing at which the Pentagon Papers were introduced into the public record. To us this claim is incontrovertible. The Speech or Debate Clause was designed to assure a co-equal branch of the government wide freedom of speech, debate, and deliberation without intimidation or threats from the Executive Branch. It thus protects Members against prosecutions that directly impinge upon or threaten the legislative process. We have no doubt that Senator Gravel may not be made to answer — either in terms of questions or in terms of defending himself from prosecution — for the events that occurred at the subcommittee meeting. . . .

Even so, the United States strongly urges that because the Speech or Debate Clause confers a privilege only upon "Senators and Representatives," Rodberg himself has no valid claim to constitutional immunity from grand jury inquiry. . . . We agree with the Court of Appeals that for the purpose of construing the privilege a Member and his aide are to be "treated as one," or, as the District Court put it: the "Speech or Debate Clause prohibits inquiry into things done by Dr. Rodberg as the Senator's agent or assistant which would have been legislative acts, and therefore privileged, if performed by the Senator personally." Both courts recognized . . . that it is literally impossible, in view of the complexities of the modern legislative process, with Congress almost constantly in session and matters of legislative concern constantly proliferating, for Members of Congress to perform their legislative tasks without the help of aides and assistants; that the day-to-day work of such aides is so critical to the Members' performance that they must be treated as the latter's alter egos; and that if they are not so recognized, the central role of the Speech or Debate Clause — to prevent intimidation of legislators by the Executive and accountability before a possibly hostile judiciary—will inevitably be diminished and frustrated. . . .

[T]o confine the protection of the Speech or Debate Clause to words spoken in debate would be an unacceptably narrow view. Committee reports, resolutions, and the act of voting are equally covered; "in short, . . . things generally done in a session of the House by one of its members in relation to the business before it." Rather than giving the Clause a cramped construction, the Court has sought to implement its fundamental purpose of freeing the legislator from executive and judicial oversight that realistically threatens to control his conduct as a legislator. . . .

[We need not distinguish] between a Senator and his personal aides with respect to legislative immunity. In *Kilbourn*-type situations, both aide and Member should be immune with respect to committee and House action leading to the illegal resolution. So, too, in *Eastland*, as in this litigation, senatorial aides should enjoy immunity for helping a Member conduct committee hearings. On the other hand, no prior case has held that Members of Congress would be immune if they executed an invalid resolution by themselves carrying out an illegal arrest, or if, in order to secure information for a hearing, themselves seized the property or invaded the privacy of a citizen. Neither they nor their aides should be immune from liability or questioning in such circumstances. . . .

[Abuses will be forestalled if] the privilege available to the aide is confined to those services that would be immune legislative conduct if performed by the Senator himself. This view places beyond the Speech or Debate Clause a variety of services characteristically performed by aides for Members of Congress, even though within the scope of their employment. It likewise provides no protection for criminal conduct threatening the security of the person or property of others, whether performed at the direction of the Senator in preparation for or in execution of a legislative act or done without his knowledge or direction. Neither does it immunize Senator or aide from testifying at trials or grand jury proceedings involving third-party crimes where the questions do not require testimony about or impugn a legislative act. Thus our refusal to distinguish between Senator and aide in applying the Speech or Debate Clause does not mean that Rodberg is for all purposes exempt from grand jury questioning.

II

We are convinced also that the Court of Appeals correctly determined that Senator Gravel's alleged arrangement with Beacon Press to publish the Pentagon Papers was not protected speech or debate. . . . Historically, the English legislative privilege was not viewed as protecting republication of an otherwise immune libel on the floor of the House. . . . [V]oting by Members and committee reports are protected; and we recognize today—as the Court has recognized before—that a Member's conduct at legislative committee hearings, although subject to judicial review in various circumstances, as is legislation itself, may not be made the basis for a civil or criminal judgment against a Member because that conduct is within the "sphere of legitimate legislative activity."

But the Clause has not been extended beyond the legislative sphere. That Senators generally perform certain acts in their official capacity as Senators does not necessarily make all such acts legislative in nature. Members of Congress are constantly in touch with the Executive Branch of the Government and with administrative agencies— they may cajole, and exhort with respect to the administration of a federal statute— but such conduct, though generally done, is not protected legislative activity. . . .

Legislative acts are not all-encompassing. The heart of the Clause is speech or debate in either House. Insofar as the Clause is construed to reach other matters, they must be an integral part of the deliberative and communicative processes by which Members participate in committee and House proceedings with respect to the consideration and passage or rejection of proposed legislation or with respect to other matters which the Constitution places within the jurisdiction of either House. . . .

Here, private publication by Senator Gravel through the cooperation of Beacon Press was in no way essential to the deliberations of the Senate; nor does questioning as to private publication threaten the integrity or independence of the Senate by impermissibly exposing its deliberations to executive influence. . . . [T]he Speech or Debate Clause . . . does not privilege either Senator or aide to violate an otherwise valid criminal law in preparing for or implementing legislative acts. If republication of these classified papers would be a crime under an Act of Congress, it would not be entitled to immunity under the Speech or Debate Clause. . . . The . . . Clause does not in our view extend immunity to Rodberg, as a Senator's aide, from testifying before the grand jury about the arrangement between Senator Gravel and Beacon Press or about his own participation, if any, in the alleged transaction, so long as legislative acts of the Senator are not impugned.

III

Similar considerations lead us to disagree with the Court of Appeals insofar as it fashioned . . . a nonconstitutional testimonial privilege protecting Rodberg from any questioning by the grand jury concerning the matter of republication of the Pentagon Papers. This privilege, thought to be similar to that protecting executive officials from liability for libel, see *Barr v. Matteo,* 360 U.S. 564 (1959), was considered advisable "to the extent that a congressman has responsibility to inform his constituents. . . ." But we cannot carry a judicially fashioned privilege so far as to immunize criminal conduct proscribed by an Act of Congress or to frustrate the grand jury's inquiry into whether publication of these classified documents violated a federal criminal statute. . . .

The judgment of the Court of Appeals is vacated and the cases are remanded to that court for further proceedings consistent with this opinion. So ordered.

Justice STEWART, dissenting in part.

The Court today holds that the Speech or Debate Clause does not protect a Congressman from being forced to testify before a grand jury about sources of information used in preparation for legislative acts. This critical question . . . was addressed only tangentially during the oral arguments. . . . I cannot join in the Court's summary resolution of so vitally important a constitutional issue.

In preparing for legislative hearings, debates, and roll calls, a member of Congress obviously needs the broadest possible range of information. Valuable information may often come from sources in the Executive Branch or from citizens in private life. And informants such as these may be willing to relate information to a Congressman only in confidence.... Thus, the acquisition of knowledge through a promise of nondisclosure of its source will often be a necessary concomitant of effective legislative conduct....

The Court, however, today decides, sua sponte, that a Member of Congress may, despite the Speech or Debate Clause, be compelled to testify before a grand jury concerning the sources of information used by him in the performance of his legislative duties, if such an inquiry *"proves relevant to investigating possible third-party crime."* (emphasis supplied). In my view, this ruling is highly dubious in view of the basic purpose of the Speech or Debate Clause....

Under the Court's ruling, a Congressman may be subpoenaed by a vindictive Executive to testify about informants who have not committed crimes and who have no knowledge of crime. Such compulsion can occur, because the judiciary has traditionally imposed virtually no limitations on the grand jury's broad investigatory powers.... But even if the Executive had reason to believe that a Member of Congress had knowledge of a specific probable violation of law, it is by no means clear to me that the Executive's interest in the administration of justice must always override the public interest in having an informed Congress. Why should we not, given the tension between two competing interests, each of constitutional dimensions, balance the claims of the Speech or Debate Clause against the claims of the grand jury in the particularized contexts of specific cases? And why are not the Houses of Congress the proper institutions in most situations to impose sanctions upon a Representative or Senator who withholds information about crime acquired in the course of his legislative duties? ...

Justice DOUGLAS, dissenting.

I would construe the Speech or Debate Clause to insulate Senator Gravel and his aides from inquiry concerning the Pentagon Papers, and Beacon Press from inquiry concerning publication of them, for that publication was but another way of informing the public as to what had gone on in the privacy of the Executive Branch concerning the conception and pursuit of the so-called "war" in Vietnam.... As to Senator Gravel's efforts to publish the Subcommittee record's contents, wide dissemination of this material as an educational service is as much a part of the Speech or Debate Clause philosophy as mailing under a frank a Senator's or a Congressman's speech across the Nation....

Justice BRENNAN, with whom Justice DOUGLAS, and Justice MARSHALL, join, dissenting.

... My concern is with the narrow scope accorded the Speech or Debate Clause by today's decision.... In holding that Senator Gravel's alleged arrangement with Beacon Press to publish the Pentagon Papers is not shielded from extra-senatorial inquiry by the Speech or Debate Clause, the Court adopts what for me is a far too narrow view of the legislative function. . . . [T]he Court excludes from the sphere of protected legislative activity a function that I had supposed lay at the heart of our democratic system . . . the legislator's duty to inform the public about matters affecting the administration of government. . . . The informing function has been cited . . . as among the most important responsibilities of legislative office. Woodrow Wilson, for example, emphasized its role in preserving the separation of powers by ensuring that the administration of public policy by the Executive is understood by the legislature and electorate. . . . Congressional Government 303 (1885) . . . .

[I]t is plain that Senator Gravel's dissemination of material placed by him in the record of a congressional hearing is itself legislative activity protected by the privilege of speech or debate. Whether or not that privilege protects the publisher from prosecution or the Senator from senatorial discipline, it certainly shields the Senator from any grand jury inquiry about his part in the publication. As we held in *United States v. Johnson*, 383 U.S. 169 (1966), neither a Congressman, nor his aides, nor third parties may be made to testify concerning privileged acts or their motives. . . . Thus, if the republication of this committee record was unauthorized or even prohibited by the Senate rules, it is up to the Senate, not the Executive or Judiciary, to fashion the appropriate sanction to discipline Senator Gravel. . . .

Equally troubling in today's decision is the Court's refusal to bar grand jury inquiry into the source of documents received by the Senator and placed by him in the hearing record. The receipt of materials for use in a congressional hearing is an integral part of the preparation for that legislative act. . . . I would hold that Senator Gravel's receipt of the Pentagon Papers, including the name of the person from whom he received them, may not be the subject of inquiry by the grand jury. I would go further, however, and also exclude from grand jury inquiry any knowledge that the Senator or his aides might have concerning how the source himself first came to possess the Papers. This immunity, it seems to me, is essential to the performance of the informing function. . . .

---

1. *Scope of the Immunity.* Since an aide's immunity derives from that of a Member of Congress, the real fight in *Gravel* is over the scope of the underlying congressional privilege. First, consider the Court's summary of preexisting cases—do they define the privilege too narrowly? As the Court emphasizes, it covers only activities relating rather closely to the processing of legislation. For example, why not include contacts with the executive, which as the Court acknowledges are constant and are clearly a vital congressional responsibility? Consider this question when we review congressional oversight of the executive in the next chapter.

2. *"Privileges and Immunities" and Evidentiary Searches.* The Speech and Debate Clause does not insulate members of Congress from prosecution for fraud or corruption, but it does have implications for the gathering of evidence that would support such prosecutions. Consider, for example, the FBI's investigation of former Rep.

William J. Jefferson of New Orleans. The FBI had received information that "Jefferson . . . had sought and in some cases already accepted financial backing and or concealed payments of cash or equity interests in business ventures located in the United States, Nigeria, and Ghana in exchange for his undertaking official acts as a Congressman while promoting the business interests of himself and the targets." *United States v. Rayburn House Office Building, Room 2113, Washington, D.C. 20515*, 497 F.3d 654, 656 (D.C. Cir. 2007). On May 20, 2006, in the first FBI search ever of the legislative office of a sitting Member of Congress, over a dozen agents executed a warrant for a search of Jefferson's office, during which the agents "reviewed every paper record and copied the hard drives on all of the computers and electronic data stored on other media in" that office. They also removed two boxes of documents, as well as copies of the hard drives and electronic data. The Deputy Attorney General, however, ordered a freeze on inspection of these materials while the legality of the search was determined. When Jefferson, on Speech and Debate grounds, demanded the return of all seized materials, the District Court rejected his argument, after determining that the Congressman had failed to show any actual impediment to his legislative functions. The D.C. Circuit reversed, reasoning that "a key purpose of the [Speech and Debate nondisclosure] privilege is to prevent intrusions in the legislative process and that the legislative process is disrupted by the disclosure of legislative material, regardless of the use to which the disclosed materials are put. The bar on compelled disclosure is absolute, and there is no reason to believe that the bar does not apply in the criminal as well as the civil context." *Id.* at 660. The Court held, therefore, that Jefferson was entitled to withhold from executive inspection any documents covered by the privilege. As a consequence, the FBI had to return to him all original and copied legislative materials. FBI agents who executed the warrant were barred from disclosing the contents of any privileged materials they inspected, and could not participate in the prosecution. Jefferson was ultimately convicted on 11 corruption charges, fueled, in part, by the discovery of $90,000 in his home freezer—decidedly outside the scope of Speech and Debate protection.

3. *A Privilege to Obtain and Disseminate Information?* The major disagreement among the Justices in *Gravel* concerns whether the privilege should protect both the confidentiality of sources of congressional information and the dissemination of information by publication outside Congress. The majority rejects both; do they or the dissenters have the better of the argument?

The Court has since returned to the "output" side of the dispute—congressional publicity. In *Hutchinson v. Proxmire*, 443 U.S. 111 (1979), the Court allowed a defamation suit by Ronald Hutchinson, a behavioral scientist, against Senator William Proxmire and his legislative aide. Proxmire had initiated a "Golden Fleece of the Month Award" to publicize what he perceived to be egregious examples of wasteful governmental spending. He announced an award to the National Science Foundation and other agencies for spending almost half a million dollars to fund Hutchinson's research into aggressive behavior patterns of primates, such as the clenching of jaws when they were exposed to various aggravating stimuli. Proxmire gave a speech to the Senate describing the award; its text was then incorporated into a press release, which was sent to 275 members of the news media. Proxmire later referred to his Golden Fleece Awards in a newsletter sent to about 100,000 people. In the speech, Proxmire's peroration was:

> Dr. Hutchinson's studies should make the taxpayers as well as his monkeys grind their teeth. . . . In view of the transparent worthlessness of Hutchinson's study of jaw-grinding and biting by angry or hard-drinking monkeys, it is time we put a stop to the bite Hutchinson and the bureaucrats who fund him have been taking of the taxpayer.

Chief Justice Burger's opinion for the Court said:

> Respondents . . . contend that in the modern day very little speech or debate occurs on the floor of either House; from this they argue that press releases and newsletters are necessary for Members of Congress to communicate with other Members. . . . Respondents also argue that an essential part of the duties of a Member of Congress is to inform constituents, as well as other Members, of the issues being considered. . . . The gloss [in our cases] going beyond a strictly literal reading of the Clause has not, however, departed from the objective of protecting only legislative activities. . . . [T]he very purpose of our Constitution [was] to provide written definitions of the powers, privileges, and immunities granted rather than rely on evolving constitutional concepts identified from diverse sources as in English law. . . .

> Indeed, the precedents abundantly support the conclusion that a Member may be held liable for republishing defamatory statements originally made in either House. We perceive no basis for departing from that long-established rule. . . . We reach a similar conclusion here. A speech by Proxmire in the Senate would be wholly immune and would be available to other Members of Congress and the public in the Congressional Record. But neither the newsletters nor the press release was "essential to the deliberations of the Senate" and neither was part of the deliberative process.

> Respondents, however, argue that newsletters and press releases are essential to the functioning of the Senate; without them, they assert, a Senator cannot have a significant impact on the other Senators. We may assume that a Member's published statements exert some influence on other votes in the Congress and therefore have a relationship to the legislative and deliberative process. . . . *United States v. Johnson*, 383 U.S. 169 (1966), carefully distinguished between what is only "related to the due functioning of the legislative process," and what constitutes the legislative process entitled to immunity under the Clause: "In its narrowest scope, the Clause is a very large, albeit essential, grant of privilege. It has enabled reckless men to slander [by speech or debate] and even destroy others with impunity, but that was the conscious choice of the Framers." 408 U.S., at 513–16. We are unable to discern any "conscious choice" to grant immunity for defamatory statements scattered far and wide by mail, press, and the electronic media.

Respondents also argue that newsletters and press releases are privileged as part of the "informing function" of Congress. Advocates of a broad reading of the "informing function" sometimes tend to confuse two uses of the term "informing." In one sense, Congress informs itself collectively by way of hearings of its committees. . . . [There is] a distinction between the informing function and the legislative function . . . It is in this narrower . . . sense that this Court has employed "informing" in previous cases holding that congressional efforts to inform itself through committee hearings are part of the legislative function.

The other sense of the term . . . perceives it to be the duty of Members to tell the public about their activities. Valuable and desirable as it may be in broad terms, the transmittal of such information by individual Members in order to inform the public and other Members is not a part of the legislative function or the deliberations that make up the legislative process. As a result, transmittal of such information by press releases and newsletters is not protected by the Speech or Debate Clause.

Doe v. McMillan, 412 U.S. 306 (1973), is not to the contrary. It dealt only with reports from congressional committees, and held that Members of Congress could not be held liable for voting to publish a report. Voting and preparing committee reports are the individual and collective expressions of opinion within the legislative process. As such, they are protected by the Speech or Debate Clause. Newsletters and press releases, by contrast, are primarily means of informing those outside the legislative forum; they represent the views and will of a single Member. It does not disparage either their value or their importance to hold that they are not entitled to the protection of the Speech or Debate Clause. . . .

So why can't a Senator have a little fun? If the Court's unwillingness to extend the congressional privilege to the "informing function" seems unduly parsimonious to you, does your answer change if you consider the activities of Senator Proxmire's predecessor from Wisconsin, Joe McCarthy? Amid the "Red scare" hysteria of the 1950s, McCarthy entered American history as an "ism" for blasting careers and lives with his reckless charges that various individuals in and out of government had Communist affiliations. It was only after several years of his outrageous behavior that the Senate censured him and he faded away in alcoholic disgrace.

Does either Congress's constitutional autonomy or the Speech or Debate Clause preclude federal courts from subjecting Members of Congress to lawsuits in which citizens claim damages for violations of their constitutional rights? For many years, Congress had never created a statutory cause of action for such suits against either its own Members or federal executives. In contrast, Congress long ago subjected *state* officials to liability for actions under color of law that deprive persons of their "rights, . . . secured by the Constitution and laws." 42 U.S.C. § 1983. The Supreme

Court partly filled the gap in *Bivens v. Six Unknown Named Agents of Federal Bureau of Narcotics*, 403 U.S. 388 (1971). The victim of an arrest and search that violated the Fourth Amendment sued the responsible federal agents for damages. The Court, stating that "[h]istorically, damages have been regarded as the ordinary remedy for an invasion of personal interests in liberty," implied a cause of action for damages from the Fourth Amendment. Justice Harlan, concurring, pointed out that traditional injunctive remedies against illegal conduct are useless where a citizen not accused of any crime has been subjected to a completed constitutional violation: in such cases, "it is damages or nothing."

In *Davis v. Passman*, 442 U.S. 228 (1979), the Court extended *Bivens* to Members of Congress. In an opinion by Justice Brennan, the Court held that a cause of action for damages could be implied from the equal protection component of the Due Process Clause to allow courts to consider claims of sex discrimination in congressional staffing decisions. Dissenting opinions by Chief Justice Burger and by Justices Stewart and Powell thought that the Court's decision presented severe separation of powers issues due to its intrusion on congressional autonomy. The case has subsequently been superseded by the Congressional Accountability Act of 1996, discussed at the end of this chapter.

2. Immunities of Executive Officers from Civil Liability

In this section we consider whether senior executive officials, including the President, should be amenable to damages for their unlawful actions. The executive branch does not enjoy any explicit constitutional privilege such as those possessed by Members of Congress. Throughout this section, consider how that fact should affect the Court's analysis.

Bivens, supra, reserved the question whether federal defendants could assert qualified or absolute immunities from damages in at least some circumstances. The Court has since been busily about that task, as the following cases reveal. Note that in limning immunities for federal executive officers, the Court has had a body of law to draw on — the immunities it had implied for state officers sued under § 1983.

a. The President

Nixon v. Fitzgerald

457 U.S. 731 (1982)

Justice POWELL delivered the opinion of the Court.

The plaintiff in this lawsuit seeks relief in civil damages from a former President of the United States. The claim rests on actions allegedly taken in the former President's official capacity during his tenure in office. The issue before us is the scope of the immunity possessed by the President of the United States.

I

In January 1970 the respondent A. Ernest Fitzgerald lost his job as a management analyst with the Department of the Air Force. Fitzgerald's dismissal occurred in the context of a departmental reorganization and reduction in force, in which his job was eliminated. In announcing the reorganization, the Air Force characterized the action as taken to promote economy and efficiency in the Armed Forces. . . . Fitzgerald had attained national prominence approximately one year earlier, . . . [when he] appeared before the Subcommittee on Economy in Government of the Joint Economic Committee of . . . Congress. To the evident embarrassment of his superiors in the Department of Defense, Fitzgerald testified that cost-overruns on the C-5A transport plane could approximate $2 billion. . . .

Concerned that Fitzgerald might have suffered retaliation for his congressional testimony, the Subcommittee . . . convened public hearings on Fitzgerald's dismissal. . . . At a news conference on December 8, 1969, President Richard Nixon was queried about Fitzgerald's impending separation from Government service. The President responded by promising to look into the matter. Shortly after the news conference the petitioner asked White House Chief of Staff H. R. Haldeman to arrange for Fitzgerald's assignment to another job within the administration. . . . Fitzgerald's proposed reassignment encountered resistance within the administration. In an internal memorandum . . . White House aide Alexander Butterfield reported to Haldeman that "Fitzgerald is no doubt a top-notch cost expert, but he must be given very low marks in loyalty; and after all, loyalty is the name of the game." Butterfield therefore recommended that "[w]e should let him bleed, for a while at least." There is no evidence of White House efforts to reemploy Fitzgerald subsequent to the Butterfield memorandum. . . .

At a news conference on January 31, 1973, the President [assumed] personal responsibility for Fitzgerald's dismissal: "I was totally aware that Mr. Fitzgerald would be fired or discharged or asked to resign. . . . No, this was not a case of some person down the line deciding he should go. It was a decision that was submitted to me. I made it and I stick by it." A day later, however, the White House press office issued a retraction of the President's statement. According to a press spokesman, the President had confused Fitzgerald with another former executive employee. On behalf of the President, the spokesman asserted that Mr. Nixon had not had "put before him the decision regarding Mr. Fitzgerald." . . .

III

A

This Court consistently has recognized that government officials are entitled to some form of immunity from suits for civil damages. In *Spalding v. Vilas*, 161 U.S. 483 (1896), the Court considered the immunity available to the Postmaster General in a [tort] suit for damages based upon his official acts. Drawing upon principles of immunity developed in English cases at common law, the Court concluded that "[t]he interests of the people" required a grant of absolute immunity to public officers.

In the absence of immunity, the Court reasoned, executive officials would hesitate to exercise their discretion . . . even when the public interest required bold and unhesitating action. Considerations of "public policy and convenience" therefore compelled a judicial recognition of immunity from suits arising from official acts. . . .

Decisions subsequent to *Spalding* have extended the defense of immunity to actions besides those at common law. . . . In *Tenney v. Brandhove*, 341 U.S. 367 (1951), the Court considered whether the passage of 42 U.S.C. § 1983, which made no express provision for immunity for any official, had abrogated the privilege accorded to state legislators at common law. *Tenney* held that it had not. . . . Similarly, the decision in *Pierson v. Ray*, 386 U.S. 547 (1967), involving a § 1983 suit against a state judge, recognized the continued validity of the absolute immunity of judges for acts within the judicial role. . . . The Court in *Pierson* also held that police officers are entitled to a qualified immunity protecting them from suit when their official acts are performed in "good faith."

In *Scheuer v. Rhodes*, 416 U.S. 232 (1974), the Court considered the immunity available to state executive officials in a § 1983 suit alleging the violation of constitutional rights. In that case we rejected the officials' claim to absolute immunity under the doctrine of *Spalding v. Vilas*, finding instead that state executive officials possessed a "good faith" immunity from § 1983 suits alleging constitutional violations. . . . *Scheuer* established a two-tiered division of immunity defenses in § 1983 suits. To most executive officers *Scheuer* accorded qualified immunity. For them the scope of the defense varied in proportion to the nature of their official functions and the range of decisions that conceivably might be taken in "good faith." This "functional" approach also defined a second tier, however, at which the especially sensitive duties of certain officials—notably judges and prosecutors—required the continued recognition of absolute immunity. *See, e.g., Imbler v. Pachtman*, 424 U.S. 409 (1976) (state prosecutors possess absolute immunity with respect to the initiation and pursuit of prosecutions); *Stump v. Sparkman*, 435 U.S. 349 (1978) (state judge possesses absolute immunity for all judicial acts).

This approach was reviewed in detail in *Butz v. Economou*, 438 U.S. 478 (1978), when we considered for the first time the kind of immunity possessed by *federal* executive officials who are sued for constitutional violations. In *Butz* the Court rejected an argument, based on decisions involving federal officials charged with common-law torts, that all high federal officials have a right to absolute immunity from constitutional damages actions. [W]e held that federal officials generally have the same qualified immunity possessed by state officials in cases under § 1983. . . . In *Butz* itself we upheld a claim of absolute immunity for administrative officials engaged in functions analogous to those of judges and prosecutors. . . .

B

Our decisions concerning the immunity of government officials from civil damages liability have been guided by the Constitution, federal statutes, and history. Additionally, at least in the absence of explicit constitutional or congressional guidance, our immunity decisions have been informed by the common law. This Court necessarily also has weighed concerns of public policy, especially as illuminated by our history and the structure of our government. . . . Because the Presidency did not exist through most of the development of common law, any historical analysis must draw its evidence primarily from our constitutional heritage and structure. Historical inquiry thus merges almost at its inception with the kind of "public policy" analysis appropriately undertaken by a federal court. This inquiry involves policies and principles that may be considered implicit in the nature of the President's office in a system structured to achieve effective government under a constitutionally mandated separation of powers.

IV

Here a former President asserts his immunity from civil damages claims of two kinds. He stands named as a defendant in a direct action under the Constitution and in two statutory actions under federal laws of general applicability. In neither case has Congress taken express legislative action to subject the President to civil liability for his official acts. Applying the principles of our cases to claims of this kind, we hold that petitioner, as a former President of the United States, is entitled to absolute immunity from damages liability predicated on his official acts. We consider this immunity a functionally mandated incident of the President's unique office, rooted in the constitutional tradition of the separation of powers and supported by our history. Justice Story's analysis remains persuasive:

> "There are . . . incidental powers, belonging to the executive department, which are necessarily implied from the nature of the functions, which are confided to it. Among these, must necessarily be included the power to perform them. . . . The president cannot, therefore, be liable to arrest, imprisonment, or detention, while he is in the discharge of the duties of his office; and for this purpose his person must be deemed, in civil cases at least, to possess an official inviolability." 3 J. Story, Commentaries on the Constitution of the United States § 1563, pp. 418–19 (1st ed. 1833).

A

The President occupies a unique position in the constitutional scheme. Article II, § 1, of the Constitution provides that "[t]he executive Power shall be vested in a President of the United States. . . ." This grant of authority establishes the President as the chief constitutional officer of the Executive Branch, entrusted with supervisory and policy responsibilities of utmost discretion and sensitivity. These include the enforcement of federal law; . . . the conduct of foreign affairs — a realm in which the Court has recognized that "[i]t would be intolerable that courts, without the relevant information, should review and perhaps nullify actions of the Executive taken on information properly held secret"; and management of the Executive Branch — a task for which "imperative reasons requir[e] an unrestricted power [in the President] to remove the most important of his subordinates in their most important duties."

In arguing that the President is entitled only to qualified immunity, the respondent relies on cases in which we have recognized immunity of this scope for governors and cabinet officers. We find these cases to be inapposite. The President's unique status under the Constitution distinguishes him from other executive officials. Because of the singular importance of the President's duties, diversion of his energies by concern with private lawsuits would raise unique risks to the effective functioning of government. As is the case with prosecutors and judges — for whom absolute immunity now is established — a President must concern himself with matters likely to "arouse the most intense feelings." Yet, as our decisions have recognized, it is in precisely such cases that there exists the greatest public interest in providing an official "the maximum ability to deal fearlessly and impartially with" the duties of his office. This concern is compelling where the officeholder must make the most sensitive and far-reaching decisions entrusted to any official under our constitutional system. Nor can the sheer prominence of the President's office be ignored. In view of the visibility of his office and the effect of his actions on countless people, the President would be an easily identifiable target for suits for civil damages. Cognizance of this personal vulnerability frequently could distract a President from his public duties, to the detriment of not only the President and his office but also the Nation that the Presidency was designed to serve.

B

Courts traditionally have recognized the President's constitutional responsibilities and status as factors counseling judicial deference and restraint. For example, while courts generally have looked to the common law to determine the scope of an official's evidentiary privilege, we have recognized that the Presidential privilege is "rooted in the separation of powers under the Constitution." It is settled law that the separation-of-powers doctrine does not bar every exercise of jurisdiction over the President of the United States. But our cases also have established that a court, before exercising jurisdiction, must balance the constitutional weight of the interest to be served against the dangers of intrusion on the authority and functions of the Executive Branch. When judicial action is needed to serve broad public interests — as when the Court acts, not in derogation of the separation of powers, but to maintain their proper balance, cf. *Youngstown Sheet & Tube Co. v. Sawyer*, or to vindicate the public interest in an ongoing criminal prosecution, see *United States v. Nixon* — the exercise of jurisdiction has been held warranted. In the case of this merely private suit for damages based on a President's official acts, we hold it is not.

C

In defining the scope of an official's absolute privilege, this Court has recognized that the sphere of protected action must be related closely to the immunity's justifying purposes. Frequently our decisions have held that an official's absolute immunity should extend only to acts in performance of particular functions of his office. But the Court also has refused to draw functional lines finer than history and reason would support. In view of the special nature of the President's constitutional office and functions, we think it appropriate to recognize absolute Presidential immunity from damages liability for acts within the "outer perimeter" of his official responsibility.

Under the Constitution and laws of the United States the President has discretionary responsibilities in a broad variety of areas, many of them highly sensitive. In many cases it would be difficult to determine which of the President's innumerable "functions" encompassed a particular action. In this case, for example, respondent argues that he was dismissed in retaliation for his testimony to Congress — a violation of 5 U.S.C. § 7211 and 18 U.S.C. § 1505. The Air Force, however, has claimed that the underlying reorganization was undertaken to promote efficiency. Assuming that petitioner Nixon ordered the reorganization in which respondent lost his job, an inquiry into the President's motives could not be avoided under the kind of "functional" theory asserted both by respondent and the dissent. Inquiries of this kind could be highly intrusive.

Here respondent argues that petitioner Nixon would have acted outside the outer perimeter of his duties by ordering the discharge of an employee who was lawfully entitled to retain his job in the absence of "such cause as will promote the efficiency of the service." 5 U.S.C. § 7512(a). . . . [He argues that] no federal official could, within the outer perimeter of his duties of office, cause Fitzgerald to be dismissed without satisfying this standard in prescribed statutory proceedings. This construction would subject the President to trial on virtually every allegation that an action was unlawful, or was taken for a forbidden purpose. Adoption of this construction thus would deprive absolute immunity of its intended effect. It clearly is within the President's constitutional and statutory authority to prescribe the manner in which the Secretary will conduct the business of the Air Force. Because this [includes] the authority to prescribe reorganizations and reductions in force, we conclude that petitioner's alleged wrongful acts lay well within the outer perimeter of his authority.

V

A rule of absolute immunity for the President will not leave the Nation without sufficient protection against misconduct on the part of the Chief Executive. There remains the constitutional remedy of impeachment. In addition, there are formal and informal checks on Presidential action that do not apply with equal force to other executive officials. The President is subjected to constant scrutiny by the press. Vigilant oversight by Congress also may serve to deter Presidential abuses of office, as well as to make credible the threat of impeachment. Other incentives to avoid misconduct may include a desire to earn reelection, the need to maintain prestige as an element of Presidential influence, and a President's traditional concern for his historical stature. The existence of alternative remedies and deterrents establishes that absolute immunity will not place the President "above the law." For the President, as for judges and prosecutors, absolute immunity merely precludes a particular private remedy for alleged misconduct in order to advance compelling public ends. . . .

Chief Justice BURGER, concurring.

I join the Court's opinion, but I write separately to underscore that the Presidential immunity . . . is mandated by the constitutional doctrine of separation of powers. . . . Absolute immunity for a President . . . is either to be found in the constitutional separation of powers or it does not exist. The Court today holds that the Constitution mandates such immunity and I agree.

Justice WHITE, with whom Justice BRENNAN, Justice MARSHALL, and Justice BLACKMUN join, dissenting.

. . . The Court now [holds that a] President, acting within the outer boundaries of what Presidents normally do, may, without liability, deliberately cause serious injury to any number of citizens even though he knows his conduct violates a statute or tramples on the constitutional rights of those who are injured. Even if the President in this case ordered Fitzgerald fired by means of a trumped-up reduction in force, knowing that such a discharge was contrary to the civil service laws, he would be absolutely immune from suit. . . . He would be immune regardless of the damage he inflicts, regardless of how violative of the statute and of the Constitution he knew his conduct to be, and regardless of his purpose. . . .

We have not taken such a scatter-gun approach in other cases. *Butz* held that absolute immunity did not attach to the office held by a member of the President's Cabinet but only to those specific functions performed by that officer for which absolute immunity is clearly essential. Members of Congress are absolutely immune under the Speech or Debate Clause of the Constitution, but the immunity extends only to their legislative acts. . . . Judges are absolutely immune from liability for damages, but only when performing a judicial function, and even then they are subject to criminal liability. The absolute immunity of prosecutors is likewise limited to the prosecutorial function. A prosecutor who directs that an investigation be carried out in a way that is patently illegal is not immune. . . . The Court . . . makes no effort to distinguish categories of Presidential conduct that should be absolutely immune from other categories of conduct that should not qualify for that level of immunity.

I

. . . [This decision] has all the earmarks of a constitutional pronouncement — absolute immunity for the President's office is mandated by the Constitution. Although the Court appears to disclaim this [in a footnote], it is difficult to read the opinion coherently as standing for any narrower proposition: Attempts to subject the President to liability either by Congress through a statutory action or by the courts through a *Bivens* proceeding would violate the separation of powers. Such a generalized absolute immunity cannot be sustained when examined in the traditional manner and in light of the traditional judicial sources. . . .

A

The Speech or Debate Clause, Art. I, § 6, guarantees absolute immunity to Members of Congress; nowhere, however, does the Constitution directly address the issue of Presidential immunity. . . . The debate at the Convention on whether or not the

President should be impeachable did touch on the potential dangers of subjecting the President to the control of another branch, the Legislature . . . . [T]he Convention debate did not focus on wrongs the President might commit against individuals, but rather on whether there should be a method of holding him accountable for what might be termed wrongs against the state. Thus, examples of the abuses that concerned delegates were betrayal, oppression, and bribery; the delegates feared that the alternative to an impeachment mechanism would be "tumults & insurrections" by the people in response to such abuses. The only conclusions that can be drawn from this debate are that the independence of the Executive was not understood to require a total lack of accountability to the other branches and that there was no general desire to insulate the President from the consequences of his improper acts . . . .

[Another] piece of historical evidence cited by petitioner is an exchange at the first meeting of the Senate, involving Vice President Adams and Senators Ellsworth and Maclay. . . . Senator Ellsworth and Vice President Adams defended the proposition that "the President, personally, was not subject to any process whatever; could have no action, whatever, brought against him; was above the power of all judges, justices, &c. For [that] would . . . put it in the power of a common justice to exercise any authority over him, and stop the whole machine of government." In their view the impeachment process was the exclusive form of process available against the President. Senator Maclay ardently opposed this view and put the case of a President committing "murder in the street." In his view, in such a case . . . there was "loyal justice." . . . Again, nothing more can be concluded from this than that the proper scope of Presidential accountability, including the question whether the President should be subject to judicial process, was no clearer then than it is now. . . .

From the history discussed above, . . . all that can be concluded is that absolute immunity from civil liability for the President finds no support in constitutional text or history, or in the explanations of the earliest commentators. This is too weak a ground to support a declaration by this Court that the President is absolutely immune from civil liability. . . .

B

No bright line can be drawn between arguments for absolute immunity based on the constitutional principle of separation of powers and arguments based on what the Court refers to as "public policy." . . . While absolute immunity might maximize executive efficiency and therefore be a worthwhile policy, lack of such immunity may not so disrupt the functioning of the Presidency as to violate the separation-of-powers doctrine. . . . The President has been held to be subject to judicial process at least since 1807. *United States v. Burr.* . . . If there is a separation-of-powers problem here, it must be found in the nature of the *remedy* and not in the *process* involved. . . . [T]he President, were he subject to civil liability, could be held liable only for an action that he knew, or as an objective matter should have known, was illegal and a clear abuse of his authority and power. In such circumstances, the question that must be answered is who should bear the cost of the resulting injury — the wrongdoer or the victim. . . .

II

handwritten note in margin: Interesting comparison made

. . . The scope of immunity is determined by function, not office. The wholesale claim that the President is entitled to absolute immunity in all of his actions stands on no firmer ground than did the claim that all Presidential communications are entitled to an absolute privilege, which was rejected in favor of a functional analysis, by a unanimous Court in *United States v. Nixon* [*infra*]. Therefore, whatever may be true of the necessity of such a broad immunity in certain areas of executive responsibility, the only question that must be answered here is whether the dismissal of employees falls within a constitutionally assigned executive function, the performance of which would be substantially impaired by the possibility of a private action for damages. I believe it does not.

Respondent has so far proceeded in this action on the basis of three separate causes of action: two federal statutes — 5 U.S.C. § 7211 and 18 U.S.C. § 1505 — and the First Amendment. . . . The first of these statutes, 5 U.S.C. § 7211, states that "[t]he right of employees . . . to . . . furnish information to either House of Congress, or to a committee or Member thereof, may not be interfered with or denied." The second, 18 U.S.C. § 1505, makes it a crime to obstruct congressional testimony. It does not take much insight to see that at least one purpose of these statutes is to assure congressional access to information in the possession of the Executive Branch, which Congress believes it requires in order to carry out its responsibilities. Insofar as these statutes implicate a separation-of-powers argument, I would think it to be just the opposite of that suggested by petitioner and accepted by the majority. In enacting these statutes, Congress sought to preserve its own constitutionally mandated functions in the face of a recalcitrant Executive. . . . It is no response to this to say that such a cause of action would disrupt the President in the furtherance of his responsibilities. That approach . . . assumes that Presidential functions are to be valued over congressional functions. . . .

Absolute immunity is appropriate when the threat of liability may bias the decisionmaker in ways that are adverse to the public interest. But as the various regulations and statutes protecting civil servants from arbitrary executive action illustrate, this is an area in which the public interest is demonstrably on the side of encouraging less "vigor" and more "caution" on the part of decisionmakers. . . . Absolute immunity would be nothing more than a judicial declaration of policy that directly contradicts the policy of protecting civil servants reflected in the statutes and regulations. . . .

Justice BLACKMUN, with whom Justice BRENNAN and Justice MARSHALL join, dissenting.

I join Justice White's dissent. . . . [N]o man, not even the President of the United States, is absolutely and fully above the law. . . . Nor can I understand the Court's holding that the absolute immunity of the President is compelled by separation-of-powers concerns, when the Court at the same time expressly leaves open the possibility that the President nevertheless may be fully subject to congressionally created forms of liability. These two concepts, it seems to me, cannot coexist. . . .

———

1. *Should (Can?) Congress Reverse* Fitzgerald*?* The majority in *Nixon v. Fitzgerald* reserves the question whether Congress could create a statutory damages remedy against the President. What do you think? What should be the major provisions of such a statute? Regarding congressional power, consider Chief Justice Burger's statement that "[a]bsolute immunity for a President . . . is either to be found in the constitutional separation of powers or it does not exist. The Court today holds that the Constitution mandates such immunity and I agree."

Constitutional history is pertinent to answering this question. The majority responded to Justice White's comments about the history in a footnote:

> [T]here is historical evidence from which it may be inferred that the Framers assumed the President's immunity from damages liability. At the Constitutional Convention several delegates expressed concern that subjecting the President even to impeachment would impair his capacity to perform his duties of office. *See 2 M. Farrand, Records of the Federal Convention of 1787,* p. 64 (1911) (remarks of Gouverneur Morris); *id.*, at 66 (remarks of Charles Pinckney). The delegates of course did agree to an Impeachment Clause. But nothing in their debates suggests an expectation that the President would be subjected to the distraction of suits by disappointed private citizens. And Senator Maclay has recorded the views of Senator Ellsworth and Vice President John Adams—both delegates to the Convention—that "the President, personally, was not the subject to any process whatever. . . . For [that] would . . . put it in the power of a common justice to exercise any authority over him and stop the whole machine of Government." Journal of William Maclay 167 (E. Maclay ed., 1890) . . . . Thomas Jefferson also argued that the President was not intended to be subject to judicial process. When Chief Justice Marshall held in *United States v. Burr*, 25 F. Cas. 30 (No. 14,692d) (CC Va.1807), that a subpoena duces tecum can be issued to a President, Jefferson protested strongly:" . . . The leading principle of our Constitution is the independence of the Legislature, executive and judiciary of each other . . . But would the executive be independent of the judiciary, if he were subject to the *commands* of the latter, & to imprisonment for disobedience; if the several courts could bandy him from pillar to post, keep him constantly trudging from north to south & east to west, and withdraw him entirely from his constitutional duties?. . . ." 10 The Works of Thomas Jefferson 404 n. (P. Ford ed., 1905).

Does this history compel an immunity for the President?

2. *A Remand to Congress?* As an alternative decision, the *Fitzgerald* Court could have declined to imply a cause of action against the President under *Bivens*, noting that Congress had legislated to forbid obstructing congressional testimony, but had provided no damages remedy, suggesting that it had decided to eschew one. Should the Court have held instead that the *separation of powers* precludes judicial implication of a *Bivens*-style damages remedy against the President, given the textual

commitment to Congress of power to discipline Presidents? *See* Stephen L. Carter, *The Political Aspects of Judicial Power: Some Notes on the Presidential Immunity Decision*, 131 U. PA. L. REV. 1341, 1366–68 (1983):

> The balance of powers among the three branches of the federal government is a delicate construct, and if any one of the branches is empowered to create new checks on the others that branch will be in the position to upset the very balance that it purports to protect. . . . That is why the federal courts cannot create a cause of action for damages running against a President. . . .

3. *Don't Get Mad, Get Even.* The *Fitzgerald* Court remarked (in a footnote) on the paucity of pre-*Bivens* suits against the President for damages. Which way does that cut? The best-known precedent is *Livingston v. Jefferson*, 15 F. Cas. 660 (No. 8,411) (C.C. Va. 1811). An old enemy of Jefferson's, who claimed land in New Orleans, sued the former President for damages for having secured possession for the United States by sending in the U.S. Marshal. The suit was dismissed by the ubiquitous John Marshall (pursuant to his circuit duties) because it was not brought where the land was. The story is engagingly told by Ronan E. Degnan, Livingston v. Jefferson — *A Freestanding Footnote*, 75 CALIF. L. REV. 115 (1987).

4. *Aiding Statutory Goals.* Under a functional analysis, what weight should be given to congressional attempts to ensure that the executive branch operates in compliance with law? Fitzgerald was a prominent example of a "whistleblower," someone who exposes illegality or at least mismanagement in government programs. Congress has since expanded protection for whistleblowers, forbidding reprisals for disclosures of information reasonably believed to evidence a violation of law or regulation, mismanagement, and the like. 5 U.S.C. § 2302(b)(8). *See* Robert Vaughn, *Statutory Protection of Whistleblowers in the Federal Executive Branch*, 1982 U. ILL. L. REV. 615. Alas, there are signs that employees still decline to reveal waste and illegality out of fear of reprisal. Congressional Research Service, *The Whistleblower Protection Act: An Overview*, available at http://www.fas.org/sgp/crs/natsec/RL33918.pdf. If the Court were informed of all this, should it imply a damages remedy to help Congress achieve its manifest aims?

What does *Fitzgerald* imply about suits against a President for conduct unrelated to his duties, or conduct that occurred before he took office? The following case addresses the latter issue:

Clinton v. Jones

520 U.S. 681 (1997)

Justice STEVENS delivered the opinion of the Court.

This case raises a constitutional and a prudential question concerning the Office of the President of the United States. Respondent, a private citizen, seeks to recover damages from the current occupant of that office based on actions allegedly taken before his term began. The President submits that in all but the most exceptional cases the Constitution requires federal courts to defer such litigation until his term ends and that, in any event, respect for the office warrants such a stay. Despite the force of the arguments supporting the President's submissions, we conclude that they must be rejected.

I

Petitioner, William Jefferson Clinton, was elected to the Presidency in 1992, and re-elected in 1996. His term of office expires on January 20, 2001. In 1991 he was the Governor of the State of Arkansas. Respondent, Paula Corbin Jones, . . . was an employee of the Arkansas Industrial Development Commission. On May 6, 1994, she commenced this action in the United States District Court for the Eastern District of Arkansas by filing a complaint naming petitioner and Danny Ferguson, a former Arkansas State Police officer, as defendants. The complaint alleges two federal claims, and two state-law claims over which the federal court has jurisdiction because of the diverse citizenship of the parties. As the case comes to us, we are required to assume the truth of the detailed—but as yet untested—factual allegations in the complaint.

Those allegations principally describe events that are said to have occurred on the afternoon of May 8, 1991, during an official conference held at the Excelsior Hotel in Little Rock, Arkansas. The Governor delivered a speech at the conference; respondent—working as a state employee—staffed the registration desk. She alleges that Ferguson persuaded her to leave her desk and to visit the Governor in a business suite at the hotel, where he made "abhorrent" sexual advances that she vehemently rejected. She further claims that her superiors at work subsequently dealt with her in a hostile and rude manner, and changed her duties to punish her for rejecting those advances. Finally, she alleges that after petitioner was elected President, Ferguson defamed her by making a statement to a reporter that implied she had accepted petitioner's alleged overtures, and that various persons authorized to speak for the President publicly branded her a liar by denying that the incident had occurred.

Respondent seeks actual damages of $75,000 and punitive damages of $100,000. Her complaint contains four counts. The first charges that petitioner, acting under color of state law, deprived her of rights protected by the Constitution, in violation of 42 U.S.C. § 1983. The second charges that petitioner and Ferguson engaged in a conspiracy to violate her federal rights, also actionable under federal law. 42 U.S.C. § 1985. The third is a state common law claim for intentional infliction of emotional distress, grounded primarily on the incident at the hotel. The fourth count, also based on state law, is for defamation, embracing both the comments allegedly made to the press by Ferguson and the statements of petitioner's agents. Inasmuch as the legal sufficiency of the claims has not yet been challenged, we assume, without deciding, that each of the four counts states a cause of action as a matter of law. With the exception of the last charge, which arguably may involve conduct within the outer perimeter of the President's official responsibilities, it is perfectly clear that the alleged misconduct of petitioner was unrelated to any of his official duties as President of the United States and, indeed, occurred before he was elected to that office.

II

In response to the complaint, petitioner promptly advised the District Court that he intended to file a motion to dismiss on grounds of Presidential immunity, and requested the court to defer all other pleadings and motions until after the immunity issue was resolved. Relying on our cases holding that immunity questions should be decided at the earliest possible stage of the litigation, our recognition of the "'singular importance of the President's duties,'" (quoting *Nixon v. Fitzgerald*), and the fact that the question did not require any analysis of the allegations of the complaint, the court granted the request. Petitioner thereupon filed a motion "to dismiss . . . without prejudice and to toll any statutes of limitation [that may be applicable] until he is no longer President, at which time the plaintiff may refile the instant suit." The District Judge denied the motion to dismiss on immunity grounds and ruled that discovery in the case could go forward, but ordered any trial stayed until the end of petitioner's Presidency. . . . [S]he concluded that the public interest in avoiding litigation that might hamper the President in conducting the duties of his office outweighed any demonstrated need for an immediate trial. Both parties appealed. A divided panel of the Court of Appeals affirmed the denial of the motion to dismiss, but because it regarded the order postponing the trial until the President leaves office as the "functional equivalent" of a grant of temporary immunity, it reversed that order. . . .

III

. . . . The representations made on behalf of the Executive Branch as to the potential impact of the precedent established by the Court of Appeals merit our respectful and deliberate consideration. . . . [We] identify two important constitutional issues . . . that we need not address today. First, because the claim of immunity is asserted in a federal court and relies heavily on the doctrine of separation of powers that restrains each of the three branches of the Federal Government from encroaching on the domain of the other two, it is not necessary to consider or decide whether a comparable claim might succeed in a state tribunal. If this case were being heard in a state forum, instead of advancing a separation-of-powers argument, petitioner would presumably rely on federalism and comity concerns,[13] as well as the interest in protecting federal officials from possible local prejudice that underlies the authority to remove certain cases brought against federal officers from a state to a federal court. Whether those concerns would present a more compelling case for immunity is a question that is not before us. Second, our decision rejecting the immunity claim

---

13. Because the Supremacy Clause makes federal law "the supreme Law of the Land," Art. VI, cl. 2, any direct control by a state court over the President, who has principal responsibility to ensure that those laws are "faithfully executed," Art. II, § 3, may implicate concerns that are quite different from the interbranch separation-of-powers questions addressed here. Cf., e. g., Hancock v. Train, 426 U. S. 167, 178–179 (1976); Mayo v. United States, 319 U. S. 441, 445 (1943). See L. Tribe, American Constitutional Law 513 (2d ed. 1988) ("[A]bsent explicit congressional consent no state may command federal officials . . . to take action in derogation of their . . . federal responsibilities").

and allowing the case to proceed does not require us to confront the question whether a court may compel the attendance of the President at any specific time or place. We assume that the testimony of the President, both for discovery and for use at trial, may be taken at the White House at a time that will accommodate his busy schedule, and that, if a trial is held, there would be no necessity for the President to attend in person, though he could elect to do so.

IV

Petitioner's principal submission—that "in all but the most exceptional cases," the Constitution affords the President temporary immunity from civil damages litigation arising out of events that occurred before he took office—cannot be sustained on the basis of precedent. Only three sitting Presidents have been defendants in civil litigation involving their actions prior to taking office. Complaints against Theodore Roosevelt and Harry Truman had been dismissed before they took office; the dismissals were affirmed after their respective inaugurations. Two companion cases arising out of an automobile accident were filed against John F. Kennedy in 1960 during the Presidential campaign. . . . The matter was settled out of court. Thus, none of those cases sheds any light on the constitutional issue before us.

The principal rationale for affording certain public servants immunity from suits for money damages arising out of their official acts is inapplicable to unofficial conduct. In cases involving prosecutors, legislators, and judges we have repeatedly explained that the immunity serves the public interest in enabling such officials to perform their designated functions effectively without fear that a particular decision may give rise to personal liability. . . . That rationale provided the principal basis for our holding that a former President of the United States was "entitled to absolute immunity from damages liability predicated on his official acts," *Fitzgerald*. . . . Petitioner's effort to construct an immunity from suit for unofficial acts grounded purely in the identity of his office is unsupported by precedent.

V

We are also unpersuaded by the evidence from the historical record to which petitioner has called our attention. He points to a comment by Thomas Jefferson protesting the subpoena duces tecum Chief Justice Marshall directed to him in the Burr trial, a statement in the diaries kept by Senator William Maclay of the first Senate debates, in which then-Vice President John Adams and Senator Oliver Ellsworth are recorded as having said that "the President personally [is] not . . . subject to any process whatever," lest it be "put . . . in the power of a common Justice to exercise any Authority over him and Stop the Whole Machine of Government," and to a quotation from Justice Story's Commentaries on the Constitution. None of these sources sheds much light on the question at hand.

Respondent, in turn, has called our attention to conflicting historical evidence. Speaking in favor of the Constitution's adoption at the Pennsylvania Convention, James Wilson—who had participated in the Philadelphia Convention at which the document was drafted — explained that, although the President "is placed [on] high," "not a single privilege is annexed to his character; far from being above the laws, he is amenable to them in his private character as a citizen, and in his public character by impeachment." 2 J. Elliot, Debates on the Federal Constitution 480 (2d ed. 1863). This description is consistent with both the doctrine of Presidential immunity as set forth in *Fitzgerald* and rejection of the immunity claim in this case. With respect to acts taken in his "public character" — that is, official acts — the President may be disciplined principally by impeachment, not by private lawsuits for damages. But he is otherwise subject to the laws for his purely private acts . . . .

VI

Petitioner's strongest argument supporting his immunity claim is based on the text and structure of the Constitution. He does not contend that the occupant of the Office of the President is "above the law," in the sense that his conduct is entirely immune from judicial scrutiny. The President argues merely for a postponement of the judicial proceedings that will determine whether he violated any law. His argument is grounded in the character of the office that was created by Article II of the Constitution, and relies on separation-of-powers principles that have structured our constitutional arrangement since the founding.

As a starting premise, petitioner contends that he occupies a unique office with powers and responsibilities so vast and important that the public interest demands that he devote his undivided time and attention to his public duties. He submits that — given the nature of the office — the doctrine of separation of powers places limits on the authority of the Federal Judiciary to interfere with the Executive Branch that would be transgressed by allowing this action to proceed.

We have no dispute with the initial premise of the argument. Former Presidents, from George Washington to George Bush, have consistently endorsed petitioner's characterization of the office. After serving his term, Lyndon Johnson observed: "Of all the 1,886 nights I was President, there were not many when I got to sleep before 1 or 2 a.m., and there were few mornings when I didn't wake up by 6 or 6:30." In 1967, the Twenty-fifth Amendment to the Constitution was adopted to ensure continuity in the performance of the powers and duties of the office; one of the sponsors of that Amendment stressed the importance of providing that "at all times" there be a President "who has complete control and will be able to perform" those duties. . . . We have, in short, long recognized the "unique position in the constitutional scheme" that this office occupies. Thus, while we suspect that even in our modern era there remains some truth to Chief Justice Marshall's suggestion that the duties of the Presidency are not entirely "unremitting," we accept the initial premise of the Executive's argument.

It does not follow, however, that separation-of-powers principles would be violated by allowing this action to proceed. . . . Rather than arguing that the decision of the case will produce either an aggrandizement of judicial power or a narrowing of executive power, petitioner contends that — as a byproduct of an otherwise traditional exercise of judicial power—burdens will be placed on the President that will hamper the performance of his official duties. We have recognized that "[e]ven when a branch does not arrogate power to itself . . . the separation-of-powers doctrine requires that a branch not impair another in the performance of its constitutional duties." *Loving v. United States*, 517 U.S. 748, 757 (1996). As a factual matter, petitioner contends that this particular case—as well as the potential additional litigation that an affirmance of the Court of Appeals judgment might spawn—may impose an unacceptable burden on the President's time and energy, and thereby impair the effective performance of his office.

Petitioner's predictive judgment finds little support in either history or the relatively narrow compass of the issues raised in this particular case. As we have already noted, in the more than 200-year history of the Republic, only three sitting Presidents have been subjected to suits for their private actions. If the past is any indicator, it seems unlikely that a deluge of such litigation will ever engulf the Presidency. As for the case at hand, if properly managed by the District Court, it appears to us highly unlikely to occupy any substantial amount of petitioner's time.

Of greater significance, petitioner errs by presuming that interactions between the Judicial Branch and the Executive, even quite burdensome interactions, necessarily rise to the level of constitutionally forbidden impairment of the Executive's ability to perform its constitutionally mandated functions . . . . Two long-settled propositions, first announced by Chief Justice Marshall, support that conclusion.

First, we have long held that when the President takes official action, the Court has the authority to determine whether he has acted within the law. Perhaps the most dramatic example of such a case is our holding that President Truman exceeded his constitutional authority when he issued an order directing the Secretary of Commerce to take possession of and operate most of the Nation's steel mills in order to avert a national catastrophe. *Youngstown*. Despite the serious impact of that decision on the ability of the Executive Branch to accomplish its assigned mission, and the substantial time that the President must necessarily have devoted to the matter as a result of judicial involvement, we exercised our Article III jurisdiction to decide whether his official conduct conformed to the law. Our holding was an application of the principle established in *Marbury*, that "[i]t is emphatically the province and duty of the judicial department to say what the law is."

Second, it is also settled that the President is subject to judicial process in appropriate circumstances. Although Thomas Jefferson apparently thought otherwise, Chief Justice Marshall, when presiding in the treason trial of Aaron Burr, ruled that a subpoena duces tecum could be directed to the President. *United States v. Burr*. We unequivocally and emphatically endorsed Marshall's position when we held that President Nixon was obligated to comply with a subpoena commanding him to produce certain tape recordings of his conversations with his aides. *United States v. Nixon*. As we explained, "neither the doctrine of separation of powers, nor the need for confidentiality of high-level communications, without more, can sustain an absolute, unqualified Presidential privilege of immunity from judicial process under all circumstances."

Sitting Presidents have responded to court orders to provide testimony and other information with sufficient frequency that such interactions between the Judicial and Executive Branches can scarcely be thought a novelty. President Monroe responded to written interrogatories, President Nixon — as noted above — produced tapes in response to a subpoena duces tecum, President Ford complied with an order to give a deposition in a criminal trial, and President Clinton has twice given videotaped testimony in criminal proceedings. Moreover, sitting Presidents have also voluntarily complied with judicial requests for testimony. President Grant gave a lengthy deposition in a criminal case under such circumstances, and President Carter similarly gave videotaped testimony for use at a criminal trial.

In sum, "[i]t is settled law that the separation-of-powers doctrine does not bar every exercise of jurisdiction over the President of the United States." *Fitzgerald.* If the Judiciary may severely burden the Executive Branch by reviewing the legality of the President's official conduct, and if it may direct appropriate process to the President himself, it must follow that the federal courts have power to determine the legality of his unofficial conduct. The burden on the President's time and energy that is a mere byproduct of such review surely cannot be considered as onerous as the direct burden imposed by judicial review and the occasional invalidation of his official actions. We therefore hold that the doctrine of separation of powers does not require federal courts to stay all private actions against the President until he leaves office.

The reasons for rejecting such a categorical rule apply as well to a rule that would require a stay "in all but the most exceptional cases." Indeed, if the Framers of the Constitution had thought it necessary to protect the President from the burdens of private litigation, we think it far more likely that they would have adopted a categorical rule than a rule that required the President to litigate the question whether a specific case belonged in the "exceptional case" subcategory. In all events, the question whether a specific case should receive exceptional treatment is more appropriately the subject of the exercise of judicial discretion than an interpretation of the Constitution. Accordingly, we turn to the question whether the District Court's decision to stay the trial until after petitioner leaves office was an abuse of discretion.

VII

The Court of Appeals described the District Court's discretionary decision to stay the trial as the "functional equivalent" of a grant of temporary immunity. Concluding that petitioner was not constitutionally entitled to such an immunity, the court held that it was error to grant the stay. Although we ultimately conclude that the stay should not have been granted, we think the issue is more difficult than the opinion of the Court of Appeals suggests.

Strictly speaking the stay was not the functional equivalent of the constitutional immunity that petitioner claimed, because the District Court ordered discovery to proceed. Moreover, a stay of either the trial or discovery might be justified by considerations that do not require the recognition of any constitutional immunity. The District Court has broad discretion to stay proceedings as an incident to its power to control its own docket . . . . Although we have rejected the argument that the potential burdens on the President violate separation-of-powers principles, those burdens are appropriate matters for the District Court to evaluate in its management of the case. The high respect that is owed to the office of the Chief Executive, though not justifying a rule of categorical immunity, is a matter that should inform the conduct of the entire proceeding, including the timing and scope of discovery.

Nevertheless, we are persuaded that it was an abuse of discretion for the District Court to defer the trial until after the President leaves office. Such a lengthy and categorical stay takes no account whatever of the respondent's interest in bringing the case to trial. The complaint was filed within the statutory limitations period—albeit near the end of that period—and delaying trial would increase the danger of prejudice resulting from the loss of evidence, including the inability of witnesses to recall specific facts, or the possible death of a party.

The decision to postpone the trial was, furthermore, premature. The proponent of a stay bears the burden of establishing its need. In this case, at the stage at which the District Court made its ruling, there was no way to assess whether a stay of trial after the completion of discovery would be warranted. Other than the fact that a trial may consume some of the President's time and attention, there is nothing in the record to enable a judge to assess the potential harm that may ensue from scheduling the trial promptly after discovery is concluded. We think the District Court may have given undue weight to the concern that a trial might generate unrelated civil actions that could conceivably hamper the President in conducting the duties of his office. If and when that should occur, the court's discretion would permit it to manage those actions in such fashion (including deferral of trial) that interference with the President's duties would not occur. But no such impingement upon the President's conduct of his office was shown here.

VIII

We add a final comment on . . . the risk that our decision will generate a large volume of politically motivated harassing and frivolous litigation. . . . Most frivolous and vexatious litigation is terminated at the pleading stage or on summary judgment, with little if any personal involvement by the defendant. Moreover, the availability of sanctions provides a significant deterrent to litigation directed at the President in his unofficial capacity for purposes of political gain or harassment. History indicates that the likelihood that a significant number of such cases will be filed is remote . . . .

The Federal District Court has jurisdiction to decide this case. Like every other citizen who properly invokes that jurisdiction, respondent has a right to an orderly disposition of her claims. Accordingly, the judgment of the Court of Appeals is affirmed.

Justice BREYER, concurring in the judgment.

I agree with the majority that the Constitution does not automatically grant the President an immunity from civil lawsuits based upon his private conduct. Nor does the "doctrine of separation of powers . . . require federal courts to stay" virtually "all private actions against the President until he leaves office. . . ." In my view, however, once the President sets forth and explains a conflict between judicial proceeding and public duties, the matter changes. At that point, the Constitution permits a judge to schedule a trial in an ordinary civil damages action (where postponement normally is possible without overwhelming damage to a plaintiff) only within the constraints of a constitutional principle—a principle that forbids a federal judge in such a case to interfere with the President's discharge of his public duties. I have no doubt that the Constitution contains such a principle applicable to civil suits, based upon Article II's vesting of the entire "executive Power" in a single individual, implemented through the Constitution's structural separation of powers, and revealed both by history and case precedent. . . . [J]udicial scheduling orders in a private civil case must not only take reasonable account of, say, a particularly busy schedule, or a job on which others critically depend, or an underlying electoral mandate. They must also reflect the fact that interference with a President's ability to carry out his public responsibilities is constitutionally equivalent to interference with the ability of the entirety of Congress, or the Judicial Branch, to carry out its public obligations.

II

. . . . Case law, particularly *Nixon v. Fitzgerald*, strongly supports the principle that judges hearing a private civil damages action against a sitting President may not issue orders that could significantly distract a President from his official duties. . . . First, the Court found that the Constitution assigns the President singularly important duties (thus warranting an "absolute," rather than a "qualified," immunity). Second, the Court held that "recognition of immunity" does not require a "specific textual basis" in the Constitution. Third, although physical constraint of the President was not at issue, the Court nevertheless considered Justice Story's constitutional analysis, "persuasive." Fourth, the Court distinguished contrary precedent on the ground that it involved criminal, not civil, proceedings. Fifth, the Court's concerns encompassed the fact that "the sheer prominence of the President's office" could make him "an easily identifiable target for suits for civil damages." Sixth, and most important, the Court rested its conclusion in important part upon the fact that civil lawsuits "could distract a President from his public duties, to the detriment of not only the President and his office but also the Nation that the Presidency was designed to serve." . . . .

The cases ultimately turn on an assessment of the threat that a civil damages lawsuit poses to a public official's ability to perform his job properly. And, whether they provide an absolute immunity, a qualified immunity, or merely a special procedure, they ultimately balance consequent potential public harm against private need. Distraction and distortion are equally important ingredients of that potential public harm. Indeed, a lawsuit that significantly distracts an official from his public duties can distort the content of a public decision just as can a threat of potential future liability. If the latter concern can justify an "absolute" immunity in the case of a President no longer in office, where distraction is no longer a consideration, so can the former justify, not immunity, but a postponement, in the case of a sitting President.

III

The majority points to the fact that private plaintiffs have brought civil damages lawsuits against a sitting President only three times in our Nation's history; and it relies upon the threat of sanctions to discourage, and "the court's discretion" to manage, such actions so that "interference with the President's duties would not occur." I am less sanguine. Since 1960, when the last such suit was filed, the number of civil lawsuits filed annually in Federal District Courts has increased from under 60,000 to about 240,000; the number of federal district judges has increased from 233 to about 650; the time and expense associated with both discovery and trial have increased; an increasingly complex economy has led to increasingly complex sets of statutes, rules, and regulations that often create potential liability, with, or without fault. And this Court has now made clear that such lawsuits may proceed against a sitting President. The consequence, as the Court warned in *Fitzgerald*, is that a sitting President, given "the visibility of his office," could well become "an easily identifiable target for suits for civil damages." The threat of sanctions could well discourage much unneeded litigation, but some lawsuits (including highly intricate and complicated ones) could resist ready evaluation and disposition; and individual district court procedural rulings could pose a significant threat to the President's official functions. . . . Yet, I agree with the majority that there is no automatic temporary immunity and that the President should have to provide the District Court with a reasoned explanation of why the immunity is needed; and I also agree that, in the absence of that explanation, the court's postponement of the trial date was premature. For those reasons, I concur in the result.

---

1. *Policy Wonks.* In both *Fitzgerald* and *Jones*, the Justices engage in what amounts to public policy analysis. Who has the better of the argument? Are the *Jones* Court's distinctions of *Fitzgerald* persuasive?

2. *Constitutional History.* The opinions in both *Fitzgerald* and *Jones* debate the pertinent constitutional history. A footnote in *Jones* said:

> Jefferson's argument provides little support for petitioner's position. As we explain later, the prerogative Jefferson claimed was denied him by the Chief Justice in the very decision Jefferson was protesting, and this Court

has subsequently reaffirmed that holding. The statements supporting a similar proposition recorded in Senator Maclay's diary are inconclusive of the issue before us here for the same reason. In addition, this material is hardly proof of the unequivocal common understanding at the time of the founding. Immediately after mentioning the positions of Adams and Ellsworth, Maclay went on to point out in his diary that he virulently disagreed with them, concluding that his opponents' view "[s]hows clearly how amazingly fond of the old leven many People are." Finally, Justice Story's comments in his constitutional law treatise provide no substantial support for petitioner's position. Story wrote that because the President's "incidental powers" must include "the power to perform [his duties], without any obstruction," he "cannot, therefore, be liable to arrest, imprisonment, or detention, while he is in the discharge of the duties of his office; and for this purpose his person must be deemed, in civil cases at least, to possess an official inviolability." Story said only that "an official inviolability," was necessary to preserve the President's ability to perform the functions of the office; he did not specify the dimensions of the necessary immunity. While we have held that an immunity from suits grounded on official acts is necessary to serve this purpose, it does not follow that the broad immunity from all civil damages suits that petitioner seeks is also necessary.

What does the history tell us? *See* Akhil Reed Amar & Neal K. Katyal, *Executive Privileges and Immunities: The* Nixon *and* Clinton *Cases*, 108 HARV. L. REV. 701 (1995), arguing that there is a much better case for immunity in *Jones* than in *Fitzgerald*.

3. *Denouement.* The subsequent history of *Jones* is instructive. Discovery commenced, and President Clinton's deposition eventually led to his impeachment trial in the Senate. In *Jones* itself, the President won on summary judgment, 990 F. Supp. 657 (E.D. Ark. 1998), and settled the case while on appeal for $850,000. (Most summary judgment victors do not settle for a multiple of the damages claimed.) After the impeachment, the District Judge found Clinton in contempt for lying in his deposition and ordered him to pay the court costs and plaintiff's attorney's fees caused by his misconduct. *Jones v. Clinton*, 36 F. Supp. 2d 1118 (E.D. Ark. 1999). As we noted earlier, Clinton eventually apologized for lying in this litigation. What do you make of this train of events? Do Presidents have sufficient protection against harassing private litigation?

4. *Lawsuits against Donald Trump.* Two lawsuits filed against Donald Trump for pre-presidential conduct have revived the immunity question. Summer Zervos, a former contestant on Trump's reality-show *The Apprentice*, alleged during the presidential campaign that Donald Trump had groped and tried to force himself upon her. Candidate Trump vigorously and disparagingly denied the charges. Zervos filed a defamation suit in New York state court against Trump three days before he was inaugurated. *See Zervos v. Trump*, No. 150522/2017 (Jan. 17, 2017). In response, President Trump filed a motion, citing footnote 13 in *Clinton v. Jones*, claiming immunity under the Supremacy Clause because the suit was filed in state court. *See id.*

Memorandum of Law in Support of President Donald J. Trump's Application (March 27, 2017). How do you think the court should rule?

Kashiya Nwanguma and two other protesters were beaten at a Trump presidential rally in 2016 after then-candidate Trump admonished the crowd to "get 'em outta here." The protesters have sued their assailants for assault and included Donald Trump as a defendant for inciting the violence. The President's lawyer not only asserted temporary immunity from this *federal* lawsuit, but cited *Clinton v. Jones* as the lone authority to support the assertion. Answer of Defendants Donald J. Trump, President of the United States and Donald J. Trump for President, Inc. at 17 (listing as fifth affirmative defense, "Mr. Trump is immune from proceedings pursuant to *Clinton v. Jones*, 520 U.S. 681 (1997)"). Is there any reading of *Clinton v. Jones* that supports the immunity claim? One of us has argued that the answer is so obviously "no" that the lawyer who made the claim should be sanctioned. *See* Neil Kinkopf, *Sanctionable*, TAKE CARE (April 24, 2017), available at https://takecareblog.com/blog/sanctionable. As this volume goes to press, the District Court has denied defense motions asserting that the protestors have failed to state a claim and that, in any event, candidate Trump's remarks were constitutionally protected speech; the judge, however, certified those rulings for interlocutory appeal. *Nwanguma v. Trump*, No. 3:16-CV-247-DJH-HBB (W.D. Ky. Aug. 9, 2017). Permission to file the appeal has been granted by the Sixth Circuit. *In re Trump*, No. 17-510 (6th Cir. Nov. 1, 2017).

b. Other Executive Officers

Harlow & Butterfield v. Fitzgerald
457 U.S. 800 (1982)

Justice POWELL delivered the opinion of the Court.

The issue in this case is the scope of the immunity available to the senior aides and advisers of the President of the United States in a suit for damages based upon their official acts.

I

In this suit for civil damages petitioners Bryce Harlow and Alexander Butterfield are alleged to have participated in a conspiracy to violate the constitutional and statutory rights of the respondent A. Ernest Fitzgerald . . . in their capacities as senior White House aides to former President Richard M. Nixon. . . . Harlow [was] the Presidential aide principally responsible for congressional relations . . . [who had] a series of conversations in which Harlow discussed Fitzgerald's dismissal with Air Force Secretary Robert Seamans. . . . Disputing Fitzgerald's contentions, Harlow . . . contends that he took all his actions in good faith.

. . . Employed as Deputy Assistant to the President and Deputy Chief of Staff to H. R. Haldeman, Butterfield circulated a White House memorandum in that month in which he claimed to have learned that Fitzgerald planned to "blow the whistle" on some "shoddy purchasing practices" by exposing these practices to public view.

Fitzgerald [alleges] that Butterfield had commenced efforts to secure Fitzgerald's retaliatory dismissal. . . . In a subsequent memorandum emphasizing the importance of "loyalty," Butterfield counseled against offering Fitzgerald another job in the administration at that time. . . .

Together with their codefendant Richard Nixon, petitioners Harlow and Butterfield moved for summary judgment. . . . In denying the motion the District Court . . . ruled that petitioners were not entitled to absolute immunity. . . . The Court of Appeals dismissed the appeal. . . .

I

. . . For executive officials in general, . . . our cases make plain that qualified immunity represents the norm. In *Scheuer v. Rhodes*, we acknowledged that high officials require greater protection than those with less complex discretionary responsibilities. Nonetheless, we held that a governor and his aides could receive the requisite protection from qualified or good-faith immunity. In *Butz v. Economou*, we extended the approach of *Scheuer* to high federal officials of the Executive Branch. [We balanced] competing values: not only the importance of a damages remedy to protect the rights of citizens, but also "the need to protect officials who are required to exercise their discretion and the related public interest in encouraging the vigorous exercise of official authority." Without discounting the adverse consequences of denying high officials an absolute immunity from private lawsuits alleging constitutional violations—consequences found sufficient in *Spalding v. Vilas*, to warrant extension to such officials of absolute immunity from suits at common law—we emphasized our expectation that insubstantial suits need not proceed to trial. . . .

III

A

Petitioners argue that they are entitled to a blanket protection of absolute immunity as an incident of their offices as Presidential aides. . . . In *Butz v. Economou*, the Secretary of Agriculture—a Cabinet official directly accountable to the President—asserted a defense of absolute official immunity from suit for civil damages. We rejected his claim. In so doing we did not question the power or the importance of the Secretary's office. Nor did we doubt the importance to the President of loyal and efficient subordinates in executing his duties of office. Yet we found these factors, alone, to be insufficient to justify absolute immunity. "[T]he greater power of [high] officials," we reasoned, "affords a greater potential for a regime of lawless conduct." . . . Having decided in *Butz* that Members of the Cabinet ordinarily enjoy only qualified immunity from suit, we conclude today that it would be equally untenable to hold absolute immunity an incident of the office of every Presidential subordinate based in the White House. Members of the Cabinet are direct subordinates of the President, frequently with greater responsibilities, both to the President and to the Nation, than White House staff. . . .

B

In disputing the controlling authority of *Butz*, petitioners rely on the principles developed in *Gravel v. United States*. In *Gravel* we endorsed the view that "it is literally impossible . . . for Members of Congress to perform their legislative tasks without the help of aides and assistants" and that "the day-to-day work of such aides is so critical to the Members' performance that they must be treated as the latter's alter egos. . . ." Having done so, we held the Speech and Debate Clause derivatively applicable to the "legislative acts" of a Senator's aide that would have been privileged if performed by the Senator himself. Petitioners contend that the rationale of *Gravel* mandates a similar "derivative" immunity for the chief aides of the President of the United States. Emphasizing that the President must delegate a large measure of authority to execute the duties of his office, they argue that recognition of derivative absolute immunity is made essential by all the considerations that support absolute immunity for the President himself.

Petitioners' argument is not without force. Ultimately, however, it sweeps too far. If the President's aides are derivatively immune because they are essential to the functioning of the Presidency, so should the Members of the Cabinet—Presidential subordinates some of whose essential roles are acknowledged by the Constitution itself—be absolutely immune. Yet we implicitly rejected such derivative immunity in *Butz*. Moreover, in general our cases have followed a "functional" approach to immunity law. We have recognized that the judicial, prosecutorial, and legislative functions require absolute immunity. But this protection has extended no further than its justification would warrant. In *Gravel*, for example, we emphasized that Senators and their aides were absolutely immune only when performing "acts legislative in nature," and not when taking other acts even "in their official capacity." *See Hutchinson v. Proxmire*, 443 U.S. 111, 125–33 (1979) . . . .

C

Petitioners also assert an entitlement to immunity based on the "special functions" of White House aides. This form of argument accords with the analytical approach of our cases. For aides entrusted with discretionary authority in such sensitive areas as national security or foreign policy, absolute immunity might well be justified to protect the unhesitating performance of functions vital to the national interest. But a "special functions" rationale does not warrant a blanket recognition of absolute immunity for all Presidential aides in the performance of all their duties. . . .

The burden of justifying absolute immunity rests on the official asserting the claim. . . . [T]he general requisites are familiar in our cases. In order to establish entitlement to absolute immunity a Presidential aide first must show that the responsibilities of his office embraced a function so sensitive as to require a total shield from liability. He then must demonstrate that he was discharging the protected function when performing the act for which liability is asserted. Applying these standards to the claims advanced by petitioners Harlow and Butterfield, we cannot conclude on the record before us that either has shown that "public policy requires [for any of the functions of his office] an exemption of [absolute] scope." . . .

IV

Even if they cannot establish that their official functions require absolute immunity, petitioners [argue for] the qualified immunity standard that would permit the defeat of insubstantial claims without resort to trial. We agree.

A

. . . In identifying qualified immunity as the best attainable accommodation of competing values, . . . we relied on the assumption that this standard would permit "[i]nsubstantial lawsuits [to] be quickly terminated." Yet petitioners advance persuasive arguments that the dismissal of insubstantial lawsuits without trial . . . requires an adjustment of the "good faith" standard established by our decisions.

B

Qualified or "good faith" immunity is an affirmative defense that must be pleaded by a defendant official. Decisions of this Court have established that the "good faith" defense has both an "objective" and a "subjective" aspect. The objective element involves a presumptive knowledge of and respect for "basic, unquestioned constitutional rights." *Wood v. Strickland*, 420 U.S. 308, 322 (1975). The subjective component refers to "permissible intentions." Characteristically the Court has defined these elements by identifying the circumstances in which qualified immunity would *not* be available. Referring both to the objective and subjective elements, we have held that qualified immunity would be defeated if an official "*knew or reasonably should have known* that the action he took within his sphere of official responsibility would violate the constitutional rights of the [plaintiff], *or* if he took the action *with the malicious intention* to cause a deprivation of constitutional rights or other injury. . . ." (emphasis added).

The subjective element of the good-faith defense frequently has proved incompatible with our admonition . . . that insubstantial claims should not proceed to trial. Rule 56 of the Federal Rules of Civil Procedure provides that disputed questions of fact ordinarily may not be decided on motions for summary judgment. And an official's subjective good faith has been considered to be a question of fact that some courts have regarded as inherently requiring resolution by a jury. . . . [I]t now is clear that substantial costs attend the litigation of the subjective good faith of government officials. Not only are there the general costs of subjecting officials to the risks of trial — distraction of officials from their governmental duties, inhibition of discretionary action, and deterrence of able people from public service. There are special costs to "subjective" inquiries of this kind. Immunity generally is available only to officials performing discretionary functions. In contrast with the thought processes accompanying "ministerial" tasks, the judgments surrounding discretionary action almost inevitably are influenced by the decisionmaker's experiences, values, and emotions. These variables explain in part why questions of subjective intent so rarely can be decided by summary judgment. Yet they also frame a background in which there often is no clear end to the relevant evidence. Judicial inquiry into subjective motivation therefore may entail broad-ranging discovery and the deposing of numerous persons, including an official's professional colleagues. Inquiries of this kind can be peculiarly disruptive of effective government.

. . . [W]e conclude today that bare allegations of malice should not suffice to subject government officials either to the costs of trial or to the burdens of broad-reaching discovery. We therefore hold that government officials performing discretionary functions generally are shielded from liability for civil damages insofar as their conduct does not violate clearly established statutory or constitutional rights of which a reasonable person would have known. . . . Where an official could be expected to know that certain conduct would violate statutory or constitutional rights, he should be made to hesitate; and a person who suffers injury caused by such conduct may have a cause of action. But where an official's duties legitimately require action in which clearly established rights are not implicated, the public interest may be better served by action taken "with independence and without fear of consequences."

C

In this case petitioners have asked us to hold that the respondent's pretrial showings were insufficient to survive their motion for summary judgment. We think it appropriate, however, to remand the case to the District Court for its reconsideration of this issue in light of this opinion. . . .

Justice BRENNAN, with whom Justice MARSHALL and Justice BLACKMUN join, concurring.

I agree with the substantive standard announced by the Court today, imposing liability when a public-official defendant "knew or should have known" of the constitutionally violative effect of his actions. This standard would not allow the official who *actually knows* that he was violating the law to escape liability for his actions, even if he could not "reasonably have been expected" to know what he actually did know. Thus the clever and unusually well-informed violator of constitutional rights will not evade just punishment for his crimes. . . . I write separately only to note that given this standard, it seems inescapable to me that some measure of discovery may sometimes be required to determine exactly what a public-official defendant did "know" at the time of his actions. . . .

Justice REHNQUIST, concurring.

At such time as a majority of the Court is willing to re-examine our holding in *Butz v. Economou*, I shall join in that undertaking with alacrity. But until that time comes, I agree that the Court's opinion in this case properly disposes of the issues presented, and I therefore join it.

Chief Justice BURGER, dissenting.

... In this case the Court decides that senior aides of the President do not have derivative immunity from the President. I am at a loss, however, to reconcile this conclusion with our holding in *Gravel v. United States*. ... We very properly recognized in *Gravel* that the central purpose of a Member's absolute immunity would be "diminished and frustrated" if the legislative aides were not also protected by the same broad immunity. ... [W]ithout absolute immunity for these "elbow aides," who are indeed "alter egos," a Member could not effectively discharge all of the assigned constitutional functions of a modern legislator.

The Court has made this reality a matter of our constitutional jurisprudence. How can we conceivably hold that a President of the United States, who represents a vastly larger constituency than does any Member of Congress, should not have "alter egos" with comparable immunity? ... The primary layer of senior aides of a President—like a Senator's "alter egos"—are literally at a President's elbow, with offices a few feet or at most a few hundred feet from his own desk. The President, like a Member of Congress, may see those personal aides many times in one day. They are indeed the President's "arms" and "fingers" to aid in performing his constitutional duty to see "that the laws [are] faithfully executed." Like a Member of Congress, but on a vastly greater scale, the President cannot personally implement a fraction of his own policies and day-to-day decisions. ...

Precisely the same public policy considerations on which the Court now relies in *Nixon v. Fitzgerald*, and that we relied on only recently in *Gravel*, are fully applicable to senior Presidential aides. ... In addition, exposure to civil liability for official acts will result in constant judicial questioning, through judicial proceedings and pretrial discovery, into the inner workings of the Presidential Office beyond that necessary to maintain the traditional checks and balances of our constitutional structure. ...

The *Gravel* Court took note of the burdens on congressional aides: the stress of long hours, heavy responsibilities, constant exposure to harassment of the political arena. Is the Court suggesting the stresses are less for Presidential aides? By construing the Constitution to give only qualified immunity to senior Presidential aides we give those key "alter egos" only lawsuits, winnable lawsuits perhaps, but lawsuits nonetheless, with stress and effort that will disperse and drain their energies and their purses. ...

Butz v. Economou does not dictate that senior Presidential aides be given only qualified immunity. ... A senior Presidential aide works more intimately with the President on a daily basis than does a Cabinet officer, directly implementing Presidential decisions literally from hour to hour. ... The Court's analysis in *Gravel* demonstrates that the question of derivative immunity does not and should not depend on a person's rank or position in the hierarchy, but on the *function* performed by the person and the relationship of that person to the superior. ... The function of senior Presidential aides, as the "alter egos" of the President, is an integral, inseparable part of the function of the President. ...

———————

Mitchell v. Forsyth

472 U.S. 511 (1985)

Justice WHITE delivered the opinion of the Court.

This is a suit for damages stemming from a warrantless wiretap authorized by petitioner, a former Attorney General of the United States. The case presents [the question] whether the Attorney General is absolutely immune from suit for actions undertaken in the interest of national security. . . .

I

In 1970, the Federal Bureau of Investigation learned that members of an antiwar group . . . had made plans to blow up heating tunnels linking federal office buildings in Washington, D.C., and had also discussed the possibility of kidnaping then National Security Adviser Henry Kissinger. [A]cting on the basis of this information, the then Attorney General John Mitchell authorized a warrantless wiretap on the telephone of William Davidon . . . a member of the group . . . in the interest of national security. [T]he Government intercepted three conversations between Davidon and respondent Keith Forsyth. . . . [Revelation of the tap to Forsyth in other litigation was accompanied by an] affidavit, sworn to by then Attorney General Richard Kleindienst, averring that the surveillance to which Forsyth had been subjected was authorized "in the exercise of [the President's] authority relating to the national security. . . ."

Shortly thereafter, this Court ruled that the Fourth Amendment does not permit the use of warrantless wiretaps in cases involving domestic threats to the national security. *United States v. United States District Court*, 407 U.S. 297 (1972) (*Keith*). In the wake of the *Keith* decision, Forsyth filed this lawsuit. . . . Forsyth alleged that the surveillance to which he had been subjected violated both the Fourth Amendment and Title III of the Omnibus Crime Control and Safe Streets Act, 18 U.S.C. §§ 2510–2520, which sets forth comprehensive standards governing the use of wiretaps and electronic surveillance by both governmental and private agents. He asserted that both the constitutional and statutory provisions provided him with a private right of action; he sought compensatory, statutory, and punitive damages. . . .

The District Court rejected Mitchell's argument that under [the *Harlow*] standard he should be held immune from suit for warrantless national security wiretaps authorized before this Court's decision in *Keith*: that decision was merely a logical extension of general Fourth Amendment principles and in particular of the ruling in *Katz v. United States*, 389 U.S. 347 (1967), in which the Court held for the first time that electronic surveillance unaccompanied by physical trespass constituted a search subject to the Fourth Amendment's warrant requirement. Mitchell and the Justice Department, the court suggested, had chosen to "gamble" on the possibility that this Court would create an exception to the warrant requirement if presented with a case involving national security. Having lost the gamble, Mitchell was not entitled to complain of the consequences. The court therefore denied Mitchell's motion for summary judgment, granted Forsyth's motion for summary judgment on the issue of liability, and scheduled further proceedings on the issue of damages. . . .

II

We first address Mitchell's claim that the Attorney General's actions in furtherance of the national security should be shielded from scrutiny in civil damage actions by an absolute immunity similar to that afforded the President, judges, prosecutors, witnesses, and officials performing "quasi-judicial" functions . . . . We conclude that the Attorney General is not absolutely immune from suit for damages arising out of his allegedly unconstitutional conduct in performing his national security functions. As the Nation's chief law enforcement officer, the Attorney General provides vital assistance to the President . . . Mitchell's argument, in essence, is that the national security functions of the Attorney General are so sensitive, so vital to the protection of our Nation's well-being, that we cannot tolerate any risk that in performing those functions he will be chilled by the possibility of personal liability for acts that may be found to impinge on the constitutional rights of citizens. . . .

Our decisions in this area leave no doubt that the Attorney General's status as a Cabinet officer is not in itself sufficient to invest him with absolute immunity. . . . Mitchell's claim, then, must rest . . . on the nature of the functions he was performing in this case. Because Mitchell was not acting in a prosecutorial capacity in this case, the situations in which we have applied a functional approach to absolute immunity questions provide scant support for blanket immunization of his performance of the "national security function."

First, in deciding whether officials performing a particular function are entitled to absolute immunity, we have generally looked for a historical or common-law basis for the immunity in question. . . . Mitchell points to no analogous historical or common-law basis for an absolute immunity for officers carrying out tasks essential to national security.

Second, the performance of national security functions does not subject an official to the same obvious risks of entanglement in vexatious litigation as does the carrying out of the judicial or "quasi-judicial" tasks that have been the primary wellsprings of absolute immunities. The judicial process is an arena of open conflict, and in virtually every case there is, if not always a winner, at least one loser. It is inevitable that many of those who lose will pin the blame on judges, prosecutors, or witnesses and will bring suit against them in an effort to relitigate the underlying conflict. National security tasks, by contrast, are carried out in secret; open conflict and overt winners and losers are rare. Under such circumstances, it is far more likely that actual abuses will go uncovered than that fancied abuses will give rise to unfounded and burdensome litigation. Whereas the mere threat of litigation may significantly affect the fearless and independent performance of duty by actors in the judicial process, it is unlikely to have a similar effect on the Attorney General's performance of his national security tasks.

Third, most of the officials who are entitled to absolute immunity from liability for damages are subject to other checks that help to prevent abuses of authority from going unredressed. Legislators are accountable to their constituents, and the judicial process is largely self-correcting: procedural rules, appeals, and the possibility of collateral challenges obviate the need for damage actions to prevent unjust results. Similar built-in restraints on the Attorney General's activities in the name of national security, however, do not exist. And despite our recognition of the importance of those activities to the safety of our Nation and its democratic system of government, we cannot accept the notion that restraints are completely unnecessary. . . .

We emphasize that the denial of absolute immunity will not leave the Attorney General at the mercy of litigants with frivolous and vexatious complaints. Under the standard of qualified immunity articulated in *Harlow v. Fitzgerald*, the Attorney General will be entitled to immunity so long as his actions do not violate "clearly established statutory or constitutional rights of which a reasonable person would have known." . . . We do not believe that the security of the Republic will be threatened if its Attorney General is given incentives to abide by clearly established law.

III

. . . [*Harlow*'s concerns] are not limited to liability for money damages; they also include . . . such pretrial matters as discovery . . . , as "(i)nquiries of this kind can be peculiarly disruptive of effective government." . . . Accordingly, we hold that a district court's denial of a claim of qualified immunity, to the extent that it turns on an issue of law, is an appealable "final decision" within the meaning of 28 U.S.C. § 1291 notwithstanding the absence of a final judgment.

IV

. . . Under *Harlow v. Fitzgerald*, Mitchell is immune unless his actions violated clearly established law. Forsyth complains that in November, 1970, Mitchell authorized a warrantless wiretap aimed at gathering intelligence regarding a domestic threat to national security—the kind of wiretap that the Court subsequently declared to be illegal. *Keith*. The question of Mitchell's immunity turns on whether it was clearly established in November, 1970, well over a year before *Keith* was decided, that such wiretaps were unconstitutional. We conclude that it was not. . . . As of 1970, the Justice Departments of six successive administrations had considered warrantless domestic security wiretaps constitutional. Only three years earlier, this Court had expressly left open the possibility that this view was correct. Two Federal District Courts had accepted the Justice Department's position. . . . In framing the issue before it, the *Keith* Court explicitly recognized that the question was one that had yet to receive the definitive answer that it demanded. . . .

The District Court's conclusion that Mitchell is not immune because he gambled and lost on the resolution of this open question departs from the principles of

Harlow. Such hindsight-based reasoning on immunity issues is precisely what *Harlow* rejected. The decisive fact is not that Mitchell's position turned out to be incorrect, but that the question was open at the time he acted. Hence, in the absence of contrary directions from Congress, Mitchell is immune from suit for his authorization of the Davidon wiretap notwithstanding that his actions violated the Fourth Amendment. . . .

[Justices POWELL and REHNQUIST took no part in the decision. Chief Justice BURGER and Justice STEVENS both concurred, arguing that the Attorney General was "entitled to absolute immunity for . . . his exercise of the discretionary power of the President in the area of national security." Justice O'CONNOR concurred, emphasizing that the denial of immunity comes within a "small class" of immediately appealable interlocutory orders. Justices BRENNAN and MARSHALL concurred that qualified immunity was the correct standard, but dissented from the holding that denials of immunity are immediately appealable.]

————

1. *Is Intent Irrelevant?* Part IV of *Harlow* recognizes that, to be of use, qualified immunity must defeat insubstantial claims without going to trial. Is the Court's reformulation of the immunity in *Harlow* likely to achieve that end? Unhappily, as then-Judge Scalia has pointed out, whether conduct violates clearly established rights "often, if not invariably, depends on the intent with which the conduct is performed." *Halperin v. Kissinger*, 807 F.2d 180, 184 (D.C. Cir. 1986). Thus, the legality of the wiretap involved in *Halperin* depended on whether its purpose was to obtain foreign intelligence. After noting that *Harlow* was "to say the least, unclear" about how to handle such problems, Scalia concluded:

> [A]t least where . . . the officials claiming immunity purported at the time . . . to have been motivated by national security concerns, a purely objective inquiry into the pretextuality of the purpose is appropriate. That is to say, if the facts establish that the purported national security motivation would have been reasonable, the immunity defense will prevail.

Do you agree?

2. *Gravel v. Harlow.* Why does the *Harlow* Court deny the executive the benefit of the "alter ego" immunity that congressional aides enjoy? Is it so that presidential aides will have an incentive to resist, and ultimately to refuse, presidential orders that they consider illegal?

3. *Who Is the Client?* A further complication exists for government lawyers trying these cases. Sometimes the terms of an agency's appropriations may be broad enough to permit the agency to settle a lawsuit against an employee sued in his or her individual capacity, although the agency would be precluded from indemnifying the employee for damages awarded after a trial. In such a case, if the Department of Justice provides representation for the employee, it is problematic whether the employee's true adversary is the plaintiff or the employee's own agency. The

Department does sometimes provide for retention of private defense counsel. 28 C.F.R § 50.15.

4. Mitchell's *Limits.* After *Mitchell,* what specific functions of presidential aides are likely to receive absolute immunity? What about those relating to defense and foreign policy? Are they sharply different from the national security functions involved in *Mitchell*? For a critique by the respondent's counsel in *Mitchell* of the Court's evolving treatment of qualified immunities, see David Rudovsky, *The Qualified Immunity Doctrine in the Supreme Court: Judicial Activism and the Restriction of Constitutional Rights,* 138 U. PA. L. REV. 23 (1989).

5. *Waiving Sovereign Immunity to Provide Redress.* In 1988, Congress amended the Federal Tort Claims Act to make the United States the sole party defendant in any covered tort action brought against an employee in his or her individual capacity, unless the alleged tort would (a) violate the Constitution or (b) violate another statute permitting direct suit against the individual employee. In any case in which the United States is substituted as the party defendant, the employee has absolute immunity. No other action against the employee or his or her estate is permitted. Federal Employees Liability Reform and Tort Compensation Act of 1988, Pub. L. No. 100-694, § 5, 102 Stat. 4564, *amending* 28 U.S.C. § 2679(b) (see appendix).

Should Congress have extended its conferral of absolute immunity and its willingness to step in as substitute defendant to alleged constitutional torts? *See* Thomas J. Madden, Nicholas W. Allard & David H. Remes, *Bedtime for* Bivens: *Substituting the United States as Defendant in Constitutional Tort Suits,* 20 HARV. J. LEGIS. 469 (1983). It has been argued that existing law provides strong incentives for risk-averse officials to avoid vigorous discharge of their duties, out of fear of liability, or at least litigation. PETER H. SCHUCK, SUING GOVERNMENT (1983); Ronald A. Cass, *Damage Suits Against Public Officers,* 129 U. Pa. L. Rev. 1110 (1981). How would you advise Congress on this subject? Would your advice to the executive be different?

6. *Proving a Damages Action.* In *Ashcroft v. Iqbal,* 556 U.S. 662 (2009), Justice Kennedy wrote a controversial 5–4 decision that increased the requisite specificity of fact pleadings needed to allow a *Bivens* action to go forward. Iqbal, a Pakistani Muslim, was arrested in the United States on criminal charges after the terror attacks of 9/11, and held under restrictive conditions of detention. He was convicted of the charges (which were not related to terrorism) and was removed to his native Pakistan. He then brought a *Bivens* action against former Attorney General John Ashcroft and FBI Director Robert Mueller, alleging that they were the "architects" of an unconstitutional policy of harsh confinement based on his race, religion, or national origin. Justice Kennedy's opinion held that a complaint must contain facts which, if true, were "plausible" grounds for the claim, not merely possible ones. Here, the majority found nothing in the complaint to negate the existence of a legitimate policy to detain those with a probable connection to foreign terror groups, a policy that would have a "disparate, incidental impact on Arab Muslims, even though the purpose of the policy was to target neither Arabs nor Muslims." The effects of *Iqbal* on

damages actions remain to be seen. A particular difficulty in many national security cases such as *Iqbal* will be the difficulties plaintiffs encounter in discovering enough facts about the conduct of government officers to plead sufficient complaints, in light of the state secrets privilege that we cover later in this chapter.

3. Judicial Immunities

Bradley v. Fisher, 80 U.S. (13 Wall.) 335 (1872) established the rule that federal judges possess an absolute immunity from damages unless they act in the "clear absence of all jurisdiction." In 1867, Bradley was defense counsel for John Suratt, who was charged with the murder of President Lincoln. The trial, presided over by Judge Fisher, was held in the Criminal Court of the District of Columbia, and ended in a hung jury. At the end of one day's proceedings, Bradley accosted Fisher, charged him with having insulted Bradley throughout the trial, and threatened the judge with "personal chastisement." After the trial, Fisher had Bradley's name struck from the court's roll of attorneys, and Bradley sued him for damages.

Justice Field's opinion for the Supreme Court extended immunity to Fisher:

> however erroneous [his] act may have been, and however injurious in its consequences it may have proved to the plaintiff. For it is a principle of the highest importance to the proper administration of justice that a judicial officer, in exercising the authority vested in him, shall be free to act upon his own convictions, without apprehension of personal consequences to himself. Liability to answer to every one who might feel himself aggrieved by the action of the judge, would be inconsistent with the possession of this freedom, and would destroy that independence without which no judiciary can be either respectable or useful. . . . [This] has been the settled doctrine of the English courts for many centuries, and has never been denied, that we are aware of, in the courts of this country. . . .

> Nor can this exemption of the judges from civil liability be affected by the motives with which their judicial acts are performed. . . . If civil actions could be maintained . . . because the losing party [in litigation] should see fit to allege in his complaint that the acts of the judge were done with partiality, or maliciously, or corruptly, the protection essential to judicial independence would be entirely swept away. . . .

> [J]udges of courts of superior or general jurisdiction are not liable to civil actions for their judicial acts, even when such acts are in excess of their jurisdiction, and are alleged to have been done maliciously or corruptly. A distinction must be here observed between excess of jurisdiction and the clear absence of all jurisdiction over the subject-matter. . . . Thus, if a probate court, invested only with authority over wills . . . should proceed to try parties for public offenses, jurisdiction . . . being entirely wanting in the court, and this being necessarily known to its judge, his commission would

afford no protection. . . . Against the consequences of [judges'] erroneous or irregular action, from whatever motives proceeding, the law has provided for private parties numerous remedies. . . . But for malice or corruption . . . within the general scope of their jurisdiction, the judges . . . can only be reached by public prosecution in the form of impeachment. . . .

Justice Field concluded that because the court in question possessed the power to disbar attorneys from practice before it, the immunity held, even though the court had erred in not granting Bradley a hearing regarding his misconduct before disciplining him. Two dissenting Justices would have allowed the suit because of the allegation of malice.

For a modern application of *Bradley*'s principles, see *Stump v. Sparkman*, 435 U.S. 349 (1978). A § 1983 action was brought against a state court judge who had approved a petition for the sterilization of a "somewhat retarded" 15-year-old girl. The immunity held because state law granted the court in question broad general jurisdiction, and no specific statute or case law foreclosed consideration of the petition for sterilization. *See also Mireles v. Waco*, 502 U.S. 9 (1991) (immunity protects a judge's intemperate order to police to forcibly bring a tardy attorney to his courtroom). Absolute immunity does not protect a judge's executive or administrative actions, however. *See Forrester v. White*, 484 U.S. 219 (1988) (immunity does not protect dismissal of a probation officer).

C. Information and Accountability

It is commonplace to observe that the accountability of an officer to the people depends on the information they can obtain about his or her activities. In our system, accountability often depends on attempts by one (or more) of the branches of government to force another to reveal information. Secrecy in the executive branch has produced most of the controversy in this regard. Mostly for purposes of comparison, we also note the capacities of Congress and the judiciary to control information about their processes.

1. Confidentiality in Congress and the Judiciary

As the immediately preceding section on judicial immunities suggests, courts are well situated to protect their own proceedings from compulsory disclosure, at least absent a statute that clearly requires it. Presumably there is a judicial privilege (paralleling executive privilege) that shields the deliberation of collegial courts, but the federal courts have never had to articulate it against legislative onslaughts. After the early failure of the impeachment of Justice Chase for his conduct on the bench, federal judges have not had to fear intrusive impeachment inquiries into their judicial decisions. In modern times, the burrowings of journalists have sometimes breached judicial confidentiality somewhat (but only after the fact), as in Bob Woodward and Scott Armstrong, The Brethren (1979), and Jeffrey Toobin, The Nine (2007). Similarly, the papers of former Justices, once released to libraries, feed the activities of court historians. A branch that still feels free to bar news cameras from its open sessions is not unable to protect the confidentiality of its most sensitive functions.

Confidentiality within Congress is a far more qualified value than within the courts. As an intensely political body, Congress operates mostly through an open process of lobbying, position-taking, and bargaining. The *Congressional Record* publishes floor debate in both houses, and many committee hearings and reports are published as well. Still, the institution has real needs to hold some matters confidential. Most obviously, the intelligence, armed service, and foreign relations committees share many of the nation's most sensitive military and diplomatic secrets with the executive. The internal rules of Congress allow such matters to be considered in secret executive session, and provide special controls on distribution of materials concerning them.

Article I, § 5, of the Constitution provides authority for secrecy. It provides that "Each House shall keep a Journal of its Proceedings, and from time to time publish the same, excepting such Parts as may in their Judgment require Secrecy. . . ." The Framers — veterans of revolutionary war and intrigue — surely understood the need for legislative secrecy. Still, it is not clear whether there is a congressional privilege to resist subpoenas seeking the legislature's papers. According to Professor David Kaye, in *Congressional Papers and Judicial Subpoenas*, 23 UCLA L. Rev. 57 (1975):

> For at least a century, prosecutors, criminal defendants, and private litigants have sought, subpoena in hand, to wrest papers from Congress. By and large, Congress has grudgingly complied. In the few instances in which Congress has withheld the subpoenaed information, the question of congressional privilege was not conclusively litigated.

Professor Kaye concludes that primary congressional concerns in these cases have been to maintain control over original copies of documents, to ensure that disclosures are authorized by the house in possession, and to protect some material gathered in executive session. As we have seen, the Speech or Debate privilege prevents courts from compelling congressional testimony about "legislative acts." A congressional privilege might also rest on the Journal clause, quoted above. Consider the routine congressional activities that are not within the Speech or Debate privilege, such as contacts with constituents. Should any of these be protected from disclosure, for reasons such as the privacy interests of citizens?

In 1992, a scandal surrounded the House of Representatives' internal bank, which was part of the Office of the Sergeant-at-Arms. The bank permitted over 300 House members to write numerous overdrafts on their accounts, sometimes totaling over $10,000 per member. The Justice Department, employing its statutory authority to

hire special counsel, hired retired Judge Malcolm Wilkey to serve as a special prosecutor to investigate possible criminal wrongdoing in connection with the bank.
Wilkey proceeded to demand virtually all House records shedding light on the bank's
operations, including microfilm copies of all checks handled by the bank for the
previous three years. Following Speaker Foley's initial refusal to comply with the
demand without a House vote, Judge Wilkey responded with a formal subpoena.
Wilkey pressed for disclosure, reminding the House that no records connected with
its deliberative or legislative functions were involved, and giving assurances of confidentiality. The House then overwhelmingly voted to comply — over the objections
of House leaders who argued that the subpoena was overbroad and unduly intrusive
into the private affairs of House members. Based in part on this vote, the U.S. District Court for the District of Columbia refused to enjoin the subpoena. The court
determined that the subpoena was not overbroad in light of the records' prima facie
relevance and the diminished expectation of privacy that accompanied the members'
use of a non-standard, congressional bank. For the exchange of correspondence
between Judge Wilkey and Congress, see *Leaders, Special Counsel Exchange Letters*,
Cong. Q. Weekly Rep., May 2, 1992, at 1193. Eventually, the Sergeant-at-Arms pled
guilty to a charge of embezzlement in connection with shoddy practices at the bank.

2. Executive Privilege

Throughout our history, the executive branch has resisted disclosure of certain
information to private parties or to other branches of government, based on a series
of justifications typically grouped under the label "executive privilege." *See generally*
Louis Fisher, The Politics of Executive Privilege (2004); Mark J. Rozell,
Executive Privilege: Presidential Power, Secrecy, and Accountability (rev.
ed. 2002). Executive privilege is not, however, a clear or unitary concept. It has encompassed claims of varying kinds, some of them having statutory support. Important
variables in assessing a claim of privilege include the nature of the information sought,
the level of government at which the information was developed, the government's
asserted interest in nondisclosure, the availability of the information from other
sources, and the impact of nondisclosure on private rights.

The three varieties of privilege most commonly asserted are for state secrets, for
information the disclosure of which would jeopardize law enforcement activities
(e.g., names of informers), and for intra-branch deliberative communications. In
United States v. Nixon, which follows, the President claimed a privilege to protect
the confidentiality of all his personal communications. This, of course, is potentially a much broader privilege than one based on state secrets or the protection of
particular executive branch functions.

Two fundamental questions underlie controversies involving executive privilege.
First, who decides the scope of the asserted privilege? Whether information should
be disclosed could be regarded as a question committed to the discretion of the executive and unreviewable in court under the political question doctrine. Second, what

difference does the identity of the requester make? Perhaps judicial and congressional subpoenas should be treated in quite different ways.

a. Courts v. The Executive

In 1974, the Court had yet to decide whether the Constitution affords the President an executive privilege, what its scope might be, and who decides its coverage. As you read its landmark decision concerning these issues, consider how persuasively and completely the Court handled them.

United States v. Nixon

418 U.S. 684 (1974)

Chief Justice BURGER delivered the opinion of the Court.

. . . On March 1, 1974, a grand jury of the United States District Court for the District of Columbia returned an indictment charging seven named individuals with various offenses, including conspiracy to defraud the United States and to obstruct justice. [The seven defendants were John N. Mitchell, H. R. Haldeman, John D. Ehrlichman, Charles W. Colson, Robert C. Mardian, Kenneth W. Parkinson, and Gordon Strachan. All were senior officials on the White House staff or the Committee for the Re-election of the President.] Although he was not designated as such in the indictment, the grand jury named the President, among others, as an unindicted coconspirator. On April 18, 1974, upon motion of the Special Prosecutor, a subpoena duces tecum was issued pursuant to Rule 17(c) to the President. . . . This subpoena required the production . . . of certain tapes, memoranda, papers, transcripts or other writings relating to certain precisely identified meetings between the President and others. . . . On April 30, the President publicly released edited transcripts of 43 conversations; portions of 20 conversations subject to subpoena in the present case were included. On May 1, 1974, the President's counsel filed a "special appearance" and a motion to quash the subpoena under Rule 17(c). This motion was accompanied by a formal claim of privilege. . . . [T]he District Court denied the motion to quash . . . [and] ordered "the President or any subordinate officer, official, or employee with custody or control of the documents or objects subpoenaed," to deliver [them] to the District Court. . . .

I

JURISDICTION

The threshold question presented is whether the . . . order of the District Court was an appealable order. . . . [The Court had granted certiorari immediately following appeal of the order to the Court of Appeals.] Here . . . the traditional contempt avenue to immediate appeal is peculiarly inappropriate due to the unique setting in which the question arises. To require a President of the United States to place himself in the posture of disobeying an order of a court merely to trigger the procedural mechanism for review of the ruling would be unseemly, and would present an unnecessary occasion for constitutional confrontation between two branches of the Government. . . . [We] conclude that the order of the District Court was an appealable order. . . .

II

JUSTICIABILITY

[T]he President's counsel argue[s] that the Court lacked jurisdiction to issue the subpoena because the matter was an intra-branch dispute between a subordinate and superior officer of the Executive Branch and hence not subject to judicial resolution [and] that the dispute does not present a "case" or "controversy" which can be adjudicated in the federal courts. . . . Since the Executive Branch has exclusive authority and absolute discretion to decide whether to prosecute a case, it is contended that a President's decision is final in determining what evidence is to be used in a given criminal case. Although his counsel concedes that the President has delegated certain specific powers to the Special Prosecutor, he has not "waived nor delegated to the Special Prosecutor the President's duty to claim privilege as to all materials . . . which fall within the President's inherent authority to refuse to disclose to any executive officer." The Special Prosecutor's demand for the items therefore presents, in the view of the President's counsel, a political question, since it involves a "textually demonstrable" grant of power under Art. II.

The mere assertion of a claim of an "intra-branch dispute," without more, has never operated to defeat federal jurisdiction; justiciability does not depend on such a surface inquiry. . . Our starting point is the nature of the proceeding for which the evidence is sought—here a pending criminal prosecution. . . . Under the authority of Art. II, § 2, Congress has vested in the Attorney General the power to conduct the criminal litigation of the United States Government. 28 U.S.C. § 516. It has also vested in him the power to appoint subordinate officers to assist him in the discharge of his duties. Acting pursuant to those statutes, the Attorney General has delegated the authority to represent the United States in these particular matters to a Special Prosecutor with unique authority and tenure. The regulation gives the Special Prosecutor explicit power to contest the invocation of executive privilege in the process of seeking evidence deemed relevant to the performance of these specially delegated duties.

So long as this regulation is extant it has the force of law. In *United States ex rel. Accardi v. Shaughnessy*, 347 U.S. 260 (1954), regulations of the Attorney General delegated certain of his discretionary powers to the Board of Immigration Appeals and required that Board to exercise its own discretion on appeals in deportation cases. The Court held that so long as the Attorney General's regulations remained operative, he denied himself the authority to exercise the discretion delegated to the Board even though the original authority was his and he could reassert it by amending the regulations. *Service v. Dulles*, 354 U.S. 363, 388 (1957), and *Vitarelli v. Seaton*, 359 U.S. 535 (1959), reaffirmed the basic holding of *Accardi*. Here, as in *Accardi*, it is theoretically possible for the Attorney General to amend or revoke the regulation defining the Special Prosecutor's authority. But he has not done so. So long as this regulation remains in force the Executive Branch is bound by it, and indeed the United States as the sovereign composed of the three branches is bound to respect and to enforce it. . . .

The demands of and the resistance to the subpoena present an obvious controversy in the ordinary sense, but that alone is not sufficient to meet constitutional standards. In the constitutional sense, controversy means more than disagreement and conflict; rather it means the kind of controversy courts traditionally resolve. Here at issue is the production or nonproduction of specified evidence deemed by the Special Prosecutor to be relevant and admissible in a pending criminal case. It is sought by one official of the Executive Branch within the scope of his express authority; it is resisted by the Chief Executive on the ground of his duty to preserve the confidentiality of the communications of the President. . . . This setting assures there is "that concrete adverseness which sharpens the presentation of issues upon which the court so largely depends for illumination of difficult constitutional questions." *Baker v. Carr*, 369 U.S. at 204. Moreover, since the matter is one arising in the regular course of a federal criminal prosecution, it is within the traditional scope of Art. III power. . . .

IV

THE CLAIM OF PRIVILEGE

A

[W]e turn to the claim that the subpoena should be quashed because it demands "confidential conversations between a President and his close advisors that it would be inconsistent with the public interest to produce." The first contention is a broad claim that the separation of powers doctrine precludes judicial review of a President's claim of privilege. The second contention is that if he does not prevail on the claim of absolute privilege, the court should hold as a matter of constitutional law that the privilege prevails over the subpoena duces tecum.

In the performance of assigned constitutional duties each branch of the Government must initially interpret the Constitution, and the interpretation of its powers by any branch is due great respect from the others. The President's counsel . . . reads the Constitution as providing an absolute privilege of confidentiality for all Presidential communications. Many decisions of this Court, however, have unequivocally reaffirmed the holding of *Marbury v. Madison*, 1 Cranch 137 (1803), that "[i]t is emphatically the province and duty of the judicial department to say what the law is."

[O]ther exercises of power by the Executive Branch and the Legislative Branch have been found invalid as in conflict with the Constitution. In a series of cases, the Court interpreted the explicit immunity conferred by express provisions of the Constitution on Members of the House and Senate by the Speech or Debate Clause. . . . And in *Baker v. Carr*, 369 U.S. at 211, the Court stated:

"[D]eciding whether a matter has in any measure been committed by the Constitution to another branch of government, or whether the action of that branch exceeds whatever authority has been committed, is itself a delicate exercise in constitutional interpretation, and is a responsibility of this Court as ultimate interpreter of the Constitution."

Notwithstanding the deference each branch must accord the others, the "judicial Power of the United States" vested in the federal courts by Art. III, § 1, of the Constitution can no more be shared with the Executive Branch than the Chief Executive, for example, can share with the Judiciary the veto power. . . . Any other conclusion would be contrary to the basic concept of separation of powers and the checks and balances that flow from the scheme of a tripartite government. We therefore reaffirm that it is the province and duty of this Court "to say what the law is" with respect to the claim of privilege presented in this case.

B

In support of his claim of absolute privilege, the President's counsel urges two grounds, one of which is common to all governments and one of which is peculiar to our system of separation of powers. The first ground is the valid need for protection of communications between high Government officials and those who advise and assist them in the performance of their manifold duties; the importance of this confidentiality is too plain to require further discussion. Human experience teaches that those who expect public dissemination of their remarks may well temper candor with a concern for appearances and for their own interests to the detriment of the decisionmaking process. Whatever the nature of the privilege of confidentiality of Presidential communications in the exercise of Art. II powers, the privilege can be said to derive from the supremacy of each branch within its own assigned area of constitutional duties. Certain powers and privileges flow from the nature of enumerated powers; the protection of the confidentiality of Presidential communications has similar constitutional underpinnings.

The second ground asserted by the President's counsel in support of the claim of absolute privilege rests on the doctrine of separation of powers. Here it is argued that the independence of the Executive Branch within its own sphere insulates a President from a judicial subpoena in an ongoing criminal prosecution, and thereby protects confidential Presidential communications.

However, neither the doctrine of separation of powers, nor the need for confidentiality of high-level communications, without more, can sustain an absolute, unqualified Presidential privilege of immunity from judicial process under all circumstances. The President's need for complete candor and objectivity from advisers calls for great deference from the courts. However, when the privilege depends solely on the broad, undifferentiated claim of public interest in the confidentiality of such conversations, a confrontation with other values arises. Absent a claim of need to protect military, diplomatic, or sensitive national security secrets, we find it difficult to accept the argument that even the very important interest in confidentiality of Presidential communications is significantly diminished by production of such material for in camera inspection with all the protection that a district court will be obliged to provide.

The impediment that an absolute, unqualified privilege would place in the way of the primary constitutional duty of the Judicial Branch to do justice in criminal prosecutions would plainly conflict with the function of the courts under Art. III. In designing the structure of our Government and dividing and allocating the sovereign power among three co-equal branches, the Framers of the Constitution sought to provide a comprehensive system, but the separate powers were not intended to operate with absolute independence. . . . To read the Art. II powers of the President as providing an absolute privilege as against a subpoena essential to enforcement of criminal statutes on no more than a generalized claim of the public interest in confidentiality of nonmilitary and nondiplomatic discussions would upset the constitutional balance of "a workable government" and gravely impair the role of the courts under Art. III.

C

Since we conclude that the legitimate needs of the judicial process may outweigh Presidential privilege, it is necessary to resolve those competing interests in a manner that preserves the essential functions of each branch. . . . The expectation of a President to the confidentiality of his conversations and correspondence, like the claim of confidentiality of judicial deliberations, for example, has . . . the necessity for protection of the public interest in candid, objective, and even blunt or harsh opinions in Presidential decisionmaking. A President and those who assist him must be free to explore alternatives in the process of shaping policies and making decisions and to do so in a way many would be unwilling to express except privately. These are the considerations justifying a presumptive privilege for Presidential communications. The privilege is fundamental to the operation of Government and inextricably rooted in the separation of powers under the Constitution. In *Nixon v. Sirica*, 487 F.2d 700 (1973), the Court of Appeals held that such Presidential communications are "presumptively privileged," and this position is accepted by both parties in the present litigation. We agree with Chief Justice Marshall's observation, therefore, that "[i]n no case of this kind would a court be required to proceed against the president as against an ordinary individual." *United States v. Burr*, 25 F. Cas., at 192.

But this presumptive privilege must be considered in light of our historic commitment to the rule of law. . . . To ensure that justice is done, it is imperative to the function of courts that compulsory process be available for the production of evidence needed either by the prosecution or by the defense. . . . The privileges . . . are designed to protect weighty and legitimate competing interests. . . . [T]hese exceptions to the demand for every man's evidence are not lightly created nor expansively construed, for they are in derogation of the search for truth.

In this case the President challenges a subpoena served on him as a third party requiring the production of materials for use in a criminal prosecution; he does so on the claim that he has a privilege against disclosure of confidential communications. He does not place his claim of privilege on the ground they are military or diplomatic secrets. As to these areas of Art. II duties the courts have traditionally shown the utmost deference to Presidential responsibilities. . . . In *United States v. Reynolds*, 345 U.S. 1 (1953), dealing with a claimant's demand for evidence in a Tort Claims Act case against the Government, the Court said:

> "It may be possible to satisfy the court, from all the circumstances of the case, that there is a reasonable danger that compulsion of the evidence will expose military matters which, in the interest of national security, should not be divulged. When this is the case, the occasion for the privilege is appropriate, and the court should not jeopardize the security which the privilege is meant to protect by insisting upon an examination of the evidence, even by the judge alone, in chambers."

No case of the Court, however, has extended this high degree of deference to a President's generalized interest in confidentiality. Nowhere in the Constitution . . . is there any explicit reference to a privilege of confidentiality, yet to the extent this interest relates to the effective discharge of a President's powers, it is constitutionally based.

The right to the production of all evidence at a criminal trial similarly has constitutional dimensions. The Sixth Amendment explicitly confers upon every defendant in a criminal trial the right "to be confronted with the witnesses against him" and "to have compulsory process for obtaining witnesses in his favor." Moreover, the Fifth Amendment also guarantees that no person shall be deprived of liberty without due process of law. It is the manifest duty of the courts to vindicate those guarantees, and to accomplish that it is essential that all relevant and admissible evidence be produced.

In this case we must weigh the importance of the general privilege of confidentiality of Presidential communications in performance of the President's responsibilities against the inroads of such a privilege on the fair administration of criminal justice. The interest in preserving confidentiality is weighty indeed and entitled to great respect. However, we cannot conclude that advisers will be moved to temper the candor of their remarks by the infrequent occasions of disclosure because of the possibility that such conversations will be called for in the context of a criminal prosecution. On the other hand, the allowance of the privilege to withhold evidence that is demonstrably relevant in a criminal trial would cut deeply into the guarantee of due process of law and gravely impair the basic function of the courts. . . . The President's broad interest in confidentiality of communications will not be vitiated by disclosure of a limited number of conversations preliminarily shown to have some bearing on the pending criminal cases.

We conclude that when the ground for asserting privilege as to subpoenaed materials sought for use in a criminal trial is based only on the generalized interest in confidentiality, it cannot prevail over the fundamental demands of due process of law in the fair administration of criminal justice. The generalized assertion of privilege must yield to the demonstrated, specific need for evidence in a pending criminal trial.

D

... If a President concludes that compliance with a subpoena would be injurious to the public interest he may properly, as was done here, invoke a claim of privilege on the return of the subpoena. Upon receiving a claim of privilege from the Chief Executive, it became the further duty of the District Court to treat the subpoenaed material as presumptively privileged and to require the Special Prosecutor to demonstrate that the Presidential material was "essential to the justice of the [pending criminal] case." *United States v. Burr*, 25 Fed. Cas., at 192. Here the District Court treated the material as presumptively privileged, proceeded to find that the Special Prosecutor had made a sufficient showing to rebut the presumption, and ordered an *in camera* examination of the subpoenaed material. On the basis of our examination of the record we are unable to conclude that the District Court erred in ordering the inspection. .... We now turn to the important question of the District Court's responsibilities in conducting the *in camera* examination of Presidential materials. ...

E

Statements that meet the test of admissibility and relevance must be isolated; all other material must be excised. .... It is elementary that *in camera* inspection of evidence is always a procedure calling for scrupulous protection against any release or publication of material not found by the court, at that stage, probably admissible in evidence and relevant to the issues of the trial for which it is sought. .... Moreover, a President's communications and activities encompass a vastly wider range of sensitive material than would be true of any "ordinary individual." It is therefore necessary ... to afford Presidential confidentiality the greatest protection consistent with the fair administration of justice. The need for confidentiality even as to idle conversations with associates in which casual reference might be made concerning political leaders within the country or foreign statesmen is too obvious to call for further treatment. .... [O]nce the decision is made to excise, the material is restored to its privileged status and should be returned under seal to its lawful custodian. ...

Affirmed.

Justice REHNQUIST took no part in ... these cases.

---

1. *Threshold Issues.* As Professor Paul Freund put it, in *Foreword: On Presidential Privilege, The Supreme Court, 1973 Term*, 88 Harv. L. Rev. 13 (1974), the *Nixon* case came to the Court "trailing clouds of jurisdictional and procedural issues." Should the Court have invoked one of them to avoid the merits?

(a) *Immunity from Process?* Review the materials in Chapter Two on the amenability of the President to judicial process, where we observe that, although *Nixon*

322   3 · AUTONOMY AND MUTUAL ACCOUNTABILITY AMONG THE BRANCHES

includes no direct analysis of the issue, related litigation probed it extensively. Obviously, the Court held that the President must comply with a subpoena in at least some circumstances. Does the Court state or imply limits to his amenability to process? After *Jones, supra,* is anything left of arguments for presidential immunity from process, at least in federal courts?

(b) *Family Feud?* Do you agree with the Court that this was not just a nonjusticiable family quarrel within the executive? The Court quoted the regulation creating the office of Special Prosecutor, which revealed the extraordinary promise of independence that the President had made:

> "[T]he Special Prosecutor will have the greatest degree of independence that is consistent with the Attorney General's statutory accountability for all matters falling within the jurisdiction of the Department of Justice. The Attorney General will not countermand or interfere with the Special Prosecutor's decisions or actions. . . . In accordance with assurances given by the President to the Attorney General that the President will not exercise his Constitutional powers to effect the discharge of the Special Prosecutor or to limit the independence that he is hereby given, the Special Prosecutor will not be removed from his duties except for extraordinary improprieties on his part. . . ."

The Court then relied on the general doctrine that agencies must obey their own regulations. *See* Joshua Schwartz, *The Irresistible Force Meets the Immovable Object: Estoppel Remedies for an Agency's Violation of its own Regulations or Other Misconduct,* 44 ADMIN. L. REV. 653 (1992); Peter Raven-Hansen, *Regulatory Estoppel: When Agencies Break Their Own "Laws,"* 64 TEXAS L. REV. 1 (1985). It is unclear that this doctrine is of constitutional dimension, however. Is it then a sufficient response? If the President could rescind the regulation and fire the Prosecutor anytime, is there an Article III "case or controversy" here? And is the President competent to bargain away his constitutional power to remove his subordinates? (We will return to these questions in Chapter Four when we consider powers of removal and statutory special prosecutors.)

Professor William Van Alstyne, in *A Political and Constitutional Review of* United States v. Nixon, 22 UCLA L. REV. 116 (1974), suggests that the Court's analysis threatens an unjustifiable fragmentation of executive power. Given that successful prosecution and the confidentiality of presidential communications can both be viewed as "executive" interests, can a court justifiably permit a subordinate official to override the President's determination as to the relative weight of those interests in a particular instance? Would your answer be different if the President were not an unindicted co-conspirator in the case?

(c) *A Political Question?* To the President's argument that the executive should decide claims of privilege, the Court responds with a cite to *Marbury*'s assertion that it is the province of the courts to say what the law is. Is that a sufficient answer?

See Gerald Gunther, *Judicial Hegemony and Legislative Autonomy: The* Nixon *Case and the Impeachment Process*, 22 UCLA L. REV. 30, 34 (1974): "[T]here is nothing in *Marbury* . . . that precludes a constitutional interpretation that gives final authority to another branch." What would be the consequences for our government if the Court had held that the executive has sole power to resolve executive privilege claims?

2. *Balancing, or a Legal Rule?* Turning to the merits of the sufficiency of the President's claim of privilege, what is the holding of *Nixon*? If a presidential communication is relevant and admissible in a criminal trial, should the generalized interest in confidentiality alone ever override the interest in disclosure? If not, does this case involve ad hoc balancing, or a categorical judgment of comparative institutional needs? Is the Court's "balancing" persuasive in *Nixon*? Why is there a threat to due process if the trial court could dismiss the prosecution for unfairness? Note that the defendants are not seeking the evidence, and that privileges such as attorney-client and husband-wife are allowed in criminal trials.

3. *The Source of Executive Privilege.* What is the constitutional basis for the Court's theory of executive privilege? In a footnote, the Court said: "*McCulloch v. Maryland*, 4 Wheat 316, [held] that that which was reasonably appropriate and relevant to the exercise of a granted power was to be considered as accompanying the grant." Is *McCulloch* correctly cited? Doesn't it stand for the proposition that, under the "necessary and proper" clause, *Congress* can exercise powers incident to *its* granted powers? What has that to do with implied presidential powers? Is the Court's ground for privilege one of necessity for the functioning of the Presidency? Can Congress promulgate statutory procedures for the exercise of executive privilege?

4. *Constitutional Crisis.* We have remarked above that the Court's great cases must be read in historical context. To what extent is the Court's approach in *Nixon* a product of the extraordinary historical circumstances of a case whose outcome produced the resignation of a President? *See* Paul J. Mishkin, *Great Cases and Soft Law: A Comment on* United States v. Nixon, 22 UCLA L. REV. 76 (1974), explaining various defects and mysteries in the Court's opinion as "dictated by the self-defensive needs of the Court as an institution." For more analysis of *Nixon*, see the other articles in *Symposium*, United States v. Nixon, 22 UCLA L. REV. 4 (1974); Archibald Cox, *Executive Privilege*, 122 U. PA. L. REV. 1383 (1974); Freund, *supra*; Christopher H. Schroeder, *The Story of* United States v. Nixon: *The President and the Tapes*, in PRESIDENTIAL POWER STORIES (Christopher H. Schroeder & Curtis A. Bradley, eds., 2009). For retrospectives, see *Symposium, Twenty-Five Years after Watergate: The Impact on Legal Ethics and the Investigation of Public Corruption*, 51 HASTINGS L. J. 599 (2000).

The standard account of the Watergate events that led to the case is provided by Washington Post reporters Bob Woodward and Carl Bernstein in ALL THE PRESIDENT'S MEN (1974) and THE FINAL DAYS (1976). A key moment in the unraveling of the Nixon presidency was the testimony by White House counsel-turned-whistleblower

John Dean, exposing a plan by former attorney General John Mitchell to tap phones at Democratic National Committee headquarters in order to gain damaging information concerning the DNC chair, Larry O'Brien.

5. *Iran-Contra and Executive Privilege.* The scope of *United States v. Nixon* was tested in the prosecutions of Lt. Col. Oliver North and former National Security Advisor John Poindexter for offenses related to the Iran-Contra episode, which we discuss in Chapter Five. *See generally* Theodore Draper, A Very Thin Line: The Iran-Contra Affair (1991). In the North case, U.S. District Judge Gerhard Gesell denied the defendant permission to subpoena the personal testimony of former President Reagan. Although Judge Gesell agreed that the court was empowered to subpoena a sitting or former President, he inferred from *Nixon* that such compulsion would be improper unless the testimony was necessary to secure a fair trial. Judge Gesell was unpersuaded that North would be able to obtain any relevant information from President Reagan personally that had not already been made available through other witnesses or in government documents. *United States v. North*, 713 F. Supp. 1448, 1450 (D.D.C. 1989).

In the Poindexter case, however, Judge Harold Greene did authorize a subpoena for President Reagan's testimony. Judge Greene accepted the argument that a President should be compelled to testify only upon a substantial showing of materiality, even without a formal claim of executive privilege, but determined that Poindexter had met this "meticulous" standard. *United States v. Poindexter*, 732 F. Supp. 142, 147–48 (D.D.C. 1990). He determined that President Reagan would be questioned on videotape, in part to permit the deletion of immaterial questions, or questions the answers to which might be privileged. President Reagan agreed to the procedure, and did not invoke executive privilege as to his testimony in general.

Reagan did invoke executive privilege, however, with respect to Poindexter's demand for his personal diaries. Prior to reaching the privilege question, Judge Greene inspected the diaries *in camera* to determine the potentially relevant portions. *United States v. Poindexter*, 727 F. Supp. 1501 (D.D.C. 1989). At the point Judge Greene identified the portions of the diaries he would be prepared to make available to Poindexter, Reagan formally invoked privilege. To assist in his weighing of the competing interests, Judge Greene permitted the President to review Poindexter's detailed explanation of the anticipated use of the diary material in his case. Concluding that Reagan's answers to interrogatories already provided the essence of the targeted information, Judge Greene upheld the claim of privilege. The ultimate convictions in both the North and Poindexter cases were vacated on other grounds. *United States v. North*, 910 F.2d 843 (D.C. Cir. 1990), *modified*, 920 F.2d 940 (D.C. Cir. 1990); *United States v. Poindexter*, 951 F.2d 369 (D.C. Cir. 1991).

6. *Executive Privilege in the Clinton Administration.* President Clinton was involved in a series of litigations involving various kinds of privilege claims, with results that were quite unfriendly to expansive views of presidential privileges. *See generally*

Symposium, Executive Privilege and the Clinton Presidency, 8 Wm. & Mary Bill Rts. J. 535 (2000); Jonathan Turley, *Paradise Lost: The Clinton Administration and the Erosion of Executive Privilege*, 60 Md. L.Rev. 205 (2001); Dawn Johnsen, *Executive Privilege Since* United States v. Nixon: *Issues of Motivation and Accommodation*, 83 Minn. L. Rev. 1127 (1999); Patricia Wald & Jonathan Siegel, *The D.C. Circuit and the Struggle for Control of Presidential Information*, 90 Geo. L. J. 737 (2002).

The first case was the only one that did not involve the President's own possible misconduct. Allegations that Secretary of Agriculture Mike Espy had received illegal gifts led to appointment of an Independent Counsel (and eventually to Espy's acquittal at trial). President Clinton ordered his White House Counsel to investigate as well, to see if disciplinary action was warranted. The Independent Counsel had the grand jury subpoena the White House Counsel's investigative records. The President asserted executive privilege for some of the documents, including some that were not prepared for his own examination. Hence the case raised an issue not present in *Nixon*: the applicability of the privilege to materials held by presidential aides in the scope of preparing advice for him, as distinguished from direct communications between aides and the President. The court of appeals upheld the applicability of the privilege to "communications authored by or solicited and received by presidential advisers." *In re Sealed Case (Espy),* 121 F.3d 729 (D.C. Cir. 1997). Judge Wald framed the issue as whether a narrower definition of privilege would "'impede the President's ability to perform his constitutional duty,'" quoting *Morrison v. Olson,* 487 U.S. 654, 691 (1988) (*infra*, Chapter Four), and concluded that it would, since the materials related to the President's constitutional power to remove Espy. Proceeding to employ the *Nixon* balance between the President's interest in confidentiality and the need for evidence in a pending trial, the court required disclosure of evidence that is "directly relevant" and not available "with due diligence" from another source. Hence *Espy* would extend the privilege from the Oval Office to the remainder of the West Wing of the White House, with qualifications.

President Clinton's struggles with Independent Counsel Starr led to assertions of four different kinds of privilege, in which Clinton was mostly unsuccessful. First, when Starr subpoenaed presidential aides Bruce Lindsey and Sidney Blumenthal to the grand jury to testify about Monica Lewinsky, Clinton interposed a claim of executive privilege. District Judge Johnson rejected the OIC's argument that the communications in question were purely private, and that *Nixon* applied only to "presidential decisionmaking and deliberation." *In re Grand Jury Proceedings,* 5 F. Supp. 2d 21 (D.D.C. 1998). She noted the difficulty of any easy distinction between the two categories, and treated the communications as presumptively privileged. Following *Espy*, the judge then asked whether the material "likely contains important evidence" that "is not available with due diligence elsewhere." After reviewing the evidence in camera, she concluded that the OIC had met its burden, and rejected the President's claim. He did not appeal this part of the decision.

Second, the circuit courts twice rejected Clinton's claim of a governmental attorney-client privilege. As part of the Whitewater investigation, the OIC subpoenaed notes taken by attorneys in the White House Counsel's office at meetings with Hillary Rodham Clinton and her private attorney during breaks in her grand jury testimony. The court rejected any executive branch attorney-client privilege in the context of a criminal investigation: "We . . . find it significant that executive branch employees, including attorneys, are under a statutory duty to report criminal wrongdoing by other employees to the Attorney General. *See* 28 U.S.C. §535(b) (1994). Even more importantly, however, the general duty of public service calls upon government employees and agencies to favor disclosure over concealment." *In re Grand Jury Subpoena Duces Tecum*, 112 F. 3d 910 (8th Cir. 1997), *cert. denied*, 521 U.S. 1105 (1997). The President then asserted an attorney-client privilege concerning Bruce Lindsey's appearance before the Lewinsky grand jury, and lost again:

> . . . [T]he principal question is whether an attorney in the Office of the President, having been called before a federal grand jury, may refuse, on the basis of a government attorney-client privilege, to answer questions about possible criminal conduct by government officials and others. To state the question is to suggest the answer, for the Office of the President is a part of the federal government, consisting of government employees doing government business, and neither legal authority nor policy nor experience suggests that a federal government entity can maintain the ordinary common law attorney-client privilege to withhold information relating to a federal criminal offense. The Supreme Court and this court have held that even the constitutionally based executive privilege for presidential communications fundamental to the operation of the government can be overcome upon a proper showing of need for the evidence in criminal trials and in grand jury proceedings. *Nixon.* In the context of federal criminal investigations and trials, there is no basis for treating legal advice differently from any other advice the Office of the President receives in performing its constitutional functions. The public interest in honest government and in exposing wrongdoing by government officials, as well as the tradition and practice, acknowledged by the Office of the President and by former White House Counsel, of government lawyers reporting evidence of federal criminal offenses whenever such evidence comes to them, lead to the conclusion that a government attorney may not invoke the attorney-client privilege in response to grand jury questions seeking information relating to the possible commission of a federal crime. The extent to which the communications of White House Counsel are privileged against disclosure to a federal grand jury depends, therefore, on whether the communications contain information of possible criminal offenses.

In re Lindsey, 148 F.3d 1100 (D.C. Cir.) (per curiam), *cert. denied*, 525 U.S. 996 (1998); *See* Nelson Lund & Douglas R. Cox, *Executive Power and Governmental Attorney-Client Privilege: The Clinton Legacy,* 17 J. OF LAW & POLITICS 631 (2001).

Third, the D.C. Circuit rejected a claim, made by the Secret Service rather than Clinton himself, of a "protective functions" privilege for the Service's contacts with the President. *In re Sealed Case*, 148 F.3d 1073 (D.C. Cir. 1998) (per curiam), *reh'g denied*, 146 F.3d 1031 (D.C. Cir. 1998), *cert. denied*, 525 U.S. 990. The court said: "As described by the Secret Service, the protective function privilege absolutely protects 'information obtained by Secret Service personnel while performing their protective function in physical proximity to the President,' except that the privilege 'does not apply, in the context of a federal investigation or prosecution, to bar testimony by an officer or agent concerning observations or statements that, at the time they were made, were sufficient to provide reasonable grounds for believing that a felony has been, is being, or will be committed.'" There was no precedent for such a privilege, and the court would not supply one. The court concluded that the Secret Service had failed to "demonstrate that recognition of the privilege in its proposed form will materially enhance presidential security by lessening any tendency of the President to 'push away' his protectors in situations where there is some risk to his safety." Evidence of misconduct, the court thought, was likely to occur in private, not out in public, where most dangers lurk.

Fourth, in the lone victory for Clinton, the Supreme Court held that the attorney-client privilege survives the death of the client. *Swidler & Berlin v. United States*, 524 U.S. 399 (1998). Deputy White House Counsel Vincent Foster, Jr., had consulted a private attorney while investigations were pending, days before he committed suicide. Independent Counsel Starr subpoenaed the attorney's notes of the conversation, and lost. The Court thought that the weight of precedent supported survival of the privilege: "Knowing that communications will remain confidential even after death encourages the client to communicate fully and frankly with counsel. While the fear of disclosure, and the consequent withholding of information from counsel, may be reduced if disclosure is limited to posthumous disclosure in a criminal context, it seems unreasonable to assume that it vanishes altogether. Clients may be concerned about reputation, civil liability, or possible harm to friends or family. Posthumous disclosure of such communications may be as feared as disclosure during the client's lifetime." The Court noted that Foster, "perhaps already contemplating suicide," might not have sought legal advice if he had doubted that the conversation would be privileged.

7. Executive Privilege in the George W. Bush Administration. The second President Bush was extremely protective of executive branch information. Notable controversies that are discussed later in this chapter concerned the scope of the state secrets privilege, an executive order relating to presidential records, confidentiality issues involving meetings of the energy task force (also mentioned in Chapter Two with the standing issues in *Walker v. Cheney*), and an executive privilege controversy with Congress concerning the firing of some United States Attorneys. In Chapter Five we consider the Bush administration's policy concerning classification of government documents, which was also controversial.

8. *Openness in the Obama Administration.* The Obama administration immediately moved to set a different tone regarding openness from that of its predecessor. On January 21, 2009, his first full day in office, President Obama issued a Memorandum on Transparency and Open Government, promising to conduct as open a government as possible, and initiating a complex process of public participation in formulation of an Open Government Directive from OMB to the agencies, which issued on December 8, 2009. The Memorandum enshrined a presumption of openness and called upon agencies to publish more information online, to improve the quality of government information, to establish a culture of open government, and to establish a framework to promote these goals. OMB, in turn, issued a directive instructing every executive agency to publish an Open Government Plan on its website and to update that plan every two years. Groups that advocate for openness and transparency in government were initially encouraged as these practices seemed to usher in an attitude toward disclosure that was distinct from previous administrations — such as the public release of White House visitor logs and permission to photograph the arrival in the United States of war dead from Afghanistan. Ultimately, however, these advocates ended up giving the Obama Administration mixed reviews. They note that OMB itself never complied with the directive to update its Open Government Plan. *See* http://www.openthegovernment.org/sites/default/files/Letter%20 to%20the%20President-OMB%20Open%20Government%20Plan.pdf. Moreover, most agencies continued to do a poor job of responding to FOIA requests. *See* Center for Effective Government, Making the Grade: Access to Information Scorecard 2015, available at http://www.foreffectivegov.org/access-to-information-scorecard-2015. The Obama Administration continued the Bush Administration's trend of over-classifying information. Ironically, President Obama himself complained that too much information was being classified. *See* "Exclusive: President Barack Obama on Fox News Sunday" (April 10, 2016), available at http://www.foxnews.com/transcript /2016/04/10/exclusive-president-barack-obama-on-fox-news-sunday.html. The Obama Administration also aggressively pursued leakers. Finally, the Obama pursued the same expansive approach to the state secrets privilege championed by the Bush Administration, which we discuss infra. On the other hand, nearing the end of his term, President Obama signed the bipartisan FOIA Improvement Act of 2016, Pub L. No. 114-185 (June 30, 2016), which among things, codified the presumption of openness established in his 2009 Memorandum.

9. *Openness in the Trump Administration.* It is much too early in the Trump Administration to draw any conclusions regarding its commitment to transparency. The early indications are, however, that it will be less forthcoming than its predecessor was. For example, the White House has announced that it will not publicly disclose visitor logs. It has been reported that "[t]he Trump administration has removed or tucked away a wide variety of information that until recently was provided to the public, limiting access, for instance, to disclosures about workplace violations, energy efficiency and animal-welfare abuses." Juliet Eilperin, Under Trump, Inconvenient

Data Is Being Sidelined, Wash. Post (May 17, 2017). And the Administration seems to be making concerted efforts to prevent leaks and to chill disclosures by prosecuting leakers. For example, NSA contractor Reality Winner has been arrested for leaking information regarding attempts by Russia to influence the 2016 presidential election.

10. *Another Fight Over White House Tapes?* After firing FBI Director James Comey, President Trump tweeted, "James Comey better hope that there are no 'tapes' of our conversations before he starts leaking to the press!" In testimony before the Senate Intelligence Committee, Comey declared "Lordy, I hope there are tapes." If there are in fact such tapes and if the Senate Intelligence Committee were to subpoena them, would the President be required to comply? Would the subpoena stand on stronger ground if it were issued by a (hypothetical) House Impeachment Committee?

The State Secrets Privilege

The state secrets privilege enables a federal executive to bar discovery of evidence whose disclosure may prejudice national security. The origins of the privilege are unclear. Chief Justice Marshall, sitting on circuit, recognized the government's authority to withhold secrets in the treason trial of Aaron Burr (*see* Freund, *supra*), and the Supreme Court, in 1876, barred a Civil War spy from suing the Government for breaching an alleged agreement to compensate him for wartime espionage services. *Totten v. United States*, 92 U.S. 105 (1876). Wigmore later observed magisterially that the existence of a state secrets privilege "has never been doubted" 8 John H. Wigmore, Evidence § 2378 at 794 (John T. McNaughten rev. 1961). Still, the Supreme Court did not establish the modern formulation of the privilege until it decided *United States v. Reynolds*, 345 U.S. 1 (1952).

Reynolds was a wrongful death action under the Federal Tort Claims Act, brought for the death of civilians in the crash of an Air Force bomber. Plaintiffs sought production of the official crash report. The government resisted, claiming in a public affidavit by the Secretary of the Air Force that the state secrets privilege barred discovery of the report. Instead, the Secretary offered to produce the surviving crew members for depositions about unclassified matters. The Court upheld the claim of privilege. Although a statute and regulations supported the Secretary's claim of privilege in this case, Chief Justice Vinson noted that the ultimate source of a state secrets privilege is "an inherent executive power which is protected in the constitutional system of separation of power." His opinion went on (345 U.S. at 7–11):

> The privilege belongs to the Government and must be asserted by it; it can neither be claimed nor waived by a private party. It is not to be lightly invoked. There must be a formal claim of privilege, lodged by the head of the department which has control over the matter, after actual personal consideration by that officer. The court itself must determine whether the circumstances are appropriate for the claim of privilege, and yet do so without forcing a disclosure of the very thing the privilege is designed to protect. . . .

Judicial control over the evidence in a case cannot be abdicated to the caprice of executive officers. Yet we will not go so far as to say that the court may automatically require a complete disclosure to the judge before the claim of privilege will be accepted in any case. It may be possible to satisfy the court, from all the circumstances of the case, that there is a reasonable danger that compulsion of the evidence will expose military matters which, in the interest of national security, should not be divulged. When this is the case, the occasion for the privilege is appropriate, and the court should not jeopardize the security which the privilege is meant to protect by insisting upon an examination of the evidence, even by the judge alone, in chambers. . . .

In each case, the showing of necessity which is made will determine how far the court should probe in satisfying itself that the occasion for invoking the privilege is appropriate. Where there is a strong showing of necessity, the claim of privilege should not be lightly accepted, but even the most compelling necessity cannot overcome the claim of privilege if the court is ultimately satisfied that military secrets are at stake. A fortiori, where necessity is dubious, a formal claim of privilege . . . will have to prevail. Here, necessity was greatly minimized by an available alternative [examination of the surviving crew members]. By their failure to pursue that alternative, respondents have posed the privilege question for decision with the formal claim of privilege set against a dubious showing of necessity.

The outcome in *Reynolds*, shielding information on the crash from families of the victims, created an obvious risk that the executive would hide embarrassing information rather than real secrets. It turns out that this was true in *Reynolds* itself— the information revealed negligence and contained no secrets. *See* Louis Fisher, In the Name of National Security: Unchecked Presidential Power and the *Reynolds* Case (2006). This potential for abuse of the privilege has bedeviled the cases ever since. The ambiguities of the state secrets doctrine and the complexities of its application are well illustrated in the following opinion:

Mohamed v. Jeppesen Dataplan, Inc.
614 F.3d 1070 (9th Cir. 2010) (en banc).

FISHER, Circuit Judge.

This case requires us to address the difficult balance the state secrets doctrine strikes between fundamental principles of our liberty, including justice, transparency, accountability and national security. Although as judges we strive to honor *all* of these principles, there are times when exceptional circumstances create an irreconcilable conflict between them. On those rare occasions, we are bound to follow the Supreme Court's admonition that "even the most compelling necessity cannot overcome the claim of privilege if the court is ultimately satisfied that [state] secrets are at stake." *United States v. Reynolds,* 345 U.S. 1, 11 (1953). After much deliberation, we reluctantly conclude this is such a case, and the plaintiffs' action must be dismissed. Accordingly, we affirm the judgment of the district court.

I. BACKGROUND

... A. Factual Background

1. The Extraordinary Rendition Program

Plaintiffs allege that the Central Intelligence Agency ("CIA"), working in concert with other government agencies and officials of foreign governments, operated an extraordinary rendition program to gather intelligence by apprehending foreign nationals suspected of involvement in terrorist activities and transferring them in secret to foreign countries for detention and interrogation by United States or foreign officials. According to plaintiffs, this program has allowed agents of the U.S. government "to employ interrogation methods that would [otherwise have been] prohibited under federal or international law." Relying on documents in the public domain, plaintiffs, all foreign nationals, claim they were each processed through the extraordinary rendition program. They also make the following individual allegations. [The court summarizes the allegations of five foreign nationals, each of whom claimed to have been subject to torture in Egypt, Pakistan, Morocco, or Afghanistan, after being transferred to the custody of U.S. officials, who had them flown to their respective sites of incarceration and subsequent mistreatment.]

2. Jeppesen's Alleged Involvement in the Rendition Program

Plaintiffs contend that publicly available information establishes that defendant Jeppesen Dataplan, Inc., a U.S. corporation, provided flight planning and logistical support services to the aircraft and crew on all of the flights transporting each of the five plaintiffs among the various locations where they were detained and allegedly subjected to torture. The complaint asserts "Jeppesen played an integral role in the forced" abductions and detentions and "provided direct and substantial services to the United States for its so-called 'extraordinary rendition' program," thereby "enabling the clandestine and forcible transportation of terrorism suspects to secret overseas detention facilities." It also alleges that Jeppesen provided this assistance with actual or constructive "knowledge of the objectives of the rendition program," including knowledge that the plaintiffs "would be subjected to forced disappearance, detention, and torture" by U.S. and foreign government officials.

B. Summary of the Claims

Plaintiffs brought suit against Jeppesen under the Alien Tort Statute, 28 U.S.C. § 1350, alleging seven theories of liability marshaled under two claims, one for "forced disappearance" and another for "torture and other cruel, inhuman or degrading treatment." ...

C. Procedural History

Before Jeppesen answered the complaint, the United States moved to intervene and to dismiss plaintiffs' complaint under the state secrets doctrine. The then-Director of the CIA, General Michael Hayden, filed two declarations in support of the motion to dismiss, one classified, the other redacted and unclassified. The public declaration states that "[d]isclosure of the information covered by this privilege assertion reasonably could be expected to cause serious—and in some instances, exceptionally grave—damage to the national security of the United States and, therefore, the information should be excluded from any use in this case." It further asserts that "because highly classified information is central to the allegations and issues in this case, the risk is great that further litigation will lead to disclosures harmful to U.S. national security and, accordingly, this case should be dismissed."

The district court granted the motions to intervene and dismiss and entered judgment in favor of Jeppesen, stating that "at the core of Plaintiffs' case against Defendant Jeppesen are 'allegations' of covert U.S. military or CIA operations in foreign countries against foreign nationals—clearly a subject matter which is a state secret." Plaintiffs appealed. A three-judge panel of this court reversed and remanded, holding that the government had failed to establish a basis for dismissal under the state secrets doctrine but permitting the government to reassert the doctrine at subsequent stages of the litigation. *Jeppesen I,* 579 F.3d at 953, 961–62. We took the case en banc to resolve questions of exceptional importance regarding the scope and application of the state secrets doctrine.

The government maintains its assertion of privilege on appeal, continuing to rely on General Hayden's two declarations. While the appeal was pending Barack Obama succeeded George W. Bush as President of the United States. On September 23, 2009, the Obama administration announced new policies for invoking the state secrets privilege, effective October 1, 2009, in a memorandum from the Attorney General. *See* Memorandum from the Attorney Gen. to the Heads of Executive Dep'ts and Agencies on Policies and Procedures Governing Invocation of the State Secrets Privilege (Sept. 23, 2009) ("Holder Memo"), http://www.justice.gov/opa/documents/state-secret-privileges.pdf. The government certified both in its briefs and at oral argument before the en banc court that officials at the "highest levels of the Department of Justice" of the new administration had reviewed the assertion of privilege in this case and determined that it was appropriate under the newly announced policies.

II. STANDARD OF REVIEW

We review de novo the interpretation and application of the state secrets doctrine and review for clear error the district court's underlying factual findings. *Al-Haramain Islamic Found., Inc. v. Bush,* 507 F.3d 1190, 1196 (9th Cir. 2007).

III. THE STATE SECRETS DOCTRINE

The Supreme Court has long recognized that in exceptional circumstances courts must act in the interest of the country's national security to prevent disclosure of state secrets, even to the point of dismissing a case entirely. *See Totten v. United States,* 92 U.S. 105 (1876). The contemporary state secrets doctrine encompasses two applications of this principle. One completely bars adjudication of claims premised on state secrets (the "Totten bar"); the other is an evidentiary privilege ("the *Reynolds* privilege") that excludes privileged evidence from the case and *may* result in dismissal of the claims. *See United States v. Reynolds*, 345 U.S. 1, 73 S.Ct. 528, 97 L.Ed. 727 (1953). We first address the nature of these applications and then apply them to the facts of this case.

A. The *Totten* Bar

In 1876 the Supreme Court stated "as a *general principle* [ ] that public policy forbids the maintenance of any suit in a court of justice, the trial of which would inevitably lead to the disclosure of matters which the law itself regards as confidential." *Totten*, 92 U.S. at 107 (emphasis added). The Court again invoked the principle in 1953, citing *Totten* for the proposition that "where the very subject matter of the action" is "a matter of state secret," an action may be "dismissed on the pleadings without ever reaching the question of evidence" because it is "so obvious that the action should never prevail over the privilege." *Reynolds*, 345 U.S. at 11 n. 26. This application of *Totten's* general principle — which we refer to as the *Totten* bar — is "designed not merely to defeat the asserted claims, but to preclude judicial inquiry" entirely. *Tenet v. Doe*, 544 U.S. 1, 7 n. 4 (2005).

The Court first applied this bar in *Totten* itself, where the estate of a Civil War spy sued the United States for breaching an alleged agreement to compensate the spy for his wartime espionage services. Setting forth the "general principle" quoted above, the Court held that the action was barred because it was premised on the existence of a "contract for secret services with the government," which was "a fact not to be disclosed." *Totten*, 92 U.S. at 107.

A century later, the Court applied the *Totten* bar in *Weinberger v. Catholic Action of Hawaii/Peace Education Project*, 454 U.S. 139, 146–47 (1981). There, the plaintiffs sued under the National Environmental Policy Act of 1969, 42 U.S.C. §4321 *et seq.,* to compel the Navy to prepare an environmental impact statement regarding a military facility where the Navy allegedly proposed to store nuclear weapons. The Court held that the allegations were "beyond judicial scrutiny" because, "[d]ue to national security reasons, . . . the Navy can neither admit nor deny that it proposes to store nuclear weapons at [the facility]." *Id.* (citing *Totten*, 92 U.S. at 107).

The Court more recently reaffirmed and explained the *Totten* bar in a case involving two former Cold War spies who accused the CIA of reneging on a commitment to provide financial support in exchange for their espionage services. Relying on "*Totten's* core concern" of "preventing the existence of the plaintiffs' relationship with the Government from being revealed," the Court held that the action was, like *Totten* and *Weinberger,* incapable of judicial review. *Tenet,* 544 U.S. at 8–10.

Plaintiffs contend that the *Totten* bar applies *only* to a narrow category of cases they say are not implicated here, namely claims premised on a plaintiff's espionage relationship with the government. We disagree. We read the Court's discussion of *Totten* in *Reynolds* to mean that the *Totten* bar applies to cases in which "the very subject matter of the action" is "a matter of state secret." *Reynolds*, 345 U.S. at 11, n.26, 73 S.Ct. 528. "[A] contract to perform espionage" is only an example. *Id.* This conclusion is confirmed by *Weinberger*, which relied on the *Totten* bar to hold that a case involving nuclear weapons secrets, and having nothing to do with espionage contracts, was "beyond judicial scrutiny." . . .

We also disagree with plaintiffs' related contention that the *Totten* bar cannot apply unless the *plaintiff* is a party to a secret agreement with the government. The environmental groups and individuals who were the plaintiffs in *Weinberger* were not parties to agreements with the United States, secret or otherwise. The purpose of the bar, moreover, is to prevent the revelation of state secrets harmful to national security, a concern no less pressing when the plaintiffs are strangers to the espionage agreement that their litigation threatens to reveal. Thus, even if plaintiffs were correct that the *Totten* bar is limited to cases premised on espionage agreements with the government, we would reject their contention that the bar is necessarily limited to cases in which the plaintiffs are themselves parties to those agreements.

B. The *Reynolds* Privilege

In addition to the *Totten* bar, the state secrets doctrine encompasses a "privilege against revealing military [or state] secrets, a privilege which is well established in the law of evidence." *Reynolds*, 345 U.S. at 6–7. A successful assertion of privilege under *Reynolds* will remove the privileged evidence from the litigation. Unlike the *Totten* bar, a valid claim of privilege under *Reynolds* does not automatically require dismissal of the case. In some instances, however, the assertion of privilege will require dismissal because it will become apparent during the *Reynolds* analysis that the case cannot proceed without privileged evidence, or that litigating the case to a judgment on the merits would present an unacceptable risk of disclosing state secrets. . . .

Analyzing claims under the *Reynolds* privilege involves three steps:

> First, we must "ascertain that the procedural requirements for invoking the state secrets privilege have been satisfied." Second, we must make an independent determination whether the information is privileged. . . . Finally, "the ultimate question to be resolved is how the matter should proceed in light of the successful privilege claim."

Al-Haramain, 507 F.3d at 1202 (citation omitted) (quoting *El-Masri v. United States*, 479 F.3d 296, 304 (4th Cir. 2007)). We discuss these steps in turn.

1. Procedural Requirements

a. Assertion of the privilege. . . . In the present case, General Michael Hayden, then-Director of the CIA, asserted the initial, formal claim of privilege and submitted detailed public and classified declarations. We were informed at oral argument that the current Attorney General, Eric Holder, has also reviewed and approved the ongoing claim of privilege. Although *Reynolds* does not require review and approval by the Attorney General when a different agency head has control of the matter, such additional review by the executive branch's chief lawyer is appropriate and to be encouraged.

b. Timing. Plaintiffs contend that the government's assertion of privilege was premature, urging that the *Reynolds* privilege cannot be raised before an obligation to produce specific evidence subject to a claim of privilege has actually arisen. We disagree. The privilege may be asserted at any time, even at the pleading stage.

The privilege indisputably may be raised with respect to discovery requests seeking information the government contends is privileged. Courts have repeatedly sustained claims of privilege under those circumstances. We also conclude that the government may assert a *Reynolds* privilege claim prospectively, even at the pleading stage, rather than waiting for an evidentiary dispute to arise during discovery or trial. In some cases, the court may be able to determine with certainty from the nature of the allegations and the government's declarations in support of its claim of secrecy that litigation must be limited or cut off in order to protect state secrets, even before any discovery or evidentiary requests have been made. In such cases, waiting for specific evidentiary disputes to arise would be both unnecessary and potentially dangerous. The showing the government must make to prevail on a claim of state secrets privilege may be especially difficult when attempted before any request for specific information or evidence has actually been made, but foreclosing the government from even trying to make that showing would be inconsistent with the need to protect state secrets.

2. The Court's Independent Evaluation of the Claim of Privilege

When the privilege has been properly invoked, "we must make an independent determination whether the information is privileged." *Al-Haramain,* 507 F.3d at 1202. . . . This step in the *Reynolds* analysis "places on the court a special burden to assure itself that an appropriate balance is struck between protecting national security matters and preserving an open court system." 507 F.3d at 1203. In evaluating the need for secrecy, "we acknowledge the need to defer to the Executive on matters of foreign policy and national security and surely cannot legitimately find ourselves second guessing the Executive in this arena." *Id.* But "the state secrets doctrine does not represent a surrender of judicial control over access to the courts." *El-Masri,* 479 F.3d at 312. . . .

We do not offer a detailed definition of what constitutes a state secret. The Supreme Court in *Reynolds* found it sufficient to say that the privilege covers "matters which, in the interest of national security, should not be divulged." We do note, however, that an executive decision to *classify* information is insufficient to establish that the information is privileged. Although classification may be an indication of the need for secrecy, treating it as conclusive would trivialize the court's role, which the Supreme Court has clearly admonished "cannot be abdicated to the caprice of executive officers."

3. How Should the Matter Proceed?

When a court sustains a claim of privilege, it must then resolve " 'how the matter should proceed in light of the successful privilege claim.' " *Al-Haramain,* 507 F.3d at

1202. . . . Ordinarily, simply excluding or otherwise walling off the privileged information may suffice to protect the state secrets and "'the case will proceed accordingly, with no consequences save those resulting from the loss of evidence.'" In some instances, however, application of the privilege may require dismissal of the action. When this point is reached, the *Reynolds* privilege converges with the *Totten* bar, because both require dismissal. There are three circumstances when the *Reynolds* privilege would justify terminating a case.

First, if "the plaintiff cannot prove the *prima facie* elements of her claim with nonprivileged evidence, then the court may dismiss her claim as it would with any plaintiff who cannot prove her case." Second, "'if the privilege deprives the defendant of information that would otherwise give the defendant a valid defense to the claim, then the court may grant summary judgment to the defendant.'"

Third, and relevant here, even if the claims and defenses might theoretically be established without relying on privileged evidence, it may be impossible to proceed with the litigation because—privileged evidence being inseparable from nonprivileged information that will be necessary to the claims or defenses—litigating the case to a judgment on the merits would present an unacceptable risk of disclosing state secrets.

IV. APPLICATION

We therefore turn to the application of the state secrets doctrine in this case. The government contends that plaintiffs' lawsuit should be dismissed, whether under the *Totten* bar or the *Reynolds* privilege, because "state secrets are so central to this case that permitting further proceeding[s] would create an intolerable risk of disclosure that would jeopardize national security." Plaintiffs argue that the *Totten* bar does not apply and that, even if the government is entitled to some protection under the *Reynolds* privilege, at least some claims survive. The district court appears to have dismissed the action under the *Totten* bar, making a "threshold determination" that "the very subject matter of the case is a state secret." Having dismissed on that basis, the district court did not address whether application of the *Reynolds* privilege would require dismissal.

We do not find it quite so clear that the very subject matter of this case is a state secret. Nonetheless, having conducted our own detailed analysis, we conclude that the district court reached the correct result because dismissal is warranted even under *Reynolds*. Recognizing the serious consequences to plaintiffs of dismissal, we explain our ruling so far as possible within the considerable constraints imposed on us by the state secrets doctrine itself.

A. The *Totten* Bar

The categorical, "absolute protection [the Court] found necessary in enunciating the *Totten* rule" is appropriate only in narrow circumstances. The *Totten* bar applies only when the "very subject matter" of the action is a state secret — i.e., when it is "obvious" without conducting the detailed analysis required by *Reynolds* "that the action [c]ould never prevail over the privilege." *Reynolds,* 345 U.S. at 11 n.26. The Court has applied the *Totten* bar on just three occasions, involving two different kinds of state secrets: In *Tenet* and *Totten* the Court applied the *Totten* bar to "the distinct class of cases that depend upon clandestine spy relationships," and in *Weinberger* the Court applied the *Totten* bar to a case that depended on whether the Navy proposed to store nuclear weapons at a particular facility. Although the Court has not limited the *Totten* bar to cases premised on secret espionage agreements or the location of nuclear weapons, neither has it offered much guidance on when the *Totten* bar applies beyond these limited circumstances. Because the *Totten* bar is rarely applied and not clearly defined, because it is a judge-made doctrine with extremely harsh consequences and because conducting a more detailed analysis will tend to improve the accuracy, transparency and legitimacy of the proceedings, district courts presented with disputes about state secrets should ordinarily undertake a detailed *Reynolds* analysis before deciding whether dismissal on the pleadings is justified.

Here, some of plaintiffs' claims might well fall within the *Totten* bar. In particular, their allegations that Jeppesen conspired with agents of the United States in plaintiffs' forced disappearance, torture and degrading treatment are premised on the existence of an alleged covert relationship between Jeppesen and the government — a matter that the Fourth Circuit has concluded is "practically indistinguishable from that categorically barred by *Totten* and *Tenet.*" *El-Masri,* 479 F.3d at 309. On the other hand, allegations based on plaintiffs' theory that Jeppesen should be liable simply for what it "should have known" about the alleged unlawful extraordinary rendition program while participating in it are not so obviously tied to proof of a secret agreement between Jeppesen and the government.

We do not resolve the difficult question of precisely which claims may be barred under *Totten* because application of the *Reynolds* privilege leads us to conclude that this litigation cannot proceed further. We rely on the *Reynolds* privilege rather than the *Totten* bar for several reasons. First, the government has asserted the *Reynolds* privilege along with the *Totten* bar, inviting the further inquiry *Reynolds* requires and presenting a record that compels dismissal even on this alternate ground. Second, we have discretion to affirm on any basis supported by the record. Third, resolving this case under *Reynolds* avoids difficult questions about the precise scope of the *Totten* bar and permits us to conduct a searching judicial review, fulfilling our obligation under *Reynolds* "to review the [government's claim] with a very careful, indeed a skeptical, eye, and not to accept at face value the government's claim or justification of privilege." *Al-Haramain,* 507 F.3d at 1203.

B. The *Reynolds* Privilege

There is no dispute that the government has complied with *Reynolds'* procedural requirements for invoking the state secrets privilege by filing General Hayden's formal claim of privilege in his public declaration. We therefore focus on the second and third steps in the *Reynolds* analysis . . .

1. Whether and to What Extent the Evidence Is Privileged

The government asserts the state secrets privilege over four categories of evidence. In particular, the government contends that neither it nor Jeppesen should be compelled, through a responsive pleading, discovery responses or otherwise, to disclose: "[1] information that would tend to confirm or deny whether Jeppesen or any other private entity assisted the CIA with clandestine intelligence activities; [2] information about whether any foreign government cooperated with the CIA in clandestine intelligence activities; [3] information about the scope or operation of the CIA terrorist detention and interrogation program; [or 4] any other information concerning CIA clandestine intelligence operations that would tend to reveal intelligence activities, sources, or methods." These indisputably are matters that the state secrets privilege may cover.

We have thoroughly and critically reviewed the government's public and classified declarations and are convinced that at least some of the matters it seeks to protect from disclosure in this litigation are valid state secrets, "which, in the interest of national security, should not be divulged." *Reynolds,* 345 U.S. at 10. The government's classified disclosures to the court are persuasive that compelled or inadvertent disclosure of such information in the course of litigation would seriously harm legitimate national security interests. In fact, every judge who has reviewed the government's formal, classified claim of privilege in this case agrees that in this sense the claim of privilege is proper, although we have different views as to the scope of the privilege and its impact on plaintiffs' case. The plaintiffs themselves "do not dispute that, during the course of litigation, there may well be relevant evidence that may be properly withheld pursuant to the privilege."

We are precluded from explaining precisely which matters the privilege covers lest we jeopardize the secrets we are bound to protect. We can say, however, that the secrets fall within one or more of the four categories identified by the government and that we have independently and critically confirmed that their disclosure could be expected to cause significant harm to national security.

2. Effect on the Proceedings

Having determined that the privilege applies, we next determine whether the case must be dismissed under the *Reynolds* privilege. We have thoroughly considered plaintiffs' claims, several possible defenses and the prospective path of this litigation. We also have carefully and skeptically reviewed the government's classified submissions, which include supplemental information not presented to the district court. We rely heavily on these submissions, which describe the state secrets implicated here, the harm to national security that the government believes would result from explicit or implicit disclosure and the reasons why, in the government's view, further litigation would risk that disclosure.

Given plaintiffs' extensive submission of public documents and the stage of the litigation, we do not rely on the first two circumstances in which the *Reynolds* privilege requires dismissal—that is, whether plaintiffs could prove a prima facie case without privileged evidence, or whether the privilege deprives Jeppesen of evidence that would otherwise give it a valid defense to plaintiffs' claims. Instead, we assume without deciding that plaintiffs' prima facie case and Jeppesen's defenses may not inevitably depend on privileged evidence. Proceeding on that assumption, we hold that dismissal is nonetheless required under *Reynolds* because there is no feasible way to litigate Jeppesen's alleged liability without creating an unjustifiable risk of divulging state secrets.

As the dissent correctly notes, we have previously disapproved of *El-Masri* for conflating the *Totten* bar's "very subject matter" inquiry with the *Reynolds* privilege. *See Al-Haramain,* 507 F.3d at 1201. We adhere to that approach today by maintaining a distinction between the *Totten* bar on the one hand and the *Reynolds* privilege on the other. Maintaining that distinction, however, does not mean that the *Reynolds* privilege can never be raised prospectively or result in a dismissal at the pleading stage. As we explained in *Al-Haramain* (as do we in the text), the *Totten* bar and the *Reynolds* privilege form a "continuum of analysis." 507 F.3d at 1201. A case may fall outside the *Totten* bar because its "very subject matter" is not a state secret, and yet it may become clear in conducting a *Reynolds* analysis that plaintiffs cannot establish a prima facie case, that defendants are deprived of a valid defense or that the case cannot be litigated without presenting either a certainty or an unacceptable risk of revealing state secrets. When that point is reached, including, if applicable, at the pleading stage, dismissal is appropriate under the *Reynolds* privilege. Notwithstanding its erroneous conflation of the *Totten* bar and the *Reynolds* privilege, we rely on *El-Masri* because it properly concluded—with respect to allegations comparable to those here—that "virtually any conceivable response to [plaintiffs'] allegations would disclose privileged information," and, therefore, that the action could not be litigated "without threatening the disclosure" of state secrets. *El-Masri,* 479 F.3d at 308, 310.

We reach this conclusion because all seven of plaintiffs' claims, even if taken as true, describe Jeppesen as providing logistical support in a broad, complex process, certain aspects of which, the government has persuaded us, are absolutely protected by the state secrets privilege. Notwithstanding that some information about that process has become public, Jeppesen's alleged role and its attendant liability cannot be isolated from aspects that are secret and protected. Because the facts underlying plaintiffs' claims are so infused with these secrets, *any* plausible effort by Jeppesen to defend against them would create an unjustifiable risk of revealing state secrets, even if plaintiffs could make a prima facie case on one or more claims with non-privileged evidence.

Here, further litigation presents an unacceptable risk of disclosure of state secrets no matter what legal or factual theories Jeppesen would choose to advance during a defense. Whether or not Jeppesen provided logistical support in connection with the extraordinary rendition and interrogation programs, there is precious little Jeppesen could say about its relevant conduct and knowledge without revealing information about how the United States government does *or does not* conduct covert operations. Our conclusion holds no matter what protective procedures the district court might employ. Adversarial litigation, including pretrial discovery of documents and witnesses and the presentation of documents and testimony at trial, is inherently complex and unpredictable. Although district courts are well equipped to wall off isolated secrets from disclosure, the challenge is exponentially greater in exceptional cases like this one, where the relevant secrets are difficult or impossible to isolate and even efforts to define a boundary between privileged and unprivileged evidence would risk disclosure by implication. In these rare circumstances, the risk of disclosure that further proceedings would create cannot be averted through the use of devices such as protective orders or restrictions on testimony.

Dismissal at the pleading stage under *Reynolds* is a drastic result and should not be readily granted. We are not persuaded, however, by the dissent's views that the state secrets privilege can never be "asserted during the pleading stage to excise entire allegations," or that the government must be required "to make its claims of state secrets with regard to specific items of evidence or groups of such items as their use is sought in the lawsuit."

. . . [O]ur detailed *Reynolds* analysis reveals that the claims and possible defenses are so infused with state secrets that the risk of disclosing them is both apparent and inevitable. Dismissal under these circumstances, like dismissal under the *Totten* bar, reflects the general principle that "public policy forbids the maintenance of any suit in a court of justice, the trial of which would inevitably lead to the disclosure of matters which the law itself regards as confidential, and respecting which it will not allow the confidence to be violated." *Totten,* 92 U.S. at 107. * * *

Although we are necessarily precluded from explaining precisely why this case cannot be litigated without risking disclosure of state secrets, or the nature of the harm to national security that we are convinced would result from further litigation, we are able to offer a few observations.

First, we recognize that plaintiffs have proffered hundreds of pages of publicly available documents . . . that they say corroborate some of their allegations concerning Jeppesen's alleged participation in aspects of the extraordinary rendition program. As the government has acknowledged, its claim of privilege does not extend to public documents. Accordingly, we do not hold that any of the documents plaintiffs have submitted are subject to the privilege; rather, we conclude that even assuming plaintiffs could establish their entire case *solely* through nonprivileged evidence — unlikely as that may be — any effort by Jeppesen to defend would unjustifiably risk disclosure of state secrets.

Second, we do not hold that the existence of the extraordinary rendition program is itself a state secret. The program has been publicly acknowledged by numerous government officials including the President of the United States. . . .

Third, we acknowledge the government's certification at oral argument that its assertion of the state secrets privilege comports with the revised standards set forth in the current administration's September 23, 2009 memorandum, adopted several years after the government first invoked the privilege in this case. Those standards require the responsible agency to show that "assertion of the privilege is necessary to protect information the unauthorized disclosure of which reasonably could be expected to cause significant harm to the national defense or foreign relations." They also mandate that the Department of Justice "will not defend an invocation of the privilege in order to: (i) conceal violations of the law, inefficiency, or administrative error; (ii) prevent embarrassment to a person, organization, or agency of the United States government; (iii) restrain competition; or (iv) prevent or delay the release of information the release of which would not reasonably be expected to cause significant harm to national security." That certification here is consistent with our independent conclusion, having reviewed the government's public and classified declarations, that the government is not invoking the privilege to avoid embarrassment or to escape scrutiny of its recent controversial transfer and interrogation policies, rather than to protect legitimate national security concerns.

V. OTHER REMEDIES

Our holding today is not intended to foreclose—or to pre-judge—possible *non-judicial* relief, should it be warranted for any of the plaintiffs. Denial of a judicial forum based on the state secrets doctrine poses concerns at both individual and structural levels. For the individual plaintiffs in this action, our decision forecloses at least one set of judicial remedies, and deprives them of the opportunity to prove their alleged mistreatment and obtain damages. At a structural level, terminating the case eliminates further judicial review in this civil litigation, one important check on alleged abuse by government officials and putative contractors. Other remedies may partially mitigate these concerns, however, although we recognize each of these options brings with it its own set of concerns and uncertainties.

First, that the judicial branch may have deferred to the executive branch's claim of privilege in the interest of national security does not preclude the government from honoring the fundamental principles of justice. The government, having access to the secret information, can determine whether plaintiffs' claims have merit and whether misjudgments or mistakes were made that violated plaintiffs' human rights. Should that be the case, the government may be able to find ways to remedy such alleged harms while still maintaining the secrecy national security demands. For instance, the government made reparations to Japanese Latin Americans abducted from Latin America for internment in the United States during World War II.

Second, Congress has the authority to investigate alleged wrongdoing and restrain excesses by the executive branch.

Third, Congress also has the power to enact private bills. . . . When national security interests deny alleged victims of wrongful governmental action meaningful access to a judicial forum, private bills may be an appropriate alternative remedy.

Fourth, Congress has the authority to enact remedial legislation authorizing appropriate causes of action and procedures to address claims like those presented here. When the state secrets doctrine "compels the subordination of appellants' interest in the pursuit of their claims to the executive's duty to preserve our national security, this means that remedies for ... violations that cannot be proven under existing legal standards, if there are to be such remedies, must be provided by Congress. That is where the government's power to remedy wrongs is ultimately reposed." *Halkin v. Helms,* 690 F.2d at 1001 (footnote omitted).

VI. CONCLUSION

We, like the dissent, emphasize that it should be a rare case when the state secrets doctrine leads to dismissal at the outset of a case. Nonetheless, there are such cases—not just those subject to *Totten*'s per se rule, but those where the mandate for dismissal is apparent even under the more searching examination required by *Reynolds.* This is one of those rare cases. For the reasons stated, we hold that the government's valid assertion of the state secrets privilege warrants dismissal of the litigation, and affirm the judgment of the district court. The government shall bear all parties' costs on appeal.

AFFIRMED.

[Judge Bea's concurrence, preferring to resolve the case on *Totten* grounds, is omitted.]

MICHAEL DALY HAWKINS, Circuit Judge, with whom Judges SCHROEDER, CANBY, THOMAS, and PAEZ, Circuit Judges, join, dissenting:

A Flawed Procedure

I agree with my colleagues in the majority that *United States v. Reynolds,* 345 U.S. 1, 73 S.Ct. 528, 97 L.Ed. 727 (1953), is a rule of evidence, requiring courts to undertake a careful review of evidence that might support a claim or defense to determine whether either could be made without resort to legitimate state secrets. I part company concerning when and where that review should take place.

The majority dismisses the case in its entirety before Jeppesen has even filed an answer to Plaintiffs' complaint. Outside of the narrow *Totten* context, the state secrets privilege has never applied to prevent parties from litigating the truth or falsity of allegations, or facts, or information simply because the government regards the truth or falsity of the allegations to be secret. Within the *Reynolds* framework, dismissal is justified if and only if specific privileged evidence is itself indispensable to establishing either the truth of the plaintiffs' allegations or a valid defense that would otherwise be available to the defendant.

This is important, because an approach that focuses on specific evidence after issues are joined has the benefit of confining the operation of the state secrets doctrine so that it will sweep no more broadly than clearly necessary. The state secrets doctrine is a judicial construct without foundation in the Constitution, yet its application often trumps what we ordinarily consider to be due process of law. This case now presents a classic illustration. Plaintiffs have alleged facts, which must be taken as true for purposes of a motion to dismiss, that any reasonable person would agree to be gross violations of the norms of international law, remediable under the Alien Tort Statute. They have alleged in detail Jeppesen's complicity or recklessness in participating in these violations. The government intervened, and asserted that the suit would endanger state secrets. The majority opinion here accepts that threshold objection by the government, so Plaintiffs' attempt to prove their case in court is simply cut off. They are not even allowed to attempt to prove their case by the use of nonsecret evidence in their own hands or in the hands of third parties.

It is true that, judicial construct though it is, the state secrets doctrine has become embedded in our controlling decisional law. Government claims of state secrets therefore must be entertained by the judiciary. But the doctrine is so dangerous as a means of hiding governmental misbehavior under the guise of national security, and so violative of common rights to due process, that courts should confine its application to the narrowest circumstances that still protect the government's essential secrets. When, as here, the doctrine is successfully invoked at the threshold of litigation, the claims of secret are necessarily broad and hypothetical. The result is a maximum interference with the due processes of the courts, on the most general claims of state secret privilege. It is far better to require the government to make its claims of state secrets with regard to specific items of evidence or groups of such items as their use is sought in the lawsuit. An official certification that evidence is truly a state secret will be more focused if the head of a department must certify that specific evidence sought in the course of litigation is truly a secret and cannot be revealed without danger to overriding, essential government interests. And when responsive pleading is complete and discovery under way, judgments as to whether secret material is essential to Plaintiffs' case or Jeppesen's defense can be made more accurately.

By refusing to examine the voluminous public record materials submitted by Plaintiffs in support of their claims, and by failing to undertake an analysis of Jeppesen's ability to defend against those claims, the district court forced every judge of the court of appeals to undertake that effort. This was no small undertaking. Materials the government considers top secret had to be moved securely back and forth across the country and made available in a "cone of silence" environment to first the three-judge panel assigned the case and then the twenty-seven active judges of this court to evaluate whether the case merited en banc consideration. This quite literally put the cart before the horse, depriving a reviewing court of a record upon which its traditional review function could be carried out. This is more than a matter of convenience. Making factual determinations is the particular province of trial courts and for sound reason: they are good at it. Not directing the district court to do that work sends exactly the wrong message in the handling of these critical and sensitive cases. Finding remand "unnecessary," as the majority does here, not only rewards district courts for failing to do their job, but ensures that future appeals courts will have to do that job for them.

. . . [T]the majority assumes that even if Plaintiffs' prima facie case and Jeppesen's defense did not depend on privileged evidence, dismissal is required "because there is no feasible way to litigate Jeppesen's alleged liability without creating an unjustifiable risk of divulging state secrets." But Jeppesen has yet to answer or even to otherwise plead, so we have no idea what those defenses or assertions might be. Making assumptions about the contours of future litigation involves mere speculation, and doing so flies straight in the face of long standing principles of Rule 12 law by extending the inquiry to what *might* be divulged in future litigation.

We should have remanded this matter to district court to do the *Reynolds* work that should have been done in the first place. . . .

The Totten *Bar*

. . . Courts have applied the *Totten* bar in one of two scenarios: (1) The plaintiff is party to a secret agreement with the government; or (2) The plaintiff sues to solicit information from the government on a "state secret" matter.

More generally, the *Totten* bar has been applied to suits against the government, and never to a plaintiff's suit against a third-party/non-governmental entity. . . . Here, the "very subject matter" of this lawsuit is Jeppesen's involvement in an overseas detention program. Plaintiffs are neither parties to a secret agreement with the government, nor are they attempting, as the result of this lawsuit, to solicit information from the government on a "state secret" matter. Rather, they are attempting to remedy "widespread violations of individual constitutional rights" occurring in a program whose existence has been made public. *See Hepting v. AT & T*, 439 F. Supp. 2d 974, 993 (N.D.Cal.2006).

Totten's logic simply cannot be stretched to encompass the claims here, as they are brought by third-party plaintiffs against non-government defendant actors for their involvement in tortious activities. Nothing Plaintiffs have done supports a conclusion that their "lips [are] to be for ever sealed respecting" the claim on which they sue, such that filing this lawsuit would in itself defeat recovery. Instead of "avoid[ing] difficult questions about the precise scope of the *Totten* bar," the majority ought to have found the *Totten* bar inapplicable, and rejected the district court's analysis. *Totten* cannot and does not apply to Plaintiffs' claims.

The Reynolds *Evidentiary Privilege*

. . . Whatever validity there may be to the idea that evidentiary privileges can apply at the pleadings stage, it is wrong to suggest that such an application would permit the removal of *entire allegations* resulting in out-and-out dismissal of the entire suit. Instead, the state secrets privilege operates at the pleadings stage to except from the implications of Rule 8(b)(6) the refusal to answer certain allegations, not, as the government contends, to permit the government or Jeppesen to avoid filing a responsive pleading at all. In the Fifth Amendment context, the Fourth Circuit has explained that the privilege against self-incrimination "protects an individual . . . from answering specific allegations in a complaint or filing responses to interrogatories in a civil action where the answers" would violate his rights under the privilege. *N. River Ins.*

Co., Inc. v. Stefanou, 831 F.2d 484, 486–87 (4th Cir. 1987). Accordingly, "when properly invoked, the fifth amendment privilege against self-incrimination . . . can avoid the operation of Rule [8(b)(6)]." *Id.* at 487.

But a proper invocation of the privilege does not excuse a defendant from the requirement to file a responsive pleading; the obligation is to answer those allegations that can be answered and to make a specific claim of the privilege as to the rest, so the suit can move forward.

According to this rationale, Plaintiffs are correct that the government moving forward may assert the state secrets privilege to prevent Jeppesen from answering any allegations, where the answer would constitute evidence properly protected by the privilege. But, recognizing that the privilege may apply at the pleadings stage to prevent defendants from answering certain allegations vis-a-vis operation of Rule 8(b)(6) does not mean the privilege can be used to remove altogether certain subject matters from a lawsuit. Observing that pleadings may constitute evidence, in other words, does not transform an evidentiary privilege into an immunity doctrine. The state secrets privilege, as an evidentiary privilege, is relevant not to the sufficiency of the *complaint,* but only to the sufficiency of evidence available to later *substantiate* the complaint.

Because the *Reynolds* privilege, like any other evidentiary privilege, "'extends only to [evidence] and not to facts,'" it cannot be invoked to prevent a litigant from persuading a jury of the truth or falsity of an allegation by reference to non-privileged evidence, regardless whether privileged evidence might also be probative of the truth or falsity of the allegation.

Reynolds *and Rule 12(b)(6)*

The majority claims there is "no feasible way to litigate Jeppesen's alleged liability *without creating an unjustifiable risk of divulging state secrets,*" ignoring well-established principles of civil procedure which, at this stage of the litigation, do not permit the prospective evaluation of hypothetical claims of privilege that the government has yet to raise and the district court has yet to consider.

Our task in reviewing the grant of a Rule 12 motion to dismiss "is necessarily a limited one." We are not to determine whether a particular party will ultimately prevail, but instead only whether the complaint "state[s] a claim upon which relief can be granted," Fed. R. Civ. Pro. 12(b)(6). If Plaintiffs here have stated a claim on which relief can be granted, they should have an opportunity to present evidence in support of their allegations, without regard for the likelihood of ultimate success.

This limited inquiry—a long-standing feature of the Rules of Civil Procedure—serves a sensible judicial purpose. We simply cannot resolve whether the *Reynolds* evidentiary privilege applies without (1) an actual request for discovery of specific evidence, (2) an explanation from Plaintiffs of their need for the evidence, and (3) a formal invocation of the privilege by the government with respect to that evidence, explaining why it must remain confidential. Nor can we determine whether the parties will be able to establish their cases without use of privileged evidence without also knowing what non-privileged evidence they will marshal. Thus neither the Federal Rules nor *Reynolds* would permit us to dismiss this case for "failure to state a claim upon which relief can be granted," Fed. R. Civ. Pro. 12(b)(6), on the basis of an evidentiary privilege relevant, not to the sufficiency of the complaint, but only to the sufficiency of evidence available to later substantiate the complaint.

A decision to remand would have the additional benefit of conforming with "the general rule . . . that a federal appellate court does not consider an issue not passed on below," and will allow the district court to apply *Reynolds* in the first instance. The majority's analysis here is premature. . . . We should remand for the government to assert the privilege with respect to secret evidence, and for the district court to determine what evidence is privileged and whether any such evidence is indispensable either to Plaintiffs' prima facie case or to a valid defense otherwise available to Jeppesen. Only if privileged evidence is indispensable to either party should it dismiss the complaint.

Conclusion

The majority concludes its opinion with a recommendation of alternative remedies. Not only are these remedies insufficient, but their suggestion understates the severity of the consequences to Plaintiffs from the denial of judicial relief. Suggesting, for example, that the Executive could "honor [ ] the fundamental principles of justice" by determining "whether plaintiffs' claims have merit," disregards the concept of checks and balances. Permitting the executive to police its own errors and determine the remedy dispensed would not only deprive the judiciary of its role, but also deprive Plaintiffs of a fair assessment of their claims by a neutral arbiter. The majority's suggestion of payment of reparations to the victims of extraordinary rendition, such as those paid to Japanese-Americans for the injustices suffered under Internment during World War II, over fifty years after those injustices were suffered, elevates the impractical to the point of absurdity. Similarly, a congressional investigation, private bill, or enacting of "remedial legislation," leaves to the legislative branch claims which the federal courts are better equipped to handle.

---

1. *State Secrets and Domestic Surveillance During the Vietnam War.* Prior to 9/11, the most important contemporary state secrets cases followed disclosure in the 1970s of illegal surveillance directed against the antiwar movement. Specifically, individuals and organizations who had actively opposed the Vietnam War sued the former and present directors of the National Security Agency, Central Intelligence Agency, Defense Intelligence Agency, Federal Bureau of Investigation, and Secret Service, claiming that the defendants had violated their statutory and constitutional rights. They alleged that the National Security Agency (NSA) conducted warrantless interceptions of their international communications at the request of the other defendants. In addition to damages, plaintiffs sought declaratory and injunctive relief against

further illegal surveillance by the government. *Halkin v. Helms*, 598 F.2d 1 (D.C. Cir. 1978).

The suit was filed in October 1975, after the President's Commission on CIA Activities Within the United States revealed that defendants had conducted illegal surveillance of anti-war activists. The Commission disclosed that NSA had furnished other agencies reports of the foreign communications of Americans, to assist investigations of possible foreign influence over domestic peace groups. NSA obtained the intelligence by scanning electronic communications worldwide. Its computers were programmed with "watchlists," words or phrases designed to identify communications of intelligence interest. Using this technique, NSA established two surveillance operations: MINARET, to intercept foreign communications, and SHAMROCK, to intercept communications entering or leaving the United States. Between 1967 and 1973, NSA added the names of approximately 1,200 Americans to its watchlists under these operations. The acquired communications were disseminated in 2,000 reports to other intelligence agencies.

Plaintiffs sought to discover whether their communications had been intercepted by NSA and disseminated to other defendants. Defendants responded with a motion to dismiss based on a formal claim of the state secrets privilege. In a public affidavit to the District Court, the Secretary of Defense asserted: "Civil discovery or a responsive pleading which would (1) confirm the identity of individuals or organizations whose foreign communications were acquired by NSA, (2) disclose the dates and contents of such communications, or (3) divulge the methods and techniques by which the communications were acquired by NSA, would severely jeopardize the intelligence collection mission of NSA by identifying present communications collection and analysis capabilities." The Secretary also submitted a classified affidavit and gave ex parte testimony for *in camera* examination by the court. On the basis of this information, the court upheld the claim of privilege for operation MINARET, but denied the privilege with respect to operation SHAMROCK because extensive public disclosure of operation SHAMROCK had defeated the purpose behind the privilege.

On appeal, the Court of Appeals held that both NSA operations were privileged as state secrets. Judge Robb rejected plaintiff's argument that it would not reveal state secrets to discover whether NSA had acquired their communications, without more. The court ruled that a standard of "utmost deference" should guide any assessment of the executive's claim of the state secrets privilege. Despite the plaintiffs' strong showing of need, the court held that the District Court's *in camera* examination of the basis for the claim of privilege satisfied the scrutiny required by *Reynolds*. The test of "reasonable danger" in this case, the court posited, was whether discovery would reveal "useful information to a sophisticated analyst." This standard gave the Secretary's claim of privilege a presumption of validity. The court found that the

[p]laintiffs' argument is naive. A number of inferences flow from the confirmation or denial of acquisition of a particular individual's communications. What may seem trivial to the uninformed, may appear of great moment to one who has a broad view of the scene and may put the questioned item of information in its proper context. The courts, of course, are ill-equipped to become sufficiently steeped in foreign intelligence matters to serve effectively in the review of secrecy classifications in that area.

The court also rejected the District Court's finding that "congressional committees investigating intelligence matters had revealed so much information about SHAMROCK that such a disclosure would pose no threat to the NSA mission." Instead, the court concluded that further disclosures could pose a reasonable danger to national security.

On remand, plaintiffs amended their complaint to expand its allegations of unwarranted surveillance. They averred that, in addition to NSA's interception of their international communications, the CIA had engaged in unwarranted surveillance of Americans under operation CHAOS, an intelligence project designed to determine whether foreign governments influenced domestic anti-war activists. Operation CHAOS employed three methods of surveillance. First, it enlisted the aid of foreign intelligence agencies to spy on American dissidents traveling abroad. Second, it infiltrated foreign and domestic anti-war groups. Third, the CIA expanded its existing projects to obtain intelligence about American dissidents. Project MERRIMAC infiltrated domestic anti-war and radical groups believed to pose a threat to CIA property or personnel. Project RESISTANCE gathered information about the activities of anti-war groups without infiltration. The Director of the CIA moved to block further discovery under the state secrets privilege. The District Court granted the motion and dismissed the complaint.

Appealing again, plaintiffs challenged the adequacy of the CIA's justification for raising the state secrets privilege to bar discovery of operation CHAOS. *Halkin v. Helms*, 690 F.2d 977 (D.C. Cir. 1982). Ironically, the court enlisted one of plaintiffs' own arguments—that public disclosure of operation CHAOS had defeated any justification for the privilege—to uphold the District Court's decision to grant the CIA immunity from discovery. The court thought that new discovery of operation CHAOS, coupled with prior public disclosure, would pose a reasonable danger to American diplomatic interests:

> It is self-evident that the disclosures sought here pose a "reasonable danger" to the diplomatic and military interests of the United States. Revelation of particular instances in which foreign governments assisted the CIA in conducting surveillance of dissidents could strain diplomatic relations in a number of ways—by generally embarrassing foreign governments who may wish to avoid or may even explicitly disavow allegations of CIA or United States involvements, or by rendering foreign governments or their officials

subject to political or legal action by those among their own citizens who may have been subjected to surveillance in the course of dissident activity.

Discovery would also endanger CIA agents: "the identities of CIA operatives who contributed information to CHAOS . . . are self-evidently the sort of information which if disclosed could harm national security or diplomatic interests."

Plaintiffs also argued that the requirements for withholding documents under FOIA apply to discovery under the state secrets privilege. The court, however, distinguished FOIA on the ground that it serves a fundamentally different purpose from the privilege:

> The most important difference is that the claim of the state secrets privilege is a decision of policy made at the highest level of the executive branch after consideration of the facts of the particular case. The Reynolds requirements compel that it fulfill these requisites. Consequently, the risk of permitting relatively unaccountable "invisible" bureaucratic decisions as to the national security value of information (specifically, the decisions to classify information that trigger FOIA Exemption 1) to bar disclosure of information on a wholesale basis is not presented in a state secrets case.

The court said that, although FOIA and the privilege are distinguishable in purpose, both bar disclosure of the sort of information sought here. Since the information fit within FOIA's national security exemption, the panel concluded that there was no reason to order the CIA further to justify the redactions in documents it had produced for plaintiffs.

Once the court had upheld the CIA's invocation of the state secrets privilege, it turned to the question of available remedies. Plaintiffs sought injunctive and declaratory relief against submission of their names by the CIA to watchlists for interception by NSA. The court held that plaintiffs lacked standing to seek this relief. Since submission of names to a watchlist is not a violation of the Fourth Amendment, and since plaintiffs were barred from discovering whether their communications were actually intercepted (*Halkin I*), they could not show the requisite injury for standing. Therefore, plaintiffs' only recourse was legislation.

Another prominent state secrets case is *Ellsberg v. Mitchell*, 709 F.2d 51 (D.C. Cir. 1983). Daniel Ellsberg—the former Rand analyst who disclosed the Pentagon Papers—and others sued for damages for warrantless electronic surveillance by various federal officials. Plaintiffs sought to discover the identity of the official who authorized the wiretaps. Defendants admitted that plaintiffs had been overheard on wiretaps, but claimed that the state secrets privilege barred further discovery. The District Court upheld the claim of privilege and dismissed plaintiffs' claim. On appeal, the judgment was affirmed in part and reversed in part. The court, per Judge Edwards, said (at 56–60):

It is now well established that the United States, by invoking its state secrets privilege, may block discovery in a lawsuit of any information that, if disclosed, would adversely affect national security. Prior to World War Two, the government rarely had occasion to exercise this prerogative, and, consequently, the scope of the privilege remained somewhat in doubt. In recent years, however, the state secrets privilege has been asserted in a growing number of cases, and the resultant bevy of judicial decisions assessing the legitimacy of its invocation has brought its lineaments into reasonably sharp focus. The following principles may be distilled from the case law . . . .

When properly invoked, the state secrets privilege is absolute. No competing public or private interest can be advanced to compel disclosure of information found to be protected by a claim of privilege. However, because of the broad sweep of the privilege, the Supreme Court has made clear that "[i]t is not to be lightly invoked." Thus, the privilege may not be used to shield any material not strictly necessary to prevent injury to national security; and, whenever possible, sensitive information must be disentangled from nonsensitive information to allow for the release of the latter.

It has been argued that certain limitations on the capacity of the judicial branch safely and reliably to evaluate invocations of the state secrets privilege should induce the courts to renounce any role in this area, i.e., to accept without question a privilege claim made by a ranking executive officer. Such an extreme solution, however, would have grave drawbacks. As noted by Professor McCormick [HANDBOOK OF THE LAW OF EVIDENCE (Edward W. Cleary ed., 1972)]:

> The head of an executive department can appraise the public interest of secrecy as well (or perhaps in some cases better) than the judge, but his official habit and leaning tend to sway him toward a minimizing of the interest of the individual. Under the normal administrative routine the question will come to him with recommendations from cautious subordinates against disclosure and in the press of business the chief is likely to approve the recommendation about such a seemingly minor matter without much independent consideration.

Although there can be no abdication of a judicial role in connection with proposed applications of the state secrets doctrine, it is nevertheless frequently noted that the trial judge should accord considerable deference to recommendations from the executive department. Moreover, it is recognized that the government need not demonstrate that injury to the national interest will inevitably result from disclosure; a showing of "reasonable danger" that harm will ensue is sufficient. Finally, when assessing claims of a state secrets privilege, a trial judge properly may rely on affidavits and other secondary sources more often than he might when evaluating assertions of other evidentiary privileges.

Whether (and in what spirit) the trial judge in a particular case should examine the materials sought to be withheld depends upon two critical considerations. First, the more compelling a litigant's showing of need for the information in question, the deeper "the court should probe in satisfying itself that the occasion for invoking the privilege is appropriate." Second, the more plausible and substantial the government's allegations of danger to national security, in the context of all the circumstances surrounding the case, the more deferential should be the judge's inquiry into the foundations and scope of the claim. Neither of these two factors can affect the judge's response, however, if he is "ultimately satisfied" that disclosure of the material *would* damage national security.

With these principles in mind, we turn to the objections made by the plaintiffs to the positions taken by the defendants, the government, and the District Court. The plaintiffs' first argument—a challenge to the scope of the privilege claim—is necessarily somewhat vague. Ignorant of what in fact has been withheld, they are able to say only that "too much" has been shielded. The tasks of posing and answering more specific questions therefore devolve on us. We have examined all of the various affidavits and exhibits submitted to the District Court for *in camera* inspection. For the most part, the documents contained therein indicate what the defendants' responses to the plaintiffs' interrogatories would be, and why such responses cannot be made public. With regard to almost all of the material, we find that the District Court was correct in concluding that invocation of the state secrets privilege was proper. In other words, we conclude that there is a "reasonable danger" that revelation of the information in question would either enable a sophisticated analyst to gain insights into the nation's intelligence-gathering methods and capabilities or would disrupt diplomatic relations with foreign governments. . . .

The court went on to discuss the effect of its partial reversal:

The effect of the government's successful invocation of the state secrets privilege, when the government is not itself a party to the suit in question, is well established: "[T]he result is simply that the evidence is unavailable, as though a witness had died, and the case will proceed accordingly, with no consequences save those resulting from the loss of the evidence." Likewise, it is now settled that, when the government is a defendant in a civil suit, its invocation of the privilege results in no alteration of pertinent substantive or procedural rules; the effect is the same, in other words, as if the government were not involved in the controversy. The rationale for this doctrine is that the United States, while waiving its sovereign immunity for many purposes, has never consented to an increase in its exposure to liability when it is compelled, for reasons of national security, to refuse to release relevant evidence. . . .

Under these conditions, dismissal of the relevant portion of the suit would be proper only if the plaintiffs were manifestly unable to make out a *prima facie* case without the requested information. Are the plaintiffs thus incapacitated? With regard to those whom the government has not admitted overhearing, the answer is clearly yes. An essential element of each plaintiff's case is proof that he himself has been injured. . . . Dismissal of the claims of those parties was therefore proper. With regard to the five plaintiffs whom the government has conceded overhearing, the answer is far less obvious. Unlike their colleagues, they can demonstrate injury to themselves. . . . [T]he defendants have acknowledged that none of those taps was instituted pursuant to a warrant. . . .

The court concluded that:

the burden is on those seeking an exemption from the Fourth Amendment warrant requirement to show the need for it. Accordingly, to make out a prima facie case of a constitutional violation, the plaintiffs need not disprove the defendants' allegation that their actions are excused by the "foreign agent" exemption; rather, the defendants must prove their contention. As the defendants have not yet made such a showing in the instant case, dismissal of the claims of the five plaintiffs whom the defendants have acknowledged overhearing would be improper.

What conclusions do you draw from these cases? The plaintiffs in *Halkin I* and *II*, denied standing because they could not prove the injuries that they sought to discover, might have perceived a Catch-22. Was the Court of Appeals faithful to the *Reynolds* formula? Does *Ellsberg* take a significantly different tack?

2. *State Secrets and Warrantless Surveillance After 9/11*. In late 2005, the press disclosed the existence of a secret government program of warrantless surveillance of terror suspects that had been initiated in the wake of the 9/11 attacks. We consider the legality of that program in Chapter Seven. The litigations that challenged the program were affected by two major developments since the 1970s: a Supreme Court decision, *United States v. U.S. Dist. Court (Keith)*, 407 U.S. 297 (1972), requiring warrants for domestic national security surveillance, and a statute, the Foreign Intelligence Surveillance Act (FISA), Pub. L. No. 95-511, 92 Stat. 1783, 50 U.S.C. §§ 1801–71, requiring special warrants for gathering intelligence from foreign agents. As explained in Chapter Seven, the plaintiffs in only one case so far have been able, notwithstanding the state secrets doctrine, to establish standing. *In re National Security Agency Telecommunications Records Litigation*, 700 F. Supp. 2d 1182 (N. D. Cal. 2010). *See also Al-Haramain Islamic Foundation v. Bush*, 451 F. Supp. 2d 1215 (D. Or. Sep 07, 2006), *rev'd*, 507 F.3d 1190 (9th Cir. 2007), *dismissed on remand, In re National Security Agency Telecommunications Records Litigation*, 564 F. Supp. 2d 1109 (N.D. Cal. 2008). That is because the Court of Appeals agreed with the District

Court's determination that, given the President's public acknowledgment that a program of warrantless surveillance existed, no harm to national security could occur from concession of the fact of surveillance in this case. Unfortunately for the plaintiffs, however, their claims were ultimately dismissed on grounds of sovereign immunity. *Al-Haramain Islamic Foundation v. Obama*, 705 F.3d 845 (9th Cir. 2012).

3. *State Secrets Reform in the Obama Administration*. The George W. Bush administration invoked the state secrets privilege more than twice as many times as had occurred in the previous twenty-four years. Holly Wells, *The State Secrets Privilege: Overuse Causing Unintended Consequences*, 50 ARIZ. L. REV. 967, 968 (2008). Many political supporters of Senator Obama hoped that President Obama would significantly change that pattern. As noted in *Mohamed v. Jeppesen Dataplan*, the Obama Justice Department responded to this concern with a change in litigation procedure. Under a policy announced on September 23, 2009, Attorney General Holder committed the Department to invoking the privilege only to prevent "significant" harm. He pledged that the privilege would not be invoked to conceal violations of law or merely embarrassing behavior. Should any agency wish the privilege to be invoked on its behalf, it would have to provide to the Justice Department a detailed justification, which, in turn, would have to be endorsed by the Assistant Attorney General in charge of the relevant litigating division. Should the AAG recommend invocation, that recommendation would be reviewed by a newly constituted State Secret Review Committee, whose recommendation, in turn, would go to the Deputy Attorney General and, if approved, to the Attorney General. The privilege would not be invoked without the Attorney General's signoff, and the Attorney General, if he or she invokes the privilege, would report the matter to the relevant agency Inspector General should the Attorney General find plausible the underlying assertions of wrongdoing.

This change in policy did not lead the Obama Administration to abandon the state secrets claims made by the Bush Administration in any still-pending litigation. Do you think intrabranch procedural reform goes far enough — or too far — in limiting use of the state secrets privilege? Could Congress constitutionally make such a procedure mandatory? Could Congress prescribe the judicial procedure to be followed in evaluating state secrets privilege claims — including a mandatory *in camera* review of any evidence claimed to be privileged? See, e.g., the proposed State Secrets Protection Act, S. 417, 111th Cong., 1st Sess. (2009).

4. Totten *v.* Reynolds. As the Ninth Circuit notes, there is virtually no difference between judicial invocation of the *Totten* bar and the conclusion, under *Reynolds*, that a case cannot move forward for the plaintiff, the defense, or both, without revealing state secrets. Although courts nominally treat *Totten* as relevant only in limited circumstances, any distinction between *Totten* and *Reynolds* vanishes altogether when a court applies *Reynolds* without even looking at the assertedly privileged evidence. For example, in *El-Masri v. United States*, 479 F. 3d 296 (4th Cir. 2007), cert. denied, 552 U.S. 947 (2007), an innocent German citizen was kidnapped by the CIA while on vacation in Macedonia. He was taken to a secret prison in Afghanistan where he was tortured and imprisoned under brutal conditions. Six months later, the CIA

realized that this was a case of mistaken identity. They took El-Masri from the prison to Albania and abandoned him along a road. He sued the CIA for violations of due process and international law. The CIA Director responded with affidavits invoking the state secrets privilege. El-Masri rejoined that there had been various public disclosures of "extraordinary renditions" such as his, and that President Bush himself had revealed the existence of the secret CIA prisons.

Nevertheless, the Fourth Circuit affirmed dismissal of the case without in camera review of the secrets involved. The court, per Judge King, stressed that judges are ill-equipped to assess the importance of state secrets. It accepted the CIA's "mosaic theory," that an item of information "that may seem trivial to the uninformed, may appear of great moment to one who has a broad view of the scene and may put the questioned item of information in its proper context." The court thought that in camera review could not cure this problem. Does the "mosaic theory, if accepted, allow any meaningful limit to the privilege? Is it enough to justify judicial refusals even to inspect the information in question?

b. Congress v. The Executive

Because of the institutional competition between the executive and Congress, both branches are highly sensitive about legislative access to executive branch information. Actual executive branch refusals to provide requested information to Congress are matters of legal, as well as political delicacy. Judicial decisions on the scope of executive privilege against Congress are rare because the executive finds it difficult to mount court challenges to congressional demands for information, as we shall see. Ordinarily, to obtain judicial review, an executive official must accept a citation for contempt of Congress and await court action to enforce it. (Prior to 1857, Congress, in citing persons for contempt, set the punishment on an ad hoc basis. In 1857, Congress enacted the original version of 2 U.S.C. § 192, imposing criminal liability for refusing any congressional demand for information.) To avoid extreme "brinksmanship" on the part of both branches, most disputes over requested information are resolved through negotiation, without a formal privilege claim.

Executive privilege disputes between President and Congress have a substantial history. *See* LOUIS FISHER, THE POLITICS OF EXECUTIVE PRIVILEGE (2004). For a good summary, we turn to Professor — and former Watergate Special Prosecutor — Archibald Cox, in *Executive Privilege*, 122 U. PA. L. REV. 1383, 1395–1405 (1974):

> Senate and House Committees and less often the Senate and House themselves have been demanding information from the Executive Branch since the administration of George Washington. Nearly always the requests were satisfied, but one finds interspersed through history occasions on which Presidents declined to comply with congressional requests. Some of the refusals were accompanied by messages asserting a very broad presidential discretion to withhold any papers or other material the President thinks it in the public interest to withhold. Some Attorneys General gave opinions

supporting the claim. Some Senators and Representatives and some committee reports acquiesced in the claim. Others resisted it . . .

Historians, judges and lawyers differ over the proper description and analysis of these incidents. All ended inconclusively because there was not in the past and may not be today any method of resolving the conflict short of impeachment. One gets a useful picture of the kinds of occasions on which information has been withheld by Chief Executives, however, by classifying each of the twenty-seven occasions listed in a purportedly complete compilation of prior claims of executive privilege made by the Department of Justice under President Eisenhower, not by what was said, but by what was done. [Memorandum by Attorney General William P. Rogers, reprinted in Hearing on S. 921 Before the Subcomm. on Constitutional Rights of the Sen. Comm. on the Judiciary, 85th Cong., 2d Sess., at 33–146 (1958).]

At the very outset four of the seventeen Presidents and five of the twenty-seven instances compiled must be stricken from the list upon the ground that the congressional request explicitly stated that the President should decide whether furnishing the papers would be in the public interest. In these instances there was no need for a claim of constitutional right because there was no resistance to a congressional demand. President Jefferson, for example, is often said to have claimed executive privilege in withholding from the House information regarding the Burr conspiracy. The House request shows on its face that the House asked for information "except such as [the President] may deem the public welfare to require not to be disclosed." . . .

A number of Presidents withheld information from the Senate or House as a method of challenging the power of the particular body to deal with the subject matter upon which the information was said to bear. Analytically, these cases have no bearing upon any possible privilege of executive secrecy with respect to matters admittedly within the jurisdiction of the House making the demand. The most notable example is George Washington's firm declination in 1796 to deliver to the House of Representatives documents pertaining to the negotiation of the Jay Treaty. Washington relied in his rebuff of the House, not upon the need for secrecy but upon the principle that the Constitution assigns no role to the House in relation to treaties. All the papers requested by the House were "in fact . . . laid before the Senate," to aid that body in the performance of its legitimate role in the treaty-making function.

[Cox includes in the same category presidential refusals to produce information regarding removals of executive officers. He then identifies a category of presidential withholding of investigative files.] All nine instances can honestly be described as assertions of the confidentiality of papers in the Executive Branch, but it is equally plain that the claim was not based upon an undifferentiated interest in preserving confidentiality among executive officials. . . . The chief purpose of the withholding was to protect possibly innocent persons . . . against disclosure of the rumors and loose allegations often found in investigative reports. [Citing 40 Op. A.G. 45 (1941) (Jackson).] . . .

If this reading of history is fair, four conclusions follow:

(1) Over a period of a century and a half thirteen Presidents found a total of twenty occasions on which to refuse to turn over information demanded by an arm of Congress. Sometimes Presidents bespoke a broad discretion. Attorneys General wrote broad opinions to support them. Commentators often accepted their views.

(2) If one looks at what was done and confines the words to the events, nothing appears which even approaches a solid historical practice of recognizing claims of executive privilege based upon an undifferentiated need for preserving the secrecy of internal communications within the Executive Branch. Only two Presidents, Andrew Jackson and Theodore Roosevelt, can be said to have withheld information under circumstances in which the withholding could not easily be justified upon some other, specialized ground.

(3) So far as one can judge from the history of past occasions for claiming power to withhold, President Nixon would have not done the slightest damage to the Presidency by an immediate, full disclosure. President Jackson, surely a strong Chief Executive, wrote that if the Congress could

> point to any case where there is the slightest reason to suspect corruption or abuse of trust, no obstacle which I can remove shall be interposed to prevent the fullest scrutiny by all legal means. The offices of all the departments will be opened to you, and every proper facility furnished for this purpose.

(4) There is no settled executive practice of giving Congress whatever it wishes from the Executive Branch.

The materials that follow are used to illuminate the processes by which legal and policy issues involved in a dispute over Congress's right to executive branch information are resolved. We begin with a 1982 executive branch policy statement concerning the invocation of executive privilege. We then include excerpts from Judge Leventhal's opinion in *United States v. A.T. & T.*, asserting that the Constitution contemplates a process of good faith negotiation and compromise between the branches in such a dispute. Finally, a recent and typically inconclusive litigation shows the rough road that negotiation sometimes takes. As you read the materials, consider the competing traditions of legal interpretation in Congress and the executive branch. How well does the process you see here comport with the ideal of a "government of laws"?

1.) Executive Branch Procedure for Invoking Executive Privilege

Modern executive branch procedures for responding to congressional requests for information were initiated by the following memorandum issued by President Reagan (reprinted in H.R. Rep. No. 435, 99th Cong., 1st Sess. 1106 (1985)):

Memorandum for the Heads
of Executive Departments and Agencies
November 4, 1982

SUBJECT: Procedures Governing Responses to Congressional Requests for Information

The policy of this Administration is to comply with Congressional requests for information to the fullest extent consistent with the constitutional and statutory obligations of the Executive Branch. While this Administration, like its predecessors, has an obligation to protect the confidentiality of some communications, executive privilege will be asserted only in the most compelling circumstances, and only after careful review demonstrates that assertion of the privilege is necessary. Historically, good faith negotiations between Congress and the Executive Branch have minimized the need for invoking executive privilege, and this tradition of accommodation should continue as the primary means of resolving conflicts between the Branches. To ensure that every reasonable accommodation is made to the needs of Congress, executive privilege shall not be invoked without specific Presidential authorization.

The Supreme Court has held that the Executive Branch may occasionally find it necessary and proper to preserve the confidentiality of national security secrets, deliberative communications that form a part of the decision-making process, or other information important to the discharge of the Executive Branch's constitutional responsibilities. Legitimate and appropriate claims of privilege should not thoughtlessly be waived. However, to ensure that this Administration acts responsibly and consistently in the exercise of its duties, with due regard for the responsibilities and prerogatives of Congress, the following procedures shall be followed whenever Congressional requests for information raise concerns regarding the confidentiality of the information sought:

1. Congressional requests for information shall be complied with as promptly and as fully as possible, unless it is determined that compliance raises a substantial question of executive privilege. A "substantial question of executive privilege" exists if disclosure of the information requested might significantly impair the national security (including the conduct of foreign relations), the deliberative processes of the Executive Branch or other aspects of the performance of the Executive Branch's constitutional duties.

2. If the head of an executive department or agency ("Department Head") believes, after consultation with department counsel, that compliance with a Congressional

request for information raises a substantial question of executive privilege, he shall promptly notify and consult with the Attorney General through the Assistant Attorney General for the Office of Legal Counsel, and shall also promptly notify and consult with the Counsel to the President. If the information requested of a department or agency derives in whole or in part from information received from another department or agency, the latter entity shall also be consulted as to whether disclosure of the information raises a substantial question of executive privilege.

3. Every effort shall be made to comply with the Congressional request in a manner consistent with the legitimate needs of the Executive Branch. The Department Head, the Attorney General and the Counsel to the President may, in the exercise of their discretion in the circumstances, determine that executive privilege shall not be invoked and release the requested information.

4. If the Department Head, the Attorney General or the Counsel to the President believes, after consultation, that the circumstances justify invocation of executive privilege, the issue shall be presented to the President by the Counsel to the President, who will advise the Department Head and the Attorney General of the President's decision.

5. Pending a final Presidential decision on the matter, the Department Head shall request the Congressional body to hold its request for the information in abeyance. The Department Head shall expressly indicate that the purpose of this request is to protect the privilege pending a Presidential decision, and that the request itself does not constitute a claim of privilege.

6. If the President decides to invoke executive privilege, the Department Head shall advise the requesting Congressional body that the claim of executive privilege is being made with the specific approval of the President.

Any questions concerning these procedures or related matters should be addressed to the Attorney General, through the Assistant Attorney General for the Office of Legal Counsel, and to the Counsel to the President.

Ronald Reagan

————————

The Reagan memorandum was the first new presidential directive on the subject since a March 24, 1969, memorandum by President Nixon. The primary changes made by Reagan were: the inclusion of the second unnumbered prefatory paragraph, a requirement in paragraph 2 that the head of a department concerned about privilege consult White House counsel in addition to the Attorney General, and the addition of the White House counsel to the decisionmaking process outlined in paragraphs 3 and 4. What do you think these changes are meant to accomplish? Do they pose potential problems for the President?

As an adviser to an incoming administration, would you suggest altering the policy? President Clinton's White House counsel Lloyd Cutler issued a Memorandum to All Executive Departments and Agency General Counsels (Sept. 28, 1994), stating that Congressional requests should be granted "to the fullest extent consistent with the constitutional and statutory obligations of the executive branch." Although executive privilege would be claimed to protect "the confidentiality of deliberations within the White House," it would not be asserted "relating to investigations of personal wrongdoing by government officials, . . . either in judicial proceedings or in congressional investigations and hearings." Did the President keep this promise?

In both June and October, 2017 testimony to the Senate Judiciary Committee, Attorney General Jeff Sessions refused to answer questions about communications with the President on the ground that the President, at some point, might wish to invoke executive privilege. On the latter occasion, Sessions reaffirmed the applicability of the 1982 Reagan Memorandum, but insisted he wished to continue preserving the President's right to claim privilege at a later time. This drew the following response from one Senator: "What I'm worried about is that this administration is de facto rewriting Ronald Reagan's executive order about executive privilege so that the period of abeyance has no end to it and Congress is stonewalled on information without ever getting an assertion of executive privilege, an assertion to which I believe we are entitled if we're going to be prevented from getting information." Jeremy Stahl, *Jeff Sessions Is Using Phony Executive Privilege to Shield Trump, and GOP Senators Are Letting Him*, SLATE (Oct. 18 2017), http://www.slate.com/blogs/the_slatest/2017/10/18/why_jeff_sessions_testimony_about_executive_privilege_was_so_important.html. Does the Reagan Memorandum imply that the President's period for deliberation will not be of indefinite duration?

2.) A Constitutional Requirement of Compromise?

A dispute that led to United States v. American Telephone & Telegraph Co., 567 F.2d 121 (D.C. Cir. 1977), arose when the Subcommittee on Oversight and Investigations of the House Interstate and Foreign Commerce Committee subpoenaed documents from A.T. & T. The documents concerned warrantless wiretapping that the United States, with the assistance of A.T. & T., assertedly conducted for national security reasons. The Department of Justice sued A.T. & T. to enjoin compliance with the subpoena on the ground that public disclosure of the Attorney General's letters requesting foreign intelligence surveillance of particular targets would harm national security. The chair of the House subcommittee intervened, on behalf of the House, as the real party defendant.

Rather than resolve the dispute on its merits, the Court of Appeals, when the case first reached it, remanded with a suggestion that the parties negotiate a settlement under guidelines proposed by the court. The Justice Department then proceeded — unsuccessfully — to attempt to negotiate a procedure under which, instead of receiving the Attorney General's letters, the subcommittee would receive expurgated copies of the backup memoranda upon which the Attorney General based his decisions to authorize wiretaps. Information identifying the wiretap targets would be replaced by generic descriptive language fashioned by the Department. Negotiations broke down, however, over the proper procedure for assuring the subcommittee of the accuracy of the generic descriptions. The Department of Justice would permit subcommittee staff to inspect a substantial sample of unexpurgated memoranda for purposes of comparison, but, for fear of a leak, would neither turn over to the subcommittee the unexpurgated memos themselves, nor notes that the subcommittee staff might take upon inspecting the memos.

When the case returned to the Court of Appeals, it ordered a procedure that, although closer to the executive's "final offer," represented a genuine compromise of the two branches' positions. Judge Leventhal justified his concededly delicate balancing approach as follows:

> As Judge Friendly recalled in his 1976 Bicentennial lecture, it is one of the major strengths of the Constitution, and far from a weakness, that conflicting viewpoints have been resolved through intermediate positions. Much of this spirit of compromise is reflected in the generality of language found in the Constitution—generality which allows for dispute as to which of the coordinate branches may exercise authority in a particular fact situation.

> The framers, rather than attempting to define and allocate all governmental power in minute detail, relied, we believe, on the expectation that where conflicts in scope of authority arose between the coordinate branches, a spirit of dynamic compromise would promote resolution of the dispute in the manner most likely to result in efficient and effective functioning of our governmental system. Under this view, the coordinate branches do not exist in an exclusively adversary relationship to one another when a conflict in authority arises. Rather, each branch should take cognizance of an implicit constitutional mandate to seek optimal accommodation through a realistic evaluation of the needs of the conflicting branches in the particular fact situation. This aspect of our constitutional scheme avoids the mischief of polarization of disputes. Professor Freund has cautioned that "[i]n the eighteenth-century Newtonian universe that is the Constitution, an excessive force in one direction is apt to produce a corresponding counterforce." . . . [Freund, *supra*, at 20.]

> An . . . instance of judicial balancing of executive and legislative interests emerged when the Senate Committee investigating improper activities in the 1972 presidential campaign issued a subpoena directing the President to deliver certain relevant tapes and documents. The President declined on the ground of executive privilege. The Committee sought to enforce the subpoena. This court weighed the public interest protected by the President's claim of privilege against the interest that would be served by disclosure to the Committee, and declined to enforce the congressional subpoena. *Senate Select Committee on Presidential Campaign Activities v. Nixon*, 498 F.2d 725 (D.C. Cir. 1974) . . . .

Judge Leventhal also rejected a claim that the case involved a nonjusticiable political question (as had the court in *Senate Select Committee*):

> The simple fact of a conflict between the legislative and executive branches over a congressional subpoena does not preclude judicial resolution. . . . Normally, when the court abstains on political question grounds it acquiesces in a "commitment of the issue" to one of the political branches for resolution of the merits. . . . That branch is recognized as having the constitutional authority to make a decision that settles the dispute. Where the dispute consists of a clash of authority between two branches, however, judicial abstention does not lead to orderly resolution of the dispute. No one branch is identified as having final authority in the area of concern.

Finding that there were manageable standards for resolution of the controversy, he concluded: "In our view, neither the traditional political question doctrine nor any close adaptation thereof is appropriate where neither of the conflicting political branches has a clear and unequivocal constitutional title."

———————

Required Accommodation? For analysis of this case, see Comment, United States v. AT&T: *Judicially Supervised Negotiation and Political Questions*, 77 COLUM. L. REV. 466 (1977). The author concludes that in the presence of constitutional conflict, "the constitutional scheme would seem to require no less than that the line between [the branches] be drawn at the point of optimal accommodation." Assuming that Professor Pareto is not available to draw such a line, how is a court to do so? Without judicial prodding, what would you suppose is the likelihood of the branches successfully achieving, in Judge Leventhal's words, "optimal accommodation through a realistic evaluation of the needs of the conflicting branches in the particular fact situation?" What factors would likely affect the success of negotiations? What factors should shape the executive's negotiating strategy? Consider the litigation that follows.

3.) Litigating Executive Responses to Congressional Subpoenas
Committee on the Judiciary, U.S. House of Representatives v. Miers
558 F. Supp. 2d 53 (D.D.C. 2008).

JOHN D. BATES, District Judge.

This dispute pits the political branches of the federal government against one another in a case all agree presents issues of extraordinary constitutional significance. The heart of the controversy is whether senior presidential aides are absolutely immune from compelled congressional process. But as is often true of lawsuits that raise important separation of powers concerns, there are many obstacles to the invocation of the jurisdiction of the federal courts that must first be addressed.

The Committee on the Judiciary ("Committee"), acting on behalf of the entire House of Representatives, asks the Court to declare that former White House Counsel Harriet Miers must comply with a subpoena and appear before the Committee to testify regarding an investigation into the forced resignation of nine United States Attorneys in late 2006, and that current White House Chief of Staff Joshua Bolten must produce a privilege log in response to a congressional subpoena. Ms. Miers and Mr. Bolten (collectively "the Executive") have moved to dismiss this action in its entirety on the grounds that the Committee lacks standing and a proper cause of action, that disputes of this kind are non-justiciable, and that the Court should exercise its discretion to decline jurisdiction. On the merits, the Executive argues that sound principles of separation of powers and presidential autonomy dictate that the President's closest advisors must be absolutely immune from compelled testimony before Congress, and that the Committee has no authority to demand a privilege log from the White House.

Notwithstanding that the opposing litigants in this case are co-equal branches of the federal government, at bottom this lawsuit involves a basic judicial task— subpoena enforcement—with which federal courts are very familiar. The executive privilege claims that form the foundation of the Executive's resistance to the Committee's subpoenas are not foreign to federal courts either. After all, . . . the Supreme Court has confirmed the fundamental role of the federal courts to resolve the most sensitive issues of separation of powers. In the thirty-four years since *United States v. Nixon* was decided, the courts have routinely considered questions of executive privilege or immunity, and those issues are now "of a type that are traditionally justiciable," in federal courts, *United States v. Nixon*, 418 U.S. at 697, and certainly not unprecedented, as the Executive contends.

Indeed, the aspect of this lawsuit that is unprecedented is the notion that Ms. Miers is absolutely immune from compelled congressional process. The Supreme Court has reserved absolute immunity for very narrow circumstances, involving the President's personal exposure to suits for money damages based on his official conduct or concerning matters of national security or foreign affairs. The Executive's current claim of absolute immunity from compelled congressional process for senior presidential aides is without any support in the case law. The fallacy of that claim was presaged in *United States v. Nixon* itself (id. at 706):

> neither the doctrine of separation of powers, nor the need for confidentiality
> of high-level communications, without more, can sustain an absolute, unqual-
> ified Presidential privilege of immunity from judicial [or congressional]
> process under all circumstances.

It is important to note that the decision today is very limited. To be sure, most of this lengthy opinion addresses, and ultimately rejects, the Executive's several reasons why the Court should not entertain the Committee's lawsuit, but on the merits of the Committee's present claims the Court only resolves, and again rejects, the claim by the Executive to absolute immunity from compelled congressional process for senior presidential aides. The specific claims of executive privilege that Ms. Miers and Mr. Bolten may assert are not addressed—and the Court expresses no view on such claims. Nor should this decision discourage the process of negotiation and accommodation that most often leads to resolution of disputes between the political branches. Although standing ready to fulfill the essential judicial role to "say what the law is" on specific assertions of executive privilege that may be presented, the Court strongly encourages the political branches to resume their discourse and negotiations in an effort to resolve their differences constructively, while recognizing each branch's essential role . . . .

BACKGROUND

. . . Fortunately, . . . the operative facts are not significantly in dispute, notwithstanding each side's attempt to put its own gloss on the relevant events. In early December 2006, the Department of Justice ("DOJ") requested and received resignations from seven U.S. Attorneys: Daniel Bogden (D.Nev.), Paul K. Charlton (D.Ariz.), Margaret Chiara (W.D.Mich.), David Iglesias (D.N.M.), Carol Lam (S.D.Cal.), John McKay (W.D.Wash.), and Kevin Ryan (N.D.Cal.). At some point earlier in the year, DOJ had also asked for and received resignations from two other U.S. Attorneys: H.E. "Bud" Cummins III (E.D.Ark.) and Todd Graves (W.D.Mo.). The circumstances surrounding these forced resignations aroused almost immediate suspicion. Few of the U.S. Attorneys, for instance, were given any explanation for the sudden request for their resignations. Many had no reason to suspect that their superiors were dissatisfied with their professional performance; to the contrary, most had received favorable performance reviews.

Additional revelations further fueled speculation that improper criteria had motivated the dismissals. Carol Lam, for example, had successfully prosecuted Republican Congressman Randy "Duke" Cunningham for bribery following a high-profile investigation and was "in the midst" of pursuing additional high-ranking Republican officials when she was terminated. See Report of the Committee on the Judiciary, House of Representatives, H.R.Rep. No. 110-423 (2007) (hereinafter "Contempt Report"), at 17. John McKay had refused requests by Republican officials to pursue accusations of voter fraud during the 2004 Washington gubernatorial race. Similarly, David Iglesias was contacted by two Republican Members of Congress from New Mexico (Senator Pete Domenici and Representative Heather Wilson) who were disappointed to learn that Iglesias had no plans to seek indictments against members of the opposing political party in the run-up to the 2006 congressional elections.

As these events came to light, the Committee on the Judiciary—a standing Committee of the House of Representatives—commenced an investigation into the forced resignations in early 2007. Citing its authority under House Rule X, which provides that the Judiciary Committee's oversight responsibilities extend to issues relating to judicial proceedings and criminal law enforcement, the Committee declared that it aimed to:

investigat[e] and expos[e] any possible malfeasance, abuse of authority, or violation of existing laws on the part of the Executive Branch related to these concerns, and (2) consider[ ] whether the conduct uncovered may warrant additions or modifications to existing Federal Law, such as more clearly prohibiting the kinds of improper political interference with prosecutorial decisions as have been alleged here.

The Committee heard the testimony of six of the dismissed U.S. Attorneys during the first hearing held on March 6, 2007. Shortly thereafter, Committee Chairman John Conyers, Jr., and Linda T. Sanchez, Chairwoman of the Subcommittee on Commercial and Administrative Law, wrote to officials at DOJ and the White House requesting that certain individuals, among them Ms. Miers, be made available for questioning by the Committee.

In response, the Executive, "[i]n order to accommodate the Committee's interests . . . [,] made available to Congress a very substantial number of witnesses and documents." Thus, the Executive made "then-Principal Associate Deputy Attorney General William Moschella available to Congress as a witness, and subsequently made available thirteen additional Executive Branch witnesses for testimony or interviews, including the Attorney General, the Chief of Staff to the Attorney General, incumbent and former Deputy Attorneys General, and serving U.S. Attorneys." Mr. Moschella testified that "the forced resignations were all performance related and that any White House involvement was minimal and occurred only at the end of the process." Similarly, then-Attorney General Alberto Gonzales initially indicated that he was not involved in the process at all but later testified that he had very little recollection of the entire matter. [In a footnote, the court added: Indeed, by one count Mr. Gonzales testified no fewer than sixty-four times that he could not recall particular details concerning the events in question. See Eric Lichtblau, Bush's Law 295–96 (2008).]

On May 23, 2007, Monica Goodling, former Senior Counsel to Attorney General Gonzales and DOJ's White House Liaison, testified before the Committee pursuant to limited use immunity. Similarly, on July 11, 2007, former White House Political Director Sara M. Taylor testified before the Senate Committee on the Judiciary pursuant to a duly issued subpoena. Ms. Taylor invoked executive privilege as necessary on a question-by-question basis. Moreover, in addition to the live testimony provided, DOJ produced to Congress "over 7,850 pages of documents, including more than 2,200 pages from the Office of the Attorney General and 2,800 pages from the Office of the Deputy Attorney General." DOJ made available another 3,750 pages of documents, bringing the total number of pages produced to Congress to "nearly 12,000."

According to the Committee, however, "[s]ubsequent testimony and documents provided by Department officials . . . suggested that the Gonzales and Moschella statements were false and misleading, thus still leaving unresolved precisely what the reasons were for the terminations and what role the White House played in them."

Most importantly, none of the DOJ officials who testified before the Committee could identify who at DOJ had recommended the dismissal of the majority of the terminated U.S. Attorneys. Former Deputy Attorney General James B. Comey, who had supervised the dismissed U.S. Attorneys, had not recommended their removal—with the apparent exception of Kevin Ryan—and "could not credit the reasons offered for the terminations of the others." The Committee concluded that it is "well established that, in the opening days of President Bush's second term, then Senior Presidential Advisor Karl Rove raised the idea with officials in the White House Counsel's office of replacing some or all U.S. Attorneys." The Committee has not been able to determine, however, "why Mr. Rove was interested in this issue." Similarly, the Committee determined that "[n]ewly installed White House Counsel Harriet Miers apparently took up Mr. Rove's idea, and over the next two years received repeated drafts of the firing list." But likewise, "the Committee has learned very little as to why Ms. Miers believed that an effort to replace sitting U.S. Attorneys should be launched."

After deciding that Ms. Miers had played a significant personal role in the termination decision-making, the Committee intensified its efforts to obtain her testimony. Ms. Miers, however, had not responded to the initial letter from the Committee requesting a voluntary interview. Hence, on March 9, 2007, Chairman Conyers and Chairwoman Sanchez wrote to Fred F. Fielding, Counsel to the President, requesting that the administration produce documents relating to the investigation and "make certain White House officials available for interviews and questioning."

Mr. Fielding responded by letter dated March 20, 2007. He indicated that the White House was willing to "make available for interviews the President's former Counsel; current Deputy Chief of Staff and Senior Advisor; Deputy Counsel; and Special Assistant in the Office of Political Affairs." That offer was conditioned, however, upon several terms and restrictions. To begin with, the interviews were to be limited to "the subject of (a) communications between the White House and persons outside the White House concerning the request for resignations of the U.S. Attorneys in question; and (b) communications between the White House and Members of Congress concerning those reports." Moreover, the Executive indicated that the interviews were to be "private and conducted without the need for an oath, transcript, subsequent testimony, or the subsequent issuance of subpoenas." The White House also offered to provide to the Committee two categories of documents: "(a) communications between the White House and the Department of Justice concerning the request for resignations for the U.S. Attorneys in question; and (b) communications on the same subject between White House staff and third parties, including Members of Congress or their staffs on the subject."

The Committee did not receive Mr. Fielding's offer warmly. In particular, the Committee viewed the proposal as "unreasonably restrictive" in part because "no matter what was revealed [through the document production or interviews], no other testimony or documents could be requested from the White House." Moreover, the documents the White House offered to produce "excluded all internal White House communications regarding the firing of the U.S. Attorneys, even though some documents reflecting such internal communications had already been provided by the Justice Department." Thus, pursuant to House rules, on March 21, 2007, the Subcommittee voted to authorize Chairman Conyers to "issue subpoenas for the testimony of former White House Counsel Harriet Miers . . . and other specified White House officials." In addition, the Subcommittee also authorized Chairman Conyers to issue "subpoenas for documents in the custody or control of . . . White House Chief of Staff Joshua Bolten."

Chairman Conyers and Chairwoman Sanchez wrote to Mr. Fielding on March 22, 2007 to inform him that the Committee could not "accept your proposal for a number of reasons." Specifically, the letter stated that:

> [T]he failure to permit any transcript of our interviews with White House officials is an invitation to confusion and will not permit us to obtain a straightforward and clear record. Also, limiting the questioning (and document production) to discussions by and between outside parties will further prevent our Members from learning the full picture concerning the reasons for the firings and related issues. As we are sure you are aware, limitations of this nature are completely unsupported by precedents applied to prior Administrations—both Democratic and Republican.

Nevertheless, the Committee indicated that it remained "committed to seeking a cooperative resolution to this matter on a voluntary basis." For that reason, Chairman Conyers refrained from immediately issuing subpoenas in the hope that a negotiated solution would obviate the need to rely upon compulsory process.

Chairman Conyers and Senator Leahy, Chairman of the Senate Committee on the Judiciary, wrote to Mr. Fielding again on March 28, 2007 in an effort to reach an agreeable accommodation. The Chairmen requested that the White House abandon its "all or nothing" approach and instead produce the documents that it had already offered to make available. They also suggested that the parties narrow the dispute to "internal" White House documents and then focus on developing a process to deal with production. Mr. Fielding responded by letter dated April 12, 2007. He asked the Committees to "reconsider [their] rejection of the President's proposal." Mr. Fielding also "respectfully decline[d] [the Chairmen's] suggestion to immediately produce the documents that we are prepared to release." In conclusion, he indicated that the Executive "continue[d] to believe that the accommodation we offered on March 20 . . . will satisfy the Committees' interests."

Finally, Chairman Conyers and Chairwoman Sanchez wrote to Mr. Fielding on May 21, 2007 to "make one last appeal for . . . voluntary cooperation." They indicated that the Committee had been "willing and able to meet to consider other means of resolving our dispute, but we have received no response to our letters or proposals to you." Explaining that "it is becoming increasingly clear that we will not be able to complete our investigation absent full and complete cooperation from the White House," they emphasized the Committee's willingness to work out a voluntary resolution to the dispute but noted that it would "be constitutionally irresponsible to accept your 'all or nothing' limitations that would completely preclude any access to on-the-record statements by current and former White House personnel or access to internal White House communications." Thus, they stated that absent an effort by the White House to accommodate the Committee's request, "we will have no alternative but to begin to resort to compulsory process to carry out our oversight responsibilities."

Mr. Fielding responded to Chairman Leahy, Chairman Conyers, and Chairwoman Sanchez on June 7, 2007. He noted that the Executive had "made efforts to resolve our differences on this issue in a mutually acceptable fashion" by meeting with members from both Committees to discuss proposals. Moreover, he cited to various disclosures made by DOJ without objection from the White House. In addition, Mr. Fielding expressed his aspiration to "avoid the prospect of 'subpoenas' and 'compulsory process' referred to in your recent letters and statement." He concluded by reiterating, once again, the terms of the Executive's initial proposal, explaining that "[i]t is difficult to see how this proposal will not provide your Committees with all information necessary to evaluate the White House's connection to the Department's request for U.S. Attorney resignations."

Apparently viewing Mr. Fielding's June 7, 2007 letter as evidence of the Executive's intransigence, the Committee issued subpoenas to Mr. Bolten and Ms. Miers on June 13, 2007. Mr. Bolten was directed to produce responsive documents to the Committee by June 28, 2007 and to deliver a privilege log with respect to any documents withheld on the grounds of privilege. Ms. Miers was directed to appear to testify before the Committee on July 12, 2007 and to produce relevant documents in her possession; she, too, was advised to supply a privilege log for any documents withheld as privileged.

On June 27, 2007, Solicitor General and then-Acting Attorney General Paul Clement wrote to the President indicating that "[i]t is my considered legal judgment that you may assert executive privilege over the subpoenaed documents and testimony." Mr. Clement explained that the "Office of Legal Counsel of the Department of Justice . . . reviewed the documents identified by the Counsel to the President as responsive to subpoenas." Those responsive documents fell into "three broad categories": "(1) internal White House communications; (2) communications by White House officials with individuals outside the Executive Branch, including with individuals in the Legislative Branch; and (3) communications between White House officials and Department of Justice officials." Mr. Clement concurred with the conclusion of the Office of Legal Counsel ("OLC") that the documents "fall within the scope of executive privilege . . . [and] that Congress's interests in the documents and related testimony would not be sufficient to override an executive privilege claim."

Based upon Mr. Clement's letter and OLC's analysis, Mr. Fielding wrote to Chairmen Leahy and Conyers on June 28, 2007 advising them that the "President has decided to assert Executive Privilege and therefore the White House will not be making any production in response to these subpoenas for documents." In addition, Mr. Fielding indicated that the President had also directed Ms. Miers not to produce any responsive documents to the Committee; George Manning, counsel for Ms. Miers, confirmed that instruction by letter dated June 28, 2007. Mr. Bolten did not provide any documents to the Committee when his response date came due on June 28, 2007. The next day, Chairmen Leahy and Conyers wrote to Mr. Fielding seeking to obtain the specific bases for the Executive's assertion of privilege. They also requested that the White House provide a personal signed statement by the President confirming that he had decided to invoke executive privilege. Mr. Fielding denied both requests on July 9, 2007. On that same day, Mr. Fielding wrote to counsel for Ms. Miers informing him that the President had decided to assert executive privilege over the substance of Ms. Miers's testimony, and hence she was instructed not to provide any testimony before the Committee. In a July 10, 2007 letter to Mr. Manning, Mr. Fielding explained that OLC had concluded that Ms. Miers was absolutely immune from compelled congressional testimony. He again directed Mr. Manning to ensure that Ms. Miers did not appear to testify before the Committee on July 12, 2007, and attached a copy of OLC's opinion — also dated July 10, 2007 — to his letter.

Mr. Manning promptly informed the Committee that Ms. Miers had been instructed not to provide any testimony in response to her subpoena. Chairman Conyers and Chairwoman Sanchez objected to this development, urging Mr. Manning that "[w]e are aware of absolutely no court decision that supports the notion that a former White House official has the option of refusing to even appear in response to a Congressional subpoena." They warned that Ms. Miers ran the risk of being held in contempt of Congress if she declined to appear. By letter dated July 11, 2007, Mr. Manning confirmed that Ms. Miers would not appear to testify before the Committee on July 12, 2007.

When Ms. Miers failed to appear on July 12th, Chairwoman Sanchez decided to reject "Ms. Miers's privilege and immunity claims." The Subcommittee sustained that determination by a vote of 7–5. Chairman Conyers then delivered a copy of that ruling to Mr. Manning, along with a letter again warning that Ms. Miers could face contempt of Congress charges if she did not comply with the substance of the subpoena. In response, Mr. Manning restated that Ms. Miers would not appear to testify before the Committee or produce any responsive documents. On July 19, 2007, Chairman Sanchez again rejected Mr. Bolten's claims of executive privilege and his refusal to produce a privilege log. That decision was also sustained by the Subcommittee. Chairman Conyers then provided Mr. Fielding with a copy of that ruling and inquired as to whether the White House would comply with the subpoena. On July 23, 2007, Mr. Fielding informed Chairman Conyers that "the President's position remains unchanged."

Frustrated by the Executive's actions, the full Committee met on July 25, 2007 and adopted a resolution "recommending that the House of Representatives find that former White House Counsel Harriet Miers and White House Chief of Staff Joshua Bolten be cited for contempt of Congress for refusal to comply with subpoenas issued by the Committee." See 153 Cong. Rec. D1051-01 (2007). Chairman Conyers provided Mr. Fielding with a copy of the Committee's report in the hope that it might prompt the White House voluntarily to change its position. He received no response. So, on November 5, 2007, the Committee filed its report with the full House of Representatives. Once again, Chairman Conyers wrote to Mr. Fielding to inform him of that development and to reiterate that the Committee still hoped "to resolve the issue on a cooperative basis"; Chairman Conyers even included "a proposal for resolving the dispute." This time, Mr. Fielding responded by rejecting Chairman Conyers's offer, explicitly noting that "[w]e are therefore at a most regrettable impasse." He urged the Committee to "reconsider its proposed actions" and to accept the President's initial proposal.

With no negotiated solution in sight, the full House of Representatives voted to hold Ms. Miers and Mr. Bolten in contempt of Congress on February 14, 2008 by a vote of 223–32. [Note: Republican House Members boycotted the vote.] The House also passed three accompanying resolutions — H.Res. 979, 980, and 982 — that were meant to guide the next steps in the process. Resolution 979, for instance, provided that the Speaker of the House shall certify a copy of the Contempt Report "to the U.S. Attorney for the District of Columbia, 'to the end that Ms. Miers be proceeded against in the manner and form provided by law.'" It also provided analogous treatment for Mr. Bolten. Resolution 980 authorized Chairman Conyers to initiate a civil action in federal court to seek declaratory and injunctive relief "affirming the duty of any individual to comply with any subpoena."

On February 28, 2008, Speaker of the House Nancy Pelosi certified the Contempt Report to Jeffrey A. Taylor, U.S. Attorney for the District of Columbia. Pursuant to the terms of 2 U.S.C. §§ 192 and 194, Mr. Taylor was directed to present the contempt charges against Ms. Miers and Mr. Bolten to a grand jury. See 2 U.S.C. § 194. On that same day, Speaker Pelosi wrote to Attorney General Michael B. Mukasey. The Attorney General had previously indicated that he would not permit Mr. Taylor to bring the contempt citations before a grand jury, and Speaker Pelosi "urged him to reconsider his position." The next day, however, the Attorney General responded that because Ms. Miers and Mr. Bolten were acting pursuant to the direct orders of the President, "the Department has determined that noncompliance . . . with the Judiciary Committee subpoenas did not constitute a crime, and therefore the Department will not bring the congressional contempt citations before a grand jury or take any other action to prosecute Mr. Bolten or Ms. Miers." With criminal enforcement of its subpoenas foreclosed, the Committee — invoking Resolution 980 — filed this action seeking a declaratory judgment and other injunctive relief.

The undisputed factual record, then, establishes the following. Notwithstanding a prolonged period of negotiation, the parties reached a self-declared impasse with respect to the document production and testimony at issue here. Faced with that reality, the full House of Representatives voted to hold Ms. Miers and Mr. Bolten in contempt of Congress and certified the Contempt Report to the U.S. Attorney for the District of Columbia to pursue criminal enforcement of the contempt citations. The

Attorney General then directed the U.S. Attorney not to proceed against Ms. Miers and Mr. Bolten. The Committee, then, filed this suit seeking civil enforcement of its subpoena authority by way of declaratory and injunctive relief.

The only real factual "dispute" here is which party is responsible for the impasse. Unsurprisingly, each side blames the other. The Committee contends that the Executive proposed an untenable "take it or leave it" offer that would have significantly curtailed the Committee's capacity to perform its oversight duties, and then would not budge from its initial position. The Executive insists that the Committee's proposals "have been substantially the same and one-sided: they propose accommodations on the part of the White House without signaling any willingness on the part of the Committee to accommodate itself to the Presidential interests at stake." Hence, it is the Committee (in the Executive's view) that has stonewalled the accommodation process by pressing unreasonable demands that, if accepted, would amount to "incremental Executive Branch abandonment of [the President's] constitutional obligations." Although it is relevant that the political branches have reached an impasse, it is not important to assign blame for purposes of the motions now before the Court.

DISCUSSION

Because the Executive's motion to dismiss raises threshold issues that may preclude the need to reach the merits of the Committee's claims, the Court will address its motion first. There is one preliminary matter to discuss briefly however. Both sides concede, and the Court agrees, that 28 U.S.C. § 1331 provides subject matter jurisdiction over this lawsuit. Because this dispute concerns an allegation that Ms. Miers and Mr. Bolten failed to comply with duly issued congressional subpoenas, and such subpoena power derives implicitly from Article I of the Constitution, this case arises under the Constitution for purposes of § 1331 . . . .

I. The Executive's Motion to Dismiss

The Executive launches three distinct attacks in its motion to dismiss, raising considerations of standing, cause of action, and equitable discretion. The Court will address each contention in turn, but none provides a basis to dismiss this action.

A. Standing

[The court upheld the Committee's standing to bring the action, and moved on to broader issues of justiciability.]

The Executive also maintains that this dispute is not the sort that is traditionally amenable to judicial resolution. The Court disagrees for two primary reasons: (1) in essence, this lawsuit merely seeks enforcement of a subpoena, which is a routine and quintessential judicial task; and (2) the Supreme Court has held that the judiciary is the final arbiter of executive privilege, and the grounds asserted for the Executive's refusal to comply with the subpoena are ultimately rooted in executive privilege. Whatever merit there once was to the contention that questions of executive privilege are inherently non-justiciable, it can no longer be maintained in light of *United States v. Nixon* and its progeny . . . .

The mere fact that the President himself—let alone his advisors, as here—is the subject of the subpoena in question has not been viewed historically as an insurmountable obstacle to judicial resolution. Indeed, in *Burr,* Chief Justice Marshall explained that "the obligation [to comply with a subpoena] . . . is general; and it would seem that no person could claim an exemption from [it]." "The guard" that protects the Executive from "vexatious and unnecessary subpoenas," in Chief Justice Marshall's view, "is . . . the conduct of a court after those subpoenas have issued; not in any circumstance which is to precede their being issued." Any claim that compliance with a subpoena would jeopardize national security or privileged presidential information "will have its due consideration on the return of the subpoena," Chief Justice Marshall noted. Thus, federal precedent dating back as far as 1807 contemplates that even the Executive is bound to comply with duly issued subpoenas. The Supreme Court emphatically reaffirmed that proposition in *United States v. Nixon* in 1974.

The Committee correctly points out that "courts have decided countless cases that involve the allocation of power between the political branches (not to mention between the political branches and the judiciary)." The Committee cites a litany of cases in support of that proposition, all of which deal with important separation of powers concerns in their own right. Hence, in the Committee's view, federal courts have a long history of resolving cases that involve significant (and often contentious) separation of powers disputes between the branches of the federal government, thus refuting the Executive's assertion that this dispute is non-justiciable because it is not amenable to judicial resolution.

The Executive makes two arguments to rebut these points, neither of which is convincing. First, the Executive contends, *United States v. Nixon* is limited to the context of grand jury subpoenas and thus does not inform the present case. Grand jury proceedings, the argument goes, fall well within the traditional scope of an Article III court whereas this dispute does not. The Court disagrees. To be sure, the Supreme Court in *United States v. Nixon* explicitly cabined its opinion to the criminal arena. But in identifying "the kind of controversy courts traditionally resolve," the Court focused on the issue of the production of specific evidence deemed to be relevant, and the resolution of a claim of executive privilege raised to resist production-noting that "these issues are 'of a type which are traditionally justiciable.'" Although the setting here is a civil subpoena enforcement proceeding, the issues parallel those in *Nixon* and the setting is sufficient to ensure sharp presentation of the issues. . . .

It is readily apparent . . . that the justiciability principles underlying the Supreme Court's decision in *United States v. Nixon* have been extended beyond the limited realm of grand jury subpoenas. Most significantly, of course, the D.C. Circuit has confronted this issue in precisely the context presented by the instant case. In *Senate Select Comm. III*, a Senate committee brought a civil action to enforce subpoenas that it had issued to President Nixon to produce certain taped recordings of conversations between President Nixon and his White House counsel. 498 F.2d at 727. President Nixon declined to comply with the subpoena, asserting absolute executive privilege. Relying heavily upon *Nixon v. Sirica*, 487 F.2d 700 (D.C.Cir. 1973), the court rejected President Nixon's claim of absolute privilege and instead held that he was entitled only to a presumptive privilege. The court ultimately concluded that the Select Committee had not satisfied the "demonstrably critical" showing required to overcome the presumptive privilege because: (1) the House Judiciary Committee, which had "begun an inquiry into presidential impeachment," had already received copies of the tapes, thus rendering the Select Committee's oversight investigation "merely cumulative"; and (2) the Select Committee had already received written transcripts of the recordings and its asserted interest in ensuring the accuracy of the transcripts was not powerful enough to overcome the President's interest in confidentiality. . . .

[A]lthough Congress does not have the authority to enforce the laws of the nation, it does have the "power of inquiry." *See McGrain v. Daugherty*, 273 U.S. 135 (1927). And according to the Supreme Court, "the power of inquiry—with process to enforce it—is an essential and appropriate auxiliary to the legislative function." Indeed, the Court has indicated that the "issuance of a subpoena pursuant to an authorized investigation is . . . an indispensable ingredient of lawmaking." *See Eastland v. United States Servicemen's Fund*, 421 U.S. 491 (1975). "Just as the power to issue subpoenas is a necessary part of the Executive Branch's authority to execute federal laws," so too is Congress's need to enforce its subpoenas a necessary part of its power of inquiry.

Two significant OLC opinions issued during the Reagan administration warrant examination at this point. In 1984, an opinion by Acting Assistant Attorney General Theodore Olson confirmed the viability of a federal civil suit brought by a House of Congress to enforce subpoenas issued to executive officials. *See Prosecution for Contempt of Congress of an Executive Branch Official Who Has Asserted a Claim of Executive Privilege*, 8 U.S. Op. Off. Legal Counsel 101, 137 (1984) (hereinafter "Olson OLC Opinion"). As OLC opined, Congress has three options available to enforce a subpoena against a recalcitrant respondent: (1) referral to the U.S. Attorney for prosecution of a criminal contempt of Congress charge; (2) detention and prosecution pursuant to Congress's inherent contempt authority; or (3) a civil action to enforce the subpoena in a federal district court. When the respondent is a member of the executive branch who refuses to comply on the basis of executive privilege, however, OLC stated that the "contempt of Congress statute does not require and could not constitutionally require a prosecution of that official, or even, we believe, a referral to a grand jury of the facts relating to the alleged contempt." That conclusion is rooted in concerns over both the Executive's traditional prosecutorial discretion, as well as the "concomitant chilling effect" that might impair presidential advice if the possibility of criminal prosecution loomed over the President's close advisors. Significantly, OLC also determined that "the same reasoning that suggests that the statute could not constitutionally be applied against a Presidential assertion of privilege applies to Congress' inherent contempt powers as well. Thus, neither criminal prosecution nor inherent contempt could be employed against a recalcitrant executive branch official, as OLC saw it.

Instead, "Congress [can] obtain a judicial resolution of the underlying privilege claim and vindicate its asserted right to obtain any documents by a civil action for enforcement of a congressional subpoena." As OLC put it, a civil action would be superior because:

> Congress has a legitimate and powerful interest in obtaining any unprivileged documents necessary to assist it in its lawmaking function ... [and] [a] civil suit to enforce the subpoena would be aimed at the congressional objective of obtaining the documents, not at inflicting punishment on an individual who failed to produce them. Thus, even if criminal sanctions were not available against an executive official who asserted the President's claim of privilege, Congress would be able to vindicate its legitimate desire to obtain documents if it could establish that its need for the records outweighed the Executive's interest in preserving confidentiality.

In fact, after examining *Senate Select Comm. III*, OLC concluded that "there is little doubt that, at the very least, Congress may authorize civil enforcement of its subpoenas and grant jurisdiction to the courts to entertain such cases." There is no suggestion whatsoever in the Olson OLC Opinion that such a civil suit would encounter any Article III obstacles because Congress (or a committee) would lack standing or because the dispute would not be considered traditionally amenable to judicial resolution. To the contrary, OLC rather emphatically concluded that a civil action would be the least controversial way for Congress to vindicate its investigative authority.

A 1986 OLC opinion authored by Assistant Attorney General Charles Cooper reached the same conclusion. See *Response to Congressional Requests for Information Regarding Decisions Made Under the Independent Counsel Act*, 10 U.S. Op. Off. Legal Counsel 68 (1986) (hereinafter "Cooper OLC Opinion"). In that opinion, OLC restated its position that Congress may institute "a civil suit seeking declaratory enforcement of [a] subpoena." Likewise, OLC indicated that although inherent contempt is theoretically available to Congress and could ultimately be challenged by the executive branch through a writ of habeas corpus brought by the detained official, "it seems most unlikely that Congress could dispatch the Sergeant-at-Arms to arrest and imprison an Executive Branch official who claimed executive privilege." Ultimately, OLC concluded that "although the civil enforcement route has not been tried by the House, it would appear to be a viable option." ... There can be no doubt, then, that at least one prior administration regarded a civil suit by Congress to enforce a subpoena as presenting a justiciable controversy—and, indeed, to be the preferred method for resolving such inter-branch disputes. ("[O]nly judicial intervention can prevent a stalemate between the other two branches that could result in a particular paralysis of government operations.") ....

Turning to the legitimacy of this investigation, *McGrain* itself is enlightening. There, the investigation at issue involved:

> [T]he administration of the Department of Justice — whether its functions were being properly discharged or were being neglected or misdirected, and particularly whether the Attorney General and his assistants were performing or neglecting their duties in respect of the institution and prosecution of proceedings to punish crimes and enforce appropriate remedies against the wrongdoers.

The Court held that such a "subject [is] one on which legislation could be had and would be materially aided by the information which the investigation was calculated to elicit." So, too, here — in fact, it is nearly the identical subject matter that the Committee is investigating. Simply put, the Executive characterizes the Committee's investigation far too narrowly. It is not merely an investigation into the Executive's use of his removal power but rather a broader inquiry into whether improper partisan considerations have influenced prosecutorial discretion .... It defies both reason and precedent to say that the Committee, which is charged with oversight of DOJ generally, cannot permissibly employ its investigative resources on this subject. Indeed, given its "unique ability to address improper partisan influence in the prosecutorial process . . . [n]o other institution will fill the vacuum if Congress is unable to investigate and respond to this evil." Brief of Former United States Attorneys at 10–11 . . . .

To recap, the Committee has issued subpoenas to two high-ranking executive branch officials who have refused to comply, citing executive privilege. The Committee's attempt to pursue criminal prosecution of its contempt of Congress citation was thwarted by the Executive. Exercise of Congress's inherent contempt power through arrest and confinement of a senior executive official would provoke an unseemly constitutional confrontation that should be avoided. Thus, the Committee filed this suit to vindicate both its right to the information that is the subject of the subpoena and its institutional prerogative to compel compliance with its subpoenas. A harm to either interest satisfies the injury-in-fact standing requirement. Clear judicial precedent, along with persuasive reasoning in OLC opinions, establishes that the Committee has standing to pursue this action and, moreover, that this type of dispute is justiciable in federal court. Consequently, the Executive's motion to dismiss for lack of standing will be denied.

B. Cause of Action

Even if the Committee can satisfy the Article III prerequisites to bringing a case in federal court, the Executive argues, the complaint must nonetheless be dismissed because there is no cause of action that authorizes this lawsuit. Although the complaint identifies the Declaratory Judgment Act, 28 U.S.C. §§ 2201–2202 ("DJA" or "Act"), as the basis for the Committee's requested relief, the Executive insists that the Act "does not create a cause of action." Moreover, the Executive urges, this Court should decline to recognize an implied cause of action in favor of the Committee derived from the Constitution. [The court rejected both of these contentions.]

C. Equitable Discretion

That leaves the Executive's final basis for dismissal. Even if the Committee has either the requisite right pursuant to the DJA or an implied cause of action, the Executive contends that this Court nevertheless has the discretion to decline to hear the case, and should do so here. The Executive is correct that the Court has such discretion. The DJA provides that a court "may declare the rights and other legal relations of any party seeking such declaration." See 28 U.S.C. § 2201(a). The Supreme Court has held that the Act's textual commitment to discretion indicates that "district courts possess discretion in determining whether and when to entertain an action under the Declaratory Judgment Act, even when the suit satisfies subject matter jurisdictional prerequisites." Wilton v. Seven Falls, 515 U.S. 277, 283 . . . . Thus, the question here is not whether the Court can entertain this suit, but whether it should do so. There are no dispositive factors to consider in this analysis. Instead, there are several factors that help to guide the Court's determination:

> Among the factors relevant to the propriety of granting a declaratory judgment are the following: whether it would finally settle the controversy between the parties; whether other remedies are available or other proceedings pending; the convenience of the parties; the equity of the conduct of the declaratory judgment plaintiff; prevention of "procedural fencing"; the state of the record; the degree of adverseness between the parties; and the public importance of the question to be decided.

Hanes Corp., 531 F.2d at 591 n. 4.

The Executive presents a litany of reasons why the Court should decline to decide this case. But the crux of the Executive's position is that the federal judiciary should not enter into this dispute between the political branches. "[F]or more than 200 years," the Executive asserts, "the political branches have resolved their disputes over congressional requests for information without Congress invoking the aid of the federal judiciary to adjudicate Congress's claims." And if this Court were to reach the merits of the case, a decision "would inexorably alter the separation of powers and forever change how the political branches deal with each other and the nature of accommodation, if any, between them." Moreover, a "definitive judicial resolution of these issues would invite further judicial involvement in an area where it is settled that courts should tread lightly, if at all." In short, according to the Executive, this Court should leave this dispute to resolution by the political process, which is what the Framers intended.

There is some force to the Executive's position, but the Court is not persuaded. To begin with, whatever way this Court decides the issues before it may impact the balance between the political branches in this and future settings. . . . Hence, a decision to foreclose access to the courts, as the Executive urges, would tilt the balance in favor of the Executive here, the very mischief the Executive purports to fear. Moreover, the Executive is mistaken in the contention that judicial intervention in this arena at the request of Congress would be unprecedented in the nation's history.

The 1974 decision by the Supreme Court in *United States v. Nixon* adjusted this balance by clarifying that the judiciary must be available to resolve executive privilege claims . . . . The Court does not understand why separation of powers principles are more offended when the Article I branch sues the Article II branch than when the Article II branch sues the Article I branch.

OLC itself has noted that the Supreme Court confirmed in *United States v. Nixon* that the judiciary is the ultimate arbiter of claims of executive privilege. Ever since then, it has been apparent that issues relating to claims of executive privilege are subject to at least some judicial oversight. Moreover, the judiciary has a long history of deciding cases that involve various separation of powers issues and, indeed, cases such as *AT & T I, United States v. House of Representatives,* and *Senate Select Comm. III* mark judicial involvement in congressional subpoena disputes between the executive and legislative branches. The status quo in the light of which the political branches have operated — at least since *United States v. Nixon* — is the availability of ultimate judicial intervention in exactly this sort of controversy. That fact was made abundantly clear in both the Olson and Cooper OLC opinions, and things have not changed since then. Put another way, the historical record dating back to *United States v. Nixon* suggests that the political branches have negotiated with one another against the backdrop of presumptive judicial review, mindful of that very real possibility. Thus, contrary to the Executive's contention, declining to decide this case would be the action most likely to "alter" the accommodations process between the political branches.

Nor would hearing this case open the floodgates for similar litigation that would overwhelm the federal courts and paralyze the accommodations process between the political branches. . . . [T]here have been very few lawsuits brought in federal court raising this issue — certainly no rush to the courthouse by either political branch is evident. The process of negotiation between the executive and legislative branches has functioned as always. Indeed, there are powerful reasons to believe that most disputes of this nature will continue to be resolved through the informal processes of negotiation and accommodation. Resort to the judicial process is, after all, not a particularly expedient way to obtain prompt access to sought-after information, especially if a full House or Senate resolution is a necessary part of the process. The lengthy delays in the history of this case are a testament to the inefficiency of resort to the judicial process. Finally, the prospect of ultimate judicial resolution will help to ensure that the parties continue to negotiate in good faith rather than rewarding intransigence.

. . . [T]he Committee presents persuasive reasons why the Court should exercise its discretion to decide the issues raised in its motion for partial summary judgment. First, judicial resolution would settle this dispute between the parties as to whether Ms. Miers is absolutely immune from congressional process and whether Mr. Bolten must respond further. Resolution of the immunity issue will determine the next steps (if any) the parties must take in this matter. Second, contrary to the

Executive's suggestion that the Committee did not make any serious counter-offers, the record reflects that it was the Executive and not the Committee that refused to budge from its initial bargaining position. Mr. Fielding himself stated that the Committee had written to him "on eight previous occasions, three of which letters contain or incorporate specific proposals involving terms for a possible agreement." The Executive, by contrast, apparently continued to adhere to its original proposal without modification. Thus, the "equity of the conduct of the declaratory judgment plaintiff" supports the exercise of the Court's discretion in favor of the Committee. Third, the record is fully developed for purposes of the issues presented by these motions . . . . Fourth, the parties are most surely sufficiently adverse. Fifth, both sides agree that this case raises issues of enormous "public importance." Finally, there is a strong possibility that this sort of dispute could routinely "recur." Indeed, it already has: on July 10, 2008, former White House advisor Karl Rove asserted absolute immunity in response to a congressional subpoena and on July 30, 2008 the Committee voted to hold him in contempt. See David Stout, Democrats Call for Contempt Charges Against Rove, *N.Y. Times*, July 31, 2008.

Still, the timing of this dispute gives the Court some pause. The 110th Congress expires on January 3, 2009. Unlike the Senate, the House is not a continuing body. This House ends on January 3, 2009. Significantly, the subpoenas issued by this House will also expire on that date. Moreover, a new executive administration will take office in January 2009 following the presidential elections that will be held in November. There is, therefore, the question of mootness possibly looming on the horizon that threatens both parties here . . . . To be sure, the incoming House of Representatives may elect to re-issue similar subpoenas, but that remains speculative at this juncture. Similarly, the incoming executive administration may decline to pursue the assertions of immunity and executive privilege that form the foundation of this dispute. A former President may still assert executive privilege, but the claim necessarily has less force, particularly when the sitting President does not support the claim of privilege. . . . [T]here is no way to predict whether the new administration will support the assertions of privilege made in this case. There is also the likelihood of appeal of this decision and, given the significance of the issues involved, a stay pending appeal is at least possible. Thus, although proceedings before this Court could be concluded prior to January 2009, any appeals process may not run its course before that date. At that point, the case would arguably become moot.

Nevertheless, the Court concludes that this concern does not counsel against entertaining this case. . . . [T]here are over five months of live controversy remaining. Furthermore, this mootness concern is likely to be present in nearly every controversy of this nature. Because the Congress expires every two years, and a subpoena issued by the House remains valid only for the duration of that Congress, it would be difficult for any House subpoena dispute to fit into that two-year window once the time for appeal is factored into the equation. The process contemplates a long period of negotiation with resort to the judiciary, if at all, only in the case of a legitimate impasse. The combination of the congressional process and litigation time (including appeal) means that every subpoena dispute of this nature would likely run up against the two-year window. That may present a problem that is capable of repetition yet evading review, a well-recognized exception to mootness. But in any event, it is not necessary to decide that question now because this case is not presently moot and, significantly, neither side has asked the Court to stay its hand due to mootness considerations.

The Court re-emphasizes its limited involvement at this point. The Court has addressed only traditional legal issues — standing, causes of action, equitable discretion — and has not yet been asked to rule on any particular assertion of executive privilege. Indeed, the ultimate disposition that the Court reaches today — that Ms. Miers is not absolutely immune from congressional process and that Mr. Bolten must produce more detailed documentation concerning privilege claims — still does not address the merits of any particular assertion of presidential privilege. . . . Quite frankly, this decision does not foreclose the accommodations process; if anything, it should provide the impetus to revisit negotiations . . . . Two parties cannot negotiate in good faith when one side asserts legal privileges but insists that they cannot be tested in court in the traditional manner. That is true whether the negotiating partners are private firms or the political branches of the federal government. Accordingly, the Court will deny the Executive's motion to dismiss.

II. The Committee's Motion for Partial Summary Judgment

The Executive cannot identify a single judicial opinion that recognizes absolute immunity for senior presidential advisors in this or any other context. That simple yet critical fact bears repeating: the asserted absolute immunity claim here is entirely unsupported by existing case law. In fact, there is Supreme Court authority that is all but conclusive on this question and that powerfully suggests that such advisors do not enjoy absolute immunity. The Court therefore rejects the Executive's claim of absolute immunity for senior presidential aides.

A. Absolute Immunity

The Committee's primary argument on this point is incredibly straight-forward. Ms. Miers was the recipient of a duly issued congressional subpoena. Hence, she was legally obligated to appear to testify before the Committee on this matter, at which time she could assert legitimate privilege claims to specific questions or subjects. The Supreme Court has made it abundantly clear that compliance with a congressional subpoena is a legal requirement. *United States v. Bryan*, 339 U.S. 323, 331, (1950). Indeed, the Court noted:

> A subpoena has never been treated as an invitation to a game of hare and hounds, in which the witness must testify only if cornered at the end of the chase. If that were the case, then, indeed, the great power of testimonial compulsion, so necessary to the effective functioning of courts and legislatures, would be a nullity. We have often iterated the importance of this public

duty, which every person within the jurisdiction of the Government is bound to perform when properly summoned.

With her duty to appear thus established, the Committee asserts that the burden rests with Ms. Miers to explain why compliance was excused in this instance.

The Executive maintains that absolute immunity shields Ms. Miers from compelled testimony before Congress. Although the exact reach of this proposed doctrine is not clear, the Executive insists that it applies only to "a very small cadre of senior advisors." The argument starts with the assertion that the President himself is absolutely immune from compelled congressional testimony. There is no case that stands for that exact proposition, but the Executive maintains that the conclusion flows logically from *Nixon v. Fitzgerald*, where the Supreme Court held that the President "is entitled to absolute immunity from damages liability predicated on his official acts." [The court rejected this contention, noting the holding of *Harlow, supra*.]

The Executive's concern that "[a]bsent immunity . . . there would be no effective brake on Congress's discretion to compel the testimony of the President's advisers at the highest level of government" is also unfounded. To begin with, the process of negotiation and accommodation will ensure that most disputes over information and testimony are settled informally. Moreover, political considerations—including situations where Congress or one House of Congress is controlled by the same political party that holds the Presidency—will surely factor into Congress's decision whether to deploy its compulsory process over the President's objection. In any event, the historical record produced by the Committee reveals that senior advisors to the President have often testified before Congress subject to various subpoenas dating back to 1973. Thus, it would hardly be unprecedented for Ms. Miers to appear before Congress to testify and assert executive privilege where appropriate. . . . [A] claim of absolute immunity from compulsory process cannot be erected by the Executive as a surrogate for the claim of absolute executive privilege already firmly rejected by the courts. Presidential autonomy, such as it is, cannot mean that the Executive's actions are totally insulated from scrutiny by Congress. That would eviscerate Congress's historical oversight function . . . . Permitting the Executive to determine the limits of its own privilege would impermissibly transform the presumptive privilege into an absolute one, yet that is what the Executive seeks through its assertion of Ms. Miers's absolute immunity from compulsory process. That proposition is untenable and cannot be justified by appeals to Presidential autonomy.

Tellingly, the only authority that the Executive can muster in support of its absolute immunity assertion are two OLC opinions authored by Attorney General Janet Reno and Principal Deputy Assistant Attorney General Steven Bradbury, respectively. See *Assertion of Executive Privilege With Respect to Clemency Decision*, 1999 WL 33490208 (O.L.C. 1999); *Immunity of Former Counsel to the President From Compelled Congressional Testimony*, 2007 WL 5038035 (O.L.C. 2007). Those opinions conclude that immediate advisors to the President are immune from compelled congressional testimony. The question, then, is how much credence to give to those opinions. Like the Olson and Cooper OLC opinions, the Reno and Bradbury opinions represent only persuasive authority. (Hence, the Court concludes that the opinions are entitled to only as much weight as the force of their reasoning will support.)

With that established, the Court is not at all persuaded by the Reno and Bradbury opinions. Unlike the Olson and Cooper OLC opinions, which are exhaustive efforts of sophisticated legal reasoning, bolstered by extensive citation to judicial authority, the Reno and Bradbury OLC opinions are for the most part conclusory and recursive. Neither cites to a single judicial opinion recognizing the asserted absolute immunity. Indeed, the three-page Bradbury OLC opinion was hastily issued on the same day that the President instructed Ms. Miers to invoke absolute immunity, and it relies almost exclusively upon the conclusory Reno OLC opinion and a statement from a memorandum written by then-Assistant Attorney General William Rehnquist in 1971. Mr. Rehnquist wrote:

> The President and his immediate advisers — that is, those who customarily meet with the President on a regular or frequent basis — should be deemed absolutely immune from testimonial compulsion by a congressional committee. They not only may not be examined with respect to their official duties, but they may not even be compelled to appear before a congressional committee.

Mr. Rehnquist also wrote that the rationale supporting the proposed immunity for senior advisors is grounded in the fact that those individuals "are presumptively available to the President 24 hours a day, and the necessity of either accommodating a congressional committee or persuading a court to arrange a more convenient time, could impair that availability." Significantly, Mr. Rehnquist referred to his conclusions as "tentative and sketchy," and then later apparently recanted those views. In *Clinton v. Jones*, then-Chief Justice Rehnquist joined in holding that even the demands of the President's schedule could not relieve him of the duty to give a civil deposition. Whatever force the Rehnquist memorandum had when written, then, it retains little vitality in light of *Clinton v. Jones*. If the President must find time to comply with compulsory process in a civil lawsuit, so too must his senior advisors for a congressional subpoena.

[The court appended a footnote discussing the President's involvement in this case: There is some ambiguity over the scope of the President's involvement in the decision to terminate the U.S. Attorneys in this case. The Committee contends that the White House has asserted that the "President was not involved in any way . . . and that he did not receive advice from his aides about the U.S. Attorneys and he did not make a decision to fire any of them." That assertion is based on a statement made by Acting White House Press Secretary Dana Perino on March 27, 2007. The Executive, however, now maintains that the Committee "substantially overstates the record on this point." As the Executive sees it, the record simply indicates that "the President was not involved in decisions about who would be asked to resign from the department," but "does not reflect that the President had no future involvement" in any capacity. Given the Court's limited decision here, it is unnecessary to address this factual dispute at this time. The Court notes, however, that the degree and nature of the President's involvement may be relevant to the proper executive privilege characterization . . . .]

. . . Congress . . . is acting pursuant to a legitimate use of its investigative authority. Notwithstanding its best efforts, the Committee has been unable to discover the underlying causes of the forced terminations of the U.S. Attorneys. The Committee has legitimate reasons to believe that Ms. Miers's testimony can remedy that deficiency. There is no evidence that the Committee is merely seeking to harass Ms. Miers by calling her to testify. Importantly, moreover, Ms. Miers remains able to assert privilege in response to any specific question or subject matter. For its part, the Executive has not offered any independent reasons that Ms. Miers should be relieved from compelled congressional testimony beyond its blanket assertion of absolute immunity. The Executive's showing, then, does not support either absolute or qualified immunity in this case . . . .

[I]f the Executive's absolute immunity argument were to prevail, Congress could be left with no recourse to obtain information that is plainly not subject to any colorable claim of executive privilege. For instance, surely at least some of the questions that the Committee intends to ask Ms. Miers would not elicit a response subject to an assertion of privilege; so, too, for responsive documents, many of which may even have been produced already. The Executive's proposed absolute immunity would thus deprive Congress of even non-privileged information. That is an unacceptable result.

Clear precedent and persuasive policy reasons confirm that the Executive cannot be the judge of its own privilege and hence Ms. Miers is not entitled to absolute immunity from compelled congressional process. Ms. Miers is not excused from compliance with the Committee's subpoena by virtue of a claim of executive privilege that may ultimately be made. Instead, she must appear before the Committee to provide testimony, and invoke executive privilege where appropriate.

B. Privilege Log Production

That leaves one final issue—whether Ms. Miers and Mr. Bolten are legally obligated to produce privilege logs in response to the Committee's subpoenas. The Court will not belabor this point. At oral argument, counsel for the Committee candidly admitted that there is "no statute or case law" that dictates that those individuals must produce privilege logs. Instead, the Committee asserts that producing a privilege log is simply a very pragmatic practice that should be required here.

The Committee is certainly correct that privilege logs have great practical utility. Beyond their legal usefulness, the Court believes that a more detailed description of the documents withheld and the privileges asserted would be a tremendous aid during the negotiation and accommodation process. A more fulsome description, for instance, may lead the Committee to conclude that it has no need for certain categories of documents, thus helping to narrow the dispute between the parties and enhance the possibility of resolution. Notwithstanding such obvious benefits, however, in the absence of an applicable statute or controlling case law, the Court does not have a ready ground by which to force the Executive to make such a production strictly in response to a congressional subpoena. But . . . if the Court is called upon to decide the merits of any specific claim of privilege, it will need a better description of the documents withheld than the one found in Mr. Clement's letter of June 27, 2007. But the Court will stop short of requiring the Executive to produce a full privilege log. Instead, the Executive should produce a more detailed list and description of the nature and scope of the documents it seeks to withhold on the basis of executive privilege sufficient to enable resolution of any privilege claims. . . .

———————

1. *Running Out the Clock*. Note the timing problem that the court struggled with in *Miers*, and the potential for it to recur. This controversy occurred toward the end of the Bush administration. After the court's decision in the summer of 2008, the court of appeals issued a stay in October, and the case was voluntarily dismissed in 2009, after the administration left office. An agreement was ultimately reached in March 2009 with the House Judiciary Committee to permit questioning of both Harriet Miers and Karl Rove, with transcripts provided for all parties. *See* "Agreement Concerning Accommodation, *Committee on the Judiciary v. Harriet Miers*," http:// judiciary.house.gov/hearings/pdf/Agreement090304.pdf. As the court noted, the two-year cycle of each House term makes it hard to litigate these issues, at least if the executive can stall successfully for a substantial period. Was that happening in this case? How would you expect this problem to affect negotiations generally?

2. *Applicability of the* Cheney *Test*. In *Cheney v. United States District Court for the District of Columbia*, 542 U.S. 367 (2004), excerpted later in this chapter, the Court considered how executive privilege should operate in civil litigation rather than in response to congressional subpoenas. As we will see, the Court instructed district courts to manage discovery to avoid the "unwarranted impairment" of executive functions that would attend forcing multiple invocations of executive privilege in response to broad subpoenas. Was overbreadth a problem in *Miers*? How much intrusion on executive functions did the case entail?

3. *Testimonial Immunity*. Should there be any absolute zone of testimonial immunity for some officers? Which ones? What does the *Nixon* case suggest?

4. *Grading Performances*. What do you think of the behavior of the executive and congressional personnel in this case? Was the executive stonewalling? Should the committee have accepted the offer of testimony without oaths or follow-up opportunities? What were the legitimate interests of each branch here? For a defense of the Bush Administration's handling of executive privilege in the Miers matter (and vis-à-vis Congress in general) by lawyers who had served, respectively, as President Bush's White House Counsel and Associate White House Counsel, see Fred F. Fielding and Heath P. Tarbert, *Principled Accommodation: The Bush Administration's Approach to Congressional Oversight and Executive Privilege*, 32 J.L. & POL. 95 (2016).

One of your authors was highly critical of executive branch lawyering in an earlier executive privilege imbroglio with Congress that led to the first-ever full House of Representatives vote of contempt against a sitting agency head. Peter M. Shane, *Legal Disagreement and Negotiation in a Government of Laws: The Case of Executive Privilege Claims Against Congress*, 71 Minn. L. Rev. 461 (1987). The dispute arose when two committees of the House launched an investigation of suspected corruption in the administration of the Superfund — a trust fund created for the cleanup of toxic waste sites — under EPA Administrator Anne Gorsuch and Superfund Administrator Rita Lavelle. Although providing a large volume of records to the Committees in response to their requests, the Justice Department withheld other documents on the ground that it would be improper to release open law enforcement files. President Reagan formally asserted executive privilege. After negotiations broke down, a citation of contempt was voted first by the Public Works and Transportation Committee, then by the full House. As it turns out, however, the Justice Department and White House, within two months, became persuaded that Rita Lavelle had been guilty of improper administration of the superfund and perjury in her testimony to Congress. The White House ultimately released to the House all of the documents it had demanded.

In the course of the dispute, Attorney General William French Smith issued letters to the relevant subcommittee chairs, justifying the nondisclosure of the disputed records in order to forestall the appearance of political influence over ongoing law enforcement investigations, protect law enforcement sources and methods, and maintain the privacy of innocent parties who might be named in law enforcement documents. Perhaps unfortunately, however, these relatively measured claims followed an earlier Smith opinion in another executive privilege dispute, which was rather less measured. Opining on a refusal by Secretary of the Interior James Watt to disclose documents to Congress related to the status of Canada under the Mineral Lands Leasing Act, Smith had asserted that (1) Congress's interests in information "for oversight purposes are . . . considerably weaker than its interest when specific legislative proposals are in question," and (2) "the congressional oversight interest will support a demand for predecisional, deliberative documents in the possession of the Executive Branch only in the most unusual circumstances." 5 Op. O.L.C. 27 (1981). These assertions, unaccompanied by any citation to judicial authority, were both targets of a vigorous response by the chief House lawyer, Stanley Brand, who was then General Counsel to the Clerk of the House. And, ultimately, in order to avoid a House contempt vote against Secretary Watt, the White House agreed to permit Members to inspect all the documents withheld; none appeared even to the Republicans on the subcommittee to be sensitive. Louis Fisher, The Politics of Executive Privilege 126 (2004). Professor Shane argues that the overzealous lawyering of the Watt dispute weakened Attorney General Smith's negotiating position in the Superfund matter. Shane, *Legal Disagreement.* 71 Minn. L. Rev., at 514.

5. *Vehicles for review.* Note the traditional (and understandable) position of the executive that it will not bring a criminal contempt proceeding against an officer who

has executed a presidential order to invoke executive privilege against Congress, and OLC's concession at various times that a civil action as in *Miers* is the appropriate step for Congress to take. In the complete version of a 1976 statement to Congress that is excerpted in Chapter Four, Assistant Attorney General Rex Lee suggested the creation of jurisdiction in the federal courts to hear civil actions for the enforcement of congressional subpoenas. For a similar proposal, see James Hamilton & John C. Grabow, *A Legislative Proposal for Resolving Executive Privilege Disputes Precipitated by Congressional Subpoenas*, 21 Harv. J. Legis. 145 (1984). Arguably, the availability of a clear judicial route for the adjudication of interbranch executive privilege claims would leave the executive branch better off because it can now offer such claims for judicial validation only by way of defending a contempt action. See *United States v. House of Representatives of the United States*, 556 F. Supp. 150 (D.D.C. 1983), rebuffing the Reagan Administration's request for a declaratory judgment upholding the refusal of EPA Administrator Gorsuch to withhold documents from the House in the episode recounted above.

For an argument that a criminal enforcement provision is preferable, and that Congress should have resort to independent counsel to enforce its subpoenas, see Stanley M. Brand & Sean Connelly, *Constitutional Confrontations: Preserving a Prompt and Orderly Means By Which Congress May Enforce Investigative Demands Against Executive Branch Officials*, 36 Cath. U. L. Rev. 71 (1986). Would it be permissible for Congress to insist (by statute) on criminal contempt prosecutions against executive branch officials who withhold information based on a President's formal claim of executive privilege? Professor Todd Peterson has argued, in *Prosecuting Executive Branch Officials for Contempt of Congress*, 66 N.Y.U. L. Rev. 563 (1991), that Congress may not compel the Attorney General to bring such prosecutions because they would be institutionally unnecessary to protect Congress's access to information. Thus, depriving the Attorney General of discretion not to prosecute would allow Congress to target individuals for criminal sanctions without compelling justification and in violation of the intended separation of prosecutorial and legislative decision making. OLC had earlier taken a similar position, arguing also that the contempt of Congress law should be read, as a matter of ordinary statutory construction, as leaving intact the Justice Department's discretion not to prosecute for contempt any executive branch official or employee whose noncompliance with a congressional subpoena is simply carrying out a presidential order to assert executive privilege. *Memorandum Opinion for the Attorney General re: Prosecution for Contempt of Congress of an Executive Branch Official Who Has Asserted a Claim of Executive Privilege*, 8 Op. O.L.C. 101 (1984).

6. *Where Do We Go from Here?* For an extensive analysis of the competing views of the three branches on executive privilege, and a critical assessment of the executive's handling of executive privilege controversies from the Reagan administration, see Professor Shane's Minnesota article, cited above. Shane argues that the political branches should establish a *modus vivendi* to permit the maximum resolution of these disputes through "problem-solving negotiation," rather than through "hard

bargaining" or resort to the courts. In a June 1987, resolution, the Administrative Law Section of the American Bar Association recommended that the ABA endorse this approach. In 1990, the Administrative Conference of the United States followed suit. 55 Fed. Reg. 52369 (1990). The ACUS recommendations are based upon Peter M. Shane, *Negotiating for Knowledge: Administrative Responses to Congressional Demands for Information*, 44 Admin. L. Rev. 197–243 (1992).

D. Congressional Power to Regulate Accountability

The "necessary and proper" clause grants power to Congress not only to implement its own powers conferred by Article I, § 8, but also to "carry[] into Execution . . . all other Powers vested by this Constitution in the Government of the United States, or in any Department or Officer thereof." This second part of the clause gives Congress wide power to determine the structure, powers, process, and personnel of the other two branches. Here we look at how Congress regulates the upper reaches of the executive branch, where the likelihood of constitutional limits to congressional discretion is greatest. We then note some controversial aspects of its regulation of the judiciary. Finally, to come full circle, we examine Congress's recent efforts at improving its self-regulation by internal rules or statutes.

1. Regulating the Executive

To what extent may Congress control the institutional presidency? To what extent should generally applicable administrative procedure statutes be interpreted to apply to the President and his immediate staff? A series of cases has begun outlining answers to these important questions.

a. Control of Presidential Documents

Until the Nixon Presidency, it was the custom of Presidents leaving office to collect their papers and to dispose of them as they liked. The following case reveals an abrupt change in that practice.

———————

Nixon v. Administrator of General Services
433 U.S. 425 (1977)

[Following his resignation as President, Richard Nixon reached an agreement with the Administrator of General Services, governing access to and care and storage of 42 million pages of presidential papers and nearly 900 tape recordings of presidential conversations. Under the agreement, Nixon retained title to the documents with the express purpose of eventually donating them to the United States. The tapes were to remain on deposit for five years, after which the U.S. would take title, but Nixon could direct that certain tapes be destroyed, and, in any event, the tapes would be destroyed at the time of his death or on September 1, 1984, whichever came first.

Largely to abrogate this agreement, Congress, within months, enacted the Presidential Recordings and Materials Preservation Act, note following 44 U.S.C. §2111, directing the Administrator to "receive, obtain, or retain . . . complete possession and control" over the Nixon materials, and to promulgate regulations governing public access to them, taking account of the following factors:

> (1) the need to provide the public with the full truth, at the earliest reasonable date, of the abuses of governmental power popularly identified under the generic term "Watergate";
>
> (2) the need to make such recordings and materials available for use in judicial proceedings; . . .
>
> (5) the need to protect any party's opportunity to assert any legally or constitutionally based right or privilege which would prevent or otherwise limit access to such recordings and materials; . . . and;
>
> (7) the need to give to Richard M. Nixon, or his heirs, for his sole custody and use, tape recordings and other materials which are not likely to be related to the need described in paragraph (2) and are not otherwise of general historical significance.

Nixon sued to enjoin the enforcement of the Act and its implementing regulations. The three-judge District Court considered and rejected only facial challenges to the Act; regulations were yet to be drafted. The Supreme Court, in an opinion by Justice BRENNAN, affirmed the judgment:]

IV

Claims Concerning the Autonomy of the Executive Branch

A

Separation of Powers

We reject at the outset appellant's argument that the Act's regulation of the disposition of Presidential materials within the Executive Branch constitutes, without more, a violation of the principle of separation of powers. . . . The Executive Branch became a party to the Act's regulation when President Ford signed the Act into law, and the administration of President Carter . . . vigorously supports . . . its constitutionality. Moreover, the control over the materials remains in the Executive Branch. The Administrator of General Services, who must promulgate and administer the regulations that are the keystone of the statutory scheme, is himself an official of the Executive Branch, appointed by the President. The career archivists appointed to do the initial screening for the purpose of selecting out and returning to appellant his private and personal papers similarly are Executive Branch employees.

Appellant's argument is in any event based on an interpretation of the separation-of-powers doctrine inconsistent with the origins of that doctrine, recent decisions of the Court, and the contemporary realities of our political system. True, it has been said that "each of the three general departments of government [must remain] entirely free from the control or coercive influence, direct or indirect, of either of the others . . . ," *Humphrey's Executor v. United States*, 295 U.S. 602, 629 (1935), and that "[t]he sound application of a principle that makes one master in his own house precludes him from imposing his control in the house of another who is master there." *Id.*, at 630. But the more pragmatic, flexible approach . . . was expressly affirmed by this Court only three years ago in *United States v. Nixon*. There . . . the Court squarely rejected the argument that the Constitution contemplates a complete division of authority between the three branches. . . . [W]e therefore find that appellant's argument rests upon an "archaic view of the separation of powers as requiring three airtight departments of government."

Rather, in determining whether the Act disrupts the proper balance between the coordinate branches, the proper inquiry focuses on the extent to which it prevents the Executive Branch from accomplishing its constitutionally assigned functions. *United States v. Nixon*, 418 U.S., at 711–12. Only where the potential for disruption is present must we then determine whether that impact is justified by an overriding need to promote objectives within the constitutional authority of Congress.

It is therefore highly relevant that the Act provides for custody of the materials in officials of the Executive Branch. . . . For it is clearly less intrusive to place custody and screening of the materials within the Executive Branch itself than to have Congress or some outside agency perform the screening function. While the materials may also be made available for use in judicial proceedings, this provision is expressly qualified by any rights, defense, or privileges that any person may invoke including, of course, a valid claim of executive privilege. Similarly, although some of the materials may eventually be made available for public access, the Act expressly recognizes . . . defenses or privileges available to appellant or the Executive Branch. . . .

Thus, whatever are the future possibilities for constitutional conflict in the promulgation of regulations respecting public access to particular documents, nothing contained in the Act renders it unduly disruptive of the Executive Branch and, therefore, unconstitutional on its face. And, of course, there is abundant statutory precedent for the regulation and mandatory disclosure of documents in the possession of the Executive Branch. *See, e.g.*, the Freedom of Information Act, 5 U.S.C. § 552; the Privacy Act of 1974, 5 U.S.C. § 552a; the Government in the Sunshine Act, 5 U.S.C. § 552b; the Federal Records Act, 44 U.S.C. § 2101 *et seq.* Such regulation of material generated in the Executive Branch has never been considered invalid as an invasion of its autonomy. Similar congressional power to regulate Executive Branch documents exists in this instance, a power that is augmented by the important interests that the Act seeks to attain.

B

Presidential Privilege

[W]e next consider appellant's more narrowly defined claim that the Presidential privilege shields these records from archival scrutiny. We start with what was established in *United States v. Nixon*—that the privilege is a qualified one. . . . [T]his case initially involves appellant's assertion of a privilege against the very Executive Branch in whose name the privilege is invoked. The nonfederal appellees . . . contend that only an incumbent President can assert the privilege of the Presidency. . . . Nevertheless, we think that the Solicitor General states the sounder view, and we adopt it:

> ". . . Unless he can give his advisers some assurance of confidentiality, a President could not expect to receive the full and frank submissions of facts and opinions upon which effective discharge of his duties depends. The confidentiality necessary to this exchange cannot be measured by the few months or years between the submission of the information and the end of the President's tenure; the privilege is not for the benefit of the President as an individual, but for the benefit of the Republic. Therefore the privilege survives the individual President's tenure."

At the same time, however, the fact that neither President Ford nor President Carter supports appellant's claim detracts from the weight of his contention that the Act impermissibly intrudes into the executive function and the needs of the Executive Branch. . . .

The appellant may legitimately assert the Presidential privilege, of course, only as to those materials whose contents fall within the scope of the privilege. . . . [In *Nixon*,] the Court held that the privilege is limited to communications "in performance of [a President's] responsibilities," . . . "of his office," . . . and made "in the process of shaping policies and making decisions." Of the estimated 42 million pages of documents and 880 tape recordings whose custody is at stake, the District Court concluded that the appellant's claim of Presidential privilege could apply at most to the 200,000 items with which the appellant was personally familiar.

The appellant bases his claim of Presidential privilege in this case on the assertion that the potential disclosure of communications given to the appellant in confidence would adversely affect the ability of future Presidents to obtain the candid advice necessary for effective decision-making. We are called upon to adjudicate that claim, however, only with respect to the process by which the materials will be screened and catalogued by professional archivists. For any eventual public access will be governed by the guidelines of § 104, which direct the Administrator to take into account "the need to protect any party's opportunity to assert any . . . constitutionally based right or privilege," § 104(a)(5), and the need to return purely private materials to the appellant, § 104(a)(7).

In view of these specific directions, there is no reason to believe that the restriction on public access ultimately established by regulation will not be adequate to preserve executive confidentiality. [An absolute barrier to all outside disclosure is not practically or constitutionally necessary. . .]. [T]here has never been an expectation that the confidences of the Executive Office are absolute and unyielding. All former Presidents from President Hoover to President Johnson have deposited their papers in Presidential libraries (an example appellant has said he intended to follow) for governmental preservation and eventual disclosure. The screening processes for . . . these libraries also involved comprehensive review by archivists, often involving materials upon which access restrictions ultimately have been imposed. The expectation of the confidentiality of executive communications thus has always been limited and subject to erosion over time after an administration leaves office. . . .

The screening constitutes a very limited intrusion by personnel in the Executive Branch sensitive to executive concerns. These very personnel have performed the identical task in each of the Presidential libraries without any suggestion that such activity has in any way interfered with executive confidentiality. Indeed, in light of this consistent historical practice, past and present executive officials must be well aware of the possibility that, at some time in the future, their communications may be reviewed on a confidential basis by professional archivists. . . .

Moreover, adequate justifications are shown for this limited intrusion into executive confidentiality comparable to those held to justify the *in camera* inspection of the District Court sustained in *United States v. Nixon*. . . . The legislative history of the Act clearly reveals that . . . Congress acted to . . . deal with the perceived need to preserve the materials for legitimate historical and governmental purposes. An incumbent President should not be dependent on happenstance or the whim of a prior President when he seeks access to records of past decisions that define or channel current governmental obligations. Nor should the American people's ability to reconstruct and come to terms with their history be truncated by an analysis of Presidential privilege that focuses only on the needs of the present. Congress can legitimately act to rectify the hit-or-miss approach that has characterized past attempts to protect these substantial interests by entrusting the materials to expert handling by trusted and disinterested professionals . . . .

Thus, as in the Presidential libraries, the intermingled state of the materials requires the comprehensive review and classification contemplated by the Act if Congress' important objectives are to be furthered. . . . [G]iven the safeguards built into the Act . . . and the minimal nature of the intrusion into the confidentiality of the Presidency, we believe that the claims of Presidential privilege clearly must yield to the important congressional purposes of preserving the materials and maintaining access to them for lawful governmental and historical purposes. . . . If the broadly written protections of the Act should nevertheless prove inadequate to safeguard appellant's rights or to prevent usurpation of executive powers, there will be time enough to consider that problem in a specific factual context. For the present, we hold, in agreement with the District Court, that the Act on its face does not violate the Presidential privilege. . . .

[The Court concluded that the Act did not violate Nixon's First Amendment rights, because there was no less restrictive way to meet the compelling need to screen the documents. Nor did the Act constitute a bill of attainder: it did not impose legislative punishment as historically understood, it served legitimate purposes in maintaining evidence for criminal trials and assuring the preservation of historical records, and no punitive intent appeared from the legislative history.

Justices STEVENS, WHITE, POWELL, and BLACKMUN wrote concurring opinions.

Chief Justice BURGER dissented, arguing that the Act violated the separation of powers principle by coercing the president in his disposition of presidential papers, that the act usurped exclusively presidential functions of controlling presidential files, records, and papers, and that it violated the President's privilege in confidential communications. He further argued that the Act amounted to a "Bill of Attainder" by singling out a class of one for detrimental treatment.

Justice REHNQUIST dissented because the Act would "restrain the necessary free flow of information to and from the present President and future Presidents," and that so substantial an intrusion upon the effective discharge of presidential duties violated the separation of powers.]

---

1. *The Role of Functional Analysis.* Note the majority's separation of powers analysis. The Court defines the issue as whether the executive is prevented "from accomplishing its constitutionally assigned functions." The Court then appears to balance the Act's intrusion on executive functions against the justifications advanced for them. Is this "functional" analysis similar to the Court's approach in *United States v. Nixon*? Compare the Court's use of formalist analysis in cases such as *Chadha*. What outcome would a formalist approach produce here? Presumably, functional analysis allows more mixing of the powers of the branches than does formalism. For historical support, the Court gave these cites in a footnote:

> Madison in The Federalist No. 47, reviewing the origin of the separation-of-powers doctrine, remarked that Montesquieu, the "oracle" always consulted on the subject, "did not mean that these departments ought to have no *partial agency* in, or no *control* over the acts of each other. His meaning, as his own words import . . . can amount to no more than this, that where the *whole* power of one department is exercised by the same hands which possess the *whole* power of another department, the fundamental principles of a free constitution, are subverted." (emphasis in original).

Similarly, Justice Story wrote:

> "[W]hen we speak of a separation of the three great departments of government, and maintain that that separation is indispensable to public

liberty, we are to understand this maxim in a limited sense. It is not meant to affirm that they must be kept wholly and entirely separate and distinct, and have no common link of connection or dependence, the one upon the other, in the slightest degree." 1 J. Story, Commentaries on the Constitution § 525 (M. Bigelow 5th ed., 1905).

2. *Executive Waiver?* Do you agree with Justice Powell that the positions of Presidents Ford and Carter should be dispositive on the question of the executive interests at stake in this case? Consider, in this respect, that the Court partly supports its conclusion about the Act's minimal intrusion into the executive's functions by noting that the Act contemplates the availability of executive privilege as a shield against the ultimate public disclosure of particular presidential documents.

3. *Nixon's Revenge.* Final regulations under the Presidential Recordings and Materials Preservation Act were promulgated on December 16, 1977. The D.C. Circuit upheld summary judgment for GSA in President Nixon's legal challenge to the regulations. *Nixon v. Freeman*, 670 F.2d 346 (D.C. Cir.), *cert. denied*, 459 U.S. 1035 (1982). Subsequently, the court of appeals held that President Nixon was entitled to just compensation for those of his papers that the government kept. *Nixon v. United States*, 978 F.2d 1269 (D.C. Cir. 1992).

4. *A Long-Run Solution?* In 1978, President Carter signed the Presidential Records Act (PRA), 44 U.S.C. § 2201–07, which establishes government ownership of presidential records, except for the private papers of the President. There are restrictions on access to certain categories of information (such as classified material and the President's deliberations with his advisers) for not more than 12 years. Thereafter, access is permitted under the Freedom of Information Act, but exemption 5, shielding policy deliberations, is not available. The Department of Justice testified in support of the constitutionality of the Act. Presidential Records Act of 1978, Hearings on H.R. 10998 and Related Bills Before a Subcomm. of the House Comm. on Government Operations, 95th Cong., 2d Sess. (1978). Would even wider access be desirable? Advise the Attorney General on the constitutionality of proposed legislation requiring that, 15 years after issuance, all unclassified government documents shall be available for public inspection.

5. *"Don't Worry, Dad, Your Secret's Safe With Me."* Like the statute crafted for the Nixon records, the Presidential Records Act preserves any constitutionally-based privilege against access to presidential documents that a former or incumbent President may possess. 44 U.S.C. § 2204(c)(2). President George W. Bush issued a controversial executive order making the most of this provision. Under Executive Order No. 13,233, 3 C.F.R. 815 (2002), former Presidents could invoke executive privilege throughout their lifetimes, and could even assign the authority to invoke the privilege to a third party, such as a family member. The order would even have allowed former Vice Presidents to claim executive privilege for their records—is there any legal basis for such a claim? Without explicit statutory authority, the order allowed withholding on grounds of attorney-client or attorney work-product

privileges. It also required persons seeking privileged materials to show a "demonstrated, specific need" for them. For an argument that the order was invalid under the PRA, for shifting too much authority from the Archivist to former Presidents and other private persons, see Jonathan Turley, *Presidential Papers and Popular Government: The Convergence of Constitutional and Property Theory in Claims of Ownership and Control of Presidential Records*, 88 CORN. L. REV. 651 (2003). For a full analysis of issues under the Act, including the controversies during the Bush presidency, see PETER M. SHANE, MADISON'S NIGHTMARE, *supra* at 127–32. On his first day in office, President Obama revoked the Bush order. Executive Order No. 13,489, 74 Fed. Reg. 4669 (2009). The Obama order provides procedures for the assertion of executive privilege concerning presidential records by sitting or former Presidents.

b. The Administrative Procedure Act

The Administrative Procedure Act (APA), 5 U.S.C. § 551 *et seq.*, enacted in 1946, provides a code of rulemaking and adjudicative procedure that is widely applicable to federal agencies. Whether the APA applies to the President's statutory decisions was in doubt until recently. *See* Jonathan R. Siegel, *Suing the President: Nonstatutory Review Revisited*, 97 Colum. L. Rev. 1612 (1997). To introduce the issues, we turn to Harold H. Bruff, *Judicial Review and the President's Statutory Powers*, 68 VA. L. REV. 1, 17–21 (1982):

> [P]residential actions implementing statutes fall into two broad functional categories, law-making and law-applying. [Although the line between them is indistinct, the essential difference is that law-making actions establish a general policy to govern a class of persons or situations; law-applying actions determine how a general policy should apply to a particular set of facts.] Presidential law-making is functionally similar to administrative rulemaking, for which the APA provides minimum procedural prerequisites. An agency must usually notify the public of a proposed rulemaking, afford an opportunity for written comment on the proposed rule, and accompany the rule it finally adopts with a statement of its basis and purpose. [§ 553] In practice, these simple requirements have developed into a rather elaborate and time-consuming process that tends to produce a massive public record of information, analysis, and opinion, and that culminates in a detailed explanation of the factual basis and policy rationale for the final rule. In contrast, Presidents perform their rulemaking activities simply by issuing executive orders or proclamations, without any prior public procedure, and often without any accompanying explanation.
>
> Presidential law-applying is functionally similar to "informal" decision-making by administrative officials (so called because the APA requires no special procedures for administrative actions other than rulemaking and adjudication). Agencies, under the pressure of judicial review, normally

accompany announcements of their informal statutory decisions with explanations similar to those used for rulemaking. Presidents sometimes furnish contemporaneous explanations of their law-applying decisions, but there is no consistent practice.

The presidential actions of interest here are procedurally and functionally similar to decisions of cabinet-level administrative officers, for which the APA provides both minimum procedural requirements and a well-understood standard for judicial review. . . . Under the APA, a court reviewing agency action must first decide whether the action is reviewable at all. The Supreme Court has established a "basic presumption of review," under which "only upon a showing of 'clear and convincing evidence' of a contrary legislative intent should the courts restrict access to judicial review." [*Abbott Laboratories v. Gardner*, 387 U.S. 136, 141 (1967).] Where review occurs, a court examines agency action for its constitutionality, statutory authorization, procedural regularity, and substantive rationality. [APA § 706(2)(A)-(D).] The APA's standard of judicial review for rulemaking and for informal agency actions is much the same, except for procedural issues relating to rulemaking.

Constitutional and procedural issues aside, the courts focus on the presence of statutory authority for a challenged action and on the rationality of the judgments of fact and policy that underlie it. On issues of statutory authority, courts often state — but do not always follow — a doctrine that they should defer to an administrator's statutory interpretation within the bounds of reason and ascertainable legislative intent. [*Chevron, U.S.A., Inc. v. Natural Resources Defense Council, Inc.*, 467 U.S. 837 (1984).] This deference is based on the administrator's presumed expertise and a related notion that Congress commits these leeway issues (which are intermixed with policy concerns) to the agency and not to the courts.

On issues of fact and policy, the APA requires courts to set aside agency actions that are "arbitrary, capricious, [or] an abuse of discretion." [§ 706(2)(A).] The Supreme Court has parsed this terminology to require a "searching and careful" inquiry into the agency's judgments, although a reviewing court is not to "substitute its judgment for that of the agency." [*Citizens to Preserve Overton Park, Inc. v. Volpe*, 401 U.S. 402, 416 (1971).] The effort is to ensure that agency actions are "based on a consideration of the relevant factors" and have a "rational basis" in fact.

Courts exercise this review for statutory authority and rationality by comparing any formal explanation adopted at the time of the decision with the "administrative record" on which the agency based the decision. Substantial indeterminacies attend this process, however. First, administrative records are not self-defining, because there are often no formal agency procedures for determining in advance which documents will be considered in reaching a final decision. Accordingly, efforts to link the morass of documents in an agency with a final decision usually require a process of post hoc reconstruction.

Second, an agency may not provide a formal explanation that suffices to reveal the factual and policy judgments that underlie its decision. The APA does not require formal findings and reasons for informal actions, although it does require the equivalent for rulemaking, in a statement of basis and purpose. To facilitate review, courts frequently have implied requirements for findings and reasons from particular program statutes. Where they have done so, or where administrators have furnished explanations on their own initiative, courts have restricted review to a comparison of the formal explanation with the administrative record. Absent particular indications of "bad faith or improper behavior," the court does not inquire further into the "actual" basis of decision. If the explanation does not sufficiently justify the action on the basis of the administrative record, the usual remedy is a remand to the agency for further consideration.

The Court addressed the issue of the APA's applicability to the President in *Franklin v. Massachusetts*, 505 U.S. 788 (1992), a case which also illustrates the doctrinal complexity attending judicial review when both the President and a subordinate administrator (as in *Youngstown*, the Commerce Secretary) are charged with implementing an administrative function.

Franklin was a challenge by Massachusetts to the transfer from it to the State of Washington of one congressional seat, pursuant to returns from the 1990 census. The transfer occurred when the Commerce Department decided to count as residents of a state any overseas military personnel who listed that state as their "home of record." Usually, however, the Commerce Department had previously excluded overseas federal employees from state enumerations. A three-judge district court held the 1990 enumeration unlawful under the APA. As a remedy, the panel directed the Commerce Secretary to eliminate the overseas federal employees from the apportionment counts, directed the President to recalculate the number of Representatives per State and to transmit the new calculation to Congress, and directed the Clerk of the House of Representatives to inform the States of the change.

As the Supreme Court explained, the statutory process for determining state enumerations is a complex one:

> Under the automatic reapportionment statute, the Secretary of Commerce takes the census [via the Bureau of the Census], "in such form and content as she may determine." 13 U.S.C. § 141(a). . . . "The tabulation of total population by States . . . as required for the apportionment of Representatives in Congress . . . shall be . . . reported by the Secretary to the President of the United States." § 141(b). After receiving the Secretary's report, the President "shall transmit to the Congress a statement showing the whole

number of persons in each State . . . as ascertained under the . . . decennial census of the population, and the number of Representatives to which each State would be entitled . . . by the method . . . of equal proportions. . . ." 2 U.S.C. § 2a(a). "Each State shall be entitled . . . to the number of Representatives shown" in the President's statement, and the Clerk of the House of Representatives must "send to the executive of each State a certificate of the number of Representatives to which such State is entitled." § 2a(b).

Massachusetts, and two of its voters suing individually, challenged the post-1990 state enumeration as unlawfully arbitrary under the APA and as violative of the constitutional requirement that the apportionment of Representatives be determined by an "actual Enumeration" of persons "in each State." U.S. Const., art. I, § 2, cl. 3; U.S. Const., amend. XIV, § 2.

Four Justices — O'Connor, White, Rehnquist, and Thomas — found that the Secretary's report to the President was not reviewable under the APA because it did not constitute "final agency action," which the APA requires as the basis for review:

> An agency action is not final if it is only "the ruling of a subordinate official," or "tentative." The core question is whether the agency has completed its decisionmaking process, and whether the result of that process is one that will directly affect the parties. In this case, the action that creates an entitlement to a particular number of Representatives and has a direct effect on the reapportionment is the President's statement to Congress, not the Secretary's report to the President.

The four Justices regarded the President's involvement as rendering the Secretary's report "tentative," because "§ 2 [of the Act] does not curtail the President's authority to direct the Secretary in making policy judgments that result in 'the decennial census;' he is not expressly required to adhere to the policy decisions reflected in the Secretary's report":

> [T]he Department of Commerce . . . was explicit that the data presented to the President was still subject to correction. Moreover, there is no statute that rules out an instruction by the President to the Secretary to reform the census, even after the data is submitted to him. It is not until the President submits the information to Congress that the target stops moving, because only then are the States entitled by § 2a to a particular number of Representatives. Because the Secretary's report to the President carries no direct consequences for the reapportionment, it serves more like a tentative recommendation than a final and binding determination.

Based on this reasoning, the only action that would qualify as final agency action reviewable under the APA was the President's report to Congress. The O'Connor quartet, however, found that report unreviewable under the APA because the President is not an "agency" that the APA exposes to judicial review:

[W]e can only review the APA claims here if the President, not the Secretary of Commerce, is an "agency" within the meaning of the Act. The APA defines "agency" as "each authority of the Government of the United States, whether or not it is within or subject to review by another agency, but does not include—(A) the Congress; (B) the courts of the United States; . . ." 5 U.S.C. §§ 701(b)(1), 551(1). The President is not explicitly excluded from the APA's purview, but he is not explicitly included, either. Out of respect for the separation of powers and the unique constitutional position of the President, we find that textual silence is not enough to subject the President to the provisions of the APA. We would require an express statement by Congress before assuming it intended the President's performance of his statutory duties to be reviewed for abuse of discretion. As the APA does not expressly allow review of the President's actions, we must presume that his actions are not subject to its requirements. Although the President's actions may still be reviewed for constitutionality, we hold that they are not reviewable for abuse of discretion under the APA.

Their conclusion, however, did leave the order open to constitutional review, assuming the plaintiffs had standing. The executive branch had challenged standing, in part on the ground that the court could not issue an injunction against the President, and without any possibility of such redress, the plaintiffs could not bring an Article III case. Justice O'Connor, observing that the Supreme Court had never enjoined a President (although the *Nixon* case upheld a subpoena to him), elided the question whether "extraordinary" injunctive relief against the President would have been proper. She concluded "that the injury alleged is likely to be redressed by declaratory relief against the Secretary alone." "[I]t is substantially likely," she wrote, "that the President and other executive and congressional officials would abide by an authoritative interpretation of the census statute and constitutional provision by the District Court, even though they would not be directly bound by such a determination." She then proceeded to find the President's report constitutional.

Justice Scalia, in a solo appearance, agreed both that the Commerce Secretary had not implemented "final agency action," and that the President is not an APA agency. He would have found the plaintiffs without standing, however, on the constitutional question. Also, he would have held the President categorically immune from an injunctive order regarding the performance of a nonministerial duty.

Justices Stevens, Blackmun, Kennedy, and Souter would have found a route around all issues of presidential susceptibility to review. In their judgment, the Commerce Secretary's report was "final agency action" because:

The plain language of the statute demonstrates that the President has no substantive role in the computation of the census. . . . In the face of this clear statutory mandate, the Court must fall back on an argument based on statutory silence. The Court insists that there is no law prohibiting the President from changing the census figures after he receives them from the

> Secretary.... The Court's argument cannot be harmonized with a statutory scheme that directs the Secretary to take the "decennial census" and the President to report to Congress figures "as ascertained under the . . . decennial census." This language cannot support the Court's view that the statute endows the President with discretion to modify the census results reported by the Secretary.... [T]he Executive involvement in the process is to be wholly ministerial.

In Justice Stevens' view, the O'Connor opinion mistakenly regarded the President's census activities as discretionary because it confused the sources and nature of his powers regarding his subordinates:

> The Court confuses two duties of the President: (1) the general duty to supervise the actions of the Secretary of Commerce, and (2) the statutory duty to transmit the Census Report and the apportionment calculations to Congress. This confusion is evident from the Court's statement, "It is hard to imagine a purpose for involving the President if he is to be prevented from exercising his accustomed supervisory powers over his executive officers." It may be true that the statute does not purport to limit the President's "accustomed supervisory powers" over the Secretary of Commerce. The President would enjoy these "accustomed powers," however, whether or not he was responsible for transmitting the census and apportionment calculations to Congress. These "accustomed powers," therefore, cannot be relevant in deciding whether agency action is final for the purposes of the APA, or else no action of an Executive department would ever be final. The Court's argument then depends on construing the statute to grant discretion to the President that he would not otherwise enjoy.... The statutory language here will not bear this interpretation. Moreover, whatever purpose the Court wishes to "imagine" for the statute's designating the President as the official responsible for performing the apportionment calculations, the legislative record makes it absolutely clear that the purpose was not to give the President any new discretionary authority over the census.

Justice Stevens agreed with O'Connor, et al., that the reapportionment order was constitutional. After finding the Secretary's action reviewable under the APA, moreover, he proceeded to find it lawful under APA standards.

What are the results of this case? At least a majority of the Court thinks the President is not an "agency" under the APA. (Justice Stevens reserves the question.) No one on the Court thinks the action of a subordinate administrator is reviewable final action if it is preliminary to implementation by the President, subject to the President's own discretion. A majority on the Court apparently presumes that a statute requiring the President to act upon a subordinate's report, but not expressly prohibiting his own exercise of policy judgment, renders the President's acts nonministerial. One Justice would immunize the President categorically from injunctive or declaratory relief in any lawsuit implicating nonministerial functions.

Franklin was a very poor vehicle for deciding whether the APA should apply to the President. In fact, under this statute Presidents have seemed to regard their function as rather ministerial, simply passing the Commerce Secretary's figures along to Congress without change. The administrative record and policy justifications on which the action would pass or fail judicial review had been compiled in the Department before anything was sent to the President. The courts at all levels reviewed the action of the Secretary or the President on the basis of that record.

Franklin was followed by *Dalton v. Specter*, 511 U.S. 462 (1994), a case involving the Defense Base Closure and Realignment Act, note following 10 U.S.C. § 2687. The Act provided for an independent Commission to recommend particular military base closures to the President, after considering a list provided by the Department of Defense. The President could approve or disapprove the recommendations in their entirety; upon his approval, Congress could stop the closures by enacting a joint resolution of disapproval. The Commission and the President approved a list including the Philadelphia Navy Yard, and Congress did not disapprove. Affected workers and their representatives challenged the action of the Department and the Commission substantively and procedurally under the Act and the APA. In an opinion by Chief Justice Rehnquist, the Court refused to grant review. As in *Franklin*, the actions challenged were not final. And the President's actions were not reviewable because he was not an agency under the APA. The Court also explicitly disapproved a statement by the Court of Appeals, interpreting *Franklin*, that constitutional review could be granted on any claim that the President had exceeded statutory authority. The claim here was purely statutory, and could not be converted into a constitutional one without destroying the distinction between them. Four Justices concurred, finding that the Act precluded judicial review. Justice Blackmun wrote separately to emphasize that the case presented no direct challenge to any allegedly ultra vires action of the President.

Hence neither *Franklin* nor *Dalton* tells us how the courts should review instances of *presidential* discretion. The Bruff article *supra*, after concluding that the APA should not apply to the President directly because of the danger of losing sight of the unique features of the Presidential office, goes on to recommend a style of judicial review that is quite similar to that of the APA:

> The administrative record against which a court should compare a President's decision usually is generated principally in one or more executive agencies; White House materials are likely to be mostly policy memoranda that are protected by executive privilege. Therefore, a central task for the courts is to see that appropriate links exist between a record developed in one place and a decision reached in another. Performed correctly, judicial review can help to ensure bureaucratic regularity, with particular tasks being performed at appropriate levels in the bureaucracy. The primary effect on executive branch decisionmaking should be to force the White House to consult with agencies having relevant program responsibilities, and with counsel. The agencies may already possess an administrative record

pertinent to an upcoming decision; at any rate, they—not the White House—are the appropriate place to compile one. The function of compiling and reviewing an administrative record within an agency is to discover, and explain to the ultimate policymakers, the limits of defensible discretion. Similarly, the role of the President's counsel is to render opinions on the permissibility of postulated policy choices, given certain fact assumptions and the terms and legislative history of the relevant statute.

If legal review of a proposed decision reveals that certain factual judgments or policy rationales must underlie a decision if it is to be legal, these matters ought to accompany the proposal all the way to the President's desk. The effect, however, should never be to increase the workload of the President himself. All that need reach the President is an indication in the options memorandum (or in oral discussion) that a particular decision would require certain fact and policy underpinning, a summary of those conclusions, and a statement that the appropriate officials believe them to be adequately supported. The President's selection of a particular option will then also select the basis for it that will be advanced on judicial review. . . .

[A]n officer's accountability to Congress and the public is ensured if he or she must demonstrate that a statutory decision is based on judgments of fact and policy that are rational and within statutory parameters. If, for example, announcement of a rationale that is politically unpalatable is a legally necessary precondition to a particular option, another option may be selected. Moreover, from the standpoint of the President's political accountability to Congress and the public, a requirement that he reveal his rationale for a decision clearly is preferable to a system that would allow him to select an option without explanation, leaving all concerned to speculate on the reasons for it. Thus, if the courts exercise their review function in a way that makes the President take responsibility for an action by stating a legally sufficient rationale for it, they will have done all they can to clarify the respective responsibilities of the two policymaking branches of government. . . .

Explanation requirements can also increase the efficacy of executive branch checks on presidential action. The President bears a constitutional responsibility to ensure the legality of his actions, which is discharged by the ordinary processes of bureaucratic review that precede his decisions. Thus, the bureaucracy constitutes an important check on both the policy and legal bases of presidential action. Although administrative officials ordinarily are prepared to judge both the facts and the law in a fashion that is sympathetic to known presidential desires, there are limits to what they will approve. If the responsible agency officials and lawyers are consulted in advance of a presidential decision, they can urge caution or advance alternatives without having to threaten to refuse their assent to a proposed decision until it is necessary to do so. After the fact, the situation changes radically—especially for the President's lawyers, who are left with the unappetizing question of whether they should refuse to defend in court an action they would not have approved in advance. . . .

The exercise of presidential discretion became a point of particular controversy during the Obama presidency. Some critics of the President argued that his use of prosecutorial discretion in areas such as foregoing enforcement of the federal prohibition on the possession and use of marijuana in states that allow its medicinal use overstepped the limits of prosecutorial discretion and represented a refusal to enforce the law that violated the President's constitutional duty to "take care that the laws be faithfully executed." We consider these issues in connection with presidential non-enforcement, *infra*, in Chapter 4D.

The State of Texas and other litigants challenging the authority of the executive branch to suspend deportation proceedings against certain classes of parents of U.S. citizens framed their challenge as an APA claim. The decision to suspend deportation for the various classes of aliens was taken by the Department of Homeland Security pursuant to guidance President Obama offered to DHS. Texas asserted that DHS's decision was subject to the APA's requirement of notice and comment and was invalid for failure to comply with that requirement. The District Court and Fifth Circuit Court of Appeals both indicated their preliminary agreement with Texas in imposing a preliminary injunction. *See Texas v. United States,* 787 F.3d 733 (5th Cir. 2015). The Supreme Court agreed to hear the challenge. While the case was pending, Justice Scalia died, leaving the Court deadlocked. By a 4–4 vote, the preliminary injunction was upheld without further opinion. *See United States v. Texas,* 579 U.S. ___ (2016).

c. Freedom of Information Act

Kissinger v. Reporters Committee for Freedom of the Press

445 U.S. 136 (1980)

[During his tenure as Assistant to the President for National Security Affairs (1969–1975) and as Secretary of State (1973–1977), Henry Kissinger followed the practice of having his secretaries monitor all of his telephone conversations and record their contents by shorthand or on tape. The notes or tapes were used to prepare detailed summaries or verbatim transcripts of the conversations, and then destroyed. In late 1976, while still Secretary of State, Kissinger arranged—without consulting the Department of State office responsible for record maintenance and disposal—to move the telephone notes from his State Department office to the New York estate of Nelson Rockefeller.

In December, 1976, Kissinger donated the notes to the Library of Congress under an agreement substantially delaying public access to them. Several weeks later, a Kissinger aide extracted portions of the notes for the Department of State files, indicating "significant policy decisions or actions not otherwise reflected in the Department's records." Kissinger declined, however, to subject the notes themselves to inspection by the Government Archivist to determine which, if any, were properly Department records.

This case involved three Freedom of Information Act (FOIA) requests for the notes. The plaintiffs asked the District Court to require the Library of Congress, not an "agency" under the FOIA, to return the notes to the Department of State with directions to process them for FOIA disclosure. The District Court granted most of the relief requested. In an opinion by Justice REHNQUIST, the Supreme Court held that no statute authorized an order to produce the materials that had been donated to the Library of Congress:]

II

... The question must be, of course, whether Congress has conferred jurisdiction on the federal courts to impose this remedy. Two statutory schemes are relevant to this inquiry. First, if Congress contemplated a private right of action under the Federal Records Act and the Federal Records Disposal Act, this would in itself justify the remedy imposed if Kissinger in fact wrongfully removed the documents. In the alternative, the lower court order could be sustained if authorized by the FOIA.

A

The Federal Records Act of 1950, 44 U.S.C. §§ 2901 et seq., authorizes the "head of each Federal agency" to establish a "records management program" and to define the extent to which documents are "appropriate for preservation" as agency records. The records management program requires that adequate documentation of agency policies and procedures be retained. The Records Disposal Act, a complementary records management Act, provides the exclusive means for record disposal. 44 U.S.C. § 3314. Under the Records Disposal Act, once a document achieves the status of a "record" as defined by the Act, it may not be alienated or disposed of without the consent of the Administrator of General Services, who has delegated his authority in such matters to the Archivist of the United States. 44 U.S.C. §§ 3303, 3303a, 3308–3314. Thus if Kissinger's telephone notes were "records" within the meaning of the Federal Records Act, a question we do not reach, then Kissinger's transfer might well violate the Act since he did not seek the approval of the Archivist prior to transferring custody to himself and then to the Library of Congress. We assume such a wrongful removal arguendo for the purposes of this opinion.

But the Federal Records Act establishes only one remedy for the improper removal of a "record" from the agency. The head of the agency is required under 44 U.S.C. § 3106 to notify the Attorney General if he determines or "has reason to believe" that records have been improperly removed from the agency. . . . [T]he Attorney General may bring suit to recover the records. . . . [N]o suit has been instituted against Kissinger to retrieve the records under 44 U.S.C. § 3106. . . . No provision of either Act, . . . expressly confers a right of action on private parties. Nor do we believe that such a private right of action can be implied. . . . Congress expressly recognized the need for devising adequate statutory safeguards against the unauthorized removal of agency records, and opted in favor of a system of administrative standards and enforcement. . . .

B

. . . [FOIA] authorizes federal courts to ensure private access to requested materials when three requirements have been met. Under 5 U.S.C. § 552(a)(4)(B) federal jurisdiction is dependent upon a showing that an agency has (1) "improperly"; (2) "withheld"; (3) "agency records." Judicial authority to devise remedies and enjoin agencies can only be invoked . . . if the agency has contravened all three components of this obligation. We find it unnecessary to decide whether the telephone notes were "agency records" since we conclude that a covered agency — here the State Department — has not "withheld" those documents from the plaintiffs. . . . Congress did not mean that an agency improperly withholds a document which has been removed from the possession of the agency prior to the filing of the FOIA request. In such a case, the agency has neither the custody or control necessary to enable it to withhold. . . .

The conclusion that possession or control is a prerequisite to FOIA disclosure duties is reinforced by an examination of the purposes of the Act. The Act does not obligate agencies to create or retain documents; it only obligates them to provide access to those which it in fact has created and retained. It has been settled by decision of this Court that only the Federal Records Act, and not the FOIA, requires an agency to actually create records, even though the agency's failure to do so deprives the public of information which might have otherwise been available to it. . . .

III

The Safire request raises a separate question. At the time when Safire submitted his request for certain notes of Kissinger's telephone conversations, all the notes were still located in Kissinger's office at the State Department. . . . We conclude that the Safire request sought disclosure of documents which were not "agency records" within the meaning of the FOIA. Safire's request sought . . . all transcripts of telephone conversations made by Kissinger from his White House office between January 21, 1969, and February 12, 1971, in which (1) Safire's name appeared; or (2) in which Kissinger discussed the subject of information "leaks" with General Alexander Haig, Attorney General John Mitchell, President Richard Nixon, J. Edgar Hoover, or any other official of the FBI.

The FOIA does render the "Executive Office of the President" an agency subject to the Act. 5 U.S.C. § 552(e). The legislative history is unambiguous, however, in explaining that the "Executive Office" does not include the Office of the President. The Conference Report for the 1974 FOIA Amendments indicates that "the President's immediate personal staff or units in the Executive Office whose sole function is to advise and assist the President" are not included within the term "agency" under the FOIA. H. R. Conf. Rep. No. 93-1380, p. 15 (1974). Safire's request was limited to a period of time in which Kissinger was serving as Assistant to the President. Thus these telephone notes were not "agency records" when they were made.

The RCFP requesters have argued that since some of the telephone notes made while Kissinger was adviser to the President may have related to the National Security Council they may have been National Security Council records and therefore subject to the Act. *See* H. R. Rep. No. 93-876, p. 8 (1974), indicating that the National Security Council is an executive agency to which the FOIA applies. We need not decide when records which, in the words of the RCFP requesters, merely "relate to" the affairs of an FOIA agency become records of that agency. To the extent Safire sought discussions concerning information leaks which threatened the internal secrecy of White House policymaking, he sought conversations in which Kissinger had acted in his capacity as a Presidential adviser, only. . . .

[Justices BRENNAN and STEVENS concurred in part and dissented in part. Justices MARSHALL and BLACKMUN took no part in the case.]

———————

1. *Perverse Incentives?* In his separate opinion, Justice Stevens lamented the effect of the Court's decision in creating "an incentive for outgoing agency officials to remove potentially embarrassing documents from their files in order to frustrate future FOIA requests." He would have defined "withholding" to include documents that an agency "has a legal right to possess or control." Do you agree? Note that after the 1978 legislation concerning presidential records, subordinate officers may be able to exert more control over their official records than the President can. Is that appropriate?

2. *Archives Reform.* In the National Archives and Records Administration Act of 1984, Pub. L. No. 98-497, codified at 44 U.S.C. § 2101 *et seq.*, Congress established an independent National Archives and Records Administration, and transferred to it the record-keeping functions previously exercised by the GSA. Congress hoped to ensure professional rather than political records management. The legislative history noted the Kissinger imbroglio; in response, Congress authorized the Archivist to seek the initiation of action by the Attorney General to recover improperly removed records, with notice to Congress. Does that solve the problem?

3. *FOIA and Executive Privilege.* Is FOIA's inapplicability to the President and his immediate advisers compelled by the constitutional executive privilege? If so, is the scope of the FOIA exception correctly drawn? On the other hand, since FOIA contains exemptions for classified documents and policy deliberations, did Congress need to create any special blanket exception for the President?

4. *Categorizing White House Entities for FOIA Purposes.* In *Meyer v. Bush*, 981 F.2d 1288 (D.C. Cir. 1993), the court, applying *Kissinger*, held that FOIA did not apply to President Reagan's Task Force on Regulatory Relief, a cabinet body chaired by the Vice President that reviewed agency regulations for consistency with cost-benefit principles. The *Meyer* court identified "three interrelated factors" for determining whether

entities that both advise the President and supervise others in the Executive Branch exercise "substantial independent authority" and hence are agencies subject to FOIA: (1) "how close operationally the group is to the President," (2) "whether it has a self-contained structure," and (3) "the nature of its delegat[ed]" authority. *Armstrong v. Executive Office of the President*, 90 F.3d 553 (D.C. Cir. 1996), *cert. denied*, 520 U.S. 1239 (1997), culminated a long-running litigation over the preservation of electronic records within the White House. The plaintiffs sued on the final day of the Reagan Administration to enjoin deletion of the contents of its electronic message system. *Armstrong* eventually held that the National Security Council was not an agency subject to FOIA. The court found that the NSC is "proximate" to the President: "The President chairs the statutory Council, and his National Security Adviser, working in close contact with and under the direct supervision of the President, controls the NSC staff. The intimate organizational and operating relationship between the President and the NSC is, in our view, entitled to significantly greater weight in evaluating the NSC's arguable status as an agency than is the self-contained structure of the entity." Nor was the nature of its delegated authority sufficient to alter the court's conclusion that "the close working relationship between the NSC and the President indicates that the NSC is more like 'the President's immediate personal staff' than it is like an agency exercising authority, independent of the President."

5. *The Early Bird* . . . The D.C. Circuit followed *Kissinger* in *National Security Archive v. Archivist of United States*, 909 F.2d 541 (D.C. Cir. 1990), rebuffing a request for documents relating to the investigation of the Iran/Contra affair by the President's Special Review Board (also known as the Tower Commission). The plaintiff sought documents from the White House counsel, to whom the records were transferred once the Tower Commission disbanded. The court held that, because White House counsel served within the Office of the President and because that office is not an "agency" under FOIA, counsel did not have to provide any of the requested records. The plaintiff had erred by failing to direct its records request to the Tower Commission, which, while it existed, plainly did have custody of its own records.

6. *Policy Fluctuations.* Since 1977, incoming Attorneys General have issued memoranda setting forth the administration's general approach to FOIA requests. Over the years, there have been wide variations in the openness of the policies pursued. (The story is told in Nancy V. Baker, General Ashcroft: Attorney at War 181–82 (2006).) President Clinton's Attorney General, Janet Reno, encouraged disclosure in the absence of "foreseeable harm." President George W. Bush's Attorney General, John Ashcroft, took a sharply more restrictive tack, shifting from "maximum responsible disclosure" under Reno to "careful consideration" of requests. He was prepared to defend nondisclosures "unless they lack a sound legal basis." President Obama's Attorney General, Eric Holder, reversed course again. His FOIA guidelines reinstated a presumption of disclosure, and said that withholding should occur only for cases involving harm to an interest protected by one of the exemptions. See usdoj.gov/ag/foia-memo-March2009.pdf.

d. Federal Advisory Committee Act

The Federal Advisory Committee Act (FACA), 5 U.S.C. App.2 § 1 *et seq.*, requires meetings between federal agencies and private advisory groups to be held openly. In *Public Citizen v. U.S. Department of Justice*, 491 U.S. 440 (1989), the Court held that FACA did not apply to the American Bar Association Standing Committee on the Federal Judiciary, which advised the Justice Department on potential judicial nominees until the George W. Bush Administration ended the practice. The majority held that to read the Act otherwise would pose a serious separation of powers issue regarding congressional intrusion into the President's judicial nomination power. To sustain its conclusion, the Court had to rely on legislative history to avoid the strong contrary implications of the FACA's text, which includes within the category of regulated "advisory committees":

> any committee . . . which is . . . utilized by the President, or . . . by one or more agencies, in the interest of obtaining advice or recommendations for the President or one or more agencies or officers of the Federal Government. . . .

§ 3(2)(C). Although the history indicated that the language of the Act did not fairly convey Congress's intent, the Court also stressed the importance of construing the FACA to avoid "formidable constitutional difficulties." Such difficulties would have arisen had the Court found that Congress had attempted to control the processes by which the President solicits advice concerning the exercise of his constitutional appointment power. Justice Kennedy, writing also for Chief Justice Rehnquist and Justice O'Connor, would have held that the Act, by its plain terms, did apply, and that it violated the President's power to nominate federal judges:

> The essential feature of the separation-of-powers issue in this suit, and the one that dictates the result, is that this application of the statute encroaches upon a power that the text of the Constitution commits in explicit terms to the President. . . . By its terms, the [Appointments] Clause divides the appointment power into two separate spheres: the President's power to "nominate," and the Senate's power to give or withhold its "Advice and Consent." No role whatsoever is given either to the Senate or to Congress as a whole in the process of choosing the person who will be nominated for appointment. . . .
>
> In some of our more recent cases involving the powers and prerogatives of the President, we have employed something of a balancing approach, asking whether the statute at issue prevents the President "'from accomplishing [his] constitutionally assigned functions.'" *Morrison v. Olson*, 487 U.S. 654, 695 (1988), quoting *Nixon v. Administrator of General Services*, 433 U.S. 425, 443 (1977), and whether the extent of the intrusion on the President's powers "is justified by an overriding need to promote objectives within the constitutional authority of Congress." In each of these cases, the power at issue was not explicitly assigned by the text of the Constitution to be within the

sole province of the President, but rather was thought to be encompassed within the general grant to the President of the "executive Power . . . .

In a line of cases of equal weight and authority, however, where the Constitution by explicit text commits the power at issue to the exclusive control of the President, we have refused to tolerate any intrusion by the Legislative Branch. For example, the Constitution confers upon the President the "Power to grant Reprieves and Pardons for Offenses against the United States, except in Cases of Impeachment." In *United States v. Klein*, 13 Wall. 128 (1872), the Court . . . held that the Congress could not in any manner limit the full legal effect of the President's power. . . . *INS v. Chadha*, 462 U.S. 919 (1983), is another example of the Court's refusal to apply a balancing test to assess the validity of an enactment which interferes with a power that the Constitution, in express terms, vests within the exclusive control of the President. In *Chadha*, the Court struck down a legislative veto provision . . . on the ground, inter alia, that it violated the explicit constitutional requirement that all legislation be presented to the President for his signature before becoming law. In so holding, the Court did not ask whether the "overriding need to promote objectives within the constitutional authority of Congress" justified this intrusion upon the Executive's prerogative, but rather stated that the lawmaking process must adhere in strict fashion to the "explicit and unambiguous provisions of the Constitution [which] prescribe and define the respective functions of the Congress and of the Executive in the legislative process."

The justification for our refusal to apply a balancing test in these cases, though not always made explicit, is clear enough. Where a power has been committed to a particular Branch of the Government in the text of the Constitution, the balance already has been struck by the Constitution itself. It is improper for this Court to arrogate to itself the power to adjust a balance settled by the explicit terms of the Constitution. . . . [W]here the Constitution draws a clear line, we may not engage in such tinkering. . . .

These considerations are decisive of the suit before us. The President's power to nominate principal officers falls within the line of cases in which a balancing approach is inapplicable. The Appointments Clause sets out the respective powers of the Executive and Legislative Branches with admirable clarity. The President has the sole responsibility for nominating these officials, and the Senate has the sole responsibility of consenting to the President's choice. . . . It is . . . plain that the application of FACA would constitute a direct and real interference with the President's exclusive responsibility to nominate federal judges. The District Court found, "at minimum, that the application of FACA to the ABA Committee would potentially inhibit the President's freedom to investigate, to be informed, to evaluate, and to consult during the nomination process," and that these consequences create an "obvious and significant potential for 'disruption' of the President's constitutional prerogative during the nomination process," and these findings are not contested here. . . . The mere fact that FACA would regulate so as to interfere with the manner in which the President obtains information necessary to discharge his duty assigned under the Constitution to nominate federal judges is enough to invalidate the Act.

Justice Scalia did not participate in the consideration or decision of the case. Although Justices do not give reasons for such recusals, it may be relevant that, while assistant attorney general in charge of the Office of Legal Counsel, he opined that the FACA did not apply to the ABA's advisory functions.

What do you think of Justice Kennedy's approach? Is it a good explanation — and guide — for the Court's use of formalism? Review our notes after *Chadha* for some pertinent commentary on relatively clear constitutional text and formalism, and consider this approach as you read the Court's cases on the President's powers of appointment and removal in the next chapter.

A unique controversy under FACA arose early in the Clinton presidency. A few days after he took office, the new President announced the creation of the President's Task Force on National Health Care Reform, an advisory body comprised of six Cabinet secretaries, several senior White House officials, and, as chairperson, First Lady Hillary Rodham Clinton. He charged the Task Force with preparing a comprehensive health care reform proposal for submission to Congress. When it became clear that the Task Force intended to hold many of its meetings in secret, excluded organizations sought to force it to comply with FACA.

Ass'n of American Physicians and Surgeons v. Clinton
997 F.2d 898 (D.C. Cir. 1993)

SILBERMAN, Circuit Judge:

This expedited appeal presents the question whether the President's Task Force on National Health Care Reform ("Task Force") . . . [is an] advisory committee for purposes of the Federal Advisory Committee Act ("FACA"). If [it is], we are asked to decide whether FACA unconstitutionally encroaches on the President's Article II executive powers. We hold that the Task Force is not an advisory group subject to FACA. . . .

I.

On January 25, 1993, President Clinton established the President's Task Force on National Health Care Reform . . . [and] charged this body with the task of "listening to all parties" and then "preparing health care reform legislation to be submitted to Congress. . . ." . . . [T]he Task Force met behind closed doors at least 20 times in April and May to "formulate" and "deliberate" on its advice to the President. . . . [T]he Association of American Physicians and Surgeons [and other groups] sought access to the Task Force's meetings under [FACA]. Their efforts were rebuffed by the Counsel to the President, who informed them that the Task Force was not an advisory committee subject to FACA. Appellees thereupon brought suit ... [claiming] that the Task Force was a FACA committee because it was chaired by Mrs. Clinton, a private citizen, and that ... FACA permitted them to attend all of the meetings of the Task Force and of any of its subgroups. .... The government responded that the Task Force was exempt from FACA because all of its members—including Mrs. Clinton—were government officers and employees. The government alternatively challenged any application of FACA to the Task Force as an unconstitutional infringement on the President's executive power.

... [T]he district court granted in part appellees' motion for a preliminary injunction. .... Mrs. Clinton, the court held, was not an officer or employee of the federal government merely by virtue of her status as "First Lady." Therefore, the Task Force could not qualify for an exemption from FACA as an advisory group composed solely of "full-time officers or employees" of the government. *See* 5 U.S.C. App. 1 § 3(2)(iii). The court, however, agreed with the government that FACA encroached on the President's constitutional authority to receive confidential advice for the purpose of recommending legislation. But the court thought that executive prerogatives were implicated only when the Task Force was advising the President, not when it engaged in information-gathering. The district court accordingly granted a preliminary injunction requiring the Task Force to meet all the requirements of FACA except when it met to formulate advice or recommendations for the President. ...

III.

Congress passed FACA in 1972 to control the growth and operation of the "numerous committees, boards, commissions, councils, and similar groups which have been established to advise officers and agencies in the executive branch of the Federal Government." 5 U.S.C. App. 1, § 2(a). ... FACA places a number of restrictions on the advisory committees themselves. Before it can meet or take any action, a committee first must file a detailed charter. The committee must give advance notice in the Federal Register of any meetings, and it must hold all meetings in public. Under section 10, the committee must keep detailed minutes of each meeting, and make the records available—along with any reports, records, or other documents used by the committee—to the public, provided they do not fall within the exemptions of the Freedom of Information Act (FOIA). Under section 5, an advisory committee established by the President or by legislation must be "fairly balanced in terms of the points of view represented," § 5(b)(2). The Act also requires that precautions be taken to ensure that the advice and recommendations of the committee "will not be inappropriately influenced by the appointing authority or by any special interest."

The Act's definition of an "advisory" committee is apparently rather sweeping. ... FACA's definition contains one important proviso, however. Section 3(2)(iii) exempts "any committee which is composed wholly of full-time officers or employees of the

Federal Government." And, according to the government, . . . subjecting the Task Force to FACA would fall outside Congress' purpose of regulating the growth and use of committees composed of outsiders called in to advise government officials. . . . Appellees contend that [Mrs. Clinton] is not an officer or employee of the federal government despite her traditional and ceremonial status as "First Lady." This is not just a technicality according to appellees; she is statutorily barred from appointment as an officer because of the Anti-Nepotism Act. *See* 5 U.S.C. § 3110(b).

The district court, finding no definition of officer or employee of the federal government in FACA itself, quite reasonably turned to Title 5 of the U.S. Code to find a definition. *See* 5 U.S.C. §§ 2104 & 2105. An officer or employee according to those sections must be: (i) appointed to the civil service; (ii) engaged in the performance of a federal function; and (iii) subject to supervision by a higher elected or appointed official. As the district court held, and as appellees correctly point out, Mrs. Clinton has not been appointed to the civil service. Reading these definitions in pari materia with FACA would seem to suggest that the Task Force is not exempt . . . .

The government would have us conclude that the traditional, if informal, status and "duties" of the President's wife as "First Lady" gives her de facto officer or employee status. The government invokes what it describes as "a longstanding tradition of public service" by First Ladies — including, we are told, Sarah Polk, Edith Wilson, Eleanor Roosevelt, Rosalynn Carter, and Nancy Reagan — who have acted (albeit in the background) as advisers and personal representatives of their husbands. . . . More persuasive, however, is the government's argument that Congress itself has recognized that the President's spouse acts as the functional equivalent of an assistant to the President. The legislative authorization to the President to pay his White House aides includes [a provision authorizing the provision of government services to the spouse of the President "in connection with assistance provided by such spouse to the President in the discharge of the President's duties and responsibilities."] 3 U.S.C. § 105(e). . . . We see no reason why a President could not use his or her spouse to carry out a task that the President might delegate to one of his White House aides. It is reasonable, therefore, to construe section 105(e) as treating the presidential spouse as a de facto officer or employee. Otherwise, if the President's spouse routinely attended, and participated in, cabinet meetings, he or she would convert an all-government group, established or used by the President, into a FACA advisory committee. . . .

Suffice it to say that the question whether Mrs. Clinton's membership on the Task Force triggers FACA is not an easy one. The government argues, therefore, that we should construe the statute not to apply here, because otherwise we would face a serious constitutional issue. . . . Only a few years ago the Court employed that very maxim of statutory construction . . . [in *Public Citizen*]. The government there argued that applying FACA would impair the effectiveness of the committee's deliberations (by exposing them to public examination), and thus would interfere with the advice that the committee provided to the Attorney General and ultimately, it was assumed, to the President. Such interference would encroach on the President's appointment power — his sole responsibility to nominate federal judges. In order to escape that constitutional question, the Court held that the ABA committee was not "utilized" by the President because it was established and run by a private organization, even though the Act covers advisory committees established or utilized by the executive branch. The Court adopted, we think it is fair to say, an extremely strained construction of the word "utilized" in order to avoid the constitutional question. . . .

It is, of course, necessary before considering the maxim of statutory construction to determine whether the government's constitutional argument in this case is a powerful one. In other words, are we truly faced, as the Court thought it was in *Public Citizen*, with a grave question of constitutional law? The government relies primarily on the claim that an explicit presidential power is implicated. Article II of the Constitution provides that the President "shall from time to time give to the Congress Information of the State of the Union, and recommend to their Consideration such Measures as he shall judge necessary and expedient." U.S. Const. art. II, § 3, cl.1. According to the government, this clause gives the President the sole discretion to decide what measures to propose to Congress, and it leaves no room for congressional interference. To exercise this power, the government claims, the President also must have the constitutional right to receive confidential advice on proposed legislation.

Under the government's theory, FACA would interfere with the President's unbounded discretion to propose legislation. President Clinton formed the Task Force specifically to recommend legislation dealing with health care reform. FACA's requirement of public meetings would inhibit both candid discussion within the Task Force and its presentation of advice to the President. Challenging the district court's ruling, the government argues that this encroachment occurs regardless of whether the Task Force is engaged in information-gathering or internal deliberation. In either situation, the glare of publicity would inhibit the free flow of frank advice and would handicap the President's ability to develop legislation.

Appellees point out that the concurring opinion in *Public Citizen* commanded the votes of only three justices and rely, instead, on the Court's opinion in *Morrison v. Olson*, 487 U.S. 654 (1988) [excerpted *infra* Chapter Four]. *Morrison* upheld the Ethics in Government Act's creation of an independent counsel because it did not prevent the President "from accomplishing [his] constitutionally assigned functions," even though the counsel was largely immune from the executive branch's operational control (she was appointed by a panel of judges and was removable only for good cause). Applying FACA to the Task Force, according to appellees, has a rather minor impact on the institution of the presidency compared to the much greater encroachment on the President's core executive function sanctioned in *Morrison*.

Nevertheless, the government maintains that *Morrison* is not directly on point. Picking up on Justice Kennedy's concurrence in *Public Citizen*, the government contends that the *Morrison* Court's imprecise balancing test, which is apparently less favorable to the President, does not apply when a textual grant of presidential authority is implicated. In distinguishing *Morrison*, Justice Kennedy said [that the removal power is not conferred by the text of the Constitution] . . . . But because *Public Citizen* involved the President's textually granted power to appoint federal judges, the concurrence would have struck FACA down. . . . The government argues that here, as in *Public Citizen*, but unlike in *Morrison*, we have an explicit textual delegation to the President to propose legislation.

We perceive several weaknesses in the government's position. First, the government ignores the *Morrison* Court's consideration of the President's Article II, section 3 responsibility to "take Care that the Laws be faithfully executed." The Court specifically recognized that the statute before it encroached upon or burdened that responsibility, but concluded that the burden was not great enough to be unconstitutional. . . . *Morrison v. Olson,* thus, cannot be easily disposed of in accordance with the government's (and Justice Kennedy's) suggested distinction. The President's constitutional duty to take care that the laws be faithfully executed, moreover, seems far greater in importance than his authority to recommend legislation. The Framers intended the Take Care Clause to be an affirmative duty on the President and the President alone. In contrast, the Recommendation Clause is less an obligation than a right. The President has the undisputed authority to recommend legislation, but he need not exercise that authority with respect to any particular subject or, for that matter, any subject. Only the President can ensure that the laws be faithfully executed, but anyone in the country can propose legislation.

The government's focus on the Recommendation Clause seems somewhat artificial. Discussions on policy—whether they take place in executive branch groups or in pure FACA advisory committees—to some extent always implicate proposed legislation. Whenever an executive branch group considers policy initiatives, it discusses interchangeably new legislation, executive orders, or other administrative directives. Thus, virtually anytime an advisory group meets to discuss a problem, it will implicate the Recommendation Clause, from which all executive branch authority to recommend legislation derives. Accordingly, if the application of FACA to groups advising the President or anyone else in the executive branch were constitutionally problematic, insofar as those groups were advising on proposed legislation, FACA would be problematic with regard to virtually all policy advice. Under that reasoning FACA would be constitutionally suspect on its face—an argument the government declined to make.

We do think that the government's alternative, albeit implicit, argument is more persuasive. Application of FACA to the Task Force clearly would interfere with the President's capacity to solicit direct advice on any subject related to his duties from a group of private citizens, separate from or together with his closest governmental associates. That advice might be sought on a broad range of issues in an informal or formal fashion. Presidents have created advisory groups composed of private citizens (sometimes in conjunction with government officials) to meet periodically and advise them (hence the phrase "kitchen cabinets") on matters such as the conduct of a war. Presidents have even created formal "cabinet committees" composed in part of private citizens. This case is no different. Here, the President has formed a committee of his closest advisers—cabinet secretaries, White House advisers, and his wife—to advise him on a domestic issue he considers of the utmost priority.

Applying FACA to the Task Force does not raise constitutional problems simply because the Task Force is involved in proposing legislation. Instead, difficulties arise because of the Task Force's operational proximity to the President himself—that is, because the Task Force provides advice and recommendations directly to the President. The Supreme Court has recognized that a President has a great need to receive advice confidentially: [*see*] *United States v. Nixon*, 418 U.S. 683, 705–06 (1974); *see also Nixon v. Administrator of Gen. Servs.*, 433 U.S. 425, 441–49 (1977) . . . . Article II not only gives the President the ability to consult with his advisers confidentially, but also, as a corollary, it gives him the flexibility to organize his advisers and seek advice from them as he wishes. In *Meyer v. Bush*, 981 F.2d 1288 at 1293–97, [(1993)] for example, we held that the President could create a Task Force composed of cabinet secretaries and other close advisers to study regulatory reform without having to comply with FOIA. In this regard, FACA's requirement that an advisory committee must be "fairly balanced in terms of the view represented" would—if enforceable and applied to groups of presidential advisers—restrict the President's ability to seek advice from whom and in the fashion he chooses. . . .

A statute interfering with a President's ability to seek advice directly from private citizens as a group, intermixed, or not, with government officials, therefore raises Article II concerns. This is all the more so when the sole ground for asserting that the statute applies is that the President's own spouse, a member of the Task Force, is not a government official. . . . If we were to go on to decide the constitutionality question, we would be obliged to ask whether, in *Morrison v. Olson* terms, this asserted application of FACA "impermissibly" burdens executive power. *Morrison* tells us to balance how much the interference with the President's executive power prevents the President "from accomplishing his constitutionally assigned functions," against the "overriding need to promote objectives within the constitutional authority of Congress." We readily confess that this balancing test is not one that, as judges, we can apply with confidence. This is all the more reason to view the constitutional issue soberly. We are satisfied that the application of FACA to the Task Force seriously burdens executive power. And our reading of *Morrison* does not lead us easily to a conclusion that the burden placed is a permissible one. . . .

We believe it is the Task Force's operational proximity to the President, and not its exact function at any given moment, that implicates executive powers and therefore forces consideration of the *Morrison* test. The President's confidentiality interest is strong regardless of the particular role the Task Force is playing on any given day. . . . if public disclosure of the real information-gathering process is required, the confidentiality of the advice-giving function inevitably would be compromised. If you know what information people seek, you can usually determine why they seek it. A group directly reporting and advising the President must have confidentiality at each stage in the formulation of advice to him. As we said in *Meyer*, "proximity to the President, in the sense of continuing interaction, is surely in part what Congress had in mind when it exempted [from FOIA] the President's 'immediate personal staff.'" And, as we recognized in *Soucie v. David*, 448 F.2d 1067 (D.C. Cir. 1971), FOIA's exemption may be constitutionally required to protect the President's executive powers. . . .

Prudent use of the maxim of statutory construction allows us to avoid the difficult constitutional issue posed by this case. The question whether the President's spouse is "a full-time officer or employee" of the government is close enough for us properly to construe FACA not to apply to the Task Force merely because Mrs. Clinton is a member. We follow the Supreme Court's lead, if not its strict precedent, in recognizing that [if the Act] were "read unqualifiedly, it would extend FACA's requirements to any group of two or more persons, or at least any formal organization, from which the President or an executive agency seeks advice." *Public Citizen*. Because it believed that Congress could not have intended such a result, the *Public Citizen* majority read "utilize" to exclude the ABA committee. If the Supreme Court correctly construed the statute not to cover the advice the Attorney General receives, on behalf of the President, from the ABA, the statutory construction issue we face should be resolved a fortiori in favor of the government.

We, therefore, read the phrase "full-time officer or employee of the government" in FACA to apply to Mrs. Clinton. In doing so, we express no view as to her status under any other statute. . . . The Task Force need not comply with the requirements of FACA because it is a committee composed wholly of full-time government officials. . . .

So ordered.

BUCKLEY, Circuit Judge, concurring in the judgment:

. . . I would hold that the Task Force was not exempt from the public disclosure requirements of FACA; and having done so, I would address the constitutional implications of that holding. . . . [T]he Supreme Court has acknowledged a Presidential right to confidentiality that "is fundamental to the operation of Government and inextricably rooted in the separation of powers under the Constitution." *Nixon* . . . [T]he Court [has] permitted only the most limited intrusions on the privilege. FACA, by contrast, would have required that the Task Force operate in the full glare of provisions requiring public meetings and disclosure of records. It is hard to imagine conditions better calculated to suppress the "candid, objective, and even blunt or harsh opinions," *Nixon*, that the President was entitled to receive from the twelve advisors he had appointed to his Task Force. Because none of Congress's purposes in enacting FACA are of a gravity that would justify overriding the Presidential privilege in this case, I would conclude that FACA is unconstitutional as applied to the Task Force. . . .

---

1. *Input v. Output*. What do you think of the district court's distinction between Task Force meetings to gather information, which were to be opened under FACA,

and meetings to formulate advice to the President, which could not be subjected to the Act? Is the rationale offered by the Court of Appeals for rejecting the distinction persuasive?

2. *The Kennedy Theory.* Is the critique offered by the Court of Appeals of Justice Kennedy's theory of executive power from *Public Citizen* persuasive? If the court is right that applying a textual approach to the Recommendations Clause would produce overly sweeping effects, are there other constitutional provisions of which the same might be said? *See* Jay S. Bybee, *Advising the President: Separation of Powers and the Federal Advisory Committee Act,* 104 YALE L.J. 51 (1994).

3. *"What, no more dinner parties?"* As the court observes, the broadest literal reading of FACA would apply it to any two persons advising the President, unless both were government employees. That would abolish such time-honored institutions as "kitchen cabinets" of a President's valued friends from private life. Should FACA be amended to exclude applicability to the President and his immediate circle, like FOIA?

———————

As you read the case that follows, consider whether a combination of separation of powers, executive privilege, and mandamus principles have carved a de facto exception to FACA for the upper levels of the executive branch.

Cheney v. United States District Court for the District of Columbia

542 U.S. 367 (2004)

Justice KENNEDY delivered the opinion of the Court.

The United States District Court for the District of Columbia entered discovery orders directing the Vice President and other senior officials in the Executive Branch to produce information about a task force established to give advice and make policy recommendations to the President. This case requires us to consider the circumstances under which a court of appeals may exercise its power to issue a writ of mandamus to modify or dissolve the orders when, by virtue of their overbreadth, enforcement might interfere with the officials in the discharge of their duties and impinge upon the President's constitutional prerogatives.

I

A few days after assuming office, President George W. Bush issued a memorandum establishing the National Energy Policy Development Group (NEPDG or Group). The Group was directed to "develo[p] . . . a national energy policy designed to help the private sector, and government at all levels, promote dependable, affordable, and environmentally sound production and distribution of energy for the future." The President assigned a number of agency heads and assistants—all employees of the Federal Government—to serve as members of the committee. He authorized the Vice President, as chairman of the Group, to invite "other officers of the Federal

Government" to participate "as appropriate." Five months later, the NEPDG issued a final report and, according to the Government, terminated all operations. Following publication of the report, respondents Judicial Watch and the Sierra Club filed these [actions, alleging that] the NEPDG had failed to comply with the procedural and disclosure requirements of the Federal Advisory Committee Act. . . .

Respondents do not dispute the President appointed only Federal Government officials to the NEPDG. . . . The complaint alleges, however, that "non-federal employees," including "private lobbyists," "regularly attended and fully participated in nonpublic meetings." Relying on *Association of American Physicians & Surgeons, Inc. v. Clinton*, 997 F.2d 898 (C.A.D.C. 1993) (*AAPS*), respondents contend that the regular participation of the non-Government individuals made them *de facto* members of the committee. According to the complaint, their "involvement and role are functionally indistinguishable from those of the other [formal] members." As a result, respondents argue, the NEPDG . . . is subject to FACA's requirements. . . . The suit seeks declaratory relief and an injunction requiring them to produce all materials allegedly subject to FACA's requirements . . . .

The District Court held . . . that FACA's substantive requirements could be enforced against the Vice President and other Government participants on the NEPDG under the Mandamus Act, 28 U.S.C. § 1361, and against the agency defendants under the Administrative Procedure Act (APA), 5 U.S.C. § 706. The District Court recognized the disclosure duty must be clear and nondiscretionary for mandamus to issue, and there must be, among other things, "final agency actions" for the APA to apply. According to the District Court, it was premature to decide these questions. It held only that respondents had alleged sufficient facts to keep the Vice President and the other defendants in the case.

The District Court deferred ruling on the Government's contention that to . . . apply FACA to the NEPDG would violate principles of separation of powers and interfere with the constitutional prerogatives of the President and the Vice President. Instead, the court allowed respondents to conduct a "tightly-reined" discovery to ascertain the NEPDG's structure and membership, and thus to determine whether the *de facto* membership doctrine applies. While acknowledging that discovery itself might raise serious constitutional questions, the District Court explained that the Government could assert executive privilege to protect sensitive materials from disclosure. . . . Furthermore, the District Court explained, even were it appropriate to address constitutional issues, some factual development is necessary to determine the extent of the alleged intrusion into the Executive's constitutional authority. The court denied in part the motion to dismiss and ordered respondents to submit a discovery plan [which the court approved] . . . .

Petitioners sought a writ of mandamus in the Court of Appeals to vacate the discovery orders, to direct the District Court to rule on the basis of the administrative record, and to dismiss the Vice President from the suit. . . . A divided panel of the Court of Appeals dismissed the petition for a writ of mandamus and the Vice

President's attempted interlocutory appeal. *In re Cheney*, 334 F.3d 1096 (C.A.D.C. 2003). With respect to mandamus, the majority declined to issue the writ on the ground that alternative avenues of relief remained available. Citing *United States v. Nixon*, the majority held that petitioners, to guard against intrusion into the President's prerogatives, must first assert privilege. Under its reading of *Nixon*, moreover, privilege claims must be made "'with particularity.'" .... The majority acknowledged the scope of respondents' requests is overly broad, because it seeks far more than the "limited items" to which respondents would be entitled if "the district court ultimately determines that the NEPDG is subject to FACA." ... It nonetheless agreed with the District Court that petitioners "'shall bear the burden'" of invoking executive privilege and filing objections to the discovery orders with "'detailed precision.'". .... In the majority's view, the Vice President was not forced to choose between disclosure and suffering contempt for failure to obey a court order. The majority held that to require the Vice President to assert privilege does not create the unnecessary confrontation between two branches of Government described in *Nixon*.

We now vacate the judgment of the Court of Appeals and remand the case for further proceedings to reconsider the Government's mandamus petition. ...

III

We now come to the central issue in the case—whether the Court of Appeals was correct to conclude it "ha[d] no authority to exercise the extraordinary remedy of mandamus," on the ground that the Government could protect its rights by asserting executive privilege in the District Court. The common-law writ of mandamus against a lower court is codified at 28 U.S.C. § 1651(a): "The Supreme Court and all courts established by Act of Congress may issue all writs necessary or appropriate in aid of their respective jurisdictions and agreeable to the usages and principles of law." This is a "drastic and extraordinary" remedy "reserved for really extraordinary causes." *Ex parte Fahey*, 332 U.S. 258, 259–260 (1947) ....

Were the Vice President not a party in the case, the argument that the Court of Appeals should have entertained an action in mandamus, notwithstanding the District Court's denial of the motion for certification, might present different considerations. Here, however, the Vice President and his comembers on the NEPDG are the subjects of the discovery orders. The mandamus petition alleges that the orders threaten "substantial intrusions on the process by which those in closest operational proximity to the President advise the President." These facts and allegations remove this case from the category of ordinary discovery orders where interlocutory appellate review is unavailable, through mandamus or otherwise. It is well established that ... the public interest requires that a coequal branch of Government "afford Presidential confidentiality the greatest protection consistent with the fair administration of justice," and give recognition to the paramount necessity of protecting the Executive Branch from vexatious litigation that might distract it from the energetic performance of its constitutional duties.

These separation-of-powers considerations should inform a court of appeals' evaluation of a mandamus petition involving the President or the Vice President. Accepted mandamus standards are broad enough to allow a court of appeals to prevent a lower court from interfering with a coequal branch's ability to discharge its constitutional responsibilities.

IV

The Court of Appeals dismissed these separation-of-powers concerns. Relying on *United States v. Nixon*, it held that even though respondents' discovery requests are overbroad and "go well beyond FACA's requirements," the Vice President and his former colleagues on the NEPDG "shall bear the burden" of invoking privilege with narrow specificity and objecting to the discovery requests with "detailed precision." . . . *Nixon* cannot bear the weight the Court of Appeals puts upon it. First, unlike this case, which concerns respondents' requests for information for use in a civil suit, *Nixon* involves the proper balance between the Executive's interest in the confidentiality of its communications and the "constitutional need for production of relevant evidence in a criminal proceeding." . . . The distinction *Nixon* drew between criminal and civil proceedings is not just a matter of formalism. As the Court explained, the need for information in the criminal context is much weightier because "our historic[al] commitment to the rule of law . . . is nowhere more profoundly manifest than in our view that 'the twofold aim [of criminal justice] is that guilt shall not escape or innocence suffer.'" . . . . The need for information for use in civil cases, while far from negligible, does not share the urgency or significance of the criminal subpoena requests in *Nixon*. As *Nixon* recognized, the right to production of relevant evidence in civil proceedings does not have the same "constitutional dimensions."

. . . . Withholding materials from a tribunal in an ongoing criminal case when the information is necessary to the court in carrying out its tasks "conflict[s] with the function of the courts under Art. III." Such an impairment of the "essential functions of [another] branch" is impermissible. Withholding the information in this case, however, does not hamper another branch's ability to perform its "essential functions" in quite the same way . . . . Even if FACA embodies important congressional objectives, the only consequence from respondents' inability to obtain the discovery they seek is that it would be more difficult for private complainants to vindicate Congress' policy objectives under FACA. And even if, for argument's sake, . . . FACA's statutory objectives would be to some extent frustrated, it does not follow that a court's Article III authority or Congress' central Article I powers would be impaired. . . .

A party's need for information is only one facet of the problem. An important factor weighing in the opposite direction is the burden imposed by the discovery orders. This is not a routine discovery dispute. The discovery requests are directed to the Vice President and other senior Government officials who served on the NEPDG to give advice and make recommendations to the President. . . . The observation in *Nixon* that production of confidential information would not disrupt the functioning of the Executive Branch cannot be applied in a mechanistic fashion to civil litigation. In the criminal justice system, there are various constraints, albeit imperfect, to filter out insubstantial legal claims. The decision to prosecute a criminal case, for example, is made by a publicly accountable prosecutor subject to budgetary considerations and under an ethical obligation, not only to win and zealously to advocate for his client but also to serve the cause of justice. . . . Although under Federal Rule of Civil Procedure 11, sanctions are available, and private attorneys also owe an obligation of candor to the judicial tribunal, these safeguards have proved insufficient to discourage the filing of meritless claims against the Executive Branch. "In view of the visibility of" the Offices of the President and the Vice President and "the effect of their actions on countless people," they are "easily identifiable target[s] for suits for civil damages." *Nixon v. Fitzgerald.*

Finally, the narrow subpoena orders in *United States v. Nixon* stand on an altogether different footing from the overly broad discovery requests approved by the District Court in this case. . . . The very specificity of the subpoena requests serves as an important safeguard against unnecessary intrusion into the operation of the Office of the President.

In contrast to *Nixon*'s subpoena orders that "precisely identified" and "specific[ally] . . . enumerated" the relevant materials, the discovery requests here, as the panel majority acknowledged, ask for everything under the sky:

"1. All documents identifying or referring to any staff, personnel, contractors, consultants or employees of the Task Force.

"2. All documents establishing or referring to any Sub-Group.

"3. All documents identifying or referring to any staff, personnel, contractors, consultants or employees of any Sub-Group.

"4. All documents identifying or referring to any other persons participating in the preparation of the Report or in the activities of the Task Force or any Sub-Group.

"5. All documents concerning any communication relating to the activities of the Task Force, the activities of any Sub-Groups, or the preparation of the Report. . . .

"6. All documents concerning any communication relating to the activities of the Task Force, the activities of the Sub-Groups, or the preparation of the Report between any person . . . and [a list of agencies]." . . .

Given the breadth of the discovery requests in this case compared to the narrow subpoena orders in *United States v. Nixon*, our precedent provides no support for the proposition that the Executive Branch "shall bear the burden" of invoking executive privilege with sufficient specificity and of making particularized objections. . . . Here, as the Court of Appeals acknowledged, the discovery requests . . . provide respondents all the disclosure to which they would be entitled in the event they prevail on the merits, and much more besides. In these circumstances, *Nixon* does not require the Executive Branch to bear the onus of critiquing the unacceptable discovery requests line by line. . . .

The Government, however, did in fact object to the scope of discovery and asked the District Court to narrow it in some way. Its arguments were ignored . . . . Executive privilege is an extraordinary assertion of power "not to be lightly invoked." Once executive privilege is asserted, coequal branches of the Government are set on a collision course. The Judiciary is forced into the difficult task of balancing the need for information in a judicial proceeding and the Executive's Article II prerogatives. This inquiry places courts in the awkward position of evaluating the Executive's claims of confidentiality and autonomy, and pushes to the fore difficult questions of separation of powers and checks and balances. These "occasion[s] for constitutional confrontation between the two branches" should be avoided whenever possible. . . .

As this case implicates the separation of powers, the Court of Appeals must . . . ask . . . whether the District Court's actions constituted an unwarranted impairment of another branch in the performance of its constitutional duties. This is especially so here because the District Court's analysis of whether mandamus relief is appropriate should itself be constrained by principles similar to those we have outlined that limit the Court of Appeals' use of the remedy. The panel majority, however, failed to ask this question. Instead, it labored under the mistaken assumption that the assertion of executive privilege is a necessary precondition to the Government's separation-of-powers objections.

V

. . . [W]e decline petitioners' invitation to direct the Court of Appeals to issue the writ against the District Court. . . . [T]his is not a case where, after having considered the issues, the Court of Appeals abused its discretion by failing to issue the writ. Instead, the Court of Appeals, relying on its mistaken reading of *United States v. Nixon*, prematurely terminated its inquiry after the Government refused to assert privilege and did so without even reaching the weighty separation-of-powers objections raised in the case, much less exercised its discretion to determine whether "the writ is appropriate under the circumstances." . . . [W]e leave it to the Court of Appeals to address the parties' arguments with respect to the challenge to *AAPS* and the discovery orders. . . . We note only that all courts should be mindful of the burdens imposed on the Executive Branch in any future proceedings . . . . The judgment of the Court of Appeals for the District of Columbia is vacated, and the case is remanded for further proceedings consistent with this opinion.

Justice STEVENS, concurring. . . .

[R]espondents sought to obtain, through discovery, information about the NEP-DG's work in order to establish their entitlement to the same information. Thus, granting broad discovery in this case effectively prejudged the merits of respondents' claim for mandamus relief—an outcome entirely inconsistent with the extraordinary nature of the writ. Under these circumstances, instead of requiring petitioners to object to particular discovery requests, the District Court should have required respondents to demonstrate that particular requests would tend to establish their theory of the case. . . .

Justice THOMAS, with whom Justice SCALIA joins, concurring in part and dissenting in part.

. . . The question with which the Court of Appeals was faced . . . necessarily had to account for the fact that respondents sought mandamus relief in the District Court. Because they proceeded by mandamus, respondents had to demonstrate in the District Court a clear and indisputable right to the Federal Advisory Committee Act (FACA) materials. If respondents' right to the materials was not clear and indisputable, then petitioners' right to relief in the Court of Appeals was clear. One need look no further than the District Court's opinion to conclude respondents' right to relief in the District Court was unclear and hence that mandamus would be unavailable . . . . Because the District Court clearly exceeded its authority in this case, I would reverse the judgment of the Court of Appeals and remand the case with instruction to issue the writ.

Justice GINSBURG, with whom Justice SOUTER joins, dissenting.

. . . Given the Government's decision to resist all discovery, mandamus relief based on the exorbitance of the discovery orders is at least "premature." I would therefore affirm the judgment of the Court of Appeals denying the writ, and allow the District Court, in the first instance, to pursue its expressed intention "tightly [to] rei[n] [in] discovery," should the Government so request. . . .

The Government's bottom line was firmly and consistently that "review, limited to the administrative record, should frame the resolution of this case." That administrative record would "consist of the Presidential Memorandum establishing NEPDG, NEPDG's public report, and the Office of the Vice President's response to . . . Judicial Watch's request for permission to attend NEPDG meetings"; it would not include anything respondents could gain through discovery. . . . In accord with the Court of Appeals, I am "confident that [were it moved to do so] the district court here [would] protect petitioners' legitimate interests and keep discovery within appropriate limits." I would therefore affirm the judgment of the Court of Appeals.

---

1. *Executive Privilege.* Executive privilege was never invoked in this case. (Do you see why not?) Nevertheless, the Court thought it important to distinguish this case from *Nixon*. How much guidance can we draw from *Cheney* for the resolution of executive privilege claims in civil litigation? Does executive privilege doctrine merge with general separation of powers principles in a civil case? On remand, the court of appeals got the hint and issued the writ of mandamus the Vice President

had requested. *In re Cheney*, 406 F. 3d 723 (D.C. Cir. 2005) (en banc). The court reasoned that the private parties would count as members of the NEPDG—thus rendering the NEPDG subject to disclosure requirements—only if they could vote regarding, or exercise a veto over, the decisions of the group. Because Judicial Watch and the Sierra Club had not even alleged either possibility, they could not win their suit, and the discovery orders were unjustified.

2. *Litigation Strategy.* Did the plaintiffs err by making their discovery requests so broad? The Court detected an attempt on their part to obtain a win on the merits in the guise of discovery—what else could they have done? In a footnote, Justice Stevens suggested an answer: "A few interrogatories or depositions might have determined, for example, whether any non-Government employees voted on NEPDG recommendations or drafted portions of the committee's report. In my view, only substantive participation of this nature would even arguably be suffi-cient to warrant classifying a non-Government employee as a *de facto* committee member."

3. *Fending Off Congress, Too.* Vice President Cheney was successful also in invoking separation of powers concerns—but not formally claiming executive privilege—to ward off a congressional investigation of the NEPDG:

> In spring, 2001 the Congressional Government Accountability Office (GAO) asked the Vice President to provide information concerning the membership and operations of the NEPDG, based on the request of two Congressmen, John D. Dingell, the ranking Democrat on the House Commit-tee on Energy and Commerce, and Henry A. Waxman, the ranking Democrat on the House Committee on Government Reform. David Addington, the Vice President's Counsel, provided some general information about the task force, but would not disclose "the names of NEPDG staff members, the names of persons in attendance at the NEPDG meetings or at meetings between staff and persons outside of the government, or the dates, locations, and subjects of any meetings with non-federal employees." Addington also questioned the legal basis for the GAO investigation. When the Comptroller Gen-eral, the head of the GAO, demanded the information not yet provided, Vice President Cheney sent letters to both the House and Senate indicating that the GAO was exceeding its investigative authority and that, if its investigation were carried forth, it would "unconstitutionally interfere with the functioning of the executive branch." As negotiations over some degree of possible disclosure proceeded, the Vice President's office did pro-vide the names of the staff members who were government employees, but not the private parties who had met with the NEPDG.
>
> With Democrats in control of the Senate from 2001 to early 2003, key Democratic Senators wrote the Comptroller General in early 2002 to urge him to press forward. When the Vice President persisted in his

nondisclosure, the GAO filed suit in February 2002. The executive branch responded that the investigation was unconstitutional because the NEPDG operated pursuant to two of the President's explicit constitutional authorities, the power to "require the Opinion, in writing, of the principal Officer in each of the executive Departments, upon any Subject relating to the Duties of their respective Offices," and the power to "recommend to [Congress's] Consideration such Measures as he shall judge necessary and expedient." According to Cheney, how a President seeks information in connection with these authorities cannot be overseen by either Congress or the judiciary. Congress could not, according to this argument, legislate how the President fulfills these powers, so it cannot investigate how he does so, either through a congressional committee or through the Government Accountability Office.

Avoiding what it took to be difficult constitutional arguments, the U.S. District Court for the District of Columbia dismissed the case in December 2002 on the ground that Comptroller General, on these particular facts, could not constitutionally be allowed to sue the executive branch. Employing the highly technical constitutional doctrine of standing, the court held that GAO had no right to sue where the denial of the information sought would not actually inflict an injury on Congress. Walker v. Cheney, 230 F. Supp. 2d 51 (D.D.C. 2002). Given GOP legislative victories in November 2002 and the impending Republican takeover of the Senate, the GAO then declined to pursue an appeal from this ruling, presumably realizing that it would not have the political backing of either the Republican-controlled House or the Republican-controlled Senate.

Peter M. Shane, Madison's Nightmare: How Executive Power Threatens American Democracy 125–126 (2009).

4. *There Are Victories and There Are . . .* In 2007, a "former White House official" leaked to the Washington Post a list of everyone who met with the NEPDG. Michael Abramowitz and Steven Mufson, *Papers Detail Industry's Role in Cheney's Energy Report*, Wash. Post, at A1 (July 18, 2007). The lists disclosed that "about 300 groups and individuals met with staff members of the energy task force"; of the 300, 13 were representatives of environmental groups.

e. Other Statutory Restrictions

In *Andrus v. Sierra Club*, 442 U.S. 347 (1979), the Supreme Court held that § 102(2)(C) of the National Environmental Policy Act (NEPA), 42 U.S.C. § 4321-4370a, which requires that environmental impact statements ("EIS's") be included in recommendations or reports of federal agencies on "proposals for legislation and other major Federal actions significantly affecting the quality of the human environment," does not require agencies to file EIS's with their appropriations requests, which are considered and processed originally by OMB, which is part of the Executive Office of the President. At the time of the Court of Appeals decision, which had gone the other way, guidelines issued by the Council on Environmental Quality (CEQ), another part of the Executive Office of the President, included a contrary interpretation of NEPA.

CEQ reversed its position in 1978, in the process of re-promulgating the guidelines as regulations to be binding on government agencies, arguing that not requiring EIS's for appropriations requests was consistent with traditional procedural distinctions in the handling of appropriations and substantive legislation. The Supreme Court accepted this reading of NEPA, on statutory grounds. Perhaps significantly, however, there was no hint in the Court's opinion of any constitutional limitation on Congress's power to regulate the process by which agencies prepare policy recommendations for presidential review. Do the FACA cases suggest a new sensitivity to this problem?

In *Common Cause v. Nuclear Regulatory Commission*, 674 F. 2d 921 (D.C. Cir. 1982), the Court of Appeals held that the Government in the Sunshine Act, 5 U.S.C. § 552b, which generally requires meetings of multi-member federal agencies to be open to the public, does not exempt agency budget deliberations from its requirements. Although an independent agency, the NRC is required to participate in OMB's centralized budget review process. The Commission, in arguing for a blanket exemption for budget deliberations, relied partly on the "[l]ongstanding practice of confidentiality for Executive Branch discussions leading to the formulation of the President's budget," and partly on the President's statutory rulemaking authority for budget preparation.

The court rejected both these arguments, stating that the President's statutory rulemaking authority was limited by other applicable statutes, including the Sunshine Act, and that public disclosure of agency deliberations did not, on its face, interfere with the President's ability to revise agency requests and prepare a unified budget. The court did recognize "that specific items discussed at Commission budget meetings might be exempt from the open meetings requirement of the act," and expressed "no view with regard to any constitutional issue of Executive privilege, a question," according to the court, "which is narrower than the . . . general claim based on separation of powers." The court added that only the President, and not an agency, may assert presidential privilege.

If this case seems inconsistent with those immediately preceding it in this chapter, perhaps the NRC's status as an independent agency, "outside the pale" of the Cabinet, has something to do with that.

f. Subjecting Presidential Advisers to Advice and Consent

Although the question has not been adjudicated, the executive has historically taken the position that the separation of powers bars Congress from demanding the testimony of the President's Cabinet and special assistants. The general practice, however, has been to permit such persons to testify "voluntarily." Should questions arise that might require divulging privileged information, the testifying official can assert privilege as to particular answers.

Partly in order to secure greater cooperation from the President's advisers in congressional testimony, Congress has considered subjecting particular advisers to appointment with the Senate's advice and consent. Nominees to such positions could then be questioned during confirmation hearings about their willingness to supply information to Congress. We outline the issues regarding two kinds of sensitive advisers, those for budgetary and national security matters.

In 1974 the Director and Deputy Director of OMB were made subject to advice and consent. The Senate's committee report on the legislation explained (S. Rep. No. 93-7, 93d Cong., 1st Sess. (1973)):

> The objective of the bill is to afford the Senate an opportunity to inquire into the qualifications, background, and fitness of these officials in the same manner as is required for virtually all other policy-making officials in the executive branch. . . . [T]he Budget and Accounting Act, 1921, established a national budget system and a Bureau of the Budget to advise and assist the President in developing a unified budget for submission to the Congress. . . . [The Conference Committee deleted a requirement] that appointments to the offices of Director and Assistant Director of the Bureau of the Budget should be subject to Senate confirmation, . . . on the theory that these positions were personal to the President and that he should be allowed to "appoint men whom he believed he could trust to do his will in the preparation of the budget." . . .

> Since 1939, vast changes have occurred in the structure, responsibilities and authority of [what is now] the Office of Management and Budget. . . . With a current staff of nearly 700 persons, this agency, originally established by the Congress as a management tool and institutional aid for the President, has developed into a super department with enormous authority over all of the activities of the Federal Government. Its Director has become, in effect, a Deputy President who exercises vital Presidential powers. OMB determines line by line budget limitations for each agency, including the regulatory commissions. Following authorization by the Congress of programs and activities, and the funding of such activities, the Office of Management and Budget develops impoundment actions, limiting the expenditures of funds for programs approved by law to those falling within the President's priorities, rather than those established by the Congress. By statute, the Director of OMB has authority to apportion appropriations, approve agency systems for the control of appropriated funds and establish reserves. . . .

> Under numerous . . . statutes, or by Presidential delegations, the Director of OMB has been given a vast number of additional functions. . . . The Director . . . exercises control over the nature and types of questionnaires,

surveys, reports, and forms which may be issued and utilized by Government agencies. . . . Finally, the Director and his staff exercise oversight and control over the management of, and expenditures for, national security programs, international programs, defense expenditures, natural resources programs, and many others having a direct impact upon the economy and security of the Nation. . . .

An even more sensitive role than that of the OMB director is played by the Assistant to the President for National Security Affairs, popularly known as the National Security Adviser. Then-Deputy Secretary of State Warren Christopher testified in opposition to altering the status of the Adviser, in The National Security Adviser: Role and Accountability, Hearing Before the Senate Comm. on Foreign Relations, 96th Cong., 2d Sess. (1980):

> . . . As part of these hearings, I understand that the committee is once again considering whether the positions of Assistant and Deputy Assistant to the President for National Security Affairs should be subject to the advice and consent of the Senate. . . . [T]he Administration opposes this proposal. We believe it would intrude upon the authority of the President in international affairs and complicate the conduct of our foreign relations. It would do so without significant compensating value to the Congress.
>
> Let me begin my discussion by reviewing briefly the development of the position of the National Security Adviser and its relationship to the National Security Council. [The NSC] was created . . . to coordinate the many strands of national policy set by various departments, all of which bore upon our global posture. The [National Security Act] specified statutory members of the National Security Council, including the President and the Secretaries of State and Defense, and it provided for a civilian staff headed by an executive secretary. There was no mention of an Assistant to the President for National Security Affairs. That position was created by Presidential statement in 1953.
>
> I do not propose to trace the intervening history in any depth. From it, however, some broad observations emerge. First, the function of the NSC and its staff has varied widely, depending primarily on the needs and preferences of the President in office. During the Eisenhower Administration, for example, the Council structure was highly developed and extensively used. President Kennedy, by contrast, preferred a less formal approach. Second, the requirement which inspired the creation of the National Security Council—for interdepartmental coordination on foreign affairs—remains its most important role. . . .
>
> Within the NSC system, the National Security Adviser has a dual responsibility. First, at the President's request, he provides advice on foreign and defense policy. He also directs the NSC system in order to bring options to the President's attention and to assure that the President's decisions are

appropriately followed. Finally, like all Presidential advisers, the National Security Adviser performs additional duties, such as conducting fact-finding missions, on behalf of the President and at his direction. . . .

The Administration recognizes that the United States can have an effective and durable foreign policy only if the Congress is fully informed and involved. . . . [W]e also believe there is agreement that the President of the United States requires a personal and confidential staff of his own choosing. He must be able to draw upon advisers who, within the law, answer only to him. He must be able to hear a wide range of views and consider all possible options when he makes his decisions. The availability of the unfettered advice of persons the President trusts serves not just the convenience of the President, but the interests of the country as well. . . .

State Department officials have been readily available for formal testimony and have conducted countless informal briefings and consultations. . . . These are the officials with direct responsibility for our policy and our programs in the world. . . . By contrast, the Assistant to the President for National Security Affairs does not administer statutory programs. He does not expend public funds. Rather, the principal roles of the National Security Adviser are to provide confidential advice to the President and to coordinate foreign policy. His appearance to testify on the Hill would impinge upon the President's right to obtain confidential advice from individuals responsible only to him. . . . [T]he proposal . . . would directly impinge upon the Office of the President by limiting his necessary flexibility in foreign policy. . . .

As the chief architect of American foreign policy, the President must be able to choose his personal and confidential advisers without the searching inquiry that confirmation hearings entail. It is inappropriate for the Senate to pass on the qualifications of intimate Presidential advisers. For only the President is in a position to adjudge the needs of his immediate office and to decide what, if any, advice he requires and who, if anyone will provide it. Just as it is unthinkable that the selection of personal aides of Senators would be subject to outside scrutiny, it is equally unthinkable that the appointment of the President's personal advisers should be subject to the advice and consent of the Senate. . . . Moreover, as the Nation's chief diplomat, the President should have flexibility to decide the level and formality of our contacts with other countries, including the use of personal emissaries when he deems it appropriate. So long as the Congress is informed and the Administration is answerable for the results, the prerogatives of the Congress are in no way impaired. . . . Our system provides ample opportunity to question and challenge the President's decisions. But if our government is to operate effectively, it must accord the President breathing space. . . . The proposal under consideration is an unwarranted intrusion by the Congress that will needlessly hamper future Presidents.

———————

1. *Drawing the Inner Circle.* Has the President a constitutional right, in the exercise of his "core functions," to some advisers and agents of his own selection, not subject to senatorial advice and consent and not ordinarily amenable to congressional subpoenas? If so, how many and for which functions? Could the Counsel to the President be subjected to advice and consent?

2. *National Security Adviser, Part 2.* In the wake of the Iran/Contra scandal, calls for subjecting the National Security Adviser to confirmation were made anew. The President's Special Review Board (Tower Commission), however, took essentially the same position in 1987 as had Warren Christopher in his testimony. The Board's Recommendation 2 was: "We urge the Congress not to require Senate confirmation of the National Security Adviser." In explanation, the Board urged that:

> confirmation is inconsistent with the role the National Security Adviser should play. He should not decide, only advise. He should not engage in policy implementation or operations. He should serve the President, with no collateral and potentially diverting loyalties. Confirmation would tend to institutionalize the natural tension that exists between the Secretary of State and the National Security Adviser. Questions would increasingly arise about who really speaks for the President in national security matters. . . . Several [officials we interviewed] suggested that [requiring confirmation] could induce the President to turn to other internal staff or to people outside government to play that role.

3. *National Security Adviser, Part 3.* The presidential commission inquiring into the causes of the 9/11 terrorist attacks, formally known as the National Commission on Terrorist Attacks Upon the United States, desired the testimony of President Bush's National Security Adviser, Condoleezza Rice. After an extended standoff with attendant negative publicity in the press, the President agreed to allow her to testify under oath to the Commission. The President's consent—and his reservations and conditions—were communicated in a letter from his Counsel, Alberto R. Gonzales, to the Commission's Chairman, Thomas H. Kean, and Vice Chairman, Lee H. Hamilton. In part, the letter said:

> As you know, based on principles underlying the Constitutional separation of powers, Presidents of both parties have long taken the position that White House advisors and staff are not subject to the jurisdiction of legislative bodies and do not provide testimony—even on a voluntary basis—on policy matters discussed within the White House or advice given to the President. Indeed, I am not aware of any instance of a *sitting* National Security Advisor testifying in public to a legislative body (such as the Commission) concerning policy matters. We continue to believe, as I advised you by letter dated March 25, 2004, that the principles underlying the Constitutional separation of powers counsel strongly against such public testimony, and that Dr. Rice's testimony before the Commission can occur only with

recognition that the events of September 11, 2001 present the most extraordinary and unique circumstances, and with conditions and assurances designed to limit harm to the ability of future Presidents to receive candid advice.

Nevertheless, the President recognizes the truly unique and extraordinary circumstances underlying the Commission's responsibility to prepare a detailed report on the facts and circumstances of the horrific attacks on September 11, 2001. Furthermore, we have now received assurances from the Speaker of the House and the Majority Leader of the Senate that, in their view, Dr. Rice's public testimony in connection with the extraordinary events of September 11, 2001 does not set, and should not be cited as, a precedent for future requests for a National Security Advisor or any other White official to testify before a legislative body. In light of the unique nature of the Commission and these additional assurances, the President has determined that, although he retains the legal authority to decline to make Dr. Rice available to testify in public, he will agree, as a matter of comity and subject to the conditions set forth below, to the Commission's request for Dr. Rice to testify publicly regarding matters within the Commission's statutory mandate.

The necessary conditions are as follows. First, the Commission must agree in writing that Dr. Rice's testimony before the Commission does not set a precedent for future Commission requests, or requests in any other context, for testimony by a National Security Advisor or any other White House official. Second, the Commission must agree in writing that it will not request additional public testimony from any White House official, including Dr. Rice. . . . Other White House officials with information relevant to the commission's inquiry . . . will continue to provide the Commission with information through private meetings, briefings, and documents, consistent with our previous practice.

Letter of Hon. Alberto Gonzales to Chairman Kean and Chairman Hamilton (Mar. 30, 2004), available at http://www.usatoday.com/news/washington/2004-03-30-rice-letter_x.htm.

Clearly, the President hoped to minimize the precedential effect of Dr. Rice's testimony. Do you think that attempt succeeded? In the absence of any obvious damage to the executive branch as a result of the testimony, won't it be more difficult in the future to argue that it must never be allowed? In addressing these questions, consider the evolution of the office of National Security Adviser over time. As you'll recall from our description of the executive branch in Chapter One, the New Deal led to the creation of various confidential assistants to the President. These were originally intended to be anonymous, rather faceless functionaries. Maybe they never were: FDR's Harry Hopkins was ubiquitous, for example. At any rate, at least since the not notably self-effacing Henry Kissinger, National Security Advisers have usually been conspicuous public figures, contesting for power with cabinet secretaries and often prevailing. Should we then rethink the no-testimony tradition? If so, the Rice testimony will be an important precedent, notwithstanding the President's protestations to the contrary.

g. The Foreign Emoluments Clause

The Constitution aims to secure the President's independence by insulating the office from external financial inducements. First, the Constitution provides that "The President shall, at stated Times, receive for his services, a Compensation, which shall neither be increased nor diminished during the period for which he shall have been elected, and he shall not receive within that period any other emolument from the United States or any of them." U.S. Const. art. 2, § 2, cl. 7. Thus, Congress may not bring the President to heel by threatening a reduction in salary (a threat that would be largely hollow given the President's veto power) or by promising a raise. As Alexander Hamilton put it, "It is evident that without proper attention to this article, the separation of the executive from the legislative department would be nominal and nugatory. The legislature, with a discretionary power over the salary and emoluments of the Chief Magistrate, could render him as obsequious to their will as they might think proper to make him." The Federalist No. 73, at 492 (Clinton Rossiter, ed. 1961). Similarly, states, which have no power to alter the President's salary, may not seek to purchase influence through financial inducements. The framers harbored the same concern about improper influence by of foreign nations, and that concern was not limited to the office of the President but extended to all officers. In response, they adopted the Foreign Emoluments Clause, which provides "no person holding any office of profit or trust under [the United States] shall, without the consent of Congress, accept of any present, emolument, office, or title of any kind whatever from any king, prince, or foreign state." U.S. Const. art. 1, § 9, cl. 8. Because the Foreign Emoluments Clause expressly authorizes Congress to allow exceptions, it is an element of Congress's overall power to regulate accountability of the executive branch.

1. *Flawed Design?* Doesn't the Foreign Emoluments Clause create a serious loophole in the Domestic Emoluments Clause? Note that the Domestic Emoluments Clause is absolute; it forbids Congress to vary the President's compensation without exception or qualification. But couldn't Congress "render [the President] obsequious" by offering to allow the President to accept foreign emoluments?

2. *Application to the Trump Financial Empire.* President Donald Trump has holdings and business interests around the globe. These business interests inevitably receive payments from foreign governments, for example, when an official of a foreign government stays at a Trump hotel or when a foreign mission rents office space in the Trump Tower or one of his other properties. The President and his companies also receive valuable property rights and other accommodations from foreign governments. For example, the People's Republic of China granted trademark rights to President Trump after his inauguration. *See* Sui-Lee Wee, *Trump Adds More Trademarks in China*, N.Y. Times (June 13, 2017).

Several lawsuits have been brought against the President asserting that he has violated the Foreign Emoluments Clause. *See, e.g., CREW v. Trump*, No. 1:17-cv-00458-RA (S.D.N.Y. April 18, 2017). The plaintiffs assert that the Clause is violated whenever an officer receives any thing of value from a foreign government or an entity controlled by a foreign government. *See id.* First Amended Complaint at 11. In its motion to dismiss, the Department of Justice has argued that the Foreign Emoluments Clause only "prohibits benefits arising from the U.S. official's provision of service pursuant to an office or employment." *See id.* Motion to Dismiss at 27 (June 9, 2017).

Each of these interpretations is problematic. If CREW's interpretation is correct, then payments no one has ever thought to raise a Foreign Emoluments Clause issue are in fact unconstitutional. For example, President Barack Obama would have violated the Clause by receiving, while in office, royalty checks from his books, which include the proceeds from their sale to the National Library of Russia or to any other public library in a foreign nation. Moreover, any President who has held stock in a corporation that receives income from a foreign government has violated the Clause. If, on the other hand, the DOJ view is correct, the Foreign Emoluments Clause is rendered a dead letter. A foreign government need only funnel its emoluments through a private corporation in which the President has a financial stake.

The interpretation advocated for in DOJ's motion to dismiss is inconsistent with the Department's longstanding interpretation of the Foreign Emoluments Clause. The Office of Legal Counsel has consistently taken a functional view of the Clause that seeks to steer a middle course between the extreme interpretations that are dueling in the *CREW* lawsuit. OLC has specifically concluded that benefits that derive from foreign governments may be forbidden under the Clause even though they have no nexus to a person's federal role. *See, e.g., Applicability of the Emoluments Clause to Non-Government Members of ACUS*, 17 Op. O.L.C. 114, 119 (1993) (the Clause prohibited private lawyers serving on a federal advisory committee from drawing shares of their law firms' profits because those firms had foreign governmental clients, even though the officers "did not personally represent a foreign government, . . . had no personal contact with that client of the firm, [and] could not be said to be subject to the foreign government's 'control' in his or her activities on behalf of the partnership").

3. *Enforcement.* How is the Foreign Emoluments Clause to be enforced? As noted, several lawsuits are pending in which various plaintiffs seek a court order to enjoin the President from violating the Clause. The plaintiffs include a non-profit advocacy group concerned with government ethics (Committee for Responsibility and Ethics in Washington), businesses in the hospitality industry that claim to have lost the business of foreign governments to Trump-related companies, individuals employed in the hospitality industry, the State of Maryland and the District of Columbia (which own convention centers that may have lost business to Trump hotels), and members of Congress. Do you think any of these individuals have standing? In particular, are their injuries within the "zone of interests" that the Foreign Emoluments Clause is designed to protect? Is the proper remedy impeachment? Thinking back to the materials above on impeachment, do you believe that violations of the

Foreign Emoluments Clause represent "high crimes and misdemeanors"? Would it depend on the magnitude of the "emolument" or the nature of the conduct apparently induced by it?

2. Regulating the Judiciary

We have already encountered Congress's fundamental power to determine the structure and jurisdiction of the federal courts. Now we pause to look at an innovative means that Congress chose for regulating judicial behavior: the creation of an independent agency, partly composed of judges, to promulgate sentencing guidelines for federal criminal cases. After the *Mistretta* case, which follows, the Supreme Court held that the sentencing guidelines it considered could not bind federal judges, for reasons related to jury rights and not the separation of powers. Are there identifiable limits to the power of Congress to burden the everyday functioning of the federal courts?

<hr>

Mistretta v. United States

488 U.S. 361 (1989)

[In Chapter Two, we noted that the Court rejected a delegation doctrine challenge to this scheme. Justice BLACKMUN then turned to general separation of power analysis.]

. . . In adopting [our] flexible understanding of separation of powers, we simply have recognized Madison's teaching that the greatest security against tyranny—the accumulation of excessive authority in a single branch—lies not in a hermetic division between the Branches, but in a carefully crafted system of checked and balanced power within each Branch. . . . Accordingly, . . . the Framers "built into the tripartite Federal Government . . . a self-executing safeguard against the encroachment or aggrandizement of one branch at the expense of the other." . . . [W]e have upheld statutory provisions that to some degree commingle the functions of the Branches, but that pose no danger of either aggrandizement or encroachment. In *Nixon v. Administrator of General Services,* . . . we described our separation-of-powers inquiry as focusing "on the extent to which [a provision of law] prevents the Executive Branch from accomplishing its constitutionally assigned functions." In cases specifically involving the Judicial Branch, we have expressed our vigilance against two dangers: first, that the Judicial Branch neither be assigned nor allowed "tasks that are more appropriately accomplished by [other] branches," and, second, that no provision of law "impermissibly threatens the institutional integrity of the Judicial Branch." *Commodity Futures Trading Comm'n v. Schor.*

Mistretta argues that the Act suffers from each of these constitutional infirmities. He argues that Congress, in constituting the Commission as it did, effected an unconstitutional accumulation of power within the Judicial Branch while at the same time undermining the Judiciary's independence and integrity. Specifically, petitioner claims that in delegating to an independent agency within the Judicial Branch the power to promulgate sentencing guidelines, Congress unconstitutionally has required the Branch, and individual Article III judges, to exercise not only their judicial authority, but legislative authority—the making of sentencing policy—as well. Such rulemaking authority, petitioner contends, may be exercised by Congress, or delegated by Congress to the Executive, but may not be delegated to or exercised by the Judiciary. At the same time, petitioner asserts, Congress unconstitutionally eroded the integrity and independence of the Judiciary by requiring Article III judges to sit on the Commission, by requiring that those judges share their rulemaking authority with nonjudges, and by subjecting the Commission's members to appointment and removal by the President. . . .

Although the unique composition and responsibilities of the Sentencing Commission give rise to serious concerns about a disruption of the appropriate balance of governmental power among the coordinate Branches, we [uphold] . . . Congress' considered scheme for resolving the seemingly intractable dilemma of excessive disparity in criminal sentencing.

The Sentencing Commission unquestionably is a peculiar institution within the framework of our Government. Although placed by the Act in the Judicial Branch, it is not a court and does not exercise judicial power. Rather, the Commission is an "independent" body comprised of seven voting members including at least three federal judges, entrusted by Congress with the primary task of promulgating sentencing guidelines. . . . Congress' decision to create an independent rulemaking body to promulgate sentencing guidelines and to locate that body within the Judicial Branch is not unconstitutional unless Congress has vested in the Commission powers that are more appropriately performed by the other Branches or that undermine the integrity of the Judiciary.

According to express provision of Article III, the judicial power of the United States is limited to "Cases" and "Controversies." . . . As a general principle, we [have] stated . . . that "'executive or administrative duties of a nonjudicial nature may not be imposed on judges holding office under Article III of the Constitution.'" Nonetheless, we have recognized significant exceptions to this general rule and have approved the assumption of some nonadjudicatory activities by the Judicial Branch. . . .

None of our cases indicate that rulemaking per se is a function that may not be performed by an entity within the Judicial Branch, either because rulemaking is inherently nonjudicial or because it is a function exclusively committed to the Executive Branch. On the contrary, . . . [i]n *Sibbach v. Wilson & Co.*, 312 U.S. 1 (1941), we upheld . . . the Rules Enabling Act of 1934 which conferred upon the Judiciary the power to promulgate federal rules of civil procedure. . . . [That reflected a view held since] *Wayman v. Southard*, 23 U.S. (10 Wheat.) 1 (1825), decided more than a century earlier, where Chief Justice Marshall wrote for the Court that rulemaking power pertaining to the Judicial Branch may be "conferred on the judicial department." . . . Pursuant to this power to delegate rulemaking authority to the Judicial Branch, Congress expressly has authorized this Court to establish rules for the conduct of its own business and to prescribe rules of procedure for lower federal courts in bankruptcy cases, in other civil cases, and in criminal cases, and to revise the federal rules of evidence. . . .

[W]e can discern no separation-of-powers impediment to the placement of the Sentencing Commission within the Judicial Branch. As we described at the outset, the sentencing function long has been a peculiarly shared responsibility among the Branches of government and has never been thought of as the exclusive constitutional province of any one Branch. . . . Indeed, the legislative history of the Act makes clear that Congress' decision to place the Commission within the Judicial Branch reflected Congress' "strong feeling" that sentencing has been and should remain "primarily a judicial function." That Congress should vest such rulemaking in the Judicial Branch, far from being "incongruous" or vesting within the Judiciary responsibilities that more appropriately belong to another Branch, simply acknowledges the role that the Judiciary always has played, and continues to play, in sentencing. Indeed, had Congress decided to confer responsibility for promulgating sentencing guidelines on the Executive Branch, we might face the constitutional questions whether Congress unconstitutionally had assigned judicial responsibilities to the executive or unconstitutionally had united the power to prosecute and the power to sentence within one Branch. . . .

Given the consistent responsibility of federal judges to pronounce sentence within the statutory range established by Congress, we find that the role of the Commission in promulgating guidelines for the exercise of that judicial function bears considerable similarity to the role of this Court in establishing rules of procedure under the various enabling acts. . . . Petitioner nonetheless objects that the analogy between the Guidelines and the rules of procedure is flawed: Although the Judicial Branch may participate in rulemaking and administrative work that is "procedural" in nature, it may not assume, it is said, the "substantive" authority over sentencing policy that Congress has delegated to the Commission. Such substantive decisionmaking, petitioner contends, entangles the Judicial Branch in essentially political work of the other Branches and unites both judicial and legislative power in the Judicial Branch. . . .

Although we are loathe to enter the logical morass of distinguishing between substantive and procedural rules, . . . we recognize that the task of promulgating rules regulating practice and pleading before federal courts does not involve the degree of political judgment integral to the Commission's formulation of sentencing guidelines. . . . We do not believe, however, that the significantly political nature of the Commission's work renders unconstitutional its placement within the Judicial Branch. . . . In this case, the "practical consequences" of locating the Commission within the Judicial Branch pose no threat of undermining the integrity of the Judicial Branch or of expanding the powers of the Judiciary beyond constitutional bounds by uniting within the Branch the political or quasi-legislative power of the Commission with the judicial power of the courts.

First, although the Commission is located in the Judicial Branch, its powers are not united with the powers of the Judiciary in a way that has meaning for separation-of-powers analysis. Whatever constitutional problems might arise if the powers of the Commission were vested in a court, the Commission is not a court, does not exercise judicial power, and is not controlled by or accountable to members of the Judicial Branch. The Commission, on which members of the Judiciary may be a minority, is an independent agency in every relevant sense.... In contrast to a court, the Commission's members are subject to the President's limited powers of removal.... [B]ecause Congress vested the power to promulgate sentencing guidelines in an independent agency, not a court, there can be no serious argument that Congress combined legislative and judicial power within the Judicial Branch.

Second, although the Commission wields rulemaking power and not the adjudicatory power exercised by individual judges when passing sentence, the placement of the Sentencing Commission in the Judicial Branch has not increased the Branch's authority. Prior to the passage of the Act, the Judicial Branch, as an aggregate, decided precisely the questions assigned to the Commission: what sentence is appropriate to what criminal conduct under what circumstances. It was the everyday business of judges, taken collectively, to evaluate and weigh the various aims of sentencing and to apply those aims to the individual cases that came before them. The Sentencing Commission does no more than this, albeit basically through the methodology of sentencing guidelines, rather than entirely individualized sentencing determinations. Accordingly, in placing the Commission in the Judicial Branch, Congress cannot be said to have aggrandized the authority of that Branch or to have deprived the Executive Branch of a power it once possessed. Indeed, because the Guidelines have the effect of promoting sentencing within a narrower range than was previously applied, the power of the Judicial Branch is, if anything, somewhat diminished by the Act.... Thus, ... this authorization does nothing to upset the balance of power among the Branches. ...

We now turn to petitioner's claim that Congress' decision to require at least three federal judges to serve on the Commission and to require those judges to share their authority with nonjudges undermines the integrity of the Judicial Branch.... Petitioner urges us to strike down the Act on the ground that its requirement of judicial participation on the Commission unconstitutionally conscripts individual federal judges for political service and thereby undermines the essential impartiality of the Judicial Branch. We find Congress' requirement of judicial service somewhat troublesome, but we do not believe that the Act impermissibly interferes with the functioning of the Judiciary.

The text of the Constitution contains no prohibition against the service of active federal judges on independent commissions such as that established by the Act. The Constitution does include an Incompatibility Clause applicable to national legislators.... No comparable restriction applies to judges, and we find it at least inferentially meaningful that at the Constitutional Convention two prohibitions against plural officeholding by members of the judiciary were proposed, but did not reach the floor of the Convention for a vote.

Our inferential reading that the Constitution does not prohibit Article III judges from undertaking extrajudicial duties finds support in the historical practice of the Founders after ratification. Our early history indicates that the Framers themselves did not read the Constitution as forbidding extrajudicial service by federal judges. The first Chief Justice, John Jay, served simultaneously as Chief Justice and as Ambassador to England, where he negotiated the treaty that bears his name. Oliver Ellsworth served simultaneously as Chief Justice and as Minister to France. While he was Chief Justice, John Marshall served briefly as Secretary of State and was a member of the Sinking Fund Commission with responsibility for refunding the Revolutionary War debt.

All these appointments were made by the President with the "Advice and Consent" of the Senate. Thus, at a minimum, both the Executive and Legislative Branches acquiesced in the assumption of extrajudicial duties by judges. In addition, although the records of Congress contain no reference to the confirmation debate, Charles Warren, in his history of this Court, reports that the Senate specifically rejected by a vote of 18–8 a resolution proposed during the debate over Jay's nomination to the effect that such extrajudicial service was "contrary to the spirit of the Constitution." 1 C. Warren, The Supreme Court in United States History 119 (rev. ed. 1926). This contemporaneous practice by the Founders themselves is significant evidence that the constitutional principle of separation of powers does not absolutely prohibit extrajudicial service.

Subsequent history, moreover, reveals a frequent and continuing, albeit controversial, practice of extrajudicial service. In 1877, five Justices served on the Election Commission that resolved the hotly contested Presidential election of 1876, where Samuel J. Tilden and Rutherford B. Hayes were the contenders. Justices Nelson, Fuller, Brewer, Hughes, Day, Roberts, and Van Devanter served on various arbitral commissions. Justice Roberts was a member of the commission organized to investigate the attack on Pearl Harbor. Justice Jackson was one of the prosecutors at the Nuremberg trials; and Chief Justice Warren presided over the commission investigating the assassination of President Kennedy. Such service has been no less a practice among lower court federal judges. While these extrajudicial activities spawned spirited discussion and frequent criticism, and although some of the judges who undertook these duties sometimes did so with reservation and may have looked back on their service with regret, "traditional ways of conducting government . . . give meaning" to the Constitution. *Youngstown Sheet & Tube Co. v. Sawyer* (concurring opinion) . . . .

In light of the foregoing history and precedent, we conclude that the principle of separation of powers does not absolutely prohibit Article III judges from serving on commissions such as that created by the Act. The judges serve on the Sentencing Commission not pursuant to their status and authority as Article III judges, but solely because of their appointment by the President as the Act directs. Such power as these judges wield as Commissioners is not judicial power; it is administrative power derived from the enabling legislation. Just as the nonjudicial members of the Commission act as administrators, bringing their experience and wisdom to bear on the problems of sentencing disparity, so too the judges, uniquely qualified on the subject of sentencing, assume a wholly administrative role upon entering into the deliberations of the Commission. In other words, the Constitution, at least as a per se matter, does not forbid judges from wearing two hats; it merely forbids them from wearing both hats at the same time. . . .

Finally, we reject petitioner's argument that the mixed nature of the Commission violates the Constitution by requiring Article III judges to share judicial power with nonjudges. As noted earlier, the Commission is not a court and exercises no judicial power. Thus, the Act does not vest Article III power in nonjudges or require Article III judges to share their power with nonjudges.

The Act empowers the President to appoint all seven members of the Commission with the advice and consent of the Senate. . . . The Act also grants the President authority to remove members of the Commission, although "only for neglect of duty or malfeasance in office or for other good cause shown." . . . [W]e do not believe that the President's appointment and removal powers over the Commission afford him influence over the functions of the Judicial Branch or undue sway over its members. . . .

We conclude that in creating the Sentencing Commission—an unusual hybrid in structure and authority—Congress neither delegated excessive legislative power nor upset the constitutionally mandated balance of powers among the coordinate Branches. . . . Accordingly, we hold that the Act is constitutional. . . .

Justice SCALIA, dissenting.

. . . Henceforth there may be agencies "within the Judicial Branch" (whatever that means), exercising governmental powers, that are neither courts nor controlled by courts, nor even controlled by judges. If an "independent agency" such as this can be given the power to fix sentences previously exercised by district courts, I must assume that a similar agency can be given the powers to adopt Rules of Procedure and Rules of Evidence previously exercised by this Court. The bases for distinction would be thin indeed . . . . [I]t seems to me far from a marginal question whether our constitutional structure allows for a body which is not the Congress, and yet exercises no governmental powers except the making of rules that have the effect of laws. . . . [I]n the long run the improvisation of a constitutional structure on the basis of currently perceived utility will be disastrous. . . .

––––––––––

1. *A Balancing Act.* In *Mistretta*, the majority perceived no statutory alteration of the preexisting balance of power among the branches. It also saw a positive value for the Commission's independence from the branch it served. When we examine the

constitutional status of the independent regulatory agencies in the next chapter, consider the pertinence to that question of this aspect of *Mistretta*. For commentary, see Mark Tushnet, *The Sentencing Commission and Constitutional Theory: Bowls and Plateaus in Separation of Powers Theory*, 66 S. Cal. L. Rev. 581 (1992); Stephen L. Carter, *Constitutional Improprieties: Reflections on* Mistretta, Morrison, *and Administrative Government*, 57 U. Chi. L. Rev. 357 (1990).

2. *One Robe, Two Hats.* Consider the Court's history of extrajudicial performance by judges. Has the practice redounded to the credit of the judiciary? If not, perhaps the Constitution should have an incompatibility clause for judges too. Failing that, where should the Supreme Court draw the line?

3. Congressional Self-Regulation

For several reasons, Members of Congress often are accountable only to each other and to the electorate. As we have seen, they possess a constitutional privilege surrounding their "legislative acts"; they are exempt from the impeachment process that can remove officers of the other two branches; they can except themselves from the application of laws of general applicability. We review here the methods Congress has evolved for disciplining its members, and for subjecting itself to the legal strictures that bind ordinary citizens.

Under Article I, section 5 of the Constitution, Congress has the responsibility to judge and punish the misconduct of its Members. Ethics committees in both houses receive complaints, investigate the facts, and recommend sanctions ranging from reprimands to expulsion. Review the historical discussion of expulsions in *Powell v. McCormack, supra*. Clearly, Members need have little fear of expulsion (at least if they refrain from joining the Confederacy). Nor have the lesser sanctions been imposed frequently. If self-enforcement has meant underenforcement of ethical norms in Congress, lawyers should not be surprised when they consider the record of their own efforts at self-regulation.

Nixon v. United States, supra, holding nonjusticiable a challenge to Senate Rule XI on impeachment procedures, suggests that congressional disciplinary procedures are not subject to judicial review. Hence Congress is probably free to structure its standards and processes for self-regulation largely as it thinks best, as long as it retains the final decision to sanction a Member. What Congress *should* responsibly do within its zone of exclusive power is, of course, another matter. Any system for self-regulation incorporates values of collegial empathy and professional solidarity that present both benefits and costs. The advantages lie in an assurance that those who judge will possess a full understanding of the fact and policy issues involved in particular cases. The disadvantages lie in assuming the disagreeable task of judging one's peers and in restricting the amount of public confidence that the process can generate.

Self-discipline in bodies as small as the houses of Congress, and especially the Senate, can create outright conflicts of interest. The present or future support of fellow Members is needed for a myriad of bills and other matters. It is hard for anyone to lay these daily concerns to one side when judging a colleague. The affections or animosities of party politics only increase the strains. In addition, special functional conflicts result from the historic role of members of the ethics committees as both investigators and judges of their colleagues.

Congressional self-regulation presents the dilemma that an acquittal or lenient sentence seems a whitewash and automatically erodes public confidence in the process, while a severe sentence seems harsh or partisan. The rarity of the actual imposition of sanctions by Congress suggests to some observers that the process is toothless. This conclusion may not take account, however, of the special role of disclosure as a sanction in electoral politics. If the disciplinary process can reliably expose questionable conduct, the importance of having sanctions imposed by Congress diminishes as the public assumes the ultimate role of judging its servants.

The recent upsurge of interest in reforming Congress generally has produced a blizzard of proposals that the ethics committees be reformed. For a summary and analysis by a respected former Representative, see LEE H. HAMILTON, STRENGTHENING CONGRESS, ch. 6 (2009). A major scandal involving relations between lobbyist Jack Abramoff and Members and staff of Congress resulted in the Honest Leadership and Open Government Act of 2007, Pub. L. No. 110-81, 121 Stat. 735 (2007). The Act is primarily aimed at tightening lobbyist activities and contacts with legislators, including limiting campaign contributions and gifts from lobbyists to Members. Also in response, the House created the Office of Congressional Ethics with H.R. Res. 895, 110th Cong. (2008). (The Senate did not take similar action, although the Senate Select Committee on Ethics published several new rules following the passage of the Act.) An eight person Board of Directors who are nominated by the Speaker and the Minority Leader controls the OCE. It is composed of private citizens who cannot be Members of Congress or federal employees. Hence the process of ethics review now involves non-lawmakers for the first time, although the Office has no power to take formal action. According to its website (http://oce.house.gov/about.shtml):

> The OCE's investigations have two stages: (1) a preliminary review, which is completed in 30 days and (2) a second-phase review which is completed in 45 days, with the possibility of a 14 day extension. The Board must authorize each preliminary and second-phase review. At the end of any second phase review, the Board must recommend to the Ethics Committee either that the matter requires the Committee's further review or that it should dismiss the matter. When it makes its recommendation, the OCE Board may also transmit to the Ethics Committee a report that includes, among other things, findings of fact and citations to laws, rules or regulations that may have been violated.

The Office began meeting in early 2009 and immediately launched inquiries into the activities of 10 Representatives. The Office does not disclose the names of persons it investigates, and has no power to compel cooperation with investigations. The Office cannot initiate a formal complaint but can recommend a formal investigation to the House Ethics Committee. However, as of early 2010, no Member of Congress has been punished under the new ethics regime, despite a variety of scandals over the past several years. There were, though, a few reprimands to Members following the Abramoff scandal.

A separate means for policing Congress is criminal enforcement by executive branch or independent prosecutors. Again, recall from *Powell v. McCormack* that Congressmen are generally subject to the criminal law for activities outside of the Speech or Debate privilege. Traditionally, the Justice Department has handled these prosecutions, although as we saw with the House bank scandal, independent counsel has sometimes been used. Which method do you favor?

For many years, when Congress enacted major legislation regulating private conduct, for example statutes promoting health and safety or civil rights, it exempted itself from the law's coverage. This practice became sharply controversial. *See Application of Laws and Administration of the Hill, Hearings Before the Joint Committee on the Organization of Congress*, 103d Cong., 1st Sess. (1993). Initially, while technically exempting itself from various statutes, Congress created "shadow regulation" for itself by internal rule. This practice had the advantage of allowing Congress to tailor enforcement processes to its special institutional nature, while subjecting itself to the same substantive norms that govern us all.

At the outset of the 104th Congress, with passage of the Congressional Accountability Act (CAA), Pub. L. No. 104-1, 109 Stat. 3, 2 U.S.C. §§ 1301–1438, Congress took steps to subject itself more directly to federal regulatory statutes. *See* Charles Grassley with Jennifer Shaw Schmidt, *Practicing What We Preach: A Legislative History of Congressional Accountability*, 35 Harv. J. Legis. 33 (1998); Harold H. Bruff, *That the Laws Shall Bind Equally on All: Congressional and Executive Roles in Applying Laws to Congress*, 48 Ark. L. Rev. 105 (1995); Christina L. Deneka, *Congressional Anti-Accountability and the Separation of Powers: A Survey of the Congressional Accountability Act's Problems*, 52 Rutgers L. Rev. 855 (2000). The Act applies to the employees of the House and Senate and to such immediate support organizations as the Capitol Police and the Congressional Budget Office. For the most part, it excepts the Library of Congress, the Government Accountability Office, and the Government Printing Office, which were already partially covered by law. As a result, the Act regulates the core of the legislative branch, and excludes some of the outlying functions for which there is relatively little justification for legislative branch enforcement techniques.

The CAA directly applies the core substantive provisions of eleven federal statutes to Congress. The most important of these are: The Fair Labor Standards Act, Title VII of the Civil Rights Act, the Americans With Disabilities Act, the Age Discrimination Act, the Family and Medical Leave Act, the Rehabilitation Act, the Occupational Safety and Health Act, and the statutes defining labor-management relations in the federal service. Thus, Congress has invoked the statutes that govern terms of employment, protections from discrimination, and guarantees of employee health and safety.

The CAA is administered by an Office of Compliance within the legislative branch, headed by a Board of Directors who are congressional appointees. There is a complex scheme for the Board's adoption of substantive regulations, which is obviously designed to allay constitutional concerns. First, most of the provisions that apply particular federal statutes to congressional employees contain a requirement that the Board's regulations "shall be the same as" those promulgated by the executive branch official who usually administers the statute, "except insofar as the Board may determine, for good cause shown . . . that a modification . . . would be more effective for the implementation of the rights and protections under this section." Second, after the Board adopts regulations, they are approved by any of three methods: simple resolution of the house to which they apply, concurrent resolution of both houses, or joint resolution. The Board's recommendation to Congress regarding which method to apply will doubtless depend on whether there is enough variance from the text of the statute and the regulations of the executive to support an argument that new law is being made, so that presentation to the President is required under *Chadha*.

The CAA also contains a process for complaints and hearings. The Office appoints hearing officers to hold adjudications. On appeal, the Board reviews the records of the hearings. Judicial review follows in the Federal Circuit, under a normal administrative law "substantial evidence" standard. (In civil rights cases, an employee can elect an action in district court instead of the Board's adjudicatory process.) The Act authorizes judicial review of the Board's regulations under the Administrative Procedure Act's normal criteria. (Regulations that have been adopted by joint resolution are, however, only to be reviewed for constitutionality, since they are the equivalent of statutes.)

Is this scheme safe from constitutional invalidation? The Act applies norms to Congress by statute rather than by rules of the houses, as earlier proposals had provided. Still, the Act authorizes congressional employees to promulgate regulations to implement the statutes. Under *Buckley v. Valeo, infra* Chapter Four, this might constitute execution of the law that must be performed by executive branch officers. Several considerations suggest, however, that *Buckley* should not invalidate the Act. First, the Act stays sufficiently near the core support functions of Congress for the regulations to derive some support from the constitutional rulemaking power of Congress. In contrast, *Buckley* involved regulation of many persons having no current affiliation with Congress. Second, the Act requires the regulations to conform to the executive branch's substantive regulations unless there is good reason to vary them. Hence, executive enforcement policy will have at least indirect influence within Congress, and will often have binding force.

Surely it is appropriate for the Act to contain a mechanism for adapting executive regulations to the special institutional nature of Congress. When there is a need for substantial addition to statutory text or substantial variation from an executive branch regulation, Congress can adopt a joint resolution that is the equivalent of a new statute. Otherwise, the congressional regulations can have the ambiguous legal effect of interpretive regulations of the executive branch. These regulations lack the force of law, but courts defer to any persuasive effect that they possess. *See generally* ADMINISTRATIVE CONFERENCE OF THE UNITED STATES, A GUIDE TO FEDERAL AGENCY RULEMAKING 52–69 (2d ed. 1991). The fact that they will be administered by congressional rather than executive officers should be adequately justified by the reluctance of Congress to subject its personnel to the enforcement efforts of a rival branch of government. The Office also adopts procedural rules and investigates and adjudicates complaints. The process for considering alleged violations of law is to include informal stages such as mediation, followed by hearings before independent boards composed of neutrals who are recommended by professional organizations. The boards have subpoena power and hold hearings on the record. They can order compensation to be paid from funds to be set aside by each house. Their decisions are subject to review within the Office, after which any aggrieved employee may seek judicial review. That review, in the Court of Appeals for the Federal Circuit, may set aside decisions for errors of fact, law, or procedure.

The CAA's complex scheme, resembling executive branch statutory administration but not employing it, has proved difficult to administer. *See* James J. Brudney, *Congressional Accountability and Denial: Speech or Debate Clause and Conflict of Interest Challenges to Unionization of Congressional Employees*, 36 HARV. J. LEGIS. 1 (1999); James T. O'Reilly, *Collision in the Congress: Congressional Accountability, Workplace Conflict, and the Separation of Powers*, 5 GEO. MASON L. REV. 1 (1996). The office of Compliance maintains a website with reports of its activities and progress: http://www.compliance.gov.

Extending the premise of the CAA, Congress enacted an Executive Branch Accountability Act, 3 U.S.C. §401 note, applying labor laws to the executive, and has considered doing so for the judiciary. *See* JUDICIAL CONFERENCE OF THE UNITED STATES, STUDY OF JUDICIAL BRANCH COVERAGE PURSUANT TO THE CONGRESSIONAL ACCOUNTABILITY ACT OF 1995 (1996). Are there concerns surrounding such legislation that do not apply to congressional self-regulation?

A different kind of congressional self-regulation consists of the adoption of rules for processing legislation. The Senate has long honored the "filibuster," by which one senator may indefinitely extend debate, effectively killing a bill, unless a three-fifths supermajority invokes cloture. The Senate also requires a three-fifths majority to exceed budget spending limits; the House requires a two-thirds vote to suspend its rules. At the outset of the 104th Congress, the House adopted a new rule requiring a three-fifths majority to pass legislation increasing federal income tax rates.

Are these provisions constitutional? The problem is one of reconciling two portions of Article I, section 5 of the Constitution: each house of Congress may "determine the Rules of its Proceedings," and "a Majority of each shall constitute a Quorum to do Business." Since Article I, §7 explicitly requires a supermajority to override a Presidential veto, and since other supermajority provisions appear (e.g., for expulsion of congressmen, proposal of constitutional amendments, or ratification of treaties by the Senate), is there a persuasive implication that Congress may not add other supermajority requirements? Does the fact that the framers decided not to impose a constitutional requirement of more than a simple majority for ordinary legislation mean that Congress may never do so by rule? *See generally* John O. McGinnis & Michael B. Rappaport, *Supermajority Rules as a Constitutional Solution*, 40 Wm. & Mary L. Rev. 365 (1999). If these rules, or some of them, are unconstitutional, is there any way to litigate the issues? *See Michel v. Anderson*, 14 F.3d 623 (D.C. Cir. 1994), which reached the merits of a challenge to a House rule allowing territorial delegates to vote in Committee of the Whole, and upheld the rule.

The use of the filibuster in the Senate has evolved over the years. The story, alas, is one of escalating noncooperation between the two major parties. See Thomas E. Mann & Norman J. Ornstein, The Broken Branch 80–82 (2006). By the late twentieth century, the Senate, like the House, had experienced a shift of power from centrists toward the ideological poles. With partisan strife increasing, use of the filibuster accelerated. It had once been reserved for occasional use against especially controversial legislation. The unsuccessful filibuster of the Civil Rights Act of 1964 is the classic example. By the time of the Clinton administration, half of all major legislation was being subjected to filibuster. By the outset of the Obama administration, it was generally understood that all major legislation needed 60 votes in the Senate, the number needed to invoke cloture and end a filibuster. Does the practical existence of a routine supermajority rule in the Senate affect your view of the constitutional issue? Consider this question when we return to the filibuster in the next chapter in the context of judicial nominations, where it has been especially prominent and controversial.

Chapter 4

Control of Administration by the Elected Branches

Congress and the executive constantly battle for control of our "administrative state." In this chapter we explore the various constitutional and other means they employ in the contest. We begin with control of personnel through powers of appointment and removal, a topic that introduces the special status of the independent agencies. A section on prosecution independent of executive control shows the stakes over independence at their highest. We then examine the role of both branches in supervising policymaking in the agencies. Finally, we outline the residuum of executive discretion in domestic affairs, once Congress's powers are subtracted.

A. Personnel

1. The Appointments Clause

Buckley v. Valeo
424 U.S. 1 (1976)

[In a long per curiam opinion, the Court decided a series of constitutional challenges to the Federal Election Campaign Act of 1971, which was a comprehensive attempt to reform the processes of electing federal officials by limiting political contributions and expenditures, establishing public funding for campaigns, and requiring financial recordkeeping and disclosures by candidates and political committees. After considering these features of the Act, the Court turned to the constitutionality of the structure and operation of the Federal Election Commission, which was created by Congress to administer the Act:]

IV. The Federal Election Commission

The 1974 amendments to the Act create an eight-member Federal Election Commission, and vest in it primary and substantial responsibility for administering and enforcing the Act. The question . . . is whether, in view of the manner in which a majority of its members are appointed, the Commission may under the Constitution exercise the powers conferred upon it. . . . Beyond . . . recordkeeping, disclosure, and investigative functions, . . . the Commission is given extensive rulemaking and adjudicative powers. . . . [It may] "formulate general policy with respect to the administration of this Act" and enumerated sections of Title 18's Criminal Code, as to all of which provisions the Commission "has primary jurisdiction with respect to [their] civil enforcement." The Commission is authorized . . . to render advisory opinions with respect to activities possibly violating the Act, the Title 18 sections, or the campaign funding provisions of Title 26; [those relying on advisory opinions are] "presumed to be in compliance with the [statutory provision] with respect to which such advisory opinion is rendered." . . .

The Commission's enforcement power is both direct and wide ranging. It may institute a civil action for [declaratory or injunctive relief to enforce the campaign laws.] . . . In no respect do the foregoing civil actions require the concurrence of or participation by the Attorney General; conversely, the decision not to seek judicial relief in the above respects would appear to rest solely with the Commission. . . . Finally, . . . the Commission, after notice and opportunity for hearing, [may] make "a finding that a person . . . failed to file" a required report of contributions or expenditures. [The candidate is thereby disqualified from seeking federal office for a year.] . . .

The body in which this authority is reposed consists of eight members. The Secretary of the Senate and the Clerk of the House of Representatives are ex officio members of the Commission without the right to vote. Two members are appointed by the President pro tempore of the Senate "upon the recommendations of the majority leader of the Senate and the minority leader of the Senate." Two more are to be appointed by the Speaker of the House of Representatives, likewise upon the recommendations of its respective majority and minority leaders. The remaining two members are appointed by the President. Each of the six voting members of the Commission must be confirmed by the majority of both Houses of Congress, and each of the three appointing authorities is forbidden to choose both of their appointees from the same political party. . . .

B. The Merits

Appellants urge that since Congress has given the Commission wide-ranging rule-making and enforcement powers with respect to the substantive provisions of the Act, Congress is precluded under the principle of separation of powers from vesting in itself the authority to appoint those who will exercise such authority. Their argument is based on the language of Art. II, § 2, cl. 2, of the Constitution. . . . Appellants' argument is that this provision is the exclusive method by which those charged with executing the laws of the United States may be chosen. . . .

Appellee Commission . . . urge[s] that the Framers of the Constitution, while mindful of the need for checks and balances among the three branches of the National Government, had no intention of denying to the Legislative Branch authority to appoint its own officers. Congress, either under the Appointments Clause or under its grants of substantive legislative authority and the Necessary and Proper Clause in Art. I, is in their view empowered to provide for the appointment to the Commission in the manner which it did because the Commission is performing "appropriate legislative functions." . . .

1. Separation of Powers

. . . Our inquiry of necessity touches upon the fundamental principles of the Government established by the Framers of the Constitution, and all litigants . . . start on common ground in the recognition of the intent of the Framers that the powers of the three great branches of the National Government be largely separate from one another. James Madison, writing in the Federalist No. 47, defended the work of the Framers against the charge that these three governmental powers were not *entirely* separate from one another in the proposed Constitution. He asserted that while there was some admixture, the Constitution was nonetheless true to Montesquieu's well-known maxim that the legislative, executive, and judicial departments ought to be separate and distinct. . . .

Yet it is also clear from the provisions of the Constitution itself, and from the Federalist Papers, that the Constitution by no means contemplates total separation of each of these three essential branches of Government. The President is a participant in the law-making process by virtue of his authority to veto bills enacted by Congress. The Senate is a participant in the appointive process by virtue of its authority to refuse to confirm persons nominated to office by the President. The men who met in Philadelphia in the summer of 1787 were practical statesmen, experienced in politics, who viewed the principle of separation of powers as a vital check against tyranny. But they likewise saw that a hermetic sealing off of the three branches of Government from one another would preclude the establishment of a Nation capable of governing itself effectively. . . . The Framers regarded the checks and balances that they had built into the tripartite Federal Government as a self-executing safeguard against the encroachment or aggrandizement of one branch at the expense of the other. . . . [Similar] to the facts of the present case is this Court's decision in *Springer v. Philippine Islands*, 277 U.S. 189 (1928), where the Court held that the legislature of the Philippine Islands could not provide for legislative appointment to executive agencies.

2. The Appointments Clause

The principle of separation of powers was not simply an abstract generalization in the minds of the Framers: it was woven into the document that they drafted in Philadelphia in the summer of 1787. [The Court quoted the "vesting" provisions of Articles I–III.] . . . The further concern of the Framers of the Constitution with maintenance of the separation of powers is found in the so-called "Ineligibility" and "Incompatibility" Clauses contained in Art. I, § 6. . . . It is in the context of these cognate provisions of the document that we must examine the language of Art. II, § 2, cl. 2, which appellants contend provides the only authorization for appointment of those to whom substantial executive or administrative authority is given by statute. . . . The Appointments Clause could, of course, be read as merely dealing with etiquette or protocol in describing "Officers of the United States," but the drafters had a less frivolous purpose in mind . . . .

We think that the term "Officers of the United States" as used in Art. II, defined to include "all persons who can be said to hold an office under the government" in

[*United States v. Germaine*, 99 U.S. 508 (1879)] is a term intended to have substantive meaning. We think its fair import is that any appointee exercising significant authority pursuant to the laws of the United States is an "Officer of the United States," and must, therefore, be appointed in the manner prescribed by § 2, cl. 2, of that Article. . . . If a postmaster first class, *Myers v. United States*, 272 U.S. 52 (1926), and the clerk of a district court, *Ex parte Hennen*, 38 U.S. 225, 13 Pet. 230 (1839), are inferior officers of the United States within the meaning of the Appointments Clause, as they are, surely the Commissioners before us are at the very least such "inferior Officers" within the meaning of that Clause.

Although two members of the Commission are initially selected by the President, his nominations are subject to confirmation not merely by the Senate, but by the House of Representatives as well. The remaining four voting members of the Commission are appointed by the President pro tempore of the Senate and by the Speaker of the House. While the second part of the Clause authorizes Congress to vest the appointment of the officers described in that part in "the Courts of Law, or in the Heads of Departments," neither the Speaker of the House nor the President pro tempore of the Senate comes within this language. The phrase "Heads of Departments," used as it is in conjunction with the phrase "Courts of Law," suggests that the Departments referred to are themselves in the Executive Branch or at least have some connection with that branch. While the Clause expressly authorizes Congress to vest the appointment of certain officers in the "Courts of Law," the absence of similar language to include Congress must mean that neither Congress nor its officers were included within the language "Heads of Departments" in this part of cl. 2.

Thus with respect to four of the six voting members of the Commission, neither the President, the head of any department, nor the Judiciary has any voice in their selection. . . . [The] Commission has argued, . . . that the Appointments Clause of Art. II should not be read to exclude the "inherent power of Congress" to appoint its own officers to perform functions necessary to that body as an institution. But there is no need to read the Appointments Clause contrary to its plain language in order to reach [that] result. . . . Ranking nonmembers, such as the Clerk of the House of Representatives, are elected under the internal rules of each House and are designated by statute as "officers of the Congress." [N]othing in our holding with respect to Art. II, § 2, cl. 2, will deny to Congress "all power to appoint its own inferior officers to carry out appropriate legislative functions." . . .

[T]he debates of the Constitutional Convention, and the Federalist Papers, are replete with expressions of fear that the Legislative Branch of the National Government will aggrandize itself at the expense of the other two branches. The debates during the Convention, and the evolution of the draft version of the Constitution, seem to us to lend considerable support to our reading of the language of the Appointments Clause itself. An interim version of the draft Constitution had vested in the Senate the authority to appoint Ambassadors, public Ministers, and Judges of the Supreme Court, and the language of Art. II as finally adopted is a distinct change in this regard. We believe that it was a deliberate change made by the Framers with the intent to deny Congress any authority itself to appoint those who were "Officers of the United States." The debates on the floor of the Convention reflect at least in part the way the change came about.

On Monday, August 6, 1787, the Committee on Detail to which had been referred the entire draft of the Constitution reported its draft to the Convention, including the following two articles that bear on the question before us:

> Article IX, § 1: "The Senate of the United States shall have power . . . to appoint Ambassadors, and Judges of the Supreme Court."

> Article X, § 2: "[The President] shall commission all the officers of the United States; and shall appoint officers in all cases not otherwise provided for by this Constitution."

It will be seen from a comparison of these two articles that the appointment of Ambassadors and Judges of the Supreme Court was confided to the Senate, and that the authority to appoint—not merely nominate, but to actually appoint—all other officers was reposed in the President. . . .

[O]n Friday, August 31, a motion had been carried without opposition to refer such parts of the Constitution as had been postponed or not acted upon to a Committee of Eleven. Such reference carried with it both Arts. IX and X. The following week the Committee of Eleven made its report to the Convention, in which the present language of Art. II, § 2, cl. 2, dealing with the authority of the President to nominate is found, virtually word for word, as § 4 of Art. X. The same Committee also reported a revised article concerning the Legislative Branch to the Convention. The changes are obvious. In the final version, the Senate is shorn of its power to appoint Ambassadors and Judges of the Supreme Court. The President is given, not the power to *appoint* public officers of the United States, but only the right to *nominate* them, and a provision is inserted by virtue of which Congress may require Senate confirmation of his nominees. It would seem a fair surmise that a compromise had been made. But no change was made in the concept of the term "Officers of the United States," which since it had first appeared in Art. X had been taken by all concerned to embrace all appointed officials exercising responsibility under the public laws of the Nation.

Appellee Commission and amici urge that because of what they conceive to be the extraordinary authority reposed in Congress to regulate elections, this case stands on a different footing than if Congress had exercised its legislative authority in another field. There is, of course, no doubt that Congress has express authority to regulate congressional elections, by virtue of the power conferred in Art. I, § 4. This Court has also held that it has very broad authority to prevent corruption in national Presidential elections. But Congress has plenary authority in all areas in which it has substantive legislative jurisdiction, *McCulloch v. Maryland*, 17 U.S. 316, 4 Wheat. 316 (1819), so long as the exercise of that authority does not offend some other constitutional restriction. We see no reason to believe that the authority of Congress over federal election practices is of such a wholly different nature from the other grants of authority to Congress that it may be employed in such a manner as to offend well-established constitutional restrictions stemming from the separation of powers.

The position that because Congress has been given explicit and plenary authority to regulate a field of activity, it must therefore have the power to appoint those who are to administer the regulatory statute is both novel and contrary to the language of the Appointments Clause. Unless their selection is elsewhere provided for, all Officers of the United States are to be appointed in accordance with the Clause. . . . No class or type of officer is excluded because of its special functions. The President appoints judicial as well as executive officers. Neither has it been disputed and apparently it is not now disputed that the Clause controls the appointment of the members of a typical administrative agency even though its functions, as this Court recognized in *Humphrey's Executor v. United States*, 295 U.S. 602, 624 (1935), may be "predominantly quasi-judicial and quasi-legislative" rather than executive. The Court in that case carefully emphasized that although the members of such agencies were to be independent of the Executive in their day-to-day operations, the Executive was not excluded from selecting them. . . .

We are also told . . . that Congress had good reason for not vesting in a Commission composed wholly of Presidential appointees the authority to administer the Act, since the administration of the Act would undoubtedly have a bearing on any incumbent President's campaign for re-election. While one cannot dispute the basis for this sentiment as a practical matter, it would seem that those who sought to challenge incumbent Congressmen might have equally good reason to fear a Commission which was unduly responsive to members of Congress whom they were seeking to unseat. But such fears, however rational, do not by themselves warrant a distortion of the Framers' work.

Appellee Commission . . . finally contend[s] . . . that . . . Congress had ample authority under the Necessary and Proper Clause of Art. I to effectuate this result. We do not agree. The proper inquiry when considering the Necessary and Proper Clause is not the authority of Congress to create an office or a commission, which is broad indeed, but rather its authority to provide that its own officers may make appointments to such office or commission. . . . Congress could not, merely because it concluded that such a measure was "necessary and proper" to the discharge of its substantive legislative authority, pass a bill of attainder or ex post facto law contrary to the prohibitions contained in §9 of Art. I. No more may it vest in itself, or in its officers, the authority to appoint officers of the United States when the Appointments Clause by clear implication prohibits it from doing so.

The . . . cases from this Court dealing with the constitutional authority of Congress to circumscribe the President's power to *remove* officers of the United States [are] entirely consistent with this conclusion. In . . . *Humphrey's Executor*, where it was held that Congress could circumscribe the President's power to remove members of independent regulatory agencies, the Court was careful to note that it was dealing with an agency intended to be independent of executive authority "*except in its selection.*" (emphasis in original) . . . .

3. The Commission's Powers

Thus, on the assumption that all of the powers granted in the statute may be exercised by an agency whose members have been appointed in accordance with the Appointments Clause, the ultimate question is which, if any, of those powers may be exercised by the present voting Commissioners, none of whom was appointed as provided by that Clause. Our previous description of the statutory provisions disclosed that the Commission's powers fall generally into three categories: functions relating to the flow of necessary information — receipt, dissemination, and investigation; functions with respect to the Commission's task of fleshing out the statute — rulemaking and advisory opinions; and functions necessary to ensure compliance with the statute and rules — informal procedures, administrative determinations and hearings, and civil suits.

Insofar as the powers confided in the Commission are essentially of an investigative and informative nature, falling in the same general category as those powers which Congress might delegate to one of its own committees, there can be no question that the Commission as presently constituted may exercise them. . . . But when we go beyond this type of authority to the more substantial powers exercised by the Commission, we reach a different result. The Commission's enforcement power, exemplified by its discretionary power to seek judicial relief, is authority that cannot possibly be regarded as merely in aid of the legislative function of Congress. A lawsuit is the ultimate remedy for a breach of the law, and it is to the President, and not to the Congress, that the Constitution entrusts the responsibility to "take Care that the Laws be faithfully executed." Art. II, § 3.

Congress may undoubtedly under the Necessary and Proper Clause create "offices" in the generic sense and provide such method of appointment to those "offices" as it chooses. But Congress' power under that Clause is inevitably bounded by the express language of Art. II, § 2, cl. 2, and unless the method it provides comports with the latter, the holders of those offices will not be "Officers of the United States." They may, therefore, properly perform duties only in aid of those functions that Congress may carry out by itself, or in an area sufficiently removed from the administration and enforcement of the public law as to permit their being performed by persons not "Officers of the United States." . . .

We hold that these provisions of the Act, vesting in the Commission primary responsibility for conducting civil litigation in the courts of the United States for vindicating public rights, violate Art. II, § 2, cl. 2, of the Constitution. Such functions may be discharged only by persons who are "Officers of the United States" within the language of that section. All aspects of the Act are brought within the Commission's broad administrative powers: rulemaking, advisory opinions, and determinations of eligibility for funds and even for federal elective office itself. These functions, exercised free from day-to-day supervision of either Congress or the Executive Branch, are more legislative and judicial in nature than are the Commission's enforcement powers, and are of kinds usually performed by independent regulatory agencies or by some department in the Executive Branch under the direction of an

Act of Congress. Congress viewed these broad powers as essential to effective and impartial administration of the entire substantive framework of the Act. Yet each of these functions also represents the performance of a significant governmental duty exercised pursuant to a public law. While the President may not insist that such functions be delegated to an appointee of his removable at will, *Humphrey's Executor v. United States,* none of them operates merely in aid of congressional authority to legislate or is sufficiently removed from the administration and enforcement of public law to allow it to be performed by the present Commission. These administrative functions may therefore be exercised only by persons who are "Officers of the United States." . . .

————————

1. *Defining Federal Office.* The *Buckley* Court said that "any appointee exercising significant authority pursuant to the laws of the United States" is an Officer of the United States and must be appointed in conformity with Article II. (In a footnote, the Court said that "[e]mployees are lesser functionaries subordinate to officers.") The Court then provided some further definition by distinguishing investigative and informative functions, which Congress may perform itself or through its agents, from enforcement powers, exercised through litigation, administrative adjudication, and rulemaking, which must be performed by Officers of the United States because they constitute "the performance of a significant governmental duty exercised pursuant to a public law." Note the Court's unwillingness to characterize some administrative functions, such as adjudication and rulemaking, as outside the scope of the Appointments Clause. Compare the Court's similar approach in *Chadha, supra* Chapter Two. In each case, the Court finds the operation of a constitutional procedure (bicameralism and presentment in *Chadha* and the Appointments Clause in *Buckley*) is premised on the exercise of significant authority, which each case understands as the power to alter legal rights and duties. Also, note the Court's attempts to distinguish its earlier cases concerning *removal* of officers. We will explore these matters in connection with the removal cases below.

The *Buckley* Court's view of the scope and effect of the Appointments Clause is congruent with executive branch views that were first articulated in the nineteenth century. *See* Attorney General H.S. Legare, *Appointment and Removal of Inspectors of Customs,* 4 Op. Att'y Gen. 162 & 165 (two opinions) (1843); Attorney General A.T. Akerman, *Civil-Service Commission,* 13 Op. Att'y Gen. 516 (1871), *reprinted in* H. Jefferson Powell, The Constitution and the Attorneys General 64–67, 203–09 (1999).

2. *Formalism. Buckley* is at least superficially formalist—the Court started with the text of the appointments clause, added a premise about what officers do, and concluded that Congress may not share this power. The Court did not ask the question usually associated with functional analysis: whether core executive functions are threatened. The Court could easily have written a purely functionalist opinion, because the President would have little control of administration if Congress could place ordinary regulation in the hands of its own agents. So the choice of analytic

method probably did not affect the outcome. In that case, why did the Court employ formalism? Should Congress retain some authority to appoint officers having clearly executive responsibilities, where "core" presidential powers are not threatened?

Recall Justice Kennedy's endorsement of formalism in his refusal in *Public Citizen, supra* Chapter Three, to countenance statutory restrictions on the President's process for selecting judicial nominees. His opinion went on to say:

> By its terms, the Clause divides the appointment power into two separate spheres: the President's power to "nominate," and the Senate's power to give or withhold its "Advice and Consent." No role whatsoever is given either to the Senate or to Congress as a whole in the process of choosing the person who will be nominated for appointment. As Hamilton emphasized:
>
>> "In the act of nomination, [the President's] judgment *alone* would be exercised; and as it would be his *sole* duty to point out the man who, with the approbation of the Senate, should fill an office, his responsibility would be as *complete* as if he were to make the final appointment." The Federalist No. 76, 456–57 (C. Rossiter ed., 1961) (emphasis added).
>
> And again:
>
>> "It will be the office of the President to *nominate*, and, with the advice and consent of the Senate, to *appoint*. There will, of course, be no exertion of *choice* on the part of the Senate. They may defeat one choice of the Executive, and oblige him to make another; but they cannot themselves *choose* — they can only ratify or reject the choice he may have made." *Id.*, No. 66, at 405 (emphasis in original).
>
> Indeed, the sole limitation on the President's power to nominate these officials is found in the Incompatibility Clause, which provides that "no Senator or Representative shall, during the Time for which he was elected, be appointed to any civil Office under the Authority of the United States, which shall have been created, or the Emoluments whereof shall have been increased during such time." U.S. Const., Art. I, §6, cl. 2.

Would Justice Kennedy's reasoning cast doubt on such congressional restrictions on nominations as limitations on the number of members of any major party who may be appointed to independent agencies such as the FEC?

3. *Who Is an Officer?* What is the scope of the *Buckley* holding? Consider the case of the United States Commission on Civil Rights. Under 42 U.S.C. §1975, the Commission's duties are to "study and collect information" and to "make appraisals of the laws and policies of the Federal Government" concerning civil rights violations, and to report its findings to Congress and the President. Following a controversy over President Reagan's removal of several Commission members, the Commission was reconstituted by Congress. *See* Comment, *The Rise and Fall of the United States Commission on Civil Rights*, 22 Harv. C.R.-C.L. L. Rev. 449 (1987). Under the statute, four members are appointed by the President, two by the President pro

tempore of the Senate, and two by the Speaker of the House. Is this statute constitutional? Even though the Commission's activities are investigative, has the President a good argument that he should be able to appoint all the members of a body that functions as a watchdog over federal civil rights enforcement? Or is that a good reason for the current composition of the Commission? For a provocative originalist critique of the *Buckley* approach, arguing that the category of "officers" should be understood to include all government officials with responsibility for an ongoing governmental duty, see Jennifer L. Mascott, *Who are "Officers of the United States?"* 70 STAN. L. REV. ___ (forthcoming 2018).

4. *Identifying "Heads of Departments."* Among the authorities in whom article II permits Congress to vest the appointment of "inferior officers" are "Heads of Departments." Beyond the heads of cabinet departments, it is not clear just who these may be. In *United States v. Freytag*, 501 U.S. 868 (1991), the Court unanimously upheld the authority of the Chief Judge of the United States Tax Court, an Article I tribunal, to appoint special trial judges. Although the latter are indubitably "inferior officers," the Court split five to four as to whether their appointment was permissible because the Chief Judge is the head of a "Department" within the meaning of Article II, or instead, because the Tax Court is a "court of law." The majority took the latter approach, concluding that the appointments clause reference to "Courts of Law" was not limited to Article III courts, and that "a holding that every organ in the Executive Branch is a department would multiply indefinitely the actors eligible to appoint."

Justice Blackmun's majority opinion seemed to be saying that the only heads of departments who could name inferior officers were the members of the cabinet, "limited in number and easily identified." Why? Because "[t]heir heads are subject to political oversight and share the President's accountability to the people." This statement appears to refer to an assignment of responsibility for oversight to the President, which if missing breaks the necessary link to the people. There are broad implications here for the constitutionality of the independent commissions, for whom presidential oversight is limited. Of course, *Freytag* involved no such grand issues. The concurring Justices found it implausible to regard article I tribunals as "Courts of Law" for constitutional purposes, and thought the reference to "Heads of Departments" logically and historically must comprise "the heads of all agencies immediately below the President in the organizational structure of the Executive Branch."

A later case, *Edmond v. United States*, 520 U.S. 651 (1997), allowed the Secretary of Transportation to appoint civilian members of the Coast Guard Court of Appeals. The case gave Justice Scalia, writing for a new majority, an opportunity to correct Justice Blackmun's rhetorical excess. He did so, arguing that "in the context of a clause designed to preserve political accountability . . . we think it evident that 'inferior officers' are officers whose work is directed and supervised at some level by others who were appointed by presidential nomination with the advice and consent of the Senate." This simple formulation is more consistent with the text of Article II than is the creative Blackmun version. It also carries a broad implication—that anyone who *is* a principal officer in the formal sense *may* be supervised by the President to preserve political accountability. Again, neither *Freytag* nor *Edmond* was an appropriate vehicle for resolving such large issues, which we consider later in this chapter. The cases certainly showed, though, that concern about constitutional architecture was in the air.

5. *What Does an Officer Do?* In *Buckley*, the Court noted in passing that the Secretary of the Senate and the Clerk of the House were ex officio members of the FEC, without the right to vote. In *Federal Election Commission v. NRA Political Victory Fund*, 6 F.3d 821 (D.C. Cir. 1993), *cert. pet. dism'd for lack of juris.*, 513 U.S. 88 (1994), the court held that these congressional agents could not constitutionally sit on the Commission and participate in its deliberations. Did this decision strain at gnats, or was it a salutary protection against the placing of congressional moles within executive agencies?

6. *What's a New Appointment?* Congress, reacting to a profound crisis in the savings and loan industry, enacted the Financial Institutions Reform, Recovery, and Enforcement Act of 1989, Pub. L. No. 101-73, 103 Stat. 183. The Act abolished the preexisting regulatory agency—the Federal Home Loan Bank Board (FHLBB)—and established in its place a new Office of Thrift Supervision (OTS) in the Treasury Department. Congress provided that the President would appoint the OTS Director with Senate advice and consent, but that the chair of the FHLBB as of the date of the new statute would automatically become OTS's first director. When OTS sought to appoint a receiver for Olympic Federal Savings and Loan, Olympic successfully enjoined the OTS action on the ground that the designation of its director by statute constituted an impermissible congressional appointment, in violation of Article II. The district court distinguished this challenge from cases in which service in a new agency became a new duty for a person already holding another office. *Olympic Federal Savings & Loan v. Director, Office of Thrift Supervision*, 732 F. Supp. 1183 (D.D.C. 1990).

7. *What's a New Appointment, Part II?* Congress, by statute, frequently adds new duties to an existing office. Generally speaking this is unexceptionable. It is conceivable, however, that Congress could add duties in a way that undermines the President's appointment authority or even in a way that amounts to a congressional appointment. Imagine, as happens from time to time, that the head of an agency is at odds with the President. Congress might add or transfer from another agency significant new duties to the agency at odds with the President. Imagine further that the head of the agency (whether an individual or a commission) is independent from the President, because it is insulated from the President's removal power. In this instance, Congress might be said to have undermined the discretion and control the Appointments Clause means to grant the President. Is there any limit on Congress's ability to employ this tactic?

The Supreme Court provided an answer in *Shoemaker v. United States*, 147 U.S. 282 (1893). The Court held that Congress may add new duties to an existing office without raising Appointments Clause issues as long as the new duties are germane to the office's pre-existing duties. If the new duties are not germane, then Congress has created a new office, and the new office must be filled in accordance with the Appointments Clause.

8. *What's a New Office, Part III?* Congress might also work an end-run around the constitutional prohibition, expressed in *Buckley*, against congressional appointments to federal office by enacting legislation to extend the term of a sitting officer. (Again, imagine an officer who is at odds with the President.) The issue was most recently posed when Congress considered legislation extending the term of the Director of the Federal Bureau of Investigation. The Director at the time, Robert Mueller, was appointed by President George W. Bush in 2001. In 2011, while Barack Obama was President, (the Republican-controlled) Congress considered legislation to extend Director Mueller's term by two years. The Office of Legal Counsel determined that the legislation would be constitutionally permissible. "The traditional position of the Executive Branch has been that Congress, by extending an incumbent officer's term, does not displace and take over the President's appointment authority, as long as the President remains free to remove the officer at will and make another appointment." *Constitutionality of Legislation Extending the Term of the FBI Director*, 35 Op. O.L.C. (2011); *see also Displaced Persons Commission — Terms of Members*, 41 Op. Att'y Gen. 88, 89–90 (1951).

In 1987 OLC departed from the traditional view. It opined that a statutory extension of the terms of United States Parole Commissioners constituted "an unconstitutional interference with the President's appointment power," because "[b]y extending the term of office for incumbent Commissioners appointed by the President for a fixed term, the Congress will effectively reappoint those Commissioners to new terms." *Reappointment of United States Parole Commissioners*, 11 Op. O.L.C. 135, 136 (1987). OLC's 2011 opinion rejected the 1987 opinion and returned the executive branch to the traditional view.

The courts have been even more deferential to Congress. For example, three federal appellate courts have upheld the extension of the terms of sitting Bankruptcy Judges. *See In re Investment Bankers, Inc.*, 4 F.3d 1556, 1562–63 (10th Cir. 1993); *In re Benny*, 812 F.2d 1133, 1141–42 (9th Cir. 1987); *In re Koerner*, 800 F.2d 1358, 1366–67 (5th Cir. 1986). These courts upheld the term extensions despite the fact that Bankruptcy Judges are not subject to Presidential removal at-will.

2. Alternatives to the Appointments Clause

The process of nominating and confirming officers has encountered sharp criticism. *See generally* Michael J. Gerhardt, The Federal Appointments Process (rev. ed., 2003); Obstacle Course: The Report of the Twentieth Century Fund Task Force on the Presidential Appointment Process (1996); Stephen L. Carter, The Confirmation Mess: Cleaning Up the Federal Appointments Process (1994). Much of the concern surrounds judicial appointments, yet many of the difficulties apply to executive appointments as well. Presidents and Senators have frequently battled over nominations. There are several untoward consequences. First, there have been extended delays in the process, with new administrations finding it difficult to staff a government and with federal courts carrying vacancies for long periods. Second, as the two major parties have rotated in the presidency and in control of the Senate, each has engaged in retaliation for the perceived sins of the other in defeating nominees. Third, the contentiousness of the process had led to "confirmation hell" for nominees, who dangle in uncertainty for extended periods and endure hostile and intrusive inquiries into their private lives. The acrimony, inefficiency, and misbehavior that the confirmation wars have produced go on and on, with no end in sight. This dysfunction has increased the importance of alternative methods for filling vacancies, particularly interim (or acting) and recess appointments.

a. *Interim Appointments.* In the *Olympic Federal* case, after Olympic's lawsuit was filed, President George H.W. Bush appointed a new OTS director under the Vacancies Act, 5 U.S.C. §§ 3345–47. The Act permits the President to appoint agency heads or other presidential appointees needing Senate advice and consent to fill certain vacancies temporarily created by death, resignation, sickness, or other absence. The court held that the successor's appointment under this act was impermissible because Congress did not authorize the President to fill on an emergency basis a vacancy left by the resignation of a person never properly appointed as an officer of the United States. The court rejected the existence of any inherent Presidential power to make limited emergency appointments even in the absence of statutory authorization. *Accord, Franklin Savings Association v. Director of the Office of Thrift Supervision,* 740 F. Supp. 1535 (D. Kan. 1990).

President Clinton also created a controversy under the Vacancies Act. After the Senate Judiciary Committee rejected his nomination of Bill Lann Lee to head the Civil Rights Division of the Department of Justice, Clinton named Lee an Acting Assistant Attorney General. Clinton argued that Lee was not subject to the short periods of temporary service authorized by the Act because of an exception for the Attorney General, which he read to refer to the Department of Justice generally. *See* Brandon P. Denning, *Article II, the Vacancies Act and the Appointment of "Acting" Executive Branch Officials,* 76 Wash. U. L.Q. 1039 (1998). Congress got even, though, by passing the Federal Vacancies Reform Act (FVRA), Pub. L. No. 105-277, 112 Stat. 2681, tightening controls on filling vacancies generally and clarifying the applicability of the Vacancies Act to DOJ. *See* Joshua L. Stayn, *Vacant Reform: Why the Federal Vacancies Reform Act of 1998 is Unconstitutional,* 50 Duke L.J. 1511 (2001). Under the restrictions of the FVRA, the Supreme Court held invalid President Obama's 2010 appointment of an acting general counsel to the National Labor Relations Board after he subsequently nominated that same individual to fill the post permanently; a 7–2 majority read the Act as precluding the President from temporarily filling an advice-and-consent position with an individual the President has also nominated for that office. *NLRB v. SW General,* 137 S. Ct. 929 (2017).

b. *Recess Appointments.* Article II, § 2, clause 3 authorizes the President to "fill up all Vacancies that may happen during the Recess of the Senate, by granting Commissions which shall expire at the End of their next Session." The Clause has raised two major interpretive challenges. First, what counts as a "recess"? Does the Clause refer exclusively to the intersession recess that (*i.e.*, the interval between the formal final adjournment *sine die* of one session of the Senate and the start of a new session) or does it also include intrasession recesses (*i.e.*, those that occur when the Senate adjourns to take a break during an on-going session)? The first occasion for the executive branch to issue a formal opinion on this question did not arise until 1901. (President Andrew Johnson made numerous recess appointments at least some of which were made during an intrasession recess. Attorney General Evarts opined on their validity, but he did not address the question of inter- versus intrasession recesses. *See President's Power to Fill Vacancies in Recess of the Senate*, 12 Op. Att'y Gen. 32 (1866).) Attorney General Philander Knox embraced the narrow view that the Clause applies only with respect to intersession recesses, so that the President was not authorized to use the recess appointment power to fill vacancies during an intrasession Senate recess. *See President—Appointment of Officers—Holiday Recess*, 23 Op. Att'y Gen. 599 (1901). Professor Powell comments that Knox's opinion "was arguably in tension with his predecessors' understanding of the purpose of the recess appointments clause—to avoid any interruption in the functioning of the executive—and with Attorney General Miller's rejection of any constitutional distinction between an adjournment and a recess in the context of the pocket veto clause." H. Jefferson Powell, The Constitution and the Attorneys General 244 (1999). In 1921, Attorney General Harry Daugherty disavowed Knox's position and adopted the broader interpretation, concluding that the President may make recess appointments during a recess regardless of whether the recess is an inter- or an intrasession recess. *See Executive Power—Recess Appointments*, 33 Op. Att'y Gen. 20 (1921). This has been the consistent position of the executive branch, through presidents of both political parties, ever since.

This position raises a subsidiary question: will any recess—even one lasting a few days or a few minutes—suffice to provide the predicate for invoking the recess appointment power? The executive branch has consistently answered this question "no." Instead, the executive branch has taken a functional view of the Recess Appointments Clause and the executive branch must determine when "there is a real and genuine recess making it impossible for him to receive the advice and consent of the Senate." 33 Op. Att'y Gen. at 25. The question then is how long must a recess be to render the advice-and-consent process impracticable. Published opinions approved appointments under the Clause during recesses as brief as fifteen days. *See Recess Appointments during an Intrasession Recess*, 16 Op. O.L.C. 15 (1992).

The second interpretive question regarding the Recess Appointments Clause concerns the meaning of "vacancies that may happen" during a recess. Does this refer only to vacancies that arise during the Senate's recess (for example, when an officer resigns or dies during a recess) or does it also encompass vacancies that may have arisen when the Senate was in session but that continue to exist when the Senate recesses? This question arose much earlier than the issue of what sort of adjournment constitutes a recess. Attorney General William Wirt, in 1823, established what has remained the uniform position of the executive branch: the Recess Appointments Clause authorizes the President to fill any vacancy that exists while the Senate is in recess regardless of whether the Senate was in session or in recess when vacancy first came to exist. *See* 1 Op. Att'y Gen. 631 (1823).

Under the executive branch's interpretation, the recess appointment power is quite expansive. As we discussed *supra* in section 1, the dysfunctionality of the confirmation process has rendered regular appointments increasingly cumbersome and fraught. Presidents of both political parties have found the Recess Appointments Clause to be an attractive end-run around the minefield of Senate confirmation, and have increasingly resorted to this power. The Senate has devised its own tactic for short-circuiting the President's recess appointment power: the *pro forma* session. Instead of taking a recess that would be long enough to implicate the recess appointment power (as interpreted by the executive branch), the Senate reconvenes every few days for a session that lasts a few minutes or even a few seconds. No actual business is transacted during these sessions; rather the chair gavels the Senate into session and, after announcing the date of the next (*pro forma*) meeting, gavels the Senate back into recess. Thus, the Senate may go weeks or months without holding a substantive session, but it will have formally been in recess only a few days at a time. The only reason for proceeding in this manner is to thwart the President's ability to invoke the Recess Appointments Clause.

The executive branch reaction was predictable. The Office of Legal Counsel opined that these *pro forma* sessions do not toll the clock when computing the length of a recess. Since the Senate is functionally unavailable to provide advice and consent, the purpose of the Recess Appointments Clause would be vitiated by recognizing the *pro forma* session. *See Lawfulness of Recess Appointments during a Recess of the Senate Notwithstanding Periodic Pro Forma Sessions*, 36 Op. O.L.C. ___, 2012 WL 168645 (2012). The Senate adjourned on December 17, 2011 and did not hold another substantive session until January 23, 2012. During this interval, the Senate held *pro forma* sessions every Tuesday and Friday. President Obama on January 4, 2012—between the Senate's January 3 and January 6 *pro forma* sessions—recess-appointed three members of the National Labor Relations Board. The NLRB took action that adversely affected Noel Canning. Noel Canning then brought a lawsuit asserting that the Board was invalidly composed. This lawsuit gave the Supreme Court its first opportunity to interpret the Recess Appointments Clause.

National Labor Relations Bd. v. Noel Canning

134 S. Ct. 2550 (2014).

Justice BREYER delivered the opinion of the Court.

* * *

II

Before turning to the specific questions presented, we shall mention two background considerations that we find relevant to all three. First, *the Recess Appointments*

Clause sets forth a subsidiary, not a primary, method for appointing officers of the United States. The immediately preceding Clause—Article II, Section 2, Clause 2—provides the primary method of appointment. It says that the President "shall nominate, *and by and with the Advice and Consent of the Senate,* shall appoint Ambassadors, other public Ministers and Consuls, Judges of the supreme Court, and all other Officers of the United States" (emphasis added).

The Federalist Papers make clear that the Founders intended this method of appointment, requiring Senate approval, to be the norm (at least for principal officers). Alexander Hamilton wrote that the . . .

> "ordinary power of appointment is confided to the President and Senate *jointly,* and can therefore only be exercised during the session of the Senate; but as it would have been improper to oblige this body to be continually in session for the appointment of officers; and as vacancies might happen *in their recess,* which it might be necessary for the public service to fill without delay, the succeeding clause is evidently intended to authorise the President *singly* to make temporary appointments." *Id.,* No. 67, at 455.

Thus the Recess Appointments Clause reflects the tension between, on the one hand, the President's continuous need for "the assistance of subordinates," *Myers v. United States,* 272 U.S. 52, 117 (1926), and, on the other, the Senate's practice, particularly during the Republic's early years, of meeting for a single brief session each year. We seek to interpret the Clause as granting the President the power to make appointments during a recess but not offering the President the authority routinely to avoid the need for Senate confirmation.

Second, *in interpreting the Clause, we put significant weight upon historical practice.* For one thing, the interpretive questions before us concern the allocation of power between two elected branches of Government. Long ago Chief Justice Marshall wrote that

> "a doubtful question, one on which human reason may pause, and the human judgment be suspended, in the decision of which the great principles of liberty are not concerned, but the respective powers of those who are equally the representatives of the people, are to be adjusted; if not put at rest by the practice of the government, ought to receive a considerable impression from that practice." *McCulloch v. Maryland,* 4 Wheat. 316, 401, 4 L.Ed. 579 (1819).

And we later confirmed that "[l]ong settled and established practice is a consideration of great weight in a proper interpretation of constitutional provisions" regulating the relationship between Congress and the President. *The Pocket Veto Case,* 279 U.S. 655, 689 (1929).

We recognize, of course, that the separation of powers can serve to safeguard individual liberty, *Clinton v. City of New York,* 524 U.S. 417, 449–450 (1998) (Kennedy, J., concurring), and that it is the "duty of the judicial department"—in a separation-of-powers case as in any other—"to say what the law is," *Marbury v.*

Madison, 1 Cranch 137, 177 (1803). But it is equally true that the longstanding "practice of the government," *McCulloch, supra,* at 401, can inform our determination of "what the law is," *Marbury, supra,* at 177.

There is a great deal of history to consider here. Presidents have made recess appointments since the beginning of the Republic. Their frequency suggests that the Senate and President have recognized that recess appointments can be both necessary and appropriate in certain circumstances. We have not previously interpreted the Clause, and, when doing so for the first time in more than 200 years, we must hesitate to upset the compromises and working arrangements that the elected branches of Government themselves have reached.

III

The first question concerns the scope of the phrase "*the recess* of the Senate." Art. II, § 2, cl. 3 (emphasis added). The Constitution provides for congressional elections every two years. And the 2–year life of each elected Congress typically consists of two formal 1–year sessions, each separated from the next by an "inter-session recess." The Senate or the House of Representatives announces an inter-session recess by approving a resolution stating that it will "adjourn *sine die,*" *i.e.,* without specifying a date to return (in which case Congress will reconvene when the next formal session is scheduled to begin).

The Senate and the House also take breaks in the midst of a session. The Senate or the House announces any such "intra-session recess" by adopting a resolution stating that it will "adjourn" to a fixed date, a few days or weeks or even months later. All agree that the phrase "the recess of the Senate" covers inter-session recesses. The question is whether it includes intra-session recesses as well.

In our view, the phrase "the recess" includes an intra-session recess of substantial length. Its words taken literally can refer to both types of recess. Founding-era dictionaries define the word "recess," much as we do today, simply as "a period of cessation from usual work." 13 The Oxford English Dictionary 322–323 (2d ed. 1989) (hereinafter OED) . . . .

We recognize that the word "the" in "*the* recess" might suggest that the phrase refers to the single break separating formal sessions of Congress. That is because the word "the" frequently (but not always) indicates "a particular thing." S. Johnson, A Dictionary of the English Language 1602–2003 (4th ed. 1773). But the word can also refer "to a term used generically or universally." 17 OED 879. The Constitution, for example, directs the Senate to choose a President *pro tempore* "in *the* Absence of the Vice–President." Art. I, § 3, cl. 5 (emphasis added). And the Federalist Papers refer to the chief magistrate of an ancient Achaean league who "administered the government in *the* recess of the Senate." The Federalist No. 18, at 113 (J. Madison) (emphasis added). Reading "the" generically in this way, there is no linguistic problem applying the Clause's phrase to both kinds of recess. And, in fact, the phrase "the recess" was used to refer to intra-session recesses at the time of the founding. See, *e.g.,* 3 Farrand 76 (letter from Washington to Jay).

The constitutional text is thus ambiguous. And we believe the Clause's purpose demands the broader interpretation. The Clause gives the President authority to make appointments during "the recess of the Senate" so that the President can ensure the continued functioning of the Federal Government when the Senate is away. The Senate is equally away during both an inter-session and an intra-session recess, and its capacity to participate in the appointments process has nothing to do with the words it uses to signal its departure.

History also offers strong support for the broad interpretation. We concede that pre-Civil War history is not helpful. But it shows only that Congress generally took long breaks between sessions, while taking no significant intra-session breaks at all (five times it took a break of a week or so at Christmas). Obviously, if there are no significant intra-session recesses, there will be no intra-session recess appointments. In 1867 and 1868, Congress for the first time took substantial, nonholiday intra-session breaks, and President Andrew Johnson made dozens of recess appointments. . . . [T]hough the 40th Congress impeached President Johnson on charges relating to his appointment power, he was not accused of violating the Constitution by making intra-session recess appointments.

In all, between the founding and the Great Depression, Congress took substantial intra-session breaks (other than holiday breaks) in four years: 1867, 1868, 1921, and 1929. And in each of those years the President made intra-session recess appointments.

Since 1929, and particularly since the end of World War II, Congress has shortened its inter-session breaks as it has taken longer and more frequent intra-session breaks; Presidents have correspondingly made more intra-session recess appointments. Indeed, if we include military appointments, Presidents have made thousands of intra-session recess appointments . . . .

Not surprisingly, the publicly available opinions of Presidential legal advisers that we have found are nearly unanimous in determining that the Clause authorizes these appointments

The upshot is that restricting the Clause to inter-session recesses would frustrate its purpose. It would make the President's recess-appointment power dependent on a formalistic distinction of Senate procedure. Moreover, the President has consistently and frequently interpreted the word "recess" to apply to intra-session recesses, and has acted on that interpretation. The Senate as a body has done nothing to deny the validity of this practice for at least three-quarters of a century. And three-quarters of a century of settled practice is long enough to entitle a practice to "great weight in a proper interpretation" of the constitutional provision. *The Pocket Veto Case*, 279 U.S. 689.

We are aware of, but we are not persuaded by, important arguments to the contrary. First, some argue that the Founders would likely have intended the Clause to apply only to inter-session recesses, for they hardly knew any other. Indeed, from the founding until the Civil War inter-session recesses were the only kind of significant recesses that Congress took. The problem with this argument, however, is that it does not fully describe the relevant founding intent. The question is not: Did the Founders at the time think about intra-session recesses? Perhaps they did not. The question is: Did the Founders intend to restrict the scope of the Clause to the form of congressional recess then prevalent, or did they intend a broader scope permitting the Clause to apply, where appropriate, to somewhat changed circumstances? The Founders knew they were writing a document designed to apply to ever-changing circumstances over centuries. After all, a Constitution is "intended to endure for ages to come," and must adapt itself to a future that can only be "seen dimly," if at all. *McCulloch,* 4 Wheat., at 415. We therefore think the Framers likely did intend the Clause to apply to a new circumstance that so clearly falls within its essential purposes, where doing so is consistent with the Clause's language . . . .

The greater interpretive problem is determining how long a recess must be in order to fall within the Clause. Is a break of a week, or a day, or an hour too short to count as a "recess"? The Clause itself does not say. And Justice Scalia claims that this silence itself shows that the Framers intended the Clause to apply only to an inter-session recess.

We disagree. For one thing, the most likely reason the Framers did not place a textual floor underneath the word "recess" is that they did not foresee the *need* for one. They might have expected that the Senate would meet for a single session lasting at most half a year. The Federalist No. 84, at 596 (A. Hamilton). And they might not have anticipated that intra-session recesses would become lengthier and more significant than inter-session ones. The Framers' lack of clairvoyance on that point is not dispositive. Unlike Justice Scalia, we think it most consistent with our constitutional structure to presume that the Framers would have allowed intra-session recess appointments where there was a long history of such practice.

Moreover, the lack of a textual floor raises a problem that plagues *both* interpretations — Justice Scalia's and ours. Today a brief inter-session recess is just as possible as a brief intra-session recess. And though Justice Scalia says that the "notion that the Constitution empowers the President to make unilateral appointments every time the Senate takes a half-hour lunch break is *so absurd as to be self-refuting,*" he must immediately concede (in a footnote) that the President "can make recess appointments during any break *between* sessions, *no matter how short.*"

. . . The Recess Appointments Clause seeks to permit the Executive Branch to function smoothly when Congress is unavailable. And though Congress has taken short breaks for almost 200 years, and there have been many thousands of recess appointments in that time, we have not found a single example of a recess appointment made during an intra-session recess that was shorter than 10 days. Nor has the Solicitor General. Indeed, the Office of Legal Counsel once informally advised against making a recess appointment during a 6–day intra-session recess. The lack of examples suggests that the recess-appointment power is not needed in that context. (The length of a recess is "ordinarily calculated by counting the calendar days running from the day after the recess begins and including the day the recess ends.")

There are a few historical examples of recess appointments made during inter-session recesses shorter than 10 days . . . . But when considered against 200 years of settled practice, we regard these few scattered examples as anomalies. We therefore conclude, in light of historical practice, that a recess of more than 3 days but less than 10 days is presumptively too short to fall within the Clause. We add the word "pre-sumptively" to leave open the possibility that some very unusual circumstance—a national catastrophe, for instance, that renders the Senate unavailable but calls for an urgent response—could demand the exercise of the recess-appointment power during a shorter break. (It should go without saying—except that Justice Scalia compels us to say it—that political opposition in the Senate would not qualify as an unusual circumstance.)

IV

The second question concerns the scope of the phrase "vacancies *that may hap-pen* during the recess of the Senate." All agree that the phrase applies to vacancies that initially occur during a recess. But does it also apply to vacancies that initially occur before a recess and continue to exist during the recess? In our view the phrase applies to both kinds of vacancy.

We believe that the Clause's language, read literally, permits, though it does not nat-urally favor, our broader interpretation. We concede that the most natural meaning of "happens" as applied to a "vacancy" (at least to a modern ear) is that the vacancy "hap-pens" when it initially occurs. But that is not the only possible way to use the word.

We can still understand this earlier use of "happen" if we think of it used together with another word that, like "vacancy," can refer to a continuing state, say, a financial crisis. A statute that gives the President authority to act in respect to "any financial crisis that may happen during his term" can easily be interpreted to include crises that arise before, and continue during, that term. Perhaps that is why the Oxford English Dictionary defines "happen" in part as "chance *to be,*" rather than "chance to occur."

In any event, the linguistic question here is not whether the phrase can be, but whether it must be, read more narrowly. The question is whether the Clause is ambig-uous. And the broader reading, we believe, is at least a permissible reading of a "doubtful" phrase. We consequently go on to consider the Clause's purpose and his-torical practice.

The Clause's purpose strongly supports the broader interpretation. That purpose is to permit the President to obtain the assistance of subordinate officers when the Senate, due to its recess, cannot confirm them. Attorney General Wirt clearly described how the narrower interpretation would undermine this purpose:

> "Put the case of a vacancy occurring in an office, held in a distant part of the country, on the last day of the Senate's session. Before the vacancy is made known to the President, the Senate rises. The office may be an important one; the vacancy may paralyze a whole line of action in some essential branch of our internal police; the public interests may imperiously demand that it shall be immediately filled. But the vacancy happened to occur during the

session of the Senate; and if the President's power is to be limited to such vacancies only as happen to occur during the recess of the Senate, the vacancy in the case put must continue, however ruinous the consequences may be to the public." 1 Op. Atty. Gen., at 632.

Examples are not difficult to imagine: An ambassadorial post falls vacant too soon before the recess begins for the President to appoint a replacement; the Senate rejects a President's nominee just before a recess, too late to select another. Wirt explained that the "substantial purpose of the constitution was to keep these offices filled," and "if the President shall not have the power to fill a vacancy thus circumstanced, . . . the substance of the constitution will be sacrificed to a dubious construction of its letter." *Ibid.*

We do not agree with [the] suggestion that the Framers would have accepted the catastrophe envisioned by Wirt because Congress can always provide for acting officers, see 5 U.S.C. § 3345, and the President can always convene a special session of Congress, see U.S. Const., Art. II, § 3. Acting officers may have less authority than Presidential appointments. 6 Op. OLC 119, 121 (1982). Moreover, to rely on acting officers would lessen the President's ability to staff the Executive Branch with people of his own choosing, and thereby limit the President's control and political accountability. Special sessions are burdensome (and would have been especially so at the time of the founding). The point of the Recess Appointments Clause was to *avoid* reliance on these inadequate expedients.

At the same time, we recognize one important purpose-related consideration that argues in the opposite direction. A broad interpretation might permit a President to avoid Senate confirmations as a matter of course. If the Clause gives the President the power to "fill up all vacancies" that occur before, and continue to exist during, the Senate's recess, a President might not submit any nominations to the Senate. He might simply wait for a recess and then provide all potential nominees with recess appointments. He might thereby routinely avoid the constitutional need to obtain the Senate's "advice and consent."

Wirt thought considerations of character and politics would prevent Presidents from abusing the Clause in this way. He might have added that such temptations should not often arise. It is often less desirable for a President to make a recess appointment. A recess appointee only serves a limited term. That, combined with the lack of Senate approval, may diminish the recess appointee's ability, as a practical matter, to get a controversial job done. And even where the President and Senate are at odds over politically sensitive appointments, compromise is normally possible. Indeed, the 1940 Pay Act amendments represent a general compromise, for they foresee payment of salaries to recess appointees where vacancies occur *before* the recess began but not *too long* before (namely, within 30 days before). Moreover, the Senate, like the President, has institutional "resources," including political resources, "available to protect and assert its interests." In an unusual instance, where a matter is important enough to the Senate, that body can remain in session, preventing recess appointments by refusing to take a recess. In any event, the Executive Branch has adhered to the broader interpretation for two centuries, and Senate confirmation has always remained the norm for officers that require it.

[Justice Breyer next canvassed the historical practice of recess appointments that arose before and continued during a Senate recess. He concluded that] "practice over the last 200 years strongly favors the broader interpretation."

V

The third question concerns the calculation of the length of the Senate's "recess." On December 17, 2011, the Senate by unanimous consent adopted a resolution to convene "*pro forma* session[s]" only, with "no business . . . transacted," on every Tuesday and Friday from December 20, 2011, through January 20, 2012.

The President made the recess appointments before us on January 4, 2012, in between the January 3 and the January 6 *pro forma* sessions. We must determine the significance of these sessions—that is, whether, for purposes of the Clause, we should treat them as periods when the Senate was in session or as periods when it was in recess. If the former, the period between January 3 and January 6 was a 3–day recess, which is too short to trigger the President's recess-appointment power. If the latter, however, then the 3–day period was part of a much longer recess during which the President did have the power to make recess appointments.

In our view, however, the *pro forma* sessions count as sessions, not as periods of recess. We hold that, for purposes of the Recess Appointments Clause, the Senate is in session when it says it is, provided that, under its own rules, it retains the capacity to transact Senate business. The Senate met that standard here.

The standard we apply is consistent with the Constitution's broad delegation of authority to the Senate to determine how and when to conduct its business. The Constitution explicitly empowers the Senate to "determine the Rules of its Proceedings." And we have held that "all matters of method are open to the determination" of the Senate, as long as there is "a reasonable relation between the mode or method of proceeding established by the rule and the result which is sought to be attained" and the rule does not "ignore constitutional restraints or violate fundamental rights." *United States v. Ballin*, 144 U.S. 1, 5 (1892).

. . . [W]e conclude that we must give great weight to the Senate's own determination of when it is and when it is not in session. But our deference to the Senate cannot be absolute. When the Senate is without the *capacity* to act, under its own rules, it is not in session even if it so declares. In that circumstance, the Senate is not simply unlikely or unwilling to act upon nominations of the President. It is *unable* to do so. The purpose of the Clause is to ensure the continued functioning of the Federal Government while the Senate is unavailable. This purpose would count for little were we to treat the Senate as though it were in session even when it lacks the ability to provide its "advice and consent." Art. II, § 2, cl. 2. Accordingly, we conclude that when the Senate declares that it is in session and possesses the capacity, under its own rules, to conduct business, it is in session for purposes of the Clause.

Applying this standard, we find that the *pro forma* sessions were sessions for purposes of the Clause . . . .

It is so ordered.

Justice SCALIA, with whom THE CHIEF JUSTICE, Justice THOMAS, and Justice ALITO join, concurring in the judgment.

To prevent the President's recess-appointment power from nullifying the Senate's role in the appointment process, the Constitution cabins that power in two significant ways. First, it may be exercised only in "the Recess of the Senate," that is, the intermission between two formal legislative sessions. Second, it may be used to fill only those vacancies that "happen during the Recess," that is, offices that become vacant during that intermission. Both conditions are clear from the Constitution's text and structure, and both were well understood at the founding . . . .

II. Intra–Session Breaks
A. Plain Meaning

A sensible interpretation of the Recess Appointments Clause should start by recognizing that the Clause uses the term "Recess" in contradistinction to the term "Session."

In the founding era, the terms "recess" and "session" had well-understood meanings in the marking-out of legislative time. The life of each elected Congress typically consisted (as it still does) of two or more formal sessions separated by adjournments "*sine die,*" that is, without a specified return date. The period *between* two sessions was known as "the recess." By contrast, other provisions of the Constitution use the verb "adjourn" rather than "recess" to refer to the commencement of breaks *during* a formal legislative session. See, *e.g.,* Art. I, § 5, cl. 1; *id.,* § 5, cl. 4.

To be sure, in colloquial usage both words, "recess" and "session," could take on alternative, less precise meanings. A session could include any short period when a legislature's members were "assembled for business," and a recess could refer to any brief "suspension" of legislative "business." But as even the majority acknowledges, the Constitution's use of "the word 'the' in '*the* [R]ecess'" tends to suggest "that the phrase refers to the single break separating formal sessions."

More importantly, neither the Solicitor General nor the majority argues that the Clause uses "session" in its loose, colloquial sense. And if "the next Session" denotes a *formal* session, then "the Recess" must mean the break *between* formal sessions. [T]he "Recess" and the "Session" to which the Clause refers are mutually exclusive, alternating states. It is linguistically implausible to suppose—as the majority does—that the Clause uses one of those terms ("Recess") informally and the other ("Session") formally in a single sentence, with the result that an event can occur during *both* the "Recess" *and* the "Session."

Besides being linguistically unsound, the majority's reading yields the strange result that an appointment made during a short break near the beginning of one official session will not terminate until the end of the *following* official session, enabling the appointment to last for up to two years. The Clause's self-evident design is to have the President's unilateral appointment last only until the Senate has "had an *opportunity* to act on the subject." 3 J. Story, Commentaries on the Constitution of the United States § 1551, p. 410 (1833) (emphasis added) . . . .

The boundlessness of the colloquial reading of "the Recess" refutes the majority's assertion that the Clause's "purpose" of "ensur[ing] the continued functioning of the Federal Government" demands that it apply to intra-session breaks as well as inter-session recesses. *Ante,* at 2561. The majority disregards another self-evident purpose of the Clause: to preserve the Senate's role in the appointment process — which the founding generation regarded as a critical protection against "despotism," *Freytag,* 501 U.S., at 883 — by clearly delineating the times when the President can appoint officers without the Senate's consent. Today's decision seriously undercuts *that* purpose.

To avoid the absurd results that follow from its colloquial reading of "the Recess," the majority is forced to declare that some intra-session breaks — though undisputedly within the phrase's colloquial meaning — are simply "too short to trigger the Recess Appointments Clause." But it identifies no textual basis whatsoever for limiting the length of "the Recess," nor does it point to any clear standard for determining how short is too short. It is inconceivable that the Framers would have left the circumstances in which the President could exercise such a significant and potentially dangerous power so utterly indeterminate . . . .

The majority says that a break of four to nine days is "presumptively too short" but that the presumption may be rebutted in an "unusual circumstance," such as a "national catastrophe . . . that renders the Senate unavailable but calls for an urgent response." The majority must hope that the *in terrorem* effect of its "presumptively too short" pronouncement will deter future Presidents from making any recess appointments during 4–to–9–day breaks and thus save us from the absurd spectacle of unelected judges evaluating (after an evidentiary hearing?) whether an alleged "catastrophe" was sufficiently "urgent" to trigger the recess-appointment power.

Even if the many questions raised by the majority's failure to articulate a standard could be answered, a larger question would remain: If the Constitution's text empowers the President to make appointments during any break in the Senate's proceedings, by what right does the majority subject the President's exercise of that power to vague, court-crafted limitations with no textual basis? The majority claims its temporal guideposts are informed by executive practice, but a President's self-restraint cannot "bind his successors by diminishing their powers." *Free Enterprise Fund,* 561 U.S. at 497.

B. Historical Practice

For the foregoing reasons, the Constitution's text and structure unambiguously refute the majority's freewheeling interpretation of "the Recess." It is not plausible that the Constitution uses that term in a sense that authorizes the President to make unilateral appointments during *any* break in Senate proceedings, subject only to hazy, atextual limits crafted by this Court centuries after ratification. The majority, however, insists that history "offers strong support" for its interpretation. The historical practice of the political branches is, of course, irrelevant when the Constitution is clear. But even if the Constitution were thought ambiguous on this point, history does not support the majority's interpretation. [Justice Scalia reviewed the history of Recess Appointments Clause practice. He concluded that it does not support the understanding that the power applies to intrasession recesses, primarily because this was not the established position of the executive branch until 1921 and because the practice was criticized by individual senators, though never condemned by the body as a whole.]

III. Pre–Recess Vacancies

. . . I would hold that the recess-appointment power is limited to vacancies that arise during the recess in which they are filled . . . .

A. Plain Meaning

As the majority concedes, "the most natural meaning of 'happens' as applied to a 'vacancy' . . . is that the vacancy 'happens' when it initially occurs." "Happen" meant [in the founding era], as it does now, "to fall out; to chance; to come to pass." 1 Johnson, Dictionary of the English Language 913. Thus, a vacancy that *happened* during the Recess was most reasonably understood as one that *arose* during the recess. It was, of course, possible in certain contexts for the word "happen" to mean "happen to be" rather than "happen to occur," as in the idiom "it so happens." But that meaning is not at all natural when the subject is a vacancy, a state of affairs that comes into existence at a particular moment in time.

In any event, no reasonable reader would have understood the Recess Appointments Clause to use the word "happen" in the majority's "happen to be" sense, and thus to empower the President to fill all vacancies that might *exist* during a recess, regardless of when they arose.

[T]he majority's reading not only strains the Clause's language but distorts its constitutional role, which was meant to be subordinate. As Hamilton explained, appointment with the advice and consent of the Senate was to be "the general mode of appointing officers of the United States." The Federalist No. 67, at 455. The Senate's check on the President's appointment power was seen as vital because "manipulation of official appointments had long been one of the American revolutionary generation's greatest grievances against executive power." *Freytag*, 501 U.S., at 883. The unilateral power conferred on the President by the Recess Appointments Clause was therefore understood to be "nothing more than a supplement" to the "general method" of advice and consent. The Federalist No. 67, at 455 . . . .

More fundamentally, the majority [is] mistaken to say that the Constitution's "substantial purpose" is to "keep . . . offices filled." The Constitution is not a road map for maximally efficient government, but a system of "carefully crafted restraints" designed to "protect the people from the improvident exercise of power." *Chadha*, 462 U.S., at 957, 959. . . .

[Justice Scalia canvassed historical practice. He summarized it as follows:] Washington's and Adams' Attorneys General read the Constitution to restrict recess appointments to vacancies arising during the recess, and there is no evidence that any of the first four Presidents consciously departed from that reading. The contrary reading was first defended by an executive official in 1823, was vehemently rejected by the Senate in 1863, was vigorously resisted by legislation in place from 1863 until 1940, and is arguably inconsistent with legislation in place from 1940 to the present. The Solicitor General has identified only about 100 appointments that have ever been made under the broader reading, and while it seems likely that a good deal more have been made in the last few decades, there is good reason to doubt that many were made before 1940 (since the appointees could not have been compensated). I can conceive of no sane constitutional theory under which this evidence of "historical practice" — which is actually evidence of a long-simmering inter-branch conflict — would require us to defer to the views of the Executive Branch.

IV. Conclusion

What the majority needs to sustain its judgment is an ambiguous text and a clear historical practice. What it has is a clear text and an at-best-ambiguous historical practice. Even if the Executive could accumulate power through adverse possession by engaging in a *consistent* and *unchallenged* practice over a long period of time, the oft-disputed practices at issue here would not meet that standard. Nor have those practices created any justifiable expectations that could be disappointed by enforcing the Constitution's original meaning. There is thus no ground for the majority's deference to the unconstitutional recess-appointment practices of the Executive Branch . . . .

I concur in the judgment only.

———————

1. *Formalism v. Functionalism.* Note that Justice Kennedy, a formalist in *Public Citizen v. Dep't of Justice, supra* Chapter 3, joins the functionalist opinion of Justice Breyer here. Below, in *Zivotofsky v. Kerry*, we will see Justice Kennedy himself author a highly functionalist opinion for the Court. Although the Court ultimately does not uphold the recess appointments to the NLRB, the *Noel Canning* opinion is largely favorable to the executive branch in that it affirms the executive branch's expansive reading of the Recess Appointments Clause with respect to both what counts as a "recess" and when a vacancy "happens." These cases are similar to one another in employing functionalism that is less deferential to Congress and more indulgent of executive power. In this respect, however, they represent a departure from previous cases that employ functionalism almost uniformly in a way that is highly deferential to Congress and much less accommodating of the executive branch. Which is the more appropriate stance for the Court to take?

2. *Dicta*. Did the Court go out of its way to affirm the executive branch's position on the meaning of "recess" and "happen"? The majority decided the case on the narrow ground that a *pro forma* session counts as a session (as long as the Senate *could* do business during the *pro forma* session) and therefore the recess was too brief to allow the President to make a recess appointment. Is the balance of Justice Breyer's opinion (interpreting "recess" and "happen") *dicta*? The Court's majority may have viewed resolving these issues as a predicate for deciding on the effects of a *pro forma* session. On the other hand, the majority could have assumed the resolution of these issues *arguendo*, only for purposes of answering the *pro forma* issue, in which case it would not have needed to reach the constitutional questions over the meaning of "recess" and "happen." Should it have done so? If so, should we regard the Court's treatment of these questions as binding precedent or as *dicta*?

And what are the implications, if any, of *Noel Canning* for *intersession* recess appointments? Do you interpret the Court's ten-day rule as applicable to all periods of Senate adjournment, whether within or between sessions? If so, should the President regard the opinion as limiting presidential discretion to make intersession recess appointments — a question not raised in *Noel Canning* — even during a break between sessions of only nine days or, for that matter, ten seconds?

3. Appointment of Judges

The power of judicial appointment allows a President to work an enduring influence on the course of American government. Yet this power is subject to very little law. Aspirants even to the Supreme Court, unlike presidential, vice-presidential, and congressional candidates, are not subject to any constitutional limitations regarding age, citizenship, or residency. Indeed, no judge or Justice need even be a lawyer. Congress has considered bills to limit Supreme Court appointments to persons under a particular age or with prior judicial experience, but no limitation has been enacted. The history of judicial appointments is consequently one of presidential discretion, limited formally only by the Senate confirmation process, which also proceeds without direct constitutional guidance.

For the most part, we do not consider legal issues here. Instead, we consider a variety of policy questions that attend the judicial appointments process. We begin with a brief discussion of presidential criteria for choosing Supreme Court Justices, and of the processes for identifying, evaluating, and confirming nominees. We then examine the controversy that surrounded President Franklin D. Roosevelt's court-packing plan of 1937. We also note current debate over the appropriate nature of Senate inquiry into the ideology of Supreme Court nominees. Turning to the lower courts, we summarize both an innovative Carter administration process for the selection of Court of Appeals judges and more recent battles over the use of the filibuster in the confirmation process for lower court judges. Finally, we consider the permissibility and appropriateness of presidential use of the recess appointment power for judges.

a. Appointments to the Supreme Court
Note on Supreme Court Appointments

All but four Presidents have appointed at least one Supreme Court Justice. Presidents have sometimes made their purported criteria explicit; more often, the criteria have been tacit and ad hoc. Nonetheless, history allows us to catalogue several factors that are likely to count in virtually all nominations. *See generally* Henry J. Abraham, Justices, Presidents, and Senators: A History of Supreme Court Appointments from Washington to Bush (2008); David Yalof, Pursuit of Justices: Presidential Politics and the Selection of Supreme Court Nominees (1999).

Ability and Character. Every President, in explaining nominations publicly, has cited ability and character among his criteria for selection. The appropriate measure of merit, however, may well vary with the needs of the country and of the Court when a vacancy occurs. Sometimes, the Court's greatest need may be an exceptional intellectual leader. At other times, a catalytic administrator or effective advocate may be better. In any event, because there is always a surplus of highly capable individuals for the available vacancies, rarely has a candidate's outstanding ability seemed to have decided the nomination (except, perhaps for Holmes and Cardozo). Indeed, a few of the nation's greatest justices appear to have been chosen without primary regard for their intellectual capacity. For example, James Madison nominated Joseph Story to the Court only after two confirmed appointees declined the position and a third nominee had been rejected by the Senate. It is uncertain what led Madison to Story, although it is known that Story's uncle and Madison were close friends.

An obvious potential measure of merit is prior distinguished judicial experience. About 60 per cent of the Justices have had prior judicial experience; in the twentieth century, Republican Presidents appointed proportionately more former judges than did Democrats. All but one Justice, however, reached the Court only after a substantial career in politics or public service of some sort. Some history of functioning in a high-pressure environment may help to assure that public criticism or the magnitude of a Justice's tasks will not compromise the nominee's judicial effectiveness and independence.

Political and Legal Philosophy. A *sine qua non* for nomination is likely to be the acceptability to the President of a candidate's personal philosophy. On occasion, the importance of a single issue to the nation's welfare or to a President's program may loom so large that a candidate's position on it becomes the litmus test of acceptability. Examples include the cause of the Union under Lincoln, the constitutionality of paper money under Grant, and the legitimacy of federal regulation of the economy under Franklin Roosevelt. At other times, acceptability may be measured more in terms of general party affiliation.

Even if either partisan identification or single-issue politics predominates, however, the Justice's performance may not be predictable. Examples of Justices whose rulings have been at odds with the philosophies of their appointing Presidents include James McReynolds, whom Woodrow Wilson appointed based largely on McReynolds's fervent antitrust position, and Earl Warren, whom Eisenhower appointed based largely on Warren's political service to Eisenhower and the Republican Party. (President George H.W. Bush appointed both David Souter and Clarence Thomas to the Court, Justices whose views diverged so substantially, it would be hard to imagine that both tracked the likely views of President Bush.) Such disappointments may convince a President of the importance of examining a nominee's overall pattern of values and opinions as closely as possible.

One reason why a Justice's performance may surprise the appointing President is possible confusion in the recruitment process between a candidate's political and legal philosophies. Felix Frankfurter was, in terms of political philosophy, the ardent New Dealer that Franklin Roosevelt had expected. The central theme of Frankfurter's judicial philosophy, however, was one of judicial restraint, thus distinguishing his Court performance dramatically from those of other FDR appointees such as Douglas, Black, and Murphy.

Enhancing the Representativeness of the Court. In narrowing the pool of potential nominees, Presidents have frequently sought individuals who would enhance public perceptions of the representativeness of the Court. The primary measure of representativeness has been geographical — especially in the Nineteenth Century — although partisan affiliation and, more recently, religion, race, and gender have entered as considerations. Of the 113 Justices to date, 109 have been men, two have been African-American, and one Latina-American. 107 have been native-born, and 91 have been Protestant. Since 1894, at least one seat on the Court has been held by a Catholic (except for the period 1949–1956), and at least one seat has been held by a Jewish Justice from 1916 to 1969, and from 1994 to date. (Indeed, between 2010 and 2017, every Justice was either Catholic or Jewish.)

Other Criteria. Additional criteria for selection have included age, health, friendship, the elimination of a potential opponent from electoral politics, placating political opposition, and securing political support. The presence of such motives need not correlate with the unsuitability of a candidate on other grounds. Among the Justices appointed in part because of close personal friendship with a President are Taney, Field, Stone, and Frankfurter, all of whom would have been qualified under any likely set of criteria.

Identifying and Evaluating Potential Nominees. Potential sources of the names of prospects for the Court are almost endless. Solicited or unsolicited suggestions may come from the President's advisers, members of Congress, sitting judges or Justices, legal scholars, state bar representatives, concerned private citizens, and from candidates themselves. Once potential nominees are identified, someone must evaluate the serious contenders. A tradition has arisen of active Department of Justice participation in the process of assessing Supreme Court candidates. The Department may initiate its own study of potential candidates, and plays a leading role in marshalling assessments from private groups and individuals.

Beginning in 1952 in the Eisenhower administration, a special advisory role has been played by the American Bar Association Standing Committee on the Federal Judiciary, as we saw in *Public Citizen, supra*. The mode of ABA participation has varied. The ABA-Justice Department relationship was especially stormy during the Nixon Administration. For undisclosed reasons, Nixon initially abandoned his predecessors' practice of consulting the ABA prior to announcing nominees. The ABA wound up in the embarrassing posture of favorably evaluating two Nixon nominees whom the Senate refused to confirm. When the Administration changed policy in 1971 and asked the ABA for its views on two candidates prior to their public designation, the ABA returned the embarrassment by reviewing the candidates unfavorably and disclosing its report to the press. Such extensive ABA participation led to criticism that an organization that is not responsible to any public political process exercised undue influence in the appointments process. The presumed benefit of ABA review is its potential for nonpartisan professional evaluation of a nominee. President George W. Bush declined to seek the views of the ABA about his nominees, but President Obama resumed the practice. President Trump has again opted out.

Senate Confirmation. Once the President nominates, he submits his choice for the "advice and consent" of the Senate. Whether a nominee can secure the support of a majority of the Senate may depend on a host of factors, none of which need necessarily relate to the President's criteria for making an appointment. Typically the reasons for rejection include doubts about a candidate's ability or good character, dislike of a nominee's partisanship or ideology, or disfavor due to a candidate's prior identification with the unpopular side of a significant popular controversy.

During the first half of the twentieth century, the Senate seldom materially influenced the selection of a Justice. Since the conditional resignation of Earl Warren in 1968, however, presidential nominations for the Court have repeatedly been defeated by the Senate or have been withdrawn in part because of Senate pressure. Judge Harrold Carswell's nomination failed because of his visible lack of ability and apparent insensitivity to civil rights concerns. Judge Clement Haynesworth's failed because of his participation in lower court cases in which he arguably had or had created a financial conflict of interest. Justice Abe Fortas failed to become Chief Justice because while on the Court he accepted paid employment by a university, maintained a close advisory relationship with the President, and received fees from a private foundation.

In October, 1987, following a bitter confirmation battle, the Senate rejected the nomination to the Supreme Court of Judge Robert H. Bork of the U.S. Court of Appeals for the D.C. Circuit, whom President Reagan had chosen to succeed retiring Justice Lewis Powell. The White House and Judge Bork's defenders argued that he was qualified by virtue of his abilities and his extensive public service, and characterized attacks on him as ideologically motivated distortions of his record. Judge Bork's critics argued that he had long advocated a view of constitutional law that was both historically indefensible and stridently hostile to many of the key Supreme Court decisions in recent decades expanding the scope of judicially protected rights. The vigor of the Bork confirmation fight provoked considerable commentary on the Senate's use of its confirmation power. *See* Symposium, *Confirmation Controversy: The Selection of a Supreme Court Justice*, 84 Nw. U. L. Rev. 832 (1990).

Bork's defeat by an unprecedented margin in the full Senate was followed by the short-lived nomination of Judge Douglas Ginsburg, also of the D.C. Circuit, a conservative who had less clear constitutional views than Judge Bork. Judge Ginsburg's nomination was withdrawn after it was disclosed to the White House's embarrassment that, while a law professor, Judge Ginsburg had engaged in marijuana use. Justice Powell was ultimately succeeded by Judge Anthony Kennedy of the Ninth Circuit, widely perceived upon confirmation as a moderate conservative more akin in outlook to Powell than to Judges Bork or Ginsburg.

The Senate's role in confirming Justices again became the focus of extraordinary attention upon Justice William Brennan's July, 1990, resignation from the Court. Commentators expected that the replacement of Justice Brennan by a conservative could have a profound impact on the resolution of constitutional cases in a great many areas. President George H.W. Bush's choice to succeed Justice Brennan was Judge David Souter, who had only recently been appointed to the U.S. Court of Appeals for the First Circuit from the Supreme Court of New Hampshire. Although clearly falling within the broad category of "conservative," Judge Souter proved a challenging nominee to scrutinize because, while New Hampshire Attorney General and then as a judge, he made extraordinarily few public statements of his personal views on social and political issues. His nomination sailed through, helped largely by his eloquent and balanced disquisitions on constitutional law before the Judiciary Committee and by his support from New Hampshire Senator Warren Rudman, a widely respected Republican moderate.

In 1991, President George H.W. Bush settled on a far more controversial nominee to succeed retiring Justice Thurgood Marshall. He appointed Clarence Thomas, a young and relatively new member of the D.C. Circuit, who, as a staunchly conservative African-American, had served a controversial term as chair of the Equal Employment Opportunity Commission. Judge Thomas's record and testimony were more vulnerable to challenge than Judge Souter's, but his greatest obstacle came when news leaked that University of Oklahoma law professor Anita Hill had accused Thomas of sexually harassing her during her tenure as his special assistant at EEOC. After riveting public hearings, the Senate narrowly confirmed Thomas.

Confirmations without substantial controversy or acrimony finally occurred when President Clinton nominated Judge Ruth Bader Ginsburg of the D.C. Circuit to replace retiring Justice Byron White, and Judge Stephen Breyer of the First Circuit to replace Justice Harry Blackmun. Although Judge Ginsburg was relatively forthcoming about her views on women's rights, she met little opposition. Judge Breyer's sometimes cautionary writings about regulation caused some grumbling from liberals, but no significant challenge appeared.

President George W. Bush made two Supreme Court appointments and suffered one false start. Judge John G. Roberts, Jr. of the D.C. Circuit replaced Chief Justice William Rehnquist as Chief Justice. He was originally nominated to replace Justice O'Connor, but the President withdrew that nomination upon the death of Chief Justice Rehnquist and nominated him to replace the late chief. Relatively uncontroversial hearings followed party lines. Roberts, who possessed extremely strong professional credentials, was widely praised by Republicans and conservatives, and was only mildly challenged by Democrats and liberals. He was confirmed by a 78–22 vote. The confirmation hearings focused mostly on his faith and the possibility that Catholicism would play a role in his jurisprudence. Specifically, questions relating to his views on abortion, on the beginning of life and the right to privacy, and on the role of religion in deciding cases were prominent in his hearings before the Senate Judiciary Committee. Judge Roberts espoused a judicial minimalist approach when discussing his views. He likened himself to an umpire, claiming that his "job is to call balls and strikes, not to pitch or bat."

Judge Samuel A. Alito, Jr., of the Third Circuit replaced Justice Sandra Day O'Connor. The Senate voted 58–42 to confirm him. More controversy surfaced than with Roberts. Some Democrats threatened a filibuster before the conclusion of the confirmation hearings. As with Roberts, abortion was a key focus of confirmation hearing questions. He was also questioned sharply about broad views of executive power that he had expressed while in the Office of Legal Counsel.

Before turning to Alito, President Bush had nominated White House Counsel Harriet E. Miers to replace Justice O'Connor. Miers was the first failed nominee since Judges Robert Bork and Douglas Ginsburg. Ten days before confirmation hearings were to begin, Miers withdrew her nomination after criticism from both liberals and conservatives. She had never been a judge, and there was concern from both sides because of her inexperience and lack of a track record. Robert Bork thought her nomination was a "disaster," leading some to say Miers was "Borked" by Bork!

President Barack Obama made two appointments to the Court. Judge Sonia M. Sotomayor of the Second Circuit replaced Justice David H. Souter. She was confirmed by a vote of 68–31. Following the trend of other recent Supreme Court nominations, support for Sotomayor was largely along party lines. As with Roberts and Alito, the opposition was concerned with her ability to be impartial. Opponents questioned her ability to set aside her personal views and convictions in interpreting the Constitution. Like Roberts and Alito, Sotomayor gave partial and restrained answers stressing that judges do not make law. The main controversy surrounded a 2001 statement she made: "I would hope that a wise Latina woman with the richness of her experiences would more often than not reach a better conclusion than a white male who hasn't lived that life." She faced significant questioning from the Committee related to this remark and tried to distance herself from the statement, asserting that it was meant only to inspire women and Latinos pursuing legal careers.

In May, 2010, President Obama nominated Solicitor General and former Harvard Law School dean Elena Kagan to succeed Justice John Paul Stevens. She was confirmed in August, 2010 by a vote of 63–37, with only one Democrat in opposition. At age 50, she became the first Justice in 38 years—since the appointment of then-Associate Justice Rehnquist—to join the Court without having served on any other bench. Opponents criticized her lack of judicial experience or significant private practice background. Moreover, because she had been a senior policy adviser in the Clinton White House, some opponents suggested she would be an activist for a liberal political agenda. Ironically, because Kagan had not been especially notable as a law professor for her political activism and because Justice Stevens, especially in his later years, had become so outspoken a progressive voice on the Court, Obama was also criticized from the left for not appointing a more conspicuously left-wing legal thinker to fill the Stevens seat.

Over the decades, many commentators have noted the breakdown in norms of bipartisan comity in the vetting and confirmation of Justices. It seems fair to say that any comity that remained was lost, however, following the unexpected death of Justice Antonin Scalia in February, 2016. His passing created the first genuine prospect of a judicial appointee replacing a Justice of a distinctly different judicial philosophy since Clarence Thomas succeeded Thurgood Marshall in 1991. To fill the vacancy, President Obama nominated Merrick B. Garland, chief judge of the U.S. Court of Appeals for the D.C. Circuit. Despite apparent admiration for Judge Garland among Senators of both parties—Senator Orrin Hatch (R-UT) had earlier urged his nomination—Senate Republicans declared their unwillingness to consider any nomination by President Obama to succeed Justice Scalia. Their declared rationale was a supposed tradition of Presidents in the final year of their terms not nominating candidates for Supreme Court vacancies. In fact, there is no such tradition, and no elected President had ever been similarly blocked. Prior to the Garland nomination, there were only six instances since the country began when the Senate held a Supreme Court vacancy open for a new President—three times when the appointing President had not been elected (Tyler, Fillmore, and Andrew Johnson) and three times when the nomination was made after a new President had already been elected—most recently in 1881. Robin Bradley Kar and Jason Mazzone, *The Garland Affair: What History and the Constitution Really Say About President Obama's Powers to Appoint a Replacement for Justice Scalia*, NYU LAW REVIEW: ON-LINE FEATURES (2016), http://www.nyulawreview.org/online-features/garland-affair-what-history-and-constitution-really-say-about-president-obamas. The Senate's stance sparked a debate among its critics whether the refusal was a regrettable, but permissible, exercise of discretionary power, e.g., Miguel A. Estrada and Benjamin Wittes, *There no longer are any rules in the Supreme Court nomination process*, WASH. POST (Feb. 19, 2016), http://tinyurl.com/yauqx7k2, or a violation of the Senate's constitutional obligation at least to consider nominees on their merits, Peter M. Shane, *The Constitution as a Code of Honor* HUFFINGTON POST (Apr. 06, 2016), http://www.huffingtonpost.com/peter-m-shane/the-constitution-as-a-cod_b_9611628.html.

The 2016 election, of course, meant that a Republican-controlled Senate would next consider a potential Scalia successor chosen by a Republican President, and, on

January 31, 2017, President Trump nominated Judge Neil A. Gorsuch of the U.S. Court of Appeals for the Tenth Circuit. Having insufficient votes in the Senate to overcome a filibuster, however, Senate Republicans exercised what had been called "the nuclear option" and changed Senate rules so that no judicial nominations at all would any longer require the approval of more than a bare majority. Justice Gorsuch was confirmed on April 7, 2017. His early opinions suggest a jurist much in line with the Justice he succeeded.

It seems almost quaint at this point to consider whether Senators should look beyond a prospective Justice's educational, professional and civic credentials to determine whether or not to support a judicial nominee. It remains an important question, however, how closely the Senate should question prospective Justices about their positions on particular legal or political issues? Consider the views of Professor Robert N. Clinton, in *Judges Must Make Law: A Realistic Appraisal of the Judicial Function in a Democratic Society*, 67 Iowa L. Rev. 711 (1982):

> The plain and simple fact is that judges, of necessity, must from time to time make, rather than interpret, law and that they are perfectly justified in so doing. Indeed, no clear line actually can be drawn between making and interpreting law and the distinction is therefore illusory. . . .

> [T]he observed distinctions between liberals and conservatives or between activists and proponents of self-restraint on the bench are actuated by a judge's personal perceptions of the society and by personal values. These differences indicate that it is vital that such matters be explored in the process of selecting and approving justices of the United States Supreme Court and judges of any other court . . . .

> To suggest that an in-depth exploration of a potential nominee's social, political, and moral values is appropriate is not to suggest, however, that the President or the Senate should or can secure iron-clad guarantees as to how judicial nominees will decide particular cases in the future. Such efforts are simply inappropriate. The judicial process is a deliberative one in which the judges are requested to suspend judgment until they have heard the arguments on both sides of the case. . . . Because the argument between two adverse parties, each having an important stake in the controversy, often illuminates the policy considerations that underlie constitutional decision-making, federal courts are constitutionally prohibited from rendering advisory opinions. Similarly, a nominee for the federal bench is justified in refusing to answer or evading questions about how he or she would in the future decide particular issues or cases. Thus, Justice Sandra Day O'Connor is to be applauded for her dogged efforts to resist such questioning. . . .

> On the other hand, because some inquiry into the social, political, and moral values of a nominee is appropriate and necessary, it may be that Justice O'Connor legitimately can be criticized, insofar as she refused to respond to specific questions dealing with her political philosophy, which were framed

in a manner that could not implicate a case that could come before the Court. For example, there is an important difference between asking a judge, "Would you vote to overrule the decision in *Roe v. Wade*?" and asking the nominee to respond to the following question: "If constitutionally permissible, would you as a legislator vote to prohibit abortions in all cases or, possibly, except in cases of rape or incest?" While the former question is plainly inappropriate, the latter question, while hypothetical, does test the nominee's political and social value structure in a context divorced from any potential judicial decisionmaking and, for that reason, seems justified and appropriate. . . . [S]uch information is vital to the Senate if it is effectively to exercise one of the few democratic checks available in our system of government to shape the course and direction of the federal judiciary.

Does Clinton endorse questioning nominees about matters unrelated to judging ("If you were a legislator, . . ."), while excluding questions that *are* related to the job? Should a nominee be expected to answer whether he or she thought a particular case had been correctly decided? ("How would you have voted in *Roe v. Wade*?") How far could such probing extend without calling for a promised vote in a future case?

———————

Politics, like law, has precedents that confine later decisions. Some modern limits to a President's ability to shape the Supreme Court through use of the appointments power are demonstrated by the history of FDR's ill-fated "Court-packing" plan in 1937. The full story is told in James M. Burns, Roosevelt: The Lion and the Fox, Ch. 15 (1956); *see also* William E. Leuchtenburg, *The Origins of Franklin D. Roosevelt's "Court-Packing Plan,"* 1966 Sup. Ct. Rev. 347. We provide excerpts from the President's argument to the nation in favor of the plan, and the Senate Judiciary Committee's adverse report on it.

———————

The Coming Crisis in Recovery and What Can Be Done About It

President Roosevelt, by Radio from Washington, March 9, 1937

S. Rep. No. 711, 75th Cong., 1st Sess. 41–45 (1937)

. . . Tonight, sitting at my desk in the White House, I make my first radio report to the people in my second term of office. The American people have learned from the depression. For in the last three national elections an overwhelming majority of them voted a mandate that the Congress and the President begin the task of providing [a program of] protection — not after long years of debate, but now. The courts, however, have cast doubts on the ability of the elected Congress to protect us against catastrophe, by meeting squarely our modern social and economic conditions. We are at a crisis in our ability to proceed with that protection. . . . [Here the President made his analogy of the government to a three-horse team, with one of the horses — the Court — not pulling in unison, which we quoted in Chapter One.]

I hope that you have re-read the Constitution of the United States. Like the Bible, it ought to be read again and again. It is an easy document to understand when you remember that it was called into being because the Articles of Confederation under which the original thirteen States tried to operate after the Revolution showed the need of a national government with power enough to handle national problems. . . . But the framers went further. Having in mind that in succeeding generations many other problems then undreamed of would become national problems, they gave to the Congress the ample broad powers "to levy taxes . . . and provide for the common defense and general welfare of the United States." . . . [S]ince the rise of the modern movement for social and economic progress through legislation, the Court has more and more often and more and more boldly asserted a power to veto laws passed by the Congress and State Legislatures. . . . In the last four years the sound rule of giving statutes the benefit of all reasonable doubt has been cast aside. The Court has been acting not as a judicial body but as a policy-making body.

When the Congress has sought to stabilize national agriculture, to improve the conditions of labor, to safeguard business against unfair competition, to protect our national resources, and in many other ways to serve our clearly national needs, the majority of the Court has been assuming power to pass on the wisdom of these acts of Congress—and to approve or disapprove the public policy written into these laws. That is not only my accusation. It is the accusation of most distinguished justices of the present Supreme Court. I have not the time to quote to you all the language used by dissenting justices in many of these cases. . . . [I]t is perfectly clear, that as Chief Justice Hughes has said: "We are under a Constitution but the Constitution is what the judges say it is."

The Court . . . has improperly set itself up as a third house of the Congress—a super-legislature, as one of the justices has called it—reading into the Constitution words and implications which are not there, and which were never intended to be there. We have, therefore, reached the point as a nation where we must take action to save the Constitution from the Court and the Court from itself. We must find a way to take an appeal from the Supreme Court to the Constitution itself. . . . When I commenced to review the situation . . . I [decided] that short of amendments the only method which was clearly constitutional, and would at the same time carry out other much-needed reforms, was to infuse new blood into all our courts. We must have men worthy and equipped to carry out impartial justice. But, at the same time, we must have judges who will bring to the courts a present-day sense of the Constitution—judges who will retain in the courts the judicial functions of a court and reject the legislative powers which the courts have today assumed.

In forty-five out of the forty-eight States of the Union, judges are chosen not for life but for a period of years. In many States judges must retire at the age of 70. Congress has provided financial security by offering life pensions at full pay for Federal judges on all courts who are willing to retire at 70. . . . But all Federal judges, once appointed, can, if they choose, hold office for life, no matter how old they may get to be.

What is my proposal? It is simply this: Whenever a judge or justice of any Federal court has reached the age of 70 and does not avail himself of the opportunity to retire on a pension, a new member shall be appointed by the President then in office, with the approval, as required by the Constitution, of the Senate of the United States. That plan has two chief purposes. By bringing into the judicial system a steady and continuing stream of new and younger blood I hope, first, to make the administration of all Federal justice speedier and, therefore, less costly; secondly, to bring to the decision of social and economic problems younger men who have had personal experience and contact with modern facts and circumstances under which average men have to live and work. This plan will save our national Constitution from hardening of the judicial arteries. . . .

If, for instance, any one of the six Justices of the Supreme Court now over the age of 70 should retire as provided under the plan, no additional place would be created. Consequently, although there never can be more than fifteen, there may be only fourteen, or thirteen, or twelve. And there may be only nine. There is nothing novel or radical about this idea. . . . It has been discussed and approved by many persons of high authority ever since a similar proposal passed the House of Representatives in 1869. . . . Those opposing this plan have sought to arouse prejudice and fear by crying that I am seeking to "pack" the Supreme Court and that a baneful precedent will be established. . . . If by that phrase . . . the charge is made that I would appoint and the Senate would confirm justices worthy to sit beside present members of the Court who understand those modern conditions—that I will appoint justices who will not undertake to override the judgment of the Congress or legislative policy— . . . if the appointment of such justices can be called "packing the courts," then I say that I and with me the vast majority of the American people favor doing just that thing—now.

Is it a dangerous precedent for the Congress to change the number of the justices? The Congress has always had, and will have, that power. The number of justices has been changed several times before—in the administrations of John Adams and Thomas Jefferson, both signers of the Declaration of Independence—Andrew Jackson, Abraham Lincoln and Ulysses S. Grant. . . .

We think it so much in the public interest to maintain a vigorous judiciary that we encourage the retirement of elderly judges by offering them a life pension at full salary. . . . But chance and the disinclination of individuals to leave the Supreme bench have now given us a court in which five justices will be over seventy-five years of age before next June and one over seventy. Thus a sound public policy has been defeated. . . .

During the past half century the balance of power between the three great branches of the Federal Government has been tipped out of balance by the courts in direct contradiction of the high purposes of the framers of the Constitution. It is my purpose to restore that balance. . . .

———————

Reorganization of the Federal Judiciary

S. Rep. No. 711, 75th Cong., 1st Sess. (1937)

The Committee on the Judiciary, to whom was referred the bill (S. 1392) to reorganize the judicial branch of the Government, after full consideration, . . . hereby report the bill adversely with the recommendation that it do not pass. . . . The bill . . . may be summarized in the following manner:

By section 1(a) the President is directed to appoint an additional judge to any court of the United States when and only when three contingencies arise: (a) That a sitting judge shall have attained the age of 70 years; (b) That he shall have held a Federal judge's commission for at least 10 years; (c) That he has neither resigned nor retired within 6 months after the happening of the two contingencies first named. . . . By section 1(b) it is provided that in event of the appointment of judges under the provisions of section 1(a), then the size of the court to which such appointments are made is "permanently" increased by that number. But . . . [r]egardless of the age or service of the members of the Federal judiciary, . . . the Supreme Court may not be increased beyond 15 members; no circuit court of appeals . . . may be increased by more than 2 members; and . . . the number of judges now authorized to be appointed for any district or group of districts may not be more than doubled. . . .

The next question is to determine to what extent "the persistent infusion of new blood" may be expected from this bill. It will be observed that the bill before us does not and cannot compel the retirement of any judge. . . . It will be remembered that the mere attainment of three score and ten by a particular judge does not, under this bill, require the appointment of another . . . unless he has served as a judge for 10 years. In other words, age itself is not penalized; the penalty falls only when age is attended with experience. . . . [T]he introduction of old and inexperienced blood into the courts is not prevented by this bill. . . .

Take the Supreme Court as an example. As constituted at the time this bill was presented to the Congress, there were six members of that tribunal over 70 years of age. If all six failed to resign or retire . . . then the Supreme Court would consist of 15 members. These 15 would then serve, regardless of age, at their own will, during good behavior, in other words, for life. Though as a result we had a court of 15 members 70 years of age or over, nothing could be done about it under this bill, and there would be no way to infuse "new" blood or "young" blood except by a new law further expanding the Court, unless, indeed, Congress and the Executive should be willing to follow the course defined by the framers of the Constitution for such a contingency and submit to the people a constitutional amendment limiting the terms of Justices or making mandatory their retirement at a given age.

It thus appears that the bill before us does not with certainty provide for increasing the personnel of the Federal judiciary, does not remedy the law's delay, does not serve the interest of the "poorer litigant" and does not provide for the "constant" or "persistent infusion of new blood" into the judiciary. What does it do? The answer is clear. It applies force to the judiciary. It is an attempt to impose upon the courts a course of action, a line of decision which, without that force, without that imposition, the judiciary might not adopt. . . . Increasing the personnel is not the object of this measure; infusing young blood is not the object. . . .

Can reasonable men by any possibility differ about the constitutional impropriety of such a course? . . . That judges should hold office during good behavior is the prescription. It is founded upon historic experience of the utmost significance. Compensation at stated times, which compensation was not to be diminished during their tenure, was also ordained. Those comprehensible terms were the outgrowths of experience which was deep-seated. . . . [The framers] sought to correct an abuse and to prevent its recurrence. . . .

The effect of this bill is not to provide for an increase in the number of Justices composing the Supreme Court. The effect is to provide a forced retirement or, failing in this, to take from the Justices affected a free exercise of their independent judgment. . . . Let us, for the purpose of the argument, grant that the Court has . . . substituted its will for the congressional will in the matter of legislation. May we nevertheless safely punish the Court? . . . Manifestly, if we may force the hand of the Court to secure our interpretation of the Constitution, then some succeeding Congress may repeat the process to secure another and a different interpretation and one which may not sound so pleasant in our ears as that for which we now contend.

There is a remedy for usurpation or other judicial wrongdoing. If this bill be supported by the toilers of this country upon the ground that they want a Court which will sustain legislation limiting hours and providing minimum wages, they must remember that the procedure employed in the bill could be used in another administration to lengthen hours and to decrease wages. . . . When members of the Court usurp legislative powers or attempt to exercise political power, they lay themselves open to the charge of having lapsed from that "good behavior" which determines the period of their official life. . . . But, if the fault of the judges is not so grievous as to warrant impeachment, if their offense is merely that they have grown old, and we feel, therefore, that there should be a "constant infusion of new blood", then obviously the way to achieve that result is by constitutional amendment fixing definite terms for the members of the judiciary or making mandatory their retirement at a given age. Such a provision would indeed provide for the constant infusion of new blood, not only now but at all times in the future. The plan before us is but a temporary expedient which operates once and then never again, leaving the Court as permanently expanded to become once more a court of old men, gradually year by year falling behind the times. . . .

----

1. *Unwise or Unconstitutional?* What is your assessment of FDR's Court-packing plan? Do you agree with the Committee that it was unconstitutional? Does your answer depend on the motive behind the plan? If so, was Roosevelt's error merely one of how he structured and explained the plan?

2. *Bad Timing?* Apart from the crisis that stemmed from the Court's repeated invalidation of New Deal legislation, is there a real need for "a steady and continuing stream of new and younger blood" on the Court? In short, did FDR pick a bad time to advance a good idea? If so, what measures would be appropriate, and by what process (legislation or constitutional amendment) should they be adopted?

3. *Precedential Value.* What is the enduring historical lesson of the Court-packing plan? Is it that the Court is sacrosanct from blatant political manipulation by the President? Or is the message exactly to the contrary—Roosevelt eventually abandoned the plan, but it may have spurred the Court's rather abrupt switch to approving New Deal legislation. (*E.g., NLRB v. Jones & Laughlin Steel Corp.,* 301 U.S. 1 (1937), decided while the debate raged.) Was Roosevelt correct in his later assessment that he lost the battle but won the war?

b. Appointments to the Courts of Appeals and District Courts

In 1978, President Carter issued Executive Order 12059, which created a "United States Circuit Judge Nominating Commission." *See* LARRY C. BERKSON & SUSAN B. CARBON, THE UNITED STATES CIRCUIT JUDGE NOMINATING COMMISSION: ITS MEMBERS, PROCEDURES, AND CANDIDATES (1980). The Commission was composed of thirteen panels, organized regionally. Each panel was to recommend for nomination as circuit judges "persons whose character, experience, ability and commitment to equal justice under law, fully qualify them to serve in the Federal judiciary." The panels were to "include members of both sexes and members of minority groups." Upon notification of the President's need for a nominee, a panel was to give public notice of the vacancy, search for candidates, and report its recommendations to the President. The criteria for selection were:

(1) That those persons are members in good standing of at least one state bar, or the District of Columbia bar, and members in good standing of any other bars of which they may be members;

(2) That they possess, and have reputations for, integrity and good character;

(3) That they are of sound health;

(4) That they possess, and have demonstrated, outstanding legal ability and commitment to equal justice under law; and

(5) That their demeanor, character, and personality indicate that they would exhibit judicial temperament if appointed to the position of United States Circuit Judge.

Panels were encouraged to consider "whether the training, experience, or expertise of certain of the well qualified individuals would help to meet a perceived need of the court of appeals on which the vacancy or vacancies exist," and "to make special efforts to seek out and identify well qualified women and members of minority groups as potential nominees."

President Reagan revoked the order, thereby returning judicial selection to a more politicized process, as it has remained since. *See generally* SHELDON GOLDMAN, PICKING FEDERAL JUDGES: LOWER COURT SELECTION FROM ROOSEVELT THROUGH REAGAN (1997); Carl Tobias, *The Bush Administration and Appeals Courts Nominees*, 10 WM. & MARY BILL RTS. J. 103 (2001); William Ross, *The Questioning of Lower Federal Court Nominees at Senate Confirmation Hearings*, *id.* at 119.

Nominations of lower federal court judges have traditionally been affected by a custom usually referred to as "senatorial courtesy." *See generally* Brandon Denning, *The 'Blue Slip': Enforcing the Norms of the Judicial Confirmation Process*, *id.* at 75. Presidents have usually deferred to a Senator of their own party when choosing a nominee for a federal office, including judicial office, in the Senator's home state. This practice is enforced by the deference of the entire Senate to a Senator's opposition to a particular candidate. The consequence of this custom is to shift the choice of nominees from the President to the Senate, whatever the Appointments Clause might say.

Presidents Bill Clinton and George W. Bush tried to regain some control of the selection of lower court judges from the Senate, touching off an intermittent war over nominations that featured extensive use of the filibuster. The story is told in THOMAS E. MANN & NORMAN J. ORNSTEIN, THE BROKEN BRANCH: HOW CONGRESS IS FAILING AMERICA AND HOW TO GET IT BACK ON TRACK 162–69 (2006). The use of filibusters to defeat nominees who had majority support in the Senate became routine, dropping confirmation rates for circuit judges to just over fifty percent for these two Presidents. (It had formerly been far higher.) As Majority Leader, Republican Senator Bill Frist finally proposed an earlier version of the "nuclear option" to resolve the stalemate. It would have worked as follows. To avoid the supermajority needed to force cloture of debate, a Senator would have raised a point of order that extended debate on pending judicial nominations is out of order. As President of the Senate, Vice President Cheney would have upheld the point of order. Because challenges to rulings of the chair are resolved by simple majority, the longtime frustrations caused by the filibuster would have been ended by majority rule. Two factors caused Frist and others to draw back, however. First, there was fear of the loss of this useful weapon when majority control of the Senate eventually switched. Second, Minority Leader Harry Reid threatened to shut down the Senate by the simple expedient of refusing the usual unanimous consent to take routine actions. The nuclear weapons were shelved, and the courts are not likely to intervene. See *Judicial Watch, Inc. v. U. S. Senate*, 432 F.3d 359 (D.C. Cir. 2005), upholding the dismissal on standing grounds of a challenge to the constitutionality of the filibuster rule as applied to judicial nominations.

The battle over lower court nominations intensified during the Obama Administration. In large part because he faced a larger number of lower court vacancies than earlier Presidents, President Obama appointed as many lower court judges as President George W. Bush and almost as many as President Reagan. The rate of approval, however, eighty-three percent, was the lowest of any of the two-term Presidents since 1945. Senate Democrats' frustration with what they perceived to be the slow-walking of both judicial nominees and nominees to executive branch positions led them in November, 2013, to trigger the "nuclear option" Senator Frist had earlier contemplated, eliminating the prospect of filibusters for any nominees other than for Supreme Court vacancies. Barry J. McMillion, U.S. Circuit and District Court Nominations: Comparative Statistics of Two-Term Presidencies Since 1945 (Congressional Research Service Apr. 24, 2017), https://fas.org/sgp/crs/misc/IN10694.pdf. For a helpful historical review of the ebb and flow of Senate procedures as they affect nominations to the lower federal courts, see DENIS STEVEN RUTKUS, THE APPOINTMENT PROCESS FOR U.S. CIRCUIT AND DISTRICT COURT NOMINATIONS: AN OVERVIEW (Congressional Research Service No. R43762, 2016), https://fas.org/sgp/crs/misc/R43762.pdf. As noted above, the filibuster was eliminated for Supreme Court nominations in early 2017.

Should Presidents — or the public — be wary of excessive partisanship or other forms of homogeneity in judicial appointments? Empirical studies have shown a dismaying correlation between the judges' orientation toward the validity of federal regulation and the politics of the President who appointed them. Richard L. Revesz, *Environmental Regulation, Ideology, and the D.C. Circuit*, 83 VA. L. REV. 1717 (1997); and *Congressional Influence on Judicial Behavior? An Empirical Examination of Challenges to Agency Action in the D.C. Circuit*, 76 N.Y.U. L. REV. 1100 (2001); Thomas J. Miles & Cass R. Sunstein, *The Real World of Arbitrariness Review*, 75 U. CHI. L. REV. 761 (2008); Cass R. Sunstein, David Schkade & Lisa Michelle Ellman, *Ideological Voting on Federal Courts of Appeals: A Preliminary Investigation*, 90 VA. L. REV. 301 (2004). The solution for this problem might seem to be for Presidents to show more restraint in nominating active ideological partisans to the federal bench, although it may not be clear where the line is to be drawn between the kinds of partisan loyalty that have presumably figured in judicial nominations forever and the sorts of ideological precommitment that count as inappropriately "activist." Unfortunately, to the extent any President does elevate ideological activists for the bench, his success would likely strengthen the incentive for successor Presidents of the other party to counter by nominating activists of their own.

c. Recess Appointments of Judges

As we noted above, Article II, § 2, authorizes the President to fill vacancies during recesses of the Senate by granting commissions that expire at the end of the session. Does this power to make temporary appointments include federal judges, who are guaranteed life tenure by Article III? This raises an interesting problem in structural interpretation of two apparently clashing provisions of the Constitution. Our history also bears on resolution of the problem.

In *United States v. Woodley,*751 F.2d 1008 (9th Cir. 1985) (en banc), *cert. denied*, 475 U.S. 1048 (1986), the court struggled with the issues. In 1980, Walter Heen was nominated to fill a vacancy in the United States District Court for Hawaii. When the Senate recessed on December 16, 1980, the nomination had not come before the Senate for its advice and consent. During the Senate's recess, on December 31, 1980,

President Carter gave Heen a recess appointment, and he then took the oath and assumed his duties as district court judge. On January 21, 1981, Heen's nomination was withdrawn by President Reagan. Heen continued sitting as a district judge pursuant to his recess commission until December 16, 1981, when the 97th Congress ended its First Session. While Heen was on the bench, he presided over a trial of a Ms. Woodley on narcotics charges. She challenged his authority to preside.

In an opinion by Judge Beezer, the court held that the recess appointment clause extends to judicial officers and that a recess appointee to the federal bench could exercise the judicial power of the United States. The court was strongly influenced by historical practice:

> In 1789, shortly after ratification of the Constitution, George Washington, who had served as President of the Constitutional Convention, exercised his power under the recess provision. During the recess between the sessions of the First Congress, he conferred three recess district judge commissions. . . . Moreover, the district court judges were confirmed upon the return of the Senate without objection to their recess appointments. It is further noteworthy that President Washington's recess appointments of Justice Johnson in 1791 and of Chief Justice Rutledge in 1795 went unchallenged. One commentator has aptly noted that "the most significant historical fact is that by the end of 1823, there had been five recess appointments to the Supreme Court. During this period, when those who wrote the Constitution were alive and active, not one dissenting voice was raised against the practice." Note, *Recess Appointments to the Supreme Court—Constitutional but Unwise?* 10 Stan. L. Rev. 124, 132 (1957).

> The actions of the three branches of our government have consistently confirmed the President's power to make recess appointments. The Executive Branch has made extensive use of the recess power. Approximately 300 judicial recess appointments have been made in our nation's history. Presidents Eisenhower and Kennedy alone made fifty-three such appointments during their Administrations. *See* H. Chase, Federal Judges, The Appointing Process 86–88, 114–15 (1972).

> The Legislative Branch has consistently confirmed judicial recess appointees without dissent. Moreover, Congress has passed legislation providing for the salaries of recess appointees, without excluding judges. 5 U.S.C. § 5503.

> Finally, we turn to the Judicial Branch. The only direct challenge, prior to the present action, to the President's power to make judicial recess appointments was rejected by the Second Circuit in *United States v. Allocco*, 305 F.2d 704 (2d Cir. 1962), *cert. denied*, 371 U.S. 964 (1963). Although the United States Supreme Court has never passed on the issue, numerous Justices have been recess appointees. Chief Justice Rutledge sat as a recess appointee for six months and participated in two decisions. . . . Altogether, fifteen recess appointments have been made to the Supreme Court. Staff of House Comm.

on the Judiciary, 86th Cong., 1st Sess., Recess Appointments of Federal Judges 40 (Comm. Print 1959). Of these, at least four appointees sat on the Court prior to their confirmation. There is no evidence that any member of the Supreme Court ever objected to this practice on constitutional grounds.

With some reservations, the court accordingly upheld the practice:

> A recess appointee lacks life tenure and is not protected from salary diminution. As a result, such an appointee is in theory subject to greater political pressure than a judge whose nomination has been confirmed. Yet our Constitution has bestowed upon the Executive the power to make interim judicial appointments. This power is not unfettered, however, but is subject to its own limitations and safeguards. It may only be invoked when the Senate is in recess, and recess commissions expire at the end of the next congressional session. We must therefore view the recess appointee not as a danger to the independence of the judiciary, but as the extraordinary exception to the prescriptions of article III. The judicial recess appointee, who has sworn to uphold the Constitution, fills a void left by those preceding in office, thereby permitting the unbroken orderly functioning of our judicial system. . . .

The dissent by Judge Norris cited some history of its own:

> I agree with the majority that there is a direct conflict between the Recess Appointments Clause of Article II and the tenure and salary provisions of Article III of the Constitution. I also agree with the majority that in deciding which clause should prevail, we must look beyond the Constitution itself. . . . We need only look to recent history to appreciate that there is genuine tension between the values underlying the two opposing constitutional provisions. President Eisenhower's recess appointments to the Supreme Court of Chief Justice Earl Warren in 1953 and Justice Brennan in 1956 both created controversy about the legitimacy of recess appointments to that Court. Senator Joseph McCarthy's public interrogation of Justice Brennan while the latter was a sitting Justice of the Court tells its own cautionary tale:

>> Senator McCarthy. You, of course, I assume, will agree with me and a number of the members of the committee — that communism is not merely a political way of life, it is a conspiracy designed to overthrow the United States Government.

>> Mr. Brennan. Will you forgive me an embarrassment, Senator. You appreciate that I am a sitting Justice of the Court. There are presently pending before the Court some cases in which I believe will have to be decided the question what is communism, at least in the frame of reference in which those particular cases have come before the Court. I know, too, that you appreciate that having taken an oath of office it is my obligation not to discuss any of those pending matters. With that qualification, whether the label communism or any other label, any conspiracy

to overthrow the Government of the United States is a conspiracy that I not only would do anything appropriate to aid suppressing, but a conspiracy which, of course, like every American, I abhor.

Senator McCarthy. Mr. Brennan, I don't want to press you unnecessarily, but the question was simple. You have not been confirmed yet as a member of the Supreme Court. There will come before that Court a number of questions involving the all-important issue of whether or not communism is merely a political party or whether it represents a conspiracy to overthrow this Government. I believe that the Senators are entitled to know how you feel about that and you won't be prejudicing then any cases by answering the question.

Hearings Before the Senate Committee on the Judiciary on Nomination of William Joseph Brennan, Jr., 85th Cong., 1st Sess., 17–18 (1957).

Even before Justice Brennan's ordeal, the recess appointment of Chief Justice Warren provoked [an objection from the eminent Professor Henry Hart, who] noted that Warren's permanent appointment would be

subject to three future contingencies: (1) the decision of the President to forward his nomination to the Senate; (2) the decision of the President not to withdraw the nomination before it has been acted upon; and (3) the decision of the Senate to confirm the nomination. The Senate will be entirely free . . . to postpone its action until near the close of the session in order to see how the new nominee is going to vote.

Hart then stated, "I cannot believe that the Constitution contemplates that any Federal judge . . . should hold office, and decide cases, with all these strings tied to him." Recognizing that, as the majority here stresses, recess appointments had been made in the past and that Attorneys General had assumed such appointments to be valid, Hart stressed that "occasional practice backed by mere assumption cannot settle a basic question of constitutional principle." Looking to "the spirit and purpose of the Constitution," Hart observed,

the impropriety [of recess appointments to the federal judiciary] becomes unmistakable. On few other points in the Constitutional Convention were the framers in such complete accord as on the necessity of protecting judges from every kind of extraneous influence upon their decisions.

Hart concluded, a judge

cannot possibly have this independence if his every vote, indeed his every question from the bench, is subject to the possibility of inquiry in later committee hearings and floor debates to determine his fitness to continue in judicial office . . . .

[T]he constitutional plan of separation of powers rests on clear institutional protections for judicial independence. The concerns for efficiency, convenience, and expediency that underlie the Recess Appointments Clause pale in comparison. The purpose served by the President's power to fill judicial vacancies during a recess of the Senate is obviously to avoid delay in the administration of justice in federal courts. . . . There are ways, however, of coping with pressing caseloads without compromising the principle of judicial independence. . . .

If *Woodley* had reached the Supreme Court, how should it have been decided? Assuming that the recess appointments power applies to judges, how would you advise a President regarding the wisdom of its use? Perhaps the answer depends on just how the power is used. Consider the following two case studies:

After a period of over twenty years without the recess appointment of a judge, President Clinton made one. He had been repeatedly thwarted by holds on nominees to a North Carolina seat on the Fourth Circuit Court of Appeals, placed by the irascible Senator Jesse Helms of North Carolina. In late December, 2000, Clinton named a Virginian, Roger Gregory, as a recess appointee to the seat. Both of Virginia's Republican Senators subsequently endorsed Gregory and asked President George W. Bush to nominate him for a permanent position, as Bush then did! The story is told by Michael J. Gerhardt, in *Norm Theory and the Future of the Federal Appointments Process*, 50 DUKE L.J. 1687, 1710–12 (2001).

President Bush also used the recess appointment power strategically, and in a way that led to a temporary truce in the confirmation wars over judicial appointments. Frustrated by the refusal of Senate Democrats to agree to confirmation of two of his nominees to the Courts of Appeals, Charles W. Pickering, Sr., and William H. Pryor, Jr., Bush gave each a recess appointment in early 2004. In May, 2004, the Democrats agreed to allow votes on 25 noncontroversial nominations to the district and appeals courts, in exchange for the President's promise to make no more recess appointments before the next inaugural day. Recess appointments controversies continued in Bush's second term. After a particularly controversial recess appointment of an executive officer (John Bolton as U.S. representative to the United Nations), Senate Democrats blocked all recess appointments for the balance of Bush's time in office. At this early stage, President Trump has also made no judicial recess appointments. President Obama made 32 recess appointments, but none to any court.

4. Removals (Herein of Independent Agencies)

a. Separation of Powers

The Supreme Court has decided a series of important cases on the power of the President to remove executive officers, three of which appear below. The prominence of these cases stems partly from the fact that the Court has not directly addressed the President's power to supervise officers; therefore, whether he can dismiss them is generally thought to determine whether he may direct their behavior in office.

There may, however, be differences between removal and supervision—keep the distinction in mind as you read the cases, and we will explore it later.

The prominence of the removal cases has another, related source: the Court has taken the occasion to spin broad theories about the separation of powers, which have important implications in many other contexts. Yet the theories of the next three cases contain marked inconsistencies. As you read them, notice the modes of separation of powers analysis that the Justices employ, and try to identify the vision of executive power that seems to lie behind each of the various positions. Modern separation of powers scholars have also spun broad theories from the removal cases. The scholars tend to divide into two great realms, the presidentialists and the congressionalists, the two labels indicating which of the two branches they tend to support in interbranch clashes. There are also some scholars in the middle, including the authors of this casebook, who bravely assert: "It depends." (A relatively formalist version of the "middle" way is exemplified by Peter M. Shane, Madison's Nightmare: How Executive Power Threatens American Democracy (2009), which ties the scope of congressional control over removals to the substantive scope of Congress's regulatory powers. The superb work of Peter Strauss exemplifies a more fully functionalist middle way, attending to the general goal of maintaining policy parity between the elected branches. See *The Place of Agencies in Government: Separation of Powers and the Fourth Branch*, 84 Colum. L. Rev. 573 (1984), and *Overseer, or "The Decider"? The President in Administrative Law*, 75 Geo. Wash. L. Rev. 696 (2007).)

The fiercest presidentialists, citing the clause in Article II vesting the executive power in a President, adhere to the "unitary executive" theory, which demands very strong presidential powers of appointment and removal as guarantees of the individual political responsibility that the framers placed in the President. See Steven G. Calabresi & Christopher Yoo, The Unitary Executive (2008); for some extreme presidentialist views, see John Yoo, The Powers of War and Peace: The Constitution and Foreign Affairs after 9/11 (2005). These scholars envision a simpler organization chart for the executive branch than the one that exists, with presidential control and responsibility flowing down many lines into the heart of the bureaucracy.

The fiercest congressionalists, citing the Take Care Clause, argue that the President must generally rest content with the powers that Congress chooses to confer by statute, so that constraints on appointment and removal are usually valid. For a thoughtful congressionalist approach, see the work of Louis Fisher, *e.g.* The Constitution and 9/11: Recurring Threats to America's Freedoms (2008), and Constitutional Conflicts between Congress and the President, (5th rev. ed., 2007). *See also* David Gray Adler and Larry N. George, eds., The Constitution and the Conduct of American Foreign Policy (1996). They are happy with a quite pluralist—even messy—organization chart that reflects varying congressional judgments about independence over the years, resulting from the political climate of the moment.

Those in the middle want to know more about the particular situation. In particular, they want to know what the sum total of the relationships of each constitutional branch is regarding an agency, whereupon they assess the appropriateness of the arrangement for the functions to be performed. This approach forfeits the predictability and elegance of the more polar positions. Taken seriously, it demands some difficult empirical and legal judgments. It can, nonetheless, claim legitimacy from a structural constitutional characteristic. The Constitution's first three articles outline ties between the constitutional branches and the agencies, implying that the role of all three is pertinent to constitutional analysis.

For its part, the Supreme Court wobbles back and forth between "formal" opinions that historically have pleased the presidentialists and "functional" opinions that historically have pleased the congressionalists. See Peter L. Strauss, *Formal and Functional Approaches to Separation-of-Powers Questions—A Foolish Inconsistency?* 72 Cornell L. Rev. 488 (1987); Neil Kinkopf, *Of Devolution, Privatization, and Globalization: Separation of Powers Limits on Congressional Authority to Assign Federal Power to Non-Federal Actors,* 50 Rutgers L. Rev. 331 (1998); Harold H. Bruff, *The Incompatibility Principle,* 59 Admin. L. Rev. 225 (2007). The Court has never satisfactorily explained why it selects one approach or the other, probably because it does not know. The scholars have helpfully offered their speculations, but the Court majestically ignores them.

Recall that before any of the Supreme Court cases arose, a removal controversy eventuated in our first impeachment of a President. Andrew Johnson was impeached for defying the Tenure of Office Act of 1867, which forbade presidential removal of certain cabinet members without the consent of the Senate. Johnson removed Secretary of War Stanton, amid a battle over Reconstruction. Although disputed at the time, the constitutionality of the Act was not resolved by the courts. Sixty years later, successor legislation finally produced a case that reached the Supreme Court. Although the official removed was minor—a postmaster—the Court gave extensive and scholarly attention to the underlying issues. The result must have comforted the ghost of Andrew Johnson.

Myers v. United States

272 U.S. 52 (1926)

Chief Justice TAFT delivered the opinion of the Court.

This case presents the question whether under the Constitution the President has the exclusive power of removing executive officers of the United States whom he has appointed by and with the advice and consent of the Senate.

Myers ... was on July 21, 1917, appointed by the President, by and with the advice and consent of the Senate, to be a postmaster of the first class at Portland, Oregon, for a term of four years. On January 20, 1920, Myers' resignation was demanded. He refused the demand. ... [H]e was removed from office by order of the Postmaster

General, acting by direction of the President. . . . [H]e brought this suit in the Court of Claims for his salary from the date of his removal. . . . The Court of Claims gave judgment against Myers and this is an appeal from that judgment. . . .

By the . . . Act of Congress . . . under which Myers was appointed with the advice and consent of the Senate as a first-class postmaster, it is provided that "Postmasters of the first, second, and third classes shall be appointed and may be removed by the President by and with the advice and consent of the Senate, and shall hold their offices for four years unless sooner removed or suspended according to law." The Senate did not consent to the President's removal of Myers during his term. If this statute . . . is valid, the appellant . . . is entitled to recover his unpaid salary. . . . The government maintains that the requirement is invalid, for the reason that . . . the President's power of removal of executive officers appointed by him with the advice and consent of the Senate is full and complete without consent of the Senate. If this view is sound, the removal of Myers by the President without the Senate's consent was legal. . . . We are therefore confronted by the constitutional question and cannot avoid it. . . .

Senate has to consent to removal

The question where the power of removal of executive officers . . . was vested, was presented early in the first session of the First Congress. There is no express provision respecting removals in the Constitution, except as section 4 of Article II . . . provides for removal from office by impeachment. The subject was not discussed in the Constitutional Convention. . . . In the House of Representatives of the First Congress, on Tuesday, May 18, 1789, Mr. Madison moved in the committee of the whole that there should be established three executive departments, one of Foreign Affairs, another of the Treasury, and a third of War, at the head of each of which there should be a Secretary, to be appointed by the President by and with the advice and consent of the Senate, and to be removable by the President. The committee agreed to the establishment of a Department of Foreign Affairs, but a discussion ensued as to making the Secretary removable by the President. "The question was now taken and carried, by a considerable majority, in favor of declaring the power of removal to be in the President." 1 Annals of Congress, 383.

On June 16, 1789, the House resolved itself into a committee of the whole on a bill proposed by Mr. Madison for establishing an executive department to be denominated the Department of Foreign Affairs, [the head of which was] "to be removable from office by the President of the United States." After a very full discussion the question was put: Shall the words "to be removable by the President" be struck out? It was determined in the negative — yeas 20, nays 34.

On June 22, in the renewal of the discussion: Mr. Benson moved to amend the bill . . . so as to imply the power of removal to be in the President alone. . . . "Mr. Benson stated that his objection to the clause 'to be removable by the President' arose from an idea that the power of removal by the President hereafter might appear to be exercised by virtue of a legislative grant only, and consequently be subjected to legislative instability, when he was well satisfied in his own mind that it was fixed by a fair legislative construction of the Constitution." Mr. Madison admitted the objection. . . . He said: "They certainly may be construed to imply a legislative grant of the power. He wished everything like ambiguity expunged, . . . and therefore seconded the motion. Gentlemen have all along proceeded on the idea that the Constitution vests the power in the President." . . . Mr. Benson's first amendment to alter the second clause by the insertion of the italicized words, made that clause read as follows:

> "That there shall be in the State Department an inferior officer . . . to be called the chief clerk . . . *and who, whenever the principal officer shall be removed from office by the President of the United States*, or in any other case of vacancy, shall . . . have charge and custody of all records, books and papers appertaining to said department."

The first amendment was then approved by a vote of 30 to 18. . . . The bill as amended . . . was then passed by a vote of 29 to 22. . . .

After the bill as amended had passed the House, it was sent to the Senate, where it was discussed in secret session, without report. The critical vote there was upon the striking out of the clause recognizing and affirming the unrestricted power of the President to remove. The Senate divided by 10 to 10, requiring the deciding vote of the Vice President, John Adams, who voted against striking out, and in favor of the passage of the bill as it had left the House. Ten of the Senators had been in the Constitutional Convention, and of them 6 voted that the power of removal was in the President alone. The bill, having passed as it came from the House, was signed by President Washington and became a law. Act of July 27, 1789, 1 Stat. 28. . . .

[T]he . . . reasonable construction of the Constitution must be that the branches should be kept separate in all cases in which they were not expressly blended, and the Constitution should be expounded to blend them no more than it affirmatively requires. . . . The vesting of the executive power in the President was essentially a grant of the power to execute the laws. But the President alone and unaided could not execute the laws. He must execute them by the assistance of subordinates. . . . As he is charged specifically to take care that they be faithfully executed, the reasonable implication, even in the absence of express words, was that as part of his executive power he should select those who were to act for him under his direction in the execution of the laws. The further implication must be, in the absence of any express limitation respecting removals, that as his selection of administrative officers is essential to the execution of the laws by him, so must be his power of removing those for whom he cannot continue to be responsible. It was urged that the natural meaning of the term "executive power" granted the President included the appointment and removal of executive subordinates. If such appointments and removals were not an exercise of the executive power, what were they? They certainly were not the exercise of legislative or judicial power in government as usually understood. . . .

The requirement of the second section of Article II that the Senate should advise and consent to the presidential appointments, was to be strictly construed. . . . The executive power was given in general terms, strengthened by specific terms where emphasis was regarded as appropriate, and was limited by direct expressions where limitation was needed, and the fact that no express limit was placed on the power of removal by the executive was convincing indication that none was intended. This is the same construction of Article II as that of Alexander Hamilton. . . .

The history of the clause by which the Senate was given a check upon the President's power of appointment makes it clear that it was not prompted by any desire to limit removals. . . . [T]he important purpose of those who brought about the restriction was to lodge in the Senate, where the small states had equal representation with the larger states, power to prevent the President from making too many appointments from the larger states. . . . The formidable opposition to the Senate's veto on the President's power of appointment indicated that in construing its effect, it should not be extended beyond its express application to the matter of appointments. . . .

real purpose

It was pointed out in this great debate that the power of removal, though equally essential to the executive power, is different in its nature from that of appointment. A veto by the Senate . . . upon removals is a much greater limitation upon the executive branch, and a much more serious blending of the legislative with the executive, than a rejection of a proposed appointment. It is not to be implied. The rejection of a nominee of the President for a particular office does not greatly embarrass him in the conscientious discharge of his high duties . . . because the President usually has an ample field from which to select for office, according to his preference, competent and capable men. The Senate has full power to reject newly proposed appointees whenever the President shall remove the incumbents. Such a check enables the Senate to prevent the filling of offices with bad or incompetent men, or with those against whom there is tenable objection. . . .

Another argument urged against the constitutional power of the President alone to remove executive officers . . . is that, in the absence of an express power of removal granted to the President, power to make provision for removal of all such officers is vested in the Congress by section 8 of Article I. Mr. Madison, mistakenly thinking that an argument like this was advanced by Roger Sherman, took it up and answered it as follows:

> "He seems to think . . . that the power of displacing from office is subject to legislative discretion, because, it having a right to create, it may limit or modify as it thinks proper. . . . [W]hen I consider that the Constitution clearly intended to maintain a marked distinction between the legislative, executive and judicial powers of government, and when I consider that, if the Legislature has a power such as is contended for, they may subject and transfer at discretion powers from one department of our government to another, they may, on that principle, exclude the President altogether from exercising any authority in the removal of officers, they may . . . vest it in the whole Congress, or they may reserve it to be exercised by this house. When I consider the consequences of this doctrine, and compare them with the true principles of the Constitution, I own that I cannot subscribe to it. . . ."
> 1 Annals of Congress, 495, 496.

. . . The constitutional construction that excludes Congress from legislative power to provide for the removal of superior officers finds support in the second section of Article II. . . . This is "but the Congress may by law vest the appointment of such inferior officers, as they think proper, in the President alone, in the Courts of Law, or in the Heads of Departments." These words, it has been held by this court, give to Congress the power to limit and regulate removal of such inferior officers by heads of departments when it exercises its constitutional power to lodge the power of appointment with them. . . . By the plainest implication it excludes Congressional dealing with appointments or removals of executive officers not falling within the exception and leaves unaffected the executive power of the President to appoint and remove them. . . .

It could never have been intended to leave to Congress unlimited discretion to vary fundamentally the operation of the great independent executive branch of government and thus most seriously to weaken it. It would be a delegation by the convention to Congress of the function of defining the primary boundaries of another of the three great divisions of government. . . . It is reasonable to suppose also that had it been intended to give to Congress power to regulate or control removals in the manner suggested, it would have been . . . specifically enumerated. . . .

It is argued that the denial of the legislative power to regulate removals in some way involves the denial of power to prescribe qualifications for office, or reasonable classification for promotion, and yet that has been often exercised. We see no conflict between the latter power and that of appointment and removal, provided of course that the qualifications do not so limit selection and so trench upon executive choice as to be in effect legislative designation . . . .

Made responsible under the Constitution for the effective enforcement of the law, the President needs as an indispensable aid to meet it the disciplinary influence upon those who act under him of a reserve power of removal. But it is contended that executive officers appointed by the President with the consent of the Senate are bound by the statutory law, and are not his servants to do his will, and that his obligation to care for the faithful execution of the laws does not authorize him to treat them as such. The degree of guidance in the discharge of their duties that the President may exercise over executive officers varies with the character of their service as prescribed in the law under which they act. The highest and most important duties which his subordinates perform are those in which they act for him. In such cases they are exercising not their own but his discretion. This field is a very large one. It is sometimes described as political. Each head of a department is and must be the President's alter ego in the matters of that department where the President is required by law to exercise authority. . . .

But . . . the President should have a like power to remove his appointees charged with other duties than those above described. The ordinary duties of officers prescribed by statute come under the general administrative control of the President by virtue of the general grant to him of the executive power, and he may properly supervise and guide their construction of the statutes under which they act in order to

secure that unitary and uniform execution of the laws which Article II o.
stitution evidently contemplated in vesting general executive power in the .
alone. Laws are often passed with specific provision for adoption of regulati
department or bureau head to make the law workable and effective. The abil.
judgment manifested by the official thus empowered, as well as his energy and sti.
tion of his subordinates, are subjects which the President must consider and supe.
in his administrative control. Finding such officers to be negligent and inefficie
the President should have the power to remove them. Of course there may be dut.
so peculiarly and specifically committed to the discretion of a particular officer as
to raise a question whether the President may overrule or revise the off   iter-
pretation of his statutory duty in a particular instance   T¹   s of
a quasi judicial character imposed on executive office   ive
tribunals whose decisions after hearing affect interests   ge
of which the President cannot in a particular case prope   it
even in such a case he may consider the decision after i   r
removing the officer, on the ground that the discretion re‿
officer by statute has not been on the whole intelligently or wise₁,
wise he does not discharge his own constitutional duty of seeing that the .
faithfully executed. . . .

For the reasons given, we must therefore hold that the provision of the law of 1876
by which the unrestricted power of removal of first-class postmasters is denied to
the President is in violation of the Constitution and invalid. This leads to an affirmance of the judgment of the Court of Claims. . . .

The separate opinion of Justice McREYNOLDS.

. . . Nothing short of language clear beyond serious disputation should be held to
clothe the President with authority wholly beyond congressional control arbitrarily
to dismiss every officer whom he appoints except a few judges. There are no such
words in the Constitution. . . . The Legislature may create post offices and prescribe
qualifications, duties, compensation, and term. And it may protect the incumbent
in the enjoyment of his term unless in some way restrained therefrom. The real question, therefore, comes to this: Does any constitutional provision definitely limit the
otherwise plenary power of Congress over postmasters, when they are appointed by
the President with the consent of the Senate? . . . Congress, in the exercise of its
unquestioned power, may deprive the President of the right either to appoint or to
remove any inferior officer, by vesting the authority to appoint in another. . . . He
must utilize the force which Congress gives. He cannot, without permission, appoint
the humblest clerk or expend a dollar of the public funds . . . .

[I]f it were possible to spell out of the debate and action of the first Congress on
the bill to establish the Department of Foreign Affairs some support for the present
claim of the United States, this would be of little real consequence, for the same Congress on at least two occasions took the opposite position, and time and time again
subsequent Congresses have done the same thing. It would be amazing for this
court to base the interpretation of a constitutional provision upon a single doubtful

congressional interpretation, when there have been dozens of them extending through 135 years, which are directly to the contrary effect. . . . Congress has long and vigorously asserted its right to restrict removals and there has been no common executive practice based upon a contrary view. . . .

It is beyond the ordinary imagination to picture 40 or 50 capable men, presided over by George Washington, vainly discussing, in the heat of a Philadelphia summer, whether express authority to require opinions in writing should be delegated to a President in whom they had already vested the illimitable executive power here claimed. . . .

The Federalist, Article LXXVI, by Mr. Hamilton, says:

"It has been mentioned as one of the advantages to be expected from the cooperation of the Senate, in the business of appointments, that it would contribute to the stability of the administration. The consent of that body would be necessary to displace as well as to appoint. A change of the Chief Magistrate, therefore, would not occasion so violent or so general a revolution in the officers of the government as might be expected, if he were the sole disposer of offices. Where a man in any station had given satisfactory evidence of his fitness for it, a new President would be restrained from attempting a change in favor of a person more agreeable to him, by the apprehension that a discountenance of the Senate might frustrate the attempt, and bring some degree of discredit upon himself. Those who can best estimate the value of a steady administration will be most disposed to prize a provision, which connects the official existence of public men with the approbation or disapprobation of that body, which, from the greater permanency of its own composition, will in all probability be less subject to inconstancy than any other member of the government." . . .

The claim advanced for the United States is supported by no opinion of this court, and conflicts with *Marbury v. Madison.* . . . The court must have appreciated that, unless it found Marbury had the legal right to occupy the office irrespective of the President's will, there would be no necessity for passing upon the much-controverted and far-reaching power of the judiciary to declare an act of Congress without effect. . . .

If the framers of the Constitution had intended "the executive power," . . . to include all power of an executive nature, they would not have added the carefully defined grants of section 2. . . . That the general words of a grant are limited, when followed by those of special import, is an established canon; and an accurate writer would hardly think of emphasizing a general grant by adding special and narrower ones without explanation. . . . Those who maintain that Art. II § 1, was intended as a grant of every power of executive nature not specifically qualified or denied must show that the term "executive power" had some definite and commonly accepted meaning in 1787. This court has declared that it did not include all powers exercised by the King of England; and, considering the history of the period, none can say that it had then (or afterwards) any commonly accepted and practical definition. If any one of the descriptions of "executive power" known in 1787 had been substituted for it, the whole plan would have failed. Such obscurity would have been intolerable to thinking men of that time. . . .

Justice BRANDEIS, dissenting:

. . . The separation of the powers of government did not make each branch completely autonomous. It left each in some measure, dependent upon the others. . . . Obviously the President cannot secure full execution of the laws, if Congress denies to him adequate means of doing so. Full execution may be defeated because Congress declines to create offices indispensable for that purpose. Or, because Congress having created the office, declines to make the indispensable appropriation. . . . If, in any such way, adequate means are denied to the President, the fault will lie with Congress. The President performs his full constitutional duty, if, with the means and instruments provided by Congress and within the limitations prescribed by it, he uses his best endeavors to secure the faithful execution of the laws enacted.

Checks and balances were established in order that this should be a "government of laws and not of men." As White said in the House in 1789, an uncontrollable power of removal in the Chief Executive "is a doctrine not to be learned in American governments." Such power had been denied in Colonial Charters, and even under Proprietary Grants and Royal Commissions. It had been denied in the thirteen States before the framing of the Federal Constitution. The doctrine of the separation of powers was adopted by the Convention of 1787 not to promote efficiency but to preclude the exercise of arbitrary power. The purpose was not to avoid friction, but, by means of the inevitable friction incident to the distribution of the governmental powers among three departments, to save the people from autocracy . . . .

Justice HOLMES, dissenting:

. . . We have to deal with an office that owes its existence to Congress and that Congress may abolish tomorrow. Its duration and the pay attached to it while it lasts depend on Congress alone. Congress alone confers on the President the power to appoint to it and at any time may transfer the power to other hands. With such power over its own creation, I have no more trouble in believing that Congress has power to prescribe a term of life for it free from any interference than I have in accepting the undoubted power of Congress to decree its end. I have equally little trouble in accepting its power to prolong the tenure of an incumbent until Congress or the Senate shall have assented to his removal. The duty of the President to see that the laws be executed is a duty that does not go beyond the laws or require him to achieve more than Congress sees fit to leave within his power.

———————

1. *Superformalism.* The Court's opinion by Chief Justice Taft, himself a former President, has always been a favorite of the executive in briefs and Attorney General opinions. Do you see why? Taft's approach is quite formalist: no branch should have implied powers to participate in functions assigned by the Constitution to another;

because removal is an executive function, the Senate may not share it. Therefore the President has an illimitable power to remove those executive officers whom he has appointed.

As is typical of formalism, however, much remains unanswered. *Why* is removal an exclusively executive function? It is not mentioned in the Constitution, except for Congress's power to impeach. Taft answers that the President needs removal power in order to perform his own constitutional duties, for which he must have loyal subordinates. Surely there is a core of truth to this, but *which* subordinates must he control, and for *what* executive functions? In short, why does the President need a removal power that extends down the hierarchy to the Portland postmaster?

The approach of the dissenters resembles a modern functional one. They argue that the President does not need a removal power that extends to this level of government in order to discharge his responsibilities. They point out that Congress often places appointment power in the heads of departments, and then limits removal through the civil service laws. They also stress Congress's undoubted power to define the terms and powers of offices and to determine appropriations for them. The majority thinks that senatorial participation in a removal is different — do the dissents adequately answer that point? *See generally* Saikrishna Prakash, *The Story of* Myers *and its Wayward Successors: Going Postal on the Removal Power*, in PRESIDENTIAL POWER STORIES (Christopher H. Schroeder & Curtis A. Bradley eds., 2009)

2. *The "Decision of 1789."* The Court lavishes attention on the "decision of 1789." What do you think it stands for? For example, was the Tenure of Office Act of 1867 unconstitutional as applied to the Secretary of War? Taft's version of the "decision of 1789" is quite incomplete, in two ways. He minimizes the ambiguity of the decision itself, which was consistent with both a constitutional removal power and one conferred by Congress. And he neglects to mention that, although the First Congress created the new Departments of State and War with characteristics consistent with broad supervision by the President, it also created a Treasury Department with more detailed statutory controls, including limits on Presidential removal of its Comptroller. *See* Lawrence Lessig & Cass R. Sunstein, *The President and the Administration*, 94 COLUM. L. REV. 1, 22–32 (1994). Nevertheless, a robust interpretation of the President's power to supervise executive officers was articulated within the executive branch as early as an opinion by Attorney General Caleb Cushing, *Relation of the President to the Executive Departments*, 7 Op. Att'y Gen. 453 (1855), *reprinted in* H. JEFFERSON POWELL, THE CONSTITUTION AND THE ATTORNEYS GENERAL 131–48 (1999). This opinion prefigures much of the *Myers* analysis.

3. *The Unitary Executive.* Taft appears to have a vision of a completely unitary executive branch, organized hierarchically under the President. He says, in language dear to the hearts of later executive advisers, that the President may "supervise and guide" subordinates in pursuit of a "unitary and uniform" execution of the laws. Taft then includes a dictum that apparently refers to regulatory commissions such as the Interstate Commerce Commission and the Federal Trade Commission. He says that the President might not be able to overrule matters "committed to the discretion of

a particular officer." (How are we to identify those?) And he refers to "quasi judicial" activities as beyond the President's influence. Nevertheless, Taft would allow the President to remove such officers afterwards, for their unwisdom. He views that as a necessary component of the President's duty to "take Care that the Laws be faithfully executed." Do you agree? As you read the next case, see whether you think the Court adequately responds to Taft.

The *Myers* dissenters seemed to have a much more pluralist view of the executive. This view is captured in the quote from Hamilton's Federalist No. 77, which seemed to envision a semipermanent bureaucracy at the highest levels, which the President could not unilaterally displace. (Hamilton later recanted.) Do you agree with Hamilton that the "stability of the administration" that would result would be beneficial? What if the Cabinet were composed of a group having little sympathy for the President or for each other? Do you agree with the apparent position of the dissenters that Congress should be able to organize the executive largely as it pleases, under the grant of power in the "necessary and proper" clause?

The Court's next removal case occurred at the height of its war with Franklin D. Roosevelt, who removed an FTC Commissioner on the advice that *Myers* meant that Congress could not restrict the President's power to discharge presidential appointees. The Court unanimously rebuked the President in an opinion issued the same day as its invalidation of the NIRA in *Schechter Poultry, supra* Chapter Two. Viewing the juxtaposition, the future Justice Scalia wrote that "the same mistrust of New Deal executive freewheeling aroused by the truly sweeping NRA proposals addressed in *Schechter* colored the companion case as well." (*Historical Anomalies in Administrative Law*, YEARBOOK 1985, 103, 108.) As you will see, the Court's hostility produced a broad opinion that contrasted sharply with *Myers*. To what extent does the Court state principles that should govern today?

Humphrey's Executor v. United States
295 U.S. 602 (1935)

Justice SUTHERLAND delivered the opinion of the Court.

. . . William E. Humphrey, the decedent, . . . was nominated by President Hoover to succeed himself as a member of the Federal Trade Commission, and was confirmed by the United States Senate . . . for a term of seven years. . . . On July 25, 1933, President Roosevelt addressed a letter to the commissioner asking for his resignation, on the ground "that the aims and purposes of the Administration with respect to the work of the Commission can be carried out most effectively with personnel of my own selection," but disclaiming any reflection upon the commissioner personally or upon his services. . . . The commissioner declined to resign; [the President removed him.] Humphrey never acquiesced in this action. . . . [His executor sued for his salary from the date of removal to the date of death.] Upon these facts, . . . the following questions are certified:

"1. Do the provisions of section 1 of the Federal Trade Commission Act, stating that 'any commissioner may be removed by the President for inefficiency, neglect of duty, or malfeasance in office', restrict or limit the power of the President to remove a commissioner except upon one or more of the causes named?

"If the foregoing question is answered in the affirmative, then—

"2. If the power of the President to remove a commissioner is restricted or limited as shown by the foregoing interrogatory and the answer made thereto, is such a restriction or limitation valid under the Constitution of the United States?"

The Federal Trade Commission Act, 15 U.S.C. §§ 41, 42, creates a commission of five members to be appointed by the President by and with the advice and consent of the Senate. . . . In exercising [its power under § 5 of the Act to prevent "unfair methods of competition"], the commission must issue a complaint stating its charges and giving notice of hearing. . . . A person, partnership, or corporation proceeded against is given the right to appear . . . and show cause why an order to cease and desist should not be issued. . . . If the commission finds the method of competition is one prohibited by the act, it is directed to [state] its findings as to the facts, and to issue and cause to be served a cease and desist order. If the order is disobeyed, the commission may apply to the appropriate Circuit Court of Appeals for its enforcement. The party subject to the order may seek and obtain a review in the Circuit Court of Appeals in a manner provided by the act. . . .

First. The question . . . is whether, by the provisions of section 1 of the [Act], the President's power is limited to removal for the specific causes enumerated therein. . . . [I]f the intention of Congress that no removal should be made during the specified term except for one or more of the enumerated causes were not clear upon the face of the statute, as we think it is, it would be made clear by a consideration of the character of the commission and the legislative history which accompanied and preceded the passage of the act.

The commission is to be nonpartisan; and it must, from the very nature of its duties, act with entire impartiality. It is charged with the enforcement of no policy except the policy of the law. Its duties are neither political nor executive, but predominantly quasi-judicial and quasi-legislative. Like the Interstate Commerce Commission, its members are called upon to exercise the trained judgment of a body of experts "appointed by law and informed by experience." . . .

Thus, the language of the act, the legislative reports, and the general purposes of the legislation as reflected by the debates, all combine to demonstrate the congressional intent to create a body of experts who shall gain experience by length of service; a body which shall be independent of executive authority, *except in its selection*, and free to exercise its judgment without the leave or hindrance of any other official or any department of the government. To the accomplishment of these purposes, it is clear that Congress was of opinion that length and certainty of tenure would vitally contribute. And to hold that, nevertheless, the members of the commission continue in office at the mere will of the President, might be to thwart, in large measure, the very ends which Congress sought to realize by definitely fixing the term of office.

We conclude that the intent of the act is to limit the executive power of removal to the causes enumerated, the existence of none of which is claimed here; and we pass to the second question.

Second. To support its contention that the removal provision of section 1, as we have just construed it, is an unconstitutional interference with the executive power of the President, the government's chief reliance is *Myers v. United States*. . . . Nevertheless, the narrow point actually decided was only that the President had power to remove a postmaster of the first class, without the advice and consent of the Senate as required by act of Congress. In the course of the opinion of the court, expressions occur which tend to sustain the government's contention, but these are beyond the point involved and, therefore, do not come within the rule of stare decisis. In so far as they are out of harmony with the views here set forth, these expressions are disapproved. . . .

The office of a postmaster is so essentially unlike the office now involved that the decision in the *Myers* case cannot be accepted as controlling our decision here. A postmaster is an executive officer restricted to the performance of executive functions. He is charged with no duty at all related to either the legislative or judicial power. The actual decision in the *Myers* case finds support in the theory that such an officer is merely one of the units in the executive department and, hence, inherently subject to the exclusive and illimitable power of removal by the Chief Executive, whose subordinate and aid he is. Putting aside dicta, . . . the necessary reach of the decision goes far enough to include all purely executive officers. It goes no farther; much less does it include an officer who occupies no place in the executive department and who exercises no part of the executive power vested by the Constitution in the President.

The Federal Trade Commission is an administrative body created by Congress to carry into effect legislative policies embodied in the statute in accordance with the legislative standard therein prescribed, and to perform other specified duties as a legislative or as a judicial aid. Such a body cannot in any proper sense be characterized as an arm or an eye of the executive. Its duties are performed without executive leave and, in the contemplation of the statute, must be free from executive control. In administering the provisions of the statute in respect of "unfair methods of competition,"—that is to say, in filling in and administering the details embodied by that general standard—the commission acts in part quasi-legislatively and in part quasi-judicially. . . . To the extent that it exercises any executive function, as distinguished from executive power in the constitutional sense, it does so in the discharge and effectuation of its quasi-legislative or quasi-judicial powers, or as an agency of the legislative or judicial departments of the government.

If Congress is without authority to prescribe causes for removal of members of the trade commission and limit executive power of removal accordingly, that power at once becomes practically all-inclusive in respect of civil officers with the exception of the judiciary provided for by the Constitution. The Solicitor General, at the bar, apparently recognizing this to be true, with commendable candor, agreed that his view in respect of the removability of members of the Federal Trade Commission necessitated a like view in respect of the Interstate Commerce Commission and the Court of Claims. We are thus confronted with the serious question whether not only the members of these quasi-legislative and quasi-judicial bodies, but the judges of the legislative Court of Claims, exercising judicial power, continue in office only at the pleasure of the President.

We think it plain under the Constitution that illimitable power of removal is not possessed by the President in respect of officers of the character of those just named. The authority of Congress, in creating quasi-legislative or quasi-judicial agencies, to require them to act in discharge of their duties independently of executive control, cannot well be doubted; and that authority includes, as an appropriate incident, power to fix the period during which they shall continue, and to forbid their removal except for cause in the meantime. For it is quite evident that one who holds his office only during the pleasure of another cannot be depended upon to maintain an attitude of independence against the latter's will.

The fundamental necessity of maintaining each of the three general departments of government entirely free from the control or coercive influence, direct or indirect, of either of the others, has often been stressed and is hardly open to serious question. So much is implied in the very fact of the separation of the powers of these departments by the Constitution; and in the rule which recognizes their essential coequality. The sound application of a principle that makes one master in his own house precludes him from imposing his control in the house of another who is master there. . . . The power of removal here claimed for the President falls within this principle, since its coercive influence threatens the independence of a commission, which is not only wholly disconnected from the executive department, but which, as already fully appears, was created by Congress as a means of carrying into operation legislative and judicial powers, and as an agency of the legislative and judicial departments.

In the light of the question now under consideration, we have re-examined the precedents referred to in the *Myers* case, and find nothing in them to justify a conclusion contrary to that which we have reached. . . . [In the "decision of 1789," regarding the Secretary of State, the office] was not only purely executive, but the officer one who was responsible to the President, and to him alone, in a very definite sense. A reading of the debates shows that the President's illimitable power of removal was not considered in respect of other than executive officers. And it is pertinent to observe that when, at a later time, the tenure of office for the Comptroller of the Treasury was under consideration, Mr. Madison quite evidently thought that, since the duties of that office were not purely of an executive nature but partook of the judiciary quality as well, a different rule in respect of executive removal might well apply. 1 Annals of Congress, cols. 611–612.

In *Marbury v. Madison*, it is made clear that Chief Justice Marshall was of opinion that a justice of the peace for the District of Columbia was not removable at the will of the President; and that there was a distinction between such an officer and officers appointed to aid the President in the performance of his constitutional duties. In the latter case, the distinction he saw was that "their acts are his acts" and his will, therefore, controls; and, by way of illustration, he adverted to the act establishing the Department of Foreign Affairs, which was the subject of the "decision of 1789."

The result of what we now have said is this: Whether the power of the President to remove an officer shall prevail over the authority of Congress to condition the power by fixing a definite term and precluding a removal except for cause will depend upon the character of the office; the *Myers* decision, affirming the power of the President alone to make the removal, is confined to purely executive officers; and as to officers of the kind here under consideration, we hold that no removal can be made during the prescribed term for which the officer is appointed, except for one or more of the causes named in the applicable statute. To the extent that, between the decision in the *Myers* case, . . . and our present decision . . . there shall remain a field of doubt, we leave such cases as may fall within it for future consideration and determination as they may arise.

In accordance with the foregoing, the questions submitted are answered: [Yes].

———————

1. *Regulation Without Politics.* Notice why the Court construes the FTC Act to forbid removal for reasons other than the statutory grounds. It reads the Act as embodying a premise associated with the Progressive movement, that regulation should be a neutral and expert process, above the unseemly strife of politics. For the Court, itself in sympathy with the Progressive view, it was then only a short step to the conclusion that it is constitutional for Congress to minimize the political influence of the President on the regulators. Yet the independent agencies have never been totally isolated from politics—consider, for example, the nature of *congressional* oversight, which we explore below. Today, the Progressive view seems both an impossible and an undesirable dream. Inescapably, regulation is rife with politics. Indeed, political oversight is crucial to the legitimacy of regulation by unelected bureaucrats. Thus, the Court's opinion now rests partly on discredited political science.

2. *A Due Process Basis?* If the Court's theory of administrative expertise seems too unrealistic today to justify the Court's conclusions, is there another available basis? The case seems to rest in large part on a procedural value: the need to recognize congressional power to protect officers engaged in adjudication from summary removal without cause. This is a clearly appropriate ground for restrictions on presidential intervention, isn't it? Indeed, concepts of due process and statutes codifying them (e.g., 5 U.S.C. § 557(d)) forbid *ex parte* intervention in administrative adjudication by anyone. And compare the Court's emphasis on fair process in its delegation doctrine analysis in its contemporaneous decision in *Schechter Poultry*. So perhaps Chief Justice Taft was wrong to opine that the President should be able to fire an adjudicator

for decisions he disapproves. (If the President's views on a matter in adjudication are known in advance, there would be a risk of influence on the outcome of the case.) But what about rulemaking and other informal executive actions, for which neither due process nor statutes forbid ex parte contacts? We will consider this issue in connection with presidential supervision of executive branch policymaking.

3. *Implying Removal Restrictions.* Procedural values appeared again in *Wiener v. United States*, 357 U.S. 349 (1958). Congress established the War Claims Commission to "adjudicate according to law" certain claims arising from enemy action in World War II. The Commissioners were presidential appointees; there was no provision regarding their removal. President Eisenhower, asserting a need to complete the Commission's task "with personnel of my own selection," removed Commissioner Myron Wiener, who then sued for lost salary. Justice Frankfurter's opinion for a unanimous Court found that Congress intended the Commission to decide claims on the merits, entirely free of influence from any other branch of government. Wiener's removal was illegal because Congress would not want the Commissioners to fear "the Damocles' sword of removal by the President for no reason other than that he preferred to have . . . men of his own choosing."

4. *The Meaning of "Cause."* What is the precise holding of *Humphrey's Executor*? Is it that Congress may constitutionally forbid presidential removals of FTC Commissioners without cause? If so, and considering that specific cause was not asserted in any of the removal cases, what is the meaning of the typical statutory formulation of "inefficiency, neglect of duty, or malfeasance in office"? We consider this issue below, with presidential supervision of agency policymaking.

5. *Holding v. Dicta. Humphrey's Executor* describes a special constitutional status for the independent agencies. In dicta, the Court accords them a position entirely outside the executive branch, without textual support in the Constitution for doing so. For justification, the Court points to the "quasi-judicial" and "quasi-legislative" functions performed by the FTC, and distinguishes them from activities performed by "purely executive officers." This attempt to draw a functional distinction is, however, belied by practice: executive branch agencies often perform "quasi-judicial" and "quasi-legislative" functions. (For example, the Food and Drug Administration issues many rules, and the Department of Veterans Affairs performs many adjudications.) Similarly, independent agencies often perform such executive duties as prosecution (for example, the FTC has concurrent jurisdiction to enforce the antitrust laws with the Department of Justice). Thus, the Court's constitutional distinction is highly oversimplified and unrealistic. Can you supply a better basis for protecting some functions from presidential interference? Which ones should qualify?

Whatever the soundness of these dicta in *Humphrey's Executor*, Congress has embraced them with a fervor equal to the executive's attachment to *Myers*. Congressional committees never tire of reminding nominees to the independent agencies that they are "arms of Congress." Then-Judge Scalia lamented that "the holding of the case has been expanded to embrace its entire rationale . . . [it] continues to induce the Executive to leave the policy control of the independent agencies to congressional committees, and fastidiously to avoid any appearance of influence in those entities." Antonin Scalia, *Historical Anomalies in Administrative Law*, 1985 Sup. Ct. Hist. Soc'y Y.B. 110.

6. *Defining Executive Power.* Have the Court's subsequent decisions in *Buckley* and *Chadha* undercut the rationale of *Humphrey's Executor*? Recall the *Buckley* Court's statement that although the FEC's rulemaking and adjudicative functions "are more legislative and judicial in nature than are the Commission's enforcement powers," they must be performed by presidential appointees because "none of them operates merely in aid of congressional authority to legislate or is sufficiently removed from the administration and enforcement of public law to allow it to be performed by the present Commission." Still, the *Buckley* Court insisted that its decision was "entirely consistent" with the removal cases. Do you agree? If these activities are not purely executive, why need they be performed by Officers of the United States?

As for *Chadha*, review the Court's characterization of administrative functions. The Court would not create a special preserve for the legislative veto either for the independent agencies or for rulemaking. Isn't that inconsistent with *Humphrey's Executor*? We will have more to say on these matters after the next removal case.

Bowsher v. Synar

478 U.S. 714 (1986)

Chief Justice BURGER delivered the opinion of the Court.

The question presented by these appeals is whether the assignment by Congress to the Comptroller General of the United States of certain functions under the Balanced Budget and Emergency Deficit Control Act of 1985 violates the doctrine of separation of powers.

I

A

. . . [T]he Balanced Budget and Emergency Deficit Control Act of 1985, 2 U.S.C. § 901 et seq. (Supp. 1986), popularly known as the "Gramm-Rudman-Hollings Act," [attempts] to eliminate the federal budget deficit. To that end, the Act sets a "maximum deficit amount" for federal spending for each of fiscal years 1986 through 1991. The size of that maximum deficit amount progressively reduces to zero in fiscal year 1991. If in any fiscal year the federal budget deficit exceeds the maximum deficit amount by more than a specified sum, the Act requires across-the-board cuts in federal spending to reach the targeted deficit level. . . .

These "automatic" reductions are accomplished through a rather complicated procedure, spelled out in § 251, the so-called "reporting provisions" of the Act. Each year, the Directors of the Office of Management and Budget (OMB) and the Congressional Budget Office (CBO) independently estimate the amount of the federal budget deficit for the upcoming fiscal year. If that deficit exceeds the maximum targeted deficit amount for that fiscal year by more than a specified amount, the Directors of OMB and CBO independently calculate, on a program-by-program basis, the budget reductions necessary to ensure that the deficit does not exceed the maximum deficit amount. The Act then requires the Directors to report jointly their deficit estimates and budget reduction calculations to the Comptroller General.

The Comptroller General, after reviewing the Directors' reports, then reports his conclusions to the President. The President in turn must issue a "sequestration" order mandating the spending reductions specified by the Comptroller General. There follows a period during which Congress may by legislation reduce spending to obviate, in whole or in part, the need for the sequestration order. If such reductions are not enacted, the sequestration order becomes effective and the spending reductions included in that order are made . . . .

B

. . . Congressman Synar, who had voted against the Act, filed a complaint seeking declaratory relief that the Act was unconstitutional. . . . A virtually identical lawsuit was also filed by the National Treasury Employees Union [because the Act] suspended certain cost-of-living benefit increases to the Union's members. A three-judge District Court . . . invalidated the reporting provisions. *Synar v. United States*, 626 F. Supp. 1374 (DC 1986) (Scalia, Johnson, Gasch, JJ.) . . . . The District Court . . . rejected appellees' challenge that the Act violated the delegation doctrine. The court expressed no doubt that the Act delegated broad authority, but delegation of similarly broad authority has been upheld in past cases. . . . [The court] held that the role of the Comptroller General in the deficit reduction process violated the constitutionally imposed separation of powers. . . . We affirm. . . .

III

. . . [T]he famous warning of Montesquieu [was] quoted by James Madison in The Federalist No. 47, that "'there can be no liberty where the legislative and executive powers are united in the same person, or body of magistrates'. . . ." Unlike parliamentary systems such as that of Great Britain, no person who is an officer of the United States may serve as a Member of the Congress. Art. I, § 6. Moreover, unlike parliamentary systems, the President, under Article II, is responsible not to the Congress but to the people. . . . The Constitution does not contemplate an active role for Congress in the supervision of officers charged with the execution of the laws it enacts. The President appoints "Officers of the United States" with the "Advice and Consent of the Senate . . ." Article II, § 2. Once the appointment has been made and confirmed, however, the Constitution explicitly provides for removal of Officers of the United States by Congress only upon impeachment. . . . A direct congressional role in the removal of officers charged with the execution of the laws beyond this limited one is inconsistent with separation of powers. . . .

This Court first directly addressed this issue in *Myers v. United States. Humphrey's Executor* involved an issue not presented either in the *Myers* case or in this case—i.e., the power of Congress to limit the President's powers of removal of a Federal

Trade Commissioner. . . . The Court distinguished *Myers*, reaffirming its holding that congressional participation in the removal of executive officers is unconstitutional. . . . In light of these precedents, we conclude that Congress cannot reserve for itself the power of removal of an officer charged with the execution of the laws except by impeachment. To permit the execution of the laws to be vested in an officer answerable only to Congress would, in practical terms, reserve in Congress control over the execution of the laws. As the District Court observed, "Once an officer is appointed, it is only the authority that can remove him, and not the authority that appointed him, that he must fear and, in the performance of his functions, obey." The structure of the Constitution does not permit Congress to execute the laws; it follows that Congress cannot grant to an officer under its control what it does not possess.

Our decision in *INS v. Chadha* supports this conclusion. In *Chadha*, we struck down a one house "legislative veto" provision by which each House of Congress retained the power to reverse a decision Congress had expressly authorized the Attorney General to make. . . . To permit an officer controlled by Congress to execute the laws would be, in essence, to permit a congressional veto. Congress could simply remove, or threaten to remove, an officer for executing the laws in any fashion found to be unsatisfactory to Congress. This kind of congressional control over the execution of the laws, *Chadha* makes clear, is constitutionally impermissible. . . .

IV

Appellants urge that the Comptroller General performs his duties independently and is not subservient to Congress. . . . The critical factor lies in the provisions of the statute defining the Comptroller General's office relating to removability. Although the Comptroller General is nominated by the President from a list of three individuals recommended by the Speaker of the House of Representatives and the President pro tempore of the Senate, *see* 31 U.S.C. § 703(a)(2), and confirmed by the Senate, he is removable only at the initiative of Congress. He may be removed not only by impeachment but also by Joint Resolution of Congress "at any time" resting on any one of the following bases:

"(i) permanent disability; (ii) inefficiency; (iii) neglect of duty; (iv) malfeasance; or (v) a felony or conduct involving moral turpitude."

31 U.S.C. § 703(e)(1). This provision was included, as one Congressman explained in urging passage of the Act, because Congress "felt that [the Comptroller General] should be brought under the sole control of Congress, so that Congress at the moment when it found he was inefficient and was not carrying on the duties of his office as he should and as the Congress expected, could remove him without the long, tedious process of a trial by impeachment." 61 Cong. Rec. 1081 (1921). . . .

The statute permits removal for "inefficiency," "neglect of duty," or "malfeasance." These terms are very broad and, as interpreted by Congress, could sustain removal of a Comptroller General for any number of actual or perceived transgressions of the legislative will. The Constitutional Convention chose to permit impeachment of executive officers only for "Treason, Bribery, or other high Crimes and Misdemeanors." It rejected language that would have permitted impeachment for "maladministration," with Madison arguing that "[s]o vague a term will be equivalent to a tenure during pleasure of the Senate." 2 Farrand 550. . . . The Framers recognized that, in the long term, structural protections against abuse of power were critical to preserving liberty. In constitutional terms, the removal powers over the Comptroller General's office dictate that he will be subservient to Congress.

. . . [T]he dissent is simply in error to suggest that the political realities reveal that the Comptroller General is free from influence by Congress. The Comptroller General heads the General Accounting Office, "an instrumentality of the United States Government independent of the executive departments," 31 U.S.C. §702(a), which was created by Congress in 1921 as part of the Budget and Accounting Act of 1921, 42 Stat. 23. Congress created the office because it believed that it "needed an officer, responsible to it alone, to check upon the application of public funds in accordance with appropriations." H. Mansfield, The Comptroller General: A Study in the Law and Practice of Financial Administration 65 (1939). It is clear that Congress has consistently viewed the Comptroller General as an officer of the Legislative Branch. The Reorganization Acts of 1945 and 1949, for example, both stated that the Comptroller General and the GAO are "a part of the legislative branch of the Government." . . . Over the years, the Comptrollers General have also viewed themselves as part of the Legislative Branch. . . .

[B]ecause Congress has retained removal authority over the Comptroller General, he may not be entrusted with executive powers. The remaining question is whether the Comptroller General has been assigned such powers in the . . . Act of 1985.

V

. . . Appellants suggest that the duties assigned to the Comptroller General in the Act are essentially ministerial and mechanical so that their performance does not constitute "execution of the law" in a meaningful sense. On the contrary, we view these functions as plainly entailing execution of the law in constitutional terms. Interpreting a law enacted by Congress to implement the legislative mandate is the very essence of "execution" of the law. Under §251, the Comptroller General must exercise judgment concerning facts that affect the application of the Act. He must also interpret the provisions of the Act to determine precisely what budgetary calculations are required. Decisions of that kind are typically made by officers charged with executing a statute . . . [Indeed, the Comptroller General commands the President himself to carry out, without the slightest variation (with exceptions not relevant to the constitutional issues presented), the directive of the Comptroller General as to the budget reductions . . .] By placing the responsibility for execution of the Balanced Budget and Emergency Deficit Control Act in the hands of an officer who is subject to removal only by itself, Congress in effect has retained control over the execution of the Act and has intruded into the executive function. The Constitution does not permit such intrusion. . . .

Justice STEVENS, with whom Justice MARSHALL joins, concurring in the judgment.

. . . I disagree with the Court . . . on the reasons why the Constitution prohibits the Comptroller General from exercising the powers assigned to him by . . . the Act. It is not the dormant, carefully circumscribed congressional removal power that represents the primary constitutional evil. Nor do I agree with the conclusion of both the majority and the dissent that the analysis depends on a labeling of the functions assigned to the Comptroller General as "executive powers." Rather, I am convinced that the Comptroller General must be characterized as an agent of Congress because of his longstanding statutory responsibilities; that . . . when Congress, or a component or an agent of Congress, seeks to make policy that will bind the Nation, it must follow the procedures mandated by Article I of the Constitution. . . .

I

The fact that Congress retained for itself the power to remove the Comptroller General is important evidence supporting the conclusion that he is a member of the Legislative Branch of the Government. Unlike the Court, however, I am not persuaded that the congressional removal power is either a necessary, or a sufficient, basis for concluding that his statutory assignment is invalid. . . . The notion that the removal power at issue here automatically creates some kind of "here-and-now subservience" of the Comptroller General to Congress is belied by history. There is no evidence that Congress has ever removed, or threatened to remove, the Comptroller General for reasons of policy. . . .

II

In assessing the role of the Comptroller General, it is appropriate to consider his already existing statutory responsibilities. . . . In the statutory section that identifies the Comptroller General's responsibilities for investigating the use of public money, four of the five enumerated duties specifically describe an obligation owed to Congress. . . . The Comptroller General's current statutory responsibilities on behalf of Congress are fully consistent with the historic conception of the Comptroller General's office. . . . On at least three occasions since 1921, moreover, in considering the structure of government, Congress has defined the Comptroller General as being a part of the Legislative Branch. . . . This is not to say, of course, that the Comptroller General has no obligations to the Executive Branch, or that he is an agent of the Congress in quite so clear a manner as the Doorkeeper of the House. . . . It is at least clear that, in most, if not all, of his statutory responsibilities, the Comptroller General is properly characterized as an agent of the Congress.

III

. . . One reason that the exercise of legislative, executive, and judicial powers cannot be categorically distributed among three mutually exclusive branches of government is that governmental power cannot always be readily characterized with only one of those three labels. On the contrary, as our cases demonstrate, a particular function, like a chameleon, will often take on the aspect of the office to which it is assigned. . . . The *Chadha* case itself illustrates this basic point. The governmental decision that was being made was whether a resident alien who had overstayed his student visa should be deported. From the point of view of the administrative law judge who conducted a hearing on the issue—or as Justice Powell saw the issue in his concurrence—the decision took on a judicial coloring. From the point of view of the Attorney General . . . to whom Congress had delegated the authority to suspend deportation of certain aliens, the decision appeared to have an executive character. But, as the Court held, when the House of Representatives finally decided that Chadha must be deported, its action "was essentially legislative in purpose and effect."

. . . Under the District Court's analysis, and the analysis adopted by the majority today, it would therefore appear that the function at issue is "executive" if performed by the Comptroller General but "legislative" if performed by the Congress. In my view, however, the function may appropriately be labeled "legislative" even if performed by the Comptroller General or by an executive agency. [I]t is far from novel to acknowledge that independent agencies do indeed exercise legislative powers. . . . [T]he District Court had no difficulty in concluding that Congress could delegate the performance of those functions to another branch of the Government. If the delegation to a stranger is permissible, why may not Congress delegate the same responsibilities to one of its own agents? That is the central question before us today.

IV

. . . The Gramm-Rudman-Hollings Act assigns to the Comptroller General the duty to make policy decisions that have the force of law. . . . It is the Comptroller General's Report that the President must follow and that will have conclusive effect. It is, in short, the Comptroller General's report that will have a profound, dramatic, and immediate impact on the government and on the Nation at large. Article I of the Constitution specifies the procedures that Congress must follow when it makes policy that binds the Nation: its legislation must be approved by both Houses of Congress and presented to the President. . . . If Congress were free to delegate its policymaking authority to one of its components, or to one of its agents, it would be able to evade "the carefully crafted restraints spelled out in the Constitution." That danger—congressional action that evades constitutional restraints—is not present when Congress delegates lawmaking power to the executive or to an independent agency. . . .

In my opinion, Congress itself could not exercise the Gramm-Rudman-Hollings functions through a concurrent resolution. . . . I think it equally clear that Congress may not simply delegate those functions to an agent such as the Congressional Budget Office. Since I am persuaded that the Comptroller General is also fairly deemed to be an agent of Congress, he too cannot exercise such functions. . . . In short, even though it is well settled that Congress may delegate legislative power to independent agencies or to the Executive, and thereby divest itself of a portion of its lawmaking power, when it elects to exercise such power itself, it may not authorize a lesser representative of the Legislative Branch to act on its behalf. . . .

Justice WHITE, dissenting.

. . . Before examining the merits of the Court's argument, I wish to emphasize what it is that the Court quite pointedly and correctly does not hold: namely, that "executive" powers of the sort granted the Comptroller by the Act may only be exercised by officers removable at will by the President. The Court's apparent unwillingness to accept this argument, which has been tendered in this Court by the Solicitor General, is fully consistent with the Court's longstanding recognition that it is within the power of Congress under the "Necessary and Proper" Clause, Art. I, §8, to vest authority that falls within the Court's definition of executive power in officers who are not subject to removal at will by the President and are therefore not under the President's direct control. . . . [W]ith the advent and triumph of the administrative state and the accompanying multiplication of the tasks undertaken by the Federal Government, the Court has been virtually compelled to recognize that Congress may reasonably deem it "necessary and proper" to vest some among the broad new array of governmental functions in officers who are free from the partisanship that may be expected of agents wholly dependent upon the President. . . .

In determining whether a limitation on the President's power to remove an officer performing executive functions constitutes a violation of the constitutional scheme of separation of powers, a court must "focu[s] on the extent to which [such a limitation] prevents the Executive Branch from accomplishing its constitutionally assigned functions." *Nixon v. Administrator of General Services* . . . It is evident (and nothing in the Court's opinion is to the contrary) that the powers exercised by the Comptroller General under the Gramm-Rudman Act are not such that vesting them in an officer not subject to removal at will by the President would in itself improperly interfere with Presidential powers. Determining the level of spending by the Federal Government is not by nature a function central either to the exercise of the President's enumerated powers or to his general duty to ensure execution of the laws; rather, appropriating funds is a peculiarly legislative function, and one expressly committed to Congress by Art. I, §9, which provides that "[n]o Money shall be drawn from the Treasury, but in Consequence of Appropriations made by Law." . . . Delegating the execution of this legislation—that is, the power to apply the Act's criteria and make the required calculations—to an officer independent of the President's will does not deprive the President of any power that he would otherwise have or that is essential to the performance of the duties of his office. Rather, the result of such a delegation, from the standpoint of the President, is no different from the result of more traditional forms of appropriation: under either system, the level of funds available to the Executive branch to carry out its duties is not within the President's discretionary control. . . .

II

. . . [T]he question remains whether, as the Court concludes, the fact that the officer to whom Congress has delegated the authority to implement the Act is removable by a joint resolution of Congress should require invalidation of the Act. The Court's decision . . . is based on a syllogism: the Act vests the Comptroller with "executive power"; such power may not be exercised by Congress or its agents; the Comptroller is an agent of Congress because he is removable by Congress; therefore the Act is invalid. I have no quarrel with the proposition that the powers exercised by the Comptroller under the Act may be characterized as "executive" in that they involve the interpretation and carrying out of the Act's mandate. I can also accept the general proposition that although Congress has considerable authority in designating the officers who are to execute legislation, the constitutional scheme of separated powers does prevent Congress from reserving an executive role for itself or for its "agents." *Buckley v. Valeo.* I cannot accept, however, that the exercise of authority by an officer removable for cause by a joint resolution of Congress is analogous to the impermissible execution of the law by Congress itself, nor would I hold that the congressional role in the removal process renders the Comptroller an "agent" of the Congress, incapable of receiving "executive" power. . . .

[The] procedural and substantive limitations on the removal power militate strongly against the characterization of the Comptroller as a mere agent of Congress by virtue of the removal authority. Indeed, similarly qualified grants of removal power are generally deemed to protect the officers to whom they apply and to establish their independence from the domination of the possessor of the removal power. Removal authority limited in such a manner is more properly viewed as motivating adherence to a substantive standard established by law than as inducing subservience to the particular institution that enforces that standard. That the agent enforcing the standard is Congress may be of some significance to the Comptroller, but Congress' substantively limited removal power will undoubtedly be less of a spur to subservience than Congress' unquestionable and unqualified power to enact legislation reducing the Comptroller's salary, cutting the funds available to his department, reducing his personnel, limiting or expanding his duties, or even abolishing his position altogether.

More importantly, the substantial role played by the President in the process of removal through joint resolution reduces to utter insignificance the possibility that the threat of removal will induce subservience to the Congress. [A] joint resolution must be presented to the President and is ineffective if it is vetoed by him, unless the veto is overridden by the constitutionally prescribed two-thirds majority of both Houses of Congress. The requirement of presidential approval obviates the possibility that the Comptroller will perceive himself as so completely at the mercy of Congress that he will function as its tool. If the Comptroller's conduct in office is not so unsatisfactory to the President as to convince the latter that removal is required under the statutory standard, Congress will have no independent power to coerce the Comptroller unless it can muster a two-thirds majority in both Houses—a feat of bipartisanship more difficult than that required to impeach and convict. The incremental *in terrorem* effect of the possibility of congressional removal in the face of a presidential veto is therefore exceedingly unlikely to have any discernible impact on the extent of congressional influence over the Comptroller. The practical result of the removal provision is not to render the Comptroller unduly dependent upon or subservient to Congress, but to render him one of the most independent officers in the entire federal establishment. . . .

The Act vesting budget-cutting authority in the Comptroller General represents Congress' judgment that the delegation of such authority to counteract ever-mounting deficits is "necessary and proper" to the exercise of the powers granted the Federal Government by the Constitution; and the President's approval of the statute signifies his unwillingness to reject the choice made by Congress. Under such circumstances, the role of this Court should be limited to determining whether the Act so alters the balance of authority among the branches of government as to pose a genuine threat to the basic division between the lawmaking power and the power to execute the law. Because I see no such threat, I cannot join the Court in striking down the Act.

Justice BLACKMUN, dissenting.

. . . Appellees have not sought invalidation of the 1921 provision that authorizes Congress to remove the Comptroller General by joint resolution. . . . The only relief sought in this case is nullification of the automatic budget-reduction provisions of the Deficit Control Act, and that relief should not be awarded even if the Court is correct that those provisions are constitutionally incompatible with Congress' authority to remove the Comptroller General by joint resolution. Any incompatibility, I feel, should be cured by refusing to allow congressional removal — if it ever is attempted — and not by striking down the central provisions of the Deficit Control Act. . . .

———————

1. *Who Nominates?* The *Bowsher* Court remarked in passing that the Comptroller General is nominated by the President from a list of three individuals recommended by a group of Members of Congress. The statute calls for Congressional recommendation to the President of "at least three individuals." And it adds that "the President may ask [the Congressional group] to recommend additional individuals." 31 U.S.C. § 703(a)(3). Does that infringe the President's appointments power under *Buckley*, in view of the limited choice available to the President? Recall that in *Myers* the Court remarked that the Senate's rejection of a nominee "does not greatly embarrass" the President's discharge of his constitutional duties, "because [he] usually has an ample field from which to select for office, according to his preference, competent and capable" replacements. Consider Justice Kennedy's views on appointments in *Public Citizen, supra* — would he condemn this provision?

2. *Bringing the Comptroller in from the Cold.* Would the Court have been well advised to accept Justice Blackmun's invitation to strike down the removal provision rather than the Deficit Control Act? In the wake of *Bowsher*, constitutional doubts surround the GAO's other statutory functions. Should Congress amend the removal provision to make the Comptroller removable by the President for cause? *See* Paul R. Verkuil, *The Status of Independent Agencies After* Bowsher v. Synar, 1986 DUKE L.J. 779, 802–04. Would that radically alter the Comptroller's relationships with the two branches?

In at least some settings, Congress has taken a different tack. In the years since *Bowsher*, Congress has reassigned some of the Comptroller General's statutory powers to officers who are not removable by Congress. For example, Congress has amended the Judgment Fund to reallocate the Comptroller General's role to the Secretary of the Treasury. *See* 31 U.S.C. § 1304(a)(2). Prior to 1996, the Comptroller General had the authority to certify payments from the fund, and therefore to determine whether the fund would be available. *See* Pub. L. 104-316 § 202(m).

3. *Tying the President's Hands.* The 1985 Act apparently placed the President in a ministerial role, charged with executing an order drafted by an officer not responsible to him. Was it constitutional for Congress to reduce the President's role in controlling spending to this degree? *See* E. Donald Elliott, *Regulating the Deficit After Bowsher v. Synar*, 4 YALE J. ON REG. 317 (1987).

4. *The Meaning of "Cause," Again.* Note that the removal statute involved in *Bowsher* contains the core provisions usually found in statutes restricting *presidential* removal: "inefficiency, neglect of duty, malfeasance." The Court says that "[t]hese terms are very broad and, as interpreted by Congress, could sustain removal . . . for any number of actual or perceived transgressions of the legislative will." Does that mean that the President has broad discretion under the cognate statutes? That certainly isn't what *Humphrey's Executor* suggests. Samuel Alito, when he was still an appellate judge, embraced an expansive view of what constitutes cause. *See* Samuel A. Alito, Jr., *Panel Discussion at Federalist Society 2000 National Lawyer's Convention: Administrative Law & Regulation: Presidential Oversight and the Administrative State*, 2 ENGAGE 11, 12 (2001).

At this point, we pause to examine three illustrative statutory provisions on presidential removal. As you read each, consider how much guidance you can infer regarding permissible grounds for removal and the President's managerial prerogatives over the agency:

Nuclear Regulatory Commission (42 U.S.C. § 5841(e)):

> Any member of the commission may be removed by the President for inefficiency, neglect of duty, or malfeasance in office.

Consumer Product Safety Commission (15 U.S.C. § 2053(a)):

> An independent regulatory commission is hereby established, to be known as the Consumer Product Safety Commission, consisting of five Commissioners who shall be appointed by the President, by and with the advice and consent of the Senate. . . . *The Chairman shall be appointed by the President, by and with the advice and consent of the Senate, from among the members of the Commission. An individual may be appointed as a member of the Commission and as Chairman at the same time.* Any member of the Commission may be removed by the President for neglect of duty or malfeasance in office but for no other cause.

(Emphasis added). Section 2 of the Act of Nov. 10, 1978, Pub. L. No. 95-631, amended this subsection by adding the italicized language. The immediately preceding sentence originally read: "Senate, one of whom shall be designated by the President as Chairman." The next sentence, which the amendment deleted, read: The Chairman, when so designated, shall act as Chairman until the expiration of his term of office as Commissioner. *See* Act of Oct. 27, 1972, Pub. L. No. 92-573, Sec. 4(a), 86 Stat. 1210.

Environmental Protection Agency (5 U.S.C. App., Reorg. Plan No. 3 of 1970, 1(b)):

> There shall be at the head of the Agency the Administrator of the Environmental Protection Agency. . . . The Administrator shall be appointed by the President, by and with the advice and consent of the Senate. . . .

How do you interpret those statutes that explicitly require cause for removal? Can a member of the Nuclear Regulatory Commission be dismissed for drunkenness at NRC meetings? For taking bribes? For handing in decisions tardily, i.e., "inefficiently?" For interpreting the law contrary to an opinion on point issued by the Attorney General?

Do limited removability and agency independence go hand in hand? Do you infer from the absence of express limitations on the President's power to remove the Administrator of EPA that it is meant to be less "independent" than the Consumer Product Safety Commission? Notice the amendment to the CPSC statute. The chair of a multi-member agency normally has substantial managerial responsibilities within the agency, for example the power to hire important staff members. For some independent agencies, the practice is for the President to designate or demote a chair at will. What implication do you draw from the amendment changing the process for designating the CPSC chair?

5. *Who Holds the Leash Owns the Dog?* Note that Justice White's dissent referred to the fact that the executive had made an unqualified "unitary executive" argument for the proposition that anyone who executes the law must be removable at will by the President, and that the majority had not endorsed the argument. Actually, the majority responded to this argument obliquely in a footnote, denying that its holding cast any doubt on the constitutional status of the independent agencies—the case involved "nothing like" the statutes qualifying presidential removal, said the Court, because the statute at hand involved congressional removal. Do you agree that there is no such implication? The Court approvingly quoted the District Court's conclusion that "[o]nce an officer is appointed, it is only the authority that can remove him . . . that he must fear, and, in the performance of his functions, obey." The Court later said that "[i]n constitutional terms, the removal powers over the Comptroller General's office dictate that he will be subservient to Congress." If control follows removability for constitutional purposes, may the President now control the independent agencies? The answer depends on how one reads the removal provisions. That leads to a trap, doesn't it: if *Humphrey's Executor* still means that these agencies are independent of the President "except in their selection," what are they doing executing the law?

Plainly, bigger game is afoot than the *Bowsher* Court wished to hunt. Academics have filled the air with potshots. *See generally* Symposium, Bowsher v. Synar,

72 Cornell L. Rev. 421 (1987); David P. Currie, *The Distribution of Powers After Bowsher*, 1986 Sup. Ct. Rev. 19; Paul R. Verkuil, *supra*.

Recall the Court's decision in *Wiener,* in which it implied restrictions on removal from a statute that contained none, because of the adjudicative functions of the officers. Does *Bowsher* suggest that the courts should avoid implying removal restrictions in order to minimize Article II concerns? Consider the U.S. Commission on Civil Rights, around which controversy swirled during the Reagan administration. In the notes following *Buckley, supra,* we raised questions about the way the Commission is appointed under a statutory reconstitution in 1983. Previously, its members were all presidential appointees and there was no statutory restriction on their removal. In an effort to reshape the Commission to accord with his views, President Reagan removed three of its members. (The full story is told in Comment, *The Rise and Fall of the United States Commission on Civil Rights*, 22 Harv. C.R.-C.L. L. Rev. 449, 476–80 (1987).) They obtained a preliminary injunction against the removal, *Berry v. Reagan*, 32 Empl. Prac. Dec. (CCH); pg. 33,898 (D.D.C.), *vacated as moot,* 732 F.2d 949 (D.C. Cir. 1983). The District Court concluded that Congress intended the Commission to be free of presidential control, because "[w]hen performing its fact-finding, investigatory, and monitoring functions . . . the Commission is often required to criticize the policies of the Executive that are contrary to existing civil rights legislation." Does *Bowsher* undermine this result, or is there special reason to insulate "watchdog" functions within the executive? We return to this question when we consider "special prosecutors" in the next section.

6. *Aggrandizement.* The Court provided some further explanation of *Bowsher* in a decision issued the same day, *Commodity Futures Trading Commission v. Schor,* excerpted in Chapter Two. In *Schor,* the Court upheld allocation of potential Article III adjudicative authority (over a counterclaim arising under state law) to an administrative agency rather than to a federal court. The Court employed functional analysis, in sharp contrast to the formalism of *Bowsher.* Justice O'Connor explained:

> Unlike *Bowsher,* this case raises no question of the aggrandizement of congressional power at the expense of a coordinate branch. Instead, the separation of powers question presented in this case is whether Congress impermissibly undermined, without appreciable expansion of its own power, the role of the Judicial Branch. . . . [W]e have also been faithful to our Article III precedents, which counsel that bright line rules cannot effectively be employed to yield broad principles applicable in all Article III inquiries.

Is "aggrandizement" then the key to the Court's choice of approach — and outcome?

7. *Bowsher II or Chadha II?* In *Metropolitan Washington Airports Authority v. Citizens for the Abatement of Aircraft Noise,* 501 U.S. 252 (1991), the Supreme Court overturned what it took to be an impermissible extension of congressional involvement in administration, but one that had nothing to do with the institutional competition between President and Congress that lies at the core of earlier cases. In 1986, Congress authorized the transfer of federal operating control over two major airports

near the District of Columbia to the Metropolitan Washington Airport Authority, a regional authority established by Virginia-D.C. compact. To assume control of the airports, however, the MWAA Board of Directors would have to create a nine-member Board of Review with the power to veto certain actions of the Directors. The nine members of the Board of Review were required to be members of Congress, "serving in their individual capacities, as representatives of the users of the Metropolitan Washington Airports." The MWAA Board of Directors was required further to select eight of the nine Board of Review members from the membership of designated congressional committees having jurisdiction over transportation and related matters. One of the first matters subjected to the Board of Review's potential veto was a "master plan" providing for the enhanced usage of National Airport, an airport especially convenient to Capitol Hill and already the chronic target of citizen complaints about aircraft noise. If upheld, the scheme for congressional membership on the MWAA Board of Directors would have given some Members of Congress the opportunity to bring a congressional point of view to MWAA policy making, including the master plan, to prevent the adoption of policies that would reduce the convenience of National. Six members of the Court held that the Board of Review's power to veto decisions by the MWAA Directors represented federal action taken on behalf of Congress. The Court, per Justice Stevens, noted the framers' fears of the legislature:

> To forestall the danger of encroachment "beyond the legislative sphere," the Constitution imposes two basic and related constraints on Congress. It may not "invest itself or its Members with either executive power or judicial power." And, when it exercises its legislative power, it must follow the "single, finely wrought and exhaustively considered procedures" specified in Article I. . . . The Court of Appeals found it unnecessary to discuss the second constraint because the court was satisfied that the power exercised by the Board of Review over "key operational decisions is quintessentially executive." We need not agree or disagree with this characterization [to] conclude that the Board of Review's power is constitutionally impermissible. If the power is executive, the Constitution does not permit an agent of Congress to exercise it. If the power is legislative, Congress must exercise it in conformity with the bicameralism and presentment requirements. . . .

Curiously, the majority appended a footnote disclaiming reliance on the Incompatibility Clause of Article I, section 6, which forbids members of Congress from holding executive offices, or the Appointments Clause, Article II, section 2.

Justice White vigorously dissented, joined by the Chief Justice and by Justice Marshall. He argued that separation of powers analysis was inapplicable to the functions of members of Congress serving in their individual capacities on a body created under state law. In any event, it was implausible to regard Board of Review members as agents of Congress when (a) Congress did not appoint them, (b) continuity in Congress or on any committee was not a condition for completion of service on the Board, (c) Congress could not remove Board members, and (d) Board members had no legal obligations to Congress. The majority, however, regarded the challenged Act as "a blueprint for extensive expansion of the legislative power. . . ." It said Congress could use similar structures "to enable its Members or its agents to retain control, outside the ordinary legislative process, of the activities of state grant recipients charged with executing virtually every aspect of national policy."

Congress responded to *MWAA* by removing the requirement that the Board be composed of Members of Congress, although its members were still to be congressional nominees. Congress also removed the Board's veto authority, but allowed the members to have nonvoting participation at meetings of the airport Directors. Congress also authorized the Board to make recommendations to the Directors, which, if not adopted, would subject the Directors' actions to joint resolutions of disapproval by Congress. In *Hechinger v. Metropolitan Washington Airports Authority*, 36 F.3d 97 (D.C. Cir. 1994), *cert. denied*, 513 U.S. 1126 (1995), the court struck down the new arrangement. It concluded that the Board was still an agent of Congress, and that it was still exercising federal power as defined in *MWAA*.

B. Modern Syntheses of Appointment and Removal Powers

Morrison v. Olson

487 U.S. 654 (1988)

Chief Justice REHNQUIST delivered the opinion of the Court.

This case presents us with a challenge to the independent counsel provisions of the Ethics in Government Act of 1978, 28 U.S.C. §§ 49, 591 et seq. (Supp. 1988). We hold today that these provisions of the Act do not violate the appointments clause of the Constitution, art. II, § 2, cl. 2, or the limitations of article III, nor do they impermissibly interfere with the President's authority under article II in violation of the constitutional principle of separation of powers.

I

. . . [T]he Ethics in Government Act allows for the appointment of an "independent counsel" to investigate and, if appropriate, prosecute certain high ranking government officials for violations of federal criminal laws. The Act requires the Attorney General, upon receipt of information that he determines is "sufficient to constitute grounds to investigate whether any person (covered by the Act) may have violated any Federal criminal law," to conduct a preliminary investigation of the matter. When the Attorney General has completed this investigation, or 90 days has elapsed, he is required to report to a special court (the Special Division) created by the Act "for the purpose of appointing independent counsels." [This is a Special Division of the Court of Appeals for the District of Columbia, consisting of three judges appointed by the Chief Justice.] If the Attorney General determines that "there are no reasonable grounds to believe that further investigation is warranted," then he must notify the Special Division of this result. In such a case, "the division of the court shall have no power to appoint an independent counsel." If, however, the Attorney General has determined that there are "reasonable grounds to believe that further investigation or prosecution is warranted," then he "shall apply to the division of the court for the appointment of an independent counsel." The Attorney General's application to the court "shall contain sufficient information to assist the (court) in selecting an independent counsel and in defining that independent counsel's prosecutorial jurisdiction." Upon receiving this application, the Special Division "shall appoint an appropriate independent counsel and shall define that independent counsel's prosecutorial jurisdiction."

With respect to all matters within the independent counsel's jurisdiction, the Act grants the counsel "full power and independent authority to exercise all investigative and prosecutorial functions and powers of the Department of Justice, the Attorney General, and any other officer or employee of the Department of Justice." The functions of the independent counsel include conducting grand jury proceedings and other investigations, participating in civil and criminal court proceedings and litigation, and appealing any decision in any case in which the counsel participates in an official capacity. . . . The counsel may appoint employees. . . . [A]n independent counsel "shall, except where not possible, comply with the written or other established policies of the Department of Justice respecting enforcement of the criminal laws." . . .

Two statutory provisions govern the length of an independent counsel's tenure in office. The first defines the procedure for removing an independent counsel. Section 596(a)(1) provides:

> An independent counsel appointed under this chapter may be removed from office, other than by impeachment and conviction, only by the personal action of the Attorney General and only for good cause, physical disability, mental incapacity, or any other condition that substantially impairs the performance of such independent counsel's duties.

If an independent counsel is removed pursuant to this section, . . . an independent counsel can obtain judicial review of the Attorney General's action by filing a civil action in the United States District Court for the District of Columbia. . . . The reviewing court is authorized to grant reinstatement or "other appropriate relief." The other provision governing the tenure of the independent counsel defines the procedures for "terminating" the counsel's office. Under section 596(b)(1), the office of an independent counsel terminates when he notifies the Attorney General that he has completed or substantially completed any investigations or prosecutions undertaken pursuant to the Act. In addition, the Special Division, acting either on its own or on the suggestion of the Attorney General, may terminate the office of an independent counsel at any time if it finds that "the investigation of all matters within the prosecutorial jurisdiction of such independent counsel . . . have been completed or so substantially completed that it would be appropriate for the Department of Justice to complete such investigations and prosecutions." . . .

The proceedings in this case provide an example of how the Act works in practice. In 1982 two subcommittees of the House of Representatives issued subpoenas directing the Environmental Protection Agency (EPA) to produce certain documents relating to the efforts of the EPA and the Land and Natural Resources Division of the Justice Department to enforce the "superfund law." At that time, appellee Olson was the Assistant Attorney General for the Office of Legal Counsel (OLC), appellee Schmults was Deputy Attorney General, and appellee Dinkins was the Assistant Attorney General for the Land and Natural Resources Division. Acting on the advice of the Justice Department, the President ordered the Administrator of EPA to invoke executive privilege to withhold certain of the documents on the ground that they contained "enforcement sensitive information." ... In response, the House voted to hold the Administrator in contempt. ... The conflict abated in March 1983, when the Administration agreed to give the House committees limited access to the documents.

The following year, the House Judiciary Committee began an investigation into the Justice Department's role in the controversy over the EPA documents. During this investigation, appellee Olson testified before a House subcommittee on March 10, 1983. ... [Some] documents were at first withheld, although these documents were eventually disclosed by the Department after the Committee learned of their existence. In 1985, the majority members of the Judiciary Committee published a lengthy report on the Committee's investigation. The report ... suggested that appellee Olson had given false and misleading testimony to the subcommittee on March 10, 1983, and that appellees Schmults and Dinkins had wrongfully withheld certain documents from the Committee, thus obstructing the Committee's investigation. The Chairman of the Judiciary Committee forwarded a copy of the report to the Attorney General with a request, pursuant to [§ 592(g)], that he seek the appointment of an independent counsel to investigate the allegations against Olson, Schmults, and Dinkins.

The Attorney General directed the Public Integrity Section of the Criminal Division to conduct a preliminary investigation. The Section's report concluded that the appointment of an independent counsel was warranted to investigate the Committee's allegations with respect to all three appellees. After consulting with other Department officials, however, the Attorney General chose to apply to the Special Division for the appointment of an independent counsel solely with respect to appellee Olson. The Attorney General accordingly requested appointment of an independent counsel to investigate whether Olson's March 10, 1983, testimony "regarding the completeness of (OLC's) response to the Judiciary Committee's request for OLC documents, and regarding his knowledge of EPA's willingness to turn over certain disputed documents to Congress, violated 18 U.S.C. § 1505, § 1001, or any other provision of federal criminal law." The Attorney General also requested that the independent counsel have authority to investigate "any other matter related to that allegation." ...

[Eventually, the Special Division appointed appellant, Alexia Morrison, as independent counsel, with jurisdiction reflecting the Attorney General's request.] In

January 1987, appellant asked the Attorney General pursuant to section 594(e) to refer to her as "related matters" the Committee's allegations against appellees Schmults and Dinkins. The Attorney General refused to refer the matters, concluding that his decision not to request the appointment of an independent counsel in regard to those matters was final. . . . Appellant then asked the Special Division to order that the matters be referred to her. . . . On April 2, 1987, the Division ruled that the Attorney General's decision not to seek appointment of an independent counsel with respect to Schmults and Dinkins was final and unreviewable . . . , and that therefore the court had no authority to make the requested referral. *In re Olson*, 818 F.2d 34. The court ruled, however, that its original grant of jurisdiction to appellant was broad enough to permit inquiry into whether Olson may have conspired with others, including Schmults and Dinkins, to obstruct the Committee's investigation.

Following this ruling, in May and June 1987, appellant caused a grand jury to issue and serve subpoenas ad testificandum and duces tecum on appellees. All three appellees moved to quash the subpoenas, claiming, among other things, that the independent counsel provisions of the Act were unconstitutional and that appellant accordingly had no authority to proceed. On July 20, 1987, the District Court upheld the constitutionality of the Act and denied the motions to quash. A divided Court of Appeals reversed. . . . We now reverse [the court of appeals].

II

[The Court first concluded that the independent counsel waived her contention that the constitutional issues addressed by the Court of Appeals could not be reviewed on appeal from the District Court's contempt judgment.]

III

. . . The parties do not dispute that "[t]he Constitution for purposes of appointment . . . divides all its officers into two classes." *United States v. Germaine*, 99 U.S. 508, 509 (1879). . . . The initial question is, accordingly, whether appellant is an "inferior" or a "principal" officer. If she is the latter, as the Court of Appeals concluded, then the Act is in violation of the Appointments Clause. . . . [I]n our view appellant clearly falls on the "inferior officer" side of that line. Several factors lead to this conclusion.

First, appellant is subject to removal by a higher Executive Branch official. Although appellant may not be "subordinate" to the Attorney General (and the President) insofar as she possesses a degree of independent discretion to exercise the powers delegated to her under the Act, the fact that she can be removed by the Attorney General indicates that she is to some degree "inferior" in rank and authority. Second, appellant is empowered by the Act to perform only certain, limited duties. An independent counsel's role is restricted primarily to investigation and, if appropriate, prosecution for certain federal crimes. Admittedly, the Act delegates to appellant "full power and independent authority to exercise all investigative and prosecutorial functions and powers of the Department of Justice," but this grant of authority does not include any authority to formulate policy for the Government or the Executive Branch, nor does it give appellant any administrative duties outside of those necessary to operate her office. The Act specifically provides that in policy matters appellant is to comply to the extent possible with the policies of the Department.

Third, appellant's office is limited in jurisdiction. Not only is the Act itself restricted in applicability to certain federal officials suspected of certain serious federal crimes, but an independent counsel can only act within the scope of the jurisdiction that has been granted by the Special Division pursuant to a request by the Attorney General. Finally, appellant's office is limited in tenure. There is concededly no time limit on the appointment of a particular counsel. Nonetheless, the office of independent counsel is "temporary" in the sense that an independent counsel is appointed essentially to accomplish a single task, and when that task is over the office is terminated, either by the counsel herself or by action of the Special Division. . . . All of this is consistent with our reference in *United States v. Nixon*, 418 U.S. 683, 694, 696 (1974), to the office of Watergate Special Prosecutor whose authority was similar to that of appellant as a "subordinate officer."

This does not, however, end our inquiry under the Appointments Clause. Appellees argue that even if appellant is an "inferior" officer, the Clause does not empower Congress to place the power to appoint such an officer outside the Executive Branch. They contend that the Clause does not contemplate congressional authorization of "interbranch appointments," in which an officer of one branch is appointed by officers of another branch. . . . On its face, the language of [the final proviso of the appointments clause] admits of no limitation on interbranch appointments. Indeed, the inclusion of "as they think proper" seems clearly to give Congress significant discretion to determine whether it is "proper" to vest the appointment of, for example, executive officials in the "courts of Law." We recognized as much in one of our few decisions in this area, *Ex parte Siebold*, 100 U.S. 371 (1879), where we stated:

> It is no doubt usual and proper to vest the appointment of inferior officers in that department of the government, executive or judicial, or in that particular executive department to which the duties of such officers appertain. But there is no absolute requirement to this effect in the Constitution; and, if there were, it would be difficult in many cases to determine to which department an office properly belonged. . . . But as the Constitution stands, the selection of the appointing power, as between the functionaries named, is a matter resting in the discretion of Congress. And, looking at the subject in a practical light, it is perhaps better that it should rest there, than that the country should be harassed by the endless controversies to which a more specific direction on this subject might have given rise. 100 U.S., at 397–98. . . .

We also note that the history of the clause provides no support for appellees' position. . . . [T]here was little or no debate [at the Constitutional Convention] on the question of whether the Clause empowers Congress to provide for interbranch appointments, and there is nothing to suggest that the Framers intended to prevent Congress from having that power.

(We do not mean to say that Congress' power to provide for interbranch appointments of "inferior officers" is unlimited.) In addition to separation of powers concerns, which would arise if such provisions for appointment had the potential to impair the constitutional functions assigned to one of the branches, *Siebold* itself suggested that Congress' decision to vest the appointment power in the courts would be improper if there was some "incongruity" between the functions normally performed by the courts and the performance of their duty to appoint. In this case, however, we do not think it impermissible for Congress to vest the power to appoint independent counsels in a specially created federal court. We thus disagree with the Court of Appeals' conclusion that there is an inherent incongruity about a court having the power to appoint prosecutorial officers. . . . Lower courts have . . . upheld interim judicial appointments of United States Attorneys, and Congress itself has vested the power to make these interim appointments in the district courts.

Congress of course was concerned when it created the office of independent counsel with the conflicts of interest that could arise in situations when the Executive Branch is called upon to investigate its own high-ranking officers. If it were to remove the appointing authority from the Executive Branch, the most logical place to put it was in the Judicial Branch. In the light of the Act's provision making the judges of the Special Division ineligible to participate in any matters relating to an independent counsel they have appointed, we do not think that appointment of the independent counsels by the court runs afoul of the constitutional limitation on "incongruous" interbranch appointments.

IV

Appellees next contend that the powers vested in the Special Division by the Act conflict with Article III of the Constitution. . . . As a general rule, we have broadly stated that "executive or administrative duties of a nonjudicial nature may not be imposed on judges holding office under Art. III of the Constitution." The purpose of this limitation is to help ensure the independence of the Judicial Branch and to prevent the judiciary from encroaching into areas reserved for the other branches.

With this in mind, we address in turn the various duties given to the Special Division by the Act. Most importantly, the Act vests in the Special Division the power to choose who will serve as independent counsel and the power to define his or her jurisdiction. Clearly, once it is accepted that the Appointments Clause gives Congress the power to vest the appointment of officials such as the independent counsel in the "courts of Law," there can be no Article III objection to the Special Division's exercise of that power, as the power itself derives from the Appointments Clause, a source of authority for judicial action that is independent of Article III. Appellees contend, however, that the Division's Appointments Clause powers do not encompass the power to define the independent counsel's jurisdiction. We disagree. In our view, Congress' power under the Clause to vest the "Appointment" of inferior officers in the courts may, in certain circumstances, allow Congress to give the courts some discretion in defining the nature and scope of the appointed official's authority.

Particularly when, as here, Congress creates a temporary "office" the nature and duties of which will by necessity vary with the factual circumstances giving rise to the need for an appointment in the first place, it may vest the power to define the scope of the office in the court as an incident to the appointment of the officer pursuant to the Appointments Clause. . . . [T]he jurisdiction that the court decides upon must be demonstrably related to the factual circumstances that gave rise to the Attorney General's investigation and request for the appointment of the independent counsel in the particular case. . . .

We are more doubtful about the Special Division's power to terminate the office of the independent counsel pursuant to section 596(b)(2). As appellees suggest, the power to terminate, especially when exercised by the Division on its own motion, is "administrative" to the extent that it requires the Special Division to monitor the progress of proceedings of the independent counsel and come to a decision as to whether the counsel's job is "completed." . . . Nonetheless, we do not, as did the Court of Appeals, view this provision as a significant judicial encroachment upon executive power or upon the prosecutorial discretion of the independent counsel. . . . As we see it, "termination" . . . is basically a device for removing from the public payroll an independent counsel who has served her purpose, but is unwilling to acknowledge the fact. So construed, the Special Division's power to terminate does not pose a sufficient threat of judicial intrusion into matters that are more properly within the Executive's authority to require that the Act be invalidated as inconsistent with Article III. . . .

V

We now turn to consider whether the Act is invalid under the constitutional principle of separation of powers. Two related issues must be addressed: The first is whether the provision of the Act restricting the Attorney General's power to remove the independent counsel to only those instances in which he can show "good cause," taken by itself, impermissibly interferes with the President's exercise of his constitutionally appointed functions. The second is whether, taken as a whole, the Act violates the separation of powers by reducing the President's ability to control the prosecutorial powers wielded by the independent counsel.

A

. . . Unlike both *Bowsher* and *Myers*, this case does not involve an attempt by Congress itself to gain a role in the removal of executive officials other than its established powers of impeachment and conviction. The Act instead puts the removal power squarely in the hands of the Executive Branch; an independent counsel may be removed from office, "only by the personal action of the Attorney General, and only for good cause." There is no requirement of congressional approval of the Attorney General's removal decision, though the decision is subject to judicial review. In our view, the removal provisions of the Act make this case more analogous to *Humphrey's Executor v. United States*, and *Weiner v. United States*, than to *Myers* or *Bowsher*. . . .

Appellees contend that *Humphrey's Executor* and *Wiener* are distinguishable from this case because they did not involve officials who performed a "core executive function." They argue that our decision in *Humphrey's Executor* rests on a distinction between "purely executive" officials and officials who exercise "quasi-legislative" and "quasi-judicial" powers. In their view, when a "purely executive" official is involved, the governing precedent is *Myers*, not *Humphrey's Executor*. And, under *Myers*, the President must have absolute discretion to discharge "purely executive" officials at will. We undoubtedly did rely on the terms "quasi-legislative" and "quasi-judicial" to distinguish the officials involved in *Humphrey's Executor* and *Wiener* from those in *Myers*, but our present considered view is that the determination of whether the Constitution allows Congress to impose a "good cause"-type restriction on the President's power to remove an official cannot be made to turn on whether or not that official is classified as "purely executive."

The analysis contained in our removal cases is designed not to define rigid categories of those officials who may or may not be removed at will by the President, but to ensure that Congress does not interfere with the President's exercise of the "executive power" and his constitutionally appointed duty to "take care that the laws be faithfully executed" under Article II. *Myers* was undoubtedly correct in its holding, and in its broader suggestion that there are some "purely executive" officials who must be removable by the President at will if he is to be able to accomplish his constitutional role. . . . At the other end of the spectrum from *Myers*, the characterization of the agencies in *Humphrey's Executor* and *Wiener* as "quasi-legislative" or "quasi-judicial" in large part reflected our judgment that it was not essential to the President's proper execution of his Article II powers that these agencies be headed up by individuals who were removable at will. We do not mean to suggest that an analysis of the functions served by the officials at issue is irrelevant. But the real question is whether the removal restrictions are of such a nature that they impede the President's ability to perform his constitutional duty, and the functions of the officials in question must be analyzed in that light.

Considering for the moment the "good cause" removal provision in isolation from the other parts of the Act at issue in this case, we cannot say that the imposition of a "good cause" standard for removal by itself unduly trammels on executive authority. There is no real dispute that the functions performed by the independent counsel are "executive" in the sense that they are law enforcement functions that typically have been undertaken by officials within the Executive Branch. As we noted above, however, the independent counsel is an inferior officer under the Appointments Clause, with limited jurisdiction and tenure and lacking policy-making or significant administrative authority. Although the counsel exercises no small amount of discretion and judgment in deciding how to carry out her duties under the Act, we simply do not see how the President's need to control the exercise of that discretion is so central to the functioning of the Executive Branch as to require as a matter of constitutional law that the counsel be terminable at will by the President.

Nor do we think that the "good cause" removal provision at issue here impermissibly burdens the President's power to control or supervise the independent counsel, as an executive official, in the execution of her duties under the Act. This is not a case in which the power to remove an executive official has been completely stripped from the President, thus providing no means for the President to ensure the "faithful execution" of the laws. Rather, because the independent counsel may be terminated for "good cause," the Executive, through the Attorney General, retains ample authority to assure that the counsel is competently performing her statutory responsibilities in a manner that comports with the provisions of the Act. Although we need not decide in this case exactly what is encompassed within the term "good cause" under the Act, the legislative history of the removal provision also makes clear that the Attorney General may remove an independent counsel for "misconduct." Here, as with the provision of the Act conferring the appointment authority of the independent counsel on the special court, the congressional determination to limit the removal power of the Attorney General was essential, in the view of Congress, to establish the necessary independence of the office. . . .).

B

The final question to be addressed is whether the Act, taken as a whole, violates the principle of separation of powers by unduly interfering with the role of the Executive Branch. . . . [T]he system of separated powers and checks and balances established in the Constitution was regarded by the Framers as "a self-executing safeguard against the encroachment or aggrandizement of one branch at the expense of the other." . . . On the other hand, we have never held that the Constitution requires that the three Branches of Government "operate with absolute independence."

We observe first that this case does not involve an attempt by Congress to increase its own powers at the expense of the Executive Branch. . . . [T]his case simply does not pose a "dange[r] of congressional usurpation of Executive Branch functions." Indeed, with the exception of the power of impeachment—which applies to all officers of the United States—Congress retained for itself no powers of control or supervision over an independent counsel. . . . Congress' role under the Act is limited to receiving reports or other information and oversight of the independent counsel's activities, functions that we have recognized generally as being incidental to the legislative function of Congress.

Similarly, we do not think that the act works any judicial usurpation of properly executive functions. . . . [T]he Special Division has no power to appoint an independent counsel sua sponte; it may only do so upon the specific request of the Attorney General, and the courts are specifically prevented from reviewing the Attorney General's decision not to seek appointment. In addition, once the court has appointed a counsel and defined her jurisdiction, it has no power to supervise or control the activities of the counsel. . . .

Finally, we do not think that the Act "impermissibly undermine[s]" the powers of the Executive Branch, or "disrupts the proper balance between the coordinate branches [by] prevent[ing] the Executive Branch from accomplishing its constitutionally assigned functions." It is undeniable that the Act reduces the amount of control or supervision that the Attorney General and, through him, the President exercises over the investigation and prosecution of a certain class of alleged criminal activity. . . . Nonetheless, the Act does give the Attorney General several means of supervising or controlling the prosecutorial powers that may be wielded by an independent counsel. Most importantly, the Attorney General retains the power to remove the counsel for "good cause," a power that we have already concluded provides the Executive with substantial ability to ensure that the laws are "faithfully executed" by an independent counsel. No independent counsel may be appointed without a specific request by the Attorney General, and the Attorney General's decision not to request appointment if he finds "no reasonable grounds to believe that further investigation is warranted" is committed to his unreviewable discretion. The Act thus gives the Executive a degree of control over the power to initiate an investigation by the independent counsel. In addition, the jurisdiction of the independent counsel is defined with reference to the facts submitted by the Attorney General, and once a counsel is appointed, the Act requires that the counsel abide by Justice Department policy unless it is not "possible" to do so. Notwithstanding the fact that the counsel is to some degree "independent" and free from Executive supervision to a greater extent than other federal prosecutors, in our view these features of the Act give the Executive Branch sufficient control over the independent counsel to ensure that the President is able to perform his constitutionally assigned duties.

VI

. . . The decision of the Court of Appeals is . . . Reversed.

Justice KENNEDY took no part in the consideration or decision of this case.

Justice SCALIA, dissenting.

The framers of the Federal Constitution . . . viewed the principle of separation of powers as the absolutely central guarantee of a just government. . . . [T]he founders conspicuously and very consciously declined to sap the executive's strength in the same way they had weakened the legislature: by dividing the executive power. Proposals to have multiple executives, or a council of advisors with separate authority were rejected. . . . Thus, while "[a]ll legislative Powers herein granted shall be vested in a Congress of the United States, which shall consist of a Senate *and* House of Representatives," U.S. Const., Art. I, § 1 (emphasis added), "[t]he executive Power shall be vested in *a President of the United States*," Art. II, § 1, cl. 1 (emphasis added).

That is what this suit is about. Power. The allocation of power among Congress, the President, and the courts in such fashion as to preserve the equilibrium the Constitution sought to establish—so that "a gradual concentration of the several powers in the same department," Federalist No. 51, p. 321 (J. Madison), can effectively be resisted. Frequently an issue of this sort will come before the Court clad, so to speak, in sheep's clothing: the potential of the asserted principle to effect important change in the equilibrium of power is not immediately evident, and must be discerned by a careful and perceptive analysis. But this wolf comes as a wolf.

I

. . . As a practical matter, it would be surprising if the Attorney General had any choice [assuming this statute is constitutional] but to seek appointment of an independent counsel to pursue the charges against the principal object of the congressional request, Mr. Olson. Merely the political consequences (to him and the President) of seeming to break the law by refusing to do so would have been substantial. . . . The context of this statute is acrid with the smell of threatened impeachment. Where, as here, a request for appointment of an independent counsel has come from the Judiciary Committee of either House of Congress, the Attorney General must, if he decides not to seek appointment, explain to that Committee why.

Thus, by the application of this statute in the present case, Congress has effectively compelled a criminal investigation of a high-level appointee of the President in connection with his action arising out of a bitter power dispute between the President and the Legislative Branch. Mr. Olson may or may not be guilty of a crime; we do not know. But we do know that the investigation of him has been commenced, not necessarily because the President or his authorized subordinates believe it is in the interest of the United States, in the sense that it warrants the diversion of resources from other efforts, and is worth the cost in money and in possible damage to other governmental interests; and not even, leaving aside those normally considered factors, because the President or his authorized subordinates necessarily believe that an investigation is likely to unearth a violation worth prosecuting; but only because the Attorney General cannot affirm, as Congress demands, that there are no reasonable grounds to believe that further investigation is warranted. The decision regarding the scope of that further investigation, its duration, and, finally, whether or not prosecution should ensue, are likewise beyond the control of the President and his subordinates.

II

If to describe this case is not to decide it, the concept of a government of separate and coordinate powers no longer has meaning. . . . Our opinions are full of the recognition that it is the principle of separation of powers, and the inseparable corollary that each department's "defense must . . . be made commensurate to the danger of attack," Federalist No. 51 (Madison), which gives comprehensible content to the appointments clause, and determines the appropriate scope of the removal power. . . . To repeat, Art. II, section 1, cl. 1 of the Constitution provides: "The executive Power shall be vested in a President of the United States." . . . [T]his does not mean some of the executive power, but all of the executive power. It seems to me, therefore, that the decision of the Court of Appeals invalidating the present statute must be upheld on fundamental separation-of-powers principles if the following two questions are answered affirmatively: (1) Is the conduct of a criminal prosecution (and of an investigation to decide whether to prosecute) the exercise of purely executive power?

(2) Does the statute deprive the President of the United States of exclusive control over the exercise of that power? Surprising to say, the Court appears to concede an affirmative answer to both questions, but seeks to avoid the inevitable conclusion that since the statute vests some purely executive power in a person who is not the President of the United States it is void. . . .

In what other sense can one identify "the executive Power" that is supposed to be vested in the President (unless it includes everything the Executive Branch is given to do) except by reference to what has always and everywhere if conducted by Government at all been conducted never by the legislature, never by the courts, and always by the executive. . . . Governmental investigation and prosecution of crimes is a quintessentially executive function.

As for the second question, whether the statute before us deprives the President of exclusive control over that quintessentially executive activity: The Court does not, and could not possibly, assert that it does not. That is indeed the whole object of the statute. Instead, the Court points out that the President, through his Attorney General, has at least some control. That concession is alone enough to invalidate the statute, but I cannot refrain from pointing out that the Court greatly exaggerates the extent of that "some" presidential control. "Most importan[t]" among these controls, the Court asserts, is the Attorney General's "power to remove the counsel for 'good cause.'" This is somewhat like referring to shackles as an effective means of locomotion. . . . What we in *Humphrey's Executor* found to be a means of eliminating presidential control, the Court today considers the "most importan[t]" means of assuring presidential control. . . . As I have said, however, it is ultimately irrelevant how much the statute reduces presidential control. . . . It is not for us to determine, and we have never presumed to determine, how much of the purely executive powers of government must be within the full control of the President. The Constitution prescribes that they all are. . . .

We should say here that the President's constitutionally assigned duties include complete control over investigation and prosecution of violations of the law, and that the inexorable command of Article II is clear and definite: the executive power must be vested in the President of the United States. Is it unthinkable that the President should have such exclusive power, even when alleged crimes by him or his close associates are at issue? No more so than that Congress should have the exclusive power of legislation, even when what is at issue is its own exemption from the burdens of certain laws. No more so than that this Court should have the exclusive power to pronounce the final decision on justiciable cases and controversies, even those pertaining to the constitutionality of a statute reducing the salaries of the Justices. A system of separate and coordinate powers necessarily involves an acceptance of exclusive power that can theoretically be abused. . . . While the separation of powers may prevent us from righting every wrong, it does so in order to ensure that we do not lose liberty. The checks against any Branch's abuse of its exclusive powers are twofold: First, retaliation by one of the other Branch's use of its exclusive powers: Congress, for example, can impeach the Executive who willfully fails to enforce the laws; the Executive can decline to prosecute under unconstitutional statutes; and the courts can dismiss malicious prosecutions; Second, and ultimately, there is the political check that the people will replace those in the political branches (the branches more "dangerous to the political rights of the Constitution," Federalist No. 78,) who are guilty of abuse⟨ Political pressures produced special prosecutors—for Teapot Dome and for Watergate, for example—long before this statute created the independent counsel. ⟩

The Court has, nonetheless, replaced the clear constitutional prescription that the executive power belongs to the President with a "balancing test." . . . [The Court] simply announces, with no analysis, that the ability to control the decision whether to investigate and prosecute the President's closest advisors, and indeed the President himself, is not "so central to the functioning of the Executive Branch" as to be constitutionally required to be within the President's control. Apparently that is so because we say it is so. Having abandoned as the basis for our decision-making the text of Article II that "the executive Power" must be vested in the President, the Court does not even attempt to craft a substitute criterion a "justiciable standard," however remote from the Constitution that today governs, and in the future will govern, the decision of such questions. . . .

[E]ven as an ad hoc, standardless judgment the Court's conclusion must be wrong. Before this statute was passed, the President, in taking action disagreeable to the Congress, or an executive officer giving advice to the President or testifying before Congress concerning one of those many matters on which the two branches are from time to time at odds, could be assured that his acts and motives would be adjudged insofar as the decision whether to conduct a criminal investigation and to prosecute is concerned in the Executive Branch, that is, in a forum attuned to the interests and the policies of the Presidency. That was one of the natural advantages the Constitution gave to the Presidency, just as it gave Members of Congress (and their staffs) the advantage of not being prosecutable for anything said or done in their legislative capacities. It is the very object of this legislation to eliminate that assurance of a sympathetic forum. Unless it can honestly be said that there are "no reasonable grounds to believe" that further investigation is warranted, further investigation must ensue; and the conduct of the investigation, and determination of whether to prosecute, will be given to a person neither selected by nor subject to the control of the President who will in turn assemble a staff by finding out, presumably, who is willing to put aside whatever else they are doing, for an indeterminate period of time, in order to investigate and prosecute the President or a particular named individual in his administration. The prospect is frightening . . . even outside the context of a bitter, interbranch political dispute. Perhaps the boldness of the President himself will not be affected though I am not even sure of that. (How much easier it is for Congress, instead of accepting the political damage attendant to the commencement of impeachment proceedings against the President on trivial grounds or, for that matter, how easy it is for one of the President's political foes outside of Congress simply to trigger a debilitating criminal investigation of the Chief Executive under this law.)

But as for the President's high-level assistants, who typically have no political base of support, it is as utterly unrealistic to think that they will not be intimidated by this prospect, and that their advice to him and their advocacy of his interests before a hostile Congress will not be affected, as it would be to think that the Members of Congress and their staffs would be unaffected by replacing the Speech or Debate Clause with a similar provision. It deeply wounds the President, by substantially reducing the President's ability to protect himself and his staff. That is the whole object of the law, of course, and I cannot imagine why the Court believes it does not succeed. . . .

III

. . . I fail to see how the fact that appellant is more difficult to remove than most principal officers helps to establish that she is an inferior officer. . . . [I]t seems to me impossible to maintain that appellant's authority is so "limited" as to render her an inferior officer. The Court seeks to brush this away by asserting that the independent counsel's power does not include any authority to "formulate policy for the Government or the Executive Branch." But the same could be said for all officers of the Government, with the single exception of the President. . . . I find nothing unusually limited about the independent counsel's tenure. To the contrary, unlike most high-ranking Executive Branch officials, she continues to serve until she (or the Special Division) decides that her work is substantially completed. This particular independent prosecutor has already served more than two years, which is at least as long as many cabinet officials. As to the scope of her jurisdiction, there can be no doubt that is small (though far from unimportant). But within it she exercises more than the full power of the Attorney General. . . . If the mere fragmentation of Executive responsibilities into small compartments suffices to render the heads of each of those compartments inferior officers, then Congress could deprive the President of the right to appoint his chief law-enforcement officer by dividing up the Attorney General's responsibilities among a number of "lesser" functionaries.

. . . [T]he text of the Constitution and the division of power that it establishes . . . demonstrate, I think, that the independent counsel is not an inferior officer because she is not subordinate to any officer in the Executive Branch (indeed, not even to the President). . . . That "inferior" means "subordinate" is . . . consistent with what little we know about the evolution of the Appointments Clause . . . . [The clause] was intended merely to make clear . . . that those officers appointed by the President with Senate approval could on their own appoint their subordinates, who would, of course, by chain of command still be under the direct control of the President. . . . Because appellant is not subordinate to another officer, she is not an "inferior" officer and her appointment other than by the President with the advice and consent of the Senate is unconstitutional . . . .

V

The purpose of the separation and equilibration of powers in general, and of the unitary Executive in particular, was not merely to assure effective government but to preserve individual freedom. Those who hold or have held offices covered by the Ethics in Government Act are entitled to that protection as much as the rest of us. . . . Only someone who has worked in the field of law enforcement can fully appreciate the vast power and the immense discretion that are placed in the hands of a prosecutor with respect to the objects of his investigation. . . .

Under our system of government, the primary check against prosecutorial abuse is a political one. The prosecutors who exercise this awesome discretion are selected and can be removed by a President, whom the people have trusted enough to elect. Moreover, when crimes are not investigated and prosecuted fairly, nonselectively, with a reasonable sense of proportion, the President pays the cost in political damage to his administration. . . . I leave it to the reader to recall the examples of this in recent years. That result, of course, was precisely what the Founders had in mind when they provided that all executive powers would be exercised by a single Chief Executive. . . . The President is directly dependent on the people, and since there is only one President, he is responsible. . . .

That is the system of justice the rest of us are entitled to, but what of that select class consisting of present or former high-level executive-branch officials? If an allegation is made against them . . . a process is set in motion that is not in the full control of persons "dependent on the people," and whose flaws cannot be blamed on the President. An independent counsel is selected, and the scope of her authority prescribed, by a panel of judges. . . . So if there is anything wrong with the selection, there is effectively no one to blame. The independent counsel thus selected proceeds to assemble a staff. . . . Can one imagine a less equitable manner of fulfilling the Executive responsibility to investigate and prosecute? . . .

As described in the brief filed on behalf of three ex-Attorneys General from each of the last three administrations:

> The problem . . . is that the institutional environment of the independent counsel, specifically, her isolation from the Executive Branch and the internal checks and balances it supplies is designed to heighten, not to check, all of the occupational hazards of the dedicated prosecutor; the danger of too narrow a focus, of the loss of perspective, of preoccupation with the pursuit of one alleged suspect to the exclusion of other interests.

Brief for Edward H. Levi, Griffin B. Bell, and William French Smith as Amici Curiae 11.

It is, in other words, an additional advantage of the unitary Executive that it can achieve a more uniform application of the law. Perhaps that is not always achieved, but the mechanism to achieve it is there. The mini-Executive that is the independent counsel, however, operating in an area where so little is law and so much is discretion, is intentionally cut off from the unifying influence of the Justice Department, and from the perspective that multiple responsibilities provide. What would normally be regarded as a technical violation (there are no rules defining such things), may in her small world assume the proportions of an indictable offense. . . . How frightening it must be to have your own independent counsel and staff appointed, with nothing else to do but to investigate you until investigation is no longer worthwhile — with whether it is worthwhile not depending upon what such judgments usually hinge on, competing responsibilities. And to have that counsel and staff decide, with no basis for comparison, whether what you have done is bad enough, willful enough, and provable enough, to warrant an indictment. How admirable the constitutional system that provides the means to avoid such a distortion. And how unfortunate the judicial decision that has permitted it.

———————

1. *A Unitary Executive for Prosecution?* Note the central premise of the Scalia dissent — that the vesting clause of Article II gives the President exclusive control over all exercises of executive power, including all functions typically performed by members of the executive branch. Would any of the decisions you have read have to be reversed under this premise? How do you assess this premise in light of the following argument:

> That the founding generation conceptualized criminal prosecution as an inherently executive function, necessarily encompassed by the vesting clause of article II is extremely unlikely. In England, criminal prosecution was not reserved to the Crown. In the colonies and in some states with constitutions worded identically in all relevant respects to the federal constitution, there were judicially appointed prosecutors as well as executive appointed prosecutors functioning with apparent policy independence. I am unaware of evidence that the faithful execution clause was intended at all as a power-conferring clause. Its origination in the English bill of rights and the lack of debate surrounding its adoption in this country suggest strongly that it was understood chiefly as an uncontroversial prohibition on the executive suspension of statutes, not an aggrandizement of the President's role in policymaking. If I am right about that, then creating independent counsel to prevent a *de facto* suspension of statutes through executive branch corruption strongly vindicates the clause, rather than violating it.

Peter M. Shane, *The Separation of Powers and the Rule of Law: The Virtues of "Seeing the Trees,"* 30 Wm. & Mary L. Rev. 375, 379–80 (1989). *Accord* William Gwyn, *The Indeterminacy of the Separation of Powers and the Federal Courts*, 57 Geo. Wash. L. Rev. 474 (1989). *See also* John H. Langbein, *The Origins of Public Prosecution at Common Law*, 17 Am. J. Legal Hist. 313 (1973).

Professor Susan Low Bloch, in *The Early Role of the Attorney General in Our Constitutional Scheme: in the Beginning There Was Pragmatism*, 1989 Duke L.J. 561, 567, points out that an early draft of the Judiciary Act of 1789, which created the office of Attorney General, would have had the Supreme Court appoint the Attorney General and the lower federal courts appoint district attorneys! As enacted, this provision deleted court-appointment and assigned the Attorney General to represent the United

States in the Supreme Court, while the district attorneys were to conduct lower court litigation, with no provision for the Attorney General to supervise them. So the First Congress does not seem to have seen the prosecutorial function as purely executive. If the founding generation did not conceive of criminal prosecution as an inherently executive function, would that be enough to answer Justice Scalia? On the early Congress's pragmatic eclecticism in the design of administrative institutions generally, see Jerry L. Mashaw, Creating the Administrative Constitution: The Lost One Hundred Years of American Administrative Law (2012).

2. *Judicial Prosecutions of Criminal Contempt.* The majority's position in *Morrison* was foreshadowed by the Court's opinion in *Young v. United States ex rel. Vuitton et Fils S.A.*, 481 U.S. 787 (1987). The petitioners had been convicted of criminal contempt for violating an injunction barring their further infringement of the trademark of Louis Vuitton, S.A., a French handbag manufacturer. To prosecute the criminal contempt, the U.S. district court had appointed two private attorneys, both counsel to Vuitton. The Supreme Court held that such appointments were within the inherent power of the judiciary, but, in a split vote, reversed the petitioners' convictions. Four members of the Court regarded it as impermissible to appoint counsel for an interested party as contempt prosecutors. Four members of the Court regarded the practice as disfavored, but harmless here. Justice Scalia, the deciding vote, was the only Justice to argue that judicial appointment of the prosecutors was impermissible.

3. Morrison *and Citizen Enforcement of Public Law.* Does Congress impermissibly undermine executive authority over prosecutions by permitting *qui tam* actions, that is, prosecutions of public statutes by private persons, even in cases when the executive has declined to prosecute or has filed suit, but withdrawn? The Supreme Court has upheld the authority of Congress to grant standing to private parties to pursue *qui tam* actions, but has yet to reach the Article II issues. *Vermont Agency of Natural Resources v. United States*, 529 U.S. 765 (2000). *See United States ex rel. Kelly v. Boeing Co.*, 9 F.3d 743 (9th Cir. 1993) (upholding *qui tam* provisions of the False Claims Act against separation of powers challenge); *U.S. Department of Housing and Urban Development ex rel. Givler v. Smith*, 775 F. Supp. 172 (E.D. Pa. 1991) (same). The history of *qui tam* actions is discussed in Note, *The False Claims Act, Qui Tam Relators, and the Government: Which Is the Real Party to the Action?* 43 Stan. L. Rev. 1061 (1991). For an attack on the constitutionality of such suits, see Comment, *"Missing the Analytical Boat": The Unconstitutionality of the Qui Tam Provisions of the False Claims Act*, 27 Idaho L. Rev. 319 (1990–91). For a defense, see Robin Kundis Craig, *Will Separation of Powers Challenges "Take Care" of Environmental Citizen Suits? Article II, Injury-in-Fact, Private "Enforcers," and Lessons from Qui Tam Litigation*, 72 U. Colo. L. Rev. 93 (2001).

4. *Reviews. Morrison* prompted considerable scholarly commentary. *See generally* Kevin M. Stack, *The Story of* Morrison v. Olson*: The Independent Counsel and Independent Agencies in Watergate's Wake*, in Presidential Power Stories, *supra* at 401; Stephen L. Carter, *The Independent Counsel Mess*, 102 Harv. L. Rev. 105 (1988);

Symposium: Separation of Powers and the Executive Branch: The Reagan Era in Retrospect, 57 Geo. Wash. L. Rev. 401 (1989) (most notably, articles by Gwyn, Shane, and Rosenberg). Post mortems included as much discussion of the *Morrison* Court's method as of its result, with self-described formalists on both sides of the issue. *Compare* Lee Liberman, Morrison v. Olson: *A Formalistic Perspective on Why the Court was Wrong*, 38 Am. U. L. Rev. 313 (1989), *with* Peter M. Shane, *Independent Policymaking and Presidential Power: A Constitutional Analysis*, 57 Geo. Wash. L. Rev. 596, 598–608 (1989) (see discussion headed, "*Morrison v. Olson:* An Easy Formalist Case?"). Should *Morrison* be viewed as a "functionalist" decision, Note, Morrison v. Olson: *Renewed Acceptance For a Functional Approach to Separation of Powers?*, 16 Hastings Const. L.Q. 603 (1989), a hybrid decision, Keith M. Werhan, *Toward an Eclectic Approach to Separation of Powers:* Morrison v. Olson *Examined*, 16 Hastings Const. L.Q. 393 (1989), or proof that the categories of "functionalist" and "formalist" are overdrawn?

5. Morrison *and the Independent Agencies.* Where does the Court's reformulation of the *Humphrey's Executor* test for the constitutionality of removal restrictions leave us? In a footnote, the Court discussed its precedents:

> The difficulty of defining such categories of "executive" or "quasi-legislative" officials is illustrated by a comparison of our decisions in cases such as *Humphrey's Executor, Buckley v. Valeo,* and *Bowsher.* In *Buckley,* we indicated that the functions of the Federal Election Commission are "administrative," and "more legislative and judicial in nature," and are "of kinds usually performed by independent regulatory agencies or by some department in the Executive Branch under the direction of an Act of Congress." In *Bowsher,* we found that the functions of the Comptroller General were "executive" in nature, in that he was required to "exercise judgment concerning facts that affect the application of the Act," and he must "interpret the provisions of the Act to determine precisely what budgetary calculations are required." Compare this with the description of the FTC's powers in *Humphrey's Executor,* which we stated "occupie[d] no place in the executive department": "The [FTC] is an administrative body created by Congress to carry into effect legislative policies embodied in the statute in accordance with the legislative standard therein prescribed, and to perform other specified duties as a legislative or as a judicial aid." . . . [I]t is hard to dispute that the powers of the FTC at the time of *Humphrey's Executor* would at the present time be considered "executive," at least to some degree.

In that case, what functional distinction between executive and independent agencies remains?

In 1996, Assistant Attorney General Walter Dellinger of the Office of Legal Counsel attempted a restatement of the law in a comprehensive and very valuable memorandum on *The Constitutional Separation of Powers Between the President and Congress, reprinted in* H. Jefferson Powell, The Constitution and the Attorneys General 617–73 (1999). He concludes (at 662):

The Supreme Court's removal cases establish a spectrum of potential conclusions about specific removal limitations. At one end of the spectrum, restrictions on the President's power to remove officers with broad policy responsibilities in areas Congress does not or cannot shelter from presidential policy control clearly should be deemed unconstitutional. We think, for example, that a statute that attempts to limit the President's authority to discharge the Secretary of Defense would be plainly unconstitutional and that the courts would so hold. As the Court stated in *Morrison, Myers* "was undoubtedly correct . . . in its broader suggestion that there are some 'purely executive' officials who must be removable by the President at will if he is to be able to accomplish his constitutional role." At the other end of the spectrum, we believe that for cause and fixed term limitations on the power to remove officers with adjudicatory duties affecting the rights of private individuals will continue to meet with consistent judicial approval: the contention that the essential role of the executive branch would be imperiled by giving a measure of independence to such officials is untenable under both precedent and principle. Between these two extremes, the arguments are less clear, and it is imperative that the executive branch carefully examine removal limitations in pending legislation for their impact on the President's ability to exercise his or her constitutional powers and carry out his or her duties.

Is this a durable formulation of the law? Note that the Clinton OLC abandoned the position asserted, but not reached, in *Bowsher, supra,* that executive power may only be exercised by officers removable at will by the President.

6. *The Clinton Impeachment and the Demise of the Independent Counsel Statute.* The most prominent and controversial Independent Counsel investigation was that led by Kenneth Starr, which culminated in the impeachment and acquittal of President Clinton. The Independent Counsel Act expired after the investigation, and there is no prospect in sight that it will be revived. Not surprisingly, there has been a flood of academic commentary about *l'affaire* Clinton; some of it is cited with our materials on the impeachment in Chapter Three. For a sampling of symposia, see *Symposium, The Independent Counsel Statute: Reform or Repeal?* (Christopher H. Schroeder, special ed.), 62 Law & Contemp. Probs. 1 (1999); *Panel, The Independent Counsel Statute,* 51 Admin. L. Rev. 627 (1999); *Symposium, The Independent Counsel Act: From Watergate to Whitewater and Beyond,* 86 Geo. L.J. 2011 (1998). The principal issues that have been debated are:

a) *The Wisdom of Court-Appointment of Prosecutors.* The events leading to Starr's selection were controversial. During a time that the Independent Counsel statute was in abeyance, the Attorney General had employed her statutory authority to appoint special attorneys (28 U.S.C. § 543) to select Robert B. Fiske, Jr., as an independent counsel to investigate the Whitewater matter. Once the Act had revived, she applied to the Special Division for an appointment under the Act, and requested that Fiske continue his investigation. The court rejected her advice and appointed Starr to the post. The press then reported that while the Attorney General's application was pending before the Special Division, one of its members lunched with two Senators, one of whom had been vocally critical of Fiske's performance. Complaints of judicial misconduct were filed pursuant to the statutory procedures described in Chapter Three. The Chief Judge of the Circuit rejected the complaints, *Matter of Charge of Judicial Misconduct or Disability*, 39 F.3d 374 (D.C. Cir. 1994). He explained that there had been no conduct "prejudicial to the . . . business of the courts," as prohibited by 28 U.S.C. §372(c)(1). The appointment responsibility was mostly an ancillary Article II power of the court, so the complaint was peripheral to the statute's core concern. Moreover, outside consultation was appropriate to the discretionary function of appointment, when it would not be in an adversary litigation. Does this explanation satisfy you? For a review and critique of the Special Division's performance, see John Q. Barrett, *Special Division Agonistes*, 5 WIDENER LAW SYMPOSIUM J. 17 (2000).

b) *The Behavior of Independent Prosecutors.* Starr's conduct of the Clinton investigation received sharp criticism for exceeding the bounds of normal prosecutorial conduct. *See Symposium, The Independent Counsel Investigation, the Impeachment Proceedings, and President Clinton's Defense: Inquiries into the Role and Responsibilities of Lawyers*, 68 FORDHAM L. REV. 559 (1999). The indictment against Starr is summarized by Robert W. Gordon, *Imprudence and Partisanship: Starr's OIC and the Clinton-Lewinsky Affair, id.* at 646:

> I argue that the OIC was imprudent when it failed to act on its opportunity to prevent Clinton from lying in his deposition and Lewinsky from filing a false affidavit in the *Jones* case; when it expanded its jurisdiction to investigate Clinton's affair with Lewinsky and his attempts to conceal the affair after it ended; when it deployed massively intrusive and disruptive investigative techniques to uncover evidence against Clinton; when it deployed prosecutorial powers against people whose main offense was criticizing the OIC and its tactics; when it refused to consider, or at any rate drastically discounted, the damage its investigations would inflict on witnesses and other innocent and not-so-innocent persons, and to the effective functioning of the Presidency and the business of the country; and finally, when it used the evidence it had gathered as the basis for a referral of impeachment of a sitting President to the Congress.

In fairness, it is clear that some of Starr's actions were provoked by President Clinton's aggressive defense during the investigation and impeachment. Should Starr have shown greater resistance to the temptation to do battle?

c) *The IC's Involvement with Impeachment.* There was also substantial criticism of Starr's relationship to the impeachment proceedings. *See* MICHAEL J. GERHARDT, THE FEDERAL IMPEACHMENT PROCESS: A CONSTITUTIONAL AND HISTORICAL ANALYSIS 189–90 (2d ed. 2000), arguing that Starr attempted to influence the impeachment

> through a series of actions, including but not limited to the strong characterizations and brief-like quality of his office's referral, aggressive advocacy

on behalf of the wording or characterizations of the referral in his testimony before the Judiciary committee, submission to the committee in response to White House attacks on the eve of the impeachment vote, public response to criticisms of his testimony from his former ethics advisor (who had quit in protest to the tenor of the testimony), and assisting the House Managers on the eve of the impeachment trial's conclusion to meet informally with Monica Lewinsky to determine her feasibility as a witness. These actions undermined Starr's claims of impartiality.

See also Ken Gormley, *Impeachment and the Independent Counsel: a Dysfunctional Union*, 51 Stan. L. Rev. 309 (1999). How could Starr have been appropriately helpful to the impeachment inquiry without seeming to be its adjunct?

d) *What to Do?* Now that the independent counsel provisions of the Ethics in Government Act have lapsed, the mechanism for investigating allegations of high-level executive branch wrong-doing reverts to the former, administrative model. The Attorney General, or Acting Attorney General if the Attorney General is recused, may appoint a Special Counsel whenever an investigation raises a conflict of interest. *See* 28 U.S.C. 600.1. The regulations also provide a Special Counsel with a meaningful degree of independence. A Special Counsel is not subject to the day-to-day supervision of the Attorney General or any other Department of Justice official. However, DOJ regulations allow that the Attorney General "may after review conclude that [an] action [by a Special Counsel] is so inappropriate or unwarranted under established Departmental practices that it should not be pursued." 28 U.S.C. 600.7(b). Finally, a Special Counsel may be removed "only by the personal action of the Attorney General" and the grounds for removal are limited to "misconduct, dereliction of duty, incapacity, conflict of interest, or for other good cause, including violation of Departmental policies." 28 U.S.C. 600.7(d).

A Special Counsel, then, differs from an Independent Counsel in a number of ways. First, they appointed differently. An Independent Counsel was appointed by a panel of judges, the Special Division, whereas a Special Counsel is appointed directly by the Attorney General. A Special Counsel is instructed to follow DOJ policies and the Special Counsel's actions can be overridden by the Attorney General if "inappropriate or unwarranted." An Independent Counsel was statutorily required to follow DOJ policies to the extent possible. If an Independent Counsel were to determine it appropriate to deviate from those policies, the statute did not authorize the Attorney General to override the Independent Counsel. The grounds for removing an Independent Counsel were substantially the same as the grounds, mentioned above, for removing a Special Counsel. There is one final, and crucially important difference. The rules setting forth the scope of authority and independence of a Special Counsel are set forth by regulation and, therefore, can be rescinded or revised at the discretion of the Attorney General. The powers and independence of the Independent Counsel were set forth by statute and so could be altered only by act of Congress.

e) *What To Do Next?* Might there be a better way of dealing with allegations of wrong-doing by high-level executive branch officials? A good place to begin is with some comprehensive histories and analyses of the Act, *see* Katy J. Harriger, The Special Prosecutor in American Politics (2d ed. 2000); Charles A. Johnson & Danette Brickman, Independent Counsel: The Law and the Investigations (2001); Benjamin J. Priester, Paul G. Rozelle & Mirah A Horowitz, *The Independent Counsel Statute: A Legal History*, 62 Law & Contemp. Probs. 5 (1999). Some have bravely suggested that the statute be renewed, with adjustments reflecting experience. *See* Erwin Chemerinsky, *Learning the Wrong Lessons from History: Why There Must be an Independent Counsel Law*, 5 Widener Law Symposium J. 1 (2000). Others think the statute is better left dead, *see* Herbert J. Miller, Jr. & John P. Elwood, *The Independent Counsel Statute: An Idea Whose Time Has Passed*, 62 Law & Contemp. Probs. 111 (1999); Cass R. Sunstein, *Bad Incentives and Bad Institutions,* 86 Geo. L. J. 2267 (1998). Finally, a careful set of recommendations is provided by a blue-ribbon, bipartisan task force report, American Enterprise Institute and The Brookings Institution, Robert Dole & George J. Mitchell, Co-chairs, Project on the Independent Counsel Statute, Report and Recommendations (1999). The Report calls for statutory clarification of the Attorney General's responsibility to appoint special counsel when conflicts of interest are presented, regulations to guide special counsel investigations, and guarantees of independent authority to investigate and prosecute wrongdoing balanced with authority to remove a counsel or terminate an investigation—in short, a return to the overall model used for the Watergate investigation!

7. *Investigating the Trump Administration.* The Department of Justice has been investigating the attempts by Russia to influence the 2016 presidential election. We described the specifics of this matter *supra* in chapter 3A. Attorney General Sessions has recused himself from that investigation. For purposes of this investigation, then, Deputy Attorney General Rod Rosenstein is the Acting Attorney General. On May 17, 2017, Rosenstein appointed former FBI Director Robert Mueller to be Special Counsel in charge of investigating the matter of Russian influence into the 2016 presidential election. Mueller's investigation has reportedly expanded to include an investigation of President Trump personally for obstruction of justice. *See* Michael S. Schmidt and Matt Appuzzo, *Mueller Interview List is Said to Point at Trump Inquiry*, N.Y. Times (June 15, 2017). Simultaneously, President Trump was said to have been giving consideration to firing the Special Counsel. *See* Michael Shear and Maggie Haberman, *Friend Says Trump Is Considering Firing Mueller as Special Counsel*, N.Y. Times (June 12, 2017). Do you think the administrative Special Counsel mechanism for investigating misconduct by the President, in particular, is sufficient?

8. *The Unitary Executive after* Morrison. Justice Scalia's opinion is the iconic favorite of the unitary executive movement. In the wake of the Clinton investigation, the opinion garnered new attention as many observers found it quite prescient. For a response, here is Peter M. Shane in Madison's Nightmare: How Executive Power Threatens American Democracy 41–2 (2009):

Morrison v. Olson represents a powerful statement as to the limits of Presidential authority. The kind of administrative activity at stake in this activity—criminal prosecution—was certainly known to the framers of the Constitution. If the framers had in mind a definition of "executive power" that gave the President constitutional authority to control all policy making discretion that Congress delegates to anyone within the executive branch, that definition would necessarily have extended to the control of all policy making discretion inherent in prosecuting the criminal laws that Congress enacted. The Court correctly determined, however, that policy control over criminal prosecution is historically not part of the "executive power" constitutionally vested in the President, even though criminal prosecution was a government function well known to the framers. For presidentialists to argue in the face of that history that the framers nonetheless implicitly prohibited congressional delimitation of presidential authority over matters they could hardly have envisioned—such as the Nuclear Regulatory Commission or the Federal Communications Commission, for example—is utterly fanciful.

In short, the Constitution simply does not command the unitary presidency in domestic affairs that the presidentialists imagine. How unitary the Presidency should be in terms of supervising the administration of domestic affairs is legitimately a matter of debate and decision within Congress; if the President exceeds the boundaries Congress sets, courts are entitled to enforce those limits against him. The "unitary presidency" of presidentialist theory is a myth.

Professors Steven G. Calabresi and Christopher S. Yoo, authors of THE UNITARY EXECUTIVE, *supra*, have argued for an overruling of *Morrison*, on grounds that the decision is "inconsistent with the text of the Constitution, the original meaning of the Constitution's Framers, the practice of the last 220 years, and good public policy." *Remove* Morrison v. Olson, 62 VAND. L. REV. EN BANC 103, 119 (2009), available at www.vanderbilt.edu/lawreview/enbanc/roundtable. Their policy argument for an unrestricted presidential power of removal appears in *id.* at 116–17:

The arguments from text, original history, and practice supporting the President's constitutional power to remove are also supported by policy considerations. First, ensuring that the President can exercise control over the entire executive branch promotes energy in the executive, a quality widely regarded as essential to good government. Energy in the executive helps in military and foreign-affairs matters and it leads to the control and suppression of factions and special interests at home.

Second, giving the President responsibility for all aspects of executing federal law enhances political accountability by making clear precisely who is responsible for the executive branch's performance. Moreover, dividing executive authority increases information costs, which inevitably decreases the public's ability to hold executive officials accountable. The existence of multiple executive entities also increases bargaining costs and can create debilitating collective action problems.

Finally, the more executive branch officials become independent of the President, the more they fall under the control of congressional committees. Such committees are dominated by chairs who are responsive to the needs of a small congressional district or a single state and thus are more likely to be influenced by special interests than the President, who represents a diffuse national majority and is necessarily harder to capture.

Thus, permitting Congress to place limits on the President's removal power threatens to upset the Madisonian conception of the separation of powers, which envisions all three branches constantly engaged in a state of dynamic tension. By reducing the President's role in this balance, limitations on the removal power inevitably tip the balance in Congress's favor.

For a response, see Harold H. Bruff, *Bringing the Independent Agencies in from the Cold, id.* at 63.

These issues returned to the Supreme Court in a case that concerned a minor agency, but that raised large issues about the constitutional structure of the executive.

Free Enterprise Fund v. Public Company Accounting Oversight Board

561 U.S. 477 (2010)

Chief Justice ROBERTS delivered the opinion of the Court.

Our Constitution divided the "powers of the new Federal Government into three defined categories, Legislative, Executive, and Judicial." Article II vests "[t]he executive Power . . . in a President of the United States of America," who must "take Care that the Laws be faithfully executed." Art. II, § 1, cl. 1; id., § 3. In light of "[t]he impossibility that one man should be able to perform all the great business of the State," the Constitution provides for executive officers to "assist the supreme Magistrate in discharging the duties of his trust." 30 Writings of George Washington 334 (J. Fitzpatrick ed.1939).

Since 1789, the Constitution has been understood to empower the President to keep these officers accountable — by removing them from office, if necessary. *See generally Myers v. United States,* 272 U.S. 52 (1926). This Court has determined, however, that this authority is not without limit. In *Humphrey's Executor v. United States,* 295 U.S. 602 (1935), we held that Congress can, under certain circumstances, create independent agencies run by principal officers appointed by the President, whom the President may not remove at will but only for good cause. Likewise, in *United States v. Perkins,* 116 U.S. 483 (1886), and *Morrison v. Olson,* 487 U.S. 654 (1988), the Court sustained similar restrictions on the power of principal executive officers — themselves responsible to the President — to remove their own inferiors. The parties do not ask us to reexamine any of these precedents, and we do not do so.

We are asked, however, to consider a new situation not yet encountered by the Court. The question is whether these separate layers of protection may be combined. May the President be restricted in his ability to remove a principal officer, who is in turn restricted in his ability to remove an inferior officer, even though that inferior officer determines the policy and enforces the laws of the United States? We hold that such multilevel protection from removal is contrary to Article II's vesting of the executive power in the President. The President cannot "take Care that the Laws be faithfully executed" if he cannot oversee the faithfulness of the officers who execute them. Here the President cannot remove an officer who enjoys more than one level of good-cause protection, even if the President determines that the officer is neglecting his duties or discharging them improperly. That judgment is instead committed to another officer, who may or may not agree with the President's determination, and whom the President cannot remove simply because that officer disagrees with him. This contravenes the President's "constitutional obligation to ensure the faithful execution of the laws."

I

A

After a series of celebrated accounting debacles, Congress enacted the Sarbanes-Oxley Act of 2002 (or Act), 116 Stat. 745. Among other measures, the Act introduced tighter regulation of the accounting industry under a new Public Company Accounting Oversight Board. The Board is composed of five members, appointed to staggered 5-year terms by the Securities and Exchange Commission. It was modeled on private self-regulatory organizations in the securities industry — such as the New York Stock Exchange — that investigate and discipline their own members subject to Commission oversight. Congress created the Board as a private "nonprofit corporation," and Board members and employees are not considered Government "officer[s] or employee[s]" for statutory purposes. 15 U.S.C. §§ 7211(a), (b). The Board can thus recruit its members and employees from the private sector by paying salaries far above the standard Government pay scale. [The salary for the Chairman is $673,000. Other Board members receive $547,000.]

Unlike the self-regulatory organizations, however, the Board is a Government-created, Government-appointed entity, with expansive powers to govern an entire industry. Every accounting firm — both foreign and domestic — that participates in auditing public companies under the securities laws must register with the Board, pay it an annual fee, and comply with its rules and oversight. The Board is charged with enforcing the Sarbanes-Oxley Act, the securities laws, the Commission's rules, its own rules, and professional accounting standards. To this end, the Board may regulate every detail of an accounting firm's practice, including hiring and professional development, promotion, supervision of audit work, the acceptance of new business and the continuation of old, internal inspection procedures, professional ethics rules, and "such other requirements as the Board may prescribe."

The Board promulgates auditing and ethics standards, performs routine inspections of all accounting firms, demands documents and testimony, and initiates formal investigations and disciplinary proceedings. The willful violation of any Board rule is treated as a willful violation of the Securities Exchange Act of 1934, 48 Stat. 881, 15 U.S.C. § 78a et seq. — a federal crime punishable by up to 20 years' imprisonment or $25 million in fines ($5 million for a natural person). And the Board itself can issue severe sanctions in its disciplinary proceedings, up to and including the permanent revocation of a firm's registration, a permanent ban on a person's associating with any registered firm, and money penalties of $15 million ($750,000 for a natural person). Despite the provisions specifying that Board members are not Government officials for statutory purposes, the parties agree that the Board is "part of the Government" for constitutional purposes, *Lebron v. National Railroad Passenger Corporation*, 513 U.S. 374 (1995), and that its members are "'Officers of the United States'" who "exercis[e] significant authority pursuant to the laws of the United States," *Buckley v. Valeo*, 424 U.S. 1, 125–126 (1976) (per curiam) (quoting Art. II, § 2, cl. 2).

The Act places the Board under the SEC's oversight, particularly with respect to the issuance of rules or the imposition of sanctions (both of which are subject to Commission approval and alteration). But the individual members of the Board — like the officers and directors of the self-regulatory organizations — are substantially insulated from the Commission's control. The Commission cannot remove Board members at will, but only "for good cause shown," "in accordance with" certain procedures. § 7211(e)(6).

Those procedures require a Commission finding, "on the record" and "after notice and opportunity for a hearing," that the Board member

"(A) has willfully violated any provision of th[e] Act, the rules of the Board, or the securities laws; (B) has willfully abused the authority of that member; or (C) without reasonable justification or excuse, has failed to enforce compliance with any such provision or rule, or any professional standard by any registered public accounting firm or any associated person thereof." § 7217(d)(3).

Removal of a Board member requires a formal Commission order and is subject to judicial review. Similar procedures govern the Commission's removal of officers and directors of the private self-regulatory organizations. The parties agree that the Commissioners cannot themselves be removed by the President except under the *Humphrey's Executor* standard of "inefficiency, neglect of duty, or malfeasance in office," and we decide the case with that understanding.

B

Beckstead and Watts, LLP, is a Nevada accounting firm registered with the Board. The Board inspected the firm, released a report critical of its auditing procedures, and began a formal investigation. Beckstead and Watts and the Free Enterprise Fund, a nonprofit organization of which the firm is a member, then sued the Board and its members, seeking (among other things) a declaratory judgment that the Board is unconstitutional and an injunction preventing the Board from exercising its powers.

Before the District Court, petitioners argued that the Sarbanes-Oxley Act contravened the separation of powers by conferring wide-ranging executive power on Board members without subjecting them to Presidential control. Petitioners also challenged the Act under the Appointments Clause, which requires "Officers of the United States" to be appointed by the President with the Senate's advice and consent. Art. II, § 2, cl. 2. The Clause provides an exception for "inferior Officers," whose appointment Congress may choose to vest "in the President alone, in the Courts of Law, or in the Heads of Departments." Because the Board is appointed by the SEC, petitioners argued that (1) Board members are not "inferior Officers" who may be appointed by "Heads of Departments"; (2) even if they are, the Commission is not a "Departmen[t]"; and (3) even if it is, the several Commissioners (as opposed to the Chairman) are not its "Hea[d]." The United States intervened to defend the Act's constitutionality. Both sides moved for summary judgment; the District Court determined that it had jurisdiction and granted summary judgment to respondents. A divided Court of Appeals affirmed. 537 F.3d 667 (C.A.D.C. 2008). . . . We granted certiorari. 556 U.S. ___ (2009).

II

We first consider whether the District Court had jurisdiction. We agree with both courts below that the statutes providing for judicial review of Commission action did not prevent the District Court from considering petitioners' claims. . . .

III

We hold that the dual for-cause limitations on the removal of Board members contravene the Constitution's separation of powers.

A

The Constitution provides that "[t]he executive Power shall be vested in a President of the United States of America." Art. II, § 1, cl. 1. As Madison stated on the floor of the First Congress, "if any power whatsoever is in its nature Executive, it is the power of appointing, overseeing, and controlling those who execute the laws." 1 Annals of Cong. 463 (1789).

The removal of executive officers was discussed extensively in Congress when the first executive departments were created. The view that "prevailed, as most consonant to the text of the Constitution" and "to the requisite responsibility and harmony in the Executive Department," was that the executive power included a power to oversee executive officers through removal; because that traditional executive power was not "expressly taken away, it remained with the President." Letter from James Madison to Thomas Jefferson (June 30, 1789), 16 Documentary History of the First Federal Congress 893 (2004). "This Decision of 1789 provides contemporaneous and weighty evidence of the Constitution's meaning since many of the Members of the First Congress had taken part in framing that instrument." *Bowsher v. Synar*, 478 U.S.

714, 723–724 (1986) And it soon became the "settled and well understood construction of the Constitution." *Ex parte Hennen*, 13 Pet. 230, 259 (1839).

The landmark case of *Myers v. United States* reaffirmed the principle that Article II confers on the President "the general administrative control of those executing the laws." It is his responsibility to take care that the laws be faithfully executed. The buck stops with the President, in Harry Truman's famous phrase. As we explained in *Myers,* the President therefore must have some "power of removing those for whom he can not continue to be responsible."

Nearly a decade later in *Humphrey's Executor*, this Court held that *Myers* did not prevent Congress from conferring good-cause tenure on the principal officers of certain independent agencies. That case concerned the members of the Federal Trade Commission, who held 7-year terms and could not be removed by the President except for "inefficiency, neglect of duty, or malfeasance in office." . . . *Humphrey's Executor* did not address the removal of inferior officers, whose appointment Congress may vest in heads of departments. If Congress does so, it is ordinarily the department head, rather than the President, who enjoys the power of removal. This Court has upheld for-cause limitations on that power as well.

In *Perkins,* a naval cadet-engineer was honorably discharged from the Navy because his services were no longer required. He brought a claim for his salary under statutes barring his peacetime discharge except by a court-martial or by the Secretary of the Navy "for misconduct." This Court adopted verbatim the reasoning of the Court of Claims, which had held that when Congress "'vests the appointment of inferior officers in the heads of Departments[,] it may limit and restrict the power of removal as it deems best for the public interest.'" Because Perkins had not been "'dismissed for misconduct . . . [or upon] the sentence of a court-martial,'" the Court agreed that he was "'still in office and . . . entitled to [his] pay.'"

We again considered the status of inferior officers in *Morrison*. . . . [T]he Court sustained the statute. *Morrison* did not, however, address the consequences of more than one level of good-cause tenure—leaving the issue, as both the court and dissent below recognized, "a question of first impression" in this Court.

B

As explained, we have previously upheld limited restrictions on the President's removal power. In those cases, however, only one level of protected tenure separated the President from an officer exercising executive power. It was the President—or a subordinate he could remove at will—who decided whether the officer's conduct merited removal under the good-cause standard.

The Act before us does something quite different. It not only protects Board members from removal except for good cause, but withdraws from the President any decision on whether that good cause exists. That decision is vested instead in other tenured officers—the Commissioners—none of whom is subject to the President's direct control. The result is a Board that is not accountable to the President, and a President who is not responsible for the Board. The added layer of tenure protection makes a difference. Without a layer of insulation between the Commission and the Board, the Commission could remove a Board member at any time, and therefore would be fully responsible for what the Board does. The President could then hold the Commission to account for its supervision of the Board, to the same extent that he may hold the Commission to account for everything else it does.

A second level of tenure protection changes the nature of the President's review. Now the Commission cannot remove a Board member at will. The President therefore cannot hold the Commission fully accountable for the Board's conduct, to the same extent that he may hold the Commission accountable for everything else that it does. The Commissioners are not responsible for the Board's actions. They are only responsible for their own determination of whether the Act's rigorous good-cause standard is met. And even if the President disagrees with their determination, he is powerless to intervene—unless that determination is so unreasonable as to constitute "inefficiency, neglect of duty, or malfeasance in office."

This novel structure does not merely add to the Board's independence, but transforms it. Neither the President, nor anyone directly responsible to him, nor even an officer whose conduct he may review only for good cause, has full control over the Board. The President is stripped of the power our precedents have preserved, and his ability to execute the laws—by holding his subordinates accountable for their conduct—is impaired.

That arrangement is contrary to Article II's vesting of the executive power in the President. Without the ability to oversee the Board, or to attribute the Board's failings to those whom he can oversee, the President is no longer the judge of the Board's conduct. He is not the one who decides whether Board members are abusing their offices or neglecting their duties. He can neither ensure that the laws are faithfully executed, nor be held responsible for a Board member's breach of faith. This violates the basic principle that the President "cannot delegate ultimate responsibility or the active obligation to supervise that goes with it," because Article II "makes a single President responsible for the actions of the Executive Branch." *Clinton v. Jones*, 520 U.S. 681, 712–713 (1997). Indeed, if allowed to stand, this dispersion of responsibility could be multiplied. If Congress can shelter the bureaucracy behind two layers of good-cause tenure, why not a third? At oral argument, the Government was unwilling to concede that even five layers between the President and the Board would be too many. The officers of such an agency—safely encased within a Matryoshka doll of tenure protections—would be immune from Presidential oversight, even as they exercised power in the people's name . . . . The President can always choose to restrain himself in his dealings with subordinates. He cannot, however, choose to bind his successors by diminishing their powers, nor can he escape responsibility for his choices by pretending that they are not his own.

The diffusion of power carries with it a diffusion of accountability. The people do not vote for the "Officers of the United States." They instead look to the President to guide the "assistants or deputies . . . subject to his superintendence." The Federalist No. 72, p. 487 (J. Cooke ed.1961) (A. Hamilton). Without a clear and effective chain of command, the public cannot "determine on whom the blame or the punishment of a pernicious measure, or series of pernicious measures ought really to fall." Id. That is why the Framers sought to ensure that "those who are employed in the execution of the law will be in their proper situation, and the chain of dependence be preserved; the lowest officers, the middle grade, and the highest, will depend, as they ought, on the President, and the President on the community." 1 Annals of Cong., at 499 (J. Madison).

By granting the Board executive power without the Executive's oversight, this Act subverts the President's ability to ensure that the laws are faithfully executed—as well as the public's ability to pass judgment on his efforts. The Act's restrictions are incompatible with the Constitution's separation of powers.

C

Respondents and the dissent resist this conclusion, portraying the Board as "the kind of practical accommodation between the Legislature and the Executive that should be permitted in a 'workable government.'" According to the dissent, Congress may impose multiple levels of for-cause tenure between the President and his subordinates when it "rests agency independence upon the need for technical expertise." The Board's mission is said to demand both "technical competence" and "apolitical expertise," and its powers may only be exercised by "technical professional experts." In this respect the statute creating the Board is, we are told, simply one example of the "vast numbers of statutes governing vast numbers of subjects, concerned with vast numbers of different problems, [that] provide for, or foresee, their execution or administration through the work of administrators organized within many different kinds of administrative structures, exercising different kinds of administrative authority, to achieve their legislatively mandated objectives."

No one doubts Congress's power to create a vast and varied federal bureaucracy. But where, in all this, is the role for oversight by an elected President? The Constitution requires that a President chosen by the entire Nation oversee the execution of the laws . . . . One can have a government that functions without being ruled by functionaries, and a government that benefits from expertise without being ruled by experts. Our Constitution was adopted to enable the people to govern themselves, through their elected leaders. The growth of the Executive Branch, which now wields vast power and touches almost every aspect of daily life, heightens the concern that it may slip from the Executive's control, and thus from that of the people. This concern is largely absent from the dissent's paean to the administrative state.

For example, the dissent dismisses the importance of removal as a tool of supervision, concluding that the President's "power to get something done" more often depends on "who controls the agency's budget requests and funding, the relationships between one agency or department and another, . . . purely political factors (including Congress' ability to assert influence)," and indeed whether particular unelected officials support or "resist" the President's policies. The Framers did not rest our liberties on such bureaucratic minutiae . . . . In fact, the multilevel protection that the dissent endorses "provides a blueprint for extensive expansion of the legislative power." In a system of checks and balances, "[p]ower abhors a vacuum," and one branch's handicap is another's strength. 537 F.3d, at 695, n. 4 (Kavanaugh, J., dissenting). "Even when a branch does not arrogate power to itself," therefore, it must not "impair another in the performance of its constitutional duties." *Loving v. United States*, 517 U.S. 748, 757 (1996). Congress has plenary control over the salary, duties, and even existence of executive offices. Only Presidential oversight can counter its influence. That is why the Constitution vests certain powers in the President that "the Legislature has no right to diminish or modify." 1 Annals of Cong., at 463 (J. Madison).

The Framers created a structure in which "[a] dependence on the people" would be the "primary controul on the government." The Federalist No. 51, at 349 (J. Madison). That dependence is maintained, not just by "parchment barriers," id., No. 48, at 333 (same), but by letting "[a]mbition . . . counteract ambition," giving each branch "the necessary constitutional means, and personal motives, to resist encroachments of the others," id., No. 51, at 349. A key "constitutional means" vested in the President — perhaps the key means — was "the power of appointing, overseeing, and controlling those who execute the laws." 1 Annals of Cong., at 463. And while a government of "opposite and rival interests" may sometimes inhibit the smooth functioning of administration, The Federalist No. 51, at 349, "[t]he Framers recognized that, in the long term, structural protections against abuse of power were critical to preserving liberty."

Calls to abandon those protections in light of "the era's perceived necessity" are not unusual. Nor is the argument from bureaucratic expertise limited only to the field of accounting. The failures of accounting regulation may be a "pressing national problem," but "a judiciary that licensed extraconstitutional government with each issue of comparable gravity would, in the long run, be far worse." Neither respondents nor the dissent explains why the Board's task, unlike so many others, requires more than one layer of insulation from the President — or, for that matter, why only two. The point is not to take issue with for-cause limitations in general; we do not do that. The question here is far more modest. We deal with the unusual situation, never before addressed by the Court, of two layers of for-cause tenure. And though it may be criticized as "elementary arithmetical logic," two layers are not the same as one.

The President has been given the power to oversee executive officers; he is not limited, as in Harry Truman's lament, to "persuad[ing]" his unelected subordinates "to do what they ought to do without persuasion." In its pursuit of a "workable government," Congress cannot reduce the Chief Magistrate to a cajoler-in-chief.

D

The United States concedes that some constraints on the removal of inferior executive officers might violate the Constitution. It contends, however, that the removal restrictions at issue here do not. To begin with, the Government argues that the Commission's removal power over the Board is "broad," and could be construed as broader still, if necessary to avoid invalidation. But the Government does not contend that simple disagreement with the Board's policies or priorities could constitute "good cause" for its removal. Nor do our precedents suggest as much. *Humphrey's Executor*, for example, rejected a removal premised on a lack of agreement " 'on either the policies or the administering of the Federal Trade Commission,' " because the FTC was designed to be " 'independent in character' And here there is judicial review of any effort to remove Board members, see 15 U.S.C. § 78y(a)(1), so the Commission will not have the final word on the propriety of its own removal orders. The removal restrictions set forth in the statute mean what they say.

Indeed, this case presents an even more serious threat to executive control than an "ordinary" dual for-cause standard. Congress enacted an unusually high standard that must be met before Board members may be removed. A Board member cannot be removed except for willful violations of the Act, Board rules, or the securities laws; willful abuse of authority; or unreasonable failure to enforce compliance — as determined in a formal Commission order, rendered on the record and after notice and an opportunity for a hearing. The Act does not even give the Commission power to fire Board members for violations of other laws that do not relate to the Act, the securities laws, or the Board's authority. The President might have less than full confidence in, say, a Board member who cheats on his taxes; but that discovery is not listed among the grounds for removal under § 7217(d)(3).

Alternatively, respondents portray the Act's limitations on removal as irrelevant, because — as the Court of Appeals held — the Commission wields "at-will removal power over Board functions if not Board members." The Commission's general "oversight and enforcement authority over the Board," § 7217(a), is said to "blun[t] the constitutional impact of for-cause removal," and to leave the President no worse off than "if Congress had lodged the Board's functions in the SEC's own staff," Broad power over Board functions is not equivalent to the power to remove Board members. The Commission may, for example, approve the Board's budget, issue binding regulations, relieve the Board of authority, amend Board sanctions, or enforce Board rules on its own. But altering the budget or powers of an agency as a whole is a problematic way to control an inferior officer. The Commission cannot wield a free hand to supervise individual members if it must destroy the Board in order to fix it . . . .

Finally, respondents suggest that our conclusion is contradicted by the past practice of Congress. But the Sarbanes-Oxley Act is highly unusual in committing substantial executive authority to officers protected by two layers of for-cause removal — including at one level a sharply circumscribed definition of what constitutes "good cause," and rigorous procedures that must be followed prior to removal . . . . The dissent here suggests that other such positions might exist, and complains that we do not resolve their status in this opinion. The dissent itself, however, stresses the very size and variety of the Federal Government, and those features discourage general pronouncements on matters neither briefed nor argued here. In any event, the dissent fails to support its premonitions of doom; none of the positions it identifies are similarly situated to the Board. For example, many civil servants within independent agencies would not qualify as "Officers of the United States," who "exercis[e] significant authority pursuant to the laws of the United States." The parties here concede that Board members are executive "Officers," as that term is used in the Constitution. We do not decide the status of other Government employees, nor do we decide whether "lesser functionaries subordinate to officers of the United States" must be subject to the same sort of control as those who exercise "significant authority pursuant to the laws."

Nor do the employees referenced by the dissent enjoy the same significant and unusual protections from Presidential oversight as members of the Board. Senior or policymaking positions in government may be excepted from the competitive service to ensure Presidential control, and members of the Senior Executive Service may be reassigned or reviewed by agency heads (and entire agencies may be excluded from that Service by the President). While the full extent of that authority is not before us, any such authority is of course wholly absent with respect to the Board. Nothing in our opinion, therefore, should be read to cast doubt on the use of what is colloquially known as the civil service system within independent agencies.

Finally, the dissent wanders far afield when it suggests that today's opinion might increase the President's authority to remove military officers. Without expressing any view whatever on the scope of that authority, it is enough to note that we see little analogy between our Nation's armed services and the Public Company Accounting Oversight Board. Military officers are broadly subject to Presidential control through the chain of command and through the President's powers as Commander in Chief. . . .

There is no reason for us to address whether these positions identified by the dissent, or any others not at issue in this case, are so structured as to infringe the President's constitutional authority. Nor is there any substance to the dissent's concern that the "work of all these various officials" will "be put on hold . . . . The only issue in this case is whether Congress may deprive the President of adequate control over the Board, which is the regulator of first resort and the primary law enforcement authority for a vital sector of our economy. We hold that it cannot.

IV

Petitioners' complaint argued that the Board's "freedom from Presidential oversight and control" rendered it "and all power and authority exercised by it" in violation of the Constitution. We reject such a broad holding. Instead, we agree with the Government that the unconstitutional tenure provisions are severable from the remainder of the statute . . . . Concluding that the removal restrictions are invalid leaves the Board removable by the Commission at will, and leaves the President separated from Board members by only a single level of good-cause tenure. The Commission is then fully responsible for the Board's actions, which are no less subject than the Commission's own functions to Presidential oversight . . . .

V

Petitioners raise three more challenges to the Board under the Appointments Clause. None has merit.

First, petitioners argue that Board members are principal officers requiring Presidential appointment with the Senate's advice and consent. We held in *Edmond v. United States*, 520 U.S. 651 (1997), that "[w]hether one is an 'inferior' officer depends on whether he has a superior," and that "'inferior officers' are officers whose work is directed and supervised at some level" by other officers appointed by the President with the Senate's consent. In particular, we noted that "[t]he power to remove officers" at will and without cause "is a powerful tool for control" of an inferior. As explained above, the statutory restrictions on the Commission's power to remove Board members are unconstitutional and void. Given that the Commission is properly viewed, under the Constitution, as possessing the power to remove Board members at will, and given the Commission's other oversight authority, we have no hesitation in concluding that under *Edmond* the Board members are inferior officers whose appointment Congress may permissibly vest in a "Hea[d] of Departmen[t]."

But, petitioners argue, the Commission is not a "Departmen[t]" like the "Executive departments" (e.g., State, Treasury, Defense) listed in 5 U.S.C. § 101. In *Freytag*, 501 U.S., at 887, n. 4, we specifically reserved the question whether a "principal agenc[y], such as . . . the Securities and Exchange Commission," is a "Departmen[t]" under the Appointments Clause. Four Justices, however, would have concluded that the Commission is indeed such a "Departmen [t]," because it is a "free-standing, self-contained entity in the Executive Branch."

Respondents urge us to adopt this reasoning as to those entities not addressed by our opinion in *Freytag*, and we do. Respondents' reading of the Appointments Clause is consistent with the common, near-contemporary definition of a "department" as a "separate allotment or part of business; a distinct province, in which a class of duties are allotted to a particular person." 1 N. Webster, American Dictionary of the English Language (1828). It is also consistent with the early practice of Congress, which in 1792 authorized the Postmaster General to appoint "an assistant, and deputy postmasters, at all places where such shall be found necessary," § 3, 1 Stat. 234 — thus treating him as the "Hea [d] of [a] Departmen[t]" without the title of Secretary or any role in the President's Cabinet. And it is consistent with our prior cases, which have never invalidated an appointment made by the head of such an establishment. Because the Commission is a freestanding component of the Executive Branch, not subordinate to or contained within any other such component, it constitutes a "Departmen[t]" for the purposes of the Appointments Clause.

But petitioners are not done yet. They argue that the full Commission cannot constitutionally appoint Board members, because only the Chairman of the Commission is the Commission's "Hea[d]." The Commission's powers, however, are generally vested in the Commissioners jointly, not the Chairman alone. The Commissioners do not report to the Chairman, who exercises administrative and executive functions subject to the full Commission's policies. . . .

As a constitutional matter, we see no reason why a multimember body may not be the "Hea[d]" of a "Departmen[t]" that it governs. The Appointments Clause necessarily contemplates collective appointments by the "Courts of Law," and each

House of Congress, too, appoints its officers collectively. . . . Practice has also sanctioned the appointment of inferior officers by multimember agencies. We conclude that the Board members have been validly appointed by the full Commission.

In light of the foregoing, petitioners are not entitled to broad injunctive relief against the Board's continued operations. But they are entitled to declaratory relief sufficient to ensure that the reporting requirements and auditing standards to which they are subject will be enforced only by a constitutional agency accountable to the Executive.

The Constitution that makes the President accountable to the people for executing the laws also gives him the power to do so. That power includes, as a general matter, the authority to remove those who assist him in carrying out his duties. Without such power, the President could not be held fully accountable for discharging his own responsibilities; the buck would stop somewhere else. . . . While we have sustained in certain cases limits on the President's removal power, the Act before us imposes a new type of restriction — two levels of protection from removal for those who nonetheless exercise significant executive power. Congress cannot limit the President's authority in this way.

The judgment of the United States Court of Appeals for the District of Columbia Circuit is affirmed in part and reversed in part, and the case is remanded for further proceedings consistent with this opinion.

Justice BREYER, with whom Justice STEVENS, Justice GINSBURG, and Justice SOTOMAYOR join, dissenting.

. . . I agree that the Accounting Board members are inferior officers. But in my view the statute does not significantly interfere with the President's "executive Power." It violates no separation-of-powers principle. And the Court's contrary holding threatens to disrupt severely the fair and efficient administration of the laws. I consequently dissent.

I

A

The legal question before us arises at the intersection of two general constitutional principles. On the one hand, Congress has broad power to enact statutes "necessary and proper" to the exercise of its specifically enumerated constitutional authority. Art. I, § 8, cl. 18. . . . On the other hand, the opening sections of Articles I, II, and III of the Constitution . . . imply a structural separation-of-powers principle. And that principle, along with the instruction in Article II, § 3 that the President "shall take Care that the Laws be faithfully executed," limits Congress' power to structure the Federal Government. . . . But neither of these two principles is absolute in its application to removal cases. . . . Rather, depending on, say, the nature of the office, its function, or its subject matter, Congress sometimes may, consistent with the Constitution, limit the President's authority to remove an officer from his post. And we must here decide whether the circumstances surrounding the statute at issue justify such a limitation.

In answering the question presented, we cannot look to more specific constitutional text, such as the text of the Appointments Clause or the Presentment Clause, upon which the Court has relied in other separation-of-powers cases. That is because, with the exception of the general "vesting" and "take care" language, the Constitution is completely "silent with respect to the power of removal from office." Nor does history offer significant help. The President's power to remove Executive Branch officers "was not discussed in the Constitutional Convention." The First Congress enacted federal statutes that limited the President's ability to oversee Executive Branch officials, including the Comptroller of the United States, federal district attorneys (precursors to today's United States Attorneys), and, to a lesser extent, the Secretary of the Treasury. See, e.g., Lessig, *Readings By Our Unitary Executive*, 15 Cardozo L. Rev. 175, 183–184 (1993); H. Bruff, Balance of Forces: Separation of Powers in the Administrative State 414–417 (2006). But those statutes did not directly limit the President's authority to remove any of those officials — "a subject" that was "much disputed" during "the early history of this government," "and upon which a great diversity of opinion was entertained." Scholars, like Members of this Court, have continued to disagree, not only about the inferences that should be drawn from the inconclusive historical record, but also about the nature of the original disagreement. Nor does this Court's precedent fully answer the question presented. At least it does not clearly invalidate the provision in dispute. . . .

B

When previously deciding this kind of nontextual question, the Court has emphasized the importance of examining how a particular provision, taken in context, is likely to function . . . . Federal statutes now require or permit Government officials to provide, regulate, or otherwise administer, not only foreign affairs and defense, but also a wide variety of such subjects as taxes, welfare, social security, medicine, pharmaceutical drugs, education, highways, railroads, electricity, natural gas, nuclear power, financial instruments, banking, medical care, public health and safety, the environment, fair employment practices, consumer protection and much else besides. Those statutes create a host of different organizational structures. Sometimes they delegate administrative authority to the President directly, sometimes they place authority in a long-established Cabinet department, sometimes they delegate authority to an independent commission or board, sometimes they place authority directly in the hands of a single senior administrator, sometimes they place it in a sub-cabinet bureau, office, division or other agency, sometimes they vest it in multimember or multiagency task groups, sometimes they vest it in commissions or advisory committees made up of members of more than one branch, sometimes they divide it among groups of departments, commissions, bureaus, divisions, and administrators, and sometimes they permit state or local governments to participate as well. Statutes similarly grant administrators a wide variety of powers — for example, the power to make rules, develop informal practices, investigate, adjudicate, impose sanctions, grant licenses, and provide goods, services, advice, and so forth. . . .

The functional approach required by our precedents recognizes this administrative complexity and, more importantly, recognizes the various ways presidential power operates within this context—and the various ways in which a removal provision might affect that power. As human beings have known ever since Ulysses tied himself to the mast so as safely to hear the Sirens' song, sometimes it is necessary to disable oneself in order to achieve a broader objective. Thus, legally enforceable commitments—such as contracts, statutes that cannot instantly be changed, and, as in the case before us, the establishment of independent administrative institutions— hold the potential to empower precisely because of their ability to constrain. If the President seeks to regulate through impartial adjudication, then insulation of the adjudicator from removal at will can help him achieve that goal. And to free a technical decisionmaker from the fear of removal without cause can similarly help create legitimacy with respect to that official's regulatory actions by helping to insulate his technical decisions from nontechnical political pressure.

Neither is power always susceptible to the equations of elementary arithmetic. A rule that takes power from a President's friends and allies may weaken him. But a rule that takes power from the President's opponents may strengthen him. And what if the rule takes power from a functionally neutral independent authority? In that case, it is difficult to predict how the President's power is affected in the abstract. . . . Compared to Congress and the President, the Judiciary possesses an inferior understanding of the realities of administration, and the manner in which power, including and most especially political power, operates in context.

There is no indication that the two comparatively more expert branches were divided in their support for the "for cause" provision at issue here. In this case, the Act embodying the provision was passed by a vote of 423 to 3 in the House of Representatives and a by vote of 99 to 0 in the Senate. The creation of the Accounting Board was discussed at great length in both bodies without anyone finding in its structure any constitutional problem. The President signed the Act. And, when he did so, he issued a signing statement that critiqued multiple provisions of the Act but did not express any separation-of-powers concerns. See President's Statement on Signing the Sarbanes-Oxley Act of 2002, 30 Weekly Comp. of Pres. Doc. 1286 (2002). Thus, here, as in similar cases, we should decide the constitutional question in light of the provision's practical functioning in context. And our decision should take account of the Judiciary's comparative lack of institutional expertise.

II

A

To what extent then is the Act's "for cause" provision likely, as a practical matter, to limit the President's exercise of executive authority? In practical terms no "for cause" provision can, in isolation, define the full measure of executive power. This is because a legislative decision to place ultimate administrative authority in, say, the

Secretary of Agriculture rather than the President, the way in which the statute defines the scope of the power the relevant administrator can exercise, the decision as to who controls the agency's budget requests and funding, the relationships between one agency or department and another, as well as more purely political factors (including Congress' ability to assert influence) are more likely to affect the President's power to get something done. That is why President Truman complained that "'the powers of the President amount to'" bringing "'people in and try[ing] to persuade them to do what they ought to do without persuasion.'" C. Rossiter, The American Presidency 154 (2d rev. ed.1960). And that is why scholars have written that the President "is neither dominant nor powerless" in his relationships with many Government entities, "whether denominated executive or independent." Strauss, *The Place of Agencies in Government: Separation of Powers and the Fourth Branch,* 84 Colum. L.Rev. 573, 583 (1984). Those entities "are all subject to presidential direction in significant aspects of their functioning, and [are each] able to resist presidential direction in others."

Indeed, notwithstanding the majority's assertion that the removal authority is "the key" mechanism by which the President oversees inferior officers in the independent agencies, it appears that no President has ever actually sought to exercise that power by testing the scope of a "for cause" provision. See Bruff, *Bringing the Independent Agencies in from the Cold*, 62 Vanderbilt L.Rev. En Banc 63, 68 (2009), online at http://vanderbiltlawreview. org/articles/2009/11/Bruff-62-Vand-L-Rev-En-Banc-63.pdf (noting that "Presidents do not test the limits of their power by removing commissioners . . .").

But even if we put all these other matters to the side, we should still conclude that the "for cause" restriction before us will not restrict presidential power significantly. For one thing, the restriction directly limits, not the President's power, but the power of an already independent agency. . . . [S]o long as the President is legitimately foreclosed from removing the Commissioners except for cause (as the majority assumes), nullifying the Commission's power to remove Board members only for cause will not resolve the problem the Court has identified: The President will still be "powerless to intervene" by removing the Board members if the Commission reasonably decides not to do so. In other words, the Court fails to show why two layers of "for cause" protection — Layer One insulating the Commissioners from the President, and Layer Two insulating the Board from the Commissioners — impose any more serious limitation upon the President's powers than one layer . . . .

[O]nce we leave the realm of hypothetical logic and view the removal provision at issue in the context of the entire Act, its lack of practical effect becomes readily apparent. That is because the statute provides the Commission with full authority and virtually comprehensive control over all of the Board's functions. . . .

[T]he Court is simply wrong when it says that "the Act nowhere gives the Commission effective power to start, stop, or alter" Board investigations. On the contrary, the Commission's control over the Board's investigatory and legal functions is virtually absolute. Moreover, the Commission has general supervisory powers over the

Accounting Board itself: It controls the Board's budget; it can assign to the Board any "duties or functions" that it "determines are necessary or appropriate"; it has full "oversight and enforcement authority over the Board," including the authority to inspect the Board's activities whenever it believes it "appropriate" to do so. And it can censure the Board or its members, as well as remove the members from office, if the members, for example, fail to enforce the Act, violate any provisions of the Act, or abuse the authority granted to them under the Act.

What is left? The Commission's inability to remove a Board member whose perfectly reasonable actions cause the Commission to overrule him with great frequency? What is the practical likelihood of that occurring, or, if it does, of the President's serious concern about such a matter? Everyone concedes that the President's control over the Commission is constitutionally sufficient. And if the President's control over the Commission is sufficient, and the Commission's control over the Board is virtually absolute, then, as a practical matter, the President's control over the Board should prove sufficient as well.

B

At the same time, Congress and the President had good reason for enacting the challenged "for cause" provision. First and foremost, the Board adjudicates cases. This Court has long recognized the appropriateness of using "for cause" provisions to protect the personal independence of those who even only sometimes engage in adjudicatory functions. Indeed, as early as 1789 James Madison stated that "there may be strong reasons why an" executive "officer" such as the Comptroller of the United States "should not hold his office at the pleasure of the Executive branch" if one of his "principal dut[ies]" "partakes strongly of the judicial character." 1 Annals of Congress 611–612. The Court, however, all but ignores the Board's adjudicatory functions when conducting its analysis . . . .

Moreover, in addition to their adjudicative functions, the Accounting Board members supervise, and are themselves, technical professional experts. This Court has recognized that the "difficulties involved in the preparation of" sound auditing reports require the application of "scientific accounting principles." And this Court has recognized the constitutional legitimacy of a justification that rests agency independence upon the need for technical expertise. Here, the justification for insulating the "technical experts" on the Board from fear of losing their jobs due to political influence is particularly strong. Congress deliberately sought to provide that kind of protection. It did so for good reason. And historically, this regulatory subject matter — financial regulation — has been thought to exhibit a particular need for independence. And Congress, by, for example, providing the Board with a revenue stream independent of the congressional appropriations process, helped insulate the Board from congressional, as well as other, political influences.

In sum, Congress and the President could reasonably have thought it prudent to insulate the adjudicative Board members from fear of purely politically based removal. And in a world in which we count on the Federal Government to regulate matters as complex as, say, nuclear-power production, the Court's assertion that we should simply learn to get by "without being" regulated "by experts" is, at best, unrealistic — at worst, dangerously so.

C

Where a "for cause" provision is so unlikely to restrict presidential power and so likely to further a legitimate institutional need, precedent strongly supports its constitutionality. First, in considering a related issue in *Nixon v. Administrator of General Services,* 433 U.S. 425 (1977), the Court made clear that when "determining whether the Act disrupts the proper balance between the coordinate branches, the proper inquiry focuses on the extent to which it prevents the Executive Branch from accomplishing its constitutionally assigned functions." The Court said the same in *Morrison,* where it upheld a restriction on the President's removal power. Here, the removal restriction may somewhat diminish the Commission's ability to control the Board, but it will have little, if any, negative effect in respect to the President's ability to control the Board, let alone to coordinate the Executive Branch. . . . [T]he Accounting Board's adjudicatory responsibilities, the technical nature of its job, the need to attract experts to that job, and the importance of demonstrating the nonpolitical nature of the job to the public strongly justify a statute that assures that Board members need not fear for their jobs when competently carrying out their tasks, while still maintaining the Commission as the ultimate authority over Board policies and actions. . . .

In sum, the Court's prior cases impose functional criteria that are readily met here. Once one goes beyond the Court's elementary arithmetical logic (i.e., "one plus one is greater than one") our precedent virtually dictates a holding that the challenged "for cause" provision is constitutional.

D

We should ask one further question. Even if the "for cause" provision before us does not itself significantly interfere with the President's authority or aggrandize Congress' power, is it nonetheless necessary to adopt a bright-line rule forbidding the provision lest, through a series of such provisions, each itself upheld as reasonable, Congress might undercut the President's central constitutional role? The answer to this question is that no such need has been shown. Moreover, insofar as the Court seeks to create such a rule, it fails. And in failing it threatens a harm that is far more serious than any imaginable harm this "for cause" provision might bring about.

The Court fails to create a bright-line rule because of considerable uncertainty about the scope of its holding — an uncertainty that the Court's opinion both reflects and generates. The Court suggests, for example, that its rule may not apply where an inferior officer "perform[s] adjudicative . . . functions." But the Accounting Board performs adjudicative functions. What, then, are we to make of the Court's potential exception? And would such an exception apply to an administrative law judge who also has important administrative duties beyond pure adjudication? The Court elsewhere suggests that its rule may be limited to removal statutes that provide for "judicial review of a[n] effort to remove" an official for cause. But we have previously stated that all officers protected by a for-cause removal provision and later subject to termination are entitled to "notice and [a] hearing" in the "courts," as without such review "the appointing power" otherwise "could remove at pleasure or for such cause as [only] it deemed sufficient." What weight, then, should be given to this hint of an exception?

The Court further seems to suggest that its holding may not apply to inferior officers who have a different relationship to their appointing agents than the relationship between the Commission and the Board. But the only characteristic of the "relationship" between the Commission and the Board that the Court apparently deems relevant is that the relationship includes two layers of for-cause removal. Why then would any different relationship that also includes two layers of for-cause removal survive where this one has not? In a word, what differences are relevant? . . .

The Court begins to reveal the practical problems inherent in its double for-cause rule when it suggests that its rule may not apply to "the civil service." The "civil service" is defined by statute to include "all appointive positions in . . . the Government of the United States," excluding the military, but including all civil "officer[s]" up to and including those who are subject to Senate confirmation. The civil service thus includes many officers indistinguishable from the members of both the Commission and the Accounting Board . . . . [T]he Court's "double for-cause" rule applies to appointees who are "inferior officer [s]." And who are they? Courts and scholars have struggled for more than a century to define the constitutional term "inferior officers," without much success. The Court does not clarify the concept. But without defining who is an inferior officer, to whom the majority's new rule applies, we cannot know the scope or the coherence of the legal rule that the Court creates. . . .

I see no way to avoid sweeping hundreds, perhaps thousands of high level government officials within the scope of the Court's holding, putting their job security and their administrative actions and decisions constitutionally at risk. To make even a conservative estimate, one would have to begin by listing federal departments, offices, bureaus and other agencies whose heads are by statute removable only "for cause." I have found 48 such agencies, which I have listed in Appendix A. Then it would be necessary to identify the senior officials in those agencies (just below the top) who themselves are removable only "for cause." I have identified 573 such high-ranking officials, whom I have listed in Appendix B. They include most of the leadership of the Nuclear Regulatory Commission (including that agency's executive director as well as the directors of its Office of Nuclear Reactor Regulation and Office of Enforcement), virtually all of the leadership of the Social Security Administration, the executive directors of the Federal Energy Regulatory Commission and the Federal Trade Commission, as well as the general counsels of the Chemical Safety Board, the Federal Mine Safety and Health Review Commission, and the National Mediation Board.

This list is a conservative estimate because it consists only of career appointees in the Senior Executive Service (SES), a group of high-ranking officials distinct from the "competitive service," who "serve in the key positions just below the top Presidential appointees," and who are, without exception, subject to "removal" only for cause. SES officials include, for example, the Director of the Bureau of Prisons, the Director of the National Drug Intelligence Center, and the Director of the Office of International Monetary Policy in the Treasury Department. And by virtually any definition, essentially all SES officials qualify as "inferior officers," for their duties, as defined by statute, require them to "direc[t] the work of an organizational unit," carry out high-level managerial functions, or "otherwise exercis[e] important policy-making, policy-determining, or other executive functions." Is the SES exempt from today's rule or is it not? The Court, after listing reasons why the SES may be different, simply says that it will not "addres[s]" the matter. Perhaps it does not do so because it cannot do so without revealing the difficulty of distinguishing the SES from the Accounting Board and thereby also revealing the inherent instability of the legal rule it creates.

The potential list of those whom today's decision affects is yet larger. As Justice SCALIA has observed, administrative law judges (ALJs) "are all executive officers." And ALJs are each removable "only for good cause established and determined by the Merit Systems Protection Board," But the members of the Merit Systems Protection Board are themselves protected from removal by the President absent good cause. My research reflects that the Federal Government relies on 1,584 ALJs to adjudicate administrative matters in over 25 agencies. See Appendix C, infra. These ALJs adjudicate Social Security benefits, employment disputes, and other matters highly important to individuals. Does every losing party before an ALJ now have grounds to appeal on the basis that the decision entered against him is unconstitutional?

And what about the military? Commissioned military officers "are 'inferior officers.'" There are over 210,000 active-duty commissioned officers currently serving in the armed forces. Numerous statutory provisions provide that such officers may not be removed from office except for cause (at least in peacetime). And such officers can generally be so removed only by other commissioned officers, who themselves enjoy the same career protections. The majority might simply say that the military is different. But it will have to explain how it is different. It is difficult to see why the Constitution would provide a President who is the military's "commander-in-chief," Art. II, §2, cl. 1, with less authority to remove "inferior" military "officers" than to remove comparable civil officials.

The majority sees "no reason . . . to address whether" any of "these positions," "or any others," might be deemed unconstitutional under its new rule, preferring instead to leave these matters for a future case. But what is to happen in the meantime? Is the work of all these various officials to be put on hold while the courts of appeals determine whether today's ruling applies to them? . . . Thus, notwithstanding the majority's assertions to the contrary, the potential consequences of today's holding are worrying. The upshot, I believe, is a legal dilemma. To interpret the Court's decision as applicable only in a few circumstances will make the rule less harmful but arbitrary. To interpret the rule more broadly will make the rule more rational, but destructive.

III

One last question: How can the Court simply assume without deciding that the SEC Commissioners themselves are removable only "for cause?" Unless the Commissioners themselves are in fact protected by a "for cause" requirement, the Accounting Board statute, on the Court's own reasoning, is not constitutionally defective. I am not aware of any other instance in which the Court has similarly (on its own or through stipulation) created a constitutional defect in a statute and then relied on that defect to strike a statute down as unconstitutional. It is certainly not obvious that the SEC Commissioners enjoy "for cause" protection. Unlike the statutes establishing the 48 federal agencies listed in Appendix A, infra, the statue that established the Commission says nothing about removal. It is silent on the question. As far as its text is concerned, the President's authority to remove the Commissioners is no different from his authority to remove the Secretary of State or the Attorney General.

Nor is the absence of a "for cause" provision in the statute that created the Commission likely to have been inadvertent. Congress created the Commission during the 9-year period after this Court decided *Myers*, and thereby cast serious doubt on the constitutionality of all "for cause" removal provisions, but before it decided *Humphrey's Executor*, which removed any doubt in respect to the constitutionality of making commissioners of independent agencies removable only for cause. In other words, Congress created the SEC at a time when, under this Court's precedents, it would have been unconstitutional to make the Commissioners removable only for cause. And, during that 9-year period, Congress created at least three major federal agencies without making any of their officers removable for cause. By way of contrast, only one month after Humphrey's Executor was decided, Congress returned to its pre-*Myers* practice of including such provisions in statutes creating independent commissions. See § 3, 49 Stat. 451, 29 U.S.C. § 153 (establishing National Labor Relations Board with an explicit removal limitation).

The fact that Congress did not make the SEC Commissioners removable "for cause" does not mean it intended to create a dependent, rather than an independent agency. Agency independence is a function of several different factors, of which "for cause" protection is only one. Those factors include, inter alia, an agency's separate (rather than presidentially dependent) budgeting authority, its separate litigating authority, its composition as a multimember bipartisan board, the use of the word "independent" in its authorizing statute, and, above all, a political environment, reflecting tradition and function, that would impose a heavy political cost upon any President who tried to remove a commissioner of the agency without cause.

The absence of a "for cause" provision is thus not fatal to agency independence. Indeed, a "Congressional Research Service official suggests that there are at least 13 'independent' agencies without a removal provision in their statutes." But it does draw the majority's rule into further confusion. For not only are we left without a definition of an "inferior officer," but we are also left to guess which department heads will be deemed by the majority to be subject to for-cause removal notwithstanding statutes containing no such provision. If any agency deemed "independent" will be similarly treated, the scope of the majority's holding is even broader still. See Appendix D, infra (listing agencies potentially affected).

The Court then, by assumption, reads into the statute books a "for cause removal" phrase that does not appear in the relevant statute and which Congress probably did not intend to write. And it does so in order to strike down, not to uphold, another statute. This is not a statutory construction that seeks to avoid a constitutional question, but its opposite. I do not need to decide whether the Commissioners are in fact removable only "for cause" because I would uphold the Accounting Board's removal provision as constitutional regardless. But were that not so, a determination that the silent SEC statute means no more than it says would properly avoid the determination of unconstitutionality that the Court now makes.

———————

1. *Who won?* The plaintiffs had hoped to dismantle the powers of the PCAOB entirely, or even to obtain an overruling of *Morrison*. Despite executive-friendly rhetoric, however, the Court's holding just made the Board members subject to removal by the SEC, without otherwise affecting its regulatory powers. By itself, this outcome has little importance. Instead, the significance of the decision lies in its implications for other, apparently similar arrangements, as the Justices debated at length. If you were a lawyer for the Free Enterprise Fund, what case would you bring next in an effort to promote the theory of the unitary executive? If you were a lawyer for the President, what would you tell him is the significance of the case for executive power?

2. *Edmond.* In *Edmond v. United States*, 520 U.S. 651 (1997), which the majority cites above, the Court unanimously upheld the appointment by the Secretary of Transportation of civilian members of the Coast Guard Court of Criminal Appeals, on the ground that the latter were "inferior officers" rather than principal officers. The case gave Justice Scalia an opportunity to express his unhappiness with *Morrison*— his unhappiness, in particular, with the Court's apparent turn to balancing in the earlier case to decide on what counts as constitutional "inferiority." As in the *PCAOB* case, however, the Court's holding had little, if any implication for the durability of *Morrison*. Although the Court rested on the formal test for "inferiority," on which it relies also in *PCAOB*, it noted that the balancing approach of *Morrison*—focusing on the appointees' breadth of jurisdiction, term of office, and scope for discretion— would have produced an identical outcome.

3. *Adding the PCAOB to the Government.* The Court readily and unanimously rejected the effort by Congress to designate the PCAOB as a private entity, because of its numerous statutory functions. Any other decision would have cut a very large hole in the *Buckley* principle, wouldn't it? This is not the only example of the Supreme Court refusing to accept Congress's designation of an entity as private. In a case presenting the question whether Amtrak was a state actor for First Amendment purposes,

the Supreme Court held that Amtrak was a government agency despite a statute chartering Amtrak as a corporation and not as a government entity. *See Lebron v. Nat'l R.R. Passenger Corp.*, 513 U.S. 374 (1995).

4. *Adding a For-Cause Limit to the SEC.* The majority agreed with the parties that the SEC is subject to a for-cause removal restriction like the one in *Humphrey's Executor*, although the statute contains none. Consider Justice Breyer's argument on this score. Should the Court have just held that the President has plenary removal power over the SEC itself? What would the implications of that holding have been?

5. *Making Matroyshkas.* Should the then-Solicitor General, Elena Kagan, have responded to a question by conceding that a five-layer removal scheme would be valid in her view? What line could she have drawn? Indeed, why did the executive not side with the plaintiffs in this case?

6. *Appointing Inferior Officers.* Note that all nine Justices agreed that the members of the Board were validly appointed, rejecting several assaults by the plaintiffs. Does this clear away all prior confusion about such appointments?

7. *What Is the Reach of the Decision?* The dissent assails the majority for trying to have it both ways. The Court's opinion contains a lot of unitary executive theory in its discussion of accountability to the President, yet it repeatedly disclaims any intent to have sweeping, government-wide effects. Well, which is it? Do you agree with Justice Breyer that many existing structures are thrown into doubt by the Court's decision? (Examine the appendices he attached to his opinion if you want to get a flavor of the possible effects.) One way out of this dilemma may lie in the Chief Justice's statement that the President may "hold the Commission to account for its supervision of the Board, to the same extent that he may hold the Commission to account for everything else it does." What does *that* mean? Can the President assert invigorated powers to supervise the top layer in other multi-layered removal restrictions? In other passages, however, the Court makes clear its endorsement for its existing precedents on removals. So — what may the President do to the SEC if he concludes that the PCAOB is misbehaving?

A judicial desire to have it both ways might also be seen in *PHH Corp. v. Consumer Finance Protection Bureau*, 839 F.3d 1 (D.C. Cir. 2016), *vacated and reh'g en banc ordered*, No. 15-1177 (D.C. Cir. Feb. 16, 2017). The Consumer Finance Protection Bureau (CFPB) is one of the relatively rare federal agencies headed by a single administrator — in this case, the Director — who enjoys statutory protection against at-will presidential removal. In *PHH*, a D.C. Circuit panel opinion written by Judge Kavanaugh held that the structure was unconstitutional because limitations on removal are permissible only for multi-member agencies. The premise of Judge Kavanaugh's unprecedented argument is that the Constitution subjects all administrators to at-will presidential removal as a protection against arbitrary government and that, where the president is limited in his removal authority, only a multimember structure provides an equivalent level of anti-arbitrariness protection. The opinion is unusual in a number of respects, not least of which is the suggestion that presidents have more influence over multimember bodies than they do over single-headed agencies. But it is also striking that Judge Kavanaugh, who has not been reluctant to express constitutional reservations about *Humphrey's Executor*, offers—in support of his thesis—perhaps the most robust policy defense of the independent agency structure in administrative law jurisprudence:

> How do multi-member independent agencies fare better than single-Director independent agencies in protecting individual liberty? As compared to single-Director independent agencies, multi-member independent agencies help prevent arbitrary decisionmaking and abuses of power, and thereby help protect individual liberty, because they do not concentrate power in the hands of one individual. . . . In a multi-member independent agency, no single commissioner or board member possesses authority to do much of anything. Before the agency can infringe your liberty in some way— for example, initiating an enforcement action against you or issuing a rule that affects your liberty or property—a majority of commissioners must agree. That in turn makes it harder for the agency to infringe your liberty. . . . In a multi-member agency, even though each individual commissioner is not accountable to or checked by the President, each commissioner is at least still accountable to his or her fellow commissioners and needs the assent of a majority of commissioners to take significant action.

> In addition, unlike single-Director independent agencies, multi-member independent agencies "can foster more deliberative decision making." Relatedly, multi-member independent agencies benefit from diverse perspectives and different points of view among the commissioners and board members. The multiple voices and perspectives make it more likely that the costs and downsides of proposed decisions will be more fully ventilated. In short, the deliberative process and multiple viewpoints in a multi-member independent agency can help ensure that an agency does not wrongly bring an enforcement action or adopt rules that unduly infringe individual liberty.

> As compared to a single-Director structure, a multi-member independent agency also helps to avoid arbitrary decisionmaking and to protect individual liberty because the multi-member structure—and its inherent requirement for compromise and consensus—will tend to lead to decisions that are not as extreme, idiosyncratic, or otherwise off the rails. A multi-member independent agency can only go as far as the middle vote is willing to go. Conversely, under a single-Director structure, an agency's policy goals "will be subject to the whims and idiosyncratic views of a single individual."

> Relatedly, as compared to a single-Director independent agency, a multi-member independent agency provides the added benefit of "a built-in monitoring system for interests on both sides because that type of body is more likely to produce a dissent if the agency goes too far in one direction."

> Moreover, multi-member independent agencies are better structured than single-Director independent agencies to guard against "capture" of—that is, undue influence over—the independent agencies by regulated entities or interest groups, for example. . . . Capture can infringe individual liberty because capture can prevent a neutral, impartial agency assessment of what rules to issue and what enforcement actions to undertake. In a multi-member agency, however, the capturing parties "must capture a majority of the membership rather than just one individual."

839 F.3d at 26–28. Are you persuaded? Or is it too doctrinally unstable to conclude that independent agencies are presumptively unconstitutional, but that, to the extent the Constitution permits them, they must fit a particular institutional design? As this volume goes to press, the *PHH* case has been reargued to the D.C. Circuit en banc, but not yet decided.

C. Supervision and Coordination of Policymaking

Both President and Congress oversee statutory administration in the myriad agencies. This section reviews the law and policy of oversight by both branches, and then closes with some analysis of the special status of the independent agencies.

1. The President's Power to Manage Administration

a. *Formative Years: Groping for Principles*

The Constitution does not specify the internal organization of the Executive Branch. At the Convention, a proposal to do so was wisely rejected. Article II, after vesting the executive power in the President, contains three provisions that appear to assume that subordinate officers will perform ordinary law administration. (Of course, modern government affords no practical alternative to such an arrangement.) First, the injunction to the President to "take Care that the Laws be faithfully executed" is in the passive mood. The President, apparently, is to superintend someone else's activities. Similarly, the President is empowered to "require the Opinion, in writing, of the principal Officer in each of the executive Departments, upon any subject relating to the Duties of their respective Offices." This curious provision is the remnant of the proposal for a constitutional specification of executive organization. Once disparaged as "trifling" by Justice Jackson (in *Youngstown*), the Opinions Clause suggests both that the President is not to be a stranger to administration, and that other officers will make the decisions that underlie opinions they may furnish the President. Finally, the appointments clause authorizes "Heads of Departments" to appoint inferior officers, saving the time and energy of the President for weightier matters.

Early practice under the Constitution set an enduring pattern. Opinions rendered by Attorneys General to the President concluded that assumption of an officer's statutory authority by the President was more difficult to justify than was supervision, which could be enforced by the officer's removal and replacement if necessary. Therefore, a congressional decision to assign a particular statutory decision to a subordinate executive officer, rather than to the President himself, has always been considered significant. The opinions also decided that the extent of presidential supervision should depend on the subject matter. Thus, one opinion advised the President that he should not countermand the adjudicative decisions of accounting officers about the amount owing a particular claimant. *The President and Accounting Officers*, 1 Op. Att'y Gen. 624 (1823). President Monroe asked Attorney General William Wirt whether Monroe could legally and properly revise the Treasury Department's settlement of the account of Major Joseph Wheaton for the period of his tenure in the Quartermaster's Department. The Attorney General opined that the President was powerless to overturn the Department's decision. He read the faithful execution clause to contemplate that subordinate officers should perform duties assigned to them by law. The President, he concluded, would have neither the responsibility nor the power to perform those tasks himself. This opinion was sound, and would be compelled by statute today.

On the larger question about the President's relationship to administration, a point of view rather different from Wirt's emerges in an opinion rendered eight years later, by Attorney General (later Chief Justice) Roger B. Taney to Andrew Jackson's Secretary of State.

The Jewels of the Princess of Orange

2 Op. Att'y Gen. 482 (1831)

[Apparently on behalf of the President, the Secretary of State asked Taney whether the President could direct the federal district attorney (now the United States Attorney) in New York to discontinue the prosecution of an action to condemn certain stolen jewels brought into the United States in violation of the revenue laws. The true owner, the Princess of Orange, a member of the royal family of the Netherlands, had asked for their return. After concluding that the jewels were not liable to forfeiture, Taney turned to the questions whether the proceeding could be terminated, and whether the President could so direct. Taney concluded that a district attorney had legal authority to discontinue any suit when termination would be in the interest of the United States:]

Assuming that the district attorney possesses the power to discontinue a prosecution, the next inquiry is, Can the President lawfully direct him, in any case, to do so? ... I think the President does possess the power. The interest of the country and the purposes of justice manifestly require that he should possess it; and its existence is necessarily implied by the duties imposed upon him in that clause of the constitution ... which enjoins him to take care that the laws be faithfully executed. ... There is no specific grant of power in the constitution which authorizes the President to order the discontinuance of a prosecution against the public property of a foreign nation; and the circumstances that such a prosecution would endanger the peace of the United States . . . would be a strong reason for exercising the power if he possessed it. And if he does possess it in such cases, and it is not specifically granted by the constitution, it must be derived from the general supervisory powers which belong to his office, and which are necessary to enable him to perform the duty imposed upon him, of seeing that the law is faithfully executed. . . .

[T]he direction of the President is not required to communicate any new authority to the district attorney, but to direct him or aid him in the execution of the power he is admitted to possess. It might, indeed, happen that a district attorney was prosecuting a suit in the name of the United States, against their interest and against justice, and for the purpose of oppressing an individual; such a prosecution would not be a faithful execution of the law; and upon the President being satisfied that the forms of law were abused for such a purpose, and being bound to take care that the law was faithfully executed, it would become his duty to take measures to correct the procedure. And the most natural and proper measure to accomplish that object would be, to order the district attorney to discontinue the prosecution. The district attorney might refuse to obey the President's order; and if he did refuse, the prosecution, while he remained in office, would still go on; because the President could give no order to the court or the clerk to make any particular entry. He could only act through his subordinate officer, the district attorney, who is responsible to him, and who holds his office at his pleasure. And if that officer still continued a prosecution which the President was satisfied ought to be discontinued, the removal of the disobedient officer, and the substitution of one more worthy in his place, would enable the President, through him, faithfully to execute the law. And it is for this, among other reasons, that the power of removing the district attorney resides in the President. . . .

The district attorney stands in relation to the President on very different grounds from that of the court. The judicial power is wholly independent of the Executive. . . . He has no right to interfere with their proceedings; and if they misbehave themselves in office, they are not responsible to him. . . . Upon the whole, I consider the district attorney as under the control and direction of the President, . . . and that it is within the legitimate power of the President to direct him to institute or to discontinue a pending suit, and to point out to him his duty, whenever the interest of the United States is directly or indirectly concerned. And I find, on examination, that the practice of the government has conformed to this opinion; and that, in many instances where the interference of the Executive was asked for, the cases have been referred to the Attorney General, and, in every case, the right to interfere and direct the district attorney is assumed or asserted. . . .

———————

1. *An Opinion or a Club?* Why do you think the Secretary of State requested Attorney General Taney's opinion? At this time, the district attorneys were within the State Department. Do you suppose the Secretary needed a favorable opinion to secure his subordinate's compliance with his wishes?

2. *Taking Care, Again.* Why do you think Taney eschews a foreign affairs basis for his opinion? Do you infer that Taney agrees or disagrees with the Wirt opinion mentioned earlier?

3. *Ministerial Duties.* Does Taney suggest that Congress may not deprive the President of power to direct his subordinates even in the exercise of nondiscretionary duties? The Supreme Court, seven years after the Taney opinion, rejected the notion that the President could forbid a subordinate to perform a ministerial task vested in the officer by Congress. *Kendall v. United States ex rel. Stokes*, 37 U.S. (12 Pet.) 524 (1838), discussed in the *Note on Obtaining Judicial Review of Executive Actions* in Chapter Two. In *Kendall*, the Court issued a famous dictum: "To contend, that the obligation imposed on the president to see the laws faithfully executed, implies a power to forbid their execution, is a novel construction of the constitution, and entirely inadmissible." Does this ringing statement beg the important question—what if the President and his subordinate disagree on what the law requires? For example, suppose a United States Attorney and the President disagree over whether a forfeiture action may legally be dismissed—who will or should prevail?

4. *Plus Ça Change . . .* Lest the foregoing opinion appear to be of only quaint historical significance, it should be recalled that, in June 1988, Secretary of State George P. Shultz and Attorney General Edwin Meese reached an informal agreement under which federal prosecutors would have to obtain the President's approval before seeking a grand jury indictment against a foreign leader. The unusual step was prompted by the Administration's apparent embarrassment at its inability to prompt the removal from office of Panamanian leader General Manuel Antonio Noriega, who had been indicted by a federal grand jury on charges related to drug smuggling. Is there any doubt as to the President's authority to impose such a requirement on federal prosecutors?

5. *Jackson, the Treasury Department and the National Bank.* A famous controversy early in our history demonstrated in operation the competing principles emanating from the opinions of Attorneys General Wirt and Taney: President Andrew Jackson's dismissal of Treasury Secretary William J. Duane. Leonard D. White, The Jacksonians: A Study in Administrative History, 1829–1861, ch. 2 (1954), tells the full story. After Jackson's veto of the bill to reauthorize the Bank of the United States and in anticipation of the Bank's termination, Jackson decided to remove deposits of government funds, sending them to state banks. Congress, however, had provided that "the deposits of the money of the United States . . . shall be made in said bank or branches thereof, unless the Secretary of the Treasury shall at any time otherwise order and direct." 3 Stat. 266, § 16 (April 10, 1816). Treasury Secretary Louis McLane opposed removal of the funds, and was transferred to State. His successor, Duane, immediately doubted both the legality and wisdom of removal. A series of letters and interviews with the President followed. Somewhat surprisingly (considering his volatility), Jackson did not simply try to command the decision. Instead, he tried to persuade Duane. White, *supra* at 38, says:

[Eventually] Duane told the President he would not remove the deposits, in a conversation which was "long and occasionally animated," and in which Jackson sought to avoid a break. "A secretary, sir," said Jackson, "is merely an executive agent, a subordinate, and you may say so in self-defence." To which Duane replied, "In this particular case, congress confers a discretionary power, and requires reasons if I exercise it. Surely this contemplates responsibility on my part." Here was the heart of the matter. On September 23, 1833, Jackson solved the problem by summarily removing Duane. . . . Taney became Secretary of the Treasury, and the deposits were removed. . . . The ambiguous position of the Secretary of the Treasury, growing out of the organic act of 1789, was thus brought to an end. Whatever responsibility to Congress the Secretary may have had by the terms of the act of 1789 or the Second Bank Act, it was clear that he had a more immediate and direct responsibility to the President, and that duties enjoined upon him by law had to be exercised within the framework of presidential policy.

That was not the end of the matter, however. In the Senate, Daniel Webster argued that Congress could place independent authority in the hands of the Secretary of the Treasury. Webster distinguished the President's power to dismiss Duane, which he conceded, from the power to direct the performance of the Secretary's statutory duties, which he denied. White, *id.* at 42, quotes his argument:

> "The law," he declared, "charges the officer, whoever he may be, with the performance of certain duties. The President, with the consent of the Senate, appoints an individual to be such an officer; and this individual he may remove, if he so please; but, until he is removed, he is the officer, and remains charged with the duties of his station, duties which nobody else can perform, and for the neglect or violation of which he is liable to be impeached."

The Senate then passed a Resolution of Censure, condemning Jackson's actions forcing removal of the government deposits from the Bank. Jackson responded with a "Protest." The Senate refused to receive it. After years of further maneuvering, the Senate formally expunged the censure. White concludes, *id.* at 44: "Thus Jackson earned a personal triumph, and thus symbolically his reading of executive powers gained political confirmation." The eminent Edward Corwin was more blunt: "Never before and never since has the Senate so abased itself before a President." THE PRESIDENT: OFFICE AND POWERS 267 (1941).

The lesson of the Duane affair is that a President may obtain the statutory interpretation that he desires from a subordinate officer, *if* he possesses and is willing to exercise removal power over the officer, and *if* the Senate is willing to confirm a successor who will do the President's bidding! If removal authority is restricted, a suit to test the legality of the President's directive will ensue, addressing questions left over from *Humphrey's Executor.* And whether or not removal authority is restricted, the President's action draws the attention of Congress to the underlying statutory interpretation, inviting a clarification or correction—if a presidential veto can be overridden. The power of the veto means that the need for senatorial confirmation of a successor officer is a readier check on presidential law-interpretation than is amendment of the statute. In any event, the controversial interpretation is evident to the courts, which can accept or reject it under the usual standards.

6. *The National Bank and Presidential Authority to Appoint and Remove.* Although rarely discussed in contemporary debates over the President's appointment and removal powers, the Bank of the United States, in Professor Shane's view, is instructive as to both:

> [An] insufficiently-appreciated blow to the . . . originalist case for a hard unitary presidency is the First Bank of the United States. Separation of powers theorists have largely ignored the Bank, presumably because, as a kind of public-private partnership, it so obviously does not fit comfortably within any traditional view of the administrative state. . . . Yet there is no doubt the Bank wielded government power. As Professor Mashaw recounts, the Bank of the United States—strongly urged by Framer Alexander Hamilton and modeled after the Bank of England—effectively regulated the money supply. . . .

> The precise degree of government influence in the selection of the directors of the First Bank of the United States is difficult to measure. Directors were to be chosen according to a plurality of shareholder votes, and the United States was limited to subscribing to no more than a fifth of the Bank's stock. Although the number of votes given to each shareholder depended on a complex formula, the United States bloc was presumably large enough to be influential, although the statute was silent as to who would vote on behalf of the United States. The government's minority status was cemented, however, when the Bank was re-chartered in 1816. Under the Second Bank Bill, the President was explicitly authorized to appoint five of the Bank's directors, with the Senate's advice and consent, not even enough by themselves to constitute a quorum for doing business; private shareholders would choose the remaining twenty. Under both statutes, the Treasury Department enjoyed some limited supervisory authority over the Bank in the sense that the Secretary could demand reports and inspect Bank records. There was, however, no provision for presidential or Treasury authority to direct the bank in its operations.

> What makes this example of attenuated presidential influence so telling was that enactment of the Bank's charter in 1791 was very much the subject of constitutional debate. James Madison famously opposed the Bank as going beyond the enumerated powers of Congress, recalling that the Philadelphia Convention specifically declined to give Congress an express power of incorporation precisely to avoid the establishment of a national bank. The measure was debated vigorously in the House on constitutional grounds, even though unanimously approved by the Senate. Nor did Congress's adoption of the Bank bill end the intra-governmental deliberations. President Washington, who, of course, had presided over the Constitutional

Convention, thought the issue of sufficient moment that, prior to signing the Bank's charter, he sought the formal opinions of his Attorney General and Secretaries of State and of the Treasury on the constitutional issue. We thus have four major statements by leading contemporary figures — Hamilton, Jefferson, Madison, and Edmund Randolph — all formally assessing the constitutionality of the bank bill.

Here's the rub: Not one of these opinions mentions the separation of powers as a source of objection or concern. Jefferson, Madison, and Randolph all thought the Bank unconstitutional as going beyond Congress's Article I powers, but none says a word about the lack of presidential supervisory authority or indeed anything about the Bank's attenuated accountability to even the Treasury Department. Hamilton does not acknowledge the Executive's attenuated influence over the Bank as something that needs to be constitutionally explained away. He does not mention it at all. . . .

In this respect, . . . it is enlightening to look at the Bank debate at a later stage in history. As is well known, Congress failed to re-charter the Bank when the first charter lapsed in 1811, leaving the U.S. to fight the War of 1812 without the aid of a central fiscal institution. The resulting fiscal difficulties prompted Congress in 1816 to charter a Second Bank of the United States for another twenty years, again much to the chagrin of the agricultural states. Congressional Whigs voted in 1832 to extend the charter four years early thinking the move would help them in the 1832 election. Instead, Andrew Jackson made his vehement opposition to the Bank a central campaign issue and sent Congress a vigorous and detailed veto message.

Key portions of Jackson's message, reminiscent of earlier statements in opposition to the Bank, again challenged the Bank as unconstitutional. While taking note that the Supreme Court had approved Congress's exertion of an implicit incorporation power, Jackson took the position that the Supreme Court had been appropriately deferential to the elected branches in applying the Necessary and Proper Clause, but that he, as President, need not be. . . . But Jackson — who had every reason to attack the Bank on any plausible constitutional basis and who was, at that stage in history, our most pro-executive Chief Executive, did not object to the Bank on any separation of powers ground.

Peter M. Shane, *The Originalist Myth of the Unitary Executive*, 19 U. Pa. J. Const. L. 323, 354–359 (2016). It is intriguing in light of this history that Professors Walter Dellinger and H. Jefferson Powell — at the time of their writing the Assistant Attorney General in charge of OLC and his former deputy, respectively — have observed that a modern-day OLC opinion on the constitutionality of a national bank would have focused immediately on possible separation of powers objections to the bill. Walter Dellinger & H. Jefferson Powell, *The Constitutionality of the Bank Bill: The Attorney General's First Constitutional Law Opinions*, 44 Duke L.J. 110, 131 (1994). Why would contemporary government lawyers be more attuned to such issues than government lawyers in the early decades of the Republic?

b. The President's Statutory Powers to Manage the Executive Branch

A number of statutes confer managerial authority on the President. Their existence feeds the current debate over the President's power to control executive policymaking in statutory interstices. We have already examined the most important of these statutory powers, regarding the budgetary and spending processes of the government. We return to them here to make the overall picture complete and because they relate to arguments about the President's implied statutory powers.

In general, OMB controls both the budgetary and legislative requests of federal agencies, including the independent agencies. Congress has occasionally granted an exception from one or both of these requirements, however (e.g., 15 U.S.C. § 2076(k), Consumer Product Safety Commission). OMB has specified procedures for submittal and clearance of agency requests. Congress further strengthened OMB's oversight of executive agencies by enacting the Chief Financial Officers Act of 1990, Pub. L. No. 101-576, 104 Stat. 2838. That Act not only creates the position of presidentially appointed Chief Financial Officer for every agency, with extensive powers to monitor agency revenues, expenditures, and accounting, but also an OMB Office of Federal Financial Management to coordinate their activities.

Thus, Congress has recognized both the need for coordination of government policy and the President's unique capacity to provide it. As a practical matter, OMB derives considerable leverage from its power to review the agencies' requests to Congress. As we shall see, OMB has not been loath to exercise this leverage in pursuit of the President's policy agenda.

OMB also has power to control the agencies' demands for information from the public, under the Paperwork Reduction Act of 1980, Pub. L. No. 96-511, 94 Stat. 2812 (codified in scattered sections of 5, 20, 30, 42, and 44 U.S.C.). The independent agencies may overrule OMB directives under this statute by majority vote. 44 U.S.C. § 3507(f). The component of OMB that administers the Paperwork Reduction Act, the Office of Information and Regulatory Affairs (OIRA), also administers the executive order programs for coordinating policymaking that we explore below. Stormy relations between OIRA and Congress due to the executive orders have led Congress to subject the head of the office to advice and consent (Pub. L. No. 99-591, Oct. 30, 1986). After introducing you to the executive order programs, we will examine their relationship to the powers conferred by the Paperwork Reduction Act.

Since the New Deal, Congress has authorized the President to prepare government reorganization plans, which, within certain limits, may transfer, consolidate, or abolish agency functions. 5 U.S.C. § 901 *et seq*. The current statute, for example, forbids abolishing or transferring all the functions of an executive department or independent regulatory agency. For many years, Congress subjected presidential reorganization plans to legislative veto (recall Justice White's historical summary in *Chadha*). In 1984, Congress amended the statute to require the plans to be approved by joint resolution. 5 U.S.C. §§ 908–12. This continuing congressional desire to keep a close control on reorganization authority recognizes that it is not just a matter of pigeon-holing government functions. Instead, the placement of a function in one agency rather than another can have important effects on substantive policy. *See generally* Barry D. Karl, *Executive Reorganization and Presidential Power*, 1977 Sup. Ct. Rev. 1. For example, the Environmental Protection Agency was created by reorganization plan in 1970. To see Karl's point, consider what difference it makes that pesticide regulation resides in EPA rather than the Agriculture Department.

Finally, some statutes vest substantive authority directly in the President. Under 3 U.S.C. § 301, he may subdelegate these powers to any agency in the executive branch, "*[p]rovided*, That nothing contained herein shall relieve the President of his responsibility . . . for the acts of any such . . . official." The legislative history of the statute recognized that "the President cannot delegate many functions because delegation would be inappropriate due to their character." (S. Rep. No. 1867, 81st Cong., 2d Sess. (1950)). Which statutory functions should the President exercise directly?

The foregoing is not an exhaustive catalogue of the President's statutory powers to manage the government. For more detail, *see* Peter L. Strauss, *The Place of Agencies in Government: Separation of Powers and the Fourth Branch*, 84 Colum. L. Rev. 573, 587–91 (1984), reminding us of such managerial powers as the Department of Justice's control of most government litigation and the Office of Personnel Management's employment functions. For a political scientist's analysis of the relative effectiveness of the various tools that Presidents possess to influence administration, including case studies of Presidents' attempts to influence particular agencies, see Richard W. Waterman, Presidential Influence and the Administrative State (1989).

c. Participation in Administrative Rulemaking

Sierra Club v. Costle

657 F.2d 298 (D.C. Cir. 1981)

[In an extensive opinion, the court reviewed and upheld the Environmental Protection Agency's new source performance standards for coalfired power plants. The standards, issued pursuant to the Clean Air Act, were intended to reduce sulfur dioxide and particulate emissions from new facilities through the use of expensive "scrubber" technology. After rejecting substantive challenges to the standards by both industry and environmental groups, including the Environmental Defense Fund (EDF), the court turned to procedural issues concerning EPA's rulemaking. Here it considered the legality of meetings between EPA officials and private groups, White House officials, and members of Congress, which occurred after the formal period for public comment on the proposed rules had ended.

Section 553 of the Administrative Procedure Act, which governs most agency rule-making, contains no ban on "ex parte" contacts between rulemakers and interested persons, occurring outside the "administrative record" that is compiled for judicial review. (Other statutes, such as the Clean Air Act, sometimes modify the APA's basic procedures.) Nevertheless, case law in the late 1970's began evincing concerns that the administrative record faithfully reflect the facts and policy arguments actually available to the agency, and that all interested persons be treated fairly. *Sierra Club* is an important development in this line of cases, and is of special interest here because of its consideration of contacts from the executive branch and Congress. Excerpts from Judge WALD's opinion follow.]

2. Meetings Held With Individuals Outside EPA

The [Clean Air Act] does not explicitly treat the issue of post-comment period meetings with individuals outside EPA. Oral face-to-face discussions are not prohibited anywhere, anytime, in the Act. The absence of such prohibition may have arisen from the nature of the informal rulemaking procedures Congress had in mind. Where agency action resembles judicial action, where it involves formal rulemaking, adjudication, or quasi-adjudication among "conflicting private claims to a valuable privilege," the insulation of the decisionmaker from ex parte contacts is justified by basic notions of due process to the parties involved. But where agency action involves informal rulemaking of a policymaking sort, the concept of ex parte contacts is of more questionable utility.

Under our system of government, the very legitimacy of general policymaking performed by unelected administrators depends in no small part upon the openness, accessibility, and amenability of these officials to the needs and ideas of the public from whom their ultimate authority derives, and upon whom their commands must fall. As judges we are insulated from these pressures because of the nature of the judicial process in which we participate; but we must refrain from the easy temptation to look askance at all face-to-face lobbying efforts, regardless of the forum in which they occur, merely because we see them as inappropriate in the judicial context. Furthermore, the importance to effective regulation of continuing contact with a regulated industry, other affected groups, and the public cannot be underestimated. Informal contacts may enable the agency to win needed support for its program, reduce future enforcement requirements by helping those regulated to anticipate and shape their plans for the future, and spur the provision of information which the agency needs. The possibility of course exists that in permitting ex parte communications with rulemakers we create the danger of "one administrative record for the public and this court and another for the Commission." Under the Clean Air Act procedures, however, "[t]he promulgated rule may not be based (in part or whole) on any information or data which has not been placed in the docket. . . ." Thus EPA must justify its rulemaking solely on the basis of the record it compiles and makes public.

Regardless of this court's views on the need to restrict all post-comment contacts in the informal rulemaking context, however, it is clear to us that Congress has decided not to do so in the statute which controls this case. As we have previously noted:

> . . . If Congress wanted to forbid or limit ex parte contact in every case of informal rulemaking, it certainly had a perfect opportunity of doing so when it enacted the Government in the Sunshine Act, Pub. L. No. 94-409, 90 Stat. 1241 (Sept. 13, 1976). . . . That it did not extend the ex parte contact provisions of the amended section 557 [which governs adjudication] to section 553 — even though such an extension was urged upon it during the hearing — is a sound indication that Congress still does not favor a per se prohibition or even a "logging" requirement in all such proceedings.

. . . It still can be argued, however, that if oral communications are to be freely permitted after the close of the comment period, then at least some adequate summary of them must be made in order to preserve the integrity of the rulemaking docket, which under the statute must be the sole repository of material upon which EPA intends to rely. The statute does not require the docketing of all post-comment period conversations and meetings, but we believe that a fair inference can be drawn that in some instances such docketing may be needed in order to give practical effect to section 307(d)(4)(B)(i), which provides that all *documents* "of central relevance to the rulemaking" shall be placed in the docket as soon as possible after their availability. This is so because unless oral communications of central relevance to the rulemaking are also docketed in some fashion or other, information central to the justification of the rule could be obtained without ever appearing on the docket, simply by communicating it by voice rather than by pen, thereby frustrating the command of section 307 that the final rule not be "based (in part or whole) on any information or data which has not been placed in the docket. . . ."

a. Intra-Executive Branch Meetings

We have already held that a blanket prohibition against meetings during the post-comment period with individuals outside EPA is unwarranted, and this perforce applies to meetings with White House officials. We have not yet addressed, however, the issue whether such oral communications with White House staff, or the President himself, must be docketed on the rulemaking record, and we now turn to that issue. The facts . . . present us with a single undocketed meeting held on April 30, 1979, at 10:00 a.m., attended by the President, White House staff, other high ranking members of the Executive Branch, as well as EPA officials, and which concerned the issues and options presented by the rulemaking.

We note initially that section 307 makes specific provision for including in the rulemaking docket the . . . drafts of the final rule submitted to an executive review process prior to promulgation, as well as all "written comments," "documents," and "written responses" resulting from such interagency review process. . . . This specific requirement does not mention informal meetings or conversations concerning the rule which are not part of the initial or final review processes, nor does it refer to oral comments of any sort. Yet it is hard to believe Congress was unaware that intra-executive meetings and oral comments would occur throughout the rule-making process. We assume, therefore, that unless expressly forbidden by Congress, such intra-executive contacts may take place, both during and after the public comment period; the only real issue is whether they must be noted and summarized in the docket.

The court recognizes the basic need of the President and his White House staff to monitor the consistency of executive agency regulations with Administration policy. He and his White House advisers surely must be briefed fully and frequently about rules in the making, and their contributions to policymaking considered. The executive power under our Constitution, after all, is not shared — it rests exclusively with the President. The idea of a "plural executive," or a President with a council of state, was considered and rejected by the Constitutional Convention. Instead the Founders chose to risk the potential for tyranny inherent in placing power in one person, in order to gain the advantages of accountability fixed on a single source. To ensure the President's control and supervision over the Executive Branch, the Constitution — and its judicial gloss — vests him with the powers of appointment and removal, the power to demand written opinions from executive officers, and the right to invoke executive privilege to protect consultative privacy. In the particular case of EPA, Presidential authority is clear since it has never been considered an "independent agency," but always part of the Executive Branch.

The authority of the President to control and supervise executive policymaking is derived from the Constitution; the desirability of such control is demonstrable from the practical realities of administrative rulemaking. Regulations such as those involved here demand a careful weighing of cost, environmental, and energy considerations. They also have broad implications for national economic policy. Our form of government simply could not function effectively or rationally if key executive policymakers were isolated from each other and from the Chief Executive. Single mission agencies do not always have the answers to complex regulatory problems. An overworked administrator exposed on a 24-hour basis to a dedicated but zealous staff needs to know the arguments and ideas of policymakers in other agencies as well as in the White House.

We recognize, however, that there may be instances where the docketing of conversations between the President or his staff and other Executive Branch officers or rulemakers may be necessary to ensure due process. This may be true, for example, where such conversations directly concern the outcome of adjudications or quasi-adjudicatory proceedings; there is no inherent executive power to control the rights of individuals in such settings. Docketing may also be necessary in some circumstances where a statute like this one *specifically requires* that essential "information or data" upon which a rule is based be docketed. But in the absence of any further Congressional requirements, we hold that it was not unlawful in this case for EPA not to docket a face-to-face policy session involving the President and EPA officials during the post-comment period, since EPA makes no effort to base the rule on any "information or data" arising from that meeting. Where the President himself is directly involved in oral communications with Executive Branch officials, Article II considerations . . . require that courts tread with extraordinary caution in mandating disclosure beyond that already required by statute.

The purposes of full-record review which underlie the need for disclosing ex parte conversations in some settings do not require that courts know the details of every White House contact, including a Presidential one, in this informal rulemaking setting. After all, any rule issued here with or without White House assistance must have the requisite *factual support* in the rulemaking record, and under this particular statute the Administrator may not base the rule in whole or in part on any "*information or data*" which is not in the record, no matter what the source. The courts will monitor all this, but they need not be omniscient to perform their role effectively. Of course, it is always possible that undisclosed Presidential prodding may direct an outcome that *is* factually based on the record, but different from the outcome that would have obtained in the absence of Presidential involvement. In such a case, it would be true that the political process did affect the outcome in a way the courts could not police. But we do not believe that Congress intended that the courts convert informal rulemaking into a rarified technocratic process, unaffected by political considerations or the presence of Presidential power. In sum, we find that the existence of intra-Executive Branch meetings during the post-comment period, and the failure to docket one such meeting involving the President, violated neither the procedures mandated by the Clean Air Act nor due process.

---

1. *Presidential Jawboning.* Declining to require disclosure of the White House meeting, the court says that it is permissible for "undisclosed Presidential prodding" to "direct an outcome that *is* factually based on the record, but different from the outcome that would have obtained" otherwise. Do you agree? In general, what is the significance of a statutory delegation directly to an agency, rather than to the President? One could argue that, when Congress delegates power to an executive agency rather than an independent one, it contemplates presidential supervision. On the other hand, perhaps a delegation to EPA is meant to take advantage of both the expertise and the political orientation of that agency.

2. *Opening up the Process?* Could Congress, consistent with the President's executive privilege, require disclosure of White House-agency contacts in rulemaking? If such a statute would be constitutional, would it improve the administrative process? How should it deal with the problem of "conduit" communications, in which administration or inter-agency contacts serve as conduits for private parties in order to get the latter's off-the-record views into the proceeding?

3. *Word from Above.* In *Portland Audubon Soc'y v. Endangered Species Committee*, 984 F.2d 1534 (9th Cir. 1993), the court held that the proceedings of the Endangered Species Committee, which can exempt federal agencies from the requisites of the Endangered Species Act, were subject to the ban on ex parte contacts in § 557 of the APA. The Committee, a cabinet-level group informally known as the "God squad"

due to its power over species survival, was alleged to have yielded to pressure from White House staff members in deciding to exempt actions involving the spotted owl. The court held that the Committee's decisions were adjudicatory in nature, and emphasized that the governing statute required decisions to be made on the record. It would not create a special statutory or constitutional right for the President or his aides to communicate with the Committee. Should it have done so?

4. *Setting Priorities. Sierra Club* is the fullest judicial discussion to date of ad hoc presidential intervention in rulemaking. For more analysis of the issues, see Harold H. Bruff, *Presidential Power and Administrative Rulemaking*, 88 YALE L.J. 451 (1979). It is easy to see what drew the President's attention in *Sierra Club*. This was a very high-stakes rulemaking, with millions of dollars, large aggregate environmental effects, and perhaps thousands of jobs in the balance. It also had implications for a highly complex and wide-ranging set of national policy issues about energy and the environment. In a footnote, the court quoted a passage from a perceptive book by CHARLES SCHULTZE, THE PUBLIC USE OF PRIVATE INTEREST 9–10 (1977):

> In the field of energy and the environment the generally accepted objectives of national policy imply a staggeringly complex and interlocking set of actions, directly affecting the production and consumption decisions of every citizen and every business firm. Consider for a moment the chain of collective decisions and their effects just in the case of electric utilities. Petroleum imports can be conserved by switching from oil-fired to coal-fired generation. But barring other measures, burning high-sulfur Eastern coal substantially increases pollution. Sulfur can be "scrubbed" from coal smoke in the stack, but at a heavy cost, with devices that turn out huge volumes of sulfur wastes that must be disposed of and about whose reliability there is some question. Intermittent control techniques (installing high smokestacks and switching off burners when meteorological conditions are adverse) can, at lower cost, reduce local concentrations of sulfur oxides in the air, but cannot cope with the growing problem of sulfates and widespread acid rainfall. Use of low-sulfur Western coal would avoid many of these problems, but this coal is obtained by strip mining. Strip-mining reclamation is possible, but substantially hindered in large areas of the West by lack of rainfall. Moreover, in some coal-rich areas the coal beds form the underground aquifer and their removal could wreck adjacent farming or ranching economies. Large coal-burning plants might be located in remote areas far from highly populated urban centers in order to minimize the human effects of pollution. But such areas are among the few left that are unspoiled by pollution and both environmentalists and the residents (relatively few in number compared with those in metropolitan localities but large among the voting population in the particular states) strongly object to this policy. Fears, realistic or imaginary, about safety and about accumulation of radioactive waste have increasingly hampered the nuclear option.

How can the nation best manage these tradeoffs?

Among recent Presidents, only Bill Clinton regularly and actively intervened in rulemaking. His actions provided a model for aggressive presidential molding of federal rules — and have sparked sharp controversy about the appropriateness, and the legality, of his actions. Justice Elena Kagan, who was part of the White House staff that supported Clinton's efforts, explains and defends the program in *Presidential Administration*, 114 HARV. L. REV. 2245 (2001). She summarizes a prominent example of Clinton's activity, id. at 2282–83:

> On August 10, 1995, President Clinton began a press conference by announcing publication of a proposed rule to reduce youth smoking. He explained his action as follows:
>
>> Today I am announcing broad executive action to protect the young people of the United States from the awful dangers of tobacco. . . . Today and every day this year, 3,000 young people will begin to smoke. One thousand of them ultimately will die of . . . diseases caused by smoking. . . . Therefore, by executive authority, I will restrict sharply the advertising, promotion, distribution, and marketing of cigarettes to teenagers. I do this on the basis of the best available scientific evidence. . . . Fourteen months of study by the Food and Drug Administration confirms what we all know: Cigarettes and smokeless tobacco are harmful, highly addictive, and aggressively marketed to our young people. . . . So today I am authorizing the Food and Drug Administration to initiate a broad series of steps all designed to stop sales and marketing of cigarettes and smokeless tobacco to children.
>
> With that, Clinton laid out the six principal measures proposed in the rule to limit the marketing and advertising of tobacco to children, and noted that Congress could make the rule unnecessary by passing legislation containing these restrictions. The announcement by the President effectively opened the public comment period (here, lasting ninety days) that the APA requires for regulations. Following the comment period, the Food and Drug Administration (FDA) (a component of an executive branch agency), with the participation of White House, OMB, and Justice Department staff, spent some nine months preparing the 921-page final rule and supporting annex. Although the final rule incorporated a number of changes, none went to the heart of the regulatory proposal (or to the President's public comments). The final documents, containing new proscriptions on tobacco manufacturers and vendors, a statement of the health-related justifications for those proscriptions, and a lengthy defense of FDA jurisdiction over the issue, nowhere mentioned the President; rules, as a historic matter, very rarely have done so, and this one was no exception. Nonetheless, Clinton stepped up again to announce the issuance of the rule, this time in a Rose Garden ceremony.

Overall, President Clinton issued 107 directives to agency heads concerning regulatory policy, compared to nine for President Reagan and four for President George H.W.

Bush, *id.* at 2294–95. These actions blurred traditional understandings of the boundaries between agency heads and the President, she acknowledges (*id.* at 2306):

> As these directives and announcements show, Clinton effectively placed himself in the position of a department head with respect to nearly every possible method of administrative policymaking. In rulemakings, he ordered and announced the issuance of proposed regulations for public comment, as well as the issuance of final regulations after the legally prescribed comment period had ended. If he never technically directed the issuance of a final regulation prior to a public comment period (though he certainly made this result more likely), he merely followed in this respect the legal strictures, imposed by the APA, applicable to any secretary. He additionally took full advantage of the opportunities the APA provided for more informal policymaking, by ordering and announcing, just as a department head might, final agency action through guidance, policy statements, and the like. And he involved himself in the development and implementation of enforcement policy, even (albeit rarely) as to decisions to prosecute identifiable parties like manufacturers of handguns or tobacco products. The only mode of administrative action from which Clinton shrank was adjudication. At no time in his tenure did he attempt publicly to exercise the powers that a department head possesses over an agency's on-the-record determinations.
>
> Clinton simultaneously used his central position in the governmental structure to direct administrative action transcending individual departments. Many of the matters in which he took a special interest, evident again in the spheres of health care and firearms regulation, involved multiple agency heads possessing partial or competing jurisdictions. Here, Clinton's actions demanded simple coordination or, perhaps still more often, joint adoption of new policy goals, as in his efforts to enhance protections for patients or increase the tracing of firearms.

Clinton avoided rulemaking on technical subjects, such as the one in *Sierra Club*, and rulemaking by the independent agencies. For staff, he relied on the small domestic policy units in the White House. His focus on administration rather than legislation reflected the world of divided government in which he found himself—it was difficult for him to achieve new legislation, and difficult for Congress to override his actions. Justice Jackson's twilight zone again?

For critiques of the Clinton program see Peter L. Strauss, *Presidential Rulemaking*, 72 Chi.-Kent L. Rev. 965 (1997); Cynthia R. Farina, *The Consent of the Governed: Against Simple Rules for a Complex World*, *id.* at 987, and *Undoing the New Deal Through the New Presidentialism*, 22 Harv. J.L. & Pub. Pol'y 227 (1998). Professors Strauss and Farina emphasize the careful set of controls that modern administrative law has evolved to control rulemaking. Agencies must examine the issues surrounding a proposed rule carefully and with full responsiveness to comments from affected interests; they must justify final rules on the basis of an elaborate administrative record and must articulate the statutory basis for their rules. (You can see these processes at work in *Sierra Club*.) Congressional committees and individual Members add their oversight, as does the OMB bureaucracy in the coordination process that we discuss below. And finally, the courts review final rules for their basis in fact, policy, and law. The concern shared by Strauss and Farina is that the President's "bully pulpit" gives him so much power that he can derange the careful balances and relationships of the administrative state, replacing them with what may be personal whims, half-baked policies, or the preferences of powerful supporters. Do you agree, or is this a good way to cut through the many entanglements that beset federal rulemaking?

Whether or not the Clinton program was a good idea, was it within a President's prerogatives? In other words, were the Clinton directives concerning rulemaking legal? Recall a question we have been asking in this Chapter: when Congress places authority in an executive agency rather than an independent one, does it contemplate — and authorize — Presidential supervision? This question suggests another: what *kind* of Presidential supervision does this placement allow? Justice (then, Professor) Kagan argues that the Opinions Clause surely supports at least "procedural" supervision, consisting of consultation and dialogue, *supra* at 2324. This much is not very controversial, and *Sierra Club* can be cited in its favor. For the more problematic substantive supervision, such as the youth smoking rule, she calls for a default rule of statutory construction that would allow the President to act unless Congress clearly forbids him to do so, for example by using an independent agency or by otherwise signaling its intent in the statute, *id.* at 2320. In other words, the President owns the twilight zone. Is that the right answer?

President George W. Bush issued some directives, albeit with less publicity than his predecessor employed. For example, he asked the Secretary of Health and Human Services to implement regulations on the privacy of medical records that had been inherited from the Clinton administration, but to recommend "appropriate modifications to the rule." Statement on Federal Regulations on Privacy of Medical Records, 37 Weekly Comp. Pres. Docs 611–12 (April 16, 2001). The resulting regulation is at 67 Fed. Reg. 53182-01 (Aug. 14, 2002). The agency complied without formally mentioning presidential participation in the change. Most controversial was his August, 2001 determination that federal funding should be available for embryonic stem-cell research, but only using embryonic stem cell lines that were already in existence at that time — a presidential command delivered through a press conference.

The Bush administration also employed a new tool that was implemented by OIRA, the "prompt letter." This was "a public request by OIRA, to a regulator, that a rulemaking be initiated or completed, that information relevant to a regulatory program be disclosed to the public, or that a piece of research or analysis relevant to rulemaking be conducted." John D. Graham, *Saving Lives Through Administrative Law and Economics*, 157 U. Pa. L. Rev. 395, 460 (2008). The letters were used in a variety of contexts, for example food labeling and workplace safety. They were a salutary way for the administration to communicate priorities to the regulators.

In the first weeks of his presidency, Barack Obama issued a series of policy instructions to federal regulatory agencies. Obama's brief memoranda to the agencies were carefully restrained. In each case, he "requested" an agency to pursue a particular rulemaking under its statutes, but in no case did he direct any outcome for the agency to reach. First, he asked the Environmental Protection Agency to reconsider a Bush administration denial of a requested waiver for California and other states that would have allowed state emission standards for new motor vehicles to be more stringent than federal standards. 74 Fed. Reg. 4905 (Jan. 28, 2009). He also asked the Secretary of Transportation to speed the promulgation of new automobile fuel economy standards. 74 Fed. Reg. 4907 (Jan. 28, 2009). And he requested the Secretary of Energy to issue new appliance energy efficiency standards. 74 Fed. Reg. 6537 (Feb. 9, 2009).

Specific directives, such as those by Presidents Clinton, Bush, and Obama, can overcome the ossification of rulemaking and galvanize agency action on particular topics. They are a way for Presidents to cut through the complex web of relationships with public and private entities that any agency inhabits and give it a direction to follow. For the complexities of these webs, see Edward L. Rubin, Beyond Camelot: Rethinking Politics and Law for the Modern State (2005). These directives are surely within presidential powers when they select priorities from the vast statutory menu and set a general policy direction. Within our government, the President is in the unique position of ensuring that a "mass of legislation" be executed. (The quotation is from *Youngstown Sheet & Tube Co. v. Sawyer*, 343 U.S. 579, 688 (1952) (Vinson, C.J., dissenting)). Setting priorities for the executive branch and spurring new initiatives are core presidential responsibilities.

There are, however, three legal risks to avoid. All of these risks have presented enduring problems for executive order programs that manage regulation generally, as we will see in the next section of this chapter. First, a particular directive can induce a violation of statutory limits. President Clinton's tobacco initiative had exactly that effect. The FDA had long taken the view that it had no jurisdiction over tobacco. Clinton impatiently overrode the FDA's caution, and the Supreme Court struck down the regulation on the jurisdictional ground. *FDA v. Brown & Williamson Tobacco Corp.*, 529 U.S. 120 (2000). Thus, in crafting their administration's legal policies, Presidents should respect the knowledge and experience that agency lawyers possess.

The second legal risk is the dictation of policies that are not supported by the administrative records to which the government's experts contribute. Any final administrative implementation of a statute requires careful analysis of issues of fact, policy, and law, to which both staff experts and political appointees in the agencies can contribute. Short-circuiting that process can produce ill-considered or even illegal decisions. Thus, dictating a particular agency action is fundamentally different from initiating a rulemaking process that will have a general direction but not a preordained outcome.

Third, there is the risk that, at some point, presidential command may seem to displace the statutory vesting of decisional authority in a different administrator. As the materials below reveal, the Justice Department approved what has now become the routine system for OMB oversight of agency rulemaking only on the understanding that White House review would not displace what is decreed by law to be "an agency's ultimate judgment."

There are also policy risks. First, unless the President is quite sparing about the number of these directives he issues to a particular agency, the chronically underfunded regulatory agencies may find themselves overwhelmed, unable to meet their normal statutory responsibilities. Second, every presidential action carries various White House communications in its wake. This follow-up activity can generate conflicting or incoherent commands to agencies. Over the years, various White House officers have intervened sporadically in important rulemakings to inject their views. Lisa Schultz Bressman & Michael P. Vandenbergh, *Inside the Administrative State: A Critical Look at the Practice of Presidential Control*, 105 MICH. L. REV. 47 (2006) (reviewing White House contacts with the Environmental Protection Agency by the George H.W. Bush and Clinton administrations). Therefore, a President who wishes to coordinate federal regulatory policy must first coordinate the activities of both his own staff and the heads of all the agencies. Finally, to the degree he is perceived to command agency performance, a President necessarily makes the resulting administrative policy decisions his own. Prior to the Clinton Administration, at least, it would frequently have been conventional political advice to a President not to leave his "fingerprints" too conspicuously on the day-to-day work of the regulatory bureaucracy.

d. Coordinating the Regulatory Process

Each President since Nixon has tried to achieve some systematic coordination of rulemaking by executive branch agencies, to make it more responsive to the President's policy concerns. From President Ford on, each initiative has taken the form of one or more executive orders. Before considering the orders, we provide some background. First, we outline efforts through the years to identify the causes of, and solutions to, the imperfections of government regulation. (The French are said to define regulation as "the substitution of error for chance.") Then we turn to competing arguments concerning the need for greater executive coordination of policy.

Various study commissions, most of them presidential, have analyzed the administrative "malaise" and have recommended cures. They reveal a surprising (and depressing) similarity of perceptions about the problems and necessary reforms. First came the "Brownlow Commission" in the New Deal, famous for its condemnation of independent agencies as a "headless 'fourth branch' of Government, a haphazard deposit of irresponsible agencies and uncoordinated powers." PRESIDENT'S COMM. ON ADMINISTRATIVE MANAGEMENT, REPORT 40 (1937). Shortly thereafter, THE FINAL REPORT OF THE ATTORNEY GENERAL'S COMMITTEE, S. Doc. No. 8, 77th Cong., 1st Sess. (1941), laid the basis for the federal APA. Alone among the study groups, it could claim landmark results.

In 1955, the Hoover Commission recommended the creation of an administrative court to hear and decide enforcement actions. Commission on the Organization of the Executive Branch of the Government, Legal Services and Procedure (1955).

Its views were repeated in part by the Ash Council in 1971. THE PRESIDENT'S ADVISORY COUNCIL ON EXECUTIVE ORGANIZATION, A NEW REGULATORY FRAMEWORK (1971). Thus observers have repeatedly called for a separation of adjudicative from policymaking functions in the agencies. WILLIAM CARY, POLITICS AND THE REGULATORY AGENCIES 125–34 (1967). Agency independence has been attacked as the villain by some and defended by others.

In 1960, James Landis, a former dean of the Harvard Law School, Chairman of the Civil Aeronautics Board, and member of the FTC, prepared a report for the new President examining alleged internal deficiencies of the agencies—delay, costs, personnel, ethics, policy coordination and formulation, and administrative organization. REPORT ON REGULATORY AGENCIES TO THE PRESIDENT-ELECT, reprinted in Sen. Comm. on the Judiciary, 86th Cong., 2d Sess. (Comm. Print 1960).

Almost twenty years later agencies were still being criticized for taking too much time, for adopting inconsistent or otherwise counterproductive requirements, for ignoring elementary requirements of fairness, and so forth. *See generally* SEN. COMM. ON GOVERNMENTAL AFFAIRS, STUDY ON FEDERAL REGULATION, 95th Cong., 1st Sess., vols. I–V (1977). Nevertheless, as we will see below, the Committee did not think that increased presidential management was the answer to regulation's problems.

The American Bar Association created a prestigious Commission on Law and the Economy, whose final report, FEDERAL REGULATION: ROADS TO REFORM (1979), contained a series of recommendations on improving federal regulation. The Commission favored stronger presidential management of the regulatory process to achieve policy coordination and to avoid unnecessary cost, duplication, and conflict. The Commission said (at 68):

> Our government has adopted a wide variety of national goals. Many of these goals—checking inflation, spurring economic growth, reducing unemployment, protecting our national security, assuring equal opportunity, increasing social security, cleaning up the environment, improving energy sufficiency—conflict with one another, and all of them compete for the same resources. One of the central tasks of modern democratic government is to make wise balancing choices among courses of action that pursue one or more of these conflicting and competing objectives.
>
> While Congress establishes the goals, it cannot legislate the details of every action taken in pursuit of each goal, or make the balancing choices that each such decision requires. It has therefore delegated this task to the regulatory agencies. But we have given each of the regulatory agencies one set of primary goals, with only limited responsibility for balancing a proposed action in pursuit of its own goals against adverse impacts on the pursuit of other goals. For most of these agencies, no effective mechanisms exist for coordinating the decisions of one agency with those of other agencies, or conforming them to the balancing judgments of elected generalists, such as the President and Congress. Appointed rather than elected, specialist rather

than generalist, regulatory agency officials enjoy an independence from the political process—and from one another—that weakens the national ability to make balancing choices, or to hold anyone politically accountable when choices are made badly or not at all.

To illustrate the problem, the Commission noted that, as of 1979, at least 16 federal agencies bore regulatory responsibilities that directly affected the price and supply of energy. This diffusion of policymaking authority persisted despite the earlier consolidation of several energy-oriented agencies into a Department of Energy. Similar multiplicity problems presented themselves with respect to antitrust, equal employment, industrial safety, and natural resources policymaking. From this, the Commission concluded (at 73):

> Congress cannot perform these [balancing] tasks by legislating the details of one regulation after another; that is why Congress delegated rulemaking power to the agencies in the first place, and gave them a wide degree of discretion as to the content of the rules to be issued. The President is the elected official most capable of making the needed balancing decisions as critical issues arise, while the most appropriate and effective role for Congress is to review and, where necessary, to curb unwise presidential intervention.

Accordingly, the Commission recommended passage of a statute authorizing the President to direct agencies to decide certain "critical" regulatory issues, and to order changes in their decisions. *See also* Lloyd N. Cutler & David R. Johnson, *Regulation and the Political Process*, 84 YALE L.J. 1395 (1975). Congress has not accepted the invitation; presidential coordination has proceeded, as before, by executive order.

For a congressional perspective, one markedly less receptive to presidential coordination, we utilize the Study on Federal Regulation, which has a thorough analysis that cites the classic literature on this subject.

Regulatory Organization

5 Study on Federal Regulation, Senate Comm. on Governmental Affairs,
95th Cong., 1st Sess. 6–7, 67–81 (1977)

... Freedom from executive domination was ... the prime motivating force for the creation by Congress of the independent regulatory commissions. More than anything else, they were intended to be independent of the White House. That mainspring, expressed often in terms of the "arm of Congress" idea, also emphasized the special relationship of the commissions to Congress. ... As a general proposition, Presidents have respected the independent status of the commissions. There is an expectation that, in discharging their adjudicatory functions in particular, those agencies should be free of interference or direction from the White House. ... In this area, appearance is as important as reality; and the President must be and appear to be at an arm's length distance from these quasi-judicial commissions. ...

For years the commission form has been bombarded with . . . criticisms. . . . [M]uch of the coordination that presently exists can be traced to the Roosevelt area: executive control of budgets and legislative recommendations, supervision of information gathering plans, and the power to reorganize these bodies in whole or part all first occurred during his presidency. . . . In the 1950s Marver Bernstein viewed efficient coordination of policy in an independent setting as improbable [Regulating Business by Independent Commission, 144 (1955)]:

> In an age which throws upon the President an unmanageable burden of political leadership and administrative management, the survival of islands of administrative independence, however qualified, only serves to increase the difficulties of integration.

On the eve of the Kennedy Administration, James Landis in less stringent terms raised the same question of accountability and coordination in his report to the President-elect. And as recently as 1970, the Ash Council reported to President Nixon that multi-member commissions precluded effective regulatory action [President's Advisory Council on Executive Organization, A New Regulatory Framework, Report on Selected Independent Regulatory Agencies, 40 (1971)]:

> The overseeing of economic regulation by responsible public officials, necessary to assure effective discharge of agency responsibilities, cannot exist if the decisionmakers are immune from public concerns as expressed through their elected representatives . . . commissioners [have] a degree of independence that may serve to protect them from improper influence but was not intended to allow them to become unresponsive.

What is needed, according to a leading member of the bar, is "*continuous* political monitoring of all government regulation to ensure its responsiveness to the changing economic and social needs that the political process reflects." [Lloyd N. Cutler & David R. Johnson, *Regulation and the Political Process*, 84 Yale L.J. 1395, 1397 (1975).] Independence of course precludes that monitoring by the Executive Branch.

Independence, it has also been argued, weakens the agencies, by removing them from the benefits of Presidential support and making them more vulnerable to domination by the regulated industries. Marver Bernstein viewed the private sector as the major beneficiary of the independent form:

> . . . Maintenance of the myth of commission independence represents a conscious effort by regulated groups to confine regulatory authority to an agency that is somewhat more susceptible than an executive department to influence, persuasion, and, eventually, capture and control.

Originally independence from partisan control was considered to be a guarantee of strong regulatory policy; has the reverse occurred? . . .

According to opponents of independence, there are other negative impacts of isolation from the President: the more these agencies are removed from the budget process, the less Administration support they receive on this important matter. The result may be commissions that are budgetarily weak; which again works to the advantage of those private interests that have no enthusiasm for vigorous regulatory activities. [See Roger Noll, Reforming Regulation: An Evaluation of Ash Council Proposals, pp. 6–7 (1972).] In short the theory goes that independence from the President means that the agencies lack a champion—a void that, at no small cost, is filled by the regulated industries . . . .

The foregoing arguments against the independent form are, at first blush, considerable. But does a far too close association with the regulated industries, or a lack of systematic Congressional oversight, necessarily suggest abandonment of the independent form? We think not. The private sector carefully monitors the work of these commissions, very simply because it has so much at stake. Would not the same resources and energy be expended, regardless of where these agencies were located? And what is there—in fact, not supposition—to suggest that executive departments or agencies are any less independent from the sustained efforts of those interests? We wonder whether, in that regard, there are any significant differences between an independent commission and a Presidential regulatory agency. . . .

Congress can be faulted for its lack of interest in these quasi-legislative agencies. But the executive branch has also failed to effectively utilize the powers it has to properly influence these commissions. . . . In the scheme of things, it is understandable that the President and his top advisors have more pressing concerns to occupy their time. As Judge Friendly has pointed out [The Federal Administrative Agencies: The Need for Better Definition of Standards 154 (1962)]:

> The spectacle of a chief executive, burdened to the limit of endurance with decisions on which the very existence of mankind may depend, personally taking on the added task of determining to what extent newspapers should be allowed to own television stations or whether railroads should be allowed to reduce rates only to or somewhat below the truck level, is pure mirage.

In point of fact, Presidential concern over such matters, when it exists at all, is delegated to often middle-level White House assistants. And the relatively hum-drum issues that mark day-to-day regulation rarely capture the attention of top advisors to the President. In addition to the press of other business, it is also probably true that there is very little political gain for Presidents from properly-functioning regulatory agencies. . . . Therefore it is something short of accurate to characterize independence as a barrier to a continuing Presidential interest in the commissions.

Much of what there is has not been competently used by either legislative or executive branch to coordinate the independent agencies. There is truth in Professor Cary's assertion that the independent commissions are really "stepchildren whose custody is contested by both the Congress and the Executive, but without very much affection from either one." The dispute over structure, over where these agencies fit in the federal scheme, is really a diversion from a much more difficult issue; . . . the real problem is the development of coherent national policies on regulation itself. In that quandary, neither legislative nor executive branches have shown much sustained interest.

At present the greatest degree of systematic attention the agencies receive from Congress and the President occurs in the budget process. The budget is the single oversight mechanism the agencies can expect on a regular basis from either Congress or the White House. The Office of Management and Budget does deliberately and carefully review agency funding requests, and the same is true of the appropriation committees of Congress. . . . OMB and Congressional review is expected to remain as searching as it is at present.

In addition there is nothing, to our knowledge, which prevents the President from taking a greater interest either in the independent commission or broad regulatory policy. As President Kennedy, in his regulatory message to Congress in 1961, asserted an affirmative duty to oversee the proper functioning of federal agencies, whether independent or otherwise ["Regulatory Agencies—Message from the President of the United States", *Congressional Record*, April 13, 1961, p. 5357]:

> . . . The President's responsibilities require him to know and evaluate how efficiently these agencies dispatch their business, including any lack of prompt decision of the thousands of cases they are called upon to decide, any failure to evolve policy in areas where they have been charged by the Congress to do so, or any other difficulties that militate against the performance of their statutory duties . . . .

In point of fact the argument against independence, as a Hoover Commission task force observed in 1949, frequently is "based mainly on theoretical or doctrinal grounds and not on actual failures of coordination or conflicts among agencies." Coordination is not of course a commandment, and instead is required only when it is justified. Coordination is necessary only to the extent that there are direct unresolved conflicts between, or unnecessary duplication of, agency functions. To a substantial extent, independent commissions exercise functions that are not closely related to the rest of government, and that require no extensive coordination. For example the regulation of security exchanges and issuance of new securities can be carried on by the Securities and Exchange Commission without active coordination by any other Federal department or agency. The same is true of other independent commissions . . . .

Are these commissions in fact unaccountable, a kind of "miniature independent government" adrift without guidance or purpose? Our examination suggests that is not the case. As previously discussed, there are a series of formal limitations upon the independent status of the commissions: Congress charts their regulatory mandate in the statutes; OMB and the President examine and typically revise their budgets, which in turn are subject to adoption by Congress; OMB also reviews their recommendation concerning legislative action; [OMB] screens their information-gathering plans; the Justice Department coordinates, even conducts, their litigation; and the President with the advice and consent of the Senate appoints their commissioners. Indeed, unlike almost all top-level Executive Branch officials, agency chairmen are appointed solely by the President without Senate concurrence, and may be removed from that office for any reason by the White House. Thus the top official of the independent commissions is very much accountable to the President. As such, how much accuracy is there in the assertion that these agencies constitute a "headless 'fourth branch'"? . . .

Independence does have its positive advantages . . . .

Presidential commissions would necessarily mean that the policies of those bodies would change with the occupant of the White House; regulation, affecting as it does major aspects of the economy, ought not be subject to such abrupt changes. The multiple membership of these agencies, with terms expiring at staggered intervals, does tend to serve as a buffer against Presidential control and direction. Finally the notion of government officials gaining expertise as a result of comparatively lengthy terms is not without validity. The turnover for commissions . . . is considerably less frequent than that of executive officials serving at the pleasure of the President. Experience gained from that longer service undoubtedly serves the public interest. . . .

What are the appropriate circumstances for the creation of an independent regulatory commission? It is a question that admits of no definite answer outside the context of a given situation. Even strictly regulatory tasks involving quasi-judicial functions need not necessarily be vested in an independent collegial structure. The Agriculture Department as well as other executive agencies, such as the EPA, are proof of that proposition. In no small part it depends on who is creating the structure: Presidents have generally tended toward a single administrator form, while Congress has an inclination favoring multimember commissions; but neither branch has consistently favored one structure over the other. A decision on structure is after all a political issue, very much influenced by the prevailing political situation. And that situation can neither be quantified nor predicted.

Yet, there are general guidelines drawn from past experience which do merit consideration in such structural decisions. Chief among them is the relative importance to be attached to group decision-making. A commission form obviously requires a majority vote for adoption of policy. Necessarily one commissioner must convince his fellow members of the desirability of a course of action — a process that usually and properly involves compromise and accommodation of varying viewpoints and opinions. On the other hand, a single administrator does not need the approval, as such, of other members of his agency in order to act. . . . In certain situations group deliberation in a nonpartisan setting requires a commission form. One obvious example is federal supervision of communications. There it is generally agreed that the commission form is appropriate. [T]he Ash Council . . . concluded:

> A single administrator for the Federal Communications Commission would be in an exceptionally vulnerable position which, because of its appearances, could impair public trust. The public is entitled to assume that the information it obtains through the broadcast media is not distorted by the political perspectives of the party in favor.

Other responsibilities suggest the appropriateness of the commission form. For example the power to award long-term licenses among competing applicants, or to set rates and prices for commodities is often thought to require a collegial body; group decision-making is considered appropriate for that authority. The rate-fixing consideration was of pivotal importance in the recent decision by Congress to establish the new Federal Energy Regulatory Commission. As this Committee's report on that measure stated, "No single official should have sole responsibility for both proposing and setting such prices" for oil and natural gas. . . .

In summary the Committee believes that the independent status of the regulatory commissions should be continued. However, the situation concerning the characteristics of independence is, at present, confusing. In a patchwork, even haphazard fashion, certain independent regulatory commissions have been excepted, sometimes for only specific purposes, from certain requirements of central coordination. . . .

We believe the situation warrants a single piece of legislation. To as great an extent as possible, that legislation should apply at least to the [sixteen] independent regulatory commissions [Board of Governors of the Federal Reserve System; Commodity Futures Trading Commission; Consumer Product Safety Commission; Federal Communications Commission; Federal Deposit Insurance Corporation; Federal Energy Regulatory Commission; Federal Housing Finance Board; Federal Maritime Commission; Federal Trade Commission; Interstate Commerce Commission; Mine Enforcement Safety and Health Review Commission; National Labor Relations Board; Nuclear Regulatory Commission; Occupational safety and Health Review Commission; Postal Rate Commission; and the Securities and Exchange Commission]. . . . The major components of that proposal would include:

(1) The selection by the independent regulatory commissions of individuals for positions classed as . . . Noncareer Executive Assignments would not be subject to clearance or approval by any executive branch official. . . .

(2) Independent regulatory commissions located outside executive departments should concurrently transmit to Congress any budget request, testimony or comments, intended for the legislative branch, at the same time they are submitted to an official or agency of the executive department.

(3) Legislative messages originating with independent regulatory commissions and intended for submission to Congress should be exempted from prior clearance by any official or agency of the executive branch.

(4) The independent regulatory commissions should be authorized to sue and be sued, in their own name and by their own attorneys, in any civil actions brought in connection with their jurisdiction and functions. That authority should apply to all civil cases, other than those before the Supreme Court.

———————

1. *The Virtues of Independence.* Who has the better of the argument, the proponents of consolidation or those of independence? Or is each right some of the time?

2. *How Independent Are They?* The Study remarks that it is difficult to tell how much more independent of the President these agencies are than are some executive

agencies. For a variety of views on that issue, some of them skeptical of sharp differences, see Symposium: *The Independence of Independent Agencies*, 1988 Duke L.J. 215 (1988). *See also* Glen O. Robinson, *On Reorganizing the Independent Regulatory Agencies*, 57 Va. L. Rev. 947 (1971). For another valuable study of the federal independent agencies, see Marshall J. Breger & Gary J. Edles, Independent Agencies in the United States: Law, Structure, and Politics (2015).

3. *A Plural Executive?* Do the Senate Committee's justifications for independence rise to *constitutional* distinctions? Put another way, what is the *minimum* residuum of executive control required by the Constitution? Appointment only? In *Morrison v. Olson, supra*, the Supreme Court declared that restrictions on removal of officers are valid unless they "impede the President's ability to perform his constitutional duty." Are any of the traditional independent agencies vulnerable under this test? Professor Shane has argued that the President's Faithful Execution responsibilities mandate that he be allowed to fire all principal officers for cause, but that Congress has the authority—whether or not a good idea—to preclude policy-based removals for agency heads whose only job is implementing administrative discretion delegated by Congress (and not conferred on the executive branch by Article II directly). Peter M. Shane, Madison's Nightmare, *supra*, at 33–34.

4. *Removal v. Supervision.* How do removal powers bear on issues of supervision? Does the President's "faithful execution" obligation encompass more than a duty to assure the sobriety and punctuality of federal officers? Is removal, in any event, a good management tool? Putting aside the imposition of policy, how should the President react when a commission puts out sloppily reasoned decisions after prolonged and unjustified delays? Should he remove some or all of the commissioners? Demote the chair? What if he considers the delays unjustified, but the results good, or vice versa?

Recent presidential efforts to impose some overall coordination on regulation began when the Reagan Administration adopted the first program with comprehensive central review of regulations. Later Presidents have retained the basic structure of the Reagan program, with adjustments reflecting their own approach to regulation. Peter M. Shane, in *Presidential Regulatory Oversight and the Separation of Powers: The Constitutionality of Executive Order No. 12,291*, 23 Ariz. L. Rev. 1235, 1235–42 (1981), outlines this management technique:

> Executive Order No. 12,291, "Federal Regulation," requires executive agencies, to the extent permitted by statute, to observe cost-benefit principles in implementing regulations. In order to assure agency compliance for regulations that have a significant effect on the economy, the order requires executive agencies also to evaluate proposed "major rules" according to a prescribed "regulatory impact analysis." . . . [W]ith the Reagan order, the President has finally both articulated a set of overarching policy principles to guide the regulatory process and explicitly required his subordinates to be bound by those principles to the extent permitted by law. The order is not a break with the past in that, through it, the President attempts to assert

significant control over administrative rulemaking. Rather, the key innovations of Executive Order No. 12,291 are the mandatory character of the requirements it imposes and the comprehensive management system that the order creates to effect the President's goals. . . . The most notable of the new provisions are the requirements in section 3 of the order for agencies to issue preliminary and final Regulatory Impact Analyses (RIA's) in connection with "major rules." An RIA must include statements of the anticipated costs and benefits of the proposed major rule, the anticipated incidence of those costs and benefits, the net anticipated benefits of the regulation, and other potentially more cost-effective regulatory possibilities, with an explanation, if appropriate, of the legal reasons why the most cost-effective means of achieving the anticipated benefits cannot be adopted. The cost-benefit analysis mandated by the order expressly requires the inclusion of beneficial or adverse regulatory effects that cannot be quantified in monetary terms. . . .

A second category of requirements, appearing in section 2 of the order, is most clearly substantive in nature. [S]ection 2 requires agencies, to the extent permitted by law, to "adhere" to five general principles "[i]n promulgating new regulations, reviewing existing regulations, and developing legislative proposals concerning regulation." These principles require agencies to base administrative decisions on "adequate information concerning the need for and consequences of proposed government action" and to set regulatory objectives, order regulatory priorities, and undertake regulatory action in a way that will maximize the net benefits to society when costs and benefits are compared. These provisions, as drafted, do not dictate particular regulatory decisions. Even in a particular context, they may do no more than set a range of permissible options, rather than pointing to a necessary result. The terms "cost" and "benefit" are not defined by the order, and the mandatory inclusion of even unquantifiable costs and benefits in the required calculus can afford agencies significant leeway in exercising their own policy judgment in identifying the beneficial or adverse effects of regulation.

The section 2 principles are, however, expressly intended to require agencies to weigh competing values in a particular direction and to be prepared to justify regulatory decisions according to a generally prescribed form of analysis. In this sense, section 2 is not neutrally "procedural." Its requirements would obviously be of no effect if agencies did not treat them as foreclosing at least some regulatory possibilities. . . .

[A]n agency must transmit each proposed major rule, together with a preliminary RIA, to the Director of OMB sixty days prior to the publication of any notice of proposed rulemaking. The Director then has sixty days to review such a submission, and may require the agency to consult with him concerning the preliminary RIA and notice of proposed rulemaking, and to refrain, subject to judicial or statutory deadlines, from publishing its proposal until the Director's review is concluded. . . . The prospects of protracted high-level "jawboning" and delay in the regulatory process may be effective sanctions to procure agency compliance with OMB regulatory policy. The potential exists, in particular cases, for the Director to abuse his discretion and overstep his legal authority despite the order's general provision that the Director's review powers shall not "be construed as displacing the agencies' responsibilities delegated by law."

See also Cass R. Sunstein, *Cost-Benefit Analysis and the Separation of Powers*, 23 Ariz. L. Rev. 1267 (1981).

Before the executive order was issued, the Assistant Attorney General for the Office of Legal Counsel issued the following opinion, concluding that the proposed order was legal on its face, and could be applied to the independent agencies if the President chose to do so (which he did not):

Memorandum for Honorable David Stockman, Director, Office of Management and Budget

Re: Proposed Executive Order on Federal Regulation

I. Legal Authority: Executive Branch Agencies

The President's authority to issue the proposed Executive Order derives from his constitutional power to "take Care that the Laws be faithfully executed." U.S. Const., Art. II. § 3. It is well established that this provision authorizes the President, as head of the Executive Branch, to "supervise and guide" Executive officers in "their construction of the statutes under which they act in order to secure that unitary and uniform execution of the laws which Article II of the Constitution evidently contemplated in vesting general executive power in the President alone." *Myers v. United States*, 272 U.S. 52, 135 (1926).

The supervisory authority recognized by *Myers* is based on the distinctive constitutional role of the President. The "take Care" clause charges the President with the function of coordinating the execution of many statutes simultaneously: "Unlike an administrative commission confined to the enforcement of the statute under which it was created . . . the President is a constitutional officer charged with taking care that a 'mass of legislation' be executed," *Youngstown Sheet & Tube Co. v. Sawyer*, 343 U.S. 579, 702 (1952) (Vinson, C.J., dissenting). Moreover, because the President is the only elected official who has a national constituency, he is uniquely situated to design and execute a uniform method for undertaking regulatory initiatives that responds to the will of the public as a whole. In fulfillment of the President's constitutional responsibilities, the proposed Order promotes a coordinated system of regulation, ensuring a measure of uniformity in the interpretation and execution of a number of diverse statutes. If no such guidance were permitted, confusion and inconsistency could result as agencies interpreted open-ended statutes in differing ways.

Nevertheless, it is clear that the President's exercise of supervisory powers must conform to legislation enacted by Congress. In issuing directives to govern the Executive Branch, the President may not, as a general proposition, require or permit agencies to transgress boundaries set by Congress. *Youngstown Sheet & Tube Co. v. Sawyer*, 343 U.S. 579 (1952). It is with these basic precepts in mind that the proposed Order must be approached.

We believe that an inquiry into congressional intent in enacting statutes delegating rulemaking authority will usually support the legality of presidential supervision of rulemaking by Executive Branch agencies. When Congress delegates legislative power to Executive Branch agencies, it is aware that those agencies perform their functions subject to presidential supervision on matters of both substance and procedure. This is not to say that Congress never intends in a specific case to restrict presidential supervision of an Executive agency; but it should not be presumed to have done so whenever it delegates rulemaking power directly to a subordinate Executive Branch official rather than the President. Indeed, after *Myers* it is unclear to what extent Congress may insulate Executive Branch agencies from presidential supervision. Congress is also aware of the comparative insulation given to the independent regulatory agencies, and it has delegated rulemaking authority to such agencies when it has sought to minimize presidential interference. By contrast, the heads of non-independent agencies hold their positions at the pleasure of the President, who may remove them from office for any reason. It would be anomalous to attribute to Congress an intention to immunize from presidential supervision those who are, by force of Art. II, subject to removal when their performance in exercising their statutory duties displeases the President. . . . This Office has often taken the position that the President may consult with those having statutory decisionmaking responsibilities, and may require them to consider statutorily relevant matters that he deems appropriate, as long as the President does not divest the officer of ultimate statutory authority. Of course, the President has the authority to inform an appointee that he will be discharged if he fails to base his decisions on policies the President seeks to implement. . . .

We believe that the President would not exceed any limitations on his authority by authorizing the . . . Director to supervise agency rulemaking as the Order would provide. The Order does not empower the Director . . . to displace the relevant agencies in discharging their statutory functions or in assessing and weighing the costs and benefits of proposed actions. The function of the Director would be supervisory in nature. It would include such tasks as the supplementation of factual data, the development and implementation of uniform systems of methodology, the identification of incorrect statements of fact, and the placement in the administrative record of a statement disapproving agency conclusions that do not appear to conform to the principles expressed in the President's Order. Procedurally, the Director . . . would be authorized to require an agency to defer rulemaking while it responded to . . . statements of disapproval of proposed agency action. This power of consultation would not, however, include authority to reject an agency's ultimate judgment, delegated to it by law, that potential benefits outweigh costs, that priorities under the statute compel a particular course of action, or that adequate information is available to justify regulation. . . .

II. Independent Regulatory Commissions

We now consider whether the proposed Order may legally be applied to the independent regulatory commissions in certain respects. Principally, the Order would require independent agencies to prepare RIA's and would authorize the Director or the Task Force to exercise limited supervision over the RIA's. For reasons stated below, we believe that, under the best view of the law, these and some other requirements of the Order can be imposed on the independent agencies. We would emphasize, however, that an attempt to exercise supervision of these agencies through techniques such as those in the proposed Order would be lawful only if the Supreme Court is prepared to repudiate certain expansive dicta in the leading case on the subject, and that an attempt to infringe the autonomy of the independent agencies is very likely to produce a confrontation with Congress, which has historically been jealous of its prerogatives with regard to them. . . .

The holding of *Humphrey's Executor* is that Congress may constitutionally require cause for the removal of an FTC Commissioner; the Court's opinion, however, contains broad dicta endorsing a perceived congressional purpose to insulate the FTC almost entirely from Presidential supervision. . . . If the dicta of *Humphrey's Executor* are taken at face value, the President's constitutional power to supervise the independent agencies is limited to his power of appointment, and none of the proposed Order's requirements may legally be applied to the independent agencies. We believe, however, that there are several reasons to conclude that the Supreme Court would today retreat from these dicta. First, the Court in *Humphrey's Executor* and *Wiener* focused primarily on the inappropriateness of Presidential interference in agency adjudication, a concern not pertinent to supervision of rulemaking. Second, insofar as the Court was concerned about rulemaking, it did not take account of the fact that Executive Branch and independent agencies engage in rulemaking in a functionally indistinguishable fashion. Third, the Court espoused what is now an outmoded view about the "apolitical" nature of regulation. It is now recognized that rulemaking may legitimately reflect political influences of certain kinds from a number of sources, including Congress and the affected public. Fourth, the President has today a number of statutory powers over the independent agencies, which recognize the legitimacy of his influence in their activities. . . .

We believe that the foregoing constitutional and statutory analysis supports the application to the independent agencies of those portions of the Order that would be extended to them. The principal requirement is that independent agencies prepare RIA's. These analyses would have only an indirect effect on substantive discretion, since the identification of costs and benefits and the particular balance struck would be for the agency to make. It should also be possible for OMB to prescribe criteria for independent agencies to follow in preparing their RIA's, to consult with them in the process, and to disagree with an independent agency's analysis on the administrative record. None of these actions would directly displace the agencies' ultimate discretion to decide what rule best fulfills their statutory responsibilities. . . .

1. *Constitutionality.* Is Executive Order No. 12,291 lawful on its face? What constitutional support exists for the reportorial requirements of Sections 4 and 5 of the order? For the substantive provisions of Section 2? In analyzing the order under *Youngstown*, what weight should be given to Congress' statutory decisions to vest regulatory authority under various programs in officers other than the President? Of what relevance is it that the APA does not provide for any centralized presidential review of executive agency rulemaking? On these questions, *see* Shane, *supra*, at 1255–62. What is the relevance of continuing appropriations for the administering office of OMB, the OIRA?

For analyses of the legal issues surrounding the executive order, see Symposium, *Cost-Benefit Analysis and Agency Decision-Making: An Analysis of Executive Order No. 12,291*, 23 Ariz. L. Rev. 1195 (1981). The debate was extensive: *compare* Alan B. Morrison, *OMB Interference with Agency Rulemaking: The Wrong Way to Write a Regulation*, 99 Harv. L. Rev. 1059 (1986), *with* Christopher C. DeMuth & Douglas H. Ginsburg, *White House Review of Agency Rulemaking, id.* at 1075.

2. *Accountability.* Note that the order was most potent in application to programs operating under broad delegations. For an argument favoring broad statutory delegations precisely because they facilitate political accountability to the President, see Jerry L. Mashaw, *Prodelegation: Why Administrators Should Make Political Decisions*, 1 Yale J. of Law, Econ. & Org. 81 (1985).

3. *Independent Agencies.* Could the order have been applied to independent agencies? (The definition of "agency" in § 1(d) of the final version of the order excluded what are commonly considered the independent regulatory commissions from its purview.) Was President Reagan too timid? What advice would you have given the President on whether he *should* have applied the order to the independent agencies, assuming that he had the power to do so?

4. *Ex Parte Contacts.* The implementation of the order involved considerable intra-branch ex parte contacts. To what extent are these legally problematic after *Sierra Club v. Costle*? What advice would you give OMB regarding ex parte contacts with agencies before, during, and after the comment period in informal rulemaking? *See* Paul R. Verkuil, *Jawboning Administrative Agencies: Ex Parte Contacts by the White House*, 80 Colum. L. Rev. 943 (1980). In *Portland Audubon Society v. Endangered Species Committee, supra*, the court considered whether the APA's statutory limits on ex parte contacts applied to the "God squad," a cabinet-level committee empowered to grant exemptions from the requisites of the Endangered Species Act. Because the statute required the committee's decisions to be made "on the record," the court held that the APA's ban on ex parte contacts applied.

5. *Judicial Review.* Section 9 of the order provided that it was "intended only to improve the internal management of the Federal government, and is not intended to create any right or benefit, substantive or procedural, enforceable at law. . . ." Review the *Note on Private Enforcement of Executive Orders* in Chapter Two. Should

the President be allowed to control whether his subordinates' compliance with his directions is judicially reviewable? What is the source of existing limitations on judicial review of compliance with executive orders—the Constitution, prudential concerns, or a reading of presidential intent? Assuming that no statute expressly authorized the order, could the President have authorized courts to invalidate rules found to be inconsistent with its requirements?

Note: Post-Reagan Presidential Regulatory Oversight

As it happens, the legality of Executive Order No. 12,291, which remained in effect through the George H.W. Bush Administration, was never tested in court. Its implementation, however, proved controversial. Professor Bruff published one of the earliest studies of OIRA in operation, identifying several problems in the administration of the executive order program. Harold H. Bruff, *Presidential Management of Agency Rulemaking*, 57 GEO. WASH. L. REV. 533, 552–61 (1989). First, although OMB review did not delay most rulemaking substantially, long delays attended review of some especially controversial rules. In some instances, the result was that statutory deadlines for issuing rules were exceeded. Second, policy-based pressure from OMB sometimes caused final rules to stray from fidelity to the governing statutes, especially in terms of whether the statutes allowed cost to be considered. Third, OMB pressure sometimes resulted in the selection of a final rule that was not among the alternatives supported by the administrative record. Based on Professor Bruff's report, the Administrative Conference of the United States (ACUS) recommended several improvements in the oversight process, including (1) additional guarantees that material relevant to the rulemaking process would become public in a timely manner and (2) the extension of the oversight program to independent agency rulemaking. 54 Fed. Reg. 5207 (1989), reprinted at 1 C.F.R. § 305.99-9 (1990).

Although independent agencies remain largely outside the OIRA program, Congress clearly shared the widely expressed concerns about delay and secrecy in regulatory oversight. Not surprisingly, many Democrats—including 1992 presidential candidate Bill Clinton—also disdained the conspicuously anti-regulatory rhetorical tilt embodied in Executive Order No. 12,291. Consequently, the Clinton Administration undertook a significant rewrite of the program. The result, Executive Order No. 12,866 appears in the Appendix.

The two orders employ strikingly similar strategies, although they also exhibit sometimes subtle, but often important, differences. For example, President Reagan's objectives, stated in the preamble to his executive order, suggested a wide-ranging critique of the existing regulatory process. President Clinton, by contrast, while reaffirming much of the Reagan language, made clear his belief that the regulatory system can "protect and improve . . . health, safety, the environment, and well-being [as well as] improve the performance of the economy. . . ." The Clinton preamble went on to underline the Administration's commitment not to compromise the decision-making primacy of line agencies, not to cloak the regulatory oversight process in secrecy, and not to allow the integrity of the regulatory review process to be jeopardized.

Leaving the hortatory language of the preambles, the Reagan executive order directed agencies to regulate only where regulatory benefits outweigh the costs and to choose regulatory means that minimize the net costs of any administrative initiative. The Clinton order kept that mandate, but added both nuance and additional values. For example, the Clinton order cautions against over-reliance on "hard variables," and articulates a number of regulatory benefits that are not easily monetizable. In addition, agencies are meant to consider a host of factors that are not directly related to the costliness of regulation, including innovation, consistency, predictability, flexibility, distributive impacts, and equity. This broader value structure is much less against the grain of the underlying values that were the predicate for much of the regulatory state whose actions OMB is to oversee.

In setting out regulatory review procedures, the Clinton order also made some important changes from the Reagan model. The Reagan order, for example, like the Clinton order, targeted OMB resources on significant regulations. But under the Reagan order, significance was measured entirely in monetary terms. By contrast, the Clinton order treated as significant not only those regulations of high monetary value, but any regulation that could "significantly hurt the environment, public health, or safety, or diminish the rights of individuals receiving government entitlements, grants, or loans."

Moreover, the Clinton order was sensitive to the delay critique of Reagan and George H.W. Bush regulatory review, that is, that it was interminable and resulted in "paralysis by analysis." The Clinton order included a tight time table within which the review process had to proceed. If the Office of Information and Regulatory Affairs (OIRA) at OMB failed to meet the deadlines, the executive order gave agencies the green light to proceed. Moreover, any analysis or objections raised by OIRA were required to be provided in writing and to set forth the pertinent provision of the executive order on which OMB was relying.

The Clinton order tried to make the regulatory review process more transparent. It contained disclosure provisions and protections against ex parte contacts by interested parties. The Clinton order thus sought to protect agencies' rulemaking processes from undisclosed pressures brought to bear through OMB rather than through the notice and comment proceeding at the agency. It also required disclosure of significant information while the review process is ongoing.

Finally, the Clinton order did apply to all agencies, including the independent agencies, a requirement to participate in an information-sharing initiative called the Unified Regulatory Agency: "Each agency shall prepare an agenda of all regulations under development or review, at a time and in a manner specified by the Administrator of OIRA."

Surprising to some, the George W. Bush Administration kept Executive Order No. 12,866 in place with only minor adjustments, some of which, in turn, were undone by the Obama Administration. For its part, the primary process change instituted by the Obama Administration appears to have been an increased emphasis on agencies' retrospective analysis of the effectiveness of their existing rules, plans for which must be shared with OIRA by all agencies, including the independents. § 4(b).

The Trump Administration took no early position on the future of Executive Order No. 12,866. The Administration's opening weeks, however, brought an ambitious executive order to complement the process that would dramatically intensify OMB's role in coordinating administrative rulemaking in two distinct ways. First, the order, entitled "Reducing Regulation and Controlling Regulatory Costs," Exec. Order No. 13,771, 82 Fed. Reg. 9339 (2017), purports to authorize OMB to impose a regulatory budget on administrative agencies. Under this system: "For fiscal year 2017, which is in progress, the heads of all agencies are directed that the total incremental cost of all new regulations, including repealed regulations, to be finalized this year shall be no greater than zero." § 2(b). In future years, the Director of OMB would determine for each agency, as part of the overall budget process, the net incremental cost that its regulatory initiatives could impose on the economy. § 3(d). (Benefits would not enter this calculation.)

Second, the order would impose what its advocates have called a "cut-go" system for rulemaking: "Unless prohibited by law, whenever an executive department or agency (agency) publicly proposes for notice and comment or otherwise promulgates a new regulation, it shall identify at least two existing regulations to be repealed." § 2(a). The order leaves it to OMB to issue clarifying guidance as to how cut-go is to be implemented.

Although, like 12,291 and 12,866, the Trump order requires its commands to be implemented only to the extent "permitted" or "not prohibited" by law, its requirements are plainly substantive, not just procedural or informational. It is thus striking that, at least as of the time of this writing, there is no federal statute that authorizes OMB to impose either cut-go or a regulatory budget. It is also not surprising that the order was immediately subjected to legal challenge. *Public Citizen v. Trump,* 1:17-cv-00253 (D.D.C. 2017). As Professor Shane has written: "Trump's order raises the puzzling question whether a presidential command, in effect, to ignore the law 'unless prohibited by law' is lawful." Peter M. Shane, *The GOP's Radical Assault on Regulations Has Already Begun,* WASH. MONTHLY (Feb. 27, 2017), http://washingtonmonthly .com/2017/02/27/the-gops-radical-assault-on-regulations-has-already-begun/. As it happens, the U.S. District Court for the Northern District of California has answered that question, "No," with regard to another early Trump order, Executive Order 13,768, 82 Fed. Reg. 8799 (2017), which directed the Attorney General and Secretary of Homeland Security to cut federal funding to so-called sanctuary jurisdictions — that is, jurisdictions declining to cooperate with federal immigration enforcement — "to the extent consistent with law." Because there appeared to be no statutory support for the directive, the District Court upheld the plaintiff jurisdiction's facial challenge to its validity. *County of Santa Clara v. Trump*, Case Nos. 17-cv-00574-WHO, 17-cv-00485-WHO (N.D. Cal., Apr. 25, 2017).

Of course, even if overturned, Executive Order No. 13,771 sent a powerful signal of the Administration's radically different view of regulation as compared to its predecessor. If asked as a government lawyer to approve the drafting of Executive Order No. 13,771, would you have felt comfortable signing off as to the order's legality?

2. Congressional Oversight

Some basic ground rules for congressional oversight of administration were set in *D.C. Federation of Civic Ass'ns v. Volpe*, 459 F.2d 1231 (D.C. Cir. 1971), *cert. denied*, 405 U.S. 1030 (1972). The court considered whether the Secretary of Transportation had acted properly in approving construction of a controversial bridge that was supported by an influential Congressman. Judge Bazelon's opinion said:

> [T]he controversy concerns a projected bridge between the Georgetown waterfront in the District of Columbia and Spout Run in Virginia. The bridge, which would be part of the Interstate Highway System and would be built largely with federal funds, would traverse the Three Sisters Islands . . . and would use some parkland. . . . The bridge was [finally approved] after Representative Natcher, Chairman of the Subcommittee on the District of Columbia of the House Appropriations Committee, indicated unmistakably that money for construction of the District's subway system would be withheld if the bridge plan were not revived. To satisfy the Chairman, . . . a decision by Transportation Secretary Volpe [was needed] that the project should go ahead. . . .
>
> [T]he Secretary's approval of the bridge must be predicated on compliance with a number of statutory provisions. Plaintiffs . . . maintain that the Secretary's determinations under the statute were tainted by his consideration of extraneous factors unrelated to the merits of the questions presented. They allege . . . that pressures exerted by Representative Natcher contributed to the decision to approve the bridge. . . . When funds for the subway were, in fact, blocked, Representative Natcher made his position perfectly clear, stating that "as soon as the freeway project gets under way beyond recall then we will come back to the House and recommend that construction funds for rapid transit be approved." The author of this opinion is convinced that the impact of this pressure is sufficient, standing alone, to invalidate the Secretary's action. . . . [R]eversal would be required, in my opinion, because extraneous pressure intruded into the calculus of considerations on which the Secretary's decision was based. Judge Fahy, on the other hand, has concluded that since critical determinations cannot stand irrespective of the allegations of pressure, he finds it unnecessary to decide the case on this independent ground. . . . The Secretary's testimony indicated . . . that "his decision was based on the merits of the project and not *solely* on the extraneous political pressures."

. . . Judge Fahy . . . has authorized me to note his concurrence in my discussion of the controlling principle of law: namely, that the decision would be invalid if based in whole or in part on the pressures emanating from Representative Natcher. Judge Fahy agrees, and we therefore hold, that on remand the Secretary must make new determinations based strictly on the merits and completely without regard to any considerations not made relevant by Congress in the applicable statutes. . . . If he had been acting in [a quasi-judicial] capacity, plaintiffs could have forcefully argued that the decision was invalid because of the decisionmaker's bias, or because he had received ex parte communications. Well-established principles could have been invoked to support these arguments, and plaintiffs might have prevailed even without showing that the pressure had actually influenced the Secretary's decision. With regard to judicial decisionmaking, whether by court or agency, the appearance of bias or pressure may be no less objectionable than the reality. But since the Secretary's action was not judicial, that rationale has no application here.

If, on the other hand, the Secretary's action had been purely legislative, we might have agreed with the District Court that his decision could stand in spite of a finding that he had considered extraneous pressures. Beginning with *Fletcher v. Peck*, [10 U.S. 87 (1810)] the Supreme Court has maintained that a statute cannot be invalidated merely because the legislature's action was motivated by impermissible considerations (except, perhaps, in special circumstances not applicable here [citing race discrimination cases]). . . .

. . . [T]he underlying problem cannot be illuminated by a simplistic effort to force the Secretary's action into a purely judicial or purely legislative mold. His decision was not "judicial" in that he was not required to base it solely on a formal record established at a public hearing. At the same time, it was not purely "legislative" since Congress had already established the boundaries within which his discretion could operate. But even though his action fell between these two conceptual extremes, it is still governed by principles that we had thought elementary and beyond dispute. If, in the course of reaching his decision, Secretary Volpe took into account "considerations that Congress could not have intended to make relevant," his action proceeded from an erroneous premise and his decision cannot stand. The error would be more flagrant, of course, if the Secretary had based his decision solely on the pressures generated by Representative Natcher. But it should be clear that his action would not be immunized merely because he also considered some relevant factors. . . . We hold only that the Secretary must reach his decision strictly on the merits and in the manner prescribed by statute, without reference to irrelevant or extraneous considerations. . . . Secretary Volpe . . . was placed, through the action of others, in an extremely treacherous position. Our holding is designed, if not to extricate him from that position, at least to enhance his ability to obey the statutory command notwithstanding the difficult position in which he was placed. . . . Accordingly, the District Court is directed to enjoin construction of the bridge until the defendants have complied with the applicable statutory provisions as set forth in our opinion.

Judge McKinnon, dissenting in part, argued that:

> if Judge Bazelon's individual view as to the position of Congress in this and other matters were to prevail, the result would come close to setting up legalistic standards which are practically impossible of compliance. Judge Bazelon's opinion would do that here by deciding . . . that because a member of the Cabinet had *knowledge* of the position of Congress on appropriations for subways and highways in the District of Columbia that his decision with respect to the merits of a highway project must necessarily have been improperly influenced by that information.
>
> Actually any member of the Cabinet worthy of his position would necessarily know the position of Congress on such matters. No person with the position and ability to make the decision with respect to the Three Sisters Bridge would be ignorant of the publicly expressed congressional position on such matters. What Judge Bazelon fails to consider is that there were congressional pressures both ways. . . . I do not find it unusual for a Cabinet member to be capable of resisting such pressures.

----

1. *The* Pillsbury *Doctrine.* In *Pillsbury Co. v. FTC*, 354 F.2d 952 (5th Cir. 1966), the court vacated and remanded an FTC decision after an antitrust subcommittee of the House of Representatives had held an oversight hearing while the Commission was considering whether to order Pillsbury to divest a corporate acquisition. At the hearing, the *Pillsbury* case was referred to repeatedly by Members of Congress, who urged the Commission to alter the interpretation of antitrust law it had tentatively adopted in that case. The court held that this was "an improper intrusion into the adjudicatory processes of the Commission" because "when such an investigation focuses directly and substantially upon the mental decisional processes of a Commission *in a case which is pending before it*, Congress is no longer intervening in the agency's legislative function, but rather, in its *judicial* function." The court was not swayed by the fact that the FTC never had adopted the policy position that the subcommittee urged upon it. After *Pillsbury*, congressional committees have learned to oversee general policy issues that are contained in agency adjudications by inquiring into the policies without mentioning the cases by name. Is this the right thing to do?

2. *Law v. Politics.* The majority in *D.C. Federation* emphasizes the constraints imposed by the pertinent statutes and the Secretary's duty under *Overton Park* to rest decision only on "relevant factors." Do you agree with the majority that this means that the administrator must ignore extraneous political pressure entirely in making an informal decision? Is that realistic? What if the administrator admits considering the congressional pressure but insists that the same decision would have been

602   4 · CONTROL OF ADMINISTRATION BY THE ELECTED BRANCHES

made without it? For an argument that an administrator should be allowed to consider any congressional policy pressure that is not forbidden by the governing statute, see Richard J. Pierce, Jr., *Political Control Versus Impermissible Bias In Agency Decisionmaking: Lessons from* Chevron *and* Mistretta, 57 U. Chi. L. Rev. 481 (1990).

All three judges appear to believe that if Congressman Natcher had simply urged approval of the bridge based on highway needs that were addressed by the statutes, nothing impermissible would have occurred. Indeed, is that sort of pressure affirmatively desirable, because it brings appointed bureaucrats into closer touch with elected officials—and indirectly, with the people?

3. *Congress v. Executive Branch.* Do your answers to any of the foregoing questions change if the pressure comes from someone in OMB? For a comparison of the two kinds of oversight, see Sidney A. Shapiro, *Political Oversight and the Deterioration of Regulatory Policy*, 46 Admin. L. Rev. 1 (1994).

4. *Irrelevant Factors v. Bias.* In *Koniag, Inc. v. Andrus*, 580 F.2d 601 (D.C. Cir. 1978), the Secretary of the Interior found certain native Alaskan villages ineligible to take land and revenues under the Alaska Native Claims Settlement Act. Two days before the Secretary determined that the villages were ineligible, Congressman Dingell sent him a letter asking him to postpone decision pending a review by the Comptroller General, on grounds that agency regulations had misinterpreted the statute and that some unspecified villages should not have been certified. Citing *D.C. Federation*, the court said that the letter "compromised the appearance of the Secretary's impartiality." Is that a correct citation? Does it matter that the Secretary did not accede to the Congressman's request?

DCP Farms v. Yeutter, 957 F.2d 1183 (5th Cir. 1992), involved a controversy that arose under federal crop subsidy programs. DCP Farms had used a series of family trusts to evade statutory limits of $50,000 per person and to qualify for $1.4 million in subsidies. After USDA decided to review DCP Farms' eligibility, its Office of Inspector General identified the case as an egregious violation of the statutory limit. Meetings between USDA officials and Congressional staff followed, in which DCP Farms was specifically discussed. The Chairman of the House subcommittee then wrote the Secretary of Agriculture, warning that if trusts were treated as persons, he would introduce legislation to override that interpretation, and arguing that DCP Farms' large subsidy "violates both the spirit and letter of the law." A response from USDA assured the Chairman that "the Department will take a very aggressive position in dealing with this case," but promised no particular outcome. USDA then sent DCP Farms letter rulings concluding that they had evaded payment limits and were ineligible to receive any payments for several years. Before resorting to an administrative hearing, DCP Farms sought to enjoin the participation of all officials of the national office from further participation. The court refused the injunction. It distinguished *Pillsbury* on grounds that the case at bar had yet to reach an adjudicatory stage when the congressional intervention occurred. An opposite conclusion, the court thought, would "erect no small barrier to Congressional oversight." Does *DCP Farms* or *Koniag* take the better approach to these issues?

5. *Controlling Constituent Casework.* Congress encountered ethical questions raised by the intervention of five senators with federal thrift regulators on behalf of savings and loan executive Charles Keating. Keating raised $1.3 million for the campaigns and causes of the five senators. In two meetings in 1987, the senators pressed regulators to refrain from enforcing a strict regulation against Keating's Lincoln Savings, which subsequently failed. For all but one of the senators, the Senate Ethics Committee later concluded that there was insufficient "linkage" between the contributions and the interventions to violate the Senate's rule against "improper conduct which may reflect upon the Senate." The Committee recommended consideration of more specific standards to guide and confine constituent service. *Investigation of Senator Alan Cranston*, Sen. Rep. No. 103-223, 102d Cong., 1st Sess (1991). What should these standards be? Would you require disclosure of constituent contacts? Should they be barred in some circumstances? How can we prevent "improper" conduct without destroying Congress' representative function? *See* Ronald M. Levin, *Congressional Ethics and Constituent Advocacy in an Age of Mistrust*, 95 Mich. L. Rev. 1 (1996).

In *Sierra Club v. Costle, supra*, after reviewing the legality of ex parte contacts between executive branch officials and EPA rulemakers, the court considered the effect of congressional oversight:

> Finally, EDF challenges the rulemaking on the basis of alleged Congressional pressure, citing principally two meetings with Senator Byrd. EDF asserts that under the controlling case law the political interference demonstrated in this case represents a separate and independent ground for invalidating this rulemaking. But among the cases EDF cites in support of its position, [*Pillsbury, Koniag*] only *D.C. Federation of Civic Associations v. Volpe* seems relevant to the facts here.... *D.C. Federation* ... requires that two conditions be met before an administrative rulemaking may be overturned simply on the grounds of Congressional pressure. First, the content of the pressure upon the Secretary is designed to force him to decide upon factors not made relevant by Congress in the applicable statute. Representative Natcher's threats were of precisely that character, since deciding to approve the bridge in order to free the "hostage" mass transit appropriation was not among the decision-making factors Congress had in mind when it enacted the highway approval provisions of Title 23 of the United States Code. Second, the Secretary's determination must be affected by those extraneous considerations.

> In the case before us, there is no persuasive evidence that either criterion is satisfied. Senator Byrd requested a meeting in order to express "strongly" his already well-known views that the ... standards' impact on coal reserves was a matter of concern to him. EPA initiated a second responsive meeting to report its reaction to the reserve data submitted by the NCA. In neither meeting is there any allegation that EPA made any commitments to Senator Byrd. The meetings did underscore Senator Byrd's deep concerns for EPA, but there

is no evidence he attempted actively to use "extraneous" pressures to further his position. Americans rightly expect their elected representatives to voice their grievances and preferences concerning the administration of our laws. We believe it entirely proper for Congressional representatives vigorously to represent the interests of their constituents before administrative agencies engaged in informal, general policy rulemaking, so long as individual Congressmen do not frustrate the intent of Congress as a whole as expressed in statute, nor undermine applicable rules of procedure. Where Congressmen keep their comments focused on the substance of the proposed rule—and we have no substantial evidence to cause us to believe Senator Byrd did not do so here—administrative agencies are expected to balance Congressional pressure with the pressures emanating from all other sources. To hold otherwise would deprive the agencies of legitimate sources of information and call into question the validity of nearly every controversial rulemaking. . . .

---

1. *Adjudication v. Rulemaking.* The Sierra Club court distinguished *Pillsbury* and *Koniag* on grounds that they did not involve rulemaking (657 F.2d 298 n.533). Is the distinction fully persuasive?

2. *Congressional v. Executive Oversight. Sierra Club* wound up treating congressional and executive oversight the same, in terms of the governing legal rules. Is that appropriate?

3. A Unitary or Plural Executive? The Special Status of the Independent Agencies Revisited

Now that we have seen the full range of relationships between the elected branches and the agencies, we can address two kinds of basic legal questions. First, what is the constitutional nature of the executive branch: is it unitary, and therefore subject to broad presidential supervision into which Congress may not intrude? Or is it plural, and therefore subject to broad congressional authority to dictate both the structure of the agencies and their relationships to the President? The second question, which may provide an answer to the first question or at least a method of applying one's answer to specific issues, is the choice between formal and functional analytic approaches to separation of powers issues. As we have seen, formal analysis tends to reinforce unitariness and to condemn innovative arrangements such as agency independence, whereas functional analysis tends to support fragmentary arrangements.

By now, you may be inclined to one of the following possible answers to the first question:

1. *The executive branch is unitary because that was the original intent of the framers.* Steven G. Calabresi & Saikrishna B. Prakash, *The President's Power to Execute the*

Laws, 104 YALE L.J. 541 (1994); Steven G. Calabresi & Kevin H. Rhodes, *The Structural Constitution: Unitary Executive, Plural Judiciary*, 105 HARV. L. REV. 1153 (1992).

2. *The executive branch is unitary because modern conditions demand it.* Professor Sunstein rejects a unitary executive as a matter of original intent, Cass R. Sunstein, *The Myth of the Unitary Executive*, 7 ADMIN. L.J. AM.U. 299 (1993). Nevertheless, the conception Americans hold of the presidency and its relation to administration has evolved substantially, as has the nation and its government. Perhaps this means that a modest original view of the constitutional role of the President should expand to meet modern needs. For just such an argument, see Lawrence Lessig & Cass R. Sunstein, *The President and the Administration*, 94 COLUM. L. REV. 1 (1994). *See also* Steven G. Calabresi, *Some Normative Arguments for the Unitary Executive*, 48 ARK. L. REV. 23 (1995).

3. *The executive branch is plural because that was the original intent of the framers.* Martin Flaherty, *The Most Dangerous Branch*, 105 YALE L.J. 1725 (1996); A. Michael Froomkin, *The Imperial Presidency's New Vestments*, 88 NW. U. L. REV. 1346 (1994).

4. *The executive branch is plural because modern conditions demand it.* Perhaps the increase in presidential lawmaking in modern America requires a hospitable interpretation of the checks to his power; *see* Abner S. Greene, *Checks and Balances in an Era of Presidential Lawmaking*, 61 U. CHI. L. REV. 123 (1994); Michael Fitts, *The Paradox of Power in the Modern State: Why A Unitary, Centralized Presidency May Not Exhibit Effective or Legitimate Leadership*, 144 U. PA. L. REV. 827 (1996); Robert V. Percival, *Presidential Management of the Administrative State: The Not-So-Unitary Executive*, 51 DUKE L.J. 963 (2001).

How do these premises translate into the formal/functional analytic choice? Here is a sampling of views. Professor Peter L. Strauss, in *Formal and Functional Approaches to Separation-of-Powers Questions — A Foolish Inconsistency?* 72 CORNELL L. REV. 488, 492–94, 519–21 (1987), summarizes his own functional approach, adopted in his fine earlier article, *The Place of Agencies in Government: Separation of Powers and the Fourth Branch*, 84 COLUM. L. REV. 573 (1984):

> The Constitution does not define the administrative, as distinct from the political, organs of the federal government; it leaves that *entirely* to Congress. What the Constitution describes instead are three generalist national institutions (Congress, President, and Supreme Court) which, together with the states, serve as the principal heads of political and legal authority. Each of these three generalist institutions serves as the ultimate authority for a distinctive governmental authority-type (legislative, executive, or judicial). Each may be thought of as having a paradigmatic relationship, characterized by that authority-type, with the working government that Congress creates.
>
> Although these heads of government serve distinct functions, employing distinctive procedures, . . . the same cannot be said of the administrative level of government. Virtually every part of the government Congress has

created—the Department of Agriculture as well as the Securities and Exchange Commission—exercises *all three* of the governmental functions the Constitution so carefully allocates among Congress, President, and Court. These agencies adopt rules having the shape and impact of statutes, mold governmental policy through enforcement decisions and other initiatives, and decide cases in ways that determine the rights of private parties. If in 1787 such a merger of function was unthinkable, in 1987 it is unavoidable given Congress's need to delegate at some level the making of policy for a complex and interdependent economy, and the equal incapacity (and undesirability) of the courts to resolve all matters appropriately characterized as involving "adjudication." A formal theory of separation of powers that says these functions cannot be joined is unworkable; that being so, a theory that locates each agency "in" one or another of the three conventional "branches" of American government, according to its activities, fares no better. . . .

Rather than describe agencies in terms of branches, in other words, the analysis suggested one could examine their relationships with each of the three named heads of government, to see whether those relationships undermine the intended distribution of authority *among those three*. . . . [T]his analysis of separation-of-powers issues proposes examining the quality of relationships between an agency and each of the three named heads of government. It is not necessary to insist that there be particular relationships between an agency and any of the named constitutional actors (beyond the few specified in the constitutional text) in order to require relationships of a certain overall character or quality. . . .

Harold H. Bruff, in *On the Constitutional Status of the Administrative Agencies*, 36 Am. U. L. Rev. 491, 493–94 (1987), begins by arguing that "the optimal level of specificity for constitutional rules that organize the government is low," because

[t]he government is vast and diverse; perforce, even statutes that have government-wide effect are cast in generalities. Moreover, predicting the effects of rules on institutions is hazardous, even in the short run. Also, the obstacles to altering constitutional rules are considerable, even when they are generated by the courts. Not only does constitutional ambiguity serve these needs for flexibility, it also aids the operation of government. Mutual uncertainties about the limits of power foster cooperation between the branches. Where there is clarity, the incentive to compromise disappears.

What about the special constitutional status of the independent agencies? Bruff concludes that there is no justification for granting independent agencies *constitutional* status different from executive agencies with respect to presidential oversight. The effect, Bruff argues, of treating all agencies as having equivalent constitutional status subordinate to the President is "to prevent Congress from denying the President a supervisory role that is appropriate to the function involved." This distinction between independent *agencies* and independent *functions* runs through the analysis of several commentators. *See, e.g.*, Professor Strauss' Columbia article, *supra*, in which he argues that limits on presidential policy-based removals of agency heads are constitutional if they do not disturb the overall parity of political influence on administration between Congress and the President. That is, under a rule of parity, both political branches may oversee a particular function if either may do so.

In *The Incompatibility Principle*, 59 ADMIN. L. REV. 225 (2007), Bruff defines a role for formalism:

> In its appointment and removal cases, the Court has strictly enforced the incompatibility principle that Congress and the executive must employ separate personnel. Although the Court has always invoked other provisions of the Constitution in explaining these rulings, prohibiting incompatibility has provided both a common thread and a link to a firm purpose of the framers. Congress may not control executive officers by assuming the President's power to nominate or remove them *(Buckley, Myers, Bowsher)*. Congress may, however, constrain presidential removal in ways compatible with his duty to ensure faithful execution of the law *(Humphrey's Executor, Morrison)*. The Court has been strict in drawing the line between legislative and executive functions. Congress may not participate in execution by overriding executive actions with nonstatutory processes *(Chadha, MWAA)*. Yet Congress is free to employ innovative structural arrangements that do not draw its Members into execution *(Mistretta)*. Thus the Court has largely contented itself with preventing our government from evolving into a parliamentary model at the instance of Congress.

> Overall, the constitutional law that governs separation of powers remains unconfining. Many of the largest issues remain unresolved. For example, what is the set of executive functions that Congress may shield from plenary presidential supervision? For purposes of maintaining a system of separated powers, it is enough to know that the President retains his constitutional claim to exert enough supervision to ensure that he can perform his constitutional duties *(Morrison)*. What this may mean in a particular context awaits assessment in the light of the facts of a particular controversy.

> If Congress had been allowed to blur the line between the branches, the Madisonian competition of loyalties and values would have weakened or evaporated as well. An "executive" officer who had been appointed by Congress, was removable by Congress, and whose decisions were subject to legislative veto would be unlikely to display significant loyalty to the executive or meaningful resistance to informal congressional pressure. Perhaps there would have evolved the kind of legislative dominance that marked the revolutionary state governments. Even if that had not happened, our system could be fundamentally different from its present form.

> In short, good fences make good neighbors. If the Court reserves its formalist rigor for situations that fit the incompatibility principle, it will have done almost enough by way of constitutional definition of the essential

separations of power. The possibility of aggrandizement beyond these situations remains, however. The Court can remain alert to such dangers, reviewing statutes with appropriate deference, as it so often does today.

Is this a good way to understand and predict the caselaw?

Adherents to the unitary executive theory believe that an unrestricted presidential power to remove officers must be accompanied by a parallel authority to direct their activities within statutory limits. A good summary of this point of view comes from Professor Geoffrey Miller, in *Independent Agencies*, 1986 Sup. Ct. Rev. 41, 44–45:

> The thesis of this article is that Congress may not constitutionally deny the President the power to remove a policy-making official who has refused an order of the President to take an action within the officer's statutory authority. This thesis rests on a model of the President's relationship to the federal administrative state. Congress, in this model, has power to create federal agencies, to vest substantial discretion in agency heads, and to provide that action by the agency head is a necessary precondition to the effective exercise of the authority in question. The President retains the constitutional power to direct the officer to take particular actions within his or her discretion or to refrain from acting when the officer has discretion not to act. Such presidential directives can either be specific to the action in question or general programmatic instruction applicable to a range of actions or agencies. Congress may not constitutionally restrict the President's power to remove officials who fail to obey these presidential instructions, but may prohibit the President from removing officers for other reasons, such as personal animus or refusing to obey an order to do something outside the officer's statutory authority.
>
> This thesis — that the President may not be denied the power to remove an officer who has failed to comply with a presidential directive to take an action within the scope of the officer's discretion — may sound revolutionary. In fact, the thesis could be implemented without wholesale invalidation of federal statutes. Most statutes establishing independent agencies can easily be construed as including disobedience of the President's lawful instructions within the varieties of "cause" for which presidential removal is already authorized. In the relatively infrequent cases where the statutes cannot be so construed, the unconstitutionality of the removal provision would not ordinarily invalidate the agency's substantive and enforcement powers.

Do you regard Miller's thesis as viable after *Morrison v. Olson*? Does *Morrison* remove all doubt as to the constitutionality of protecting the tenure of "independent agency" administrators through "for cause" limitations on their removability by the President? Even if court-appointed prosecutors are permissible for historical reasons, are Justice Scalia's arguments in favor of a unitary executive more compelling in the independent agency context? Do you believe Justice Scalia would agree or disagree with Professor Miller's argument?

Professor William Luneburg has attempted to add a significant dimension to the debate in *Civic Republicanism, the First Amendment, and Executive Branch Policy-making*, 43 ADMIN. L. REV. 367 (1991). Luneburg argues that both conventional first amendment doctrine and the so-called "civic republicanism" school of constitutional interpretation emphasize deliberation as a critical virtue of effective government. Yet, he argues:

> The unitary executive theory of the Presidency, if adopted, would further erode the ability to insure the existence of a deliberative process capable of receiving and considering differing points of view and would do so at the point where it is most needed — at the very apex of governmental structure, in the dialogue of agency heads with the President.

See also Yvette M. Barksdale, *The Presidency and Administrative Value Selection*, 42 AM. U. L. REV. 273 (1993). Do you believe that the quality of government policy deliberation would be enhanced by increasing the relative policy independence of the heads of administrative agencies?

Consider whether you agree with the following doctrinal synthesis by Professor Shane:

> [R]ecent Supreme Court opinions cast substantial doubt on the proposition that there are constitutionally distinct categories of agencies called "executive" or "independent." . . .

> [First,] the Constitution provides that the President shall appoint all non-inferior administrative officers "by and with the Advice and Consent of the Senate." The Supreme Court has held this provision fully applicable to the Federal Election Commission, an "independent agency," . . . . Congress may not, by labeling an agency "independent," deprive the President of his appointments role.

> Second, the Constitution — as read by the Supreme Court since *Myers v. United States* — limits the permissible scope of Congress's power to participate in the removal of any officer of the United States. Congress may remove an officer of the United States only through impeachment. . . .

> Third, because the President is charged to "take Care that the Laws be faithfully executed," Congress must permit the President to remove, directly or through a subordinate he fully controls, any administrator who is not faithfully executing the laws. Although the full scope of this power has not been elaborated, it presumably includes the power to discharge an official who has broken the law, who refuses to implement the law, or who is performing so poorly as to undermine Congress's purposes in delegating power in the first place.

> Fourth, however, even if an administrator is performing power of a sort historically performed almost entirely by officers universally regarded as executive, Congress need not render the administrator susceptible to "at will" discharge by the President. It may be that the President must have

plenary removal power to supervise fully the exercise of administrative functions by any official—such as the Secretary of State—who assists the President in discharging an inherent article II function. If an administrator, however, is implementing delegated authority that is not within the scope of the President's inherent article II functions, then any discretion the President has to discharge the administrator depends upon congressional permission—except for the constitutionally guaranteed authority to discharge an officer for failing faithfully to execute the laws.

The foregoing propositions, all squarely affirmed by recent Supreme Court decisions, assure the President a constitutionally prescribed minimum level of authority with respect to every agency. That an agency has multiple administrators, with lengthy, staggered terms, or that Congress has limited the number of agency administrators who may be members of a particular party, would have no impact on the President's appointment power or on his authority to take care that the laws be faithfully executed. Nor would Congress have more authority to supervise the administrators within such an agency. . . . In these respects, all agencies are "executive."

On the other hand, the relationship that the Constitution promises to the President falls far short of plenary policy control. Only if an administrator is involved in discharging functions constitutionally vested in the President is such control a probable constitutional mandate. Otherwise, the scope of such supervisory power and the scope of authority the President has to remove an executive official are judgments within the discretion of Congress.

Peter M. Shane, *Negotiating for Knowledge: Administrative Responses to Congressional Demands for Information*, 44 ADMIN. L. REV. 197, 235–37 (1992). Would a more avowedly functionalist approach better capture recent developments? Can the above principles be justified as following a conventionalist reading of constitutional text?

The usual analytic dichotomy, formal v. functional, has engendered increasing criticism for a reason you can appreciate: formal analysis is too strict, and functional analysis is too permissive. As you can see from some of the excerpts above, scholars have begun the task of outlining alternative approaches. *See* Thomas W. Merrill, *The Constitutional Principle of Separation of Powers*, 1991 SUP. CT. REV. 225 (arguing for a "minimal" conception of separation of powers, consisting of "a simple rule: there are only three branches of government, and every federal office must be accountable to one of these branches."); M. Elizabeth Magill, *The Real Separation in Separation of Powers Law*, 86 VA. L. REV. 1127 (2000) (arguing that separation of powers analysis really divides into concerns over keeping "the three government powers in different departments" and "the need to balance the departments"); M. Elizabeth Magill, *Beyond Powers and Branches in Separation of Powers Law*, 150 U. PA. L. REV. 603 (2001) (critiquing the two components of analysis she identified in her earlier article and calling for new approaches).

D. The Faithful Execution of the Laws

1. Faithful Execution: Duty or Authority?

As elaborated earlier in this chapter, disputes over administrative appointments and removals (and Congress's authority to structure those processes) have provided most of the judicial guidance available to the elected branches regarding the President's constitutional position with regard to the executive bureaucracy. Yet as the Justice Department memo to Director Stockman reveals, when the President (and the President's lawyers) look for constitutional "hooks" on which to hang the President's claims to administrative authority, a typical starting point, along with the Executive Power Vesting Clause, is the Faithful Execution Clause (often called also the "Take Care Clause"), which provides that the President "shall take Care that the Laws be faithfully executed." Having studied how all the Presidents thus far have construed their powers, Professor Bruff concludes that Presidents have consistently treated the clause "as 'central' and 'essential' to their concept of the office." Harold H. Bruff, *The President's Faithful Execution Duty*, 87 U. Colo. L. Rev. 1107, 1109 (2016). Champions of unitary executive theory tout the Clause as underscoring personal presidential responsibility for (and control over) law execution, e.g., Saikrishna Prakash, Imperial from the Beginning 84–109 (2015), although Professor Bruff advances only the more modest claim that the clause in some manner "extends the President's responsibility beyond the conduct of his or her own office to a more general accountability for the actions of the subordinate executive officers who will perform most administrative actions." Bruff, *supra*, at 1108–09. In any event, the Clause would seem to underscore the President's mandatory duty, stated in the oath, to "faithfully execute the Office of President of the United States." In this sense, it seems a source more of obligation than of power.

The Jackson concurrence in *Youngstown* strongly implies, however, why the Faithful Execution Clause could be important, especially in domestic affairs, as a source of authority as well as a reiteration of duty. When presidents pursue domestic initiatives, they have very few explicit Article II powers on which to rely. The domestic powers that Article II specifies, e.g., the veto power or the pardon power, do not augur the sort of affirmative policy-generating punch signaled by such authorities as the President's power to negotiate treaties or the President's role as commander in chief. That means, on the domestic front, unless the President has a statutory basis for a particular undertaking, the "zone of twilight" is the only hospitable "zone" within which to defend his or her initiatives. Arguments in the "zone of twilight" logically require some plausible starting point in Article II. Hence, the Vesting and Faithful Execution Clauses will almost invariably be where presidents are tempted to look for at least credible authority to act without clear congressional imprimatur. As discussed below, two contexts for such an argument might seem especially inviting.

Emergency Action. One such context would involve presidential action in the face of national emergency. Recall from the discussion of *Youngstown* in Chapter 2 an important argument by Professor Henry Monaghan that "presidential authority to invade the 'private rights' of American citizens *absent legislative authority*—that is, presidential authority independently to alter negatively what in common legal understanding would be viewed as a prior liberty or property baseline," is "virtually nonexistent." Henry P. Monaghan, *The Protective Power of the Presidency*, 93 Colum. L. Rev. 1, 9 (1993). The only exception Professor Monaghan discerns from this rule is a narrow "executive 'protective' power," encompassing "a general authority to protect and defend the personnel, property, and instrumentalities of the United States from harm." *Id.* at 10–11.

As argued by Professor Monaghan, this "general power" is profoundly limited. It could not be exercised merely to protect the rights of private parties under federal law; nor could it properly be used to protect the personnel, property, and instrumentalities of the United States from harm that is entirely the indirect consequence of a third-party controversy. *Id.* at 70–72. Professor Monaghan does not think Presidents are empowered to "determin[e] the content of the primary legal duties of American citizens," or to subject American citizens to drastic and massive invasions of civil liberties contrary to our traditions. *Id.* at 72–74.

Is this conception of the executive, however, unduly modest? Professor Monaghan draws his theory from what he calls "the constitutional conception of a Chief Executive authorized to enforce the laws." *Id.* at 11. The clearest authority for this argument is surely *In re Neagle*, excerpted in Chapter 2, which upheld the President's vesting of authority in a deputy U.S. marshal to serve as bodyguard to a Supreme Court Justice. Yet, the actual language of *Neagle*, which speaks of enforcing "the rights, duties, and obligations growing out of the Constitution . . . ," would obviously extend further than the "protective power" Professor Monaghan identifies.

In December 2008, facing what was widely believed to be the potential collapse of the U.S. auto industry, President George W. Bush decided to grant loans to the auto companies to permit, if possible, their restructuring outside bankruptcy. In announcing his decision, President Bush said the following:

> [T]here's too great a risk that bankruptcy now would lead to a disorderly liquidation of American auto companies. . . . A more responsible option is to give the auto companies an incentive to restructure outside of bankruptcy— and a brief window in which to do it. And that is why my administration worked with Congress on a bill to provide automakers with loans to stave off bankruptcy while they develop plans for viability. This legislation earned bipartisan support from majorities in both houses of Congress.
>
> Unfortunately, despite extensive debate and agreement that we should prevent disorderly bankruptcies in the American auto industry, Congress was unable to get a bill to my desk before adjourning this year.
>
> This means the only way to avoid a collapse of the U.S. auto industry is for the executive branch to step in.

President Bush Discusses Administration's Plan to Assist Automakers, 2008 WL 5266402 (White House) (Dec. 19, 2008). In other words, something needs to be done, Congress did not get around to doing it, and so the President has to intervene. The loans the President authorized were to be provided under the Emergency Economic Stabilization Act of 2008, Pub. Law No. 110-343 (2008). That Act, however, authorizes the Secretary of the Treasury only to purchase or insure the "troubled assets" of "financial institutions." 12 U.S.C. §§ 5211–12. A loan would not seem to be either a form of purchase or insurance. Likewise, it is hardly obvious that a car manufacturer would qualify as a "financial institution," which the Act defines as "any institution, including, but not limited to, any bank, savings association, credit union, security broker or dealer, or insurance company, established and regulated under the laws of the United States or any State, territory, or possession of the United States. . . ." 12 U.S.C. §§ 5202. Did the President thus have statutory authority under the Emergency Economic Stabilization Act of 2008 to create an Automotive Industry Financing Program? (President Obama, it should be noted, kept the program in place.) Did he have any constitutionally vested "protective power" that expanded the scope of his discretion under the statute?

Constitutional Enforcement. A second potential context would involve executive action to protect constitutional rights, even without statutory authority to do so. After all, the Constitution is law. Presidents swear to defend the Constitution. Taking care that the Constitution "be faithfully executed" might seem a natural fit for the text.

The Third Circuit, however, rejected just such an argument in *United States v. City of Philadelphia*, 644 F.2d 187 (3d Cir. 1980). The Justice Department alleged that (1) Philadelphia police officers had engaged in a widespread practice of violating the rights of persons they encountered on the streets and elsewhere in the city and (2) high-ranking city and Police Department officials had deliberately encouraged discriminatory police treatment of blacks and Hispanics. A three-judge panel concluded that the government lacked an implied right of action under the criminal law statutes protecting civil rights. Moreover, according to the court, the Attorney General had no standing to advance the civil rights of third persons absent an express statutory grant of the necessary authority:

> Section 5 of the fourteenth amendment confers on Congress, not on the Executive or the Judiciary, the "power to enforce, by appropriate legislation, the provisions of this article." The Supreme Court has repeatedly recognized the central role of Congress in establishing appropriate mechanisms to enforce the fourteenth amendment. "It is not said the *judicial power* of the general government shall extend to enforcing the prohibitions and to protecting the rights and immunities guaranteed . . . . It is the power of Congress which has been enlarged." *Ex parte Virginia*, 100 U.S. 339, 345 (1879). Congress has exercised its power to "enforc[e] the prohibitions" on many occasions, but it has refused to grant the Executive and the Judiciary the authority that now is asserted. . . .

In addition, the Supreme Court in the last decade has repeatedly recognized the importance of a proper respect for the independent roles of state and local governments in our federal system. Judge Ditter wrote eloquently and persuasively for the court below that to permit this action to proceed "would be to vest an excessive and dangerous degree of power in the hands of the Attorney General" . . . .

Id., at 200. The panel opinion drew a sharp, extended dissent from the court's subsequent refusal to rehear the case en banc. Writing for himself and three other judges, Judge John J. Gibbons cited a string of cases in which the Supreme Court had previously approved a nonstatutory cause of action for the executive branch to sue in order to protect the interests of the United States, broadly conceived. The Justice Department's civil rights complaint, he argued did not "involve the creation of new rights conflicting with legislative and judicial precedent in the 'national interest.' Rather, it falls comfortably into the category of decisions upholding non-specific statutory authority to supply a new remedy for an established scheme of rights." *Id.*, at 226.

Somewhat oddly, as Judge Gibbons notes, the panel omitted any mention of the *Debs* decision, discussed in Chapter 2. One might well ask whether the facts of *Debs*— involving the asserted protection of interstate commerce—or the facts of *City of Philadelphia* presented a stronger case for reading the faithful execution clause broadly and which better illustrated the dangers of an expansive interpretation of inherent executive power. For a vigorous defense of an executive role in enforcing fourteenth amendment rights, *see* Bruce Ledewitz, *The Power of the President to Enforce the Fourteenth Amendment*, 52 Tenn. L. Rev. 605 (1985).

It is worth noting, despite the Third Circuit's emphasis on Congress's role in enforcing Fourteenth Amendment rights, that its opinion might have been equally driven by two other sources of constitutional anxiety—the implications for federalism of sanctioning a broad nonstatutory power for the executive branch to sue state and local governments and the judiciary's lack of enthusiasm for involving itself in the grant of structural remedies in public litigation. Since the heyday of structural remedies in the 1960s and 1970s, federal courts have sharply cut back on their use, whether because their implementation has appeared too taxing for the courts, judges are unhappy with the consequences of earlier-imposed remedies, procedural doctrines make their imposition less likely, or courts are simply less persuaded that executive agencies are systemically inhospitable to the claims of particular subcommunities. See Samuel Issacharoff and Robert H. Klonoff, *The Public Value of Settlement*, 78 Ford. L. Rev. 1177, 1192–93 (2009).

2. Faithful Nonexecution?

Whether or not the Faithful Execution Clause expands executive authority to act independently, it is frequently read by scholars as importing into the Constitution a prohibition against the executive suspension of statutes analogous to the bar against royal suspension that Parliament enacted in 1689. English Bill of Rights, 1689, 1 W. & M., c. 2 (Eng.). Although a Pennsylvania Constitution of 1682 had included a "Take Care" provision even before the English Bill of Rights, it seems far more likely that the federal framers were primarily influenced by state constitutions written much closer to 1787 — state constitutions that the English Bill of Rights is quite likely to have influenced. An obvious problem with this understanding, however, is that no one — inside or outside government — expects or even wants the law to be enforced on every plausible occasion. "Faithful" cannot plausibly mean "comprehensive." On the contrary, extreme adherence to legal requirements is as likely to be a form of intentional disruption as a display of fidelity to office. Jessica Bulman-Pozen and David E. Pozen, *Uncivil Obedience*, 115 Colum. L. Rev. 809 (2015). The implausibility of comprehensive enforcement thus necessarily raises the question of how much non-enforcement of the laws can be reconciled with the duty of faithful execution. Alternatively, at what point does the limited enforcement of a statute become its impermissible suspension?

a. Unconstitutional Statutes

As noted earlier, one obvious question with regard to the President's duty to "take Care that the Laws be faithfully executed" lies in the scope of the word "Laws." Does "Laws" include the Constitution? If the President is obligated to enforce the Constitution, how should he react to legislative enactments he deems to be unconstitutional? What if his interpretation of the Constitution conflicts with a Supreme Court decision?

The proposition that the President need not enforce an unconstitutional law was voiced early by Thomas Jefferson, with respect to the Alien and Sedition Laws. In a letter to Abigail Adams, he wrote:

> You seem to think it devolved on the judges to decide on the validity of the sedition law. But nothing in the Constitution has given them a right to decide for the Executive, more than to the Executive to decide for them. Both magistracies are equally independent in the sphere of action assigned to them. The judges, believing the law constitutional, had a right to pass a sentence of fine and imprisonment; because that power was placed in their hands by the Constitution. But the Executive, believing the law to be unconstitutional, was bound to remit the execution of it; because that power has been confided to him by the Constitution. That instrument meant that its co-ordinate branches should be checks on each other. But the opinion which gives to the judges the right to decide what laws are constitutional, and what not, not only for themselves in their own sphere of action, but for the Legislature & Executive also, in their spheres, would make the judiciary a despotic branch.

VIII Writings of Thomas Jefferson 310 (P. Ford ed., 1897).

In an October, 1986 address cited earlier, Attorney General Edwin Meese III discussed, in terms reminiscent of Jefferson's letter, the relationship between the executive and the Supreme Court on constitutional issues. Meese asserted: "[C]onstitutional interpretation is not the business of the Court only, but also properly the business of all branches of government." Edwin M. Meese, III, *The Law of the Constitution*, 61 Tul. L. Rev. 979, 985 (1987). He argued that there is a "necessary distinction between the Constitution and constitutional law." *Id.* at 981. The former, the document itself, is the nation's supreme law. The latter, "constitutional law," is "that body of law that has resulted from the Supreme Court's adjudications involving disputes over constitutional provisions or doctrines." *Id.* at 982. The distinction, Meese argued, must be recognized in order to preserve the possibility that each branch of government, including the Supreme Court, may appeal to the Constitution as a source of authority for correcting past errors in the law: "If a constitutional decision is not the same as the Constitution itself, if it is not binding in the same way that the Constitution is, we as citizens may respond to a decision with which we disagree." *Id.* at 985. In illustration of the point, Meese cited Abraham Lincoln's stance on *Dred Scott v. Sandford*, 60 U.S. (19 How.) 393 (1856). Although agreeing that the decision bound the parties to the immediate case, Lincoln said:

> We nevertheless do oppose [*Dred Scott*] ... as a political rule which shall be binding on the voter, to vote for nobody who thinks it wrong, which shall be binding on the members of Congress or the President to favor no measure that does not actually concur with the principles of that decision.

3 Collected Works of Abraham Lincoln 255 (Roy P. Basler ed., 1953).

Despite Jefferson's opinion on independent executive authority to construe the Constitution, Attorneys General traditionally refrain from rendering opinions as to the constitutionality of statutes once they are enacted, whether or not those statutes had the approval of the President. This is so, even though it is generally recognized that the Attorney General, through the power to issue formal opinions of law, may constrain executive agencies to follow those opinions unless they are withdrawn or overruled in court. *Smith v. Jackson*, 246 U.S. 388, 390–91 (1918); *Public Citizen v. Burke*, 655 F. Supp. 318, 321–22 (D.D.C. 1987). With regard to possibly unconstitutional statutes, however, Attorney General Cummings said in 1937 that the head of an administrative agency is:

> under no duty to question or to inquire into the constitutional power of the Congress. .... Assuming, therefore, that in the administrative branch of the Government only the President ordinarily can have proper interest in questioning the validity of a measure passed by the Congress, and that such interest ceases when he has expressed his approval or disapproval, it necessarily follows that there rarely can be proper occasion for the rendition of an opinion by the Attorney General upon its constitutionality after it has become law.

39 Op. Att'y Gen. 12, 13–14 (1937). *See generally* Note, *The Authority of Administrative Agencies to Consider the Constitutionality of Statutes*, 90 Harv. L. Rev. 1682 (1977). The one exception noted by Cummings encompasses laws that involve "conflict

between the prerogatives of the legislative department and those of the executive department," that is, acts that may violate the separation of powers. 39 Op. Att'y Gen. at 16. That position was more recently amplified by Attorney General Civiletti as follows: "[T]he Executive's duty faithfully to execute the law embraces a duty to enforce the fundamental law set forth in the Constitution as well as a duty to enforce the law founded in the Acts of Congress, and cases arise in which the duty to the one precludes the duty to the other." In such cases, according to Civiletti, enforcement of the unconstitutional acts "would constitute an abdication of the responsibility of the Executive Branch, as an equal and coordinate branch of Government with the Legislative Branch, to preserve the integrity of its functions against constitutional encroachment." 43 Op. Att'y Gen. No. 25 at 11–12 (June 5, 1980).

In 1994, Walter Dellinger, then-Assistant Attorney General in charge of OLC, sought to distill from the history of Executive branch practice and judicial reaction a set of seven "propositions" that would provide guidance in implementing the "unassailable" conclusion that "in some situations the President may decline to enforce unconstitutional statutes":

Presidential Authority to Decline to Execute Unconstitutional Statutes

18 Op. O.L.C. 199, 200–203 (1994).

1. The President's office and authority are created and bounded by the Constitution; he is required to act within its terms. Put somewhat differently, in serving as the executive created by the Constitution, the President is required to act in accordance with the laws—including the Constitution, which takes precedence over other forms of law. This obligation is reflected in the Take Care Clause and in the President's oath of office.

2. When bills are under consideration by Congress, the executive branch should promptly identify unconstitutional provisions and communicate its concerns to Congress so that the provisions can be corrected. Although this may seem elementary, in practice there have been occasions in which the President has been presented with enrolled bills containing constitutional flaws that should have been corrected in the legislative process.

3. The President should presume that enactments are constitutional. There will be some occasions, however, when a statute appears to conflict with the Constitution. In such cases, the President can and should exercise his independent judgment to determine whether the statute is constitutional. In reaching a conclusion, the President should give great deference to the fact that Congress passed the statute and that Congress believed it was upholding its obligation to enact constitutional legislation. Where possible, the President should construe provisions to avoid constitutional problems.

4. The Supreme Court plays a special role in resolving disputes about the constitutionality of enactments. As a general matter, if the President believes that the Court

would sustain a particular provision as constitutional, the President should execute the statute, notwithstanding his own beliefs about the constitutional issue. If, however, the President exercising his independent judgment, determines both that a provision would violate the Constitution and that it is probable that the Court would agree with him, the President has the authority to decline to execute the statute.

5. Where the President's independent constitutional judgment and his determination of the Court's probable decision converge on a conclusion of unconstitutionality, the President must make a decision about whether or not to comply with the provision. That decision is necessarily specific to context, and it should be reached after careful weighing of the effect of compliance with the provision on the constitutional rights of affected individuals and on the executive branch's constitutional authority. Also relevant is the likelihood that compliance or non-compliance will permit judicial resolution of the issue. That is, the President may base his decision to comply (or decline to comply) in part on a desire to afford the Supreme Court an opportunity to review the constitutional judgment of the legislative branch.

6. The President has enhanced responsibility to resist unconstitutional provisions that encroach upon the constitutional powers of the Presidency. Where the President believes that an enactment unconstitutionally limits his powers, he has the authority to defend his office and decline to abide by it, unless he is convinced that the Court would disagree with his assessment. If the President does not challenge such provisions (i.e., by refusing to execute them), there often will be no occasion for judicial consideration of their constitutionality; a policy of consistent Presidential enforcement of statutes limiting his power thus would deny the Supreme Court the opportunity to review the limitations and thereby would allow for unconstitutional restrictions on the President's authority.

Some legislative encroachments on executive authority, however, will not be justiciable or are for other reasons unlikely to be resolved in court. If resolution in the courts is unlikely and the President cannot look to a judicial determination, he must shoulder the responsibility of protecting the constitutional role of the presidency. This is usually true, for example, of provisions limiting the President's authority as Commander in Chief. Where it is not possible to construe such provisions constitutionally, the President has the authority to act on his understanding of the Constitution. . . .

7. The fact that a sitting President signed the statute in question does not change this analysis. The text of the Constitution offers no basis for distinguishing bills based on who signed them; there is no constitutional analogue to the principles of waiver and estoppel. Moreover, every President since Eisenhower has issued signing statements in which he stated that he would refuse to execute unconstitutional provisions. . . . In accordance with these propositions, we do not believe that a President is limited to choosing between vetoing, for example, the Defense Appropriations Act and executing an unconstitutional provision in it. In our view, the President has the authority to sign legislation containing desirable elements while refusing to execute a constitutionally defective provision.

———————————

1. *Power to Suspend Statutes?* Do you agree in general with the proposition that the executive branch is entitled to suspend execution of laws that violate the separation of powers? Would it matter that a President had signed a disputed enactment? Consider the Attorney General's argument that an unconstitutional provision "may be a part of a larger and vitally necessary piece of legislation." Should it matter whether the provision is central or peripheral to the legislation, or whether Congress has provided that the legislation is severable? Should it matter whether the President who signed the legislation objected to it during the legislative process or in a signing statement? If it does matter, would this affect your view of the controversy, discussed in Chapter Two, regarding the presidential use of signing statements to object to arguably unconstitutional provisions of a statute he is nonetheless prepared to sign into law? Is the case stronger for allowing the President to waive the constitutional prerogatives of the executive branch than for allowing the President to waive objections to infringements on individual rights? For a supportive general analysis of independent presidential review of the constitutionality of laws he is charged to enforce, see Frank H. Easterbrook, *Presidential Review*, 40 Case W. Res. L. Rev. 905 (1989–90).

2. *Provoking Litigation Through Legal Compliance.* Should it make a difference in your view whether executive branch compliance or noncompliance with a possibly unconstitutional statute might facilitate a lawsuit that could result in an authoritative judicial resolution of the controversy? Recall, in this respect, the stance of the Department of Justice with respect to defending or opposing the legislative veto, discussed in Chapter Two, above. Consider also the executive branch's handling of *United States v. Lovett*, 328 U.S. 303 (1946). Lovett arose from an appropriations rider that prohibited the payment of salary to three government employees who had been accused informally of disloyalty; they could be paid only if they were reappointed to office with the advice and consent of the senate. The Department of Justice successfully contested the constitutionality of the statute, but the executive branch, in part to produce a justiciable controversy, did enforce the statute in order not to moot the litigation. See John Hart Ely, United States v. Lovett: *Litigating the Separation of Powers*, 10 Harv. C. R.-C. L. L. Rev. 1 (1975). Are presidents on stronger ground in disobeying statutes that violate the separation of powers when compliance would injure no one with standing to seek judicial invalidation of such statutes?

3. *Signing, Then Seeking to Repeal.* In *Presidential Non-Enforcement of Constitutionally Objectionable Statutes*, 63 Law & Contemp. Probs. 7 (2000), Dawn Johnsen relates President Clinton's dilemma regarding the National Defense Authorization Act for Fiscal Year 1996, which included a provision requiring the armed forces to discharge individuals infected with the human immunodeficiency virus ("HIV"), even if asymptomatic. Clinton concluded that this provision violated equal protection, and vetoed an early version of the law. He decided against a second veto of a revised version that still included the objectionable provision because of the necessity, in his judgment, to assure orderly continued funding for the military: "President Clinton decided that the constitutionally appropriate response was to seek repeal of the provision and, if unsuccessful, to comply with the law but not defend it in the

already-planned legal challenge. Congress would be free to file a brief defending the law. The President was successful in working with Congress to repeal the provision before the law's effective date, when the President would have been required to discharge the service members." In Johnsen's view:

> The system worked at its best in this case. The President encouraged debate over the law's constitutionality and promoted his constitutional view through the lawmaking process, rather than by unilaterally blocking the provision, which in this case also would have rendered the dispute over the law's constitutionality nonjusticiable. The success of the repeal effort, however, masks the extraordinary closeness of the question. Had the repeal effort failed, more than a thousand HIV-positive individuals faced the loss of their jobs and benefits. Also weighing in favor of non-enforcement, the President in a sense was better situated than the courts to protect the constitutional interests of the service members. The President possessed expertise as commander in chief relevant to assessing the constitutionality of the provision, while the courts probably would have upheld the provision under judicial doctrines that reflect deference to Congress, which in this instance did not explicitly consider the constitutional issue during the legislative process.

Id. at 13–14.

b. Nonexecution and Administrative Discretion

Although incidents of constitutionally based nonexecution exist, laws are much more likely to go un- or underenforced as a matter of administrative discretion. As Professor Saikrishna Prakash has written: "In a world with constrained resources and so many laws and scofflaws, the Faithful Execution Clause supplies no easy answers [to questions of administrative discretion]. The pardon power . . . further complicates matters, for it suggests that the Constitution does not require the unyielding execution of all laws." Saikrishna Bangalore Prakash, Imperial from the Beginning: The Constitution of the Original Executive 97 (2015).

In fact, instances of incomplete enforcement are a ubiquitous feature of federal public administration. The following excerpt from an article by Professor Shane offers a taxonomy of incomplete enforcement.

Faithful Nonexecution
Peter M. Shane
Ohio State Public Law Working Paper No. 300,
available at SSRN: https://ssrn.com/abstract=2637827
(2017)

I. Varieties of Nonexecution

A. General Definition

Cataloguing all forms of under-implementation of the law that are potentially anxiety-provoking from a rule-of-law point of view requires a broad definition of "nonexecution." It makes sense to use "nonexecution" to refer to any government decision:

(a) To forego the application of penal or other regulatory law in circumstances that, to the knowledge of the government, would technically support the application of that law;

(b) To forego investigative activity despite the government's expectation that such activity would likely bring to the government's attention circumstances that would support the imposition of penal or regulatory law; or

(c) To forego the implementation of a statutorily authorized program of public benefit.

The first of these categories presumably covers what would most often strike observers as the underenforcement of law. There are circumstances, that is, in which government is aware of activities within its jurisdiction that it could regulate or penalize, but it fails to do so. It is necessary, however, to add the second category. The largest volume of potentially regulable activity untouched by government is presumably activity of which government is simply unaware. Yet ignorance cannot completely assuage rule-of-law anxieties because some of that ignorance may be intentional. That is, the government's unawareness of some potentially regulable activity may result from deliberate investigative decisions that insulate such activity from probable discovery. Anyone concerned with the possible faithlessness of legal execution needs to be worried not only by government decisions to ignore regulable activity it sees, but also by government decisions not to investigate activity that, if discovered, would be subject to regulation or penalty. The third category simply recognizes that not all the law that the government executes is regulatory. Congress enacts programs, as well, for the conferral of public benefits. They regulate only those persons who seek to obtain the proffered benefits. Yet, should an Administration refuse to send out social security checks or tax refunds, it could betray the faithful execution ideal as easily as if it were to forebear from the regulation of air pollution or securities fraud.

B. Quasi-Adjudicative Nonexecution

Courts have confronted questions of nonexecution within each of the categories I have named, but implicitly make a threshold distinction between what might be called quasi-adjudicative nonexecution and programmatic nonexecution.[1] In the

---

1. Cf., Heckler v. Chaney, 470 U.S. 821, 838 (1985) (Brennan, J., concurring) ("Today the Court holds that *individual* decisions of the Food and Drug Administration not to take enforcement action in response to citizen requests are presumptively not reviewable under the Administrative Procedure Act, 5 U.S.C. §§ 701–706. . . . This general presumption is based on the view that, in the normal course of events, Congress intends to allow broad discretion for its administrative agencies to make *particular enforcement decisions*, and there often may not exist readily discernible "law to apply" for courts to conduct judicial review of nonenforcement decisions.") (emphasis supplied)

domain of criminal law, what I mean by quasi-adjudicative nonexecution covers much of what is typically described as "prosecutorial discretion." For example, in a particular criminal case, federal prosecutors may believe that an offense has occurred, but that the offense is excusable under the circumstances, that proof would be difficult, that a jury would be unlikely to convict for some reason other than the evidence, or that the offender's cooperation in another criminal investigation justifies lowering or dropping the charges.[2] It has been argued that such discretion inevitably inheres in the executive by the very nature of executive power or by necessary implication from specific obligations or powers mentioned in Article II, including the pardon power.[3] One could reach the same conclusion by treating criminal statutes as implicitly conferring prosecutorial discretion on the executive branch given what is surely the near-universal expectation that such discretion is an ordinary feature of criminal law enforcement.[4] Whatever the source of the executive branch's prosecutorial discretion, it has a long and all-but-unquestioned pedigree. Nonexecution of this kind is quasi-adjudicative because it is based on contextual factors peculiar to an individual case, not to more general considerations.

The Supreme Court has recognized an analogous and similarly longstanding form of non-implementation discretion in the civil context. In the canonical case of *Heckler v. Chaney*,[5] the Supreme Court held nonreviewable a decision by the Food and Drug Administration not to pursue enforcement actions based upon allegations that Oklahoma and Texas were violating the Federal Food, Drug and Cosmetic Act in their use of drugs for lethal injection that the FDA had not approved for that purpose. The Court determined that agency decisions not to initiate civil enforcement proceedings were presumptively within the category of "agency action committed to agency discretion by law,"[6] and thus ordinarily beyond judicial review under the Administrative Procedure Act. It cited a number of earlier decisions that it took to establish an agency's "absolute discretion" "not to enforce [law], whether through criminal or civil process."[7] The Court noted that Congress, in particular civil statutes, might withdraw "discretion from the agency and provide[] guidelines for exercise of its enforcement power."[8] Absent such statutory constraints, however, agencies could simply exercise their own judgment. Action "committed to agency discretion" includes

---

2. *See generally* Michael Edmund O'Neill, *Understanding Federal Prosecutorial Declinations: An Empirical Analysis of Predictive Factors*, 41 Am. Crim. L. Rev. 1439 (2004).

3. In re Aiken Cty., 725 F.3d 255, 262 (D.C. Cir. 2013) ("The Presidential power of prosecutorial discretion is rooted in Article II, including the Executive Power Clause, the Take Care Clause, the Oath of Office Clause, and the Pardon Clause.").

4. *Prosecution for Contempt of Cong. of an Exec. Branch Official Who Has Asserted a Claim of Exec. Privilege*, 8 Op. O.L.C. 101, 122 (1984) ("Because of the wide scope of a prosecutor's discretion in determining which cases to bring, courts, as a matter of law, do not ordinarily interpret a statute to limit that discretion unless the intent to do so is clearly and unequivocally stated.").

5. 470 U.S. 821 (1985).

6. 5 U.S.C. § 701(a)(2).

7. 470 U.S. at 831.

8. *Id.*, at 833.

agency refusals to institute investigative or enforcement proceedings, unless Congress has indicated otherwise.

In explaining why individual cases of nonexecution are generally unsuited for judicial review, the Court emphasized the highly contextual nature of case-by-case decision making:

> [A]n agency decision not to enforce often involves a complicated balancing of a number of factors which are peculiarly within its expertise. Thus, the agency must not only assess whether a violation has occurred, but whether agency resources are best spent on this violation or another, whether the agency is likely to succeed if it acts, whether the particular enforcement action requested best fits the agency's overall policies, and, indeed, whether the agency has enough resources to undertake the action at all. An agency generally cannot act against each technical violation of the statute it is charged with enforcing. [9]

As long as case-by-case nonexecution is not motivated by corrupt or legitimate factors, such as bribery, personal or political favoritism or animosity, or unconstitutional animus, quasi-adjudicative nonexecution — even if it involves large numbers of cases — is not constitutionally faithless. It is worth noting that, even with regard to [a program of deferred action for some classes of undocumented immigrants], opponents concede that the Department of Homeland Security would have unreviewable discretion to grant deferred action on an individuated basis to each of the applicants covered by that program.[10] It is the program's categorical approach to priority setting that supposedly raises anxieties about faithful execution.

C. Programmatic Nonexecution

Unlike prosecutorial discretion, what could be called "programmatic nonexecution" involves a categorical determination to forego legal implementation with relatively little regard to the nuances of individual cases. The distinction between programmatic and quasi-adjudicative nonexecution is analogous to the rulemaking/adjudication distinction around which much administrative law doctrine and practice are organized.[11] The distinction is concededly imperfect. After all, one could characterize a prosecutor's exercise of quasi-adjudicative discretion not to prosecute an individual case based on weak circumstantial evidence as implementing a

---

9. *Id.* at 831.

10. Texas v. United States, 809 F.3d 134, 166 (5th Cir. 2015), as revised (Nov. 25, 2015), aff'd by equally divided Court, 136 S.Ct. 2271 (2016) ("[N]either the preliminary injunction nor compliance with the APA requires the Secretary to remove any alien or to alter his enforcement priorities.")

11. *Compare* Londoner v. Denver, 210 U.S. 373 (1908) (requiring administrative hearings on request before the levying of taxes on individual properties based on value of improvements), *with* Bi–Metallic Investment Co. v. State Board of Equalization, 239 U.S. 441, 445 (1915) (holding that Denver property owners were not entitled to administrative hearings prior to an across-the-board upward evaluation of the value of all Denver taxable property).

programmatic determination to prefer prosecutions based on direct evidence. Conversely, it is almost always the case that formal policies of "programmatic non-execution" reserve to the relevant agency the discretion to execute the law fully in particular cases.[12] Moreover, the more flexible the programmatic criteria for nonexecution, the more quasi-adjudicative judgment is entailed in deciding whether a particular case qualifies. . . \ — thus potentially commingling programmatic and quasi-adjudicative judgments. Nonetheless, the distinction has a common-sense appeal and enables us to distinguish between nonexecution driven primarily by the kinds of considerations administrative lawyers customarily call adjudicative facts and nonexecution based primarily on broader considerations of policy.

Within the general category of programmatic nonexecution, it is possible to identify at least six different familiar varieties. They are by no means mutually exclusive, but each arguably raises somewhat different issues regarding fidelity to law.

1. [Professor Shane's first category involves the problem of unconstitutional laws, discussed above.]

2. *Statutorily Authorized Waivers*. A second category of nonexecution somewhat confounds the execution/nonexecution distinction because the same underenforced statute that makes conduct regulable simultaneously confers on the executive branch discretion with regard to limiting enforcement. For example, the Personal Responsibility and Work Opportunity Reconciliation Act of 1996[13] authorized the Secretary of Health and Human Services to waive certain requirements that would otherwise limit state flexibility in administering the federally funded public assistance program called Temporary Assistance to Needy Families. In 2012, Kathleen Sebelius, the Obama Administration's first HHS Secretary, issued a so-called "Information Memorandum" intended "to notify states of the Secretary's willingness to exercise her waiver authority . . . to allow states to test alternative and innovative strategies, policies, and procedures that are designed to improve employment outcomes for needy families."[14] Controversially, the demonstration projects HHS suggested as possible "alternative . . . strategies" included hypothetical initiatives that would appear to relax work-participation requirements for TANF recipients that states would otherwise be required to enforce.[15] The Department of Education has issued similar guidance

---

12. *E.g.*, Dual and Successive Prosecution Policy ("Petite Policy"), U.S. Attorney's Manual §9-2.031, https://www.justice.gov/usam/usam-9-2000-authority-us-attorney-criminal-division -mattersprior-approvals#9-2.031 ("Satisfaction of the three substantive prerequisites [for initiating federal prosecution] does not mean that a proposed prosecution must be approved or brought. The traditional elements of federal prosecutorial discretion continue to apply.")

13. Pub.L. 104–193, 110 Stat. 2105 (1996).

14. Memorandum from Earl Johnson, Director, Office of Family Assistance, to States administering the TANF Program and other interested parties (July 12, 2012), at 1, *available at* http://www. acf.hhs.gov/programs/ofa/policy/im-ofa/2012/im201203/im201203.html.

15. For example, HHS might look favorably upon "[p]rojects that test systematically extending the period in which vocational educational training or job search/readiness programs count toward participation rates, either generally or for particular subgroups, such as an extended

that would have the effect of relieving states from obligations otherwise enforceable as a condition of federal funding under the No Child Left Behind Act.[16]

These examples of administrative initiative exemplify what Professors David Barron and Todd D. Rakoff have called "big waiver."[17] As they describe in a paper generally favorable to the practice, Congress sometimes will enact "a fully reticulated, legislatively defined regulatory framework" that contains within it a delegation of "broad, discretionary power to determine whether the rule or rules that Congress has established should be dispensed with."[18] Authorizations of "big waiver" seem to confound the execution/nonexecution distinction because the implementation of a waiver program simultaneously does away with legal requirements that might otherwise have been enforced, but does so pursuant to explicit congressional license. It is important, however, to include authorized waiver programs as instances of nonexecution because even explicit waiver authority may be exercised beyond permissible bounds and thus in derogation of the law.

3. *Maximizing the Effectiveness of the Underenforced Statute With Limited Resources.* Likely the most common category of underenforcement is nonexecution to advance program effectiveness. Agencies typically lack the resources for comprehensive administration of even those programs with which they are sympathetic as a matter of policy and about which they harbor no constitutional doubts. Nonexecution in this context simply reflects priority setting to get the most bang for Congress's appropriated buck, consistent with Congress's own explicit or imputed priorities. Thus, for example, the Occupation Safety and Health Administration (OSHA) lists on its website[19] and in its operations manual a set of workplace inspection priorities:

- Imminent danger
- Catastrophes / fatalities
- Worker complaints and referrals
- Targeted inspections — high injury/illness rates, severe violators
- Follow-up inspections.

As explained in the manual: "OSHA's priority system for conducting inspections is designed to allocate available OSHA resources as effectively as possible to ensure that maximum feasible protection is provided to working men and women."[20]

---

training period for those pursuing a credential. The purpose of such a waiver would be to determine through evaluation whether a program that allows for longer periods in certain activities improves employment outcomes." *Id.*

16. Pub. L. No. 107-110, 115 Stat. 1425 (2001), superseded by the Every Child Succeeds Act, Pub. L. 114-95,129 Stat. 1802 (2015).

17. David J. Barron and Todd D. Rakoff, *In Defense of Big Waiver*, 113 COLUM. L. REV. 265 (2013).

18. *Id.*, at 268.

19. https://www.osha.gov/dep/index.html.

20. OSHA Field Operations Manual (Aug. 2, 2016), at 2–3, https://www.osha.gov/OshDoc/Directive_pdf/CPL_02-00-160.pdf.

Presumably, many, if not all administrative agencies with enforcement powers have policies of this sort, although there is variance no doubt in their explicitness and availability to the public. Following such priorities will presumably mean that some violations, deemed less serious, will effectively be ignored. Nonetheless, each agency's implicit rationale amounts to: "We're doing the best we can to achieve the specific objectives of this assignment with the funds Congress provided to achieve its objectives."

The same program-optimizing rationale may apply in certain contexts that where the concern is not chiefly budgetary. For example, even policy sympathizers have criticized the Obama Administration for failing in a number of respects to implement the Affordable Care Act (ACA)[21] on the timetable or with the stringency that Act apparently dictated. The Administration never issued a thoroughgoing explanation for its policies, tending to refer only to the exercise of "prosecutorial discretion."[22] Because the ACA, however, represented the first Obama Administration's foremost political priority, it seems safe to assume that its partial nonexecution of the ACA — whether or not lawful — was likely motivated by an expectation that relaxing execution would ultimately make accomplishment of the program's overall objectives more, not less likely. As it happens, this kind of ambiguity can arise whenever any Administration casts a nonexecution policy under a regulatory regime as a matter of postponement.[23] Not implementing a statutory deadline may reflect less the necessity to accommodate resource constraints than a reflection of an agency's determination that regulatory action, if deliberated longer and implemented later, may turn out to be sounder and more effective.

In *Commonwealth of Pa. v. Lynn,*[24] the D.C. Circuit did confront an intriguing, but likely rare example in which an agency put a program on permanent hold because the agency thought Congress had authorized a tool inconsistent with its explicit statutory objectives. Specifically, the court overturned a grant of summary judgment that would have required the Secretary of the Department of Housing and Urban Development (HUD) to resume accepting, processing, and approving applications for federal subsidies under three different programs established under national housing laws[25] that he had suspended on the ground that they were not accomplishing Congress' intended purposes. It was undisputed that the Secretary suspended the programs for reasons related to the feasibility of accomplishing their goals and not for reasons of policy extrinsic to the operation of the programs (such as political

---

21. Patient Protection and Affordable Care Act, Pub. L. 111–148, 124 Stat. 119 (2010).

22. Nicholas Bagley, Legal *Limits and the Implementation of the Affordable Care Act*, 164 U. PENN. L. REV. 1715 (2016).

23. Cass R. Sunstein and Adrien Vermeule, The Law of "Not Now": When Agencies Defer Decisions, 103 GEO. L.J. 157 (2014).

24. 501 F.2d 848 (D.C. Cir. 1974),

25. HUD Act of 1965, § 101, 12 U.S.C. § 1701s; HUD Act of 1968, §§ 235 and 236, 12 U.S.C. §§ 1715z, 1715z-1.

opposition to government intervention in the housing market).[26] The court's canvass of a range of statutes that HUD administered, as well as the explicit purposes of the specific programs at issue, persuaded the court that Congress had implicitly granted the Secretary limited discretion to suspend the programs when he had adequate reason to believe that they were frustrating national housing policy and not serving Congress's express statutory intent to aid low-income persons.[27] In sum, HUD's non-implementation of the subsidies program was treated as faithfully executing the housing statutes in the sense that its nonexecution was intended to promote, not impede Congress's goals, and the court inferred Congress delegated authority to the Secretary to make such a determination.

4. *Optimizing the Accomplishment of Competing Missions.* When they have budgetary flexibility to do so, an agency's nonexecution decisions may reflect a slightly different rationale — not to maximize the effectiveness of the program that is under-implemented, but to conserve resources for higher priority programs. One example is the Reagan Administration's "passive enforcement" strategy after President Carter, pursuant to his authority under the Military Selective Service Act,[28] had reinstituted draft registration in the wake of the Soviet Union's invasion of Afghanistan.[29] Between 1981 and 1983, despite "[g]overnment estimates of noncompliance with the Act in 1980 and 1981 [that] ranged from just over half a million to one million men,"[30] the Justice Department decided to prosecute persons for failing to register with the Selective Service only if they themselves reported their nonregistration to the Federal government or were reported by unsolicited third parties. This directly affected a very small number of young men who were legally required to register, but who instead wrote to the Selective Service System, providing their names and addresses, but refusing — as a form of political protest — to put the same information on the prescribed registration form. As a result:

> the so-called 'passive enforcement' policy resulted in the prosecution by 1985 of only seventeen draft resisters, sixteen of whom were self-declared nonregistrants. All seventeen were vocal opponents of the requirement for Selective Service registration, having protested that requirement through their inculpatory letters, statements to the general public, or both.[31]

---

26. Com. of Pa. v. Lynn, 501 F.2d 848, 852 (D.C. Cir. 1974) ("While it may be doubted whether mere 'concern about the equity and efficiency' of a program duly established by Congress could, without more, support an executive decision to suspend its operation, it is clear that this is not the usual case of claimed authority 'to defer approval for reasons totally collateral and remote' to the purpose of the authorizing legislation.")

27. *Id.*, at 851–856.

28. 50 U.S.C. § 3801, et seq.

29. Proclamation No. 4771, 3 C.F.R. 82 (1981).

30. Peter M. Shane, *Equal Protection, Free Speech, and the Selective Prosecution of Draft Nonregistrants*, 72 Iowa L. Rev. 359, 361 (1987)

31. *Id.*, at 359.

The "passive enforcement" policy could hardly have been intended by the Justice Department to represent an optimal level of Selective Service enforcement; on the contrary, "[a] memorandum from the then-assistant attorney general in charge of the Justice Department's criminal division expressly recognized that any public awareness of the government's policy would provide 'a disincentive, until the last possible moment, to registration.'"[32] At most, with regard to the Selective Service System, the program of drastically limited law execution represented a way "to promote general deterrence, . . . since failing to proceed against publicly known offenders would encourage others to violate the law."[33] The Supreme Court's approval of the program[34] notwithstanding, the Department was not prioritizing the use of prosecutorial resources to have the maximum impact on Military Selective Service Act enforcement. It presumably was trying instead to focus its time and material resources on infractions of other criminal laws deemed to be targeting more serious social harms.

5. *Promoting Non-Program Values.* Whenever an agency decides not to pursue a particular class of cases, it can almost always characterize its decision as one of focusing resources as effectively as possible to accomplish the objectives of one or another program within its purview. It sometimes appears, however, that the agency's non-execution policy is motivated at least as significantly by other values — values that the agency may even regard as constitutionally embedded.

A well-known example is the Justice Department's longstanding policy on the federal prosecution of defendants who have already been subjected to state prosecution for substantially the same acts.[35] In essence, this so-called "*Petite* Policy"[36] precludes a dual or successive federal prosecution unless the matter involves a distinct and substantial federal interest that the state prosecution leaves "demonstrably unvindicated."[37] Because overlapping state and federal prosecutions do not violate the Double Jeopardy Clause,[38] the Department's nonexecution decisions under the policy are not constitutionally mandated. The policy lists "[p]romot[ing the] efficient utilization of Department resources" among its purposes.[39] But the policy is also intended "to protect persons charged with criminal conduct from the burdens associated with multiple prosecutions and punishments for substantially the same act(s)

---

32. *Id.*, at 365, discussing Memorandum from Assistant Attorney General D. Lowell Jensen to United States Attorneys, Prosecution of Selective Service Non-Registrants 2 (July 9, 1982).

33. Wayte v. United States, 470 U.S. 598, 613 (1985).

34. *Id.*

35. Formally called the "Dual and Successive Prosecution Policy," 9 U.S. Attorney's Manual §2.031(1), https://www.justice.gov/usam/usam-9-2000-authority-us-attorney-criminal-division-mattersprior-approvals#9-2.031.

36. *Id.* The policy is also called the "*Petite* Policy" because an earlier version had resulted in the dismissal with Justice Department consent of a federal indictment challenged as a violation of the Double Jeopardy Clause. *See* Petite v. United States, 361 U.S. 529 (1960).

37. *Id.*

38. Abbate v. United States, 359 U.S. 187 (1959).

39. *Id.*

or transaction(s),"[40] a fairness value reflective of the double jeopardy concern, and "to promote coordination and cooperation between federal and state prosecutors,"[41] which is essentially a concern for values of federalism. A similar federalism concern apparently motivates Justice Department policy regarding marijuana enforcement, which takes into account that state laws now frequently authorize at least some marijuana cultivation and distribution, subject to effective state regulation.[42]

6. *Policy Resistance.* A final category — and, by definition, the most problematic — would comprise the non-implementation of any statutory duty because the Administration opposes the statute. The classic litigated case involved a failure of the former Department of Health, Education and Welfare to pursue enforcement of title VI of the Civil Rights Act of 1964[43] against federally funded school districts and institutions of higher education that remained racially segregated. HEW was ordered to:

> commence enforcement proceedings against seventy-four secondary and primary school districts found either to have reneged on previously approved desegregation plans or to be otherwise out of compliance with Title VI, commence enforcement proceedings against forty-two districts previously deemed by HEW to be in presumptive violation of the Supreme Court's ruling in *Swann v. Charlotte-Mecklenburg Board of Education*, 402 U.S. 1, 91 (1971), demand of eighty-five other secondary and primary districts an explanation of racial disproportion in apparent violation of *Swann*, implement an enforcement program to secure Title VI compliance with respect to vocational and special schools, [and] monitor all school districts under court desegregation orders to the extent that HEW resources permit. . . . [44]

HEW offered no official explanation of its behavior, offering only the claim of unreviewable prosecutorial discretion as its ultimately unsuccessful defense. It was generally understood, however, that the Nixon Administration favored voluntary desegregation, rather than government-enforced desegregation, especially if it involved mandatory student reassignments and busing to achieve racial balance.[45] The central import of the opinions rendered in the case lay in the implicit rejection of the notion that the Administration's policy agenda could trump Congress's imposition of a mandatory duty.

---

40. *Id.*

41. *Id.*

42. Memorandum from James M. Cole, Deputy Attorney General, to All United States Attorneys, re: Guidance Regarding Marijuana Enforcement (Aug. 19, 2013), https://www.justice.gov/iso/opa/resources/3052013829132756857467.pdf.

43. 42 U.S.C. § 2000d *et seq.*

44. Adams v. Richardson, 480 F.2d 1159, 1161 (D.C. Cir. 1973).

45. *See, e.g.,* Statement by President Richard Nixon About the Busing of Schoolchildren (Aug. 3, 1971), http://www.presidency.ucsb.edu/ws/?pid=3098 ("I am against busing as that term is commonly used in school desegregation cases. I have consistently opposed the busing of our Nation's schoolchildren to achieve a racial balance, and I am opposed to the busing of children simply for the sake of busing.")

To a similar effect was the Supreme Court's 2007 decision taking EPA to task for failing under the Bush Administration to regulate greenhouse gas emissions from new automobiles.[46] The EPA defended its inaction on two grounds. First, it denied that it had jurisdiction under the Clean Air Act to regulate carbon emissions from new motor vehicles. Its fallback defense was the assertion that it had discretion to forbear from regulatory activity because the President thought such regulation imprudent. The Supreme Court rejected both claims, interpreting the Clean Air Act as imposing a mandatory duty to regulate under certain prescribed circumstances that took no account of the President's estimate of regulatory prudence.[47]

Mixed Motives. Of course, particular programs of nonexecution can easily spring from more than one motivation. A stark example involved the Carter Administration's policy on the now forgotten legal exclusion from the United States of gay and lesbian aliens. Under the Immigration and Nationality Act of 1952, Congress had required the exclusion from the United States of aliens "afflicted with psychopathic personality, epilepsy, or a mental defect."[48] The legislative history of this provision indicated unambiguously Congress's intent to encompass homosexuality within the mental health category of "psychopathic personality,"[49] as did a 1965 amendment that substituted "sexual deviation" for "epilepsy."[50] In short, the statute precluded the lawful immigration of gay men and lesbians on putative grounds of mental health.

The Act divided administrative responsibility for enforcing health-based exclusionary provisions between the Immigration and Naturalization Service (INS), which was then an agency within the Justice Department,[51] and the Public Health Service (PHS), which would assist the INS.[52] As offensive as it now sounds, if the INS suspected an alien of homosexuality and the alien would not voluntarily withdraw his or her application for admission, the INS ordinarily would refer the alien to the PHS for a mental health examination.[53] A PHS finding of homosexuality would inevitably lead to the alien's exclusion because the Act provided that a PHS certificate, unlike

---

46. Massachusetts v. EPA, 549 U.S. 497 (2007).

47. *Id.*, at 522–523. ("The alternative basis for EPA's decision — that even if it does have statutory authority to regulate greenhouse gases, it would be unwise to do so at this time — rests on reasoning divorced from the statutory text. While the statute does condition the exercise of EPA's authority on its formation of a 'judgment,' 42 U.S.C. § 7521(a)(1), that judgment must relate to whether an air pollutant 'cause[s], or contribute[s] to, air pollution which may reasonably be anticipated to endanger public health or welfare,' ibid. Put another way, the use of the word 'judgment' is not a roving license to ignore the statutory text. It is but a direction to exercise discretion within defined statutory limits.")

48. Immigration and Nationality Act of 1952, 66 Stat. 182, then codified at 8 U.S.C. § 1182 (a) (4), quoted at Fleuti v. Rosenberg, 302 F.2d 652, 654 n. 2 (9th Cir. 1962), *vacated*, Rosenberg v. Fleuti, 374 U.S. 449 (1963).

49. Boutilier v. INS, 387 U.S. 118, 120–121 (1967).

50. The amendment is discussed in Matter of Longstaff, 716 F.2d 1439, 1445 (5th Cir. 1983).

51. 8 U.S.C. § 1551 and note.

52. Immigration and Nationality Act of 1952, § 234, 66 Stat. 198.

53. Hill v. U.S.I.N.S., 714 F.2d 1470, 1472 (9th Cir. 1983).

an INS inspector's assessment, would be a dispositive certification of any "mental disease, defect, or disability."[54]

After the American Psychiatric Association in 1973 removed homosexuality from the list of psychiatric disorders in its Diagnostic and Statistical Manual,[55] opponents of the exclusion provision put pressure on the Surgeon General, as head of the Public Health Service, to stop certifying "homosexuality" as a mental defect.[56] On August 2, 1979, the Surgeon General finally issued such an order resting, first, on the change in psychiatric understanding of homosexuality, and, second, on the contention that the determination of homosexuality is not made through a medical diagnostic procedure.[57]

The PHS order required the Justice Department to reevaluate its enforcement policy. In doing so, it faced a significant conundrum. On one hand, the Office of Legal Counsel had advised the INS that it technically did not need PHS assistance to enforce the exclusion;[58] Justice Department lawyers were reluctant to claim authority to ignore a law because of an executive determination that it was simply bad policy.[59] On the other hand, INS leadership shared PHS's lack of enthusiasm for the exclusion and was leery of leaving determinations of sexual orientation to the judgment of individual border agents.

After significant deliberation, the Department issued a statement so limiting enforcement that the new process would likely exclude, if anyone, only a volunteer seeking purposefully to challenge the law.[60] Specifically, no questions about sexual orientation would be asked, and the exclusion would be enforced only against an individual who voluntarily self-identified as gay or lesbian or was so identified by a third party, but only after the alien verifies his or sexual orientation during a private

---

54. Immigration and Nationality Act of 1952, § 236, 66 Stat. 200.

55. Petition of Hill, 775 F.2d 1037, 1039 (9th Cir. 1985).

56. Joseph B. Treaster, "Homosexuals Still Fight U.S. Immigration Limits," N.Y. Times, at A20 (Aug. 12, 1979).

57. Memorandum from Dr. Julius B. Richmond, Assistant Secretary for Health and Surgeon General, to Drs. William H. Foege and George I. Lythcott (Aug. 2, 1979).

58. Robert Pear, "Ban is Affirmed on Homosexuals Entering Nation," N.Y. TIMES, at A16 (Dec. 27, 1979).

59. Having served as an Attorney-Adviser in the Office of Legal Counsel at the time, my characterizations of attitudes within the Department concerning this debate is based on my personal recollection.

60. 57 Interpreter Releases 440 (1980); Such test cases presented themselves in short order, resulting in Ninth Circuit opinions holding that the exclusion could not be enforced without a PHS certificate.

Lesbian/Gay Freedom Day Comm., Inc. v. U.S. I. N. S., 541 F. Supp. 569 (N.D. Cal. 1982), aff'd sub nom. Hill v. U.S.I.N.S., 714 F.2d 1470 (9th Cir. 1983); but see In re Longstaff, 716 F.2d 1439 (5th Cir. 1983) (upholding an administrative decision to deny naturalization to resident alien determined, without PHS certification, to have been gay and thus properly excludable when he entered the U.S. in 1965). The Reagan Administration appears not to have pursued exclusions further, likely in anticipation of the exclusion's repeal, which occurred in 1986.

"secondary inspection."[61] In an accompanying background paper, the Department justified its limited enforcement regime on four grounds: the asserted lack of any "generally agreed-upon definition of homosexuality," the arbitrary enforcement pattern that could arise from "reliance upon subjective indicia (such as attire or mannerisms)," the invasion of personal privacy entailed in inquiring into sexual preference, and the lack of agency expertise in determining sexual orientation.[62] Although the policy could be characterized as reflecting an administrative judgment that Congress's immigration goals would be better served by redirecting elsewhere the resources of time and effort that might have been devoted to this particular exclusion, it is safe to say that the limits on execution also reflected a widespread administrative sentiment that the exclusion was an affront to values of dignity and equality. Intriguingly, after the Ninth Circuit rejected the argument that the INS, without PHS certification, could exclude gay and lesbian aliens based on mental health,[63] there is no indication of which I am aware that the Reagan Administration tried to compel PHS to reverse its nonenforcement stand. The Administration may have hoped for fairly prompt legislative repeal of the exclusion as part of a larger overhaul of the Immigration and Naturalization Act; the exclusion was not repealed, however, until the Immigration Act of 1990, enacted under the George H.W. Bush Administration.[64]

---

1. *Constitutional or Administrative Law? Dalton v. Specter,* 511 U.S. 462 (1994), involved an unsuccessful challenge to President Bill Clinton's decision to approve closing the Philadelphia Naval Shipyard pursuant to the Defense Base Closure and Realignment Act of 1990. Presidential decisions under that Act come at the end of an elaborate administrative process in which the Secretary of Defense prepares a list of recommended closures for review by Congress and the Defense Base Closure and Realignment Commission, an eight-member independent agency. The Commission, in turn, holds hearings and conducts its own assessment, which is transmitted to the President for a final decision, which may only be to approve or reject the Commission's recommendations *in toto.* Anticipating (correctly) that a President's decision might not be reviewable under the Administrative Procedure Act because the President is not an APA "agency," the plaintiffs also contended that presidential approval of base closures in excess of statutory authority would raise a reviewable constitutional claim, as a violation of the separation of powers. The Supreme Court explicitly rejected this argument: "[C]laims simply alleging that the President has exceeded his statutory authority are not 'constitutional' claims . . . ." 511 U.S. at 473.

---

61. Department of Justice Press Release of Sept. 9, 1980, reprinted in Peter M. Shane and Harold H. Bruff, Separation of Powers Law: Cases and Materials 591 (2d ed. 2005)
62. Justice Department Background Paper on Homosexual Exclusion Policy (Sept. 9, 1980), reprinted in Shane and Bruff, *supra* note 79, at 591–592.
63. Lesbian/Gay Freedom Day Comm., Inc. v. U.S. I. N. S., 541 F. Supp. 569 (N.D. Cal. 1982), *aff'd sub nom.* Hill v. U.S.I.N.S., 714 F.2d 1470 (9th Cir. 1983).
64. Immigration Act of 1990, § 601(a), Pub. L. 101-649, 104 Stat. 5067 (1990).

Dalton adds a potentially important dimension to our consideration of the non-execution phenomenon because a seeming implication of Professor Shane's taxonomy is that the underenforcement of law should generally be considered a problem of statutory, rather than constitutional law. For example, when an agency acts under his second category, "statutorily authorized waivers," the legal question presented is whether the agency's proffered waiver of the law properly interprets the scope of that statutory waiver authority. No larger constitutional issue seems to be implicated. Conversely, the problem with the final category—nonexecution based on flat-out resistance to congressional policy—would seem to be the irreconcilability of flat-out resistance with any plausible interpretation of Congress's intent in granting administrative authority to the executive branch in the first place. The intermediate categories of priority-setting can likewise be analyzed under the familiar administrative law standard, i.e., whether the decision was "arbitrary, capricious, [or] an abuse of discretion," 5 U.S.C. § 706. Implementing a statute properly under this standard generally requires that the relevant agency (a) consider all policy factors that the governing statute makes mandatory, (b) forego consideration of any policy factor that the governing statute prohibits, (c) reach a reasonable decision based on relevant factors, and (d) explain its decision adequately. See generally *Citizens to Preserve Overton Park v. Volpe*, 401 U.S. 402 (1971).

If administrative law does provide the right framework for analyzing these issues, consider your intuitions about the *statutory* defensibility of the specific examples Professor Shane mentions—are any more or less problematic, in your view, as a challenge to the rule of law? What would it take to make a persuasive case that the following initiatives were not "arbitrary and capricious?"

- HHS's relaxation of work standards under the Temporary Assistance for Needy Families Act?

- OSHA's refraining from inspections of workplaces about which it has not received worker complaints?

- Treasury's effective postponement of what would otherwise have been employer obligations to provide insurance under the Affordable Care Act?

- Limiting criminal prosecution of draft nonregistrants to vocal "refuseniks" only?

- Not prosecuting marijuana offenses against individuals in compliance with their respective states' marijuana laws?

2. *How Much Persistence Does Faithfulness Require?* In the episode Professor Shane recounts concerning gay and lesbian immigration, there was disagreement between the Fifth and Ninth Circuits as to the correctness of the Justice Department's legal position that the INS could enforce the exclusion without the benefit of a PHS certificate. To the best of your authors' knowledge, however, the Reagan Administration did not seek Supreme Court review of the Ninth Circuit's unfavorable view of its position and simply gave up on enforcing the ban. Were these decisions, in your view, consistent with the faithful execution ideal? In other words, should the Administration

have considered itself duty-bound to pursue Supreme Court review? Alternatively, should the Attorney General have felt compelled to seek presidential involvement to force PHS performance of mental health inspections, notwithstanding the change in the Diagnostic and Statistical Manual of Mental Disorders? Would you imagine the President would have welcomed such an invitation?

3. *Accountability for Nonexecution.* Even if (a) the executive branch frequently underenforces statutes and (b) underenforcement is analytically susceptible to conventional administrative law analysis, that does not mean such practices are necessarily subject to effective accountability measures. As Professor Shane notes, when nonexecution occurs on a "quasi-adjudicative" basis—that is, pursuant to prosecutorial discretion in either its criminal or civil enforcement forms—courts will rarely review it. On the criminal side, courts have long protected prosecutorial discretion as a matter of common law, sometimes suggesting that judicial review of individual criminal prosecution decisions would violate the separation of powers. *See, e.g., Inmates of Attica Correctional Facility v. Rockefeller,* 477 F.2d 375 (2d Cir. 1973); *Powell v. Katzenbach,* 359 F.2d 234 (D.C. Cir. 1965), *cert. denied,* 384 U.S. 906 (1966). On the civil side, as noted above, *Heckler v. Chaney,* 470 U.S. 821, 832 (1985) holds that an agency's decision not to take enforcement action should be presumed "committed to agency discretion" under the Administrative Procedure Act, 5 U.S.C.§ 701(a)(2), and thus immune to judicial review.

As for what Professor Shane calls "programmatic nonexecution," judicial review may be available, but only under certain conditions. First, the decision not to enforce must be crystallized in some form that a court would recognize as constituting reviewable "final agency action" under the Administrative Procedure Act, 5 U.S.C. § 704. An arguably amorphous pattern of executive branch indifference towards a set of statutory obligations may well not be enough. *Lujan v. National Wildlife Federation,* 497 U.S. 871 (1990). Moreover, a complaining party will need to meet the requirements of standing—a showing that nonenforcement is injuring them in a concrete, particularized way and that a requirement of more vigorous legal implementation would redress their injury. For example, even if HHS were funding state programs of public assistance under the Temporary Assistance for Needy Families Act that were insufficiently robust in their work requirements, who could bring suit?

Given the hurdles to judicial review, the obvious alternative is congressional oversight. Note, however, the likely difficulty of relying on robust oversight in a polarized political environment. For example, would a GOP-dominated Congress provide tough oversight of a Republican President determined not to enforce the Affordable Care Act? Would a Democrat-dominated Congress provide tough oversight of a Democratic President determined not to enforce immigration laws against undocumented persons who were otherwise in compliance with the law? Questions of accountability, as well as legality, loom large over the following case study:

Case Study: Obama Administration Deferred Action Policies for Undocumented Immigrants

The Department of Homeland Security has estimated that in 2009, Barack Obama's first year as president, the "unauthorized immigrant" population in the United States comprised 10.8 million people who had either entered the U.S. illegally or overstayed their visas. Michael Hoefer, Nancy Rytina, and Bryan Baker, Estimates of the Unauthorized Immigrant Population Residing in the United States: January 2011 (DHS, March 2012), available at https://www.dhs.gov/sites/default/files/publications/ois_ill_pe_2011_0.pdf. Despite an unprecedented volume of DHS enforcement actions, that population continued to increase through 2010 before starting to fall back.

Given an unauthorized immigrant population of that magnitude, President Obama tried twice to persuade Congress to enact legislation that would shield many undocumented persons from forced removal and provide a path for otherwise law-abiding immigrants to achieve lawful residence. In 2010, the Democratic House passed a bill first introduced during the George W. Bush Administration—the so-called DREAM (Development, Relief and Education for Alien Minors) Act—which would have protected hundreds of thousands of undocumented individuals who had been brought to the U.S. illegally as children, but who had essentially lived their lives as Americans. Specifically, the bill would have created a path to lawful resident status for immigrants between the ages of 12 and 35, who arrived in the U.S. before the age of 16, who were of good moral character, and who had resided continuously in the U.S. for at least 5 consecutive years since the date of their arrival. A Republican filibuster in the Senate, however, prevented the bill from coming to a vote. After Obama was reelected in 2012, Senate Democrats, now with some Republican support, managed to pass a bipartisan comprehensive immigration reform bill that would have provided a 13-year path to citizenship for unauthorized, but otherwise law-abiding immigrants in the U.S., provided that certain measures to toughen border security were taken first. House Republicans, now in the majority, refused to vote on the legislation.

The Obama Administration reacted in turn to each of these defeats with administrative programs based on "prosecutorial discretion." As the Supreme Court has recognized, although "[r]emoval is a civil, not criminal, matter," a "principal feature of the removal system is the broad discretion exercised by immigration officials" over decisions whether to forcibly remove undocumented persons from the United States. *Arizona v. United States*, 567 U.S. 387, 396 (2012). The Court has even gone so far as to state that the "concerns" prompting judicial deference to criminal prosecutorial discretion are "greatly magnified in the deportation context." *Reno v. American-Arab Anti-Discrimination Committee*, 525 U.S. 471, 490 (1999).

The variety of enforcement discretion which the Obama Administration proposed to implement on a broad basis is known as "deferred action." Kate M. Manuel and Todd Garvey, Prosecutorial Discretion in Immigration Enforcement: Legal Issues 11–12 (Congressional Research Service, Dec. 27, 2013). Deferred action "constitutes nonbinding, revocable notification that [immigration] authorities have chosen not to seek the removal of a particular individual." Anil Kalhan, *Deferred Action, Supervised Enforcement Discretion, and the Rule of Law Basis for Executive Action on Immigration*, 63 UCLA L. Rev. Disc. 58, 67 (2015). Prior to the mid-1970s, some individuals received such notifications pursuant to a so-called "nonpriority program," described only in internal "operations instructions" of what used to be called the Immigration and Naturalization Service. The first publication of such instructions came in 1975, as a result of litigation involving the late John Lennon. Shoba S. Wadhia, *The Role of Prosecutorial Discretion in Immigration Law*, 9 Conn. Pub. Int. L.J. 243, 246–248 (2010). The term "deferred action" has since been incorporated into the Immigration and Naturalization Act. 8 U.S.C. § 1227(d)(2).

Unlike the bills that failed in Congress, deferred action does not directly change the legal status of any immigrant. If someone either entered the U.S. unlawfully or overstayed their visa, they remain susceptible to forced removal because the grant of deferred action is revocable. Over the years, however, changes in the law have meant that recipients of deferred action receive certain collateral benefits aside from the reduced anxiety resulting from the official notification of low-priority status. For example, aliens who leave the U.S., voluntarily or otherwise, after having been present in the U.S. without legal authority for at least one year become inadmissible for lawful re-entry for ten years thereafter. 8 U.S.C. § 1182(a)(9)(B)(i)(II). But a grant of "deferred action" tolls the period of "unlawful presence." Thus, any undocumented persons who receive deferred action within a year of their unauthorized entry or overstaying a grant of lawful presence could leave the United States and apply for reentry without waiting the statutory ten years. Likely significant for many more aliens, however, under immigration regulations adopted in 1981, an alien who has been granted deferred action may also apply for a discretionary grant of work authorization in the U.S. immediately "if the alien establishes an economic necessity for employment." 8 C.F.R. § 274a.12(c)(14) (2015).

The Obama Administration's first initiative to implement deferred action on a programmatic basis followed the legislative impasse over the DREAM Act. The so-called "Deferred Action for Childhood Arrivals (DACA)" program. It was embodied in a memorandum entitled, "Exercising Prosecutorial Discretion with Respect to Individuals Who Came to the United States as Children," sent by Secretary of Homeland Security Janet Napolitano to the Acting Commissioner of U.S. Customs and Border Protection (CBP) and the Directors of U.S. Citizenship and Immigration Services (UCSIS) and of Immigration and Customs Enforcement (ICE), all sub-agencies within DHS. The memo essentially covered most of the individuals who would have benefitted from the DREAM Act, although applicants needed to be under 30. Furthermore, an applicant would be required either to be in school, to have graduated from high school or obtained a general education development certificate, or to be an honorably discharged veteran. Relief would not be provided under the DACA Program for anyone convicted of a felony offense, a significant misdemeanor offense, or multiple misdemeanor offenses, or who would otherwise posed a threat to national security or public safety. Successful applicants would receive deferred action for a two-year renewable period, but no change in legal status. The memo repeatedly stated that DHS was not waiving any discretion to make decisions about applicants on an individuated basis, providing, for example: "No individual should receive deferred action under this memorandum unless they first pass a background check and requests for relief pursuant to this memorandum are to be decided on a case by case basis. DHS cannot provide any assurance that relief will be granted in all cases." Secretary Napolitano characterized her directive as guidance for the exercise of prosecutorial discretion to help ensure that "enforcement resources are not expended on . . . low priority cases but are instead appropriately focused on people who meet our enforcement priorities."

The DACA program was politically controversial, but the litigation it triggered in opposition proved inconsequential. A challenge by ICE agents and deportation officers, along with the State of Mississippi, was thrown out for lack of standing. *Crane v. Johnson*, 783 F.3d 244 (5th Cir. 2015). A similar challenge by an Arizona sheriff met the same fate. *Arpaio v. Obama*, 797 F.3d 11 (D.C. Cir. 2015), *cert. denied*, 136 S. Ct. 900 (2016).

The history of the Obama Administration's second programmatic initiative regarding deferred action has proved, however, to be far more complex. Following the President's reelection, the Senate passed a bipartisan comprehensive immigration reform bill, but the GOP-controlled House — despite the likelihood of majority support — refused to put the bill to a vote. As explained by New York Times reporter Charlie Savage, the White House, in mid-2014, coordinated a process of interagency consultation intended to identify how far the Administration could go in extending deferred action to immigrants whose forced removal would be a low enforcement priority. CHARLIE SAVAGE, POWER WARS: INSIDE OBAMA'S POST-9/11 PRESIDENCY 659–666 (2015). Key Administration officials in designing the strategy included White House Counsel Neil Eggleston, Karl Thompson, then the new acting head of OLC, and Lucas Guttentag, a law professor and long-time advocate for immigrant rights, who had become Senior Counselor to Leon Rodriguez, the then-recently confirmed Director of USCIS. They developed a plan to extend deferred action to as many as four million undocumented immigrants whose children were citizens by virtue of their birth on U.S. soil. Under existing immigration law, those children, upon reaching the age of 21, would be entitled to seek legal residency for their close relatives. Deferred action for the parents could keep them in the U.S. until then. The legal policy group also considered extending deferred action to the young people who received deferred action under the DACA program, but rejected the idea based on Mr. Thompson's legal analysis.

The new program was formalized through two memoranda that DHS Secretary Jeh Johnson issued on November 20, 2014. The first, entitled, "Policies for the Apprehension, Detention and Removal of Undocumented Immigrants," set forth "Department-wide guidance" on DHS civil enforcement priorities. It created three enforcement categories. Of greatest concern would be persons identified as "threats to national security, border security, and public safety." Second-highest priority would be accorded to "misdemeanants and new immigration violators." Lowest priority would attach to persons who committed other immigration violations, although even those aliens, according to the memo, "should generally be removed unless they qualify for asylum or another form of relief under our laws or, unless, in the judgment of an immigration officer, the alien is not a threat to the integrity of the immigration system or there are factors suggesting the alien should not be an enforcement priority."

The second memo, entitled, "Exercising Prosecutorial Discretion with Respect to Individuals Who Came to the United States as Children and with Respect to Certain Individuals Who Are the Parents of U.S. Citizens or Permanent Residents," was, like the Napolitano DACA memo, issued to the three key DHS officials in charge of immigration enforcement. The new policy, called "Deferred Action for Parents of Americans" or DAPA, for short, soon entered a tortuous route through the federal courts. During the 2016 presidential campaign, Donald Trump promised, as President, to undo DACA and DAPA. As you will see from the notes below, undoing DAPA would be easier because the government would simply have to abandon its plans to defend it from hostile lower courts. Nonetheless, analyzing the way in which the Office of Legal Counsel sought to defend DAPA surfaces the kinds of issues likely to face any Administration seeking to defend a programmatic underenforcement of any regulatory statute. A survey of the issues raised follows this excerpt from the OLC opinion.

The Department of Homeland Security's Authority to Prioritize Removal of Certain Aliens Unlawfully Present in the United States and to Defer Removal of Others

38 Op. O.L.C. ___ (2014)

MEMORANDUM OPINION FOR THE SECRETARY OF HOMELAND SECURITY
AND THE COUNSEL TO THE PRESIDENT

You have asked two questions concerning the scope of the Department of Homeland Security's discretion to enforce the immigration laws. First, you have asked whether, in light of the limited resources available to the Department ("DHS") to remove aliens unlawfully present in the United States, it would be legally permissible for the Department to implement a policy prioritizing the removal of certain categories of aliens over others. DHS has explained that although there are approximately 11.3 million undocumented aliens in the country, it has the resources to remove fewer than 400,000 such aliens each year. DHS's proposed policy would prioritize the removal of aliens who present threats to national security, public safety, or border security. . . .

Second, you have asked whether it would be permissible for DHS to extend deferred action, a form of temporary administrative relief from removal, to certain aliens who are the parents of children who are present in the United States. Specifically, DHS has proposed to implement a program under which an alien could apply for, and would be eligible to receive, deferred action if he or she is not a DHS removal priority under the policy described above; has continuously resided in the United States since before January 1, 2010; has a child who is either a U.S. citizen or a lawful permanent resident; is physically present in the United States both when DHS announces its program and at the time of application for deferred action; and presents "no other factors that, in the exercise of discretion, make[] the grant of deferred action inappropriate." You have also asked whether DHS could implement a similar program for parents of individuals who have received deferred action under the Deferred Action for Childhood Arrivals ("DACA") program.

As has historically been true of deferred action, these proposed deferred action programs would not "legalize" any aliens who are unlawfully present in the United States: Deferred action does not confer any lawful immigration status, nor does it provide a path to obtaining permanent residence or citizenship. Grants of deferred action under the proposed programs would, rather, represent DHS's decision not to seek an alien's removal for a prescribed period of time. Under decades-old regulations promulgated pursuant to authority delegated by Congress, see 8 U.S.C. §§ 1103(a)(3), 1324a(h)(3), aliens who are granted deferred action—like certain other categories of aliens who do not have lawful immigration status, such as asylum applicants— may apply for authorization to work in the United States in certain circumstances, 8 C.F.R. § 274a.12(c)(14) (providing that deferred action recipients may apply for work authorization if they can show an "economic necessity for employment"); see also 8 C.F.R. § 109.1(b)(7) (1982). Under DHS policy guidance, a grant of deferred action also suspends an alien's accrual of unlawful presence for purposes of [statutory] provisions that restrict the admission of aliens who have departed the United States after having been unlawfully present for specified periods of time. A grant of deferred action under the proposed programs would remain in effect for three years, subject to renewal, and could be terminated at any time at DHS's discretion.

For the reasons discussed below, we conclude that DHS's proposed prioritization policy and its proposed deferred action program for parents of U.S. citizens and lawful permanent residents would be permissible exercises of DHS's discretion to enforce the immigration laws. We further conclude that, as it has been described to us, the proposed deferred action program for parents of DACA recipients would not be a permissible exercise of enforcement discretion.

I.

We first address DHS's authority to prioritize the removal of certain categories of aliens over others. We begin by discussing some of the sources and limits of DHS's enforcement discretion under the immigration laws, and then analyze DHS's proposed prioritization policy in light of these considerations.

A.

DHS's authority to remove aliens from the United States rests on the Immigration and Nationality Act of 1952 ("INA"), as amended, 8 U.S.C. §§ 1101 et seq. In the INA, Congress established a comprehensive scheme governing immigration and naturalization. The INA specifies certain categories of aliens who are inadmissible to the United States. *See* 8 U.S.C. § 1182. It also specifies "which aliens may be removed from the United States and the procedures for doing so." *Arizona v. United States*, 132 S. Ct. 2492, 2499 (2012). . . .

Before 2003, the Department of Justice, through the Immigration and Naturalization Service ("INS"), was also responsible for providing immigration-related administrative services and generally enforcing the immigration laws. In the Homeland Security Act of 2002, Congress transferred most of these functions to DHS, giving it primary responsibility both for initiating removal proceedings and for carrying out final orders of removal. The Act divided INS's functions among three different agencies within DHS: U.S. Citizenship and Immigration Services ("USCIS"), which oversees legal immigration into the United States and provides immigration and naturalization services to aliens; ICE, which enforces federal laws governing customs, trade, and immigration; and U.S. Customs and Border Protection ("CBP"), which monitors and secures the nation's borders and ports of entry. The Secretary of Homeland Security is thus now "charged with the administration and enforcement of [the INA] and all other laws relating to the immigration and naturalization of aliens." 8 U.S.C. § 1103(a)(1).

As a general rule, when Congress vests enforcement authority in an executive agency, that agency has the discretion to decide whether a particular violation of the law warrants prosecution or other enforcement action. This discretion is rooted in the President's constitutional duty to "take Care that the Laws be faithfully executed," U.S. Const. art. II, § 3, and it reflects a recognition that the "faithful[]" execution of the law does not necessarily entail "act[ing] against each technical violation of the statute" that an agency is charged with enforcing. *Heckler v. Chaney*, 470 U.S. 821, 831 (1985). Rather, as the Supreme Court explained in *Chaney*, the decision whether to initiate enforcement proceedings is a complex judgment that calls on the agency to "balanc[e] . . . a number of factors which are peculiarly within its expertise." *Id*. . . .

The principles of enforcement discretion discussed in *Chaney* apply with particular force in the context of immigration. Congress enacted the INA against a background understanding that immigration is "a field where flexibility and the adaptation of the congressional policy to infinitely variable conditions constitute the essence of the program." *United States ex rel. Knauff v. Shaughnessy*, 338 U.S. 537, 543 (1950) (internal quotation marks omitted). Consistent with this understanding, the INA vested the Attorney General (now the Secretary of Homeland Security) with broad authority to "establish such regulations; . . . issue such instructions; and perform such other acts as he deems necessary for carrying out his authority" under the statute. 8 U.S.C. § 1103(a)(3). Years later, when Congress created the Department of Homeland Security, it expressly charged DHS with responsibility for "[e]stablishing national immigration enforcement policies and priorities." Homeland Security Act of 2002, Pub. L. No. 107-296, § 402(5), 116 Stat. 2135, 2178 (codified at 6 U.S.C. § 202(5)).

With respect to removal decisions in particular, the Supreme Court has recognized that "the broad discretion exercised by immigration officials" is a "principal feature of the removal system" under the INA. *Arizona*, 132 S. Ct. at 2499. The INA expressly authorizes immigration officials to grant certain forms of discretionary relief from removal for aliens, including parole, 8 U.S.C. § 1182(d)(5)(A); asylum, *id.* § 1158(b)(1)(A); and cancellation of removal, *id.* § 1229b. But in addition to administering these statutory forms of relief, "[f]ederal officials, as an initial matter, must decide whether it makes sense to pursue removal at all." *Arizona*, 132 S. Ct. at 2499. And, as the Court has explained, "[a]t each stage" of the removal process "commenc[[ing] proceedings, adjudicat[ing] cases, [and] execut[ing] removal orders" immigration officials have "discretion to abandon the endeavor." *Am.-Arab Anti-Discrim. Comm.*, 525 U.S. at 483 (quoting 8 U.S.C. § 1252(g) (alterations in original)). . . .

Immigration officials' discretion in enforcing the laws is not, however, unlimited. Limits on enforcement discretion are both implicit in, and fundamental to, the Constitution's allocation of governmental powers between the two political branches. These limits, however, are not clearly defined. The open-ended nature of the inquiry under the Take Care Clause"—whether a particular exercise of discretion is "faithful[]" to the law enacted by Congress—does not lend itself easily to the application of set formulas or bright-line rules. And because the exercise of enforcement discretion generally is not subject to judicial review, *see Chaney*, 470 U.S. at 831–33, neither the Supreme Court nor the lower federal courts have squarely addressed its constitutional bounds. Rather, the political branches have addressed the proper allocation of enforcement authority through the political process. As the Court noted in *Chaney*, Congress "may limit an agency's exercise of enforcement power if it wishes, either by setting substantive priorities, or by otherwise circumscribing an agency's power to discriminate among issues or cases it will pursue." *Id.* at 833. The history of immigration policy illustrates this principle: Since the INA was enacted, the Executive Branch has on numerous occasions exercised discretion to extend various forms of immigration relief to categories of aliens for humanitarian, foreign policy, and other reasons. When Congress has been dissatisfied with Executive action, it has responded, as *Chaney* suggests, by enacting legislation to limit the Executive's discretion in enforcing the immigration laws.

Nonetheless, the nature of the Take Care duty does point to at least four general (and closely related) principles governing the permissible scope of enforcement discretion that we believe are particularly relevant here. First, enforcement decisions should reflect "factors which are peculiarly within [the enforcing agency's] expertise." *Chaney*, 470 U.S. at 831. Those factors may include considerations related to agency resources, such as "whether the agency has enough resources to undertake the action," or "whether agency resources are best spent on this violation or another." *Id.* Other relevant considerations may include "the proper ordering of [the agency's] priorities," *id.* at 832, and the agency's assessment of "whether the particular enforcement action [at issue] best fits the agency's overall policies," *id.* at 831.

Second, the Executive cannot, under the guise of exercising enforcement discretion, attempt to effectively rewrite the laws to match its policy preferences. In other words, an agency's enforcement decisions should be consonant with, rather than contrary to, the congressional policy underlying the statutes the agency is charged with administering. . . .

Third, the Executive Branch ordinarily cannot, as the Court put it in *Chaney*, "consciously and expressly adopt[] a general policy" that is so extreme as to amount to an abdication of its statutory responsibilities." 470 U.S. at 833 n.4. Abdication of the duties assigned to the agency by statute is ordinarily incompatible with the constitutional obligation to faithfully execute the laws. . . .

Finally, lower courts, following *Chaney*, have indicated that non-enforcement decisions are most comfortably characterized as judicially unreviewable exercises of enforcement discretion when they are made on a case-by-case basis. That reading of *Chaney* reflects a conclusion that case-by-case enforcement decisions generally avoid the concerns mentioned above. Courts have noted that "single-shot non-enforcement decisions" almost inevitably rest on "the sort of mingled assessments of fact, policy, and law . . . that are, as *Chaney* recognizes, peculiarly within the agency's expertise and discretion." *Crowley Caribbean Transp.*, 37 F.3d at 676–77 (emphasis omitted). Individual enforcement decisions made on the basis of case-specific factors are also unlikely to constitute "general polic[ies] that [are] so extreme as to amount to an abdication of [the agency's] statutory responsibilities." That does not mean that all "general policies" respecting non-enforcement are categorically forbidden: Some "general policies" may, for example, merely provide a framework for making individualized, discretionary assessments about whether to initiate enforcement actions in particular cases. *Cf. Reno v. Flores*, 507 U.S. 292, 313 (1993) (explaining that an agency's use of "reasonable presumptions and generic rules" is not incompatible with a requirement to make individualized determinations). But a general policy of non-enforcement that forecloses the exercise of case-by-case discretion poses "special risks" that the agency has exceeded the bounds of its enforcement discretion.

B.

We now turn, against this backdrop, to DHS's proposed prioritization policy. In their exercise of enforcement discretion, DHS and its predecessor, INS, have long employed guidance instructing immigration officers to prioritize the enforcement of the immigration laws against certain categories of aliens and to deprioritize their enforcement against others. The policy DHS proposes, which is similar to but would supersede earlier policy guidance, is designed to "provide clearer and more effective guidance in the pursuit" of DHS's enforcement priorities; namely, "threats to national security, public safety and border security." Johnson Prioritization Memorandum at 1.

Under the proposed policy, DHS would identify three categories of undocumented aliens who would be priorities for removal from the United States. *See generally id.* at 3–5. The highest priority category would include aliens who pose particularly serious threats to national security, border security, or public safety, including aliens engaged in or suspected of espionage or terrorism, aliens convicted of offenses related to participation in criminal street gangs, aliens convicted of certain felony offenses, and aliens apprehended at the border while attempting to enter the United States unlawfully. *See id*. at 3. The second-highest priority would include aliens convicted of multiple or significant misdemeanor offenses; aliens who are apprehended after unlawfully entering the United States who cannot establish that they have been continuously present in the United States since January 1, 2014; and aliens determined to have significantly abused the visa or visa waiver programs. *See id*. at 3–4. The third priority category would include other aliens who have been issued a final order of removal on or after January 1, 2014. *See id*. at 4. The policy would also provide that none of these aliens should be prioritized for removal if they "qualify for asylum or another form of relief under our laws." *Id*. at 3–5.

The policy would instruct that resources should be directed to these priority categories in a manner "commensurate with the level of prioritization identified." *Id*. at 5. It would, however, also leave significant room for immigration officials to evaluate the circumstances of individual cases. For example, the policy would permit an ICE Field Office Director, CBP Sector Chief, or CBP Director of Field Operations to deprioritize the removal of an alien falling in the highest priority category if, in her judgment, "there are compelling and exceptional factors that clearly indicate the alien is not a threat to national security, border security, or public safety and should not therefore be an enforcement priority." *Id*. at 3. Similar discretionary provisions would apply to aliens in the second and third priority categories. The policy would also provide a non-exhaustive list of factors DHS personnel should consider in making such deprioritization judgments.[65] In addition, the policy would expressly state that its terms should not be construed "to prohibit or discourage the apprehension, detention, or removal of aliens unlawfully in the United States who are not identified as priorities," and would further provide that "[i]mmigration officers and attorneys may pursue removal of an alien not identified as a priority" if, "in the judgment of an ICE Field Office Director, removing such an alien would serve an important federal interest." *Id*. at 5.

DHS has explained that the proposed policy is designed to respond to the practical reality that the number of aliens who are removable under the INA vastly exceeds the resources Congress has made available to DHS for processing and carrying out removals. The resource constraints are striking. As noted, DHS has informed us that there are approximately 11.3 million undocumented aliens in the country, but that Congress has appropriated sufficient resources for ICE to remove fewer than 400,000

---

65. These factors include "extenuating circumstances involving the offense of conviction; extended length of time since the offense of conviction; length of time in the United States; military service; family or community ties in the United States; status as a victim, witness or plaintiff in civil or criminal proceedings; or compelling humanitarian factors such as poor health, age, pregnancy, a young child or a seriously ill relative." Johnson Prioritization Memorandum at 6.

aliens each year, a significant percentage of whom are typically encountered at or near the border rather than in the interior of the country. The proposed policy explains that, because DHS "cannot respond to all immigration violations or remove all persons illegally in the United States," it seeks to "prioritize the use of enforcement personnel, detention space, and removal assets" to "ensure that use of its limited resources is devoted to the pursuit of" DHS's highest priorities.

In our view, DHS's proposed prioritization policy falls within the scope of its lawful discretion to enforce the immigration laws. To begin with, the policy is based on a factor clearly "within [DHS's] expertise." *Chaney*, 470 U.S. at 831. Faced with sharply limited resources, DHS necessarily must make choices about which removals to pursue and which removals to defer. DHS's organic statute itself recognizes this inevitable fact, instructing the Secretary to establish "national immigration enforcement policies and priorities." 6 U.S.C. § 202(5). And an agency's need to ensure that scarce enforcement resources are used in an effective manner is a quintessential basis for the use of prosecutorial discretion.

The policy DHS has proposed, moreover, is consistent with the removal priorities established by Congress. In appropriating funds for DHS's enforcement activities—which, as noted, are sufficient to permit the removal of only a fraction of the undocumented aliens currently in the country" Congress has directed DHS to "prioritize the identification and removal of aliens convicted of a crime by the severity of that crime." Department of Homeland Security Appropriations Act, 2014, Pub. L. No. 113-76, div. F, tit. II, 128 Stat. 5, 251 ("DHS Appropriations Act"). Consistent with this directive, the proposed policy prioritizes individuals convicted of criminal offenses involving active participation in a criminal street gang, most offenses classified as felonies in the convicting jurisdiction, offenses classified as "aggravated felonies" under the INA, and certain misdemeanor offenses. Johnson Prioritization Memorandum at 3–4. The policy ranks these priority categories according to the severity of the crime of conviction. The policy also prioritizes the removal of other categories of aliens who pose threats to national security or border security, matters about which Congress has demonstrated particular concern. The policy thus raises no concern that DHS has relied "on factors which Congress had not intended it to consider." *Nat'l Ass'n of Home Builders*, 551 U.S. at 658.

Further, although the proposed policy is not a "single-shot non-enforcement decision," neither does it amount to an abdication of DHS's statutory responsibilities, or constitute a legislative rule overriding the commands of the substantive statute. The proposed policy provides a general framework for exercising enforcement discretion in individual cases, rather than establishing an absolute, inflexible policy of not enforcing the immigration laws in certain categories of cases. Given that the resources Congress has allocated to DHS are sufficient to remove only a small fraction of the total population of undocumented aliens in the United States, setting forth written guidance about how resources should presumptively be allocated in particular cases is a reasonable means of ensuring that DHS's severely limited resources are systematically directed to its highest priorities across a large and diverse agency, as well as ensuring consistency in the administration of the removal system. The proposed policy's identification of categories of aliens who constitute removal priorities is also consistent with the categorical nature of Congress's instruction to prioritize the removal of criminal aliens in the DHS Appropriations Act.

And, significantly, the proposed policy does not identify any category of removable aliens whose removal may not be pursued under any circumstances. Although the proposed policy limits the discretion of immigration officials to expend resources to remove non-priority aliens, it does not eliminate that discretion entirely. It directs immigration officials to use their resources to remove aliens in a manner "commensurate with the level of prioritization identified," but (as noted above) it does not "prohibit or discourage the apprehension, detention, or removal of aliens unlawfully in the United States who are not identified as priorities." Instead, it authorizes the removal of even non-priority aliens if, in the judgment of an ICE Field Office Director, "removing such an alien would serve an important federal interest," a standard the policy leaves open-ended. Accordingly, the policy provides for case-by-case determinations about whether an individual alien's circumstances warrant the expenditure of removal resources, employing a broad standard that leaves ample room for the exercise of individualized discretion by responsible officials. For these reasons, the proposed policy avoids the difficulties that might be raised by a more inflexible prioritization policy and dispels any concern that DHS has either undertaken to rewrite the immigration laws or abdicated its statutory responsibilities with respect to non-priority aliens.

II.

We turn next to the permissibility of DHS's proposed deferred action programs for certain aliens who are parents of U.S. citizens, lawful permanent residents ("LPRs"), or DACA recipients, and who are not removal priorities under the proposed policy discussed above. We begin by discussing the history and current practice of deferred action. We then discuss the legal authorities on which deferred action relies and identify legal principles against which the proposed use of deferred action could be evaluated. Finally, we turn to an analysis of the proposed deferred action programs themselves . . . .

A.

In immigration law, the term "deferred action" refers to an exercise of administrative discretion in which immigration officials temporarily defer the removal of an alien unlawfully present in the United States. It is one of a number of forms of discretionary relief—in addition to such statutory and non-statutory measures as parole, temporary protected status, deferred enforced departure, and extended voluntary departure—that immigration officials have used over the years to temporarily prevent the removal of undocumented aliens.

The practice of granting deferred action dates back several decades. For many years after the INA was enacted, INS exercised prosecutorial discretion to grant "non-priority" status to removable aliens who presented "appealing humanitarian factors." This form of administrative discretion was later termed "deferred action."

Although the practice of granting deferred action "developed without express statutory authorization," it has become a regular feature of the immigration removal system that has been acknowledged by both Congress and the Supreme Court. Deferred action "does not confer any immigration status" "i.e., it does not establish any enforceable legal right to remain in the United States" and it may be revoked by immigration authorities at their discretion. USCIS SOP at 3, 7. Assuming it is not revoked, however, it represents DHS's decision not to seek the alien's removal for a specified period of time.

Under longstanding regulations and policy guidance promulgated pursuant to statutory authority in the INA, deferred action recipients may receive two additional benefits. [The opinion identifies the potential to apply for work permits and the tolling of the period of "unlawful presence," for purposes of re-entry after departure.]

Immigration officials today continue to grant deferred action in individual cases for humanitarian and other purposes, a practice we will refer to as "ad hoc deferred action." Recent USCIS guidance provides that personnel may recommend ad hoc deferred action if they "encounter cases during [their] normal course of business that they feel warrant deferred action." USCIS SOP at 4. An alien may also apply for ad hoc deferred action by submitting a signed, written request to USCIS containing "[a]n explanation as to why he or she is seeking deferred action" along with supporting documentation, proof of identity, and other records. *Id.* at 3.

For decades, INS and later DHS have also implemented broader programs that make discretionary relief from removal available for particular classes of aliens. In many instances, these agencies have made such broad-based relief available through the use of parole, temporary protected status, deferred enforced departure, or extended voluntary departure. . . . [I]n 1990, INS implemented a "Family Fairness" program that authorized granting extended voluntary departure and work authorization to the estimated 1.5 million spouses and children of aliens who had been granted legal status under the Immigration Reform and Control Act of 1986, Pub. L. No. 99-603, 100 Stat. 3359 ("IRCA"). *See* Memorandum for Regional Commissioners, INS, from Gene McNary, Commissioner, INS, *Re: Family Fairness: Guidelines for Voluntary Departure under 8 CFR 242.5 for the Ineligible Spouses and Children of Legalized Aliens* (Feb. 2, 1990) ("Family Fairness Memorandum").

On at least five occasions since the late 1990s, INS and later DHS have also made discretionary relief available to certain classes of aliens through the use of deferred action. . . .

Congress has long been aware of the practice of granting deferred action, including in its categorical variety, and of its salient features; and it has never acted to disapprove or limit the practice. On the contrary, it has enacted several pieces of legislation that have either assumed that deferred action would be available in certain circumstances, or expressly directed that deferred action be extended to certain categories of aliens. . . . These classes include certain immediate family members of LPRs who were killed on September 11, 2001, and certain immediate family members of certain U.S. citizens killed in combat. In the same legislation, Congress made these individuals eligible to obtain lawful status as "family-sponsored immigrant[s]" or "immediate relative[s]" of U.S. citizens.

Finally, Congress acknowledged the practice of granting deferred action in the REAL ID Act of 2005, Pub. L. No. 109-13, div. B, 119 Stat. 231, 302 (codified at 49 U.S.C. § 30301 note), which makes a state-issued driver's license or identification card acceptable for federal purposes only if the state verifies, among other things, that the card's recipient has "[e]vidence of [l]awful [s]tatus." Congress specified that, for this purpose, acceptable evidence of lawful status includes proof of, among other things, citizenship, lawful permanent or temporary residence, or "approved deferred action status." *Id.* § 202(c)(2)(B)(viii).

B.

. . . Deferred action differs in at least three respects from more familiar and widespread exercises of enforcement discretion. First, unlike (for example) the paradigmatic exercise of prosecutorial discretion in a criminal case, the conferral of deferred action does not represent a decision not to prosecute an individual for past unlawful conduct; it instead represents a decision to openly tolerate an undocumented alien's continued presence in the United States for a fixed period (subject to revocation at the agency's discretion). Second, unlike most exercises of enforcement discretion, deferred action carries with it benefits in addition to non-enforcement itself . . . . Third, class-based deferred action programs, like those for VAWA recipients and victims of Hurricane Katrina, do not merely enable individual immigration officials to select deserving beneficiaries from among those aliens who have been identified or apprehended for possible removal — as is the case with ad hoc deferred action — but rather set forth certain threshold eligibility criteria and then invite individuals who satisfy these criteria to apply for deferred action status.

While these features of deferred action are somewhat unusual among exercises of enforcement discretion, the differences between deferred action and other exercises of enforcement discretion are less significant than they might initially appear. The first feature — the toleration of an alien's continued unlawful presence — is an inevitable element of almost any exercise of discretion in immigration enforcement. . . . Deferred action arguably goes beyond such tacit acknowledgment by expressly communicating to the alien that his or her unlawful presence will be tolerated for a prescribed period of time. This difference is not, in our view, insignificant. But neither does it fundamentally transform deferred action into something other than an exercise of enforcement discretion: As we have previously noted, deferred action confers no lawful immigration status, provides no path to lawful permanent residence or citizenship, and is revocable at any time in the agency's discretion.

With respect to the second feature, the additional benefits deferred action confers — the ability to apply for work authorization and the tolling of unlawful presence — do not depend on background principles of agency discretion under DHS's general immigration authorities or the Take Care Clause at all, but rather depend on independent and more specific statutory authority rooted in the text of the INA. The first of those authorities, DHS's power to prescribe which aliens are authorized to work in the United States, is grounded in 8 U.S.C. § 1324a(h)(3), which defines an "unauthorized alien" not entitled to work in the United States as an alien who is neither an LPR nor "authorized to be . . . employed by [the INA] or by the Attorney General [now the Secretary of Homeland Security]." This statutory provision has long been understood to recognize the authority of the Secretary (and the Attorney General before him) to grant work authorization to particular classes of aliens. Although the INA requires the Secretary to grant work authorization to particular classes of aliens, it places few limitations on the Secretary's authority to grant work authorization to other classes of aliens. Further, and notably, additional provisions of the INA expressly contemplate that the Secretary may grant work authorization to aliens lacking lawful immigration status — even those who are in active removal proceedings or, in certain circumstances, those who have already received final orders of removal. *See id.* § 1226(a)(3) (permitting the Secretary to grant work authorization to an otherwise work-eligible alien who has been arrested and detained pending a decision whether to remove the alien from the United States); *id.* § 1231(a)(7) (permitting the Secretary under certain narrow circumstances to grant work authorization to aliens who have received final orders of removal). Consistent with these provisions, the Secretary has long permitted certain additional classes of aliens who lack lawful immigration status to apply for work authorization, including deferred action recipients who can demonstrate an economic necessity for employment.

The Secretary's authority to suspend the accrual of unlawful presence of deferred action recipients is similarly grounded in the INA. The relevant statutory provision treats an alien as "unlawfully present" for purposes of 8 U.S.C. § 1182(a)(9)(B)(i) and (a)(9)(C)(i)(I) if he "is present in the United States after the expiration of the period of stay authorized by the Attorney General." 8 U.S.C. § 1182(a)(9)(B)(ii). That language contemplates that the Attorney General (and now the Secretary) may authorize an alien to stay in the United States without accruing unlawful presence under section 1182(a)(9)(B)(i) or section 1182(a)(9)(C)(i). And DHS regulations and policy guidance interpret a "period of stay authorized by the Attorney General" to include periods during which an alien has been granted deferred action. *See* 8 C.F.R. § 214.14(d)(3); 28 C.F.R. § 1100.35(b)(2); USCIS Consolidation of Guidance at 42.

The final unusual feature of deferred action programs is particular to class-based programs. The breadth of such programs, in combination with the first two features of deferred action, may raise particular concerns about whether immigration officials have undertaken to substantively change the statutory removal system rather than simply adapting its application to individual circumstances. But the salient feature of class-based programs — the establishment of an affirmative application process with threshold eligibility criteria — does not in and of itself cross the line between executing the law and rewriting it. Although every class-wide deferred action program that has been implemented to date has established certain threshold eligibility criteria, each program has also left room for case-by-case determinations, giving immigration officials discretion to deny applications even if the applicant fulfills all of the program criteria. Like the establishment of enforcement priorities discussed in Part I, the establishment of threshold eligibility criteria can serve to avoid arbitrary enforcement decisions by individual officers, thereby furthering the goal of ensuring consistency across a large agency. The guarantee of individualized, case-by-case review helps avoid potential concerns that, in establishing such eligibility criteria, the Executive is attempting to rewrite the law by defining new categories of aliens who are automatically entitled to particular immigration relief. Furthermore, while permitting potentially eligible individuals to apply for an exercise of enforcement discretion is not especially common, many law enforcement agencies have developed programs that invite violators of the law to identify themselves to the authorities in exchange for leniency. Much as is the case with those programs, inviting eligible aliens to identify themselves through an application process may serve the agency's law enforcement interests by encouraging lower-priority individuals to identify themselves to the agency. In so doing, the process may enable the agency to better focus its scarce resources on higher enforcement priorities.

Apart from the considerations just discussed, perhaps the clearest indication that these features of deferred action programs are not per se impermissible is the fact that Congress, aware of these features, has repeatedly enacted legislation appearing to endorse such programs. As discussed above, Congress has not only directed that certain classes of aliens be made eligible for deferred action programs—and in at least one instance, in the case of VAWA beneficiaries, directed the expansion of an existing program—but also ranked evidence of approved deferred action status as evidence of "lawful status" for purposes of the REAL ID Act. These enactments strongly suggest that when DHS in the past has decided to grant deferred action to an individual or class of individuals, it has been acting in a manner consistent with congressional policy "rather than embarking on a frolic of its own." *United States v. Riverside Bayview Homes, Inc.*, 474 U.S. 121, 139 (1985). Congress's apparent endorsement of certain deferred action programs does not mean, of course, that a deferred action program can be lawfully extended to any group of aliens, no matter its characteristics or its scope, and no matter the circumstances in which the program is implemented. Because deferred action, like the prioritization policy discussed above, is an exercise of enforcement discretion rooted in the Secretary's broad authority to enforce the immigration laws and the President's duty to take care that the laws are faithfully executed, it is subject to the same four general principles previously discussed. . . .

Furthermore, because deferred action programs depart in certain respects from more familiar and widespread exercises of enforcement discretion, particularly careful examination is needed to ensure that any proposed expansion of deferred action complies with these general principles, so that the proposed program does not, in effect, cross the line between executing the law and rewriting it. In analyzing whether the proposed programs cross this line, we will draw substantial guidance from Congress's history of legislation concerning deferred action. In the absence of express statutory guidance, the nature of deferred action programs Congress has implicitly approved by statute helps to shed light on Congress's own understandings about the permissible uses of deferred action. Those understandings, in turn, help to inform our consideration of whether the proposed deferred action programs are "faithful[]" to the statutory scheme Congress has enacted. U.S. Const. art. II, § 3.

C.

We now turn to the specifics of DHS's proposed deferred action programs. . . .

1.

We begin by considering whether the proposed program for the parents of U.S. citizens and LPRs reflects considerations within the agency's expertise. . . .

With respect to DHS's first justification, the need to efficiently allocate scarce enforcement resources is a quintessential basis for an agency's exercise of enforcement discretion. *See Chaney*, 470 U.S. at 831. Because, as discussed earlier, Congress has appropriated only a small fraction of the funds needed for full enforcement, DHS can remove no more than a small fraction of the individuals who are removable under the immigration laws. The agency must therefore make choices about which violations of the immigration laws it will prioritize and pursue. And as *Chaney* makes clear, such choices are entrusted largely to the Executive's discretion. 470 U.S. at 831.

The deferred action program DHS proposes would not, of course, be costless. Processing applications for deferred action and its renewal requires manpower and resources. But DHS has informed us that the costs of administering the proposed program would be borne almost entirely by USCIS through the collection of application fees. DHS has indicated that the costs of administering the deferred action program would therefore not detract in any significant way from the resources available to ICE and CBP—the enforcement arms of DHS—which rely on money appropriated by Congress to fund their operations. DHS has explained that, if anything, the proposed deferred action program might increase ICE's and CBP's efficiency by in effect using USCIS's fee-funded resources to enable those enforcement divisions to more easily identify non-priority aliens and focus their resources on pursuing aliens who are strong candidates for removal. The proposed program, in short, might help DHS address its severe resource limitations, and at the very least likely would not exacerbate them.

DHS does not, however, attempt to justify the proposed program solely as a cost-saving measure, or suggest that its lack of resources alone is sufficient to justify creating a deferred action program for the proposed class. Rather, . . . DHS has explained that the program would also serve a particularized humanitarian interest in promoting family unity by enabling those parents of U.S. citizens and LPRs who are not otherwise enforcement priorities and who have demonstrated community and family ties in the United States (as evidenced by the length of time they have remained in the country) to remain united with their children in the United States.

Like determining how best to respond to resource constraints, determining how to address such "human concerns" in the immigration context is a consideration that is generally understood to fall within DHS's expertise. *Arizona*, 132 S. Ct. at 2499.

This second justification for the program also appears consonant with congressional policy embodied in the INA. Numerous provisions of the statute reflect a particular concern with uniting aliens with close relatives who have attained lawful immigration status in the United States. The INA provides a path to lawful status for the parents, as well as other immediate relatives, of U.S. citizens: U.S. citizens aged twenty-one or over may petition for parents to obtain visas that would permit them to enter and permanently reside in the United States, and there is no limit on the overall number of such petitions that may be granted. And although the INA contains no parallel provision permitting LPRs to petition on behalf of their parents, it does provide a path for LPRs to become citizens, at which point they too can petition to obtain visas for their parents. Additionally, the INA empowers the Attorney General to cancel the removal of, and adjust to lawful permanent resident status, aliens who have been physically present in the United States for a continuous period of not less than ten years, exhibit good moral character, have not been convicted of specified offenses, and have immediate relatives who are U.S. citizens or LPRs and who would suffer exceptional hardship from the alien's removal. DHS's proposal to focus on the parents of U.S. citizens and LPRs thus tracks a congressional concern, expressed in the INA, with uniting the immediate families of individuals who have permanent legal ties to the United States.

At the same time, because the temporary relief DHS's proposed program would confer to such parents is sharply limited in comparison to the benefits Congress has made available through statute, DHS's proposed program would not operate to circumvent the limits Congress has placed on the availability of those benefits. The statutory provisions discussed above offer the parents of U.S. citizens and LPRs the prospect of permanent lawful status in the United States. The cancellation of removal provision, moreover, offers the prospect of receiving such status immediately, without the delays generally associated with the family-based immigrant visa process. DHS's proposed program, in contrast, would not grant the parents of U.S. citizens and LPRs any lawful immigration status, provide a path to permanent residence or citizenship, or otherwise confer any legally enforceable entitlement to remain in the United States. It is true that, as we have discussed, a grant of deferred action would confer eligibility to apply for and obtain work authorization, pursuant to the Secretary's statutory authority to grant such authorization and the longstanding regulations promulgated thereunder. But unlike the automatic employment eligibility that accompanies LPR status, this authorization could be granted only on a showing of economic necessity, and would last only for the limited duration of the deferred action grant.

The other salient features of the proposal are similarly consonant with congressional policy. The proposed program would focus on parents who are not enforcement priorities under the prioritization policy discussed above — a policy that, as explained earlier, comports with the removal priorities set by Congress. The continuous residence requirement is likewise consistent with legislative judgments that extended periods of continuous residence are indicative of strong family and community ties.

We also do not believe DHS's proposed program amounts to an abdication of its statutory responsibilities, or a legislative rule overriding the commands of the statute. As discussed earlier, DHS's severe resource constraints mean that, unless circumstances change, it could not as a practical matter remove the vast majority of removable aliens present in the United States. The fact that the proposed program would defer the removal of a subset of these removable aliens—a subset that ranks near the bottom of the list of the agency's removal priorities—thus does not, by itself, demonstrate that the program amounts to an abdication of DHS's responsibilities. And the case-by-case discretion given to immigration officials under DHS's proposed program alleviates potential concerns that DHS has abdicated its statutory enforcement responsibilities with respect to, or created a categorical, rule-like entitlement to immigration relief for, the particular class of aliens eligible for the program. An alien who meets all the criteria for deferred action under the program would receive deferred action only if he or she "present[ed] no other factors that, in the exercise of discretion," would "make[] the grant of deferred action inappropriate." Johnson Deferred Action Memorandum at 4. The proposed policy does not specify what would count as such a factor; it thus leaves the relevant USCIS official with substantial discretion to determine whether a grant of deferred action is warranted. In other words, even if an alien [meets the specified criteria for deferred action], the USCIS official evaluating the alien's deferred action application must still make a judgment, in the exercise of her discretion, about whether that alien presents any other factor that would make a grant of deferred action inappropriate. This feature of the proposed program ensures that it does not create a categorical entitlement to deferred action that could raise concerns that DHS is either impermissibly attempting to rewrite or categorically declining to enforce the law with respect to a particular group of undocumented aliens.

Finally, the proposed deferred action program would resemble in material respects the kinds of deferred action programs Congress has implicitly approved in the past, which provides some indication that the proposal is consonant not only with interests reflected in immigration law as a general matter, but also with congressional understandings about the permissible uses of deferred action. As noted above, the program uses deferred action as an interim measure for a group of aliens to whom Congress has given a prospective entitlement to lawful immigration status. While Congress has provided a path to lawful status for the parents of U.S. citizens and LPRs, the process of obtaining that status "takes time." The proposed program would provide a mechanism for families to remain together, depending on their circumstances, for some or all of the intervening period. Immigration officials have on several occasions deployed deferred action programs as interim measures for other classes of aliens with prospective entitlements to lawful immigration status, including VAWA self-petitioners, bona fide T and U visa applicants, certain immediate family members of certain U.S. citizens killed in combat, and certain immediate family members of aliens killed on September 11, 2001. As noted above, each of these programs has received Congress's implicit approval — and, indeed, in the case of VAWA self-petitioners, a direction to expand the program beyond its original bounds.[15] In addition, much like these and other programs Congress has implicitly endorsed, the program serves substantial and particularized humanitarian interests. Removing the parents of U.S. citizens and LPRs — that is, of children who have established permanent legal ties to the United States — would separate them from their nuclear families, potentially for many years, until they were able to secure visas through the path Congress has provided. During that time, both the parents and their U.S. citizen or LPR children would be deprived of both the economic support and the intangible benefits that families provide.

We recognize that the proposed program would likely differ in size from these prior deferred action programs. Although DHS has indicated that there is no reliable way to know how many eligible aliens would actually apply for or would be likely to receive deferred action following individualized consideration under the proposed program, it has informed us that approximately 4 million individuals could be eligible to apply. We have thus considered whether the size of the program alone sets it at odds with congressional policy or the Executive's duties under the Take Care Clause. In the absence of express statutory guidance, it is difficult to say exactly how the program's potential size bears on its permissibility as an exercise of executive enforcement discretion. But because the size of DHS's proposed program corresponds to the size of a population to which Congress has granted a prospective entitlement to lawful status without numerical restriction, it seems to us difficult to sustain an argument, based on numbers alone, that DHS's proposal to grant a limited form of administrative relief as a temporary interim measure exceeds its enforcement discretion under the INA. Furthermore, while the potential size of the program is large, it is nevertheless only a fraction of the approximately 11 million undocumented aliens who remain in the United States each year because DHS lacks the resources to remove them; and, as we have indicated, the program is limited to individuals who would be unlikely to be removed under DHS's proposed prioritization policy. There is thus

---

15. Several extended voluntary departure programs have been animated by a similar rationale, and the most prominent of these programs also received Congress's implicit approval. In particular, as noted above, the Family Fairness policy, implemented in 1990, authorized granting extended voluntary departure and work authorization to the estimated 1.5 million spouses and children of aliens granted legal status under IRCA — aliens who would eventually "acquire lawful permanent resident status" and be able to petition on behalf of their family members. Family Fairness Memorandum at 1; see supra pp. 1415. Later that year, Congress granted the beneficiaries of the Family Fairness program an indefinite stay of deportation. See Immigration Act of 1990, Pub. L. No. 101649, § 301, 104 Stat. 4978, 5030. Although it did not make that grant of relief effective for nearly a year, Congress clarified that "the delay in effectiveness of this section shall not be construed as reflecting a Congressional belief that the existing family fairness program should be modified in any way before such date." Id. § 301(g). INS's policies for qualifying Third Preference visa applicants and nurses eligible for H1 nonimmigrant status likewise extended to aliens with prospective entitlements to lawful status.

little practical danger that the program, simply by virtue of its size, will impede removals that would otherwise occur in its absence. And although we are aware of no prior exercises of deferred action of the size contemplated here, INS's 1990 Family Fairness policy, which Congress later implicitly approved, made a comparable fraction of undocumented aliens—approximately four in ten" potentially eligible for discretionary extended voluntary departure relief. This suggests that DHS's proposed deferred action program is not, simply by virtue of its relative size, inconsistent with what Congress has previously considered a permissible exercise of enforcement discretion in the immigration context.

In light of these considerations, we believe the proposed expansion of deferred action to the parents of U.S. citizens and LPRs is lawful. . . .

2.

We now turn to the proposed deferred action program for the parents of DACA recipients. The relevant considerations are, to a certain extent, similar to those discussed above: Like the program for the parents of U.S. citizens and LPRs, the proposed program for parents of DACA recipients would respond to severe resource constraints that dramatically limit DHS's ability to remove aliens who are unlawfully present, and would be limited to individuals who would be unlikely to be removed under DHS's proposed prioritization policy. And like the proposed program for LPRs and U.S. citizens, the proposed program for DACA parents would preserve a significant measure of case-by-case discretion not to award deferred action even if the general eligibility criteria are satisfied.

But the proposed program for parents of DACA recipients is unlike the proposed program for parents of U.S. citizens and LPRs in two critical respects. First, although DHS justifies the proposed program in large part based on considerations of family unity, the parents of DACA recipients are differently situated from the parents of U.S. citizens and LPRs under the family-related provisions of the immigration law. Many provisions of the INA reflect Congress's general concern with not separating individuals who are legally entitled to live in the United States from their immediate family members. But the immigration laws do not express comparable concern for uniting persons who lack lawful status (or prospective lawful status) in the United States with their families. DACA recipients unquestionably lack lawful status in the United States. Although they may presumptively remain in the United States, at least for the duration of the grant of deferred action, that grant is both time-limited and contingent, revocable at any time in the agency's discretion. Extending deferred action to the parents of DACA recipients would therefore expand family-based immigration relief in a manner that deviates in important respects from the immigration system Congress has enacted and the policies that system embodies.

Second, as it has been described to us, the proposed deferred action program for the parents of DACA recipients would represent a significant departure from deferred action programs that Congress has implicitly approved in the past. Granting deferred action to the parents of DACA recipients would not operate as an interim measure for individuals to whom Congress has given a prospective entitlement to lawful status. Such parents have no special prospect of obtaining visas, since Congress has not enabled them to self-petition—as it has for VAWA self-petitioners and individuals eligible for T or U visas—or enabled their undocumented children to petition for visas on their behalf. Nor would granting deferred action to parents of DACA recipients, at least in the absence of other factors, serve interests that are comparable to those that have prompted implementation of deferred action programs in the past. Family unity is, as we have discussed, a significant humanitarian concern that underlies many provisions of the INA. But a concern with furthering family unity alone would not justify the proposed program, because in the absence of any family member with lawful status in the United States, it would not explain why that concern should be satisfied by permitting family members to remain in the United States. The decision to grant deferred action to DACA parents thus seems to depend critically on the earlier decision to make deferred action available to their children. But we are aware of no precedent for using deferred action in this way, to respond to humanitarian needs rooted in earlier exercises of deferred action. The logic underlying such an expansion does not have a clear stopping point: It would appear to argue in favor of extending relief not only to parents of DACA recipients, but also to the close relatives of any alien granted deferred action through DACA or any other program, those relatives' close relatives, and perhaps the relatives (and relatives' relatives) of any alien granted any form of discretionary relief from removal by the Executive.

For these reasons, the proposed deferred action program for the parents of DACA recipients is meaningfully different from the proposed program for the parents of U.S. citizens and LPRs. It does not sound in Congress's concern for maintaining the integrity of families of individuals legally entitled to live in the United States. And unlike prior deferred action programs in which Congress has acquiesced, it would treat the Executive's prior decision to extend deferred action to one population as justifying the extension of deferred action to additional populations. DHS, of course, remains free to consider whether to grant deferred action to individual parents of DACA recipients on an ad hoc basis. But in the absence of clearer indications that the proposed class-based deferred action program for DACA parents would be consistent with the congressional policies and priorities embodied in the immigration laws, we conclude that it would not be permissible.

III.

In sum, for the reasons set forth above, we conclude that DHS's proposed prioritization policy and its proposed deferred action program for parents of U.S. citizens and lawful permanent residents would be legally permissible, but that the proposed deferred action program for parents of DACA recipients would not be permissible.

Karl R. Thompson
Principal Deputy Assistant Attorney General
Office of Legal Counsel

———————

1. *Structuring the Advisory Process.* As Presidents often do, the Obama Administration disseminated the above-excerpted OLC opinion to coincide with the release of Secretary Johnson's memo establishing DAPA. Administrations may release Justice Department opinions — sometimes formal opinions of the Attorney General, but more often opinions from OLC — to substantiate the legality of controversial initiatives. The imprimatur of the Justice Department is presumably intended to elicit confidence in some degree of independent judgment, that is, that it is not only White House Counsel who thinks the President is on solid legal ground.

What then should be made of the model of legal decision making actually followed in this case? Not only was OLC in contact with DHS as the details of DAPA were worked out, but their consultation was coordinated under apparently close White House supervision. According to Mr. Savage's account, OLC's negative judgment on extending DAPA to parents of all DACA beneficiaries was left in the public opinion — an unusual move — at the urging of White House Counsel, to "show that they had really thought about [an even broader program] and obeyed legal limits." SAVAGE, POWER WARS, at 662. So closely was President Obama identified with DAPA as "his" initiative that commenters frequently referred to an "Obama executive order on immigration," even though, technically speaking, there was none. The White House typically referred to the program as an "executive action."

In thinking about the role of law in disciplining executive action, the questions of when and how to involve Justice Department lawyers in the President's decision making are arguably critical. Structuring the advice-giving function is presumably within the President's discretion, but should Presidents think themselves better served by preserving some degree of arm's-length relationship with the Justice Department or by treating OLC as a part of a White House-organized policy team? What impact might the latter model have on the role of the Attorney General? Presumably, the Assistant Attorney General in charge of OLC reports to the Attorney General in the first instance. How and when should an Attorney General intercede upon determining that a White House-led team is heading in a legal direction with which the Attorney General is uncomfortable? Is the choice of one model or the other likely to make a meaningful difference in the constraining force of law on presidential action? An arms-length DOJ model preserves a special role for the AG and OLC, whereas the "legal team" model moves more control to the White House. Should the move towards a "legal team" model be viewed as just one more slice of a move towards centralization evident also in OMB rulemaking oversight or the White House's use of policy czars?

2. *Deferred Action for Childhood Arrivals.* The excerpt above omits the details OLC provided regarding the "five occasions since the late 1990s" when category-based deferred action programs were implemented. The fifth of them was DACA, for which the Obama Administration had not provided an OLC opinion. Footnote 8 in OLC's DAPA memo, however, recounted the advice OLC had given regarding the earlier program:

Before DACA was announced, our Office was consulted about whether such a program would be legally permissible. As we orally advised, our preliminary view was that such a program would be permissible, provided that immigration officials retained discretion to evaluate each application on an individualized basis. We noted that immigration officials typically consider factors such as having been brought to the United States as a child in exercising their discretion to grant deferred action in individual cases. We explained, however, that extending deferred action to individuals who satisfied these and other specified criteria on a class-wide basis would raise distinct questions not implicated by ad hoc grants of deferred action. We advised that it was critical that, like past policies that made deferred action available to certain classes of aliens, the DACA program require immigration officials to evaluate each application for deferred action on a case-by-case basis, rather than granting deferred action automatically to all applicants who satisfied the threshold eligibility criteria. We also noted that, although the proposed program was predicated on humanitarian concerns that appeared less particularized and acute than those underlying certain prior class-wide deferred action programs, the concerns animating DACA were nonetheless consistent with the types of concerns that have customarily guided the exercise of immigration enforcement discretion.

3. *The OLC Framework for Analyzing DAPA.* OLC's opinion explicitly acknowledges the Janus-faced character of the Faithful Execution Clause, which it cites both as a basis for presidential law enforcement discretion and as a source of the President's law enforcement duty. What is less clear, however, is the degree to which OLC is offering primarily a constitutional argument for DAPA or a statutory defense.

For example, as the opinion notes, 6 U.S.C. § 202 explicitly provides: "The Secretary [of Homeland Security] shall be responsible for the following: . . . (5) Establishing national immigration enforcement policies and priorities." In the face of so explicit a delegation, defending the Secretary's prioritization memo on statutory grounds would seem to be quite straightforward. Does the analysis in Part I of the opinion go further than necessary to substantiate the legality of the prioritization memo? What role, if any, does the Faithful Execution Clause play in the analysis?

Defending DAPA, of course, is more complex — and presumably does require an explanation of the legality of deferred action, in general, and the reasonableness of the specific DAPA program as an implementation of deferred action, in particular. Here, the statutory and constitutional arguments seem to be deliberately conflated. Part II promises to "discuss the legal authorities on which deferred action relies," and concedes that "the practice of granting deferred action 'developed without express statutory authorization.'" Part II-B then describes the power to implement deferred action as "rooted in the Secretary's broad authority to enforce the immigration laws *and* the President's duty to take care that the laws are faithfully executed" (emphasis added). How those authorities intermix, however, is never really explained. Consider two other potential avenues for structuring the OLC analysis.

OLC might have argued for a view of DAPA as fundamentally a presidential initiative in the Jackson "zone of twilight." That is, the President would rest the DHS initiative primarily on an exercise of Article II power when the initiative has been neither explicitly authorized, nor prohibited by statute. Based on this premise, the point of reciting prior examples of deferred action would be more "Frankfurterian," i.e., to show that the President was not upsetting Congress's view of the proper exercise of administrative power and thus not destabilizing the separation of powers in any way. Indeed, the four limiting principles that OLC identifies for the exercise of enforcement discretion are explicitly offered as principles rooted, not in the immigration statutes per se, but in "the nature of the Take Care duty" more generally. Do you find this explication of the "Take Care duty" persuasive? Would an opinion defending DAPA more emphatically on Article II grounds have been any more or less persuasive than the actual OLC opinion?

Alternatively, OLC might have characterized DAPA primarily as a straightforward implementation of Secretary Johnson's statutory powers. As the opinion notes early on, except as other statutes may confer immigration-related powers on some other officer, 8 U.S.C. § 1103(a)(1) "charge[s the Secretary of Homeland Security] with the administration and enforcement of . . . all . . . laws relating to the immigration and naturalization of aliens." Under 8 U.S.C. § 1103(a)(2), the Secretary is explicitly authorized to "establish such regulations . . . and perform such other acts as he deems necessary for carrying out his authority . . . ." Given the breadth of these provisions and the usual inference that law enforcement statutes permit discretion in the design of enforcement actions, the history recounted in Part IIA would chiefly be used to demonstrate that the inference of implicit statutory authorization for deferred action is not "arbitrary and capricious" under the Administrative Procedure Act. But the analysis might well then have been wise to emphasize some additional points— specifically, the unlikelihood that DAPA will actually decrease the deterrent effect of our immigration laws and the contributions DAPA would make to the Secretary's ability to carry out its authorities more generally under the immigration laws. Would the statutory argument be incomplete in any way? How, if at all, is the Faithful Execution Clause relevant to this analysis?

There is an important, practical reason for considering the alternative paths of analysis. Specifically, OLC thought a deferred action program for parents of DACA beneficiaries was beyond the Secretary's powers because such a program would not echo "Congress's concern for maintaining the integrity of families of individuals legally entitled to live in the United States." That concern seems especially salient if one thinks of DAPA as an initiative supportable chiefly by the President's Article II power exercised in the zone of twilight. If all the Secretary needs to justify a deferred action initiative under the law is a rationale for the program that is not "arbitrary and capricious" as a mode of exercising his or her explicit powers under the immigration statutes, could not a case not have been made in defense of the broader proposed program? Would such an approach go too far in deferring to executive branch discretion to underenforce law?

4. *DAPA in Court.* Whether or not OLC reached a sound legal conclusion, DAPA received a chilly judicial reception:

The District Court Injunction. On behalf of itself and 25 other states, Texas sued to challenge DAPA largely on procedural grounds shortly after its announcement. (Opponents suggested Texas strategically filed suit in the Brownsville Division of the United States District Court for the Southern District of Texas—a "division" comprising a single judge widely viewed as antagonistic to the Obama Administration's immigration policies.) Texas argued for a preliminary injunction against DAPA on the ground that Secretary Johnson improperly by-passed the APA's notice and public comment procedures in issuing his DAPA memorandum.

In granting Texas's requested relief, Judge Andrew Hanen had to deal with a lengthy and complex series of procedural issues. The United States (ultimately supported also by 15 states and the District of Columbia) argued that Texas lacked standing to sue, that the program for various reasons was not judicially reviewable, and that, in any event, the APA notice-and-comment requirements were inapplicable.

The court upheld Texas's standing based on the asserted burden of having to issue drivers licenses to DAPA beneficiaries, which would be required under Texas law for any DAPA beneficiary who also applied successfully for work authorization. Texas alleged that it issues drivers licenses at a financial loss, although the Government argued unsuccessfully that Texas's injuries were thus self-inflicted by virtue of its control over its own laws and license fees. The court found that the burden on Texas satisfied the Article III-based injury requirement. Moreover, Texas fell within the "zone of interests" to be protected by the immigration laws because "it is the duty of the federal government to protect the border and enforce the immigration laws," partially to the benefit of the states. *Texas v. United States*, 86 F. Supp. 3d 591, 624 (S.D. Tex.). The court likewise accepted two other standing theories Texas had asserted: its entitlement to sue as *parens patriae* on behalf of its citizens and a theory the court called "abdication standing," under which a state might challenge the federal government for failing to enforce federal law in an area where states lacked constitutional authority to protect themselves and their citizens from injury.

The reviewability and "notice-and-comment" questions are complex and intertwined. The Government argued that DAPA was an exercise of prosecutorial discretion, which is exempt from judicial review under the Administrative Procedure Act. First, the Government argued, the DAPA memo was simply a "policy statement" concerning the allocation of agency enforcement resources and therefore exempt from the notice-and-comment requirements of 5 U.S.C. § 553. Moreover, because the statement did not commit DHS to the conferral of deferred action on every applicant meeting the general criteria, it did not constitute reviewable "final agency action." The court disagreed. It found that the DAPA memo amounted to a substantive rule intended to have binding consequences for both DHS and the program's beneficiaries—a characterization that the Government vigorously denied. Once characterized as a substantive rule, moreover, DAPA also amounted, in the court's analysis, to "final agency action" subject to judicial review, as opposed to mere policy guidance, which would not be.

The Government's remaining procedural argument was that DAPA, as an exercise of prosecutorial decision making, was within the category that the APA calls "agency action . . . committed to agency discretion by law," citing *Heckler v. Chaney*, 470 U.S. 821 (1985), discussed extensively in the OLC excerpt. The court agreed that it lacked power to review either the Secretary's enforcement priorities or individual non-prosecution decisions. It insisted, however, that DAPA went further. In the court's view, the program represented a positive grant of benefits to a specified class of undocumented immigrants. It thus did not represent, in the court's view, non-enforcement, but rather affirmative policymaking.

Having jumped the procedural hurdles of standing, finality, reviewability, the court then granted a preliminary injunction on the basis that the executive branch unlawfully bypassed the APA's notice-and-comment requirements. The order stayed the DAPA memo (and, as part of that memo, an extension of DACA deferred action from two to three years), presumably until the Government subjected the DAPA rule to notice and comment. The court's analysis, however, is curious in at least two respects. First, although Judge Hanen was at pains to insist that he was "specifically not addressing Plaintiffs' likelihood of success on their substantive APA claim or their constitutional claims under the Take Care Clause/separation of powers doctrine," *id.* at 677, he stated, in the course of his opinion, that "[t]he DHS Secretary is not just rewriting the laws; he is creating them from scratch," *id.* at 663. Doesn't that statement indicate Judge Hanen's view on the substantive claim he insists he is not addressing? Moreover, although Judge Hanen rested his conclusion significantly upon a determination that DAPA amounts to an affirmative conferral of benefits upon its potential applicants, his opinion nowhere mentions that the APA exempts from notice-and-comment requirements any "matter relating to agency management or personnel or to public property, loans, grants, benefits, or contracts."

Fifth Circuit Denial of Stay. Following the District Court opinion, the Government immediately sought a stay of the injunction pending a full hearing on Texas's challenges—a request denied by a split panel. The majority thought Texas likely to prevail ultimately on its "driver's license" theory of standing and characterized DAPA as changing its potential recipients' legal status in the United States, which the Government (and OLC's opinion) denied. *Texas v. United States*, 787 F.3d 733 (5th Cir. 2015). It found inapplicable the presumption of nonreviewability for challenges to prosecutorial discretion because, like the district court, the majority characterized DAPA as an affirmative conferral of benefits. The court also found the DAPA criteria sufficiently binding on DHS and its employees to belie the Government's characterization of DAPA as a mere policy statement exempt from notice-and-comment. Reaching the question whether DAPA might be issued without notice-and-comment because of the APA's "benefits" exception, the majority reached the issue, but defined the exception narrowly to apply only to agencies that manage programs of public benefits.

Fifth Circuit Judge Stephen Higginson dissented, concluding that Texas's challenge was nonreviewable under *Heckler v. Chaney*. He denied both that DAPA changed its beneficiaries' legal status and that it bound DHS sufficiently to make it a substantive rule subject to notice-and-comment.

Fifth Circuit Affirmance. Given the opinion denying the Government's requested stay, it was unsurprising that a subsequent panel which included the two judges in the earlier majority likewise affirmed on its merits the grant of the preliminary injunction. Rather remarkably, however, the two judges went beyond their earlier opinion to find for Texas on the substantive claim that DAPA was "manifestly contrary to" the Immigration and Nationality Act. *Texas v. United States*, 809 F.3d 134, 186 (5th Cir. 2015). The new third judge on the panel, Judge King, dissented. While expressing "serious misgivings" about Texas's theory of standing, she emphatically reiterated Judge Higginson's position that DAPA was a nonjusticiable exercise in prosecutorial discretion. She likewise agreed that DAPA qualified as a policy statement exempt from notice-and-comment rulemaking requirements. Judge King finally chastised the majority for reaching the substantive claim on which Judge Hanen had not ruled, but argued that, in any event, Secretary Johnson's interpretation of his statutory authority was reasonable.

Grant of Certiorari. In light of the matter's importance, the Government sought a writ of certiorari from the Supreme Court, posing three questions: the question of Texas's standing, whether DAPA was "arbitrary and capricious or otherwise not in accordance with law," and whether DAPA was subject to the APA's notice-and-comment requirement. In granting the petition, the Court perhaps ominously (for the Government, that is), added a fourth question: "Whether the Guidance violates the Take Care Clause of the Constitution, Art. II, § 3," an issue on which there had been no lower court ruling and which Texas, in opposing certiorari, had not raised. *United States v. Texas*, 136 S. Ct. 906 (2016).

Death of Justice Scalia and the Court's 4–4 Affirmance. As if the case were not yet singular enough in its complexity and political importance, the sudden death of Justice Antonin Scalia on February 13, 2016 appeared to dramatically change the landscape for litigation. The case was orally argued on April 18, 2016. On June 23, the decision below was affirmed without opinion by an equally divided Court. *United States v. Texas*, 136 S. Ct. 2271 (2016). As one of us has written, this outcome had the unfortunate consequence of leaving much legal confusion in its wake:

> Unfortunately, the Supreme Court's 4–4 tie . . . offers no clues as to the justices' reactions to the wide-ranging analyses offered by both of the lower courts—analyses with implications going far beyond the immigration context to all of administrative regulation. The litigants in this case—and potentially in others yet to come—can reach no confident conclusions about the weightiness of the lower courts' lengthy legal pronouncements. Logically,

the four justices who voted to uphold the injunction must have agreed that Texas has standing to bring its lawsuit. Presumably, they also agreed with the lower courts' determination that DAPA could not legally be issued without notice and comment. It would be useful, for the sake of a wide range of future cases, to know what arguments for these propositions the four justices found persuasive. It would certainly be helpful to know if any or all of them approved of the substantive doubts cast by the Fifth Circuit on Johnson's reading of his statutory authority to issue DAPA at all.

Because of the lack of detail in the decision, we also do not know the views of the four justices who would have voided the injunction, and we do not know their views about Johnson's statutory authority. They might simply think Texas lacked standing to sue. They might think Johnson was within his rights in not conducting a formal notice-and-comment process. Administrative lawyers—including the Obama administration's lawyers—really have no idea what to infer from these four justices' unexplained stance.

Peter M. Shane, *The U.S. Supreme Court's Big Immigration Case Wasn't About Presidential Power*, TheAtlantic.com (June 28, 2016), http://www.theatlantic.com/politics/archive/2016/06/us-v-texas-wasnt-really-about-presidential-power/489047/.

Eight Is Not Enough (to Save DAPA). Because of this uncertainty, and anticipating that Justice Scalia's replacement might well be seated before the end of the Obama Administration, the Government then made the unusual move of petitioning for rehearing in the Supreme Court following the appointment of a new Justice. On March 16, 2016—and in the face of the Senate Republican majority's already announced determination to leave the Scalia seat vacant until the election of Obama's successor—President Obama nominated Merrick Garland, Chief Judge of the U.S. Court of Appeals for the D.C. Circuit, to succeed Justice Scalia. On October 3, however, the Supreme Court denied the petition for rehearing. United States v. Texas, No. 15-674 (U.S. Oct. 3, 2016). On June 15, 2017, the Trump Administration formally rescinded the DAPA memorandum. As this book goes to press, DACA is still in effect.

"Nonexecution" and the Trump Administration. As a presidential candidate, Donald J. Trump promised that, if elected, there would follow some significant relief for businesses from the burdens of government regulation. Some of that relief could come from deregulatory statutes that a Republican Congress might enact for the signature of the new Republican president. Some might come from notice-and-comment rulemaking rescinding existing regulations. The question posed by the DAPA episode, however, is whether relief might also come from the nonexecution of regulatory programs still formally in effect. Should the Trump (or any other) Administration drastically reduce the number of plant inspections under various worker safety statutes or ignore prima facie evidence of Clean Air Act violations, or the like, could such underenforcement be successfully challenged? Consider the arguments available to the Administration to defend underenforcement, who (if anyone) would have standing to mount a judicial challenge, and the procedural hurdles that might face challengers. If, for example, a new Administration thinks corporate taxes too high, could it simply decline to collect them? Would that be different from DAPA and, if so, how?

5. *Presidential "Ownership" of Regulatory Activity.* As noted above, President Obama was so personally identified with the DACA and DAPA programs that these administrative actions were widely reported as his "executive orders." In the *Atlantic* essay, quoted above, Professor Shane bemoaned this confusion as an unfortunate development:

> In her law-professor days, now-Justice Elena Kagan wrote a much-noted article arguing that presidents should, in effect, take ownership of their administrations' bureaucratic policymaking. EPA environmental regulation should be embraced as presidential environmental regulation. FDA public-health regulation should be seen as presidential health regulation. Presidents should be encouraged to make regulation their own in both how they engage with the bureaucracy and how they discuss an administration's regulatory output. She argued: "[P]residential leadership enhances transparency, enabling the public to comprehend more accurately the sources and nature of bureaucratic power."
>
> *United States v. Texas* . . . shows that the opposite is true. Both the media and the public appear confused about "the sources and nature of [DHS's] power." Far from promoting public comprehension, President Obama, no doubt abetted by his opponents, has muddled public understanding by aggressively branding the program as his own.

Id. Professor Shane further suggests that the President intensified opposition to the program by blurring the lines of legal accountability:

> When Obama says he was "left with little choice but to take steps within my existing authority to make our immigration system smarter, fairer, and more just," he is thus not promoting transparency about legal responsibility. He is intensifying confusion. As president, he no doubt has constitutional authority to consult with the secretary of homeland security, help shape DHS's agenda, and inform the secretary of his strongly preferred policy outcomes. He could not have forced Johnson to promulgate a program, however; in the face of impasse, Obama would be able only to fire this secretary and try to appoint another. When Obama refers to "his" powers or "my" actions, he mainly insures that all the opposition to the program, both legal and political, will get focused with laser-like intensity on him, rather than Johnson.

Id. Do you think the Administration might have done better in mobilizing support for the program if it were depicted more forcefully as an implementation not of presidential power, but of bureaucratic strategy? Is there any generalizable lesson for presidents inclined to take rhetorical ownership of administrative initiatives?

6. *Any Work for the Faithful Execution Clause?* As you reflect on the DAPA case study and the examples of nonexecution Professor Shane catalogues, does it appear

to you that there is *any* work to be done by the Faithful Execution (or "Take Care") Clause in measuring the legality of a President's efforts at legal implementation? Professor Shane argues that an agency's *de facto* suspension of a particular statute could most sensibly be challenged as a violation of that statute. What about a President's order that an agency stop enforcing a particular law? Could a President constitutionally prevent the execution of law by failing to nominate the agency officials necessary for law to be executed? As noted above, with regard to the *Noel Canning* controversy, the five-member National Labor Relations Board requires a quorum of three to act. Could a president constitutionally decide to leave three vacancies on the Board vacant? How, if at all, could any such duty be enforced?

Professor Gillian Metzger has suggested that the Faithful Execution Clause implies a constitutional duty of supervision, which might be used, among other things, to undergird some manner of new institutional reform litigation. The argument is both complex and speculative, but a central premise is that "the duty is a systemic and structural one. It requires systems and structures of supervision adequate to preserve overall hierarchical control and accountability of governmental power." Gillian Metzger, *The Constitutional Duty to Supervise*, 124 YALE L.J. 1836, 1900 (2015). Whether or not a duty to supervise may be persuasively crafted from Article II, are their refusals to implement the law of a *systemic* character that might be constitutionally problematic, even if discrete instances of nonexecution might not be?

c. Prosecutorial Discretion and Criminal Law Enforcement

As our discussion of the Obama Administration's immigration policies reflects, the paradigm example of nonreviewable executive enforcement discretion is prosecutorial discretion with regard to crime. How far Congress can go in tying the executive branch's hands in this domain was at the heart of the following OLC opinion. It resulted from the 1982 fight, discussed in Chapter Three, between the Reagan Administration and the House of Representatives over executive privilege and the investigation of corruption in the administration of EPA's Superfund program—an episode that also led to *Morrison v. Olson*, excerpted earlier in this chapter.

Prosecution for Contempt of Congress of an Executive Branch Official Who Has Asserted a Claim of Executive Privilege

Memorandum Opinion for the Attorney General
8 O.P. OLC 101 (1984)

I. Introduction

This memorandum memorializes our formal response to your request for our opinion whether, pursuant to the criminal contempt of Congress statute, 2 U.S.C. §§ 192, 194, a United States Attorney must prosecute or refer to a grand jury a citation for contempt of Congress issued with respect to an executive official who has asserted a claim of executive privilege in response to written instructions from the President of the United States. Your inquiry originally arose in the context of a resolution adopted by the House of Representatives on December 16, 1982, during the final days of the 97th Congress, which instructed the Speaker of the House of Representatives to certify the report of the Committee on Public Works and Transportation concerning the "contumacious conduct of the Administrator, United States Environmental Protection Agency, in failing and refusing to furnish certain documents in compliance with a subpoena duces tecum of a duly constituted subcommittee of said committee . . . to the United States Attorney for the District of Columbia, to the end that the Administrator . . . may be proceeded against in the manner and form provided by law." H.R. Res. 632, 97th Cong., 2d Sess. (1982). Section 192 of Title 2, United States Code, provides, in general, that willful failure to produce documents in response to a congressional subpoena shall be a misdemeanor. Section 194 provides that if such a failure is reported to either house of Congress it "shall" be certified to the "appropriate United States attorney whose duty it shall be to bring the matter before the grand jury for its action." . . .

[W]e have concluded that, as a matter of both statutory construction and the Constitution's structural separation of powers, a United States Attorney is not required to refer a contempt citation in these circumstances to a grand jury or otherwise to prosecute an Executive Branch official who is carrying out the President's instruction in a factual context such as that presented by the December 16, 1982, contempt citation. First, as a matter of statutory interpretation reinforced by compelling separation of powers considerations, we believe that Congress may not direct the Executive to prosecute a particular individual without leaving any discretion to the Executive to determine whether a violation of the law has occurred. Second, as a matter of statutory interpretation and the constitutional separation of powers, we believe that the contempt of Congress statute was not intended to apply and could not constitutionally be applied to an Executive Branch official who asserts the President's claim of executive privilege in this context.

Our conclusions are predicated upon the proposition, endorsed by a unanimous Supreme Court less than a decade ago, that the President has the authority, rooted inextricably in the separation of powers under the Constitution, to preserve the confidentiality of certain Executive Branch documents. . . .

II. Background

[The opinion begins with a detailed account of the House's 1982 investigation of Superfund enforcement and the claim of executive privilege regarding some of the EPA documents House committees had subpoenaed.] The President's assertion of executive privilege, and the Attorney General's explanation of the law enforcement considerations and constitutional justification for the decision not to release the documents outside the Executive Branch while enforcement proceedings were ongoing, did not dissuade the congressional subcommittees from pressing their demands for the withheld material. After the EPA Administrator asserted the President's claim of privilege at a December 2, 1982, Public Works Subcommittee hearing, the Subcommittee immediately approved a contempt of Congress resolution against her. The full Committee did likewise on December 10, 1982, and rejected a further proposal by the Department of Justice to establish a formal screening process and briefings regarding the contents of the documents. The full House adopted the contempt of Congress resolution on December 16, 1982, and the following day Speaker O'Neill certified the contempt citation to the United States Attorney for the District of Columbia for prosecution under the criminal contempt of Congress statute.

D. The Criminal Contempt of Congress Statute

The criminal contempt of Congress statute contains two principal sections, 2 U.S.C. §§ 192 & 194. Section 192, which sets forth the criminal offense of contempt of Congress, provides in pertinent part:

> Every person who having been summoned as a witness by the authority of either House of Congress to give testimony or to produce papers upon any matter under inquiry before either House . . . or any committee of either House of Congress, willfully makes default, or who, having appeared, refuses to answer any question pertinent to the question under inquiry, shall be deemed guilty of a misdemeanor, punishable by a fine of not more than $1,000 nor less than $100 and imprisonment in a common jail for not less than one month nor more than twelve months.

Section 194 purports to impose mandatory duties on the Speaker of the House or the President of the Senate, as the case may be, and the United States Attorney, to take certain actions leading to the prosecution of persons certified by a house of Congress to have failed to produce information in response to a subpoena. It provides:

> Whenever a witness summoned as mentioned in section 192 of this title fails to appear to testify or fails to produce any books, papers, records, or documents, as required, or whenever any witness so summoned refuses to answer any question pertinent to the subject under inquiry before either House . . . or any committee or subcommittee of either House of Congress, and the fact of such failure or failures is reported to either House while Congress is in session or when Congress is not in session, a statement of fact constituting such failure is reported and filed with the President of the Senate or the Speaker of the House, *it shall be the duty of the said President of the Senate or the Speaker of the House,* as the case may be, *to certify, and he shall so certify, the statement of facts* aforesaid under the seal of the Senate or House, as the case may be, *to the appropriate United States attorney, whose duty it shall be to bring the matter before the grand jury for its action.*(Emphasis added.)

[The opinion goes on to describe the unsuccessful executive branch attempt in the U.S. District Court for the District of Columbia to enjoin the House of Representatives from pursuing contempt against EPA Administrator Anne Gorsuch, and the compromise agreement under which the congressional subcommittee originating the vote of contempt was given limited access to the withheld documents and sponsored a resolution to withdraw the contempt citation against the EPA Administrator.] During the pendency of the lawsuit and the subsequent settlement negotiations, the United States Attorney for the District of Columbia refrained from referring the contempt citation to the grand jury. The United States Attorney took the position that referral would have been inappropriate during that period and that the statute left him with discretion to withhold referral. Following the passage of the resolution withdrawing the contempt citation, "the relevant facts and documents were presented . . . to a federal grand jury, which voted unanimously not to indict the EPA Administrator."

III. Generally Applicable Legal Principles: The Separation of Powers, the Duties of the Executive to Enforce the Law, and the Derivation and Scope of the Principles of Prosecutorial Discretion and Executive Privilege . . .

[OLC's general discussion of the separation of powers is omitted.]

C. The Derivation and Scope of Prosecutorial Discretion and Executive Privilege

The issues addressed by this memorandum involve two important constitutional doctrines that spring from the constitutional limits imposed by the separation of powers and the Executive's duty to enforce the laws: prosecutorial discretion and executive privilege.

1. Prosecutorial Discretion

The doctrine of prosecutorial discretion is based on the premise that because the essential core of the President's constitutional responsibility is the duty to enforce the laws, the Executive Branch has exclusive authority to initiate and prosecute actions to enforce the laws adopted by Congress. That principle was reaffirmed by the Supreme Court in *Buckley v. Valeo*, 424 U.S. 1 (1976), in which the Court invalidated the provision of the Federal Election Act that vested the appointment of certain members of the Federal Election Commission in the President pro tempore of the Senate and the Speaker of the House. In so holding, the Court recognized the exclusively executive nature of some of the Commission's powers, including the right to commence litigation:

> The Commission's enforcement power, exemplified by its discretionary power to seek judicial relief, is authority that cannot possibly be regarded as merely in aid of the legislative function of Congress. A lawsuit is the ultimate remedy for a breach of the law, and it is to the President, and not to the Congress, that the Constitution entrusts the responsibility to "take care that the laws be faithfully executed." Art. II, s 3.

424 U.S. at 138.

The Executive's exclusive authority to prosecute violations of the law gives rise to the corollary that neither the Judicial nor Legislative Branches may directly interfere with the prosecutorial discretion of the Executive by directing the Executive Branch to prosecute particular individuals. This principle was explained in *Smith v. United States*, 375 F.2d 243 (5th Cir.), *cert. denied*, 389 U.S. 841 (1967), in which the court considered the applicability of the Federal Tort Claims Act to a prosecutorial decision not to arrest or prosecute persons injuring plaintiff's business. The court ruled that the government was immune from suit under the discretionary decision exception of the Act on the ground that the Executive's prosecutorial discretion was rooted in the separation of powers under the Constitution:

> The President of the United States is charged in Article 2, Section 3, of the Constitution with the duty to "take Care that the Laws be faithfully executed." The Attorney General is the President's surrogate in the prosecution of all offenses against the United States. . . . The discretion of the Attorney General in choosing whether to prosecute or not to prosecute, or to abandon a prosecution already started, is absolute. . . . This discretion is required in all cases. We emphasize that this discretion, exercised in even the lowliest and least consequential cases, can affect the policies, duties, and success of a function placed under the control of the Attorney General by our Constitution and statutes.

375 F.2d at 246–47. The court went on to state that this prosecutorial discretion is protected "no matter whether these decisions are made during the investigation or prosecution of offenses." Id. at 248.

[The opinion next discusses the constitutional basis for executive privilege, relying on *United States v. Nixon*, 418 U.S. 683, 708 (1974).]

IV. The Duty of the Executive Branch When an Executive Official Has Been Cited for Contempt of Congress for Asserting the President's Claim of Executive Privilege

A. Prosecutorial Discretion

The first specific question that is presented by the circumstances that gave rise to this memorandum is whether the United States Attorney is required to refer every contempt of Congress citation to a grand jury. This question raises issues of statutory construction as well as the constitutional limits of prosecutorial discretion. We deal first with the statutory questions.

As a preliminary matter, we note that § 194 does not on its face actually purport to require the United States Attorney to proceed with the prosecution of a person cited by a house of Congress for contempt; by its express terms the statute discusses only referral to a grand jury. Even if a grand jury were to return a true bill, the United States Attorney could refuse to sign the indictment and thereby prevent the case from going forward. *United States v. Cox*, 342 F.2d 167 (5th Cir.) (en banc), *cert. denied*, 381 U.S. 935 (1965). Thus, as a matter of statutory interpretation, there is no doubt that the contempt of Congress statute does not require a prosecution; the only question is whether it requires referral to the grand jury. . . .

2. Judicial Opinions Interpreting the Language of § 194

Section 194 imposes similarly worded, nominally mandatory, referral obligations on both the Speaker of the House (or the President of the Senate) and the United States Attorney once a contempt of Congress resolution has been adopted by the House or Senate:

> *it shall be the duty* of the said President of the Senate or the Speaker of the House as the case may be, to certify, and *he shall so certify*, the statement of facts aforesaid under the seal of the Senate or House, as the case may be, to the appropriate United States attorney, *whose duty it shall be* to bring the matter before the grand jury for its action.

(Emphasis added.)

Although the language, "it shall be the duty of" and "whose duty it shall be," might suggest a nondiscretionary obligation, the United States Court of Appeals for the District of Columbia Circuit has expressly held, at least with respect to the Speaker of the House, that the duty is not mandatory, and that, in fact, the Speaker has an obligation under the law, at least in some cases, to exercise his discretion in determining whether to refer a contempt citation. *Wilson v. United States*, 369 F.2d 198 (D.C. Cir. 1966). In Wilson, the court reversed a conviction for contempt of Congress on the ground that the Speaker had assumed that the statute did not permit any exercise of discretion by him and he had therefore automatically referred a contempt citation to the United States Attorney while Congress was not in session. The court based its conclusion that the Speaker was required to exercise his discretion on the longstanding practice of both the House and Senate and on congressional debates on contempt citations in which the houses had recognized their own discretion not to approve a contempt resolution. The court concluded that because full House approval of a contempt citation is necessary when Congress was in session, the Speaker is required to exercise some discretion when the House is not in session.

Although the reasons underlying the court's decision not to impose a mandatory duty on the Speaker in Wilson do not necessarily require the same conclusion with respect to the United States Attorney, the decision at least supports the proposition that the seemingly mandatory language of § 194 need not be construed as divesting either the Speaker or the United States Attorney of all discretion.

In several cases, the United States Court of Appeals for the District of Columbia Circuit has at least assumed that the United States Attorney retains discretion not to refer a contempt of Congress citation to a grand jury. In these cases, the court refused to entertain challenges to congressional subpoenas, at least in part on the ground that the prospective witnesses would have adequate subsequent opportunities to challenge a committee's contempt finding, including the opportunity to persuade the United States Attorney not to refer the case to a grand jury. . . . These cases emphasize the particular significance of prosecutorial discretion in the context of the contempt of Congress statute. In general, with respect to any criminal allegation, prosecutorial discretion plays an important role in protecting the rights of the accused by providing an additional level of review with respect to the factual and legal sufficiency of the charges. This role is even more important when dealing with the contempt of Congress statute because, as the above cases demonstrate, witnesses generally have no opportunity to challenge congressional subpoenas directly. Thus, as the cases indicate, prosecutorial discretion serves a vital purpose in protecting the rights of the accused in contempt cases by mitigating the otherwise stern consequences of asserting a right not to respond to a congressional subpoena. . . .

3. Common-Law Prosecutorial Discretion

In addition to the court decisions that suggest that the United States Attorney may decide not to refer a contempt citation to a grand jury, the common-law doctrine of prosecutorial discretion weighs heavily against and, in our opinion, precludes an interpretation that the statute requires automatic referral. Because of the wide scope of a prosecutor's discretion in determining which cases to bring, courts, as a matter of law, do not ordinarily interpret a statute to limit that discretion unless the intent to do so is clearly and unequivocally stated. The general rule is that "the Executive Branch has exclusive authority and absolute discretion to decide whether to prosecute a case." *United States v. Nixon*, 418 U.S. 683, 693 (1974). The Attorney General and his subordinates, including the United States Attorneys, have the authority to exercise this discretion reserved to the Executive. *United States v. San Jacinto Tin Co.*, 125 U.S. 273 (1888); *The Gray Jacket*, 72 U.S. (5 Wall.) 370 (1866). . . .

Courts have applied this general principle of prosecutorial discretion in refusing to interfere with a prosecutor's decision not to initiate a case, despite the specific language of 28 U.S.C. § 547, which states in part that "each United States Attorney, within his district, *shall* . . . prosecute *for all* offenses against the United States." (Emphasis added.) . . .

Courts exhibit the same deference to prosecutorial discretion even when the specific statute involved uses words that would otherwise have mandatory, nondiscretionary implications. For example, 42 U.S.C. § 1987 states that United States Attorneys are "authorized *and required* . . . to initiate prosecutions against all persons violating any of the provisions of the federal criminal civil rights statutes." (Emphasis added.) Although a number of cases have been initiated to force a United States Attorney to bring civil rights actions on the ground that this statute imposes a nondiscretionary duty to prosecute, the courts uniformly have rejected the contention that the statute limits a prosecutor's normal discretion to decide not to bring a particular case. . . .

4. Constitutional Considerations

Our construction of § 194 is reinforced by the need to avoid the constitutional problems that would result if § 194 were read to require referral to a grand jury. . . . [T]he constitutionally prescribed separation of powers requires that the Executive retain discretion with respect to whom it will prosecute for violations of the law. Although most cases expressly avoid this constitutional question by construing statutes not to limit prosecutorial discretion, the cases that do discuss the subject make it clear that common law prosecutorial discretion is strongly reinforced by the constitutional separation of powers.

A number of courts have expressly relied upon the constitutional separation of powers in refusing to force a United States Attorney to proceed with a prosecution. For example, in *Pugach v. Klein*, 193 F. Supp. 630 (S.D.N.Y. 1961), the court declined to order the United States Attorney to commence a prosecution for violation of federal wiretap laws on the ground that it was clear beyond question that it is not the business of the Courts to tell the United States Attorney to perform what they conceive to be his duties. . . .

The Fifth Circuit, sitting en banc, has underscored the constitutional foundations of prosecutorial discretion. *United States v. Cox*, 342 F.2d 167 (5th Cir.) (en banc), cert. denied, 381 U.S. 935 (1965). In Cox, the court overturned a district court's order that a United States Attorney prepare and sign an indictment that a grand jury had voted to return. The plurality opinion stated:

> The executive power is vested in the President of the United States, who is required to take care that the laws be faithfully executed. The Attorney General is the hand of the President in taking care that the laws of the United States in legal proceedings and in the prosecution of offenses, be faithfully executed. The role of the grand jury is restricted to a finding as to whether or not there is probable cause to believe that an offense has been committed. The discretionary power of the attorney for the United States in determining whether a prosecution shall be commenced or maintained may well depend upon matters of policy wholly apart from any question of probable cause. Although as a member of the bar, the attorney for the United States is an officer of the court, he is nevertheless an executive official of the Government, and it is as an officer of the executive department that he exercises a discretion as to whether or not there shall be a prosecution in a particular case. It follows, as an incident of the constitutional separation of powers, that courts are not to interfere with the free exercise of the discretionary powers of the attorneys of the United States in their control over criminal prosecutions.

342 F.2d at 171 (footnotes omitted). Even the three dissenting judges in *Cox* conceded that, although they believed that the United States Attorney could be required to sign the indictment, "once the indictment is returned, the Attorney General or the United States Attorney can refuse to go forward." Id. at 179.

Although prosecutorial discretion may be regulated to a certain extent by Congress and in some instances by the Constitution, the decision not to prosecute an individual may not be controlled because it is fundamental to the Executive's prerogative. For example, the individual prosecutorial decision is distinguishable from instances in which courts have reviewed the legality of general Executive Branch policies. See *Nader v. Saxbe*, 497 F.2d 676 (D.C. Cir. 1974); *Adams v. Richardson*, 480 F.2d 1159 (D.C. Cir. 1973) (en banc) (per curiam); *NAACP v. Levi*, 418 F. Supp. 1109 (D.D.C. 1976). In these cases the courts accepted jurisdiction to rule whether an entire enforcement program was being implemented based on an improper reading of the law. . . . Similarly distinguishable are the cases concerning the constitutional limits on selective prosecution, which hold that prosecutorial discretion may not be exercised on the basis of impermissible factors such as race, religion, or the exercise of free speech.

If the congressional contempt statute were interpreted to divest the United States Attorney of discretion, then the statute would create two distinct problems with respect to the separation of powers. . . . Divesting the United States Attorney of discretion would run afoul of . . . the separation of powers by stripping the Executive of its proper constitutional authority and by vesting improper power in Congress. . . .

[I]f Congress could specify an individual to be prosecuted, it would be exercising powers that the Framers intended not be vested in the legislature. A legislative effort to require prosecution of a specific individual has many of the attributes of a bill of attainder and would seem to be inconsistent with many of the policies upon which the Constitution's prohibition against bills of attainder was based. See *United States v. Brown*, 381 U.S. 437 (1965); *United States v. Lovett*, 328 U.S. 303 (1946). The constitutional role of Congress is to adopt general legislation that will be applied and implemented by the Executive Branch. . . . [T]he Legislative Branch, which is assigned the role of passing laws of general applicability and specifically excluded from questions of individual guilt or innocence, may not decide on an individual basis who will be prosecuted.

These constitutional principles of prosecutorial discretion apply even though the issue here is referral to the grand jury and not commencement of a criminal case after indictment. A referral to a grand jury commences the criminal prosecution process. That step is as much a part of the function of executing the laws as is the decision to sign an indictment. . . . Moreover, if the Executive has already determined that, as a matter of law, no violation of the law has occurred, it would serve no practical purpose to refer a case to the grand jury. Given the importance of these constitutional principles and the fundamental need to preserve the Executive's power to enforce the laws, we see no reason for distinguishing between the decision to prosecute and the decision to refer to the grand jury in this case. . . .

For all of the above reasons, as a matter of statutory construction strongly reinforced by constitutional separation of powers principles, we believe that the United States Attorney and the Attorney General, to whom the United States Attorney is responsible, retain their discretion not to refer a contempt of Congress citation to a grand jury. It follows, of course, that we believe that even if the provision of a statute requiring reference to a grand jury were to be upheld, the balance of the prosecutorial process could not be mandated.

B. Whether the Criminal Contempt of Congress Statute Applies to an Executive Official Who Asserts, On Direct Orders of the President, the President's Claim of Executive Privilege

[Having concluded that the history and separation of powers implications of prosecutorial discretion both argue in favor of not reading the criminal contempt of Congress statutes as mandating grand jury referral, the remainder of the opinion argues that the statute was intended to apply and could not constitutionally be applied to an official asserting presidential claims of executive privilege.]

The balancing required by the separation of powers demonstrates that the contempt of Congress statute cannot be constitutionally applied to an executive official in the context under consideration. On the one hand, Congress has no compelling need to employ criminal prosecution in order to vindicate its rights. The Executive, however, must be free from the threat of criminal prosecution if its right to assert executive privilege is to have any practical substance. Thus, when the major impact on the President's ability to exercise his constitutionally mandated function is balanced against the relatively slight imposition on Congress in requiring it to resort to a civil rather than a criminal remedy to pursue its legitimate needs, we believe that the constitutionally mandated separation of powers requires the statute to be interpreted so as not to apply to Presidential assertions of executive privilege. . . .

In the narrow and unprecedented circumstances presented here, in which an Executive Branch official has acted to assert the President's privilege to withhold information from a congressional committee concerning open law enforcement files, based upon the written legal advice of the Attorney General, the contempt of Congress statute does not require and could not constitutionally require a prosecution of that official, or even, we believe, a referral to a grand jury of the facts relating to the alleged contempt. Congress does not have the statutory or constitutional authority to require a particular case to be referred to the grand jury. In addition, because the Congress has an alternative remedy both to test the validity of the Executive's claim of privilege and to obtain the documents if the courts decide that the privilege is outweighed by a valid and compelling legislative need, a criminal prosecution and the concomitant chilling effect that it would have on the ability of a President to assert a privilege, is an unnecessary and unjustified burden that, in our judgment, is inconsistent with the Constitution.

Theodore B. Olson
Assistant Attorney General
Office of Legal Counsel

———————

1. *A Statutory Stretch?* The OLC opinion refers to "constitutional problems" that would be posed were 2 U.S.C. § 194 read to require the referral to a grand jury of EPA Administrator Anne Gorsuch's refusal to testify (although it nowhere refers explicitly — even in its original unedited version — to the so-called "constitutional avoidance" canon of statutory construction). Given the potential relevance of that canon, perhaps the most striking feature of the opinion is the lengths to which it goes to argue that, notwithstanding the seemingly mandatory character of the text, Congress should not be regarded as having prohibited the ordinary exercise of prosecutorial discretion and that the statute, in any event, should not be read as encompassing the refusal of an administration official (current or past) to testify based on a presidential claim of executive privilege. One of your authors has written of this memo: "Measured by any literal reading of the contempt statute, Mr. Olson's conclusion sounds like a stretch, to be sure. But his conclusion, rooted in traditional tools of

statutory analysis, stands up to any reasonable standard of responsible government lawyering. It is persuasive nontextualism." Peter M. Shane, *The Presidential Statutory Stretch and the Rule of Law*, 87 U. Colo. L. Rev. 1231, 1236 (2016). Are you persuaded?

2. *Revisiting Independent Counsel.* Does not *Morrison v. Olson*, excerpted above, cast doubt on the executive branch's frequent assertion of plenary constitutional policy authority over criminal prosecutions. After all, if the judicial appointment of a criminal prosecutor leaves the President's constitutional authorities intact—even when the prosecutor cannot be removed by the President on policy grounds—then the scope of policy authority over criminal prosecutions constitutionally vested in the executive must be something less than comprehensive. On the other hand, in cases other than those covered by special prosecutor-type statutory arrangements, the executive is typically successful arguing that no other branch may interfere with its decisions whether or not to charge violations of the criminal law in particular cases. All criminal law enforcement displays a traditional—and largely unquestioned—practice of discretionary nonenforcement with which courts hardly ever interfere.

3. *Judicial Deference to Prosecutorial Decision Making.* In withholding judicial oversight from particular prosecutorial decisions, the courts are presumably recognizing that, rightly or wrongly, the executive branch's criminal law enforcement decisions may be rooted in policies apart from the merits of particular cases. A dramatic example is *Smith v. United States*, 375 F.2d 243 (5th Cir. 1967), in which the white plaintiff, who had served as a juror in a black plaintiff's unsuccessful civil rights action against a Georgia sheriff, sued to challenge the federal government's failure to prosecute civil rights groups for mounting a retaliatory boycott of his grocery store. Smith charged that the government's failure to arrest or prosecute those who injured his business violated the Federal Tort Claims Act. The Fifth Circuit found that the decision whether or not to prosecute the boycotters was a decision within the "discretionary function" exemption from liability under the FTCA, and thus not susceptible to judicial review in an FTCA suit—a conclusion that the court deemed reinforced by separation of powers considerations. Quoting from its earlier decision in *United States v. Cox*, 342 F.2d 167, 171 (5th Cir. 1965), the court said:

> "The discretionary power of the attorney for the United States in determining whether a prosecution shall be commenced or maintained may well depend upon matters of policy wholly apart from any question of probable cause. Although as a member of the bar, the attorney for the United States is an officer of the court, he is nevertheless an executive official of the Government, and it is as an officer of the executive department that he exercises a discretion as to whether or not there shall be a prosecution in a particular case. It follows, as an incident of the constitutional separation of powers, that the courts are not to interfere with the free exercise of the discretionary powers of the attorneys of the United States in their control over criminal prosecutions."

This discretion is required in all cases. The present case provides, however, a most compelling example of the soundness of the rule. "All must be aware now that there are times when the interests of the nation require that a prosecution be foregone." Concurring opinion of Judge Brown in *United States v. Cox, supra*, 342 F.2d at 182.

The national wellbeing has been in balance during the recent struggle for racial equality, of which the present action is a piece. The federal government's decisions concerning enforcement of its criminal statutes comprise a part of its pursuit of national policy. If the government could be held liable for prosecuting or failing to prosecute such a case, its choices in this area could quite conceivably be affected by such a suit. Thus, a policy decision of the federal government might be influenced by a plaintiff with no governmental responsibility.

The plain implication here is that the executive branch would have been within its proper discretion in deciding not to prosecute Smith's boycotters if the U.S. Attorney had been concerned that such a prosecution, whether or not likely to succeed on the evidence, would have exacerbated local racial tensions. Do you agree that such a decision should not be judicially reviewable?

In the mid-1970s, a federal district court judge in the District of Columbia took a different stance regarding the reviewability of the Justice Department's prosecutorial policies. In *NAACP v. Levi*, 418 F. Supp. 1109 (D.D.C. 1976), the NAACP challenged what it asserted was the federal government's failure "to conduct an affirmative and exhaustive investigation" of an African-American "citizen's death from gunshot wounds while in custody of Arkansas law enforcement officers." Alabama investigated the shooting immediately after it happened and prosecuted the state trooper responsible, but he was acquitted by a jury in state court. The local U.S. Attorney declined to sue under any federal civil rights statutes.

In refusing to dismiss the suit for failure to state a claim, Judge Barrington Parker distinguished *Levi* on the ground that it challenged a general policy with regard to the federal prosecution of acts that were criminal also under state law. He quoted the D.C. Circuit's opinion in *Nader v. Saxbe*, 497 F.2d 676, 679 (D.C. Cir. 1974), as follows:

The instant complaint does not ask the court to assume the essentially Executive function of deciding whether a particular alleged violator should be prosecuted. Rather, the complaint seeks a conventionally judicial determination of whether certain fixed policies allegedly followed by the Justice Department and the United States Attorney's office lie outside the constitutional and statutory limits of "prosecutorial discretion."

In a continuing footnote he further commented:

The Executive's constitutional duty to "take Care that the Laws be faithfully executed," Art. II, § 3, applies to all laws, not merely to criminal statutes, *see In re Neagle*, 135 U.S. 1, 63–64 (1890). It would seem to follow that the exercise of prosecutorial discretion, like the exercise of Executive discretion generally, is subject to statutory and constitutional limits enforceable through judicial review (citations omitted). The law has long recognized the distinction between judicial usurpation of discretionary authority and judicial review of the statutory and constitutional limits to that authority (citations omitted). Judicial review of the latter sort is normally available unless Congress has expressly withdrawn it (citations omitted) 497 F.2d at 679, 680, fn. 19.

In 1977, the case was dismissed by agreement of the parties, *NAACP v. Bell*, 76 F.R.D. 134 (D.D.C. 1977), after then-Attorney General Griffin Bell committed to a policy under which, with regard to potential federal prosecutions of civil rights crimes that might also have been prosecuted under state law, every such prosecution would be evaluated on its own merits to determine if a federal prosecution would help to vindicate rights sought to be protected by those laws. Ellen S. Podgor, *Department of Justice Guidelines: Balancing "Discretionary Justice"*, 13 CORNELL J.L. & PUB. POL'Y 167, 181 (2004).

The *Smith* case, above, is fairly representative of the deferential stance of the federal judiciary toward prosecutorial decision making. The Supreme Court has regarded prosecutorial discretion as all but nonreviewable in a host of contexts, for example: (1) discretion to prosecute only a subclass of all suspected violators of a federal law, *Wayte v. United States*, 470 U.S. 598 (1985); (2) discretion to prosecute under the more punitive of two statutes under which the same conduct could be prosecuted, *United States v. Batchelder*, 442 U.S. 114 (1979); and (3) discretion to delay prosecution for strategic reasons, *United States v. Lovasco*, 431 U.S. 783 (1977). The Court has further limited the judicial role in reviewing prosecutorial discretion by restricting plaintiff standing to challenge nonprosecution decisions, *Linda R. S. v. Richard D.*, 410 U.S. 614 (1973), and by granting prosecutors absolute immunity from personal damages liability for actions performed within the scope of their prosecutorial duties, *Imbler v. Pachtman*, 424 U.S. 409 (1976).

It is generally perceived that the federal courts' deference towards federal prosecutors stems, at least in part, from separation of powers concerns. The question remains, what are they? To understand the problem, it is necessary to distinguish between two distinct sets of concerns, both served by the separation of powers, which have different implications for prosecutorial decision making and its review.

One set of issues might be called "separation of powers proper," that is, a concern that the core "legislative," "executive," and "judicial" powers each be retained by the respective branch involved. Recall Justice Scalia's position in *Morrison v. Olson*, excerpted above, for example, that criminal prosecution is a core executive function. On that ground, judicial deference would be required to avoid usurpation of prerogatives that belong categorically within the executive branch.

A different set of concerns is usually captured in the phrase, "separation of functions." These concerns, closely related to concepts of due process, focus on the unfairness of melding the powers to make rules, to enforce rules, to interpret rules, and to impose sanctions for rule violations all in the same actor. Because modern administrative agencies typically exercise each of these functions somewhere within each agency, structural protections such as guaranteed tenure for administrative law judges are used to assure fairness. What is critical from this point of view is not that the executive branch have plenary discretion regarding prosecution, but that Article III judges who may be finders of fact, adjudicators of law, and sentencers do not become unduly involved in the decisions whether and with what to charge individuals in the first place.

In the cases cited above, it would seem to make little difference whether the Court's animating concern was the separation of powers proper or a separation of functions. Either concern would have yielded deferential judicial review. If the Court's philosophy is one of separation of powers proper, however, that would make a difference on other issues — for example, whether Congress could vest in the courts the power to appoint special prosecutors.

Do you think the Court has entertained more deference towards prosecutors than a "separation of functions" theory warrants? After all, the separation of functions is intended chiefly as a protection against governmental unfairness towards individual defendants. How far should a court go, in the name of fairness produced by a separation of functions, in *not* policing more particularized claims that a prosecutor has behaved unfairly?

3. Faithful Execution and the Courts

a. A Duty to Defend Congress?

The ideal of legal fidelity embodied in the Faithful Execution Clause arguably extends further than to issues of direct legal implementation. It may also be read to imply constitutional norms affecting the behavior of the executive branch in court, especially (but not necessarily limited to) when the executive branch is called upon to defend laws Congress has enacted. On the other hand, even if the executive is presumptively required — and the presumption is a strong one — to implement the enactments of Congress, there might not be an equal presumption that the executive must defend a statute attacked in court as unconstitutional. Indeed, the position of executive branch lawyers as "officers of the Court" might suggest a wholly different role.

This issue arose in connection with *Buckley v. Valeo*, 424 U.S. 1 (1976) (per curiam), a case challenging the constitutionality of the Federal Election Commission. The Justice Department refused in *Buckley*, on separation of powers grounds, to defend Congress's authority to appoint four of the Commission's six voting members — authority that the Court invalidated, as reflected in the excerpt *supra*. Consider, as you read the following statements offered at a congressional hearing spurred by Justice's position, whether the Attorney General must defend every law the government carries out. Could he be obligated to defend a law that the executive branch refuses to implement on constitutional grounds? The following excerpted statements addressing these issues were offered by former Assistant Attorney General (later Solicitor General) Rex Lee and Simon Lazarus, later a member of the Domestic Policy Staff under President Carter.

Representation of Congress and Congressional Interests in Court

Hearings Before the Subcomm. on Separation of Powers of the Senate Comm. on the Judiciary, 94th Cong., 2d Sess. 4–6, 150–52 (1976)

Statement of Rex Lee

. . . The defense of statutes attacked on constitutional grounds is an important part of the Justice Department's work. There are essentially two situations in which the Department will not defend the constitutionality of a statute. The first situation involves those cases in which upholding the statute would have the effect of limiting the President's constitutional powers or prerogatives. It is neither shocking nor surprising that the Congress in enacting legislation occasionally takes a different view from that of the President concerning the President's rights. It is equally clear that the President is entitled to a defense of his perceived rights.

The litigation now before the Supreme Court in *Buckley v. Valeo* is illustrative. . . . The Attorney General is . . . a named party in that case. On his own behalf and as counsel for the Federal Election Commission, he is defending the constitutionality of the Federal Election Campaign laws as amended by the Federal Election Campaign Act Amendments of 1974, 88 Stat. 1263, insofar as those statutes are being challenged under the first, fourth, or ninth amendments, or the due process clause of the fifth amendment. However, the brief the Department has filed for the Federal Election Commission does not address any of the issues arising out of the law enforcement powers of the Commission. With respect to these, the Attorney General has filed a separate brief urging the Supreme Court not to decide the constitutionality of the Commission's enforcement powers. The separate brief urges that this issue is not ripe for adjudication. Should the Court reach it, however, our position is that the statute unconstitutionally vests in the Federal Election Commission, as essentially an arm of the Congress, enforcement responsibilities reserved by article II of the Constitution to the executive branch. On this aspect of the case the Commission is represented by its own special counsel.

The second situation in which the Department will not defend against a claim of unconstitutionality involves cases where the Attorney General believes, not only personally as a matter of conscience, but also in his official capacity as the chief legal officer of the United States, that a law is so patently unconstitutional that it cannot be defended. Such a situation is thankfully most rare. In fact, the only instance of which I am aware is the case of *United States v. Lovett*. The statute in that case, in effect, dismissed three named executive officials. There were two grounds on which the Department declined to defend its constitutionality, first, that it unconstitutionally infringed on the President's control over executive personnel, and second, that it worked a bill of attainder. The House of Representatives hired special counsel to defend the statute. A majority of the Senate also believing it to be unconstitutional had passed the bill only because it was a rider to a necessary appropriations bill and after several conferences the House refused to recede. The United States Supreme Court unanimously held the statute unconstitutional.

These situations should not be confused with situations in which the Department defends the constitutionality of a statute unsuccessfully in lower courts but does not seek an appeal. The Supreme Court cannot and will not give plenary review to every lower court decision declaring a statute unconstitutional. By limiting the cases in which review is sought, the Solicitor General is more likely to obtain plenary review in those cases where it is most important. The decision not to appeal a finding that a law is unconstitutional is, of course, not made lightly. In both of these contexts—congressional representation and defense of constitutionality—the factor which dictates non-participation of the Department of Justice is a conflict of interest. The result of this disqualification of Justice Department lawyers is not that congressional defendants are unrepresented, or that the constitutionality of congressional legislation is not vigorously and ably asserted. In either situation, outside counsel is always available. . . .

Testimony of Simon Lazarus, Arnold and Porter Law Firm, Washington, D.C.

. . . My purpose this morning is to discuss the question of the obligation, if there is one, of the Department of Justice to uphold the constitutionality of statutes passed by Congress and signed by the President when they are challenged in court and to consider whether it is appropriate or when it is appropriate for the Department to fail to support the constitutionality of Federal laws, what problems that raises, and what remedies there might be, and in particular, whether there is reason for concern that the interests of Congress are not adequately being represented by the manner in which this problem is dealt with now. . . .

I don't think that one can legitimately construe any of the various provisions of the United States Code defining the Attorney General's obligations and authority or any provision of the Constitution to require the Attorney General or the Solicitor General to support the constitutionality of laws that are challenged in the courts.

However, I think that it has always been understood, as a matter of practice, that that is what the Solicitor General is there for. He is there to be a responsible and distinguished advocate for the interests of the U.S. Government, which is generally understood to include the Congress, as well as the executive branch. And I think this is reflected in our practice. . . . The Department, and the Solicitor General's Office, in particular, does not always blindly push for the narrow interests of the agency it happens to be defending at a particular moment and that's also understood.

However, the standard by which the Department and the Solicitor General's Office has historically determined whether it should uphold the position that has been taken by an executive agency or an administrative agency has always been, according to Robert L. Stern, who is one of the most eminent authorities on the Solicitor General's Office, that the position taken by the agency would be supportive unless there was "no respectable argument" in favor of the agency's position.

If that standard were applied to the Federal Election Campaign Act, I think it's quite clear that the Justice Department would have taken a position in support of the law, because there's no question that even the most vulnerable provisions of the Federal Election Campaign Act could be supported by very respectable, if not very strong, arguments. . . .

What would be the consequences, if it were understood that it was part of the Attorney General's function when he thought a constitutional issue was important enough to simply go to court and say, "These are my views" and represent that those views are the views of the United States.

The amicus curiae brief that was filed in the Supreme Court [in *Buckley v. Valeo*] which, in effect, revealed that the Justice Department was taking at one and the same time an advocate's and a neutral position on the law—was filed in the name of the United States. And I think that that is a very disturbing issue. To be sure it's perfectly clear what authority the Attorney General has when he comes to court to defend an action of the Government, such as the passage of a law. It's even reasonably clear what authority he has to come in and represent the interests of the executive branch, if they conflict with the law, which is a very rare occurrence, I would say.

But I see no basis for coming into court and simply giving an opinion which is a personal opinion, such as he might express in a law review article, where it would be perfectly appropriate for him to express such an opinion. . . .

———

Solicitors General. A complete picture of the Justice Department's litigating function requires some discussion of the Solicitor General of the United States, an official mentioned by both Simon Lazarus and Rex Lee (who served as Solicitor General throughout the first Reagan Administration). Under 28 U.S.C. § 505, the Solicitor General (known in Washington as "the S.G.") is to be a person "learned in the law" appointed by the President to assist the Attorney General. As the Justice Department has long been organized, the Solicitor General is charged with representing the United States before the Supreme Court and deciding whether to approve the appeal, on behalf of the United States, of any adverse decision by a lower court.

Traditionally, presidents have selected especially eminent lawyers to be Solicitors General, including former judges and prominent scholars. It is perceived as a good job to have if one is to be considered seriously for a Supreme Court appointment. (In recent decades, Justices Thurgood Marshall and Elena Kagan, for example, had each served as Solicitor General.) There have been extensive debates, however, regarding the Solicitor General's role. Should the S.G. be a detached, relatively dispassionate presenter of the law to the Supreme Court, or is the S.G. simply the President's chief advocate in litigation? Critics of the Reagan Administrations—especially of Solicitor General Charles Fried—argued that the Solicitor General's Office became too willing to advance ideologically driven positions in the Supreme Court, at some cost to the credibility of the Office. Defenders insisted that the Office maintained a consistent, high degree of professionalism and that its legal arguments, even when unsuccessful, were institutionally appropriate. Professor Fried defended his role as Solicitor General in a memoir, CHARLES FRIED, ORDER AND LAW: ARGUING THE REAGAN REVOLUTION—A FIRSTHAND ACCOUNT (1991).

———————

Among the most controversial refusals of the executive branch to defend a statute's constitutionality in Court was the Obama Administration's decision to abandon the legal defense of the federal Defense of Marriage Act (DOMA), Pub. L. 104-199, 100 Stat. 2419 (1996), which both adopted a federal definition of marriage that limits the term to heterosexual couples and purported to exempt states not recognizing same-sex marriage from any obligation to give effect to same-sex marriages that are recognized in other jurisdictions. What follows is Attorney General's explanation of his (and the President's) decision not to defend DOMA:

Letter from Attorney General Eric H. Holder to Congress on Litigation Involving the Defense of Marriage Act
February 23, 2011

The Honorable John A. Boehner Speaker
U.S. House of Representatives
Washington, DC 20515
Re: *Defense of Marriage Act*

Dear Mr. Speaker:

After careful consideration, including review of a recommendation from me, the President of the United States has made the determination that Section 3 of the Defense of Marriage Act ("DOMA"), 1 U.S.C. §7,[1] as applied to same-sex couples who are legally married under state law, violates the equal protection component of the Fifth Amendment. Pursuant to 28 U.S.C. §530D, I am writing to advise you of the Executive Branch's determination and to inform you of the steps the Department will take in two pending DOMA cases to implement that determination.

While the Department has previously defended DOMA against legal challenges involving legally married same-sex couples, recent lawsuits that challenge the constitutionality of DOMA Section 3 have caused the President and the Department to

———————

1. DOMA Section 3 states: "In determining the meaning of any Act of Congress, or of any ruling, regulation, or interpretation of the various administrative bureaus and agencies of the United States, the word 'marriage' means only a legal union between one man and one woman as husband and wife, and the word 'spouse' refers only to a person of the opposite sex who is a husband or a wife."

conduct a new examination of the defense of this provision. In particular, in November 2010, plaintiffs filed two new lawsuits challenging the constitutionality of Section 3 of DOMA in jurisdictions without precedent on whether sexual-orientation classifications are subject to rational basis review or whether they must satisfy some form of heightened scrutiny. *Windsor v. United States*, No. 1:10-cv-8435 (S.D.N.Y.); *Pedersen v. OPM*, No. 3:10-cv-1750 (D. Conn.). Previously, the Administration has defended Section 3 in jurisdictions where circuit courts have already held that classifications based on sexual orientation are subject to rational basis review, and it has advanced arguments to defend DOMA Section 3 under the binding standard that has applied in those cases.

These new lawsuits, by contrast, will require the Department to take an affirmative position on the level of scrutiny that should be applied to DOMA Section 3 in a circuit without binding precedent on the issue. As described more fully below, the President and I have concluded that classifications based on sexual orientation warrant heightened scrutiny and that, as applied to same-sex couples legally married under state law, Section 3 of DOMA is unconstitutional.

Standard of Review

The Supreme Court has yet to rule on the appropriate level of scrutiny for classifications based on sexual orientation. It has, however, rendered a number of decisions that set forth the criteria that should inform this and any other judgment as to whether heightened scrutiny applies: (1) whether the group in question has suffered a history of discrimination; (2) whether individuals "exhibit obvious, immutable, or distinguishing characteristics that define them as a discrete group"; (3) whether the group is a minority or is politically powerless; and (4) whether the characteristics distinguishing the group have little relation to legitimate policy objectives or to an individual's "ability to perform or contribute to society." *See Bowen v. Gilliard*, 483 U.S. 587, 602–03 (1987); *City of Cleburne v. Cleburne Living Ctr.*, 473 U.S. 432, 441–42 (1985).

Each of these factors counsels in favor of being suspicious of classifications based on sexual orientation. First and most importantly, there is, regrettably, a significant history of purposeful discrimination against gay and lesbian people, by governmental as well as private entities, based on prejudice and stereotypes that continue to have ramifications today. Indeed, until very recently, states have "demean[ed] the[] existence" of gays and lesbians "by making their private sexual conduct a crime." *Lawrence v. Texas*, 539 U.S. 558, 578 (2003).

Second, while sexual orientation carries no visible badge, a growing scientific consensus accepts that sexual orientation is a characteristic that is immutable, it is undoubtedly unfair to require sexual orientation to be hidden from view to avoid discrimination, *see* Don't Ask, Don't Tell Repeal Act of 2010, Pub. L. No. 111-321, 124 Stat. 3515 (2010).

Third, the adoption of laws like those at issue in *Romer v. Evans*, 517 U.S. 620 (1996), and *Lawrence*, the longstanding ban on gays and lesbians in the military, and the absence of federal protection for employment discrimination on the basis of sexual orientation show the group to have limited political power and "ability to attract the [favorable] attention of the lawmakers." *Cleburne*, 473 U.S. at 445. And while the enactment of the Matthew Shepard Act and pending repeal of Don't Ask, Don't Tell indicate that the political process is not closed *entirely* to gay and lesbian people, that is not the standard by which the Court has judged "political powerlessness." Indeed, when the Court ruled that gender-based classifications were subject to heightened scrutiny, women already had won major political victories such as the Nineteenth Amendment (right to vote) and protection under Title VII (employment discrimination).

Finally, there is a growing acknowledgment that sexual orientation "bears no relation to ability to perform or contribute to society." *Frontiero v. Richardson*, 411 U.S. 677, 686 (1973) (plurality). Recent evolutions in legislation (including the pending repeal of Don't Ask, Don't Tell), in community practices and attitudes, in case law (including the Supreme Court's holdings in *Lawrence* and *Romer*), and in social science regarding sexual orientation all make clear that sexual orientation is not a characteristic that generally bears on legitimate policy objectives.

To be sure, there is substantial circuit court authority applying rational basis review to sexual-orientation classifications. We have carefully examined each of those decisions. Many of them reason only that if consensual same-sex sodomy may be criminalized under *Bowers v. Hardwick*, then it follows that no heightened review is appropriate—a line of reasoning that does not survive the overruling of *Bowers* in *Lawrence v. Texas*, 538 U.S. 558 (2003). Others rely on claims regarding "procreational responsibility" that the Department has disavowed already in litigation as unreasonable, or claims regarding the immutability of sexual orientation that we do not believe can be reconciled with more recent social science understandings. And none engages in an examination of all the factors that the Supreme Court has identified as relevant to a decision about the appropriate level of scrutiny. Finally, many of the more recent decisions have relied on the fact that the Supreme Court has not recognized that gays and lesbians constitute a suspect class or the fact that the Court has applied rational basis review in its most recent decisions addressing classifications based on sexual orientation, *Lawrence* and *Romer*. But neither of those decisions reached, let alone resolved, the level of scrutiny issue because in both the Court concluded that the laws could not even survive the more deferential rational basis standard.

Application to Section 3 of DOMA

In reviewing a legislative classification under heightened scrutiny, the government must establish that the classification is "substantially related to an important government objective." *Clark v. Jeter*, 486 U.S. 456, 461 (1988). Under heightened scrutiny, "a tenable justification must describe actual state purposes, not rationalizations for actions in fact differently grounded." *United States v. Virginia*, 518 U.S. 515, 535–36 (1996). "The justification must be genuine, not hypothesized or invented post hoc in response to litigation." *Id*. at 533.

In other words, under heightened scrutiny, the United States cannot defend Section 3 by advancing hypothetical rationales, independent of the legislative record, as it has done in circuits where precedent mandates application of rational basis review. Instead, the United States can defend Section 3 only by invoking Congress' actual justifications for the law.

Moreover, the legislative record underlying DOMA's passage contains discussion and debate that undermines any defense under heightened scrutiny. The record contains numerous expressions reflecting moral disapproval of gays and lesbians and their intimate and family relationships—precisely the kind of stereotype-based thinking and animus the Equal Protection Clause is designed to guard against. *See Cleburne*, 473 U.S. at 448 ("mere negative attitudes, or fear" are not permissible bases for discriminatory treatment); *see also Romer*, 517 U.S. at 635 (rejecting rationale that law was supported by "the liberties of landlords or employers who have personal or religious objections to homosexuality"); *Palmore v. Sidotti*, 466 U.S. 429, 433 (1984) ("Private biases may be outside the reach of the law, but the law cannot, directly or indirectly, give them effect.").

Application to Second Circuit Cases

After careful consideration, including a review of my recommendation, the President has concluded that given a number of factors, including a documented history of discrimination, classifications based on sexual orientation should be subject to a heightened standard of scrutiny. The President has also concluded that Section 3 of DOMA, as applied to legally married same-sex couples, fails to meet that standard and is therefore unconstitutional. Given that conclusion, the President has instructed the Department not to defend the statute in *Windsor* and *Pedersen* now pending in the Southern District of New York and the District of Connecticut. I concur in this determination.

Notwithstanding this determination, the President has informed me that Section 3 will continue to be enforced by the Executive Branch. To that end, the President has instructed Executive agencies to continue to comply with Section 3 of DOMA, consistent with the Executive's obligation to take care that the laws be faithfully executed, unless and until Congress repeals Section 3 or the judicial branch renders a definitive verdict against the law's constitutionality. This course of action respects the actions of the prior Congress that enacted DOMA, and it recognizes the judiciary as the final arbiter of the constitutional claims raised.

As you know, the Department has a longstanding practice of defending the constitutionality of duly-enacted statutes if reasonable arguments can be made in their defense, a practice that accords the respect appropriately due to a coequal branch of government. However, the Department in the past has declined to defend statutes despite the availability of professionally responsible arguments, in part because the Department does not consider every plausible argument to be a "reasonable" one. "[D]ifferent cases can raise very different issues with respect to statutes of doubtful constitutional validity," and thus there are "a variety of factors that bear on whether the Department will defend the constitutionality of a statute." Letter to Hon. Orrin G. Hatch from Assistant Attorney General Andrew Fois at 7 (Mar. 22, 1996). This is the rare case where the proper course is to forgo the defense of this statute. Moreover, the Department has declined to defend a statute "in cases in which it is manifest that the President has concluded that the statute is unconstitutional," as is the case here. Seth P. Waxman, *Defending Congress*, 79 N.C. L.Rev. 1073, 1083 (2001).

In light of the foregoing, I will instruct the Department's lawyers to immediately inform the district courts in *Windsor* and *Pedersen* of the Executive Branch's view that heightened scrutiny is the appropriate standard of review and that, consistent with that standard, Section 3 of DOMA may not be constitutionally applied to same-sex couples whose marriages are legally recognized under state law. If asked by the district courts in the Second Circuit for the position of the United States in the event those courts determine that the applicable standard is rational basis, the Department will state that, consistent with the position it has taken in prior cases, a reasonable argument for Section 3's constitutionality may be proffered under that permissive standard. Our attorneys will also notify the courts of our interest in providing Congress a full and fair opportunity to participate in the litigation in those cases. We will remain parties to the case and continue to represent the interests of the United States throughout the litigation.

Furthermore, pursuant to the President's instructions, and upon further notification to Congress, I will instruct Department attorneys to advise courts in other pending DOMA litigation of the President's and my conclusions that a heightened standard should apply, that Section 3 is unconstitutional under that standard and that the Department will cease defense of Section 3. . . .

Sincerely yours,
Eric H. Holder, Jr.
Attorney General

————————

1. *A Standard for Nondefense.* What is Attorney General Holder's standard for when a legal argument is strong enough to present in defense of a statute? Is it the same as the standard Solicitor General Rex Lee advanced? Which do you think is the appropriate standard, and was that standard met in the DOMA cases?

A major source of disagreement in the 2016 presidential election campaign was the fate of the Affordable Care Act, frequently called Obamacare. Its most controversial provision, the individual mandate to buy health insurance, was upheld in the Supreme Court in a 5–4 vote, which depended critically on a somewhat surprising opinion by Chief Justice Roberts that upheld the mandate as an exercise of Congress's taxing power. *National Federation of Independent Businesses v. Sebelius*, 567 U.S. 519 (2012). Five Justices, including Roberts, found the Commerce Clause an insufficient basis for upholding the mandate. Should Chief Justice Roberts unexpectedly resign and a conservative Justice fill the vacancy, one could imagine a new lawsuit brought to challenge the constitutionality of the Affordable Care Act, essentially asking the Supreme Court to reverse its decision in *NFIB v. Sebelius*. Could the Justice Department, faced with such a suit, legitimately decline to defend the ACA? How would its nondefense of the ACA be distinguishable, if it is, from the nondefense of DOMA? For an argument that the executive branch actually has a distinct duty not to defend laws that violate equal protection principles, see Parker Rider-Longmaid, *Take Care That The Laws Be Faithfully Litigated*, 161 U. Penn. L. Rev. 291 (2012).

2. *Shifting Grounds*. Note that the Supreme Court did invalidate Section 3 of DOMA, but not on the basis of the argument the Attorney General embraced. Rather than explicitly deploy any heightened standard of constitutional scrutiny, the Court concluded that the "principal purpose and the necessary effect of [DOMA were] to demean those persons who are in a lawful same-sex marriage"; as a consequence, "DOMA is unconstitutional as a deprivation of the liberty of the person protected by the Fifth Amendment of the Constitution." *United States v. Windsor*, 133 S. Ct. 2675, 2695 (2013). Do you think the Attorney General's decision any more or less defensible in light of the Court's approach?

3. *In Which Court?* Note that the Justice Department took its anti-DOMA stance while the challenges were posed in District Court. Should Justice have at least defended DOMA at the trial level and reconsidered at the appellate stage? Edith Windsor, as it happens, won her case at the District Court level. Once the Justice Department loses in the trial court, does the norm in favor of defending Congress's enactments create any presumption in favor of appealing?

4. *Any Duty at All?* In a notable 2012 article, Professors Neal Devins and Saikrishna Prakash argued that Presidents have no duty to enforce any statute they deem unconstitutional and, in any event, that the executive branch has no duty at all to defend such statutes. Neal Devins and Saikrishna Prakash, *The Indefensible Duty to Defend*, 112 Colum. L. Rev. 507 (2012). In their view:

> There is no plausible argument that the Constitution obliges the President to press constitutional claims that he finds unpersuasive or objectionable, especially where others stand ready to make sincere arguments in defense of a law If the goal is to have the courts judge the constitutionality of laws, the duty to enforce largely satisfies this goal, making the duty to defend pointless. Hence, even if one supposes that our broad claim is misguided, almost everyone should embrace our narrow reform to abolish the unnecessary duty to defend.

Id. at 508. Their argument is rooted in a strong "departmentalist" view of each branch's independent authority to interpret the Constitution for itself: "First, nothing in the Constitution requires any one branch to accept the constitutional conclusions of another. Second, Presidents have long acted on their own understanding of the Constitution, believing that they had no duty to follow the constitutional readings of either Congress or the courts." *Id*. at 526.

Former Solicitor General Seth Waxman takes a different view: "Vigorously defending congressional legislation serves the institutional interests and constitutional judgments of all three branches. It ensures that proper respect is given to Congress's policy choices. It preserves for the courts their historic function of judicial review. And it reflects an important premise in our constitutional system — that when Congress passes a law and the President signs it, their actions reflect a shared judgment about the constitutionality of the statute." Seth P. Waxman, *Defending Congress*, 79 N.C. L. Rev. 1073 (2001). See also Daniel J. Meltzer, *Executive Defense of Congressional Acts*, 61 Duke L.J. 1183 (2012) (arguing that the duty of defense is not derived directly from constitutional text, but is a matter of judgment informed by weighty historical and institutional concerns). What is your view?

Note: Raines v. Byrd *and Congressional Standing*

According to Rex Lee's testimony, *supra*, one reason why Congress need not be unduly concerned by occasional refusals by the executive branch to defend statutes is that Congress has independent means of litigating constitutional issues. In the face of executive branch refusal to defend congressional authority in a separation of powers case, each House of Congress might be granted the status of a party, as in *Chadha*, *supra*. The constitutionality of the legislative veto was vigorously (if unsuccessfully) argued by Senate Legal Counsel Michael Davidson and Stanley M. Brand, General Counsel to the Clerk of the House, teamed with House Special Counsel Eugene Gressman. Even if the constitutional challenge is not on separation of powers grounds, Congress might be allowed to intervene as an interested party under Fed. Rule Civ. Proc. 24(a)(2).) This was the course followed in *United States v. Windsor*, in which a Bipartisan Legal Advisory Group (BLAG) in the House hired former Solicitor General Paul D. Clement to present the House's defense of DOMA.

Congress or its members may be tempted also to initiate their own lawsuits challenging executive branch action they consider unconstitutional. The difficulty facing federal courts is distinguishing between cases in which executive action truly threatens a congressional interest in a way that satisfies the constitutional requirement that litigation be based on relatively concrete, particularized injuries and cases that merely attempt to relitigate political disputes that the congressional plaintiffs lost in the political arena. The D.C. Circuit has repeatedly granted standing to members of Congress to sue, in their institutional capacity, on separation of powers grounds. Examples include a series of cases involving the pocket veto, discussed in Chapter 2. *See Kennedy v. Sampson*, 511 F.2d 430, 435–436 (C.A.D.C.1974); *Moore v. United States House of Representatives*, 733 F.2d 946, 951 (C.A.D.C.1984); id., at 956 (Scalia, J., concurring in result); *Barnes v. Kline*, 759 F.2d 21 (D.C. Cir. 1985), *vacated sub nom. Burke v. Barnes*, 107 S. Ct. 734 (1987), the pocket veto case excerpted in Chapter Two. *But see Holtzman v. Schlesinger*, 484 F.2d 1307, 1315 (C.A.2 1973) (Member of Congress has no standing to challenge constitutionality of American military operations in Vietnam war*); Harrington v. Schlesinger*, 528 F.2d 455, 459 (C.A.4 1975) (same).

At the same time, the D.C. Circuit has invoked what it has called "equitable discretion" to avoid ruling in yet other disputes. In *Melcher v. Federal Open Market Committee*, 836 F.2d 561, 563 (D.C. Cir. 1987), *cert. denied*, 486 U.S. 1042 (1988), *quoting*

Riegle v. Federal Open Market Committee, 656 F.2d 873, 881 (D.C. Cir.), *cert. denied*, 454 U.S. 1082 (1981), the court said: "Where a congressional plaintiff could obtain substantial relief from his fellow legislators through the enactment, repeal, or amendment of a statute, this court should exercise its equitable discretion to dismiss the legislator's action." On this ground, the court refused to hear a Senator's challenge to the constitutionality of the method for appointing five of the twelve members of the Federal Reserve System's Federal Open Market Committee. *See also Humphrey v. Baker*, 848 F.2d 211 (D.C. Cir. 1988), *cert. denied*, 488 U.S. 966 (1988) (denying members of Congress standing on equitable discretion grounds to challenge constitutionality of the Salary Act). "Equitable discretion" could go a long way to precluding congressional suits without erecting a constitutional barrier to such suits whenever it could be argued that, because the plaintiff members of Congress could rely on existing legislative powers to seek redress against the executive, they have not been injured by the executive branch in a way that justifies judicial intervention. A plaintiff-legislator's dispute, seen in this light, is not truly with the executive, but with other legislators who might join the plaintiff's cause, but have chosen not to do so.

The court's line-drawing has not been much aided by the Supreme Court, which, as analyzed by Professor Jonathan Nash, has offered only "scarce and inconsistent guidance on congressional standing." Jonathan Remy Nash, *A Functional Theory of Congressional Standing*, 114 Mich. L. Rev. 339 (2015). The Supreme Court's most recent foray into that subject is *Raines v. Byrd*, 521 U.S. 811 (1997), in which the Court disallowed a congressional challenge to the Line Item Veto Act, which the Court ultimately invalidated in *Clinton v. City of New York*, excerpted in Chapter Two, *supra*. The Court first pointed out that the Act worked no personal harm to the four Senator and two House Member-plaintiffs. What the plaintiffs argued, instead, was the nullification of their votes on appropriations measures that the President had altered by use of the line-item veto. They analogized their injury to that of Kansas legislators opposed to a proposed Child Labor Amendment to the U.S. Constitution who were given standing to challenge Kansas's supposed ratification notwithstanding a deadlock in the state Senate, which, according to the legislator plaintiffs, meant that no ratification had occurred. *Coleman v. Miller*, 307 U.S. 433 (1939). The Supreme Court was unpersuaded:

> [A]ppellees' claim does not fall within our holding in *Coleman*. . . . They have not alleged that they voted for a specific bill, that there were sufficient votes to pass the bill, and that the bill was nonetheless deemed defeated. In the vote on the [Line-Item Veto] Act, their votes were given full effect. They simply lost that vote. Nor can they allege that the Act will nullify their votes in the future in the same way that the votes of the *Coleman* legislators had been nullified. In the future, a majority of Senators and Congressmen can pass or reject appropriations bills; the Act has no effect on this process. In addition, a majority of Senators and Congressmen can vote to repeal the

Act, or to exempt a given appropriations bill (or a given provision in an appropriations bill) from the Act; again, the Act has no effect on this process. . . .

Nevertheless, appellees rely heavily on our statement in *Coleman* that the Kansas senators had "a plain, direct and adequate interest in maintaining the effectiveness of their votes." Appellees claim that this statement applies to them because their votes on future appropriations bills (assuming a majority of Congress does not decide to exempt those bills from the Act) will be less "effective" than before, and that the "meaning" and "integrity" of their vote has changed. . . . Even taking appellees at their word about the change in the "meaning" and "effectiveness" of their vote for appropriations bills which are subject to the Act, we think their argument pulls *Coleman* too far from its moorings. . . . There is a vast difference between the level of vote nullification at issue in *Coleman* and the abstract dilution of institutional legislative power that is alleged here. To uphold standing here would require a drastic extension of *Coleman*.

Id. at 824–825. Do you find this distinction persuasive? Should a court be more willing to adjudicate an issue of constitutional process on behalf of a plaintiff with an interest in only one particular appropriation than on behalf of a plaintiff, such as a member of Congress, with a long-run stake in the operation of the legislative system? One policy typically associated with the Supreme Court's elaboration of standing rules is the Court's desire to secure the best possible plaintiff to bring a concrete, well-focused dispute. Who — the disappointed payee or the member of Congress — is likely to be the more useful litigant in this respect?

It is not clear that *Raines* casts any doubt on the standing of congressional committees to seek civil enforcement of their subpoenas. Such an argument was rejected in *Committee on Judiciary, U.S. House of Representatives v. Miers*, 558 F. Supp. 2d 53 (D.D.C. 2008), *stayed*, 542 F.3d 909 (D.C.Cir. 2008), *case voluntarily dismissed*, 2009 WL 3568649 (D.C.Cir. Oct 14, 2009) (NO. 08-5357). At issue was the subpoena to the George W. Bush Administration's former White House counsel to testify before the House Judiciary Committee concerning U.S. Attorney dismissals that were alleged to have been politically motivated. The District Court concluded that the Supreme Court's reluctance in *Raines* to allow individual members of Congress to sue based on the personalized injuries there asserted did not disqualify a committee chair from suing to redress the institutional injury to his or her committee. The district court laid additional stress on the facts that "the Committee [had] plainly undertaken efforts to obtain the documents and testimony at issue pursuant to an official investigation, a congressional subpoena [had] been issued seeking precisely that information, and the full House [had] specifically authorized filing suit." 558 F. Supp. 2d, at 70. For a supportive analysis resting also on the unavailability of other practicable remedies, see Una Lee, *Reinterpreting* Raines: *Legislator Standing to Enforce Congressional Subpoenas*, 98 Geo. L.J. 1165 (2010).

b. The Conduct of Civil Litigation

The conduct of civil litigation can pose yet further complicated questions about the relationship of the Justice Department's role in representing the United States in court and the executive branch's obligation faithfully to execute the laws.

Settling Suits Against the Government. For example, private parties' use of litigation against the government to enforce the government's putative statutory obligations can pose difficult questions of what constitutes faithful execution of the laws in the context of settlement.

For example, to what extent is the Attorney General—as head of the Department of Justice and as executive branch lawyer—bound by the statutes of another agency in settling private litigation against that agency? The Attorney General enjoys broad statutory power to conduct litigation in furtherance of "the interests of the United States." 28 U.S.C. § 518 (1982). Attorneys General have claimed that, under this power, they have plenary authority to compromise disputes against the United States. *See* 4B Op. O.L.C. 756 (1980). The only admitted "limitation" upon this power is that it be "exercised with wise discretion and resorted to only to promote the Government's best interest or to prevent flagrant injustice. . . ." 38 Op. Att'y Gen. 98, 102 (1934).

Is such a broad inference of settlement authority consistent with the faithful execution of the laws? Suppose that Congress has authorized mineral leases on public lands only under certain conditions, and that the Department of the Interior has disqualified a particular applicant on statutory grounds. If the Attorney General determines (a) that the private applicant is otherwise a qualified lessee, (b) that the statutory disability is of little consequence, and (c) that the government's defense of a lawsuit would be unduly expensive, may he waive the statutory requirement as part of his settlement of a lawsuit for the lease? Would recognition of such authority create too great a likelihood of "sweetheart deals" between private parties and the Department of Justice, to the detriment of a faithful execution of Congress's intended policies? Or, because Congress could presumably limit the Attorney General's settlement discretion by statute, should it be assumed that, unless Congress has done so explicitly, it intends the Attorney General's authority to be as broad as the language of 28 U.S.C. § 518 implies?

In *Executive Business Media v. U.S. Department of Defense*, 3 F.3d 759 (4th Cir. 1993), the court held that the Defense Department and a potential contractor could not agree in a settlement to the effectuation of a contract between them when Department regulations provided that a competitive bidding process should precede the awarding of the contract involved. In *U.S. v. Carpenter*, 526 F.3d 1237 (9th Cir. 2008), *cert. denied sub nom., Elko County, Nev. v. Wilderness Soc.*, 556 U.S. 1147 (2009), the Ninth Circuit allowed environmental groups to intervene in a Quiet Title Act action between the United States and a county relating to the repair of a road on Forest Service land. The court held that the groups stated a cognizable claim for review whether, in settling litigation over the land, the United States purported to grant the

County a property interest in public land without complying with the procedural mechanisms for relinquishing title or issuing rights-of-way set forth in the Federal Land Policy and Management Act, 43 U.S.C. § 1701 *et seq.* Are these both sensible results?

This knotty question is made all the thornier once a court has become involved. In *Cascade Natural Gas Corp. v. El Paso Natural Gas Co.*, 386 U.S. 129 (1967), the Supreme Court held the Department of Justice may not use its settlement authority to circumscribe the power of the courts to see that their orders are carried out. In a prior decision, *United States v. El Paso Natural Gas Co.*, 376 U.S. 651 (1964), the Supreme Court had held that the acquisition of Pacific Northwest Pipeline Corporation by the El Paso Natural Gas Company violated Section 7 of the Clayton Act, and it directed the District Court "to order the divestiture without delay." Subsequent to this decision, the United States agreed to a settlement of the litigation that would have permitted interests aligned with El Paso to obtain stock in the newly formed company. The Supreme Court, in rejecting the "settlement" decree, said: "We do not question the authority of the Attorney General to settle suits after, as well as before, they reach here. The Department of Justice, however, by stipulation or otherwise has no authority to circumscribe the power of the courts to see that our mandate is carried out. No one, except this court, has authority to alter or modify our mandate." 386 U.S. at 136.

Should the Department of Justice understand from this opinion that its settlement authority after a judicial decree is more circumscribed than when a case is first filed? That is, would the agreement by the United States to the settlement decree in *Cascade Natural Gas Corp.* have been more acceptable before the Supreme Court "educated" the executive branch as to the proper interpretation of the Clayton Act in the context of this particular case? Or, assuming that the United States thought the acquisition unlawful, should it have thought itself barred at all times from settling the lawsuit in a way that would permit a reacquisition of the disputed assets by the putative antitrust violator?

An issue that focused unusual attention on Justice Department settlement policy during the 1980s involved so-called "discretion-binding" consent decrees. These decrees typically include settlement promises by the United States involving budgeting, the allocation of law enforcement resources, or decisions whether to issue or amend administrative regulations—areas over which administrative agencies usually enjoy unreviewable discretion. For example, in one controversial instance, the Environmental Protection Agency settled a lawsuit that charged it with using improper criteria in deciding which toxic pollutants to regulate, by agreeing on "a detailed, comprehensive regulatory program for implementation . . . of the toxic pollutant control and pretreatment objectives" of the Federal Water Pollution Control Act (now called the Clean Water Act, 33 U.S.C. § 1251 [1982]). *Natural Resources Defense Council v. Costle*, 12 Env't Rptr. Cas. (BNA) 1833, 1834 (D.D.C. 1979). *See Citizens for a Better Environment v. Gorsuch*, 718 F.2d 1117 (D.C. Cir. 1983), *cert. denied*, 467 U.S. 1219 (1984) (upholding settlement against separation of powers challenge).

On March 13, 1986, Attorney General Meese issued a set of guidelines purporting to forbid Justice Department attorneys from agreeing to such decrees. The Attorney General asserted that such decrees in the past had:

> forfeited the prerogatives of the Executive in order to preempt the exercise of those prerogatives by a subsequent Administration. These errors sometimes have resulted in an unwarranted expansion of the powers of [the] judiciary—often with the consent of government parties—at the expense of the executive and legislative branches.

Memorandum from Attorney General Edwin Meese, III to All Assistant Attorneys General and All United States Attorneys Re: Department Policy Regarding Consent Decrees and Settlement Agreements 1 (Mar. 13, 1986), *reprinted in* Review of Nixon Presidential Materials Access Regulations, Hearing Before a Subcomm. of the House Comm. on Gov't Operations, 99th Cong., 2d Sess. 180 (1986). Some observers, however, regarded the guidelines simply as an attempt to deter agencies from settling litigation brought against them by public interest groups seeking the vigorous enforcement of regulatory legislation to which the Reagan Administration was hostile.

The Attorney General's Guidelines were puzzling for two reasons. First, the Attorney General asserted that discretion-limiting consent decrees violate the constitutional separation of powers, but seemingly purported to retain authority to approve them in certain circumstances. Second, the Attorney General expressly permitted Justice Department attorneys to approve certain discretion-limiting settlement agreements, that is, settlements not embodied in judicial orders, even though such agreements are also judicially enforceable, and thus equally binding on the executive branch. In 1994, the Clinton Administration proposed such a settlement agreement in a lawsuit charging nonenforcement of laws designed to eliminate cancer causing residues from processed foods. EPA promised to regulate within two years as many as three dozen pesticides suspected of leaving such residues. John H. Cushman, Jr., *E.P.A. Settles Suit and Agrees to Move Against 36 Pesticides*, N.Y. Times, Oct. 13, 1994, at A24.

For a full review of the fairly arcane issues surrounding the constitutional limits on discretion-binding consent decrees, see Symposium, *Consent Decrees: Practical Problems and Legal Dilemmas*, 1987 U. Chi. Legal F. 241–351 (articles by Peter M. Shane, Michael W. McConnell, and Robert V. Percival). The Justice Department formally abandoned the Meese position in 1999. *Authority of the United States to Enter Settlements Limiting the Future Exercise of Executive Branch Discretion* (June 15, 1999), available at 1999 WL 1262049 (O.L.C.).

Private Attorneys General. The question has also arisen whether the Faithful Execution Clause ought to be interpreted as barring so-called qui tam litigation, i.e., civil actions brought by private parties on behalf of the United States to recover fines for the federal treasury and a bounty for the private litigant or "relator." That is, if the President is constitutionally charged with taking care that the laws be faithfully executed, is it permissible for Congress to authorize private parties to bring suits, the whole objective of which is to ensure the execution of the laws?

Qui tam litigation is now authorized most importantly by the False Claims Act, 31 U.S.C. §§ 3729–3733 (1994), which provides remedies for fraud against the federal government. Under the FCA, a person who presents or causes to be made a false or fraudulent claim for payment to the United States is subject to up to treble damages, as well as a civil fine of up to $10,000. The FCA *qui tam* provision authorizes "a private person (the 'relator') [to] bring a qui tam civil action 'for the person and for the United States Government' against the alleged false claimant, and 'in the name of the Government.'" *Vermont Agency of Natural Resources v. United States*, 529 U.S. 765, 769 (2000). As summarized by the Supreme Court:

> If a relator initiates the FCA action, he must deliver a copy of the complaint, and any supporting evidence, to the Government, which then has 60 days to intervene in the action. If it does so, it assumes primary responsibility for prosecuting the action, though the relator may continue to participate in the litigation and is entitled to a hearing before voluntary dismissal and to a court determination of reasonableness before settlement. If the Government declines to intervene within the 60-day period, the relator has the exclusive right to conduct the action, and the Government may subsequently intervene only on a showing of "good cause." The relator receives a share of any proceeds from the action—generally ranging from 15 to 25 percent if the Government intervenes (depending upon the relator's contribution to the prosecution), and from 25 to 30 percent if it does not (depending upon the court's assessment of what is reasonable)—plus attorney's fees and costs.

Id. at 770–771.

In *Vermont Agency,* the Supreme Court upheld qui tam litigation under the False Claims Act against the claim that qui tam plaintiffs lack Article III standing. Writing for a unanimous Court on this question, Justice Scalia concluded that, for Article III purposes, it did not matter that the injury asserted in *qui tam* suits is not an injury personal to the plaintiff. It was enough that the United States had been injured, and that the United States, by statutory implication, had "assigned" part of its right of recovery to the qui tam relator, or plaintiff. The Court relied heavily on the history of *qui tam* actions in both England and the American colonies to conclude that qui tam suits are "'cases and controversies of the sort traditionally amenable to, and resolved by, the judicial process," thus giving rise to Article III standing. *Id.* at 777. As we noted after *Morrison v. Olson*, supra, the Court nonetheless purported to reserve the questions whether qui tam suits are reconcilable with Article II's Appointments and Faithful Execution Clauses.

It is not easy to see, however, that history could entirely vindicate the constitutionality of *qui tam* litigation under one part of the Constitution and not another. Thus, shortly after *Vermont Agency,* in *Riley v. St. Luke's Episcopal Hospital*, 252 F.3d 749 (5th Cir. 2001) (en banc), the Fifth Circuit expressly upheld the False Claims Act on Article II grounds as well. With regard to the compatibility of *qui tam* litigation and Article II authority, the court said:

> That a private citizen may pursue qui tam litigation under the FCA, whether the government chooses to intervene or does not choose, does not interfere with the President's constitutionally assigned functions under Article II's Take Care Clause. Although the Clause states that the Executive must "take Care that the Laws be faithfully executed," it does not require Congress to prescribe litigation by the Executive as the *exclusive* means of enforcing federal law. . . . [T]he Executive retains significant control over litigation pursued under the FCA by a qui tam relator. First, there is little doubt that the Executive retains such control when it intervenes in an action initiated by a relator. Second, even in cases where the government does not intervene, there are a number of control mechanisms present in the qui tam provisions of the FCA so that the Executive nonetheless retains a significant amount of control over the litigation.
>
> [N]ot only may the government take over a case within 60 days of notification, but it may also intervene at a date beyond the 60-day period upon a showing of good cause. . . . [T]he government retains the unilateral power to dismiss an action "notwithstanding the objections of the person." . . . [A]lthough the government does not intervene, its involvement in the litigation nonetheless continues. [F]or example, . . . the government "may request that it be served with copies of pleadings and be sent deposition transcripts . . . [and it] may pursue alternative remedies, such as administrative proceedings." [D]espite the government's non-intervention, it "receives the larger share of any recovery," amounting to up to 70% of the proceeds of a lawsuit. Furthermore, the FCA itself describes several additional ways in which the United States retains control over a lawsuit filed by a qui tam plaintiff. In the area of settlement, for example, the government may settle a case over a relator's objections if the relator receives notice and hearing of the settlement. Additionally, in the area of discovery, if the government shows that discovery initiated by a qui tam plaintiff "would interfere with the Government's investigation or prosecution of a criminal or civil matter arising out of the same facts, the court may stay the discovery for sixty days or more," whether or not the government intervenes.

Id. at 753–754.

Are the mechanisms of ongoing executive authority to affect the course of *qui tam* litigation, described in the Fifth Circuit's opinion, constitutionally necessary to assure that *qui tam* suits respect the separation of powers? It might be observed that there is functionally little difference between *qui tam* suits to enforce federal statutes and ordinary citizen suits under generous statutory provisions that typically grant standing to "any person aggrieved" to file such suits. See, for example, *Federal Election Commission v. Akins*, 524 U.S. 11 (1998), upholding broad citizen standing to challenge the Federal Election Commission's alleged failure to enforce properly the Federal

Election Campaign Act. "Citizen suits" do differ from *qui tam* litigation in that plaintiffs must plead some concrete injury personal to themselves, and cannot rely on the putative assignment to them of the right of the United States to sue for some injury to itself. On the other hand, that "personal injury" can seem pretty tenuous.

Consider *Friends of the Earth v. Laidlaw Environmental Services,* 528 U.S. 167 (2000), in which an environmental group was found to have standing to challenge a private defendant for its past violations of the Clean Water Act. The defendant had achieved substantial legal compliance by the time of trial, but the lower court imposed a civil fine of $405,800, which went to the U.S. treasury, not to the plaintiff, and awarded significant costs to the plaintiffs. Over a vigorous Scalia dissent, joined by Justice Thomas, seven Justices found that Friends of the Earth had standing, as private parties, to sue for the purpose of enforcing a fine for the defendant's past civil violations. Various Friends members had alleged that they used the recreational area affected by Laidlaw's polluted water discharge, and that Laidlaw's activities not only reduced the aesthetic and recreational appeal of the area, but aroused the plaintiffs' personal concerns about environmental harms and impact on their property values. The court held: "To the extent that [civil fines] encourage defendants to discontinue current violations and deter them from committing future ones, they afford redress to citizen plaintiffs who are injured or threatened with injury as a consequence of ongoing unlawful conduct." *Id*. at 187. In short, Friends of the Earth was deemed entitled to seek civil fines on behalf of the United States in the context of a lawsuit over which the executive branch had no effective degree of control whatsoever. For an analysis supporting this result, *see* Peter M. Shane, *Returning Separation of Powers Analysis to its Normative Roots: The Constitutionality of* Qui Tam *Actions and Other Private Suits to Enforce Civil Penalties*, 30 Environmental L. Reporter 11,081–11,103 (2000).

c. Obedience to Judgments

Notwithstanding the Faithful Execution Clause, whether, and in what ways, judicial pronouncements of law bind the executive branch turns out to be a surprisingly multilayered question. Two noncontroversial propositions delimit the areas of controversy: First, the executive concedes its obligation to implement the final judgment in a case to which the United States is a party. Edwin M. Meese, III, *The Law of the Constitution*, 61 Tul. L. Rev. 979 (1987). Thus, for example, if a discharged government employee were to challenge successfully the constitutionality of his or her particular discharge and a court ordered reinstatement, the executive would traditionally acknowledge an obligation to reinstate the employee.

Second, the executive is not obliged to agree with the correctness of judicial pronouncements and to maximize their reach in unrelated cases. For example, the President may urge that an earlier Supreme Court decision be overruled, or may urge that plausibly distinguishable future cases be distinguished from, rather than governed by a decision with which he disagrees. Thus, following the employment case just hypothesized, the President might legitimately discharge another employee in a context arguably similar to, but not legally identical with the situation already litigated. Or, even less controversially, a President could veto on grounds of asserted unconstitutionality a bill that is all but identical to another that the Court upheld, but in an opinion that the President thought wrong. (President Jackson's veto of the rechartering of the Bank of the United States, notwithstanding *McCulloch v. Maryland*, 17 U.S. 316 (1819), illustrates the point.) None of this would amount to genuine defiance of judicial authority.

Between these poles, however, more complex cases present themselves. Is the President bound, for example, to follow a Supreme Court decision he disapproves in a subsequent case that he does acknowledge to be functionally identical? A claim of presidential authority to treat de novo every functionally identical dispute that generates the same constitutional controversy could substantially undermine the courts' capacity to uphold the rule of law. On the other hand, improper judicial interpretations of the Constitution could obviously hobble the Presidency. Consider the following hypotheticals:

1. Imagine that the President believes categorically that it is too risky to afford "top secret" clearances to the spouses of foreign nationals. Imagine that the Supreme Court were to invalidate such a rule as unconstitutionally irrational. Should the President be bound by such a judgment in cases other than that of the employee who brought his or her successful challenge to the Court?

2. Imagine that the President believes categorically that no government employee should be able to publish any book that uses even unclassified information secured by the author while in government employment. He orders the Attorney General to fire a Criminal Division lawyer who writes a best-selling book about life in the FBI; the lawyer successfully obtains reinstatement on the ground that his discharge violated the First Amendment. When another Criminal Division lawyer writes a best-selling book about life in the Drug Enforcement Administration, would the President be disrespecting the separation of powers by ordering her discharge, as well?

3. Imagine that the Supreme Court holds that the plaintiff in a civil case is entitled in discovery to some White House deliberative memos, notwithstanding the President's argument of executive privilege. Would it be unconstitutional for the President to invoke executive privilege to protect functionally identical memos at issue in a different, but essentially indistinguishable case?

Do your reactions to these hypotheticals imply any helpful set of principles to guide Presidents on these issues?

It should be noted that the issue of executive branch obligation to follow judicial doctrine is generally regarded somewhat differently when statutory issues are at stake and only lower court opinions have issued. For example, agencies commonly do not regard themselves as bound nationally by the decisions of single lower courts. Indeed, upon an unfavorable decision in one circuit, an agency may well persist in its challenged practice elsewhere in the hope of achieving a conflict among circuits and consequent Supreme Court review. The proper scope of this so-called "nonacquiescence" doctrine is a matter of considerable debate. See Stephen P. Eichel, *"Respectful Dis-agreement": Nonacquiescence by Federal Administrative Agencies in United States Court of Appeals Precedents*, 18 Colum. J. L. & Soc. Prob. 463 (1985); Samuel Estreicher & Richard L. Revesz, *Nonacquiescence by Federal Administrative Agencies*, 98 Yale L.J. 679 (1989); Note, *Executive Nonacquiescence: Problems of Statutory Interpretation and Separation of Powers*, 60 S. Cal. L. Rev. 1143 (1987); Joseph F. Weis, Jr., *Agency Non-Acquiescence—Respectful Lawlessness or Legitimate Disagreement?*, 48 U. Pitt. L. Rev. 845 (1987).

Commentators have been most critical, however, of a practice called "intracircuit nonacquiescence," in which an agency facing some administrative challenge refuses to follow relevant precedent in the circuit it knows will have jurisdiction over that challenge. A heated dispute occurred during the early 1980s concerning this prac-tice between the Ninth Circuit and the U.S. Department of Health and Human Ser-vices (HHS). In two decisions, in 1981 and 1982, the Ninth Circuit disapproved two HHS policies designed to help eliminate ineligible recipients from the federal dis-ability rolls. *Finnegan v. Matthews*, 641 F.2d 1340 (9th Cir. 1981); *Patti v. Schweiker*, 669 F.2d 582 (9th Cir. 1982). HHS reacted by indicating that, although it would fol-low the Ninth Circuit decisions in the two individual cases, it did not consider itself bound by those decisions in any other eligibility determinations. Instead, HHS deemed itself bound to modify its procedures only to conform to Supreme Court decisions. The Ninth Circuit subsequently affirmed an injunction in a class action, requiring HHS to reinstate, as eligible persons, all those residents of the Ninth Cir-cuit whose disability payments had been terminated by HHS as a result of its nonac-quiescence policy. *Lopez v. Heckler*, 713 F.2d 1432 (9th Cir. 1983). Justice Rehnquist subsequently stayed the judgment in part on the ground that the order significantly interfered "with the distribution between administrative and judicial responsibility for enforcement of the Social Security Act which Congress has established." *Heckler v. Lopez*, 463 U.S. 1328, 1331 (1983). Without shedding further light on the separa-tion of powers issues involved, the Supreme Court ultimately granted certiorari and vacated the judgment, with directions that the district court remand the cases of unnamed class members to the Secretary of HHS for an exhaustion of administra-tive remedies. 469 U.S. 1082 (1984).

Is an intracircuit nonacquiescence policy consistent with the faithful execution of the laws? Does the executive branch's disagreement with a lower court's statutory interpretation justify noncompliance? Alternatively, should a lower court decree be deemed binding on a coequal branch of the government beyond the particular case adjudicated? For further discussion of these issues see Richard J. Pierce, Sidney A. Shapiro & Paul R. Verkuil, Administrative Law and Process 404–408 (4th ed. 2004); Dan T. Coenen, *The Constitutional Case Against Intracircuit Nonac-quiescence*, 75 Minn. L. Rev. 1339 (1991); Note, *Administrative Agency Intracircuit Nonacquiescence*, 85 Colum. L. Rev. 582 (1985).

4. Pardons and Reprieves

An express presidential power with the potential to override Congress's exercise of legislative judgment and the courts' exercise of judicial power in particular cases is the power "to Grant Reprieves and Pardons for Offenses against the United States, except in cases of impeachment." Art. II, § 3. The pardon power:

> embraces all "offenses against the United States," except cases of impeachment, and includes the power to remit fines, penalties, and forfeitures, except as to money covered into the Treasury or paid an informer,[66] the power to pardon absolutely or conditionally, and the power to commute sentences.[67] . . . It was early assumed [but not adjudicated until after the Civil War* that the power included] the power to pardon specified classes or communities wholesale, in short, the power of amnesty, which is usually exercised by proclamation. General amnesties were issued by Washington in 1795, by Adams in 1800, by Madison in 1815, by Lincoln in 1863, by Johnson in 1865, 1867, and 1868, and by the first Roosevelt—to Aguinaldo's followers—in 1902.[68]

THE CONSTITUTION OF THE UNITED STATES OF AMERICA: ANALYSIS AND INTERPRETATION, S. Doc. No. 82, 92d Cong., 2d Sess. 476 (1973) [hereafter, "Library of Congress Analysis"]. The Justice Department has determined that an unconditional pardon also precludes deportation on the ground of criminal conviction, removes state legal disabilities that result from conviction of a federal crime, and extends to the remission of judicially ordered criminal restitution not yet received by the victim of the pardoned offender. Effects of a Presidential Pardon (June 19, 1995), 19 Op. O.L.C. 160 (1995).

Chief Justice Marshall declared in *United States v. Wilson*, 32 U.S. 150, 160–161 (1833), that the legal nature of federal pardons would be determined according to the usages of English common law. On that basis, the Court early regarded the pardon as an "act of grace," *id.*, which might be declined by its intended recipient. *Burdick v. United States*, 236 U.S. 79 (1915). This view has been modified, however, at least with respect to the commutation of sentences. In *Biddle v. Perovich*, 274 U.S. 480 (1927), the Court sustained the right of the President to commute a sentence of death to one of life imprisonment, against the will of the prisoner. "A pardon in our days," the Court said, "is not a private act of grace from an individual happening to possess

---

66. 23 *Ops. Atty. Gen.* 360, 363 (1901); *Illinois Central Railroad v. Bosworth*, 133 U.S. 92 (1890).

67. *Ex parte William Wells*, 18 How. (59 U.S.) 307 (1856). For the contrary view, *see* some early opinions of the Attorney General, 1 *Ops. Atty. Gen.* 341 (1820); 2 *Ops. Atty. Gen.* 275 (1829); 5 *Ops. Atty. Gen.* 687 (1795); *cf.* 4 *Ops. Atty. Gen.* 458 (1845); *United States v. Wilson*, 7 Pet. (32 U.S.) 150, 161 (1833).

* *United States v. Klein*, 13 Wall. (80 U.S.) 128, 147 (1872). *See also United States v. Padelford*, 9 Wall. (76 U.S.) 531 (1870).

68. *See* 1 J. Richardson, Messages and Papers of the Presidents, (Washington: 1897), 173, 293; 2 *id.*, 543; 7 *id.*, 3414, 3508; 8 *id.*, 3853; 14 *id.*, 6690.

power. It is a part of the Constitutional scheme. When granted it is the determination of the ultimate authority that the public welfare will be better served by inflicting less than what the judgment fixed." *Id.* at 486.

Ex parte Garland, 71 U.S. 333 (1867), is the leading case on the effect of a pardon:

> By an act passed in 1865 Congress had prescribed that before any person should be permitted to practice in a federal court he must take oath asserting that he had never voluntarily borne arms against the United States, had never given aid or comfort to enemies of the United States, and so on. Garland, who had been a Confederate sympathizer and so was unable to take the oath, had however received from President Johnson the same year "a full pardon 'for all offenses by him committed, arising from participation, direct or implied, in the Rebellion,' ...." The question before the Court was whether, armed with this pardon, Garland was entitled to practice in the federal courts despite the act of Congress just mentioned. Said Justice Field for a divided Court: "The inquiry arises as to the effect and operation of a pardon, and on this point all the authorities concur. A pardon reaches both the punishment prescribed for the offence and the guilt of the offender; and when the pardon is full, it releases the punishment and blots out of existence the guilt, so that in the eye of the law the offender is as innocent as if he had never committed the offence. If granted before conviction, it prevents any of the penalties and disabilities consequent upon conviction from attaching [thereto]; if granted after conviction, it removes the penalties and disabilities, and restores him to all his civil rights; it makes him, as it were, a new man, and gives him a new credit and capacity." [69] ...

> [Further,] Congress cannot limit the effects of a presidential amnesty. Thus the act of July 12, 1870, making proof of loyalty necessary to recover property abandoned and sold by the Government during the Civil War, notwithstanding any executive proclamation, pardon, amnesty, or other act of condonation or oblivion, was pronounced void. [Under the 1870 Act, acceptance of pardon for offenses connected with participation in the Confederate war effort was to be treated as conviction for treason, disqualifying the

---

69. 71 U.S. (4 Wall.) at 380. [*But see Carlesi v. New York*, 233 U.S. 51 (1914): "Carlesi had been convicted several years before of committing a federal offense. In the instant case the prisoner was being tried for a subsequent offense committed in New York. He was convicted as a second offender, although the President had pardoned him for the earlier offense. In other words, the fact of prior conviction by a federal court was considered in determining the punishment for a subsequent state offense. This conviction and sentence were upheld by the Supreme Court. While this case involved offenses against different sovereignties, the Court declared by way of dictum that its decision 'must not be understood as in the slightest degree intimating that a pardon would operate to limit the power of the United States in punishing crimes against its authority to provide for taking into consideration past offenses committed by the accused as a circumstance of aggravation even although for such past offenses there had been a pardon granted.'" Library of Congress Analysis, at 478.]

recipient from recovering property seized during the Civil War. In *United States v. Klein*, a case challenging the Act,] Chief Justice Chase [said]: "... [T]he legislature cannot change the effect of such a pardon any more than the executive can change a law. Yet this is attempted by the provision under consideration. The Court is required to receive special pardons as evidence of guilt and to treat them as null and void. It is required to disregard pardons granted by proclamation on condition, though the condition has been fulfilled, and to deny them their legal effect. This certainly impairs the executive authority and directs the Court to be instrumental to that end."[70] On the other hand, Congress itself, under the necessary and proper clause, may enact amnesty laws remitting penalties incurred under the national statutes.[71]

Library of Congress Analysis, at 477–80.

It would, we assume, be tenuous to characterize any exercise of the President's plenary pardon power as a technical violation of his duty to take care that the laws be faithfully executed. The impact of a pardon on law enforcement may, however, be considerable, extending beyond the particular case addressed. Controversial uses of the pardon power have become common.

Perhaps most controversially, on September 8, 1974, President Gerald Ford granted his predecessor, Richard Nixon, "a full, free, and absolute pardon ... for all offenses against the United States which he, Richard Nixon, has committed or may have committed or taken part in during the period from January 20, 1969 through August 9, 1974." Proclamation No. 4311, 3A C.F.R. 66 (1974). He explained the pardon as follows:

> [Watergate] is an American tragedy in which we all have played a part. It could go on and on and on, or someone must write the end to it. I have concluded that only I can do that, and if I can, I must.

> There are no historic or legal precedents to which I can turn in this matter, none that precisely fit the circumstances of a private citizen who has resigned the Presidency of the United States. But it is common knowledge that serious allegations and accusations hang like a sword over our former President's head, threatening his health as he tries to reshape his life, a great part of which was spent in the service of this country and by the mandate of its people.

> After years of bitter controversy and divisive national debate, I have been advised, and I am compelled to conclude that many months and perhaps more years will have to pass before Richard Nixon could obtain a fair trial by jury in any jurisdiction of the United States under governing decisions of the Supreme Court. ...

> The facts, as I see them, are that a former President of the United States, instead of enjoying equal treatment with any other citizen accused of violating

---

70. *United States v. Klein*, 80 U.S. (13 Wall.) 128, 143, 148 (1872).
71. *The Laura*, 114 U.S. 411 (1885).

the law, would be cruelly and excessively penalized either in preserving the presumption of his innocence or in obtaining a speedy determination of his guilt in order to repay a legal debt to society.

During this long period of delay and potential litigation, ugly passions would again be aroused. And our people would again be polarized in their opinions. And the credibility of our free institutions of government would again be challenged at home and abroad.

In the end, the courts might well hold that Richard Nixon had been denied due process, and the verdict of history would even more be inconclusive with respect to those charges arising out of the period of his Presidency, of which I am presently aware.

But it is not the ultimate fate of Richard Nixon that most concerns me, though surely it deeply troubles every decent and every compassionate person. My concern is the immediate future of this great country. . . .

My conscience tells me clearly and certainly that I cannot prolong the bad dreams that continue to reopen a chapter that is closed. My conscience tells me that only I, as President, have the constitutional power to firmly shut and seal this book. My conscience tells me it is my duty, not merely to proclaim domestic tranquility but to use every means that I have to insure it. . . .

Finally, I feel that Richard Nixon and his loved ones have suffered enough and will continue to suffer, no matter what I do, no matter what we, as a great and good Nation, can do together to make his goal of peace come true.

Pub. Papers: Gerald R. Ford, 101 (1974).

On the first day of his Administration, January 21, 1977, President Jimmy Carter granted "a full, complete and unconditional pardon" to all persons other than agents, officers, or employees of the Military Selective Service system (1) who may have committed any nonviolent offense between August 4, 1964 and March 28, 1973 in violation of the Military Selective Service Act or any rule or regulation promulgated thereunder; or (2) who were convicted, irrespective of the date of conviction, of any nonviolent offense committed between August 4, 1964 and March 28, 1973 in violation of the Military Selective Service Act, or any rule or regulation promulgated thereunder. Proclamation No. 4483, 3 C.F.R. 4 (1978). *See also* Executive Order No. 11967, 3 C.F.R. 91 (1978), implementing the pardon.

Four years later, Carter's successor, President Ronald Reagan, issued "full and unconditional pardons to W. Mark Felt and Edward S. Miller," two former FBI agents convicted for unlawful "black-bag jobs" or break-ins at the homes of people thought to be connected in the 1970s with the Weather Underground. On signing the pardon, Reagan stated:

[Felt's and Miller's] convictions . . . grew out of their good-faith belief that their actions were necessary to preserve the security interests of our country. The record demonstrates that they acted not with criminal intent, but in the belief that they had grants of authority reaching to the highest levels of government.

America was at war in 1972, and Messrs. Felt and Miller followed procedures they believed essential to keep the Director of the FBI, the Attorney General, and the President of the United States advised of the activities of hostile foreign powers and their collaborators in this country. They have never denied their actions, but, in fact, came forward to acknowledge them publicly in order to relieve their subordinate agents from criminal actions.

Four years ago, thousands of draft evaders and others who violated the Selective Service laws were unconditionally pardoned by my predecessor. America was generous to those who refused to serve their country in the Vietnam war. We can be no less generous to two men who acted on high principle to bring an end to the terrorism that was threatening our Nation.

Pub. Papers: Ronald Reagan 358 (1981).

What is your assessment of the appropriateness, as a matter of policy, of the Ford, Carter, and Reagan pardons?

President George H.W. Bush, rather than starting his term with a controversial pardon, saved his blockbusters for his final months in office. He effectively used the pardon power to terminate the efforts of independent counsel Lawrence Walsh to investigate further the so-called Iran-Contra affair, discussed in detail in Chapter Five. Defenders of the pardons characterized them as a laudable effort to terminate what they perceived as a dangerous subversion of executive authority by a rogue independent counsel. *See, e.g.,* Kmiec, *Pardoning Weinberger Was Right*, Nat'l L.J., Feb. 8, 1993. One of your authors took a decidedly different view:

> A "rule of law" assessment of the Iran-Contra affair must take account of the presumably near-final chapter: President Bush's pardon of Caspar Weinberger, Elliot Abrams, Duane Clarridge, Alan Fiers, Clair George, and Robert MacFarlane.[72] President Bush explained these pardons on five grounds. He asserted that (a) the named individuals were motivated by patriotism, not by hope of private gain, in any alleged malfeasance; (b) their prosecutions were tantamount to the "criminalization of policy differences";[73] (c) pardons are often used to put national political traumas to rest; (d) all those pardoned had been punished enough by the criminal process for any wrongdoing in which they might have been involved; and (e) Weinberger, at least, is so distinguished a public servant, that his prior record alone argues for leniency.

---

72. Presidential Proclamation 6518, 28 Weekly Comp. Pres. Doc. 2382 (Dec. 23, 1992).

73. *Id.* at 2383. It is more than a little revealing, I think, about the deliberative process that presumably animated these pardons that the President's proclamation embraced Oliver North's characterization of Congress's Iran-Contra investigation: "It is mind-boggling to me that . . . some here have attempted to criminalize policy differences. . . ." North Hearing, *supra* note 144, at 191.

Yet, each of these arguments is tainted by the very cast of mind that nurtured the Iran-Contra affair in the first place. Consider, first, the President's stress on the defendants' patriotism. The obligations of public office—the fiduciary role of office holders—fairly demand that public officials weigh the widest range of consequences in deciding the proper course of their own conduct. Their capacity to do harm compels it. To accept our officials' general character or overall intentions as the full measure of their moral responsibility in the discharge of their functions, however, would excuse them of any obligation to anticipate reasonably or assess plausibly the consequences of their acts.[74] Especially because people in power rarely distrust their own motives, licensing our officials to treat their own sincerity as exculpatory without attention to consequences could operationally all but extinguish the possibility of rigorous administrative ethical standards in the executive bureaucracy.

As for the alleged "criminalization of political differences," no one—certainly not President Bush—has offered a serious argument that lying to Congress for the specific purposes of avoiding executive political accountability and, later, impeding the investigation of executive wrongdoing is anything other than a serious and morally culpable act.[75] Bush's treatment of obviously plausible allegations of corrupt deception as acts of mere political vindictiveness by the prosecutor implicitly accepts the strategy of lying as itself a mere act of politics, and a justifiable act at that.[76] It comes close to claiming that the President can do no wrong[77] because what he does is political, and can be objected to only on political grounds.

---

74. Dennis F. Thompson, *The Possibility of Administrative Ethics*, Pub. Administration Rev., Sept.–Oct. 1985, at 555, 560; D.F. THOMPSON, POLITICAL ETHICS AND PUBLIC OFFICE 5–6 (1987).

75. Dennis Thompson argues that official deception in a democracy may well be morally acceptable if necessary to accomplish an objective that the people, if informed, would approve, and (a) if steps are taken to permit citizens the promptest possible review of the decisions being concealed, (b) if the deception is of a kind that the public has generally endorsed as morally justifiable, without reference to the facts of the specific deception (such as the use of undercover narcotics investigators), or (c) the true circumstances hidden by the deception are shared in advance with a smaller group that effectively replicates the public debate that would likely occur if the deception were not necessary. D.F. THOMPSON, POLITICAL ETHICS AND PUBLIC OFFICE 22–31 (1987). With respect to the instances of concealment or deception at issue in Iran-Contra, none of these conditions pertains.

76. Bush might have adopted a rationale for the pardons that would have been far less morally objectionable. At least for those officials charged with making unsworn false statements to Congress, he might have asserted that—in light of a lengthy history of widely acknowledged, but never prosecuted executive deceptions of Congress—the false statement statute did not fairly put the relevant officials on notice that their deceptive unsworn statements were, in fact, felonious. *See generally* Peter W. Morgan, *The Undefined Crime of Lying to Congress: Ethics Reform and the Rule of Law*, 86 Nw. L. REV. 177 (1992). This rationale might logically sustain a legal pardon, although it would not have amounted to the statement of moral and political approval for the deception of Congress that Bush apparently also wanted to provide.

77. *Cf.* Richard Nixon's famous statement: "If the President does it, it's legal." Facts on File World Dig., May 28, 1977, at 405 B3 (reporting on Nixon interview with David Frost).

Pardons can put national traumas to rest. The technique is especially effective when victors pardon the vanquished, or when those with standing to take offense offer forgiveness instead.[78] The Lincoln/Johnson pardons of confederate soldiers[79] and the Truman/Carter pardons of those who violated selective service laws[80] illustrate the point. Here, however, the President did not have identical standing to judge the defendants. His act was more akin to President Ford's pardon of Richard Nixon or President Reagan's pardon of rogue FBI agents, pardons with an unfortunately partisan cast. Worse yet, the Bush pardons violated the fundamental due process precept that no one should judge their own cause. Presidents Ford and Reagan at least were not suspected of being unindicted coconspirators in the acts being pardoned.

As for the defendants' distinguished pasts or the calculation that they suffered enough, we may ask what high-level wrongdoer would not say this of his or her equally lofty colleagues? It is never surprising to find that powerful officials regard themselves as self-sacrificing, are tempted to treat inconveniences imposed on them as punishment, and view themselves in comparison to perhaps wealthier friends as deserving of extra consideration in light of their preference for power over salary.[81] Should these be factors relevant to a pardon at all, they should at least be weighed only once a record has been established that permits the public to make an assessment of the moral culpability of the defendants' acts. Waiting for a trial would serve the public interest in fact-finding. There is no evidence in President Bush's proclamation, however, that he reached his judgments based on a serious weighing of the moral culpability of the individuals involved.

Peter M. Shane, *Presidents, Pardons, and Prosecutors: Legal Accountability and the Separation of Powers*, 11 YALE L. & POL'Y REV. 361, 401–04 (1993).

President Clinton, one of the stingiest Presidents in history in terms of exercising the pardon power, stirred controversy on a variety of grounds through several uses of his pardon. For example, in 1999, he granted pardons to 16 Puerto Rican nationalists, 11 of whom had been convicted for their involvement in crimes related to a campaign of terrorist bombings; the latter pardons were conditioned upon the offenders' renunciation of the use of violence. Critics charged that the pardons had been opposed by law enforcement, and were timed to help first lady Hillary Rodham Clinton in what proved to be a successful campaign to become a U.S. Senator from New York. In 2001, Clinton's final round of presidential pardons included one to Marc

---

78. Garry Wills, *Why Bush's Pardons are Unpardonable*, Wash. Post Nat'l Weekly Edition, Jan. 4–10, 1993, at 24.

79. J. T. DORRIS, PARDON AND AMNESTY UNDER LINCOLN AND JOHNSON 34–38, 108–115 (1953).

80. Pres. Proc. No. 2676, 10 Fed. Reg. 15,409 (1945); Pres. Proc. No. 4483, 42 Fed. Reg. 4391 (1977).

81. *Cf.* "I have never profited from public service. . . . I am not a crook," Richard Nixon, quoted in Carl Bernstein, *Conspiracy Without End: The Legacy of Watergate*, L.A. Times, Jan. 10, 1993, at 1, *available in* LEXIS, Nexis Library, Majpaps File.

Rich, a financier and fugitive from prosecution, who faced more than 300 years in prison for alleged crimes related to an oil-pricing scheme during the 1973 oil crisis. Critics noted that Rich's former wife was a major Democratic Party fund-raiser, his file had not received the full review ordinarily conducted by the Justice Department, and he was represented in his pursuit of the pardon by an attorney who formerly served as chief of staff to then-Vice President Al Gore. For his part, President Clinton vigorously denied that there was any irregularity in the granting of the Rich pardon or that he based his decision on anything other than his best judgment as to the merits. William Jefferson Clinton, *My Reasons for the Pardons*, N.Y. Times, Sec. 4, at 13 (Feb. 18, 2001). For a scathing analysis of the Clinton record by the lawyer who served as Pardon Attorney in the Justice Department from 1990 to 1997, see Margaret Colgate Love, *The Pardon Paradox: Lessons of Clinton's Last Pardons,* 31 Cap. U. L. Rev. 185 (2003).

What is your view? Do you think any of the pardons discussed in this section were wrongly conferred? If the President abuses his discretion in granting pardons, is there any legal recourse available to undo them? Perhaps the most obvious candidate for a constitutional limitation on the pardon power would be a rule precluding Presidents from pardoning themselves. As Professor Shane noted in the above-cited article:

> [C]ourts could conceivably determine . . . that Presidents are without power to pardon themselves. General Haig reportedly presented this option to Richard Nixon, who rejected it. *Pardon of Richard M. Nixon, and Related Matters: Hearings Before the Subcomm. on Criminal Justice of the House Judiciary Comm.*, 93d Cong., 2d Sess. 94 (1974) (testimony of Pres. Ford), *discussed in* Daniel Schorr, *Will Bush Pardon Himself?*, N.Y. Times, Dec. 29, 1992, at A15. The "rule of law" arguments in favor of the President's amenability to criminal prosecution prior to impeachment, *see* Eric M. Freedman, *The Law as King and the King as Law: Is a President Immune from Criminal Prosecution Before Impeachment?*, 20 Hastings Const. L.Q. 7 (1992), obviously counsel against any power of self-pardon. Indeed, a President's capacity to pardon himself would seem to violate flagrantly the cornerstone premise of due process and the separation of powers that no person should be judge in his or her own cause.

> Interestingly, the chief objection to conferring the pardon power on the President was the fear of some critics that the President might use his authority to shield his confederates in treason. W. H. Humbert, The Pardoning Power of the President 18 (1941); The Federalist, No. 74, at 448–49 (C. Rossiter ed., 1961) (A. Hamilton). Although reasoning from snippets is problematic, it is worth noting the response of James Wilson to Edmund Randolph's unsuccessful proposal during the Philadelphia Convention to bar presidential pardons in treason cases. Wilson contended that a pardon power was needed even as to the crime of treason, and if the President "himself be a party to the guilt he can be impeached and prosecuted." 2 Records of the Federal Convention of 1787 (M. Farrand ed.) 626 (1937).

11 YALE L. & POL'Y REV. at 404 n.196. *Accord*, Note, *Pardon Me?: The Constitutional Case Against President Self-Pardons*, 106 YALE L. J. 779 (1996) (Brian Kalt).

More controversially, Professor Harold J. Krent has argued that courts may review extreme cases of abuse in the exercise of conditional pardons. He argues that "presidents lack power under the Constitution to impose conditions that shock the conscience, such as requiring an organ donation." Harold J. Krent, *Conditioning the President's Conditional Pardon Power*, 89 CALIF. L. REV. 1665, 1717 (2001). Similarly, "review is warranted to ensure that the president through pardons has not violated any . . . structural restraint in the Constitution on his power. A court should invalidate a condition that the offender attend Presbyterian services or make payment to the president's Reelection Committee." Do you agree? Who, exactly, would have standing to bring such a suit? What would be the appropriate remedy? In demanding that the FALN members seeking pardons "renounce violence," would President Clinton have overstepped the bounds of his power, in Professor Krent's view, had he demanded that they issue a statement encouraging other supporters of Puerto Rican independence to rely solely on lawful, nonviolent means of pursuing that objective?

Is it possible to read into the Pardon Clause any other limitations on the President's power that would constrain his ability to forgive executive corruption? Should the Constitution be amended in this respect? *See* Christopher E. Smith & Scott P. Johnson, *Presidential Pardons and Accountability in the Executive Branch*, 35 WAYNE L. REV. 1113 (1989); Note, *Federal Executive Clemency Power: The President's Prerogative to Escape Accountability*, 27 U. RICH. L. REV. 345 (1993) (by James N. Jorgenson).

Attorney Margaret C. Love has argued that the most serious problem with the pardon power is not its abusive over-deployment, but its under-use. She recounts the declining number of pardons in the late 20th Century:

> Between 1932 and 1980, there were well over a hundred post-sentence pardons granted almost every year; in some years, the President signed more than 300 separate pardon warrants. These grants were generally made on a regular basis through the year, evidence that the business of pardoning was regarded as part of the ordinary housekeeping work of the Presidency. More significantly, the percentage of pardon petitions acted on favorably remained high, approaching or exceeding thirty percent in every administration from Franklin Roosevelt's to Jimmy Carter's. Even the number of commutations remained surprisingly high throughout this period, given the availability of alternative early release mechanisms like parole.
>
> During the Reagan Administration the number of clemency grants each year began to dwindle, both in absolute terms and relative to the total number of applications acted on. President Reagan pardoned a total of 393 individuals in eight years, compared to the 534 pardoned by his predecessor in four, and commuted only thirteen sentences. The percentage of Reagan's favorable actions in pardon cases dipped to a low point for the century of twenty percent, and his overall grant rate to thirteen percent. President Bush granted

even fewer pardons: his sixty-eight grants represented only seven percent of the pardon petitions acted on during his four years in office. Factoring in his three commutations, his overall grant rate is four percent. President Clinton's record at this point in his presidency [that is, through the end of 1999] is about the same as that of President Bush.

Margaret Colgate Love, *Of Pardons, Politics and Collar Buttons: Reflections on the President's Duty to Be Merciful*, 27 Fordham Urb. L.J. 1483, 1492–93 (2000). In her judgment, this decline is regrettable because of the important public welfare goals she identifies with the pardon power:

> The political duty to be merciful "if the good of the community require[s] it" may be inferred from the several ways in which pardon helps the President carry out his other constitutional duties. First, pardon serves the purpose of checking the legislature when the criminal law is static and inflexible, by signaling the need for changes in the law itself. Thus, for example, the President's decision to commute a sentence mandated by the terms of a statute, based on his conclusion that the punishment was disproportionately harsh in light of all the circumstances (including some that the law could not take into account), might encourage legislative inquiry into the possible need for changes in the law to allow individual circumstance to be considered. A grant of clemency might also reveal shortcomings in the appeals process that limit a court's ability to consider new evidence or changed circumstance. But, because pardon is a political duty and not a duty of justice, the President would be under no obligation to grant clemency to all offenders with arguably similar equitable claims.

> Pardon also serves as an executive check on courts' discretionary decisions. While much of the current interest in federal clemency arises precisely from the limits on judicial discretion imposed by the federal sentencing guidelines and statutory mandatory minimum sentences, it is possible that an act of executive mercy might lead a court to rethink its own discretionary powers and interpret them more broadly.

> Within the executive branch, pardon can play an important role in carrying out the President's obligation to take care that the laws are faithfully executed in two ways. First, it enables the President to intercede directly to change the outcome of a case that he believes was wrongly handled by his subordinates, where no judicial remedy is available. Second, it permits him to send a very direct and powerful message to his subordinates about how he wishes the law to be enforced in the future, including in particular the manner in which they should exercise their discretion.

> Finally, the President's personal intervention in a case through the pardon power reassures the public that the legal system is capable of just and moral application. It enables him to correct legal errors that for one reason or another could not be corrected by the courts, and to make equitable accommodation

where a sentence has been imposed according to the strict requirements of the law but nonetheless seems unfair. It is especially important that the public be confident in clemency as the "fail safe" of the justice system in capital cases, which are now moving forward through the federal system for the first time in many years. At the other end of the clemency spectrum, the President can use the opportunity provided by post-sentence pardons to emphasize the rehabilitative goals of the justice system by recognizing criminal justice success stories.

Id. at 1506–08. Do you agree with this assessment?

The record of President George W. Bush continued the pattern of pardon decline that Attorney Love bemoans. In eight years, he granted a total of 189 pardons (and 11 commutations), roughly half the rate of either Presidents Reagan or Clinton. Only one case—that of former vice presidential chief of staff I. Lewis ("Scooter") Libby—stirred much controversy. Libby was sentenced in 2007 to 30 months in prison and a $ 250,000 fine after his conviction in federal court of perjury, obstruction of justice and lying to investigators in the probe of the leak of Valerie Plame's identity as a CIA operative. Bush commuted Libby's prison sentence, but left the conviction and fine intact; Libby also had to serve two years' probation. Critics on the left and right (most prominently among the latter, former Vice President Cheney) challenged, respectively, the commutation as alleged political favoritism and the failure to pardon as alleged political betrayal.

Towards the end of his time in office, however, President Barack Obama sharply broke from his recent predecessors' practice. In 2014, the Justice Department announced a Clemency Initiative to prioritize applications from federal inmates incarcerated for at least a decade who would likely have received a substantially lower sentence if convicted of the same offense(s) today. The inmates would have to be "non-violent, low-level offenders without significant ties to large scale criminal organizations, gangs or cartels" and "without a significant criminal history" or "history of violence." Most of its intended beneficiaries were non-violent drug offenders. In identifying candidates for clemency, the Justice Department and Federal Bureau of Prisons partnered with a coalition called Clemency Project 2014, comprising the American Bar Association, the National Association of Criminal Defense Lawyers, the Federal Defenders, the American Civil Liberties Union, and Families Against Mandatory Minimums, as well as individual volunteers. By the end of his presidency, Barack Obama had issued some form of executive clemency to 1,927 individuals. Obama commuted the sentences of 1,715 individuals, including 504 serving life sentences, and granted 212 full pardons. His record on commutations exceeds that of every President from Truman through George W. Bush—combined.

For a comprehensive review of presidential clemency authorities, *see* Jeffrey P. Crouch, The Presidential Pardon Power (2009).

Chapter 5

Foreign Policy and National Security

After an initial broad look at the theory of separation of powers, we have now considered a variety of contests over authority between the elected branches in the domestic context. It remains to be considered whether the insights we have thus far developed apply to policymaking relevant to our dealings with other nations.

Of course, the phrases "foreign affairs" and "national security" do not appear in the constitutional text. Instead, each of the two elected branches has specific powers with obvious foreign policy relevance. For example, Article I, Section 8 of the Constitution empowers Congress to provide "for the common defense," "to regulate commerce with foreign nations," "to establish a uniform rule of naturalization," "to define and punish piracies and felonies committed on the high seas, and offenses against the Law of Nations," "to declare war, grant letters of marque and reprisal, and make rules concerning captures on land and water," "to raise and support armies," "to provide and maintain a Navy," and "to make rules for the government and regulation of the land and naval forces." The potential relevance of each of these powers to foreign affairs is transparent.

The President enjoys, under Article II, the power of Commander in Chief, the authority to appoint ambassadors, other public ministers, and consuls, and the power, "by and with the advice and consent of the Senate," to make treaties, provided two-thirds of the Senators present concur." As with the President's domestic powers, however, the import and scope of foreign affairs functions are not delimited by the constitutional text alone. For example, the unadorned constitutional text does not clearly signal whether the President alone may recognize the government of another nation; yet early precedent and subsequent history ratified this interpretation of Article II.*

---

* The Supreme Court has recently added its concurrence to this understanding. See *Zivotofsky v. Kerry*, 576 U.S. ___, 135 S. Ct. 2076 (2015). A 1988 Office of Legal Counsel opinion purported to identify another foreign affairs power that is exclusively presidential, namely, the power to extend for international purposes U.S. jurisdiction and, indeed, sovereignty over the territorial sea. Douglas Kmiec, *Legal Issues Raised By the Proposed Presidential Proclamation to Extend the Territorial Sea*, 1 TERRITORIAL SEA J. 1 (1990). The opinion relied significantly upon historical precedent in asserting both that the President possesses such powers, and that serious doubts exist whether Congress may regulate in this area. Acting in reliance on OLC's advice, President Reagan extended the U.S. territorial sea by Proclamation No. 5928, 54 Fed. Reg. 777 (1989).

The judiciary does not have any explicit power to make foreign policy. The text of Article III, however, makes clear that the framers had foreign affairs in mind even in delimiting federal jurisdiction. Recall that the Supreme Court is given original jurisdiction in "all cases affecting ambassadors, other public ministers, and consuls." Presumably, the framers were contemplating the risk to our foreign relations if ambassadors and public ministers were relegated to state courts to litigate matters that might well involve sensitive issues of state.

This chapter examines the way in which law has affected the distribution of foreign policy and national security authority against the backdrop of this constitutional framework. Part A reviews the general groping for principles we can discern as far back as the struggle over President Washington's proclamation of neutrality. Part B reviews a number of areas in which presidential claims to inherent and exclusive foreign policy power have been most prominent. Part C considers a number of areas in which Congress has explicitly taken the initiative to legislate concerning foreign policy. Parts B and C thus reveal how the discretion of each elected branch turns out to be a guide for interpreting the powers of the other. Finally, Section D briefly discusses the indirect potential impacts of the judiciary on foreign policy—with special reference to cases in which the foreign policy powers of the government exist in tension with individual rights concerns.

A. Analytic Framework: Sorting the Elected Branches' Claims to Power

Citizens of the new United States of America did not have to wait long before events were to precipitate a major debate concerning the respective powers of President and Congress regarding foreign affairs. On April 22, 1793, President Washington proclaimed that "the duty and interests of the United States require that they should with sincerity and good faith adopt and pursue a conduct friendly and impartial towards" France, on one hand, and Great Britain and its allies, on the other, who were in a state of war. The proclamation further declared that citizens of the United States would render themselves liable to punishment or forfeiture under the Law of Nations, and would forfeit the protection of the United States against such punishment or forfeiture, should they commit, aid, or abet hostilities against any of the warring powers.

In defense of the President, Alexander Hamilton—under the pen name Pacificus—published a series of seven letters. The first, excerpted below, argues for the constitutionality of the President's initiative. In response, James Madison, using the pen name Helvidius, published five responsive letters vigorously challenging Hamilton's every point. They evidence not only a long-standing tradition of debate on these subjects, but an equally venerable tradition of political invective. Madison/Helvidius says: "Several pieces with a signature of Pacificus were lately published, which had been read with singular pleasure and applause, by the foreigners and degenerate citizens among us, who hate our republican government and the French revolution." Vitriol notwithstanding, it is worth considering whose views have chiefly prevailed.

Letters of Pacificus, No. I (A. Hamilton)

The objections which have been raised against the proclamation of neutrality, lately issued by the president, have been urged in a spirit of acrimony and invective, which demonstrates that more was in view than merely a free discussion of an important public measure. They exhibit evident indications of a design to weaken the confidence of the people in the author of the measure, in order to remove or lessen a powerful obstacle to the success of an opposition to the government, which, however it may change its form according to circumstances, seems still to be persisted in with unremitting industry. . . .

The objections in question fall under four heads:

1. That the proclamation was without authority.

2. That it was contrary to our treaties with France.

3. That it was contrary to the gratitude which is due from this to that country, for the succours afforded to us in our own revolution.

4. That it was out of time and unnecessary.

In order to judge of the solidity of the first of these objections, it is necessary to examine what is the nature and design of a proclamation of neutrality.

It is to *make known* to the powers at war, and to the citizens of the country whose government does the act, that such country is in the condition of a nation at peace with the belligerent parties, and under no obligations of treaty to become an *associate in the war* with either, and that this being its situation, its intention is to observe a correspondent conduct, by performing towards each the duties of neutrality; to warn all persons within the jurisdiction of that country, to abstain from acts that shall contravene those duties, under the penalties which the laws of the land, of which the *jus gentium* [law of nations] is part, will inflict. . . .

It does not imply, that the nation which makes the declaration, will forbear to perform to either of the warring powers any stipulations in treaties which can be executed, without becoming a *party* in the war. . . .

In stating that the proclamation of neutrality does not imply the non-performance of any stipulations of treaties, which are not of a nature to make the nation an associate in the war, it is conceded that an execution of the clause of guaranty, contained in the eleventh article of our treaty of alliance with France, would be contrary to the sense and spirit of the proclamation; because it would engage us with our whole force, as an *auxiliary* in the war; it would be much more than the case of a definite succour, previously ascertained.

It follows, that the proclamation is virtually a manifestation of the sense of the government, that the United States are, *under the circumstances of the case, not bound* to execute the clause of guaranty.

If this be a just view of the force and import of the proclamation, it will remain to see, whether the president, in issuing it, acted within his proper sphere, or stepped beyond the bounds of his constitutional authority and duty.

It will not be disputed, that the management of the affairs of this country with foreign nations, is confided to the government of the United States.

It can as little be disputed, that a proclamation of neutrality, when a nation is at liberty to decline or avoid a war in which other nations are engaged, and means to do so, is a *usual* and a *proper* measure. *Its main object is to prevent the nation's being responsible for acts done by its citizens, without the privity or connivance of the government, in contravention of the principles of neutrality;* an object of the greatest moment to a country, whose true interest lies in the preservation of peace.

The inquiry then is, what department of our government is the proper one to make a declaration of neutrality, when the engagements of the nation permit, and its interests require that it should be done? . . .

The legislative department is not the *organ* of intercourse between the United States and foreign nations. It is charged neither with *making* nor *interpreting* treaties. It is therefore not naturally that member of the government, which is to pronounce the existing condition of the nation, with regard to foreign powers, or to admonish the citizens of their obligations and duties in consequence; still less is it charged with enforcing the observance of those obligations and duties.

It is equally obvious, that the act in question is foreign to the judiciary department. . . . It must then of necessity belong to the executive department to exercise the function in question, when a proper case for it occurs.

It appears to be connected with that department in various capacities: As the *organ* of intercourse between the nation and foreign nations; as the *interpreter* of the national treaties, in those cases in which the judiciary is not competent, that is, between government and government; as the *power*, which is charged with the execution of the laws, of which treaties form a part; as that which is charged with the command and disposition of the public force.

This view of the subject is so natural and obvious, so analogous to general theory and practice, that no doubt can be entertained of its justness, unless to be deduced from particular provisions of the constitution of the United States.

Let us see, then, if cause for such doubt is to be found there.

The second article of the constitution of the United States, section first, establishes this general proposition, that "the Executive Power shall be vested in a president "of the United States of America."

The same article, in a succeeding section, proceeds to delineate particular cases of executive power. It declares, among other things that the president shall be commander in chief of the army and navy of the United States, and of the militia of the several States, when called into the actual service of the United States; that he shall have power, by and with the advice and consent of the senate, to make treaties; that it shall be his duty to receive ambassadors and other public ministers, *and to take care that the laws be faithfully executed.*

It would not consist with the rules of sound construction, to consider this enumeration of particular authorities as derogating from the more comprehensive grant in the general clause, further than as it may be coupled with express restrictions or limitations; as in regard to the cooperation of the senate in the appointment of officers, and the making of treaties; which are plainly qualifications of the general executive powers of appointing officers and making treaties. The difficulty of a complete enumeration of all the cases of executive authority, would naturally dictate the use of general terms, and would render it improbable, that a specification of certain particulars was designed as a substitute for those terms, when antecedently used. The different mode of expression employed in the constitution, in regard to the two powers, the legislative and the executive, serves to confirm this inference. In the article which gives the legislative powers of the government, the expressions are, "All legislative powers herein granted 'shall be vested in' a congress of the United States." In that which grants the executive power, the expressions are, "*The executive power* shall be vested in a president of the United States."

The enumeration ought therefore to be considered, as intended merely to specify the principal articles implied in the definition of executive power; leaving the rest to flow from the general grant of that power, interpreted in conformity with other parts of the constitution, and with the principles of the free government.

The general doctrine of our constitution then is, that the *executive power* of the nation is vested in the president; subject only to the *exceptions* and *qualifications*, which are expressed in the instrument.

Two of these have been already noticed; the participation of the senate in the appointment of officers, and in the making of treaties. A third remains to be mentioned; the right of the legislature "to declare war," and grant letters "of marque and reprisal."

With these exceptions, the *executive power* of the United States is completely lodged in the president. This mode of construing the constitution has indeed been recognised by congress in formal acts, upon full consideration and debate; of which the power of removal from office is an important instance. It will follow, that if a proclamation of neutrality is merely an executive act, as, it is believed, has been shown, the step which has been taken by the president is liable to no just exception on the score of the authority.

It may be said, that this inference would be just, if the power of declaring war had not been vested in the legislature; but that this power naturally includes the right of judging, whether the nation is or is not under obligations to make war.

The answer is, that however true this position may be, it will not follow, that the executive is in any case excluded from a similar right of judgment, in the execution of its own functions.

If on the one hand, the legislature have a right to declare war, it is, on the other, the duty of the executive to preserve peace, till the declaration is made; and in fulfilling this duty, it must necessarily possess a right of judging what is the nature of the obligations which the treaties of the country impose on the government: and when it has concluded that there is nothing in them inconsistent with neutrality, it becomes both its province and its duty to enforce the laws incident to that state of the nation. The executive is charged with the execution of all laws, the law of nations, as well as the municipal law, by which the former are recognised and adopted. It is consequently bound, by executing faithfully the laws of neutrality, when the country is in a neutral position, to avoid giving cause of war to foreign powers.

This is the direct end of the proclamation of neutrality. It declares to the United States their situation with regard to the contending parties, and makes known to the community, that the laws incident to that state will be enforced. In doing this, it conforms to an established usage of nations, the operation of which, as before remarked, is to obviate a responsibility on the part of the whole society, for secret and unknown violations of the rights of any of the warring powers by its citizens.

Those who object to the proclamation will readily admit, that it is the right and duty of the executive to interpret those articles of our treaties which give to France particular privileges, in order to permit the enforcement of them: but the necessary consequence of this is, that the executive must judge what are their proper limits; what rights are given to other nations, by our contracts with them; what rights the law of nature and nations gives, and our treaties permit, in respect to those countries with which we have none; in fine, what are the reciprocal rights and obligations of the United States, and of all and each of the powers at war.

The right of the executive to receive ambassadors and other public ministers, may serve to illustrate the relative duties of the executive and legislative departments. This right includes that of judging, in the case of a revolution of government in a foreign country, whether the new rulers are competent organs of the national will, and ought to be recognised, or not; which, where a treaty antecedently exists between the United States and such nation, involves the power of continuing or suspending its operation. For until the new government is *acknowledged*, the treaties between the nations, so far at least as regards *public* rights, are of course suspended.

This power of determining virtually upon the operation of national treaties, as a consequence of the power to receive public ministers, is an important instance of the right of the executive, to decide upon the obligations of the country with regard to foreign nations. To apply it to the case of France, if there had been a treaty of alliance, *offensive* and defensive, between the United States and that country, the unqualified acknowledgment of the new government would have put the United States in a condition to become an associate in the war with France, and would have laid the legislature under an obligation, if required, and there was otherwise no valid excuse, of exercising its power of declaring war.

This serves as an example of the right of the executive, in certain cases, to determine the condition of the nation, though it may, in its consequences, affect the exercise of the power of the legislature to declare war. Nevertheless, the executive cannot thereby control the exercise of that power. The legislature is still free to perform its duties, according to its own sense of them; though the executive, in the exercise of its constitutional powers, may establish an antecedent state of things, which ought to weigh in the legislative decisions.

The division of the executive power in the constitution, creates a *concurrent* authority in the cases to which it relates.

Hence, in the instance stated, treaties can only be made by the president and senate jointly; but their activity may be continued or suspended by the president alone. . . .

While, therefore, the legislature can alone declare war, can alone actually transfer the nation from a state of peace to a state of hostility, it belongs to the "executive power" to do whatever else the law of nations, cooperating with the treaties of the country, enjoin in the intercourse of the United States with foreign powers.

In this distribution of authority, the wisdom of our constitution is manifested. It is the province and duty of the executive to preserve to the nation the blessings of peace. The legislature alone can interrupt them by placing the nation in a state of war.

But though it has been thought advisable to vindicate the authority of the executive on this broad and comprehensive ground, it was not absolutely necessary to do so. That clause of the constitution which makes it his duty to "take care that the laws be faithfully executed," might alone have been relied upon, and this simple process of argument pursued.

The president is the constitutional EXECUTOR of the laws. Our treaties, and the laws of nations, form a part of the law of the land. He, who is to execute the laws, must first judge for himself of their meaning. In order to the observance of that conduct which the laws of nations, combined with our treaties, prescribed to this country, in reference to the present war in Europe, it was necessary for the president to judge for himself, whether there was any thing in our treaties, incompatible with an adherence to neutrality. Having decided that there was not, he had a right, and if in his opinion the interest of the nation required it, it was his duty as executor of the laws, to proclaim the neutrality of the nation, to exhort all persons to observe it, and to warn them of the penalties which would attend its non-observance.

The proclamation has been represented as enacting some new law. This is a view of it entirely erroneous. It only proclaims a *fact*, with regard to the *existing state* of the nation; informs the citizens of what the laws previously established require of them in that state, and notifies them that these laws will be put in execution against the infractors of them.

Responses of Helvidius. Because Madison was less succinct in his replies than Hamilton was in his defense of President Washington, his arguments are more easily paraphrased than excerpted.

In his first letter, Madison strongly attacks Hamilton's position that sovereign powers of war and peace are presumptively lodged in the executive. He cites a variety of then-contemporary writers on international law and political theory to the effect that "the powers to declare war, to conclude peace, and to form alliances, [are] among the highest acts of the sovereignty; of which the legislative power must at least be an integral and preeminent part." In Madison's view, it is therefore absurd to regard a mechanism such as the requirement of Senate concurrence in treaties as an exception to a general rule that foreign affairs are to be handled by the executive. Instead, treaty making should be viewed as lawmaking and, according to Madison, the President's involvement in treaties should be regarded as an exception to the predominance of legislative power over the same subject.

As for the specific powers granted to the President concerning foreign affairs, Madison finds none of them relevant. The fact that the President is limited to serving as Commander in Chief demonstrates, to Madison, that policymaking with respect to war was regarded as predominantly legislative. Likewise, the charge to take care that the laws faithfully be executed does not, in Madison's view, empower the President to make laws that shall be executed. It is Madison's conclusion that Hamilton can rest an argument for executive determinations regarding neutrality only by confusing the royal prerogatives of the British monarch with the intended grant of executive power to a republican President.

In his second letter, Madison argues that the express vesting in Congress of the power to determine when conditions warrant the declaration of war necessarily implies that Congress is empowered to judge when circumstances demand the observation of neutrality. He likewise rejects Hamilton's arguments to the effect that there can be concurrent authority on particular subjects that is shared by both Congress and President. Such a distribution of powers, according to Madison, "would be as awkward in practice, as it is unnatural in theory." He observes: "If the legislature and executive have both a right to judge of the obligations to make war or not, it must sometimes happen, through not at present, that they will judge differently." He then asks: "In what light would it present to the world a nation thus speaking through two different organs, equally constitutional and authentic, two opposite languages, on the same subject, and under the same existing circumstances?"

In his third letter, Madison disputes the scope given by Hamilton to the President's power to receive ambassadors. He argues: "[L]ittle, if anything, more was intended by the clause, than to provide for a particular mode of communication almost grown into a right among modern nations; by pointing out the department of the government, most proper for the ceremony of admitting public ministers, of examining their credentials, and of authenticating their title to the privileges annexed to their character by the law of nations." Madison concedes that the executive, in fulfilling its duties, must determine whether a foreign minister possesses credentials from an existing and acting government of a country, and if they are authentic. He counters, however, that these inquiries do not permit the President to consider whether "those exercising the government (of the foreign nation) have the right along with the possession. This belongs to the nation, and to the nation alone, on whom the government operates." In other words, he would deny to the President the power—successfully claimed since Jefferson's time—to recognize who is in fact the lawful government of a foreign nation.

The fourth letter of Helvidius insists that Hamilton's arguments in favor of the President's power to determine a condition of peace or neutrality would likewise imply an executive authority to determine that existing conditions between the United States and another nation would also warrant the use of military force. He proceeds to dismiss any such argument, discussing at some length a variety of reasons why military authority of such scope would be too much power to entrust to any single individual.

> War is in fact the true nurse of executive aggrandizement. In war, a physical force is to be created; and it is the executive will, which is to direct it. In war, the public treasuries are to be unlocked; and it is the executive hand which is to dispense them. . . . The strongest passions and most dangerous weaknesses of a human beast; ambition, avarice, vanity, the honorable or venerable love of fame, are all in conspiracy against the desire and duty of peace. Hence it has grown into an axiom that the executive is the department of power most distinguished by its propensity to war: Hence it is the practice of all states, in proportion as they are free, to disarm this propensity of its influence.

Madison's fifth letter is devoted to demonstrating that the proclamation of neutrality is inconsistent with the treaty obligations owed by the United States to France. How do you assess the competing constitutional positions of these two pivotal figures in the framing of the Constitution? Whose views do you discern have prevailed historically?

Note: The History of Foreign Affairs and National Security Powers

In a recent book, Professor Saikrishna Prakash presents a strongly pro-executive view of the original understanding of the foreign affairs power and, in particular, how the Constitution allocates that power as between the President and Congress:

> In the eighteenth century, executive power was often thought to have an internal component—law execution—and an external component—foreign relations. From this usage, two insights emerge. First, the Constitution is not incomplete or full of gaps on the subject of foreign affairs, as some imagine. Rather, the Constitution explicitly grants the federal government the full spectrum of foreign-relations authorities. Congress has specific foreign affairs powers related to war, foreign commerce, and the

law of nations; the president must act with the Senate's consent in two areas, treaties and appointments; and the president enjoys all other foreign-relations powers by virtue of his executive power. Second and relatedly, the grant of executive power justifies the broad foreign affairs authority that early presidents routinely exercised. Though Article II contains but three specific foreign-relations clauses—concerning appointing and receiving ambassadors and making treaties—the first president exercised a far broader foreign affairs jurisdiction. Among other things, he formulated foreign policy, essentially monopolized diplomatic communications, and controlled America's diplomats. Washington exercised these powers (and others) because they were uncontroversial elements of his generic grant of executive power.

We can better grasp how the Constitution's text completely vests foreign affairs powers with the federal government if we keep in mind four principles. First, the president's grant of "executive Power" included a general foreign affairs power. . . . Locke, Montesquieu, Blackstone, and others noted that foreign affairs powers were components of the "executive power." Americans likewise voiced this understanding before, during, and after the Constitution's ratification. When the Constitution conferred the "executive Power," that grant meant that the president not only could execute the laws, but also had power over international relations.

Second, the Constitution incorporates broad exceptions to its grant of executive power. Many at the founding believed that the English Constitution ceded too much foreign affairs power to the Crown and that some aspects of foreign affairs had legislative overtones (such as the war power). Acting on this belief, the delegates to the Philadelphia Convention created exceptions to the executive power. Sometimes the president would have but a veto over foreign affairs, and Congress would have the primary role (for example, in matters of war, foreign commerce, and the law of nations). At other times, the president might have the initiative, with final action requiring Senate consent (Treaty making and diplomatic appointments). These exceptions to the grant of executive power ensured that the president would have fewer foreign affairs powers than the English monarch.

Third, the president cannot make foreign-relations law, that is, law that regulates individuals. With limited exceptions, the Crown relied on Parliament for funds and legislation to implement its foreign policy, including treaties. Because the Constitution evinces a more thoroughgoing distrust of executive lawmaking, the president generally lacks authority to make foreign-relations law. The one exception—treaty making—is express and requires the Senate's supermajority consent.

Fourth, Congress lacks a generic foreign affairs authority. To be sure, it enjoys significant foreign affairs powers, most prominently the powers to regulate foreign commerce and declare war. These powers can be exercised even in the face of fierce executive opposition by overriding a presidential veto. Yet even when considered in the aggregate, the powers to declare was, regulate commerce, and define and punish violations of international law, along with the authority to enact laws necessary and proper for the implementation of federal powers, do not convey a generic foreign affairs power. Hence, Congress has no claim on the foreign affairs powers not specifically mentioned in the Constitution.

Saikrishna Bangalore Prakash, Imperial from the Beginning: The Constitution of the Original Executive 110–112 (2015).

The claim, however, that the Constitution, by vesting the President with the executive power, was originally understood broadly to grant the President all foreign affairs powers unless there is an express exception is contestable. As we will see below, Justice Scalia asserts:

> Before this country declared independence, the law of England entrusted the King with the exclusive care of his kingdom's foreign affairs. The royal prerogative included the "sole power of sending ambassadors to foreign states, and receiving them at home," the sole authority to "make treaties, leagues, and alliances with foreign states and princes," "the sole prerogative of making war and peace," and the "sole power of raising and regulating fleets and armies." The People of the United States had other ideas when they organized our Government. They considered a sound structure of balanced powers essential to the preservation of just government, and international relations formed no exception to that principle.

Zivotofsky v. Kerry, 576 U.S. ___, 135 S. Ct. 2076, 2116 (2015) (Scalia, J., dissenting).

Which view do you believe better approximates the founders' design? Professor Prakash's view is also subject to the same textual rejoinder we saw Justice Jackson raise in the *Steel Seizure* case. If the vesting of the executive power were as extensive as claimed, then why does the Constitution bother to add trifling powers that would certainly have been conveyed the bulk grant of executive power? With respect to foreign affairs, why would the Constitution specifically authorize the President to receive ambassadors? Perhaps this calls to mind Justice Jackson's critique of originalism: "Just what our forefathers did envision, or would have envisioned had they foreseen modern conditions, must be divined from materials almost as enigmatic as the dreams Joseph was called upon to interpret for Pharaoh . . . . [The materials] supply more or less apt quotations . . . on each side of any question. They largely cancel each other." *Youngstown Sheet & Tube Co. v. Sawyer*, 343 U.S. 579, 634–35 (1951) (Jackson, J., concurring). *See* Neil Kinkopf, *Originalism and the Executive*, Lawfare (Jan. 19, 2016).

In a much celebrated earlier book, Dean Harold Koh seeks to draw principles from a different source—the history of how the President and Congress have exercised foreign affairs powers in practice. Koh dubs the result, "the National Security Constitution," which refers to "a normative vision of the foreign policymaking process that emerges only partially from the text of the Constitution itself." He states: "The

National Security Constitution creates the basic governmental institutions to deal with national security matters, defines the fundamental power relationship between those institutions, and places limitations upon the powers of each branch." HAROLD H. KOH, THE NATIONAL SECURITY CONSTITUTION: SHARING POWER AFTER THE IRAN-CONTRA AFFAIR 68 (1990). Dean Koh's framework is an enormously useful one; in a sense, the materials explored in this chapter represent an attempt to delineate this "National Security Constitution."

Koh argues effectively that the shape of the National Security Constitution has not been constant over time. Instead, various periods of American history have exhibited tendencies in favor of either executive or legislative predominance over foreign policy. The following brief summary of some of the highlights of that history draws heavily on Dean Koh's narrative.

America's original practices with respect to foreign policy and national security occurred, of course, in a context of relative weakness and isolation on the world scene. Prior to the culmination of the War of 1812, our survival was hardly taken for granted by the community of nations. Against this background, it is true that President Washington took a number of measures that appeared to bolster the case for presidential power in the foreign affairs area. Yet, it is probably also fair to say that his overriding goal was not the establishment of a particular set of interbranch relationships, but rather the pursuit of what he took to be sound policy regarding Great Britain, the hegemonic world power of the late 18th Century. These actions included rejecting Citizen Genet as a foreign emissary, withholding certain documents from the House regarding the Jay Treaty, employing special agents to conduct diplomacy on behalf of the United States, and issuing the neutrality proclamation of 1793, discussed earlier.

As related by Dean Koh, President Washington did once engage in military action against the Wabash Indians without congressional authorization. In that case, however, Congress arguably ratified his action. More generally, his separation of powers position was that the President enjoyed a sole constitutional power for *communicating* with foreign nations. It was precisely this power that John Marshall, then a member of the House of Representatives, sought to defend in an 1800 speech to the House, referring to the President as "the sole organ of the federal government in the field of international relations."

Not only did Washington not claim inherent presidential power to set the substantive terms of our foreign policy; he conceded that it was up to Congress whether to "correct, improve, or enforce" even his cherished policy of neutrality. And, indeed, Congress responded to this invitation. It enacted in 1794 the Neutrality Act, which imposed criminal penalties in the United States for persons who would assist a military expedition against any country with which the U.S. was at peace.

According to Koh, Presidents Adams, Jefferson, Madison and Monroe "did not fundamentally alter the basic pattern laid down in the Washington years." Adams led the United States into undeclared war with France, Jefferson entered into the Louisiana Purchase and authorized naval retaliation against the Barbary pirates, and

Madison and Monroe sought to seize West Florida. Yet, these Presidents all presumed a need for congressional ratification to legitimate their exercise of authority. Even President Jackson, according to Koh, "institutionalized a practice of information sharing with Congress and frequently requested legislative authorization of his particular acts."

The predominant authority of Congress to decide on matters of military policy is also echoed in Supreme Court opinions at the turn of the 19th Century. For example, in *Little v. Barreme*, excerpted in Chapter Six, the Court held that a Navy captain following a presidential order to seize ships during our undeclared war with France was nevertheless liable to those he had injured when he proceeded in violation of statute.

Matters began to change notably, however, as American concern shifted from protecting its territorial integrity to the pursuit of its manifest destiny. Territorial expansion under Presidents Tyler and Polk, and the Presidents' predisposition to provoke external conflict in the hope of territorial conquest, elicited seemingly easy congressional assent to unilateral executive action. Thus, by the time Supreme Court Justice Nelson, sitting as a Circuit Justice, was called upon to adjudicate an action for damages against an American naval commander who bombarded a Nicaraguan town in retaliation against a local attack on an American consul, he was able to write that the presidential duty to protect American citizens in Nicaragua "belonged to the executive to determine; and his decision is final and conclusive." *Durand v. Hollins*, 8 F. Cas. 111, 112 (C.C.S.D. N.Y. 1860) (No. 4186).

The growth of executive power reached an apotheosis under President Lincoln, who expanded presidential authority in unprecedented ways in order to preserve the Union. Lincoln's assassination, however, and a succession of weak presidents facing a particularly aggressive Congress led to a period of exceptional congressional assertiveness in foreign affairs. In 1869, the Senate refused President Grant's treaty that would have permitted the de facto annexation of Santo Domingo. Indeed, the Senate refused to ratify any important treaty in the middle part of the 19th Century, outside the field of immigration.

As summarized by Dean Koh, "by the end of the 19th Century, the effective institutional balance of power in foreign affairs had shifted far in Congress's favor, but international pressures were already forcing a transformation of American foreign relations and in the process, spurring the pendulum's return swing." In particular, soaring economic growth and the glutting of U.S. domestic markets spurred unprecedented American interest in markets abroad. The desire for markets motivated interventionist executive measures in Latin America in the 1890s, just as the push for land and natural resources spurred a series of internal wars against Native American tribes between 1870 and 1890. It is perhaps unsurprising to find in the language of such late 19th Century cases as *In re Neagle* arguments that sound much like Hamilton in the voice of Pacificus. Recall the Court's dictum in *Neagle* that the President's duty to take care that the laws shall be faithfully executed includes all the "rights, duties and obligations growing out of . . . our international relations." The contrast between this premise and the premises of a case like *Little v. Barreme* could not be more stark.

The emergence of the United States as a world power at the turn of this century was accompanied by a full-blown resurgence of presidential power. President McKinley dispatched troops to China to help put down the Boxer Rebellion without congressional authority. When he could not muster a two-thirds vote in the Senate to annex Hawaii by treaty, McKinley sponsored a statutory effort to accomplish the same result through a majority of both houses.

Theodore Roosevelt, who boldly articulated the view that "every executive officer" is a "steward of the people" unconstrained except by the most specific constitutional and statutory restrictions, intervened unilaterally in Cuba and Santo Domingo, built the Panama Canal without legislative authority, and sent the U.S. fleet around the world without congressional approval. He was unprecedented also in the degree to which he used executive agreements, rather than treaties, to establish the position of the United States on critical matters of foreign affairs. Indeed, his 1904 executive agreement with Santo Domingo, which asserted U.S. control over its custom houses, occurred after the Senate had declined to ratify a similar treaty.

President Taft's far more moderate Madisonian stance was soon eclipsed by the different views of Woodrow Wilson, which of course came into play most forcefully in the context of a world conflict of unprecedented scope. His aggressiveness, however, provoked a backlash, which manifested itself most famously in the Senate's repeated failures to approve the Treaty of Versailles establishing the League of Nations. The presidencies of Harding, Coolidge and Hoover witnessed a major reassertion of congressional government, largely under the leadership of Senator Henry Cabot Lodge.

If, however, the pendulum swung regularly between presidential and congressional assertiveness from 1789 to 1932, what Dean Koh calls our National Security Constitution was substantially reinvented, along with major aspects of our domestic constitution, with the presidency of Franklin Roosevelt. The key judicial decisions ratifying these changes appear below. For now, it is sufficient to remark that Roosevelt engaged in a level of international presidential activism that truly was novel. In an era of profound instability on the international scene, Roosevelt frequently acted independently in the hope both of stimulating international economic development and securing a dominant U.S. position in international, military and political affairs. Among his many celebrated acts in this respect was a decision to acquire rights from the British government to establish naval and air bases in exchange for so-called "over-age destroyers and obsolescent military material," a fairly transparent means of helping to arm Great Britain in 1941 without a formal declaration of war against Germany. The President's initiative in this regard was certified by then-Attorney General Robert Jackson, who commented rather dubiously on his own handiwork when concurring in *Youngstown*.

Dean Koh notes that the Roosevelt administration was important in part because FDR "did not simply centralize national power unto himself, he institutionalized it into a bureaucracy that would wield executive power." Congress substantially deferred to this bureaucracy in legislating on national security affairs in the wake of World War II. Thus, it was the National Security Act of 1947 that created the modern institutions of the Department of Defense, the Joint Chiefs of Staff, the Central Intelligence Agency, and the National Security Council. In arming the executive with a network of permanently authorized agencies subject to presidential control and constrained only by broad statutory delegations, Congress erected the machinery of what Arthur Schlesinger would ultimately call "the imperial presidency."

In the wake of the Vietnam War, and then following the Iran-Contra affair and the end of the Cold War, America seemed to be headed towards a period of renewed congressional assertiveness. As this edition of the text is written, however, the balance of powers seems very much in doubt. In the wake of September 11, 2001, three Presidents have undertaken national security initiatives of arguably unprecedented scope and ambition, often without clear congressional authorization. It is not beyond possibility that the cumulative results of these initiatives could again swing the pendulum in Congress's favor. You should ask yourself, as you review the following materials, whether Dean Koh or Professor Prakash presents a more compelling vision of the constitutional foreign affairs power. Would a greater congressional role be desirable or, potentially, disastrous?

––––––––

Against the backdrop of a genuinely complex history of political struggle, the epigrammatic quality of the following decision may seem startling. Yet, *United States v. Curtiss-Wright Corp.* has become a ubiquitously cited legal authority for the executive branch's most ambitious claims of foreign affairs powers. It was decided within two years of *Panama Refining Co. v. Ryan*, 293 U.S. 388 (1935), and *Schechter Poultry Corp. v. United States*, 295 U.S. 495 (1935), the only two Supreme Court decisions ever to overturn federal statutes as overbroad delegations of legislative authority to the federal executive branch. Because of those earlier decisions, the delegation question presented in *Curtiss-Wright* loomed as a serious issue; today, in light of the cases reviewed in Chapter Two, it would not. Although much of Justice Sutherland's discourse on the President's foreign affairs powers thus today appears to be dictum, it merits close analysis because, for reasons that will become apparent, the opinion has been a favorite among executive branch lawyers. Why would the Court be so much more supportive here than in the context of domestic regulation of broad delegations of policymaking power?

United States v. Curtiss-Wright Corp.

299 U.S. 304 (1936)

Justice SUTHERLAND delivered the opinion of the Court.

. . . [A]n indictment was returned in the court below, the first count of which charges that appellees . . . conspired to sell in the United States certain arms of war, namely fifteen machine guns, to Bolivia, a country then engaged in armed conflict in the Chaco, in violation of the Joint Resolution of Congress approved May 28, 1934, and the provisions of a proclamation issued on the same day by the President of the United States pursuant to authority conferred by § 1 of the resolution. . . . The Joint Resolution (c. 365, 48 Stat. 811) follows:

"... [I]f the President finds that the prohibition of the sale of arms and munitions of war in the United States to those countries now engaged in armed conflict in the Chaco may contribute to the reestablishment of peace between those countries, and if after consultation with the governments of other American Republics and with their cooperation, as well as that of such other governments as he may deem necessary, he makes proclamation to that effect, it shall be unlawful to sell, except under such limitations and exceptions as the President prescribes, any arms or munitions of war in any place in the United States to the countries now engaged in that armed conflict . . . until otherwise ordered by the President or by Congress.

"Sec. 2. Whoever sells any arms or munitions of war in violation of section 1 shall, on conviction, be punished by a fine not exceeding $10,000 or by imprisonment not exceeding two years, or both."

The President's proclamation (48 Stat. 1744), after reciting the terms of the Joint Resolution, declares:

"Now, therefore, I, Franklin D. Roosevelt, President of the United States of America, acting under and by virtue of the authority conferred in me by the said joint resolution of Congress, do hereby declare and proclaim that I have found that the prohibition of the sale of arms and munitions of war in the United States to those countries now engaged in armed conflict in the Chaco may contribute to the reestablishment of peace between those countries, and that I have consulted with the governments of other American Republics . . . ; and I do hereby admonish all citizens of the United States and every person to abstain from every violation of the provisions of the joint resolution. . . . [The President delegated to the Secretary of State his power to prescribe exceptions and limitations to the application of the joint resolution.]

Appellees severally demurred to the first count of the indictment on the grounds . . . first, that the joint resolution effects an invalid delegation of legislative power to the executive; second, that the joint resolution never became effective because of the failure of the President to find essential jurisdictional facts; . . . .

The court below sustained the demurrers. . . . The government appealed to this court [under a statute authorizing a direct government appeal in any criminal case in which a court invalidates the statute on which an indictment was founded.]

First. It is contended that by the Joint Resolution, the going into effect and continued operation of the resolution was conditioned (a) upon the President's judgment as to its beneficial effect upon the reestablishment of peace between the countries engaged in armed conflict in the Chaco; (b) upon the making of a proclamation, which was left to his unfettered discretion, thus constituting an attempted substitution of the President's will for that of Congress; (c) upon the making of a proclamation putting an end to the operation of the resolution, which again was left to the President's unfettered discretion; and (d) further, that the extent of its operation in particular cases was subject to limitation and exception by the President, controlled by no standard. In each of these particulars, appellees urge that Congress abdicated its essential functions and delegated them to the Executive.

Whether, if the Joint Resolution had related solely to internal affairs it would be open to the challenge that it constituted an unlawful delegation of legislative power to the Executive, we find it unnecessary to determine. The whole aim of the resolution is to affect a situation entirely external to the United States, and falling within the category of foreign affairs. . . . In other words, assuming (but not deciding) that the challenged delegation, if it were confined to internal affairs, would be invalid, [the question this Court faces is] may it nevertheless be sustained on the ground that its exclusive aim is to afford a remedy for a hurtful condition within foreign territory?

It will contribute to the elucidation of the question if we first consider the differences between the powers of the federal government in respect of foreign or external affairs and those in respect of domestic or internal affairs. . . .

The two classes of powers are different, both in respect of their origin and their nature. The broad statement that the federal government can exercise no powers except those specifically enumerated in the Constitution, and such implied powers as are necessary and proper to carry into effect the enumerated powers, is categorically true only in respect of our internal affairs. In that field, the primary purpose of the Constitution was to carve from the general mass of legislative powers *then possessed by the states* such portions as it was thought desirable to vest in the federal government, leaving those not included in the enumeration still in the states. That this doctrine applies only to powers which the states had, is self evident. And since the states severally never possessed international powers, such powers could not have been carved from the mass of state powers but obviously were transmitted to the United States from some other source. During the colonial period, those powers were possessed exclusively by and were entirely under the control of the Crown. By the Declaration of Independence, "the Representatives of the United States of America" declared the United [not the several] Colonies to be free and independent states, and as such to have "full Power to levy War, conclude Peace, contract Alliances, establish Commerce and to do all other Acts and Things which Independent States may of right do."

As a result of the separation from Great Britain by the colonies acting as a unit, the powers of external sovereignty passed from the Crown not to the colonies severally, but to the colonies in their collective and corporate capacity as the United States of America. Even before the Declaration, the colonies were a unit in foreign affairs, acting through a common agency—namely the Continental Congress, composed of delegates from the thirteen colonies. That agency exercised the powers of war and peace, raised an army, created a navy, and finally adopted the Declaration of Independence. Rulers come and go; governments end and forms of government change; but sovereignty survives. A political society cannot endure without a supreme will somewhere. Sovereignty is never held in suspense. When, therefore, the external sovereignty of Great Britain in respect of the colonies ceased, it immediately passed to the Union. That fact was given practical application almost at once. . . .

The Union existed before the Constitution, which was ordained and established among other things to form "a more perfect Union." Prior to that event, it is clear that the Union, declared by the Articles of Confederation to be "perpetual," was the sole possessor of external sovereignty and in the Union it remained without change save in so far as the Constitution in express terms qualified its exercise. The Framers' Convention was called and exerted its powers upon the irrefutable postulate that though the states were several their people in respect of foreign affairs were one. Compare *The Chinese Exclusion Case*, 130 U.S. 581, 604, 606. In that convention, the entire absence of state power to deal with those affairs was thus forcefully stated by Rufus King:

> "The states were not 'sovereigns' in the sense contended for by some. They did not possess the peculiar features of sovereignty,—they could not make war, nor peace, nor alliances, nor treaties. Considering them as political beings, they were dumb, for they could not speak to any foreign sovereign whatever. They were deaf, for they could not hear any propositions from such sovereign. They had not even the organs or faculties of defence or offence, for they could not of themselves raise troops, or equip vessels, for war." 5 Elliott's Debates 212.

It results that the investment of the federal government with the powers of external sovereignty did not depend upon the affirmative grants of the Constitution. The powers to declare and wage war, to conclude peace, to make treaties, to maintain diplomatic relations with other sovereignties, if they had never been mentioned in the Constitution, would have vested in the federal government as necessary concomitants of nationality. Neither the Constitution nor the laws passed in pursuance of it have any force in foreign territory unless in respect of our own citizens; and operations of the nation in such territory must be governed by treaties, international understandings and compacts, and the principles of international law. As a member of the family of nations, the right and power of the United States . . . are equal to the right and power of the other members of the international family. Otherwise, the United States is not completely sovereign. The power to acquire territory by discovery and occupation (*Jones v. United States*, 137 U.S. 202, 212), the power to expel undesirable aliens (*Fong Yue Ting v. United States*, 149 U.S. 698, 705 *et seq.*), the power to make such international agreements as do not constitute treaties in the constitutional sense, none of which is expressly affirmed by the Constitution, nevertheless exist as inherently inseparable from the conception of nationality. This the court recognized, and in each of the cases cited found the warrant for its conclusions not in the provisions of the Constitution, but in the law of nations.

Not only, as we have shown, is the federal power over external affairs in origin and essential character different from that over internal affairs, but participation in the exercise of the power is significantly limited. In this vast external realm, with its important, complicated, delicate and manifold problems, the President alone has the power to speak or listen as a representative of the nation. He *makes* treaties with the advice and consent of the Senate; but he alone negotiates. Into the field of negotiation the Senate cannot intrude; and Congress itself is powerless to invade it. As Marshall said in his great argument of March 7, 1800, in the House of Representatives, "The President is the sole organ of the nation in its external relations, and its sole representative with foreign nations." Annals, 6th Cong., col. 613. The Senate Committee on Foreign Relations at a very early day in our history (February 15, 1816), reported to the Senate, among other things, as follows:

> "The President is the constitutional representative of the United States with regard to foreign nations. He manages our concerns with foreign nations and must necessarily be most competent to determine when, how, and upon what subjects negotiation may be urged with the greatest prospect of success. For his conduct he is responsible to the Constitution. The committee consider this responsibility the surest pledge for the faithful discharge of his duty. They think the interference of the Senate in the direction of foreign negotiations calculated to diminish that responsibility and thereby to impair the best security for the national safety. The nature of transactions with foreign nations, moreover, requires caution and unity of design, and their success frequently depends on secrecy and dispatch."

U.S. Senate, Reports, Committee on Foreign Relations, vol. 8, p. 24.

It is important to bear in mind that we are here dealing not alone with an authority vested in the President by an exertion of legislative power, but with such an authority plus the very delicate, plenary and exclusive power of the President as the sole organ of the federal government in the field of international relations—a power which does not require as a basis for its exercise an act of Congress, but which, of course, like every other governmental power, must be exercised in subordination to the applicable provisions of the Constitution. It is quite apparent that if, in the maintenance of our international relations, embarrassment—perhaps serious embarrassment—is to be avoided and success for our aims achieved, congressional legislation which is to be made effective through negotiation and inquiry within the international field must often accord to the President a degree of discretion and freedom from statutory restriction which would not be admissible were domestic affairs alone involved. Moreover, he, not Congress, has the better opportunity of knowing the conditions which prevail in foreign countries, and especially is this true in time of war. He has his confidential sources of information. He has his agents in the form of diplomatic, consular and other officials. Secrecy in respect of information gathered by them may be highly necessary, and the premature disclosure of it productive of harmful results. Indeed, so clearly is this true that the first President refused to accede to a request to lay before the House of Representatives the instructions, correspondence and documents relating to the negotiation of the Jay Treaty — a refusal the wisdom of which was recognized by the House itself and has never since been doubted. In his reply to the request, President Washington said:

> "The nature of foreign negotiations requires caution, and their success must often depend on secrecy; and even when brought to a conclusion a full disclosure of all the measures, demands, or eventual concessions which may have been proposed or contemplated would be extremely impolitic; for this might have a pernicious influence on future negotiations, or produce immediate inconveniences, perhaps danger and mischief, in relation to other powers. The necessity of such caution and secrecy was one cogent reason for vesting the power of making treaties in the President, with the advice and consent of the Senate, the principle on which that body was formed confining it to a small number of members. To admit, then, a right in the House of Representatives to demand and to have as a matter of course all the papers respecting a negotiation with a foreign power would be to establish a dangerous precedent."

1 Messages and Papers of the Presidents, p. 194. . . .

When the President is to be authorized by legislation to act in respect of a matter intended to affect a situation in foreign territory, the legislator properly bears in mind the important consideration that the form of the President's action — or, indeed, whether he shall act at all — may well depend, among other things, upon the nature of the confidential information which he has or may thereafter receive, or upon the effect which his action may have upon our foreign relations. This consideration, in connection with what we have already said on the subject, discloses the unwisdom of requiring Congress in this field of governmental power to lay down narrowly definite standards by which the President is governed. . . .

In the light of the foregoing observations, it is evident that this court should not be in haste to apply a general rule which will have the effect of condemning legislation like that under review as constituting an unlawful delegation of legislative power. The principles which justify such legislation find overwhelming support in the unbroken legislative practice which has prevailed almost from the inception of the national government to the present day. . . .

Practically every volume of the United States Statutes contains one or more acts or joint resolutions of Congress authorizing action by the President in respect of subjects affecting foreign relations, which either leave the exercise of the power to his unrestricted judgment, or provide a standard far more general than that which has always been considered requisite with regard to domestic affairs. . . .

We had occasion to review these embargo and kindred acts in connection with an exhaustive discussion of the general subject of delegation of legislative power in a recent case, *Panama Refining Co. v. Ryan*, 293 U.S. 388, 421–22, and in justifying such acts, pointed out that they confided to the President "an authority which was cognate to the conduct by him of the foreign relations of the government."

The result of holding that the joint resolution here under attack is void and unenforceable as constituting an unlawful delegation of legislative power would be to stamp this multitude of comparable acts and resolutions as likewise invalid. And while this court may not, and should not, hesitate to declare acts of Congress, however many times repeated, to be unconstitutional if beyond all rational doubt it finds them to be so, an impressive array of legislation such as we have just set forth, enacted by nearly every Congress from the beginning of our national existence to the present day, must be given unusual weight in the process of reaching a correct determination of the problem. . . .

The uniform, long-continued and undisputed legislative practice just disclosed rests upon an admissible view of the Constitution which, even if the practice found far less support in principle than we think it does, we should not feel at liberty at this late day to disturb.

We deem it unnecessary to consider, *seriatim*, the several clauses which are said to evidence the unconstitutionality of the Joint Resolution as involving an unlawful delegation of legislative power. It is enough to summarize by saying that, both upon principle and in accordance with precedent, we conclude there is sufficient warrant for the broad discretion vested in the President to determine whether the enforcement of the statute will have a beneficial effect upon the reestablishment of peace in the affected countries; whether he shall make proclamation to bring the resolution into operation; whether and when the resolution shall cease to operate and to make proclamation accordingly; and to prescribe limitations and exceptions to which the enforcement of the resolution shall be subject. . . .

The judgment of the court below must be reversed and the cause remanded for further proceedings in accordance with the foregoing opinion.

Reversed.

Justice McREYNOLDS does not agree. He is of opinion that the court below reached the right conclusion and its judgment ought to be affirmed.

Justice STONE took no part in the consideration or decision of this case.

———————

1. *Professor or Justice Sutherland? Curtiss-Wright* gave Justice Sutherland the opportunity to propound as law a theory of U.S. foreign relations powers he first put forth as a Senator. Sutherland, The Internal and External Powers of the National Government, S. Doc. No. 417, 61st Cong., 2d Sess. (1910); George Sutherland, Constitutional Power and World Affairs (1919). For further background on *Curtiss-Wright*, see Charles A. Lofgren, United States v. Curtiss-Wright Export Corporation: *An Historical Reassessment*, 83 YALE L.J. 1 (1973).

2. *National Sovereignty and Executive Power.* Sutherland argues in *Curtiss-Wright* that the government's foreign affairs powers derive not from the states, but from the

nature of national sovereignty. (His argument that sovereignty never rested in state governments is forcefully challenged in David M. Levitan, *The Foreign Relations Power: An Analysis of Mr. Sutherland's Theory*, 55 YALE L.J. 467 (1946).) Would it follow, even if Sutherland is correct, that the executive branch would be the sole repository of those sovereign powers? Sutherland notes that, in some respects, the Constitution limits Congress's participation in foreign affairs decisionmaking. Congress's enumerated powers, however, include several with undeniable foreign affairs implications. How far, therefore, is Congress limited in regulating Presidents in their capacity as "sole organ of the federal government in the field of international relations?" If Congress, under its foreign trade power, prohibits strategic U.S. military goods from being sold to a country the President now wishes to befriend, would the President have constitutional power to disregard the legislative prohibition? (*See* section C-1 of this chapter, below.) How critical to the persuasiveness of Sutherland's legal views is the correctness of his history?

3. *Foreign Policy and Administrative Agencies.* May Congress vest regulatory authority with the potential to affect our foreign relations in an official subordinate to the President, and legislatively proscribe presidential supervision of that authority? Consider the material in section C of this chapter on foreign policy and administrative agencies.

4. *Judicial Oversight and Presidential Review of Administrative Decisions Involving Foreign Affairs.* Occasionally, when Congress recognizes the foreign affairs implications of some administrative decision, it may subject that decision to presidential approval. The question is then posed whether presidential involvement in the final decision making process somehow precludes judicial review. In a 5–4 opinion, the Supreme Court answered affirmatively in *Chicago & Southern Airlines, Inc. v. Waterman Steamship Corp.*, 333 U.S. 103 (1948). Under the then-current version of the Civil Aeronautics Act, an airline seeking an overseas and foreign air route had to obtain from the Civil Aeronautics Board (CAB) "certificates of convenience and necessity by showing a public interest in establishment of the route and the applicant's ability to serve it." Before orders granting or denying such certificates became final, however, they had to be sent to the President for his approval. When the CAB denied Waterman Steamship Corporation a certificate of convenience and necessity for a desired route air route and granted one instead to Chicago & Southern Air Lines, Waterman sued. The CAB and the victorious applicant both argued that the CAB decisions, once approved by the President, were beyond judicial review.

Under contemporary administrative law, the question presented would be treated as one of "finality." The Administrative Procedure Act authorizes judicial review only of "[a]gency action made reviewable by statute and final agency action for which there is no other adequate remedy in a court." 5 U.S.C. § 704. Where a statute is otherwise silent, a recommendation that an agency sends to the President is not deemed "final agency action," for the precise reason that only the President's decision makes it final; whether the decision involves foreign or domestic affairs makes no difference. *Franklin v. Massachusetts*, 505 U.S. 788 (1992) (denying review of Commerce Department's census report to the President, on the basis of which the President certifies to Congress the number of representatives to which each state is entitled); *Dalton v. Specter*, 511 U.S. 462 (1994) (denying review of the report to the President by the Defense Base Closure and Realignment Commission).

In *Chicago & Southern Airlines,* both the majority and the dissent regarded the President's decisions, based as they were on foreign affairs grounds, as beyond judicial review. The dissenters argued, however, that the President's foreign affairs imprimatur should be read to insulate the CAB's actions from review on conventional administrative law grounds, e.g., whether the CAB properly followed statutory criteria, based its decisions on substantial evidence, followed legally required procedures, and was otherwise not arbitrary. The majority, per Justice Jackson, on the other hand, appeared to regard the CAB's orders, once approved by the President, as so implicating the President's foreign affairs powers that it would be improper to second-guess them:

> The President, both as Commander-in-Chief and as the Nation's organ for foreign affairs, has available intelligence services whose reports are not and ought not to be published to the world. It would be intolerable that courts, without the relevant information, should review and perhaps nullify actions of the Executive taken on information properly held secret. Nor can courts sit *in camera* in order to be taken into executive confidences. But even if courts could require full disclosure, the very nature of executive decisions as to foreign policy is political, not judicial. Such decisions are wholly confided by our Constitution to the political departments of the government, Executive and Legislative. They are delicate, complex, and involve large elements of prophecy. They are and should be undertaken only by those directly responsible to the people whose welfare they advance or imperil. They are decisions of a kind for which the Judiciary has neither aptitude, facilities nor responsibility and which has long been held to belong in the domain of political power not subject to judicial intrusion or inquiry. We therefore agree that whatever of this order emanates from the President is not susceptible of review by the Judicial Department.

333 U.S. at 111. Could such reasoning be read to suggest that the President has power to legalize an otherwise unlawful order by an administrative agency by deciding it accords with our foreign policy interests? *But see Rainbow Navigation, Inc. v. Department of the Navy*, 620 F. Supp. 534 (D.D.C. 1985), *aff'd*, 783 F.2d 1072 (D.C. Cir. 1986) (Secretary of the Navy could not, on foreign affairs grounds, prefer Icelandic vessels to U.S. shipper for military supplies when Congress precluded foreign affairs criteria from influencing preference for U.S. shippers). *See also* Charles B. Hochman, *Judicial Review of Administrative Processes in Which the President Participates*, 74 HARV. L. REV. 684 (1961), and on unreviewability generally, Harvey Saferstein, *Nonreviewability: A Functional Analysis of "Committed to Agency Discretion,"* 82 HARV. L. REV. 367 (1968).

Congress eventually took a different view of the matter. The Federal Aviation Act of 1958 amended Section 801 to permit the President to disapprove CAB decisions for foreign policy reasons; should he approve of a decision, however, that decision would now, by statute, be judicially reviewable. In 1984, Congress abolished the CAB and transferred its functions in granting certificates for air transport to the Secretary of Transportation. Civil Aeronautics Board Sunset Act of 1984, Pub. L. 98-443, 98 Stat. 1703. The requirement for limited presidential review of such decisions on foreign policy grounds remains intact. 49 U.S.C. § 41307.

5. *Further Readings.* Besides the texts referred to above, other important discussions of the allocations of foreign affairs powers appear in Gerhard Casper, Separating Power (1997); Edward S. Corwin, The President 1787–1984 (Randall Bland et al. eds., 5th ed. 1984); John Hart Ely, On Constitutional Ground 149 (1996); Jack L. Goldsmith, *Federal Courts, Foreign Affairs and Federalism*, 83 Va. L. Rev. 1617 (1997); Louis Henkin, Foreign Affairs and the U.S. Constitution 14–15 (2d ed. 1996); H. Jefferson Powell, The President's Authority Over Foreign Affairs (2002); and Michael D. Ramsey, *The Myth of Extraconstitutional Foreign Affairs Power*, 42 Wm. & Mary L. Rev. 379 (2000).

Note: The Logan Act and the Federal Government's Monopoly in Foreign Policy

Whether it is the President or Congress who dominates our foreign policy making, there is little doubt that, between them, they hold all governmental power in the United States with regard to foreign affairs. *See* U.S. Const. art. I, § 10. Of obvious concern in this connection is the prospect for the disruption of our foreign relations—or the frustration of current governmental policy objectives—by actions of private citizens that may affect our relationship with other nations.

A statute that tries to preserve the federal government's monopoly in foreign affairs is the Logan Act, 18 U.S.C. § 953, adopted in 1799, which provides as follows:

> Any citizen of the United States, wherever he may be, who, without authority of the United States, directly or indirectly commences or carries on any correspondence or intercourse with any foreign government or any officer or agent thereof, with intent to influence the measures or conduct of any foreign government or of any officer or agent thereof, in relation to any disputes or controversies with the United States, or to defeat the measures of the United States, shall be fined not more than $5,000 or imprisoned not more than three years, or both.

> This section shall not abridge the right of a citizen to apply, himself or his agent, to any foreign government or the agents thereof for redress of any injury which he may have sustained from such government or any of its agents or subjects.

(A related statute aimed at protecting the government's monopoly over military policy is the Neutrality Act, 18 U.S.C. § 960, explored in Chapter Six.)

The statute is named after Dr. George Logan, a Philadelphia Quaker, a doctor and a Republican, who sailed to France in the 1790s to speak with French officials in order to help relax tensions with America. Although the French greeted his efforts with enthusiasm, President Adams successfully recommended that Congress take action to curb the "temerity and impudence of individuals affecting to interfere in public affairs between France and the United States." Although Logan's name was immortalized through this bill, most historians have noted that he accomplished little or nothing by his efforts and may even have done positive harm by his interference. *See generally* Detlev F. Vagts, *The Logan Act: Paper Tiger or Sleeping Giant?* 60 Am. J. Int'l L. 268 (1966).

The Government has occasionally invoked the possibility of Logan Act indictments, and in a few instances, prosecutions were actually commenced and abandoned. After more than two centuries on the books, however, there is no reported decision of any conviction under this statute. May the Government still constitutionally rely on it consistently with due process? Until 1960, the State Department had a regulation under which Americans who proposed to advise foreign governments with respect to disputes with the United States could obtain clearance. At present, however, there is no established procedure through which any party can obtain approval of such activities. How then, is a citizen to learn what the Act technically permits or proscribes? Does the Act's facial breadth in proscribing speech make it void for vagueness under the First Amendment? What does it mean to "defeat a measure" of the United States? Is it always possible, for example, to distinguish correspondence relevant to a legitimate business deal from the conduct of foreign policy? Because the Act poses First Amendment problems, its threatened use — and the consequent chilling effect on speech — may be more consequential than the actual prospect of a conviction.

The Act came into play during the transition from the Obama to Trump Administration. After being advised that the Russian government had attempted to influence the 2016 presidential election, President Barack Obama imposed sanctions on Moscow in December 2016. Then-President-Elect Trump's designee to serve as National Security Adviser once the Trump Administration had been inaugurated was retired General Michael Flynn. Flynn called Russian Ambassador Sergey Kislyak and, among other matters, discussed the sanctions with him. Do you believe this violates the Logan Act? Does it matter (and should it matter) that, although Flynn was technically a private citizen at the time, he was poised to (and actually did) become National Security Adviser just a few weeks later on January 20, 2017?

After the inauguration, General Flynn apparently told White House officials including the press secretary and the Vice President that he had not discussed sanctions with the Russian ambassador. When the White House repeated these assertions, Acting Attorney General Sally Yates was informed by the FBI, which monitors the phone calls of the Russian ambassador, that sanctions had, in fact, been discussed. Yates then met with the President to inform him of the conversations. The reason the Acting Attorney General did so was concern that Flynn was now subject to

Russian blackmail, in part because the Russians now had knowledge that Flynn may have violated the Logan Act. This knowledge, it was feared, could have been used as leverage over Flynn. Flynn was subsequently removed from office for having misled the Vice President. *See* Peter Baker, *et al.*, *Flynn's Downfall Sprang from "Eroding Level of Trust*," N.Y. Times (Feb. 14, 2017). Does this episode provide a further argument for the importance of the Logan Act: to keep make sure that the Administration-in-waiting respects the status of the Administration that is still in office and so to enforce the principle that there is only one President and one Administration at a time? Or does the episode provide further reason to repeal the Logan Act — because it might actually arm a hostile foreign power with blackmail leverage over government officials?

Youngstown Sheet & Tube Co. v. Sawyer

343 U.S. 579 (1952)

[Excerpted at Chapter 2A(2)]

———

1. *Are Foreign Affairs Powers Different from Domestic Powers?* Our introductory domestic cases, *Marbury* and *Youngstown*, might be thought to have established two critical analytical principles:

a. Courts may ordinarily review the legality of presidential actions, unless those actions are constitutionally committed to the President's political discretion;

b. Only the President or Congress may act within their respective spheres of exclusive authority, but either may act in areas of arguably concurrent authority, unless both act in contrary ways, in which case Congress prevails.

Does it follow, in contrast to these principles in domestic policymaking, that all presidential foreign policy decisions are unreviewable? Do *Curtiss-Wright* and *Waterman Steamship* erect a presumption opposite to the last clause of "Principle (b)" in foreign policy matters? In other words, if congressional and presidential initiatives with foreign policy impact conflict, does the President always prevail? Presumptively prevail? Ever prevail? Does the outcome depend on the "specificity" of the foreign policy power on which the President's initiative assertedly rests? In other words, to what extent does Justice Jackson's *Youngstown* opinion provide authoritative guidance in foreign as well as domestic policy contexts?

Professors Saikrishna B. Prakash and Michael D. Ramsey have argued for an interesting set of answers to these questions. They urge that constitutional text yields a comprehensible allocation of foreign affairs powers to both President and Congress, which also recognizes limits on both sides. In *The Executive Power over Foreign Affairs*, 111 Yale L.J. 231 (2001), they urge "four basic principles" that represent, in their view, a comprehensive framework for assessing the branches' respective claims to foreign affairs authority. The first, and perhaps most controversial, is that the vesting of executive power in Article II signals that the starting point for analysis is that foreign affairs powers reside in the President. The second is that the Constitution sometimes specifically allocates specific foreign affairs powers elsewhere, such as war powers, thus limiting the President. The third is that the President's foreign affairs powers cannot exceed the King's; hence, they do not include any powers either to appropriate funds or to make law binding on third parties, both of which would have been parliamentary. Finally, although Congress lacks general foreign affairs power, it may legislate fully within those of its explicit competencies that bear on foreign affairs (such as the power to regulate foreign commerce), and it may exercise its "Necessary and Proper Clause" powers to regulate *in support of* the President's foreign policy goals. *Id.* at 252–256.

Justice Sutherland's treatment of the President's authority in *Curtiss-Wright* starkly contrasts with the Court's treatment of the President's authority in *Youngstown*, and especially with Justice Jackson's famous concurring opinion. One potential ground of distinction is that *Curtiss-Wright* clearly dealt with a matter of foreign affairs, while the rights asserted by the steel mills in *Youngstown* were ordinary property rights that had been seized in order to resolve a labor dispute. Do you find this distinction persuasive? Consider its continuing vitality as you read the following case.

Zivotofsky v. Kerry

576 U.S. ___, 135 S. Ct. 2076 (2015)

Justice KENNEDY delivered the opinion of the Court.

I

Jerusalem's political standing has long been, and remains, one of the most sensitive issues in American foreign policy . . . . In 1948, President Truman formally recognized Israel in a signed statement of "recognition." That statement did not recognize Israeli sovereignty over Jerusalem. Over the last 60 years, . . . the Executive Branch has maintained that "the status of Jerusalem . . . should be decided not unilaterally but in consultation with all concerned."

The . . . State Department's Foreign Affairs Manual instructs its employees, in general, to record the place of birth on a passport as the "country [having] present sovereignty over the actual area of birth." If a citizen objects to the country listed as sovereign by the State Department, he or she may list the city or town of birth rather than the country. The FAM, however, does not allow citizens to list a sovereign that conflicts with Executive Branch policy. Because the United States does not recognize any country as having sovereignty over Jerusalem, the [Foreign Affairs Manual (FAM)] instructs employees to record the place of birth for citizens born there as "Jerusalem."

In 2002, Congress passed the Foreign Relations Authorization Act, Fiscal Year 2003. Section 214 of the Act is titled "United States Policy with Respect to Jerusalem as the Capital of Israel." The subsection that lies at the heart of this case, § 214(d), addresses passports. That subsection seeks to override the FAM by allowing citizens born in Jerusalem to list their place of birth as "Israel." Titled "Record of Place of Birth as Israel for Passport Purposes," § 214(d) states "[f]or purposes of the registration of birth, certification of nationality, or issuance of a passport of a United States citizen born in the city of Jerusalem, the Secretary shall, upon the request of the citizen or the citizen's legal guardian, record the place of birth as Israel."

In 2002, petitioner Menachem Binyamin Zivotofsky was born to United States citizens living in Jerusalem. Zivotofsky's mother . . . asked that his place of birth be listed as "'Jerusalem, Israel.'" The Embassy clerks [refused to list Israel]. Zivotofsky's parents objected and, as his guardians, brought suit.

II

In considering claims of Presidential power this Court refers to Justice Jackson's familiar tripartite framework from *Youngstown Sheet & Tube Co.* v. *Sawyer.* . . .

In this case the Secretary contends that § 214(d) infringes on the President's exclusive recognition power by "requiring the President to contradict his recognition position regarding Jerusalem in official communications with foreign sovereigns." Because the President's refusal to implement § 214(d) falls into Justice Jackson's third category, his claim must be "scrutinized with caution," and he may rely solely on powers the Constitution grants to him alone.

A

Recognition is a "formal acknowledgement" that a particular "entity possesses the qualifications for statehood" or "that a particular regime is the effective government of a state." It may also involve the determination of a state's territorial bounds.

Legal consequences follow formal recognition. Recognized sovereigns may sue in United States courts, and may benefit from sovereign immunity when they are sued. The actions of a recognized sovereign committed within its own territory also receive deference in domestic courts under the act of state doctrine. Recognition at international law, furthermore, is a precondition of regular diplomatic relations. Recognition is thus "useful, even necessary," to the existence of a state.

Despite the importance of the recognition power in foreign relations, the Constitution does not use the term "recognition," either in Article II or elsewhere.

At the time of the founding, prominent international scholars suggested that receiving an ambassador was tantamount to recognizing the sovereignty of the sending state. It is a logical and proper inference, then, that a Clause directing the President alone to receive ambassadors would be understood to acknowledge his power to recognize other nations.

This in fact occurred early in the Nation's history when President Washington recognized the French Revolutionary Government by receiving its ambassador. After this incident the import of the Reception Clause became clear — causing Hamilton to change his earlier view. He wrote that the Reception Clause "includes th[e power] of judging, in the case of a revolution of government in a foreign country, whether the new rulers are competent organs of the national will, and ought to be recognised, or not." As a result, the Reception Clause provides support, although not the sole authority, for the President's power to recognize other nations.

The inference that the President exercises the recognition power is further supported by his additional Article II powers. It is for the President, "by and with the Advice and Consent of the Senate," to "make Treaties, provided two thirds of the Senators present concur." In addition, "he shall nominate, and by and with the Advice and Consent of the Senate, shall appoint Ambassadors" as well as "other public Ministers and Consuls."

As a matter of constitutional structure, these additional powers give the President control over recognition decisions. At international law, recognition may be effected by different means, but each means is dependent upon Presidential power. In addition to receiving an ambassador, recognition may occur on "the conclusion of a bilateral treaty," or the "formal initiation of diplomatic relations," including the dispatch of an ambassador. The President has the sole power to negotiate treaties, and the Senate may not conclude or ratify a treaty without Presidential action. The President, too, nominates the Nation's ambassadors and dispatches other diplomatic agents. Congress may not send an ambassador without his involvement. Beyond that, the President himself has the power to open diplomatic channels simply by engaging in direct diplomacy with foreign heads of state and their ministers. The Constitution thus assigns the President means to effect recognition on his own initiative. Congress, by contrast, has no constitutional power that would enable it to initiate diplomatic relations with a foreign nation.

The text and structure of the Constitution grant the President the power to recognize foreign nations and governments. The question then becomes whether that power is exclusive. The various ways in which the President may unilaterally effect recognition—and the lack of any similar power vested in Congress—suggest that it is. So, too, do functional considerations. Put simply, the Nation must have a single policy regarding which governments are legitimate in the eyes of the United States and which are not.

Recognition is a topic on which the Nation must " 'speak . . . with one voice.' " That voice must be the President's. Between the two political branches, only the Executive has the characteristic of unity at all times. And with unity comes the ability to exercise, to a greater degree, "[d]ecision, activity, secrecy, and dispatch." The Federalist No. 70. The President is capable, in ways Congress is not, of engaging in the delicate and often secret diplomatic contacts that may lead to a decision on recognition. He is also better positioned to take the decisive, unequivocal action necessary to recognize other states at international law. These qualities explain why the Framers listed the traditional avenues of recognition—receiving ambassadors, making treaties, and sending ambassadors—as among the President's Article II powers.

[T]he President since the founding has exercised this unilateral power to recognize new states—and the Court has endorsed the practice. Texts and treatises on international law treat the President's word as the final word on recognition.

It remains true, of course, that many decisions affecting foreign relations—including decisions that may determine the course of our relations with recognized countries—require congressional action. Congress may "regulate Commerce with foreign Nations," "establish an uniform Rule of Naturalization," "define and punish Piracies and Felonies committed on the high Seas, and Offences against the Law of Nations," "declare War," "grant Letters of Marque and Reprisal," and "make Rules for the Government and Regulation of the land and naval Forces." In addition, the President cannot make a treaty or appoint an ambassador without the approval of the Senate. The President, furthermore, could not build an American Embassy abroad without congressional appropriation of the necessary funds. Under basic separation-of-powers principles, it is for the Congress to enact the laws, including "all Laws which shall be necessary and proper for carrying into Execution" the powers of the Federal Government.

In practice, then, the President's recognition determination is just one part of a political process that may require Congress to make laws. The President's exclusive recognition power encompasses the authority to acknowledge, in a formal sense, the legitimacy of other states and governments, including their territorial bounds. Albeit limited, the exclusive recognition power is essential to the conduct of Presidential duties. The formal act of recognition is an executive power that Congress may not qualify. If the President is to be effective in negotiations over a formal recognition determination, it must be evident to his counterparts abroad that he speaks for the Nation on that precise question.

B

The Secretary now urges the Court to define the executive power over foreign relations in even broader terms. He contends that under the Court's precedent the President has "exclusive authority to conduct diplomatic relations," along with "the bulk of foreign-affairs powers." In support of his submission that the President has broad, undefined powers over foreign affairs, the Secretary quotes *United States* v. *Curtiss-Wright Export Corp.*, which described the President as "the sole organ of the federal government in the field of international relations." This Court declines to acknowledge that unbounded power.

The *Curtiss-Wright* case does not extend so far as the Secretary suggests. In *Curtiss-Wright*, the Court considered whether a congressional delegation of power to the President was constitutional. The Court held that the delegation was constitutional, reasoning that Congress may grant the President substantial authority and discretion in the field of foreign affairs. Describing why such broad delegation may be appropriate, the opinion stated:

"In this vast external realm, with its important, complicated, delicate and manifold problems, the President alone has the power to speak or listen as a representative of the nation. He *makes* treaties with the advice and consent of the Senate; but he alone negotiates. Into the field of negotiation the Senate cannot intrude; and Congress itself is powerless to invade it. As Marshall said in his great argument of March 7, 1800, in the House of Representatives, 'The President is the sole organ of the nation in its external relations, and its sole representative with foreign nations.'"

This description of the President's exclusive power was not necessary to the holding of *Curtiss-Wright*—which, after all, dealt with congressionally authorized action, not a unilateral Presidential determination. Indeed, *Curtiss-Wright* did not hold that the President is free from Congress' lawmaking power in the field of international relations. The President does have a unique role in communicating with foreign governments, as then-Congressman John Marshall acknowledged. But whether the realm is foreign or domestic, it is still the Legislative Branch, not the Executive Branch, that makes the law.

In a world that is ever more compressed and interdependent, it is essential the congressional role in foreign affairs be understood and respected. For it is Congress that makes laws, and in countless ways its laws will and should shape the Nation's course. The Executive is not free from the ordinary controls and checks of Congress merely because foreign affairs are at issue. It is not for the President alone to determine the whole content of the Nation's foreign policy.

That said, judicial precedent and historical practice teach that it is for the President alone to make the specific decision of what foreign power he will recognize as legitimate, both for the Nation as a whole and for the purpose of making his own position clear within the context of recognition in discussions and negotiations with foreign nations. Recognition is an act with immediate and powerful significance for international relations, so the President's position must be clear. Congress cannot require him to contradict his own statement regarding a determination of formal recognition.

C

[This section of the opinion surveys "accepted understandings and practice." Justice Kennedy prefaced this survey by setting forth his conclusion: "Here, history is not all on one side, but on balance it provides strong support for the conclusion that the recognition power is the President's alone." In 1793, President Washington received the ambassador from France's Revolutionary Government. In deliberation with his cabinet, Washington determined that reception would constitute formal recognition and that consultation with Congress was unnecessary. The issue came to a head again in 1818 in connection with the independence of a number of former Spanish colonies. Speaker of the House Henry Clay proposed a law to recognize present-day Argentina. The bill failed—in part, according to Justice Kennedy, because "Congress agreed the recognition power rested solely with the President."

In 1835 the Texas Republic broke away from Mexico and presented the U.S. with another recognition issue. Congress urged President Jackson to recognize the breakaway republic. Reserving the question of who holds the power of recognition, the

President declared that "on the grounds of expediency, I am disposed to concur." Congress then enacted an appropriation for a diplomatic agent to Texas "whenever the President . . . shall deem it expedient . . . ." Thus, according to Justice Kennedy, the formal act of recognition was left to the President. Decades later, President Lincoln sought to recognize Haiti and Liberia but stated that he was unwilling to do so "without the approbation of Congress." Congress agreed and appropriated funds for diplomatic agents. As with Texas, the formal act of recognition was left to the President.

In 1898, Congress and the President disagreed over whether to recognize Spain or the insurgent government as the legitimate sovereign of Cuba, with President McKinley seeking to support the Spanish colonial government. Congress enacted and President McKinley signed a joint resolution that "the people of the Island of Cuba are, and of right ought to be, free and independent." Justice Kennedy regarded this language as a "compromise" because the joint resolution "made no mention of recognizing a new Cuban Government."

Over the ensuing eight decades, Presidents frequently exercised the recognition power and Congress made no serious effort to involve itself. This period of harmony ended in the late 1970s when President Carter recognized the People's Republic of China, the Communist government capitaled in Beijing, and rescinded recognition from the Republic of China in Taiwan. The President and Congress negotiated a statute, the Taiwan Relations Act, which treated Taiwan as a distinct entity from China. According to Justice Kennedy, "[t]hroughout the legislative process, however, no one raised a serious question regarding the President's exclusive authority to recognize the PRC—or to decline to grant formal recognition to Taiwan. Rather, Congress accepted the President's recognition determination as a completed, lawful act . . . ." "From the first Administration forward, the President has claimed unilateral authority to recognize foreign sovereigns."]

III

As the power to recognize foreign states resides in the President alone, the question becomes whether § 214(d) infringes on the Executive's consistent decision to withhold recognition with respect to Jerusalem. See *Nixon* v. *Administrator of General Services*, 433 U. S. 425, 443 (1977) (action unlawful when it "prevents the Executive Branch from accomplishing its constitutionally assigned functions").

Section 214(d) requires that, in a passport or consular report of birth abroad, "the Secretary shall, upon the request of the citizen or the citizen's legal guardian, record the place of birth as Israel" for a "United States citizen born in the city of Jerusalem." That is, § 214(d) requires the President, through the Secretary, to identify citizens born in Jerusalem who so request as being born in Israel. But according to the President, those citizens were not born in Israel. As a matter of United States policy, neither Israel nor any other country is acknowledged as having sovereignty over Jerusalem. In this way, § 214(d) "directly contradicts" the "carefully calibrated and longstanding Executive branch policy of neutrality toward Jerusalem."

If the power over recognition is to mean anything, it must mean that the President not only makes the initial, formal recognition determination but also that he may maintain that determination in his and his agent's statements. This conclusion is a matter of both common sense and necessity. If Congress could command the President to state a recognition position inconsistent with his own, Congress could override the President's recognition determination. Under international law, recognition may be effected by "written or oral declaration of the recognizing state." In addition an act of recognition must "leave no doubt as to the intention to grant it." Thus, if Congress could alter the President's statements on matters of recognition or force him to contradict them, Congress in effect would exercise the recognition power.

As Justice Jackson wrote in *Youngstown*, when a Presidential power is "exclusive," it "disabl[es] the Congress from acting upon the subject." Here, the subject is quite narrow: The Executive's exclusive power extends no further than his formal recognition determination. But as to that determination, Congress may not enact a law that directly contradicts it. This is not to say Congress may not express its disagreement with the President in myriad ways. For example, it may enact an embargo, decline to confirm an ambassador, or even declare war. But none of these acts would alter the President's recognition decision.

If Congress may not pass a law, speaking in its own voice, that effects formal recognition, then it follows that it may not force the President himself to contradict his earlier statement. That congressional command would not only prevent the Nation from speaking with one voice but also prevent the Executive itself from doing so in conducting foreign relations.

Although the statement required by § 214(d) would not itself constitute a formal act of recognition, it is a mandate that the Executive contradict his prior recognition determination in an official document issued by the Secretary of State. As a result, it is unconstitutional. This is all the more clear in light of the longstanding treatment of a passport's place-of-birth section as an official executive statement implicating recognition.

The flaw in § 214(d) is further underscored by the undoubted fact that that the purpose of the statute was to infringe on the recognition power — a power the Court now holds is the sole prerogative of the President. The statute is titled "United States Policy with Respect to Jerusalem as the Capital of Israel." The House Conference Report proclaimed that § 214 "contains four provisions related to the recognition of Jerusalem as Israel's capital." And, indeed, observers interpreted § 214 as altering United States policy regarding Jerusalem — which led to protests across the region. From the face of § 214, from the legislative history, and from its reception, it is clear that Congress wanted to express its displeasure with the President's policy by, among other things, commanding the Executive to contradict his own, earlier stated position on Jerusalem. This Congress may not do.

Affirmed

Justice SCALIA, with whom The CHIEF JUSTICE and Justice ALITO join, dissenting.

Before this country declared independence, the law of England entrusted the King with the exclusive care of his kingdom's foreign affairs. The royal prerogative included the "sole power of sending ambassadors to foreign states, and receiving them at home," the sole authority to "make treaties, leagues, and alliances with foreign states and princes," "the sole prerogative of making war and peace," and the "sole power of raising and regulating fleets and armies." The People of the United States had other ideas when they organized our Government. They considered a sound structure of balanced powers essential to the preservation of just government, and international relations formed no exception to that principle.

This case arises out of a dispute between the Executive and Legislative Branches about whether the United States should treat Jerusalem as a part of Israel. The Constitution contemplates that the political branches will make policy about the territorial claims of foreign nations the same way they make policy about other international matters: The President will exercise his powers on the basis of his views, Congress its powers on the basis of its views. That is just what has happened here.

I

Before turning to Presidential power under Article II, I think it well to establish the statute's basis in congressional power under Article I. Congress's power to "establish an uniform Rule of Naturalization" enables it to grant American citizenship to someone born abroad. The naturalization power also enables Congress to furnish the people it makes citizens with papers verifying their citizenship — say a consular report of birth abroad (which certifies citizenship of an American born outside the United States) or a passport (which certifies citizenship for purposes of international travel).

II

Recognition is more than an announcement of a policy. Like the ratification of an international agreement or the termination of a treaty, it is a formal legal act with effects under international law.

§ 214(d) has nothing to do with recognition. Section 214(d) does not require the Secretary to make a formal declaration about Israel's sovereignty over Jerusalem. And nobody suggests that international custom infers acceptance of sovereignty from the birthplace designation on a passport or birth report, as it does from bilateral treaties or exchanges of ambassadors. Recognition would preclude the United States (as a matter of international law) from later contesting Israeli sovereignty over Jerusalem. But making a notation in a passport or birth report does not encumber the Republic with any international obligations. It leaves the Nation free (so far as international law is concerned) to change its mind in the future. That would be true even if the statute required *all* passports to list "Israel."

Section 214(d) performs a more prosaic function than extending recognition. Just as foreign countries care about what our Government has to say about their borders, so too American citizens often care about what our Government has to say about their identities. The State Department does not grant or deny recognition in order to accommodate these individuals, but it does make exceptions to its rules about how it records birthplaces. Although normal protocol requires specifying the bearer's country of birth in his passport, the State Department will, if the bearer protests, specify the city of birth instead—so that an Irish nationalist may have his birthplace recorded as "Belfast" rather than "United Kingdom." Granting a request to specify "Israel" rather than "Jerusalem" does not recognize Israel's sovereignty over Jerusalem, just as granting a request to specify "Belfast" rather than "United Kingdom" does not derecognize the United Kingdom's sovereignty over Northern Ireland.

III

Even if the Constitution gives the President sole power to extend recognition, it does not give him sole power to make all decisions relating to foreign disputes over sovereignty. To the contrary, a fair reading of Article I allows Congress to decide for itself how its laws should handle these controversies. Read naturally, power to "regulate Commerce with foreign Nations," includes power to regulate imports from Gibraltar as British goods or as Spanish goods. Read naturally, power to "regulate the Value . . . of foreign Coin," includes power to honor (or not) currency issued by Taiwan. And so on for the other enumerated powers.

The Constitution likewise does not give the President exclusive power to determine which claims to statehood and territory "are legitimate in the eyes of the United States". Congress may express its own views about these matters by declaring war, restricting trade, denying foreign aid, and much else besides. To take just one example, in 1991, Congress responded to Iraq's invasion of Kuwait by enacting a resolution authorizing use of military force. No doubt the resolution reflected Congress's views about the legitimacy of Iraq's territorial claim. The preamble referred to Iraq's "illegal occupation" and stated that "the international community has demanded . . . that Kuwait's independence and legitimate government be restored." These statements are far more categorical than the caption "United States Policy with Respect to Jerusalem as the Capital of Israel." Does it follow that the authorization of the use of military force invaded the President's exclusive powers? Or that it would have done so had the President recognized Iraqi sovereignty over Kuwait?

History does not even support an exclusive Presidential power to make what the Court calls "formal statements" about "the legitimacy of a state or government and its territorial bounds". For a long time, the Houses of Congress have made formal statements announcing their own positions on these issues, again without provoking constitutional objections. A recent resolution expressed the House of Representatives' "strong support for the legitimate, democratically-elected Government of Lebanon" and condemned an "illegitimate" and "unjustifiable" insurrection by "the terrorist group Hizballah." An earlier enactment declared "the sense of the Congress that . . . Tibet . . . is an occupied country under the established principles of international law" and that "Tibet's true representatives are the Dalai Lama and the Tibetan Government in exile." After Texas won independence from Mexico, the Senate resolved that "the State of Texas having established and maintained an independent Government, . . . it is expedient and proper . . . that the independent political existence of the said State be acknowledged by the Government of the United States."

In the final analysis, the Constitution may well deny Congress power to recognize— the power to make an international commitment accepting a foreign entity as a state, a regime as its government, a place as a part of its territory, and so on. But whatever else § 214(d) may do, it plainly does not make (or require the President to make) a commitment accepting Israel's sovereignty over Jerusalem.

IV

The Court does not try to argue that § 214(d) extends recognition; nor does it try to argue that the President holds the exclusive power to make all nonrecognition decisions relating to the status of Jerusalem. As just shown, these arguments would be impossible to make with a straight face.

The Court instead announces a rule that is blatantly gerrymandered to the facts of this case. It concludes that, in addition to the exclusive power to make the "formal recognition determination," the President holds an ancillary exclusive power "to control . . . formal statements by the Executive Branch acknowledging the legitimacy of a state or government and its territorial bounds." It follows, the Court explains, that Congress may not "requir[e] the President to contradict an earlier recognition determination in an official document issued by the Executive Branch." So requiring imports from Jerusalem to be taxed like goods from Israel is fine, but requiring Customs to issue an official invoice to that effect is not? Nonsense.

Recognition is a type of legal act, not a type of statement. It is a leap worthy of the Mad Hatter to go from exclusive authority over making legal commitments about sovereignty to exclusive authority over making statements or issuing documents about national borders. The Court may as well jump from power over issuing declaratory judgments to a monopoly on writing law-review articles.

No consistent or coherent theory supports the Court's decision. At times, the Court seems concerned with the possibility of congressional interference with the President's ability to extend or withhold legal recognition. The Court concedes, as it must, that the notation required by § 214(d) "would not itself constitute a formal act of recognition." *Ante,* at 27. It still frets, however, that Congress *could* try to regulate the President's "statements" in a way that "override[s] the President's recognition determination." But "[t]he circumstance, that . . . [a] power may be abused, is no answer. All powers may be abused." What matters is whether *this* law interferes with the President's ability to withhold recognition. It would be comical to claim that it does.

The Court elsewhere objects that § 214(d) interferes with the autonomy and unity of the Executive Branch, setting the branch against itself. The Court suggests, for instance, that the law prevents the President from maintaining his neutrality about Jerusalem in "his and his agent's statements." That is of no constitutional significance. Congress has power to legislate without regard to recognition, and where Congress has the power to legislate, the President has a duty to "take Care" that its legislation "be faithfully executed," Art. II, § 3. It is likewise "the duty of the secretary of state to conform to the law". The Executive's involvement in carrying out this law does not affect its constitutionality; the Executive carries out every law.

In the end, the Court's decision does not rest on text or history or precedent. It instead comes down to "functional considerations"—principally the Court's perception that the Nation "must speak with one voice" about the status of Jerusalem. The vices of this mode of analysis go beyond mere lack of footing in the Constitution. Functionalism of the sort the Court practices today will *systematically* favor the unitary President over the plural Congress in disputes involving foreign affairs. It is possible that this approach will make for more effective foreign policy, perhaps as effective as that of a monarchy. It is certain that, in the long run, it will erode the structure of separated powers that the People established for the protection of their liberty.

I dissent.

[The opinion of Justice THOMAS concurring in part and dissenting in part is omitted.]

---

1. *Domestic v. Foreign Affairs.* In a separate dissent, Chief Justice Roberts expressed his view that the holding was a significant departure from precedent: "Today's decision is a first: Never before has this Court accepted a President's direct defiance of an Act of Congress in the field of foreign affairs. We have instead stressed that the President's power reaches 'its lowest ebb' when he contravenes the express will of Congress, 'for what is at stake is the equilibrium established by our constitutional system.' . . . For our first 225 years, no President prevailed when contradicting a statute in the field of foreign affairs." Citing *Medellin v. Texas*, 552 U.S. 491 (2008); *Hamdan v. Rumsfeld*, 548 U.S. 557 (2006); *Youngstown Sheet & Tube Co. v. Sawyer*, 343 U.S. 579 (1952); *Little v. Barreme*, 6 U.S. 170 (1804). Of course, the Court has upheld the President's direct defiance of an Act of Congress in the domestic affairs context. *See Myers v. United States*, 272 U.S. 52 (1926). Moreover, in the context of domestic affairs, we have seen that the Court has struck down Acts of Congress that limit presidential power in a variety of ways, even though the President did not defy or, in some instances, even oppose them. *See, e.g., Free Enterprise Fund v. Public Co. Accounting Oversight Bd.*, 561 U.S. 477 (2010); *Bowsher v. Synar*, 478 U.S. 714 (1986); *INS v. Chadha*, 462 U.S. 919 (1983); *Buckley v. Valeo*, 424 U.S. 1 (1976). Is Chief Justice Roberts suggesting that assertions of presidential power are on *weaker* footing when made in the context of foreign affairs as opposed to domestic affairs? If so, is he correct?

2. *A Unified Field Theory of Separation of Powers?* Regardless of whether the President should be understood to hold a greater quantum of power in the realm of domestic or foreign affairs, *Zivotofsky* raises the separate question of whether a different framework is to be utilized to resolve foreign affairs controversies as opposed to those arising in the domestic affairs context. Justice Kennedy's opinion for the Court begins by laying out Justice Jackson's tripartite framework from *Youngstown*. This has been the standard approach for determining the scope of the President's foreign affairs power since at least *Dames & Moore v. Regan*. You may have noticed that the cases in chapters 2–4 of this book (other than *Youngstown* itself) do not use the Jackson framework in the domestic affairs setting. This may suggest that the Court employs a different analytical framework for foreign affairs cases than it employs for domestic cases.

Justice Kennedy's opinion in *Zivotofsky*, however, suggests that the Court will apply a single standard to resolve claims that a statute unconstitutionally infringes upon executive authority. The issue in *Zivotofsky* falls within category 3 of the Jackson framework, because the President acts in defiance of a statutory command. To determine whether the President may prevail in category 3, Justice Kennedy asks whether the statute "prevents the Executive Branch from accomplishing its constitutionally assigned functions." This standard is quoted from a domestic affairs case—*Nixon v. Administrator of General Services* (chapter 3D(1)(a))—and appears in other domestic separation of powers cases, *e.g.*, *Morrison v. Olson* (chapter 4B).

3. *Formalism versus Functionalism.* Justice Kennedy's analysis is highly functionalist. In other words, he focuses on how the statute would actually impact the President's ability to exercise the recognition power. "If the [recognition power] is to mean anything," Congress, in Justice Kennedy's estimation, cannot require Presidents to make official statements that contradict their recognition determinations. Is this persuasive?

In separation of powers cases, the Court's analytical approach has alternated between formalism and functionalism. In cases where the Court has engaged in functional analysis, it has typically done so in a way that accords a great deal of deference to Congress. Put somewhat differently, the Court's analysis in these cases has sought to demonstrate that the obligations imposed by statutes can be reconciled with the President's constitutional office. In this sense, functionalism has been deferential and pro-Congress. Consider *Morrison v. Olson*, 487 U.S. 654 (1988); *Humphrey's Executor v. United States*, 295 U.S. 602 (1935); *Nixon v. Admin. Gen. Servs.*, 433 U.S. 425 (1977); *Clinton v. Jones*, 520 U.S. 681 (1997); *United States v. Nixon*, 418 U.S. 683 (1974).

Zivotofsky stands in contrast to this line of cases. Although it employs functional analysis—in that it turns on how the Court thinks the statute will actually operate in practice—it lacks the usual deference to Congress. Indeed, the Court seems more concerned about making sure that the statute not encroach upon the President than it does about affirming the obligation of Presidents to conform to statutory limits on their power. Does this strike you as a positive development?

Note: Statutory Interpretation in the Context of the President's Foreign Policy and National Security Powers

After *Zivotofsky* the Court is poised to apply Justice Jackson's framework to resolve separation of powers controversies in the context of foreign and military affairs. Applying the framework requires attention to the statutory background. Whether the President is acting in category one or three may depend upon the application of statutes that are subject to various and conflicting interpretations. Indeed, there may be several potentially relevant statutes, one or more of which may be understood to authorize presidential action others of which may be understood to prohibit it. For example, President George W. Bush claimed authority to detain enemy combatants captured in Afghanistan based not only on his status as Commander in Chief, but also based on the Authorization of Use of Military Force enacted in response to the attacks of September 11, 2001. A United States citizen detained as such an enemy combatant asserted that the President's authority did not extend to U.S. citizens because of a law, the Non-Detention Act, prohibiting executive detention of U.S. citizens without specific statutory authorization. *See Hamdi v. Rumsfeld*, 542 U.S. 507 (2004), excerpted in Chapter 7.

In approaching statutes bearing on the President's constitutional authority, the Court frequently invokes a doctrine known as the avoidance canon. This canon holds that a statute should be interpreted to avoid a constitutional issue if two conditions are met. First, the issue to be avoided must be serious or substantial as opposed to frivolous. Second, the alternative interpretation of the statute — the one that avoids the constitutional difficulty — must be a reasonable interpretation of the statute. You may recall that the Supreme Court applied this canon in *Public Citizen v. Dep't of Justice*, 491 U.S. 440 (1989). There, Justice Brennan read the Federal Advisory Committee Act as not applying to American Bar Association committee that advised the executive branch on potential federal judicial nominees because such a reading would raise a serious question as to whether the law impermissibly invaded the President's constitutional appointment power. Justice Kennedy wrote separately because he did not regard Justice Brennan's alternative interpretation as reasonable. (Because Justice Kennedy did not regard the constitutional question as avoidable through interpretation, he reached the merits and would have held FACA unconstitutional as applied to the ABA committee.)

The Court also applied the canon to determine whether the President is an agency under the Administrative Procedure Act. "Out of respect for the separation of powers and the unique constitutional position of the President, we find that textual silence is not enough to subject the President to [the APA]. We would require an express statement by Congress before assuming it had intended the President's performance of his statutory duties to be reviewed for abuse of discretion." *Franklin v. Massachusetts*, 491 U.S. 440, 465–467 (1989).

In the areas of foreign and military affairs, executive branch lawyers sometimes make the claim that the canon applies with particular force. The argument is that in this setting courts should defer to the executive branch, which has much greater institutional competence to address such issues. There is some judicial support for this argument. For example, in *Dep't of Navy v. Egan*, the Supreme Court stated: "Unless Congress specifically has provided otherwise, courts traditionally have been reluctant to intrude upon the authority of the Executive in military and national security affairs." 484 U.S. 518, 530 (1988).

The Court nevertheless does not always emphasize the need for deference. In some cases, the Court focuses on the importance of the rule of law and ensuring that the President and the Administration comply with statutory requirements. In a dispute over whether the Administration was properly enforcing a fishing treaty, for example, the Court had this to say: "The Secretary, of course, may not act contrary to the will of Congress when exercised within the bounds of the Constitution. If Congress has directly spoken to the precise issue in question, if the intent of Congress is clear, that is the end of the matter." *Japan Whaling Ass'n v. American Cetacean Soc'y*, 478 U.S. 221, 233 (1986).

As you read the cases in the remaining chapters, consider whether the Court is interpreting statutes in a manner that accords deference to the executive branch. To the extent that it does, consider whether you think the deference justified or whether the Court should enforce rule of law values.

Of course, not all the materials in the following chapters are judicial. We have included executive branch legal opinions as well. A number of commentators have pointed out that the case for the avoidance canon or for deference does not apply to the executive branch's own legal interpretation. These are best understood as doctrines of *judicial* restraint or as recognition of the executive's greater competence in foreign and military affairs. These considerations have no application to the executive branch's own legal analyses. *See* H. Jefferson Powell, *The Executive and the Avoidance Canon*, 81 IND. L.J. 1313 (2006); Trevor Morrison, *Constitutional Avoidance in the Executive Branch*, 106 COLUM. L. REV. 1189 (2006).

B. Executive Claims to Inherent and Exclusive Powers

1. The President's Power of Recognition and Role as "Sole Organ" of Foreign Affairs

The Supreme Court in *Zivotofsky* said little about the scope and content of the President's power over foreign affairs. It ruled that the President possesses exclusively the recognition power and that Congress may not render that power meaningless by requiring the President to issue official statements that contradict the President's recognition determinations. What, beyond this, is the President's authority over the nation's foreign relations? To what extent is the President authorized to determine the substance of United States foreign policy? To what extent is the President authorized to determine the "means and mode" by which our foreign relations will be conducted? When Presidents exercise powers in these areas, to what extent must they comply with limitations and regulations that Congress sets forth in statutes? The following two opinions of the Justice Department's Office of Legal Counsel are representative of the executive branch's position on these questions.

Bill to Relocate United States Embassy from Tel Aviv to Jerusalem
19 Op. O.L.C. 123 (1995)

This is to provide you with our views on S. 770, 104th Cong. (1995), a bill . . . "[t]o provide for the relocation of the United States Embassy in Israel to Jerusalem, and for other purposes." The provisions of this bill that render the executive branch's ability to obligate appropriated funds conditional upon the construction and opening in Jerusalem of the United States Embassy to Israel invade exclusive presidential authorities in the field of foreign affairs and are unconstitutional. The bill states that [i]t is the policy of the United States that — (1) Jerusalem should be recognized as the capital of the State of Israel; (2) groundbreaking for construction of the United States Embassy in Jerusalem should begin no later than December 31, 1996; and (3) the United States Embassy should be officially open in Jerusalem no later than May 31, 1999. S. 770, § 3(a). The bill requires that not more than fifty percent of the funds appropriated to the State Department for FY 1997 for "Acquisition and Maintenance of Buildings Abroad" may be obligated until the Secretary of State determines and reports to Congress that construction has begun on the site of the United States Embassy in Jerusalem. Id. § 3(b). Further, not more than fifty percent of the funds appropriated to the State Department for FY 1999 for "Acquisition and Maintenance of Buildings Abroad" may be obligated until the Secretary determines and reports to Congress that the United States Embassy in Jerusalem has officially opened. Id. § 3(c). Of the funds appropriated for FY 1995 for the State Department and related agencies, not less than $5,000,000 "shall be made available until expended" for costs associated with relocating the United States Embassy in Israel to Jerusalem. 123 Opinions of the Office of Legal Counsel in Volume 19 Id. § 4 . . . .

It is well settled that the Constitution vests the President with the exclusive authority to conduct the Nation's diplomatic relations with other States. This authority flows, in large part, from the President's position as Chief Executive, U.S. Const, art. II, § 1, cl. 1, and as Commander in Chief, id. art. II, § 2, cl. 1. It also derives from the President's more specific powers to "make Treaties," id. art. II, § 2, cl. 2; to "appoint Ambassadors . . . and Consuls," id.\ and to "receive Ambassadors and other public Ministers," id. art. II, § 3. The Supreme Court has repeatedly recognized the President's authority with respect to the conduct of diplomatic relations. *See, e.g., Department of Navy v. Egan*, 484 U.S. 518, 529 (1988) (the Supreme Court has " recognized 'the generally accepted view that foreign policy was the province and responsibility of the Executive'") (quoting *Haig v. Agee*, 453 U.S. 280, 293–94 (1981)); *Alfred Dunhill of London, Inc. v. Republic of Cuba*, 425 U.S. 682, 705–06 n.18 (1976) ("[T]he conduct of [foreign policy] is committed primarily to the Executive Branch."); *United States v. Louisiana*, 363 U.S. 1, 35 (1960) (the President is "the constitutional representative of the United States in its dealings with foreign nations"); *see also Ward v. Skinner*, 943 F.2d 157, 160 (1st Cir. 1991) (Breyer, C.J.) ("[T]he Constitution makes the Executive Branch . . . primarily responsible" for the exercise of "the foreign affairs power."), *cert. denied*, 503 U.S. 959 (1992); *Sanchez Espinoza v. Reagan*, 770 F.2d 202, 210 (D.C. Cir. 1985) (Scalia, J.) ("[B]road leeway" is "traditionally accorded the Executive in matters of foreign affairs."). Accordingly, we have affirmed that the Constitution "authorize[s] the President to determine the form and manner in which the United States will maintain relations with foreign nations." Issues Raised by Provisions Directing Issuance of Official or Diplomatic Passports, 16 Op. O.L.C. 18, 21 (1992). Furthermore, the President's recognition power is exclusive. *See Banco Nacional de Cuba v. Sabbatino*, 376 U.S. 398, 410 (1964) ("Political recognition is exclusively a function of the Executive."); see also Restatement (Third) of the Foreign Relations Law of the United States § 204 (1987) ("[T]he President has exclusive authority to recognize or not to recognize a foreign state or government, and to maintain or not to maintain diplomatic relations with a foreign 124 Bill to Relocate United States Embassy from Tel Aviv to Jerusalem government."). It is well established, furthermore, that this power is not limited to the bare act of according diplomatic recognition to a particular government, but encompasses as well the authority to take such actions as are necessary to make the power of recognition an effective tool of United States foreign policy. *United States v. Pink*, 315 U.S. 203, 229 (1942) (The authority to recognize governments "is not limited to a determination of the government to be recognized. It includes the power to determine the policy which is to govern the question of recognition.").

The proposed bill would severely impair the President's constitutional authority to determine the form and manner of the Nation's diplomatic relations. The bill seeks to effectuate the policy objectives that "Jerusalem should be recognized as the capital of the State of Israel" and that "the United States Embassy should be officially open in Jerusalem no later than May 31, 1999." To those ends, it would prohibit the executive branch from obligating more than a fixed percentage of the funds appropriated to the State Department for " Acquisition and Maintenance of Buildings Abroad" in FY 1997 until the Secretary determines and reports to Congress that construction has begun on the site of the United States Embassy in Jerusalem. It would also prohibit the executive branch from obligating more than a fixed percentage of the funds appropriated for the same purpose for FY 1999 until the Secretary determines and reports to Congress that the United States Embassy in Jerusalem has "officially opened." By thus conditioning the executive branch's ability to obligate appropriated funds, the bill seeks to compel the President to build and to open a United States Embassy to Israel at a site of extraordinary international concern and sensitivity.

We believe that Congress cannot constitutionally constrain the President in such a manner. In general, because the venue at which diplomatic relations occur is itself often diplomatically significant, Congress may not impose on the President its own foreign policy judgments as to the particular sites at which the United States' diplomatic relations are to take place. More specifically, Congress cannot trammel the President's constitutional authority to conduct the Nation's foreign affairs and to recognize foreign governments by directing the relocation of an embassy. This is particularly true where, as here, the location of the embassy is not only of great significance in establishing the United States' relationship with a single country, but may well also determine our relations with an entire region of the world.

Finally, to the extent that S. 770 is intended to affect recognition policy with respect to Jerusalem, it is inconsistent with the exclusivity of the President's recognition power. Our conclusions are not novel. With respect to the Foreign Relations Authorization Act, FY 1994 & 1995, Pub. L. No. 103-236, § 221, 108 Stat. 382, 421 (1994), which included provisions purporting to require the establishment of an office in Lhasa, Tibet, the President stated that he would "implement them to the extent consistent with [his] constitutional responsibilities." 1 Pub. Papers of William J. Clinton 807, 808 (1994). The Reagan Administration objected in 1984 to a bill to compel the relocation of the United States Embassy from Tel Aviv to Jerusalem, on the grounds that the decision was "so closely connected with the President's exclusive constitutional power and responsibility to recognize, and to conduct ongoing relations with, foreign governments as to, in our view, be beyond the proper scope of legislative action." Letter for Dante B. Fascell, Chairman, Committee on Foreign Affairs, United States House of Representatives, from George P. Shultz, Secretary of State at 2 (Feb. 13, 1984). Again, in 1987, President Reagan stated that he would construe certain provisions of the Foreign Relations Authorization Act, FY 1988 & 1989, including those that forbade "the closing of any consulates," in a manner that would avoid unconstitutional interference with the President's authority with respect to diplomacy. 2 Pub. Papers of Ronald Reagan 1541, 1542 (1987). Indeed, as long ago as 1876, President Grant declared in a signing statement that he would construe legislation in such a way as to avoid "implying a right in the legislative branch to direct the closing or discontinuing of any of the diplomatic or consular offices of the Government," because if Congress sought to do so, it would "invade the constitutional rights of the Executive." 7 Messages and Papers of the Presidents 377, 378 (James D. Richardson ed., 1898).

Finally, it does not matter in this instance that Congress has sought to achieve its objectives through the exercise of its spending power, because the condition it would impose on obligating appropriations is unconstitutional. *See United States v. Butler*, 297 U.S. 1, 74 (1936); 16 Op. O.L.C. at 28–29 ("As we have said on several prior occasions, Congress may not use its power over appropriation of public funds 'to attach conditions to Executive Branch appropriations requiring the President to relinquish his constitutional discretion in foreign affairs.'") (quoting Issues Raised by Foreign

Relations Authorization Bill, 14 Op. O.L.C. 37, 42 n.3 (1990)) (quoting Constitutionality of Proposed Statutory Provision Requiring Prior Congressional Notification for Certain CIA Covert Actions, 13 Op. O.L.C. 258, 261–62 (1989)). For the above reasons, we believe that the bill's provisions conditioning appropriated funds on the building and opening of a United States Embassy in Jerusalem are unconstitutional.

Constitutionality of Section 7054 of the Fiscal Year 2009 Foreign Appropriations Act
33 Op. O.L.C. ___ (June 1, 2009)

* * * * *

I.

Section 7054 provides as follows:

> None of the funds made available under title I of this Act may be used to pay expenses for any United States delegation to any specialized agency, body, or commission of the United Nations if such commission is chaired or presided over by a country, the government of which the Secretary of State has determined, for purposes of section 6(j)(1) of the Export Administration Act of 1979 (50 U.S.C. app. 2405(j)(1)), supports international terrorism.

Section 6(j)(1) of the Export Administration Act ("EAA") mandates a license for the export of goods to a country the government of which the Secretary has determined "has repeatedly provided support for acts of international terrorism" ("terrorist list state"). The limitation imposed by section 7054 applies only to funds made available by title I of the Foreign Appropriations Act. You have informed us, however, that title I is the only source of appropriated funds currently available to the State Department for a number of purposes related to the administration of foreign affairs, including the carrying out of diplomatic and consular programs. You have further explained that title I appropriations are the only operating funds available to pay for State Department delegations to specialized U.N. entities. Section 7054 would thus effectively preclude the State Department from including any representatives in U.S. delegations to any specialized U.N. agency, commission or body chaired by a terrorist list state. You have also informed us that most such government delegations are headed by a State Department official and include one or more additional State Department officials.

In signing the Omnibus Act, President Obama issued the following statement:

> Certain provisions of the bill, in titles I and IV of Division B, title IV of Division E, and title VII of Division H, would unduly interfere with my constitutional authority in the area of foreign affairs by effectively directing the Executive on how to proceed or not proceed in negotiations or discussions with international organizations and foreign governments. I will not treat these provisions as limiting my ability to negotiate and enter into agreements with foreign nations.

Daily Comp. Pres. Doc. No. 2009-00145 (Mar. 11, 2009) (President Obama's Statement on Signing the Omnibus Appropriations Act, 2009). Section 7054 is within title VII of division H, and purports to "effectively direct[] the Executive on how to proceed or not proceed in negotiations or discussions with international organizations and foreign governments." Thus, although the President's signing statement did not identify section 7054 specifically, it encompasses that provision.

The same restriction on the use of appropriated funds has appeared in successive appropriations acts since fiscal year 2005. President Bush indicated in signing statements accompanying these appropriations acts that the Executive Branch would construe such restrictions as "advisory." Consistent with President Bush's direction, the Department sent representatives to participate from January 19, 2009 through January 23, 2009 in a session of a U.N. specialized body—the executive board of the United Nations Development Program ("UNDP") and the United Nations Population Fund ("UNFPA")—that was chaired at the time by Iran, a terrorist list state. Another meeting of the executive board of UNDP/UNFPA, which Iran still chairs, is scheduled for May 26, 2009 to June 5, 2009, and the State Department—the lead U.S. participant in the proceedings of this body—believes it would be advantageous to United States foreign policy objectives to send State Department officials to accompany the U.S. delegation. Moreover, because the State Department is contemplating participation in other upcoming meetings of specialized U.N. entities that may fall within the restriction imposed by section 7054, and because the Department may receive little prior notice that a terrorist list state will chair a particular U.N. entity in the future, you have asked for more general guidance on whether and under what conditions the Department must comply with section 7054. * * *

III.

In our view, section 7054 impermissibly interferes with the President's authority to manage the Nation's foreign diplomacy. To be sure, a determination that a duly enacted statute unconstitutionally infringes on Executive authority must be "well-founded," Memorandum for the Heads of Executive Departments and Agencies, Re: Presidential Signing Statements, 74 Fed. Reg. 10669 (2009); see also Presidential Authority to Decline to Execute Unconstitutional Statutes, 18 Op. O.L.C. 199, 200–01 (1994), and Congress quite clearly possesses significant article I powers in the area of foreign affairs, including with respect to questions of war and neutrality, commerce and trade with other nations, foreign aid, and immigration. As ample precedent demonstrates, however, Congress's power to legislate in the foreign affairs area does not include the authority to attempt to dictate the modes and means by which the President engages in international diplomacy with foreign countries and through international fora. Section 7054 constitutes an attempt to exercise just such authority: It effectively denies the President the use of his preferred agents—representatives of the State Department—to participate in delegations to specified U.N. entities chaired or presided over by certain countries. As this Office has explained, such statutory restrictions are impermissible because the President's constitutional authority to conduct diplomacy bars Congress from attempting to determine the "form and manner in which the United States . . . maintain[s] relations with foreign nations." Issues Raised by Provisions Directing Issuance of Official or Diplomatic Passports, 16 Op. O.L.C. 18, 21 (1992) (citing Issues Raised by Foreign Relations Authorization Bill, 14 Op. O.L.C. 37, 38 (1990)).

The President's basic authority to conduct the Nation's diplomatic relations derives from his specific constitutional authorities to "make Treaties," to "appoint Ambassadors . . . and Consuls" (subject to Senate advice and consent), U.S. Const. art. II, § 2, cl. 2, and to "receive Ambassadors and other public Ministers," id. art. II, § 3. It also flows more generally from the President's status as Chief Executive, id. art. II, § 1, cl. 1, and from the requirement in article II, section 3 of the Constitution that the President "shall take Care that the Laws be faithfully executed." As a result of these authorities, it is well established that the President is "the constitutional representative of the United States in its dealings with foreign nations." *United States v. Louisiana*, 363 U.S. 1, 35 (1960); *see also Ex parte Hennen*, 38 U.S. (13 Pet.) 225, 235 (1839) ("As the executive magistrate of the country, [the President] is the only functionary intrusted with the foreign relations of the nation."). As John Marshall noted in his famous speech of March 7, 1800 before the House of Representatives (while still a member of that body), the Executive Branch is "entrusted with the whole foreign intercourse of the nation, with the negotiation of all its treaties, with the power of demanding a reciprocal performance of the article, which is accountable to the nation for the violation of its engagements, with foreign nations, and for the consequences resulting from such violation." John Marshall, Speech of March 7, 1800, in 4 The Papers of John Marshall 104–05 (Charles T. Cullen ed., 1984). The President is, in other words, the "organ" of the Nation's diplomatic relations. Pacificus No. 1 (June 29, 1793), reprinted in 15 The Papers of Alexander Hamilton 33, 38 (Harold C. Syrett ed., 1969) (italics removed). * * *

Congress may by statute affirm the President's authority to determine whether, how, when, and through whom to engage in foreign diplomacy. But when Congress takes the unusual step of purporting to impose statutory restrictions on this well recognized authority, the Executive Branch has resisted. For example, Congress enacted an appropriations rider in 1913, providing that "[h]ereafter the Executive shall not extend or accept any invitation to participate in any international congress, conference, or like event, without first having specific authority of law to do so." Act of Mar. 4, 1913, ch. 149, 37 Stat. 913 (1913) (codified at 22 U.S.C. § 262 (2006)). The Executive has not acted in accord with that requirement, see Henry M. Wriston, American Participation in International Conferences, 20 Am. J. Int'l L. 33, 40 (1926) (observing that "there is not a single case [since 1913] where the President secured from Congress authorization to accept an invitation to a conference of a political or diplomatic character," and that "since 1917 the whole practice of requesting Congress for authority to accept invitations to any sort of international conference has virtually fallen into disuse"), and the measure is now a "known dead letter," Louis Henkin, Foreign Affairs and the United States Constitution 118 (2d ed. 1996). Indeed, when first informed of the provision's existence (more than three years after its enactment), President Wilson reportedly termed it "utterly futile." Wriston at 39. Wilson's dismissive characterization accorded with the view, expressed in a leading treatise of the day, that the President "cannot be compelled by a resolution of either house or of both houses of Congress to exercise" his constitutional powers with respect to "instituting negotiations." Samuel B. Crandall, Treaties: Their Making and Enforcement 74 (2d ed. 1916).

In more recent decades, the Executive has continued to object when Congress has attempted to impose limits on the form and manner by which the President exercises his diplomatic powers. In particular, the Executive has asserted on numerous occasions that the President possesses the "'exclusive authority to determine the time, scope, and objectives'" of international negotiations or discussions, including the authority "to determine the individuals who will" represent the United States in those diplomatic exchanges. And this Office has "repeatedly objected on constitutional grounds to Congressional attempts to mandate the time, manner and content of diplomatic negotiations," including in the context of potential engagement with international fora. See Memorandum for Alan Kreczko, Legal Adviser, National Security Council, from Walter Dellinger, Assistant Attorney General, Office of Legal Counsel, Re: WTO Dispute Settlement Review Commission Act at 3 (Feb. 9, 1995) ("Dellinger WTO Memo").

For example, we concluded that it would be unconstitutional for Congress to adopt joint resolutions mandating that the President enter negotiations to modify the rules of the World Trade Organization. See id. Relatedly, we determined that a legislative provision purporting to prevent the State Department from expending appropriated funds on delegates to an international conference unless legislative representatives were included in the delegation was an "impermissibl[e] interfere[nce]" with the President's "constitutional responsibility to represent the United States abroad and thus to choose the individuals through whom the Nation's foreign affairs are conducted." 14 Op. O.L.C. at 38, 41. And the Executive Branch has objected numerous times on constitutional grounds to legislative provisions purporting to preclude any U.S. government employee from negotiating with (or recognizing) the Palestine Liberation Organization ("PLO") or its representatives until the PLO had met certain conditions.

In objecting to one such provision, this Office explained that Congress "possesses no constitutional authority to forbid the President from engaging in diplomatic contacts." Memorandum for Carol T. Crawford, Assistant Attorney General, Office of Legislative Affairs, from John O. McGinnis, Deputy Assistant Attorney General, Office of Legal Counsel, Re: H.R. 2939 at 3 (Oct. 19, 1989). Other Executive Branch precedents are to similar effect. See Bill to Relocate United States Embassy from Tel Aviv to Jerusalem, 19 Op. O.L.C. 123, 126 (1995).[11]

---

11. See also Placing of United States Armed Forces Under United Nations Operational or Tactical Control, 20 Op. O.L.C. 182, 186 (1996) (proposed bill prohibiting the obligation or expenditure of appropriated funds by the Department of Defense for the activities of elements of the armed

Judicial support for the Executive Branch's position can be found in *Earth Island Institute v. Christopher*, 6 F.3d 648 (9th Cir. 1993). In that case, the United States Court of Appeals for the Ninth Circuit struck down a statute purporting to require the Secretary of State to initiate negotiations with, and otherwise engage, foreign governments for the purposes of developing and entering into international agreements for the protection of sea turtles. The court deemed the statute an unconstitutional "intru[sion] upon the conduct of foreign relations by the Executive." Id. at 653. Additional judicial support can be found in the Supreme Court's clear dicta in *United States v. Curtiss-Wright Export Corp.*, 299 U.S. 304 (1936): "[T]he President alone has the power to speak or listen as a representative of the nation. . . . Into the field of negotiation the Senate cannot intrude; and Congress itself is powerless to invade it," id. at 319.

That the President possesses the exclusive power to determine how to conduct diplomacy with other nations does not mean that Congress is without relevant authority. For example, the Senate must approve the treaties the President negotiates, see U.S. Const. art. II, § 2, cl. 2, and Congress can, by a subsequently enacted statute, limit the effect of treaties, see *Whitney v. Robertson*, 124 U.S. 190, 194 (1888). The Senate may even refuse its consent to a treaty if an international organization makes entry into such treaty a necessary precondition of United States participation in the proceedings of that organization. The statutory limitation at issue here, however, does not constitute such an exercise of Congress's legitimate authority in the area of foreign affairs; rather, it purports to restrict the President from engaging in diplomacy through international fora that are organized pursuant to a treaty to which the United States is a party. See United Nations Charter, Jun. 26, 1945, 59 Stat. 1031, 1031. Section 7054, in other words, seeks to regulate who may participate in the delegations the President may send to the international fora of an organization to which the United States belongs, and at which the United States would be received were its delegations to be sent. * * *

For these reasons, section 7054's prevention of the inclusion of State Department representatives in delegations to the specified U.N. entities is unconstitutional.

IV.

Our conclusion is not affected by the fact that Congress has drafted its restriction as a prohibition on the use of appropriated funds rather than as a direct prohibition. Congress's spending power is undoubtedly broad, and, as a general matter, Congress may decline to appropriate money altogether for a particular function, or place binding conditions on the appropriations it does make. But as the Executive Branch has repeatedly observed, "it does not necessarily follow that [Congress] may attach whatever condition it desires to an appropriation," for "Congress may not deploy [the spending power] to accomplish unconstitutional ends." The Supreme Court has affirmed this fundamental proposition on a number of occasions. The most notable

---

forces placed under the United Nations' operational or tactical control would "impermissibly undermin[e] the President's constitutional authority with respect to the conduct of diplomacy") . . . .

case is *United States v. Lovett*, 328 U.S. 303 (1946). There, the Court expressly rejected the proposition that the appropriations power is "plenary and not subject to judicial review," and struck down as an unconstitutional bill of attainder a provision in an appropriations act that barred the payment of salaries to named federal employees. Id. at 305, 307; *see also United States v. Klein*, 80 U.S. 128, 147–48 (1871) (deeming an appropriations proviso that "impair[ed] the effect of a [presidential] pardon" void as an unconstitutional "infring[ement]" on "the constitutional power of the Executive"); *Office of Personnel Mgmt. v. Richmond*, 496 U.S. 414, 435 (1990) (White, J., concurring) (noting that "the [majority] does not state that statutory restrictions on appropriations may never fall even . . . if they encroach on the powers reserved to another branch of the Federal Government").

Consistent with these precedents, the Executive Branch has long adhered to the view that "Congress cannot use the appropriations power to control a Presidential power that is beyond its direct control." Presidential Certification Regarding the Provision of Documents to the House of Representatives Under the Mexican Debt Disclosure Act of 1995, 20 Op. O.L.C. 253, 267 (1996) (internal quotation marks omitted); Mutual Security Program—Cutoff of Funds from Office of Inspector General and Comptroller, 41 Op. Att'y Gen. 507, 530 (1960) (Att'y Gen. Rogers).[16] This proposition applies with equal force in the foreign affairs context. . . .

V.

Accordingly, the Secretary would be justified in disregarding section 7054—and using funds appropriated in title I for the purpose of paying the expenses of delegations to U.N. entities chaired by terrorist list states.

---

1. *Bold Claims of Exclusive Power?* These opinions assert exclusive presidential authority to determine the "manner and mode" of conducting the nation's foreign affairs and seem to go a long way toward asserting an exclusive power to determine the substance of the nation's foreign policy. This may not be surprising given that these are the views of the executive branch. Do the opinions provide a persuasive argument for their assertions?

2. *Limited Leverage Through Appropriations?* Only Congress can create federal offices and only Congress can appropriate funds. Why should Congress not be able to determine that it will create an office (an ambassadorship, for example) but only

---

16. The Supreme Court suggested in South Dakota v. Dole, 483 U.S. 203 (1987), that "the constitutional limitations on Congress when exercising its spending power" vis á vis the States "are less exacting than those on its authority to regulate directly." Id. at 209. But the Court has since made clear that Congress does not enjoy such heightened latitude when it purports to impose spending conditions on the Executive Branch, for "Dole did not involve separation-of-powers principles." Metro. Wash. Airports Auth. v. Citizens for the Abatement of Aircraft Noise, Inc., 501 U.S. 252, 271 (1991); see also 16 Op. O.L.C. at 29 (Dole does not apply to spending conditions in the separation-of-powers context).

to perform certain functions and only to pursue certain ends? Why should Congress not be able to appropriate funds but only for specified purposes? *Zivotofsky* seems to affirm Congress's power: "it is Congress that makes laws, and in countless ways its laws will and should shape the Nation's course. The Executive is not free from the ordinary controls and checks of Congress merely because foreign affairs are at issue. It is not for the President alone to determine the whole content of the Nation's foreign policy. . . . Congress may [] express its disagreement with the President in myriad ways. For example, it may enact an embargo, decline to confirm an ambassador, or even declare war."

On the other hand, the spending power seems different. No government action is possible without the expenditure of some funds. Congress's power of the purse, then, could allow it to exercise practical and effective control over all aspects of military and foreign affairs, even those that seem exclusively committed to the President. This concern permeates the two OLC opinions above. Do you think they strike the right balance between the legitimate institutional interests of Congress and the President?

2. Treaty Processes

a. Overview of Treaty Powers

Powers of the President and Senate

The Constitution states that the President shall have the power to make treaties, provided two-thirds of the members of the Senate present advise and consent in each case. U.S. Const., art. II, sec. 2, par. 2. The requirement for a two-thirds vote testifies to an apparent wariness of international entanglements; recall that advice and consent to presidential appointments requires only a bare majority.

Although the treaty-making power is thus expressly shared between the Senate and the President, the precise boundaries of each participant's responsibilities are unclear. Treaty-making consists of negotiation, approval, ratification, the exchange of ratifications and proclamation. Although the last two steps may be considered merely administrative requirements for the formal completion of an international pact, the Constitution is silent as to how the first and critical discretionary step — negotiation — is conducted. Historically, the President has acquired the task of negotiating treaties, while the Senate has played a more passive role, entering the process at the approval stage. The Senate has managed to continue to be influential in treaty-making, however, by refusing approval, placing restrictions on treaties, or purporting to aid the President in treaty interpretation. *See generally* Cong. Research Serv., Treaties and Other International Agreements: The Role of the United States Senate (1984).

President Washington originally interpreted the Senate's "advise and consent" power to mean that, before a treaty is negotiated, the Senate's advice must be sought on a preliminary basis. In Untrodden Ground: How Presidents Interpret the Constitution 35–36 (2015), Professor Bruff explains what happened to that notion:

During the process of forming the Constitution, concerns surfaced that the role of the Senate in advising and consenting to nominations and treaties would blur the separation of powers between the branches. [But] the Senate might be a wise advisory council on foreign relations, perhaps even playing an active role in negotiating treaties as well as approving them. Early in his presidency, George Washington explored this possibility. The results foreclosed an active role for the Senate in advising on treaty negotiations, shifting that power into the executive branch exclusively.

In the summer of 1789, President Washington and Secretary of War Henry Knox were formulating the new nation's initial policy regarding the Indian tribes. The two men shared a view that would later seem relatively advanced and humane, that Indian relations should be managed through purchase or treaty acquisition of land and not through brutal and uncompensated conquest. They were also attempting to seize the initiative in forming Indian policy, leaving Congress in a reactive role.

Secretary Knox informed the president that he had drafted a treaty providing for a three-person commission to negotiate peace between the Creek Indians and Georgia. Washington thought he should consult the Senate regarding the instructions for the envoys. Both the president and the Senate expected consultation to occur before the final terms of a treaty were set. What ensued would foreclose any formal prior consultation of the Senate by presidents.

Armed with a message containing seven complex questions for the Senate, Washington proceeded to their chamber. He gave the treaty papers to Vice President Adams (sitting in his constitutional role as president of the Senate). Adams read them, trying to make himself heard over street noise. The senators, who were unprepared to respond, began asking questions. More ominously, Senator Maclay, an early and determined opponent of Washington's, made a series of motions to obstruct or delay the provision of advice.

Eventually, after much discomfort all around, a proposal arose to refer the questions to a committee. This triggered an outburst of Washington's famous (and usually suppressed) temper. Declaring that "this defeats my every purpose in coming here," Washington stormed out of the chamber. He did return some days later and obtained the Senate's approval to sending the commissioners, but he never again sought its advice on treaty negotiations. Henceforth, presidents have communicated with the full Senate only in writing and usually only for its consent to treaties already negotiated.

For institutional reasons, even the early Senate of twenty six members was unsuited to a role as an advisory council. Four intrinsic problems were evident in the Creek treaty fiasco. First, the quality of advice depends on the information available to the adviser, but the executive branch cannot bring the Senate fully into its everyday activities. Second, because the Senate has always been far less hierarchical than the larger House of Representatives, harnessing it to a particular task is notoriously difficult. Third, the presence of the "loyal" opposition, personified by Maclay in 1789, makes confidentiality difficult to preserve and offers ample opportunities for obstructionism. Fourth, senators have political bases independent of the president and cannot be controlled like an executive council.

Washington was used to hierarchical military advice from generals who were loyal to him and fully acquainted with the facts. He could replicate that system within the executive branch but not with the Senate. Today's Senate, four times as large as the original body and a deeply fractured institution, cannot provide reliable, confidential, and cogent advice in advance of negotiations, even with the organizational advantages of the committee system. Washington had made a misstep, but he rapidly learned his lesson.

The Senate now does not formally advise on treaties before or during negotiations. Instead, the President appoints and instructs the negotiators and follows their progress in negotiations. If the President approves what they have negotiated and obtains the advice and consent of the Senate, the President may "ratify" or "make" the treaty. Because ratification is thus a discretionary power, the President may decline to make a treaty even after obtaining the Senate's consent.

This is not to minimize the extraordinary potential impact of the Senate approval process. The lack of consent to a treaty has played havoc in more than a few Presidents' foreign policy plans. An important example is the Senate's rejection of the Treaty of Versailles. President Wilson referred to the Senate thereafter as the "graveyard of treaties."

The Senate, of course, is not constrained to base its approval or disapproval decisions on any particular criteria. Thus, the Senate may deny its consent not because it thinks a proposed treaty would contravene the national interest, but because, for example, of partisan politics.

The Senate has also managed to forestall some potential agreements through inaction. A familiar example is the International Convention on the Prevention and Punishment of the Crime of Genocide, which was placed before the Senate in 1949, but not consented to until 1986. In fact, because the Senate conditioned final ratification on the enactment of implementing legislation, ratification did not occur until 1988, following passage of the Genocide Convention Implementation Act of 1987, 18 U.S.C. § 1091 *et seq.*

The Senate may modify a treaty through the use of reservations, giving it another important source of influence in the treaty-making process. A reservation is a unilateral statement purporting to exclude or modify the legal effect of certain treaty provisions as they might be applied to the United States. International law permits such reservations unless expressly precluded by treaty or "incompatible with the object or the purpose of the treaty." *See* Vienna Convention on the Law of

Treaties, arts. 2, 17–23, U.N. Doc. No. A/Conf. 39/27, *reprinted in* 63 Am. J. Int. L. 875 (1969). The constitutional authority of the Senate to impose reservations has not been questioned seriously. If the Senate may give or withhold consent, it is thought to follow that the Senate may also give its consent based on the condition that changes be made.

Conditions may be imposed not only to modify international obligations of a treaty but also to control its effect in the United States. Such reservations, for example, include Senate insistence that a treaty not take effect or that action not be taken under it by United States officials without the approval of Congress. Other reservations have required the President to perform some domestic act to affect the treaty's impact. For example, the Senate Reservation to the Reciprocal Military Service Convention with Great Britain, June 3, 1918, 40 Stat. 1620, required the President, before ratifying the Convention, to issue a general certificate exempting from military service citizens of the United States in Great Britain who were outside the ages of military service specified in United States laws. He fulfilled his obligation through an exchange of diplomatic notes.

For international purposes, the President determines the United States' position as to the meaning of a treaty, but domestically, Congress and the courts also contribute. Congress interprets a treaty when it considers implementing legislation or other legislation on the same subject. The result is that, even though Congress admits to giving the executive interpretation "great weight," Congress effectively asserts an independent right of interpretation. Courts, for their part, may be called upon to interpret treaties in the course of adjudicating cases arising under their terms. As illustrated in the Supreme Court's post-9/11 jurisprudence, the courts may reject executive branch treaty interpretations, just as they may reject executive interpretations of ordinary statutes. *See, e.g., Hamdan v. Rumsfeld*, 548 U.S. 557, 630–31 (2006) (rejecting the executive branch's interpretation of the Geneva Conventions as inapplicable to the armed conflict between the United States and al Qaeda).

During the 1980s, a notable controversy emerged concerning the relevance to treaty interpretation of the Senate's understanding of a treaty at the time it gave its consent, when that understanding was not codified in a series of conditions or reservations. In 1972, the United States concluded an Anti-ballistic Missile (ABM) treaty with the Soviet Union, Treaty on the Limitation of Anti-Ballistic Missile Systems, May 26, 1972, United States-U.S.S.R., 23 U.S.T. 3435, T.I.A.S. No. 7503. That treaty was then interpreted as imposing a perpetual ban on the development, testing, or deployment of mobile or space-based ABM systems. Notwithstanding this view, the Defense Department, in late 1985, began to argue that the treaty did not ban the testing and development of exotic, so-called "Star Wars" space-based defense systems. The interpretation, supported by State Department Legal Adviser Abraham Sofaer, precipitated strong dissent both within the Administration and Congress. Critics, including all but one of the eight key negotiators of the ABM treaty, charged first that the text and negotiating record of the treaty simply did not support the Sofaer view. David C. Morrison, *Rereading ABM*, 19 Nat'l J. 2304 (1987); S. Rep. No. 164,

100th Cong., 1st Sess. 28–36 (1987). Equally important, Senators insisted that, even if records of secret negotiations did support the Sofaer view, the executive could not constitutionally reinterpret the treaty in a manner that differed from the executive's original presentation of the treaty to the Senate. Any such power of unilateral rein-terpretation, it was argued, would undermine the contemplated role of the Senate in consenting to a treaty before it could be formally made and ratified. *But see Rainbow Navigation v. Department of the Navy*, 911 F.2d 797 (D.C. Cir. 1990), *cert. denied*, 499 U.S. 906 (1991) (in light of plain treaty language, Navy not bound by alleged execu-tive representations to Senate, in seeking advice and consent on U.S.-Icelandic trade treaty, that U.S. flag shipper to Iceland would not be disadvantaged as con-sequence of treaty). For a challenge to the Reagan Administration ABM interpreta-tion by one of the treaty's negotiators, see RAYMOND L. GARTHOFF, POLICY VERSUS THE LAW: THE REINTERPRETATION OF THE ABM TREATY (1987). *See also Review of ABM Treaty Interpretation Dispute and SDI: Hearing Before the Subcomm. on Arms Control, Int'l Security and Science of the House Comm. on Foreign Relations*, 100th Cong., 1st Sess. (1987). The contending positions are explored thoroughly in *Symposium: Arms Control Treaty Interpretation*, 137 U. PA. L. REV. 1353 (1989).

Congress undertook a variety of legislative measures to prevent the Administra-tion from implementing its reinterpretation. After both the House and Senate adopted amendments to the 1988 defense authorization bill that would have required U.S. adherence to the traditional interpretation of the ABM treaty, White House advisers and congressional leaders agreed on a compromise. Without naming the ABM treaty, the compromise act prohibited for one year those specific Star Wars tests that would be in violation of the traditional interpretation, and the purchase of hardware nec-essary to conduct those tests. National Defense Authorization Act for Fiscal Years 1988 and 1989, Pub. L. No. 100-180, § 225, 101 Stat. 1019, 1056 (1987).

With the concurrence of the Reagan Administration, Congress subsequently incorporated language in the National Defense Authorization Act for Fiscal Year 1989 extending the ban on Strategic Defense Initiative (SDI) tests that would violate the traditional interpretation of the ABM treaty. Pub. L. No. 100-456, § 223, 102 Stat. 1942 (1988). The George H.W. Bush Administration left this deal between Congress and the President on SDI testing intact. National Defense Authorization Act for Fiscal Years 1990 and 1991, Pub. L. No. 101-189, § 223, 103 Stat. 1397–98 (1989). Although the implications of the ABM Treaty for U.S. defense policy remained contested in other respects as late as the summer of 1991, *see* Morrison, *Reviving the ABM Debate*, NAT'L J., Aug. 10, 1991, at 1984, the breakup of the Soviet Union seemed likely to ren-der moot much of the previous decade's debate over the desirability of space-based anti-ballistic weapons. The Clinton Administration informed Congress in July 1993 that it intended to follow the "traditional" or "review" reading of the ABM Treaty. The George W. Bush Administration finally resolved the matter, however, in a largely unanticipated move — it announced that the United States was simply withdrawing from the ABM pact, a position the treaty explicitly authorized the President to adopt.

Miles A. Pomper, *Bush's Move to Void ABM Pact Has Democrats Looking for Options*, C.Q. WEEKLY, Dec. 15, 2001, at 2986.

At different times, the power to terminate a treaty has been claimed for the President, for the President and Senate jointly, and for Congress alone. Presidents have claimed authority, presumably under their foreign affairs powers, to act for the United States to terminate treaties, whether in accordance with their terms or in violation of international law. In some situations, a President has invited another party to terminate a treaty, achieving the same result.

Whether or not Congress has any treaty termination power as a formal matter, it does have the capacity effectively to breach treaties. It can accomplish termination by refusing to pass legislation necessary to the implementation of treaty obligations, passing legislation inconsistent with a treaty, or seeking indirectly to compel the President to terminate a treaty or induce another party to do so.

Permissible Scope of Treaties

The Constitution does not expressly impose substantive limits on the treaty power, nor does it directly imply that any exist. The Supreme Court has not held any provision of any treaty unconstitutional, and few have been seriously challenged there. It is likely, however, that treaties are subject to the constitutional limitations that apply to all exercises of federal power, principally the prohibitions contained in the Bill of Rights. The leading case is *Reid v. Covert*, 354 U.S. 1 (1957), involving the overseas courts-martial of civilian wives for killing their serviceman husbands. Military jurisdiction assertedly rested, in part, on executive agreements providing military jurisdiction over civilian dependents of U.S. servicepeople overseas. A Supreme Court plurality said: "[W]e reject the idea that when the United States acts against citizens abroad it can do so free of the Bill of Rights. The United States is entirely a creature of the Constitution. Its power and authority have no other source." *Id*. at 5–6. Therefore: "It would be manifestly contrary to the . . . Constitution . . . to . . . [permit] the United States to exercise power under an international agreement without observing constitutional prohibitions." *Id*. at 17. The holding of *Reid*, however, was that the asserted jurisdiction was unauthorized, not that the executive agreement was unconstitutional.

In addition to the Bill of Rights, it has been argued that structural provisions of the Constitution likewise limit the treaty power. For example, although the Constitution does not give the states any role in the treaty-making process, the claim was made early in this century that the Tenth Amendment protects the states by forbidding treaties to be made on subjects constitutionally reserved to the states. This argument was rejected by the Supreme Court in *Missouri v. Holland*, 252 U.S. 416 (1920), involving a treaty between Canada and the United States to protect migratory birds through hunting regulations. Although this subject matter would today not be viewed as reserved to the states even vis-a-vis Congressional enactments, Justice Holmes went so far as to imply that, even if the tenth amendment were a limit on Congress's regulatory power, it would not similarly limit the treaty power. In recent years, scholars have questioned this contention. *See, e.g.,* Curtis A. Bradley, *The Treaty Power and American Federalism*, 97 Mich. L. Rev. 390, 400–09 (1998). The Supreme Court recently took a case that gave it the opportunity to reconsider *Missouri v. Holland*. In *Bond v. United States*, 134 S. Ct. 2077 (2014), a Pennsylvania woman was charged with violating the Chemical Weapons Convention Implementation Act. The woman had determined to take revenge on her husband's pregnant mistress by smearing dangerous chemicals on the handle of the door to the mistress's home. The mistress suffered a burned thumb. The Supreme Court instead avoided the constitutional issue and interpreted the Implementation Act as not covering the situation.

Similarly, members of the House of Representatives have argued that treaties may not be used to dispose of federal property because article IV of the Constitution expressly vests the property disposition power in both Houses of Congress. In a suit seeking to block the transfer of federal property to Panama under treaties negotiated by President Carter, the U.S. Court of Appeals rejected that position. *Edwards v. Carter*, 580 F.2d 1055 (D.C. Cir. 1978), *cert. denied*, 436 U.S. 907 (1978).

Legal Impact of Treaties

The laws of nations differ as to the domestic legal status of a treaty invoked as the source of governing law in a lawsuit. England regards treaties as only international obligations, without effect as domestic law unless so implemented by Parliament. Other countries may regard most treaties as providing rules of decision in domestic cases without further legislative action.

The Supremacy Clause includes treaties among the sources of law that represent "the supreme Law of the Land." U.S. Const. art. VI, cl. 2. Article VI was designed principally to assure the supremacy of treaties to state law, but it has also been interpreted to mean that treaties may become domestic law upon ratification, if they are "self-executing."

The distinction between "self-executing" and "non-self-executing" treaties recognizes that, although treaties bind the United States internationally, U.S. courts may not always implement the treaties directly as sources of decisional rules in relevant domestic cases. A non-self-executing treaty is not a source of domestic law without implementing legislation. To determine whether or not a treaty is self-executing, courts purport to examine the intent of the negotiating parties. In fact, courts may give predominant consideration to whether regarding a treaty as self-executing will prove impracticable or derogate from Congress's legislative authority. Thomas Buergenthal & Harold G. Maier, Public International Law in a Nutshell 194–200 (1985); *see also* Iwasawa, *The Doctrine of Self-Executing Treaties in the United States: A Critical Analysis*, 26 Va. J. Int'l L. 627 (1986). Chief Justice Marshall, in *Foster v. Neilson*, 27 U.S. (2 Pet.) 253 (1829), *overruled on other grounds, United States v. Percheman*, 32 U.S. (7 Pet.) 51 (1833), recognized that a treaty must be regarded as equivalent to an act of legislation, when the treaty operates of itself without the aid of any legislative provision. Thus, for example, the Peace Treaty of 1783 and the Jay Treaty of 1794 were self-executing in restoring Tory land rights. *Fairfax's Devisee v.*

Hunter's Lessee, 11 U.S. (7 Cranch) 603 (1813). Marshall said, however: "[W]hen the terms of the stipulation import a contract—when either of the parties engages to perform a particular act, the treaty addresses itself to the political, not the judicial department; and the legislature must execute the contract before it can become a rule for the court." *Foster*, 27 U.S. at 314.

Because of our constitutional distribution of power, there are presumably some measures which cannot be authorized by a self-executing treaty. A treaty may not appropriate funds; the Constitution expressly provides: "No money shall be drawn from the Treasury, but in Consequence of Appropriations made by Law." U.S. Const. art. I, § 9, cl. 7. Therefore, any financial undertaking by the United States will require appropriation by Congress. A treaty likewise may not enact criminal law; only Congress may prescribe penal sanctions. It has also been said that the United States cannot declare war by treaty; Congress must declare it.

A treaty of any kind lacks status as law if it is not binding internationally, it is invalid under international law, or if expired, or terminated, or destroyed by breach.

Congress presumably has power to do what is "necessary and proper" to implement a treaty even if its actions are otherwise not within its expressly enumerated powers. There is still debate as to whether Congress is constitutionally and morally obligated to implement treaties once made. It has been urged that the House of Representatives may not refuse to execute a treaty because the treaty amounts to a national pledge—although such refusal would surely be judicially unreviewable. The opposing viewpoint is that the House of Representatives must use its own judgment as to what is most conducive to the public good. This debate still exists in principle, although Congress has not yet failed to carry out international obligations in practice, at least at the time of original commitment. Although Congress may later enact legislation inconsistent with an old treaty, it typically goes no farther following ratification than shaping and limiting important details of implementation, sometimes not giving the President the precise authorities or as much money as he may urge that a treaty requires.

Because treaties are law and often deal with matters within the purview of congressional legislation, it has sometimes happened that a treaty and an act of Congress are inconsistent. The legal consequences have long been settled by the Supreme Court. In *Whitney v. Robertson*, 124 U.S. 190, 194 (1888) the Court held that a treaty is on the same footing as legislation; because both are the supreme law of the land, if the two are inconsistent, the more recent controls. There is, however, a strong presumption against the implied repeal of a treaty. *Compare Palestine Information Office v. Schultz*, 853 F.2d 932 (D.C. Cir. 1988) (upholding the closing of PLO's Washington, D.C. Palestine Information Office under the Foreign Missions Office), *with United States v. Palestine Liberation Organization*, 695 F. Supp. 1456 (S.D.N.Y. 1988) (holding that Anti-Terrorism Act of 1987 did not require U.S. to close PLO's permanent observer office at United Nations, in violation of the "Agreement Between the United States and the United Nations Regarding the Headquarters of the United Nations").

b. Presidential Treaty Implementation

Medellín v. Texas

552 U.S. 491 (2008)

Chief Justice ROBERTS delivered the opinion of the Court.

The International Court of Justice (ICJ), located in the Hague, is a tribunal established pursuant to the United Nations Charter to adjudicate disputes between member states. In the *Case Concerning Avena and Other Mexican Nationals* (*Mex. v. U.S.*), 2004 I.C.J. 12 (Judgment of Mar. 31) (*Avena*), that tribunal considered a claim brought by Mexico against the United States. The ICJ held that, based on violations of the Vienna Convention, 51 named Mexican nationals were entitled to review and reconsideration of their state-court convictions and sentences in the United States. This was so regardless of any forfeiture of the right to raise Vienna Convention claims because of a failure to comply with generally applicable state rules governing challenges to criminal convictions.

In *Sanchez-Llamas v. Oregon*, 548 U.S. 331 (2006) — issued after *Avena* but involving individuals who were not named in the *Avena* judgment — we held that, contrary to the ICJ's determination, the Vienna Convention did not preclude the application of state default rules. After the *Avena* decision, President George W. Bush determined, through a Memorandum to the Attorney General (Feb. 28, 2005), App. to Pet. for Cert. 187a (Memorandum or President's Memorandum), that the United States would "discharge its international obligations" under *Avena* "by having State courts give effect to the decision."

Petitioner José Ernesto Medellín, who had been convicted and sentenced in Texas state court for murder, is one of the 51 Mexican nationals named in the *Avena* decision. Relying on the ICJ's decision and the President's Memorandum, Medellín filed an application for a writ of habeas corpus in state court. The Texas Court of Criminal Appeals dismissed Medellín's application as an abuse of the writ under state law, given Medellín's failure to raise his Vienna Convention claim in a timely manner under state law. We granted certiorari to decide two questions. *First,* is the ICJ's judgment in *Avena* directly enforceable as domestic law in a state court in the United States? *Second,* does the President's Memorandum independently require the States to provide review and reconsideration of the claims of the 51 Mexican nationals named in *Avena* without regard to state procedural default rules? We conclude that neither *Avena* nor the President's Memorandum constitutes directly enforceable federal law that pre-empts state limitations on the filing of successive habeas petitions. We therefore affirm the decision below.

I

A

In 1969, the United States, upon the advice and consent of the Senate, ratified the Vienna Convention on Consular Relations (Vienna Convention or Convention),

Apr. 24, 1963, [1970] 21 U.S.T. 77, T.I.A.S. No. 6820, and the Optional Protocol Concerning the Compulsory Settlement of Disputes to the Vienna Convention (Optional Protocol or Protocol), Apr. 24, 1963, [1970] 21 U.S.T. 325, T.I.A.S. No. 6820. The preamble to the Convention provides that its purpose is to "contribute to the development of friendly relations among nations." 21 U.S.T., at 79; *Sanchez-Llamas, supra*, at 337, 126 S.Ct. 2669. Toward that end, Article 36 of the Convention was drafted to "facilitat[e] the exercise of consular functions." Art. 36(1), 21 U.S.T., at 100. It provides that if a person detained by a foreign country "so requests, the competent authorities of the receiving State shall, without delay, inform the consular post of the sending State" of such detention, and "inform the [detainee] of his righ[t]" to request assistance from the consul of his own state. Art. 36(1)(b), *id.*, at 101.

The Optional Protocol provides a venue for the resolution of disputes arising out of the interpretation or application of the Vienna Convention. Art. I, 21 U.S.T., at 326. Under the Protocol, such disputes "shall lie within the compulsory jurisdiction of the International Court of Justice" and "may accordingly be brought before the [ICJ] . . . by any party to the dispute being a Party to the present Protocol." *Ibid.*

The ICJ is "the principal judicial organ of the United Nations." United Nations Charter, Art. 92, 59 Stat. 1051, T.S. No. 993 (1945). It was established in 1945 pursuant to the United Nations Charter. The ICJ Statute-annexed to the U.N. Charter-provides the organizational framework and governing procedures for cases brought before the ICJ. Statute of the International Court of Justice (ICJ Statute), 59 Stat. 1055, T.S. No. 993 (1945).

Under Article 94(1) of the U.N. Charter, "[e]ach Member of the United Nations undertakes to comply with the decision of the [ICJ] in any case to which it is a party." 59 Stat. 1051. The ICJ's jurisdiction in any particular case, however, is dependent upon the consent of the parties. See Art. 36, 59 Stat. 1060. The ICJ Statute delineates two ways in which a nation may consent to ICJ jurisdiction: It may consent generally to jurisdiction on any question arising under a treaty or general international law, Art. 36(2), *ibid.*, or it may consent specifically to jurisdiction over a particular category of cases or disputes pursuant to a separate treaty, Art. 36(1), *ibid.* The United States originally consented to the general jurisdiction of the ICJ when it filed a declaration recognizing compulsory jurisdiction under Art. 36(2) in 1946. The United States withdrew from general ICJ jurisdiction in 1985. By ratifying the Optional Protocol to the Vienna Convention, the United States consented to the specific jurisdiction of the ICJ with respect to claims arising out of the Vienna Convention. On March 7, 2005, subsequent to the ICJ's judgment in *Avena*, the United States gave notice of withdrawal from the Optional Protocol to the Vienna Convention. Letter from Condoleezza Rice, Secretary of State, to Kofi A. Annan, Secretary-General of the United Nations.

B

Petitioner José Ernesto Medellín, a Mexican national, has lived in the United States since preschool. A member of the "Black and Whites" gang, Medellín was convicted of capital murder and sentenced to death in Texas for the gang rape and brutal murders of two Houston teenagers.

On June 24, 1993, 14-year-old Jennifer Ertman and 16-year-old Elizabeth Pena were walking home when they encountered Medellín and several fellow gang members. Medellín attempted to engage Elizabeth in conversation. When she tried to run, petitioner threw her to the ground. Jennifer was grabbed by other gang members when she, in response to her friend's cries, ran back to help. The gang members raped both girls for over an hour. Then, to prevent their victims from identifying them, Medellín and his fellow gang members murdered the girls and discarded their bodies in a wooded area. Medellín was personally responsible for strangling at least one of the girls with her own shoelace.

Medellín was arrested at approximately 4 a.m. on June 29, 1993. A few hours later, between 5:54 and 7:23 a.m., Medellín was given *Miranda* warnings; he then signed a written waiver and gave a detailed written confession. Local law enforcement officers did not, however, inform Medellín of his Vienna Convention right to notify the Mexican consulate of his detention. Brief for Petitioner 6–7. Medellín was convicted of capital murder and sentenced to death; his conviction and sentence were affirmed on appeal.

Medellín first raised his Vienna Convention claim in his first application for state postconviction relief. The state trial court held that the claim was procedurally defaulted because Medellín had failed to raise it at trial or on direct review. The trial court also rejected the Vienna Convention claim on the merits, finding that Medellín had "fail[ed] to show that any non-notification of the Mexican authorities on the validity of his conviction or punishment." *Id.,* at 62. The Texas Court of Criminal Appeals affirmed. *Id.,* at 64–65.

Medellín then filed a habeas petition in Federal District Court. The District Court denied relief, holding that Medellín's Vienna Convention claim was procedurally defaulted and that Medellín had failed to show prejudice arising from the Vienna Convention violation. See *Medellín v. Cockrell,* Civ. Action No. H-01-4078 (SD Tex., June 26, 2003), App. to Brief for Respondent 86–92.

While Medellín's application for a certificate of appealability was pending in the Fifth Circuit, the ICJ issued its decision in *Avena.* The ICJ held that the United States had violated Article 36(1)(b) of the Vienna Convention by failing to inform the 51 named Mexican nationals, including Medellín, of their Vienna Convention rights. 2004 I.C.J., at 53–55. In the ICJ's determination, the United States was obligated "to provide, by means of its own choosing, review and reconsideration of the convictions and sentences of the [affected] Mexican nationals." *Id.,* at 72. The ICJ indicated that such review was required without regard to state procedural default rules. *Id.,* at 56–57.

The Fifth Circuit denied a certificate of appealability. *Medellín v. Dretke,* 371 F.3d 270, 281 (2004). The court concluded that the Vienna Convention did not confer individually enforceable rights. *Id.,* at 280. The court further ruled that it was in any event bound by this Court's decision in *Breard v. Greene,* 523 U.S. 371, 375, 118 S.Ct.

1352, 140 L.Ed.2d 529 (1998) (*per curiam*), which held that Vienna Convention claims are subject to procedural default rules, rather than by the ICJ's contrary decision in *Avena*. 371 F.3d, at 280.

This Court granted certiorari. *Medellín v. Dretke*, 544 U.S. 660, 661, 125 S.Ct. 2088, 161 L.Ed.2d 982 (2005) (*per curiam*) (*Medellín I*). Before we heard oral argument, however, President George W. Bush issued his Memorandum to the United States Attorney General, providing:

> I have determined, pursuant to the authority vested in me as President by the Constitution and the laws of the United States of America, that the United States will discharge its international obligations under the decision of the International Court of Justice in [*Avena*], by having State courts give effect to the decision in accordance with general principles of comity in cases filed by the 51 Mexican nationals addressed in that decision.

Medellín, relying on the President's Memorandum and the ICJ's decision in *Avena,* filed a second application for habeas relief in state court. *Ex parte Medellín*, 223 S.W.3d 315, 322–323 (Tex.Crim.App.2006). Because the state-court proceedings might have provided Medellín with the review and reconsideration he requested, and because his claim for federal relief might otherwise have been barred, we dismissed his petition for certiorari as improvidently granted.

The Texas Court of Criminal Appeals subsequently dismissed Medellín's second state habeas application as an abuse of the writ. 223 S.W.3d, at 352. In the court's view, neither the *Avena* decision nor the President's Memorandum was "binding federal law" that could displace the State's limitations on the filing of successive habeas applications. *Ibid*. We again granted certiorari. 550 U.S. 917, 127 S.Ct. 2129, 167 L. Ed.2d 862 (2007).

II

Medellín first contends that the ICJ's judgment in *Avena* constitutes a "binding" obligation on the state and federal courts of the United States. He argues that "by virtue of the Supremacy Clause, the treaties requiring compliance with the *Avena* judgment are *already* the 'Law of the Land' by which all state and federal courts in this country are 'bound.'" Reply Brief for Petitioner 1. Accordingly, Medellín argues, *Avena* is a binding federal rule of decision that pre-empts contrary state limitations on successive habeas petitions.

No one disputes that the *Avena* decision — a decision that flows from the treaties through which the United States submitted to ICJ jurisdiction with respect to Vienna Convention disputes — constitutes an *international* law obligation on the part of the United States. But not all international law obligations automatically constitute binding federal law enforceable in United States courts. The question we confront here is whether the *Avena* judgment has automatic *domestic* legal effect such that the judgment of its own force applies in state and federal courts.

[The majority proceeds to determine that, under the Optional Protocol, the *Avena* decision does not have a binding domestic legal effect in United States courts.]

III

Medellín next argues that the ICJ's judgment in *Avena* is binding on state courts by virtue of the President's February 28, 2005 Memorandum. The United States contends that while the *Avena* judgment does not of its own force require domestic courts to set aside ordinary rules of procedural default, that judgment became the law of the land with precisely that effect pursuant to the President's Memorandum and his power "to establish binding rules of decision that preempt contrary state law." Accordingly, we must decide whether the President's declaration alters our conclusion that the *Avena* judgment is not a rule of domestic law binding in state and federal courts.

A

The United States maintains that the President's constitutional role "uniquely qualifies" him to resolve the sensitive foreign policy decisions that bear on compliance with an ICJ decision and "to do so expeditiously." In this case, the President seeks to vindicate United States interests in ensuring the reciprocal observance of the Vienna Convention, protecting relations with foreign governments, and demonstrating commitment to the role of international law. These interests are plainly compelling.

Such considerations, however, do not allow us to set aside first principles. The President's authority to act, as with the exercise of any governmental power, "must stem either from an act of Congress or from the Constitution itself." *Youngstown*, 343 U.S. 579, 585 (1952). Justice Jackson's familiar tripartite scheme provides the accepted framework for evaluating executive action in this area. . . .

B

The United States marshals two principal arguments in favor of the President's authority "to establish binding rules of decision that preempt contrary state law." The Solicitor General first argues that the relevant treaties give the President the authority to implement the *Avena* judgment and that Congress has acquiesced in the exercise of such authority. The United States also relies upon an "independent" international dispute-resolution power wholly apart from the asserted authority based on the pertinent treaties. Medellín adds the additional argument that the President's Memorandum is a valid exercise of his power to take care that the laws be faithfully executed.

1

The United States maintains that the President's Memorandum is authorized by the Optional Protocol and the U.N. Charter. That is, because the relevant treaties "create an obligation to comply with *Avena*," they "*implicitly* give the President authority to implement that treaty-based obligation." As a result, the President's Memorandum is well grounded in the first category of the *Youngstown* framework.

We disagree. The President has an array of political and diplomatic means available to enforce international obligations, but unilaterally converting a non-self-executing treaty into a self-executing one is not among them. The responsibility for transforming an international obligation arising from a non-self-executing treaty into domestic law falls to Congress. As this Court has explained, when treaty stipulations are "not self-executing they can only be enforced pursuant to legislation to carry them into effect." *Whitney, supra,* at 194, 8 S.Ct. 456. Moreover, "[u]ntil such act shall be passed, the Court is not at liberty to disregard the existing laws on the subject." *Foster, supra,* at 315.

The requirement that Congress, rather than the President, implement an executing treaty derives from the text of the Constitution, which divides the treaty-making power between the President and the Senate. The Constitution vests the President with the authority to "make" a treaty. Art. II, §2. If the Executive determines that a treaty should have domestic effect of its own force, that determination may be implemented "in mak[ing]" the treaty, by ensuring that it contains language plainly providing for domestic enforceability. If the treaty is to be self-executing in this respect, the Senate must consent to the treaty by the requisite two-thirds vote, *ibid.,* consistent with all other constitutional restraints.

Once a treaty is ratified without provisions clearly according it domestic effect, however, whether the treaty will ever have such effect is governed by the fundamental constitutional principle that "'[t]he power to make the necessary laws is in Congress; the power to execute in the President.'" *Hamdan v. Rumsfeld,* 548 U.S. 557, 591 (2006). As already noted, the terms of a non-self-executing treaty can become domestic law only in the same way as any other law — through passage of legislation by both Houses of Congress, combined with either the President's signature or a congressional override of a Presidential veto. Indeed, "the President's power to see that the laws are faithfully executed refutes the idea that he is to be a lawmaker." *Youngstown,* 343 U.S., at 587.

A non-self-executing treaty, by definition, is one that was ratified with the understanding that it is not to have domestic effect of its own force. That understanding precludes the assertion that Congress has implicitly authorized the President-acting on his own-to achieve precisely the same result. We therefore conclude, given the absence of congressional legislation, that the non-self-executing treaties at issue here did not "express[ly] or implied[ly]" vest the President with the unilateral authority to make them self-executing. See *id.,* at 635 (Jackson, J., concurring). Accordingly, the President's Memorandum does not fall within the first category of the *Youngstown* framework.

Indeed, the preceding discussion should make clear that the non-self-executing character of the relevant treaties not only refutes the notion that the ratifying parties vested the President with the authority to unilaterally make treaty obligations binding on domestic courts, but also implicitly prohibits him from doing so. When the President asserts the power to "enforce" a non-self-executing treaty by unilaterally creating domestic law, he acts in conflict with the implicit understanding of the ratifying Senate. His assertion of authority, insofar as it is based on the pertinent non-self-executing treaties, is therefore within Justice Jackson's third category, not the first or even the second.

Each of the two means described above for giving domestic effect to an international treaty obligation under the Constitution — for making law — requires joint action by the Executive and Legislative Branches: The Senate can ratify a self-executing treaty "ma[de]" by the Executive, or, if the ratified treaty is not self-executing, Congress can enact implementing legislation approved by the President. It should not be surprising that our Constitution does not contemplate vesting such power in the Executive alone. As Madison in The Federalist No. 47, under our constitutional system of checks and balances, "[t]he magistrate in whom the whole executive power resides cannot of himself make a law." J. Cooke ed., p. 326 (1961). That would, however, seem an apt description of the asserted executive authority unilaterally to give the effect of domestic law to obligations under a non-self-executing treaty.

The United States nonetheless maintains that the President's Memorandum should be given effect as domestic law because "this case involves a valid Presidential action in the context of Congressional 'acquiescence'." Under the *Youngstown* tripartite framework, congressional acquiescence is pertinent when the President's action falls within the second category — that is, when he "acts in absence of either a congressional grant or denial of authority." 343 U.S., at 637 (Jackson, J., concurring). Here, however, as we have explained, the President's effort to accord domestic effect to the *Avena* judgment does not meet that prerequisite.

In any event, even if we were persuaded that congressional acquiescence could support the President's asserted authority to create domestic law pursuant to a non-self-executing treaty, such acquiescence does not exist here. The United States first locates congressional acquiescence in Congress's failure to act following the President's resolution of prior ICJ controversies. A review of the Executive's actions in those prior cases, however, cannot support the claim that Congress acquiesced in this particular exercise of Presidential authority, for none of them remotely involved transforming an international obligation into domestic law and thereby displacing state law.

The United States also directs us to the President's "related" statutory responsibilities and to his "established role" in litigating foreign policy concerns as support for the President's asserted authority to give the ICJ's decision in *Avena* the force of domestic law. Congress has indeed authorized the President to represent the United States before the United Nations, the ICJ, and the Security Council, 22 U.S.C. § 287, but the authority of the President to represent the United States before such bodies speaks to the President's *international* responsibilities, not any unilateral authority to create domestic law. The authority expressly conferred by Congress in the international realm cannot be said to "invite" the Presidential action at issue here. See *Youngstown, supra,* at 637 (Jackson, J., concurring). At bottom, none of the sources of authority identified by the United States supports the President's claim that Congress has acquiesced in his asserted power to establish on his own federal law or to override state law.

None of this is to say, however, that the combination of a non-self-executing treaty and the lack of implementing legislation precludes the President from acting to comply with an international treaty obligation. It is only to say that the Executive cannot unilaterally execute a non-self-executing treaty by giving it domestic effect. That is, the non-self-executing character of a treaty constrains the President's ability to comply with treaty commitments by unilaterally making the treaty binding on domestic courts. The President may comply with the treaty's obligations by some other means, so long as they are consistent with the Constitution. But he may not rely upon a non-self-executing treaty to "establish binding rules of decision that preempt contrary state law."

2

We thus turn to the United States' claim that—independent of the United States' treaty obligations—the Memorandum is a valid exercise of the President's foreign affairs authority to resolve claims disputes with foreign nations. The United States relies on a series of cases in which this Court has upheld the authority of the President to settle foreign claims pursuant to an executive agreement. In these cases this Court has explained that, if pervasive enough, a history of congressional acquiescence can be treated as a "gloss on 'Executive Power' vested in the President by § 1 of Art. II."

This argument is of a different nature than the one rejected above. Rather than relying on the United States' treaty obligations, the President relies on an independent source of authority in ordering Texas to put aside its procedural bar to successive habeas petitions. Nevertheless, we find that our claims-settlement cases do not support the authority that the President asserts in this case.

The claims-settlement cases involve a narrow set of circumstances: the making of executive agreements to settle civil claims between American citizens and foreign governments or foreign nationals. They are based on the view that "a systematic, unbroken, executive practice, long pursued to the knowledge of the and never before questioned," can "raise a presumption that the [action] had been [taken] in pursuance of its consent." *Dames & Moore, supra,* at 686 (some internal quotation marks omitted). As this Court explained in *Garamendi,*

> Making executive agreements to settle claims of American nationals against foreign governments is a particularly longstanding practice . . . . Given the fact that the practice goes back over 200 years, and has received congressional acquiescence throughout its history, the conclusion that the President's control of foreign relations includes the settlement of claims is indisputable.

539 U.S., at 415.

Even still, the limitations on this source of executive power are clearly set forth and the Court has been careful to note that "[p]ast practice does not, by itself, create power." *Dames & Moore, supra,* at 686.

The President's Memorandum is not supported by a "particularly longstanding practice" of congressional acquiescence, see *Garamendi, supra,* at 415, 123 S.Ct. 2374, but rather is what the United States itself has described as "unprecedented action," Indeed, the Government has not identified a single instance in which the President has attempted (or Congress has acquiesced in) a Presidential directive issued to state courts, much less one that reaches deep into the heart of the State's police powers and compels state courts to reopen final criminal judgments and set aside neutrally applicable state laws. The Executive's narrow and strictly limited authority to settle international claims disputes pursuant to an executive agreement cannot stretch so far as to support the current Presidential Memorandum.

3

Medellín argues that the President's Memorandum is a valid exercise of his "Take Care" power. The United States, however, does not rely upon the President's responsibility to "take Care that the Laws be faithfully executed." U.S. Const., Art. II, § 3. We think this a wise concession. This authority allows the President to execute the laws, not make them. For the reasons we have stated, the *Avena* judgment is not domestic law; accordingly, the President cannot rely on his Take Care powers here.

The judgment of the Texas Court of Criminal Appeals is affirmed.

[The opinion of Justice STEVENS, concurring in the judgment, is omitted.]

Justice BREYER, with whom Justice SOUTER and Justice GINSBURG join, dissenting.

[Most of Justice Breyer's dissent is devoted to his conclusion that, under the Optional Protocol, the *Avena* decision is automatically binding in domestic courts.]

Because the majority concludes that the Nation's international legal obligation to enforce the ICJ's decision is not automatically a domestic legal obligation, it must then determine whether the President has the constitutional authority to enforce it. And the majority finds that he does not.

In my view, that second conclusion has broader implications than the majority suggests. The President here seeks to implement treaty provisions in which the United States agrees that the ICJ judgment is binding with respect to the *Avena* parties. Consequently, his actions draw upon his constitutional authority in the area of foreign affairs. In this case, his exercise of that power falls within that middle range of Presidential authority where Congress has neither specifically authorized nor specifically forbidden the Presidential action in question. At the same time, if the President were to have the authority he asserts here, it would require setting aside a state procedural law.

It is difficult to believe that in the exercise of his Article II powers pursuant to a ratified treaty, the President can *never* take action that would result in setting aside state law. Cf. *United States v. Pink,* 315 U.S. 203 (1942) ("No State can rewrite our foreign policy to conform to its own domestic policies"). Suppose that the President believes it necessary that he implement a treaty provision requiring a prisoner exchange involving someone in state custody in order to avoid a proven military threat. Or suppose he believes it necessary to secure a foreign consul's treaty-based rights to move freely or to contact an arrested foreign national. Cf. Vienna Convention, Art. 34, 21 U.S.T., at 98. Does the Constitution require the President in each and every such instance to obtain a special statute authorizing his action? On the other hand, the Constitution must impose significant restrictions upon the President's ability, by invoking Article II treaty-implementation authority, to circumvent ordinary legislative processes and to pre-empt state law as he does so.

Previously this Court has said little about this question. It has held that the President has a fair amount of authority to make and to implement executive agreements, at least in respect to international claims settlement, and that this authority can require contrary state law to be set aside. It has made clear that principles of foreign sovereign immunity trump state law and that the Executive, operating without explicit legislative authority, can assert those principles in state court. See *Ex parte Peru*, 318 U.S. 578 (1943). It has also made clear that the Executive has inherent power to bring a lawsuit "to carry out treaty obligations." *Sanitary Dist. of Chicago v. United States*, 266 U.S. 405, 425 (1925). But it has reserved judgment as to "the scope of the President's power to preempt state law pursuant to authority delegated by . . . a ratified treaty"—a fact that helps to explain the majority's inability to find support in precedent for its own conclusions. *Barclays Bank PLC v. Franchise Tax Bd. of Cal.*, 512 U.S. 298, 329 (1994).

Given the Court's comparative lack of expertise in foreign affairs; given the importance of the Nation's foreign relations; given the difficulty of finding the proper constitutional balance among state and federal, executive and legislative, powers in such matters; and given the likely future importance of this Court's efforts to do so, I would very much hesitate before concluding that the Constitution implicitly sets forth broad prohibitions (or permissions) in this area.

I would thus be content to leave the matter in the constitutional shade from which it has emerged. Given my view of this case, I need not answer the question. And I shall not try to do so. That silence, however, cannot be taken as agreement with the majority's Part III conclusion.

The majority's two holdings taken together produce practical anomalies. They unnecessarily complicate the President's foreign affairs task insofar as, for example, they increase the likelihood of Security Council *Avena* enforcement proceedings, of worsening relations with our neighbor Mexico, of precipitating actions by other nations putting at risk American citizens who have the misfortune to be arrested while traveling abroad, or of diminishing our Nation's reputation abroad as a result of our failure to follow the "rule of law" principles that we preach. The holdings also encumber Congress with a task (postratification legislation) that, in respect to many decisions of international tribunals, it may not want and which it may find difficult to execute. At the same time, insofar as today's holdings make it more difficult to enforce the judgments of international tribunals, including technical non-politically-controversial judgments, those holdings weaken that rule of law for which our Constitution stands.

These institutional considerations make it difficult to reconcile the majority's holdings with the workable Constitution that the Founders envisaged. They reinforce the importance, in practice and in principle, of asking Chief Justice Marshall's question: Does a treaty provision address the "Judicial" Branch rather than the "Political Branches" of Government. And they show the wisdom of the well-established precedent that indicates that the answer to the question here is "yes."

————————

1. *Self-Executing v. Non-Self-Executing Treaties.* In terms of intellectual context, the *Medellín* decision arose at the intersection of two significant jurisprudential debates. One of those debates concerns the appropriate interpretation of the President's Article II foreign affairs powers. Professor Michael Stokes Paulsen has suggested that "the Constitution's grant of 'the executive power' is rightly understood as embracing the power to *determine and direct* the content of the United States's policies with respect to relations with other nations." Michael Stokes Paulsen, *The Constitutional Power to Interpret International Law*, 118 Yale L. J. 1762, 1812 (2009) (emphasis added). (To be fair, the quoted phrase is contained within a subjunctive clause that merely assumes, for argument's sake, that the President's power is as described.) A more modest explication of the "sole organ" power asserts:

> [T]o say that the President has the "power to speak or listen as a representative of the nation" or that he is the "sole organ" of the federal government in international relations does not mean that the President has exclusive authority over the nation's foreign affairs. The power to communicate does not of necessity imply a unilateral power to make foreign policy. Instead, it means something quite a bit more limited: the President is empowered to act as the formal legal representative of the United States and is therefore uniquely empowered to speak with foreign entities on behalf of the United States.

Oona A. Hathaway, *Presidential Power Over International Law: Restoring the Balance*, 119 Yale L. J. 140, 208 (2009). *Medellín* seems clearly to support the latter view.

A second and equally complex debate, however, involves the degree to which the United States should regard itself as bound domestically by international law. The Paulsen article cited above states the anti-internationalist thesis most starkly:

> [I]nternational law is not binding law on the United States, and cannot be binding law except to the extent provided in the U.S. Constitution. That extent is very limited and subject to several important constitutional overrides—empowerments or restrictions that nearly always permit international law requirements to be superseded by contrary enactments or actions of U.S. governmental actors. The result is that international law is primarily a political constraint on the exercise of U.S. power, not a true legal constraint; it is chiefly a policy consideration of international relations—of international politics. International law may be quite relevant in that sense. But it is largely irrelevant as a matter of U.S. law. While the legal regime of international law may consider international law supreme over the law of every nation, the U.S. Constitution does not.

118 Yale L. J. at 1770. *See also* Jack L. Goldsmith and Eric A. Posner, The Limits of International Law (2005).

Such a provocatively stated thesis, of course, drew heated dissents. Although Professor Paulsen's first premise—the supremacy of constitutional law in determining the domestic impact of international law—is widely shared, it is not clear why this fact deprives international law of the character of law A series of responsive essays noted (a) the ubiquity of international law as a source of rules both routinely invoked by the U.S. government and relied upon by private parties, (b) the availability of international institutions to enforce international law obligations and impose liability for violations, and (c) the fact that "U.S. participation in the international legal system operates smoothly and in ways largely indistinguishable from the application of domestic laws." Margaret E. McGinness, *Old W(h)ine, Old Bottles: A Response to Professor Paulsen*, 119 Yale L. J. Online 31, 33 (2009). See also Julian Ku, *The Prospects for the Peaceful Co-Existence of Constitutional and International Law*, 119 Yale L. J. Online 15 (2009); Peter J. Spiro, *Wishing International Law Away*, 119 Yale L. J. Online 23 (2009); and Robert Ahdieh, *The Fog of Certainty*, 119 Yale L. J. Online 41 (2009).

This latter debate might well have implications for the process of deciding whether treaties are "self-executing." In portions of the *Medellín* opinions we omit, the majority and dissent debate whether the judgment of the International Court of Justice in *Avena* should be deemed binding in the U.S., absent additional legislation. The majority focuses on the absence of treaty language "plainly providing for domestic enforceability"; it is reluctant to find self-executing status absent a clear statement to that effect. In dissent, however, Justice Breyer insists: "[T]he absence or presence of language in a treaty about a provision's self-execution proves nothing at all. At best the Court is hunting the snark. At worst it erects legalistic hurdles that can threaten the application of provisions in many existing commercial and other treaties and make it more difficult to negotiate new ones." 552 U. S., at 549 (Breyer, J., dissenting). It is not hard to infer from these approaches a greater and lesser anxiety, respectively, about making international norms binding as a matter of domestic law.

2. The Geneva Conventions and Limits to "Interpretation." Medellín appears to limit the President's power to implement non-self-executing treaties to those powers he enjoys by virtue of congressional authorization. In a variety of contexts, however, the President clearly has powers of treaty "interpretation" that are important. Under the "sole organ" power, for example, Presidents may articulate to other countries what they understand to be our treaty obligations under international law. As a matter of domestic law, either where a treaty is self-executing or where Congress has incorporated treaty terms into legislation—whether explicitly or implicitly—Presidents may have to construe a treaty's meaning, just as would be the case for any other legislation subject to executive enforcement.

The question necessarily arises, however, as to the scope of this interpretive power. Following the attacks of September 11 and the U.S. invasion of Afghanistan, a host of difficult issues arose — more of which are discussed in Chapter Six — concerning the applicability of the Geneva Conventions both to al Qaeda and the Taliban. There are four Geneva conventions, the most important of which in this context is the Convention Relative to the Treatment of Prisoners of War, 6 U.S.T. 3517 ("Geneva Convention III"). Geneva III, like the other three Geneva Conventions contains what is called — confusingly enough — Common Article 3. (It is a "Common Article" because present in each of the Conventions.) Common Article III provides some minimal protections, falling short of full prisoner of war protections, to individuals who are involved in a conflict in the territory of a signatory state. Article 4 of Geneva III, however, goes on to define who shall be considered to be "prisoners of war." Article 5 provides that, should "any doubt arise as to whether persons, having committed a belligerent act and having fallen into the hands of the enemy" are entitled to POW status, they are to be treated as POW's under Article 4 until an appropriate tribunal decides otherwise.

In a highly controversial opinion, the Justice Department's Office of Legal Counsel opined, however, that the President could deprive Taliban prisoners of POW status through simple "interpretation":

> Even if the President declines to suspend our obligations under Geneva III toward Afghanistan, it is possible that Taliban detainees still might not receive the legal status of POWs. Geneva III provides that once a conflict falls within common article 2, combatants must fall within one of several categories in order to receive POW status. Article 4(A)(l)-(3) sets out the three categories relevant here: i) members of the armed forces of a party to the conflict, along with accompanying militia and volunteer forces; ii) members of militia or volunteer corps who are commanded by an individual responsible to his subordinates, who have a distinctive sign recognizable from a distance, who carry arms openly, and who obey the laws of war; and iii) members of regular armed forces who profess allegiance to a government or authority that is not recognized by the detaining power. Should "any doubt arise as to whether persons, having committed a belligerent act and having fallen into the hands of the enemy," Article 5 of Geneva III requires that these individuals "enjoy the protections of" the Convention until a tribunal has their status. As we understand it, as a matter of practice prisoners are presumed to have article 4 POW status until a tribunal determines otherwise.

> Although these provisions seem to contemplate a case-by-case determination of an individual detainee's status, the President could determine categorically that all Taliban prisoners fall outside Article 4. Under Article II of the Constitution, the President possesses the power to interpret treaties on behalf of the nation. "' He could interpret Geneva III, in light of the known facts concerning the operation of Taliban forces during the Afghanistan conflict, to find that all of the Taliban forces do not fall within the legal definition of prisoners of war as defined by Article 4. A presidential determination of this nature would eliminate any legal "doubt" as to the prisoners'

status, as a matter of domestic law, and would therefore obviate the need for Article 5 tribunals.

Memorandum for Alberto R. Gonzales, Counsel to the President, and William J. Haynes II, General Counsel, Department of Defense, from Jay S. Bybee, Assistant Attorney General, Office of Legal Counsel, *Re: Application of Treaties and Laws to al Qaeda and Taliban Detainees* (Jan. 22, 2002), reprinted in KAREN J. GREENBERG AND JOSHUA L. DRATEL, THE TORTURE PAPERS: THE ROAD TO ABU GHRAIB 81, 110 (2005). The obvious problem with the proposed act of "interpretation" is that it would seem, in effect, to be "suspending" Article 5, rather than "interpreting" Article IV—effectively making the President alone the sole tribunal for deciding POW status. As one of us has put the matter: "Article 5 was written to preserve a right of adjudication by 'a competent tribunal' in cases of factual doubt about captured combatants, and the President's lawyers were permitting him to remove doubt regarding the facts by simply asserting that he personally had none." PETER M. SHANE, MADISON'S NIGHTMARE: HOW EXECUTIVE POWER THREATENS AMERICAN DEMOCRACY 100 (2009). The power of suspension is discussed in the notes after the *Goldwater v. Carter* opinions, below.

---

c. Presidential Treaty Termination

As noted earlier, the President is now regarded by all branches of government as having exclusive power to establish (or break) diplomatic relations with other nations. EDWARD S. CORWIN, THE PRESIDENT: OFFICE AND POWERS, 1787–1957 177–93 (4th ed. 1957). Establishing diplomatic relations, however, typically requires attention to a variety of additional problems, such as the resolution of outstanding claims by U.S. nationals against the nationals of the other country, and vice versa, or adjustments in our foreign policy with regard to third countries. As you review the following case and the cases on claims settlement through executive agreement, consider how far the President's exclusive power over diplomatic recognition should be deemed to imply exclusive power over other aspects of foreign affairs implicated in the recognition process.

Goldwater v. Carter

444 U.S. 996 (1979)

ORDER

Dec. 13, 1979. The petition for a writ of certiorari is granted. The judgment of the Court of Appeals is vacated and the case is remanded to the District Court with directions to dismiss the complaint.

Justice MARSHALL concurs in the result. . . .

Justice WHITE and Justice BLACKMUN join in the grant of the petition for a writ of certiorari but would set the case for argument and give it plenary consideration. . . .

Justice POWELL, concurring.

Although I agree with the result reached by the Court, I would dismiss the complaint as not ripe for judicial review.

I

This Court has recognized that an issue should not be decided if it is not ripe for judicial review. Prudential considerations persuade me that a dispute between Congress and the President is not ready for judicial review unless and until each branch has taken action asserting its constitutional authority. Differences between the President and the Congress are commonplace under our system. The differences should, and almost invariably do, turn on political rather than legal considerations. The Judicial Branch should not decide issues affecting the allocation of power between the President and Congress until the political branches reach a constitutional impasse. Otherwise, we would encourage small groups or even individual Members of Congress to seek judicial resolution of issues before the normal political process has the opportunity to resolve the conflict.

In this case, a few Members of Congress claim that the President's action in terminating the treaty with Taiwan has deprived them of their constitutional role with respect to a change in the supreme law of the land. Congress has taken no official action. In the present posture of this case, we do not know whether there ever will be an actual confrontation between the Legislative and Executive Branches. . . . If the Congress chooses not to confront the President, it is not our task to do so. I therefore concur in the dismissal of this case.

II

Justice Rehnquist suggests, however, that the issue presented by this case is a nonjusticiable political question which can never be considered by this Court. I cannot agree. In my view, reliance upon the political-question doctrine is inconsistent with our precedents. As set forth in the seminal case of *Baker v. Carr*, 369 U.S. 186, 217 (1962), the doctrine incorporates three inquiries: (i) Does the issue involve resolution of questions committed by the text of the Constitution to a coordinate branch of Government? (ii) Would resolution of the question demand that a court move beyond areas of judicial expertise? (iii) Do prudential considerations counsel against judicial intervention? In my opinion the answer to each of these inquires would require us to decide this case if it were ready for review.

First, the existence of "a textually demonstrable constitutional commitment of the issue to a coordinate political department," *ibid.*, turns on an examination of the constitutional provisions governing the exercise of the power in question. No constitutional provision explicitly confers upon the President the power to terminate treaties. Further, Art. II, § 2, of the Constitution authorizes the President to make treaties with the advice and consent of the Senate. Article VI provides that treaties shall be a part of the supreme law of the land. These provisions add support to the view that the text of the Constitution does not unquestionably commit the power to terminate treaties to the President alone.

Second, there is no "lack of judicially discoverable and manageable standards for resolving" this case; nor is a decision impossible "without an initial policy determination of a kind clearly for nonjudicial discretion." *Baker v. Carr*, 369 U.S., at 217. We are asked to decide whether the President may terminate a treaty under the Constitution without congressional approval. Resolution of the question may not be easy, but it only requires us to apply normal principles of interpretation to the constitutional provisions at issue. The present case involves neither review of the President's activities as Commander in Chief nor impermissible interference in the field of foreign affairs. Such a case would arise if we were asked to decide, for example, whether a treaty required the President to order troops into a foreign country. But "it is error to suppose that every case or controversy which touches foreign relations lies beyond judicial cognizance." *Baker v. Carr*, 369 U.S., at 211. This case "touches" foreign relations, but the question presented to us concerns only the constitutional division of power between Congress and the President.

A simple hypothetical demonstrates the confusion that I find inherent in Justice Rehnquist's opinion concurring in the judgment. Assume that the President signed a mutual defense treaty with a foreign country and announced that it would go into effect despite its rejection by the Senate. Under Justice Rehnquist's analysis that situation would present a political question even though Art. II, § 2, clearly would resolve the dispute. Although the answer to the hypothetical case seems self-evident because it demands textual rather than interstitial analysis, the nature of the legal issue presented is no different from the issue presented in the case before us. In both cases, the Court would interpret the Constitution to decide whether congressional approval is necessary to give a Presidential decision on the validity of a treaty the force of law. Such an inquiry demands no special competence or information beyond the reach of the Judiciary.

Finally, the political-question doctrine rests in part on prudential concerns calling for mutual respect among the three branches of Government. Thus, the Judicial Branch should avoid "the potentiality of embarrassment [that would result] from multifarious pronouncements by various departments on one question." Similarly, the doctrine restrains judicial action where there is an "unusual need for unquestioning adherence to a political decision already made." *Baker v. Carr*, 369 U.S., at 217.

If this case were ripe for judicial review, none of these prudential considerations would be present. Interpretation of the Constitution does not imply lack of respect for a coordinate branch. If the President and the Congress had reached irreconcilable positions, final disposition of the question presented by this case would eliminate, rather than create, multiple constitutional interpretations. The specter of the Federal Government brought to a halt because of the mutual intransigence of the President and the Congress would require this Court to provide a resolution pursuant to our duty " 'to say what the law is.' " *United States v. Nixon*, 418 U.S. 683, 703 (1974), quoting *Marbury v. Madison*, 1 Cranch 137, 177 (1803).

III

In my view, the suggestion that this case presents a political question is incompatible with this Court's willingness on previous occasions to decide whether one branch of our Government has impinged upon the power of another. . . . If the Congress, by appropriate formal action, had challenged the President's authority to terminate the treaty with Taiwan, the resulting uncertainty could have serious consequences for our country. In that situation, it would be the duty of this Court to resolve the issue.

Justice REHNQUIST, with whom THE CHIEF JUSTICE, Justice STEWART, and Justice STEVENS join, concurring in the judgment.

I am of the view that the basic question presented by the petitioners in this case is "political" and therefore nonjusticiable because it involves the authority of the President in the conduct of our country's foreign relations and the extent to which the Senate or the Congress is authorized to negate the action of the President. In *Coleman v. Miller*, 307 U.S. 433, a case in which members of the Kansas Legislature brought an action attacking a vote of the State Senate in favor of the ratification of the Child Labor Amendment, . . . Chief Justice Hughes' opinion concluded that "Congress in controlling the promulgation of the adoption of a constitutional amendment has the final determination of the question whether by lapse of time its proposal of the amendment had lost its vitality prior to the required ratifications."

I believe it follows *a fortiori* from *Coleman* that the controversy in the instant case is a nonjusticiable political dispute that should be left for resolution by the Executive and Legislative Branches of the Government. Here, while the Constitution is express as to the manner in which the Senate shall participate in the ratification of a treaty, it is silent as to that body's participation in the abrogation of a treaty. In this respect the case is directly analogous to *Coleman, supra*. . . . In light of the absence of any constitutional provision governing the termination of a treaty, and the fact that different termination procedures may be appropriate for different treaties, the instant case in my view also "must surely be controlled by political standards."

I think that the justifications for concluding that the question here is political in nature are even more compelling than in *Coleman* because it involves foreign relations—specifically a treaty commitment to use military force in the defense of a foreign government if attacked.

The present case differs in several important respects from *Youngstown Sheet & Tube Co. v. Sawyer*, 343 U.S. 579 (1952), cited by petitioners as authority both for reaching the merits of this dispute and for reversing the Court of Appeals. In *Youngstown*, private litigants brought a suit contesting the President's authority under his war powers to seize the Nation's steel industry, an action of profound and demonstrable domestic impact. Here, by contrast, we are asked to settle a dispute between coequal branches of our Government, each of which has resources available to protect and assert its interests, resources not available to private litigants outside the judicial forum. Moreover, as in *Curtiss-Wright*, the effect of this action, as far as we can tell, is "entirely external to the United States, and [falls] within the category of foreign affairs." Finally, as already noted, the situation presented here is closely akin to that presented in *Coleman*, where the Constitution spoke only to the procedure for ratification of an amendment, not to its rejection. . . . Since the political nature of the questions presented should have precluded the lower courts from considering or deciding the merits of the controversy, the prior proceedings in the federal courts must be vacated, and the complaint dismissed.

[The opinion of Justice BLACKMUN is omitted.]

Justice BRENNAN, dissenting.

I . . . would affirm the judgment of the Court of Appeals insofar as it rests upon the President's well-established authority to recognize, and withdraw recognition from, foreign governments.

In stating that this case presents a non-justiciable "political question," Justice Rehnquist, in my view, profoundly misapprehends the political-question principle as it applies to matters of foreign relations. Properly understood, the political-question doctrine restrains courts from reviewing an exercise of foreign policy judgment by the coordinate political branch to which authority to make that judgment has been "constitutional[ly] commit[ted]." *Baker v. Carr*, 369 U.S. 186, 211–13 (1962). But the doctrine does not pertain when a court is faced with the *antecedent* question whether a particular branch has been constitutionally designated as the repository of political decisionmaking power. The issue of decisionmaking authority must be resolved as a matter of constitutional law, not political discretion; accordingly, it falls within the competence of the courts.

The constitutional question raised here is prudently answered in narrow terms. Abrogation of the defense treaty with Taiwan was a necessary incident to Executive recognition of the Peking Government, because the defense treaty was predicated upon the now-abandoned view that the Taiwan Government was the only legitimate political authority in China. Our cases firmly establish that the Constitution commits to the President alone the power to recognize, and withdraw recognition from, foreign regimes. That mandate being clear, our judicial inquiry into the treaty rupture can go no further.

----

1. *Reviewing the Constitutional Options.* There are a host of plausible positions as to where the Constitution assigns treaty-termination power. Which of the following is most persuasive:

a. The constitutional requirement of Senate treaty approval implies a requirement of Senate approval for treaty termination?

b. The President's constitutional foreign policy powers include the power of treaty termination:

(1) Always?

(2) When treaty termination is a necessary incident to the recognition of a foreign government?

(3) Unless the treaty expressly reserves to the legislature a role in termination?

(4) As long as treaty termination does not implicate our participation in a congressionally approved military alliance?

c. The only constitutional language that could be thought to cover termination expressly is the necessary and proper clause, and, therefore, treaty termination requires ordinary legislation?

2. *Parsing the Political Question.* Treaty termination conceivably poses at least two separate questions: first, whether the treaty was terminated by the branch of government with power to terminate treaties; second, whether the terminating branch acted on permissible grounds. Does Rehnquist persuade you that the latter question is a political question? Would Powell disagree? What about the former question?

3. *Do Congress's Responses Affect Reviewability?* Note that, following President Carter's announcement that the United States would recognize the PRC, Congress enacted legislation to govern future U.S. relations with Taiwan. Should it be relevant to a federal court's decision whether to adjudicate any legal issue regarding treaty termination that Congress did not take the occasion of that statute to object to the termination of the Mutual Defense Treaty of 1954?

4. *Congressional "Vetoes" of Treaty Termination?* Could a two-thirds vote of each House of Congress constitutionally prevent the President's termination of a treaty? How could or should Congress resist if a President were unilaterally to withdraw from NATO without the derecognition of any signatory to the NATO treaty?

5. *The Original Understanding Treaty Termination.* After reviewing the founding era evidence, Professor Saikrishna Prakash concludes that "[t]here seems to have been no consensus on these matters, leaving us the text and structure of the document, and scattered claims about treaty withdrawals and violations." SAIKRISHNA BANGALORE PRAKASH, IMPERIAL FROM THE BEGINNING: THE CONSTITUTION OF THE ORIGINAL EXECUTIVE (2015).

5. *For Further Reading.* For historical perspectives on the treaty termination power, see Arthur Bestor, *Respective Roles of Senate and President in the Making and Abrogation of Treaties—The Original Intent of the Framers of the Constitution Historically Examined,* 55 WASH. L. REV. 1 (1979); Raoul Berger, *The President's Unilateral Termination of the Taiwan Treaty,* 75 Nw. U. L. REV. 577 (1980). For a thorough discussion of the issues surrounding judicial review of foreign affairs-related claims, with particular attention to the *Goldwater v. Carter* litigation, see Theodore Y. Blumoff, *Judicial Review, Foreign Affairs, and Legislative Standing,* 25 GA. L. REV. 227 (1991). Thorough discussion of the treaty powers appear in Louis Henkin, FOREIGN AFFAIRS AND THE CONSTITUTION (1972), and MICHAEL J. GLENNON, CONSTITUTIONAL DIPLOMACY (1990).

2. Executive Agreements

Note: International Non-Treaty Agreements

Although the Constitution does not mention executive agreements, the instrument was known even in President Washington's day, and has become the predominant form of international agreement for the U.S. Its use has been vastly expanded by practice and judicial sanction. Congress has recognized the constitutionality of negotiating executive agreements by enacting the Case Act, 1 U.S.C. § 112b (1972), which requires the Secretary of State to transmit the text of agreements other than treaties to each chamber for informational purposes. More than 6,000 executive agreements are in force today as compared to roughly 1,000 treaties. Between 1980 and 2000 alone, the United States entered into 2744 executive agreements specifically authorized by statute, as compared to 375 treaties. Oona A. Hathaway, *Treaties' End: The Past, Present and Future of International Lawmaking in the United States*, 117 YALE L. J. 1236, 1258, 1260 (2008).

There are three types of executive agreement: treaty-based executive agreements, congressional-executive agreements and unilateral-executive agreements.

Treaty-based executive agreements, made, as the term implies, pursuant to treaties, enjoy the same legal status as the treaties that authorize them so long as they are consistent with and within the scope of those treaties.

Congressional-executive agreements are those authorized by statute. On some particular subjects, such as postal relations, reciprocal trade, and foreign assistance, Congress has authorized the President in advance to negotiate and conclude executive agreements. Congress has also authorized the President to conclude certain agreements that have already been negotiated, as in the case of the Headquarters Agreement with the United Nations and various multilateral agreements establishing international organizations, e.g., UNRA, the International Bank and the International Monetary Fund, and the International Refugee Organization. There is no express constitutional basis for such interbranch collaboration. The Constitution expressly prescribes the treaty procedure, but does not mention other methods for negotiating foreign relations.

It is often asserted that the congressional-executive agreement is a complete alternative to a treaty; instead of seeking approval from the Senate only, approval is sought from both houses of Congress. Like a treaty, such an agreement becomes the law of the land, superseding inconsistent state laws as well as inconsistent provisions in earlier treaties, other international agreements or acts of Congress. Nonetheless, the interchangeability of the two forms of agreement has been disputed from time to time. The following excerpt from an Office of Legal Counsel opinion by Assistant Attorney General Walter Dellinger defends the adoption of international agreements by statute, rather than by Senate ratification. It responds to Senate hearing testimony by Professor Laurence Tribe challenging the use of legislation to implement the latest round of trade agreements adopted pursuant to the General Agreement on Tariffs and Trade.

Memorandum Opinion for the United States Trade Representative: Whether Uruguay Round Agreements Required Ratification as a Treaty

18 Op. O.L.C. 232 (1994)

This memorandum supplements our earlier opinion on the question whether the Uruguay Round Agreements concluded under the auspices of the General Agreement on Tariffs and Trade (the "GATT") must be ratified as a treaty. It replies to two later papers by Professor Laurence H. Tribe, and his testimony before the Senate Committee on Commerce, Science, and Transportation, that have disputed our conclusion on that subject. After considering Professor Tribe's arguments, we again conclude that the Uruguay Round Agreements may constitutionally be adopted by the passage of implementing legislation by both Houses of Congress, together with signing by the President.

I. The Treaty Clause

. . . Like Professor Tribe, we find that neither the text of the Constitution, nor the materials surrounding its drafting and ratification, nor subsequent Supreme Court case law interpreting it, provide clear-cut tests for deciding when an international agreement must be regarded as a "treaty" in the constitutional sense, and submitted to the Senate for its "Advice and Consent" under the Treaty Clause, U.S. Const. art. II, §2, cl. 2. In such circumstances, a significant guide to the interpretation of the Constitution's requirements is the practical construction placed on it by the executive and legislative branches acting together. . . .

Such practical construction has long established (and Professor Tribe acknowledges) that "there are many classes of agreements with foreign countries which are not required to be formulated as treaties" for constitutional purposes. Most pertinently here, practice under the Constitution has established that the United States can assume major international trade obligations such as those found in the Uruguay Round Agreements when they are negotiated by the President and approved and implemented by Act of Congress pursuant to procedures such as those set forth in 19 U.S.C. §§ 2902 & 2903. In following these procedures, Congress acts under its broad Foreign Commerce Clause powers, and the President acts pursuant to his constitutional responsibility for conducting the Nation's foreign affairs. The use of these procedures, in which both political branches deploy sweeping constitutional powers, fully satisfies the Constitution's requirements; the Treaty Clause's provision for concurrence by two-thirds of the Senators present is not constitutionally mandatory for international agreements of this kind.

Professor Tribe recognizes the existence of these decades-old practices, which have resulted in the approval of such fundamental trade pacts as the North American Free Trade Agreement (the "NAFTA"). But he disparages the use of Congressional-Executive agreements as merely a matter of "political leaders' casual approach to the Constitution." This dismissive characterization gives virtually no weight to the considered constitutional judgments of the political branches. We believe that that approach is mistaken. Disagreements and uncertainties surrounding the scope of the Treaty Clause—including its interaction with Congress's power to regulate commerce—are two centuries old. Congress's Foreign Commerce Clause authority and the President's responsibility for foreign affairs are unquestionably broad. In such circumstances, the political branches can fairly conclude—and have in fact concluded—that even major trade agreements such as the Uruguay Round Agreements may be approved and implemented by Acts of Congress, rather than ratified as treaties. Indeed, Professor Tribe himself wrote in 1988 that "it does appear settled that a hybrid form of international agreement—that in which the President is supported by a Joint Resolution of Congress—is coextensive with the treaty power. Such Congressional-Executive agreements are the law of the land, superseding inconsistent state or federal laws." Laurence H. Tribe, American Constitutional Law 228 n.18 (2d ed. 1988) (emphasis added).

Historically, the scope of the Treaty Clause, and its interplay with other constitutional clauses, have provoked controversies of several different kinds. The persistence of these controversies (which trace back to the eighteenth century), and the nearly complete absence of judicial decisions resolving them, underscore the necessity of relying on congressional precedent to interpret the relevant constitutional provisions. No one could deny that "congressional practice alone cannot justify abandonment of the Constitution's structural provisions," but it begs the question to assume that the treaty ratification process is structurally required by the Constitution in cases such as this. . . .

One recurring kind of dispute over the Treaty Clause has been whether international agreements could be given effect by Executive action alone, or whether they required submission to the Senate for its concurrence. *See, e.g.,* 2 Messages and Papers of the Presidents 33 (James D. Richardson ed., 1896) (President Monroe's message to the Senate of April 6, 1818, expressing uncertainty whether the Executive alone could make an international agreement for the naval disarmament of the Great Lakes, or whether Senate advice and consent was required). A second type of recurring dispute, more pertinent here, centered on the respective powers of the Senate and the House of Representatives in such areas as the regulation of foreign trade, where different clauses of the Constitution assign responsibilities either to one House alone or to both Houses together. As Secretary of State Dulles explained in testimony before the Senate Judiciary Committee in 1953, there is an

> undefined, and probably undefinable, borderline between international agreements which require two-thirds Senate Concurrence, but no House concurrence, as in the case of treaties, and agreements which should have the majority concurrence of both Chambers of Congress. . . . This is an area to be dealt with by friendly cooperation between the three departments of Government which are involved, rather than by attempts at constitutional definition, which are futile, or by the absorption, by one branch of Government, of responsibilities which are presently and properly shared.

Treaties and Executive Agreements: Hearings Before a Subcomm. of the Senate Comm. on the Judiciary, 83d Cong. 828 (1953).

Intra-branch disputes over the Treaty Clause can be traced as far back as 1796, when Representative Albert Gallatin argued that the "[t]reaty-making power . . . may be considered as clashing" with Congress's "authority of regulating trade," and that "[a] difference of opinion may exist as to the proper construction of the several articles of the Constitution, so as to reconcile those apparently contradictory provisions." 5 Annals of Cong. 437 (1796).

Again, in 1844, the Senate Foreign Relations Committee, under Senator Rufus Choate, presented a report on the Prussian and Germanic Confederation Treaty, in which the Committee urged rejection of the treaty because "the legislature is the department of government by which commerce should be regulated and laws of revenue be passed. The Constitution, in terms, communicates the power to regulate commerce and to impose duties to that department. It communicates it, in terms, to no other. Without engaging at all in an examination of the extent, limits, and objects of the power to make treaties, the committee believe that the general rule of our system is indisputably that the control of trade and the function of taxing belong, without abridgement or participation, to Congress." Compilation of Reports of the Senate Committee on Foreign Relations, 1789–1901, S. Doc. No. 56-231, pt. 8, at 36 (2d Sess. 1901).

From time to time, the House of Representatives has also insisted that a treaty be made dependent on the consent of both Houses of Congress. This has occurred when, for example, the House's power over appropriations has been at issue, as in the Gadsden purchase treaty of 1853 and the Alaskan purchase treaty of 1867. In 1880, the House asserted that the negotiation of a commercial treaty that fixed duties on foreign imports would be an unconstitutional invasion of its prerogatives over the origination of revenues; in 1883, it demanded, in connection with a proposed commercial treaty with Mexico, to have a voice in treaties affecting revenue.

In 1898, the United States annexed Hawaii by joint resolution, Joint Res. 55, 55th Cong., 30 Stat. 750 (1898), even though the Senate had previously rejected an annexation treaty, and even though opponents of the measure argued strenuously both in Congress and in the press that such an annexation could be accomplished only by treaty, and not by a simple legislative act.

More recently, the court in Edwards v. Carter, 580 F.2d 1055 (D.C. Cir.) (per curiam), cert. denied, 436 U.S. 907 (1978), rejected the claim by members of the House of Representatives that the treaty power could not be used to transfer the Panama Canal to Panama. The plaintiffs relied on the Constitution's Property Clause, U.S. Const. art. IV, § 3, cl. 2, which commits to "[t]he Congress" the power "to dispose of and make all needful Rules and Regulations respecting the Territory or other Property belonging to the United States." The court answered this claim by pointing out that

> [t]he grant of authority to Congress under the property clause states that
> "The Congress shall have Power . . . ," not that only the Congress shall have

power, or that the Congress shall have exclusive power. In this respect the property clause is parallel to Article I, § 8, which also states that "The Congress shall have Power . . . ." Many of the powers thereafter enumerated in § 8 involve matters that were at the time the Constitution was adopted, and that are at the present time, also commonly the subject of treaties. The most prominent example of this is the regulation of commerce with foreign nations, Art. [I], § 8, cl. 3, and appellants do not go so far as to contend that the treaty process is not a constitutionally allowable means for regulating foreign commerce. It thus seems to us that, on its face, the property clause is intended not to restrict the scope of the treaty clause, but, rather, is intended to permit Congress to accomplish through legislation what may concurrently be accomplished through other means provided in the Constitution.

580 F.2d at 1057–58. As the court noted, the Constitution on its face permits foreign commerce to be regulated either through the Treaty Clause or through the Foreign Commerce Clause. Nothing in the language of the Constitution privileges the Treaty Clause as the "sole" or "exclusive" means of regulating such activity. In actual practice, Congress and the President, understanding that nothing in the Constitution constrained them to choose one procedure rather than the other, have followed different procedures on different occasions.

In general, these inter- and intra-branch disputes over the scope of the Treaty Clause have been resolved through the political process, occasionally with marked departures from prior practices. *See* Goldwater v. Carter, 444 U.S. 996, 1004 n.1 (1979) (Rehnquist, J., concurring in judgment); John O. McGinnis, Constitutional Review by the Executive in Foreign Affairs and War Powers: A Consequence of Rational Choice in the Separation of Powers, 56 Law & Contemp. Probs. 293, 305–08 (1993). For example, after the House of Representatives objected to the concentration of power over Indian affairs in the hands of the Senate through the Treaty Clause, Congress in 1871 enacted a rider to an Indian appropriation bill declaring that no fresh treaties were to be made with the Indian nations. Act of Mar. 3, 1871, ch. 120, 16 Stat. 544, 566. Although the United States had been making Indian treaties for almost a century before that enactment, *see* United States v. Kagama, 118 U.S. 375, 382 (1886), after 1871 "the federal government continued to make agreements with Indian tribes, many similar to treaties, that were approved by both Senate and House," but "the House's action sounded the death knell for treaty making." Felix S. Cohen, Handbook of Federal Indian Law 107 & n.370 (1982 ed.). The policy of the 1871 enactment remains in effect. *See* 25 U.S.C. § 71. We are uncertain whether this longstanding legislation would be constitutional by Professor Tribe's lights.

The existence of such recurring disputes over the scope and meaning of the Treaty Clause undermines any dogmatic claim that a major trade agreement such as the Uruguay Round Agreements, which stands at the intersection of the foreign affairs, revenue raising and commerce powers, must be ratified as a treaty and cannot be implemented by the action of both Houses of Congress. The distinctions between the Federal government's treaty power and the other constitutional powers in play are simply too fluid and dynamic to dictate the conclusion that one method must be followed to the complete exclusion of the other. Here, if anywhere, is an area where the sound judgment of the political branches, acting in concert and accommodating the interests and prerogatives of one another, should be respected. It is simply mistaken to suggest that this established practice of mutual adjustment and cooperation on a constitutional question of inherent uncertainty reflects mere "political convenience rather than constitutional commitment." Tribe Prepared Statement at 300. None of the three political branches involved in working out the procedure for Congressional-Executive agreements has abdicated its constitutional responsibility; none has endangered the basic, structural provisions of Articles I and II. . . .

WALTER DELLINGER
Assistant Attorney General
Office of Legal Counsel

---

1. *Why Prefer Legislation?* According to Professor Oona Hathaway, treaties—as compared to congressional-executive agreements—have "weaker democratic legitimacy, are more cumbersome and politically vulnerable, and create less reliable legal commitments." Oona A. Hathaway, *Treaties' End: The Past, Present and Future of International Lawmaking in the United States*, 117 YALE L. J. 1236, 1241 (2008). These asserted virtues are rooted in the involvement of the House in authorizing congressional-executive agreements and the inapplicability of the constitutional supermajority requirement for Senate ratification. Of course, many international agreements require legislative implementation, if only the appropriation of funds. If approval of an agreement is sought from both houses before ratification, the danger that the House of Representatives might later refuse to join in the agreement is all but eliminated. For a concurring view by two political scientists as to the relative virtues of executive agreements, see GLEN S. KRUTZ AND JEFFREY S. PEAKE, TREATY POLITICS AND THE RISE OF EXECUTIVE AGREEMENTS: INTERNATIONAL COMMITMENTS IN A SYSTEM OF SHARED POWERS (2009).

2. *Standards.* Does the OLC Memo suggest any general principles, traceable to the Constitution, that may usefully be used to distinguish between treaties and international agreements that are implemented through legislation? In *Laws as Treaties? The Constitutionality of Congressional-Executive Agreements,* 99 MICH. L. REV. 757 (2001), Professor John C. Yoo argues against the thesis of complete interchangeability. He argues that constitutional text, original design, and historical practice support the following distinction:

> Congress can resort to congressional-executive agreements in areas over which Congress already possesses plenary constitutional authority, such as international trade and finance. Treaties, however, still remain the required instrument of national policy when the federal government reaches international agreements on matters outside of Article I, Section 8, or over which the President and Congress possess concurrent and potentially conflicting

powers. As I have argued elsewhere, treaties may still be concluded in areas
of Congressional authority, but such treaties must be non-self-executing, in
order to preserve the Constitution's separation of the executive and legislative powers.

Id. at 821. If Professor Yoo is correct, should courts be prepared to step in and invalidate congressional-executive agreements concluded in domains where only treaties
would be proper?

Professor Hathaway dissents emphatically from the Yoo position. Her historical
analysis of the use of treaties versus congressional-legislative agreements finds no reliable, principled basis on which to distinguish the contexts in which they have been
employed. The State Department has attempted to set standards for the use of different international law making processes, State Dept. Circular 175, "Procedures on
Treaties and Other International Agreements," 11 F.A.M. 700; Hathaway agrees such
standards may be helpful in suggesting when *unilateral* executive agreements are
inappropriate. In her view, however, the Department's criteria provide virtually no
guidance for choosing between treaties and congressional-executive agreements. This
is unsurprising, she thinks, because the exceptional procedures contemplated by the
Treaty Clause are chiefly rooted in two historical considerations that no longer bear
weight—first, the Framers' expectation that the Senate would function in a close
advisory role to the President, and second, the southern states' concern that they
needed a potential veto power in the Senate to prevent the adoption of treaties that
might affect the legality of slavery. Oona A. Hathaway, 117 Yale L. J. at 1276–1278.
It would better suit contemporary circumstances, she argues, to prefer recourse to
the congressional-executive agreement process in all cases, except three contexts in
which the Treaty Clause "has been used beyond the ordinary jurisdiction of the federal government, as defined by existing or contemporary jurisprudence, scholarly
commentary, and historical practice: (1) cession of territory, (2) extradition, and
(3) disabilities of aliens." *Id.* at 1344–1345.

3. *Modifying Treaties.* Because many international agreements are negotiated in
order to modify the terms of earlier agreements, it is reasonable to ask whether the
form must remain consistent over time. That is, once the United States concludes a
treaty with another nation, may the President modify the treaty through a legislatively approved executive agreement, or does it require a treaty to modify a treaty?

In a 1996 opinion, the Office of Legal Counsel concluded that Congress may authorize the President to modify, through an executive agreement, prior treaty obligations. Its reasoning was as follows: For domestic purposes, treaties are part of the
Supreme Law of the land, equivalent to statutes, and hence subject to congressional
modification through statutes enacted later. If Congress may modify directly a treaty
through statute, it may statutorily delegate to the President the power to negotiate
modifications. Congressional authorization, of course, does not relieve the United
States of international obligations it shoulders under the earlier treaty. If, however,
the President achieves agreement with the treaty's co-signatory, such an agreement
will suffice to change the nature of the United States' obligations under international

law. Do you agree? Whatever the logic of OLC's position, it was able to cite very little historical precedent for its result. Acting Assistant Attorney General Christopher Schroeder, *Validity of Congressional-Executive Agreements That Substantially Modify the United States' Obligations under an Existing Treaty*, 20 Op. O.L.C. 389 (1996).

4. *Unilateral President Agreements.* Executive agreements may also be made solely under the President's authority. While no one has doubted that the President has the power to make some such executive agreements, there has been constitutional controversy surrounding others. It is accepted, for example, that the President, as commander-in-chief, may make armistice agreements; viewed broadly, the commander in chief power might support many other agreements as well, including war-time commitments on territorial and political issues for the post-war era, as at Yalta and Potsdam. The President also has sole responsibility for the recognition of foreign governments, and the Supreme Court has held this power sufficient to authorize unilateral-executive agreements to settle issues that are necessary to establish diplomatic relations. *See United States v. Belmont*, 301 U.S. 324 (1937). Additionally, it is sometimes suggested that executive agreements, unlike treaties, do not involve long-term relationships or obligations. *See* Robert H. Jackson, *Acquisition of Naval Air Bases in Exchange for Over-Age Destroyers*, 39 Op. Att'y Gen. 484, 487 (1940), reprinted in H. JEFFERSON POWELL, THE CONSTITUTION AND THE ATTORNEYS GEN- ERAL 307, 309 (1999) (purporting to differentiate executive agreements from treaties, which "involve commitments as to the future which would carry an obligation to exercise powers vested in the Congress").

It is unclear, however, that any principled line identifies in practice those unilateral executive agreements that do not improperly trespass on the Senate's role. Yet, historical practice alone does not establish that the President is wholly free from constitutional constraints in making any agreement on any matter involving our relations with another country. This would remove the express "check" of Senate consent to treaties that appears in article II. An argument that the forms of international agreement can and should be distinguished based on the source of power they implement appears in Kenneth C. Randall, *The Treaty Power*, 51 OHIO ST. L.J. 1089 (1990).

The Supreme Court has not yet held any executive agreement ultra vires for lack of Senate consent, nor has it given other guidelines that might define the President's power to act alone. Members of the Senate have periodically charged presidential usurpation, but have not articulated plausible limits to presidential power. *See, e.g., Dole v. Carter*, 444 F. Supp. 1065 (D. Kan. 1977) (denying Senator's petition to enjoin return to Hungary, absent a treaty, of Hungarian coronation regalia). Presidential practice, too, has not reflected any principle of limitation. Numerous agreements have been made ranging over the entire field of foreign relations.

State Department Circular 175, cited earlier, was drafted in 1974 in order to help insure that treaties and other international agreements for the United States are carried out within constitutional and other appropriate limits. (It carefully notes, however, that deviation from its provisions will not invalidate actions taken by government officers nor affect the validity of negotiations engaged in or of treaties or other agreements concluded.) In addition to citing the President's authority to conclude executive agreements pursuant to statutory or treaty authority, the Circular states that the President may conclude agreements to implement inherent presidential powers, including: (a) the President's authority as Chief Executive to represent the nation in foreign affairs; (b) the President's authority to receive ambassadors and other public ministers; (c) the President's authority as commander in chief and (d) the President's authority "to take care that the laws be faithfully executed."*

It is possible to identify at least one likely limitation on the unilateral executive agreement power that does not apply to treaties. Unless an executive agreement may be connected to at least implicit statutory authorization, it is probable that, unlike a treaty, it may not override prior statutes. Thus, in *United States v. Guy W. Capps*, 204 F.2d 655 (4th Cir. 1953), *aff'd on other grounds*, 348 U.S. 296 (1955), the court refused to give effect to an executive agreement regulating the export of potatoes from Canada to the United States. The court regarded the agreement, effecting a regulation of interstate and foreign commerce, as not within Presidential authority alone, but also within Congress's power to regulate such trade. Because the agreement conflicted with provisions of the Agricultural Act of 1948, the Court held that the agreement was invalid; the President's inherent foreign affairs powers were insufficient to permit an override of Congress's determinations as to trade. *Cf. South Puerto Rico Sugar Co. Trading Corp. v. United States*, 334 F.2d 622 (Ct. Cl. 1964), *cert. denied*, 379 U.S. 964 (1965).

This requirement that Presidents respect prior statutes has not, however, been thought to prevent Presidents altogether from making executive agreements as to matters on which Congress could legislate, but has not. In some circumstances, the domestic legal impact of an executive agreement may be identical to that of an article II treaty. *See, e.g., Weinberger v. Rossi*, 456 U.S. 25 (1982) (construing "treaty" exception to antidiscrimination statute as extending to executive agreements).

If an executive agreement is within the President's power, there seem to be no formal requirements as to how it must be made. It may be signed by the President or on his behalf; it may be made by Secretaries of State, ambassadors or lesser authorized officials; and there is no reason why it must be formal or even written.

Finally, it should be noted that executive agreements—like treaties—may not contravene constitutional protections for individual rights. *Ozonoff v. Berzak*, 744 F.2d 224 (1st Cir. 1984) (prohibiting loyalty check of World Health Organization physician under executive order, the terms of which violated the First Amendment).

---

* In order to decide which constitutionally authorized procedure for international agreement ought to be chosen, other guidelines mention: (a) the extent to which the agreement involves commitments or risks affecting the nation as a whole; (b) whether the agreement is intended to affect state laws; and (c) whether the agreement may be given effect without the enactment of subsequent legislation by the Congress. Other variables include the formality needed, the anticipated duration of the agreement and past practice. The Circular further urges the President to consult Congress as to process before making an international agreement.

For additional discussion, see LAWRENCE MARGOLIS, EXECUTIVE AGREEMENTS AND PRESIDENTIAL POWER IN FOREIGN POLICY (1986).

United States v. Pink

315 U.S. 203 (1942)

Justice DOUGLAS delivered the opinion of the Court.

This action was brought by the United States to recover the assets of the New York branch of the First Russian Insurance Co. which remained in the hands of respondent after the payment of all domestic creditors. . . .

The First Russian Insurance Co., organized under the laws of the former Empire of Russia, established a New York branch in 1907. It deposited with the Superintendent of Insurance, pursuant to the laws of New York, certain assets to secure payment of claims resulting from transactions of its New York branch. By certain laws, decrees, enactments and orders, in 1918 and 1919, the Russian Government nationalized the business of insurance and all of the property, wherever situated, of all Russian insurance companies (including the First Russian Insurance Co.), and discharged and cancelled all the debts of such companies and the rights of all shareholders in all such property. The New York branch of the First Russian Insurance Co. continued to do business in New York until 1925. At that time, respondent, pursuant to an order of the Supreme Court of New York, took possession of its assets for a determination and report upon the claims of the policyholders and creditors in the United States. Thereafter, all claims of domestic creditors, *i.e.*, all claims arising out of the business of the New York branch, were paid by respondent, leaving a balance in his hands of more than $1,000,000. In 1931, the New York Court of Appeals directed respondent to dispose of that balance as follows: first, to pay claims of foreign creditors who had filed attachment prior to the commencement of the liquidation proceeding . . . ; and second, to pay any surplus to a quorum of the board of directors of the company. Pursuant to that mandate, respondent proceeded with the liquidation of the claims of the foreign creditors. Some payments were made thereon. The major portion of the allowed claims, however, were not paid, a stay having been granted pending disposition of the claim of the United States. On November 16, 1933, the United States recognized the Union of Soviet Socialist Republics as the *de jure* Government of Russia and as an incident of that recognition accepted an assignment (known as the Litvinov Assignment) of certain claims. The Litvinov Assignment was in the form of a letter, dated November 16, 1933, to the President of the United States from Maxim Litvinov, People's Commissar for Foreign Affairs, reading as follows:

> "Following our conversations I have the honor to inform you that the Government of the Union of Soviet Socialist Republics agrees that . . . the Government of the Union of Soviet Socialist Republics will not take any steps to [litigate] . . . for the amounts admitted to be due or that may be found to be due it, as the successor of prior Governments of Russia, or otherwise, from

American nationals, including corporations, . . . does hereby release and assign all such amounts to the Government of the United States, the Government of the Union of Soviet Socialist Republics to be duly notified in each case of any amount realized . . . from such release and assignment.

"The Government of the Union of Soviet Socialist Republics further agrees . . . not to make any claims with respect to:

"(a) judgments rendered or that may be rendered by American courts in so far as they relate to property, or rights, or interests therein, in which the Union of Soviet Socialist Republics or its nationals may have had or may claim to have an interest; or,

"(b) acts done or settlements made by or with the Government of the United States, or public officials in the United States, or its nationals, relating to property, credits, or obligations of any Government of Russia or nationals thereof."

This was acknowledged by the President on the same date. The acknowledgment, after setting forth the terms of the assignment, concluded:

"I am glad to have these undertakings by your Government and I shall be pleased to notify your Government in each case of any amount realized by the Government of the United States from the release and assignment to it of the amounts admitted to be due, or that may be found to be due, the Government of the Union of Soviet Socialist Republics. . . ."

On November 14, 1934, the United States brought an action in the federal District Court for the Southern District of New York, seeking to recover the assets in the hands of respondent. This Court held in *United States v. Bank of New York & Trust Co.*, 296 U.S. 463, that . . . " . . . the jurisdiction of the state court should be respected"; and that, whatever might be "the effect of recognition" of the Russian Government, it did not terminate the state proceedings. The United States was remitted to the state court for determination of its claim, no opinion being intimated on the merits. . . .

Thereafter, the present suit was instituted in the Supreme Court of New York. The defendants, other than respondent, were certain designated policyholders and other creditors who had presented in the liquidation proceedings claims against the corporation. The complaint prayed, *inter alia*, that the United States be adjudged to be the sole and exclusive owner entitled to immediate possession of the entire surplus fund in the hands of the respondent.

Respondent's answer denied the allegations of the complaint that title to the funds in question passed to the United States and that the Russian decrees had the effect claimed. It also set forth various affirmative defenses—that the order of distribution pursuant to the decree in 255 N.Y. 415, 175 N.E. 114, could not be affected by the Litvinov Assignment; . . . that the Russian decrees had no extraterritorial effect, according to Russian law; that if the decrees were given extraterritorial effect, they were confiscatory and their recognition would be unconstitutional and contrary to the public policy of the United States and of the State of New York; and that the United States, under the Litvinov Assignment, acted merely as a collection agency for the Russian Government and hence was foreclosed from asserting any title to the property in question.

The answer was filed in March, 1938. In April, 1939, the New York Court of Appeals decided *Moscow Fire Ins. Co. v. Bank of New York & Trust Co.*, 280 N.Y. 286, 20 N.E. 2d 758. . . . The New York Court of Appeals held in the *Moscow* case that the Russian decrees in question had no extraterritorial effect. If that is true, it is decisive of the present controversy. For the United States acquired, under the Litvinov Assignment, only such rights as Russia had. *Guaranty Trust Co. v. United States*, 304 U.S. 126, 143. If the Russian decrees left the New York assets of the Russian insurance companies unaffected, then Russia had nothing here to assign. But that question of foreign law is not to be determined exclusively by the state court. The claim of the United States based on the Litvinov Assignment raises a federal question. *United States v. Belmont*, 301 U.S. 324. This Court will review or independently determine all questions on which a federal right is necessarily dependent. Here, title obtained under the Litvinov Assignment depends on a correct interpretation of Russian law. As in cases arising under the full faith and credit clause, these questions of foreign law on which the asserted federal right is based are not peculiarly within the cognizance of the local courts. While deference will be given to the determination of the state court, its conclusion is not accepted as final.

We do not stop to review all the evidence in the voluminous record of the *Moscow* case bearing on the question of the extraterritorial effect of the Russian decrees of nationalization, except to note that the expert testimony tendered by the United States gave great credence to its position. Subsequently to the hearings in that case, however, the United States, through diplomatic channels, requested the Commissariat for Foreign Affairs of the Russian Government to obtain an official declaration by the Commissariat for Justice of the R.S.F.S.R. which would make clear, as a matter of Russian law, the intended effect of the Russian decree nationalizing insurance companies upon the funds of such companies outside of Russia. The official declaration, dated November 28, 1937, [certified that all property of the insurance companies had been nationalized, wherever located].

The referee in the *Moscow* case found, and the evidence supported his finding, that the Commissariat for Justice has power to interpret existing Russian law. That being true, this official declaration is conclusive so far as the intended extraterritorial effect of the Russian decree is concerned.

We hold that, so far as its intended effect is concerned, the Russian decree embraced the New York assets of the First Russian Insurance Co.

The question of whether the decree should be given extraterritorial effect is, of course, a distinct matter. One primary issue raised in that connection is whether, under our constitutional system, New York law can be allowed to stand in the way.

The decision of the New York Court of Appeals in the *Moscow* case is unequivocal. It held that "under the law of this State such confiscatory decrees do not affect the property claimed here" . . . . It is one thing to hold, as was done in *Guaranty Trust Co. v. United States, supra*, 304 U.S. at p. 142, that under the Litvinov Assignment the United States did not acquire "a right free of preexisting infirmity," such as the running of the statute of limitations against the Russian Government, its assignor. Unlike the problem presented here and in the *Moscow* case, that holding in no way sanctions the asserted power of New York to deny enforcement of a claim under the Litvinov Assignment because of an overriding policy of the State which denies validity in New York of the Russian decrees on which the assigned claim rests. That power was denied New York in *United States v. Belmont, supra*, 301 U.S. 324. With one qualification, to be noted, the *Belmont* case is determinative of the present controversy.

That case involved the right of the United States under the Litvinov Assignment to recover, from a custodian or stakeholder in New York, funds which had been nationalized and appropriated by the Russian decrees.

This Court, speaking through Justice Sutherland, held that the conduct of foreign relations is committed by the Constitution to the political departments of the Federal Government; that the propriety of the exercise of that power is not open to judicial inquiry; and that recognition of a foreign sovereign conclusively binds the courts and "is retroactive and validates all actions and conduct of the government so recognized from the commencement of its existence." It further held (p. 330) that recognition of the Soviet Government, the establishment of diplomatic relations with it, and the Litvinov Assignment were "all parts of one transaction, resulting in an international compact between the two governments." After stating that, "in respect of what was done here, the Executive had authority to speak as the sole organ" of the national government, it added: "The assignment and the agreements in connection therewith did not, as in the case of treaties, as that term is used in the treaty making clause of the Constitution (Art. II, § 2), require the advice and consent of the Senate." It held that the "external powers of the United States are to be exercised without regard to state laws or policies. The supremacy of a treaty in this respect has been recognized from the beginning." And it added that "all international compacts and agreements" are to be treated with similar dignity for the reason that "complete power over international affairs is in the national government and is not and cannot be subject to any curtailment or interference on the part of the several states." This Court did not stop to inquire whether in fact there was any policy of New York which enforcement of the Litvinov Assignment would infringe since "no state policy can prevail against the international compact here involved."

The New York Court of Appeals, in the *Moscow* case (280 N.Y. 309, 20 N.E. 2d 758), distinguished the *Belmont* case on the ground that it was decided on the sufficiency of the pleadings, the demurrer to the complaint admitting that under the Russian decree the property was confiscated by the Russian Government and then transferred to the United States under the Litvinov Assignment. But, as we have seen, the Russian decree in question was intended to have an extraterritorial effect and to embrace funds of the kind which are here involved. Nor can there be any serious doubt that claims of the kind here in question were included in the Litvinov Assignment. It is broad and inclusive. It should be interpreted consonantly with the purpose of the compact to eliminate all possible sources of friction between these two great nations. Strict construction would run counter to that national policy. For, as we shall see, the existence of unpaid claims against Russia and its nationals, which were held in this country, and which the Litvinov Assignment was intended to secure, had long been one impediment to resumption of friendly relations between these two great powers.

The holding in the *Belmont* case is therefore determinative of the present controversy, unless the stake of the foreign creditors in this liquidation proceeding and the provision which New York has provided for their protection call for a different result.

The *Belmont* case forecloses any relief to the Russian corporation. For this Court held in that case (301 U.S. at p. 332): ". . . our Constitution, laws and policies have no extraterritorial operation, unless in respect of our own citizens. . . . What another country has done in the way of taking over property of its nationals, and especially of its corporations, is not a matter for judicial consideration here. Such nationals must look to their own government for any redress to which they may be entitled."

But it is urged that different considerations apply in case of the foreign creditors to whom the New York Court of Appeals ordered distribution of these funds. The argument is that their rights in these funds have vested by virtue of the New York decree; that to deprive them of the property would violate the Fifth Amendment which extends its protection to aliens as well as to citizens; and that the Litvinov Assignment cannot deprive New York of its power to administer the balance of the fund in accordance with its laws for the benefit of these creditors.

At the outset, it should be noted that, so far as appears, all creditors whose claims arose out of dealing with the New York branch have been paid. Thus we are not faced with the question whether New York's policy of protecting the so-called local creditors by giving them priority in the assets deposited with the State should be recognized within the [full faith and credit interpretation] of *Clark v. Willard*, 294 U.S. 211, or should yield to the Federal policy expressed in the international compact or agreement. We intimate no opinion on that question. The contest here is between the United States and creditors of the Russian corporation who, we assume, are not citizens of this country and whose claims did not arise out of transactions with the New York branch. The United States is seeking to protect not only claims which it holds but also claims of its nationals. H. Rep. No. 865, 76th Cong., 1st Sess. Such claims did not arise out of transactions with this Russian corporation; they are, however, claims against Russia or its nationals. The existence of such claims and their non-payment had for years been one of the barriers to recognition of the Soviet regime by the Executive Department. The purpose of the discussions leading to the policy of recognition was to resolve "all questions outstanding" between the two nations. Settlement of all American claims against Russia was one method of removing some of the prior objections to recognition based on the Soviet policy of nationalization. The Litvinov Assignment was not only part and parcel of the new policy of recognition, it was also the method adopted by the Executive Department for alleviating in this country the rigors of nationalization. Congress tacitly recognized that policy. Acting in anticipation of the realization of funds under the Litvinov Assignment (H. Rep. No. 865, 76th Cong., 1st Sess.), it authorized the appointment of a Commissioner to determine the claims of American nationals against the Soviet Government. Joint Resolution of August 4, 1939, 53 Stat. 1199.

If the President had the power to determine the policy which was to govern the question of recognition, then the Fifth Amendment does not stand in the way of giving full force and effect to the Litvinov Assignment. To be sure, aliens as well as citizens are entitled to the protection of the Fifth Amendment. *Russian Volunteer Fleet v. United States*, 282 U.S. 481. A State is not precluded, however, by the Fourteenth Amendment from according priority to local creditors as against creditors who are nationals of foreign countries and whose claims arose abroad. *Disconto Gesellschaft v. Umbreit*, 208 U.S. 570. By the same token, the Federal Government is not barred by the Fifth Amendment from securing for itself and our nationals priority against such creditors. And it matters not that the procedure adopted by the Federal Government is globular and involves a regrouping of assets. There is no Constitutional reason why this Government need act as the collection agent for nationals of other countries when it takes steps to protect itself or its own nationals on external debts. There is no reason why it may not, through such devices as the Litvinov Assignment, make itself and its nationals whole from assets here before it permits such assets to go abroad in satisfaction of claims of aliens made elsewhere and not incurred in connection with business conducted in this country. The fact that New York has marshaled the claims of the foreign creditors here involved and authorized their payment does not give them immunity from that general rule.

If the priority had been accorded American claims by treaty with Russia, there would be no doubt as to its validity. The same result obtains here. The powers of the President in the conduct of foreign relations included the power, without consent of the Senate, to determine the public policy of the United States with respect to the Russian nationalization decrees. "What government is to be regarded here as representative of a foreign sovereign state is a political rather than a judicial question, and is to be determined by the political department of the government." *Guaranty Trust Co. v. United States, supra*, 304 U.S. at p. 137. That authority is not limited to a determination of the government to be recognized. It includes the power to determine the policy which is to govern the question of recognition. Objections to the underlying policy as well as objections to recognition are to be addressed to the political department and not to the courts. As we have noted, this Court in the *Belmont* case recognized that the Litvinov Assignment was an international compact which did not require the participation of the Senate. It stated: "There are many such compacts, of which a protocol, a modus vivendi, a postal convention, and agreements like that now under consideration are illustrations." Recognition is not always absolute; it is sometimes conditional. 1 Moore, International Law Digest (1906), pp. 73–74; 1 Hackworth, Digest of International Law (1940), pp. 192–95. Power to remove such obstacles to full recognition as settlement of claims of our nationals (Levitan, Executive Agreements, 35 Ill. L. Rev. 365, 382–85) certainly is a modest implied power of the President who is the "sole organ of the federal government in the field of international relations." *United States v. Curtiss-Wright Corp., supra*, p. 320. Effectiveness in handling the delicate problems of foreign relations requires no less. Unless such a power exists, the power of recognition might be thwarted or seriously diluted. No such obstacle can be placed in the way of rehabilitation of relations between this country and another nation, unless the historic conception of the powers and responsibilities of the President in the conduct of foreign affairs is to be drastically revised. It was the judgment of the political department that full recognition of the Soviet Government required the settlement of all outstanding problems including the claims of our nationals. Recognition and the Litvinov Assignment were interdependent. We would usurp the executive function if we held that that decision was not final and conclusive in the courts.

"All constitutional acts of power, whether in the executive or in the judicial department, have as much legal validity and obligation as if they proceeded from the legislature, ..." The Federalist, No. 64. A treaty is a "Law of the Land" under the supremacy clause (Art. VI, Cl. 2) of the Constitution. Such international compacts and agreements as the Litvinov Assignment have a similar dignity. *United States v. Belmont, supra*, 301 U.S. at p. 331. *See* Corwin, The President, Office & Powers (1940), pp. 228–40.

It is, of course, true that even treaties with foreign nations will be carefully construed so as not to derogate from the authority and jurisdiction of the States of this nation unless clearly necessary to effectuate the national policy. *Guaranty Trust Co. v. United States, supra*, p. 143 and cases cited. For example, in *Todok v. Union State Bank*, 281 U.S. 449, this Court took pains in its construction of a treaty, relating to the power of an alien to dispose of property in this country, not to invalidate the provisions of state law governing such dispositions. Frequently the obligation of a treaty will be dependent on state law. But state law must yield when it is inconsistent with, or impairs the policy or provisions of, a treaty or of an international compact or agreement. Then, the power of a State to refuse enforcement of rights based on foreign law which runs counter to the public policy of the forum must give way before the superior Federal policy evidenced by a treaty or international compact or agreement.

Enforcement of New York's policy as formulated by the *Moscow* case would collide with and subtract from the Federal policy, whether it was premised on the absence of extraterritorial effect of the Russian decrees, the conception of the New York branch as a distinct juristic personality, or disapproval by New York of the Russian program of nationalization. For the *Moscow* case refuses to give effect or recognition in New York to acts of the Soviet Government which the United States by its policy of recognition agreed no longer to question. Enforcement of such state policies would indeed tend to restore some of the precise impediments to friendly relations which the President intended to remove on inauguration of the policy of recognition of the Soviet Government. . . .

We recently stated in *Hines v. Davidowitz*, 312 U.S. 52, 68, that the field which affects international relations is "the one aspect of our government that from the first has been most generally conceded imperatively to demand broad national authority"; and that any state power which may exist "is restricted to the narrowest of limits." There, we were dealing with the question as to whether a state statute regulating aliens survived a similar federal statute. We held that it did not. Here, we are dealing with an exclusive federal function. If state laws and policies did not yield before the exercise of the external powers of the United States, then our foreign policy might be thwarted. These are delicate matters. If state action could defeat or alter our foreign policy, serious consequences might ensue. The nation as a whole would be held to answer if a State created difficulties with a foreign power. Certainly, the conditions for "enduring friendship" between the nations, which the policy of recognition in this instance was designed to effectuate, are not likely to flourish where, contrary to national policy, a lingering atmosphere of hostility is created by state action.

Such considerations underlie the principle of *Oetjen v. Central Leather Co.*, 246 U.S. 297, 302–03, that when a revolutionary government is recognized as a *de jure* government, "such recognition is retroactive in effect and validates all the actions and conduct of the government so recognized from the commencement of its existence." They also explain the rule expressed in *Underhill v. Hernandez*, 168 U.S. 250, 252, that "the courts of one country will not sit in judgment on the acts of the government of another done within its own territory." . . .

We hold that the right to the funds or property in question became vested in the Soviet Government as the successor to the First Russian Insurance Co.; that this right has passed to the United States under the Litvinov Assignment; and that the United States is entitled to the property as against the corporation and the foreign creditors.

The judgment is reversed and the cause is remanded to the Supreme Court of New York for proceedings not inconsistent with this opinion.

Reversed.

Justice REED and Justice JACKSON did not participate in the consideration or decision of this case.

[Justice FRANKFURTER wrote a separate concurrence. Justice STONE dissented.]

---

1. *Reviewing the Issues.* Among the more instructive aspects of the *Pink* case is the hint it gives of the factual and legal complexity of claims settlement litigation. Can you summarize the procedural history of this litigation and the question that differentiates this case from *Belmont*?

2. *The Scope of Unilateral Presidential Power?* The court holds that the executive agreement at issue, accepting the Litvinov Assignment, did not require Senate consent. Does *Pink* cast doubt on the statement in *United States v. Guy W. Capps, Inc.*, 204 F.2d 655 (4th Cir. 1953), *aff'd on other grounds*, 348 U.S. 296 (1955), cited earlier, that the President may not enter into executive agreements inconsistent with prior federal legislation? What if the agreement is part and parcel of the United States' recognition of another country?

3. *Act of State Doctrine.* Claims litigation often involves a challenge to the expropriatory or other injurious acts of foreign governments in foreign territory. In the United States, as well as in other countries, litigants raising such claims may find adjudication barred by the so-called Act of State Doctrine, a judicially-imposed rule of self-restraint, by which courts do not inquire into the validity of acts of other governments within their own territory. The doctrine, given modern explanation in *Banco Nacional de Cuba v. Sabbatino*, 376 U.S. 398 (1964), respects the separation of powers because it seeks to prevent courts from undermining the political branches. The contours of the doctrine are not always clear, however. Both Congress and the executive branch, for example, may try to prevent its application. In 1964, Congress enacted the Hickenlooper Amendment, 22 U.S.C. § 2370(e)(2) (1982), seeking to limit the use of the doctrine, unless the President determines and suggests to a court that, because of U.S. foreign policy interests, the doctrine ought to be applied.* The Amendment has been strictly construed by the courts, and has not always prevented courts from following the Act of State doctrine on their own initiative. The Supreme Court has decided that the doctrine does not apply to litigation that ascribes unlawful motivations to foreign officials, so long as the objective of the suit is not to invalidate an official foreign act. *W.S. Kirkpatrick & Co. v. Environmental Tectonics Corp., International*, 493 U.S. 400 (1990).

In 1972, three of the five majority Justices in *First National City Bank v. Banco Nacional de Cuba*, 406 U.S. 759, expressed approval of the so-called *Bernstein* exception [based on *Bernstein v. N.V. Nederlandsche-Amerikaansche Stoomvaart-Maatschappij*, 210 F.2d 375 (2d Cir. 1954)] to the doctrine. In *Bernstein*, the Court of Appeals, on separation of powers grounds, respected a request from the State Department to refrain from applying the doctrine and examine the legal issues raised by an otherwise protected foreign sovereign act. Six of the nine Justices disapproved of the exception, however, and it is not followed as law. Nonetheless, courts may give some weight to the Department of State's views in deciding, in a particular case, whether invocation of the doctrine is appropriate.

---

* In a variety of contexts, the State Department provides courts with specific "suggestions" or instructions as to U.S. foreign policy. Such suggestions, for example, are used to inform courts as to the U.S. recognition policy with respect to a particular foreign government. The State Department may supply its views on its own initiative, and, in rare cases, a court may seek them *sua sponte*; typically, however, they are sought by one of the parties to pending litigation. With respect to recognition, the current judicial practice is to rely on these views conclusively.

This tortuous history raises several separation of powers puzzles. First, should the Act of State doctrine be regarded as a judicial statement that the validity of other governments' acts in their own territory is a question constitutionally committed to the political branches of government to determine? If so, the doctrine would then appear to be a branch of the political question doctrine, and the political branches presumably could not delegate their constitutionally vested decisionmaking authority to the courts. Alternatively, should the doctrine be viewed as a prudential practice to avoid undermining foreign relations in particular cases? If so, then assurances in a particular case that foreign relations would not be adversely affected by judicial inquiry into another government's acts should have weight. Perhaps, given that the courts have no foreign affairs powers, they should be determinative. But, from whom may those assurances come—from the President or from Congress? May Congress limit the President's ability to command either the application or nonapplication of the doctrine? Must Congress authorize such commands?

For a more thorough exploration of the Act of State doctrine, see Henry J. Steiner & Detlev F. Vagts, Transnational Legal Problems: Materials and Text 672–728 (1976); Thomas M. Franck & Michael J. Glennon, Foreign Relations and National Security Law 202–14 (1987).

4. *Further Reading.* For further discussion of the separation of powers implications of international claims settlements, see Note, *The Executive Claims Settlement Power: Constitutional Authority and Foreign Affairs Applications*, 85 Colum. L. Rev. 155 (1985).

———————

Dames & Moore v. Regan

453 U.S. 654 (1981)

[In the waning hours of the Carter Administration, executive branch officials worked feverishly to reach a settlement of the Iranian hostage crisis, which began in November 1979. As a part of a deal for the hostages' release, President Carter agreed both to nullify certain attachments that courts had awarded U.S. creditors against assets of the Iranian government, and to suspend certain claims against Iran pending their resolution in an international claims tribunal. Only the former action purported to rest on statutory authority. Carter's agreement did not involve our recognition of Iran. Although the U.S. recognized the revolutionary government in 1979, we subsequently broke diplomatic relations (which did not affect the prior recognition). As you read this decision, consider how you would have advised President Carter in advance regarding the legality of the settlement. Which sources of authority would you have invoked, with what weight for each? Also, consider the decision's effect on precedent. Does this case breathe new life into *Midwest Oil*? What guidance does Justice Rehnquist derive from *Youngstown*?]

Justice REHNQUIST delivered the opinion of the Court.

The questions presented by this case touch fundamentally upon the matter in which our Republic is to be governed. Throughout the nearly two centuries of our Nation's existence under the Constitution, this subject has generated considerable debate. . . . As [various] writings reveal it is doubtless both futile and perhaps dangerous to find any epigrammatical explanation of how this country has been governed. Indeed, as Justice Jackson noted, "[a] judge . . . may be surprised at the poverty of really useful and unambiguous authority applicable to concrete problems of executive power as they actually present themselves." *Youngstown Sheet & Tube Co. v. Sawyer*, 343 U.S. 579, 634 (1952) (concurring opinion).

Our decision today will not dramatically alter this situation, for the Framers "did not make the judiciary the overseer of our government." *Id.*, at 594 (Frankfurter, J., concurring). We are confined to a resolution of the dispute presented to us. That dispute involves various Executive Orders and regulations by which the President nullified attachments and liens on Iranian assets in the United States, directed that these assets be transferred to Iran, and suspended claims against Iran that may be presented to an International Claims Tribunal. This action was taken in an effort to comply with an Executive Agreement between the United States and Iran. We granted certiorari before judgment in this case, and set an expedited briefing and argument schedule, because lower courts had reached conflicting conclusions on the validity of the President's actions and, as the Solicitor General informed us, unless the Government acted by July 19, 1981, Iran could consider the United States to be in breach of the Executive Agreement.

But before turning to the facts and law which we believe determine the result in this case, we stress that the expeditious treatment of the issues involved by all of the courts which have considered the President's actions makes us acutely aware of the necessity to rest decision on the narrowest possible ground capable of deciding the case. This does not mean that reasoned analysis may give way to judicial fiat. It does mean that the statement of Justice Jackson — that we decide difficult cases presented to us by virtue of our commissions, not our competence — is especially true here. We attempt to lay down no general "guidelines" covering other situations not involved here, and attempt to confine the opinion only to the very questions necessary to decision of the case.

Perhaps it is because it is so difficult to reconcile the foregoing definition of Art. III judicial power with the broad range of vitally important day-to-day questions regularly decided by Congress or the Executive, without either challenge or interference by the Judiciary, that the decisions of the Court in this area have been rare, episodic, and afford little precedential value for subsequent cases. . . .

As we now turn to the factual and legal issues in this case, we freely confess that we are obviously deciding only one more episode in the never-ending tension between the President exercising the executive authority in a world that presents each day some new challenge with which he must deal and the Constitution under which we all live and which no one disputes embodies some sort of system of checks and balances.

I

On November 4, 1979, the American Embassy in Tehran was seized and our diplomatic personnel were captured and held hostage. In response to that crisis, President Carter, acting pursuant to the International Emergency Economic Powers Act, 91 Stat. 1626, 50 U.S.C. §§ 1701–1706 (hereinafter IEEPA), declared a national emergency on November 14, 1979, and blocked the removal or transfer of "all property and interests in property of the Government of Iran, its instrumentalities and controlled entities and the Central Bank of Iran which are or become subject to the jurisdiction of the United States. . . ." Exec. Order No. 12170. President Carter authorized the Secretary of the Treasury to promulgate regulations carrying out the blocking order. On November 15, 1979, the Treasury Department's Office of Foreign Assets Control issued a regulation providing that "[u]nless licensed or authorized . . . any attachment, judgment, decree, lien, execution, garnishment, or other judicial process is null and void with respect to any property in which on or since [November 14, 1979,] there existed an interest of Iran." 31 C.F.R. § 535.203(e) (1980). The regulations also made clear that any licenses or authorizations granted could be "amended, modified, or revoked at any time." § 535.805.

On November 26, 1979, the President granted a general license authorizing certain judicial proceedings against Iran but which did not allow the "entry of any judgment or of any decree or order of similar or analogous effect . . ." On December 19, 1979, a clarifying regulation was issued stating that "the general authorization for judicial proceedings contained . . . includes pre-judgment attachment." § 535.418.

On December 19, 1979, petitioner Dames & Moore filed suit in the United States District Court for the Central District of California against the Government of Iran, the Atomic Energy Organization of Iran, and a number of Iranian banks. In its complaint, petitioner alleged that its wholly owned subsidiary . . . was a party to a written contract with the Atomic Energy Organization. . . . [T]he subsidiary was to conduct site studies for a proposed nuclear power plant in Iran. As provided in the terms of the contract, the Atomic Energy Organization terminated the agreement for its own convenience on June 30, 1979. Petitioner contended, however, that it was owed $3,436,694.30 plus interest for services performed under the contract prior to the date of termination. The District Court issued orders of attachment directed against property of the defendants, and the property of certain Iranian banks was then attached to secure any judgment that might be entered against them.

On January 20, 1981, the Americans held hostage were released by Iran pursuant to an Agreement entered into the day before and embodied in two Declarations of the Democratic and Popular Republic of Algeria. The Agreement stated that "[i]t is the purpose of [the United States and Iran] . . . to terminate all litigation as between the Government of each party and the nationals of the other, and to bring about the settlement and termination of all such claims through binding arbitration." In furtherance of this goal, the Agreement called for the establishment of an Iran-United States Claims Tribunal which would arbitrate any claims not settled within six months. Awards of the Claims Tribunal are to be "final and binding" and "enforceable . . . in the courts of any nation in accordance with its laws." Under the Agreement, the United States is obligated

> "to terminate all legal proceedings in United States courts involving claims of United States persons and institutions against Iran and its state enterprises, to nullify all attachments and judgments obtained therein, to prohibit all further litigation based on such claims, and to bring about the termination of such claims through binding arbitration."

In addition, the United States must "act to bring about the transfer" by July 19, 1981, of all Iranian assets held in this country by American banks. One billion dollars of these assets will be deposited in a security account in the Bank of England, to the account of the Algerian Central Bank, and used to satisfy awards rendered against Iran by the Claims Tribunal.

On January 19, 1981, President Carter issued a series of Executive Orders implementing the terms of the agreement. Exec. Orders Nos. 12276–12285, 46 Fed. Reg. 7913–7932. These Orders revoked all licenses permitting the exercise of "any right, power, or privilege" with regard to Iranian funds, securities, or deposits; "nullified" all non-Iranian interests in such assets acquired subsequent to the blocking order of November 14, 1979; and required those banks holding Iranian assets to transfer them "to the Federal Reserve Bank of New York, to be held or transferred as directed by the Secretary of the Treasury."

On February 24, 1981, President Reagan issued an Executive Order in which he "ratified" the January 19th Executive Orders. Exec. Order No. 12294, 46 Fed. Reg. 14111. Moreover, he "suspended" all "claims which may be presented to the . . . Tribunal" and provided that such claims "shall have no legal effect in any action now pending in any court of the United States." The suspension of any particular claim terminates if the Claims Tribunal determines that it has no jurisdiction over that claim; claims are discharged for all purposes when the Claims Tribunal either awards some recovery and that amount is paid, or determines that no recovery is due.

Meanwhile, on January 27, 1981, petitioner moved for summary judgment in the District Court[, which] . . . awarded petitioner the amount claimed under the contract plus interest. . . . The District Court [later] ordered that all prejudgment attachments obtained against the Iranian defendants be vacated and that further proceedings against the bank defendants be stayed in light of the Executive Orders discussed above.

. . . [P]etitioner [subsequently] filed this action in the District Court for declaratory and injunctive relief against the United States and the Secretary of the Treasury, seeking to prevent enforcement of the Executive Orders and Treasury Department regulations implementing the Agreement with Iran. In its complaint, petitioner alleged that the actions of the President and the Secretary of the Treasury implementing the Agreement with Iran were beyond their statutory and constitutional powers and, in any event, were unconstitutional to the extent they adversely affect petitioner's final judgment against the Government of Iran and the Atomic Energy

Organization, its execution of that judgment in the State of Washington, its prejudgment attachments, and its ability to continue to litigate against the Iranian banks. On May 28, 1981, the District Court denied petitioner's motion for a preliminary injunction and dismissed petitioner's complaint for failure to state a claim upon which relief could be granted. Prior to the District Court's ruling, the United States Courts of Appeals for the First and the District of Columbia Circuits upheld the President's authority to issue the Executive Orders and regulations challenged by petitioner. *See Chas. T. Main Int'l, Inc. v. Khuzestan Water & Power Authority*, 651 F.2d 800 (CA1 1981); *American Int'l Group, Inc. v. Islamic Republic of Iran*, 211 U.S. App. D.C. 468, 657 F.2d 430 (1981).

On June 3, 1981, petitioner filed a notice of appeal from the District Court's order, and the appeal was docketed in the United States Court of Appeals for the Ninth Circuit. On June 4, the Treasury Department amended its regulations to mandate "the transfer of bank deposits and certain other financial assets of Iran in the United States to the Federal Reserve Bank of New York by noon, June 19." The District Court, however, entered an injunction pending appeal prohibiting the United States from requiring the transfer of Iranian property that is subject to "any writ of attachment, garnishment, judgment, levy, or other judicial lien" issued by any court in favor of petitioner. Arguing that this is a case of "imperative public importance," petitioner then sought a writ of certiorari before judgment. *See* 28 U.S.C. § 2101(e); this Court's Rule 18. Because the issues presented here are of great significance and demand prompt resolution, we granted the petition for the writ, adopted an expedited briefing schedule, and set the case for oral argument on June 24, 1981. 452 U.S. 932 (1981).

II.

The parties and the lower courts, confronted with the instant questions, have all agreed that much relevant analysis is contained in *Youngstown Sheet & Tube Co. v. Sawyer*, 343 U.S. 579 (1952). Justice Black's opinion for the Court in that case, involving the validity of President Truman's effort to seize the country's steel mills in the wake of a nationwide strike, recognized that "[t]he President's power, if any, to issue the order must stem either from an act of Congress or from the Constitution itself." Justice Jackson's concurring opinion elaborated in a general way the consequences of different types of interaction between the two democratic branches in assessing Presidential authority to act in any given case. . . .

Although we have in the past found and do today find Justice Jackson's classifications of executive actions into three general categories analytically useful, we should be mindful of Justice Holmes' admonition, . . . that "[t]he great ordinances of the Constitution do not establish and divide fields of black and white." *Springer v. Philippine Islands*, 277 U.S. 189, 209 (1928) (dissenting opinion). Justice Jackson himself recognized that his three categories represented "a somewhat over-simplified grouping," and it is doubtless the case that executive action in any particular instance falls, not neatly in one of three pigeonholes, but rather at some point along a spectrum running from explicit congressional authorization to explicit congressional prohibition. This is particularly true as respects cases such as the one before us, involving responses to international crises the nature of which Congress can hardly have been expected to anticipate in any detail.

III

In nullifying post-November 14, 1979, attachments and directing those persons holding blocked Iranian funds and securities to transfer them to the Federal Reserve Bank of New York for ultimate transfer to Iran, President Carter cited five sources of express or inherent power. The Government, however, has principally relied on § 203 of the IEEPA, 50 U.S.C. § 1702(a)(1), as authorization for these actions. Section 1702(a)(1) provides in part:

> "At the times and to the extent specified in section 1701 of this title, the President may, under such regulations as he may prescribe, by means of instructions, licenses, or otherwise—
>
> "(A) investigate, regulate, or prohibit—
>
> "(i) any transactions in foreign exchange,
>
> "(ii) transfers of credit or payments between, by, through, or to any banking institution, to the extent that such transfers or payments involve any interest of any foreign country or a national thereof,
>
> "(iii) the importing or exporting of currency or securities, and
>
> "(B) investigate, regulate, direct and compel, nullify, void, prevent or prohibit, any acquisition, holding, withholding, use, transfer, withdrawal, transportation, importation or exportation of, or dealing in, or exercising any right, power, or privilege with respect to, or transactions involving, any property in which any foreign country or a national thereof has any interest;
>
> "by any person, or with respect to any property, subject to the jurisdiction of the United States."

The Government contends that the acts of "nullifying" the attachments and ordering the "transfer" of the frozen assets are specifically authorized by the plain language of the above statute. The two Courts of Appeals that have considered the issue agreed with this contention. In *Chas. T. Main Int'l, Inc. v. Khuzestan Water & Power Authority*, the Court of Appeals for the First Circuit explained:

> "The President relied on his IEEPA powers in November 1979, when he 'blocked' all Iranian assets in this country, and again in January 1981, when he 'nullified' interests acquired in blocked property, and ordered that property's transfer. The President's actions, in this regard, are in keeping with the language of IEEPA: initially he 'prevent[ed] and prohibit[ed]' 'transfers' of Iranian assets; later he 'direct[ed] and compel[led]' the 'transfer' and 'withdrawal' of the assets, 'nullify[ing]' certain 'rights' and 'privileges' acquired in them.

"Main argues that IEEPA does not supply the President with power to override judicial remedies, such as attachments and injunctions, or to extinguish 'interests' in foreign assets held by United States citizens. But we can find no such limitation in IEEPA's terms. The language of IEEPA is sweeping and unqualified. It provides broadly that the President may void or nullify the 'exercising [by *any* person of] *any* right, power or privilege with respect to . . . any property in which any foreign country has any interest. . . .' 50 U.S.C. § 1702(a)(1)(B)."

651 F.2d, at 806–07 (emphasis in original). In *American Int'l Group, Inc. v. Islamic Republic of Iran*, the Court of Appeals for the District of Columbia Circuit employed a similar rationale in sustaining President Carter's action. . . .

Petitioner contends that we should ignore the plain language of this statute because an examination of its legislative history as well as the history of § 5(b) of the Trading With the Enemy Act (hereinafter TWEA), 40 Stat. 411, as amended, 50 U.S.C. App. § 5(b) (1976 ed. and Supp. III), from which the pertinent language of § 1702 is directly drawn, reveals that the statute was not intended to give the President such extensive power over the assets of a foreign state during times of national emergency. According to petitioner, once the President instituted the November 14, 1979, blocking order, § 1702 authorized him "only to continue the freeze or to discontinue controls."

We do not agree and refuse to read out of § 1702 all meaning to the words "transfer," "compel," or "nullify." Nothing in the legislative history of either § 1702 or § 5(b) of the TWEA requires such a result. To the contrary, we think both the legislative history and cases interpreting the TWEA fully sustain the broad authority of the Executive when acting under this congressional grant of power. *See, e.g., Orvis v. Brownell*, 345 U.S. 183 (1953). Although Congress intended to limit the President's emergency power in peacetime, we do not think the changes brought about by the enactment of the IEEPA in any way affected the authority of the President to take the specific actions taken here. We likewise note that by the time petitioner instituted this action, the President had already entered the freeze order. Petitioner proceeded against the blocked assets only after the Treasury Department had issued revocable licenses authorizing such proceedings and attachments. The Treasury Regulations provided that "unless licensed" any attachment is null and void, 31 CFR § 535.203(e) (1980), and all licenses "may be amended, modified, or revoked at any time." § 535.805. As such, the attachments obtained by petitioner were specifically made subordinate to further actions which the President might take under the IEEPA. Petitioner was on notice of the contingent nature of its interest in the frozen assets.

This Court has previously recognized that the congressional purpose in authorizing blocking orders is "to put control of foreign assets in the hands of the President. . . ." *Propper v. Clark*, 337 U.S. 472, 493 (1949). Such orders permit the President to maintain the foreign assets at his disposal for use in negotiating the resolution of a declared national emergency. The frozen assets serve as a "bargaining chip" to be used by the President when dealing with a hostile country. Accordingly, it is difficult to accept petitioner's argument because the practical effect of it is to allow individual claimants throughout the country to minimize or wholly eliminate this "bargaining chip" through attachments, garnishments, or similar encumbrances on property. Neither the purpose the statute was enacted to serve nor its plain language supports such a result.

Because the President's action in nullifying the attachments and ordering the transfer of the assets was taken pursuant to specific congressional authorization, it is "supported by the strongest of presumptions and the widest latitude of judicial interpretation, and the burden of persuasion would rest heavily upon any who might attack it." *Youngstown*, 343 U.S., at 637 (Jackson, J., concurring). Under the circumstances of this case, we cannot say that petitioner has sustained that heavy burden. A contrary ruling would mean that the Federal Government as a whole lacked the power exercised by the President, and that we are not prepared to say.

IV

Although we have concluded that the IEEPA constitutes specific congressional authorization to the President to nullify the attachments and order the transfer of Iranian assets, there remains the question of the President's authority to suspend claims pending in American courts. Such claims have, of course, an existence apart from the attachments which accompanied them. In terminating these claims through Executive Order No. 12294 the President purported to act under authority of both the IEEPA and 22 U.S.C. § 1732, the so-called "Hostage Act."

We conclude that although the IEEPA authorized the nullification of the attachments, it cannot be read to authorize the suspension of the claims. The claims of American citizens against Iran are not in themselves transactions involving Iranian property or efforts to exercise any rights with respect to such property. An *in personam* lawsuit, although it might eventually be reduced to judgment and that judgment might be executed upon, is an effort to establish liability and fix damages and does not focus on any particular property within the jurisdiction. The terms of the IEEPA therefore do not authorize the President to suspend claims in American courts. This is the view of all the courts which have considered the question.

The Hostage Act, passed in 1868, provides:

> "Whenever it is made known to the President that any citizen of the United States has been unjustly deprived of his liberty by or under the authority of any foreign government, it shall be the duty of the President forthwith to demand of that government the reasons of such imprisonment; and if it appears to be wrongful and in violation of the rights of American citizenship, the President shall forthwith demand the release of such citizen, and if the release so demanded is unreasonably delayed or refused, the President shall use such means, not amounting to acts of war, as he may think necessary and proper to obtain or effectuate the release; and all the facts and proceedings relative thereto shall as soon as practicable be communicated by the President to Congress."

We are reluctant to conclude that this provision constitutes specific authorization to the President to suspend claims in American courts. Although the broad language of the Hostage Act suggests it may cover this case, there are several difficulties with such a view. The legislative history indicates that the Act was passed in response to a situation unlike the recent Iranian crisis. Congress in 1868 was concerned with the activity of certain countries refusing to recognize the citizenship of naturalized Americans travelling abroad, and repatriating such citizens against their will. These countries were not interested in returning the citizens in exchange for any sort of ransom. This also explains the reference in the Act to imprisonment "in violation of the rights of American citizenship." Although the Iranian hostage-taking violated international law and common decency, the hostages were not seized out of any refusal to recognize their American citizenship—they were seized precisely *because of* their American citizenship. The legislative history is also somewhat ambiguous on the question whether Congress contemplated Presidential action such as that involved here or rather simply reprisals directed against the offending foreign country and *its* citizens.

Concluding that neither the IEEPA nor the Hostage Act constitutes specific authorization of the President's action suspending claims, however, is not to say that these statutory provisions are entirely irrelevant to the question of the validity of the President's action. We think both statutes highly relevant in the looser sense of indicating congressional acceptance of a broad scope for executive action in circumstances such as those presented in this case. . . . [T]he IEEPA delegates broad authority to the President to act in times of national emergency with respect to property of a foreign country. The Hostage Act similarly indicates congressional willingness that the President have broad discretion when responding to the hostile acts of foreign sovereigns. . . . An original version of the Act, which authorized the President to suspend trade with a foreign country and even arrest citizens of that country in the United States in retaliation, was rejected because "there may be a great variety of cases arising where other and different means would be equally effective, and where the end desired could be accomplished without resorting to such dangerous and violent measures."

Although we have declined to conclude that the IEEPA or the Hostage Act directly authorizes the President's suspension of claims for the reasons noted, we cannot ignore the general tenor of Congress's legislation in this area in trying to determine whether the President is acting alone or at least with the acceptance of Congress. As we have noted, Congress cannot anticipate and legislate with regard to every possible action the President may find it necessary to take or every possible situation in which he might act. Such failure of Congress specifically to delegate authority does not, "especially . . . in the areas of foreign policy and national security," imply "congressional disapproval" of action taken by the Executive. *Haig v. Agee*, 453 U.S. 280, 291. On the contrary, the enactment of legislation closely related to the question of the President's authority in a particular case which evinces legislative intent to accord the President broad discretion may be considered to "invite" "measures on independent presidential responsibility," *Youngstown*, 343 U.S., at 637 (Jackson, J., concurring). At least this is so where there is no contrary indication of legislative intent and when, as here, there is a history of congressional acquiescence in conduct of the sort engaged in by the President. It is to that history which we now turn.

Not infrequently in affairs between nations, outstanding claims by nationals of one country against the government of another country are "sources of friction" between the two sovereigns. *United States v. Pink*, 315 U.S. 203, 225 (1942). To resolve these difficulties, nations have often entered into agreements settling the claims of their respective nationals. As one treatise writer puts it, international agreements settling claims by nationals of one state against the government of another "are established international practice reflecting traditional international theory." L. Henkin, Foreign Affairs and the Constitution 262 (1972). Consistent with that principle, the United States has repeatedly exercised its sovereign authority to settle the claims of its nationals against foreign countries. Though those settlements have sometimes been made by treaty, there has also been a longstanding practice of settling such claims by executive agreement without the advice and consent of the Senate.[8] Under such agreements, the President has agreed to renounce or extinguish claims of United States nationals against foreign governments in return for lump-sum payments or the establishment of arbitration procedures. To be sure, many of these settlements were encouraged by the United States claimants themselves, since a claimant's only hope of obtaining any payment at all might lie in having his Government negotiate a diplomatic settlement on his behalf. But it is also undisputed that the "United States has sometimes disposed of the claims of its citizens without their consent, or even without consultation with them, usually without exclusive regard for their interests, as distinguished from those of the nation as a whole." Henkin, *supra*, at 262–63. It is clear that the practice of settling claims continues today. Since 1952, the President has entered into at least 10 binding settlements with foreign nations, including an $80 million settlement with the People's Republic of China.

Crucial to our decision today is the conclusion that Congress has implicitly approved the practice of claim settlement by executive agreement. This is best demonstrated by Congress's enactment of the International Claims Settlement Act of 1949, 22 U.S.C. § 1621. The Act had two purposes: (1) to allocate to United States nationals funds received in the course of an executive claims settlement with Yugoslavia, and (2) to provide a procedure whereby funds resulting from future settlements could be distributed. To achieve these ends Congress created the International Claims Commission, now the Foreign Claims Settlement Commission, and gave it jurisdiction to make final and binding decisions with respect to claims by United States nationals against settlement funds. 22 U.S.C. § 1623(a). By creating a procedure to implement future settlement agreements, Congress placed its stamp of approval on such agreements. . . .

---

8. At least since the case of the "Wilmington Packet" in 1799, Presidents have exercised the power to settle claims of United States nationals by executive agreement.

Over the years Congress has frequently amended the International Claims Settlement Act to provide for particular problems arising out of settlement agreements, thus demonstrating Congress's continuing acceptance of the President's claim settlement authority. With respect to the Executive Agreement with the People's Republic of China, for example, Congress established an allocation formula for distribution of the funds received pursuant to the Agreement. 22 U.S.C. § 1627(f). As with legislation involving other executive agreements, Congress did not question the fact of the settlement or the power of the President to have concluded it. In 1976, Congress authorized the Foreign Claims Settlement Commission to adjudicate the merits of claims by United States nationals against East Germany, so that the Executive would "be in a better position to negotiate an adequate settlement . . . of these claims." S. Rep. No. 94-1188, p. 2 (1976); 22 U.S.C. § 1644b. Similarly, Congress recently amended the International Claims Settlement Act to facilitate the settlement of claims against Vietnam. 22 U.S.C. §§ 1645, 1645a(5) (1976 ed., Supp. IV). The House Report stated that the purpose of the legislation was to establish an official inventory of losses of private United States property in Vietnam so that recovery could be achieved "through future direct Government-to-Government negotiation of private property claims." H.R. Rep. No. 96-915, pp. 2–3, U. S. Code Cong. & Admin. News, 1980, pp. 7328, 7329–7330. Finally, the legislative history of the IEEPA further reveals that Congress has accepted the authority of the Executive to enter into settlement agreements. Though the IEEPA was enacted to provide for some limitation on the President's emergency powers, Congress stressed that "[n]othing in this act is intended . . . to interfere with the authority of the President to [block assets], or to impede the settlement of claims of U.S. citizens against foreign countries." S. Rep. No. 95-466, p. 6 (1977); 50 U.S.C. § 1706(a)(1).

In addition to congressional acquiescence in the President's power to settle claims, prior cases of this Court have also recognized that the President does have some measure of power to enter into executive agreements without obtaining the advice and consent of the Senate. In *United States v. Pink*, 315 U.S. 203 (1942), for example, the Court upheld the validity of the Litvinov Assignment, which was part of an Executive Agreement whereby the Soviet Union assigned to the United States amounts owed to it by American nationals so that outstanding claims of other American nationals could be paid. The Court explained that the resolution of such claims was integrally connected with normalizing United States' relations with a foreign state. . . .

Petitioner raises two arguments in opposition to the proposition that Congress has acquiesced in this longstanding practice of claims settlement by executive agreement. First, it suggests that all pre-1952 settlement claims, and corresponding court cases such as *Pink*, should be discounted because of the evolution of the doctrine of sovereign immunity. Petitioner observes that prior to 1952 the United States adhered to the doctrine of absolute sovereign immunity, so that absent action by the Executive there simply would be no remedy for a United States national against a foreign government. When the United States in 1952 adopted a more restrictive notion of sovereign immunity, by means of the so-called "Tate" letter, it is petitioner's view that United States nationals no longer needed executive aid to settle claims and that, as a result, the President's authority to settle such claims in some sense "disappeared." Though petitioner's argument is not wholly without merit, it is refuted by the fact that since 1952 there have been at least 10 claims settlements by executive agreement. Thus, even if the pre-1952 cases should be disregarded, congressional acquiescence in settlement agreements since that time supports the President's power to act here.

Petitioner next asserts that Congress divested the President of the authority to settle claims when it enacted the Foreign Sovereign Immunities Act of 1976 (hereinafter FSIA), 28 U.S.C. §§ 1330, 1602 *et seq.* The FSIA granted personal and subject-matter jurisdiction in the federal district courts over commercial suits brought by claimants against those foreign states which have waived immunity. 28 U.S.C. § 1330. Prior to the enactment of the FSIA, a foreign government's immunity to suit was determined by the Executive Branch on a case-by-case basis. According to petitioner, the principal purpose of the FSIA was to depoliticize these commercial lawsuits by taking them out of the arena of foreign affairs — where the Executive Branch is subject to the pressures of foreign states seeking to avoid liability through a grant of immunity — and by placing them within the exclusive jurisdiction of the courts. Petitioner thus insists that the President, by suspending its claims, has circumscribed the jurisdiction of the United States courts in violation of Art. III of the Constitution.

We disagree. In the first place, we do not believe that the President has attempted to divest the federal courts of jurisdiction. Executive Order No. 12294 purports only to "suspend" the claims, not divest the federal court of "jurisdiction." As we read the Executive Order, those claims not within the jurisdiction of the Claims Tribunal will "revive" and become judicially enforceable in United States courts. This case, in short, illustrates the difference between modifying federal-court jurisdiction and directing the courts to apply a different rule of law. The President has exercised the power, acquiesced in by Congress, to settle claims and, as such, has simply effected a change in the substantive law governing the lawsuit. Indeed, the very example of sovereign immunity belies petitioner's argument. No one would suggest that a determination of sovereign immunity divests the federal courts of "jurisdiction." Yet, petitioner's argument, if accepted, would have required courts prior to the enactment of the FSIA to reject as an encroachment on their jurisdiction the President's determination of a foreign state's sovereign immunity.

Petitioner also reads the FSIA much too broadly. The principal purpose of the FSIA was to codify contemporary concepts concerning the scope of sovereign immunity and withdraw from the President the authority to make binding determinations of the sovereign immunity to be accorded foreign states. The FSIA was thus designed to remove one particular barrier to suit, namely sovereign immunity, and cannot be fairly read as *prohibiting* the President from settling claims of United States nationals against foreign governments. It is telling that the Congress which enacted the FSIA considered but rejected several proposals designed to limit the power of the President to enter into executive agreements, including claims settlement agreements. It is quite unlikely that the same Congress that rejected proposals to limit the President's authority to conclude executive agreements sought to accomplish that very purpose *sub silentio* through the FSIA. And, as noted above, just one year after enacting the FSIA, Congress enacted the IEEPA, where the legislative history stressed that nothing in the IEEPA was to impede the settlement of claims of United States citizens. It would be surprising for Congress to express this support for settlement agreements had it intended the FSIA to eliminate the President's authority to make such agreements.

In light of all of the foregoing — the inferences to be drawn from the character of the legislation Congress has enacted in the area, such as the IEEPA and the Hostage Act, and from the history of acquiescence in executive claims settlement — we conclude that the President was authorized to suspend pending claims pursuant to Executive Order No. 12294. As Justice Frankfurter pointed out in *Youngstown*, "a systematic, unbroken, executive practice, long pursued to the knowledge of the Congress and never before questioned . . . may be treated as a gloss on 'Executive Power' vested in the President by § 1 of Art. II." Past practice does not, by itself, create power, but "long-continued practice, known to and acquiesced in by Congress, would raise a presumption that the [action] had been [taken] in pursuance of its consent. . . ." *United States v. Midwest Oil Co.*, 236 U.S. 459, 474 (1915). *See Haig v. Agee*, 453 U.S., at 291, 292. Such practice is present here and such a presumption is also appropriate. In light of the fact that Congress may be considered to have consented to the President's action in suspending claims, we cannot say that action exceeded the President's powers.

Our conclusion is buttressed by the fact that the means chosen by the President to settle the claims of American nationals provided an alternative forum, the Claims Tribunal, which is capable of providing meaningful relief. The Solicitor General also suggests that the provision of the Claims Tribunal will actually *enhance* the opportunities for claimants to recover their claims, in that the Agreement removes a number of jurisdictional and procedural impediments faced by claimants in United States courts. Although being overly sanguine about the chances of United States claimants before the Claims Tribunal would require a degree of naiveté which should not be demanded even of judges, the Solicitor General's point cannot be discounted. Moreover, it is important to remember that we have already held that the President has the *statutory* authority to nullify attachments and to transfer the assets out of the country. The President's power to do so does not depend on his provision of a forum whereby claimants can recover on those claims. The fact that the President has provided such a forum here means that the claimants are receiving something in return for the suspension of their claims, namely, access to an international tribunal before which they may well recover something on their claims. Because there does appear to be a real "settlement" here, this case is more easily analogized to the more traditional claim settlement cases of the past.

Just as importantly, Congress has not disapproved of the action taken here. Though Congress has held hearings on the Iranian Agreement itself, Congress has not enacted legislation, or even passed a resolution, indicating its displeasure with the Agreement. Quite the contrary, the relevant Senate Committee has stated that the establishment of the Tribunal is "of vital importance to the United States." S. Rep. No. 97-71, p. 5 (1981). We are thus clearly not confronted with a situation in which Congress has in some way resisted the exercise of Presidential authority.

Finally, we re-emphasize the narrowness of our decision. We do not decide that the President possesses plenary power to settle claims, even as against foreign governmental entities. As the Court of Appeals for the First Circuit stressed, "[t]he sheer magnitude of such a power, considered against the background of the diversity and complexity of modern international trade, cautions against any broader construction of authority than is necessary." *Chas. T. Main Int'l, Inc. v. Khuzestan Water & Power Authority*, 651 F.2d, at 814. But where, as here, the settlement of claims has been determined to be a necessary incident to the resolution of a major foreign policy dispute between our country and another, and where, as here, we can conclude that Congress acquiesced in the President's action, we are not prepared to say that the President lacks the power to settle such claims.

V

We do not think it appropriate at the present time to address petitioner's contention that the suspension of claims, if authorized, would constitute a taking of property in violation of the Fifth Amendment to the United States Constitution in the absence of just compensation. Both petitioner and the Government concede that the question whether the suspension of the claims constitutes a taking is not ripe for review. However, this contention, and the possibility that the President's actions may effect a taking of petitioner's property, make ripe for adjudication the question whether petitioner will have a remedy at law in the Court of Claims under the Tucker Act, 28 U.S.C. § 1491, in such an event. That the fact and extent of the taking in this case is yet speculative is inconsequential because "there must be at the time of taking 'reasonable, certain and adequate provision for obtaining compensation.'" *Regional Rail Reorganization Act Cases*, 419 U.S. 102, 124–25 (1974), quoting *Cherokee Nation v. Southern Kansas R. Co.*, 135 U.S. 641, 659 (1890).

It has been contended that the "treaty exception" to the jurisdiction of the Court of Claims, 28 U.S.C. § 1502, might preclude the Court of Claims from exercising jurisdiction over any takings claims the petitioner might bring. At oral argument, however, the Government conceded that § 1502 would not act as a bar to petitioner's action in the Court of Claims. We agree. Accordingly, to the extent petitioner believes it has suffered an unconstitutional taking by the suspension of the claims, we see no jurisdictional obstacle to an appropriate action in the United States Court of Claims under the Tucker Act.

The judgment of the District Court is accordingly affirmed, and the mandate shall issue forthwith.

It is so ordered.

Justice STEVENS, concurring in part.

In my judgment the possibility that requiring this petitioner to prosecute its claim in another forum will constitute an unconstitutional "taking" is so remote that I would not address the jurisdictional question considered in Part V of the Court's opinion. However, I join the remainder of the opinion.

Justice POWELL, concurring and dissenting in part.

I join the Court's opinion except its decision that the nullification of the attachments did not effect a taking of property interests giving rise to claims for just compensation. The nullification of attachments presents a separate question from whether the suspension and proposed settlement of claims against Iran may constitute a taking. I would leave both "taking" claims open for resolution on a case-by-case basis in actions before the Court of Claims. The facts of the hundreds of claims pending against Iran are not known to this Court and may differ from the facts in this case. I therefore dissent from the Court's decision with respect to attachments. The decision may well be erroneous, and it certainly is premature with respect to many claims.

. . . The Court holds that parties whose valid claims are not adjudicated or not fully paid may bring a "taking" claim against the United States in the Court of Claims, the jurisdiction of which this Court acknowledges. The Government must pay just compensation when it furthers the Nation's foreign policy goals by using as "bargaining chips" claims lawfully held by a relatively few persons and subject to the jurisdiction of our courts. The extraordinary powers of the President and Congress upon which our decision rests cannot, in the circumstances of this case, displace the Just Compensation Clause of the Constitution.

---

1. *Congressional Limits on Settlement Powers.* To what extent could Congress have legislatively proscribed claims settlements by executive agreement, or at least claims settlements that are not part of a process of recognition? Note the Court's apparently greater tentativeness in *Dames & Moore* in endorsing presidential authority, as compared to *Pink*. (Could that tentativeness be the consequence of the time pressure the federal courts faced for decision — time pressure we have observed in other important separation of powers cases?) Did the President have any constitutional power to nullify claims against Iranian assets apart from IEEPA? Is that power tied to national emergencies? On what constitutional authority is it based? *See* Lee R. Marks & John C. Grabow, *The President's Foreign Economic Powers After* Dames & Moore v. Regan: *Legislation by Acquiescence*, 68 CORNELL L. REV. 68 (1982).

In footnotes we have omitted, the Court observed that Congress had only rarely objected to the "longstanding practice of claim settlement by executive agreement, even when it has had an opportunity to do so." 453 U.S. at 682 n.10. For example, when Congress in 1972 required that texts of significant executive agreements henceforth be transmitted into Congress, it declined to impose any substantive limitation on the President's claims settlement authority. Yet, the following year, when President Nixon sought to settle over $105 million in claims against Czechoslovakia for $20.5 million, "Congress quickly demonstrated its displeasure by enacting legislation requiring that the Agreement be renegotiated." *Id.* at 688 n. 13 (citing R. B. Lillich, *The Gravel Amendment to the Trade Reform Act of 1974*, 69 Am. J. Int'l L. 837, 839– 840 (1975)).

2. *International Settlements as "Takings."* The Court explicitly declined to express any views on the claim of the petitioner that it had suffered a constitutional taking. Justice Powell, in partial dissent, obviously thought the question a serious one, and sought to hold open the possibility that the executive orders making attachments available on only a conditional basis might have effected a taking, whether or not the actual nullification of the attachments did so. On what basis, if any, could it be argued that, to the extent claimants against Iran do not recover 100 per cent of their claims through the international tribunal, those claimants still do *not* have any "tak- ings" claim against the United States? What if the U.S. had provided, instead of the possibility of arbitration, a fixed settlement of all outstanding private claims against Iran for 75 cents on the dollar? 50 cents? 10 cents? *See Shanghai Power Co. v. United States*, 4 Cl. Ct. 237 (Ct. Cl. 1983), *aff'd*, 765 F.2d 159 (Fed. Cir. 1985), *cert. denied*, 474 U.S. 909 (1985) (Presidential act in recognition of People's Republic of China set- tling corporation's claim against PRC for one-sixth its value held not a taking). The unavailability of such claims is strongly implied in *United States v. Sperry Corpora- tion*, 493 U.S. 52 (1989), which held that a statutory requirement that successful claim- ants in the Iran-United States Claims Tribunal pay a portion of any award to the United States did not impose any obligation of just compensation. Explaining why Sperry suffered no compensable loss, the Court reasoned, in part: "Had the Presi- dent not agreed to the Tribunal . . . , Sperry would have had no assurance that it could have pursued its action against Iran to judgment or that a judgment would have been readily collectible." *See also Belk v. United States*, 858 F.2d 706 (Fed. Cir. 1988) (exec- utive agreement, in seeking hostage release, not to permit U.S. hostages to sue Iran for seizure, detention, and subsequent injuries held not a compensable taking).

Consider, in this connection, the Supreme Court's holding that the Constitution creates no "property" protected by the due process clauses of the fifth and fourteenth amendments; rather, property interests "are created and their dimensions are defined by existing rules or understandings that stem from an independent [legal] source . . . [and] that secure certain benefits and that support claims of entitlement to those ben- efits." *Board of Regents of State Colleges v. Roth*, 408 U.S. 564, 577 (1972). Did Dames & Moore face a situation in which the "existing understanding" was (and is) that U.S. nationals who do business abroad take their chances with the political branches in securing their claims against other nations? (Intriguingly, the Dames & Moore sub- sidiary whose claim was at issue in the above case had contractually agreed to liti- gate its contract claims in Iran. Should that affect the takings analysis?)

3. *Should Banks Trust the President?* If, under the *mistaken* impression that the Pres- ident has the authority to nullify attachments of foreign assets, U.S. banks holding attached assets release them to the foreign government, would the domestic claim- ants have a successful claim against the banks? If so, would the banks have a good claim against the United States? Should the Supreme Court have written a stronger

endorsement of executive power in international emergencies, to avoid future doubts from interfering with the resolution of similar crises?

4. *Foreign Sovereign Immunities Act.* Prior to 1976, the President had judicially recognized authority to grant immunity to foreign governments involved in U.S. litigation. In 1976, Congress enacted the Foreign Sovereign Immunities Act, 28 U.S.C. §§ 1602–1611, proscribing immunities in certain classes of cases, including any case in which the action is based on a foreign state's commercial activities in the U.S. Is the Act conclusive as to the President's authority? Consider, in reading the next chapter, if it would make a difference if the President's purpose in conferring immunity were to permit a friendly foreign power to marshal its assets in wartime.

5. *Post-*Dames & Moore *Litigation.* The Supreme Court's decision in *Dames & Moore* hardly halted the tide of litigation prompted by the Iranian hostage crisis. At least two courts reached the takings question reserved in *Dames & Moore*, and found that, as a matter of law, no taking occurred. *E-Systems Inc. v. United States*, 2 Cl. Ct. 271 (1983); *American Int'l Group v. Islamic Republic of Iran*, 657 F.2d 430 (D.C. Cir. 1981). *See also Itek Corporation v. First National Bank of Boston*, 730 F.2d 19 (1st Cir. 1984).

Complex litigation likewise followed concerning a host of substantive and procedural issues that defy brief summary. For example, standby letters of credit were originally exempted from coverage by the blocking regulations, but were covered in subsequent amendments. Litigation concerning these multi-party international arrangements generally involved an American corporation attempting to enjoin an American bank from making payment on letters of credit in favor of an Iranian party to which the American corporation would ultimately be liable. *See* Herbert A. Getz, *Enjoining the International Standby Letter of Credit: The Iranian Letter of Credit Cases*, 21 Harv. Int'l L.J. 189, 198–200 (1980). Similarly, on the status of possessory liens against Iranian property, *see E-Systems Inc., supra*.

As of November 1985, about 130 American companies had won a total of about $370 million from Iran through the Iran-United States Claims Tribunal. A Westlaw check showed nearly 780 decisions and awards rendered by the end of 1994. The nine-member panel, consisting of three American, three Iranian, and three neutral judges, are responsible for resolving over 3,800 claims filed with the tribunal. Approximately 86 per cent of the claims are private claims by individuals or companies against the government of the other country—overwhelmingly suits by American parties against Iran. Other claims involve disputes between the two governments or between banks of the two countries. Ironically, the time taken by the tribunal to begin processing the claims had at least one beneficial effect; the $1 billion security fund initially created for the settlement of claims grew substantially beyond $1 billion because interest on the fund exceeded the amount of the awards paid out. *See* Henderson, *Bringing It All Back Home*, Wash. Post Nat'l Weekly Edition, Nov. 4, 1985, at 22.

6. *For Further Reading.* For overviews of the legal issues, international and domestic, raised by the Iranian Hostage Agreement, see Note, *The Iranian Hostage Agreement Under International and United States Law*, 81 Colum. L. Rev. 822 (1981);

Symposium, Dames & Moore v. Regan, 29 U.C.L.A. L. Rev. 977 (1982); Harold H. Bruff, *The Story of* Dames & Moore: *Resolution of an International Crisis by Executive Agreement*, in Presidential Power Stories 369 (Christopher H. Schroeder & Curtis A. Bradley, eds., 2009). For a critical view of the Supreme Court's acquiescence, based on legislative silence, in the President's removal of U.S. citizens' commercial claims from the jurisdiction of U.S. courts, see Lee R. Marks and John C. Grabow, *The President's Foreign Economic Powers After* Dames & Moore v. Regan: *Legislation by Acquiescence*, 68 Cornell L. Rev. 68 (1982). On the takings issues not reached by the Court, see also Phillip R. Trimble, *Foreign Policy Frustrated*—Dames & Moore, *Claims Court Jurisdiction and a New Raid on the Treasury*, 84 Colum. L. Rev. 317 (1984). On the unavailability of a private right of action to require the executive to pursue inquiries authorized by the Hostage Act, see *Smith v. Reagan*, 844 F.2d 195 (4th Cir. 1988), *cert. denied*, 488 U.S. 954 (1988).

Note: The Iran Nuclear Agreement of 2015

On July 14, 2015, the United States, along with China, Russia, Great Britain, Germany, and France, entered into an agreement with the Islamic Republic of Iran. Under the agreement, known as the Joint Comprehensive Plan of Action (or JCPOA), Iran agreed to a range of limits on its nuclear program designed to prevent or substantially delay Iran's ability to develop nuclear weapons. In return, the United States and the other nations agreed to lift a wide range of economic sanctions that had been imposed on Iran over the preceding three decades.

Within the United States, the JCPOA has been enormously controversial. Congress responded to news that the Obama Administration was close to concluding an agreement by enacting the Iran Nuclear Agreement Review Act, Pub. L. No. 114-17 (May 22, 2015). The INARA required the President to submit any agreement to Congress and to wait 30 days until implementing any agreement. The Act contemplated that, during the 30 day waiting period, Congress would vote to approve or disapprove the agreement. To date, however, Congress has not held a vote.

On March 9, 2015, while the agreement was being negotiated, 47 Republican Senators sent an "open letter to the leaders of [Iran]."

> It has come to our attention while observing your nuclear negotiations with our government that you may not fully understand our constitutional system. Thus, we are writing to bring to your attention two features of our Constitution—the power to make binding international agreements and the different character of federal offices—which you should seriously consider as negotiations progress.

> First, under our Constitution, while the president negotiates international agreements, Congress plays the significant role of ratifying them. In the case of a treaty, the Senate must ratify it by a two-thirds vote. A so-called congressional-executive agreement requires a majority vote in both the

House and the Senate (which, because of procedural rules, effectively means a three-fifths vote in the Senate). Anything not approved by Congress is a mere executive agreement.

Second, the offices of our Constitution have different characteristics. For example, the president may serve only two 4-year terms, whereas senators may serve an unlimited number of 6-year terms. As applied today, for instance, President Obama will leave office in January 2017, while most of us will remain in office well beyond then—perhaps decades.

What these two constitutional provisions mean is that we will consider any agreement regarding your nuclear-weapons program that is not approved by the Congress as nothing more than an executive agreement between President Obama and Ayatollah Khamenei. The next president could revoke such an executive agreement with the stroke of a pen and future Congresses could modify the terms of the agreement at any time.

We hope this letter enriches your knowledge of our constitutional system and promotes mutual understanding and clarity as nuclear negotiations progress.

The Open Letter accurately sets forth three types of international agreements: treaties, congressional-executive agreements, and unilateral executive agreements. (It omits treaty-based executive agreements, presumably because it is irrelevant to this situation.) The status of the JCPOA itself is exceedingly complicated. First, the agreement was clearly not concluded as a treaty or treaty-based executive agreement. Some commentators have argued that an agreement of such magnitude must be ratified as a treaty. *See, e.g.*, Lee A. Casey & David Rivkin, *The Lawless Underpinnings of the Iran Nuclear Deal*, Wall St. J. (July 26, 2015). The reading included in this chapter has covered a wide range of international agreements that have been concluded outside the constitutional treaty process. Do you agree that the JCPOA is of surpassing importance in comparison to those other agreements?

It turns out to be unclear whether the agreement is best understood as a congressional-executive agreement, a unilateral executive agreement, or something else entirely. At first blush, it may appear to be a unilateral executive agreement. There is no statute that specifically authorizes the President to enter into an agreement with Iran regarding its nuclear program. On the other hand, the JCPOA does not rest solely on the President's own constitutional authority. The highly complex sanctions regime results from, broadly speaking, two types of sources. First, many sanctions are imposed by executive orders issued by Presidents pursuant to statutory authorization, such as the International Emergency Economic Powers Act and the National Emergency Act. Second, many other sanctions are imposed by directly by statute. For a comprehensive listing of the specific sanctions imposed on Iran and the authority under which they have been imposed, see Diane Rennack, Iran: U.S. Economic Sanctions and Authority to Lift or Waive Restrictions (Congressional Research Service No. R43311, 2016). Generally, sanctions imposed in the first category are within the President's discretion and so may be revoked by the President. As to the second category, the statutes imposing sanctions also authorize the President to suspend or revoke them if the President makes certain findings. For the most part, the President may waive sanctions when the President makes a determination that doing so is in the national interest. Some of these sanctions, however, may only be waived if the President certifies that Iran should no longer be listed as a state-sponsor of terrorism and has abandoned its program to develop nuclear weapons. This last set of sanctions may reside outside the President's authority to waive or revoke, given that Iran continues to qualify as a state-sponsor of terrorism. To the extent the JCPOA revokes sanctions in this last category, it seems to be a unilateral executive agreement. As to the vast majority of sanctions, there appears to be a statutory basis for removing sanctions and thus that the JCPOA is a congressional-executive agreement.

For its part, the State Department asserted that the JCPOA was neither a treaty, nor an executive agreement. In a November 19, 2015 letter from Julia Frifield, assistant secretary for legislative affairs, to then-Representative Mike Pompeo: The Joint Comprehensive Plan of Action (JCPOA) is not a treaty or an executive agreement, and is not a signed document. The JCPOA reflects political commitments between Iran, the P5+1 (the United States, the United Kingdom, France, Germany, Russia, China), and the European Union. As you know, the United States has a long-standing practice of addressing sensitive problems in negotiations that culminate in political commitments.

The difference between a "political commitment" and a unilateral executive agreement is presumably that the former is not intended to be binding even under international law in any but a normative or moral sense. *See* Duncan B. Hollis & Joshua J. Newcomer, *"Political" Commitments and the Constitution*, 49 Va. J. Int. L. 507 (2009). In the case of the JCPOA, however, that distinction might have been blurred by the adoption of Resolution 2231 by the United Nations Security Council, which approves the deal and "[c]alls upon all Members States, regional organizations and international organizations to take such actions as may be appropriate to support the implementation of the JCPOA, including by taking actions commensurate with the implementation plan set out in the JCPOA and this resolution and by refraining from actions that undermine implementation of commitments under the JCPOA." On the potentially transformative impact of Security Council resolutions on political commitments, see Jack Goldsmith, *How a U.N. Security Council Resolution Transforms a Non-Binding Agreement with Iran Into a Binding Obligation Under International Law (Without Any New Senatorial or Congressional Vote)*, Lawfare (Mar. 12, 2015), https://www.lawfareblog.com/how-un-security-council-resolution-transforms-non-binding-agreement-iran-binding-obligation-under.

For contrasting expert judgments on whether UNSCR 2231, as worded, actually does bind U.S. presidents, *compare* Colum Lynch and John Hudson, *Obama Turns to U.N. to Outmaneuver Congress*, Foreign Policy (July 15, 2015), http://foreignpolicy.com/2015/07/15/obama-turns-to-u-n-to-outmaneuver-congress-iran-nuclear-deal/ (binding), *with* John B. Bellinger III, The new UNSCR on Iran: Does it bind the

United States (and future presidents)? Brookings (July 21, 2015), https://www
.brookings.edu/blog/markaz/2015/07/21/the-new-unscr-on-iran-does-it-bind-the
-united-states-and-future-presidents/ (not binding).

On January 16, 2016, the International Atomic Energy Agency verified that Iran
had implemented the measures required by the JCPOA regarding its nuclear capabilities. In response, the United States began to lift sanctions. For a listing of those
sanctions lifted and those remaining in place at the end of the Obama Administration, see U.S. Department of the Treasury, "Frequently Asked Questions Relating to
the Lifting of Certain U.S. Sanctions Under the Joint Comprehensive Plan of Action
(JCPOA) on Implementation Day" (Dec. 15, 2016), https://www.treasury.gov/resource
-center/sanctions/Programs/Documents/jcpoa_faqs.pdf. These events tee up the
issue that the Open Letter raised: May President Trump renounce the JCPOA and
re-impose sanctions? That may prove more difficult than the Open Letter indicates.
In order to do so, the President would have to review the many different statutes that
authorize each distinct sanction. These statutes require the President to make findings and the facts would have to justify such findings at the time a new President
would seek to re-impose the sanctions. On the legal issues posed by any renunciation of the JCPOA, see Stephen P. Mulligan, Withdrawal from International
Agreements: Legal Framework, the Paris Agreement, and the Iran Nuclear
Agreement (2017).

3. Control of Sensitive Information

Presidential claims of executive agreement power do not exhaust the range of
executive branch assertions of inherent and exclusive national security powers that
go beyond constitutional text. Since World War II, the executive has been particularly adamant that the President has discretionary powers to withhold sensitive
information on foreign policy grounds from both Congress and the public. Recall,
from Chapter Three, that the Supreme Court has ratified the existence of a state
secrets privilege that authorizes the executive to withhold certain categories of sensitive information from disclosure in judicial proceedings. An important issue is
how far this notion of "privilege" extends in terms of executive power to insist on
national security secrecy. A celebrated test of executive power in this context
occurred during the Vietnam War. On June 13, 1971, the *New York Times* published
its first installment of excerpts from a secret government study entitled *History of
United States Decision Making Process on Vietnam Policy.* The study, better known as
the Pentagon Papers, had been commissioned by Secretary of Defense Robert
McNamara in June 1967 to present an "encyclopedic and objective" history of
America's Vietnam policy between 1945 and 1968. Thirty-six historians, among
them Daniel Ellsberg, researched for more than a year and a half to complete a massive document of several thousand pages in forty-seven volumes. Although classified "secret" and "top secret," the Pentagon Papers disclosed very little information
that had not been publicly reported about the Vietnam War. But to Ellsberg, who
leaked the Pentagon Papers to *The New York Times* and later *The Washington Post,*

the study confirmed the growing impression that the government had failed at each escalation of the war to justify continued American involvement in Vietnam. He defended disclosure of the Pentagon Papers as an act of patriotism that served the national interest. To President Richard Nixon, however, it was an indefensible breach of national security.

The Justice Department moved quickly to enjoin further publication of the Pentagon Papers. (The Supreme Court's hurried disposition of the case appears below.) Meanwhile, the Nixon White House launched its own assault against Daniel Ellsberg and press leaks. President Nixon ordered his chief domestic advisor, John Ehrlichman, to form a Special Investigations Unit, dubbed the Plumbers. Ehrlichman assigned two White House staff members, Egil Krogh and David Young, to the Plumbers. They in turn hired Gordon Liddy and Howard Hunt, men trained in surveillance by the FBI and CIA. Their first objective was to discredit Daniel Ellsberg by leaking derogatory information to the press. On September 3, 1971, with Ehrlichman's approval and technical support from the CIA, Libby and Hunt led a burglary of the office of Ellsberg's psychiatrist. Taking Ellsberg's medical records back to the White House, Hunt drafted a damaging psychological profile of Ellsberg. Ehrlichman authorized Charles Colson, special counsel to the President, to leak the Ellsberg profile to the press.

Domestic espionage was not new to the Nixon White House. A year before the Pentagon Papers controversy, President Nixon had approved the "Huston Plan," under which White House employees wiretapped the private telephones of news reporters, infiltrated and disrupted anti-war groups, and mounted smear campaigns against the administration's detractors. The Plumbers, however, were much more threatening: once established, they enabled the President and his advisers to attempt ever more daring plots against their opponents.

Within a year of the Ellsberg break-in, the Plumbers, funded by Nixon campaign contributions, tried twice to bug the McGovern presidential campaign headquarters and successfully wiretapped some telephones at the Democratic National Committee Headquarters in the Watergate building. When former Attorney General John Mitchell, then serving as President Nixon's campaign director, complained that the wiretaps at the Watergate were useless, Liddy and Hunt reassembled the Ellsberg burglary team for a second Watergate break-in on June 17, 1972—this time to bug the telephone of Larry O'Brien, chair of the Democratic National Committee. The break-in was foiled, however, when police officers apprehended the burglars in O'Brien's office as they attempted to photograph documents.

Much of the Watergate affair following the June 17th arrests involved White House attempts to cover up the illegal activities of the Plumbers. John Dean, the President's Counsel, gave Hunt's psychological profile of Ellsberg to L. Patrick Gray, acting FBI director, who burned it along with other Plumbers' documents in the fireplace of his Connecticut home. FBI agents investigating the Watergate break-in traced checks in possession of the burglars to a slush fund maintained by the Committee to Reelect the President. Jailed for his part in the Watergate break-in, Hunt threatened to "bring down Ehrlichman" by revealing the Ellsberg break-in unless he received a substantial payment of "hush money." On March 21, 1973, President Nixon, in a taped conversation with John Dean in the oval office, planned the payment of hush money to the Watergate burglars in exchange for their silence about the Ellsberg break-in.

By 1974 President Nixon had resigned from the Presidency in the face of certain impeachment by the House of Representatives. His aides had been jailed or granted immunity for their parts in the Ellsberg and Watergate burglaries and for the obstruction of justice and perjury. American ground forces left Vietnam; the Republic of South Vietnam fell the next year.

———————

New York Times Co. v. United States
403 U.S. 713 (1971)

PER CURIAM.

We granted certiorari in these cases in which the United States seeks to enjoin the New York Times and the Washington Post from publishing the contents of a classified study entitled "History of U.S. Decision-Making Process on Viet Nam Policy."

"Any system of prior restraints of expression comes to this Court bearing a heavy presumption against its constitutional validity." The Government "thus carries a heavy burden of showing justification for the imposition of such a restraint." The District Court[s] held that the Government had not met that burden. We agree.

[The Court summarily affirmed the District Courts.]

So ordered.

Justice BLACK, with whom Justice DOUGLAS joins, concurring.

I adhere to the view that the Government's case against the Washington Post should have been dismissed and that the injunction against the New York Times should have been vacated without oral argument when the cases were first presented to this Court. I believe that every moment's continuance of the injunctions against these newspapers amounts to a flagrant, indefensible, and continuing violation of the First Amendment. . . .

[T]he Government argues in its brief that in spite of the First Amendment, "[t]he authority of the Executive Department to protect the nation against publication of information whose disclosure would endanger the national security stems from two interrelated sources: the constitutional power of the President over the conduct of foreign affairs and his authority as Commander-in-Chief." . . .

The Government does not even attempt to rely on any act of Congress. Instead it makes the bold and dangerously far-reaching contention that the courts should take it upon themselves to "make" a law abridging freedom of the press in the name of equity, presidential power and national security, even when the representatives of the people in Congress have adhered to the command of the First Amendment and refused to make such a law.[5] To find that the President has "inherent power" to halt the publication of news by resort to the courts would wipe out the First Amendment and destroy the fundamental liberty and security of the very people the Government hopes to make "secure." No one can read the history of the adoption of the First Amendment without being convinced beyond any doubt that it was injunctions like those sought here that Madison and his collaborators intended to outlaw in this Nation for all time.

The word "security" is a broad, vague generality whose contours should not be invoked to abrogate the fundamental law embodied in the First Amendment. The guarding of military and diplomatic secrets at the expense of informed representative government provides no real security for our Republic. . . .

Justice DOUGLAS, with whom Justice BLACK joins, concurring.

. . . It should be noted at the outset that the First Amendment provides that "Congress shall make no law . . . abridging the freedom of speech, or of the press." That leaves, in my view, no room for governmental restraint on the press. There is, moreover, no statute barring the publication by the press of the material which the Times and the Post seek to use. . . . So any power that the Government possesses must come from its "inherent power."

The power to wage war is "the power to wage war successfully." But the war power stems from a declaration of war. The Constitution by Art. I, § 8, gives Congress, not the President, power "[t]o declare War." Nowhere are presidential wars authorized. We need not decide therefore what leveling effect the war power of Congress might have.

These disclosures may have a serious impact. But that is no basis for sanctioning a previous restraint on the press. The Government says that it has inherent powers to go into court and obtain an injunction to protect the national interest, which in this case is alleged to be national security. *Near v. Minnesota*, 283 U.S. 697 (1931), repudiated that expansive doctrine in no uncertain terms.

The dominant purpose of the First Amendment was to prohibit the widespread practice of governmental suppression of embarrassing information. It is common knowledge that the First Amendment was adopted against the widespread use of the common law of seditious libel to punish the dissemination of material that is embarrassing to the powers-that-be. *See* T. Emerson, The System of Freedom of Expression, c. V (1970); Z. Chafee, Free Speech in the United States, c. XIII (1941). The

---

5. Compare the views of the Solicitor General with those of James Madison, the author of the First Amendment. When speaking of the Bill of Rights in the House of Representatives, Madison said: "If they [the first ten amendments] are incorporated into the Constitution, independent tribunals of justice will consider themselves in a peculiar manner the guardians of those rights; they will be an impenetrable bulwark against every assumption of power in the Legislative or Executive; they will be naturally led to resist every encroachment upon rights expressly stipulated for in the Constitution by the declaration of rights." 1 Annals of Cong. 439.

present cases will, I think, go down in history as the most dramatic illustration of that principle. A debate of large proportions goes on in the Nation over our posture in Vietnam. That debate antedated the disclosure of the contents of the present documents. The latter are highly relevant to the debate in progress.

Secrecy in government is fundamentally anti-democratic, perpetuating bureaucratic errors. Open debate and discussion of public issues are vital to our national health. . . .

Justice BRENNAN, concurring.

. . . The error that has pervaded these cases from the outset was the granting of any injunctive relief whatsoever, interim or otherwise. The entire thrust of the Government's claim throughout these cases has been that publication of the material sought to be enjoined "could," or "might," or "may" prejudice the national interest in various ways. But the First Amendment tolerates absolutely no prior judicial restraints of the press predicated upon surmise or conjecture that untoward consequences may result. Our cases, it is true, have indicated that there is a single, extremely narrow class of cases in which the First Amendment's ban on prior judicial restraint may be overridden. Our cases have thus far indicated that such cases may arise only when the Nation "is at war," *Schenck v. United States*, 249 U.S. 47, 52 (1919), during which times "[n]o one would question but that a government might prevent actual obstruction to its recruiting service or the publication of the sailing dates of transports or the number and location of troops." *Near v. Minnesota*, 283 U.S. 697, 716 (1931). Even if the present world situation were assumed to be tantamount to a time of war, or if the power of presently available armaments would justify even in peacetime the suppression of information that would set in motion a nuclear holocaust, in neither of these actions has the Government presented or even alleged that publication of items from or based upon the material at issue would cause the happening of an event of that nature. . . . Thus, only governmental allegation and proof that publication must inevitably, directly, and immediately cause the occurrence of an event kindred to imperiling the safety of a transport already at sea can support even the issuance of an interim restraining order. In no event may mere conclusions be sufficient: for if the Executive Branch seeks judicial aid in preventing publication, it must inevitably submit the basis upon which that aid is sought to scrutiny by the judiciary. And therefore, every restraint issued in this case, whatever its form, has violated the First Amendment—and not less so because that restraint was justified as necessary to afford the courts an opportunity to examine the claim more thoroughly. Unless and until the Government has clearly made out its case, the First Amendment commands that no injunction may issue.

Justice STEWART, with whom Justice WHITE joins, concurring.

. . . If the Constitution gives the Executive a large degree of unshared power in the conduct of foreign affairs and the maintenance of our national defense, then under the Constitution the Executive must have the largely unshared duty to determine and preserve the degree of internal security necessary to exercise that power successfully. . . . [I]t is the constitutional duty of the Executive—as a matter of sovereign prerogative and not as a matter of law as the courts know law—through the promulgation and enforcement of executive regulations, to protect the confidentiality necessary to carry out its responsibilities in the fields of international relations and national defense.

This is not to say that Congress and the courts have no role to play. Undoubtedly Congress has the power to enact specific and appropriate criminal laws to protect government property and preserve government secrets. . . . But in the cases before us we are asked neither to construe specific regulations nor to apply specific laws. We are asked, instead, to perform a function that the Constitution gave to the Executive, not the Judiciary. We are asked, quite simply, to prevent the publication by two newspapers of material that the Executive Branch insists should not, in the national interest, be published. I am convinced that the Executive is correct with respect to some of the documents involved. But I cannot say that disclosure of any of them will surely result in direct, immediate, and irreparable damage to our Nation or its people. That being so, there can under the First Amendment be but one judicial resolution of the issues before us. I join the judgments of the Court.

Justice WHITE, with whom Justice STEWART joins, concurring.

I concur in today's judgments, but only because of the concededly extraordinary protection against prior restraints enjoyed by the press under our constitutional system. I do not say that in no circumstances would the First Amendment permit an injunction against publishing information about government plans or operations. Nor, after examining the materials the Government characterizes as the most sensitive and destructive, can I deny that revelation of these documents will do substantial damage to public interests. Indeed, I am confident that their disclosure will have that result. But I nevertheless agree that the United States has not satisfied the very heavy burden that it must meet to warrant an injunction against publication in these cases, at least in the absence of express and appropriately limited congressional authorization for prior restraints in circumstances such as these.

The Government's position is simply stated: The responsibility of the Executive for the conduct of the foreign affairs and for the security of the Nation is so basic that the President is entitled to an injunction against publication of a newspaper story whenever he can convince a court that the information to be revealed threatens "grave and irreparable" injury to the public interest; and the injunction should issue whether or not the material to be published is classified, whether or not publication would be lawful under relevant criminal statutes enacted by Congress, and regardless of the circumstances by which the newspaper came into possession of the information.

At least in the absence of legislation by Congress, based on its own investigations and findings, I am quite unable to agree that the inherent powers of the Executive and the courts reach so far as to authorize remedies having such sweeping potential for inhibiting publications by the press. Much of the difficulty inheres in the "grave and irreparable danger" standard suggested by the United States. If the United States were to have judgment under such a standard in these cases, our decision would be of little guidance to other courts in other cases, for the material at issue here would not be available from the Court's opinion or from public records, nor would it be published by the press. . . .

It is not easy to reject the proposition urged by the United States and to deny relief on its good-faith claims in these cases that publication will work serious damage to the country. But that discomfiture is considerably dispelled by the infrequency of prior-restraint cases. Normally, publication will occur and the damage be done before the Government has either opportunity or grounds for suppression. So here, publication has already begun and a substantial part of the threatened damage has already occurred. The fact of a massive breakdown in security is known, access to the documents by many unauthorized people is undeniable, and the efficacy of equitable relief against these or other newspapers to avert anticipated damage is doubtful at best.

What is more, terminating the ban on publication of the relatively few sensitive documents the Government now seeks to suppress does not mean that the law either requires or invites newspapers or others to publish them or that they will be immune from criminal action if they do. . . .

When the Espionage Act was under consideration in 1917, Congress eliminated from the bill a provision that would have given the President broad powers in time of war to proscribe, under threat of criminal penalty, the publication of various categories of information related to the national defense.[3] Congress at that time was unwilling to clothe the President with such far-reaching powers to monitor the press, and those opposed to this part of the legislation assumed that a necessary concomitant of such power was the power to "filter out the news to the people through some man." 55 Cong. Rec. 2008 (remarks of Sen. Ashurst). However, these same members of Congress appeared to have little doubt that newspapers would be subject to criminal prosecution if they insisted on publishing information of the type Congress had itself determined should not be revealed. Senator Ashurst, for example, was quite sure that the editor of such a newspaper "should be punished if he did publish information as to the movements of the fleet, the troops, the aircraft, the location of powder factories, the location of defense works, and all that sort of thing."

The Criminal Code contains numerous provisions potentially relevant to these cases. Section 797 makes it a crime to publish certain photographs or drawings of military installations. Section 798, also in precise language, proscribes knowing and willful publication of any classified information concerning the cryptographic systems or communication intelligence activities of the United States as well as any information obtained from communication intelligence operations. . . . I would have

---

3. "Whoever, in time of war, in violation of reasonable regulations to be prescribed by the President, which he is hereby authorized to make and promulgate, shall publish any information with respect to the movement, . . . description, . . . or disposition of any of the armed forces . . . of the United States, . . . or any other information relating to the public defense calculated to be useful to the enemy, shall be punished by a fine . . . or by imprisonment. . . ." 55 Cong. Rec. 2100.

no difficulty in sustaining convictions under these sections on facts that would not justify the intervention of equity and the imposition of a prior restraint.

The same would be true under those sections of the Criminal Code casting a wider net to protect the national defense. Section 793(e) makes it a criminal act for any unauthorized possessor of a document "relating to the national defense" either (1) willfully to communicate or cause to be communicated that document to any person not entitled to receive it or (2) willfully to retain the document and fail to deliver it to an officer of the United States entitled to receive it. . . . Of course, in the cases before us, the unpublished documents have been demanded by the United States and their import has been made known at least to counsel for the newspapers involved. In *Gorin v. United States*, 312 U.S. 19, 28 (1941), the words "national defense" as used in a predecessor of § 793 were held by a unanimous Court to have "a well understood connotation" — a "generic concept of broad connotations, referring to the military and naval establishments and the related activities of national preparedness" — and to be "sufficiently definite to apprise the public of prohibited activities" and to be consonant with due process. Also, as construed by the Court in *Gorin*, information "connected with the national defense" is obviously not limited to that threatening "grave and irreparable" injury to the United States.

It is thus clear that Congress has addressed itself to the problems of protecting the security of the country and the national defense from unauthorized disclosure of potentially damaging information. It has not, however, authorized the injunctive remedy against threatened publication. It has apparently been satisfied to rely on criminal sanctions and their deterrent effect on the responsible as well as the irresponsible press. . . .

Justice MARSHALL, concurring.

. . . The issue is whether this Court or the Congress has the power to make law. In these cases there is no problem concerning the President's power to classify information as "secret" or "top secret." Congress has specifically recognized Presidential authority, which has been formally exercised in Exec. Order 10501 (1953), to classify documents and information. *See, e.g.,* 18 U.S.C. § 798; 50 U.S.C. § 783. Nor is there any issue here regarding the President's power as Chief Executive and Commander in Chief to protect national security by disciplining employees who disclose information and by taking precautions to prevent leaks.

The problem here is whether in these particular cases the Executive Branch has authority to invoke the equity jurisdiction of the courts to protect what it believes to be the national interest. *See In re Debs*, 158 U.S. 564, 584 (1895). . . . It would . . . be utterly inconsistent with the concept of separation of powers for this Court to use its power of contempt to prevent behavior that Congress has specifically declined to prohibit. . . . The Constitution . . . did not provide for government by injunction in which the courts and the Executive Branch can "make law" without regard to the action of Congress. It may be more convenient for the Executive Branch if it need only convince a judge to prohibit conduct rather than ask the Congress to pass a law, and it may be more convenient to enforce a contempt order than to seek a criminal conviction in a jury trial. Moreover, it may be considered politically wise to get a court to share the responsibility for arresting those who the Executive Branch has probable cause to believe are violating the law. But convenience and political considerations of the moment do not justify a basic departure from the principles of our system of government.

In these cases we are not faced with a situation where Congress has failed to provide the Executive with broad power to protect the Nation from disclosure of damaging state secrets. Congress has on several occasions given extensive consideration to the problem of protecting the military and strategic secrets of the United States. This consideration has resulted in the enactment of statutes making it a crime to receive, disclose, communicate, withhold, and publish certain documents, photographs, instruments, appliances, and information. . . . Congress has provided penalties ranging from a $10,000 fine to death for violating the various statutes. . . .

If the Government had attempted to show that there was no effective remedy under traditional criminal law, it would have had to show that there is no arguably applicable statute. Of course, at this stage this Court could not and cannot determine whether there has been a violation of a particular statute or decide the constitutionality of any statute. Whether a good-faith prosecution could have been instituted under any statute could, however, be determined. . . .

It is true that Judge Gurfein found that Congress had not made it a crime to publish the items and material specified in § 793(e). He found that the words "communicates, delivers, transmits . . ." did not refer to publication of newspaper stories. And that view has some support in the legislative history and conforms with the past practice of using the statute only to prosecute those charged with ordinary espionage. . . .

On at least two occasions Congress has refused to enact legislation that would have made the conduct engaged in here unlawful and given the President the power that he seeks in this case. In 1917 during the debate over the original Espionage Act, still the basic provisions of § 793, Congress rejected a proposal to give the President in time of war or threat of war authority to directly prohibit by proclamation the publication of information relating to national defense that might be useful to the enemy. The proposal provided that:

> "During any national emergency resulting from a war to which the United States is a party, or from threat of such a war, the President may, by proclamation, declare the existence of such emergency and, by proclamation, prohibit the publishing or communicating of, or the attempting to publish or communicate any information relating to the national defense which, in his judgment, is of such character that it is or might be useful to the enemy. Whoever violates any such prohibition shall be punished by a fine of not more than $10,000 or by imprisonment for not more than 10 years, or both: *Provided*, that nothing in this section shall be construed to limit or restrict

any discussion, comment, or criticism of the acts or policies of the Government or its representatives or the publication of the same." 55 Cong. Rec. 1763.

Congress rejected this proposal after war against Germany had been declared even though many believed that there was a grave national emergency and that the threat of security leaks and espionage was serious. . . . [T]he Executive Branch comes to this Court and asks that it be granted the power Congress refused to give.

In 1957 the United States Commission on Government Security found that "[a] irplane journals, scientific periodicals, and even the daily newspaper have featured articles containing information and other data which should have been deleted in whole or in part for security reasons." In response to this problem the Commission proposed that "Congress enact legislation making it a crime for any person willfully to disclose without proper authorization, for any purpose whatever, information classified 'secret' or 'top secret,' knowing, or having reasonable grounds to believe, such information to have been so classified." Report of Commission on Government Security 619–20 (1957). After substantial floor discussion on the proposal, it was rejected. *See* 103 Cong. Rec. 10447–10450. . . . The Government is here asking this Court to remake that decision. This Court has no such power. . . .

Justice HARLAN, with whom THE CHIEF JUSTICE and Justice BLACKMUN join, dissenting.

These cases forcefully call to mind the wise admonition of Mr. Justice Holmes, dissenting in *Northern Securities Co. v. United States*, 193 U.S. 197, 400–401 (1904):

> "Great cases, like hard cases, make bad law. For great cases are called great, not by reason of their real importance in shaping the law of the future, but because of some accident of immediate overwhelming interest which appeals to the feelings and distorts the judgment. These immediate interests exercise a kind of hydraulic pressure which makes what previously was clear seem doubtful, and before which even well settled principles of law will bend."

With all respect, I consider that the Court has been almost irresponsibly feverish in dealing with these cases.

Both the Court of Appeals for the Second Circuit and the Court of Appeals for the District of Columbia Circuit rendered judgment on June 23. The New York Times' petition for certiorari, its motion for accelerated consideration thereof, and its application for interim relief were filed in this Court on June 24 at about 11 a.m. . . . The briefs of the parties were received less than two hours before argument on June 26.

This frenzied train of events took place in the name of the presumption against prior restraints created by the First Amendment. Due regard for the extraordinarily important and difficult questions involved in these litigations should have led the Court to shun such a precipitate timetable. In order to decide the merits of these cases properly, some or all of the following questions should have been faced:

1. Whether the Attorney General is authorized to bring these suits in the name of the United States. Compare *In re Debs*, 158 U.S. 564 (1895), with *Youngstown Sheet & Tube Co. v. Sawyer*, 343 U.S. 579 (1952). This question involves as well the construction and validity of a singularly opaque statute—the Espionage Act, 18 U.S.C. § 793(e).

2. Whether the First Amendment permits the federal courts to enjoin publication of stories which would present a serious threat to national security. *See Near v. Minnesota*, 283 U.S. 697, 716 (1931) (dictum).

3. Whether the threat to publish highly secret documents is of itself a sufficient implication of national security to justify an injunction on the theory that regardless of the contents of the documents harm enough results simply from the demonstration of such a breach of secrecy.

4. Whether the unauthorized disclosure of any of these particular documents would seriously impair the national security.

5. What weight should be given to the opinion of high officers in the Executive Branch of the Government with respect to questions 3 and 4.

6. Whether the newspapers are entitled to retain and use the documents notwithstanding the seemingly uncontested facts that the documents, or the originals of which they are duplicates, were purloined from the Government's possession and that the newspapers received them with knowledge that they had been feloniously acquired.

7. Whether the threatened harm to the national security or the Government's possessory interest in the documents justifies the issuance of an injunction against publication in light of—

a. The strong First Amendment policy against prior restraints on publication;

b. The doctrine against enjoining conduct in violation of criminal statutes; and

c. The extent to which the materials at issue have apparently already been otherwise disseminated. . . .

Forced as I am to reach the merits of these cases, I dissent from the opinion and judgments of the Court. . . . It is plain to me that the scope of the judicial function in passing upon the activities of the Executive Branch of the Government in the field of foreign affairs is very narrowly restricted. This view is, I think, dictated by the concept of separation of powers upon which our constitutional system rests.

In a speech on the floor of the House of Representatives, Chief Justice John Marshall, then a member of that body, stated: "The President is the sole organ of the nation in its external relations, and its sole representative with foreign nations." 10 Annals of Cong. 613. From that time, shortly after the founding of the Nation, to this, there has been no substantial challenge to this description of the scope of executive power.

From this constitutional primacy in the field of foreign affairs, it seems to me that certain conclusions necessarily follow. Some of these were stated concisely by

President Washington, declining the request of the House of Representatives for the papers leading up to the negotiation of the Jay Treaty:

> "The nature of foreign negotiations requires caution, and their success must often depend on secrecy; and even when brought to a conclusion a full disclosure of all the measures, demands, or eventual concessions which may have been proposed or contemplated would be extremely impolitic; for this might have a pernicious influence on future negotiations, or produce immediate inconveniences, perhaps danger and mischief, in relation to other powers." 1 J. Richardson, Messages and Papers of the Presidents 194–195 (1896).

The power to evaluate the "pernicious influence" of premature disclosure is not, however, lodged in the Executive alone. I agree that, in performance of its duty to protect the values of the First Amendment against political pressures, the judiciary must review the initial Executive determination to the point of satisfying itself that the subject matter of the dispute does lie within the proper compass of the President's foreign relations power. Constitutional considerations forbid "a complete abandonment of judicial control." Moreover, the judiciary may properly insist that the determination that disclosure of the subject matter would irreparably impair the national security be made by the head of the Executive Department concerned — here the Secretary of State or the Secretary of Defense — after actual personal consideration by that officer. This safeguard is required in the analogous area of executive claims of privilege for secrets of state.

But in my judgment the judiciary may not properly go beyond these two inquiries and redetermine for itself the probable impact of disclosure on the national security. . . . Even if there is some room for the judiciary to override the executive determination, it is plain that the scope of review must be exceedingly narrow. I can see no indication in the opinions [below] that the conclusions of the Executive were given even the deference owing to an administrative agency, much less that owing to a co-equal branch of the Government operating within the field of its constitutional prerogative. . . .

Pending further hearings in each case conducted under the appropriate ground rules, I would continue the restraints on publication. I cannot believe that the doctrine prohibiting prior restraints reaches to the point of preventing courts from maintaining the status quo long enough to act responsibly in matters of such national importance as those involved here.

Justice BLACKMUN, dissenting.

I join Justice Harlan in his dissent. I also am in substantial accord with much that Justice White says, by way of admonition, in the latter part of his opinion. . . .

———————

1. *Was* Pentagon Papers *an Easy Case?* Garnering legal guidance from the *Pentagon Papers* case is not easy because the Court's nine opinions offer as many as seven

different approaches to the case, differing in either nuance or overall theory. The terse *per curiam* opinion stresses the extraordinary threshold showing that the executive must make to justify a prior restraint. In this case, however, whatever the standard, the executive branch faced somewhat unhelpful facts in making a case for secrecy. There were numerous sets of the papers, and they were no longer under any controlled custody. Indeed, the President had sent a set to Congress. Moreover, the material was entirely historical, recounting events up to 1968. Where does that leave us for prior restraints on material under a court's custody, relating to current secrets?

2. Pentagon Papers *in the World of New Media*. Recent decades have witnessed an explosion in the information and communication technologies available for facilitating the unauthorized disclosure of government information. No project dramatizes the possibilities better than WikiLeaks, which describes itself on its web site as "a multi-jurisdictional public service designed to protect whistleblowers, journalists and activists who have sensitive materials to communicate to the public. . . . WikiLeaks combines the protection and anonymity of cutting-edge cryptographic technologies with the comfortable presentation style of Wikipedia, although the two are not otherwise related." In other words, WikiLeaks acts as an intermediary between government "leakers" and the public, making confidential documents available online in the form of an online compendium.

In early July, 2010, WikiLeaks made available to three news publications—The New York Times, The Guardian (UK), and Der Spiegel—92,000 individual reports (about 75,000 of them classified) concerning the progress of the Afghanistan War between 2004 and 2009. The news organizations involved each agreed not to write about or otherwise disclose the documents until July 25, 2010, when the entire set would be made available online. In part, the New York Times described the tenor of the documents as follows:

> The documents . . . illustrate in mosaic detail why, after the United States has spent almost $300 billion on the war in Afghanistan, the Taliban are stronger than at any time since 2001.

> As the new American commander in Afghanistan, Gen. David H. Petraeus, tries to reverse the lagging war effort, the documents sketch a war hamstrung by an Afghan government, police force and army of questionable loyalty and competence, and by a Pakistani military that appears at best uncooperative and at worst to work from the shadows as an unspoken ally of the very insurgent forces the American-led coalition is trying to defeat. . . .

> The reports—usually spare summaries but sometimes detailed narratives—shed light on some elements of the war that have been largely hidden from the public eye:

> • The Taliban have used portable heat-seeking missiles against allied aircraft, a fact that has not been publicly disclosed by the military. This type of weapon helped the Afghan mujahedeen defeat the Soviet occupation in the 1980s.

- Secret commando units like Task Force 373 — a classified group of Army and Navy special operatives — work from a "capture/kill list" of about 70 top insurgent commanders. These missions, which have been stepped up under the Obama administration, claim notable successes, but have sometimes gone wrong, killing civilians and stoking Afghan resentment.

- The military employs more and more drone aircraft to survey the battlefield and strike targets in Afghanistan, although their performance is less impressive than officially portrayed. Some crash or collide, forcing American troops to undertake risky retrieval missions before the Taliban can claim the drone's weaponry.

- The Central Intelligence Agency has expanded paramilitary operations inside Afghanistan. The units launch ambushes, order airstrikes and conduct night raids. From 2001 to 2008, the C.I.A. paid the budget of Afghanistan's spy agency and ran it as a virtual subsidiary.

Over all, the documents do not contradict official accounts of the war. But in some cases the documents show that the American military made misleading public statements — attributing the downing of a helicopter to conventional weapons instead of heat-seeking missiles or giving Afghans credit for missions carried out by Special Operations commandos.

C. J. Chivers, Carlotta Gall, *et al.*, *View Is Bleaker Than Official Portrayal of War in Afghanistan*, N.Y. Times, at A1 (July 25, 2010). Suspicion focused on a 22-year-old military intelligence officer, who was accused also of earlier leaking a video depicting a helicopter attack in Iraq that resulted in the deaths of civilians, including a press photographer and his driver. The New York Times quoted the reaction of Secretary of Defense Robert Gates to the documents as follows: "The battlefield consequences of the release of these documents are potentially severe and dangerous for our troops, our allies and Afghan partners, and may well damage our relationships and reputation in that key part of the world. Intelligence sources and methods, as well as military tactics, techniques and procedures, will become known to our adversaries." Charlie Savage, *Gates Assails WikiLeaks Over Release of Reports*, N.Y. Times, at A1 (July 29, 2010). For its part, The Times insisted: "The Times has taken care not to publish information that would harm national security interests or disclose anything that was likely to put lives at risk or jeopardize military or antiterrorist operations, withholding any names of operatives in the field and informants cited in the reports. It also has not linked to the archives of raw material." *Id.*

Had the Defense Department known of the WikiLeaks release prior to July 25, could it have successfully enjoined the publication of the documents involved by WikiLeaks? By the New York Times? How exposed is the New York Times to potential criminal prosecution?

3. *United States v. Progressive, Inc.* In his *Pentagon Papers* opinion, Justice Brennan cites the famous dictum from *Near v. Minnesota* that the Government might prevent

publication of such matters as troop locations in wartime. He argues that only proof of such direct threats to national security can justify a prior restraint, and that the courts can review the persuasiveness of the executive's factual submissions. Do you agree? What standard of judicial review would be appropriate? Compare Justice Harlan's argument that the courts should stop once they have ascertained that the subject matter pertains to the foreign relations power, and that the determination of necessity to suppress it has been made after "actual personal consideration" by an officer of appropriate rank. Would such a test sufficiently protect First Amendment values, in light of the incentives for government officers to resist disclosure of materials that are merely embarrassing?

In light of this debate, consider an extraordinary case that arose in 1979. A District Court granted the Government a preliminary injunction against publication by *The Progressive* of an article detailing the basic design of the American hydrogen bomb. *United States v. Progressive, Inc.*, 467 F. Supp. 990 (W.D. Wis. 1979). The author, Howard Morland, deduced the information entirely from unclassified materials: interviews with government employees, visits to nuclear weapons facilities, and the study of government documents—all with the knowledge and consent of the U.S. Department of Energy. The Government argued that the way this unclassified material was synthesized in the article could provide new insights to building an H-bomb.

Solely on the basis of affidavits and counsels' briefs and oral arguments, the District Court issued the injunction based on the *possibility* of "grave, direct, immediate and irreparable harm" to the national interest. Six months later, while the preliminary injunction was still in effect, the Government moved to dismiss the case as moot after another author succeeded in publishing an article elsewhere with substantially the same information. *United States v. Progressive, Inc.*, 610 F. 2d 819 (7th Cir. 1979) (appeal dismissed without opinion). For a critical review of the court's rationale and its fact-finding procedure, see Note, United States v. Progressive, Inc.: *The Faustian Bargain and the First Amendment*, 75 Nw. U. L. Rev. 538 (1980). More recent commentary includes Lucas A. Powe, Jr., *The H-Bomb Injunction*, 61 U. Colo. L. Rev. 55 (1990), and John Cary Sims, *Triangulating the Boundaries of Pentagon Papers*, 2 Wm. & Mary Bill Rts J. 341 (1993).

Did the District Court apply the correct standard for reviewing the executive's claims? How can the executive address the "cat-out-of-the-bag" problem in these cases?

4. *Congress's Role in Protecting Secrets.* Justice White seemingly entertains little doubt that, consistent with the First Amendment, Congress may provide criminal liability for the publication of material that could not constitutionally be restrained prior to publication. Does this make sense? Why?

In the same vein, Justice Marshall insists that the *Pentagon Papers* case implicates not only First Amendment principles, but serious separation of powers questions as well. Note that both he and Justice White cite Congress' refusal to pass bills that would have made it a crime to publish information "relating to the national defense" in violation of presidential orders. Is this case like *Youngstown*, then? If the bills had been enacted, would they justify prior restraints? (And why, by the way, did Congress decline to pass these bills? Would it have been wise to enact them?) What result should follow here if Congress had authorized the executive to sue for injunctive relief against the possible publication of materials, "the revelation of which will substantially damage the national security?"

Problem: *Applying* New York Times *After September 11*

The September 11, 2001 terrorist attacks on New York City and Washington, D.C. understandably spawned intense anxiety about the relationship between government openness and national security. This concern has nowhere been more evident than in the conduct of law enforcement investigations after September 11. The United States detained over 1,000 people in the wake of the attacks. Over three-quarters were held for possible immigration law violations, while 129 were charged with federal criminal offenses and others were held as material witnesses for grand jury proceedings. The government refused to publicize any details about the detainees, including their identities. Indeed, when the government started deportation proceedings against some of the detained aliens, Chief Immigration Judge Michael Creppy issued an unpublished order that the public and the press be excluded from immigration hearings in cases of "special interest."

The federal lower courts split on the executive's entitlement to preserve this degree of secrecy. In *Center for National Security Studies v. U.S. Department of Justice*, 331 F.3d 918 (D.C. Cir. 2003), *cert. denied*, 540 U.S. 1104 (2004), the D.C. Circuit overturned a lower court ruling that the Justice Department was required by the Freedom of Information Act to disclose the names of its detainees and their attorneys. The majority held that the government could rely on the Act's Exemption 7(A), which excludes from mandatory disclosure "records or information compiled for law enforcement purposes . . . to the extent that the production of such law enforcement records or information . . . could reasonably be expected to interfere with enforcement proceedings." The majority was likewise of the view that there was no First Amendment right to the information. Judge Tatel dissented, most strenuously on the ground that the Justice Department had not offered any detailed explanation why the release of each and every detainee's identity would pose a threat to law enforcement. He also disputed the government's justification for withholding attorney identities, namely, that making those names public would permit easy identification of the clients. Because a lawyer's release of a client's identity without consent is unethical, and because the detainees are free, if they want, to disclose the fact of their detention, Tatel would have rejected the government's reasoning.

The government succeeded also in defending the closing of deportation hearings in *North Jersey Media Group v. Ashcroft*, 308 F.3d 198 (3d Cir. 2002), *cert. denied*, 538 U.S. 1056 (2003). The court, following the Supreme Court's reasoning in *Richmond Newspapers v. Virginia*, 448 U.S. 555 (1980), held that there was an insufficient tradition of open deportation hearings to support a First Amendment claim to openness and that, even if there were, requiring openness in this context threatened to undermine immigration law enforcement with regard to would-be terrorists.

The Sixth Circuit, however, came to the opposite conclusion in *Detroit Free Press v. Ashcroft*, 303 F.3d 681 (6th Cir. 2002), holding that there is a first amendment right to open deportation hearings, and that, while preventing terrorism is a compelling government interest, a blanket order closing all deportation hearings involving persons suspected of aiding in terrorism was not narrowly tailored to serving that purpose. As a result, the government was required to hold an open hearing for Rabih Haddad, an Ann Arbor man investigated for possible terrorist fund-raising, who was deported to Lebanon in 2003.

Imagine that a Justice Department employee were to leak to the Washington Post (a) a list of aliens currently detained in connection with the investigation of terrorism, (b) a list of their lawyers, or (c) the transcript of a closed deportation hearing. After the Pentagon Papers case, could the United States hope to succeed in a suit to enjoin publication of any of this material? Again, would it make any difference if Congress had expressly authorized the withholding of the identity information, the closing of deportation hearings, or executive branch suits to enjoin publication of information about either?

———————

For further ruminations on questions such as these, see Harold Edgar & Benno C. Schmidt, Curtiss-Wright *Comes Home: Executive Power and National Security Secrecy*, 21 Harv. Civ. Rts.-Civ. Lib. L. Rev. 349, 360–61 (1986):

When the Nixon Administration sought to enjoin publication of the "Pentagon Papers" fifteen years ago, we were struck by what seemed the bizarre institutional premises of the Administration's main legal position. The government argued that without any statutory authorization, the President, in his role as commander-in-chief and steward of foreign relations, could create a legal norm of secrecy and enlist the injunctive powers of the federal courts to enforce his norm against publications that posed a "grave and irreparable danger" to national security. The government's brief in the Supreme Court did not even mention the statutory situation.

Even if the Executive could sue for injunctive relief without statutory authorization, he cannot create the legal rule that he seeks to enforce in the domestic arena. Since Congress had made no law, what possible basis could there have been even to consider the first amendment?

The absence of legislative authorization was noted in the questions at oral argument and in several of the Justices' opinions, although only Marshall argued that it should be decisive. Of the six Justices who concurred in the judgment against the government, all but Justice Brennan relied to some degree on the absence of statutory authority for injunctive relief. Moreover, considerable interest was expressed on the different issue of criminal sanctions for publication of classified government documents. A number of the Justices volunteered readings of the espionage statutes in relation to hypothetical criminal proceedings against the publishers, reporters and information sources involved, even though such questions had not been briefed, were dreadfully difficult, and were quite unnecessary to a ruling about the injunction.

These speculative dicta addressing the potential capacity of the espionage statutes to criminalize publication of the "Pentagon Papers," when added to our own institutional predispositions, led us fifteen years ago to exaggerate the extent to which the Court accepted the premise of legislative hegemony over national security secrecy issues. [Edgar & Schmidt, *The Espionage Statutes and Publication of Defense Information*, 73 Colum. L. Rev. 929 (1973).] With hindsight, we now believe that the central theme of the *Pentagon Papers* opinions, at least in institutional terms, was the surprising willingness of many of the Justices to contemplate scenarios set in a statutory vacuum, where executive power backed by judicial support would govern issues of national security secrecy, at least so long as Congress remained a passive bystander

Edgar and Schmidt explain the evolution of their views as follows (*id.* at 351):

We [believed] that Congress should be the controlling institution in striking a tolerable balance between secrecy needs and the value of public debate about foreign and military policy. We . . . assumed that the Supreme Court in particular would see the virtues of legislative resolution of secrecy questions. Contrary to our predictions and prescriptions, the years since the *Pentagon Papers* have seen a considerable enhancement of executive power in areas of national security secrecy, an aggrandizement significantly assisted by the Supreme Court, with Congress noticeably absent from the discourse.

Note on Classification and Protection of Government Documents

No statute sets overall government policy concerning the classification, or the handling of documents that are sensitive with respect to national security. Instead, each administration has the opportunity to form its own policy by executive order. Perhaps unsurprisingly, what has resulted is a process of ongoing modulation, from Administration to Administration, in the standards and processes governing both classification and declassification. President Carter, for example, thought information otherwise classifiable should be declassified if "the need to protect such information [is] outweighed by the public interest in disclosure. . . ." Executive Order No. 12,065, 3 C.F.R. 190 (1979). President Reagan disagreed. He further revoked a Carter requirement that the potential danger posed by release be "identifiable" before information may be classified, a requirement reinstituted by President Clinton. Executive Order No. 12958, 60 Fed. Reg. 19,825 (1995).

On December 29, 2009, President Obama issued an executive order on classification that followed the now-familiar pattern of fine-tuning his predecessor's handiwork. Exec, Order No. 13526, 75 Fed. Reg. 707 (2010). Perhaps most significant, the order bars classification if there is "significant doubt" as to the need to classify, and directs classification at a lower level if there is a "significant doubt" as to the appropriate level of classification. The order restores the requirement (which President George W. Bush had deleted) that information be classified only if its unauthorized disclosure could cause damage that is "identifiable or describable." It further creates a National Declassification Center in order to help "streamline" the declassification process.

It is worth noting that, especially after 9/11, supporters of declassification have been worried, in part, that overclassification might weaken national security by impeding the flow of important information among relevant law enforcement and intelligence agencies. With that concern in mind, Congress enacted the Reducing Over-Classification Act, Pub. L. 11-258, 111th Cong., 2d Sess. (2010). It creates procedures to promote information sharing with state, local, tribal, and private sector entities, and to foster training and incentives to promote more accurate classification. For example, the Act requires the Department of Homeland Security to designate a Classified Information Advisory Officer to disseminate educational materials and administer training programs to assist state, local, tribal, and private sector entities. It also directs the Director of National Intelligence to establish guidance to standardize formats for intelligence products, and directs Inspectors General to assess the effectiveness of agency classification policies.

Once a document has been classified, the Freedom of Information Act (FOIA), 5 U.S.C. § 552, exempts it from the mandatory disclosure to which most agency records are subject, under certain conditions. Exemption 1 of FOIA, § 552(b)(1), protects documents that are "(A) specifically authorized under criteria established by an Executive order to be kept secret in the interest of national defense or foreign policy and (B) are in fact properly classified pursuant to such Executive order." The courts are authorized to review documents *in camera* as part of a *de novo* review of the agency's decision to withhold; the burden of proof is on the agency to justify classification on both substantive and procedural grounds. Courts are also authorized to order the release of information contained in classified documents if it is both nonclassifiable and segregable from protected portions of the documents. *See Goldberg v. U.S. Dept. of State*, 818 F.2d 71 (D.C. Cir. 1987), *cert. denied*, 485 U.S. 904 (1988). Comment, *A Nation Less Secure: Diminished Public Access to Information*, 21 Harv. Civ. Rts.-Civ. Lib. L. Rev. 409 (1986).

Agencies may also be able to protect documents under the authority of their governing statutes. Exemption 3 of FOIA allows the withholding of materials that are "specifically exempted from disclosure by statute." (§ 552(b)(3)) In *CIA v. Sims*, 471 U.S. 159 (1985), the Court held that the National Security Act of 1947, by authorizing the CIA Director to protect "intelligence sources and methods," was an exempting statute for FOIA purposes. In addition, the Central Intelligence Agency Information Act, 50 U.S.C. §§ 431–32, protects CIA "operational files," with some limitations. *See* Karen A. Winchester & James W. Zirkle, *Freedom of Information and the CIA Information Act*, 21 U. RICH. L. REV. 231 (1987). Congress has also enacted the Intelligence Identities Protection Act, 50 U.S.C. §§ 421–26, which attaches criminal sanctions to the unauthorized disclosure of the names of covert agents.

The attacks of September 11, 2001 spawned intense concern within both Congress and the executive for a new category of information, which might be considered "sensitive, but unclassified." President Bush's chief of staff, Andrew H. Card, Jr., forwarded guidance to the heads of all executive agencies, stating: "[D]epartments and agencies maintain and control sensitive information related to America's homeland security that might not meet one or more of the standards for classification set forth in Part 1 of Executive Order 12958. The need to protect such sensitive information from inappropriate disclosure should be carefully considered, on a case-by-case basis, together with the benefits that result from the open and efficient exchange of scientific, technical, and like information." Memorandum for Heads of Executive Departments and Agencies from Andrew H. Card, Jr., Assistant to the President and Chief of Staff re: *Action to Safeguard Information Regarding Weapons of Mass Destruction and Other Sensitive Documents Related to Homeland Security* (Mar. 19, 2002), available at http://www.usdoj.gov/oip/foiapost /2002foiapost10.htm.

In a similar vein, a portion of the Homeland Security Act of 2002, Pub.L. 107-296, Title II, § 212, 116 Stat. 2150, created a category of information called "critical infrastructure information," defined as:

> information not customarily in the public domain and related to the security of critical infrastructure or protected systems—
>
> > (A) actual, potential, or threatened interference with, attack on, compromise of, or incapacitation of critical infrastructure or protected systems by either physical or computer-based attack or other similar conduct (including the misuse of or unauthorized access to all types of communications and data transmission systems) that violates Federal, State, or local law, harms interstate commerce of the United States, or threatens public health or safety;
> >
> > (B) the ability of any critical infrastructure or protected system to resist such interference, compromise, or incapacitation, including any planned or past assessment, projection, or estimate of the vulnerability of critical infrastructure or a protected system, including security testing, risk evaluation thereto, risk management planning, or risk audit; or
> >
> > (C) any planned or past operational problem or solution regarding critical infrastructure or protected systems, including repair, recovery,

> reconstruction, insurance, or continuity, to the extent it is related to
> such interference, compromise, or incapacitation.

6 U.S.C. § 131. To the extent private parties now voluntarily submit "critical infrastructure information" to a federal agency, such information is categorically exempt from mandatory disclosure under the FOIA, without regard to its classification status. 6 U.S.C. § 133(a)(1). Moreover, the legally unauthorized disclosure of any such information is a crime. 6 U.S.C. § 133(f).

In short, the United States protects its secrets through a mosaic of statutes and executive orders. In 1986, Edgar and Schmidt recalled their 1973 review of the statutes discussed in the *Pentagon Papers* opinions, and concluded, *supra* at 357, that:

> even though it is common knowledge that the current statutes are hopelessly muddled, Congress has found it impossible to enact more coherent general legislation protecting national defense information against revelation. The effort to clarify would have required firm answers to too many difficult questions.

This statement seems no less true more than three decades later.

Still, sometimes a muddle is better than the alternatives. Unlike the British, we do not have a simple, comprehensive Official Secrets Act, criminalizing unauthorized release and possession of government information. *See* Evan J. Wallach, *Executive Powers of Prior Restraint over Publication of National Security Information: the UK and USA Compared*, 32 Int'l & Comp. L.Q. 424 (1983). Would such a statute be consistent with the First Amendment?

Protecting Classified Information After Snepp. In *Snepp v. United States*, 444 U.S. 507 (1980), a former CIA agent challenged the validity of a nondisclosure clause in his employment contract that required him to secure the CIA's preclearance before publishing any book. The contractual provision was designed to prevent the publication of classified information. Snepp asserted that the provision was a prior restraint in violation of the First Amendment. The Supreme Court disagreed, holding that enforcing such a voluntary contractual provision in the context of legitimate national security interests is permissible. The executive branch wasted little time after *Snepp* in expanding its use of nondisclosure agreements to protect classified information from unauthorized disclosure. In addition to beefing up (from his perspective) the executive order on the classification of national security information, President Reagan issued National Security Decision Directive 84 (NSDD-84), reprinted in *National Security Decision Directive 84, Hearing Before the Senate Comm. on Governmental Affairs*, 98th Cong., 1st Sess. 85–86 (1983), which required all agencies handling classified information to "adopt internal procedures to safeguard against unlawful disclosures of classified information." *Id.* at § 1. Under NSDD-84, those procedures were required to provide at a minimum that all persons with access to classified information sign a nondisclosure agreement, and that such nondisclosure agreements include provisions for prepublication review whenever the signatory had access to Sensitive Compartmented Information (SCI). *Id.*

NSDD-84 also directed agencies to "adopt internal procedures to govern the reporting and investigation of unauthorized disclosures of such information." *Id.* at § 2. To further such investigations, the directive, in its most controversial provision, stated:

> The Office of Personnel Management and all departments and agencies with employees having access to classified information are directed to revise existing regulations and policies, as necessary, so that employees may be required to submit to polygraph examinations, when appropriate, in the course of investigations of unauthorized disclosures of classified information. As a minimum, such regulations shall permit an agency to decide that appropriate adverse consequences will follow an employee's refusal to cooperate with a polygraph examination that is limited in scope to the circumstances of the unauthorized disclosure under investigation. Agency regulations may provide that only the head of the agency, or his delegate, is empowered to order an employee to submit to a polygraph examination. Results of polygraph examinations should not be relied upon to the exclusion of other information obtained during investigations.

Id. at § 5.

In defending NSDD-84 before the Senate Governmental Affairs Committee, Assistant Attorney General Richard Willard expressed the view that protective administrative procedures were essential to the security of classified information because threatened criminal prosecutions were not effective enough to deter or remedy unauthorized disclosures of classified information. The preclearance requirements intended to be implemented under the directive would be comprehensive in scope: "The agreement not to disclose classified information extends to any method by which such information can be communicated, including oral disclosures. The prepublication review obligation extends only to 'materials' that contain or purport to contain certain kinds of information. This could include reports, correspondence or lecture notes. Implementing regulations recognize that oral statements cannot be subject to prepublication review in the same manner as writings." Moreover, former employees, in addition to agreeing not to disclose classified information, also had to agree not to "speak or write in a manner that expressly or impliedly confirms the accuracy of classified information that may have entered the public domain as the consequence of an unauthorized disclosure." *Id.* at 23–30 (1983).

Another potentially key advantage of preclearance agreements, according to Mr. Willard, was their susceptibility to enforcement through injunction. Although he acknowledged "an unresolved question as to the legal standard that should be applied," Willard pointed out that courts had not treated government attempts to enforce prepublication agreements with the same hostility as traditional prior restraints.

NSDD-84 received a hostile reaction in Congress, which legislated to delay implementation of both the prepublication clearance and polygraph provisions of the order. The administration subsequently suspended the order, with a view to its possible later reinstatement. The story is told in Comment, *The Constitutionality of Expanding Prepublication Review of Government Employees' Speech*, 72 Calif. L. Rev. 962, 973–74 (1984). *See also* Mary M. Cheh, *Judicial Supervision of Executive Secrecy: Rethinking Freedom of Expression for Government Employees and the Public Right of Access to Government Information*, 69 Cornell L. Rev. 690 (1984); Lucas Powe, Jr., *The Constitutional Implications of President Reagan's Censorship Directive* 84, 17 The Center Magazine 2 (1984).

The Reagan Administration eventually promulgated Standard Form 189, which all government employees and contractors with access to classified information were required to sign, on pain of losing their security classifications—and their jobs. The form's signatories were bound never to divulge in a "direct or indirect" fashion "classified or classifiable" data. "Classifiable" information was that which "as a result of negligence, time constraints, error, or lack of opportunity or oversight has not been marked as classified information," and disclosures violate SF 189 if the person "knew or reasonably should have known" that material was classifiable. 52 Fed. Reg. 28802 (1987). Any information to which signatories gained access was to remain government property "forever."

SF 189 was subsequently replaced with SF 312, available at http://www.archives.gov/isoo/security-forms/sf312.pdf, which deleted the term "classifiable information," and now covers "marked or unmarked classified information, including oral communications; and unclassified information that meets the standards for classification and is in the process of a classification determination, as provided in Sections 1.2 and 1.4(e) of Executive Order 12958 or under any other Executive order or statute that requires interim protection for certain information while a classification determination is pending. 'Classified information' does not include unclassified information that may be subject to possible classification at some future date, but is not currently in the process of a classification determination." Information Security Oversight Office, Classified Information Nondisclosure Agreement Standard Form 312 Briefing Booklet (Spring, 2001).

4. Power to Conduct Investigations (Herein, of Foreign Intelligence Surveillance)

a. Electronic Surveillance, Executive Power, and the Fourth Amendment Prior to FISA

Claims of inherent executive authority to protect national security involve not only withholding information, but also acquiring it. The following committee report excerpt summarizes some of the history of electronic surveillance that Presidents have authorized under assertedly inherent executive power.

Foreign Intelligence Surveillance Act of 1977[*]

S. Rep. No. 604, 95th Cong., 1st Sess. (1977)

In 1928, the Supreme Court in *Olmstead v. United States*[5] held that wiretapping was not within the coverage of the Fourth Amendment. Three years later, Attorney General William D. Mitchell authorized telephone wiretapping, upon the personal approval of bureau chiefs, of syndicated bootleggers and in "exceptional cases where the crimes are substantial and serious, and the necessity is great and [the bureau chief and the Assistant Attorney General] are satisfied that the persons whose wires are to be tapped are of the criminal type." These general guidelines governed the Department's practice through the thirties and telephone wiretapping was considered to be an important law enforcement tool.

Congress placed the first restrictions on wiretapping in the Federal Communications Act of 1934, which made it a crime for any person "to intercept and divulge or publish the contents of wire and radio communications."[7] The Supreme Court construed this section to apply to Federal agents and held that evidence obtained from the interception of wire and radio communications, and the fruits of that evidence, were inadmissible in court.[8] However, the Justice Department did not interpret the Federal Communications Act or the *Nardone* decision as prohibiting the interception of wire communications *per se*; rather only the interception and divulgence of their contents outside the Federal establishment was considered to be unlawful. Thus, the Justice Department found continued authority for its national security wiretaps.

In 1940, President Roosevelt issued a memorandum to the Attorney General stating his view that electronic surveillance would be proper under the Constitution where "grave matters involving defense of the nation" were involved. The President authorized and directed the Attorney General "to secure information by listening devices [directed at] the conversation or other communications of persons suspected of subversive activities against the Government of the United States, including suspected spies." The Attorney General was requested "to limit these investigations so conducted to a minimum and to limit them insofar as possible as to aliens."

This practice was continued in successive administrations. In 1946, Attorney General Tom C. Clark sent President Truman a letter informing him of President

---

[*] Congress did not pass legislation on electronic surveillance for foreign intelligence purposes until 1978. Foreign Intelligence Act of 1978, Pub. L. No. 95-511, 92 Stat. 1783, *codified at* 50 U.S.C. § 1801 *et seq*. There is substantial continuity, however, between the 1977 and 1978 bills and legislative reports. *See* H.R. Rep. No. 1283, 95th Cong., 2d Sess. (1978); S. Rep. No. 701, 95th Cong., 2d Sess. (1978); H.R. Rep. No. 1720, 95th Cong., 2d Sess. (1978) (conference report).

5. 277 U.S. 468.

7. 47 U.S.C. 605 (1964 ed.), 48 Stat. 1103.

8. *Nardone v. United States*, 302 U.S. 379 (1937); 308 U.S. 338 (1939).

Roosevelt's directive. Clark's memorandum, however, omitted the portion of President Roosevelt's directive limiting wiretaps "insofar as possible to aliens." Instead, he recommended that the directive "be continued in force" in view of the "increase in subversive activities" and "a very substantial increase in crime." President Truman approved.[10]

In the early fifties, however, Attorney General J. Howard McGrath took the position that he would not approve or authorize the installation of microphone surveillances by means of trespass. This policy was quickly reversed by Attorney General Herbert Brownell in 1954 in a sweeping memorandum to FBI Director Hoover instructing him that the Bureau was indeed authorized to conduct such trespassory surveillances regardless of the fact of surreptitious entry, and without the need to first acquire the Attorney General's authorization. Such surveillance was simply authorized whenever the Bureau concluded that the "national interest" so required. The Brownell memorandum is instructive:

> It is my opinion that the department should adopt that interpretation which will permit microphone coverage by the FBI in a manner most conducive to our national interest. I recognize that for the FBI to fulfill its important intelligence function, considerations of internal security and the national interest are paramount; and, therefore, may compel the unrestricted use of this technique in the national interest.

From the relatively limited authorization of warrantless electronic surveillance under President Roosevelt, then, the mandate for the FBI was quickly expanded to the point where the only criterion was the FBI's subjective judgment that the "national interest" required the electronic surveillance. . . .

In *Katz v. United States*, 389 U.S. 347 (1967), the Supreme Court finally discarded the *Olmstead* doctrine and held that the Fourth Amendment's warrant provision did apply to electronic surveillance. The Court explicitly declined, however, to extend its holding to cases "involving the national security." 389 U.S. at 358, n.23. The next year, Congress followed suit: responding to the *Katz* case, Congress enacted the Omnibus Crime Control and Safe Streets Act (18 U.S.C. sections 2510–2520). Title III of that Act established a procedure for the judicial authorization of electronic surveillance for the investigation and prevention of specified types of serious crimes and the use of the product of such surveillance in court proceedings. It prohibited wiretapping and electronic surveillance by persons other than duly authorized law enforcement officers, personnel of the Federal Communications Commission, or communication common carriers monitoring communications in the normal course of their employment. Title III, however, disclaimed any intention of legislating in the national security area. . . .

---

10. In 1950, aides to President Truman discovered Clark's incomplete quotation, and the President considered returning to the terms of the original 1940 authorization. However, the 1946 directive was never rescinded.

United States v. United States District Court (Keith)

407 U.S. 297 (1972)

Justice POWELL delivered the opinion of the Court.

The issue before us is an important one for the people of our country and their Government. It involves the delicate question of the President's power, acting through the Attorney General, to authorize electronic surveillance in internal security matters without prior judicial approval. Successive Presidents for more than one-quarter of a century have authorized such surveillance in varying degrees, without guidance from the Congress or a definitive decision of this Court. This case brings the issue here for the first time. Its resolution is a matter of national concern, requiring sensitivity both to the Government's right to protect itself from unlawful subversion and attack and to the citizen's right to be secure in his privacy against unreasonable Government intrusion.

This case arises from a criminal proceeding in the United States District Court for the Eastern District of Michigan, in which the United States charged three defendants with conspiracy to destroy Government property in violation of 18 U.S.C. § 371. One of the defendants, Plamondon, was charged with the dynamite bombing of an office of the Central Intelligence Agency in Ann Arbor, Michigan.

During pretrial proceedings, the defendants moved to compel the United States to disclose certain electronic surveillance information and to conduct a hearing to determine whether this information "tainted" the evidence on which the indictment was based or which the Government intended to offer at trial. In response, the Government filed an affidavit of the Attorney General, acknowledging that its agents had overheard conversations in which Plamondon had participated. The affidavit also stated that the Attorney General approved the wiretaps "to gather intelligence information deemed necessary to protect the nation from attempts of domestic organizations to attack and subvert the existing structure of the Government." The logs of the surveillance were filed in a sealed exhibit for *in camera* inspection by the District Court.

On the basis of the Attorney General's affidavit and the sealed exhibit, the Government asserted that the surveillance was lawful, though conducted without prior judicial approval, as a reasonable exercise of the President's power (exercised through the Attorney General) to protect the national security. The District Court held that the surveillance violated the Fourth Amendment, and ordered the Government to make full disclosure to Plamondon of his overheard conversations. 321 F. Supp. 1074 (ED Mich. 1971).

The Government then filed in the Court of Appeals for the Sixth Circuit a petition for a writ of mandamus to set aside the District Court order, which was stayed. . . . [T]hat court held that the surveillance was unlawful and that the District Court had properly required disclosure of the overheard conversations, 444 F.2d 651 (1971).

I

Title III of the Omnibus Crime Control and Safe Streets Act, 18 U.S.C. §§ 2510–2520, authorizes the use of electronic surveillance for classes of crimes carefully specified in 18 U.S.C. § 2516. Such surveillance is subject to prior court order. Section 2518 sets forth the detailed and particularized application necessary to obtain such an order as well as carefully circumscribed conditions for its use. The Act represents a comprehensive attempt by Congress to promote more effective control of crime while protecting the privacy of individual thought and expression. Much of Title III was drawn to meet the constitutional requirements for electronic surveillance enunciated by this Court in *Berger v. New York*, 388 U.S. 41 (1967), and *Katz v. United States*, 389 U.S. 347 (1967).

Together with the elaborate surveillance requirements in Title III, there is the following proviso, 18 U.S.C. § 2511 (3):

> "Nothing contained in this chapter or in section 605 of the Communications Act of 1934 (48 Stat. 1143; 47 U.S.C. 605) shall limit the constitutional power of the President to take such measures as he deems necessary to protect the Nation against actual or potential attack or other hostile acts of a foreign power, to obtain foreign intelligence information deemed essential to the security of the United States, or to protect national security information against foreign intelligence activities. *Nor shall anything contained in this chapter be deemed to limit the constitutional power of the President to take such measures as he deems necessary to protect the United States against the overthrow of the Government by force or other unlawful means, or against any other clear and present danger to the structure or existence of the Government.* The contents of any wire or oral communication intercepted by authority of the President in the exercise of the foregoing powers may be received in evidence in any trial hearing, or other proceeding only where such interception was reasonable, and shall not be otherwise used or disclosed except as is necessary to implement that power." (Emphasis supplied.)

The Government relies on § 2511 (3). It argues that "in excepting national security surveillances from the Act's warrant requirement Congress recognized the President's authority to conduct such surveillances without prior judicial approval." Brief for United States 7, 28. The section thus is viewed as a recognition or affirmance of a constitutional authority in the President to conduct warrantless domestic security surveillance such as that involved in this case.

We think the language of § 2511 (3), as well as the legislative history of the statute, refutes this interpretation. The relevant language is that:

> "Nothing contained in this chapter . . . shall limit the constitutional power of the President to take such measures as he deems necessary to protect . . ."

against the dangers specified. At most, this is an implicit recognition that the President does have certain powers in the specified areas. Few would doubt this, as the section refers—among other things—to protection "against actual or potential attack or other hostile acts of a foreign power." But so far as the use of the President's electronic surveillance power is concerned, the language is essentially neutral.

Section 2511 (3) certainly confers no power, as the language is wholly inappropriate for such a purpose. It merely provides that the Act shall not be interpreted to limit or disturb such power as the President may have under the Constitution. In short, Congress simply left presidential powers where it found them. . . .

[I]t would have been incongruous for Congress to have legislated with respect to the important and complex area of national security in a single brief and nebulous paragraph. This would not comport with the sensitivity of the problem involved or with the extraordinary care Congress exercised in drafting other sections of the Act. We therefore think the conclusion inescapable that Congress only intended to make clear that the Act simply did not legislate with respect to national security surveillances.

The legislative history of § 2511 (3) supports this interpretation. . . . [V]iewing § 2511 (3) as a congressional disclaimer and expression of neutrality, we hold that the statute is not the measure of the executive authority asserted in this case. Rather, we must look to the constitutional powers of the President.

II

It is important at the outset to emphasize the limited nature of the question before the Court. This case raises no constitutional challenge to electronic surveillance as specifically authorized by Title III of the Omnibus Crime Control and Safe Streets Act of 1968. Nor is there any question or doubt as to the necessity of obtaining a warrant in the surveillance of crimes unrelated to the national security interest. *Katz v. United States*, 389 U.S. 347 (1967); *Berger v. New York*, 388 U.S. 41 (1967). Further, the instant case requires no judgment on the scope of the President's surveillance power with respect to the activities of foreign powers, within or without this country. The Attorney General's affidavit in this case states that the surveillances were "deemed necessary to protect the nation from attempts of *domestic organizations* to attack and subvert the existing structure of Government" (emphasis supplied). There is no evidence of any involvement, directly or indirectly, of a foreign power.[8]

---

8. Section 2511 (3) refers to "the constitutional power of the President" in two types of situations: (i) where necessary to protect against attack, other hostile acts or intelligence activities of a "foreign power"; or (ii) where necessary to protect against the overthrow of the Government or other clear and present danger to the structure or existence of the Government. Although both of the specified situations are sometimes referred to as "national security" threats, the term "national security" is used only in the first sentence of § 2511 (3) with respect to the activities of foreign powers. This case involves only the second sentence of § 2511 (3), with the threat emanating—according to the Attorney General's affidavit—from "domestic organizations." Although we attempt no precise definition, we use the term "domestic organization" in this opinion to mean a group or organization (whether formally or informally constituted) composed of citizens of the United States and which has no significant connection with a foreign power, its agents or agencies. No doubt there are cases where it will be difficult to distinguish between "domestic" and "foreign" unlawful activities

Our present inquiry, though important, is therefore a narrow one. It addresses a question left open by *Katz, supra*, at 358 n.23:

> "Whether safeguards other than prior authorization by a magistrate would satisfy the Fourth Amendment in a situation involving the national security . . ."

The determination of this question requires the essential Fourth Amendment inquiry into the "reasonableness" of the search and seizure in question, and the way in which that "reasonableness" derives content and meaning through referent to the warrant clause.

. . . [T]he President of the United States has the fundamental duty, under Art. II, § 1, of the Constitution, to "preserve, protect and defend the Constitution of the United States." Implicit in that duty is the power to protect our Government against those who would subvert or overthrow it by unlawful means. In the discharge of this duty, the President—through the Attorney General—may find it necessary to employ electronic surveillance to obtain intelligence information on the plans of those who plot unlawful acts against the Government. The use of such surveillance in internal security cases has been sanctioned more or less continuously by various Presidents and Attorneys General since July 1946 . . .

Though the Government and respondents debate their seriousness and magnitude, threats and acts of sabotage against the Government exist in sufficient number to justify investigative powers with respect to them. The covertness and complexity of potential unlawful conduct against the Government and the necessary dependency of many conspirators upon the telephone make electronic surveillance an effective investigatory instrument in certain circumstances. The marked acceleration in technological developments and sophistication in their use have resulted in new techniques for the planning, commission, and concealment of criminal activities. It would be contrary to the public interest for Government to deny to itself the prudent and lawful employment of those very techniques which are employed against the Government and its law-abiding citizens. . . .

But a recognition of these elementary truths does not make the employment by Government of electronic surveillance a welcome development—even when employed with restraint and under judicial supervision. There is, understandably, a deep-seated uneasiness and apprehension that this capability will be used to intrude upon cherished privacy of law-abiding citizens. We look to the Bill of Rights to safeguard this privacy. Though physical entry of the home is the chief evil against which the wording of the Fourth Amendment is directed, its broader spirit now shields private speech from unreasonable surveillance. Our decision in *Katz* refused to lock the Fourth Amendment into instances of actual physical trespass. Rather, the

---

directed against the Government of the United States where there is collaboration in varying degrees between domestic groups or organizations and agents or agencies of foreign powers. But this is not such a case.

Amendment governs "not only the seizure of tangible items, but extends as well to the recording of oral statements . . . without any 'technical trespass under . . . local property law.'" . . .

National security cases, moreover, often reflect a convergence of First and Fourth Amendment values not present in cases of "ordinary" crime. Though the investigative duty of the executive may be stronger in such cases, so also is there greater jeopardy to constitutionally protected speech. "Historically the struggle for freedom of speech and press in England was bound up with the issue of the scope of the search and seizure power," *Marcus v. Search Warrant*, 367 U.S. 717, 724 (1961). History abundantly documents the tendency of Government — however benevolent and benign its motives — to view with suspicion those who most fervently dispute its policies. Fourth Amendment protections become the more necessary when the targets of official surveillance may be those suspected of unorthodoxy in their political beliefs. The danger to political dissent is acute where the Government attempts to act under so vague a concept as the power to protect "domestic security." Given the difficulty of defining the domestic security interest, the danger of abuse in acting to protect that interest becomes apparent. . . .

III

As the Fourth Amendment is not absolute in its terms, our task is to examine and balance the basic values at stake in this case: the duty of Government to protect the domestic security, and the potential danger posed by unreasonable surveillance to individual privacy and free expression. If the legitimate need of Government to safeguard domestic security requires the use of electronic surveillance, the question is whether the needs of citizens for privacy and free expression may not be better protected by requiring a warrant before such surveillance is undertaken. We must also ask whether a warrant requirement would unduly frustrate the efforts of Government to protect itself from acts of subversion and overthrow directed against it.

Though the Fourth Amendment speaks broadly of "unreasonable searches and seizures," the definition of "reasonableness" turns, at least in part, on the more specific commands of the warrant clause. . . . [W]here practical, a governmental search and seizure should represent both the efforts of the officer to gather evidence of wrongful acts and the judgment of the magistrate that the collected evidence is sufficient to justify invasion of a citizen's private premises or conversation. Inherent in the concept of a warrant is its issuance by a "neutral and detached magistrate." The further requirement of "probable cause" instructs the magistrate that baseless searches shall not proceed.

These Fourth Amendment freedoms cannot properly be guaranteed if domestic security surveillances may be conducted solely within the discretion of the Executive Branch. The Fourth Amendment does not contemplate the executive officers of Government as neutral and disinterested magistrates. Their duty and responsibility are to enforce the laws, to investigate, and to prosecute. But those charged with this investigative and prosecutorial duty should not be the sole judges of when to utilize constitutionally sensitive means in pursuing their tasks. The historical judgment, which the Fourth Amendment accepts, is that unreviewed executive discretion may yield too readily to pressures to obtain incriminating evidence and overlook potential invasions of privacy and protected speech.

It may well be that, in the instant case, the Government's surveillance of Plamondon's conversations was a reasonable one which readily would have gained prior judicial approval. But this Court "has never sustained a search upon the sole ground that officers reasonably expected to find evidence of a particular crime and voluntarily confined their activities to the least intrusive means consistent with that end." The Fourth Amendment contemplates a prior judicial judgment, not the risk that executive discretion may be reasonably exercised. This judicial role accords with our basic constitutional doctrine that individual freedoms will best be preserved through a separation of powers and division of functions among the different branches and levels of Government. The independent check upon executive discretion is not satisfied, as the Government argues, by "extremely limited" post-surveillance judicial review. Indeed, post-surveillance review would never reach the surveillances which failed to result in prosecutions. Prior review by a neutral and detached magistrate is the time-tested means of effectuating Fourth Amendment rights.

It is true that there have been some exceptions to the warrant requirement. But those exceptions are few in number and carefully delineated; in general, they serve the legitimate needs of law enforcement officers to protect their own well-being and preserve evidence from destruction. Even while carving out those exceptions, the Court has reaffirmed the principle that the "police must, whenever practicable, obtain advance judicial approval of searches and seizures through the warrant procedure," *Terry v. Ohio*, 392 U.S. 1, 20 (1968).

The Government argues that the special circumstances applicable to domestic security surveillances necessitate a further exception to the warrant requirement. It is urged that the requirement of prior judicial review would obstruct the President in the discharge of his constitutional duty to protect domestic security. We are told further that these surveillances are directed primarily to the collecting and maintaining of intelligence with respect to subversive forces, and are not an attempt to gather evidence for specific criminal prosecutions. It is said that this type of surveillance should not be subject to traditional warrant requirements which were established to govern investigation of criminal activity, not ongoing intelligence gathering.

The Government further insists that courts "as a practical matter would have neither the knowledge nor the techniques necessary to determine whether there was probable cause to believe that surveillance was necessary to protect national security." These security problems, the Government contends, involve "a large number of complex and subtle factors" beyond the competence of courts to evaluate.

As a final reason for exemption from a warrant requirement, the Government believes that disclosure to a magistrate of all or even a significant portion of the information involved in domestic security surveillances "would create serious potential dangers to the national security and to the lives of informants and agents. . . . Secrecy is the essential ingredient in intelligence gathering; requiring prior judicial authorization would create a greater 'danger of leaks . . . , because in addition to the judge, you have the clerk, the stenographer and some other officer like a law assistant or bailiff who may be apprised of the nature' of the surveillance."

. . . There is, no doubt, pragmatic force to the Government's position. But we do not think a case has been made for the requested departure from Fourth Amendment standards. The circumstances described do not justify complete exemption of domestic security surveillance from prior judicial scrutiny. Official surveillance, whether its purpose be criminal investigation or ongoing intelligence gathering, risks infringement of constitutionally protected privacy of speech. Security surveillances are especially sensitive because of the inherent vagueness of the domestic security concept, the necessarily broad and continuing nature of intelligence gathering, and the temptation to utilize such surveillances to oversee political dissent. We recognize, as we have before, the constitutional basis of the President's domestic security role, but we think it must be exercised in a manner compatible with the Fourth Amendment. In this case we hold that this requires an appropriate prior warrant procedure.

We cannot accept the Government's argument that internal security matters are too subtle and complex for judicial evaluation. Courts regularly deal with the most difficult issues of our society. There is no reason to believe that federal judges will be insensitive to or uncomprehending of the issues involved in domestic security cases. Certainly courts can recognize that domestic security surveillance involves different considerations from the surveillance of "ordinary crime." If the threat is too subtle or complex for our senior law enforcement officers to convey its significance to a court, one may question whether there is probable cause for surveillance.

Nor do we believe prior judicial approval will fracture the secrecy essential to official intelligence gathering. The investigation of criminal activity has long involved imparting sensitive information to judicial officers who have respected the confidentialities involved. Judges may be counted upon to be especially conscious of security requirements in national security cases. Title III of the Omnibus Crime Control and Safe Streets Act already has imposed this responsibility on the judiciary in connection with such crimes as espionage, sabotage, and treason, §§ 2516(1)(a) and (c), each of which may involve domestic as well as foreign security threats. Moreover, a warrant application involves no public or adversary proceedings: it is an *ex parte* request before a magistrate or judge. Whatever security dangers clerical and secretarial personnel may pose can be minimized by proper administrative measures, possibly to the point of allowing the Government itself to provide the necessary clerical assistance.

Thus, we conclude that the Government's concerns do not justify departure in this case from the customary Fourth Amendment requirement of judicial approval prior to initiation of a search or surveillance. Although some added burden will be imposed upon the Attorney General, this inconvenience is justified in a free society to protect constitutional values. Nor do we think the Government's domestic surveillance powers will be impaired to any significant degree. A prior warrant establishes presumptive validity of the surveillance and will minimize the burden of justification in post-surveillance judicial review. By no means of least importance will be the reassurance of the public generally that indiscriminate wiretapping and bugging of law-abiding citizens cannot occur.

IV

. . . [W]e do not hold that the same type of standards and procedures prescribed by Title III are necessarily applicable to this case. We recognize that domestic security surveillance may involve different policy and practical considerations from the surveillance of "ordinary crime." The gathering of security intelligence is often long range and involves the interrelation of various sources and types of information. The exact targets of such surveillance may be more difficult to identify than in surveillance operations against many types of crime specified in Title III. Often, too, the emphasis of domestic intelligence gathering is on the prevention of unlawful activity or the enhancement of the Government's preparedness for some possible future crisis or emergency. Thus, the focus of domestic surveillance may be less precise than that directed against more conventional types of crime.

Given these potential distinctions between Title III criminal surveillances and those involving the domestic security, Congress may wish to consider protective standards for the latter which differ from those already prescribed for specified crimes in Title III. Different standards may be compatible with the Fourth Amendment if they are reasonable both in relation to the legitimate need of Government for intelligence information and the protected rights of our citizens. For the warrant application may vary according to the governmental interest to be enforced and the nature of citizen rights deserving protection. . . .

We . . . hold . . . that prior judicial approval is required for the type of domestic security surveillance involved in this case and that such approval may be made in accordance with such reasonable standards as the Congress may prescribe.

V

As the surveillance of Plamondon's conversations was unlawful, because conducted without prior judicial approval, the courts below correctly held that *Alderman v. United States*, 394 U.S. 165 (1969), is controlling and that it requires disclosure to the accused of his own impermissibly intercepted conversations. As stated in *Alderman*, "the trial court can and should, where appropriate, place a defendant and his counsel under enforceable orders against unwarranted disclosure of the materials which they may be entitled to inspect."

The judgment of the Court of Appeals is hereby

Affirmed.

———————

1. *The Relevance of History.* Justice Powell observes that Presidents and Attorneys General had all but continuously, since July 1946, sanctioned the warrantless use of electronic surveillance for national security purposes, resting on assertedly inherent presidential authority. In footnote 10, he elaborated: "In that month Attorney General Tom Clark advised President Truman of the necessity of using wiretaps 'in cases vitally affecting the domestic security.' In May 1940 President Roosevelt had authorized Attorney General Jackson to utilize wiretapping in matters 'involving the defense of the nation,' but it is questionable whether this language was meant to apply to solely domestic subversion. The nature and extent of wiretapping apparently varied under different administrations and Attorneys General, but, except for the sharp curtailment under Attorney General Ramsey Clark in the latter years of the Johnson administration, electronic surveillance has been used both against organized crime and in domestic security cases at least since the 1946 memorandum from Clark to Truman. Brief for United States 16–18; Brief for Respondents 51–56; 117 Cong. Rec. 14056." Should the Court have given more weight to this history in deciding the scope of executive power?

2. *Distinguishing Domestic from Foreign National Security Threats.* In the critical footnote 8 above, Justice Powell purports to limit the foregoing decision to domestic national security threats, reserving questions as to the scope of inherent presidential authority with respect to gathering national security information on foreign powers and the standards that might govern implementation of the warrant clause, if it applies. How easy a distinction is this for government agents to implement, especially before they have received the information they seek to obtain?

b. The Foreign Intelligence Surveillance Act, 1978–2001

In the wake of *Keith*, Congress sought to preempt the constitutional questions concerning foreign intelligence gathering by enacting the Foreign Intelligence Surveillance Act of 1978 (FISA), 50 U.S.C. § 1801 *et seq.* (1982). That Act established warrant requirements to govern certain instances of foreign intelligence gathering, and a process for assembling a panel of judges, now called the Foreign Intelligence Surveillance Court, to enforce them. The warrant procedure of FISA is unusual. The Foreign Intelligence Surveillance Court operates in secret, and, in cases in which a warrant is challenged, the court may "review in camera and ex parte the [warrant] application, order, and such other materials . . . as may be necessary to determine whether the surveillance . . . was lawfully authorized and conducted." 50 U.S.C. § 1806(f).

As explained in the Senate Judiciary Committee report accompanying the bill that became FISA, Congress viewed FISA—the terms of which were subject to intense negotiation with the Carter Administration—as striking a critical balance. The Senate Select Committee to Study Government Operations with Respect to Intelligence Activities, chaired by Senator Frank Church of Idaho, had revealed a troubling history of "illegal or improper national security taps and bugs." Congress consequently thought it imperative to "curb the practice by which the Executive Branch may conduct warrantless electronic surveillance on its own unilateral determination that national security justifies it." At the same time, Congress understood the importance of electronic surveillance to U.S. counterintelligence work. The Senate Judiciary Committee quoted with approval the finding of the Church Committee that the use of covert surveillance had "provided the Government with vital intelligence, which would be difficult to acquire through other means, about the activities and intentions of foreign powers and has provided important leads in counterespionage cases." Foreign Intelligence Surveillance Act of 1977, S. Rep. No. 604, 95th Cong., 1st Sess. (1977). In this connection, you may recall the conclusion, reported above, of Professors Prakash and Ramsey that Congress may exercise its "Necessary and Proper Clause" powers to regulate the President's foreign affairs powers, but only *in support of* the President's foreign policy goals. The Judiciary Committee took a somewhat different view: "The basis for this legislation is the understanding—concurred in by the Attorney General—that even if the President has an 'inherent' constitutional power to authorize warrantless surveillance for foreign intelligence purposes, Congress has the power to regulate the exercise of this authority by legislating a reasonable warrant procedure governing foreign intelligence surveillance."

Given the intricate structure of FISA, the following roadmap may be helpful in understanding what Congress perceived to be its critical legal and policy choices, and how it resolved them:

Replacing Probable Cause. Of critical importance was Congress's decision to accept, at least partly, the Supreme Court's invitation in *Keith* to create "protective standards" for national security investigations different from the standard governing ordinary law enforcement warrants. (Law enforcement warrants require that the government show probable cause that its desired search would unearth evidence of a crime.) Instead, in applying for a FISA warrant, the Attorney General would have to certify that "the purpose of the surveillance is to obtain foreign intelligence information" and the information sought is "deem[ed to be] the information sought to be foreign intelligence information." 50 U.S.C. § 1804(7).

Critical to understanding this standard, of course, is the definition of "foreign intelligence information," which FISA specifies as follows:

(1) information that relates to, and if concerning a United States person is necessary to, the ability of the United States to protect against—,

(A) actual or potential attack or other grave hostile acts of a foreign power or an agent of a foreign power;

(B) sabotage or international terrorism by a foreign power or an agent of a foreign power; or

(C) clandestine intelligence activities by an intelligence service or network of a foreign power or by an agent of a foreign power; or

(2) information with respect to a foreign power or foreign territory that relates to, and if concerning a United States person is necessary to —,

(A) the national defense or the security of the United States; or

(B) the conduct of the foreign affairs of the United States.

50 U.S.C. § 1801(e). In 2008, "sabotage or international terrorism" in subparagraph (1)(B) was deleted and "sabotage, international terrorism, or the international proliferation of weapons of mass destruction" inserted in its place.

Persons Covered. It is not enough to sustain a FISA warrant application, however, that the information sought be foreign intelligence information. A FISA warrant — and thus the relaxation of the probable cause standard — is available to the government only if "the target of the electronic surveillance is a foreign power or an agent of a foreign power." 50 U.S.C. § 1804(7). This brings into play two more complex definitions:

"Foreign power" means —,

(1) a foreign government or any component thereof, whether or not recognized by the United States;

(2) a faction of a foreign nation or nations, not substantially composed of United States persons;

(3) an entity that is openly acknowledged by a foreign government or governments to be directed and controlled by such foreign government or governments;

(4) a group engaged in international terrorism or activities in preparation therefor;

(5) a foreign-based political organization, not substantially composed of United States persons; or

(6) an entity that is directed and controlled by a foreign government or governments.

50 U.S.C. § 1801(a).

"Agent of a foreign power" means —

(1) any person other than a United States person, who —

(A) acts in the United States as an officer or employee of a foreign power, or as a member of a foreign power as defined in subsection (a) (4);

(B) acts for or on behalf of a foreign power which engages in clandestine intelligence activities in the United States contrary to the interests of the United States, when the circumstances of such person's presence in the United States indicate that such person may engage in such activities in the United States, or when such person knowingly aids or abets any person in the conduct of such activities or knowingly conspires with any person to engage in such activities; or

(2) any person who—,

(A) knowingly engages in clandestine intelligence gathering activities for or on behalf of a foreign power, which activities involve or may involve a violation of the criminal statues of the United States;

(B) pursuant to the direction of an intelligence service or network of a foreign power, knowingly engages in any other clandestine intelligence activities for or on behalf of such foreign power, which activities involve or are about to involve a violation of the criminal statutes of the United States;

(C) knowingly engages in sabotage or international terrorism, or activities that are in preparation therefor, for or on behalf of a foreign power; or

(D) knowingly aids or abets any person in the conduct of activities described in subparagraph (A), (B), or (C) or knowingly conspires with any person to engage in activities described in subparagraph (A), (B), or (C).

50 U.S.C. § 1801(b).

Despite the complexity of these definitions, two major points should not be lost. First, FISA does not provide an alternative to conventional law enforcement warrants unless there is some connection between the target of surveillance and activity that is foreign or international in character. In a wholly domestic case like *Keith*, the requisite warrant is still a probable cause warrant. Second, different definitions and standards apply depending on whether the target of surveillance is what FISA calls a "United States person." Under FISA, "United States person" means "a citizen of the United States, an alien lawfully admitted for permanent residence (as defined in section 101(a) (20) of the Immigration and Nationality Act), an unincorporated association a substantial number of members of which are citizens of the United States or aliens lawfully admitted for permanent residence, or a corporation which is incorporated in the United States, but does not include a corporation or an association which is a foreign power . . . ." 50 U.S.C. § 1801(j).[1]

What Is Electronic Surveillance? The scope of FISA's warrant requirement is further delimited by FISA's very definition of electronic surveillance. Under FISA, as originally drafted:

"Electronic surveillance" means—,

(1) the acquisition by an electronic, mechanical, or other surveillance device of the contents of any wire or radio communication surveillance

---

1. In 1999, "agent of a foreign power" was amended to include anyone who "knowingly enters the United States under a false or fraudulent identity for or on behalf of a foreign power or, while in the United States, knowingly assumes a false or fraudulent identity for or on behalf of a foreign power." The definitions of "foreign power" and "agent of a foreign power" were amended in 2008 to include persons involved in the international proliferation of weapons of mass destruction.

device of the contents of any wire or radio communication sent by or intended to be received by a particular, known United States person who is in the United States, if the contents are acquired by intentionally targeting that United States person, under circumstances in which a person has a reasonable expectation of privacy and a warrant would be required for law enforcement purposes;

(2) the acquisition by an electronic, mechanical, or other surveillance device of the contents of any wire communication to or from a person in the United States, without the consent of any party thereto, if such acquisition occurs in the United States;

(3) the intentional acquisition by an electronic, mechanical, or other surveillance device of the contents of any radio communication, under circumstances in which a person has a under circumstances in which a person has a reasonable expectation of privacy and a warrant would be required for law enforcement purposes, and if both the sender and all intended recipients are located within the United States; or

(4) the installation or use of an electronic, mechanical, or other surveillance device in the United States for monitoring to acquire information, other than from a wire or radio communication, under circumstances in which a person has a reasonable expectation of privacy and a warrant would be required for law enforcement purposes.

50 U.S.C. § 1801(f).

What this definition may well obscure for the uninitiated reader are the categories of what is, in fact, electronic surveillance, but that FISA apparently permits to proceed without warrants. *Most notably, communications wholly outside the United States are exempt, no matter who participates.* Also, acquisitions of radio (i.e., wireless) communications are not covered unless they occur "under circumstances in which a person has a reasonable expectation of privacy," circumstances that generally are not deemed to exist under law for wholly wireless communications. The only category of surveillance in which FISA warrants are required without regard to any additional analysis of "reasonable expectations of privacy" is the acquisition in the United States of wire communications to or from a person in the United States without their content. Technological changes in telephony created unanticipated problems for the executive branch under this definition, however; these are discussed below with regard to the Terrorist Surveillance Program.

Safe Harbors for Warrantless Surveillance. In striking the balance between presidential authority and civil liberties protection, Congress appears to have accepted the view that, in some cases, presidents may constitutionally engage in warrantless surveillance and, in at least some such cases, it would be inappropriate to impose a warrant requirement by statute. Specifically, the President is allowed to conduct warrantless surveillance for up to a year at a time if the Attorney General certifies in writing that the surveillance is directed solely at:

(i) the acquisition of the contents of communications transmitted by means of communications used exclusively between or among foreign powers . . . or

(ii) the acquisition of technical intelligence other than the spoken communications of individuals, from property or premises under the open and exclusive control of a foreign power . . .

50 U.S.C. § 1802. FISA provides, however, that this exception is not available if there is a "substantial likelihood that the surveillance will acquire the contents of any communication to which a United States person is a party." If not, and if the Attorney General makes the necessary certification, the Attorney General must also impose what FISA calls "minimization procedures" to insure the proper handling of any information acquired through surveillance, and notice must be sent to the House Permanent Select Committee on Intelligence and the Senate Select Committee on Intelligence.

Congress also authorized warrantless surveillance in certain emergency situations. Thus, if the Attorney General determines that the basis for a FISA warrant is present, but "an emergency situation exists with respect to the employment of electronic surveillance to obtain foreign intelligence information before an order authorizing such surveillance can with due diligence be obtained," the Attorney General was allowed to conduct surveillance for 24 hours (expanded in 2001 to 72 hours and in 2008 to seven days) while the warrant application is being prepared. 50 U.S.C. § 1805(e). Further, the Attorney General is allowed to conduct warrantless electronic surveillance to acquire foreign intelligence information "for a period not to exceed fifteen calendar days following a declaration of war by the Congress." 50 U.S.C. § 1811.

Foreign Intelligence Surveillance Court. As noted above, in circumstances where FISA requires the Attorney General to seek a warrant for electronic surveillance, FISA permits recourse to a specially created Foreign Intelligence Surveillance Court. To hear the Attorney General's original applications, the court comprises seven district judges from seven different Circuits, each chosen for a term of seven years by the Chief Justice of the United States. The Chief Justice also chooses three Court of Appeals Judges for seven-year terms to constitute a review panel for appeals from judgments of the FISC. 50 U.S.C. § 1803.

Minimization Procedures. In order to avoid the abuse of what FISA appears to authorize as an easier route to obtaining electronic surveillance warrants, the statute generally requires the Attorney General, when implementing surveillance, to follow "minimization procedures." When the Attorney General applies for a warrant, the minimization procedures intended to be followed must be spelled out. "Minimization procedures" under FISA means:

(1) specific procedures, which shall be adopted by the Attorney General, that are reasonably designed in light of the purpose and technique of the particular surveillance, to minimize the acquisition and retention, and prohibit the dissemination, of nonpublicly available information concerning

unconsenting United States persons consistent with the need of the United States to obtain, produce, and disseminate foreign intelligence information;

(2) procedures that require that nonpublicly available information, which is not foreign intelligence information, as defined in subsection (e) (1), shall not be disseminated in a manner that identifies any United States person, without such person's consent, unless such person's identity is necessary to understand foreign intelligence information or assess its importance;

(3) notwithstanding paragraphs (1) and (2), procedures that allow for the retention and dissemination of information that is evidence of a crime which has been, is being, or is about to be committed and that is to be retained or disseminated for law enforcement purposes; and

(4) notwithstanding paragraphs (1), (2), and (3), with respect to any electronic surveillance approved pursuant to section 102(a), procedures that require that no contents of any communication to which a United States person is a party shall be disclosed, disseminated, or used for any purpose or retained for longer than twenty-four [now, seventy-two] hours unless a court order . . . is obtained or unless the Attorney General determines that the information indicates a threat of death or serious bodily harm to any person.

18 U.S.C. § 1801(h).

Oversight. As an additional safeguard, Congress enacted provisions aimed at insuring its effective oversight of foreign intelligence surveillance. The Attorney General is required to report annually the total number of applications made for orders and extensions of orders approving electronic surveillance and the total number of such orders and extensions either granted, modified, or denied. 18 U.S.C. § 1807. The Attorney General is also required to "fully inform" the Intelligence Committees of the House and Senate concerning foreign intelligence surveillance on at least a semi-annual basis. 18 U.S.C. § 1808. An obvious concern exists, of course, with regard to the potential for oversight when (a) there are no actual statutory standards governing the conduct of national security investigations, and (b) briefings are limited to a relatively few Members of Congress.

––––––––––––

1. *FISA Warrants and Criminal Proceedings.* Under 50 U.S.C. § 1806, the Attorney General must give personal approval before information acquired pursuant to FISA warrants may be used in ordinary criminal proceedings. Courts have repeatedly held FISA warrant procedures sufficiently protective to sustain the constitutional use in criminal prosecutions of evidence secured pursuant to FISA warrants originally for foreign intelligence purposes. *See, e.g., United States v. Posey,* 864 F.2d 1487 (9th Cir. 1989); *United States v. Isa,* 923 F.2d 1300 (8th Cir. 1991).

2. *Extending FISA to Physical Searches.* FISA did not originally provide authorization for the use of any counterintelligence technique other than electronic surveillance. The executive branch consequently took the position that it retained

inherent authority to conduct so-called "black bag jobs," i.e., surreptitious physical entries onto premises to search for tangible items. It tested that theory in 1981 by actually applying to the Foreign Intelligence Surveillance Court for a warrant to support a physical search. In a publicly released opinion, the FISC held that it lacked jurisdiction to issue such a warrant, relying on the plain language of FISA, the meaning of which it found to be confirmed by the relevant committee reports. Speaking for the Court, Judge Hart said, "In view of the clearly expressed intent of Congress to withhold authority to issue orders approving physical searches, it would be idle to consider whether a judge of the FISC nevertheless has some implied or inherent authority to do so. Obviously, where a given authority is denied it cannot be supplied by resort to principles of inherent, implied or ancillary jurisdiction." *In the Matter of the Application of the United States for an Order Authorizing the Physical Search of Nonresidential Premises and Personal Property*, Unnumbered Slip Opinion, (U.S. Foreign Intelligence Surveillance Court, Jun. 11, 1981), reprinted in S. Rep. No. 280, 97th Cong., 1st Sess. 16 (1981).

Congress subsequently amended FISA to encompass physical searches, Pub.L. 103-359, Title VIII, § 807(a)(3), 108 Stat. 3444 (1994), codified at 50 U.S.C. § 1822. Yet later revisions extended the Act to pen register and trap-and-trace orders (listings of the telephone numbers that a dialer calls, and similar information about incoming phone contacts), and to subpoenas for business records in the hands of third parties. Should Congress's earlier failure to provide for FISA warrants for these kinds of national security searches have prompted the conclusion that they remained within the President's inherent authority, or, rather, that, absent probable cause to sustain an application for a criminal warrant, such searches would have been unconstitutional for any reason?

3. *Internal Checks.* In its report on FISA, the Senate Judiciary Committee described the statute's operation as subject to both "internal" and "external" checks. In operation, it would appear that the internal checks rested on more than just the formal requirement that the Executive follow "a method of written accountability" for surveillance warrants. Prior to the mid-1970s, the FBI, seeking legal approval within the Justice Department for a contemplated national security investigation, would apparently shop around the Department for an amenable forum until it could locate a lawyer likely to "sign off" on the FBI's plans. James McGee, Main Justice: The Men and Women Who Enforce the Nation's Criminal Laws and Guard its Liberties 311 (1996). To end this practice, Attorney General Levi created an Office of Intelligence Policy and Review (OIPR), which began to provide both continuity and consistency to Justice Department oversight, under a new set of department guidelines, discussed further below. When Congress, during the Carter Administration, was finally persuaded to enact FISA, OIPR took over the gatekeeping function with regard to applications for FISA warrants. The centrality of its role was significantly enhanced by the appointment to head the office of Mary Lawton, a senior career attorney whose legal skill and legendary integrity gave the Department an extraordinary measure of credibility during both Democratic and Republican presidencies

until her death in 1993. *See id.* at 303–319. Given the nature of FISC proceedings, how much importance do you imagine such informal factors play in the robustness of FISA as a genuine check on executive discretion?

After 9/11, the executive branch became yet more aggressive in its approach to foreign intelligence surveillance, purporting to draw authority not only from FISA but from Congress's enactment of an Authorization to Use Military Force against al Qaeda and the Taliban. The complex legal issues posed are taken up in Chapter 7D, below.

C. Congress's Role in Regulating Foreign Policy

We noted, in starting this chapter, that Congress's several express constitutional authorities regarding foreign trade, military affairs, naturalization, international law, and war amply belie any general claim of Presidential monopoly over global affairs. The Supreme Court, in the *Keith* case, required the executive to deal with Congress in constructing a framework for national security investigations, as well. Having examined in the previous section the degree to which legislative authority is a prerequisite to executive initiative, we now consider situations in which Congress *has* legislated, either with direct reference to foreign affairs or in ways that produce indirect foreign policy impacts. Does Article II limit the permissible scope of such legislation? Should solicitousness for presidential discretion in foreign affairs guide statutory interpretation in ambiguous cases?

1. Direct Regulation of Foreign Affairs and National Security Policy

a. Presidential and Congressional Oversight of CIA and FBI Intelligence Gathering

No area of government activity has raised more profound questions of delegated authority and effective oversight than the enterprise of intelligence gathering. The FISA materials excerpted in the previous section are best understood against this background, but represent only a thin slice of Congress's concerns. The ebb and flow of interest in oversight can perhaps best be understood by tracing its general contours through three historical periods, from the founding of the CIA through Watergate and the Church Committee, from the mid-1970s through 9/11, and the post-9/11 period.

Intelligence Oversight: Early Decades. Since its creation in 1947, the Central Intelligence Agency has conducted its activities under a very broad statutory mandate, subject, until 2004, to the general direction of only the National Security Council. National Security Act of 1947, § 102(d), 61 Stat. 497 (1947), *codified with amendments at* 50 U.S.C. §§ 403(2000). *See generally* Note, *The Central Intelligence Agency: Present Authority and Proposed Legislative Change*, 62 VA. L. REV. 332 (1976). More remarkably, the Federal Bureau of Investigation (FBI) has never been subject to any substantive statutory restrictions at all as to the scope of its permissible intelligence activities; the Bureau derives its investigative authority entirely from the general statutory powers of the Attorney General regarding investigations. 28 U.S.C. § 533 (1982). *See generally* John T. Elliff, *The Attorney General's Guidelines for FBI Investigations*, 69 Cornell L. Rev. 785 (1984).

For nearly 30 years, congressional oversight of the intelligence community was practically nonexistent. Between 1947 and 1975, Congress either rejected or ignored 200 legislative proposals to increase its oversight over the CIA. In 1975, however, that immunity from oversight came to an abrupt end. (*See generally* 1975 Cong. Q. Almanac 361–412; 1976 Cong. Q. Almanac 294–308, 415–21.) The CIA, FBI, and other intelligence-gathering units within the executive branch became the focus of intense governmental investigations chiefly because of a series of *New York Times* articles disclosing massive, illegal domestic intelligence operations during the Nixon administration. The alleged activities, in apparent violation of the National Security Act, were aimed at antiwar and dissident groups. The newspaper's startling disclosures followed close upon the heels of alleged CIA links to the Watergate scandal and allegations of CIA efforts to "destabilize" the government of deposed Chilean President Salvador Allende, episodes which had likewise spurred calls for deeper scrutiny.

The Church and Rockefeller Inquiries. Reports of CIA abuse provoked responses from both the President and Congress. On January 5, 1975, following the resignation of James Angleton, the CIA counterintelligence chief, President Ford named an eight-member commission (including future President Reagan) under Vice President Rockefeller ("Rockefeller Commission") to investigate alleged CIA statutory violations.

On January 15, CIA Director William Colby sent a lengthy report to the Senate Appropriations Intelligence Operations Subcommittee, acknowledging that the CIA had carried out surveillance of journalists and political activists, opened the mail of U.S. citizens, infiltrated domestic protest groups and gathered information for secret files on more than 10,000 Americans. Twelve days later, the Senate established an eleven-member select committee under Senator Frank Church ("Church Committee") to investigate the activities of the CIA, FBI, and other law enforcement and intelligence agencies to determine if they had engaged in any illegal or unethical intelligence activities during the Vietnam period. (A parallel study was later undertaken in the House of Representatives, under Rep. Otis G. Pike, of New York.)

The Rockefeller Commission reported that, although most CIA intelligence operations were within statutory bounds, some were "plainly unlawful and constituted improper invasions upon the rights of Americans." The commission revealed the existence from 1962–72 of a special group within the CIA called Operation CHAOS, charged with collecting information on dissident groups within the United States. CHAOS developed a computerized index with the names of more than 300,000 persons and organizations, and compiled files on 7,200 Americans. The Commission found further that the CIA exceeded its authority by investigating journalists and

5 · FOREIGN POLICY AND NATIONAL SECURITY

American citizens who had no relationship with the Agency. In five instances, the CIA investigated American newsmen to identify their sources of classified information.

The CIA also provided "supplies" (alias documents, tape recorder and photography equipment) to former CIA employee E. Howard Hunt, Jr., who had used some of these in his Watergate activities. Additionally, the CIA turned over classified information to President Nixon for use towards political ends.

The Commission reported numerous incidents of improper wiretapping, bugging, break-ins, obtaining federal tax returns, and opening mail. From the late 1940s until 1967, the CIA had conducted an illegal drug experimentation program on persons without their consent. In addition, the Agency participated in law enforcement activities, such as recruitment for the Bureau of Narcotics and Dangerous Drugs, which are prohibited by the CIA charter. In addition to the 7,200 CHAOS files, the CIA kept 57,000 open files on United States citizens.

The Rockefeller Commission made some thirty recommendations to prevent future abuses. It recommended that the practice of gathering intelligence on domestic activities by the CIA be generally prohibited, with exceptions for the domestic monitoring of U.S. citizens who pose a "clear threat" to the agency's facilities or personnel, of citizens suspected of espionage, and of persons currently or formerly affiliated with the CIA or CIA applicants. The Rockefeller Commission recommended that the 1947 National Security Act be amended to define "foreign intelligence" as information concerning the activities and intentions of foreign nations, *wherever* that information might be found, and that the CIA not be able to infiltrate organizations in the United States in the absence of written approval by the Director after a determination that such action is necessary to meet a clear danger.

The revelations of the Rockefeller Commission were but a hint, however, of the more comprehensive findings to be reported by the Church Committee. On September 16, 1975, CIA Director William E. Colby admitted in public hearings that agency employees had violated a 1970 presidential order requiring the destruction of two deadly poisons. Other testimony revealed the existence of a twenty-year mail surveillance program undertaken by the CIA even though the Agency knew it to be illegal and regarded it as of little value. The mail included correspondence of several prominent figures including Richard Nixon, Senators Edward Kennedy and Hubert Humphrey, Martin Luther King, Jr., Federal Reserve Board Chairman Arthur Burns, and even Senator Church. Between 1970 and 1972 alone, the CIA examined about 2 million pieces of mail a year.

In relation to foreign policy, the CIA's involvement in attempts to assassinate foreign leaders was no longer speculation. The Committee reported plots to kill Fidel Castro of Cuba and Patrice Lumumba of the Congo. The CIA also conducted covert operations against General Raphael Trujillo of the Dominican Republic and President Ngo Dinh Diem of South Vietnam. Although both were eventually assassinated, no direct links connected the CIA to their deaths. The CIA also supported groups in Chile attempting to kidnap Chilean General Rene Schneider. Schneider was killed in 1970 by an unrelated group.

The aid to Chilean insurgents went far beyond aid to the group trying to kidnap Schneider. Massive intervention was reportedly aimed at overthrowing the government of President Salvador Allende.

The Church Committee also revealed extraordinary FBI abuses. The FBI had employed blackmail, bugging, and intimidation tactics in a campaign initiated by former director J. Edgar Hoover to discredit Martin Luther King, Jr. Sixteen separate bugs were placed in hotel rooms used by King during 1964–65. Wiretaps were placed in the offices of King's Southern Christian Leadership Conference in Atlanta and New York from 1963–66. In 1964, just before King was to receive the Nobel Peace Prize, FBI agents sent him an anonymous letter containing compromising transcripts from the hotel bugging and suggesting the only way out for him was suicide. During a sanitation strike in Memphis, which included a boycott of white-owned businesses, the bureau leaked information to the press that King was staying at a white-owned hotel. King moved to a black-owned hotel where he was later assassinated.

Even after King's death the harassment tactics continued. The Bureau devised a plan to prevent congressional support for a national holiday on King's birthday. The testimony before the Committee did not reveal whether this plan was ever implemented.

The Church Committee reported numerous FBI break-ins in connection with the Bureau's counterintelligence operations. From 1942 to 1968, the Bureau conducted 238 burglaries against "domestic subversive targets" and kept records of such break-ins in secret files. In addition, surveillance of prominent figures was undertaken during the 1964 Democratic National Convention. During the 1970s, campus surveillance was also expanded to disrupt political movements. During some point in the history of campus surveillance, the FBI had an actual plan to disrupt leftist college groups. Some of the techniques suggested were starting rumors that student leaders were FBI informants, sending letters to members' parents or employers, and harassing students through narcotics enforcement.

The FBI also tried "divide and conquer" tactics against dissident groups. The Bureau, for example, tried to promote tensions between two black militant groups in Chicago by anonymously tipping the leader of the Blackstone Rangers that the Black Panthers planned on having him killed. On another occasion, the FBI sent letters to suspected Mafia-owned businesses, chastising them for allegedly discriminatory employment practices and then forging a suspected Communist's name to the letters, apparently hoping for reprisals against him.

The Ku Klux Klan was one of the FBI's main targets. In order to infiltrate the Klan effectively, however, the Bureau allowed (but did not instruct) its agents to participate in violence against blacks and civil rights activists.

The Committee reported widespread use of the FBI by past Presidents for personal political ends. The Committee concluded that Presidents Roosevelt, Truman, Eisenhower, Kennedy, Johnson, and Nixon had all received reports from the FBI on journalists, political opponents, and critics of administration policy. Although the practice began in the Roosevelt Administration, the committee reported that it "grew to unprecedented" dimensions during the Johnson and Nixon eras.

According to Senator Church, the lack of congressional oversight was a basic reason for the intelligence community's failures and misdeeds. The committee set out ninety-six recommendations, most intended to be included in legislation improving congressional oversight of intelligence gathering. The committee proposed to allow only limited activity within the United States by the CIA and to centralize domestic activities under the FBI. *See generally* COMMISSION ON CIA ACTIVITIES WITHIN THE UNITED STATES, REPORT TO THE PRESIDENT (1975); FINAL REPORT OF THE SENATE SELECT COMM. TO STUDY GOVERNMENTAL OPERATIONS WITH RESPECT TO INTELLIGENCE ACTIVITIES, S. Rep. No. 755, 94th Cong., 2d Sess. (1976) (6 vols.).

Intelligence Oversight from Ford Through September 11. Despite the calls for increased oversight, Congress never enacted a substantive charter for the FBI or revised the CIA's statutory mandate to clarify the permissible bounds of intelligence activities. Prior to the Iran-Contra affair, reviewed in subpart b, *infra*, the most significant legislative reform was the reorganization of legislative oversight of intelligence pursuant to provisions included in the Fiscal 1981 Intelligence Authorization Act, Pub. L. No. 96-450, 94 Stat. 1975 (1980). That Act created a single intelligence oversight committee in each House of Congress, and required the executive branch to keep each committee "fully and currently informed" of all current intelligence activities. 50 U.S.C. § 413 (1982). Each committee was specifically to be notified of all covert operations, although the President, in extraordinary circumstances, could limit notification to the chair and ranking members, plus the House Speaker and minority leader, and the majority and minority leaders of the Senate.

Some significant reform of intelligence operations occurred, however, under executive order. Responding modestly to the Rockefeller and Church investigations, President Ford issued an order in 1976 intended to clarify the responsibilities of the various investigative agencies of government with respect to intelligence gathering, all of which would be coordinated by a Committee on Foreign Intelligence, chaired by the Director of Central Intelligence (DCI), and an Operations Advisory Group. Although placing no new restrictions on foreign covert operations, the Order did seek to clarify the scope of domestic intelligence activities the President regarded as unlawful. Exec. Order No. 11,905, 3 C.F.R. 90 (1977).

Less than two years later, President Carter overhauled the executive order process, providing much more extensive substantive guidance on proscribed intelligence-gathering techniques. Carter created an Intelligence Oversight Board consisting of advisors from outside the government to assist him in overseeing the intelligence agencies. He abolished the Committee on Foreign Intelligence and the Operations

Advisory Group, instead coordinating policy through committees of the National Security Council. The Carter order provided additional detail on the respective duties of the various intelligence agencies, and created a central role for the Attorney General to ensure legal compliance in the conduct of all intelligence activities. Exec. Order No. 12,036, 3 C.F.R. 112 (1979).

In December 1981, President Reagan replaced the Carter order with a new order intended to streamline executive branch oversight. The Order eliminated much of the Carter order's codification of restricted or prohibited intelligence practices, and greatly reduced the Attorney General's express role in intelligence oversight. Exec. Order No. 12,333, 3 C.F.R. 200 (1982). These moves were controversial, especially because Congress, in enacting the Foreign Intelligence Surveillance Act of 1978, had foregone the regulation of some aspects of intelligence gathering because of assurances that the executive branch would establish and implement effective internal guidelines. Nonetheless, Executive Order 12,333 has now remained in place, with minor amendments, under both Republican and Democratic administrations for nearly three decades.

Paralleling these developments, Attorney General William French Smith, in 1983, issued new guidelines for FBI domestic security investigations, replacing 1976 guidelines that had been implemented by Attorney General Levi in the wake of Watergate, and which were followed throughout the Carter Administration, as well. There was substantial continuity, however, between the two sets of guidelines. Perhaps the main difference was that the newer standards permitted a full domestic security investigation based on a "reasonable indication" of political action based on violence and a violation of federal laws, while the former standards required "specific and articulable facts giving reason" to suspect such activity. The Carter Administration, however, had recommended that the broader standard be adopted for domestic security investigations in a statutory FBI charter. The changes are described in detail in John T. Elliff, *The Attorney General's Guidelines for FBI Investigations*, 69 Cornell L. Rev. 785 (1984).

Oversight Since September 11. The George W. Bush Administration revised the guidelines yet again. On May 30, 2002, Attorney General Ashcroft issued revised Guidelines on General Crimes, Racketeering Enterprise and Terrorism Enterprise Investigations and, on October 31, 2003, he issued revised Guidelines for FBI National Security Investigations and Foreign Intelligence Collection. The latter are classified, but a November 5, 2003 Justice Department fact sheet, indicated that the changes made by the latter document are similar to those made by the former. Among the more notable changes were these:

- The 2002 directive included authorization to subscribe to any commercial or non-profit profiling and data mining service. It also authorized investigators to visit any place (including web-surfing) and attend any event that is open to the public. These actions could be undertaken in the absence of any minimal suspicion of illegal activity.

- The period for preliminary inquiries with no supervisory review was increased from 90 to 180 days. Preliminary inquiries could go on for up to one year without notifying Headquarters. Correspondingly, the initial period for full investigations increased from 180 days to one year.

- Authorization for extending preliminary inquiries or launching full inquiries could now occur at lower levels in the FBI.

- The prior guidelines allowed the use of highly intrusive techniques only in "compelling circumstances." New wording stated that the FBI should not hesitate to use any lawful techniques, even if intrusive, where the intrusiveness is warranted in light of the seriousness of the possible crime.

Jerry Berman and James X. Dempsey, CDT's Guide to the FBI Guidelines: Impact on Civil Liberties and Security——The Need for Congressional Oversight (June 26, 2002), available at http://www.cdt.org/wiretap/020626guidelines.shtml. While the 1976 Levi Guidelines were drafted significantly in consultation with the House and Senate Judiciary Committees, the 2002 guidelines appeared to be entirely the product of the Justice Department's internal deliberations. Id.

In its waning months, the George W. Bush Administration overhauled the entire system of Attorney General Guidelines. On September 29, 2008, Attorney General Michael Mukasey issued the "Attorney General's Guidelines for Domestic FBI Operations," replacing what had been six separate sets of FBI guidelines, including the Attorney General's Guidelines on General Crimes, Racketeering Enterprise and Terrorism Enterprise Investigations, and on FBI National Security Investigations and Foreign Intelligence Collection. Set to take effect on December 31, 2008, the new Guidelines were intended to "effect a more complete integration and harmonization of standards, thereby providing the FBI and other affected Justice Department components with clearer, more consistent, and more accessible guidance for their activities, and making available to the public in a single document the basic body of rules for the FBI's domestic operations." Attorney General's Guidelines for Domestic FBI Operations (Sept. 29, 2008), available at http://www.justice.gov/ag/readingroom/guidelines.pdf.

A detailed comparison of the succeeding versions of the Guidelines would go beyond the scope of this note, but, as of 2010, the Justice Department's Inspector General was already posing the question whether, in certain respects, the 2008 Guidelines went too far in relaxing civil liberties checks on the FBI. Specifically, in September 2010, the OIG released a 209-page report concerning its review of the FBI's investigations from 2001–2006 of five domestic advocacy groups and one individual. Although concluding that these targets were not chosen on constitutionally prohibited grounds, the OIG found that the FBI had misled the public about these investigations and that they were affected by some irregularities. In its recommendation section, the report states:

> The 2008 Attorney General's Guidelines and the FBI's Domestic and Investigative and Operational Guidelines [DIOG] in various places address First

Amendment issues in connection with federal criminal investigations. The 2008 Attorney General's Guidelines loosened the limitation on the FBI's retention of information collected in connection with attendance at public events. . . . [T]he FBI formerly was prohibited from retaining any such information unless it relates to potential criminal or terrorist activity. This limitation has been removed from the most recent guidelines. Therefore, some of the violations of policy we found in this review would not be violations if they occurred today. We recommend that the Department reexamine the Guidelines and the DIOG to determine whether to reinstate the prohibition on retaining information from public events that is not related to potential criminal or terrorist activity.

U.S. Department of Justice Office of Inspector General, A Review of the FBI's Investigation of Certain Domestic Advocacy Groups 187 (Sept. 2010), available at http://www.justice.gov/oig/special/s1009r.pdf. The Obama Administration left the Attorney General's 2008 Guidelines in place. In October 2011, however, the FBI issued a revision of its Domestic Investigations and Operations Guide. The Guide loosens restrictions on FBI agents in a number of minor respects. https://vault.fbi.gov/FBI%20Domestic%20Investigations%20and%20Operations%20Guide%20(DIOG).

Congressional and public oversight of the intelligence agencies has undoubtedly been impeded by ambiguities in the substantive missions of the intelligence agencies, and the reluctance of any decisionmaker to appear to be impeding efforts to protect national security. Yet, lurking behind this complex story are at least two other critical problems. One is the chronic uncertainty as to the constitutional locus of authority for intelligence gathering and national security generally. The question arises pointedly in this context whether the President's foreign affairs and military powers imply limits, either constitutional or policy-based, on the appropriate role of Congress in overseeing intelligence operations? The second, and arguably worsening problem, is the dizzying organizational complexity of the post-9/11 intelligence sector. In a lengthy 2010 investigation, two Washington Post reporters concluded: "The top-secret world the government created in response to the terrorist attacks of Sept. 11, 2001, has become so large, so unwieldy and so secretive that no one knows how much money it costs, how many people it employs, how many programs exist within it or exactly how many agencies do the same work." Dana Priest and William M. Arkin, *Top-Secret America: A Hidden World, Growing Beyond Control*, Wash. Post, at A1 (July 19, 2010). Stunningly, the reporters found: "Some 1,271 government organizations and 1,931 private companies work on programs related to counterterrorism, homeland security and intelligence in some 10,000 locations across the United States." Id. Partly in order to address this problem, Congress, in 2004, authorized the creation of a new institution, the Office of the Director of National Intelligence, which would have authority to bring the intelligence sector under control. The ODNI, however, was not given clear legal or budgetary authority with regard to the agencies within its supposed purview. As a result, law professor Samuel Rascoff has suggested a major reconceptualization of the entire enterprise of intelligence oversight:

Samuel J. Rascoff, *Domesticating Intelligence*

83 S. Cal. L. Rev. 575 (2010)[1]

The experience of the [Terrorist Surveillance Program] is indicative of a larger problem for national security law and policy: the widening chasm between domestic intelligence practice and domestic intelligence governance. It is no secret that domestic intelligence is back with a vengeance. Whether employing electronic surveillance, human intelligence, data mining, or terrorism "watch-lists," the government has significantly increased its domestic intelligence efforts as part of a broader counterterrorism strategy. In the wake of 9/11, new government agencies with domestic intelligence responsibilities have been created, and others have been substantially retooled to focus on intelligence. State and local governments have also become heavily involved in domestic intelligence activities, either collaboratively with the federal government or independently. The resurgence of domestic intelligence has not been accompanied by a corollary growth in intelligence governance, which has created a troubling chasm at the heart of domestic intelligence. The vacuum is, in fact, doubly troubling. First, and most obviously, the gap between intelligence practice and governance raises the specter of widespread abuse and diminishment in civil liberties. The history of domestic intelligence in America (and across the world) is replete with instances of the government invoking questionable ends to justify increasingly expansive—and legally troubling—intelligence practices. Indeed, the current vacuum can be seen as the latest development in a historical pattern aptly named the "boom-and-bust cycle" of intelligence governance, where the resurgence of interest in intelligence (motivated by concerns about a particular threat) has typically meant a relaxation of the rules restraining intelligence agencies. This relaxation of limits has, in turn, typically generated periods of abusive practices, followed by inquests and periods of tighter regulation.

The governance vacuum also carries a risk to security: without appropriately scaled and designed governance, intelligence is likely to become nonrigorous and ultimately ineffective at providing policymakers with the informational advantage they need to keep terrorist threats at bay. In other words, the current governance gap in domestic intelligence is a problem not only for people who worry about liberty, but also for those primarily concerned with security. . . .

[T]he current vacuum has three main dimensions. First, there is a doctrinal aspect to the vacuum: current law exempts numerous and increasingly relevant categories of intelligence gathering, such as human intelligence and data mining, from meaningful judicial scrutiny. This is at least partly the result of the Supreme Court's

---

ongoing unwillingness to express a view about the status and permissible scope of intelligence under the Constitution. Second, there is an institutional component. Increasingly, important practitioners of contemporary domestic intelligence—including agencies formerly devoted exclusively to foreign intelligence matters, as well as local and state police—function without meaningful oversight. At the same time, organizations that have been called on for a generation to provide governance of intelligence—such as the FISC and the congressional intelligence committees—are not well positioned to shoulder the burden of governing the newly ascendant domestic intelligence apparatus.

Third, and most centrally, the vacuum in intelligence governance has conceptual dimensions. The current patchwork of intelligence governance, which grew up in response to the abuses uncovered in the mid-1970s, continues to focus on the prevention of illegality and the politicization of intelligence. But intelligence governance ought to take broader aim, not just at illegally obtained or badly motivated intelligence, but also at unreliable or inefficient intelligence. In other words, the purpose of intelligence governance should not merely be to ward off bad intelligence; it should also be to promote good intelligence.

More fundamentally still, the current vacuum in intelligence governance is connected to a conceptual problem that has plagued domestic intelligence over the course of its century-old history in the United States: Just what sort of activity is domestic intelligence? At different points in the last century, most notably in the wake of 1970s-era revelations of abusive practices within the intelligence community, American officials and commentators on domestic intelligence imported the tools and conceptual frameworks of criminal law to the universe of domestic intelligence. The intelligence process was assimilated to the investigation of crime, and the modalities of checking state power in this area were largely borrowed from criminal procedure. Neither approach was a very good fit, but they nevertheless endured for a quarter-century of relative stability until they came under increased pressure from the post-9/11 counterterrorism imperative and, specifically, the need to design an intelligence regime equipped to anticipate and help prevent certain high-impact, low-probability events. While as a practical matter the criminal standard has given out, conceptually it continues to dominate thinking about domestic intelligence and its governance.

If the analogy to criminal law has obscured the deep meaning of intelligence and interfered with its proper governance, how should we organize our thinking about domestic intelligence? . . . I argue that domestic intelligence is properly regarded as a form of risk assessment, a familiar feature from various regulatory regimes across the administrative state. Domestic intelligence as risk assessment is characterized by three main features. First, it is proactive—it seeks to acquire and make sense of information about a hazard before the underlying risk materializes. Second, it is aggregative, meaning that domestic intelligence seeks to acquire vast quantities of data from which to draw informed conclusions. Aggregation is evident in the mass acquisition and computer-driven analysis of telephonic communications, electronic mail, and business records, from which patterns of activity potentially suggesting a terrorist threat can be discerned. The aggregative tendency in intelligence collection and analysis is not, however, limited to electronic communications. It also finds expression in human intelligence, where a newfound focus on identifying social patterns (for example, concerning the "radicalization" of young Muslims) has led officials to collect and analyze intelligence relative to whole communities or neighborhoods in search of meaningful trends (as opposed to intelligence regarding specific individuals about whom officials had already nurtured suspicions). Third, and relatedly, domestic intelligence as risk assessment places a premium on the rigorous analysis of data. . . .

To address the vacuum in domestic intelligence governance, we need to employ a regime that is suited to the activities and institutions that require governing. In view of the regulatory nature of domestic intelligence discussed above, I argue . . . that the basic features of administrative law—specifically a particularly expansive conception of cost-benefit analysis that I refer to as rationality review, (judicial) review for compliance with regulatory mandates, and pluralism underwritten by transparency— should assume a central role in the governance of domestic intelligence. . . .

A. Rationality Review

. . . Employing rationality review as a standard tool for proposed intelligence programs would represent an important development in the governance of intelligence in a number of respects. First, and most basically, rationality review would help promote more accurate and cost-effective intelligence. Second, and somewhat more controversially, I argue that rationality review may actually prove to be a more effective tool for the protection of basic rights than the current governance regime. Third, . . . rationality review will help supply the methodological foundations of a centralized regulatory review process in the intelligence sphere akin to the role that OIRA has come to play in the regulatory state. . . .

1. Accurate Intelligence

Rationality review of intelligence programs may be conducive to more accurate intelligence in three significant ways. First, rationality review promises heightened scientific rigor in the intelligence process by revealing submerged analytic assumptions and forcing intelligence officials to articulate rationales for preferring one course of action over another. Second, and relatedly, rationality review of intelligence raises consciousness of, and helps to combat, the role of heuristic biases and bureaucratic pathologies prevalent among intelligence professionals. Rationality review functions as a potential bulwark against the politicization of intelligence, a notorious problem during the Cold War, as well as in more recent times.

While a veneer of scientific rigor attends intelligence analysis—for example, intelligence estimates, especially those that involve "assigning precise numerical ratings," are frequently marked with levels of confidence ranging from "high probability" to "'cannot rule out'"—intelligence has been surprisingly untouched by thorough risk-based analysis. As the anthropologist of intelligence Rob Johnston has lamented, intelligence officials "quite often use[] the word 'tradecraft' to describe intelligence analysis," that Johnston juxtaposes with "scientific process." Rationality review takes aim at precisely this phenomenon and forces officials to move from inherently unreliable intuitionism to more rational methods of assessment and analysis. Sen has explained, "[E]xplicitness . . . present[s] some kind of . . . barrier against [the] implicit railroading of unacceptable decisions that would be widely rejected if properly articulated."

Not only would rationality review play a role in rooting out the distorting influences of personal bias, it would perform a valuable function in addressing specific kinds of heuristic and institutional biases endemic to intelligence, which impede clear thinking about a threat and the best approaches to tackling it. One basic form of institutional bias (well documented in the case of intelligence analysis) is tunnel vision: the tendency of intelligence professionals to overstate the importance of addressing the full implications of risk A while risk B goes unattended to. Tunnel vision may affect individual analysts, but it is just as likely to take root in whole organizations. For example, an intelligence agency (especially one that combines intelligence and law enforcement functions) may attempt to run all possible leads on a threatening individual or group without stopping to consider that other, potentially much more threatening, individuals may go undetected as a function of resource allocation. Another worrisome heuristic bias is groupthink: the tendency of members of an organization to converge on an approach to a particular problem due to social pressure and convention rather than considered judgment. Meanwhile, cognitive biases, such as probability neglect, rate attempts to assess accurately the nature of the threat (and, by implication, to select the precise tools needed to combat it). A properly designed regime of rationality review for these biases, not only by drawing attention to their distorting influences, but also by directing intelligence agencies to address relatively unheralded problems.

Finally, rationality review would promote more accurate intelligence by locating and helping to weed out overtly politicized intelligence. History teaches that the politicization of intelligence can be irresistible to some powerful public figures. Whether intended to maximize political advantage by engaging in demagoguery of the terrorist threat or by spying on (and blackmailing) political foes, politicization threatens the integrity of the intelligence process itself. While it is possible that even a searching rationality review analysis will fail to take note of (or be able to handle) certain forms of politicization, the rationality review process at a minimum gives a boost to the opponents of politicization by giving them a voice in a formal review process and creates the possibility of a neutral ground on which to resolve internal conflicts.

2. Rights-Protecting Intelligence

While rationality review is not vulnerable to the criticism lodged against narrower conceptions of cost-benefit analysis to the effect that they (inappropriately and inadequately) attempt to monetize all costs and benefits including those that correspond to basic rights, it is potentially subject to the more general critique that it furnishes the basis for downplaying rights protection in the national security area. But rationality review need not entail this bias against rights protection. As a theoretical matter, even cost-benefit analysis can operate under certain deontological constraints. More practically, even a balancing regime unconstrained by deontological limits may promote rights compliance more effectively than the present regime in a number of respects.

First, precisely because its scope is not limited by the present contours of First or Fourth Amendment doctrine, rationality review is well positioned to supply more wide-ranging protections against potentially overbearing intelligence programs. For example, a widespread human intelligence program might flunk cost-benefit review because the information sought is publicly available in academic literature and a costly invasion of privacy is therefore not justified. Such a claim would not be cognizable under current constitutional doctrine. Similarly, a data-mining program could run afoul of rationality review, even if current constitutional law furnishes no basis for enjoining the government from engaging in it. In other words, rationality review shows the way to an intelligence governance regime that could expand on the relatively paltry array of rights currently protected under constitutional law. . . .

Second, the rationality review I advocate could (and should) be wielded to review a wider range of intelligence programs from a larger set of institutions than are currently subject to federal governance. In particular, state and local intelligence regimes, which have grown in scale and prominence in recent years, would be part of a centralized review process. For example, rationality review could be employed to reject a proposed state-led initiative to gather certain kinds of intelligence on the grounds that the FBI was already engaged in the sort of intelligence analysis under discussion and that duplicating the national-level effort could not be justified in view of the costs of the proposed program. Increasing the number of agencies practicing domestic intelligence that are subject to a governance regime represents an important gain for overall rights protection.

Third, and perhaps most significantly, rationality review protects rights more effectively than the current regime by being more attuned to questions of efficiency. Important intelligence gains do not necessarily flow from the most ambitious or far-reaching programs. Indeed, as critics of data mining have argued, for example, casting the widest possible intelligence net is frequently misguided from the standpoint of generating useful intelligence. Indiscriminate human intelligence operations are similarly likely to yield relatively little useful intelligence. In addition to being ineffective, these broad-gauged intelligence programs tend to correlate with being highly invasive of rights: the less precision built into the intelligence program, the more likely it is to acquire information about individuals removed from any threat, which, in turn, unhelpfully occupies the time of more intelligence professionals. Thus, as what might be described as an ancillary benefit, rationality review affords substantial rights protections by being attuned to the need for more focused intelligence programs. In the language of a leading European student of intelligence governance, oversight of "efficiency" and "propriety" are inherently complimentary and are not two unrelated categories.

3. Coordinated Intelligence

Not only does rationality review pave the way for more accurate and more rights-protective intelligence, it also lays the methodological foundation for a more coordinated and consistent intelligence process, and one with more robust and centralized accountability mechanisms. "Information sharing"—or its absence—has been one of the key motifs in discussions of intelligence after 9/11. The problem may arise because of bureaucratic infighting or because the right mechanisms (technological and administrative) do not exist to pool intelligence. Rationality review takes aim at both. It reduces the risk of egregious husbanding of intelligence within agencies by forcing information about proposed intelligence programs into the (relative) open. It inevitably also leads to more dialogue between agencies by creating a "common language" spoken by all elements of the intelligence community regardless of their particular specialties or mandates.

This common language, in turn, furnishes the starting point for a reviewing body (patterned on OIRA) to "check the agency's work" in the sense of reviewing underlying calculations (as appropriate), while also noting where whole categories of costs and benefits have been ignored. The record generated by rationality review is of potentially more widespread use. It may also be employed by intelligence managers and strategists trying to understand the long-term consequences of a program or to refine the way that intelligence is practiced and governed.

B. Judicial Review for Compliance

Central to American administrative law and practice is judicial review of agency action: the idea that decisions taken by agencies are subject to oversight by the courts. Agency actions are subject to review on a number of bases. Parties may challenge the constitutionality of an agency action—for example, on the ground that it violates the separation of powers or the nondelegation doctrine or the right of free speech. They may raise an objection rooted in the agency's interpretation of law, causing the court to consider application of so-called *Chevron* deference. Alternatively, they may seek to overturn an agency decision by asserting a defect in the agency's process. The court may also entertain a challenge based on a different sort of claim: that in view of the agency's stated (and putatively legitimate) ends, the means it selected for regulating were misguided. Whether setting aside the agency action as "arbitrary and capricious" or as failing to withstand a judicial "hard look," the court has the power to police the ways in which the agency complies with its own stated regulatory agenda.

To the extent that judicial review has figured in the governance of intelligence, it has been in the loose sense that judges have figured in some aspects of intelligence oversight. For example, Article III judges who sit on the FISC play an important role in the review of applications for electronic surveillance for compliance with the statute's requirements (as well as with bedrock constitutional guaranties). As discussed above, however, this role is highly circumscribed, as in the case of the issuance of search warrants. Once the FISC judge has given assent to a government surveillance application, the judge's job as an intelligence overseer is basically done. Typically, there is no opportunity to test the constitutionality of the intelligence at trial as there is (at least in concept) in criminal law. More generally, courts may entertain civil suits alleging violations of rights stemming from intelligence programs. As discussed above, suits of this sort immediately run into a number of practical and doctrinal obstacles.

The regulatory model of intelligence governance implies a different way to conceptualize judicial review of intelligence in a manner that resonates with the experience of courts in administrative law. At some regular interval after an agency has implemented a particular intelligence program (following successful rationality review), a court should review the agency's program for fidelity to the agency's own stated (and previously approved) objectives. In focusing on how the agency has implemented the intelligence program in practice, a court could determine whether, in view of empirical evidence, the actual costs and benefits of the program are roughly in line with those that were anticipated prior to the program's implementation. Even more basically, the court could determine whether the agency was remaining true to the stated goals and limitations of the program's mandate.

In reviewing compliance with the program's mandate, the court would take aim at one of the core problems with intelligence (and one of the core liabilities of the current regime of intelligence governance): intelligence drift. By "intelligence drift," I mean to refer to two subtly different but interrelated phenomena. The first is the tendency of an intelligence program to begin by focusing on assessing risk A and later to morph insidiously into a program focusing on a totally different risk B. While drift of this sort may be justified on some occasions as an appropriate response to an evolving risk (or, at any rate, an evolving understanding of a constant risk), it is just as likely to come about because the intelligence officials running a program suffer from the bureaucratic equivalent of a wandering eye. The second type of drift implicates the extreme reluctance with which intelligence agencies acknowledge that a program has outlived its utility. The tendency for intelligence agencies to want to keep drilling in dry wells is precisely what has led to abusive and ineffective intelligence in the past.

Judicial review of this sort would play an important role in the overall governance of domestic intelligence. In addition to having to justify prospective intelligence programs for cost-benefit rationality ex ante, intelligence agencies would be required to stand by their initial plans (or put forth compelling justifications for any departure from them) ex post. Furthermore, Article III judges are well positioned to engage in this sort of judicial review. Because the scope of the review is limited to the agency's compliance with its original plan (concerning which there will have been a developed record stemming from rationality review), the court need not develop expertise in the utility of one or another form of intelligence gathering. No different from the D.C. Circuit sitting in review of agency action across the regulatory state, the reviewing court would simply be looking for the agency's compliance with its own carefully delineated plan.

C. Pluralism

... Pluralism in the form of consulting interested parties can play numerous important roles in the intelligence arena. First, it can help shape the normative framework for determining the proper scope of an inevitably contested process like domestic intelligence as risk assessment. As John Graham notes, "The important role of values in risk analysis is not an argument against risk analysis." Interest group contestation in this area can be an important tool for allowing multiple viewpoints to be aired and normative judgments to be appropriately calibrated. This is especially true in view of the prevalence and salience of various heuristic biases in the area of counterterrorism more broadly.

Second, pluralism in the form of input from the community of subject matter experts can help improve the scientific integrity—and hence, the ultimate utility—of intelligence. While members of the intelligence community must shoulder the ultimate responsibility for "getting it right," a process akin to "peer review" may prove beneficial....

Third, pluralism would afford communities disproportionately affected by domestic intelligence the opportunity to share their particular concerns with the government. As former senior FBI official Michael Rolince has observed, although:

> there is concern that [the new guidelines] may encourage the violation of U.S. civil rights through the harassment of innocent persons, particularly in Muslim and Arab communities ... [t]he new guidelines may place FBI agents in greater contact with Arab Americans and other ethnic minority groups; this would, indeed, be a positive outcome.

Outreach of this sort is vital not only because of the profound civil rights issues at stake, but also because outreach ensures the ongoing willingness of members of these communities to provide the vital information they possess to security officials.

D. Transparency

Related to—and underwriting the possibility of–pluralism in domestic intelligence governance is the concept of transparency. At first blush, transparency seems like an odd fit with an intelligence community that inevitably carries out much of its work in secret; but as Director of National Intelligence Dennis Blair testified at his confirmation hearing, "There is a need for transparency and accountability in a mission where most work necessarily remains hidden from public view." Blair further testified that he intends to "communicate frequently and candidly with the oversight committees, and as much as possible with the American people."

One respect in which the domestic intelligence state can move in the direction of greater transparency is in the disclosure of the nature and scope of the legal authority it exercises. The very fact that the current Attorney General's Guidelines covering domestic intelligence (as well as the recently revised executive order governing foreign and domestic intelligence) are published (almost in their entirety) and are available on the Internet represents a break from past tradition. Another sense in which the domestic intelligence apparatus could achieve greater transparency is in the continued publication of its analytic findings where senior intelligence officials offer insights into the major threats of the day and nonclassified versions of National Intelligence Estimates are made public. For example, Blair recently testified that the "primary near-term security concern of the United States is the global economic crisis and its geopolitical implications." The point would be for the domestic intelligence apparatus to more candidly describe the nature and the intensity of the threat, past the superficial and frequently misleading color-coded alerts of the sort issued for the last six years by the DHS. A good example is supplied by the MI5's website, which contains thoughtful, detailed information about the terrorist threat to the United Kingdom, as well as the government's policy for countering it.

Disclosures of this sort do, to be sure, entail certain risks. For example, politicians may be inclined to exaggerate a threat that has been reported by the intelligence agency for narrow political gain, or to minimize an intelligence-driven analysis that undercuts a preferred political platform. Citizens (who will typically lack a context for understanding the threat baseline) may fail to understand the nature of the assessment and may tend to overreact to it. To the extent that the threat tracks defined religious or ethnic groups, certain civil liberty concerns might be implicated. Additionally, the intelligence apparatus itself may take advantage of opportunities to disclose information in order to promote the agency's own perceived self-interest, or perhaps even to engage in disinformation. In general, a more robust regime of regulatory governance of domestic intelligence requires greater emphasis on peeling back layers of secrecy.

THE INSTITUTIONAL LIFE OF REGULATORY GOVERNANCE

. . . If a regulatory approach to intelligence governance is to succeed, however, these ideas must be instantiated in a set of concrete institutions and practices. Rationality review must be implemented by an agency with the right mixture of expertise and objectivity; judicial review must have teeth but also sensitivity to context; and pluralist processes must be allowed to develop within a habitually secretive intelligence apparatus. . . .

A. ODNI: Rationality Review

Created in 2004 by the Intelligence Reform and Terrorism Prevention Act ("IRTPA"), the ODNI [Office of the Director of National Intelligence] is perched atop the sixteen agencies that make up the loosely knit intelligence community. With a staff of around 1500, the ODNI was designed in large part to coordinate the efforts of these various organizations, encourage the flow of information between and among them, and synthesize intelligence for the president. Predictably, the ODNI has had trouble getting off the ground and establishing its superagency status. Even before the ink on the intelligence law was dry, the ODNI had been stripped of a good deal of the budgeting authority that had been contemplated in response to the 9/11 Commission's complaint that the CIA director had historically faced the impossible task of "direct[ing] agencies without controlling them . . . [or] control[ling] their purse strings." The fierce independence of the agencies, most notably of the CIA, has made intelligence community integration exceedingly difficult, and without having succeeded at that defining role, the ODNI has found itself grasping for a purpose. . . .

Faced with the daunting challenge of carving out a meaningful institutional niche, the ODNI ought to embrace the mission of regulatory governance of intelligence. First, the ODNI's authorizing statute and legal authorities make the office (or some part of it to which the DNI assigns the task) uniquely well positioned to consider the costs and benefits of proposed intelligence programs. Second, the office possesses the requisite mix of expertise and detachment to make informed but dispassionate decisions about intelligence programs. Third, embracing the role of regulatory governance would contribute meaningfully to the furtherance of the ODNI's twin goals of facilitating information sharing across the intelligence community and providing overarching strategic management of American intelligence. In sum, the ODNI—or some office within it—ought to aspire to play the role for the intelligence community that OIRA has played for the administrative state beginning with Reagan's Order 12,866. . . .

Not only does the DNI have the necessary statutory power to engage in rationality review, but the DNI's office also possesses the core competences to discharge that role effectively. First, the DNI's office (which has a sufficiently large staff to tackle the daunting task of intelligence governance) possesses the requisite expertise in intelligence matters to provide meaningful governance. Steeped in the culture and technical capacities of intelligence, the ODNI is considerably more likely than congressional or judicial overseers to ask the right sorts of questions (without which governance approaches a rubber stamp). At the same time, the DNI enjoys sufficient distance from the various intelligence agencies that are subordinate to the ODNI to be relatively free from fear of agency capture. While the ODNI's initial employees generally came from the constituent intelligence agencies and may well have brought to their new jobs the professional biases of their former workplaces, increasingly, the ODNI staff is comprised of direct hires.

Finally, embracing the role of rationality review will not only strengthen intelligence governance, but it will also simultaneously help the DNI realize the two most important strategic objectives of intelligence, both derived from the 9/11 Commission Report (which supplied a conceptual roadmap for the ITRPA). First, the DNI must facilitate information sharing—the lack of which, in the estimation of the 9/11 Commission, was a major contributing factor to the success of the attacks. Above and beyond the ordinary flow of intelligence from the agencies to the DNI (for inclusion in the President's Daily Brief, for example), rationality review provides an important channel for generating information flows about intelligence programs from the agencies to the DNI. . . .

B. FISA: Judicial Review of Intelligence Programs

. . . The rise of a risk-assessment model of domestic intelligence has brought about a fundamental addition to FISA practice. Central to the FISA Amendments Act of 2008 is a provision that gives the FISC authority to issue what amounts to a "programmatic" or "basket" warrant for an entire intelligence program. In order to conduct basket warrant-type surveillance in accord with the FISA Amendments Act, the government must seek an order of approval from the FISC, which requires the submission to the FISC of attestations (signed by the Attorney General, as well as the DNI) of its compliance with statutory requirements, as well as of the details of procedures it has adopted in order to ensure such compliance. If the government fails to convince the FISC that it satisfies the statutory requirements, the FISC can deny approval of a basket warrant, and the government may take an appeal to the FISA Court of Review.

The issuance of programmatic warrants is in some respects analogous to the well-established practice of issuing administrative warrants in other areas, such as public health. What is nevertheless surprising about the new law is that it assigns to the FISC a role in the judicial review of compliance with the terms of basket warrants. This power is, in turn, largely bound up with the FISC's supervision of the government's compliance with its stated plans for targeting foreigners overseas and differentiating potentially valuable intelligence from reams of innocuous information about individuals not suspected of terrorist involvement. (Other parts of the government's certification, such as its general claim that "a significant purpose of the acquisition is to obtain foreign intelligence information," are likely to be treated deferentially.) As Senator Dianne Feinstein explained during an exchange before the Senate Judiciary Committee, the issuance of programmatic warrants calls for "court oversight," by which the FISC could "set the strictures, say [']I want you to report to me every 3 months, every 30 days,['] [and thus] provide oversight protection."

In other hearings, senior government officials reiterated this role of the FISC in post hoc judicial review. For example, in testimony before the House Judiciary Committee, Assistant Attorney General for National Security Ken Wainstein observed that "[t]he FISA Court is receiving the procedures by which we conduct this surveillance," which places the court in a position to detect a government program, and "that doesn't fit with the law." Opponents of the new law remarked on the departure from historical practice. During congressional debates, Senator Kit Bond, relying on a report issued by the Republicans on the Senate Intelligence Committee, and referring obliquely to the differences between individualized and more aggregative warrants, said:

> [T]he FISA Court has little, if any, historical experience with assessing compliance with minimization in the context of foreign targeting. There are significant differences between the scope, purpose, and means by which the acquisition of foreign intelligence is conducted in the domestic and foreign targeting contexts. While the FISA Court is well-suited to assess compliance

with minimization procedures in the domestic context, such assessment is better left to the Executive branch in the foreign targeting context.

How this process has played out in practice is thus far difficult to say. But, especially when viewed in light of the fact that the FISC now receives semiannual reports on the status of collection under program warrants, a new model of judicial review of intelligence programs appears to be emerging: one that assigns to the court a role not only in the ex ante issuance of warrants (even basket warrants), but also in the substantive hard look-style review of agency compliance with stated intelligence programs. Although the court's purview is limited (by the terms of FISA) to the supervision of electronic surveillance conducted by the federal intelligence community, the kind of judicial review that the FISC is now engaged in brings contemporary practice much closer to the sort of judicial review that I advocate.

One major difference between judicial review before the FISC and traditional judicial review of agency action stands out: the absence of a meaningful adversarial process within the intelligence review process. This difference—the result of a structural feature of intelligence gathering—is at least partially addressed by the FISA Amendments Act in that the law provides for the possibility of judicial review of directives to compel the participation of telecommunications firms in electronic surveillance. Thus, Section 702(h)(6) of the new law authorizes a service provider who receives such a directive to "file a petition with the [FISA] Court of Review," following which "[t]he Court of Review shall have jurisdiction to consider such petition and shall provide a written statement for the record of the reasons for a decision under this subparagraph."

While promising in concept (because telecommunications firms are arguably in a better position than government officials, both technically and institutionally, to uncover potential abuse), and potentially helpful in addressing a constitutional concern pertaining to the absence of a case or controversy before the FISA Court of Review, participation by telecommunications carriers in litigation before the FISC may prove less useful in practice. In a much debated provision, the FISA Amendments Act immunizes telecoms from liability arising from following directives issued from the government, making it unlikely that any communications provider will challenge any directive it receives.

A slightly different, and slightly more promising, approach has recently been explored by the Second Circuit in a case surrounding the use of national security letters ("NSLs")—essentially administrative subpoenas by which the government requests information from providers of telephone or electronic communications services (such as Internet providers). While the original statutory authority for NSLs required that the recipient of such a letter strictly comply with its terms without disclosing to anyone (including counsel) the fact that the letter was received—let alone its contents—a number of district courts found the statute's nondisclosure requirement to violate the First Amendment. Congress subsequently revisited the law in the course of amending the PATRIOT Act and provided for the possibility of judicial review of the NSL's nondisclosure order at the initiation of the letter's recipient. The Second Circuit found that by placing the burden on the recipient to challenge the nondisclosure order, the NSLs continued to run afoul of the First Amendment. Rather than strike down the statute as written, the court came up with a novel remedy. The recipient could merely notify the government of its intent to challenge the nondisclosure requirement, following which the government would be accorded a period of time within which "to initiate a judicial review proceeding to maintain the nondisclosure requirement." While not eliminating the problem of the absence of incentives on the part of third parties to challenge government requests for information (and the corresponding requirement that secrecy be maintained), the Second Circuit approach has the benefit of placing the burden on the government to initiate the proceedings and to overcome a presumption against it.

C. The Attorney General's Guidelines: Public Participation

Owing to its secretive nature, interest groups are significantly less prominent in the intelligence process than they are across the regulatory state, where legal mechanisms such as informal notice-and-comment rulemaking create meaningful opportunities for pluralist participation. Some modicum of change may be occurring with respect to this critical feature of regulatory governance. The process by which the new Attorney General's Guidelines were issued bore at least a passing resemblance to traditional informal agency rulemaking. FBI general counsel Valerie Caproni recently observed that the new guidelines were "signed after unprecedented consultation" with interest groups, including civil liberties advocates such as the American Civil Liberties Union. She further explained that "historically the Attorney General has not brought Congress or outside groups into the process of drafting guidelines. Having the consultation process is new, and I believe it was extremely helpful." director Robert Mueller underscored that the FBI not only sought suggestions from outside groups in a spirit of openness that went much further than the sets of guidelines that had gone before, but that the FBI was also incorporating suggestions that were made. Beyond the groups that were present for the consultation process, Mueller committed to making the FBI internal rules issued pursuant to the new guidelines "[publicly] available . . . to the greatest extent possible."

Not everyone was convinced of the adequacy of the new approach. In particular, certain politicians argued for even greater transparency and public participation in the formulation of the new guidelines. Senator Russ Feingold challenged the process, asking Director Mueller during a Senate committee hearing, "Why can't you at least solicit . . . suggestions in a meaningful process that involves more than a single meeting where the participants aren't even allowed . . . to keep a copy [of the draft guidelines]?" Regardless of the fact that it did not represent as robust an instance of popular participation in rulemaking as many would have liked, the process's very existence suggests the possible emergence in the domestic intelligence arena of a new ethic of interest group representation—a hallmark of agency rulemaking across the administrative state for a generation.

1. *Applying Administrative Law Concepts to Intelligence Operations.* Professor Rascoff's analysis asks us to understand domestic intelligence gathering as a form of public administration and to apply to its management those techniques of internal and external bureaucratic control that are thought, in other contexts, to promote sound regulatory behavior. Professor Shane has urged a similar approach in the more limited context of managing the antiterrorist watch list system, which functions most famously for screening passenger access to air travel. The *Bureaucratic Due Process of Government Watch Lists*, 75 Geo. WASH L. REV. 804–855 (2007). To what degree do such techniques hold genuine promise of both promoting better intelligence work and reducing abuses? Do you think it likely that intelligence agencies would voluntarily adopt such methods absent any legislative command to do so?

2. *Article III and the FISC.* Professor Rascoff would grant the Foreign Intelligence Surveillance Court a role in reviewing compliance by intelligence agencies with their approved intelligence plans. Is this consistent with Article III limits on judicial power? Judge Posner thinks the absence of an adversarial proceeding may point to a constitutional infirmity with such a system. Richard A. Posner, *Privacy, Surveillance, and Law,* 75 U. CHI. L. REV. 245, 255 (2008). In a footnote, Professor Rascoff opines: "The best counterargument is probably that the review process ought to be regarded from the standpoint of constitutional law as the equivalent to reconsideration by the court of a search warrant." Is this persuasive? If there is a problem with programmatic review by the FISC, does the infirmity also taint the 2008 provisions for "basket warrants," i.e., FISC initial approval of foreign intelligence surveillance on a programmatic basis?

3. *Further Reading.* The document that has most profoundly shaped debate (if not always results) concerning intelligence reform since 9/11 is the 9/11 Commission Report: FINAL REPORT OF THE NATIONAL COMMISSION ON TERRORIST ATTACKS UPON THE UNITED STATES (2004). In addition, Professor Rascoff's article is rich in citations on the intelligence agencies and the issues relating to oversight. Notable among the sources cited are James Burch, *A Domestic Intelligence Agency for the United States? A Comparative Analysis of Domestic Intelligence Agencies and Their Implications for Homeland Security,* HOMELAND SECURITY AFF., June 2007, art. 1, http://www.hsaj.org/pages/volume3/issue2/pdfs/3.2.2.pdf; William E. Odom, FIXING INTELLIGENCE: FOR A MORE SECURE AMERICA (2003); Anne Joseph O'Connell, *The Architecture of Smart Intelligence: Structuring and Overseeing Agencies in the Post-9/11 World,* 94 CAL. L. REV. 1655 (2006); RICHARD A. POSNER, COUNTERING TERRORISM: BLURRED FOCUS, HALTING STEPS (2007); RICHARD A. POSNER, REMAKING DOMESTIC INTELLIGENCE (2005); and GREGORY F. TREVERTON, RAND CORP., REORGANIZING U.S. DOMESTIC INTELLIGENCE: ASSESSING THE OPTIONS (2008).

b. The Iran-Contra Affair

In November 1986, President Reagan confirmed reports that the United States had in 1985 and 1986 facilitated six sales of TOW anti-tank missiles, Hawk anti-aircraft missiles, and spare parts for missile systems to Iran. Certain of the missiles had been previously sold to Israel; Israel agreed to sell their missiles to Iran if the U.S. approved and agreed to replenish the Israeli arsenal. Other missiles and parts were sold directly by the U.S. government to Iran. The Administration originally defended all of the transactions as part of an attempt to improve relations generally with Iran. Critics charged that the sales were, in fact, an attempt to buy the release of Americans held hostage in Lebanon by Islamic revolutionary groups believed to be under Iranian influence. It was further alleged that the operation was conducted by the staff of the National Security Council, rather than by the Central Intelligence Agency, for the central purpose of avoiding legally required congressional oversight of the operations involved.

Among the issues raised by these sales was their legality under various statutes regulating the international sale of arms, statutes clearly within Congress's power to regulate foreign trade. *See* Raymond J. Celada, Laws Implicated By Shipments of Military Materials to Iran (Congressional Research Service, 1986). A hint of the complexities involved appears in the following passage from the report of a Special Review Board ("Tower Commission") established by President Reagan on December 1, 1986 to review the controversial activities of the National Security Council staff:

> The Arms Export Control Act, the principal U.S. statute governing arms sales abroad, makes it unlawful to export arms without a license. Exports of arms by U.S. government agencies, however, do not require a license if they are otherwise authorized by law. Criminal penalties—fines and imprisonment—are provided for willful violations.
>
> The initial arms transfers in the Iran initiative involved the sale and shipment by Israel of U.S.-origin missiles. The usual way for such international retransfer of arms to be authorized under U.S. law is pursuant to the Arms Export Control Act. This Act requires that the President consent to any transfers by another country of arms exported under the Act and imposes three conditions before such Presidential consent may be given:
>
>> (a) the United States would itself transfer the arms in question to the recipient country;
>>
>> (b) a commitment in writing has been obtained from the recipient country against unauthorized retransfer of significant arms, such as missiles; and
>>
>> (c) a prior written certification regarding the retransfer is submitted to the Congress if the defense equipment, such as missiles, has an acquisition cost of 14 million dollars or more. 22 U.S.C. 2753 (a), (d).
>
> In addition, the Act generally imposes restrictions on which countries are eligible to receive U.S. arms and on the purposes for which arms may be sold.[2]

---

2. It may be possible to authorize transfers by another country under the Arms Export Control Act without obtaining the President's consent. As a practical matter, however, the legal requirements may not differ significantly. For example, section 614(2) permits the President to waive the

The other possible avenue whereby government arms transfers to Iran may be authorized by law would be in connection with intelligence operations conducted under the National Security Act. This Act requires that the Director of Central Intelligence and the heads of other intelligence agencies keep the two Congressional intelligence committees "fully and currently informed" of all intelligence activities under their responsibility. 50 U.S.C. 413. Where prior notice of significant intelligence activities is not given, the intelligence committees are to be informed "in a timely fashion." In addition, the so-called Hughes-Ryan Amendment to the Foreign Assistance Act requires that "significant anticipated intelligence activities" may not be conducted by the CIA unless and until the President finds that "each such operation is important to the national security of the United States." 22 U.S.C. 2422.

When the Israelis began transferring arms to Iran in August 1985, they were not acting on their own. U.S. officials had knowledge about the essential elements of the proposed shipments. The United States shared some common purpose in the transfers and received a benefit from them—the release of a hostage. Most importantly, Mr. McFarlane [the National Security Adviser] communicated prior U.S. approval to the Israelis for the shipments, including an undertaking for replenishment. But for this U.S. approval, the transactions may not have gone forward. In short, the United States was an essential participant in the arms transfers to Iran that occurred in 1985.

Whether this U.S. involvement in the arms transfers by the Israelis was lawful depends fundamentally upon whether the President approved the transactions before they occurred. In the absence of Presidential approval, there does not appear to be any authority in this case for the United States to engage in the transfer of arms or consent to the transfer by another country. The arms transfers to Iran in 1985 and hence the Iran initiative itself would have proceeded contrary to U.S. law.

The Attorney General reached a similar judgment with respect to the activities of the CIA in facilitating the November 1985 shipment by the Israelis of HAWK missiles. In a letter to the Board, the Attorney General concluded that with respect to the CIA assistance, "a finding under the Hughes-Ryan Amendment would be required."[4]

---

requirements of the Act. But this waiver authority may not be exercised unless it is determined that the international arms sales are "vital to the national security interests of the United States." Moreover, before granting a waiver, the President must consult with and provide written justification to the foreign affairs and appropriations committees of the Congress. 22 U.S.C. 2374(3).

4. Apparently no determination was made at the time as to the legality of these activities even though serious concerns about legality were expressed by the Deputy Director of CIA, a Presidential finding was sought by CIA officials before any further CIA activities in support of the Iran initiative were undertaken, and the CIA counsel, Mr. Stanley Sporkin, advised that as a matter of prudence any new finding should seek to ratify the prior CIA activities.

The Board was unable to reach a conclusive judgment about whether the 1985 shipments of arms to Iran were approved in advance by the President. On balance the Board believes that it is plausible to conclude that he did approve them in advance.

Yet even if the President in some sense consented to or approved the transactions, a serious question of law remains. It is not clear that the form of the approval was sufficient for purposes of either the Arms Export Control Act or the Hughes-Ryan Amendment. The consent did not meet the conditions of the Arms Export Control Act, especially in the absence of a prior written commitment from the Iranians regarding unauthorized retransfer.

Under the National Security Act, it is not clear that mere oral approval by the President would qualify as a Presidential finding that the initiative was vital to the national security interests of the United States. The approval was never reduced to writing. It appears to have been conveyed to only one person. The President himself has no memory of it. And there is contradictory evidence from the President's advisors about how the President responded when he learned of the arms shipments which the approval was to support. In addition, the requirement for Congressional notification was ignored. In these circumstances, even if the President approved of the transactions, it is difficult to conclude that his actions constituted adequate legal authority.

. . . [T]he legal underpinning of the Iran initiative during 1985 was at best highly questionable. The Presidential Finding of January 17, 1986, formally approved the Iran initiative as a covert intelligence operation under the National Security Act. This ended the uncertainty about the legal status of the initiative and provided legal authority for the United States to transfer arms directly to Iran.

The National Security Act also requires notification of Congress of covert intelligence activities. If not done in advance, notification must be "in a timely fashion." The Presidential finding of January 17 directed that Congressional notification be withheld, and this decision appears to have never been reconsidered. While there was surely justification to suspend Congressional notification in advance of a particular transaction relating to a hostage release, the law would seem to require disclosure where, as in the Iran case, a pattern of relative inactivity occurs over an extended period. To do otherwise prevents the Congress from fulfilling its proper oversight responsibilities.

John Tower, et al., Report of the President's Special Review Board IV 8–9 (1987).

Assuming that at least some of the arms transfers to Iran occurred under procedures that did not comply with all relevant provisions of law, could the President argue (a) persuasively or even (b) plausibly that he had inherent authority to effect the arms transfers in pursuit of his foreign policy without respect to the statutes involved? What would be the constitutional basis for such authority? Review the cases earlier in this chapter. Could you have written a memorandum responsibly supporting the President's authority to make the transfers based solely on his constitutional powers? How does *Youngstown* shape your analysis? The Tower Commission had this to say about the apparent involvement of Administration lawyers in decisionmaking relevant to the Iran initiative:

> Throughout the Iran initiative, significant questions of law do not appear to have been adequately addressed. In the face of a sweeping statutory prohibition and explicit requirements relating to Presidential consent to arms transfers by third countries, there appears to have been at the outset in 1985 little attention, let alone systematic analysis, devoted to how Presidential actions would comply with U.S. law. The Board has found no evidence that an evaluation was ever done during the life of the operation to determine whether it continued to comply with the terms of the January 17 Presidential Finding. Similarly, when a new prohibition was added to the Arms Export Control Act in August of 1986 to prohibit exports to countries on the terrorism list (a list which contained Iran), no evaluation was made to determine whether this law affected authority to transfer arms to Iran in connection with intelligence operations under the National Security Act. This lack of legal vigilance markedly increased the chances that the initiative would proceed contrary to law.

Id. at IV 9. What is your assessment? Is the Commission "pussyfooting" in the last quoted sentence? Over a vigorous dissent, the majority joint report for the congressional committees investigating the Iran-Contra affair went further than the Tower Commission in condemning what it perceived as a "disdain" for law shared by key Reagan Administration officials. *See generally* S. Rep. No. 216, 100th Cong., 1st Sess. (1987); H.R. Rep. No. 433, 100th Cong., 1st Sess. (1987).

While the committees in both Houses conducted their investigations, President Reagan announced a comprehensive review of executive branch procedures concerning covert operations in order to implement the recommendations of the Tower Commission. On August 7, 1987, the President promised specific reform measures, including the reduction of all future "Findings" pertaining to national security operations to writing, except in cases of "extreme emergency"; forbearance from issuing any retroactive "Findings"; and a requirement that agencies designated by the President for the discharge of covert operations comply with all procedures applicable to the President in notifying Congress concerning such operations. *See* Letter to the Chairman and Vice Chairman of the Senate Select Committee on Intelligence Regarding Procedures for Presidential Approval and Notification of Congress, 23 Weekly Comp. Pres. Doc. 910 (Aug. 7, 1987). The joint congressional report, however, suggested stronger reform, recommending that Congress enact a requirement of advance notification, except in emergencies, of all covert operations. As you review the discussion of the War Powers Resolution in Chapter Six, consider the degree to which notification requirements effectively foster legal and political accountability. How might you draft such requirements for covert operations both to facilitate effective oversight and to respect the constitutional authority of the President?

Two weeks after initial U.S. confirmation of the Iranian arms deals, it was further revealed that National Security Council (NSC) staff had facilitated the diversion of profits from the arms sales to the support of military forces (the "Contras") seeking to overthrow the government of Nicaragua. This funding occurred during a period for which Congress had imposed a series of restrictions on military and intelligence appropriations (the so-called "Boland Amendments") proscribing the use of those appropriations for the military or paramilitary assistance of the Contra forces. These limitations were imposed despite the vigorous opposition of the Administration, for which support of the Contras was considered a foreign policy priority. (These amendments may be viewed as part of a trend over the last 15 years toward congressional resort to appropriations riders to impose substantive limitations on the statutory authority of the executive branch. Recall *Brown v. Califano*, reprinted in Chapter Two, concerning the use of appropriations statutes to regulate the implementation of Title VI of the Civil Rights Act of 1964.)

Whether the use of National Security Council staff to facilitate Contra support violated the then-current Boland Amendment is a complex question, in no small part because the various Contra aid restrictions enacted by Congress differed in their precise terms, and those differences make for rich argument over legislative intent. In order to further debate on the issue, Rep. William V. Alexander, Jr. of Arkansas took the unusual step on June 15, 1987 of inserting into the Congressional record the legislative history of each of these provisions. 133 Cong. Rec. H4585–4987 (daily ed. June 15, 1987). This compilation includes a chart of the twelve Contra aid restrictions enacted between December 1982 and October 1986. During fiscal year 1985 — the period chiefly relevant to the initiation of the Contra funding initiative — Congress provided:

> [N]o funds available to the Central Intelligence Agency, the Department of Defense, or any other agency or entity of the United States involved in intelligence activities may be obligated or expended for the purpose or which would have the effect of supporting, directly or indirectly, military or paramilitary operations in Nicaragua by any nation, group, organization, movement, or individual.

Department of Defense Appropriations Act 1985, § 8066, enacted in Further Continuing Appropriations Act, Pub. L. No. 98-473, 98 Stat. 1935 (1984). Whether this proscription applied to the NSC's 1985 activities involving the Contras depends, statutorily, on whether the NSC is to be viewed as "agency or entity of the United States," and, if so, whether it is "involved in intelligence activities," within the intent of the statute. See the discussion of the National Security Council in Chapter Three, above.

Note that the appropriations act was a so-called "continuing resolution," funding all those government agencies that had not been funded by the beginning of the fiscal year, October 1, 1984. Recall that, without this appropriation, most administrative operations of the executive branch would have had to shut down. It is in this context that President Reagan signed the statute containing the fiscal year 1985 Boland Amendment. Does this example help explain the temptation to use appropriations acts to impose substantive limits on government authority? Would the context in which the President signed the act excuse any failure scrupulously to obey it?

Whatever the proper resolution of these questions, it is clear that the Contra support initiative raises important constitutional questions concerning both presidential and congressional authorities.

For example, on the congressional side, are there limits to Congress's power to regulate presidential attempts to raise money from private citizens or from other countries in support of his foreign affairs objectives? Presumably, the Boland Amendment is unproblematic if it is simply a limitation on the government accounts on which the President may properly draw for such a fund-raising effort. Congress could surely tell the President to use the State Department, but not the Treasury Department for such an effort. Some members of Congress have argued, however, that the Boland Amendment was essentially a comprehensive ban on attempts by anyone involved in government intelligence work to undertake any initiative in support of the Contras. Could Congress have provided: "No officer of the Government of the United States may raise funds from any source in support of military or paramilitary activity in Nicaragua?" What would be the source of Congress's authority for such a statute? If Congress lacks authority for such a statute, could it permissibly enact the same proscription in the form of an appropriations rider? That is, does its spending power for the general welfare give it greater leeway in this context than when it legislates pursuant to its substantive regulatory powers? Would such a view undermine any notion of inherent presidential authority to accomplish anything that he cannot accomplish on his own salary?* Cf., *The Sufficiency of the President's Certification Under the Mexican Debt Disclosure Act*, 20 Op. O.L.C. 253 (1996), reprinted in H. JEFFERSON POWELL, THE CONSTITUTION AND THE ATTORNEYS GENERAL 673 (arguing that the Justice Department properly gives statutory conditions on the President's exercise of foreign policy discretion a narrow construction in order to avoid "grave doubts about the constitutionality" of such measures).

On the executive side, does the President have inherent authority to undertake covert fund-raising initiatives in support of his foreign affairs objectives? (For example, would the Contra initiative have been lawful even if the executive found itself,

---

* In 1988, a suit by 15 House members and one Senator seeking a declaratory judgment that Congress, through these restrictions, was unconstitutionally interfering with the President's policy of supporting the Nicaraguan contras was dismissed both for lack of standing and under the D.C. Circuit's rule of equitable discretion. *Dornan v. U.S. Secretary of Defense*, 851 F.2d 450 (D.C. Cir. 1988).

The Senate, for its part, adopted in July 1989 a version of the State Department authorization bill for fiscal 1990 that would have made it a felony for a government official to solicit funds from private sources or foreign countries to advance activities prohibited by Congress. No such provision was included in the foreign relations authorization act finally passed by Congress.

because of the Boland Amendment, in its weakest legal position under Justice Jackson's *Youngstown* analysis?) If so, what are the implications for the Article I vesting of the appropriations power in Congress as a source of "checks and balances"? Even if the Boland Amendment did not expressly proscribe the NSC activities that took place, is the argument for inherent presidential authority strong enough to withstand the suggestion that the NSC initiative undermined the "faithful execution of the laws" given the policy of non-aid to the Contras implicit in that amendment? Would it be relevant to the legal analysis whether the fund-raising was covert, and hence, resistant to ordinary mechanisms of governmental accountability, or public, and thus subject to a full and educated congressional response?

On November 18, 1987, the House and Senate committees investigating the Iran-Contra affair issued their final report. S. Rep. No. 216, 100th Cong., 1st Sess. (1987); H.R. Rep. No. 433, 100th Cong., 1st Sess. (1987). The Democratic majorities of both committees, together with three Republican Senators, concluded that the Administration had engaged in "an evasion of the letter and the spirit" of the law, and laid blame partially with President Reagan, whose solicitation of foreign donations for the Contras assertedly "set the stage" for his subordinates' "disdain" for legal restrictions. Two Senate and the six House Republicans contended that the Boland amendments were unconstitutional. A helpful summary of the lengthy report appears at 45 CONG. Q. 2847–59 (1987). *See also* JOHN TOWER, ET AL., REPORT OF THE PRESIDENT'S SPECIAL REVIEW BOARD (1987); PRELIMINARY INQUIRY INTO THE SALE OF ARMS TO IRAN AND POSSIBLE DIVERSION OF FUNDS TO THE NICARAGUAN RESISTANCE, S. Rep. No. 100-7, 100th Cong., 1st Sess. (1987). Note that the preceding discussion has focused entirely on the constitutional issues lurking behind this episode; testimony before Congress also established that executive branch officials had intentionally lied to congressional committees to prevent their discovery of the Contra funding operation. (Do this and the Watergate episode suggest that perjury and obstruction of justice charges are likely the inevitable outgrowths of secret policy gone wrong?) For a highly critical history of the Iran-Contra affairs, see T. DRAPER, A VERY THIN LINE: THE IRAN-CONTRA AFFAIRS (1991). A more condensed version of Theodore Draper's analysis of the constitutional implications of Iran-Contra appears as *The Constitution in Danger*, N.Y. REV. OF BOOKS, Mar. 1, 1990, at 41. A response co-authored by a Justice Department attorney and a member of the Bush White House Counsel's office appears in Lawrence J. Block & David B. Rivkin, Jr., *'The Constitution in Danger': An Exchange*, N.Y. REV. OF BOOKS, May 17, 1990, at 50.

Although prosecutions for perjury before Congress would seem to pose no separation of powers problem in principle, Congress's Iran-Contra investigation did ultimately prove problematic for the successful criminal prosecution of two major figures connected with the affair. Lawrence Walsh, the Iran/Contra special prosecutor, secured jury convictions of former National Security Adviser John M. Poindexter and former NSC staff member Oliver North for obstructing Congress, among other offenses. The D.C. Circuit, however, vacated both sets of convictions on the ground that insufficient steps were taken to ensure that the defendants' immunized testimony to Congress during the Iran/Contra hearings did not taint their criminal trials. *United States v. North*, 910 F.2d 843 (D.C. Cir. 1990), *modified*, 920 F.2d 940 (D.C. Cir. 1990), *cert. denied*, 500 U.S. 941 (1991); *United States v. Poindexter*, 951 F.2d 369 (D.C. Cir. 1991), *cert. denied*, 506 U.S. 1021 (1992). The court held that (a) any alteration in a trial witness's testimony by virtue of exposure to a defendant's immunized testimony or (b) the use of immunized testimony even to refresh a witness's recollection would violate the privilege against self-incrimination. Strict adherence to this principle could make the contemporaneous exploration of executive branch scandals before both congressional and judicial tribunals exceedingly difficult.

c. Iran-Contra and Congressional Oversight of Covert Operations

Congress's response to the Iran-Contra scandal did not envision systemic reforms as thoroughgoing as those more recently proposed by Professor Rascoff. Instead, as has been its preference in recent decades, Congress turned to possible reforms in the processes of presidential reporting to Congress. Indeed, the 100th Congress came close to enacting legislation that would have required the President to notify Congress within 48 hours of all covert operations. The Senate passed such a bill, S. 1721, 100th Cong., 2d Sess. (1988), and a version was approved by the House Intelligence Committee. H.R. 3822, 100th Cong., 2d Sess. (1988). President Reagan threatened to veto any such legislation, however, and the House—slowed by a controversy over whether former Speaker Jim Wright had improperly leaked intelligence data—never brought the bill to a vote. *See Intelligence Oversight Act of 1988: Hearings and Markup on H.R. 3822 Before the House Comm. on Foreign Affairs*, 100th Cong., 2d Sess (1988); Symposium: Intelligence Oversight, National Security, and Democracy, 12 Harv. J.L. & Pub. Pol. 285 (1989); Note, *Congressional Assertiveness, Executive Authority and the Intelligence Oversight Act: A New Threat to the Separation of Powers*, 64 Notre Dame L. Rev. 571 (1989). *See* Assistant Attorney General Charles Cooper, *The President's Compliance with the "Timely Notification" Requirement of Section 501(B) of the National Security Act*, 10 Op. O.L.C. 158 (Dec. 17, 1986), *reprinted in* H. Jefferson Powell, The Constitution and the Attorneys General 483 (1999) (defending President's Reagan delay in notifying Congress of his Iran initiatives, and insisting that statutory reporting requirements must be so construed as to avoid interference with the President foreign policy powers).

In another effort to strengthen CIA oversight, Congress did amend the statutory office of CIA Inspector General to make that officer a presidential appointee subject to Senate advice and consent. The new statute provides that the chair or ranking member of either Intelligence Committee may demand from the Director of Central Intelligence any Inspector General report—a provision that the Administration argued was unconstitutional, but which ultimately did not provoke a veto. Intelligence Authorization Act, Fiscal Year 1990, 50 U.S.C. § 403q. Should the President have vetoed this law?

After several abortive attempts at compromise, Congress finally, in 1991, repealed the Hughes-Ryan Amendment and enacted a new statutory framework for the presidential use of covert actions. Until 2010, amendments were chiefly technical or cosmetic, reflecting that the Director of National Intelligence, not the CIA director, is now responsible for reporting to Congress. On October 7, 2010, President Obama signed into law the Intelligence Authorization Act for Fiscal Year 2010, Pub. L. 111-259, 111th Cong., 2d Sess., 124 Stat 2654 (2010). The key provisions on intelligence oversight from Title 50, U.S.C., currently read as follows:

Title 50, Chapter One — National Security
Subchapter III — Accountability for Intelligence Activities

§ 413. General Congressional oversight provisions

(a) Reports to Congressional committees of intelligence activities and anticipated activities

(1) The President shall ensure that the congressional intelligence committees are kept fully and currently informed of the intelligence activities of the United States, including any significant anticipated intelligence activity as required by this subchapter.

(2) Nothing in this subchapter shall be construed as requiring the approval of the congressional intelligence committees as a condition precedent to the initiation of any significant anticipated intelligence activity.

(b) Reports concerning illegal intelligence activities

The President shall ensure that any illegal intelligence activity is reported promptly to the congressional intelligence committees, as well as any corrective action that has been taken or is planned in connection with such illegal activity.

(c) Procedures for reporting information

The President and the congressional intelligence committees shall each establish such written procedures as may be necessary to carry out the provisions of this subchapter.

(d) Procedures to protect from unauthorized disclosure

The House of Representatives and the Senate shall each establish, by rule or resolution of such House, procedures to protect from unauthorized disclosure all classified information, and all information relating to intelligence sources and methods, that is furnished to the intelligence committees or to Members of Congress under this subchapter. Such procedures shall be established in consultation with the Director of National Intelligence. In accordance with such procedures, each of the congressional intelligence committees shall promptly call to the attention of its respective House, or to any appropriate committee or committees of its respective House, any matter relating to intelligence activities requiring the attention of such House or such committee or committees.

(e) Construction of authority conferred

Nothing in this Act shall be construed as authority to withhold information from the congressional intelligence committees on the grounds that providing the information to the intelligence committees would constitute the unauthorized disclosure of classified information or information relating to intelligence sources and methods.

(f) "Intelligence activities" defined

As used in this section, the term "intelligence activities" includes covert actions as defined in section 413b(e) of this title, and includes financial intelligence activities.

§413a. Reporting of congressional intelligence committees other than covert actions

(a) In general

To the extent consistent with due regard for the protection from unauthorized disclosure of classified information relating to sensitive intelligence sources and methods or other exceptionally sensitive matters, the Director of National Intelligence and the heads of all departments, agencies, and other entities of the United States Government involved in intelligence activities shall—

(1) keep the congressional intelligence committees fully and currently informed of all intelligence activities, other than a covert action (as defined in section 413b(e) of this title), which are the responsibility of, are engaged in by, or are carried out for or on behalf of, any department, agency, or entity of the United States Government, including any significant anticipated intelligence activity and any significant intelligence failure; and

(2) furnish the congressional intelligence committees any information or material concerning intelligence activities (including the legal basis under which the intelligence activity is being or was conducted), other than covert actions, which is within their custody or control, and which is requested by either of the congressional intelligence committees in order to carry out its authorized responsibilities.

(b) Form and contents of certain reports

Any report relating to a significant anticipated intelligence activity or a significant intelligence failure that is submitted to the congressional intelligence committees for purposes of subsection (a)(1) of this section shall be in writing, and shall contain the following:

(1) A concise statement of any facts pertinent to such report.

(2) An explanation of the significance of the intelligence activity or intelligence failure covered by such report.

(c) Standards and procedures for certain reports

The Director of National Intelligence, in consultation with the heads of the departments, agencies, and entities referred to in subsection (a) of this section, shall establish standards and procedures applicable to reports covered by subsection (b) of this section.

§ 413b. Presidential approval and reporting of covert actions

(a) Presidential findings

The President may not authorize the conduct of a covert action by departments, agencies, or entities of the United States Government unless the President determines such an action is necessary to support identifiable foreign policy objectives of the United States and is important to the national security of the United States, which determination shall be set forth in a finding that shall meet each of the following conditions:

(1) Each finding shall be in writing, unless immediate action by the United States is required and time does not permit the preparation of a written finding, in which case a written record of the President's decision shall be contemporaneously made and shall be reduced to a written finding as soon as possible but in no event more than 48 hours after the decision is made.

(2) Except as permitted by paragraph (1), a finding may not authorize or sanction a covert action, or any aspect of any such action, which already has occurred.

(3) Each finding shall specify each department, agency, or entity of the United States Government authorized to fund or otherwise participate in any significant way in such action. Any employee, contractor, or contract agent of a department, agency, or entity of the United States Government other than the Central Intelligence Agency directed to participate in any way in a covert action shall be subject either to the policies and regulations of the Central Intelligence Agency, or to written policies or regulations adopted by such department, agency, or entity, to govern such participation.

(4) Each finding shall specify whether it is contemplated that any third party which is not an element of, or a contractor or contract agent of, the United States Government, or is not otherwise subject to United States Government policies and regulations, will be used to fund or otherwise participate in any significant way in the covert action concerned, or be used to undertake the covert action concerned on behalf of the United States.

(5) A finding may not authorize any action that would violate the Constitution or any statute of the United States.

(b) Reports to congressional intelligence committees; production of information

To the extent consistent with due regard for the protection from unauthorized disclosure of classified information relating to sensitive intelligence sources and methods or other exceptionally sensitive matters, the Director of National Intelligence and the heads of all departments, agencies, and entities of the United States Government involved in a covert action—

(1) shall keep the congressional intelligence committees fully and currently informed of all covert actions which are the responsibility of, are engaged in by, or are carried out for or on behalf of, any department, agency, or entity of the United States Government, including significant failures; and

(2) shall furnish to the congressional intelligence committees any information or material concerning covert actions (including the legal basis under which the covert action is being or was conducted) which is in the possession, custody, or control of any department, agency, or entity of the United States Government and which is requested by either of the congressional intelligence committees in order to carry out its authorized responsibilities.

(c) Timing of reports; access to finding

(1) The President shall ensure that any finding approved pursuant to subsection (a) of this section shall be reported in writing to the congressional intelligence committees as soon as possible after such approval and before the initiation of the covert action authorized by the finding, except as otherwise provided in paragraph (2) and paragraph (3).

(2) If the President determines that it is essential to limit access to the finding to meet extraordinary circumstances affecting vital interests of the United States, the finding may be reported to the chairmen and ranking minority members of the congressional intelligence committees, the Speaker and minority leader of the House of Representatives, the majority and minority leaders of the Senate, and such other member or members of the congressional leadership as may be included by the President.

(3) Whenever a finding is not reported pursuant to paragraph (1) or (2) of this section, the President shall fully inform the congressional intelligence committees in a timely fashion and shall provide a statement of the reasons for not giving prior notice.

(4) In a case under paragraph (1), (2), or (3), a copy of the finding, signed by the President, shall be provided to the chairman of each congressional intelligence committee.

(5)(A) When access to a finding or a notification provided under subsection (d)(1) is limited to the Members of Congress specified in paragraph (2), a written statement of the reasons for limiting such access shall also be provided.

(B) Not later than 180 days after a statement of reasons is submitted in accordance with subparagraph (A) or this subparagraph, the President shall ensure that—(i) all members of the congressional intelligence committees are provided access to the finding or notification; or (ii) a statement of reasons that it is essential to continue to limit access to such finding or such notification to meet extraordinary circumstances affecting vital interests of the United States is submitted to the Members of Congress specified in paragraph (2).

(d) Changes in previously approved actions

(1) The President shall ensure that the congressional intelligence committees, or, if applicable, the Members of Congress specified in subsection (c) (2) of this section, are notified in writing of any significant change in a previously approved covert action, or any significant undertaking pursuant to a previously approved finding, in the same manner as findings are reported pursuant to subsection (c) of this section.

(2) In determining whether an activity constitutes a significant undertaking for purposes of paragraph (1), the President shall consider whether the activity — (A) involves significant risk of loss of life; (B) requires an expansion of existing authorities, including authorities relating to research, development, or operations; (C) results in the expenditure of significant funds or other resources; (D) requires notification under section 504; (E) gives rise to a significant risk of disclosing intelligence sources or methods; or (F) presents a reasonably foreseeable risk of serious damage to the diplomatic relations of the United States if such activity were disclosed without authorization.

(e) "Covert action" defined

As used in this subchapter, the term "covert action" means an activity or activities of the United States Government to influence political, economic, or military conditions abroad, where it is intended that the role of the United States Government will not be apparent or acknowledged publicly, but does not include —

(1) activities the primary purpose of which is to acquire intelligence, traditional counterintelligence activities, traditional activities to improve or maintain the operational security of United States Government programs, or administrative activities;

(2) traditional diplomatic or military activities or routine support to such activities;

(3) traditional law enforcement activities conducted by United States Government law enforcement agencies or routine support to such activities; or

(4) activities to provide routine support to the overt activities (other than activities described in paragraph (1), (2), or (3)) of other United States Government agencies abroad.

(f) Prohibition on covert actions intended to influence United States political processes, etc.

No covert action may be conducted which is intended to influence United States political processes, public opinion, policies, or media.

(g)(1) In any case where access to a finding reported under subsection (c) or notification provided under subsection (d)(1) is not made available to all members of a congressional intelligence committee in accordance with subsection (c)(2), the President shall notify all members of such committee that such finding or such notification has been provided only to the members specified in subsection (c)(2).

(2) In any case where access to a finding reported under subsection (c) or notification provided under subsection (d)(1) is not made available to all members of a congressional intelligence committee in accordance with subsection (c)(2), the President shall provide to all members of such committee a general description regarding the finding or notification, as applicable, consistent with the reasons for not yet fully informing all members of such committee.

(3) The President shall maintain—(A) a record of the members of Congress to whom a finding is reported under subsection (c) or notification is provided under subsection (d)(1) and the date on which each member of Congress receives such finding or notification; and (B) each written statement provided under subsection (c)(5).

§ 414. Funding of intelligence activities

(a) Obligations and expenditures for intelligence or intelligence-related activity; prerequisites

Appropriated funds available to an congressional intelligence committees may be obligated or expended for an intelligence or intelligence-related activity only if—

(1) those funds were specifically authorized by the Congress for use for such activities; or

(2) in the case of funds from the Reserve for Contingencies of the Central Intelligence Agency and consistent with the provisions of section 413b of this title concerning any significant anticipated intelligence activity, the Director of the Central Intelligence Agency has notified the appropriate congressional committees of the intent to make such funds available for such activity; or

(3) in the case of funds specifically authorized by the Congress for a different activity—

(A) the activity to be funded is a higher priority intelligence or intelligence-related activity;

(B) the use of such funds for such activity supports an emergent need, improves program effectiveness, or increases efficiency; and

(C) the Director of National Intelligence, the Secretary of Defense, or the Attorney General, as appropriate, has notified the appropriate congressional committees of the intent to make such funds available for such activity;

(4) nothing in this subsection prohibits obligation or expenditure of funds available to an intelligence agency in accordance with sections 1535 and 1536 of Title 31.

(b) Activities denied funding by Congress

Funds available to an intelligence agency may not be made available for any intelligence or intelligence-related activity for which funds were denied by the Congress.

(c) Presidential finding required for expenditure of funds on covert action

No funds appropriated for, or otherwise available to, any department, agency, or entity of the United States Government may be expended, or may be directed to be expended, for any covert action, as defined in section 413b(e) of this title, unless and until a Presidential finding required by subsection (a) of section 413b of this title has been signed or otherwise issued in accordance with that subsection.

(d) Report to congressional committees required for expenditure of nonappropriated funds for intelligence activity

(1) Except as otherwise specifically provided by law, funds available to an intelligence agency that are not appropriated funds may be obligated or expended for an intelligence or intelligence-related activity only if those funds are used for activities reported to the appropriate congressional committees pursuant to procedures which identify—

(A) the types of activities for which nonappropriated funds may be expended; and

(B) the circumstances under which an activity must be reported as a significant anticipated intelligence activity before such funds can be expended.

(2) Procedures for purposes of paragraph (1) shall be jointly agreed upon by the congressional intelligence committees and, as appropriate, the Director of National Intelligence or the Secretary of Defense.

(e) Definitions

As used in this section—

(1) the term "intelligence agency" means any department, agency, or other entity of the United States involved in intelligence or intelligence-related activities;

(2) the term "appropriate congressional committees" means the Permanent Select Committee on Intelligence and the Committee on Appropriations of the House of Representatives and the Select Committee on Intelligence and the Committee on Appropriations of the Senate; and

(3) the term "specifically authorized by the Congress" means that—

(A) the activity and the amount of funds proposed to be used for that activity were identified in a formal budget request to the Congress, but funds shall be deemed to be specifically authorized for that activity only to the extent that the Congress both authorized the funds to be appropriated for that activity and appropriated the funds for that activity; or

(B) although the funds were not formally requested, the Congress both specifically authorized the appropriation of the funds for the activity and appropriated the funds for the activity.

---

1. *"Timely Notice" and Other Contentious Issues.* When President George H.W. Bush signed the FY1991 version of these provisions, a key point of interbranch contention was the meaning of "timely notice." In his signing statement, Bush reiterated his intention to comply with the Act as outlined in an October 30, 1989 letter he had sent to the then chair and ranking member of the Senate Intelligence Committee. That letter read, in part:

> I am aware of your concerns regarding the provision of notice to Congress of covert action and the December 17, 1986 opinion of the Office of Legal Counsel of the Department of Justice, with which you strongly disagree primarily because of the statement that "a number of factors combine to support the conclusion that the 'timely notice' language should be read to leave the President with virtually unfettered discretion to choose the right moment for making the required notification."

> I can assure you that I intend to provide notice to Congress of covert action in a fashion sensitive to these concerns. The statute requires prior notice or, when no prior notice is given, timely notice. I anticipate that in almost all instances, prior notice will be possible. In those rare instances where prior notice is not provided, I anticipate that notice will be provided within a few days. Any withholding beyond this period will be based upon my assertion of authorities granted this office by the Constitution.

Statement on Signing the Intelligence Authorization Act, Fiscal Year 1991, 27 WEEKLY COMP. PRES. DOC. 1137 (Aug. 14, 1991). Bush's statement addressed other points of tension as follows:

> Several provisions in the Act requiring the disclosure of certain information to the Congress raise constitutional concerns. These provisions cannot be construed to detract from the President's constitutional authority to withhold information the disclosure of which could significantly impair foreign relations, the national security, the deliberative processes of the Executive, or the performance of the Executive's constitutional duties.

> I believe that the Act's definition of "covert action" is unnecessary. In determining whether particular military activities constitute covert actions, I shall continue to bear in mind the historic missions of the Armed Forces to protect the United States and its interests, influence foreign capabilities and intentions, and conduct activities preparatory to the execution of operations.

Congress's conference report on the 1991 Act disputed what Members took to be President Bush's understanding of his constitutional prerogatives with regard to notice:

> In re-enacting the phrase "in a timely fashion," . . . it is the intent of the conferees that this provision be interpreted in a manner consistent with whatever authority the Constitution may provide. If the Constitution in fact provides the President authority to withhold notice of covert actions for longer periods, then the conferees' interpretation cannot be legally binding upon the President. In his letter to the committees, reprinted above, the President asserts that the Constitution, in his view, does provide such authority.
>
> Neither committee has ever accepted this assertion. The conferees recognize that this is a question that neither they nor the Congress itself can resolve. Congress cannot diminish by statute powers that are granted by the Constitution. Nor can either the legislative or executive branch authoritatively interpret the Constitution, which is the exclusive province of the judicial branch.
>
> Congress is, however, free to interpret the meaning of statutes which it enacts. While the conferees recognize that they cannot foreclose by statute the possibility that the President may assert a constitutional basis for withholding notice of covert actions for periods longer than "a few days," they believe that the President's stated intention to act under the "timely notice" requirement of existing law to make a notification "within a few days" is the appropriate manner to proceed under this provision, and is consistent with what the conferees believe is its meaning and intent.

Conference Report on H.R. 1455, 102d Cong., 1st Sess. 1990, 137 Cong. Rec. H5898, H5905 (daily ed. July 25, 1991).

2. *Assessing Congress's Handiwork — Constitutionality.* Do the provisions quoted above raise any constitutional concerns? Would an earlier proposal to require notification of covert actions within 48 hours of inception have exceeded Congress's powers?

3. *Assessing Congress's Handiwork — Efficacy.* On which issues would it appear that the elected branches have simply "agreed to disagree"? Despite these disagreements, the 1991 Act left some observers hopeful that the reforms would forestall future abuses. William E. Conner, *Reforming Oversight of Covert Actions After the Iran-Contra Affair: A Legislative History of the Intelligence Authorization Act for FY 1991*, 32 VA. J. INT'L L. 871 (1992).

In his article excerpted above, Professor Rascoff outlines a series of "structural obstacles" that he believes were foreordained to limit the effectiveness of the congressional Intelligence Committees as overseers:

> First, membership on the committees was term limited. As the 9/11 Commission Report observed, many intelligence committee members "believed

term limits prevent them from developing the necessary expertise to conduct effective oversight." Second, the purview of the committees was limited to the oversight of very specific aspects of intelligence practice, such as covert action undertaken by the Central Intelligence Agency ("CIA"). Third, to the extent that the committees also functioned as watchdogs on the lookout for abuse, the investigative powers they wielded would typically not be used until after alleged abusive practices were publicly revealed. As recent events amply demonstrate, committee members (regardless of party) are poorly incentivized to question intelligence practices that come close to the line of legality, if they do not cross it. Fourth, intelligence committees lack the budgeting authority that can provide oversight with teeth. Fifth, the committees lack robust staffing, putting them at a disadvantage in attempting to govern a vast and unwieldy intelligence arm, and what staff is on hand is frequently denied access to the most classified briefings. In addition to the evident limitations of these specialized committees, there is the larger problem that domestic intelligence oversight is furnished by a wide range of committees and subcommittees—a congressional mirror image of the fragmentation that exists within the intelligence community itself. According to a recent study, no fewer than seventeen committees have oversight responsibilities for intelligence matters. Although substantive overlap may have certain benefits, it tends to sap the vitality of the oversight function by diffusing responsibility.

Rascoff, *Domesticating Intelligence*, 83 S. CAL. L. REV. at 597–98. Do you agree with his diagnosis? Could these defects be remedied effectively? Professor Rascoff might have added yet one more problem—that the executive branch has long insisted that certain intelligence information not be shared with congressional staff, regardless of their level of security clearance. Professor Kathleen Clark argues that such insistence trammels on Congress's constitutional right to share information with staff when necessary for the effective execution of its functions, and that the intelligence committees should amend their rules to clarify the scope of that entitlement. Kathleen Clark, *Congress's Right to Counsel in Intelligence Oversight*, 2011 U. ILL. L. REV. 915 (2011). Do you agree? Why do you think Congress has acquiesced in the executive's demands?

4. *Leaving the Constitution as They Found It.* In reporting on the 2010 amendments, the Senate Intelligence Committee indicated:

The modifications to the notification provisions . . . are intended to clarify and improve certain specific and important elements of this practice, but should not be construed to be anything more than specific requirements that procedures, findings, and reasons be in writing, and information on legality be provided. The modifications contained in this section do not alter the fundamental compact between the Executive and Legislative branches with respect to national security oversight. Moreover, nothing in these provisions is intended to infringe on the President's constitutional authority in this area or on the constitutional authority of Congress to conduct oversight of U.S. intelligence activities. S. Rept. 111-223, 111th Cong., 2d Sess. 27 (2010).

2. Foreign Policy and Foreign Commerce

a. The International Emergency Economic Powers Act

Despite the Court's expansive reading in *Dames & Moore* of the International Emergency Economic Powers Act (IEEPA), IEEPA was enacted in 1977 to limit the broad emergency powers previously delegated to the President under the Trading with the Enemy Act (TWEA), § 301(1), 55 Stat. 838, 839–40 (1941). Prior to the amendment of the TWEA, that act conferred extensive powers on the President both in wartime and in "any other period of national emergency" that the President might declare. Congress repealed the peacetime powers delegated by the TWEA, Trading With the Enemy Act Amendments, Pub. L. No. 95-223, 91 Stat. 1625 (1977), and adopted the IEEPA in its place. The basic change enacted in the IEEPA was not in the range of powers delegated to the President, which was nearly identical in both acts, but rather a seeming change in the scope of the power delegated to declare national emergencies.[*] Congress authorized the declaration of a national emergency based only on "any unusual and extraordinary threat, which has its source in whole or substantial part outside the United States, to the national security, foreign policy, or the economy of the United States. . . ." 50 U.S.C. § 1701 (1982).

How much, however, did this statutory change really change the scope of presidential power? Consider in this connection a pre-IEEPA case concerning the President's peacetime TWEA powers, *United States v. Yoshida International, Inc.*, 526 F.2d 560 (C.C.P.A. 1975). Yoshida sought to invalidate an import duty surcharge imposed by President Nixon because of "an exceptionally severe and worsening balance of payments deficit" experienced by the U.S. in the summer of 1971. As described by the court:

> The gold reserve backing of the U.S. dollar had dropped from $17.8 billion in 1960 to less than $10.4 billion in June of 1971, reflecting a growing lack of confidence in the U.S. dollar abroad. Foreign exchange rates were being controlled by some of our major trading partners in such a way as to overvalue the U.S. dollar. That action, by stimulating U.S. imports and restraining U.S. exports, contributed substantially to the balance of payments deficit. As one

---

[*] A related effort to circumscribe the President's powers regarding national emergencies was the National Emergencies Act, Pub. L. No. 94-412, 90 Stat. 1255 (1976). That act prescribed procedures for the declaration of national emergencies, for their termination, and for presidential reporting to Congress in connection with national emergencies. To end the practice of declaring national emergencies of unjustifiably indefinite duration, Congress provided that any emergency not otherwise terminated would terminate one year after its declaration unless the President should "publish in the Federal Register and transmit to the Congress a notice stating that such emergency is to continue in effect" beyond its anniversary. 50 U.S.C. § 1622(d) (1982).

step in a program designed to meet the economic crisis, the President issued Proclamation 4074, which in relevant part stated:

WHEREAS, there has been a prolonged decline in the international monetary reserves of the United States, and our trade and international competitive position is seriously threatened and, as a result, our continued ability to assure our security could be impaired;

WHEREAS, the balance of payments position of the United States requires the imposition of a surcharge on dutiable imports;

A. I hereby declare a national emergency during which I call upon the public and private sector to make the efforts necessary to strengthen the international economic position of the United States.

B. (1) I hereby terminate in part for such period as may be necessary and modify prior Presidential Proclamations which carry out trade agreements insofar as such proclamations are inconsistent with . . . the terms of this Proclamation.

(2) Such proclamations are suspended only insofar as is required to assess a surcharge in the form of a supplemental duty amounting to 10 percent ad valorem. Such supplemental duty shall be imposed on all dutiable articles [with certain exceptions,] . . . .

526 F.2d at 567.

The court commenced its legal analysis with the following premise:

The people of the new United States, in adopting the Constitution, granted the power to "lay and collect duties" and to "regulate commerce" to the Congress, not to the Executive. U.S. Constitution, Art. I, Sec. 8, clauses 1 and 3. Nonetheless, . . . Congress, beginning as early as 1794 and continuing into 1974, has delegated the exercise of much of the power to regulate foreign commerce to the Executive. . . . It is nonetheless clear that no undelegated power to regulate *commerce*, or to set tariffs, inheres in the Presidency.

526 F.2d at 571–72. The court then concluded that no delegated power sufficient to sustain the Nixon proclamation could be found in either the Tariff Act of 1930, 19 U.S.C. § 1351(a)(6), or the Trade Expansion Act of 1962, 19 U.S.C. § 1885(b) (1982).

The court nonetheless upheld the proclamation as an exercise of "national emergency" power under the TWEA. Because the TWEA did not expressly limit the President's power to declare an emergency, the propriety of that declaration did not present a hard question. Would it present any harder a question under the IEEPA, which permits a declaration of emergency in the face of an "unusual and extraordinary threat, which has its source in whole or substantial part outside the United States, to . . . the economy of the United States . . . ?"

The more difficult question, the court believed, was:

whether Congress, having itself regulated imports by employing duties as a regulatory tool, and having delegated to the President, for use in national emergencies, the power to regulate imports, intended to permit the President to employ the same regulatory tool, and what, if any, limitations lay upon his use thereof.

526 F.2d at 574. The court concluded, however, that the language of the TWEA — which in this respect is identical to the language of the IEEPA — did not categorically prohibit the use of tariffs as a form of import "regulation," so long as the measure was facially a reasonable response to the emergency presented. Because the proclamation was so tailored, the court upheld it.

Again, does the IEEPA change the analysis? It seems unlikely that courts will relish an intense role in reviewing the President's determinations whether a national emergency exists or whether particular measures represent an appropriate response. Would the Nixon tariff surcharge fare any less well under the IEEPA than it did under the TWEA? If the IEEPA were not construed to permit a tariff surcharge as a response to a national economic emergency caused by foreign sources, would the President have any inherent article II authority to sustain his initiative under *Youngstown*?

b. Trade Expansion Act

Independent Gasoline Marketers Council v. Duncan
492 F. Supp. 614 (D.D.C. 1980)

AUBREY E. ROBINSON, JR., District Judge.

In these consolidated actions Plaintiffs Independent Gasoline Marketers Council, Inc. . . . and Marathon Oil Corporation, seek to enjoin [implementation of] the Petroleum Import Adjustment Program ("PIAP" or "the Program") proclaimed by the President of the United States in Proclamation 4744 (45 Fed. Reg. 22864; April 3, 1980), as amended. This Program was created as a result of the report to the President on March 14, 1979, by the Treasury Secretary, acting pursuant to Section 232(b) of the Trade Expansion Act of 1962 as amended (TEA), that oil was being imported into the United States "in such quantities and under such circumstances as to threaten to impair the national security." 44 Fed. Reg. 18818 (March 29, 1979). The investigation upon which this determination was founded had been initiated on March 15, 1978, by W. Michael Blumenthal, former Secretary of the Treasury, in the exercise of his authority under Section 232. Information and advice were solicited from the Secretary of Defense, the Secretary of Energy, the Secretary of State, the Secretary of Commerce, the Federal Reserve Board, the Central Intelligence Agency and other appropriate officers of the United States regarding the effects on national security of the imports of petroleum and petroleum products. Those matters specified in Section 232(c) of the TEA and other relevant factors were considered.

The Treasury Secretary found that the level of imported oil threatened our national security. He recommended that President Carter take action. The President's response was the enactment of the PIAP, which was implemented primarily to lower domestic gasoline consumption by raising the retail price of all gasoline by $.10 per gallon.

Its mechanism may be summarized as follows: Under the PIAP, a license fee would be imposed on imported crude oil and gasoline. The amount of the fee (presently estimated at $4.62 per barrel of crude oil and $4.35 per barrel of gasoline) would float, and would be determined by the effect of the fee on the retail price of gasoline. The PIAP would be terminated if and when Congress increases the present $.04 per gallon excise tax to $.14 per gallon.

In economic terms, the PIAP may best be viewed as a demand-side disincentive. [Ed. Note: That is, it lowers demand for a given good by artificially raising its price, instead of lowering the supply, as with a quota.] . . . The PIAP mechanism completely undermines this demand-side disincentive, however, by contemplating that the cost of the fee would eventually be paid by consumers of both domestic and imported gasoline. Thus, the imposition of the fee would not put imported oil at a competitive disadvantage with domestic oil, and the demand for imported oil would not decrease proportionately to domestic oil. Rather, the specific demand-side disincentive initially placed on imported oil is, under the PIAP, transformed into a generalized demand-side disincentive on the purchase of all gasoline.

Because of the displacement of the initial import fee onto both domestic and imported oil, and the nature of the fee itself, the PIAP could not act as a disincentive to reduce imports. . . . Rather than attempt to directly decrease the amount of oil imported into the United States, the PIAP attempts to decrease the total amount of oil consumed, and therefore could have only a collateral effect on the retailing of foreign oil.

Under Section 232 of the Trade Expansion Act, 19 U.S.C. § 1862(b), if the Secretary of Commerce [Ed. Note: or, prior to 1980, the Treasury Secretary] has found after an appropriate investigation that imports of an article "threaten to impair the national security," the President is authorized to "take such action, and for such time, as he deems necessary to adjust the imports of such article" so as to lessen the threat to national security. Defendants argue that the TEA standing alone authorizes the Petroleum Import Adjustment Program. They contend first that Section 232 empowers the President to impose license fees as he has done in the PIAP. They argue further that the TEA gives the President authority to channel the impact of that fee to gasoline sales because doing so will (a) enable the program to have the desired effect on imports and (b) equitably distribute the burden of the program throughout the nation.

In *FEA v. Algonquin, SNG, Inc.*, 426 U.S. 548 (1976), the Supreme Court held that Section 232 authorizes the President to impose a system of license fees as a means of controlling imports. In that case, respondents had argued that the section empowers the President to control imports only by imposing "direct" controls such as quotas and not through the use of license fees. In holding to the contrary, the Court found that the statute authorizes not only quantitative restraints that affect the supply of imported goods, but also monetary measures, such as license fees, that control imports by affecting demand. The Court noted that a license fee itself "as much as a quota has its initial and direct impact on imports, albeit on their price as opposed to their quantity." Although concluding that the statute authorizes a license fee, the Court cautioned that its conclusion does not mean that "*any* action the President might take, as long as it has even a remote impact on imports, is also so authorized."

Algonquin is not dispositive of the instant action. The import fee approved by the Supreme Court in that case directly affected the price of imported oil relative to domestic oil. Standing alone, the import fee component of the PIAP would have a similar effect. In the context of the PIAP mechanism as a whole, however, the import fee has no "initial and direct impact on imports" similar to that of the fee approved in *Algonquin*. Nor is it intended to have such a result. . . . No monetary burden is imposed on imported oil that is not imposed on domestic oil. . . . Any impact on imports will be indirect and will result from the general gasoline conservation fee, not from the initial import fee.

To determine whether the Trade Expansion Act authorizes the PIAP, the Court must look to the design of the program as a whole. Analysis of the manner in which PIAP would function belies Defendants' contention that it is structured to lower demand for imported oil in particular rather than demand for oil generally. Two aspects of the program undercut Defendants' argument. First, . . . the initial import fee is completely offset by [PIAP's pricing] mechanism. Second, assuming a stable level of domestic oil production, the per barrel import fee would decrease if the level of imports rose. The rationale underlying PIAP thus reduces to the contention that TEA empowers the President to impose a $.10 per gallon "conservation fee" on all gasoline so as to lower demand for the product. The TEA provides no such authority.

TEA does not authorize the President to impose general controls on domestically produced goods either through a monetary mechanism or through a quantitative device. The statute provides for regulation of imports. A regulation on imports may incidentally regulate domestic goods. The regulation of domestic oil contemplated by PIAP, however, is not incidental to regulation of imported oil. Rather, it is a primary purpose of the program, and is essential to the goal of reducing demand for all gasoline regardless of its source. Moreover, the impact of the oil conservation fee is greater on domestically produced oil than on imported oil since the former comprises roughly sixty (60) per cent of all crude oil utilized today, and Defendants acknowledge that the PIAP's effect on import levels will be slight.

In *Algonquin*, the Supreme Court indicated that TEA does not authorize "any action the President might take, as long as it has even a remote impact on imports." Any possible benefits of the PIAP on levels of oil imports are far too remote and indirect for the TEA alone to support the program. The remoteness of the program's effect on imports is apparent from three factors. First, the quantitative impact of the program on import levels will admittedly be slight. Second, the program imposes broad controls on domestic goods to achieve that slight impact. Third, Congress has thus far denied the President authority to reduce gasoline consumption through a gasoline conservation levy. PIAP is an attempt to circumvent that stumbling block in the guise of an import control measure. TEA alone does not sanction this attempt to exercise authority that has been deliberately withheld from the President by the Congress.

[The court next rejected government arguments that any portions of the PIAP not authorized by the TEA were sustainable under the Emergency Petroleum Allocation Act (EPAA), 15 U.S.C. § 751, et seq. Whether or not the EPAA could authorize such a program, the President had not complied with the prescribed procedures for invoking EPAA authority.]

Defendants finally contend that, because of the national security aspects presented by this nation's consumption of imported oil, the President has authority, independent of Congress, to impose a gasoline conservation fee. The extent of the "inherent" nature of Presidential power was delineated by the Supreme Court in *Youngstown Sheet & Tube Co. v. Sawyer*, 343 U.S. 579 (1952). [The court quoted Justice Black's passage emphasizing the vesting of lawmaking powers in Congress.] It is clear that Congress, not the President, must decide whether the imposition of a gasoline conservation fee is good policy.

On this issue, Congress has already spoken. The Energy Policy and Conservation Act, (EPCA) 42 U.S.C. § 6201, et seq., gives the President the authority to prescribe a "plan which imposes reasonable restrictions on the public or private use of energy which are necessary to reduce energy consumption." 42 U.S.C. § 6262(a)(1). Section 202 of that Act provides that

(2) An energy conservation contingency plan under this section may not

(A) impose rationing or any tax, tariff, or user fee;

(B) contain any provision respecting the price of petroleum products. . . .

42 U.S.C. § 6262(a)(2). Congress has thus precluded the use of demand-side disincentives to lower overall gasoline consumption. It is imperative to note that the EPCA is not effective until the President has found the existence of a severe energy supply interruption. 42 U.S.C. § 6261(b). Thus, even in times of severe energy supply interruptions, the President may not use monetary measures to decrease demand. The imposition of the gasoline conservation fee is contrary to manifest Congressional intent.

The gasoline conservation fee at issue in the instant litigation does not fall within the inherent powers of the President, is not sanctioned by the statutes cited by Defendants, and is contrary to manifest Congressional intent. The Court has no choice but to grant Plaintiffs the relief they seek.

———————

1. *What Did President Carter Do Wrong?* Did the *Independent Gasoline Marketers Council* court improperly confuse questions as to the scope of power delegated by the TEA and questions whether the President properly implemented those powers that were delegated? Consider this critique:

The court's opinion . . . did not articulate the standard of review it was applying to factual judgments about the likely effect of the program on imports, which the court correctly regarded as vital to the legality of the program under the TEA. Because the year-old Treasury report had recommended no particular action, it did not provide support for the intended effects of the President's program. To fill the gap in the record, the Government filed an affidavit by Secretary of Energy Duncan, which argued that the program would "maximize the conservation effect and the reduction of imports" resulting from the initial fee on imported oil. Secretary Duncan appended a copy of a brief memorandum he and Treasury Secretary Miller had sent the President formally recommending adoption of the program on grounds that it would reduce gasoline consumption, "thereby reducing the level of oil imports." The court cited neither document and, in the end, apparently simply disagreed with the President's judgment.

Finally, the court found that the President's action contravened a statute forbidding the imposition of fees on gasoline as part of contingency plans for conservation in case of supply disruptions.[243] The court viewed the President's program as "an attempt to circumvent" this restriction on his authority "in the guise of an import control measure."[244]

The court's analysis was flawed. It should first have decided whether the President's action would have been legal if it had produced the effects claimed for it, or whether it exceeded his statutory authority on its face. If the court were prepared to conclude that the President's program was in conflict with the statutory limitation on his authority to include fees on gasoline in contingency plans, it should have rested its holding squarely on that provision. The resulting precedent would have had minimal effect on the President's import authority under the TEA. Instead, the court confused its determination of the extent of the President's statutory authority with its review of the factual basis for his action in a fashion that led to creation of an unnecessarily narrow statutory precedent. The court should have relied on the Government's affidavits for the purpose of elaborating the President's rationale that a fee applied to retail sales of all gasoline would reduce imports, and it should have deferred to that judgment if the Government could have supported the order's rationality on the administrative record.

Harold H. Bruff, *Judicial Review and the President's Statutory Powers*, 68 VA. L. REV. 1, 54–55 (1982).

---

243. Energy Policy and Conservation Act, 42 U.S.C. §§ 6201–6422 (Supp. III 1979).

244. 492 F. Supp. at 618. The Government subsequently appealed; Congress responded with legislation, passed over the President's veto, specifically repealing the program. 126 Cong. Rec. S6376–87 (daily ed. June 6, 1980); 126 Cong. Rec. H4600–02 (daily ed. June 5, 1980).

2. *Presidential Authority Over Foreign Investment.* For another important example of presidential statutory authority in the field of foreign commerce, see the Omnibus Trade and Competitiveness Act of 1988, 19 U.S.C. § 2901 et seq., authorizing the President to suspend or prohibit mergers, acquisitions, or takeovers that would result in foreign control of U.S. corporations, where such control would threaten to impair national security. *See* Patrick DeSouza, *Executive Discretion to Regulate Foreign Investment in the United States,* 7 J.L. & Pol. 289 (1991).

3. Immigration and Foreign Policy

Yet another area of congressional federal authority with obvious ramifications for our foreign policy concerns the regulation of immigration. The full import of immigration law for foreign affairs could only be assessed in a work as long as this entire book. For the sake of completeness, however, at least some mention of the foreign affairs aspects of immigration law is warranted. For a comprehensive review of American immigration law, see T. Alexander Aleinikoff, David A. Martin, Hiroshi Motomura, Maryellen Fullerton & Juliet P. Stumpf, Immigration and Citizenship: Process and Policy (8th ed. 2016). For an outstanding review of the separation of powers issues lurking in this area, see Adam B. Cox and Cristina M. Rodríguez, *The President and Immigration Law,* 119 Yale L. J. 458 (2009).

There remains, however, considerable doctrinal ambiguity about the locus of constitutional authority to control immigration. As explained by Professors Cox and Rodríguez:

> The courts have never precisely delineated the relative powers of the political branches over immigration regulation. . . . Though the Court forged the plenary power doctrine [sharply limiting judicial scrutiny of immigration rules adopted by the political branches] in the late nineteenth century, the jurisprudential separation-of-powers story is largely a twentieth-century one, not only because complex congressionally driven immigration regulation did not really begin until the 1890s, but also because the expansion of the administrative state in the twentieth century changed the separation-of-powers terrain. In broad outlines, in the formative period of U.S. immigration law in the 1890s, the Court treated the regulatory authority of the political branches as largely interchangeable, eliding important questions about the distribution of authority between the branches, but occasionally alluding to an inherent executive power to implement sovereign prerogatives. Over time, as Congress increasingly engaged in immigration regulation, the Court more frequently emphasized the legitimacy conferred on executive actions by congressional authorization. Nonetheless, hints of inherent executive authority persisted in the Court's reasoning. The Court's treatment of the interbranch relationship ultimately has been too thin and confused to provide definitive answers to the separation-of-powers question we pose. But the jurisprudential

history at least suggests that conceptions of inherent and delegated authority have both shaped the way in which the Court has characterized the relationship between the political branches.

119 YALE L. J., at 465–66. The following case remains a leading example:

United States ex rel. Knauff v. Shaughnessy
338 U.S. 537 (1950)

JUSTICE MINTON delivered the opinion of the Court.

May the United States exclude without hearing, solely upon a finding by the Attorney General that her admission would be prejudicial to the interests of the United
States, the alien wife of a citizen who had served honorably in the armed forces of
the United States during World War II?

On August 14, 1948, petitioner sought to enter the United States to be naturalized. On that day, she was temporarily excluded from the United States and detained
at Ellis Island. On October 6, 1948, the Assistant Commissioner of Immigration and
Naturalization recommended that she be permanently excluded without a hearing
on the ground that her admission would be prejudicial to the interests of the United
States. On the same day, the Attorney General adopted this recommendation and
entered a final order of exclusion.

The authority of the Attorney General to order the exclusion of aliens without
a hearing flows from [an Act of Congress providing] that the President might,
upon finding that the interests of the United States required it, impose additional
restrictions and prohibitions on the entry into and departure of persons from the
United States during the national emergency proclaimed May 27, 1941. Pursuant to
this Act of Congress, the President issued Proclamation 2523, and authorized the
promulgation of regulations jointly by the Secretary of State and the Attorney General. It was also provided that no alien should be permitted to enter the United
States if it were found that such entry would be prejudicial to the interest of the
United States.

Pursuant to the authority of this proclamation, the Secretary of State and the
Attorney General issued regulations specif[ying] the classes of aliens whose entry into
the United States was deemed prejudicial to the public interest [and] provid[ing] that
the Attorney General might deny an alien a hearing before a board of inquiry in special cases where he determined that the alien was excludable under the regulations
on the basis of information of a confidential nature, the disclosure of which would
be prejudicial to the public interest.

At the outset, we wish to point out that an alien who seeks admission to this country may not do so under any claim of right. Admission of aliens to the United States
is a privilege granted by the sovereign United States Government. Such privilege is
granted to an alien only upon such terms as the United States shall prescribe. It must
be exercised in accordance with the procedure which the United States provides.

Petitioner contends that the 1941 Act and the regulations thereunder are void to the extent that they contain unconstitutional delegations of legislative power. But there is no question of inappropriate delegation of legislative power involved here. The exclusion of aliens is a fundamental act of sovereignty. The right to do so stems not alone from legislative power, but is inherent in the executive power to control the foreign affairs of the nation. *United States v. Curtiss-Wright Export Corp.,* 299 U. S. 304. When Congress prescribes a procedure concerning the admissibility of aliens, it is not dealing alone with a legislative power. It is implementing an inherent executive power.

Thus, the decision to admit or to exclude an alien may be lawfully placed with the President, who may, in turn, delegate the carrying out of this function to a responsible executive officer of the sovereign, such as the Attorney General. The action of the executive officer under such authority is final and conclusive. Whatever the rule may be concerning deportation of persons who have gained entry into the United States, it is not within the province of any court, unless expressly authorized by law, to review the determination of the political branch of the Government to exclude a given alien.

Whatever the procedure authorized by Congress is, it is due process as far as an alien denied entry is concerned.

We find no substantial merit to petitioner's contention that the regulations were not "reasonable," as they were required to be by the 1941 Act. We think them reasonable in the circumstances of the period for which they were authorized, namely, the national emergency of World War II. However, 22 U.S.C. §§ 223 authorizes these special restrictions on the entry of aliens only when the United States is at war or during the existence of the national emergency proclaimed May 27, 1941. For ordinary times, Congress has provided aliens with a hearing. And the contention of petitioner is that she is entitled to the statutory hearing because, for purposes of the War Brides Act, within which she comes, the war terminated when the President proclaimed the cessation of hostilities. She contends that the War Brides Act, applicable portions of which are set out in the margin, discloses a congressional intent that special restrictions on the entry of aliens should cease to apply to war brides upon the cessation of hostilities. [The War Brides Act states:

> "That, notwithstanding any of the several clauses of section 3 of the Act of February 5, 1917, excluding physically and mentally defective aliens, and notwithstanding the documentary requirements of any of the immigration laws or regulations, Executive orders, or Presidential proclamations issued thereunder, alien spouses or alien children of United States citizens serving in, or having an honorable discharge certificate from the armed forces of the United States during the Second World War shall, if otherwise admissible under the immigration laws and if application for admission is made within three years of the effective date of this Act, be admitted to the United States. . . ."]

The War Brides Act provides that World War II is the period from December 7, 1941, until the proclaimed termination of hostilities. This has nothing to do with the period for which the regulations here acted under were authorized. The beginning and end of the war are defined by the War Brides Act, we assume, for the purpose of ascertaining the period within which citizens must have served in the armed forces in order for their spouses and children to be entitled to the benefits of the Act. The special procedure followed in this case was authorized not only during the period of actual hostilities, but during the entire war and the national emergency proclaimed May 27, 1941. The national emergency has never been terminated. Indeed, a state of war still exists. Thus, the authority upon which the Attorney General acted remains in force.

There is nothing in the War Brides Act or its legislative history to indicate that it was the purpose of Congress, by partially suspending compliance with certain requirements and the quota provisions of the immigration laws, to relax the security provisions of the immigration laws. There is no indication that Congress intended to permit members or former members of the armed forces to marry and bring into the United States aliens who the President, acting through the Attorney General in the performance of his sworn duty, found should be denied entry for security reasons. As all other aliens, petitioner had to stand the test of security. This she failed to meet.

JUSTICE DOUGLAS and JUSTICE CLARK took no part in the consideration or decision of this case.

JUSTICE JACKSON, whom JUSTICE BLACK and JUSTICE FRANKFURTER join, dissenting.

I do not question the constitutional power of Congress to authorize immigration authorities to turn back from our gates any alien or class of aliens. But I do not find that Congress has authorized an abrupt and brutal exclusion of the wife of an American citizen without a hearing.

Congress held out a promise of liberalized admission to alien brides, taken unto themselves by men serving in or honorably discharged from our armed services abroad, as the Act, set forth in the Court's opinion, indicates. The petitioning husband is honorably discharged, and remained in Germany as a civilian employee. Our military authorities abroad required their permission before marriage. The Army in Germany is not without a vigilant and security-conscious intelligence service. This woman was employed by our European Command, and her record is not only without blemish, but is highly praised by her superiors. The marriage of this alien woman to this veteran was approved by the Commanding General at Frankfurt-on-Main.

Now this American citizen is told he cannot bring his wife to the United States, but he will not be told why.

He must abandon his bride to live in his own country or forsake his country to live with his bride.

So he went to court and sought a writ of habeas corpus, which we never tire of citing to Europe as the unanswerable evidence that our free country permits no arbitrary official detention. And the Government tells the Court that not even a court can find out why the girl is excluded. But it says we must find that Congress authorized this treatment of war brides, and, even if we cannot get any reasons for it, we must say it is legal; security requires it.

Security is like liberty, in that many are the crimes committed in its name. The menace to the security of this country, be it great as it may, from this girl's admission is as nothing compared to the menace to free institutions inherent in procedures of this pattern. In the name of security, the police state justifies its arbitrary oppressions on evidence that is secret, because security might be prejudiced if it were brought to light in hearings. The plea that evidence of guilt must be secret is abhorrent to free men, because it provides a cloak for the malevolent, the misinformed, the meddlesome, and the corrupt to play the role of informer undetected and uncorrected.

I am sure the officials here have acted from a sense of duty, with full belief in their lawful power, and no doubt upon information which, if it stood the test of trial, would justify the order of exclusion. But not even they know whether it would stand this test. And anyway, as I have said before, personal confidence in the officials involved does not excuse a judge for sanctioning a procedure that is dangerously wrong in principle.

Congress will have to use more explicit language than any yet cited before I will agree that it has authorized an administrative officer to break up the family of an American citizen or force him to keep his wife by becoming an exile. Likewise, it will have to be much more explicit before I can agree that it authorized a finding of serious misconduct against the wife of an American citizen without notice of charges, evidence of guilt and a chance to meet it.

I should direct the Attorney General either to produce his evidence justifying exclusion or to admit Mrs. Knauff to the country.

---

1. *She Persisted*. Ellen Knauff was not the "girl" being passively imported as a war bride that Justice Jackson's opinion portrays. She tells the story of her remarkable life in her autobiography. ELLEN KNAUFF, THE ELLEN KNAUFF STORY (1952). Her cause was taken up by members of Congress and in newspapers across the country. Eventually, the political pressure forced the Attorney General to authorize a hearing before the Board of Immigration Appeals. The basis for her exclusion turns out to have been a charge that she engaged in espionage for Czechoslovakia while working as a civilian employee of the U.S. Army's Civil Censorship Division in occupied Germany. Knauff and her attorneys were able to prove that she had not provided secret information to Czechoslovakia. (Indeed, the Civil Censorship Division did not handle secret information.) The BIA ordered Knauff admitted to the United States for permanent residence. See Charles D. Weisselberg, *The Exclusion and Detention of Aliens: Lessons from the Lives of Ellen Knauff and Ignatz Mezei*, 143 U. PENN. L. REV. 933, 958–964 (1995). What does this say about the need for deference in the immigration context?

2. *Deferential Review of Final Decisions. Knauff* involved a challenge to the process established by the statute and implementing regulations. The Court is even more deferential when the challenge is to a determination made under these procedures to an individual determination. If, in such a case, the determination is made "on the basis of a facially legitimate and bona fide reason, the courts will [not] look behind the exercise of that discretion." *Kleindienst v. Mandel*, 408 U.S. 753 (1972).

3. *Is* Knauff *Still Good Law?* Justice Minton's opinion for the Court makes some sweeping claims about executive authority, particularly that "[t]he exclusion of aliens is a fundamental act of sovereignty. The right to do so stems not alone from legislative power, but is inherent in the executive power to control the foreign affairs of the nation." Not surprisingly, his cite for the proposition is *Curtiss-Wright.* But the Supreme Court has repudiated *Curtiss-Wright*'s extravagant claims of executive authority in *Zivotofsky v. Clinton, supra.* The Court has not had occasion to consider the consequences of its repudiation of *Curtiss-Wright* for immigration law, though President Trump's executive orders on immigration (which we discuss below) could provide an opportunity to do just that. If we remove the *Curtiss-Wright* strand of the Court's reasoning, the case becomes a standard application of the framework Justice Jackson set forth two years later in his *Steel Seizure* concurrence. The question is in which category to place the executive action (exclusion without a hearing). Justice Minton, for the Court, places it in Category One as authorized by the statute allowing the President to exclude aliens. Justice Jackson sees it as prohibited by the War Brides Act. Who has the better argument?

4. *De Facto Delegated Authority. Knauff* demonstrates the judiciary's inclination to rely on both inherent executive authority and on delegated statutory authority and broadly to defer to the actions of the executive branch on these grounds. An additional source of authority is what Professors Cox and Rodríguez call "de facto delegated authority." The last phenomenon results from the convergence of two realities: congressional enactment of detailed and highly stringent immigration rules, and the existence of an unauthorized population in the United States that is simply much too large to make universal enforcement practicable. This combination of factors "functionally gives the President the power to exert control over the number and types of immigrants inside the United States." 119 YALE L.J. at 463. This is the context in which President Obama, as had Presidents Reagan and George H.W. Bush before him, exercised authority to defer immigration enforcement action against large classes of undocumented aliens. (We discuss that action in detail in connection with the President's authority to decline to enforce the law *supra* in Chapter Four.)

Note: The Trump Executive Orders on Immigration

As a candidate for President, Donald Trump channeled the backlash against immigration. He famously promised to build a wall along the length of the border with Mexico, to implement mass deportation of undocumented aliens, to put an end to "sanctuary cities," and to establish a "Muslim ban." As President, Donald Trump has taken steps toward fulfilling each of these promises. The wall remains a matter of negotiation with Congress. President Trump has declared that all undocumented aliens are subject to deportation and has rescinded the status that President Obama's immigration deferrals had conferred on many such aliens. Within days of taking office, President Trump issued an executive order implementing a travel ban that prohibited, at least temporarily, citizens of seven majority-Muslim nations to travel to the United States and another executive order declaring sanctuary cities ineligible to receive federal grants. These executive orders were immediately challenged in court.

The Travel Ban Order(s)

On January 27, 2017, one week after assuming office, President Trump issued Executive Order 13769, entitled "Protecting the Nation from Foreign Terrorist Entry into the United States." As is usual, the order began by identifying, in general terms, the source of the President's authority to issue it. The Order followed the standard template and declared that it was issued "[b]y the authority vested in me as President by the Constitution and laws of the United States of America, including the Immigration and Nationality Act (INA), 8 U.S.C. 1101 et seq., and section 301 of title 3, United States Code." The section of the INA cited included the authority cited by the executive branch above in *Knauff* to exclude anyone whose admission the President or his delegee determines would be detrimental to the interests of the United States. Section 1 set forth the purpose of the order:

> Numerous foreign-born individuals have been convicted or implicated in terrorism-related crimes since September 11, 2001, including foreign nationals who entered the United States after receiving visitor, student, or employment visas, or who entered through the United States refugee resettlement program. Deteriorating conditions in certain countries due to war, strife, disaster, and civil unrest increase the likelihood that terrorists will use any means possible to enter the United States. The United States must be vigilant during the visa-issuance process to ensure that those approved for admission do not intend to harm Americans and that they have no ties to terrorism.

The Order directed the Secretaries of State and Homeland Security to undertake a review of screening procedures as well as the security situation in a number of foreign nations. Pending that review, the Order imposed a number of changes on the process and eligibility for entry of non-citizens into the United States. Section 3(c) suspended for 90 days the entry of any citizen or national of Iran, Iraq, Libya, Somalia, Sudan, Syria, or Yemen. Section 5(a) suspended for 120 days the admission of refugees through the United States Refugee Admissions Program. The Order, in section 5(b), provided that when USRAP resumes, the Secretaries should "prioritize refugee claims made by individuals on the basis of religious-based persecution, provided that the religion of the individual is a minority religion in the individual's country of nationality." The Order also barred indefinitely the entry of all refugees from Syria. *Id.* 5(c). The Order authorized the Secretaries to make case-by-case exceptions to the travel ban where entry of an alien would serve the national interest. The Order specifies that an exception would be in the national interest if the alien seeking entry "is a religious minority in his country of nationality facing religious persecution." 82 Fed. Reg. 8979.

The Order took effect immediately. It is fair to characterize the enforcement of the Order as chaotic. It was not immediately clear, for example, whether the order applied to lawful permanent resident aliens of the United States whose citizenship was with one of the seven listed countries. It was also unclear whether the Order was supposed to apply to those traveling to the United States whose flight was en route while the order was issued or who landed before the Order was issued but who had not yet cleared customs. Initially, the Order was applied to exclude each of these categories of travelers, leaving hundreds of foreign nationals stranded and detained at United States airports.

Dozens of suits were brought seeking to enjoin enforcement of the travel ban. One judge refused to issue a temporary restraining order. *See Louhghalam v. Trump*, 17-10154-NMG (D. Ma. Feb. 3, 2017). But virtually every other court ruled against the executive branch, with a nation-wide restraining order issued in *Washington v. Trump*, No. C17-0141-JLR (W.D. Wa., Feb. 3, 2017), *aff'd* No. 17-35105 (9th Cir. Feb 7, 2017). The Ninth Circuit's opinion upholding the restraining order summarizes the legal issues the Executive Order raised:

Due Process

The Fifth Amendment of the Constitution prohibits the Government from depriving individuals of their "life, liberty, or property, without due process of law." U.S. Const. amend. V. The Government may not deprive a person of one of these protected interests without providing "notice and an opportunity to respond," or, in other words, the opportunity to present reasons not to proceed with the deprivation and have them considered.

The Government has not shown that the Executive Order provides what due process requires, such as notice and a hearing prior to restricting an individual's ability to travel. Indeed, the Government does not contend that the Executive Order provides for such process. Rather, in addition to the arguments addressed in other parts of this opinion, the Government argues that most or all of the individuals affected by the Executive Order have no rights under the Due Process Clause.

The procedural protections provided by the Fifth Amendment's Due Process Clause are not limited to citizens. Rather, they "appl[y] to all 'persons' within the United States, including aliens," regardless of "whether their presence here is lawful, unlawful, temporary, or permanent." Zadvydas v. Davis, 533 U.S. 678, 693 (2001). These rights also apply to certain aliens attempting to reenter the United States after travelling abroad. Landon v. Plasencia, 459 U.S. 21, 33–34 (1982). The Government has provided no affirmative argument showing that the States' procedural due process claims fail as to these categories of aliens.

For example, the Government has failed to establish that lawful permanent residents have no due process rights when seeking to re-enter the United States. Nor has the Government established that the Executive Order provides lawful permanent residents with constitutionally sufficient process to challenge their denial of re-entry.

Even if the claims based on the due process rights of lawful permanent residents were no longer part of this case, the States would continue to have potential claims regarding possible due process rights of other persons who are in the United States, even if unlawfully, see Zadvydas, 533 U.S. 693; non-immigrant visaholders who have been in the United States but temporarily departed or wish to temporarily depart, and applicants who have a relationship with a U.S. resident or an institution that might have rights of its own to assert. Accordingly, the Government has not demonstrated that the States lack viable claims based on the due process rights of persons who will suffer injuries to protected interests due to the Executive Order.

Religious Discrimination

The First Amendment prohibits any "law respecting an establishment of religion." U.S. Const. amend. I. A law that has a religious, not secular, purpose violates that clause, as does one that "officially prefer[s] [one religious denomination] over another," Larson v. Valente, 456 U.S. 228, 244 (1982). The States argue that the Executive Order violates the Establishment and Equal Protection Clauses because it was intended to disfavor Muslims. In support of this argument, the States have offered evidence of numerous statements by the President about his intent to implement a "Muslim ban" as well as evidence they claim suggests that the Executive Order was intended to be that ban, including sections 5(b) and 5(e) of the Order. The States' claims raise serious allegations and present significant constitutional questions. In light of the sensitive interests involved, the pace of the current emergency proceedings, and our conclusion that the Government has not met its burden of showing likelihood of success on appeal on its arguments with respect to the due process claim, we reserve consideration of these claims until the merits of this appeal have been fully briefed.

Washington v. Trump, No. 17-35105 (9th Cir., Feb. 7, 2017).

President Trump issued a revised travel ban, Executive Order No. 13780, on March 6, 2017. The revised Order was designed to avoid at least some of the legal difficulties encountered by the original version. The revision deleted Iraq from the list of countries whose nationals would be temporarily barred from traveling to the United States, clarified that it does not apply to legal permanent residents, and eliminated any reference to religion (particularly eliminating any reference to religious-minority status as a basis for granting a case-by-case waiver of the ban). On March 15, 2017, District Judge Derrick Watson issued a nation-wide Temporary Restraining Order enjoining enforcement of the revised Order. *See Hawaii v. Trump*, No. 17-00050 DKW-KSC (D. Hi., Mar. 15, 2017), *aff'd*, ___ F. 3d ___, 2017 WL 2529640 (9th Cir. 2017) (per curiam). Judge Watson ruled that despite the revisions the plaintiffs were likely to succeed on the merits of their Establishment Clause claim because the revised order was motivated by anti-Muslim animus:

> Because a reasonable, objective observer—enlightened by the specific historical context, contemporaneous public statements, and specific sequence of events leading to its issuance—would conclude that the Executive Order was issued with a purpose to disfavor a particular religion, in spite of its stated, religiously-neutral purpose, the Court finds that Plaintiffs are likely to succeed on the merits of their Establishment Clause claim.

> It is undisputed that the Executive Order does not facially discriminate for or against any particular religion, or for or against religion versus non-religion. There is no express reference, for instance, to any religion nor does the Executive Order—unlike its predecessor—contain any term or phrase that can be reasonably characterized as having a religious origin or connotation. Indeed, the Government defends the Executive Order principally because of its religiously neutral text. [It is a] flawed notion that the Executive Order cannot be found to have targeted Islam because it applies to all individuals in the six referenced countries. It is undisputed, using the primary source upon which the Government itself relies, that these six countries have overwhelmingly Muslim populations that range from 90.7% to 99.8%. It would therefore be no paradigmatic leap to conclude that targeting these countries likewise targets Islam

> A review of the historical background here makes plain why the Government wishes to focus on the Executive Order's text, rather than its context. The record before this Court is unique. It includes significant and unrebutted evidence of religious animus driving the promulgation of the Executive Order and its related predecessor. For example—In March 2016, Mr. Trump said, during an interview, "I think Islam hates us." Mr. Trump was asked, "Is there a war between the West and radical Islam, or between the West and Islam itself?" He replied: "It's very hard to separate. Because you don't know who's who." In that same interview, Mr. Trump stated: "But there's a tremendous hatred. And we have to be very vigilant. We have to be very careful. And we can't allow people coming into this country who have this hatred of the United States . . . [a]nd of people that are not Muslim." Plaintiffs allege that "[l]ater, as the presumptive Republican nominee, Mr. Trump began using facially neutral language, at times, to describe the Muslim ban." For example, they point to a July 24, 2016. Mr. Trump was asked: "The Muslim ban. I think you've pulled back from it, but you tell me." Mr. Trump responded:

"I don't think it's a rollback. In fact, you could say it's an expansion. I'm looking now at territories. People were so upset when I used the word Muslim. Oh, you can't use the word Muslim. Remember this. And I'm okay with that, because I'm talking territory instead of Muslim." And during an October 9, 2016 televised presidential debate, Mr. Trump was asked: "Your running mate said this week that the Muslim ban is no longer your position. Is that correct? And if it is, was it a mistake to have a religious test?" Mr. Trump replied: "The Muslim ban is something that in some form has morphed into a[n] extreme vetting from certain areas of the world." When asked to clarify whether "the Muslim ban still stands," Mr. Trump said, "It's called extreme vetting."

The Government appropriately cautions that, in determining purpose, courts should not look into the "veiled psyche" and "secret motives" of government decisionmakers and may not undertake a "judicial psychoanalysis of a drafter's heart of hearts." The Government need not fear. The remarkable facts at issue here require no such impermissible inquiry. For instance, there is nothing "veiled" about this press release: "Donald J. Trump is calling for a total and complete shutdown of Muslims entering the United States. []" (Press Release, Donald J. Trump for President, Donald J. Trump Statement on Preventing Muslim Immigration (Dec. 7, 2015).

Nor is there anything "secret" about the Executive's motive specific to the issuance of the Executive Order: Rudolph Giuliani explained on television how the Executive Order came to be. He said: "When [Mr. Trump] first announced it, he said, 'Muslim ban.' He called me up. He said, 'Put a commission together. Show me the right way to do it legally.'" On February 21, 2017, commenting on the then-upcoming revision to the Executive Order, the President's Senior Adviser, Stephen Miller, stated, "Fundamentally, [despite "technical" revisions meant to address the Ninth Circuit's concerns in Washington,] you're still going to have the same basic policy outcome [as the first]."

These plainly-worded statements, made in the months leading up to and contemporaneous with the signing of the Executive Order, and, in many cases, made by the Executive himself, betray the Executive Order's stated secular purpose. Any reasonable, objective observer would conclude, as does the Court for purposes of the instant Motion for TRO, that the stated secular purpose of the Executive Order is, at the very least, "secondary to a religious objective" of temporarily suspending the entry of Muslims.

To emphasize these points, Plaintiffs assert that the stated national security reasons for the Executive Order are pretextual. While these additional assertions certainly call the motivations behind the Executive Order into greater question, they are not necessary to the Court's Establishment Clause determination.

Here, it is not the case that the Administration's past conduct must forever taint any effort by it to address the security concerns of the nation.

Based upon the current record available, however, the Court cannot find the actions taken during the interval between revoked Executive Order No. 13,769 and the new Executive Order to be "genuine changes in constitutionally significant conditions." The Court recognizes that "purpose needs to be taken seriously under the Establishment Clause and needs to be understood in light of context; an implausible claim that governmental purpose has changed should not carry the day in a court of law any more than in a head with common sense." Yet, context may change during the course of litigation, and the Court is prepared to respond accordingly.

In a unanimous per curiam opinion, the Ninth Circuit upheld the lower court's judgment, but eschewed its constitutional analysis. The court held instead that the executive order likely exceeded the President's statutory authority under the Immigration and Nationality Act because it was not supported by findings sufficient to justify the exercise of discretion under the statute. *Hawaii v. Trump*, No. 17-15589, 2017 WL 2529640 (9th Cir. June 12, 2017), *cert. granted sub nom.* Trump v. Int'l Refugee Assistance Project, No. 16-1436, 2017 WL 2722580 (U.S. June 26, 2017).

The District Court's willingness to examine the President's actual motive, as opposed to the purposes set forth in the Order itself and those represented by counsel during the legal proceedings, was extraordinary. Was this a proper inquiry? Judge Watson seemed to regard the inquiry as justified in this case because of the consistency and clarity of candidate and President Trump's statements and because Establishment Clause doctrine demands an inquiry into intent. The Fourth Circuit, in a lengthy 10–3 en banc decision, followed much the same approach in May 2017, reaching the same result. *International Refugee Assistance Project v. Trump*, No. 17-1351 (4th Cir., May 2, 2017), *affirming, International Refugee Assistance Project v. Trump*, No. TDC-17-0361, 2017 WL 1018235 (D. Md. Mar. 16, 2017) (referring to the executive order as a "text [that] speaks with vague words of national security, but in context drips with religious intolerance, animus, and discrimination").

On June 26, 2017, the Supreme Court consolidated the Fourth and Ninth Circuit cases and granted certiorari regarding both. *Trump v. International Refugee Assistance Project*, Nos. 16–1436 (16A1190) and 16–1540 (16A1191) (U.S., June 26, 2017). By a 6–3 vote, the Court, in a per curiam opinion, granted the Government's applications to stay the lower courts' injunctions against implementing the travel ban, to the "extent the injunctions prevent enforcement of § 2(c) with respect to foreign nationals who lack any bona fide relationship with a person or entity in the United States." *Id.* at 9. The Court noted that the plaintiffs in both cases exemplified the kinds of "bona fide relationship" protected by the modified injunction, e.g., immigrants having a close familial relationship with a U.S. person and students admitted to enrollment in a U.S. university. The Court struck the same balance of equities with regard to the Order's refugee cap: "An American individual or entity that has a bona fide relationship with a particular person seeking to enter the country as a refugee can legitimately claim concrete hardship if that person is excluded." *Id.* at 13. Justices Thomas, Alito and Gorsuch would have lifted the injunctions in their entirety, asserting that the Government had demonstrated a likelihood of prevailing ultimately on the merits. Justice Thomas also objected to the majority's tailoring of the injunctions on the ground that the Court's judgment "will burden executive officials with the task of deciding—on peril of contempt—whether individuals from the six affected nations who wish to enter the United States have a sufficient connection to a person or entity in this country." 582 U.S. at ___ (Thomas, J., concurring in part and dissenting in part). On the eve of the October 2017 Supreme Court term, President Trump issued Presidential Proclamation 9645. The proclamation rescinded the March Executive Order and reissued it in expanded form. Under the terms of the proclamation, the travel ban is permanent, rather than limited to 90 days. The list of countries to which the ban applies was also changed: Chad, Iran, North Korea, Somalia, Syria, Venezuela, and Yemen. This list adds North Korea and Venezuela and removes Sudan from the countries covered in the previous order. The Administration has asserted that this Proclamation is "the result of a deliberative, rigorous examination of security risks that was designed to avoid the chaotic rollout of his first ban." Michael D. Shear, *New Order Bars Almost All Travel from Seven Countries*, N.Y. Times (Sept. 24, 2017). The Supreme Court has remanded the pending travel ban cases and directed them to be dismissed as moot. As this book goes to press, there has been no judicial ruling on Proclamation 9465.

Should courts take the President's motives into account when presidential action is challenged on grounds other than the Establishment Clause? Consider, once again, the *Steel Seizure* case. President Truman claimed that he had nationalized the steel industry to avoid an imminent military emergency should a strike interrupt the production of steel. The situation was somewhat more complicated than that, "the President and many of his advisers saw no legitimate labor-management dispute, but instead believed that the steel companies were using the specter of a strike to strong-arm the government into raising steel prices. The seizure was a way to maintain steel production while bringing the industry back to the bargaining table . . . ." Patricia Bellia, *The Story of the* Steel Seizure *Case*, in Presidential Power Stories 233 (Christopher Schroeder & Curtis Bradley, eds., 2009). You will recall that the Court accepted President Truman's assertion of an emergency. Should the Court have considered that the President was actually motivated by bargaining strategy and financial considerations?

Sanctuary Cities

On January 25, 2017, two days before issuing the travel ban, President Trump signed Executive Order 13768, which sets forth the Administration's immigration enforcement policies and priorities generally and which deals with sanctuary cities particularly. A sanctuary city, for purposes of the Order, is one that maintains a policy of not exchanging or sharing with federal law enforcement agencies information relating to the immigration status of individuals that the local jurisdiction gathers in the course of providing services or enforcing state and local law. Federal law forbids state and local jurisdictions from maintaining a policy that forbids the exchange of such information. *See* 8 U.S.C. 1373. The Executive Order purports to bar sanctuary cities from eligibility to receive federal grants:

Sec. 9. Sanctuary Jurisdictions. It is the policy of the executive branch to ensure, to the fullest extent of the law, that a State, or a political subdivision of a State, shall comply with 8 U.S.C. 1373.

(a) In furtherance of this policy, the Attorney General and the Secretary, in their discretion and to the extent consistent with law, shall ensure that jurisdictions that willfully refuse to comply with 8 U.S.C. 1373 (sanctuary jurisdictions) are not eligible to receive Federal grants, except as deemed necessary for law enforcement purposes by the Attorney General or the Secretary. The Secretary has the authority to designate, in his discretion and to the extent consistent with law, a jurisdiction as a sanctuary jurisdiction. The Attorney General shall take appropriate enforcement action against any entity that violates 8 U.S.C. 1373, or which has in effect a statute, policy, or practice that prevents or hinders the enforcement of Federal law.

San Francisco and Santa Clara County are sanctuary jurisdictions and brought an action to retain their eligibility to receive federal grants. They argued that the Order represents an unconstitutional condition because the amount of federal grants represents such a large percentage of each jurisdiction's budget that they would have no choice but to accede to the terms of the Order. This would violate an element of the constitutional system of federalism—the anti-commandeering doctrine—which holds that the federal government may not compel state or local governments to enforce federal law or federal programs. *See National Federation of Independent Business v. Sebelius*, 567 U.S. 519 (2012); *Printz v. United States*, 521 U.S. 898 (1997). The Justice Department lawyers representing the Administration did not attempt to defend the Order. Instead, they offered a narrow construction to save its constitutionality. They claimed that the Order applied only to three rather small law enforcement grant programs that are already expressly conditioned on compliance with 8 U.S.C. 1373. The textual basis for this interpretation of the Order is its direction that sanctuary cities be denied federal grants "to the extent consistent with law." Because it would be unconstitutional to condition the receipt of all federal grants on compliance with section 1373, the Order should not be understood to be so all-encompassing. The District Court rejected the Department of Justice's construction of the Order. According to the Court, the language of the Order is directed at all federal grants, not just the three small law enforcement grants. Moreover, the Court cited numerous statements by candidate and President Trump to the effect that he meant to bar sanctuary cities from receiving any federal grants. The Court also cited statements by the Attorney General and the President's spokesman to the same effect. *See Santa Clara v. Trump*, No. 17-cv-00574 (N.D.Ca., April 25, 2017). The court granted an injunction barring the enforcement of the Order.

Here again, the District Court took the extraordinary step of examining the public record for statements by the President and members of the Administration to determine the actual motive behind the Order. It is not unusual for a court to seek to interpret a law according to the intent of the authority that issued the law. This is a more familiar inquiry when a court seeks to discern the legislative intent as a means of interpreting a statute. In interpreting executive branch rules, the more familiar posture of courts is that they defer to reasonable agency interpretations under the famous *Chevron* doctrine. Indeed, when an agency interprets its own regulation, it is accorded even greater deference. *See Auer v. Robbins*, 519 U.S. 452 (1997). In the sanctuary cities case, the judge did not accord any deference whatsoever to the executive branch's interpretation of its own Order. Does this trouble you?

In general, a Court will engage in serious interpretive contortions to avoid a constitutional issue. *See, e.g., Public Citizen v. Department of Justice*, 491 U.S. 440 (1989). The *Santa Clara* court, by contrast, turned to the public record to justify reading the Order in a way that violates the Constitution. Was the court right to do so? Consider the issue from the perspective of an executive branch lawyer reviewing the Order for form and legality before it was issued. Would you have read the "to the extent consistent with law" language as sufficient to narrow the scope of the order to avoid the constitutional question? If so, can any executive order pass review as long as it contains the boilerplate "to the extent consistent with law" caveat?

4. Regulatory Programs Affecting Foreign Policy

Westinghouse Electric Corp. v. U.S. Nuclear Regulatory Commission

598 F.2d 759 (3d Cir. 1979)

ADAMS, Circuit Judge.

On December 23, 1977, the United States Nuclear Regulatory Commission (NRC) suspended for approximately two years its decisionmaking process regarding proposals for the recycling of spent nuclear fuel and the use in nuclear reactors of plutonium recovered from that fuel. This suspension was announced in an order terminating informal rulemaking and related licensing proceedings concerning this subject. In part, the decision to place a moratorium upon these deliberations was taken in deference to President Carter's stated objective of deferring domestic plutonium recycling while the United States initiated a multinational evaluation of alternative fuel cycles that would pose a lesser risk of international proliferation of nuclear weapons. Petitions for review were filed requesting us to set aside and enjoin the NRC's order on the grounds that, in terminating these proceedings, the NRC violated the Atomic Energy Act (AEA)[1] and the National Environmental Policy Act (NEPA).[2] Because we conclude that the NRC acted within the scope of its authority and that there is no requirement to have a NEPA statement at this time, the petitions for review will be denied.

---

1. 42 U.S.C. §§ 2011–2296 (1976).
2. 42 U.S.C. §§ 4321–4347 (1976).

I.

For over two decades, the federal government, initially through the Atomic Energy Commission (AEC) and later through the NRC, a successor agency to the AEC, has been exploring, together with the private sector, the feasibility of reprocessing spent nuclear fuel and employing the plutonium recovered from such fuel in nuclear reactors utilized to generate electricity. Commercial implementation of the plutonium recycling process would have the advantages of conserving uranium resources and of alleviating the problem of disposing of radioactive wastes, but might also pose the dangers of a proliferation of nuclear weapons and the possible sabotage of reprocessing facilities. This is so because, unlike the slightly "enriched" uranium currently used in nuclear reactors, plutonium can be employed in the production of nuclear explosives and might be diverted to that end by foreign governments or by terrorists.

Recognizing that a decision to implement a wide-scale program for the commercial recycling of plutonium constitutes a major federal action significantly affecting the environment, and thereby necessitating an environmental impact statement (EIS) in order to comply with § 102(2)(C) of NEPA, the AEC in 1974 commenced work on a Generic Environmental Statement on the Use of Recycled Plutonium in Mixed Oxide Fuel in Light Water Cooled Reactors (GESMO). Concomitant with the GESMO informal rulemaking proceeding, the Commission . . . conducted adjudicatory licensing proceedings on applications by private companies dealing with the construction and operation of nuclear fuel reprocessing plants, some of which were already pending when GESMO was undertaken. Among the applications before the Commission were those of Allied-General Nuclear Services . . . for a license to operate the nearly-completed fuel reprocessing plant that it had permission to construct at Barnwell, South Carolina, and of Westinghouse Electric Corp. . . . for a license to construct a similar plant at Anderson, South Carolina.

One of the concerns expressed while the rulemaking and adjudicatory proceedings were progressing was that dangers to world security might ensue from the commercial reprocessing of nuclear fuel. For example, the AEC staff's first draft of GESMO, which was published on August 21, 1974, prompted a number of critical comments by the public. These included a letter from the President's Council on Environmental Quality that was directed at GESMO's failure (a) to address the proliferation dangers, (b) to explore what safeguards were available, and (c) to weigh the possibility of developing alternative sources of energy. In response to this criticism, the staff undertook to reassess its study and to supplement the draft GESMO with an analysis of proliferation risks and safeguards.[10] And, on October 28, 1976, President Ford discussed the

---

10. In November 1975, after an earlier announcement and the receipt of comments, the NRC published a policy statement declaring that a study of safeguard alternatives would be included in GESMO and weighed in NRC's final decision on the subject of wide-scale commercial recycling of plutonium. That statement also specified the procedures and schedule to be followed for GESMO hearings and set forth criteria under which interim licensing of non-experimental, recycle-related activities would be considered. *See* 40 Fed. Reg. 53056 (1975), *corrected*, 40 Fed. Reg. 59497 (1975). Various environmental groups sought review of this policy statement in the Court of Appeals for the

risks entailed in plutonium recycling in a statement on nuclear policy. He declared that the nation "should pursue reprocessing and recycling in the future only if they are found to be consistent with our international (non-proliferation) objectives."

President Carter disclosed his administration's policy concerning plutonium recycling on April 7, 1977. Noting with alarm the serious proliferation risks of plutonium recycling, the President stated that part of the government's response would be to "defer indefinitely the commercial reprocessing and recycling of plutonium produced in the U.S. nuclear power programs," and to sponsor an international nuclear fuel cycle evaluation (INFCE) program aimed at developing alternative processes with lower proliferation risks.

Almost immediately thereafter, a motion was filed to terminate the GESMO proceeding, and . . . the NRC announced its intention to reassess "the future course and scope of GESMO, the review of recycle-related applications, and the matter of interim licensing," and invited GESMO participants, the Executive Branch, and other interested persons to submit their views on the subject. President Carter's position was explained on October 4, 1977, in a letter by Stuart Eizenstat, Assistant to the President for Domestic Affairs and Policy.[15] The NRC then solicited further public comment on the President's position and on several alternative courses of action.[16]

Second Circuit. That court affirmed the NRC's hearing procedures but held that the interim licensing of recycle-related activities on a commercial basis violated NEPA. The Supreme Court vacated and remanded that judgment for consideration of mootness after the NRC's order of December 23, 1977.

 15. Mr. Eizenstat's letter stated in pertinent part:

 The President believes that our goal of stopping the spread of nuclear weapons capability among non-weapons states can be significantly improved by a halt in purex reprocessing. Last April 7, he stated that the U.S. should "defer indefinitely the commercial reprocessing and recycling of the plutonium produced in U.S. nuclear power programs". The Administration has proposed an accelerated research and development program to examine alternative fuel cycles not involving direct access to plutonium. The President has also asked other countries to join us in an International Nuclear Fuel Cycle Evaluation to examine alternative approaches to advanced nuclear technologies. The GESMO proceedings and related licensing requests may impact these non-proliferation initiatives. While the studies and analyses done by the Commission staff, if available in published form, may be of value to the International Nuclear Fuel Cycle Evaluation, the President believes that his non-proliferation initiatives would be assisted both domestically and internationally if the Commission were to terminate the GESMO proceedings. Specifically, the President believes that the following actions would be helpful in achieving the Administration's goals:

 * Publication of the Commission's assessment of safeguards issues.

 * Termination of staff reviews and hearings relating to recycle activities. (Continuation of these activities could lead other nations to question the United States commitment to deter commercial reprocessing and plutonium recycle.)

 * Denial of interim licensing of fuel cycle facilities.

 * Denial of interim licensing for use of mixed oxide fuel in reactors, except in small quantities for experimental purposes.

The letter is reprinted at 42 Fed. Reg. 57186 (1977).

 16. *See* 42 Fed. Reg. 57185 (1977). The notice described four possible courses of action: (1) terminating GESMO and denying the related license applications; (2) continuing as before; (3) taking

Thereafter, on December 23, 1977, the NRC issued an order terminating the GESMO proceeding as well as most proceedings relating to pending or future plutonium-recycle license applications. Among other things, the order also committed the NRC "to re-examine the above matter after the completion of the ongoing alternative fuel cycle studies, now expected to take about two years," and to publish shortly after the decision a statement of the reasons underlying the decision.

. . . Westinghouse filed petitions in this Court . . . challenging the termination of both GESMO and the licensing proceedings with respect to its Anderson, South Carolina facility. Four days later, Allied-General . . . filed a similar petition. . . .

As explained by the NRC in considerable detail in its May 8 Memorandum of Decision, the December 23 Order terminating GESMO and related licensing proceedings was prompted by the President's policy initiatives as well as by the pendency of studies into alternative fuel cycles. With respect to the first reason for termination, the NRC noted in its Memorandum that although the proceedings in question concern domestic activities, it is appropriate for the NRC to weigh the foreign policy implications as well, because the AEA requires that the common defense and security be considered in making any domestic licensing decision. "[I]n the absence of a clear statutory mandate to the contrary" and in view of Congress' reception of the Administration's nuclear policy,[38] the NRC deemed it proper to accord "substantial deference" to the President's request that it terminate the proceedings, since "the President is the national spokesman in the area of foreign policy." In addition, the NRC examined the President's request and reasoned that indeed the country's international prerogatives would be compromised were the proceedings to continue.[40] . . .

The NRC carefully examined policy-based arguments tendered by various commenters that the proceedings ought to be continued, but was not persuaded by them.

---

an intermediate course of action, such as deferring further consideration of GESMO and the related proceedings pending completion of ongoing national and international studies; or (4) continuing GESMO to some convenient stopping point, such as completion of the health, safety, and environmental hearings.

38. Congress explicitly supported the alternative fuel cycle studies proposed by the President in § 105 of the Nuclear Non-Proliferation Act of 1978, Pub. L. No. 95-242, 92 Stat. 120, which was pending in the Senate at the time of the December 23 decision (having already passed the House of Representatives) and was enacted before the May 8 Memorandum was released. Section 105 states:

> The President shall take immediate initiatives to invite all nuclear supplier and recipient nations to reevaluate all aspects of the nuclear fuel cycle, with emphasis on alternatives to an economy based on the separation of pure plutonium or the presence of high enriched uranium, methods to deal with spent fuel storage, and methods to improve the safeguards for existing nuclear technology. . . .

22 U.S.C. § 3224 (Supp. 1979). In addition, Congress endorsed the non-proliferation goals of the Administration, as well as its efforts to encourage international cooperation, in §§ 2 and 3 of that Act, 22 U.S.C. §§ 3201–02. . . .

40. The NRC recognized that the United States' initiatives to discourage other nations from reprocessing spent fuel would be undermined if at the same time it continued to pursue domestic commercial reprocessing, since American arguments that the marginal economic benefits are outweighed by the grave security dangers would lose their credibility.

It emphasized that its decision to terminate the GESMO and related licensing proceedings "does not involve their final disposition on the merits," and is taken because "the present state of studies and national fuel cycle policy evaluations precludes an informed decision on the merits of plutonium recycle at this time." Finally, the NRC noted that the President and Congress have indicated that they may reassess their positions after the studies are completed, and that the NRC is committed to reexamine its December 23 decision "in light of the completed studies, expected to take about two years, and any revisions of the Administration's policies." . . .

In passing the Atomic Energy Act of 1954, Congress enacted "a regulatory scheme which is virtually unique in the degree to which broad responsibility is reposed in the administering agency, free of close prescription in its charter as to how it shall proceed in achieving the statutory objectives." . . . Given this broad delegation of authority to the NRC to choose the necessary means by which to implement the general policy objectives of the AEA, we cannot say that the NRC must inexorably proceed with the processing of license applications and the development of a final GESMO when in its judgment to do so would endanger the attainment of its statutory objectives. . . .

Inasmuch as we conclude that the NRC may, in its discretion, delay processing applications and refuse to accept new ones when there are sound reasons for doing so, we must now examine whether in the present case this discretion was abused or was exercised in a manner not in conformity with statutory dictates. [W]e are satisfied, at least for now, that the NRC has not abused its discretion in refusing to continue the pending proceedings on the ground that it cannot yet formulate a generic standard or make a determination on the question of inimicality [to national security and public safety]. When and if it ever becomes apparent that the NRC has *de facto* denied the license applications despite the applicants' compliance with the pertinent regulations and without making a finding of inimicality, or that the moratorium is of unreasonable duration, judicial recourse will be available to the aggrieved parties.

Petitioners also maintain that the NRC impermissibly terminated the GESMO and related licensing proceedings at the request of the President and in deference to his foreign policy pronouncement. They charge that in failing to act independently of the Executive Branch, the NRC contravened Congress' express intent that the Commission be completely free from presidential influence and control.[65] According to petitioners, the fact that the President has primary responsibility over foreign affairs does not justify the NRC's derogation from Congress' plan, since foreign affairs powers are vested in Congress as well. And, petitioners assert, Congress exercised its

---

65. Expressions of congressional intent that the Commission be independent of the Executive Branch may be found throughout the debates surrounding the passage of the AEA, which took place against the backdrop of the Dixon-Yates controversy. That controversy arose when the President attempted to instruct the Commission to enter into a contract with particular utilities for the provision of electricity to certain Commission facilities. . . .

share of those powers by legislating that with respect to nuclear energy, which inevitably touches upon the sensitive area of foreign affairs, a strict separation is to prevail between the President and the Commission. This is particularly so, petitioners declare, in the context of domestic licensing. In contrast, in the area of international arrangements, such as export licensing, Congress has legislated a divergence from this scheme by making Commission decisions subject to approval by the President.

Although petitioners' argument is resonant with constitutional subtleties concerning the "twilight zone" in which congressional and presidential powers overlap, neither the authority reposed in the NRC nor the agency's exercise of that authority in this case require us to venture into that largely uncharted area. The legislative history produced by petitioners makes clear that Congress intended that the Commission be independent not only from pressures brought to bear by the President, but from all external pressures. Representative is the view expressed by Senator Magnuson:

> Actually, the AEC was established by Congress with the hope and aim of making it the most sensitive agency of Government, more independent than any other, and to be protected from Congress itself, and from all other interference, including Executive interference.

Independence, however, does not mean that the Commission must ignore or reject positions espoused by the President, by Congress or by other parties. The Commission was "charged with a most sensitive and most vital responsibility," a responsibility that cannot possibly be performed properly if the Commission is oblivious or nonresponsive to actions being taken by others, whether within or outside the government. When it created independent administrative agencies, Congress undoubtedly desired that they interact with the three branches of the government much as the legislative body interacts with the executive branch, with "separateness but interdependence, autonomy but reciprocity," so that "practice will integrate the dispersed powers into a workable government."

As previously set forth, the NRC is directed in many provisions of the AEA to consider "the common defense and security." Any contemplation of these sensitive matters necessarily touches upon areas that are also within the domain of the President and of Congress. It was therefore appropriate for the NRC to take note of the relevant developments in the executive and legislative branches and to ascertain, with the help of interested parties, what bearing these developments may have on its own agenda. As we understand the NRC's actions here, that is all it did, and it maintained its independence from both those branches while making an informed decision to suspend its proceedings.

There is no evidence that the President improperly interfered with the NRC's decisionmaking process, or that the NRC capitulated to the President. Instead, the agency appears to have examined the President's position, and agreed with the President's contention that continuation of the proceedings would adversely affect the President's nonproliferation efforts. Then, after determining that Congress had not exercised its constitutional powers in this area in a contrary manner, neither through the AEA nor through subsequent legislation, the NRC decided that it would be prudent to terminate the proceedings for a time so that the President might pursue his objectives. Given this record, we cannot say that the NRC abused its discretion or acted arbitrarily, capriciously, or not in accordance with the law when it rested its decision in part on a desire not to obstruct the goal of securing international nonproliferation. . . .

[T]he petitions for review will be denied.

---

1. *How Directive May a President Be?* As the preceding case illustrates, the "independence" of "independent agencies" does not preclude presidential communication with such agencies (indeed, the President, like any "interested person," may submit comments with respect to informal rulemaking under 5 U.S.C. § 553), and does not preclude such agencies from basing administrative decisions on factors brought to their attention through executive communications. Recall, from Chapter Four, *Sierra Club v. Costle*, in which Judge Wald stated that presidential jawboning did not invalidate a statutorily authorized administrative decision, even if the decision was different from another statutorily authorized decision the agency might have made without such pressure.

But was this the only issue involved in this case? Although Stuart Eizenstat reported on October 4, 1977 that it was President Carter's position that the commercial reprocessing and recycling of plutonium "should" be deferred (see note 15), the court more accurately reports that the President, on April 4, 1977, said that such processes "would" be deferred. As a Department of Justice lawyer, how would you have responded on April 3, 1977 if asked whether the President had the authority to make his intended statement on April 4? Could the President lawfully have directed a 20-year moratorium on U.S. commercial reprocessing and recycling of plutonium? Could the President lawfully have directed the action that the Nuclear Regulatory Commission took in this case? Assuming that Congress did not provide by statute for presidential review of the foreign policy aspects of NRC licensing decisions, how should a Presidential attempt to prevent licensing on foreign policy grounds be analyzed under *Youngstown*, *Curtiss-Wright*, and *Zivotofsky*? To use the APA's judicial review standard, 5 U.S.C. § 706(2)(A), would it be "arbitrary and capricious" for the NRC to decline licenses on the ground that, in considering the "common defense and security" under statute, it will treat as conclusive any presidential determination that a license would not serve the interests of the "common defense and security"?

2. *Agency "Independence" and Foreign Policy.* The court states in *Westinghouse* that "Congress intended the Commission be independent not only from pressures brought to bear by the President, but from all external pressures." This characterization is reminiscent of Justice White's description of the General Accounting Office in *Bowsher v. Synar*, discussed in Chapter Four. Which, if any, functions of the Nuclear Regulatory Commission could Congress vest in an office structured like the position of

Comptroller General, in the interest of "total" independence? Did the NRC's actions regarding the recycling issue exhibit such independence? Would the agency have conformed as readily to the policy views of President Carter had Congress not endorsed them?

3. *Towards a Canon of Statutory Construction?* The *Westinghouse* case implicates the question we asked after *Curtiss-Wright* and *Waterman Steamship* whether Congress may vest regulatory authority with the potential to affect our foreign relations in an official subordinate to the President, but proscribe presidential supervision of that authority. If such legislation would be constitutionally problematic — an open question — then it might also follow that statutes conferring regulatory authority with the potential to affect our foreign relations should be interpreted, in the absence of contrary language, to imply a power *pro tanto* of presidential review. Conversely, if a regulatory statute expressly precludes presidential review, perhaps the agency's implied powers should be construed narrowly whenever a broader construction would give the agency power to affect our foreign relations. You may find the following note useful to assess the wisdom of these hypotheses.

D. Judicial Review and Foreign Policy

To our knowledge, no commentator has ever interpreted the judicial power vested by Article III as encompassing affirmative authority to make foreign policy. Yet, as is evident in various decisions excerpted in this Chapter, the courts are acutely aware that the role of the judiciary in reviewing both legislative enactments and executive initiatives can have significant foreign policy impacts. Anxiety on this score is manifest in the plurality opinion in *Goldwater v. Carter, supra*, which treated the allocation of treaty termination authority as a political question. The Act of State Doctrine, reviewed after *United States v. Pink, supra*, is a judicial invention designed to restrain the courts from meddling, even inadvertently, in foreign policy decisions of the elected branches. Chapter Six, dealing with war powers, includes prominent examples of judicial recourse to other procedural doctrines, such as standing and nonjusticiability, to avoid pronouncements of law that could limit the policy making capacities of Congress and the President.

Besides rules of procedure, there exist two other mechanisms — one obvious, one subtle — through which courts could affect foreign affairs at least indirectly. The more obvious mechanism would be judicial willingness to apply "the law of nations" as a source of law to constrain our government's actions. Despite an oft-quoted sentiment, however, that "[i]nternational law is part of our law," *The Paquete Habana*, 175 U.S. 677, 700 (1900), international law has enjoyed at most a checkered career as a source of decisional authority in federal courts. On some such occasions, the Court has merely implemented a congressional decision, pursuant to its express constitutional powers, either to define offenses against the law of nations or otherwise to incorporate international law into our own, art. I, § 8, cl. 10, *e.g. United States v. Smith*,

18 U.S. 153 (1820) (upholding piracy prosecution). On yet other occasions, especially in admiralty, courts have incorporated customary international law into U.S. common law, even without statutory authorization. As summed up by two noted authors, "The courts have tended to apply the law of nations in five subject-areas: the protection of human rights, the protection of diplomats, the punishment of piracy and terrorism, the punishment of war-related crimes, and the settlement of claims arising out of the seizure of alien property without adequate compensation." THOMAS M. FRANCK & MICHAEL J. GLENNON, FOREIGN RELATIONS AND NATIONAL SECURITY LAW 175(4th ed. 2012). In addition, the Supreme Court has relied heavily on international law, especially the law of war, to determine the scope of power accorded to the President by the Authorization for the Use of Military Force and the Uniform Code of Military Justice. *See Hamdan v. Rumsfeld*, 548 U.S. 557 (2006); *Hamdi v. Rumsfeld*, 542 U.S. 507 (2004). May courts legitimately turn to customary international law to create U.S. common law? Is common law of this sort more problematic in some of these areas than in others?

The more subtle mechanism through which courts may affect foreign policy is through an expansion or contraction of the deference afforded the executive in interpreting Congress's delegations of statutory authority. Courts, that is, could substantially limit executive discretion by requiring statutory authority for presidential initiatives and by applying the nondelegation doctrine vigorously. Likewise where executive initiatives arguably impinge on individual rights, courts might read statutes narrowly under the guise of avoiding difficult constitutional issues.

One can see these possibilities played out explicitly, for example, in litigation where the government's foreign policy concerns pose tensions with individual rights. Cases involving international travel are illustrative. The scope of the executive's powers in constraining such travel has been clouded by the silence of the relevant statutes concerning standards for withholding or revoking passports. In *Kent v. Dulles*, 357 U.S. 116 (1958), the Court reviewed a challenge to a State Department regulation denying passports to applicants because of their alleged Communist beliefs and associations and their refusals to file affidavits concerning present or past membership in the Communist Party. Rather than confront difficult issues concerning the permissible grounds for passport denial, the Court held that, absent a clear statement from Congress, it would not conclude that Congress had granted the executive branch administrative authority with such serious individual rights implications. Seven years later, however, in *Zemel v. Rusk*, 381 U.S. 1 (1965), the Court held that the Secretary of State could restrict travel for all citizens to Cuba, but only after finding implicit authority for area travel restrictions in light of congressional acquiescence in a long-standing executive branch practice of implementing them. Such acquiescence was deemed a clear statement of legislative intent. (*See also Regan v. Wald*, 468 U.S. 222 (1984), upholding Treasury Department regulations restricting travel-related economic transactions—and hence travel—in an effort to prevent Cuba from earning hard currency through U.S. tourism.) *Kent* and *Zemel* are the focus of the following decision, which poses the question whether the Court still perceives international travel restrictions as posing difficult constitutional issues and whether it still follows a restrictive approach to statutory interpretation in divining authority to limit that travel.

Haig v. Agee

453 U.S. 280 (1981)

Chief Justice BURGER delivered the opinion of the Court.

The question presented is whether the President, acting through the Secretary of State, has authority to revoke a passport on the ground that the holder's activities in foreign countries are causing or are likely to cause serious damage to the national security or foreign policy of the United States.

I

A

Philip Agee, an American citizen, currently resides in West Germany.[1] From 1957 to 1968, he was employed by the Central Intelligence Agency. He held key positions in the division of the Agency that is responsible for covert intelligence gathering in foreign countries. In the course of his duties at the Agency, Agee received training in clandestine operations, including the methods used to protect the identities of intelligence employees and sources of the United States overseas. He served in undercover assignments abroad and came to know many Government employees and other persons supplying information to the United States. The relationships of many of these people to our Government are highly confidential; many are still engaged in intelligence gathering.

In 1974, Agee called a press conference in London to announce his "campaign to fight the United States CIA wherever it is operating." He declared his intent "to expose CIA officers and agents and to take the measures necessary to drive them out of the countries where they are operating." Since 1974, Agee has, by his own assertion, devoted consistent effort to that program, and he has traveled extensively in other countries in order to carry it out. To identify CIA personnel in a particular country, Agee goes to the target country and consults sources in local diplomatic circles whom he knows from his prior service in the United States Government. He recruits collaborators and trains them in clandestine techniques designed to expose the "cover" of CIA employees and sources. Agee and his collaborators have repeatedly and publicly identified individuals and organizations located in foreign countries as undercover CIA agents, employees, or sources. The record reveals that the identifications divulge classified information, violate Agee's express contract not to make any

---

1. Agee has been deported from Great Britain, France, and the Netherlands. Dirty Work: The CIA in Western Europe 286–300 (P. Agee & L. Wolf eds., 1978).

public statements about Agency matters without prior clearance by the Agency,[5] have prejudiced the ability of the United States to obtain intelligence, and have been followed by episodes of violence against the persons and organizations identified.[7]

In December 1979, the Secretary of State revoked Agee's passport and delivered an explanatory notice to Agee in West Germany. The notice states in part:

> "The Department's action is predicated upon a determination made by the Secretary under the provisions of [22 CFR] Section 51.70(b)(4) that your activities abroad are causing or are likely to cause serious damage to the national security or the foreign policy of the United States. The reasons for the Secretary's determination are, in summary, as follows: Since the early 1970s it has been your stated intention to conduct a continuous campaign to disrupt the intelligence operations of the United States. In carrying out that campaign you have travelled in various countries (including, among others, Mexico, the United Kingdom, Denmark, Jamaica, Cuba, and Germany), and your activities in those countries have caused serious damage to the national security and foreign policy of the United States. Your stated intention to continue such activities threatens additional damage of the same kind."

The notice also advised Agee of his right to an administrative hearing and offered to hold such a hearing in West Germany on 5 days' notice.

Agee at once filed suit against the Secretary. He alleged that the regulation invoked by the Secretary, 22 CFR § 51.70(b)(4) (1980), has not been authorized by Congress

---

5. As a condition for his employment by the Agency, Agee contracted that "[i]n consideration of my employment by CIA I undertake not to publish or to participate in the publication of any information or material relating to the Agency, its activities or intelligence activities generally, either during or after the term of my employment by the Agency without specific prior approval by the Agency." This language is identical to the clause which we construed in *Snepp v. United States*, 444 U.S. 507, 508 (1980).

7. In December 1975, Richard Welch was murdered in Greece after the publication of an article in an English-language newspaper in Athens naming Welch as CIA Chief of Station. In July 1980, two days after a Jamaica press conference at which Agee's principal collaborator identified Richard Kinsman as CIA Chief of Station in Jamaica, Kinsman's house was strafed with automatic gunfire. Four days after the same press conference, three men approached the Jamaica home of another man similarly identified as an Agency officer. Police challenged the men and gunfire was exchanged. In January 1981, two American officials of the American Institute for Free Labor Development, previously identified as a CIA front by Agee and discussed extensively in Agee's book Inside the Company: CIA Diary, were assassinated in El Salvador.

The Secretary does not assert that Agee has specifically incited anyone to commit murder. However, affidavits of the CIA's Deputy Director for Operations set out and support his judgment that Agee's purported identifications are "thinly-veiled invitations to violence," that "Agee's actions could, in today's circumstances, result in someone's death," and that Agee's conduct has "markedly increased the likelihood of individuals so identified being the victims of violence." One of those affidavits also shows that the ultimate effectiveness of Agee's program depends on activities of hostile foreign groups, and that such groups can be expected to engage in physical surveillance, harassment, kidnaping, and, in extreme cases, murder of United States officials abroad.

and is invalid; that the regulation is impermissibly overbroad; that the revocation prior to a hearing violated his Fifth Amendment right to procedural due process; and that the revocation violated a Fifth Amendment liberty interest in a right to travel and a First Amendment right to criticize Government policies. He sought declaratory and injunctive relief, and he moved for summary judgment on the question of the authority to promulgate the regulation and on the constitutional claims. For purposes of that motion, Agee conceded the Secretary's factual averments and his claim that Agee's activities were causing or were likely to cause serious damage to the national security or foreign policy of the United States. The District Court held that the regulation exceeded the statutory powers of the Secretary under the Passport Act of 1926, 22 U.S.C. § 211a, granted summary judgment for Agee, and ordered the Secretary to restore his passport.

A divided panel of the Court of Appeals affirmed. *Agee v. Muskie*, 629 F.2d 80 (D.C. Cir. 1980). It held that the Secretary was required to show that Congress had authorized the regulation either by an express delegation or by implied approval of a "substantial and consistent" administrative practice, *Zemel v. Rusk*, 381 U.S. 1, 12 (1965). The court found no express statutory authority for the revocation. It perceived only one other case of actual passport revocation under the regulation since it was promulgated and only five other instances prior to that in which passports were actually denied "even arguably for national security or foreign policy reasons." The Court of Appeals took note of the Secretary's reliance on "a series of statutes, regulations, proclamations, orders and advisory opinions dating back to 1856," but declined to consider those authorities, reasoning that "the criterion for establishing congressional assent by inaction is the actual imposition of sanctions and not the mere assertion of power." The court also regarded it as material that most of the Secretary's authorities dealt with powers of the Executive Branch "during time of war or national emergency" or with respect to persons "engaged in criminal conduct."

II

The principal question before us is whether the statute authorizes the action of the Secretary pursuant to the policy announced by the challenged regulation.[17]

A

1

. . . [W]e begin with the language of the statute. The Passport Act of 1926 provides in pertinent part:

---

17. In light of our decision on this issue, we have no occasion in this case to determine the scope of "the very delicate, plenary and exclusive power of the President as the sole organ of the federal government in the field of international relations — a power which does not require as a basis for its exercise an act of Congress, but which, of course, like every other governmental power, must be exercised in subordination to the applicable provisions of the Constitution." *See United States v. Curtiss-Wright Export Corp.*, 299 U.S. 304 (1936).

"The Secretary of State may grant and issue passports, and cause passports to be granted, issued, and verified in foreign countries by diplomatic representatives of the United States . . . under such rules as the President shall designate and prescribe for and on behalf of the United States, and no other person shall grant, issue, or verify such passports." 22 U.S.C. § 211a.

This language is unchanged since its original enactment in 1926.

The Passport Act does not in so many words confer upon the Secretary a power to revoke a passport. Nor, for that matter, does it expressly authorize denials of passport applications. Neither, however, does any statute expressly limit those powers. It is beyond dispute that the Secretary has the power to deny a passport for reasons not specified in the statutes. For example, in *Kent v. Dulles*, 357 U.S. 116 (1958), the Court recognized congressional acquiescence in Executive policies of refusing passports to applicants "participating in illegal conduct, trying to escape the toils of the law, promoting passport frauds, or otherwise engaging in conduct which would violate the laws of the United States." In *Zemel*, the Court held that "the weightiest considerations of national security" authorized the Secretary to restrict travel to Cuba at the time of the Cuban missile crisis. Agee concedes that if the Secretary may deny a passport application for a certain reason, he may revoke a passport on the same ground.

2

Particularly in light of the "broad rule making authority granted in the [1926] Act," a consistent administrative construction of that statute must be followed by the courts "'unless there are compelling indications that it is wrong.'" *E. I. du Pont de Nemours & Co. v. Collins*, 432 U.S. 46, 55 (1977). This is especially so in the areas of foreign policy and national security, where congressional silence is not to be equated with congressional disapproval. . . .

Applying these considerations to statutory construction, the *Zemel* Court observed:

"[B]ecause of the changeable and explosive nature of contemporary international relations, and the fact that the Executive is immediately privy to information which cannot be swiftly presented to, evaluated by, and acted upon by the legislature, *Congress—in giving the Executive authority over matters of foreign affairs—must of necessity paint with a brush broader than that it customarily wields in domestic areas.*"

381 U.S., at 17 (emphasis supplied). Matters intimately related to foreign policy and national security are rarely proper subjects for judicial intervention. . . .

B

1

A passport is, in a sense, a letter of introduction in which the issuing sovereign vouches for the bearer and requests other sovereigns to aid the bearer. Very early, the Court observed:

"[A passport] is a document, which, from its nature and object, is addressed to foreign powers; purporting only to be a request, that the bearer of it may pass safely and freely; and is to be considered rather in the character of a political document, by which the bearer is recognised, in foreign countries, as an American citizen; and which, by usage and the law of nations, is received as evidence of the fact." *Urtetiqui v. D'Arcy*, 9 Pet. 692, 698 (1835).

With the enactment of travel control legislation making a passport generally a requirement for travel abroad,[22] a passport took on certain added characteristics. Most important for present purposes, the only means by which an American can lawfully leave the country or return to it—absent a Presidentially granted exception— is with a passport. *See* 8 U.S.C. § 1185(b) (1976 ed., Supp. IV). As a travel control document, a passport is both proof of identity and proof of allegiance to the United States. Even under a travel control statute, however, a passport remains in a sense a document by which the Government vouches for the bearer and for his conduct.

The history of passport controls since the earliest days of the Republic shows congressional recognition of Executive authority to withhold passports on the basis of substantial reasons of national security and foreign policy. Prior to 1856, when there was no statute on the subject, the common perception was that the issuance of a passport was committed to the sole discretion of the Executive and that the Executive would exercise this power in the interests of the national security and foreign policy of the United States. This derived from the generally accepted view that foreign policy was the province and responsibility of the Executive. From the outset, Congress endorsed not only the underlying premise of Executive authority in the areas of foreign policy and national security, but also its specific application to the subject of passports. Early Congresses enacted statutes expressly recognizing the Executive authority with respect to passports.

The first Passport Act, adopted in 1856, provided that the Secretary of State "shall be authorized to grant and issue passports . . . under such rules as the President shall designate and prescribe for and on behalf of the United States. . . ." § 23, 11 Stat. 60. This broad and permissive language worked no change in the power of the Executive to issue passports; nor was it intended to do so. The Act was passed to centralize passport authority in the Federal Government and specifically in the Secretary of State. In all other respects, the 1856 Act "merely confirmed an authority already possessed and exercised by the Secretary of State. This authority was ancillary to his broader authority to protect American citizens in foreign countries and was necessarily incident to his general authority to conduct the foreign affairs of the United States under the Chief Executive." Senate Committee on Government Operations, Reorganization of the Passport Functions of the Department of State, 86th Cong., 2d Sess., 13 (Comm. Print 1960).

The President and the Secretary of State consistently construed the 1856 Act to preserve their authority to withhold passports on national security and foreign

---

22. With exceptions during the War of 1812 and the Civil War, passports were not mandatory until 1918. It was not until 1978 that passports were required by statute in nonemergency peacetime.

policy grounds. Thus, as an emergency measure in 1861, the Secretary issued orders prohibiting persons from going abroad or entering the country without passports; denying passports to citizens who were subject to military service unless they were bonded; and absolutely denying passports to persons "on errands hostile and injurious to the peace of the country and dangerous to the Union." 3 J. Moore, A Digest of International Law 920 (1906); U.S. Dept. of State, The American Passport 49–54 (1898). An 1869 opinion of Attorney General Hoar held that the granting of a passport was not "obligatory in any case." 13 Op. Atty. Gen. 89, 92. . . .

In 1903, President Theodore Roosevelt promulgated a rule providing that "[t]he Secretary of State has the right in his discretion to refuse to issue a passport, and will exercise this right towards anyone who, he has reason to believe, desires a passport to further an unlawful or improper purpose." Subsequent Executive Orders issued between 1907 and 1917 cast no doubt on this position. This policy was enforced in peacetime years to deny passports to citizens whose conduct abroad was "likely to embarrass the United States" or who were "disturbing, or endeavoring to disturb, the relations of this country with the representatives of foreign countries."

By enactment of the first travel control statute in 1918, Congress made clear its expectation that the Executive would curtail or prevent international travel by American citizens if it was contrary to the national security. The legislative history reveals that the principal reason for the 1918 statute was fear that "renegade Americans" would travel abroad and engage in "transference of important military information" to persons not entitled to it. The 1918 statute left the power to make exceptions exclusively in the hands of the Executive, without articulating specific standards. Unless the Secretary had power to apply national security criteria in passport decisions, the purpose of the Travel Control Act would plainly have been frustrated.

Against this background, and while the 1918 provisions were still in effect, Congress enacted the Passport Act of 1926. The legislative history of the statute is sparse. However, Congress used language which is identical in pertinent part to that in the 1856 statute, as amended, and the legislative history clearly shows congressional awareness of the Executive policy. There is no evidence of any intent to repudiate the longstanding administrative construction. Absent such evidence, we conclude that Congress, in 1926, adopted the longstanding administrative construction of the 1856 statute.

The Executive construed the 1926 Act to work no change in prior practice and specifically interpreted it to authorize denial of a passport on grounds of national security or foreign policy. Indeed, by an unbroken line of Executive Orders, regulations, instructions to consular officials, and notices to passport holders, the President and the Department of State left no doubt that likelihood of damage to national security or foreign policy of the United States was the single most important criterion in passport decisions. . . . This history of administrative construction was repeatedly communicated to Congress, not only by routine promulgation of Executive Orders and regulations, but also by specific presentations. . . .

In 1966, the Secretary of State promulgated the regulations at issue in this case. 22 CFR §§ 51.70(b)(4), 51.71(a) (1980). Closely paralleling the 1956 regulation, these provisions authorize revocation of a passport where "[t]he Secretary determines that the national's activities abroad are causing or are likely to cause serious damage to the national security or the foreign policy of the United States."

Zemel recognized that congressional acquiescence may sometimes be found from nothing more than silence in the face of an administrative policy. Here, however, the inference of congressional approval "is supported by more than mere congressional inaction." Twelve years after the promulgation of the regulations at issue and 22 years after promulgation of the similar 1956 regulation, Congress enacted the statute making it unlawful to travel abroad without a passport even in peacetime. 8 U.S.C. § 1185(b) (1976 ed., Supp. IV). Simultaneously, Congress amended the Passport Act of 1926 to provide that "[u]nless authorized by law," in the absence of war, armed hostilities, or imminent danger to travelers, a passport may not be geographically restricted.[48] Title 8 U.S.C. § 1185(b) must be read *in pari materia* with the Passport Act.

The 1978 amendments are weighty evidence of congressional approval of the Secretary's interpretation, particularly that in the 1966 regulations. Despite the long-standing and officially promulgated view that the Executive had the power to withhold passports for reasons of national security and foreign policy, Congress in 1978, "though it once again enacted legislation relating to passports, left completely untouched the broad rule-making authority granted in the earlier Act." *Zemel, supra,* at 12.

3

Agee argues that the only way the Executive can establish implicit congressional approval is by proof of longstanding and consistent *enforcement* of the claimed power: that is, by showing that many passports were revoked on national security and foreign policy grounds. For this proposition, he relies on *Kent*. A necessary premise for Agee's contention is that there were frequent occasions for revocation and that the claimed Executive power was exercised in only a few of those cases. However, if there were no occasions — or few — to call the Secretary's authority into play, the absence of frequent instances of enforcement is wholly irrelevant. The exercise of a power emerges only in relation to a factual situation, and the continued validity of the power is not diluted simply because there is no need to use it.

---

48. Act of Oct. 7, 1978, § 124, 92 Stat. 971, 22 U.S.C. § 211a (1976 ed., Supp. IV). This amendment added the following language to the Passport Act:

> "Unless authorized by law, a passport may not be designated as restricted for travel to or for use in any country other than a country with which the United States is at war, where armed hostilities are in progress, or where there is imminent danger to the public health or the physical safety of United States travellers."

The statute provides that the purpose of this amendment is "achieving greater United States compliance with the provisions of the Final Act of the Conference on Security and Cooperation in Europe (signed at Helsinki on August 1, 1975)." 92 Stat. 971.

The history is clear that there have been few situations involving substantial likelihood of serious damage to the national security or foreign policy of the United States as a result of a passport holder's activities abroad, and that in the cases which have arisen, the Secretary has consistently exercised his power to withhold passports. Perhaps the most notable example of enforcement of the administrative policy, which surely could not have escaped the attention of Congress, was the 1948 denial of a passport to a Member of Congress who sought to go abroad to support a movement in Greece to overthrow the existing government. Another example was the 1954 revocation of a passport held by a man who was supplying arms to groups abroad whose interests were contrary to positions taken by the United States. In 1970, the Secretary revoked passports of two persons who sought to travel to the site of an international airplane hijacking.

there haven't even been many cases

The Secretary has construed and applied his regulations consistently, and it would be anomalous to fault the Government because there were so few occasions to exercise the announced policy and practice. Although a pattern of actual enforcement is one indicator of Executive policy, it suffices that the Executive has "openly asserted" the power at issue. *Kent* is not to the contrary. There, it was shown that the claimed governmental policy had not been enforced consistently. The Court stressed that "as respects Communists these are scattered rulings and not consistently of one pattern." In other words, the Executive had allowed passports to some Communists, but sought to deny one to Kent. The Court had serious doubts as to whether there was in reality any definite policy in which Congress could have acquiesced. Here, by contrast, there is no basis for a claim that the Executive has failed to enforce the policy against others engaged in conduct likely to cause serious damage to our national security or foreign policy. . . .

Agee also contends that the statements of Executive policy are entitled to diminished weight because many of them concern the powers of the Executive in wartime. However, the statute provides no support for this argument. History eloquently attests that grave problems of national security and foreign policy are by no means limited to times of formally declared war.

4

Relying on the statement of the Court in *Kent* that "illegal conduct" and problems of allegiance were, "so far as relevant here, the only [grounds] which it could fairly be argued were adopted by Congress in light of prior administrative practice," Agee argues that this enumeration was exclusive and is controlling here. This is not correct.

Kent ∅ about conduct its

The *Kent* Court had no occasion to consider whether the Executive had the power to revoke the passport of an individual whose *conduct* is damaging the national security and foreign policy of the United States. *Kent* involved denials of passports solely on the basis of political beliefs entitled to First Amendment protection. Although finding it unnecessary to reach the merits of that constitutional problem, the *Kent* Court emphasized the fact that "[w]e deal with *beliefs*, with *associations*, with *ideological* matters." 357 U.S., at 130 (emphasis supplied) . . . .

about political beliefs

The protection accorded beliefs standing alone is very different from the protection accorded conduct. Thus, in *Aptheker v. Secretary of State*, [378 U.S. 500 (1964)], the Court held that a statute which, like the policy at issue in *Kent*, denied passports to Communists solely on the basis of political beliefs unconstitutionally "establishes an irrebuttable presumption that individuals who are members of the specified organizations will, if given passports, engage in activities inimical to the security of the United States." The Court recognized that the legitimacy of the objective of safeguarding our national security is "obvious and unarguable." The Court explained that the statute at issue was not the least restrictive alternative available: "The prohibition against travel is supported only by a tenuous relationship between the bare fact of organizational membership and the activity Congress sought to proscribe."

Beliefs and speech are only part of Agee's "campaign to fight the United States CIA." In that sense, this case contrasts markedly with the facts in *Kent* and *Aptheker*. No presumptions, rebuttable or otherwise, are involved, for Agee's conduct in foreign countries presents a serious danger to American officials abroad and serious danger to the national security.

enforcement was consistent. ✓

We hold that the policy announced in the challenged regulations is "sufficiently substantial and consistent" to compel the conclusion that Congress has approved it.

III

Agee also attacks the Secretary's action on three constitutional grounds: first, that the revocation of his passport impermissibly burdens his freedom to travel; second, that the action was intended to penalize his exercise of free speech and deter his criticism of Government policies and practices; and third, that failure to accord him a prerevocation hearing violated his Fifth Amendment right to procedural due process.

In light of the express language of the passport regulations, which permits their application only in cases involving likelihood of "serious damage" to national security or foreign policy, these claims are without merit.

Revocation of a passport undeniably curtails travel, but the freedom to travel abroad with a "letter of introduction" in the form of a passport issued by the sovereign is subordinate to national security and foreign policy considerations; as such, it is subject to reasonable governmental regulation. The Court has made it plain that the *freedom* to travel outside the United States must be distinguished from the *right* to travel within the United States. . . .

It is "obvious and unarguable" that no governmental interest is more compelling than the security of the Nation. Protection of the foreign policy of the United States is a governmental interest of great importance, since foreign policy and national security considerations cannot neatly be compartmentalized. Measures to protect the secrecy of our Government's foreign intelligence operations plainly serve these interests.

National Security = top priority

Not only has Agee jeopardized the security of the United States, but he has also endangered the interests of countries other than the United States—thereby creating serious problems for American foreign relations and foreign policy. Restricting Agee's foreign travel, although perhaps not certain to prevent all of Agee's harmful activities, is the only avenue open to the Government to limit these activities.

restricting his travel is only way to stop him

Assuming, *arguendo*, that First Amendment protections reach beyond our national boundaries, Agee's First Amendment claim has no foundation. The revocation of Agee's passport rests in part on the content of his speech: specifically, his repeated disclosures of intelligence operations and names of intelligence personnel. Long ago, however, this Court recognized that "[n]o one would question but that a government might prevent actual obstruction to its recruiting service or the publication of the sailing dates of transports or the number and location of troops." *Near v. Minnesota ex rel. Olson*, 283 U.S. 697, 716 (1931). Agee's disclosures, among other things, have the declared purpose of obstructing intelligence operations and the recruiting of intelligence personnel. They are clearly not protected by the Constitution. The mere fact that Agee is also engaged in criticism of the Government does not render his conduct beyond the reach of the law.

his speech ∅ protected by Constitution

To the extent the revocation of his passport operates to inhibit Agee, "it is an inhibition of *action*," rather than of speech. *Zemel*, 381 U.S., at 16–17 (emphasis supplied). Agee is as free to criticize the United States Government as he was when he held a passport—always subject, of course, to express limits on certain rights by virtue of his contract with the Government.

restricting action, ∅ speech

On this record, the Government is not required to hold a prerevocation hearing. In *Cole v. Young*, 351 U.S. 536 (1956), we held that federal employees who hold "sensitive" positions "where they could bring about any discernible adverse effects on the Nation's security" may be suspended without a presuspension hearing. For the same reasons, when there is a substantial likelihood of "serious damage" to national security or foreign policy as a result of a passport holder's activities in foreign countries, the Government may take action to ensure that the holder may not exploit the sponsorship of his travels by the United States. . . . The Constitution's due process guarantees call for no more than what has been accorded here: a statement of reasons and an opportunity for a prompt postrevocation hearing.[62]

We reverse the judgment of the Court of Appeals and remand for further proceedings consistent with this opinion.

Reversed and remanded.

Justice BLACKMUN, concurring.

There is some force, I feel, in Justice Brennan's observations, that today's decision cannot be reconciled fully with all the reasoning of *Zemel v. Rusk* and, particularly,

---

62. We do not decide that these procedures are constitutionally required.

of *Kent v. Dulles*, and that the Court is cutting back somewhat upon the opinions in those cases *sub silentio*. I would have preferred to have the Court disavow forthrightly the aspects of *Zemel* and *Kent* that may suggest that evidence of a longstanding Executive policy or construction in this area is not probative of the issue of congressional authorization. Nonetheless, believing this is what the Court in effect has done, I join its opinion.

Justice BRENNAN, with whom Justice MARSHALL joins, dissenting.

. . . This is not a complicated case. The Court has twice articulated the proper mode of analysis for determining whether Congress has delegated to the Executive Branch the authority to deny a passport under the Passport Act of 1926. The analysis is hardly confusing, and I expect that had the Court faithfully applied it, today's judgment would affirm the decision below.

In *Kent v. Dulles*, . . . [b]ecause the Passport Act of 1926—the same statute at issue here—did not expressly authorize the denial of passports to alleged Communists, the Court examined cases of actual passport refusals by the Secretary to determine whether "it could be fairly argued" that this category of passport refusals was "adopted by Congress in light of prior administrative practice." The Court was unable to find such prior administrative practice, and therefore held that the regulation was unauthorized.

In *Zemel v. Rusk*, the issue was whether the Secretary could restrict travel for all citizens to Cuba. In holding that he could, the Court expressly approved the holding in *Kent*. . . . In reaching its decision, the Court in *Zemel* relied upon numerous occasions when the State Department had restricted travel to certain international areas. . . . As in *Kent* and *Zemel*, there is no dispute here that the Passport Act of 1926 does not *expressly* authorize the Secretary to revoke Agee's passport. Therefore, the sole remaining inquiry is whether there exists "with regard to the sort of passport [revocation] involved [here], an administrative *practice* sufficiently substantial and consistent to warrant the conclusion that Congress had implicitly approved it." *Zemel v. Rusk*, 381 U.S., at 12 (emphasis added). The Court today, citing to this same page in *Zemel* applies a test markedly different from that of *Zemel* and *Kent* and in fact expressly disavowed by the latter. . . . [N]either *Zemel* nor *Kent* holds that a longstanding Executive *policy* or *construction* is sufficient proof that Congress has implicitly authorized the Secretary's action. The cases hold that an administrative *practice* must be demonstrated; in fact *Kent* unequivocally states that mere *construction* by the Executive—no matter how longstanding and consistent—is *not* sufficient. . . .

The Court's requirement in *Kent* of evidence of the Executive's *exercise* of discretion as opposed to its possession of discretion may best be understood as a preference for the strongest proof that Congress knew of and acquiesced in that authority. The presence of sensitive constitutional questions in the passport revocation context cautions against applying the normal rule that administrative constructions in cases of statutory construction are to be given great weight. Only when Congress had maintained its silence in the face of a consistent and substantial pattern of actual passport denials or revocations—where the parties will presumably object loudly, perhaps through legal action, to the Secretary's exercise of discretion—can this Court be sure that Congress is aware of the Secretary's actions and has implicitly approved that exercise of discretion. Moreover, broad statements by the Executive Branch relating to its discretion in the passport area lack the precision of definition that would follow from concrete applications of that discretion in specific cases. Although Congress might register general approval of the Executive's overall policy, it still might disapprove of the Executive's pattern of applying that broad rule in specific categories of cases.

Not only does the Court ignore the *Kent-Zemel* requirement that Executive discretion be supported by a consistent administrative practice, but it also relies on the very Executive construction and policy deemed irrelevant in *Kent*. Thus, noting that "[t]he President and the Secretary of State consistently construed the 1856 (Passport) Act to preserve their authority to withhold passports on national security and foreign policy grounds," the Court reaches out to hold that "Congress, in 1926, adopted the longstanding administrative construction of the 1856 statute." The Court quotes from 1869 and 1901 opinions of the Attorneys General. But *Kent* expressly cited both of these opinions as examples of Executive constructions *not* relevant to the determination whether Congress had implicitly approved the Secretary's exercise of authority. The Court similarly relies on four Executive Orders issued between 1907 and 1917 to buttress its position, even though *Kent* expressly cited the same four Orders as examples of Executive constructions inapposite to the proper inquiry. Where the Court in *Kent* discounted the constructions of the Act made by "[t]he scholars, the courts, the Chief Executive, and the Attorneys General," today's Court decides this case on the basis of constructions evident from "an unbroken line of Executive Orders, regulations, instructions to consular officials, and notices to passport holders."[7] The Court's reliance on material expressly abjured in *Kent* becomes understandable only when one appreciates the paucity of recorded administrative practice—the only evidence upon which *Kent* and *Zemel* permit reliance—with respect to passport denials or revocations based on foreign policy or national security considerations relating to an individual. The Court itself identifies only three occasions over the past 33 years when the Secretary has revoked passports for such reasons. And only one of these cases involved a revocation pursuant to the

---

7. Even if the Court were correct to use administrative constructions of passport legislation, it is by no means certain that the Executive *did* construe the Acts to give it the discretion alleged here, since it sometimes referred to the unqualified rights of citizens to passports. *See, e.g.,* 15 Op. Atty. Gen. 114, 117 (1876); 13 Op. Atty. Gen. 397, 398 (1871). Indeed the State Department has sought legislation from Congress to provide the sort of authority exercised in this case. See S. 4110, § 103(6), 85th Cong., 2d Sess. (1958); Hearings on S. 2770, S. 3998, S. 4110, and S. 4137 before the Senate Committee on Foreign Relations, 85th Cong., 2d Sess., 1, 4 (1958); see also H.R. 14895, § 205(e), 89th Cong., 2d Sess. (1966). This hardly suggests that the Executive thought it had such authority.

regulations challenged in this case. Yet, in 1979 alone, there were 7,835,000 Americans traveling abroad.

... [N]o one is "faulting" the Government because there are only few occasions when it has seen fit to deny or revoke passports for foreign policy or national security reasons. The point that *Kent* and *Zemel* make, and that today's opinion should make, is that the Executive's authority to revoke passports touches an area fraught with important constitutional rights, and that the Court should therefore "construe narrowly all delegated powers that curtail or dilute them." The presumption is that Congress must expressly delegate authority to the Secretary to deny or revoke passports for foreign policy or national security reasons before he may exercise such authority....

III

I suspect that this case is a prime example of the adage that "bad facts make bad law." Philip Agee is hardly a model representative of our Nation. And the Executive Branch has attempted to use one of the only means at its disposal, revocation of a passport, to stop respondent's damaging statements. But . . . it is important to remember that this decision applies not only to Philip Agee, whose activities could be perceived as harming the national security, but also to other citizens who may merely disagree with Government foreign policy and express their views.[9]

... [T]he Court professes to rely on, but in fact departs from, the two precedents in the passport regulation area, *Zemel* and *Kent*. Of course it is always easier to fit oneself within the safe haven of *stare decisis* than boldly to overrule precedents of several decades' standing. Because I find myself unable to reconcile those cases with the decision in this case, however, and because I disagree with the Court's *sub silentio* overruling of those cases, I dissent.[10]

----

9. An excerpt from the petitioner's portion of the oral argument is particularly revealing:
"QUESTION: General McCree, supposing a person right now were to apply for a passport to go to Salvador, and when asked the purpose of his journey, to say, to denounce the United States policy in Salvador in supporting the junta. And the Secretary of State says, I just will not issue a passport for that purpose. Do you think that he can consistently do that in the light of our previous cases?
"MR. McCREE: I would say, yes, he can. Because we have to vest these — The President of the United States and the Secretary of State working under him are charged with conducting the foreign policy of the Nation, and the freedom of speech that we enjoy domestically may be different from that that we can exercise in this context."
The reach of the Secretary's discretion is potentially staggering.
10. Because I conclude that the regulation is invalid as an unlawful exercise of authority by the Secretary under the Passport Act of 1926, I need not decide the important constitutional issues presented in this case. However, several parts of the Court's whirlwind treatment of Agee's constitutional claims merit comment, either because they are extreme oversimplifications of constitutional doctrine or mistaken views of the law and facts of this case.
First, the Court states [that the revocation of Agee's passport inhibits *action*, not *speech*]. Under the Court's rationale, . . . a 40 year prison sentence imposed upon a person who criticized the

1. *Where Are the Statutory Criteria?* This case does not involve an executive claim of inherent constitutional power to revoke passports on national security grounds; the issue presented was one of the scope of a statutory delegation. Why was it not dispositive that the Passport Act not only did not specify criteria for the revocation of passports, but it did not expressly confer any passport revocation authority at all? Why, if the statute tacitly confers standardless revocation authority, is the resulting delegation of legislative power nevertheless constitutional? (Does the absence of express statutory support for the majority view suggest that the majority perceives, but does not wish to rely on, an Article II basis for the Secretary of State's regulation?) Is there any constitutional obligation of the executive branch to promulgate criteria for passport revocation before purporting to exercise such authority?

2. *Deferring to Executive Branch Legal Interpretation in Foreign Affairs Cases. Haig v. Agee* would appear to support a proposition, frequently voiced by legal scholars, that the judiciary is (and ought to be) deferential to the executive branch in reviewing its interpretation of foreign affairs statutes. Yet, *Kent v. Dulles* points the other way, as does the *Medellin* case, excerpted earlier in this chapter, with regard to reviewing executive branch treaty interpretation. Several more conspicuous "exceptions" appear in the cases excerpted in Chapter Seven that arose from the incarceration of alleged enemy combatants in Guantanamo. In the view of Deborah N. Pearlstein, these examples, among others, cast doubt on whether the courts are any more or less predictably deferential in foreign affairs law as compared to the general run of cases involving judicial review of executive branch legal interpretation. Deborah N. Pearlstein, *After Deference: Formalizing the Judicial Power for Foreign Relations Law*, 159 U. Penn L. Rev. 784 (2011).

Observing doctrinal instability in this regard, several prominent legal scholars have recommended that federal courts approach executive branch legal interpretation in the foreign affairs area with so-called *Chevron* deference, following the Supreme Court's decision in *Chevron U.S.A., Inc. v. Natural Resources Defense Council*, 467 U.S. 837 (1984). If the Court were to follow this approach, then the federal judiciary

---

Government's food stamp policy would represent only an "inhibition of action." After all, the individual would remain free to criticize the United States Government, albeit from a jail cell.

... [Moreover, t]he Court seems to misunderstand the prior precedents of this Court, for Agee's speech is undoubtedly protected by the Constitution.... [I]t may be that respondent's First Amendment right to speak is outweighed by the Government's interest in national security, [but] revocation of his passport obviously does implicate First Amendment rights by chilling his right to speak, and therefore the Court's responsibility must be to balance that infringement against the asserted governmental interests to determine whether the revocation contravenes the First Amendment....

Second, ... [t]he District Court nowhere held that respondent lacked standing to contend vagueness and overbreadth.... [I]t is strange indeed to suggest that an individual whose activities admittedly fall within the core of the challenged regulation does not have standing to argue overbreadth. After all, the purpose of the overbreadth doctrine in First Amendment cases is precisely to permit a person who falls within the legislation nevertheless to challenge the wide sweep of the legislation as it affects another's protected activity....

would defer to any interpretation proffered by the executive with respect to a legally ambiguous text, if that interpretation is not clearly unreasonable. See Eric A. Posner and Cass R. Sunstein, *Chevronizing Foreign Relations Law*, 116 Yale L. J. 1170 (2007); Curtis A. Bradley, Chevron *Deference and Foreign Affairs*, 86 Va. L. Rev. 649 (2000). But see Derek Jinks and Neal Katyal, *Disregarding Foreign Relations Law*, 116 Yale L. J. 1230 (2007); Neil Kinkopf, *The Statutory Commander in Chief*, 81 Ind. L.J. 1169 (2006). Pearlstein is unpersuaded on both descriptive and normative grounds. First, she notes that the Supreme Court's application of *Chevron* has itself been so irregular as to cast doubt on the capacity of that doctrine to lend stability to foreign affairs law. (The irregularity point is well documented in William N. Eskridge, Jr. and Lauren E. Baer, *The Continuum of Deference: Supreme Court Treatment of Agency Statutory Interpretations from* Chevron *to* Hamdan, 96 Geo. L. J. 1083 (2008).) Second, she does not believe *Chevron* deference would advance, in the foreign affairs area, either of the values with which it is most often associated—deference to expertise and executive branch accountability. That is because it is by no means certain that the executive interpretations offered to the federal courts emanate from expert, as opposed to politically driven voices. Further, deference in an area of law where the executive already operates with extraordinary discretion would reduce even further the degree to which executive initiatives are subject to any meaningful external review. What is your assessment? Are there criteria that can usefully distinguish between foreign affairs cases in which courts should be deferential to the executive and those in which more intense review is appropriate?

3. *In the Shadow of the First Amendment.* The Justices disagree on what needs to be shown in *Agee* to demonstrate congressional knowledge of and acquiescence in an administrative interpretation. Perhaps the burden each side would place on the executive reflects its appraisal of the seriousness of the constitutional issues posed by the revocation of Agee's passport or of passports in general. In your view, which side is right?

4. *Relevance of the Logan Act.* The majority attributes the scant administrative history of national security-based passport controls to the relative lack of instances in which a passport holder's activities abroad involved "substantial likelihood of serious damage to the national security or foreign policy of the United States." Does the Logan Act history support this view?

5. *Interpreting Interbranch History.* Do you agree with footnote 7 to the dissent that executive branch efforts to secure *express* statutory authority for particular activities belie arguments on behalf of the executive that *implicit* statutory authority already exists for those activities? Would the Court's adoption of this position as a rule of statutory construction deter salutary executive branch efforts to prompt Congress to clarify executive authority?

6. *Agee's Procedural Rights.* On what ground does the majority deny that Agee had a right to a hearing before the termination of his passport? Is a post-revocation hearing constitutionally required? If a hearing is due, should Agee be entitled to challenge at that hearing the State Department's *general* position that activities of the sort

alleged against Agee violate national security, or should he only be allowed to challenge the charges *as applied* in his case? *See United States v. Helmy*, 712 F. Supp. 1423 (E.D. Cal. 1989) (defendants denied any opportunity to challenge administrative listing of certain commodities as controlled commodities under Arms Export Control Act and Export Administration Act of 1979 not denied due process; decision to place defense articles on commodities control list implicates commander-in-chief power and is judicially unreviewable).

7. *Unlimited Foreign Policy Discretion to Revoke Passports?* Note from footnote 9 to the dissent the Solicitor General's answer on the scope of the Secretary of State's power. Did he give the correct answer? Would there have been a preferable answer?

8. *Intelligence Identities Protection Act.* Passport revocation has proven an almost wholly ineffectual response to the sort of problem posed by Philip Agee. What else could or should the government do? In 1982, Congress enacted the Intelligence Identities Protection Act, 50 U.S.C. § 421 *et seq.* As slightly amended, that Act provides, in part:

> Whoever, having or having had authorized access to classified information that identifies a covert agent, intentionally discloses any information identifying such covert agent to any individual not authorized to receive classified information, knowing that the information disclosed so identifies such covert agent and that the United States is taking affirmative measures to conceal such covert agent's intelligence relationship to the United States, shall be fined under Title 18 or imprisoned not more than ten years, or both.

50 U.S.C. § 421(a) (2000). The Act also creates lesser included offenses for persons who commit disclosures of the kind outlawed in § 421(a), if (1) such persons have authorized access to classified information, whether or not that information identified the covert agent in question, § 421(b), or (2) such persons are engaged "in the course of a pattern of activities intended to identify and expose covert agents and with reason to believe that such activities would impair or impede the foreign intelligence activities of the United States," § 421 (c). Opponents of the legislation insisted it was unconstitutional to criminalize the publication of agents' names if such information is derived from public documents, on which Agee and others have claimed to rely. Herman Schwartz, *A Constitutional Disaster*, THE NATION, July 3, 1982, at 11–13. The argument has yet to be tested in court. What do you think? For a largely negative assessment of the Act's effectiveness in protecting CIA agent identities, see Andrew M. Szilagyi, *Blowing Its Cover: How the Intelligence Identities Protection Act Has Masqueraded as an Effective Law and Why It Must Be Amended*, 51 WM. & MARY L. REV. 2269 (2010).

9. *Subsequent Developments.* Phillip Agee, who died in 2008, never did recover his U.S. passport. *Agee v. Baker*, 753 F. Supp. 373 (D.D.C. 1990). Between 1976 and 1990, he traveled on passports from Grenada and Nicaragua; Germany gave him a passport in 1990. Interestingly, the lack of a U.S. passport apparently did not prevent his travel without arrest to and from the United States, although he made his

permanent home, in the last years of his life, in Havana. Duncan Campbell, *The Spy Who Stayed Out in the Cold*, THE GUARDIAN, at G2-14 (Jan. 10, 2007).

10. *Foreign Policy and the First Amendment.* Another much contested area of executive power involving individual rights concerns the President's authority, pursuant to statute, to prohibit or regulate the import or export of informational material that would threaten national security. In *Meese v. Keene*, 481 U.S. 465 (1987), the Supreme Court upheld against first amendment challenge a requirement in the Foreign Agents Registration Act, 22 U.S.C. § 611, that certain foreign informational materials be circulated only with the label "political propaganda." Treasury Department regulations banning travel to Cuba for the purpose of importing informational material were upheld in *Walsh v. Brady*, 927 F.2d 1229 (D.C. Cir. 1991). Do such cases manifest undue judicial solicitude for the discretion of the political branches? Insufficient concern for counter-balancing first amendment interests?

Chapter 6

War Powers

Closely related to the political branches' struggle over foreign policy making has been the tension, since our founding, over their respective authorities to control military policy. At first glance, the text seems clearly to favor congressional primacy—an interpretation buttressed by early sources. Article I, section 8, expressly authorizes Congress to "provide for the common Defence," as well as:

To declare war, grant letters of marque and reprisal, and make rules concerning captures on land and water;

To raise and support armies, . . .

To provide and maintain a navy;

To make rules for the government and regulation of the land and naval forces;

To provide for calling forth the militia to execute the laws of the union, suppress insurrections and repel invasions; (and)

To provide for organizing, arming, and disciplining, the militia, and for governing such part of them as may be employed in the service of the United States. . . .

Against this impressive array of powers, the President's sole explicit military role under the Constitution is to serve as "Commander in Chief of the Army and Navy of the United States, and of the Militia of the several states, when called into actual Service of the United States." U.S. Const., art. II, § 2.

Yet, even the briefest reflection on U.S. military history since World War II suggests that it is the President, not Congress, who has exercised the primary initiative in military policy making. Indeed, the Executive has adhered to a constitutional view, first fully elaborated during the Vietnam period, that the President has unreviewable authority (a) to determine when the interests of the United States demand U.S. military action and (b) to commit our troops to the protection of U.S. interests, even without clear legislative authority.

How the distribution of powers has evolved—and the legality of current practices—cannot usefully be assessed without an historical framework. Part A of this chapter, which focuses on the respective branches' powers with respect to committing U.S. troops to military action, thus takes an historical focus. First, we present some early documents indicating the strong originalist case for legislative primacy, as well as the Supreme Court opinion that accepted, by a single vote margin,

Lincoln's defense of the Union as falling within his inherent military powers. We then present a series of materials that review the debate over war powers during what is undoubtedly the watershed experience in reaching our current *modus operandi*: Vietnam. In terms of legal developments, the key event culminating that episode was the enactment of the War Powers Resolution of 1973.

Sections B and C look at the evolution of war powers doctrine in the post-Vietnam period. Section B considers, in light of the War Powers Resolution, the wide variety of limited-scale military deployments that Presidents have initiated without explicit statutory authority since the resolution was enacted. The obvious issue posed by the frequency of these undertakings is whether the War Powers Resolution has accomplished anything. That issue is considered, along with proposals for substantially revising its terms.

Section C reviews what may be a watershed of equal significance to Vietnam — the Gulf War of 1990–1991 and the Iraq War of 2003. Both of these conflicts occurred pursuant to express legislative authority; yet, significant questions persist as to whether such resolutions were necessary or sufficient to legalize America's military efforts.

Section D considers the scope of the President's wartime powers off the battlefield. First, we review those powers as they affect the civil liberties of civilians on the home front and the organization of the economy. This section also reviews some of the difficult questions of law and policy raised with regard to the aftermath of the post-September 11 military action in Afghanistan — questions that challenge whether "wartime" and "peacetime" remain legally adequate categories to capture what is at stake in this field. Finally, Sections E and F briefly discuss the President's peacetime use of troops in law enforcement and federalism issues raised in the context of military authority.

The secondary literature discussing the allocation of war powers between the President and Congress is immense. Major book-length contributions to the war powers debate include JOHN HART ELY, WAR AND RESPONSIBILITY: CONSTITUTIONAL LESSONS OF VIETNAM AND ITS AFTERMATH (1993); LOUIS FISHER, PRESIDENTIAL WAR POWER (2004); MICHAEL J. GLENNON, CONSTITUTIONAL DIPLOMACY (1990); STEPHEN M. GRIFFIN, LONG WARS AND THE CONSTITUTION (2013); LOUIS HENKIN, CONSTITUTIONALISM, DEMOCRACY, AND FOREIGN AFFAIRS (1990); HAROLD H. KOH, THE NATIONAL SECURITY CONSTITUTION: SHARING POWER AFTER THE IRAN-CONTRA AFFAIR (1990); David J. Barron & Martin S. Lederman, *The Commander in Chief at the Lowest Ebb — Framing the Problem, Doctrine, and Original Understanding*, 121 HARV. L. REV. 689 (2008); David J. Barron & Martin S. Lederman, *The Commander in Chief at the Lowest Ebb — A Constitutional History*, 121 HARV. L. REV. 941 (2008); H. JEFFERSON POWELL THE PRESIDENT AS COMMANDER IN CHIEF: AN ESSAY IN CONSTITUTIONAL VISION (2013); and MARIAH ZEISBERG, WAR POWERS: THE POLITICS OF CONSTITUTIONAL AUTHORITY (2013). For an historical perspective on presidential accountability for war making, see RICHARD J. BARNET, THE ROCKETS'

RED GLARE: WHEN AMERICA GOES TO WAR—THE PRESIDENTS AND THE PEOPLE (1990). A good, though now somewhat dated, sampling of other work is cited in David G. Adler, *The Constitution and Presidential Warmaking: The Enduring Debate*, 103 POL. SCI. Q. 1 (1988), and Gary B. Born, *Review Essay: The President's War Powers*, 23 TEX. INT'L L.J. 153 (1988) (critically reviewing FRANCIS D. WORMUTH & EDWIN B. FIRMAGE, TO CHAIN THE DOG OF WAR: THE WAR POWER OF CONGRESS IN HISTORY AND LAW (1986).) Professor Firmage's views are presented also in *The War Power of Congress and Revision of the War Powers Resolution*, 17 J. CONTEMP. L. 237 (1991).

A. Power to Commit Troops—From the Founding to Vietnam

1. Scope of the Commander in Chief Clause: Early Views

THE FEDERALIST, No. 69 (Hamilton)

The President is to be the "commander-in-chief of the army and navy of the United States, and of the militia of the several States, when called into the actual service of the United States. . . ." In most . . . particulars the power of the President will resemble equally that of the king of Great Britain and of the governor of New York. The most material points of difference are these: *First.* The President will have only the occasional command of such part of the militia of the nation as by legislative provision may be called into the actual service of the Union. The king of Great Britain and the governor of New York have at all times the entire command of all the militia within their several jurisdictions. In this article, therefore, the power of the President would be inferior to that of either the monarch or the governor. *Secondly.* The President is to be commander-in-chief of the army and navy of the United States. In this respect his authority would be nominally the same with that of the king of Great Britain, but in substance much inferior to it. It would amount to nothing more than the supreme command and direction of the military and naval forces, as first General and admiral of the Confederacy; while that of the British king extends to the *declaring* of war and to the *raising* and *regulating* of fleets and armies; all of which, by the Constitution under consideration, would appertain to the legislature. The governor of New York, on the other hand, is by the constitution of the State vested only with the command of its militia and navy. But the constitutions of several of the States expressly declare their governors to be commanders-in-chief as well of the army as navy; and it may well be a question, whether those of New Hampshire and Massachusetts, in particular, do not, in this instance, confer larger powers upon their respective governors than could be claimed by a President of the United States.

Little v. Barreme

6 U.S. 170 (1804)

Chief Justice MARSHALL delivered the opinion of the Court.

The Flying-Fish, a Danish vessel having on board Danish and neutral property, was captured on the 2d of December 1799, on a voyage from Jeremie to St. Thomas's, by the United States frigate Boston, commanded by Captain Little, and brought into the port of Boston, where she was libelled as an American vessel that had violated the non-intercourse law. The judge before whom the cause was tried, directed a restoration of the vessel and cargo as neutral property, but refused to award damages for the capture and detention, because in his opinion, there was probable cause to suspect the vessel to be American. On an appeal to the circuit court this sentence was reversed, because the Flying-Fish was on a voyage from, not to, a French port, and was therefore, had she even been an American vessel, not liable to capture on the high seas.

During the hostilities between the United States and France, an act for the suspension of all intercourse between the two nations was annually passed. That under which the Flying-Fish was condemned, declared every vessel, owned, hired or employed wholly or in part by an American, which should be employed in any traffic or commerce with or for any person resident within the jurisdiction or under the authority of the French republic, to be forfeited together with her cargo; the one half to accrue to the United States, and the other to any person or persons, citizens of the United States, who will inform and prosecute for the same.

The 5th section of this act authorizes the president of the United States, to instruct the commanders of armed vessels, "to stop and examine any ship or vessel of the United States on the high sea, which there may be reason to suspect to be engaged in any traffic or commerce contrary to the true tenor of the act, and if upon examination it should appear that such ship or vessel is bound or sailing to any port or place within the territory of the French republic or her dependencies, it is rendered lawful to seize such vessel, and send her into the United States for adjudication."

It is by no means clear that the president of the United States whose high duty it is to "take care that the laws be faithfully executed," and who is commander in chief of the armies and navies of the United States, might not, without any special authority for that purpose, in the then existing state of things, have empowered the officers commanding the armed vessels of the United States, to seize and send into port for adjudication, American vessels which were forfeited by being engaged in this illicit commerce. But when it is observed that the general clause of the first section of the act, which declares that such vessels may be seized, and may be prosecuted in any district or circuit court, which "shall be holden within or for the district where the seizure shall be made," obviously contemplates a seizure within the United States; and that the 5th section gives a special authority to seize on the high seas, and limits that authority to the seizure of vessels bound or sailing to a French port, the legislature seem to have prescribed that the manner in which this law shall be carried into execution, was to exclude a seizure of any vessel not bound to a French port. Of consequence, however strong the circumstances might be, which induced Captain Little to suspect the Flying-Fish to be an American vessel, they could not excuse the detention of her, since he would not have been authorized to detain her had she been really American.

It was so obvious, that if only vessels sailing to a French port could be seized on the high seas, that the law would be very often evaded, that this act of congress appears to have received a different construction from the executive of the United States; a construction much better calculated to give it effect.

A copy of this act was transmitted by the secretary of the navy, to the captains of the armed vessels, who were ordered to consider the 5th section as a part of their instructions. The same letter contained the following clause. "A proper discharge of the important duties enjoined on you, arising out of this act, will require the exercise of a sound and an impartial judgment. You are not only to do all that in you lies, to prevent all intercourse, whether direct or circuitous, between the ports of the United States, and those of France or her dependencies, where the vessels are apparently as well as really American, and protected by American papers only, but you are to be vigilant that vessels or cargoes really American, but covered by Danish or other foreign papers, and bound to or from French ports, do not escape you."

These orders given by the executive under the construction of the act of congress made by the department to which its execution was assigned, enjoin the seizure of American vessels sailing from a French port. Is the officer who obeys them liable for damages sustained by this misconstruction of the act, or will his orders excuse him? If his instructions afford him no protection, then the law must take its course, and he must pay such damages as are legally awarded against him; if they excuse an act not otherwise excusable, it would then be necessary to inquire whether this is a case in which the probable cause which existed to induce a suspicion that the vessel was American, would excuse the captor from damages when the vessel appeared in fact to be neutral.

I confess the first bias of my mind was very strong in favor of the opinion that though the instructions of the executive could not give a right, they might yet excuse from damages. I was much inclined to think that a distinction ought to be taken between acts of civil and those of military officers; and between proceedings within the body of the country and those on the high seas. That implicit obedience which military men usually pay to the orders of their superiors, which indeed is indispensably necessary to every military system, appeared to me strongly to imply the principle that those orders, if not to perform a prohibited act, ought to justify the person whose general duty it is to obey them, and who is placed by the laws of his country in a situation which in general requires that he should obey them. I was strongly inclined to think that where, in consequence of orders from the legitimate authority, a vessel is seized with pure intention, the claim of the injured party for damages would be against that government from which the orders proceeded, and would be a proper subject for negotiation. But I have been convinced that I was mistaken, and

I have receded from this first opinion. I acquiesce in that of my brethren, which is, that the instructions cannot change the nature of the transaction, or legalize an act which without those instructions would have been a plain trespass.

It becomes therefore unnecessary to inquire whether the probable cause afforded by the conduct of the Flying-Fish to suspect her of being an American, would excuse Captain Little from damages for having seized and sent her into port, since had she actually been an American, the seizure would have been unlawful?

Captain Little then must be answerable in damages to the owner of this neutral vessel, and as the account taken by order of the circuit court is not objectionable on its face, and has not been excepted to by counsel before the proper tribunal, this court can receive no objection to it.

There appears then to be no error in the judgment of the circuit court, and it must be affirmed with costs.

---

1. *War Powers — Legislative Preemption?* Note the similarity between Chief Justice Marshall's analysis and the approach of several of the *Youngstown* Justices concerning the President's emergency powers. That is, he raises the possibility that, in the face of congressional silence, the President could have lawfully authorized the seizure of U.S. ships traveling from France. He treats the relevant statute, however, as embodying a congressional preemption of presidential discretion on this question. Are you persuaded? Even if the legislative act controlled the President's powers, should the authority to seize ships traveling to France have been interpreted to imply authority to seize ships traveling from a hostile nation?

2. *Just Following Orders?* Was it appropriate to hold Captain Little personally liable for this incident? Would it be good policy for the government to indemnify from liability those who rely on superior orders? You may wish to recall the immunity cases from Chapter Three in this regard.

The Prize Cases
67 U.S. (2 Black) 635 (1863)

[Abraham Lincoln's victory in the 1860 election was a culmination of a series of events leading to the secession of the Southern states, and on December 20, 1860, South Carolina became the first state to withdraw from the Union. Other states of the deep South followed. Efforts on the part of the Buchanan administration to check secession failed, and one by one most of the federal forts in the South were taken over by secessionists. On February 4, 1861 — a month before Lincoln's inauguration — six Southern states sent representatives to Montgomery, Alabama, to set up a new, independent government. With Jefferson Davis at its head, the Confederate States of America came into being.

Lincoln was prepared to conciliate the South, but would not recognize that the Union could be divided. The test of his position came early in his Administration

when he learned that the federal troops at Fort Sumter, South Carolina, a
few military installations in the South still in federal control, had to be promp.
plied or withdrawn. Lincoln determined that supplies must be sent even if do.
provoked the Confederates into firing on the fort. (In fact, some historians con,
this decision was made *because* it would provoke just such a response.) On April 1
1861, just before Federal supply ships arrived, Confederate guns opened fire upon For,
Sumter, precipitating a war which is still the most costly in American lives of any in
the nation's history.

By proclamations of April 19 and 27, 1861, President Lincoln established a blockade of Southern ports and provided that any vessel attempting to violate the blockade could be taken as prize. 12 Stat. 1258, 1259. Although subsequently ratified, the
blockade was declared before Congress had a chance to assemble and take action on
the matter. The immediate purpose of the blockade was to cripple the Confederacy
because it needed foreign markets for its crops and manufactured goods, and required
food and military supplies that it could not produce.

Because the United States never admitted that the southern ports were not ports
of the United States, it would have been legally possible to proclaim them closed and
thereby avoid the international law implications of a blockade. This was, in fact, the
course of action recommended to President Lincoln by Secretary of the Navy Welles.

But serious difficulties stood in the way of relying exclusively on such a measure.
Most notably, such a closing would have been impossible to enforce because the
United States did not control the land on which the ports were located or by which
they were surrounded. The only means by which the United States Navy could act
against neutral shipping was to resort to international law and the law of the
blockade.

The four vessels involved in the Prize Cases had been captured by public vessels
of the United States for attempting to violate the blockade. They were taken on behalf
of the United States and in each case condemned by the district court exercising its
jurisdiction as provided in the proclamations.]

Justice GRIER.

There are certain propositions of law which must necessarily affect the ultimate
decision of these cases. . . . They are, 1st. Had the President a right to institute a blockade of ports in possession of persons in armed rebellion against the Government, on
the principles of international law, as known and acknowledged among civilized
States?

2d. Was the property of persons domiciled or residing within those States a proper
subject of capture on the sea as "enemies' property?"

I. Neutrals have a right to challenge the existence of a blockade *de facto*, and also
the authority of the party exercising the right to institute it. They have a right to enter
the ports of a friendly nation for the purposes of trade and commerce, but are bound
to recognize the rights of a belligerent engaged in actual war, to use this mode of coercion, for the purpose of subduing the enemy.

That a blockade *de facto* actually existed, and was formally declared and notified by the President on the 27th and 30th of April, 1861, is an admitted fact in these cases.

That the President, as the Executive Chief of the Government and Commander-in-chief of the Army and Navy, was the proper person to make such notification, has not been, and cannot be disputed.

The right of prize and capture has its origin in the "*jus belli*," and is governed and adjudged under the law of nations. To legitimate the capture of a neutral vessel or property on the high seas, a war must exist *de facto*, and the neutral must have a knowledge or notice of the intention of one of the parties belligerent to use this mode of coercion against a port, city, or territory, in possession of the other.

Let us enquire whether, at the time this blockade was instituted, a state of war existed which would justify a resort to these means of subduing the hostile force. [I]t is not necessary to constitute war, that both parties should be acknowledged as independent nations or sovereign States. A war may exist where one of the belligerents claims sovereign rights as against the other.

. . . A civil war is never solemnly declared; it becomes such by its accidents — the number, power, and organization of the persons who originate and carry it on. When the party in rebellion occupy and hold in a hostile manner a certain portion of territory; have declared their independence; have cast off their allegiance; have organized armies; have commenced hostilities against their former sovereign, the world acknowledges them as belligerents, and the contest a *war*. *They* claim to be in arms to establish their liberty and independence, in order to become a sovereign State, while the sovereign party treats them as insurgents and rebels who owe allegiance, and who should be punished with death for their treason. . . . [T]he parties to a civil war usually concede to each other belligerent rights. They exchange prisoners, and adopt the other courtesies and rules common to public or national wars. . . . As a civil war is never publicly proclaimed, *eo nomine* against insurgents, its actual existence is a fact in our domestic history which the Court is bound to notice and to know. . . .

By the Constitution, Congress alone has the power to declare a national or foreign war. It cannot declare war against a State, or any number of States, by virtue of any clause in the Constitution. The Constitution confers on the President the whole Executive power. He is bound to take care that the laws be faithfully executed. He is Commander-in-chief of the Army and Navy of the United States, and of the militia of the several States when called into the actual service of the United States. He has no power to initiate or declare a war either against a foreign nation or a domestic State. But by the Acts of Congress of February 28th, 1795, and 3d of March, 1807, he is authorized to call out the militia and use the military and naval forces of the United States in case of invasion by foreign nations, and to suppress insurrection against the government of a State or of the United States.

If a war be made by invasion of a foreign nation, the President is not only authorized but bound to resist force by force . . . without waiting for any special legislative authority. And whether the hostile party be a foreign invader, or States organized in rebellion, it is none the less a war, although the declaration of it be "*unilateral.*" . . .

The battles of Palo Alto and Resaca de la Palma had been fought before the passage of the Act of Congress of May 13th, 1846, which recognized "*a state of war as existing by the act of the Republic of Mexico.*" This act not only provided for the future prosecution of the war, but was itself a vindication and ratification of the Act of the President in accepting the challenge without a previous formal declaration of war by Congress.

This greatest of civil wars was not gradually developed by popular commotion, tumultuous assemblies, or local unorganized insurrections. However long may have been its previous conception, it nevertheless sprung forth suddenly from the parent brain, a Minerva in the full panoply of *war*. The President was bound to meet it in the shape it presented itself, without waiting for Congress to baptize it with a name; and no name given to it by him or them could change the fact.

. . . Foreign nations acknowledge it as war by a declaration of neutrality. The condition of neutrality cannot exist unless there be two belligerent parties. . . . As soon as the news of the attack on Fort Sumter, and the organization of a government by the seceding States, assuming to act as belligerents, could become known in Europe, to wit, on the 13th of May, 1861, the Queen of England issued her proclamation of neutrality, "recognizing hostilities as existing between the Government of the United States of American and *certain States* styling themselves the Confederate States of America." This was immediately followed by similar declarations or silent acquiescence by other nations. After such an official recognition by the sovereign, a citizen of a foreign State is estopped to deny the existence of a war with all its consequences as regards neutrals. . . .

Whether the President in fulfilling his duties, as Commander-in-chief, in suppressing an insurrection, has met with such armed hostile resistance, and a civil war of such alarming proportions as will compel him to accord to them the character of belligerents, is a question to be decided *by him*, and this Court must be governed by the decisions and acts of the political department of the Government to which this power was entrusted. "He must determine what degree of force the crisis demands." The proclamation of blockade is itself official and conclusive evidence to the Court that a state of war existed which demanded and authorized a recourse to such a measure, under the circumstances peculiar to the case.

If it were necessary to the technical existence of a war, that it should have a legislative sanction, we find it in almost every act passed at the extraordinary session of the Legislature of 1861, which was wholly employed in enacting laws to enable the Government to prosecute the war with vigor and efficiency. And finally, in 1861, we find Congress . . . passing an act "approving, legalizing, and making valid all the acts, proclamations, and orders of the President, &c., as if they had been *issued and done under the previous express authority* and direction of the Congress of the United States."

Without admitting that such an act was necessary under the circumstances, it is plain that if the President had in any manner assumed powers which it was necessary should have the authority or sanction of Congress, . . . this ratification has operated to perfectly cure the defect. . . .

The objection made to this act of ratification, that it is *ex post facto*, and therefore unconstitutional and void, might possibly have some weight on the trial of an indictment in a criminal Court. But precedents from that source cannot be received as authoritative in a tribunal administering public and international law.

On this first question therefore we are of the opinion that the President had a right, *jure belli*, to institute a blockade of ports in possession of the States in rebellion, which neutrals are bound to regard.

[In the remainder of the majority opinion, Justice Grier concluded that the property of all persons residing within the territory of the States in rebellion that is captured on the high seas may lawfully be treated as enemy property.]

Justice NELSON, dissenting.

[An] objection taken to the seizure of this vessel and cargo is, that there was no existing war between the United States and the States in insurrection within the meaning of the law of nations, which drew after it the consequences of a public or civil war[, which,] . . . when duly commenced by proclamation or otherwise, entitles both of the belligerent parties to all the rights of war against each other, and as respects neutral nations. . . . Chancellor Kent . . . observes, "as war cannot lawfully be commenced on the part of the United States without an act of Congress, such act is, of course, a formal notice to all the world, and equivalent to the most solemn declaration."

The legal consequences resulting from a state of war between two countries at this day are well understood, and will be found described in every approved work on the subject of international law. The people of the two countries become immediately the enemies of each other—all intercourse commercial or otherwise between them unlawful—all contracts existing at the commencement of the war suspended, and all made during its existence utterly void. . . . [I]nterdiction of trade and intercourse direct or indirect is absolute and complete by the mere force and effect of war itself. All the property of the people of the two countries on land or sea are subject to capture and confiscation by the adverse party as enemies' property. . . . The ports of the respective countries may be blockaded, and letters of marque and reprisal granted as rights of war, and the law of prizes as defined by the law of nations comes into full and complete operation, resulting from maritime captures, *jure belli*. . . . [T]he same code which has annexed to the existence of a war all these disturbing consequences has declared that the right of making war belongs exclusively to the supreme or sovereign power of the State.

This power in all civilized nations is regulated by the fundamental laws or municipal constitution of the country. By our Constitution this power is lodged in

Congress. Congress shall have power "to declare war, grant letters of marque and reprisal, and make rules concerning captures on land and water." . . .

In the case of a rebellion or resistance of a portion of the people of a country against the established government, there is no doubt, if in its progress and enlargement the government thus sought to be overthrown sees fit, it may by the competent power recognize or declare the existence of a state of civil war, which will draw after it all the consequences and rights of war between the contending parties as in the case of a public war. . . . It is not to be denied, therefore, that if a civil war existed between that portion of the people in organized insurrection to overthrow this Government at the time this vessel and cargo were seized, and if she was guilty of a violation of the blockade, she would be lawful prize of war. But before this insurrection against the established Government can be dealt with on the footing of a civil war, within the meaning of the law of nations and the Constitution of the United States, and which will draw after it belligerent rights, it must be recognized or declared by the war-making power of the Government. No power short of this can change the legal status of the Government or the relations of its citizens from that of peace to a state of war, or bring into existence all those duties and obligations of neutral third parties growing out of a state of war. . . . There is no difference in this respect between a civil or a public war.

. . . [S]ome confusion existed on the argument [in these cases] as to the definition of a war that drew after it all the rights of prize of war. . . . An idea seemed to be entertained that all that was necessary to constitute a war was organized hostility in the district of country in a state of rebellion. . . . With a view to enforce this idea, we had, during the argument, an imposing historical detail of the several measures adopted by the Confederate States to enable them to resist the authority of the general Government, and of many bold and daring acts of resistance and of conflict. It was said that war was to be ascertained by looking at the armies and navies or public force of the contending parties, and the battles lost and won. . . .

Now, in one sense, no doubt this is war, and may be a war of the most extensive and threatening dimensions and effects, but it is a statement simply of its existence in a material sense, and has no relevancy or weight when the question is what constitutes war in a legal sense, in the sense of the law of nations, and of the Constitution of the United States? For it must be a war in this sense to attach to it all the consequences that belong to belligerent rights. Instead, therefore, of inquiring after armies and navies, and victories lost and won, or organized rebellion against the general Government, the inquiry should be into the law of nations and into the municipal fundamental laws of the Government. . . . [C]ivil war, . . . under our system of government, can exist only by an act of Congress, which requires the assent of two of the great departments of the Government, the Executive and Legislative.

We have thus far been speaking of the war power under the Constitution of the United States, and as known and recognized by the law of nations. But we are asked, what would become of the peace and integrity of the Union in case of an insurrection at home or invasion from abroad if this power could not be exercised by the President in the recess of Congress, and until that body could be assembled?

The framers of the Constitution fully comprehended this question, and provided for the contingency. Indeed, it would have been surprising if they had not, as a rebellion had occurred in the State of Massachusetts while the Convention was in session, and which had become so general that it was quelled only by calling upon the military power of the State. The Constitution declares that Congress shall have power "to provide for calling forth the militia to execute the laws of the Union, suppress insurrections, and repel invasions." Another clause, "that the President shall be Commander-in-chief of the Army and Navy of the United States, and of the militia of the several States when called into the actual service of the United States;" and, again, "He shall take care that the laws shall be faithfully executed." Congress passed laws on this subject in 1792 and 1795. 1 United States Laws, pp. 264, 424.

The last Act provided that whenever the United States shall be invaded or be in imminent danger of invasion from a foreign nation, it shall be lawful for the President to call forth such number of the militia most convenient to the place of danger, and in case of insurrection in any State against the Government thereof, it shall be lawful for the President, on the application of the Legislature of such State, if in session, or if not, of the Executive of the State, to call forth such number of militia of any other State or States as he may judge sufficient to suppress such insurrection.

The 2d section provides, that when the laws of the United States shall be opposed, or the execution obstructed in any State by combinations too powerful to be suppressed by the course of judicial proceedings, it shall be lawful for the President to call forth the militia of such State, or of any other State or States as may be necessary to suppress such combinations; and by the Act 3 March, 1807, (2 U.S. Laws, 443,) it is provided that in case of insurrection or obstruction of the laws, either in the United States or of any State or Territory, where it is lawful for the President to call forth the militia for the purpose of suppressing such insurrection, and causing the laws to be executed, it shall be lawful to employ for the same purpose such part of the land and naval forces of the United States as shall be judged necessary. It will be seen, therefore, that ample provision has been made under the Constitution and laws against any sudden and unexpected disturbance of the public peace from insurrection at home or invasion from abroad. The whole military and naval power of the country is put under the control of the President to meet the emergency. He may call out a force in proportion to its necessities, one regiment or fifty, one ship-of-war or any number at his discretion. If, like the insurrection in the State of Pennsylvania in 1793, the disturbance is confined to a small district of country, a few regiments of the militia may be sufficient to suppress it. If of the dimension of the present, when it first broke out, a much larger force would be required. But whatever its numbers, whether great or small, that may be required, ample provision is here made; and whether great or small, the nature of the power is the same. It is the exercise of a power under the municipal laws of the country and not under the law of nations; and, as we see, furnishes the most ample means of repelling attacks from abroad or suppressing disturbances at home until the assembling of Congress, who can, if it be deemed necessary, bring into operation the war power, and thus change the nature and character of the contest. Then, instead of being carried on under the municipal law of 1795, it would be under the law of nations, and the Acts of Congress as war measures with all the rights of war.

. . . It has also been argued that [the] power of the President from necessity should be construed as vesting him with the war power, or the Republic might greatly suffer or be in danger from the attacks of the hostile party before the assembling of Congress. But we have seen that the whole military and naval force are in his hands under the municipal laws of the country. He can meet the adversary upon land and water with all the forces of the Government. The truth is, this idea of the existence of any necessity for clothing the President with the war power, under the Act of 1795, is simply a monstrous exaggeration; for, besides having the command of the whole of the army and navy, Congress can be assembled within any thirty days, if the safety of the country requires that the war power shall be brought into operation.

. . . Certainly it cannot rightfully be said that the President has the power to convert a loyal citizen into a belligerent enemy or confiscate his property as enemy's property. Congress assembled on the call for an extra session the 4th of July, 1861, and among the first acts passed was one in which the President was authorized by proclamation to interdict all trade and intercourse between all the inhabitants of States in insurrection and the rest of the United States, subjecting vessel and cargo to capture and condemnation as prize, and also to direct the capture of any ship or vessel belonging in whole or in part to any inhabitant of a State whose inhabitants are declared by the proclamation to be in a state of insurrection, found at sea or in any part of the rest of the United States. Act of Congress of 13th of July, 1861, secs. 5, 6. . . . The President's Proclamation was issued on the 16th of August following, and embraced Georgia, North and South Carolina, part of Virginia, Tennessee, Alabama, Louisiana, Texas, Arkansas, Mississippi and Florida. This Act of Congress, we think, recognized a state of civil war between the Government and the Confederate States, and made it territorial. . . .

[W]hen the Government of the United States recognizes a state of civil war to exist between a foreign nation and her colonies, but remaining itself neutral, the Courts are bound to consider as lawful all those acts which the new Government may direct against the enemy, and we admit the President who conducts the foreign relations of the Government may fitly recognize or refuse to do so, the existence of civil war in the foreign nation under the circumstances stated. But this is a very different question from the one before us, which is whether the President can recognize or declare a civil war, under the Constitution, with all its belligerent rights, between his own Government and a portion of its citizens in a state of insurrection. That power, as we have seen, belongs to Congress. We agree when such a war is recognized or declared to exist by the war-making power, but not otherwise, it is the duty of the Courts to follow the decision of the political power of the Government. . . .

Congress on the 6th of August, 1862, passed an Act confirming all acts, proclamations, and orders of the President, after the 4th of March, 1861, respecting the army and navy, and legalizing them, so far as was competent for that body, and it has been suggested, but scarcely argued, that this legislation on the subject had the effect to bring into existence an *ex post facto* civil war with all the rights of capture and confiscation, *jure belli*, from the date referred to. An *ex post facto* law is defined, when, after an action, indifferent in itself, or lawful, is committed, the Legislature then, for the first time, declares it to have been a crime and inflicts punishment upon the person who committed it. The principle is sought to be applied in this case. Property of the citizen or foreign subject engaged in lawful trade at the time, and illegally captured, which must be taken as true if a confirmatory act be necessary, may be held and confiscated by subsequent legislation. Here the captures were without any Constitutional authority, and void; and, on principle, no subsequent ratification could make them valid. . . .

Chief Justice TANEY, Justice CATRON and Justice CLIFFORD, concurred in the dissenting opinion of Justice Nelson.

———

1. *Law Enforcement or War Making?* Note that the issue dividing the majority and dissent in *The Prize Cases* was not whether the President had authority to close Southern ports in response to the Confederate insurrection, but whether he could lawfully designate that closure a "blockade." Prior to *The Prize Cases*, it was arguable that blockades were permissible under international law only in cases of war between sovereign states. Plainly, Lincoln did not concede the Confederacy's status as a sovereign state; nor did he want any other nation to do so. On the other hand, had Lincoln merely "closed" ports pursuant to his statutory law enforcement powers, then foreign shippers, even if neutral, would run the risk of being treated as smugglers. The British insisted their shippers be able to exercise the rights of neutrals. Thus, for this reason at least, Lincoln felt it imperative to declare a blockade and to insist that international law justified his actions.

When *The Prize Cases* were argued, it was by no means clear that the Supreme Court would accept the theory that the Confederate insurrection counted as "war" for international law purposes. That it did so apparently owed much, if not everything, to the lawyerly skill of the U.S. Attorney from Boston, somewhat belatedly called in to assist with the case. This was Richard Henry Dana, Jr., today better known as author of Two Years Before the Mast (1840), the story of his sea voyage around Cape Horn to California. For an essay that well recounts the drama surrounding the case, see Jeffrey L. Amestoy, *The Supreme Court Argument That Saved the Union: Richard Henry Dana, Jr., and the* Prize Cases, 35 J. Sup. Ct. History 10 (2010). A Supreme Court holding that the blockade was unlawful could have resulted, during a highly vulnerable moment, in huge damage awards against the United States, and cast into doubt the legality of both Lincoln's suspension of habeas corpus and the Emancipation Proclamation.

2. *Must Emergency Presidential Measures Always Rest on Statutory Authority?* The dissent in *The Prize Cases* does not dispute that Lincoln possessed statutory authority to respond to the insurrection by force. The difference seems to be that the dissent, regarding the President's exercise of his authority as law enforcement, believes that any taking of property that resulted from that exercise must be justly compensated. The Court's holding, however, that both the insurrection and the President's response to it are covered by the international law of war, renders any enemy property seized as liable to capture without compensation.

The majority is arguably ambiguous, however, as to whether President Lincoln's blockade needed to rest on *both* his commander in chief power and preexisting statutory authority, or would have been authorized entirely on the basis of his inherent authorities under Article II. Justice Grier famously wrote: "If a war be made by invasion of a foreign nation, the President is not only authorized but bound to resist force by force . . . without waiting for any special legislative authority." But note that this statement came after his observation that: "[B]y the Acts of Congress of February 28th, 1795, and 3d of March, 1807, [the President] is authorized to call out the militia and use the military and naval forces of the United States in case of invasion by foreign nations, and to suppress insurrection against the government of a State or of the United States." In drawing the analogy between Lincoln's blockade and his authority to respond to invasion, Justice Grier could thus be interpreted to mean: "If a war be made by invasion of a foreign nation, the President is not only authorized (by Congress, as he was in the Civil War) but bound (by his commander-in-chief role, which is triggered by the fact of foreign invasion) to resist force by force. . . ." Or, perhaps he meant: "If a war be made by invasion of a foreign nation, the President is not only authorized (by Article II of the Constitution, as he was in the Civil War) but bound (by Article II of the Constitution, as he was in the Civil War) to resist force by force?" For a defense of the former reading, see Stephen I. Vladeck, Note, *Emergency Power and the Militia Acts*, 114 YALE L.J. 149, 177–180 (2004). Note that this reading would represent a significant limitation on the emergency powers the President can claim domestically without congressional authorization,

Presumably, in prescribing a constitutional separation of powers for the prosecution of war, the Constitution is concerned with serious dangers that would attend allowing the President unilaterally to raise an army, declare war, and command the troops. What are those dangers? Are they absent in cases of civil insurrection?

3. *The Scope of Judicial Review over Presidential War Making.* Should *The Prize Cases* be read as holding that any legal challenge to a presidential determination of military emergency should be regarded as presenting a nonjusticiable political question? What about a legal challenge to the degree of presidential response to a military emergency?

4. *Congress's Role in Delimiting Executive Power.* Should the Court have resolved *The Prize Cases* differently if Congress had not yet statutorily ratified Lincoln's

actions? Although the point appears not have been argued, do the statutes on insurrection to which the opinions refer clearly pertain to cases of insurrection by the states? If not, where would the dissent leave executive power in such a case?

5. *Court-Packing: The Lincoln Precedent.* Franklin Roosevelt's court-packing plan, discussed above in Chapter Four, had its precedent in the first Lincoln Administration. Although Lincoln prevailed in *The Prize Cases* on a 5 to 4 vote, he was concerned that a precariously balanced Supreme Court — the Court that wrote *Dred Scott v. Sandford*, 60 U.S. (19 How.) 393 (1857) — could undermine the war effort. Just a week before the announcement of the judgment in *The Prize Cases*, Congress authorized the addition to the Court of a tenth justice. Lincoln appointed Stephen J. Field of California, a pro-Union Westerner who was assigned to ride the new far western Tenth Circuit. When Justice Catron, a dissenter in *The Prize Cases*, died in 1865, the Court reverted permanently to its membership of nine. Do you assess Lincoln's court-packing effort as being any more or less legitimate than Roosevelt's?

Note: The 2001 Authorization to Use Military Force

Justice Grier wrote: "If a war be made by invasion of a foreign nation, the President is not only authorized but bound to resist force by force . . . without waiting for any special legislative authority." An obvious question is how to understand this presidential obligation in the context of international terrorism. Is an attack of the scale of September 11, 2001 the legal equivalent of invasion by a foreign "nation"? What "resistance" may the President deploy unilaterally? May he do more than repel the "incursion"? We examine the legal implications of the 9/11 terrorist attacks more fully in Chapter 7.

Note, however, that Congress obviated such questions with regard to the U.S. response to the September 11 attacks by enacting a resolution the following week. The resolution, entitled "Authorization for the Use of Military Force," empowered the President "to use all necessary and appropriate force against those nations, organizations, or persons he determines" were responsible for the attacks. The full text of the resolution is reproduced in the Appendix.

To what extent does the resolution provide the President authority he lacked under Article II alone? Is the breadth of the delegation troubling? The President relied on this authority in organizing a coalition to overthrow the Taliban in Afghanistan. Is there any doubt he had legal authority sufficient for that purpose? How many other countries might succeeding presidents also invade under this authority?

2. The Vietnam Watershed

The confident early assertions of congressional primacy in military policy making are obviously at odds with much of our military history. Indeed, the most protracted military engagement in U.S. history — the Vietnam War — is also a marked example of unilateral executive initiative in leading U.S. military affairs. Because that engagement proved both costly and unsuccessful, it aroused the most profound opposition to the executive's increasing dominance of military policy. Tensions between the political branches elicited both the executive's strongest assertion ever of the scope of its inherent authorities and Congress's vigorous rebuttal.

Because Vietnam truly provides the experiential backdrop to all political conflicts that have occurred more recently over military policy, it is especially important to study the political branches' interpretations of their respective power at that time. Discontent with executive policy during the Watergate-weakened Nixon presidency ultimately produced the War Powers Resolution, Congress's formal attempt to reassert its prerogatives. These materials pose the obvious questions: Has the War Powers Resolution made any difference? How should all three branches interact on those issues?

a. Debating Executive Claims to Power

Meeker,[*] The Legality of United States Participation in the Defense of Viet-Nam

54 Dept. State Bull. 474 (1966)

IV. THE PRESIDENT HAS FULL AUTHORITY TO COMMIT UNITED STATES FORCES IN THE COLLECTIVE DEFENSE OF SOUTH VIET-NAM

There can be no question in present circumstances of the President's authority to commit United States forces to the defense of South Viet-Nam. The grant of authority to the President in article II of the Constitution extends to the actions of the United States currently undertaken in Viet-Nam. In fact, however, it is unnecessary to determine whether this grant standing alone is sufficient to authorize the actions taken in Viet-Nam. These actions rest not only on the exercise of Presidential powers under article II but on the SEATO treaty — a treaty advised and consented to by the Senate — and on actions of the Congress, particularly the joint resolution of August 10, 1964. When these sources of authority are taken together . . . there can be no question of the legality under domestic law of United States actions in Viet-Nam.

A. THE PRESIDENT'S POWER UNDER ARTICLE II OF THE CONSTITUTION EXTENDS TO THE ACTIONS CURRENTLY UNDERTAKEN IN VIET-NAM

Under the Constitution, the President, in addition to being Chief Executive, is Commander in Chief of the Army and Navy. He holds the prime responsibility for the conduct of United States foreign relations. These duties carry very broad powers, including the power to deploy American forces abroad and commit them to military operations when the President deems such action necessary to maintain the security and defense of the United States.

At the Federal Constitutional Convention in 1787, it was originally proposed that Congress have the power "to make war." There were objections that legislative

---

[*] The author of this article, Leonard Meeker, was then Legal Adviser to the U.S. Department of State.

proceedings were too slow for this power to be vested in Congress; it was suggested that the Senate might be a better repository. Madison and Gerry then moved to substitute "to declare war" for "to make war," "leaving to the Executive the power to repel sudden attacks." It was objected that this might make it too easy for the Executive to involve the nation in war, but the motion carried with but one dissenting vote.

In 1787 the world was a far larger place, and the framers probably had in mind attacks upon the United States. In the 20th century, the world has grown much smaller. An attack on a country far from our shores can impinge directly on the nation's security. In the SEATO treaty, for example, it is formally declared that an armed attack against Viet-Nam would endanger the peace and safety of the United States.

Since the Constitution was adopted there have been at least 125 instances in which the President has ordered the armed forces to take action or maintain positions abroad without obtaining prior congressional authorization, starting with the "undeclared war" with France (1798–1800). For example, President Truman ordered 250,000 troops to Korea during the Korean war of the early 1950's. President Eisenhower dispatched 14,000 troops to Lebanon in 1958.

The Constitution leaves to the President the judgment to determine whether the circumstances of a particular armed attack are so urgent and the potential consequences so threatening to the security of the United States that he should act without formally consulting the Congress.

B. THE SOUTHEAST ASIA COLLECTIVE DEFENSE TREATY AUTHORIZES THE PRESIDENT'S ACTIONS

Under article VI of the United States Constitution, "all treaties made, or which shall be made, under the Authority of the United States, shall be the supreme Law of the Land." Article IV, paragraph 1, of the SEATO treaty establishes as a matter of law that a Communist armed attack against South Viet-Nam endangers the peace and safety of the United States. In this same provision the United States has undertaken a commitment in the SEATO treaty to "act to meet the common danger in accordance with its constitutional processes" in the event of such an attack.

Under our Constitution it is the President who must decide when an armed attack has occurred. He has also the constitutional responsibility for determining what measures of defense are required when the peace and safety of the United States are endangered. If he considers that deployment of U.S. forces to South Viet-Nam is required, and that military measures against the source of Communist aggression in North Viet-Nam are necessary, he is constitutionally empowered to take those measures.

The SEATO treaty specifies that each party will act "in accordance with its constitutional processes."

It has recently been argued that the use of land forces in Asia is not authorized under the treaty because their use to deter armed attack was not contemplated at the time the treaty was considered by the Senate. Secretary Dulles testified at that time that we did not intend to establish (1) a land army in Southeast Asia capable of deterring Communist aggression, or (2) an integrated headquarters and military organization like that of NATO; instead, the United States would reply on "mobile striking power" against the sources of aggression. However, the treaty obligation in article IV, paragraph 1, to meet the common danger in the event of armed aggression, is not limited to particular modes of military action. What constitutes an adequate deterrent or an appropriate response, in terms of military strategy, may change; but the essence of our commitment to act to meet the common danger, as necessary at the time of an armed aggression, remains. In 1954 the forecast of military judgment might have been against the use of substantial United States ground forces in Viet-Nam. But that does not preclude the President from reaching a different military judgment in different circumstances, 12 years later.

C. THE JOINT RESOLUTION OF CONGRESS OF AUGUST 10, 1964, AUTHORIZES UNITED STATES PARTICIPATION IN THE COLLECTIVE DEFENSE OF SOUTH VIET-NAM

. . . Following the North Vietnamese attacks in the Gulf of Tonkin against United States destroyers, Congress adopted, by a Senate vote of 88–2 and a House vote of 416–0, a joint resolution containing a series of important declarations and provisions of law.

Section 1 resolved that "the Congress approves and supports the determination of the President, as Commander in Chief, to take all necessary measures to repel any armed attack against the forces of the United States and to prevent further aggression." Thus, the Congress gave its sanction to specific actions by the President to repel attacks against United States naval vessels in the Gulf of Tonkin and elsewhere in the western Pacific. Congress further approved the taking of "all necessary measures . . . to prevent further aggression." . . .

The joint resolution then went on to provide in section 2:

> The United States regards as vital to its national interest and to world peace the maintenance of international peace and security in southeast Asia. Consonant with the Constitution of the United States and the Charter of the United Nations and in accordance with its obligations under the Southeast Asia Collective Defense Treaty, the United States is, therefore, prepared, as the President determines, to take all necessary steps, including the use of armed force, to assist any member or protocol state of the Southeast Asia Collective Defense Treaty requesting assistance in defense of its freedom.

Section 2 thus constitutes an authorization to the President, in his discretion, to act — using armed force if he determines that is required — to assist South Viet-Nam at its request in defense of its freedom. . . .

It has been suggested that the legislative history of the joint resolution shows an intention to limit United States assistance to South Viet-Nam to aid, advice, and training. This suggestion is based on an amendment offered from the floor by Senator [Gaylord] Nelson which would have added the following to the text:

> The Congress also approves and supports the efforts of the President to bring the problem of peace in Southeast Asia to the Security Council of the United Nations, and the President's declaration that the United States, seeking no extension of the present military conflict, will respond to provocation in a manner that is "limited and fitting." Our continuing policy is to limit our role to the provision of aid, training assistance, and military advice, and it is the sense of Congress that, except when provoked to a greater response, we should continue to attempt to avoid a direct military involvement in the Southeast Asian conflict.[25]

Senator [J. W.] Fulbright, who had reported the joint resolution from the Foreign Relations Committee, spoke on the amendment as follows:

> It states fairly accurately what the President has said would be our policy, and what I stated my understanding was as to our policy; also what other Senators have stated. In other words, it states that our response should be appropriate and limited to the provocation, which the Senator states as "respond to provocation in a manner that is limited and fitting," and so forth. . . .

> The Senator has put into his amendment a statement of policy that is unobjectionable. However, I cannot accept the amendment under the circumstances. I do not believe it is contrary to the joint resolution, but it is an enlargement. I am informed that the House is now voting on this resolution. The House joint resolution is about to be presented to us. I cannot accept the amendment and go to conference with it, and thus take responsibility for delaying matters.

> I do not object to it as a statement of policy. I believe it is an accurate reflection of what I believe is the President's policy, judging from his own statements. . . .

Senator Nelson's amendment related the degree and kind of U.S. response in Viet-Nam to "provocation" on the other side; the response should be "limited and fitting." The greater the provocation, the stronger are the measures that may be characterized as "limited and fitting." Bombing of North Vietnamese naval bases was a "limited and fitting" response to the attacks on U.S. destroyers in August 1964, and the subsequent actions taken by the United States and South Viet-Nam have been an appropriate response to the increased war of aggression carried on by North Viet-Nam since that date. Moreover, Senator Nelson's proposed amendment did not purport to be a restriction on authority available to the President but merely a statement concerning what should be the continuing policy of the United States.

---

25. 110 Cong. Rec. 18459 (Aug. 7, 1964).

Congressional realization of the scope of authority being conferred by the joint resolution is shown by the legislative history of the measure as a whole. The following exchange between Senators Cooper and Fulbright is illuminating:

> Mr. COOPER [John Sherman Cooper]. . . . The Senator will remember that the SEATO Treaty, in article IV, provides that in the event an armed attack is made . . . upon one of the protocol states such as South Vietnam, the . . . United States, would then take such action as might be appropriate, after resorting to their constitutional processes. I assume that would mean, in the case of the United States, that Congress would be asked to grant the authority to act.
>
> Does the Senator consider that in enacting this resolution we are satisfying that requirement of article IV of the Southeast Asia Collective Defense Treaty? In other words, are we now giving the President advance authority to take whatever action he may deem necessary respecting South Vietnam and its defense, or with respect to the defense of any other country included in the treaty?
>
> Mr. FULBRIGHT. I think that is correct.
>
> Mr. COOPER. Then, looking ahead, if the President decided that it was necessary to use such force as could lead into war, we will give that authority by this resolution?
>
> Mr. FULBRIGHT. That is the way I would interpret it. If a situation later developed in which we thought the approval should be withdrawn it could be withdrawn by concurrent resolution.

The August 1964 joint resolution continues in force today. Section 2 of the resolution provides that it shall expire "when the President shall determine that the peace and security of the area is reasonably assured by international conditions created by action of the United Nations or otherwise, except that it may be terminated earlier by concurrent resolution of the Congress." The President has made no such determination, nor has Congress terminated the joint resolution.[28]

Instead, Congress in May 1965 approved an appropriation of $700 million to meet the expense of mounting military requirements in Viet-Nam. (Public Law 89-18, 79 Stat. 109.) The President's message asking for this appropriation states that this was "not a routine appropriation. For each Member of Congress who supports this request is also voting to persist in our efforts to halt Communist aggression in South Vietnam." The appropriation act constitutes a clear congressional endorsement and approval of the actions taken by the President.

On March 1, 1966, the Congress continued to express its support of the President's policy by approving a $4.8 billion supplemental military authorization by votes of

---

28. On March 1, 1966, the Senate voted, 92–5, to table an amendment that would have repealed the joint resolution.

392–4 and 93–2. An amendment that would have limited the President's authority to commit forces to Viet-Nam was rejected in the Senate by a vote of 94–2.

D. NO DECLARATION OF WAR BY THE CONGRESS IS REQUIRED TO AUTHORIZE UNITED STATES PARTICIPATION IN THE COLLECTIVE DEFENSE OF SOUTH VIET-NAM

No declaration of war is needed to authorize American actions in Viet-Nam. As shown in the preceding sections, the President has ample authority to order the participation of United States armed forces in the defense of South Viet-Nam.

Over a very long period in our history, practice and precedent have confirmed the constitutional authority to engage United States forces in hostilities without a declaration of war. This history extends from the undeclared war with France and the war against the Barbary pirates at the end of the 18th century to the Korean war of 1950–53.

James Madison, one of the leading framers of the Constitution, and Presidents John Adams and Jefferson all construed the Constitution, in their official actions during the early years of the Republic, as authorizing the United States to employ its armed forces abroad in hostilities in the absence of any congressional declaration of war. Their views and actions constitute highly persuasive evidence as to the meaning and effect of the Constitution. History has accepted the interpretation that was placed on the Constitution by the early Presidents and Congresses in regard to the lawfulness of hostilities without a declaration of war. The instances of such action in our history are numerous.

In the Korean conflict, where large-scale hostilities were conducted with an American troop participation of a quarter of a million men, no declaration of war was made by the Congress. The President acted on the basis of his constitutional responsibilities. While the Security Council, under a treaty of this country—the United Nations Charter—recommended assistance to the Republic of Korea against the Communist armed attack, the United States had no treaty commitment at that time obligating us to join in the defense of South Korea. In the case of South Viet-Nam we have the obligation of the SEATO treaty and clear expressions of congressional support. If the President could act in Korea without a declaration of war, *a fortiori* he is empowered to do so now in Viet-Nam. It may be suggested that a declaration of war is the only available constitutional process by which congressional support can be made effective for the use of United States armed forces in combat abroad. But the Constitution does not insist on any rigid formalism. It gives Congress a choice of ways in which to exercise its powers. In the case of Viet-Nam the Congress has supported the determination of the President by the Senate's approval of the SEATO treaty, the adoption of the joint resolution of August 10, 1964, and the enactment of the necessary authorizations and appropriations.

V. CONCLUSION

. . . The United States has commitments to assist South Viet-Nam in defending itself against Communist aggression from the North. The United States gave undertakings to this effect at the conclusion of the Geneva conference in 1954. Later that year the United States undertook an international obligation in the SEATO treaty to defend South Viet-Nam against Communist armed aggression. And during the past decade the United States has given additional assurance to the South Vietnamese Government.

The Geneva accords of 1954 provided for a cease-fire and regroupment of contending forces, a division of Viet-Nam into two zones, and a prohibition on the use of either zone for the resumption of hostilities or to "further an aggressive policy." From the beginning, North Viet-Nam violated the Geneva accords through a systematic effort to gain control of South Viet-Nam by force. In the light of these progressive North Vietnamese violations, the introduction into South Viet-Nam beginning in late 1961 of substantial United States military equipment and personnel, to assist in the defense of the South, was fully justified; substantial breach of an international agreement by one side permits the other side to suspend performance of corresponding obligations under the agreement. United States actions in Viet-Nam, taken by the President and approved by the Congress, do not require any declaration of war, as shown by a long line of precedents for the use of United States armed forces abroad in the absence of any congressional declaration of war.

National Commitments

S. Rep. No. 129 (Comm. on Foreign Relations),
91st Cong., 1st Sess. (1969)

• • •

1. THE INTENT OF THE FRAMERS

There is no uncertainty or ambiguity about the intent of the framers of the Constitution with respect to the war power. Greatly dismayed by the power of the British Crown to commit Great Britain—and with it the American colonies—to war, fearful of the possible development of monarchical tendencies in their new republic, and fearful as well of the dangers of large standing armies and military defiance of civilian authority, they vested the power to commit the United States to war exclusively in Congress. This power was not, like certain others, divided between the executive and the legislature; it was conferred upon Congress and Congress alone.

It was understood by the framers—and subsequent usage confirmed their understanding—that the President in his capacity as Commander in Chief of the Armed Forces would have the right, indeed the duty, to use the Armed Forces to repel sudden attacks on the United States, even in advance of Congressional authorization to do so. It was further understood that he would direct and lead the Armed Forces and put them to any use specified by Congress but that this did not extend to the initiation of hostilities. As Senator Ervin said in his statement to the committee, ". . . a distinction must be drawn between defensive warfare and offensive warfare."

The Constitutional Convention had at first proposed to give Congress the power to "*make war*" but changed this to "*declare war.*" The purpose of the change was not to enlarge Presidential power in any significant degree (it was supported by delegates who subsequently refused to sign the Constitution on the ground that it gave too much power to the President) but to permit him to take action to repel sudden attacks. Madison's notes on the proceedings of the convention report the change of wording as follows:

> Mr. Madison and Mr. Gerry *moved* to insert "*declare,*" striking out "*make*" war; leaving to the Executive the power to repel sudden attacks.[15]

It should be remembered as well that the Congress was not expected to be in session for more than 1 month a year and that it was thought that it would be dangerous to leave the country defenseless during the long adjournment. Were the matter being considered now, in our age of long congressional sessions, rapid transportation, and instantaneous communication, one may wonder whether it would be thought necessary to concede the Executive any authority at all in this field. In any case it was authority to repel sudden attacks—that and nothing more—that the framers conceded to the President.

Relatively little attention was given by the Constitutional Convention to the comparative roles of President and Congress in making war. The probable reason, a recent scholar suggests, is that the full power to initiate the use of the armed forces was assumed by everyone to rest with Congress; seeing no issue of separation of powers, they gave the matter scant attention.[17]

The evidence is abundant that the framers did not intend the executive to have the power to initiate war. . . .

2. THE WAR POWER FROM 1789 TO 1900

The early Presidents carefully respected Congress's authority to initiate war. President Adams took action to protect American ships from French attacks on the Atlantic only to the extent that Congress authorized him to do so; even in the case of this "limited war" between the United States and revolutionary France the President did not regard himself as free to use the Armed Forces without authorization by Congress.

Early in his term of office President Jefferson sent a naval squadron to the Mediterranean to protect American commerce against piracy, but it was not at first permitted to engage in offensive action against the Barbary pirates. On December 8, 1801, President Jefferson, having judged that offensive action was necessary, sent the following message to Congress:

---

15. The Records of the Federal Convention of 1787, 4 volumes. (Max Farrand ed., New Haven and London: Yale University Press, 1966), vol. 2, p. 318.

17. Robert William Russell, *The United States Congress and the Power To Use Military Force Abroad*, Ph.D. thesis, Fletcher School of Law and Diplomacy, 1967, pp. 58–59.

Tripoli, the least considerable of the Barbary States, had come forward with demands unfounded either in right or in compact, and had permitted itself to denounce war on our failure to comply before a given day. The style of the demand admitted but one answer. I sent a small squadron of frigates into the Mediterranean . . . with orders to protect our commerce against the threatened attack. . . . Our commerce in the Mediterranean was blockaded and that of the Atlantic in peril.

Then, referring to the capture of one of the Tripolitan ships by the American ship *Enterprise*, Jefferson continued:

. . . Unauthorized by the Constitution, without the sanction of Congress, to go beyond the line of defense, the vessel, being disabled from committing further hostilities, was liberated with its crew. The Legislature will doubtless consider whether, by authorizing measures of offense also, they will place our force on an equal footing with that of its adversaries. I communicate all material information on this subject, that in the exercise of this important function confided by the Constitution to the Legislature exclusively their judgment may form itself on a knowledge and consideration of every circumstance of weight.[19]

The Monroe Doctrine is often cited as an instance and precedent for the making of foreign commitments by executive action. In fact a distinction was made at the time between a statement of policy and its implementation, the latter being regarded as falling within the province of Congress. In reply to an inquiry by the Government of Colombia in 1824 as to what action the United States might take in response to possible European intervention against the New Latin American republics, Secretary of State John Quincy Adams replied:

With respect to the question, "in what manner the Government of the United States intends to resist on its part any interference of the Holy Alliance for the purpose of subjugating the new republics or interfering in their political forms" you understand that by the Constitution of the United States, the ultimate decision of this question belongs to the Legislative Department of the Government. . . .[20]

In 1846 President Polk sent American forces into the disputed territory between Corpus Christi and the Rio Grande River, precipitating the clash which began the Mexican War. The constitutionality of this act is uncertain but Abraham Lincoln, then a Congressman from Illinois, was certain that it was unconstitutional. He wrote:

---

19. U.S. Congress, Joint Committee on Printing, Compilation of Messages and Papers of the Presidents, 20 volumes (James D. Richardson, ed., New York: Bureau of National Literature, Inc., 1897), vol. 1, p. 314.

20. John Quincy Adams to Don Jose Maria Salazar, Aug. 6, 1824, quoted in *The Record of American Diplomacy* (Ruhl J. Bartlett, editor, third edition, New York: Alfred A. Knopf, 1954), p. 185.

... Allow the President to invade a neighboring nation, whenever *he* shall deem it necessary to repel an invasion, and you allow him to do so, *whenever he may choose to say* he deems it necessary for such purpose — and you allow him to make war at pleasure. Study to see if you can fix *any limit* to his power in this respect, after you have given him so much as you propose. . . .

The provision of the Constitution giving the warmaking power to Congress, was dictated, as I understand it, by the following reasons. Kings had always been involving and impoverishing their people in wars, pretending generally, if not always, that the good of the people was the object. This, our Convention undertook to be the most oppressive of all Kingly oppressions; and they resolved to so frame the Constitution that *no one man* should hold the power of bringing this oppression upon us.[21]

During the 19th century American Armed Forces were used by the President on his own authority for such purposes as suppressing piracy, suppressing the slave trade by American ships, "hot pursuit" of criminals across frontiers, and protecting American lives and property in backward areas or areas where government had broken down. Such limited uses of force without authorization by Congress, not involving the initiation of hostilities against foreign governments, came to be accepted practice, sanctioned by usage though not explicitly by the Constitution.

Some Presidents, notably Polk, Grant, and McKinley, interpreted their powers as Commander in Chief broadly, while others, such as the early Presidents and Buchanan and Cleveland, were scrupulously deferential to the war power of Congress. Summarizing the war power in the 19th century, Robert William Russell writes:

It is not a simple matter to arrive at conclusions concerning this period in which the constitutional interpretation was far from consistent, where Grant's extreme view is sandwiched between the conservative views of Buchanan and Cleveland. But there was one opinion that enjoyed wide acceptance: the President could constitutionally employ American military force outside the nation as long as he did not use it to commit "acts of war." While the term was never precisely defined, an "act of war" in this context usually meant *the use of military force against a sovereign nation* without that nation's *consent* and without that nation's having declared war upon or used force against the United States. To perform acts of war the President needed the authorization of Congress. Even when a foreign state initiated military acts of war, the President always sought *post hoc* congressional approval for his response.

This dividing line between the proper spheres of legislative and executive authority was sufficiently flexible to permit the President to use military

21. Letter to William H. Herndon, Feb. 15, 1848, in The Collected Works of Abraham Lincoln, 9 volumes (New Brunswick: Rutgers University Press, 1953), vol. 1, pp. 451–52.

force in the unimportant cases, while preserving the role of Congress in important decisions. The acts of war doctrine was probably a step beyond what the framers intended when they changed the congressional power from "make" war to "declare" war, and was certainly a move in the direction of Presidential power compared to the cautious stance of Washington, Adams, Jefferson, and Madison. The central objective which the Constitution sought—congressional authority to approve the initiation of major conflicts—was undamaged, but a certain fraying of the edges had occurred. This slight deterioration was greatly accelerated during the following 50 years.[22]

3. THE EXPANSION OF EXECUTIVE POWER IN THE 20TH CENTURY, 1900–41

The use of the Armed Forces against sovereign nations without authorization by Congress became common practice in the 20th century. President Theodore Roosevelt used the Navy to prevent Colombian forces from suppressing insurrection in the province of Panama and intervened militarily in Cuba and the Dominican Republic. Presidents Taft and Wilson also sent armed forces to the Caribbean and Central America without Congressional authorization. In Haiti, the Dominican Republic, and Nicaragua these interventions resulted in the establishment of American military governments.

President Wilson seized the Mexican port of Vera Cruz in 1914 as an act of reprisal, in order, he said, to "enforce respect" for the government of the United States. The two Houses of Congress adopted separate resolutions in support of President Wilson's action but the Senate did not complete action on its resolution until after the seizure of Vera Cruz. After the Mexican bandit Pancho Villa raided the town of Columbus, N. Mex., in 1916, President Wilson sent a force under General Pershing into Mexico in "hot pursuit" of the bandits; the expedition turned into a prolonged intervention of nearly 2 years and almost brought about war with Mexico. The Senate adopted a resolution supporting the President after General Pershing's force had entered Mexico; this resolution was never reported out of the Foreign Affairs Committee of the House of Representatives.

The military powers which had been acquired by Presidents in the 19th century—for purposes of "hot pursuit" and the protection of American lives and property, and under treaties which conferred rights and obligations on the United States—were not serious infringements on Congress' war power because they had been used for the most part against individuals or bands of pirates or bandits and not against sovereign states. Roosevelt, Taft, and Wilson used these powers to engage in military action against sovereign states, thereby greatly expanding the scope of executive power over the use of the armed forces and setting precedents for the greater expansions of executive power which were to follow. The Congresses of that era did

---

22. Russell, *The United States Congress and the Power To Use Military Force Abroad*, pp. 242–43.

not see fit to resist or oppose these incursions of their constitutional authority; indeed, as we have noted, one or both Houses of Congress gave retroactive approval to President Wilson's unauthorized interventions in Mexico.

Roosevelt, Taft, and Wilson asserted no general or "inherent" Presidential power to make war. Indeed, when it came to full-scale conflict with Germany, President Wilson explicitly acknowledged the war power of the Congress. *Advising* Congress to declare war on Germany in his war message of April 2, 1917, the President said:

> I have called the Congress into extraordinary session because there are serious, very serious, choices of policy to be made, and made immediately, which it is neither right nor constitutionally permissible that I should assume the responsibility of making.[23]

President Franklin Roosevelt expanded executive power over the use of the Armed Forces to an unprecedented degree. The exchange of overaged American destroyers for British bases in the Western Hemisphere was accomplished by executive agreement, in violation of the Senate's treaty power, and was also a violation of the international law of neutrality, giving Germany legal cause, had she chosen to take it, to declare war on the United States. The transaction was an *emergency* use of Presidential power, taken in the belief that it might be essential to save Great Britain from invasion.

In 1941 President Roosevelt, on his own authority, committed American forces to the defense of Greenland and Iceland and authorized American naval vessels to escort convoys to Iceland provided that at least one ship in each convoy flew the American or Icelandic flag. When the American destroyer *Greer* was fired on by a German submarine, . . . President Roosevelt utilized the occasion to announce that thereafter American naval vessels would shoot on sight against German and Italian ships west of the 26th meridian. By the time Germany and Italy declared war on the United States, in the wake of the Japanese attack on Pearl Harbor, the United States had already been committed by its President, acting on his own authority, to an undeclared naval war in the Atlantic. Roosevelt, however, achieved his objective without asserting a general or "inherent" Presidential power to commit the Armed Forces abroad.

4. THE PASSING OF THE WAR POWER FROM CONGRESS TO THE EXECUTIVE AFTER WORLD WAR II

The trend initiated by Theodore Roosevelt, Taft, and Wilson, and accelerated by Franklin Roosevelt, continued at a rapid rate under Presidents Truman, Eisenhower, Kennedy, and Johnson, bringing the country to the point at which the real power to commit the country to war is now in the hands of the President. The trend which began in the early 20th century has been consummated and the intent of the framers of the Constitution as to the war power substantially negated.

---

23. The Public Papers of Woodrow Wilson: War and Peace, 2 volumes (Ray Stannard Baker & William E. Dodd eds., New York and London: Harper Bros.), vol. 1, p. 6.

By the late 1940s there had developed a kind of ambivalence as to the war power in the minds of officials in the executive branch, Members of Congress and, presumably, the country at large. On the one hand, it was and still is said that Congress alone has the power to declare war; on the other hand it was widely believed, or at least conceded, that the President in his capacity as Commander in Chief had the authority to use the Armed Forces in any way he saw fit. Noting that the President has in fact exercised power over the Armed Forces we have come to assume that he is entitled to do so. The actual possession of a power has given rise to a belief in its constitutional legitimacy.

The fact that Congress has acquiesced in, or at the very least has failed to challenge, the transfer of the war power from itself to the executive, is probably the most important single fact accounting for the speed and virtual completeness of the transfer. Why has Congress agreed to this rearrangement of powers which is without constitutional justification, and at its own expense?

To some degree, it seems to be the result of the unfamiliarity of the United States with its new role as a world power. Lacking guidelines of experience for the accommodation of our constitutional system to the new demands that have been made upon it, Congress has acquiesced in the resort to expedients in foreign policy making which we have already noted. In addition, the fact that so many of the great policy decisions of the postwar era have been made in an atmosphere of real or contrived urgency has put tremendous pressure on Members of Congress to set aside apprehensions as to the exercise of power by the executive lest they cause some fatal delay or omission in the nation's foreign policy.

Another possible factor in congressional passivity is that Congress may have permitted itself to be overawed by the cult of executive expertise. Like the newly rich who go beyond the bounds of good taste in material display, the newly powerful may go beyond the bounds of good judgment in their intellectual display. A veritable army of foreign policy experts has sprung up in government and in the universities in recent years, contributing greatly to our knowledge and skill in foreign relations but also purveying the belief that foreign policy is an occult science which ordinary citizens, including Members of Congress, are simply too stupid to grasp. Many Members of Congress seem to have accepted this viewpoint, forgetting the point made by Professor Bartlett that "there are no experts in wisdom concerning human affairs or in determining the national interest, and there is nothing in the realm of foreign policy that cannot be understood by the average American citizen."[24]

There may also be a historical memory at work in Congress' acceptance of executive predominance in foreign relations. The Senate, it has long been widely agreed, acted with disastrous irresponsibility in its rejection of the Covenant of the League of Nations in 1919. Since at least 1945, when the Senate ratified the United Nations Charter with virtually no debate, Congress has been doing a kind of penance for its

---

24. *U.S. Commitments to Foreign Powers*, p. 20.

prewar isolationism, and that penance has sometimes taken the form of overly hasty acquiescence in proposals for the acceptance of one form or another of international responsibility. Congress, it seems clear, was deficient in vision during the 1920's and 1930's, but so were Presidents Harding, Coolidge, Hoover, and — prior to 1938 — Roosevelt. . . . In its deference to the executive in foreign affairs, Congress has conceded him, and the experts around him, a kind of infallibility which the wisest among them would readily acknowledge they do not have. Versailles, like Munich, has conveyed more lessons than were in it; its only lesson, as far as the workings of the American government are concerned, is the need not of congressional diffidence but of congressional responsibility — and the same counsel could profitably be heeded by the executive as well.

Returning to our chronology, we can detect the ambivalence about the executive's control of the armed forces in events of the post-World War II period. . . .

There seems to have been general agreement that the United Nations Charter, the NATO Treaty, and the other postwar security treaties did not change the relative powers of Congress and the President with respect to the use of the Armed Forces. There was little agreement, however, on what exactly those relative powers were — not, in the committee's opinion, because there could be any real doubt on constitutional grounds but because, as the trend toward executive control accelerated, constitutional considerations were neglected and the *de facto* power of the President came to be accepted as a constitutional power. As E. S. Corwin wrote in 1949, in many American minds —

> . . . the President's power to repel sudden attacks had developed into an undefined power . . . to employ without congressional authorization the Armed Forces in the protection of American rights and interests abroad whenever necessary.[27]

Dr. Russell comments:

> . . . The intriguing aspect of this new interpretation of the constitutional division of powers is that it occurred at a point in American history when the older, specific categories under which force had been used by Presidents had disappeared. The right to intervene in Latin America was no longer maintained and the right to protect lives and property by armed force had been renounced. The areas where Presidents wished to use armed force were no longer primitive nations, but major powers against whom the use of armed force could not be easily disguised as anything but acts of war. If Presidents wished to exercise the power to use armed force abroad for general purposes without the consent of Congress they needed to assert a broader explanation of the President's constitutional authority than the right to use armed force in all cases except acts of war. What they needed to establish complete independence from congressional control was to assert that the President had

---

27. Edward S. Corwin, *Who Has the Power to Make War?* N.Y. Times, July 31, 1949, p. 14.

a general constitutional power to use armed force to protect U.S. "interests" or "security." With no established limits on when Presidents might use force or on the quantity used, there would be no need to go to Congress.[28]

President Truman committed American Armed Forces to Korea in 1950 without Congressional authorization. Congressional leaders and the press were simultaneously informed of the decision but the decision had already been made.

President Truman himself made no public explanation of his use of the war power but an article in the Department of State Bulletin asserted that "the President, as Commander in Chief of the Armed Forces of the United States, has full control over the use thereof." The article pointed to past instances in which the President had used the Armed Forces in what was said to be "the broad interests of American foreign policy" and also asserted that there was a "traditional power of the President to use the Armed Forces of the United States without consulting Congress."[29] Here, clearly expostulated, is a doctrine of general or "inherent" Presidential power — something which had not been claimed by previous Presidents. [Yet, s]carcely a voice of dissent was raised in Congress at the time of Truman's action. . . .

In 1951 the Senate Committees on Foreign Relations and Armed Services held joint hearings to discuss President Truman's plan for sending six divisions of American soldiers to Europe. Secretary of State Acheson gave the committees the following interpretation of the President's powers:

> Not only has the President the authority to use the Armed Forces in carrying out the broad foreign policy of the United States and implementing treaties, but it is equally clear that this authority may not be interfered with by the Congress in the exercise of powers which it has under the Constitution.

Acheson thought it inappropriate even to discuss constitutional matters:

> We are in a position in the world today where the argument as to who has the power to do this, that, or the other thing, is not exactly what is called for from America in this very critical hour.[32]

President Eisenhower exhibited some ambivalence as to his authority to use the Armed Forces. He conceded the authority of Congress, for example in the following statement at a press conference on March 10, 1954:

> There is going to be no involvement of America in war unless it is a result of the constitutional process that is placed upon Congress to declare it. Now let us have that clear. . . .[33]

---

28. *The United States Congress and the Power to Use Military Force Abroad*, p. 389.

29. *Department of State Bulletin*, vol. 23, No. 578, July 31, 1950, pp. 173–77.

32. *Assignment of Ground Forces of the United States to Duty in the European Area, Hearing by Committees on Foreign Relations and Armed Services*, U.S. Senate, 82nd Cong., 1st Sess., on S. Con. Res. 8, Feb. 1–28, 1951 (Washington: U.S. Government Printing Office, 1951), pp. 92–93.

33. Public Papers of the Presidents of the United States: Eisenhower, 1954 (Washington: U.S. Government Printing Office, 1960), p. 306.

But, in asking Congress for "presidential authority to use American Armed Forces to protect Formosa and the Pescadores," he said:

> Authority for some of the action which might be required would be inherent in the authority of the Commander in Chief. Until congress can act I would not hesitate, so far as my constitutional powers extend, to take whatever emergency action might be forced upon us in order to protect the rights and security of the United States.

> However, a suitable congressional resolution would clearly and publicly establish the authority of the President as Commander in Chief to employ the Armed Forces of this Nation promptly and effectively for the purposes indicated if in his judgment it became necessary.[34]

The burden of President Eisenhower's message seems to have been that, although he regarded himself as having some authority to dispose of the Armed Forces, he did not regard it as entirely certain that he did have it or in what amount. It was presumably in order to put this authority on an unquestionable basis that he asked for a congressional resolution.

It is significant that in the case of the Formosa resolution President Eisenhower asked for *authority* rather than mere approval or support and that under the resolution adopted by Congress the President was "*authorized* to employ the Armed Forces," upon his own finding of necessity, for the defense of Formosa and the Pescadores. The use of the word *authorize* by both President and Congress strongly implied recognition by both that the authority to commit the armed forces lay with the Congress, to grant or withhold. The committee emphasizes this point as one which may have significance in possible future congressional action on resolutions pertaining to the use of the Armed Forces.

Although the word *authorize* was used in the Formosa resolution, the authorization was an extremely broad one, empowering the President to employ the Armed Forces to defend Formosa and the Pescadores "as he determines necessary." It can be argued that an authorization so general and imprecise amounts to an unconstitutional alienation of its war power on the part of the Congress. Indeed, Senate opposition to the Formosa resolution centered on the contention that the language of the resolution sought to enable the President to wage war without a declaration of war by Congress. During the debate on the resolution Senator Morse said that, "under the Constitution of the United States, no President has the right to commit an act of war against a sovereign power."[35]

Subsequent resolutions involving the possible use of armed force abandoned the principle of *authorization*, demonstrating not only ambivalence as to the extent of the President's authority but a lack of attention to the underlying constitutional question. The Middle East resolution of 1957, the Cuba resolution of 1962, and the Gulf

---

34. *Congressional Record*, 84th Cong., 1st Sess., vol. 101, pt. 1, Senate, Jan. 24, 1955, p. 601.
35. *Congressional Record*, 84th Cong., 1st Sess., vol. 101, pt. 1, Senate, Jan. 24, 1955, p. 766.

of Tonkin resolution of 1964 dropped the vital concept of congressional authorization and instead used terminology which, by failing to express a grant of power by Congress, implied acceptance of the view that the President already had the power to use the Armed Forces in the ways proposed and that, the resolutions were no more than expressions of congressional support and national unity. The prevailing attitude in each instance seems to have been one of concern not with constitutional questions but with the problem at hand and with the need for a method of dealing with it, heightened in all three cases by a sense of urgency. Nonetheless, precedents were set.

The debate on the Middle East resolution of 1957 revealed two dominant attitudes on the war power; first, a reluctance to define it with precision, and, second, growing senatorial acceptance of the view that the President, in his capacity as Commander in Chief, could commit the Armed Forces to defend what he might regard as the "vital interest" of the nation. In testimony before the Committees on Foreign Relations and Armed Services, Secretary of State Dulles refused to express an opinion as to whether or not the President could commit the Armed Forces in the absence of the resolution. Senator Fulbright, whose view has changed with time and experience, thought at the time that the President had power as Commander in Chief to use the Armed Forces to defend the "vital interests" of the country and that the resolution would have the effect of limiting that power.[36] This viewpoint was widely shared at the time. In their report the two committees struck out the word "authorize" and expressed satisfaction at having avoided the necessity of defining the relative powers of Congress and the President.[37] The debate on the floor of the Senate showed preponderant, but far from unanimous, support for this expansive view of Presidential authority.[38] The final resolution said that, "if the President determines the necessity thereof, the United States is prepared to use armed force" to defend Middle Eastern nations against Communist aggression, "provided that such employment shall be consonant with the treaty obligations of the United States and with the Constitution of the United States." What exactly was thought to be required for the use of force to be "consonant with the Constitution" was by this time more obscure than ever. When President Eisenhower sent 14,000 American troops to Lebanon in 1958, he said that they were being sent "to protect American lives and by their presence there to encourage the Lebanese Government in defense of Lebanese sovereignty and integrity." No reference was made to the resolution of the previous year.

In September 1962 Congress adopted a joint resolution pertaining to Cuba. The Kennedy administration favored a concurrent resolution expressing the sense of

---

36. *The President's Proposal on the Middle East, Hearings before the Committees on Foreign Relations and Armed Services*, U.S. Senate, 85th Cong., 1st Sess., Jan. 14 to Feb. 11, 1957 (Washington: U.S. Government Printing Office, 1957), pp. 111–19.

37. To Promote Peace and Stability in the Middle East, S. Rep. No. 70, 85th Cong., 1st Sess. (Washington: U.S. Government Printing Office, 1957), p. 9.

38. Russell, *The United States Congress and the Power To Use Military Force Abroad*, pp. 416–20.

Congress that the President "possesses all necessary authority" to prevent Cuba, "by whatever means may be necessary, including the use of arms," from "exporting its aggressive purposes" in the hemisphere, to prevent the establishment of a foreign, i.e., Soviet, military base in Cuba, and to support Cuban aspirations for self-determination. Senator Russell opposed the concurrent resolution favored by the administration. "I do not believe," he said, "that the Armed Services Committee is going to make a constitutional assertion that the President of the United States has the right to declare war, and that is what this does."[39] The resolution as finally adopted was a joint resolution, stating that "the United States is determined" to do those things spelled out in the abandoned concurrent resolution.

The Cuban missile crisis occurred 1 month later. Two hours before he went on television on October 22, 1962, to announce the "quarantine" on shipments of offensive missiles to Cuba, President Kennedy met with the congressional leadership and briefed them on the decisions which had, of course, already been made. In the belief that they had a *duty* to give the President their best judgment, certain Senators expressed opinions as to possible wise courses of action. This was the extent of congressional participation in the greatest crisis of the postwar era, the one crisis which brought the world to the brink of nuclear war. Finding the congressional advice in some cases "captious and inconsistent," Theodore Sorensen later wrote that the President's meeting with the congressional leadership was the "only sour note of the day."[40] . . .

The Gulf of Tonkin resolution represents the extreme point in the process of constitutional erosion that began in the first years of this century. Couched in broad terms, the resolution constitutes an acknowledgment of virtually unlimited Presidential control of the Armed Forces. It is of more than historical importance that the Congress now ask itself why it was prepared to acquiesce in the transfer to the executive of a power which, beyond any doubt, was intended by the Constitution to be exercised by Congress.

Several answers suggest themselves:

First, in the case of each of the resolutions discussed, Congress was confronted with a situation that seemed to be urgent and, lacking firm historical guidelines for the discharge of its foreign policy responsibilities in a real or seeming emergency, it acquiesced in an expedient which seemed to meet the needs of the moment, the foremost of which at the time of each of the resolutions seemed to be an expression of national unity. In the case of the Gulf of Tonkin resolution, the Senate responded to the administration's contention that the effect of the resolution would be lost if it were not enacted quickly. The desired effect was a resounding expression of national unity and support for the President at a moment when it was felt that the country

39. *Situation in Cuba, Hearings before the Senate Foreign Relations and Armed Services Committees*, U.S. Senate, 87th Cong., 2d Sess., Sept. 1962 (Washington: U.S. Government Printing Office, 1962), p. 72.

40. Kennedy (New York: Harper & Row, 1965), p. 702.

had been attacked. In order, therefore, to avoid the delay that would arise from a careful analysis of the language of the resolution and the further delay that would arise if the resolution had to go to a Senate-House conference to reconcile differing versions, the Foreign Relations Committee and the entire Senate speedily approved the resolution in the language in which it had already been adopted by the House of Representatives. The prevailing attitude was not so much that Congress was granting or acknowledging the executive's authority to take certain actions but that it was expressing unity and support for the President in a moment of national crisis and, therefore, that the exact words in which it expressed those sentiments were not of primary importance.

Second, in the course of two decades of cold war the country and its leaders became so preoccupied with questions of national security as to have relatively little time or thought for constitutional matters. . . .

Third, in the case of the Gulf of Tonkin resolution, there was a discrepancy between the language of the resolution and the intent of Congress. Although the language of the resolution lends itself to the interpretation that Congress was consenting in advance to a full-scale war in Asia should the President think it necessary, that was not the expectation of Congress at the time. In adopting the resolution Congress was closer to believing that it was helping to *prevent* a large-scale war by taking a firm stand than it was laying the legal basis for the conduct of such a war. . . . Its expectations were shaped by events outside of the formal legislative record, notably the national election campaign then in progress, in which President Johnson's basic position as to Vietnam was expressed in his assertion that ". . . we are not about to send American boys 9,000 or 10,000 miles away from home to do what Asian boys ought to be doing for themselves."[44] It is difficult, therefore, to credit Under Secretary of State Katzenbach's contention that the Gulf of Tonkin resolution, combined with the SEATO Treaty, was the "functional equivalent" of a declaration of war.[45] In adopting a resolution with such sweeping language, however, Congress committed the error of making a *personal* judgment as to how President Johnson would implement the resolution when it had a responsibility to make an *institutional* judgment, first, as to what *any* President would do with so great an acknowledgment of power, and, second, as to whether, under the Constitution, Congress had the right to grant or concede the authority in question.

From the executive's point of view these questions are academic, because every President since World War II has asserted at one time or another that he had the authority to commit the Armed Forces to conflict without the consent of Congress. The Johnson administration was not entirely consistent in its interpretations of the Gulf of Tonkin resolution, but on a number of occasions it was asserted that the

---

44. Remarks in Memorial Hall, Akron University, Akron, Ohio, Oct. 21, 1964.
45. *U.S. Commitments to Foreign Powers*, p. 82.

President would have full authority to conduct the war in Vietnam on its full scale even in the absence of the resolution. . . .

The exact view of the executive as to the meaning of Congress constitutional power to "declare war" remains somewhat obscure. In his testimony before the Foreign Relations Committee on August 17, 1967, Under Secretary Katzenbach referred to a declaration of war as something which is "outmoded in the international arena" and also as something that would not "correctly reflect the limited objectives of the United States with respect to Vietnam."[48] The Under Secretary . . . asked: "What could a declaration of war have done that would have given the President more authority and a clearer voice of the Congress of the United States than that did?"[49] . . .

The burden of the Under Secretary's remarks seems to have been, first, that the Gulf of Tonkin resolution was not a declaration of war but its "functional equivalent," and, second, that declarations of war are inappropriate when the nation's purposes are "limited" and in any case are "outmoded in the international arena." . . . The committee is reluctant to believe that the executive feels itself free to alter on its own authority a provision of the Constitution which it believes to be "outmoded in the international arena." Nor can the committee accept the view that "limited" wars can be undertaken by the executive without the consent of Congress; neither the Constitution nor the conduct of American Presidents prior to 1950—with one or two possible exceptions—justify that interpretation of the Constitution. It is obvious that the question of authority to commit the United States to war is in need of clarification.

One final occurrence must be mentioned to complete our chronology. On April 28, 1965, after consulting his advisers and briefing the leaders of Congress, President Johnson sent American Armed Forces to the Dominican Republic. As in the instances of Korea in 1950 and Lebanon in 1958, American forces were sent to a foreign country without reference to any resolution or other act or expression of Congress. The congressional leadership were informed but that cannot be equated with obtaining the consent of Congress.

Great emphasis has been placed by the Executive on its diligence in "informing" and "consulting" the Congress on foreign policy decisions. "Consistently," says the Department of State . . . , "Congress is informed and consulted concerning both the implementation of existing commitments and policy and the planning of new initiatives." Unfortunately, the terms "consult" and "inform" are used interchangeably, although the distinction between solicitation of advice in advance of a decision and the provision of information in the wake of a decision would seem to be a significant one. In fact, recent administrations have been fairly conscientious about "informing" the congressional leadership—although not the Congress itself—of their foreign policy decisions. . . . [I]n matters involving the commitment of the Armed Forces

---

48. *U.S. Commitments to Foreign Powers*, p. 81.
49. *Ibid.* pp. 81, 83.

to hostilities abroad, the Constitution requires that the consent of Congress be obtained in advance of action by the executive. . . .

President Nixon's four immediate predecessors—Eisenhower a shade less than the others—all asserted unrestricted executive authority to commit the Armed Forces without the consent of Congress, and Congress, for the most part, has acquiesced in the transfer of its war power to the executive. The evolution traced in these pages is the basis of the committee's contention that the intent of the framers of the Constitution with respect to the exercise of the war power has been virtually nullified. . . .

6. CONCLUSION: THE RESTORATION OF CONSTITUTIONAL BALANCE

. . . The committee is strongly of the view that a restoration of the division of war powers specified by the Constitution and generally adhered to during more than a century of national experience is both compatible with modern conditions and essential to constitutional government. . . .

Claims to unlimited executive authority over the use of armed force are made on grounds of both legitimacy and necessity. . . . Failing of constitutional and historical legitimacy, the case for unlimited executive power over the Armed Forces has final resort to the spurious and dangerous doctrine of "inherent powers of the Presidency." . . . [Besides the arguments for executive power based on executive branch expertise in foreign affairs, t]he other principal argument made in support of emergency powers over foreign policy is the necessity of speed in response to a grave threat to the nation's security or survival. To this the committee has two responses:

> First, a useful distinction can be made between speed and haste. In a number of situations in recent years which were characterized as emergencies, American policy would have profited from brief delays to permit deliberation and consultation with the Congress. In the case of the joint resolutions adopted by Congress pertaining to Formosa, the Middle East, Cuba and the Gulf of Tonkin, not one was a matter of the greatest urgency although that did not in each case seem clear at the time. In the case of the Gulf of Tonkin resolution, a delay of a week or two would have permitted Congress both to ascertain the facts regarding the occurrence in the Gulf of Tonkin and to record its intentions in a legislative record; the retaliatory attacks on the North Vietnamese ports had already been made when the resolution was put before Congress, so that a delay would have had no military consequences.

Second, the committee is well aware that there have been, and may in the future again be, instances of great national emergency such as the Cuban missile crisis when prompt action is essential. In such instances consultation with the Congress is by no means out of the question; Congress has demonstrated on many occasions that it is capable of acting as speedily as the executive. Should the urgency or the need of secrecy be judged so great, however, as to preclude any form of consultation with Congress, the President, as we have noted, has unchallenged authority to respond to a sudden attack upon the United States. This authority is recognized as nothing less than a duty and it is inconceivable that the Congress would fail to support the President in response to a direct attack on the United States.

Finally, should the President find himself confronted with a situation of such complexity and ambiguity as to leave him without guidelines for constitutional action, it would be far better for him to take the action he saw fit without attempting to justify it in advance and leave it to Congress or the courts to evaluate his action in retrospect. A single unconstitutional act, later explained or pronounced unconstitutional, is preferable to an act dressed up in some spurious, precedent-setting claim of legitimacy. As a member of the Nation's first Congress, Alexander White, of Virginia, said:

> It would be better for the President to extend his powers on some extraordinary occasions, even where he is not strictly justified by the Constitution, than the legislature should grant an improper power to be exercised at all times. . . .[58]

For all of the foregoing reasons the committee rejects the contention that the war powers as spelled out in the Constitution are obsolete and strongly recommends that the Congress reassert its constitutional authority over the use of the Armed Forces. No constitutional amendment or legislative enactment is required for this purpose; all that is required is the restoration of constitutional procedures which have been permitted to atrophy.

. . . If Congress makes clear that it intends to exercise these powers, it is most unlikely that the executive will fail to respect that intention. Napoleon is credited with the maxim that "the tools belong to the man that can use them." Only Congress, by exercising its constitutional powers, can prevent them from passing into other hands.

The committee does not believe that formal declarations of war are the only available means by which Congress can authorize the President to initiate limited or general hostilities. Joint resolutions such as those pertaining to Formosa, the Middle East, and the Gulf of Tonkin are a proper method of granting authority, provided that they are precise as to what is to be done and for what period of time, and provided that they do in fact *grant authority* and not merely express approval of undefined action to be taken by the President. That distinction is of the greatest importance. As used in the recent past, joint resolutions have been instruments of political control over the Congress in the hand of the President, enabling him to claim support for any action he may choose to take and so phrased as to express Congressional acquiescence in the constitutionally unsound contention that the President in his capacity as Commander in Chief has the authority to commit the country to war.

The committee therefore recommends that, in considering future resolutions involving the use or possible use of the Armed Forces, Congress—

---

58. The Annals of Congress, June 18, 1789, vol. 1, p. 537.

(1) debate the proposed resolution at sufficient length to establish a legislative record showing the intent of Congress;

(2) use the words *authorize* or *empower* or such other language as will leave no doubt that Congress alone has the right to authorize the initiation of war and that, in granting the President authority to use the Armed Forces, Congress is granting him power that he would not otherwise have;

(3) state in the resolution as explicitly as possible under the circumstances the kind of military action that is being authorized and the place and purpose of its use; and

(4) put a time limit on the resolution, thereby assuring Congress the opportunity to review its decision and extend or terminate the President's authority to use military force. . . .

Notes and Questions on Vietnam

1. *Implications of the Meeker Thesis.* On what bases does Leonard Meeker assert that the President was empowered to conduct the war in Southeast Asia? Does it follow, even if the war was lawful, that it was a "war" within the meaning of article I? For example, would the lawfulness of the war justify legislatively unauthorized domestic emergency measures to assure the prosecution of the war? (Recall *Youngstown.*) If not, does it follow that the Vietnam experience has left a purpose for declaring war more important than gratuitous formality?

2. *What is a "Declaration of War"?* Why, given the history of legislative acquiescence in the Vietnam War, did Congress never issue a document formally declaring war on Vietnam? Note that it has always been understood that Congress may authorize limited hostile engagements short of a declared war. *Cf. Bas v. Tingy*, 4 U.S. (4 Dall.) 37 (1800) (awarding shipowner compensation under federal statute dealing with recapture of ships from "the enemy"; France deemed "the enemy" although Congress never declared war in naval hostilities with France between 1798 and 1800). Because the United States has issued no such formal declarations since World War II, and yet has plainly engaged in numerous military encounters, the common view has been that (a) only explicit declarations of war amount to exercises of the Article I "declare war" power, and (b) such formal declarations of war by the United States are not to be favored as the instrument for authorizing the use of military force. This could be because formal declarations of war might be thought to trigger legal consequences that we would not wish to attend every hostile U.S. military engagement, or because the difficulty of getting Congress to take such categorical action would lead Congress to exercise less, rather than more regulatory vigilance over presidential military deployments.

In an intriguing pair of articles, Professor Sai Prakash has argued that the conventional view is entirely wrong. As he reads history, Congress, whenever it grants authority to deploy military force, is exercising its "declare war" power. It need not use the word "declare" for this to be so. Saikrishna Bangalore Prakash, *Exhuming the Seemingly Moribund Declaration of War*, 77 Geo. W. L. Rev. 89 (2008). Under the Prakash view of things, enactments such as the Authorization for the Use of Military Force, enacted after 9/11 or the Gulf of Tonkin Resolution, would thus count as declarations of war for constitutional purposes.

Professor Prakash further asserts that, without an authorizing declaration of some sort, the President is simply not authorized to "make war." That is, he may deploy or even use the military abroad to protect U.S. interests, but not to the extent that his use would amount to a declaration of war, albeit of an informal sort. Saikrishna Bangalore Prakash, *The Separation and Overlap of War and Military Powers*, 87 Tex. L. Rev. 299, 358–362 (2008). Professor Prakash defends this view historically, as representing the best understanding of how declarations of war were understood at the time of the Founding and for a considerable period thereafter.

For a dramatically different view, see John Yoo, The Powers of War and Peace: The Constitution and Foreign Affairs After 9/11, at 151 (2005) ("Declarations do simply what they say they do: they declare. To use the eighteenth century understanding, they make public, show openly, and make known the state of international legal relations between the United States and another nation. . . . Declarations are also important for domestic constitutional purposes. Textually, a declaration of war places the nation in a state of total war, which triggers enhanced powers on the part of the federal government.") On Professor Yoo's constitutional reading, the President may wage war without any prior authorization from Congress. *Accord Authority of the President under Domestic and International Law to Use Military Force against Iraq*, 26 Op. O.L.C. 143, 151 (2002)("Article II vests in the President, as Chief Executive and Commander in Chief, the constitutional authority to use such military forces as are provided to him by Congress to engage in military hostilities to protect the national interest of the United States. The Constitution nowhere requires for the exercise of such authority the consent of Congress.")

Putting aside the historical debate, is one or the other understanding of "declarations of war" more functionally appropriate or more attractive on normative grounds? Should there be some sort of legal instrument for the authorization of war that automatically carries implications for the enhanced powers of the federal government that other forms of legal authorization do not? Are declarations of war more likely to reflect the kind of popular consensus behind a war effort that would make the collateral consequences of a declaration of war more legitimate on the domestic front? (If national consensus were the sole prerequisite for a declaration of war, however, it would be hard to understand why Congress, on September 12, 2001, did not declare one.) Should it be a legitimate objection to the imposition of extraordinary wartime burdens on particular individuals, for example, the draft, that such burdens are legitimate only if there is sufficient popular backing to produce a declaration of war? *See Orlando v. Laird*, 443 F.2d 1039 (2d Cir.), *cert. denied*, 404 U.S. 869 (1971) (Congressional action ratifying Vietnam military operations sufficient to justify compelling soldiers to participate in hostilities); *but cf. Mitchell v. Laird*, 488 F.2d 611 (D.C. Cir. 1973) (dismissing suit to enjoin Vietnam War as presenting political question, but opining in dictum that Congress had not authorized Vietnam War in a "Constitutionally satisfactory form"). Should this issue be regarded as justiciable? *Compare Atlee v. Laird*, 347 F. Supp. 689 (E.D. Pa. 1972) (three-judge court), *aff'd sub nom. Atlee v. Richardson*, 411 U.S. 911 (1973), *with Massachusetts v. Laird*, 400 U.S. 886 (1970) (Douglas, J., dissenting from denial of motion for leave to file a bill of complaint). So long as the President's war-making powers, in the absence of an explicit declaration of war, are limited by appropriations and substantive legislation, should we be worried that the United States can become engaged in *de facto* war without a declaration of war? Is the current practice more salutary than requiring a declaration of war in each instance of international belligerency?

For an analysis supporting formal declarations of war as the sole appropriate means for authorizing hostilities tantamount to war — but simultaneously granting the President significant authority for the unilateral deployment of military force, see J. Gregory Sidak, *To Declare War*, 41 DUKE L.J. 27 (1991). For a rebuttal, see Harold H. Koh, *The Coase Theorem and the War Power: A Response*, 41 DUKE L.J. 122 (1991).

3. *Limits to Formalism?* Following Professor Prakash's argument, would it be plausible or useful for Congress and the President today to try to settle on the constitutional understanding that Dr. Russell finds in nineteenth century practice, that "the President could constitutionally employ American military force outside the nation as long as he did not use it to commit 'acts of war'"? Professor Prakash would appear to limit such employment of force to repelling attacks, attacking pirates and bandits, and rescuing U.S. citizens abroad. Do such bright-line categories, in your view, account for all the cases in which presidents should be able to deploy force abroad without or in advance of congressional authority?

4. *Limits to Functionalism?* To what extent is the linchpin of Meeker's argument his observation that the world has "grown much smaller" since 1787? How much military and foreign affairs power should this circumstance be deemed to have vested in the President? Does it strengthen or weaken the case for unilateral presidential power to terminate treaties? Does the advent of the nuclear age help explain the growth of executive power since World War II? Does it justify those developments?

5. *The Constitutionality of the Tonkin Gulf Resolution.* Note that the Tonkin Gulf resolution provided that it could be terminated by concurrent resolution of Congress. Would such a termination be constitutional under *Chadha*? If not, how could Congress rescind any grant of warmaking power to the President? In the Vietnam period, Congress ultimately found the most effective check on executive power to be limitations on the use of appropriations. Are such limitations on the use of funds for conducting hostilities constitutional? Are they appropriate? We will return at length in Section D of this chapter to questions regarding Congress's authority to regulate how Presidents prosecute the wars that Congress authorizes.

6. *Does History Amend the Constitution?* Does history confirm Meeker's argument that the Constitution supported the President's authority to commit troops to Vietnam? Do he and the Senate read history consistently? As you read the War Powers Resolution, which follows, consider whether Congress, through explicit legislation, can overcome the historical gloss on constitutional text. Alternatively, should the President ever be able to argue that he has accrued war powers originally vested in Congress through a kind of adverse possession?

7. *Asking Forgiveness, Not Permission.* The Senate report cites with approval Jefferson's constitutionally punctilious handling of the Barbary Pirates. Do modern circumstances in any way limit the attractiveness or practicability of his approach?

8. *Practical Alternatives?* How useful do you believe are the various suggestions in the Senate report for a more responsible congressional exercise of its war powers? Is it a meaningful check on the President to require congressional authorization for the use of military force if Congress is likely to grant such authority in extremely broad terms? Is it realistic to expect Congress, in a crisis situation, to draft such authorizations more closely or with any greater precision than it has in the past? Should Congress ever put time limits on its grants of authority?

b. Congress's Efforts to Limit the President's Authority to Commit Troops: The War Powers Resolution

The key separation of powers development emanating from the Vietnam experience was Congress's enactment of the War Powers Resolution. The following materials are intended to provoke analysis of that Resolution, its rationale, and the prospects for its successful implementation.

War Powers Resolution

Pub. L. 93-148, 87 Stat. 555, codified at 50 U.S.C. 1541 *et seq.*

Section 1. This joint resolution may be cited as the "War Powers Resolution."

PURPOSE AND POLICY

Sec. 2. (a) It is the purpose of this joint resolution to fulfill the intent of the framers of the Constitution of the United States and insure that the collective judgment of both the Congress and the President will apply to the introduction of United States Armed Forces into hostilities, or into situations where imminent involvement in hostilities is clearly indicated by the circumstances, and to the continued use of such forces in hostilities or in such situations.

(b) Under article I, section 8, of the Constitution, it is specifically provided that the Congress shall have the power to make all laws necessary and proper for carrying into execution, not only its own powers but also all other powers vested by the

Constitution in the Government of the United States, or in any department or officer thereof.

(c) The constitutional powers of the President as Commander-in-Chief to introduce United States Armed Forces into hostilities, or into situations where imminent involvement in hostilities is clearly indicated by the circumstances, are exercised only pursuant to (1) a declaration of war, (2) specific statutory authorization, or (3) a national emergency created by attack upon the United States, its territories or possessions, or its armed forces.

CONSULTATION

Sec. 3. The President in every possible instance shall consult with Congress before introducing United States Armed Forces into hostilities or into situations where imminent involvement in hostilities is clearly indicated by the circumstances, and after every such introduction shall consult regularly with the Congress until United States Armed Forces are no longer engaged in hostilities or have been removed from such situations.

REPORTING

Sec. 4. (a) In the absence of a declaration of war, in any case in which United States Armed Forces are introduced—

(1) into hostilities or into situations where imminent involvement in hostilities is clearly indicated by the circumstances;

(2) into the territory, airspace or waters of a foreign nation, while equipped for combat, except for deployments which relate solely to supply, replacement, repair, or training of such forces; or

(3) in numbers which substantially enlarge United States Armed Forces equipped for combat already located in a foreign nation;

the President shall submit within 48 hours to the Speaker of the House of Representatives and to the President pro tempore of the Senate a report, in writing, setting forth—

(A) the circumstances necessitating the introduction of United States Armed Forces;

(B) the constitutional and legislative authority under which such introduction took place; and

(C) the estimated scope and duration of the hostilities or involvement.

(b) The President shall provide such other information as the Congress may request in the fulfillment of its constitutional responsibilities with respect to committing the Nation to war and to the use of United States Armed Forces abroad.

(c) Whenever United States Armed Forces are introduced into hostilities or into any situation described in subsection (a) of this section, the President shall, so long as such armed forces continue to be engaged in such hostilities or situation, report to the Congress periodically on the status of such hostilities or situation as well as on the scope and duration of such hostilities or situation, but in no event shall he report to the Congress less often than once every six months.

CONGRESSIONAL ACTION

Sec. 5. (a) Each report submitted pursuant to section 4(a)(1) shall be transmitted to the Speaker of the House of Representatives and to the President pro tempore of the Senate on the same calendar day. . . . If, when the report is transmitted, the Congress has adjourned sine die or has adjourned for any period in excess of three calendar days, the Speaker of the House of Representatives and the President pro tempore of the Senate, if they deem it advisable (or if petitioned by at least 30 percent of the membership of their respective Houses) shall jointly request the President to convene Congress in order that it may consider the report and take appropriate action pursuant to this section.

(b) Within sixty calendar days after a report is submitted or is required to be submitted pursuant to section 4(a)(1), whichever is earlier, the President shall terminate any use of United States Armed Forces with respect to which such report was submitted (or required to be submitted), unless the Congress (1) has declared war or has enacted a specific authorization for such use of United States Armed Forces, (2) has extended by law such sixty-day period, or (3) is physically unable to meet as a result of an armed attack upon the United States. Such sixty-day period shall be extended for not more than an additional thirty days if the President determines and certifies to the Congress in writing that unavoidable military necessity respecting the safety of United States Armed Forces requires the continued use of such armed forces in the course of bringing about a prompt removal of such forces.

(c) Notwithstanding subsection (b), at any time that United States Armed Forces are engaged in hostilities outside the territory of the United States, its possessions and territories without a declaration of war or specific statutory authorization, such forces shall be removed by the President if the Congress so directs by concurrent resolution.

[Sections 6 and 7 of the Resolution provide for expedited consideration of legislative action to be taken pursuant to the Resolution in the event of U.S. military engagements.]

INTERPRETATION OF JOINT RESOLUTION

Sec. 8. (a) Authority to introduce United States Armed Forces into hostilities or into situations wherein involvement in hostilities is clearly indicated by the circumstances shall not be inferred—

(1) from any provision of law (whether or not in effect before the date of the enactment of this joint resolution) including any provision contained in any appropriation Act, unless such provision specifically authorizes the introduction of United States Armed Forces into hostilities or into such situations and states that it is intended to constitute specific statutory authorization within the meaning of this joint resolution; or

(2) from any treaty heretofore or hereafter ratified unless such treaty is implemented by legislation specifically authorizing the introduction of United States Armed Forces into hostilities or into such situations and stating that it is intended to constitute specific statutory authorization within the meaning of this joint resolution.

. . .

(c) For purposes of this joint resolution, the term "introduction of United States Armed Forces" includes the assignment of members of such armed forces to command, coordinate, participate in the movement of, or accompany the regular or irregular military forces of any foreign country or government when such military forces are engaged, or there exists an imminent threat that such forces will become engaged, in hostilities.

(d) Nothing in this joint resolution—

(1) is intended to alter the constitutional authority of the Congress or of the President, or the provisions of existing treaties; or

(2) shall be construed as granting any authority to the President with respect to the introduction of United States Armed Forces into hostilities or into situations wherein involvement in hostilities is clearly indicated by the circumstances which authority he would not have had in the absence of this joint resolution.

SEPARABILITY CLAUSE

Sec. 9. If any provision of this joint resolution or the application thereof to any person or circumstance is held invalid, the remainder of the joint resolution and the application of such provision to any other person or circumstance shall not be affected thereby.

———————

President Nixon's Veto of the War Powers Resolution
H. Doc. No. 171, 93d Cong., 1st Sess. (1973)

To the House of Representatives:

I hereby return without my approval House Joint Resolution 542—the War Powers Resolution. While I am in accord with the desire of the Congress to assert its proper role in the conduct of our foreign affairs, the restrictions which this resolution would impose upon the authority of the President are both unconstitutional and dangerous to the best interests of our Nation.

The proper roles of the Congress and the Executive in the conduct of foreign affairs have been debated since the founding of our country. Only recently, however, has there been a serious challenge to the wisdom of the Founding Fathers in choosing not to draw a precise and detailed line of demarcation between the foreign policy powers of the two branches.

The Founding Fathers understood the impossibility of foreseeing every contingency that might arise in this complex area. They acknowledged the need for flexibility in responding to changing circumstances. They recognized that foreign policy decisions must be made through close cooperation between the two branches and not through rigidly codified procedures.

These principles remain as valid today as they were when our Constitution was written. Yet House Joint Resolution 542 would violate those principles by defining the President's powers in ways which would strictly limit his constitutional authority.

CLEARLY UNCONSTITUTIONAL

House Joint Resolution 542 would attempt to take away, by a mere legislative act, authorities which the President has properly exercised under the Constitution for almost 200 years. One of its provisions would automatically cut off certain authorities after sixty days unless the Congress extended them. Another would allow the Congress to eliminate certain authorities merely by the passage of a concurrent resolution — an action which does not normally have the force of law, since it denies the President his constitutional role in approving legislation.

I believe that both these provisions are unconstitutional.

UNDERMINING OUR FOREIGN POLICY

While I firmly believe that a veto of House Joint Resolution 542 is warranted solely on constitutional grounds, I am also deeply disturbed by the practical consequences of this resolution. For it would seriously undermine this Nation's ability to act decisively and convincingly in time of international crisis. As a result, the confidence of our allies in our ability to assist them could be diminished and the respect of our adversaries for our deterrent posture could decline. A permanent and substantial element of unpredictability would be injected into the world's assessment of American behavior, further increasing the likelihood of miscalculation and war.

If this resolution had been in operation, America's effective response to a variety of challenges in recent years would have been vastly complicated or even made impossible. We may well have been unable to respond in the way we did during the Berlin crisis of 1961, the Cuban missile crisis of 1962, the Congo rescue operation in 1964, and the Jordanian crisis of 1970 — to mention just a few examples.

While all the specific consequences of House Joint Resolution 542 cannot yet be predicted, it is clear that it would undercut the ability of the United States to act as an effective influence for peace. For example, the provision automatically cutting off certain authorities after 60 days unless they are extended by the Congress could work to prolong or intensify a crisis. Until the Congress suspended the deadline, there would be at least a chance of United States withdrawal and an adversary would be tempted therefore to postpone serious negotiations until the 60 days were up. Only after the Congress acted would there be a strong incentive for an adversary to negotiate. In addition, the very existence of a deadline could lead to an escalation of hostilities in order to achieve certain objectives before the 60 days expired.

The measure would jeopardize our role as a force for peace in other ways as well. It would, for example, strike from the President's hand a wide range of important peacekeeping tools by eliminating his ability to exercise quiet diplomacy backed by subtle shifts in our military deployments. It would also cast into doubt authorities which Presidents have used to undertake certain humanitarian relief missions in conflict areas, to protect fishing boats from seizure, to deal with ship or aircraft hijackings, and to respond to threats of attack. Not the least of the adverse consequences of this resolution would be the prohibition contained in section 8 against fulfilling our obligations under the NATO treaty as ratified by the Senate. Finally, since the bill is somewhat vague as to when the 60 day rule would apply, it could lead to extreme confusion and dangerous disagreements concerning the prerogatives of the two branches, seriously damaging our ability to respond to international crises.

FAILURE TO REQUIRE POSITIVE CONGRESSIONAL ACTION

I am particularly disturbed by the fact that certain of the President's constitutional powers as Commander in Chief of the Armed Forces would terminate automatically under this resolution 60 days after they were invoked. No overt Congressional action would be required to cut off these powers — they would disappear automatically unless the Congress extended them. In effect, the Congress is here attempting to increase its policy-making role through a provision which requires it to take absolutely no action at all.

In my view, the proper way for the Congress to make known its will on such foreign policy questions is through a positive action, with full debate on the merits of the issue and with each member taking the responsibility of casting a yes or no vote after considering those merits. The authorization and appropriations process represents one of the ways in which such influence can be exercised. I do not, however, believe that the Congress can responsibly contribute its considered, collective judgment on such grave questions without full debate and without a yes or no vote. Yet this is precisely what the joint resolution would allow. It would give every future Congress the ability to handcuff every future President merely by doing nothing and sitting still. In my view, one cannot become a responsible partner unless one is prepared to take responsible action.

STRENGTHENING COOPERATION BETWEEN THE CONGRESS AND THE EXECUTIVE BRANCHES

The responsible and effective exercise of the war powers requires the fullest cooperation between the Congress and the Executive and the prudent fulfillment by each branch of its constitutional responsibilities. House Joint Resolution 542 includes certain constructive measures which would foster this process by enhancing the flow of information from the executive branch to the Congress. Section 3, for example, calls for consultations with the Congress before and during the involvement of the United

States forces in hostilities abroad. This provision is consistent with the desire of this Administration for regularized consultations with the Congress in an even wider range of circumstances.

RICHARD NIXON.
THE WHITE HOUSE, *October 24, 1973*

War Powers: A Test of Compliance—Relative to the Danang Sealift, the Evacuation of Phnom Penh, the Evacuation of Saigon, and the Mayaguez Incident

Hearings Before the House Comm. on Int'l Rel.,
94th Cong., 1st Sess. 46–48 (1975)

Legislative History of the Consultation Provision of the War Powers Resolution

• • •

Explanation of Consultation Provision in H.J. Res. 542 from House Report 93-287

Section 2. Consultation

This section directs that the President "*in every possible instance shall consult with the leadership and appropriate committees of the Congress before committing United States Armed Forces to hostilities or to situations where hostilities may be imminent.*

The use of the word "every" reflects the committee's belief that such consultation *prior* to the commitment of armed forces should be inclusive. In other words, it should apply in extraordinary and emergency circumstances—even when it is not possible to get formal congressional approval in the form of a declaration of war or other specific authorization. At the same time, through use of the word "possible" it recognizes that a situation may be so dire, e.g. hostile missile attack underway, and require such instantaneous action that no prior consultation will be possible.

The second element of section 2 relates to situations *after* a commitment of forces has been made (with or without prior consultation). In that instance, it imposes upon the President, through use of the word "shall," the obligation to "*consult regularly. . . .*"

A considerable amount of attention was given to the definition of *consultation*. Rejected was the notion that consultation should be synonymous with merely being informed. Rather, consultation in this provision means that a decision is pending on a problem and that Members of Congress are being asked by the President for their advice and opinions and, in appropriate circumstances, their approval of action contemplated. Furthermore, for consultation to be meaningful, the President himself must participate and all information relevant to the situation must be made available.

In the context of this and following sections of the resolution, a *commitment* of armed forces commences when the President makes the final decision to act and issues orders putting that decision into effect.

The word *hostilities* was substituted for the phrase *armed conflict* during the subcommittee drafting process because it was considered to be somewhat broader in scope. In addition to a situation in which fighting actually has begun, *hostilities* also encompasses a state of confrontation in which no shots have been fired but where there is a clear and present danger of armed conflict. "*Imminent hostilities*" denotes a situation in which there is a clear potential either for such a state of confrontation or for actual armed conflict.

Explanation by Senator Jacob Javits of the Conference Report
Congressional Record, October 10, 1973, p. 33549

Consultation

Section 3, the provisions establishing a statutory requirement of advance consultation as well as continuing consultation with the Congress, [is] to be read as maximal rather than minimal. The consultation requirement is not discretionary for the President; he is obliged by law to consult before the introduction of forces into hostilities and to continue consultations so long as the troops are engaged. This section does take account of the contingency that there may be instances of such great suddenness in which it is not possible to consult in advance. . . .

It is important to note that, while consultation is a statutorily established requirement in this legislation, the President does not acquire or derive any authority respecting the use of the Armed Forces through the consultation process per se—although "consultation" may lead to a declaration of war or the enactment of specific statutory authorization. In other words, consultation is not a substitute for specific statutory authorization.

Section 3 is rather intended to reestablish the historic, consultative tradition between the executive and the Congress respecting foreign affairs and international security matters, which has generally prevailed throughout our Nation's history. The breakdown in recent years of this consultative tradition has contributed heavily to strains between the executive and the Congress, and in my judgment is an important contributory element in the constitutional crisis now confronting our Nation with respect to the war powers.

Questions on the War Powers Resolution

1. *Facial Constitutionality?* As a general matter, is Congress constitutionally empowered to define its own and the President's war powers? *See* Stephen L. Carter, *The Constitutionality of the War Powers Resolution*, 70 Va. L. Rev. 101 (1984). If so, are any of the provisions of the War Powers Resolution constitutionally objectionable on their face: the cataloguing of the President's powers; the consultation requirements; the reporting requirements; the 60-day cut-off provisions; the legislative

veto provision? How does section 8(d)(1), added in conference, affect the constitutionality of section (2)(c)? How does it affect the impact of (2)(c)?

2. *Impact of* Chadha. Is the legislative veto provision constitutional after *Chadha*? If not, how would you rule on the severability question? *See* Comment, *Congressional Control of Presidential Warmaking Under the War Powers Act: The Status of a Legislative Veto after* Chadha, 132 U. PA. L. REV. 1217 (1984).

3. *Protecting U.S. Persons and Property Generally.* Note that the circumstances Congress describes in section 2(c) of the resolution as permitting the President to introduce U.S. armed forces into hostilities do not concede any general authority to use military force for the protection of U.S. persons and property abroad. Presidents, however, have asserted such power, relying on 19th century precedent. Consider the following excerpt from a massive treatise on the Constitution produced by the Congressional Research Service in the Library of Congress, THE CONSTITUTION OF THE UNITED STATES OF AMERICA: ANALYSIS AND INTERPRETATION, S. Doc. No. 82, 92d Cong., 2d Sess. 562–63 (1973):

> In 1854, one Lieutenant Hollins, in command of a United States warship, bombarded the town of Greytown, Nicaragua because of the refusal of local authorities to pay reparations for an attack by a mob on the United States consul. Upon his return to the United States, Hollins was sued in a federal court by Durand for the value of certain property which was alleged to have been destroyed in the bombardment. His defense was based upon the orders of the President and Secretary of the Navy and was sustained by Justice Nelson, on circuit.[2] "As the Executive head of the nation, the President is made the only legitimate organ of the General Government, to open and carry on correspondence or negotiations with foreign nations, in matters concerning the interests of the country or of its citizens. It is to him, also, the citizens abroad must look for protection of person and of property, and for the faithful execution of the laws existing and intended for their protection. . . .
>
> "Now, as it respects the interposition of the Executive abroad, for the protection of the lives or property of the citizen, the duty must, of necessity, rest in the discretion of the President. Acts of lawless violence, or of threatened violence to the citizen or his property, cannot be anticipated and provided for; and the protection, to be effectual or of any avail, may, not unfrequently, require the most prompt and decided action. Under our system of Government, the citizen abroad is as much entitled to protection as the citizen at home. The great object and duty of Government is the protection of the lives, liberty, and property of the people composing it, whether abroad or at home; and any Government failing in the accomplishment of the object, or the performance of the duty, is not worth preserving."

---

2. *Durand* v. *Hollins*, 8 Fed. Cas. 111 (No. 4186) (C.C.S.D.N.Y. 1860).

This incident and this case were but two items in the 19th century advance of the concept that the President had the duty and the responsibility to protect American lives and property abroad through the use of armed forces if deemed necessary.[4] The duty could be said to grow out of the inherent powers of the Chief Executive or perhaps out of his obligation to "take Care that the Laws be faithfully executed." Although there were efforts made at times to limit this presidential power narrowly to the protection of persons and property rather than to the promotion of broader national interests,[7] no such distinction was observed in practice and so grew the concepts which have become the source of serious national controversy in the 1960's and 1970's, the power of the President to use troops abroad to observe national commitments and protect the national interest without seeking prior approval from Congress.[8]

See also In re Neagle, 135 U.S. 1 (1890), discussed in Chapter Two. Should Congress have included the general protection of U.S. persons and property abroad as a constitutionally sufficient ground for presidential use of military force? If the President has any such power, does its omission from section 2 render the resolution unconstitutional? Why not? (Note that Presidents have taken the position that War Powers Resolution is simply inapplicable to military actions for the protection of U.S. persons and property abroad.)

4. *Relevance to Ultimate War Making?* For an intriguing set of essays analyzing the implications of the separation of powers for nuclear warfare, partly against the backdrop of Congress's experience with the War Powers Resolution, *see* First Use of Nuclear Weapons: Under the Constitution, Who Decides? (Peter Raven-Hansen ed., 1987). A helpful bibliography of war powers literature generally appears *id.* at 233–42.

5. *Suggestions for Reform.* In the nearly four decades since its enactment, the War Powers Resolution has attracted numerous proposals for reform. We highlight a number of them in Section B of this chapter, after we review the history of the Resolution's implementation. Even before delving into that history, are there aspects of the Resolution you think could be improved or should be eliminated?

---

4. *See* United States Solicitor of the Department of State, Right to Protect Citizens in Foreign Countries by Landing Forces (Washington: 3d. rev. ed. 1934); M. Offutt, The Protection of Citizens Abroad by the Armed Forces of the United States (Baltimore: 1928).

7. E. Corwin, The President: Office and Powers 1787–1957 (New York: 4th ed. 1957), 198–201.

8. In 1965, President Johnson landed troops in the Dominican Republic during a revolution, assertedly to protect the lives of United States citizens threatened by the rebels, 52 Dept. State Bull. 738 (1965), but no doubt also to serve other interests, i.e., "to help prevent another Communist state in this hemisphere." *Id.* 743. It should be noted that after evacuation of United States citizens had been completed, the United States military presence was increased from 400 Marines to over 20,000 troops. N.Y. Times, Sept. 5, 1965, p. 1, col. 4.

Note: Covert Warmaking and the Neutrality Act

The legislative history of the War Powers Resolution makes clear that it addresses only conventional military operations—the introduction by the President of "United States Armed Forces" into hostilities or situations where hostilities are imminent. Increasingly, however, the twentieth century has witnessed the growth of covert paramilitary action as a tool of U.S. foreign policy. This phenomenon poses equally profound questions as to the proper allocation of constitutional responsibility for national policymaking.

As in foreign policy (see the discussion of the Logan Act in Chapter Five), Congress early attempted by statute to secure a government monopoly over military policy. In 1794, Congress adopted the Neutrality Act, which provides in its current form:

> Whoever, within the United States, knowingly begins or sets on foot or provides or prepares a means for or furnishes the money for, or takes part in, any military or naval expedition or enterprise to be carried on from thence against the territory or dominion of any foreign prince or state, or of any colony, district, or people with whom the United States is at peace, shall be fined under this title or imprisoned not more than three years, or both.

18 U.S.C. § 960 (1982), as amended.

The Neutrality Act, unlike the Logan Act, continues to be the basis of criminal prosecutions. *See, e.g.*, U.S. v. Khan, 461 U.S. 477 (4th Cir. 2006) (defendant trained co-conspirators who had traveled to Kashmir and joined with terrorist group to fire on Indian positions); U.S. v Jack, No. 2:07-cr-00266 FCD DAD, 2010 WL 4718613 (E.D.Cal. Nov. 12, 2010) (defendants allegedly plotted the acquisition and transfer of military arms, munitions, materiel, personnel, and money from the United States to insurgents attempting to overthrow the government of Laos). Undoubtedly, the most famous of these remains the prosecution of Aaron Burr for allegedly preparing a military expedition against Mexico. *United States v. Burr*, 25 F. Cas. 201 (C.C.D. Va. 1807) (No. 14,694a) (upholding indictment as charging acts violative of Neutrality Act).

Besides their differing histories, there is arguably an important difference between the constitutional underpinnings of the two acts. The Logan Act, in proscribing the private conduct of foreign diplomacy, protects *executive* management of foreign policy. Private persons who secure from the State Department the "authority of the United States" to communicate with foreign governments do not run afoul of the Act. 18 U.S.C. § 963. The President is thus protected against interference with his initiatives by unauthorized private persons, but has flexibility under the Act regarding the deployment of private persons to assist in those initiatives.

The Neutrality Act, however, is a blanket prohibition against the conduct of military operations against countries with which the United States is at peace. The difference in wording likely reflects an early understanding (persisting through the Act's several reenactments) that the Act's function was to protect Congress' control of military policy. This inference is buttressed by the date of the statutory enactment—a time roughly contemporaneous with the original decision to vest in Congress the power to declare war, and a time during which Congress (and the Continental Congress before it) exercised its power to issue "Letters of Marque and Reprisal," U.S. Const., art. I, § 8, cl. 11. These letters were instruments authorizing private persons to conduct military hostilities for the United States. For a comprehensive review of the "letters of marque and reprisal" power and its current implications for covert warmaking, *see* Jules Lobel, *Covert War and Congressional Authority: Hidden War and Forgotten Power*, 134 U. Pa. L. Rev. 1035 (1986). For an equally global treatment of the history and interpretation of the Neutrality Act, see Jules Lobel, *The Rise and Decline of the Neutrality Act: Sovereignty and Congressional War Powers in United States Foreign Policy*, 24 Harv. Int'l L.J. 1 (1983).

If this analysis of the Neutrality Act and its underlying theory is correct, an important issue arises whether the Act circumscribes covert warmaking by government officials, even with presidential backing. A corollary issue is whether such a prohibition could be enforced effectively. The Ninth Circuit has held that a member of Congress and private citizens lack standing to secure review of an Attorney General decision under the Ethics in Government Act not to seek the appointment of independent counsel to investigate alleged Neutrality Act violations by government officials making war against Nicaragua. *Dellums v. Smith*, 797 F.2d 817 (9th Cir. 1986), *rev'g*, 573 F. Supp. 1489 (N.D. Cal. 1983). Likewise, the District of Columbia Circuit has barred private suits under the Neutrality Act for damages or injunctive relief. *Sanchez-Espinoza v. Reagan*, 770 F.2d 202 (D.C. Cir. 1985).

In your view, is the Neutrality Act relevant to an assessment whether the President may lawfully authorize covert paramilitary operations? Whether he may engage in fund-raising from private parties and third countries to support such operations? Are your answers any different with respect to actions by the Director of Central Intelligence, the National Security Adviser, or one of their ambitious subordinates, should they conduct a paramilitary operation that is not revealed to the President?

Note: War Powers and Impeachment

Should the War Powers Resolution prove ineffectual and the federal judiciary reluctant to intervene, what other tools exist to enforce legal limits to the President's war powers? The most obvious potential constraint is Congress's impeachment power, but the impracticability of its exercise raises equally plain questions.

In recommending that the House of Representatives impeach President Nixon, the House Judiciary Committee in 1974 expressly rejected an article of impeachment based on his alleged abuse of war powers. As recounted in the Committee report:

> On July 30, 1974, the Committee considered a proposed Article of Impeachment dealing with the unauthorized bombing of Cambodia and the concealment from the Congress of that bombing:
>
> > In his conduct of the office of President of the United States, Richard M. Nixon, in violation of his constitutional oath faithfully to execute the office of President of the United States and, to the best of his ability,

preserve, protect, and defend the Constitution of the United States, and in disregard of his constitutional duty to take care that the laws be faithfully executed, on and subsequent to March 17, 1969, authorized, ordered, and ratified the concealment from the Congress of the facts and the submission to the Congress of false and misleading statements concerning the existence, scope and nature of American bombing operations in Cambodia in derogation of the power of the Congress to declare war, to make appropriations and to raise and support armies, and by such conduct warrants impeachment and trial and removal from office.

The Committee, by a vote of 26–12, decided not to report the proposed Article to the House.

The article charged that the President had concealed the bombing in Cambodia from the Congress and that he had submitted, personally and through his aides, false and misleading statements to the Congress concerning that bombing. The investigation of those allegations centered upon the initial decision to bomb Cambodia; the type, scope, extent and nature of the bombing missions; the reporting and recording system used internally within the military and the Administration; and the statements made by Administration officials to Congress and to the public both during the military operation and after it had ceased.

On February 11, 1969, the President received the initial request to institute the bombing from his military advisors. On March 17, 1969, after a series of National Security Council meetings, the President approved the request and directed that the operation be undertaken under tight security.

On March 18, 1969, the bombing of Cambodia commenced with B-52 strikes under the code name MENU OPERATION. These strikes continued until May 26, 1970, almost one month after the American incursion into Cambodia. The operational reports prepared after each mission stated that these strikes had taken place in South Vietnam rather than in Cambodia.

Between April 24 and May 24, 1970, American planes conducted tactical air strikes in Cambodia under the code name "regular" PATIO. No operational reports were made with respect to these strikes. Similarly, prior to June 30, 1970, an unspecified number of tactical air strikes occurred in various parts of Cambodia. Again no regular reports were prepared.

On May 14, 1970, a one day series of "special" PATIO sorties were conducted, operational reports stated that the strikes had occurred in Laos rather than Cambodia. The tactical air sorties with the code name "regular" FREEDOM DEAL were accurately reported as having occurred in Cambodia. A series of tactical air bombing missions in Cambodia called "special" FREEDOM DEAL occurred outside the boundaries designated for FREEDOM DEAL bombing, although the operational reports indicated otherwise.

On July 1, 1973, Congress enacted P.L. 93-50 and P.L. 93-52 providing for the cessation of all bombing in Cambodia by August 15, 1973. At that time the bombing had not been formally acknowledged by the President or his representatives.

Later, during the Senate Armed Services Committee hearings on the Cambodian bombing, military and Administration officials explained that the bombing was not publicized because of the delicate diplomatic and military situation in Southeast Asia prior to the American incursion into Cambodia. They stated that it was their understanding that Cambodia's ruler, Prince Sihanouk, had privately agreed to the bombing of Cambodia prior to his overthrow. It was further stated that certain Members of Congress had been informed of the military action and that this constituted sufficient notice to Congress of the President's military decision. Finally, the submission of false data to Congress was said to have resulted from the highly classified nature of the accurate bombing statistics.

The Committee considered the views of the supporters of this proposed Article of Impeachment that the President's conduct constituted ground for impeachment because the Constitution vests the power to make war in Congress and implicitly prohibits the Executive from waging an undeclared war. Stating that impeachment is a process for redefining the powers of the President, the supporters argued that the President, by issuing false and misleading statements, failed to provide Congress with complete and accurate information and thereby prevented Congress from responsibly exercising its powers to declare war, to raise and support armies, and to make appropriations. They stated that informing a few selected members of the Congress about the Cambodian bombing did not constitute the constitutionally required notice, particularly inasmuch as the President's contemporaneous public statements were contrary to the facts and the selected Members were committed to a course of action involving war that did not represent the views of a substantial portion of American citizens. The supporters also stated that Congress had not ratified the President's conduct through inaction or by its 1973 limitation on bombing because Congress did not know of the bombing until after it voted the authorization. Finally, they asserted that the technicalities or merits of the war in Southeast Asia, the acquiescence or protests of Prince Sihanouk, and the arguably similar conduct of past Presidents were irrelevant to the question of President Nixon's constitutional accountability in usurping Congress' war-making and appropriations powers.

The Committee did not agree to the article for a variety of reasons. The two principal arguments in opposition to it were that President Nixon was performing his constitutional duty in ordering the bombing and that Congress had been given sufficient notice of the bombing. Several Members stated that the president as Commander-in-Chief was acting to protect American troops and that other Presidents had engaged in similar military activities without prior Congressional consent. Examining the bombing of Cambodia from the perspective of Congressional responsibility, the opponents of the Article concluded that, even if President Nixon usurped Congressional power, Congress shared the blame through acquiescence or ratification of his actions. They stated that the President had provided sufficient notice of the military actions to Congress by informing key Members. Finally, they said that the passage of the War Powers Resolution in 1973 mooted the question raised by the Article.

IMPEACHMENT OF RICHARD M. NIXON, PRESIDENT OF THE UNITED STATES, H. REPT. No. 1305, 93d Cong., 2d Sess. (1974).

Recalling our discussion in Chapter Three of President Nixon's travails, it might well be argued that none of the recommended articles of impeachment charged abuses of power as serious as the allegations in the proposed but rejected article on the concealment of information about bombing operations in Cambodia. That was emphatically the judgment of Professor Ely. JOHN HART ELY, WAR AND RESPONSIBILITY: CONSTITUTIONAL LESSONS OF VIETNAM AND ITS AFTERMATH 104 (1993). His judgment is implicitly confirmed by a highly critical assessment of U.S. military and foreign policy in Southeast Asia and its impact on Cambodia, WILLIAM SHAWCROSS, SIDESHOW (1979). Are you persuaded by the majority's arguments for rejecting that article? Would you regard presidential complicity in the events discussed in Chapter Five with respect to the diversion of funds from Iranian arms sales to the Contras as an impeachable offense? Would the majority's arguments on the proposed Cambodia article apply to a proposed impeachment article based on the Contra episode?

B. Unilateral Presidential Initiative After the War Powers Resolution

1. Presidential War-making in the Post-Vietnam Era

Whatever its drafters' expectations, enactment of the War Powers Resolution did not end either unilateral presidential military initiative or legal debate about the allocation of war powers under the Constitution. Between 1973 and 2016, Presidents had issued at least 142 letters to Congress pursuant to the War Powers Resolution. *See* ROBERT F. GRIMMETT, CONG. RESEARCH SERV., WAR POWERS RESOLUTION: PRESIDENTIAL COMPLIANCE (2012); www.whitehouse.gov/briefing-room/presidential-actions/presidential-memoranda. Deployments had occurred in each of the following places: Afghanistan, Albania, Bosnia, Cambodia, Central African Republic, Djibouti, East Timor, Ethiopia, Eritrea, Granada, Guinea-Bissau, Haiti, Iran, Iraq, Ivory Coast, Kenya/Tanzania, Kosovo, Lebanon, Liberia, Libya, Panama, Persian Gulf, Rwanda, Sierra Leone, Somalia, and Yemen/Aden. Few of these involved explicit congressional authorization.

In the wake of many of these episodes, one of us in the late 1990s provided the following menu of plausible war powers doctrines available in the academic literature:

Nearly all recent academic articles on war powers—as well as two important recent books—focus on the ultimate question of law on this subject: Whom does the Constitution authorize to commit United States troops to military hostilities? There exist at least five different positions on this question:

John Hart Ely,[2] Louis Fisher,[3] and Jules Lobel[4] argue that the President is constitutionally empowered to deploy military force on his own initiative only in emergencies that preclude the pursuit of advance congressional authorization. They acknowledge no general presidential power to use military force to protect national security. Each specifically resists making a lawyerly leap from the President's universally recognized authority to repel sudden attacks to any broader power to respond unilaterally to national security threats wherever they may arise. These authors acknowledge a history of episodes in which Presidents have deployed military force unilaterally, but each insists either that such episodes are beyond the purview of the legal war powers debate or, if they are not, that a history of usurpatious practice cannot change our constitutional framework.

At the other end of the spectrum, Robert Turner[7] and John Yoo[8] argue that the President enjoys unilateral authority to deploy United States forces in any situation other than the initiation on a major scale of offensive hostilities. Their positions echo official State Department doctrine articulated during the Vietnam War. . . .

Between these two positions, at least three others exist in the literature. Acting Solicitor General Walter Dellinger, formerly assistant attorney general in charge of the Office of Legal Counsel, has argued for a *Youngstown*-like approach. Unlike Legal Advisor Meeker, Professor Dellinger concedes that Congress could, if it so desired, expressly constrain the President in

---

2. See John Hart Ely, War and Responsibility: Constitutional Lessons of Vietnam and Its Aftermath 3, 7 (1993).

3. *See* Louis Fisher, Presidential War Power 11 (1995).

4. *See* Jules Lobel, *"Little Wars" and the Constitution*, 50 U. Miami L. Rev. 61, 75 (1995).

7. *See* Robert F. Turner, *War and the Forgotten Executive Power Clause of the Constitution: A Review Essay of John Hart Ely's War and Responsibility*, 34 Va. J. Int'l L. 903, 906–10 (1994).

8. Actually, I am here understating Professor Yoo's conclusion as to the scope of presidential discretion in war making. Professor Yoo argues that the framers did not understand the declaration of war as an authorization for war, but rather as a declaration of a state of affairs between the United States and other nations intended to settle their "formal, legal relationship," and to justify different standards of American government behavior towards United States citizens with regard to their rights and duties. John C. Yoo, *The Continuation of Politics By Other Means: The Original Understanding of War Powers*, 84 Calif. L. Rev. 167, 245 (1996). Thus, under Professor Yoo's interpretation, the President never needs advance authorization for military initiative, but is subject always to congressional control through its funding powers. *See* id. at 295.

exercising military force in most situations.[12] Absent such constraints, however, whether the President may use armed forces in particular circumstances depends — à la Justice Jackson — on the nature, intent, and impact of the President's actions and on the full legislative context in which his initiative would go forward.

Professor Peter Spiro has taken a more historically oriented approach, urging that long-standing historical practice has categorically confirmed both the requirement of congressional authorization for "the massive use of force against an enemy capable . . . of marshaling substantial force," as well as the President's unilateral power to engage in small-scale "strike operations" in defense of American interests.[14] Between these poles lie the problematic cases: open-ended deployments of United States troops in unstable or hostile environments. Presidents may initiate these deployments "for protective, humanitarian, or peacekeeping purposes," but, because of their sometimes protracted nature, as well as their potential to create war, history confirms that they are subject to congressional regulation.

Professor Jane Stromseth, while pursuing interpretive methods akin to those of Professor Spiro, finds less play in the constitutional scheme for wholly discretionary presidential action. She finds historical confirmation for the President's powers to initiate peacetime deployments of troops for foreign policy purposes, as well as to engage in the limited use of force "to rescue American citizens abroad whose lives are in imminent danger."[17] She disagrees with Professor Spiro's conclusion that the President is otherwise authorized to engage in "strike operations" for non-rescue purposes.

Peter M. Shane, *Learning McNamara's* Lessons: *How the War Powers Resolution Advances the Rule of Law,* 47 Case W. Res. L. Rev. 1281, 1281–84 (1997). Professor Prakash's position, discussed in Section A, above, probably comes closest to that of Professor Stromseth.

Below are accounts of just a few of the post-1973 presidential military deployments, chosen to represent the varying rationales Presidents have offered for such ventures: the rescue of Americans, stabilizing governments whose precariousness could undermine foreign policy interests of the United States, retaliation for attacks on United

---

12. *See* Walter Dellinger, *After the Cold War: Presidential Power and the Use of Military Force,* 50 U. Miami L. Rev. 107, 113 (1995). [Ed. Note: The position of then-Assistant Attorney General Dellinger, asserted on behalf of the Clinton Administration, echoed the position also of John M. Harmon, assistant attorney general in charge of the Office of Legal Counsel during most of the Carter Administration. *Presidential Power to Use Armed Forces Abroad Without Statutory Authorization,* 4A Op. O.L.C. 185 (1980), reprinted in H. Jefferson Powell, The Constitution and the Attorneys General 402 (1999).]

14. Peter J. Spiro, War *Powers and the Sirens of Formalism,* 68 N.Y.U. L. Rev. 1338, 1348, 1352–53 (1993) (reviewing Ely, *supra* note 2).

17. Jane E. Stromseth, *Understanding Constitutional War Powers Today: Why Methodology Matters,* 106 Yale L.J. 845, 882 (1996) (reviewing Fisher, *supra* note 3).

States persons, humanitarian intervention, the protection of U.S. persons and property, and international peacekeeping. As you read the following historical snippets, consider whether the chronicle of executive branch practice buttresses any of the contending constitutional positions. Is the history reconcilable with the views of the founding generation, as expressed by Hamilton and Marshall? Following the historical narrative, we return to the question whether the War Powers Resolution has accomplished anything, or whether a different statutory framework would be preferable.

a. Rescuing Americans

The first formal invocation of the Resolution came in 1975, when President Ford had three occasions to file brief reports with Congress concerning the evacuation of U.S. citizens from Cambodia and from Saigon, and the seizure of the *S.S. Mayaguez*, a U.S. merchant vessel. Each of these reports was facially consistent with obligations imposed on the President by Section 4 of the War Powers Resolution, although none of the reports conceded the authority of Congress to impose such requirements. Furthermore, some members of Congress complained that the reports and the limited congressional consultation that preceded them did not represent a serious effort by the executive branch to involve Congress in military decision making. Former New York Senator Jacob Javits, a primary author of the War Powers Resolution, testified before a congressional committee:

> To a disturbing extent, consultations with the Congress prior to the Mayaguez incident resembled the old, discredited practice of informing selected members of Congress a few hours in advance at the implementation of decisions already taken within the Executive Branch. It is unclear whether this relapse was from force of habit or was calculated to test the mettle and resoluteness of the Congress.

War Powers: A Test of Compliance—Relative to the Danang Sealift, the Evacuation of Phnom Penh, the Evacuation of Saigon, and the Mayaguez Incident, Hearings Before the House Comm. on Int'l Rel., 94th Cong., 1st Sess. 61 (1975). The seriousness of the executive branch's commitment to the War Powers Resolution process was further called into question regarding President Carter's decision to attempt a military rescue in 1980 of American hostages held in Iran. The President's report to Congress and his counsel's legal opinion on the requirement for consultation with Congress follow:

President Carter's Report to Speaker O'Neill Concerning the Abortive Rescue Attempt in Iran

(Apr. 26, 1980)

Public Papers of the Presidents: Jimmy Carter, 1980–81, at 777

Dear Mr. Speaker: Because of my desire that Congress be informed on this matter and consistent with the reporting provisions of the War Powers Resolution of 1973 (Public Law 93-148), I submit this report.

On April 24, 1980, elements of the United States Armed Forces under my direction commenced the positioning stage of a rescue operation which was designed, if the subsequent stages had been executed, to effect the rescue of the American hostages who have been held captive in Iran since November 4, 1979, in clear violation of international law and the norms of civilized conduct among nations. The subsequent phases of the operation were not executed. Instead, for the reasons described below, all these elements were withdrawn from Iran and no hostilities occurred.

The sole objective of the operation that actually occurred was to position the rescue team for the subsequent effort to withdraw the American hostages. The rescue team was under my overall command and control and required my approval before executing the subsequent phases of the operation designed to effect the rescue itself. . . .

Beginning approximately 10:30 AM EST on April 24, six U.S. C-130 transport aircraft and eight RH-53 helicopters entered Iran airspace. Their crews were not equipped for combat. Some of the C-130 aircraft carried a force of approximately 90 members of the rescue team equipped for combat, plus various support personnel.

From approximately 2 to 4 PM EST the six transports and six of the eight helicopters landed at a remote desert site in Iran approximately 200 miles from Teheran where they disembarked the rescue, commenced refueling operations and began to prepare for the subsequent phases.

During the flight to the remote desert site, two of the eight helicopters developed operating difficulties. . . . Of the six helicopters which landed at the remote desert site, one developed a serious hydraulic problem and was unable to continue with the mission. The operational plans called for a minimum of six helicopters in good operational condition able to proceed from the desert site. . . . When the number of helicopters available to continue dropped to five, . . . I decided to cancel the mission and ordered the United States Armed Forces involved to return from Iran.

During the process of withdrawal, one of the helicopters accidentally collided with one of the C-130 aircraft, which was preparing to take off, resulting in the death of eight personnel and the injury of several others. At this point, the decision was made to load all surviving personnel aboard the remaining C-130 aircraft and to abandon the remaining helicopters at the landing site. . . . No United States Armed Forces remain in Iran.

The remote desert area was selected to conceal this phase of the mission from discovery. At no time during the temporary presence of United States Armed Forces in Iran did they encounter Iranian forces of any type. . . .

At one point during the period in which United States Armed Forces elements were on the ground at the desert landing site a bus containing forty-four Iranian civilians happened to pass along a nearby road. The bus was stopped and then disabled. Its occupants were detained by United States Armed Forces elements until their departure, and then released unharmed. One truck closely followed by a second vehicle also passed by while United States Armed Forces elements were on the ground. These elements stopped the truck by a shot into its headlights. The driver ran to the second vehicle which then escaped across the desert. Neither of these incidents affected the subsequent decision to terminate the mission.

Our rescue team knew, and I knew, that the operation was certain to be dangerous. We were all convinced that if and when the rescue phase of the operation had been commenced, it had an excellent chance of success. . . . The mission on which they were embarked was a humanitarian mission. It was not directed against Iran. It was not directed against the people of Iran. It caused no Iranian casualties.

This operation was ordered and conducted pursuant to the President's powers under the Constitution as Chief Executive and as Commander-in-Chief of the United States Armed Forces, expressly recognized in Section 8(d)(1) of the War Powers Resolution. In carrying out this operation, the United States was acting wholly within its right, in accordance with Article 51 of the United Nations Charter, to protect and rescue its citizens where the government of the territory in which they are located is unable or unwilling to protect them.

Sincerely, Jimmy Carter.

Legal Opinion by Lloyd Cutler, President's Counsel, on War Powers Consultation Relative to the Iran Rescue Mission (May 9, 1980)

Subcomm. on Int'l Security and Scientific Affairs of the House Comm. on Foreign Affairs, War Powers Resolution: Relevant Documents, Correspondence, Reports, 98th Cong., 1st Sess. 50 (1983)

1. In my opinion, the President's decision to use the armed forces in an attempt to rescue the American hostages in Iran, without consulting Congress before taking this action, was a lawful exercise of his constitutional powers as President and Commander-in-Chief, and did not violate the War Powers Resolution of 1973.

2. The President's constitutional power to use the armed forces to rescue Americans illegally detained abroad is clearly established. *In re Neagle*, 135 U.S. 1, *Durand v. Hollins*, 8 Fed. Cases 111. This power was expressly recognized in the Senate version of the War Powers Resolution, and is not negated by the final version of the Resolution, especially where, as here, those to be rescued include United States Marines.

3. His inherent constitutional power to conduct this kind of rescue operation, which depends on total surprise, includes the power to act before consulting Congress, if the President concludes, as he did in this case, that to do so would unreasonably endanger the success of the operation and the safety of those to be rescued.

4. Section 3 of the War Powers Resolution does require consulting with Congress "in every possible instance" before introducing United States Armed Forces into "hostilities or into situations where imminent involvement in hostilities is clearly indicated by the circumstances." In this case, the first stage of the operation — introducing the

rescue team into Iran during the night of April 24—did not involve any hostilities. The rescue effort itself was not to be initiated before the following night, and could have been aborted before any involvement in hostilities was "clearly indicated," and this is in fact what occurred.

5. In any event, Section 8(d)(1) of the War Powers Resolution provides that nothing in it "is intended to alter the constitutional authority of the Congress or of the President." If Section 3 were read to require prior consultation in these precise circumstances—where the President has inherent constitutional authority to conduct a rescue operation dependent on surprise and reasonable grounds to believe that prior consultation would unreasonably endanger the success of the operation and the safety of those to be rescued—this would raise grave issues as to the constitutionality of Section 3. Since statutes and joint resolutions are to be read where possible in a manner that does not raise such grave constitutional issues, Section 3 and Section 8(d)(1), read together, should not be construed to require prior consultation under the precise circumstances of this case.

"Implementation" or Charade? Do you agree with the Cutler opinion? In particular, is there force to his argument in paragraph 5? If so, how far does the argument extend?

---

b. Stabilizing Other Governments in Furtherance of American Foreign Policy

The most serious controversy during the Reagan Administration concerning the War Powers Resolution concerned the President's authority to deploy Marines in Lebanon to help stabilize the Lebanese Government:

> The Administration decided in August 1982, to send a contingent of U.S. Marines to Beirut as part of a multinational force to help facilitate the PLO's evacuation from the Lebanese capital. On August 20, 1982, following consultations with President Reagan on the use of U.S. forces in such a role, Senators Percy and Pell wrote to the President, recommending that he report this deployment under Section 4(a)(1) of the War Powers Resolution. On August 21, 800 French troops arrived, the first contingent of the Multinational Forces (MNF), and on August 25, 800 U.S. Marines landed in Beirut. President Reagan reported to the Congress "consistent with the War Powers Resolution" but stated the Marines would not be in a hostile situation and would be withdrawn within 30 days. . . . On September 11, the Marines were withdrawn.
>
> On September 16, President Bashir Gemayal of Lebanon was assassinated, and on September 16–18, a massacre took place at the Sabra and Shatila Palestinian refugee camps. President Reagan announced on September 21 that U.S. Marines would return to Lebanon as part of an international

force. On September 24, Senators Percy and Pell again wrote to the President recommending that the reintroduction of U.S. troops be reported under Section 4(a)(1). On September 29, U.S. Marines took over the Beirut airport area and President Reagan submitted a report "consistent with the War Powers Resolution" but insisting that the Marines were "not expected to become engaged in hostilities." On December 15, 1982, 14 Committee Members wrote to the President to say they "would expect Congress to be involved at the earliest possible stage . . . and that formal Congressional authorization would be sought before undertaking long-term or expanded commitments or extending indefinitely the present level of operations."

S. Rep. No. 98-242, 98th Cong., 1st Sess. 1–2 (1983).

Within a year of the Marines' initial deployment, Congress appropriated $151 million in economic and military assistance for Lebanon, requiring, however, that the President seek the earliest possible authorization by Congress for any significant expansion in the number or role of U.S. troops. Lebanon Emergency Assistance Act, Pub. L. 98-43, 97 Stat. 214 (1983). Two months later, in August, 1983, two Marines died in hostile fire directed at their position at the Beirut airport. Although President Reagan reported the event "consistent with section four of the War Powers Resolution," he declined to regard the resolution as "triggered," on the ground that the danger posed to the Marines was only "temporary." The Senate nonetheless initiated a debate on legislation aimed at certifying the Resolution as having been triggered on August 29, 1983, which would have resulted in an automatic pullout date of October 29, unless extended by the President.

In response to Congress's new-found vigilance, President Reagan entered into negotiations that prompted the enactment of the Multinational Force in Lebanon Resolution (MFLR), Pub. L. 98-119, 97 Stat. 805 (1983), and his signing of that legislation on October 12, 1983. The MFLR "determined" that the War Powers Resolution had been triggered on August 29, 1983, but expressly authorized the continued presence of U.S. forces in Lebanon for 18 months, unless extended, following the date of the MFLR's enactment. The MFLR also stated the general terms of the Marines' authorized mission, and provided that authority for their continued presence would expire in less than 18 months if any of a number of specified conditions occurred that would obviate their deployment.

Not surprisingly, President Reagan's signing statement tried to limit the Resolution's precedential significance. He stated his disagreement with a number of its findings, and declared that his signature did not "cede any of the authority vested in [the President] under the Constitution," or concede the constitutionality of the 60-day cutoff provision in the War Powers Resolution. *See* PAPERS OF THE PRESIDENTS: RONALD REAGAN, 1983, at 1444.

Proponents of the MFLR, however, asserted that it was vitally significant in a number of ways. First, it supposedly showed Congress's capacity to act meaningfully within the framework established by the War Powers Resolution. It would stand as precedent for Congress's authority to prescribe the specific duration of an authorized military deployment. The MFLR's requirements for presidential reports and for the expeditious treatment of proposed subsequent legislation on Lebanon envisioned and thus legitimated an expectation of continuing congressional oversight. The MFLR's limited mandate in terms of the numbers and role of troops was a first, as were the express limitations on the President's authority to expand the Marines' role. Under the MFLR, the only extension of role that would have *not* required additional authorization would involve measures by the Marines to ensure their own safety. Finally, the MFLR set a precedent defining "hostilities" broadly for purposes of interpreting the War Powers Resolution. *See generally* MULTINATIONAL FORCE IN LEBANON RESOLUTION, S. REP. No. 98-242, 98th Cong., 1st Sess. (1983).

Detractors, of course, disagreed. Senate dissenters argued that a resolution simply recognizing that the War Powers Resolution had been triggered would have placed the onus on the President effectively to seek authorization for military involvement in Lebanon based on specific policy objectives. In their view, the MFLR "compromise" allowed Congress to blink the President's repeated failures to recognize the applicability of congressional limits on his military authority. Moreover, they regarded the 18 months' authority as an insufficient guarantee of congressional vigilance.

As it happens, reality in the field overtook the domestic political-legal debate. Within two weeks after the President signed the Resolution, 241 U.S. Marines were killed in an attack on Marine barracks at the Beirut airport. Further casualties and mounting public and congressional criticism of U.S. policy resulted in an offshore evacuation of the Marines in February, 1984, and their withdrawal less than two months later from the Multinational Force.

The Clinton Administration also undertook a major deployment of U.S. military forces in order to stabilize a foreign country — considerably closer than Lebanon — whose instability was perceived as threatening to U.S. interests. Specifically, in October 1993, U.S. naval forces implemented a petroleum and arms embargo of Haiti, in response to the refusal of the Haitian military to fulfill its agreement to restore rule in that country to its elected President, Jean-Bertrand Aristide. President Clinton issued reports "consistent with the War Powers Resolution" concerning the embargo on October 20, 1993, and April 20, 1994.

On September 21, 1994, President Clinton reported a potentially far more dangerous mission — albeit one that ultimately succeeded (in the short term) with very little armed resistance. Two days earlier, substantial airborne and seaborne U.S. forces entered Haitian territorial waters and airspace, and finally secured entry into the Port-au-Prince airport and seaport facilities. The purpose of the mission was to secure the departure of the military government, and to maintain peace in Haiti pending the arrival of a U.N. mission to stabilize the country until further elections in 1996. President Clinton described the troops as having been assigned to the multinational force authorized by U.N. Security Council Resolution 940. A Justice Department defense of the President's authority to deploy military forces was offered in a letter by then-Assistant Attorney General Walter Dellinger to Senators Dole, Simpson,

Thurmond, and Cohen. *Deployment of United States Armed Forces into Haiti,* 18 Op. O.L.C. 173 (1994), *reprinted in* H. JEFFERSON POWELL, THE CONSTITUTION AND THE ATTORNEYS GENERAL 572 (1999).

Unlike U.S. missions to Somalia and Bosnia, the Haitian effort had a clear and relatively discrete military objective. On the other hand, the Haiti intervention was originally planned to involve 20,000 U.S. troops in what could have been extended combat. Because of the low level of resistance, fewer troops were expected to be required, but the total cost of the enterprise probably amounted to at least a half-billion dollars.

Reactions in Congress to Clinton's Haiti initiatives were mixed. Although the President successfully headed off efforts to prohibit the use of appropriated funds for military intervention in Haiti, Congress was clearly displeased by his unwillingness to condition his initiatives upon express congressional authority. Thus, in November 1993, Congress recorded its "sense" that funds appropriated for the Department of Defense for Fiscal 1994 should not "be obligated or expended for United States military operations in Haiti unless authorized in advance by Congress." Echoing that sentiment, Congress expressed its sense in October 1994, that "the President should have sought and welcomed congressional approval before deploying United States armed forces to Haiti."

The Haiti intervention dramatized the malaise commonly attending our processes for making military policy. On one hand, a presidential commitment of 20,000 troops to depose the de facto government of another nation is a bold act to undertake without explicit congressional authorization. On the other hand, President Clinton—partly in hope of securing the voluntary departure of Haiti's military leaders—was publicly and completely explicit about his precise intentions. In the Haiti context, Congress could not plausibly rely on any asserted legislative ignorance of presidential intentions to excuse either its failure to trigger the War Powers Resolution or, more directly, to regulate the scope of military confrontation with Haiti.

On October 25, 1994, Congress enacted a joint resolution finally stating the "sense of Congress regarding United States armed forces operations in Haiti." Pub. L. 103-423, 103rd Cong., 2d Sess. (1994). That post-invasion resolution required the President to report to Congress "the national security objectives to be achieved by operation Uphold Democracy, and a detailed description of United States policy, the military mission and the general rules of engagement under which operations of the United States armed forces are conducted in and around Haiti. . . ." The resolution further required: "Changes or modifications to such objectives, policy, military mission, or general rules of engagement shall be submitted to Congress within forty-eight hours of approval." It demanded monthly reports to Congress (until the cessation of the operation) concerning a variety of details regarding the Haiti deployment and its costs.

There was, however, not a word in the resolution about the War Powers Resolution. In customarily tepid terms, the resolution concludes: "Nothing in this resolution should be construed or interpreted to constitute congressional approval or disapproval of the participation of the United States armed forces in the United Nations mission in Haiti." U.S. military personnel were fully withdrawn from the U.N. Mission in Haiti by April, 1996. (President George W. Bush redeployed a small number of U.S. military forces to Haiti in late February, 2004, when an uprising resulted in the ouster of President Aristede and an outbreak of violent lawlessness that threatened both a humanitarian disaster and an outpouring of Haitians seeking refuge in the United States.)

c. Retaliation for Attacks on United States Persons

The Libya bombing in April, 1986, followed a heightening of tension between Libya and the United States resulting from U.S. charges of Libyan-sponsored international terrorism and a naval confrontation in the Libyan-claimed Gulf of Sidra. President Reagan stated that he finally ordered the air strike against five military targets on April 16 after "irrefutable" proof linked Libya to sponsorship of an April 5 bombing of a Berlin discotheque, which killed an American soldier and wounded 50 others. The asserted rationale for the bombing was the national right of self-defense.

The Administration briefed about a dozen members of Congress concerning the attack several hours before the strike. At the time of the briefing, the U.S. Air Force planes involved in the strike had already left their bases in England; the Administration later said the planes would have been recalled in the face of any strong congressional objections to the plan. President Reagan sent a report to Congress on April 16, "consistent with the War Powers Resolution," formally noting the strike and its rationale. While the report satisfied some members of Congress that the War Powers Resolution had been respected, others charged that it amounted to mere notification and not the consultation that the Resolution requires.

In general, congressional reaction to the attack itself mixed support for retaliation against Libya with concern about the decisionmaking process that led to the attack. The latter concern, however, was not entirely in one direction. While some asserted the need for tightening the War Powers Resolution's consultation requirements, others called for new legislation expressly authorizing greater presidential flexibility in responding to asserted acts of international terrorism. One House member has argued that Congress' failure to invoke the resolution in connection with the Libya bombing—an initiative with consensus support—does not belie the resolution's potential force in the face of more controversial initiatives. Robert G. Torricelli, *The War Powers Resolution After the Libya Crisis*, 7 PACE L. REV. 661 (1987). For one commentator's analysis of the minimal consultation necessary to mount a Libya-style attack constitutionally, see Note, *Self Defense or Presidential Pretext? The Constitutionality of Unilateral Preemptive Military Action*, 78 GEO. L.J. 415 (1989).

d. Protecting U.S. Persons and Property

The first major military venture of the George H.W. Bush Administration was an invasion of Panama on December 20, 1989, that ended the rule in that country of General Manuel Noriega. Noriega, for several years the target of allegations of murder, corruption, and electoral fraud, was indicted in the U.S. in 1988 for drug offenses. A range of economic and diplomatic sanctions during 1988 and 1989 failed to topple his regime. In May, 1989, Noriega conducted a presidential election, in which he claimed victory for his candidate despite widespread reports that the anti-Noriega opposition had won by a wide margin. A faction of the Panamanian Defense Force failed in a coup against Noriega in October, 1989, resulting in stiff criticism of the Bush Administration for failing to support the dissidents effectively. In December, a new National Assembly of Representatives, composed largely of Noriega loyalists, designated Noriega head of the government and "maximum leader" of the struggle for liberation. The Assembly also declared that there existed a state of war between Panama and the United States.[1] In attacks on U.S. military personnel, a Marine lieutenant was killed, another officer wounded, and a third officer beaten while his wife was interrogated and threatened.

Seven hours prior to the invasion, President Bush informed congressional leaders of the planned venture. He deployed 12,000 troops to Panama on December 20, followed by 2,000 additional troops three days later. The publicly declared objectives of the invasion were the protection of Americans living in Panama, preservation of legal control over the Panama Canal, and enforcement of U.S. drug laws against Noriega. An hour prior to the invasion, the anti-Noriega presidential candidate was sworn in as head of government at a U.S. military installation.

Noriega eluded detection for four days, and spent another 10 in refuge in the Vatican Embassy, before surrendering to U.S. authorities. (The legality of his ultimately successful prosecution on drug charges was upheld in *United States v. Noriega*, 746 F. Supp. 1506 (S.D. Fla. 1990).) Twenty-three U.S. soldiers and three U.S. civilians died in the invasion. Varying U.S. counts placed Panamanian losses somewhere in the hundreds. One day following the invasion, President Bush addressed a letter to the Speaker of the House and President Pro Tempore of the Senate reporting on the invasion "consistent with the War Powers Resolution."

The U.S. withdrew the last of its invasion troops on February 13, 1990. Probably because there existed popular support for the invasion, there had been little congressional criticism of President Bush's modest "consultation" prior to the venture. Subsequently, however, commentators did challenge the legality of the invasion, Alan Berman, *In Mitigation of Illegality: The U.S. Invasion of Panama*, 79 Ky. L.J. 735 (1991), and the high ratio of civilian to military deaths. *See* Physicians for Human Rights, Operation "Just Cause": The Human Cost of Military Action in Panama (1991).

---

1. Although widely reported as a declaration of war, there is ambiguity whether the statement was intended as a legal declaration or as a rhetorical assessment of the state of U.S.-Panama relations that Panama regarded the United States as initiating. Theodore Draper, *Did Noriega Declare War?* N.Y. Rev. of Books, Mar. 29, 1990, at 13.

e. Humanitarian Intervention

In 1991, the deposing of Somali strongman Mohammed Siad Barre after 22 years in power precipitated inter-clan fighting, fueled by arms that had been stockpiled by the now-defunct government. The consequent civil war resulted in a famine threatening starvation to nearly one third of the country's population.

The U.N. responded in 1992 by endorsing plans for an airlift to take food and medical supplies to Somalia. In support of the effort, the Bush Administration announced its commitment in September, 1992, to deploy over 2,000 Marines to provide offshore support for the airlift. After the November elections, the lame-duck President offered the U.N. 28,000 additional troops to help stabilize Somalia and permit effective food and relief deliveries. In December, 1992, the Security Council resolved "to use all necessary means to establish as soon as possible a secure environment for humanitarian relief operations in Somalia." Both the resolution and President Bush's commitment of troops were endorsed by President-elect Clinton. The Justice Department's defense of President Bush's authority to deploy troops to Somalia appears in Assistant Attorney General Timothy E. Flanigan, *Authority to Use United States Military Forces in Somalia*, 16 Op. O.L.C. 8 (1992), *reprinted in* H. Jefferson Powell, The Constitution and the Attorneys General 552 (1999).

By the spring of 1993, both the House and the Senate had approved their respective versions of a resolution authorizing the use of U.S. forces to support the U.N.-sponsored operation in Somalia. Before Congress could concur on a single legislative text, however, the military situation in Somalia grew substantially more precarious. With the government in collapse, the dominant force in Somalia clearly belonged to warlord Mohammed Farrah Aidid, whose gunmen, in September, 1993, wounded three U.S. troops in a gun battle with U.N. forces. On October 3 and 4, a further gun battle with Aidid's forces left an additional 18 U.S. troops dead. In the face of mounting political pressure at home, President Clinton announced that U.S. troops would be withdrawn from Somalia by March 31, 1994.

Congress finally codified its views on the Somalia crisis through amendments to the Department of Defense Appropriations Act for Fiscal Year 1994, *supra*, and the National Defense Authorization Act, Fiscal Year 1994, Pub. L. No. 103-160, 107 Stat. 1547 (1993). The Appropriations Act stated the purposes for which Congress approved the use of United States forces in Somalia, but generally cut off the availability of appropriations for Somali operations after March 31, 1994—the withdrawal date President Clinton had already announced. The National Defense Authorization Act required the President to report to Congress by October 15, 1993, "the goals and objectives supporting deployment of United States forces to Somalia and a description of the mission, command arrangements, size, functions, location and anticipated duration in Somalia of those forces." (The Act was signed on November 30, 1993!) Congress also required that the report include the status of "planning to transfer" the functions of United States forces to the United Nations. § 1512(a)(3). The next subsection stated: "Congress believes the President should by November 15, 1993, seek and receive congressional authorization in order for the deployment of United States forces to Somalia to continue." The statement of Congress's "belief" in this respect obscured whether the provision was mandatory or hortatory. In any event, the United States officially ended its 15-month mission on March 25, 1994, with the withdrawal of the final contingent of troops from Mogadishu. Only a handful of soldiers remained to protect a dozen diplomats at the U.S. liaison office.

Sporadic fighting among rival clans continued throughout 1994, and the United Nations proved unsuccessful in motivating the parties to adopt a lasting cease-fire. In late February, 1995, 1,800 Marines were again briefly deployed to Somalia to assist in evacuating the final remnant of U.N. forces. By March 2, 1995, the U.N. attempt to stabilize Somalia and to end the suffering of the Somali peoples was over.

The fact that Congress, over a year after the initial U.S. development, felt compelled to demand a presidential explanation of U.S. objectives evidences the uncertainty surrounding U.S. goals. Were we trying to weaken Aidid, assure the delivery of humanitarian aid, restore stable government, or some or all of the above? Nor does the War Powers Resolution seem to have played a major role in structuring policy making. In the roughly fourteen months he had command of the troops in Somalia, President Clinton communicated regularly, though most often informally, with congressional leaders. He reported to Congress in a manner purporting to be "consistent with the War Powers Resolution," only once, however, in June, 1993.

f. Antiterrorism Operations

Throughout their respective terms, Presidents George W. Bush and Obama both regularly sent to Congress what amount to consolidated reports giving details of U.S. military deployments and operations related to terrorism. Although the Obama Administration has declined to refer to these operations as part of what the Bush Administration variously called the "global war on terrorism," or just the "war on terror," the reports of both Administrations concern the deployment of combat-equipped forces to various locations "in the Central, Pacific, Southern and African Command areas of operation," in support of actions against al Qaeda and its supporters. The following paragraph from a June, 2010 report is typical:

> In furtherance of U.S. efforts against terrorists who pose a continuing and imminent threat to the United States, its friends, its allies, and U.S. forces abroad, the United States continues to work with partners around the globe, with a particular focus on the U.S. Central Command's area of operations. In this context, the United States has deployed U.S. combat-equipped forces to assist in enhancing the counterterrorism capabilities of our friends and allies, including special operations and other forces for sensitive operations in various locations around the world. In addition, the U.S. forces headquarters element in Djibouti provides command and control support as necessary to U.S. forces in the Horn of Africa region. The United States is committed to thwarting the efforts of al-Qa'ida and its affiliates to carry out

future acts of international terrorism and we have continued to work with our counterterrorism partners to disrupt and degrade the capabilities of al-Qa'ida and its affiliates. As necessary, in response to the terrorist threat, I will direct additional measures in the exercise of the right of the United States to self-defense and to protect U.S. citizens and interests. It is not possible to know at this time the precise scope or the duration of the deployments of U.S. Armed Forces necessary to counter the terrorist threat to the United States.

Letter of President Barack H. Obama to Speaker Pelosi and Senate President Biden, 2010 WL 2379241 (June 15, 2010).

g. International Peacekeeping

Few events have tested the United States' capacity for coherent policy-making more than the disintegration of Yugoslavia and the consequent outbreak of war. In 1980, the death of Marshall Tito, Yugoslavia's leader since 1946, helped generate a period of profound economic and political crisis. An experiment in power-sharing within the government unraveled as regional leaders tightened control over their respective states, often subjecting ethnic minorities within the republics to discriminatory measures. Slobodan Milosevic, a hard-line Serbian nationalist, won control of the Communist Party organization (and, therefore, the government) in Serbia in 1987. He promised to promote Serbian ethnic rights, particularly with respect to the Kosovo province of Serbia, in which ethnic Albanians made up 90 percent of the population. Although he succeeded both in crushing Albanian protests and extending Serbian influence in Montenegro, his aggressiveness fueled movements for secession in both Slovenia and Croatia.

By 1990, Yugoslavia was clearly headed toward dissolution. Croatian and Slovenian leaders were arguing for at most a loose confederation, with Serbia and Montenegro still pushing for a strong union, and Bosnia and Macedonia arguing a middle course. In early 1991, leaders in both Slovenia and Croatia announced plans to secede from Yugoslavia if a political agreement on confederation were not reached. Milosevic responded with an armed attack on Slovenia, the failure of which enabled the Slovenes finally to secure their independence. A fiercer conflict broke out in Croatia, where local Serbs—remembering the Croatians' massacres of Serbs during World War II—started militias to secure the autonomy of Serbian areas against the Croatian government. With the support of the Yugoslav army, the militias overran nearly one third of Croatian territory.

War next erupted in Bosnia, the most ethnically mixed republic of the former Yugoslavia. A majority of Bosnian voters, in February 1992, supported a referendum to break away from Yugoslavia. Bosnian Serbs, however, roughly one-third of the population, boycotted the referendum. The creation of a new government with the Bosnian Muslims firmly in control precipitated a war between the new government and Bosnian Serb forces, armed substantially by Milosevic. Within two years, over

100,000 people had been killed, and 1,500,000 people had been rendered refugees in the Bosnia fighting.

The capacity of the Bosnian Muslims to respond effectively to Serb attacks had been significantly weakened by the United Nations arms embargo imposed over Yugoslavia in 1991. In early 1992, the United Nations commenced an effort to protect minority Serbs in Croatia and the Bosnian Muslims. When the Yugoslav army and Serb irregulars began a siege of Sarajevo in April, 1992, President Bush permitted two U.S. Air Force planes to break through the siege, marking the first delivery of U.S. humanitarian aid.

What followed from 1992 through the signing of peace accords in November, 1995 was a frequently frustrating series of diplomatic and military efforts involving the United Nations and NATO, aimed at prompting a negotiated settlement of the Bosnian conflict. During that time, President Clinton proved unsuccessful in persuading U.S. allies to cooperate in lifting the arms embargo on behalf of the Bosnian Muslims. Indeed, the Serbs showed their first signs of interest in a lasting cease-fire and a negotiated settlement just as Congress appeared on the verge of threatening to overturn the embargo unilaterally.

U.S. military cooperation in both U.N. and NATO efforts prompted at least seven separate public reports to Congress, "consistent with the War Powers resolution." These reports concerned:

(1) U.S. participation in NATO's airborne enforcement of a no-fly zone over Bosnia;

(2) The augmentation of U.N. armed forces in Macedonia with U.S. forces to ensure the stability of that former Yugoslav republic;

(3) Providing U.S. air power to assist in NATO air strikes against heavy weapons located within 20 kilometers of the center of Sarajevo after February 20, 1994, a NATO-imposed deadline for their removal;

(4) Conducting airlift and aid-drop missions in Sarajevo and throughout Bosnia to deliver medical and other supplies; and

(5) Deploying U.S. aircraft in neutralizing Bosnian Serb gunners who were attacking U.N. personnel in Gorazde, in Bosnia.

Throughout this period, Congress authorized U.S. assistance to Bosnia, chiefly through appropriations measures. Congress additionally expressed its "sense" that "the President should terminate the United States arms embargo of the government of Bosnia and Herzegovina." By late 1994, however, Congress was clearly becoming restive with the Clinton Administration's lack of success in facilitating an end to the armed conflict. Section 8100 of the Department of Defense appropriations for Fiscal 1995 expressed "the sense of Congress" that appropriated funds should not be used to participate in implementation of a Bosnian peace settlement "unless previously authorized by the Congress," and further, that none of the funds appropriated should be spent for costs incurred by the United States armed forces while serving in international peace-keeping or peace enforcement operations under U.N. command. Query: As the President's Counsel, would you regard the "sense of Congress" as to how appropriated funds "should" be spent as indicating legally binding limitations on the expenditure of appropriated funds?

Congress's assertiveness had some impact. Although prospects brightened for a negotiated settlement in fall, 1995, President Clinton and Secretary of State Warren Christopher asserted that U.S. ground troops would be necessary to enforce any agreement that might be forthcoming. While claiming his constitutional prerogatives were intact, President Clinton promised he would seek congressional approval for any such deployment. With United Nations resolutions continuing to authorize international participation in a NATO-lead "stabilization" force for the area, the United States, as of 2004, has continued to contribute under 2,000 troops to the effort — with the President reporting to Congress every six months on the extent of the deployment.

Resolution of the Bosnia conflict did not, unfortunately, end the violence in the remaining portions of Yugoslavia. In addition to confronting separationist sentiment in areas of Yugoslavia beyond its borders, Serbia during the 1990s found itself contending with Kosovo, a Serbian province in which ethnic Albanians are the majority and which had been given autonomous status under Yugoslavia's 1974 constitution. With the rise of Serbian nationalism in the 1980s and the election, in 1987, of Slobodan Milosevic as President of Serbia, Kosovo, in 1990, found its autonomy revoked, government institutions suspended, and Albanian officials removed from their posts. These moves provoked increasingly strident Albanian resistance, including the formation of a Kosovo Liberation Army, which began a campaign of armed attacks against Serbian security forces. Serbia retaliated through a brutal military repression of the Albanian population, which, in turn, displaced tens of thousands of Kosovars from their homes and led to a potentially destabilizing out-migration to Bosnia, Albania, and Macedonia. Following a NATO statement of concern in 1997, a so-called "Contact Group" comprising the United States, France, Germany, Great Britain, Italy, and Russia stepped up diplomatic efforts to produce a peaceful resolution.

Great Britain's then-Defense Secretary, Lord Robertson, has described as follows the events of the ensuing fifteen months:

> Throughout 1998 diplomatic efforts to find a peaceful, negotiated solution were taken forward by the Contact Group. But the international community became aware that this might not be enough. NATO Defence Ministers therefore decided in June 1998 to task NATO military planners to produce a range of options, both ground and air, for military support to the diplomatic process, and by early August the results had been reviewed by the NAC [North Atlantic Council]. NATO also undertook a series of air and ground exercises to demonstrate the Alliance's ability to project power rapidly into the region. Four RAF strike aircraft participated.

By mid September 1998 an estimated 250,000 Kosovo Albanians had been driven from their homes and some 50,000 were still in the open as the winter approached. It was clear many might die. On 23 September the UN Security Council adopted resolution 1199, which highlighted the impending human catastrophe in Kosovo, and demanded a cease-fire and the start of real political dialogue. The following day NATO Defence Ministers, meeting in Vilamoura in Portugal, affirmed their resolve and determination to take action if required. NATO also agreed to begin the formal build-up and readying of forces to conduct air strikes. On 8 October a Contact Group meeting in London gave US envoy [Assistant Secretary of State] Richard Holbrooke a mandate for his mission to Belgrade to secure agreement to the requirements of SCR 1199. On 13 October NATO agreed Activation Orders for air strikes. The same day Holbrooke reported to NATO that Milosevic had agreed to the deployment of an unarmed OSCE [Organisation for Security and co-operation in Europe] verification mission to Kosovo and to the establishment of a NATO aerial verification mission. Following negotiations with senior NATO military representatives, the Federal Republic of Yugoslavia (FRY) authorities also agreed to reduce the numbers of security forces personnel in Kosovo to pre-crisis levels. On 27 October, NATO agreed to keep compliance of the agreements, which were underpinned by UN Security Council resolution 1203, under continuous review and to remain prepared to carry out air strikes should they be required, given the continuing threat of a humanitarian crisis. . . .

But despite an initial stabilisation of the situation, the violence continued. Following a massacre in the village of Racak on 15 January 1999, NATO increased its state of readiness for action. . . . On 28 January, NATO issued a "solemn warning" to Milosevic and the Kosovo Albanian leadership. This increased military pressure was paralleled by accelerated activity on the diplomatic front. On 29 January, the FRY/Serbian and Kosovo Albanian leaderships were summoned to talks at Rambouillet in France. This summons was given added emphasis the next day when NATO issued a statement reaffirming its demands, and delegating to the NATO Secretary General, Javier Solana, authority to commence air strikes against targets on FRY territory.

The negotiations at Rambouillet in February 1999, co-chaired by the UK and France, presented the FRY/Serbian governments and the Kosovo Albanian delegation with proposals for an equitable and balanced agreement on interim self-administration for Kosovo. The proposals, which reflected previous rounds of consultations with the parties, would have protected the rights of all sides. They recalled the international community's commitment to the sovereignty and territorial integrity of the FRY, provided for democratic self-government in Kosovo and specified that amendments would require the consent of all parties. The first round of talks was suspended on 23 February, with both sides expressing broad agreement to the principle of substantial autonomy for Kosovo. In the light of this progress a second round of talks was convened in Paris on 15 March to discuss implementation. We had made clear at Rambouillet that this would involve a NATO-led military force on the ground. But while the Kosovo Albanians were able to accept the documents negotiated at Rambouillet, it became clear that the FRY/Serbian side was under instructions not to agree. Indeed, they reneged on the commitment they had made. The talks were suspended on 19 March against a background of intensifying violence on the ground, clearly instigated by the FRY security forces, and evidence of a massive build up of FRY/ Serbian forces in and around Kosovo. . . .

It was known that a spring offensive against the KLA had been planned, and experience from Summer 1998 — when a quarter of a million Kosovo Albanians were driven from their homes — indicated the likelihood of it being accompanied by civilian casualties, destruction and displacement. It was for this reason that NATO had to act without delay. We were conscious that military action might be seized upon by Milosevic as an excuse to accelerate the offensive already underway. But while we had anticipated that the offensive could involve operations against the KLA and violent repression of the civilian population, we could not have predicted the full horror and extent of the brutality, which was to include scenes reminiscent of the 1930s and 1940s. This was no improvised brutality. My German colleague, Rudolf Scharping revealed on 9 April details of a covert Serbian plan, code-named Operation Horseshoe, to expel Kosovo Albanians from their homeland. The plan had been drawn up months before and showed that while Milosevic was pretending to negotiate, his forces had been preparing to annihilate. Had we not been prepared to launch the air strikes and continue them for as long as was necessary, the atrocities could still be continuing.

The Kosovo Crisis: A Paper by Lord Robertson of Ellen, available at http://www .kosovo.mod.uk/account/intro.htm.

Following upon the March 19 suspension of the Rambouillet talks, President Clinton committed U.S. military forces to begin, on March 24, 1999, assisting in NATO air strikes against Yugoslavia to end the Serb offensive against Kosovo and force its participation in peace talks. The bombing and our attendant support, entailing approximately 2,500 soldiers and aviators, went on until June 10, 1999, when Yugoslavia accepted NATO's conditions for a withdrawal of FRY forces from Kosovo. NATO determined to deploy a security force in Kosovo to maintain peace, to which the United States committed between 7,000 and 8,500 troops. As of late 2003, U.S. deployment was ongoing, although the number of troops involved had declined to roughly 2,100.

As with the U.S. deployment in Bosnia and the other seceding Yugoslav regions, which at one point reached over 25,000 troops, Congress's ratification of President Clinton's initiatives — such as it was — came entirely through annual appropriations measures. A concurrent resolution was introduced in Congress that would have purported to require the President to withdraw U.S. troops from Kosovo, but it was defeated in the house, 139 to 290. *Campbell v. Clinton*, 203 F.3d 19, 23 (D.C. Cir. 2000), cert. denied, 531 U.S. 815 (2000). The OLC memo excerpted below is widely regarded as the furthest-reaching Justice Department attempt since the War Powers Resolution to find authorization for hostilities to which the President had committed troops:

MEMORANDUM FOR THE ATTORNEY GENERAL RE: AUTHORIZATION FOR CONTINUING HOSTILITIES IN KOSOVO

24 Op. O.L.C. 327 (2000)

. . . This Memorandum memorializes and explains advice we provided to you in May of 1999 regarding whether Pub. L. No. 106-31, 113 Stat. 57 (May 21, 1999), the emergency supplemental appropriation for military operations in Kosovo, constituted authorization for continuing hostilities after the expiration of sixty days under section 5(b) of the War Powers Resolution, Pub. L. No. 93-148, 87 Stat. 555 (1973), codified at 50 U.S.C. §§ 1541–1548 (1994) (the "WPR"). . . .

II. Appropriations and Authorization of Military Combat

The Supreme Court has recognized that, as a general matter, appropriation statutes may "stand[] as confirmation and ratification of the action of the Chief Executive." Fleming v. Mohawk Wrecking & Lumber Co., 331 U.S. 111, 116 (1947). Congress may also "amend substantive law in an appropriations statute, as long as it does so clearly." Robertson v. Seattle Audubon Soc., 503 U.S. 429, 440 (1992). . . . Indeed, on numerous occasions, the Supreme Court has applied this general principle to find that Congress had authorized or ratified executive branch action through appropriation measures. . . . The notion that Congress can authorize hostilities through appropriation laws follows directly from this general principle. . . . Indeed, Congress has on numerous occasions authorized U.S. involvement in armed conflict at least in part through appropriation laws.

. . . In several instances in early Administrations, appropriation laws played an important role in authorizing or ratifying Presidential use of the Armed Forces in situations of conflict. For example, President George Washington "used force against the Wabash Indians pursuant to a statute that provided forces and authorized the call-up of militia to protect frontier inhabitants from the hostile incursions of Indians. This statute, along with the requests and debates that accompanied it, and the appropriations that followed its adoption, made clear that Congress approved the military engagements Washington undertook against the Wabash." Abraham D. Sofaer, The Power Over War, 50 U. Miami L. Rev. 33, 41 (1995) (emphasis added) (footnote omitted). . . . Congress also authorized President Adams to conduct the undeclared Quasi-War against France in part by appropriating funds to strengthen the military. Id. at 139–66 (describing appropriation laws and other measures by which Congress authorized hostilities against France). . . .

The most conspicuous example of Congress authorizing hostilities through its appropriations power occurred during the War in Vietnam. See William C. Banks & Peter Raven-Hansen, National Security Law and the Power of the Purse 119 (1994) ("The paradigm of what we have called legitimating appropriations–appropriation measures from which the executive infers authority for national security actions–is the succession of appropriations for military activities in Southeast Asia during the Vietnam War."). In that war, the State Department Legal Adviser argued that Congress had authorized the conflict, not only through the Gulf of Tonkin Resolution, 78 Stat. 384 (1964), but also by enacting supplemental appropriations bills. . . . Five years later, the Solicitor General Erwin Griswold made similar arguments. . . .

Some have argued that, on the contrary, appropriation statutes that fund ongoing war efforts do not constitute authorization of those war efforts. . . . This argument can take one of two forms. First, one could argue that a general defense-related appropriation statute does not authorize the ongoing hostilities because it provides only general defense-related funds and does not indicate any approval of the specific hostilities at issue. While this might be true, it does not undermine the basic principle explained above—that an appropriation statute specifically and conspicuously aimed at funding hostilities may constitute authorization of those hostilities. Second, some have argued that appropriations, regardless of how specific they may be with respect to ongoing war efforts, should not be interpreted to authorize continuing military operations because those appropriations could just as easily be understood as providing resources for men and women already in combat, simply to ensure that they do not suffer as a result of a disagreement between the Executive and the Congress regarding the wisdom of the deployment.

Although this may be true in some cases, in other cases, as Ely explains, this proposition "doesn't make sense . . . [[because] Congress could [phrase] its funds cut-off as a phase out, providing for the protection of the troops as they [are] withdrawn." John Hart Ely, War and Responsibility: Constitutional Lessons of Vietnam and its Aftermath 29 (1995). Congress took such a step with respect to hostilities in Somalia in November of 1993, when it provided that funds could be obligated beyond March of 1994 only "to protect American diplomatic facilities and American citizens, and noncombat personnel to advise the United Nations commander in Somalia." Pub. L. No. 103-139, § 8151(b)(2)(B), 107 Stat. 1418, 1476 (1993). Alternatively, Congress could preclude the use of funds to introduce additional troops, as it did through the 1971 Cooper-Church Amendment, which provided that "none of the funds authorized or appropriated pursuant to this or any other Act may be used to finance the introduction of United States ground combat troops into Cambodia, or to provide United States advisers to or for Cambodian military forces in Cambodia." Pub. L. No. 91-652, § 7(a), 84 Stat. 1942, 1943 (1971). In the end, the question whether a particular targeted appropriation constitutes authorization for continuing hostilities will turn on the specific circumstances of each case. . . .

III. Appropriations and the War Powers Resolution

... Section 8(a) of the WPR, however, provides that authority "shall not be inferred ... from any provision of law ... including any provision contained in any appropriations Act, unless such provision specifically authorizes the introduction of United States Armed Forces into hostilities or into such situations and states that it is intended to constitute specific statutory authorization within the meaning of this chapter." 50 U.S.C. § 1547(a). In assessing whether an appropriation statute can constitute authorization, the critical question thus becomes how to understand section 8(a)(1).

The precursor of section 8(a)(1) is section 3(4) of S. 440, the version of the WPR passed by the Senate. That section provided that a specific statutory authorization:

shall not be inferred (A) from any provision of law hereafter enacted, including any provision contained in any appropriations Act, unless such provision specifically authorizes the introduction of such Armed Forces in hostilities ... and specifically exempts the introduction of such Armed Forces from compliance with the provisions of this Act.

... The House version of the WPR did not contain an analogous provision. The Conference report indicates that the Senate version was the source of the "specific statutory authorization" language in the final bill. See H.R. Conf. Rep. No. 93-547 at 2 (1973). That language, according to the Senate report on S. 440, was intended to "guard against the passage of another resolution of the Tonkin Gulf type" by requiring that "any area resolutions, to qualify under this bill as a grant of authority to introduce the armed forces into hostilities ... meet certain carefully drawn criteria—as spelled out in the language of [§ 8(a)(1)]." S. Rep. No. 93-220, at 24. ... Congress thus required that authorizing legislation expressly reference the WPR to avoid "any ambiguities" regarding congressional intent to sanction continued hostilities.

To the extent, however, that this interpretation would take from Congress a constitutionally permissible method of authorizing war, it runs afoul of the axiom that one Congress cannot bind a later Congress. See, e.g., Fletcher v. Peck, 10 U.S. (6 Cranch) 87, 135 (1810) (noting that "[t]he correctness of [the] principle," "that one legislature is competent to repeal any [law] which a former legislature was competent to pass, and that one legislature cannot abridge the powers of a succeeding legislature," "can never be controverted"). Underlying this axiom is the principle that one Congress cannot surrender through legislation power that the Constitution vests in Congress....

Applying this general principle to the issue of section 8(a)(1)'s constitutionality, Professor Philip Bobbitt has argued that, were section 8(a)(1) read to bind subsequent Congresses, it would be unconstitutional: "[F]ramework statutes ... cannot bind future Congresses. If Congress can constitutionally authorize the use of force through its appropriations and authorization procedures, an interpretive statute that denies this inference–as does ... the original War Powers Resolution–is without legal effect. ..."

This argument is compelling. If section 8(a)(1) were read to block all possibility of inferring congressional approval of military action from any appropriation, unless that appropriation referred in terms to the WPR and stated that it was intended to constitute specific authority for the action under that statute, then it would be unconstitutional. . . . One statute, such as the WPR, cannot mandate that certain types of appropriation statutes that would otherwise constitute authorization for conflict cannot do so simply because a subsequent Congress does not use certain "magical passwords." . . .

In order to avoid this constitutional problem, we do not interpret section 8(a)(1) as binding future Congresses but instead as having the effect of establishing a background principle against which Congress legislates. In our view, section 8(a)(1) continues to have operative legal effect, but only so far as it operates to inform how an executive or judicial branch actor should interpret the intent of subsequent Congresses that enact appropriation statutes that do not specifically reference the WPR. On the question whether an appropriation statute enacted by a subsequent Congress constitutes authorization for continued hostilities, it is the intent of the subsequent Congress, as evidenced by the text and legislative history of the appropriation statute, that controls the analysis. The existence of section 8(a)(1) might affect this analysis. If the appropriation statute is entirely ambiguous as to whether it constitutes authorization for continuing hostilities, for example, it might be proper for a judicial or executive branch actor to conclude that, because the subsequent Congress was aware of the background principle established by section 8(a)(1), its failure to refer specifically back to the WPR evidences an intent not to authorize continuing hostilities. If, however, Congress, in enacting an appropriation statute, demonstrates a clear intent to authorize continuing hostilities, then it would be appropriate to conclude that the appropriation statute does authorize those hostilities, even though the statute does not specifically refer back to the WPR. Under these circumstances, the appropriation statute would supersede or work an implied partial repeal of section 8(a)(1). In other words, section 8(a)(1) establishes procedural requirements that, under the statute, Congress must follow to authorize hostilities; nonetheless, a subsequent Congress remains free to choose in a particular instance to enact legislation that clearly authorizes hostilities and, in so doing, it can decide not to follow the WPR's procedures. . . . This reading of section 8(a)(1) finds support in a series of cases interpreting statutes similar in form to section 8(a)(1). . . . Academic commentators have understood section 8(a)(1) in a similar fashion. . . . [W]here Congress, in passing an appropriations bill, clearly intends to authorize conflict, the WPR cannot be read to deny legal effect to that clear intent.

IV. Pub. L. No. 106-31 and Congressional Authorization of the War in Kosovo

. . . The "clock" established in section 5(b) of the WPR began running in the present case on March 26, 1999, when the President, citing national security concerns, informed Congress that U.S. military forces had begun a series of air strikes in the Federal Republic of Yugoslavia. . . . Approximately three weeks after sending this letter, the President, through the White House budget office, formally submitted a request to Congress for $6 billion to fund continuing efforts in Kosovo. . . . Of this amount, close to $5 billion was to be used for continued air operations and war material through September 30, 1999, and the rest was intended to assist the hundreds of thousands of ethnic Albanian refugees who were fleeing from Kosovo. The congressional leadership promptly made clear their intention to use the request as a vehicle to augment defense spending more generally and called for defense funding far in excess of the requested $6 billion.

Debate over the continuing military operations in Kosovo intensified on April 28, 1999, when the House considered and voted on four different Kosovo-related measures. First, the House defeated . . . a concurrent resolution directing the President to remove the Armed Forces from Serbia within 30 days, and [a resolution] declaring a state of war between the United States and Serbia. The House also voted 249–180 to support . . . blocking funding for ground troops without additional specific authorization from Congress, and tied, 213–213, on . . a concurrent resolution stating that the President "is authorized to conduct military air operations and missile strikes" against Serbia. As highlighted by the debates concerning these measures, there can be no doubt that members of Congress were fully cognizant of the WPR and the 60-day time clock.

Despite these votes, the appropriation effort moved forward. Following testimony by Secretary of Defense Cohen before the Subcommittee on Defense on April 21, and after a public markup on April 29, the House Appropriations Committee reported H.R. 1664, 106th Cong. (1999), entitled "[a] bill making emergency supplemental appropriations for military operations, refugee relief, and humanitarian assistance relating to the conflict in Kosovo, and for military operations in Southwest Asia for the fiscal year ending September 30, 1999, and for other purposes," to the full House on May 4. The $12.9 billion bill provided the funds requested by the President for military operations in Kosovo, as well as over $6 billion in other military funding, for such things as spare parts, depot maintenance, recruiting, and readiness training. Following a floor debate on May 6, the House passed H.R. 1664 the same day by a vote of 311–105.

The next week, the House and Senate held a joint conference on H.R. 1664 and H.R. 1141, 106th Cong. (1999), another emergency supplemental funding bill that up to that point had focused on providing relief to Central American nations devastated by hurricanes. During the three day conference, the conferees stripped H.R. 1664 of the appropriations relating to Kosovo and other military funding and added those appropriations to H.R. 1141. . . . The House debated H.R. 1141 on May 18 and passed the bill by a 269–158 vote on the same day. The Senate debated the bill on May 20 and passed it by a 64–36 vote on the same day.

The bill signed by the President, entitled "[a]n Act [m]aking emergency supplemental appropriations for the fiscal year ending September 30, 1999, and for other purposes," appropriated well over $5 billion to fund efforts in Kosovo. . . . [T]he congressional debates and the text of Pub. L. No. 106-31 make clear that Congress was unquestionably aware that it was funding the hostilities in Kosovo. Moreover, the appropriations bill was specifically targeted in substantial degree to the President's request for funds to continue the military action in Kosovo. Congress, in other words, used its constitutional authority to appropriate funds to allow the President to continue hostilities in the Federal Republic of Yugoslavia. In light of the nature of the bill and the historical precedent, discussed above, for Congress to authorize hostilities through appropriations measures, Pub. L. No. 106-31 would, in the absence of the WPR, have constituted constitutionally adequate authorization for continued bombing in the region.

[The remainder of this section argues in greater detail that various aspects of the text of Pub. L. No. 106-31 make sense only if Congress intended to authorize operations in Kosovo, a conclusion supported also by the relevant committee hearings and floor debate.]

V. Pub. L. No. 106-31 and the War Powers Resolution

As described in the preceding section, the text of Pub. L. No. 106-31 and the legislative record as a whole make clear that Congress intended, by enacting the President's request, to enable the President to continue U.S. participation in Operation Allied Force for as long as funding remained available, i.e., through at least the end of the fiscal year on September 30, and indeed even longer. Congress was repeatedly advised of this effect by its own Members (both supporters and opponents of continuing the operation) and by Administration witnesses. For at least the month that the Administration's request was pending, and at a time when the duration of hostilities was uncertain, Congress was aware that a vote for the bill would be a vote to authorize the campaign.

In this context, the concerns that have been voiced about finding congressional authorization in general appropriation statutes are not applicable. The purposes of both H.R. 1664 and H.R. 1141 were plain on the face of the bills. Nor was this a case in which the Committees with jurisdiction over war powers "would [have been] somewhat surprised to learn that their careful work on the substantive legislation had been undone by the simple—and brief—insertion of some inconsistent language in Appropriations Committees' Reports." The bill was surely among the most visible and important pieces of legislation introduced before the first session of the 106th Congress, and both the Administration and individual members pointedly and publicly underscored its significance. . . . H.R. 1141 was a freestanding bill that, in the form in which it was presented by the Administration, focused narrowly on military spending for Operation Allied Force. In sum, H.R. 1141 was intended to enable the President to continue Operation Allied Force, and to furnish him with the necessary funds for doing so, even if that operation were not brought to a successful conclusion by May 25. . . .

The House's votes on the four other Kosovo-related measures on April 28 do not lead us to change our conclusion. Although the House did defeat the resolution declaring a state of war between the United States and Serbia and passed a resolution blocking funding for ground troops without additional specific authorization, it also defeated a resolution that would have directed the President to remove the Armed Forces from the region and tied on the resolution that would have specifically authorized the President to conduct military air operations against Serbia. The message of all these votes is ambiguous. The only clear message that Congress sent regarding the continuation of military operations in Serbia is Pub. L. No. 106-31, which appropriated over $5 billion to continue these operations. As we have already explained, this was sufficient to constitute specific authorization within the meaning of the WPR.

Moreover, the argument, explained earlier, . . . that appropriation statutes should not be understood as authorizing hostilities because they might just as easily be intended to protect troops already committed, carries little weight here. . . . The United States did not have ground troops in combat in Serbia or Kosovo at the time Pub. L. No. 106-31 was enacted, but rather was engaged in an air campaign in which U.S. forces were in harm's way only for the length of each sortie flown. If Congress did not intend to authorize continuing hostilities, but instead intended only to protect previously deployed troops, it could have, and most likely would have, styled its rejection of authorization for continuing hostilities by either phasing out appropriated funds over time, as it did in the case of Somalia, or by prohibiting the use of funds for certain purposes, as it did with the Cooper-Church amendment. Here, Congress chose neither option. Instead, it appropriated funds "until expended" without placing any limitations on the use of those funds. . . .

Section 8(a)(1) does not lead to a contrary conclusion. As discussed above, that section cannot constitutionally be read to take from Congress a mechanism for authorizing war permitted by the Constitution. Instead, it has the effect of establishing a background principle against which Congress legislates. Section 8(a)(1) means, then, that it cannot be "inferred"–to quote the language of the provision–that Congress has authorized the continuation of conflicts from the mere fact that it has enacted an appropriation statute (unless the statute references the WPR). Nonetheless, if the text and legislative history of the appropriation statute make clear that it was Congress's clear intent to authorize continued operations, that intent is controlling, even if the statute does not reference the WPR. Such an appropriation statute is an implied partial repeal of section 8(a)(1) (or a supersession of section 8(a)(1)). . . .

Finally, it is worth observing that, in this case, the underlying purpose of the WPR's "clock" was fully satisfied. That clock functions to ensure that, where the President commits U.S. troops to hostilities without first obtaining congressional authorization, Congress has the opportunity to consider the merits of the President's actions and to decide whether those hostilities may continue. Here, the President ordered a series of air strikes in the Federal Republic of Yugoslavia "to demonstrate the seriousness of NATO's purpose so that the Serbian leaders understand the imperative of reversing course; to deter an even bloodier offensive against innocent civilians in Kosovo; and, if necessary, to seriously damage the Serbian military's capacity to harm the people of Kosovo." Congress then had the opportunity to deliberate on the wisdom of the President's actions, which it did, considering several resolutions relating to the military efforts in Kosovo. After all of those deliberations, Congress decided to use one of its most important constitutional powers over war and peace — its appropriation power — specifically to fund the ongoing military effort. By doing so, it authorized the President to continue military activities in the region. . . .

Randolph D. Moss

Assistant Attorney General

———————

1. *Canons v. Cannons?* AAG Moss was on incontrovertible ground in asserting that one Congress may not legislate away the constitutional authorities of later Congresses. Deciding, however, that legislation enacted by a later Congress is actually intended to be understood as departing from the dictates of a prior Congress presumably requires attention to the venerable presumption against implied statutory repeals. Footnotes to the opinion excerpted above acknowledge, and assert the irrelevance of, that presumption in this matter. OLC's argument consists of three propositions. First, "[a]lthough the law disfavors implied repeals, particularly with respect to appropriation statutes, *see Tennessee Valley Auth. v. Hill*, 437 U.S. 153, 190 (1978), the presumption against implied repeals can be overcome if the statutory language or legislative history evidences an intent to repeal the prior statute." Second, the maxim does not apply in this instance because Members of Congress were well aware of "the discrepancy between section 8(a)(1) and Pub. L. No. 106-31." Finally, the text and history of the enactment make clear that "both the Administration and individual Members of Congress strongly and visibly underscored the significance of the legislation," i.e., the provision of funding to support the President's military initiative in Kosovo. Are you persuaded? If so, under what circumstances would you not find the existence of appropriations to meet the requirement for congressional authorization of hostilities? If not, do you regard the advice as so implausible as to be unethical, or simply as the weaker side of a close argument? In other words, do you regard the opinion as one that the Justice Department could responsibly provide to the President even if it is not what you would regard as the best view of the law?

2. *Memorializing Legal Advice.* You may be puzzled that the December 19, 2000 Moss memorandum "memorializes and explains advice" OLC provided to the Attorney General in May, 1999. It may be worth noting that, in May 1999, Randolph Moss was the Acting Assistant Attorney General in charge of OLC, having succeeded Dawn Johnsen and Beth Nolan, each of whom served as an Acting Assistant Attorney General following Walter Dellinger's move from OLC to the Solicitor General's Office in 1994. After Moss served in an acting capacity for over a year and a half, President Clinton gave him a recess appointment as OLC head in August, 2000. The Senate actually confirmed him on December 15, 2000, with a month and five days left to go in the Administration. How might these events explain the 19-month delay in issuing the memo? (Postscript: Moss was appointed a judge on the United States District Court for the District of Columbia on November 14, 2014.)

Case Study: The Libya No-Fly Zone

Beginning in December 2010, a wave of uprisings and protests seeking democratic change swept across North Africa and the Middle East. By mid-February 2011, protesters in Libya had taken control over the eastern part of the country. Libya's autocratic leader, Colonel Muammar Qadhafi, responded by directing violence against protesters, including strafing and bombing operations. The United Nations Security Council adopted a resolution condemning Qadhafi's human rights abuses. By mid-March, Qadhafi had prepared to retake control over the eastern part of his country and threatened to have his troops go door-to-door to kill civilians. To prevent this threatened massacre, the U.N. Security Council authorized member states to impose a no-fly zone over Libya in order to prevent Col. Qadhafi's troops from advancing on the eastern part of the country. The United States and various coalition partners then enforced the no-fly zone by conducting a series of airstrikes against the Libyan military. President Obama explained the U.S. role as follows:

> Now, here is why this matters to us. Left unchecked, we have every reason to believe that Qaddafi would commit atrocities against his people. Many thousands could die. A humanitarian crisis would ensue. The entire region could be destabilized, endangering many of our allies and partners. The calls of the Libyan people for help would go unanswered. The democratic values that we stand for would be overrun. Moreover, the words of the international community would be rendered hollow.

Barack Obama, Remarks by the President on the Situation in Libya (Mar. 18, 2011), https://obamawhitehouse.archives.gov/the-press-office/2011/03/18/remarks-president-situation-libya.

Authority to Use Military Force in Libya
35 Op. O.L.C. ___, 2011 WL 1459998 (April 1, 2011)

II.

* * *

A.

Earlier opinions of this Office and other historical precedents establish the framework for our analysis. As we explained in 1992, Attorneys General and this Office "have concluded that the President has the power to commit United States troops abroad," as well as to "take military action," "for the purpose of protecting important national interests," even without specific prior authorization from Congress. *Authority to Use United States Military Forces in Somalia*, 16 Op. O.L.C. 6, 9 (1992) ("*Military Forces in Somalia*"). This independent authority of the President, which exists at least insofar as Congress has not specifically restricted it, *See Deployment of United States Armed Forces into Haiti*, 18 Op. O.L.C. 173, 176 n.4, 178 (1994) ("*Haiti Deployment*"), derives from the President's "unique responsibility," as Commander in Chief and Chief Executive, for "foreign and military affairs," as well as national security. . . .

"Our history," this Office observed in 1980, "is replete with instances of presidential uses of military force abroad in the absence of prior congressional approval." *Presidential Power*, 4A Op. O.L.C. at 187. Since then, instances of such presidential initiative have only multiplied, with Presidents ordering, to give just a few examples, bombing in (1986), an intervention in Panama (1989), troop deployments to Somalia (1992), Bosnia (1995), and Haiti (twice, 1994 and 2004), air patrols and airstrikes in Bosnia (1993–1995), and a bombing campaign in Yugoslavia (1999), without specific prior authorizing legislation. *See* Grimmett, *supra*, at 13–31. This historical practice is an important indication of constitutional meaning, because it reflects the two political branches' practical understanding, developed since the founding of the Republic, of their respective roles and responsibilities with respect to national defense, and because "[m]atters intimately related to foreign policy and national security are rarely proper subjects for judicial intervention." *Haig*, 453 U.S. at 292. In this context, the "pattern of executive conduct, made under claim of right, extended over many decades and engaged in by Presidents of both parties, 'evidences the existence of broad constitutional power.'" *Haiti Deployment*, 18 Op. O.L.C. at 178 (quoting *Presidential Power*, 4A Op. O.L.C. at 187).

Indeed, Congress itself has implicitly recognized this presidential authority. The War Powers Resolution ("WPR"), 50 U.S.C. §§ 1541–1548 (2006), a statute Congress described as intended "to fulfill the intent of the framers of the Constitution of the United States," *id.* § 1541(a), provides that, in the absence of a declaration of war, the President must report to Congress within 48 hours of taking certain actions, including introduction of U.S. forces "into hostilities or into situations where imminent involvement in hostilities is clearly indicated by the circumstances." *Id.* § 1543(a). The Resolution further provides that the President generally must terminate such use of force within 60 days (or 90 days for military necessity) unless Congress extends this deadline, declares war, or "enact[s] a specific authorization." *Id.* § 1544(b). As this Office has explained, although the WPR does not itself provide affirmative statutory authority for military operations, *See id.* § 1547(d)(2), the Resolution's "structure . . . recognizes and presupposes the existence of unilateral presidential authority to deploy armed forces" into hostilities or circumstances presenting an imminent risk of hostilities. *Haiti Deployment*, 18 Op. O.L.C. at 175. That structure—requiring a report within 48 hours after the start of hostilities and their termination within 60 days after that—"makes sense only if the President may introduce troops into hostilities or potential hostilities without prior authorization by the Congress." *Haiti Deployment*, 18 Op. O.L.C. at 175–76.

We have acknowledged one possible constitutionally-based limit on this presidential authority to employ military force in defense of important national interests—a planned military engagement that constitutes a "war" within the meaning of the Declaration of War Clause may require prior congressional authorization. *See Proposed Bosnia Deployment*, 19 Op. O.L.C. at 331; *Haiti Deployment*, 18 Op. O.L.C. at

177. But the historical practice of presidential military action without congressional approval precludes any suggestion that Congress's authority to declare war covers every military engagement, however limited, that the President initiates. In our view, determining whether a particular planned engagement constitutes a "war" for constitutional purposes instead requires a fact-specific assessment of the "anticipated nature, scope, and duration" of the planned military operations. *Haiti Deployment*, 18 Op. O.L.C. at 179. This standard generally will be satisfied only by prolonged and substantial military engagements, typically involving exposure of U.S. military personnel to significant risk over a substantial period. Again, Congress's own key enactment on the subject reflects this understanding. By allowing United States involvement in hostilities to continue for 60 or 90 days, Congress signaled in the WPR that it considers congressional authorization most critical for "major, prolonged conflicts such as the wars in Vietnam and Korea," not more limited engagements. *Id.* at 176. . . .

B.

[T]he President's legal authority to direct military force in Libya turns on two questions: first, whether United States operations in Libya would serve sufficiently important national interests to permit the President's action as Commander in Chief and Chief Executive and pursuant to his authority to conduct U.S. foreign relations; and second, whether the military operations that the President anticipated ordering would be sufficiently extensive in "nature, scope, and duration" to constitute a "war" requiring prior specific congressional approval under the Declaration of War Clause.

In prior opinions, this Office has identified a variety of national interests that, alone or in combination, may justify use of military force by the President. In 2004, for example, we found adequate legal authority for the deployment of U.S. forces to Haiti based on national interests in protecting the lives and property of Americans in the country, preserving "regional stability," and maintaining the credibility of United Nations Security Council mandates. Memorandum for Alberto R. Gonzales, Counsel to the President, from Jack L. Goldsmith III, Assistant Attorney General, Office of Legal Counsel, *Re: Deployment of United States Armed Forces to Haiti* at 3–4 (Mar. 17, 2004) ("2004 Haiti Opinion"). In 1995, we similarly concluded that the President's authority to deploy approximately 20,000 ground troops to Bosnia, for purposes of enforcing a peace agreement ending the civil war there, rested on national interests in completing a "pattern of inter-allied cooperation and assistance" established by prior U.S. participation in NATO air and naval support for peacekeeping efforts, "preserving peace in the region and forestalling the threat of a wider conflict," and maintaining the credibility of the UNSC. *Proposed Bosnia Deployment*, 19 Op. O.L.C. at 332–33. And in 1992, we explained the President's authority to deploy troops in Somalia in terms of national interests in providing security for American civilians and military personnel involved in UNSC-supported humanitarian relief efforts and (once again) enforcing UNSC mandates. *Military Forces in Somalia*, 16 Op. O.L.C. at 10–12.

In our view, the combination of at least two national interests that the President reasonably determined were at stake here—preserving regional stability and supporting the UNSC's credibility and effectiveness—provided a sufficient basis for the President's exercise of his constitutional authority to order the use of military force.[3] First, the United States has a strong national security and foreign policy interest in security and stability in the Middle East that was threatened by Qadhafi's actions in Libya. As noted, we recognized similar regional stability interests as justifications for presidential military actions in Haiti and Bosnia. With respect to Haiti, we found "an obvious interest in maintaining peace and stability," "[g]iven the proximity of Haiti to the United States," and particularly considering that "past instances of unrest in Haiti have led to the mass emigration of refugees attempting to reach the United States." 2004 Haiti Opinion at 3. In the case of Bosnia, we noted (quoting prior statements by President Clinton justifying military action) the longstanding commitment of the United States to the " 'principle that the security and stability of Europe is of fundamental interest to the United States,' " and we identified, as justification for the military action, the President's determination that "[i]f the war in the former Yugoslavia resumes, 'there is a very real risk that it could spread beyond Bosnia, and involve Europe's new democracies as well as our NATO allies." ' *Proposed Bosnia Deployment*, 19 Op. O.L.C. at 333. In addition, in another important precedent, President Clinton justified extensive airstrikes in the Federal Republic of Yugoslavia ("FRY") in 1999—military action later ratified by Congress but initially conducted without specific authorization, *See Authorization for Continuing Hostilities in Kosovo*, 24 Op. O.L.C. 327 (2000)—based on concerns about the threat to regional security created by that government's repressive treatment of the ethnic Albanian population in Kosovo. "The FRY government's violence," President Clinton explained, "creates a conflict with no natural boundaries, pushing refugees across borders and potentially drawing in neighboring countries. The Kosovo region is a tinderbox that could ignite a wider European war with dangerous consequences to the United States." *Letter to Congressional Leaders Reporting on Airstrikes Against Serbian Targets in the Federal Republic of Yugoslavia (Serbia and Montenegro)*, 35 Weekly Comp. Pres. Doc. 527, 527 (Mar. 26, 1999).

As his statements make clear, President Obama determined in this case that the Libyan government's actions posed similar risks to regional peace and security. Much as violence in Bosnia and Kosovo in the 1990s risked creating large refugee movements, destabilizing neighboring countries, and inviting wider conflict, here the Libyan government's "illegitimate use of force . . . [was] forcing many [civilians] to flee to neighboring countries, thereby destabilizing the peace and security of the region." Obama March 21, 2011 Report to Congress. "Left unaddressed," the President noted in his report to Congress, "the growing instability in Libya could ignite wider instability in the Middle East, with dangerous consequences to the national security interests of the United States." *Id.* Without outside intervention, Libya's civilian population faced a "humanitarian catastrophe," *id.*; as the President put it on another occasion, "innocent people" in Libya were "being brutalized" and Qadhafi "threaten[ed] a bloodbath that could destabilize an entire region." The risk of regional destabilization in this case was also recognized by the UNSC, which determined in Resolution 1973 that the "situation" in Libya "constitute[d] a threat to international peace and security." S.C. Res. 1973. As this Office has previously observed, "[t]he President is entitled to rely on" such UNSC findings "in making his determination that the interests of the United States justify providing the military assistance that [the UNSC resolution] calls for." *Military Forces in Somalia*, 16 Op. O.L.C. at 12.

Qadhafi's actions not only endangered regional stability by increasing refugee flows and creating a humanitarian crisis, but, if unchecked, also could have encouraged the repression of other democratic uprisings that were part of a larger movement in the Middle East, thereby further undermining United States foreign policy goals in the region. Against the background of widespread popular unrest in the region, events in Libya formed "just one more chapter in the change that is unfolding across the Middle East and North Africa." Obama March 18, 2011 Remarks. Qadhafi's campaign of violence against his own country's citizens thus might have set an example for others in the region, causing "[t]he democratic impulses that are dawning across the region [to] be eclipsed by the darkest form of dictatorship, as repressive leaders concluded that violence is the best strategy to cling to power." Obama March 28, 2011 Address.

At a minimum, a massacre in Libya could have imperiled transitions to democratic government underway in neighboring Egypt and Tunisia by driving "thousands of additional refugees across Libya's borders." *Id.* Based on these factors, we believe the President could reasonably find a significant national security interest in preventing Libyan instability from spreading elsewhere in this critical region.

The second important national interest implicated here, which reinforces the first, is the longstanding U.S. commitment to maintaining the credibility of the United Nations Security Council and the effectiveness of its actions to promote international peace and security. Since at least the Korean War, the United States government has recognized that " '[t]he continued existence of the United Nations as an effective international organization is a paramount United States interest.' " *Military Forces in Somalia*, 16 Op. O.L.C. at 11 (quoting *Authority of the President to Repel the Attack in Korea*, 23 Dep't St. Bull. 173, 177 (1950)). . . . Here, the UNSC's credibility and effectiveness as an instrument of global peace and stability were at stake in Libya once the UNSC took action to impose a no-fly zone and ensure the safety of civilians—particularly after Qadhafi's forces ignored the UNSC's call for a cease fire and for the cessation of attacks on civilians. As President Obama noted, without military action to stop Qadhafi's repression, "[t]he writ of the United Nations Security Council would have been shown to be little more than empty words, crippling that institution's future credibility to uphold global peace and security." We think the President could legitimately find that military action by the United States to assist the international coalition in giving effect to UNSC Resolution 1973 was needed to secure "a substantial national foreign policy objective." *Military Forces in Somalia*, 16 Op. O.L.C. at 12.

We conclude, therefore, that the use of military force in Libya was supported by sufficiently important national interests to fall within the President's constitutional power. At the same time, turning to the second element of the analysis, we do not believe that anticipated United States operations in Libya amounted to a "war" in the constitutional sense necessitating congressional approval under the Declaration of War Clause. This inquiry, as noted, is highly fact-specific and turns on no single factor. *See Proposed Bosnia Deployment*, 19 Op. O.L.C. at 334 (reaching conclusion based on specific "circumstances"); *Haiti Deployment*, 18 Op. O.L.C. at 178 (same). Here, considering all the relevant circumstances, we believe applicable historical precedents demonstrate that the limited military operations the President anticipated directing were not a "war" for constitutional purposes.

As in the case of the no-fly zone patrols and periodic airstrikes in Bosnia before the deployment of ground troops in 1995 and the NATO bombing campaign in connection with the Kosovo conflict in 1999 — wo military campaigns initiated without a prior declaration of war or other specific congressional authorization — President Obama determined that the use of force in Libya by the United States would be limited to airstrikes and associated support missions; the President made clear that "[t]he United States is not going to deploy ground troops in Libya." Obama March 18, 2011 Remarks. The planned operations thus avoided the difficulties of withdrawal and risks of escalation that may attend commitment of ground forces — two factors that this Office has identified as "arguably" indicating "a greater need for approval [from Congress] at the outset," to avoid creating a situation in which "Congress may be confronted with circumstances in which the exercise of its power to declare war is effectively foreclosed." *Proposed Bosnia Deployment*, 19 Op. O.L.C. at 333. Furthermore, also as in prior operations conducted without a declaration of war or other specific authorizing legislation, the anticipated operations here served a "limited mission" and did not "aim at the conquest or occupation of territory." *Id.* at 332. . . . Considering the historical practice of even intensive military action — such as the 17-day-long 1995 campaign of NATO airstrikes in Bosnia and some two months of bombing in Yugoslavia in 1999 — without specific prior congressional approval, as well as the limited means, objectives, and intended duration of the anticipated operations in Libya, we do not think the "anticipated nature, scope, and duration" of the use of force by the United States in Libya rose to the level of a "war" in the constitutional sense, requiring the President to seek a declaration of war or other prior authorization from Congress.

Accordingly, we conclude that President Obama could rely on his constitutional power to safeguard the national interest by directing the anticipated military operations in Libya — which were limited in their nature, scope, and duration — without prior congressional authorization.

Caroline D. Krass
Principal Deputy Assistant Attorney General

———————

1. *Any Limits Left?* The opinion asserts that "the President has the power to commit United States troops abroad, as well as to take military action, for the purpose of protecting important national interests." The opinion also makes clear that this force may not be of such a scale as to amount to war. Nonetheless, can you perceive any meaningful legal limit on the President's power to order the use of military force short of war? Will there ever be an instance in which the President could not articulate an important national interest in ordering military force?

2. *Is a Humanitarian Justification Sufficient?* Do you agree that the no-fly zone fits within the precedents OLC cites? Note that preventing regional stability has factored into other uses of military force, notably in Kosovo and Haiti. But these are different regions of the world. Haiti is a geographic neighbor of the U.S. and a Haitian refugee crisis would directly implicate the territory of the U.S. Kosovo is in Europe and borders NATO allies with whom the U.S. has mutual defense treaty obligations. Is the threat of instability in North Africa and the Middle East an interest of the same order? Do you agree that the very real threat of a humanitarian catastrophe justifies the President in using military force abroad without prior congressional approval?

3. *From Lebanon to Syria.* On April 6, 2017, the Trump Administration announced that 59 Tomahawk cruise missiles had been fired at the Al Shayrat airfield in Syria in response to the Assad regime's use of chemical weapons against a civilian population two days earlier, which had killed 80 people. Although the U.S. has been militarily involved in Syria because of the fight against the Islamic State, a topic we explore in Chapter 7, this was clearly different—an attack on the Assad regime itself. The Administration provided neither a formal legal opinion defending the legality of the strike, nor a formal explanation of its justification under international law. Jack Goldsmith, who headed OLC during part of the George W. Bush Administration, had written critically of the Libya opinion, but thought the Syria intervention ignored even the vague limits on presidential power that DAAG Krass set forth:

> A key document for understanding OLC's view of the legality of the Syria strike is the 2011 OLC opinion justifying the intervention in Libya. The Libya opinion clarified several lines of Executive branch precedent . . . and for the first time (for the Executive branch) publicly invoked the 1999 NATO intervention in Kosovo as a "precedent" (a term used in the opinion) under the Constitution for uses of force. It sets forth a two-part test for determining when a presidential use of military force abroad is consistent with the Constitution.
>
> The *first* part asks whether the President has presumptive authority to use force unilaterally. For OLC, this authority turns on whether the "national interest" vindicated by the use of force sufficiently important? That sounds vague and easy to satisfy, but as we'll see in a moment, OLC has (at least until the Syria strike) pointed to some objective limits. If the president perceives that "national interest" would be vindicated by a use of force, OLC says that he can presumptively use force abroad under his powers as "Commander in

Chief and Chief Executive, for foreign and military affairs, as well as national security."

However, OLC acknowledged "one possible constitutionally-based limit on this presidential authority to employ military force in defense of important national interests—a planned military engagement that constitutes a 'war' within the meaning of the Declaration of War Clause may require prior congressional authorization." This *second* part of the test turns on the "anticipated nature, scope, and duration of the planned military operations." The idea is that relatively short-term and small-scale operations abroad are not "war" and thus do not implicate the Declare War clause, but larger-scale, longer-term operations might be "war" and thus might implicate the clause.

Applying this test to Syria, consider the "scale of operations" prong first. . . . As long as the military intervention in Syria is short term and limited and does not involve ground troops against Assad forces, it breaks no new legal ground.

The same cannot be said of the other prong of the test, which asks whether the President has authority to strike in the first place. What is the important national interest in intervening in Syria? No U.S. persons or property are at stake. That fact alone distinguishes most executive branch precedents. In the Libya opinion, OLC argued that "at least two national interests that the President reasonably determined were at stake here—preserving regional stability and supporting the UNSC's credibility and effectiveness." The second interest—the "credibility and effectiveness" of a Security Council Resolution—is a controversial basis for justifying presidential unilateralism because it seems to substitute international institutional approval for congressional approval. This line of reasoning began with Truman's unilateral initiation of the Korean war in response to North Korea's international aggression. In that instance, in 1950, the State Department argued (among other things) that the President as Commander in Chief could deploy U.S. armed forces, consistent with the Constitution, for the purpose of upholding the "paramount United States interest" in the "continued existence of the United Nations as an effective international organization." Moreover, the Kosovo precedent arguably extends this reasoning from the Security Council to NATO, which supported (and indeed conducted) the Kosovo strikes.

Whatever one thinks about this part of OLC's reasoning, it at least makes presidential power turn on the consent and validation of other countries with different interests, which provides some measure of limitation, however weak. And yet even this weak limitation is missing in last night's strikes. The President barely consulted with other countries in advance, much less got their approval through an important international security-related organization.

That leaves the Executive branch to rely on the weakest and easiest-to-satisfy of all possible interests: preservation of "regional stability" and maintenance of "peace and stability." We can discern how the Executive branch will shape this part of the test to Syria in the President's remarks last night:

> It is in this vital *national security interest* of the United States to prevent and deter the spread and use of deadly chemical weapons.
>
> There can be no dispute that Syria used banned chemical weapons, violated its obligations under the Chemical Weapons Convention and ignored the urging of the U.N. Security Council. . . .
>
> As a result the refugee crisis continues to deepen and the *region continues to destabilize,* threatening the United States and its allies.

This passage contains the seeds of the Trump administration's legal rationale for the strike. First, the administration will argue that Assad's human rights abuses and the civil war in Syria has created regional instability that creates an important interest justifying unilateral presidential force. And second, it will argue that the United States has an important interest in deterring the spread of chemical weapons and in enforcing a norm against the use of chemical weapons. . . .

There are at least two points to note about this rationale. First, the interests invoked—protecting regional security and in upholding or enforcing important treaty norms—will *always be present* when the President is considering military intervention. Taken alone—and they are all we have here—these interests provide no practical limitation on presidential power. To be sure, the regional security interest has been invoked in Libya and in many earlier OLC opinions, but they were always invoked in connection with other factors (such as the consent of the nation in question) or other more concrete and limited interests (such as the protection of U.S. persons or property, or the preservation of the U.N. Charter or a regional security treaty commitment), and never as sufficient by themselves. . . .

Second, it seems pretty clear that the Trump team will rely heavily on Obama administration legal analysis. . . .

In sum, while it is impossible to know yet for sure, the Trump administration appears to have pushed out the OLC and other executive branch opinions and precedents to justify unilateral presidential military force based only on regional instability and the desire to uphold important international norms. As I wrote of this rationale when it was being considered by the Obama administration,

> Its main problem is that it places no limit at all on the president's ability to use significant military force unilaterally. Future presidents will easily be able to invoke regional stability and the need to protect

important international norms whenever they want to intervene abroad with strikes like the one expected against Syria. . . .

Jack Goldsmith, *The Constitutionality of the Syria Strike Through the Eyes of OLC (and the Obama Administration)*, LAWFARE (Apr. 7, 2017), https://www.lawfareblog.com /constitutionality-syria-strike-through-eyes-olc-and-obama-administration. What is your view? Would you expect the Syria bombing to have long-term significance for the unilateral exercise of presidential war powers?

4. *The 60-Day Cutoff Debate.* After the initial airstrikes in Libya, the U.S. ceded control of the operation to allies and played what the State Department has described as a supporting role. When the operation reached its 60th day, it seemed that the War Powers Resolution would require U.S. participation to cease altogether as there had not been an express authorization enacted by Congress. As the War Powers Resolution clock was ticking down, President Obama sought the views of his legal advisers as to whether U.S. involvement with the no-fly zone could continue despite the WPR. According to press accounts, the Office of Legal Counsel and the General Counsel of the Defense Department each advised the President that U.S. activities in connection with the no-fly zone represented hostilities and therefore could not continue beyond the time limit of the WPR without congressional authorization. The State Department's Legal Adviser, Harold Koh, advised that the U.S.'s supporting role in enforcing the no-fly zone did not represent hostilities under the WPR. Here is Dean Koh's testimony on the issue:

Harold Hongju Koh, U.S. Department of State, Washington, D.C.

Libya and War Powers, Hearing Before the
Senate Committee on Foreign Relations,
112th Cong., 1st Sess., at 11–16.

June 28, 2011

. . . We believe that the President is acting lawfully in Libya, consistent with both the Constitution and the War Powers Resolution, as well as with international law. Our position is carefully limited to the facts of the present operation, supported by history, and respectful of both the letter of the Resolution and the spirit of consultation and collaboration that underlies it.

* * * * *

. . . The legal debate has focused on the Resolution's 60-day clock, which directs the President—absent express Congressional authorization (or the applicability of other limited exceptions) and following an initial 48-hour reporting period—to remove United States Armed Forces within 60 days from "hostilities" or "situations where imminent involvement in hostilities is clearly indicated by the circumstances." But as virtually every lawyer recognizes, the operative term, "hostilities," is an ambiguous standard, which is nowhere defined in the statute. Nor has this standard ever been defined by the courts or by Congress in any subsequent war powers legislation.

Indeed, the legislative history of the Resolution makes clear there was no fixed view on exactly what the term "hostilities" would encompass. Members of Congress understood that the term was vague, but specifically declined to give it more concrete meaning, in part to avoid unduly hampering future Presidents by making the Resolution a "one size fits all" straitjacket that would operate mechanically, without regard to particular circumstances.

From the start, lawyers and legislators have disagreed about the meaning of this term and the scope of the Resolution's 60-day pullout rule. Application of these provisions often generates difficult issues of interpretation that must be addressed in light of a long history of military actions abroad, without guidance from the courts, involving a Resolution passed by a Congress that could not have envisioned many of the operations in which the United States has since become engaged. Because the War Powers Resolution represented a broad compromise between competing views on the proper division of constitutional authorities, the question whether a particular set of facts constitutes "hostilities" for purposes of the Resolution has been determined more by interbranch practice than by a narrow parsing of dictionary definitions. Both branches have recognized that different situations may call for different responses, and that an overly mechanical reading of the statute could lead to unintended automatic cutoffs of military involvement in cases where more flexibility is required.

In the nearly 40 years since the Resolution's enactment, successive Administrations have thus started from the premise that the term "hostilities" is "definable in a meaningful way only in the context of an actual set of facts." And successive Congresses and Presidents have opted for a process through which the political branches have worked together to flesh out the law's meaning over time. By adopting this approach, the two branches have sought to avoid construing the statute mechanically, divorced from the realities that face them.

In this case, leaders of the current Congress have stressed this very concern in indicating that they do not believe that U.S. military operations in Libya amount to the kind of "hostilities" envisioned by the War Powers Resolution's 60-day pullout provision. The historical practice supports this view. In 1975, Congress expressly invited the Executive Branch to provide its best understanding of the term "hostilities." My predecessor Monroe Leigh and Defense Department General Counsel Martin Hoffmann responded that, as a general matter, the Executive Branch understands the term "to mean a situation in which units of the U.S. armed forces are actively engaged in exchanges of fire with opposing units of hostile forces." On the other hand, as Leigh and Hoffmann suggested, the term should not necessarily be read to include situations where the nature of the mission is limited (i.e., situations that do not "involve the full military engagements with which the Resolution is primarily concerned"; where the exposure of U.S. forces is limited (e.g., situations involving "sporadic military or paramilitary attacks on our armed forces stationed abroad," in which the overall threat faced by our military is low); and where the risk of escalation is therefore limited. Subsequently, the Executive Branch has reiterated the distinction between full military encounters and more constrained operations, stating that "intermittent military engagements" do not require withdrawal of forces under the Resolution's 60-day rule. In the thirty-six years since Leigh and Hoffmann provided their analysis, the Executive Branch has repeatedly articulated and applied these foundational understandings. The President was thus operating within this long-standing tradition of Executive Branch interpretation when he relied on these understandings in his legal explanation to Congress on June 15, 2011.

In light of this historical practice, a combination of four factors present in Libya suggests that the current situation does not constitute the kind of "hostilities" envisioned by the War Powers Resolution's 60-day automatic pullout provision.

First, the mission is limited: By Presidential design, U.S. forces are playing a constrained and supporting role in a NATO-led multinational civilian protection operation, which is implementing a U.N. Security Council Resolution tailored to that limited purpose. This is a very unusual set of circumstances, not found in any of the historic situations in which the "hostilities" question was previously debated, from the deployment of U.S. armed forces to Lebanon, Grenada, and El Salvador in the early 1980s, to the fighting with Iran in the Persian Gulf in the late 1980s, to the use of ground troops in Somalia in 1993. Of course, NATO forces as a whole are more deeply engaged in Libya than are U.S. forces, but the War Powers Resolution's 60-day pullout provision was designed to address the activities of the latter.

Second, the exposure of our armed forces is limited: To date, our operations have not involved U.S. casualties or a threat of significant U.S. casualties. Nor do our current operations involve active exchanges of fire with hostile forces, and members of our military have not been involved in significant armed confrontations or sustained confrontations of any kind with hostile forces. Prior administrations have not found the 60-day rule to apply even in situations where significant fighting plainly did occur, as in Lebanon and Grenada in 1983 and Somalia in 1993.[15] By highlighting this point, we in no way advocate a legal theory that is indifferent to the loss of non-American lives. But here, there can be little doubt that the greatest threat to Libyan civilians comes not from NATO or the United States military, but from Qadhafi. The Congress that adopted the War Powers Resolution was principally concerned with the safety of U.S. forces, and with the risk that the President would entangle them in an overseas conflict from which they could not readily be extricated. In this instance, the absence of U.S. ground troops, among other features of the Libya

---

15. In Lebanon, the Reagan Administration argued that U.S. armed forces were not in "hostilities," though there were roughly 1,600 U.S. marines equipped for combat on a daily basis and roughly 2,000 more on ships and bases nearby; U.S. marine positions were attacked repeatedly; and four marines were killed and several dozen wounded in those attacks. See Richard F. Grimmett, Congressional Research Service, The War Powers Resolution: After Thirty Six Years 13–15 (Apr. 22, 2010). In Grenada, the Administration did not acknowledge that "hostilities" had begun under the War Powers Resolution after 1,900 members of the U.S. armed forces had landed on the island, leading to combat that claimed the lives of nearly twenty Americans and wounded nearly 100 more. See Grimmett, supra, at 15; Ben Bradlee, Jr., A Chronology on Grenada, Boston Globe, Nov. 6, 1983.

operation, significantly reduces both the risk to U.S. forces and the likelihood of a protracted entanglement that Congress may find itself practically powerless to end.

Third, the risk of escalation is limited: U.S. military operations have not involved the presence of U.S. ground troops, or any significant chance of escalation into a broader conflict characterized by a large U.S. ground presence, major casualties, sustained active combat, or expanding geographical scope. Contrast this with the 1991 Desert Storm operation, which although also authorized by a United Nations Security Council Resolution, presented "over 400,000 [U.S.] troops in the area—the same order of magnitude as Vietnam at its peak—together with concomitant numbers of ships, planes, and tanks." Prior administrations have found an absence of "hostilities" under the War Powers Resolution in situations ranging from Lebanon to Central America to Somalia to the Persian Gulf tanker controversy, although members of the United States Armed Forces were repeatedly engaged by the other side's forces and sustained casualties in volatile geopolitical circumstances, in some cases running a greater risk of possible escalation than here.

Fourth and finally, the military means we are using are limited: This situation does not present the kind of "full military engagement[] with which the [War Powers] Resolution is primarily concerned." The violence that U.S. armed forces have directly inflicted or facilitated after the handoff to NATO has been modest in terms of its frequency, intensity, and severity. The air-to-ground strikes conducted by the United States in Libya are a far cry from the bombing campaign waged in Kosovo in 1999, which involved much more extensive and aggressive aerial strike operations led by U.S. armed forces. The U.S. contribution to NATO is likewise far smaller than it was in the Balkans in the mid-1990s, where U.S. forces contributed the vast majority of aircraft and air strike sorties to an operation that lasted over two and a half years, featured repeated violations of the no-fly zone and episodic firefights with Serb aircraft and gunners, and paved the way for approximately 20,000 U.S. ground troops. Here, by contrast, the bulk of U.S. contributions to the NATO effort has been providing intelligence capabilities and refueling assets. A very significant majority of the overall sorties are being flown by our coalition partners, and the overwhelming majority of strike sorties are being flown by our partners. American strikes have been confined, on an as-needed basis, to the suppression of enemy air defenses to enforce the no-fly zone, and to limited strikes by Predator unmanned aerial vehicles against discrete targets in support of the civilian protection mission; since the handoff to NATO, the total number of U.S. munitions dropped has been a tiny fraction of the number dropped in Kosovo. All NATO targets, moreover, have been clearly linked to the Qadhafi regime's systematic attacks on the Libyan population and populated areas, with target sets engaged only when strictly necessary and with maximal precision.

Had any of these elements been absent in Libya, or present in different degrees, a different legal conclusion might have been drawn. But the unusual confluence of these four factors, in an operation that was expressly designed to be limited—limited in mission, exposure of U.S. troops, risk of escalation, and military means employed—led the President to conclude that the Libya operation did not fall within the War Powers Resolution's automatic 60-day pullout rule.

Nor is this action inconsistent with the spirit of the Resolution. Having studied this legislation for many years, I can confidently say that we are far from the core case that most Members of Congress had in mind in 1973. The Congress that passed the Resolution in that year had just been through a long, major, and searing war in Vietnam, with hundreds of thousands of boots on the ground, secret bombing campaigns, international condemnation, massive casualties, and no clear way out. In Libya, by contrast, we have been acting transparently and in close consultation with Congress for a brief period; with no casualties or ground troops; with international approval; and at the express request of and in cooperation with NATO, the Arab League, the Gulf Cooperation Council, and Libya's own Transitional National Council. We should not read into the 1973 Congress's adoption of what many have called a "No More Vietnams" resolution an intent to require the premature termination, nearly forty years later, of limited military force in support of an international coalition to prevent the resumption of atrocities in Libya. Given the limited risk of escalation, exchanges of fire, and U.S. casualties, we do not believe that the 1973 Congress intended that its Resolution be given such a rigid construction—absent a clear Congressional stance—to stop the President from directing supporting actions in a NATO-led, Security Council-authorized operation, for the narrow purpose of preventing the slaughter of innocent civilians. . . .

---

1. *Too Great a Stretch*? Are you persuaded? Were a foreign power to participate in supporting the imposition of a no-fly zone over the territory of the U.S., wouldn't the U.S. consider that a hostile act or even an act of war? Given Col. Qadhafi's past support of terrorist attacks on the U.S., isn't it the case that U.S. participation in the enforcing the Libyan no-fly zone ran a significant risk of involving the U.S. in a potentially escalating round of hostilities?

2. *Forum Shopping by Presidents?* The Obama Administration's formulation of its legal position on the 60-day cutoff represents an extraordinary departure from the usual process for executive branch legal interpretation. Typically, agencies submit their views to the Office of Legal Counsel, which then provides final legal advice to the President. The President is not required to accept OLC's advice, though it is exceedingly rare that a President would overrule OLC's legal interpretation. What is truly unprecedented is that the process appears to have reduced OLC to one legal interpreter among several. The problem with this way of proceeding is that it is subject to the view that the President is shopping for the legal advice that suits him. It also has the potential to create an incentive among the President's legal advisers to tailor their legal advice to the President's liking. Why stand up to the President if the President can simply ask other lawyers until the President secures the desired interpretation?

3. *The Ethics of Statutory Interpretation*. Imagine that you are an executive branch lawyer. The President has made clear a determination to follow through on a national security initiative that you do not regard as unethical, but as to which statutory authority is problematic. Is there a case to be made that you would be serving the rule of law better by helping the President advance a questionable claim to statutory authority, rather than argue for a yet more expansive reading of the President's Article II powers? Professor Shane thinks so, if done rarely, transparently, and in sufficiently compelling circumstances. Peter M. Shane, *The Presidential Statutory Stretch and the Rule of Law*, 87 Colo. L. Rev. 1231 (2015). Professor Dawn Johnsen, who served as acting head of OLC during the Clinton Administration, appears to think not. Dawn Johnsen, *Power Wars Symposium: A Study in Contrasting Views of Executive Authority*, Just Security (Nov. 25, 2015), https://www.justsecurity .org/27891/contrasting-views-executive-authority/ ("[P]residential legal advisors . . . should offer their best, honest, accurate interpretations — as opposed to merely reasonable or plausible interpretations. . . . Law does not answer all questions and, particularly on national security matters, relevant legal authorities may not be susceptible to one best interpretation. Often, though, there is a best answer.").

2. Judicial Review of Presidential War-Making

The Supreme Court never ruled whether the Vietnam War was legal, or even whether its legality was a political question. As you read the following dissent from a denial of certiorari in a case that would have presented these issues, consider whether the Court behaved responsibly in failing to exercise its discretionary review powers. *Compare* Louis Henkin, *On Drawing Lines*, 82 Harv. L. Rev. 63, 90–91 (1968) (defending denials of certiorari), *with* Graham Hughes, *Civil Disobedience and the Political Question Doctrine*, 43 N.Y.U. L. Rev. 1, 15 (1968) (criticizing Court's failure to give reasoned response to civil disobedients protesting legality of war). *See also* Note, *Congress, the President, and the Power to Commit Forces to Combat*, 81 Harv. L. Rev. 1771 (1968); William Van Alstyne, *Congress, the President, and the Power to Declare War*, 121 U. Pa. L. Rev. 1 (1972).

Mora v. McNamara

389 U.S. 934 (1967)

Petition for writ of certiorari to the United States Court of Appeals for the District of Columbia Circuit. Denied.

Justice MARSHALL took no part in the consideration or decision of this petition.

Justice STEWART, with whom Justice DOUGLAS joins, dissenting.

The petitioners were drafted into the United States Army in late 1965, and six months later were ordered to a West Coast replacement station for shipment to Vietnam. They brought this suit to prevent the Secretary of Defense and the Secretary of the Army from carrying out those orders, and requested a declaratory judgment that the present United States military activity in Vietnam is "illegal." The District Court dismissed the suit, and the Court of Appeals affirmed.

There exist in this case questions of great magnitude. Some are akin to those referred to by Justice Douglas in *Mitchell v. United States*, 386 U.S. 972.* But there are others:

> I. Is the present United States military activity in Vietnam a "war" within the meaning of Article I, Section 8, Clause 11 of the Constitution?

> II. If so, may the Executive constitutionally order the petitioners to participate in that military activity, when no war has been declared by the Congress?

> III. Of what relevance to Question II are the present treaty obligations of the United States?

> IV. Of what relevance to Question II is the joint Congressional ("Tonkin Gulf") Resolution of August 10, 1964?

> (a) Do present United States military operations fall within the terms of the Joint Resolution?

> (b) If the Joint Resolution purports to give the Chief Executive authority to commit United States forces to armed conflict limited in scope only by his own absolute discretion, is the Resolution a constitutionally impermissible delegation of all or part of Congress' power to declare war?

These are large and deeply troubling questions. Whether the Court would ultimately reach them depends, of course, upon the resolution of serious preliminary issues of justiciability. We cannot make these problems go away simply by refusing to hear the case of three obscure Army privates. I intimate not even tentative views upon any of these matters, but I think the Court should squarely face them by granting certiorari and setting this case for oral argument.

Justice DOUGLAS, with whom Justice STEWART concurs, dissenting.

The questions posed by Mr. Justice Stewart cover the wide range of problems which the Senate Committee on Foreign Relations recently explored,[1] in connection with the SEATO Treaty of February 19, 1955, and the Tonkin Gulf Resolution. Mr. Katzenbach, representing the Administration, testified that he did not regard the Tonkin Gulf Resolution to be "a declaration of war" and that while the Resolution was not "constitutionally necessary" it was "politically, from an international viewpoint and from a domestic viewpoint, extremely important." He added:

---

* In *Mitchell*, the convicted defendant in a prosecution for failure to report for induction contended that the war in Vietnam was being conducted in violation of various treaties. Justice Douglas dissented from the denial of certiorari.

1. Hearings on S. Res. No. 151, 90th Cong., 1st Sess. (1967).

The use of the phrase "to declare war" as it was used in the Constitution of the United States had a particular meaning in terms of the events and the practices which existed at the time it was adopted. . . .

[I]t was recognized by the Founding Fathers that the President might have to take emergency action to protect the security of the United States, but that if there was going to be another use of the armed forces of the United States, that was a decision which Congress should check the Executive on, which Congress should support. It was for that reason that the phrase was inserted in the Constitution.

Now, over a long period of time, . . . there have been many uses of the military forces of the United States for a variety of purposes without a congressional declaration of war. But it would be fair to say that most of these were relatively minor uses of force. . . .

A declaration of war would not, I think, correctly reflect the very limited objectives of the United States with respect to Vietnam. It would not correctly reflect our efforts there, what we are trying to do, the reasons why we are there, to use an outmoded phraseology, to declare war.

The view that Congress was intended to play a more active role in the initiation and conduct of war than the above statements might suggest has been espoused by Senator Fulbright (Cong. Rec., Oct. 11, 1967, p. 14683–14690), quoting Thomas Jefferson who said:

We have already given . . . one effectual check to the Dog of War by transferring the power of letting him loose from the Executive to the Legislative body, from those who are to spend to those who are to pay.

These opposed views are reflected in the *Prize Cases*, 2 Black 635, a five-to-four decision rendered in 1863. Justice Grier, writing for the majority, emphasized the arguments for strong presidential powers. Justice Nelson, writing for the minority of four, read the Constitution more strictly, emphasizing that what is war in actuality may not constitute war in the constitutional sense. During all subsequent periods in our history—through the Spanish-American War, the Boxer Rebellion, two World Wars, Korea, and now Vietnam—the two points of view urged in the *Prize Cases* have continued to be voiced.

A host of problems is raised. Does the President's authority to repel invasions and quiet insurrections, do his powers in foreign relations and his duty to execute faithfully the laws of the United States, including its treaties, justify what has been threatened of petitioners? What is the relevancy of the Gulf of Tonkin Resolution and the yearly appropriations in support of the Vietnam effort?

The London Treaty (59 Stat. 1546), the SEATO Treaty (6 U.S.T. 81, 1955), the Kellogg-Briand Pact (46 Stat. 2343), and Article 39 of Chapter VII of the UN Charter [59 Stat. 1043 (1945)] deal with various aspects of wars of "aggression." Do any of them embrace hostilities in Vietnam, or give rights to individuals affected to complain, or in other respects give rise to justiciable controversies?

There are other treaties or declarations that could be cited. Perhaps all of them are wide of the mark. There are sentences in our opinions which, detached from their context, indicate that what is happening is none of our business:

> Certainly it is not the function of the Judiciary to entertain private litigation — even by a citizen — which challenges the legality, the wisdom, or the propriety of the Commander-in-Chief in sending our armed forces abroad or to any particular region.

Johnson v. Eisentrager, 339 U.S. 763, 789.

We do not, of course, sit as a committee of oversight or supervision. What resolutions the President asks and what the Congress provides are not our concern. With respect to the Federal Government, we sit only to decide actual cases or controversies within judicial cognizance that arise as a result of what the Congress or the President or a judge does or attempts to do to a person or his property.

In *Ex parte Milligan*, 4 Wall. 2, the Court relieved a person of the death penalty imposed by a military tribunal, holding that only a civilian court had power to try him for the offense charged. Speaking of the purpose of the Founders in providing constitutional guarantees, the Court said:

> They knew . . . the nation they were founding, be its existence short or long, would be involved in war; how often or how long continued, human foresight could not tell; and that unlimited power, wherever lodged at such a time, was especially hazardous to freemen. For this, and other equally weighty reasons, they secured the inheritance they had fought to maintain, by incorporating in a written constitution the safeguards which *time* had proved were essential to its preservation. Not one of these safeguards can the President, or Congress, or the Judiciary disturb, except the one concerning the writ of *habeas corpus*.

. . . These petitioners should be told whether their case is beyond judicial cognizance. If it is not, we should then reach the merits of their claims, on which I intimate no views whatsoever.

---

1. *Should Courts Judge Wars?* Do courts have any proper role to play in keeping military operations within statutorily authorized bounds? Consider in this regard, *Holtzman v. Schlesinger*, 414 U.S. 1304 (Marshall, Circuit Justice, 1973) (declining to vacate court of appeals stay of district court order enjoining Cambodia bombing). Courts revisited that issue with respect to military operations in Central America. *Ramirez de Arellano v. Weinberger*, 745 F.2d 1500 (D.C. Cir. 1984) (en banc), *vacated*, 471 U.S. 1113 (1985), *on remand*, 788 F.2d 762 (D.C. Cir. 1986) (holding justiciable the claim of a U.S. citizen that his private ranch in Honduras was being unlawfully used for U.S. military operations); *Sanchez-Espinoza v. Reagan*, 568 F. Supp. 596 (D.D.C. 1983), *aff'd*, 770 F.2d 202 (D.C. Cir. 1985) (holding challenges to military operations in Nicaragua nonjusticiable); *Crockett v. Reagan*, 558 F. Supp. 893 (D.D.C.

1982) *aff'd*, 720 F.2d 1355 (D.C. Cir. 1983), *cert. denied*, 467 U.S. 1251 (1984) (holding challenge to military aid to El Salvador nonjusticiable). *See also* John Norton Moore, Law and The Indo-China War (1972); Abner J. Mikva, *The Political Question Revisited: War Powers and the "Zone of Twilight,"* 76 Ky. L.J. 329 (1987–88).

2. *Continuing Debate.* Intriguingly, the issue of the Vietnam War's constitutionality seemed to receive new attention during the George H.W. Bush Administration. The constitutionality of the war pursuant to congressional authorization—and the appropriateness of Congress' level of oversight was defended in David C. Wright, *America in Vietnam: A Model for the Exercise of the War Powers*, 15 J. Contemp. L. 253 (1989). John Hart Ely concurred that Congress provided sufficient constitutional authority for those portions of the war effort made public, but not for aspects of the war as to which the public was not advised. John H. Ely, *The American War in Indochina, Part I: The (Troubled) Constitutionality of the War They Told Us About*, 42 Stan. L. Rev. 877 (1990); John H. Ely, *The American War in Indochina, Part II: The Unconstitutionality of the War They Didn't Tell Us About*, 42 Stan. L. Rev. 1093 (1990). *See also* John Hart Ely, War and Responsibility: Constitutional Lessons of Vietnam and Its Aftermath (1993).

Campbell v. Clinton

203 F.3d 19 (D.C. Cir. 2000), *cert. denied*, 531 U.S. 815.

Before: SILBERMAN, RANDOLPH, and TATEL, Circuit Judges.

SILBERMAN, Circuit Judge:

A number of congressmen, led by Tom Campbell of California, filed suit claiming that the President violated the War Powers Resolution and the War Powers Clause of the Constitution by directing U.S. forces' participation in the recent NATO campaign in Yugoslavia. The district court dismissed for lack of standing. We agree with the district court and therefore affirm.

On March 24, 1999, President Clinton announced the commencement of NATO air and cruise missile attacks on Yugoslav targets. Two days later he submitted to Congress a report, "consistent with the War Powers Resolution," detailing the circumstances necessitating the use of armed forces, the deployment's scope and expected duration, and asserting that he had "taken these actions pursuant to [his] authority . . . as Commander in Chief and Chief Executive." On April 28, Congress voted on four resolutions related to the Yugoslav conflict: It voted down a declaration of war 427 to 2 and an "authorization" of the air strikes 213 to 213, but it also voted against requiring the President to immediately end U.S. participation in the NATO operation and voted to fund that involvement. The conflict between NATO and Yugoslavia continued for 79 days, ending on June 10 with Yugoslavia's agreement to withdraw its forces from Kosovo and allow deployment of a NATO-led peacekeeping force. Throughout this period Pentagon, State Department, and NATO spokesmen informed the public on a frequent basis of developments in the fighting.

Appellants, 31 congressmen opposed to U.S. involvement in the Kosovo intervention, filed suit prior to termination of that conflict seeking a declaratory judgment that the President's use of American forces against Yugoslavia was unlawful under both the War Powers Clause of the Constitution and the War Powers Resolution ("the WPR"). *See* 50 U.S.C. § 1541 *et seq.* The WPR requires the President to submit a report within 48 hours "in any case in which United States Armed Forces are introduced . . . into hostilities or into situations where imminent involvement in hostilities is clearly indicated by the circumstances," and to "terminate any use of United States Armed Forces with respect to which a report was submitted (or required to be submitted), unless the Congress . . . has declared war or has enacted a specific authorization for such use of United States Armed Forces" within 60 days. Appellants claim that the President did submit a report sufficient to trigger the WPR on March 26, or in any event was required to submit a report by that date, but nonetheless failed to end U.S. involvement in the hostilities after 60 days. The district court granted the President's motion to dismiss, *see Campbell v. Clinton,* 52 F. Supp. 2d 34 (D.D.C.1999), and this appeal followed.

II.

The government does not respond to appellants' claim on the merits. Instead the government challenges the jurisdiction of the federal courts to adjudicate this claim on three separate grounds: the case is moot; appellants lack standing, as the district court concluded; and the case is nonjusticiable. Since we agree with the district court that the congressmen lack standing it is not necessary to decide whether there are other jurisdictional defects.

The question whether congressmen have standing in federal court to challenge the lawfulness of actions of the executive was answered, at least in large part, in the Supreme Court's recent decision in *Raines v. Byrd,* 521 U.S. 811 (1997). *Raines* involved a constitutional challenge to the President's authority under the short-lived Line Item Veto Act. . . . Observing it had never held that congressmen have standing to assert an institutional injury as against the executive, the Court held that petitioners in the case lacked "legislative standing" to challenge the Act. The Court noted that petitioners already possessed an adequate political remedy, since they could vote to have the Line Item Veto Act repealed, or to provide individual spending bills with a statutory exemption.

Thereafter in *Chenoweth v. Clinton,* 181 F.3d 112, 115 (D.C.Cir. 1999), emphasizing the separation-of-powers problems inherent in legislative standing, we held that congressmen had no standing to challenge the President's introduction of a program through executive order rather than statute. . . .

There remains, however, a soft spot in the legal barrier against congressional legal challenges to executive action, and it is a soft spot that appellants sought to penetrate. In 1939 the Supreme Court in *Coleman v. Miller* voted 5–4 to recognize the standing of Kansas State legislators in the Supreme Court to challenge the actions of the Kansas Secretary of State and the Secretary of the State Senate. That case arose out of a State Senate vote on the ratification of a constitutional amendment, the Child Labor Amendment, proposed by Congress in 1924. The State Senate split 20 to 20, and the Lieutenant Governor, the presiding officer of the Senate, then cast a deciding vote in favor. The State House subsequently also passed a ratification resolution. Thereupon the twenty State Senators who voted against ratification plus one more (who presumably had voted for the resolution) brought a mandamus action in the State Supreme Court challenging the Lieutenant Governor's right to vote. They sought an order compelling the Secretary of the Senate to erase the endorsement on the resolution and restraining the Secretary of State from authenticating the resolution and passing it on to the Governor. The Supreme Court of Kansas entertained the action but ruled against the plaintiffs on the merits. Granting certiorari, the United States Supreme Court determined that "at least the twenty senators whose votes, if their contention were sustained, would have been sufficient to defeat the resolution . . . have an interest . . . sufficient to give the Court jurisdiction," because they have a legal interest "in maintaining the effectiveness of their votes."

In *Raines* the plaintiff congressmen had relied on *Coleman* to argue that they had standing because the presidential veto had undermined the "effectiveness of their votes." The Supreme Court noted that *Coleman* might be distinguished on grounds that the federal constitutional separation of powers concerns that underlay its decision in *Raines* (and which we emphasized in *Chenoweth*) were not present, or that if the Court in *Coleman* had not taken the case a question of federal law—the ratification *vel non* by the Kansas Legislature—would remain as decided by the Kansas Court. But the Court thought it unnecessary to cabin *Coleman* on those grounds. Instead, the Court emphasized that the congressmen were not asserting that their votes had been "completely nullified". . . .

Here the plaintiff congressmen, by specifically defeating the War Powers Resolution authorization by a tie vote and by defeating a declaration of war, sought to fit within the *Coleman* exception to the *Raines* rule. This parliamentary tactic led to an extensive argument before us as to exactly what the Supreme Court meant by a claim that a legislator's vote was completely "nullified."

It is, to be sure, not readily apparent what the Supreme Court meant by that word. It would seem the Court used nullify to mean treating a vote that did not pass as if it had, or vice versa. The "nullification" alleged in this case therefore differs from *Coleman* in a significant respect. In that case state officials endorsed a defeated ratification, treating it as approved, while the President here did not claim to be acting pursuant to the defeated declaration of war or a statutory authorization, but instead "pursuant to [his] constitutional authority to conduct U.S. foreign relations and as Commander-in-Chief and Chief Executive." *See* Letter to Congressional Leaders Reporting on Airstrikes Against Serbian Targets in the Federal Republic of Yugoslavia (Serbia and Montenegro), 35 Weekly Comp. Pres. Doc. 528 (March 26, 1999). The Court did not suggest in *Raines* that the President "nullifies" a congressional vote and thus legislators have standing whenever the government does something Congress voted against, still less that congressmen would have standing anytime a

President allegedly acts in excess of statutory authority. As the government correctly observes, appellants' statutory argument, although cast in terms of the nullification of a recent vote, essentially is that the President violated the quarter-century old War Powers Resolution. Similarly, their constitutional argument is that the President has acted illegally—in excess of his authority—because he waged war in the constitutional sense without a congressional delegation. Neither claim is analogous to a *Coleman* nullification.

We think the key to understanding the Court's treatment of *Coleman* and its use of the word nullification is its implicit recognition that a ratification vote on a constitutional amendment is an unusual situation. It is not at all clear whether once the amendment was "deemed ratified," *see Raines*, 521 U.S. at 822, the Kansas Senate could have done anything to reverse that position. We think that must be what the Supreme Court implied when it said the *Raines* plaintiffs could not allege that the "[Line Item Veto Act] would nullify their votes *in the future*," and that, after all, a majority of senators and congressmen could always repeal the Line Item Veto Act. The *Coleman* senators, by contrast, may well have been powerless to rescind a ratification of a constitutional amendment that they claimed had been defeated. In other words, they had no legislative remedy. Under that reading—which we think explains the very narrow possible *Coleman* exception to *Raines*—appellants fail because they continued, after the votes, to enjoy ample legislative power to have stopped prosecution of the "war."

In this case, Congress certainly could have passed a law forbidding the use of U.S. forces in the Yugoslav campaign; indeed, there was a measure—albeit only a concurrent resolution—introduced to require the President to withdraw U.S. troops. Unfortunately, however, for those congressmen who, like appellants, desired an end to U.S. involvement in Yugoslavia, this measure was *defeated* by a 139 to 290 vote. Of course, Congress always retains appropriations authority and could have cut off funds for the American role in the conflict. Again there was an effort to do so but it failed; appropriations were authorized. And there always remains the possibility of impeachment should a President act in disregard of Congress' authority on these matters.

* * *

Appellants' constitutional claim stands on no firmer footing. Appellants argue that the War Powers Clause of the Constitution proscribes a President from using military force except as is necessary to repel a sudden attack. But they also argue that the WPR "implements" or channels congressional authority under the Constitution. It may well be then that since we have determined that appellants lack standing to enforce the WPR there is nothing left of their constitutional claim. Assuming, however, that appellants' constitutional claim should be considered separately, the same logic dictates they do not have standing to bring such a challenge. That is to say Congress has a broad range of legislative authority it can use to stop a President's war making, *see generally* John C. Yoo, *The Continuation of Politics by Other Means: The Original Understanding of War Powers*, 84 Cal. L. Rev. 167 (1996), and therefore under *Raines* congressmen may not challenge the President's war-making powers in federal court.

Judge Randolph asserts that appellants lack standing because they do not claim that the President violated various statutes that depend on the existence of a war or the *imminence* of war. But that position sidesteps appellants' basic claim that the President unconstitutionally conducted a war without authority, and the logic of Judge Randolph's reasoning ("There is no suggestion that despite the vote, President Clinton *invaded* Yugoslavia by land or took some other action authorized only during a declared war.") is that if there had been a "war" appellants would have had standing. He therefore presents as an alternate reason for denying standing that the President did not "nullify" the vote against the declaration of war because he did not take any actions that constitute "war" in the constitutional sense. That analysis, however, conflates standing with the merits. At the standing stage we must take as correct appellants' claim that the President violated the Constitution simply by ordering U.S. forces to attack Yugoslavia.

In our view Judge Randolph's criticism of our analysis does not give sufficient attention to *Raines'* focus on the political self-help available to congressmen. *See infra* at 22 (Randolph, J., concurring). Even though the congressmen in *Raines* sought review before the Court of what was soon after determined in *Clinton v. City of New York*, 524 U.S. 417 (1998), to be an unconstitutional statute, the Court denied them standing as congressmen because they possessed political tools with which to remedy their purported injury. Our colleague notes a distinction drawn by *Raines* between "the right to vote in the future [and] the nullification of a vote in the past," *see infra* at 22 (Randolph, J., concurring), and asserts that the former does not remedy the latter. But *Raines* rejected this argument, which is why the congressmen in *Raines* lacked standing whereas petitioners in *New York* were allowed to contest the President's "nullification" of particular appropriations line items. Indeed, *Raines* explicitly rejected Judge Randolph's argument that legislators should not be required to turn to politics instead of the courts for their remedy. Although the plaintiff legislators in *Raines* had already failed to stop passage of the Line Item Veto Act, the Court's response was the equivalent of "if at first you don't succeed, try and try again"—either work for repeal of the Act, or seek to have individual spending bills made exempt. *See Raines,* 521 U.S. at 824–25, 825 n. 9, 830. Judge Randolph overlooks this key portion of *Raines* when he disagrees with our conclusion that plaintiffs lack standing because they may "fight again tomorrow." *Infra* at 22 (Randolph, J., concurring).

• • •

Accordingly, the district court is affirmed; appellants lack standing.

SILBERMAN, Circuit Judge, concurring:

. . . [I]n my view, no one is able to bring this challenge because the two claims are not justiciable. We lack "judicially discoverable and manageable standards" for addressing them, and the War Powers Clause claim implicates the political question doctrine.

Prior litigation under the WPR has turned on the threshold test whether U.S. forces are engaged in hostilities or are in imminent danger of hostilities. But the question posed by appellants—whether the President's refusal to discontinue American activities in Yugoslavia violates the WPR—necessarily depends on the statute having been triggered in the first place. It has been held that the statutory threshold standard is not precise enough and too obviously calls for a political judgment to be one suitable for judicial determinations. *See, e.g., Sanchez-Espinoza v. Reagan,* 770 F.2d 202, 209 (D.C.Cir. 1985) (aid to Contras); *Crockett v. Reagan,* 720 F.2d 1355, 1356–57 (D.C.Cir. 1983) (U.S. advisors in El Salvador); *see also Ange v. Bush,* 752 F.Supp. 509, 514 (D.D.C.1990) (pre-Gulf War buildup); *Lowry v. Reagan,* 676 F.Supp. 333, 340 n. 53 (D.D.C.1987) (reflagging operations in the Persian Gulf). I think that is correct. Appellants point to a House Report suggesting that hostilities for purposes of the WPR include all situations "where there is a reasonable expectation that American military personnel will be subject to hostile fire." *See* H.R. Rep. No. 287, 93rd Cong., 1st Sess. 7 (1973). That elaboration hardly helps. It could reasonably be thought that anytime American soldiers are confronted by armed or potentially armed forces of a non-ally there is a reasonable expectation that they will be subject to hostile fire. Certainly any competent military leader will assume that to be so.

Appellants argue that here there is no real problem of definition because this air war was so overwhelming and indisputable. It is asserted that the President implicitly conceded the applicability of the WPR by sending the report to Congress. In truth, the President only said the report was "consistent" with the WPR. In any event, I do not think it matters how clear it is in any particular case that "hostilities" were initiated if the statutory standard is one generally unsuited to judicial resolution.

Nor is the constitutional claim justiciable. Appellants contend this case is governed by *Mitchell v. Laird,* 488 F.2d 611, 614 (D.C.Cir. 1973), where we said that "[t]here would be no insuperable difficulty in a court determining whether" the Vietnam conflict constituted a war in the Constitutional sense. *See also Dellums v. Bush,* 752 F. Supp. 1141, 1146 (D.D.C.1990) ("[T]he Court has no hesitation in concluding that an offensive entry into Iraq by several hundred thousand United States servicemen . . . could be described as a 'war' within the meaning . . . of the Constitution."). But a careful reading of both cases reveals that the language upon which appellants rely is only dicta. (In *Laird* the Court ultimately held that the resolution of the issues was a political question. *See* 488 F.2d at 616.)

Appellants cannot point to any constitutional test for what is war. *See, e.g., Holtzman v. Schlesinger,* 414 U.S. 1316, 94 S.Ct. 8, 38 L.Ed.2d 28 (1973) (Justice Douglas, in chambers, vacating order of Court of Appeals granting stay of district court's injunction against bombing of Cambodia), 414 U.S. at 1321, 94 S.Ct. 8 (1973) (Justice Marshall, in chambers, granting stay the same day with the concurrence of the other Justices); *Holtzman v. Schlesinger,* 484 F.2d 1307 (2d Cir. 1973) (holding legality of Cambodia bombing nonjusticiable because courts lack expertise to determine import of various military actions). Instead, appellants offer a rough definition of war provided in 1994 by an Assistant Attorney General to four Senators with respect to a planned intervention in Haiti, as well as a number of law review articles each containing its own definition of war. I do not think any of these sources, however, offers a coherent test for judges to apply to the question what constitutes war, a point only accentuated by the variances, for instance, between the numerous law review articles. For that reason, I disagree with Judge Tatel's assertion that we can decide appellants' constitutional claim because it is somehow obvious in this case that our country fought a war. *See infra* at 40 (Tatel, J., concurring). *Baker v. Carr* speaks of a case involving "a lack of judicially discoverable and manageable standards for resolving" the issue presented, *see* 369 U.S. at 217, not just a case the facts of which are obscure; the focus is on the standards. Even if this court knows all there is to know about the Kosovo conflict, we still do not know what standards to apply to those facts.

Judge Tatel points to numerous cases in which a court has determined that our nation was at war, but none of these cases involved the question whether the President had "declared war" in violation of the Constitution. For instance, in *Bas v. Tingy*, 4 U.S. (4 Dall.) 37, 1 L.Ed. 731 (1800), the question whether there was a "war" was only relevant to determining whether France was an "enemy" within the meaning of a prize statute. *See id.* at 37 ("[T]he argument turned, principally, upon two inquiries: 1st. Whether the Act of March 1799, applied only to the event of a future general war? 2d. Whether France was *an enemy* of the United States, within the meaning of the law?"). Indeed, Justice Washington's opinion in that case, upon which Judge Tatel principally relies, suggests that whether there was a war in the constitutional sense was irrelevant. *See id.* at 42 ("Besides, it may be asked, why should the rate of salvage be different in such a war as the present, from the salvage in a war more solemn [*i.e.* a declared war] or general?"). It is similarly irrelevant that courts have determined the existence of a war in cases involving insurance policies and other contracts, the Federal Tort Claims Act, and provisions of the military criminal code applicable in "time of war." *See infra* at 39 (Tatel, J., concurring). None of these cases asked whether there was a war as the Constitution uses that word, but only whether a particular statutory or contractual provision was triggered by some instance of fighting. Comparing *Bas v. Tingy*'s lengthy discussion whether our quarrel with France constituted a solemn or imperfect, general or limited war, *see* 4 U.S. at 40–41, with today's propensity to label any widespread conflict an undifferentiated war, it would not be surprising if an insurance contract's "war" provisions, or even a statute's for that matter, were triggered before the Constitution's.

Even assuming a court could determine what "war" is, it is important to remember that the Constitution grants Congress the power to declare war, which is not necessarily the same as the power to determine whether U.S. forces will fight in a war. This distinction was drawn in the *Prize Cases,* 67 U.S. (2 Black) 635, 17 L.Ed. 459 (1862). There, petitioners challenged the authority of the President to impose a blockade on the secessionist States, an act of war, where Congress had not declared war against the Confederacy. The Court, while recognizing that the President "has no power to initiate or declare a war," observed that "war may exist without a declaration on either side." *Id.* at 668. In instances where war is declared against the United States by the actions of another country, the President "does not initiate the war, but is bound to accept the challenge without waiting for any special legislative authority."

Id. Importantly, the Court made clear that it would not dispute the President on measures necessary to repel foreign aggression. The President alone

> must determine what degree of force the crisis demands. The proclamation of blockade is itself official and conclusive evidence to the Court that a state of war existed which demanded and authorized a recourse to such a measure, under the circumstances peculiar to the case.

Id. at 670. And, to confirm the independent authority of the President to meet foreign aggression, the Court noted that while Congress had authorized the war, it may not have been required to: "*If* it were necessary to the technical existence of a war, that it should have a legislative sanction, we find it. . . ." *Id.* (emphasis added).

I read the *Prize Cases* to stand for the proposition that the President has independent authority to repel aggressive acts by third parties even without specific congressional authorization, and courts may not review the level of force selected. *See* Geoffrey Corn, *Presidential War Power: Do the Courts Offer Any Answers?* 157 Mil. L. Rev. 180, 214 (1998); J. Gregory Sidak, *To Declare War,* 41 Duke L.J. 27, 54 (1991); Cyrus R. Vance, *Striking the Balance: Congress and the President Under the War Powers Resolution,* 133 U. Pa. L. Rev. 79, 85 (1984). Therefore, I assume, *arguendo,* that appellants are correct and only Congress has authority to *initiate* "war." If the President may direct U.S. forces in response to third-party initiated war, then the question any plaintiff who challenges the constitutionality of a war must answer is, who started it? The question of who is responsible for a conflict is, as history reveals, rather difficult to answer, and we lack judicial standards for resolving it. *See, e.g., Greenham Women Against Cruise Missiles v. Reagan,* 591 F.Supp. 1332, 1337–38 (S.D.N.Y.1984) (court lacked judicially manageable standards to decide if placement of U.S. cruise missiles in England was a war-like, "aggressive" act). Then there is the problem of actually discovering the necessary information to answer the question, when such information may be unavailable to the U.S. or its allies, or unavailable to courts due to its sensitivity. *See id.* at 1338. Perhaps Yugoslavia did pose a threat to a much wider region of Europe and to U.S. civilian and military interests and personnel there. . . .

In most cases this will also be an issue of the greatest sensitivity for our foreign relations. Here, the President claimed on national television that our country needed to respond to Yugoslav aggression to protect our trading interests in Europe, and to prevent a replay of World War I. A pronouncement by another branch of the U.S. government that U.S. participation in Kosovo was "unjustified" would no doubt cause strains within NATO. *Cf. United States v. New,* 50 M.J. 729, 739–40 (Army Ct.Crim.App.1999) (lawfulness of U.N. peacekeeping operation in Macedonia was a political question).

In sum, there are no standards to determine either the statutory or constitutional questions raised in this case, and the question of whether the President has intruded on the war-declaring authority of Congress fits squarely within the political question doctrine. We therefore have another basis for our affirming the district court's dismissal of appellants' case.

RANDOLPH, Circuit Judge, concurring in the judgment:

The majority opinion does not, I believe, correctly analyze plaintiffs' standing to sue. It misconceives the holding of *Raines v. Byrd,* 521 U.S. 811 (1997), and conflicts with the law of this circuit. I believe plaintiffs lack standing, at least to litigate their constitutional claim, but for reasons the majority opinion neglects. I also believe that the case is moot, an optional disposition of the appeal. The serious questions about the constitutionality of the War Powers Resolution must therefore be put off for still another day.

I. Standing

. . . The Members of Congress appearing as plaintiffs contend that President Clinton violated the Constitution and the War Powers Resolution and that they are entitled to a judicial declaration so stating. They have standing, they say, because President Clinton's prosecution of the war "completely nullified" their votes against declaring war and against authorizing a continuation of the hostilities.

A.

The quoted phrase — "completely nullified" — is from *Raines v. Byrd,* 521 U.S. 811, 823 (1997), giving the Court's appraisal of the rule in *Coleman v. Miller,* 307 U.S. 433 (1939). The majority opinion in our case seems to assume that the only thing left of legislative standing is whatever *Raines* preserves. I will not quarrel with the assumption, at least for cases in which a legislator is claiming that his vote has been illegally nullified. . . .

Here, plaintiffs had the votes "sufficient to defeat" "a specific legislative action" — they defeated a declaration of war (their constitutional claim) and they blocked a resolution approving the President's continuation of the war (their statutory claim). To follow precisely the formulation in *Raines,* they would have standing only if the legislative actions they defeated went "into effect." Obviously, this did not happen: war was not declared, and the President never maintained that he was prosecuting the war with the House's approval.

Plaintiffs' reply is that the President's military action against Yugoslavia without congressional authorization had the effect of completely nullifying their votes, of making their votes worthless. With respect to their vote against declaring war, that clearly is not true. A congressional declaration of war carries with it profound consequences.[6] The United States Code is thick with laws expanding executive power "in time of war." *See* Office of the Judge Advocate General, United States Air Force, Digest of War and Emergency Legislation Affecting the Department of Defense 171–84 (1996) (listing statutes "effective in time of war"); *cf. id.* at 185–91 (listing statutes "effective in time of national emergency declared by the President"); *id.* at

---

6. Although the United States has committed its armed forces into combat more than a hundred times, Congress has declared war only five times: the War of 1812, the Mexican-American War of 1848, the Spanish-American War of 1898, World War I, and World War II.

192–98 (listing statutes "effective in time of national emergency declared by Congress").[7] Under these laws, the President's authority over industries, the use of land, and the terms and conditions of military employment is greatly enhanced.[8] A declaration of war may also have the effect of decreasing commercial choices and curtailing civil liberties.[9] *See* William H. Rehnquist, All the Laws But One: Civil Liberties in Wartime 218–19 (1998) ("Without question the government's authority to engage in conduct that infringes civil liberty is greatest in time of declared war—the *Schenck* and *Hirabayashi* opinions make this clear. . . . [B]ut from the point of view of governmental authority under the Constitution, it is clear that the President may do many things in carrying out a congressional directive that he may not be able to do on his own.").

The vote of the House on April 28, 1999, deprived President Clinton of these powers. The vote against declaring war followed immediately upon the vote not to require immediate withdrawal. Those who voted against a declaration of war did so to deprive the President of the authority to expand hostilities beyond the bombing campaign and, specifically, to deprive him of the authority to introduce ground troops into the conflict. *See* 145 Cong. Rec. H2427-41 (daily ed. Apr. 28, 1999). There is no suggestion that despite the vote, President Clinton invaded Yugoslavia by land or took

---

7. In the early days of the Republic, the power of the executive in time of war was constrained by an absence of legislation. For example, in *Brown v. United States,* 12 U.S. (8 Cranch) 110, 3 L.Ed. 504 (1814), the Court rejected the argument that the President had the authority to confiscate enemy property found within the United States without explicit statutory authority even during a declared war. *See id.* at 129. The same reasoning was applied to the taking of ships on the high seas in *Little v. Barreme,* 6 U.S. (2 Cranch) 170, 2 L.Ed. 243 (1804). Even in the wake of World War II, after Congress passed a large number of war-related measures, the Court strictly construed the President's authority. The most notable example, of course, is *Youngstown Sheet & Tube Co. v. Sawyer,* 343 U.S. 579, 585, 72 S.Ct. 863, 96 L.Ed. 1153 (1952) ("The President's power, if any, to issue the order must stem either from an act of Congress or from the Constitution itself."); *cf. also Dames & Moore v. Regan,* 453 U.S. 654, 101 S.Ct. 2972, 69 L.Ed.2d 918 (1981).

8. *See, e.g.,* 10 U.S.C. § 2538 (authorizing the President to "take immediate possession of any plant that is equipped to manufacture, or that . . . is capable of manufacturing" war material "in time of war or when war is imminent"); 10 U.S.C. § 2644 ("In time of war, the President, through the Secretary of Defense, may take possession and assume control of all or part of any system of transportation to transport troops, war material, and equipment, or for other purposes related to the emergency."); 10 U.S.C. § 2663(b) ("In time of war or when war is imminent, the United States may, immediately upon the filing of a petition for condemnation under subsection (a), take and use the land to the extent of the interest sought to be acquired."); 50 U.S.C. § 1829 ("Notwithstanding any other provision of law, the President, through the Attorney General, may authorize physical searches without a court order . . . to acquire foreign intelligence information for a period not to exceed 15 calendar days following a declaration of war by the Congress.").

9. *See, e.g.,* 18 U.S.C. § 2388(a) ("Whoever, when the United States is at war, willfully causes or attempts to cause insubordination, disloyalty, mutiny, or refusal of duty, in the military or naval forces of the United States, or willfully obstructs the recruiting or enlistment service of the United States, to the injury of the service or the United States, or attempts to do so—Shall be fined under this title or imprisoned not more than twenty years, or both."); 18 U.S.C. § 3287 (tolling statute of limitations for any offense involving fraud against the property of the United States until three years after the termination of hostilities).

some other action authorized only during a declared war. It follows that plaintiffs' votes against declaring war were not for naught. For that reason, plaintiffs do not have standing to sue on their constitutional claim.

As to their claim under the War Powers Resolution, the beauty of this measure, or one of its defects is in its automatic operation: unless a majority of both Houses declares war, or approves continuation of hostilities beyond 60 days, or Congress is "physically unable to meet as a result of an armed attack upon the United States," the Resolution requires the President to withdraw the troops. 50 U.S.C. § 1544(b). The President has nothing to veto. Congress may allow the time to run without taking any vote, or it may—as the House did here—take a vote and fail to muster a majority in favor of continuing the hostilities.

To put the matter in terms of *Raines* once again, plaintiffs had the votes "sufficient to defeat" "a specific legislative action"—they blocked a resolution authorizing the President's continuation of the war with Yugoslavia—but it is not true, in the language of *Raines,* that this "legislative action" nevertheless went "into effect." Congressional authorization simply did not occur. The President may have acted as if he had Congress's approval, or he may have acted as if he did not need it. Either way, plaintiffs' real complaint is not that the President ignored their votes; it is that he ignored the War Powers Resolution, and hence the votes of an earlier Congress, which enacted the law over President Nixon's veto. It is hard for me to see that this amounts to anything more than saying: "We, the members of Congress, have standing because the President violated one of our laws." To hold that Members of Congress may litigate on such a basis strikes me as highly problematic, not only because the principle is unconfined but also because it raises very serious separation-of-powers concerns. *See Raines,* supra; *Barnes v. Kline,* 759 F.2d 21, 41 (D.C.Cir. 1985) (Bork, J., dissenting), *vacated as moot,* 479 U.S. 361 (1987). But because the case is moot, I need say no more.

B.

The majority opinion analyzes standing rather differently than I do. It says plaintiffs lack standing to pursue their statutory claim because "they continued, after the votes, to enjoy ample legislative power to have stopped prosecution of the 'war.' " Maj. op. at 23. For specifics, the opinion points out that Congress defeated House Concurrent Resolution 82, a resolution requiring immediate disengagement from the conflict in Yugoslavia; that "Congress always retains appropriations authority and could have cut off funds for the American role in the conflict";[10] and that "there

---

10. The majority attaches some importance to Congress's decision to authorize funding for Operation Allied Force and argues that Congress could have denied funding if it wished to end the war. However, in *Mitchell v. Laird,* 488 F.2d 611, 616 (D.C.Cir. 1973), we held that, as "every schoolboy knows," Congress may pass such legislation, not because it is in favor of continuing the hostilities, but because it does not want to endanger soldiers in the field. The War Powers Resolution itself makes the same point: "Authority to introduce United States Armed Forces into hostilities or into situations wherein involvement in hostilities is clearly indicated by the circumstances *shall not be*

always remains the possibility of impeachment." *Id.* The same reason—the possibility of future legislative action—is used to defeat plaintiffs' standing with respect to their constitutional claim.

The majority has, I believe, confused the right to vote in the future with the nullification of a vote in the past, a distinction *Raines* clearly made. To say that your vote was not nullified because you can vote for other legislation in the future is like saying you did not lose yesterday's battle because you can fight again tomorrow. The Supreme Court did not engage in such illogic. When the Court in *Raines* mentioned the possibility of future legislation, it was addressing the argument that "the [Line Item Veto] Act will nullify the [Congressmen's] votes in the future. . . ." *Id.* This part of the Court's opinion, which the majority adopts here, is quite beside the point to our case. No one is claiming that their votes on future legislation will be impaired or nullified or rendered ineffective.

Besides, as long as Congress and the Constitution exist, Members will always be able to vote for legislation. And so the majority's decision is tantamount to a decision abolishing legislative standing. I have two problems with this. First, if we are going to get rid of legislative standing altogether, we ought to do so openly and not under the cover of an interpretation, or rather misinterpretation, of a phrase in *Raines.* If the Supreme Court had meant to do away with legislative standing, it would have said so and it would have given reasons for taking that step.

My second problem is just as serious, perhaps more so: the majority's decision conflicts with this court's latest legislative standing decision. In *Chenoweth v. Clinton,* 181 F.3d 112, 116–17 (D.C.Cir. 1999), we interpreted *Raines* consistently with my analysis in this case and concluded that a previous legislative standing decision of this court—*Kennedy v. Sampson,* 511 F.2d 430 (D.C.Cir. 1974)—upholding legislative standing to challenge the legality of a pocket veto was still good law. The plaintiff in *Kennedy* had standing under the proper interpretation of *Raines,* we held, because the "pocket veto challenged in that case had made ineffective a bill that both houses of the Congress had approved. Because it was the President's veto—not a lack of legislative support—that prevented the bill from becoming law (either directly or by the Congress voting to override the President's veto), those in the majority could plausibly describe the President's action as a complete nullification of their votes." 181 F.3d at 116–17. If *Chenoweth* is correct, the majority opinion in this case must be wrong. If *Chenoweth* is correct, it is no answer to say—as the majority says in this case—that standing is lacking because, despite the pocket veto, Congress could pass

---

inferred . . . from any provision of law (whether or not in effect before November 7, 1973), *including any provision contained in any appropriation Act,* unless such provision specifically authorizes the introduction of United States Armed Forces into hostilities or into such situations and states that it is intended to constitute specific statutory authorization within the meaning of this chapter." 50 U.S.C. § 1547(a)(1) (emphasis added). Those portions of the Emergency Supplemental Appropriations Act, Pub.L. No. 106-31, 113 Stat. 57, relating to the attacks on Yugoslavia specified the limited purpose for the emergency appropriations, but contained no language even roughly approximating that required by the War Powers Resolution. *See id.,* ch. 3, 113 Stat. 76-83.

the same law again, or it could retaliate by cutting off appropriations for the White House or it could impeach the President.

C.

My position, the majority complains, "sidesteps" plaintiffs' merits "claim that the President unconstitutionally conducted a war without authority," Maj. op. at 23. This is meant to be criticism? A properly-conducted standing analysis almost always avoids—sidesteps—a decision on the merits. In the next breath, the majority turns around and contradicts itself, proclaiming that my analysis "conflates standing with the merits." *Id.* I am familiar with what I have written. I do not recall having rendered a judgment about whether the President violated the Constitution. The careful reader will, I think, agree with me. Nor do I present "as an alternative reason for denying standing that the President did not . . . take any actions constituting war in the constitutional sense." *Id.* The majority's sentence is doubly misleading. Here is my alternative reason for denying standing, pure and simple: regardless whether President Clinton waged a "war," plaintiffs never claimed that he exercised statutory authority reserved to him only when Congress has declared a war; and so their votes against declaring war cannot be considered a nullity. Thus, one, I have taken no position on whether the President engaged in a "war," and two, I say only that plaintiffs never *alleged* that the President utilized these statutory powers. Too often a strategy in legal argumentation is to pretend to answer an argument by misstating it. My argument remains unanswered. All the majority has done is to misstate it almost as badly as it has misread *Raines.*

II. Mootness

The amended complaint, filed on May 19, 1999, sought a declaratory judgment "that no later than May 25, 1999, the President must terminate the involvement of the United States Armed Forces in such hostilities unless Congress declares war, or enacts other explicit authorization, or has extended the sixty day period." Amended Complaint at 12; *see* 50 U.S.C. § 1544(b)(1)-(2). All agree that the "hostilities" ended by June 21, 1999, after NATO's Secretary General announced the official termination of the air campaign and Secretary of Defense Cohen announced the redeployment of more than 300 U.S. aircraft back to their home bases.

To save their case from mootness, plaintiffs therefore invoke the rule regarding issues "capable of repetition, yet evading review." *Southern Pacific Terminal Co. v. ICC,* 219 U.S. 498, 515 (1911); *Christian Knights of the Ku Klux Klan v. District of Columbia,* 972 F.2d 365, 369–71 (D.C.Cir. 1992). Plaintiffs must, but cannot, satisfy both elements to prevail. Their constitutional and statutory claims are at cross purposes.

The "evading review" part of the formulation is temporal. How quickly must an activity begin and end to evade judicial review? This depends on which court does the reviewing. The Supreme Court has treated the matter in terms of itself. Hence evading review means evading Supreme Court review, which can be (though usually is not) swift review. Some undeclared wars, or in the euphemism of the day, "hostilities," are over quickly; others, like the Korean War and the war in Vietnam, last for years. Circuit precedent requires us to determine whether the activity challenged is "inherently" of a sort that evades review; circuit precedent also holds that "offensive wars initiated without congressional approval" are not in that category. *Conyers v. Reagan,* 765 F.2d 1124, 1128 (D.C.Cir. 1985). That holding, which remains the law of the circuit, means that we must treat plaintiffs' claims as moot.

Plaintiffs' statutory claim — that President Clinton continued the war for more than 60 days without congressional authorization, in violation of the War Powers Resolution — also may not satisfy the "capable of repetition" element. There is an aspect of probability involved here. "By 'capable of repetition' the Supreme Court means 'a reasonable expectation that the same complaining party would be subject to the same action again.'" This introduces some complications. Who should be considered the "same complaining parties"? And what is the "same action again"?

The same "complaining parties" must refer to the individual Members of Congress who brought this suit. They have sued in their official capacity and the injury they allege relates to their conduct as legislators. Thus, in assessing the likelihood of a recurrence of "the same action," the inquiry must be restricted only to the period in which these Congressmen would likely remain in office. As to the "same action," this refers to President Clinton's alleged violation of the War Powers Resolution by continuing hostilities for more than 60 days without Congress's affirmative approval. How likely is that to recur? Not very, if history is any guide. The War Powers Resolution has been in effect for a quarter of a century. Yet President Clinton is the first President who arguably violated the 60-day provision. In order to show why their claims will "evade review," plaintiffs tell us that, in modern times, United States attacks on foreign nations will be over quickly, by which they mean less than 60 days.[15] Accepting that prediction as accurate dooms their case. It means that the likelihood of this President, or some other, violating the 60-day provision of the War Powers Resolution is remote, not only because we can expect other Presidents to obtain congressional approval for wars lasting more than 60 days, but also because most military actions in the future (as plaintiffs agree) will be over before the 60-day limit for undeclared or unauthorized wars has been exceeded.

TATEL, Circuit Judge, concurring:

Although I agree with Judge Silberman that *Raines v. Byrd,* 521 U.S. 811 (1997), as interpreted by this court in *Chenoweth v. Clinton,* 181 F.3d 112 (D.C.Cir. 1999), deprives plaintiffs of standing to bring this action, I do not share his view that the case poses a nonjusticiable political question. In my view, were this case brought by plaintiffs with standing, we could determine whether the President, in undertaking the air campaign in Yugoslavia, exceeded his authority under the Constitution or the War Powers Resolution.

---

15. "The 1998 air attack against Afghanistan and Sudan, the December 1998 air attacks against Iraq, the 1995 air assault against the Bosnian Serbs, the 1994 Haitian invasion, the 1991 Persian Gulf War, the 1989 Panama invasion, the 1986 air attack against Libya, the 1983 Grenada attack were all completed in less than 60 days." Reply Brief for Plaintiffs-Appellants at 5–6.

To begin with, I do not agree that courts lack judicially discoverable and manageable standards for "determining the existence of a 'war.'" Whether the military activity in Yugoslavia amounted to "war" within the meaning of the Declare War Clause, U.S. Const. art. I, § 8, cl. 11, is no more standardless than any other question regarding the constitutionality of government action. . . .

Since the earliest years of the nation, courts have not hesitated to determine when military action constitutes "war." In *Bas v. Tingy*, 4 U.S. (4 Dall.) 37 (1800), the Supreme Court had to decide whether hostilities between France and the United States amounted to a state of war in order to resolve disputes over captured ships. Because outright war had not been declared, the justices examined both the facts of the conflict ("the scene of bloodshed, depredation and confiscation, which has unhappily occurred," *id.* at 39) and the acts of Congress that had authorized limited military action:

> In March 1799, congress had raised an army; stopped all intercourse with France; dissolved our treaty; built and equipt ships of war; and commissioned private armed ships; enjoining the former, and authorising the latter, to defend themselves against the armed ships of France, to attack them on the high seas, to subdue and take them as prize, and to re-capture armed vessels found in their possession.

Id. at 41. Given these events, Justice Bushrod Washington concluded that France and the United States were at war both "[i]n fact and in law." *Id.* at 42. "If they were not our enemies," he said, "I know not what constitutes an enemy." *Id.* at 41. One year later, Chief Justice Marshall, focusing on the same conflict with France, said: "The whole powers of war being, by the constitution of the United States, vested in congress, the acts of that body can alone be resorted to as our guides in this enquiry. . . . To determine the real situation of America in regard to France, the acts of congress are to be inspected." *Talbot v. Seeman*, 5 U.S. (1 Cranch) 1, 28 (1801).

Half a century later, in *The Prize Cases*, 67 U.S. (2 Black) 635, 666 (1862), the Court had to determine whether a state of war, though undeclared, existed "*de facto*" between the United States and the confederacy, and if so, whether it justified the U.S. naval blockade of confederate ports. "As a civil war is never publicly proclaimed, . . . its actual existence is a fact in our domestic history which the Court is bound to notice and to know." *Id.* at 667. There was no formal declaration of war, the Court explained, because the Constitution does not permit Congress to "declare war against a State, or any number of States." *Id.* at 668. Yet the Court, guided by the definition of war as "[t]hat state in which a nation prosecutes its right by force," *id.* at 666, determined that a state of war actually existed. . . . In making this determination, the Court looked to the facts of the conflict, *id.*, to the acts of foreign governments recognizing the war and declaring their neutrality, *id.* at 669, and to congressional action authorizing the President's use of force, *id.* at 670–71. Given these facts, the Court refused "to affect a technical ignorance of the existence of a war, which all the world acknowledges to be the greatest civil war known in the history of the human race." *Id.* at 669.

More recent cases have also recognized the competence of courts to determine whether a state of war exists. Responding to a challenge to the constitutionality of the Vietnam War, this circuit confronted "the critical question . . . whether the hostilities in Indo-China constitute *in the Constitutional sense* a 'war,' both within and beyond the meaning of that term in Article I, Section 8, Clause 11." *Mitchell v. Laird*, 488 F.2d 611, 614 (D.C.Cir. 1973) (emphasis added). The court found "no insuperable difficulty in a court determining whether," given the extent of the hostilities, "there has been a war in Indo-China." *Id.* Once the war was recognized as such, the court saw no problem in "facing up to the question as to whether because of the war's duration and magnitude the President is or was without power to continue the war without Congressional approval," or "whether Congress has given, in a Constitutionally satisfactory form, the approval requisite for a war of considerable duration and magnitude." *Id.* Nor did the court hesitate to determine that once the Gulf of Tonkin resolution had been repealed, later congressional actions appropriating funds for the war and extending the draft were insufficient to "serve as a valid assent to the Vietnam war." *Id.* at 615. Given this absence of congressional approval for the war's continuation, the President had a duty to try "in good faith and to the best of his ability, to bring the war to an end as promptly as was consistent with the safety of those fighting and with a profound concern for the durable interests of the nation — its defense, its honor, its morality." *Id.* at 616. Although the court ultimately declined to answer the question whether President Nixon was in fact fulfilling his duty to end the Vietnam War, *see id.*, it nonetheless made clear that courts are competent to adjudge the existence of war and the allocation of war powers between the President and Congress. Regardless of whether this language is dicta, *Mitchell* supports my view that this court could resolve the war powers claims presented here. Without undue difficulty, courts have also determined whether hostilities amount to "war" in other contexts. These have included insurance policies and other contracts, the Federal Tort Claims Act, and provisions of military criminal law applicable "in time of war."

Although courts have thus determined the existence of war as defined by the Constitution, statutes, and contracts, in this case plaintiffs' War Powers Resolution claim would not even require that we do so. We would need to ask only whether, and at what time, "United States Armed Forces [were] introduced into hostilities or into situations where imminent involvement in hostilities [was] clearly indicated by the circumstances." 50 U.S.C. § 1543(a)(1). On this question, the record is clear. In his report to the Speaker of the House and the President pro tempore of the Senate, transmitted "consistent with the War Powers Resolution," President Clinton stated: "on March 24, 1999, U.S. military forces, at my direction . . . began a series of air strikes in the Federal Republic of Yugoslavia. . . ." 35 Weekly Comp. Pres. Doc. 527 (March 26, 1999), available at 1999 WL 12654381. Pursuant to the priority procedures of the War Powers Resolution, 50 U.S.C. §§ 1545–46, both houses of Congress responded by expediting consideration of resolutions to declare war, H.J. Res 44, to authorize airstrikes, S.J. Res. 20, and to withdraw troops, H. Con. Res. 82. Defense Secretary William Cohen told the Senate Armed Services Committee: "We're certainly engaged in hostilities, we're engaged in combat." Hearing on Kosovo, Senate Armed Services Comm., 106th Cong., April 15, 1999, 1999 WL 221637 (testimony of William Cohen, Secretary of Defense). President Clinton issued an Executive Order designating the region a U.S. combat zone and March 24 as "the date of the commencement of combatant activities in such zone." Exec. Order No. 13,119, 64 Fed.Reg. 18797 (Apr. 13, 1999).

The undisputed facts of this case are equally compelling with respect to plaintiffs' constitutional claim. If in 1799 the Supreme Court could recognize that sporadic battles between American and French vessels amounted to a state of war, and if in 1862 it could examine the record of hostilities and conclude that a state of war existed with the confederacy, then surely we, looking to similar evidence, could determine whether months of daily airstrikes involving 800 U.S. aircraft flying more than 20,000 sorties and causing thousands of enemy casualties amounted to "war" within the meaning of Article I, section 8, clause 11.

Determining whether a state of war exists would certainly be more difficult in situations involving more limited military force over a shorter period of time. But just as we never shrink from deciding a First Amendment case simply because we can imagine a more difficult one, the fact that a challenge to a different military action might present a closer question would not justify abdicating our responsibility to construe the law and apply it to the facts of this case.

Nor is the question nonjusticiable because the President, as Commander in Chief, possesses emergency authority to use military force to defend the nation from attack without obtaining prior congressional approval. . . . President Clinton does not claim that the air campaign was necessary to protect the nation from imminent attack. In his report to Congress, the President explained that the military action was "in response to the FRY government's continued campaign of violence and repression against the ethnic Albanian population in Kosovo." 35 Weekly Comp. Pres. Doc. 527 (Mar. 26, 1999), available at 1999 WL 12654381. Although the President also said that military action would prevent an expanded war in Europe, *see* Radio Address of the President to the Nation, March 27, 1999, available at 1999 WL 170552, he never claimed that an emergency required him to act without congressional authorization; in fact, the Kosovo issue had been festering for years.

The government also claims that this case is nonjusticiable because it "requires a political, not a judicial, judgment." The government has it backwards. Resolving the issue in this case would require us to decide not whether the air campaign was wise — a "policy choice[ ] and value determination [ ] constitutionally committed for resolution to the halls of Congress or the confines of the Executive Branch," *Japan Whaling Ass'n v. American Cetacean Soc'y,* 478 U.S. 221, 230 (1986) — but whether the President possessed legal authority to conduct the military operation. Did the President exceed his constitutional authority as Commander in Chief? Did he intrude on Congress's power to declare war? Did he violate the War Powers Resolution? Presenting purely legal issues, these questions call on us to perform one of the most important functions of Article III courts: determining the proper constitutional allocation of power among the branches of government. Although our answer could well have political implications, "the presence of constitutional issues with significant political overtones does not automatically invoke the political question doctrine. Resolution of litigation challenging the constitutional authority of one of the three branches cannot be evaded by courts because the issues have political implications. . . ." *INS v. Chadha,* 462 U.S. 919, 942–43 (1983). This is so even where. . . . the issue relates to foreign policy. If "we cannot shirk [our] responsibility" to decide whether an Act of Congress requires the President to impose economic sanctions on a foreign nation for diminishing the effectiveness of an international treaty, a question rife with "political overtones," *Japan Whaling Ass'n,* 478 U.S. at 230, then surely we cannot shirk our responsibility to decide whether the President exceeded his constitutional or statutory authority by conducting the air campaign in Yugoslavia.

The Government's final argument—that entertaining a war powers challenge risks the government speaking with "multifarious voices" on a delicate issue of foreign policy—fails for similar reasons. Because courts are the final arbiters of the constitutionality of the President's actions, "there is no possibility of 'multifarious pronouncements' on this question." *Chadha,* 462 U.S. at 942. Any short-term confusion that judicial action might instill in the mind of an authoritarian enemy, or even an ally, is but a small price to pay for preserving the constitutional separation of powers and protecting the bedrock constitutional principle that "[i]t is emphatically the province and duty of the judicial department to say what the law is." *Marbury v. Madison,* 5 U.S. (1 Cranch), 137, 177 (1803).

Litigating the Persian Gulf War. As discussed below, by the time the United States finally engaged in hostilities with Iraqi forces in the 1991 Persian Gulf War, Congress had enacted legislative authority for the military deployment. On October 23, 1990, however, Congress enacted a bill providing for "imminent danger" pay for U.S. troops in the Persian Gulf, special pay for reserve medical and dental officers and a number of other personnel and procurement matters. At roughly the same time, a substantial number of Senators and Representatives issued statements expressing concern about the possibility of a presidentially initiated war without congressional authorization, and demanding consultation. The Administration initially refused to concede a need on its part for legislative authority to pursue any further response to Iraq, and instead pursued international support for an offensive against Iraq.

As a consequence, two lawsuits were filed to enjoin the use of military force (or non-volunteer service members) against Iraq without a declaration of war. The challengers in *Dellums v. Bush,* 752 F. Supp. 1141 (D.D.C. 1990), were members of Congress, thus raising the knotty issue of congressional standing. The plaintiff in *Ange v. Bush,* 752 F. Supp. 509 (D.D.C. 1990), however, was a sergeant in a National Guard unit deployed in the Gulf. The judges in the two cases took distinctively different approaches to whether the issue sought to be litigated was a "political question." In *Ange,* Judge Lamberth found the suit lacked ripeness and presented a political question. He concluded that the delineation of the war powers was textually committed to elected branches, that the ramifications of military decisions require that full accountability be vested in elected officials, that the judiciary lacks relevant expertise, and that Congress has ample mechanisms for checking a president who exceeds constitutional bounds on his authority. In *Dellums*, Judge Greene—who concluded that the members of Congress did have standing to protect their entitlement to vote whether to authorize war—agreed that the suit lacked ripeness because Congress had taken no position yet on the conflict and the executive was not irreversibly committed to a course of action that would eliminate a congressional vote. He insisted, however, that the lawfulness of going to war without legislative authority did not present a political question. His argument was much the same as Judge Tatel's above.

What is your view? Should courts entertain war powers suits on behalf of members of Congress? Do such suits present political questions? Is any such suit more likely to present a political question the "riper" it becomes?

3. Reform of the War Powers Resolution

If its backers hoped the War Powers Resolution would lessen presidential interest in military initiative, the existence of 129 reports to Congress between 1973 and 2010 suggests a disappointing outcome. Further, a Congressional Research Service (CRS) report quoted below finds 18 examples during the same period—other than "routine" training programs or extensions of military assistance, covert operations, or humanitarian deployments—where U.S. armed forces were sent into potentially hostile situations without a report to Congress. ROBERT F. GRIMMETT, CONGRESSIONAL RESEARCH SERVICE, THE WAR POWERS RESOLUTION: AFTER THIRTY-SIX YEARS 70–71 (2010). With this record, it is not surprising various calls have been made for changes to the WPR, most to augment Congress's authority, some to give the President even more flexibility. CRS Specialist in International Relations Robert Grimmett sums them up as follows:

ROBERT F. GRIMMETT, THE WAR POWERS RESOLUTION: AFTER THIRTY-SIX YEARS

Congressional Research Service No. R41199, at 44–48 (2011).

Proposed Amendments

After 34 years of experience with it in practice, controversy continues over the War Powers Resolution's effectiveness and appropriateness as a system for maintaining a congressional role in the use of armed forces in conflict. One view is that the War Powers Resolution is basically sound and does not need amendment. Those who hold this opinion believe it has brought about better communication between the two branches in times of crisis, and has given Congress a vehicle by which it can act when a majority of Members wish to do so. The Resolution served as a restraint on the use of armed forces by the President in some cases because of awareness that certain actions might invoke its provisions. For example, the threat of invoking the War

Powers Resolution may have been helpful in getting U.S. forces out of Grenada, in keeping the number of military advisers in El Salvador limited to 55, and in prodding Congress to take a stand on authorizing the war against Iraq.

A contrary view is that the War Powers Resolution is an inappropriate instrument that restricts the President's effectiveness in foreign policy and should be repealed. Those with this perspective believe that the basic premise of the War Powers Resolution is wrong because in it, Congress attempts excessive control of the deployment of U.S. military forces, encroaching on the responsibility of the President. Supporters of repeal contend that the President needs more flexibility in the conduct of foreign policy and that the time limitation in the War Powers Resolution is unconstitutional and impractical. Some holding this view contend that Congress has always had the power, through appropriations and general lawmaking, to inquire into, support, limit, or prohibit specific uses of U.S. Armed Forces if there is majority support. The War Powers Resolution does not fundamentally change this equation, it is argued, but it complicates action, misleads military opponents, and diverts attention from key policy questions.

A third view is that the War Powers Resolution has not been adequate to accomplish its objectives and needs to be strengthened or reshaped. Proponents of this view assert that Presidents have continued to introduce U.S. armed forces into hostilities without consulting Congress and without congressional authorization. Presidents have cited section 4(a)(1) on only one occasion—Mayaguez—and by the time the action was reported, it was virtually over. Holders of this third view have proposed various types of amendments to the War Powers Resolution. These include returning to the version originally passed by the Senate, establishing a congressional consultation group, adding a cutoff of funds, and providing for judicial review. A general discussion of these categories of possible changes follows.

Return to Senate Version: Enumerating Exceptions for Emergency Use

In 1977, Senator Thomas Eagleton proposed that the War Powers Resolution return to the original language of the version passed by the Senate, and this proposal has been made several times since. This would require prior congressional authorization for the introduction of forces into conflict abroad without a declaration of war except to respond to or forestall an armed attack against the United States or its forces or to protect U.S. citizens while evacuating them. The amendment would eliminate the construction that the President has 60 to 90 days in which he can militarily act without authorization. Opponents fear the exceptions to forestall attacks or rescue American citizens abroad would serve as a blanket authorization and might be abused, yet might not allow the needed speed of action and provide adequate flexibility in other circumstances.

Shorten or Eliminate Time Limitation

Another proposal is to shorten the time period that the President could maintain forces in hostile situations abroad without congressional authorization from 60 to 30 days, or eliminate it altogether. Some proponents of this amendment contend the current War Powers Resolution gives the President 60 to 90 days to do as he chooses and that this provides too much opportunity for mischief or irreversible action. The original Senate version provided that the use of armed forces in hostilities or imminent hostilities in any of the emergency situations could not be sustained beyond 30 days without specific congressional authorization, extendable by the President upon certification of necessity for safe disengagement. Opponents of this and related measures argue that they induce military opponents to adopt strategies to win given conflicts in Congress that they could not win in the field over time.

Replace Automatic Withdrawal Requirement

The War Powers Resolution has an automatic requirement for withdrawal of troops 60 days after the President submits a section 4(a)(1) report. Some Members of Congress favor replacing this provision with expedited procedures for a joint resolution to authorize the action or require disengagement. One of the main executive branch objections to the War Powers Resolution has been that the withdrawal requirement could be triggered by congressional inaction, and that adversaries can simply wait out the 60 days. By providing for withdrawal by joint resolution, this amendment would also deal with the provision for withdrawal by concurrent resolution, under a cloud because of the *Chadha* decision. On the other hand, a joint resolution requiring disengagement could be vetoed by the President and thus would require a two-thirds majority vote in both Houses for enactment.

Cutoff of Funds

Some proposals call for prohibiting the obligation or expenditure of funds for any use of U.S. armed forces in violation of the War Powers Resolution or laws passed under it except for the purpose of removing troops. Congress could enforce this provision by refusing to appropriate further funds to continue the military action. This has always been the case, some contend, and would not work because Congress would remain reluctant to withhold financial support for U.S. Armed Forces once they were abroad.

Elimination of Action by Concurrent Resolution

Many proposed amendments eliminate section 5(c) providing that U.S. forces engaged in hostilities abroad without congressional authorization are to be removed if Congress so directs by concurrent resolution, and section 7 providing priority procedures for a concurrent resolution. Those who hold this view contend the concurrent resolution section is invalid because of the *Chadha* decision.

Expedited Procedures

Several proposals call for new and more detailed priority procedures for joint resolutions introduced under the War Powers Resolution. These would apply to joint resolutions either authorizing a military action or calling for the withdrawal of forces, and to congressional action to sustain or override a presidential veto of the joint resolution.

Consultation Group

Several proposed amendments have focused on improving consultation under the War Powers Resolution, particularly by establishing a specific consultation group in Congress for this purpose. Senators Byrd, Nunn, Warner, and Mitchell have proposed the President regularly consult with an initial group of 6 Members—the majority and minority leaders of both Chambers plus the Speaker of the House and President pro tempore of the Senate. Upon a request from a majority of this core group, the President is to consult with a permanent consultative group of 18 Members consisting of the leadership and the ranking and minority members of the Committees on Foreign Relations, Armed Services, and Intelligence. The permanent consultative group would also be able to determine that the President should have reported an introduction of forces and to introduce a joint resolution of authorization or withdrawal that would receive expedited procedures.

Other Members have favored a consultation group, but consider that amendment of the War Powers Resolution is not required for Congress to designate such a group. On October 28, 1993, House Foreign Affairs Chairman Lee Hamilton introduced H.R. 3405 to establish a Standing Consultative Group. Its purpose would be to facilitate improved interaction between the executive branch and Congress on the use of U.S. military forces abroad, including under the War Powers Resolution or United Nations auspices. Members of the Consultative Group would be appointed by the Speaker of the House and the Majority Leader of the Senate, after consultation with the minority leaders. The Group would include majority and minority representatives of the leadership and the committees on foreign policy, armed services, intelligence, and appropriations.

Another proposal would attempt to improve consultation by broadening the instances in which the President is required to consult. This proposal would cover all situations in which a President is required to report, rather than only circumstances that invoke the time limitation, as is now the case.

Judicial Review

Proposals have been made that any Member of Congress may bring an action in the United States District Court for the District of Columbia for judgment and injunctive relief on the grounds that the President or the U.S. Armed Forces have not complied with any provision of the War Powers Resolution. The intent of this legislation is to give standing to Members to assert the interest of the House or Senate, but whether it would impel courts to exercise jurisdiction is uncertain. Most recent federal court decisions have rejected War Powers lawsuits by congressional litigants on the grounds they lacked standing to sue. Proposals have also called for the court not to decline to make a determination on the merits, on the grounds that the issue of compliance is a political question or otherwise nonjusticiable; to accord expedited consideration to the matter; and to prescribe judicial remedies including that the President submit a report or remove Armed Forces from a situation.

Change of Name

Other proposals would construct a Hostilities Act or Use of Force Act and repeal the War Powers Resolution. A possible objection to invoking the War Powers Resolution is reluctance to escalate international tension by implying that a situation is war. Some would see this as a step in the wrong direction; in the Korean and Vietnam conflicts, some contend, it was self-deceptive and ultimately impractical not to recognize hostilities of that magnitude as war and bring to bear the Constitutional provision giving Congress the power to declare war.

United Nations Actions

With the increase in United Nations actions since the end of the Cold War, the question has been raised whether the War Powers Resolution should be amended to facilitate or restrain the President from supplying forces for U.N. actions without congressional approval. Alternatively, the United Nations Participation Act might be amended, or new legislation enacted, to specify how the War Powers Resolution is to be applied, and whether the approval of Congress would be required only for an initial framework agreement on providing forces to the United Nations, or whether Congress would be required to approve an agreement to supply forces in specified situations, particularly for U.N. peacekeeping operations.

———————

1. *A Premature Requiem for the WPR?* Do the foregoing proposals draw too negative an historical lesson as to the importance of the War Powers Resolution? Several commentators have argued that the chief function of the Resolution has not been constitutional, but political, giving Congress an added, useful tool to coordinate its formal response to presidential war making with public opinion in a way that protects Congress institutionally. Note, *Congress, the War Powers Resolution, and the Secret Political Life of a "Dead Letter,"* 7 J. L. & POL. 177 (1990).

Professor Shane has argued that the political role of the War Powers Resolution has served the rule of law in the domain of military policy making:

> It is clear that, since the enactment of the War Powers Resolution ("WPR") the executive branch has often resisted technical compliance with its formal textual commands. From this point of view, the WPR has failed as law. And yet, . . . if one reviews the actual behavior of the two branches, it is clear that they have achieved a modus vivendi, an "effective law" of war powers that balances a de facto legislative delegation of "strike operation" discretion to the executive against a significantly constraining process within which the executive must proceed if it is intent on any lengthy or massive military deployment. The WPR has supported, in other words, an interbranch dynamic that has made each branch more accountable to its institutional obligations.
>
> The WPR embodies three key commands to the executive. In committing United States military forces to hostilities or to situations in which

hostilities may be imminent, the executive must: (1) consult Congress to the extent practicable, (2) report within forty-eight hours of the relevant commitment, and (3) withdraw within sixty or ninety days, if Congress does not affirmatively authorize the military deployment.

For military operations intended to take but a few days to execute, the WPR essentially leaves the President to his own discretion. President Reagan's invasion of Grenada and bombing of Libya, President Bush's invasion of Panama, and President Clinton's bombing of Iraq and expedition to Haiti exemplify such operations. In none of these cases did the President acknowledge that he was legally bound by the WPR. Nonetheless, in each of these cases, the President did make a report to Congress within 48 hours of the commencement of the operation — just as the WPR would require.

In contrast, the WPR explicitly asserts Congress's entitlement to decide whether the United States should go to war or place itself on a war footing. Again, although President [George H.W.] Bush denied his need for legislative authorization, the fact that he sought explicit congressional authority for Operation Desert Storm paid obvious respect to Congress's understanding of its own powers. He did not seriously seek to deny that the deployment of tens of thousands of American troops in defense against what was then believed to be a genuinely powerful military adversary implicated Congress's war policy prerogatives. Moreover, despite what must surely have been the temptation to do otherwise, President Bush . . . [did not go] beyond the scope of Congress's authorizing resolution.

It is true, of course, that various Presidents engaged in strike operations without advance congressional approval. What is not clear, however, is that Congress adheres to a view of the Constitution that renders such operations unlawful. Although Congress has never ceded to the President any formal acknowledgement of constitutionally based executive discretion in such endeavors, Congress has routinely tolerated strike operations — correctly perceiving that they pose no genuine threat to Congress's capacity to regulate more substantial forms of military deployment.

As for Lebanon, Somalia, and Bosnia, it seems clear that each of the elected branches used the ambiguity of its own powers — and the ambiguity of the legal status of our military deployments — to help leverage its bargaining position over the course of events. A less vigilant Congress — the Congress of the 1960s, for example — could easily have allowed any of these engagements to become a version of Vietnam. In each case, however, Congress used the WPR and its own claims to authority to force the executive to sharpen its articulation of American objectives, respond to contrary positions with regard to the executive branch's foreign policy analyses, and share substantial information with Congress. In every case, the country experienced a better informed and more substantial intragovernment debate over military policy than the executive mustered in the Vietnam era. In the cases of Lebanon and Somalia, Congress helped set the stage for a relatively early withdrawal of ground troops. In the case of Bosnia, congressional pressure presumably helped curtail what might have been a temptation to commit United States ground troops even prior to the Dayton accords. With the Dayton accords in place, the United States deployment had a far better defined mission than would have been the case had the Clinton Administration moved earlier in that direction. It also seems to be a mission that the American people accepts. . . .

If the process were now to be reformed, it seems unlikely that the key improvement needed is a requirement of formal congressional approval prior to strike operations. What we need is a genuine congressional commitment after strike operations to an intensive and independent factual post-mortem regarding every military deployment. The knowledge that Congress is reliably committed to such investigations would help assure that, in planning even strike operations, the executive branch would truly confront and question the key assumptions underlying its proposed initiatives, test the information available to it, force key executive policy makers to address seriously the disagreements among them, and engage in intrabranch debate sufficiently open and receptive to dissent to merit public confidence in the decisions ultimately reached.

Of course, from at least one substantive point of view this version of the rule of law is truly disappointing. If you believe that strike operation deployments of American military power are virtually never going to serve the interests of international justice, then the process I would permit will seem an insufficient constraint on American militarism. But conflating the goals of legality and sound policy is, especially in this context, a mistake. There is apparently a substantial consensus within Congress that the current "exigencies of life . . . demand some degree of executive and military flexibility." In the face of such consensus, although law is a form of politics, it is not a form of politics plausibly sufficient to protect the world against improper assertions of American force. That is what elections are for.

In short, for those military engagements that are unambiguously "war," the WPR has effectively affirmed Congress's authority to authorize or to forbear from military hostilities. In other deployments that portend lengthy and dangerous commitments of United States troops, the WPR has created a framework for interbranch negotiation that has helped to assure Congress a more significant role in the regulation of military force. In strike operations, the WPR has effectively delegated discretion to the executive, but it is in these cases that the costs of Vietnam-style policy making pathology loom least. Congress can reduce even these costs by investigating such operations closely after the fact. Through such investigations, Congress would more effectively be asserting what it believes to be the primacy of its authority without formally denying the executive a degree of discretion that, if experience is any guide, Congress wants the President to have.

Peter M. Shane, *Learning McNamara's* Lessons: *How the War Powers Resolution Advances the Rule of Law,* 47 CASE W. RES. L. REV. 1281, 1300–1303 (1997). A then-Yale law student, Christopher Ford, offered a similar analysis in, *War Powers as We Live Them: Congressional-Executive Bargaining Under the Shadow of the War Powers Resolution,* 11 J.L. & POL. 609, 613–620 (1995). Is this perspective too sanguine as to the effects of the WPR on the distribution of war powers between Congress and the President? Early perspectives on this issue still notable for their thoughtfulness include Michael J. Glennon, *The War Powers Resolution Ten Years Later: More Politics Than Law,* 78 AM. J. INT'L L. 571 (1984); Note, *A Defense of the War Powers Resolution,* 93 YALE L.J. 1330 (1984); Note, *The Future of the War Powers Resolution,* 36 STAN. L. REV. 1407 (1984); Note, *The War Powers Resolution: A Tool for Balancing Power Through Negotiation,* 70 VA. L. REV. 1037 (1984); Symposium, *The War Powers Resolution,* 17 LOYOLA L.A. L. REV. 579 (1984); and Cyrus R. Vance, *Striking the Balance: Congress and the President Under the War Powers Resolution,* 133 U. PA. L. REV. 79 (1984).

2. *The Post-Cold War World.* Although military confrontation remains as a major feature of international affairs, the end of the Cold War redrew the map of world conflict in especially challenging ways. Presidents have wrestled mightily with the need to define an appropriate U.S. military policy in a world beset by regional, often inter-ethnic, armed conflagration.

In addition to concerns whether the WPR is working, recent experiences seem to have galvanized at least two other distinct anxieties about the interplay of the separation of powers and military policy-making. The first has been whether either political branch alone, or both in tandem, can succeed in articulating a coherent post-Cold War mission for U.S. military deployment related to regional peace-keeping.

The second is anxiety about the role of multinational command in directing U.S. troops. Congress, for example, "found," through the Department of Defense Appropriations Act for Fiscal Year 1994, Pub. L. No. 103-139, 107 Stat. 1418 (1993), that, "any special agreement negotiated by the President with the United Nations Security Council to make units of the United States Armed Forces available on call to the United Nations must be approved by the Congress pursuant to the United Nations' Participation Act, enacted into law in 1945." Reacting to the Somalia operations, the Act additionally "found" that the United Nations had not "yet acquired the expertise or infrastructure to enable it to effectively manage 'peace enforcement' operations." *Id.,* § 9001(5)-(6). What significance, if any, should the President attach to such a finding?

C. Congressionally Authorized Wars After Vietnam: The Persian Gulf and Iraq Wars

Many observers thought presidential military deployments of the kind described above in the previous section largely discredited the effectiveness of the War Powers Resolution in establishing or restoring (depending on your historical interpretation) Congress's control over the power to make war. Perhaps even more intriguing in this respect are our two post-Vietnam experiences of massive and open-ended military engagement, the Persian Gulf War of 1991 and the Iraq War of 2003. In both cases, Presidents Bush started by insisting that they possessed constitutional authority, without congressional augmentation, sufficient to conduct the military initiatives they desired. In both cases also, however, each President ultimately sought explicit congressional authorization in advance of engaging in hostilities, and Congress provided the authorization that the Presidents sought. The obvious question is whether these events testify to an actual shift of power back toward the legislative branch with regard to warmaking, or simply provide thin cover for a continuing concentration in the President of the power to direct our military affairs.

1. The Persian Gulf War: A New Watershed?

a. Managing the Crisis Under Presidential Authority Alone

The first Persian Gulf crisis began with the Iraqi invasion of Kuwait on August 2, 1990. President Bush responded almost immediately with both military deployment and economic sanctions. He reported on those responses in the following two letters to Congress:

Letter to the Speaker of the House and the President Pro Tempore of the Senate on the Deployment of United States Armed Forces to Saudi Arabia and the Middle East

26 WEEKLY COMP. PRES. DOC. 1225 (Aug. 9, 1990)

Dear Mr. Speaker: (Dear Mr. President:)

On August 2, 1990, Iraq invaded and occupied the sovereign state of Kuwait in flagrant violation of the Charter of the United Nations. In the period since August 2, Iraq has massed an enormous and sophisticated war machine on the Kuwaiti-Saudi Arabian border and in southern Iraq, capable of initiating further hostilities with little or no additional preparation. Iraq's actions pose a direct threat to neighboring countries and to vital U.S. interests in the Persian Gulf region.

In response to this threat and after receiving the request of the Government of Saudi Arabia, I ordered the forward deployment of substantial elements of the United States Armed Forces into the region. I am providing this report on the deployment and mission of our Armed Forces in accordance with my desire that Congress be fully informed and consistent with the War Powers Resolution.

Two squadrons of F-15 aircraft, one brigade of the 82nd Airborne Division, and other elements of the Armed Forces began arriving in Saudi Arabia at approximately 9:00 a.m. (EDT) on August 8, 1990. Additional U.S. air, naval, and ground Forces also will be deployed. The Forces are equipped for combat, and their mission is defensive. They are prepared to take action in concert with Saudi forces, friendly regional forces, and others to deter Iraqi aggression and to preserve the integrity of Saudi Arabia.

I do not believe involvement in hostilities is imminent; to the contrary, it is my belief that this deployment will facilitate a peaceful resolution of the crisis. If necessary, however, the Forces are fully prepared to defend themselves. Although it is not possible to predict the precise scope and duration of this deployment, our Armed Forces will remain so long as their presence is required to contribute to the security of the region and desired by the Saudi government to enhance the capability of Saudi armed forces to defend the Kingdom.

I have taken these actions pursuant to my constitutional authority to conduct our foreign relations and as Commander in Chief. These actions are in exercise of our inherent right of individual and collective self-defense. I look forward to cooperation with the Congress in helping to restore peace and stability to the Persian Gulf region.

Sincerely, George Bush

Letter to the Speaker of the House and the President Pro Tempore of the Senate on Additional Economic Measures Taken with Respect to Iraq and Kuwait

26 WEEKLY COMP. PRES. DOC. 1229 (Aug. 9, 1990)

Dear Mr. Speaker: (Dear Mr. President:)

On August 2, 1990, I reported to the Congress that, pursuant to section 204(b) of the International Emergency Economic Powers Act, 50 U.S.C. section 1703(b), and section 201 of the National Emergencies Act, 50 U.S.C. section 1621, I exercised my statutory authority to declare a national emergency and to issue two executive orders that imposed a comprehensive economic embargo against Iraq and blocked both Iraqi and Kuwaiti government property within the jurisdiction of the United States or under the control of U.S. persons.

In the days after the imposition of U.S. economic sanctions, the Iraqi government has tightened its unlawful grip over the territory of Kuwait and has installed a puppet regime that in no way represents the people or legitimate Government of Kuwait. On August 6, the United Nations Security Council, to bring the invasion and occupation of Kuwait to an end and to restore the sovereignty, independence, and territorial integrity of Kuwait, decided that all nations shall impose sweeping economic sanctions against both Iraq and Kuwait.

Today, I have taken additional steps to respond to these developments and to ensure that the economic measures we are taking with respect to Iraq and Kuwait conform to United Nations Security Council Resolution 661 of August 6, 1990. Specifically, pursuant to section 204(b) of the International Emergency Economic Powers Act, 50 U.S.C. section 1703(b), section 201 of the National Emergencies Act, 50 U.S.C. section 1621, and the United Nations Participation Act, 22 U.S.C. section 287(c), I have issued two new Executive orders.

The order I have issued with respect to Iraq:

—prohibits exports and imports of goods and services between the United States and Iraq, and any activity that promotes or is intended to promote such exportation and importation;

—prohibits any dealing by a U.S. person in connection with property of Iraqi origin exported from Iraq after August 6, 1990, or intended for exportation to or from Iraq to any country, and related activities;

—prohibits transactions related to travel to or from Iraq or to activities by any such person within Iraq, except for transactions necessary for prompt departure from Iraq, the conduct of official business of the United States Government or of the United Nations, or journalistic travel;

—prohibits transactions related to transportation to or from Iraq, or the use of vessels or aircraft registered in Iraq by U.S. persons;

—prohibits the performance by any U.S. person of any contract in support of certain categories of projects in Iraq;

—prohibits the commitment or transfer of funds or other financial or economic resources by any U.S. person to the Government of Iraq, or any other person in Iraq;

—blocks all property of the Government of Iraq now or hereafter located in the United States or in the possession or control of U.S. persons, including their foreign branches; and

—clarifies that the definition of U.S. persons includes vessels of U.S. registry.

In a separate order, I have extended to Kuwait all economic sanctions currently in effect against Iraq. Specifically, that order:

—prohibits exports and imports of goods and services between the United States and Kuwait, and any activity that promotes or is intended to promote such exportation or importation;

—prohibits any dealing by a U.S. person in connection with property of Kuwaiti origin exported from Kuwait after August 6, 1990, or intended for exportation to or from Kuwait to any country, and related activities;

—prohibits transactions related to travel to or from Kuwait or to activities by any such person within Kuwait, except for transactions necessary for prompt departure from Kuwait, the conduct of official business of the United States Government or of the United Nations, or journalistic travel;

—prohibits transactions related to transportation to or from Kuwait, or the use of vessels or aircraft registered in Kuwait by U.S. persons;

—prohibits the performance by any U.S. person of any contract in support of certain categories of projects in Kuwait;

—prohibits the commitment or transfer of funds or other financial or economic resources by any U.S. person to the Government of Kuwait, or any other person in Kuwait;

—blocks all property of the Government of Kuwait now or hereafter located in the United States or in the possession or control of U.S. persons, including their foreign branches; and

—clarifies that definition of U.S. persons includes vessels of U.S. registry.

Today's orders provide that the Secretary of the Treasury, in consultation with the Secretary of State, is authorized to take such actions, including the promulgation of rules and regulations, as may be necessary to carry out the purposes of those orders. The orders were effective at 8:55 p.m. e.d.t., August 9, 1990.

The declarations of national emergency made by Executive Orders 12722 and 12723, and any other provision of those orders not inconsistent with today's orders, remain in force and are unaffected by today's orders.

I am enclosing a copy of each of today's orders.

Sincerely, George Bush

b. The United Nations Authorizes Force

By August 11, the United States had imposed a military blockade on Iraq with the aim of preventing all shipping to Iraq of products other than medical supplies. According to the Defense Department, over 3,600 ships were intercepted by November, over 400 of which were boarded and 16 of which were diverted. By late October, the Bush Administration was explicitly warning Iraq that the United States was prepared to use force to end the Iraqi occupation of Kuwait. By early November, the United States had deployed 230,000 troops to the region, and President Bush announced a significant increase in deployment to provide "an adequate offensive military option."

President Bush's apparent determination to address the Persian Gulf crisis solely on his own authority provoked two lawsuits challenging the scope of his unilateral military powers. Before those suits were decided, however, the legal basis for possible military intervention changed with the adoption by the United Nations of the following resolution:

United Nations Security Council Resolution 678

Adopted by the Security Council at its 2963rd meeting,
on 29 November 1990

THE SECURITY COUNCIL,

RECALLING, AND REAFFIRMING its resolutions 660 (1990) of 2 August 1990, 661 (1990) of 6 August 1990, 662 (1990) of 9 August 1990, 664 (1990) of 18 August 1990,

665 (1990) of 25 August 1990, 666 (1990) of 13 September 1990, 667 (1990) of 16 September 1990, 669 (1990) of 24 September 1990, 670 (1990) of 25 September 1990, 674 (1990) of 29 October 1990, and 677 (1990) of 28 November 1990,

NOTING THAT, despite all efforts by the United Nations, Iraq refuses to comply with its obligation to implement resolution 660 (1990) and the above-mentioned subsequent relevant resolutions, in flagrant contempt of the Security Council,

MINDFUL of its duties and responsibilities under the Charter of the United Nations for the maintenance and preservation of international peace and security,

DETERMINED to secure full compliance with its decisions,

ACTING under Chapter VII of the Charter,

1. DEMANDS that Iraq comply fully with resolution 660 (1990) and all subsequent relevant resolutions, and decides, while maintaining all its decisions, to allow Iraq one final opportunity, as a pause of goodwill, to do so;

2. AUTHORIZES Member States co-operating with the Government of Kuwait, unless Iraq on or before 15 January fully implements, as set forth in paragraph 1 above, the foregoing resolutions, to use all necessary means to uphold and implement resolution 660 (1990) and all subsequent relevant resolutions and to restore international peace and security in the area;

3. REQUESTS all States to provide appropriate support for the actions undertaken in pursuance of paragraph 2 of the present resolution;

4. REQUESTS the States concerned to keep the Security Council regularly informed on the progress of actions undertaken pursuant to paragraphs 2 and 3 of the present resolution;

5. DECIDES to remain seized of the matter.

———

1. *Impact of U.N. Treaty on U.S. War Powers?* Although the Security Council resolution authorizes member states "to use all necessary means to uphold and implement resolution 660," Professor Thomas Franck argued that the only use of force properly authorized by the resolution was a U.N.-sponsored police action. In his view, an actual declaration of war against Iraq by a member state would not only have exceeded the terms of the resolution, but would have violated the U.N. Charter's ban on the use of military aggression to settle grievances. Thomas M. Franck, *Declare War? Congress Can't*, N.Y. Times, Dec. 11, 1990, at A27. Whether the United States is engaged in a police action or "war" may have important domestic legal consequences, as *The Prize Cases* and *Youngstown* would suggest. Moreover, acceptance of Professor Franck's argument would presumably limit the objectives that member states could have lawfully pursued in deploying force against Iraq. Is his view persuasive?

2. *Further Reading.* For positive and negative views, respectively, of the legitimacy of Resolution 678 and the diplomacy that provoked it, see Eugene V. Rostow, *Until What? Enforcement Action or Collective Self-Defense*, 85 Am. J. Int'l L. 506 (1991),

and Burns H. Weston, *Security Council Resolution 678 and Persian Gulf Decision Making: Precarious Legitimacy*, 85 Am. J. Int'l L. 516 (1991).c. Congress Acts (and the President Responds)

For whatever reason—whether out of concern for principle, or to strengthen its hand politically, or because it believed it would solidify the war effort, or because it was sure of victory—the executive ultimately acquiesced in a congressional debate over proposed legislation to authorize the offensive use of military force in the Persian Gulf. Congress subsequently enacted the following statute, the first military authorization of its kind since World War II:

Authorization for Use of Military Force Against Iraq Resolution
Public Law 102-01, 105 Stat. 3 (Jan. 14, 1991)

Whereas the Government of Iraq without provocation invaded and occupied the territory of Kuwait on August 2, 1990;

Whereas both the House of Representatives (in H.J. Res. 658 of the 101st Congress) and the Senate (in S. Con. Res. 147 of the 101st Congress) have condemned Iraq's invasion of Kuwait and declared their support for international action to reverse Iraq's aggression;

Whereas, Iraq's conventional, chemical, biological, and nuclear weapons and ballistic missile programs and its demonstrated willingness to use weapons of mass destruction pose a grave threat to world peace;

Whereas the international community has demanded that Iraq withdraw unconditionally and immediately from Kuwait and that Kuwait's independence and legitimate government be restored;

Whereas the United Nations Security Council repeatedly affirmed the inherent right of individual or collective self-defense in response to the armed attack by Iraq against Kuwait in accordance with Article 51 of the United Nations Charter;

Whereas, in the absence of full compliance by Iraq with its resolutions, the United Nations Security Council in Resolution 678 has authorized member states of the United Nations to use all necessary means, after January 15, 1991, to uphold and implement all relevant Security Council resolutions and to restore international peace and security in the area; and Whereas Iraq has persisted in its illegal occupation of, and brutal aggression against Kuwait:

Now, therefore, be it Resolved by the Senate and House of Representatives of the United States of America in Congress assembled, . . .

SEC. 2. AUTHORIZATION FOR USE OF UNITED STATES ARMED FORCES.

(a) AUTHORIZATION.—The President is authorized, subject to subsection (b), to use United States Armed Forces pursuant to United Nations Security Council Resolution 678 (1990) in order to achieve implementation of Security Council Resolutions 660, 661, 662, 664, 665, 666, 667, 669, 670, 674, and 677.

(b) REQUIREMENT FOR DETERMINATION THAT USE OF MILITARY FORCE IS NECESSARY.—Before exercising the authority granted in subsection (a), the President shall make available to the Speaker of the House of Representatives and the President pro tempore of the Senate his determination that—

(1) the United States has used all appropriate diplomatic and other peaceful means to obtain compliance by Iraq with the United Nations Security Council resolutions cited in subsection (a); and

(2) that those efforts have not been and would not be successful in obtaining such compliance.

(c) WAR POWERS RESOLUTION REQUIREMENTS.—

(1) SPECIFIC STATUTORY AUTHORIZATION.—Consistent with section 8(a)(1) of the War Powers Resolution, the Congress declares that this section is intended to constitute specific statutory authorization within the meaning of section 5(b) of the War Powers Resolution.

(2) APPLICABILITY OF OTHER REQUIREMENTS.—Nothing in this resolution supersedes any requirement of the War Powers Resolution.

SEC. 3. REPORTS TO CONGRESS.

At least once every 60 days, the President shall submit to the Congress a summary on the status of efforts to obtain compliance by Iraq with the resolutions adopted by the United Nations Security Council in response to Iraq's aggression.

———————

Statement on Signing the Resolution Authorizing the Use of Military Force Against Iraq

27 Weekly Comp. Pres. Doc. 48 (Jan. 14, 1991)

Today I am signing H.J. Res. 77, the "Authorization for Use of Military Force Against Iraq Resolution." By passing H.J. Res. 77, the Congress of the United States has expressed its approval of the use of U.S. Armed Forces consistent with U.N. Security Council Resolution 678. I asked the Congress to support implementation of U.N. Security Council Resolution 678 because such action would send the clearest possible message to Saddam Hussein that he must withdraw from Kuwait without condition or delay. I am grateful to those of both political parties who joined in the expression of resolve embodied in this resolution. To all, I emphasize again my conviction that this resolution provides the best hope for peace.

The debate on H.J. Res. 77 reflects the profound strength of our constitutional democracy. In coming to grips with the issues at stake in the Gulf, both Houses of Congress acted in the finest traditions of our country. This resolution provides unmistakable support for the international community's determination that Iraq's ongoing aggression against, and occupation of, Kuwait shall not stand. As I made clear to congressional leaders at the outset, my request for congressional support did not, and my signing this resolution does not, constitute any change in the long-standing positions of the executive branch on either the President's constitutional authority to use the Armed Forces to defend vital U.S. interests or the constitutionality of the War Powers Resolution. I am pleased, however, that differences on these issues between the President and many in the Congress have not prevented us from uniting in a common objective. I have had the benefit of extensive and meaningful consultations with the Congress throughout this crisis, and I shall continue to consult closely with the Congress in the days ahead.

George Bush
The White House, January 14, 1991.

1. *A New (or Old) "Separation of Powers" Order?* Do you interpret the foregoing as a victory for Congress in asserting its military authority and, in particular, in reasserting the legitimacy of the War Powers Resolution? Why or why not?

2. *Statutes v. Declaration of War.* Is statutory authorization of the sort enacted on January 14, 1991 an improvement over a formal declaration of war? *See* J. Gregory Sidak, *To Declare War*, 41 Duke L.J. 27 (1991), and Harold H. Koh, *The Coase Theorem and the War Power: A Response*, 41 Duke L.J. 122 (1991).d. The Conduct of the War

The diplomatic and military history of the Persian Gulf War defy quick summary. The United States commenced an air offensive against Iraq on January 17, 1991. Although Iraq possessed one of the world's largest armies and apprehension was great concerning the possible use of chemical and biological weapons, Iraqi military commanders accepted the cease-fire terms of the U.S.-led coalition forces on March 3, 1991. The coalition had sustained only a handful of casualties, while civilian and military casualties in Iraq numbered in the thousands.

The conduct of the war raised numerous issues. Although many applauded the Administration's efforts on its own terms, some observers continued to believe that economic sanctions could have achieved any proper U.S. objectives vis-a-vis Iraqi aggression. Others thought that military force was appropriate, but should have been deployed for objectives broader than the liberation of Kuwait, including the overthrow of Iraqi president Saddam Hussein and independence for the much-beleaguered Iraqi Kurdish population. Although the war was unique in terms of the round-the-clock television coverage made available to U.S. viewers, many journalists argued that the news was unconstitutionally suppressed through excessive restrictions on press access and prepublication review. *See* Note, *Assessing the Constitutionality of Press Restrictions in the Persian Gulf War*, 44 Stan. L. Rev. 675 (1992). The Bush Administration also faced questions whether inept U.S. diplomacy had imprudently strengthened Iraq and encouraged its invasion of Kuwait, and whether the armed services had purposely published false reports concerning the performance of high-priced military hardware during the war. For helpful background and contesting assessments of the U.S. position, see *Symposium on International Law and the Rules of War: The Crisis Over Kuwait*, 1991 Duke J. Comp. & Int'l L. 1; *Gulf War Legal and*

Diplomatic Documents, 13 Hous. J. Int'l L. 281 (1991); and the numerous books reviewed in Theodore Draper, "The Gulf War Reconsidered," N.Y. Rev. of Books, Jan. 16, 1992, at 46, and, Theodore Draper, "The True History of the Gulf War," N.Y. Rev. of Books, Jan. 30, 1992, at 38.

In terms of assessing the interaction between the President and Congress, the controversies over the proper objectives of the war pose difficult questions. By restricting its express objective to the liberation of Kuwait, the United States was able to engage Iraq as the leader of a multinational coalition with the United Nations imprimatur. If the President had determined to press on until the overthrow of Saddam Hussein, would he have needed further congressional authorization? Would his overstepping the bounds of Security Council Resolution 678 have raised compelling problems in defending the legality of the war? For Congress, does the quick success of the U.S.-led military effort portend likely legislative willingness in the future to "stampede to approve the next war that comes along," or will "the heady smell of accountability . . . prove so sweet . . . that [Members] will be moved to reclaim their constitutional prerogatives even when they are not essentially forced to?" John H. Ely, *Kuwait, the Constitution, and the Courts: Two Cheers for Judge Greene*, 8 Const. Comm. 1, 7–8 (1991).

2. The Iraq Invasion of 2003

On March 20, 2003, a U.S. military strike on a target south of Baghdad initiated the first "preemptive war" in American history, a campaign, that is, to attack "another nation so as to prevent or mitigate a presumed *military* attack or use of force by that nation against the United States." Richard F. Grimmett, U.S. Use of Preemptive Military Force (Congressional Research Service No. RS21311, 2003), available at http://www.dtic.mil/dtic/tr/fulltext/u2/a463017.pdf. As summarized seven months earlier by Congressional Research Service National Defense Specialist Richard Grimmett:

> The historical record indicates that the United States has never, to date, engaged in a "preemptive" military attack against another nation. Nor has the United States ever attacked another nation militarily *prior* to its first having been attacked or *prior* to U.S. citizens or interests first having been attacked, with the singular exception of the Spanish-American War. The Spanish-American War is unique in that the principal goal of United States military action was to compel Spain to grant Cuba its political independence. An act of Congress passed just prior to the U.S. declaration of war against Spain explicitly declared Cuba to be independent of Spain, demanded that Spain withdraw its military forces from the island, and authorized the President to use U.S. military force to achieve these ends. Spain rejected these demands, and an exchange of declarations of war by both countries soon followed. Various instances of the use of force . . . could, using a less stringent definition, be argued by some as historic examples of "preemption" by

the United States. The . . . Cuban Missile crisis of 1962, represents a threat situation which some may argue had elements more parallel to those presented by Iraq today–but it was resolved without a "preemptive" military attack by the United States.

The circumstances surrounding the origins of the Mexican War are somewhat controversial in nature–but the term "preemptive" attack by the United States does not apply to this conflict. During, and immediately following the First World War, the United States, as part of allied military operations, sent military forces into parts of Russia to protect its interests, and to render limited aid to anti-Bolshevik forces during the Russian civil war. In major military actions since the Second World War, the President has either obtained Congressional authorization for use of military force against other nations, in advance of using it, or has directed military actions abroad on his own initiative in support of multinational operations such as those of the United Nations or of mutual security arrangements like the North Atlantic Treaty Organization (NATO). Examples of these actions include participation in the Korean War, the 1990–1991 Persian Gulf War, and the Bosnian and Kosovo operations in the 1990s. Yet in all of these varied instances of the use of military force by the United States, such military action was a "response," *after the fact*, and was not "preemptive" in nature.

Id. at 2–3.

How the United States reached this point is a complex tale, many of the details of which are currently either unknown or under strenuous debate. At first blush, however, the questions that would appear interesting to a separation of powers specialist might well seem to have been settled by the Authorization for Use of Military Force Against Iraq Resolution of 2002, Pub.L. No. 107-243, 116 Stat. 1498, enacted by Congress on October 16, 2002. That resolution, reprinted below, provides that the President "is authorized to use the Armed Forces of the United States as he determines to be necessary and appropriate in order to — (1) defend the national security of the United States against the continuing threat posed by Iraq; and (2) enforce all relevant United Nations Security Council resolutions regarding Iraq." § 3, reprinted note following 50 U.S.C. § 1541. One might have thought that such a resolution would have settled the key constitutional questions attending the Iraq War.

The issues presented, however, are considerable. First, as detailed below, debate persists about the legality of the Iraq invasion under international law. This raises the question whether the Constitution authorizes Congress to declare wars in violation of international norms. Second, the resolution raises important nondelegation questions: May Congress delegate to the President the power to launch a massive military attack on a wholly preemptive basis without abdicating its Article I authority? Or, for that matter, did the President, as a constitutional matter, need Congress's 2002 resolution in order to support his invasion of Iraq? Fourth, should it appear that significant errors in intelligence gathering affected the American decision to go to war, how may Congress investigate mistakes or abuses in light of executive privilege? What forms of executive accountability are consistent with a proper reading of Article II?

a. From the Persian Gulf War to the 2003 Invasion

Following the first Persian Gulf War, on April 3, 1991, the United Nations Security Council adopted Resolution 687. That resolution not only reaffirmed the inviolability of Kuwait's borders, but required Iraq (1) to destroy, remove, or render harmless all of its chemical and biological weapons and all ballistic missiles with a range greater than 150 kilometers and related major parts, and (2) to agree unconditionally "not to acquire or develop nuclear weapons or nuclear-weapons-usable material or any subsystems or components or any [related] research, development, support or manufacturing facilities." The resolution provided further for a program of international supervision to insure that the provisions regarding weapons of mass destruction (WMD) would be implemented.

Although Saddam Hussein claimed to comply, the United Nations accused Iraq of cheating throughout the 1990s. Escalating tensions over his lack of cooperation resulted in the withdrawal of UN weapons inspectors in December 1998 and four days of air and missile strikes by the United States and Britain to punish his recalcitrance. *See* Arms Control Association, Iraq: A Chronology of UN Inspections And an Assessment of Their Accomplishments, 1990–2002, available at http://www.armscontrol.org/act/2002_10/iraqspecialoct02.asp?print. The attack prompted months of additional debate on the Security Council, which, early in 1999, authorized a formal review of UN policy toward Iraq, including the status of Iraq's disarmament. As recounted by the Arms Control Association, a US "NGO" (non-governmental organization) devoted to arms control issues, "The panel charged with assessing Iraq's disarmament reports at the end of March [1999] that 'the bulk of Iraq's proscribed weapons programmes has been eliminated,' but it also notes that 'important elements still have to be resolved.'"

The Security Council divided over how best to respond to this assessment, especially given claims by Iraq that it had fully complied with Resolution 687 and was entitled to a lifting of all sanctions before it would permit any return of UN weapons inspectors. While the United States and Britain continued to insist that full disarmament would have to precede a lifting of sanctions, China, France and Russia argued that sanctions should be eased in light of the Iraqi compliance to date. On December 17, 1999, the Security Council passed Resolution 1284, creating a new UN Monitoring, Verification, and Inspection Commission (UNMOVIC), erasing limits on the amount of oil Iraq can sell under the oil-for-food program and holding out "the possibility that sanctions could be suspended for 120-day increments if Iraq cooperates with the new UN team, which is to be given unconditional and unrestricted access." *Id.* Iraq refused, however, to comply with this resolution.

When George W. Bush assumed the Presidency in 2001, matters between Iraq and the UN stood very much at a stalemate. Weapons inspections had not resumed (other than a routine inspection by the International Atomic Energy Agency in 2000). The United States and Britain led an effort in the Security Council to revise the sanctions process to focus more on military goods, and less on civilian goods. This initiative was intended to recognize some measure of compliance by Iraq, without relaxing pressure to resume the WMD inspection program.

At this point, the precise relationship between particular events and the path towards war becomes more difficult to specify. Although the Administration began seriously to make its case for war against Iraq only in 2002, there are indications that "regime change" was an earlier Administration goal. In a 2004 authorized biography of President Bush's first Treasury Secretary Paul O'Neill, Ronald Suskind attributes to O'Neill the observation that, as early as an January 30, 2001 National Security Council meeting, "Rumsfeld, Cheney and Wolfowitz . . . were already planning the next war in Iraq and the shape of a post-Saddam country." RON SUSKIND, THE PRICE OF LOYALTY: GEORGE W. BUSH, THE WHITE HOUSE, AND THE EDUCATION OF PAUL O'NEILL 96 (2004). At a meeting of National Security Council "principals" on February 1, 2001 — still less than two weeks into the new Administration — Secretary of Defense Donald Rumsfeld had already begun speaking of how to accomplish the goal of "going after Saddam" and "freeing the Iraqi people." *Id.* at 85. Paul Wolfowitz, who, as Undersecretary of Defense for Policy in 1991, had opposed the decision of President George H.W. Bush to withdraw from Iraq while Saddam remained in power, was now Deputy Secretary of Defense. He had co-signed a 1998 letter to President Clinton already advocating Saddam's ouster as an aim of American foreign policy. Letter of Elliot Abrams, *et al.* to President William J. Clinton re: American Policy on Iraq (January 28, 1998), available at http://www.newamericancentury .org/iraqclintonletter.htm. When terrorist attacks on September 11, 2001 riveted American attention to the Mideast, members of the Administration began linking Saddam to Al Qaeda, although, as of March, 2004, it was still the view of the Central Intelligence Agency that no such link could be confirmed. Douglas Jehl, *C.I.A. Chief Says He's Corrected Cheney Privately*, N.Y. TIMES, Mar. 10, 2004, at 1. BOB WOODWARD, PLAN OF ATTACK (2004), verifies these assertions.

The United States campaign to intensify pressure on Iraq began in earnest with President Bush's January, 2002 State of the Union Address, at which he referred to Iraq, along with Iran and North Korea, as part of an "axis of evil." The Administration's policy for Iraq, and its rationale, received varying elaborations. On April 4, 2002, President Bush said, "I made up my mind that Saddam needs to go . . . The policy of my Government is that he goes. . . ." On August 1, he reaffirmed that his goal was "regime change." The need for regime change was variously defended on the grounds that Iraq was not complying with United Nations Security Council resolutions, that Saddam had tried to assassinate then-former President George H.W. Bush, and that Saddam had inflicted brutality on the Iraqi people, especially its Shiite and Kurdish populations. In October, 2002, however, President Bush said that Hussein could remain in power by complying with all UN mandates. If he did so, according to the President, "that in itself will signal the regime has changed." Louis

Fisher, *Deciding on War Against Iraq: Institutional Failures*, 118 Pol. Sci. Q. 389, 393 (2003).

The United States appeared to move closer to war, when President Bush, in September, 2002, issued a new National Security Strategy (NSS) of the United States of America, available at http://www.whitehouse.gov/nsc/nss.pdf. Under the goal, "Prevent Our Enemies from Threatening Us, Our Allies, and Our Friends with Weapons of Mass Destruction," the NSS declared that preemptive military action would be a legitimate tool of protecting American security:

> For centuries, international law recognized that nations need not suffer an attack before they can lawfully take action to defend themselves against forces that present an imminent danger of attack. Legal scholars and international jurists often conditioned the legitimacy of preemption on the existence of an imminent threat — most often a visible mobilization of armies, navies, and air forces preparing to attack.
>
> We must adapt the concept of imminent threat to the capabilities and objectives of today's adversaries. Rogue states and terrorists do not seek to attack us using conventional means. They know such attacks would fail. Instead, they rely on acts of terror and, potentially, the use of weapons of mass destruction — weapons that can be easily concealed, delivered covertly, and used without warning.
>
> The targets of these attacks are our military forces and our civilian population, in direct violation of one of the principal norms of the law of warfare. As was demonstrated by the losses on September 11, 2001, mass civilian casualties is the specific objective of terrorists and these losses would be exponentially more severe if terrorists acquired and used weapons of mass destruction.
>
> The United States has long maintained the option of preemptive actions to counter a sufficient threat to our national security. The greater the threat, the greater is the risk of inaction — and the more compelling the case for taking anticipatory action to defend ourselves, even if uncertainty remains as to the time and place of the enemy's attack. To forestall or prevent such hostile acts by our adversaries, the United States will, if necessary, act preemptively. . . .
>
> The purpose of our actions will always be to eliminate a specific threat to the United States or our allies and friends.

Id. at 15–16.

Although the NSS made clear the Administration's obvious contemplation of preemptive military action against Iraq, the Administration seemed to change tacks. In a September 12, 2002 speech to the United Nations, President Bush offered the prospect of a peaceful resolution if, among other things, Iraq immediately and unconditionally pledged to remove or destroy all of its WMD. Iraq announced four days later that it would allow arms inspectors to return "without conditions," but asked for a meeting to discuss final arrangements. The United States accused Saddam of stalling, and urged the Security Council to approve a new resolution authorizing the use of force if Iraq did not disarm.

At the same time, urging that Iraq posed an immediate threat to the United States, Bush sought a congressional resolution that would also authorize the use of force against Iraq should it fail to comply with the demands for disarmament. As indicated above, Congress enacted the Authorization for Use of Military Force Against Iraq Resolution of 2002 on October 16, 2002. The Security Council also achieved consensus around a new resolution, Resolution 1441, which it adopted on November 8. The resolution insisted that "Iraq shall provide UNMOVIC and the IAEA immediate, unimpeded, unconditional, and unrestricted access to any and all, including underground, areas, facilities, buildings, equipment, records, and means of transport which they wish to inspect," and "recall[ed]" "that the Council has repeatedly warned Iraq that it will face serious consequences as a result of its continued violations of its obligations."

As a consequence, Iraq finally readmitted UN inspectors for the first time since 1998 on November 27, 2002, and two weeks later delivered a lengthy declaration to the United Nations purporting to account for its weapons programs, and denying the current possession of WMD. The United States rejected the declaration as incomplete and untruthful. After three months of continuing diplomatic pressure, the United States, Britain and Spain proposed on March 7, 2003 that Saddam give up Iraq's banned weapons by March 17 or face war. It had become evident, however, that the United States could not secure an agreement on the Security Council to pass any further resolution that would authorize military action explicitly. On March 17, the United States and its two allies declared that the time for diplomacy had passed, that they were withdrawing their proposal for an additional UN resolution, and that Saddam had 48 hours to leave Iraq. Iraq rejected this ultimatum on March 18, while also offering unlimited access for American and British weapons inspectors. "[P]rivately Iraq went well beyond this. In several back-channel contacts with U.S. officials, Iraq offered the U.S. 'direct U.S. involvement on the ground in disarming Iraq,' oil concessions, the turn-over of a wanted terrorist, cooperation on the Israeli-Palestinian peace-process, and even internationally-supervised elections within two years." James Risen, *Iraq Said to Have Tried to Reach Last-Minute Deal to Avert War*, N.Y TIMES, Nov. 6, 2003.

The United States commenced its military strike against Iraq on March 20 and entered Baghdad on April 9. The aftermath of this invasion is covered in Chapter Seven.

b. Constitutional War Powers and International Law

It is conventional contemporary understanding that customary international law does not limit, for domestic purposes, the constitutional authorities of the President or Congress. Whether that understanding is faithful to the original Constitution has, however, been challenged. For a thorough review, see Jules Lobel, *The Limits of Constitutional Power: Conflicts Between Foreign Policy and International Law*, 71 Va. L. Rev. 1071 (1985).

The issue is significant because of arguments whether the United Nations Security Council's Iraq resolutions were sufficient to authorize the U.S. attack and whether, if not, the United States acted in violation of constitutional law. Consider the following brief readings:

David Ackerman, International Law and the Preemptive Use of Force Against Iraq

Congressional Research Service Report No. RS21314, at 6 (2003)

[I]n both theory and practice the preemptive use of force appears to have a home in current international law; but its boundaries are not wholly determinate. Its clearest legal foundation is in Chapter VII of the UN Charter. Under Article 39 the Security Council has the authority to determine the existence not only of breaches of the peace or acts of aggression that have already occurred but also of threats to the peace; and under Article 42 it has the authority to "take such action by air, sea, or land forces as may be necessary to maintain or restore international peace and security." These authorities clearly seem to encompass the possibility of the preemptive use of force. As a consequence, the preemptive use of force by the United States against Iraq or any other sovereign nation pursuant to an appropriate authorization by the Security Council would seem to be consonant with international law. Less clear is whether international law currently allows the preemptive use of force by a nation or group of nations without Security Council authorization. That would seem to be permissible only if Article 51 is not read literally but expansively to preserve as lawful the use of force in self-defense as traditionally allowed in customary international law. As noted, the construction of Article 51 remains a matter of debate. But so construed, Article 51 would not preclude the preemptive use of force by the U.S. against Iraq or other sovereign nations. To be lawful, however, such uses of force would need to meet the traditional requirements of necessity and proportionality.

If customary international law governing the preemptive use of force does remain valid, a primary difficulty still remains of determining what situations meet the test of necessity. . . . [T]hat requirement is most easily met when an armed attack is clearly imminent, as in the case of the Arab-Israeli War of 1967. But beyond such obvious situations, as Abram Chayes argued, the judgment of necessity becomes increasingly subjective; and there is at present no consensus either in theory or practice about whether the possession or development of weapons of mass destruction by a rogue state justifies the preemptive use of force. Most analysts recognize that if overwhelmingly lethal weaponry is possessed by a nation willing to use that weaponry directly or through surrogates, some kind of anticipatory self-defense may be a matter of national survival; and many contend that international law ought, if it does not already do so, to allow for the preemptive use of force in that situation. But many states and analysts are decidedly reluctant to legitimate the preemptive use of force even in that situation on the grounds the justification can easily be abused. Moreover, it remains a fact that the international community judged Israel's destruction of Iraq's nuclear reactor site in 1981 to be an aggressive act rather than an act of self-defense. An attack on Iraq, if done apart from authorization by the Security Council, likely will give the international community a renewed opportunity to determine whether traditional international law regarding preemption still applies or whether it ought to be reformulated.

UN Resolution 687. The case under international law for the legality of invading Iraq was stated succinctly in Ruth Wedgwood, *Legal Authority Exists for a Strike on Iraq,* FIN. TIMES, Mar. 14, 2003, at 19. According to Professor Wedgwood, Iraq was, as of mid-March, 2003, still in violation of the 1991 United Nations Resolution 687, which required "that Iraq give up its weapons of mass destruction and permit verification." Not only was Iraq's acquiescence to this requirement a condition of the ceasefire in the Persian Gulf War, but an earlier resolution, Resolution 678, authorized the use of force in support of all "subsequent relevant resolutions" needed to restore regional peace and security. In her judgment, force was necessary because neither economic sanctions, nor the perpetual maintenance of an armed force to sustain the authority of the weapons inspectors was a viable option. The following essay, which appeared on-line in November, 2002, responds to the central points in the Wedgwood analysis:

Mary Ellen O'Connell, *UN Resolution 1441: Compelling Saddam, Restraining Bush*

http://jurist.law.pitt.edu/forum/forumnew73.php

. . . Before Resolution 1441, some in the Bush Administration had maintained that the US could launch a major invasion of Iraq to change the regime without Security Council authorization. They either argued that the US had the authority under existing Security Council resolutions on Iraq, or, in a dramatic departure from 55 years of legal doctrine, some argued the US has the right to use force against Iraq to preempt potential future threats. Both arguments lacked foundation. Any basis they might have had has been largely undercut by Resolution 1441.

The first argument, that the Council has authorized force in prior resolutions, has three versions. Supporters of the first version acknowledge that no prior resolutions on Iraq provides explicit authorization for using armed force, but they nevertheless find implicit authority. The argument is that the ceasefire resolution, 687 (1991), and subsequent resolutions all tie back to the one resolution, 678 (1990), which did explicitly authorize the use of force to oust Iraq from Kuwait and establish peace in the region. Further, members of the Security Council for about a year after the adoption of the ceasefire resolution apparently acquiesced in the interpretation that it implied authority to do more than liberate Kuwait. Few protested the creation of the Kurdish protection zone in northern Iraq or in using force to establish no fly zones in northern and southern sectors of the country. So while Resolution 687 paragraph 34 explicitly reserves to the UN Security Council the decision to take any measures against Iraq beyond sanctions, using force in the no-fly zones is arguably permissible.

On the other hand, members of the Security Council have not acquiesced in using force in connection with Iraqi weapons inspections. The ceasefire resolution declares that sanctions will remain on Iraq until inspectors certify it is free of weapons of mass destruction. The debate since 1991 has been about lifting or leaving the sanctions, not whether states should be able to use military force to rid Iraq of weapons of mass destruction and the means to produce them.

When the US and UK carried out bombing in Iraq in connection with weapons inspections during Operation Desert Fox in December 1998, that use of force was heavily condemned. No acquiescence has occurred to allow force for enforcing weapons inspections, and certainly none has developed to authorize ousting Saddam Hussein.

This conclusion was underscored when President Bush acknowledged as much in his speech to the UN on September 12. He said the US would pursue the *necessary* resolutions in the Security Council, meaning that new resolutions, authorizing force, would be necessary before the US or any other country could carry out lawful enforcement action in respect to any Iraqi weapons of mass destruction.

Resolution 1441 provides no new authorization for using force. It states in paragraph 12 that a meeting of the Security Council will be the first step upon a report by inspectors that Iraq has obstructed their activities. Consequences will follow a meeting. Syria has confirmed that it received a letter from US Secretary of State Colin Powell "in which he stressed that there is nothing in the resolution to allow it to be used as a pretext to launch a war on Iraq." Thus, if and when a meeting is called, Security Council members will have an opportunity to state their assessment of whether serious consequences are called for *or not*.

Yet, if the Council is silent on consequences or even decides affirmatively not to use force, the US and UK may try to argue that once a meeting has been held they are free to act, that holding the meeting is all that is required. The resolution does not state explicitly that results of the meeting will determine future action. The US has stated repeatedly it will use force in Iraq. President Bush said to the UN on September 12: "If Iraq's regime defies us again, the world must move deliberately, decisively, to hold Iraq to account." The US made this position clear throughout the negotiations of Resolutions 1441 and can point to the fact that Resolution 1441, unlike the ceasefire resolution (687), does not explicitly state it will be for the Security Council to decide on measures to take in response Iraqi non-compliance. Other members of the Security Council, however, have consistently taken the position that the Security Council must decide on consequences. That position tracks both the explicit terms of the United Nations Charter and the general law, discussed further below. As it stands, none of the Security Council resolutions authorize the US or UK to use force to enforce Iraq's obligations to rid itself of weapons of mass destruction, including Resolution 1441.

One of the vaguer passages of Resolution 1441 is related to the controversy over implicit authorization. As discussed above, the US and UK generally assert the right to use force in the no-fly zones on the basis of implied authorization. US Secretary of Defense Donald Rumsfeld has suggested that Iraqi firing on US planes policing the no-fly zones could be part of a "pattern of behavior" that might be taken to the Security Council. Paragraph 8 of Resolution 1441 may or may not support his view. It states: "Iraq shall not take or threaten hostile acts directed against any representative or personnel of the United Nations or the IAEA or of any member State taking action to uphold any Council resolution. . . ." Since Council resolutions do not establish the no-fly zones, some will argue that the US and UK flights are not upholding any Council resolution. Secretary Rumsfeld sees it differently.

The second version of the argument that prior Security Council resolutions authorize force centers on the "material breach" argument. This argument apparently originated in the UK, but US officials have also mentioned it in recent months. Blair government officials argue that the ceasefire resolution and subsequent resolutions are like any other international agreement. In the case of material breach of a multilateral treaty, in some cases, all the parties may respond, including, where appropriate, by coercive countermeasures.

This is indeed a curious argument. Its main concept "material breach" has made its way into Resolution 1441. The problem is that "material breach" never was a viable basis for using force against Iraq. Security Council resolutions are not like treaties or other agreements reached through negotiations aimed at achieving consensus. Rather, Security Council resolutions are mandates upon parties and must be respected with or without their consent. They are enforced, modified, or terminated by the Security Council, not by states in general. Neither the explicit terms of the UN Charter nor the practice of the Security Council supports any other interpretation. Under the UN Charter, states may only use force in individual or collective self-defense in the face of an armed attack or with the authorization of the Security Council when the Council finds a threat or breach of international peace. Thus, without Security Council authorization, states do not have the right to use force to enforce the Council's resolutions, whether a breach is material or immaterial. The Security Council's history with respect to its resolutions on Iraq make clear that it has not relinquished to the US the right to enforce its resolutions unilaterally.

The concept of material breach, therefore, provides no independent basis for the US or UK to invade Iraq. The concept is, however, now part of Resolution 1441. As noted above, paragraph 1 of the resolution states that in the Security Council's view Iraq is already in material breach, and in paragraph 4 the Council:

> *Decides* that false statements or omissions in the declarations submitted by Iraq pursuant to this resolution and failure by Iraq at any time to comply with, and cooperate fully in the implementation of, this resolution shall constitute a further material breach of Iraq's obligations and will be reported to the Council for assessment in accordance with paragraphs 11 and 12 below. . . .

Paragraph 11 requires the reporting of *any* interference with inspection activities and paragraph 12 contains the Security Council's decision to convene immediately upon receipt of a report. Hans Blix, the chief UN weapons inspector, has said a delay of as little as 30 minutes in allowing access will result in a report, as will four flat tires, though not one flat tire.

But then it will be for the Security Council to decide the consequences. Under the international law governing enforcement, all coercive measures are limited by the principles of necessity and proportionality, including those mandated by the Security Council itself. Consequences should be commensurate with the nature of the breach. To this extent the "materiality" of the breach is not as important as finding a remedy that fits the wrong. It will be for Security Council members to calibrate response to any failure to comply. Thus, if the inspectors report even minor obstruction by Iraq, the Security Council should not necessarily authorize major military force.

The third version of the argument that authority existed to invade before the adoption of Resolution 1441 is promoted by the UK alone and not supported by the Bush Administration. The British argue that some of their uses of force against Iraq following the Gulf War are justified as humanitarian intervention. They argue that the doctrine of humanitarian intervention could also support force against Iraq for regime change. The argument is difficult to sustain. To the extent force has been used in Iraq until 1999, the UK has tended to argue it had implied authority. Humanitarianism alone surfaced after Kosovo. To date, no government is on record as recognizing a crystallized rule permitting the use of force to pursue humanitarian aims. Certainly, the United States does not support such a rule.

In addition to pre-existing authority, we also hear that the some in the Bush Administration espouse the right of preemptive self-defense. They believe that this doctrine would support invading Iraq regardless of what the Security Council says or even of what Iraq does to comply. The doctrine of preemptive force has been described in the new National Security Strategy, in Secretary Rumsfeld's August report, and in President Bush's June speech at West Point. It purports to allow the United States to use military force against a perceived threat or even to prevent threats from developing. They see Iraq as posing just such a future threat.

As already explained, international law restricts the right to use military force unilaterally to cases of self-defense against an armed attack. Once an attack is underway or will be imminently, the victim nation can use force, provided that the force is proportional and necessary. In cases of threat that lack the objective evidence of an armed attack, either under way or imminent, the defender needs Security Council authorization to use significant military force.

In conclusion, Resolution 1441 is designed to ensure that Saddam Hussein does not have weapons of mass destruction nor the capability to produce them. If applied reasonably by the Security Council, consistently with principles of international law, it is possible for Saddam to comply. To that extent, the resolution is not a cynical exercise to provide legal cover for a US invasion. Indeed, it requires restraint on the part of the US, too. The resolution weakens US arguments of authority to use force under prior resolutions, in the face of material breach or to pre-empt threats. However, Resolution 1441 does open the door for Security Council authorized action, including force, should Saddam fail to comply in good faith.

c. The Necessity and Scope of Congressional Authorization

If international law, for domestic purposes, does not limit the war powers of the respective branches, then the key legal questions presented by the Iraq War were (a) whether the President needed legislative authority to launch the war, and (b), if so, whether Congress adequately provided such authority. Despite its initial insistence that the President had authority to launch a preemptive attack without further congressional authorization, President Bush successfully campaigned for an authorizing resolution in early fall, 2002. The text of that resolution, and the decision resolving a legal challenge to its constitutionality follow:

Authorization for Use of Military Force Against Iraq Resolution of 2002

Public Law No. 107-243, 116 Stat 1498.

JOINT RESOLUTION to authorize the use of United States Armed Forces against Iraq.

Whereas in 1990 in response to Iraq's war of aggression against and illegal occupation of Kuwait, the United States forged a coalition of nations to liberate Kuwait and its people in order to defend the national security of the United States and enforce United Nations Security Council resolutions relating to Iraq;

Whereas after the liberation of Kuwait in 1991, Iraq entered into a United Nations sponsored cease-fire agreement pursuant to which Iraq unequivocally agreed, among other things, to eliminate its nuclear, biological, and chemical weapons programs and the means to deliver and develop them, and to end its support for international terrorism;

Whereas the efforts of international weapons inspectors, United States intelligence agencies, and Iraqi defectors led to the discovery that Iraq had large stockpiles of chemical weapons and a large scale biological weapons program, and that Iraq had an advanced nuclear weapons development program that was much closer to producing a nuclear weapon than intelligence reporting had previously indicated;

Whereas Iraq, in direct and flagrant violation of the cease-fire, attempted to thwart the efforts of weapons inspectors to identify and destroy Iraq's weapons of mass destruction stockpiles and development capabilities, which finally resulted in the withdrawal of inspectors from Iraq on October 31, 1998;

Whereas in Public Law 105-235 (August 14, 1998), Congress concluded that Iraq's continuing weapons of mass destruction programs threatened vital United States interests and international peace and security, declared Iraq to be in "material and unacceptable breach of its international obligations" and urged the President "to take appropriate action, in accordance with the Constitution and relevant laws of the United States, to bring Iraq into compliance with its international obligations";

Whereas Iraq both poses a continuing threat to the national security of the United States and international peace and security in the Persian Gulf region and remains in material and unacceptable breach of its international obligations by, among other things, continuing to possess and develop a significant chemical and biological weapons capability, actively seeking a nuclear weapons capability, and supporting and harboring terrorist organizations;

Whereas Iraq persists in violating resolution of the United Nations Security Council by continuing to engage in brutal repression of its civilian population thereby threatening international peace and security in the region, by refusing to release, repatriate, or account for non-Iraqi citizens wrongfully detained by Iraq, including an American serviceman, and by failing to return property wrongfully seized by Iraq from Kuwait;

Whereas the current Iraqi regime has demonstrated its capability and willingness to use weapons of mass destruction against other nations and its own people;

Whereas the current Iraqi regime has demonstrated its continuing hostility toward, and willingness to attack, the United States, including by attempting in 1993 to assassinate former President Bush and by firing on many thousands of occasions on United States and Coalition Armed Forces engaged in enforcing the resolutions of the United Nations Security Council;

Whereas members of al Qaeda, an organization bearing responsibility for attacks on the United States, its citizens, and interests, including the attacks that occurred on September 11, 2001, are known to be in Iraq;

Whereas Iraq continues to aid and harbor other international terrorist organizations, including organizations that threaten the lives and safety of United States citizens;

Whereas the attacks on the United States of September 11, 2001, underscored the gravity of the threat posed by the acquisition of weapons of mass destruction by international terrorist organizations;

Whereas Iraq's demonstrated capability and willingness to use weapons of mass destruction, the risk that the current Iraqi regime will either employ those weapons to launch a surprise attack against the United States or its Armed Forces or provide them to international terrorists who would do so, and the extreme magnitude of harm that would result to the United States and its citizens from such an attack, combine to justify action by the United States to defend itself;

Whereas United Nations Security Council Resolution 678 (1990) authorizes the use of all necessary means to enforce United Nations Security Council Resolution 660 (1990) and subsequent relevant resolutions and to compel Iraq to cease certain activities that threaten international peace and security, including the development of weapons of mass destruction and refusal or obstruction of United Nations weapons inspections in violation of United Nations Security Council Resolution 687 (1991), repression of its civilian population in violation of United Nations Security Council Resolution 688 (1991), and threatening its neighbors or United Nations operations in Iraq in violation of United Nations Security Council Resolution 949 (1994);

Whereas in the Authorization for Use of Military Force Against Iraq Resolution (Public Law 102-1), Congress has authorized the President "to use United States Armed Forces pursuant to United Nations Security Council Resolution 678 (1990) in order to achieve implementation of Security Council Resolution 660, 661, 662, 664, 665, 666, 667, 669, 670, 674, and 677";

Whereas in December 1991, Congress expressed its sense that it "supports the use of all necessary means to achieve the goals of United Nations Security Council Resolution 687 as being consistent with the Authorization of Use of Military Force Against Iraq Resolution (Public Law 102-1)," that Iraq's repression of its civilian population violates United Nations Security Council Resolution 688 and "constitutes a continuing threat to the peace, security, and stability of the Persian Gulf region," and that Congress, "supports the use of all necessary means to achieve the goals of United Nations Security Council Resolution 688";

Whereas the Iraq Liberation Act of 1998 (Public Law 105-338) expressed the sense of Congress that it should be the policy of the United States to support efforts to remove from power the current Iraqi regime and promote the emergence of a democratic government to replace that regime;

Whereas on September 12, 2002, President Bush committed the United States to "work with the United Nations Security Council to meet our common challenge" posed by Iraq and to "work for the necessary resolutions," while also making clear that "the Security Council resolutions will be enforced, and the just demands of peace and security will be met, or action will be unavoidable";

Whereas the United States is determined to prosecute the war on terrorism and Iraq's ongoing support for international terrorist groups combined with its development of weapons of mass destruction in direct violation of its obligations under the 1991 cease-fire and other United Nations Security Council resolutions make clear that it is in the national security interests of the United States and in furtherance of the war on terrorism that all relevant United Nations Security Council resolutions be enforced, including through the use of force if necessary;

Whereas Congress has taken steps to pursue vigorously the war on terrorism through the provision of authorities and funding requested by the President to take the necessary actions against international terrorists and terrorist organizations, including those nations, organizations, or persons who planned, authorized, committed, or aided the terrorist attacks that occurred on September 11, 2001, or harbored such persons or organizations;

Whereas the President and Congress are determined to continue to take all appropriate actions against international terrorists and terrorist organizations, including those nations, organizations, or persons who planned, authorized, committed, or aided the terrorist attacks that occurred on September 11, 2001, or harbored such persons or organizations;

Whereas the President has authority under the Constitution to take action in order to deter and prevent acts of international terrorism against the United States, as Congress recognized in the joint resolution on Authorization for Use of Military Force (Public Law 107-40); and

Whereas it is in the national security interests of the United States to restore international peace and security to the Persian Gulf region: Now, therefore, be it, Resolved by the Senate and House of Representatives of the United States of America in Congress assembled,

SECTION 1. SHORT TITLE.

This joint resolution may be cited as the "Authorization for Use of Military Force Against Iraq Resolution of 2002".

SEC. 2. SUPPORT FOR UNITED STATES DIPLOMATIC EFFORTS.

The Congress of the United States supports the efforts by the President to—

(1) strictly enforce through the United Nations Security Council all relevant Security Council resolutions regarding Iraq and encourages him in those efforts; and

(2) obtain prompt and decisive action by the Security Council to ensure that Iraq abandons its strategy of delay, evasion and noncompliance and promptly and strictly complies with all relevant Security Council resolutions regarding Iraq.

SEC. 3. AUTHORIZATION FOR USE OF UNITED STATES ARMED FORCES.

(a) AUTHORIZATION.—The President is authorized to use the Armed Forces of the United States as he determines to be necessary and appropriate in order to—

(1) defend the national security of the United States against the continuing threat posed by Iraq; and

(2) enforce all relevant United Nations Security Council resolutions regarding Iraq.

(b) PRESIDENTIAL DETERMINATION.—In connection with the exercise of the authority granted in subsection (a) to use force the President shall, prior to such exercise or as soon thereafter as may be feasible, but no later than 48 hours after exercising such authority, make available to the Speaker of the House of Representatives and the President pro tempore of the Senate his determination that—

(1) reliance by the United States on further diplomatic or other peaceful means alone either (A) will not adequately protect the national security of the United States against the continuing threat posed by Iraq or (B) is not likely to lead to enforcement of all relevant United Nations Security Council resolutions regarding Iraq; and

(2) acting pursuant to this joint resolution is consistent with the United States and other countries continuing to take the necessary actions against international terrorist and terrorist organizations, including those nations, organizations, or persons who planned, authorized, committed or aided the terrorist attacks that occurred on September 11, 2001.

(c) WAR POWERS RESOLUTION REQUIREMENTS.—

(1) SPECIFIC STATUTORY AUTHORIZATION.—Consistent with section 8(a)(1) of the War Powers Resolution, the Congress declares that this section is intended to constitute specific statutory authorization within the meaning of section 5(b) of the War Powers Resolution.

(2) APPLICABILITY OF OTHER REQUIREMENTS.—Nothing in this joint resolution supersedes any requirement of the War Powers Resolution.

SEC. 4. REPORTS TO CONGRESS.

(a) REPORTS.—The President shall, at least once every 60 days, submit to the Congress a report on matters relevant to this joint resolution, including actions taken pursuant to the exercise of authority granted in section 3 and the status of planning for efforts that are expected to be required after such actions are completed, including those actions described in section 7 of the Iraq Liberation Act of 1998 (Public Law 105-338).

(b) SINGLE CONSOLIDATED REPORT.—To the extent that the submission of any report described in subsection (a) coincides with the submission of any other report on matters relevant to this joint resolution otherwise required to be submitted to Congress pursuant to the reporting requirements of the War Powers Resolution (Public Law 93-148), all such reports may be submitted as a single consolidated report to the Congress.

(c) RULE OF CONSTRUCTION.—To the extent that the information required by section 3 of the Authorization for Use of Military Force Against Iraq Resolution (Public Law 102-1) is included in the report required by this section, such report shall be considered as meeting the requirements of section 3 of such resolution.

Approved October 16, 2002.

Doe v. Bush

323 F.3d 133 (1st Cir. 2003).

Before LYNCH, Circuit Judge, CYR and STAHL, Senior Circuit Judges.

LYNCH, Circuit Judge.

Plaintiffs are active-duty members of the military, parents of military personnel, and members of the U.S. House of Representatives. They filed a complaint in district court seeking a preliminary injunction to prevent the defendants, President George W. Bush and Secretary of Defense Donald Rumsfeld, from initiating a war against Iraq. They assert that such an action would violate the Constitution. The district court dismissed the suit, and plaintiffs appeal. We affirm the dismissal.

In October 2002, Congress passed the Authorization for Use of Military Force Against Iraq Resolution of 2002 (the "October Resolution"), Pub L. No. 107-243, 116 Stat. 1498. Plaintiffs argue that the October Resolution is constitutionally inadequate to authorize the military offensive that defendants are now planning against Iraq. *See* U.S. Const. art. I, § 8, cl. 11 (granting Congress the power "[t]o declare war"). They base this argument on two theories. They argue that Congress and the President are in collision—that the President is about to act in violation of the October Resolution. They also argue that Congress and the President are in collusion—that Congress has handed over to the President its exclusive power to declare war.

In either case, plaintiffs argue, judicial intervention is necessary to preserve the principle of separation of powers which undergirds our constitutional structure. Only the judiciary, they argue, has the constitutionally assigned role and the institutional competence to police the boundaries of the constitutional mandates given to the other branches: Congress alone has the authority to declare war and the President alone has the authority to make war.

The plaintiffs argue that important and increasingly vital interests are served by the requirement that it be Congress which decides whether to declare war. Quoting Thomas Jefferson, they argue that congressional involvement will slow the "dogs of war"; that Congress, the voice of the people, should make this momentous decision, one which will cost lives; and that congressional support is needed to ensure that the country is behind the war, a key element in any victory. They also argue that, absent an attack on this country or our allies, congressional involvement must come prior to war, because once war has started, Congress is in an uncomfortable default position where the use of its appropriations powers to cut short any war is an inadequate remedy.

The defendants are equally eloquent about the impropriety of judicial intrusion into the "extraordinarily delicate foreign affairs and military calculus, one that could be fatally upset by judicial interference." Such intervention would be all the worse here, defendants say, because Congress and the President are in accord as to the threat to the nation and the legitimacy of a military response to that threat.

The case before us is a somber and weighty one. We have considered these important concerns carefully, and we have concluded that the circumstances call for judicial restraint. The theory of collision between the legislative and executive branches is not suitable for judicial review, because there is not a ripe dispute concerning the President's acts and the requirements of the October Resolution passed by Congress. By contrast, the theory of collusion, by its nature, assumes no conflict between the political branches, but rather a willing abdication of congressional power to an emboldened and enlarged presidency. That theory is not fit for judicial review for a different, but related, reason: Plaintiffs' claim that Congress and the President have transgressed the boundaries of their shared war powers, as demarcated by the Constitution, is presently insufficient to present a justiciable issue. Common to both is our assessment that, before courts adjudicate a case involving the war powers allocated to the two political branches, they must be presented with a case or controversy that clearly raises the specter of undermining the constitutional structure.

I.

* * * * *

On September 12, 2002, President Bush addressed the United Nations General Assembly. There he called for a renewed effort to demand Iraqi disarmament and indicated that he thought military force would be necessary if diplomacy continued to fail. In response, Iraq agreed to allow inspectors back into the country, but it has failed to comply fully with the earlier Security Council resolutions.

The week after his September 12 speech at the United Nations, President Bush proposed language for a congressional resolution supporting the use of force against Iraq. Detailed and lengthy negotiations between and among congressional leaders and the Administration hammered out a revised and much narrower version of the resolution. The House of Representatives passed this measure by a vote of 296 to 133 on October 10, 2002; the Senate followed suit on October 11 by a vote of 77 to 23. . . .

On November 8, 2002, the Security Council passed Resolution 1441, which declared that Iraq remained in material breach of its obligations and offered "a final opportunity to comply with its disarmament obligations." S.C. Res. 1441, U.N. SCOR, 57th Sess., 4644th mtg., U.N. Doc. S/RES/1441 (2002). It also noted that "the Council has repeatedly warned Iraq that it will face serious consequences as a result of its continued violations of its obligations." *Id.* In diplomatic parlance, the phrase "serious consequences" generally refers to military action. More than 200,000 United States troops are now deployed around Iraq, preparing for the possibility of an invasion.

The complaint was filed, along with motions for preliminary injunction and expedited hearing, on February 13, 2003. The district court heard oral argument on February 24 and denied the motion in an order issued that day. The court released a more detailed written opinion on February 27. *See Doe v. Bush,* 240 F. Supp. 2d 95 (D.Mass.2003). Plaintiffs appealed and this court expedited consideration, hearing oral argument on March 4, 2003 and receiving additional briefing on March 11. Because the case was dismissed on a pretrial motion, we independently review the claims afresh.

II.

The Constitution reserves the war powers to the legislative and executive branches. This court has declined the invitation to become involved in such matters once before. Over thirty years ago, the First Circuit addressed a war powers case challenging the constitutionality of the Vietnam War on the basis that Congress had not declared war. *Massachusetts v. Laird,* 451 F.2d 26 (1st Cir. 1971). The court found that other actions by Congress, such as continued appropriations to fund the war over the course of six years, *id.* at 34, provided enough indication of congressional approval to put the question beyond the reach of judicial review:

> The war in Vietnam is a product of the jointly supportive actions of the two branches to whom the congeries of the war powers have been committed. Because the branches are not in opposition, there is no necessity of deter-mining boundaries. Should either branch be opposed to the continuance of hostilities, however, and present the issue in clear terms, a court might well take a different view. This question we do not face.

Id. Applying this precedent to the case at hand today, the district court concluded, "[T]here is a day to day fluidity in the situation that does not amount to resolute con-flict between the branches — but that does argue against an uninformed judicial intervention," *Doe,* 240 F. Supp. 2d at 96.

The lack of a fully developed dispute between the two elected branches, and the consequent lack of a clearly defined issue, is exactly the type of concern which causes courts to find a case unripe. In his concurring opinion in *Goldwater v. Carter,* 444 U.S. 996 (1979), Justice Powell stated that courts should decline, on ripeness grounds, to decide "issues affecting the allocation of power between the President and Con-gress until the political branches reach a constitutional impasse." *Id.* at 997 (Powell, J., concurring). A number of courts have adopted Justice Powell's ripeness reasoning in cases involving military powers.

Ripeness doctrine involves more than simply the timing of the case. It mixes vari-ous mutually reinforcing constitutional and prudential considerations. One such consideration is the need "to prevent the courts, through avoidance of premature adjudication, from entangling themselves in abstract disagreements." *Abbott Labs. v. Gardner,* 387 U.S. 136, 148 (1967). Another is to avoid unnecessary constitutional decisions. A third is the recognition that, by waiting until a case is fully developed before deciding it, courts benefit from a focus sharpened by particular facts. The case before us raises all three of these concerns.

[margin note: if Branches ∅ in opposition, ∅ necessity to determine boundaries]

[margin note: here they lack a fully developed dispute + a clearly defined issue]

These rationales spring, in part, from the recognition that the scope of judicial power is bounded by the Constitution. "It is a principle of first importance that the federal courts are courts of limited jurisdiction." C.A. Wright & M.K. Kane, *Law of Federal Courts* 27 (6th ed.2002). Article III of the Constitution limits jurisdiction to "cases" and "controversies," and prudential doctrines may counsel additional restraint.

The ripeness of a dispute is determined de novo.... Two factors are used to evaluate ripeness: "the fitness of the issues for judicial decision and the hardship to the parties of withholding court consideration." *Abbott Labs.,* 387 U.S. at 149. Ordinarily, both factors must be present.

The hardship prong of this test is most likely satisfied here; the current mobilization already imposes difficulties on the plaintiff soldiers and family members, so that they suffer "present injury from a future contemplated event." Plaintiffs also lack a realistic opportunity to secure comparable relief by bringing the action at a later time.

The fitness inquiry here presents a greater obstacle. Fitness "typically involves subsidiary queries concerning finality, definiteness, and the extent to which resolution of the challenge depends upon facts that may not yet be sufficiently developed." *Ernst & Young,* 45 F.3d at 535. The baseline question is whether allowing more time for development of events would "significantly advance our ability to deal with the legal issues presented [or] aid us in their resolution." "[T]he question of fitness does not pivot solely on whether a court is capable of resolving a claim intelligently, but also involves an assessment of whether it is appropriate for the court to undertake the task." These prudential considerations are particularly strong in this case, which presents a politically-charged controversy involving momentous issues, both substantively (war and peace) and constitutionally (the powers of coequal branches).

One thrust of the plaintiffs' argument is that the October Resolution only permits actions sanctioned by the Security Council. In plaintiffs' view, the Resolution's authorization is so narrow that, even with Security Council approval of military force, Congress would need to pass a new resolution before United States participation in an attack on Iraq would be constitutional. At a minimum, according to plaintiffs, the October Resolution authorizes no military action "outside of a United Nations coalition."

For various reasons, this issue is not fit now for judicial review. For example, should there be an attack, Congress may take some action immediately. The purported conflict between the political branches may disappear. "[T]hat the future event may never come to pass augurs against a finding of fitness." *McInnis-Misenor,* 319 F.3d at 72.

Many important questions remain unanswered about whether there will be a war, and, if so, under what conditions. Diplomatic negotiations, in particular, fluctuate daily. The President has emphasized repeatedly that hostilities still may be averted if Iraq takes certain actions. The Security Council is now debating the possibility of passing a new resolution that sets a final deadline for Iraqi compliance. United Nations weapons inspectors continue their investigations inside Iraq. Other countries ranging from Canada to Cameroon have reportedly pursued their own proposals to broker a compromise. As events unfold, it may become clear that diplomacy has either succeeded or failed decisively. The Security Council, now divided on the issue, may reach a consensus. To evaluate this claim now, the court would need to pile one hypothesis on top of another. We would need to assume that the Security Council will not authorize war, and that the President will proceed nonetheless. *See id.* at 72–73 (outlining chain of uncertain events necessary to make case ripe); *Ernst & Young,* 45 F.3d at 538 (same).

Thus, even assuming that plaintiffs correctly interpret the commands of the legislative branch, it is impossible to say yet whether or not those commands will be obeyed. As was the situation in *Goldwater,* "[i]n the present posture of this case, we do not know whether there will ever be an actual confrontation between the Legislative and Executive Branches." 444 U.S. at 998 (Powell, J., concurring).

Our analysis is based on ripeness rather than the political question doctrine. The political question doctrine — that courts should not intervene in questions that are the province of the legislative and executive branches — is a famously murky one. It has also been used fairly infrequently to block judicial review. The modern definition of the doctrine was established in the landmark case of *Baker v. Carr,* 369 U.S. 186 (1962). In the forty years since that case, the Supreme Court has found a case nonjusticiable on the basis of the political question doctrine only twice. *See Nixon v. United States,* 506 U.S. 224, 236 (1993) (Senate procedures for impeachment of a federal judge); *Gilligan v. Morgan,* 413 U.S. 1, 12 (1973) (training, weaponry, and orders of Ohio National Guard). Our court has been similarly sparing in its reliance on the political question doctrine.

Ultimately, however, the classification matters less than the principle. If courts may ever decide whether military action contravenes congressional authority, they surely cannot do so unless and until the available facts make it possible to define the issues with clarity.

III.

Plaintiffs' collusion theory presents different concerns. We understand plaintiffs to make two distinct arguments as to why an attack under the October Resolution would be unlawful. The first argument, discussed above, is that the October Resolution placed conditions on the President's authority to order action in Iraq, and that he is preparing to disregard those conditions.

The other argument, our focus now, is that the October Resolution delegates excessive authority to the President, rendering it constitutionally inadequate as a vehicle for Congress to "declare war."[10]

---

10. The plaintiffs appropriately disavow the formalistic notion that Congress only authorizes military deployments if it states, "We declare war." This has never been the practice and it was not the understanding of the founders. *See* J.H. Ely, *War and Responsibility* 25–26 (1993). Congressional authorization for military action has often been found in the passage of resolutions that lacked

According to this second argument, the Constitution deliberately vested power to declare war in the legislative branch as a necessary check on the power of the executive branch, and Congress is not free to upset this careful balance by giving power to the President. This claim of collusion does not align precisely with the test that the political branches have yet to reach a "constitutional impasse"; the claim is that the branches have *agreed* to an unconstitutional transfer of the "war declaration" powers from Congress to the President. Some initial review of the merits of the claim is "inherent when the constitutional issue is posed in terms of scope of authority." *Laird,* 451 F.2d at 33–34.

The Supreme Court has been willing to adjudicate other cases concerning the distribution of constitutional authority between the legislative and executive branches, notwithstanding the call for restraint embodied in the political question doctrine. Sometimes it rejects the application of the political question doctrine explicitly. *See, e.g., United States v. Munoz-Flores,* 495 U.S. 385, 389–96 (1990); *Immigration & Naturalization Serv. v. Chadha,* 462 U.S. 919, 942–43 (1983). Other times the Court has merely proceeded to the merits without explicitly rejecting the political question doctrine. *See, e.g., Clinton,* 524 U.S. at 421; *Morrison v. Olson,* 487 U.S. 654 (1988); *cf. Bush v. Gore,* 531 U.S. 98, 112 (2000) (Rehnquist, C.J., concurring) (considering separation of powers between state legislature and state judiciary under U.S. Const. art. II, § 1, cl. 2).

The Supreme Court has recognized a role for judicial review of these types of separation of powers claims even when Congress appears to have agreed to the challenged arrangement. In *Clinton v. City of New York, supra,* a claim was brought by citizens deprived of the benefits of an appropriation that the President cancelled under the procedures in the Line Item Veto Act, 2 U.S.C. §§ 691–692 (2000). These citizens argued that Congress had unconstitutionally delegated to the President its authority under the Presentment Clause, U.S. Const. art. I, § 7, cl. 2. The Court reviewed the constitutionality of the Act despite apparent support for it from both of the other branches, which had jointly enacted the statute and used its procedures.

In some ways, the claims made by plaintiffs here parallel those made in *Clinton:* that the Constitution vested power in the legislative branch as a necessary check on the power of the executive branch, and that Congress is not free to upset the careful balance by giving power to the executive. *See* 524 U.S. at 452 (Kennedy, J., concurring) ("That a congressional cession of power is voluntary does not make it innocuous. . . . Abdication of responsibility is not part of the constitutional design."); *cf. New York v. United States,* 505 U.S. 144, 182 (1992) ("The Constitution's division of power among the three branches is violated where one branch invades the territory of another, whether or not the encroached-upon branch approves the encroachment.").

---

these "magic words," or in continued enactments of appropriations or extensions of the draft which were aimed at waging a particular war.

There are also, however, significant differences between *Clinton* and the case before us. For one, in *Clinton* the President had fully exercised the power that was at issue, which "removed any concern" about ripeness. 524 U.S. at 430. For another, the Line Item Veto Act contained specific provisions, accepted by both Congress and the President when they enacted the law, which not only permitted judicial review of the statute's validity but created a special expedited process for it. There was less danger of courts invading the province of these other branches, because specific statutory authority directed them to consider the case. A third difference is the scale of the purported delegation. The Line Item Veto Act gave the President wide discretion to cancel items of discretionary budget authority, direct spending, or limited tax benefits. 2 U.S.C. §691(a). The determinations required of the President in the October Resolution are much more narrowly focused.

[handwritten margin note: line item veto was different it contained provisions permitting judicial review]

Perhaps the most important difference is the shared nature of the powers in question here. The Constitution explicitly divides the various war powers between the political branches. To the Congress goes the power to "declare war," U.S. Const. art. 1, §8, cl. 11; to "raise and support armies" through appropriations of up to two years, cl. 12; to "provide and maintain a navy," cl. 13; and to "make rules for the government and regulation of the land and naval forces," cl. 14. The President's role as commander-in-chief is one of the few executive powers enumerated by the Constitution. U.S. Const. art. II, §2, cl. 1.

Given this "amalgam of powers," the Constitution overall "envisages the *joint* participation of the Congress and the executive in determining the scale and duration of hostilities." *Laird,* 451 F.2d at 31–32 (emphasis added). "The great ordinances of the Constitution do not establish and divide fields of black and white." *Youngstown Sheet & Tube Co. v. Sawyer,* 343 U.S. 579, 597 (1952) (Frankfurter, J., concurring) (quoting *Springer v. Philippine Islands,* 277 U.S. 189, 209, 48 S.Ct. 480, 72 L.Ed. 845 (1928) (Holmes, J., dissenting)). Rather, there is sometimes a "zone of twilight in which [the President] and Congress may have concurrent authority, or in which its distribution is uncertain. . . . In this area, any actual test of power is likely to depend on the imperatives of events and contemporary imponderables rather than on abstract theories of law." *Youngstown,* 343 U.S. at 637 (Jackson, J., concurring).

[handwritten margin note: They should consider war jointly]

In this zone of shared congressional and presidential responsibility, courts should intervene only when the dispute is clearly framed. An extreme case might arise, for example, if Congress gave absolute discretion to the President to start a war at his or her will. Plaintiffs' objection to the October Resolution does not, of course, involve any such claim. Nor does it involve a situation where the President acts without any apparent congressional authorization, or against congressional opposition.

[handwritten margin note: legislative + executive are in conflict here]

The mere fact that the October Resolution grants some discretion to the President fails to raise a sufficiently clear constitutional issue. The plaintiffs argue that Congress is constitutionally forbidden from deciding that certain conditions are necessary to lead to war and then yielding to the President the authority to make the determination of whether those conditions exist.[12] The President, in this view, has power to make such determinations only in the context of repelling sudden attacks on this country or its allies. The Supreme Court recently and forcefully reiterated that, notwithstanding the Constitution's vesting of "*all* legislative power" in Congress, U.S. Const. art. I, § 1 (emphasis added), enactments which leave discretion to the executive branch are permissible as long as they offer some "intelligible principle" to guide that discretion. War powers, in contrast to "*all* legislative power," are shared between the political branches. Furthermore, the Supreme Court has also suggested that the nondelegation doctrine has even less applicability to foreign affairs. The reference to nondelegation is thus of little help to plaintiffs in trying to present the type of serious issue necessary to overcome judicial restraint in the adjudication of war powers cases.

Nor is there clear evidence of congressional abandonment of the authority to declare war to the President. To the contrary, Congress has been deeply involved in significant debate, activity, and authorization connected to our relations with Iraq for over a decade, under three different presidents of both major political parties, and during periods when each party has controlled Congress. It has enacted several relevant pieces of legislation expressing support for an aggressive posture toward Iraq, including authorization of the prior war against Iraq and of military assistance for groups that would overthrow Saddam Hussein. It has also accepted continued American participation in military activities in and around Iraq, including flight patrols and missile strikes. Finally, the text of the October Resolution itself spells out justifications for a war and frames itself as an "authorization" of such a war.

It is true that "courts possess power to review either legislative or executive action that transgresses identifiable textual limits" on constitutional power. Questions about the structure of congressional power can be justiciable under the proper circumstances. But courts are rightly hesitant to second-guess the form or means by which the coequal political branches choose to exercise their textually committed constitutional powers. As the circumstances presented here do not warrant judicial intervention, the appropriate recourse for those who oppose war with Iraq lies with the political branches.

Dismissal of the complaint is *affirmed*.

———————

1. War-Making and the Nondelegation Doctrine. The idea that the nondelegation doctrine might limit the ways in which Congress may authorize presidential

———————

12. Suppose, however, that Congress did pass a law stating simply, "The United States declares war on Iraq." This would still leave to the President all determinations concerning timing, strategy, and tactics; the President would decide both when and how to start an attack and when and how to stop it. It is difficult to see how Congress could be said to shirk its constitutional responsibilities in that scenario.

military deployments obviously depends on two a͟s͟.͟ ͟ needs congressional authorization to deploy U.S. troops in ͟s͟.͟ repulsion of an invasion or its equivalent, and second, that there is a ͟.͟.͟ to draw between statutes that defer appropriately to presidential timing and ta͟.͟.͟ decisions, given his role in foreign affairs, and statutes that would amount to an unconstitutional abdication of the power to declare war. That is, it is not enough to assert that Congress could not constitutionally authorize the President "to declare war, as he may deem appropriate, upon such other nations against whom it would be in the interests of the United States to declare war." For judicial review to be meaningful, there would presumably have to be a way of distinguishing between (a) such a blanket abandonment of Congress's constitutional role and (b) the lesser forms of delegation that Congress may employ. Do you think there is a meaningful role for judicial review to play with regard to war-making and the delegation doctrine?

2. Nondelegation and International Law. The earlier readings by Wedgwood and O'Connell raised the issue whether the Iraq invasion was consistent with international law. As our notes indicated, however, the question whether a military undertaking is consistent with international law is *not* the same question as to whether it is constitutional. But might this raise a nondelegation doctrine concern?

Consider: One could argue, given the seriousness of violating international law in undertaking a particular military deployment, that the President should not be permitted to launch any such undertaking unless Congress's authorization is unambiguous. Such a rule might seem a logical extension of the vesting of authority in Congress, for domestic purposes, "[t]o define ... Offenses against the Law of Nations," Art. I, §8, cl. 10. Do you think such a rule sensible? Do you think such a rule would be susceptible to judicial enforcement?

3. Law and Politics. The invasion of Iraq and its aftermath have crystallized an intense debate over whether the war was a good idea in terms of the interests of the United States. The chart below encapsulates many of the most frequently heard arguments:

The invasion advanced American interests because . . .	The invasion was detrimental to American interests because . . .
The United States is better off without Saddam Hussein in power.	America has suffered significant casualties and will shoulder a huge economic burden in rebuilding Iraq.
The display of American military power has prompted other countries, such as Libya and Iran, to be more cooperative with international rules on WMD.	The invasion has destabilized Iraq and made it a more attractive battleground for foreign terrorists, including Al Qaeda, to operate.

The war has helped cement an alliance between the United States and Pakistan, which aids in the war on terrorism and has created an opportunity for rapprochement between Pakistan and India.	The invasion has weakened America's ties to its traditional allies and committed the U.S. military to a level of involvement that makes it difficult to devote appropriate resources to other international crises.
Removing Saddam has made Iraq less of a threat to Israel, thus laying the groundwork for an eventual resolution of the Israeli-Palestinian conflict.	The invasion has undermined American credibility and influence in the Muslim world.
The invasion strengthens the hand of reformist elements in the Arab world because authoritarian rulers now realize that limits exist to what other nations will tolerate in terms of domestic repression in the Mideast.	Our invasion of Iraq threatens to undermine the credibility of international law as a restraint on the use of state power, even though the United States is a major beneficiary of a robust international law regime.

To the extent the arguments in favor of the war are accurate, does any provide a legal justification for presidential action without prior congressional authorization? To the extent the arguments against the war are accurate, does any weaken the President's case that the invasion was lawful?

d. Interbranch Accountability for Preemptive War-Making and the Separation of Powers

Before the invasion of Iraq, a debate was already brewing about the accuracy of American claims that Iraq posed an imminent danger because of its weapons of mass destruction. In his January, 2003 State of the Union Address, President Bush made the claim that Saddam's government "recently sought significant quantities of Uranium from Africa." The document on which that claim was based, however, turned out to be a fabrication. Louis Fisher, *Deciding on War Against Iraq: Institutional Failures*, 118 POL. SCI. Q. 389, 402 (2003). Although the Administration generally ignored pre-war dissent from the proposition that Iraq continued to have WMD, Dr. David Kay, in January, 2004, resigned as the chief U.S. weapons inspector, having concluded that the United States and other nations were simply wrong on the WMD issue. The Administration had portrayed Saddam Hussein as having links to Al Qaeda, despite the lack of any hard evidence to back the connection. George Tenet, the Director of Central Intelligence, testified before Congress on March 9, 2004, that Vice President Cheney erred in relying on a Defense Department document as providing substantiation for the claim that Al Qaeda had ties with the government of Saddam Hussein. Douglas Jehl, *C.I.A. Chief Says He's Corrected Cheney Privately*, N.Y. TIMES, Mar. 10, 2004, at 1.

The United States was unable to locate WMD in Iraq or to document their existence after the Persian Gulf War. Dr. Kay's congressional testimony helped to ignite a political firestorm, raising questions whether the Administration manipulated intelligence to persuade Congress and the American public to support the invasion on false pretenses. Kay indicated that he did not believe government officials had intentionally misrepresented the facts, and it is unclear whether fault lay with the quality of the underlying intelligence, the ways in which it was shared with key decision makers, or the manner in which the White House responded to the evidence with which it was presented.

President Bush responded on February 6, 2004, by issuing an executive order creating a Commission on the Intelligence Capabilities of the United States Regarding Weapons of Mass Destruction, Exec. Order No. 13,328, 69 Fed. Reg. 6901 (2004). Under Section 5A, "To carry out this order, the Commission shall have full and complete access to information relevant to its mission . . . and in the possession, custody, or control of any executive department or agency to the maximum extent permitted by law and consistent with Executive Order 12958 of April 17, 1995, as amended."

Because each member of the Commission would be a presidential appointee, it was widely assumed that one of the President's aims in creating the new commission was to forestall a wide-ranging inquiry into White House handling of pre-war intelligence by the House and Senate intelligence committees. Helen Fessenden, *Bush Reverses Course on Prewar Intelligence Probe*, Cong. Q. Weekly Rept., Feb. 7, 2004, at 390. Nonetheless, the creation of the commission and the looming prospect of further congressional inquiry raise difficult questions about achieving accountability in this sensitive area. For example, would it be appropriate to withhold from Congress, on grounds of executive privilege, any information that is being shared with the independent commission? Under what conditions, if any, should members of the Administration, including the President and Vice President, be compelled to testify before either Congress or the commission? Recall the controversy over whether National Security Adviser Rice should testify to the 9/11 Commission that we recounted in Chapter Three. Would her testimony in that instance, notwithstanding the accompanying protestations that no precedent was set thereby, affect your judgment here?

3. *War and Political Accountability.* For purposes of domestic law, the 2002 Authorization to Use Military Force in Iraq essentially settled the question whether initiating war in 2003 was lawful. As the war dragged on, however, numerous questions arose concerning the wisdom of the invasion and the competence (or incompetence) with which the U.S. managed post-invasion affairs. Important accounts include Michael R. Gordon and General Bernard E. Trainor, Cobra II: The Inside Story of the Invasion and Occupation Of Iraq (2006); George Packer, The Assassins' Gate: America in Iraq (2006); and Thomas E. Ricks, Fiasco: The American Military Adventure in Iraq (2006). A more personal account by a highly decorated Army officer who is also a distinguished military historian is

Peter R. Mansoor, Baghdad at Sunrise: A Brigade Commander's War in Iraq (2008). Professor Shane's estimation of the Iraq initiative, based largely on the works just cited, is as follows:

America's role in Iraq has been largely defined by four colossal blunders:

1. Basing the invasion on suspicions that Saddam possessed weapons of mass destruction, notwithstanding contrary evidence, the contrary opinion of at least some weapons inspectors, doubts as to the reliability of the key intelligence sources on which we were relying, and Saddam's last minute willingness to allow UN inspectors comprehensive and unconditional access to look for WMD;

2. Invading Iraq with insufficient forces to secure the country after the toppling of Saddam;

3. Toppling Saddam without any plan to rebuild the civilian or military infrastructure of Iraq; and

4. Toppling Saddam without regard to unleashing potential sectarian violence in Iraq, the radicalization of the Muslim populace in other nations, and the inevitable enhancement of the geopolitical position of Iran.

Peter M. Shane, Madison's Nightmare: Executive Power and the Threat to American Democracy 69 (2009). Journalist Joseph Lelyveld has summarized the costs of the Iraq intervention as "more than 4,400 Americans killed in action and 30,000 wounded, many grievously; 100,000 or more Iraqi civilian casualties; several million refugees; and an overall cost to American taxpayers approaching $1 trillion." Joseph Lelyveld, *Curveballs* (Reviewing George W. Bush, Decision Points (2010)), N.Y. Rev. of Books, Jan.13, 2011, at 4. Defenders of the Bush policy argue that toppling Saddam was worth the cost, especially if it leads to the emergence of Iraq as a stable democratic nation.

In light of the serious questions with regard to the wisdom and prosecution of the Iraq war, it is not surprising that contentious issues arose as to appropriate mechanisms for establishing accountability. Consider, for example, the apparent inaccuracy of Administration claims that Iraq posed an imminent danger because of its weapons of mass destruction. In his January, 2003 State of the Union Address, President Bush asserted that Saddam's government "recently sought significant quantities of Uranium from Africa." The document on which that claim was based, however, turned out to be a fabrication. Louis Fisher, *Deciding on War Against Iraq: Institutional Failures*, 118 Pol. Sci. Q. 389, 402 (2003). Although the Administration generally ignored pre-war dissent from the proposition that Iraq continued to have WMD, Dr. David Kay, in January, 2004, resigned as the chief U.S. weapons inspector, having concluded that the United States and other nations were simply wrong on the WMD issue. The Administration had portrayed Saddam Hussein as having links to Al Qaeda, despite the lack of any hard evidence to back the connection. George Tenet, the Director of Central Intelligence, testified before Congress on March 9, 2004, that Vice President Cheney erred in relying on a Defense Department document as providing substantiation for the claim that Al Qaeda had ties with the government of Saddam Hussein. Douglas Jehl, *C.I.A. Chief Says He's Corrected Cheney Privately*, N.Y. TIMES, Mar. 10, 2004, at 1.

President Bush reacted to the apparent intelligence failure regarding WMD by establishing the bipartisan Commission on the Intelligence Capabilities of the United States Regarding Weapons of Mass Destruction discussed in the previous note. The Intelligence Capabilities Commission released its final report on March 31, 2005. COMMISSION ON THE INTELLIGENCE CAPABILITIES OF THE UNITED STATES REGARDING WEAPONS OF MASS DESTRUCTION, REPORT TO THE PRESIDENT OF THE UNITED STATES (2005), available at http://www.gpoaccess.gov/wmd/pdf/full_wmd_report.pdf. In its cover letter, the Commission stressed that it found no intentional wrongdoing by the intelligence community:

> We conclude that the Intelligence Community was dead wrong in almost all of its pre-war judgments about Iraq's weapons of mass destruction. This was a major intelligence failure. Its principal causes were the Intelligence Community's inability to collect good information about Iraq's WMD programs, serious errors in analyzing what information it could gather, and a failure to make clear just how much of its analysis was based on assumptions, rather than good evidence. On a matter of this importance, we simply cannot afford failures of this magnitude.

> After a thorough review, the Commission found no indication that the Intelligence Community distorted the evidence regarding Iraq's weapons of mass destruction. What the intelligence professionals told you about Saddam Hussein's programs was what they believed. They were simply wrong.

The Commission likewise appeared to exonerate the Administration from suspicious that the White House had induced the intelligence failure by demanding, directly or otherwise, a predetermined result. The Commission reported that it "found no evidence of political pressure to influence the Intelligence Community's pre-war assessments of Iraq's weapons programs. . . . [A]nalysts universally asserted that in no instance did political pressure cause them to skew or alter any of their analytical judgments. We conclude that it was the paucity of intelligence and poor analytical tradecraft, rather than political pressure, that produced the inaccurate pre-war intelligence assessments." *Id.* at 50–51. At the same time, the Commission regarded the intelligence process as adversely affected by the pre-existing "conventional wisdom" that Saddam possessed WMD: "Some analysts were affected by this 'conventional wisdom' and the sense that challenges to it—or even refusals to find its confirmation—would not be welcome." *Id.* at 191.

The Commission's report failed to satisfy critics of the war. Because each member of the Commission was a presidential appointee, it was widely assumed when President Bush created the Commission that one of his aims had been to forestall a wider-ranging inquiry into White House handling of pre-war intelligence by congressional committees. Helen Fessenden, *Bush Reverses Course on Prewar Intelligence*

Probe, Cong. Q. Weekly Rept., Feb. 7, 2004, at 390. In June, 2003, the Senate Select Committee on Intelligence had already begun a formal review of U.S. intelligence in the run-up to war. At about the same time, however, as President Bush set up the Intelligence Capabilities Commission, the Senate committee agreed to divide its investigation into two phases. The first, to be pursued immediately would look at:

- the collection of intelligence on Iraq from the end of the Gulf War to the commencement of Operation Iraqi Freedom;
- intelligence activities relating to Iraq conducted by the Policy Counterterrorism Evaluation Group (PCTEG) and the Office of Special Plans within the Office of the Under Secretary of Defense for Policy; and
- and the use by the Intelligence Community of information provided by the Iraqi National Congress (INC).

Senate Select Committee on Intelligence, Report on the U.S. Intelligence Community's Prewar Intelligence Assessments on Iraq, 108th Cong., 2d Sess. 2 (2004). Phase II would continue to focus on the latter two issues, but examine also:

- whether public statements, reports, and testimony regarding Iraq by U.S. Government officials made between the Gulf War period and the commencement of Operation Iraqi Freedom were substantiated by intelligence information;
- the postwar findings about Iraq's weapons of mass destruction and weapons programs and links to terrorism and how they compare with prewar assessments; and
- prewar intelligence assessments about postwar Iraq.

Id.

The committee's July, 2004 Phase I report was severely critical of the intelligence community. Among its other conclusions, the committee found that most major key judgments in a crucial October, 2002 National Intelligence Estimate were either overstated or unsupported by the underlying intelligence reporting, that policymakers were not fully briefed on the uncertainties behind those judgments, that a "group think dynamic" distorted Intelligence Community judgments, that Intelligence Community managers failed to "encourage analysts to challenge their assumptions, fully consider alternative arguments, accurately characterize the intelligence reporting, or counsel analysts who lost their objectivity," and that human intelligence collection efforts regarding WMD were largely inadequate due to "a broken corporate culture and poor management." Nonetheless, it postponed until Phase II, any consideration as to whether the White House had misled Congress or the American people about the justifications for war.

The committee's final report on whether public statements regarding Iraq by executive branch officials were substantiated by intelligence information did not issue until June, 2008. Committee Democrats asserted that Republican Senator Pat Roberts, who chaired the Phase I investigation, had deliberately slowed Phase II efforts; when Democrats took control of the Senate after the 2006 elections, they revived the investigation, with the apparent support of Republican Senators Chuck Hagel and Olympia Snowe. The committee "identified five major policy speeches" made by President Bush, Vice President Cheney, and Secretary of State Colin Powell "during this period as the most significant expressions of how the Bush Administration communicated intelligence judgments to the American people, the United States Congress, and the international community." SENATE SELECT INTELLIGENCE COMMITTEE, REPORT ON WHETHER PUBLIC STATEMENTS REGARDING IRAQ BY U.S. GOVERNMENT OFFICIALS WERE SUBSTANTIATED BY INTELLIGENCE INFORMATION, S. REPT. No. 110-345, 110th Cong., 2d Sess. 90 (2008). The committee also examined speeches by senior Administration officials to the extent they made additional assertions not included in the five key speeches.

On the veracity of the statements, the committee chairman framed his summary with evident care:

> Administration statements prior to the war often reflected the reporting of the Intelligence Community, even when the judgments underlying the reporting were based on flawed analysis or false information. However, senior Administration officials repeatedly spoke in declarative and unequivocal terms about Iraq's weapons of mass destruction programs and support for terrorists. These declarative statements were not substantiated. In the push to rally public support for the invasion of Iraq, Administration officials often failed to accurately portray what was known, what was not known, and what was suspected about Iraq and the threat it represented to our national security.

> The report documents significant instances in which the Administration went beyond what the Intelligence Community knew or believed in making public claims, most notably on the false assertion that Iraq and al-Qaida had an operational partnership and joint involvement in carrying out the attacks of September 11th. The President and his advisors undertook a relentless public campaign in the aftermath of the attacks to use the war against al-Qaida as a justification for overthrowing Saddam Hussein. Representing to the American people that the two had an operational partnership and posed a single, indistinguishable threat was fundamentally misleading and led the Nation to war on false premises.

> The Committee also found instances where a public statement selectively used that intelligence information which supported a particular policy viewpoint while ignoring contradictory information. . . .

> The Administration's misuse of intelligence . . . was aided by the selective declassification of intelligence reporting. . . . The Administration exploited [its] declassification authority . . . , knowing that others attempting to disclose additional details that might provide balance or improve accuracy would be prevented from doing so under threat of prosecution. This unlevel playing field allowed senior officials to disclose and discuss sensitive

intelligence reports when it supported the Administration's policy objectives and keep out of the public discourse information which did not.

Id. at 91–92. Note the lawyerly formulation of "representing" information that was "fundamentally misleading," which, in turn, "led the Nation to war on false premises." What the Chairman is not revealing is whether he regards the Administration as having intentionally lied.

In your judgment, are there lessons to be drawn from this episode about the adequacy of congressional oversight with regard to presidential war making? First, consider the substance of the committee's conclusions. Putting aside the electoral calendar for the moment and, assuming the majority's conclusions are both accurate and accurately described by the chairman, would there have been an appropriate basis for an impeachment investigation? If so, should the House have gone ahead and launched such an investigation with under eight months left before the end of the second Bush Administration? If not, is there anything else Congress could or should have done with regard to establishing responsibility for failing "to accurately portray what was known, what was not known, and what was suspected about Iraq and the threat it represented to our national security?" Was the appropriate accountability mechanism simply the next election cycle? (Note that, just after the Democratic congressional victories in 2006, President Bush dismissed his Secretary of Defense, Donald Rumsfeld, who would have been both partly responsible for making what turned out to be an unsubstantiated case for the invasion, and perhaps chiefly responsible for what Professor Shane characterizes above as "colossal blunders" 2–4.)

Does it strike you that partisan loyalty might result in serious problems with the committee investigation process as a source of executive accountability? Had Democrats controlled the Senate in 2003, is it not likely that the Select Committee on Intelligence would have reached its conclusions in 2006, rather than 2008 — perhaps resulting in even more dramatic results in the 2006 midterms and more serious talk of impeachment? Other nations sometimes try to promote administrative accountability by designating certain legislative committees to be chaired by whatever party does not control the chief executive position. Should the U.S. have such a system? We discuss this and other potential institutional reforms for improving checks and balances in Chapter Seven.

President Bush's Intelligence Capacities Commission did recommend 74 reforms, aimed overall at producing — in the words of the cover letter — "an Intelligence Community that is truly integrated, far more imaginative and willing to run risks, open to a new generation of Americans, and receptive to new technologies." We discuss the operations of the intelligence community and reforms in intelligence oversight more fully in Chapter Five.

4. *Status of Forces Agreement.* Yet another source of controversy surrounding the Iraq War was the unilateral executive agreement President Bush negotiated with the Iraqis in 2008 regarding eventual U.S. withdrawal from Iraq. Formally entitled, an

"Agreement Between the United States of America and the Republic of Iraq On the Withdrawal of United States Forces from Iraq and the Organization of Their Activities during Their Temporary Presence in Iraq," http://graphics8.nytimes.com /packages/pdf/world/20081119_SOFA_FINAL_AGREED_TEXT.pdf, this "status of forces agreement (SOFA)," was one of two agreements—the other called a "strategic framework agreement"—that the Bush Administration concluded in its final months to establish "the principal provisions and requirements that regulate the temporary presence, activities, and withdrawal of the United States Forces from Iraq."

Historically, perhaps the most important function of SOFA's has been to establish the degree to which foreign forces are subject to local law. Under Security Council Resolutions renewed annually from 2003 through 2007, multinational forces, international consultants, and U.S. personnel were immune from the Iraqi legal process. Under Article 8 of the U.S.-Iraq SOFA, Iraq now has "the primary right to exercise jurisdiction over members of the United States Forces and of the civilian component for the grave premeditated felonies . . . , when such crimes are committed outside agreed facilities and areas and outside duty status," as well as "the primary right to exercise jurisdiction over United States contractors and United States contractor employees." The United States retains "the primary right to exercise jurisdiction over members of the United States Forces and of the civilian component for matters arising inside agreed facilities and areas; during duty status outside agreed facilities and areas; and in circumstances not covered" the scope of Iraq's primary rights.

The constitutional issue presented by the U.S.-Iraq SOFA is whether, because of its scope, President Bush could permissibly commit the United States to its provisions without any form of legislative sanction or Senate ratification. For its part, the Iraqi Parliament ratified the agreement on November 27, 2008, but the pact was never submitted for U.S. congressional approval. Yale law professors Bruce Ackerman and Oona Hathaway have argued that the agreement "undermine[d] the constitutional powers of the next president as commander in chief," by determining the scope of Iraqi regulation to which U.S. troops would be subject. Bruce Ackerman and Oona Hathaway, *Bush's Final Illusion*, Slate, Oct. 21, 2008, available at http://www.slate .com/id/2202771/. For example, under Article IV of the SOFA, all U.S. military operations carried out pursuant to the Agreement, other than in self-defense, have to be "conducted with the agreement of the Government of Iraq," and "coordinated with Iraqi authorities," operating through a Joint Military Operations Coordination Committee. According to Ackerman and Hathaway, U.S. troops have previously been subjected to equivalent foreign control only pursuant to treaty. The Bush Administration's response to such criticisms was chiefly that SOFA's had previously been accomplished through unilateral executive agreements, giving ample historical precedent for the U.S.-Iraq agreement. Greg Bruno, *Council on Foreign Relations Backgrounder: U.S. Security Agreements and Iraq*, (Dec. 23, 2008), available at http://www .cfr.org/publication/16448/us_security_agreements_and_iraq.html.

Most political criticism of the SOFA appeared to dissipate upon public release of its final terms when it became clear that (a) the agreement did not purport to create a long-term security obligation for the United States or otherwise to provide the basis for American intervention in Iraq after 2011, and (b) the agreement did not purport to extend legal immunity for private contractors, whose activities in Iraq had proved highly controversial.

As a presidential candidate, then-Senator Barack Obama (like then-Senators Joe Biden and Hillary Clinton) had criticized Bush unilateralism on the SOFA; even as President-elect, he took the position: "Any SOFA should be subject to Congressional review to ensure it has bipartisan support here at home." The Obama-Biden Plan: Iraq, Change.gov, available at http://change.gov/agenda/iraq_agenda/. President Obama, however, neither sought congressional approval for the SOFA, nor explained his decision not to do so. Can you speculate as to his reasons?

Note: Congressional Authority to Regulate How the President Makes War

Recall William Rehnquist's statement, as head of the Office of Legal Counsel, that "Congress undoubtedly has the power in certain situations to restrict the President's power as Commander in Chief to a narrower scope than it would have had in the absence of legislation. . . . This is not to say, however, that every conceivable condition or restriction which Congress may by legislation seek to impose on the use of American military forces would be free of constitutional doubt." 1 Op. O.L.C. Supp. at 333–34. The future Chief Justice did not attempt to define the spheres of presidential and congressional authority in the abstract. Rather, as is the tradition of both the executive and judicial branches, he addressed the issue actually presented by the proposal to pursue Viet Cong into Cambodia.

The conduct of the War in Iraq presented another occasion to consider the scope of the President's power and of Congress's power to regulate the manner in which the President may prosecute an authorized military operation. By the end of 2006, it became clear that the war effort in Iraq was not going well. Indeed, the difficulties with the war effort contributed to the Democrats taking control of Congress at the 2006 midterm elections. Despite the military and electoral setbacks, President George W. Bush decided to order an escalation in our troop commitment. This plan, known as the troop surge, was highly controversial. The new Democratic majority in Congress seriously considered legislation to prohibit the surge. Defenders of the Administration argued that such a move would be unconstitutional:

> The precise line between congressional and presidential authority is sometimes unclear, and no court has jurisdiction to rule on the issue. The analysis, however, is straightforward. When the two political branches exercise their respective constitutional powers in a way that brings them into conflict—a scenario clearly envisioned by the Framers—the relevant constitutional principle is that neither branch can vitiate the ability

of the other to discharge its core constitutional responsibilities. Just as the president cannot raise his own funds (by obtaining loans unauthorized by Congress, for example), the legislature cannot attach conditions to federal spending that would destroy the president's authority to direct the military's tactical and strategic operations. This balance makes perfect sense; if Congress could closely direct how the executive branch spends appropriated funds, it would vitiate the president's core responsibilities as chief executive and commander in chief, transforming him into a cipher. This outcome would fundamentally warp the Framers' entire constitutional fabric. . . .

Although this system may seem unsatisfactory to those who disagree with President Bush's Iraq policy, it has two great virtues. First, it bolsters the Constitution's fundamental design — the separation of powers between the coequal branches of government. The Framers vested executive authority in a president for a reason. As Alexander Hamilton explained in the Federalist Papers: "Energy in the executive is a leading character in the definition of good government. It is essential to the protection of the community against foreign attacks." Second, requiring Congress to exercise its power in dramatic ways ensures political accountability. If Congress believes the war is lost, or not worth winning, it must take responsibility for the consequences of forcing a U.S. withdrawal. Otherwise, it must leave the president to direct the war and to bear responsibility for the decisions he has made and will make.

Lee A. Casey & David B. Rivkin, Jr., *What Congress Can (And Can't) Do on Iraq*, Wash. Post (Jan. 16, 2007).

A group of 23 constitutional law professors wrote congressional leaders expressing a contrary view:

Scholars' Letter to Congressional Leaders on the Proposed Iraq Troop Surge
January 17, 2007

Dear Congressional Leaders:

Since President Bush announced his intention to increase the number of troops deployed in Iraq, Americans have been debating the wisdom of his plan. Some have questioned whether Congress possesses the constitutional authority to affect that plan's implementation. Vital, therefore, to the public debate and to congressional deliberations is a clear understanding of the authority that the Constitution vests in Congress. We write as constitutional scholars to express our view that this authority is more than ample for Congress to give legal effect to its will with respect to the troop increase.

The Constitution's text is quite plain with respect to one mechanism by which Congress might give legal effect to whatever judgment it makes: Congress's spending powers. Congress clearly may cut off funds entirely and bring an armed conflict to an end. It may also take the intermediate step of providing that the President may not use military appropriations to alter the scope or nature of the conflict that Congress has authorized and funded, such as by prohibiting the President from using appropriated funds to increase troop levels or to broaden a conflict into additional nations or territories.

A question of current debate is whether Congress's spending powers provide the only check that Congress holds in the context of ongoing military hostilities. The Constitution confers on Congress the power to declare war, but it also makes the President the Commander in Chief. As Commander in Chief, the President possesses certain interstitial or inherent powers to act in the absence of congressional legislation — for example, to defend the nation even when Congress has not specifically provided authority. But as Justice Jackson famously emphasized in *Youngstown Sheet & Tube Co. v. Sawyer* (the Steel Seizure case), presidential power to act in the absence of congressional action must not be equated with presidential power to ignore statutory restrictions enacted pursuant to Congress's constitutional authorities.

The Constitution expressly grants Congress extensive powers relating to war, beyond the well-known appropriations power and the power to declare war. Specifically, the Constitution authorizes Congress to:

- Lay and collect taxes, duties, imposts and excises, to pay the debts and provide for the common defence and general welfare of the United States;

- Define and punish piracies and felonies committed on the high seas and offenses against the law of nations;

- Declare war, grant letters of marque and reprisal, and make rules concerning captures on land and water;

- Raise and support armies, but no appropriation of money to that use shall be for a longer term than two years;

- Provide and maintain a navy;

- Make rules for the government and regulation of the land and naval forces;

- Provide for calling forth the militia to execute the laws of the union, suppress insurrections and repel invasions;

- Provide for organizing, arming, and disciplining the militia and for governing such part of them as may be employed in the service of the United States, reserving to the states respectively, the appointment of the officers and the authority of training the militia according to the discipline prescribed by Congress;

- Make all laws which shall be necessary and proper for carrying into execution the foregoing powers, and all other powers vested by this Constitution in the Government of the United States or in any department or officer thereof.

These provisions plainly set forth an extensive role for Congress that goes far beyond the initial decision to declare war and subsequent decisions regarding its funding. This mass of war powers confers on Congress an ongoing regulatory authority with respect to the war. Indeed, these powers are so extensive that Chief Justice John Marshall opined (with some exaggeration, when read out of context) that "[t]he whole powers of war [are], by the Constitution of the United States, vested in Congress. . . ."[1] As Commander in Chief, the President's role is to prosecute the war that Congress has authorized within the legitimate parameters Congress sets forth. Congress has exercised precisely this power to define the parameters of armed conflict or war on a number of occasions, some of which concern recent military engagements [citations omitted].

This understanding of Congress's role has also been the consistent interpretation of the courts. Early in our country's history, the Supreme Court set forth this interpretation in a series of cases arising from the naval war with France. The statutory basis for this conflict was a set of authorizations to use force against French maritime interests. These statutes empowered the President to use military force to take specific, limited sorts of actions against French vessels; they identified the places where force could be exercised and the purposes for which force should be employed.

In *Bas v. Tingy*, Justice Samuel Chase explained that these statutes "authori[z]ed hostilities on the high seas by certain persons in certain cases," but did not give the President the authority "to commit hostilities on land; to capture unarmed French vessels, nor even to capture French armed vessels lying in a French port."[2] This meant that Congress had authorized a limited war against France—a war, in the words of Justice Bushrod Washington, "confined in its nature and extent; being limited as to places, persons, and things."[3] In such a war, those "who are authorised to commit hostilities . . . can go no farther than to the extent of their commission."[4]

In *Little v. Barreme*, Chief Justice Marshall held that the President's war powers were subject to valid statutory limitation. This case considered the statute whereby Congress had authorized the U.S. Navy to intercept vessels bound to French ports, but did not authorize the President to intercept ships bound from such ports. In *Little* a U.S. Navy ship, acting pursuant to a presidential order to intercept ships bound to or from French ports, intercepted a commercial vessel suspected of coming *from* a French port. The Supreme Court ruled the action illegal because it went beyond the military force authorized by statute.

The Supreme Court has continued to adhere to this view of the war power. In modern times, the Court has consistently held that the President is bound by statutory restrictions in wartime. In *Youngstown Sheet & Tube*, the Court struck down President Truman's order that the nation's steel mills continue operating in order to keep

---

1. Talbot v. Seeman, 5 U.S. (1 Cranch) 1, 28 (1801).
2. 4 U.S. (4 Dall.) at 43 (opinion of Chase, J.).
3. *Id.* at 40 (opinion of Washington, J.).
4. *Id.*

United States troops in the Korean War armed. Justice Jackson's famous concurring opinion—which the Court has since acknowledged "brings together as much combination of analysis and common sense as there is in this area"[5]—emphasized that the Constitution did not set forth an exclusive power in the Commander in Chief that would permit him to disregard Congress's statutory restrictions on his preferred means of conducting the war.

Most recently, the Supreme Court has applied Justice Jackson's framework to resolve challenges to President Bush's assertions of Commander-in-Chief power. In a number of recent Supreme Court cases, particularly *Rasul v. Bush*, *Hamdi v. Rumsfeld*, and *Hamdan v. Rumsfeld*, the Bush Administration has asserted broad unilateral authority to conduct military operations (in those cases dealing specifically with the detention and treatment of enemy combatants). In none of these cases did the Supreme Court vindicate the Bush Administration's position. Indeed, in each case, the Court required the President to comply with applicable statutory limits.

We recognize the dictum first enunciated by Chief Justice Salmon P. Chase in his concurring opinion in *Ex Parte Milligan*: "The power to make the necessary laws is in Congress; the power to execute in the President. Both powers imply many subordinate and auxiliary powers. Each includes all authorities essential to its due exercise. But neither can the President, in war more than in peace, intrude upon the proper authority of Congress, nor Congress upon the proper authority of the President. Both are servants of the people, whose will is expressed in the fundamental law. Congress cannot direct the conduct of campaigns. . . ."[6] This dictum is sometimes taken to mean that Congress may not enact laws designed to dictate tactical or command decisions. As the point is sometimes put, Congress may not micromanage the President's execution of a war. Wherever one comes down on the outer limits of legislative war powers, *Little v. Barreme* and *Bas v. Tingy* make clear that Congress retains substantial power to define the scope and nature of a military conflict that it has authorized, even where these definitions may limit the operations of troops on the ground. The proposed statutory restrictions relating to the war in Iraq that are the subject of this letter fall well within this long recognized authority.

Thus, Congress may limit the scope of the present Iraq War by either of two mechanisms. First, it may directly define limits on the scope of that war, such as by imposing geographic restrictions or a ceiling on the number of troops assigned to that conflict. Second, it may achieve the same objective by enacting appropriations restrictions that limit the use of appropriated funds. Indeed, the reason that the Constitution explicitly limits appropriations for the Army to two years is in order to ensure that Congress oversees ongoing military engagements.

The Constitution's drafters understood the immense national sacrifice that war entails. Moreover, they understood that during times of war presidential power tends

---

5. *Dames & Moore v. Regan*, 453 U.S. 654, 661 (1981).
6. 4 U.S. (4 Wall.) at 139–140 (Chase, C.J. concurring in the judgment). . . .

to expand. For these reasons, the Constitution assigns Congress the power to initiate war and to fund and define the parameters of military operations. As James Madison wrote, "the constitution supposes what the History of all Gov[ernments] demonstrates, that the Ex[ecutive] is the branch of power most interested in war, & most prone to it. It has accordingly with studied care, vested the question of war in the Legisl[ative branch]."[7] The Constitution's structure, then, clearly contemplates that important decisions regarding the scale of war will not necessarily be made by the President alone, but ideally should, and certainly can, be reached through the democratic process with all the deliberation that entails. Far from an invasion of presidential power, it would be an abdication of its own constitutional role if Congress were to fail to inquire, debate, and legislate, as it sees fit, regarding the best way forward in Iraq.

D. Presidential Wartime Powers Off the Battlefield

1. Civil Liberties

No crisis in U.S. history has more forcefully threatened the Constitution than our civil war, and no war has gone further in testing the limits of presidential emergency powers. *See generally* J.G. RANDALL, CONSTITUTIONAL PROBLEMS UNDER LINCOLN (1963); WILLIAM H. REHNQUIST, ALL THE LAWS BUT ONE: CIVIL LIBERTIES IN WARTIME (2000); DANIEL A. FARBER, LINCOLN'S CONSTITUTION (2003). The most celebrated of Lincoln's invocations of emergency power is the Emancipation Proclamation of January 1, 1863, by which the President purported to free all persons held as slaves in areas still in rebellion within the Confederate states. That proclamation, reprinted in the Appendix, *infra*, rested on Lincoln's power "as commander-in-chief of the army and navy . . . [to employ] a fit and necessary war measure for suppressing . . . rebellion. . . ." 12 Stat. 1268 (1861). Against arguments that the proclamation was an unauthorized taking of private property without just compensation, supporters urged that the rights of belligerents, which belonged to the government under *The Prize Cases, supra,* included the right to free an enemy's slaves. *See generally* RANDALL, *supra,* at 371–404.

Another source of profound controversy was Lincoln's decision in 1861 to suspend "the privilege of the writ of *habeas corpus.*" U.S. Const., art. I, § 9, cl. 2. The legal issue was not whether the privilege could be suspended; the Constitution expressly authorizes suspension "when in cases of rebellion or invasion the public safety may require it." *Id.* The Constitution is silent, however, as to who is empowered to make the determination of necessity and to suspend the privilege. Lincoln's determination

---

7. Letter to Thomas Jefferson (April 2, 1798), in 6 WRITINGS OF JAMES MADISON 312 (Gaillard Hunt, ed. (1900–1910).

to suspend the privilege without prior congressional authorization was an attempt to preclude judicial challenges to military arrests, the trial of civilians before military commissions, and other acts which, if unconstitutional, might have subjected the government or its officers to suits for injunctive or monetary relief. Although Lincoln asked Congress in 1861 to approve the legality of his actions, it was not until 1863 that Congress acted on the subject, passing legislation worded ambiguously as to whether Congress was approving the President's actions or exercising its own suspension powers.[1]

The seriousness of the *habeas corpus* controversy is well illustrated by the case of *Ex Parte Merryman*, 17 F.Cas. 144 (C.C.D. Md. 1861) (No. 9487). Merryman, lieutenant of a secessionist drill company, was among hundreds of persons arrested and placed under Union military custody in the first year of the war. Sitting individually on circuit, Chief Justice Taney issued a writ of *habeas corpus* to the arresting general, which the general, acting on Lincoln's suspension order, refused to honor. When a marshal sought to serve a writ of attachment for contempt against the general, Union soldiers refused him entrance to Fort McHenry. Taney responded: "I have exercised all the power which the constitution and laws confer upon me, but that power has been resisted by a force too strong for me to overcome." 17 F. Cas. at 153. As for the general's outright defiance of his order, Taney indicated he would order the proceedings in the case to be transmitted to Lincoln personally, in the hope that the President might determine that his general misconstrued the President's order: "It will then remain for that high officer, in fulfillment of his constitutional obligation to 'take care that the laws be faithfully executed,' to determine what measures he will take to cause the civil process of the United States to be respected and enforced." *Id.* For a painstaking review of the complex proceedings, see Seth Barrett Tillman, Ex Parte Merryman: *Myth, History, And Scholarship*, 224 MIL. L. REV. 481 (2016)

Intriguingly, the Supreme Court did not address the legal issues surrounding the suspension of *habeas corpus* until after the war's end. Lambdin Milligan had been arrested in 1864 and convicted by a military commission in Indiana of conspiring to release Confederate prisoners and to make war against the United States. The Supreme Court issued the following opinion, notwithstanding the reported uncertainty whether Milligan had been executed as scheduled on May 19, 1865. (According to one source, Milligan not only survived, but sued "successfully" for false imprisonment, recovering an award of five dollars. MARY ANN HARRELL, EQUAL JUSTICE UNDER LAW: THE SUPREME COURT IN AMERICAN LIFE 52 (1994)). See also Curtis A. Bradley, *The Story of* Ex parte Milligan: *Military Trials, Enemy Combatants, and Congressional Authorization*, in PRESIDENTIAL POWER STORIES 93–132 (Christopher H. Schroeder and Curtis A. Bradley, eds., 2009).

---

1. Act of March 3, 1863, 12 Stat. 755.

Ex Parte Milligan

71 U.S. (4 Wall.) 2 (1867)

Justice DAVIS delivered the opinion of the court.

On the 10th day of May, 1865, Lambdin P. Milligan presented a petition to the Circuit Court of the United States for the District of Indiana, to be discharged from an alleged unlawful imprisonment. The case made by the petition is this: Milligan is a citizen of the United States; has lived for twenty years in Indiana; and, at the time of the grievances complained of, was not, and never had been in the military or naval service of the United States. On the 5th day of October, 1864, while at home, he was arrested by order of General Alvin P. Hovey, commanding the military district of Indiana; and has ever since been kept in close confinement.

On the 21st day of October, 1864, he was brought before a military commission, convened at Indianapolis, by order of General Hovey, tried on certain charges and specifications; found guilty, and sentenced to be hanged; and the sentence ordered to be executed on Friday, the 19th day of May, 1865.

On the 2d day of January, 1865, after the proceedings of the military commission were at an end, the Circuit Court of the United States for Indiana met at Indianapolis and empanelled a grand jury, who were charged to inquire whether the laws of the United States had been violated; and, if so, to make presentments. The court adjourned on the 27th day of January, having, prior thereto, discharged from further service the grand jury, who did not find any bill of indictment or make any presentment against Milligan for any offence whatever; and, in fact, since his imprisonment, no bill of indictment has been found or presentment made against him by any grand jury of the United States. Milligan insists that said military commission had no jurisdiction to try him upon the charges preferred, or upon any charges whatever; because he was a citizen of the United States and the State of Indiana, and had not been, since the commencement of the late Rebellion, a resident of any of the States whose citizens were arrayed against the government, and that the right of trial by jury was guaranteed to him by the Constitution of the United States. The prayer of the petition was, that under the act of Congress, approved March 3d, 1863, entitled, "An act relating to *habeas corpus* and regulating judicial proceedings in certain cases," he may be brought before the court, and either turned over to the proper civil tribunal to be proceeded against according to the law of the land or discharged from custody altogether.

With the petition were filed the order for the commission, the charges and specifications, the findings of the court, with the order of the War Department reciting that the sentence was approved by the President of the United States, and directing that it be carried into execution without delay. The petition was presented and filed in open court by the counsel for Milligan; at the same time the District Attorney of the United States for Indiana appeared, and, by the agreement of counsel, the application was submitted to the court. The opinions of the judges of the Circuit Court were opposed on three questions, which are certified to the Supreme Court:

1st. "On the facts stated in said petition and exhibits, ought a writ of *habeas corpus* to be issued?"

2d. "On the facts stated in said petition and exhibits, ought the said Lambdin P. Milligan to be discharged from custody as in said petition prayed?"

3d. "Whether, upon the facts stated in said petition and exhibits, the military commission mentioned therein had jurisdiction legally to try and sentence said Milligan in manner and form as in said petition and exhibits is stated?"

The importance of the main question presented by this record cannot be overstated; for it involves the very framework of the government and the fundamental principles of American liberty. During the late wicked Rebellion, the temper of the times did not allow that calmness in deliberation and discussion so necessary to a correct conclusion of a purely judicial question. *Then*, considerations of safety were mingled with the exercise of power; and feelings and interests prevailed which are happily terminated. *Now* that the public safety is assured, this question, as well as all others, can be discussed and decided without passion or the admixture of any element not required to form a legal judgment. . . .

Milligan claimed his discharge from custody by virtue of the act of Congress "relating to *habeas corpus*, and regulating judicial proceedings in certain cases," approved March 3d, 1863. Did that act confer jurisdiction on the Circuit Court of Indiana to hear this case? . . . This law was passed in a time of great national peril, when our heritage of free government was in danger. An armed rebellion against the national authority, of greater proportions than history affords an example of, was raging; and the public safety required that the privilege of the writ of *habeas corpus* should be suspended. The President had practically suspended it, and detained suspected persons in custody without trial; but his authority to do this was questioned. It was claimed that Congress alone could exercise this power; and that the legislature, and not the President, should judge of the political considerations on which the right to suspend it rested. The privilege of this great writ had never before been withheld from the citizen; and as the exigence of the times demanded immediate action, it was of the highest importance that the lawfulness of the suspension should be fully established. . . . The President was authorized . . . to suspend the privilege of the writ of *habeas corpus*, whenever, in his judgment, the public safety required; and he did, by proclamation, bearing date the 15th of September, 1863, reciting, among other things, the authority of this statute, suspend it. The suspension of the writ does not authorize the arrest of any one, but simply denies to one arrested the privilege of this writ in order to obtain his liberty.

It is proper, therefore, to inquire under what circumstances the courts could rightfully refuse to grant this writ, and when the citizen was at liberty to invoke its aid.

The second and third sections of the law are explicit on these points. . . . The public safety demanded, if the President thought proper to arrest a suspected person, that he should not be required to give the cause of his detention on return to a writ of *habeas corpus*. But it was not contemplated that such person should be detained in custody beyond a certain fixed period, unless certain judicial proceedings, known to the common law, were commenced against him. The Secretaries of State and War were directed to furnish to the judges of the courts of the United States, a list of the names of all parties, not prisoners of war, resident in their respective jurisdictions, who then were or afterwards should be held in custody by the authority of the President, and who were citizens of states in which the administration of the laws in the Federal tribunals was unimpaired. After the list was furnished, if a grand jury of the district convened and adjourned, and did not indict or present one of the persons thus named, he was entitled to his discharge; and it was the duty of the judge of the court to order him brought before him to be discharged, if he desired it. . . .

Milligan, in his application to be released from imprisonment, averred the existence of every fact necessary under the terms of this law to give the Circuit Court of Indiana jurisdiction. . . .

[I]t is said that this case is ended, as the presumption is, that Milligan was hanged in pursuance of the order of the President. Although we have no judicial information on the subject, yet the inference is that he is alive; for otherwise learned counsel would not appear for him and urge this court to decide his case. It can never be in this country of written constitution and laws, with a judicial department to interpret them, that any chief magistrate would be so far forgetful of his duty, as to order the execution of a man who denied the jurisdiction that tried and convicted him; *after* his case was before Federal judges with power to decide it, who, being unable to agree on the grave questions involved, had, according to known law, sent it to the Supreme Court of the United States for decision. But even the suggestion is injurious to the Executive, and we dismiss it from further consideration. . . .

The controlling question in the case is this: Upon the *facts* stated in Milligan's petition, and the exhibits filed, had the military commission mentioned in it *jurisdiction*, legally, to try and sentence him? . . .

Every trial involves the exercise of judicial power; and from what source did the military commission that tried him derive their authority? Certainly no part of judicial power of the country was conferred on them; because the Constitution expressly vests it "in one supreme court and such inferior courts as the Congress may from time to time ordain and establish," and it is not pretended that the commission was a court ordained and established by Congress. They cannot justify on the mandate of the President; because he is controlled by law, and has his appropriate sphere of duty, which is to execute, not to make, the laws; and there is "no unwritten criminal code to which resort can be had as a source of jurisdiction."

But it is said that the jurisdiction is complete under the "laws and usages of war."

It can serve no useful purpose to inquire what those laws and usages are, whence they originated, where found, and on whom they operate; they can never be applied to citizens in states which have upheld the authority of the government, and where the courts are open and their process unobstructed. This court has judicial knowledge that in Indiana the Federal authority was always unopposed, and its courts always open to hear criminal accusations and redress grievances; and no usage of war could sanction a military trial there for any offence whatever of a citizen in civil life, in nowise connected with the military service. Congress could grant no such power; and to the honor of our national legislature be it said, it has never been provoked by the state of the country even to attempt its exercise. One of the plainest constitutional provisions was, therefore, infringed when Milligan was tried by a court not ordained and established by Congress, and not composed of judges appointed during good behavior.

Why was he not delivered to the Circuit Court of Indiana to be proceeded against according to law? No reason of necessity could be urged against it; because Congress had declared penalties against the offences charged, provided for their punishment, and directed that court to hear and determine them. And soon after this military tribunal was ended, the Circuit Court met, peacefully transacted its business, and adjourned. It needed no bayonets to protect it, and required no military aid to execute its judgments. It was held in a state, eminently distinguished for patriotism, by judges commissioned during the Rebellion, who were provided with juries, upright, intelligent, and selected by a marshal appointed by the President. The government had no right to conclude that Milligan, if guilty, would not receive in that court merited punishment; for its records disclose that it was constantly engaged in the trial of similar offences, and was never interrupted in its administration of criminal justice. If it was dangerous, in the distracted condition of affairs, to leave Milligan unrestrained of his liberty, because he "conspired against the government, afforded aid and comfort to rebels, and incited the people to insurrection," the *law* said arrest him, confine him closely, render him powerless to do further mischief; and then present his case to the grand jury of the district, with proofs of his guilt, and, if indicted, try him according to the course of the common law. If this had been done, the Constitution would have been vindicated, the law of 1863 enforced, and the securities for personal liberty preserved and defended.

Another guarantee of freedom was broken when Milligan was denied a trial by jury. The great minds of the country have differed on the correct interpretation to be given to various provisions of the Federal Constitution; and judicial decision has been often invoked to settle their true meaning; but until recently no one ever doubted that the right of trial by jury was fortified in the organic law against the power of attack. . . . *[T]his right* — one of the most valuable in a free country — is preserved to every one accused of crime who is not attached to the army, or navy, or militia in actual service. . . .

The discipline necessary to the efficiency of the army and navy, required other and swifter modes of trial than are furnished by the common law courts; and, in pursuance of the power conferred by the Constitution, Congress has declared the kinds of trial, and the manner in which they shall be conducted, for offences committed while the party is in the military or naval service. Every one connected with these branches of the public service is amenable to the jurisdiction which Congress has created for their government, and, while thus serving, surrenders his right to be tried by the civil courts. *All other persons*, citizens of states where the courts are open, if charged with crime, are guaranteed the inestimable privilege of trial by jury. . . .

It is claimed that martial law covers with its broad mantle the proceedings of this military commission. The proposition is this: that in a time of war the commander of an armed force (if in his opinion the exigencies of the country demand it, and of which he is to judge), has the power, within the lines of his military district, to suspend all civil rights and their remedies, and subject citizens as well as soldiers to the rule of *his will*; and in the exercise of his lawful authority cannot be restrained, except by his superior officer or the President of the United States.

If this position is sound to the extent claimed, then when war exists, foreign or domestic, and the country is subdivided into military departments for mere convenience, the commander of one of them can, if he chooses, within his limits, on the plea of necessity, with the approval of the Executive, substitute military force for and to the exclusion of the laws, and punish all persons, as he thinks right and proper, without fixed or certain rules. The statement of this proposition shows its importance; for, if true, republican government is a failure, and there is an end of liberty regulated by law. Martial law, established on such a basis, destroys every guarantee of the Constitution, and effectually renders the "military independent of and superior to the civil power"—the attempt to do which by the King of Great Britain was deemed by our fathers such an offence, that they assigned it to the world as one of the causes which impelled them to declare their independence. Civil liberty and this kind of martial law cannot endure together; the antagonism is irreconcilable; and, in the conflict, one or the other must perish.

This nation, as experience has proved, cannot always remain at peace, and has no right to expect that it will always have wise and humane rulers, sincerely attached to the principles of the Constitution. Wicked men, ambitious of power, with hatred of liberty and contempt of law, may fill the place once occupied by Washington and Lincoln; and if this right is conceded, and the calamities of war again befall us, the dangers to human liberty are frightful to contemplate. If our fathers had failed to provide for just such a contingency, they would have been false to the trust reposed in them. They knew—the history of the world told them—the nation they were founding, be its existence short or long, would be involved in war; how often or how long continued, human foresight could not tell; and that unlimited power, wherever lodged at such a time, was especially hazardous to freemen. For this, and other equally weighty reasons, they secured the inheritance they had fought to maintain, by incorporating in a written constitution the safeguards which *time* had proved were essential to its preservation. Not one of these safeguards can the President, or Congress, or the Judiciary disturb, except the one concerning the writ of *habeas corpus*.

It is essential to the safety of every government that, in a great crisis, like the one we have just passed through, there should be a power somewhere of suspending the writ of *habeas corpus*. In every war, there are men of previously good character, wicked enough to counsel their fellow-citizens to resist the measures deemed necessary by a good government to sustain its just authority and overthrow its enemies; and their influence may lead to dangerous combinations. In the emergency of the times, an immediate public investigation according to law may not be possible; and yet, the peril to the country may be too imminent to suffer such persons to go at large. The Constitution goes no further. It does not say after a writ of *habeas corpus* is denied a citizen, that he shall be tried otherwise than by the course of the common law; if it had intended this result, it was easy by the use of direct words to have accomplished it. . . .

It will be borne in mind that this is not a question of the power to proclaim martial law, when war exists in a community and the courts and civil authorities are overthrown. Nor is it a question what rule a military commander, at the head of his army, can impose on states in rebellion to cripple their resources and quell the insurrection. The jurisdiction claimed is much more extensive. The necessities of the service, during the late Rebellion, required that the loyal states should be placed within the limits of certain military districts and commanders appointed in them; and, it is urged, that this, in a military sense, constituted them the theater of military operations; and, as in this case, Indiana had been and was again threatened with invasion by the enemy, the occasion was furnished to establish martial law. The conclusion does not follow from the premises. If armies were collected in Indiana, they were to be employed in another locality, where the laws were obstructed and the national authority disputed. On *her* soil there was no hostile foot; if once invaded, that invasion was at an end, and with it all pretext for martial law. Martial law cannot arise from a *threatened* invasion. The necessity must be actual and present; the invasion real, such as effectually closes the courts and deposes the civil administration. It is difficult to see how the *safety* of the country required martial law in Indiana. If any of her citizens were plotting treason, the power of arrest could secure them, until the government was prepared for their trial, when the courts were open and ready to try them. It was as easy to protect witnesses before a civil as a military tribunal; and as there could be no wish to convict, except on sufficient legal evidence, surely an ordained and established court was better able to judge of this than a military tribunal composed of gentlemen not trained to the profession of the law.

It follows, from what has been said on this subject, that there are occasions when martial rule can be properly applied. If, in foreign invasion or civil war, the courts are actually closed, and it is impossible to administer criminal justice according to law, *then*, on the theatre of active military operations, where war really prevails, there is a necessity to furnish a substitute for the civil authority, thus overthrown, to preserve the safety of the army and society; and as no power is left but the military, it is allowed to govern by martial rule until the laws can have their free course. As necessity creates the rule, so it limits its duration; for, if this government is continued *after* the courts are reinstated, it is a gross usurpation of power. Martial rule can never exist where the courts are open, and in the proper and unobstructed exercise of their jurisdiction. It is also confined to the locality of actual war. Because, during the late Rebellion it could have been enforced in Virginia, where the national authority was overturned and the courts driven out, it does not follow that it should obtain in

Indiana, where that authority was never disputed, and justice was always administered. And so in the case of a foreign invasion, martial rule may become a necessity in one state, when, in another, it would be "mere lawless violence." . . . To the third question, then, on which the judges below were opposed in opinion, an answer in the negative must be returned. . . .

The two remaining questions in this case must be answered in the affirmative. The suspension of the privilege of the writ of *habeas corpus* does not suspend the writ itself. The writ issues as a matter of course; and on the return made to it the court decides whether the party applying is denied the right of proceeding any further with it.

If the military trial of Milligan was contrary to law, then he was entitled, on the facts stated in his petition, to be discharged from custody by the terms of the act of Congress of March 3d, 1863. . . .

But it is insisted that Milligan was a prisoner of war, and, therefore, excluded from the privileges of the statute. It is not easy to see how he can be treated as a prisoner of war, when he lived in Indiana for the past twenty years, was arrested there, and had not been, during the late troubles, a resident of any of the states in rebellion. If in Indiana he conspired with bad men to assist the enemy, he is punishable for it in the courts of Indiana; but, when tried for the offence, he cannot plead the rights of war; for he was not engaged in legal acts of hostility against the government, and only such persons, when captured, are prisoners of war. If he cannot enjoy the immunities attaching to the character of a prisoner of war, how can he be subject to their pains and penalties? . . .

(The CHIEF JUSTICE, with Justices WAYNE, SWAYNE, and MILLER concurred separately in the judgment.)

---

1. *Military Law v. Martial Law.* As the preceding case indicates, military law — the ordinary law that applies to military affairs — is a discrete subject, which we do not pursue here. *See generally* Eugene R. Fidell, et al., Military Justice: Cases and Materials (2d ed. 2012). It should not be confused with "martial law," which is the extraordinary rule of civilians by military authorities because of military emergency. "It is an unbending rule of law, that the exercise of military power, where the rights of the citizen are concerned, shall never be pushed beyond that which the exigency requires." *Raymond v. Thomas*, 91 U.S. 712, 716 (1876).

Democratic supporters of now-President Andrew Johnson and the Radical Republicans in the post-Civil War Congress vigorously disputed the relevance of *Milligan* to Reconstruction. Democrats, including President Johnson, thought *Milligan* implicitly required the prompt readmission of Southern states to the Union with all sovereign powers intact. Congressional Republicans, however, enacted the Reconstruction Acts of 1867 and 1868 over Johnson's vetoes, dividing the South into military districts, and gave military commanders significant authority over state government. From the end of the war until January 1, 1869, the Union army conducted 1,435 military trials in the South. Mark E. Neely, Jr., The Fate of Liberty: Abraham Lincoln and Civil Liberties 176–77 (1991).

2. *Preserving Recourse to Habeas.* What does the Court mean by stating that suspension of the "privilege of the Writ" does not suspend the writ itself?

3. Milligan *in World War II.* Justice Black relied on *Milligan* in deciding *Duncan v. Kahanamoku,* 327 U.S. 304 (1946), in which the Court held invalid a declaration of martial law by the governor of the Territory of Hawaii on December 7, 1941, suspending, with the President's subsequent approval, the writ of habeas corpus in that territory. The animating event, of course, was the bombing of Pearl Harbor, which set off considerable panic as to the vulnerability of Hawaii and the west coast to Japanese attack. Can the two cases be reconciled with *Ex parte Quirin,* 317 U.S. 1 (1942), in which the Court upheld the trial and condemnation of a group of Nazi saboteurs by a presidentially convened tribunal of military officers, although the United States was not in the war zone and civilian courts were operating? (The *Quirin* court summarily held *Milligan* inapplicable to "enemy belligerents," including belligerents who are citizens of the United States.) A common feature of *Milligan* and *Quirin* was the apparent judicial uncertainty, at the time the Court acted in each case, whether the petitioners were still alive. A common feature of *Milligan* and *Duncan* was the fact that each case was decided during peacetime.

4. *Consequences for Judicial Power.* Does *Milligan* stand for the proposition that federal courts have inherent jurisdiction to determine the limits of their own jurisdiction?

Korematsu v. United States
323 U.S. 214 (1944)

Justice BLACK delivered the opinion of the Court.

The petitioner, an American citizen of Japanese descent, was convicted in a federal district court for remaining in San Leandro, California, a "Military Area," contrary to Civilian Exclusion Order No. 34 of the Commanding General of the Western Command, U.S. Army, which directed that after May 9, 1942, all persons of Japanese ancestry should be excluded from that area. No question was raised as to petitioner's loyalty to the United States. . . .

It should be noted, to begin with, that all legal restrictions which curtail the civil rights of a single racial group are immediately suspect. That is not to say that all such restrictions are unconstitutional. It is to say that courts must subject them to the most rigid scrutiny. Pressing public necessity may sometimes justify the existence of such restrictions; racial antagonism never can.

In the instant case prosecution of the petitioner was begun by information charging violation of an Act of Congress, of March 21, 1942, 56 Stat. 173, which provides that

> . . . whoever shall enter, remain in, leave, or commit any act in any military area or military zone prescribed, under the authority of an Executive order of the President, by the Secretary of War, or by any military commander designated by the Secretary of War, contrary to the restrictions applicable to

any such area or zone or contrary to the order of the Secretary of War or any such military commander, shall, if it appears that he knew or should have known of the existence and extent of the restrictions or order and that his act was in violation thereof, be guilty of a misdemeanor and upon conviction shall be liable to a fine of not to exceed $5,000 or to imprisonment for not more than one year, or both, for each offense.

Exclusion Order No. 34, which the petitioner knowingly and admittedly violated was one of a number of military orders and proclamations, all of which were substantially based upon Executive Order No. 9066, 7 Fed.Reg. 1407. That order, issued after we were at war with Japan, declared that "the successful prosecution of the war requires every possible protection against espionage and against sabotage to national-defense material, national-defense premises, and national-defense utilities. . . ."

One of the series of orders and proclamations, a curfew order, which like the exclusion order here was promulgated pursuant to Executive Order 9066, subjected all persons of Japanese ancestry in prescribed West Coast military areas to remain in their residences from 8 p.m. to 6 a.m. As is the case with the exclusion order here, that prior curfew order was designed as a "protection against espionage and against sabotage." In *Hirabayashi v. United States*, 320 U.S. 81, we sustained a conviction obtained for violation of the curfew order. The Hirabayashi conviction and this one thus rest on the same 1942 Congressional Act and the same basic executive and military orders, all of which orders were aimed at the twin dangers of espionage and sabotage.

The 1942 Act was attacked in the *Hirabayashi* case as an unconstitutional delegation of power; it was contended that the curfew order and other orders on which it rested were beyond the war powers of the Congress, the military authorities and of the President, as Commander in Chief of the Army; and finally that to apply the curfew order against none but citizens of Japanese ancestry amounted to a constitutionally prohibited discrimination solely on account of race. . . . We upheld the curfew order as an exercise of the power of the government to take steps necessary to prevent espionage and sabotage in an area threatened by Japanese attack.

In the light of the principles we announced in the *Hirabayashi* case, we are unable to conclude that it was beyond the war power of Congress and the Executive to exclude those of Japanese ancestry from the West Coast war area at the time they did. True, exclusion from the area in which one's home is located is a far greater deprivation than constant confinement to the home from 8 p.m. to 6 a.m. Nothing short of apprehension by the proper military authorities of the gravest imminent danger to the public safety can constitutionally justify either. But exclusion from a threatened area, no less than curfew, has a definite and close relationship to the prevention of espionage and sabotage. The military authorities, charged with the primary responsibility of defending our shores, concluded that curfew provided inadequate protection and ordered exclusion. They did so, as pointed out in our *Hirabayashi* opinion, in accordance with Congressional authority to the military to say who should, and who should not, remain in the threatened areas. In this case the petitioner challenges the assumptions upon which we rested our conclusions in the *Hirabayashi* case. He also urges that by May 1942, when Order No. 34 was promulgated, all danger of Japanese invasion of the West Coast had disappeared. After careful consideration of these contentions we are compelled to reject them.

Here, as in the *Hirabayashi* case, ". . . we cannot reject as unfounded the judgment of the military authorities and of Congress that there were disloyal members of that population, whose number and strength could not be precisely and quickly ascertained. We cannot say that the war-making branches of the Government did not have ground for believing that in a critical hour such persons could not readily be isolated and separately dealt with, and constituted a menace to the national defense and safety, which demanded that prompt and adequate measures be taken to guard against it."

Like curfew, exclusion of those of Japanese origin was deemed necessary because of the presence of an unascertained number of disloyal members of the group, most of whom we have no doubt were loyal to this country. It was because we could not reject the finding of the military authorities that it was impossible to bring about an immediate segregation of the disloyal from the loyal that we sustained the validity of the curfew order as applying to the whole group. In the instant case, temporary exclusion of the entire group was rested by the military on the same ground. The judgment that exclusion of the whole group was for the same reason a military imperative answers the contention that the exclusion was in the nature of group punishment based on antagonism to those of Japanese origin. That there were members of the group who retained loyalties to Japan has been confirmed by investigations made subsequent to the exclusion. Approximately five thousand American citizens of Japanese ancestry refused to swear unqualified allegiance to the United States and to renounce allegiance to the Japanese Emperor, and several thousand evacuees requested repatriation to Japan.[2]

We uphold the exclusion order as of the time it was made and when the petitioner violated it. In doing so, we are not unmindful of the hardships imposed by it upon a large group of American citizens. But hardships are part of war, and war is an aggregation of hardships. All citizens alike, both in and out of uniform, feel the impact of war in greater or lesser measure. Citizenship has its responsibilities as well as its privileges, and in time of war the burden is always heavier. Compulsory exclusion of large groups of citizens from their homes, except under circumstances of direst emergency and peril, is inconsistent with our basic governmental institutions. But when under conditions of modern warfare our shores are threatened by hostile forces, the power to protect must be commensurate with the threatened danger.

---

2. Hearings before the Subcommittee on the National War Agencies Appropriation Bill for 1945, Part II, 608–726; Final Report, Japanese Evacuation from the West Coast, 1942, 309–327; Hearings before the Committee on Immigration and Naturalization, House of Representatives, 78th Cong., 2d Sess., on H.R. 2701 and other bills to expatriate certain nationals of the United States, pp. 37–42, 49–58.

It is argued that on May 30, 1942, the date the petitioner was charged with remaining in the prohibited area, there were conflicting orders outstanding, forbidding him both to leave the area and to remain there. Of course, a person cannot be convicted for doing the very thing which it is a crime to fail to do. But the outstanding orders here contained no such contradictory commands.

There was an order issued March 27, 1942, which prohibited petitioner and others of Japanese ancestry from leaving the area, but its effect was specifically limited in time "until and to the extent that a future proclamation or order should so permit or direct." 7 Fed. Reg. 2601. That "future order," the one for violation of which petitioner was convicted, was issued May 3, 1942, and it did "direct" exclusion from the area of all persons of Japanese ancestry, before 12 o'clock noon, May 9; furthermore it contained a warning that all such persons found in the prohibited area would be liable to punishment under the March 21, 1942 Act of Congress. Consequently, the only order in effect touching the petitioner's being in the area on May 30, 1942, the date specified in the information against him, was the May 3 order which prohibited his remaining there, and it was that same order, which he stipulated in his trial that he had violated, knowing of its existence. There is therefore no basis for the argument that on May 30, 1942, he was subject to punishment, under the March 27 and May 3rd orders, whether he remained in or left the area.

It does appear, however, that on May 9, the effective date of the exclusion order, the military authorities had already determined that the evacuation should be effected by assembling together and placing under guard all those of Japanese ancestry, at central points, designated as "assembly centers," in order "to insure the orderly evacuation and resettlement of Japanese voluntarily migrating from military area No. 1 to restrict and regulate such migration." Public Proclamation No. 4, 7 Fed. Reg. 2601. And on May 19, 1942, eleven days before the time petitioner was charged with unlawfully remaining in the area, Civilian Restrictive Order No. 1, 8 Fed. Reg. 982, provided for detention of those of Japanese ancestry in assembly or relocation centers. It is now argued that the validity of the exclusion order cannot be considered apart from the orders requiring him, after departure from the area, to report and to remain in an assembly or relocation center. The contention is that we must treat these separate orders as one and inseparable; that, for this reason, if detention in the assembly or relocation center would have illegally deprived the petitioner of his liberty, the exclusion order and his conviction under it cannot stand.

We are thus being asked to pass at this time upon the whole subsequent detention program in both assembly and relocation centers, although the only issues framed at the trial related to petitioner's remaining in the prohibited area in violation of the exclusion order. Had petitioner here left the prohibited area and gone to an assembly center we cannot say either as a matter of fact or law that his presence in that center would have resulted in his detention in a relocation center. Some who did report to the assembly center were not sent to relocation centers, but were released upon condition that they remain outside the prohibited zone until the military orders were modified or lifted. This illustrates that they pose different problems and may be governed by different principles. The lawfulness of one does not necessarily determine the lawfulness of the others. This is made clear when we analyze the requirements of the separate provisions of the separate orders. These separate requirements were that those of Japanese ancestry (1) depart from the area; (2) report to and temporarily remain in an assembly center; (3) go under military control to a relocation center there to remain for an indeterminate period until released conditionally or unconditionally by the military authorities. . . . There is no reason why violations of these orders, insofar as they were promulgated pursuant to congressional enactment, should not be treated as separate offenses. The *Endo* case (*Ex parte Mitsuye Endo*) 323 U.S. 283,* graphically illustrates the difference between the validity of an order to exclude and the validity of a detention order after exclusion has been effected. Since the petitioner has not been convicted of failing to report or to remain in an assembly or relocation center, we cannot in this case determine the validity of those separate provisions of the order. It is sufficient here for us to pass upon the order which petitioner violated. To do more would be to go beyond the issues raised, and to decide momentous questions not contained within the framework of the pleadings or the evidence in this case. It will be time enough to decide the serious constitutional issues which petitioner seeks to raise when an assembly or relocation order is applied or is certain to be applied to him, and we have its terms before us.

Some of the members of the Court are of the view that evacuation and detention in an Assembly Center were inseparable. After May 3, 1942, the date of Exclusion Order No. 34, Korematsu was under compulsion to leave the area not as he would choose but via an Assembly Center. The Assembly Center was conceived as a part of the machinery for group evacuation. The power to exclude includes the power to do it by force if necessary. And any forcible measure must necessarily entail some degree of detention or restraint whatever method of removal is selected. But whichever view is taken, it results in holding that the order under which petitioner was convicted was valid. It is said that we are dealing here with the case of imprisonment of a citizen in a concentration camp solely because of his ancestry, without evidence or inquiry concerning his loyalty and good disposition towards the United States. Our task would be simple, our duty clear, were this a case involving the imprisonment of a loyal citizen in a concentration camp because of racial prejudice. Regardless of the true nature of the assembly and relocation centers — and we deem it unjustifiable to call them concentration camps with all the ugly connotations that term implies — we are dealing specifically with nothing but an exclusion order. . . . Korematsu was not excluded from the Military Area because of hostility to him or his race. He *was* excluded because we are at war with the Japanese Empire, because the properly constituted military authorities feared an invasion of our West Coast and felt constrained

---

* *Endo* held that neither the relevant statutes or executive orders permitted a U.S. citizen of Japanese ancestry, whose loyalty was conceded, to be detained at a relocation camp by civilian authorities.

to take proper security measures, because they decided that the military urgency of the situation demanded that all citizens of Japanese ancestry be segregated from the West Coast temporarily, and finally, because Congress, reposing its confidence in this time of war in our military leaders—as inevitably it must—determined that they should have the power to do just this. There was evidence of disloyalty on the part of some, the military authorities considered that the need for action was great, and time was short. We cannot—by availing ourselves of the calm perspective of hindsight—now say that at that time these actions were unjustified.

Affirmed.

Justice FRANKFURTER, concurring.

. . . I am unable to see how the legal considerations that led to the decision in *Hirabayashi*, fail to sustain the military order which made the conduct now in controversy a crime. And so I join in the opinion of the Court. . . .

The provisions of the Constitution which confer on the Congress and the President powers to enable this country to wage war are as much part of the Constitution as provisions looking to a nation at peace. . . . [T]he validity of action under the war power must be judged wholly in the context of war. That action is not to be stigmatized as lawless because like action in times of peace would be lawless. . . . The respective spheres of action of military authorities and of judges are of course very different. But within their sphere, military authorities are no more outside the bounds of obedience to the Constitution than are judges within theirs. . . . To recognize that military orders are "reasonably expedient military precautions" in time of war and yet to deny them constitutional legitimacy makes of the Constitution an instrument for dialectic subtleties not reasonably to be attributed to the hard-headed Framers, of whom a majority had had actual participation in war. If a military order such as that under review does not transcend the means appropriate for conducting war, such action by the military is as constitutional as would be any authorized action by the Interstate Commerce Commission within the limits of the constitutional power to regulate commerce. And being an exercise of the war power explicitly granted by the Constitution for safeguarding the national life by prosecuting war effectively, I find nothing in the Constitution which denies to Congress the power to enforce such a valid military order by making its violation an offense triable in the civil courts. To find that the Constitution does not forbid the military measures now complained of does not carry with it approval of that which Congress and the Executive did. That is their business, not ours.

Justice ROBERTS.

I dissent, because I think the indisputable facts exhibit a clear violation of Constitutional rights.

This is not a case of keeping people off the streets at night as was *Hirabayashi*, 320 U.S. 81, nor a case of temporary exclusion of a citizen from an area for his own safety or that of the community, nor a case of offering him an opportunity to go temporarily out of an area where his presence might cause danger to himself or to his fellows. On the contrary, it is the case of convicting a citizen as a punishment for not submitting to imprisonment in a concentration camp, based on his ancestry, and solely because of his ancestry, without evidence or inquiry concerning his loyalty and good disposition towards the United States. . . .

A chronological recitation of events will make it plain that the petitioner's supposed offense did not, in truth, consist in his refusal voluntarily to leave the area which included his home in obedience to the order excluding him therefrom. Critical attention must be given to the dates and sequence of events.

December 8, 1941, the United States declared war on Japan.

February 19, 1942, the President issued Executive Order No. 9066. . . .

February 20, 1942, Lieutenant General DeWitt was designated Military Commander of the Western Defense Command embracing the westernmost states of the Union,—about one-fourth of the total area of the nation.

March 2, 1942, General DeWitt promulgated Public Proclamation No. 1, which recites that the entire Pacific Coast is "particularly subject to attack, to attempted invasion . . . and, in connection therewith, is subject to espionage and acts of sabotage." It states that "as a matter of military necessity" certain military areas and zones are established known as Military Areas Nos. 1 and 2. It adds that "Such persons or classes of persons as the situation may require" will, by subsequent orders, "be excluded from all of Military Area No. 1" and from certain zones in Military Area No. 2. Subsequent proclamations were made which, together with Proclamation No. 1, included in such areas and zones all of California, Washington, Oregon, Idaho, Montana, Nevada and Utah, and the southern portion of Arizona. The orders required that if any person of Japanese, German or Italian ancestry residing in Area No. 1 desired to change his habitual residence he must execute and deliver to the authorities a Change of Residence Notice.

San Leandro, the city of petitioner's residence, lies in Military Area No. 1. On March 2, 1942, the petitioner, therefore, had notice that, by Executive Order, the President, to prevent espionage and sabotage, had authorized the Military to exclude him from certain areas and to prevent his entering or leaving certain areas without permission. He was on notice that his home city had been included, by Military Order, in Area No. 1, and he was on notice further that, at sometime in the future, the Military Commander would make an order for the exclusion of certain persons, not described or classified, from various zones including that in which he lived. March 21, 1942, Congress enacted [18 U.S.C. § 97a]. . . . This is the Act under which the petitioner was charged.

March 24, 1942, General DeWitt instituted the curfew for certain areas within his command, by an order the validity of which was sustained in *Hirabayashi v. United States, supra.*

March 24, 1942, General DeWitt began to issue a series of exclusion orders relating to specified areas.

March 27, 1942, by Proclamation No. 4, the General recited that "it is necessary, in order to provide for the welfare and to insure the orderly evacuation and resettlement of Japanese *voluntarily migrating* from Military Area No. 1 to restrict and regulate such migration"; and ordered that, as of March 29, 1942, "all alien Japanese and persons of Japanese ancestry who are within the limits of Military Area No. 1, be and they are hereby prohibited from leaving that area for any purpose until and to the extent that a future proclamation or order of this headquarters shall so permit or direct."[5] . . .

May 3, 1942, General DeWitt issued Civilian Exclusion Order No. 34 providing that, after 12 o'clock May 8, 1942, all persons of Japanese ancestry, both alien and non-alien, were to be excluded from a described portion of Military Area No. 1, which included the County of Alameda, California. The order required a responsible member of each family and each individual living alone to report, at a time set, at a Civil Control Station for instructions to go to an Assembly Center, and added that any person failing to comply with the provisions of the order who was found in the described area after the date set would be liable to prosecution under the Act of March 21, 1942. It is important to note that the order, by its express terms, had no application to persons within the bounds "of an established Assembly Center pursuant to instructions from this Headquarters. . . ." The obvious purpose of the orders made, taken together, was to drive all citizens of Japanese ancestry into Assembly Centers within the zones of their residence, under pain of criminal prosecution.

The predicament in which the petitioner thus found himself was this: He was forbidden, by Military Order, to leave the zone in which he lived; he was forbidden, by Military Order, after a date fixed, to be found within that zone unless he were in an Assembly Center located in that zone. General DeWitt's report to the Secretary of War concerning the programme of evacuation and relocation of Japanese makes it entirely clear, if it were necessary to refer to that document,—and, in the light of the above recitation, I think it is not, that an Assembly Center was a euphemism for a prison. No person within such a center was permitted to leave except by Military Order. In the dilemma that he dare not remain in his home, or voluntarily leave the area, without incurring criminal penalties, and that the only way he could avoid punishment was to go to an Assembly Center and submit himself to military imprisonment, the petitioner did nothing.

. . . [Following his conviction, Korematsu] was at once taken into military custody and lodged in an Assembly Center. We further know that, on March 18, 1942, the President had promulgated Executive Order No. 9102 establishing the War Relocation Authority under which so-called Relocation Centers, a euphemism for concentration camps, were established pursuant to cooperation between the military authorities of the Western Defense Command and the Relocation Authority, and that the petitioner has been confined either in an Assembly Center, within the zone in which he had

---

5. The italics in the quotation are mine. The use of the word 'voluntarily' exhibits a grim irony probably not lost on petitioner and others in like case. Either so, or its use was a disingenuous attempt to camouflage the compulsion which was to be applied.

lived or has been removed to a Relocation Center where, as the facts disclosed in Ex parte Endo, 323 U.S. 283, demonstrate, he was illegally held in custody.

The Government has argued this case as if the only order outstanding at the time the petitioner was arrested and informed against was Exclusion Order No. 34 ordering him to leave the area in which he resided, which was the basis of the information against him. . . . This, I think, is a substitution of an hypothetical case for the case actually before the court. . . . This case cannot . . . be decided on any such narrow ground as the possible validity of a Temporary Exclusion Order under which the residents of an area are given an opportunity to leave and go elsewhere in their native land outside the boundaries of a military area. To make the case turn on any such assumption is to shut our eyes to reality. . . .

[The] stark realities are met by the suggestion that it is lawful to compel an American citizen to submit to illegal imprisonment on the assumption that he might, after going to the Assembly Center, apply for his discharge by suing out a writ of habeas corpus, as was done in the *Endo* case. . . . [I]t is a new doctrine of constitutional law that one indicted for disobedience to an unconstitutional statute may not defend on the ground of the invalidity of the statute but must obey it though he knows it is no law and, after he has suffered the disgrace of conviction and lost his liberty by sentence, then, and not before, seek, from within prison walls, to test the validity of the law. . . . I would reverse the judgment of conviction.

Justice MURPHY, dissenting.

This exclusion of "all persons of Japanese ancestry, both alien and non-alien," from the Pacific Coast area on a plea of military necessity in the absence of martial law ought not to be approved. Such exclusion goes over "the very brink of constitutional power" and falls into the ugly abyss of racism. In dealing with matters relating to the prosecution and progress of a war, we must accord great respect and consideration to the judgments of the military authorities who are on the scene and who have full knowledge of the military facts. The scope of their discretion must, as a matter of necessity and common sense, be wide. And their judgments ought not to be overruled lightly by those whose training and duties ill-equip them to deal intelligently with matters so vital to the physical security of the nation.

At the same time, however, it is essential that there be definite limits to military discretion, especially where martial law has not been declared. Individuals must not be left impoverished of their constitutional rights on a plea of military necessity that has neither substance nor support. Thus, like other claims conflicting with the asserted constitutional rights of the individual, the military claim must subject itself to the judicial process of having its reasonableness determined and its conflicts with other interests reconciled. "What are the allowable limits of military discretion, and whether or not they have been overstepped in a particular case, are judicial questions." *Sterling v. Constantin*, 287 U.S. 378, 401.

The judicial test of whether the Government, on a plea of military necessity, can validly deprive an individual of any of his constitutional rights is whether the deprivation is reasonably related to a public danger that is so "immediate, imminent, and impending" as not to admit of delay and not to permit the intervention of ordinary constitutional processes to alleviate the danger. *United States v. Russell*, 13 Wall. 623, 627–28. Civilian Exclusion Order No. 34, banishing from a prescribed area of the Pacific Coast "all persons of Japanese ancestry, both alien and non-alien," clearly does not meet that test. Being an obvious racial discrimination, the order deprives all those within its scope of the equal protection of the laws as guaranteed by the Fifth Amendment. It further deprives these individuals of their constitutional rights to live and work where they will, to establish a home where they choose and to move about freely. In excommunicating them without benefit of hearings, this order also deprives them of all their constitutional rights to procedural due process. Yet no reasonable relation to an "immediate, imminent, and impending" public danger is evident to support this racial restriction which is one of the most sweeping and complete deprivations of constitutional rights in the history of this nation in the absence of martial law.

It must be conceded that the military and naval situation in the spring of 1942 was such as to generate a very real fear of invasion of the Pacific Coast, accompanied by fears of sabotage and espionage in that area. The military command was therefore justified in adopting all reasonable means necessary to combat these dangers. In adjudging the military action taken in light of the then apparent dangers, we must not erect too high or too meticulous standards; it is necessary only that the action have some reasonable relation to the removal of the dangers of invasion, sabotage and espionage. But the exclusion, either temporarily or permanently, of all persons with Japanese blood in their veins has no such reasonable relation. And that relation is lacking because the exclusion order necessarily must rely for its reasonableness upon the assumption that all persons of Japanese ancestry may have a dangerous tendency to commit sabotage and espionage and to aid our Japanese enemy in other ways. It is difficult to believe that reason, logic or experience could be marshalled in support of such an assumption.

That this forced exclusion was the result in good measure of this erroneous assumption of racial guilt rather than bona fide military necessity is evidenced by the Commanding General's Final Report on the evacuation from the Pacific Coast area.[1] In it he refers to all individuals of Japanese descent as "subversive," as belonging to "an enemy race" whose "racial strains are undiluted," and as constituting "over 112,000 potential enemies... at large today" along the Pacific Coast.[2] In support of this

---

1. Final Report, Japanese Evacuation from the West Coast, 1942, by Lt. Gen. J. L. DeWitt. This report is dated June 5, 1943, but was not made public until January, 1944.

2. Further evidence of the Commanding General's attitude toward individuals of Japanese ancestry is revealed in his voluntary testimony on April 13, 1943, in San Francisco before the House Naval Affairs Subcommittee to Investigate Congested Areas, Part 3, pp. 739–40 (78th Cong., 1st Sess.):

> I don't want any of them [persons of Japanese ancestry] here. They are a dangerous element. There is no way to determine their loyalty. The west coast contains too many vital installations essential to the defense of the country to allow any Japanese on this coast... The danger of the Japanese was, and is now—if they are permitted to come

blanket condemnation of all persons of Japanese descent, however, no reliable evidence is cited to show that such individuals were generally disloyal,[3] or had generally so conducted themselves in this area as to constitute a special menace to defense installations or war industries, or had otherwise by their behavior furnished reasonable ground for their exclusion as a group.

Justification for the exclusion is sought, instead, mainly upon questionable racial and sociological grounds not ordinarily within the realm of expert military judgment, supplemented by certain semi-military conclusions drawn from an unwarranted use of circumstantial evidence. Individuals of Japanese ancestry are condemned because they are said to be "a large, unassimilated, tightly knit racial group, bound to an enemy nation by strong ties of race, culture, custom and religion."[4] They are claimed to be given to "emperor worshipping ceremonies[5] and to "dual citizenship."[6] Japanese language schools and allegedly pro-Japanese organizations are cited as evidence of possible group disloyalty, together with facts as to certain persons being educated and residing at length in Japan. It is intimated that many of these individuals deliberately resided "adjacent to strategic points," thus enabling them "to carry into execution a tremendous program of sabotage on a mass scale should any considerable number of them have been inclined to do so."[9] The need for protective custody is also asserted. The report refers without identity to "numerous incidents of violence" as well as to other admittedly unverified or cumulative incidents. From this, plus certain other

---

back—espionage and sabotage. It makes no difference whether he is an American citizen, he is still a Japanese. American citizenship does not necessarily determine loyalty. . . . But we must worry about the Japanese all the time until he is wiped off the map. Sabotage and espionage will make problems as long as he is allowed in this area. . . .

3. The Final Report, p. 9, casts a cloud of suspicion over the entire group by saying that "while it was *believed* that *some* were loyal, it was known that many were not." (Italics added.)

4. Final Report, p. vii; see also pp. 9, 17. To the extent that assimilation is a problem, it is largely the result of certain social customs and laws of the American general public. Studies demonstrate that persons of Japanese descent are readily susceptible to integration in our society if given the opportunity. Strong, The Second-Generation Japanese Problem (1934); Smith, Americans in Process (1937); Mears, Resident Orientals on the American Pacific Coast (1928); Millis, The Japanese Problem in the United States (1942). The failure to accomplish an ideal status of assimilation, therefore, cannot be charged to the refusal of these persons to become Americanized or to their loyalty to Japan. And the retention by some persons of certain customs and religious practices of their ancestors is no criterion of their loyalty to the United States.

5. Final Report, pp. 10–11. No sinister correlation between the emperor worshipping activities and disloyalty to America was shown.

6. Final Report, p. 22. The charge of "dual citizenship" springs from a misunderstanding of the simple fact that Japan in the past used the doctrine of *jus sanguinis*, as she had a right to do under international law, and claimed as her citizens all persons born of Japanese nationals wherever located. Japan has greatly modified this doctrine, however, by allowing all Japanese born in the United States to renounce any claim of dual citizenship and by releasing her claim as to all born in the United States after 1925. . . .

9. Final Report, p. 10; see also pp. vii, 9, 15–17. This insinuation, based purely upon speculation and circumstantial evidence, completely overlooks the fact that the main geographic pattern of Japanese population was fixed many years ago with reference to economic, social and soil conditions. . . .

events not shown to have been connected with the Japanese Americans, it is concluded that the "situation was fraught with danger to the Japanese population itself" and that the general public "was ready to take matters into its own hands."[10] Finally, it is intimated, though not directly charged or proved, that persons of Japanese ancestry were responsible for three minor isolated shellings and bombings of the Pacific Coast area,[11] as well as for unidentified radio transmissions and night signalling.

The main reasons relied upon by those responsible for the forced evacuation, therefore, do not prove a reasonable relation between the group characteristics of Japanese Americans and the dangers of invasion, sabotage and espionage. The reasons appear, instead, to be largely an accumulation of much of the misinformation, half-truths and insinuations that for years have been directed against Japanese Americans by people with racial and economic prejudices—the same people who have been among the foremost advocates of the evacuation.[12] A military judgment based upon such racial and sociological considerations is not entitled to the great weight ordinarily given the judgments based upon strictly military considerations. Especially is this so when every charge relative to race, religion, culture, geographical location, and legal and economic status has been substantially discredited by independent studies made by experts in these matters.

The military necessity which is essential to the validity of the evacuation order thus resolves itself into a few intimations that certain individuals actively aided the enemy, from which it is inferred that the entire group of Japanese Americans could not be trusted to be or remain loyal to the United States. No one denies, of course, that there were some disloyal persons of Japanese descent on the Pacific Coast who did all in their power to aid their ancestral land. Similar disloyal activities have been engaged in by many persons of German, Italian and even more pioneer stock in our country. But to infer that examples of individual disloyalty prove group disloyalty and justify discriminatory action against the entire group is to deny that under our system of law individual guilt is the sole basis for deprivation of rights. Moreover,

---

10. Final Report, pp. 8–9. This dangerous doctrine of protective custody, as proved by recent European history, should have absolutely no standing as an excuse for the deprivation of the rights of minority groups. In this instance, moreover, there are only two minor instances of violence on record involving persons of Japanese ancestry.

11. Final Report, p. 18. One of these incidents (the reputed dropping of incendiary bombs on an Oregon forest) occurred on Sept. 9, 1942, a considerable time after the Japanese Americans had been evacuated from their homes and placed in Assembly Centers.

12. Special interest groups were extremely active in applying pressure for mass evacuation. Mr. Austin E. Anson, managing secretary of the Salinas Vegetable Grower-Shipper Association, has frankly admitted that "We're charged with wanting to get rid of the Japs for selfish reasons. . . . We do. It's a question of whether the white man lives on the Pacific Coast or the brown men. They came into this valley to work, and they stayed to take over. . . . They undersell the white man in the markets. . . . They work their women and children while the white farmer has to pay wages for his help. If all the Japs were removed tomorrow, we'd never miss them in two weeks, because the white farmers can take over and produce everything the Jap grows. And we don't want them back when the war ends, either." Quoted by Taylor in his article "The People Nobody Wants," 214 Sat. Eve. Post 24, 66 (May 9, 1942).

this inference, which is at the very heart of the evacuation orders, has been used in support of the abhorrent and despicable treatment of minority groups by the dictatorial tyrannies which this nation is now pledged to destroy. To give constitutional sanction to that inference in this case, however well-intentioned may have been the military command on the Pacific Coast, is to adopt one of the cruelest of the rationales used by our enemies to destroy the dignity of the individual and to encourage and open the door to discriminatory actions against other minority groups in the passions of tomorrow.

No adequate reason is given for the failure to treat these Japanese Americans on an individual basis by holding investigations and hearings to separate the loyal from the disloyal, as was done in the case of persons of German and Italian ancestry. *See* House Report No. 2124 (77th Cong., 2d Sess.) 247–52. It is asserted merely that the loyalties of this group "were unknown and time was of the essence." Yet nearly four months elapsed after Pearl Harbor before the first exclusion order was issued; nearly eight months went by until the last order was issued; and the last of these "subversive" persons was not actually removed until almost eleven months had elapsed. Leisure and deliberation seem to have been more of the essence than speed. And the fact that conditions were not such as to warrant a declaration of martial law adds strength to the belief that the factors of time and military necessity were not as urgent as they have been represented to be.

Moreover, there was no adequate proof that the Federal Bureau of Investigation and the military and naval intelligence services did not have the espionage and sabotage situation well in hand during this long period. Nor is there any denial of the fact that not one person of Japanese ancestry was accused or convicted of espionage or sabotage after Pearl Harbor while they were still free,[15] a fact which is some evidence of the loyalty of the vast majority of these individuals and of the effectiveness of the established methods of combatting these evils. It seems incredible that under these circumstances it would have been impossible to hold loyalty hearings for the mere 112,000 persons involved—or at least for the 70,000 American citizens—especially when a large part of this number represented children and elderly men and women.[16] Any inconvenience that may have accompanied an attempt to conform to procedural due process cannot be said to justify violations of constitutional rights of individuals.

---

15. The Final Report, p. 34, makes the amazing statement that as of February 14, 1942, "The very fact that no sabotage has taken place to date is a disturbing and confirming indication that such action will be taken." Apparently, in the minds of the military leaders, there was no way that the Japanese Americans could escape the suspicion of sabotage.

16. During a period of six months, the 112 alien tribunals or hearing boards set up by the British Government shortly after the outbreak of the present war summoned and examined approximately 74,000 German and Austrian aliens. These tribunals determined whether each individual enemy alien was a real enemy of the Allies or only a "friendly enemy." About 64,000 were freed from internment and from any special restrictions, and only 2,000 were interned. Kempner, *The Enemy Alien Problem in the Present War*, 34 Amer. Journ. of Int. Law 443, 444–46; House Report No. 2124 (77th Cong., 2d Sess.), 280–1.

I dissent, therefore, from this legalization of racism. . . .

Justice JACKSON, dissenting.

Korematsu was born on our soil, of parents born in Japan. The Constitution makes him a citizen of the United States by nativity and a citizen of California by residence. No claim is made that he is not loyal to this country. There is no suggestion that apart from the matter involved here he is not law-abiding and well disposed. Korematsu, however, has been convicted of an act not commonly a crime. It consists merely of being present in the state whereof he is a citizen, near the place where he was born, and where all his life he has lived.

Even more unusual is the series of military orders which made this conduct a crime. They forbid such a one to remain, and they also forbid him to leave. They were so drawn that the only way Korematsu could avoid violation was to give himself up to the military authority. This meant submission to custody, examination, and transportation out of the territory, to be followed by indeterminate confinement in detention camps.

A citizen's presence in the locality, however, was made a crime only if his parents were of Japanese birth. Had Korematsu been one of four—the others being, say, a German alien enemy, an Italian alien enemy, and a citizen of American-born ancestors, convicted of treason but out on parole—only Korematsu's presence would have violated the order. The difference between their innocence and his crime would result, not from anything he did, said, or thought, different than they, but only in that he was born of different racial stock.

Now, if any fundamental assumption underlies our system, it is that guilt is personal and not inheritable. Even if all of one's antecedents had been convicted of treason, the Constitution forbids its penalties to be visited upon him, for it provides that "no attainder of treason shall work corruption of blood, or forfeiture except during the life of the person attainted." [Article 3, § 3, cl. 2.] But here is an attempt to make an otherwise innocent act a crime merely because this prisoner is the son of parents as to whom he had no choice, and belongs to a race from which there is no way to resign. If Congress in peace-time legislation should enact such a criminal law, I should suppose this Court would refuse to enforce it.

But the "law" which this prisoner is convicted of disregarding is not found in an act of Congress, but in a military order. Neither the Act of Congress nor the Executive Order of the President, nor both together, would afford a basis for this conviction. It rests on the orders of General DeWitt. And it is said that if the military commander had reasonable military grounds for promulgating the orders, they are constitutional and become law, and the Court is required to enforce them. There are several reasons why I cannot subscribe to this doctrine.

It would be impracticable and dangerous idealism to expect or insist that each specific military command in an area of probable operations will conform to conventional tests of constitutionality. When an area is so beset that it must be put under military control at all, the paramount consideration is that its measures be successful, rather than legal. The armed services must protect a society, not merely its Constitution. Defense measures will not, and often should not, be held within the limits that bind civil authority in peace. No court can require such a commander in such circumstances to act as a reasonable man; he may be unreasonably cautious and exacting. Perhaps he should be. But a commander in temporarily focusing the life of a community on defense is carrying out a military program; he is not making law in the sense the courts know the term. He issues orders, and they may have a certain authority as military commands, although they may be very bad as constitutional law. But if we cannot confine military expedients by the Constitution, neither would I distort the Constitution to approve all that the military may deem expedient. That is what the Court appears to be doing, whether consciously or not. I cannot say, from any evidence before me, that the orders of General DeWitt were not reasonably expedient military precautions, nor could I say that they were. But even if they were permissible military procedures, I deny that it follows that they are constitutional. If, as the Court holds, it does follow, then we may as well say that any military order will be constitutional and have done with it.

The limitation under which courts always will labor in examining the necessity for a military order are illustrated by this case. How does the Court know that these orders have a reasonable basis in necessity? No evidence whatever on that subject has been taken by this or any other court. There is sharp controversy as to the credibility of the DeWitt report. So the Court, having no real evidence before it, has no choice but to accept General DeWitt's own unsworn, self-serving statement, untested by any cross-examination, that what he did was reasonable. And thus it will always be when courts try to look into the reasonableness of a military order.

In the very nature of things military decisions are not susceptible of intelligent judicial appraisal. They do not pretend to rest on evidence, but are made on information that often would not be admissible and on assumptions that could not be proved. Information in support of an order could not be disclosed to courts without danger that it would reach the enemy. Neither can courts act on communications made in confidence. Hence courts can never have any real alternative to accepting the mere declaration of the authority that issued the order that it was reasonably necessary from a military viewpoint. Much is said of the danger to liberty from the Army program for deporting and detaining these citizens of Japanese extraction. But a judicial construction of the due process clause that will sustain this order is a far more subtle blow to liberty than the promulgation of the order itself. A military order, however unconstitutional, is not apt to last longer than the military emergency. Even during that period a succeeding commander may revoke it all. But once a judicial opinion rationalizes such an order to show that it conforms to the Constitution, or rather rationalizes the Constitution to show that the Constitution sanctions such an order, the Court for all time has validated the principle of racial discrimination in criminal procedure and of transplanting American citizens. The principle then lies about like a loaded weapon ready for the hand of any authority that can bring forward a plausible claim of an urgent need. Every repetition imbeds that principle more deeply in our law and thinking and expands it to new purposes. Nothing better illustrates this danger than does the Court's opinion in this case. It argues that we are bound to uphold the conviction of Korematsu because we upheld one in *Hirabayashi*, when we sustained these orders in so far as they applied a curfew requirement to a citizen of Japanese ancestry. I think we should learn something from that experience.

In that case we were urged to consider only the curfew feature, that being all that technically was involved, because it was the only count necessary to sustain Hirabayashi's conviction and sentence. We yielded, and the Chief Justice guarded the opinion as carefully as language will do. However, in spite of our limiting words we did validate a discrimination of the basis of ancestry for mild and temporary deprivation of liberty. Now the principle of racial discrimination is pushed from support of mild measures to very harsh ones, and from temporary deprivations to indeterminate ones. And the precedent which it is said requires us to do so is *Hirabayashi*. How far the principle of this case would be extended before plausible reasons would play out, I do not know.

I should hold that a civil court cannot be made to enforce an order which violates constitutional limitations even if it is a reasonable exercise of military authority. The courts can exercise only the judicial power, can apply only law, and must abide by the Constitution, or they cease to be civil courts and become instruments of military policy.

Of course the existence of a military power resting on force, so vagrant, so centralized, so necessarily heedless of the individual, is an inherent threat to liberty. But I would not lead people to rely on this Court for a review that seems to me wholly delusive. The military reasonableness of these orders can only be determined by military superiors. If the people ever let command of the war power fall into irresponsible and unscrupulous hands, the courts wield no power equal to its restraint. The chief restraint upon those who command the physical forces of the country, in the future as in the past, must be their responsibility to the political judgments of their contemporaries and to the moral judgments of history.

My duties as a justice as I see them do not require me to make a military judgment as to whether General DeWitt's evacuation and detention program was a reasonable military necessity. I do not suggest that the courts should have attempted to interfere with the Army in carrying out its task. But I do not think they may be asked to execute a military expedient that has no place in law under the Constitution. I would reverse the judgment and discharge the prisoner.

Notes and Questions on Japanese Internment and Its Aftermath

1. *Judicial Review of Military Emergencies: What Standards?* What standard of review did the Court apply in assessing the facts alleged in justification of the military orders that Korematsu disobeyed? How *should* the Court have determined

whether the facts of *Korematsu* demonstrated the taking of "proper security measures" based on a reasonable assessment of "military urgency" or "the imprisonment of a citizen in a concentration camp solely because of his ancestry"? Even if, contrary to Justice Jackson, the military legitimacy of security measures taken in wartime will be deemed by courts to afford those measures a presumption of legal validity, did not Korematsu demonstrate enough to overcome that presumption? Did the military meet even a burden of going forward with evidence?

2. *Justice Jackson's "Clean Hands" Approach.* How much good would Jackson's "lend no aid" position have done actually to protect Japanese-Americans against unlawful detention? Insofar as his argument rests on the fact that Korematsu's conviction rested wholly on disobedience of a military order, would that conviction, under Jackson's analysis, stand on better ground if the President and Congress had more clearly authorized that order? (Recall *Kent v. Dulles* and *Hampton v. Mow Sun Wong*, reviewed in the materials on delegation in Chapter Two, in which the Court invalidated administrative decisions with foreign policy and national security implications on the ground that they had not been authorized with sufficient clarity by those political actors most competent to assess foreign policy and national security.)

3. *Fact Finding Under Pressure.* Imagine that, before any of the *Korematsu* events had occurred, you had been asked to advise the Department of the Army in 1942 on the following question: If military authorities determine the existence of a situation of grave imminent danger to public safety, may the Army constitutionally impose restrictions on the movements of a local U.S. population if, in the view of the Army, such restrictions are closely and definitely related to avoiding sabotage and espionage? How would you proceed to address the question at hand?

4. *Conviction Overturned.* In the 1980s, Korematsu succeeded in having his conviction overturned. *Korematsu v. United States*, 584 F. Supp. 1406 (N.D. Cal. 1984). A federal district court in California granted a writ of *coram nobis* based on findings that the government deliberately omitted relevant information and provided misleading information in papers submitted to the Supreme Court concerning whether the military orders at issue were reasonably related to the security and defense of the nation and to the prosecution of the war. The government's assertions as to mootness and the statute of limitations failed; the court found that Korematsu continued to suffer the consequences of his conviction and that the statute of limitations was not a bar because much of the evidence needed for his post-conviction challenge had only recently been discovered by a Commission on Wartime Relocation and Internment of Civilians, established by Congress in 1980. Wartime Relocation and Internment Act, Pub. L. No. 96-317, 52, 95 Stat. 964 (1980). *See also* Peter Irons, *Return of the Yellow Peril*, THE NATION, Oct. 19, 1985, at 361, discussing the 1985 reversal of the conviction of Gordon Hirabayashi for violation of a curfew order, upheld by the Supreme Court in *Hirabayashi v. United States*, 320 U.S. 81 (1943).

In *Hohri v. United States*, 782 F.2d 227 (D.C. Cir. 1986), a group of Japanese-American victims of the evacuation sued the U.S. to recover damages for injuries arising out of the wartime internment. They persuaded the D.C. Circuit that the government's fraudulent concealment of facts undermining its claims of military necessity tolled the applicable statute of limitations on at least certain of their claims until 1980. (The Supreme Court, however, vacated the judgment on the ground that the district court's decision adverse to the plaintiffs should have been appealed to the U.S. Court of Appeals for the Federal Circuit. *United States v. Hohri*, 482 U.S. 64 (1987).) The Court of Appeals rejected the government's argument that, unlike Korematsu's post-conviction petition, the plaintiffs' damage actions could have been filed timely based on information available prior to the work of the 1980 commission. The Court was not moved by the fact that the plaintiffs had had other options for relief available to them earlier. In 1948, Congress created a mechanism for the reimbursement of Japanese-American victims through the American Japanese Evacuation Claims Act. Claims were permitted against the government for property loss, resulting in the filing of 26,000 claims and the distribution of $37 million in damages.

Congress ultimately settled the claims pending in *Hohri* by authorizing $1.25 billion to establish a trust fund in the Treasury Department from which $20,000 payments tax-free would be made in reparations to approximately 60,000 Japanese-American internees who are still alive. Civil Liberties Act of 1988, Pub. L. No. 100-383, 102 Stat. 903, *codified at* 50 App. U.S.C. § 1989 *et seq.* Among the Act's express purposes were to "apologize" for and "acknowledge the fundamental injustice of the evacuation, relocation, and internment" of Japanese-American citizens and Japanese permanent resident aliens during World War II. Despite the apology, it took Congress over a year actually to appropriate the money to be spent pursuant to its authorization of compensation. Pub. L. No. 101-162, 103 Stat. 988, 996 (1989).

5. *Ethics of Government Lawyering.* In overturning Korematsu's conviction and holding the statute of limitations tolled on takings claims, the federal courts found, through the report by the Commission on Wartime Relocation and Internment of Civilians, Personal Justice Denied (1983), that the U.S. Department of Justice had information at its disposal directly contradictory to the report by General DeWitt that military necessity justified exclusion and internment of persons of Japanese ancestry without regard to individual identity.

Executive Order 9066, upon which the military relied as authority for the evacuation and internment of Japanese Americans, was adopted at the behest of General DeWitt. DeWitt's so-called Final Report of June 5, 1943, based the War Department's anti-espionage program on a number of alleged facts: supposed signaling from shore to enemy submarines; the FBI's discovery of arms and contraband during raids on Japanese-American homes and businesses on the West Coast; the danger posed to evacuees by vigilantes; the concentration of a number of Japanese ethnic organizations which might allegedly shelter pro-Japanese attitudes or activities such as emperor-worship.

Reading the Final Report while preparing to defend the exclusion before the Supreme Court, Justice Department attorneys were, of course, drawn to the signaling contention as directly relevant to military operations. The claim was investigated by the FCC and found to be so utterly unsubstantiated that, in its brief to the Supreme Court, the Justice Department was careful not to rely on DeWitt's Final Report as a factual basis for the military decision it had to defend. There had not been any identifiable shore-to-ship signaling. Similarly, the arms and contraband argument had earlier been dismissed. The Department of Justice concluded that, although the FBI did confiscate arms and contraband from some ethnic Japanese, most items were those frequently in the possession of law-abiding citizens. Thus, neither of these "facts" justified military exclusion.

DeWitt's third argument, protecting the Japanese Americans against vigilantism, had some factual credibility. There were serious episodes of violent crimes against ethnic Japanese on the West Coast. The obvious issue raised by these incidents, however, is whether the government could properly discharge its duty to the victims of crime by imprisoning the victims. Would such police protection, in any event, be relevant to the operations of military authorities?

Finally, an argument that the Japanese were dangerously located near sensitive military installations failed to take account of similar circumstances concerning other ethnic groups. The 1980 Commission concluded that Italian-Americans were located in more strategic coastal locations than the Japanese.

Although the Government's brief in *Korematsu* thus contained few hard facts, Justice Black asserts in his opinion that the military orders were not based on "racial prejudice." The data relied on by the Court, however, derived in part from allegations of disloyalty based on cultural characteristics of the Japanese, such as their alleged community solidarity and commitment to separate language schools. These allegations are scorned in Justice Murphy's dissent, which notes that "not one person of Japanese ancestry was accused or convicted of espionage or sabotage after Pearl Harbor while they were still free."

A. Imagine that you, as a Justice Department lawyer in 1942, were aware that key facts asserted by the military in justification for the Japanese evacuation orders were unsubstantiated. Does your ethical obligation to the courts require you (1) to refrain from relying on those facts in making your argument? (2) to divulge your factual understanding to the courts? (3) to confess error?

B. Imagine that you, as a Justice Department lawyer in 1942, believe that the military's actions—even if justified in fact—were *motivated* by racial prejudice, would your conclusion affect your participation in a conduct of the Government's defense?

6. *Further Reading.* Two excellent books providing additional background information on the Japanese internment cases are JACOBUS tenBROEK *ET AL.*, PREJUDICE,

WAR AND THE CONSTITUTION (1954), and PETER H. IRONS, JUSTICE AT WAR (1983). For a fascinating comparative study, see A. W. B. Simpson, *Detention Without Trial in the Second World War: Comparing the British and American Experiences*, 16 FLA. ST. U. L. REV. 225 (1988). Professor Simpson concludes that, for reasons of racism and despite the greater military threat to England, war time detention of civilians was more widespread and long term in the United States than in Great Britain. In both countries, however, the judiciary failed to afford any meaningful relief during the course of the war.

2. Mobilization and Regulation of the Economy

Note: Presidential Economic Controls During World War II

The power normally associated with the President's constitutional role as Commander in Chief of the Armed Forces is the power to command military troops in wartime. Presidents have also, however, asserted wartime domestic power to regulate the economy in support of the war effort.

The most innovative uses of economic controls occurred during World War II, under President Roosevelt. Some of these and their judicial reception are summarized in the following excerpt from Constitution of the United States of America: Analysis and Interpretation, S. Doc. No. 6, 103d Cong., 1st Sess. 441, 443–446 (1973).

> [I]n exercising both the powers which he claimed as Commander-in-Chief and those which Congress conferred upon him to meet the emergency, Mr. [Franklin] Roosevelt employed new emergency agencies, created by himself and responsible directly to him, rather than the established departments or existing independent regulatory agencies.[121] . . .
>
> **Presidential Government of Labor Relations.** The most important segment of the home front regulated by what were in effect presidential edicts was the field of labor relations. Exactly six months before Pearl Harbor, on June 7, 1941, Mr. Roosevelt, citing his proclamation thirteen days earlier of an unlimited national emergency, issued an Executive Order seizing the North American Aviation Plant at Inglewood, California, where, on account of a strike, production was at a standstill.[129] Attorney General Jackson justified the seizure as growing out of the "duty constitutionally and inherently rested upon the President to exert his civil and military as well as his moral authority to keep the defense efforts of the United States a going concern," as well as "to obtain supplies for which Congress has appropriated the money, and

---

121. For a listing of the agencies and an account of their creation to the close of 1942, *see* Vanderbilt, *War Powers and Their Administration*, in 1942 Annual Survey of American Law (New York Univ.), 106

129. E.O. 8773, 6 *Fed. Reg.* 2777 (1941).

which it has directed the President to obtain."[130] Other seizures followed, and on January 12, 1942, Mr. Roosevelt, by Executive Order 9017, created the National War Labor Board. "Whereas," the order read in part, "by reason of the state of war declared to exist by joint resolution of Congress, . . . the national interest demands that there shall be no interruption of any work which contributes to the effective prosecution of the war; and Whereas as a result of a conference of representatives of labor and industry which met at the call of the President on December 17, 1941, it has been agreed that for the duration of the war there shall be no strikes or lockouts, and that all labor disputes shall be settled by peaceful means, and that a National War Labor Board be established for a peaceful adjustment of such disputes. Now, therefore, by virtue of the authority vested in me by the Constitution and the statutes of the United States, it is hereby ordered: 1. There is hereby created in the Office for Emergency Management a National War Labor Board. . . ."[131] In this field, too, Congress intervened by means of the War Labor Disputes Act of June 25, 1943,[132] which, however, still left ample basis for presidential activity of a legislative character.[133]

Sanctions Implementing Presidential Directives. To implement his directives as Commander-in-Chief in wartime, and especially those which he issued in governing labor disputes, President Roosevelt often resorted to "sanctions," which may be described as penalties lacking statutory authorization. Ultimately, the President sought to put sanctions in this field on a systematic basis. The order empowered the Director of Economic Stabilization, on receiving a report from the National War Labor Board that someone was not complying with its orders, to issue "directives" to the appropriate department or agency requiring that privileges, benefits, rights, or preferences enjoyed by the noncomplying party be withdrawn.[134]

Sanctions were also occasionally employed by statutory agencies, such as OPA, to supplement the penal provisions of the Emergency Price Control Act of January 30, 1942.[135] In the case of *Steuart & Bro. v. Bowles*,[136] the Supreme Court had the opportunity to regularize this type of executive emergency legislation. Here a retail dealer in fuel oil was charged with having violated a rationing order of OPA by obtaining large quantities of oil from its supplier without surrendering ration coupons, by delivering many thousands of gallons of fuel oil without requiring ration coupons, and so on,

---

130. Edward S. Corwin, Total War and the Constitution (New York: 1946), 47–48.
131. 7 *Fed. Reg.* 237 (1942).
132. 57 Stat. 163 (1943).
133. *See* Vanderbilt, *War Powers and their Administration*, 1945 Annual Survey of American Law (N.Y. Univ.), 254, 271–73.
134. E.O. 9370, 8 *Fed. Reg.* 11463 (1943).
135. 56 Stat. 23 (1942).
136. 322 U.S. 398 (1944).

and was prohibited by the agency from receiving oil for resale or transfer for the ensuing year. The offender conceded the validity of the rationing order in support of which the suspension order was issued but challenged the validity of the latter as imposing a penalty that Congress had not enacted and asked the district court to enjoin it.

The court refused to do so and was sustained by the Supreme Court in its position. Said Justice Douglas, speaking for the Court: "Without rationing, the fuel tanks of a few would be full; the fuel tanks of many would be empty. Some localities would have plenty; communities less favorably situated would suffer. Allocation or rationing is designed to eliminate such inequalities and to treat all alike who are similarly situated. . . . But middlemen— wholesalers and retailers—bent on defying the rationing system could raise havoc with it. From the viewpoint of a rationing system a middleman who distributes the product in violation and disregard of the prescribed quotas is an inefficient and wasteful conduit. . . . Certainly we would not say that the President would lack the power under this Act to take away from a wasteful factory and route to an efficient one a previous supply of material needed for the manufacture of articles of war. . . . Yet if the President has the power to channel raw materials into the most efficient industrial units and thus save scarce materials from wastage it is difficult to see why the same principle is not applicable to the distribution of fuel oil."[137] Sanctions were, therefore, constitutional when the deprivations they wrought were a reasonably implied amplification of the substantive power which they supported and were directly conservative of the interests which this power was created to protect and advance. It is certain, however, that sanctions not uncommonly exceeded this pattern.[138]

Constitutional Status of Presidential Agencies. The question of the legal status of the presidential agencies was dealt with judicially but once. This was in the decision of the United States Court of Appeals of the District of Columbia in *Employers Group v. National War Labor Board*, [143 F.2d 145 (D.C. Cir. 1944)] which was a suit to annul and enjoin a "directive order" of the War Labor Board. The Court refused the injunction on the ground that at the time when the directive was issued any action of the Board was "informatory," "at most advisory." In support of this view the Court quoted approvingly a statement by the chairman of the Board itself: "These orders are in reality mere declarations of the equities of each industrial dispute, as determined by a tripartite body in which industry, labor, and the public share equal responsibility; and the appeal of the Board is to the moral obligation of employers and workers to abide by the nonstrike, no-lock-out agreement and . . . to carry out the directives of the tribunal created under that

137. *Id.* 404–05.
138. E. Corwin, The President: Office and Powers 1787–1957 (New York: 4th ed. 1957), 249–250.

agreement by the Commander in Chief." Nor, the Court continued, had the later War Labor Disputes Act vested War Labor Boards orders with any greater authority, with the result that they were still judicially unenforceable and unreviewable. Following this theory, the War Labor Board was not an office wielding power, but a purely advisory body, such as Presidents have frequently created in the past without the aid or consent of Congress. Congress itself, nevertheless, both in its appropriation acts and in other legislation, treated the presidential agencies as in all respects offices. . . .

The Postwar Period. The end of active hostilities did not terminate either the emergency or the federal-governmental response to it. President Truman proclaimed the termination of hostilities on December 31, 1946,[139] and Congress enacted a joint resolution which repealed a great variety of wartime statutes and set termination dates for others in July, 1947.[140] Signing the resolution, the President said that the emergencies declared in 1939 and 1940 continued to exist and that it was "not possible at this time to provide for terminating all war and emergency powers."[141] The hot war was giving way to the Cold War.

Congress thereafter enacted a new Housing and Rent Act to continue the controls begun in 1942[142] and continued the draft.[143] With the outbreak of the Korean War, legislation was enacted establishing general presidential control over the economy again[144] and by executive order the President created agencies to exercise the power.[145] The Court continued to assume the existence of a state of wartime emergency prior to Korea but with misgivings. In *Woods v. Cloyd W. Miller Co.*,[146] the Court held constitutional the new rent control law on the ground that cessation of hostilities did not conclude the Government's powers but that the power continued to remedy the evil arising out of the emergency. Yet for the Court, Justice Douglas noted: "We recognize the force of the argument that the effects of war under modern conditions may be felt in the economy for years and years, and that if the war power can be used in days of peace to treat all the wounds which war inflicts on our society, it may not only swallow up all other powers of Congress but largely obliterate the Ninth and Tenth Amendments as well. There are no such implications in today's decision." Justice Jackson, while concurring, noted that he found the war power "the most dangerous one to free government in the whole catalogue of powers" and cautioned that its

139. Proc. 2714, 12 *Fed. Reg.* 1 (1947).
140. S.J. Res. 123, 61 Stat. 449 (1947).
141. *Woods v. Cloyd W. Miller Co.*, 333 U.S. 138, 140 n.3 (1948).
142. 61 Stat. 193 (1947).
143. 62 Stat. 604 (1948), as amended, 50 U.S.C. App. § 451 *et seq.*
144. Defense Production Act of 1950, 64 Stat. 798.
145. E.O. 10161, 15 Fed. Reg. 6105 (1950).
146. 333 U.S. 138 (1948).

exercise should "be scrutinized with care." And in *Ludecke v. Watkins*,[149] four Justices were prepared to hold that the presumption in the statute under review of continued war with Germany was fiction and not be utilized.

But the postwar was a time of reaction against the wartime exercise of power by President Roosevelt and President Truman was not permitted the same liberties. The Twenty-second Amendment writing into permanent law the two term custom, the "Great Debate" about our participation in NATO, the attempt to limit the treaty-making power, and other actions, bespoke the reaction. The Supreme Court signalized this reaction when it struck down the President's action in seizing the steel industry while it was struck during the Korean War.

Powers of the President under the War Labor Disputes Act to Seize Properties Affected by Strikes
40 Op. Att'y Gen. 312 (1944)

MY DEAR MR. PRESIDENT: My opinion has been requested on the legality of a proposed Executive order directing the Secretary of Commerce to take possession of and to operate certain plants and facilities of Montgomery Ward and Company in Chicago, Illinois, in which a strike is now in progress. . . . In my opinion, the facts . . . justify the following conclusions:

(1) Montgomery Ward and Company is engaged in activities of a kind essential to the maintenance of our war economy. An interruption or stoppage of the Company's activities would have an adverse effect upon the war effort.

(2) There is a real and present danger that the labor dispute that is now interrupting the operations of the plants and facilities of the Company in Chicago may extend throughout the nation and interrupt the operations of other plants and facilities of the Company. There is an equally real and present danger that the dispute will breed other labor controversies that will interrupt the operations of plants and facilities of other companies, both in the Chicago area and elsewhere, that are engaged in making or distributing goods or performing services that are essential to the war effort.

(3) There is now no reason to expect that the disputes between the Company and its employees in Chicago and elsewhere in the United States will be settled promptly and peacefully either by agreement or by the machinery that Congress has set up in the War Labor Disputes Act.

The basic legal question is whether you have the authority to take possession of and to operate the plants and facilities of Montgomery Ward and Company in Chicago in order to prevent a serious interference with the war effort. Section 3 of

----

149. 335 U.S. 160 (1948).

the War Labor Disputes Act provides in part as follows: "The power of the President under the foregoing provisions of this section to take immediate possession of any plant upon a failure to comply with any such provisions, and the authority granted by this section for the use and operation by the United States or in its interests of any plant of which possession is so taken, shall also apply as hereinafter provided to any plant, mine, or facility equipped for the manufacture, production, or mining of any articles or materials which may be required for the war effort or which may be useful in connection therewith. Such power and authority may be exercised by the President through such department or agency of the Government as he may designate, and may be exercised with respect to any such plant, mine, or facility whenever the President finds, after investigation, and proclaims that there is an interruption of the operation of such plant, mine, or facility as a result of a strike or other labor disturbance, that the war effort will be unduly impeded or delayed by such interruption, and that the exercise of such power and authority is necessary to insure the operation of such plant, mine, or facility in the interest of the war effort. . . ."

On the basis of the facts that have been summarized, and the conclusions that those facts justify, it is my opinion, first, that the plants and facilities of Montgomery Ward are the kind of plants and facilities whose seizure is authorized by section 3 and, second, that you may properly make the findings required by section 3 as a condition precedent to the exercise of the power that it confers. I believe, therefore, that section 3 of the War Labor Disputes Act authorizes you to take possession of and to operate the plants and facilities of Montgomery Ward and Company.

It is not necessary, however, to rely solely upon the provisions of section 3 of the War Labor Disputes Act. As Chief Executive and as Commander-in-Chief of the Army and Navy, the President possesses an aggregate of powers that are derived from the Constitution and from various statutes enacted by the Congress for the purpose of carrying on the war. The Constitution lays upon the President the duty "to take care that the laws be faithfully executed." The Constitution also places on the President the responsibility and invests in him the powers of Commander-in-Chief of the Army and Navy. In time of war when the existence of the nation is at stake, this aggregate of powers includes authority to take reasonable steps to prevent nation-wide labor disturbances that threaten to interfere seriously with the conduct of the war. The fact that the initial impact of these disturbances is on the production or distribution of essential civilian goods is not a reason for denying the Chief Executive and the Commander-in-Chief of the Army and Navy the power to take steps to protect the nation's war effort. In modern war the maintenance of a healthy, orderly, and stable civilian economy is essential to successful military effort. The Congress has recognized this fact by enacting such statutes as the Emergency Price Control Act of 1942; the act of October 2, 1942, entitled "An Act to Amend the Emergency Price Control Act of 1942, to aid in preventing inflation, and for other purposes"; the Small Business Mobilization Law of June 11, 1942; and the War Labor Disputes Act. Even in the absence of section 3 of the War Labor Disputes Act, therefore, I believe that by the exercise of the aggregate of your powers as Chief Executive and Commander-in-Chief, you could lawfully take possession of and operate the plants and facilities of Montgomery Ward and Company if you found it necessary to do so to prevent injury to the country's war effort.

I conclude that in the circumstances of this case section 3 of the War Labor Disputes Act and your constitutional and statutory powers as Chief Executive and Commander-in-Chief of the Army and of the Navy, considered either separately or together, authorize you to direct the Secretary of Commerce to take possession of and to operate the plants and facilities of Montgomery Ward and Company in Chicago, Illinois.

The proposed Executive order, presented by the Chairman of the National War Labor Board and forwarded for my consideration by the Director of the Bureau of the Budget, has my approval as to form and legality.

Respectfully yours, FRANCIS BIDDLE.

Montgomery Ward v. Youngstown. The strike that precipitated the preceding opinion is perhaps best known for the newspaper photograph it produced of U.S. army troops carrying the head of Montgomery Ward out of his office. Do you agree with Attorney General Biddle's interpretation of the Constitution? Should this opinion provoke any reassessment of *Youngstown*?

Chapter 7

The "Long War" and the Separation of Powers

The stability of virtually any body of formal law depends on the coherence of the categories on which it is built. We have already seen how much separation of powers law — especially law concerning the powers of the President — turns on distinctions made between war and peace, battlefield and home front, and international and domestic affairs. Consider, for example, the apparent difference it made in *Korematsu* that Congress had declared war on Japan, as opposed to the context of *Youngstown*, in which the President acted without any such declaration. *Ex parte Milligan* confined the constitutional permissibility of martial law to "the theatre of active military operations," where "the courts are actually closed, and it is [otherwise] impossible to administer criminal justice according to law." This holding gave martial law geographic as well as situational limits. The Court has cautioned that its famous reference in *United States v. Curtiss-Wright* to "the very delicate, plenary and exclusive power of the President as the sole organ of the federal government in the field of international relation" should not be over-interpreted as sanctioning unlimited presidential authority to do anything in foreign, as compared to domestic, affairs. Yet that warning appears in a decision, *Zivotofsky v. Kerry*, 576 U.S. ___ , 135 S.Ct. 2076, 2089 (2015), which (a) affirms a rare grant of power to the President that is not only constitutionally vested, but beyond congressional control and (b) rests directly on the importance of the President's role on the international stage:

> [J]udicial precedent and historical practice teach that it is for the President alone to make the specific decision of what foreign power he will recognize as legitimate, both for the Nation as a whole and for the purpose of making his own position clear within the context of recognition in discussions and negotiations with foreign nations.

Id. In short, war/peace, battlefield/home front, and domestic/international have been salient markers for centuries in analyzing the constitutional distribution of national authorities.

Nevertheless, just as the Internet blew open the media categories — text, voice, and video — around which communications law had been organized prior to the 1990s, the aftermath of September 11 has challenged fundamental doctrinal markers in constitutional law. The horrors of that day awakened the United States to the long-term global challenge posed by al Qaeda and other extreme jihadist groups — a challenge that would entail both military and nonmilitary responses, as well as vigilance both within and beyond our borders. In 2004, Gen. John P. Abizaid, then the Central Command chief overseeing U.S. military operations in the Middle East, used the phrase "the Long War" to underscore the nature of the struggle, and the phrase has stuck—although some have suggested that "Forever War" might be more appropriate. Bradley Graham and Josh White, *Abizaid Credited With Popularizing the Term 'Long War,'* WASH. POST (Feb. 3, 2006). Deciding when war is "over" has become complicated even as a matter of international law. DUSTIN A. LEWIS, GABRIELLA BLUM, AND NAZ K. MODIRZADEH, INDEFINITE WAR: UNSETTLED INTERNATIONAL LAW ON THE END OF ARMED CONFLICT (2017). With no settled end in sight, the Long War thus challenges the conventional building blocks of separation of powers doctrine. To tweak slightly a critical question posed by legal historian Mary Dudziak, how does the law of peace work in an era of widespread military conflict? Mary L. Dudziak, *War and Peace in Time and Space*, 13 SEATTLE J. FOR SOC. JUST. 381 (2014). That question is the focus of this chapter.

A. Wartime Powers During the "War" on Terror

1. The Treatment of Enemy Combatants

Although not technically in conflict, there seems to be a dissonance in decisions like *Milligan* and *Korematsu* that Chief Justice Rehnquist, in his history of wartime civil liberties cases, expressed as follows: "The laws will . . . not be silent in time of war, but they will speak with a somewhat different voice." WILLIAM H. REHNQUIST, ALL THE LAWS BUT ONE: CIVIL LIBERTIES IN WARTIME 224–225 (1998). As suggested above, a statement like this presupposes that it is possible to discern the difference between a time of war and a time of peace. In deciding the scope of the President's authorities to respond to September 11, should the powers at issue be viewed as war powers or peacetime powers?

What follows first is a brief summary of the attacks and the government's response, including President George W. Bush's order regarding the detention and trial of potential enemy combatants. The order is limited by its terms to persons other than U.S. citizens, and was presumably intended to have its greatest impact on persons captured outside the United States. The order has been applied, however, to at least one alien captured while lawfully in the United States, and, although not within the purview of the order, at least one U.S. citizen has been detailed as an "enemy combatant." We will explore the legal issues raised by these cases, as well as by the use of detention pursuant to material witness warrants as an instrument of our counterterrorism policies. Despite the bluntness of the national security challenges that elicited our government's response, the legal issues are dauntingly complex, given that the relevant variables include the grounds for presidential authority (statutory or constitutional), the identity of the persons detained (citizen or noncitizen), the location of the hostile conduct (within the U.S. or beyond), and the conduct charged (war crime or ordinary criminal offense).

Stephen J. Shapiro, et al., Report of the Bar of the City of New York

Committee on Military Affairs and Justice (December 2001)

[T]he September 11, 2001 terrorist attacks [were committed] against the World Trade Center and the Pentagon ("September 11 attacks") by 18 foreign nationals believed by the U.S. Government to have been associated with the al Qaeda organization based primarily in Afghanistan. Al Qaeda has been accused of providing the inspiration, training, financing and control of the September 11 attacks, as well as assaults on two U.S. embassies in Africa, and on the *U.S.S. Cole* in Yemeni waters. In response to the September 11 attacks, the Congress on September 18 authorized military action but did not declare war. The United States' decision to use force was supported generally by resolutions of the United Nations Security Council and specifically by the North Atlantic Treaty Organization, as well as by many national governments. On September 21, the President declared that a National Emergency had been in existence since September 11. After the Islamic fundamentalist Taliban "government" of Afghanistan refused to surrender the al Qaeda leaders, U.S. and U.K. armed forces launched a military campaign against Taliban forces in Afghanistan.

Almost simultaneously with issuance of the Military Order on November 13, Afghan units opposing the Taliban and assisted by U.S. air support expelled the Taliban from the country's major cities, including from its capital Kabul. . . . [It is foreseeable] that some al Qaeda leaders (as opposed to soldiers or leaders from the Taliban's armed forces) may be captured and come within the control of U.S. armed forces, at which time it would have to be determined when, where and how they might be tried. . . .

Moreover, a large number of foreign nationals have been detained within the U.S.—according to Justice Department officials exceeding 1,000 in number but whose actual number remains undisclosed—many of whom are still in custody. It appears that some if not all of these detainees may be transferred from the control and custody of the Department of Justice (*i.e.*, Immigration and Naturalization Service) to the control and custody of the Department of Defense, as such transfer is directed by the Order.

Notice, Detention Treatment, and Trial of Certain Non-Citizens in the War Against Terrorism

66 Fed. Reg. 57833 (2001).

By the authority vested in me as President and as Commander in Chief of the Armed Forces of the United States by the Constitution and the laws of the United States of America, including the Authorization for Use of Military Force Joint Resolution (Public Law 107-40, 115 Stat. 224) and sections 821 and 836 of title 10, United States Code, it is hereby ordered as follows:

Section 1. Findings.

(a) International terrorists, including members of al Qaeda, have carried out attacks on United States diplomatic and military personnel and facilities abroad and on citizens and property within the United States on a scale that has created a state of armed conflict that requires the use of the United States Armed Forces.

(b) In light of grave acts of terrorism and threats of terrorism, including the terrorist attacks on September 11, 2001, on the headquarters of the United States Department of Defense in the national capital region, on the World Trade Center in New York, and on civilian aircraft such as in Pennsylvania, I proclaimed a national emergency on September 14, 2001 (Proc. 7463, Declaration of National Emergency by Reason of Certain Terrorist Attacks).

(c) Individuals acting alone and in concert involved in international terrorism possess both the capability and the intention to undertake further terrorist attacks against the United States that, if not detected and prevented, will cause mass deaths, mass injuries, and massive destruction of property, and may place at risk the continuity of the operations of the United States Government.

(d) The ability of the United States to protect the United States and its citizens, and to help its allies and other cooperating nations protect their nations and their citizens, from such further terrorist attacks depends in significant part upon using the United States Armed Forces to identify terrorists and those who support them, to disrupt their activities, and to eliminate their ability to conduct or support such attacks.

(e) To protect the United States and its citizens, and for the effective conduct of military operations and prevention of terrorist attacks, it is necessary for individuals subject to this order pursuant to section 2 hereof to be detained, and, when tried, to be tried for violations of the laws of war and other applicable laws by military tribunals.

(f) Given the danger to the safety of the United States and the nature of international terrorism, and to the extent provided by and under this order, I find consistent with section 836 of title 10, United States Code, that it is not practicable to apply in military commissions under this order the principles of law and the rules of evidence generally recognized in the trial of criminal cases in the United States district courts.

(g) Having fully considered the magnitude of the potential deaths, injuries, and property destruction that would result from potential acts of terrorism against the United States, and the probability that such acts will occur, I have determined that an extraordinary emergency exists for national defense purposes, that this emergency constitutes an urgent and compelling government interest, and that issuance of this order is necessary to meet the emergency.

Sec. 2. Definition and Policy.

(a) The term "individual subject to this order" shall mean any individual who is not a United States citizen with respect to whom I determine from time to time in writing that:

(1) there is reason to believe that such individual, at the relevant times,

(i) is or was a member of the organization known as al Qaeda;

(ii) has engaged in, aided or abetted, or conspired to commit, acts of international terrorism, or acts in preparation therefor, that have caused, threaten to cause, or have as their aim to cause, injury to or adverse effects on the United States, its citizens, national security, foreign policy, or economy; or

(iii) has knowingly harbored one or more individuals described in subparagraphs (i) or (ii) of subsection 2(a)(1) of this order; and

(2) it is in the interest of the United States that such individual be subject to this order.

(b) It is the policy of the United States that the Secretary of Defense shall take all necessary measures to ensure that any individual subject to this order is detained in accordance with section 3, and, if the individual is to be tried, that such individual is tried only in accordance with section 4.

(c) It is further the policy of the United States that any individual subject to this order who is not already under the control of the Secretary of Defense but who is under the control of any other officer or agent of the United States or any State shall, upon delivery of a copy of such written determination to such officer or agent, forthwith be placed under the control of the Secretary of Defense.

Sec. 3. Detention Authority of the Secretary of Defense. Any individual subject to this order shall be—

(a) detained at an appropriate location designated by the Secretary of Defense outside or within the United States;

(b) treated humanely, without any adverse distinction based on race, color, religion, gender, birth, wealth, or any similar criteria;

(c) afforded adequate food, drinking water, shelter, clothing, and medical treatment;

(d) allowed the free exercise of religion consistent with the requirements of such detention; and

(e) detained in accordance with such other conditions as the Secretary of Defense may prescribe.

Sec. 4. Authority of the Secretary of Defense Regarding Trials of Individuals Subject to this Order.

(a) Any individual subject to this order shall, when tried, be tried by military commission for any and all offenses triable by military commission that such individual is alleged to have committed, and may be punished in accordance with the penalties provided under applicable law, including life imprisonment or death.

(b) As a military function and in light of the findings in section 1, including subsection (f) thereof, the Secretary of Defense shall issue such orders and regulations, including orders for the appointment of one or more military commissions, as may be necessary to carry out subsection (a) of this section.

(c) Orders and regulations issued under subsection (b) of this section shall include, but not be limited to, rules for the conduct of the proceedings of military commissions, including pretrial, trial, and post-trial procedures, modes of proof, issuance of process, and qualifications of attorneys, which shall at a minimum provide—

(1) military commissions to sit at any time and any place, consistent with such guidance regarding time and place as the Secretary of Defense may provide;

(2) a full and fair trial, with the military commission sitting as the triers of both fact and law;

(3) admission of such evidence as would, in the opinion of the presiding officer of the military commission (or instead, if any other member of the commission so requests at the time the presiding officer renders that opinion, the opinion of the commission rendered at that time by a majority of the commission), have probative value to a reasonable person;

(4) in a manner consistent with the protection of information classified or classifiable under Executive Order 12958 of April 17, 1995, as amended, or any successor Executive Order, protected by statute or rule from unauthorized disclosure, or otherwise protected by law, (A) the handling of, admission into evidence of, and access to materials and information, and (B) the conduct, closure of, and access to proceedings;

(5) conduct of the prosecution by one or more attorneys designated by the Secretary of Defense and conduct of the defense by attorneys for the individual subject to this order;

(6) conviction only upon the concurrence of two-thirds of the members of the commission present at the time of the vote, a majority being present;

(7) sentencing only upon the concurrence of two-thirds of the members of the commission present at the time of the vote, a majority being present; and

(8) submission of the record of the trial, including any conviction or sentence, for review and final decision by me or by the Secretary of Defense if so designated by me for that purpose.

Sec. 5. Obligation of Other Agencies to Assist the Secretary of Defense.

Departments, agencies, entities, and officers of the United States shall, to the maximum extent permitted by law, provide to the Secretary of Defense such assistance as he may request to implement this order.

Sec. 6. Additional Authorities of the Secretary of Defense.

(a) As a military function and in light of the findings in section 1, the Secretary of Defense shall issue such orders and regulations as may be necessary to carry out any of the provisions of this order.

(b) The Secretary of Defense may perform any of his functions or duties, and may exercise any of the powers provided to him under this order (other than under section 4(c)(8) hereof) in accordance with section 113(d) of title 10, United States Code.

Sec. 7. Relationship to Other Law and Forums.

(a) Nothing in this order shall be construed to—

(1) authorize the disclosure of state secrets to any person not otherwise authorized to have access to them;

(2) limit the authority of the President as Commander in Chief of the Armed Forces or the power of the President to grant reprieves and pardons; or

(3) limit the lawful authority of the Secretary of Defense, any military commander, or any other officer or agent of the United States or of any State to detain or try any person who is not an individual subject to this order.

(b) With respect to any individual subject to this order—

(1) military tribunals shall have exclusive jurisdiction with respect to offenses by the individual; and

(2) the individual shall not be privileged to seek any remedy or maintain any proceeding, directly or indirectly, or to have any such remedy or proceeding sought on the individual's behalf, in (i) any court of the United States, or any State thereof, (ii) any court of any foreign nation, or (iii) any international tribunal.

(c) This order is not intended to and does not create any right, benefit, or privilege, substantive or procedural, enforceable at law or equity by any party, against the United States, its departments, agencies, or other entities, its officers or employees, or any other person.

(d) For purposes of this order, the term "State" includes any State, district, territory, or possession of the United States.

(e) I reserve the authority to direct the Secretary of Defense, at any time hereafter, to transfer to a governmental authority control of any individual subject to this order. Nothing in this order shall be construed to limit the authority of any such governmental authority to prosecute any individual for whom control is transferred.

Sec. 8. Publication.

This order shall be published in the Federal Register.

GEORGE W. BUSH
THE WHITE HOUSE,
November 13, 2001.

————————

1. *Military Commissions.* This order provides that "[a]ny individual subject to this order shall, when tried, be tried by military commission for any and all offenses

triable by military commission." As explained by a Defense Department fact sheet: "Military Commissions have historically been used to prosecute enemy combatants who violate the laws of war; the last time the United States used the Military Commission process was during World War II." Department of Defense Fact Sheet: Military Commission Procedures, available at http://www.defenselink.mil/news/Aug2003 /d20030812factsheet.pdf. The limitation of military commissions to tribunals that try enemy combatants for violations of the laws of war thus distinguishes them from either (1) ad hoc tribunals that provide civil justice during martial law because ordinary courts are unavailable, and (2) courts-martial, which are courts constituted pursuant to the Uniform Code of Military Justice, chiefly to try to military personnel for specified offenses. The "laws of war" refer to "the part of international law relating to the conduct of armed conflict and military occupations, including the protection of civilians, wounded, and prisoners of war," ADAM ROBERTS AND RICHARD GUELFF, DOCUMENTS ON THE LAWS OF WAR 1 (3d ed. 2000), and are thus generally embodied in treaties and other international documents. When Congress promulgated the Uniform Code of Military Justice, it expressly preserved recognition for the role of military commissions in enforcing this body of law:

> The provisions of this chapter conferring jurisdiction upon courts-martial do not deprive military commissions, provost courts, or other military tribunals of concurrent jurisdiction with respect to offenders or offenses that by statute or by the law of war may be tried by military commissions, provost courts, or other military tribunals.

18 U.S.C. § 821 (2000). A helpful guide to the nature of military tribunals and to sources that elucidate their history and practices is Stephen Young, United States Military Commissions: A Quick Guide to Available Resources (March 1, 2002), available at http://tinyurl.com/ybvwby45.

2. *Implementing Regulations.* The President's Order originally raised an uproar, in part because of possibilities it seemed to open for adjudication that would fall short of international norms of fairness. Especially troubling was the implication of Section 4(c)(7) that a death sentence might be imposed based on a less than unanimous verdict. That last prospect was eliminated by the trial procedures subsequently adopted by the Defense Department, Military Commission Order No. 1, Procedures for Trials by Military Commissions of Certain Non-United States Citizens in the War Against Terrorism (Mar. 21, 2002), which considerably fleshed out the protections to be afforded the accused.

Among the key remaining differences between trials by military commission and courts-martial is that, for military commissions:

> Evidence shall be admitted if, in the opinion of the Presiding Officer (or instead, if any other member of the Commission so requests at the time the Presiding Officer renders that opinion, the opinion of the Commission rendered at that time by a majority of the Commission), the evidence would have probative value to a reasonable person.

Id., § 6(D)(1). By contrast, the Uniform Code of Military Justice directs the President to provide rules of proof at courts-martial that "apply the principles of law and the rules of evidence generally recognized in the trial of criminal cases in the United States district courts." 10 U.S.C. § 836 (2000). This difference presumably reflects that the acts tried before military commissions frequently occur on the battlefield or in venues that preclude application of ordinary rules of evidence, such as a strict chain of custody.

3. *Judicial Review.* Given the absence of time limits in the President's order, its imposition could result in the indefinite detention of an individual whom the President designates an "enemy combatant." The right of the United States to detain enemy combatants, without recourse to habeas corpus, was affirmed in *Johnson v. Eisentrager*, 339 U.S. 763 (1950), involving German nationals who, after Germany's surrender on May 8, 1945, but before the surrender of Japan, assisted Japanese forces fighting against the United States and were captured. The question arises, however, whether non-citizens who deny that they are "enemy combatants" are entitled to judicial review of that determination.

In a 6–3 opinion, the Supreme Court resolved this question affirmatively in *Rasul v. Bush*, 542 U.S. 466 (2004). The petitioners were two Australian and twelve Kuwaiti citizens who were captured in Afghanistan during hostilities between the United States and the Taliban. The majority distinguished the *Rasul* petitioners from those in *Eisentrager* on three grounds: "They are not nationals of countries at war with the United States, and they deny that they have engaged in or plotted acts of aggression against the United States; they have never been afforded access to any tribunal, much less charged with and convicted of wrongdoing; and for more than two years they have been imprisoned in territory over which the United States exercises exclusive jurisdiction and control." Equally important, the Court limited *Eisentrager* to the question whether its petitioners were *constitutionally* entitled to habeas review, absent a statute recognizing that right. Over a vigorous dissent by Justice Scalia, joined by the Chief Justice and by Justice Thomas, *Rasul* held that the individuals suing in *Rasul* were entitled to the benefit of 28 U.S.C. § 2241, the general federal habeas statute. Justice Kennedy concurred only in the judgment, limiting his approval of habeas jurisdiction to cases (1) in which the noncitizen petitioners are being held in territory over which the United States exerts plenary jurisdiction and control, and (2) in which their detention is indefinite and "without benefit of any legal proceeding to determine their status."

The Supreme Court eventually got to answer the question whether the trial of alleged enemy combatants by military commission was permissible, but not before a habeas petition brought it an equally complex issue, namely, whether U.S. citizens can be designated "enemy combatants." The answer during a declared war is apparently positive because one of the Nazi saboteurs whose trial by military tribunal was upheld in *Ex parte Quirin*, 317 U.S. 1 (1942), held U.S. citizenship. But that defendant was captured violating the laws of war during a declared war with Germany, not as part of an ongoing struggle against a non-state-based terrorist enterprise.

In addressing this question, the Courts of Appeals divided, but in cases that were factually distinguishable. In *Hamdi v. Rumsfeld*, 316 F.3d 450 (4th Cir. 2003), the Fourth Circuit held that the executive was authorized to detain as an enemy combatant an American citizen seized within the zone of combat in Afghanistan. In *Padilla v. Rumsfeld*, 352 F.3d 695 (2d Cir. 2003), the Second Circuit found such authority lacking with regard to a U.S. citizen so detained, but by law enforcement authorities arresting him in the United States. Although it granted certiorari in both cases, the Supreme Court did not immediately reach the merits in *Padilla*. Instead, the Court decided, 5–4, that the Second Circuit did not have habeas jurisdiction in Padilla's case because the proper respondent was the commander of a naval brig in Charleston, South Carolina, in which Padilla was incarcerated. Thus, the Court has yet to address the question whether the executive has authority outside the zone of combat to seize a U.S. citizen (or, indeed, a non-citizen) as an enemy combatant. The Court did address in the following opinion the scope of executive authority within the zone of combat:

Hamdi v. Rumsfeld

542 U.S. 507 (2004).

Justice O'CONNOR announced the judgment of the Court and delivered an opinion, in which THE CHIEF JUSTICE, Justice KENNEDY, and Justice BREYER join.

• • •

I

On September 11, 2001, the al Qaeda terrorist network used hijacked commercial airliners to attack prominent targets in the United States. Approximately 3,000 people were killed in those attacks. One week later, in response to these "acts of treacherous violence," Congress passed a resolution authorizing the President to "use all necessary and appropriate force against those nations, organizations, or persons he determines planned, authorized, committed, or aided the terrorist attacks" or "harbored such organizations or persons, in order to prevent any future acts of international terrorism against the United States by such nations, organizations or persons." Authorization for Use of Military Force ("the AUMF"), 115 Stat. 224. Soon thereafter, the President ordered United States Armed Forces to Afghanistan, with a mission to subdue al Qaeda and quell the Taliban regime that was known to support it.

This case arises out of the detention of a man whom the Government alleges took up arms with the Taliban during this conflict. His name is Yaser Esam Hamdi. Born an American citizen in Louisiana in 1980, Hamdi moved with his family to Saudi Arabia as a child. By 2001, the parties agree, he resided in Afghanistan. At some point that year, he was seized by members of the Northern Alliance, a coalition of military groups opposed to the Taliban government, and eventually was turned over to the United States military. The Government asserts that it initially detained and interrogated Hamdi in Afghanistan before transferring him to the United States Naval Base in Guantanamo Bay in January 2002. In April 2002, upon learning that Hamdi is an American citizen, authorities transferred him to a naval brig in Norfolk, Virginia, where he remained until a recent transfer to a brig in Charleston, South Carolina. The Government contends that Hamdi is an "enemy combatant," and that this status justifies holding him in the United States indefinitely—without formal charges or proceedings—unless and until it makes the determination that access to counsel or further process is warranted.

In June 2002, Hamdi's father, Esam Fouad Hamdi, filed the present petition for a writ of habeas corpus under 28 U.S.C. § 2241 in the Eastern District of Virginia, naming as petitioners his son and himself as next friend. The elder Hamdi alleges in the petition that he has had no contact with his son since the Government took custody of him in 2001, and that the Government has held his son "without access to legal counsel or notice of any charges pending against him." The petition contends that Hamdi's detention was not legally authorized. It argues that, "[a]s an American citizen, . . . Hamdi enjoys the full protections of the Constitution," and that Hamdi's detention in the United States without charges, access to an impartial tribunal, or assistance of counsel "violated and continue[s] to violate the Fifth and Fourteenth Amendments to the United States Constitution." The habeas petition asks that the court, among other things, (1) appoint counsel for Hamdi; (2) order respondents to cease interrogating him; (3) declare that he is being held in violation of the Fifth and Fourteenth Amendments; (4) "[t]o the extent Respondents contest any material factual allegations in this Petition, schedule an evidentiary hearing, at which Petitioners may adduce proof in support of their allegations"; and (5) order that Hamdi be released from his "unlawful custody." Although his habeas petition provides no details with regard to the factual circumstances surrounding his son's capture and detention, Hamdi's father has asserted in documents found elsewhere in the record that his son went to Afghanistan to do "relief work," and that he had been in that country less than two months before September 11, 2001, and could not have received military training. The 20-year-old was traveling on his own for the first time, his father says, and "[b]ecause of his lack of experience, he was trapped in Afghanistan once that military campaign began."

The District Court found that Hamdi's father was a proper next friend, appointed the federal public defender as counsel for the petitioners, and ordered that counsel be given access to Hamdi. The United States Court of Appeals for the Fourth Circuit reversed that order, holding that the District Court had failed to extend appropriate deference to the Government's security and intelligence interests. It directed the District Court to consider "the most cautious procedures first," and to conduct a deferential inquiry into Hamdi's status. It opined that "if Hamdi is indeed an 'enemy combatant' who was captured during hostilities in Afghanistan, the government's present detention of him is a lawful one."

On remand, the Government filed a response and a motion to dismiss the petition. It attached to its response a declaration from one Michael Mobbs (hereinafter "Mobbs Declaration"), who identified himself as Special Advisor to the Under Secretary of Defense for Policy. Mobbs indicated that in this position, he has been "substantially involved with matters related to the detention of enemy combatants in the current war against the al Qaeda terrorists and those who support and harbor them (including the Taliban)." He expressed his "familiar[ity]" with Department of Defense and United States military policies and procedures applicable to the detention, control, and transfer of al Qaeda and Taliban personnel, and declared that "[b]ased upon my review of relevant records and reports, I am also familiar with the facts and circumstances related to the capture of . . . Hamdi and his detention by U.S. military forces."

Mobbs then set forth what remains the sole evidentiary support that the Government has provided to the courts for Hamdi's detention. The declaration states that Hamdi "traveled to Afghanistan" in July or August 2001, and that he thereafter "affiliated with a Taliban military unit and received weapons training." It asserts that Hamdi "remained with his Taliban unit following the attacks of September 11" and that, during the time when Northern Alliance forces were "engaged in battle with the Taliban," "Hamdi's Taliban unit surrendered" to those forces, after which he "surrender[ed] his Kalishnikov assault rifle" to them. The Mobbs Declaration also states that, because al Qaeda and the Taliban "were and are hostile forces engaged in armed conflict with the armed forces of the United States," "individuals associated with" those groups "were and continue to be enemy combatants." Mobbs states that Hamdi was labeled an enemy combatant "[b]ased upon his interviews and in light of his association with the Taliban." According to the declaration, a series of "U.S. military screening team[s]" determined that Hamdi met "the criteria for enemy combatants," and "a subsequent interview of Hamdi has confirmed that he surrendered and gave his firearm to Northern Alliance forces, which supports his classification as an enemy combatant."

After the Government submitted this declaration, the Fourth Circuit directed the District Court to proceed in accordance with its earlier ruling and, specifically, to " 'consider the sufficiency of the Mobbs Declaration as an independent matter before proceeding further.' " The District Court found that the Mobbs Declaration fell "far short" of supporting Hamdi's detention. It criticized the generic and hearsay nature of the affidavit, calling it "little more than the government's 'say-so.' " It ordered the Government to turn over numerous materials for *in camera* review, including copies of all of Hamdi's statements and the notes taken from interviews with him that related to his reasons for going to Afghanistan and his activities therein; a list of all interrogators who had questioned Hamdi and their names and addresses; statements by members of the Northern Alliance regarding Hamdi's surrender and capture; a list of the dates and locations of his capture and subsequent detentions; and the names and titles of the United States Government officials who made the determinations that Hamdi was an enemy combatant and that he should be moved to a naval brig. The court indicated that all of these materials were necessary for "meaningful judicial review" of whether Hamdi's detention was legally authorized and whether Hamdi had received sufficient process to satisfy the Due Process Clause of the Constitution and relevant treaties or military regulations.

The Government sought to appeal the production order, and the District Court certified the question of whether the Mobbs Declaration, "'standing alone, is sufficient as a matter of law to allow meaningful judicial review of [Hamdi's] classification as an enemy combatant.'" The Fourth Circuit reversed, but did not squarely answer the certified question. It instead stressed that, because it was "undisputed that Hamdi was captured in a zone of active combat in a foreign theater of conflict," no factual inquiry or evidentiary hearing allowing Hamdi to be heard or to rebut the Government's assertions was necessary or proper. Concluding that the factual averments in the Mobbs Declaration, "if accurate," provided a sufficient basis upon which to conclude that the President had constitutionally detained Hamdi pursuant to the President's war powers, it ordered the habeas petition dismissed. The Fourth Circuit emphasized that the "vital purposes" of the detention of uncharged enemy combatants—preventing those combatants from rejoining the enemy while relieving the military of the burden of litigating the circumstances of wartime captures halfway around the globe—were interests "directly derived from the war powers of Articles I and II." In that court's view, because "Article III contains nothing analogous to the specific powers of war so carefully enumerated in Articles I and II," separation of powers principles prohibited a federal court from "delv[ing] further into Hamdi's status and capture." Accordingly, the District Court's more vigorous inquiry "went far beyond the acceptable scope of review."

On the more global question of whether legal authorization exists for the detention of citizen enemy combatants at all, the Fourth Circuit rejected Hamdi's arguments that 18 U.S.C. § 4001(a) and Article 5 of the Geneva Convention rendered any such detentions unlawful. The court expressed doubt as to Hamdi's argument that § 4001(a), which provides that "[n]o citizen shall be imprisoned or otherwise detained by the United States except pursuant to an Act of Congress," required express congressional authorization of detentions of this sort. But it held that, in any event, such authorization was found in the post-September 11 Authorization for Use of Military Force. . . . The court likewise rejected Hamdi's Geneva Convention claim, concluding that the convention is not self-executing and that, even if it were, it would not preclude the Executive from detaining Hamdi until the cessation of hostilities.

Finally, the Fourth Circuit rejected Hamdi's contention that its legal analyses with regard to the authorization for the detention scheme and the process to which he was constitutionally entitled should be altered by the fact that he is an American citizen detained on American soil. Relying on *Ex parte Quirin,* 317 U.S. 1 (1942), the court emphasized that "[o]ne who takes up arms against the United States in a foreign theater of war, regardless of his citizenship, may properly be designated an enemy combatant and treated as such." "The privilege of citizenship," the court held, "entitles Hamdi to a limited judicial inquiry into his detention, but only to determine its legality under the war powers of the political branches. At least where it is undisputed that he was present in a zone of active combat operations, we are satisfied that the Constitution does not entitle him to a searching review of the factual determinations underlying his seizure there."

The Fourth Circuit denied rehearing en banc, and we granted certiorari. We now vacate the judgment below and remand.

II

The threshold question before us is whether the Executive has the authority to detain citizens who qualify as "enemy combatants." There is some debate as to the proper scope of this term, and the Government has never provided any court with the full criteria that it uses in classifying individuals as such. It has made clear, however, that, for purposes of this case, the "enemy combatant" that it is seeking to detain is an individual who, it alleges, was " 'part of or supporting forces hostile to the United States or coalition partners' " in Afghanistan and who " 'engaged in an armed conflict against the United States' " there. We therefore answer only the narrow question before us: whether the detention of citizens falling within that definition is authorized.

The Government maintains that no explicit congressional authorization is required, because the Executive possesses plenary authority to detain pursuant to Article II of the Constitution. We do not reach the question whether Article II provides such authority, however, because we agree with the Government's alternative position, that Congress has in fact authorized Hamdi's detention, through the AUMF.

Our analysis on that point, set forth below, substantially overlaps with our analysis of Hamdi's principal argument for the illegality of his detention. He posits that his detention is forbidden by 18 U.S.C. § 4001(a). Section 4001(a) states that "[n]o citizen shall be imprisoned or otherwise detained by the United States except pursuant to an Act of Congress." Congress passed § 4001(a) in 1971 as part of a bill to repeal the Emergency Detention Act of 1950, 50 U.S.C. § 811 *et seq.*, which provided procedures for executive detention, during times of emergency, of individuals deemed likely to engage in espionage or sabotage. Congress was particularly concerned about the possibility that the Act could be used to reprise the Japanese internment camps of World War II. The Government again presses two alternative positions. First, it argues that § 4001(a), in light of its legislative history and its location in Title 18, applies only to "the control of civilian prisons and related detentions," not to military detentions. Second, it maintains that § 4001(a) is satisfied, because Hamdi is being detained "pursuant to an Act of Congress" — the AUMF. Again, because we conclude that the Government's second assertion is correct, we do not address the first. In other words, for the reasons that follow, we conclude that the AUMF is explicit congressional authorization for the detention of individuals in the narrow category we describe (assuming, without deciding, that such authorization is required), and that the AUMF satisfied § 4001(a)'s requirement that a detention be "pursuant to an Act of Congress" (assuming, without deciding, that § 4001(a) applies to military detentions).

The AUMF authorizes the President to use "all necessary and appropriate force" against "nations, organizations, or persons" associated with the September 11, 2001, terrorist attacks. 115 Stat. 224. There can be no doubt that individuals who fought against the United States in Afghanistan as part of the Taliban, an organization known to have supported the al Qaeda terrorist network responsible for those attacks, are individuals Congress sought to target in passing the AUMF. We conclude that detention of individuals falling into the limited category we are considering, for the duration of the particular conflict in which they were captured, is so fundamental and accepted an incident to war as to be an exercise of the "necessary and appropriate force" Congress has authorized the President to use.

The capture and detention of lawful combatants and the capture, detention, and trial of unlawful combatants, by "universal agreement and practice," are "important incident[s] of war." *Ex parte Quirin,* 317 U.S., at 28. The purpose of detention is to prevent captured individuals from returning to the field of battle and taking up arms once again.

There is no bar to this Nation's holding one of its own citizens as an enemy combatant. In *Quirin,* one of the detainees, Haupt, alleged that he was a naturalized United States citizen. 317 U.S., at 20. We held that "[c]itizens who associate themselves with the military arm of the enemy government, and with its aid, guidance and direction enter this country bent on hostile acts, are enemy belligerents within the meaning of . . . the law of war." *Id.,* at 37–38. While Haupt was tried for violations of the law of war, nothing in *Quirin* suggests that his citizenship would have precluded his mere detention for the duration of the relevant hostilities. See *id.,* at 30–31. Nor can we see any reason for drawing such a line here. A citizen, no less than an alien, can be "part of or supporting forces hostile to the United States or coalition partners" and "engaged in an armed conflict against the United States," Brief for Respondents 3; such a citizen, if released, would pose the same threat of returning to the front during the ongoing conflict.

In light of these principles, it is of no moment that the AUMF does not use specific language of detention. Because detention to prevent a combatant's return to the battlefield is a fundamental incident of waging war, in permitting the use of "necessary and appropriate force," Congress has clearly and unmistakably authorized detention in the narrow circumstances considered here.

Hamdi objects, nevertheless, that Congress has not authorized the *indefinite* detention to which he is now subject. The Government responds that "the detention of enemy combatants during World War II was just as 'indefinite' while that war was being fought." We take Hamdi's objection to be not to the lack of certainty regarding the date on which the conflict will end, but to the substantial prospect of perpetual detention. We recognize that the national security underpinnings of the "war on terror," although crucially important, are broad and malleable. As the Government concedes, "given its unconventional nature, the current conflict is unlikely to end with a formal cease-fire agreement." The prospect Hamdi raises is therefore not far-fetched. If the Government does not consider this unconventional war won for two generations, and if it maintains during that time that Hamdi might, if released, rejoin forces fighting against the United States, then the position it has taken throughout the litigation of this case suggests that Hamdi's detention could last for the rest of his life.

It is a clearly established principle of the law of war that detention may last no longer than active hostilities. *See* Article 118 of the Geneva Convention (III) Relative to the Treatment of Prisoners of War, Aug. 12, 1949, [1955] 6 U.S.T. 3316, 3406, T.I.A.S. No. 3364 ("Prisoners of war shall be released and repatriated without delay after the cessation of active hostilities"). *See also* Article 20 of The Hague Convention (II) on Laws and Customs of War on Land, July 29, 1899, 32 Stat. 1817 (as soon as possible after "conclusion of peace"); Hague Convention (IV), *supra*, Oct. 18, 1907, 36 Stat. 2301("conclusion of peace" (Art. 20)); Geneva Convention, *supra*, July 27, 1929, 47 Stat.2055 (repatriation should be accomplished with the least possible delay after conclusion of peace (Art. 75)).

Hamdi contends that the AUMF does not authorize indefinite or perpetual detention. Certainly, we agree that indefinite detention for the purpose of interrogation is not authorized. Further, we understand Congress' grant of authority for the use of "necessary and appropriate force" to include the authority to detain for the duration of the relevant conflict, and our understanding is based on longstanding law-of-war principles. If the practical circumstances of a given conflict are entirely unlike those of the conflicts that informed the development of the law of war, that understanding may unravel. But that is not the situation we face as of this date. Active combat operations against Taliban fighters apparently are ongoing in Afghanistan. *See, e.g.,* Constable, U.S. Launches New Operation in Afghanistan, Washington Post, Mar. 14, 2004, p. A22 (reporting that 13,500 United States troops remain in Afghanistan, including several thousand new arrivals); J. Abizaid, Dept. of Defense, Gen. Abizaid Central Command Operations Update Briefing, Apr. 30, 2004, http://www.defense link.mil /transcripts/2004/ tr20040430-1402.html (as visited June 8, 2004, and available in the Clerk of Court's case file) (media briefing describing ongoing operations in Afghanistan involving 20,000 United States troops). The United States may detain, for the duration of these hostilities, individuals legitimately determined to be Taliban combatants who "engaged in an armed conflict against the United States." If the record establishes that United States troops are still involved in active combat in Afghanistan, those detentions are part of the exercise of "necessary and appropriate force," and therefore are authorized by the AUMF.

Ex parte Milligan, 4 Wall. 2, 125 (1866), does not undermine our holding about the Government's authority to seize enemy combatants, as we define that term today. In that case, the Court made repeated reference to the fact that its inquiry into whether the military tribunal had jurisdiction to try and punish Milligan turned in large part on the fact that Milligan was not a prisoner of war, but a resident of Indiana arrested while at home there. That fact was central to its conclusion. Had Milligan been captured while he was assisting Confederate soldiers by carrying a rifle against Union troops on a Confederate battlefield, the holding of the Court might well have been different. The Court's repeated explanations that Milligan was not a prisoner of war suggest that had these different circumstances been present he could have been detained under military authority for the duration of the conflict, whether or not he was a citizen.[17]

Moreover, as Justice Scalia acknowledges, the Court in *Ex parte Quirin*, 317 U.S. 1 (1942), dismissed the language of *Milligan* that the petitioners had suggested prevented them from being subject to military process. Clear in this rejection was a disavowal of the New York State cases cited in *Milligan*, on which Justice Scalia relies. Both *Smith v. Shaw*, 12 Johns. 257 (N.Y.1815), and *M'Connell v. Hampton*, 12 Johns. 234 (N.Y.1815), were civil suits for false imprisonment. Even accepting that these cases once could have been viewed as standing for the sweeping proposition for which Justice Scalia cites them—that the military does not have authority to try an American citizen accused of spying against his country during wartime—*Quirin* makes undeniably clear that this is not the law today. Haupt, like the citizens in *Smith* and *M'Connell*, was accused of being a spy. The Court in *Quirin* found him "subject to trial and punishment by [a] military tribunal[ ]" for those acts, and held that his citizenship did not change this result. 317 U.S., at 31, 37–38.

Quirin was a unanimous opinion. It both postdates and clarifies *Milligan*, providing us with the most apposite precedent that we have on the question of whether citizens may be detained in such circumstances. Brushing aside such precedent—particularly when doing so gives rise to a host of new questions never dealt with by this Court—is unjustified and unwise.

To the extent that Justice Scalia accepts the precedential value of *Quirin*, he argues that it cannot guide our inquiry here because "[i]n *Quirin* it was uncontested that the petitioners were members of enemy forces," while Hamdi challenges his classification as an enemy combatant. But it is unclear why, in the paradigm outlined by Justice Scalia, such a concession should have any relevance. Justice Scalia envisions a system in which the only options are congressional suspension of the writ of habeas corpus or prosecution for treason or some other crime. He does not explain how his historical analysis supports the addition of a third option—detention under some other process after concession of enemy-combatant status—or why a concession should carry any different effect than proof of enemy-combatant status in a proceeding that comports with due process. To be clear, our opinion only finds legislative authority to detain under the AUMF once it is sufficiently clear that the individual is, in fact, an enemy combatant; whether that is established by concession or by some other process that verifies this fact with sufficient certainty seems beside the point.

Further, Justice Scalia largely ignores the context of this case: a United States citizen captured in a *foreign* combat zone. Justice Scalia refers to only one case involving this factual scenario—a case in which a United States citizen-POW (a member of the Italian army) from World War II was seized on the battlefield in Sicily and

---

17. Here the basis asserted for detention by the military is that Hamdi was carrying a weapon against American troops on a foreign battlefield; that is, that he was an enemy combatant. The legal category of enemy combatant has not been elaborated upon in great detail. The permissible bounds of the category will be defined by the lower courts as subsequent cases are presented to them.

then held in the United States. The court in that case held that the military detention of that United States citizen was lawful. *See In re Territo,* 156 F.2d, at 148.

Justice Scalia's treatment of that case—in a footnote—suffers from the same defect as does his treatment of *Quirin:* Because Justice Scalia finds the fact of battlefield capture irrelevant, his distinction based on the fact that the petitioner "conceded" enemy combatant status is beside the point. Justice Scalia can point to no case or other authority for the proposition that those captured on a foreign battlefield (whether detained there or in U.S. territory) cannot be detained outside the criminal process.

Moreover, Justice Scalia presumably would come to a different result if Hamdi had been kept in Afghanistan or even Guantanamo Bay. This creates a perverse incentive. Military authorities faced with the stark choice of submitting to the full-blown criminal process or releasing a suspected enemy combatant captured on the battlefield will simply keep citizen-detainees abroad. Indeed, the Government transferred Hamdi from Guantanamo Bay to the United States naval brig only after it learned that he might be an American citizen. It is not at all clear why that should make a determinative constitutional difference. . . .

[Part III of the Court's opinion, discussing the scope of judicial authority to scrutinize Hamdi's challenge to his designation as an "enemy combatant" is discussed in the notes following this excerpt.]

IV

Hamdi asks us to hold that the Fourth Circuit also erred by denying him immediate access to counsel upon his detention and by disposing of the case without permitting him to meet with an attorney. Brief for Petitioners 19. Since our grant of certiorari in this case, Hamdi has been appointed counsel, with whom he has met for consultation purposes on several occasions, and with whom he is now being granted unmonitored meetings. He unquestionably has the right to access to counsel in connection with the proceedings on remand. No further consideration of this issue is necessary at this stage of the case.

*   *   *

The judgment of the United States Court of Appeals for the Fourth Circuit is vacated, and the case is remanded for further proceedings.

It is so ordered.

Justice SOUTER, with whom Justice GINSBURG joins, concurring in part, dissenting in part, and concurring in the judgment.

. . . The plurality . . . [accepts] the Government's position that if Hamdi's designation as an enemy combatant is correct, his detention (at least as to some period) is authorized by an Act of Congress as required by § 4001(a), that is, by the Authorization for Use of Military Force, 115 Stat. 224 (hereinafter Force Resolution). *Ante,* at 9–14. Here, I disagree and respectfully dissent. The Government has failed to demonstrate that the Force Resolution authorizes the detention complained of here even on the facts the Government claims. If the Government raises nothing further than the record now shows, the Non-Detention Act entitles Hamdi to be released.

I

The Government's first response to Hamdi's claim that holding him violates § 4001(a), prohibiting detention of citizens "except pursuant to an Act of Congress," is that the statute does not even apply to military wartime detentions, being beyond the sphere of domestic criminal law. Next, the Government says that even if that statute does apply, two Acts of Congress provide the authority § 4001(a) demands: a general authorization to the Department of Defense to pay for detaining "prisoners of war" and "similar" persons, 10 U.S.C. § 956(5), and the Force Resolution, passed after the attacks of 2001. At the same time, the Government argues that in detaining Hamdi in the manner described, the President is in any event acting as Commander in Chief under Article II of the Constitution, which brings with it the right to invoke authority under the accepted customary rules for waging war. On the record in front of us, the Government has not made out a case on any theory.

II

The threshold issue is how broadly or narrowly to read the Non-Detention Act, the tone of which is severe: "No citizen shall be imprisoned or otherwise detained by the United States except pursuant to an Act of Congress." Should the severity of the Act be relieved when the Government's stated factual justification for incommunicado detention is a war on terrorism, so that the Government may be said to act "pursuant" to congressional terms that fall short of explicit authority to imprison individuals? With one possible though important qualification, *see infra*, at 10–11, the answer has to be no. For a number of reasons, the prohibition within § 4001(a) has to be read broadly to accord the statute a long reach and to impose a burden of justification on the Government.

First, the circumstances in which the Act was adopted point the way to this interpretation. The provision superseded a cold-war statute, the Emergency Detention Act of 1950 (formerly 50 U.S.C. § 811 *et seq.* (1970 ed.)), which had authorized the Attorney General, in time of emergency, to detain anyone reasonably thought likely to engage in espionage or sabotage. That statute was repealed in 1971 out of fear that it could authorize a repetition of the World War II internment of citizens of Japanese ancestry; Congress meant to preclude another episode like the one described in *Korematsu v. United States*, 323 U.S. 214(1944). *See* H.R.Rep. No. 92-116, pp. 2, 4–5 (1971). While Congress might simply have struck the 1950 statute, in considering the repealer the point was made that the existing statute provided some express procedural protection, without which the Executive would seem to be subject to no statutory limits protecting individual liberty. It was in these circumstances that a proposed limit on Executive action was expanded to the inclusive scope of § 4001(a) as enacted.

The fact that Congress intended to guard against a repetition of the World War II internments when it repealed the 1950 statute and gave us § 4001(a) provides a powerful reason to think that § 4001(a) was meant to require clear congressional authorization before any citizen can be placed in a cell. It is not merely that the legislative history shows that § 4001(a) was thought necessary in anticipation of times just like the present, in which the safety of the country is threatened. To appreciate what is most significant, one must only recall that the internments of the 1940s were accomplished by Executive action. Although an Act of Congress ratified and confirmed an Executive order authorizing the military to exclude individuals from defined areas and to accommodate those it might remove, *see Ex parte Endo*, 323 U.S. 283, 285–288 (1944), the statute said nothing whatever about the detention of those who might be removed; internment camps were creatures of the Executive, and confinement in them rested on assertion of Executive authority. When, therefore, Congress repealed the 1950 Act and adopted § 4001(a) for the purpose of avoiding another *Korematsu*, it intended to preclude reliance on vague congressional authority (for example, providing "accommodations" for those subject to removal) as authority for detention or imprisonment at the discretion of the Executive (maintaining detention camps of American citizens, for example). In requiring that any Executive detention be "pursuant to an Act of Congress," then, Congress necessarily meant to require a congressional enactment that clearly authorized detention or imprisonment.

Second, when Congress passed § 4001(a) it was acting in light of an interpretive regime that subjected enactments limiting liberty in wartime to the requirement of a clear statement and it presumably intended § 4001(a) to be read accordingly. This need for clarity was unmistakably expressed in *Ex parte Endo*, decided the same day as *Korematsu*. *Endo* began with a petition for habeas corpus by an interned citizen claiming to be loyal and law-abiding and thus "unlawfully detained." 323 U.S., at 294. The petitioner was held entitled to habeas relief in an opinion that set out this principle for scrutinizing wartime statutes in derogation of customary liberty:

> In interpreting a wartime measure we must assume that [its] purpose was to allow for the greatest possible accommodation between . . . liberties and the exigencies of war. We must assume, when asked to find implied powers in a grant of legislative or executive authority, that the law makers intended to place no greater restraint on the citizen than was clearly and unmistakably indicated by the language they used.

Id., at 300. Congress's understanding of the need for clear authority before citizens are kept detained is itself therefore clear, and § 4001(a) must be read to have teeth in its demand for congressional authorization.

Finally, even if history had spared us the cautionary example of the internments in World War II, even if there had been no *Korematsu*, and *Endo* had set out no principle of statutory interpretation, there would be a compelling reason to read § 4001(a) to demand manifest authority to detain before detention is authorized. The defining character of American constitutional government is its constant tension between security and liberty, serving both by partial helpings of each. In a government of separated powers, deciding finally on what is a reasonable degree of guaranteed liberty whether in peace or war (or some condition in between) is not well entrusted to the

Executive Branch of Government, whose particular responsibility is to maintain security. For reasons of inescapable human nature, the branch of the Government asked to counter a serious threat is not the branch on which to rest the Nation's entire reliance in striking the balance between the will to win and the cost in liberty on the way to victory; the responsibility for security will naturally amplify the claim that security legitimately raises. A reasonable balance is more likely to be reached on the judgment of a different branch, just as Madison said in remarking that "the constant aim is to divide and arrange the several offices in such a manner as that each may be a check on the other—that the private interest of every individual may be a sentinel over the public rights." The Federalist No. 51, p. 349 (J. Cooke ed. 1961). Hence the need for an assessment by Congress before citizens are subject to lockup, and likewise the need for a clearly expressed congressional resolution of the competing claims.

III

Under this principle of reading § 4001(a) robustly to require a clear statement of authorization to detain, none of the Government's arguments suffices to justify Hamdi's detention.

A

First, there is the argument that § 4001(a) does not even apply to wartime military detentions, a position resting on the placement of § 4001(a) in Title 18 of the United States Code, the gathering of federal criminal law. The text of the statute does not, however, so limit its reach, and the legislative history of the provision shows its placement in Title 18 was not meant to render the statute more restricted than its terms. . . .

B

Next, there is the Government's claim, accepted by the Court, that the terms of the Force Resolution are adequate to authorize detention of an enemy combatant under the circumstances described, a claim the Government fails to support sufficiently to satisfy § 4001(a) as read to require a clear statement of authority to detain. Since the Force Resolution was adopted one week after the attacks of September 11, 2001, it naturally speaks with some generality, but its focus is clear, and that is on the use of military power. It is fairly read to authorize the use of armies and weapons, whether against other armies or individual terrorists. But, like the statute discussed in *Endo*, it never so much as uses the word detention, and there is no reason to think Congress might have perceived any need to augment Executive power to deal with dangerous citizens within the United States, given the well-stocked statutory arsenal of defined criminal offenses covering the gamut of actions that a citizen sympathetic to terrorists might commit. *See, e.g.,* 18 U.S.C. § 2339A (material support for various terrorist acts); § 2339B (material support to a foreign terrorist organization); § 2332a (use of a weapon of mass destruction, including conspiracy and attempt); § 2332b(a)(1) (acts of terrorism "transcending national boundaries," including threats, conspiracy, and attempt); 18 U.S.C.A. § 2339C (Supp. 2004) (financing of certain terrorist acts); see also 18 U.S.C. § 3142(e) (pretrial detention). *See generally* Brief for Janet Reno et al. as *Amici Curiae* in *Rumsfeld v. Padilla,* O.T.2003, No. 03-1027, pp. 14–19, and n. 17 (listing the tools available to the Executive to fight terrorism even without the power the Government claims here); Brief for Louis Henkin et al. as *Amici Curiae* in *Rumsfeld v. Padilla,* O.T.2003, No. 03-1027, p. 23, n. 27.

C

Even so, there is one argument for treating the Force Resolution as sufficiently clear to authorize detention of a citizen consistently with § 4001(a). Assuming the argument to be sound, however, the Government is in no position to claim its advantage.

Because the Force Resolution authorizes the use of military force in acts of war by the United States, the argument goes, it is reasonably clear that the military and its Commander in Chief are authorized to deal with enemy belligerents according to the treaties and customs known collectively as the laws of war. Accordingly, the United States may detain captured enemies, and *Ex parte Quirin,* 317 U.S. 1 (1942), may perhaps be claimed for the proposition that the American citizenship of such a captive does not as such limit the Government's power to deal with him under the usages of war. *Id.,* at 31, 37–38. Thus, the Government here repeatedly argues that Hamdi's detention amounts to nothing more than customary detention of a captive taken on the field of battle: if the usages of war are fairly authorized by the Force Resolution, Hamdi's detention is authorized for purposes of § 4001(a).

There is no need, however, to address the merits of such an argument in all possible circumstances. For now it is enough to recognize that the Government's stated legal position in its campaign against the Taliban (among whom Hamdi was allegedly captured) is apparently at odds with its claim here to be acting in accordance with customary law of war and hence to be within the terms of the Force Resolution in its detention of Hamdi. In a statement of its legal position cited in its brief, the Government says that "the Geneva Convention applies to the Taliban detainees." Office of the White House Press Secretary, Fact Sheet, Status of Detainees at Guantanamo (Feb. 7, 2002), www.whitehouse.gov/news/releases/2002/02/20020207-13 .html (as visited June 18, 2004, and available in Clerk of Court's case file) (hereinafter White House Press Release) (cited in Brief for Respondents 24, n. 9). Hamdi presumably is such a detainee, since according to the Government's own account, he was taken bearing arms on the Taliban side of a field of battle in Afghanistan. He would therefore seem to qualify for treatment as a prisoner of war under the Third Geneva Convention, to which the United States is a party. Article 4 of the Geneva Convention (III) Relative to the Treatment of Prisoners of War, Aug. 12, 1949, [1955] 6 U.S. T. 3316, 3320, T. I. A. S. No. 3364.

By holding him incommunicado, however, the Government obviously has not been treating him as a prisoner of war, and in fact the Government claims that no Taliban detainee is entitled to prisoner of war status. This treatment appears to be a violation of the Geneva Convention provision that even in cases of doubt, captives are entitled to be treated as prisoners of war "until such time as their status has been determined by a competent tribunal." Art. 5, 6 U.S. T., at 3324. The Government answers that the President's determination that Taliban detainees do not qualify as prisoners of war is conclusive as to Hamdi's status and removes any doubt that would trigger application of the Convention's tribunal requirement. But reliance on this categorical pronouncement to settle doubt is apparently at odds with the military regulation, Enemy Prisoners of War, Retained Personnel, Civilian Internees and Other Detainees, Army Reg. 190-8, §§ 1-5, 1-6 (1997), adopted to implement the Geneva Convention, and setting out a detailed procedure for a military tribunal to determine an individual's status. See, e.g., id., § 1-6 ("A competent tribunal shall be composed of three commissioned officers"; a "written record shall be made of proceedings"; "[p]roceedings shall be open" with certain exceptions; "[p]ersons whose status is to be determined shall be advised of their rights at the beginning of their hearings," "allowed to attend all open sessions," "allowed to call witnesses if reasonably available, and to question those witnesses called by the Tribunal," and to "have a right to testify"; and a tribunal shall determine status by a "[p]reponderance of evidence"). One of the types of doubt these tribunals are meant to settle is whether a given individual may be, as Hamdi says he is, an "[i]nnocent civilian who should be immediately returned to his home or released." Id., 1-6e (10)(c). The regulation, jointly promulgated by the Headquarters of the Departments of the Army, Navy, Air Force, and Marine Corps, provides that "[p]ersons who have been determined by a competent tribunal not to be entitled to prisoner of war status may not be executed, imprisoned, or otherwise penalized without further proceedings to determine what acts they have committed and what penalty should be imposed." Id., § 1-6g. The regulation also incorporates the Geneva Convention's presumption that in cases of doubt, "persons shall enjoy the protection of the . . . Convention until such time as their status has been determined by a competent tribunal." Id., § 1-6a. Thus, there is reason to question whether the United States is acting in accordance with the laws of war it claims as authority.

Whether, or to what degree, the Government is in fact violating the Geneva Convention and is thus acting outside the customary usages of war are not matters I can resolve at this point. What I can say, though, is that the Government has not made out its claim that in detaining Hamdi in the manner described, it is acting in accord with the laws of war authorized to be applied against citizens by the Force Resolution. I conclude accordingly that the Government has failed to support the position that the Force Resolution authorizes the described detention of Hamdi for purposes of § 4001(a).

It is worth adding a further reason for requiring the Government to bear the burden of clearly justifying its claim to be exercising recognized war powers before declaring § 4001(a) satisfied. Thirty-eight days after adopting the Force Resolution, Congress passed the statute entitled Uniting and Strengthening America by Providing Appropriate Tools Required to Intercept and Obstruct Terrorism Act of 2001 (USA PATRIOT ACT), 115 Stat. 272; that Act authorized the detention of alien terrorists for no more than seven days in the absence of criminal charges or deportation proceedings, 8 U.S.C. § 1226a(a)(5) (2000 ed., Supp. I). It is very difficult to believe that the same Congress that carefully circumscribed Executive power over alien terrorists on home soil would not have meant to require the Government to justify clearly its detention of an American citizen held on home soil incommunicado.

D

Since the Government has given no reason either to deflect the application of § 4001(a) or to hold it to be satisfied, I need to go no further; the Government hints of a constitutional challenge to the statute, but it presents none here. I will, however, stray across the line between statutory and constitutional territory just far enough to note the weakness of the Government's mixed claim of inherent, extrastatutory authority under a combination of Article II of the Constitution and the usages of war. It is in fact in this connection that the Government developed its argument that the exercise of war powers justifies the detention, and what I have just said about its inadequacy applies here as well. Beyond that, it is instructive to recall Justice Jackson's observation that the President is not Commander in Chief of the country, only of the military. *Youngstown Sheet & Tube Co. v. Sawyer,* 343 U.S. 579, 643–644 (1952) (concurring opinion); see also *id.,* at 637–638 (Presidential authority is "at its lowest ebb" where the President acts contrary to congressional will).

There may be room for one qualification to Justice Jackson's statement, however: in a moment of genuine emergency, when the Government must act with no time for deliberation, the Executive may be able to detain a citizen if there is reason to fear he is an imminent threat to the safety of the Nation and its people (though I doubt there is any want of statutory authority). This case, however, does not present that question, because an emergency power of necessity must at least be limited by the emergency; Hamdi has been locked up for over two years. Cf. *Ex parte Milligan,* 4 Wall. 2, 127 (1866) (martial law justified only by "actual and present" necessity as in a genuine invasion that closes civilian courts).

Whether insisting on the careful scrutiny of emergency claims or on a vigorous reading of § 4001(a), we are heirs to a tradition given voice 800 years ago by Magna Carta, which, on the barons' insistence, confined executive power by "the law of the land."

IV

Because I find Hamdi's detention forbidden by § 4001(a) and unauthorized by the Force Resolution, I would not reach any questions of what process he may be due in litigating disputed issues in a proceeding under the habeas statute or prior to the habeas enquiry itself. . . . Since this disposition does not command a majority of the Court, however, the need to give practical effect to the conclusions of eight members of the Court rejecting the Government's position calls for me to join with the plurality in ordering remand on terms closest to those I would impose. Although I think litigation of Hamdi's status as an enemy combatant is unnecessary, the terms of the plurality's remand will allow Hamdi to offer evidence that he is not an enemy combatant, and he should at the least have the benefit of that opportunity. . . .

Subject to these qualifications, I join with the plurality in a judgment of the Court vacating the Fourth Circuit's judgment and remanding the case.

Justice SCALIA, with whom Justice STEVENS joins, dissenting.

. . . Where the Government accuses a citizen of waging war against it, our constitutional tradition has been to prosecute him in federal court for treason or some other crime. Where the exigencies of war prevent that, the Constitution's Suspension Clause, Art. I, § 9, cl. 2, allows Congress to relax the usual protections temporarily. Absent suspension, however, the Executive's assertion of military exigency has not been thought sufficient to permit detention without charge. No one contends that the congressional Authorization for Use of Military Force, on which the Government relies to justify its actions here, is an implementation of the Suspension Clause. Accordingly, I would reverse the decision below. . . .

The absence of military authority to imprison citizens indefinitely in wartime — whether or not a probability of treason had been established by means less than jury trial — was confirmed by three cases decided during and immediately after the War of 1812. In the first, *In re Stacy,* 10 Johns. 328 (N.Y.1813), a citizen was taken into military custody on suspicion that he was "carrying provisions and giving information to the enemy." *Id.,* at 330 (emphasis deleted). Stacy petitioned for a writ of habeas corpus, and, after the defendant custodian attempted to avoid complying, Chief Justice Kent ordered attachment against him. Kent noted that the military was "without any color of authority in any military tribunal to try a citizen for that crime" and that it was "holding him in the closest confinement, and contemning the civil authority of the state." *Id.,* at 333–334.

Two other cases, later cited with approval by this Court in *Ex parte Milligan,* 4 Wall. 2, 128–129, upheld verdicts for false imprisonment against military officers. In *Smith v. Shaw,* 12 Johns. 257 (N.Y.1815), the court affirmed an award of damages for detention of a citizen on suspicion that he was, among other things, "an enemy's spy in time of war." *Id.,* at 265. The court held that "[n]one of the offences charged against *Shaw* were cognizable by a court-martial, except that which related to his being a spy; and if he was an *American* citizen, he could not be charged with such an offence. He might be amenable to the civil authority for treason; but could not be punished, under martial law, as a spy." *Ibid.* "If the defendant was justifiable in doing what he did, every citizen of the *United States* would, in time of war, be equally exposed to a like exercise of military power and authority." *Id.,* at 266. Finally, in *M'Connell v. Hampton,* 12 Johns. 234 (N.Y.1815), a jury awarded $9,000 for false imprisonment after a military officer confined a citizen on charges of treason; the judges on appeal did not question the verdict but found the damages excessive, in part because "it does not appear that [the defendant] . . . knew [the plaintiff] was a citizen." *Id.,* at 238 (Spencer, J.).

President Lincoln, when he purported to suspend habeas corpus without congressional authorization during the Civil War, apparently did not doubt that suspension was required if the prisoner was to be held without criminal trial. In his famous message to Congress on July 4, 1861, he argued only that he could suspend the writ, not that even without suspension, his imprisonment of citizens without criminal trial was permitted. *See* Special Session Message, 6 Messages and Papers 20–31.

Further evidence comes from this Court's decision in *Ex parte Milligan, supra.* There, the Court issued the writ to an American citizen who had been tried by military commission for offenses that included conspiring to overthrow the Government, seize munitions, and liberate prisoners of war. The Court rejected in no uncertain terms the Government's assertion that military jurisdiction was proper "under the 'laws and usages of war,'" *id.,* at 121:

> "It can serve no useful purpose to inquire what those laws and usages are, whence they originated, where found, and on whom they operate; they can never be applied to citizens in states which have upheld the authority of the government, and where the courts are open and their process unobstructed." Ibid. . . .

The Government argues that our more recent jurisprudence ratifies its indefinite imprisonment of a citizen within the territorial jurisdiction of federal courts. It places primary reliance upon *Ex parte Quirin,* 317 U.S. 1 (1942), a World War II case upholding the trial by military commission of eight German saboteurs, one of whom, Hans Haupt, was a U.S. citizen. The case was not this Court's finest hour. The Court upheld the commission and denied relief in a brief *per curiam* issued the day after oral argument concluded; a week later the Government carried out the commission's death sentence upon six saboteurs, including Haupt. The Court eventually explained its reasoning in a written opinion issued several months later.

Only three paragraphs of the Court's lengthy opinion dealt with the particular circumstances of Haupt's case. The Government argued that Haupt, like the other petitioners, could be tried by military commission under the laws of war. In agreeing with that contention, *Quirin* purported to interpret the language of *Milligan* quoted above (the law of war "can never be applied to citizens in states which have upheld the authority of the government, and where the courts are open and their process unobstructed") in the following manner:

> "Elsewhere in its opinion . . . the Court was at pains to point out that Milligan, a citizen twenty years resident in Indiana, who had never been a resident of any of the states in rebellion, was not an enemy belligerent either entitled to the status of a prisoner of war or subject to the penalties imposed upon unlawful belligerents. We construe the Court's statement as to the inapplicability of the law of war to Milligan's case as having particular reference to the facts before it. From them the Court concluded that Milligan, not being a part of or associated with the armed forces of the enemy, was a non-belligerent, not subject to the law of war . . . ." 317 U.S., at 45.

In my view this seeks to revise *Milligan* rather than describe it. . . . But even if *Quirin* gave a correct description of *Milligan,* or made an irrevocable revision of it, *Quirin* would still not justify denial of the writ here. In *Quirin* it was uncontested that the petitioners were members of enemy forces. They were "*admitted* enemy invaders," 317 U.S., at 47 (emphasis added), and it was "undisputed" that they had landed in the United States in service of German forces, *id.,* at 20. The specific holding of the Court was only that, "upon the *conceded* facts," the petitioners were "plainly within [the] boundaries" of military jurisdiction, *id.,* at 46 (emphasis added). But where those jurisdictional facts are *not* conceded—where the petitioner insists that he is *not* a belligerent—*Quirin* left the pre-existing law in place: Absent suspension of the writ, a citizen held where the courts are open is entitled either to criminal trial or to a judicial decree requiring his release.

It follows from what I have said that Hamdi is entitled to a habeas decree requiring his release unless (1) criminal proceedings are promptly brought, or (2) Congress has suspended the writ of habeas corpus. A suspension of the writ could, of course, lay down conditions for continued detention, similar to those that today's opinion prescribes under the Due Process Clause. Cf. Act of Mar. 3, 1863, 12 Stat. 755. But there is a world of difference between the people's representatives' determining the need for that suspension (and prescribing the conditions for it), and this Court's doing so.

The plurality finds justification for Hamdi's imprisonment in the Authorization for Use of Military Force. . . . This is not remotely a congressional suspension of the writ, and no one claims that it is. Contrary to the plurality's view, I do not think this statute even authorizes detention of a citizen with the clarity necessary to satisfy the interpretive canon that statutes should be construed so as to avoid grave constitutional concerns, or with the clarity necessary to overcome the statutory prescription that "[n]o citizen shall be imprisoned or otherwise detained by the United States except pursuant to an Act of Congress." But even if it did, I would not permit it to overcome Hamdi's entitlement to habeas corpus relief. The Suspension Clause of the Constitution, which carefully circumscribes the conditions under which the writ can be withheld, would be a sham if it could be evaded by congressional prescription of requirements *other than the common-law requirement of committal for criminal prosecution* that render the writ, though available, unavailing. If the Suspension Clause does not guarantee the citizen that he will either be tried or released, unless the conditions for suspending the writ exist and the grave action of suspending the writ has been taken; if it merely guarantees the citizen that he will not be detained unless Congress by ordinary legislation says he can be detained; it guarantees him very little indeed.

It should not be thought, however, that the plurality's evisceration of the Suspension Clause augments, principally, the power of Congress. As usual, the major effect of its constitutional improvisation is to increase the power of the Court. Having found a congressional authorization for detention of citizens where none clearly exists; and having discarded the categorical procedural protection of the Suspension Clause; the plurality then proceeds, under the guise of the Due Process Clause, to prescribe what procedural protections *it* thinks appropriate. It "weigh[s] the private interest . . . against the Government's asserted interest," *ante,* at 22 (internal quotation marks omitted), and—just as though writing a new Constitution—comes up with an unheard-of system in which the citizen rather than the Government bears the burden of proof, testimony is by hearsay rather than live witnesses, and the presiding officer may well be a "neutral" military officer rather than judge and jury. *See ante,* at 26–27. It claims authority to engage in this sort of "judicious balancing" from *Mathews v. Eldridge,* 424 U.S. 319(1976), a case involving . . . *the withdrawal of disability benefits!* Whatever the merits of this technique when newly recognized property rights are at issue (and even there they are questionable), it has no place where the Constitution and the common law already supply an answer.

Having distorted the Suspension Clause, the plurality finishes up by transmogrifying the Great Writ—disposing of the present habeas petition by remanding for the District Court to "engag[e] in a factfinding process that is both prudent and incremental," *ante,* at 32. "In the absence of [the Executive's prior provision of procedures that satisfy due process], . . . a court that receives a petition for a writ of habeas corpus from an alleged enemy combatant must itself ensure that the minimum requirements of due process are achieved." *Ante,* at 31–32. This judicial remediation of executive default is unheard of. It is not the habeas court's function to make illegal detention legal by supplying a process that the Government could have provided, but chose not to. If Hamdi is being imprisoned in violation of the Constitution (because without due process of law), then his habeas petition should be granted; the Executive may then hand him over to the criminal authorities, whose detention for the purpose of prosecution will be lawful, or else must release him.

There is a certain harmony of approach in the plurality's making up for Congress's failure to invoke the Suspension Clause and its making up for the Executive's failure to apply what it says are needed procedures—an approach that reflects what might be called a Mr. Fix-it Mentality. The plurality seems to view it as its mission to Make Everything Come Out Right, rather than merely to decree the consequences, as far as individual rights are concerned, of the other two branches' actions and omissions. Has the Legislature failed to suspend the writ in the current dire emergency? Well, we will remedy that failure by prescribing the reasonable conditions that a suspension should have included. And has the Executive failed to live up to those reasonable conditions? Well, we will ourselves make that failure good, so that this dangerous fellow (if he is dangerous) need not be set free. The problem with this approach is not only that it steps out of the courts' modest and limited role in a democratic society; but that by repeatedly doing what it thinks the political branches ought to do it encourages their lassitude and saps the vitality of government by the people.

VI

Several limitations give my views in this matter a relatively narrow compass. They apply only to citizens, accused of being enemy combatants, who are detained within the territorial jurisdiction of a federal court. This is not likely to be a numerous group; currently we know of only two, Hamdi and Jose Padilla. Where the citizen is captured outside and held outside the United States, the constitutional requirements may be different. Moreover, even within the United States, the accused citizen-enemy combatant may lawfully be detained once prosecution is in progress or in contemplation. The Government has been notably successful in securing conviction, and hence long-term custody or execution, of those who have waged war against the state.

I frankly do not know whether these tools are sufficient to meet the Government's security needs, including the need to obtain intelligence through interrogation. It is far beyond my competence, or the Court's competence, to determine that. But it is not beyond Congress's. If the situation demands it, the Executive can ask Congress to authorize suspension of the writ — which can be made subject to whatever conditions Congress deems appropriate, including even the procedural novelties invented by the plurality today. To be sure, suspension is limited by the Constitution to cases of rebellion or invasion. But whether the attacks of September 11, 2001, constitute an "invasion," and whether those attacks still justify suspension several years later, are questions for Congress rather than this Court. If civil rights are to be curtailed during wartime, it must be done openly and democratically, as the Constitution requires, rather than by silent erosion through an opinion of this Court. . . .

Many think it not only inevitable but entirely proper that liberty give way to security in times of national crisis — that, at the extremes of military exigency, *inter arma silent leges.* Whatever the general merits of the view that war silences law or modulates its voice, that view has no place in the interpretation and application of a Constitution designed precisely to confront war and, in a manner that accords with democratic principles, to accommodate it. Because the Court has proceeded to meet the current emergency in a manner the Constitution does not envision, I respectfully dissent.

Justice THOMAS, dissenting.

The Executive Branch, acting pursuant to the powers vested in the President by the Constitution and with explicit congressional approval, has determined that Yaser Hamdi is an enemy combatant and should be detained. This detention falls squarely within the Federal Government's war powers, and we lack the expertise and capacity to second-guess that decision. As such, petitioners' habeas challenge should fail, and there is no reason to remand the case. The plurality reaches a contrary conclusion by failing adequately to consider basic principles of the constitutional structure as it relates to national security and foreign affairs and by using the balancing scheme of *Mathews v. Eldridge,* 424 U.S. 319 (1976). I do not think that the Federal Government's war powers can be balanced away by this Court. Arguably, Congress could provide for additional procedural protections, but until it does, we have no right to insist upon them. But even if I were to agree with the general approach the plurality takes, I could not accept the particulars. The plurality utterly fails to account for the Government's compelling interests and for our own institutional inability to weigh competing concerns correctly. I respectfully dissent. . . .

1. *What Process is Due to an Alleged Enemy Combatant?* Having determined that Congress authorized the executive to seize U.S. citizen enemy combatants in the zone of combat, the Court had next to decide what process was due to such individuals, so detained, who disputed their "enemy combatant" status.

The Bush Administration had argued that Hamdi was entitled to no more than the most cursory judicial examination of a sworn executive branch affidavit—the Mobbs Declaration—that, largely through hearsay, asserted a prima facie justification for Hamdi's classification. The Fourth Circuit agreed: "The factual averments in the affidavit, if accurate, are sufficient to confirm that Hamdi's detention conforms with a legitimate exercise of the war powers given the executive by Article II, Section 2 of the Constitution . . . ." *Hamdi v. Rumsfeld*, 16 F.3d 450, 473 (4th Cir. 2003). The court vacated a district court discovery order that would have supported a searching inquiry into the factual basis for Hamdi's status, concluding, "[N]o evidentiary hearing or factual inquiry on our part is necessary or proper, because it is undisputed that Hamdi was captured in a zone of active combat operations in a foreign country and because any inquiry must be circumscribed to avoid encroachment into the military affairs entrusted to the executive branch."

The Supreme Court disagreed. It held first that, as a matter of law, the Mobbs Declaration was insufficient to justify Hamdi's detention as an enemy combatant:

[T]he circumstances surrounding Hamdi's seizure cannot in any way be characterized as "undisputed," as "those circumstances are neither conceded in fact, nor susceptible to concession in law, because Hamdi has not been permitted to speak for himself or even through counsel as to those circumstances." 337 F.3d 335, 357 (C.A.4 2003) (Luttig, J., dissenting from denial of rehearing en banc); see also *id.*, at 371–372 (Motz, J., dissenting from denial of rehearing en banc). Further, the "facts" that constitute the alleged concession are insufficient to support Hamdi's detention. Under the definition of enemy combatant that we accept today as falling within the scope of Congress' authorization, Hamdi would need to be "part of or supporting forces hostile to the United States or coalition partners" and "engaged in an armed conflict against the United States" to justify his detention in the United States for the duration of the relevant conflict. The habeas petition states only that "[w]hen seized by the United States Government, Mr. Hamdi resided in Afghanistan." An assertion that one *resided* in a country in which combat operations are taking place is not a concession that one was "*captured* in a zone of active combat operations in a foreign theater of war," 316 F.3d, at 459 (emphasis added), and certainly is not a concession that one was "part of or supporting forces hostile to the United States or coalition partners" and "engaged in an armed conflict against the United States."

124 S. Ct. at 2644–45.

Second, the Court rejected the executive branch's position on the appropriate conduct of judicial review:

Under the Government's most extreme rendition of this argument, "[r]espect for separation of powers and the limited institutional capabilities of courts in matters of military decision-making in connection with an ongoing conflict" ought to eliminate entirely any individual process, restricting the courts to investigating only whether legal authorization exists for the broader detention scheme. At most, the Government argues, courts should review its determination that a citizen is an enemy combatant under a very deferential "some evidence" standard. Under this review, a court would assume the accuracy of the Government's articulated basis for Hamdi's detention, as set forth in the Mobbs Declaration, and assess only whether that articulated basis was a legitimate one.

Id. at 2645. The Court instead held the Government's suggested process insufficient to meet the requirements of due process, as articulated in *Mathews v. Eldridge,* 424 U.S. 319 (1976).

The invocation of *Mathews v. Eldridge* struck a surprising note. That case involved the sufficiency of administrative procedures for adjudicating the entitlement to disability benefits, and has generally been deployed in cases involving administrative contexts far more mundane than *Hamdi.* In such contexts:

> *Mathews* dictates that the process due in any given instance is determined by weighing "the private interest that will be affected by the official action" against the Government's asserted interest, "including the function involved" and the burdens the Government would face in providing greater process. The *Mathews* calculus then contemplates a judicious balancing of these concerns, through an analysis of "the risk of an erroneous deprivation" of the private interest if the process were reduced and the "probable value, if any, of additional or substitute safeguards."

542 U.S. at 529. Applying *Mathews* to Hamdi, the Supreme Court found that the private and public interests competing in *Hamdi* were, quite predictably, of the very highest order. It analyzed the procedures that properly balanced those interests as follows:

> We . . . hold that a citizen-detainee seeking to challenge his classification as an enemy combatant must receive notice of the factual basis for his classification, and a fair opportunity to rebut the Government's factual assertions before a neutral decisionmaker. . . . At the same time, the exigencies of the circumstances may demand that, aside from these core elements, enemy combatant proceedings may be tailored to alleviate their uncommon potential to burden the Executive at a time of ongoing military conflict. Hearsay, for example, may need to be accepted as the most reliable available evidence from the Government in such a proceeding. Likewise, the Constitution would not be offended by a presumption in favor of the Government's evidence, so long as that presumption remained a rebuttable one and fair opportunity for rebuttal were provided. Thus, once the Government puts forth

credible evidence that the habeas petitioner meets the enemy-combatant criteria, the onus could shift to the petitioner to rebut that evidence with more persuasive evidence that he falls outside the criteria. A burden-shifting scheme of this sort would meet the goal of ensuring that the errant tourist, embedded journalist, or local aid worker has a chance to prove military error while giving due regard to the Executive once it has put forth meaningful support for its conclusion that the detainee is in fact an enemy combatant. . . .

We think it unlikely that this basic process will have the dire impact on the central functions of warmaking that the Government forecasts. The parties agree that initial captures on the battlefield need not receive the process we have discussed here; that process is due only when the determination is made to *continue* to hold those who have been seized. The Government has made clear in its briefing that documentation regarding battlefield detainees already is kept in the ordinary course of military affairs. Any factfinding imposition created by requiring a knowledgeable affiant to summarize these records to an independent tribunal is a minimal one. Likewise, arguments that military officers ought not have to wage war under the threat of litigation lose much of their steam when factual disputes at enemy-combatant hearings are limited to the alleged combatant's acts. This focus meddles little, if at all, in the strategy or conduct of war, inquiring only into the appropriateness of continuing to detain an individual claimed to have taken up arms against the United States. While we accord the greatest respect and consideration to the judgments of military authorities in matters relating to the actual prosecution of a war, and recognize that the scope of that discretion necessarily is wide, it does not infringe on the core role of the military for the courts to exercise their own time-honored and constitutionally mandated roles of reviewing and resolving claims like those presented here. Cf. *Korematsu v. United States*, 323 U.S. 214, 233–234 (1944) (Murphy, J., dissenting) ("[L]ike other claims conflicting with the asserted constitutional rights of the individual, the military claim must subject itself to the judicial process of having its reasonableness determined and its conflicts with other interests reconciled"). . . .

In so holding, we necessarily reject the Government's assertion that separation of powers principles mandate a heavily circumscribed role for the courts in such circumstances. Indeed, the position that the courts must forgo any examination of the individual case and focus exclusively on the legality of the broader detention scheme cannot be mandated by any reasonable view of separation of powers, as this approach serves only to *condense* power into a single branch of government. We have long since made clear that a state of war is not a blank check for the President when it comes to the rights of the Nation's citizens. *Youngstown Sheet & Tube*, 343 U.S., at 587. Whatever power the United States Constitution envisions for the Executive in its exchanges with other nations or with enemy organizations in times of conflict, it most assuredly envisions a role for all three branches when individual liberties are at stake. *Mistretta v. United States,* 488 U.S. 361, 380 (1989) (it was "the central judgment of the Framers of the Constitution that, within our political scheme, the separation of governmental powers into three coordinate Branches is essential to the preservation of liberty"). Likewise, we have made clear that, unless Congress acts to suspend it, the Great Writ of habeas corpus allows the Judicial Branch to play a necessary role in maintaining this delicate balance of governance, serving as an important judicial check on the Executive's discretion in the realm of detentions. Thus, while we do not question that our due process assessment must pay keen attention to the particular burdens faced by the Executive in the context of military action, it would turn our system of checks and balances on its head to suggest that a citizen could not make his way to court with a challenge to the factual basis for his detention by his government, simply because the Executive opposes making available such a challenge. Absent suspension of the writ by Congress, a citizen detained as an enemy combatant is entitled to this process.

. . . Aside from unspecified "screening" processes, and military interrogations in which the Government suggests Hamdi could have contested his classification, Hamdi has received no process. An interrogation by one's captor, however effective an intelligence-gathering tool, hardly constitutes a constitutionally adequate factfinding before a neutral decisionmaker. That even purportedly fair adjudicators "are disqualified by their interest in the controversy to be decided is, of course, the general rule." Plainly, the "process" Hamdi has received is not that to which he is entitled under the Due Process Clause.

There remains the possibility that the standards we have articulated could be met by an appropriately authorized and properly constituted military tribunal. Indeed, it is notable that military regulations already provide for such process in related instances, dictating that tribunals be made available to determine the status of enemy detainees who assert prisoner-of-war status under the Geneva Convention. *See* Enemy Prisoners of War, Retained Personnel, Civilian Internees and Other Detainees, Army Regulation 190-8, § 1-6 (1997). In the absence of such process, however, a court that receives a petition for a writ of habeas corpus from an alleged enemy combatant must itself ensure that the minimum requirements of due process are achieved. . . .

542 U.S. at 533–538. Justices Souter and Ginsburg dissented on two aspects of the proposed procedures: "I do not mean to imply agreement that the Government could claim an evidentiary presumption casting the burden of rebuttal on Hamdi, or that an opportunity to litigate before a military tribunal might obviate or truncate enquiry by a court on habeas." *Id.* at 2660. On the other hand, because Justice Thomas found no requirement for procedures more protective than those the executive had already

offered, there are presently five votes on the court for giving Hamdi no more procedural protection than the plurality sets forth.

In response to the decisions in *Rasul* and *Hamdi, supra,* the Defense Department, on July 7, 2004, announced the creation of Combatant Status Review Tribunals, to provide an administrative determination of the status of Guantanamo detainees, which could then be appealed to the federal courts. The Pentagon order provided that detainees held at Guantanamo Bay would be notified within 10 days of their opportunity to contest their enemy combatant status under this process. (They would likewise be told of their right to seek release through federal habeas corpus.) Individual tribunals would consist of three neutral officers, none of whom had prior involvement with the detainee. Each detainee would be assigned a military officer as a personal representative. That officer is assigned to assist the detainee in preparing for a tribunal hearing. Detainees have the right to testify, call witnesses, and introduce evidence. Any detainee determined not to be an enemy combatant is to be transferred to their country of citizenship or subjected to "other disposition consistent with domestic and international obligations and the foreign policy of the United State." Memorandum of Deputy Secretary of Defense Paul Wolfowitz to the Secretary of the Navy, re: Order Establishing Combatant Status Review Tribunal, par. I (Jul. 7, 2004), available at http://www.dod.gov/news/Jul2004/d20040707review.pdf.

2. Constitutional Authority to Seize U.S. Citizens as Enemy Combatants. The Bush Administration was presumably hoping for two outcomes in the *Hamdi* case: a broad affirmation of the President's constitutional war powers and a highly deferential stance with regard to judicial review of executive determinations regarding alleged enemy combatants. It got neither. And, although the Court was explicit (a) in avoiding any analysis of the scope of presidential war powers and (b) in limiting its *Hamdi* holding to the zone-of-combat context, the opinion did not augur favorably for the government's position in the *Padilla* case, involving a U.S. citizen-alleged enemy combatant arrested in the United States.

First, in the *Padilla* case, the sole plausible source of statutory authority for the arrest of a citizen-enemy combatant in the United States was again the Authorization for the Use of Military Force Resolution. By its very name, however, that resolution seems inapplicable to the chartering of law enforcement authorities. With regard to Mr. Hamdi, who was captured in Afghanistan, the Supreme Court said: "There can be no doubt that individuals who fought against the United States in Afghanistan as part of the Taliban . . . are individuals Congress sought to target in passing the AUMF. We conclude that detention of individuals falling into the limited category we are considering, for the duration of the particular conflict in which they were captured, is so fundamental and accepted an incident to war as to be an exercise of the 'necessary and appropriate force' Congress has authorized the President to use." Is it likely that the Court would have said the same for American citizens who might be conspiring with enemies of the United States, but who remain outside the zone of combat?

If the AUMF does not apply, the President would seem to be in his least propitious position under *Youngstown*. That is, given the Non-Detention Act, the President would presumably be entitled to arrest U.S. citizens as enemy combatants outside the zone of combat only (a) if his constitutional powers as commander in chief embrace such authority, *and* (b) if his commander in chief authority with regard to the arrest of U.S. citizens is beyond the regulatory power of Congress. Four Justices on the Court — Ginsburg, Scalia, Souter, and Stevens — have effectively answered at least one of those questions negatively in *Hamdi*. Given the circumspection of the four-Justice plurality who upheld the arrest of Hamdi in Afghanistan, it seems quite likely that one or more of them would have substantial doubts about extending the President's authority to domestic arrests.

In rejecting the Administration's authority to detain Padilla as an enemy combatant, the Second Circuit, in *Padilla v. Rumsfeld*, 352 F.3d 695 (2d Cir. 2003), *rev'd*, 124 S. Ct. 2711 (2004), followed an ambitious route. Rather than ask whether the President had sufficient commander-in-chief authority to allow him to proceed in violation of the Non-Detention Act, the court took on the seemingly harder question whether the commander-in-chief power provided the President *any* inherent authority *at all* to detain U.S. citizens on American soil as enemy combatants. The court concluded that he did not, finding that a variety of constitutional provisions signaled a constitutional design to empower Congress exclusively to specify when U.S. citizens may be detained domestically for acts hostile to the United States. In reaching this conclusion, the court relied on the vesting of power in Congress to punish offenses against the law of Nations, U.S. Const., art. I, § 8, cl. 10, and to suspend the writ of habeas corpus, id. at art. 1, § 9, cl. 2, as well as on "the need to prevent military intrusion into civilian life," 352 F. 3d, at 714–15, embodied in the Third Amendment's prohibition on a peacetime quartering of troops. U.S. Const., amend. III.

Rather than pursue this route further, the Government effectively mooted the dispute by transferring Padilla to civilian custody and trying him on conventional criminal charges in an Article III court. In August 2007, Padilla was convicted of conspiracy to murder, kidnap and maim people and two counts of providing material support to terrorists. He was subsequently sentenced to 17 years and 4 months in federal prison.

4. *Authority to Seize Non-Citizens in the United States as Enemy Combatants.* None of the cases litigated thus far deals with the detention of non-citizen enemy combatants outside the zone of combat. Such persons would not have the protection of the Non-Detention Act. If they are lawfully present in the United States, does the AUMF apply to them? Is there a stronger case that the President has inherent power to provide for the domestic detention of lawfully present non-citizens than he would of U.S. citizens?

5. *Material Witness Warrants.* Jose Padilla, the petitioner in *Rumsfeld v. Padilla*, 542 U.S. 426 (2004), was arrested first as a material witness, and might have been held in that status even if he had been released as an enemy combatant and not otherwise

prosecuted. The federal material witness statute, 18 U.S.C. § 1844 (2000), "authorizes the government to detain witnesses in situations where the witness possesses information deemed material to a criminal proceeding, and the court finds that it may become impracticable to secure his testimony by subpoena. The impracticability determination is based on whether or not the witness poses a high flight risk." Heidee Stoller, et al., *Developments in Law and Policy: The Costs of Post-9/11 National Security Strategy*, 22 YALE L. & POL'Y REV. 197, 198 (2004). As recounted in the article by Stoller, et al.: "[R]ecent jurisprudence has not abated Fourth Amendment concerns about the appropriate standard for determining materiality, the risk of erroneous detention in the grand jury context, the possibility of pretextual detentions, the role of depositions, and the harsh conditions of confinement." Id. at 217.

In *Ashcroft v. al-Kidd*, 563 U.S. 731 (2011), however, the Court unanimously upheld Attorney General Ashcroft's claim to immunity in a suit by a U.S. citizen detained under the material witness statute, who argued that the detention was a mere pretext to investigate him, without probable cause, on potential terrorism charges. Because "not a single judicial opinion had held that pretext could render an objectively reasonable arrest pursuant to a material-witness warrant unconstitutional," *id.* at 741, the Attorney General—even if al-Kidd's detention was pretextual—had not violated clearly established law and was thus entitled to qualified immunity in a suit for damages. The Court did not address the Attorney General's claim for absolute immunity.

It bears noting that the Roberts Court has generally not been receptive to constitutional torts claims brought pursuant to *Bivens v. Six Unknown Fed. Narcotics Agents*, 403 U.S. 388 (1971). In a 4–2 decision, *Ziglar v. Abbasi*, 137 S. Ct. 1843 (2017), the Court held no cause of action existed on behalf of six undocumented aliens, five of whom were of Arab or South Asian descent, who had been detained under harsh conditions at the Metropolitan Detention Center (MDC) in Brooklyn, New York in the immediate wake of September 11, but who had nothing to do with the attacks. According to their complaint, which the Court accepted as true for purposes of its analysis:

> Conditions in the Unit were harsh. Pursuant to official Bureau of Prisons policy, detainees were held in "'tiny cells for over 23 hours a day.'" 789 F.3d, at 228. Lights in the cells were left on 24 hours. Detainees had little opportunity for exercise or recreation. They were forbidden to keep anything in their cells, even basic hygiene products such as soap or a toothbrush. When removed from the cells for any reason, they were shackled and escorted by four guards. They were denied access to most forms of communication with the outside world. And they were strip searched often—any time they were moved, as well as at random in their cells. Some of the harsh conditions in the Unit were not imposed pursuant to official policy. According to the complaint, prison guards engaged in a pattern of "physical and verbal abuse." Ibid. Guards allegedly slammed detainees into walls; twisted their arms, wrists, and fingers; broke their bones; referred to them as terrorists;

threatened them with violence; subjected them to humiliating sexual comments; and insulted their religion.

Id. at *7. To the extent the former detainees sought damages against high-level Justice Department officials who failed to prevent their subordinates' assertedly unconstitutional behavior, Justice Kennedy, writing for a four-Justice plurality (with Justices Kagan, Sotomayor, and Gorsuch not participating), concluded that a *Bivens* remedy was inappropriate. The Court remanded, however, for the Court of Appeals to determine whether "special factors" would justify a Fifth Amendment-based *Bivens* remedy against the MDC's warden for allowing prison guards to abuse the detainees. Noting, however, an apparent trend to leave to Congress the creation of damages actions for official misconduct, Justice Kennedy wrote: "Given the notable change [since 1971] in the Court's approach to recognizing implied causes of action, . . . the Court has made clear that expanding the *Bivens* remedy is now a 'disfavored' judicial activity." *Id.* at *12. Justice Breyer dissented, joined by Justice Ginsburg.

———————

In sending alleged enemy combatants to Guantanamo, the George W. Bush Administration had plainly hoped to create a situation of maximum legal discretion with regard to the detention, interrogation, and conditions of confinement for alleged enemy combatants. Part of that strategy had been the geographical choice of Guantanamo, in what turned out to be an unsuccessful plan to deny detainees access to habeas review of their detention. Another key decision was adopting an interpretation of the Geneva Conventions as inapplicable to the detainees. The following excerpt describes the contentious political process within the administration that surrounded this question of legal interpretation:

Harold H. Bruff, Bad Advice: Bush's Lawyers in the War on Terror

200–212 (2009).

On January 9, 2002, John Yoo and OLC Special Counsel Robert Delahunty sent a draft opinion to the Pentagon, titled *Application of Treaties and Laws to al Qaeda and Taliban Detainees.* . . . [T]he draft triggered a sharp controversy within the administration. A final version of the opinion differed only in detail.

The 40-page length and dry, analytic tone of the *Application of Treaties* opinion mask the extraordinary nature of the positions it takes. . . . It concludes that the President can either suspend the Geneva Conventions in Afghanistan or, in a lesser step, determine that they do not apply to al Qaeda and Taliban prisoners.

The particular arguments that appear in *Application of Treaties* flow from two aspects of John Yoo's unusual theories about the law of foreign relations. Both of these positions would be readily apparent in the President's decisions about the treaties. First, Yoo believes that the treaty power is executive except as specifically stated in the Constitution (as in the Senate's role in ratification). . . . [M]ainstream foreign relations scholars usually recognize a broad power of executive initiative, conditioned on congressional acquiescence—that the President proposes, but Congress disposes. Yoo finds a much broader set of executive powers that cannot be overridden by Congress, and a more limited role for the courts, than do most others.

Second, and corollary to the first position, Yoo claims that the President enjoys an apparently unlimited power to interpret existing treaties. . . . He argues that "treaty interpretation is so tied up in the setting of foreign policy that the power has come to rest with the executive branch." The President can also "interpret, and even violate, international law in the course of executing foreign policy." Yoo is correct that a President's constitutional powers should include some discretion in interpreting our nation's international obligations (Presidents do violate international law or suspend treaties on occasion). The question is, how much discretion? Yoo states no limits, perhaps believing that the obligation of the President's oath and the existence of his political accountability provide enough of a check on baseless interpretation.

. . . Somewhat surprisingly, the *Application of Treaties* opinion does not begin with an analysis of the Geneva Conventions themselves. Instead, it focuses on the federal War Crimes Act, which criminalizes certain violations of the Geneva Conventions and other law of war treaties. There is a reason for this strategy, and it requires a bit of explanation. . . . Unlike most scholars of foreign relations law, John Yoo is very reluctant to consider any treaty to be self-executing, absent the clearest evidence of that intention. This is because "treaties exert an impact in the realm of international politics and foreign policy, rather than in constitutional law." This position minimizes the force of the Supremacy Clause, which has long been understood to make self-executing treaty obligations part of federal law, with the same stature as statutes. Instead, Yoo believes the President is ordinarily unconstrained by international law unless it has been codified by Congress.

This background explains why *Application of Treaties* does not analyze the direct force of the Geneva Conventions in American law. Instead, it parses the War Crimes Act without stopping to acknowledge that the Conventions have been treated as self-executing within the American military ever since their ratification. The opinion does discuss international law at some length, but supposedly always in the context of understanding the WCA's partial codification of it.

This strategy has three crucial interpretive advantages for the executive. First, since the WCA is a criminal statute, the opinion invokes the canon of construction called the rule of lenity, which calls for interpreting criminal statutes favorably to defendants—who could be American officials. Therefore, to the extent that incorporated treaty provisions could be read to shelter either the detainees from their captors or the captors from prosecution, it is the captors who will receive special solicitation. This stance is difficult to reconcile with the purposes of the Geneva Conventions.

Second and more broadly, the strategy deflects attention away from both the international law of war, of which the Conventions are a part, and the ingrained traditions in our own military of honoring the law of war even when it may not technically apply. The opinion does mention the option of extending rights to detainees when it is not mandatory to do so, and reviews instances of that practice, for example regarding the Viet Cong. What the opinion omits is any recognition that the military's "voluntary" grant of rights may have been strategic. Following international law without conceding its binding effect prevents any resolution of the question whether the rights are indeed mandatory—even if they are. And that was the central question regarding the al Qaeda and Taliban detainees.

Third, since the WCA codifies only a few central parts of the Conventions, other protections could be left out of the analysis entirely. Of particular importance was Article 5 of the POW Convention, which provides: "Should any doubt arise as to whether persons, having committed a belligerent act and having fallen into the hands of the enemy [merit POW status], such persons shall [be treated as POWs] until such time as their status has been determined by a competent tribunal." On its face, Article 5 appears to have been applicable to the detainees. Having no intention of according them Article 5 hearings, however, the administration simply ignored this provision. The draft OLC opinion encouraged this approach by leaving Article 5 out of its analysis.

The War Crimes Act forbids both grave breaches of the Geneva Conventions and certain violations of Common Article 3. The four Conventions similarly define grave breaches. Thus, the POW Convention forbids "willful killing, torture or inhuman treatment, . . . willfully causing great suffering or serious injury to body or health . . . or willfully depriving a prisoner of war of the rights of fair and regular trial . . . ." The Civilian Convention appears to provide residual protections to anyone not covered by the others, since it explicitly applies to "those who, at a given moment and in any manner whatsoever, find themselves, in case of a conflict or occupation, in the hands of a Party to the conflict . . . of which they are not nationals." Both the POW Convention and the Civilian Convention forbid coercion to obtain information. Finally, there is the overarching protection of Common Article 3, with its bans on cruel treatment or the use of irregular and unfair courts.

Thus, the portions of the Geneva Conventions that the WCA explicitly adopted contain two kinds of essential protections for persons detained in armed conflicts. First, they forbid torture, cruelty, inhumanity, and coercion. Second, they guarantee basic rights to due process. The Bush administration wanted to treat the detainees in ways inconsistent with both these kinds of rights. It wanted to employ harsh interrogation methods, many of which would have violated Geneva strictures. And it wanted to craft its own procedures for prosecuting war criminals, regardless of any prevailing conceptions that might be drawn from international law. Therefore, to meet the administration's goals the detainees would have to fall outside all of the Geneva protections codified by the WCA. *Application of Treaties* supports the legality of precisely that conclusion.

Application of Treaties takes an advocate's approach that acknowledges contrary precedent only as a prelude to rejecting its applicability. The opinion's analytic technique combines very broad assertions about presidential power with very narrow, often literal interpretations of Geneva provisions. For example, it eliminates Common Article 3 by noting its applicability to conflicts "not of an international character" and arguing that the terror war does involve an international organization, al Qaeda. This reading is plausible, given the text quoted above. There were at the time, though, widely accepted arguments that the article is meant to be a catchall, covering all unconventional conflicts. *Application of Treaties* rejects these arguments by taking the narrow position that as codified in the WCA, the article covers only civil wars.

To buttress this conclusion, the opinion deploys the avoidance canon: "We believe that the Congress must state explicitly its intention to take the constitutionally dubious step of restricting the President's plenary power over military operations (including the treatment of prisoners), and that unless Congress clearly demonstrates such an intent, the WCA must be read to avoid such constitutional problems." This statement exaggerates the President's powers over military operations in general and prisoners in particular. Congress has enacted much valid legislation regarding both. Also, it illustrates the opinion's strategy of bringing international obligations into a domestic framework where broad views of executive power can be asserted to limit them.

The opinion goes on to argue that because al Qaeda is not a nation but "merely a violent political movement or organization," Common Article 2 does not protect its members by triggering POW status for them. This too is plausible as a reading of the text, but it does stand in some tension with the administration's declaration of a War on Terrorism and its conduct of conventional military operations against al Qaeda. In any event, the opinion's interpretations of the common articles recognize protections for detainees only in wars between nations and in civil wars. Members of al Qaeda, falling in neither category, are excluded from the protections the Conventions provide.

These initial conclusions suggest, however, that the Taliban would receive protection, since the United States was engaging in armed conflict in Afghanistan. The opinion responds by citing the fact that the Taliban (like al Qaeda) do not meet the Conventions' definition of regular armed forces that merit POW protections because they are irregulars who do not wear uniforms or obey the laws of war. This is a sound argument, although it is somewhat confounded by the fact that the Taliban were the closest approximation to an army that Afghanistan had at the time.

The opinion places greater emphasis on a more strained argument about the Taliban. It relies on various statements by Defense Secretary Rumsfeld that the Taliban were not really the government of Afghanistan. The opinion asserts that it is well within the President's foreign affairs powers to declare that Afghanistan is a "failed state" with no functioning government. In that case, it would lack capacity to sustain international agreements, and would not receive their protection. Therefore, the President can suspend the operation of the Geneva Conventions with regard to Afghanistan.

Presidents do suspend treaties for various reasons, such as a material breach by another nation. Yet the United States had never before characterized a major nation as a failed state, in part because we could not then hold its putative rulers to international obligations. More important, the United States had never before considered suspending the Geneva Conventions for any reason. To do so would be a step of the greatest gravity. The opinion's breezy discussion of suspension omits these major considerations.

The opinion then notes (and rejects) the widely-held view that human rights treaties may not be suspended. It concludes that even if suspension would violate international law, the President may proceed: "We emphasize that the resolution of that question, however, has no bearing on domestic constitutional issues, or on the application of the WCA." The opinion asserts that according the Geneva Conventions domestic legal effect would interfere with the President's constitutional powers in foreign affairs. For the same reason, the "customary" international law of war does not bind the President and cannot supply protections for either group of detainees. Nonetheless, the opinion says that the President's constitutional authority to interpret customary law and to apply it if he chooses to do so allows him to extend protections to either or both groups. It is a matter of discretion, though, not law.

Application of Treaties makes both al Qaeda and Taliban detainees international outlaws, possessing only those rights the President chooses to grant them. This stance ignores a fundamental purpose of the four Geneva Conventions: to leave no one without some form of international protection, varying with the particular status of the individual. In place of an approach that honors the basic thrust of the Conventions, the opinion expends much effort arguing that the detainees fall outside each of several potential categories of protected persons, until at the end they are left with nothing. . . .

The draft *Application of Treaties* opinion created "quite a bit of havoc" among government lawyers. For the State Department, Legal Adviser Taft wrote a 40-page response to the OLC opinion, objecting that "the most important factual assumptions on which your draft is based and its legal analysis [are] seriously flawed." In particular, Taft objected to Yoo's "failed state" argument as "without support" and "contrary to the official position of the United States, the United Nations and all other states that have considered the issue." Taft was right—Yoo had transported the doctrine from the political science literature, "without support in international law and without precedent."

It should surprise no one that State would defend the binding effect of treaties. The Department daily tries to induce other nations to obey their international obligations, and is quite sensitive to the effect of any appearance that the United States is not honoring its own. Therefore, State took the position that al Qaeda captives were entitled to Common Article 3 protections, and that Taliban prisoners were entitled to POW protections, pending hearings in particular cases of doubt.

From the opposite direction came pressure to allow effective intelligence-gathering. As John Yoo put it, if the POW Convention applied we "would be able to ask Osama bin Laden loud questions, and nothing more." "Consensus eluded the group," he reports, although [White House Counsel] Alberto Gonzales made every effort to achieve it. Someone then decided to override State's objections and issue the opinion. A couple of weeks after its issuance in draft, *Application of Treaties* was edited somewhat and sent to . . . Gonzales as an opinion bearing the same title, but over the signature of Assistant Attorney General Jay Bybee. The overall analysis is the same in the two memos. The State Department had been steamrolled.

The final OLC opinion, given the luxury of a bit more time, adds a few points. For example, it observes that even if the basic requirements from Geneva that are codified in the WCA are regarded as binding, the details of confinement would not have to follow full POW norms because those are found elsewhere in the Conventions. This distinction offered the possibility of a middle way between the alternatives of applying the Conventions fully to the detainees and denying that they apply at all. This middle way would have honored the fundamental ideas in the grave breach and Common Article 3 formulas, while allowing for some flexibility in conditions of confinement. It was not pursued, because it would have foreclosed some of the harsh interrogation techniques that the administration wanted to employ. . . .

On January 18th, President Bush initially decided against granting POW status to the captives, but that was not the end of the matter. Secretary of State Colin Powell asked for reconsideration of the decision. . . . Secretary Powell's concerns were shared by General Richard Myers, the current Chairman of the Joint Chiefs of Staff, who had not been consulted regarding the President's initial decision about Geneva. Myers feared that "it would open the door for mistreatment" of U.S. prisoners. During the period of reconsideration that had been initiated by Powell, Myers and Rumsfeld disagreed openly, a rarity. Myers made his point in a National Security Council meeting with Bush and Cheney present, saying "I don't think this is a legal issue." He understood the legal argument against applying Geneva, he said, but stressed that we would be treated as we treated others.

The Pentagon's military lawyers, the Judge Advocate Generals (JAGs), shared Myers's concern about reciprocity under Geneva — if we refused to follow it, others would use the excuse to abuse our troops. They argued that the principles of Geneva "applied to any war and to anyone that the United States fought." John Yoo says that these arguments were fully aired, including participation by the uniformed lawyers. The OLC lawyers disagreed with them, arguing that this was a policy issue. Citing history, OLC noted that our enemies in Korea and Vietnam had abused our troops despite the existence of Geneva. Thus it appears that having characterized reciprocity as a policy issue, OLC nevertheless dove in on one side of the debate, contradicting those who knew far more about it than did the civilian lawyers. OLC also argued that Geneva principles had not become customary international law that bound the United States. The State Department disagreed.

The two kinds of objections that arose over the President's initial decision about the detainees flowed from two sources for which Cheney, Rumsfeld, Addington, and Yoo had little respect: international law and military tradition. The underlying tensions went well beyond issues about the status of the detainees. International law was a primary instrument of lawfare against the United States. And John Yoo had fully imbibed the longstanding hostility of the other three toward a recalcitrant military bureaucracy. It soon became apparent that their dismissive attitude toward international and military values had found another adherent: White House Counsel Alberto Gonzales.

In late January, Gonzales felt ready to write a memorandum to the President, summarizing the debate and preparing Bush for a final decision. The four-page memo avoids detailed legal discussion. Instead, it supplies bulleted points of both law and policy in favor of and against applying Geneva protections to the detainees, and then gives Gonzales's own conclusions. After reciting the earlier OLC conclusion that the Prisoner of War Convention does not apply to al Qaeda or the Taliban and Powell's disagreement with those conclusions, Gonzales states his view that the President has the constitutional authority to decide that the POW Convention does not apply to either group. He concedes that the Taliban present a more difficult case, since they were in control of Afghanistan when the United States invaded in late 2001. He passes along OLC's judgment that the President can escape Geneva by determining either that Afghanistan was a "failed state" at the time hostilities commenced, or that the Taliban were not a government but a "terrorist-like" group.

Gonzales then asserts that "OLC's interpretation of this legal issue is definitive." Its opinion binds the Executive Branch, he says, notwithstanding that the Legal Adviser to the Secretary of State "has expressed a different view." This stance that OLC advice is binding on the executive had been asserted frequently in the past — especially by the Justice Department. The difficulty with advancing it in this controversy is that it gave supremacy to the lawyers who had the least actual experience with problems involving war and its prisoners. The Departments of Defense and State had many lawyers who possessed that experience, but they had been shouldered aside.

Gonzales continues by reviewing the consequences of adhering to the earlier decision not to apply the POW Convention to the captives. The first positive consequence would be to preserve "flexibility." Avoiding Geneva would also avoid "foreclosing options," especially regarding "nonstate actors." In the "new kind of war" against terrorism, the need to obtain information from captives and to try some of them for war crimes renders obsolete Geneva's strict limitations on questioning of enemy prisoners and renders quaint some of its provisions requiring the captured enemy be afforded such things as commissary privileges."

This reference to some Geneva provisions as "obsolete" or "quaint" caused a storm of criticism when the memo was subsequently leaked to the press. There is no sign that it created similar reverberations within the administration.

Gonzales also argued that avoiding Geneva "[s]ubstantially reduces the threat of domestic criminal prosecution under the War Crimes Act." He notes that the Act's prohibition of grave Geneva breaches would include such offenses as "outrages against personal dignity" and "inhuman treatment." These terms are undefined, he says.

Moreover, it is "difficult to predict the needs" that might arise in combating terror-ism. A presidential determination that Geneva does not apply "would provide a solid defense to any future prosecution."

Turning to the potential negative effects of the earlier decision, Gonzales sum-marizes the objections he has heard. These include arguments that since 1949 the United States has never denied the applicability of the Geneva Conventions, and that the first Bush administration stated a policy of applying Geneva "whenever armed hostilities occur with regular foreign armed forces," whatever the technicalities. Gon-zales admits that if the President's decision stands, the United States cannot invoke Geneva or the War Crimes Act against mistreatment of our own forces. The deci-sion would also "likely provoke widespread condemnation" here and abroad, and could "undermine U.S. military culture which emphasizes maintaining the highest standards of conduct in combat."

Turning to his own views, Gonzales concludes that the objections to the earlier decision are "unpersuasive." This is a "new type of warfare," not contemplated at the time of Geneva. He thinks that the President's "policy of providing humane treat-ment to enemy detainees" provides the credibility to insist on reciprocity. Of course, terrorists will not follow Geneva in any event. Criticism there will be, but military culture will be preserved by the President's proposed directive to apply the "princi-ples" of Geneva although not the letter.

Colin Powell shot back a response to Gonzales's memorandum, urging that the Conventions should apply to the conflict. His memo stresses that pursuant to Geneva, the President can still determine that al Qaeda and some or all of the Taliban do not merit POW status. Even so, all captives should be treated consistently with the princi-ples of the POW Convention. Adhering to the earlier decision would "reverse over a century of U.S. policy and practice" and would "undermine the protections of the law of war for our troops, both in this specific conflict and in general." Not surpris-ingly, Powell finds a "high cost in terms of negative international reaction" if Geneva is not applied. By contrast, following Geneva would provide a "more defensible legal framework" and a "positive international posture" as a result of "taking the high ground." As for OLC, its opinion would likely be rejected by foreign governments or tribunals, whatever its effect might be domestically.

The State Department followed up with a strongly phrased memorandum to Gon-zales from Legal Adviser Taft. It argues that a decision to apply Geneva is consistent with both the "plain language" of the Conventions and "the unvaried practice of the United States" for over fifty years. He reiterates the reciprocity argument and con-cludes that from a policy standpoint, applying Geneva "provides the best legal basis" for treating the captives "in the way we intend to treat them." Thus, he finds the boundary between law and policy to be blurrier than it seems to OLC.

Attorney General Ashcroft also weighed in with a letter to the President that he prepared personally, not by his staff. Having been on the sidelines for most of the controversy, he now rushed into the game. His letter argues that a determination against applying Geneva creates the least legal jeopardy, because courts will not review it. The alternative, applying Geneva but concluding that al Qaeda and perhaps the Taliban are unlawful combatants not entitled to POW status, might not receive judicial deference. He concludes that rejecting Geneva will minimize "the legal risks of liability, litigation and criminal prosecution."

OLC followed the Attorney General's letter with a substantial memorandum regarding the status of the Taliban under Geneva, arguing that they could be denied POW status even if the Conventions apply generally, because the Taliban are "unlawful combatants" who wear no uniforms and ignore the laws of war. Like the earlier OLC opinions in this extended war of memoranda, the final OLC opinion assures the President that he can make categorical determinations that detainees held as members of al Qaeda and the Taliban are not entitled to Geneva protections, because they are unlawful combatants. That is a justifiable conclusion regarding POW status, and a more dubious one concerning other Geneva protections.

On February 7, 2002, the President issued an order titled *Humane Treatment of al Qaeda and Taliban Detainees*, modifying his earlier decision. His order accepts "the legal conclusion of the Department of Justice" that no part of the Geneva Conventions applies to al Qaeda. He decides that Geneva will apply to the Taliban even though he shares Justice's legal opinion that this is not mandatory. (He is declining to rely on the dubious "failed state" theory.) Nevertheless, the Taliban are unlawful combatants not entitled to POW status. He also accepts Justice's conclusion that Common Article 3 does not apply to either group, because this is an international conflict and Article 3 governs internal ones. The President then stresses that "our values as a Nation . . . call for us to treat detainees humanely." He directs that:

> As a matter of policy, the United States Armed Forces shall continue to treat detainees humanely and, to the extent appropriate and consistent with military necessity, in a manner consistent with the principles of Geneva.

It has been said of General Ulysses Grant that his military orders had such clarity that no subordinate could mistake his directions. The same cannot be said of President Bush's order of February 2002. A lawyer's formulation, it looks in both directions at once: Geneva "principles" apply, if "consistent with military necessity." Somewhat more clearly, treatment is to be "humane." John Yoo would later conclude optimistically that "[a]ny concerns about a decline in military discipline were cured by President Bush's order that the detainees be treated humanely." That judgment is belied by the reality of the disconnect that occurred between the President's order and its execution in the field. Jack Goldsmith noted more accurately that the formula President Bush used in his order was "very vague" and left "all of the hard issues about 'humane' and 'appropriate' treatment to unknown officials."

Four years after President Bush's determination regarding the Geneva Conventions and two years after the *Hamdi* decision, the Supreme Court was called upon to resolve the fundamental question whether the executive branch could try alleged enemy combatants being held at Guantanamo by military commission:

Hamdan v. Rumsfeld

548 U.S. 557 (2006).

Justice STEVENS announced the judgment of the Court and delivered the opinion of the Court with respect to Parts I through IV, Parts VI through VI-D-iii, Part VI-D-v, and Part VII, and an opinion with respect to Parts V and VI-D-iv, in which Justice SOUTER, Justice GINSBURG, and Justice BREYER join.

Petitioner Salim Ahmed Hamdan, a Yemeni national, is in custody at an American prison in Guantanamo Bay, Cuba. In November 2001, during hostilities between the United States and the Taliban (which then governed Afghanistan), Hamdan was captured by militia forces and turned over to the U.S. military. In June 2002, he was transported to Guantanamo Bay. Over a year later, the President deemed him eligible for trial by military commission for then-unspecified crimes. After another year had passed, Hamdan was charged with one count of conspiracy "to commit . . . offenses triable by military commission."

Hamdan filed petitions for writs of habeas corpus and mandamus to challenge the Executive Branch's intended means of prosecuting this charge. He concedes that a court-martial constituted in accordance with the Uniform Code of Military Justice (UCMJ), 10 U.S.C. § 801 *et seq.* (2000 ed. and Supp. III), would have authority to try him. His objection is that the military commission the President has convened lacks such authority, for two principal reasons: First, neither congressional Act nor the common law of war supports trial by this commission for the crime of conspiracy—an offense that, Hamdan says, is not a violation of the law of war. Second, Hamdan contends, the procedures that the President has adopted to try him violate the most basic tenets of military and international law, including the principle that a defendant must be permitted to see and hear the evidence against him. . . . [W]e conclude that the military commission convened to try Hamdan lacks power to proceed because its structure and procedures violate both the UCMJ and the Geneva Conventions. Four of us also conclude, see Part V, *infra,* that the offense with which Hamdan has been charged is not an "offens[e] that by . . . the law of war may be tried by military commissions." 10 U.S.C. § 821.

I

[In Part I, the Court recounts the issuance of President Bush's November 13, 2001 order, and the details of the charges against Hamdan. These charges were contained in two paragraphs of a "charging document."]

Only the final two paragraphs, entitled "Charge: Conspiracy," contain allegations against Hamdan. Paragraph 12 charges that "from on or about February 1996 to on or about November 24, 2001," Hamdan "willfully and knowingly joined an enterprise of persons who shared a common criminal purpose and conspired and agreed with [named members of al Qaeda] to commit the following offenses triable by military commission: attacking civilians; attacking civilian objects; murder by an unprivileged belligerent; and terrorism." There is no allegation that Hamdan had any command responsibilities, played a leadership role, or participated in the planning of any activity.

Paragraph 13 lists four "overt acts" that Hamdan is alleged to have committed sometime between 1996 and November 2001 in furtherance of the "enterprise and conspiracy": (1) he acted as Osama bin Laden's "bodyguard and personal driver," "believ[ing]" all the while that bin Laden "and his associates were involved in" terrorist acts prior to and including the attacks of September 11, 2001; (2) he arranged for transportation of, and actually transported, weapons used by al Qaeda members and by bin Laden's bodyguards (Hamdan among them); (3) he "drove or accompanied [O]sama bin Laden to various al Qaeda-sponsored training camps, press conferences, or lectures," at which bin Laden encouraged attacks against Americans; and (4) he received weapons training at al Qaeda-sponsored camps.

After this formal charge was filed, the United States District Court for the Western District of Washington transferred Hamdan's habeas and mandamus petitions to the United States District Court for the District of Columbia. Meanwhile, a Combatant Status Review Tribunal (CSRT) convened pursuant to a military order issued on July 7, 2004, decided that Hamdan's continued detention at Guantanamo Bay was warranted because he was an "enemy combatant." Separately, proceedings before the military commission commenced.

On November 8, 2004, however, the District Court granted Hamdan's petition for habeas corpus and stayed the commission's proceedings. It concluded that the President's authority to establish military commissions extends only to "offenders or offenses triable by military [commission] under the law of war," 344 F. Supp. 2d, at 158; that the law of war includes the Geneva Convention (III) Relative to the Treatment of Prisoners of War, Aug. 12, 1949, [1955] 6 U.S.T. 3316, T.I.A.S. No. 3364 (Third Geneva Convention); that Hamdan is entitled to the full protections of the Third Geneva Convention until adjudged, in compliance with that treaty, not to be a prisoner of war; and that, whether or not Hamdan is properly classified as a prisoner of war, the military commission convened to try him was established in violation of both the UCMJ and Common Article 3 of the Third Geneva Convention because it had the power to convict based on evidence the accused would never see or hear. 344 F. Supp. 2d, at 158–172.

The Court of Appeals for the District of Columbia Circuit reversed. Like the District Court, the Court of Appeals declined the Government's invitation to abstain from considering Hamdan's challenge. On the merits, the panel rejected the District Court's further conclusion that Hamdan was entitled to relief under the Third Geneva Convention. All three judges agreed that the Geneva Conventions were not "judicially enforceable," 415 F.3d, at 38, and two thought that the Conventions did not in any event apply to Hamdan, *id.,* at 40–42; but see *id.,* at 44 (Williams, J., concurring). In other portions of its opinion, the court concluded that our decision in *Quirin* foreclosed any separation-of-powers objection to the military commission's jurisdiction, and held that Hamdan's trial before the contemplated commission would violate neither the UCMJ nor U.S. Armed Forces regulations intended to implement the Geneva Conventions. 415 F.3d, at 38, 42–43. . . .

II

[The Court rejected the government's argument that it lacked jurisdiction under the then-recently enacted Detainee Treatment Act of 2005 (DTA), Pub.L. 109-148, 119 Stat. 2739. The Court held that the DTA's curtailment of habeas corpus jurisdiction in connection with applications for "a writ of habeas corpus filed by or on behalf of an alien detained by the Department of Defense at Guantanamo Bay, Cuba" was not intended to apply retroactively to habeas petitions pending at the time the DTA was enacted.]

III

[The Court next rejected the argument, based on *Schlesinger v. Councilman,* 420 U.S. 738 (1975) that, even if the Court has statutory jurisdiction, it should apply the "judge-made rule that civilian courts should await the final outcome of on-going military proceedings before entertaining an attack on those proceedings." As read by the Court, *Councilman* identified "two considerations of comity that together favor abstention pending completion of ongoing court-martial proceedings against service personnel": (1) "military discipline and, therefore, the efficient operation of the Armed Forces are best served if the military justice system acts without regular inter-ference from civilian courts," and (2) "federal courts should respect the balance that Congress struck between military preparedness and fairness to individual service members when it created 'an integrated system of military courts and review proce-dures, a critical element of which is the Court of Military Appeals, consisting of civil-ian judges "completely removed from all military influence or persuasion . . . ." ' " The Court concluded that neither of these comity considerations applied to *Hamdan* because the petitioner was not a member of the U.S. armed forces, and "the tribunal convened to try Hamdan is not part of the integrated system of military courts, com-plete with independent review panels, that Congress has established."]

IV

The military commission, a tribunal neither mentioned in the Constitution nor created by statute, was born of military necessity. See W. Winthrop, Military Law and Precedents 831 (rev. 2d ed. 1920) (hereinafter Winthrop). Though foreshadowed in some respects by earlier tribunals like the Board of General Officers that General Washington convened to try British Major John Andre for spying during the Revo-lutionary War, the commission "as such" was inaugurated in 1847. *Id.,* at 832; G. Davis, A Treatise on the Military Law of the United States 308 (2d ed. 1909) (hereinafter Davis). As commander of occupied Mexican territory, and having available to him no other tribunal, General Winfield Scott that year ordered the estab-lishment of both " '*military commissions*' " to try ordinary crimes committed in the occupied territory and a "*council of war*" to try offenses against the law of war. Win-throp 832 (emphases in original). . . .

Exigency alone, of course, will not justify the establishment and use of penal tribunals not contemplated by Article I, §8 and Article III, §1 of the Constitution unless some other part of that document authorizes a response to the felt need. And that authority, if it exists, can derive only from the powers granted jointly to the President and Congress in time of war.

The Constitution makes the President the "Commander in Chief" of the Armed Forces, Art. II, §2, cl. 1, but vests in Congress the powers to "declare War . . . and make Rules concerning Captures on Land and Water," Art. I, §8, cl. 11, to "raise and support Armies," *id.,* cl. 12, to "define and punish . . . Offences against the Law of Nations," *id.,* cl. 10, and "To make Rules for the Government and Regulation of the land and naval Forces," *id.,* cl. 14. The interplay between these powers was described by Chief Justice Chase in the seminal case of *Ex parte Milligan:* "The power to make the necessary laws is in Congress; the power to execute in the President. Both powers imply many subordinate and auxiliary powers. Each includes all authorities essential to its due exercise. But neither can the President, in war more than in peace, intrude upon the proper authority of Congress, nor Congress upon the proper authority of the President . . . . Congress cannot direct the conduct of campaigns, nor can the President, or any commander under him, without the sanction of Congress, institute tribunals for the trial and punishment of offences, either of soldiers or civilians, unless in cases of a controlling necessity, which justifies what it compels, or at least insures acts of indemnity from the justice of the legislature." 4 Wall., at 139–140.

Whether Chief Justice Chase was correct in suggesting that the President may constitutionally convene military commissions "without the sanction of Congress" in cases of "controlling necessity" is a question this Court has not answered definitively, and need not answer today. For we held in *Quirin* that Congress had, through Article of War 15, sanctioned the use of military commissions in such circumstances. 317 U.S., at 28. . . . Contrary to the Government's assertion, however, even *Quirin* did not view the authorization as a sweeping mandate for the President to "invoke military commissions when he deems them necessary." Rather, the *Quirin* Court recognized that Congress had simply preserved what power, under the Constitution and the common law of war, the President had had before 1916 to convene military commissions—with the express condition that the President and those under his command comply with the law of war. . . .

The Government would have us . . . find in either the AUMF or the DTA specific, overriding authorization for the very commission that has been convened to try Hamdan. Neither of these congressional Acts, however, expands the President's authority to convene military commissions. . . . Together, the UCMJ, the AUMF, and the DTA at most acknowledge a general Presidential authority to convene military commissions in circumstances where justified under the "Constitution and laws," including the law of war. Absent a more specific congressional authorization, the task of this Court is, as it was in *Quirin,* to decide whether Hamdan's military commission is so justified. . . .

V*

The common law governing military commissions may be gleaned from past practice and what sparse legal precedent exists. Commissions historically have been used in three situations. First, they have substituted for civilian courts at times and in places where martial law has been declared. Their use in these circumstances has raised constitutional questions, see *Duncan v. Kahanamoku,* 327 U.S. 304, but is well recognized. See Winthrop 822, 836–839. Second, commissions have been established to try civilians "as part of a temporary military government over occupied enemy territory or territory regained from an enemy where civilian government cannot and does not function." *Duncan,* 327 U.S., at 314; see *Milligan,* 4 Wall., at 141–142 (Chase, C. J., concurring in judgment) (distinguishing "MARTIAL LAW PROPER" from "MILITARY GOVERNMENT" in occupied territory). Illustrative of this second kind of commission is the one that was established, with jurisdiction to apply the German Criminal Code, in occupied Germany following the end of World War II. See *Madsen v. Kinsella,* 343 U.S. 341, 356 (1952).

The third type of commission, convened as an "incident to the conduct of war" when there is a need "to seize and subject to disciplinary measures those enemies who in their attempt to thwart or impede our military effort have violated the law of war," *Quirin,* 317 U.S., at 28–29, has been described as "utterly different" from the other two. Not only is its jurisdiction limited to offenses cognizable during time of war, but its role is primarily a factfinding one—to determine, typically on the battlefield itself, whether the defendant has violated the law of war. The last time the U.S. Armed Forces used the law-of-war military commission was during World War II. In *Quirin,* this Court sanctioned President Roosevelt's use of such a tribunal to try Nazi saboteurs captured on American soil during the War. And in *Yamashita,* we held that a military commission had jurisdiction to try a Japanese commander for failing to prevent troops under his command from committing atrocities in the Philippines. . . .

Quirin is the model the Government invokes most frequently to defend the commission convened to try Hamdan. That is both appropriate and unsurprising. Since Guantanamo Bay is neither enemy-occupied territory nor under martial law, the law-of-war commission is the only model available. At the same time, no more robust model of executive power exists; *Quirin* represents the high-water mark of military power to try enemy combatants for war crimes.

The classic treatise penned by Colonel William Winthrop, whom we have called "the 'Blackstone of Military Law,'" *Reid v. Covert,* 354 U.S. 1, 19, n. 38 (1957) (plurality opinion), describes at least four preconditions for exercise of jurisdiction by a tribunal of the type convened to try Hamdan. First, "[a] military commission, (except where otherwise authorized by statute), can legally assume jurisdiction only of

---

* [Note that, because Justice Kennedy does not join this part of the opinion, it represents the views of only four Justices.]

offenses committed within the field of the command of the convening commander."
Winthrop 836. The "field of command" in these circumstances means the "theatre
of war." *Ibid.* Second, the offense charged "must have been committed within the
period of the war." *Id.,* at 837. No jurisdiction exists to try offenses "committed either
before or after the war." *Ibid.* Third, a military commission not established pursuant to martial law or an occupation may try only "[i]ndividuals of the enemy's army
who have been guilty of illegitimate warfare or other offences in violation of the laws
of war" and members of one's own army "who, in time of war, become chargeable
with crimes or offences not cognizable, or triable, by the criminal courts or under
the Articles of war." *Id.,* at 838. Finally, a law-of-war commission has jurisdiction to
try only two kinds of offense: "Violations of the laws and usages of war cognizable
by military tribunals only," and "[b]reaches of military orders or regulations for
which offenders are not legally triable by court-martial under the Articles of war."
Id., at 839. . . .

The charge against Hamdan, described in detail in Part I, *supra,* alleges a conspiracy extending over a number of years, from 1996 to November 2001. All but two
months of that more than 5-year-long period preceded the attacks of September 11,
2001, and the enactment of the AUMF—the Act of Congress on which the Government relies for exercise of its war powers and thus for its authority to convene military
commissions. Neither the purported agreement with Osama bin Laden and others
to commit war crimes, nor a single overt act, is alleged to have occurred in a theater
of war or on any specified date after September 11, 2001. None of the overt acts that
Hamdan is alleged to have committed violates the law of war.

These facts alone cast doubt on the legality of the charge and, hence, the commission; as Winthrop makes plain, the offense alleged must have been committed both
in a theater of war and *during,* not before, the relevant conflict. But the deficiencies
in the time and place allegations also underscore—indeed are symptomatic of—the
most serious defect of this charge: The offense it alleges is not triable by law-of-war
military commission.

There is no suggestion that Congress has, in exercise of its constitutional authority to "define and punish . . . Offences against the Law of Nations," U.S. Const., Art.
I, § 8, cl. 10, positively identified "conspiracy" as a war crime. As we explained in
Quirin, that is not necessarily fatal to the Government's claim of authority to try the
alleged offense by military commission; Congress, through Article 21 of the UCMJ,
has "incorporated by reference" the common law of war, which may render triable
by military commission certain offenses not defined by statute. 317 U.S., at 30. When,
however, neither the elements of the offense nor the range of permissible punishments
is defined by statute or treaty, the precedent must be plain and unambiguous. To
demand any less would be to risk concentrating in military hands a degree of adjudicative and punitive power in excess of that contemplated either by statute or by
the Constitution. . . .

At a minimum, the Government must make a substantial showing that the crime
for which it seeks to try a defendant by military commission is acknowledged to be

an offense against the law of war. That burden is far from satisfied here. The crime of "conspiracy" has rarely if ever been tried as such in this country by any law-of-war military commission not exercising some other form of jurisdiction, and does not appear in either the Geneva Conventions or The Hague Conventions—the major treaties on the law of war. . . .

Finally, international sources confirm that the crime charged here is not a recognized violation of the law of war. As observed above, none of the major treaties governing the law of war identifies conspiracy as a violation thereof. And the only "conspiracy" crimes that have been recognized by international war crimes tribunals (whose jurisdiction often extends beyond war crimes proper to crimes against humanity and crimes against the peace) are conspiracy to commit genocide and common plan to wage aggressive war, which is a crime against the peace and requires for its commission actual participation in a "concrete plan to wage war." 1 Trial of the Major War Criminals Before the International Military Tribunal: Nuremberg, 14 November 1945–1 October 1946, p. 225 (1947). . . .

The charge's shortcomings are not merely formal, but are indicative of a broader inability on the Executive's part here to satisfy the most basic precondition—at least in the absence of specific congressional authorization—for establishment of military commissions: military necessity. Hamdan's tribunal was appointed not by a military commander in the field of battle, but by a retired major general stationed away from any active hostilities. Hamdan is charged not with an overt act for which he was caught redhanded in a theater of war and which military efficiency demands be tried expeditiously, but with an *agreement* the inception of which long predated the attacks of September 11, 2001 and the AUMF. That may well be a crime, but it is not an offense that "by the law of war may be tried by military commissio[n]." 10 U.S.C. § 821. None of the overt acts alleged to have been committed in furtherance of the agreement is itself a war crime, or even necessarily occurred during time of, or in a theater of, war. Any urgent need for imposition or execution of judgment is utterly belied by the record; Hamdan was arrested in November 2001 and he was not charged until mid-2004. These simply are not the circumstances in which, by any stretch of the historical evidence or this Court's precedents, a military commission established by Executive Order under the authority of Article 21 of the UCMJ may lawfully try a person and subject him to punishment.

VI

Whether or not the Government has charged Hamdan with an offense against the law of war cognizable by military commission, the commission lacks power to proceed. The UCMJ conditions the President's use of military commissions on compliance not only with the American common law of war, but also with the rest of the UCMJ itself, insofar as applicable, and with the "rules and precepts of the law of nations," *Quirin*, 317 U.S., at 28—including, *inter alia*, the four Geneva Conventions signed in 1949. See *Yamashita*, 327 U.S., at 20–21, 23–24. The procedures that the Government has decreed will govern Hamdan's trial by commission violate these laws.

A

. . . Every commission established pursuant to Commission Order No. 1 must have a presiding officer and at least three other members, all of whom must be commissioned officers. § 4(A)(1). . . . The accused is entitled to appointed military counsel and may hire civilian counsel at his own expense so long as such counsel is a U.S. citizen with security clearance "at the level SECRET or higher." §§ 4(C)(2)–(3).

The accused also is entitled to a copy of the charge(s) against him, both in English and his own language (if different), to a presumption of innocence, and to certain other rights typically afforded criminal defendants in civilian courts and courts-martial. See §§ 5(A)–(P). These rights are subject, however, to one glaring condition: The accused and his civilian counsel may be excluded from, and precluded from ever learning what evidence was presented during, any part of the proceeding that either the Appointing Authority or the presiding officer decides to "close." Grounds for such closure "include the protection of information classified or classifiable . . . ; information protected by law or rule from unauthorized disclosure; the physical safety of participants in Commission proceedings, including prospective witnesses; intelligence and law enforcement sources, methods, or activities; and other national security interests." § 6(B)(3). Appointed military defense counsel must be privy to these closed sessions, but may, at the presiding officer's discretion, be forbidden to reveal to his or her client what took place therein.

Another striking feature of the rules governing Hamdan's commission is that they permit the admission of *any* evidence that, in the opinion of the presiding officer, "would have probative value to a reasonable person." § 6(D)(1). Under this test, not only is testimonial hearsay and evidence obtained through coercion fully admissible, but neither live testimony nor witnesses' written statements need be sworn. See §§ 6(D)(2)(b), (3). Moreover, the accused and his civilian counsel may be denied access to evidence in the form of "protected information" (which includes classified information as well as "information protected by law or rule from unauthorized disclosure" and "information concerning other national security interests," §§ 6(B)(3), 6(D)(5)(a)(v)), so long as the presiding officer concludes that the evidence is "probative" under § 6(D)(1) and that its admission without the accused's knowledge would not "result in the denial of a full and fair trial." § 6(D)(5)(b). Finally, a presiding officer's determination that evidence "would not have probative value to a reasonable person" may be overridden by a majority of the other commission members. § 6(D)(1).

Once all the evidence is in, the commission members (not including the presiding officer) must vote on the accused's guilt. A two-thirds vote will suffice for both a verdict of guilty and for imposition of any sentence not including death (the imposition of which requires a unanimous vote). § 6(F). Any appeal is taken to a three-member review panel composed of military officers and designated by the Secretary of Defense, only one member of which need have experience as a judge. § 6(H)(4). The review panel is directed to "disregard any variance from procedures specified in this Order or elsewhere that would not materially have affected the outcome of the trial before the Commission." *Ibid.* Once the panel makes its recommendation to the Secretary of Defense, the Secretary can either remand for further proceedings or forward the record to the President with his recommendation as to final disposition. §6(H)(5). The President then, unless he has delegated the task to the Secretary, makes the "final decision." §6(H)(6). He may change the commission's findings or sentence only in a manner favorable to the accused. *Ibid.*

B

Hamdan raises both general and particular objections to the procedures set forth in Commission Order No. 1. His general objection is that the procedures' admitted deviation from those governing courts-martial itself renders the commission illegal. Chief among his particular objections are that he may, under the Commission Order, be convicted based on evidence he has not seen or heard, and that any evidence admitted against him need not comply with the admissibility or relevance rules typically applicable in criminal trials and court-martial proceedings. . . . [The majority rejects the Government's arguments that Hamdan's procedural challenges are premature.]

C

. . . [T]he procedures governing trials by military commission historically have been the same as those governing courts-martial. . . . There is a glaring historical exception to this general rule. The procedures and evidentiary rules used to try General Yamashita near the end of World War II deviated in significant respects from those then governing courts-martial. See 327 U.S. 1. The force of that precedent, however, has been seriously undermined by post-World War II developments.

Yamashita, from late 1944 until September 1945, was Commanding General of the Fourteenth Army Group of the Imperial Japanese Army, which had exercised control over the Philippine Islands. On September 3, 1945, after American forces regained control of the Philippines, Yamashita surrendered. Three weeks later, he was charged with violations of the law of war. A few weeks after that, he was arraigned before a military commission convened in the Philippines. He pleaded not guilty, and his trial lasted for two months. On December 7, 1945, Yamashita was convicted and sentenced to hang. This Court upheld the denial of his petition for a writ of habeas corpus.

The procedures and rules of evidence employed during Yamashita's trial departed so far from those used in courts-martial that they generated an unusually long and vociferous critique from two Members of this Court. See *id.*, at 41–81 (Rutledge, J., joined by Murphy, J., dissenting). Among the dissenters' primary concerns was that the commission had free rein to consider all evidence "which in the commission's opinion 'would be of assistance in proving or disproving the charge,' without any of the usual modes of authentication." *Id.*, at 49 (Rutledge, J.).

The majority, however, did not pass on the merits of Yamashita's procedural challenges because it concluded that his status disentitled him to any protection under the Articles of War . . . At least partially in response to subsequent criticism of General Yamashita's trial, the UCMJ's codification of the Articles of War after World War II expanded the category of persons subject thereto to include defendants in Yamashita's (and Hamdan's) position, and the Third Geneva Convention of 1949 extended prisoner-of-war protections to individuals tried for crimes committed before their capture. The most notorious exception to the principle of uniformity, then, has been stripped of its precedential value.

The uniformity principle is not an inflexible one; it does not preclude all departures from the procedures dictated for use by courts-martial. But any departure must be tailored to the exigency that necessitates it. . . .

Article 36 places two restrictions on the President's power to promulgate rules of procedure for courts-martial and military commissions alike. First, no procedural rule he adopts may be "contrary to or inconsistent with" the UCMJ—however practical it may seem. Second, the rules adopted must be "uniform insofar as practicable." That is, the rules applied to military commissions must be the same as those applied to courts-martial unless such uniformity proves impracticable.

. . . Among the inconsistencies Hamdan identifies is that between §6 of the Commission Order, which permits exclusion of the accused from proceedings and denial of his access to evidence in certain circumstances, and the UCMJ's requirement that "[a]ll . . . proceedings" other than votes and deliberations by courts-martial "shall be made a part of the record and shall be in the presence of the accused." 10 U.S.C.A. §839(c) (Supp. 2006). Hamdan also observes that the Commission Order dispenses with virtually all evidentiary rules applicable in courts-martial. . . .

The President here has determined, pursuant to subsection (a), that it is impracticable to apply the rules and principles of law that govern "the trial of criminal cases in the United States district courts," §836(a), to Hamdan's commission. We assume that complete deference is owed that determination. The President has not, however, made a similar official determination that it is impracticable to apply the rules for courts-martial. And even if subsection (b)'s requirements may be satisfied without such an official determination, the requirements of that subsection are not satisfied here.

Nothing in the record before us demonstrates that it would be impracticable to apply court-martial rules in this case. There is no suggestion, for example, of any logistical difficulty in securing properly sworn and authenticated evidence or in applying the usual principles of relevance and admissibility. Assuming *arguendo* that the reasons articulated in the President's Article 36(a) determination ought to be considered in evaluating the impracticability of applying court-martial rules, the only reason offered in support of that determination is the danger posed by international terrorism. Without for one moment underestimating that danger, it is not evident to us why it should require, in the case of Hamdan's trial, any variance from the rules that govern courts-martial.

The absence of any showing of impracticability is particularly disturbing when considered in light of the clear and admitted failure to apply one of the most fundamental protections afforded not just by the Manual for Courts-Martial but also by the UCMJ itself: the right to be present. See 10 U.S.C.A. §839(c) (Supp. 2006). Whether or not that departure technically is "contrary to or inconsistent with" the terms of the UCMJ, 10 U.S.C. §836(a), the jettisoning of so basic a right cannot lightly be excused as "practicable."

Under the circumstances, then, the rules applicable in courts-martial must apply. Since it is undisputed that Commission Order No. 1 deviates in many significant respects from those rules, it necessarily violates Article 36(b). . . .

D

The procedures adopted to try Hamdan also violate the Geneva Conventions. . . .

i

The Court of Appeals relied on *Johnson v. Eisentrager,* 339 U.S. 763 (1950), to hold that Hamdan could not invoke the Geneva Conventions to challenge the Government's plan to prosecute him in accordance with Commission Order No. 1. *Eisentrager* involved a challenge by 21 German nationals to their 1945 convictions for war crimes by a military tribunal convened in Nanking, China, and to their subsequent imprisonment in occupied Germany. The petitioners argued, *inter alia,* that the 1929 Geneva Convention rendered illegal some of the procedures employed during their trials, which they said deviated impermissibly from the procedures used by courts-martial to try American soldiers. We rejected that claim on the merits because the petitioners (unlike Hamdan here) had failed to identify any prejudicial disparity "between the Commission that tried [them] and those that would try an offending soldier of the American forces of like rank," and in any event could claim no protection, under the 1929 Convention, during trials for crimes that occurred before their confinement as prisoners of war.

Buried in a footnote of the opinion, however, is this curious statement suggesting that the Court lacked power even to consider the merits of the Geneva Convention argument:

> "We are not holding that these prisoners have no right which the military authorities are bound to respect. The United States, by the Geneva Convention of July 27, 1929, 47 Stat.2021, concluded with forty-six other countries, including the German Reich, an agreement upon the treatment to be accorded captives. These prisoners claim to be and are entitled to its protection. It is, however, the obvious scheme of the Agreement that responsibility for observance and enforcement of these rights is upon political and military authorities. Rights of alien enemies are vindicated under it only through protests and intervention of protecting powers as the rights of our citizens against foreign governments are vindicated only by Presidential intervention."

Id., at 789, n. 14. The Court of Appeals, on the strength of this footnote, held that "the 1949 Geneva Convention does not confer upon Hamdan a right to enforce its provisions in court." 415 F.3d, at 40.

Whatever else might be said about the *Eisentrager* footnote, it does not control this case. We may assume that "the obvious scheme" of the 1949 Conventions is identical in all relevant respects to that of the 1929 Convention, and even that that scheme would, absent some other provision of law, preclude Hamdan's invocation of the Convention's provisions as an independent source of law binding the Government's actions and furnishing petitioner with any enforceable right. For, regardless of the nature of the rights conferred on Hamdan, they are, as the Government does not dispute, part of the law of war. And compliance with the law of war is the condition upon which the authority set forth in Article 21 is granted.

ii

For the Court of Appeals, acknowledgment of that condition was no bar to Hamdan's trial by commission. As an alternative to its holding that Hamdan could not invoke the Geneva Conventions at all, the Court of Appeals concluded that the Conventions did not in any event apply to the armed conflict during which Hamdan was captured. The court accepted the Executive's assertions that Hamdan was captured in connection with the United States' war with al Qaeda and that that war is distinct from the war with the Taliban in Afghanistan. It further reasoned that the war with al Qaeda evades the reach of the Geneva Conventions. We, like Judge Williams, disagree with the latter conclusion.

The conflict with al Qaeda is not, according to the Government, a conflict to which the full protections afforded detainees under the 1949 Geneva Conventions apply because Article 2 of those Conventions (which appears in all four Conventions) renders the full protections applicable only to "all cases of declared war or of any other armed conflict which may arise between two or more of the High Contracting Parties." 6 U.S.T., at 3318. Since Hamdan was captured and detained incident to the conflict with al Qaeda and not the conflict with the Taliban, and since al Qaeda, unlike Afghanistan, is not a "High Contracting Party" — *i.e.*, a signatory of the Conventions, the protections of those Conventions are not, it is argued, applicable to Hamdan.

We need not decide the merits of this argument because there is at least one provision of the Geneva Conventions that applies here even if the relevant conflict is not one between signatories. Article 3, often referred to as Common Article 3 because, like Article 2, it appears in all four Geneva Conventions, provides that in a "conflict not of an international character occurring in the territory of one of the High Contracting Parties, each Party to the conflict shall be bound to apply, as a minimum," certain provisions protecting "[p]ersons taking no active part in the hostilities, including members of armed forces who have laid down their arms and those placed *hors de combat* by . . . detention." One such provision prohibits "the passing of sentences and the carrying out of executions without previous judgment pronounced by a regularly constituted court affording all the judicial guarantees which are recognized as indispensable by civilized peoples."

The Court of Appeals thought, and the Government asserts, that Common Article 3 does not apply to Hamdan because the conflict with al Qaeda, being "'international in scope,'" does not qualify as a "'conflict not of an international character.'" That reasoning is erroneous. The term "conflict not of an international character" is used here in contradistinction to a conflict between nations. So much is demonstrated by the "fundamental logic [of] the Convention's provisions on its application." Common Article 2 provides that "the present Convention shall apply to all cases of declared war or of any other armed conflict which may arise between two or more of the High Contracting Parties." 6 U.S.T., at 3318 (Art. 2, ¶ 1). High Contracting Parties (signatories) also must abide by all terms of the Conventions vis-à-vis one another even if one party to the conflict is a nonsignatory "Power," and must so abide vis-à-vis the nonsignatory if "the latter accepts and applies" those terms. *Ibid.* (Art. 2, ¶ 3). Common Article 3, by contrast, affords some minimal protection, falling short of full protection under the Conventions, to individuals associated with neither a signatory nor even a nonsignatory "Power" who are involved in a conflict "in the territory of" a signatory. The latter kind of conflict is distinguishable from the conflict described in Common Article 2 chiefly because it does not involve a clash between nations (whether signatories or not). In context, then, the phrase "not of an international character" bears its literal meaning.

Although the official commentaries accompanying Common Article 3 indicate that an important purpose of the provision was to furnish minimal protection to rebels involved in one kind of "conflict not of an international character," *i.e.*, a civil war, the commentaries also make clear "that the scope of the Article must be as wide as possible." In fact, limiting language that would have rendered Common Article 3 applicable "especially [to] cases of civil war, colonial conflicts, or wars of religion," was omitted from the final version of the Article, which coupled broader scope of application with a narrower range of rights than did earlier proposed iterations.

iii

Common Article 3, then, is applicable here and, as indicated above, requires that Hamdan be tried by a "regularly constituted court affording all the judicial guarantees which are recognized as indispensable by civilized peoples." 6 U.S.T., at 3320 (Art. 3, ¶ 1(d)). While the term "regularly constituted court" is not specifically defined in either Common Article 3 or its accompanying commentary, other sources disclose its core meaning. The commentary accompanying a provision of the Fourth Geneva Convention, for example, defines "'regularly constituted'" tribunals to include "ordinary military courts" and "definitely exclud[e] all special tribunals." GCIV Commentary 340 (defining the term "properly constituted" in Article 66, which the commentary treats as identical to "regularly constituted"). . . .

The Government offers only a cursory defense of Hamdan's military commission in light of Common Article 3. As Justice KENNEDY explains, that defense fails because "[t]he regular military courts in our system are the courts-martial established by congressional statutes." At a minimum, a military commission "can be 'regularly constituted' by the standards of our military justice system only if some practical need explains deviations from court-martial practice." As we have explained, no such need has been demonstrated here.

iv**

Inextricably intertwined with the question of regular constitution is the evaluation of the procedures governing the tribunal and whether they afford "all the judicial guarantees which are recognized as indispensable by civilized peoples." 6 U.S.T., at 3320 (Art. 3, ¶ 1(d)). Like the phrase "regularly constituted court," this phrase is not defined in the text of the Geneva Conventions. But it must be understood to incorporate at least the barest of those trial protections that have been recognized by customary international law. . . .

We agree with Justice KENNEDY that the procedures adopted to try Hamdan deviate from those governing courts-martial in ways not justified by any "evident practical need," and for that reason, at least, fail to afford the requisite guarantees. We add only that, as noted in Part VI-A, *supra*, various provisions of Commission Order No. 1 dispense with the principles, articulated in Article 75 and indisputably part of the customary international law, that an accused must, absent disruptive conduct or consent, be present for his trial and must be privy to the evidence against him. See §§ 6(B)(3), (D). That the Government has a compelling interest in denying Hamdan access to certain sensitive information is not doubted. But, at least absent express statutory provision to the contrary, information used to convict a person of a crime must be disclosed to him.

v

Common Article 3 obviously tolerates a great degree of flexibility in trying individuals captured during armed conflict; its requirements are general ones, crafted to accommodate a wide variety of legal systems. But *requirements* they are nonetheless. The commission that the President has convened to try Hamdan does not meet those requirements.

VII

We have assumed, as we must, that the allegations made in the Government's charge against Hamdan are true. We have assumed, moreover, the truth of the message implicit in that charge—viz., that Hamdan is a dangerous individual whose beliefs, if acted upon, would cause great harm and even death to innocent civilians, and who would act upon those beliefs if given the opportunity. It bears emphasizing that Hamdan does not challenge, and we do not today address, the Government's power to detain him for the duration of active hostilities in order to prevent such harm. But in undertaking to try Hamdan and subject him to criminal punishment, the Executive is bound to comply with the Rule of Law that prevails in this jurisdiction.

The judgment of the Court of Appeals is reversed, and the case is remanded for further proceedings.

** [Justice Kennedy's concurrence does not extend to this subpart.]

It is so ordered.

THE CHIEF JUSTICE took no part in the consideration or decision of this case.

Justice BREYER, with whom Justice KENNEDY, Justice SOUTER, and Justice GINS-BURG join, concurring.

. . . The Court's conclusion ultimately rests upon a single ground: Congress has not issued the Executive a "blank check." Indeed, Congress has denied the President the legislative authority to create military commissions of the kind at issue here. Nothing prevents the President from returning to Congress to seek the authority he believes necessary.

Where, as here, no emergency prevents consultation with Congress, judicial insistence upon that consultation does not weaken our Nation's ability to deal with danger. To the contrary, that insistence strengthens the Nation's ability to determine — through democratic means — how best to do so. The Constitution places its faith in those democratic means. Our Court today simply does the same.

Justice KENNEDY, with whom Justice SOUTER, Justice GINSBURG, and Justice BREYER join as to Parts I and II, concurring in part.

I

. . . The Court is correct to concentrate on one provision of the law of war that is applicable to our Nation's armed conflict with al Qaeda in Afghanistan and, as a result, to the use of a military commission to try Hamdan. That provision is Common Article 3 of the four Geneva Conventions of 1949. . . . Assuming the President has authority to establish a special military commission to try Hamdan, the commission must satisfy Common Article 3's requirement of a "regularly constituted court affording all the judicial guarantees which are recognized as indispensable by civilized peoples," 6 U.S.T., at 3318. The terms of this general standard are yet to be elaborated and further defined, but Congress has required compliance with it by referring to the "law of war" in § 821. The Court correctly concludes that the military commission here does not comply with this provision. . . .

II

. . . [T]he circumstances of Hamdan's trial present no exigency requiring special speed or precluding careful consideration of evidence. For roughly four years, Hamdan has been detained at a permanent United States military base in Guantanamo Bay, Cuba. And regardless of the outcome of the criminal proceedings at issue, the Government claims authority to continue to detain him based on his status as an enemy combatant.

Against this background, the Court is correct to conclude that the military commission the President has convened to try Hamdan is unauthorized. . . . To begin with, the structure and composition of the military commission deviate from conventional court-martial standards. Although these deviations raise questions about the fairness of the trial, no evident practical need explains them. . . .

Against the background of . . . significant powers for the Appointing Authority, which in certain respects at least conform to ordinary court-martial standards, the regulations governing the commissions at issue make several noteworthy departures. At a general court-martial—the only type authorized to impose penalties of more than one year's incarceration or to adjudicate offenses against the law of war, the presiding officer who rules on legal issues must be a military judge. A military judge is an officer who is a member of a state or federal bar and has been specially certified for judicial duties by the Judge Advocate General for the officer's Armed Service. To protect their independence, military judges at general courts-martial are "assigned and directly responsible to the Judge Advocate General or the Judge Advocate General's designee." They must be detailed to the court, in accordance with applicable regulations, "by a person assigned as a military judge and directly responsible to the Judge Advocate General or the Judge Advocate General's designee." Here, by contrast, the Appointing Authority selects the presiding officer, and that officer need only be a judge advocate, that is, a military lawyer.

The Appointing Authority, moreover, exercises supervisory powers that continue during trial. Any interlocutory question "the disposition of which would effect a termination of proceedings with respect to a charge" is subject to decision not by the presiding officer, but by the Appointing Authority. . . . While in some circumstances the Government may appeal certain rulings at a court-martial—including "an order or ruling that terminates the proceedings with respect to a charge or specification," the appeals go to a body called the Court of Criminal Appeals, not to the convening authority. The Court of Criminal Appeals functions as the military's intermediate appeals court; it is established by the Judge Advocate General for each Armed Service and composed of appellate military judges. This is another means in which, by structure and tradition, the court-martial process is insulated from those who have an interest in the outcome of the proceedings.

Finally, in addition to these powers with respect to the presiding officer, the Appointing Authority has greater flexibility in appointing commission members. While a general court-martial requires, absent a contrary election by the accused, at least five members, the Appointing Authority here is free, as noted earlier, to select as few as three. This difference may affect the deliberative process and the prosecution's burden of persuasion.

As compared to the role of the convening authority in a court-martial, the greater powers of the Appointing Authority here—including even the resolution of dispositive issues in the middle of the trial—raise concerns that the commission's decisionmaking may not be neutral. If the differences are supported by some practical need beyond the goal of constant and ongoing supervision, that need is neither apparent from the record nor established by the Government's submissions. . . .

These structural differences between the military commissions and courts-martial—the concentration of functions, including legal decisionmaking, in a single executive official; the less rigorous standards for composition of the tribunal; and the creation of special review procedures in place of institutions created and regulated by Congress—remove safeguards that are important to the fairness of the proceedings and the independence of the court. Congress has prescribed these guarantees for courts-martial; and no evident practical need explains the departures here. For these reasons the commission cannot be considered regularly constituted under United States law and thus does not satisfy Congress' requirement that military commissions conform to the law of war.

Apart from these structural issues, moreover, the basic procedures for the commissions deviate from procedures for courts-martial, in violation of § 836(b). As the Court explains, the Military Commission Order abandons the detailed Military Rules of Evidence, which are modeled on the Federal Rules of Evidence in conformity with § 836(a)'s requirement of presumptive compliance with district-court rules. . . . [T]he Government has made no demonstration of practical need for these special rules and procedures, either in this particular case or as to the military commissions in general; nor is any such need self-evident. For all the Government's regulations and submissions reveal, it would be feasible for most, if not all, of the conventional military evidence rules and procedures to be followed.

In sum, as presently structured, Hamdan's military commission exceeds the bounds Congress has placed on the President's authority in §§ 836 and 821 of the UCMJ. Because Congress has prescribed these limits, Congress can change them, requiring a new analysis consistent with the Constitution and other governing laws. At this time, however, we must apply the standards Congress has provided. By those standards the military commission is deficient.

III

In light of the conclusion that the military commission here is unauthorized under the UCMJ, I see no need to consider several further issues addressed in the plurality opinion by Justice STEVENS and the dissent by Justice THOMAS. . . .

[Justices Scalia, Thomas, and Alito each wrote a separate dissent, in which the other two dissenting Justices joined, at least in part. Justice Scalia's dissent argued that the Detainee Treatment Act eliminated jurisdiction over Hamdan's habeas petition. Justice Alito's dissent added the argument that "Common Article 3 is satisfied . . . because the military commissions (1) qualify as courts, (2) that were appointed and established in accordance with domestic law, and (3) any procedural improprieties that might occur in particular cases can be reviewed in those cases." Justice Thomas' dissent argued that the President's authority with regard to military commissions was enhanced by the Authorization to Use Military Force in Afghanistan (a point not joined by Justice Alito). He then argues that the military commission properly had jurisdiction given "the (1) time and (2) place of the offense, (3) the status of the offender, and (4) the nature of the offense charged." On the last point, he not only challenges Justice Stevens' view of the conspiracy charge, but urges (in a point also not joined by Justice Alito) that Hamdan was adequately charged with a separate war crime, "membership in a war-criminal enterprise." He disputes the majority view that the military commission trying Hamdan fails to measure up to conditions specified in the UCMJ, and finds that Common Article III is not judicially enforceable and, in any event, Hamdan's claim under that article is not yet ripe for adjudication. (Justice Alito does not join a portion of Justice Thomas' provision arguing that, even if Common Article III is enforceable, its requirements have been met because the President has authoritatively determined that Article III does not apply to al Qaeda. Chief Justice Roberts, while serving as a D.C. Court of Appeals judge on the panel overruled by this decision, had agreed with the position that the Bush interpretation of Article III was reasonable and entitled to deference.)]

––––––––––

Congress reacted to *Hamdan* by enacting the Military Commissions Act of 2006, Pub. L. No. 109-366, 120 Stat. 2600. The MCA provides a statutory definition of "unlawful combatant," and authorizes the President to try alien unlawful combatants by military tribunal, which Congress declares to be a "regularly constituted court." The MCA provides, in addition, a circumscribed process for the judicial review of such proceedings, and otherwise eliminates habeas access for non-citizens subject to the MCA. It also makes yet clearer than did the Detainee Treatment Act of 2005 (at issue in *Hamdan*) that its limitations apply to habeas actions pending at the time of its enactment. In 2008, the Supreme Court addressed the constitutionality of the MCA limitations on judicial review.

Boumediene v. Bush

553 U.S. 723 (2007)

Justice KENNEDY delivered the opinion of the Court.

Petitioners are aliens designated as enemy combatants and detained at the United States Naval Station at Guantanamo Bay, Cuba. There are others detained there, also aliens, who are not parties to this suit.

Petitioners present a question not resolved by our earlier cases relating to the detention of aliens at Guantanamo: whether they have the constitutional privilege of habeas corpus, a privilege not to be withdrawn except in conformance with the Suspension Clause, Art. I, §9, cl. 2. We hold these petitioners do have the habeas corpus privilege. Congress has enacted a statute, the Detainee Treatment Act of (DTA), 119 Stat. 2739, that provides certain procedures for review of the detainees' status. We hold that those procedures are not an adequate and effective substitute for habeas corpus. Therefore §7 of the Military Commissions Act of 2006 (MCA), 28 U.S.C.A. §2241(e) (Supp. 2007), operates as an unconstitutional suspension of the writ. We do not address whether the President has authority to detain these petitioners nor do we hold that the writ must issue. These and other questions regarding the legality of the detention are to be resolved in the first instance by the District Court. . . .

[The Court reviewed the background to this case, including its rulings in *Hamdi* and *Hamdan,* and decided that MCA §7 strips the federal courts of statutory jurisdiction to hear habeas corpus actions pending at the time of its enactment.]

III

In deciding the constitutional questions now presented we must determine whether petitioners are barred from seeking the writ or invoking the protections of the Suspension Clause either because of their status, *i.e.,* petitioners' designation by the Executive Branch as enemy combatants, or their physical location, *i.e.,* their presence at Guantanamo Bay. The Government contends that noncitizens designated as enemy combatants and detained in territory located outside our Nation's borders have no constitutional rights and no privilege of habeas corpus. Petitioners contend they do have cognizable constitutional rights and that Congress, in seeking to eliminate recourse to habeas corpus as a means to assert those rights, acted in violation of the Suspension Clause. . . .

A

The Framers viewed freedom from unlawful restraint as a fundamental precept of liberty, and they understood the writ of habeas corpus as a vital instrument to secure that freedom. Experience taught, however, that the common-law writ all too often had been insufficient to guard against the abuse of monarchial power. That history counseled the necessity for specific language in the Constitution to secure the writ and ensure its place in our legal system.

Magna Carta decreed that no man would be imprisoned contrary to the law of the land. Art. 39, in Sources of Our Liberties 17 (R. Perry & J. Cooper eds. 1959) ("No free man shall be taken or imprisoned or dispossessed, or outlawed, or banished, or in any way destroyed, nor will we go upon him, nor send upon him, except by the legal judgment of his peers or by the law of the land"). Important as the principle was, the Barons at Runnymede prescribed no specific legal process to enforce it. Holdsworth tells us, however, that gradually the writ of habeas corpus became the means by which the promise of Magna Carta was fulfilled. 9 W. Holdsworth, A History of English Law 112 (1926). . . .

Still, the writ proved to be an imperfect check. Even when the importance of the writ was well understood in England, habeas relief often was denied by the courts or suspended by Parliament. Denial or suspension occurred in times of political unrest, to the anguish of the imprisoned and the outrage of those in sympathy with them. . . .

This history was known to the Framers. It no doubt confirmed their view that pendular swings to and away from individual liberty were endemic to undivided, uncontrolled power. The Framers' inherent distrust of governmental power was the driving force behind the constitutional plan that allocated powers among three independent branches. This design serves not only to make Government accountable but also to secure individual liberty. Because the Constitution's separation-of-powers structure, like the substantive guarantees of the Fifth and Fourteenth Amendments, protects persons as well as citizens, foreign nationals who have the privilege of litigating in our courts can seek to enforce separation-of-powers principles.

That the Framers considered the writ a vital instrument for the protection of individual liberty is evident from the care taken to specify the limited grounds for its suspension: "The Privilege of the Writ of Habeas Corpus shall not be suspended, unless when in Cases of Rebellion or Invasion the public Safety may require it." Art. I, § 9, cl. 2. The word "privilege" was used, perhaps, to avoid mentioning some rights to the exclusion of others. (Indeed, the only mention of the term "right" in the Constitution, as ratified, is in its clause giving Congress the power to protect the rights of authors and inventors. See Art. I, § 8, cl. 8.)

Surviving accounts of the ratification debates provide additional evidence that the Framers deemed the writ to be an essential mechanism in the separation-of-powers scheme. . . .

B

The broad historical narrative of the writ and its function is central to our analysis, but we seek guidance as well from founding-era authorities addressing the specific question before us: whether foreign nationals, apprehended and detained in distant countries during a time of serious threats to our Nation's security, may assert the privilege of the writ and seek its protection. The Court has been careful not to foreclose the possibility that the protections of the Suspension Clause have expanded along with post-1789 developments that define the present scope of the writ. See *INS v. St. Cyr*, 533 U.S. 289, 300–301 (2001). But the analysis may begin with precedents as of 1789, for the Court has said that "at the absolute minimum" the Clause protects the writ as it existed when the Constitution was drafted and ratified. . . .

Each side in the present matter argues that the very lack of a precedent on point supports its position. The Government points out there is no evidence that a court sitting in England granted habeas relief to an enemy alien detained abroad; petitioners respond there is no evidence that a court refused to do so for lack of jurisdiction.

Both arguments are premised, however, upon the assumption that the historical record is complete and that the common law, if properly understood, yields a definite answer to the questions before us. There are reasons to doubt both assumptions. Recent scholarship points to the inherent shortcomings in the historical record. See Halliday & White 14–15 (noting that most reports of 18th-century habeas proceedings were not printed). And given the unique status of Guantanamo Bay and the particular dangers of terrorism in the modern age, the common-law courts simply may not have confronted cases with close parallels to this one. We decline, therefore, to infer too much, one way or the other, from the lack of historical evidence on point.

IV

Drawing from its position that at common law the writ ran only to territories over which the Crown was sovereign, the Government says the Suspension Clause affords petitioners no rights because the United States does not claim sovereignty over the place of detention.

Guantanamo Bay is not formally part of the United States. See DTA § 1005(g), 119 Stat. 2743. And under the terms of the lease between the United States and Cuba, Cuba retains "ultimate sovereignty" over the territory while the United States exercises "complete jurisdiction and control." Under the terms of the 1934 Treaty, however, Cuba effectively has no rights as a sovereign until the parties agree to modification of the 1903 Lease Agreement or the United States abandons the base. See Treaty Defining Relations with Cuba, May 29, 1934, U.S.-Cuba, Art. III, 48 Stat. 1683, T.S. No. 866.

The United States contends, nevertheless, that Guantanamo is not within its sovereign control. This was the Government's position well before the events of September 11, 2001. And in other contexts the Court has held that questions of sovereignty are for the political branches to decide. Even if this were a treaty interpretation case that did not involve a political question, the President's construction of the lease agreement would be entitled to great respect.

We therefore do not question the Government's position that Cuba, not the United States, maintains sovereignty, in the legal and technical sense of the term, over Guantanamo Bay. But this does not end the analysis. Our cases do not hold it is improper for us to inquire into the objective degree of control the Nation asserts over foreign territory. . . . [F]or purposes of our analysis, we accept the Government's position that Cuba, and not the United States, retains *de jure* sovereignty over Guantanamo Bay. As we did in *Rasul,* however, we take notice of the obvious and uncontested fact that the United States, by virtue of its complete jurisdiction and control over the base, maintains *de facto* sovereignty over this territory.

Were we to hold that the present cases turn on the political question doctrine, we would be required first to accept the Government's premise that *de jure* sovereignty is the touchstone of habeas corpus jurisdiction. This premise, however, is unfounded. . . . [T]he history of common-law habeas corpus provides scant support for this proposition; and, for the reasons indicated below, that position would be inconsistent with our precedents and contrary to fundamental separation-of-powers principles.

A

The Court has discussed the issue of the Constitution's extraterritorial application on many occasions. These decisions undermine the Government's argument that, at least as applied to noncitizens, the Constitution necessarily stops where *de jure* sovereignty ends. . . .

Practical considerations weighed heavily . . . in *Johnson v. Eisentrager,* 339 U.S. 763 (1950), where the Court addressed whether habeas corpus jurisdiction extended to enemy aliens who had been convicted of violating the laws of war. The prisoners were detained at Landsberg Prison in Germany during the Allied Powers' post-war occupation. The Court stressed the difficulties of ordering the Government to produce the prisoners in a habeas corpus proceeding. It "would require allocation of shipping space, guarding personnel, billeting and rations" and would damage the prestige of military commanders at a sensitive time. In considering these factors the Court sought to balance the constraints of military occupation with constitutional necessities.

True, the Court in *Eisentrager* denied access to the writ, and it noted the prisoners "at no relevant time were within any territory over which the United States is sovereign, and [that] the scenes of their offense, their capture, their trial and their punishment were all beyond the territorial jurisdiction of any court of the United States." 339 U.S., at 778. The Government seizes upon this language as proof positive that the *Eisentrager* Court adopted a formalistic, sovereignty-based test for determining the reach of the Suspension Clause. We reject this reading for three reasons.

First, we do not accept the idea that the above-quoted passage from *Eisentrager* is the only authoritative language in the opinion and that all the rest is dicta. The Court's determinations, based on practical considerations, were integral to Part II of its opinion and came before the decision announced its holding.

Second, because the United States lacked both *de jure* sovereignty and plenary control over Landsberg Prison, it is far from clear that the *Eisentrager* Court used the term sovereignty only in the narrow technical sense and not to connote the degree of control the military asserted over the facility. The Justices who decided *Eisentrager* would have understood sovereignty as a multifaceted concept. . . .

Third, if the Government's reading of *Eisentrager* were correct, the opinion would have marked not only a change in, but a complete repudiation of [earlier cases'] functional approach to questions of extraterritoriality. We cannot accept the Government's view. Nothing in *Eisentrager* says that *de jure* sovereignty is or has ever been the only relevant consideration in determining the geographic reach of the Constitution or of habeas corpus. A constricted reading of *Eisentrager* overlooks what we see as a common thread . . . : the idea that questions of extraterritoriality turn on objective factors and practical concerns, not formalism.

B

The Government's formal sovereignty-based test raises troubling separation-of-powers concerns as well. The political history of Guantanamo illustrates the deficiencies of this approach. The United States has maintained complete and uninterrupted control of the bay for over 100 years. At the close of the Spanish-American War, Spain ceded control over the entire island of Cuba to the United States and specifically "relinquishe[d] all claim[s] of sovereignty . . . and title." See Treaty of Paris, Dec. 10, 1898, U.S.-Spain, Art. I, 30 Stat. 1755, T.S. No. 343. From the date the treaty with Spain was signed until the Cuban Republic was established on May 20, 1902, the United States governed the territory "in trust" for the benefit of the Cuban people. *v. Henkel*, 180 U.S. 109, 120 (1901); H. Thomas, Cuba or The Pursuit of Freedom 436, 460 (1998). And although it recognized, by entering into the 1903 Lease Agreement, that Cuba retained "ultimate sovereignty" over Guantanamo, the United States continued to maintain the same plenary control it had enjoyed since 1898. Yet the

Government's view is that the Constitution had no effect there, at least as to non-citizens, because the United States disclaimed sovereignty in the formal sense of the term. The necessary implication of the argument is that by surrendering formal sovereignty over any unincorporated territory to a third party, while at the same time entering into a lease that grants total control over the territory back to the United States, it would be possible for the political branches to govern without legal constraint.

Our basic charter cannot be contracted away like this. The Constitution grants Congress and the President the power to acquire, dispose of, and govern territory, not the power to decide when and where its terms apply. Even when the United States acts outside its borders, its powers are not "absolute and unlimited" but are subject "to such restrictions as are expressed in the Constitution." *Murphy v. Ramsey*, 114 U.S. 15 (1885). Abstaining from questions involving formal sovereignty and territorial governance is one thing. To hold the political branches have the power to switch the Constitution on or off at will is quite another. The former position reflects this Court's recognition that certain matters requiring political judgments are best left to the political branches. The latter would permit a striking anomaly in our tripartite system of government, leading to a regime in which Congress and the President, not this Court, say "what the law is." *Marbury v. Madison*, 1 Cranch 137, 177 (1803).

These concerns have particular bearing upon the Suspension Clause question in the cases now before us, for the writ of habeas corpus is itself an indispensable mechanism for monitoring the separation of powers. The test for the scope of this provision must not be subject to manipulation by those whose power it is designed to restrain.

C

As we recognized in *Rasul*, 542 U.S., at 476 (KENNEDY, J., concurring in judgment), the outlines of a framework for determining the reach of the Suspension Clause are suggested by the factors the Court relied upon in *Eisentrager*. In addition to the practical concerns discussed above, the *Eisentrager* Court found relevant that each petitioner:

"(a) is an enemy alien; (b) has never been or resided in the United States; (c) was captured outside of our territory and there held in military custody as a prisoner of war; (d) was tried and convicted by a Military Commission sitting outside the United States; (e) for offenses against laws of war committed outside the United States; (f) and is at all times imprisoned outside the United States." 339 U.S., at 777.

Based on this language from *Eisentrager*, and the reasoning in our other extraterritoriality opinions, we conclude that at least three factors are relevant in determining the reach of the Suspension Clause: (1) the citizenship and status of the detainee and the adequacy of the process through which that status determination was made; (2) the nature of the sites where apprehension and then detention took place; and (3) the practical obstacles inherent in resolving the prisoner's entitlement to the writ.

Applying this framework, we note at the onset that the status of these detainees is a matter of dispute. Petitioners, like those in *Eisentrager,* are not American citizens. But the petitioners in *Eisentrager* did not contest, it seems, the Court's assertion that they were "enemy alien[s]." In the instant cases, by contrast, the detainees deny they are enemy combatants. They have been afforded some process in CSRT proceedings to determine their status; but, unlike in *Eisentrager,* there has been no trial by military commission for violations of the laws of war. The difference is not trivial. The records from the *Eisentrager* trials suggest that, well before the petitioners brought their case to this Court, there had been a rigorous adversarial process to test the legality of their detention. . . . In comparison the procedural protections afforded to the detainees in the CSRT hearings are far more limited, and, we conclude, fall well short of the procedures and adversarial mechanisms that would eliminate the need for habeas corpus review. . . .

As to the second factor relevant to this analysis, the detainees here are similarly situated to the *Eisentrager* petitioners in that the sites of their apprehension and detention are technically outside the sovereign territory of the United States. As noted earlier, this is a factor that weighs against finding they have rights under the Suspension Clause. But there are critical differences between Landsberg Prison, circa 1950, and the United States Naval Station at Guantanamo Bay in 2008. Unlike its present control over the naval station, the United States' control over the prison in Germany was neither absolute nor indefinite. Like all parts of occupied Germany, the prison was under the jurisdiction of the combined Allied Forces. The United States was therefore answerable to its Allies for all activities occurring there. The Allies had not planned a long-term occupation of Germany, nor did they intend to displace all German institutions even during the period of occupation. *Eisentrager* was thus consistent with the Insular Cases, where it had held there was no need to extend full constitutional protections to territories the United States did not intend to govern indefinitely. Guantanamo Bay, on the other hand, is no possession. In every practical sense Guantanamo is not abroad; it is within the constant jurisdiction of the United States.

As to the third factor, we recognize, as the Court did in *Eisentrager,* that there are costs to holding the Suspension Clause applicable in a case of military detention abroad. Habeas corpus proceedings may require expenditure of funds by the Government and may divert the attention of military personnel from other pressing tasks. While we are sensitive to these concerns, we do not find them dispositive. Compliance with any judicial process requires some incremental expenditure of resources. Yet civilian courts and the Armed Forces have functioned alongside each other at various points in our history. The Government presents no credible arguments that the military mission at Guantanamo would be compromised if habeas corpus courts had jurisdiction to hear the detainees' claims. And in light of the plenary control the United States asserts over the base, none are apparent to us.

The situation in *Eisentrager* was far different, given the historical context and nature of the military's mission in post-War Germany. When hostilities in the

European Theater came to an end, the United States became responsible for an occupation zone encompassing over 57,000 square miles with a population of 18 million. In addition to supervising massive reconstruction and aid efforts the American forces stationed in Germany faced potential security threats from a defeated enemy. . . .

Similar threats are not apparent here; nor does the Government argue that they are. The United States Naval Station at Guantanamo Bay consists of 45 square miles of land and water. The base has been used, at various points, to house migrants and refugees temporarily. At present, however, other than the detainees themselves, the only long-term residents are American military personnel, their families, and a small number of workers. The detainees have been deemed enemies of the United States. At present, dangerous as they may be if released, they are contained in a secure prison facility located on an isolated and heavily fortified military base. There is no indication, furthermore, that adjudicating a habeas corpus petition would cause friction with the host government. . . . Under the facts presented here, . . . there are few practical barriers to the running of the writ. To the extent barriers arise, habeas corpus procedures likely can be modified to address them.

It is true that before today the Court has never held that noncitizens detained by our Government in territory over which another country maintains *de jure* sovereignty have any rights under our Constitution. But the cases before us lack any precise historical parallel. They involve individuals detained by executive order for the duration of a conflict that, if measured from September 11, 2001, to the present, is already among the longest wars in American history. The detainees, moreover, are held in a territory that, while technically not part of the United States, is under the complete and total control of our Government. Under these circumstances the lack of a precedent on point is no barrier to our holding.

We hold that Art. I, §9, cl. 2, of the Constitution has full effect at Guantanamo Bay. If the privilege of habeas corpus is to be denied to the detainees now before us, Congress must act in accordance with the requirements of the Suspension Clause. The MCA does not purport to be a formal suspension of the writ; and the Government, in its submissions to us, has not argued that it is. Petitioners, therefore, are entitled to the privilege of habeas corpus to challenge the legality of their detention.

V

In light of this holding the question becomes whether the statute stripping jurisdiction to issue the writ avoids the Suspension Clause mandate because Congress has provided adequate substitute procedures for habeas corpus. [The Court goes on to find the DTA review process an inadequate substitute for habeas review because "the Court of Appeals has jurisdiction not to inquire into the legality of the detention generally but only to assess whether the CSRT complied with the 'standards and procedures specified by the Secretary of Defense' and whether those standards and procedures are lawful." Moreover, the CSRT's place significant "constraints upon the detainee's ability to rebut the factual basis for the Government's assertion that he is an enemy combatant. . . . [T]he detainee has limited means to find or present evidence to challenge the Government's case against him. He does not have the assistance of counsel and may not be aware of the most critical allegations that the Government relied upon to order his detention. The detainee can confront witnesses that testify during the CSRT proceedings. But given that there are in effect no limits on the admission of hearsay evidence—the only requirement is that the tribunal deem the evidence "relevant and helpful," the detainee's opportunity to question witnesses is likely to be more theoretical than real."]

The Government defends the CSRT process, arguing that it was designed to conform to the procedures suggested by the plurality in *Hamdi*. Setting aside the fact that the relevant language in *Hamdi* did not garner a majority of the Court, it does not control the matter at hand. None of the parties in *Hamdi* argued there had been a suspension of the writ. Nor could they. The § 2241 habeas corpus process remained in place. Accordingly, the plurality concentrated on whether the Executive had the authority to detain and, if so, what rights the detainee had under the Due Process Clause. True, there are places in the *Hamdi* plurality opinion where it is difficult to tell where its extrapolation of § 2241 ends and its analysis of the petitioner's Due Process rights begins. But the Court had no occasion to define the necessary scope of habeas review, for Suspension Clause purposes, in the context of enemy combatant detentions. The closest the plurality came to doing so was in discussing whether, in light of separation-of-powers concerns, § 2241 should be construed to prohibit the District Court from inquiring beyond the affidavit Hamdi's custodian provided in answer to the detainee's habeas petition. The plurality answered this question with an emphatic "no."

Even if we were to assume that the CSRTs satisfy due process standards, it would not end our inquiry. Habeas corpus is a collateral process that exists, in Justice Holmes' words, to "cu[t] through all forms and g[o] to the very tissue of the structure. . . . Even when the procedures authorizing detention are structurally sound, the Suspension Clause remains applicable and the writ relevant. This is so, . . . even where the prisoner is detained after a criminal trial conducted in full accordance with the protections of the Bill of Rights.

Although we make no judgment whether the CSRTs, as currently constituted, satisfy due process standards, we agree with petitioners that, even when all the parties involved in this process act with diligence and in good faith, there is considerable risk of error in the tribunal's findings of fact. This is a risk inherent in any process that, in the words of the former Chief Judge of the Court of Appeals, is "closed and accusatorial." And given that the consequence of error may be detention of persons for the duration of hostilities that may last a generation or more, this is a risk too significant to ignore.

For the writ of habeas corpus, or its substitute, to function as an effective and proper remedy in this context, the court that conducts the habeas proceeding must have the means to correct errors that occurred during the CSRT proceedings. This includes some authority to assess the sufficiency of the Government's evidence against the detainee. It also must have the authority to admit and consider relevant exculpatory evidence that was not introduced during the earlier proceeding. Federal habeas petitioners long have had the means to supplement the record on review, even in the postconviction habeas setting. Here that opportunity is constitutionally required.

Consistent with the historic function and province of the writ, habeas corpus review may be more circumscribed if the underlying detention proceedings are more thorough than they were here. . . . The extent of the showing required of the Government in these cases is a matter to be determined. We need not explore it further at this stage. We do hold that when the judicial power to issue habeas corpus properly is invoked the judicial officer must have adequate authority to make a determination in light of the relevant law and facts and to formulate and issue appropriate orders for relief, including, if necessary, an order directing the prisoner's release.

C

We now consider whether the DTA allows the Court of Appeals to conduct a proceeding meeting these standards. "[W]e are obligated to construe the statute to avoid [constitutional] problems" if it is "'fairly possible'" to do so. There are limits to this principle, however. The canon of constitutional avoidance does not supplant traditional modes of statutory interpretation. We cannot ignore the text and purpose of a statute in order to save it.

The DTA does not explicitly empower the Court of Appeals to order the applicant in a DTA review proceeding released should the court find that the standards and procedures used at his CSRT hearing were insufficient to justify detention. This is troubling. Yet, for present purposes, we can assume congressional silence permits a constitutionally required remedy. In that case it would be possible to hold that a remedy of release is impliedly provided for. The DTA might be read, furthermore, to allow petitioners to assert most, if not all, of the legal claims they seek to advance, including their most basic claim: that the President has no authority under the AUMF to detain them indefinitely. (Whether the President has such authority turns on whether the AUMF authorizes–and the Constitution permits–the indefinite detention of "enemy combatants" as the Department of Defense defines that term. Thus a challenge to the President's authority to detain is, in essence, a challenge to the Department's definition of enemy combatant, a "standard" used by the CSRTs in petitioners' cases.) At oral argument, the Solicitor General urged us to adopt both these constructions, if doing so would allow MCA § 7 to remain intact.

The absence of a release remedy and specific language allowing AUMF challenges are not the only constitutional infirmities from which the statute potentially suffers, however. The more difficult question is whether the DTA permits the Court of Appeals to make requisite findings of fact. The DTA enables petitioners to request "review" of their CSRT determination in the Court of Appeals, DTA § 1005(e)(2)(B)(i); but the "Scope of Review" provision confines the Court of Appeals' role to reviewing whether the CSRT followed the "standards and procedures" issued by the Department of Defense and assessing whether those "standards and procedures" are lawful, § 1005(e)(2)(C). Among these standards is "the requirement that the conclusion of the Tribunal be supported by a preponderance of the evidence . . . allowing a rebuttable presumption in favor of the Government's evidence." § 1005(e)(2)(C)(i).

Assuming the DTA can be construed to allow the Court of Appeals to review or correct the CSRT's factual as opposed to merely certifying that the tribunal applied the correct standard of proof, we see no way to construe the statute to allow what is also constitutionally required in this context: an opportunity for the detainee to present relevant exculpatory evidence that was not made part of the record in the earlier proceedings. . . .

Under the DTA the Court of Appeals has the power to review CSRT determinations by assessing the legality of standards and procedures. This implies the power to inquire into what happened at the CSRT hearing and, perhaps, to remedy certain deficiencies in that proceeding. But should the Court of Appeals determine that the CSRT appropriate and lawful standards and procedures, it will have reached the limits of its jurisdiction. There is no language in the DTA that can be construed to allow the Court of Appeals to admit and consider newly discovered evidence that could not have been made part of the CSRT record because it was unavailable to either the Government or the detainee when the CSRT made its findings. This evidence, however, may be critical to the detainee's argument that he is not an enemy combatant and there is no cause to detain him.

This is not a remote hypothetical. One of the petitioners, Mohamed Nechla, requested at his CSRT hearing that the Government contact his employer. Petitioner claimed the employer would corroborate Nechla's contention he had no affiliation with al Qaeda. Although the CSRT determined this testimony would be relevant, it also found the witness was not reasonably available to testify at the time of the hearing. Petitioner's counsel, however, now represents the witness is available to be heard. If a detainee can present reasonably available evidence demonstrating there is no basis for his continued detention, he must have the opportunity to present this evidence to a habeas corpus court. Even under the Court of Appeals' generous construction of the DTA, however, the evidence identified by Nechla would be inadmissible in a DTA review proceeding. The role of an Article III court in the exercise of its habeas corpus function cannot be circumscribed in this manner.

By foreclosing consideration of evidence not presented or reasonably available to the detainee at the CSRT proceedings, the DTA disadvantages the detainee by limiting the scope of collateral review to a record that may not be accurate or complete. In other contexts, *e.g.,* in post-trial habeas cases where the prisoner already has had a full and fair opportunity to develop the factual predicate of his claims, similar limitations on the scope of habeas review may be permissible. In this context, however, where the underlying detention proceedings lack the necessary adversarial character, the detainee cannot be held responsible for all deficiencies in the record. . . .

We do not imply DTA review would be a constitutionally sufficient replacement for habeas corpus but for these limitations on the detainee's ability to present exculpatory evidence. For even if it were possible, as a textual matter, to read into the statute each of the necessary procedures we have identified, we could not overlook the cumulative effect of our doing so. To hold that the detainees at Guantanamo may, under the DTA, challenge the President's legal authority to detain them, contest the CSRT's findings of fact, supplement the record on review with exculpatory evidence, and request an order of release would come close to reinstating the § 2241 habeas corpus process Congress sought to deny them. The language of the statute, read in light of Congress' reasons for enacting it, cannot bear this interpretation. Petitioners have met their burden of establishing that the DTA review process is, on its face, an inadequate substitute for habeas corpus.

Although we do not hold that an adequate substitute must duplicate § 2241 in all respects, it suffices that the Government has not established that the detainees' access to the statutory review provisions at issue is an adequate substitute for the writ of habeas corpus. MCA § 7 thus effects an unconstitutional suspension of the writ. In view of our holding we need not discuss the reach of the writ with respect to claims of unlawful conditions of treatment or confinement.

VI

[The Court goes on to analyze "whether there are prudential barriers to habeas corpus review under these circumstances."]

In cases involving foreign citizens detained abroad by the Executive, it likely would be both an impractical and unprecedented extension of judicial power to assume that habeas corpus would be available at the moment the prisoner is taken into custody. If and when habeas corpus jurisdiction applies, as it does in these cases, then proper deference can be accorded to reasonable procedures for screening and initial detention under lawful and proper conditions of and treatment for a reasonable period of time. Domestic exigencies, furthermore, might also impose such onerous burdens on the Government that here, too, the Judicial Branch would be required to devise sensible rules for staying habeas corpus proceedings until the Government can comply with its requirements in a responsible way. Here, as is true with detainees apprehended abroad, a relevant consideration in determining the courts' role is whether there are suitable alternative processes in place to protect against the arbitrary exercise of governmental power.

The cases before us, however, do not involve detainees who have been held for a short period of time while awaiting their CSRT determinations. Were that the case, or were it probable that the Court of Appeals could complete a prompt review of their applications, the case for requiring temporary abstention or exhaustion of alternative remedies would be much stronger. These qualifications no longer pertain here. In some of these cases six years have elapsed without the judicial oversight that habeas corpus or an adequate substitute demands. And there has been no showing that the Executive faces such onerous burdens that it cannot respond to habeas corpus actions. To require these detainees to complete DTA review before proceeding with their habeas corpus actions would be to require additional months, if not years, of delay. The first DTA review applications were filed over two years ago, but no decisions on the merits have been issued. While some delay in fashioning new is unavoidable, the costs of delay can no longer be borne by those who are held in custody. The detainees in these cases are entitled to a prompt habeas corpus hearing.

Our decision today holds only that petitioners before us are entitled to seek the writ; that the DTA review procedures are an inadequate substitute for habeas corpus; and that petitioners in these cases need not exhaust the review procedures in the Court of Appeals before proceeding with their habeas actions in the District Court. The only law we identify as unconstitutional is MCA § 7, 28 U.S.C.A. § 2241(e) (Supp. 2007). Accordingly, both the DTA and the CSRT process remain intact. Our holding with regard to exhaustion should not be read to imply that a habeas court should intervene the moment an enemy combatant steps foot in a territory where the writ runs. The Executive is entitled to a reasonable period of time to determine a detainee's status before a court entertains that detainee's habeas corpus petition. The CSRT process is the mechanism Congress and the President set up to deal with these issues. Except in cases of undue delay, federal courts should refrain from entertaining an enemy combatant's habeas corpus petition at least until after the Department, acting via the CSRT, has had a chance to review his status.

B

Although we hold that the DTA is not an adequate and effective substitute for habeas corpus, it does not follow that a habeas corpus court may disregard the dangers the detention in these cases was intended to prevent. . . . [T]he Suspension Clause does not resist innovation in the field of habeas corpus. Certain accommodations can be made to reduce the burden habeas corpus proceedings will place on the military without impermissibly diluting the protections of the writ.

In the DTA Congress sought to consolidate review of petitioners' claims in the Court of Appeals. Channeling future cases to one district court would no doubt reduce administrative burdens on the Government. This is a legitimate objective that might be advanced even without an amendment to § 2241. If, in a future case, a detainee files a habeas petition in another judicial district in which a proper respondent can be served, the Government can move for change of venue to the court that will hear these petitioners' cases, the United States District Court for the District of Columbia.

Another of Congress' reasons for vesting exclusive jurisdiction in the Court of Appeals, perhaps, was to avoid the widespread dissemination of classified information. The Government has raised similar concerns here and elsewhere. We make no attempt to anticipate all of the evidentiary and access-to-counsel issues that will arise during the course of the detainees' habeas corpus proceedings. We recognize, however, that the Government has a legitimate interest in protecting sources and methods of intelligence gathering; and we expect that the District Court will use its discretion to accommodate this interest to the greatest extent possible.

These and the other remaining questions are within the expertise and competence of the District Court to address in the first instance.

Justice SOUTER, with whom Justice GINSBURG and Justice BREYER join, concurring.

Four years ago, this Court in *Rasul v. Bush*, held that statutory habeas jurisdiction extended to claims of foreign nationals imprisoned by the United States at Guantanamo Bay, "to determine the legality of the Executive's potentially indefinite detention" of them. . . . But no one who reads the Court's opinion in *Rasul* could seriously doubt that the jurisdictional question must be answered the same way in purely constitutional cases, given the Court's reliance on the historical background of habeas generally in answering the statutory question. . . . [W]hether one agrees or disagrees with today's decision, it is no bolt out of the blue.

A second fact insufficiently appreciated by the dissents is the length of the disputed imprisonments, some of the prisoners represented here today having been locked up for six years. Hence the hollow ring when the dissenters suggest that the Court is somehow precipitating the judiciary into reviewing claims that the military (subject to appeal to the Court of Appeals for the District of Columbia Circuit) could handle within some reasonable period of time. . . . [S]uggestions of judicial haste are all the more out of place given the Court's realistic acknowledgment that in periods of exigency the tempo of any habeas review must reflect the immediate peril facing the country. . . .

Chief Justice ROBERTS, with whom Justice SCALIA, Justice THOMAS, and Justice ALITO join, dissenting.

Today the Court strikes down as inadequate the most generous set of procedural protections ever afforded aliens detained by this country as enemy combatants. The political branches crafted these procedures amidst an ongoing military conflict, after much careful investigation and thorough debate. . . .

It is grossly premature to pronounce on the detainees' right to habeas without first assessing whether the remedies the DTA system provides vindicate whatever rights petitioners may claim. . . . If the CSRT procedures meet the minimal due process requirements outlined in *Hamdi,* and if an Article III court is available to ensure that these procedures are followed in future cases, there is no need to reach the Suspension Clause question. Detainees will have received all the process the Constitution could possibly require, whether that process is called "habeas" or something else. The question of the writ's reach need not be addressed. . . .

[T]he Court finds the DTA system an inadequate habeas substitute, for one central reason: Detainees are unable to introduce at the appeal stage exculpatory evidence discovered after the conclusion of their CSRT proceedings. The Court hints darkly that the DTA may suffer from other infirmities, but it does not bother to name them, making a response a bit difficult. As it stands, I can only assume the Court regards the supposed defect it did identify as the gravest of the lot. . . .

The majority rests its decision on abstract and hypothetical concerns. Step back and consider what, in the real world, Congress and the Executive have actually granted aliens captured by our Armed Forces overseas and found to be enemy combatants:

- The right to hear the bases of the charges against them, including a summary of any classified evidence.

- The ability to challenge the bases of their detention before military tribunals modeled after Geneva Convention procedures. Some 38 detainees have been released as a result of this process.

- The right, before the CSRT, to testify, introduce evidence, call witnesses, question those the Government calls, and secure release, if and when appropriate.

- The right to the aid of a personal representative in arranging and presenting their cases before a CSRT.

- Before the D.C. Circuit, the right to employ counsel, challenge the factual record, contest the lower tribunal's legal determinations, ensure compliance with the and laws, and secure release, if any errors below establish their entitlement to such relief.

In sum, the DTA satisfies the majority's own criteria for assessing adequacy. This statutory scheme provides the combatants held at Guantanamo greater procedural protections than have ever been afforded alleged enemy detainees—whether citizens or aliens—in our national history. . . . I respectfully dissent.

Justice SCALIA, with whom THE CHIEF JUSTICE, Justice THOMAS, and Justice ALITO join, dissenting.

Today, for the first time in our Nation's history, the Court confers a constitutional right to habeas corpus on alien enemies detained abroad by our military forces in the course of an ongoing war. THE CHIEF JUSTICE's dissent, which I join, shows that the procedures prescribed by Congress in the Detainee Treatment Act provide the essential protections that habeas corpus guarantees; there has thus been no suspension of the writ, and no basis exists for judicial intervention beyond what the Act allows. My problem with today's opinion is more fundamental still: The writ of habeas corpus does not, and never has, run in favor of aliens abroad; the Suspension Clause thus has no application, and the Court's intervention in this military matter is entirely *ultra vires.* . . .

The Court purports to derive from our precedents a "functional" test for the extraterritorial reach of the writ, *ante,* at 2258, which shows that the Military Commissions Act unconstitutionally restricts the scope of habeas. That is remarkable because the most pertinent of those precedents, *Johnson v. Eisentrager,* conclusively establishes the opposite. . . . Writing for the Court, Justice Jackson held that American courts lacked habeas jurisdiction:

"We are cited to *[sic]* no instance where a court, in this or any other country where the writ is known, has issued it on behalf of an alien enemy who, at no relevant time and in no stage of his captivity, has been within its territorial jurisdiction. Nothing in the text of the Constitution extends such a right, nor does anything in our statutes." *Id.,* at 768. . . .

III

Putting aside the conclusive precedent of *Eisentrager,* it is clear that the original understanding of the Suspension Clause was that habeas corpus was not available to aliens abroad . . . . It is entirely clear that, at English common law, the writ of habeas corpus did not extend beyond the sovereign territory of the Crown. To be sure, the writ had an "extraordinary territorial ambit," because it was a so-called "prerogative writ," which, unlike other writs, could extend beyond the realm of England to other places where the Crown was sovereign. But prerogative writs could not issue to foreign countries, even for British subjects; they were confined to the King's dominions–those areas over which the Crown was sovereign. . . .

What history teaches is confirmed by the nature of the limitations that the Constitution places upon suspension of the common-law writ. It can be suspended only "in Cases of Rebellion or Invasion." Art. I, § 9, cl. 2. The latter case (invasion) is plainly limited to the territory of the United States; and while it is conceivable that a rebellion could be mounted by American citizens abroad, surely the overwhelming majority of its occurrences would be domestic. If the extraterritorial scope of habeas turned on flexible, "functional" considerations, as the Court holds, why would the Constitution limit its suspension almost entirely to instances of domestic crisis? Surely there is an even greater justification for suspension in foreign lands where the United States might hold prisoners of war during an ongoing conflict. And correspondingly, there is less threat to liberty when the Government suspends the writ's (supposed) application in foreign lands, where even on the most extreme view prisoners are entitled to fewer constitutional rights. It makes no sense, therefore, for the Constitution generally to forbid suspension of the writ abroad if indeed the writ has application there.

It may be objected that the foregoing analysis proves too much, since this Court has already suggested that the writ of habeas corpus *does* run abroad for the benefit of United States citizens. . . . The reason for that divergence is not difficult to discern. The common-law writ, as received into the law of the new constitutional Republic, took on such changes as were demanded by a system in which rule is derived from the consent of the governed, and in which citizens (not "subjects") are afforded defined protections against the Government. . . . It accords with that principle to say: "When the Government reaches out to punish a citizen who is abroad, the shield which the Bill of Rights and other parts of the Constitution provide to protect his life and liberty should not be stripped away just because he happens to be in another land." On that analysis, "[t]he distinction between citizens and aliens follows from the undoubted proposition that the Constitution does not create, nor do general principles of law create, any juridical relation between our country and some undefined, limitless class of noncitizens who are beyond our territory." In sum, because I conclude that the text and history of the Suspension Clause provide no basis for our jurisdiction, I would affirm the Court of Appeals even if *Eisentrager* did not govern these cases.

———————

Notes and Questions on the Guantanamo Detainee Cases

1. *Reflecting on the Bush Administration's Legal Decision Making.* *Hamdan* and *Boumediene* repudiated the Bush Administration's positions that the Geneva Conventions were inapplicable to the Guantanamo detainees and that, in any event, the Conventions were not judicially enforceable at their behest. On the former point, though, the Administration appears to have had the support of Chief Justice Roberts and Justices Scalia and Thomas. Justice Alito would have joined on the second point. So, reflecting on the tale of lawyering related by the Professor Bruff excerpt, do you see any relationship between the way in which the Administration crafted its legal position and the losses it sustained in the Supreme Court? Or, were these just matters on which reasonable people could reasonably disagree and the way in which the internal legal debate was conducted, while dramatic, did not make it any more or less likely to reach an answer that the Supreme Court would agree with?

2. *Procedural Due Process and Habeas Corpus.* At first blush, it may seem puzzling that the *Boumediene* majority rejects as an inadequate substitute for habeas review the CSRT procedures adopted following the Court's due process analysis in *Hamdi*. The move is less puzzling if one considers that the due process analysis in *Hamdi* appears to have assumed the availability of judicial review via habeas petitions as a final, formal check on the soundness of any administrative determination that a particular detainee could properly be classified as an enemy combatant. In domestic procedural due process cases, the government is typically excused, as a constitutional matter, from holding highly formal pre-deprivation administrative hearings where a claimant (to government employment, for example) is entitled to formal review after being denied whatever "liberty" or "property" interest is in dispute; if no such formal review is available, the initial administrative determination would have to be more exacting. *Cleveland Board of Education v. Loudermill*, 470 U.S. 552 (1985). In cases involving Guantanamo detainees, without habeas review, there apparently would be no guarantee of a full-blown formal adjudication of enemy combatant status after the CSRT proceeding because the detainee might never actually be tried (by military commission or otherwise). By analogy to the domestic due process cases, it would seem to follow that, without habeas review, the CSRT proceedings would likewise have to be more formal than the Court inferred in *Hamdi*.

3. *Habeas After* Boumediene. After deciding in *Rasul v. Bush* that federal courts have jurisdiction over habeas petitions brought by non-citizens detained at Guantánamo, the Supreme Court granted certiorari, vacated, and remanded a Ninth Circuit decision that had actually reached the same conclusion, *Gherebi v. Bush*, 352 F.3d 1278 (9th Cir. 2003), *vacated*, 542 U.S. 952 (2004). The Court directed reconsideration in light of

Rumsfeld v. Padilla, supra, presumably implying that "there was only one appropriate venue for such suits—the federal courts in and for the District of Columbia." Stephen I. Vladeck, *The D.C. Circuit After* Boumediene, 41 Seton Hall L. Rev. 1451, 1452 (2011). The career of *Boumediene* in the D.C. Circuit since 2007 has generated what Professor Vladeck quite understatedly calls "a remarkably interesting and complex body of case law." In the estimation of some observers, some of that complexity is the result of an agenda among at least some of the D.C. Circuit's members to give the Supreme Court's habeas holdings "as narrow a compass as is remotely defensible." Id. at 1454. The factual and doctrinal detail of these cases defies easy paraphrase, but a sense of the D.C. Circuit's general support for the Government's position may be gleaned from a 2014 summary prepared by the Congressional Research Service:

- the Executive may lawfully detain persons who are "part of" Al Qaeda, the Taliban, and affiliated groups, and possibly also persons who provide a sufficient degree of support to such entities in their hostilities against the United States and its allies;

- a functional approach is appropriate when assessing whether a person is "part of" Al Qaeda, meaning that judges should consider the significance of a person's activities in relation to the organization, rather than requiring formal proof of membership, such as evidence the petitioner received orders from the organization's hierarchy;

- the government may satisfy its evidentiary burden in support of a person's detention when its factual claims are supported by a preponderance of evidence, but a lower standard might be constitutionally permissible;

- it is proper for a habeas court to assess the cumulative weight and effect of proffered evidence according to a "conditional probability analysis" when determining whether the government has demonstrated factual grounds for detaining a habeas petitioner;

- consideration of hearsay evidence in habeas cases is not determined by the Federal Rules of Evidence;

- official government records, including government intelligence reports, are entitled to a presumption of regularity in Guantanamo habeas litigation;

- the writ of habeas affords Guantanamo detainees with a limited right to challenge their proposed transfer to the custody of a foreign government as well as matters related to their conditions of confinement;

- habeas courts lack authority, absent an authorizing statute, to compel the Executive to release non-citizen detainees into the United States, even if such persons have been determined by the court to be unlawfully detained;

- it is unlikely that noncitizens who have been transferred to foreign custody may seek judicial review of their designation as enemy combatants by the U.S. government; and

- the constitutional writ of habeas does not presently extend to noncitizen detainees held at U.S.-operated facilities in Afghanistan.

Jennifer K. Elsea and Michael John Garcia, Judicial Activity Concerning Enemy Combatant Detainees: Major Court Rulings 7–8 (Congressional Research Service No. R41156, 2014) (citations omitted), available at https://fas.org/sgp/crs/natsec/R41156.pdf.

4. *Military Commissions in Practice.* To the extent that the Bush Administration hoped for "swift justice" from Guantanamo military commissions, it was surely disappointed—not least, it would appear, because of the perhaps unanticipated independence and tenacity of military defense lawyers. Between 2002 and 2008, 779 individuals were detained at Guantanamo, of whom 530 were transferred or released from U.S. custody prior to the Obama Administration. Guantanamo Review Task Force, Final Report 1 (Jan. 22, 2010), available at http://www.justice.gov/ag/guantanamo-review-final-report.pdf. As of early 2017, only eight military commission proceedings had resulted in convictions, one of which was subsequently set aside in part and three others of which were vacated on appeal. *Guantánamo by the Numbers*, Miami Herald (Oct. 25, 2016), http://www.miamiherald.com/news/nation-world/world/americas/guantanamo/article2163210.html. Seven other detainees were involved in ongoing proceedings. They included the alleged mastermind behind the 9/11 attacks, Khalid Sheik Mohammed, and his four alleged co-conspirators. The magnitude of the legal complexities involved are well signaled by the headline in a January 2017 news article, Carol Rosenberg, *Guantánamo prosecutor wants to start 9/11 trial in March 2018*, Miami Herald (Jan. 24, 2017), http://www.miamiherald.com/news/nation-world/world/americas/guantanamo/article128527924.html. The story quotes the attorney for one of the alleged co-conspirators as calling a March 2018 start date "hopelessly optimistic."

Both Congress and the Obama Administration tried in significant respects to reform the military commissions system at Guantanamo to enhance their legitimacy and effectiveness. Congress enacted the Military Commissions Act of 2009 (MCA 2009) as part of the Department of Defense Authorization Act for FY2010, codifying some reforms the executive branch supported and in various respects amending the Military Commissions Act of 2006. For a detailed review, see Jennifer K. Elsea The Military Commissions Act of 2009 (MCA 2009): Overview and Legal Issues (Congressional Research Service No. R41163, 2014), available at https://fas.org/sgp/crs/natsec/R41163.pdf.

Important separation of powers questions remain, however, concerning the military commission system. First, although Congress, in response to *Hamdan*, defined inchoate conspiracy as an offense triable by military commission, 10 U.S.C. § 950t(29), it remains the case that conspiracy was not an offense under international law when allegedly committed by Guantanamo detainees. It is thus uncertain whether Congress can permit the military trial of inchoate conspiracy in the face of Article III's provision for a jury trial "of all crimes, except in cases of impeachment." A D.C.

Circuit panel decision answering this question negatively was overturned by a 6–3 per curiam en banc decision, with the majority writing five separate opinions. *Al-Bahlul v. United States*, 840 F.3d 757 (D.C. Cir. 2016), *reh'g denied*, (Nov. 28, 2016), *overturning, Al-Bahlul v. United States*, 792 F.3d 1 (D.C. Cir. 2015). But this holding seems to go beyond *Ex parte Quirin*, 317 U.S. 1 (1942), which held only that the Article III guarantee did not apply to foreign belligerents allegedly engaged in violation of the international laws of war.

Moreover, the 2009 reform left intact the structure for post-trial appeals Congress created in 2006, including a Court of Military Commission Review (CMCR). The CMCR's separation of powers challenge arises from its unusual status as an Article I military court comprising both military and civilian members that is apparently reviewable only by the U.S. Court of Appeals for the D.C. Circuit. Unlike the court's civilian members, the military members are not appointed to their CMCR roles by the President with the advice and consent of the Senate, but rather assigned by the Secretary of Defense. Yet it is not clear that they are merely inferior officers. That is, the court is not subject to higher level review within the executive branch, and the Defense Secretary can remove military judges from the CMCR for only "good cause" or "military necessity." *In re al-Nashiri*, 791 F.3d 71, 83 (D.C. Cir. 2015), *subsequent mandamus proceeding sub nom. In re al-Nashiri*, 835 F.3d 110 (D.C. Cir. 2016). As of 2016, however, the issue had been raised only in mandamus proceedings, and the D.C. Circuit found the question sufficiently murky to preclude mandamus, at the same time observing (if not pleading):

> [T]he President and the Senate could decide to put to rest any Appointments Clause questions regarding the CMCR's military judges. They could do so by re-nominating and re-confirming the military judges to be CMCR judges. Taking these steps — whether or not they are constitutionally required — would answer any Appointments Clause challenge to the CMCR.

Id. at 86. For a scathing review of the CMCR's performance, see Steve Vladeck, The Misbegotten Court of Military Commission Review, Lawfare (May 24, 2016), https://www.lawfareblog.com/misbegotten-court-military-commission-review.

5. *The Campaigns to Close Guantanamo (and Keep It Open)*. President Obama campaigned on a promise to close Guantanamo. His January 22, 2009 executive order directed a comprehensive review of the Guantanamo detainees and called for closure of the facility "as soon as practicable, and no later than 1 year from the date of this order." Exec. Order No. 13,492, § 3, 74 Fed. Reg. 4897, 4898 (2009). Yet this turned out to be an objective beyond Obama's reach. Year after year, Congress enacted various prohibitions against the use of appropriations either to transfer Guantanamo detainees to the territorial United States or to "construct, acquire, or modify any facility" other than Guantanamo to hold those incarcerated there.

President Obama explained his rationale for seeking the closure of Guantanamo as follows:

Guantanamo set back the moral authority that is America's strongest currency in the world. Instead of building a durable framework for the struggle against al Qaeda that drew upon our deeply held values and traditions, our government was defending positions that undermined the rule of law. In fact, part of the rationale for establishing Guantanamo in the first place was the misplaced notion that a prison there would be beyond the law — a proposition that the Supreme Court soundly rejected. Meanwhile, instead of serving as a tool to counter terrorism, Guantanamo became a symbol that helped al Qaeda recruit terrorists to its cause. Indeed, the existence of Guantanamo likely created more terrorists around the world than it ever detained.

So the record is clear: Rather than keeping us safer, the prison at Guantanamo has weakened American national security. It is a rallying cry for our enemies. It sets back the willingness of our allies to work with us in fighting an enemy that operates in scores of countries. By any measure, the costs of keeping it open far exceed the complications involved in closing it.

Remarks by the President at the National Archives on National Security (May 21, 2009). As for his reaction to the statutory impediments to fulfilling his commitment, President Obama's signing statement regarding the National Defense Authorization Act for Fiscal Year 2017, 2016 WL 7438431 (White House), was similar to those before it:

As I have said in the past, the restrictions . . . concerning the detention facility at Guantanamo are unwarranted and counterproductive. In particular, section 1033 renews the bar against using appropriated funds to construct or modify any facility in the United States, its territories, or possessions to house any Guantanamo detainee in the custody or under the control of the Department of Defense unless authorized by the Congress. Section 1032 also renews the bar against using appropriated funds to transfer Guantanamo detainees into the United States for any purpose. . . .

As I have said repeatedly, the provisions in this bill concerning detainee transfers would, in certain circumstances, violate constitutional separation of powers principles. Additionally, section 1034 could in some circumstances interfere with the ability to transfer a detainee who has been granted a writ of habeas corpus. In the event that the restrictions on the transfer of detainees in sections 1032 and 1034 operate in a manner that violates these constitutional principles, my Administration will implement them in a manner that avoids the constitutional conflict.

Despite his reservations, President Obama did not endeavor to transfer any detainees to the United States in violation of these restrictions.

By way of contrast, throughout his 2016 campaign, candidate Trump repeatedly voiced his deep disagreement with this view. As of April 2017, a draft executive order was being circulated that would revoke the Obama order and declare: "The detention operations at U.S. Naval Station Guantánamo Bay, are legal, safe, and humane, and are in the interests of justice and consistent with U.S. and international law." *Protecting America Through Lawful Detention of Terrorists and Other Designated Enemy Elements*, https://assets.documentcloud.org/documents/3455640/Revised -draft-Trump-EO-on-detainees-and-Gitmo.pdf. See Charlie Savage, *ISIS Detainees May Be Held at Guantánamo, Document Shows*, N.Y. Times (Feb. 8, 2017), https:// www.nytimes.com/2017/02/08/us/politics/guantanamo-islamic-state-detainees .html?_r=0. The draft order also describes "individuals and networks associated with the Islamic State," as "associated forces" in connection with al Qaeda and the Taliban, thus suggesting the hypothetical — but legally adventurous possibility — that the Trump Administration would want to incarcerate captured Islamic State fighters at Guantanamo. The contested applicability of the 2001 AUMF to the Islamic State is discussed in Section B, below.

President Obama's ambition to close Guantanamo was actually in line with a policy conclusion that the George W. Bush Administration had also reached. In his 2010 memoir, President Bush wrote: "While I believe opening Guantanamo after 9/11 was necessary, the detention facility had become a propaganda tool for our enemies and a distraction for our allies. I worked to find a way to close the prison without compromising security." George W. Bush, Decision Points 180 (2010).

John Bellinger, who served first as an associate counsel to the President during the first Gorge W. Bush Administration and then as Legal Advisor to the Department of State throughout the second, has similarly defended the opening of Guantanamo while calling for its closing:

> The Trump Administration should learn from the bitter legal and policy experiences of the Bush Administration: adding new detainees to Guantanamo will produce more (and more risky) lawsuits; difficult practical problems down the road as to what to do with the detainees; and unnecessary friction with allies. Guantanamo detainees have prevailed in numerous challenges to their detention in federal courts (including four cases before the Supreme Court). Any new ISIS detainees in Guantanamo would undoubtedly claim in habeas petitions that the 2001 AUMF does not authorize their detention because it is limited to the organizations responsible for the 9-11 attacks. . . . [O]ur allies are likely to cut back on intelligence, law enforcement, and military cooperation if they believe the United States is not acting consistent with international law and our shared democratic values.

John Bellinger, *Guantanamo Redux: Why It Was Opened and Why It Should Be Closed (and not Enlarged)*, Lawfare (Mar. 12, 2017), https://www.lawfareblog.com/guanta namo-redux-why-it-was-opened-and-why-it-should-be-closed-and-not-enlarged. What is your assessment?

6. *The Article III Alternative.* The controversy between Congress and the Obama Administration focused both on the security risks that might be entailed in moving Guantanamo detainees to the territorial United States and on the wisdom of trying alleged enemy combatants in regular federal courts. Attorney General Holder

vigorously defended the plan to do so, including among such potential defendants Khalid Sheikh Mohammed, the alleged mastermind of the September 11 attacks, and five others accused of having significant roles in facilitating the attacks. In testimony to the Senate Judiciary Committee, he said: "I am a prosecutor, and as a prosecutor my top priority was simply to select the venue where the government will have the greatest opportunity to present the strongest case in the best forum." Testimony of Attorney General Eric Holder to the Senate Judiciary Committee (Nov. 18, 2009), available at http://www.justice.gov/ag/testimony/2009/ag-testimony-091118 .html. The Justice Department nonetheless postponed bringing KSM to trial in the face of stiff congressional resistance. The Justice Department did bring to trial in the Southern District of New York Ahmed Ghailani, who had been indicted for his alleged role in the 1998 bombings of U.S. embassies in Kenya and Tanzania. A jury acquitted him on all major terrorism charges, convicting him only on a single count of conspiracy to destroy government buildings. Again, not surprisingly, opponents of federal court trials for Guantanamo detainees pointed to the acquittals as evidence of the unsuitability of civilian tribunals for these defendants. Supporters pointed to Ghailani's conviction, pursuant to strict due process, of a crime that carries a 20-year-to-life sentence. It was widely argued that a significant reason for the acquittals was the judge's decision to exclude a key witness, whose existence, the judge determined, had become known to the government only through an improperly coercive interrogation. Of course, it was by no means clear that the witness would have been allowed to testify before a military commission either.

Conceding the advantages of hindsight over foresight, does this record suggest that the Bush Administration was ill-advised, on policy grounds, to pursue the Guantanamo military commission system as its vehicle for the detention and punishment of enemy combatants? Is it relevant that, during the years the commissions have been open, prosecutions in federal court on anti-terrorism charges have led to over 500 convictions? Introduction to The National Security Division's Chart of Public/ Unsealed International Terrorism and Terrorism-Related Convictions from 9/11/2001 to 12/31/2014, http://www.humanrightsfirst.org/sites/default/files/NSD-Terrorism -Related-Convictions.pdf. John Bellinger, who was Senior Associate Counsel to the President and Legal Adviser to the National Security Council on 9/11 and throughout its immediate aftermath, has insisted that Guantanamo was "*not* chosen primarily because it was outside the United States and not subject to the jurisdiction of U.S. courts," but rather because of "the need to find a completely secure facility outside Afghanistan that was available immediately, convenient to the United States, relatively low-cost, and that had sufficient supporting infrastructure for both the detainees and guard force." John Bellinger, *Guantanamo Redux: Why It was Opened and Why It Should Be Closed (and not Enlarged)*, Lawfare (Mar. 12, 2017), https://www.law fareblog.com/guantanamo-redux-why-it-was-opened-and-why-it-should-be-closed -and-not-enlarged. Nonetheless, he acknowledges that the Administration's hope of fending off legal challenges by the detainees was "certainly one factor" in the decision making. Should the Administration (and Congress) have been more receptive to the prospect of holding detainees in domestic military brigs and pursuing alleged crimes through Article III courts?

7. *Where to Send Detainees Approved for Release?* The 530 or so detainees that the Bush Administration transferred voluntarily out of Guantanamo were sent to other countries, "mostly to the countries of their nationality, so that they could be prosecuted, detained, or monitored by their own governments." John Bellinger, *supra*. For its part, although President Obama failed to close Guantanamo, the Task Force created pursuant to his 2009 executive order issued a report in January 2010, Guantanamo Review Task Force, Final Report (Jan. 22, 2010), available at http://www.justice.gov/ag/guantanamo-review-final-report.pdf, which indicated how the Administration hoped to move forward despite the delays. Of 240 persons subject to review, 126 were approved for transfer to countries outside the United States, and an additional 30 Yemenis were approved for repatriation depending on the security environment in Yemen or the availability of other third-country hosts.[1]

However, in addition to enacting appropriations and authorization provisions designed to keep Guantanamo open during the Obama Administration, Congress also repeatedly enacted restrictions aimed at limiting the President's authority to move Guantanamo detainees to third countries. Typical of Congress's approach was Section 1035 of the National Defense Authorization Act for Fiscal Year 2014, P.L. 113-66, 127 Stat 672 (2013), which authorized the Secretary of Defense "to transfer or release any individual detained at Guantanamo to the individual's country of origin, or any other foreign country," if, after a legally prescribed review, the Secretary determines "that the individual is no longer a threat to the national security of the United States; or ... such transfer or release outside the United States is to effectuate an order affecting disposition of the individual by a court or competent tribunal of the United States having jurisdiction." Any other such transfer would be authorized only if "actions that have been or are planned to be taken will substantially mitigate the risk of such individual engaging or reengaging in any terrorist or other hostile activity that threatens the United States or United States persons or interests," and if the Secretary determines that the transfer is in the national security interests of the United States. The latter determination, however, would have to be reported to Congress and would have to take into account a series of specific factors:

(c) FACTORS TO BE CONSIDERED IN MAKING DETERMINATION.—
In making the determination specified in subsection (b), the Secretary of Defense shall specifically evaluate and take into consideration the following factors:

---

1. That left 84 persons, of whom 36 were subjects of active cases or investigations. The report indicated that the Attorney General had decided to try six of these 36 in federal court in the Southern District of New York and another six by military commission, with the status of the remaining 24 still under review. This left a residual category of 48 detainees "determined to be too dangerous to transfer but not feasible for prosecution." The Report asserted that detention of this last group without trial was authorized by the post-9/11 authorization to use military force.

(1) The recommendations of the Guantanamo Detainee Review Task Force established pursuant to Executive Order No. 13492 and the recommendations of the Periodic Review Boards established pursuant to No. Executive Order 13567, as applicable.

(2) The security situation in the foreign country to which the individual is to be transferred, including whether or not the country is a state sponsor of terrorism, the presence of foreign terrorist groups, and the threat posed by such groups to the United States.

(3) Any confirmed case in which an individual transferred to the foreign country to which the individual is to be transferred subsequently engaged in terrorist or other hostile activity that threatened the United States or United States persons or interests.

(4) Any actions taken by the United States or the foreign country to which the individual is to be transferred, or change in circumstances in such country, that reduce the risk of reengagement of the type described in paragraph (3).

(5) Any assurances provided by the government of the foreign country to which the individual is to be transferred, including that—

    (A) such government maintains control over any facility at which the individual is to be detained if the individual is to be housed in a government-controlled facility; and

    (B) such government has taken or agreed to take actions to substantially mitigate the risk of the individual engaging or reengaging in any terrorist or other hostile activity that threatens the United States or United States persons or interests.

(6) An assessment of the capacity, willingness, and past practices (if applicable) of the foreign country described in paragraph (5) in meeting any assurances it has provided, including assurances under paragraph (5) regarding its capacity and willingness to mitigate the risk of reengagement.

(7) Any record of cooperation by the individual to be transferred with United States intelligence and law enforcement authorities, pursuant to a pre-trial agreement, while in the custody of or under the effective control of the Department of Defense, and any agreements and effective mechanisms that may be in place, to the extent relevant and necessary, to provide continued cooperation with United States intelligence and law enforcement authorities.

(8) In the case of an individual who has been tried in a court or competent tribunal of the United States having jurisdiction on charges based on the same conduct that serves as a basis for the determination that the individual is an enemy combatant, whether or not the individual has been acquitted of such charges or has been convicted and has completed serving the sentence pursuant to the conviction.

For his part, President Obama objected to these conditions in signing each NDAA containing them, but chiefly on what sounded like policy, rather than constitutional grounds. For Fiscal Year 2014, he actually expressed appreciation that the Section 1035 conditions were more flexible than in prior years, but added: "Section 1035 does not . . . eliminate all of the unwarranted limitations on foreign transfers and, in certain circumstances, would violate constitutional separation of powers principles."

The Obama Administration's one act of seeming defiance of these restrictions occurred during May 2014, when President Obama, without the required notice to Congress, agreed to release five Taliban detainees, including two military commanders, in exchange for Sgt. Bowe Bergdahl, the one U.S. prisoner of war held by the Taliban. (Upon his return to the U.S., Bergdahl was subsequently charged with desertion — he was captured by the Taliban after apparently leaving his post. Following a guilty plea in October, 2017, Bergdahl was dishonorably discharged at a reduced rank and required to pay a $1,000 fine from his salary for ten months.) There are at least four different hypothetical assessments of the legality of the Bergdahl exchange:

- A 2002 OLC memo had asserted that the president had Article II authority, beyond Congress's control, to determine all questions concerning the treatment of wartime detainees. If this were true, then the president had authority within the *Youngstown* framework to ignore any restriction Congress would have imposed that would interfere with the president's determination whether the exchange and its confidentiality were in the national interest. This memo, however, was one of the George W. Bush OLC opinions specifically withdrawn by Steven G. Bradbury, principal deputy assistant attorney general for the OLC and its acting head from 2005–2009, as memorialized in a January 15, 2009, "Memorandum for the Files," just before the end of the George W. Bush Administration.

- The Obama Administration may have believed that, given the specific context for the Bergdahl exchange, the President had Article II authority to defy the advance notification requirement under the precise circumstances presented. At least, such a claim of authority would be sufficiently plausible to counsel against reading the NDAA as a prohibition on its exercise. On June 3, 2014, Deputy Assistant to the President Caitlin Hayden released a statement asserting that Congress would not have intended the 30-day notice requirement to be binding in the unique circumstances in which 30 days' delay could have endangered Bergdahl's life:

  > In these circumstances, delaying the transfer in order to provide the 30-day notice would interfere with the Executive's performance of two related functions that the Constitution assigns to the President: protecting the lives of Americans abroad and protecting U.S. soldiers. Because such interference would significantly alter the balance between Congress and the President, and could even raise constitutional concerns, we believe it is fair to conclude that Congress did not intend that

the Administration would be barred from taking the action it did in
these circumstances.

- One of your authors took the position that the release actually was not even a
  technical statutory violation. The argument would be that such a confidential
  prisoner exchange amounts to the very sort of "fundamental and accepted . . .
  incident to war" that the President was authorized to undertake by the 2001
  AUMF. In a circumstance where advance notice would have put Bergdahl's life
  in danger, the Administration could have argued that the NDAA could not properly be read as an implied limit on the President's AUMF authority, nor on his
  authority under the Hostage Act to "use such means, not amounting to acts of
  war and not otherwise prohibited by law, as he may think necessary and proper
  to obtain or effectuate the release" of an American citizen "unjustifiably deprived
  of his liberty by or under the authority of any foreign government." Peter M.
  Shane, *The Non-Constitutional Non-Crisis*, Slate (June 5, 2014), http://www
  .slate.com/articles/news_and_politics/jurisprudence/2014/06/stop_saying
  _that_the_exchange_of_prisoners_for_bergdahl_was_illegal_the.html. Under
  this interpretation, the President was acting pursuant to the most favorable of
  the three *Youngstown* categories.

- Finally, it could be argued that the President impermissibly disregarded an
  explicit limitation on his authority to deal with enemy detainees that Congress
  constitutionally imposed pursuant to its authority to "declare war, grant letters
  of marque and reprisal, and *make rules concerning captures on land* and water."
  U.S. Const., Art. I, § 8 (emphasis added).

Which of these views do you find most persuasive?

Nearly a year-and-a-half later, Congress enacted yet tighter restraints on third-
party transfers as part of a National Defense Authorization Act for Fiscal Year 2016.
It added a categorical ban on transfers to Libya, Somalia, Syria or Yemen, and made
the certifications required of the Secretary of Defense yet more demanding. It
required, for example, if a Guantanamo detainee had previously been transferred to
a particular country and had then engaged in later acts of terrorism, that the Secretary could vouch that the country in question was committed now to appropriate
steps that would mitigate the risk of recidivism by any newly released detainee. On
this occasion, President Obama vetoed the measure—but not exclusively because of
the Guantanamo restrictions. Obama objected chiefly to a proposed method of
defense funding that would evaded an interbranch deal on both domestic and military spending ceilings. Following the negotiation of a budgetary compromise, the
President signed a revised version of the NDAA FY 2016 into law. His signing statement was one of the relatively few in which Obama raised constitutional doubts about
statutory provisions he was signing into law:

> Sections 1033 and 1034 impose additional restrictions on foreign transfers
> of detainees—in some cases purporting to bar such transfers entirely. As

I have said repeatedly, the executive branch must have the flexibility, with regard to the detainees who remain at Guantanamo, to determine when and where to prosecute them, based on the facts and circumstances of each case and our national security interests, and when and where to transfer them consistent with our national security and our humane treatment policy. Under certain circumstances, the provisions in this bill concerning detainee transfers would violate constitutional separation of powers principles. Additionally, section 1033 could in some circumstances interfere with the ability to transfer a detainee who has been granted a writ of habeas corpus. In the event that the restrictions on the transfer of detainees in sections 1031, 1033, and 1034 operate in a manner that violates these constitutional principles, my Administration will implement them in a manner that avoids the constitutional conflict.

Statement by the President, 2015 WL 7566732, at *2

8. Kiyemba v. Obama *and Releases into the United States.* A complex line of Guantanamo-related litigation involved a group of 22 detainees who were Chinese citizens of Uighur ethnicity, members of "a Turkic Muslim minority whose members reside in the Xinjiang province of far-west China." *Kiyemba v. Obama*, 555 F.3d 1022, 1023 (D.C.Cir. 2009), *judgment vacated*, 559 U.S. 131 (2010). Before September 11, they had traveled to a Uigher camp in Afghanistan's Tora Bora mountains in Afghanistan. They were detained as enemy combatants after aerial strikes destroyed the camp, which had been run by the Eastern Turkistan Islamic Movement (ETIM), a Uighur independence group that American military officials believed was associated with al Qaeda or the Taliban, and which our State Department had designated a terrorist organization. Evidence indicated that at least some of those captured intended to fight the Chinese government, and that they had received firearms training at the Tora Bora camp. After aerial strikes destroyed the camp, which had been run by the Eastern Turkistan Islamic Movement (ETIM), a Uighur independence group that American military officials believed was associated with al Qaeda or the Taliban, and which our State Department had designated a terrorist organization. Evidence indicated that at least some of those captured intended to fight the Chinese government, and that they had received firearms training at the Tora Bora camp.

In 2008, the D.C. Circuit held that, for at least one of the Uighers, the evidence offered to a CSRT in order to show that the ETIM was associated with al Qaeda or the Taliban or that the detainee had engaged in hostilities against the United States was insufficient to justify enemy combatant status. *Parhat v. Gates*, 532 F.3d 834 (D.C.Cir. 2008). Because the government saw no material differences between its evidence against Parhat and its evidence against the other Uighurs, it designated all the Uighurs for potential release. The problem was finding a new home. The Uighur detainees objected that, if returned to China, they would face arrest, torture or execution. If no other country would take them, they argued they had a legal entitlement to be released in the United States.

In 2009, the D.C. Circuit rejected the Uighurs' argument, holding that the decision whether or not to exclude particular aliens from the United States was a political question, not subject to judicial review. The Supreme Court granted certiorari on the question whether federal courts had authority to order the detainees' release into the United States "where the Executive detention is indefinite and without authorization in law, and release into the continental United States is the only possible effective remedy." *Kiyemba v. Obama*, 555 F.3d 1022 (D.C.Cir. 2009), *cert. granted*, 558 U.S. 969 (2009).

Prior to argument, however, the government managed to procure settlement offers for the detainees, and seventeen were resettled to Bermuda (4), Albania (5), Switzerland (2), and the Pacific island of Palau (6). Five, however, refused resettlement. In light of these circumstances, the Supreme Court vacated its grant of certiorari and remanded for further lower court proceedings. The D.C. Circuit reiterated its original conclusion, which the Supreme Court declined to review. *Kiyemba v. Obama*, 605 F.3d 1046 (D.C.Cir. May 28, 2010), *on remand from*, 559 U.S. 131 (2010), *cert. denied*, 563 U.S. 954 (2011). Congress, as noted above, has enacted appropriations riders that would deny the government authority to effect their transfer to the United States, even if the government were persuaded to do so.

9. *Detainees at Bagram Air Force Base.* Notwithstanding President Obama's commitment to close Guantanamo, the Obama Administration successfully continued the Bush Administration stance of opposing judicial review of detentions at Bagram Air Field in Afghanistan. In *Al-Maqaleh v. Gates*, 605 F.3d 84 (D.C. Cir. 2010), the D.C. Court of Appeals held that "the practical obstacles inherent in resolving the prisoner's entitlement to the writ" weigh "overwhelmingly in favor of the position of the United States . . . , Bagram, indeed the entire nation of Afghanistan, remains a theater of war. . . . [T]he position of the United States is even stronger in this case than it was in *Eisentrager*." In January 2010, however, the Administration did agree to release the names of its Bagram detainees, a position the Bush Administration had opposed.

10. *What Does Suspension Suspend?* Because the Court in *Rasul* and *Boumediene* affirmed the availability of habeas review, it did not have to consider the question — had habeas been lawfully suspended — of what the suspension of habeas actually suspends. That is, does it simply eliminate the possibility of securing judicial review of a petitioner's detention or conditions of confinement, or does it actually remove substantive constitutional restrictions that would normally apply to the government? For example, would a lawful suspension of habeas actually permit Congress to authorize the arrest and detention of terrorism suspects on mere suspicion? Or, would an individual subjected to arrest in violation of fourth amendment standards be able to sue at some point for damages, even if they could not pursue habeas? For a defense of the more limited view of detention, see Trevor W. Morrison, *Suspension and the Extrajudicial Constitution*, 107 COLUM. L. REV. 1533 (2007). The broader view is advanced in Amanda L. Tyler, *Suspension as an Emergency Power*, 118 YALE L. J. 600 (2009).

11. *War, Law Enforcement, or All of the Above?* If the review of the Guantanamo cases and our subsequent notes persuades you of nothing else, you should now be convinced that the legal issues surrounding the detention, interrogation and trial of alleged enemy combatants were numerous, complex, and hotly contested. Many supporters of the Bush Administration (and, thus, critics of the Obama Administration) sought to frame the debate as a difference in viewpoint over whether America's antiterrorism efforts are best understood as warfare or law enforcement. In the former view, the primary value would be defeating an enemy and preventing future attack. In the latter view, supposedly, the primary values would be bringing wrongdoers to justice and upholding the rule of law. In his Judiciary Committee testimony quoted above, however, Attorney General Holder challenged the dichotomy: "Prosecuting the 9/11 defendants in federal court does not represent some larger judgment about whether or not we are at war. We are at war, and we will use every instrument of national power—civilian, military, law enforcement, intelligence, diplomatic, and others—to win." For a prominent defense of the "preventive war" framing to the problem of terrorism, see RICHARD A. POSNER, PREVENTING SURPRISE ATTACKS: INTELLIGENCE REFORM IN THE WAKE OF 9/11 (2005). For an equally vigorous response, see DAVID COLE AND JULES LOBEL, LESS SAFE, LESS FREE: WHY AMERICA IS LOSING THE WAR ON TERROR (2007).

Note: Government Lawyering, September 11 and the Iraq War

In responding to the attacks of September 11, 2001, the Bush Administration typically staked out expansive claims for unfettered presidential discretion to decide how best to protect U.S. national security. On some issues, such as the availability of habeas corpus and application of certain treaty obligations to noncitizen detainees in Guantanamo, reasonable minds plainly could and did differ. Yet, in light of the Supreme Court's seeming rebuke to presidential unilateralism in both *Rasul* and *Hamdi*, one wonders whether the President would have been better served had his lawyers staked out a more nuanced position on behalf of his authority. Recall, for example, Justice Souter's argument in *Hamdi* that the Government ought not be able to rely on the customary laws of war as authorizing Mr. Hamdi's detention when the executive's refusal to treat the Afghanistan detainees as prisoners of war demonstrates (to Justice Souter) that the executive had repudiated the customary laws of war in the context of Afghanistan. It is not clear that lawyering style alone would lead any Justice to a more or less sympathetic bottom line regarding the Administration's legal claims, but it is not hard to suspect such impacts over time. As a Justice Department lawyer asked to make the most ambitious arguments possible on behalf of the executive branch, what ought you to do if you believe that more modest claims might equally well accomplish the President's immediate objectives and could avoid antagonizing moderate judges and Justices?

On some issues, however, the Justice Department is widely regarded, across the political spectrum, as having gone further in asserting presidential authority (and minimizing statutory limits) than was consistent with professional standards. The controversy that surfaced this question most profoundly focused on legal advice concerning the interrogation of U.S. detainees from both Afghanistan and Iraq. In a lengthy and now notorious August 1, 2002 memorandum to White House Counsel Alberto Gonzales, U.S. Court of Appeals Judge Jay S. Bybee, then assistant attorney general in charge of the Office of Legal Counsel, offered two conclusions—in a memorandum authored primarily by John Yoo—that have struck subsequent observers as unsupportable:

- The federal statutory prohibition against committing torture outside the United States pertains only to the intentional infliction of physical pain "equivalent in intensity to the pain accompanying serious physical injury, such as organ failure, impairment of bodily function, or even death," or "significant psychological harm of significant duration, e.g., lasting for months or even years"; and

- That statutory prohibition "must be construed as not applying to interrogations undertaken pursuant to [the President's] commander-in-chief authority," because "Congress may no more regulate the President's ability to detain and interrogate enemy combatants than it may regulate his ability to direct troop movements on the battlefield."

Memorandum from Jay S. Bybee, Assistant Attorney General, to Alberto R. Gonzales, Counsel to the President, re: Standards of Conduct for Interrogation under 18 U.S.C. §§ 2340–2340A, at 1, 34–35 (Aug. 1, 2002). It followed from these conclusions that numerous interrogation techniques, albeit "cruel, inhuman or degrading," *id.* at 2, do not amount to "torture," and, even if they did, Congress would be without authority to bar their use against any "enemy combatant" in wartime.

One noted scholar of legal ethics has characterized the August 1, 2002 opinion as "riddled with weird arguments, cherry-picked quotations, and inexplicable omissions." David Luban, *Margolis is Wrong*, SLATE.COM (Feb. 22, 2010), available at http://www.slate.com/id/2245531/pagenum/all/. Professor Shane has called its analysis of "serious physical harm," "implausible." PETER M. SHANE, MADISON'S NIGHTMARE: HOW EXECUTIVE POWER THREATENS AMERICAN DEMOCRACY 102 (2009). Devastating critiques, by liberal and conservative legal scholars, respectively, of the position that Congress may not regulate the President's prosecution of war appear in David Barron and Martin S. Lederman, *The Commander in Chief at the Lowest Ebb? Framing the Problem, Doctrine, and Original Understanding*, 121 HARV. L. REV. 689 (2008), and Saikrishna Bangalore Prakash, *The Separation and Overlap of War and Military Powers*, 87 TEX. L. REV. 299 (2008). Although Professor Yoo has steadfastly defended his positions, the overwhelming peer consensus appears to be that the opinion is not merely wrong, but egregiously so, in both conclusions and reasoning. If this consensus view is correct, then the August 1 memo poses problems that go beyond matters of legal strategy, to profound questions of personal and professional ethics.

The following excerpt from Professor Bruff's BAD ADVICE provides a careful parsing of the August 1 memo, and places the issuance of that opinion in an historical and bureaucratic context that may help explain the relevant lawyers' mindset.

Written before the Justice Department's subsequent ethics investigation, the discussion lays a detailed groundwork for analyzing the scope and enforceability of government lawyers' ethical responsibilities when acting in their advisory capacity.

Harold H. Bruff, Bad Advice: Bush's Lawyers in the War on Terror
230–262 (2009).

The events that sent the Bush administration into [the] quicksand [of drawing lines around permissible interrogation techniques] began soon after 9/11. Vice President Cheney set the tone, saying that we would soon have to work on the "dark side" of intelligence, using "any means at our disposal." . . .

On September 17, 2001, President Bush signed a memorandum authorizing the CIA to capture, detain, and interrogate terrorism suspects. Eventually, the CIA would maintain an entire secret prison system overseas. There were both legal and practical reasons for designating the CIA as the jailer for selected terrorism suspects. Legally, the CIA is exempt from many strictures that bind the other potential jailer, the military. For example, military law forbids both coercive interrogation and general mistreatment of prisoners. By contrast, the CIA is accustomed to operating on the dark side under a vague statutory charter. Practically, the agency is usually better able to operate in secret than is the U.S. military. The administration did not want anyone to know whom we held, what we were doing to them, or what we were learning from them.

President Bush's initial directive to the CIA did not contain guidelines regarding interrogation techniques. CIA had some experience in conducting interrogations, but not on this new scale. The agency's venerable "KUBARK" manual for counterintelligence interrogation, dating from the 1960s, reflects judgments that were still in place on 9/11. The manual catalogues interrogation techniques, many of them coercive, that are thought to produce reliable information. It gives practical (not moral) advice against inflicting torture, physical brutality, or intense pain, because they induce false confessions and increase the hostility of the subject. Instead, the manual suggests techniques such as disorientation, fatigue, humiliation, and sensory deprivation. The purpose is to destroy the psychological will to resist. Apparently, success is common. An update, the *"Human Resource Exploitation Training Manual,"* came out in 1983 (given the title, 1984 would have been a better date). The new manual elaborates many fine points of the earlier techniques, but mostly stops short of brute force except for remarking that the use of "pain" might be helpful. These limits would not survive the impatience created by the terror war.

After receiving the President's memo, the agency quickly cobbled a program together. It did so "by consulting Egyptian and Saudi intelligence officials and copying Soviet interrogation methods long used in training American servicemen to withstand capture." CIA officers in the field soon barraged headquarters at Langley with questions about the limits to approved interrogation methods. They were deeply concerned about lawfare if revelation of their actions broke the rules as later understood. The agency could easily be made to look quite bad. Although it is in the nature of CIA's mission to consort with unsavory characters around the world and to break numerous local laws wherever it operates, adopting interrogation methods from such notorious sources might exceed our nation's tolerance. Also, officers who lacked field experience had little practical or legal sense for the boundaries.

It is not surprising that CIA felt unguided. The part of the President's order of February 7, 2002, that required humane treatment of detainees was addressed to the armed forces, a category that excludes CIA. In addition, OLC's early *Habeas* and *Application of Treaties* opinions had created large law-free zones outside the United States and had eliminated Geneva protections for the prisoners. Given all that, what law—if any—limited interrogation?

In late 2001, U.S. forces went into Afghanistan and started to gather prisoners. Among them, some "high-value" captives soon began to appear. These were usually assigned to CIA custody; the military held everyone else. The first senior al Qaeda operative to be captured was Abu Zubaydah, the group's travel and logistics manager, who was taken in a firefight in early 2002. While Zubaydah recovered from wounds suffered during his capture, he was flown to a secret CIA prison near Bangkok. FBI agents conducted some preliminary interrogations. The FBI is deeply ingrained with the strictures against coercive questioning that suffuse American criminal law. Hence it employed normal noncoercive techniques. Zubaydah revealed some information, including the critical fact that the architect of 9/11 was Khalid Sheikh Mohammed ("KSM"), but also displayed resistance. Impatient CIA agents then intervened, and Zubaydah soon "was stripped, held in an icy room and jarred by ear-splittingly loud music." The shift to coercive techniques had begun, opening a rift between CIA and FBI that has never closed in the terror war. Zubaydah was waterboarded, which ended his resistance. He was later transferred to another CIA "black site" in Poland, and eventually to Guantanamo. . . .

Early guidance from the principals

As prisoners and problems accumulated, CIA Director George Tenet told his General Counsel, Scott Mueller, that standards were needed to guide interrogations. "We need guidance from Justice and the White House on what we're allowed to do," he said. As it happened, there was a high-level structure in place to respond to Tenet's concerns. After 9/11, the National Security Council created a Principals Committee, a cabinet-level group that met frequently to advise President Bush on issues of national security policy. National Security Adviser Rice chaired the Committee; its members were Vice President Cheney, Defense Secretary Rumsfeld, Secretary of State Powell, Attorney General Ashcroft, and CIA Director Tenet.

The Principals Committee met frequently in the small White House Situation Room. The group began reviewing and approving the use of particular "enhanced interrogation techniques" against individual al Qaeda captives. (They may have been reviewing renditions as well.) The discussion and instructions were very detailed;

for example, they specified whether a captive could be slapped, deprived of sleep, or waterboarded. A combination of techniques was sometimes approved.

Khalid Sheikh Mohammed was a subject of intense interest for his possible knowledge of terror plots. After an informant revealed his location, he was captured and transported first to Afghanistan and then to the CIA black site in Poland. KSM was initially defiant. In response, "a variety of tough techniques were used about 100 times over two weeks" on him, including waterboarding. Interrogators then desisted and asked for advice, fearing they might have crossed the line into torture. He eventually produced a great deal of information, some of it as a result of harsh interrogation and some of it from traditional noncoercive practices. Eventually he was transferred to Guantanamo, where he awaits trial for his crimes.

The urgent desire to forestall future attacks drove these meetings and approvals. Pressure to obtain information from the captives was intense—by the summer of 2002, "threat reports were pulsing." Eventually, the Attorney General demurred. He was troubled by the discussions. He agreed with the general policy decision to allow aggressive tactics and had repeatedly advised that they were legal. But he argued that senior White House advisers should not be involved in the grim details of interrogations, sources said. According to a top official, Ashcroft asked aloud after one meeting: "Why are we talking about this in the White House? History will not judge this kindly."

Ashcroft's growing discomfort with the operations of the Principals Committee was well-founded. It appears that urgent requests for approvals were flowing from risk-averse CIA officials in the field almost directly to the Committee. Missing was the usual bureaucratic process of staff review of policy and legal issues that ordinarily precedes cabinet-level decisions, even urgent ones. Therefore, the Committee's decisions always risked being ill-informed. Except for Colin Powell and John Ashcroft, no one in the group had the kind of military or law enforcement experience that might have given them a feel for the issues. Perhaps Ashcroft's discomfort also stemmed from the fact that the Committee "took care to insulate President Bush" from their deliberations and decisions. Still, this was not Iran/Contra, which was a rogue operation shielded from the President and almost everyone else. Instead, senior officials gamely tried to manage the terror war on the fly.

It appears that by the time a formal opinion request went to OLC sometime in 2002, the Principals Committee had made a significant number of decisions. The Attorney General had given his opinion that the techniques in use were legal. It would have been natural for him to have discussed these matters informally with White House Counsel Gonzales and with his own aides Bybee and Yoo. Whether he did so or not, he certainly knew that the Department had already placed the interrogators deep in legal limbo.

In any event, by the time OLC formulated its opinion on interrogation practices, both the administration and the Justice Department were seriously committed to a course of conduct. In essence, OLC was backed into a corner. It would have been extremely difficult for the Office to have written an opinion negating the legality of decisions taken by the administration's senior leadership and exposing the CIA to yet another round of retroactive condemnation of its actions. We should not be very surprised that no such opinion emerged. Instead, OLC wrote an opinion that was meant to remain secret, and that tried to navigate its way around some formidable legal obstacles.

A wall of law against torture

As they crafted their opinions, the executive's lawyers had to know that both international and domestic law erected formidable barriers to torture, and more broadly to most forms of harsh interrogation. Hence the context was quite unlike that in which OLC lawyers commonly find themselves. Many opinion requests place OLC in Justice Jackson's twilight zone, where both constitutional and statutory materials are inconclusive. (For example, the *Habeas* opinion dwelt in that zone.) But not this one. The difficulty of eradicating torture and lesser forms of cruelty has driven the law to state firm prohibitions, not flexible standards that regulate but do not forbid conduct. In practice, these bans may be more aspirational than effective, but they are firmly in place and may not be ignored by lawyers. Here is a brief catalogue.

. . . [T]he Geneva Conventions require nations to criminalize "grave breaches" of their protections, including "willful killing, torture or inhuman treatment, . . . willfully causing great suffering or serious injury to body or health." Common Article 3 requires "humane treatment" of prisoners of all kinds and forbids "cruel treatment and torture" or "outrages on personal dignity, in particular humiliating and degrading treatment." Prisoners of war and civilians cannot be subjected to coercive interrogation of any kind; hence the administration's urgent desire to classify al Qaeda and Taliban captives as "unlawful enemy combatants" instead.

Domestically, the federal War Crimes Act discharged the Geneva obligation by criminalizing both grave breaches of the Conventions and violations of Common Article 3. OLC's *Application of Treaties* opinion, however, had already attempted to remove all WCA jeopardy for the terror war by eliminating all Geneva protections for the detainees.

A greater obstacle to harsh interrogation lay in the fact that both international and domestic law contained another explicit and unconditional ban on torture. The international Convention Against Torture and Other Cruel, Inhuman or Degrading Treatment or Punishment (CAT), which the United States signed, took force in 1987. Although many international agreements have prohibited torture over the years, none had defined it until the CAT provided that it is "any act by which severe pain or suffering, whether physical or mental, is intentionally inflicted on a person for such purposes as obtaining . . . information or a confession, [or] punishing him . . . [by a public official]." The ban on torture is unconditional: "no exceptional circumstances whatsoever, whether a state of war or a threat of war, internal political instability or any other public emergency, may be invoked as a justification of torture." Thus, the CAT rejects the ticking bomb scenario and all other emergency arguments for torture. The Convention also requires state parties to take effective steps to prevent torture, forbids them to send captives to nations where they are likely to face torture, and requires them to "undertake to prevent . . . other acts of cruel, inhuman, or degrading treatment or punishment which do not amount to torture."

The United States Senate's 1994 ratification of CAT attached a reservation stating that none of the Convention's provisions would be self-executing. To meet its obligations under the CAT, Congress then enacted a criminal statute that forbids torture performed outside the United States and closely tracks the CAT's definitions of prohibited conduct. Under federal law, torture is "an act committed by a person acting under the color of law specifically intended to inflict severe physical or mental pain or suffering (other than pain or suffering incidental to lawful sanctions) upon another person within his custody or physical control." There are two principal differences between the international and domestic definitions: Congress added the specific intent requirement and narrowed the meaning of mental suffering. I discuss both changes below.

Torture within the United States has long been illegal under general constitutional and statutory provisions. The Constitution's Eighth Amendment forbids the "cruel and unusual" punishment of prisoners. This includes torture, "unnecessary cruelty," and the "wanton infliction of physical pain." The Supreme Court has also held that the due process clauses of the Fifth and Fourteenth Amendments forbid government agents to inflict physical abuse on prisoners. The best-known case is *Rochin v. California* [342 U.S. 165 (1952)], in which the Court condemned the forced stomach pumping of a criminal suspect, saying that this police conduct "shocks the conscience." Since what shocks the conscience is both subjective and fact-dependent, this constitutional test has proved difficult for the Supreme Court to apply consistently. Therefore, it is also difficult for lawyers to predict what will cross the line into unconstitutional brutality. Equally important, the moral relativity of the "shocks the conscience" test puts our domestic constitutional law at odds with the absolute ban on torture in the CAT.

In addition, the Fifth Amendment's guarantee against self-incrimination forbids coercive interrogations. Both federal and state criminal laws denounce murder, mayhem, and assault, as does the Uniform Code of Military Justice. There is also a special federal civil remedy for damages for victims of torture, in the Torture Victims Protection Act (TVPA).

This barricade of laws against torture should have engendered an attitude of great caution about harsh interrogation in the minds of the President's lawyers. In addition, a few months previously both the State Department and the uniformed military lawyers had reminded them of the importance of our nation's traditions of complying fully with Geneva protections in all conflicts, whether or not the Conventions technically applied. Yet all of this was overborne by the great pressure to approve practices already in use and to produce intelligence, no matter the cost.

A golden shield for the CIA

On August 1, 2002, OLC's Assistant Attorney General, Jay Bybee, sent an opinion to White House Counsel Alberto Gonzales, titled *Standards of Conduct for Interrogation under 18 U.S.C. §§ 2340-2340A*. A . . . memo listing specific approved techniques of interrogation accompanied it. Some months later, quite similar advice was rendered to the Pentagon . . . .

The prosaic title of the *Interrogation* opinion belies its fate as the centerpiece of legal debate about the War on Terrorism—it is commonly condemned as the "torture memo." The principal author of the opinion was John Yoo. He worked closely with David Addington, who ensured that Vice President Cheney's theories of executive power would be reflected. He also shared drafts with the offices of Attorney General Ashcroft and his Deputy Larry Thompson, and received suggestions from them. Yoo says that no one suggested significant changes or disagreed with the conclusions in the *Interrogation* memo.

Jack Goldsmith has explained that there may have been a good reason for the lack of opposition: the draft opinion was not shared with the State Department, which would have "strenuously objected." Goldsmith says that "Gonzales made it a practice to limit readership of controversial legal opinions to a very small group of lawyers." This was done "to control outcomes in the opinions and minimize resistance to them." The result of excluding those who might have offered constructive criticism was bad advice that would spark impressive levels of resistance and acrimony after the fact. Unrestrained, *Interrogation*'s authors provided some remarkably creative analysis. The opinion has received sharp criticism for that quality, because of the conclusions it supports.

Interrogation is long—just over 50 pages in reprinted form—and is obviously meant to be definitive. It bears the hallmarks of John Yoo's point of view: minimization of obligations imposed by international law, maximization of the executive's constitutional power, highly restrictive interpretation of statutes that might bind the executive, and willingness to compress statutes by invoking the avoidance canon. Its overall purpose is to immunize American agents who employ harsh interrogation tactics from successful prosecution or even the fear of prosecution, as the reader can readily gather from the memo's detailed discussion of available defenses to prosecution. *Interrogation* is designed to comfort the interrogator and not to warn him or her to steer clear of actions that may produce criminal jeopardy. Its basic thrust runs counter to the formidable bodies of law that attempt to eliminate torture and cruelty.

In the usual fashion of OLC opinions, *Interrogation* begins by restating the question asked, in this case by White House Counsel Gonzales. The issue is the "standards of conduct" under the CAT "as implemented by" the federal criminal code. Thus, a strategy found in the earlier *Application of Treaties* opinion appears again. International law will be viewed only through the lens of its limited incorporation into domestic law. Consequently, every element of domestic law that tends to confine the substantive reach of international principles can be deployed. Broad concepts of executive power and available materials that suggest narrow statutory interpretation will be especially useful.

Interrogation focuses on the two critical issues about the statutory terminology that OLC was asked to address: the meaning of "specifically intended to inflict" and the meaning of "severe pain or suffering," either physical or mental. Its overall conclusion is that acts must be "of an extreme nature"—the opinion repeats the word extreme many times—to constitute crimes. Actions "may be cruel, inhuman, or degrading, but still not produce pain and suffering of the requisite intensity" to be criminal. Along the way, the opinion erects four separate barriers to the successful prosecution of American interrogators. In its own way, *Interrogation*'s wall against prosecution is as impressive as the walls against torture that it tears down.

The opinion's first focus is on the specific intent requirement in the torture statute. OLC opines that a criminal actor "must expressly intend to achieve the forbidden act . . . . [that is] the infliction of [severe] pain must be the defendant's precise objective." It is not enough to know that severe pain will occur as long as inflicting it is not the interrogator's purpose. It is easy to understand why this distinction is important in many contexts. For example, doctors know when their procedures will inflict pain, but they are not torturers because their purpose is to heal, and they would eliminate the pain if they could. In support of its interpretation of specific intent, OLC accurately cites standard sources at some length, including Black's Law Dictionary and some Supreme Court cases. All of these sources do in fact support a narrow view of the specific intent requirement under various statutes. The opinion also warns that proof of a person's knowledge of consequences allows a jury to infer the intent to produce them.

In the context of harsh interrogation, however, all of this is quite artificial. Knowledge and intention are no longer separate, because inflicting pain is the intended means to the end of acquiring intelligence. Calibrating the subject's level of distress is central to the interrogator's attempt to break his or her will, not an unintended byproduct. Perhaps, then, *Interrogation* is aiming at a point it does not mention. Although the opinion does not quite say so, it suggests strongly that the presence of a purpose to gather intelligence negates criminal specific intent. If so, an interrogator who seeks information rather than sadistic pleasure is safe. Given the premises of the terror war, this would be a very broad shield. Until interrogation occurs, no one can tell what a detainee knows that might be of value. If an interrogator were prosecuted and claimed a legitimate purpose, how could a jury say beyond a reasonable doubt that none had been present?

Interrogation quotes without comment the Senate report that explains the addition of the specific intent requirement. The report says: "For an act to be 'torture,' it must . . . be intended to cause severe pain and suffering." The absence of any qualification implies that if the specific intent to cause suffering is present, it does not matter *why* the interrogator inflicts it. This interpretation is consistent with the purposes of both the CAT and the torture statute, because they do not recognize a purpose to obtain intelligence as a defense. Any such defense would gut both the

Convention and the statute. OLC, presumably aware of this problem and having narrowed the intent requirement as much as possible, moves along to the next issue.

Interrogation's substantive definition of "severe pain or suffering" has become notorious for its unpersuasiveness. It says: "Physical pain amounting to torture must be equivalent in intensity to the pain accompanying serious physical injury, such as organ failure, impairment of bodily function, or even death." Mental pain or suffering "must result in significant psychological harm of significant duration, e.g., lasting for months or even years." These definitions are extreme for a reason: they provide a way to negate the specific intent to torture. Since interrogators will routinely intend to inflict suffering, they can escape conviction only if there are significant levels of evident suffering that do not constitute torture. The opinion notes that interrogators can defend themselves on grounds that they held a good faith belief that their conduct would not produce the prohibited harm. The more extreme the harm must be, the more effective the defense.

More particularly, these definitions of physical and mental suffering were probably crafted to avoid condemning what the CIA was already doing. Waterboarding was probably on OLC's mind. An inability to breathe combined with apprehension of immediate death from drowning certainly creates impressive levels of physical and mental suffering, as it is intended to do. The procedure can be continued until the subject's resistance is overborne, and repeated as necessary. But there is no clear connection to pain as defined in the opinion, or to long-term psychological damage. Similarly, many of the other "enhanced" interrogation techniques do not involve either the intense pain that typifies classic tortures or provable psychological carryovers. They do seem to be well within anyone's definition of treatment that is "cruel, inhuman, or degrading." Two examples of reported CIA techniques should suffice: "Long Time Standing" (forcing prisoners to stand, handcuffed and with their feet shackled to the floor, for more than 40 hours), and "The Cold Cell" (forcing prisoners to stand naked in a cell kept at 50 degrees, while being continuously doused with cold water).

The opinion's definition of severity has led to much criticism, and fairly so. The language about impending organ failure and death was drawn from a wholly unrelated source, the federal statutes that use similar terms to define indicia of an emergency medical condition for purposes of providing health benefits. Apparently, the OLC lawyers ran a computer word search of the federal statutes, and this is what turned up. Yet the point of the medical definition, which uses the presence of severe pain as one indicator, is to say when it is reasonable for a person in distress to go to an emergency room. The definition may be ungenerous, but it is easy to see that its purpose is to deny benefits to those who respond to minor aches and pains by repairing to the hospital. The context of the federal torture statute is fundamentally different, because it concerns the intentional infliction of pain on another person, not the need to endure what nature does to us. There is no reason the think that the level of pain a person should be asked to endure before seeking medical help bears any relation to the level of pain that another person may permissibly inflict on him or her.

Interrogation also cites the dictionary definition of severe as "hard to endure." Perhaps this is the common ground between the two kinds of federal statutes that the opinion discusses, but I think that most people find pain hard to endure long before it approaches organ failure or death. (Certainly, we spend a lot of money on palliatives for ordinary levels of pain.) It is easy to see why the opinion seeks to modify the dictionary definition with a more extreme concept of severity. The whole point of using harsh interrogation techniques is to make them hard to endure, and many of them may constitute felonious torture if there is no added element. Therefore, the memo concludes its discussion of definitions by emphasizing that torture "is not the mere infliction of pain or suffering on another, but is instead a step well removed." Citing more dictionary definitions, this time of the term torture, the memo says it must involve "intense pain" or "excruciating pain" caused by "extreme acts."

Interrogation discusses the definition of "severe mental pain or suffering" at some length. The federal torture statute incorporated the Senate's addition of the phrase "prolonged mental harm" to the CAT's definition. To OLC, this meant that criminal acts "must cause some lasting, though not necessarily permanent, damage." There was no medical definition of the statutory phrase, but OLC thought that post-traumatic stress disorder might be an example. To limit the reach of this provision, OLC argued that a defendant must specifically intend the harm, not the actions giving rise to it, and that a good faith defense would be available. Therefore, no matter how intense the mental suffering might be from repeated waterboarding or any other enhanced technique, if lasting damage was uncertain there would be no criminal liability.

Interrogation then turns to the history of the CAT, since it is clear that the torture statute was enacted to fulfill the obligations of the United States to implement the Convention. Here the memo emphasizes the CAT's distinction between torture and "other acts of cruel, inhuman, or degrading treatment." The Convention required signatory states to "undertake to prevent" such actions, but did not require their criminalization. Because Congress had taken no action to implement this duty, there was no available statutory definition of cruel, inhuman, or degrading treatment. Had there been one, identifying the border with torture would have been easier.

The opinion begins its analysis of the ratification process by asserting the President's responsibility to interpret treaties. Therefore, an executive interpretation that the Senate had accepted would be due special deference. The Reagan administration had told the Senate that it understood torture to mean "a deliberate and calculated act of an extremely cruel and inhuman nature, specifically intended to inflict excruciating and agonizing physical or mental pain or suffering." As examples it gave "sustained systematic beatings, application of electric currents to sensitive parts of the body and tying up or hanging in positions that cause extreme pain." Concerned about the vagueness of the terms "cruel, inhuman or degrading," the administration decided they should refer to conduct prohibited by the Fifth, Eighth, and Fourteenth Amendments to the Constitution. That would include the cruel and unusual punishments barred by the Eighth Amendment and the "shocking" mistreatment barred by the due process clauses of the other two amendments.

The ratification process continued into the administration of the first President Bush, which softened the tone of the Reagan interpretation somewhat without seeming to alter its substance. New testimony defined torture as "that barbaric cruelty which lies at the top of the pyramid of human rights misconduct." To OLC, the common ground was "the extraordinary or extreme acts required to constitute torture." OLC thought that the Senate understanding at the time of ratification embraced this view, since it referred to torture as "an extreme form of cruel and inhuman treatment." *Interrogation* concludes that the CAT and its history confirm that the implementing statute meant to prohibit "only the most egregious conduct," "only the most heinous acts."

For two reasons, the OLC reading of the ratification history finds more clarity than the history contains. First, everyone agrees that by definition, torture is an extreme form of cruelty. Therefore, references to that fact do not explain how extreme the conduct must be. Second, no one relishes the explicit drawing of nice distinctions between cruelty and torture. Therefore, attempts to give examples of torture tend to stay well away from mistreatment that might be only cruel. In the end, the administration retreated to a cross-reference. Cruelty would consist of conduct already prohibited by the Constitution. However comforting that strategy was as a way to avoid an ugly subject, it failed to aid in line-drawing, because the Constitution prohibits both torture and various kinds of cruelty.

Interrogation notes that the courts had yet to interpret the federal statute, there having been no prosecutions under it. Hence, OLC sought guidance from cases under the Torture Victims Protection Act. Since the TVPA uses the CAT's definition of torture, its caselaw is pertinent. The courts had not performed "any lengthy analysis of what acts constitute torture." OLC, in an appendix to its opinion, summarizes the facts of the cases to provide examples of torture. The appendix reveals why the cases did not search out the border: the acts giving rise to the lawsuits were torture in anyone's conception of the term. These included savage beatings, pulling of teeth, death threats, deprivation of food and water, electric shocks, and rape. On the other hand, there was some evidence of what courts did not consider torture. For example, the European Court of Human Rights had upheld as merely inhuman and degrading the use of wall standing, hooding, subjection to noise, sleep deprivation, and reduced diets.

The third barrier to prosecution that *Interrogation* erects is the President's constitutional power. OLC asserts that the federal torture statute would be unconstitutional "if it impermissibly encroached on the President's constitutional power to conduct a military campaign." The premise is that the interrogation of terror suspects is within the "core" of executive war powers. Reciting the history of the 9/11 attacks and the war with al Qaeda, the opinion stresses the "imperative" need to gain information about future attacks through interrogation. OLC argues that the President's warmaking authority is exclusive, not shared with Congress: "Congress may no more regulate the President's ability to detain and interrogate enemy combatants than it may regulate his ability to direct troop movements on the battlefield."

To avoid a constitutional confrontation, OLC invokes the avoidance canon. "In light of the President's complete authority over the conduct of war, without a clear statement otherwise, we will not read a criminal statute as infringing on the President's ultimate authority in these areas." Arguing that the canon has "special force" for foreign affairs and war, the opinion concludes that the torture statute "must be construed as not applying to interrogations undertaken pursuant to [the President's] Commander-in-Chief authority."

OLC's use of the avoidance canon masks the sweeping implications of its constitutional argument. Everyone agrees that the Commander in Chief Clause gives Presidents some power exclusive of congressional direction to command our military in combat. The actual *extent* of that power is, however, quite uncertain. For Congress has a group of explicit war powers, including the raising and regulating of military forces. Statutes control actual military operations in many ways: by determining the number of troops available, procuring their weapons, and even setting or ratifying strategic goals (such as the "Germany first" strategy in World War II). Congress does not, however, try to dictate day-to-day tactics. *Interrogation,* ignoring the actual existence of shared power to control the military, asserts that the zone of exclusive executive power is very broad, extending to interrogation techniques.

Interrogation, unlike troop movements, is amenable to general rules set in advance by legislation. The existence of the Geneva Conventions and the CAT presuppose this as an international matter; the existence of the federal torture statute presupposes it as a domestic matter. The implication of the OLC opinion is that the torture statute is unconstitutional on its face, because the President may order torture whenever he believes it necessary. Use of the avoidance canon saves the opinion from asserting this astonishing proposition directly, but it is there in the logic, just under the surface of the prose. The opinion's immensely sweeping and unsupported claim of executive authority parallels John Yoo's attempt to free the President from congressional supervision in the terror war in his initial *Constitutional Authority* opinion of September 2001.

In its final section, *Interrogation* erects its fourth barrier to prosecution of interrogators. It reviews "certain justification defenses" that "would potentially eliminate criminal liability." These are necessity and self defense. Both defenses are recognized in American law, although no federal statute establishes and defines them. The necessity defense allows imposing harm that avoids a greater harm—killing one person to save many others. . . . OLC could find a Supreme Court case recognizing the necessity defense. The context of that case was rather remote from the torture statute; it involved prison escapees urging the necessity of escape from threats and violence. Also, there appear to be no cases in which the defense has ever prevailed. Nevertheless, OLC argues gamely that the defense could be "successfully maintained" where "any harm that might occur during an interrogation would pale to insignificance" compared to that threatened by a terror attack. The facts would matter: the more certain the evidence that a suspect possesses information, the more imminent an attack, and the more grave the feared damage, the sturdier the defense would be.

Interrogation fails to mention a much more fundamental problem with the necessity defense it posits than its thin pedigree in federal law. Both the CAT and the federal torture statute ban torture without qualification. The text and history of both reject the notion that torture can be justified. Therefore, whatever the status of the necessity defense generally, this was an inappropriate context in which to claim its applicability.

Interrogation observes that a claim of self-defense is well-established in federal law. The doctrine allows the use of force to save either oneself or another person when that is reasonably believed to be necessary. From this premise, OLC argues that the defense could also insulate interrogations, given a national right of self-defense. This line of argument transports self-defense far from its roots and normal application. (It is really just a recasting of OLC's version of the necessity defense.) The self-defense doctrine ordinarily justifies the use of force against a dangerous assailant, not a helpless prisoner. In the absence of conventional legal support for its new version of the defense, OLC could only cite generalized materials in misleading ways.

Interrogation concludes that even if a government defendant "were to harm" an enemy combatant in interrogation, there would be justification. For both this and the necessity defense, the opinion says euphemistically that "harm" may be justified. It never squarely defends the use of "torture." The delicacy of euphemism is, however, the thinnest of veils for what the opinion really does. It carves out a wide swath of protection for harsh interrogation practices that verge on, but do not quite include, techniques that always and everywhere have been known as torture.

A retreat under fire

Interrogation could not stand the light of day. Alberto Gonzales disapproved it publicly immediately after its release in June 2004, in the wake of the Abu Ghraib prison abuse scandal. He explained that the memo "explored broad legal theories," and that some of the discussion "quite frankly, is irrelevant and unnecessary to support any action taken by the President." He then said that "overbroad" discussions "that address abstract legal theories, or discussions subject to misinterpretation, but not relied upon by decision-makers are under review, and may be replaced, if appropriate, with more concrete guidance addressing only those issues necessary for the legal analysis of actual practices." (The memorandum was certainly overbroad and certainly not irrelevant.)

In late 2004, a week before Gonzales's confirmation hearings for Attorney General, Acting OLC head Daniel Levin issued a replacement opinion with a more temperate analysis. Although OLC sometimes qualifies or supersedes one of its prior opinions, this instance of public repudiation is unprecedented, as it would be in most bureaucracies.

The official retraction of *Interrogation* had actually occurred before Gonzales repudiated it, during the tenure at OLC of Jack Goldsmith. When Goldsmith became head of OLC in the fall of 2003, Jay Bybee and John Yoo had both left the Office. As he reviewed OLC's recent work, Goldsmith found that two memos "stood out" as problematic, *Interrogation* and its counterpart for military interrogations. *Interrogation* was certainly important. Goldsmith knew that it was the basis for what President Bush later called "alternative" interrogation procedures for "key architects" of 9/11 and other attacks: KSM, Abu Zubaydah, and others. A CIA official had called the opinion a "golden shield." It would not be easy to modify or rescind the opinion; obviously there had been considerable reliance on it.

Still, Goldsmith found that *Interrogation* defined torture "too narrowly" using "questionable statutory interpretations." There was an "unusual lack of care and sobriety" in its legal analysis, especially in the assertion that any congressional effort to regulate interrogation would an unconstitutional interference with the commander in chief power. Goldsmith could find no foundation for this claim in prior OLC opinions or "any other source of law." It would overturn many laws, for example the UCMJ. *Interrogation* "rested on cursory and one-sided legal arguments" that failed to consider congressional power or "the many Supreme Court decisions" in tension with it. Moreover, Goldsmith thought that when a conclusion that Congress is disabled is taken "in secret, respect for separation of powers demands a full consideration of competing congressional and judicial prerogatives," which was not there.

Another problem was the "tendentious tone." "It reads like a bad defense counsel's brief, not an OLC opinion," a senior government lawyer said to Goldsmith. He concluded that the two opinions "lacked the tenor of detachment and caution that usually characterizes OLC work, and that is so central to the legitimacy of OLC." Instead, they appeared "designed to confer immunity for bad acts." They were also "wildly broader than was necessary to support what was actually being done." Usually, he knew, OLC "has precise actions in mind" and conforms its analysis to them. *Interrogation,* however, was "untied to any concrete practices." In December 2003, he concluded he must withdraw and replace the opinion, and the military one as well.

The CIA techniques that *Interrogation* approved had, however, "been vetted in the highest circles of government." (That would be the Principals Committee.) In early June 2004, the memos started leaking. Within the administration, only David Addington defended them. After Goldsmith decided on withdrawal, Deputy Attorney General James Comey came to his aid. Attorney General Ashcroft was "understandably shaken" to hear the news. When Ashcroft accepted the withdrawal, Goldsmith submitted his resignation to make it "stick." During this period Addington confronted Goldsmith with a list of opinions that he had rescinded or modified, and said sarcastically that he needed to know which OLC opinions "you still stand by."

Revelation of the OLC opinion led to an impassioned debate. At Gonzales's confirmation hearings, *Interrogation* received bad reviews. OLC veteran and Yale Law Dean Harold Koh called it "perhaps the most clearly erroneous legal opinion I have ever read." Its "absurdly narrow" definition of torture, he said, "flies in the face of the plain meaning of the term." Koh also stated that the opinion's international law positions were erroneous, that it "grossly overreads the inherent power of the President," and that the failure to mention *Steel Seizure* was a "stunning failure of lawyerly craft."

Interrogation has spawned a large legal literature, most of it highly critical. In August 2004, the American Bar Association adopted a resolution condemning "any use of torture or other cruel, inhuman or degrading treatment or punishment upon persons within the custody or under the physical control of the United States government . . . and any endorsement or authorization of such measures by government lawyers . . . ." A group of over a hundred prominent lawyers, retired judges and law school professors signed a statement condemning *Interrogation,* declaring that it sought to "circumvent long established and universally acknowledged principles of law and common decency."

Characteristically, John Yoo has defended the OLC opinion without reservation. To him, retraction of the *Interrogation* memorandum "was really just politics." The replacement memo "changed little in actual administration policy" but gave political cover by intruding vagueness. It undercut our efforts to prevent attacks by forcing agents in the field "to operate in a vacuum of generalizations. Our intent in the Justice Department's original research was to give clear legal guidance on what constituted 'torture' under the law, so that our agents would know exactly what was prohibited, and what was not." Thus the memorandum's main points, if not some of its legal details, were crafted as field guidance. The specific examples of torture in the appendix would tell agents what not to do.

With Yoo's description in mind, I would summarize the opinion's message to a field agent as follows: "If you are trying to get information not torturing for its own sake, almost anything goes. Only the most extreme treatment should raise doubt in your mind. And the law and the President's power form your shield rather than a sword to be used against you for what you do." This was a prescription for the abuses soon to follow.

Yoo's discussion of the finer points of the law of interrogation stresses President Bush's order that prisoners be treated humanely as a sufficient guarantee against abuse. Yoo fails to understand, however, that the opinion he wrote looks in the opposite direction, and in many places encourages harsh conduct that threatens to cross the line into outright torture. For example, Yoo notes that our ratification of the CAT did require the criminalization of torture, but distinguished "cruel, inhuman, or degrading treatment," for which the Convention merely required prevention efforts. Since Congress had not legislated to prohibit cruelty, he converts the distinction from a duty to a license.

Turning the law on its head, Yoo cites the Senate definition of cruelty as incorporating actions already prohibited by the Constitution, and then emphasizes that these bans apply to our criminal justice system not to enemy aliens outside the country.

This line of reasoning removes any barrier to cruelty, even though the Senate had thought that the Constitution provided one. Yoo concludes happily that the opinion allowed our prisons to be rather like boot camps, allowing uncomfortable physical positions, limited sleep, and similar discomforts.

Yoo quotes Anthony Lewis's comparison of the opinion's discussion of defenses to "a mob lawyer to a mafia don on how to skirt the law and stay out of prison." He has said that in response to the CIA's request to know how far interrogators could go, the client needed to know the full range of his options, and to offer any less would have been irresponsible. The advice he provided, however, was misleading to the client due to its refusal to discuss or even acknowledge the existence of serious arguments against all of its major positions.

For example, critics have charged that the opinion's assertion that the President's war power could override the torture statute was a breach of professional responsibility because the opinion did not discuss *Steel Seizure*, and especially Justice Jackson's famous opinion. That is correct. Yoo asserts that the opinion did not cite Jackson because "earlier OLC opinions, reaching across several administrations, had concluded that it had no application to the President's conduct of foreign affairs and national security." He sees *Steel Seizure* as a case about "labor disputes." Citing an opinion by Walter Dellinger, the head of OLC in the Clinton Administration, asserting that the President can refuse to enforce unconstitutional statutes (especially when they limit the commander in chief power), Yoo concludes that the Bybee opinion was "really doing little more than following in the footsteps of the Clinton Justice Department and all prior Justice Departments."

Not so. Yoo's apologia misrepresents the traditions of the Justice Department, and of American constitutional law as well. . . . *Steel Seizure* is a framework decision for separation of powers analysis—it is far from just a case about "labor disputes." Within OLC, *Steel Seizure* is ordinarily regarded as providing fundamental guidance. Jackson's opinion in particular is full of wisdom about emergency powers in wartime, and Yoo would have done well to heed its instruction. His failure even to cite it is a failure to give candid advice to a client, because the case stands in the way of the facile analysis that is typical of *Interrogation*. *Steel Seizure* teaches that statutes are not lightly to be set aside even under the pressures of wartime, and that is precisely the point that *Interrogation* rejects. It does so without grappling with, or even mentioning, the primary Supreme Court precedent. Some years after issuance of the *Interrogation* opinion, the Supreme Court would reinforce *Steel Seizure* in *Hamdan*, reminding everyone about separation of powers fundamentals.

Yoo also chides his critics that they do not understand the need to "innovate and take risks." Although Yoo notes the common argument that torture does not work because it produces unreliable information, he asserts that coercive interrogation is effective and has provided much useful intelligence in the terror war. What this omits is that there is a wide zone of conduct between outright torture and those coercive actions that would bar the admission of evidence in a normal American criminal trial. The *Interrogation* opinion used advocacy rather than analysis to bring the legal line for permitted conduct as close to torture as possible, never admitting the extraordinary nature of the advice being given.

An OLC opinion that hewed to the lawyer's duty of professional detachment would have outlined the substantial legal and consequential risks created by a very narrow definition of torture. The consequential risks were soon to appear at Guantanamo and Abu Ghraib. Above all, there would have been a quality totally absent from the *Interrogation* opinion and from John Yoo's defense of it: a sense of humility and doubt in the face of the great imponderables that the torture issue presents. An OLC lawyer who is asked to opine on mixed issues of constitutional and statutory law is often on firm ground. For example, whether military commissions comport with American law is a question that can be addressed by looking at conventional legal materials.

The question of what constitutes torture is different. Any lawyer asked to address it should feel the need for resources beyond the lawbooks, and for the utmost caution in providing an answer. Of course, no ultimate answer is available, as people have known for centuries. Therefore, the lawyer's duty is to look to our own history and traditions, to international understandings, and to the views of those who have struggled with the limits to interrogation in the field. This is an issue along the borderline between policy and law. The lawyers should have deferred more than they did to those having pertinent experience. In the next chapter, I consider what happened when that deference was both most merited and most lacking—the provision of advice concerning interrogation by the military rather than the CIA.

Of all the legal opinions that were provided to President Bush in the terror war, *Interrogation* is the most deficient in legal right and moral conscience. Its legal conclusions are almost wholly antithetical to existing bodies of law and their manifest purposes. John Yoo's opinion displays little respect for statutes and treaties in its rush to confirm apparently unlimited executive power over interrogation. In good conscience, the opinion should have admitted the novelty of its major positions and their inconsistency with major precedents such as *Steel Seizure*. Instead, the opinion verges on violation of the weakest conception of the advocate's duty—the avoidance of frivolous arguments. In the end, *Interrogation* fails most fundamentally in its absence of a quality that lawyers are not required to have but that the President's lawyers should always strive to display, wisdom.

Holding the line

Jack Goldsmith notes that the replacement opinion by his temporary successor, Dan Levin, took months to complete. It gave the torture law "a much more rigorous and balanced interpretation" than did *Interrogation*. To maintain the golden shield, it stated that none of the conclusions in earlier memos would be different under this one. Goldsmith concludes sadly: "The opinion that had done such enormous harm was completely unnecessary to the tasks at hand."

The imbroglio surrounding the release, retraction, and replacement of *Interrogation* did not end the Bush administration's battles over CIA interrogation techniques. The replacement opinion, sent to Deputy Attorney General Comey by Daniel Levin at the end of 2004, is *Legal Standards Applicable Under 18 U.S.C. 2340-2340A*. This opinion is a careful retreat, not a capitulation. Running only 16 pages, it is much shorter and less tendentious than *Interrogation*. It begins with a firm policy statement of the kind that appropriately informs legal analysis: "Torture is abhorrent both to American law and values and to international norms." After noting that "questions" had arisen about the earlier memo, it says that the opinion request had asked for a document that could be released to the public. OLC's expectation of a wider audience than the client agency and its knowledge of the furor that had surrounded *Interrogation* are evident throughout the new opinion.

Getting down to business, *Legal Standards* states that it "supersedes" *Interrogation* "in its entirety." Lest the clients in CIA lose heart, though, the opinion quickly drops the footnote that Jack Goldsmith mentioned and everyone else soon noticed, providing that none of the conclusions in OLC's earlier memos "would be different under the standards set forth in this memorandum." In short, although the supporting analysis was about to change, the authorized behaviors would be the same. The essential strategy of *Legal Standards* is to prune away some of John Yoo's most luxuriant foliage, and to adopt a more cautious interpretation of the federal torture statute.

Legal Standards eliminates entirely *Interrogation*'s discussion of both the President's war powers and available defenses to prosecution. It finds this analysis "unnecessary" and "inconsistent with the President's unequivocal directive that United States personnel not engage in torture." It is true that OLC, like a court, usually conforms its analysis to the questions raised by the opinion request. For a topic as sensitive as torture, the less said, the better. This opinion takes the President's directive at face value, and steers the clients farther away from conduct that might be torture than did *Interrogation*. The earlier opinion had responded to the administration's secret subtext—urgent signals emanating from the Principals Committee, calling for approval of harsh interrogation techniques.

By simply eliding these two topics, OLC avoided any need to say what parts of the earlier analysis were defective. It would have been hard to find anything good to say about the fabricated discussion of defenses. The President's war powers were surely overstated as well, but OLC always asserts that there is a zone of exclusive executive power to command the military. Not wishing to make concessions it might regret by paring down Yoo's claims, OLC simply and understandably avoided the topic.

Legal Standards does revisit the statutory definitions of severe pain or suffering and specific intent. The analysis of severity, pulling in both directions, winds up lacking clarity, as do so many attempts to address this issue. First, the opinion disapproves the notorious "organ failure" definition of severe pain. It then parallels *Interrogation* by quoting both dictionary definitions of severity and the ratification history's definition of torture as involving "extreme, deliberate and unusually cruel practices." On the other hand, the new opinion concludes that a definition of severe pain as "excruciating and agonizing" would set too high a threshold. The examples of torture that it gives, though, are drawn from the TVPA cases and all involve extreme brutality (such as severe beatings, pulling of teeth, and cutting off fingers).

Unlike the earlier memo, *Legal Standards* does not conclude that severe suffering must always include severe pain to constitute torture. Admitting the subjectivity of attempts to define pain and suffering, the opinion emphasizes the duration and intensity of mistreatment and the need to distinguish it as beyond cruelty. It may be that adding the durational requirement is a quiet way to endorse waterboarding, which usually breaks its victims quickly. For mental pain and suffering, *Legal Standards* retreats from the earlier, strained interpretation of "prolonged," and defines it to mean "some lasting duration." The examples it gives, however, mostly involve harm lasting several years or more.

Turning to specific intent, the opinion notes inconsistency in the caselaw (knowledge of consequences not desire to produce them is sometimes enough to satisfy the requirement). OLC is reluctant to give a precise meaning to the intent element, because the President's directive against torture should not be met by "parsing the specific intent element . . . to approve as lawful conduct that might otherwise amount to torture." This is an implicit rebuke to John Yoo. It would be enough for criminal liability, OLC now says, if there is a "conscious desire" to inflict severe pain or suffering. A good faith defense that such suffering would not occur would be available. Concluding, *Legal Standards* removes an ambiguity left by its predecessor by saying explicitly that a motive to protect national security or any other "good reason" does not justify torture.

Legal Standards is a better and more responsible opinion than *Interrogation*. Both opinions are unsatisfactory in the ways that abstract attempts to define torture usually are. The later opinion's rather muddled discussion of severity is an example of that characteristic. The opinion does, though, set a lower threshold for torture than did *Interrogation* (it would be difficult to set the bar *higher*). *Legal Standards* also gives clear and restrained advice about the specific intent requirement. Most important, it avoids the strained efforts of its predecessor to erect all conceivable barriers to torture prosecutions. . . .

Changing the guard

The tenure of Alberto Gonzales as Attorney General was troubled and brief. . . . He resigned under fire in September 2007, after about two and a half years in his post. He left a Justice Department that was in substantial disarray. Many senior positions were filled on an acting basis, and portions of the career staff were in open revolt.

Needing a successor of unquestioned integrity, the President settled on retired federal judge Michael Mukasey, who was confirmed in October 2007. Mukasey's confirmation process was contentious. He assured the Senate Judiciary Committee that he would be more independent from the White House than his predecessor. He condemned the *Interrogation* opinion as "a mistake" and "unnecessary." Yet he irritated the Committee by holding firm to the Department's traditional view that Presidents have some constitutional authority to take actions that conflict with statutory limits, especially in national security matters. The problem was the usual one, that Attorneys General will not concede the absence of such authority, but cannot say in advance exactly when it exists.

Most of the controversy attending Mukasey's confirmation resulted from a very unsatisfactory dialogue about torture. The Committee repeatedly pressed Mukasey to say whether he considered waterboarding to be torture. He would not answer the question, because he could not do so without making one of two serious errors. If he said waterboarding is not torture, he might not be confirmed; at the least, he would open himself to widespread derision. Besides, he might be lying. If he testified that waterboarding is torture, he would expose the CIA to serious lawfare for actions the Justice Department had approved. Mukasey did say that he found waterboarding "repugnant," and explained his concerns about exposing interrogators to lawfare. Some members of the Committee, though, were having too much self-righteous fun to let him off the hook and seek a clear understanding for the future. In the end, Mukasey was confirmed by an unusually close vote of 53–40.

The new Attorney General soon found himself responding to an uproar caused by disclosures that the CIA had taken and later destroyed videotapes of hundreds of hours of interrogations of two senior al Qaeda captives, Abu Zubaydah and Abd al-Rahim al-Nashiri. CIA had been warned not to destroy the tapes by White House and Justice Department officials and by Members of Congress, but the head of CIA's Directorate of Operations ordered the destruction anyway, without informing either the agency's Director or its General Counsel. It appeared that CIA officials may have lied about the existence of the tapes both to federal judges and to the 9/11 Commission. Investigations of possible obstruction of justice were soon initiated by the CIA Inspector General, the Justice Department, and the congressional intelligence committees. Although the golden shield that OLC had originally constructed for CIA would probably still protect the interrogators themselves, those who covered up the facts would be fully exposed to prosecution.

"Exactly what they feared is what's happening. The winds change, and the recriminations begin," observed Jack Goldsmith No, not exactly. Both political branches had continued to support CIA. The executive had continued to churn out opinions supporting enhanced interrogations; Congress had twice ratified CIA actions within limits, and had erected defenses to prosecution for past interrogations. CIA's misbehavior concerning destruction of the tapes was its own fault. By the twenty-first century, anyone working in the executive should understand the danger of a cover-up.

Some changes were in the wind, though. The new Attorney General had an incentive to distance himself from his predecessor by showing the kind of independence that the Bush White House had never previously tolerated. Within the Department, the Office of Professional Responsibility initiated an internal review of the OLC opinions concerning harsh interrogation, with a special emphasis on approval of waterboarding. The Office was examining "whether the legal advice in these memoranda was consistent with the professional standards that apply to Department of

Justice attorneys." After investigating, the Office could reprimand miscreant lawyers or even seek their disbarment. . . .

---

1. *The Aftermath.* On July 29, 2009, the Justice Department's Office of Professional Responsibility (OPR) issued a 261-page report on possible professional misconduct related to the so-called "torture memos." Department of Justice Office of Professional Responsibility, Investigation into the Office of Legal Counsel's Memoranda Concerning Issues Relating to the Central Intelligence Agency's Use of "Enhanced Interrogation Techniques" on Suspected Terrorists (July 29, 2009), available at http://judiciary.house.gov/hearings/pdf/OPRFinalReport090729.pdf. Although OPR considered whether a number of former OLC officials had committed professional misconduct—and specifically cleared Steven Bradbury, Patrick Philbin, and an unnamed "relatively inexperienced" OLC attorney—its investigation was essentially focused on John Yoo and Jay Bybee. OPR found that Yoo committed intentional professional misconduct (254) and Bybee committed reckless professional misconduct (257).

Under OPR's analytic framework, attorneys commit professional misconduct if they intentionally violate or act in reckless disregard of a known, unambiguous obligation imposed by law, the rules of professional conduct, or DOJ policy (18). OPR concluded that both Yoo and Bybee were bound by rules of the District of Columbia Bar, including Rule 2.1 ("Advisor") which imposes a duty to "exercise independent professional judgment and render candid advice" (21–22), and Rule 1.1, the general competence rule (22–24). In order to determine whether any DOJ official failed to meet these standards, OPR evaluated the legal arguments and conclusions proffered by Messrs. Bybee and Yoo, premising its analysis on the assumption that "the right to be free from official torture is fundamental and universal, a right deserving the highest status under international law." (24)

OPR made five separate findings concerning John Yoo: (1) he "knowingly provided incomplete and one-sided advice in his analysis of the Constitution's Commander-in-Chief Clause . . . ,"(252) (2) he "knew that the Commander-in-Chief section [of the Bybee memo] might be used in an effort to provide immunity to CIA officers engaged in acts that might be construed as torture," (252) (3) he "was aware that the Bybee Memo's discussion of specific intent was insufficient," (252) (4) he "knowingly provided incomplete advice to the client," (253) and (5) he "knowingly misstated the strength of the Bybee Memo's argument 'that interrogation of [prisoners] using methods that might violate [the torture statute] would be justified under the doctrine of self-defense . . . .'" (253) *Id.* at 252–53.

OPR determined that Bybee was "responsible for ensuring that the advice provided [by OLC] to the clients presented a thorough, objective, and candid view of the law" and that he "assumed responsibility for verifying" that the memos bearing his signature met this standard, even though he did not draft the documents. *Id.* at 255. With this in mind OPR made three findings with regard to Bybee: (1) he "should have known that the memoranda were not thorough, objective, or candid in terms of the legal advice they were providing to clients . . . ," (256) (2) he "should have recognized and questioned the unprecedented nature of his conclusion that acts of outright torture could not be prosecuted under certain circumstances," (257) and (3) he "should have questioned the logic and utility of applying language from the medical benefits statutes to the torture statute." (257)

Notwithstanding these findings, the Justice Department ultimately did not pursue sanctions. Instead, David Margolis, the Associate Deputy Attorney General to whom OPR reports, rejected substantial portions of the OPR analysis. Memorandum for the Attorney General and the Deputy Attorney General from David Margolis, Associate Deputy Attorney General re: Memorandum of Decision Regarding Objections to the Findings of Professional Misconduct in the Office of Professional Responsibility's Report of Investigation into the Office of Legal Counsel's Memoranda Concerning Issues Relating to the Central Intelligence Agency's Use of "Enhanced Interrogation Techniques" on Suspected Terrorists (Jan. 5, 2010), available at http://judiciary.house.gov/hearings/pdf/DAGMargolisMemo100105.pdf. Mr. Margolis criticized OPR for providing the Attorney General as well as Professor Yoo and Judge Bybee what he regarded as insufficient time to review and comment on its final draft, and asserted that earlier drafts of the report erred in not providing a clear analytical framework for determining violations of professional conduct, finding that this was a significant departure from standard practice. His rejection of OPR's substantive conclusions, however, defies easy summary. Mr. Margolis states, at one point, that OPR failed to identify any known, unambiguous obligation imposed by "law, rule of professional conduct, or Department regulation" (11) that applied to Bybee and Yoo, but then concedes, at another, that such obligations did arise under D.C. bar rules (26–27). These obligations included a duty, under Rule 1.2, "not to provide advice . . . that was knowingly or recklessly false or issued in bad faith." Bybee and Yoo also shouldered, under Rule 1.1, a duty of "competence," but, according to Margolis, work would violate this duty only if it contained "serious deficiencies" that "prejudiced or could have prejudiced the client." (27) Beyond these, Margolis found in Rule 1.4, a duty to "explain a matter to the extent reasonably necessary to permit the client to make informed decisions regarding the representation." (Id.)

Applying what he took to be the D.C. bar standards, Mr. Margolis then analyzed how the Bybee-Yoo memos dealt with matters criticized by OPR. Although he repeatedly found the work "flawed," he found that none of the flaws warranted discipline. He treats the interpretation of severe pain as "a performance deficiency." (34) On the commander in chief power, he found it unclear whether applicable rules of professional responsibility or Justice Department policy unambiguously required John Yoo to note in his memorandum any counterarguments to his position. (45) On a series of other issues, Margolis finds that the Bybee-Yoo analyses "were most susceptible to criticism because they slanted toward a narrow interpretation of the torture statute at every turn." (64) Yet, he did not believe there was a preponderance of evidence to find that incorrect advice had been given knowingly and recklessly or in bad faith (id.). Likewise, although their errors were "more than minor," the failings of Bybee and Yoo did not amount to "serious deficiencies that could have prejudiced the client." (65)

The Margolis memo was most critical of John Yoo. Because Professor Yoo's "expansive view of executive power" antedated his service in the Bush Administration, Margolis thought he could not be credibly accused of trying merely to "please" his client. Nonetheless, he found the issue of Yoo's intent to be "a close question":

> I fear that John Yoo's loyalty to his own ideology and convictions clouded his view of his obligation to his client and led him to author opinions that reflected his own extreme, if sincerely held, views of executive power while speaking for an institutional client. These memoranda suggest that he failed to appreciate the enormous responsibility that comes with the authority to issue institutional opinions that carried the authoritative weight of the Department of Justice. (67)

This is hardly the exoneration for which an attorney accused of misconduct might wish.

The Margolis memo itself came in for some withering criticism. See, e.g., David Luban, *Margolis is Wrong*, SLATE.COM (Feb. 22, 2010), available at http://www.slate.com/id/2245531/pagenum/all/; Brian Tamanaha, *Why Yoo's Sincere Extremist Excuse Doesn't Work*, BALKINIZATION (Feb. 20, 2010), available at http://balkin.blogspot.com/2010/02/why-yoos-sincere-extremist-excuse.html. Writing before the OPR investigation, Professor Bruff, in BAD ADVICE, at 295–296, nominated Alberto Gonzales, David Addington, and John Yoo, each for bar discipline. (He reaches this conclusion after considering the possibility that the lawyers involved in the torture memos might be exposed to criminal or civil liability, an outcome he would disfavor because of the chill such liability might impose on the provision of candid, forthright legal advice to future administrations. Do you agree?)

2. *Further Reflection (and Reading)*. Looking back on this episode, how far do you think a Justice Department lawyer should go in creating theories that would give the executive branch unfettered authority to resort to extraordinary measures in America's efforts to thwart terrorism? In exploring such theories, is the lawyer obligated, or entitled, to provide moral, as well as legal counsel? The Bybee memo unleashed considerable debate on this question, as well. For example, the New York Times summarized the view of Harvard Law Professor and former solicitor general Charles Fried: " 'When a government is faced with a situation and is faced with options, 'surely one of the questions it asks—but only one of them—is, what does the law require? Another question is, is it effective? Another is, is it moral? Those are not the same questions.' The lawyer's role, he said, is to answer the first question." Adam Liptak, *Torture and Legal Ethics; How Far Can a Government Lawyer Go?* N.Y. TIMES, June 27, 2004. (Professor Fried's answer is especially poignant in light of a book he subsequently wrote with his son, the philosopher Gregory Fried, the title of which strongly signals the Frieds' moral view. CHARLES FRIED AND GREGORY FRIED, BECAUSE IT IS

WRONG: TORTURE, PRIVACY, AND PRESIDENTIAL POWER IN THE AGE OF TERROR (2010).) The news story quoting Professor Fried also quotes the rather different view of New York University law professor Stephen Gillers: "A good lawyer does not think of himself as merely a technician. A good lawyer advises on the wisdom of a particular course of conduct. The consequences of being a technician and not a conscience are stunning." Liptak, *supra*.

The literature relevant to these debates is mountainous. Readers who wish to peruse the primary documents should consult KAREN J. GREENBERG AND JOSHUA L. DRATEL, THE TORTURE PAPERS: THE ROAD TO ABU GHRAIB (2005). Important collections of essays on these issues include MARJORIE COHN, ED., THE UNITED STATES AND TORTURE: INTERROGATION, INCARCERATION, AND ABUSE (2011); SANFORD LEVINSON, ED., TORTURE: A COLLECTION (2004); and *"Symposium: War, Terrorism, and Torture: Limits on Presidential Power in the 21st Century,"* 81 IND. L. REV. 1139 (2006). For George W. Bush's defense of his Administration's stance on interrogation, see GEORGE W. BUSH, DECISION POINTS 169–170 (2010).

2. Targeted Killing

The ongoing three-branch "trialogue" over Guantanamo that has now persisted throughout the Obama Administration and beyond has carried forward a series of legal and policy controversies that had started to take shape very soon after 9/11. Between 2009 and 2017, however, as the Obama Administration started to implement its own strategy for the war against al-Qaeda and its associates, additional controversies rose to public attention—controversies raised both by Congress's failure to update its 2001 and 2002 AUMFs (a topic taken up in the next section) and by President Obama's shift in tactics from large and expensive new military deployments to what the Defense Department's 2012 strategic document called "small-footprint" approaches. DEPARTMENT OF DEFENSE, SUSTAINING U.S. GLOBAL LEADERSHIP: PRIORITIES FOR 21ST CENTURY DEFENSE 3 (2012), http://archive.defense.gov/news /Defense_Strategic_Guidance.pdf. As explained by Professors Jack Goldsmith and Matthew Waxman:

> Under Obama, "drone strikes, cyber attacks and Special Operations raids that made use of America's technological superiority" became "the new, quick-and-dirty expression of military and covert power," says David Sanger of the New York Times. While President Bush deployed these tactics to some extent, President Obama expanded their use significantly and made them central to U.S. counterterrorism operations and to projecting U.S. military force more generally.

Jack Goldsmith and Matthew Waxman, *The Legal Legacy of Light-Footprint Warfare*, 39 WASH. Q. 7 (2016). In their view, the Obama strategy was "undergird[ed]" by "constitutional and statutory innovations that enhance the President's discretion to start and continue military interventions that deploy these tools." Id., at 7–8.

"Small-footprint" certainly did not mean "noncontroversial." Perhaps the starkest issue was raised by an April 2010, Los Angeles Times report that the Obama administration had authorized the capture or killing of Anwar al-Aulaqi, a Muslim cleric born to Yemeni parents in New Mexico, and thus a U.S. citizen. Nothing in our war powers jurisprudence clearly answers the question whether and under what circumstances a President might be authorized "to single out a person or group for attack by U.S. forces when the target consists of individuals, some of whom may be American citizens, who have not been tried and convicted for a capital crime." Phillip Bobbitt, *Foreword*, in H. Jefferson Powell, Targeting Americans: The Constitutionality of the U.S. Drone War x (2016). Nor in 2010 did the Obama Administration provide a clear statement of its legal position regarding either targeted killing in general or the scope of constitutional protections, if any, that might be applicable to U.S. citizens abroad suspected of taking up arms against the United States.[2] News of an OLC opinion purporting to justify the targeting of al-Aulaqi did not emerge until late 2011, after the drone strike that did, indeed, kill al-Aulaqi.

Yet identifying the Administration's legal analysis was suddenly made easier by the release in December 2016 of a remarkable White House document entitled, "Report on the Legal and Policy Frameworks Guiding the United States' Use of Military Force and Related National Security Operations," https://www.justsecurity.org/wp-content/uploads/2016/12/framework.Report_Final.pdf. As explained in a Foreword by President Obama, the report was offered in an effort to demonstrate that the Administration's "uses of force overseas [were] supported by a solid domestic law framework and consistent with an international legal framework predicated on the concepts of sovereignty and self-defense embedded in the United Nations Charter."

Two document excerpts follow. The first is a portion of an opinion issued by the U.S. District Court for the District of Columbia dismissing a suit brought by the father of Anwar al-Aulaqi to enjoin his son's inclusion on an alleged "kill list." The court held the challenge nonjusticiable for a host of reasons including the father's lack of standing (asserted under multiple theories), the D.C. Circuit's doctrine of "equitable discretion," the lack of a cause of action under the Alien Tort Statute, and the state secrets privilege. Perhaps most telling for separation of powers purposes, however, was the court's treatment of the political question doctrine, which we include. Following the excerpt is the portion of the 2016 White House Legal and Policy Framework Report that outlines the Administration's position on the law of targeting.

---

2. For most of Obama's two terms—and despite repeated calls from within and beyond the academy for a systematic presentation of its legal views—the Administration's positions on key controversies were chiefly conveyed through various speeches delivered by senior Administration officials addressing one or another point of controversy. See Kenneth Anderson and Benjamin Wittes, eds., Speaking the Law: The Obama Administration's Addresses on National Security Law (2015).

Al-Aulaqi v. Obama

727 F. Supp. 2d 1 (D.D.C. 2010).

MEMORANDUM OPINION

BATES, District Judge.

On August 30, 2010, plaintiff Nasser Al-Aulaqi ("plaintiff") filed this action, claiming that the President, the Secretary of Defense, and the Director of the CIA (collectively, "defendants") have unlawfully authorized the targeted killing of plaintiff's son, Anwar Al-Aulaqi, a dual U.S.-Yemeni citizen currently hiding in Yemen who has alleged ties to al Qaeda in the Arabian Peninsula ("AQAP"). Plaintiff seeks an injunction prohibiting defendants from intentionally killing Anwar Al-Aulaqi "unless he presents a concrete, specific, and imminent threat to life or physical safety, and there are no means other than lethal force that could reasonably be employed to neutralize the threat." Defendants have responded with a motion to dismiss plaintiff's complaint on five threshold grounds: standing, the political question doctrine, the Court's exercise of its "equitable discretion," the absence of a cause of action under the Alien Tort Statute ("ATS"), and the state secrets privilege.

This is a unique and extraordinary case. Both the threshold and merits issues present fundamental questions of separation of powers involving the proper role of the courts in our constitutional structure. Leading Supreme Court decisions from *Marbury v. Madison*, 5 U.S. (1 Cranch) 137, 2 L.Ed. 60 (1803), through Justice Jackson's celebrated concurrence in *Youngstown Sheet & Tube Co. v. Sawyer*, 343 U.S. 579 (1952), to the more recent cases dealing with Guantanamo detainees have been invoked to guide this Court's deliberations. Vital considerations of national security and of military and foreign affairs (and hence potentially of state secrets) are at play.

Stark, and perplexing, questions readily come to mind, including the following: How is it that judicial approval is required when the United States decides to target a U.S. citizen overseas for electronic surveillance, but that, according to defendants, judicial scrutiny is prohibited when the United States decides to target a U.S. citizen overseas for death? Can a U.S. citizen—himself or through another—use the U.S. judicial system to vindicate his constitutional rights while simultaneously evading U.S. law enforcement authorities, calling for "jihad against the West," and engaging in operational planning for an organization that has already carried out numerous terrorist attacks against the United States? Can the Executive order the assassination of a U.S. citizen without first affording him any form of judicial process whatsoever, based on the mere assertion that he is a dangerous member of a terrorist organization? How can the courts, as plaintiff proposes, make real-time assessments of the nature and severity of alleged threats to national security, determine the imminence of those threats, weigh the benefits and costs of possible diplomatic and military responses, and ultimately decide whether, and under what circumstances, the use of military force against such threats is justified? When would it ever make sense for the United States to disclose in advance to the "target" of contemplated military action the precise standards under which it will take that military action? And how does the evolving AQAP relate to core al Qaeda for purposes of assessing the legality of targeting AQAP (or its principals) under the September 18, 2001 Authorization for the Use of Military Force?

. . . Before reaching the merits of plaintiff's claims, . . . this Court must decide whether plaintiff is the proper person to bring the constitutional and statutory challenges he asserts, and whether plaintiff's challenges, as framed, state claims within the ambit of the Judiciary to resolve. . . . Because these questions of justiciability require dismissal of this case at the outset, the serious issues regarding the merits of the alleged authorization of the targeted killing of a U.S. citizen overseas must await another day or another (non-judicial) forum.

BACKGROUND

This case arises from the United States' alleged policy of "authorizing, planning, and carrying out targeted killings, including of U.S. citizens, outside the context of armed conflict." Specifically, plaintiff, a Yemeni citizen, claims that the United States has authorized the targeted killing of plaintiff's son, Anwar Al-Aulaqi, in violation of the Constitution and international law.

Anwar Al-Aulaqi is a Muslim cleric with dual U.S.-Yemeni citizenship, who is currently believed to be in hiding in Yemen. Anwar Al-Aulaqi was born in New Mexico in 1971, and spent much of his early life in the United States, attending college at Colorado State University and receiving his master's degree from San Diego State University before moving to Yemen in 2004. On July 16, 2010, the U.S. Treasury Department's Office of Foreign Assets Control ("OFAC") designated Anwar Al-Aulaqi as a Specially Designated Global Terrorist ("SDGT") in light of evidence that he was "acting for or on behalf of al-Qa'ida in the Arabian Peninsula (AQAP)" and "providing financial, material or technological support for, or other services to or in support of, acts of terrorism[.]" In its designation, OFAC explained that Anwar Al-Aulaqi had "taken on an increasingly operational role" in AQAP since late 2009, as he "facilitated training camps in Yemen in support of acts of terrorism" and provided "instructions" to Umar Farouk Abdulmutallab, the man accused of attempting to detonate a bomb aboard a Detroit-bound Northwest Airlines flight on Christmas Day 2009. *See* OFAC Designation. Media sources have also reported ties between Anwar Al-Aulaqi and Nidal Malik Hasan, the U.S. Army Major suspected of killing 13 people in a November 2009 shooting at Fort Hood, Texas. According to a January 2010 *Los Angeles Times* article, unnamed "U.S. officials" have discovered that Anwar Al-Aulaqi and Hasan exchanged as many as eighteen e-mails prior to the Fort Hood shootings.

Recently, Anwar Al-Aulaqi has made numerous public statements calling for "jihad against the West," praising the actions of "his students" Abdulmutallab and Hasan, and asking others to "follow suit." Michael Leiter, Director of the National Counterterrorism Center, has explained that Anwar Al-Aulaqi's "familiarity with the West" is a "key concern[ ]" for the United States, and media sources have similarly cited Anwar Al-Aulaqi's ability to communicate with an English-speaking audience as a source of "particular concern" to U.S. officials. But despite the United States' expressed "concern" regarding Anwar Al-Aulaqi's "familiarity with the West" and his "role in AQAP," the United States has not yet publicly charged Anwar Al-Aulaqi with any crime. For his part, Anwar Al-Aulaqi has made clear that he has no intention of making himself available for criminal prosecution in U.S. courts, remarking in a May 2010 AQAP video interview that he "will never surrender" to the United States, and that "[i]f the Americans want me, [they can] come look for me."

Plaintiff does not deny his son's affiliation with AQAP or his designation as a SDGT. Rather, plaintiff challenges his son's alleged unlawful inclusion on so-called "kill lists" that he contends are maintained by the CIA and the Joint Special Operations Command ("JSOC"). In support of his claim that the United States has placed Anwar Al-Aulaqi on "kill lists," plaintiff cites a number of media reports, which attribute their information to anonymous U.S. military and intelligence sources. For example, in January 2010, *The Washington Post* reported that, according to unnamed military officials, Anwar Al-Aulaqi was on "a shortlist of U.S. citizens" that JSOC was authorized to kill or capture. *See* Wizner Decl., Ex. F. A few months later, *The Washington Post* cited an anonymous U.S. official as stating that Anwar Al-Aulaqi had become "the first U.S. citizen added to a list of suspected terrorists the CIA is authorized to kill." And in July 2010, National Public Radio announced—on the basis of unidentified "[i]ntelligence sources"—that the United States had already ordered "almost a dozen" unsuccessful drone and air-strikes targeting Anwar Al-Aulaqi in Yemen.

Based on these news reports, plaintiff claims that the United States has placed Anwar Al-Aulaqi on the CIA and JSOC "kill lists" without "charge, trial, or conviction." Plaintiff alleges that individuals like his son are placed on "kill lists" after a "closed executive process" in which defendants and other executive officials determine that "secret criteria" have been satisfied. Plaintiff further avers "[u]pon information and belief" that once an individual is placed on a "kill list," he remains there for "months at a time." Consequently, plaintiff argues, Anwar Al-Aulaqi is "now subject to a standing order that permits the CIA and JSOC to kill him . . . without regard to whether, at the time lethal force will be used, he presents a concrete, specific, and imminent threat to life, or whether there are reasonable means short of lethal force that could be used to address any such threat."

The United States has neither confirmed nor denied the allegation that it has issued a "standing order" authorizing the CIA and JSOC to kill plaintiff's son. Additionally, the United States has neither confirmed nor denied whether—if it has, in fact, authorized the use of lethal force against plaintiff's son—the authorization was made with regard to whether Anwar Al-Aulaqi presents a concrete, specific, and imminent threat to life, or whether there were reasonable means short of lethal force that could be used to address any such threat. The United States has, however, repeatedly stated that if Anwar Al-Aulaqi "were to surrender or otherwise present himself to the proper authorities in a peaceful and appropriate manner, legal principles with which the United States has traditionally and uniformly complied would prohibit using lethal force or other violence against him in such circumstances."

Nevertheless, plaintiff alleges that due to his son's inclusion on the CIA and JSOC "kill lists," Anwar Al-Aulaqi is in "hiding under threat of death and cannot access counsel or the courts to assert his constitutional rights without disclosing his whereabouts and exposing himself to possible attack by Defendants." Plaintiff therefore brings four claims—three constitutional, and one statutory—on his son's behalf. He asserts that the United States' alleged policy of authorizing the targeted killing of U.S. citizens, including plaintiff's son, outside of armed conflict, "in circumstances in which they do not present concrete, specific, and imminent threats to life or physical safety, and where there are means other than lethal force that could reasonably be employed to neutralize any such threat," violates (1) Anwar Al-Aulaqi's Fourth Amendment right to be free from unreasonable seizures and (2) his Fifth Amendment right not to be deprived of life without due process of law. Plaintiff further claims that (3) the United States' refusal to disclose the criteria by which it selects U.S. citizens like plaintiff's son for targeted killing independently violates the notice requirement of the Fifth Amendment Due Process Clause. Finally, plaintiff brings (4) a statutory claim under the Alien Tort Statute ("ATS"), 28 U.S.C. § 1350, alleging that the United States' "policy of targeted killings violates treaty and customary international law."

Plaintiff seeks both declaratory and injunctive relief. First, he requests a declaration that, outside of armed conflict, the Constitution prohibits defendants "from carrying out the targeted killing of U.S. citizens," including Anwar Al-Aulaqi, "except in circumstances in which they present a concrete, specific, and imminent threat to life or physical safety, and there are no means other than lethal force that could reasonably be employed to neutralize the threat." Second, plaintiff requests a declaration that, outside of armed conflict, "treaty and customary international law" prohibit the targeted killing of all individuals—regardless of their citizenship—except in those same, limited circumstances. Third, plaintiff requests a preliminary injunction prohibiting defendants from intentionally killing Anwar Al-Aulaqi "unless he presents a concrete, specific, and imminent threat to life or physical safety, and there are no means other than lethal force that could reasonably be employed to neutralize the threat." Finally, plaintiff seeks an injunction ordering defendants to disclose the criteria that the United States uses to determine whether a U.S. citizen will be targeted for killing. . . .

DISCUSSION

[Judge Bates's opinion first traverses a series of theories under which Nasser al-Aulaqi sought to assert standing to pursue declaratory or injunctive relief in defense of constitutional rights belonging either to his son or to himself. The court finds merit in none of them. As analyzed by Judge Bates, Nasser al-Aulaqi cannot sue as his son's next friend because he has not identified any insuperable barrier to his son filing suit on his own behalf; nor has he established that his adult son regards a federal suit as serving his own best interests. For closely related reasons, Judge Bates also regards the father as providing insufficient grounds to assert third-party standing within the acknowledged exceptions to the usual rule that limits plaintiffs to asserting only their own legal rights. Judge Bates would not recognize the father as having Article III standing to pursue any constitutional right of his own, because (a) he regards the emotional anxiety provoked by the government's alleged actions as an insufficient injury-in-fact to qualify for standing and (b) the potential injury to the parent's interest in maintaining a relationship with an adult child does not constitute an injury to a legally protected interest.[1] Nasser al-Aulaqi also tried to assert a claim under the Alien Tort Statute ("ATS"), which provides that "[t]he district courts shall have original jurisdiction of any civil action by an alien for a tort only, committed in violation of the law of nations or a treaty of the United States." 28 U.S.C. § 1350. Judge Bates concluded that no cause of action existed because "plaintiff cites no case in which a court has ever recognized a 'customary international law norm' against a threatened future extrajudicial killing, nor does he cite a single case in which an alien has ever been permitted to recover under the ATS for the extrajudicial killing of his U.S. citizen child." Judge Bates also found that the suit was not covered by the Administrative Procedure Act.]

III. *The Political Question Doctrine*

Defendants argue that even if plaintiff has standing to bring his constitutional claims or states a cognizable claim under the ATS, his claims should still be dismissed because they raise non-justiciable political questions. Like standing, the political question doctrine is an aspect of "the concept of justiciability, which expresses the jurisdictional limitations imposed on the federal courts by the 'case or controversy' requirement of Article III of the Constitution." The political question doctrine "is 'essentially a function of the separation of powers,'" and "'excludes from judicial review those controversies which revolve around policy choices and value determinations constitutionally committed for resolution to the halls of Congress or the confines of the Executive Branch.'" The precise "'contours'" of the political question doctrine remain "'murky and unsettled.'" Still, the Supreme Court has articulated six factors which are said to be "[p]rominent on the surface" of cases involving non-justiciable political questions:

> [1] a textually demonstrable constitutional commitment of the issue to a coordinate political department; or [2] a lack of judicially discoverable and manageable standards for resolving it; or [3] the impossibility of deciding without an initial policy determination of a kind clearly for nonjudicial discretion; or [4] the impossibility of a court's undertaking independent resolution without expressing lack of respect due coordinate branches of government; or [5] an unusual need for unquestioning adherence to a

---

1. [Ed.: This last conclusion may well conflate the standing inquiry with the court's view of the substantive constitutional claim.]

political decision already made; or [6] the potentiality of embarrassment from multifarious pronouncements by various departments on one question.

Baker [v. Carr], 369 U.S. at 217, 82 S.Ct. 691. The first two factors—a textual commitment to another branch of government and a lack of judicially manageable standards—are considered "the most important," but in order for a case to be non-justiciable, the court "need only conclude that one factor is present, not all."

Unfortunately, the *Baker* factors are much easier to enumerate than they are to apply, and it is perhaps for this reason that the political question doctrine "continues to be the subject of scathing scholarly attack." Dean Erwin Chemerinsky has gone so far as to remark that the *Baker* criteria "seem useless in identifying what constitutes a political question." *See* Erwin Chemerinsky, *Federal Jurisdiction* 149 (5th ed. 2007). According to him, the political question doctrine cannot be understood by mechanically applying the factors enumerated in *Baker,* but "only by examining the specific areas where the Supreme Court has invoked [the doctrine]." Although Dean Chemerinsky's derogation of the *Baker* factors is extreme, it is true that "the category of political questions is more amenable to description by infinite itemization than by generalization."

An examination of the specific areas in which courts have invoked the political question doctrine reveals that national security, military matters and foreign relations are "'quintessential sources of political questions.'" As the D.C. Circuit recently explained, cases involving national security and foreign relations "raise issues that 'frequently turn on standards that defy judicial application' or 'involve the exercise of a discretion demonstrably committed to the executive or legislature.'" Unlike the political branches, the Judiciary has "no covert agents, no intelligence sources, and no policy advisors." Courts are thus institutionally ill-equipped "to assess the nature of battlefield decisions," or to "define the standard for the government's use of covert operations in conjunction with political turmoil in another country," These types of decisions involve "delicate, complex" policy judgments with "large elements of prophecy," and "are decisions of a kind for which the Judiciary has neither aptitude, facilities, nor responsibility." *Chicago & S. Air Lines v. Waterman Corp.,* 333 U.S. 103, 111 (1948). The difficulty that U.S. courts would encounter if they were tasked with "ascertaining the 'facts' of military decisions exercised thousands of miles from the forum, lies at the heart of the determination whether the question [posed] is a 'political' one."

At the same time, the Supreme Court has also made clear that "it is error to suppose that every case or controversy which touches foreign relations lies beyond judicial cognizance." Although "'attacks on foreign policymaking are nonjusticiable, claims alleging non-compliance with the law are justiciable, even though the limited review that the court undertakes may have an effect on foreign affairs.'" The political question doctrine, the Supreme Court has warned, was only designed to cover a "narrow" category of "carefully defined" cases, and should not be employed as "an ad hoc litmus test of [courts'] reactions to the desirability of and need for judicial application of constitutional or statutory standards to a given type of claim." Hence, in order to decide whether a particular legal challenge constitutes an impermissible "attack on foreign policymaking" or is instead a justiciable claim with a permissible "effect on foreign affairs," a court "must conduct 'a discriminating analysis of the particular question posed' in the 'specific case.'"

Judicial resolution of the "particular questions" posed by plaintiff in this case would require this Court to decide: (1) the precise nature and extent of Anwar Al-Aulaqi's affiliation with AQAP; (2) whether AQAP and al Qaeda are so closely linked that the defendants' targeted killing of Anwar Al-Aulaqi in Yemen would come within the United States' current armed conflict with al Qaeda; (3) whether (assuming plaintiff's proffered legal standard applies) Anwar Al-Aulaqi's alleged terrorist activity renders him a "concrete, specific, and imminent threat to life or physical safety," *see* Compl., Prayer for Relief (c); and (4) whether there are "means short of lethal force" that the United States could "reasonably" employ to address any threat that Anwar Al-Aulaqi poses to U.S. national security interests. Such determinations, in turn, would require this Court, in defendants' view, to understand and assess "the capabilities of the [alleged] terrorist operative to carry out a threatened attack, what response would be sufficient to address that threat, possible diplomatic considerations that may bear on such responses, the vulnerability of potential targets that the [alleged] terrorist [ ] may strike, the availability of military and nonmilitary options, and the risks to military and nonmilitary personnel in attempting application of non-lethal force." Viewed through these prisms, it becomes clear that plaintiff's claims pose precisely the types of complex policy questions that the D.C. Circuit has historically held non-justiciable under the political question doctrine.

Most recently, in *El-Shifa v. United States*[, 607 F.3d 836 (2010)], the D.C. Circuit examined whether the political question doctrine barred judicial resolution of claims by owners of a Sudanese pharmaceutical plant who brought suit seeking to recover damages after their plant was destroyed by an American cruise missile. President Clinton had ordered the missile strike in light of intelligence indicating that the plant was "'associated with the [Osama] bin Ladin network' and 'involved in the production of materials for chemical weapons.'" The plaintiffs maintained that the U.S. government had been negligent in determining that the plant was tied "to chemical weapons and Osama bin Laden," and therefore sought "a declaration that the government's failure to compensate them for the destruction of the plant violated customary international law, a declaration that statements government officials made about them were defamatory, and an injunction requiring the government to retract those statements." Dismissing the plaintiffs' claims as non-justiciable under the political question doctrine, the D.C. Circuit explained that "[i]n military matters . . . the courts lack the competence to assess the strategic decision to employ force or to create standards to determine whether the use of force was justified or well-founded." Rather than endeavor to resolve questions beyond the Judiciary's institutional competence, the court held that "[i]f the political question doctrine means anything in the arena of national security and foreign relations, it means the courts cannot assess the merits of the President's decision to launch an attack on a foreign target."

Here, plaintiff asks this Court to do exactly what the D.C. Circuit forbid (sic) in *El-Shifa*—assess the merits of the President's (alleged) decision to launch an attack on a foreign target. Although the "foreign target" happens to be a U.S. citizen, the same reasons that counseled against judicial resolution of the plaintiffs' claims in *El-Shifa* apply with equal force here. Just as in *El-Shifa,* any judicial determination as to the propriety of a military attack on Anwar Al-Aulaqi would " 'require this court to elucidate the . . . standards that are to guide a President when he evaluates the veracity of military intelligence.' " Indeed, that is just what plaintiff has asked this Court to do. But there are no judicially manageable standards by which courts can endeavor to assess the President's interpretation of military intelligence and his resulting decision—based on that intelligence—whether to use military force against a terrorist target overseas. Nor are there judicially manageable standards by which courts may determine the nature and magnitude of the national security threat posed by a particular individual. In fact, the D.C. Circuit has expressly held that the question whether an organization's alleged "terrorist activity" threatens "the national security of the United States" is "nonjusticiable." Given that courts may not undertake to assess whether a particular organization's alleged terrorist activities threaten national security, it would seem axiomatic that courts must also decline to assess whether a particular individual's alleged terrorist activities threaten national security. But absent such a judicial determination as to the nature and extent of the alleged national security threat that Anwar Al-Aulaqi poses to the United States, this Court cannot possibly determine whether the government's alleged use of lethal force against Anwar Al-Aulaqi would be "justified or well-founded." Thus, the second *Baker* factor—a "lack of judicially discoverable and manageable standards" for resolving the dispute—strongly counsels against judicial review of plaintiff's claims.

The type of relief that plaintiff seeks only underscores the impropriety of judicial review here. Plaintiff requests both a declaration setting forth the standard under which the United States can select individuals for targeted killing as well as an injunction prohibiting defendants from intentionally killing Anwar Al-Aulaqi unless he meets that standard—i.e., unless he "presents a concrete, specific, and imminent threat to life or physical safety, and there are no means other than lethal force that could reasonably be employed to neutralize the threat." Yet plaintiff concedes that the " 'imminence' requirement" of his proffered legal standard would render any "real-time judicial review" of targeting decisions "infeasible," and he therefore urges this Court to issue his requested preliminary injunction and then enforce the injunction "through an after-the-fact contempt motion or an after-the-fact damages action." But as the D.C. Circuit has explained, "[i]t is not the role of judges to second-guess, with the benefit of hindsight, another branch's determination that the interests of the United States call for military action." Such military determinations are textually committed to the political branches. Moreover, any post hoc judicial assessment as to the propriety of the Executive's decision to employ military force abroad "would be anathema to . . . separation of powers" principles. The first, fourth, and sixth *Baker* factors thus all militate against judicial review of plaintiffs' claims, since there is a "textually demonstrable constitutional commitment" of the United States' decision to employ military force to coordinate political departments (Congress and the Executive), and any after-the-fact judicial review of the Executive's decision to employ military force abroad would reveal a "lack of respect due coordinate branches of government" and create "the potentiality of embarrassment of multifarious pronouncements by various departments on one question."

The mere fact that the "foreign target" of military action in this case is an individual—rather than alleged enemy property—does not distinguish plaintiff's claims from those raised in *El-Shifa* for purposes of the political question doctrine. The D.C. Circuit has on several occasions dismissed claims on political question grounds where resolution of those claims would require a judicial determination as to the propriety of the use of force by U.S. officials against a specific individual abroad. For example, the court in *Harbury v. Hayden* dismissed as non-justiciable the claims of an American widow who alleged that her husband—a Guatemalan rebel fighter—had been tortured and killed by Guatemalan army officers working in conjunction with the CIA in Guatemala. Notwithstanding the plaintiff's contention that "U.S. officials were responsible for physically abusing and killing" her husband, the D.C. Circuit concluded that "the political question doctrine plainly applies to this case."

Similarly, in *Schneider v. Kissinger,* the D.C. Circuit deemed non-justiciable the claims raised by the decedents of a Chilean general, who alleged that the United States had caused the general's kidnaping, torture, and death in furtherance of its Cold War efforts to overthrow the leftist Chilean leader Salvador Allende. As the *Schneider* court explained, "in order to determine whether the covert operations which allegedly led to the tragic death of [the general] were wrongful," it would first need to determine "whether, 35 years ago, at the height of the Cold War . . . 'it was proper for an Executive Branch official . . . to support covert actions against' a committed Marxist who was set to take power in a Latin American country." The court conceded that it may have been a "drastic measure" for the United States to ally itself with "dissidents in another country to kidnap a national of that country," but nonetheless concluded that any determination as to "whether drastic measures should be taken in matters of foreign policy and national security is not the stuff of adjudication, but of policymaking." Because there were no judicially "discoverable and manageable standards for the resolution" of the plaintiffs' claims, the court dismissed the case as posing a non-justiciable political question. *See also Gonzalez–Vera,* 449 F.3d at 1264 (holding non-justiciable claims alleging that Henry Kissinger and other U.S. executive officials cooperated with Chilean dictator Augusto Pinochet to commit human rights abuses in Chile, since "[w]hatever Kissinger did as National Security Advisor or Secretary of State 'can hardly be called anything other than foreign policy'") (internal citation omitted); *Bancoult,* 445 F.3d at 436 (dismissing claims by former residents of the Chagos Archipelago, who alleged that the United States had caused the forcible relocation and killing of island residents in the 1960s in order to establish a military base on the island, on the ground that the "specific tactical measures" employed by the United States in depopulating the island were "inextricably intertwined with the underlying strategy of establishing a regional military presence"—an unreviewable political question).

Plaintiff's claim is distinguishable from those asserted in these cases in only one meaningful respect: Anwar Al-Aulaqi—unlike the Guatemalan rebel fighter in *Harbury,* the Chilean general in *Schneider,* the other Chileans in *Gonzalez–Vera,* or the Chagos Archipelago inhabitants in *Bancoult*—is a U.S. citizen. The significance of Anwar Al-Aulaqi's U.S. citizenship is not lost on this Court. Indeed, it does not appear that any court has ever—on political question doctrine grounds—refused to hear a U.S. citizen's claim that his personal constitutional rights have been violated as a result of U.S. government action taken abroad.

Nevertheless, there is inadequate reason to conclude that Anwar Al-Aulaqi's U.S. citizenship—standing alone—renders the political question doctrine inapplicable to plaintiff's claims. Plaintiff cites two contexts in which courts have found claims asserting violations of U.S. citizens' constitutional rights to be justiciable despite the fact that those claims implicate grave national security and foreign policy concerns. Courts have been willing to entertain habeas petitions from U.S. citizens detained by the United States as enemy combatants, and they have also heard claims from U.S. citizens alleging unconstitutional takings of their property by the U.S. military abroad. But habeas petitions and takings claims are both much more amenable to judicial resolution than the claims raised by plaintiff in this case.

Courts have been willing to hear habeas petitions (from both U.S. citizens and aliens) because "the Constitution specifically contemplates a judicial role" for claims by individuals challenging their detention by the Executive. While the Suspension Clause reflects a "textually demonstrable commitment" of habeas corpus claims to the Judiciary, there is no "constitutional commitment to the courts for review of a military decision to launch a missile at a foreign target." Indeed, such military decisions are textually committed not to the Judiciary, but to the political branches. Moreover, the resolution of habeas petitions does not require expertise beyond the purview of the Judiciary. Although plaintiff is correct to point out that habeas cases involving Guantanamo detainees often involve judicial scrutiny of highly sensitive military and intelligence information, such information is only used to determine whether "the United States has unjustly deprived an American citizen of liberty through acts it has already taken." *Abu Ali v. Ashcroft,* 350 F. Supp. 2d 28, 65 (D.D.C. 2004). These post hoc determinations are "precisely what courts are accustomed to assessing." But courts are certainly not accustomed to assessing claims like those raised by plaintiff here, which seek to prevent future U.S. military action in the name of national security against specifically contemplated targets by the imposition of judicially-prescribed legal standards enforced through "after-the-fact contempt motion[s]" or "after-the-fact damages action[s]." Hence, the *Baker* factors dictate a different outcome for plaintiff's claims than for habeas petitions filed by detainees at Guantanamo Bay.

Plaintiff's claims are also fundamentally distinct from those in which U.S. citizens have been permitted to sue the United States for alleged unconstitutional takings of their property by the U.S. military abroad. In *Ramirez de Arellano,* the D.C. Circuit declined to dismiss as non-justiciable the claims brought by U.S. citizens who asserted that the U.S. military had unlawfully expropriated their cattle ranch in Honduras in violation of the Fifth Amendment. The D.C. Circuit, ruling en banc, explained that the plaintiffs' claims did not constitute a challenge "to the United States military presence in Honduras" but instead were "narrowly focused on the lawfulness of the United States defendants' occupation and use of the plaintiffs' cattle ranch." Once the court characterized the case as a land dispute between the plaintiffs and the U.S. government, it had little difficulty concluding that "adjudication of the defendants' constitutional authority to occupy and use the plaintiffs' property" did not require "expertise beyond the capacity of the Judiciary" or "unquestioning adherence to a political decision by the Executive."

Unlike *Ramirez,* the questions posed in this case do require both "expertise beyond the capacity of the Judiciary" and the need for "unquestioning adherence to a political decision by the Executive." Here, plaintiff asks the Judiciary to limit the circumstances under which the United States may employ lethal force against an individual abroad whom the Executive has determined "plays an operational role in AQAP planning terrorist attacks against the United States." The injunctive and declaratory relief sought by plaintiff would thus be vastly more intrusive upon the powers of the Executive than the relief sought in *Ramirez,* where the court was only called upon to adjudicate "the defendants' constitutional authority to occupy and use the plaintiffs' property." Moreover, although resolution of the plaintiffs' claims in *Ramirez* only required "interpretations of the Constitution and of federal statutes," which are "quintessential tasks of the federal Judiciary," *see id.,* resolution of the claims in this case would require assessment of "strategic choices directing the nation's foreign affairs [that] are constitutionally committed to the political branches."

To be sure, this Court recognizes the somewhat unsettling nature of its conclusion — that there are circumstances in which the Executive's unilateral decision to kill a U.S. citizen overseas is "constitutionally committed to the political branches" and judicially unreviewable. But this case squarely presents such a circumstance. The political question doctrine requires courts to engage in a fact-specific analysis of the "particular question" posed by a specific case, and the doctrine does not contain any "carve-out" for cases involving the constitutional rights of U.S. citizens. While it may be true that "the political question doctrine wanes" where the constitutional rights of U.S. citizens are at stake, it does not become inapposite. Indeed, in one of the only two cases since *Baker v. Carr* in which the Supreme Court has dismissed a case on political question grounds, the plaintiffs were U.S. citizens alleging violations of their constitutional rights. *See Gilligan v. Morgan,* 413 U.S. 1, 3 (1973).

In *Gilligan,* students at Kent State University brought suit in the wake of the "Kent State massacre," seeking declaratory and injunctive relief that would prohibit the

Ohio Governor from "prematurely ordering National Guard troops to duty in civil disorders" and "restrain leaders of the National Guard from future violation of the students' constitutional rights." According to the Court, the plaintiffs were, in essence, asking for "initial judicial review and continuing surveillance by a federal court over the training, weaponry, and orders of the Guard." Dismissing the plaintiffs' claims as presenting non-justiciable political questions, the Court noted that "[i]t would be difficult to think of a clearer example of the type of governmental action that was intended by the Constitution to be left to the political branches." As the Court explained, the Judiciary lacks the "competence" to make "complex subtle, and professional decisions as to the composition, training, equipping, and control of a military force," and "[t]he ultimate responsibility for these decisions is appropriately vested in branches of the government which are periodically subject to electoral accountability."

So, too, does the Constitution place responsibility for the military decisions at issue in this case "in the hands of those who are best positioned and most politically accountable for making them." "Judges, deficient in military knowledge . . . and sitting thousands of miles away from the field of action, cannot reasonably or appropriately determine" if a specific military operation is necessary or wise. Whether the alleged "terrorist activities" of an individual so threaten the national security of the United States as to warrant that military action be taken against that individual is a "political judgment[ ] . . . [which] belong[s] in the domain of political power not subject to judicial intrusion or inquiry."

Contrary to plaintiff's assertion, in holding that the political question doctrine bars plaintiff's claims, this Court does not hold that the Executive possesses "unreviewable authority to order the assassination of any American whom he labels an enemy of the state." Rather, the Court only concludes that it lacks the capacity to determine whether a specific individual in hiding overseas, whom the Director of National Intelligence has stated is an "operational" member of AQAP, presents such a threat to national security that the United States may authorize the use of lethal force against him. This Court readily acknowledges that it is a "drastic measure" for the United States to employ lethal force against one of its own citizens abroad, even if that citizen is currently playing an operational role in a "terrorist group that has claimed responsibility for numerous attacks against Saudi, Korean, Yemeni, and U.S. targets since January 2009." But as the D.C. Circuit explained in *Schneider,* a determination as to whether "drastic measures should be taken in matters of foreign policy and national security is not the stuff of adjudication, but of policymaking." Because decision-making in the realm of military and foreign affairs is textually committed to the political branches, and because courts are functionally ill-equipped to make the types of complex policy judgments that would be required to adjudicate the merits of plaintiff's claims, the Court finds that the political question doctrine bars judicial resolution of this case. . . .

[Judge Bates further concluded that the state secrets privilege also required that the claim be dismissed.]

CONCLUSION

For the foregoing reasons, the Court will grant defendants' motion to dismiss. A separate order has been filed on this date.

White House Report on the Legal and Policy Frameworks Guiding The United States' Use of Military Force and Related National Security Operations

December 2016

Targeting

The U.S. Government makes extensive efforts to ensure that its targeting efforts comply with all applicable international obligations, domestic laws, and policies. This section of the report does not discuss all of the legal and policy considerations relevant to these efforts, but instead focuses on (1) the law of armed conflict framework underlying U.S. targeting efforts; (2) two key topics relevant to the legal framework— constitutional constraints on the targeting of U.S. persons and law of armed conflict rules applicable to the targeting of money and revenue-generating objects; and (3) key policies concerning targeting military objectives and reducing incidental civilian casualties.

A. The Law of Armed Conflict and Targeting

It is well-and long-established that under the law of armed conflict, States may target specific, identified individual members of an enemy force as well as individuals directly participating in hostilities. For example, during World War II, U.S. Navy forces lawfully shot down the aircraft of Admiral Yamamoto, the commander of the Japanese navy, specifically because he was on board. His loss was a significant setback for the Japanese war effort. Today, just as in 1943, the use of lethal force against an identified member of the enemy force in an ongoing armed conflict is consistent with law of armed conflict principles governing who may be made the object of attack.

Removing the senior leadership of terrorist groups against which the United States is engaged in hostilities—including those in charge of plotting attacks against the United States and its partners—is an important piece of the overall U.S. strategy for defeating these groups. It is also consistent with the U.S. commitment to minimizing civilian casualties. Indeed, targeting particular individuals serves to narrow the focus when force is employed and to avoid broader harm to civilians and civilian objects.

Under the law of armed conflict, States may also use technologically advanced weapons systems—including unmanned aerial vehicles, commonly referred to as "drones"—so long as they are employed in conformity with applicable law of armed conflict principles and rules.

Technologically advanced weapons systems can often enhance the United States' ability to implement its obligations under the law of armed conflict. Precision-guided munitions, enhanced sensors, and the ability to monitor targets for extended periods of time can allow the United States to distinguish more effectively between a member of the enemy forces and a civilian. It is U.S. policy to develop, acquire, and field weapons systems and other technological capabilities that further enable the discriminate use of force in different operational contexts.

Additionally, using targeted lethal force against an enemy consistent with the law of armed conflict does not constitute an "assassination." Assassinations are unlawful killings and are prohibited by Executive Order. There is no requirement under international law to provide legal process before a State may use lethal force in accordance with the law of armed conflict.

None of the above diminishes longstanding and important obligations under both domestic and international law that constrain how and in what circumstances force may be used in the course of an armed conflict. In its targeting practices in the context of both international and non-international armed conflicts, the United States complies with—and in many important respects has policies that provide greater safeguards than—the requirements of all applicable law, including the law of armed conflict.

First, U.S. targeting practices comply with the principle of distinction, which in the targeting context requires that attacks be limited to military objectives and that civilians or civilian objects not be made the object of attack. Even when the United States is dealing with enemy forces that do not wear uniforms or carry their arms openly, the United States goes to great lengths to apply this principle. In particular, the United States considers all available information about a potential target's current and historical activities to inform an assessment of whether the individual is a lawful target. For example, an individual who is formally or functionally a member of an armed group against which the United States is engaged in an armed conflict is generally targetable. Determining that someone is a "functional" member of an armed group may include looking to, among other things, the extent to which that person performs functions for the benefit of the group that are analogous to those traditionally performed by members of a country's armed forces; whether that person is carrying out or giving orders to others within the group; and whether that person has undertaken certain acts that reliably connote meaningful integration into the group.

Second, U.S. targeting practices comply with the principle of proportionality, which, among other things, prohibits attacks in which the expected loss of life or injury to civilians and damage to civilian objects incidental to the attack would be excessive in relation to the concrete and direct military advantage expected to be gained. Additionally, feasible precautions must be taken in conducting an attack to reduce the risk of harm to civilians and other protected persons and objects, such as, in certain circumstances when it is appropriate to do so, warning civilians before bombardments. In U.S. operations against enemy forces, great care is taken to adhere to the principle of proportionality in both planning and execution to ensure that collateral damage is kept to a minimum. Indeed, as discussed below, the United States routinely applies certain heightened policy standards that are more protective of civilians than is required under the law of armed conflict.

Third, U.S. targeting practices conform to the principle of necessity, which requires that the use of military force (including all measures needed to defeat the enemy as quickly and efficiently as possible that are not prohibited by the law of armed conflict) be directed at accomplishing a legitimate military purpose. Individuals who are part of enemy forces are generally legitimate military targets, and the United States may use lethal force against enemy forces in the armed conflict in which it is engaged, subject to other applicable law of armed conflict rules. The law of armed conflict does not require that enemy combatants be warned before being made the object of attack, and it does not require that enemy combatants be given an opportunity to surrender before being made the object of attack.

Fourth, U.S. targeting practices conform to the principle of humanity, which prohibits the infliction of suffering, injury, or destruction unnecessary to accomplish a legitimate military purpose. For example, it is forbidden to use weapons that are calculated to cause superfluous injury.

Finally, and as discussed further below, there is a robust review process before the United States uses military force against members of enemy forces, and that review process includes rigorous safeguards to protect civilians. Throughout the military chain of command, commanders, advised by trained and experienced staffs — including intelligence officers, operations officers, and judge advocates — review operations for compliance with applicable U.S. domestic and international law, including the law of armed conflict, and for consistency with the policies and orders of superiors in the military chain of command.

B. Selected Topics Regarding Targeting

1. U.S. Constitutional Constraints Regarding Targeting U.S. Citizens Who Are Abroad and Part of an Enemy Force

... [T]he 2001 AUMF provides the primary domestic legal framework for targeting enemy forces in the context of the current hostilities. Additional constitutional considerations are implicated by the targeting of U.S. citizens abroad who are part of an enemy force.

In a small number of instances, U.S. citizens have joined enemy forces and planned attacks against the United States from abroad. This situation has historical precedent. In previous conflicts, U.S. citizens have fought in foreign armies against the United States, including with the Axis countries during World War II. Longstanding legal principles and court decisions confirm that being a U.S. citizen does not immunize a member of the enemy from attack. As a plurality of the U.S. Supreme Court made clear in 2004 with respect to detention authority, "[a] citizen, no less than an alien, can be 'part of or supporting forces hostile to the

United States or coalition partners' and 'engaged in an armed conflict against the United States.'"

However, the United States must take into account all relevant constitutional considerations with respect to U.S. citizens. When the United States knows in advance that the specific object of its attack is an individual U.S. citizen, it proceeds on the basis that constitutional rights—in particular, the Fifth Amendment's Due Process Clause and the Fourth Amendment's prohibition on unreasonable searches and seizures—attach to the U.S. citizen even while the individual is abroad.[3] Those rights are considered in assessing whether it is lawful to target the individual.

The United States has publicly provided this constitutional analysis in detail on numerous occasions.[4] In particular, these publicly released materials discuss how the United States has applied a due process balancing analysis to determine the circumstances under which it may use lethal force against a U.S. citizen who is a senior operational leader of an enemy force planning violent attacks against Americans, and how, under this analysis, the United States would be able to use force against the senior operational leader in at least the following circumstances: (1) where an informed, high-level official of the U.S. Government has determined that the targeted individual poses an imminent threat of violent attack against the United States; (2) where a capture operation would be infeasible and where those conducting the operation continue to monitor whether capture becomes feasible; and (3) where such an operation would be conducted consistent with applicable law of armed conflict principles.

The United States applied these three criteria for the use of force against a U.S. citizen in the only specific, targeted strike against an identified U.S. citizen that it has conducted—the strike that targeted Anwar al-Aulaqi. First, Anwar al-Aulaqi posed an imminent threat of violent attack on U.S. persons. He was the chief of external operations of AQAP, one of the most dangerous regional affiliates of al-Qa'ida and a group that has committed numerous terrorist attacks overseas and attempted multiple times to conduct terrorist attacks against the U.S. homeland. In this role, al-Aulaqi repeatedly made clear his intent to attack U.S. persons; he was also directly and personally involved in the continued planning and execution of terrorist attacks against the U.S. homeland. Based on this information, high-level U.S. Government officials appropriately concluded that al-Aulaqi posed an imminent threat of violent attack against the United States. Second, before carrying out the operation that killed al-Aulaqi, senior officials conducted a careful evaluation of the circumstances at the

---

3. *See* David J. Barron, Acting Assistant Attorney General, Office of Legal Counsel, U.S. Department of Justice, to the Attorney General, *Applicability of Federal Criminal Laws and the Constitution to Contemplated Lethal Operations Against Shaykh Anwar al-Aulaqi* (July 16, 2010) ("Aulaqi Memo"), *available at* https://www.justice.gov/sites/default/files/olc/pages/attachments/2015/04/02/2010-07-16_-_olc_aaga_barron_-_al-aulaqi.pdf.

4. *See, e.g., id.*; Letter from Attorney General Eric Holder to the Hon. Patrick J. Leahy, May 22, 2013 ("Holder Letter"), *available at* https://www.justice.gov/sites/default/files/ag/legacy/2013/05/28/AG-letter-5-22-13.pdf.

time and determined that it was not feasible to capture al-Aulaqi. Third, senior officials determined that the operation would be conducted consistent with applicable law of armed conflict principles. In addition, the operation was undertaken with the consent of the Government of Yemen.

Beyond the Fifth Amendment's Due Process Clause, the United States has also proceeded on the basis that a lethal operation targeting a U.S. citizen abroad who is planning attacks against the United States would result in a "seizure" under the Fourth Amendment. The U.S. Supreme Court has made clear that the constitutionality of a seizure is determined by "balanc[ing] the nature and quality of the intrusion on the individual's Fourth Amendment interests against the importance of the governmental interests alleged to justify the intrusion." Even in domestic law enforcement operations, the Court has noted that "[w]here the officer has probable cause to believe that the suspect poses a threat of serious physical harm, either to the officer or to others, it is not constitutionally unreasonable to prevent escape by using deadly force." Thus, "if the suspect threatens the officer with a weapon or there is probable cause to believe that he has committed a crime involving the infliction or threatened infliction of serious physical harm, deadly force may be used if necessary to prevent escape, and if, where feasible, some warning has been given."

At least in circumstances where the targeted person is an operational leader of an enemy force and an informed, high-level U.S. Government official has determined that the individual poses an imminent threat of violent attack against the United States, and those conducting the operation would carry out the operation only if capture were infeasible, the use of lethal force would not violate the Fourth Amendment. Under such circumstances, the intrusion on any Fourth Amendment interests would be outweighed by the "importance of the governmental interests [that] justify the intrusion" — the interests in protecting the lives of U.S. nationals.

Notably, although the three circumstances outlined above are sufficient to render a lethal operation against a U.S. citizen lawful under the circumstances described, they are not necessarily required. In particular, the three circumstances may not apply to operations that take place on traditional battlefields. Rather, the United States has concluded only that the stated circumstances would be sufficient to make lawful a lethal operation in a foreign country directed against a specific individual U.S. citizen.

———————

1. *Policy Shifts on Drone Warfare.* While the turn to drone warfare was dramatic under President Obama, its use decreased over time. Professor David Cole, writing in the summer of 2016, explained:

> It is . . . important to note that Obama's policy and practice of using drones have evolved significantly over the course of his presidency. His initial years in office were marked by an aggressive expansion of the drone program. In Pakistan, for example, according to the New America Foundation, President Bush oversaw forty-eight drone strikes, killing between 377 and 558 people,

whereas President Obama has overseen 355 strikes, killing between 1,907 and 3,067 people. But the number of drone strikes in Pakistan under Obama peaked at 122 in 2010, and has dropped every year since then. There were only ten strikes in Pakistan in 2015, and thus far only three in 2016. The number of strikes has also dropped in Yemen, from a high of forty-seven in 2012 to twenty-four in 2015 and nine thus far this year. In short, President Obama has shown significantly less proclivity to rely on drones in his second term than in his first.

David Cole, *The Drone Presidency*, N.Y. Rev. of Books (Aug. 18, 2016), at 19. The early months of the Trump Administration, however, have witnessed a return to a more aggressive policy. As of April 2017, according to Micah Zenko, a senior fellow with the Council on Foreign Relations:

During President Obama's two terms in office, he approved 542 such targeted strikes in 2,920 days—one every 5.4 days. From his inauguration through today, President Trump had approved at least 75 drone strikes or raids in 74 days—about one every day. These include three drone strikes in Yemen on January 20, 21, and 22; the January 28 Navy SEAL raid in Yemen; more than seventy strikes in Yemen since February 28; and one reported strike in Pakistan on March 1.

Micah Zenko, *The (Not-So) Peaceful Transition of Power: Trump's Drone Strikes Outpace Obama*, Council on Foreign Relations Politics, Power, and Preventive Action Blog (Mar. 2, 2017, updated), http://blogs.cfr.org/zenko/2017/03/02/the-not-so-peaceful-transition-of-power/.

2. *The Applicability of Due Process.* One of the more intriguing and perhaps surprising elements in the Obama Administration's legal framework on targeted killing is that it concedes that an enemy combatant on foreign soil who has taken up arms against the United States is still protected, if a U.S. citizen, by Fourth and Fifth Amendment rights. Not everyone agrees. Among the dissenters are two former Deputy Assistant Attorneys General in the Office of Legal Counsel, the already-discussed John Yoo, see John Yoo, *The Real Problem with Obama's Drone Memo*, Wall. St. J. (Feb. 7, 2013), https://www.wsj.com/articles/SB10001424127887323951904578288380180346300, but also Jeff Powell, who held his position during the Clinton Administration. Professor Powell writes:

In making war, the federal government is not governing the community, but defending it, and this fundamental shift in constitutional role is reflected in sound constitutional thinking. The Bill of Rights imposes limitations on domestic governance as part of the fundamental constitutional commitments to limited government and the protection of liberty, but those commitments are not in question when the government acts against those whom it cannot as a practical matter govern. The relevant constitutional commitment in that circumstance is to the principle that the federal government the power to wage war successfully. When the political branches are constitutionally authorized to direct the war powers against a citizen as an enemy, therefore, they are not subject to Bill of Rights constraints.

H. JEFFERSON POWELL, TARGETING AMERICANS: THE CONSTITUTIONALITY OF THE U.S. DRONE WAR 70 (2016). Professor Powell takes as key precedents a series of Supreme Court opinions involving the Civil War. For example, *Miller v. United States*, 78 U.S. 268 (1870), dealt with the question whether Congress could constitutionally authorize the summary seizure of railroad stock belonging to a Virginian who had adhered to the confederacy. Answering that question in the affirmative, the Court wrote:

> [I]f the statutes were not enacted under the municipal power of Congress to legislate for the punishment of crimes against the sovereignty of the United States, if, on the contrary, they are an exercise of the war powers of the government, it is clear they are not affected by the restrictions imposed by the fifth and sixth amendments. . . . The Constitution confers upon Congress expressly power to declare war, grant letters of marque and reprisal, and make rules respecting captures on land and water. Upon the exercise of these powers no restrictions are imposed. Of course the power to declare war involves the power to prosecute it by all means and in any manner in which war may be legitimately prosecuted. It therefore includes the right to seize and confiscate all property of an enemy and to dispose of it at the will of the captor. . . . The confiscation is not because of crime, but because of the relation of the property to the opposing belligerent, a relation in which it has been brought in consequence of its ownership. It is immaterial to it whether the owner be an alien or a friend, or even a citizen or subject of the power that attempts to appropriate the property. In either case the property may be liable to confiscation under the rules of war. It is certainly enough to warrant the exercise of this belligerent right that the owner be a resident of the enemy's country, no matter what his nationality. The whole doctrine of confiscation is built upon the foundation that it is an instrument of coercion, which, by depriving an enemy of property within reach of his power, whether within his territory or without it, impairs his ability to resist the confiscating government, while at the same time it furnishes to that government means for carrying on the war. Hence any property which the enemy can use, either by actual appropriation or by the exercise of control over its owner, or which the adherents of the enemy have the power of devoting to the enemy's use, is a proper subject of confiscation.

Id. at 304–306. Applying similar reasoning to the case of targeted killing, Professor Powell would argue that, in the context of a constitutionally authorized war, the government is permitted to exercise its war powers against citizen-enemies without respecting the constitutional rights that would apply if the same individuals were subject to domestic legal processes, such as a trial for treason. POWELL, *supra*, at 72.

Professor Powell does recognize a possible tension between his stance and a decision like *Hamdi*, which extended Fifth Amendment due process rights to a U.S. citizen alleged to be an enemy combatant. He gives *Hamdi* a limited reading, however, under which the only reason due process applied was that Hamdi was contesting the fact of enemy combatant status: "O'Connor's reasoning allows the treatment of a citizen as an enemy pursuant to the lawful exercise of war powers without regard to due process or other procedural guarantees in the Bill of Rights 'once it is sufficiently clear that the individual is, in fact, an enemy combatant.'" Id., at 76. Is that a persuasive reading? Recall that Nasser al-Aulaqi did not contest his son's classification as a "Specially Designated Global Terrorist."

3. *What Process is Due?* In referring to "a due process balancing analysis" as the basis for the constitutionally permissible legal targeting of a citizen-enemy, the 2016 White House Legal and Policy Framework Report is presumably basing its analysis on the three-factor approach set forth in *Mathews v. Eldridge*, 424 US 319 (1976), which was also the basis for the plurality opinion in *Hamdi*. Two of those factors—the government's interest in expeditious decision making and the individual's interest in avoiding an erroneous decision—undoubtedly balance each other out because both are surely at their weightiest. The third factor—the soundness of the decision making process in avoiding error—would thus be determinative. The closest thing we have to a publicly available description of that process appears in a 2013 Presidential Policy Guidance (PPG), entitled, "Procedures for Approving Direct Action Against Terrorist Targets Located Outside the United States and Areas of Active Hostilities." That document became public in 2016 following a FOIA suit brought by the American Civil Liberties Union. As summarized by reporter Charlie Savage:

> [The PPG] shows, for example, that the operational agencies of the National Security Council—meaning the Defense Department and the C.I.A.—may nominate someone for proposed killing after a review by their top lawyers.
>
> The National Counterterrorism Center then develops a report analyzing the intelligence about that person, and top lawyers across different security agencies deliberate over whether the person meets legal standards for attack.
>
> The process then goes to the "deputies committee," made up of the No. 2 officials at national security departments and agencies. They weigh such factors as whether it is feasible to halt the perceived threat short of killing a terror suspect, and the impact of a strike on "the broader regional and international political interests of the United States."
>
> The deputies make recommendations to their agency directors or department secretaries, who make up the "principals committee." If they unanimously agree—and if the target is not an American citizen—the strike can proceed with notice to the president. Otherwise, the president must make the decision.
>
> But the document also says the president may waive the rules in "extraordinary cases." It cites when there is a "fleeting opportunity" and no time to follow the full review procedures, or a proposal to kill a suspect who "poses a continuing, imminent threat to another country's persons."

Charlie Savage, *U.S. Releases Rules for Airstrike Killings of Terror Suspects*, N.Y. Times (Aug. 6, 2016), https://www.nytimes.com/2016/08/07/us/politics/us-releases-rules -for-airstrike-killings-of-terror-suspects.html?_r=0. It is notable that the PPG provides guidance extending much further than drone strikes: "The principal value of the release is that it reveals the extraordinarily detailed and comprehensive procedural requirements the President and Congress have established for all uses of force, including capture operations, against terrorist targets outside the United States and areas of active hostilities. I can't say for sure, but I suspect that there's never been anything, in any nation, quite like the interagency and interbranch review reflected here." Marty Lederman, *The Presidential Policy Guidance for targeting and capture outside Afghanistan, Iraq and Syria*, Just Security (Aug. 6, 2016), https://www.just security.org/32298/presidential-policy-guidance-targeting-capture-afghanistan-iraq -syria/.

Objectors, however, have asserted two possible grounds on which the *Mathews* functional approach, if operationalized entirely within the executive branch, might be categorically inadequate. One argument is that no procedure can count as due process that precludes any form of notice or opportunity to be heard before a neutral decision maker. Professor Powell takes this position, quoting *Hamdi*:

> "An essential principle of due process is that a deprivation of life, liberty, or property 'be preceded by notice and opportunity for hearing appropriate to the nature of the case.'" "[D]ue process requires a 'neutral and detached judge in the first instance.'" "For more than a century the central meaning of procedural due process has been clear: 'Parties whose rights are to be affected are entitled to be heard; and in order that they may enjoy that right they must first be notified.' It is equally fundamental that the right to notice and an opportunity to be heard 'must be granted at a meaningful time and in a meaningful manner.'" These essential constitutional promises may not be eroded.

Hamdi v. Rumsfeld, 542 U.S. 507, 533 (2004) (internal citations omitted).

The second argument asserts that constitutional due process must entail some form of judicial process: "[A]uthority from the preconstitutional and Founding eras supports the position that the phrase 'due process of law' at the time of the Fifth Amendment's ratification referred specifically to judicial procedures." Jane Y. Chong, *Targeting the Twenty-First-Century Outlaw*, 122 Yale L.J. 724, 735 (2012). As Ms. Chong details, scholars have offered a number of proposals for judicial involvement, including a post hoc *Bivens* action, trial in absentia, and some form of "targeted killing court," each of which has also been the subject of fairly obvious practical objections. She suggests as yet another alternative a proceeding based on the historical practice of outlawry—in essence, a process to declare targeted individuals beyond the protection of the law:

> At a conceptual level, modern-day outlawry proceedings amount to an uncommonly straightforward death-eligibility process. In a departure from

the legal norm, the death eligibility of the prospective target would turn not on his proven guilt but instead on his apparent recalcitrance, as evidenced by his failure to respond to the measures taken by each of the three branches. As a threshold matter, Congress would need to craft the outlawing process. In the case of a particular prospective target, the Executive could then initiate the process, while the courts would be charged with ensuring adherence to the process.

In more concrete terms, under an outlawry statute, the Executive would be able to exercise its traditional prosecutorial discretion in deciding whether and when to bring a special category of charges against suspected citizen-terrorists. Once the government has fulfilled, at minimum [specified] procedural protections . . . , a suspect's failure to submit himself to legal authorities would empower a court to issue a judgment of outlawry against him.

Meanwhile, the judiciary would hold the power to declare a citizen an "outlaw" based on a procedural definition of a legitimate target of lethal force: a suspect who refuses to submit to the legal process, as defined by a set of procedural requisites specified under statute, or perhaps left to the courts' design. This form of judicial review is most notable for what it would not involve: outlawry proceedings would not compel the judiciary to make real-time assessments of the threat posed by individual targets, to determine when the use of military force against such threats is justified, or to demand from the Executive comprehensive proof that use of lethal force is warranted.

Id. at 754–755.

Ms. Chong's creative proposal understandably raises a number of questions. Among them is the threshold issue whether due process can be satisfied by a potential target's waiver of his or her right to defend against a declaration of outlawry. Another, if Judge Bates's analysis of the political question doctrine is sound, is whether any judicial involvement in military targeting would be consistent with the separation of powers. A third is what the executive branch can or should do absent congressional authorization. Ms. Chong recognizes that her proposal would require Congress to enact a statutory process that does not now exist. If no court currently has jurisdiction to serve as an arbiter on targeted killing decisions, might that excuse the executive branch's exclusive reliance on internal decision making—or prompt the conclusion that targeted killing of U.S. citizens is simply not now a constitutionally available option?

For a proposal of judicial involvement modeled on the Foreign Intelligence Surveillance Court, see Samuel S. Adelsberg, *Bouncing the Executive's Blank Check: Judicial Review and the Targeting of Citizens*, 6 Harv. L. & Pol. Rev. 437 (2012). Former White House Counsel and Attorney General Alberto Gonzales, who remains closely identified with the counterterrorism policies of the George W. Bush Administration, has proposed a quasi-judicial process modeled on the Combatant Status Review

Tribunals, which would remain within the executive branch. Alberto R. Gonzales, *Drones: The Power to Kill*, 82 Geo. Wash. L. Rev. 1 (2013).

4. *OLC Advice.* As noted earlier, prior to publication of the 2016 White House Legal and Policy Framework Report, the Obama Administration's legal positions on counterterrorism issues were mainly discernible from official speeches, congressional testimony, and the occasional leaked document. One such document was an undated Department of Justice White Paper, leaked in 2013, entitled, "Lawfulness of a Lethal Operation Directed Against a U.S. Citizen Who is a Senior Operational Leader of Al-Qa'ida or an Associated Force." The document apparently was prepared to share with members of Congress. As it turned out, Attorney General Holder had previously offered much of its analysis in a 2012 address to the Northwestern University School of Law. It was not until a successful FOIA suit against the Justice Department brought by the New York Times and the ACLU, however, that the Administration finally released a redacted version of the July 2010 OLC opinion analyzing the legality of targeting al-Aulaqi. *N.Y. Times Co. v. U.S. Dep't of Justice*, 756 F.3d 100 (2d Cir.), *opinion amended on denial of reh'g*, 758 F.3d 436 (2d Cir. 2014), *supplemented*, 762 F.3d 233 (2d Cir. 2014). See Office of Legal Counsel, Applicability of Federal Criminal Laws and the Constitution to Contemplated Lethal Operations Against Shaykh Anwar al-Aulaqi (July 16, 2010), https://fas.org/irp/agency/doj/olc/aulaqi.pdf. It now seems clear that the 2013 White Paper was largely based on the 2010 opinion, which is, in turn, reflected in the 2016 White House Report. Much of the analysis is statutory, but perhaps its most revealing detail is its date, nearly a year before the first unsuccessful attempt to kill al-Aulaqi.

5. *Oversight and Accountability: Elected Branches.* Debates over both the legality and moral legitimacy of drone strikes during the Obama Administration were of course made more complex and speculative by the secrecy surrounding drone policy. As of 2013, one commentator voiced a common perception in writing: "The main obstacle to acknowledging the scope, legality, and oversight of U.S. targeted killings beyond traditional or 'hot' battlefields [was] the division of lead executive authority between the Joint Special Operations Command (JSOC)—a subunit of the Department of Defense (DOD) Special Operations Command—and the Central Intelligence Agency (CIA)." Micah Zenko, Transferring CIA Drone Strikes to the Pentagon (Council on Foreign Relations Policy Innovation Memorandum No. 31, Apr. 2013), http://www.cfr.org/drones/transferring-cia-drone-strikes-pentagon/p30434. News reports suggested that, as early as 2011, President Obama sought to shift more operational control to the Pentagon, a move that he sought to accelerate in 2013 with the help of his 2008 election opponent, Sen. John McCain (R-AZ). Senator McCain was quoted as saying that the move "would be a nice, first measure to assure the American people that there is sufficient oversight of who we are going to kill and not kill." Carlo Muñoz, *McCain: Senate to tee up armed drone ops in defense authorization debate*, The Hill (July 31, 2013), http://thehill.com/policy/defense/314737-mccain-senate-to-tee-up-armed-drone-ops-in-defense-authorization-debate. By the

end of the Obama Administration, the shift seemed to have gained traction, as evidenced perhaps by the declining number of CIA-directed strikes.

If the change yields any difference in transparency, it might be because of a stronger norm of openness in the Defense Department or because, if a drone strike represents a covert action under 50 U.S.C. § 3093(e), official reporting is likely to be limited to Congress. It is by no means clear, however, that the transfer really portends significant changes in terms of overall accountability. First, it appears that, irrespective of who is in charge of the operation, the drone is operated by Air Force personnel. Moreover, Professor Goldsmith has argued that "the Intelligence Committees are much more informed about CIA drone strikes than the Armed Services Committees are about DOD drone strikes, and appear to exercise more rigorous oversight." Jack Goldsmith, *Questions About CIA v. DOD Drone Strikes*, LAWFARE (May 13, 2014), https://www.lawfareblog.com/questions-about-cia-v-dod-drone -strikes. He likewise argues that the CIA has a record of fewer targeting mistakes. The most important point, however, may be the drone warfare is now such a well-integrated operation between the Defense Department and the CIA that even a transfer of responsibility to Defense hardly betokens a reduced role for CIA involvement. Rather, it is likely that the CIA remains "a central component of an overall system in which the strike itself is simply the apex of a complicated intelligence collection-and-analysis process." Robert Chesney, *Shift to JSOC on Drone Strikes Does Not Mean CIA Has Been Sidelined*, LAWFARE (June 16, 2016), https://www.lawfareblog.com/shift-jsoc -drone-strikes-does-not-mean-cia-has-been-sidelined.

Perhaps unsurprisingly, the Trump Administration may be giving renewed leeway to the CIA to conduct drone strikes, although the scope of the new policy, as of spring, 2017, is not clear. Gordon Lubold and Shane Harris, *Trump Broadens CIA Powers, Allows Deadly Drone Strikes*, Wall St. J. (Mar. 13, 2017), https://www.wsj.com/ articles/trump-gave-cia-power-to-launch-drone-strikes-1489444374. According to reporters Lubold and Harris, this could make a difference in targeting practice: "Both agencies take steps to determine the validity of targets before striking. When it comes to vetting targets, the CIA uses a higher, or 'near certainty,' standard, while the Defense Department relies on 'reasonable certainty' in war zones, though it adheres to the higher standard when operating elsewhere." Professor Chesney has summarized other potential impacts of any responsibility shift as follows:

1. CIA drone strikes take place under color of Title 50, and official public statements about the consequences of particular strikes accordingly are difficult to make and cannot be done as a matter of course. Identical operations conducted by JSOC under color of Title 10 don't pose this problem. Of course, it's not clear that the Trump administration will continue Obama-era policies pursuant to which the government will take advantage of this freedom in order to make such disclosures.

2. Some host governments will tolerate a CIA presence but not a military presence.

3. Even under a policy forbidding CIA from playing the trigger-pulling role, the CIA will remain a significant if not dominant part of the kill chain because of the central role played by intelligence collection and analysis in that kill chain. The fight over who pulls the trigger, from this point of view, concerns which type of official is in a position at the final moment to apply distinction and proportionality principles to the evolving fact pattern. In that respect, recall the quote above regarding the stricter deliberative standard CIA reportedly applies.

Robert Chesney, *A Revived CIA Drone Strike Program? Comments on the New Policy,* LAWFARE (Mar. 14, 2017), https://www.lawfareblog.com/revived-cia-drone-strike-program-comments-new-policy.

For its part, Congress did, in the National Defense Authorization Act for Fiscal Year 2014, adopt a new provision for Title 50 to systematize congressional committee oversight of "kill/capture missions" outside a theater of major hostilities. As amended in late 2016, 50 U.S.C. § 130f now requires: "[t]he Secretary of Defense [to] promptly submit to the congressional defense committees notice in writing of any sensitive military operation conducted under this title no later than 48 hours following such operation." That section defines "sensitive military operation" to include "(1) A lethal operation or capture operation—conducted by the armed forces outside a declared theater of active armed conflict."

6. *Unintended Killings.* The White House framework carefully refers to the strike against Anwar al-Aulaqi as the Administration's "only specific, targeted strike against an identified U.S. citizen," it is known that U.S. strikes since 2010 have killed at least seven other Americans, including al-Aulaqi's son, Abdulrahman al-Aulaqi, and a Taliban hostage killed by accident, Warren Weinstein. Indeed, the Administration also acknowledged over the years that drone strikes inadvertently killed a far larger number of civilians, although estimates vary from dozens to over 1,000, in part because the category of "civilian" may be contested. Reacting to this concern, President Obama issued "United States Policy on Pre- and Post-Strike Measures to Address Civilian Casualties in U.S. Operations Involving the Use of Force," Exec. Order No. 13732, 81 Fed. 44485 (2016). The Order both directs certain measures be taken in an effort to minimize civilian casualties, but also requires annual reports by the Director of National Intelligence "or such other official as the President may designate, . . . about the number of strikes undertaken by the U.S. Government against terrorist targets outside areas of active hostilities . . , as well as assessments of combatant and non-combatant deaths resulting from those strikes, and publicly release an unclassified summary of such information . . . ." As of May 1, 2017, however, the release date specified for the first such report, none had issued. The Trump Administration has not announced whether it will follow the order.

7. *International Law.* The United States has taken the position that its drone strikes are permissible under international, as well as domestic law because (a) they are undertaken as measures in national self-defense and (b) they are undertaken in other countries either (1) with their consent or (2) because the country involved (chiefly,

Syria) is unwilling or unable to assist the U.S. in support of our self-defense. (Intriguingly, the 2016 White House Legal and Policy Framework Report does not discuss Pakistan in this respect, and Pakistan has generally been reluctant to acknowledge its consent to U.S. operations; former President Pervez Musharraf, however, acknowledged in a 2013 interview that his government gave such consent.) Of course, international law may be implicated not only by the use of drones in general, but by the circumstances surrounding particular strikes, and questions about the adequate observance of the principles of distinction, proportionality, avoidance of unnecessary suffering, and military necessity. For a survey of the international law arguments, see Vivek Sehrawat, *Legal Status of Drones Under LOAC and International Law*, 5 Penn St. J.L. & Int'l Aff. 164 (2017). See also NYC Bar Association Comm. on International Law, The Legality Under International Law of Targeted Killings by Drones Launched by the United States (2014).

8. *Oversight and Accountability: Judicial Review.* In an extraordinary opinion, the D.C. Circuit rejected on political question grounds a suit brought under the Torture Victim Protection Act and the Alien Tort Statute by two members of a Yemeni family whose relatives were killed in a drone attack for which they were not the intended targets. *Ali Jaber v. United States*, No. 16-5093 (D.C. Cir., June 30, 2017). What is extraordinary is not the panel's unanimous legal conclusion, but rather the concurrence in her own opinion by Judge Janice Rogers Brown, a concurrence that decries in strong terms what she regards as the lack of adequate oversight and accountability regarding the use of drones:

> Theory holds that courts must apply the political question doctrine to circumstances where decision-making, and the constitutional interpretation necessary to that process, properly resides in the political branches of government. But theory often does not correspond with reality. The world today looks a lot different than it did when the Supreme Court decided Baker v. Carr, 369 U.S. 186 (1962). Our latest phase in the evolution of asymmetric warfare continues to present conundrums that seem to defy solution. Today, the Global War on Terror has entered a new chapter—in part because of the availability of "sophisticated precision-strike technologies" like drones. Philip Alston, *The CIA & Targeted Killings Beyond Borders*, 2 Harv. Nat'l Sec. J. 283, 441 (2011). Yet the political question doctrine insures that effective supervision of this wondrous new warfare will not be provided by U.S. courts.
>
> In other liberal democracies, courts play (or seem to play) a significant supervisory role in policing exercises of executive power. See Kristen E. Eichensehr, *Comment, On Target? The Israeli Supreme Court & the Expansion of Targeted Killings*, 116 Yale L.J. 1873, 1873 (2007) (noting the Israeli Supreme Court had authored the "world's first judicial decision on targeted killings," holding "terrorists are civilians under the law of armed conflict and thus are lawfully subject to attack only when they directly participate in hostilities"). In this country, however, strict standing requirements, the

political question doctrine, and the state secrets privilege confer such defer-ence to the Executive in the foreign relations arena that the Judiciary has no part to play. These doctrines may be deeply flawed. In fact, I suspect that technology has rendered them largely obsolete, but the Judiciary is simply not equipped to respond nimbly to a reality that is changing daily if not hourly. * * *

El-Shifa Pharmaceutical Industries Co. v. United States, 607 F.3d 836 (D.C. Cir. 2010) (en banc), sensibly holds that a court should not second-guess an Executive's decision about the appropriate military response—avoiding the need for boots on the ground, for example—to address a singular threat that might occur once or twice at widely separated intervals. Its doctrine, how-ever, seems a wholly inadequate response to an executive decision—deployed through the CIA/JSOC targeted killing program—implementing a standard operating procedure that will be replicated hundreds if not thousands of times.

Addressing these two markedly different scenarios through a shared legal framework is simply impossible, and yet it is precisely what our precedent demands. To the extent the military sees itself as merely continuing the war declared on the U.S. by other means, the drone program may take the war to the enemy. Thus, anyone who credibly represents a threat can be targeted, and, as when armies actually clash, a certain amount of collateral damage is inevitable. See id. On the other hand, CIA/JSOC signature strike activities are covert (at least until the missile finds its target) and intended to develop intelligence that allows the U.S. to anticipate threats to interests at home and abroad. The rules of that game are tacitly assumed to be unknown. Courts are ill-equipped "to assess the nature of battlefield decisions" or "to define the standard for the government's use of covert operations in conjunction with political turmoil in another country." *Al-Aulaqi v. Obama*, 727 F. Supp. 2d 1, 45 (D.D.C. 2010).

Of course, this begs the question: if judges will not check this outsized power, then who will? No high-minded appeal to departmentalism, arguing "each [branch] must in the exercise of its functions be guided by the text of the Constitution according to [that branch's] own interpretation of it," E. Burns, James Madison: Philosopher Of The Constitution 187 (reprinted 1968), changes the fact that every other branch of government seems to be passing the buck. The President is the most equipped to police his own house. See generally Akhil Reed Amar, American's Constitution: A Biography 60–63 (2005) (discussing the President's independent obligation to ensure his actions comply with the Constitution). But, despite an impressive number of executive oversight bodies, there is pitifully little oversight within the Executive. Presidents are slow to appoint members to these boards; their operations are shrouded in secrecy; and it often seems the boards are more interested in protecting and excusing the actions of agencies than holding them accountable. Congress, perhaps? But congressional oversight is a joke—and a bad one at that. Anyone who has watched the zeal with which politicians of one party go after the lawyers and advisors of the opposite party following a change of administration can understand why neither the military nor the intelligence agencies puts any trust in congressional oversight committees. They are too big. They complain bitterly that briefings are not sufficiently in-depth to aid them in making good decisions, but when they receive detailed information, they all too often leak like a sieve.

Our democracy is broken. We must, however, hope that it is not incurably so. This nation's reputation for open and measured action is our national birthright; it is a history that ensures our credibility in the international community. The spread of drones cannot be stopped, but the U.S. can still influence how they are used in the global community—including, someday, seeking recourse should our enemies turn these powerful weapons 180 degrees to target our homeland. The Executive and Congress must establish a clear policy for drone strikes and precise avenues for accountability.

Ali Jaber v. United States, No. 16-5093 (D.C. Cir., June 30, 2017) (Brown, J., concurring).

9. *Further Reading.* The literature on the legality, ethics and wisdom of U.S. drone policy is immense. In addition to works already cited, important volumes include Peter L. Bergen and Daniel Rothenberg, eds., Drone Wars: Transforming Conflict, Law, and Policy (2014); David Cortright, Rachel Fairhurst, and Kristen Wall, eds., Drones and the Future of Armed Conflict: Ethical, Legal, and Strategic Implications (2015); Hugh Gusterson, Drone: Remote Control Warfare (2016); and Jeremy Scahill and The Staff of The Intercept, The Assassination Complex: Inside the Government's Secret Drone Warfare Program (2017). The Lawfare Blog also hosts a bibliography of significant books and articles on targeted killing at https://www.lawfareblog.com/targeted-killing-resources -bibliography.

B. Congressional War-Making Authority and the "Long War"

The preceding discussions of presidential authority with regard to enemy combatants and targeted killing take as a premise that the United States is constitutionally engaged in warfare. Yet as the 2016 White House Legal and Policy Framework Report makes clear, the primary congressional authority for our military engagements in the Middle East and Africa still emanates from the 2001 and 2002 Authorizations to Use Military Force with regard to al-Qaeda and Iraq, respectively. As one human rights attorney has succinctly summarized the situation: "These two laws, passed more than 15 years ago to address specific threats, are now being used as legal cover for new conflicts that span numerous geographic locations and include many additional groups or 'associated forces'—a term that does not appear in the text of either AUMF." Heather Brandon, *An ISIS AUMF: Where We Are Now, Where to Go Next, and Why It's So Important to Get It Right,* JUST SECURITY (May 8, 2017), https://www.justsecurity.org/40549/isis-aumf-now-next-important/. The following excerpt from the White House report sets forth the justification of the Obama Administration (and presumably, so far, of the Trump Administration) for relying on these aging authorizations:

White House Report on the Legal and Policy Frameworks Guiding The United States' Use of Military Force and Related National Security Operations
December 2016

The Domestic Law Bases for the Ongoing Use of U.S. Military Force

A. Statutory Authorization: The 2001 AUMF . . .

1. The Scope of the 2001 AUMF

All three branches of the U.S. Government have affirmed the ongoing authority conferred by the 2001 AUMF and its application to al-Qa'ida, to the Taliban, and to forces associated with those two organizations within and outside Afghanistan.

In March 2009, the Department of Justice filed a brief addressing the question of the scope of the government's detention authority under the 2001 AUMF in litigation over detention at Guantanamo Bay. The brief explained that the 2001 AUMF authorizes detention of enemy forces as an aspect of the authority to use force. With respect to the scope of detention authority under the 2001 AUMF, the brief explained that the 2001 AUMF authorized the detention of "persons who were part of, or substantially supported, Taliban or al-Qa'ida forces or associated forces that are engaged in hostilities against the United States or its coalition partners, including any person who has committed a belligerent act, or has directly supported hostilities, in aid of such enemy armed forces." The brief stated that, in applying that standard, "[p]rinciples derived from law-of-armed-conflict rules governing international armed conflicts . . . must inform the interpretation of the detention authority Congress has authorized" in the 2001 AUMF.

In the National Defense Authorization Act for Fiscal Year 2012 (2012 NDAA), Congress expressly affirmed "that the authority of the President to use all necessary and appropriate force pursuant to the [2001] Authorization for Use of Military Force includes the authority for the Armed Forces of the United States to detain covered persons (as defined in subsection (b)) pending disposition under the law of war." In turn, subsection (b) of that Act defined a "covered person" as "any person" who either "planned, authorized, committed, or aided the terrorist attacks that occurred on September 11, 2001, or harbored those responsible for those attacks" or "who was a part of or substantially supported al-Qa'ida, the Taliban, or associated forces that are engaged in hostilities against the United States or its coalition partners, including any person who has committed a belligerent act or has directly supported such hostilities in aid of such enemy forces."

Similarly, the Federal courts have issued rulings in the detention context that affirmed the President's authority to detain individuals who are part of al-Qa'ida, the Taliban, or associated forces, or who substantially supported those forces in the armed conflict against them.

2. Definition of "Associated Forces"

As noted in the previous sub-section, all three branches of government have recognized that the 2001 AUMF authorizes the use of force against "al-Qa'ida, the Taliban, or associated forces that are engaged in hostilities against the United States or its coalition partners."

To be considered an "associated force" of al-Qa'ida or the Taliban for purposes of the authority conferred by the 2001 AUMF, an entity must satisfy two conditions. First, the entity must be an organized, armed group that has entered the fight alongside al-Qa'ida or the Taliban. Second, the group must be a co-belligerent with al-Qa'ida or the Taliban in hostilities against the United States or its coalition partners. Thus, a group is not an associated force simply because it aligns with al-Qa'ida or the Taliban or embraces their ideology. Merely engaging in acts of terror or merely sympathizing with al-Qa'ida or the Taliban is not enough to bring a group within the scope of the 2001 AUMF. Rather, a group must also have entered al-Qa'ida or the Taliban's fight against the United States or its coalition partners.

3. Application of the 2001 AUMF to Particular Groups and Individuals

Consistent with the above, the 2001 AUMF does not authorize the President to use force against every group that commits terrorist acts. Rather, the U.S. military is currently taking direct action against solely the following individuals and groups under the authority of the 2001 AUMF: al-Qa'ida; the Taliban; certain other terrorist or insurgent groups affiliated with al-Qa'ida or the Taliban in Afghanistan; AQAP; al-Shabaab; individuals who are part of al-Qa'ida in Libya; al-Qa'ida in Syria; and ISIL.

A determination was made at the most senior levels of the U.S. Government that each of the groups named above is covered by the 2001 AUMF only after a careful and lengthy evaluation of the intelligence concerning each group's organization, links with al-Qa'ida or the Taliban, and participation in al-Qa'ida or the Taliban's ongoing hostilities against the United States or its coalition partners. Moreover, the Administration also regularly briefs Congress about U.S. operations against these groups and the legal basis for these operations.

Although much of the intelligence underlying a determination that a group is covered by the 2001 AUMF is necessarily sensitive, many of these groups have made plain their continued allegiance and operational ties to al-Qa'ida. For example, this determination was made recently with respect to al-Shabaab because, among other things, al-Shabaab has pledged loyalty to al-Qa'ida in its public statements; made clear that it considers the United States one of its enemies; and been responsible for numerous attacks, threats, and plots against U.S. persons and interests in East Africa. In short, al-Shabaab has entered the fight alongside al-Qa'ida and is a co-belligerent with al-Qa'ida in hostilities against the United States, making it an "associated force" and therefore within the scope of the 2001 AUMF.

A particularly prominent group that the Administration has determined to fall within the ambit of the 2001 AUMF is the enemy force now called ISIL. As discussed below, Congress has expressed support for this action.

As the Administration has explained publicly, the 2001 AUMF has authorized the use of force against the group now called ISIL since at least 2004. The facts under-lying this determination are as follows: a terrorist group founded by Abu Mu'sab al-Zarqawi—whose ties to Osama bin Laden dated from al-Zarqawi's time in Afghan-istan and Pakistan before the September 11th attacks—conducted a series of ter-rorist attacks in Iraq beginning in 2003. These attacks prompted bin Laden to ask al-Zarqawi to merge his group with al-Qa'ida. In 2004, al-Zarqawi publicly pledged his group's allegiance to bin Laden, and bin Laden publicly endorsed al-Zarqawi as al-Qa'ida's leader in Iraq. For years afterwards, al-Zarqawi's group, which adopted the name al-Qa'ida in Iraq (AQI) when it merged with al-Qa'ida, conducted deadly terrorist attacks against U.S. and coalition forces. In response to these attacks, U.S. forces engaged in combat operations against the group from 2004 until U.S. and coalition forces left Iraq in 2011. The group has continued to plot attacks against U.S. persons and interests in Iraq and the region—including the brutal murder of kid-napped American citizens in Syria and threats to U.S. military personnel that are now present in Iraq at the invitation of the Iraqi Government.

The subsequent 2014 split between ISIL and current al-Qa'ida leadership does not remove ISIL from coverage under the 2001 AUMF. Although ISIL broke its affilia-tion with al-Qa'ida, the same organization continues to wage hostilities against the United States as it has since 2004, when it joined bin Laden's al-Qa'ida organization in its conflict against the United States. As AQI, ISIL had a direct relationship with bin Laden himself and waged that conflict in allegiance to him while he was alive. ISIL now claims that it—not al-Qa'ida's current leadership—is the true executor of bin Laden's legacy. There are rifts between ISIL and parts of the network bin Laden assembled, but some members and factions of al-Qa'ida-aligned groups have pub-licly declared allegiance to ISIL. At the same time, ISIL continues to denounce the United States as its enemy and to target U.S. citizens and interests. In these circum-stances, the President is not divested of the previously available authority under the 2001 AUMF to continue using force against ISIL—a group that has been subject to that AUMF for more than a decade—simply because of conflicts between the group and al-Qa'ida's current leadership. A contrary interpretation of the statute would allow an enemy force—rather than the President and Congress—to control the scope of the 2001 AUMF by splintering into rival factions while continuing to prosecute the same conflict against the United States.

As is also true with respect to the broader conflict against al-Qa'ida, the Taliban, and associated forces, Congress has repeatedly and specifically funded the President's military actions against ISIL through an unbroken stream of appropriations over multiple years. Shortly after announcing the military operation against ISIL in 2014, the President asked for and obtained from Congress $5.6 billion for the express purpose of carrying out specific military activities against ISIL in Iraq and Syria. Congress has since appropriated an additional $5 billion in support of the U.S. counter-ISIL effort, virtually all of it in line with the specific amounts and categories requested by the President. These funds were made available over the course of two annual budget cycles, in connection with close congressional oversight of the status and scope of U.S. counter-ISIL activities, and with knowledge of the specific measures the President was taking to counter ISIL and the statutory provisions under which he was acting.

Congressional support for the military campaign against ISIL extends beyond the appropriation of funds for specific military activities. Congress has also authorized the President to provide lethal and nonlethal assistance to select groups and forces fighting ISIL in Iraq and Syria. In doing so, Congress has defined the parameters of the assistance programs and provided specific direction for the use of its appropriations. Throughout this period, Congress has also reinforced its oversight role through reporting requirements relating to the costs and status of U.S. counter-ISIL operations, including monthly reports documenting incremental costs of the operation; quarterly reports on the status of U.S. forces deployed in support of the operation; regular reporting from the inspector general for the military operation against ISIL; and reporting consistent with the requirements in the War Powers Resolution. This reporting is in addition to information Congress receives from the Executive Branch during regular oversight hearings.

These funding, oversight, and authorizing measures convey Congress's support for the President's use of force against ISIL, including his determination that he had and continues to have authority to act under prior congressional authorizations for the use of military force.

In summary, the Executive Branch's decision that a group is covered by the 2001 AUMF is not taken lightly. That determination is made at the most senior levels of the U.S. Government, and it follows careful consideration and fact-intensive reviews by senior government lawyers and is informed by departments and agencies with relevant expertise and institutional roles, including all-source intelligence from the U.S. Intelligence Community. Finally, the fact that an al-Qa'ida or Taliban-affiliated group has not been identified as covered by the 2001 AUMF does not mean that the United States has made a final determination that it lacks the statutory authority to use force against the group. The United States remains prepared to review this question whenever a situation arises in which it may be necessary to take direct action against a terrorist group. . . .

V. Application to Key Theaters

This section of the report outlines the application of these key domestic and international legal principles to the six theaters identified at the outset—Afghanistan, Iraq, Syria, Somalia, Libya, and Yemen.

A. *Afghanistan*

. . . As a matter of domestic law, the 2001 AUMF authorizes U.S. counterterrorism combat operations in Afghanistan. Congress has also repeatedly authorized U.S. support for Afghan military forces. In the National Defense Authorization Act for Fiscal Year 2016 (2016 NDAA), for example, Congress extended authorization of the Afghanistan Security Forces Fund.

B. *Iraq*

. . . As a matter of domestic law, the 2001 AUMF and the 2002 AUMF authorize the U.S. use of force against ISIL in Iraq. As previously noted, Congress has supported the President's military actions against ISIL through an unbroken stream of appropriations. Among other actions it has taken, Congress has authorized the United States to provide "the military and other security forces of or associated with the Government of Iraq, including Kurdish and tribal security forces and other local security forces, with a national security mission, with defense articles, defense services, and related training to more effectively partner with the United States and other international coalition members to defeat ISIL."

C. *Syria*

. . . The 2001 AUMF and, in certain circumstances, the 2002 AUMF authorize the use of force in Syria against al-Qa'ida in Syria and ISIL; as previously noted, Congress has also supported this military campaign through an unbroken stream of appropriations. As previously mentioned, Congress has also authorized assistance to appropriately vetted Syrian groups and individuals for certain purposes. In the 2015 NDAA, for example, Congress authorized the Secretary of Defense, in coordination with the Secretary of State, to "provide assistance, including training, equipment, supplies, stipends, construction of training and associated facilities, and sustainment, to appropriately vetted elements of the Syrian opposition and other appropriately vetted Syrian groups and individuals."

D. *Somalia*

. . . As noted above, the 2001 AUMF authorizes counterterrorism combat operations in Somalia against al-Qa'ida and al-Shabaab.

E. *Libya*

. . . As previously described, the 2001 AUMF provides authority as a matter of domestic law for U.S. airstrikes in Libya against ISIL.

F. *Yemen*

. . . As discussed above, the 2001 AUMF confers authority to use force against AQAP. And, also as noted above, the October 12, 2016, strikes were taken to protect U.S.

vessels and personnel and were directed by the President pursuant to his constitutional authority as Commander in Chief and Chief Executive. Certain statutory authorities and the President's constitutional authorities as Commander in Chief and Chief Executive and to conduct the foreign affairs of the United States authorize the provision of limited support for counter-Houthi operations by the Saudi-led coalition.

---

1. *Iraq v. Everywhere Else.* The 2002 Iraq AUMF authorizes the President "to use the Armed Forces of the United States as he determines to be necessary and appropriate in order to — (1) defend the national security of the United States against the continuing threat posed by Iraq . . . ." The U.S. has consistently interpreted "continuing threat posed by Iraq" to encompass not only the threat posed by the Saddam Hussein regime, but also continuing threats to U.S. security posed in the aftermath of the invasion. Insofar as the 2002 AUMF is thus cited as authority for ongoing military operations in Iraq, this may not seem like much of a stretch. (It should be noted, however, that in June 2012, President Obama declared, "We've ended the war in Iraq," which might seem to complicate ongoing reliance on the 2002 statute. In 2014, the Administration's United Nations ambassador, Susan Rice, actually called for its repeal.)

Relying on the 2001 AUMF as authorization for the fight against the Islamic State (called "ISIL" in Obama Administration policy documents) seems more tenuous. As explained by one observer:

> In September 2014, the Obama Administration added ISIS to the list [of al-Qaeda-associated forces] even though . . . ISIS and al Qaeda "were literally at war with each other." . . .
>
> The 60-word AUMF actually had a fairly narrow target: those who "planned, authorized, committed, or aided the terrorist attacks that occurred on September 11, 2001 or harbored such organizations or persons" — namely al Qaeda and the Taliban. . . .
>
> As Charlie Savage [has] said . . . , "Clearly no one in 2001, when Congress authorized the use of force, was thinking about Syria." . . .
>
> The most significant expansions were made when the law was extended to "associated forces" — groups fighting "alongside" al Qaeda — despite this term never appearing in the authorization's text. Later, the Obama Administration extended the 2001 AUMF to ISIS. However, . . . ISIS was fighting against al Qaeda, so could not qualify as an associated force. So the administration claimed instead that ISIS fell under the 2001 AUMF's umbrella for a different reason: ISIS essentially was al Qaeda; the two groups were "one and the same." As then-Press Secretary Josh Earnest put it, ISIS was covered by the 2001 AUMF because it was "the true inheritor of Osama bin Laden's legacy."
>
> It is worth recalling that in 2014 when this claim was first made, national security law experts from both sides of the aisle were astounded. Before the

announcement, Ryan Goodman had noted the "remarkable consensus of opinion" among experts "that ISIS is not covered by the 2001 AUMF." Ben Wittes commented that extending the 2001 AUMF to ISIS "is not a stable or sustainable reading of the law." And Harold Hongju Koh considered a new AUMF to be the only "lawful way to fight the Islamic State" and prevent a "constitutional battle over the president's prerogative to conduct unilateral war."

Heather Brandon, *An ISIS AUMF: Where We Are Now, Where to Go Next, and Why It's So Important to Get It Right*, Just Security (May 8, 2017), https://www.justsecurity.org/40549/isis-aumf-now-next-important/.

How persuasive do you find the 2016 White House Report with regard to reliance on the 2001 AUMF? Is it significant that the Administration purported to rely on tenuous statutory authority as opposed to claiming inherent Article II authority?

2. Smith v. Obama [*now*, Smith v. Trump]. In May 2016, U.S. Army Captain Nathan Michael Smith filed suit in the U.S. District Court for the District of Columbia, seeking to declare the U.S. war against the Islamic State as illegal. The plaintiff's posture with regard to his suit was unusual because he was not opposed to the war. As explained by the trial court:

> Plaintiff is a U.S. Army Captain who was deployed, until recently, to the Kuwait headquarters of the Combined Joint Task Force-Operation Inherent Resolve. Operation Inherent Resolve is the designation the U.S. Department of Defense has given to the military campaign against the Islamic State of Iraq and the Levant ("ISIL") initiated by the United States and its allies in 2014. Plaintiff considers the operation to be a "good war" and "what [he] signed up to be part of when [he] joined the military." Nonetheless, Plaintiff seeks a declaration that Operation Inherent Resolve is illegal because Congress has not authorized it. Specifically, Plaintiff alleges that President Barack H. Obama has not sought Congress' authorization for military action against ISIL in accordance with the War Powers Resolution, and that neither the President's Commander-in-Chief power, nor prior Congressional authorizations for the use of force, give the President the authority to continue these actions. Plaintiff acknowledges that whether military action has been duly authorized is generally a question "Congress is supposed to answer," but complains that Congress is "AWOL." Plaintiff also claims that the Take Care Clause requires President Obama to publish a "sustained legal justification" for Operation Inherent Resolve to enable Plaintiff to determine for himself whether this military action is consistent with his oath to preserve and protect the Constitution.

Smith v. Obama, No. CV 16-843 (CKK), 2016 WL 6839357, at *1 (D.D.C. Nov. 21, 2016), *on appeal as*, Smith v. Trump, No. 1:16-cv-00843 (CKK) (D.C. Cir. 2017). Captain Smith's argument on the merits is based substantially on the War Powers Resolution, disputing, as he does, that the 2001 or 2002 AUMF authorizes the war against the Islamic State. His attempt to gain standing is based on his alleged quandary—citing *Little v. Barreme*—in having to decide whether to obey orders that the President is not authorized to give. The District Court, however, rejected Captain Smith's theory of standing and held the issue presented to be a nonjusticiable political question:

> With regard to the 2001 AUMF, the Court would have to determine whether the President is correct that ISIL is among "those nations, organizations, or persons" that "planned, authorized, committed, or aided the terrorist attacks that occurred on September 11, 2001, or harbored such organizations or persons," and that Operation Inherent Resolve represents "necessary and appropriate force" against that group. Pub. L. No. 107–40, § 2(a). With regard to the 2002 AUMF, the Court would have to determine whether the President is correct that operations against ISIL are "necessary and appropriate in order to . . . defend the national security of the United States against the continuing threat posed by Iraq." Pub. L. No. 107-243, § 3(a)(1). For the reasons set out below, the Court finds that these are political questions [because] the issues raised are primarily ones committed to the political branches of government, and the Court lacks judicially manageable standards, and is otherwise ill-equipped, to resolve them.

Smith v. Obama, No. CV 16-843 (CKK), 2016 WL 6839357, at *11 (D.D.C. Nov. 21, 2016). Are you persuaded? The D.C. Circuit heard oral argument in the case on October 27, 2017.

Note: Competing Proposals for an AUMF Regarding the Islamic State

Recognizing the controversies over its statutory authority for fighting the Islamic State—and with the usual presidential insistence that no new authority was necessary—the Obama Administration did forward to Congress proposed text for a new Authorization to Use Military Force. Several members of Congress offered their own proposals. In November 2014, two groups of national security scholars independently developed quite similar proposals for a new AUMF. The groups recommended that any new draft include at least the following six features:

- State a clear purpose for which force is being authorized;
- Clearly define the enemy, including a precise definition of "associated forces" (if force is authorized against associated forces at all);
- Include meaningful and specific reporting requirements;
- Require compliance with international law;
- Clarify that the ISIS AUMF provides the sole source of authority to use force against ISIS; and
- Include sunset dates for both the ISIS AUMF and the 2001 AUMF.

Brandon, *supra*. As you review the two drafts below, consider how well you think these points are covered.

Obama Administration Proposed AUMF
Against ISIL (2015)
JOINT RESOLUTION

To authorize the limited use of the United States Armed Forces against the
Islamic State of Iraq and the Levant.

* * *

- Whereas the terrorist organization that has referred to itself as the Islamic State
  of Iraq and the Levant and various other names (in this resolution referred to
  as "ISIL") poses a grave threat to the people and territorial integrity of Iraq and
  Syria, regional stability, and the national security interests of the United States
  and its allies and partners;

- Whereas ISIL holds significant territory in Iraq and Syria and has stated its intention to seize more territory and demonstrated the capability to do so;

- Whereas ISIL leaders have stated that they intend to conduct terrorist attacks
  internationally, including against the United States, its citizens, and interests;

- Whereas ISIL has committed despicable acts of violence and mass executions
  against Muslims, regardless of sect, who do not subscribe to ISIL's depraved, violent, and oppressive ideology;

- Whereas ISIL has threatened genocide and committed vicious acts of violence
  against religious and ethnic minority groups, including Iraqi Christian, Yezidi,
  and Turkmen populations;

- Whereas ISIL has targeted innocent women and girls with horrific acts of violence, including abduction, enslavement, torture, rape, and forced marriage;

- Whereas ISIL is responsible for the deaths of innocent United States citizens,
  including James Foley, Steven Sotloff, Abdul-Rahman Peter Kassig, and Kayla
  Mueller;

- Whereas the United States is working with regional and global allies and
  partners to degrade and defeat ISIL, to cut off its funding, to stop the flow of
  foreign fighters to its ranks, and to support local communities as they reject
  ISIL;

- Whereas the announcement of the anti-ISIL Coalition on September 5, 2014,
  during the NATO Summit in Wales, stated that ISIL poses a serious threat and
  should be countered by a broad international coalition;

- Whereas the United States calls on its allies and partners, particularly in the
  Middle East and North Africa, that have not already done so to join and participate in the anti-ISIL Coalition;

- Whereas the United States has taken military action against ISIL in accordance
  with its inherent right of individual and collective self-defense;

- Whereas President Obama has repeatedly expressed his commitment to working with Congress to pass a bipartisan authorization for the use of military force for the anti-ISIL military campaign; and

- Whereas President Obama has made clear that in this campaign it is more effective to use our unique capabilities in support of partners on the ground instead of large-scale deployments of

- U.S. ground forces: Now, therefore, be it

- *Resolved by the Senate and House of Representatives of the United States of America in Congress assembled,* That

SECTION 1. SHORT TITLE.

This joint resolution may be cited as the "Authorization for Use of Military Force against the Islamic State of Iraq and the Levant."

SEC. 2. AUTHORIZATION FOR USE OF UNITED STATES ARMED FORCES.

(a) AUTHORIZATION. — The President is authorized, subject to the limitations in subsection (c), to use the Armed Forces of the United States as the President determines to be necessary and appropriate against ISIL or associated persons or forces as defined in section 5.

(b) WAR POWERS RESOLUTION REQUIREMENTS. —

(1) SPECIFIC STATUTORY AUTHORIZATION. — Consistent with section 8(a)(1) of the War Powers Resolution (50 U.S.C. 1547(a)(1)), Congress declares that this section is intended to constitute specific statutory authorization within the meaning of section 5(b) of the War Powers Resolution (50 U.S.C. 1544(b)).

(2) APPLICABILITY OF OTHER REQUIREMENTS. — Nothing in this resolution supersedes any requirement of the War Powers Resolution (50 U.S.C. 1541 et seq.).

(c) LIMITATIONS. — The authority granted in subsection (a) does not authorize the use of the United States Armed Forces in enduring offensive ground combat operations.

SEC. 3. DURATION OF THIS AUTHORIZATION.

This authorization for the use of military force shall terminate three years after the date of the enactment of this joint resolution, unless reauthorized.

SEC. 4. REPORTS.

The President shall report to Congress at least once every six months on specific actions taken pursuant to this authorization.

SEC. 5. ASSOCIATED PERSONS OR FORCES DEFINED.

In this joint resolution, the term "associated persons or forces" means individuals and organizations fighting for, on behalf of, or alongside ISIL or any closely-related successor entity in hostilities against the United States or its coalition partners.

SEC. 6. REPEAL OF AUTHORIZATION FOR USE OF MILITARY FORCE AGAINST IRAQ.

The Authorization for Use of Military Force Against Iraq Resolution of 2002 (Public Law 107–243; 116 Stat. 1498; 50 U.S.C. 1541 note) is hereby repealed.

Consolidated Authorization for Use of Military Force Resolution of 2017

H.J. Res. 100, 115th Cong., 1st Sess. (2017).

IN THE HOUSE OF REPRESENTATIVES

April 27, 2017

Mr. Schiff (for himself, Mr. Carson of Indiana, Ms. Castor of Florida, Mr. Evans, Ms. Hanabusa, Mr. Hastings, Mr. Lowenthal, Mr. Moulton, Mr. Pocan, and Mr. Walz) submitted the following joint resolution; which was referred to the Committee on Foreign Affairs, and in addition to the Committee on Rules, for a period to be subsequently determined by the Speaker, in each case for consideration of such provisions as fall within the jurisdiction of the committee concerned

JOINT RESOLUTION

To authorize the use of United States Armed Forces against al Qaeda, the Islamic State of Iraq and the Levant (ISIL), and the Afghan Taliban.

Resolved by the Senate and House of Representatives of the United States of America in Congress assembled,

SECTION 1. SHORT TITLE.

This joint resolution may be cited as the 'Consolidated Authorization for Use of Military Force Resolution of 2017'.

SEC. 2. AUTHORIZATION FOR USE OF FORCE.

(a) In General. The President is authorized to use all necessary and appropriate force to protect the national security of the United States against the following:

(1) Al Qaeda, the Islamic State of Iraq and the Levant (ISIL), and the Afghan Taliban.

(2) Any organized and armed group that is associated with an entity described in paragraph (1) if such group is a co-belligerent with such entity in hostilities against the United States.

(b) Sunset Clause. The authority granted in subsection (a) shall terminate on the date that is 3 years after the date of the enactment of this joint resolution.

(c) War Powers Resolution Requirements. —

(1) Specific statutory authorization. Consistent with section 8(a)(1) of the War Powers Resolution, the Congress declares that this section is intended to constitute

specific statutory authorization within the meaning of section 5(b) of the War Powers Resolution.

(2) Applicability of other requirements. Nothing in this joint resolution supersedes any requirement of the War Powers Resolution.

SEC. 3. REPORTING AND NOTIFICATIONS.

(a) Reports Pursuant to This Joint Resolution. —

(1) In general. At least once every 90 days after the date of the enactment of this joint resolution, the President shall submit to the appropriate congressional committees and publish in the Federal Register a list of entities and organized and armed groups against which such authority has been exercised and the geographic location where such authority has been exercised.

(2) Additional information. In the case in which the authority granted in section 2(a) has been exercised against an organized and armed group described in paragraph (2) of such section, the President shall submit to the appropriate congressional committees a summary of the factual predicate for concluding that such group meets the requirements of paragraph (2) of such section.

(3) Form. Any part of the list required by paragraph (1) or the additional information required by paragraph (2) may be submitted in classified form if the President determines it is necessary to protect the national security of the United States. Any such information submitted in classified form shall be accompanied by unclassified written findings to support such a determination.

(b) Rule of Construction. The requirement to submit reports under subsection (a) is in addition to all other applicable reporting requirements under the War Powers Resolution or any other provision of law.

(c) Notification With Respect to Use of Authority To Deploy Ground Forces in a Combat Role.

(1) In general. If the President exercises the authority granted in section 2(a) to deploy ground forces in a combat role against an entity or organized and armed group, the President shall notify appropriate congressional committees at the earliest possible date after such deployment consistent with the national security interests of the United States.

(2) Modification or repeal of authority. A joint resolution introduced in the House of Representatives or the Senate on or after the date on which the appropriate congressional committees receive a notification from the President pursuant to paragraph (1) that provides for the modification or repeal of the authority provided in section 2(a) with respect to the deployment of ground forces in a combat role as described in such notification shall be considered in accordance with the procedures described in section 6 of the War Powers Resolution that are applicable to a joint resolution or bill introduced pursuant to section 5(b) of the War Powers Resolution.

(3) Definition. For purposes of this subsection, 'ground forces in a combat role' does not include special operations forces or other forces that may be deployed for purposes of training, advisory roles, search and rescue, intelligence gathering, ground support for air operations, or limited duration actions against high value targets.

(d) Appropriate Congressional Committees Defined. In this section, the term 'appropriate congressional committees' means—

(1) the Committee on Armed Services, the Committee on Foreign Affairs, and the Permanent Select Committee on Intelligence of the House of Representatives; and

(2) the Committee on Armed Services, the Committee on Foreign Relations, and the Select Committee on Intelligence of the Senate.

SEC. 4. REPEAL OF PRIOR AUTHORIZATIONS FOR USE OF UNITED STATES ARMED FORCES.

The following provisions of law are hereby repealed:

(1) The Authorization for Use of Military Force Against Iraq Resolution of 2002 (Public Law 107-243; 50 U.S.C. 1541 note).

(2) The Authorization for Use of Military Force (Public Law 107-40; 50 U.S.C. 1541 note).

———————

1. *Constraint or License?* Congress's enactment of proposals like these would obviously strengthen the legal legitimacy of military action against the Islamic State. Would a new AUMF operate, however, as a meaningful source of constraint on the President or open the door to even broader war? Professor Ryan Goodman warns of the latter:

> At present, the White House needs to be careful that it has congressional support with the actions it takes because it is already operating with a tenuous legal argument that it has the statutory authority to fight ISIS. Extending its actions to groups or even individuals that are only loosely connected to ISIS is difficult in the status quo, and will find a skeptical audience among federal judges if the issue arises, for example, in habeas litigation. With a new AUMF there will be less reason for President Trump to worry about the Hill and the courts. . . .

> [A]n "ISIS-specific" AUMF will very likely open the aperture for the administration to pursue, without returning to Congress, ISIS affiliates and "associated forces" who are not part of the group itself. The legal formula was created with respect to al-Qaeda and its associated forces, but there are important factual differences in the organizational structure of ISIS which risk a much more slippery slope than what we have seen in the past.

Ryan Goodman, *The Perils of a Congressional Authorization to Fight ISIS*, JUST SECURITY (Apr. 27, 2017), https://www.justsecurity.org/40346/perils-congressional-authorization-fight-isis/. Do you agree with Professor Goodman's risk assessment?

Do you see any way to avoid it? What if Congress enacted a statute that literally said no more than this: "The President is authorized to use all necessary and appropriate force against the Islamic State." See Jack Goldsmith, *The Practical Need for an ISIL AUMF*, Lawfare (Feb. 8, 2017), https://www.lawfareblog.com/practical-legal-need -isil-aumf. For a summary and comparison of the various AUMF proposals made so far, see Matthew C. Weed, A New Authorization for Use of Military Force Against the Islamic State: Issues and Current Proposals (Congressional Research Service No.R43760, 2017), available at https://fas.org/sgp/crs/natsec/R43 760.pdf.

2. *Legality or Dialogue.* Two significant scholarly works published during the Obama years argued, albeit in different ways, for judging the legitimacy of U.S. military engagements less by criteria of formal legality than by the quality of interbranch deliberation that preceded (and persisted during) those engagements. See Stephen M. Griffin, Long Wars and the Constitution (2013), and Mariah Zeisberg, War Powers: The Politics Of Constitutional Authority (2013). Zeisberg, a political scientist, puts the point as follows: "The availability of . . . textual, ideological, and institutional resources [created by the Constitution] for ordinary politics makes it appropriate to assess constitutional fidelity not only in terms of respect for a legal framework, but also in terms of officials' relationships to a structured politics that is created and sustained through constitutional language and institutions." Id. at 9. Griffin, a legal scholar, is explicitly reluctant to view presidential initiatives as "legal" or "illegal" if undertaken in contexts largely unguided by judicial decision making. But he finds in our post-World War II legal evolution the creation of a new "constitutional order" in which the political branches' interactions are failing to generate a practice of mutual testing and deliberation over war, "an ongoing institutional practice in which both branches are held accountable." Griffin, *supra*, at 5. Judged by a quality-of-dialogue standard, how do you assess the legitimacy of the current U.S. engagements against the Islamic State?

One of us has argued that, if the aim of our constitutional system is to generate inter-branch dialogue and accountability regarding the use of war power, we should not ignore the pressure for dialogue that comes from stressing that warfare must be *legal*:

> [H]aving the branches pursue their interaction in a more conspicuously legal frame would not only be appropriate as a matter of principle, but it could also help advance what I take to be each author's animating project, namely, revitalizing the elected branches' deliberative interactions regarding war making. . . .
>
> I would argue that instead of urging decision makers to regard themselves as part of a "nonlegalized" constitutional domain, we should want government actors habitually to understand their official behaviors with regard to war making as acts of legal obligation or legally delimited discretion. . . .
>
> A mutual commitment to the kind of legally framed, problem-solving negotiation regime I am advocating would do much to help restore the cycle of

accountability central to Professor Griffin's analysis. Framing interbranch negotiation as enacting a governing regime of law could function not as a distraction from politics, but as a rubric to motivate more responsible politics.

Peter M. Shane, *Constitutionalism and War Making*, 92 Texas L. Rev. 689, 704, 707, 709 (2014). What is your assessment?

3. *Back to Article II*? If Congress persists in not providing specific statutory authority for the U.S. fight against the Islamic State, is it inevitable that President Trump and perhaps successors will eventually just insist that they need no authority beyond Article II to deploy military forces as they fit? Would this make any practical difference? Professor Shane has argued that the public is better served when presidents assert the existence of statutory authority, even if tenuously, than if they rely on unabashed Article II arguments:

> My central claim is . . . that a President's relative modesty in asserting exclusive constitutional power does the public a major service by strengthening the ethos of accountability in the executive bureaucracy more generally. It buttresses [an] organizational psychology . . . in which government lawyers routinely impute constraining force to even broadly worded texts. In contrast, an executive establishment that views itself as having broad constitutional authority to work its will without regard to Congress is, I believe, far more likely to engage in arbitrary and ill-considered ventures than an Administration that speaks of itself as beholden in nearly all matters to congressional approval. A government of laws looks for such approval preferably in the form of positive law or at least in legislative acquiescence made manifest in some largely uncontroversial way. A president's rhetorical attentiveness to statutory constraint, even when counterintuitive, can reinforce these values.

Peter M. Shane, *The Presidential Statutory Stretch and the Rule of Law*, 87 Colo. L. Rev. 1231, 1260 (2015). What is your assessment?

C. Foreign Intelligence Surveillance After 9/11

1. FISA After September 11 and the Wall of Separation Problem

Hardly had the air started to clear after the disasters of September 11 than debate began on the apparent inability of the federal government to detect and prevent the worst terrorist attack ever launched in the continental United States. The Bush Administration immediately requested an expansion of its investigative authorities, arguing that enhanced powers were essential to forestall future such occurrences. Critics argued that legal restrictions on FBI and CIA activity had not been a factor in their pre-September 11 performance, and, further, that the enhanced authorities sought by the Justice Department—most of which had been advocated for many years prior to September 11—would not actually increase U.S. security.

The Justice Department succeeded in eliciting its sought-after amendments to FISA, which were incorporated into the Uniting and Strengthening America by Providing Appropriate Tools Required to Intercept and Obstruct Terrorism Act (USA PATRIOT) of 2001, Pub. L. No. 107-56, 115 Stat. 272. The key changes were these:

- As originally enacted, FISA required that the collection of foreign intelligence be "the purpose" of a FISA warrant. The USA-PATRIOT Act expanded the application of FISA to those situations where foreign intelligence gathering is merely "a significant" purpose of the investigation. 50 U.S.C. § 1804(a)(7)(B). "Significant" is not defined.

- FISA was amended to permit "roving wiretap" authority, which allows the interception of any communications made to or by an intelligence target without specifying the particular telephone line, computer or other facility to be monitored. 50 U.S.C. § 1805(c).

- The USA-PATRIOT Act made it easier to obtain pen register and trap and trace orders. The government can now obtain a pen register or use a trap and trace device "for any investigation to gather foreign intelligence information," without a showing that the device has, is or will be used by a foreign agent or by an individual engaged in international terrorism or clandestine intelligence activities. 50 U.S.C. § 1842(a)(1).[5]

Because of the controversy surrounding these expansions of investigative authority, Congress provided that they would "sunset" on December 31, 2005, unless extended. Most of the changes were, in fact, then extended in 2005 and 2006 on a permanent basis, although the "roving wiretap" authority was one of several that sunsets periodically. The authority currently extends to December, 2019.

To appreciate fully the significance of the first of these changes—making FISA warrants available when foreign intelligence information is not "*the* purpose" of the warrant but only "*a* significant purpose," it is necessary to understand that, as it originally implemented FISA, the Justice Department deemed this particular phrase to have a critical implication for the proper organization of foreign intelligence investigations. In particular, Justice took the view in the 1980s that this section signaled Congress's significant concern that the executive not use its new statutory investigative authorities to circumvent the standards that applied to ordinary criminal law enforcement investigations. As explained by one author, the point of the internal accountability system that FISA created within the Justice Department was "to assure the federal judge sitting in the FISA court that a national security wiretap was being

---

5. The devices that capture information about communications one initiates are called "pen registers." Devices that capture such information about communications people receive are called "trap and trace" devices.

sought for 'intelligence purposes' and for no other reason—not to discredit political enemies of the White House, not to obtain evidence for a criminal case through
the back door or a FISA counterintelligence inquiry." JAMES MCGEE, MAIN JUSTICE:
THE MEN AND WOMEN WHO ENFORCE THE NATION'S CRIMINAL LAWS AND GUARD
ITS LIBERTIES 318 (1996). In operation, where FISA required warrant applications to
represent "that the purpose of the surveillance is to obtain foreign intelligence information," the department effectively read "the purpose," to mean "the sole or at least
primary purpose."

This reading, in the Department's judgment, was buttressed by another feature of
FISA, the minimization procedures described in Chapter 6. In order to curb potential
abuses of FISA authority, the act required that, for all electronic surveillance, the
department develop "specific procedures, which shall be adopted by the Attorney
General, that are reasonably designed in light of the purpose and technique of the
particular surveillance, to minimize the acquisition and retention, and prohibit
the dissemination, of nonpublicly available information concerning unconsenting
United States persons consistent with the need of the United States to obtain, produce,
and disseminate foreign intelligence information." 50 U.S.C. § 1801(h). In reviewing an application for a FISA warrant, the FISC is required to review and approve
such minimization procedures.

The department concluded that (1) if the sole or primary purpose of a FISA warrant had to be the acquisition of foreign intelligence information and (2) if the Attorney General was to prohibit the dissemination of nonpublicly available information
derived from FISA searches, then, by statutory implication, (3) there had to be strict
limitations on the capacity of the FBI FI (foreign intelligence) and FCI (foreign counterintelligence) investigators to consult with members of the Justice Department's
Criminal Division, whose responsibilities revolve chiefly around the prosecution of
crimes.

The Justice Department codified this separation of functions in a set of guidelines
issued by Attorney General Reno on July 19, 1995, entitled, "Procedures for Contacts
Between the FBI and Criminal Division Concerning FI and Foreign Counterintelligence Investigations," which were expanded in some respects in 2000 and 2001. The
Justice Department notified the Foreign Intelligence Surveillance Court of these
procedures, and the FISC started including them as standard elements of the minimization procedures approved in connection with FISA warrant applications. These
procedures did not cut off consultation between the FBI and the Criminal Division,
but subjected such contents to the following rules:

> a. reasonable indications of significant federal crimes in FISA cases are to
> be reported to the Criminal Division of the Department of Justice;
>
> b. the Criminal Division may then consult with the FBI and give guid-
> ance to the FBI aimed at preserving the option of criminal prosecution,
> *but may not direct or control* the FISA investigation toward law enforcement
> objectives;

c. the Criminal Division may consult further with the appropriate U.S. Attorney's Office about such FISA cases;

d. on a monthly basis senior officials of the FBI provide briefings to senior officials of the Justice Department, including OIPR and the Criminal Division, about intelligence cases, including those in which FISA is or may be used;

e. all FBI 90-day interim reports and annual reports of counterintelligence investigations, including FISA cases, are being provided to the Criminal Division, and must now contain a section explicitly identifying any possible federal criminal violations;

f. all requests for *initiation or renewal of FISA authority* must now contain a section devoted explicitly to identifying any possible federal criminal *violations;*

g. the FBI is to provide monthly briefings directly to the Criminal Division concerning all counterintelligence investigations in which there is a reasonable indication of a significant federal crime;

h. prior to each briefing the Criminal Division is to identify (from FBI reports) those intelligence investigations about which it requires additional information and the FBI is to provide the information requested; and

i. since September 11, 2001, the requirement that OIPR be present at all meetings and discussions between the FBI and Criminal Division involving certain FISA cases has been suspended; instead, OIPR reviews a daily briefing book to inform itself and [the Foreign Intelligence Surveillance] Court about those discussions.

In re All Matters Submitted to the Foreign Intelligence Surveillance Court, 218 F. Supp. 2d 611, 619 (U.S.F.I.S.C. 2002), *rev'd*, *In re Sealed Case*, 310 F.3d 717 (U.S.F.I.S.C.R. 2002).

On March 2, 2002, however, Attorney General John Ashcroft issued a memorandum revoking the 1995 rules and significantly expanding the sharing of information between criminal investigation and foreign intelligence units. The memo provided: "The Criminal Division and OIPR shall have access to all information developed in full field FI [foreign intelligence] and FCI [foreign counterintelligence] investigations except as limited by orders issued by the Foreign Intelligence Surveillance Court, controls imposed by the originators of sensitive material, and restrictions established by the Attorney General or the Deputy Attorney General in particular cases." Memorandum from the Attorney General to the Director, FBI, et al., re: Intelligence Sharing Procedures for Foreign Intelligence and Foreign Counterintelligence Investigations Conducted by the FBI (March 6, 2002). The Department so notified the Foreign Intelligence Surveillance Court, which responded in an opinion—its first published opinion ever—rejecting the change as a legally insufficient implementation of FISA's implementation procedures. *In re All Matters Submitted to the Foreign Intelligence Surveillance Court*, 218 F. Supp. 2d 611, 619 (U.S.F.I.S.C.

2002). Nonetheless, the department relied on the Ashcroft memo in setting forth minimization procedures in a subsequent FISA warrant application. When the FISC predictably approved that application only upon the adoption of minimization procedures consistent with the 1995 memo, the Department brought its first appeal ever to the appellate panel constituted by FISA, the Foreign Intelligence Surveillance Court of Review (FISCR).The FISCR reversed. *In re: Sealed Case*, 310 F.3d 717 (U.S.F.I.S.C.R. 2002). That court determined, first, that FISA as enacted in 1978 did not actually require the separation of functions between criminal law enforcement and intelligence/counterintelligence operations that the Justice Department imposed. The court observed that the definition of "foreign intelligence information" would obviously include evidence of crimes "such as espionage, sabotage or terrorism." Further, in terms of protecting national security, the court accepted the Government's position that "arresting and prosecuting terrorist agents of, or spies for, a foreign power may well be the best technique to prevent them from successfully continuing their terrorist or espionage activity."

The court further discerned that the Department may have instituted its separation of functions in reaction to what the FISCR regarded as an improper reading of *United States v. Truong Dinh Hung,* 629 F.2d 908 (4th Cir. 1980). The Fourth Circuit there approved the exclusion of evidence obtained through warrantless surveillance because "the government's investigation became 'primarily' driven by law enforcement objectives," and, in the view of the Fourth Circuit, "the Executive Branch should be excused from securing a warrant only when 'the object of the search or the surveillance is a foreign power, its agents or collaborators,' and 'the surveillance is conducted "primarily" for foreign intelligence reasons.'" The FISCR noted, however, that *Truong Dinh Hung* was a pre-FISA case. Hence, its conclusion that warrantless surveillance was permissible only in investigations whose "primary purpose" was the gathering of foreign intelligence was a measure of the President's inherent constitutional power, not the scope of his power under FISA.

From this point of view, Congress's post-9/11 effort to liberalize the availability of FISA warrants took an ironic turn. The FISCR recounted the key changes intended to signal greater latitude for the Department:

> In October 2001, Congress amended FISA to change "the purpose" language in § 1804(a)(7)(B) to "a significant purpose." It also added a provision allowing "Federal officers who conduct electronic surveillance to acquire foreign intelligence information" to "consult with Federal law enforcement officers to coordinate efforts to investigate or protect against" attack or other grave hostile acts, sabotage or international terrorism, or clandestine intelligence activities, by foreign powers or their agents. 50 U.S.C. § 1806(k)(1). And such coordination "shall not preclude" the government's certification that a significant purpose of the surveillance is to obtain foreign intelligence information, or the issuance of an order authorizing the surveillance. *Id.* § 1806(k)(2).

310 F.3d at 728–729. Because, in the FISCR's view, the phrase "the purpose" had not actually been limited to a substantial, much less primary purpose, the new requirement of "a significant purpose" actually narrowed the grounds for FISA warrants: "The addition of the word 'significant' to section 1804(a)(7)(B) imposed a requirement that the government have a measurable foreign intelligence purpose, other than just criminal prosecution of even foreign intelligence crimes." Id. at 735.

Having thus construed FISA as amended, however, the FISCR went on to conclude that Attorney General Ashcroft was correct in thinking the Department had discretion to abandon the 1995 separation requirements in the formulation of its minimization procedures. Even if FISA warrants had to have the acquisition of foreign intelligence as a "measurable" purpose, that purpose still did not have to be "primary." Further, the entire thrust of the post-9/11 changes to FISA had been to encourage the integrated efforts of law enforcement and intelligence and counterintelligence investigators. In the view of the appellate panel, the FISC had thus simply overstepped its bounds in insisting on a separation of functions that the statute did not mandate. The FISCR's conclusion required it, however, to probe an additional issue: Given the difference between FISA warrant procedures and law enforcement warrant procedures under Title III of the Safe Streets and Omnibus Crime Control Act of 1968, would investigations pursuant to FISA warrants be constitutional under the Fourth Amendment if their "primary" purpose was, in fact, prosecutorial?

On this point, however, the FISCR turned somewhat Delphic. It started its analysis by indicating that the only difference between FISA and Title III warrants of potential constitutional significance would seem to be the standards for their issuance. Insofar as the Fourth Amendment simply demands that warrant applications receive prior approval from a "neutral and detached magistrate," the FISC would amply satisfy that requirement. As to whether FISA orders based on this different standard amount to constitutionally sufficient "warrants" in the Fourth Amendment sense, the FISCR said this:

> [T]o the extent the two statutes diverge in constitutionally relevant areas— in particular, in their probable cause and particularity showings—a FISA order may not be a "warrant" contemplated by the Fourth Amendment. The government itself does not actually claim that it is, instead noting only that there is authority for the proposition that a FISA order is a warrant in the constitutional sense. We do not decide the issue but note that to the extent a FISA order comes close to meeting Title III, that certainly bears on its reasonableness under the Fourth Amendment.

310 F.3d at 741–742. Of course, an affirmative answer to the question whether warrants based on the FISA standard meets the Fourth Amendment requirements—an answer one might have thought clearly implied by the *Keith* case—would have ended the FISCR's inquiry.

Instead, the FISCR advanced two alternative conclusions to support the constitutionality of using FISA warrants where a "significant" purpose of the search is the gathering of foreign intelligence information, even if the "primary" purpose is prosecutorial. One conclusion appears to be that the President has constitutional authority to conduct warrantless surveillance for national security purposes and "FISA could not encroach on the President's constitutional power." Id. at 742. The second is that the Supreme Court has approved warrantless searches "designed to serve the government's 'special needs, beyond the normal need for law enforcement.'" Id. at 745. The court then took "FISA's general programmatic purpose, to protect the nation against terrorists and espionage threats directed by foreign powers" to represent a "special need" that justifies searches that meet the standard of "reasonableness," even if not based on a warrant meeting Fourth Amendment probable cause standards. What is puzzling about the FISCR's disquisition on these points is that the court seemed to think they operate in tandem to justify its bottom line, even though either conclusion, if correct, would seem sufficient all by itself to justify the FISCR's determination that FISA searches are reasonable even when primarily prosecutorial in intent. In any event, a subsequent ruling of the FISCR explicitly interprets *In re Sealed Case* as confirming the existence of a "foreign intelligence exception" to the warrant requirement, at least where surveillance is directed at a foreign power or agent of a foreign power reasonably believed to be located outside the United States. *In re Directives Pursuant to Section 105B of the Foreign Intelligence Surveillance Act*, 551 F.3d 1004, 1011–12 (FISCR 2008).

The FISCR opinion in *In re Sealed Case* left unresolved important questions of both law and policy. The court seemed to regard the judicial imposition of any mandatory separation of criminal and intelligence functions as being not merely unwarranted, but unconstitutional. It refers, at one point, to "the impropriety of an Article III court imposing such organizational strictures." Id. at 743. If Congress were actually persuaded that the Justice Department's approach to separation of functions in the 1990s was the preferable approach, would it have authority to impose a separation of functions by statute?

As for policy, imagine that you are the next Attorney General and now understand that the FISC cannot mandate any particular internal Justice Department process for organizing FI and FCI investigations. Would you adopt the Reno or Ashcroft approaches, or something in between? In your judgment, do the forms of interaction between the criminal and intelligence sides of Justice allowed by the Reno guidelines exclude possible avenues of collaboration that you think are important? Conversely, did the Ashcroft approach relax any degree of internal constraint that you think might be important in forestalling the government's abuse of its foreign intelligence authorities? We will discuss below how the "wall of separation" problem has perhaps become more urgent with the enactment of further amendments to FISA.

2. Warrantless Surveillance Under George W. Bush, 2001–2007[6]

In enacting FISA in 1978, Congress made clear that it regarded its legislative handiwork as covering all permissible avenues for conducting the electronic surveillance of United States persons, whether for law enforcement or foreign intelligence purposes. Under 50 U.S.C. § 1809, FISA made any person guilty of a felony who "engages in electronic surveillance under color of law except as authorized by statute." FISA also amended 18 U.S.C. § 2511 to provide that "procedures [under Title III] and the Foreign Intelligence Surveillance Act of 1978 shall be the exclusive means by which electronic surveillance, as defined in section 101 of [FISA], and the interception of domestic wire and oral communications may be conducted." Against this legal background, a major controversy erupted in 2005 when it became known that the Bush Administration, since 2002, had been conducting an extensive program of foreign intelligence surveillance without warrants and, it appeared, without recourse to FISA. The full scope of that surveillance did not come to light, however, until 2013, when The Guardian began to publish a stream of news stories about NSA activities based on documents leaked by Edward Snowden, an employee of NSA contractor Booz Allen Hamilton.

a. Targeted Surveillance of Telephone and Internet Communications

September 11, for obvious reasons, prompted NSA's interest in substantially expanding its acquisition of telephony and Internet content that might reveal foreign intelligence information. On September 14, 2001, NSA Director General Michael Hayden "approved the targeting of terrorist associated foreign telephone numbers on communication links between the United States and foreign countries where terrorists were known to be operating." At first, calls originating in the United States were collected only if communicating with specified, pre-approved numbers, but this net was expanded. By September 26, because al Qaeda's leadership was in Afghanistan, General Hayden had determined that any Afghan telephone number in contact with a U.S. telephone number "was presumed to be of foreign intelligence value and could be disseminated to the FBI."

During this period, General Hayden was apparently in discussions with CIA Director George Tenet and the White House about the feared inadequacy of existing legal authorities to permit the kinds of expanded acquisition that could be useful in the wake of September 11. As a consequence, President Bush, on October 4, 2011, issued a secret memorandum entitled, "Authorization for Specified Electronic Surveillance

---

6. Portions of this section are excerpted from Peter M. Shane, *Foreword: The NSA and the Legal Regime for Foreign Intelligence Surveillance*, 10 I/S: J. L. & Pol'y for Info. Soc'y 259 (2014), which provides citations to all material quoted below.

Activities During a Limited Period to Detect and Prevent Acts of Terrorism Within the United States." As summarized in a 2009 report by the NSA Inspector General, leaked by Edward Snowden,[7] under the President's order:

> NSA could collect the content and associated metadata of telephony and Internet communications for which there was probable cause to believe that one of the communicants was in Afghanistan or that one communicant was engaged in or preparing for acts of international terrorism. In addition, NSA was authorized to acquire telephony and Internet metadata for communications with at least one communicant outside the United States or for which no communicant was known to be a citizen of the United States. NSA was also allowed to retain, process, analyze and disseminate intelligence from the communications acquired under the authority.

This authorization was subsequently modified from time-to-time depending, one presumes, on the White House's assessment of the scope of national security needs.

With regard to both telephony and Internet content, the acquisition permitted by the Bush order went beyond FISA in a number of respects. For example, certain communications originating or received in the United States might be intercepted without warrant even though they were unambiguously covered by the FISA definition of "electronic surveillance." The NSA could collect in the United States Internet content for foreign communications that simply "transited" U.S. electronic networks; thus, communications between foreign nationals might be intercepted in the United States if they were using an email service that resides on U.S. territory, even if the interception also captured content involving U.S. "communicants" having a reasonable expectation of privacy.

After the warrantless surveillance of electronic communications content was divulged in *The New York Times*, President Bush acknowledged in a December 17, 2005 radio address what the Administration called the Terrorist Surveillance Program (TSP). The Administration's description of that program, however, was limited to the interception of individual communications. A Congressional Research Service report helpfully quotes the Justice Department's public statement of January 27, 2006:

> The NSA program is narrowly focused, aimed only at international calls and targeted at al Qaeda and related groups. Safeguards are in place to protect the civil liberties of ordinary Americans.
>
> • The program only applies to communications where one party is located outside of the United States.
>
> • The NSA terrorist surveillance program described by the President is only focused on members of Al Qaeda and affiliated groups. Communications

---

7. Office of the Inspector General, National Security Agency Central Security Service, ST-09-0002 Working Draft (Mar. 24, 2009), available at http://www.aclu.org/files/natsec/nsa/20130816/NSA%20IG%20Report.pdf.

are only intercepted if there is a reasonable basis to believe that one party to the communication is a member of al Qaeda, affiliated with al Qaeda, or a member of an organization affiliated with al Qaeda.

- The program is designed to target a key tactic of al Qaeda: infiltrating foreign agents into the United States and controlling their movements through electronic communications, just as it did leading up to the September 11 attacks.

- The NSA activities are reviewed and reauthorized approximately every 45 days. In addition, the General Counsel and Inspector General of the NSA monitor the program to ensure that it is operating properly and that civil liberties are protected, and the intelligence agents involved receive extensive training.

Jeffrey W. Seifert, Data Mining and Homeland Security: An Overview 23–24 (Congressional Research Service Report No. RL31798, 2008). In a subsequent written statement for a Senate Committee on the Judiciary hearing, U.S. Attorney General Gonzalez defended the program and its accountability:

> The terrorist surveillance program targets communications where one party to the communication is outside the U.S. and the government has "reasonable grounds to believe" that at least one party to the communication is a member or agent of al Qaeda, or an affiliated terrorist organization. This program is reviewed and reauthorized by the President approximately every 45 days. The Congressional leadership, including the leaders of the Intelligence Committees of both Houses of Congress, has been briefed about this program more than a dozen times since 2001. The program provides the United States with the early warning system we so desperately needed on September 10th.

b. Telephone Metadata

A major part of what the Bush Administration left undisclosed was its bulk collection of what is typically called "telephony metadata," information identifying the calling and receiving devices involved in a communication and indicating the length of that communication, but not its content. Technically, however, most bulk collection did not fall within the confines of FISA. That's because, under Section 215 of the USA PATRIOT Act, Congress authorizes the FBI Director or a designee to seek:

> an order requiring the production of any tangible things (including books, records, papers, documents, and other items) for an investigation to protect against international terrorism or clandestine intelligence activities, provided that such investigation of a United States person is not conducted solely upon the basis of activities protected by the first amendment to the Constitution.

The application for such authority need only "specify that the records concerned are sought for an authorized investigation . . . to protect against international terrorism or clandestine intelligence activities." As it turns out, the Bush and Obama Administrations have relied on Section 215 to acquire telephone company records of the metadata concerning millions and millions of phone calls. Because the NSA did not acquire this information through government electronic surveillance, no limitations were imposed regarding the location of callers or participation of non-U.S. persons. The information is regularly collected by telephone companies for their own business purposes and was thus requested pursuant to the PATRIOT Act Section 215's authority for the acquisition of "tangible things," namely, business records. At one point during the Obama Administration, the NSA's Inspector General reported that the NSA "could gain access to approximately 81% of the international calls into and out of the United States through three corporate partners."

c. Internet Metadata

Until March 2004, telephone companies were also providing the NSA with metadata concerning Internet communications. In March 2004, however, the Justice Department's Office of Legal Counsel, under new leadership, determined that the collection of Internet metadata could not be squared with either FISA or the PATRIOT Act. Although no memorandum of its advice has been made public, two propositions probably led to this conclusion. First, because Internet metadata are not routinely kept by the cooperating companies, its acquisition would not fit under Section 215; collecting the metadata would amount to electronic surveillance. Second, because there was likely no way to exclude the collection of metadata regarding millions of emails from U.S. communicants, their bulk acquisition plainly violated the terms of FISA. In a much-publicized and dramatic episode, Attorney General Ashcroft, lying in a hospital bed, refused to sign off on President Bush's March 11, 2004 authorization for Internet metadata collection. The NSA initially continued the interception anyway, based on approval by White House Counsel, rather than the Attorney General. On March 26, 2004, however, President Bush temporarily discontinued the authorization for bulk Internet metadata collection.

3. The FISC and Congressional Responses: The 702 Programs

President Bush's acknowledgement of NSA warrantless content collection programs did not precipitate anything like the extended public discussion and systematic congressional investigations that preceded the enactment of FISA. Instead, the Administration proceeded to consult with the Foreign Intelligence Surveillance Court to develop rationales under which programs first developed under President Bush's 2001 order could be legitimated instead by orders of the FISC.

The first of these transitions actually occurred with regard to the Internet metadata program that had been suspended in March 2004. By July 2004, the Administration was able to secure from the FISC a "pen register/trap and trace" order to permit the Internet metadata collection: "[T]he order essentially gave NSA the same authority to collect bulk Internet metadata that it had under the PSP, except that it specified the datalinks from which NSA could collect, and it limited the number of people that could access the data." Orin Kerr, *Problems with the FISC's Newly-Declassified Opinion on Bulk Collection of Internet Metadata,* LAWFARE (Nov. 19, 2013), http://www.lawfareblog.com/2013/11/problems-with-the-fiscs-newly-declassified -opinion-on-bulk-collection-of-internet-metadata.

As for telephony metadata, on March 9, 2006, Congress enacted the USA PATRIOT Improvement and Reauthorization Act of 2005, which amended Section 215 to require only that the "records [pursued under that section] are sought for an authorized investigation . . . to obtain foreign intelligence information not concerning a United States person or to protect against international terrorism or clandestine intelligence activities." A FISC Order covering telephone metadata was instituted in May 2006, producing no reduction in metadata acquisition, limiting only who could access the data and requiring somewhat more stringent oversight.

The orders covering telephone and Internet content proved more complex because of the large volume of telephone numbers and email addresses — "selectors," in NSA parlance — that the NSA wanted to include. The documentation that the FISC demanded to justify the inclusion of specific selectors reduced the number of foreign addresses available from 11,000 to 3,000 and the number of domestic addresses to essentially just one. The unworkability of the FISC orders, especially for content, led the Administration in 2007 to seek amendments to FISA. Congress's initial, short-term solution was the Protect America Act of 2007. The PAA:

> authorized the Director of National Intelligence and the Attorney General to acquire foreign intelligence information concerning persons outside the United States for one year, if the acquisition involved the assistance of a communication service provider, custodian or other person, and a significant purpose of the collection was the acquisition of foreign intelligence information. The Act was set to sunset after 180 days, on February 1, 2008.

S. Rept. No. 110-209, 110th Cong., 1st Sess. 6 (2007). The PAA was highly controversial in a number of respects. For those skeptical of the TSP, the Act seemed to go too far in relaxing judicial oversight of electronic surveillance and creating loopholes through which warrantless surveillance might be directed at persons within the United States.

Congress ultimately replaced the PAA with the Foreign Intelligence Surveillance Act of 1978 Amendments of 2008. The Amendments accomplished a number of key things. Among its more controversial sections, it provided a path to immunity from liability for telecommunications companies that may have violated FISA by cooperating with Bush Administration surveillance programs between 2001 and 2007. Even more important for the future, however, Section 702 of the Amendments added a new title to FISA providing so-called, "Additional Procedures for Targeting Communications of Certain Persons Outside the United States," which were to remain in effect until December 31, 2012, but which have since been extended, but which were later extended until December 31, 2017, 50 U.S.C. §§ 1881a–1881g.

Under Section 702, when a targeted individual is reasonably believed to be outside the United States, the Attorney General may apply for an order approving the acquisition from that person of foreign intelligence information under conditions slightly more relaxed than those specified by 50 U.S.C. §§ 1804 and 1805. For example, if the targeted person is "an officer or employee" of a foreign power, they need not themselves be a "foreign power," or an "agent of a foreign power." Alternatively, when a targeted person is reasonably believed to be outside the United States, but the Attorney General wishes to conduct electronic surveillance of the target, or to acquire the target's stored electronic data or communications, within the United States, the Attorney General may seek an order from the FISC that not only approves the acquisition in question, but compels the cooperation of private "electronic communication service providers" in the acquisition.

The most dramatic new procedures, however, categorically allow the Attorney General and the Director of National Intelligence to institute legally authorized programs of surveillance of up to one year "of persons reasonably believed to be located outside the United States." Such programs do not require that targeted individuals be named to the FISC, but only that the Attorney General and the DNI certify that procedures are in place that are reasonably designed to limit surveillance to persons in general who are reasonably believed to be outside the United States, and that would prevent the intentional acquisition of communications among persons all of whom are known to be inside the United States. It is required also that minimization procedures be in place and that "a significant purpose" of the acquisition be obtaining foreign intelligence information. The Attorney General and DNI may jointly initiate such acquisitions even without judicial certification if they jointly determine "that exigent circumstances exist because, without immediate implementation of an authorization . . . intelligence important to the national security of the United States may be lost or not timely acquired and time does not permit the issuance" of a judicial order. These procedures essentially eliminate the documentation complexities that made the FISC's 2007 orders on content acquisition impracticable from NSA's point of view. The new Section 702 also appears to eliminate the statutory barrier to the collection of Internet metadata. Yet the Obama Administration reportedly shut down the program, for unspecified reasons, in 2011.

The Snowden leaks, together with subsequently declassified documents, revealed the scope of surveillance that Section 702 unleashed:

> Intelligence collection under Section 702 is conducted through two different programs. The first program, known as PRISM, collects communications from what are known as "edge providers," that is, companies that provide Internet content as opposed to Internet connections. The IC obtains access to edge provider communications after the Attorney General and the Director of National Intelligence issue directives, pursuant to guidelines approved by the Foreign Intelligence Surveillance Court, mandating that companies turn over certain information. After these directives are issued, a somewhat obscure branch of the FBI known as the Data Intercept Technology Unit

(DITU) coordinates with edge providers, on behalf of the NSA, to collect content such as emails, video chats, and social media posts. This content is then transmitted by the DITU to the NSA, which then disseminates it to other intelligence agencies.

In addition to PRISM, the IC also obtains information through a program called Upstream. Upstream collects "all e-mail and voice data flowing through the Internet 'backbone'—large fiber optic networks owned and operated by private companies like AT&T." The NSA's Special Source Operations (SSO) division partners with the corporate owners of these networks to gather data at certain key points, like at network routers or switches. The companies filter the data passing through these points according to directions they receive from the SSO, and this filtered data is then stored in NSA databases, from which it can be disseminated to other members of the IC. . . .

The scope of PRISM and Upstream cannot be overstated. These programs sift through massive quantities of data in an effort to find terrorist communications. in doing so, they are able to look at far more information than before in order to find the national security threat information they need.

Mieke Eoyang and Gary Ashcroft, *Why Electronic Surveillance Report is Necessary*, Lawfare (Feb. 28, 2017), https://www.lawfareblog.com/why-electronic-surveillance -reform-necessary. At one point, although PRISM gathers only information that is to or from a selector, Upstream would also collect information that is about a selector: "For example, if the NSA were targeting baddude@qaedamail.com, PRISM collection would only collect communications that were to or from that email address. However, Upstream, in addition to collecting such to or from communications, would also collect any communications that contained the email address baddude@qae damail.com, even if they weren't to or from that address." Id. In April 2017, however, the NSA acknowledged that it had stopped surveilling so-called "about" communications because it was inadvertently gathering too many communications from U.S. persons who were not actually in contact with foreign intelligence targets.

As this volume headed to press, a bipartisan group of House members had introduced a bill titled the USA Liberty Act that would simultaneously extend (through September 30, 2023), and amend parts of FISA, including Section 702. Not surprisingly, the proposal has generated intense debate whether the proposed amendments do enough to assuage concerns about mass surveillance. Much of the 2017 controversy seems to focus less on the national security uses of Section 702 searches, than on the government's ability without a warrant to review the raw communications collected pursuant to Section 702 for evidence of crime. With less than two months to go before the expiration of Section 702, it remains difficult to predict under what terms, if any, the authority will again be extended.

4. The Administration's Legal Defense for Ignoring FISA

The legal theories underpinning the TSP revealed in 2005 apparently underwent a considerable evolution between 2001 and 2007. OLC opinions written during the initial phase, from 2001–2003, remain classified; what we know about them appears most authoritatively through a summary prepared by an interagency Inspectors General report issued in July 2009. These opinions appear to have suggested that FISA was all but irrelevant to assessing the legality of the TSP because (a) the true source of presidential authority in this area is Article II, and (b) Congress is not empowered to limit the President's Article II powers. In 2003, however, the Justice Department took a new primary tack—relying chiefly on the Authorization to Use Military Force against al-Qaeda as a source of statutory authority for the TSP (although, as you will see, with an overlay of interpretive reasoning purporting to have constitutional roots). That defense was publicly presented for the first time in a December 2005 letter from Assistant Attorney General William Moschella to the leadership of the House and Senate Select Committees on Intelligence. Several weeks later, that position was presented in greater detail in a memorandum of unattributed authorship, entitled, "Legal Authorities Supporting the Activities of the National Security Agency Described by the President."[8] What follows are excerpts from the Inspectors General report and the Moschella letter:

Unclassified Report on the President's Surveillance Program
10–14 (July 10, 2009).[9]

DOJ Office of Legal Counsel (OLC) Deputy Assistant Attorney General John Yoo was responsible for drafting the first series of legal memoranda supporting the program. Yoo was the only OLC official "read into" the PSP from the program's inception in October 2001 until Yoo left DOJ in May 2003. The only other non-FBI DOJ officials read into the program during this period were Attorney General Ashcroft and Counsel for Intelligence Policy James Baker. . . .

In September and early October 2001, Yoo prepared several preliminary opinions relating to hypothetical random domestic electronic surveillance activities, but the first OLC opinion explicitly addressing the legality of the PSP was not drafted until after the program had been formally authorized by President Bush in October 2001. Attorney General Ashcroft approved the first Presidential Authorization for the PSP as to "form and legality" on the same day that he was read into the program.

---

8. U.S. Department of Justice, Legal Authorities Supporting the Activities of the National Security Agency Described by the President (Jan. 19, 2006), *reprinted in* David Cole and Martin S. Lederman, *The National Security Agency's Domestic Spying Program: Framing the Debate*, 81 Ind. L. Rev. 1355, 1374 (2006).

9. Pursuant to Title III of the Foreign Intelligence Surveillance Act Amendments of 2008, the report was prepared by the Inspectors General of the CIA and NSA, the Office of the Director of National Intelligence, and the Departments of Justice and of Defense. The report appears online at https://fas.org/irp/eprint/psp.pdf.

The first OLC opinion directly supporting the legality of the PSP was dated November 2, 2001, and was drafted by Yoo. . . . Yoo's . . memorandum focused almost exclusively on the activity that the President later publicly confirmed as the Terrorist Surveillance Program. Yoo acknowledged that FISA "purports to be the exclusive statutory means for conducting electronic surveillance for foreign intelligence," but opined that "[s]uch a reading would be an unconstitutional infringement on the President's Article II authorities. Yoo characterized FISA as merely providing a "safe harbor for electronic surveillance," adding that it "cannot restrict the President's ability to engage in warrantless searches that protect the national security." According to Yoo, the ultimate test of whether the government may engage in warrantless electronic surveillance activities is whether such conduct is consistent with the Fourth Amendment, not whether it meets the standards of FISA. Yoo wrote that "unless Congress made a clear statement in FISA that it sought to restrict presidential authority to conduct warrantless searches in the national security area—which it has not—then the statute must be construed to avoid such a reading. . . .

Yoo's memorandum also analyzed Fourth Amendment issues raised by the Presidential Authorizations. Yoo dismissed Fourth Amendment concerns regarding the PSP to the extent that the Authorizations applied to non-U.S. persons outside the United States. Regarding those aspects of the program that involved interception of the international communications of U.S. persons in the United States, Yoo asserted that Fourth Amendment jurisprudence allowed for searches of persons crossing the border and that interceptions of communications into or out of the United States fell within the "border crossing exception." Yoo further opined that electronic surveillance in "direct support of military operations" did not trigger constitutional rights against illegal searches and seizures, in part because the Fourth Amendment is primarily aimed at curbing law enforcement abuses.

Yoo also wrote that the activity described in the Presidential Authorizations was "reasonable" under the Fourth Amendment and therefore did not require a warrant. In support of this position, Yoo cited Supreme Court opinions upholding warrantless searches in a variety of contexts, such as drug testing of employees and sobriety checkpoints to detect drunk drivers, and in other circumstances "when special needs, beyond the normal need for law enforcement, make the warrant and probable-cause requirement impracticable." *Veronia School Dist. 47J v. Acton*, 515 U.S. 464, 562 (1995). Yoo wrote that in these situations the government's interest was found to have outweighed the individual's privacy interest, and that in this regard "no governmental interest is more compelling that the security of the Nation." *Haig v. Agee*, 435 U.S. 280, 307 (1981). According to Yoo, the activity authorized by the Presidential Authorizations advanced this governmental security interest.

Yoo's legal memorandum omitted any discussion of *Youngstown* . . . Yoo also discussed in his memoranda the legal rationale for Other Intelligence Activities authorized as part of the PSP. To the extent that particular statutes might appear to preclude these activities, Yoo concluded that "we do not believe that Congress may restrict the President's inherent constitutional powers, which allow him to gather intelligence necessary to defend the nation from direct attack."

––––––––––

Repudiation. As recounted in the Inspectors General report, the elevation of now-Harvard law professor Jack Goldsmith to head OLC following the confirmation to the Ninth Circuit of John Yoo's nominal superior, Assistant Attorney General Jay Bybee, began a reexamination of the entire body of OLC opinions supporting the Bush Administration's antiterror initiatives. In an extraordinary memo penned the week before he left office, Steven G. Bradbury, OLC's then-Principal Deputy Assistant Attorney General, acknowledged "that certain propositions stated in several opinions issued by the Office of Legal Counsel in 2001–2003 respecting the allocation of authorities between the President and Congress in matters of war and national security do not reflect the current views of this Office." OLC had "previously withdrawn or superseded a number of opinions that depended upon one or more of these propositions." Memorandum for the Files by Steven G. Bradbury, Principal Deputy Assistant Attorney General, Office of Legal Counsel re: Status of Certain OLC Opinions Issued in the Aftermath of the Terrorist Attacks of September 11, 2001 (Jan 15, 2009).

Among the propositions OLC repudiated was Professor Yoo's contention that Congress failed to include in FISA a clear statement "that it sought to restrict presidential authority to conduct warrantless surveillance activities in the national security area." According to Bradbury, "The proposition paraphrased above interpreting FISA and its applicability to presidential authority does not reflect the current analysis of the Department of Justice and should not be relied upon or treated as authoritative for any purpose."

The Bradbury memo recounted—and rejected—a further argument that appeared in a John Yoo memorandum of September 25, 2001. That memo apparently reasoned that, because the Government's post-9/11 interest in "preventing terrorist attacks against American citizens and property within the continental United States" implicated the "right to self-defense . . . of the nation and of its citizens," and because the courts had recognized that "deadly force is reasonable under the Fourth Amendment if used in self-defense or to protect others," it was appropriate to conclude that "[i]f the government's heightened interest in self-defense justifies the use of deadly force, then it certainly would also justify warrantless searches." Although Bradbury reasserted the possibility that national security searches might fall within the "special needs" justification for warrantless searches, he rejected the "lesser included" logic based on deadly force: "[T]he circumstances in which deadly force may be employed are highly fact-dependent and require a showing that the officer believed that the suspect posed an imminent threat of harm. The 9/25/01 FISA Opinion's assertion . . . does not expressly recognize that the circumstantial factors relevant to the . . . self-defense analysis are not necessarily the same as those that may determine the constitutional reasonableness of a particular search, both in its inception and in its scope."

Letter from William E. Moschella, Assistant Attorney General in charge of the Office of Legislative Affairs, U.S. Department of Justice, to Hon. Pat Roberts, Chairman, Senate Select Committee on Intelligence, et al.

(Dec. 22, 2005).[10]

Dear Chairmen Roberts and Hoekstra, Vice Chairman Rockefeller, and Ranking Member Harman:

. . . As described by the President, the NSA intercepts certain international communications into and out of the United States of people linked to al Qaeda or an affiliated terrorist organization. The purpose of these intercepts is to establish an early warning system to detect and prevent another catastrophic terrorist attack on the United States. . . .

Under Article II of the Constitution, including in his capacity as Commander in Chief, the President has the responsibility to protect the Nation from further attacks, and the Constitution gives him all necessary authority to fulfill that duty. See, e.g., *Prize Cases*, 67 U.S. (2 Black) 635, 668 (1863). The Congress recognized this constitutional authority in the preamble to the Authorization for the Use of Military Force ("AUMF") of September 18, 2001, 115 Stat. 224 (2001) ("[T]he President has authority under the Constitution to take action to deter and prevent acts of international terrorism against the United States."), and in the War Powers Resolution, see 50 U.S.C. 8 1541(c) ("The constitutional powers of the President as Commander in Chief to introduce United States Armed Forces into hostilities[] . . . [extend to] a national emergency created by attack upon the United States, its territories or possessions, or its armed forces.").

This constitutional authority includes the authority to order warrantless foreign intelligence surveillance within the United States, as all federal appellate courts, including at least four circuits, to have addressed the issue have concluded. See, e.g., *In re Sealed Case*, 310 F.3d 7 17, 742 (FISA Ct. of Review 2002) ("[A]ll the other courts to have decided the issue [have] held that the President did have inherent authority to conduct warrantless searches to obtain foreign intelligence information. . . . We take for granted that the President does have that authority. . . ."). The Supreme Court has said that warrants are generally required in the context of purely domestic threats. but it expressly distinguished foreign threats. As Justice Byron White recognized almost 40 years ago, Presidents have long exercised the authority to conduct warrantless surveillance for national security purposes, and a warrant is unnecessary "if the President of the United States or his chief legal officer, the Attorney General, has considered the requirements of national security and authorized electronic surveillance as reasonable." *Katz v. United States*, 389 U.S. 347, 363–64 (1967) (White, J., concurring).

---

10. The letter appears online at http://epic.org/privacy/nsa/olc_release1.pdf.

The President's constitutional authority to direct the NSA to conduct the activities he described is supplemented by statutory authority under the AUMF. The AUMF authorizes the President "to use all necessary and appropriate force against those nations, organizations, or persons he determines planned, authorized, committed, or aided the terrorist attacks of September 11, 2001, . . . in order to prevent any future acts of international terrorism against the United States." 5 2(a), The AUMF clearly contemplates action within the United States, See also id. pmbl. (the attacks of September 11 "render it both necessary and appropriate that the United States exercise its rights to self-defense and to protect United States citizens both at home and abroad").

The AUMF cannot be read as limited to authorizing the use of force against Afghanistan, as some have argued. Indeed, those who directly "committed" the attacks of September 11 resided in the United States for months before those attacks. The reality of the September 11 plot demonstrates that the authorization of force covers activities both on foreign soil and in America.

In *Hamdi* v. *Rumsfeld,* 542 U.S. 507 (2004), the Supreme Court addressed the scope of the AUMF. At least five Justices concluded that the AUMF authorized the President to detain a U.S. citizen in the United States because "detention to prevent a combatant's return to the battlefield is a fundamental incident of waging war" and is therefore included in the "necessary and appropriate force" authorized by the Congress. *Id.* at 5 18–19 (plurality opinion of O'Connor, J.); *see id.* at 587 (Thomas, J., dissenting). These five Justices concluded that the AUMF "clearly and unmistakably authorize[s]" the "fundamental incident[s] of waging war." *Id.* at 5 18–19 (plurality opinion); *see id.* at 587 (Thomas, J., dissenting). Communications intelligence targeted at the enemy is a fundamental incident of the use of military force. Indeed, throughout history, signals intelligence has formed a critical part of waging war. In the Civil War, each side tapped the telegraph lines of the other. In the World Wars, the United States intercepted telegrams into and out of the country. The AUMF cannot be read to exclude this long-recognized and essential authority to conduct communications intelligence targeted at the enemy. We cannot fight a war blind. Because communications intelligence activities constitute, to use the language of *Hamdi,* a fundamental incident of waging war, the AUMF *clearly und unmistakably authorizes* such activities directed against the communications of our enemy. Accordingly, the President's "authority is at its maximum." *Youngstown Sheet & Tube Co.* v. *Sawyer,* 343 U.S. 579,635 (1952) (Jackson, J., concurring); *see Dames & Moore* v. *Regan,* 453 U.S. 654, 668 (1981); *cf: Youngstown,* 343 U.S., at 585 (noting the absence of a statute "from which [the asserted authority] c[ould] be fairly implied").

The President's authorization of targeted electronic surveillance by the NSA is also consistent with the Foreign Intelligence Surveillance Act ("FISA"). Section 2511(2) (f) of title 18 provides as relevant here, that the procedures of FISA and two chapters of title 18 "shall be the exclusive means by which electronic surveillance . . . may be conducted." Section 109 of FISA, in turn, makes it unlawful to conduct electronic surveillance, "except as authorized by statute." 50 U.S.C. § 1809(a)(l). Importantly, section 109's exception for electronic surveillance "authorized by statute" is broad, especially considered in the context of surrounding provisions. *Sec* 18 U.S.C. § 251l(1) ("Except as otherwise specifically provided *in this chapter* any person who (a) intentionally intercepts . . . any wire, oral, or electronic communication[] . . . shall be punished . . . .") (emphasis added); *id.* at § 2511(2)(e) (providing a defense to liability to individuals "conduct[ing] electronic surveillance, . . . as authorized by *that Act[FISA]*") (emphasis added). By expressly and broadly excepting from its prohibition electronic surveillance undertaken "as authorized by statute," section 109 of FISA permits an exception to the "procedures" of FISA referred to in 18 U.S.C. § 2511(2)(f) where authorized by another statute, even if the other authorizing statute does not specifically amend section 2511(2)(f). The AUMF satisfies section 109's requirement for statutory authorization of electronic surveillance, just as a majority of the Court in *Hamdi* concluded that it satisfies the requirement in 18 U.S.C. § 4001(a) that no U.S. citizen be detained by the United States "except pursuant to an Act of Congress."

Some might suggest that FISA could be read to require that a subsequent statutory authorization must come in the form of an amendment to FISA itself. But under established principles of statutory construction, the AUMF and FISA must be construed in harmony to avoid any potential conflict between FISA and the President's Article II authority as Commander in Chief. Accordingly, any ambiguity as to whether the AUMF is a statute that satisfies the requirements of FISA and allows electronic surveillance in the conflict with al Qaeda without complying with FISA procedures must be resolved in favor of an interpretation that is consistent with the President's long-recognized authority.

The NSA activities described by the President are also consistent with the Fourth Amendment and the protection of civil liberties. The Fourth Amendment's "central requirement is one of reasonableness." *Illinois* v. *McArthur,* 53 1 U.S. 326, 330 (2001) (internal quotation marks omitted). For searches conducted in the course of ordinary criminal law enforcement, reasonableness generally requires securing a warrant. Outside the ordinary criminal law enforcement context, however, the Supreme Court has, at times, dispensed with the warrant, instead adjudging the reasonableness of a search under the totality of the circumstances. In particular, the Supreme Court has long recognized that "special needs, beyond the normal need for law enforcement," can justify departure from the usual warrant requirement. *Vernonia School District 47J v. Acton,* 5 15 U.S. 646, 653 (1995); *see also City of Indianapolis v. Edmond,* 531 U.S. 32.41–42 (2000) (striking down checkpoint where "primary purpose was to detect evidence of ordinary criminal wrongdoing").

Foreign intelligence collection, especially in the midst of an armed conflict in which the adversary has already launched catastrophic attacks within the United States, fits squarely within the "special needs" exception to the warrant requirement. Foreign intelligence collection undertaken to prevent further devastating attacks on our Nation serves the highest government purpose through means other than traditional law enforcement. *See In re Sealed Case,* 310 F.3d at 745; *United States* v. *Duggan,* 743 F.2d 59. 72 (2d Cir. 1984) (recognizing that the Fourth Amendment implications of foreign intelligence surveillance are far different from ordinary wire-tapping, because they are not principally used for criminal prosecution).

Intercepting communications into and out of the United States of persons linked to al Qaeda in order to detect and prevent a catastrophic attack is clearly *reasonable.* Reasonableness is generally determined by "balancing the nature of the intrusion on the individual's privacy against the promotion of legitimate governmental interests." There is undeniably an important and legitimate privacy interest at stake with respect to the activities described by the President. That must be balanced, however, against the Government's compelling interest in the security of the Nation. *see, e.g., Haig v. Agee,* 453 U.S. 280, 307 (1981) ("It is obvious and unarguable that no governmental interest is more compelling than the security of the Nation.") (citation and quotation marks omitted). The fact that the NSA activities are reviewed and reauthorized approximately every 45 days to ensure that they continue to be necessary and appropriate further demonstrates the reasonableness of these activities.

As explained above, the President determined that it was necessary following September 11 to create an early warning detection system. FISA could not have provided the speed and agility required for the early warning detection system. In addition, any legislative change, other than the AUMF, that the President might have sought specifically to create such an early warning system would have been public and would have tipped off our enemies concerning our intelligence limitations and capabilities. Nevertheless, I want to stress that the United States makes full use of FISA to address the terrorist threat, and FISA has proven to be a very important tool, especially in longer-term investigations. In addition, the United States is constantly assessing all available legal options, taking full advantage of any developments in the law.

Just as the Administration's initial public brief for its analysis took the form of a letter to Congress, the closest thing to a reply brief was likewise a letter to Congress, penned by 13 of the nation's most prominent constitutional law scholars, along with former U.S. district judge and FBI director William Sessions:

January 9, 2006 Letter from Scholars and Former Government Officials to Congressional Leadership in Response to Justice Department Letter of December 22, 2005[11]

Reprinted in 81 Ind. L. J. 1364 (2006).

Dear Members of Congress:

We are scholars of constitutional law and former government officials. We write in our individual capacities as citizens concerned by the Bush administration's

---

11. The signatories are Curtis Bradley, David Cole, Walter Dellinger, Ronald Dworkin, Richard Epstein, Philip B. Heymann, Harold Hongju Koh, Martin Lederman, Beth Nolan, William S. Sessions, Geoffrey Stone, Kathleen Sullivan, Laurence H. Tribe, and William Van Alstyne.

National Security Agency domestic spying program, as reported in *The New York Times*, and in particular to respond to the Justice Department's December 22, 2005, letter to the majority and minority leaders of the House and Senate Intelligence Committees setting forth the administration's defense of the program. . . .

[T]he Authorization for Use of Military Force (AUMF) against al-Qaeda, Pub. L. No. 107-40, 115 Stat. 224 (2001) . . . cannot reasonably be construed to implicitly authorize warrantless electronic surveillance in the United States during wartime, where Congress has expressly and specifically addressed that precise question in FISA and limited any such warrantless surveillance to the first fifteen days of war.

The DOJ also invokes the President's inherent constitutional authority as Commander in Chief to collect "signals intelligence" targeted at the enemy, and maintains that construing FISA to prohibit the President's actions would raise constitutional questions. But even conceding that the President in his role as Commander in Chief may generally collect "signals intelligence" on the enemy abroad, Congress indisputably has authority to regulate electronic surveillance within the United States, as it has done in FISA. Where Congress has so regulated, the President can act in contravention of statute only if his authority is *exclusive*, that is, not subject to the check of statutory regulation. The DOJ letter pointedly does not make that extraordinary claim.

Moreover, to construe the AUMF as the DOJ suggests would itself raise serious constitutional questions under the Fourth Amendment. The Supreme Court has never upheld warrantless wiretapping within the United States. Accordingly, the principle that statutes should be construed to avoid serious constitutional questions provides an additional reason for concluding that the AUMF does not authorize the President's actions here.

1.

Congress did not implicitly authorize the NSA domestic spying program in the AUMF, and in fact expressly prohibited it in FISA

. . . First, and most importantly, the DOJ's argument [concerning the AUMF] rests on an unstated general "implication" from the AUMF that directly contradicts *express* and *specific* language in FISA. Specific and "carefully drawn" statutes prevail over general statutes where there is a conflict. *Morales v. TWA, Inc.*, 504 U.S. 374, 384–85 (1992) (quoting *International Paper Co. v. Ouelette*, 479 U.S. 481, 494 (1987)). In FISA, Congress has directly and specifically spoken on the question of domestic warrantless wiretapping, including during wartime, and it could not have spoken more clearly.

As noted above, Congress has comprehensively regulated all electronic surveillance in the United States, and authorizes such surveillance only pursuant to specific statutes designated as the "*exclusive* means by which electronic surveillance . . . and the interception of domestic wire, oral, and electronic communications may be conducted." 18 U.S.C. § 2511(2)(f) (emphasis added). Moreover, FISA *specifically* addresses the question of domestic wiretapping during wartime. In a provision entitled "Authorization during time of war," FISA dictates that "notwithstanding any other law, the President, through the Attorney General, may authorize electronic surveillance without a court order under this subchapter to acquire foreign intelligence information *for a period not to exceed fifteen calendar days following a declaration of war by the Congress.*" 50 U.S.C.§ 1811 (emphasis added). Thus, even where Congress has declared war—a more formal step than an authorization such as the AUMF—the law limits warrantless wiretapping to the first fifteen days of the conflict. Congress explained that if the President needed further warrantless surveillance during wartime, the fifteen days would be sufficient for Congress to consider and enact further authorization. Rather than follow this course, the President acted unilaterally and secretly in contravention of FISA's terms. The DOJ letter remarkably does not even *mention* FISA's fifteen-day war provision, which directly refutes the President's asserted "implied" authority.

In light of the specific and comprehensive regulation of FISA, especially the fifteen-day war provision, there is no basis for finding in the AUMF's general language implicit authority for unchecked warrantless domestic wiretapping. As Justice Frankfurter stated in rejecting a similar argument by President Truman when he sought to defend the seizure of the steel mills during the Korean War on the basis of implied congressional authorization:

> It is one thing to draw an intention of Congress from general language and to say that Congress would have explicitly written what is inferred, where Congress has not addressed itself to a specific situation. It is quite impossible, however, when Congress did specifically address itself to a problem, as Congress did to that of seizure, to find secreted in the interstices of legislation the very grant of power which Congress consciously withheld. To find authority so explicitly withheld is . . . to disrespect the whole legislative process and the constitutional division of authority between President and Congress. *Youngstown Sheet & Tube Co.* v. *Sawyer*, 343 U.S. 579, 609 (1952) (Frankfurter, J., concurring).

Second, the DOJ's argument would require the conclusion that Congress implicitly and *sub silentio* repealed 18 U.S.C. § 2511(2)(f), the provision that identifies FISA and specific criminal code provisions as "the exclusive means by which electronic surveillance . . . may be conducted." Repeals by implication are strongly disfavored; they can be established only by "overwhelming evidence," *J.E.M. Ag. Supply, Inc.* v. *Pioneer Hi-Bred Int'l, Inc.*, 534 U.S. 124, 137 (2001), and "the only permissible justification for a repeal by implication is when the earlier and later statutes are irreconcilable,'" *id.* at 141–142 (quoting *Morton* v. *Mancari*, 417 U.S. 535, 550 (1974)). The AUMF and § 2511(2)(f) are not irreconcilable, and there is *no* evidence, let alone overwhelming evidence, that Congress intended to repeal § 2511(2)(f).

Third, Attorney General Alberto Gonzales has admitted that the administration did not seek to amend FISA to authorize the NSA spying program because it was advised that Congress would reject such an amendment. The administration cannot argue on the one hand that Congress authorized the NSA program in the AUMF, and at the same time that it did not ask Congress for such authorization because it feared Congress would say no.

Finally, the DOJ's reliance upon *Hamdi* v. *Rumsfeld*, 542 U.S. 507 (2004), to support its reading of the AUMF is misplaced. A plurality of the Court in *Hamdi* held that the AUMF authorized military detention of enemy combatants captured on the battlefield abroad as a "fundamental incident of waging war." *Id.* at 519. The plurality expressly limited this holding to individuals who were "part of or supporting forces hostile to the United States or coalition partners *in Afghanistan and who engaged in an armed conflict against the United States there.*" *Id.* at 516 (emphasis added). It is one thing, however, to say that foreign battlefield capture of enemy combatants is an incident of waging war that Congress intended to authorize. It is another matter entirely to treat unchecked warrantless *domestic* spying as included in that authorization, especially where an existing statute specifies that other laws are the "exclusive means" by which electronic surveillance may be conducted and provides that even a declaration of war authorizes such spying only for a fifteen-day emergency period.

2.

Construing FISA to prohibit warrantless domestic wiretapping does not raise any serious constitutional question, while construing the AUMF to authorize such wiretapping would raise serious questions under the Fourth Amendment

The DOJ argues that FISA and the AUMF should be construed to permit the NSA program's domestic surveillance because there otherwise might be a "conflict between FISA and the President's Article II authority as Commander-in-Chief." The statutory scheme described above is not ambiguous, and therefore the constitutional avoidance doctrine is not even implicated. But were it implicated, it would work against the President, not in his favor. Construing FISA and the AUMF according to their plain meanings raises no serious constitutional questions regarding the President's duties under Article II. Construing the AUMF to *permit* unchecked warrantless wiretapping without probable cause, however, would raise serious questions under the Fourth Amendment.

A. FISA's Limitations are consistent with the President's Article II role

We do not dispute that, absent congressional action, the President might have inherent constitutional authority to collect "signals intelligence" about the enemy abroad. Nor do we dispute that, had Congress taken no action in this area, the President might well be constitutionally empowered to conduct domestic surveillance directly tied and narrowly confined to that goal—subject, of course, to Fourth Amendment limits. Indeed, in the years before FISA was enacted, the federal law involving wiretapping specifically provided that "nothing contained in this chapter or in section 605 of the Communications Act of 1934 shall limit the constitutional power of the President . . . to obtain foreign intelligence information deemed essential to the security of the United States." 18 U.S.C.§2511(3) (1976).

But FISA specifically *repealed* that provision, FISA §201(c), 92 Stat. 1797, and replaced it with language dictating that FISA and the criminal code are the "exclusive means" of conducting electronic surveillance. In doing so, Congress did not deny that the President has constitutional power to conduct electronic surveillance for national security purposes; rather, Congress properly concluded that "even if the President has the inherent authority *in the absence of legislation* to authorize warrantless electronic surveillance for foreign intelligence purposes, Congress has the power to regulate the conduct of such surveillance by legislating a reasonable procedure, which then becomes the exclusive means by which such surveillance may be conducted." H.R. Rep. No. 95-1283, pt. 1, at 24 (1978) (emphasis added). This analysis, Congress noted, was "supported by two successive Attorneys General." *Id.*

To say that the President has inherent authority does not mean that his authority is exclusive, or that his conduct is not subject to statutory regulations enacted (as FISA was) pursuant to Congress's Article I powers. As Justice Jackson famously explained in his influential opinion in *Youngstown Sheet & Tube Co.* v. *Sawyer*, 343 U.S. at 635 (Jackson, J., concurring), the Constitution "enjoins upon its branches separateness but interdependence, autonomy but reciprocity. Presidential powers are not fixed but fluctuate, depending upon their disjunction or conjunction with those of Congress." For example, the President in his role as Commander in Chief directs military operations. But the Framers gave Congress the power to prescribe rules for the regulation of the armed and naval forces, Art. I, §8, cl. 14, and if a duly enacted statute prohibits the military from engaging in torture or cruel, inhuman, and degrading treatment, the President must follow that dictate. As Justice Jackson wrote, when the President acts in defiance of "the expressed or implied will of Congress," his power is "at its lowest ebb." 343 U.S. at 637. In this setting, Jackson wrote, "Presidential power [is] most vulnerable to attack and in the least favorable of all constitutional postures." *Id.* at 640.

Congress plainly has authority to regulate domestic wiretapping by federal agencies under its Article I powers, and the DOJ does not suggest otherwise. Indeed, when FISA was enacted, the Justice Department agreed that Congress had power to regulate such conduct, and could require judicial approval of foreign intelligence surveillance. FISA does not prohibit foreign intelligence surveillance, but merely imposes reasonable regulation to protect legitimate privacy rights. (For example, although FISA generally requires judicial approval for electronic surveillance of persons within the United States, it permits the executive branch to install a wiretap immediately so long as it obtains judicial approval within seventy-two hours. 50 U.S.C. §1805(f).)

Just as the President is bound by the statutory prohibition on torture, he is bound by the statutory dictates of FISA. The DOJ once infamously argued that the President as Commander in Chief could ignore even the criminal prohibition on torture, and, more broadly still, that statutes may not "place *any* limits on the President's determinations as to any terrorist threat, the amount of military force to be used in response, or the method, timing, and nature of the response." But the administration withdrew the August 2002 torture memo after it was disclosed, and for good reason the DOJ does not advance these extreme arguments here. Absent a serious question about FISA's constitutionality, there is no reason even to consider construing the AUMF to have implicitly overturned the carefully designed regulatory regime that FISA establishes. See, e.g., *Reno v. Flores*, 507 U.S. 292, 314 n.9 (1993) (constitutional avoidance canon applicable only if the constitutional question to be avoided is a serious one, "not to eliminate all possible contentions that the statute *might* be unconstitutional") (emphasis in original; citation omitted).

B. Construing the AUMF to authorize warrantless domestic wiretapping would raise serious constitutional questions

The principle that ambiguous statutes should be construed to avoid serious constitutional questions works against the administration, not in its favor. Interpreting the AUMF and FISA to permit unchecked domestic wiretapping for the duration of the conflict with al-Qaeda would certainly raise serious constitutional questions. The Supreme Court has never upheld such a sweeping power to invade the privacy of Americans at home without individualized suspicion or judicial oversight.

The NSA surveillance program permits wiretapping within the United States without *either* of the safeguards presumptively required by the Fourth Amendment for electronic surveillance—individualized probable cause and a warrant or other order issued by a judge or magistrate. The Court has long held that wiretaps generally require a warrant and probable cause. *Katz v. United States*, 389 U.S. 347 (1967). And the only time the Court considered the question of national security wiretaps, it held that the Fourth Amendment prohibits domestic security wiretaps without those safeguards. *United States v. United States District Court*, 407 U.S. 297 (1972). Although the Court in that case left open the question of the Fourth Amendment validity of warrantless wiretaps for foreign intelligence purposes, its precedents raise serious constitutional questions about the kind of open-ended authority the President has asserted with respect to the NSA program.

Indeed, serious Fourth Amendment questions about the validity of warrantless wiretapping led Congress to enact FISA, in order to "provide the secure framework by which the executive branch may conduct legitimate electronic surveillance for foreign intelligence purposes within the context of this nation's commitment to privacy and individual rights." S. Rep. No. 95-604, at 15 (1978) (citing, *inter alia*, *Zweibon v. Mitchell*, 516 F.2d 594 (D.C. Cir. 1975), *cert. denied*, 425 U.S. 944 (1976), in which the court of appeals held that a warrant must be obtained before a wiretap is installed on a domestic organization that is neither the agent of, nor acting in collaboration with, a foreign power).

Relying on *In re Sealed Case No. 02-001*, the DOJ argues that the NSA program falls within an exception to the warrant and probable cause requirement for reasonable searches that serve "special needs" above and beyond ordinary law enforcement. But the existence of "special needs" has never been found to permit warrantless wiretapping. "Special needs" generally excuse the warrant and individualized suspicion requirements only where those requirements are impracticable and the intrusion on privacy is minimal. See, e.g., *Griffin* v. *Wisconsin*, 483 U.S. 868, 873 (1987). Wiretapping is not a minimal intrusion on privacy, and the experience of FISA shows that foreign intelligence surveillance can be carried out through warrants based on individualized suspicion.

The court in *Sealed Case* upheld FISA itself, which requires warrants issued by Article III federal judges upon an individualized showing of probable cause that the subject is an "agent of a foreign power." The NSA domestic spying program, by contrast, includes none of these safeguards. It does not require individualized judicial approval, and it does not require a showing that the target is an "agent of a foreign power." According to Attorney General Gonzales, the NSA may wiretap any person in the United States who so much as receives a communication from anyone abroad, if the administration deems either of the parties to be affiliated with al-Qaeda, a member of an organization affiliated with al-Qaeda, "working in support of al Qaeda," or "part of" an organization or group "that is supportive of al Qaeda." Under this reasoning, a US citizen living here who received a phone call from another US citizen who attends a mosque that the administration believes is "supportive" of al-Qaeda could be wiretapped without a warrant. The absence of meaningful safeguards on the NSA program at a minimum raises serious questions about the validity of the program under the Fourth Amendment, and therefore supports an interpretation of the AUMF that does not undercut FISA's regulation of such conduct.

In conclusion, the DOJ letter fails to offer a plausible legal defense of the NSA domestic spying program. If the administration felt that FISA was insufficient, the proper course was to seek legislative amendment, as it did with other aspects of FISA in the Patriot Act, and as Congress expressly contemplated when it enacted the wartime wiretap provision in FISA. One of the crucial features of a constitutional democracy is that it is always open to the President—or anyone else—to seek to change the law. But it is also beyond dispute that, in such a democracy, the President cannot simply violate criminal laws behind closed doors because he deems them obsolete or impracticable. . . .

5. Evaluating the Justice Department as Legal Advisor

The Justice Department's lawyering of the TSP, like the legal advice concerning the detention and interrogation of suspected enemy combatants, elicited a storm of public controversy. The fact that the Bush Justice Department itself repudiated much of its original legal analysis is striking. Whether its conclusions were legally correct—or indeed, professionally defensible—is but one aspect of the question whether the Department properly understood its role as legal advisor.

Harsh judgments of the Justice Department's handiwork were not limited to outsiders. In his book, The Terror Presidency: Law and Judgment Inside the Bush Administration (2007), Jack Goldsmith, who headed OLC after the departure of

Jay Bybee and John Yoo, said he "spent hundreds of very difficult hours at OLC, in the face of extraordinary White House resistance, trying to clean up the legal mess that then-White House Counsel Gonzales, [Vice President Cheney's senior counsel] David Addington, John Yoo, and others had created in designing the foundations of the Terrorist Surveillance Program." Id. at 180. Referring to Addington and Vice President Cheney, Goldsmith writes: "After 9/11, they and other top officials in the administration dealt with FISA the way they dealt with other laws they didn't like: they blew through them in secret based on flimsy legal opinions that they guarded closely so no one could question the legal basis for their operations." Id. at 181.

The peculiarity of the Department's lawyering is perhaps made most evident by two glaring omissions. The first, revealed in the 2009 Inspectors General Report, is that the Department's advice from 2001 to 2003 appears to have made no attempt whatever to take account of the *Youngstown* case. *Youngstown* would seem plainly relevant to any legal analysis of a presidential initiative in apparent contravention of statute, especially in the national security area. The second is the failure, in interpreting the AUMF, to take account of the FISA provision regarding warrantless surveillance following a declaration of war:

> In effect, the Bush Administration argued that, in enacting the AUMF, which . . . stopped short of a declaration of war and which does not say a word about expanding executive wiretapping, Congress implicitly authorized the President to conduct warrantless surveillance potentially for all time. This would be so even though Congress, when it explicitly considered the sensitive issue of wartime surveillance in 1978, limited the President's authority to conduct warrantless surveillance to a period 'not to exceed fifteen calendar days' following a formal declaration of war.

Peter M. Shane, Madison's Nightmare: Executive Power and the Threat to American Democracy 93 (2009). Even if one disagrees with the author that this position was "legally absurd," id., is it not obvious that a complete analysis of the AUMF and FISA would have to attend to this argument? If you were advising your White House client in confidence about the legal issues that need to be confronted, would you not be bound to include this one?

A detailed history of the TSP controversy appears as Chapter Seven in Harold H. Bruff, Bad Advice: Bush's Lawyers in the War on Terror (2009). Professor Bruff explicitly links his substantive critique of the Department's legal position with what he takes to be a misconception by the relevant lawyers of the nature of their professional role. That role, as he sees it, combines a combination of sympathy for the client and disciplined detachment, at the core of which is the capacity to give disinterested advice based on all the consequences of proposed action: "Independent judgment is a professional's usual core responsibility to a client." Id. at 80. Quoting Shakespeare's *Henry V*, Professor Bruff sees as the purpose of such advice helping the client to pursue a course of action defensible in both "right and conscience." He quotes approvingly former Yale law dean Anthony Kronman: "Kronman urges . . . that [the lawyer's] responsibility goes 'beyond the preliminary clarification of [the client's] goals and includes helping him to make a deliberatively wise choice among them.'" Id. at 82.

From this perspective, Bruff argues that the Justice Department's entire interpretive strategy fell short. That strategy, he argues, seems to have consisted largely of a four-step rhetorical framework—seen also in its work on detention and interrogation:

> Step One: set the analytic framework. The memos always emphasize the foreign and wartime aspects of the situation and downplay the domestic or criminal law aspects. The reason for this is obvious, since legal precedents involving foreign policy and war are substantially more forgiving to the executive than are precedents that most lawyers view as primarily domestic. Step Two: interpret the President's constitutional powers *very* broadly, in a way that identifies no limits to them, while interpreting possible constitutional restrictions very narrowly, to place the Constitution on the President's side. Step Three: take the same approach with statutes. That is, interpret statutes that authorize executive action very broadly, and statutes that limit executive action very narrowly. And Step Four: fire the canon! That is, invoke the lawyer's "avoidance canon" of construction that calls for reading statutes in ways that avoid constitutional difficulties. Combining the avoidance canon with a broad interpretation of the executive's constitutional powers casts a wide shadow across the meaning of statutes. Combining all four elements of the strategy makes legal constraints disappear.

Id., at 162–63. As Professor Bruff indicates, the lawyers' willingness to pursue this strategy seems to have obviated dealing seriously with critical questions. Professor Bruff believes "[t]his four-part strategy fundamentally lacked the requisites of right and conscience": "Its approach to legal doctrine often featured statements of extreme positions with little support in available legal materials. The existence of strong contrary precedents was usually not acknowledged, as the dictates of conscience should have required. The result was consistently bad advice." Id. at 63.

Professor Shane similarly describes the role of the government lawyer in engaging clients in conscientious deliberation:

> Decisions within the executive branch ... are ... frequently made in [an] insulated environment. The only voices literally present in a particular policy conversation may be those of a high-level presidential appointee, some lower-level presidential appointees, and civil servants who are most directly accountable to these presidential appointees. In such settings, it would require some form of special self-discipline for those immediately involved in the decision to actually concern themselves with perspectives and interests other than the partisan agenda they likely all share. This is especially so for the vast majority of decisions that will never be reviewed in Congress because they are too low-visibility and that will never be reviewed in court because they do not affect the specific interests of identifiable individuals in a way that would ordinarily entitle them to call those decisions into question through litigation.

Seen in this light, a critical function of the law in operation — the law as embodied for the executive branch in judicial opinions rendered by the courts and statutes enacted by Congress — is to make manifest the range of interests and concerns that would not otherwise be vigorously articulated when key decisions are made. It is precisely in this way that the rule of law is a fundamental day-to-day check on the spirit of faction in government affairs. Executive branch lawyers, residing in every agency of government, make this check real because they advise on virtually every important administrative decision and focus decision makers' attention on whatever law is relevant. When the executive branch in 2009 attends, for example, to the Voting Rights Act of 1965 or the 1969 National Environmental Policy Act or the Supreme Court's 1974 decision in *United States v. Nixon*, the Administration can, in a sense, hear the multiple voices of earlier times that themselves had to reach consensus in order to create binding public policy. These voices are virtually, even if not physically present, and their recognition can serve as a buffer against the more immediate passions of partisanship or the undisciplined pursuit of self-interest. Conscientious lawyering insures that contending perspectives are brought to bear whenever current decision makers act, and is thus a critical element in preserving the democratic legitimacy of American government.

Peter M. Shane, Madison's Nightmare, *supra*, at 12.

How well do you think the Justice Department lawyers involved in TSP advising played their role? Would it make a difference to you if the lawyers were presented with hard evidence that the TSP was producing intelligence, achievable in no other way, that was saving lives? Would it make a difference if there were reason to believe that Congress, presented with the same facts, would have readily amended FISA to enable the NSA to follow its preferred intelligence-gathering approach?

In The Terror Presidency, Professor Goldsmith attributes much of what went wrong with Bush Administration lawyering to fear: "Fear explains why OLC pushed the envelope." Id. at 166. Quoting Goldsmith, however, Shane places the blame largely on an organizational psychology of "groupthink," driven by hostility in the Office of the Vice President towards the rule of law as a constraint on executive action: "Goldsmith quotes [the] view [of the Vice President's senior counsel, David Addington] of the tribunal Congress created to oversee foreign intelligence surveillance warrants: 'We're one bomb away from getting rid of that obnoxious court.'" Shane, Madison's Nightmare, *supra*, at 91. These are not mutually exclusive hypotheses, but assuming that either or both might have some basis in reality, how might one structure the process of legal advice to mitigate their influence?

6. Litigation and Accountability

It is conceivable, and perhaps probable, that the TSP resulted in the surveillance of phone calls and other electronic communications by many thousands of

Americans without regard to the terms of the Foreign Intelligence Surveillance Act. It is also notable that the Foreign Intelligence Surveillance Act of 1978 Amendments of 2008 did nothing to curtail any government liability that might be established for earlier violations of FISA. Plaintiffs in only one case succeeded in warding off the Government's procedural defenses based on the state secrets privilege, standing, or both—only to find judgment in their favor vacated on grounds of sovereign immunity. *In re National Security Agency Telecommunications Records Litigation*, 633 F. Supp. 2d 949 (N.D. Cal. 2009), *aff'd in part and rev'd in part, Al-Haramain Islamic Found., Inc. v. Obama*, 705 F.3d 845 (9th Cir. 2012).

The procedural hurdles to judicial review proved no less problematic for challenges to surveillance under Section 702, as the following decision proved:

Clapper v. Amnesty International USA

Supreme Court of the United States
568 U.S. 398 (2013).

Justice ALITO delivered the opinion of the Court.

Section 702 of the Foreign Intelligence Surveillance Act of 1978, 50 U.S.C. § 1881a (2006 ed., Supp. V), allows the Attorney General and the Director of National Intelligence to acquire foreign intelligence information by jointly authorizing the surveillance of individuals who are not "United States persons" and are reasonably believed to be located outside the United States. Before doing so, the Attorney General and the Director of National Intelligence normally must obtain the Foreign Intelligence Surveillance Court's approval. Respondents are United States persons whose work, they allege, requires them to engage in sensitive international communications with individuals who they believe are likely targets of surveillance under § 1881a. Respondents seek a declaration that § 1881a is unconstitutional, as well as an injunction against § 1881a-authorized surveillance. The question before us is whether respondents have Article III standing to seek this prospective relief.

Respondents assert that they can establish injury in fact because there is an objectively reasonable likelihood that their communications will be acquired under § 1881a at some point in the future. But respondents' theory of *future* injury is too speculative to satisfy the well-established requirement that threatened injury must be "certainly impending." *E.g., Whitmore v. Arkansas*, 495 U.S. 149, 158 (1990). And even if respondents could demonstrate that the threatened injury is certainly impending, they still would not be able to establish that this injury is fairly traceable to § 1881a. As an alternative argument, respondents contend that they are suffering *present* injury because the risk of § 1881a-authorized surveillance already has forced them to take costly and burdensome measures to protect the confidentiality of their international communications. But respondents cannot manufacture standing by choosing to make expenditures based on hypothetical future harm that is not certainly impending. We therefore hold that respondents lack Article III standing.

I

A

[Justice Alito begins by recounting the history of FISA and its amendments, leading up to the adoption of Section 702.]

Section 1881a mandates that the Government obtain the Foreign Intelligence Surveillance Court's approval of "targeting" procedures, "minimization" procedures, and a governmental certification regarding proposed surveillance. 1881a(a), (c)(1), (i)(2), (i)(3). Among other things, the Government's certification must attest that (1) procedures are in place "that have been approved, have been submitted for approval, or will be submitted with the certification for approval by the [FISC] that are reasonably designed" to ensure that an acquisition is "limited to targeting persons reasonably believed to be located outside" the United States; (2) minimization procedures adequately restrict the acquisition, retention, and dissemination of nonpublic information about unconsenting U.S. persons, as appropriate; (3) guidelines have been adopted to ensure compliance with targeting limits and the Fourth Amendment; and (4) the procedures and guidelines referred to above comport with the Fourth Amendment. § 1881a(g)(2); see § 1801(h).

The Foreign Intelligence Surveillance Court's role includes determining whether the Government's certification contains the required elements. Additionally, the Court assesses whether the targeting procedures are "reasonably designed" (1) to "ensure that an acquisition . . . is limited to targeting persons reasonably believed to be located outside the United States" and (2) to "prevent the intentional acquisition of any communication as to which the sender and all intended recipients are known . . . to be located in the United States." § 1881a(i)(2)(B). The Court analyzes whether the minimization procedures "meet the definition of minimization procedures under section 1801(h) . . . , as appropriate." § 1881a(i)(2)(C). The Court also assesses whether the targeting and minimization procedures are consistent with the statute and the Fourth Amendment. See § 1881a(i)(3)(A).

B

Respondents are attorneys and human rights, labor, legal, and media organizations whose work allegedly requires them to engage in sensitive and sometimes privileged telephone and e-mail communications with colleagues, clients, sources, and other individuals located abroad. Respondents believe that some of the people with whom they exchange foreign intelligence information are likely targets of surveillance under § 1881a. Specifically, respondents claim that they communicate by telephone and e-mail with people the Government "believes or believed to be associated with terrorist organizations," "people located in geographic areas that are a special focus" of the Government's counterterrorism or diplomatic efforts, and activists who oppose governments that are supported by the United States Government.

Respondents claim that § 1881a compromises their ability to locate witnesses, cultivate sources, obtain information, and communicate confidential information to their clients. Respondents also assert that they "have ceased engaging" in certain telephone and email conversations. According to respondents, the threat of surveillance will compel them to travel abroad in order to have in-person conversations. In addition, respondents declare that they have undertaken "costly and burdensome measures" to protect the confidentiality of sensitive communications.

C

On the day when the FISA Amendments Act was enacted, respondents filed this action seeking (1) a declaration that § 1881a, on its face, violates the Fourth Amendment, the First Amendment, Article III, and separation-of-powers principles and (2) a permanent injunction against the use of § 1881a. Respondents assert what they characterize as two separate theories of Article III standing. First, they claim that there is an objectively reasonable likelihood that their communications will be acquired under § 1881a at some point in the future, thus causing them injury. Second, respondents maintain that the risk of surveillance under § 1881a is so substantial that they have been forced to take costly and burdensome measures to protect the confidentiality of their international communications; in their view, the costs they have incurred constitute present injury that is fairly traceable to § 1881a.

After both parties moved for summary judgment, the District Court held that respondents do not have standing. On appeal, however, a panel of the Second Circuit reversed. The panel agreed with respondents' argument that they have standing due to the objectively reasonable likelihood that their communications will be intercepted at some time in the future. In addition, the panel held that respondents have established that they are suffering "*present* injuries in fact—economic and professional harms—stemming from a reasonable fear of *future* harmful government conduct." The Second Circuit denied rehearing en banc by an equally divided vote. . . .

II

. . . The law of Article III standing, which is built on separation-of-powers principles, serves to prevent the judicial process from being used to usurp the powers of the political branches. In keeping with the purpose of this doctrine, "[o]ur standing inquiry has been especially rigorous when reaching the merits of the dispute would force us to decide whether an action taken by one of the other two branches of the Federal Government was unconstitutional." "Relaxation of standing requirements is directly related to the expansion of judicial power," and we have often found a lack of standing in cases in which the Judiciary has been requested to review actions of the political branches in the fields of intelligence gathering and foreign affairs.

To establish Article III standing, an injury must be "concrete, particularized, and actual or imminent; fairly traceable to the challenged action; and redressable by a favorable ruling." "Although imminence is concededly a somewhat elastic concept, it cannot be stretched beyond its purpose, which is to ensure that the alleged injury is not too speculative for Article III purposes—that the injury is *certainly* impending." Thus, we have repeatedly reiterated that "threatened injury must be *certainly impending* to constitute injury in fact," and that "[a]llegations of *possible* future injury" are not sufficient.

III

A

Respondents assert that they can establish injury in fact that is fairly traceable to § 1881a because there is an objectively reasonable likelihood that their communications with their foreign contacts will be intercepted under § 1881a at some point in the future. This argument fails. As an initial matter, the Second Circuit's "objectively reasonable likelihood" standard is inconsistent with our requirement that "threatened injury must be certainly impending to constitute injury in fact." *Whitmore, supra,* at 158, 110 S.Ct. 1717 (internal quotation marks omitted). Furthermore, respondents' argument rests on their highly speculative fear that: (1) the Government will decide to target the communications of non-U.S. persons with whom they communicate; (2) in doing so, the Government will choose to invoke its authority under § 1881a rather than utilizing another method of surveillance; (3) the Article III judges who serve on the Foreign Intelligence Surveillance Court will conclude that the Government's proposed surveillance procedures satisfy § 1881a's many safeguards and are consistent with the Fourth Amendment; (4) the Government will succeed in intercepting the communications of respondents' contacts; and (5) respondents will be parties to the particular communications that the Government intercepts. As discussed below, respondents' theory of standing, which relies on a highly attenuated chain of possibilities, does not satisfy the requirement that threatened injury must be certainly impending. Moreover, even if respondents could demonstrate injury in fact, the second link in the above-described chain of contingencies—which amounts to mere speculation about whether surveillance would be under § 1881a or some other authority—shows that respondents cannot satisfy the requirement that any injury in fact must be fairly traceable to § 1881a.

First, it is speculative whether the Government will imminently target communications to which respondents are parties. Section 1881a expressly provides that respondents, who are U.S. persons, cannot be targeted for surveillance under § 1881a. Accordingly, it is no surprise that respondents fail to offer any evidence that their communications have been monitored under § 1881a, a failure that substantially undermines their standing theory. Indeed, respondents do not even allege that the Government has sought the FISC's approval for surveillance of their communications. Accordingly, respondents' theory necessarily rests on their assertion that the Government will target *other individuals*—namely, their foreign contacts.

Yet respondents have no actual knowledge of the Government's § 1881a targeting practices. Instead, respondents merely speculate and make assumptions about whether their communications with their foreign contacts will be acquired under § 1881a. For example, journalist Christopher Hedges states: "I have no choice but to *assume* that any of my international communications *may* be subject to government surveillance, and I have to make decisions . . . in light of that *assumption*." Similarly, attorney Scott McKay asserts that, "[b]ecause of the [FISA Amendments Act], we now have to *assume* that every one of our international communications *may* be monitored by the government." "The party invoking federal jurisdiction bears the burden of establishing" standing—and, at the summary judgment stage, such a party "can no longer rest on . . . 'mere allegations,' but must 'set forth' by affidavit or other evidence 'specific facts.'" Respondents, however, have set forth no specific facts demonstrating that the communications of their foreign contacts will be targeted. Moreover, because § 1881a at most *authorizes*—but does not *mandate* or *direct*—the surveillance that respondents fear, respondents' allegations are necessarily conjectural. Simply put, respondents can only speculate as to how the Attorney General and the Director of National Intelligence will exercise their discretion in determining which communications to target.[4]

Second, even if respondents could demonstrate that the targeting of their foreign contacts is imminent, respondents can only speculate as to whether the Government will seek to use § 1881a-authorized surveillance (rather than other methods) to do so. The Government has numerous other methods of conducting surveillance, none of which is challenged here. Even after the enactment of the FISA Amendments Act, for example, the Government may still conduct electronic surveillance of persons abroad under the older provisions of FISA so long as it satisfies the applicable requirements, including a demonstration of probable cause to believe that the person is a foreign power or agent of a foreign power. See § 1805. The Government may also obtain information from the intelligence services of foreign nations. And, although we do not reach the question, the Government contends that it can conduct FISA-exempt human and technical surveillance programs that are governed by Executive Order 12333. Even if respondents could demonstrate that their foreign contacts will imminently be targeted— indeed, even if they could show that interception of their own communications will imminently occur—they would still need to show that their injury is fairly traceable to § 1881a. But, because respondents can only speculate as to whether any (asserted) interception would be under § 1881a or some other authority, they cannot satisfy the "fairly traceable" requirement.

Third, even if respondents could show that the Government will seek the Foreign Intelligence Surveillance Court's authorization to acquire the communications of

---

4. It was suggested at oral argument that the Government could help resolve the standing inquiry by disclosing to a court, perhaps through an *in camera* proceeding, (1) whether it is intercepting respondents' communications and (2) what targeting or minimization procedures it is using. As an initial matter, it is *respondents'* burden to prove their standing by pointing to specific facts, not the Government's burden to disprove standing by revealing details of its surveillance priorities. Moreover, this type of hypothetical disclosure proceeding would allow a terrorist (or his attorney) to determine whether he is currently under U.S. surveillance simply by filing a lawsuit challenging the Government's surveillance program. Even if the terrorist's attorney were to comply with a protective order prohibiting him from sharing the Government's disclosures with his client, the court's postdisclosure decision about whether to dismiss the suit for lack of standing would surely signal to the terrorist whether his name was on the list of surveillance targets.

respondents' foreign contacts under § 1881a, respondents can only speculate as to whether that court will authorize such surveillance. In the past, we have been reluctant to endorse standing theories that require guesswork as to how independent decisionmakers will exercise their judgment. In *Whitmore,* for example, the plaintiff's theory of standing hinged largely on the probability that he would obtain federal habeas relief and be convicted upon retrial. In holding that the plaintiff lacked standing, we explained that "[i]t is just not possible for a litigant to prove in advance that the judicial system will lead to any particular result in his case."

We decline to abandon our usual reluctance to endorse standing theories that rest on speculation about the decisions of independent actors. Section 1881a mandates that the Government must obtain the Foreign Intelligence Surveillance Court's approval of targeting procedures, minimization procedures, and a governmental certification regarding proposed surveillance. § 1881a(a), (c)(1), (i)(2), (i)(3). The Court must, for example, determine whether the Government's procedures are "reasonably designed . . . to minimize the acquisition and retention, and prohibit the dissemination, of nonpublicly available information concerning unconsenting United States persons." § 1801(h); see § 1881a(i)(2), (i)(3)(A). And, critically, the Court must also assess whether the Government's targeting and minimization procedures comport with the Fourth Amendment. § 1881a(i)(3)(A).

Fourth, even if the Government were to obtain the Foreign Intelligence Surveillance Court's approval to target respondents' foreign contacts under § 1881a, it is unclear whether the Government would succeed in acquiring the communications of respondents' foreign contacts. And fifth, even if the Government were to conduct surveillance of respondents' foreign contacts, respondents can only speculate as to whether *their own communications* with their foreign contacts would be incidentally acquired.

In sum, respondents' speculative chain of possibilities does not establish that injury based on potential future surveillance is certainly impending or is fairly traceable to § 1881a.[5]

B

Respondents' alternative argument—namely, that they can establish standing based on the measures that they have undertaken to avoid § 1881 authorized surveillance—fares no better. Respondents assert that they are suffering ongoing injuries that are fairly traceable to § 1881a because the risk of surveillance under § 1881a

---

5. Our cases do not uniformly require plaintiffs to demonstrate that it is literally certain that the harms they identify will come about. In some instances, we have found standing based on a "substantial risk" that the harm will occur, which may prompt plaintiffs to reasonably incur costs to mitigate or avoid that harm. But to the extent that the "substantial risk" standard is relevant and is distinct from the "clearly impending" requirement, respondents fall short of even that standard, in light of the attenuated chain of inferences necessary to find harm here. In addition, plaintiffs bear the burden of pleading and proving concrete facts showing that the defendant's actual action has caused the substantial risk of harm. Plaintiffs cannot rely on speculation about "'the unfettered choices made by independent actors not before the court.'" *Defenders of Wildlife,* 504 U.S., at 562, 112 S.Ct. 2130.

requires them to take costly and burdensome measures to protect the confidentiality of their communications. Respondents claim, for instance, that the threat of surveillance sometimes compels them to avoid certain email and phone conversations, to "tal[k] in generalities rather than specifics," or to travel so that they can have in-person conversations. The Second Circuit panel concluded that, because respondents are already suffering such ongoing injuries, the likelihood of interception under § 1881a is relevant only to the question whether respondents' ongoing injuries are "fairly traceable" to § 1881a. Analyzing the "fairly traceable" element of standing under a relaxed reasonableness standard, the Second Circuit then held that "plaintiffs have established that they suffered *present* injuries in fact—economic and professional harms—stemming from a reasonable fear of *future* harmful government conduct."

The Second Circuit's analysis improperly allowed respondents to establish standing by asserting that they suffer present costs and burdens that are based on a fear of surveillance, so long as that fear is not "fanciful, paranoid, or otherwise unreasonable." This improperly waters down the fundamental requirements of Article III. Respondents' contention that they have standing because they incurred certain costs as a reasonable reaction to a risk of harm is unavailing—because the harm respondents seek to avoid is not certainly impending. In other words, respondents cannot manufacture standing merely by inflicting harm on themselves based on their fears of hypothetical future harm that is not certainly impending. Any ongoing injuries that respondents are suffering are not fairly traceable to § 1881a.

If the law were otherwise, an enterprising plaintiff would be able to secure a lower standard for Article III standing simply by making an expenditure based on a non-paranoid fear. As Judge Raggi accurately noted, under the Second Circuit panel's reasoning, respondents could, "for the price of a plane ticket, . . . transform their standing burden from one requiring a showing of actual or imminent . . . interception to one requiring a showing that their subjective fear of such interception is not fanciful, irrational, or clearly unreasonable." Thus, allowing respondents to bring this action based on costs they incurred in response to a speculative threat would be tantamount to accepting a repackaged version of respondents' first failed theory of standing.

Another reason that respondents' present injuries are not fairly traceable to § 1881a is that even before § 1881a was enacted, they had a similar incentive to engage in many of the countermeasures that they are now taking. For instance, respondent Scott McKay's declaration describes—and the dissent heavily relies on—Mr. McKay's "knowledge" that thousands of communications involving one of his clients were monitored in the past. But this surveillance was conducted pursuant to FISA authority that predated § 1881a. Thus, because the Government was allegedly conducting surveillance of Mr. McKay's client before Congress enacted § 1881a, it is difficult to see how the safeguards that Mr. McKay now claims to have implemented can be traced to § 1881a.

Because respondents do not face a threat of certainly impending interception under § 1881a, the costs that they have incurred to avoid surveillance are simply the product of their fear of surveillance,[7] and our decision in *Laird* [*v. Tatum*, 408 US 1 (1972)] makes it clear that such a fear is insufficient to create standing. The plaintiffs in *Laird* argued that their exercise of First Amendment rights was being "chilled by the mere existence, without more, of [the Army's] investigative and data-gathering activity." While acknowledging that prior cases had held that constitutional violations may arise from the chilling effect of "regulations that fall short of a direct prohibition against the exercise of First Amendment rights," the Court declared that none of those cases involved a "chilling effect aris[ing] merely from the individual's knowledge that a governmental agency was engaged in certain activities or from the individual's concomitant fear that, armed with the fruits of those activities, the agency might in the future take some *other* and additional action detrimental to that individual." Because "[a]llegations of a subjective 'chill' are not an adequate substitute for a claim of specific present objective harm or a threat of specific future harm," the plaintiffs in *Laird*—and respondents here—lack standing.

For the reasons discussed above, respondents' self-inflicted injuries are not fairly traceable to the Government's purported activities under § 1881a, and their subjective fear of surveillance does not give rise to standing.

IV

• • •

B

Respondents also suggest that they should be held to have standing because otherwise the constitutionality of § 1881a could not be challenged. It would be wrong, they maintain, to "insulate the government's surveillance activities from meaningful judicial review." Respondents' suggestion is both legally and factually incorrect. First, "'[t]he assumption that if respondents have no standing to sue, no one would have standing, is not a reason to find standing.'"

Second, our holding today by no means insulates § 1881a from judicial review. As described above, Congress created a comprehensive scheme in which the Foreign Intelligence Surveillance Court evaluates the Government's certifications, targeting procedures, and minimization procedures—including assessing whether the targeting and minimization procedures comport with the Fourth Amendment. § 1881a(a), (c)(1), (i)(2), (i)(3). Any dissatisfaction that respondents may have about the Foreign Intelligence Surveillance Court's rulings—or the congressional delineation of that court's role—is irrelevant to our standing analysis.

Additionally, if the Government intends to use or disclose information obtained or derived from a § 1881a acquisition in judicial or administrative proceedings, it

---

7. Although respondents' alternative theory of standing rests primarily on choices that they have made based on their subjective fear of surveillance, respondents also assert that third parties might be disinclined to speak with them due to a fear of surveillance. To the extent that such assertions are based on anything other than conjecture, they do not establish injury that is fairly traceable to § 1881a, because they are based on third parties' subjective fear of surveillance.

must provide advance notice of its intent, and the affected person may challenge the lawfulness of the acquisition. §§ 1806, 1806(e), 1881e(a) (2006 ed. and Supp. V). Thus, if the Government were to prosecute one of respondent-attorney's foreign clients using § 1881a-authorized surveillance, the Government would be required to make a disclosure.[8] Although the foreign client might not have a viable Fourth Amendment claim, it is possible that the monitoring of the target's conversations with his or her attorney would provide grounds for a claim of standing on the part of the attorney. Such an attorney would certainly have a stronger evidentiary basis for establishing standing than do respondents in the present case. In such a situation, unlike in the present case, it would at least be clear that the Government had acquired the foreign client's communications using § 1881a-authorized surveillance.

Finally, any electronic communications service provider that the Government directs to assist in § 1881a surveillance may challenge the lawfulness of that directive before the FISC. § 1881a(h)(4), (6). Indeed, at the behest of a service provider, the Foreign Intelligence Surveillance Court of Review previously analyzed the constitutionality of electronic surveillance directives issued pursuant to a now-expired set of FISA amendments. See *In re Directives Pursuant to Section 105B of Foreign Intelligence Surveillance Act*, 551 F.3d 1004, 1006–1016 (2008) (holding that the provider had standing and that the directives were constitutional).

* * *

We hold that respondents lack Article III standing because they cannot demonstrate that the future injury they purportedly fear is certainly impending and because they cannot manufacture standing by incurring costs in anticipation of nonimminent harm. We therefore reverse the judgment of the Second Circuit and remand the case for further proceedings consistent with this opinion.

It is so ordered.

Justice BREYER, with whom Justice GINSBURG, Justice SOTOMAYOR, and Justice KAGAN join, dissenting.

The plaintiffs' standing depends upon the likelihood that the Government, acting under the authority of 50 U.S.C. § 1881a (2006 ed., Supp. V), will harm them by intercepting at least some of their private, foreign, telephone, or e-mail conversations. In my view, this harm is not "speculative." Indeed it is as likely to take place as are most future events that commonsense inference and ordinary knowledge of human nature tell us will happen. This Court has often found the occurrence of similar future events sufficiently certain to support standing. I dissent from the Court's contrary conclusion.

---

8. The possibility of judicial review in this context is not farfetched. In United States v. Damrah, 412 F.3d 618 (C.A.6 2005), for example, the Government made a pretrial disclosure that it intended to use FISA evidence in a prosecution; the defendant (unsuccessfully) moved to suppress the FISA evidence, even though he had not been the target of the surveillance; and the Sixth Circuit ultimately held that FISA's procedures are consistent with the Fourth Amendment.

. . . The Court has recognized that the precise boundaries of the "case or contro-versy" requirement are matters of "degree . . . not discernible by any precise test." At the same time, the Court has developed a subsidiary set of legal rules that help to determine when the Constitution's requirement is met. Thus, a plaintiff must have "standing" to bring a legal claim. And a plaintiff has that standing, the Court has said, only if the action or omission that the plaintiff challenges has caused, or will cause, the plaintiff to suffer an injury that is "concrete and particularized," "actual or imminent," and "redress[able] by a favorable decision."

No one here denies that the Government's interception of a private telephone or e-mail conversation amounts to an injury that is "concrete and particularized." Moreover, the plaintiffs, respondents here, seek as relief a judgment declaring uncon-stitutional (and enjoining enforcement of) a statutory provision authorizing those interceptions; and, such a judgment would redress the injury by preventing it. Thus, the basic question is whether the injury, *i.e.,* the interception, is "actual or imminent."

II

A

The addition of § 1881a in 2008 changed [the] prior law in three important ways. First, it eliminated the requirement that the Government describe to the court each specific target and identify each facility at which its surveillance would be directed, thus permitting surveillance on a programmatic, not necessarily individualized, basis. § 1881a(g). Second, it eliminated the requirement that a target be a "foreign power or an agent of a foreign power." Third, it diminished the court's authority to insist upon, and eliminated its authority to supervise, instance-specific privacy-intrusion minimization procedures (though the Government still must use court-approved general minimization procedures). § 1881a(e). Thus, using the authority of § 1881a, the Government can obtain court approval for its surveillance of electronic communications between places within the United States and targets in foreign ter-ritories by showing the court (1) that "a significant purpose of the acquisition is to obtain foreign intelligence information," and (2) that it will use general targeting and privacy-intrusion minimization procedures of a kind that the court had previously approved. § 1881a(g).

B

It is similarly important to understand the kinds of communications in which the plaintiffs say they engage and which they believe the Government will intercept. Plaintiff Scott McKay, for example, says in an affidavit (1) that he is a lawyer; (2) that he represented "Mr. Sami Omar Al-Hussayen, who was acquitted in June 2004 on terrorism charges"; (3) that he continues to represent "Mr. Al-Hussayen, who, in addi-tion to facing criminal charges after September 11, was named as a defendant in several civil cases"; (4) that he represents Khalid Sheik Mohammed, a detainee, "before the Military Commissions at Guantánamo Bay, Cuba"; (5) that in representing these clients he "communicate[s] by telephone and email with people outside the United States, including Mr. Al-Hussayen himself," "experts, investigators, attorneys, family members . . . and others who are located abroad"; and (6) that prior to 2008 "the U.S. government had intercepted some 10,000 telephone calls and 20,000 email communications involving [his client] Al-Hussayen."

Another plaintiff, Sylvia Royce, says in her affidavit (1) that she is an attorney; (2) that she "represent[s] Mohammedou Ould Salahi, a prisoner who has been held at Guantánamo Bay as an enemy combatant"; (3) that, "[i]n connection with [her] representation of Mr. Salahi, [she] receive[s] calls from time to time from Mr. Salahi's brother, . . . a university student in Germany"; and (4) that she has been told that the Government has threatened Salahi "that his family members would be arrested and mistreated if he did not cooperate."

The plaintiffs have noted that McKay no longer represents Mohammed and Royce no longer represents Ould Salahi. But these changes are irrelevant, for we assess standing as of the time a suit is filed, and in any event McKay himself continues to represent Al Hussayen, his partner now represents Mohammed, and Royce continues to represent individuals held in the custody of the U.S. military overseas.

A third plaintiff, Joanne Mariner, says in her affidavit (1) that she is a human rights researcher, (2) that "some of the work [she] do[es] involves trying to track down people who were rendered by the CIA to countries in which they were tortured"; (3) that many of those people "the CIA has said are (or were) associated with terrorist organizations"; and (4) that, to do this research, she "communicate[s] by telephone and e-mail with . . . former detainees, lawyers for detainees, relatives of detainees, political activists, journalists, and fixers" "all over the world, including in Jordan, Egypt, Pakistan, Afghanistan, [and] the Gaza Strip."

Other plaintiffs, including lawyers, journalists, and human rights researchers, say in affidavits (1) that they have jobs that require them to gather information from foreigners located abroad; (2) that they regularly communicate electronically (*e.g.*, by telephone or e-mail) with foreigners located abroad; and (3) that in these communications they exchange "foreign intelligence information" as the Act defines it.

III

Several considerations, based upon the record along with commonsense inferences, convince me that there is a very high likelihood that Government, *acting under the authority of § 1881a,* will intercept at least some of the communications just described. First, the plaintiffs have engaged, and continue to engage, in electronic communications of a kind that the 2008 amendment, but not the prior Act, authorizes the Government to intercept. These communications include discussions with family members of those detained at Guantanamo, friends and acquaintances of those persons, and investigators, experts and others with knowledge of circumstances related to terrorist activities. These persons are foreigners located outside the United States. They are not "foreign power[s]" or "agent[s] of . . . foreign power [s]." And the plaintiffs state that they exchange with these persons "foreign intelligence information," defined to include information that "relates to" "international terrorism" and "the national defense or the security of the United States." See 50 U.S.C. § 1801 (2006 ed. and Supp. V).

Second, the plaintiffs have a strong *motive* to engage in, and the Government has a strong *motive* to listen to, conversations of the kind described. A lawyer representing a client normally seeks to learn the circumstances surrounding the crime (or the civil wrong) of which the client is accused. A fair reading of the affidavit of Scott McKay, for example, taken together with elementary considerations of a lawyer's obligation to his client, indicates that McKay will engage in conversations that concern what suspected foreign terrorists, such as his client, have done; in conversations that concern his clients' families, colleagues, and contacts; in conversations that concern what those persons (or those connected to them) have said and done, at least in relation to terrorist activities; in conversations that concern the political, social, and commercial environments in which the suspected terrorists have lived and worked; and so forth. Journalists and human rights workers have strong similar motives to conduct conversations of this kind.

At the same time, the Government has a strong motive to conduct surveillance of conversations that contain material of this kind. The Government, after all, seeks to learn as much as it can reasonably learn about suspected terrorists (such as those detained at Guantanamo), as well as about their contacts and activities, along with those of friends and family members. See Executive Office of the President, Office of Management and Budget, Statement of Administration Policy on S. 2248, p. 4 (Dec. 17, 2007) ("Part of the value of the [new authority] is to enable the Intelligence Community to collect expeditiously the communications of terrorists in foreign countries who may contact an associate in the United States"). And the Government is motivated to do so, not simply by the desire to help convict those whom the Government believes guilty, but also by the critical, overriding need to protect America from terrorism.

Third, the Government's *past behavior* shows that it has sought, and hence will in all likelihood continue to seek, information about alleged terrorists and detainees through means that include surveillance of electronic communications. As just pointed out, plaintiff Scott McKay states that the Government (under the authority of the pre-2008 law) "intercepted some 10,000 telephone calls and 20,000 email communications involving [his client] Mr. Al-Hussayen." Fourth, the Government has the *capacity* to conduct electronic surveillance of the kind at issue. To some degree this capacity rests upon technology available to the Government. This capacity also includes the Government's authority to obtain the kind of information here at issue from private carriers such as AT & T and Verizon. See 50 U.S.C. § 1881a(h). We are further told by *amici* that the Government is expanding that capacity.

Of course, to exercise this capacity the Government must have intelligence court authorization. But the Government rarely files requests that fail to meet the statutory criteria. See Letter from Ronald Weich, Assistant Attorney General, to Joseph R.

Biden, Jr., 1 (Apr. 30, 2012) (In 2011, of the 1,676 applications to the intelligence court, two were withdrawn by the Government, and the remaining 1,674 were approved, 30 with some modification), online at http://www.justice.gov/nsd/foia/foia_library /2011fisa-ltr.pdf. (as visited Feb. 22, 2013, and available in Clerk of Court's case file). As the intelligence court itself has stated, its review under § 1881a is "narrowly circumscribed." In re Proceedings Required by § 702(i) of the FISA Amendments Act of 2008, No. Misc. 08-01 (Aug. 17, 2008), p. 3. There is no reason to believe that the communications described would all fail to meet the conditions necessary for approval. Moreover, compared with prior law, § 1881a simplifies and thus expedites the approval process, making it more likely that the Government will use § 1881a to obtain the necessary approval.

The upshot is that (1) similarity of content, (2) strong motives, (3) prior behavior, and (4) capacity all point to a very strong likelihood that the Government will intercept at least some of the plaintiffs' communications, including some that the 2008 amendment, § 1881a, but not the pre-2008 Act, authorizes the Government to intercept.

At the same time, nothing suggests the presence of some special factor here that might support a contrary conclusion. The Government does not deny that it has both the motive and the capacity to listen to communications of the kind described by plaintiffs. Nor does it describe any system for avoiding the interception of an electronic communication that happens to include a party who is an American lawyer, journalist, or human rights worker. One can, of course, always imagine some special circumstance that negates a virtual likelihood, no matter how strong. But the same is true about most, if not all, ordinary inferences about future events. Perhaps, despite pouring rain, the streets will remain dry (due to the presence of a special chemical). But ordinarily a party that seeks to defeat a strong natural inference must bear the burden of showing that some such special circumstance exists. And no one has suggested any such special circumstance here.

Consequently, we need only assume that the Government is doing its job (to find out about, and combat, terrorism) in order to conclude that there is a high probability that the Government will intercept at least some electronic communication to which at least some of the plaintiffs are parties. The majority is wrong when it describes the harm threatened plaintiffs as "speculative."

IV

A

The majority more plausibly says that the plaintiffs have failed to show that the threatened harm is "*certainly impending.*" But, as the majority appears to concede, *certainty* is not, and never has been, the touchstone of standing. The future is inherently uncertain. Yet federal courts frequently entertain actions for injunctions and for declaratory relief aimed at preventing future activities that are reasonably likely or highly likely, but not absolutely certain, to take place. And that degree of certainty is all that is needed to support standing here.

The Court's use of the term "certainly impending" is not to the contrary. Sometimes the Court has used the phrase "certainly impending" as if the phrase described a *sufficient,* rather than a *necessary,* condition for jurisdiction. On other occasions, it has used the phrase as if it concerned *when,* not *whether,* an alleged injury would occur. Thus, in *Lujan,* 504 U.S., at 564, n. 2, 112 S.Ct. 2130, the Court considered a threatened future injury that consisted of harm that plaintiffs would suffer when they "soon" visited a government project area that (they claimed) would suffer environmental damage. The Court wrote that a "mere profession of an intent, some day, to return" to the project area did not show the harm was "*imminent,*" for "soon" might mean nothing more than "in this lifetime." Similarly, in *McConnell v. Federal Election Comm'n,* 540 U.S. 93, 124 S.Ct. 619, 157 L.Ed.2d 491 (2003), the Court denied standing because the Senator's future injury (stemming from a campaign finance law) would not affect him until his reelection. That fact, the Court said, made the injury "too remote temporally to satisfy Article III standing."

On still other occasions, recognizing that "'imminence' is concededly a somewhat elastic concept," the Court has referred to, or used (sometimes along with "certainly impending") other phrases such as "reasonable probability" that suggest less than absolute, or literal certainty. . . . Taken together the case law uses the word "certainly" as if it emphasizes, rather than literally defines, the immediately following term "impending."

B

1

More important, the Court's holdings in standing cases show that standing exists here. The Court has often *found* standing where the occurrence of the relevant injury was far *less* certain than here. Consider a few, fairly typical, cases. Consider *Pennell, supra.* A city ordinance forbade landlords to raise the rent charged to a tenant by more than 8 percent where doing so would work an unreasonably severe hardship on that tenant. A group of landlords sought a judgment declaring the ordinance unconstitutional. The Court held that, to have standing, the landlords had to demonstrate a "*realistic danger of sustaining a direct injury* as a result of the statute's operation." "It found that the landlords had done so by showing a likelihood of enforcement and a "probability," that the ordinance would make the landlords charge lower rents—even though the landlords had not shown (1) that they intended to raise the relevant rents to the point of causing unreasonably severe hardship; (2) that the tenants would challenge those increases; or (3) that the city's hearing examiners and arbitrators would find against the landlords. Here, even more so than in *Pennell,* there is a "*realistic danger*" that the relevant harm will occur. . . .

Moreover, courts have often found *probabilistic* injuries sufficient to support standing. In *Duke Power Co. v. Carolina Environmental Study Group, Inc.,* 438 U.S. 59, 98 S.Ct. 2620, 57 L.Ed.2d 595 (1978), for example, the plaintiffs, a group of individuals living near a proposed nuclear power plant, challenged the constitutionality of the Price-Anderson Act, a statute that limited the plant's liability in the case of a nuclear accident. The plaintiffs said that, without the Act, the defendants would not build a nuclear plant. And the building of the plant would harm them, in part, by emitting "non-natural radiation into [their] environment." The Court found standing in part due to "our generalized concern about exposure to radiation and the apprehension flowing from the *uncertainty* about the health and genetic consequences of even small emissions." . . .

How could the law be otherwise? Suppose that a federal court faced a claim by homeowners that (allegedly) unlawful dam-building practices created a high risk that their homes would be flooded. Would the court deny them standing on the ground that the risk of flood was only 60, rather than 90, percent? . . .

Neither do ordinary declaratory judgment actions always involve the degree of certainty upon which the Court insists here. In some standing cases, the Court has found that a reasonable probability of *future* injury comes accompanied with *present* injury that takes the form of reasonable efforts to mitigate the threatened effects of the future injury or to prevent it from occurring. Thus, in *Monsanto Co.,* 561 U.S., at ___, 130 S.Ct., at 2754–2756 plaintiffs, a group of conventional alfalfa growers, challenged an agency decision to deregulate genetically engineered alfalfa. They claimed that deregulation would harm them because their neighbors would plant the genetically engineered seed, bees would obtain pollen from the neighbors' plants, and the bees would then (harmfully) contaminate their own conventional alfalfa with the genetically modified gene. The lower courts had found a "reasonable probability" that this injury would occur.

Without expressing views about that probability, we found standing because the plaintiffs would suffer present harm by trying to combat the threat. The plaintiffs, for example, "would have to conduct testing to find out whether and to what extent their crops have been contaminated." And they would have to take "measures to minimize the likelihood of potential contamination and to ensure an adequate supply of non-genetically-engineered alfalfa." We held that these "harms, which [the plaintiffs] will suffer even if their crops are not actually infected with" the genetically modified gene, "are sufficiently concrete to satisfy the injury-in-fact prong of the constitutional standing analysis."

Virtually identical circumstances are present here. Plaintiff McKay, for example, points out that, when he communicates abroad about, or in the interests of, a client (*e.g.,* a client accused of terrorism), he must "make an assessment" whether his "client's interests would be compromised" should the Government "acquire the communications."

Since travel is expensive, since forgoing communication can compromise the client's interests, since McKay's assessment itself takes time and effort, this case does not differ significantly from *Monsanto.* And that is so whether we consider the plaintiffs' present necessary expenditure of time and effort as a separate concrete, particularized, imminent harm, or consider it as additional evidence that the future harm (an interception) is likely to occur.

3

The majority cannot find support in cases that use the words "certainly impending" to *deny* standing. While I do not claim to have read every standing case, I have examined quite a few, and not yet found any such case. The majority refers to *Whitmore v. Arkansas,* 495 U.S. 149 (1990). But in that case the Court denied standing to a prisoner who challenged the validity of a death sentence given to a *different* prisoner who refused to challenge his own sentence. The plaintiff feared that in the absence of an appeal, his fellow prisoner's death sentence would be missing from the State's death penalty database and thereby skew the database against him, making it less likely his challenges to his own death penalty would succeed. The Court found no standing. But the fellow prisoner's lack of appeal would have harmed the plaintiff only if (1) the plaintiff separately obtained federal habeas relief and was then reconvicted and resentenced to death, (2) he sought review of his new sentence, and (3) during that review, his death sentence was affirmed only because it was compared to an artificially skewed database. *Id.,* at 156–157. These events seemed not very likely to occur.

In *DaimlerChrysler Corp. v. Cuno,* 547 U.S. 332 (2006), taxpayers challenged the constitutionality of a tax break offered by state and local governments to a car manufacturer. We found no standing. But the plaintiffs would have suffered resulting injury only if that the tax break had depleted state and local treasuries and the legislature had responded by raising their taxes. *Id.,* at 344.

In *Lujan,* the case that may come closest to supporting the majority, the Court also found no standing. But, as I pointed out, *Lujan* is a case where the Court considered *when,* not *whether,* the threatened harm would occur. The relevant injury there consisted of a visit by environmental group's members to a project site where they would find (unlawful) environmental depredation. The Court pointed out that members had alleged that they would visit the project sites "soon." But it wrote that "soon" might refer to almost any time in the future. By way of contrast, the ongoing threat of terrorism means that here the relevant interceptions will likely take place imminently, if not now. . . .

In sum, as the Court concedes, the word "certainly" in the phrase "certainly impending" does not refer to absolute certainty. As our case law demonstrates, what the Constitution requires is something more akin to "reasonable probability" or "high probability." The use of some such standard is all that is necessary here to ensure the actual concrete injury that the Constitution demands. The . . . standard is readily met in this case.

* * *

While I express no view on the merits of the plaintiffs' constitutional claims, I do believe that at least some of the plaintiffs have standing to make those claims. I dissent, with respect, from the majority's contrary conclusion.

1. *Evaluating the Foreign Intelligence Surveillance Court.* The majority opinion in *Clapper* makes much of the role of the Foreign Intelligence Surveillance Court in bringing legal accountability to foreign intelligence surveillance in general and to Section 702 surveillance, in particular. From a separation of powers viewpoint, however, it might well be asked whether the FISC role regarding 702 applications is properly a judicial, as opposed to administrative role. Who, for example, are the adverse parties if an application is sought that names no actual targets? The dissent, for its part, also notes that the FISC normally rejects very few surveillance applications — although this may reflect the applicants' conscientiousness as much as judicial deference.

Prior to the Snowden leaks, a publicly released opinion by either the FISC or its appellate forum, the Foreign Intelligence Surveillance Court of Review, was a rarity. Both the leaked memos and subsequent opinions released in redacted form by the ODNI have allowed a more fine-grained understanding of its work. As explained by Professor Shane, assessments of the FISC's performance have been mixed:

> Even in severely redacted form, the FISC opinions are especially intriguing. They display a court typically deferential to the Justice Department's statutory and constitutional arguments, but intensely engaged in the crafting and monitoring of the targeting and minimization requirements the court imposes under FISA. We learn that, at least in one instance, the court found aspects of the NSA's "upstream collection" of Internet transactions including multiple communications to be unlawful.

> Unsurprisingly given the magnitude of the programs now under scrutiny, the public's incomplete access to the assessments that drive these programs, and the extraordinary density of the documents to which we now have access, reactions to the Snowden revelations have differed markedly. Benjamin Wittes, a Brookings Institution senior fellow and editor-in-chief of the exceptional Lawfare blog, has written a generally sanguine assessment:

> > [N]othing in the current disclosures should cause us to lose faith in the essential integrity of the post-Watergate system of delegated intelligence oversight. To the contrary, those disclosures should give the public great confidence both in the oversight mechanisms within the executive branch and in the judicial oversight mechanisms that review both the Section 215 collection program and the Section 702 collection program.

> > The disclosures show no evidence of any intentional, unlawful spying on Americans or abuses of civil liberties. They show a low rate of the sort of errors any complex system of technical collection will inevitably yield. They show robust compliance procedures. They show earnest and serious efforts to keep the Congress informed — including

members not on this committee or its counterpart in the House of Representatives. And they show an ongoing dialogue with the Foreign Intelligence Surveillance Court (FISC) about the parameters of the agency's legal authorities and a commitment both to keeping the court informed of activities and to complying with its judgments as to their legality. The FISC, meanwhile, in these documents looks nothing like the rubber stamp that it is portrayed to be in countless caricatures. It looks, rather, like a judicial institution of considerable energy, one whose oversight role with respect to both Section 215 and Section 702 requires enormous time and energy on the part of the executive to satisfy.

It is not hard to find less positive views. Jennifer Granick, director of civil liberties at the Stanford Center for Internet and Society and law professor Christopher Jon Sprigman, describe the NSA surveillance program as "criminal":

> The [NSA's bulk data] programs violate both the letter and the spirit of federal law. No statute explicitly authorizes mass surveillance. Through a series of legal contortions, the Obama administration has argued that Congress, since 9/11, intended to implicitly authorize mass surveillance. But this strategy mostly consists of wordplay, fear-mongering and a highly selective reading of the law.

Law professor Martin Lederman, a former Obama Justice Department official, offers a mixed assessment of the FISC:

> The disclosures . . . have demonstrated, I think, that the FISC is extremely resolute, and careful, about ensuring that the NSA and FBI comply with the terms of the FISC's own orders, including the so-called "minimization" requirements–in part because the lawyers in . . . DOJ's National Security Division, take very seriously their responsibility to bring to the court's attention any compliance problems. When it comes to the more fundamental legal questions about the proper statutory and constitutional scope of a proposed program, however, the FISC process is not nearly as thorough or reliable, in large measure because the court hears from only one side.

Peter M. Shane, *Foreword: The NSA and the Legal Regime for Foreign Intelligence Surveillance*, 10 I/S: J. L. & Pol'y for Info. Soc'y 259, 285–287 (2014), To the extent the FISC is indulging attenuated interpretations of the surveillance statutes, would its deference be justified as an alternative to the executive purporting to proceed without supervision under an assertion of inherent Article II authority? Consider:

> Anyone delving into the newly public FISC opinions will surely notice a seemingly odd pattern recently commented on by Marty Lederman. On one hand, the court is quite "resolute" and "careful" in the imposition and monitoring of so-called minimization requirements and other orders

controlling the management and dissemination of information acquired through electronic surveillance. On the other hand, the court seems super-indulgent of executive branch readings of the Foreign Intelligence Surveillance Act and USA PATRIOT Act that supposedly undergird the Government's information acquisition authority in the first place. [Lederman] speculates that the latter attitude may be nurtured by the one-sided advocacy that the court hears.

Although the court's non-adversarial docket undoubtedly does shape its output, there is quite possibly another factor at work here. That is, the FISC may believe that acquiescing in the government's creative statutory readings while taking seriously its own regulation and monitoring role may be the best option available to it for protecting the competing values at stake, including the rule of law.

If the FISC rejected the Government's statutory arguments, it would have to face more pointedly the question whether the Constitution alone, through Article II, grants the executive branch the information-seeking authority it claims. If it answers negatively, two things follow. First, we would face the prospect of the decision going initially to the FISC Court of Review and, if upheld, then being transferred under seal to the Supreme Court, should the Government seek certiorari. How that would work in the Supreme Court is anyone's guess — no procedural option is especially attractive. Second, the court might well be disabling the executive in protecting national security through an important initiative — an assessment the court might think itself ill-positioned to second-guess.

On the other hand, if the court were to affirm some realm of electronic surveillance authority that goes beyond what Congress has approved, that would necessarily be authority that the FISC would not be entitled to supervise. This may well look less attractive than keeping the Government within a statutory rubric, albeit read very broadly, which also authorizes the FISC to impose limiting implementation requirements. These requirements enable the court to instill some protection for privacy and some legal accountability, which the court does monitor rigorously. The executive apparently acquiesces in that judicial role — even, as with regard to bulk telephone records, where the court's authority to impose such requirements might itself be deemed vulnerable to challenge.

The FISC's institutional compromise, if I have correctly identified it, is hardly perfect. Its acquiescence in novel statutory interpretations looks like a disservice to a Congress that remains largely ignorant of those interpretations. The public forum surrounding legislative authorization is likely to be the only meaningful occasion for public deliberation on the proper contours for programs of electronic surveillance because there is quite likely to be no other context in which the executive branch will publicize the scope of what it thinks it needs to protect national security. If the FISC creates secret and unanticipated readings of Congress's handiwork, the value of such public deliberation is plainly called into question. It is notable also that the Government has on several occasions violated FISC orders. One may see these lapses as evidence of system weakness. On the other hand, the government's apparent candor in revealing its lapses to the FISC and the court's seriousness in responding might reveal, as Ben Wittes has argued, an oversight system of reassuring integrity.

A real possibility exists that, as an institutional compromise, the FISC's balancing act may accomplish something quite important. As I have argued elsewhere, it is imperative as a matter of democratic, constitutional self-governance that the executive branch generally regard itself as bound by legislative delimitations of its powers. An executive branch that thinks its authority is limited only by its unilateral assessments of its inherent discretionary powers is far more likely to overreach than an executive that thinks itself beholden to legislative authorization. By helping to stabilize government surveillance practice within a statutory framework, even if creatively interpreted, the FISC may well be operationalizing that insight. If so, that's not a bad thing.

Benjamin Wittes, *Peter Shane Asks: "Can A Secret Court Advance the Rule of Law?"* Lawfare (Nov 30, 2013), https://lawfareblog.com/peter-shane-asks-can-secret-court -advance-rule-law.

2. *Technology, Bulk Collection, and the Fourth Amendment.* As Professors Steven M. Bellovin, Matt Blaze, Susan Landau, and Stephanie K. Pell have written: "For more than forty years, electronic surveillance law in the United States has drawn a strong distinction between the protections afforded to communications 'content' and those afforded to the 'non-content'—also known as 'metadata'—associated with it." *It's Too Complicated: How the Internet Upends* Katz, Smith, *and Electronic Surveillance Law*, 30 Harv. J. L. & Tech. 1 (2016). The key legal reason is the assumption that, because users of electronic communication voluntarily reveal the metadata to communications providers, they lose, under *Smith v. Maryland*, 442 U.S. 735 (1979), any reasonable expectation of privacy in information shared with third-parties. Although a full exploration of Fourth Amendment law is beyond our scope here, it is important to note that technology is rapidly casting this doctrinal architecture into doubt. First, because it has become all but impossible for most people to participate in the digital world—whether or not they believe they are engaged in communication— without leaving digital signals for third parties, even current Justices have started to question the utility of third-party doctrine for delimiting Fourth Amendment rights. See *United States v. Jones*, 565 U.S. 400, 417 (2012) (Sotomayor, J., concurring) ("[I]t may be necessary to reconsider the premise that an individual has no reasonable expectation of privacy in information voluntarily disclosed to third parties."). Second, the content-metadata distinction—often analogized to, say, the difference between the contents of a postal letter and the address information on the outside of the envelope—simply does not work well for internet communications. For

a lengthy, but accessible introduction to the technological issues posed, see Bellovin, et al., *supra*, at 100 ("The Internet disrupts the content/non-content distinction . . . arguably to the point of collapse . . . .).

3. *"Backdoor Searches" and the Wall of Separation Problem Redux*. Although surveillance authorized under Section 702 may not intentionally target any "United States person" or any person known to be in the United States, 50 U.S.C. § 1881g(b), such surveillance is quite likely to collect information about United States persons who are not the primary targets. The FISC has determined that it is permissible for the FBI, even when engaged in ordinary criminal (*i.e.*, not-national-security-related) investigations, to query Section 702 databases using terms or indicators linked to U.S. persons if the search is "reasonably designed to 'find and extract' either 'foreign intelligence information' or 'evidence of a crime.' " Memorandum Opinion and Order, In re [REDACTED], No. [REDACTED], at 26–27, (FISA Ct. Nov. 6, 2015), https://www.dni.gov/files/documents/20151106-702Mem_Opinion_Order_for_Public_Release.pdf. Such inquiries are called "backdoor searches" and do not require a warrant. An issue certain to be raised during debates over the possible reauthorization of Section 702 is whether provisions need to be added to prohibit or further regulate warrantless backdoor searches of this kind; the issue is arguably made yet more pressing because, to the degree such searches compromise privacy in the U.S., it may complicate the ability of U.S. companies to engage in cross-border data exchanges with European Union countries that impose more stringent privacy requirements. Mieke Eoyang and Gary Ashcroft, *Why Electronic Surveillance Report is Necessary*, Lawfare (Feb. 28, 2017), https://www.lawfareblog.com/why-electronic-surveillance-reform-necessary. In other words, the desire of U.S. corporations to compete effectively for business in the EU may force some reconsideration of the "wall of separation" problem as it reappeared in the wake of 9/11.

4. *Foreign Surveillance and a New AUMF*. Recall that, prior to the enactment of the 2006 PATRIOT Act Amendments, the Protect America Act, and the FISA Amendments Act of 2008, the Bush Administration had rooted the defense of its extensive electronic surveillance programs in the 2001 AUMF against al-Qaeda. Should Congress now adopt a new AUMF targeting the Islamic State and associated forces, should it address specifically whether the new AUMF encompasses electronic surveillance authority beyond the scope of FISA. Under the 2008 FISA Amendments, only "an express statutory authorization for electronic surveillance" would now permit an end-run around FISA procedures for foreign intelligence surveillance. 50 U.S.C. § 1812. If a new AUMF makes no specific reference to electronic surveillance, would the wording of § 1812 suffice to ensure that future Administrations live by FISA's limits?

Chapter 8

Power and Institutional Design: The Case of the Presidency

The drafters of the original Constitution deployed two methods of protecting us against a tyrannical national government. The first involved the careful assignment of competing authorities to each of the three co-equal branches of government. "Ambition," as Madison wrote in THE FEDERALIST, No. 51, was made "to counteract ambition." The Constitution seeks to "contriv[e] the interior structure of the government as that its several constituent parts may, by their mutual relations, be the means of keeping each other in their proper places." *Id.* The tensions and uncertainties resulting from the original assignment of powers have provided the focus for most of this text.

The second strategy involved the structural and procedural design of each of the three branches of government. For example, the choices of a bicameral Congress and, initially, of a Senate removed from direct popular control were obviously intended to reduce what the drafters perceived to be certain risks in the creation of a national legislature. (Recall, in this regard, that *Chadha*, discussed in Chapter Two, was centrally concerned about preserving bicameralism, as well as preventing legislative encroachments on executive power.) Likewise, the Framers thought it protective of liberty that federal judges would be appointed, rather than elected; vested with life tenure; and subject to removal only in extreme cases and through a burdensome procedure.

We have considered the power implications of at least some of these "institutional design" decisions at various points, *e.g.*, the congressional term limits debate discussed in Chapter Three. Although reviewing all these decisions comprehensively would require another exhaustive volume, it is worth examining more systematically at least some of the institutional design features of at least one of the branches as a way of posing two questions: How do decisions on the structure, selection, removal, and internal decision making of a branch of government affect its exercise of power? How do such decisions regarding one branch affect the relative authorities of the other two branches? We choose the Presidency as our case study, considering, in Section A, our system for presidential election; in Section B, our system for presidential and vice-presidential succession; and, in Section C, proposals for a presidency either more or less politicized, either through the adoption of a parliamentary or one-term model, respectively.

A. Presidential Elections

1. The Role of States in Presidential Selection

a. The Mechanics of the Electoral College: A Primer

Perhaps the most surprising feature of the system by which we choose the leader of our national government is the pivotal role that state governments play in shaping and implementing key features of that system. That is because, under our constitutional system, what happens on our quadrennial Election Day—the first Tuesday after the first Monday in November of every year divisible by four—is *not* the selection of the President of the United States. Instead, voters in all fifty states and in the District of Columbia go to the polls and choose slates of "electors." These are unique public officials whose sole task—occurring on the first Monday after the second Wednesday in the month of December following their appointment—is the casting of ballots for President and Vice President. Although the term is not used in the Constitution, these electors have come to be known as the Electoral College.

1. The Constitutional Basics

The Constitution provides that the electors assigned to each state shall be equal to the whole number of Senators and Representatives to which the State is entitled in Congress. Art. II, § 1, cl. 1. The Twenty-Third Amendment to the Constitution, ratified in 1961, assigned to the District of Columbia the number of electors to which it would be entitled were the District a state, provided that the number shall not exceed the representation of the least populous state. As a result, the number of electors qualified to vote in the actual selection of the President is now 538. Each state legislature (and Congress, for the District of Columbia) sets the rules by which the electors shall be chosen in each state, provided only that no federal office holder may serve as an elector.

The Electoral College never meets as a group. Instead, the electors meet in their respective states in order to cast their presidential and vice-presidential ballots. Following the Twelfth Amendment, ratified in 1804, these are separate ballots, and each elector must choose, for the two distinct offices, two candidates "one of whom, at least, shall not be an inhabitant of the same state with themselves." Amend. XII, par. 1. (It was on the basis of the non-cohabitation requirement that a group of Texas voters sought to enjoin Texas electors from casting ballots in 2000 for George W. Bush and Dick Cheney, arguing unsuccessfully that each should be deemed an "inhabitant" of Texas. *Jones v. Bush*, 122 F. Supp. 2d 713 (N.D. Tex. 2002), *aff'd*, 244 F.3d 134 (5th Cir. 2000), *cert. denied*, 531 U.S. 1062 (2001).) These ballots are then to be signed, certified, and transmitted to the District of Columbia and directed to the President of the Senate, who is, under Art. I, § 3, cl. 4, the incumbent Vice President of the United States.

On January 6, following the meetings of electors, the electoral ballots are counted by the President of the Senate with the entire Congress present. Should any presidential candidate win the votes of a majority of all those electors actually appointed, that person becomes President-elect. The same rule applies for the selection of the Vice President. If no presidential candidate has a majority, then the House of Representatives is authorized to select the President from among the three presidential candidates who received the highest number of electoral votes. Each state delegation, however, votes as a whole. The District of Columbia is excluded from this vote, and the winning candidate must have a majority of all 50 states in order to win. (A quorum consists of members from two-thirds of the states.) The same process applies to the contingent election of a Vice President, except that it is the Senate, not the House, that makes the selection, and Senators must choose between the two top vote-getters for vice president. The only other restriction on the Senators is that they may not choose as Vice President anyone who would be constitutionally ineligible to be President.

As the electoral system was originally designed in 1789, the electors did not cast separately designated ballots for President and Vice President. The framers had in mind that each elector would name two public figures, on a non-partisan basis, worthy of becoming President, and they determined that the President should be the individual receiving the most electoral votes, provided that this number of votes exceeded the number of appointed electors amounting to a majority. Should more than one candidate receive a majority vote, and should their respective votes be equal, the Framers provided that the House would choose between them. If no one received a majority, the House would choose among the top five vote-getters. With each of the Philadelphia delegates undoubtedly certain that the electors would unanimously choose George Washington for the first presidency, this seemed an altogether plausible system.

Once nascent political parties began to emerge as caucuses in the 1790s, however, the flaws in this system became obvious. First, as the election of 1796 demonstrated, it was possible for the system to generate the selection of a politically antagonistic President and Vice President—in 1796, it was Adams and Jefferson. Second, if the electors for a particular party dutifully cast their two ballots for the party's presidential and vice-presidential nominees, respectively, then there would necessarily be a tie vote, always throwing the election into the House. This is precisely what occurred in the election of 1800, in which the House required 36 ballots to break the tie between Thomas Jefferson and Aaron Burr, a debacle that led to the proposal and ratification of the Twelfth Amendment.

2. The Statutory Framework

The Twelfth Amendment leaves many questions unanswered with regard to presidential balloting, but Congress has filled some of the critical lacunae through statute. There is, for example, a detailed process for certifying the electoral rosters received from each state. 3 U.S.C. § 6. If a set of electoral votes for a particular state has been duly certified pursuant to that section, and only one such set of votes has been certified for the state, those are the votes that must be counted. 3 U.S.C. § 15.

Congress deals by statute also with a phenomenon that proved critical in the election of 1876 — namely, the submission by one or more states of different electoral counts, reflecting disputes at the state level as to who, in fact, are the duly authorized electors. In legislation adopted in 1887, Congress provides a procedure by which states may achieve some certainty in their submission of electoral votes. Specifically, Congress may not substitute its judgment as to who are a state's duly authorized electors, if the state has provided for a final adjudication of any dispute, the dispute is resolved pursuant to state law already in place, and the dispute is resolved at least six days prior to the casting of the electoral ballots.

When Congress gathers for the counting of the electoral votes, members of Congress may object to particular ballots, provided that the objections be lodged in writing, and signed by both a Senator and a Representative. If there is doubt as to the proper votes cast, notwithstanding the provisions just cited, then either the two Houses of Congress have to agree on the proper roster of electoral votes for a state, or "the votes of the electors whose appointment shall have been certified by the executive of the State, under the seal thereof, shall be counted," notwithstanding any objection. 3 U.S.C. § 15.

Another problem addressed by statute is the potential for a deadlocked election. 3 U.S.C. § 19 provides: "If, by reason of . . . failure to qualify, there is neither a President nor Vice President to discharge the powers and duties of the office of President, then the Speaker of the House of Representatives shall, upon his resignation as Speaker and as Representative in Congress, act as President." If the Speaker is not constitutionally qualified to be President or is otherwise unavailable, the position goes to the President Pro Tempore of the Senate. Should the Speaker or President Pro Tempore be called upon to serve as President because of the failure of both the President-elect and the Vice President-elect to qualify, then that individual holds office only until a President or Vice President does qualify.

3. The Nature of the Elector's Office

The original vision of the presidential elector cast that official in the role of an independent judge, a thoughtful state luminary who would be able to reflect in an informed and dispassionate way on those political leaders most likely to serve honorably as President of the United States. The advent of political parties plainly changed that role, but the constitutional fact of electors' independence has occasionally raised the problem of the so-called "faithless elector." That is, what is a state to do if an elector who won appointment by pledging to support the candidate of Party X decides instead to cast his or her electoral ballot for the candidate of Party Y — or anyone else, for that matter? There were seven faithless electors in the Twentieth

Century, but faithless electors have never affected the outcome of any presidential election.

In response to this problem, political parties may seek to exact from their slate of candidates for the electoral position a pledge to support the presidential and vice-presidential candidates of the national party. Although hinting that such pledges may be legally unenforceable against an ultimately faithless elector, the Supreme Court has upheld the power of states to authorize parties to exact such pledges, and to exclude as electors those who fail to execute such a party pledge, when the parties so require. *Ray v. Blair*, 343 U.S. 214 (1952).

———————

Further Reading. Helpful resources on the mechanics of presidential elections include John Fortier, After the People Vote: A Guide to the Electoral College (3d ed. 2004); the Electoral College Web Site maintained by the National Archives and Records Administration, at http://www.archives.gov/federal_register /electoral_college/, Kevin J. Coleman, Joseph E. Cantor, and Thomas H. Neale, Presidential Elections in the United States: A Primer (Congressional Research Service No. RL30527, 2000), available at https://www.fas.org/sgp/crs/misc/RL30527 .pdf; Thomas H. Neale, The Electoral College: How It Works in Contemporary Presidential Elections (Congressional Research Service No. RL32611, 2016); CRS Report RS20300, Thomas H. Neale, Election of the President and Vice President by Congress: Contingent Election (Congressional Research Service No. RS20300, 2001), available at http://www.au.af.mil/au/awc/awcgate/crs /rs20300.pdf.

b. The Merits of the Electoral College: A Debate

The materials that follow summarize the key arguments that have been brought on behalf of continuing the Electoral College system or abandoning it in favor of a direct election process.

Direct Popular Election of the President and Vice President of the United States

S. Rep. No. 609, 95th Cong., 1st Sess. (1977)

The Committee on the Judiciary, to which was referred the resolution (S.J. Res. 1) proposing an amendment to the Constitution of the United States relating to the direct popular election of the President and the Vice President of the United States, having considered the same, . . . recommends that the joint resolution do pass. . . .

DEFECTS AND DEFICIENCIES IN THE PRESENT SYSTEM

The appearance of political party candidates as early as 1800 meant, in effect, that Hamilton's concept of a "select assembly" of independent electors already had lost its purpose only a decade after its embodiment in the Constitution. A Senate report published in 1806 caustically noted that the free and independent electors had "degenerated into mere agents in a case which requires no agency and where the agent must be useless if he is faithful and dangerous if he is not." More than 145 years later, however, the elector still retains this constitutionally guaranteed independence. In January 1969, Congress confirmed this 18th century prerogative by accepting the vote of a popularly chosen Republican elector from North Carolina who had cast his vote in the Electoral College for George Wallace, the American Independent Party candidate. Again in 1973, a Republican elector from Virginia was allowed to cast his vote for one Dr. John Hospers of the Liberation Party. An elector from Washington, Mike Padden, cast his vote for his personal choice, Ronald Reagan in 1976.

How dangerous is the anachronistic elector? Historically, as the late Justice Jackson paraphrased Gilbert and Sullivan, "they always voted at their party's beck and call and never thought of thinking for themselves at all." The prospect of unknown electors auctioning off the Presidency to the highest bidder, nevertheless, is all too real. That is the lesson of 1968, when the present electoral system brought us to the brink of a constitutional crisis. A shift from Nixon to Humphrey of only 42,000 popular votes in three States would have denied Nixon an electoral majority and given Wallace, with his 46 electoral votes, the balance of power. As the former Alabama Governor explained in an exclusive interview with *U.S. News & World Report* (September 30, 1968):

> *Question.* If none of the three candidates get a majority, is the election going to be decided in the Electoral College or in the House of Representatives?
>
> WALLACE. I think it would be settled in the Electoral College.
>
> *Question.* Two of the candidates get together or their electors get together and determine who is to be President?
>
> WALLACE. That is right.

. . . [E]liminating the elector . . . is not a cure-all for what ails our present electoral machinery. The elector, in fact, is merely a symptom of what the American Bar Association's Special Commission on Electoral Reform aptly described as our "archaic, undemocratic, complex, ambiguous, indirect, and dangerous" method of electing a President.

After a 10 month study, the Commission concluded that the entire electoral system should be replaced, and popular choice substituted for political chance.

Among other things, the present system can elect a President who has fewer popular votes than the opponent and thus is not the first choice of the voters; awards all of a State's electoral votes to the winner of the State popular vote, whether the candidate's margin is 1 vote or 1 million votes; cancels out all of the popular votes cast for the losing candidate in a State and casts these votes for the winner; assigns to each State a minimum of three electoral votes regardless of population and voter turnout; and provides for a patently undemocratic method for choosing a President in the event no candidate receives an electoral majority.

The major defect of the present electoral system—the unit rule—is not even a constitutional provision. The unit rule or "winner-take-all" formula is the State practice of awarding all of its electoral votes to the statewide popular vote winner. In effect, millions of voters are disfranchised if they vote for the losing candidate in their State because the full voting power of the State—its electoral vote—is awarded to the candidate they opposed. . . .

A practical consequence of this disfranchisement is that it discourages the minority party in traditionally one-party States. Simply stated, where there is no hope of carrying the statewide popular vote the size of the voter turnout for the likely loser is meaningless. This necessarily leads to the atrophy of the party structure in many States. By the same token, the prospective winner has little incentive to turn out the vote because the margin of victory likewise is meaningless. In sum, the unit rule has the unhealthy political effect of both discouraging second parties in areas of one-party dominance and discouraging voting. This is reflected most clearly in the poor voter turnout in U.S. Presidential elections in comparison to most other democratic nations.

A byproduct of the unit rule is the distortions it produces in the value of individual votes. Winner-take-all means that a single voter has the power to cast the "swing" vote in his State, throwing the entire bloc of electoral votes to one candidate or the other. The voter's power is thus enhanced or diminished according to how many electoral votes the voter is able to affect, that is, whether the voter comes from a large or small electoral vote State. It is therefore possible for 11 "swing" votes in the largest States and one from the District of Columbia to decide the election, even though the candidate did not get a single popular vote in all of the other States. Ultimately, the swing voter derives influence from the inherent possibility of the electoral college system that the majority of the electoral votes will not produce the same winner as the plurality of popular votes. There is, of course, no swing vote with direct election. With direct election all votes count the same.

The most dangerous result of the unit rule of our present electoral system is the lack of guarantee that the candidate with the most popular votes will win.

This dangerous prospect, more than anything else, condemns the present system as an imperfect device for recording the sentiment of American voters. In 1824, 1876, and again in 1888 this system produced Presidents who were not the popular choice of the voters. On numerous other occasions in this century, a shift of less than 1 percent of the popular vote would have produced an electoral majority for the candidate who received fewer popular votes. In 1948, for example, a shift of less than 30,000 popular votes in three States would have given Governor Dewey an electoral vote majority—despite President Truman's 2 million-plus popular vote margin.

In a runaway election—like that of 1972—any system will produce an electoral victory for the popular vote winner. It is the accuracy of the results produced in closely contested elections, however, that determines the true soundness of an electoral system. Based on this criterion, the committee concluded that the present system is clearly defective. A computer study of Presidential elections over the last 50 years revealed, for example, that in elections as close as that of 1960 the present system offered only a 50–50 chance that the electoral result would agree with the popular vote. For an election as close as 1968, where some 500,000 popular votes separated the candidates, there was one chance in three that the electoral vote winner would not be the popular vote winner as well. According to the evidence, the danger of an electoral backfire is clear and present.

THE OPPONENTS' ARGUMENTS AND SOME COUNTERPOINTS

In the 10 years the proposal for the direct popular election of the President has been before the Congress, through many weeks of hearings and many days of floor debate, the arguments on this question have been sharpened and refined. . . .

THE EFFECT OF DIRECT ELECTION ON THE TWO-PARTY SYSTEM

Opponents of direct election have alleged that abolition of the electoral college would tend to proliferate the party structure and weaken the two major parties. They believe that the winner-take-all or unit rule feature of the present system is the most important institutional guarantee for the two-party system. A well-known political scientist has summarized their argument as follows: "Under the present system, the votes cast for a minor party candidate in any state are lost except in the unlikely event he runs ahead of the major party candidate. On the other hand all of the votes cast for a minor party under a popular vote would count toward the total vote of its candidate. Therefore, the carryover of votes from state to state, which would be possible under direct election, would cause the proliferation of third parties."

However, a careful study of the dynamics of the electoral college reveals that it does not discourage third parties, and . . . actually encourages them . . . in two respects. First, it provides incentives for the regional third party candidate such as George Wallace in 1968. Wallace perceived that by carrying a large bloc of States with a thin margin, he might be able to throw the two major candidates into a deadlock and thereby see the contest settled in the House of Representatives.

The winner-take-all rule also enhances the chances of national third-party candidates when they can gather votes in large, closely balanced states. For example, as Lawrence Longley testified before the subcommittee, Eugene McCarthy in 1976,

> with less than 1 percent of the popular vote, came close to tilting the election through his strength in close pivotal States. In four States, (Iowa, Maine, Alabama and Oregon) totaling 26 electoral votes, McCarthy's vote exceeded the margin by which Ford defeated Carter. In those States, McCarthy's candidacy may have swung those States to Carter. Even more significantly, had McCarthy been on the New York ballot, it is likely Ford would have carried that State with its 41 electoral votes, and with it the election—despite Carter's national vote majority.

Most authorities agree that the deterrence of third parties is related to factors other than the electoral college. An excellent case in point is the abortive attempt of the "peace" forces to organize a fourth party after the 1968 Democratic Convention. In 1968, "Peace Party" probably could not have garnered a plurality in enough states to have a significant impact on the electoral college, and the unit rule undoubtedly played some role in their ultimate decision not to proceed. . . .

It is much more likely that the Peace Party failed in 1968 for two reasons totally unrelated to the structure of the electoral college—two reasons why nationwide third parties will also be deterred under direct election. First, . . . the organizers realized that their efforts would take votes from the major party candidate closest to them in conviction and insure the victory of the major party candidate most undesirable to them. The Peace Party would have been more apt to garner a Humphrey vote than a Nixon vote, and thus by entering the field they would have enhanced the prospects of Nixon. Second, nationwide third party movements are discouraged by the fact that they must compete with the major parties for a single office—the Presidency. Planners of a Peace Party in 1968 were discouraged by the realization that they would have little to show for their efforts, for unlike the European coalition governments, the Presidency is held by one person and would be the exclusive prize of one of the major parties. On the other hand, if all the Peace Party wanted was to "spoil" the Democratic Party's chances, then the electoral college system was best suited to its purposes. All they needed to do was to run in New York and California to insure a Democratic defeat.

Scholars who have studied the two-party system in this country and compared it to similar systems throughout the world have a variety of theories as to its cause; but none suggest the electoral college. Most political scientists believe that the major institutional influence on the two-party system is the election of almost all officials in the U.S. in single-member districts. This theory stems originally from the writings of Maurice Duverger, who has found that almost every government in the world which elects its officials from single-member districts and by plurality vote has only two major parties, while countries that use multi-member districts and proportional representation have a multitude of parties. Duverger and other scholars have found that the electoral mechanics of the single member district, in terms of its effect on the party system, are such that they tend to force factions to combine in order to be certain of capturing a popular vote plurality and victory.

It was the conclusion of the committee's majority that direct popular election would work affirmatively to strengthen the two-party system. First, by counting every popular vote regardless of where it is cast, direct election would spread and foster two-party competition on a nationwide scale. The goal of both major parties would be to "get out the vote" in every State. Simply carrying a State, the objective under the present system, would no longer be the ultimate objective. The net result, therefore, would be increased party activity—particularly in what are now one-party States. . . .

FEDERALISM AND DIRECT ELECTION

Perhaps the most frequent argument made by opponents of direct election is that the electoral college is an important component in preserving the power of the States in our Federal system. Even at the Constitutional Convention, however, the electoral college was not intended to serve that purpose.

The electoral college was effected primarily as a compromise between advocates of popular election such as James Madison, James Wilson and Gouverneur Morris and those who wanted the executive chosen by the legislative branch. The manner of choosing the President was debated sporadically over the summer of 1787, and resolved finally by the contrivance of an appointed Committee of Eleven in the early days of September as a matter of practical politics. It worked well as an arbitration device in 1787 but quickly diminished in utility thereafter.

It is clear that the well-known Great Compromise between large and small states was not a major factor in shaping the electoral college. As Neal Peirce has explained in his book, "The People's President,"

> The Great Compromise was devised to settle the dispute over representation in Congress, not the electoral college. . . . At no point in the minutes of the Convention can one find any reference to the application of the Great Compromise to the electoral college's apportionment as important to the Federal system or to the overall structure of the Constitution which was adopted. Indeed, it was never mentioned directly at all. Only in "The Federalist Papers," where James Madison argued at one point that the electoral base for the Presidency would be a "compound" of national and state factors because of the mixed apportionment base, does the argument appear. But no more than indirect reference was made to the apportionment of the electoral college in the State ratifying conventions, or in fact by any of the Nation's leaders until some years after ratification of the Constitution. The argument that the founding fathers viewed the special Federal nature of electoral college apportionment as central to the institution of the Presidency, or to the entire Constitution, is simply false. The small States thought they would gain special advantage, but by another provision—their equal votes in the House in contingent elections.

In the latest hearings on the proposed direct election amendment before the Subcommittee on the Constitution, Professor Emeritus Paul Freund of Harvard addressed the question of whether changing to direct election as a means of electing the President would affect a change on the concept of federalism as conceived by the framers of the Constitution. His reply was that such a change would be much less radical than that of the 17th Amendment in 1913 when we abandoned the indirect election of Senators and thereby abandoned the design of the framers. The original vision of the writers of the Constitution about the selection of the Executive soon proved unworkable. A whole new set of circumstances such as the growth of political parties arose and quickly required the revision of the 12th amendment. . . .

The fundamental tenets of federalism remain today as they did in 1787; the balance between State governments and the Federal Government, and the varying representation in the two Houses of Congress. Perhaps no better response has been given to the questions about direct election which arise under the name of federalism than that of Senator Mike Mansfield in 1961:

> The Federal system is not strengthened through an antiquated device which has not worked as it was intended to work when it was included in the Constitution and which, if anything, has become a divisive force in the Federal system by pitting groups of States against groups of States. As I see the Federal system in contemporary practice, the House of Representatives is the key to the protection of district interests as to district interests, just as the Senate is the key to the protection of State interests as State interests. These instrumentalities, and particularly the Senate, are the principal constitutional safeguards of the Federal system, but the Presidency has evolved, out of necessity, into the principal political office, as the courts have become the principal legal bulwark beyond districts, beyond States, for safeguarding the interests of all the people in all the States. And since such is the case, in my opinion, the Presidency should be subject to the direct and equal control of all the people.

As Senator Robert Dole remarked in testifying before the Subcommittee for the second time in 1977, direct election serves to enhance real "commonsense" federalism. . . . Dole explains that with direct election, Presidential candidates would no longer be able to ignore areas in small as well as large States, simply because their supporters are in a clear majority or clear minority. . . .

IMPACT OF DIRECT ELECTION ON THE SMALLER STATES

. . . Under the unit rule, all of the State's electoral votes are awarded to the candidate who wins a popular vote plurality—regardless of whether the plurality is 1 vote or 1 million votes. The consequence of this "winner-take-all" system is that Presidential campaigns and political power are concentrated in the large, closely contested urban States, where entire State blocs of electoral votes can be won by the narrowest of margins. . . .

There is little doubt that with direct election, candidates will continue to travel more often to heavily populated areas than sparsely populated ones. But with direct election, at least communities of the same size will hold the same attraction whether they are in a large or a small State. . . .

DIRECT ELECTION WOULD REDUCE THE DANGER OF VOTER FRAUD

According to the minority report from the Committee on the Judiciary in 1970, "One of the most calamitous and probable consequences of direct popular election will be the increased incidence of election fraud." The argument is that if fraud occurs under the present system, the impact is limited to determining the outcome on one State alone. "The incentive to steal votes is now restricted to close contests in States which have a sufficiently large electoral vote to alter the final result. Thus, fraud can be profitable only in a few States, and is seldom capable of affecting the national outcome."

In reality, the incentive to steal votes "now" as described above is a fair argument for why the electoral college system itself encourages fraud. A relatively few irregular votes can reap a healthy reward in the form of a bloc of electoral votes, because of the unit rule. In short, under the present system, fraudulent popular votes are likely to have a greater impact than a like number of fraudulent popular votes under direct election.

We may cite New York in 1976 as an example. Cries of voting irregularities arose on election night. At stake were 41 electoral votes — more than enough to elect Ford over Carter in the electoral college. Carter's popular margin was 290,000. The calls for recount were eventually dropped, but if fraud had been present in New York, Carter's plurality of 290,000 would have been enough to determine the outcome of the election. Under direct election, at least 1.7 million votes, Carter's national margin, would have had to have been irregular to determine the outcome.

Opponents of direct election charge that a popular vote would increase the incentive for fraud because in a close election every vote would count. It is precisely for this reason that we would have better policing of the polling places by the parties themselves, and possibly even better counting methods and procedural safeguards. The kinds of fraud and voting irregularities which have occurred under the electoral college are frequently in places controlled by one party. And under the electoral college system, there is no incentive for the other party to watch the polls when there is no possibility of carrying the electoral votes.

DIRECT ELECTION AND VOTE RECOUNTS

. . . It is common sense that a candidate will desire a recount only when the candidate perceives that it may change the results in the candidate's favor. And that change of fortune is more likely with the electoral college system than it is with direct election. For example, in 1976, if Ford had carried Ohio and Hawaii he would have gained the electoral majority and would have won the election. A shift of only 9,245 votes in these two States would have accomplished that result. The number of votes nation-wide needed to change the result with a direct election was Carter's plurality of 1.7 million. . . .

Further, recounts will remain unlikely under direct election as they have been with the electoral college system in that experience has shown that overall election recounts generally reveal an almost minuscule shift in number and percent of votes and almost never change the result. . . .

RUNOFF

The proposed amendment requires the winning candidate to obtain at least 40 percent of the total vote in order to win. Failing that plurality a runoff of the top two candidates is required. The 40 percent figure was arrived at because it was felt necessary to establish a reasonable plurality requirement indicating a legitimate mandate to govern. On the other hand, it was decided that a requirement that was set too high might disrupt the stability of our political system by too easily triggering a runoff.

. . . To turn once again to some indirect method of choice such as the Congress to resolve the selection of the President would mean that the choice would be useless if it reflects the will of the people and mischievous if it does not. All the dangers of deals made with third party candidates which now exist with the electoral college would be retained, with no improvement in the means of expressing the wishes of the voters themselves.

A review of Presidential elections shows that the likelihood of a runoff is dim. Only one President, Lincoln, has received less than 40 percent of the popular vote. In 1860 Lincoln received only 39.79 percent of the vote but his name did not appear on the ballot in 10 States.

Further, it appears very unlikely that neither major party candidate would receive a 40 percent plurality—even with a third party candidate in the race. Under the terms of Senate Joint Resolution 1, a splinter party would have to poll at least 20 percent of the total popular vote—and in most instances more—before triggering the runoff. That is considered unlikely in view of the strong two-party system in the United States. In 1968, for example, the most significant third party bid since 1924 could only produce 13.5 percent of the popular vote for George Wallace.

Even more to the point, the committee reviewed the four-way race in 1912, noting that in the face of challenges by an incumbent President and a popular former President, Woodrow Wilson still received more than 40 percent of the popular vote. The four-way race in 1948, involving Truman, Dewey, Thurmond, and Wallace, likewise produced a candidate with well over 40 percent of the popular vote. The likelihood of a major party candidate receiving the required plurality, therefore, is not confined merely to third party races but to multiparty contests as well.

The question has been raised as to whether the runoff might not unnecessarily encourage third parties to enter Presidential elections. As analyzed by Prof. Paul Freund of Harvard University before the subcommittee on July 28, 1977, third parties have four motivations to place a candidate in the field. They may hope to win or at least be placed in the runoff; to register the strengths of their movement or cause; to deadlock the election or play a spoiler role; or finally to cause the defeat of a particular major party candidate.

If the motive is to win, the third party obviously must register 40 percent. If it is to place in the runoff, the party must keep both major parties from achieving 40 percent, while at the same time defeating one of the major parties, an extremely difficult task.

If the minor party's aim is to effect a deadlock and exert maximum power in a contingency election, then the electoral college is probably more attractive a system than direct election. To prevent a majority in the electoral vote is far easier for a strong regional candidate than it would be to achieve at least 20 percent of the popular vote while neither major party achieved 40 percent.

Assuming, however, that a minor party candidate or group of candidates is able to garner 20 percent of the popular vote and simultaneously preclude either major party candidate from receiving at least 40 percent of the remaining votes, the bargaining position obtained may be less than would at first appear. The ability of the candidate to control the votes of all those individuals who once claimed to support him is not tantamount to the influence held by a candidate over electors pledged to that candidate. . . .

RACIAL AND MINORITY GROUP VOTING POWER UNDER ELECTORAL COLLEGE AND DIRECT ELECTION SYSTEMS

Some have defended the present electoral college approach on the theory that the system as it operates gives disproportionate voting influence to racial or ethnic minorities, thereby offsetting some of the economic or social deprivations historically suffered by these groups. The late Prof. Alexander M. Bickel of Yale Law School was a major proponent of this view. . . . This conclusion in respect to racial groups has been undermined in recent years, however, by empirical analyses which have been done of voting power under the electoral college. . . .

Perhaps the one aspect of the electoral college system which carries with it the greatest burden for ethnic or racial minorities is the unit rule provision. This system, which awards all of a State's electoral votes to the candidate who wins a majority of the popular vote, can have an impact on minority voting strength that is little short of devastating. . . . [T]he direct election approach is the only method of insuring that minority and ethnic group voters across the country exercise the voting power which their numbers command. . . .

A final question is answered by direct election, and that is the question of fundamental fairness. With direct election every vote would count. Every vote would count the same, urban or rural, black or white, rich or poor; north, south, east or west. And the person with the most votes would win. Only direct election accomplishes this result. . . .

J. A. Best, Prepared Statement on "The Case for the Electoral College"*

The Electoral College and Direct Election, Hearings Before the Subcomm. on the Constitution of the U.S. Comm. on the Judiciary,

95th Cong., 1st Sess. (1977)

. . . The distinctive element of the electoral college system is the federal unit rule principle not the office of presidential elector. This system emerged in 1832 at the same time as the national party nominating convention system.

. . . The organizing principle of the American system of government is the principle of the concurrent majority under which coalition-building and compromise create

---

broad cross-sectional majorities that provide moderate government and are resistant to tyranny. . . .

The following case for the electoral college system is not a case for the system established by the Founders in the Constitution. Contrary to the usual understanding, the date of the emergence of our current presidential election system is approximately 1832 not 1789. The original system devised by the Founders not only did not work as they had intended but was a mere embryo of the system as we know it today. . . .

The Constitution left it to the states to decide how their presidential electors would be selected. As a result, a diversity of methods were employed during the first eleven presidential elections. As late as 1828, one fourth of the states did not use the unit rule. In 1828, Maine, Maryland, New York and Tennessee used the district method of aggregating popular votes and in Delaware and South Carolina the electors were chosen by the state legislature. By 1832, all but two states had adopted the unit rule; Maryland used the district system and in South Carolina the electors were chosen by the legislature. 1832 was the year when the system assumed its peculiar, characteristic form.

. . . Faithless electors make headlines and arouse our moral indignation, but they have had no practical effect on any election. More than 17,000 electoral votes have been cast since the founding, and less than 10 of them can be called faithless or miscast. If the office of elector alone were abolished, the system as we know it would not be altered. . . . The actual, the paramount question about the electoral college system is whether the popular vote for President should be aggregated under the federal unit rule principle.

No electoral system is neutral. Every electoral system, as a practical matter, favors certain groups and interests and discriminates against others. Therefore, the issue is not whether the electoral college has biases, but rather whether the biases of the electoral college are compatible with and supportive of the American idea of democracy, whether the electoral college is an integral part of our system of government. As Senator John Kennedy put it, when he and Senator Paul Douglas led the fight against a proposal to change the system, "It is not only the unit vote for the Presidency we are talking about, but a whole solar system of governmental power. If it is proposed to change the balance of power of one of the elements of the solar system, it is necessary to consider the others."

What, then, is this "solar system," what is the American idea of democracy? It is, has been, and was intended to be a system of concurrent majorities designed to balance two very high but frequently incompatible things—liberty and equality. We are not, have never been and were not intended to be a simple majoritarian democracy, the regime whose dedication to equality is so single-minded that it will readily sacrifice liberty to achieve its goal. No attentive reader of the constitution or of the *Federalist Papers* can fail to recognize the Founder's overwhelming fear of majority faction, of majority tyranny. . . .

Our "solar system of governmental power" is filled with devices or intermediary institutions to protect minorities, to prevent the formation of all-national majorities and to limit the power of ordinary majorities. To mention just five of the most obvious and important ones, there are the Constitution itself, the amendment procedure, the Supreme Court of the United States, the United States Senate and, of course, the electoral college system. . . . None of these institutions and procedures operates simply under the principle of one citizen, one equally weighted direct vote. . . .

As it actually operates, the electoral college system has a significant number of biases. It has a bias in favor of: (1) the winner of a cross-sectional popular plurality, (2) a single election, (3) the two-party system, (4) large, competitive two-party states and well organized or self-conscious minorities in urban-suburban areas in such states, (5) ideologically moderate candidates and parties, and (6) electoral certainty. It has a bias against: (1) sectional candidacies, (2) contingency elections, (3) third parties, (4) homogeneous regions and one-party states, (5) ideologically extremist candidates and parties, and (6) the premium on fraud. These biases must be closely examined to determine how they operate and interact. . . .

The system is essentially a plurality system that magnifies the national plurality winner's margin of victory in the electoral vote. Because the unit rule awards 100 percent of a state's electoral vote to the candidate who achieves a statewide plurality, the President-Elect will receive a higher percentage of the electoral vote than he has won in the popular vote. In the thirty-six elections held since 1832, the average increase in the national plurality winner's margin in the electoral votes is 19.3 percent. In every election but one, the multiplier effect of the unit rule worked to the advantage of the undisputed winner of the popular plurality.

This does not mean that the multiplier effect gives the plurality candidate a greater mandate. The electorate largely misses the fact of the electoral college; and election analysts know full well that the multiplier effect is artificial, that the real mandate is derived from the popular vote. What this multiplier effect does mean is that the system is biased in favor of the winner of the national popular plurality, and that it makes a contingency election highly improbable.

There is but one addendum to this bias of the electoral college system, but one exception to the advantage given to the plurality winner: the bias against a purely or predominantly sectional candidacy. A candidate whose appeal is sectional and not cross-sectional, a candidate whose popular vote support is geographically narrow and deep loses the advantage of the multiplier effect. There are no electoral vote bonuses for candidates who win a state by a landslide. The top prize is 100 percent of a state's electoral votes whether a candidate polls a simple plurality or 85 percent of the statewide popular vote.

This bias against sectional candidacies is clearly illustrated by the election of 1888, when Grover Cleveland, who had a narrow popular plurality, lost to Benjamin Harrison, after running a sectional campaign. Cleveland emphasized the sectional tariff issue and increased the Democratic party's margins in the already solid South by 5 to 17 percent over the election of 1884. The average increase in the Southern states was 9 percent. To put it mildly, this strategy was dysfunctional since the unit rule gives greater rewards to candidates who muster a statewide plurality than to candidates who win a state by a landslide, such as Cleveland's 83 percent in South Carolina. Any votes a candidate gathers in excess of a statewide plurality are "wasted" because they do not yield electoral votes. In a closely contested election, geographic concentration of the popular votes is as strategically undesirable as it is politically undesirable.

Furthermore, the multiplier effect works well, produces a plurality President, even in the closest elections, and it will continue to work well as long as our power oriented parties give as much concern to the distribution of their popular votes as to the number of their popular votes. In the closest election in our history, the election of 1880, when Garfield led Hancock by a minuscule 0.1 percent of the popular votes, Garfield won 57.9 percent of the electoral vote for a magnification of 9.6 percent over his popular vote. In 1960, the second closest election, when Kennedy apparently led Nixon by less than 0.2 percent of the popular vote, it increased Kennedy's electoral vote percentage by 6.7 percent. . . . Under the unit rule the distribution of the popular votes may be as important as the number. Not every sectional dispute can be moderated by an election system, but the antisectional bias of an electoral system . . . should be prized.

A word must be said about the shift-in-votes argument used by several analysts to suggest that the system is not a reliable plurality system. In large part this argument is a parlor game of speculation in which numbers are moved from one column to another in a political vacuum and often without regard to the election laws. Several analysts have argued that a switch of less than 1 percent of the votes in New York in the 1844 election would have made Henry Clay a runner-up President. As a simple mathematical proposition, it is true. But it abstracts from the political world where such shifts would have to occur. What would produce such a shift? Is it likely that whatever produced such a shift would have no effects in any other state? If the cause of such a shift is some political act (and if it is not, does this mean that votes are cast randomly and arbitrarily?), then the effect would not be isolated to one state but could change or reverse the results in other closely contested states. . . . Unless the proposed shifts occurs in *and are limited to* the states selected in our game of speculation, the predicted result will not obtain. . . . What experience has demonstrated is that the electoral college system is a system strongly biased in favor of the winner of a cross-sectional popular plurality.

Is this bias functional given the American idea of democracy? Plurality systems are an aberration of majoritarian theory which requires that elected officials have the support of a majority of *all* citizens. . . . In practice the majority requirement is too stringent. It would necessitate compulsory voting. Run-off elections with all their attendant cost, confusion, intrigue and delay would become the rule if the majority requirement were strictly enforced. . . .

[O]ur plurality Presidencies compare quite favorably with our majority Presidencies. For fifteen presidential terms we have been governed by a minority President, one who received a plurality rather than a majority of the popular vote. Among these terms are seven that have been rated among the best in our history: those of Polk, Lincoln, Cleveland twice, Wilson twice and Truman. . . .

We have good reason to know that sectional candidacies breed civil strife and civil war. We are a continental nation; we are a heterogeneous people with a wide variety of religious, racial, ethnic, economic and ideological interests that must be consulted and considered. The electoral college bias in favor of broad cross-sectional candidacies is highly functional in such a nation.

The federal-geographic rider works in the electoral college the same way that it does for the Congress. It incorporates the Presidency into the system of concurrent majorities. It forces candidates to create broad coalitions. It provides the incentive to our national parties, as James MacGregor Burns pointed out, "to widen and 'flatten out' their vote." In fact, Burns has concluded that this is "the historic achievement of the presidential party," the party whose strategy is shaped by the electoral college. . . .

The multiplier effect of the unit rule not only favors the plurality candidate, it produces a single election. Once the electoral college system had fully evolved, the likelihood of contingency elections became remote. We have not had one since the unit rule was adopted by almost all of the states. And, in light of recent history, it seems more probable that the Twenty-fifth Amendment, dealing with vice presidential vacancies and presidential disabilities, will be far more important to the institution of the Presidency than the contingency election procedures established by the Founders.

The contingency procedure is utilized only if no candidate receives a majority of the electoral votes. This could occur in an election with more than two serious candidates. The electoral college, however, discriminates against both sectional and national third parties, and the multiplier effect continues to magnify the plurality winner's margin of victory in the electoral vote. In years when more than two candidates won electoral votes, the average increase in the plurality candidate's electoral vote over his popular vote was 17.1 percent, only 2.2 percent less than the average for all elections. . . .

The college's bias against national third parties is widely recognized, but its bias against sectional third parties is not as clearly understood. A sectional candidate is under a severe handicap because the unit rule favors a cross-sectional vote distribution pattern. Many of the popular votes for a sectional candidate are "wasted" because of their narrow and deep distribution.

Despite the sectional third party candidate's apparent advantage over a national third party candidate, he cannot win the election. It is feared, however, that he could deadlock the college and provoke a contingency election. . . . To deadlock the college, a candidate would have to win some electoral votes. Then he would have to . . . take votes away from both of the major parties, and these votes must be strategically placed in specific states. Too much here or too little there not only will mean failure to dead-lock but also could produce an electoral vote landslide for one of the two major party candidates. While such a candidate is raiding the major parties, they are not complacent and indulgent. They rush out to secure their followers and to recapture those who have strayed. The efforts of the major parties and the prospect of casting a wasted vote in a close election create strong counter-pressures on the voters to whom the third party candidate must appeal.

The third party candidacy of George Wallace in 1968 is a classic example of the single election bias of the college. Wallace was a sectional candidate who ran a national campaign and amassed 4,100,000 votes outside the South for which he received no electoral votes. Although he won 13.5 percent of the popular vote, he won only 8 percent of the electoral vote, less than half of the average distortion of the multi-plier effect in three-way electoral vote contests. His attempt to deadlock the college was a dismal failure. . . .

The result of the 1968 Wallace deadlock strategy is merely a part of a larger pat-tern, a pattern of defeat for third party strategies. There have been eleven presiden-tial elections in which a third party candidate won electoral votes. In none of these elections were we close to a deadlock, and in five of them the victor's percentage of the electoral vote surpassed sixty percent. Several of these third party candidates polled high percentages of the popular vote: Millard Fillmore received 21 percent in 1856. Robert La Follette received 17 percent in 1924. None of these prodigious efforts were any match for the multiplier effect of the unit rule. In 1856, Buchanan won with an electoral vote of 58.7 percent for an increase of 13 percent over his popular vote. In 1860, Lincoln jumped from a popular vote of merely 38.7 percent to an electoral vote of 59.4 percent, an increase of 19.7 percent. In 1924, Coolidge won an electoral vote landslide with 71.7 percent for an increase of 17.7 percent over his popular vote.

As it actually operates, the college has a bias in favor of a single election. . . . [I]t makes for stability, reduces uncertainty, prevents intrigue, shortens the period of interregnum, and allows time for the smooth transition of power. Over and above these things, the single election bias of the college supports the two-party system, the system that, in the words of Austin Ranney and Willmore Kendall, "more than any other American Institution, consciously, actively and directly nurtures consensus."

The college's bias in favor of the two-party system is sustained not only by its bias against sectional and national third parties, but also by its bias in favor of a single election. Frequent contingency elections of any kind would weaken or destroy the two-party system whose vitality may depend, as Schattschneider argued, upon its control over nominations. If, as is the case under the current system, a contingency election is highly unlikely, disenchanted partisan factions have little to gain and a great deal to lose by bucking the party nomination procedure. But if the electoral system has no bias toward a single election, if a contingency election is probable, then the second-chance psychology will spread. The parties could fragment as factional leaders scramble to enter the contest. . . .

In this continental, heterogeneous nation, the two-party system has developed as an extra-constitutional institution to perform a critically necessary function, a coalition-building, unifying function. Madison's idea was to divide and diversify, to encourage the development of numerous contending minority factions rather than a monolithic majority faction. That could be a sound plan if and only if something would serve to create coalitions, concurrent majorities, that could govern. . . . Thus, a major problem posed by the Madisonian system of a large heterogeneous federal republic, with its cultural pluralism and its separation of powers, was to provide some unity and coherence, to provide political majorities.

The two-party system arose in response to this necessity for coalition-building. Not surprisingly, our national party nominating convention system arose at the same time that the unit rule reached full development, 1832–1836. The two-party system is an integral part of the American idea of democracy, and the electoral college's bias in its favor is highly desirable. It is especially desirable at this moment in our history when the two-party system is somewhat indisposed, when the other non-institutional supports for two-partyism have decayed, when politics is individualized and the number of Independents is rising.

The college's partiality is not simply for two-partyism; it prefers moderate candidates and parties. The federal-geographic dispersion requirement quells tendencies to organize parties on class, racial, religious, ethnic, economic or ideological lines. Such factions cannot readily combine their votes across state lines. Even if the two-party system were to survive the abandonment of the unit rule, the parties could be drastically changed becoming highly ideological and dysfunctionally immoderate. Absent the unit rule, factionalism could run wild as candidates would be relieved of the necessity to create broad coalitions. Now, a victorious strategy cannot be based on narrow appeals and extravagant promises to popular majorities in one section of the country such as the populous Eastern megalopolis, or to a dominant racial group, the whites, or to a dominant religious group, the Christians, or to a single-interest constituency such as the anti-forced-busing faction. . . .

The system also has a bias in favor of large competitive, two-party states and of urban and suburban voters in such states. Again it is the unit rule that accounts for this partiality. The most populous states have large blocs of electoral votes at their disposal, and if they are competitive, if each of the two major parties has a real chance of victory in such states, they will become the major battlegrounds. Since these states are much more representative of the diversity of the nation as a whole than the homogeneous one-party states, these are the most appropriate and functional battlegrounds. The kinds of coalitions that can win in such states are the kinds of coalitions that can win a cross-sectional victory and therefore can govern. Within such states urban-suburban voters have an apparent advantage. . . . [I]t balances the rural-small-town bias of the Congress.

Although no election system can completely prevent fraud, the current system does have a bias against fraud because of the unit rule. Under any system, the closer the election the greater the inducement to cheat. But when, as now, each state is a separate electoral arena, the state boundaries quarantine the disease. . . . Furthermore, because of the multiplier effect, close popular vote contests are not always close electoral vote contests, and the point of the fraudulent activity is to affect the electoral votes through the popular votes. . . .

As a result of this bias, few elections are likely to be contested by the loser even when he has good reason to suspect fraud in some states because the fraudulent activity does not always determine the victory. The candidate who demands a recount in the hope of reversing the results must not only pick up votes and/or invalidate some of the votes for his opponent, but he must do so in particular states. . . .

If federalism is an anachronism, if cross-sectional, concurrent majorities are no longer necessary to maintain liberty, then perhaps we should abandon federalism for the national legislature as well as for the executive. To do one without the other, particularly to make the President the recipient of the only all-national mandate could change our governmental solar system, could change the balance in executive-legislative relationships to the advantage of the President. The authenticity of the voice of the Congress, speaking for a concurrent majority, could be seriously undermined by a truly plebiscitary President claiming to speak most directly and clearly for the general will. The sobering experience of the Watergate era should make us reluctant to further aggrandize the Presidency.

Is the electoral college system compatible with and supportive of the American idea of democracy? The answer, I believe, is yes. . . . The system looks to the formation of concurrent rather than simple arithmetical majorities, but the organizing principle of the whole governmental system is the concurrent majority. But above all else, the system balances the principles of liberty and equality because it at once utilizes the numerical votes of factions while restraining their destructive potential.

———————

1. *Assessing the Arguments.* By which arguments are you more persuaded — Professor Best's or those of the committee report? How much weight do you attach to arguments stressing imagined "horribles," for example, that a single vote's difference in each of just a few states could alter the electoral outcome? Note that Donald J. Trump won the 2016 presidential election because of about 77,000 votes out of the over 136 million ballots cast: "According to the final tallies, Trump won Pennsylvania by 0.7 percentage points (44,292 votes), Wisconsin by 0.7 points (22,748 votes), Michigan by 0.2 points (10,704 votes)." John McCormack, *The Election Came Down to 77,744 Votes in Pennsylvania, Wisconsin, and Michigan (Updated)*, Weekly Standard (Nov. 10, 2016), http://tinyurl.com/jkehr8e. Hillary Clinton topped his popular vote total by almost 2.9 million votes, 65,844,954 (48.2%) to 62,979,879 (46.1%).

2. *Implications of the "Unit Rule."* Note that the virtues Professor Best attributes to the electoral college flow not from its constitutionally prescribed structure, but from the universal state adoption of the unit rule, which is a matter of discretion with each state. Is it plausible to argue that 150 years of practice have effectively amended the Constitution? Could a state legislature abandon the unit rule? Could it

constitutionally determine that it will choose the state's electors without any popular vote at all in the state? (The constitutional text permits such an outcome; should that be the end of the interpretive inquiry?)

3. *"Mend, Don't End?"* A number of proposals have been suggested to mitigate the distorting effects of the electoral college while preserving an indirect election. An unsuccessful 2004 ballot initiative in Colorado would have resulted in the proportional allocation of the state's electoral votes among all candidates receiving 15 per cent or more of the popular vote. It is unclear whether the nationwide adoption of such a system would be a good thing: "When *CQ Researcher* applied this plan to the results of the presidential elections from 1960 though 1996, they concluded that it would have thrown four of these elections into the House for a decision: 1960, 1968, 1992, and 1996." Judith A. Best, *Presidential Selection: Complex Problems and Simple Solutions*, 119 Poli. Sci. Q. 39, 55 (2004). One of us has suggested a so-called "Drop Two" plan, under which every state would lose the two electors assigned based on the state's two senators: "It is [this] allocation that most significantly causes the over-weighting of the small states' votes." Peter M. Shane, *Repair the Electoral College*, Washington Post, Oct. 31, 2004, at B07. This "repair" would have produced an Electoral College outcome in 2000 consistent with the popular vote.

Professor Edward B. Foley has suggested that the Electoral College system could be rendered far less dysfunctional and more democratic if states adopted laws that required a candidate to win the support of a majority of the state's voters in order to gain the vote of all the state's electors. He argues, in other words, that the chances of a mismatch between the Electoral College tally and the national popular vote would be greatly reduced if the winning national candidate were required to be the majority winner in each of the states he or she carried. (In 2016, for example, candidate Trump received all the electoral votes from Arizona, Florida, Michigan, North Carolina, Pennsylvania, and Wisconsin, even though majorities in each state voted for some other candidate.) As explained by Professor Foley, there are a variety of techniques available to states, including but not limited to an actual runoff, that would enable the state to determine which candidate had majority support. Such requirements, he believes, would enable the Electoral College to more reliably fulfill what he describes as the majoritarian aspirations of the Framers. Edward B Foley, *How states can fix the Electoral College and prevent future Trumps*, USA Today (Nov. 9, 2017), https://www.usatoday.com/story/opinion/2017/11/09/fix-electoral-college-prevent-future-trumps-adopt-runoff-voting-edward-foley-column/839492001/.

4. *"Fair Vote."* Responding to the obvious challenges in securing a constitutional amendment to change the Electoral College, National Popular Vote, a non-profit corporation with a distinguished bi-partisan advisory board of political heavyweights, has proposed an alternative plan. It requires a number of states whose collective electoral votes would amount to a majority in the Electoral College to form an "interstate compact." Through identical legislation enacted by all of its members, each state would promise—once the requisite number of states signed up—that it would appoint electors in each presidential election committed to voting for the national

popular vote winner. If such a compact came into being, the popular vote winner would always win the Electoral College. As of mid-2016, the bill "had been enacted by 11 jurisdictions possessing 165 electoral votes—61% of the 270 electoral votes necessary to activate it, including four small jurisdictions (RI, VT, HI, DC), three medium-size states (MD, MA, WA), and four big states (NJ, IL, NY, CA). The bill has passed a total of 33 legislative chambers in 22 states—most recently by a bipartisan 40–16 vote in the Arizona House, a 28–18 vote in the Oklahoma Senate, a 57–4 vote in New York Senate, and a 37–21 vote in Oregon House." Agreement Among the States to Elect the President by National Popular Vote, NationalPopularVote.org, available at http://www.nationalpopularvote.com/written-explanation. The idea has legislative sponsors in every state. If adopted, would the compact be constitutional?

5. *Further Reading.* Important scholarly attacks on the Electoral College include George C. Edwards, Why the Electoral College is Bad for America (2004), and Jack Rakove, *Presidential Selection: Electoral Fallacies*, 119 Poli. Sci. Q. 39 (2004). Professor Best responds to Professor Rakove in Judith A. Best, *Presidential Selection: Complex Problems and Simple Solutions*, 119 Poli. Sci. Q. 39 (2004).

2. *Bush v. Gore* and the Constitutional Law of Presidential Elections

It would not be right to say that, prior to November, 2000, there was no such thing as "presidential election law." But precious little of it—that is, the relevant constitutional provisions allocating power over the process, or the federal statutes that implement those provisions—had ever been interpreted by courts. In three opinions rendered within a month of that election, the Supreme Court effectively changed all that. The impact was to implicate the Court in determining which candidate and which of two ideologically polarized parties would be in charge of a coordinate branch of government. That the Court's intervention occurred via a 5–4 judgment, and a decision in favor of the candidate who had decisively lost the popular vote on election day, foreordained that the Court's opinions would be among the most controversial rendered in American history.

"Ground Zero" for the 2000 constitutional crisis was Florida, a state in which Vice President Al Gore and Texas Governor George W. Bush (brother of Florida Governor Jeb Bush), had produced what amounted to a statistical tie in the popular vote. The night of Election Day, television commenters predicted, based on exit polls, that Vice President Gore had carried the state, and, in retrospect, there seems little question that a majority of Floridians who voted in the 2000 election thought they had voted for Gore. Thousands of likely Gore ballots in the Palm Beach area went awry, however, as the apparent result of a confusing ballot design that led many voters either to vote for an unintended candidate or to vote twice for Gore. As a result, it looked as if the collective decision of nearly 6 million Florida voters would depend upon a margin of just a few hundred votes, and the law surrounding the counting of those votes was, to put it mildly, uncertain.

The issues first presented with regard to a proper resolution of the Florida vote were issues of state law, and the following excerpt explains them:

Peter M. Shane, Disappearing Democracy: How *Bush v. Gore* Undermined the Federal Right to Vote for Presidential Electors

29 FLA. ST. U. L. REV. 535, 553–561 (2001).

In Florida, vote counting within each county was the initial responsibility of so-called election boards, which include inspectors and clerks for every precinct who are appointed to their positions by the Supervisors of Elections in each of the respective counties. The boards in each county were required to prepare certified tallies, which were delivered, in turn, to the Supervisor of Elections and to the county court judge. In addition, each Supervisor of Elections sat on a so-called county canvassing board, along with two other members — the county court judge, who acted as chair of the canvassing board, and the chair of the board of county commissioners. It was the primary duty of each county canvassing board to canvass absentee ballots, and then prepare a canvass of the entire election result within each county, "as shown by the returns . . . on file in the office of the supervisor of elections and the office of the county court judge." The county canvassing board was then charged with certifying the county's results to the Secretary of State, who was required ultimately to certify the results of any statewide election.

Florida law vested county canvassing boards with essential responsibilities in the event of challenged elections. The relevant statute permitted "[a]ny candidate whose name appeared on the ballot" to file within seventy-two hours of an election "a written request with the county canvassing board for a manual recount." It also permitted "[a]ny candidate . . . to protest the returns of the election as being erroneous by filing with the appropriate canvassing board a sworn, written protest . . . prior to the time the canvassing board certifies the results for the office being protested or within 5 days" thereafter.

The statute provided that a county canvassing board that had been asked for a manual recount "may" authorize such a process, provided that the "[t]he manual recount must include at least three precincts and at least 1 percent of the total votes cast for such candidate or issue." Although Florida law specified no criteria for proceeding with such a preliminary manual recount, it did mandate a particular course of events should such a preliminary recount be directed:

> If the manual recount indicates an error in the vote tabulation which could affect the outcome of the election, the county canvassing board shall:
>
> > (a) Correct the error and recount the remaining precincts with the vote tabulation system;
> >
> > (b) Request the Department of State to verify the tabulation software; or
> >
> > (c) Manually recount all ballots.[81]

---

81. Fla. Stat. § 102.166 (2000) (amended 2001).

In counties using paper ballots that cannot be read properly because of uncorrectable problems with the tabulation devices involved, only the third option—manually recounting all ballots—was available to fulfill what appears to be a statutory duty under this section.

Within forty-eight hours of election day, a machine recount required under Florida law for close elections narrowed Bush's initial 1784-vote lead to 327 votes. There was no mechanism available to Gore at that point to trigger a unified statewide recount. He could have sought manual recounts in every county in Florida, but his advisers believed that such a strategy would be both chaotic and unnecessary and might appear too impolitic—too much the desperate move of a sore loser. The decision was made on November 9 to pursue recounts in only four heavily Democratic counties from which numerous complaints of irregularities had emerged—Broward, Miami-Dade, Palm Beach, and Volusia. The Gore team hoped that recounts in these counties would suffice to overcome the tissue-thin Bush lead.

By this time, it became equally clear that the Bush campaign and Republican election officials in Florida would try to prevent the outcomes of hand recounts from affecting the certification of Florida's statewide vote. In particular, Katherine Harris, Florida's Secretary of State and co-chair of the Bush campaign in Florida, announced that she would not waive the apparent November 14 statutory deadline for the submission to her of county vote totals for certification. On Saturday, November 11, the Bush campaign sought from the U.S. District Court for the Southern District of Florida an injunction to block any hand recounts.

I refer to November 14 as the "apparent" deadline because, as the Florida courts would soon discuss, Florida statutes were resolutely ambiguous on the issue of deadlines. On one hand, section 102.111, Florida Statutes, stated in seemingly unequivocal terms: "If the county returns are not received by the Department of State by 5 p.m. of the seventh day following an election, all missing counties shall be ignored, and the results shown by the returns on file shall be certified." This provision was echoed by section 102.112(1), Florida Statutes, which appeared to obligate county canvassing boards to submit county returns within seven days:

> The county canvassing board or a majority thereof shall file the county returns for the election of a federal or state officer with the Department of State immediately after certification of the election results. Returns must be filed by 5 p.m. on the 7th day following the first primary and general election and by 3 p.m. on the 3rd day following the second primary.

These two provisions seemed to dictate that the 2000 county returns would have to be returned by November 14, the seventh day following the general election.

That very same paragraph of section 102.112, however, stated equally explicitly that the decision whether or not to include in statewide totals any county returns that are submitted after the specified deadline was within the discretion of the Department of State: "If the [county] returns are not received by the department by the time specified, such returns may be ignored and the results on file at that time may be certified by the department." The confusion was compounded in the next subsection, which provided: "The department shall fine each board member $200 for each day such returns are late, the fine to be paid only from the board member's personal funds." Under this provision, it was plainly the policy of the Florida Legislature that county canvassing boards should be encouraged to submit even late returns as early as possible. This would be a puzzling concern if county returns even an hour or a day late were mandatorily to be ignored.

Notwithstanding Secretary Harris's insistence on the November 14 deadline, both Volusia and Palm Beach Counties readied to do the preliminary hand recounts authorized by section 102.166(4), Florida Statutes. Palm Beach County, home of the controversial butterfly ballot, presented the threshold question of how to discern voter intent from a punch ballot that had not been read by the vote tabulation machine. That is, how should a ballot be interpreted if the ballot, with regard to a particular office, did not exhibit a single unambiguous hole from which the perforated rectangle—the now notorious "chad"—had been completely and successfully removed? On Saturday morning, November 11, the Palm Beach County Canvassing Board (PBCCB) agreed on a "sunshine rule," under which a vote would be tallied if the impression made on an imperfectly removed chad nonetheless allowed light to pass through the ballot in the proper place. Based on that standard, at 2 a.m. on Sunday, November 12, the PBCCB voted two to one that a net gain for Gore of nineteen votes from a sample of four precincts warranted a complete manual recount of the entire county.

Before proceeding further, County Judge Charles Burton, chair of the PBCCB, nonetheless wanted an official opinion from the Florida Department of State Division of Elections on two issues: First, he wanted to know if vote totals based on the recount were to be certified to the Secretary of State after Tuesday, November 14, at 5 p.m.—whether they would be counted in the certification of statewide results. Second, Burton wanted to know if the undercount for Gore detected by the preliminary manual recount over the weekend really triggered a mandatory recount under section 102.166(5) as a matter of law. That is, he wanted to know whether the apparent under-counting of Gore votes amounted to what section 102.166 calls "an error in voting tabulation that could affect the outcome of an election," which would obligate the PBCCB to conduct a countywide hand recount.

On Monday, November 13, L. Clayton Roberts, the director of the Division of Elections of the Florida Department of State, issued a negative response to both questions. Roberts noted the apparent discrepancy between section 102.111, which seemed to make mandatory the exclusion from statewide totals of any county votes certified after the statutory deadline, and section 102.112, which seemed to render their inclusion or exclusion discretionary. He nonetheless deemed any discretion conferred by section 102.112 to be irrelevant to the problem presented. In his judgment, whatever discretion section 102.112 allowed to the Department of State was intended only "[for] unforeseen circumstances not specifically contemplated by the legislature. Such unforeseen circumstances might include a natural disaster such [sic] Hurricane

Andrew, where compliance with the law would be impossible. But a close election, regardless of the identity of the candidates, is not such a circumstance." In a separate opinion, Roberts denied that an undercount would trigger a mandatory recount where the undercount was a result of "[t]he inability of a voting systems [sic] to read an improperly marked marksense or improperly punched ballot . . . ." Instead, "An 'error in the vote tabulation' [that would trigger a mandatory recount] means a counting error in which the vote tabulation system fails to count properly marked marksense or properly punched punchcard ballots." The obvious implications of these opinions were that the undercount for Gore that the PBCCB detected did not require a countywide recount and that such a recount might be pointless because it might not be possible to complete one before the statutory deadline of November 14, 2000, at 5 p.m., which, according to Clayton, the Department had no authority to waive.

The PBCCB responded to the Clayton opinion on the mandatory recount issue by seeking an advisory opinion on the same question from Florida Attorney General Robert A. Butterworth, who like Secretary Harris was a campaign co-chair for one of the presidential candidates—in Butterworth's case, for Gore. Butterworth disagreed vehemently with Clayton's conclusion on this issue. He noted first that the error that, under section 102.166, triggers a mandatory countywide recount, is not an error in "the vote tabulation system," a phrase used elsewhere in the statute, but "an error in the vote tabulation" or enumeration itself. It was Butterworth's view that, when referring to a tabulation system rather than to a vote count, the Florida Legislature consistently used the terms "vote tabulation system" and "automatic tabulating equipment." Having rejected on plain language grounds the notion that "an error in vote tabulation" meant only an error in the vote tabulation system, Butterworth argued: "[An] error in vote tabulation might be caused by a mechanical malfunction in the operation of the vote counting system, but the error might also result from the failure of a properly functioning mechanical system to discern the choices of the voters as revealed by the ballots." Butterworth buttressed his conclusion by observing that section 102.166 dictates recount procedures that include a process for discerning voter intent from visually inspected ballots. Moreover, Clayton's distinction between failures to count "properly" marked or punched ballots and failures to count ballots that were "improperly marked" could not be sustained because Florida election law does not specify how a ballot is to be punched or marked; rather, it contemplates that the discernability of "voter intent" shall be the sole legal standard that renders a ballot countable. Butterworth demonstrated that a substantial line of Florida Supreme Court decisions dating to early in the twentieth century confirmed his reading. In short, the PBCCB's discovery of a substantial number of Gore votes that were plainly intended by the voters, but not read by the mechanical system meant that an "error in vote tabulation" had occurred, triggering the Board's obligation to conduct a comprehensive recount.

In the meantime, the Volusia County Canvassing Board had gone to Florida Circuit Court to seek a temporary injunction against Secretary Harris and the Department of State that would require them to consider—even after 5 p.m. on

November 14—the certified results from counties that could not complete by that deadline the county-wide recounts they were legally required to hold. On November 14, Circuit Judge Terry P. Lewis granted the requested relief, in part.[107] According to Judge Lewis, Secretary Harris erred in insisting that only an "Act of God" would permit her legally to consider the inclusion in state totals of county returns that were submitted after the seven-day deadline. In Judge Lewis's view, Harris's insistence on early finality ignored the legislature's countervailing interest in vote count accuracy. Florida law appeared to anticipate a number of situations in which a manual recount would be called for even if it could not be completed within seven days. "It is unlikely," he wrote, "that the Legislature would give the right to protest returns, but make it meaningless because it could not be acted upon . . . ."

To give effect to the legislature's interests in both finality and accuracy, as well as the language of the statute, Judge Lewis concluded that counties were required to report existing vote totals by 5 p.m. on the seventh day following an election. Counties were also entitled, however, to decide to file late returns, which would be included or not within the state count, as the Secretary of State would be entitled to determine within her discretion:

> [T]he Secretary of State has the authority to exercise her discretion in reviewing that decision [to submit late returns], considering all attendant facts and circumstances, and decide whether to include or to ignore the late filed returns in certifying the election results and declaring the winner . . . . [T]he Secretary cannot decide ahead of time what late returns should or should not be ignored . . . .

Judge Lewis determined, however, that he could not direct Secretary Harris as to how to exercise her discretion. He could go no further than indicate that "the exercise of discretion, by its nature, contemplates a decision based upon a weighing and [a] consideration of all attendant facts and circumstances."

Secretary Harris's response to this decision was audacious. One might have thought that among "all attendant facts and circumstances" worthy of consideration in determining whether to include late filed returns would be the substance of those returns. Yet, the afternoon of Judge Lewis's order, Secretary Harris responded by instructing all counties to report no later than 2 p.m. the following day a statement of those facts and circumstances that, in the views of the respective counties, would justify her inclusion of their late filed returns. She wrote an additional letter the following day, specifying the criteria under which she intended to exercise her discretion:

Facts & Circumstances Warranting Waiver of Statutory Deadline

1. Where there is proof of voter fraud that affects the outcome of the election.

---

107. McDermott v. Harris, No. CV-00-2700, 2000 WL 1693713 (Fla. 2d Cir. Ct. Nov. 14, 2000), *rev'd sub nom.*, Palm Beach County Canvassing Bd. v. Harris, 772 So. 2d 1220 (Fla. 2000), *vacated sub nom.*, Bush v. Palm Beach County Canvassing Bd., 531 U.S. 70 (2000).

2. Where there has been a substantial noncompliance with statutory election procedures, and reasonable doubt exists as to whether the certified results expressed the will of the voters.

3. Where election officials have made a good faith effort to comply with the statutory deadline and are prevented from timely complying with their duties as a result of an act of God, or extenuating circumstances beyond their control, by way of example, an electrical power outage, a malfunction of the transmitting equipment, or a mechanical malfunction of the voting tabulation system.

Facts & Circumstances Not Warranting Waiver of Statutory Deadline

1. Where there has been substantial compliance with statutory election procedures and the contested results relate to voter error, and there exists a reasonable expectation that the certified results expressed the will of the voters.

2. Where there exists a ballot that may be confusing because of the alignment and location of the candidates' names, but is otherwise in substantial compliance with the election laws.

3. Where there is nothing "more than a mere possibility that the outcome of the election would have been effected."[115]

Following this advice, four counties — Broward, Miami-Dade, Palm Beach, and Volusia — all filed letters expressing an intention to submit late-filed returns. That afternoon, Secretary Harris announced her rejection of each of these requests. When Volusia County protested this decision to Judge Lewis, he determined, on Friday, November 17, that Harris had "exercised her reasoned judgment to determine what relevant factors and criteria should be considered, applied them to the facts and circumstances pertinent to the individual counties involved, and made her decision." This, he concluded, fulfilled his prior order.

In the meantime, the U.S. District Court for the Southern District of Florida had refused the Bush request to block any manual recounts, a decision he appealed on November 15.[119] On November 16 and 17, the Florida Supreme Court denied a request by Harris to block the recounts,[120] agreed to resolve the dispute between Harris and Attorney General Butterworth regarding the hand counts' legal basis,[121] and stayed any certification of the election by Secretary Harris while it heard the case.[122] On

---

115. Palm Beach County Canvassing Bd. v. Harris, 772 So. 2d 1220, 1226 n. 5 (Fla. 2000), vacated sub nom. Bush v. Palm Beach County Canvassing Bd., 531 U.S. 70 (2000).

119. E.J. Dionne Jr. & William Kristol eds., *Bush v. Gore*: The Court Cases and the Commentary xii (2001).

120. Palm Beach County Canvassing Bd. v. Harris, No. SC00-2346, 2000 WL 1708520 (Fla. Nov 16, 2000).

121. Palm Beach County Canvassing Bd. v. Harris, No. SC00-2346, SC00-2348, SC00-2349, 2000 WL 1716481 (Fla. Nov 17, 2000).

122. Palm Beach County Canvassing Bd. v. Harris, No. SC00-2346, SC00-2348, SC00-2349, 2000 WL 1716480 (Fla. Nov. 17, 2000).

Friday, November 18, the final day for the counting of overseas ballots, new state-wide totals were announced, expanding the Bush lead to 930.

With these events, the ground had been laid for the first of four utterly critical judicial events—a decision on the merits by the Florida Supreme Court about the legality of hand recounts prior to a certification of a statewide winner in the presidential race. After hearing oral arguments on Monday, November 20, the Court issued on November 21 its unanimous ruling that (a) the hand counts could continue, and (b) that Secretary Harris was obliged to include in the state totals any returns submitted by the counties involved by November 26, 2000.

The reasoning of the Florida Supreme Court in overruling Secretary Harris with regard to the handcounting of votes in contested counties was assessed in the first of the U.S. Supreme Court's three opinions following the Gore-Bush contest:

Bush v. Palm Beach County Canvassing Board

531 U.S. 70 (2000).

PER CURIAM

The Supreme Court of the State of Florida interpreted its elections statutes in proceedings brought to require manual recounts of ballots, and the certification of the recount results, for votes cast in the quadrennial Presidential election held on November 7, 2000. Governor George W. Bush, Republican candidate for the Presidency, filed a petition for certiorari to review the Florida Supreme Court decision. We granted certiorari on two of the questions presented by petitioner: whether the decision of the Florida Supreme Court, by effectively changing the State's elector appointment procedures after election day, violated the Due Process Clause or 3 U.S.C. § 5, and whether the decision of that court changed the manner in which the State's electors are to be selected, in violation of the legislature's power to designate the manner for selection under Art. II, § 1, cl. 2, of the United States Constitution. . . .

The [Florida] Supreme Court, with the expedition requisite for the controversy, issued its decision on November 21. *Palm Beach County Canvassing Bd. v. Harris*, 772 So.2d 1220 (2000). As the court saw the matter, there were two principal questions: whether a discrepancy between an original machine return and a sample manual recount resulting from the way a ballot has been marked or punched is an "error in vote tabulation" justifying a full manual recount; and how to reconcile what it spoke of as two conflicts in Florida's election laws: (a) between the timeframe for conducting a manual recount under Fla. Stat. § 102.166 (2000) and the timeframe for submitting county returns under §§ 102.111 and 102.112, and (b) between § 102.111, which provides that the Secretary "shall . . . ignor[e]" late election returns, and § 102.112, which provides that she "may . . . ignor[e]" such returns.

With regard to the first issue, the court held that, under the plain text of the statute, a discrepancy between a sample manual recount and machine returns due to the way in which a ballot was punched or marked did constitute an "erro⌐ tabulation" sufficient to trigger the statutory provisions for a full manual recou⌐

With regard to the second issue, the court held that the "shall . . . ignor[e]" provision of § 102.111 conflicts with the "may . . . ignor[e]" provision of § 102.112, and that the "may . . . ignor[e]" provision controlled. The court turned to the questions whether and when the Secretary may ignore late manual recounts. The court relied in part upon the right to vote set forth in the Declaration of Rights of the Florida Constitution in concluding that late manual recounts could be rejected only under limited circumstances. The court then stated: "[B]ecause of our reluctance to rewrite the Florida Election Code, we conclude that we must invoke the equitable powers of this Court to fashion a remedy . . . ." 772 So.2d, at 1240. The court thus imposed a deadline of November 26, at 5 p.m., for a return of ballot counts. The 7-day deadline of § 102.111, assuming it would have applied, was effectively extended by 12 days. The court further directed the Secretary to accept manual counts submitted prior to that deadline.

As a general rule, this Court defers to a state court's interpretation of a state statute. But in the case of a law enacted by a state legislature applicable not only to elections to state offices, but also to the selection of Presidential electors, the legislature is not acting solely under the authority given it by the people of the State, but by virtue of a direct grant of authority made under Art. II, § 1, cl. 2, of the United States Constitution. That provision reads:

> "Each State shall appoint, in such Manner as the Legislature thereof may direct, a Number of Electors, equal to the whole Number of Senators and Representatives to which the State may be entitled in the Congress . . . ."

Although we did not address the same question petitioner raises here, in McPherson *v. Blacker*, 146 U.S. 1, 25 (1892), we said:

> "[Art. II, § 1, cl. 2,] does not read that the people or the citizens shall appoint, but that 'each State shall'; and if the words 'in such manner as the legislature thereof may direct,' had been omitted, it would seem that the legislative power of appointment could not have been successfully questioned in the absence of any provision in the state constitution in that regard. Hence the insertion of those words, while operating as a limitation upon the State in respect of any attempt to circumscribe the legislative power, cannot be held to operate as a limitation on that power itself."

There are expressions in the opinion of the Supreme Court of Florida that may be read to indicate that it construed the Florida Election Code without regard to the extent to which the Florida Constitution could, consistent with Art. II, § 1, cl. 2, "circumscribe the legislative power." The opinion states, for example, that "[t]o the extent that the Legislature may enact laws regulating the electoral process, those laws are valid only if they impose no 'unreasonable or unnecessary' restraints on the right of suffrage" guaranteed by the State Constitution. 772 So.2d, at 1236. The opinion also states that "[b]ecause election laws are intended to facilitate the right of suffrage, such laws must be liberally construed in favor of the citizens' right to vote . . . ." *Id.* at 1237.

In addition, 3 U.S.C. § 5 provides in pertinent part:

> "If any State shall have provided, by laws enacted prior to the day fixed for the appointment of the electors, for its final determination of any controversy or contest concerning the appointment of all or any of the electors of such State, by judicial or other methods or procedures, and such determination shall have been made at least six days before the time fixed for the meeting of the electors, such determination made pursuant to such law so existing on said day, and made at least six days prior to said time of meeting of the electors, shall be conclusive, and shall govern in the counting of the electoral votes as provided in the Constitution, and as hereinafter regulated, so far as the ascertainment of the electors appointed by such State is concerned."

The parties before us agree that whatever else may be the effect of this section, it creates a "safe harbor" for a State insofar as congressional consideration of its electoral votes is concerned. If the state legislature has provided for final determination of contests or controversies by a law made prior to election day, that determination shall be conclusive if made at least six days prior to said time of meeting of the electors. The Florida Supreme Court cited 3 U.S.C. §§ 1–10 in a footnote of its opinion, 772 So.2d, at 1238, n. 55, but did not discuss § 5. Since § 5 contains a principle of federal law that would assure finality of the State's determination if made pursuant to a state law in effect before the election, a legislative wish to take advantage of the "safe harbor" would counsel against any construction of the Election Code that Congress might deem to be a change in the law.

After reviewing the opinion of the Florida Supreme Court, we find "that there is considerable uncertainty as to the precise grounds for the decision." *Minnesota v. National Tea Co.,* 309 U.S. 551, 555 (1940). This is sufficient reason for us to decline at this time to review the federal questions asserted to be present.

> "It is fundamental that state courts be left free and unfettered by us in interpreting their state constitutions. But it is equally important that ambiguous or obscure adjudications by state courts do not stand as barriers to a determination by this Court of the validity under the federal constitution of state action. Intelligent exercise of our appellate powers compels us to ask for the elimination of the obscurities and ambiguities from the opinions in such cases." *Id.,* at 557, 60 S.Ct. 676.

Specifically, we are unclear as to the extent to which the Florida Supreme Court saw the Florida Constitution as circumscribing the legislature's authority under Art. II, § 1, cl. 2. We are also unclear as to the consideration the Florida Supreme Court accorded to 3 U.S.C. § 5. The judgment of the Supreme Court of Florida is therefore vacated, and the case is remanded for further proceedings not inconsistent with this opinion.

It is so ordered.

———————

Identifying the Federal Issue. The Supreme Court's initial acceptance of federal jurisdiction in the Florida dispute apparently depended on two possible questions of federal law, but it is not obvious from this opinion what they are. The first, the Court says, is a potential question whether, in empowering state legislatures to decide on the processes for choosing presidential electors, the U.S. Constitution intended to free state legislatures from such constraints as might otherwise be imposed upon them by their state constitutions. The Court, however, cites no evidence for this possibility, and it is difficult to imagine any reason for it. It seems odd, to say the least, that drafters of a federal constitution who were preeminently concerned with subjecting federal legislative authority to constitutional restraint would have wanted to free state legislatures from any such restraint with regard to the sole function of choosing presidential electors. The second potential question is whether the Florida Supreme Court gave sufficient consideration, in interpreting the intent of the Florida legislature, to the legislature's putative desire to take advantage of the "safe harbor" provision of 3 U.S.C. § 5. But why is this a federal question at all? There seems to be no plausible reading that Section 5 *requires* states to take advantage of the safe harbor, and the Florida court's inferential reasoning regarding the thinking of the Florida legislature would seem, by definition, to be a question purely of state legal interpretation.

In *Supreme Court Review of State-Court Determinations of State Law in Constitutional Cases*, 103 COLUM. L. REV. 1919 (2003), Professor Henry Monaghan offers a different approach. As noted by Professor Monaghan, circumstances may exist in which a federal constitutional right depends upon a state court's characterization at one point in time—call it T_2—of what state law was at another point in time—call it T_1. For example, in *Bush v. Palm Beach County Canvassing Board*, the Florida Supreme Court, after Election Day (T_2), may well have been entitled to interpret Florida law in order to discern whether the legislative design for choosing presidential electors, adopted prior to the election (T_1), had been followed. Whether it properly exercised that authority, however—thus respecting the Florida legislature's own authority under the federal Constitution—depended upon whether its post-election T_2 reading of the law was genuinely faithful to the T_1 law as enacted prior to the election. Discerning whether the state court's interpretation of state law had "fair support" in the prior state law was thus, according to Professor Monaghan, a federal question upon which federal appellate jurisdiction may permissibly rest. Of course, asking whether the state judicial opinion had "fair support" would be a more deferential question than asking whether the state court gave state law the best possible interpretation.

As recounted in the Supreme Court's opinion, the controversial aspects of the Florida Supreme Court's opinion were its determinations "that the 'shall . . . ignor[e]' provision of § 102.111 conflicts with the 'may . . . ignor[e]' provision of § 102.112, and that the 'may . . . ignor[e]' provision controlled. The Florida Supreme Court analyzed the issue as follows:

In addition to the conflict in the above statutes, sections 102.111 and 102.112 contain a dichotomy. Section 102.111, which sets forth general criteria governing the State Canvassing Commission, was enacted in 1951 . . . provides . . . *"If the county returns are not received by the Department of State by 5 p.m. of the seventh day following an election, all missing counties shall be ignored,* and the results shown by the returns on file shall be certified." § 102.111, Fla.Stat. (2000) (emphasis added). The Legislature in 1989 revised Chapter 102 to include section 102.112, which provides that returns not received after a certain date "may" be ignored and that members of the County Board "shall" be fined . . . The above statutes conflict. Whereas section 102.111 is mandatory, section 102.112 is permissive. While it is clear that the Boards must submit returns by 5 p.m. of the seventh day following the election or face penalties, the circumstances under which penalties may be assessed are unclear.

Legislative intent—as always—is the polestar that guides a court's inquiry into the provisions of the Florida Election Code. . . . [C]hapter 102 is unclear concerning both the time limits for submitting the results of a manual recount and the penalties that may be assessed by the Secretary. In light of this ambiguity, the Court must resort to traditional rules of statutory construction in an effort to determine legislative intent.

First, it is well-settled that where two statutory provisions are in conflict, the specific statute controls the general statute. In the present case, whereas section 102.111 in its title and text addresses the general makeup and duties of the Elections Canvassing Commission, the statute only tangentially addresses the penalty for returns filed after the statutory date, noting that such returns "shall" be ignored by the Department. Section 102.112, on the other hand, directly addresses in its title and text both the "deadline" for submitting returns and the "penalties" for submitting returns after a certain date; the statute expressly states that such returns "may" be ignored and that dilatory Board members "shall" be fined. Based on the precision of the title and text, section 102.112 constitutes a specific penalty statute that defines both the deadline for filing returns and the penalties for filing returns thereafter and section 102.111 constitutes a non-specific statute in this regard. The specific statute controls the non-specific statute.

Second, it also is well-settled that when two statutes are in conflict, the more recently enacted statute controls the older statute. In the present case, the provision in section 102.111 stating that the Department "shall" ignore returns was enacted in 1951 as part of the Code. On the other hand, the penalty provision in section 102.112 stating that the Department "may" ignore returns was enacted in 1989 as a revision to Chapter 102. The more recently enacted provision may be viewed as the clearest and most recent expression of legislative intent.

Third, a statutory provision will not be construed in such a way that it renders meaningless or absurd any other statutory provision. In the present case, section 102.112 contains a detailed provision authorizing the assessment of fines against members of a dilatory County Canvassing Board. The fines are personal and substantial, i.e., $200 for each day the returns are not received. If, as the Secretary asserts, the Department were required to ignore all returns received after the statutory date, the fine provision would be meaningless. For example, if a Board simply completed its count late and if the returns were going to be ignored in any event, what would be the point in submitting the returns? The Board would simply file no returns and avoid the fines. But, on the other hand, if the returns submitted after the statutory date would not be ignored, the Board would have good reason to submit the returns and accept the fines. The fines thus serve as an alternative penalty and are applicable only if the Department may count the returns.

Fourth, related statutory provisions must be read as a cohesive whole. As stated in *Forsythe v. Longboat Key Beach Erosion Control Dist.*, 604 So.2d 452, 455 (Fla.1992), "all parts of a statute must be read together in order to achieve a consistent whole. Where possible, courts must give effect to all statutory provisions and construe related statutory provisions in harmony with another." In this regard we consider the provisions of section 102.166 and 102.168.

Section 102.166 states that a candidate, political committee, or political party may request a manual recount any time before the County Canvassing Board certifies the results to the Department and, if the initial manual recount indicates a significant error, the Board "shall" conduct a countywide manual recount in certain cases. Thus, if a protest is filed on the sixth day following an election and a full manual recount is required, the Board, through no fault of its own, will be unable to submit its returns to the Department by 5:00 p.m. on the seventh day following the election. In such a case, if the mandatory provision in section 102.111 were given effect, the votes of the county would be ignored for the simple reason that the Board was following the dictates of a different section of the Code. The Legislature could not have intended to penalize County Canvassing Boards for following the dictates of the Code....

The text of our Florida Constitution begins with a Declaration of Rights, a series of rights so basic that the founders accorded them a place of special privilege.... The right of suffrage is the preeminent right contained in the Declaration of Rights, for without this basic freedom all others would be diminished. The importance of this right was acknowledged by the authors of the Constitution, who placed it first in the Declaration.... To the extent that the Legislature may enact laws regulating the electoral process, those laws are valid only if they impose no "unreasonable or unnecessary" restraints on the right of suffrage . . . .

Because election laws are intended to facilitate the right of suffrage, such laws must be liberally construed in favor of the citizens' right to vote . . . Courts must not lose sight of the fundamental purpose of election laws: The laws are intended to facilitate and safeguard the right of each voter to express his or her will in the context of our representative democracy. Technical statutory requirements must not be exalted over the substance of this right.

Based on the foregoing, we conclude that the authority of the Florida Secretary of State to ignore amended returns submitted by a County Canvassing Board may be lawfully exercised only under limited circumstances as we set forth in this opinion. The clear import of the penalty provision of section 102.112 is to deter Boards from engaging in dilatory conduct contrary to statutory authority that results in the late certification of a county's returns. This deterrent purpose is achieved by the fines in section 102.112, which are substantial and personal and are levied on each member of a Board. The alternative penalty, i.e., ignoring the county's returns, punishes not the Board members themselves but rather the county's electors, for it in effect disenfranchises them.

Ignoring the county's returns is a drastic measure and is appropriate only if the returns are submitted to the Department so late that their inclusion will compromise the integrity of the electoral process in either of two ways: (1) by precluding a candidate, elector, or taxpayer from contesting the certification of an election pursuant to section 102.168; or (2) by precluding Florida voters from participating fully in the federal electoral process. In either case, the Secretary must explain to the Board her reason for ignoring the returns and her action must be adequately supported by the law. To disenfranchise electors in an effort to deter Board members, as the Secretary in the present case proposes, is unreasonable, unnecessary, and violates longstanding law.

Palm Beach County Canvassing Board v. Harris, 772 S.2d 1220, 1234–37 (Fla. 2001). Accepting Professor Monaghan's thesis, what would be the argument that the Florida Supreme Court's decision on the "may ignore" and "shall ignore" provisions lacked any "fair support" in Florida law?

Bush v. Gore [I]
531 U.S. 1046 (2000)

The application for stay presented to Justice KENNEDY and by him referred to the Court granted, and it is ordered that the mandate of the Florida Supreme Court, case No. SCOO-2431, is hereby stayed pending further order of the Court. In addition, the application for stay is treated as a petition for writ of certiorari, and the petition for writ of certiorari granted. Briefs of parties, not to exceed 50 pages, to be filed with the Clerk and served upon opposing counsel on or before 4 p.m. Sunday, December 10, 2000. . . . The case is set for oral argument on Monday, December 11, 2000, at 11 a.m., and a total of 1 1/2 hours is allotted for oral argument.

Justice SCALIA, concurring.

Though it is not customary for the Court to issue an opinion in connection with its grant of a stay, I believe a brief response is necessary to Justice Stevens' dissent. I will not address the merits of the case, since they will shortly be before us in the petition for certiorari that we have granted. It suffices to say that the issuance of the stay suggests that a majority of the Court, while not deciding the issues presented, believe that petitioners have a substantial probability of success.

On the question of irreparable harm, however, a few words are appropriate. The issue is not, as the dissent puts it, whether "[c]ounting every legally cast vote ca[n] constitute irreparable harm." One of the principal issues in the appeal we have accepted is precisely whether the votes that have been ordered to be counted are, under a reasonable interpretation of Florida law, "legally cast vote[s]." The counting of votes that are of questionable legality does in my view threaten irreparable harm to petitioner Bush, and to the country, by casting a cloud upon what he claims to be the legitimacy of his election. Count first, and rule upon legality afterwards, is not a recipe for producing election results that have the public acceptance democratic stability requires. Another issue in the case, moreover, is the propriety, indeed the constitutionality, of letting the standard for determination of voters' intent — dimpled chads, hanging chads, etc. — vary from county to county, as the Florida Supreme Court opinion, as interpreted by the Circuit Court, permits. If petitioners are correct that counting in this fashion is unlawful, permitting the count to proceed on that erroneous basis will prevent an accurate recount from being conducted on a proper basis later, since it is generally agreed that each manual recount produces a degradation of the ballots, which renders a subsequent recount inaccurate.

For these reasons I have joined the Court's issuance of a stay, with a highly accelerated timetable for resolving this case on the merits.

Justice STEVENS, with whom Justices SOUTER, GINSBURG, and BREYER join, dissenting.

To stop the counting of legal votes, the majority today departs from three venerable rules of judicial restraint that have guided the Court throughout its history. On questions of state law, we have consistently respected the opinions of the highest courts of the States. On questions whose resolution is committed at least in large measure to another branch of the Federal Government, we have construed our own jurisdiction narrowly and exercised it cautiously. On federal constitutional questions that were not fairly presented to the court whose judgment is being reviewed, we have prudently declined to express an opinion. The majority has acted unwisely.

Time does not permit a full discussion of the merits. It is clear, however, that a stay should not be granted unless an applicant makes a substantial showing of a likelihood of irreparable harm. In this case, petitioners have failed to carry that heavy burden. Counting every legally cast vote cannot constitute irreparable harm. On the other hand, there is a danger that a stay may cause irreparable harm to respondents—and, more importantly, the public at large—because of the risk that "the entry of the stay would be tantamount to a decision on the merits in favor of the applicants." *National Socialist Party of America v. Skokie*, 434 U.S. 1327, 1328 (Stevens, J., in chambers). Preventing the recount from being completed will inevitably cast a cloud on the legitimacy of the election.

It is certainly not clear that the Florida decision violated federal law. The Florida Code provides elaborate procedures for ensuring that every eligible voter has a full and fair opportunity to cast a ballot and that every ballot so cast is counted. See, *e.g.,* Fla. Stat. Ann. §§ 101.5614(5), 102.166 (Supp. 2001). In fact, the statutory provision relating to damaged and defective ballots states that "[n]o vote shall be declared invalid or void if there is a clear indication of the intent of the voter as determined by the canvassing board." § 101.5614(5). In its opinion, the Florida Supreme Court gave weight to that legislative command. Its ruling was consistent with earlier Florida cases that have repeatedly described the interest in correctly ascertaining the will of the voters as paramount. Its ruling also appears to be consistent with the prevailing view in other States. See, *e.g., Pullen v. Mulligan*, 138 Ill.2d 21, 79–80, 149 Ill.Dec. 215, 561 N.E.2d 585, 611 (1990). As a more fundamental matter, the Florida court's ruling reflects the basic principle, inherent in our Constitution and our democracy, that every legal vote should be counted. See *Reynolds v. Sims*, 377 U.S. 533, 544–555 (1964).

Accordingly, I respectfully dissent.

———————

Identifying Irreparable Injury. As reflected in Justice Scalia's opinion, the grant of the Supreme Court's stay had to have been predicated upon a showing of irreparable injury to then-Governor Bush if the Florida proceedings were not halted pending U.S. Supreme Court review. As described by Justice Scalia, the threat of injury was as follows: "The counting of votes that are of questionable legality does in my view threaten irreparable harm to petitioner Bush, and to the country, by casting a cloud upon what he claims to be the legitimacy of his election." Presumably, however, such a cloud could appear only under the following circumstances: (1) votes of questionable legality were counted, (2) their inclusion in the recount produced a victory for Vice President Gore, (3) subsequent judicial review determined that the votes critical to Gore were, in fact, not lawful, and (4) the public rejected the legitimacy of those court proceedings that threw out the Gore votes after they were counted. Does this scenario threaten a darker or more enduring cloud than the prospect that the Supreme Court would render the Bush election suspect by preventing the counting of votes before a determination as to their legality? Would Bush not have been better off had the recount continued and produced a Bush victory, as was entirely plausible? The Bush campaign had earlier relied on the Scalia theory of irreparable injury in seeking a federal injunction against the hand counting of Florida votes, but without success. *Siegel v. Lepore*, 234 F.3d 1163 (11th Cir. 2000); *Touchston v. McDermott*, 234 F.3d 1133 (11th Cir. 2000), *cert. denied*, 531 U.S. 1061 (2001).

Bush v. Gore (II)

531 U.S. 98 (2000)

PER CURIAM.

I

On December 8, 2000, the Supreme Court of Florida ordered that the Circuit Court of Leon County tabulate by hand 9,000 ballots in Miami-Dade County. It also ordered the inclusion in the certified vote totals of 215 votes identified in Palm Beach County and 168 votes identified in Miami-Dade County for Vice President Albert Gore, Jr., and Senator Joseph Lieberman, Democratic candidates for President and Vice President. The State Supreme Court noted that petitioner George W. Bush asserted that the net gain for Vice President Gore in Palm Beach County was 176 votes, and directed the Circuit Court to resolve that dispute on remand. *Gore v. Harris*, 772 So.2d 1243, 1248, n. 6. The court further held that relief would require manual recounts in all Florida counties where so-called "undervotes" had not been subject to manual tabulation. The court ordered all manual recounts to begin at once. Governor Bush and Richard Cheney, Republican candidates for President and Vice President, filed an emergency application for a stay of this mandate. On December 9, we granted the application, treated the application as a petition for a writ of certiorari, and granted certiorari.

The proceedings leading to the present controversy are discussed in some detail in our opinion in *Bush v. Palm Beach County Canvassing Bd., ante,* 531 U.S. 70 (2000) *(per curiam) (Bush I)*. On November 8, 2000, the day following the Presidential election, the Florida Division of Elections reported that petitioner Bush had received 2,909,135 votes, and respondent Gore had received 2,907,351 votes, a margin of 1,784 for Governor Bush. Because Governor Bush's margin of victory was less than "one-half of a percent . . . of the votes cast," an automatic machine recount was conducted under § 102.141(4) of the election code, the results of which showed Governor Bush still winning the race but by a diminished margin. Vice President Gore then sought manual recounts in Volusia, Palm Beach, Broward, and Miami-Dade Counties, pursuant to Florida's election protest provisions. Fla. Stat. Ann. § 102.166 (Supp. 2001). A dispute arose concerning the deadline for local county canvassing boards to submit their returns to the Secretary of State (Secretary). The Secretary declined to waive the November 14 deadline imposed by statute. §§ 102.111, 102.112. The Florida Supreme Court, however, set the deadline at November 26. We granted certiorari and vacated the Florida Supreme Court's decision, finding considerable uncertainty as to the grounds on which it was based. *Bush I,* 531 U.S., at 78, 121 S.Ct. 471. On December 11, the Florida Supreme Court issued a decision on remand reinstating that date.

On November 26, the Florida Elections Canvassing Commission certified the results of the election and declared Governor Bush the winner of Florida's 25 electoral votes. On November 27, Vice President Gore, pursuant to Florida's contest provisions, filed a complaint in Leon County Circuit Court contesting the certification. Fla. Stat. Ann. § 102.168 (Supp. 2001). He sought relief pursuant to § 102.168(3)(c), which provides that "[r]eceipt of a number of illegal votes or rejection of a number of legal votes sufficient to change or place in doubt the result of the election" shall be grounds for a contest. The Circuit Court denied relief, stating that Vice President Gore failed to meet his burden of proof. He appealed to the First District Court of Appeal, which certified the matter to the Florida Supreme Court.

Accepting jurisdiction, the Florida Supreme Court affirmed in part and reversed in part. *Gore v. Harris*, 772 So.2d 1243 (2000). The court held that the Circuit Court had been correct to reject Vice President Gore's challenge to the results certified in Nassau County and his challenge to the Palm Beach County Canvassing Board's determination that 3,300 ballots cast in that county were not, in the statutory phrase, "legal votes."

The Supreme Court held that Vice President Gore had satisfied his burden of proof under § 102.168(3)(c) with respect to his challenge to Miami-Dade County's failure to tabulate, by manual count, 9,000 ballots on which the machines had failed to detect a vote for President ("undervotes"). *Id.*, at 1256. Noting the closeness of the election, the court explained that "[o]n this record, there can be no question that there are legal votes within the 9,000 uncounted votes sufficient to place the results of this election in doubt." *Id.*, at 1261. A "legal vote," as determined by the Supreme Court, is "one in which there is a 'clear indication of the intent of the voter.'" *Id.*, at 1257. The court therefore ordered a hand recount of the 9,000 ballots in Miami-Dade County. Observing that the contest provisions vest broad discretion in the circuit judge to "provide any relief appropriate under such circumstances," § 102.168(8), the Supreme Court further held that the Circuit Court could order "the Supervisor of Elections and the Canvassing Boards, as well as the necessary public officials, in all counties that have not conducted a manual recount or tabulation of the undervotes . . . to do so forthwith, said tabulation to take place in the individual counties where the ballots are located." *Id.*, at 1262.

The Supreme Court also determined that both Palm Beach County and Miami-Dade County, in their earlier manual recounts, had identified a net gain of 215 and 168 legal votes for Vice President Gore. *Id.*, at 1260. Rejecting the Circuit Court's conclusion that Palm Beach County lacked the authority to include the 215 net votes submitted past the November 26 deadline, the Supreme Court explained that the deadline was not intended to exclude votes identified after that date through ongoing manual recounts. As to Miami-Dade County, the court concluded that although the 168 votes identified were the result of a partial recount, they were "legal votes [that] could change the outcome of the election." *Ibid.* The Supreme Court therefore directed the Circuit Court to include those totals in the certified results, subject to resolution of the actual vote total from the Miami-Dade partial recount.

The petition presents the following questions: whether the Florida Supreme Court established new standards for resolving Presidential election contests, thereby violating Art. II, § 1, cl. 2, of the United States Constitution and failing to comply with 3 U.S.C. § 5, and whether the use of standardless manual recounts violates the Equal Protection and Due Process Clauses. With respect to the equal protection question, we find a violation of the Equal Protection Clause.

II

A

The closeness of this election, and the multitude of legal challenges which have followed in its wake, have brought into sharp focus a common, if heretofore unnoticed, phenomenon. Nationwide statistics reveal that an estimated 2% of ballots cast do not register a vote for President for whatever reason, including deliberately choosing no candidate at all or some voter error, such as voting for two candidates or insufficiently marking a ballot. *See* Ho, More Than 2M Ballots Uncounted, AP Online (Nov. 28, 2000); Kelley, Balloting Problems Not Rare But Only in a Very Close Election Do Mistakes and Mismarking Make a Difference, Omaha World-Herald (Nov. 15, 2000). In certifying election results, the votes eligible for inclusion in the certification are the votes meeting the properly established legal requirements.

This case has shown that punchcard balloting machines can produce an unfortunate number of ballots which are not punched in a clean, complete way by the voter. After the current counting, it is likely legislative bodies nationwide will examine ways to improve the mechanisms and machinery for voting.

B

The individual citizen has no federal constitutional right to vote for electors for the President of the United States unless and until the state legislature chooses a statewide election as the means to implement its power to appoint members of the electoral college. U.S. Const., Art. II, § 1. This is the source for the statement in *McPherson v. Blacker,* 146 U.S. 1, 35 (1892), that the state legislature's power to select the manner for appointing electors is plenary; it may, if it so chooses, select the electors itself, which indeed was the manner used by state legislatures in several States for many years after the framing of our Constitution. *Id.,* at 28–33. History has now favored the voter, and in each of the several States the citizens themselves vote for Presidential electors. When the state legislature vests the right to vote for President in its people, the right to vote as the legislature has prescribed is fundamental; and one source of its fundamental nature lies in the equal weight accorded to each vote and the equal dignity owed to each voter. The State, of course, after granting the franchise in the special context of Article II, can take back the power to appoint electors. See *id.,* at 35 ("'[T]here is no doubt of the right of the legislature to resume the power at any time, for it can neither be taken away nor abdicated' ") (quoting S.Rep. No. 395, 43d Cong., 1st Sess., 9 (1874)).

The right to vote is protected in more than the initial allocation of the franchise. Equal protection applies as well to the manner of its exercise. Having once granted the right to vote on equal terms, the State may not, by later arbitrary and disparate treatment, value one person's vote over that of another. See, *e.g., Harper v. Virginia*

Bd. of Elections, 383 U.S. 663, 665 (1966) ("[O]nce the franchise is granted to the electorate, lines may not be drawn which are inconsistent with the Equal Protection Clause of the Fourteenth Amendment"). It must be remembered that "the right of suffrage can be denied by a debasement or dilution of the weight of a citizen's vote just as effectively as by wholly prohibiting the free exercise of the franchise." *Reynolds v. Sims,* 377 U.S. 533, 555 (1964).

There is no difference between the two sides of the present controversy on these basic propositions. Respondents say that the very purpose of vindicating the right to vote justifies the recount procedures now at issue. The question before us, however, is whether the recount procedures the Florida Supreme Court has adopted are consistent with its obligation to avoid arbitrary and disparate treatment of the members of its electorate.

Much of the controversy seems to revolve around ballot cards designed to be perforated by a stylus but which, either through error or deliberate omission, have not been perforated with sufficient precision for a machine to register the perforations. In some cases a piece of the card—a chad—is hanging, say, by two corners. In other cases there is no separation at all, just an indentation.

The Florida Supreme Court has ordered that the intent of the voter be discerned from such ballots. For purposes of resolving the equal protection challenge, it is not necessary to decide whether the Florida Supreme Court had the authority under the legislative scheme for resolving election disputes to define what a legal vote is and to mandate a manual recount implementing that definition. The recount mechanisms implemented in response to the decisions of the Florida Supreme Court do not satisfy the minimum requirement for nonarbitrary treatment of voters necessary to secure the fundamental right. Florida's basic command for the count of legally cast votes is to consider the "intent of the voter." 772 So.2d, at 1262. This is unobjectionable as an abstract proposition and a starting principle. The problem inheres in the absence of specific standards to ensure its equal application. The formulation of uniform rules to determine intent based on these recurring circumstances is practicable and, we conclude, necessary.

The law does not refrain from searching for the intent of the actor in a multitude of circumstances; and in some cases the general command to ascertain intent is not susceptible to much further refinement. In this instance, however, the question is not whether to believe a witness but how to interpret the marks or holes or scratches on an inanimate object, a piece of cardboard or paper which, it is said, might not have registered as a vote during the machine count. The factfinder confronts a thing, not a person. The search for intent can be confined by specific rules designed to ensure uniform treatment.

The want of those rules here has led to unequal evaluation of ballots in various respects. See *id.,* at 1267 (Wells, C.J., dissenting) ("Should a county canvassing board count or not count a 'dimpled chad' where the voter is able to successfully dislodge the chad in every other contest on that ballot? Here, the county canvassing boards disagree"). As seems to have been acknowledged at oral argument, the standards for accepting or rejecting contested ballots might vary not only from county to county but indeed within a single county from one recount team to another.

The record provides some examples. A monitor in Miami-Dade County testified at trial that he observed that three members of the county canvassing board applied different standards in defining a legal vote. 3 Tr. 497, 499 (Dec. 3, 2000). And testimony at trial also revealed that at least one county changed its evaluative standards during the counting process. Palm Beach County, for example, began the process with a 1990 guideline which precluded counting completely attached chads, switched to a rule that considered a vote to be legal if any light could be seen through a chad, changed back to the 1990 rule, and then abandoned any pretense of a *per se* rule, only to have a court order that the county consider dimpled chads legal. This is not a process with sufficient guarantees of equal treatment.

An early case in our one-person, one-vote jurisprudence arose when a State accorded arbitrary and disparate treatment to voters in its different counties. *Gray v. Sanders,* 372 U.S. 368 (1963). The Court found a constitutional violation. We relied on these principles in the context of the Presidential selection process in *Moore v. Ogilvie,* 394 U.S. 814 (1969), where we invalidated a county-based procedure that diluted the influence of citizens in larger counties in the nominating process. There we observed that "[t]he idea that one group can be granted greater voting strength than another is hostile to the one man, one vote basis of our representative government." *Id.,* at 819.

The State Supreme Court ratified this uneven treatment. It mandated that the recount totals from two counties, Miami-Dade and Palm Beach, be included in the certified total. The court also appeared to hold *sub silentio* that the recount totals from Broward County, which were not completed until after the original November 14 certification by the Secretary, were to be considered part of the new certified vote totals even though the county certification was not contested by Vice President Gore. Yet each of the counties used varying standards to determine what was a legal vote. Broward County used a more forgiving standard than Palm Beach County, and uncovered almost three times as many new votes, a result markedly disproportionate to the difference in population between the counties.

In addition, the recounts in these three counties were not limited to so-called undervotes but extended to all of the ballots. The distinction has real consequences. A manual recount of all ballots identifies not only those ballots which show no vote but also those which contain more than one, the so-called overvotes. Neither category will be counted by the machine. This is not a trivial concern. At oral argument, respondents estimated there are as many as 110,000 overvotes statewide. As a result, the citizen whose ballot was not read by a machine because he failed to vote for a candidate in a way readable by a machine may still have his vote counted in a manual recount; on the other hand, the citizen who marks two candidates in a way discernible by the machine will not have the same opportunity to have his vote count, even if a manual examination of the ballot would reveal the requisite indicia of intent.

Furthermore, the citizen who marks two candidates, only one of which is discernible by the machine, will have his vote counted even though it should have been read as an invalid ballot. The State Supreme Court's inclusion of vote counts based on these variant standards exemplifies concerns with the remedial processes that were under way.

That brings the analysis to yet a further equal protection problem. The votes certified by the court included a partial total from one county, Miami-Dade. The Florida Supreme Court's decision thus gives no assurance that the recounts included in a final certification must be complete. Indeed, it is respondents' submission that it would be consistent with the rules of the recount procedures to include whatever partial counts are done by the time of final certification, and we interpret the Florida Supreme Court's decision to permit this. See 772 So.2d, at 1261–1262, n. 21 (noting "practical difficulties" may control outcome of election, but certifying partial Miami-Dade total nonetheless). This accommodation no doubt results from the truncated contest period established by the Florida Supreme Court in *Palm Beach County Canvassing Bd. v. Harris,* at respondents' own urging. The press of time does not diminish the constitutional concern. A desire for speed is not a general excuse for ignoring equal protection guarantees.

In addition to these difficulties the actual process by which the votes were to be counted under the Florida Supreme Court's decision raises further concerns. That order did not specify who would recount the ballots. The county canvassing boards were forced to pull together ad hoc teams of judges from various Circuits who had no previous training in handling and interpreting ballots. Furthermore, while others were permitted to observe, they were prohibited from objecting during the recount.

The recount process, in its features here described, is inconsistent with the minimum procedures necessary to protect the fundamental right of each voter in the special instance of a statewide recount under the authority of a single state judicial officer. Our consideration is limited to the present circumstances, for the problem of equal protection in election processes generally presents many complexities.

The question before the Court is not whether local entities, in the exercise of their expertise, may develop different systems for implementing elections. Instead, we are presented with a situation where a state court with the power to assure uniformity has ordered a statewide recount with minimal procedural safeguards. When a court orders a statewide remedy, there must be at least some assurance that the rudimentary requirements of equal treatment and fundamental fairness are satisfied.

Given the Court's assessment that the recount process underway was probably being conducted in an unconstitutional manner, the Court stayed the order directing the recount so it could hear this case and render an expedited decision. The contest provision, as it was mandated by the State Supreme Court, is not well calculated to sustain the confidence that all citizens must have in the outcome of elections. The State has not shown that its procedures include the necessary safeguards. The problem, for instance, of the estimated 110,000 overvotes has not been addressed, although Chief Justice Wells called attention to the concern in his dissenting opinion. See 772 So.2d, at 1264, n. 26.

Upon due consideration of the difficulties identified to this point, it is obvious that the recount cannot be conducted in compliance with the requirements of equal protection and due process without substantial additional work. It would require not only the adoption (after opportunity for argument) of adequate statewide standards for determining what is a legal vote, and practicable procedures to implement them, but also orderly judicial review of any disputed matters that might arise. In addition, the Secretary has advised that the recount of only a portion of the ballots requires that the vote tabulation equipment be used to screen out undervotes, a function for which the machines were not designed. If a recount of overvotes were also required, perhaps even a second screening would be necessary. Use of the equipment for this purpose, and any new software developed for it, would have to be evaluated for accuracy by the Secretary, as required by Fla. Stat. Ann. § 101.015 (Supp. 2001).

The Supreme Court of Florida has said that the legislature intended the State's electors to "participat[e] fully in the federal electoral process," as provided in 3 U.S.C. § 5. That statute, in turn, requires that any controversy or contest that is designed to lead to a conclusive selection of electors be completed by December 12. That date is upon us, and there is no recount procedure in place under the State Supreme Court's order that comports with minimal constitutional standards. Because it is evident that any recount seeking to meet the December 12 date will be unconstitutional for the reasons we have discussed, we reverse the judgment of the Supreme Court of Florida ordering a recount to proceed.

Seven Justices of the Court agree that there are constitutional problems with the recount ordered by the Florida Supreme Court that demand a remedy. See *post,* at 545 (Souter, J., dissenting); *post,* at 551–552 (Breyer, J., dissenting). The only disagreement is as to the remedy. Because the Florida Supreme Court has said that the Florida Legislature intended to obtain the safe-harbor benefits of 3 U.S.C. § 5, Justice Breyer's proposed remedy — remanding to the Florida Supreme Court for its ordering of a constitutionally proper contest until December 18 — contemplates action in violation of the Florida Election Code, and hence could not be part of an "appropriate" order authorized by Fla. Stat. Ann. § 102.168(8) (Supp. 2001).

. . .

None are more conscious of the vital limits on judicial authority than are the Members of this Court, and none stand more in admiration of the Constitution's design to leave the selection of the President to the people, through their legislatures, and to the political sphere. When contending parties invoke the process of the courts, however, it becomes our unsought responsibility to resolve the federal and constitutional issues the judicial system has been forced to confront.

The judgment of the Supreme Court of Florida is reversed, and the case is remanded for further proceedings not inconsistent with this opinion.

Pursuant to this Court's Rule 45.2, the Clerk is directed to issue the mandate in this case forthwith.

It is so ordered.

Chief Justice REHNQUIST, with whom Justice SCALIA and Justice THOMAS join, concurring.

We join the *per curiam* opinion. We write separately because we believe there are additional grounds that require us to reverse the Florida Supreme Court's decision.

I

We deal here not with an ordinary election, but with an election for the President of the United States. In *Burroughs v. United States,* 290 U.S. 534, 545 (1934), we said:

> "While presidential electors are not officers or agents of the federal government (*In re Green,* 134 U.S. 377, 379, 10 S.Ct. 586, 33 L.Ed. 951 [(1890)]), they exercise federal functions under, and discharge duties in virtue of authority conferred by, the Constitution of the United States. The President is vested with the executive power of the nation. The importance of his election and the vital character of its relationship to and effect upon the welfare and safety of the whole people cannot be too strongly stated."

Likewise, in *Anderson v. Celebrezze,* 460 U.S. 780, 794–795 (1983) (footnote omitted), we said: "[I]n the context of a Presidential election, state-imposed restrictions implicate a uniquely important national interest. For the President and the Vice President of the United States are the only elected officials who represent all the voters in the Nation."

In most cases, comity and respect for federalism compel us to defer to the decisions of state courts on issues of state law. That practice reflects our understanding that the decisions of state courts are definitive pronouncements of the will of the States as sovereigns. Of course, in ordinary cases, the distribution of powers among the branches of a State's government raises no questions of federal constitutional law, subject to the requirement that the government be republican in character. See U.S. Const., Art. IV, § 4. But there are a few exceptional cases in which the Constitution imposes a duty or confers a power on a particular branch of a State's government. This is one of them. Article II, § 1, cl. 2, provides that "[e]ach State shall appoint, in such Manner as the *Legislature* thereof may direct," electors for President and Vice President. (Emphasis added.) Thus, the text of the election law itself, and not just its interpretation by the courts of the States, takes on independent significance.

In *McPherson v. Blacker,* we explained that Art. II, § 1, cl. 2, "convey[s] the broadest power of determination" and "leaves it to the legislature exclusively to define the method" of appointment. 146 U.S., at 27, 13 S.Ct. 3. A significant departure from the legislative scheme for appointing Presidential electors presents a federal constitutional question.

Title 3 U.S.C. § 5 informs our application of Art. II, § 1, cl. 2, to the Florida statutory scheme, which, as the Florida Supreme Court acknowledged, took that statute into account. Section 5 provides that the State's selection of electors "shall be conclusive, and shall govern in the counting of the electoral votes" if the electors are chosen under laws enacted prior to election day, and if the selection process is completed six days prior to the meeting of the electoral college. As we noted in *Bush v. Palm Beach County Canvassing Bd.*:

> "Since § 5 contains a principle of federal law that would assure finality of the State's determination if made pursuant to a state law in effect before the election, a legislative wish to take advantage of the 'safe harbor' would counsel against any construction of the Election Code that Congress might deem to be a change in the law."

If we are to respect the legislature's Article II powers, therefore, we must ensure that postelection state-court actions do not frustrate the legislative desire to attain the "safe harbor" provided by § 5.

In Florida, the legislature has chosen to hold statewide elections to appoint the State's 25 electors. Importantly, the legislature has delegated the authority to run the elections and to oversee election disputes to the Secretary of State (Secretary), Fla. Stat. Ann. § 97.012(1) (Supp. 2001), and to state circuit courts, §§ 102.168(1), 102.168(8). Isolated sections of the code may well admit of more than one interpretation, but the general coherence of the legislative scheme may not be altered by judicial interpretation so as to wholly change the statutorily provided apportionment of responsibility among these various bodies. In any election but a Presidential election, the Florida Supreme Court can give as little or as much deference to Florida's executives as it chooses, so far as Article II is concerned, and this Court will have no cause to question the court's actions. But, with respect to a Presidential election, the court must be both mindful of the legislature's role under Article II in choosing the manner of appointing electors and deferential to those bodies expressly empowered by the legislature to carry out its constitutional mandate.

In order to determine whether a state court has infringed upon the legislature's authority, we necessarily must examine the law of the State as it existed prior to the action of the court. Though we generally defer to state courts on the interpretation of state law — see, *e.g., Mullaney v. Wilbur,* 421 U.S. 684 (1975) — there are of course areas in which the Constitution requires this Court to undertake an independent, if still deferential, analysis of state law.

For example, in *NAACP v. Alabama ex rel. Patterson,* 357 U.S. 449 (1958), it was argued that we were without jurisdiction because the petitioner had not pursued the correct appellate remedy in Alabama's state courts. Petitioner had sought a state-law writ of certiorari in the Alabama Supreme Court when a writ of mandamus, according to that court, was proper. We found this state-law ground inadequate to defeat our jurisdiction because we were "unable to reconcile the procedural holding of the Alabama Supreme Court" with prior Alabama precedent. The purported state-law ground was so novel, in our independent estimation, that "petitioner could not fairly be deemed to have been apprised of its existence."

Six years later we decided *Bouie v. City of Columbia,* 378 U.S. 347 (1964), in which the state court had held, contrary to precedent, that the state trespass law applied to black sit-in demonstrators who had consent to enter private property but were then asked to leave. Relying upon *NAACP,* we concluded that the South Carolina Supreme Court's interpretation of a state penal statute had impermissibly broadened the scope of that statute beyond what a fair reading provided, in violation of due process. See 378 U.S., at 361–362. What we would do in the present case is precisely parallel: hold that the Florida Supreme Court's interpretation of the Florida election laws impermissibly distorted them beyond what a fair reading required, in violation of Article II.

This inquiry does not imply a disrespect for state *courts* but rather a respect for the constitutionally prescribed role of state *legislatures.* To attach definitive weight to the pronouncement of a state court, when the very question at issue is whether the court has actually departed from the statutory meaning, would be to abdicate our responsibility to enforce the explicit requirements of Article II.

II

Acting pursuant to its constitutional grant of authority, the Florida Legislature has created a detailed, if not perfectly crafted, statutory scheme that provides for appointment of Presidential electors by direct election. Fla. Stat. Ann. § 103.011 (1992). Under the statute, "[v]otes cast for the actual candidates for President and Vice President shall be counted as votes cast for the presidential electors supporting such candidates." *Ibid.* The legislature has designated the Secretary as the "chief election officer," with the responsibility to "[o]btain and maintain uniformity in the application, operation, and interpretation of the election laws." Fla. Stat. Ann. § 97.012 (Supp. 2001). The state legislature has delegated to county canvassing boards the duties of administering elections. § 102.141. Those boards are responsible for providing results to the state Elections Canvassing Commission, comprising the Governor, the Secretary of State, and the Director of the Division of Elections. § 102.111. Cf. *Boardman v. Esteva,* 323 So.2d 259, 268, n. 5 (1975) ("The election process . . . is committed to the executive branch of government through duly designated officials all charged with specific duties. . . . [The] judgments [of these officials] are entitled to be regarded by the courts as presumptively correct . . .").

After the election has taken place, the canvassing boards receive returns from precincts, count the votes, and in the event that a candidate was defeated by 0.5% or less, conduct a mandatory recount. Fla. Stat. § 102.141(4) (2000). The county canvassing boards must file certified election returns with the Department of State by 5 p.m. on the seventh day following the election. § 102.112(1). The Elections Canvassing Commission must then certify the results of the election. § 102.111(1).

The state legislature has also provided mechanisms both for protesting election returns and for contesting certified election results. Section 102.166 governs protests.

Any protest must be filed prior to the certification of election results by the county canvassing board. § 102.166(4)(b). Once a protest has been filed, "[t]he county canvassing board may authorize a manual recount." § 102.166(4)(c). If a sample recount conducted pursuant to § 102.166(5) "indicates an error in the vote tabulation which could affect the outcome of the election," the county canvassing board is instructed to: "(a) Correct the error and recount the remaining precincts with the vote tabulation system; (b) Request the Department of State to verify the tabulation software; or (c) Manually recount all ballots," § 102.166(5). In the event a canvassing board chooses to conduct a manual recount of all ballots, § 102.166(7) prescribes procedures for such a recount.

Contests to the certification of an election, on the other hand, are controlled by § 102.168. The grounds for contesting an election include "[r]eceipt of a number of illegal votes or rejection of a number of legal votes sufficient to change or place in doubt the result of the election." § 102.168(3)(c). Any contest must be filed in the appropriate Florida circuit court, § 102.168(1), and the canvassing board or election board is the proper party defendant, § 102.168(4). Section 102.168(8) provides that "[t]he circuit judge to whom the contest is presented may fashion such orders as he or she deems necessary to ensure that each allegation in the complaint is investigated, examined, or checked, to prevent or correct any alleged wrong, and to provide any relief appropriate under such circumstances." In Presidential elections, the contest period necessarily terminates on the date set by 3 U.S.C. § 5 for concluding the State's "final determination" of election controversies.

In its first decision, *Palm Beach Canvassing Bd. v. Harris,* 772 So.2d 1220 (2000) (*Harris I*), the Florida Supreme Court extended the 7-day statutory certification deadline established by the legislature. This modification of the code, by lengthening the protest period, necessarily shortened the contest period for Presidential elections. Underlying the extension of the certification deadline and the shortchanging of the contest period was, presumably, the clear implication that certification was a matter of significance: The certified winner would enjoy presumptive validity, making a contest proceeding by the losing candidate an uphill battle. In its latest opinion, however, the court empties certification of virtually all legal consequence during the contest, and in doing so departs from the provisions enacted by the Florida Legislature.

The court determined that canvassing boards' decisions regarding whether to recount ballots past the certification deadline (even the certification deadline established by *Harris I*) are to be reviewed *de novo,* although the Election Code clearly vests discretion whether to recount in the boards, and sets strict deadlines subject to the Secretary's rejection of late tallies and monetary fines for tardiness. See Fla. Stat. Ann. § 102.112 (Supp. 2001). Moreover, the Florida court held that all late vote tallies arriving during the contest period should be automatically included in the certification regardless of the certification deadline (even the certification deadline established by *Harris I*), thus virtually eliminating both the deadline and the Secretary's discretion to disregard recounts that violate it.

Moreover, the court's interpretation of "legal vote," and hence its decision to order a contest-period recount, plainly departed from the legislative scheme. Florida statutory law cannot reasonably be thought to *require* the counting of improperly marked ballots. Each Florida precinct before election day provides instructions on how properly to cast a vote, Fla. Stat. Ann. § 101.46 (1992); each polling place on election day contains a working model of the voting machine it uses, Fla. Stat. Ann. § 101.5611 (Supp. 2001); and each voting booth contains a sample ballot, § 101.46. In precincts using punchcard ballots, voters are instructed to punch out the ballot cleanly: "AFTER VOTING, CHECK YOUR BALLOT CARD TO BE SURE YOUR VOTING SELECTIONS ARE CLEARLY AND CLEANLY PUNCHED AND THERE ARE NO CHIPS LEFT HANGING ON THE BACK OF THE CARD." Instructions to Voters, quoted in Brief for Respondent Harris et al. 13, n. 5.

No reasonable person would call it "an error in the vote tabulation," Fla. Stat. Ann. § 102.166(5) (Supp. 2001), or a "rejection of . . . legal votes," § 102.168(3)(c), [FN4] when electronic or electromechanical equipment performs precisely in the manner designed, and fails to count those ballots that are not marked in the manner that these voting instructions explicitly and prominently specify. The scheme that the Florida Supreme Court's opinion attributes to the legislature is one in which machines are *required* to be "capable of correctly counting votes," § 101.5606(4), but which nonetheless regularly produces elections in which legal votes are predictably *not* tabulated, so that in close elections manual recounts are regularly required. This is of course absurd. The Secretary, who is authorized by law to issue binding interpretations of the Election Code, §§ 97.012, 106.23, rejected this peculiar reading of the statutes. See DE 00-13 (opinion of the Division of Elections). The Florida Supreme Court, although it must defer to the Secretary's interpretations, see *Krivanek v. Take Back Tampa Political Committee,* 625 So.2d 840, 844 (Fla.1993), rejected her reasonable interpretation and embraced the peculiar one.

But as we indicated in our remand of the earlier case, in a Presidential election the clearly expressed intent of the legislature must prevail. And there is no basis for reading the Florida statutes as requiring the counting of improperly marked ballots, as an examination of the Florida Supreme Court's textual analysis shows. We will not parse that analysis here, except to note that the principal provision of the Election Code on which it relied, § 101.5614(5), was, as Chief Justice Wells pointed out in his dissent in *Gore v. Harris,* 772 So.2d 1243, 1267 (2000) *(Harris II),* entirely irrelevant. The State's Attorney General (who was supporting the Gore challenge) confirmed in oral argument here that never before the present election had a manual recount been conducted on the basis of the contention that "undervotes" should have been examined to determine voter intent. For the court to step away from this established practice, prescribed by the Secretary, the state official charged by the legislature with "responsibility to . . . [o]btain and maintain uniformity in the application, operation, and interpretation of the election laws," § 97.012(1), was to depart from the legislative scheme.

III

The scope and nature of the remedy ordered by the Florida Supreme Court jeopardizes the "legislative wish" to take advantage of the safe harbor provided by 3 U.S.C. § 5. *Bush v. Palm Beach County Canvassing Bd.,* 531 U.S., at 78 *(per curiam).* December 12, 2000, is the last date for a final determination of the Florida electors that will satisfy § 5. Yet in the late afternoon of December 8th — four days before this deadline — the Supreme Court of Florida ordered recounts of tens of thousands of so-called "undervotes" spread through 64 of the State's 67 counties. This was done in a search for elusive — perhaps delusive — certainty as to the exact count of 6 million votes. But no one claims that these ballots have not previously been tabulated; they were initially read by voting machines at the time of the election, and thereafter reread by virtue of Florida's automatic recount provision. No one claims there was any fraud in the election. The Supreme Court of Florida ordered this additional recount under the provision of the Election Code giving the circuit judge the authority to provide relief that is "appropriate under such circumstances." Fla. Stat. Ann. § 102.168(8) (Supp. 2001).

Surely when the Florida Legislature empowered the courts of the State to grant "appropriate" relief, it must have meant relief that would have become final by the cutoff date of 3 U.S.C. § 5. In light of the inevitable legal challenges and ensuing appeals to the Supreme Court of Florida and petitions for certiorari to this Court, the entire recounting process could not possibly be completed by that date. Whereas the majority in the Supreme Court of Florida stated its confidence that "the remaining undervotes in these counties can be [counted] within the required time frame," 772 So.2d, at 1262, n. 22, it made no assertion that the seemingly inevitable appeals could be disposed of in that time. Although the Florida Supreme Court has on occasion taken over a year to resolve disputes over local elections, see, *e.g., Beckstrom v. Volusia County Canvassing Bd.,* 707 So.2d 720 (1998) (resolving contest of sheriff's race 16 months after the election), it has heard and decided the appeals in the present case with great promptness. But the federal deadlines for the Presidential election simply do not permit even such a shortened process.

As the dissent noted:

> "In [the four days remaining], all questionable ballots must be reviewed by the judicial officer appointed to discern the intent of the voter in a process open to the public. Fairness dictates that a provision be made for either party to object to how a particular ballot is counted. Additionally, this short time period must allow for judicial review. I respectfully submit this cannot be completed without taking Florida's presidential electors outside the safe harbor provision, creating the very real possibility of disenfranchising those nearly six million voters who are able to correctly cast their ballots on election day." 772 So.2d, at 1269 (opinion of Wells, C.J.) (footnote omitted).

The other dissenters echoed this concern: "[T]he majority is departing from the essential requirements of the law by providing a remedy which is impossible to achieve and which will ultimately lead to chaos." *Id.,* at 1273 (Harding, J., dissenting, jointed by Shaw, J.).

Given all these factors, and in light of the legislative intent identified by the Florida Supreme Court to bring Florida within the "safe harbor" provision of 3 U.S.C. § 5, the remedy prescribed by the Supreme Court of Florida cannot be deemed an "appropriate" one as of December 8. It significantly departed from the statutory framework in place on November 7, and authorized open-ended further proceedings which could not be completed by December 12, thereby preventing a final determination by that date.

For these reasons, in addition to those given in the *per curiam* opinion, we would reverse.

Justice STEVENS, with whom Justice GINSBURG and Justice BREYER join, dissenting.

The Constitution assigns to the States the primary responsibility for determining the manner of selecting the Presidential electors. See Art. II, § 1, cl. 2. When questions arise about the meaning of state laws, including election laws, it is our settled practice to accept the opinions of the highest courts of the States as providing the final answers. On rare occasions, however, either federal statutes or the Federal Constitution may require federal judicial intervention in state elections. This is not such an occasion.

The federal questions that ultimately emerged in this case are not substantial. Article II provides that "[e]ach *State* shall appoint, in such Manner as the Legislature *thereof* may direct, a Number of Electors." *Ibid.* (emphasis added). It does not create state legislatures out of whole cloth, but rather takes them as they come—as creatures born of, and constrained by, their state constitutions. Lest there be any doubt, we stated over 100 years ago in *McPherson v. Blacker,* 146 U.S. 1, 25 (1892), that "[w]hat is forbidden or required to be done by a State" in the Article II context "is forbidden or required of the legislative power under state constitutions as they exist." In the same vein, we also observed that "[t]he [State's] legislative power is the supreme authority except as limited by the constitution of the State." The legislative power in Florida is subject to judicial review pursuant to Article V of the Florida Constitution, and nothing in Article II of the Federal Constitution frees the state legislature from the constraints in the State Constitution that created it. Moreover, the Florida Legislature's own decision to employ a unitary code for all elections indicates that it intended the Florida Supreme Court to play the same role in Presidential elections that it has historically played in resolving electoral disputes. The Florida Supreme Court's exercise of appellate jurisdiction therefore was wholly consistent with, and indeed contemplated by, the grant of authority in Article II.

It hardly needs stating that Congress, pursuant to 3 U.S.C. § 5, did not impose any affirmative duties upon the States that their governmental branches could "violate."

Rather, § 5 provides a safe harbor for States to select electors in contested elections "by judicial or other methods" established by laws prior to the election day. Section 5, like Article II, assumes the involvement of the state judiciary in interpreting state election laws and resolving election disputes under those laws. Neither § 5 nor Article II grants federal judges any special authority to substitute their views for those of the state judiciary on matters of state law.

Nor are petitioners correct in asserting that the failure of the Florida Supreme Court to specify in detail the precise manner in which the "intent of the voter," Fla. Stat. Ann. § 101.5614(5) (Supp. 2001), is to be determined rises to the level of a constitutional violation.[123] We found such a violation when individual votes within the same State were weighted unequally, see, *e.g., Reynolds v. Sims,* 377 U.S. 533, 568 (1964), but we have never before called into question the substantive standard by which a State determines that a vote has been legally cast. And there is no reason to think that the guidance provided to the factfinders, specifically the various canvassing boards, by the "intent of the voter" standard is any less sufficient—or will lead to results any less uniform—than, for example, the "beyond a reasonable doubt" standard employed every day by ordinary citizens in courtrooms across this country.[124]

Admittedly, the use of differing substandards for determining voter intent in different counties employing similar voting systems may raise serious concerns. Those concerns are alleviated—if not eliminated—by the fact that a single impartial magistrate will ultimately adjudicate all objections arising from the recount process. Of course, as a general matter, "[t]he interpretation of constitutional principles must not be too literal. We must remember that the machinery of government would not work if it were not allowed a little play in its joints." *Bain Peanut Co. of Tex. v. Pinson,* 282 U.S. 499, 501 (1931) (Holmes, J.). If it were otherwise, Florida's decision to leave to each county the determination of what balloting system to employ—despite enormous differences in accuracy[125]—might run afoul of equal protection. So, too, might the similar decisions of the vast majority of state legislatures to delegate to local authorities certain decisions with respect to voting systems and ballot design.

---

123. The Florida statutory standard is consistent with the practice of the majority of States, which apply either an "intent of the voter" standard or an "impossible to determine the elector's choice" standard in ballot recounts.

124. Cf. *Victor v. Nebraska,* 511 U.S. 1, 5, 114 S.Ct. 1239, 127 L.Ed.2d 583 (1994) ("The beyond a reasonable doubt standard is a requirement of due process, but the Constitution neither prohibits trial courts from defining reasonable doubt nor requires them to do so").

125. The percentage of nonvotes in this election in counties using a punchcard system was 3.92%; in contrast, the rate of error under the more modern optical-scan systems was only 1.43%. *Siegel v. LePore,* 234 F.3d 1163, 1202, 1213 (charts C and F) (C.A.11, Dec. 6, 2000). Put in other terms, for every 10,000 votes cast, punchcard systems result in 250 more nonvotes than optical-scan systems. A total of 3,718,305 votes were cast under punchcard systems, and 2,353,811 votes were cast under optical-scan systems. *Ibid.*

Even assuming that aspects of the remedial scheme might ultimately be found to violate the Equal Protection Clause, I could not subscribe to the majority's disposition of the case. As the majority explicitly holds, once a state legislature determines to select electors through a popular vote, the right to have one's vote counted is of constitutional stature. As the majority further acknowledges, Florida law holds that all ballots that reveal the intent of the voter constitute valid votes. Recognizing these principles, the majority nonetheless orders the termination of the contest proceeding before all such votes have been tabulated. Under their own reasoning, the appropriate course of action would be to remand to allow more specific procedures for implementing the legislature's uniform general standard to be established.

In the interest of finality, however, the majority effectively orders the disenfranchisement of an unknown number of voters whose ballots reveal their intent—and are therefore legal votes under state law—but were for some reason rejected by ballot-counting machines. It does so on the basis of the deadlines set forth in Title 3 of the United States Code. *Ante,* at 532. But, as I have already noted, those provisions merely provide rules of decision for Congress to follow when selecting among conflicting slates of electors. They do not prohibit a State from counting what the majority concedes to be legal votes until a bona fide winner is determined. Indeed, in 1960, Hawaii appointed two slates of electors and Congress chose to count the one appointed on January 4, 1961, well after the Title 3 deadlines. See Josephson & Ross, Repairing the Electoral College, 22 J. Legis. 145, 166, n. 154 (1996). Thus, nothing prevents the majority, even if it properly found an equal protection violation, from ordering relief appropriate to remedy that violation without depriving Florida voters of their right to have their votes counted. As the majority notes, "[a] desire for speed is not a general excuse for ignoring equal protection guarantees."

Finally, neither in this case, nor in its earlier opinion in *Palm Beach County Canvassing Bd. v. Harris,* 772 So.2d 1220 (2000), did the Florida Supreme Court make any substantive change in Florida electoral law.[6] Its decisions were rooted in long-established precedent and were consistent with the relevant statutory provisions, taken as a whole. It did what courts do—it decided the case before it in light of the legislature's intent to leave no legally cast vote uncounted. In so doing, it relied on the sufficiency of the general "intent of the voter" standard articulated by the state legislature, coupled with a procedure for ultimate review by an impartial judge, to resolve the concern about disparate evaluations of contested ballots. If we assume—as I do—that the members of that court and the judges who would have carried out its mandate are impartial, its decision does not even raise a colorable federal question.

---

6. When, for example, it resolved the previously unanswered question whether the word "shall" in Fla. Stat. Ann. § 102.111 (Supp. 2001) or the word "may" in § 102.112 governs the scope of the Secretary of State's authority to ignore untimely election returns, it did not "change the law." Like any other judicial interpretation of a statute, its opinion was an authoritative interpretation of what the statute's relevant provisions have meant since they were enacted. *Rivers v. Roadway Express, Inc.,* 511 U.S. 298, 312–313 (1994).

What must underlie petitioners' entire federal assault on the Florida election procedures is an unstated lack of confidence in the impartiality and capacity of the state judges who would make the critical decisions if the vote count were to proceed. Otherwise, their position is wholly without merit. The endorsement of that position by the majority of this Court can only lend credence to the most cynical appraisal of the work of judges throughout the land. It is confidence in the men and women who administer the judicial system that is the true backbone of the rule of law. Time will one day heal the wound to that confidence that will be inflicted by today's decision. One thing, however, is certain. Although we may never know with complete certainty the identity of the winner of this year's Presidential election, the identity of the loser is perfectly clear. It is the Nation's confidence in the judge as an impartial guardian of the rule of law.

I respectfully dissent.

Justice SOUTER, with whom Justice BREYER joins, and with whom Justice STEVENS and Justice GINSBURG join as to all but Part III, dissenting.

The Court should not have reviewed either *Bush v. Palm Beach County Canvassing Bd.,* 531 U.S., at 70 (*per curiam*), or this case, and should not have stopped Florida's attempt to recount all undervote ballots, see 531 U.S., at 102, by issuing a stay of the Florida Supreme Court's orders during the period of this review, see *Bush v. Gore,* 531 U.S. 1046. If this Court had allowed the State to follow the course indicated by the opinions of its own Supreme Court, it is entirely possible that there would ultimately have been no issue requiring our review, and political tension could have worked itself out in the Congress following the procedure provided in 3 U.S.C. § 15. The case being before us, however, its resolution by the majority is another erroneous decision.

As will be clear, I am in substantial agreement with the dissenting opinions of Justice Stevens, Justice Ginsburg, and Justice Breyer. I write separately only to say how straightforward the issues before us really are.

There are three issues: whether the State Supreme Court's interpretation of the statute providing for a contest of the state election results somehow violates 3 U.S.C. § 5; whether that court's construction of the state statutory provisions governing contests impermissibly changes a state law from what the State's legislature has provided, in violation of Article II, § 1, cl. 2, of the National Constitution; and whether the manner of interpreting markings on disputed ballots failing to cause machines to register votes for President (the undervote ballots) violates the equal protection or due process guaranteed by the Fourteenth Amendment. None of these issues is difficult to describe or to resolve.

I

The 3 U.S.C. § 5 issue is not serious. That provision sets certain conditions for treating a State's certification of Presidential electors as conclusive in the event that a dispute over recognizing those electors must be resolved in the Congress under 3 U.S.C. § 15. Conclusiveness requires selection under a legal scheme in place before the election, with results determined at least six days before the date set for casting electoral votes. But no State is required to conform to §5 if it cannot do that (for whatever reason); the sanction for failing to satisfy the conditions of §5 is simply loss of what has been called its "safe harbor." And even that determination is to be made, if made anywhere, in the Congress.

II

The second matter here goes to the State Supreme Court's interpretation of certain terms in the state statute governing election "contests," Fla. Stat. Ann. § 102.168 (Supp. 2001); there is no question here about the state court's interpretation of the related provisions dealing with the antecedent process of "protesting" particular vote counts, § 102.166, which was involved in the previous case, *Bush v. Palm Beach County Canvassing Bd.* The issue is whether the judgment of the State Supreme Court has displaced the state legislature's provisions for election contests: is the law as declared by the court different from the provisions made by the legislature, to which the National Constitution commits responsibility for determining how each State's Presidential electors are chosen? See U.S. Const., Art. II, §1, cl. 2. Bush does not, of course, claim that any judicial act interpreting a statute of uncertain meaning is enough to displace the legislative provision and violate Article II; statutes require interpretation, which does not without more affect the legislative character of a statute within the meaning of the Constitution. What Bush does argue, as I understand the contention, is that the interpretation of § 102.168 was so unreasonable as to transcend the accepted bounds of statutory interpretation, to the point of being a nonjudicial act and producing new law untethered to the legislative Act in question.

The starting point for evaluating the claim that the Florida Supreme Court's interpretation effectively rewrote § 102.168 must be the language of the provision on which Gore relies to show his right to raise this contest: that the previously certified result in Bush's favor was produced by "rejection of a number of legal votes sufficient to change or place in doubt the result of the election." Fla. Stat. Ann. § 102.168(3) (c) (Supp. 2001). None of the state court's interpretations is unreasonable to the point of displacing the legislative enactment quoted. As I will note below, other interpretations were of course possible, and some might have been better than those adopted by the Florida court's majority; the two dissents from the majority opinion of that court and various briefs submitted to us set out alternatives. But the majority view is in each instance within the bounds of reasonable interpretation, and the law as declared is consistent with Article II.

1. The statute does not define a "legal vote," the rejection of which may affect the election. The State Supreme Court was therefore required to define it, and in doing that the court looked to another election statute, § 101.5614(5), dealing with damaged or defective ballots, which contains a provision that no vote shall be disregarded "if there is a clear indication of the intent of the voter as determined by the canvassing board." The court read that objective of looking to the voter's intent as indicating that the legislature probably meant "legal vote" to mean a vote recorded on a ballot

indicating what the voter intended. *Gore v. Harris,* 772 So.2d 1243, 1256–1257 (2000). It is perfectly true that the majority might have chosen a different reading. But even so, there is no constitutional violation in following the majority view; Article II is unconcerned with mere disagreements about interpretive merits.

2. The Florida court next interpreted "rejection" to determine what act in the counting process may be attacked in a contest. Again, the statute does not define the term. The court majority read the word to mean simply a failure to count. 772 So.2d, at 1257. That reading is certainly within the bounds of common sense, given the objective to give effect to a voter's intent if that can be determined. A different reading, of course, is possible. The majority might have concluded that "rejection" should refer to machine malfunction, or that a ballot should not be treated as "reject[ed]" in the absence of wrongdoing by election officials, lest contests be so easy to claim that every election will end up in one. There is, however, nothing nonjudicial in the Florida majority's more hospitable reading.

3. The same is true about the court majority's understanding of the phrase "votes sufficient to change or place in doubt" the result of the election in Florida. The court held that if the uncounted ballots were so numerous that it was reasonably possible that they contained enough "legal" votes to swing the election, this contest would be authorized by the statute. While the majority might have thought (as the trial judge did) that a probability, not a possibility, should be necessary to justify a contest, that reading is not required by the statute's text, which says nothing about probability. Whatever people of good will and good sense may argue about the merits of the Florida court's reading, there is no warrant for saying that it transcends the limits of reasonable statutory interpretation to the point of supplanting the statute enacted by the "legislature" within the meaning of Article II.

In sum, the interpretations by the Florida court raise no substantial question under Article II. That court engaged in permissible construction in determining that Gore had instituted a contest authorized by the state statute, and it proceeded to direct the trial judge to deal with that contest in the exercise of the discretionary powers generously conferred by Fla. Stat. Ann. § 102.168(8) (Supp. 2001), to "fashion such orders as he or she deems necessary to ensure that each allegation in the complaint is investigated, examined, or checked, to prevent or correct any alleged wrong, and to provide any relief appropriate under such circumstances." As Justice Ginsburg has persuasively explained in her own dissenting opinion, our customary respect for state interpretations of state law counsels against rejection of the Florida court's determinations in this case.

III

It is only on the third issue before us that there is a meritorious argument for relief, as this Court's *per curiam* opinion recognizes. It is an issue that might well have been dealt with adequately by the Florida courts if the state proceedings had not been interrupted, and if not disposed of at the state level it could have been considered by the Congress in any electoral vote dispute. But because the course of state proceedings has been interrupted, time is short, and the issue is before us, I think it sensible for the Court to address it.

Petitioners have raised an equal protection claim (or, alternatively, a due process claim, see generally *Logan v. Zimmerman Brush Co.*, 455 U.S. 422 (1982)), in the charge that unjustifiably disparate standards are applied in different electoral jurisdictions to otherwise identical facts. It is true that the Equal Protection Clause does not forbid the use of a variety of voting mechanisms within a jurisdiction, even though different mechanisms will have different levels of effectiveness in recording voters' intentions; local variety can be justified by concerns about cost, the potential value of innovation, and so on. But evidence in the record here suggests that a different order of disparity obtains under rules for determining a voter's intent that have been applied (and could continue to be applied) to identical types of ballots used in identical brands of machines and exhibiting identical physical characteristics (such as "hanging" or "dimpled" chads). See, *e.g.*, Tr. 238-242 (Dec. 2–3, 2000) (testimony of Palm Beach County Canvassing Board Chairman Judge Charles Burton describing varying standards applied to imperfectly punched ballots in Palm Beach County during precertification manual recount); *id.*, at 497–500 (similarly describing varying standards applied in Miami-Dade County); Tr. of Hearing 8–10 (Dec. 8, 2000) (soliciting from county canvassing boards proposed protocols for determining voters' intent but declining to provide a precise, uniform standard). I can conceive of no legitimate state interest served by these differing treatments of the expressions of voters' fundamental rights. The differences appear wholly arbitrary.

In deciding what to do about this, we should take account of the fact that electoral votes are due to be cast in six days. I would therefore remand the case to the courts of Florida with instructions to establish uniform standards for evaluating the several types of ballots that have prompted differing treatments, to be applied within and among counties when passing on such identical ballots in any further recounting (or successive recounting) that the courts might order.

Unlike the majority, I see no warrant for this Court to assume that Florida could not possibly comply with this requirement before the date set for the meeting of electors, December 18. Although one of the dissenting justices of the State Supreme Court estimated that disparate standards potentially affected 170,000 votes, *Gore v. Harris*, 772 So.2d, at 1272–1273, the number at issue is significantly smaller. The 170,000 figure apparently represents all uncounted votes, both undervotes (those for which no Presidential choice was recorded by a machine) and overvotes (those rejected because of votes for more than one candidate). Tr. of Oral Arg. 61–62. But as Justice Breyer has pointed out, no showing has been made of legal overvotes uncounted, and counsel for Gore made an uncontradicted representation to the Court that the statewide total of undervotes is about 60,000. *Id.*, at 62. To recount these manually would be a tall order, but before this Court stayed the effort to do that the courts of Florida were ready to do their best to get that job done. There is no justification for denying the State the opportunity to try to count all disputed ballots now.

I respectfully dissent.

Justice GINSBURG, with whom Justice STEVENS joins, and with whom Justice SOUTER and Justice BREYER join as to Part I, dissenting.

I

The Chief Justice acknowledges that provisions of Florida's Election Code "may well admit of more than one interpretation." *Ante,* at 534 (concurring opinion). But instead of respecting the state high court's province to say what the State's Election Code means, The Chief Justice maintains that Florida's Supreme Court has veered so far from the ordinary practice of judicial review that what it did cannot properly be called judging. My colleagues have offered a reasonable construction of Florida's law. Their construction coincides with the view of one of Florida's seven Supreme Court justices. *Gore v. Harris,* 772 So.2d 1243, 1264–1270 (Fla.2000) (Wells, C. J., dissenting); *Palm Beach County Canvassing Bd. v. Harris,* 772 So.2d 1273, 1291–1292 (Fla.2000) (on remand) (confirming, 6 to 1, the construction of Florida law advanced in *Gore*). I might join The Chief Justice were it my commission to interpret Florida law. But disagreement with the Florida court's interpretation of its own State's law does not warrant the conclusion that the justices of that court have legislated. There is no cause here to believe that the members of Florida's high court have done less than "their mortal best to discharge their oath of office," *Sumner v. Mata,* 449 U.S. 539, 549 (1981), and no cause to upset their reasoned interpretation of Florida law.

This Court more than occasionally affirms statutory, and even constitutional, interpretations with which it disagrees. For example, when reviewing challenges to administrative agencies' interpretations of laws they implement, we defer to the agencies unless their interpretation violates "the unambiguously expressed intent of Congress." *Chevron U.S.A. Inc. v. Natural Resources Defense Council, Inc.,* 467 U.S. 837, 843 (1984). We do so in the face of the declaration in Article I of the United States Constitution that "All legislative Powers herein granted shall be vested in a Congress of the United States." Surely the Constitution does not call upon us to pay more respect to a federal administrative agency's construction of federal law than to a state high court's interpretation of its own state's law. And not uncommonly, we let stand state-court interpretations of *federal* law with which we might disagree. Notably, in the habeas context, the Court adheres to the view that "there is 'no intrinsic reason why the fact that a man is a federal judge should make him more competent, or conscientious, or learned with respect to [federal law] than his neighbor in the state courthouse.'" *Stone v. Powell,* 428 U.S. 465, 494, n. 35 (1976) (quoting Bator, Finality in Criminal Law and Federal Habeas Corpus for State Prisoners, 76 Harv. L.Rev. 441, 509 (1963)); O'Connor, Trends in the Relationship Between the Federal and State Courts from the Perspective of a State Court Judge, 22 Wm. & Mary L.Rev. 801, 813 (1981) ("There is no reason to assume that state court judges cannot and will not provide a 'hospitable forum' in litigating federal constitutional questions.").

No doubt there are cases in which the proper application of federal law may hinge on interpretations of state law. Unavoidably, this Court must sometimes examine state law in order to protect federal rights. But we have dealt with such cases ever mindful of the full measure of respect we owe to interpretations of state law by a State's highest court. In the Contract Clause case, *General Motors Corp. v. Romein,* 503 U.S. 181 (1992), for example, we said that although "ultimately we are bound to decide for ourselves whether a contract was made," the Court "accord [s] respectful consideration and great weight to the views of the State's highest court." *Id.,* at 187. And in *Central Union Telephone Co. v. Edwardsville,* 269 U.S. 190 (1925), we upheld the Illinois Supreme Court's interpretation of a state waiver rule, even though that interpretation resulted in the forfeiture of federal constitutional rights. Refusing to supplant Illinois law with a federal definition of waiver, we explained that the state court's declaration "should bind us unless so unfair or unreasonable in its application to those asserting a federal right as to obstruct it." *Id.,* at 195, 46 S.Ct. 90.

In deferring to state courts on matters of state law, we appropriately recognize that this Court acts as an " 'outside[r]' lacking the common exposure to local law which comes from sitting in the jurisdiction." *Lehman Brothers v. Schein,* 416 U.S. 386, 391 (1974). That recognition has sometimes prompted us to resolve doubts about the meaning of state law by certifying issues to a State's highest court, even when federal rights are at stake. Notwithstanding our authority to decide issues of state law underlying federal claims, we have used the certification device to afford state high courts an opportunity to inform us on matters of their own State's law because such restraint "helps build a cooperative judicial federalism." *Lehman Brothers,* 416 U.S., at 391.

Just last Term, in *Fiore v. White,* 528 U.S. 23 (1999), we took advantage of Pennsylvania's certification procedure. In that case, a state prisoner brought a federal habeas action claiming that the State had failed to prove an essential element of his charged offense in violation of the Due Process Clause. Instead of resolving the state-law question on which the federal claim depended, we certified the question to the Pennsylvania Supreme Court for that court to "help determine the proper state-law predicate for our determination of the federal constitutional questions raised." The Chief Justice's willingness to *reverse* the Florida Supreme Court's interpretation of Florida law in this case is at least in tension with our reluctance in *Fiore* even to interpret Pennsylvania law before seeking instruction from the Pennsylvania Supreme Court. I would have thought the "cautious approach" we counsel when federal courts address matters of state law, *Arizonans,* 520 U.S., at 77, and our commitment to "build[ing] cooperative judicial federalism," *Lehman Brothers,* 416 U.S., at 391, demanded greater restraint.

Rarely has this Court rejected outright an interpretation of state law by a state high court. *Fairfax's Devisee v. Hunter's Lessee,* 7 Cranch 603 (1813), *NAACP v. Alabama ex rel. Patterson,* 357 U.S. 449 (1958), and *Bouie v. City of Columbia,* 378 U.S. 347 (1964), cited by The Chief Justice, are three such rare instances. But those cases are embedded in historical contexts hardly comparable to the situation here. *Fairfax's Devisee,* which held that the Virginia Court of Appeals had misconstrued its own forfeiture laws to deprive a British subject of lands secured to him by federal treaties, occurred amidst vociferous States' rights attacks on the Marshall Court. G. Gunther & K. Sullivan, Constitutional Law 61–62 (13th ed.1997). The Virginia court refused to obey this Court's *Fairfax's Devisee* mandate to enter judgment for the British subject's successor in interest. That refusal led to the Court's pathmarking decision in *Martin v. Hunter's Lessee,* 1 Wheat. 304 (1816). *Patterson,* a case decided three months after *Cooper v. Aaron,* 358 U.S. 1 (1958), in the face of Southern resistance to the civil rights movement, held that the Alabama Supreme Court had irregularly applied its own procedural rules to deny review of a contempt order against the NAACP arising from its refusal to disclose membership lists. We said that "our jurisdiction is not defeated if the nonfederal ground relied on by the state court is 'without any fair or substantial support.'" 357 U.S., at 455. *Bouie,* stemming from a lunch counter "sit-in" at the height of the civil rights movement, held that the South Carolina Supreme Court's construction of its trespass laws — criminalizing conduct not covered by the text of an otherwise clear statute — was "unforeseeable" and thus violated due process when applied retroactively to the petitioners. 378 U.S., at 350, 354.

The Chief Justice's casual citation of these cases might lead one to believe they are part of a larger collection of cases in which we said that the Constitution impelled us to train a skeptical eye on a state court's portrayal of state law. But one would be hard pressed, I think, to find additional cases that fit the mold. As Justice Breyer convincingly explains, this case involves nothing close to the kind of recalcitrance by a state high court that warrants extraordinary action by this Court. The Florida Supreme Court concluded that counting every legal vote was the overriding concern of the Florida Legislature when it enacted the State's Election Code. The court surely should not be bracketed with state high courts of the Jim Crow South.

The Chief Justice says that Article II, by providing that state legislatures shall direct the manner of appointing electors, authorizes federal superintendence over the relationship between state courts and state legislatures, and licenses a departure from the usual deference we give to state-court interpretations of state law. The Framers of our Constitution, however, understood that in a republican government, the judiciary would construe the legislature's enactments. See U.S. Const., Art. III; The Federalist No. 78 (A. Hamilton). In light of the constitutional guarantee to States of a "Republican Form of Government," U.S. Const., Art. IV, § 4, Article II can hardly be read to invite this Court to disrupt a State's republican regime. Yet The Chief Justice today would reach out to do just that. By holding that Article II requires our revision of a state court's construction of state laws in order to protect one organ of the State from another, The Chief Justice contradicts the basic principle that a State may organize itself as it sees fit.

The extraordinary setting of this case has obscured the ordinary principle that dictates its proper resolution: Federal courts defer to a state high court's interpretations of the State's own law. This principle reflects the core of federalism, on which all agree. "The Framers split the atom of sovereignty. It was the genius of their idea that our citizens would have two political capacities, one state and one federal, each protected from incursion by the other." *Saenz v. Roe,* 526 U.S. 489, 504, n. 17 (1999). The Chief Justice's solicitude for the Florida Legislature comes at the expense of the more fundamental solicitude we owe to the legislature's sovereign. U.S. Const., Art. II,

§ 1, cl. 2 ("Each *State* shall appoint, in such Manner as the Legislature *thereof* may direct," the electors for President and Vice President (emphasis added)); ante, at 539–540 (Stevens, J., dissenting). Were the other Members of this Court as mindful as they generally are of our system of dual sovereignty, they would affirm the judgment of the Florida Supreme Court.

II

I agree with Justice Stevens that petitioners have not presented a substantial equal protection claim. Ideally, perfection would be the appropriate standard for judging the recount. But we live in an imperfect world, one in which thousands of votes have not been counted. I cannot agree that the recount adopted by the Florida court, flawed as it may be, would yield a result any less fair or precise than the certification that preceded that recount.

Even if there were an equal protection violation, I would agree with Justice Stevens, Justice Souter, and Justice Breyer that the Court's concern about "the December 12 deadline," is misplaced. Time is short in part because of the Court's entry of a stay on December 9, several hours after an able circuit judge in Leon County had begun to superintend the recount process. More fundamentally, the Court's reluctance to let the recount go forward—despite its suggestion that "[t]he search for intent can be confined by specific rules designed to ensure uniform treatment," ultimately turns on its own judgment about the practical realities of implementing a recount, not the judgment of those much closer to the process.

Equally important, as Justice Breyer explains, the December 12 "deadline" for bringing Florida's electoral votes into 3 U.S.C. § 5's safe harbor lacks the significance the Court assigns it. Were that date to pass, Florida would still be entitled to deliver electoral votes Congress *must* count unless both Houses find that the votes "ha [d] not been . . . regularly given." 3 U.S.C. § 15. The statute identifies other significant dates. See, *e.g.,* § 7 (specifying December 18 as the date electors "shall meet and give their votes"); § 12 (specifying "the fourth Wednesday in December"—this year, December 27—as the date on which Congress, if it has not received a State's electoral votes, shall request the state secretary of state to send a certified return immediately). But none of these dates has ultimate significance in light of Congress' detailed provisions for determining, on "the sixth day of January," the validity of electoral votes. § 15.

The Court assumes that time will not permit "orderly judicial review of any disputed matters that might arise." *Ante,* at 533. But no one has doubted the good faith and diligence with which Florida election officials, attorneys for all sides of this controversy, and the courts of law have performed their duties. Notably, the Florida Supreme Court has produced two substantial opinions within 29 hours of oral argument. In sum, the Court's conclusion that a constitutionally adequate recount is impractical is a prophecy the Court's own judgment will not allow to be tested. Such an untested prophecy should not decide the Presidency of the United States.

I dissent.

Justice BREYER, with whom Justice STEVENS and Justice GINSBURG join except as to Part I-A-1, and with whom Justice SOUTER joins as to Part I, dissenting.

The Court was wrong to take this case. It was wrong to grant a stay. It should now vacate that stay and permit the Florida Supreme Court to decide whether the recount should resume.

I

The political implications of this case for the country are momentous. But the federal legal questions presented, with one exception, are insubstantial.

A

1

The majority raises three equal protection problems with the Florida Supreme Court's recount order: first, the failure to include overvotes in the manual recount; second, the fact that *all* ballots, rather than simply the undervotes, were recounted in some, but not all, counties; and third, the absence of a uniform, specific standard to guide the recounts. As far as the first issue is concerned, petitioners presented no evidence, to this Court or to any Florida court, that a manual recount of overvotes would identify additional legal votes. The same is true of the second, and, in addition, the majority's reasoning would seem to invalidate any state provision for a manual recount of individual counties in a statewide election.

The majority's third concern does implicate principles of fundamental fairness. The majority concludes that the Equal Protection Clause requires that a manual recount be governed not only by the uniform general standard of the "clear intent of the voter," but also by uniform subsidiary standards (for example, a uniform determination whether indented, but not perforated, "undervotes" should count). The opinion points out that the Florida Supreme Court ordered the inclusion of Broward County's undercounted "legal votes" even though those votes included ballots that were not perforated but simply "dimpled," while newly recounted ballots from other counties will likely include only votes determined to be "legal" on the basis of a stricter standard. In light of our previous remand, the Florida Supreme Court may have been reluctant to adopt a more specific standard than that provided for by the legislature for fear of exceeding its authority under Article II. However, since the use of different standards could favor one or the other of the candidates, since time was, and is, too short to permit the lower courts to iron out significant differences through ordinary judicial review, and since the relevant distinction was embodied in the order of the State's highest court, I agree that, in these very special circumstances, basic principles of fairness may well have counseled the adoption of a uniform standard to address the problem. In light of the majority's disposition, I need not decide whether, or the extent to which, as a remedial matter, the Constitution would place limits upon the content of the uniform standard.

2

Nonetheless, there is no justification for the majority's remedy, which is simply to reverse the lower court and halt the recount entirely. An appropriate remedy would be, instead, to remand this case with instructions that, even at this late date, would permit the Florida Supreme Court to require recounting *all* undercounted votes in Florida, including those from Broward, Volusia, Palm Beach, and Miami-Dade Counties, whether or not previously recounted prior to the end of the protest period, and to do so in accordance with a single uniform standard.

The majority justifies stopping the recount entirely on the ground that there is no more time. In particular, the majority relies on the lack of time for the Secretary of State (Secretary) to review and approve equipment needed to separate undervotes. But the majority reaches this conclusion in the absence of *any* record evidence that the recount could not have been completed in the time allowed by the Florida Supreme Court. The majority finds facts outside of the record on matters that state courts are in a far better position to address. Of course, it is too late for any such recount to take place by December 12, the date by which election disputes must be decided if a State is to take advantage of the safe harbor provisions of 3 U.S.C. § 5. Whether there is time to conduct a recount prior to December 18, when the electors are scheduled to meet, is a matter for the state courts to determine. And whether, under Florida law, Florida could or could not take further action is obviously a matter for Florida courts, not this Court, to decide.

By halting the manual recount, and thus ensuring that the uncounted legal votes will not be counted under any standard, this Court crafts a remedy out of proportion to the asserted harm. And that remedy harms the very fairness interests the Court is attempting to protect. The manual recount would itself redress a problem of unequal treatment of ballots. As Justice Stevens points out, the ballots of voters in counties that use punchcard systems are more likely to be disqualified than those in counties using optical-scanning systems. According to recent news reports, variations in the undervote rate are even more pronounced. See Fessenden, No-Vote Rates Higher in Punch Card Count, N.Y. Times, Dec. 1, 2000, p. A29 (reporting that 0.3% of ballots cast in 30 Florida counties using optical-scanning systems registered no Presidential vote, in comparison to 1.53% in the 15 counties using Votomatic punch-card ballots). Thus, in a system that allows counties to use different types of voting systems, voters already arrive at the polls with an unequal chance that their votes will be counted. I do not see how the fact that this results from counties' selection of different voting machines rather than a court order makes the outcome any more fair. Nor do I understand why the Florida Supreme Court's recount order, which helps to redress this inequity, must be entirely prohibited based on a deficiency that could easily be remedied.

B

The remainder of petitioners' claims, which are the focus of The Chief Justice's concurrence, raise no significant federal questions. I cannot agree that The Chief

Justice's unusual review of state law in this case is justified by reference either to Art. II, § 1, or to 3 U.S.C. § 5. Moreover, even were such review proper, the conclusion that the Florida Supreme Court's decision contravenes federal law is untenable.

While conceding that, in most cases, "comity and respect for federalism compel us to defer to the decisions of state courts on issues of state law," the concurrence relies on some combination of Art. II, § 1, and 3 U.S.C. § 5 to justify its conclusion that this case is one of the few in which we may lay that fundamental principle aside. *Ante,* at 534 (opinion of Rehnquist, C.J.) The concurrence's primary foundation for this conclusion rests on an appeal to plain text: Art. II, § 1's grant of the power to appoint Presidential electors to the state "Legislature." *Ibid.* But neither the text of Article II itself nor the only case the concurrence cites that interprets Article II, *McPherson v. Blacker,* 146 U.S. 1 (1892), leads to the conclusion that Article II grants unlimited power to the legislature, devoid of any state constitutional limitations, to select the manner of appointing electors. See *id.,* at 41, 13 S.Ct. 3 (specifically referring to state constitutional provision in upholding state law regarding selection of electors). Nor, as Justice Stevens points out, have we interpreted the federal constitutional provision most analogous to Art. II, § 1 — Art. I, § 4 — in the strained manner put forth in the concurrence.

The concurrence's treatment of § 5 as "inform[ing]" its interpretation of II, § 1, cl. 2, *ante,* at 534 (opinion of Rehnquist, C. J.), is no more convincing. The Chief Justice contends that our opinion in *Bush v. Palm Beach County Canvassing Bd.,* 531 U.S., at 70 *(per curiam) (Bush I),* in which we stated that "a legislative wish to take advantage of [§ 5] would counsel against" a construction of Florida law that Congress might deem to be a change in law, 531 U.S., at 78, 121 S.Ct. 471, now means that *this* Court "must ensure that post-election state-court actions do not frustrate the legislative desire to attain the 'safe harbor' provided by § 5." However, § 5 is part of the rules that govern Congress' recognition of slates of electors. Nowhere in *Bush I* did we establish that *this* Court had the authority to enforce § 5. Nor did we suggest that the permissive "counsel against" could be transformed into the mandatory "must ensure." And nowhere did we intimate, as the concurrence does here, that a state-court decision that threatens the safe harbor provision of § 5 does so in violation of Article II. The concurrence's logic turns the presumption that legislatures would wish to take advantage of § 5's "safe harbor" provision into a mandate that trumps other statutory provisions and overrides the intent that the legislature *did* express.

But, in any event, the concurrence, having conducted its review, now reaches the wrong conclusion. It says that "the Florida Supreme Court's interpretation of the Florida election laws impermissibly distorted them beyond what a fair reading required, in violation of Article II." But what precisely is the distortion? Apparently, it has three elements. First, the Florida court, in its earlier opinion, changed the election certification date from November 14 to November 26. Second, the Florida court ordered a manual recount of "undercounted" ballots that could not have been fully completed by the December 12 "safe harbor" deadline. Third, the Florida court, in the opinion now under review, failed to give adequate deference to the determinations of canvassing boards and the Secretary.

To characterize the first element as a "distortion," however, requires the concurrence to second-guess the way in which the state court resolved a plain conflict in the language of different statutes. Compare Fla. Stat. Ann. § 102.166 (Supp. 2001) (foreseeing manual recounts during the protest period) with § 102.111 (setting what is arguably too short a deadline for manual recounts to be conducted); compare § 102.112(1) (stating that the Secretary "may" ignore late returns) with § 102.111(1) (stating that the Secretary "shall" ignore late returns). In any event, that issue no longer has any practical importance and cannot justify the reversal of the different Florida court decision before us now.

To characterize the second element as a "distortion" requires the concurrence to overlook the fact that the inability of the Florida courts to conduct the recount on time is, in significant part, a problem of the Court's own making. The Florida Supreme Court thought that the recount could be completed on time, and, within hours, the Florida Circuit Court was moving in an orderly fashion to meet the deadline. This Court improvidently entered a stay. As a result, we will never know whether the recount could have been completed.

Nor can one characterize the third element as "impermissibl[e] distort[ion]" once one understands that there are two sides to the opinion's argument that the Florida Supreme Court "virtually eliminat[ed] the Secretary's discretion." The Florida statute in question was amended in 1999 to provide that the "grounds for contesting an election" include the "rejection of a number of legal votes sufficient to . . . place in doubt the result of the election." Fla. Stat. Ann. §§ 102.168(3), (3)(c) (Supp. 2001). And the parties have argued about the proper meaning of the statute's term "legal vote." The Secretary has claimed that a "legal vote" is a vote "properly executed in accordance with the instructions provided to all registered voters." On that interpretation, punchcard ballots for which the machines cannot register a vote are not "legal" votes. *Id.*, at 14. The Florida Supreme Court did not accept her definition. But it had a reason. Its reason was that a different provision of Florida election laws (a provision that addresses damaged or defective ballots) says that no vote shall be disregarded "if there is a clear indication of the intent of the voter as determined by the canvassing board" (adding that ballots should not be counted "if it is impossible to determine the elector's choice"). Fla. Stat. Ann. § 101.5614(5) (Supp. 2001). Given this statutory language, certain roughly analogous judicial precedent, *e.g., Darby v. State ex rel. McCollough,* 73 Fla. 922, 75 So. 411 (1917) *(per curiam),* and somewhat similar determinations by courts throughout the Nation, the Florida Supreme Court concluded that the term "legal vote" means a vote recorded on a ballot that clearly reflects what the voter intended. *Gore v. Harris,* 772 So.2d 1243, 1254. That conclusion differs from the conclusion of the Secretary. But nothing in Florida law requires the Florida Supreme Court to accept as determinative the Secretary's view on such a matter. Nor can one say that the court's ultimate determination is so unreasonable as to amount to a constitutionally "impermissible distort[ion]" of Florida law.

The Florida Supreme Court, applying this definition, decided, on the basis of the record, that respondents had shown that the ballots undercounted by the voting machines contained enough "legal votes" to place "the result[s]" of the election "in doubt." Since only a few hundred votes separated the candidates, and since the "undercounted" ballots numbered tens of thousands, it is difficult to see how anyone could find this conclusion unreasonable—however strict the standard used to measure the voter's "clear intent." Nor did this conclusion "strip" canvassing boards of their discretion. The boards retain their traditional discretionary authority during the protest period. And during the contest period, as the court stated, "the Canvassing Board's actions [during the protest period] may constitute evidence that a ballot does or does not qualify as a legal vote." Whether a local county canvassing board's discretionary judgment during the protest period not to conduct a manual recount will be set aside during a contest period depends upon whether a candidate provides additional evidence that the rejected votes contain enough "legal votes" to place the outcome of the race in doubt. To limit the local canvassing board's discretion in this way is not to eliminate that discretion. At the least, one could reasonably so believe.

The statute goes on to provide the Florida circuit judge with authority to "fashion such orders as he or she deems necessary to ensure that each allegation . . . is *investigated, examined, or checked,* . . . and to provide any relief appropriate." Fla. Stat. Ann. § 102.168(8) (Supp. 2001) (emphasis added). The Florida Supreme Court did just that. One might reasonably disagree with the Florida Supreme Court's interpretation of these, or other, words in the statute. But I do not see how one could call its plain language interpretation of a 1999 statutory change so misguided as no longer to qualify as judicial interpretation or as a usurpation of the authority of the state legislature. Indeed, other state courts have interpreted roughly similar state statutes in similar ways. See, *e.g., In re Election of U.S. Representative for Second Congressional Dist.,* 231 Conn. 602, 621, 653 A.2d 79, 90–91 (1994) ("Whatever the process used to vote and to count votes, differences in technology should not furnish a basis for disregarding the bedrock principle that the purpose of the voting process is to ascertain the intent of the voters"); *Brown v. Carr,* 130 W.Va. 455, 460, 43 S.E.2d 401, 404–405 (1947) ("[W]hether a ballot shall be counted . . . depends on the intent of the voter. . . . Courts decry any resort to technical rules in reaching a conclusion as to the intent of the voter").

I repeat, where is the "impermissible" distortion?

II

Despite the reminder that this case involves "an election for the President of the United States," no preeminent legal concern, or practical concern related to legal questions, required this Court to hear this case, let alone to issue a stay that stopped Florida's recount process in its tracks. With one exception, petitioners' claims do not ask us to vindicate a constitutional provision designed to protect a basic human right. Petitioners invoke fundamental fairness, namely, the need for procedural fairness, including finality. But with the one "equal protection" exception, they rely upon law that focuses, not upon that basic need, but upon the constitutional allocation of power. Respondents invoke a competing fundamental consideration—the need to determine the voter's true intent. But they look to state law, not to federal constitutional law, to protect that interest. Neither side claims electoral fraud, dishonesty, or the like. And the more fundamental equal protection claim might have been left to the state court to resolve if and when it was discovered to have mattered. It could still be resolved through a remand conditioned upon issuance of a uniform standard; it does not require reversing the Florida Supreme Court.

Of course, the selection of the President is of fundamental national importance. But that importance is political, not legal. And this Court should resist the temptation unnecessarily to resolve tangential legal disputes, where doing so threatens to determine the outcome of the election.

The Constitution and federal statutes themselves make clear that restraint is appropriate. They set forth a road-map of how to resolve disputes about electors, even after an election as close as this one. That road-map foresees resolution of electoral disputes by *state* courts. See 3 U.S.C. §5 (providing that, where a "State shall have provided, by laws enacted prior to [election day], for its final determination of any controversy or contest concerning the appointment of . . . electors . . . by *judicial* or other methods," the subsequently chosen electors enter a safe harbor free from congressional challenge). But it nowhere provides for involvement by the United States Supreme Court.

To the contrary, the Twelfth Amendment commits to Congress the authority and responsibility to count electoral votes. A federal statute, the Electoral Count Act, enacted after the close 1876 Hayes-Tilden Presidential election, specifies that, after States have tried to resolve disputes (through "judicial" or other means), Congress is the body primarily authorized to resolve remaining disputes. See Electoral Count Act of 1887, 24 Stat. 373, 3 U.S.C. §§5, 6, and 15.

The legislative history of the Act makes clear its intent to commit the power to resolve such disputes to Congress, rather than the courts:

> "The two Houses are, by the Constitution, authorized to make the count of electoral votes. They can only count legal votes, and in doing so must determine, from the best evidence to be had, what are legal votes. . . .

. . . . .

> "The power to determine rests with the two houses, and there is no other constitutional tribunal." H.R. Rep. No. 1638, 49th Cong., 1st Sess., 2 (1886) (report submitted by Rep. Caldwell, Select Committee on the Election of President and Vice-President).

The Member of Congress who introduced the Act added:

> "The power to judge of the legality of the votes is a necessary consequent of the power to count. The existence of this power is of absolute necessity to the preservation of the Government. The interests of all the States in their

relations to each other in the Federal Union demand that the ultimate tribunal to decide upon the election of President should be a constituent body, in which the States in their federal relationships and the people in their sovereign capacity should be represented."

18 Cong. Rec. 30 (1886) (remarks of Rep. Caldwell).

"Under the Constitution who else could decide? Who is nearer to the State in determining a question of vital importance to the whole union of States than the constituent body upon whom the Constitution has devolved the duty to count the vote?"

Id., at 31.

The Act goes on to set out rules for the congressional determination of disputes about those votes. If, for example, a State submits a single slate of electors, Congress must count those votes unless both Houses agree that the votes "have not been . . . regularly given." 3 U.S.C. §15. If, as occurred in 1876, a State submits two slates of electors, then Congress must determine whether a slate has entered the safe harbor of §5, in which case its votes will have "conclusive" effect. *Ibid.* If, as also occurred in 1876, there is controversy about "which of two or more of such State authorities . . . is the lawful tribunal" authorized to appoint electors, then each House shall determine separately which votes are "supported by the decision of such State so authorized by its law." *Ibid.* If the two Houses of Congress agree, the votes they have approved will be counted. If they disagree, then "the votes of the electors whose appointment shall have been certified by the executive of the State, under the seal thereof, shall be counted." *Ibid.*

Given this detailed, comprehensive scheme for counting electoral votes, there is no reason to believe that federal law either foresees or requires resolution of such a political issue by this Court. Nor, for that matter, is there any reason to think that the Constitution's Framers would have reached a different conclusion. Madison, at least, believed that allowing the judiciary to choose the Presidential electors "was out of the question." Madison, July 25, 1787 (reprinted in 5 Elliot's Debates on the Federal Constitution 363 (2d ed. 1876)).

The decision by both the Constitution's Framers and the 1886 Congress to minimize this Court's role in resolving close federal Presidential elections is as wise as it is clear. However awkward or difficult it may be for Congress to resolve difficult electoral disputes, Congress, being a political body, expresses the people's will far more accurately than does an unelected Court. And the people's will is what elections are about.

Moreover, Congress was fully aware of the danger that would arise should it ask judges, unarmed with appropriate legal standards, to resolve a hotly contested Presidential election contest. Just after the 1876 Presidential election, Florida, South Carolina, and Louisiana each sent two slates of electors to Washington. Without these States, Tilden, the Democrat, had 184 electoral votes, one short of the number required to win the Presidency. With those States, Hayes, his Republican opponent, would have had 185. In order to choose between the two slates of electors, Congress decided to appoint an electoral commission composed of five Senators, five Representatives, and five Supreme Court Justices. Initially the Commission was to be evenly divided between Republicans and Democrats, with Justice David Davis, an Independent, to possess the decisive vote. However, when at the last minute the Illinois Legislature elected Justice Davis to the United States Senate, the final position on the Commission was filled by Supreme Court Justice Joseph P. Bradley.

The Commission divided along partisan lines, and the responsibility to cast the deciding vote fell to Justice Bradley. He decided to accept the votes by the Republican electors, and thereby awarded the Presidency to Hayes.

Justice Bradley immediately became the subject of vociferous attacks. Bradley was accused of accepting bribes, of being captured by railroad interests, and of an eleventh-hour change in position after a night in which his house "was surrounded by the carriages" of Republican partisans and railroad officials. C. Woodward, Reunion and Reaction 159–160 (1966). Many years later, Professor Bickel concluded that Bradley was honest and impartial. He thought that "'the great question' for Bradley was, in fact, whether Congress was entitled to go behind election returns or had to accept them as certified by state authorities," an "issue of principle." The Least Dangerous Branch 185 (1962). Nonetheless, Bickel points out, the legal question upon which Justice Bradley's decision turned was not very important in the contemporaneous political context. He says that "in the circumstances the issue of principle was trivial, it was overwhelmed by all that hung in the balance, and it should not have been decisive."

For present purposes, the relevance of this history lies in the fact that the participation in the work of the electoral commission by five Justices, including Justice Bradley, did not lend that process legitimacy. Nor did it assure the public that the process had worked fairly, guided by the law. Rather, it simply embroiled Members of the Court in partisan conflict, thereby undermining respect for the judicial process. And the Congress that later enacted the Electoral Count Act knew it.

This history may help to explain why I think it not only legally wrong, but also most unfortunate, for the Court simply to have terminated the Florida recount. Those who caution judicial restraint in resolving political disputes have described the quintessential case for that restraint as a case marked, among other things, by the "strangeness of the issue," its "intractability to principled resolution," its "sheer momentousness, . . . which tends to unbalance judicial judgment," and "the inner vulnerability, the self-doubt of an institution which is electorally irresponsible and has no earth to draw strength from." Those characteristics mark this case.

At the same time, as I have said, the Court is not acting to vindicate a fundamental constitutional principle, such as the need to protect a basic human liberty. No other strong reason to act is present. Congressional statutes tend to obviate the need. And, above all, in this highly politicized matter, the appearance of a split decision runs the risk of undermining the public's confidence in the Court itself. That confidence is a public treasure. It has been built slowly over many years, some of which were marked by a Civil War and the tragedy of segregation. It is a vitally necessary ingredient of any successful effort to protect basic liberty and, indeed, the rule of law itself. We run no risk of returning to the days when a President (responding to this Court's efforts to protect the Cherokee Indians) might have said, "John Marshall has made his decision; now let him enforce it!" D. Loth, Chief Justice John Marshall and The Growth of the American Republic 365 (1948). But we do risk a self-inflicted wound — a wound that may harm not just the Court, but the Nation.

I fear that in order to bring this agonizingly long election process to a definitive conclusion, we have not adequately attended to that necessary "check upon our own exercise of power," "our own sense of self-restraint." *United States v. Butler,* 297 U.S. 1, 79 (1936) (Stone, J., dissenting). Justice Brandeis once said of the Court, "The most important thing we do is not doing." Bickel, *supra,* at 71. What it does today, the Court should have left undone. I would repair the damage done as best we now can, by permitting the Florida recount to continue under uniform standards.

I respectfully dissent.

---

1. *Judicial Statesmanship and the Political Question Doctrine.* Recall from Chapter Three the case of *Nixon v. United States,* in which the Court rebuffed a constitutional challenge by an impeached and convicted federal judge to the procedures by which the Senate had removed him from office. The Supreme Court unanimously determined that it would not intervene in the matter. The majority, speaking through Chief Justice Rehnquist, held that the constitutional sufficiency of Senate procedures for adjudicating impeachment controversies was a matter to be resolved exclusively by the Senate itself. The constitutional vesting in the Senate of "the sole Power to try all Impeachments" was deemed "a textually demonstrable commitment of the issue to a coordinate political department." Moreover, the majority said, the word "try" in Article I was too general to engender "judicially manageable standards" for what would amount to a constitutionally sufficient trial.

Should the Court have regarded *Bush v. Gore* as yet another occasion to defer to the elected branches? Its decision, effectively instructing Florida as to the conditions under which it could constitutionally assemble a slate of electors, preempted Congress from playing what would have been its ordinary legal role in hearing and resolving such questions. In *Disappearing Democracy: How* Bush v. Gore *Undermined the Federal Right to Vote for Presidential Electors,* excerpted above, Professor Shane argues that the Court should have stayed out of the dispute. In his judgment, congressional resolution of the dispute would have been preferable because (a) Congress acts more transparently than does the Court, (b) Congress would have had more remedial alternatives available to it; and (c) if Congress acted in a manner deemed illegitimate by the public, they would have been susceptible to electoral accountability, which the

Supreme Court was not. Because, in Shane's judgment, the Court was not confronting any defect in our national political process that required creative judicial intervention, the occasion would have been appropriate for avoiding a judicial resolution.

Professor Robert Pushaw disagrees. In his view, invoking the political question doctrine is appropriate, as in *Nixon*, only when judicial action would usurp another branch's authority under a constitutional provision that amounts to an explicit check on the powers of another branch. Although "Article I grants Congress exclusive and unreviewable authority over impeachments by giving the House of Representatives the 'executive' power of prosecuting them and the Senate the 'judicial' power of judging them," "neither Article II nor the Twelfth Amendment contains a pure check" on another branch with which *Bush v. Gore* interfered. Robert J. Pushaw, Jr., *The Presidential Election Dispute, the Political Question Doctrine, and the Fourteenth Amendment: A Reply to Professors Krent and Shane*, 29 Fla. St. U. L. Rev. 603, 615 (2001). Is this persuasive? Has Professor Pushaw identified the only basis for avoiding judicial intervention in the powers of another branch? Is it troubling that *Bush v. Gore* directly implicates the judicial branch in determining who shall control one of the co-equal elected branches of the national government?

It has been suggested in defense of *Bush v. Gore* that judicial intervention may have been a salutary alternative to the sort of institutional embarrassment the nation experienced in resolving the 1876 election, in which the House decided in favor of the popular vote loser, accepting the decisions of a Commission that resolved along party lines all electoral vote disputes submitted to it. The sordid story is told in Roy Morris, Jr., Fraud of the Century, Rutherford B. Hayes, Samuel Tilden, and the Stolen Election of 1876 (2003), and William H. Rehnquist, Centennial Crisis: The Disputed Election of 1876 (2004). For a more comprehensive overview of electoral contests, see Edward Foley, Ballot Battles: The History of Disputed Elections in the United States (2016).

2. No Federal Right to Participate in Presidential Elections? The Supreme Court starts its legal analysis in the final *Bush v. Gore* opinion with the statement: "The individual citizen has no federal constitutional right to vote for electors for the President of the United States unless and until the state legislature chooses a statewide election as the means to implement its power to appoint members of the Electoral College." 531 U.S. at 104. Although this proposition was not directly at issue in *Bush v. Gore*, it could have proved significant. While *Bush v. Gore* was unfolding, the Florida legislature was preparing to select a slate of electors on its own, in the event, presumably, that the court proceedings did not conclude acceptably to the legislature.

Is the dictum, however, correct? This was certainly the law prior to the Civil War, but, according to Professor Shane's argument in *Disappearing Democracy, supra*, the Fourteenth Amendment created a federal right to participate in the choice of presidential electors, under either the Privileges and Immunities Clause of Section 1 or the Reduction of Representation Clause of Section 2, or a combination of both. (He also notes that the Twenty-Fourth Amendment provides that the "right of citizens to vote . . . for electors for President or Vice President" may not be conditioned on a poll tax—curious wording, if no such right exists.) In *Unduly Partial: The Supreme Court and the Fourteenth Amendment in* Bush v. Gore, 29 Fla. St. U. L. Rev. 587 (2001), Professor Pamela S. Karlan agrees with Shane's conclusion, but not with his textual sources. She would find instead that the Due Process Clause protects a "substantive liberty interest in voting to elect the President." *Id.* at 597. Should the Court have opined on this issue, even by way of dicta, without entertaining argument on it?

3. *The Court's Equal Protection Analysis.* The line between equal protection and due process claims is notoriously elusive, especially in voting rights cases. Nonetheless, the Court's equal protection focus in *Bush v. Gore* may seem odd:

> Equal protection challenges generally involve the differential treatment of persons, implicit or explicit, because of groups to which they belong, for example, groups of Bush supporters or Gore supporters. Unlike typical equal protection cases, however, *Bush v. Gore* does not exhibit any obvious link between a challenged classification or criterion for treatment and any group's systematic advantage or disadvantage. The majority opinion identifies three sources of differentiation in the treatment of voters by different counties: differential standards for evaluating contested ballots, differences between recounts limited to under-votes and recounts that reexamined all of the ballots cast, and differences between tabulations based on partial recounts versus tabulations based on completed recounts. Legally speaking, these may be phenomena worth noting, but it is hard to predict who will be hurt by them. There was no allegation that any amounted to an intentionally invidious discriminatory practice—the kind of practice that the Court normally requires before it elevates the intensity of its constitutional scrutiny of state practices under the Equal Protection Clause.

Shane, *Disappearing Democracy, supra,* 29 Fla. St. U. L. Rev. at 552. Of course, one way of reading the *Bush v. Gore* majority is that the county-to-county differences it has identified in recount procedures fail even the minimal demand of rationality. But is that so? Are they not justified—at least in terms of rational connection to a legitimate state interest—by Florida's permissible decision to defer to local authorities in the conduct of statewide elections and the Florida Supreme Court's desire to enable the state to take advantage of the "safe harbor" provision of 3 U.S.C. §5?

The other problem with the Court's equal protection analysis is that it threatens to swallow whole the entire process by which states usually administer all elections. That is, to the extent virtually all states delegate the implementation of their voting schemes to county authorities, the result is a patch quilt of varying administrative practices within states that (a) could not possibly pass muster under heightened scrutiny, and (b) dwarf, in their probable practical impact, the departures from equality diagnosed by the Court in *Bush v. Gore*. The majority seems to recognize as much, when it says, "Our consideration is limited to the present circumstances, for the problem of equal protection in election processes generally presents many complexities," and "The question before the Court is not whether local entities, in the exercise of their expertise, may develop different systems for implementing elections." Is there a principled basis for voiding a statewide *recount* based on variations in recounting procedure that cannot be justified (except by deference to local authority), but not voiding statewide *initial counts* based on variations in vote tabulation procedure (for example, optical scan versus punchcards) that cannot be justified (except by deference to local authority)?

4. *Questions About Remedy*. Assume for the sake of argument that the *Bush v. Gore* majority is persuasive in its identification of deficiencies in the court-ordered recount process below. The Court nonetheless declines to give Florida beyond December 12 to implement a constitutionally adequate recount "[b]ecause the Florida Supreme Court has said that the Florida Legislature intended to obtain the safe-harbor benefits of 3 U.S.C. §5," and allowing a recount to extend until December 18 would amount to "action in violation of the Florida Election Code, and hence could not be part of an 'appropriate' order authorized by Fla. Stat. Ann. §102.168(8) (Supp. 2001)." On what basis was the Supreme Court authorized to decide this question of Florida law? If Florida were faced with the mutually exclusive options of completing a constitutionally adequate recount faithful to its "intent of the voter" standard or completing its adjudicatory process by December 12, should the decision how to resolve that conundrum consistent with Florida law have been left to the Florida courts?

5. *A Missing Due Process Analysis?* In the wake of *Bush v. Gore,* a number of authors suggested that the issues in the case, assuming justiciability, could better have been understood as implicating questions of due process. In addition to the Shane and Karlan articles cited above, see Roy A. Schotland, Bush v. Gore: *Whatever Happened to the Due Process Ground?* 34 Loy. U. Chi. L. J. 211 (2002). The authors disagree, however, on the proper legal result. For example, Shane argues that, applying the framework of *Mathews v. Eldridge*—the same framework the Supreme Court applied in *Hamdi v. Rumsfeld,* excerpted in Chapter Six—the recount procedures approved by the Florida Supreme Court did pass constitutional muster. Moreover, he argued, it was a violation of due process not to have proceeded with the court-ordered hand recount. Professor Schotland, however, has argued that the Florida recount scheme violated due process, but for very different reasons: "the combination of (a) allowing county canvassing boards such unfettered discretion that they were prone not only to error, but also to partisan manipulation, and (b) failing to provide even a simple safeguard to cabin that discretion (e.g., requiring bi-partisan canvassing boards)." *Id.* at 211. Following Schotland's theory, what should have been the remedy?

6. Bush v. Gore *and Election Reform*. The Florida debacle did prompt reform measures at both the state and federal level. As one author recounts:

> The 2000 elections prompted a flurry of attention to the equipment that Americans use to cast their votes. Numerous studies were performed and, while not all reached the same conclusion, most concluded that improvements in voting technology were an essential component of election reform.

After considerable debate, Congress in 2002 enacted and the President signed the Help America Vote Act, commonly known as "HAVA."[5] Although HAVA does not require the elimination of punch cards or any other type of equipment, it did authorize $650 million for the replacement of punch card and lever machines. Altogether, HAVA authorizes a total of $3.65 billion for election system improvements over a four-year period. It creates a new federal agency, the Election Assistance Commission ("EAC"), whose responsibilities including making payments to states and providing for the study of election systems.

Although it does not prohibit the use of any voting technology, HAVA does include some provisions designed to improve the accuracy and accessibility of our election system. It requires that voters be given the opportunity to verify their votes before they are cast.[6] In addition, HAVA requires that voting systems produce a "permanent paper record with a manual audit capacity."[7] HAVA also requires that accessible technology be provided to people with disabilities. Specifically, the law mandates that at least one DRE [Direct Record Electronic] machine or "other voting system equipped for persons with disabilities at each polling place."[8]

Dan Tokaji, *Voting Equipment*, in MORITZ COLLEGE OF LAW ELECTION LAW @ MORITZ PROJECT, THE E-BOOK ON ELECTION LAW: AN ONLINE REFERENCE GUIDE (2004), available at http://moritzlaw.osu.edu/electionlaw/ebook/part4/equipment_mach ines01.html. The literature assessing the impacts of HAVA and the contemporary state of U.S. election administration in general is immense. A good place to start is R. MICHAEL ALVAREZ AND BERNARD GROFMAN, EDS., ELECTION ADMINISTRATION IN THE UNITED STATES: THE STATE OF REFORM AFTER *BUSH V. GORE* (2014).

7. *Judicial Ethics and* Bush v. Gore. Some portion of the distress occasioned by *Bush v. Gore* was rooted in a common perception that at least some of the majority Justices were influenced by prejudice against Vice President Gore, stemming from the alleged desire of these Justices either for advancement on the Court (from Associate to Chief, in the event of a Rehnquist retirement), or to have a Republican choose their successor should they retire. At least one legal ethics scholar has found some of the allegations sufficiently serious, under a proper understanding of the relevant canons of judicial ethics, as to warrant an investigation by some body duly empowered to resolve the issues authoritatively. Richard K. Neumann, Jr., *Conflicts of Interest in Bush v. Gore: Did Some Justices Vote Illegally?* 16 GEO. J. LEGAL ETHICS 375 (2003). Who would that body be?

---

5. Public Law 107-252.

6. Section 301(a)(1)(A). For states using punch cards or other paper-based systems, this requirement may be met by establishing a voter education program. Section 301(a)(1)(B).

7. Section 301(a)(2)(B).

8. Section 301(a)(3)(B).

8. Bush v. Gore *and the Problem of Partisan Election Administration.* Putting aside the merits of the Court's reasoning in *Bush v. Gore*, a charitably inclined observer might remark that the Court's remedy can be seen as reacting to a genuine institutional problem, quite apart from the recount mechanics on which it actually based its decision. That is, Florida's election system (and that of most states) puts critical questions of election implementation and fact-finding into the hands of partisan officials who know, when they are either making rules or deciding individual cases, just what the partisan impacts of their rulings will be. It seems a bad sign that the state's two key legal officers in 2000, Secretary of State Harris and Attorney General Butterworth, were the chairs of the Florida Bush and Gore campaigns, respectively. For a thoughtful reading of *Bush v. Gore* with this concern in mind, see Daniel P. Tokaji, *First Amendment Equal Protection: On Discretion, Inequality, and Participation*, 101 MICH. L. REV. 2409, 2487–2495 (2003).

9. *So, Who Actually Got More Votes?* Whatever legal ironies may seem to shadow *Bush v. Gore*, the largest historical irony may be this: As best we can tell, the only recount method that would have assured Florida electoral victory in 2000 to George W. Bush was the recount method being urged by the Gore campaign, i.e., focusing solely on the uncounted undervotes. As summarized by one journalist:

> When the National Opinion Research Center at the University of Chicago, hired by a consortium of eight newspapers to figure out the true winner, issued its final report, the headlines at the time read: "Study of Disputed Florida Ballots Finds Justices Did Not Cast the Deciding Vote," (The New York Times) and "Florida Recounts Would Have Favored Bush" (The Washington Post). But what the NORC researchers really discovered was the Gore legal team's incredible incompetence.

> Gore's legal advisers chose, it turned out, pretty much the only counting method available that would have lost them the election. Instead of an inclusive recount of Florida's vote—one that would have been most fair to Florida's voters, Gore's top lawyer, David Boies, asked the court to count "undervotes" only. Using that method, Bush did indeed outpoll Gore, and the court's intervention did not ultimately make a difference. It turned out to be the perfect coda to a perfectly awful campaign.

> But buried beneath this colossal error . . . was the inescapable fact that Gore was the genuine choice of a plurality of Florida's voters as well as America's. As the Associated Press reported in its examination of the NORC report, "In the review of all the state's disputed ballots, Gore edged ahead under all six scenarios for counting all undervotes and overvotes statewide." . . . No matter what, if everyone who legally voted in Florida had had a chance to see their vote counted, then Al Gore not George W. Bush, was elected president.

Eric Alterman, *"Bush v. Gore*'s Disgrace Deepens," The Daily Beast, Dec. 4, 2010, *available at* http://www.thedailybeast.com/blogs-and-stories/2010-12-04/bush-v-gore-decision-looks-even-more-disgraceful-10-years-later/.

10. *Further Reading.* The literature recounting and assessing *Bush v. Gore* is mountainous. A few titles seem especially apt at capturing the flavor of the discussion. *Compare, e.g.,* Nelson Lund, *The Unbearable Rightness of* Bush v. Gore, 23 CARDOZO L. REV. 1219 (2002), *with* Laurence H. Tribe, *The Unbearable Wrongness of* Bush v. Gore, 19 CONST. COMMENT. 571 (2002). Among valuable book-length assessments and anthologies of useful analysis and perspective are BRUCE ACKERMAN, *BUSH V. GORE*: THE QUESTION OF LEGITIMACY (2002); E. J. DIONNE AND WILLIAM KRISTOL, *BUSH V. GORE*: THE COURT CASES AND THE COMMENTARY (2001); RONALD DWORKIN, A BADLY FLAWED ELECTION: DEBATING *BUSH V. GORE*, THE SUPREME COURT, AND AMERICAN DEMOCRACY (2002); RICHARD L. HASEN, THE SUPREME COURT AND ELECTION LAW: JUDGING EQUALITY FROM *BAKER V. CARR* TO *BUSH V. GORE* (2003); CASS R. SUNSTEIN AND RICHARD ALLEN EPSTEIN, THE VOTE: BUSH, GORE, AND THE SUPREME COURT (2001); JACK N. RAKOVE, THE UNFINISHED ELECTION OF 2000 (2001); JAMIN B. RASKIN, OVERRULING DEMOCRACY: THE SUPREME COURT VS. THE AMERICAN PEOPLE (2003); RICHARD A. POSNER, BREAKING THE DEADLOCK: THE 2000 ELECTION, THE CONSTITUTION, AND THE COURTS (2001); AND JEFFREY TOOBIN, TOO CLOSE TO CALL: THE THIRTY-SIX DAY BATTLE TO DECIDE THE 2000 ELECTION (2002). Major law review symposia include *Symposium: Bush v. Gore's Legacy*, 13 STAN. L. & POL'Y REV. 15 (2002); *Symposium: The Law of Presidential Elections: Issues in the Wake of Florida 2000*, 29 FLA. ST. U. L. REV. 325 (2001); *Symposium: Litigating the Presidency: The Election 2000 Decision and its Ramifications for the Supreme Court*, 61 MD. L. REV. 505 (2002); *Symposium: Perspectives on Judicial Independence*, 64 OHIO ST. L.J. 1 (2003); and *Symposium: Votes and Voices: Reevaluations in the Aftermath of the 2000 Presidential Election*, 23 CARDOZO L. REV. 1145 (2002). The following are a few of the valuable articles that appear outside the preceding volumes: Steven K. Balman, Bush v. Gore — *A Response to Dean Belsky*, 37 TULSA L. REV. 777 (Spring 2002); Martin H. Belsky, Bush v. Gore: *A Critique of Critiques*, 37 TULSA L. REV. 45 (Fall 2001); Erwin Chererinsky, *How We Should Think About* Bush v. Gore, 34 LOY. U. CHI. L. J. 1 (2002); Jesse H. Choper, *Why the Supreme Court Should Not Have Decided the Presidential Election of 2000*, 18 CONST. COMMENT. 335 (2001); Roy A. Schotland, Bush v. Gore: *Whatever Happened to the Due Process Ground?* 34 LOY. U. CHI. L. J. 211 (2002); and Norman Vieira, *The Florida Election Cases: A Commentary on* Bush v. Gore, 11 TEMP. POL. & CIV. RTS. L. REV. 385.

B. Presidential and Vice-Presidential Succession

Besides elections and removals from office through impeachment, death and disability provide the other occasions for transfers of presidential power. Succession problems are now governed by the twenty-fifth amendment and by 3 U.S.C. § 1982, in which Congress, pursuant to art. II, § 1, cl. 6, provided "for the Case of Removal, Death, Resignation, or Inability, both of the President and the Vice President." For general histories of presidential successions as well as instances of presidential illness, see JOHN D. FEERICK, FROM FAILING HANDS: THE STORY OF PRESIDENTIAL

SUCCESSION (1965); JOHN D. FEERICK, THE TWENTY-FIFTH AMENDMENT: ITS COMPLETE HISTORY AND EARLIEST APPLICATIONS (1976); and ALLAN P. SINDLER, UNCHOSEN PRESIDENTS (1976). The fascinating story of Woodrow Wilson, whose wife, together with his chief aide, Colonel House, virtually ran the White House after Wilson suffered a paralytic stroke 18 months prior to the end of his second term, is told in ALEXANDER L. AND JULIETTE L. GEORGE, WOODROW WILSON AND COLONEL HOUSE (1964).

The following memorandum prepared shortly after ratification of the twenty-fifth amendment reviews the circumstances that prompted adoption of that amendment and the amendment's proffered reforms. The history of art. II, § 1, par. 6, and the law of succession prior to the twenty-fifth amendment is further reviewed at Attorney General Robert F. Kennedy, *Presidential Disability*, 42 OP. A.G. 69 (1961).

R. Celada, Presidential Continuity and Vice Presidential Vacancy Amendment

Congressional Research Service Memorandum (Mar. 13, 1967),
reprinted in Application of the 25th Amendment to Vacancies in the
Office of the Vice President: Legislative History, House Committee on
the Judiciary (Comm. Print), 93d Cong., 1st Sess. 451–67 (1973)

At least three times in our history, during the administrations of Garfield, who lay in the twilight zone between life and death for eighty days before succumbing to an assassin's bullet, Wilson who, after suffering a stroke, spent the last eighteen months of his term in a state of at least semi-invalidism, and Eisenhower who had three separate and serious illnesses, the President of the United States, for varying periods, has been unable to carry out the duties of his office. Although the Constitution provides that when a President is disabled the Vice President shall take over, it does this in language so ambiguous that there is disagreement about whether the Vice President becomes President for the balance of the term or simply acts as President until the disability is ended. Moreover, no specific method is set forth for determining when presidential inability begins or ends. Nor is the responsibility for making such determination clearly spelled out.

Despite the virtual unanimity of informed contemporary opinion that existing law empowers the Vice President to make the determination that a President is disabled and thereafter to assume the powers and duties of the presidential office until the inability is ended, no Vice President has ever done so. Historical precedents as well as the weight of informed opinion are inclined toward the conclusion that no Vice President will act until the constitutional ambiguities have been removed. The cries for a solution to the problem have intensified as Americans have apprehended the dread possibility of a nation immobilized in a moment of maximum peril because there might be neither a fit President nor someone unquestionably authorized to act in his stead.

Following his third illness, President Eisenhower attempted to fill in some of the constitutional gaps by entering into a working agreement with Vice President Nixon.

The terms of the agreement provided that whenever the President informed the Vice President that he was unable to act the Vice President would assume the powers and duties of the presidential office until the inability had ended. If, however, the President were unable to communicate the existence of his inability, the Vice President would assume the duties of the office after such consultation as seemed to him appropriate under the circumstances. In either case the President, himself, would determine when the inability had ended and at that time resume the powers and duties of his office. Similar agreements were made between President Kennedy and Vice President Johnson and between President Johnson and Speaker McCormack who was next in line of succession until the inauguration of Vice President-elect Humphrey. A similar agreement also exists between President Johnson and Vice President Humphrey.

There has been general agreement that however valuable these working agreements might be nothing short of an amendment to the Constitution will give the person who assumes the duties of the presidential office the air of legitimacy so indispensable to their successful execution.

Furthermore, although three Attorneys General have expressed the view that these agreements are "consistent with the correct interpretation of . .,. the Constitution" their legal standing continues to present a nagging question. Since the Supreme Court does not render advisory opinions it is extremely doubtful that the matter could ever be resolved in advance of the crisis. Not until the assassination of President Kennedy, however, had there been anything approaching a consensus on precisely what the amendment to the Constitution should provide. That consensus was embodied in the resolution proposed by the 89th Congress. . . .

Article II, section 1, clause 6 of the Constitution now provides that

> In Case of the Removal of the President from Office, or of his Death, Resignation, or Inability to discharge the Powers and Duties of the said Office, the Same shall devolve on the Vice President, and the Congress may by Law provide for the Case of Removal, Death, Resignation, or Inability, both of the President and Vice President, declaring what Officer shall then act as President, and such Officer shall act accordingly, until the Disability be removed, or a President shall be elected.

Constitutional scholars have debated for many years the meaning of Article II, section 1, clause 6. The crux of the disability problem arises from the first clause. . . . The second clause relating to the congressional power has been implemented from time to time through the enactment of statutes setting forth the succession to the office of President in the event of the removal, death, and resignation, or inability of *both* the President and Vice President. Although the latter clause also raises several problems of constitutional interpretation, these more properly relate to presidential succession and are outside the scope of this paper.[13]

---

13. The principal issue arising from the second clause concerns the legal propriety of placing legislative officers in the order of presidential succession. Despite the inclusion of such persons in

Turning to the first clause, it will be noted that it outlines four situations in which the Vice President may be called upon to act as President. Three of these, namely, removal, death, and resignation, obviously contemplate the permanent exclusion of the President for the balance of his term. The source of the uncertainty arises in connection with the fourth contingency, specifically, the "Inability to discharge the Powers and Duties of the said Office." Did the Framers intend such "inability" to permanently exclude the President, even in the event of recovery, from resuming the discharge of his powers and duties? Another question arises from the remaining language of the first clause which provides "the Same shall devolve on the Vice President." To what do the words "the Same" refer? In other words, what is it that "devolves" on the Vice President? Is it the "Office" of the President or the presidential "Powers and Duties"? If the former interpretation prevails, the contingency of inability like the other three would operate to effect a permanent exclusion. However, if the latter interpretation prevails, the powers and duties would once again attach to the office upon the President's recovery.

Historical investigation and the weight of constitutional authority tend to support the conclusion that under Article II, section 1, clause 6 of the Constitution the Vice President merely discharges the powers and duties of the Presidency during the President's inability. The sole dissenting voice in this otherwise harmonious picture springs from actual practice whereby Vice Presidents have *become* Presidents upon the latter's death. The precedent was established by John Tyler's succession upon the death of William Henry Harrison on April 4, 1841. In her authoritative volume, Presidential Succession [14 (1951)], Ruth C. Silva describes these events, in part as follows:

> ... The presidential office was vacant for the first time. It was then decided that in conformity with the Constitution, Vice President Tyler was to be the President for the remaining three years and eleven months of Harrison's term. Exactly who made this decision is uncertain. Legend tells us that the precedent was established merely because Tyler claimed presidential status. The Cabinet had decided, so the story goes, that Mr. Tyler should be officially styled "Vice President of the United States, acting President." But Tyler is supposed to have promptly determined that he would enjoy all the dignities and honors which he assumed he had inherited.

Although objections were raised in Congress and in the press, Tyler's assumption established the precedent that when the presidential office is vacant, the Vice President becomes the President for the remainder of the term. As a consequence, on each

---

two of the three succession laws passed by Congress—including that currently in effect—debate on the matter continues unabated. The specific points at issue are (1) whether the Speaker and the President pro tempore are "officers" in the sense of Article II, section 1, clause 6; (2) whether a legislative officer (named to act as President) who resigns his office thereafter is eligible to act as President; and (3) whether it violates the constitutional principle of separation of powers for a Member of Congress to act as President.

of the eight occasions that the Vice President has assumed office because of the death of the President, he has taken the presidential oath. Notwithstanding that succession in these instances arose from one of the contingencies that contemplates a permanent exclusion, namely, death, they threw a cloud on a disabled President's claim to office upon full recovery.

These precedents combined with the ambiguities of Article II, section 1, clause 6 served to throttle any action in the event of a presidential crisis. Arthur, Garfield's Vice President, emphatically declined to take any steps whatsoever to assume the powers of the President. Vice President Marshall flatly refused to assume any of the powers of the presidency because of the constitutional uncertainty as to whether Wilson could resume his office when he recovered.

Adding to this already highly uncertain situation was the recurrent and troubling problem of vice presidential vacancy. Between the years 1787 and 1965, eight Presidents died in office.[6] Seven Vice Presidents also died in office and one resigned.[7] As a result of these occurrences, the nation has been without a Vice President more than twenty percent of the time during its history.

It became apparent that in order to adequately correct the flaws in our constitutional system it was necessary to accomplish the following objectives:

(1) To establish once and for all that the Vice President *assumes* the presidential *office* upon removal from office, death, or resignation of the President;

(2) To provide that in the event of the fourth contingency, namely, inability, the Vice President shall exercise the powers and duties of the office of President;

(3) To establish the procedure for determining the existence of an inability and its termination; and

(4) To provide for filling a vacancy occurring in the Vice Presidency. . . .

After more than eighty years of study by congressional committees, attorneys general, constitutional experts and bar association committees, the Congress, in the dying moments of 1963, began to act on a presidential continuity amendment. Sparked by the assassination of President Kennedy which alerted the American people as never before to the dangerous constitutional void, hearings were scheduled for early 1964.[8] Even as the nation mourned the loss of the President many thoughts were

---

6. The eight Vice Presidents who succeeded to the Presidency were John Tyler (Harrison), Millard Fillmore (Taylor), Andrew Johnson (Lincoln), Chester A. Arthur (Garfield), Theodore Roosevelt (McKinley), Calvin Coolidge (Harding), Harry S. Truman (Roosevelt), and Lyndon B. Johnson (Kennedy).

7. The seven Vice Presidents who died in office were George Clinton, Elbridge Gerry, William R. King, Henry Wilson, Thomas A. Hendricks, Garrett A. Hobart, and James Sherman. The only Vice President to have ever resigned was John C. Calhoun.

8. Presidential Inability and Vacancies in the Office of Five Presidents. Hearings before the subcommittee on Constitutional Amendments of the Committee on the Judiciary. United States Senate, 88th Cong., 2d Sess. (1964).

troubled by the prospect of the political crisis which might have followed had the fallen leader lingered on in hopeless and permanent incapacity. . . . Also, the record of Vice President Johnson's prior heart attack and advanced ages of the two immediate successors doubtless contributed to the general desire for a prompt solution. . . .

The amendment proposed to the States by the 89th Congress meets the four basic objectives noted earlier. It affirms the historical practice by which a Vice President has become President upon the death of the President, further extending the practice to the contingencies of resignation or removal from office. In order to assure that the second highest office will always be occupied, it requires the President to nominate a person to be Vice President whenever there is a vacancy in that office. The nominee is to take office as Vice President upon confirmation by a majority in both Houses of Congress.

The proposal permits the President to declare himself disabled and to declare the end of his disability. The declarations are to be reduced to writing and transmitted to the Speaker of the House of Representatives and the President pro tempore of the Senate. In the interim, the Vice President becomes Acting President. If a President does not declare the existence of his inability, the Vice President and a majority of the "principal officers of the executive departments" may declare the President disabled by transmitting their written declaration to this effect to the presiding legislative officers of the House and Senate. In such an event the Vice President is to undertake the discharge of the presidential powers and duties as Acting President. If for any reason the Cabinet proves not to be a workable instrument in this matter, Congress is empowered to set up another body to work with the Vice President.

"Thereafter" the President may announce his own recovery and "resume the powers and duties of his office." However, if the Vice President and a majority of the Cabinet disagree with the President, they have four days to send a written declaration of the fact to the Speaker and the President pro tempore. At this point the Congress is responsible for a final decision. If Congress is not in session, it would have to assemble within forty-eight hours of receipt of the declaration. From the time of receipt Congress has twenty-one days in which to decide the issue. Pending the decision, the Vice President is to continue as Acting President. If Congress fails to arrive at a decision, or if more than one-third of the membership of either House sides with the President, the President is to resume his powers and duties. If two-thirds of the membership of each House support the Vice President and the Cabinet, the Vice President is to continue as Acting President.

———————

A Medical or Political Question? The drafters of the Twenty-Fifth Amendment no doubt anticipated that the kinds of conditions that would render a President "unable to discharge the powers and duties of his office" would relate to matters of physical and mental capacity. Might a majority of "the principal officers of the executive departments" nonetheless permissibly find a President "unable to discharge the powers and duties of his office" for reasons of character, temperament, or mental condition that would not technically amount to incapacitation? Could a Congress, if controlled by the opposition party, provide for some "other body" to render such a judgment? If so, would the constitutionality of a presidential removal under the Twenty-Fifth Amendment be justiciable? What if a two-thirds vote of Congress ratified the removal? In other words, does the Twenty-Fifth Amendment provide Congress a way to remove a President without resorting to impeachment? Would such a mechanism be desirable? Dangerous? Evan Osnos, *How Trump Could Get Fired*, THE NEW YORKER (May 8, 2017), https://www.newyorker.com/magazine/2017/05/08/how-trump-could-get-fired.

Note: Reagan-Bush Temporary Power Transfer

The first occasion for using the procedure outlined in section 3 of the 25th Amendment for a temporary transfer of power to the Vice President occurred on July 13, 1985. Just before receiving anesthesia for abdominal surgery to remove a cancerous polyp, President Reagan transferred presidential authority to Vice President George Bush by letter. Reagan's letter was carefully drafted to avoid invoking the 25th Amendment unambiguously, out of an apparent anxiety over binding future Presidents to what Reagan thought might be an unfortunate precedent. Thus, Bush was not formally designated "acting President," a phrase used in the 25th Amendment, although White House officials acknowledged that Bush played that role while Reagan was on the operating table. The texts of President Reagan's July 13th letters transferring power to Vice President Bush and then withdrawing it follow:

Dear Mr. President (Mr. Speaker):

I am about to undergo surgery during which time I will be briefly and temporarily incapable of discharging the Constitutional powers and duties of the Office of the President of the United States.

After consultations with my Counsel and the Attorney General, I am mindful of the provisions of Section 3 of the 25th Amendment to the Constitution and of the uncertainties of its application to such brief and temporary periods of incapacity. I do not believe that the drafters of this Amendment intended its application to situations such as the instant one.

Nevertheless, consistent with my longstanding arrangement with Vice President George Bush, and not intending to set a precedent binding anyone privileged to hold this Office in the future, I have determined and it is my intention and direction that Vice President George Bush shall discharge those powers and duties in my stead commencing with the administration of anesthesia to me in this instance.

I shall advise you and the Vice President when I determine that I am able to resume the discharge of the Constitutional powers and duties of this Office.

May God bless this Nation and us all.

Sincerely,

Ronald Reagan

Dear Mr. President (Mr. Speaker):

Following up on my letter to you of this date, please be advised I am able to resume the discharge of the Constitutional powers and duties of the Office of the President of the United States. I have informed the Vice President of my determination and my resumption of those powers and duties.

Sincerely,

Ronald Reagan

WEEKLY COMP. PRES. DOC. (July 13, 1985).

For a legal analysis of the delegability of presidential functions during periods of disability, prepared in the wake of the 1981 attempted assassination of President Reagan, see Acting Assistant Attorney General Larry L. Simms, *Presidential Succession and Delegation in Case of Disability*, 5 OP. O.L.C. 91 (1981). President George W. Bush twice transferred presidential authority to Vice President Cheney due to medical procedures he underwent under sedation. *Bush colonoscopy leaves Cheney in charge*, THE GUARDIAN (July 20, 2007), https://www.theguardian.com/world/2007/jul/20/usa.dickcheney.

C. Redesigning the President's Political Role

Changes in the needs of the country and of government have periodically surfaced proposals for major institutional reform of the Presidency. Although none has been undertaken since the Twenty-Second Amendment, which limited the President to two terms of office, far-reaching proposals—such as creating line-item veto power, discussed in Chapter Two—continue to be made. *See, e.g.*, CHARLES M. HARDIN, PRESIDENTIAL POWER AND ACCOUNTABILITY: TOWARDS A NEW CONSTITUTION (1974) (proposing reorganization of Congress and the executive to achieve stronger checks and balances); DONALD L. ROBINSON, "TO THE BEST OF MY ABILITY:" THE PRESIDENCY AND THE CONSTITUTION (1987) (proposing electoral reforms including establishment of council of former Presidents empowered to call elections within four-year cycle). Our constitutional bicentennial was the occasion for much academic debate concerning structural reforms to the Constitution. Two especially good representatives of the literature emanating from that period are JAMES L. SUNDQUIST, CONSTITUTIONAL REFORM AND EFFECTIVE GOVERNMENT (1986), and ROBERT A. GOLDWIN AND ART KAUFMAN EDS., SEPARATION OF POWERS—DOES IT STILL WORK? (1986). For an intriguing debate on the merits or demerits of confining the president to a single six-year term, *see* One Six-Year Presidential Term, Hearing Before the Subcommittee on Crime of the House Committee on the Judiciary, 93d Cong., 1st Sess. 4–16, 19–28, 42–46 (1973).

With the escalation of political crises surrounding the Presidency since Watergate—Iran-Contra, the Clinton impeachment, *Bush v. Gore*, and the long roster of controversies surrounding the first three twenty-first century presidents—there has been a corresponding escalation in the tone of urgency surrounding calls for constitutional reform. Among the strongest voices in this vein is that of Texas law professor Sanford Levinson, who vigorously chastises contemporary "pundits who seem to believe that we can discuss contemporary American politics without paying any attention at all to the basic institutional structures that were inflicted on us in 1787 and left remarkably unchanged (save for the 17th and 20th Amendments) since then." Sandy Levinson, "It's the Constitution, Stupid," Balkinization (Dec. 9, 2010), available at http://balkin.blogspot.com/. Professor Levinson has gone so far as to advocate a new constitutional convention to correct our constitutional pathologies. Sanford Levinson, Our Undemocratic Constitution: Where the Constitution Goes Wrong (and How We the People Can Correct It) (2006).

A conspicuous feature of contemporary calls for reform, however, is a fundamental tension in the diagnosis of the constitutional malady. Our purpose here is only to sample a number of the suggested reforms and encourage discussion of the ills they may or may not serve to remedy.

1. Diagnosis One: Presidents Can Accomplish Too Little

On one side, there is concern that the separation of powers system so hamstrings government decision making as to undermine democratic accountability. A prominent D.C. lawyer and former White House Counsel, the late Lloyd Cutler, argued in a much-noted 1980 article that the separation of powers, particularly in its impact on the President, was anachronistic. Although he did not use the article to campaign for specific reforms, Cutler recommended consideration of a variety of measures that might afford our system of government more of the virtues of government coordination he perceived in parliamentary regimes. In his view, some such reforms are necessary for three major reasons. First, the federal government now makes an unprecedented number of significant allocative choices for which it is difficult to achieve a broad political consensus. Second, the increasing interdependence of the world makes the stability and predictability of our foreign policy especially important. Third, Congress itself has undergone a decentralization of power, which makes cooperation between Congress and the executive branch increasingly difficult. The flavor of Cutler's analysis is captured in the following passage:

Lloyd N. Cutler, To Form a Government*

Foreign Affairs, Fall, 1980, at 126–29

A particular shortcoming in need of a remedy is the structural inability of our government to propose, legislate and administer a balanced program for governing. In parliamentary terms, one might say that under the U.S. Constitution it is not now feasible to "form a Government." The separation of powers between the legislative

---

* Copyright 1980, Council on Foreign Relations, Inc. Reprinted by permission.

and executive branches, whatever its merits in 1793, has become a structure that almost guarantees stalemate today. As we wonder why we are having such a difficult time making decisions we all know must be made, and projecting our power and leadership, we should reflect on whether this is the one big reason.

We elect one presidential candidate over another on the basis of our judgment of the overall program he presents, his ability to carry it out, and his capacity to adapt his program to new developments as they arise. We elected President Carter, whose program included, as one of its most important elements, the successful completion of the SALT II negotiations that his two predecessors had been conducting since 1972. President Carter did complete and sign a SALT II Treaty, in June 1979, which he and his Cabinet regarded as very much in the national security interests of the United States. . . . But because we do not "form a Government," it has not been possible for President Carter to carry out this major part of his program.

Of course the constitutional requirement of Senate advice and consent to treaties presents a special situation. The case for the two-thirds rule was much stronger in 1793, when events abroad rarely affected this isolated continent, and when "entangling foreign alliances" were viewed with a skeptical eye. Whether it should be maintained in an age when most treaties deal with such subjects as taxation and trade is open to question. No parliamentary regime anywhere in the world has a similar provision. But in the American case—at least for major issues like SALT—there is merit to the view that treaties should indeed require the careful bipartisan consultation essential to win a two-thirds majority. This is the principle that Woodrow Wilson fatally neglected in 1919. But it has been carefully observed by recent Presidents, including President Carter for the Panama Canal Treaties and the SALT II Treaty. In each of these cases there was a clear prior record of support by previous Republican Administrations, and there would surely have been enough votes for fairly rapid ratification if the President could have counted on the total or near-total support of his own party—if, in short, he had truly formed a Government, with a legislative majority which takes the responsibility for governing.

Treaties may indeed present special cases, and I do not argue here for any change in the historic two-thirds requirement. But our inability to "form a Government" able to ratify SALT II is replicated regularly over the whole range of legislation required to carry out any President's overall program, foreign and domestic. Although the enactment of legislation takes only a simple majority of both Houses, that majority is very difficult to achieve. Any part of the President's legislative program may be defeated, or amended into an entirely different measure, so that the legislative record of any presidency may bear little resemblance to the overall program the President wanted to carry out. Energy and the budget provide two current and critical examples. Indeed, SALT II itself could have been presented for approval by a simple majority of each House under existing arms control legislation, but the Administration deemed this task even more difficult than achieving a two-thirds vote in the Senate. And this difficulty is of course compounded when the President's party does not even hold the majority of the seats in both Houses, as was the case from 1946 to

1948, from 1954 to 1960 and from 1968 to 1976—or almost half the duration of the last seven Administrations.

The Constitution does not require or even permit in such a case the holding of a new election, in which those who oppose the President can seek office to carry out their own overall program. Indeed, the opponents of each element of the President's overall program usually have a different makeup from one element to another. They would probably be unable to get together on any overall program of their own, or to obtain the congressional votes to carry it out. As a result the stalemate continues, and because we do not form a Government, we have no overall program at all. We cannot fairly hold the President accountable for the success or failure of his overall program, because he lacks the constitutional power to put that program into effect.

Compare this with the structure of parliamentary governments. A parliamentary government may have no written constitution, as in the United Kingdom. Or it may have a written constitution, as in West Germany, Japan and Ireland, that in other respects—such as an independent judiciary and an entrenched Bill of Rights—closely resembles our own. But while there may be a ceremonial President or, as in Japan, an Emperor, the executive consists of those members of the legislature chosen by the elected legislative majority. The majority elects a Premier or Prime Minister from among its number, and he selects other leading members of the majority as the members of his Cabinet. The majority as a whole is responsible for forming and conducting the "government." If any key part of its overall program is rejected by the legislature, or if a vote of "no confidence" is carried, the "Government" must resign and either a new "Government" must be formed out of the existing legislature or a new legislative election must be held. If the program *is* legislated, the public can judge the results, and can decide at the next regular election whether to reelect the majority or turn it out. At all times the voting public knows who is in charge, and whom to hold accountable for success or failure.

---

1. *As Compared to What?* Do you agree with Cutler's point of view? Does the record of western parliamentary democracies since World War II sustain his confidence in parliamentary structure? For a vigorous rebuttal of the Cutler thesis, see Thomas O. Sargentich, *The Limits of the Parliamentary Critique of the Separation of Powers*, 34 WM. & MARY L. REV. 679 (1993).

2. *Senators, Heal Thyselves?* The early years of the Obama Administration seemed to offer a powerful illustration of the frequent inability of the federal executive to implement the program of the winning party in a national election. In 2008, the American people gave President Obama a 52–46 percent popular vote victory over his main opponent, Senator John McCain, thus producing for the victor a two-thirds majority in the Electoral College. His party, the Democrats, was given a 71-seat edge in the House of Representatives, and an 18-seat advantage in the Senate (including two independent Senators who caucused with the Democrats). And yet, President Obama not only had difficulty enacting huge swaths of the platform on which he

campaigned—including proposals with strong popular support in national opinion polls—but he saw dozens of relatively uncontroversial nominations languish
in the Senate, which also gave him the lowest rate of judicial confirmations in modern history for a first-term President. Yet, this circumstance seems all but entirely
unrelated to the separation of powers. What hamstrung the President was the Senate rule that requires a vote of 60 Senators to cut off debate and permit a floor vote
on any proposed legislation. One headline seemed to say it all: "372 Bills That
Have Been Passed by the House & Not Yet Acted Upon By the Senate (as of 8/23/10),"
The Hill, available at http://thehill.com/homenews/senate/83057-290-bills.

To what degree would internal reform of Senate procedures redress the problems that Mr. Cutler diagnoses? Note that, in November, 2013, the Senate, led by the
Democrats, changed the filibuster rules to permit all executive branch and judicial
nominees—except for the Supreme Court—to be confirmed with a simple up-or-
down vote rather than a supermajority. In 2017, the Senate exercised the "nuclear
option" and extended the exception to the filibuster rules to cover Supreme Court
nominees as well. The Senate has yet to modify supermajority requirements for legislation, however. Thus, nearly all legislation—an exception exists for the so-called
"reconciliation" bills that conform overall spending authorization with Congress's
initially approved targets—needs three-fifths support in the Senate to secure an up-
or-down vote.

President Trump has repeatedly urged a GOP-controlled Senate to eliminate
the filibuster although, as of November 1, 2017, Republican Senators had been
unable to muster even the fifty votes that would have sufficed (given the Vice
President's tie-breaking role) to enact some pieces of legislation deemed critical
during the 2016 presidential campaign and which could have circumvented the
filibuster through the reconciliation process.

On the history of the filibuster and arguments for its reform, see Tonja Jacobi &
Jeff VanDam, *The Filibuster and Reconciliation: The Future of Majoritarian Lawmaking in the U.S. Senate*, 47 U.C. DAVIS L. REV. 261 (2013).

3. *Removing Impediments to Democracy?* A fervent small-d democrat might be
significantly distressed by the political history of the United States since the turn of
the twenty-first century, whether focusing on *Bush v. Gore* or Congress's apparent
lack of responsiveness to popular sentiment regarding important matters of
national policy. If our separation of powers system could be made more democratically responsive, would this be responsive to Mr. Cutler's concerns? Could that
be done without going the parliamentary route? In MADISON'S NIGHTMARE, Professor Shane recommends—in addition to Electoral College reform—establishing
genuinely universal suffrage, creating national voter registration standards, and
eliminating partisan gerrymandering that reduces the electoral competitiveness of
congressional districts. PETER M. SHANE, MADISON'S NIGHTMARE, *supra*, at 195–
199. How far, if at all, might such changes go in ensuring that Presidents can pursue
their programs through Congress?

2. Diagnosis Two: "The Most Dangerous Branch"

Playing off Alexander Hamilton's reference to the federal judiciary as "the least dangerous branch," the title of Professor Martin Flaherty's article, *The Most Dangerous Branch*, 105 YALE L. J. 1725 (1996), seems to capture what, in 2010, is the more popular diagnosis of what is wrong with the contemporary presidency. In addition to Professor Shane's MADISON'S NIGHTMARE, cited throughout this volume, titles of other recent works that seem to capture the spirit of alarm at the current scope of presidential power include BRUCE ACKERMAN, THE DECLINE AND FALL OF THE AMERICAN REPUBLIC (2010), and Sanford Levinson and Jack M. Balkin, *Constitutional Dictatorship: Its Dangers and Its Design*, 94 MINN. L. REV. 1789 (2010). A detailed historical account of the George W. Bush Administration and its ideological roots by Pulitzer Prize-winning journalist Charlie Savage — TAKEOVER: THE RETURN OF THE IMPERIAL PRESIDENCY AND THE SUBVERSION OF AMERICAN DEMOCRACY (2007) — is very much in the same vein.

Professor Ackerman traces "a series of developments in politics, communications, bureaucratic and military organization," that, in his judgment, "have transformed the executive branch into a clear and present danger to our constitutional tradition." He fears an increasingly demagogic presidency, in which chief executives engage in ambitious power grabs, while civilian control of the military is compromised by a politicized military and the recruitment of both current and retired military officers to serve in policy positions that were previously key to civilian control.

The dynamics Ackerman describes are complex. In brief, the role of each party's ideological base in choosing presidential candidates, our sound-bite mass media culture, and the rise of opinion polling have combined to erode those norms and structures that steered presidents towards a moderate, centrist course. The bureaucracy, too, has lost much of its stabilizing capacity as presidents have loaded it with ever-deeper layers of political loyalists, including an expanding cadre of powerful White House advisers accountable to no one but the President. Given the vague contours of Article II power and the breadth of congressional delegations to the executive branch, the stage is set for unprecedented seizures of executive authority, often in the name of real or imagined national emergency.

Professor Ackerman's work is rich in suggestions for institutional reform, chiefly at the sub-constitutional level. He has suggested allowing Congress to delegate emergency powers to the President only under severely time-limited statutes that would require an escalating supermajority to approve. (For a critique, see Adrian Vermeule, *Self-Defeating Proposals: Ackerman on Emergency Powers*, 75 FORDHAM L. REV. 631 (2006).) He would drastically reduce the number of presidential advisors who are not subject to advice and consent appointment. He recommends a Code of Military Ethics to help calibrate the relationship between political and military leaders.

Perhaps most strikingly, Ackerman has urged the creation of a Supreme Executive Tribunal, a quasi-judicial authority within the executive branch, that — without concern for Article III standing issues — would be authorized to render independent interpretations of the President's legal authority. Unlike the Office of Legal Counsel, it would be staffed by nine "judges," serving fixed and staggered terms, who are subject to advice and consent. The Tribunal would render opinions at the behest of either the President or Members of Congress. Although they would not be binding in the sense of an Article III judgment, its opinions would, Ackerman hopes, provide an important counterweight to what he sees as the invariably overgenerous interpretations of executive power by OLC and White House counsel.

Professors Levinson and Balkin see much the same troublesome terrain as does Professor Ackerman. The Constitution positions the president to undertake ambitious unilateral initiatives without genuine accountability because oversight mechanisms are weak, arguments from inherent Article II authority are readily available, executive privilege (and the state secrets privilege, in particular) allows the President to ward off judicial scrutiny, and the impeachment power is practically useless. The following section of their article offers their own reform prescriptions, and provides a useful survey and critique of other approaches.

Sanford Levinson and Jack M. Balkin, *Constitutional Dictatorship: Its Dangers and Its Design*

94 MINN. L. REV. 2010, 1856–1865 (2010).

IV. DESIGNING ACCOUNTABILITY IN A CONSTITUTIONAL DICTATORSHIP

A. Legality and its Discontents

It is very unlikely that the United States will soon dismantle its national security apparatus, or its collection of surveillance and data mining practices we call the National Surveillance State, much less a host of emergency measures dealing with domestic affairs. If so, the question is not whether we will have emergency provisions but how the government will design them, and what additional checks and balances we can put in place to enjoy the benefits of discretion without its dangers.

The most obvious solution, at least to lawyers, is additional legal regulation, or "legalization" of the presidency. The War Powers Act is a paradigmatic example. To prevent the President from doing things we do not like, we create rules that make it difficult for him to repeat the activity in the future. We might impose either procedural or substantive hurdles to action. Take torture as an example: procedural limits would require special "torture warrants" issued by an independent Article III judge; substantive limits would simply bar these methods entirely. One might have thought that we had already done this, in the anti-torture statute and in various international law obligations; the problem, of course, is that the President's lawyers decided to read these substantive requirements away or declare them unconstitutional as impinging on the President's inherent powers as commander-in-chief.

The strategy of legalization has three major problems. The first is Jack Goldsmith's objection that laws are the enemy of discretion; increased legalization means increased bureaucracy that will hamper the President's ability to make effective policy and take effective action. (Since, as we have noted previously, the President himself is not making many of the judgment calls, legalization means that lower-level officials will spend more time processing paperwork and preparing reports.) The second problem with legalization is that it may not actually impede bad judgment, but merely give incentives for strained or disingenuous legal arguments. Determined lawyers set upon a course of finding ways around legal restraints are likely to do so, even if the arguments are very poor. In The Federalist No. 41, James Madison reminds us that "[i]t is in vain to oppose Constitutional barriers to the impulse of self-preservation. It is worse than in vain; because it plants in the constitution itself necessary usurpations of power, every precedent of which is a germ of unnecessary and multiplied repetitions." If this is true of people of the very highest character and judgment, it is probably even truer of people who are rash, foolish, or venial.

A third objection to increased legalization is that legalization has not been the enemy of discretion, but rather its enabler. When Congress creates new emergency powers for the President, it does so through passing new laws. When the President wants to build out his institutional capacities for meeting emergencies, he often does so through issuing new regulations and signing new executive orders. Our experience of the last eight years of the Bush Administration may cause us to think that evasion of law is the great danger of constitutional dictatorship. In fact it may be precisely the opposite — the proliferation of legal avenues for executive branch officials to act, which can then be defended through pointing to various laws, regulations, and executive orders that authorize the discretionary action.

Lest we be misunderstood, we do not believe that direct legal restraints on executive decisionmaking are unimportant; our point is rather that they are often a limited and incomplete solution to the problem, and in some cases may even be counterproductive. A different way of addressing the question is to focus on structural mechanisms. The first are political checks, the second are methods of accountability after the fact, and the third are methods of surveillance and oversight of executive action, either before or after the fact.

B. Structural Remedies

As a preliminary matter, we note that parliamentary systems may have some modest advantages over presidential systems in heading off the dangers of constitutional dictatorship, if only because the Prime Minister has to maintain — and answer to — a parliamentary majority coalition. Presidents, by definition, are able to create their own political base separate from the legislature. Presidents who combine the attributes of head of government with head of state have the additional advantage of being symbols of the nation itself and are well-suited to garner public support and frame social realities. In the United States, for example, the President, who enters public occasions to the playing of "Hail to the Chief" and is surrounded by an enormous retinue, increasingly combines the dignitary trappings of monarchy with the media promotions accorded a rock star.

American Presidents have been plebiscitary leaders for some time. In other countries with presidential systems, particularly in Latin America, charismatic presidents have occasionally allied with the military against the legislature and the judiciary, creating the obvious dangers of dictatorial power or degeneration into military-controlled governments. Nevertheless, Professor José Antonio Cheibub has argued that political scientists have overestimated the potential dangers of presidential as opposed to parliamentary systems. Parliamentary systems do not necessarily avoid the problems of constitutional dictatorship, especially if the Prime Minister is the strong leader at the head of the political party that controls parliament. Even if presidential systems present particular dangers, the problem of holding strong leaders truly accountable may be ubiquitous.

Turning to the American presidential system, there are ways of tinkering with the present Constitution to provide a greater measure of accountability. If one especially fears the lack of future electoral accountability in a second-term President, for example, then one might consider repealing the Twenty-Second Amendment. Doing so, however, creates a potential difficulty in the opposite direction: a charismatic President might generate crisis after crisis and keep returning to office. There is somewhat less reason, however, to think that many presidents would be able to exceed two terms, especially in modern times. The modern American presidency seems to chew up its occupants in fairly short order. It is possible that this may be partly due to the political environment created by the Twenty-Second Amendment, but the problem predates the 1950s.

Even if the public repealed the Twenty-Second Amendment, the threat of losing a future election would provide only a very modest mechanism of accountability. Rejection at the polls might occur only years later, by which point the public will have moved on to other concerns. Moreover, in our current electoral college system for selecting presidents, it is quite common for a President to be elected with less than an absolute majority of the popular vote. (Richard Nixon in 1968, Bill Clinton in 1992 and 1996, and George W. Bush in 2000 are the four most recent examples.) It is somewhat less frequent for an incumbent President to be reelected with less than an absolute majority, but it happened in 1996. As a result, there might actually be majority disapproval of, and lack of confidence in, the President from day one, or shortly thereafter. To be told that the public should have to wait another four years to register disapproval of the President's judgment on matters of life and death is an inadequate remedy.

Instead (or in addition), one might support a vote of no-confidence mechanism that would allow Congress and/or the public to remove an American President at any time before the next scheduled election. The mechanism could involve some mix of congressional and popular votes of no-confidence. For example, perhaps Congress, by a two-thirds vote of all members convened as a single body, could vote "no-confidence" and declare the office of the Presidency vacant. One might take a page from the German Constitution and Israeli legislation and allow such a vote only if that same Congress had already decided on a suitable successor (the so-called constructive vote of no-confidence). One might go even further and require that the successor be from the President's own political party to avoid the specter of a "party coup" that would change the partisan character of the government without an intervening election. In the alternative, the vote could be followed by the dissolution of Congress and public elections for both Congress and the presidency (with the "fired" President presumably free to make his case to the public). The point is to establish a mechanism for the public and Congress to monitor and respond to failures of judgment on issues of the greatest importance. In our present system, by contrast, we must endure disastrous presidents in office no matter how much damage they may cause until the next scheduled election.

Perhaps equally important, a vote of "no-confidence" would have ripple effects throughout the political system that would bolster whatever other legal requirements we might wish to employ to rein in executive discretion—whether they be congressional oversight mechanisms, reporting and internal auditing requirements, or judicial review of administrative action. Congress and the public might reject a President they believe has acted too high-handedly no matter what the courts say. When the next President takes office, Congress may impose new legal or other oversight requirements as a condition of taking office. At the very least the previous rejection becomes a precedent, or a stern warning from Congress, about the sort of activities that future presidents may not engage in, and a demand that the next President be more solicitous to Congress.

The very possibility of a no-confidence vote might have two beneficial effects. First, it may give Congress an opportunity to pass legislation regulating the President with less fear that the new President will veto it. Second, the threat of future no-confidence motions will make presidents more accountable to Congress and less likely to reject oversight mechanisms. Congress can use its advantage to pass oversight and mandatory reporting mechanisms and coax later presidents to abide by them. (One can hardly imagine George W. Bush following much of Dick Cheney's advice to maximize unilateral executive power and ignore requests for oversight and reporting if Bush could have faced a vote of "no-confidence.")

Thus, the structural reform of no-confidence motions can pay dividends for other kinds of reform. For example, presidents may use their veto less often if they fear that Congress's response will be to veto them. Even if votes of no-confidence are relatively rare, they would be sufficiently thinkable to serve as an effective deterrent. Conversely, votes of no-confidence put pressure on Congress to supervise and take responsibility for a failing presidency. Constituents will reasonably ask why Congress has allowed an incompetent or corrupt President to remain in office. Considerations like these help explain why we think that a focus on additional legal regulation by itself may be insufficient without attention to larger structural issues. Designing structures differently gives legal rules additional practical force and effect.

One might think even more boldly. Rossiter offers several suggestions, based on his overview of the various emergency regimes in the five countries he studied. He begins with the seemingly obvious point that no "constitutional dictatorship should be initiated unless it is necessary or even indispensable to the preservation of the state and its constitutional order." Although unobjectionable in principle, this suggestion is more difficult to implement than it first appears. Indeed, everything depends on how many forms of executive discretion in the modern administrative and National Security State we wish to label examples of "constitutional dictatorship." As discussed above, in a distributed dictatorship, many different agencies and individuals have unreviewable discretion, ranging from the head of the Federal Reserve to the Centers for Disease Control and Prevention.

Rossiter's second suggestion for a well-designed institution of constitutional dictatorship is adopted from ancient Rome: "the decision to institute a constitutional dictatorship should never be in the hands of the man or men who will constitute the dictator." As we have seen, the American system flunks this essential test.

To the extent that the American—or any other—constitution seemingly allows a President both to declare the existence of an emergency and to engage in effectively unreviewable action, it has moved far closer to the Schmittian conception of the sovereign dictatorship. In fact, as we have seen, this is still possible in a commissarial dictatorship, if Congress by statute places the right to declare an emergency in the President, and then directs the President to take whatever steps he deems appropriate. In fact, some American framework statutes have this very character, and they take us very close to the Schmittian notion that the President decides for himself when to make exceptions to the rules. However, in this case, the "exception" to the normal legal order is part of the normal legal order, because the power to declare an emergency and to deal with that emergency is already built into the framework statute.

One response, as suggested by the South African Constitution, is to require the legislature to vote to activate the executive's emergency powers for each particular emergency. The American system tends not to choose this path. Instead, it creates framework statutes that bestow emergency powers on the President or some other executive official, including the power to declare an emergency in the first place. So although Congress has technically authorized these powers, it may be a Congress that sat long ago. Consider the Militia Act of 1795, the Insurrection Act of 1807, and the Suppression of Rebellion Act of 1861 as examples, or the Depression-Era banking statutes that empowered Henry Paulson and Ben Bernanke in 2008. There is no contemporaneous congressional vote on whether an emergency exists; instead the framework statute leaves that question to the executive, thus doing an end run around the South African (and Roman) model. The closest that the American system comes to this model is the declaration of war, which activates the President's war powers, or, following World War II (the last declared war), authorizations for the use of military force, which, however, never seem to be repealed.

In any case, there are two additional problems with the South African and Roman model, which requires the legislature to declare emergencies and activate special powers each time the executive requests them. The first arises when we are indeed faced with a crisis that demands functionally immediate decisionmaking, when there simply is not enough time to gain legislative authorization. Although the most obvious examples may involve military attack, certain kinds of economic emergencies or health emergencies may also occur suddenly.

The second problem may be even more basic. It operates even when time is not of the essence. In his classic book on the American presidency, Clinton Rossiter emphasized that one of the six "hats" worn by the President is that of "party leader." Rick Pildes and Daryl Levinson have argued that legislative oversight of an aggressive President, even in a presidential system, may not operate adequately when the political party the President leads also dominates the legislature. In fact, it may be in the electoral interest of the President's party to argue that the country faces a particularly fearful situation, which demands the kind of radical action that can be provided only by the President and members of his party. The Bush Administration's war on terror is a recent example.

Pildes and Levinson call for emulating the German practice and guaranteeing that certain important committees in the legislature be placed in the hands of the opposition party, in order to assure some measure of significant oversight. Similarly, Professor David Fontana has suggested constitutionalizing the role of the "party in opposition" in a modern party system. But even these proposals may not respond adequately to the possibility that a legislature controlled by the President's (or Prime Minister's) own party will be more than happy to delegate to the Maximum Leader all sorts of discretionary powers associated with constitutional dictatorship.

Another solution would be to require supermajorities for the declaration of emergencies and/or the delegation of emergency powers. To this we might add fixed sunset provisions. Bruce Ackerman has suggested escalator clauses, which require larger and larger majorities to keep emergency powers in place after specified time limits. This would make dictatorial powers increasingly difficult to obtain and to keep.

Finally, another solution would be to take the decision away from the process of ordinary politics completely. The model might be the Federal Reserve Board, which is relatively independent from the President and Congress, and uses its expertise to manage the money supply in the public interest. As a thought experiment, imagine the creation of an Emergency Council whose consent would be required to declare the existence of a state of emergency that would trigger the exercise of extraordinary powers for the executive. In the United States, such a Council might consist of some number of officials subject to the Senate's advise and consent powers (perhaps requiring a two-thirds majority, to ensure bipartisan support). It might also include a number of persons who serve ex officio, for example, a group of former presidents or retired secretaries of state, former heads of the Joint Chiefs of Staff, or former heads of the Federal Reserve Board. The members of the group would be chosen for their demonstrated probity and good sense in crises as well as the public's general confidence in their judgment.

Just as we might alter who has the power to declare an emergency, we might also consider altering who is authorized to respond to it. The President might not be the right person to serve as the "constitutional dictator" for every particular kind of emergency. If the problem is staving off a threatened military invasion, one might prefer someone with demonstrated military or diplomatic experience. If, on the other hand, the threat is imminent economic collapse, military experience would presumably be irrelevant, and someone like the head of the Federal Reserve (or another senior economist with wide-ranging government experience) might be the appropriate person. Rossiter and other admirers of ancient Rome have emphasized that the Roman consuls could not select themselves for the office of dictator; hence, they had incentives to ensure that the person they chose for the office had the character, skills, and judgment needed for the particular task. Just as in the Roman context, the term of emergency power would be limited. This model of delegation to specified experts seems to fly in the face of the ideology of the unitary executive. As we have argued, however, this theory is honored more in the breach than in the observance.

3. Diagnosis 3: The Patient Is Healthy

Writing in a vein very different from those who bemoan either a hamstrung or an overreaching executive, Professors Eric A. Posner and Adrien Vermeule argue that the legal fetters on the executive branch are largely diaphanous and ineffective in constraining executive discretion, but that the consequence is nonetheless an executive branch sufficiently constrained by democratic political processes to ward off tyranny. Taking their cue from the Weimar era political theorist Carl Schmitt (while rejecting, of course, his sympathies for Nazism), Posner and Vermeule argue that the checks and balances vision of the presidency is out-of-touch with reality. Furthermore, they argue, the range of issues facing contemporary government and the pressures to "do something" mean that there will never be an effective constituency for a restrained executive. The "unbound" executive is inevitable in their view, but not a cause for worry. ERIC A. POSNER AND ADRIAN VERMEULE, THE EXECUTIVE UNBOUND: AFTER THE MADISONIAN REPUBLIC (2011).

4. Diagnosis 4: Something Is Rotten . . . and Not in Denmark

Diametrically opposed to the Posner-Vermeule institutional optimism (at least as expressed in 2011), Professor Balkin diagnoses early twenty-first century America as suffering from what he calls "constitutional rot": "[A] degradation of constitutional norms that may operate over long periods of time." Jack M. Balkin, *Constitutional Rot and Constitutional Crisis* (May 15, 2017), at 5, https://ssrn.com/abstract= https:// papers.ssrn.com/sol3/papers.cfm?abstract_id=2993320. According to Professor Balkin, the deep causes of constitutional rot involve "four interlocking features, which we might call the Four Horsemen of Constitutional Rot: (1) political polarization; (2) loss of trust in government; (3) increasing economic inequality; and (4) policy disasters, a term coined by Stephen Griffin to describe important failures in decision making by our representatives, like the Vietnam War, the Iraq War and the

2008 financial crisis." Jack M. Balkin, *Constitutional Rot* (June 14, 2017), at 3, to appear in CASS R. SUNSTEIN, ED., CAN IT HAPPEN HERE? AUTHORITARIANISM IN AMERICA (2018), available at https://ssrn.com/abstract=2992961. What "rot" portends for the presidency is a shift toward a more authoritarian executive: "A system that has become so deadlocked that politics seems futile may lead to the election of demagogues and authoritarian minded politicians who undermine democratic norms and lead a nation toward autocracy." Balkin, *Constitutional Rot and Constitutional Crisis*, at 7. Balkin cites the work of Professors Richard Pildes and Daryl Levinson, discussed further below, which argues that the current state of the political party system in American means that the separation of powers no longer works well to restrain government's "oligarchic tendencies" if Congress and the executive branch are controlled by the same party. See Daryl J. Levinson & Richard H. Pildes, *Separation of Parties, Not Powers*, 119 HARV. L. REV. 2311 (2006). In Balkin's view, what fails if "rot" goes unchecked is not the formal operation of government institutions, but their capacity to provide genuinely representative governance. Government becomes "oligarchical [and] leaders spend less and less time working for the public good. Instead, they spend more and more time enriching a small group of important backers that keep them in power. Because the general public feels abandoned by politicians, it gradually loses faith in the political system." Balkin, *Constitutional Rot*, at 2. Professor Balkin notes that the United States still has significant constitutional defenses against oligarchy, but believes we are headed for major electoral showdowns that will determine if the United States can meet "[t]he central question [of] how to preserve republican government in the face of a changing global economy." *Id.*, at 14.

5. A Model Redraft of Article II

In an intriguing paper, Professor Garrett Epps has gone so far as to propose a redraft of Article II of the Constitution that, in his judgment, would realign the design of the executive branch with the normative demands appropriate for an advanced democracy. (A shorter essay that captures the essence of his critique of the Founders' handiwork is Garrett Epps, *The Founders' Great Mistake*, THE ATLANTIC, Jan./Feb. 2009, at 68.) As you review Professor Epps's draft, consider whether changes of the magnitude he envisions are truly necessary, in your judgment, to repair shortcomings in our constitutional design. Do you envision any scenario that would precipitate this level of reform?

Garrett Epps, The Ill-Made Prince:
A Modest Proposal for a New Article II

http://papers.ssrn.com/sol3/papers.cfm?abstract_id=1445643, at 51–54 (2009).

§ 1. Office of the President

The power to execute this constitution, laws made pursuant to it, and treaties made or which shall be made under the authority of the United States, shall be vested in one president of the United States, except as provided in section ___ herein, pertaining to the election of the attorney general.

§ 2. Election and Succession

The president and vice-president of the United States shall be chosen by the people at large. Each candidate for president and vice-president shall run as a slate, such slate to be qualified for the national ballot under reasonable regulations as specified by Congress. The presidential election shall be conducted over a period, uniform across the country, to be specified by Congress adequate to permit every citizen desiring to do so to participate. In each case, the winning slate shall be the slate receiving the highest number of votes nationwide, provided only that Congress may by law provide for a second election among the two candidates receiving the largest number of votes when no candidate shall receive more than ___ percent of the votes cast at the first election.

The president shall take office one week following the final election specified by congress pursuant to section 2 above. She shall take the following oath or affirmation:—"I do solemnly swear (or affirm) that I will faithfully execute the office of President of the United States, and will to the best of my ability, preserve, protect and defend the Constitution of the United States." The vice president shall take the same oath, excepting the designation of the office assumed.

No person shall serve as president or vice-president, nor be a candidate for either office, who shall not have attained the age of 35 years at the time of her election and who shall not have been a citizen of the United States for fourteen years previous to her election. In case of the death or removal of the president, the vice president shall become president and shall take the oath specified again. The vice-president shall during her service as vice-president serve as president of the Senate.

The president and vice president shall each, at stated times, receive for their services, a compensation which shall neither be increased nor diminished during the period for which they shall have been elected, and shall not receive within that period any other emolument from the United States, or any of them.

§ 3. Powers of the President

The President shall be Commander in Chief of the armed forces of the United States, and of the militia of the several states, when called into the actual service of the United States; provided only that she shall not initiate the use of military force without prior authorization by the Congress pursuant to Article I, § 8, except in case of a sudden attack upon the United States or any of them or the territory of the United states, or of an emergency of similar exigency.

When the president shall order the use of military force by the armed forces or militia or both in response to a sudden attack or emergency, the president shall convene a special session of Congress within one week of such order, unless military necessity shall make such a session impossible, in which case the session shall be called as soon as either the president, or the speaker of the House of Representatives and the president pro tempore of the Senate jointly, shall judge such session to be possible.

The president shall be chief of the cabinet, whose members shall be specified by law, and shall have the power to convene a meeting of the cabinet or of any of its members and require in writing the opinion of its officers or any of them upon any subject relating to the duties of their respective offices.

The president shall have power, by and with the advice and consent of the Senate, to make treaties, provided two thirds of the Senators present concur. After consultation with the leaders of the majority and minority in the Senate, she shall nominate, and by and with the advice and consent of the Senate, shall appoint ambassadors, other public ministers and consuls, judges of the Supreme Court and lower federal courts, and the heads of the executive departments. All other inferior executive officials shall be appointed by the president; but the Congress may by law vest the appointment of such inferior officers as they think proper in the courts of law or the heads of the executive departments. The president shall have power to fill up all vacancies that may happen during the recess of the Senate, by granting commissions which shall expire at the end of their next session, provided only that no person shall receive two such appointments to the same office during successive recesses.

The president may, on extraordinary occasions, convene both houses, or either of them, and in case of disagreement between them, with respect to the time of adjournment, she may adjourn them to such time as she shall think proper.

The president shall conduct the foreign relations of the United States in conformity with this Constitution, laws enacted pursuant to it and with treaties made or which shall be made under the authority of the United States, provided that she shall consult with the leaders of the minority and majority in Congress except in situations that shall require secrecy, in which case the Congress shall be notified as soon as practicable thereafter.

The president shall have the power to rescind all or part of any dollar amount of any discretionary budget authority specified in an appropriation Act or conference report or joint explanatory statement accompanying a conference report on the Act. She shall notify the Congress of such rescission or veto by a special message not later than ten calendar days (not including Sundays) after the date of enactment of an appropriation act providing such budget authority or a revenue or reconciliation act containing a targeted tax benefit, and such rescission shall take effect until and unless it is re-enacted in a separate bill by both Houses of Congress, in which case it shall become law without the president's signature. All monies otherwise appropriated shall be spent as directed by law.

The president shall have power to grant reprieves and pardons for offences against the United States, except in cases of impeachment or as noted above in Amendment XIV; no such pardon shall be granted during period between the presidential election, or in the case of two such elections as hereinbefore provided, the first presidential election, and the inauguration of a new president.

§ 4. Duties

The president shall give from time to time to the Congress information of the state of the union, and recommend to their consideration such measures as she shall judge necessary and expedient; no less than seven days after such a message, the president shall appear before the two Houses of Congress for a time sufficient to answer questions from the members.

The president shall faithfully observe, obey and execute this Constitution, laws made pursuant to it, and treaties made or which shall be made under the authority of the United States; when she shall determine that the national interest requires her to act in the absence of clear authority set out in the sources of law above, she shall at the next session of Congress submit a written message outlining her reasons for taking such action and the authority therefor; and if Congress shall not by vote of both Houses approve her action, she shall immediately cease; The president shall commission all the officers of the United States.

§ 5. Immunity and removal

The president shall be immune from civil suit for official actions founded upon official actions taken during her term of office, and all civil suits pending against her upon assumption of her office for actions taken before the commencement of her term of office, or which shall be commenced against her during her term of office for such actions, shall be stayed for the duration of her service.

Neither the president nor vice-president nor any of her Cabinet members or principal advisers as designated by law shall be questioned in any other place about advice they have directly furnished the president, provided that all official papers prepared pursuant to the president's authority to require advice from members of the cabinet and legal advice from the attorney general shall be made available to Congress subject to conditions as may be specified by law to ensure the protection of confidential information, and further provided that such questioning may take place in the context of a criminal proceeding against any person where a judge shall determine that such questioning is necessary, in which case such questioning shall take place under rules set by the court to preserve insofar as practicable the confidentiality of the information provided in response.

The president, vice president and all civil officers of the United States, including the attorney general, shall be removed from office on impeachment for, and conviction of, treason, bribery, or other high crimes and misdemeanors.

When an election for members of Congress held during the president's term shall produce a loss of 40 or more seats in the House of Representatives, the president shall at her sole election have the choice of (1) resignation to be succeeded by the vice-president; or (2) designation of a government of national unity by requiring resignation of all members of the cabinet and assembling within one week a new cabinet made up of equal numbers of members of both parties. If she shall elect to designate a government of national unity, the new cabinet shall be confirmed by the House, not the Senate, as a slate, rather than individually, and if the House shall reject the slate submitted by the president, the president shall then resign and be succeeded in office by the vice-president.

§6. Office of the Attorney General

The United States shall have one attorney general, who shall be elected for a term of four years during those years in which members of Congress shall be elected but no presidential election shall be conducted. The election shall be conducted under the rules and procedures specified in § 1 of this Article.

The attorney general shall be the principal law officer of the United States and shall give legal advice to the United States government and to the president, the executive departments and all agencies of the government. The attorney general shall represent the United States in all legal proceedings and shall conduct the investigative and law-enforcement functions of the Department of Justice, as Congress shall by law direct.

The attorney general shall provide legal advice, conduct legal proceedings, and direct enforcement activities in faithful conformity with this Constitution, laws made pursuant to it and treaties made or which shall be made under the authority of the United States.

The attorney general shall give the president legal advice, in writing, at the president's request and at other appropriate times and shall inform the president of the actions taken by the Justice Department, and shall attend sessions of the Cabinet as specified above when the full cabinet meets or at other meetings requested by the president; however, the president may not require the resignation of the attorney general upon designation of a government of national unity or at any other time.

The attorney general shall from time to time give to the Congress information of the state of the legal and law-enforcement policy and actions of the United States, and shall furnish to Congress information requested concerning the same, excepting only such information as may compromise ongoing legal investigations or reveal information properly classified, in which case such information shall be provided promptly when circumstances allow.

––––––––––

1. *And While We're at It . . .* It is surely not only the executive branch that seems to its critics to fall short of the Framers' normative ambitions. In THOMAS E. MANN AND NORMAN J. ORNSTEIN, THE BROKEN BRANCH: HOW CONGRESS IS FAILING AMERICA AND HOW TO GET IT BACK ON TRACK (2006), two of America's most celebrated congressional scholars describe the recent history of the legislative branch as "unsettling and destructive." They bemoan the "escalation of the permanent campaign, the collapse of the center in Congress, the growing ideological polarization of the parties, the transformation of intense partisanship into virtually tribal politics, and the decline in accountability." *Id.* at x. Despite the promise of the book's title, however, the authors' prescriptions for countering the "[a]rrogance, greed, venality, [and] condescension toward the minority," id. at xii, by their own admission, fall somewhat short of "a solid blueprint for recovery," *id.* at 226. They emphasize the importance

of restoring competitiveness to electoral districts, and a series of reforms to internal rules and processes. They write, however: "[W]e must face the reality that even if we could get the procedural, ethics, and electoral reforms through just as we would draft them, and even if we could include serious reform of the committee structure and of the budget process, it would not change Congress dramatically unless and until the leaders of Congress change their approach to governance," *id.* at 238–239. Do you agree with this diagnosis?

Of course, it might be said that despair over changing Congress "dramatically" should not preclude modest efforts at genuinely helpful reform. Professor Adrian Vermeule has suggested that progress might be made through "a repertoire of small-scale institutional devices and innovations that promote democratic values against the background of standard large-scale institutions." ADRIAN VERMEULE, MECHA-NISMS OF DEMOCRACY: INSTITUTIONAL DESIGN WRIT SMALL 2 (2007).

2. Separation of Parties. Law professors Daryl Levinson and Richard Pildes have argued that the advent of political parties shortly after the founding utterly changed the dynamics of interbranch relations within the federal government, and that the virtues of checks and balances cannot be achieved without the benefit of reforms that take party loyalties into account. Daryl L. Levinson and Richard H. Pildes, *Separation of Parties, Not Powers*, 119 HARV. L. REV. 2311 (2006). They see the greatest danger to checks and balances arriving in periods of unified government—that is, when the same party controls the White House and both Houses of Congress—because the partisanship of the President's supporters in Congress can easily trump their vigilance to protect legislative prerogative. Among their suggestions are mechanisms to preserve minority rights in Congress, even going beyond the filibuster, such as "institutional structures that enable minority parties to engage in auditing, investigation, and information gathering" vis-à-vis the executive branch. Do our most recent experiences of unified Republican (2003–2006, 2017–?) and Democratic (2009–2010) government support their thesis?

3. And Article III? An enduring focus of constitutional criticism has been the lifetime tenure afforded to federal judges, especially as it affects the Supreme Court. A thoroughgoing contemporary critique is Steven G. Calabresi and James Lundgren, *Term Limits for the Supreme Court: Life Tenure Reconsidered*, 29 HARV. J. L. & PUB. POL. 770 (2006). As far as we are aware, lifetime tenure has received no recent vigorous defense. Yet proposals for constitutional term limits have seemingly gained no traction. Perhaps the reason is best captured in a June, 2016 Gallup poll, which found that 77 percent of Americans have at least "some" confidence (as compared to "very little" or "none") in the U.S. Supreme Court, as compared to 63 percent for the President and 44 percent for Congress. Gallup: Major Institutions, available at http://www.gallup.com/poll/1597/confidence-institutions.aspx. How might more frequent Supreme Court appointments affect the presidency? The separation of powers more generally?

And a Last Word from Benjamin Franklin. When the drafters of the Constitution adjourned their secret deliberations and emerged from Independence Hall, it was reported that Mrs. Elizabeth Powell of Philadelphia, a friend of George Washington's, inquired of Benjamin Franklin: "Well, Doctor, what have we got, a republic or a monarchy?" Franklin famously responded, "A republic, if you can keep it." Questions worthy of general reflection after all the developments we have traced are, "Have we kept it?" and "Could we do better?"

Appendix

Selected Documents

Constitution of the United States

Authorization for the Use of Force (2001)

Proclamation of January 1, 1863 (Emancipation Proclamation)

Exec. Order No. 12866, Regulatory Planning and Review

Constitution of the United States

We the People of the United States, in order to form a more perfect union, establish justice, insure domestic tranquility, provide for the common defence, promote the general welfare, and secure the blessing of liberty to ourselves and our posterity, do ordain and establish the Constitution of the United States of America.

Article I.

Sect. 1. All legislative powers herein granted shall be vested in a Congress of the United States, which shall consist of a Senate and a House of Representatives.

Sect. 2. The House of Representatives shall be composed of members chosen every second year by the people of the several states, and the electors in each state shall have the qualifications requisite for electors of the most numerous branch of the state legislature. No person shall be a representative who shall not have attained to the age of twenty-five years, and been seven years a citizen of the United States, and who shall not, when elected, be an inhabitant of that state in which he shall be chosen.

Representative and direct taxes shall be apportioned among the several states which may be included within this Union, according to their respective numbers, which shall be determined by adding to the whole number of free persons, including those bound to service for a term of years, and excluding Indians not taxed, three-fifths of all other persons. The actual enumeration shall be made within three years after the first meeting of the Congress of the United States, and within every subsequent term of ten years in such manner as they shall be law direct. The number of representative shall not exceed one for every thirty thousand, but each state shall have at least one representative; and until such enumeration shall be made, the state of New Hampshire shall be entitled to choose three, Massachusetts eight, Rhode Island and Providence Plantations one, Connecticut five, New-York six, New-Jersey four, Pennsylvania eight,

1473

Delaware one, Maryland six, Virginia ten, North-Carolina five, Carolina five, and Georgia three.

When vacancies happen in the representation from any state, the executive authority thereof shall issue writs of election to fill such vacancies.

The House of Representatives shall choose the Speaker and other officers; and shall have the sole power of impeachment.

Sect. 3. The Senate of the United States shall be composed of two senators from each state chosen by the legislature thereof, for six years and each senator shall have one vote.

Immediately after they shall be assembled in consequence of the first election, they shall be divided as equally as may be into three classes. The seats of the senators of the first class shall be vacated at the expiration of the second year, of the second class at the expiration of the fourth year, and of the third class at the expiration of the sixth year, so that one-third may be chosen every second year; and if vacancies happen by resignation, or otherwise during the recess of the legislature of any state, the Executive thereof may make temporary appointments until the next meeting of the Legislature, which shall then fill such vacancies. No person shall be a senator who shall not have attained to the age of thirty years, and been nine years a citizen of the United States, who shall not, when elected, be an inhabitant of that state for which he shall be chosen.

The Vice-President of the United States shall be President of the Senate, but shall have no vote unless they be equally divided. The Senate shall choose their other officers, and also a President pro tempore, in the absence of the Vice-President, or when he shall exercise the office of President of the United States.

The Senate shall have the sole power to try all impeachments. When sitting for that purpose, they shall be on oath or affirmation. When the President of the United States is tried, the Chief Justice shall preside: And no person shall be convicted without the concurrence of two-thirds of the members present.

Judgment in cases of impeachment shall not extend further than to removal from office and disqualification to hold and enjoy any office of honor, trust or profit under the United States; but the party convicted shall nevertheless be liable and subject to indictment, trial, judgment and punishment, according to law.

Sect. 4. The times, places and manner of holding elections for senators and representatives, shall be prescribed in each state by the legislature thereof: but the Congress may at any time by law make or alter such regulations, except as to the places of choosing senators.

The Congress shall assemble at least once in every year, and such meeting shall be on the first Monday in December, unless they shall by law appoint a different day.

Sect. 5. Each house shall be the judge of the elections, returns and qualifications of its own members, and a majority of each shall constitute a quorum to do business; but a smaller number may adjourn from day to day, and may be authorized to compel the attendance of absent members, in such manner, and under such penalties as each house may provide.

Each house may determine the rules of its proceedings, punish its members for disorderly behaviour, and with the concurrence of two-thirds, expel a member.

Each house shall keep a journal of its proceedings, and from time to time publish the same, excepting such parts as may in their judgment require secrecy; and the yeas and nays of the members either house on any question shall, at the desire of one-fifth of those present be entered on the journal.

Neither house, during the session of Congress shall, without the consent of the other, adjourn for more than three days, nor to any other place than that in which the two houses shall be sitting.

Sect. 6. The senators and representatives shall receive a compensation for their services, to be ascertained by law, and paid out of the treasury of the United States. They shall in all cases, except treason, felony and breach of the peace, be privileged from arrest during their attendance at the session of their respective houses, and in going to and returning from the same; and for any speech or debate in either house, they shall not be questioned in any other place.

No senator or representative shall, during the time for which he was elected, be appointed to any civil office under the authority of the United States, which shall have been created, or the emoluments whereof shall have been increased during such time; and no person holding any office under the United States, shall be a member of either house during his continuance in office.

Sect. 7. All bills for raising revenue shall originate in the House of Representatives; but the Senate may propose or concur with amendments as on other bills.

Every bill which shall have passed the House of Representatives and the Senate, shall, before it become a law, be presented to the President of the United States; if he approve he shall sign it, but if not he shall return it, with his objections to that house in which it shall have originated, who shall enter the objections at large on their journal, and proceed to reconsider it. If after such reconsideration two-thirds of that house shall agree to pass the bill, it shall be sent, together with the objections, to the other house, by which it shall likewise be reconsidered, and if approved by two-thirds of that house, it shall become a law. But in all such cases the votes of both houses shall be determined by yeas and nays, and the names of the persons voting for and against the bill shall be entered on the journal of each house respectively. If any bill shall not be returned by the President within ten days (Sundays excepted) after it shall have been presented to him, the same shall be a law, in like manner as if he had signed it, unless the Congress by their adjournment prevent its return, in which case it shall not be a law. Every order, resolution, or vote to which the concurrence of the Senate and House of Representative may be necessary (except on a question of adjournment) shall be presented to the President of the United States; and before the same shall take effect, shall be approved by him, or being disapproved by him, shall be repassed by two-thirds of the Senate and House of Representatives, according to the rules and limitations prescribed in the case of a bill.

Sect. 8. The Congress shall have power

To lay and collect taxes, duties, imposts and excises, to pay the debts and provide for the common defence and general welfare of the United States; but all duties, imposts and excises shall be uniform throughout the United States.

To borrow money on the credit of the United States;

To regulate commerce with foreign nations, and among the several states, and with the Indian tribes;

To establish an uniform rule of naturalization, and uniform laws on the subject of bankruptcies throughout the United States;

To coin money, regulate the value thereof, and of foreign coin, and fix the standard of weights and measures;

To provide for the punishment of counterfeiting the securities and current coin of the United States;

To establish post offices and post roads;

To promote the progress of science and useful arts, by securing for limited times to authors and inventors the exclusive right to their respective writings and discoveries;

To constitute tribunals inferior to the supreme court;

To define and punish piracies and felonies committed on the high seas, and offences against the law of nations;

To declare war, grant letters of marque and reprisal, and make rules concerning captures on land and water;

To raise and support armies, but no appropriation of money to that use shall be for a longer term than two years;

To provide and maintain a navy;

To make rules for the government and regulation of the land and naval forces;

To provide for calling forth the militia to execute the laws of the union, suppress insurrections and repel invasions;

To provide for organizing, arming, and disciplining, the militia, and for governing such part of them as may be employed in the service of the United States, reserving to the States respectively, the appointment of the officers, and the authority of training the militia according to the discipline prescribed by Congress;

To exercise exclusive legislation in all cases whatsoever, over such district (not exceeding ten miles square) as may, by cession of particular States, and the acceptance of Congress, become the seat of the government of the United States, and to exercise like authority over all places purchased by the consent of the legislature of the states in which the same shall be, for the erection of forts, magazines, arsenals, dockyards, and other needful buildings; -And

To make all laws which shall be necessary and proper for carrying into execution the foregoing powers, and all other powers vested by the Constitution in the government of the United States, or in any department or officer thereof.

Sect. 9. The migration or importation of such persons as any of the states now existing shall think proper to admit, shall not be prohibited by the Congress prior to the year one thousand eight hundred and eight, but a tax or duty may be imposed on such importation, not exceeding ten dollars for each person.

The privilege of the writ of habeas corpus shall not be suspended, unless when in cases of rebellion or invasion the public safety require it.

No bill of attainder or ex post facto law shall be passed. No capitation, or other direct, tax shall be laid, unless in proportion to the census or enumeration herein before directed to be taken. No tax or duty shall be laid on articles exported from any state. No preference shall be given by any regulation of commerce or revenue to the ports of one state over those of another: nor shall vessels bound to, or from, one state, be obliged to enter, clear, or pay duties in another. No money shall be drawn from the treasury, but in consequence of appropriations made by law; and a regular statement and account of the receipts and expenditures of all public money shall be published from time to time.

No title of nobility shall be granted by the United States: And no person holding any office of profit or trust under them, shall, without the consent of the Congress, accept of any present, emolument, office, or title, of any kind whatever, from any king, prince, or foreign state.

Sect. 10. No state shall enter into any treaty, alliance, or confederation; grant letters of marque and reprisal; coin money; emit bills of credit; make any thing but gold and silver coin a tender in payment of debts; pass any bill of attainder, ex post facto law, or law impairing the obligation of contracts, or grant any title of nobility. No state shall, without the consent of the Congress, lay any imposts or duties on imports or exports, except what may be absolutely necessary for executing its inspection laws; and the net produce of all duties and imposts, laid by any state on imports or exports, shall be for the use of the Treasury of the United States; all such laws shall be subject to the revision and control of the Congress. No state shall, without the consent of Congress, lay any duty of tonnage, keep troops, or ships of war in time of peace, enter into any agreement or compact with another state, or with a foreign power, or engage in war, unless actually invaded, or in such imminent danger as will not admit of delay.

Article II.

Sect. 1. The executive power shall be vested in a President of the United States of America. He shall hold his office during the term of four years, and, together with the Vice-President, chosen for the same term, be elected as follows.

Each state shall appoint, in such manner as the legislature thereof may direct, a number of electors, equal to the whole number of senators and representatives to which the state may be entitled in the Congress: but no senator or representative, or person holding an office of trust or profit under the United States, shall be appointed an elector.

The electors shall meet in their respective states, and vote by ballot for two persons, of whom one at least shall not be an inhabitant of the same state with themselves. And they shall make a list of all the persons voted for, and of the number of votes for each; which list they shall sign and certify, and transmit sealed to the seat of the government of the United States, directed to the President of the Senate. The President of the Senate shall, in the presence of the Senate and House of Representatives, open all the certificates, and the votes shall then be counted. The person having the greatest number of votes shall be the President, if such number be a majority of the whole number of electors appointed; and if there be more than one who have such majority, and have an equal number of electors appointed; and if there be more than one who have such majority, and have an equal number of votes, then the House of Representatives shall immediately choose by ballot one of them for President; and if no person have a majority, then from the five highest on the list the said house shall in like manner choose the President. But in choosing the President, the votes shall be taken by states, the representation from each state having one vote; a quorum for this purpose shall consist of a member or members from two-thirds of the states, and a majority of all the states shall be necessary to a choice. In every case, after the choice of the President, the person having the greatest number of votes of the electors shall be the Vice-President. But if there should remain two or more who have equal votes, the Senate shall choose from them by ballot the Vice-President.

The Congress may determine the time of the choosing the electors, and the day on which they shall give their votes; which day shall be the same throughout the United States.

No person except a natural born citizen, or a citizen of the United States, at the time of the adoption of this constitution, shall be eligible to the office of President; neither shall any person be eligible to that office who shall not have attained to the age of thirty-five years, and been fourteen years a resident within the United States. In case of the removal of the President from office, or his death, resignation, or inability to discharge the powers and duties of the said office, the same shall devolve on the Vice-President, and the Congress may by law provide for the case of removal, death, resignation or inability, both of the President and Vice-President, declaring what officer shall then act as President, and such officer shall act accordingly, until the disability be removed, or a President be elected.

The President shall, at stated times, receive for his services, a compensation, which shall neither be increased nor diminished during the period for which he shall have been elected, and he shall not receive within that period any other emolument from the United States, or any of them.

Before he enter on the execution of his office, he shall take the following oath or affirmation:

> "I do solemnly swear (or affirm) that I will faithfully execute the office of President of the United States, and will to the best of my ability, preserve, protect and defend the constitution of the United States."

Sect. 2. The President shall be commander in chief of the army and navy of the United States, and of the militia of the several States, when called into the actual service of the United States; he may require the opinion, in writing of the principal officer in each of the executive departments, upon any subject relating to the duties of their respective offices, and he shall have power to grant reprieves and pardons for offences against the United States, except in cases of impeachment. He shall have power, by and with the advice and consent of the Senate, to make treaties, provided two-thirds of the senators present concur; and he shall nominate, and by and with the advice and consent of the Senate, shall appoint ambassadors, other public ministers and consuls, judges of the Supreme Court, and all other officers of the United States, whose appointments are not herein otherwise provided for, and which shall be established by law. But the Congress may by law vest the appointment of such inferior officers, as they think proper, in the President alone, in the courts of law, or in the heads of departments.

The President shall have power to fill up all vacancies that may happen during the recess of the Senate, by granting commissions which shall expire at the end of their session.

Sect. 3. He shall from time to time give to the Congress information of the state of the union, and recommend to their consideration such measures as he shall judge necessary and expedient; he may, on extraordinary occasions, convene both houses, or either of them, and in case of disagreement between them, with respect to the time of adjournment, he may adjourn them to such time as he shall think proper; he shall receive ambassadors and other public ministers; he shall take care that the laws be faithfully executed, and shall commission all the officers of the United States.

Sect. 4. The President, Vice-President and all civil officers of the United States, shall be removed from office on impeachment for, and conviction of, treason, bribery, or other high crimes and misdemeanors.

Article III.

Sect. 1. The judicial power of the United States shall be vested in one Supreme Court, and in such inferior courts as the Congress may from time to time ordain and establish. The judges, both of the Supreme and inferior courts, shall hold their offices during good behavior, and shall, at stated times, receive for their services a compensation which shall not be diminished during their continuance in office.

Sect. 2. The judicial power shall extend to all cases, in law and equity, arising under this Constitution, the laws of the United States, and treaties made, or which shall be made, under their authority; to all cases affecting ambassadors, other public ministers, and consuls; to all cases of admiralty and maritime jurisdiction; to controversies to which the United States shall be a party; to controversies between two or more states, between a state and citizens of another state, between citizens of different states, between citizens of the same state claiming lands under grants of different states, and between a state or the citizens thereof, and foreign states, citizens, or subjects.

In all cases affecting ambassadors, other public ministers and consuls, and those in which a state shall be a party, the Supreme Court shall have original jurisdiction. In all the other cases before mentioned, the Supreme Court shall have appellate jurisdiction, both as to law and fact, with such exceptions and under such regulations as the Congress shall make.

The trial of all crimes, except in cases of impeachment, shall be by jury; and such trial shall be held in the state where the said crimes shall have been committed; but when not committed within any state the trial shall be at such place or places as the Congress may by law have directed.

Sect. 3. Treason against the United States shall consist only in levying war against them, or in adhering to their enemies, giving them aid and comfort. No person shall be convicted of treason unless on the testimony of two witnesses to the same overt act, or on confession in open court.

The Congress shall have power to declare the punishment of treason, but no attainder of treason shall work corruption of blood, or forfeiture except during the life of the person attainted.

Article IV.

Sect. 1. Full faith and credit shall be given in each state to the public act, records, and judicial proceedings of every other state. And the Congress may, by general laws, prescribe the manner in which such acts, records, and proceedings shall be proved, and the effect thereof.

Sect. 2. The citizens of each state shall be entitled to all privileges and immunities of citizens in the several states.

A person charged in any state with treason, felony, or other crime, who shall flee from justice, and be found in another state, shall, on demand of the executive authority of the State from which he fled, be delivered up, to be removed to the state having jurisdiction of the crime.

No person held to service or labor in one state, under the laws thereof, escaping into another, shall, in consequence of any law or regulation therein, be discharged from such service or labor, but shall be delivered up on claim of the party to whom such service or labor may be due.

Sect. 3. New states may be admitted by the Congress into this Union; but no new state shall be formed or erected within the jurisdiction of any other state, nor any state be formed by the junction of two or more states, or parts of states, without the consent of the legislatures of the states concerned as well as of the Congress.

The Congress shall have power to dispose of and make all needful rules and regulations respecting the territory or other property belonging to the United States; and nothing in this Constitution shall be so construed as to prejudice any claims of the United States, or of any particular state.

Sect. 4. The United States shall guarantee to every state in this Union a republican form of government, and shall protect each of them against invasion; and on application of the legislature, or of the executive (when the legislature cannot be convened), against domestic violence.

Article V.

The Congress, whenever two-thirds of both houses shall deem it necessary, shall propose amendments to this Constitution, or, on the application of the legislatures of two-thirds of the several states, shall call a convention for proposing amendments, which, in either case, shall be valid, to all intents and purposes, as part of this Constitution, when ratified by the legislatures of three-fourths of the several states, or by conventions in three-fourths thereof, as the one or the other mode of ratification may be proposed by the Congress; provided [that no amendment which may be made prior to the year one thousand eight hundred and eight shall in any manner affect the first and fourth clauses in the ninth Article;] and that no state, without its consent, shall be deprived of its equal suffrage in the Senate.

Article VI.

All debts contracted and engagements entered into, before the adoption of this Constitution, shall be as valid against the United States under this Constitution, as under the Confederation.

This Constitution, and the laws of the United States which shall be made in pursuance thereof, and all treaties made, or which shall be made, under the authority of the United States, shall be the supreme law of the land; and the judges in every state shall be bound thereby, anything in the constitution or laws of any state to the contrary notwithstanding.

The senators and representatives before mentioned, and the members of the several state legislatures, and all executive and judicial officers, both of the United States and of the several states, shall be bound, by oath or affirmation, to support this Constitution; but no religious test shall ever be required as a qualification to any office or public trust under the United States.

Article VII.

The ratification of the conventions of nine states shall be sufficient for the establishment of this Constitution between the states so ratifying the same.

Done in Convention, by the unanimous consent of the states present, the seventeenth day of September, in the year of our Lord one thousand seven hundred and eighty-seven, and of the Independence of the United States of America the twelfth. In Witness whereof, we have hereunto subscribed our names.

Attest: William Jackson, Secretary
George Washington

MASSACHUSETTS: Nathaniel Gorham, Rufus King

CONNECTICUT: Wm: Saml. Johnson, Roger Sherman

NEW YORK: Alexander Hamilton

NEW JERSEY: William Livingston, David Brearly, Willian Paterson, Jonathan Dayton

PENNSYLVANIA: Benjamin Franklin, Thomas Mifflin, Robert Morris, George-Clymer, Thomas FitzSimons, Jared Ingersoll, James Wilson, Gouvernor Morris

DELAWARE: George Read, Gunning Bedford, Jr., John Dickinson, Richard Bassett, Jacob Broom

MARYLAND: James McHenry, Dan of St Thomas Jenifer, Daniel Carroll

VIRGINIA: John Blair, James Madison Jr.

NORTH CAROLINA: William Blount, Richard Dobbs Spaight, Hugh Williamson

SOUTH CAROLINA: John Rutledge, Charles Cotesworth Pinckney, Charles Pinckney, Pierce Butler

GEORGIA: William Few, Abraham Baldwin

Amendments to the Constitution

1st Amendment

Congress shall make no law respecting an establishment of religion, or prohibiting the free exercise thereof; or abridging the freedom of speech, or of the press; or the right of the people peaceably to assemble, and to petition the government for a redress of grievances.

2nd Amendment

A well-regulated militia being necessary to the security of a free state, the right of the people to keep and bear arms shall not be infringed.

3rd Amendment

No soldier shall, in time of peace, be quarters in any house, without the consent of the owner; nor in time of war, but in a manner to be prescribed by law.

4th Amendment

The right of the people to be secure in their persons, houses, papers, and effects, against unreasonable searches and seizures, shall not be violated; and no warrants shall issue, but upon probable cause, supported by oath or affirmation, and particularly describing the place to be searched and the persons or things to be seized.

5th Amendment

No person shall be held to answer for a capital, or otherwise infamous, crime, unless on a presentment or indictment of a grand jury, except in cases arising in the land or naval forces, or in the militia, when in actual service, in time of war, or public danger; nor shall any person be subject, for the same offence, to be twice put in jeopardy of life or limb; nor shall be compelled, in any criminal case, to be a witness against himself; nor be deprived of life, liberty, or property, without due process of law; nor shall private property be taken for public use, without just compensation.

6th Amendment

In all criminal prosecutions, the accused shall enjoy the right to a speedy and public trial, by an impartial jury of the state and district wherein the crime shall have been committed, which district shall have been previously ascertained by law; and to be informed of the nature and cause of the accusation; to be confronted with the witnesses against him; to have compulsory process for obtaining witnesses in his favor; and to have the assistance of counsel for his defence.

7th Amendment

In suits at common law, where the value in controversy shall exceed twenty dollars, the right of trial by jury shall be preserved; and no fact, tried by a jury, shall be otherwise re-examined in any court of the United States than according to the rules of the common law.

8th Amendment

Excessive bail shall not be required, nor excessive fines imposed, nor cruel and unusual punishment inflicted.

9th Amendment

The enumeration in the Constitution of certain rights shall not be construed to deny or disparage others retained by the people.

10th Amendment

The powers not delegated to the United States by the Constitution, nor prohibited by it to the states, are reserved to the states respectively, or to the people.

11th Amendment

The judicial power of the United States shall not be construed to extend to any suit in law or equity, commenced or prosecuted against one of the United States by citizens of another state or by citizens or subjects of any foreign state.

12th Amendment

The electors shall meet in their respective states, and vote by ballot for President and Vice-President, one of whom, at least, shall not be an inhabitant of the same state with themselves; they shall name in their ballots the person voted for as President, and in distinct ballots the person voted for as Vice-President; and they shall make distinct lists of all persons voted for as President, and of all persons voted for as Vice-President, and of the number of votes for each, which lists they shall sign, and certify, and transmit, sealed, to the seat of the government of the United States, directed to the President of the Senate; the President of the Senate shall, in the presence of the Senate and the House of Representatives, open all the certificates, and the votes shall then be counted; the person having the greatest number of votes for President shall be the President, if such number be a majority of the whole number of electors appointed; and if no person have such a majority, then, from the persons having the highest numbers, not exceeding three, on the list of those voted for a President, the House of Representative shall choose immediately, by ballot, the President. But in choosing the President, the votes shall be taken by states, the representation from each state having one vote; a quorum for this purpose shall consist of a member or members from two-thirds of the states, and a majority of all the states shall be necessary to a choice. And if the House of Representatives shall not choose a President, whenever the right of choice shall devolve upon them, [before the fourth day of March next following] the Vice-President shall act as President, as in case of death, or other constitutional disability of the President. The person having the greatest number of votes as Vice-President, shall be the Vice-President, if such number be a majority of the whole number of electors appointed; and if no person have a majority, then, form the two highest numbers on the list, the Senate shall choose the Vice-President; a quorum for the purpose shall consist of two-thirds of the whole number of senators; a majority of the whole number shall be necessary to a choice. But no person constitutionally ineligible to the office of President shall be eligible to that of Vice-President of the United States.

13th Amendment

Sect. 1. Neither slavery nor involuntary servitude, except as a punishment for crime, whereof the party shall have been duly convicted, shall exist within the United States, or any place subject to their jurisdiction.

Sect. 2. The Congress shall have power to enforce this article by appropriate legislation.

14th Amendment

Sect. 1. All persons born or naturalized in the United States, and subject to the jurisdiction thereof, are citizens of the United States and of the state wherein they reside. No state shall make or enforce any law which shall abridge the privileges or immunities of citizens of the United States; nor shall any state deprive any person of life, liberty, or property, without due process of law, nor deny any person within its jurisdiction the equal protection of the laws.

Sect. 2. Representatives shall be apportioned among the several states according to their respective numbers, counting the whole number of persons in each state, excluding Indians not taxed. But when the right to vote at any election for the choice of electors for President and Vice-President of the United States, representatives in Congress, the executive and judicial officers of a state, or the members of the legislature thereof, is denied to any of the male inhabitants of such State, being twenty-one years of age, and citizens of the United States, or in any way abridged, except for participation in rebellion or other crime, the basis of representation therein shall be reduced in the proportion which the number of such male citizens shall bear to the whole number of male citizens twenty-one years of age in such state.

Sect. 3. No person shall be a senator or representative in Congress, or elector of President and Vice President, or hold any office, civil or military, under the United States, or under any state, who, having previously taken an oath, as a member of Congress, or as an officer of the United States, or as a member of any state legislature, or as an executive or judicial officer of any state, to support the Constitution of the United States, shall have engaged in insurrection or rebellion against the same, or given aid or comfort to the enemies thereof. But Congress may, by a vote of two-thirds of each house, remove such disability.

Sect. 4. The validity of the public debt of the United States, authorized by law, including debts incurred for payment of pensions and bounties for services in suppressing insurrection or rebellion, shall not be questioned. But neither the United States nor any State shall assume or pay any debt or obligation incurred in aid of insurrection or rebellion against the United States, or any claim for the loss or emancipation of any slave; but all such debts, obligations, and claims shall be held illegal and void.

Sect. 5. The Congress shall have power to enforce, by appropriate legislation, the provisions of this article.

15th Amendment

Sect. 1. The right of citizens of the United States to vote shall not be denied or abridged by the United States or by any state on account of race, color, or previous condition of servitude.

Sect. 2. The Congress shall have power to enforce this article by appropriate legislation.

16th Amendment

The Congress shall have power to lay and collect taxes on incomes, from whatever source derived, without apportionment among the several states and without regard to any census or enumeration.

17th Amendment

The Senate of the United States shall be composed of two senators from each state, elected by the people thereof, for six years; and each senator shall have one vote. The electors in each state shall have the qualifications requisite for electors of the most numerous branch of the state legislatures.

When vacancies happen in the representation of any state in the Senate, the executive authority of such state shall issue writs of election to fill such vacancies: Provided, that the legislature of any state may empower the executive thereof to make temporary appointment until the people fill the vacancies by election as the legislature may direct. This amendment shall not be so construed as to affect the election or term of any senator chosen before it becomes valid as part of the Constitution.

18th Amendment

Sect. 1. One year from the ratification of this article the manufacture, sale or transportation of intoxicating liquors within, the importation thereof into, or the exportation thereof from the United States and all territory subject to the jurisdiction thereof for beverage purposes is hereby prohibited.

Sect. 2. Congress and the several states shall have concurrent power to enforce this article by appropriate legislation.

Sect. 3. This article shall be inoperative unless it shall have been ratified as an amendment to the Constitution by the legislatures of the several states, as provided in the Constitution, within seven years of the date of the submission hereof to the states by Congress.

19th Amendment

The right of citizens of the United States to vote shall not be denied or abridged by the United States or by any state on account of sex. Congress shall have power to enforce this article by appropriate legislation.

20th Amendment

Sect. 1. The terms of the President and Vice President shall end at noon on the 20th day of January, and the terms of senators and representatives at noon on the 3d day of January, of the years in which such terms would have ended if this article had not been ratified; and the terms of their successors shall then begin.

Sect. 2. Congress shall assemble at least once in every year, and such meeting shall begin at noon on the 3d day of January, unless they shall by law appoint a different day.

Sect. 3. If, at the time fixed for the beginning of the term of the President, the President elect shall have died, the Vice President elect shall become President. If a President shall not have been chosen before the time fixed for the beginning of his term, or if the President elect shall have failed to qualify, then the Vice President elect shall act as President until a President shall have qualified; and the Congress may by law provide for the case wherein neither a President elect nor a Vice President elect shall have qualified, declaring who shall then act as President, or the manner in which one who is to act shall be selected, and such person shall act accordingly until a President or Vice President shall have qualified.

Sect. 4. Congress may by law provide for the case of the death of any of the persons from whom the House of Representatives may choose a President whenever the right of choice shall have devolved upon them, and for the case of the death of any of the persons from whom the Senate may choose a Vice President whenever the right of choice shall have devolved upon them.

Sect. 5. Sections 1 and 2 shall take effect on the 15th day of October following the ratification of this article.

Sect. 6. This article shall be inoperative unless it shall have been ratified as an amendment to the Constitution by three-fourths of the several states within seven years from the date of its submission.

21st Amendment

Sect. 1. The eighteenth article of amendment to the Constitution of the United States is hereby repealed.

Sect. 2. The transportation or importation into any state, territory, or possession of the United States for delivery or use therein of intoxicating liquors, in violation of the laws thereof, is hereby prohibited.

Sect. 3. This article shall be inoperative unless it shall have been ratified as an amendment to the Constitution by conventions in the several states, as provided in the Constitution, within seven years from the date of the submission hereof to the states by the Congress.

22d Amendment

Sect. 1. No person shall be elected to the office of the President more than twice, and no person who has held the office of President, or acted as President, for more than two years of a term to which some other person was elected President shall be elected to the office of the President more than once. But this Article shall not apply to any person holding the office of President when this Article was proposed by the Congress, and shall not prevent any person who may be holding the office of President, or acting as President, during the term within which his Article becomes operative from holding the office of President or acting as President during the remainder of such term.

Sect. 2. This article shall be inoperative unless it shall have been ratified as an amendment to the Constitution by the legislatures of three-fourths of the several states within seven years from the date of its submission to the states by the Congress.

23d Amendment

Sect. 1. The District constituting the seat of government of the United States shall appoint in such manner as the Congress may direct: A number of electors of President and Vice President equal to the whole number of Senators and Representatives in Congress to which the District would be entitled if it were a state, but in no event more than the least populous state; they shall be considered, for the purposes of the election of President and Vice President, to be electors appointed by a state; and they shall meet in the District and perform such duties as provided by the twelfth article of amendment.

Sect. 2. The Congress shall have power to enforce this article by appropriate legislation.

24th Amendment

Sect. 1. The right of citizens of the United States to vote in any primary or other election for President or Vice President, for electors for President or Vice President, or for senator or representative in Congress, shall not be denied or abridged by the United States or any state by reason of failure to pay any poll tax or other tax.

Sect. 2. The Congress shall have power to enforce this article by appropriate legislation.

25th Amendment

Sect. 1. In case of the removal of the President from office or of his death or resignation, the Vice President shall become President.

Sect. 2. Whenever there is a vacancy in the office of the Vice President, the President shall nominate a Vice President who shall take office upon confirmation by a majority vote of both houses of Congress.

Sect. 3. Whenever the President transmits to the President pro tempore of the Senate and the Speaker of the House of Representatives his written declaration that he is unable to discharge the powers and duties of his office, and until he transmits to them a written declaration to the contrary, such powers and duties shall be discharged by the Vice President as Acting President.

Sect. 4. Whenever the Vice President and a majority of either the principal officers of the executive departments or of such other body as Congress may by law provide, transmit to the President pro tempore of the Senate and the Speaker of the House of Representatives their written declaration that the President is unable to discharge the powers and duties of his office, the Vice President shall immediately assume the powers and duties of the office as Acting President.

Thereafter, when the President transmits to the President pro tempore of the Senate and the Speaker of the House of Representatives his written declaration that no inability exists, he shall resume the powers and duties of his office unless the Vice President and a majority of either the principal officers of the executive department or of such other body as Congress may by law provide, transmit within four days to the President pro tempore of the Senate and the Speaker of the House of Representatives their written declaration that the President is unable to discharge the powers and duties of his office. Thereupon Congress shall decide the issue, assembling within forty-eight hours for that purpose if not in session. If the Congress, within twenty-one days after Congress is required to assemble, determines by two-thirds vote of both Houses that the President is unable to discharge the powers and duties of his office, the Vice President shall continue to discharge the same as Acting President; otherwise, the President shall resume the powers and duties of his office.

26th Amendment

Sect. 1. The right of citizens of the United States, who are eighteen years of age or older, to vote shall not be denied or abridged by the United States or by any state on account of age.

Sect. 2. The Congress shall have the power to enforce this article by appropriate legislation.

27th Amendment

No law varying the compensation for the services of senators and representatives shall take effect, until an election of representatives shall have intervened.

Authorization for the Use of Force

Pub. L. No. 107-40, 107th Cong., 1st Sess. (2001), 115 Stat. 224

Whereas, on September 11, 2001, acts of treacherous violence were committed against the United States and its citizens; and

Whereas, such acts render it both necessary and appropriate that the United States exercise its rights to self-defense and to protect United States citizens both at home and abroad; and

Whereas, in light of the threat to the national security and foreign policy of the United States posed by these grave acts of violence; and

Whereas, such acts continue to pose an unusual and extraordinary threat to the national security and foreign policy of the United States; and

Whereas, the President has authority under the Constitution to take action to deter and prevent acts of international terrorism against the United States: Now, therefore, be it

Resolved by the Senate and House of Representatives of the United States of America in Congress assembled, . . .

SEC. 2. AUTHORIZATION FOR USE OF UNITED STATES ARMED FORCES.

(a) IN GENERAL- That the President is authorized to use all necessary and appropriate force against those nations, organizations, or persons he determines planned, authorized, committed, or aided the terrorist attacks that occurred on September 11, 2001, or harbored such organizations or persons, in order to prevent any future acts of international terrorism against the United States by such nations, organizations or persons.

(b) War Powers Resolution Requirements-

(1) SPECIFIC STATUTORY AUTHORIZATION- Consistent with section 8(a)(1) of the War Powers Resolution, the Congress declares that this section is intended to constitute specific statutory authorization within the meaning of section 5(b) of the War Powers Resolution.

(2) APPLICABILITY OF OTHER REQUIREMENTS- Nothing in this resolution supercedes any requirement of the War Powers Resolution.

January 1, 1863
By the President of the United States of America:
a Proclamation

Whereas, on the twenty-second day of September, in the year of our Lord one thousand eight hundred and sixty-two, a proclamation was issued by the President of the United States, containing, among other things, the following, to wit:

"That on the first day of January, in the year of our Lord one thousand eight hundred and sixty-three, all persons held as slaves within any state or designated part of a state, the people whereof shall then be in rebellion against the United States, shall be then, thenceforward, and forever, free; and the Executive Government of the United States, including the military and naval authority thereof, will recognize and maintain the freedom of such persons, and will do no act or acts to repress such persons, or any of them, in any efforts they may make for their actual freedom.

"That the Executive will on the first day of January aforesaid, by proclamation, designate the states and parts of states, if any, in which the people thereof, respectively, shall then be in rebellion against the United States; and the fact that any state, or the people thereof, shall on that day be in good faith represented in the Congress of the United States, by members chosen thereto at elections wherein a majority of the qualified voters of such states shall have participated, shall, in the absence of strong countervailing testimony, be deemed conclusive evidence that such state, and the people thereof, are not then in rebellion against the United States."

Now, therefore, I, Abraham Lincoln, President of the United States, by virtue of the power in me vested as commander-in-chief of the army and navy of the United States, in time of actual armed rebellion against the authority and Government of the United States, and as a fit and necessary war measure for suppressing said rebellion, do, on this first day of January, in the year of our Lord one thousand eight hundred and sixty-three, and in accordance with my purpose so to do, publicly proclaimed for the full period of one hundred days from the day first above mentioned, order and designate as the states and parts of states wherein the people thereof, respectively, are this day in rebellion against the United States, the following, to wit:

Arkansas, Texas, Louisiana, (except the parishes of St. Bernard, Plaquemines, Jefferson, St. John, St. Charles, St. James, Ascension, Assumption, Terre Bonne, Lafourche, St. Mary, St. Martin, and Orleans, including the city of New Orleans,) Mississippi, Alabama, Florida, Georgia, South Carolina, North Carolina, and Virginia, (except the forty-eight counties designated as West Virginia, and also the counties of Berkeley, Accomac, Northampton, Elizabeth City, York, Princess Ann, and Norfolk, including the cities of Norfolk and Portsmouth,) and which excepted parts are for the present left precisely as if this proclamation were not issued.

And by virtue of the power and for the purpose aforesaid, I do order and declare that all persons held as slaves within said designated states and parts of states are, and henceforward shall be, free; and that the Executive Government of the United

States, including the military and naval authorities thereof, will recognize and maintain the freedom of said persons.

And I hereby enjoin upon the people so declared to be free to abstain from all violence, unless in necessary self-defence; and I recommend to them that, in all cases when allowed, they labor faithfully for reasonable wages.

And I further declare and make known that such persons, of suitable condition, will be received into the armed service of the United States to garrison forts, positions, stations, and other places, and to man vessels of all sorts in said service.

And upon this act, sincerely believed to be an act of justice, warranted by the Constitution upon military necessity, I invoke the considerate judgment of mankind and the gracious favor of Almighty God.

In witness whereof, I have hereunto set my hand and caused the seal of the United States to be affixed.

Done at the city of Washington this first day of January, in the year of our Lord one thousand eight hundred and sixty-three, and of the Independence of the United States of America the eighty-seventh.

ABRAHAM LINCOLN

By the President: William H. Seward, *Secretary of State.*

Exec. Order No. 12866
Regulatory Planning and Review[1]
Sep. 30, 1993, 58 Fed.Reg. 51735.

The American people deserve a regulatory system that works for them, not against them: a regulatory system that protects and improves their health, safety, environment, and well-being and improves the performance of the economy without imposing unacceptable or unreasonable costs on society; regulatory policies that recognize that the private sector and private markets are the best engine for economic growth; regulatory approaches that respect the role of State, local, and tribal governments; and regulations that are effective, consistent, sensible, and understandable. We do not have such a regulatory system today.

With this Executive order, the Federal Government begins a program to reform and make more efficient the regulatory process. The objectives of this Executive order are to enhance planning and coordination with respect to both new and existing regulations; to reaffirm the primacy of Federal agencies in the regulatory

---

1. President George W. Bush amended this executive order through Exec. Order No. 13,258, 67 Fed. Reg. 9385 (2002), and Exec. Order No. 13,422, 72 Fed. Reg. 2763 (2007). Both these orders were revoked, in turn, by President Obama's Exec. Order No. 13,497, 74 Fed. Reg. 6113 (2009).

decision-making process; to restore the integrity and legitimacy of regulatory review and oversight; and to make the process more accessible and open to the public. In pursuing these objectives, the regulatory process shall be conducted so as to meet applicable statutory requirements and with due regard to the discretion that has been entrusted to the Federal agencies.

Accordingly, by the authority vested in me as President by the Constitution and the laws of the United States of America, it is hereby ordered as follows:

Sec. 1. Statement of Regulatory Philosophy and Principles.

(a) **The Regulatory Philosophy.** Federal agencies should promulgate only such regulations as are required by law, are necessary to interpret the law, or are made necessary by compelling public need, such as material failures of private markets to protect or improve the health and safety of the public, the environment, or the well-being of the American people. In deciding whether and how to regulate, agencies should assess all costs and benefits of available regulatory alternatives, including the alternative of not regulating. Costs and benefits shall be understood to include both quantifiable measures (to the fullest extent that these can be usefully estimated) and qualitative measures of costs and benefits that are difficult to quantify, but nevertheless essential to consider. Further, in choosing among alternative regulatory approaches, agencies should select those approaches that maximize net benefits (including potential economic, environmental, public health and safety, and other advantages; distributive impacts; and equity), unless a statute requires another regulatory approach.

(b) **The Principles of Regulation.** To ensure that the agencies' regulatory programs are consistent with the philosophy set forth above, agencies should adhere to the following principles, to the extent permitted by law and where applicable:

(1) Each agency shall identify the problem that it intends to address (including, where applicable, the failures of private markets or public institutions that warrant new agency action) as well as assess the significance of that problem.

(2) Each agency shall examine whether existing regulations (or other law) have created, or contributed to, the problem that a new regulation is intended to correct and whether those regulations (or other law) should be modified to achieve the intended goal of regulation more effectively.

(3) Each agency shall identify and assess available alternatives to direct regulation, including providing economic incentives to encourage the desired behavior, such as user fees or marketable permits, or providing information upon which choices can be made by the public.

(4) In setting regulatory priorities, each agency shall consider, to the extent reasonable, the degree and nature of the risks posed by various substances or activities within its jurisdiction.

(5) When an agency determines that a regulation is the best available method of achieving the regulatory objective, it shall design its regulations in the most cost-effective manner to achieve the regulatory objective. In doing so, each agency shall

consider incentives for innovation, consistency, predictability, the costs of enforcement and compliance (to the government, regulated entities, and the public), flexibility, distributive impacts, and equity.

(6) Each agency shall assess both the costs and the benefits of the intended regulation and, recognizing that some costs and benefits are difficult to quantify, propose or adopt a regulation only upon a reasoned determination that the benefits of the intended regulation justify its costs.

(7) Each agency shall base its decisions on the best reasonably obtainable scientific, technical, economic, and other information concerning the need for, and consequences of, the intended regulation.

(8) Each agency shall identify and assess alternative forms of regulation and shall, to the extent feasible, specify performance objectives, rather than specifying the behavior or manner of compliance that regulated entities must adopt.

(9) Wherever feasible, agencies shall seek views of appropriate State, local, and tribal officials before imposing regulatory requirements that might significantly or uniquely affect those governmental entities. Each agency shall assess the effects of Federal regulations on State, local, and tribal governments, including specifically the availability of resources to carry out those mandates, and seek to minimize those burdens that uniquely or significantly affect such governmental entities, consistent with achieving regulatory objectives. In addition, as appropriate, agencies shall seek to harmonize Federal regulatory actions with related State, local, and tribal regulatory and other governmental functions.

(10) Each agency shall avoid regulations that are inconsistent, incompatible, or duplicative with its other regulations or those of other Federal agencies.

(11) Each agency shall tailor its regulations to impose the least burden on society, including individuals, businesses of differing sizes, and other entities (including small communities and governmental entities), consistent with obtaining the regulatory objectives, taking into account, among other things, and to the extent practicable, the costs of cumulative regulations.

(12) Each agency shall draft its regulations to be simple and easy to understand, with the goal of minimizing the potential for uncertainty and litigation arising from such uncertainty.

Sec. 2. Organization. An efficient regulatory planning and review process is vital to ensure that the Federal Government's regulatory system best serves the American people.

(a) **The Agencies.** Because Federal agencies are the repositories of significant substantive expertise and experience, they are responsible for developing regulations and assuring that the regulations are consistent with applicable law, the President's priorities, and the principles set forth in this Executive order.

(b) **The Office of Management and Budget.** Coordinated review of agency rulemaking is necessary to ensure that regulations are consistent with applicable law, the

President's priorities, and the principles set forth in this Executive order, and that decisions made by one agency do not conflict with the policies or actions taken or planned by another agency. The Office of Management and Budget (OMB) shall carry out that review function. Within OMB, the Office of Information and Regulatory Affairs (OIRA) is the repository of expertise concerning regulatory issues, including methodologies and procedures that affect more than one agency, this Executive order, and the President's regulatory policies. To the extent permitted by law, OMB shall provide guidance to agencies and assist the President, the Vice President, and other regulatory policy advisors to the President in regulatory planning and shall be the entity that reviews individual regulations, as provided by this Executive order.

(c) **The Vice President.** The Vice President is the principal advisor to the President on, and shall coordinate the development and presentation of recommendations concerning, regulatory policy, planning, and review, as set forth in this Executive order. In fulfilling their responsibilities under this Executive order, the President and the Vice President shall be assisted by the regulatory policy advisors within the Executive Office of the President and by such agency officials and personnel as the President and the Vice President may, from time to time, consult.

Sec. 3. Definitions. For purposes of this Executive order:

(a) "Advisors" refers to such regulatory policy advisors to the President as the President and Vice President may from time to time consult, including, among others: (1) the Director of OMB; (2) the Chair (or another member) of the Council of Economic Advisers; (3) the Assistant to the President for Economic Policy; (4) the Assistant to the President for Domestic Policy; (5) the Assistant to the President for National Security Affairs; (6) the Assistant to the President for Science and Technology; (7) the Assistant to the President for Intergovernmental Affairs; (8) the Assistant to the President and Staff Secretary; (9) the Assistant to the President and Chief of Staff to the Vice President; (10) the Assistant to the President and Counsel to the President; (11) the Deputy Assistant to the President and Director of the White House Office on Environmental Policy; and (12) the Administrator of OIRA, who also shall coordinate communications relating to this Executive order among the agencies, OMB, the other Advisors, and the Office of the Vice President.

(b) "Agency," unless otherwise indicated, means any authority of the United States that is an "agency" under 44 U.S.C. 3502(1), other than those considered to be independent regulatory agencies, as defined in 44 U.S.C. 3502(10) .

(c) "Director" means the Director of OMB.

(d) "Regulation" or "rule" means an agency statement of general applicability and future effect, which the agency intends to have the force and effect of law, that is designed to implement, interpret, or prescribe law or policy or to describe the procedure or practice requirements of an agency. It does not, however, include:

(1) Regulations or rules issued in accordance with the formal rulemaking provisions of 5 U.S.C. 556, 557;

(2) Regulations or rules that pertain to a military or foreign affairs function of the United States, other than procurement regulations and regulations involving the import or export of non-defense articles and services;

(3) Regulations or rules that are limited to agency organization, management, or personnel matters; or

(4) Any other category of regulations exempted by the Administrator of OIRA.

(e) "Regulatory action" means any substantive action by an agency (normally published in the Federal Register) that promulgates or is expected to lead to the promulgation of a final rule or regulation, including notices of inquiry, advance notices of proposed rulemaking, and notices of proposed rulemaking.

(f) "Significant regulatory action" means any regulatory action that is likely to result in a rule that may:

(1) Have an annual effect on the economy of $ 100 million or more or adversely affect in a material way the economy, a sector of the economy, productivity, competition, jobs, the environment, public health or safety, or State, local, or tribal governments or communities;

(2) Create a serious inconsistency or otherwise interfere with an action taken or planned by another agency;

(3) Materially alter the budgetary impact of entitlements, grants, user fees, or loan programs or the rights and obligations of recipients thereof; or

(4) Raise novel legal or policy issues arising out of legal mandates, the President's priorities, or the principles set forth in this Executive order.

Sec. 4. Planning Mechanism. In order to have an effective regulatory program, to provide for coordination of regulations, to maximize consultation and the resolution of potential conflicts at an early stage, to involve the public and its State, local, and tribal officials in regulatory planning, and to ensure that new or revised regulations promote the President's priorities and the principles set forth in this Executive order, these procedures shall be followed, to the extent permitted by law:

(a) **Agencies' Policy Meeting.** Early in each year's planning cycle, the Vice President shall convene a meeting of the Advisors and the heads of agencies to seek a common understanding of priorities and to coordinate regulatory efforts to be accomplished in the upcoming year.

(b) **Unified Regulatory Agenda.** For purposes of this subsection, the term "agency" or "agencies" shall also include those considered to be independent regulatory agencies, as defined in 44 U.S.C. 3502(10). Each agency shall prepare an agenda of all regulations under development or review, at a time and in a manner specified by the Administrator of OIRA. The description of each regulatory action shall contain, at a minimum, a regulation identifier number, a brief summary of the action, the legal authority for the action, any legal deadline for the action, and the name and telephone number of a knowledgeable agency official. Agencies may incorporate the information required under 5 U.S.C. 602 and 41 U.S.C. 402 into these agendas.

(c) **The Regulatory Plan.** For purposes of this subsection, the term "agency" or "agencies" shall also include those considered to be independent regulatory agencies, as defined in 44 U.S.C. 3502(10).

(1) As part of the Unified Regulatory Agenda, beginning in 1994, each agency shall prepare a Regulatory Plan (Plan) of the most important significant regulatory actions that the agency reasonably expects to issue in proposed or final form in that fiscal year or thereafter. The Plan shall be approved personally by the agency head and shall contain at a minimum:

(A) A statement of the agency's regulatory objectives and priorities and how they relate to the President's priorities;

(B) A summary of each planned significant regulatory action including, to the extent possible, alternatives to be considered and preliminary estimates of the anticipated costs and benefits;

(C) A summary of the legal basis for each such action, including whether any aspect of the action is required by statute or court order;

(D) A statement of the need for each such action and, if applicable, how the action will reduce risks to public health, safety, or the environment, as well as how the magnitude of the risk addressed by the action relates to other risks within the jurisdiction of the agency;

(E) The agency's schedule for action, including a statement of any applicable statutory or judicial deadlines; and

(F) The name, address, and telephone number of a person the public may contact for additional information about the planned regulatory action.

(2) Each agency shall forward its Plan to OIRA by June 1st of each year.

(3) Within 10 calendar days after OIRA has received an agency's Plan, OIRA shall circulate it to other affected agencies, the Advisors, and the Vice President.

(4) An agency head who believes that a planned regulatory action of another agency may conflict with its own policy or action taken or planned shall promptly notify, in writing, the Administrator of OIRA, who shall forward that communication to the issuing agency, the Advisors, and the Vice President.

(5) If the Administrator of OIRA believes that a planned regulatory action of an agency may be inconsistent with the President's priorities or the principles set forth in this Executive order or may be in conflict with any policy or action taken or planned by another agency, the Administrator of OIRA shall promptly notify, in writing, the affected agencies, the Advisors, and the Vice President.

(6) The Vice President, with the Advisors' assistance, may consult with the heads of agencies with respect to their Plans and, in appropriate instances, request further consideration or inter-agency coordination.

(7) The Plans developed by the issuing agency shall be published annually in the October publication of the Unified Regulatory Agenda. This publication shall be made available to the Congress; State, local, and tribal governments; and the public. Any views on any aspect of any agency Plan, including whether any planned regulatory action might conflict with any other planned or existing regulation, impose any unintended consequences on the public, or confer any unclaimed benefits on the public, should be directed to the issuing agency, with a copy to OIRA.

(d) **Regulatory Working Group.** Within 30 days of the date of this Executive order, the Administrator of OIRA shall convene a Regulatory Working Group ("Working Group"), which shall consist of representatives of the heads of each agency that the Administrator determines to have significant domestic regulatory responsibility, the Advisors, and the Vice President. The Administrator of OIRA shall chair the Working Group and shall periodically advise the Vice President on the activities of the Working Group. The Working Group shall serve as a forum to assist agencies in identifying and analyzing important regulatory issues (including, among others (1) the development of innovative regulatory techniques, (2) the methods, efficacy, and utility of comparative risk assessment in regulatory decision-making, and (3) the development of short forms and other streamlined regulatory approaches for small businesses and other entities). The Working Group shall meet at least quarterly and may meet as a whole or in subgroups of agencies with an interest in particular issues or subject areas. To inform its discussions, the Working Group may commission analytical studies and reports by OIRA, the Administrative Conference of the United States, or any other agency.

(e) **Conferences.** The Administrator of OIRA shall meet quarterly with representatives of State, local, and tribal governments to identify both existing and proposed regulations that may uniquely or significantly affect those governmental entities. The Administrator of OIRA shall also convene, from time to time, conferences with representatives of businesses, nongovernmental organizations, and the public to discuss regulatory issues of common concern.

Sec. 5. Existing Regulations. In order to reduce the regulatory burden on the American people, their families, their communities, their State, local, and tribal governments, and their industries; to determine whether regulations promulgated by the executive branch of the Federal Government have become unjustified or unnecessary as a result of changed circumstances; to confirm that regulations are both compatible with each other and not duplicative or inappropriately burdensome in the aggregate; to ensure that all regulations are consistent with the President's priorities and the principles set forth in this Executive order, within applicable law; and to otherwise improve the effectiveness of existing regulations:

(a) Within 90 days of the date of this Executive order, each agency shall submit to OIRA a program, consistent with its resources and regulatory priorities, under which the agency will periodically review its existing significant regulations to determine whether any such regulations should be modified or eliminated so as to make the agency's regulatory program more effective in achieving the regulatory objectives, less burdensome, or in greater alignment with the President's priorities and the principles set forth in this Executive order. Any significant regulations selected for review shall be included in the agency's annual Plan. The agency shall also identify any legislative mandates that require the agency to promulgate or continue to impose regulations that the agency believes are unnecessary or outdated by reason of changed circumstances.

(b) The Administrator of OIRA shall work with the Regulatory Working Group and other interested entities to pursue the objectives of this section. State, local, and tribal governments are specifically encouraged to assist in the identification of regulations that impose significant or unique burdens on those governmental entities and that appear to have outlived their justification or be otherwise inconsistent with the public interest.

(c) The Vice President, in consultation with the Advisors, may identify for review by the appropriate agency or agencies other existing regulations of an agency or groups of regulations of more than one agency that affect a particular group, industry, or sector of the economy, or may identify legislative mandates that may be appropriate for reconsideration by the Congress.

Sec. 6. Centralized Review of Regulations. The guidelines set forth below shall apply to all regulatory actions, for both new and existing regulations, by agencies other than those agencies specifically exempted by the Administrator of OIRA:

(a) **Agency Responsibilities.** (1) Each agency shall (consistent with its own rules, regulations, or procedures) provide the public with meaningful participation in the regulatory process. In particular, before issuing a notice of proposed rulemaking, each agency should, where appropriate, seek the involvement of those who are intended to benefit from and those expected to be burdened by any regulation (including, specifically, State, local, and tribal officials). In addition, each agency should afford the public a meaningful opportunity to comment on any proposed regulation, which in most cases should include a comment period of not less than 60 days. Each agency also is directed to explore and, where appropriate, use consensual mechanisms for developing regulations, including negotiated rulemaking.

(2) Within 60 days of the date of this Executive order, each agency head shall designate a Regulatory Policy Officer who shall report to the agency head. The Regulatory Policy Officer shall be involved at each stage of the regulatory process to foster the development of effective, innovative, and least burdensome regulations and to further the principles set forth in this Executive order.

(3) In addition to adhering to its own rules and procedures and to the requirements of the Administrative Procedure Act, the Regulatory Flexibility Act, the

Paperwork Reduction Act, and other applicable law, each agency shall develop its regulatory actions in a timely fashion and adhere to the following procedures with respect to a regulatory action:

(A) Each agency shall provide OIRA, at such times and in the manner specified by the Administrator of OIRA, with a list of its planned regulatory actions, indicating those which the agency believes are significant regulatory actions within the meaning of this Executive order. Absent a material change in the development of the planned regulatory action, those not designated as significant will not be subject to review under this section unless, within 10 working days of receipt of the list, the Administrator of OIRA notifies the agency that OIRA has determined that a planned regulation is a significant regulatory action within the meaning of this Executive order. The Administrator of OIRA may waive review of any planned regulatory action designated by the agency as significant, in which case the agency need not further comply with subsection (a) (3) (B) or subsection (a)(3)(C) of this section.

(B) For each matter identified as, or determined by the Administrator of OIRA to be, a significant regulatory action, the issuing agency shall provide to OIRA:

(i) The text of the draft regulatory action, together with a reasonably detailed description of the need for the regulatory action and an explanation of how the regulatory action will meet that need; and

(ii) An assessment of the potential costs and benefits of the regulatory action, including an explanation of the manner in which the regulatory action is consistent with a statutory mandate and, to the extent permitted by law, promotes the President's priorities and avoids undue interference with State, local, and tribal governments in the exercise of their governmental functions.

(C) For those matters identified as, or determined by the Administrator of OIRA to be, a significant regulatory action within the scope of section 3(f) (1), the agency shall also provide to OIRA the following additional information developed as part of the agency's decision-making process (unless prohibited by law):

(i) An assessment, including the underlying analysis, of benefits anticipated from the regulatory action (such as, but not limited to, the promotion of the efficient functioning of the economy and private markets, the enhancement of health and safety, the protection of the natural environment, and the elimination or reduction of discrimination or bias) together with, to the extent feasible, a quantification of those benefits;

(ii) An assessment, including the underlying analysis, of costs anticipated from the regulatory action (such as, but not limited to, the direct cost both to the government in administering the regulation and to businesses and others in complying with the regulation, and any adverse effects on the efficient functioning of the economy, private markets (including productivity, employment, and competitiveness), health, safety, and the natural environment), together with, to the extent feasible, a quantification of those costs; and

(iii) An assessment, including the underlying analysis, of costs and benefits of potentially effective and reasonably feasible alternatives to the planned regulation, identified by the agencies or the public (including improving the current regulation and reasonably viable nonregulatory actions), and an explanation why the planned regulatory action is preferable to the identified potential alternatives.

(D) In emergency situations or when an agency is obligated by law to act more quickly than normal review procedures allow, the agency shall notify OIRA as soon as possible and, to the extent practicable, comply with subsections (a) (3) (B) and (C) of this section. For those regulatory actions that are governed by a statutory or court-imposed deadline, the agency shall, to the extent practicable, schedule rulemaking proceedings so as to permit sufficient time for OIRA to conduct its review, as set forth below in subsection (b) (2) through (4) of this section.

(E) After the regulatory action has been published in the Federal Register or otherwise issued to the public, the agency shall:

(i) Make available to the public the information set forth in subsections (a)(3)(B) and (C);

(ii) Identify for the public, in a complete, clear, and simple manner, the substantive changes between the draft submitted to OIRA for review and the action subsequently announced; and

(iii) Identify for the public those changes in the regulatory action that were made at the suggestion or recommendation of OIRA.

(F) All information provided to the public by the agency shall be in plain, understandable language.

(b) **OIRA Responsibilities.** The Administrator of OIRA shall provide meaningful guidance and oversight so that each agency's regulatory actions are consistent with applicable law, the President's priorities, and the principles set forth in this Executive order and do not conflict with the policies or actions of another agency. OIRA shall, to the extent permitted by law, adhere to the following guidelines:

(1) OIRA may review only actions identified by the agency or by OIRA as significant regulatory actions under subsection (a)(3)(A) of this section.

(2) OIRA shall waive review or notify the agency in writing of the results of its review within the following time periods:

(A) For any notices of inquiry, advance notices of proposed rulemaking, or other preliminary regulatory actions prior to a Notice of Proposed

Rulemaking, within 10 working days after the date of submission of the draft action to OIRA;

(B) For all other regulatory actions, within 90 calendar days after the date of submission of the information set forth in subsections (a) (3) (B) and (C) of this section, unless OIRA has previously reviewed this information and, since that review, there has been no material change in the facts and circumstances upon which the regulatory action is based, in which case, OIRA shall complete its review within 45 days; and

(C) The review process may be extended (1) once by no more than 30 calendar days upon the written approval of the Director and (2) at the request of the agency head.

(3) For each regulatory action that the Administrator of OIRA returns to an agency for further consideration of some or all of its provisions, the Administrator of OIRA shall provide the issuing agency a written explanation for such return, setting forth the pertinent provision of this Executive order on which OIRA is relying. If the agency head disagrees with some or all of the bases for the return, the agency head shall so inform the Administrator of OIRA in writing.

(4) Except as otherwise provided by law or required by a Court, in order to ensure greater openness, accessibility, and accountability in the regulatory review process, OIRA shall be governed by the following disclosure requirements:

(A) Only the Administrator of OIRA (or a particular designee) shall receive oral communications initiated by persons not employed by the executive branch of the Federal Government regarding the substance of a regulatory action under OIRA review;

(B) All substantive communications between OIRA personnel and persons not employed by the executive branch of the Federal Government regarding a regulatory action under review shall be governed by the following guidelines:

(i) A representative from the issuing agency shall be invited to any meeting between OIRA personnel and such person(s);

(ii) OIRA shall forward to the issuing agency, within 10 working days of receipt of the communication(s), all written communications, regardless of format, between OIRA personnel and any person who is not employed by the executive branch of the Federal Government, and the dates and names of individuals involved in all substantive oral communications (including meetings to which an agency representative was invited, but did not attend, and telephone conversations between OIRA personnel and any such persons) ; and

(iii) OIRA shall publicly disclose relevant information about such communication(s), as set forth below in subsection (b) (4) (C) of this section.

(C) OIRA shall maintain a publicly available log that shall contain, at a minimum, the following information pertinent to regulatory actions under review:

(i) The status of all regulatory actions, including if (and if so, when and by whom) Vice Presidential and Presidential consideration was requested;

(ii) A notation of all written communications forwarded to an issuing agency under subsection (b)(4)(B)(ii) of this section; and

(iii) The dates and names of individuals involved in all substantive oral communications, including meetings and telephone conversations, between OIRA personnel and any person not employed by the executive branch of the Federal Government, and the subject matter discussed during such communications.

(D) After the regulatory action has been published in the Federal Register or otherwise issued to the public, or after the agency has announced its decision not to publish or issue the regulatory action, OIRA shall make available to the public all documents exchanged between OIRA and the agency during the review by OIRA under this section.

(5) All information provided to the public by OIRA shall be in plain, understandable language.

Sec. 7. Resolution of Conflicts. To the extent permitted by law, disagreements or conflicts between or among agency heads or between OMB and any agency that cannot be resolved by the Administrator of OIRA shall be resolved by the President, or by the Vice President acting at the request of the President, with the relevant agency head (and, as appropriate, other interested government officials). Vice Presidential and Presidential consideration of such disagreements may be initiated only by the Director, by the head of the issuing agency, or by the head of an agency that has a significant interest in the regulatory action at issue. Such review will not be undertaken at the request of other persons, entities, or their agents.

Resolution of such conflicts shall be informed by recommendations developed by the Vice President, after consultation with the Advisors (and other executive branch officials or personnel whose responsibilities to the President include the subject matter at issue). The development of these recommendations shall be concluded within 60 days after review has been requested.

During the Vice Presidential and Presidential review period, communications with any person not employed by the Federal Government relating to the substance of the regulatory action under review and directed to the Advisors or their staffs or to the staff of the Vice President shall be in writing and shall be forwarded by the recipient to the affected agency(ies) for inclusion in the public docket(s). When the communication is not in writing, such Advisors or staff members shall inform the outside party that the matter is under review and that any comments should be submitted in writing.

At the end of this review process, the President, or the Vice President acting at the request of the President, shall notify the affected agency and the Administrator of OIRA of the President's decision with respect to the matter.

Sec. 8. Publication. Except to the extent required by law, an agency shall not publish in the Federal Register or otherwise issue to the public any regulatory action that is subject to review under section 6 of this Executive order until (1) the Administrator of OIRA notifies the agency that OIRA has waived its review of the action or has completed its review without any requests for further consideration, or (2) the applicable time period in section 6(b) (2) expires without OIRA having notified the agency that it is returning the regulatory action for further consideration under section 6(b) (3), whichever occurs first. If the terms of the preceding sentence have not been satisfied and an agency wants to publish or otherwise issue a regulatory action, the head of that agency may request Presidential consideration through the Vice President, as provided under section 7 of this order. Upon receipt of this request, the Vice President shall notify OIRA and the Advisors. The guidelines and time period set forth in section 7 shall apply to the publication of regulatory actions for which Presidential consideration has been sought.

Sec. 9. Agency Authority. Nothing in this order shall be construed as displacing the agencies' authority or responsibilities, as authorized by law.

Sec. 10. Judicial Review. Nothing in this Executive order shall affect any otherwise available judicial review of agency action. This Executive order is intended only to improve the internal management of the Federal Government and does not create any right or benefit, substantive or procedural, enforceable at law or equity by a party against the United States, its agencies or instrumentalities; its officers or employees, or any other person.

Sec. 11. Revocations. Executive Orders Nos. 12291 and 12498; all amendments to those Executive orders; all guidelines issued under those orders; and any exemptions from those orders heretofore granted for any category of rule are revoked.

WILLIAM J. CLINTON
The White House, September 30, 1993.

Index